EU LAW

EU LAW

Text, Cases, and Materials

SIXTH EDITION

Paul Craig

and

Gráinne de Búrca

OXFORD

UNIVERSITY PRESS

OXFORD
UNIVERSITY PRESS

Great Clarendon Street, Oxford, OX2 6DP,
United Kingdom

Oxford University Press is a department of the University of Oxford.
It furthers the University's objective of excellence in research, scholarship,
and education by publishing worldwide. Oxford is a registered trade mark of
Oxford University Press in the UK and in certain other countries

Third edition 2002
Fourth edition 2008
Fifth edition 2011

Impression: 1

Published in the United States of America by Oxford University Press
198 Madison Avenue, New York, NY 10016, United States of America

British Library Cataloguing in Publication Data
Data available

Library of Congress Control Number: 2015931992

ISBN 978–0–19–871492–7

Printed in Italy by
L.E.G.O. S.p.A.

*Do mo mháthair, a spreag mé chun an dlí a staidéar agus a spreag go mór
i mbealaí eile mé freisin; agus i gcuimhne m'athar
Gráinne de Búrca*

*To Anita and Ciaran
Paul Craig*

PREFACE TO THE SIXTH EDITION

EU law has developed significantly since the fifth edition of this book and we have incorporated these developments in the new edition. The period between the fifth and sixth editions has seen the new provisions of the Lisbon Treaty tested, in relation to topics such as the hierarchy of norms, competence, and the Charter of Rights.

It was hoped that the advent of the Lisbon Treaty, duly ratified after a decade of attempts at Treaty reform, would signal a period of relative calm, in which the EU institutions could concentrate on substantive issues of concern to Europe and its citizens. The reality proved otherwise, since the coming into effect of the new Treaty was overshadowed by the financial crisis, which has occupied a considerable part of the EU's time since 2009.

There has nonetheless been considerable legislative activity in other areas, and the EU Courts have given important decisions across the spectrum of EU law, more especially in areas such as citizenship, free movement of goods, workers, services and freedom of establishment, international relations law, human rights, and equal treatment.

The sixth edition has incorporated the changes in all these areas, and reflects also the vibrant academic literature. We have always taken the revision process for this book very seriously, and this is equally so for this edition. We have tried throughout the book to give a balanced account of this diverse material, but there have, as always, been difficult choices as to what to include, given the very large range of subject matter that now falls within the remit of EU law. For topics on which the academic literature was too extensive to permit a useful selection, we have listed only monographs and collections, and not individual academic articles.

We would like to thank all those at OUP who have helped with this edition of the work, with special thanks to Helen Swann and Sarah Stephenson. Joy Ruskin-Tompkins did an excellent job as copy-editor, as did Julie Stone with the proof reading. Thanks also to the excellent research assistants who have done so much to help with preparation of this edition: Ana Bobic, Esther Lanotte, Christina Lienen, Dimitrios Nikiforos, Thomas Streinz, Vladislav Vyhnánek, and Petra Weingerl.

Paul Craig and Gráinne de Búrca

NEW TO THIS EDITION

- Detailed coverage of the way in which the Treaty of Lisbon has been applied since ratification.
- Institutional developments flowing from the most recent elections to the European Parliament and the impact on the relationship between the Commission, the European Parliament, and the European Council.
- Discussion of the institutional and substantive impact of the financial crisis.
- Important new case law on areas such as:
  - the hierarchy of legal acts,
  - competence,
  - human rights, including *Opinion 2/13 on EU Accession to the European Convention on Human Rights*,
  - citizenship,
  - supremacy,
  - direct effect,
  - international relations law.
- Nomenclature: the Lisbon Treaty changed the name of the European Court of Justice, ECJ, to the Court of Justice of the European Union, CJEU. The terminology of ECJ is preserved for cases decided prior to the Lisbon Treaty, because we felt that it would be wrong to alter the name in the official law reports when citing a case extract, and that a different name could not then be used when discussing the case in the text. The terminology of CJEU is used for cases decided post-Lisbon, and when discussing more general issues as to the ambit of a particular Treaty Article.

OUTLINE CONTENTS

DETAILED CONTENTS

TABLE OF ABBREVIATIONS

CRPD	Convention on the Rights of Persons with Disabilities
CSDP	Common Security and Defence Policy
CSIH	Court of Session Inner House
CT	Constitutional Treaty
CYELS	Cambridge Yearbook of European Legal Studies
DAA	Draft Agreement on Accession
Dec	Decision
DG	Directorate General
Dir	Directive
DSB	Dispute Settlement Body
EAGCP	Economic Advisory Group on Competition Policy
EAW	European Arrest Warrant
EBLR	European Business Law Review
EC	European Community
ECB	European Central Bank
ECFR	European Company and Financial Law Review
ECHR	European Convention on Human Rights
ECJ	European Court of Justice
ECLR	European Competition Law Review
Ecofin	Economic and Financial Affairs Council
ECtHR	European Court of Human Rights
ECR	European Court Reports
ECSC	European Coal and Steel Community
EC Treaty	European Community Treaty
ECU	European Currency Unit
EDA	Exclusive Distribution Agreement
EDC	European Defence Community
EEA	European Economic Area
EEAS	EU External Action Service
EEC	European Economic Community
EELR	European Environmental Law Review
EEW	European Evidence Warrant
EFAR	European Foreign Affairs Review
EFSF	European Financial Stability Facility
EFSM	European Financial Stabilisation Mechanism
EFTA	European Free Trade Association
EHRLRev	European Human Rights Law Review
EIO	European Investigation Order
EJIL	European Journal of International Law
EJML	European Journal of Migration and Law
ELJ	European Law Journal
ELRev	European Law Review
EMS	European Monetary System
EMU	Economic and Monetary Union

ENP	European Neighbourhood Policy
EP	European Parliament
EPA	Exclusive Purchasing Agreement
EPC	European Political Community
EPL	European Public Law
ERM	Exchange Rate Mechanism
ERPL	European Review of Public Law
ERTA	European Road Transport Agreement
ESCB	European System of Central Banks
ESDP	European Security and Defence Policy
ESM	European Stability Mechanism
EStAL	European State Aid Law Quarterly
ETSI	European Telecommunications Standards Institute
EU	European Union
EuConst	European Constitutional Law Review
EUP	European Union Politics
Euratom	European Atomic Energy Community
Eurojust	European Judicial Cooperation Union
Europol	European Police Office
EWCA	England and Wales Court of Appeal
EWHC	England and Wales High Court
FAC	Foreign Affairs Council
Fordham Int LJ	Fordham International Law Journal
FRA	Fundamental Rights Agency
FRY	Federal Republic of Yugoslavia
GAC	General Affairs Council
GATS	General Agreement on Trade in Services
GATT	General Agreement on Tariffs and Trade
GC	General Court
GDP	Gross Domestic Product
Harv LRev	Harvard Law Review
Hastings I & Comp LJ	Hastings International and Comparative Law Journal
HL	House of Lords
HRLJ	Human Rights Law Journal
HRLR	Human Rights Law Review
ICCPR	International Covenant on Civil and Political Rights
ICESCR	International Covenant on Economic, Social and Cultural Rights
ICLQ	International and Comparative Law Quarterly
I-CON	International Journal of Constitutional Law
IGC	Intergovernmental Conference
IJEL	Irish Journal of European Law
ILJ	Industrial Law Journal
ILO	International Labour Organization
IMO	International Maritime Organization

IR	Irish Reports
JCMS	Journal of Common Market Studies
JEPP	Journal of European Public Policy
JHA	Justice and Home Affairs 'Pillar'
JIEL	Journal of International Economic Law
Jnl Cons Policy	Journal of Consumer Policy
J Pol Econ	Journal of Political Economy
JSWFL	Journal of Social Welfare and Family Law
JWTL	Journal of World Trade Law
LIEI	Legal Issues of European Integration
LQR	Law Quarterly Review
LS	Legal Studies
MCA	Monetary Compensatory Amount
MEP	Member of the European Parliament
MEQR	Measures having Equivalent Effect to a Quantitative Restriction
Mich LR	Michigan Law Review
MJ	Maastricht Journal of European and Comparative Law
MLR	Modern Law Review
NATO	North Atlantic Treaty Organization
NCA	National Competition Authority
Notre Dame LRev	Notre Dame Law Review
NWJ Int L and Bus	North Western Journal of Law and Business
NYULRev	New York University Law Review
OCT	Overseas Countries and Territories
OECD	Organisation for Economic Co-operation and Development
OEEC	Organisation for European Economic Co-operation
OJ	Official Journal of the European Communities
OJLS	Oxford Journal of Legal Studies
OLAF	Office européen de lutte antifraude (European Anti-Fraud Office)
OMC	Open Method of Coordination
OMT	Outright Monetary Transactions
OSCE	Organization for Security and Co-operation in Europe
Pens LR	Pennsylvania Law Review
PJCC	Police and Judicial Cooperation in Criminal Matters
PL	Public Law
PNR	Passenger Name Record
QB	Queen's Bench Reports
RDI	Rivista di diritto internazionale
Reg	Regulation
RHDI	Revue hellénique de droit international
RTDE	Revue trimestrielle de droit européen
SCIFA	Strategic Committee on Immigration Frontiers and Asylum
SDA	Selective Distribution Agreement
SEA	Single European Act

SGEI	Services of a General Economic Interest
SGP	Stability and Growth Pact
SLC	Substantial Lessening of Competition
SMEs	Small and Medium-Sized Enterprises
So Cal L Rev	Southern California Law Review
SPS	Agreement on the Application of Sanitary and Phytosanitary Measures
SSNIP	Small but Significant and Non-transitory Increase in Prices
Summit	European Council Meeting
TBT	Agreement on Technical Barriers to Trade
TEU	Treaty on European Union
TFEU	Treaty on the Functioning of the European Union
TFRA	Task Force for Administrative Reform
TRIPs	Agreement on Trade-Related Intellectual Property Rights
TTIP	Transatlantic Trade and Investment Partnership
U Chic Legal Forum	University of Chicago Legal Forum
UKHL	United Kingdom House of Lords
UKSC	United Kingdom Supreme Court
UN	United Nations
UNCLOS	UN Convention on the Law of the Sea
Vand L Rev	Vanderbilt Law Review
VAT	Value Added Tax
WEU	Western European Union
WLR	Weekly Law Reports
WTO	World Trade Organization
Yale LJ	Yale Law Journal
YBEL	Yearbook of European Law

ACKNOWLEDGEMENTS

Grateful acknowledgement is made to all the authors and publishers of copyright material which appears in this book, and in particular to the following for permission to reprint material from the sources indicated.

B de Witte: extract from Bruno de Witte 'Setting the Scene: How did Services get to Bolestein and Why?' EUI Working Papers 20/2007.

German Law Journal and the authors: extract from D Halberstam and C Möllers, 'The German Constitutional Court says "Ja zu Deutschland!"' (2009) 10 German LJ 1241.

MIT Press: extract from A Moravcsik, 'Negotiating the Single European Act: National Interests and Conventional Statecraft in the European Community' (1991) 45 International Organization 19, 25–7.

Oxford University Press: extracts from P Craig, 'Britain in the European Union', in J Jowell and D Oliver (eds), *The Changing Constitution* (Oxford University Press, 7th edn, 2011), ch 4; P Craig, 'Comitology, Rulemaking and the Lisbon Settlement: Tensions and Strains', in C-F Bergstrom and D Ritleng (eds), *Rulemaking by the Commission: The New System* (Oxford University Press, 2015); N MacCormick, *Questioning Sovereignty* (Oxford University Press, 1999); T Tridimas, 'Constitutional Review of Member State Action: The Virtues and Vices of an Incomplete Jurisdiction', forthcoming; N Walker, 'In Search of the Area of Freedom, Security and Justice: A Constitutional Odyssey' in N Walker (ed.), *Europe's Area of Freedom, Security and Justice* (Oxford University Press, 2004); and R Whish, *Competition Law* (Oxford University Press, 6th edn, 2009).

Perseus Books: extract from R Bork, *The Antitrust Paradox: A Policy at War with Itself* (Basic Books, 1978), 297–8, 310–11.

Rodrigues: extract from Maria João Rodrigues, 'The Open Method of Coordination as a New Governance Tool' in M Telò (ed), 'L'evoluzione della governance europea', Special Issue of 'Europa/ Europe', Rome, No 2–3, 2001.

Thomson Reuters (Professional) UK Limited: extracts from Case IV/M57, Re the Concentration between Digital Equipment International and Mannesman Kienzle GmbH [1992] 4 CMLR M99; Case IV/M53, Re the Concentration between Aérospatiale SNI and Alenia Aeritalia e Selenia SpA and de Havilland [1992] 4 CMLR M2; and L Gormley and J de Haan, 'The Democratic Deficit of the European Central Bank' (1996) 21 ELRev 95, 97–9.

Wiley–Blackwell: extracts from W Bishop, 'Price Discrimination under Article 86: Political Economy in the European Court' (1981) 44 MLR 282, 287–8, 288–9; and J Scott and D Trubek, 'Mind the Gap: Law and New Approaches to Governance in the European Union', (2002) 8 ELJ 1.

Yale Law Journal Company: extract from J Weiler, 'The Transformation of Europe', (1991) 8 The Yale Law Journal, 2403, 2454, 2476–8.

Every effort has been made to trace and contact copyright holders prior to publication. If notified the publisher will undertake to rectify any errors or omissions at the earliest opportunity.

TABLE OF CASES

EUROPEAN COURT OF FIRST INSTANCE/ GENERAL COURT (NUMERICAL)

Civil Service Tribunal

Commission Decisions

NATIONAL CASES

Czech Republic

Denmark

France

TABLE OF TREATIES, EUROPEAN LEGISLATIVE INSTRUMENTS AND NATIONAL LEGISLATION

EU INSTRUMENTS

Regulations

Council Decisions

LISBON TABLE OF EQUIVALENCES[1]

TREATY ON EUROPEAN UNION

Old numbering of the Treaty on European Union	New numbering of the Treaty on European Union
TITLE I — COMMON PROVISIONS	TITLE I — COMMON PROVISIONS
Article 1	Article 1
	Article 2
Article 2	Article 3
Article 3 (repealed)[2]	
	Article 4
	Article 5[3]
Article 4 (repealed)[4]	
Article 5 (repealed)[5]	
Article 6	Article 6
Article 7	Article 7
	Article 8
TITLE II — PROVISIONS AMENDING THE TREATY ESTABLISHING THE EUROPEAN ECONOMIC COMMUNITY WITH A VIEW TO ESTABLISHING THE EUROPEAN COMMUNITY	TITLE II — PROVISIONS ON DEMOCRATIC PRINCIPLES
Article 8 (repealed)[6]	Article 9
	Article 10[7]
	Article 11
	Article 12
TITLE III — PROVISIONS AMENDING THE TREATY ESTABLISHING THE EUROPEAN COAL AND STEEL COMMUNITY	TITLE III — PROVISIONS ON THE INSTITUTIONS
Article 9 (repealed)[8]	Article 13

[1] Tables of equivalences as referred to in Article 5 of the Treaty of Lisbon. The original centre column, which set out the intermediate numbering as used in that Treaty, has been omitted.

[2] Replaced, in substance, by Article 7 of the Treaty on the Functioning of the European Union ('TFEU') and by Articles 13(1) and 21, paragraph 3, second subparagraph of the Treaty on European Union ('TEU').

[3] Replaces Article 5 of the Treaty establishing the European Community ('TEC').

[4] Replaced, in substance, by Article 15.

[5] Replaced, in substance, by Article 13, paragraph 2.

[6] Article 8 TEU, which was in force until the entry into force of the Treaty of Lisbon (hereinafter 'current'), amended the TEC. Those amendments are incorporated into the latter Treaty and Article 8 is repealed. Its number is used to insert a new provision.

[7] Paragraph 4 replaces, in substance, the first subparagraph of Article 191 TEC.

[8] The current Article 9 TEU amended the Treaty establishing the European Coal and Steel Community. This latter expired on 23 July 2002. Article 9 is repealed and the number thereof is used to insert another provision.

Old numbering of the Treaty on European Union	New numbering of the Treaty on European Union
TITLE III – PROVISIONS AMENDING THE TREATY ESTABLISHING THE EUROPEAN COAL AND STEEL COMMUNITY *CONTINUED*	TITLE III – PROVISIONS ON THE INSTITUTIONS *CONTINUED*
	Article 14[9]
	Article 15[10]
	Article 16[11]
	Article 17[12]
	Article 18
	Article 19[13]
TITLE IV – PROVISIONS AMENDING THE TREATY ESTABLISHING THE EUROPEAN ATOMIC ENERGY COMMUNITY	TITLE IV – PROVISIONS ON ENHANCED COOPERATION
Article 10 (repealed)[14]	Article 20[15]
Articles 27a to 27e (replaced)	
Articles 40 to 40b (replaced)	
Articles 43 to 45 (replaced)	
TITLE V – PROVISIONS ON A COMMON FOREIGN AND SECURITY POLICY	TITLE V – GENERAL PROVISIONS ON THE UNION'S EXTERNAL ACTION AND SPECIFIC PROVISIONS ON THE COMMON FOREIGN AND SECURITY POLICY
	Chapter 1 – General provisions on the Union's external action
	Article 21
	Article 22
	Chapter 2 – Specific provisions on the common foreign and security policy
	Section 1 – Common provisions
	Article 23
Article 11	Article 24
Article 12	Article 25
Article 13	Article 26
	Article 27

9 – Paragraphs 1 and 2 replace, in substance, Article 189 TEC;
– paragraphs 1 to 3 replace, in substance, paragraphs 1 to 3 of Article 190 TEC;
– paragraph 1 replaces, in substance, the first subparagraph of Article 192 TEC;
– paragraph 4 replaces, in substance, the first subparagraph of Article 197 TEC.
10 Replaces, in substance, Article 4.
11 – Paragraph 1 replaces, in substance, the first and second indents of Article 202 TEC;
– paragraphs 2 and 9 replace, in substance, Article 203 TEC;
– paragraphs 4 and 5 replace, in substance, paragraphs 2 and 4 of Article 205 TEC.
12 – Paragraph 1 replaces, in substance, Article 211 TEC;
– paragraphs 3 and 7 replace, in substance, Article 214 TEC;
– paragraph 6 replaces, in substance, paragraphs 1, 3 and 4 of Article 217 TEC.
13 – Replaces, in substance, Article 220 TEC;
– the second subparagraph of paragraph 2 replaces, in substance, the first subparagraph of Article 221 TEC.
14 The current Article 10 TEU amended the Treaty establishing the European Atomic Energy Community. Those amendments are incorporated into the Treaty of Lisbon. Article 10 is repealed and the number thereof is used to insert another provision.
15 Also replaces Articles 11 and 11a TEC.

Old numbering of the Treaty on European Union	New numbering of the Treaty on European Union
TITLE V – PROVISIONS ON A COMMON FOREIGN AND SECURITY POLICY *CONTINUED*	TITLE V – GENERAL PROVISIONS ON THE UNION'S EXTERNAL ACTION AND SPECIFIC PROVISIONS ON THE COMMON FOREIGN AND SECURITY POLICY *CONTINUED*
Article 14	Article 28
Article 15	Article 29
Article 22 (moved)	Article 30
Article 23 (moved)	Article 31
Article 16	Article 32
Article 17 (moved)	*Article 42*
Article 18	Article 33
Article 19	Article 34
Article 20	Article 35
Article 21	Article 36
Article 22 (moved)	*Article 30*
Article 23 (moved)	*Article 31*
Article 24	Article 37
Article 25	Article 38
	Article 39
Article 47 (moved)	Article 40
Article 26 (repealed)	
Article 27 (repealed)	
Article 27a (replaced)[16]	*Article 20*
Article 27b (replaced)[16]	*Article 20*
Article 27c (replaced)[16]	*Article 20*
Article 27d (replaced)[16]	*Article 20*
Article 27e (replaced)[16]	*Article 20*
Article 28	Article 41
	SECTION 2 – PROVISIONS ON THE COMMON SECURITY AND DEFENCE POLICY
Article 17 (moved)	Article 42
	Article 43
	Article 44
	Article 45
	Article 46
TITLE VI – PROVISIONS ON POLICE AND JUDICIAL COOPERATION IN CRIMINAL MATTERS (REPEALED)[17]	
Article 29 (replaced)[18]	
Article 30 (replaced)[19]	
Article 31 (replaced)[20]	

[16] The current Articles 27a to 27e, on enhanced cooperation, are also replaced by Articles 326 to 334 TFEU.

[17] The current provisions of Title VI of the TEU, on police and judicial cooperation in criminal matters, are replaced by the provisions of Chapters 1, 4 and 5 of Title IV of Part Three of the TFEU.

[18] Replaced by Article 67 TFEU.

[19] Replaced by Articles 87 and 88 TFEU.

[20] Replaced by Articles 82, 83 and 85 TFEU.

Old numbering of the Treaty on European Union	New numbering of the Treaty on European Union
TITLE VI – PROVISIONS ON POLICE AND JUDICIAL COOPERATION IN CRIMINAL MATTERS (REPEALED)[17] CONTINUED	
Article 32 (replaced)[21]	
Article 33 (replaced)[22]	
Article 34 (repealed)	
Article 35 (repealed)	
Article 36 (replaced)[23]	
Article 37 (repealed)	
Article 38 (repealed)	
Article 39 (repealed)	
Article 40 (replaced)[24]	*Article 20*
Article 40 A (replaced)[24]	*Article 20*
Article 40 B (replaced)[24]	*Article 20*
Article 41 (repealed)	
Article 42 (repealed)	
TITLE VII – PROVISIONS ON ENHANCED COOPERATION (REPLACED)[25]	TITLE IV – PROVISIONS ON ENHANCED COOPERATION
Article 43 (replaced)[25]	*Article 20*
Article 43 A (replaced)[25]	*Article 20*
Article 43 B (replaced)[25]	*Article 20*
Article 44 (replaced)[25]	*Article 20*
Article 44 A (replaced)[25]	*Article 20*
Article 45 (replaced)[25]	*Article 20*
TITLE VIII – FINAL PROVISIONS	TITLE VI – FINAL PROVISIONS
Article 46 (repealed)	Article 47
Article 47 (replaced)	*Article 40*
Article 48	Article 48
Article 49	Article 49
	Article 50
	Article 51
	Article 52
Article 50 (repealed)	
Article 51	Article 53
Article 52	Article 54
Article 53	Article 55

[21] Replaced by Article 89 TFEU.
[22] Replaced by Article 72 TFEU.
[23] Replaced by Article 71 TFEU.
[24] The current Articles 40 to 40 B TEU, on enhanced cooperation, are also replaced by Articles 326 to 334 TFEU.
[25] The current Articles 43 to 45 and Title VII of the TEU, on enhanced cooperation, are also replaced by Articles 326 to 334 TFEU.

TREATY ON THE FUNCTIONING OF THE EUROPEAN UNION

Old numbering of the Treaty establishing the European Community	New numbering of the Treaty on the Functioning of the European Union
PART ONE – PRINCIPLES	PART ONE – PRINCIPLES
Article 1 (repealed)	
	Article 1
Article 2 (repealed)[1]	
	TITLE I – CATEGORIES AND AREAS OF UNION COMPETENCE
	Article 2
	Article 3
	Article 4
	Article 5
	Article 6
	TITLE II – PROVISIONS HAVING GENERAL APPLICATION
	Article 7
Article 3, paragraph 1 (repealed)[2]	
Article 3, paragraph 2	Article 8
Article 4 (moved)	*Article 119*
Article 5 (replaced)[3]	
	Article 9
	Article 10
Article 6	Article 11
Article 153, paragraph 2 (moved)	Article 12 Article 13[4]
Article 7 (repealed)[5]	
Article 8 (repealed)[6]	
Article 9 (repealed)	
Article 10 (repealed)[7]	
Article 11 (replaced)[8]	*Articles 326 to 334*
Article 11a (replaced)[8]	*Articles 326 to 334*
Article 12 (repealed)	*Article 18*
Article 13 (moved)	*Article 19*
Article 14 (moved)	Article 26

[1] Replaced, in substance, by Article 3 TEU.

[2] Replaced, in substance, by Articles 3 to 6 TFEU.

[3] Replaced, in substance, by Article 5 TEU.

[4] Insertion of the operative part of the protocol on protection and welfare of animals.

[5] Replaced, in substance, by Article 13 TEU.

[6] Replaced, in substance, by Article 13 TEU and Article 282, paragraph 1, TFEU.

[7] Replaced, in substance, by Article 4, paragraph 3, TEU.

[8] Also replaced by Article 20 TEU.

Old numbering of the Treaty establishing the European Community	New numbering of the Treaty on the Functioning of the European Union
Article 15 (moved)	Article 27
Article 16	Article 14
Article 255 *(moved)*	Article 15
Article 286 *(moved)*	Article 16
	Article 17
PART TWO – CITIZENSHIP OF THE UNION	PART TWO – NON-DISCRIMINATION AND CITIZENSHIP OF THE UNION
Article 12 (moved)	Article 18
Article 13 (moved)	Article 19
Article 17	Article 20
Article 18	Article 21
Article 19	Article 22
Article 20	Article 23
Article 21	Article 24
Article 22	Article 25
PART THREE – COMMUNITY POLICIES	PART THREE – POLICIES AND INTERNAL ACTIONS OF THE UNION
	TITLE I – THE INTERNAL MARKET
Article 14 (moved)	Article 26
Article 15 (moved)	Article 27
TITLE I – FREE MOVEMENT OF GOODS	TITLE II – FREE MOVEMENT OF GOODS
Article 23	Article 28
Article 24	Article 29
CHAPTER 1 – THE CUSTOMS UNION	CHAPTER 1 – THE CUSTOMS UNION
Article 25	Article 30
Article 26	Article 31
Article 27	Article 32
PART THREE, TITLE X, CUSTOMS COOPERATION (MOVED)	CHAPTER 2 – CUSTOMS COOPERATION
Article 135 (moved)	Article 33
CHAPTER 2 – PROHIBITION OF QUANTITATIVE RESTRICTIONS BETWEEN MEMBER STATES	CHAPTER 3 – PROHIBITION OF QUANTITATIVE RESTRICTIONS BETWEEN MEMBER STATES
Article 28	Article 34
Article 29	Article 35
Article 30	Article 36
Article 31	Article 37
TITLE II – AGRICULTURE	TITLE III – AGRICULTURE AND FISHERIES
Article 32	Article 38
Article 33	Article 39
Article 34	Article 40
Article 35	Article 41

Old numbering of the Treaty establishing the European Community	New numbering of the Treaty on the Functioning of the European Union
Article 36	Article 42
Article 37	Article 43
Article 38	Article 44
TITLE III – FREE MOVEMENT OF PERSONS, SERVICES AND CAPITAL	TITLE IV – FREE MOVEMENT OF PERSONS, SERVICES AND CAPITAL
CHAPTER 1 – WORKERS	CHAPTER 1 – WORKERS
Article 39	Article 45
Article 40	Article 46
Article 41	Article 47
Article 42	Article 48
CHAPTER 2 – RIGHT OF ESTABLISHMENT	CHAPTER 2 – RIGHT OF ESTABLISHMENT
Article 43	Article 49
Article 44	Article 50
Article 45	Article 51
Article 46	Article 52
Article 47	Article 53
Article 48	Article 54
Article 294 (moved)	Article 55
CHAPTER 3 – SERVICES	CHAPTER 3 – SERVICES
Article 49	Article 56
Article 50	Article 57
Article 51	Article 58
Article 52	Article 59
Article 53	Article 60
Article 54	Article 61
Article 55	Article 62
CHAPTER 4 – CAPITAL AND PAYMENTS	CHAPTER 4 – CAPITAL AND PAYMENTS
Article 56	Article 63
Article 57	Article 64
Article 58	Article 65
Article 59	Article 66
Article 60 (moved)	Article 75
TITLE IV – VISAS, ASYLUM, IMMIGRATION AND OTHER POLICIES RELATED TO FREE MOVEMENT OF PERSONS	TITLE V – AREA OF FREEDOM, SECURITY AND JUSTICE
	CHAPTER 1 – GENERAL PROVISIONS
Article 61	Article 67[1]
	Article 68
	Article 69
	Article 70
	Article 71[2]

[1] Also replaces the current Article 29 TEU.
[2] Also replaces the current Article 36 TEU.

Old numbering of the Treaty establishing the European Community	New numbering of the Treaty on the Functioning of the European Union
Article 64, paragraph 1 (replaced)	Article 72[1] Article 73
Article 66 (replaced) Article 60 (moved)	Article 74 Article 75 Article 76
	CHAPTER 2 – POLICIES ON BORDER CHECKS, ASYLUM AND IMMIGRATION
Article 62	Article 77
Article 63, points 1 and 2, and Article 64, paragraph 2[2]	Article 78
Article 63, points 3 and 4	Article 79 Article 80
Article 64, paragraph 1 (replaced)	*Article 72*
	CHAPTER 3 – JUDICIAL COOPERATION IN CIVIL MATTERS
Article 65	Article 81
Article 66 (replaced)	*Article 74*
Article 67 (repealed) Article 68 (repealed)	
Article 69 (repealed)	
	CHAPTER 4 – JUDICIAL COOPERATION IN CRIMINAL MATTERS
	Article 82[3]
	Article 83[3]
	Article 84
	Article 85[3]
	Article 86
	CHAPTER 5 – POLICE COOPERATION
	Article 87[4]
	Article 88[4]
	Article 89[5]
TITLE V – TRANSPORT	**TITLE VI – TRANSPORT**
Article 70	Article 90
Article 71	Article 91
Article 72	Article 92
Article 73	Article 93
Article 74	Article 94
Article 75 Article 76	Article 95 Article 96
Article 77	Article 97
Article 78	Article 98
Article 79	Article 99
Article 80	Article 100

[1] Also replaces the current Article 33 TEU.

[2] Points 1 and 2 of Article 63 EC are replaced by paragraphs 1 and 2 of Article 78 TFEU, and paragraph 2 of Article 64 is replaced by paragraph 3 of Article 78 TFEU.

[3] Replaces the current Article 31 TEU.

[4] Replaces the current Article 30 TEU.

[5] Replaces the current Article 32 TEU.

Old numbering of the Treaty establishing the European Community	New numbering of the Treaty on the Functioning of the European Union
TITLE VI – COMMON RULES ON COMPETITION, TAXATION AND APPROXIMATION OF LAWS	TITLE VII – COMMON RULES ON COMPETITION, TAXATION AND APPROXIMATION OF LAWS
CHAPTER 1 – RULES ON COMPETITION	CHAPTER 1 – RULES ON COMPETITION
SECTION 1 – RULES APPLYING TO UNDERTAKINGS	SECTION 1 – RULES APPLYING TO UNDERTAKINGS
Article 81	Article 101
Article 82	Article 102
Article 83	Article 103
Article 84	Article 104
Article 85	Article 105
Article 86	Article 106
SECTION 2 – AIDS GRANTED BY STATES	SECTION 2 – AIDS GRANTED BY STATES
Article 87	Article 107
Article 88	Article 108
Article 89	Article 109
CHAPTER 2 – TAX PROVISIONS	CHAPTER 2 – TAX PROVISIONS
Article 90	Article 110
Article 91	Article 111
Article 92	Article 112
Article 93	Article 113
CHAPTER 3 – APPROXIMATION OF LAWS	CHAPTER 3 – APPROXIMATION OF LAWS
Article 95 (moved)	Article 114
Article 94 (moved)	Article 115
Article 96	Article 116
Article 97	Article 117
	Article 118
TITLE VII – ECONOMIC AND MONETARY POLICY	TITLE VIII – ECONOMIC AND MONETARY POLICY
Article 4 (moved)	Article 119
CHAPTER 1 – ECONOMIC POLICY	CHAPTER 1 – ECONOMIC POLICY
Article 98	Article 120
Article 99	Article 121
Article 100	Article 122
Article 101	Article 123
Article 102	Article 124
Article 103	Article 125
Article 104	Article 126
CHAPTER 2 – MONETARY POLICY	CHAPTER 2 – MONETARY POLICY
Article 105	Article 127
Article 106	Article 128
Article 107	Article 129
Article 108	Article 130
Article 109	Article 131
Article 110	Article 132
Article 111, paragraphs 1 to 3 and 5 (moved)	*Article 219*
Article 111, paragraph 4 (moved)	*Article 138*
	Article 133

Old numbering of the Treaty establishing the European Community	New numbering of the Treaty on the Functioning of the European Union
CHAPTER 3 – INSTITUTIONAL PROVISIONS	CHAPTER 3 – INSTITUTIONAL PROVISIONS
Article 112 (moved)	*Article 283*
Article 113 (moved)	*Article 284*
Article 114	Article 134
Article 115	Article 135
	CHAPTER 4 – PROVISIONS SPECIFIC TO MEMBER STATES WHOSE CURRENCY IS THE EURO
	Article 136
	Article 137
Article 111, paragraph 4 (moved)	Article 138
CHAPTER 4 – TRANSITIONAL PROVISIONS	CHAPTER 5 – TRANSITIONAL PROVISIONS
Article 116 (repealed)	Article 139
Article 117, paragraphs 1, 2, sixth indent, and 3 to 9 (repealed)	
Article 117, paragraph 2, first five indents (moved)	*Article 141, paragraph 2*
Article 121, paragraph 1 (moved)	Article 140[1]
Article 122, paragraph 2, second sentence (moved)	
Article 123, paragraph 5 (moved)	
Article 118 (repealed)	
Article 123, paragraph 3 (moved)	Article 141[2]
Article 117, paragraph 2, first five indents (moved)	
Article 124, paragraph 1 (moved)	Article 142
Article 119	Article 143
Article 120	Article 144
Article 121, paragraph 1 (moved)	*Article 140, paragraph 1*
Article 121, paragraphs 2 to 4 (repealed)	
Article 122, paragraphs 1, 2, first sentence, 3, 4, 5 and 6 (repealed)	
Article 122, paragraph 2, second sentence (moved)	*Article 140, paragraph 2, first subparagraph*
Article 123, paragraphs 1, 2 and 4 (repealed)	
Article 123, paragraph 3 (moved)	*Article 141, paragraph 1*
Article 123, paragraph 5 (moved)	*Article 140, paragraph 3*
Article 124, paragraph 1 (moved)	*Article 142*
Article 124, paragraph 2 (repealed)	
TITLE VIII – EMPLOYMENT	TITLE IX – EMPLOYMENT
Article 125	Article 145
Article 126	Article 146
Article 127	Article 147
Article 128	Article 148
Article 129	Article 149
Article 130	Article 150

[1] – Article 140, paragraph 1 takes over the wording of paragraph 1 of Article 121.
  – Article 140, paragraph 2 takes over the second sentence of paragraph 2 of Article 122.
  – Article 140, paragraph 3 takes over paragraph 5 of Article 123.
[2] – Article 141, paragraph 1 takes over paragraph 3 of Article 123.
  – Article 141, paragraph 2 takes over the first five indents of paragraph 2 of Article 117.

Old numbering of the Treaty establishing the European Community	New numbering of the Treaty on the Functioning of the European Union
TITLE IX – COMMON COMMERCIAL POLICY (MOVED)	*PART FIVE, TITLE II, COMMON COMMERCIAL POLICY*
Article 131 (moved)	*Article 206*
Article 132 (repealed)	
Article 133 (moved)	*Article 207*
Article 134 (repealed)	
TITLE X – CUSTOMS COOPERATION (MOVED)	*PART THREE, TITLE II, CHAPTER 2, CUSTOMS COOPERATION*
Article 135 (moved)	Article 33
TITLE XI – SOCIAL POLICY, EDUCATION, VOCATIONAL TRAINING AND YOUTH	TITLE X – SOCIAL POLICY
CHAPTER 1 – SOCIAL PROVISIONS (REPEALED)	
Article 136	Article 151
	Article 152
Article 137	Article 153
Article 138	Article 154
Article 139	Article 155
Article 140	Article 156
Article 141	Article 157
Article 142	Article 158
Article 143	Article 159
Article 144	Article 160
Article 145	Article 161
CHAPTER 2 – THE EUROPEAN SOCIAL FUND	TITLE XI – THE EUROPEAN SOCIAL FUND
Article 146	Article 162
Article 147	Article 163
Article 148	Article 164
CHAPTER 3 -EDUCATION, VOCATIONAL TRAINING AND YOUTH	TITLE XII – EDUCATION, VOCATIONAL TRAINING, YOUTH AND SPORT
Article 149	Article 165
Article 150	Article 166
TITLE XII – CULTURE	TITLE XIII – CULTURE
Article 151	Article 167
TITLE XIII – PUBLIC HEALTH	TITLE XIV – PUBLIC HEALTH
Article 152	Article 168
TITLE XIV – CONSUMER PROTECTION	TITLE XV – CONSUMER PROTECTION
Article 153, paragraphs 1, 3, 4 and 5	Article 169
Article 153, paragraph 2 (moved)	Article 12
TITLE XV – TRANS-EUROPEAN NETWORKS	TITLE XVI – TRANS-EUROPEAN NETWORKS
Article 154	Article 170
Article 155	Article 171
Article 156	Article 172
TITLE XVI – INDUSTRY	TITLE XVII – INDUSTRY
Article 157	Article 173

Old numbering of the Treaty establishing the European Community	New numbering of the Treaty on the Functioning of the European Union
TITLE XXVII – ECONOMIC AND SOCIAL COHESION	TITLE XVIII – ECONOMIC, SOCIAL AND TERRITORIAL COHESION
Article 158	Article 174
Article 159	Article 175
Article 160	Article 176
Article 161	Article 177
Article 162	Article 178
TITLE XVIII – RESEARCH AND TECHNOLOGICAL DEVELOPMENT	TITLE XIX – RESEARCH AND TECHNOLOGICAL DEVELOPMENT AND SPACE
Article 163	Article 179
Article 164	Article 180
Article 165	Article 181
Article 166	Article 182
Article 167	Article 183
Article 168	Article 184
Article 169	Article 185
Article 170	Article 186
Article 171	Article 187
Article 172	Article 188 Article 189
Article 173	Article 190
TITLE XIX – ENVIRONMENT	TITLE XX – ENVIRONMENT
Article 174	Article 191
Article 175	Article 192
Article 176	Article 193
	TITLE XXI – ENERGY
	Article 194
	TITLE XXII – TOURISM
	Article 195
	TITLE XXIII – CIVIL PROTECTION
	Article 196
	TITLE XXIV – ADMINISTRATIVE COOPERATION
	Article 197
TITLE XX – DEVELOPMENT COOPERATION (MOVED)	PART FIVE, TITLE III, CHAPTER 1, DEVELOPMENT COOPERATION
Article 177 (moved)	Article 208
Article 178 (repealed)[1]	
Article 179 (moved)	Article 209
Article 180 (moved)	Article 210
Article 181 (moved)	Article 211
TITLE XXI – ECONOMIC, FINANCIAL AND TECHNICAL COOPERATION WITH THIRD COUNTRIES (MOVED)	PART FIVE, TITLE III, CHAPTER 2, ECONOMIC, FINANCIAL AND TECHNICAL COOPERATION WITH THIRD COUNTRIES
Article 181a (moved)	Article 212

[1] Replaced, in substance, by the second sentence of the second subparagraph of paragraph 1 of Article 208 TFEU.

Old numbering of the Treaty establishing the European Community	New numbering of the Treaty on the Functioning of the European Union
PART FOUR – ASSOCIATION OF THE OVERSEAS COUNTRIES AND TERRITORIES	PART FOUR – ASSOCIATION OF THE OVERSEAS COUNTRIES AND TERRITORIES
Article 182	Article 198
Article 183	Article 199
Article 184	Article 200
Article 185	Article 201
Article 186	Article 202
Article 187	Article 203
Article 188	Article 204
	PART FIVE – EXTERNAL ACTION BY THE UNION
	TITLE I – GENERAL PROVISIONS ON THE UNION'S EXTERNAL ACTION
	Article 205
PART THREE, TITLE IX, COMMON COMMERCIAL POLICY (MOVED)	TITLE II – COMMON COMMERCIAL POLICY
Article 131 (moved)	Article 206
Article 133 (moved)	Article 207
	TITLE III – COOPERATION WITH THIRD COUNTRIES AND HUMANITARIAN AID
PART THREE, TITLE XX, DEVELOPMENT COOPERATION (MOVED)	CHAPTER 1 – DEVELOPMENT COOPERATION
Article 177 (moved)	Article 208[1]
Article 179 (moved)	Article 209
Article 180 (moved)	Article 210
Article 181 (moved)	Article 211
PART THREE, TITLE XXI, ECONOMIC, FINANCIAL AND TECHNICAL COOPERATION WITH THIRD COUNTRIES (MOVED)	CHAPTER 2 – ECONOMIC, FINANCIAL AND TECHNICAL COOPERATION WITH THIRD COUNTRIES
Article 181a (moved)	Article 212
	Article 213
	CHAPTER 3 – HUMANITARIAN AID
	Article 214
	TITLE IV – RESTRICTIVE MEASURES
Article 301 (replaced)	Article 215
	TITLE V – INTERNATIONAL AGREEMENTS
	Article 216
Article 310 (moved)	Article 217
Article 300 (replaced)	Article 218
Article 111, paragraphs 1 to 3 and 5 (moved)	Article 219
	TITLE VI – THE UNION'S RELATIONS WITH INTERNATIONAL ORGANISATIONS AND THIRD COUNTRIES AND THE UNION DELEGATIONS
Articles 302 to 304 (replaced)	Article 220
	Article 221

[1] The second sentence of the second subparagraph of paragraph 1 replaces, in substance, Article 178 TEC.

Old numbering of the Treaty establishing the European Community	New numbering of the Treaty on the Functioning of the European Union
	TITLE VII – SOLIDARITY CLAUSE
	Article 222
PART FIVE – INSTITUTIONS OF THE COMMUNITY	PART SIX – INSTITUTIONAL AND FINANCIAL PROVISIONS
TITLE I – INSTITUTIONAL PROVISIONS	TITLE I – INSTITUTIONAL PROVISIONS
CHAPTER 1 – THE INSTITUTIONS	CHAPTER 1 – THE INSTITUTIONS
SECTION 1 – THE EUROPEAN PARLIAMENT	SECTION 1 – THE EUROPEAN PARLIAMENT
Article 189 (repealed)[1]	
Article 190, paragraphs 1 to 3 (repealed)[2]	
Article 190, paragraphs 4 and 5	Article 223
Article 191, first paragraph (repealed)[3]	
Article 191, second paragraph	Article 224
Article 192, first paragraph (repealed)[4]	
Article 192, second paragraph	Article 225
Article 193	Article 226
Article 194	Article 227
Article 195	Article 228
Article 196	Article 229
Article 197, first paragraph (repealed)[5]	
Article 197, second, third and fourth paragraphs	Article 230
Article 198	Article 231
Article 199	Article 232
Article 200	Article 233
Article 201	Article 234
	SECTION 2 – THE EUROPEAN COUNCIL
	Article 235
	Article 236
SECTION 2 – THE COUNCIL	SECTION 3 – THE COUNCIL
Article 202 (repealed)[6]	
Article 203 (repealed)[7]	
Article 204	Article 237
Article 205, paragraphs 2 and 4 (repealed)[8]	
Article 205, paragraphs 1 and 3	Article 238
Article 206	Article 239
Article 207	Article 240
Article 208	Article 241
Article 209	Article 242
Article 210	Article 243

[1] Replaced, in substance, by Article 14, paragraphs 1 and 2, TEU.
[2] Replaced, in substance, by Article 14, paragraphs 1 to 3, TEU.
[3] Replaced, in substance, by Article 11, paragraph 4, TEU.
[4] Replaced, in substance, by Article 14, paragraph 1, TEU.
[5] Replaced, in substance, by Article 14, paragraph 4, TEU.
[6] Replaced, in substance, by Article 16, paragraph 1, TEU and by Articles 290 and 291 TFEU.
[7] Replaced, in substance, by Article 16, paragraphs 2 and 9 TEU.
[8] Replaced, in substance, by Article 16, paragraphs 4 and 5 TEU.

Old numbering of the Treaty establishing the European Community	New numbering of the Treaty on the Functioning of the European Union
SECTION 3 – THE COMMISSION	SECTION 4 – THE COMMISSION
Article 211 (repealed)[1]	
	Article 244
Article 212 (moved)	*Article 249, paragraph 2*
Article 213	Article 245
Article 214 (repealed)[2]	
Article 215	Article 246
Article 216	Article 247
Article 217, paragraphs 1, 3 and 4 (repealed)[3]	
Article 217, paragraph 2	Article 248
Article 218, paragraph 1 (repealed)[4]	
Article 218, paragraph 2	Article 249
Article 219	Article 250
SECTION 4 – THE COURT OF JUSTICE	SECTION 5 – THE COURT OF JUSTICE OF THE EUROPEAN UNION
Article 220 (repealed)[5]	
Article 221, first paragraph (repealed)[6]	
Article 221, second and third paragraphs	Article 251
Article 222	Article 252
Article 223	Article 253
Article 224[7]	Article 254
	Article 255
Article 225	Article 256
Article 225a	Article 257
Article 226	Article 258
Article 227	Article 259
Article 228	Article 260
Article 229	Article 261
Article 229a	Article 262
Article 230	Article 263
Article 231	Article 264
Article 232	Article 265
Article 233	Article 266
Article 234	Article 267
Article 235	Article 268
	Article 269
Article 236	Article 270
Article 237	Article 271
Article 238	Article 272
Article 239	Article 273

[1] Replaced, in substance, by Article 17, paragraph 1 TEU.

[2] Replaced, in substance, by Article 17, paragraphs 3 and 7 TEU.

[3] Replaced, in substance, by Article 17, paragraph 6, TEU.

[4] Replaced, in substance, by Article 295 TFEU.

[5] Replaced, in substance, by Article 19 TEU.

[6] Replaced, in substance, by Article 19, paragraph 2, first subparagraph, of the TEU.

[7] The first sentence of the first subparagraph is replaced, in substance, by Article 19, paragraph 2, second subparagraph of the TEU.

Old numbering of the Treaty establishing the European Community	New numbering of the Treaty on the Functioning of the European Union
Article 240	Article 274
	Article 275
	Article 276
Article 241	Article 277
Article 242	Article 278
Article 243	Article 279
Article 244	Article 280
Article 245	Article 281
	SECTION 6 – THE EUROPEAN CENTRAL BANK
	Article 282
Article 112 (moved)	Article 283
Article 113 (moved)	Article 284
SECTION 5 – THE COURT OF AUDITORS	SECTION 7 – THE COURT OF AUDITORS
Article 246	Article 285
Article 247	Article 286
Article 248	Article 287
CHAPTER 2 – PROVISIONS COMMON TO SEVERAL INSTITUTIONS	CHAPTER 2 – LEGAL ACTS OF THE UNION, ADOPTION PROCEDURES AND OTHER PROVISIONS
	SECTION 1 – THE LEGAL ACTS OF THE UNION
Article 249	Article 288
	Article 289
	Article 290[1]
	Article 291[1]
	Article 292
	SECTION 2 – PROCEDURES FOR THE ADOPTION OF ACTS AND OTHER PROVISIONS
Article 250	Article 293
Article 251	Article 294
Article 252 (repealed)	
	Article 295
Article 253	Article 296
Article 254	Article 297
	Article 298
Article 255 (moved)	Article 15
Article 256	Article 299
	CHAPTER 3 – THE UNION'S ADVISORY BODIES
	Article 300
CHAPTER 3 – THE ECONOMIC AND SOCIAL COMMITTEE	SECTION 1 – THE ECONOMIC AND SOCIAL COMMITTEE
Article 257 (repealed)[2]	
Article 258, first, second and fourth paragraphs	Article 301
Article 258, third paragraph (repealed)[3]	

[1] Replaces, in substance, the third indent of Article 202 TEC.
[2] Replaced, in substance, by Article 300, paragraph 2 of the TFEU.
[3] Replaced, in substance, by Article 300, paragraph 4 of the TFEU.

Old numbering of the Treaty establishing the European Community	New numbering of the Treaty on the Functioning of the European Union
Article 259	Article 302
Article 260	Article 303
Article 261 (repealed)	
Article 262	Article 304
CHAPTER 4 – THE COMMITTEE OF THE REGIONS	SECTION 2 – THE COMMITTEE OF THE REGIONS
Article 263, first and fifth paragraphs (repealed)[1]	
Article 263, second to fourth paragraphs	Article 305
Article 264	Article 306
Article 265	Article 307
CHAPTER 5 – THE EUROPEAN INVESTMENT BANK	CHAPTER 4 – THE EUROPEAN INVESTMENT BANK
Article 266	Article 308
Article 267	Article 309
TITLE II – FINANCIAL PROVISIONS	TITLE II – FINANCIAL PROVISIONS
Article 268	Article 310
	CHAPTER 1 – THE UNION'S OWN RESOURCES
Article 269	Article 311
Article 270 (repealed)[2]	
	CHAPTER 2 – THE MULTIANNUAL FINANCIAL FRAMEWORK
	Article 312
	CHAPTER 3 – THE UNION'S ANNUAL BUDGET
Article 272, paragraph 1 (moved)	*Article 313*
Article 271 (moved)	*Article 316*
Article 272, paragraph 1 (moved)	Article 313
Article 272, paragraphs 2 to 10	Article 314
Article 273	Article 315
Article 271 (moved)	Article 316
	CHAPTER 4 – IMPLEMENTATION OF THE BUDGET AND DISCHARGE
Article 274	Article 317
Article 275	Article 318
Article 276	Article 319
	CHAPTER 5 – COMMON PROVISIONS
Article 277	Article 320
Article 278	Article 321
Article 279	Article 322
	Article 323
	Article 324

[1] Replaced, in substance, by Article 300, paragraphs 3 and 4, TFEU.
[2] Replaced, in substance, by Article 310, paragraph 4, TFEU.

Old numbering of the Treaty establishing the European Community	New numbering of the Treaty on the Functioning of the European Union
	CHAPTER 6 – COMBATING FRAUD
Article 280	Article 325
	TITLE III – ENHANCED COOPERATION
Articles 11 and 11a (replaced)	Article 326[1]
Articles 11 and 11a (replaced)	Article 327[1]
Articles 11 and 11a (replaced)	Article 328[1]
Articles 11 and 11a (replaced)	Article 329[1]
Articles 11 and 11a (replaced)	Article 330[1]
Articles 11 and 11a (replaced)	Article 331[1]
Articles 11 and 11a (replaced)	Article 332[1]
Articles 11 and 11a (replaced)	Article 333[1]
Articles 11 and 11a (replaced)	Article 334[1]
PART SIX – GENERAL AND FINAL PROVISIONS	**PART SEVEN – GENERAL AND FINAL PROVISIONS**
Article 281 (repealed)[2]	
Article 282	Article 335
Article 283	Article 336
Article 284	Article 337
Article 285	Article 338
Article 286 (replaced)	*Article 16*
Article 287	Article 339
Article 288	Article 340
Article 289	Article 341
Article 290	Article 342
Article 291	Article 343
Article 292	Article 344
Article 293 (repealed)	
Article 294 (moved)	*Article 55*
Article 295	Article 345
Article 296	Article 346
Article 297	Article 347
Article 298	Article 348
Article 299, paragraph 1 (repealed)[3]	
Article 299, paragraph 2, second, third and fourth subparagraphs	Article 349
Article 299, paragraph 2, first subparagraph, and paragraphs 3 to 6 (moved)	*Article 355*
Article 300 (replaced)	*Article 218*
Article 301 (replaced)	*Article 215*
Article 302 (replaced)	*Article 220*
Article 303 (replaced)	*Article 220*
Article 304 (replaced)	*Article 220*

[1] Also replaces the current Articles 27a to 27e, 40 to 40b, and 43 to 45 TEU.
[2] Replaced, in substance, by Article 47 TEU.
[3] Replaced, in substance by Article 52 TEU.

Old numbering of the Treaty establishing the European Community	New numbering of the Treaty on the Functioning of the European Union
Article 305 (repealed)	
Article 306	Article 350
Article 307	Article 351
Article 308	Article 352
	Article 353
Article 309	Article 354
Article 310 (moved)	*Article 217*
Article 311 (repealed)[1]	
Article 299, paragraph 2, first subparagraph, and paragraphs 3 to 6 (moved)	Article 355
Article 312	Article 356
Final Provisions	
Article 313	Article 357
	Article 358
Article 314 (repealed)[2]	

[1] Replaced, in substance by Article 51 TEU.

[2] Replaced, in substance by Article 55 TEU.

THE DEVELOPMENT
OF EUROPEAN INTEGRATION

1 CENTRAL ISSUES

i. EU law is a complex and fascinating subject of study. This book aims to illuminate the EU legal and constitutional processes, and to depict the dynamic relationship between the substantive policies of the European Union, their institutions and procedures, and the Member States. It is important to situate legal doctrine in its historical and political context, and this book seeks to do so. It also seeks to illustrate the strongly dynamic nature of the EU polity, whose aims, policies, institutional structures, and membership have been in a continuous process of development for several decades.

ii. Reference will be made to the 'European Community' to describe the three Communities originally established in the 1950s, even though until the amendments made by the Treaty on European Union (TEU) in 1993, the European Coal and Steel Community (ECSC, which expired in 2002), the Economic Community (EEC), and the European Atomic Energy Community (Euratom) were, properly speaking, the 'Communities'. After the Maastricht Treaty, the EEC was renamed the European Community, whereas the ECSC and the Euratom retained their original titles. The two constituent parts of the Lisbon Treaty, which came into force on 1 December 2009, are the Treaty on European Union, TEU and the Treaty on the Functioning of the European Union (TFEU).

iii. This chapter situates the emergence of the EEC in the tensions produced by nationalism in the first half of the twentieth century. While nationalism could often be a positive force for the good, it also had negative implications, more particularly when it led to use of force to subdue neighbouring states.

iv. The focus then shifts to analysis of the Treaties and the principal Treaty revisions. The ECSC Treaty is examined, followed by the EEC Treaty and the amendments in the Single European Act (SEA), the Maastricht, Amsterdam, and Nice Treaties. The chapter concludes with examination of the failed Constitutional Treaty and the successful conclusion of the Lisbon Treaty. Three themes should be borne in mind when surveying this development.

v. The first is the distinction between institutional and substantive Treaty amendments. Institutional change connotes the relative power within the EU exercised by the principal players, the Council, European Council, Commission, and European Parliament (EP). Institutional change can also impact on the EU's power in relation to the Member States. Substantive Treaty amendment connotes the subject matter over which the EU has competence.

vi.   The second theme is the way in which successive Treaty amendments have made significant changes to the inter-institutional disposition of power within the EU, and to the substantive areas over which it has competence. The relative importance of the forces that shaped these changes continues to be debated by commentators.

vii. The third theme is the enlargement of the EU. The EEC began with six Member States, and there are now twenty-eight. This enlargement has been a factor in shaping institutional and substantive Treaty amendments.

viii. The chapter ends with an overview of theories of integration to explain its evolution. An awareness of these theories is important to understand why states chose to create the EEC and the reasons for subsequent Treaty changes.

2 NATIONALISM AND THE ORIGINS OF THE EU

There is no doubt that viewed from an historical perspective ideas of European unity can be traced to the late seventeenth century, when a prominent English Quaker, William Penn, called for a European Parliament.[1] There is however also little doubt that the more immediate push for European integration can be dated to the nineteenth century. It is worth recalling that, for example, Germany and Italy only became unified states in 1871. A powerful factor in the unification process was the surge in nationalist sentiment, which resonated in politics, philosophy, and literature. It can be traced back to the beginnings of the nineteenth century, in reaction to French dominance of Europe.

There was much that was positive about this nationalist sentiment, which was initially directed towards attainment of unified states from disparate principalities, combined with the desire to be rid of foreign control. It was driven by the strong feeling that those who shared a common language and culture should naturally coexist in a single political entity, the corollary being that pre-existing boundaries between principalities were 'unnatural'.

The darker side of nationalism became apparent towards the end of the nineteenth and the beginning of the twentieth centuries. It was driven in part by economic imperatives, but in part also by the desire to assert the prominence of a particular national identity. The battles were initially fought on borrowed terrain, with the main nation states in Europe engaged in the carving up of Africa. The First and Second World Wars brought the clash of nation states to the very forefront of the European stage. While there is considerable debate about the causes of both conflicts, the aggressive effect of nationalism was a significant factor in this regard.

The culmination of the Second World War generated a widespread feeling that there had to be a way of organizing international affairs so as to reduce, if not eradicate, the possibility of such conflict recurring on this scale. This explains the founding of the United Nations in 1945, where the guiding rationale was to provide a forum in which disputes could be resolved through dialogue, rather than conflict, and to institutionalize a regime of international peacekeeping where force was required.

The founding of the EEC was another response to the horrors of two World Wars, although it was to be over a decade before it became a reality. During the war, the Resistance movement had strongly supported the idea of a united Europe, to replace the destructive forces of nationalism.[2] However, the integration movement faltered after the war, especially after the electoral defeat in the UK of

---

[1] D Urwin, *The Community of Europe: A History of European Integration* (Longman, 2nd edn, 1995); J Pinder and S Usherwood, *The European Union: A Very Short Introduction* (Oxford University Press, 3rd edn, 2013).

[2] W Lipgens (ed), *Documents of the History of European Integration* (European University Institute, 1985).

Churchill, who had been a strong proponent of European unity. There were nonetheless other moves towards European cooperation. The USA in 1947 introduced the Marshall Plan to provide financial aid for Europe, which was administered in 1948 by the Organisation for European Economic Co-operation (OEEC) and in 1960 the Organisation for Economic Co-operation and Development (OECD). Cooperation in defence was furthered by the creation of the North Atlantic Treaty Organization (NATO) in 1948 and the Western European Union (WEU) in 1954. The Statute on the Council of Europe was signed in 1949, providing for a Committee of Ministers and a Parliamentary Assembly. The international organization is best known for the European Convention on Human Rights (ECHR), which was signed in 1950 and came into force in 1953. We can now consider the more concrete moves towards the founding of the EEC.

3 FROM THE ECSC TO THE EEC

(A) ECSC: EUROPEAN COAL AND STEEL COMMUNITY

The UK was unwilling to participate in potentially far-reaching plans for European integration in 1948, and this led to more modest proposals advanced by the French Foreign Minister, Robert Schuman, that France and Germany should administer their coal and steel resources pursuant to an international agreement in which supervisory authority was given to a body termed the High Authority. The plan had been drafted by Jean Monnet, a committed federalist. The proposal was framed so that other states could also join the international agreement. The focus on coal and steel was in part economic, but also in part political. Coal and steel were still the principal materials for waging war. Placing production of such material under an international body was therefore consciously designed to assuage fears that Germany might covertly rearm. It was hoped thereby to bring Germany back into the mainstream European fold, since the political architecture in Europe had changed after 1945, with Russian dominance of Eastern Europe and the emergence of the cold war.

The ECSC Treaty was signed in 1951 by France, Germany, Italy, Belgium, the Netherlands, and Luxembourg. It had a lifespan of fifty years to expire in 2002 and established a common market in coal and steel. There were four principal institutions. The High Authority, composed of nine independent appointees of the six Member State governments, was the main executive institution with decision-making power; an Assembly made up of national parliaments' delegates had supervisory and advisory powers; a Council composed of a representative from each national government had limited decision-making powers and a broader consultative role; and the Court of Justice composed of nine judges. Its proponents saw the ECSC as a supranational authority, in which the High Authority could adopt decisions other than by unanimity, which could then serve as a step towards broader European integration.[3]

(B) EUROPEAN DEFENCE COMMUNITY AND EUROPEAN POLITICAL COMMUNITY: EDC AND EPC

The 1950s also witnessed setbacks in the moves towards European integration, which were nonetheless important in the overall story of the creation of the EEC. The proposals that failed were those for the European Defence Community (EDC) and the European Political Community (EPC).

---

[3] F Duchêne, *Jean Monnet: The First Statesman of Interdependence* (Norton, 1994) 239.

The proposal for the EDC had its origins in French opposition to German membership of NATO. The French alternative outlined in the Pleven Plan in 1950 was for the EDC, which would have a European army, a common budget, and joint institutions. The EDC Treaty was signed in 1952 by the six ECSC States, but Britain refused to participate. It was felt that a European army required some form of European foreign policy, and this was the catalyst for plans to establish the EPC.

The 1953 EPC draft statute was crafted by the ECSC Assembly as reinforced by certain additional members, with the principal work done by a Constitutional Committee. It produced far-reaching plans for a federal, parliamentary-style form of European integration, with a bicameral ('two-level') parliament, one chamber elected by direct universal suffrage, and the other senate-type body appointed by national parliaments. The parliament would have real legislative power. There was also to be an Executive Council, which would have been the government of the EPC, with responsibility to the Parliament. The draft statute contained provision for a Court of Justice and an Economic and Social Council. Although the draft received almost unanimous support in the ECSC Assembly, the reaction of the six foreign ministers of the ECSC was more circumspect, and there was significant opposition to the degree of parliamentary power that existed under the draft EPC statute.

The fate of the EPC was however inextricably linked with that of the EDC. The latter failed when the French National Assembly refused to ratify the EDC in 1954, opposition coming from both the French right and left wings.[4] This resulted in a major setback for the integration process and the shelving of plans for defence and political union.

(c) EUROPEAN ECONOMIC COMMUNITY: EEC

Movement towards European integration was not, however, halted by the failure of the EDC/EPC. The demise of these ambitious projects led proponents of European integration to focus more directly on the economic rather than the political, while drawing on ideas discussed when the EPC was drafted. Thus the Netherlands had sought to include in the EPC proposals the idea of a common market. This was felt to be too risky for several countries in the early 1950s, since they had protectionist traditions, but the idea resurfaced in discussions about the EEC. A conference of foreign ministers of the six Member States of the ECSC was held in Messina in Italy in 1955. A committee chaired by Paul-Henri Spaak, Belgian Prime Minister and a strong advocate of integration, published its report in 1956, which contained the basic plan for what became the Euratom and the EEC. The underlying long-term objective may well have been political, but the initial focus was nonetheless economic. There was no temporal limit to the EEC Treaty: the Treaty of Rome was signed in March 1957 and came into effect in January 1958. There were six Member States: France, Germany, the Netherlands, Belgium, Italy, and Luxembourg. The same Member States were signatories of the Euratom Treaty, which came into effect at the same time as the EEC Treaty.

In economic terms, the idea of a common market connotes the removal of barriers to trade, such as tariffs, which increase the cost of imports, or quotas, which limit the number of imports of a certain type of product. These barriers to trade were to be abolished and a common customs tariff was to be set up. The common market was to be established over a transitional period of several stages, but it connoted more than the removal of tariffs and quotas. It entailed also the free movement of the economic factors of production in order to ensure that they were being used most efficiently throughout the Community as a whole. This explains the centrality to the Community

---

[4] J Pinder, *The Building of the European Union* (Oxford University Press, 3rd edn, 1998).

of the 'four freedoms', which are often regarded as the core of its economic constitution: free movement of goods, workers, capital, and establishment and the provision of services. The idea was therefore that if, for example, a worker could not obtain a job in a particular country, because unemployment levels were high, he or she should be able to move freely within the EEC to search for employment within another country where there might be an excess of demand over supply of labour, with the consequence that the value of the labour resource within the Community as a whole was enhanced. The Treaty also contained key provisions to ensure that the idea of a level playing field was not undermined by the anti-competitive actions of private parties, or by national action that favoured domestic industry. The Rome Treaty was in addition designed to approximate the economic policies of the Member States, to promote harmonious development of economic activities throughout the Community, to increase stability and raise the standard of living, and to promote closer relations between the Member States. There were common policies in agriculture and transport. A European Social Fund was established to improve employment opportunities, and an Investment Bank to give loans and guarantees and to help less developed regions or sectors. A European Development Fund for overseas countries and territories of some of the Member States was also established.

In institutional terms, the Rome Treaty was a mixture of continuity with the past in terms of the institutional ordering under the ECSC, combined with novel arrangements devised for the EEC. The Parliamentary Assembly and the Court of Justice were shared with the ECSC. There was, however, a separate Council of Ministers consisting of a national representative from each Member State, which represented its interest in the Council, and a separate executive authority, the Commission, which was composed of members drawn from the Member States, who had an obligation of independence and who were to represent the Community rather than the national interest. It was not until the Merger Treaty 1965 that these institutions were merged and shared by the three Communities. An Economic and Social Committee with advisory status was set up, to be shared with the Euratom Community.

The location of legislative and executive power was crucial to the Rome Treaty. It will be recalled that the draft statute for the EPC had been parliamentary in its orientation. It will be recalled also that this aroused considerable opposition from the Member States of the ECSC. The same unwillingness to accord power to parliamentary institutions was evident in the Rome Treaty. The reality was that legislative power was divided between the Commission, which proposed legislative initiatives, and the Council of Ministers, which voted on them. The Parliamentary Assembly, which changed its name to the European Parliament in 1962, although it was not officially so named until the SEA 1986, had a bare right to be consulted, and that was only where a particular Treaty Article mandated such consultation. Voting procedure varied according to the nature of the issue: in some limited instances voting was by simple majority, in many others it was by 'qualified majority', while in yet others unanimity was required. Where qualified-majority voting applied, voting in the Council was weighted to give greater weight to the larger Member States than the smaller, although the weighting was not perfectly proportional.

Executive power was also divided in the original Rome Treaty. The Commission was accorded the role of 'watchdog' to ensure that Member States complied with the Treaty; it had responsibility to ensure that regulations, directives, and decisions enacted pursuant to the Treaty were effectively implemented; and it was the principal negotiator of international agreements on behalf of the Community. The Council nonetheless exercised certain executive responsibilities in relation to, for example, the conclusion of international agreements, the planning of the overall policy agenda, and the Community budget. The Assembly was also given some power over the budget, and in addition possessed a strong but never-used power of censure, despite the tabling of many motions of censure over the years, including one shortly before the dramatic resignation of the Commission in 1999.[5]

4 FROM EEC TO THE SINGLE EUROPEAN ACT

(A) TENSIONS WITHIN THE EEC

The Rome Treaty provided the legal framework for the EEC for almost thirty years, subject to the Merger Treaty 1965, which came into effect in 1967, and which merged the executive organs of the ECSC, Euratom, and the EEC. This is all the more remarkable given that the years after the SEA saw an almost continuous process of Treaty reform.[6] There were nonetheless important developments in the period between the EEC Treaty and the SEA.

The Community expanded through accession of new Member States. The UK had chosen to remain outside the EEC when it was initially established. It made its first application to join in 1961, but the French President, Charles de Gaulle, vetoed UK membership in 1963, and also a second UK application in 1967. It was not until de Gaulle's resignation that Britain's application for membership was accepted, together with those of Ireland and Denmark in 1973. Greece became a member of the EEC in 1981, followed by Spain and Portugal in 1986.

The almost thirty-year period between the EEC and the SEA revealed tensions between an *intergovernmental* view of the Community, championed initially by President de Gaulle of France, in which state interests were regarded as paramount, and a more *supranational* perspective espoused initially by Walter Hallstein, the Commission President, in which the overall Community good was perceived as the primary objective, even if this required sacrifice by particular Member States. The tension surfaced in 1965, at the time when the transitional provisions of the Treaty dictated a move from unanimous to qualified-majority voting in the Council, which would have affected many, although not all, areas of decision-making. De Gaulle objected to a Commission proposal that the Community should be able to raise its own resources from agricultural levies and external tariffs, rather than national contributions.[7] When compromise in the Council proved impossible, France refused to attend further Council meetings and adopted what became known as the 'empty-chair' policy. This lasted for seven months, from June 1965 until January 1966, after which a settlement was reached, which became known as the Luxembourg Compromise or the Luxembourg Accords. It was essentially an agreement to disagree over voting methods in the Council. The French asserted that even in cases where the Treaty provided for majority decision-making, discussion must continue until unanimity was reached whenever important national interests were at stake. The other five Member States declared instead that in such circumstances the Council would 'endeavour, within a reasonable time, to reach solutions which can be adopted by all'.[8] It seems nonetheless that the French view prevailed, such that if a state pleaded that its 'very important interests' were at stake, then this was akin to a veto, which the other Member States would respect.

The period between the EEC Treaty and the SEA also saw other developments that enhanced Member State power over decision-making and intergovernmentalism. In 1970 the Davignon Report

---

[5] K Bradley, 'The Institutional Law of the EU in 1999' (1999/2000) 19 YBEL 547, 584.

[6] B de Witte, 'The Closest Thing to a Constitutional Conversation in Europe: The Semi-Permanent Treaty Revision Process' in P Beaumont, C Lyons, and N Walker (eds), *Convergence and Divergence in European Public Law* (Hart, 2002) ch 3.

[7] The EEC achieved its own resources through the Treaty of Luxembourg 1970 (known as 'the first budgetary treaty'), which entered into force in 1971.

[8] Bull EC 3–1966, 9.

recommended the holding of quarterly meetings of the foreign ministers of the Member States, which became an intergovernmental forum for co-operation in foreign policy. In 1973 this became known as European Political Co-operation, which enabled the EEC to be represented as one voice in other international organizations in which all Member States participated, but also enhanced intergovernmentalism.

In 1974 the European Council was established to regularize the practice of holding summits. This body consists of the heads of government of the Member States, with the President of the Commission attending its bi-annual meetings. The European Council's 'summitry' provided the Community with much-needed direction, but represented to some a weakening in the supranational elements of the Community. The European Council was not within the framework created by the Treaties, and it was not until the SEA that it was recognized in a formal instrument. The EPC and the European Council enabled Member State interests at the highest level to impact on matters of political or economic concern, and their decisions, while not formally binding, would normally constitute the frame within which binding Community initiatives would be pursued. The Member States also assumed greater control over the detail of Community secondary legislation, through the creation of what became known as Comitology. This enabled Member States to influence secondary Community legislation in a way that had not been envisaged in the original EEC Treaty.

There were however also developments during the period between the EEC and the SEA that enhanced supranationalism. Thus 1976 saw agreement on direct elections to the Assembly, and the first such elections took place in 1979. It provided the EEC with a direct electoral mandate that it had lacked hitherto, but the downside was that voter turnout was low, and elections were often fought on national rather than Community issues. The supranational dimension to the Community was more unequivocally enhanced by developments relating to resources and the budget. In 1969 agreement was reached on funding from the Community's own resources rather than from national contributions, and on the expansion of the Parliament's role in the budgetary process. This thereby gave the Community greater financial independence and strengthened Parliament's role as a decision-maker. These developments were furthered in 1975 when a second budgetary treaty was adopted. The European Court of Justice (ECJ) also made important contributions to the supranational dynamic of the Community during this period.[9] It used the doctrine of direct effect in the 1960s and 1970s to make Community policies more effective. It interpreted Treaty provisions broadly in order to foster the overall aims of the Community, such as the free movement of goods. It created the supremacy of Community law over national law to reinforce these judicial strategies.

While there were positive developments relating to the Community from a supranational perspective, it was nonetheless the case that the decade from the mid-1970s to the mid-1980s was perceived as a period of relative political stagnation in the EEC. This was epitomized by the Commission's difficulty in securing the passage of legislation through the Council, with the consequence that Community objectives were left unfulfilled.[10] The malaise was recognized in high-level reports from the mid-1970s onwards, such as the Tindemans Report 1974–5 and that of the 'Three Wise Men' in 1978,[11] both of which recommended strengthening the supranational elements of the Community, but neither was acted on. This theme is evident in the following extract.

[9] J Weiler, 'The Transformation of Europe' (1991) 100 Yale LJ 2403.

[10] P Dankert, 'The EC—Past, Present and Future' in L Tsoukalis (ed), *The EC: Past, Present and Future* (Basil Blackwell, 1983) 7.

[11] Bull EC 11–1979, 1.5.2.

P Dankert, The EC—Past, Present and Future[12]

The dialectics of co-operation or integration have also continued to dominate the process of European unification—to an increasing extent—ever since 25th March 1957. It has been a continuous 'to and fro' for years, as can be seen from the course of development of the Community institutions. The Council of Ministers, which was originally intended to be a Community body, has now become largely an intergovernmental institution thanks to the famous Luxembourg Agreement, which, under French pressure, put an end to the majority decisions which the Council was supposed to take according to the Treaty on proposals submitted by the European Commission. This rule that decisions could only be taken unanimously had the effect of gradually transforming the Commission into a kind of secretariat for the Council which carefully checked its proposals with national officials before deciding whether or not to submit them. This in turn has a negative effect on the European Parliament which can only reach for power, under the Treaty, via the Commission. The move towards intergovernmental solutions for Community problems reached its peak—after frustrated attempts such as the Fouchet plan at the beginning of the 60s—in the creation of the European Council, the EPC and the EMS.

The European Parliament proposed radical reform in 1984 in a 'Draft Treaty on European Union', but it too was largely ignored. The catalyst for change finally came from a meeting of the heads of state in the Fontainebleau European Council in 1984. This led the 1985 European Council in Milan to establish an intergovernmental conference (IGC) to discuss Treaty amendment, and this generated the SEA. The impetus for reform was furthered by an extensive Commission 'White Paper' that set a timetable for completion of the internal market before 1992.[13]

(B) SINGLE EUROPEAN ACT: SEA

(i) *Institutional and Substantive Change*

The SEA 1986 was a disappointment to those who advocated sweeping reform. It nonetheless had a far-reaching significance, and still ranks as one of the most significant Treaty revisions in the EU's history because of the institutional and substantive changes that it introduced.

The most significant *institutional change* was that the SEA began the transformation in the role of the European Parliament. The Rome Treaty gave it scant powers, and its role in the legislative process was minimal, being limited to a right to be consulted where a particular Treaty Article so mandated. The change made by the SEA might at the time have appeared relatively minimal. A new legislative procedure was created, the 'cooperation' procedure, which applied to a defined list of Treaty Articles. It transformed the Community decision-making process. Prior to the SEA, the approach to the passage of legislation was captured by the aphorism that the 'Commission proposes, and the Council disposes', revealing the Commission's role as initiator of legislation and the Council's role in voting on such measures. The change in the SEA meant that the Commission would have to take seriously the views of the European Parliament where the cooperation procedure applied. The enactment of legislation required input from three players, not two, since the cooperation procedure meant that the European Parliament could in effect block legislative proposals provided that it had some limited support in the Council.

---

[12] L Tsoukalis (ed), *The EC: Past, Present and Future* (Basil Blackwell, 1983) 7.
[13] COM(85) 310.

There were also other institutional changes. The SEA gave a legal basis to EPC and formal recognition to the European Council, although not within the Community Treaties. A Court of First Instance (CFI) was created to assist the Court of Justice. The so-called 'Comitology' procedure, under which the Council delegates powers to the Commission on certain conditions, was formally included within what was Article 202 EC.[14]

The impact of the cooperation procedure was enhanced because of the *substantive changes* made by the SEA, in particular the creation of what was initially Article 100a EEC, which confers broad power on the EU to adopt legislation concerning the internal market. The completion of a common market requires not merely that trade barriers are prohibited, what is termed negative integration, but also that there should be European regulation of certain issues *in place of* national regulation, what is termed positive integration or harmonization. The latter is required because each country will have rules on, for example, banking that express important public interests, such as the prevention of fraud. These national rules cannot be eradicated, but their very multiplicity can hamper the creation of a common market, because traders will have to satisfy a different set of such rules in each Member State, thereby adding significantly to the costs of business. A way to meet this difficulty is to have Community rules on such issues. This was recognized in the original Rome Treaty, but Article 100 EEC required unanimity in the Council, which was difficult to secure. This was the rationale for Article 100a EEC, now Article 114 TFEU, which provided for the enactment of measures to approximate the laws of the Member States for this purpose. The cooperation procedure was applicable to this Article, thereby enhancing the EP's power, and voting within the Council was by qualified majority, rather than unanimity. The SEA amended the Rome Treaty to provide that the Community should adopt measures with the aim of 'progressively establishing the internal market over a period expiring on 31 December 1992', and defined the internal market as 'an area without internal frontiers in which the free movement of goods, persons, services and capital is ensured'.[15] What is now Article 114 TFEU became the principal vehicle for the enactment of measures to complete the internal market through legislation approximating Member State laws.

The SEA also added new substantive areas of Community competence, some of which had already been asserted by the institutions and supported by the Court, without any express Treaty basis. The additions covered cooperation in economic and monetary union, social policy, economic and social cohesion, research and technological development, and environmental policy.

(ii) *Reaction and Assessment*

The SEA represented the most important revision of the Treaties since they were first adopted, and heralded a revival of the Community momentum towards integration. The initial response to the SEA was nonetheless mixed. Some saw it as a positive step forward for the Community after a period of malaise. Others, such as Pescatore, formerly a judge on the ECJ, regarded it as a setback for the integration process.[16] Yet others stressed what was achieved under the SEA in combination with the Commission's White Paper.[17]

---

[14] The legal regime for dealing with these measures was altered by the Lisbon Treaty, Arts 290–291 TFEU.
[15] Art 8a EEC.
[16] P Pescatore, 'Some Critical Remarks on the Single European Act' (1987) 24 CMLRev 9.
[17] White Paper on the Completion of the Internal Market, COM(85) 310.

J Weiler, The Transformation of Europe[18]

Clearly, the new European Parliament and the Commission were far from thrilled with the new act.

And yet, with the hindsight of just three years, it has become clear that 1992 and the SEA do constitute an eruption of significant proportions. Some of the evidence is very transparent. First, for the first time since the very early years of the Community, if ever, the Commission plays the political role clearly intended for it by the Treaty of Rome. In stark contrast to its nature during the foundational period in the 1970s and early 1980s, the Commission in large measure both sets the Community agenda and acts as a power broker in the legislative process.

Second, the decisionmaking process takes much less time. Dossiers that would have languished and in some cases did languish in impotence for years in the Brussels corridors now emerge as legislation often in a matter of months.

For the first time, the interdependence of the policy areas at the new-found focal point of power in Brussels creates a dynamic resembling the almost forgotten predictions of neo-functionalist spillover. The ever-widening scope of the legislative and policy agenda of the Community manifests this dynamic.

The SEA thus helped to 'kick-start' fulfilment of the Community's economic objectives, more especially through the new Article 100a EC. Moreover, while the SEA was characterized primarily by its 'single market' aims, and while the new provisions on regional policy, the environment, and research might be regarded as secondary, the reality was that these changes created Community competence in these fields. This reinforced the views of those who conceived of the single market project in terms of 'a true common marketplace, which, because of the inevitable connection between the social and the economic in modern political economies, would ultimately yield the much vaunted "ever closer union of the peoples of Europe"'.[19] The debate between those on different sides of the political spectrum, between a neo-liberal conception of the EU and the 'European social model', continues to this day.

5 FROM THE SEA TO THE NICE TREATY

(A) MAASTRICHT TREATY: THE TREATY ON EUROPEAN UNION

The SEA reinvigorated the Community and many measures to complete the internal market were enacted between 1986 and 1992. It would nonetheless be mistaken to think that the internal market could be 'completed' by 1992, or any particular date thereafter. This is because factors such as technological change, industrial innovation, and changing patterns of consumer behaviour can generate the need for new EU measures to reduce obstacles to inter-state trade. The momentum generated by the SEA continued after its adoption. A committee chaired by the President of the Commission, Jacques Delors, on Economic and Monetary Union (EMU) reported in 1989 and set out a three-stage plan for reaching EMU. The European Council held an IGC on the subject, and a second IGC on political union. This led to a draft Treaty in 1991 and the Treaty on European Union (TEU) was signed by the Member States in Maastricht in February 1992.[20] It entered into force in November 1993 having survived constitutional challenge before the German Federal Constitutional Court.[21]

---

[18] Weiler (n 9) 2454.
[19] Ibid 2458.
[20] R Corbett, *The Treaty of Maastricht* (Longman, 1993).
[21] Cases 2 BvR 2134/92 and 2159/92 *Brunner v The European Union Treaty* [1994] 1 CMLR 57.

(i) *The Three-Pillar System*

The TEU made important changes to the Rome Treaty, in both institutional and substantive terms. It was also significant in terms of the overall legal architecture, because it introduced the 'three-pillar' structure for the European Union, with the Communities as the first of these pillars, and the EEC Treaty was officially renamed the European Community (EC) Treaty.[22] The Second Pillar dealt with Common Foreign and Security Policy (CFSP) and built on earlier mechanisms for European Political Cooperation. The Third Pillar dealt with Justice and Home Affairs (JHA) and built on earlier initiatives in this area. The pillar structure was preserved in subsequent Treaty amendments, but was then removed by the Lisbon Treaty, although distinct rules still apply to the CFSP. Title I of the TEU contained common provisions, which laid down basic principles for the 'Union', and set out its objectives.[23]

The European Union was therefore given new responsibilities in relation to CFSP and JHA. The key issue is therefore why these new competences were not added to those already existing, as had been done in earlier Treaty amendments. The principal rationale for creating separate Pillars for the CFSP and JHA was as follows. The Member States wished for some mechanism through which they could cooperate in relation to CFSP and JHA, since in its absence such meetings would have to be set up to discuss each new problem. This was time-consuming and cumbersome. The Member States were not, however, willing to subject these areas to the normal supranational methods of decision-making that characterized the Community Pillar. They did not wish the Commission and the ECJ to have the powers they had under the Community Pillar, because the Second and Third Pillars concerned sensitive areas of policy considered to be at the core of national sovereignty. Thus decision-making under the Second and Third Pillars was more intergovernmental, with the Member States in the Council and European Council retaining the primary reins of power. The other Community institutions, the Commission, European Parliament, and ECJ, either had no role or one that was much reduced by way of comparison with the Community Pillar.

(ii) *Institutional and Substantive Change: The Community Treaties*

The Maastricht Treaty made a number of *institutional* changes to the Rome Treaty, the most significant being further increase in the Parliament's legislative involvement, by introducing the co-decision procedure, which was amended and strengthened by the Treaty of Amsterdam. This allowed the EP to block legislation, if it was subject to this procedure. The Parliament was also given the right to request the Commission to initiate legislation and the power to block the appointment of the new Commission. There were other significant institutional changes: provision was made for a European System of Central Banks (ESCB) and a European Central Bank (ECB) to oversee economic and monetary union; for a Parliamentary Ombudsman; and for a 'Committee of the Regions'.

The Maastricht Treaty also made significant *substantive changes*. It established the principle of subsidiarity. It was introduced to alleviate fears that the EC was becoming too 'federal' by distinguishing areas where action was best taken at Community level and national level.[24] A new concept of European citizenship was introduced, which was to become a fertile source for ECJ case law.[25] There were new provisions on economic and monetary union,[26] which laid the foundations for the

---

[22] D Curtin, 'The Constitutional Structure of the Union: A Europe of Bits and Pieces' (1993) 30 CMLRev 17.

[23] There were originally seven titles in the TEU: Title I included the 'common provisions', which set out the basic objectives of the TEU. Titles II, III, and IV covered the First Pillar amendments to the EEC, ECSC, and Euratom Treaties respectively. Title V created the Second Pillar of the CFSP, Title VI the Third Pillar of JHA, and Title VII contained the final provisions.

[24] Art 5 EC.

[25] Arts 17–21 EC.

[26] Arts 98–124 EC.

introduction of the single currency.[27] The Maastricht Treaty also, like the SEA, added new areas of competence to the EC, with new titles added in areas such as culture, public health, consumer protection, trans-European networks, and development cooperation, and significant modifications made in relation to the titles on, for example, the environment.

(iii) *Common Foreign and Security Policy*

The CFSP Pillar created by the Maastricht Treaty was distinct from the Community institutional and legal structure, such that decision-making was more intergovernmental and less supranational than under the Community Pillar. The CFSP Pillar established the objectives of EU action in this area, which included preservation of peace and international security, respect for human rights, and development of democracy. The Member States had an obligation to inform and consult each other on any matter of common foreign and security policy that was of general interest, in order to ensure that their combined influence could be exercised as effectively as possible, through concerted action.

Provision was made for the Council to define a 'common position' for the Member States on such issues. It was, however, the European Council, consisting of the heads of state and government of the Member States, which was to define the principles and general guidelines for the common foreign and security policy, with the Council having responsibility for decisions to implement it. The CFSP included all questions related to the security of the Union, including the eventual framing of a common defence policy. While decision-making was concentrated in the hands of institutions in which Member State interests predominated, the Council and the European Council, there was nonetheless provision for the European Parliament to be kept informed about foreign and security policy, and the Commission was to be fully associated with work in this area.

(iv) *Justice and Home Affairs*

The JHA Pillar originally governed policies such as asylum, immigration, and 'third country' (non-EU) nationals, which were integrated into the EC Treaty by the Treaty of Amsterdam. However, prior to the Lisbon Treaty the Third Pillar also included cooperation on a range of international crime issues and various forms of judicial, customs, and police cooperation, including the establishment of a European Police Office (Europol) for exchanging information. National sensitivity about such issues meant that the Member States were not willing for them to be included within the ordinary Community Pillar and be subject to the supranational rules on decision-making. Decision-making was dominated by the Council, and the ECJ's powers were limited. The Lisbon Treaty has now brought the entirety of what was the Third Pillar into the general fabric of the Treaty.[28]

(v) *Reaction and Assessment*

The TEU, like the SEA before it, was extensively analysed and criticized. The obscurity and secrecy of the negotiation processes, the complexity of the new 'Union' structure, the mixed bag of institutional reforms, the borrowing of Community institutions for the intergovernmental pillar policy-making, and the many opt-outs and exceptions (the 'variable geometry') attracted much critical comment. The perceived loss of unity and coherence of the Community legal order and the likely effect on the *acquis*

---

[27] J Pipkorn, 'Legal Arrangements in the Treaty of Maastricht for the Effectiveness of the Economic and Monetary Union' (1994) 31 CMLRev 263.
[28] Arts 67–89 TFEU.

communautaire, which had bound all Member States to the same body of legal rules and principles, is addressed in the following extract.

D Curtin, The Constitutional Structure of the Union: A Europe of Bits and Pieces[29]

The result of the Maastricht summit is an umbrella Union threatening to lead to constitutional chaos; the potential victims are the cohesiveness and the unity and the concomitant power of a legal system painstakingly constructed over the course of some 30 odd years.... And, of course, it does contain some elements of real *progress* (co-decision and powers of control for the European Parliament, increased Community competences, sanctions against recalcitrant Member States, Community 'citizenship', EMU etc.) but a *process* of integration, if it has any meaning at all, implies that you can't take one step forward and two steps backwards at the same time. Built into the principle of an 'ever closer union among the peoples of Europe' is the notion that integration should only be one way.

It must be said, at the heart of all this chaos and fragmentation, the unique *sui generis* nature of the European Community, its true world-historical significance, is being destroyed. The whole future and credibility of the Communities as a cohesive legal unit which confers rights on individuals and which enters into their national legal systems as an integral part of those systems, is at stake.

It was evident with hindsight that the 'variable geometry', differentiation, or flexibility, which appeared in several forms in the Maastricht TEU[30] and which was perceived as undermining the cohesiveness and unity of the Community order, was not a temporary feature of European integration. The attraction of flexible or differentiated integration grew, and both the Amsterdam and Nice Treaties consolidated this trend in provisions on 'closer cooperation' and 'enhanced cooperation'.[31] The variety of labels describes a range of related ideas, including the possibility that some states may participate in certain policies while other do not, or that some will participate only partially, or possibly at a later date than others.[32] While the disadvantages of variable geometry may be a perceived lack of unity and increasing fragmentation (the dangers of '*à la carte*' integration), the advantages of providing a means for accommodating difference and reaching consensus in the face of strong divergence, for permitting progress in crucial areas such as EMU or foreign policy which might otherwise be deadlocked, are evidently considered sufficient to outweigh the former.[33]

---

[29] Curtin (n 22) 67.

[30] Examples of differentiated integration introduced by the Maastricht Treaty were the UK's opt-out from what was then the Social Policy Chapter, the exemption from defence policy provisions of Member States which are neutral or were not full WEU members, and the option for the UK and Denmark to decide later whether to join the arrangements for Economic and Monetary Union. See, for earlier discussion, C-D Ehlermann, 'How Flexible is Community Law? An Unusual Approach to the Concept of "Two Speeds"' (1984) 82 Mich LR 1274.

[31] C-D Ehlermann, 'Differentiation, Flexibility, Closer Cooperation: The New Provisions of the Amsterdam Treaty' (1998) 4 ELJ 246; J Shaw, 'The Treaty of Amsterdam: Challenges of Flexibility and Legitimacy' (1998) 4 ELJ 63; E Philippart and G Edwards, 'The Provisions on Closer Co-operation in the Treaty of Amsterdam: The Politics of Flexibility in the European Union' (1998) 37 JCMS 87; H Bribosia, 'Les coopérations renforcées au lendemain du traité de Nice' [2001] Revue du droit de l'Union européenne 111.

[32] J Usher, 'Variable Geometry or Concentric Circles: Patterns for the EU' (1997) 46 ICLQ 243; A Stubb, 'Differentiated Integration' (1996) 34 JCMS 283; G de Búrca and J Scott (eds), *Constitutional Change in the EU: From Uniformity to Flexibility* (Hart, 2000); B de Witte, D Hanf, and E Vos (eds), *The Many Faces of Differentiation in EU Law* (Intersentia, 2001).

[33] A Kolliker, 'Bringing Together or Driving Apart the Union?: Towards a Theory of Differentiated Integration' (2001) 24 WEP 125.

(B) THE TREATY OF AMSTERDAM

(i) *Institutional and Substantive Change*

The process of Treaty amendment did not halt other important developments. Membership of the EU expanded shortly after the Maastricht Treaty, with Austria, Sweden, and Finland joining in 1995. An accession agreement was also negotiated with Norway, but a national referendum opposed membership of the EU, as it had done in 1973. An Agreement on the European Economic Area (EEA) was also made between the EC and the states that were party to the European Free Trade Association (EFTA), and came into force in 1994.[34]

The ink was nonetheless scarcely dry on the Maastricht Treaty before plans were made for an IGC between the Member States that would pave the way for the next round of Treaty reform, which was the Treaty of Amsterdam. It was signed in 1997 and came into effect on 1 May 1999. It was intended to prepare the Union for enlargement through accession of East European countries, but this issue was postponed until the Nice Treaty. The result was that the Treaty of Amsterdam was a modest exercise in Treaty reform, but it did delete obsolete provisions from the EC Treaty, and renumber all the Articles, titles, and sections of the TEU and the EC Treaty.

The 1990s saw a surge of debate, political and academic, concerning the *legitimacy of the EU*. This is the rationale for amendments introduced by the Amsterdam Treaty designed to enhance the EU's legitimacy. The principle of openness was added, such that decisions were to be taken 'as openly as possible' and as closely as possible to the citizen.[35] Promotion of a high level of employment and the establishment of the area of 'freedom, security and justice' were added to the EU's objectives.[36] There were amendments the effect of which was that the Union was said to be founded on respect for human rights, democracy, and the rule of law.[37] Respect for these principles was a condition for EU membership.[38] On a related note, the Amsterdam Treaty declared that the EU should respect the fundamental rights protected in the European Convention on Human Rights (ECHR) and in national constitutions,[39] and there was provision that if the Council found a 'serious and persistent breach' by a Member State of principles concerning the rule of law, human rights, and democracy, it could suspend some of that state's rights under the Treaty.[40]

The *institutional changes* made by the Amsterdam Treaty were largely an extension of a reform process begun with the SEA. The co-decision procedure was amended to increase the European Parliament's power and the number of Treaty Articles to which it was applicable was expanded. The cooperation procedure introduced by the SEA was virtually eliminated, apart from provisions on EMU. The increase in the EP's power was also evident in the amendment whereby its assent was required for appointment of the Commission President.[41] There were moreover changes designed to enhance the Community's legitimacy in relation to its citizens.

---

[34] It provided for free-movement provisions similar to those in the EC Treaty, analogous rules on competition policy, and 'close co-operation' in other policy areas, having been declared compatible with the EC Treaty by the ECJ, *Opinion 1/91* [1991] ECR 6079; *Opinion 1/92* [1992] ECR I-2821; J Forman, 'The EEA Agreement Five Years On: Dynamic Homogeneity in Practice and its Implementation by the Two EEA Courts' (1999) 36 CMLRev 751. Since 1995, the non-EU parties to the EEA have been Iceland, Norway, and Liechtenstein. One country (Switzerland) remains a member of EFTA, but decided not to join the EEA; it has however entered into a number of separate bilateral treaties with the EU.

[35] Art 1 EU.

[36] Art 2 EU.

[37] Art 6 EU.

[38] Art 49 EU.

[39] Art 6(2) EU. This was subject to judicial oversight through Art 46 EU.

[40] Art 7 EU.

[41] Art 214(2) EC.

The same continuity with the past was evident in the trajectory of *substantive changes* concerning the scope of Community power. This was, as with the SEA and the Maastricht Treaty, further enhanced through the addition of new heads of competence, or the modification of existing heads.[42] There was also a new provision that conferred legislative competence on the Community to combat discrimination based on sex, racial or ethnic origin, religion or belief, disability, age, or sexual orientation.[43]

The Treaty of Amsterdam also *amended the Second and Third Pillars*. The changes made to the Second Pillar were modest, including the fact that the Secretary-General of the Council was nominated as 'High Representative' for the CFSP to assist the Council Presidency, and the Council was given power to 'conclude' international agreements,[44] whenever this was necessary in implementing the CFSP.

The changes made to the Third Pillar were more significant. The decision-making structure had been criticized on the ground that many JHA policies were unsuited to the intergovernmental processes established. The consequence was that those parts of JHA dealing with visas, asylum, immigration, and other aspects of free movement of persons were incorporated into Title IV EC, although the relevant legal provisions meant that decision-making was still more intergovernmental than in other areas for a certain period of time. The remaining Third Pillar provisions were subjected to institutional controls closer to those under the Community Pillar, and the Third Pillar was renamed 'Police and Judicial Cooperation in Criminal Matters'. The amended Third Pillar was to provide citizens with a high level of safety in an area of freedom, security, and justice, by developing 'common action' in three areas: police cooperation in criminal matters, judicial cooperation in criminal matters, and the prevention and combating of racism and xenophobia.[45] These objectives were pursued through legal instruments specific to the Third Pillar:[46] common positions, framework decisions, decisions, and conventions. The ECJ had some jurisdiction over certain measures adopted under this Pillar,[47] although it was not equivalent to its jurisdiction under the Community Pillar.

(ii) *Reaction and Assessment*

Assessment requires a benchmark, some criterion against which to measure what was achieved against prior aspirations. The two most salient benchmarks were institutional reform to cope with enlargement, and concerns about the EU's legitimacy. Viewed against these benchmarks, the Treaty of Amsterdam does not fare well. Institutional reform to cope with enlargement was not addressed, and there was relatively little to address broader concerns about the EU's legitimacy, although the extension of co-decision, the creation of the new Title IV EC, and provisions concerning access to documents, data protection, non-discrimination, and the like were beneficial in this respect.

The Treaty of Amsterdam nonetheless had a more general impact in two respects. It eroded the distinction between the Pillars, especially in relation to the Third Pillar. It also legitimated mechanisms for different degrees of integration and cooperation between groups of states. Article 40 EU, Article 11

---

[42] There was a new title on employment, the provisions on social policy were modified, the title on public health was replaced and enhanced, and that on consumer protection was amended.

[43] Art 13 EC.

[44] Art 24 EU; JW de Zwaan, 'Legal Personality of the European Communities and the European Union' (1999) 30 Netherlands Yearbook of International Law 75; K Lenaerts and E de Smijter, 'The European Union as an Actor under International Law' (1999/2000) 19 YBEL 95.

[45] Art 29 EU.

[46] Art 34 EU.

[47] Art 35 EU.

EC, and Title VII on closer cooperation demonstrated that differentiated integration should no longer be thought of as an aberration within the legal order.

(c) NICE TREATY

(i) *Institutional and Substantive Change*

The very fact that the Treaty of Amsterdam failed to address the institutional structure pending enlargement meant that a further IGC was inevitable. It was convened in 1999 to consider composition of the Commission, the weighting of votes in the Council, and the extension of qualified-majority voting. The Nice Treaty was concluded in December 2000 after a notoriously fractious summit, and entered into force on 1 February 2003.[48]

The Nice Treaty made a number of *institutional changes* to the EC Treaty, in particular relating to the Community's institutional structure. This had been devised for a Community of six Member States, which had expanded to fifteen. There was consensus on the need for reform of institutional arrangements pending enlargement. This was achieved and the Treaty provisions concerning the weighting of votes in the Council, the distribution of seats in the European Parliament, and the composition of the Commission were amended. These topics might sound dry, but the debates concerning reform were often fierce, precisely because these issues raised broader considerations concerning the relative power of large, medium, and small states in the Community, and also raised contentious issues as to the balance of power between the EU institutions. The detailed provisions have been superseded by those in the Lisbon Treaty, but the discourse concerning these changes was similarly contentious as those in the Nice Treaty.

The principal *substantive development* concerned the EU Charter of Rights. The initial catalyst for this came from the European Council in 1999. It established a 'body' which included national parliamentarians, European parliamentarians, and national government representatives to draft a Charter of fundamental rights for the EU.[49] This body, which renamed itself a 'Convention', began work early in 2000 and drew up a Charter by the end of 2000. The Charter received political approval at the Nice European Council in December 2000.[50] It was drafted so as to be legally binding. The Charter's legal status was not however resolved in Nice, and this issue was placed on the 'post-Nice agenda' for the 2004 IGC. The Charter was largely welcomed as a step forward for the legitimacy and human rights commitment of the EU. The mode by which it was drafted also attracted positive comment as an improvement on the method by which treaties had traditionally been negotiated.

(ii) *Reaction and Assessment*

The aspirations underlying the Nice IGC were limited, the primary aim being institutional reform in the light of enlargement, a task left unresolved in the Treaty of Amsterdam. Viewed from this limited perspective, the Treaty of Nice did the job. There was nonetheless dissatisfaction with the outcome.

This was in part procedural. There was much adverse media reaction to the ill-tempered exchanges and the late-night wrangling that accompanied the IGC and the European Council meeting in Nice. This formed part of the impetus for the European Council's decision in 2001 to establish a more open and representative Convention to prepare for the next IGC.

---

[48] [2001] OJ C80/1; K Bradley, 'Institutional Design in the Treaty of Nice' (2001) 38 CMLRev 1095; R Barents, 'Some Observations on the Treaty of Nice' (2001) 8 MJ 121.

[49] G de Búrca, 'The Drafting of the EU Charter of Fundamental Rights' (2001) 26 ELRev 126.

[50] [2000] OJ C364/1.

The lingering dissatisfaction was also in part substantive. The Nice Treaty may well have addressed the primary institutional issues, but it was readily apparent that there were equally important issues that were not touched. This was reflected in Declaration 23 on the Future of the Union appended to the Nice Treaty, which called for a 'deeper and wider debate about the future of the European Union', involving a broad range of opinion. The Declaration identified four issues for the 2004 IGC: the 'delimitation of powers' between the EU and the Member States, the status of the Charter of Fundamental Rights, simplification of the Treaties, and the role of the national parliaments.

6 FROM NICE TO THE LISBON TREATY

(A) THE LAEKEN DECLARATION

The initial expectation following the Nice Treaty was that there would be another round of piecemeal Treaty reform four years later in 2004, the intent being that it would consider issues addressed but not resolved in the Nice Treaty, as set out in Declaration 23. These issues were to be considered further at the Laeken European Council scheduled for December 2001. The nature of the reform process was however transformed during 2000, which was reflected in the conclusions of the Laeken European Council.[51]

It came to be accepted that the topics left over from the Nice Treaty were not discrete, but were connected to other issues concerning the EU institutional balance of power, and with the distribution of authority between the EU and the Member States. This led to a growing feeling that there should be a more profound re-thinking of the fundamentals of the EU. It was also accepted that if a broad range of issues was to be discussed, then the result should be legitimated by input from a broader 'constituency' than hitherto. This emerging consensus was reflected in the Laeken European Council,[52] which gave formal approval, through the Laeken Declaration, to the broadening of the issues left open post-Nice. These issues became the 'headings' within which a plethora of other questions were posed, concerning virtually every issue of importance for the EU. The Laeken Declaration also formally embraced the Convention model which had been used to draw up the Charter of Rights, and established a Convention on the Future of Europe.

(B) CONSTITUTIONAL TREATY

(i) *Proposed Institutional and Substantive Change*

The Convention[53] was composed of representatives from national governments, national parliaments, the EP, and the Commission. The accession countries were also represented. The Convention was chaired by former French President Giscard d'Estaing, with two vice-chairmen, Giuliano Amato and Jean-Luc Dehaene. The executive role in the Convention was undertaken by the Praesidium.[54] It began work in 2002, making extensive use of Working Groups for particular topics.[55]

---

[51] P Craig, 'Constitutional Process and Reform in the EU: Nice, Laeken, the Convention and the IGC' (2004) 10 EPL 653.

[52] Laeken European Council, 14–15 Dec 2001.

[53] http://european-convention.europa.eu/.

[54] It was composed of the Convention Chairman and Vice-Chairmen, and nine other members.

[55] Working groups were established on: subsidiarity, Charter of Rights, legal personality, national parliaments, competence, economic governance, external action, defence, Treaty simplification, freedom, security, and justice, and social Europe. The decision to create the first six groups was taken in May 2002; the remaining five groups were created later in autumn 2002.

The end result in 2003 was a proposal for a Constitutional Treaty, but this was not preordained. The possibility of a constitutional text was mentioned only at the end of the Laeken Declaration, in the context of Treaty simplification, and the language was cautious. Many Member States felt that the Convention might just be a talking shop, which produced recommendations.[56] It was therefore a surprise when Giscard d'Estaing, in the Convention opening ceremony, announced that he sought consensus on a Constitutional Treaty for Europe. The Convention, once established, developed its own institutional vision. The idea took hold that the Convention should produce a Constitutional Treaty.[57] The Draft Treaty Establishing a Constitution for Europe[58] was duly agreed by the Convention in June 2003 and submitted to the European Council in July.[59]

The Member States in the European Council were however divided on certain issues and agreement on the Constitutional Treaty was only secured at the European Council meeting in June 2004.[60] It was still necessary for the Constitutional Treaty[61] to be ratified in accord with the constitutional requirements of each Member State. Fifteen Member States ratified the Treaty, but progress came to an abrupt halt when France and the Netherlands rejected the Constitutional Treaty in their referenda.[62] A number of Member States therefore postponed their ratification process. The European Council in 2005 decided it was best for there to be a time for 'reflection'. The Constitutional Treaty never 'recovered' from the negative votes in France and the Netherlands, and did not become law. However, the Lisbon Treaty, which was ratified in 2009, drew heavily on the Constitutional Treaty.

(ii) *Reaction and Assessment*

There was considerable diversity of views on just about every facet of the Constitutional Treaty. The principal areas of debate were as follows.[63]

There was discourse as to *whether it was wise for the EU ever to have embarked on this ambitious project*. This was reflected in the jibe 'if it ain't broke, why fix it?' On this view, grand constitutional schemes of the kind embodied in the Constitutional Treaty were unnecessary, because the EU could function on the basis of the Nice Treaty, and dangerous, because the very construction of such a constitutional document brought to the fore contentious issues, which were best resolved through less formal mechanisms. There is force in this view. It should nonetheless be recognized that the four issues left over from the Nice Treaty were not discrete. They raised broader issues concerning the nature of the EU, its powers, mode of decision-making, and relationship with the Member States. The dissatisfaction with piecemeal IGC Treaty reform, monopolized by the Member States, should not, moreover, be forgotten. If this traditional process had been adhered to in relation to the broadened

---

[56] P Norman, 'From the Convention to the IGC (Institutions)' (Federal Trust, Sept 2003) 2.

[57] CONV 250/02, Simplification of the Treaties and Drawing up of a Constitutional Treaty, Brussels, 10 Sept 2002; CONV 284/02, Summary Report on the Plenary Session—Brussels 12 and 13 September 2002, Brussels, 17 Sept 2002.

[58] The Constitutional Treaty was divided into four parts: Part I dealt with the basic objectives and values of the EU, fundamental rights, competences, forms of lawmaking, institutional division of power, and the like; Part II contained the Charter of Rights, which had been made binding by Part I; Part III concerned the policies and functions of the EU; and Part IV contained the final provisions.

[59] CONV 850/03, Draft Treaty establishing a Constitution for Europe, Brussels, 18 July 2003.

[60] Brussels European Council, 17–18 June 2004, [4]–[5].

[61] Treaty Establishing a Constitution for Europe [2004] OJ C316/1.

[62] R Dehousse, 'The Unmaking of a Constitution: Lessons from the European Referenda' (2006) 13 Constellations 151.

[63] G de Búrca, 'The European Constitution Project after the Referenda' (2006) 13 Constellations 205; A Moravcsik, 'Europe without Illusions: A Category Error' (2005) 112 Prospect, available at www.prospectmagazine.co.uk/features/europeanwithoutillusions; A Duff, 'Plan B: How to Rescue the European Constitution', Notre Europe, Studies and Research No 52, 2006; J Ziller, 'Une constitution courte et obscure ou claire et détaillée? Perspectives pour la simplification des traités et la rationalisation de l'ordre juridique de l'union européenne', EUI Working Papers, Law 2006/31.

reform agenda there would have been criticism about the 'legitimacy and representativeness deficit' inherent in the classic IGC model.

A related, but distinct, set of issues concerned *the way in which the Convention operated*. Thus some cast doubt on the participatory credentials of the Convention, pointing to the increasing centralization of initiative in the Praesidium. This was problematic and did not conform to some 'ideal-type' vision of drafting a Constitution. The Convention did not however exist within an ideal-type world. It conducted its task against the real-world conditions laid down by the European Council. Once the European Council reaffirmed the deadline the Praesidium had little choice but to take a more proactive role, since otherwise the Constitutional Treaty would not have been presented to the European Council in June 2003.

A third area of debate concerned the *content of the Constitutional Treaty*. Some were critical about the further federalization they believed to result from the Treaty, focusing on, for example, the shift from unanimity to qualified-majority voting in the Council. Others were equally critical about what they saw as the increased intergovernmentalism in the Treaty, through for example, enhanced Member State influence in the inter-institutional distribution of power, the creation of the long-term Presidency of the European Council, and the like. There were also significant differences of view concerning particular provisions of the Constitutional Treaty. Thus, for example, some applauded the distribution of competences, while others were critical, arguing that the provisions were unclear and uncertain.

(c) THE LISBON TREATY

(i) *From the Constitutional Treaty to the Lisbon Treaty*

The failure of the Constitutional Treaty meant that the legal ordering of the EU continued to be based on the Rome Treaty as amended by later treaties, including the Nice Treaty. This Treaty architecture had to regulate an EU of twenty-five Member States, the result of the 2004 enlargement that brought ten further states into the EU: the Czech Republic, Estonia, Cyprus, Latvia, Lithuania, Hungary, Malta, Poland, Slovenia, and Slovakia. Bulgaria and Romania joined the EU in 2007, and Croatia acceded in 2013 making twenty-eight states. The policy of conditionality meant that candidate states were required to adapt their laws and institutions in significant ways before any date for accession was set, at a time when they had little or no influence on European laws and policies.[64]

The decision that there should be a 'period of reflection' after the negative results in the French and Dutch referenda was sensible, given the justified concern that more states might vote against the Constitutional Treaty. The calm phrase 'period of reflection' nonetheless concealed a far more troubled perspective in the EU institutions, which were at the time unsure whether any of the content of the Constitutional Treaty could be salvaged. The Member States were not, however, willing to allow the work that had been put into the Constitutional Treaty to be lost. To this end, the European Council in 2006 commissioned Germany, which held the Presidency of the European Council in the first half of 2007, to report on the prospects for Treaty reform. The European Council meeting in 2007[65] then considered a detailed mandate of changes to the Constitutional Treaty, in order that a revised Treaty could be successfully concluded.

---

[64] H Grabbe, 'A Partnership for Accession? The Implications of EU Conditionality for the Central and East European Applicants', EUI Robert Schuman Centre Working Paper 12/99, and 'How does Europeanization affect CEE Governance? Conditionality, Diffusion and Diversity' (2001) 8 JEPP 1013; A Williams, 'Enlargement of the Union and Human Rights Conditionality: A Policy of Distinction?' (2000) 25 ELRev 601.

[65] Brussels European Council, 21–22 June 2007.

This led to the birth of the Reform Treaty. It was agreed to convene an IGC,[66] which was to finish its deliberations by the end of 2007.[67] The Reform Treaty was to contain two principal clauses, which amended respectively the TEU and the EC Treaty, the latter of which would be renamed the Treaty on the Functioning of the European Union. The Union should have a single legal personality and the word 'Community' throughout would be replaced by the word 'Union'.[68] There was a conscious decision to excise mention of the word 'constitution' from the Reform Treaty. The principal objective was to conclude this Treaty reform, and given that the constitutional terminology of the Constitutional Treaty was problematic for some Member States it was dropped. This was also the rationale for other terminological changes where the wording in the Constitutional Treaty was felt, whether correctly or not,[69] to connote the idea of the EU as a state entity. Thus the title 'Union Minister for Foreign Affairs' was replaced by High Representative of the Union for Foreign Affairs and Security Policy; the terms 'law' and 'framework law' were abandoned; there was no flag, anthem, or motto; and the clause in the Constitutional Treaty concerning the primacy of EU law was replaced by a declaration.

Portugal held the Presidency of the European Council in the second half of 2007 and was keen that Treaty reform should be concluded during its Presidency so that the new Treaty could bear its name. Developments in the second half of 2007 were rapid. There was scant time for any detailed discussion of the draft Treaty that emerged from the IGC. What became the Lisbon Treaty was forged hurriedly by the Member States and EU institutions, since they were keen to conclude a process that had started shortly after the beginning of the new millennium. The desire to conclude the Lisbon Treaty expeditiously was moreover explicable, since it was the same in most important respects as the Constitutional Treaty. The issues had been debated in detail in the Convention on the Future of Europe after a relatively open discourse, and were considered once again in the IGC in 2004. There was therefore little appetite for those engaged in the 2007 IGC to re-open Pandora's Box,[70] even if this could not be admitted too explicitly since they would be open to the criticism that they were largely re-packaging provisions that had been rejected by voters in two prominent Member States, although it should also be noted that the negative votes in the French and Dutch referenda had relatively little to do with anything new in the Constitutional Treaty.[71]

The 2007 IGC produced a document that was signed by the Member States on 13 December 2007,[72] and the title was changed from the Reform Treaty to the Lisbon Treaty in recognition of the place of signature. The finishing post was in sight, but the Treaty required ratification by each Member State, and Ireland rejected it in a referendum. This obstacle was overcome by a second Irish referendum in October 2009, after concessions were made to Ireland. The final hurdle was the unwillingness of the Czech President to ratify the Lisbon Treaty, but he did so reluctantly after a constitutional challenge to the Treaty had been rejected by the Czech Constitutional Court, and after other Member States agreed to add at a later date a Protocol to the Treaties relating to the Czech Republic and the Charter of Rights. The Lisbon Treaty entered into force on 1 December 2009.

---

[66] Ibid [10].

[67] Ibid [11].

[68] Ibid Annex I, [2].

[69] S Griller, 'Is this a Constitution? Remarks on a Contested Concept' in S Griller and J Ziller (eds), *The Lisbon Treaty: EU Constitutionalism without a Constitutional Treaty?* (Springer, 2008) 21–56.

[70] G Tsebelis, 'Thinking about the Recent Past and Future of the EU' (2008) 46 JCMS 265.

[71] See in general, R Dehousse, 'The Unmaking of a Constitution: Lessons from the European Referenda' (2006) 13 Constellations 151.

[72] Conference of the Representatives of the Governments of the Member States, Treaty of Lisbon Amending the Treaty on European Union and the Treaty Establishing the European Community, CIG 14/07, Brussels, 3 Dec 2007 [2007] OJ C306/1.

(ii) *Form*

The Lisbon Treaty amended the Treaty on European Union and the Treaty Establishing the European Community.[73] The Lisbon Treaty has seven Articles, of which Articles 1 and 2 are the most important, plus numerous Protocols and Declarations. Article 1 amended the TEU and contained some principles that govern the EU, as well as revised provisions concerning the CFSP and enhanced cooperation. Article 2 amended the EC Treaty, which was renamed the Treaty on the Functioning of the European Union. The EU is henceforth to be founded on the TEU and the TFEU, and the two Treaties have the same legal value.[74] The Union replaces and succeeds the EC.[75] A consolidated version of the Lisbon Treaty contains the new numbering and references to the old provisions where appropriate.[76]

(iii) *Substance*

Part I of the Constitutional Treaty contained the principles of a constitutional nature that governed the EU. The Lisbon Treaty is less clear in this respect, although the revised TEU has some constitutional principles for the EU. This is especially true in relation to Title I–Common Provisions, Title II–Democratic Principles, and Title III–Provisions on the Institutions. There are nonetheless matters not included within the revised TEU, which had properly been in Part I of the Constitutional Treaty. Thus, for example, the main rules concerning competence are in the TFEU,[77] as are the provisions concerning the hierarchy of norms,[78] and those relating to budgetary planning.[79]

The Lisbon Treaty did, however, improve the architecture of the TFEU. The latter Treaty is divided into Seven Parts. Part One, entitled Principles, contains two Titles, the first of which deals with Categories of Competence, the second of which covers Provisions having General Application. Part Two deals with Discrimination and Citizenship of the Union. Part Three, which covers Policies and Internal Actions of the Union, is the largest Part of the TFEU with twenty-four Titles.[80] The provisions on Police and Judicial Cooperation in Criminal Matters, the Third Pillar of the old TEU, have been moved into the new TFEU.[81] Part Four of the TFEU covers Association of Overseas Countries and Territories. Part Five deals with EU External Action, bringing together subject matter with an external dimension. Part Six is concerned with Institutional and Budgetary Provisions, while Part Seven covers General and Final Provisions.

The Lisbon Treaty is not built on the Pillar system, and in this sense the Treaty architecture that had prevailed since the Maastricht Treaty has now gone. There are nonetheless distinctive rules relating to the CFSP which means that in reality there is still something akin to a separate 'Pillar' for such

---

[73] J-C Piris, *The Lisbon Treaty: A Legal and Political Analysis* (Cambridge University Press, 2010); P Craig, *The Lisbon Treaty: Law, Politics, and Treaty Reform* (Oxford University Press, 2010).

[74] Art 1 para 3 TEU.

[75] Art 1 para 3 TEU.

[76] Consolidated Versions of the Treaty on European Union and the Treaty on the Functioning of the European Union [2008] OJ C115/1, [2010] OJ C83/1, [2012] OJ C326/1.

[77] Arts 2–6 TFEU.

[78] Arts 288–292 TFEU.

[79] Art 312 TFEU.

[80] I–Internal Market; II–Free Movement of Goods; III–Agriculture and Fisheries; IV–Free Movement of Persons, Services and Capital; V–Area of Freedom, Security and Justice; VI–Transport; VII–Common Rules on Competition, Taxation, and Approximation of Laws; VIII–Economic and Monetary Policy; IX–Employment; X–Social Policy; XI–The European Social Fund; XII–Education, Vocational Training, Youth and Sport; XIII–Culture; XIV–Public Health; XV–Consumer Protection; XVI–Trans-European Networks; XVII–Industry; XVIII–Economic, Social and Territorial Cohesion; XIX–Research and Technological Development and Space; XX–Environment; XXI–Energy; XXII–Tourism; XXIII–Civil Protection; XXIV–Administrative Cooperation.

[81] Part Three, Title V TFEU.

matters. The approach to the CFSP in the Lisbon Treaty largely replicates that in the Constitutional Treaty, subject to the change of nomenclature, from 'Union Minister for Foreign Affairs' to 'High Representative of the Union for Foreign Affairs and Security Policy'. Executive authority continues to reside principally with the European Council and the Council.[82] The ECJ continues to be largely excluded from the CFSP.[83]

(iv) *Reaction and Assessment*

It is important to keep separate the 'official' and the 'non-official' reaction to the ratification of the Lisbon Treaty, since different considerations were relevant in the two instances.

The most prominent 'official' reaction in the EU was one of relief that the Treaty reform had been concluded. It had been on the agenda for almost a decade, since the conclusion of the Nice Treaty, Declaration 23 of which had been the catalyst for the next stage of Treaty revision, which led to Laeken, the Convention on the Future of Europe, the Constitutional Treaty, and the Lisbon Treaty. The failure of the Constitutional Treaty, more especially its rejection by two founding states, had taken its toll on the EU, sapping energy and morale. The prospect of failing twice was not therefore appealing. The prospect of re-opening the debates on the key issues was equally unappealing, more especially because many official players believed that the solutions in the Lisbon Treaty really were better than what had existed previously and/or that they were the best that could be attained in the real world of politics.

The 'non-official' reaction by academics, onlookers, EU observers, and the like was mixed, as one might have expected. Indeed, the very diversity of opinion that marked reaction to the Constitutional Treaty continued in relation to the Lisbon Treaty, primarily because the latter drew so heavily on the former. Thus debates as to whether it was wise to embark on 'general' Treaty reform, and discourse as to whether the content of the resulting Treaty was too 'federal' or too 'intergovernmental' continued in relation to the Lisbon Treaty, as did discussion of the desirability and impact of major changes, such as the creation of the long-term Presidency of the European Council. These issues will be assessed in more detail in later chapters of the book, when the changes made by the Lisbon Treaty are analysed in detail. It is only then that informed conclusions can be reached about the impact of the new Treaty.

(D) POST-LISBON: THE FINANCIAL CRISIS

The Member States and EU institutional players that had finally secured the passage and ratification of the Lisbon Treaty hoped for a period of relative calm in which the new Treaty arrangements could bed down. This was not to be. The successful conclusion of the Lisbon Treaty overlapped with the onset of the financial crisis that has had a profound political, economic, and social impact on the EU.[84]

The reasons for the crisis are complex and cannot be examined in detail here, but some idea of the causes is nonetheless important.[85] The Maastricht Treaty introduced the legal framework

---

[82] Arts 22, 24 TEU.

[83] Art 24 TEU, Art 275 TFEU. It does however have jurisdiction in relation to Art 40 TEU, which is designed to ensure that exercise of CFSP powers do not impinge on the general competences of the EU, and vice versa; the ECJ also has jurisdiction under Art 275 TFEU to review the legality of decisions imposing restrictive measures on natural or legal persons adopted by the Council under Chapter 2 of Title V TEU.

[84] M Adams, F Fabbrini, and P Larouche (eds), *The Constitutionalization of European Budgetary Constraints* (Hart, 2014).

[85] http://ec.europa.eu/economy_finance/focuson/crisis/2010-04_en.htm; H James, H-W Micklitz, and H Schweitzer, 'The Impact of the Financial Crisis on the European Economic Constitution', EUI Law Working Paper, 2010/05; Ch 20 below.

for economic and monetary union. The latter connotes the idea of a single currency overseen by a European Central Bank. The former captures the idea of control over national fiscal and budgetary policy, with the basic aim of ensuring that a Member State does not spend more than it earns. The rationale for these controls was that the stability of the Euro could be undermined if the economies of the Member States that subscribed to the currency were perceived to be weak, and the financial markets might reach this conclusion if some Member States persistently spent more than they earned. The problem was that the two parts of the Maastricht settlement were out of sync.[86] EU control over national budgetary policy was relatively weak, and thus it was unable to exert the requisite control over national economic policy.

The specific problem for the EU began in earnest with the fact that Greece's credit rating to repay its debt was downgraded. This then led to problems for the Euro, and to concerns about the budgetary health of some other countries that used the currency. The impact of these developments was downward pressure on the Euro, which was only alleviated when Euro countries provided a support package for Greece that satisfied the financial markets. The sovereign debt crisis was overlaid by, and interacted with, the banking crisis that affected some lending institutions that were heavily committed to economic sectors, such as housing, which were hit badly by the downturn in the economic markets.[87] The net effect was that a number of countries, in particular Greece, Ireland, and Portugal, required very large financial assistance from funds financed by other Member States. Italy and Spain have also been on the 'danger list'. The assistance has been subject to 'strict conditionality', which means that the funding to the recipient states is contingent on their introducing far-reaching economic and social reforms, thereby increasing unemployment at a time when the general economic outlook has been bleak.

The economic and financial crisis has had profound effects on the EU, including its constitutional architecture.[88] Nor is the problem likely to go away in the short term. It has generated a complex array of political responses, some of which have been designed to provide assistance to ailing states, others of which have increased oversight of national economic policy. The measures have assumed varying legal forms, ranging from the enactment of ordinary EU legislation, albeit in an accelerated manner as warranted by the nature of the crisis, to intergovernmental agreements made outside the formal confines of the constituent Treaties. The constitutional implications of these developments continue to unfold, with profound consequences for the legal, economic, and political dimensions of the EU, and indeed for the balance between the 'economic' and the 'social', a theme that has run through the development of the EEC from its very inception. The social dimension of EU policy has been markedly affected by austerity policies at both EU and national level. The EU may weather this particular storm, but the nature of the polity that emerges thereafter remains to be seen.

7 THEORIES OF INTEGRATION

The discussion in this chapter has shown the way in which the EEC has changed since its inception. There is, however, a related but distinct issue, which is the rationale for this integration. The original EEC Treaty has been amended on many occasions and the subject matter over which the EU has

---

[86] J-V Louis, 'Guest Editorial: The No-Bailout Clause and Rescue Packages' (2010) 47 CMLRev 971.

[87] M Maduro, 'A New Governance for the European Union and the Euro: Democracy and Justice', European Parliament, Directorate-General for Internal Policies, Policy Department C: Citizens' Rights and Constitutional Affairs, PE 462.484, 2012.

[88] P Craig, 'Economic Governance and the Euro Crisis: Constitutional Architecture and Constitutional Implications' in Adams, Fabbrini, and Larouche (n 84) Ch 2.

competence has expanded very considerably. It is therefore important to consider the rationale for this. There is a wealth of literature, principally from political science, and there is not surprisingly debate as to the causes of integration.

(A) NEOFUNCTIONALISM

Neofunctionalism was the early ideology of Community integration.[89] The central tenet of neofunctionalism was the concept of 'spillover'. Functional spillover was based on the interconnectedness of the economy. Integration in one sphere created pressure for integration in other areas. Thus, for example, removal of formal tariff barriers would generate a need to deal with non-tariff barriers, which could equally inhibit realization of a single market. The desire for a level playing field between the states would then lead to other matters being decided at Community level, in order to prevent states from giving advantages to their own industries. Political spillover was equally important and involved the build-up of political pressure in favour of further integration. In integrated areas interest groups would be expected to concentrate their attention on the Community, and apply pressure on those with regulatory power. Such groups would also become mindful of remaining barriers to inter-state trade, which prevented them from reaping the rewards of existing integration, thereby adding to the pressure for further integration. The Commission was to be a major player in this political spillover, since it would encourage the beliefs of the state players. Neofunctionalism was to be the vehicle through which Community integration, conceived of as technocratic, elite-led gradualism, was to be realized. Legitimacy was conceived of in terms of outcomes, increased prosperity, which was to be secured through technocracy, even if this meant a marginal role for elected bodies.[90]

Neofunctionalism was however challenged empirically and theoretically. The empirical challenge was based on its failure to explain the reality of the Community's development. The 1965 Luxembourg crisis had a profound impact, since Member State interests re-emerged with a vengeance. The resulting *de facto* unanimity principle signalled that Member States were not willing to allow Community development inconsistent with their vital interests. Decision-making for many years thereafter was conducted in the shadow of the veto. The Commission's role changed from emerging government for the Community to a more cautious bureaucracy.[91] Moreover, evidence of interest group pressure for greater integration was found to be equivocal.[92]

The theoretical challenge to neofunctionalism was based on the fact that its failure to accord with political reality led to theoretical modification that rendered it increasingly indeterminate,[93] and on neofunctionalism's failure to relate to general themes within international relations, which sought to explain why states engaged in international cooperation. It would nonetheless be wrong to conclude that neofunctionalism has no explanatory value for EU integration, and it is arguable that functional spillover created impetus for further integration.[94]

---

[89] E Haas, *The Uniting of Europe: Political, Social and Economic Forces 1950–1957* (Stanford University Press, 1958); L Lindberg, *The Political Dynamics of European Economic Integration* (Stanford University Press, 1963); L Lindberg and S Scheingold, *Europe's Would-Be Polity: Patterns of Change in the European Community* (Prentice-Hall, 1970); L Lindberg and S Scheingold, *Regional Integration* (Harvard University Press, 1970).

[90] Lindberg and Scheingold (n 89) 268–269.

[91] K Neunreither, 'Transformation of a Political Role: The Case of the Commission of the European Communities' (1971–72) 10 JCMS 233.

[92] S George, *Politics and Policy in the European Union* (Oxford University Press, 3rd edn, 1996) 41–43.

[93] A Moravcsik, 'Preferences and Power in the European Community: A Liberal Intergovernmentalist Approach' (1993) 31 JCMS 473, 476.

[94] George (n 92) 40–41.

(B) LIBERAL INTERGOVERNMENTALISM

An alternative theory of integration is known as liberal intergovernmentalism, championed by Moravcsik.[95] His thesis is rooted in a branch of international relations theory. The central thesis is that states are the driving forces behind integration, that supranational actors are there largely at their behest and that these actors as such have little independent impact on the pace of integration.

The demand for integration is said to depend on national preferences, which are aggregated through their political institutions.[96] The increase in cross-border flows of goods and services creates what are termed 'international policy externalities' among nations, which can have negative side effects on other states, thereby creating an incentive for policy coordination.

The supply of integration is said to be a function of inter-state bargaining and strategic interaction. Domestic preferences define 'a "bargaining space" of potentially viable agreements, each of which generates gains for one or more participants'.[97] Governments choose one such agreement, normally through negotiation. Integration is pursued through a supranational institution because it is felt to be more efficient. Constructing individual *ad hoc* bargains between states can be costly.[98] This problem is obviated by a supranational structure such as the EU. The same basic driving force of efficiency is said to explain the decision-making procedures in the EU. Thus Member States carry out a cost–benefit calculation, with the decision to delegate or pool sovereignty signalling the willingness of national governments to accept an increased risk of being outvoted on any individual issue in exchange for more efficient collective decision-making.[99]

(C) MULTI-LEVEL GOVERNANCE

Liberal intergovernmentalism was predicated on the assumption that supranational institutions enabled national governments to attain policy goals that could not be obtained by independent action.[100] This state-centric view was challenged by those who saw the EU in terms of multi-level governance.[101]

Thus Marks, Hooghe, and Blank argued that integration was a process in which authority and policy-making were shared across multiple levels of government: subnational, national, and supranational.[102] National governments were major players, but did not have a monopoly of control.

---

[95] A Moravcsik, 'Preferences and Power in the European Community: A Liberal Intergovernmentalist Approach' (1993) 31 JCMS 473; A Moravcsik, *National Preference Formation and Interstate Bargaining in the European Community, 1955–86* (Harvard University Press, 1992); A Moravcsik, 'Negotiating the Single European Act: National Interests and Conventional Statecraft in the European Community' (1991) 45 International Organization 19.

[96] Moravcsik, 'Preferences and Power' (n 95) 481.

[97] Ibid 497.

[98] J Buchanan and G Tullock, *The Calculus of Consent: Logical Foundations of Constitutional Democracy* (University of Michigan Press, 1962).

[99] Moravcsik, 'Preferences and Power' (n 95) 509–510.

[100] A Milward, *The European Rescue of the Nation State* (University of California Press, 1992); A Milward and V Sorensen, 'Independence or Integration? A National Choice' in A Milward, R Ranieri, F Romero, and V Sorensen (eds), *The Frontier of National Sovereignty: History and Theory, 1945–1992* (Routledge, 1993); P Taylor, 'The European Community and the State: Assumptions, Theories and Propositions' (1991) 17 Review of International Studies 109.

[101] See, eg, M Jachtenfuchs, 'Theoretical Perspectives on European Governance' (1995) 1 ELJ 115 and 'The Governance Approach to European Integration' (2001) 39 JCMS 245; G Marks, L Hooghe, and K Blank, 'European Integration since the 1980s: State-Centric Versus Multi-Level Governance' (1996) 34 JCMS 341; B Kohler Koch, 'The Evolution and Transformation of European Governance' (Institute for Advanced Studies, Vienna: Political Science Series No 58, 1998); K Armstrong and S Bulmer, *The Governance of the Single European Market* (Manchester, 1998); S Hix, 'The Study of the European Union II. The "New Governance" Agenda and its Rival' (1998) 5 JEPP 38; I Bache and M Flinders (eds), *Multi-Level Governance* (Oxford University Press, 2004).

[102] Marks, Hooghe, and Blank (n 101) 341, 342.

Supranational institutions, including the Commission, the EP, and the ECJ, had influence in policy-making and could not merely be regarded as agents of national governments.[103] When competence over a certain subject matter has been transferred to the EU, proponents of multi-level governance contend that there are real limits to the degree of individual and collective state control over EU decisions.[104] Thus while Member States may play the decisive role in the treaty-making process, they do not exert a monopoly of influence, and the day-to-day control exercised by the states collectively is less than that postulated by state-centric theorists. The ability of the 'principals', the Member States, to control the 'agents', the Commission and the ECJ, is limited by a range of factors, including the 'multiplicity of principals, the mistrust that exists among them, impediments to coherent principal action, informational asymmetries between principals and agents and by the unintended consequences of institutional change'.[105]

(D) RATIONAL CHOICE INSTITUTIONALISM

Rational choice institutionalism is a derivative of rational choice theory. The latter is premised on methodological individualism, whereby individuals have preferences, and choose the course of action that is the optimal method of securing them.[106] Rational choice institutionalists were critical of liberal intergovernmentalism because of the minimal role that the latter accorded to EU institutions,[107] although the gap between the two theories became narrower in the late 1990s.[108]

Proponents of rational choice institutionalism acknowledged that institutions were important. Institutions constituted the rules of the game thereby enhancing equilibrium, and they exemplified principal/agent analysis. Member State 'principals' delegated to supranational 'agents' to enhance the credibility of their commitments, and to deal with incomplete contracting, since Treaty provisions are often open to a spectrum of possible interpretations. Principal/agent literature focused on the controls that the principal might use to ensure that the agent did not deviate from the desired goals of the principal.[109]

(E) CONSTRUCTIVISM

Constructivists agree with rational choice institutionalists that institutions matter. They nonetheless dispute the foundations of much rational choice literature, more especially methodological individualism and the idea that individual or state preferences are 'given'. Constructivists contend that the relevant environment in which preferences are formed is inescapably social.[110] This inevitably impacts

---

[103] Ibid 346.

[104] Ibid 350–351.

[105] Ibid 353–354.

[106] J Jupille, J Caporaso, and J Checkel, 'Integrating Institutions: Rationalism, Constructivism, and the Study of the European Union' (2003) 36 Comparative Political Studies 7.

[107] M Pollack, 'International Relations Theory and European Integration', EUI Working Papers, RSC 2000/55.

[108] This was primarily because Moravcsik modified his theory to acknowledge that supranational institutions might have greater powers over agenda setting and the making of EU law outside major Treaty negotiations than he had posited in his earlier work, A Moravcsik, *The Choice for Europe: Social Purpose and State Power from Messina to Maastricht* (Cornell University Press, 1998) 8.

[109] M Pollack, *The Engines of European Integration: Delegation, Agency and Agenda Setting in the EU* (Oxford University Press, 2003); Pollack (n 107).

[110] T Risse, 'Exploring the Nature of the Beast: International Relations Theory and Comparative Policy Analysis Meet the European Union' (1996) 34 JCMS 53; J Checkel, 'The Constructivist Turn in International Relations Theory' (1998) 50 World Politics 324; T Christiansen, K Jorgensen, and A Wiener, 'The Social Construction of Europe' (1999) 6 JEPP 528.

on, and thus constitutes, a person's understandings of their own interests. Institutions will embody social norms and will affect a person's interests and identity.

Thus whereas rational choice institutionalism regards institutions as rules of the game that provide incentives within which players pursue their given preferences, constructivists regard institutions more broadly to include 'informal rules and intersubjective understandings as well as formal rules, and posit a more important and fundamental role for institutions, which constitute actors and shape not simply their incentives but their preferences and identities as well'.[111]

There have been attempts to soften the divide between rational choice institutionalism and constructivism.[112] Thus, for example, many rational choice theorists accept that preferences may well be altruistic as opposed to egoistic, and that preferences may be constrained by social structure. There have moreover been moves to test the relative cogency of the two approaches through carefully crafted case studies.[113]

8 CONCLUSIONS

i.   Formal Treaty amendment has not been spread evenly over the EU's history. The period between the founding of the EEC and the SEA was relatively stable in this respect. The period since the SEA has been one of almost continuous Treaty revision, with the Maastricht, Amsterdam, and Nice Treaties coming in quick succession.

ii. Treaty reform is a continuation of politics by other means. The Lisbon Treaty represents the culmination of a decade of attempts at Treaty reform.

iii. The period since the inception of the EEC has seen very significant institutional and substantive changes to its powers.

iv. In institutional terms, the European Parliament has moved from a player very much on the fringes of decision-making to become an institutional force in its own right, with a major role in the legislative process. The European Council has gone from strength to strength, beginning as an institution that existed outside the strict letter of the Treaties, to become a major institutional player, a position further reinforced by the Lisbon Treaty. Treaty amendments have also impacted on the powers and institutional dynamics of the Commission and Council.

v.   In substantive terms, the many complex Treaty changes should not mask the basic fact that each successive Treaty amendment has seen an increase in the areas over which the EU has competence. The time when the EU could be regarded as solely 'economic' in its focus, if it ever truly existed, has long gone. The rationale for this will be explored in subsequent chapters. Suffice it to say the following. There is debate as to the relative importance of Member States and other players, such as the Commission, during the process of Treaty amendment. There is however no doubt that the Member States are central to the pace and direction of Treaty amendment, and that they have been willing to accord the EU competence over an increased range of areas.

---

[111] Pollack (n 107) 14–15.

[112] J Checkel, 'Bridging the Rational-Choice/Constructivist Gap? Theorizing Social Interaction in European Institutions', University of Oslo, ARENA Working Papers 00/11.

[113] See, eg, the essays in (2003) 36 Comparative Political Studies.

9 FURTHER READING

(a) Books

ADAMS, M, FABBRINI, F, AND LAROUCHE, P (eds), *The Constitutionalization of European Budgetary Constraints* (Hart, 2014)

BOND, M, AND FEUS, K, *The Treaty of Nice Explained* (Federal Trust, 2001)

CHRYSSOCHOOU, D, *Theorizing European Integration* (Sage, 2001)

CORBETT, R, *The Treaty of Maastricht* (Longman, 1993)

CRAIG, P, *The Lisbon Treaty: Law, Politics, and Treaty Reform* (Oxford University Press, 2010)

DUFF, A (ed), *The Treaty of Amsterdam* (Sweet & Maxwell, 1997)

HOLLAND, M, *European Integration from Community to Union* (Pinter, 1993)

MACCORMICK, N, *Who's Afraid of a European Constitution?* (Imprint Academic, 2005)

MONAR, J, AND WESSELS, W, *The European Union after the Treaty of Amsterdam* (Continuum, 2001)

MORAVCSIK, A, *The Choice for Europe* (University College London Press, 1999)

—— (ed), *Europe without Illusions* (University Press of America, 2005)

NORMAN, P, *The Accidental Constitution: The Making of Europe's Constitutional Treaty* (EuroComment, 2005)

O'KEEFE, D, AND TWOMEY, P (eds), *Legal Issues of the Amsterdam Treaty* (Hart, 1999)

PINDER, J, *The Building of the European Union* (Oxford University Press, 3rd edn, 1998)

PIRIS, J-C, *The Constitution for Europe: A Legal Analysis* (Cambridge University Press, 2006)

—— *The Lisbon Treaty: A Legal and Political Analysis* (Cambridge University Press, 2010)

WINTER, J, CURTIN, D, KELLERMANN, A, AND DE WITTE, B, *Reforming the Treaty on European Union: The Legal Debate* (Kluwer, 1996)

ZILLER, J, *La nouvelle Constitution européenne* (La découverte, 2005)

(b) Articles

BELLAMY, R, 'The European Constitution is Dead, Long Live European Constitutionalism' (2006) 13 Constellations 181

CRAIG, P, 'Constitutional Process and Reform in the EU: Nice, Laeken, the Convention and the IGC' (2004) 10 EPL 653

CURTIN, D, 'The Constitutional Structure of the Union: A Europe of Bits and Pieces' (1993) 30 CMLRev 17

DE BÚRCA, G, 'The European Constitution Project after the Referenda' (2006) 13 Constellations 205

DEHOUSSE, R, 'The Unmaking of a Constitution: Lessons from the European Referenda' (2006) 13 Constellations 151

MORAVCSIK, A, 'Preferences and Power in the European Community: A Liberal Intergovernmentalist Approach' (1993) 31 JCMS 473

WALKER, N, 'A Constitutional Reckoning' (2003) 13 Constellations 140

WOUTERS, J, 'Institutional and Constitutional Challenges for the European Union: Some Reflections in the Light of the Treaty of Nice' (2001) 26 ELRev 342

YATAGANAS, X, 'The Treaty of Nice: The Sharing of Power and the Institutional Balance in the European Union—A Continental Perspective' (2001) 7 ELJ 242

ZILLER, J, 'Une constitution courte et obscure ou claire et détaillée? Perspectives pour la simplification des traités et la rationalisation de l'ordre juridique de l'union européenne', EUI Working Papers, Law 2006/31.

THE INSTITUTIONS

1 CENTRAL ISSUES

i.   There are seven principal institutions listed in Article 13 TEU entrusted with carrying out the tasks of the Union: the European Parliament, the European Council, the Council, the Commission, the Court of Justice of the European Union, the European Central Bank, and the Court of Auditors. This chapter will consider their roles and how they interrelate. We shall also consider other important institutions such as the Economic and Social Committee, the Committee of the Regions, and agencies. The EU's monetary institutions will be discussed later.[1]

ii. This chapter should not be approached with any preconceptions about the traditional division of governmental functions into categories of legislative, executive, administrative, and judicial. Many of these duties are shared between institutions, thereby rendering it impossible to describe one as the sole legislator, or the sole executive. The EU does not conform to a rigid separation-of-powers principle of the sort that has shaped some national systems.

iii. The pattern of institutional competence within the EU has not remained static. It has altered as a consequence of subsequent Treaty revisions and as a result of change in the political balance of power between the institutions over time,[2] including through the emergence of a web of committees and institutional actors beyond the original 'canonical' institutions.

iv. The Lisbon Treaty made significant changes to the internal organization of the EU institutions and their respective powers. These changes were hotly debated in the Convention on the Future of Europe that produced the Constitutional Treaty.

v.   The principal issues on which opinion was divided during the deliberations leading to the Constitutional Treaty were: the election of the Commission President; the size of the Commission; control over the Council; whether there should be a long-term head of the European Council, and if so the powers attached to this office; and the locus of responsibility for EU external relations, including the Common Foreign and Security Policy.

vi. The resolution of these issues in the Constitutional Treaty was largely taken over into the Lisbon Treaty. The discussion in this chapter will reveal the contending arguments on each of these issues and the impact of such changes for the functioning of the EU.

---

[1] Ch 20.

[2] D Curtin, *Executive Power in the European Union: Law, Practices, and the Living Constitution* (Oxford University Press, 2009); P Craig, 'Institutions, Power and Institutional Balance' in P Craig and G de Búrca (eds), *The Evolution of EU Law* (Oxford University Press, 2nd edn, 2010) ch 3.

2 THE COMMISSION

It is important to understand that the term Commission connotes both the College of Commissioners and the permanent Brussels bureaucracy which staffs the Commission services.[3] The discussion begins with the former.

(A) PRESIDENT OF THE COMMISSION

The Presidency of the Commission is of real significance. The holder is first among equals as compared with the other Commissioners, and the President's powers have increased over subsequent Treaty amendments.

The Lisbon Treaty provides for the Commission President to be indirectly elected. The Commission had hitherto been opposed to this idea, fearing the politicization that might result. Its attitude changed during the Convention on the Future of Europe,[4] primarily because it was felt that this would enhance the legitimacy of the Commission President, thereby strengthening his claim to be President of the Union as a whole.[5] The European Parliament was unsurprisingly in favour of a regime in which it would elect the Commission President. The Member States were, however, unwilling to surrender all control over choice of Commission President to the European Parliament.

The 'solution' in the Constitutional Treaty[6] was carried over directly into the Lisbon Treaty. Thus Article 14(1) TEU states that the European Parliament shall elect the President of the Commission. The retention of state power is however apparent in Article 17(7) TEU. The European Council, acting by qualified majority, after appropriate consultation,[7] and taking account of the elections to the European Parliament, puts forward to the European Parliament the European Council's candidate for Presidency of the Commission. This candidate shall then be elected by the European Parliament by a majority of its members. If the candidate does not get the requisite majority support, then the European Council puts forward a new candidate within one month, following the same procedure.

The very fact that the Commission President is indirectly elected means that the 'candidate' must secure support of the dominant grouping within the European Parliament. This was nonetheless the reality even prior to the Lisbon Treaty, as exemplified by the fact that President Barroso was the official candidate of the European People's Party (EPP) when he secured re-election in autumn 2009. The link with the results of the EP elections was nonetheless heightened in 2014 when candidates supported respectively by the EPP and the Socialist Party actively campaigned for the Commission Presidency. The EPP secured the majority of votes and its candidate Jean-Claude Juncker was duly appointed as

---

[3] N Nugent, *The European Commission* (Palgrave, 2001); A Stevens with H Stevens, *Brussels Bureaucrats? The Administration of the European Union* (Palgrave, 2001); L Hooghe, *The European Commission and the Integration of Europe* (Cambridge University Press, 2002); M Pollack, *The Engines of European Integration: Delegation, Agency, and Agenda Setting in the EU* (Oxford University Press, 2003); A Smith (ed), *Politics and the European Commission: Actors, Independence, Legitimacy* (Routledge, 2004); D Dimitrakopoulos (ed), *The Changing European Commission* (Manchester University Press, 2004); D Spence (ed), *The European Commission* (Harper, 3rd edn, 2006).

[4] CONV 448/02, For the European Union Peace, Freedom, Solidarity—Communication from the Commission on the Institutional Architecture, 5 Dec 2002, [2.3]; Peace, Freedom and Solidarity, COM(2002) 728 final.

[5] P Norman, *The Accidental Constitution: The Making of Europe's Constitutional Treaty* (EuroComment, 2nd edn, 2005) 120–121.

[6] Arts I–20(1), 27(1) CT.

[7] Lisbon Treaty, Declaration 11 emphasizes consultation between the European Council and European Parliament preceding choice of the candidate for Commission President.

Commission President by the European Council, notwithstanding opposition from the UK and Hungary. The broader implications of this development for democracy in the EU will be considered in a later chapter.[8]

It is for the Commission President to lay down guidelines for the working of the Commission, decide on its internal organization, and appoint Vice-Presidents of the Commission.[9] The Juncker Commission has six Vice-Presidents, including the High Representative for Foreign Affairs, and a First Vice-President. The Vice-Presidents head project teams composed of other Commissioners, whose work is relevant to that overall project, such as a digital single market or an energy union.[10] The responsibilities of the Commission are allocated among the Commissioners by the President, who has power to reshuffle the portfolios,[11] but there will be negotiations, often intense, between the Commissioners, the President, and the Member States about 'who gets what'. The Commission President can moreover request the resignation of a Commissioner.[12]

The President plays an important role in shaping overall Commission policy, in negotiating with the Council and the Parliament, and in determining the future direction of the EU. How much is made of the post will depend on the personality and vision of the incumbent.[13] Jacques Delors had a strong vision for the Community's development. Many of the broader Community initiatives were in no small measure the result of his leadership within the Commission.[14]

(B) COLLEGE OF COMMISSIONERS

(i) *Size*

There had been considerable debate from at least the Nice Treaty 2000 concerning the size of the Commission. In the intergovernmental conference (IGC) leading to the Nice Treaty opinion was divided as to whether there should continue to be one Commissioner from each state, or whether there should be an upper limit combined with rotation.[15] The argument for the latter view was that Commissioners do not represent their state, and that a Commission with twenty-eight Commissioners could cross the line between a collegiate body and a deliberative assembly.

The Lisbon Treaty, subject to the caveat below, opted for the slimmed-down Commission. It provides that the Commission will, until 31 October 2014, consist of one national from each Member State, including the President and the High Representative for Foreign Affairs.[16] After that date the Commission is to consist of members, including the President and the High Representative for Foreign Affairs, who correspond to two-thirds of the Member States,[17] unless the European Council, acting unanimously, decides to alter this number. Member States must be treated on a strictly equal footing as regards determination of the sequence of, and the time spent by, their nationals as members of the Commission. The composition of the Commission must reflect the demographic and geographical

---

[8] Ch 5.

[9] Art 17(6) TEU, other than the High Representative of the Union for Foreign Affairs and Security Policy.

[10] http://ec.europa.eu/about/structure/index_en.htm.

[11] Art 248 TFEU.

[12] Art 17(6) TEU.

[13] J Peterson, 'The Santer Era: The European Commission in Normative, Historical and Theoretical Perspective' (1999) 6 JEPP 46.

[14] N Nugent, 'The Leadership Capacity of the European Commission' (1995) 2 JEPP 603.

[15] CONFER 4813/00, Presidency Note, 1 Dec 2000.

[16] Art 17(4) TEU.

[17] Declaration 10 specifies that when the Commission no longer includes nationals of all Member States, the Commission should pay particular attention to the need to ensure full transparency in relations with all Member States, and to ensure that political, social, and economic realities in all Member States are fully taken into account.

range of all Member States.[18] This system is to be established by the European Council.[19] The basic position in the Lisbon Treaty is therefore that there will be a slimmed-down Commission in the medium term.

The caveat is that the European Council can modify the post-2014 system by unanimously voting to alter the number of Commissioners.[20] The European Council can therefore vote to retain one Commissioner per Member State post-2014, and it made this commitment to Ireland prior to its second referendum.[21] The commitment was honoured through a European Council decision in 2013, which provided that one Commissioner per Member State would continue.[22] This decision will be reviewed in view of its effect on the functioning of the EU before the next Commission in 2019, or before the 30th state accedes to the EU, whichever is the earlier.

(ii) *Appointment*

The Convention on the Future of Europe proposed that the President-elect of the Commission would choose Commissioners from a list of three names put forward by each Member State, and that these would be approved by the European Parliament.[23] This would have put the Commission President in the driving seat as to the choice of the Commissioners, subject to approval of the entire package by the European Parliament.

The Lisbon Treaty, however, retained greater Member State influence over choice of Commissioners. Member States make suggestions for Commissioners, and the Council, by common accord with the President-elect of the Commission, adopts the list of those who are to be Commissioners. The body of Commissioners is then subject to a vote of approval by the European Parliament. However, the formal appointment of the Commission is made by the European Council, acting by qualified majority, albeit on the basis of the approval given by the European Parliament.[24] Prospective Commissioners are commonly subject to scrutiny by the relevant parliamentary committee before approval by the European Parliament. Commissioners hold office for five years, and this term is renewable.[25]

The Commissioners must be chosen on grounds of general competence and their independence must not be in doubt. They must be independent in the performance of their duties, and can neither seek nor take instructions from a government or any other body.[26] Thus while Commissioners come from the Member States they do not represent their own state. The Commissioners meet collectively as the College of Commissioners. The Commission operates under the guidance of its President, and the Commissioners take decisions by majority vote.[27]

The Commissioners have their personal staffs (or cabinets), consisting partly of national and partly of EU officials.[28] There will be approximately fifteen officials in these teams, although the President of the Commission may have a larger cabinet. The members of the cabinet liaise with other parts of the Commission, scrutinize draft regulations and directives, and keep the Commissioner informed about developments in connected areas. There have, however, been tensions between the cabinets and

---

[18] Art 17(5) TEU, Art 244 TFEU.

[19] Art 17(7) TEU.

[20] Art 17(5) TEU.

[21] Brussels European Council, 10 July 2009, [I.2].

[22] 2013/272/EU: European Council Decision of 22 May 2013 concerning the number of members of the European Commission [2013] OJ L165/98.

[23] Art I–26(2) Draft CT.

[24] Art 17(7) TEU.

[25] Art 17(3) TEU.

[26] Art 17(3) TEU.

[27] Art 250 TFEU.

[28] Nugent (n 3) ch 5.

the Commission bureaucracy, with the former being regarded as representing national rather than EU interests.

(iii) *Removal*

An individual Commissioner can be compulsorily retired if he or she no longer fulfils the conditions for the job, or for serious misconduct. This decision is made by the Court of Justice on application by the Council.[29] The difficulty of removing Commissioners was part of the problem leading to the downfall of the Santer Commission. This is the rationale for the provision whereby a Commissioner shall resign if the President so requests.[30] There are also provisions for filling Commission vacancies in the event of resignation, compulsory retirement, or death.[31]

(iv) *Decision-Making*

The College of Commissioners operates in four different ways. First, important matters are dealt with through weekly meetings of the College, and the agenda is prepared by the Secretariat-General. These meetings will be preceded by discussion held by the Commissioners' *chefs de cabinet* to resolve differences. There may also be meetings of Commission groups, designed to coordinate its activities.

Secondly, the written procedure is used where 'deliberations in College do not seem to be necessary because all points have been agreed by the relevant DGs and approval has been given by the Legal Service'.[32] The proposal is sent to the Commissioners' cabinets, and if there is no objection within a specified period the decision is made. Any Commissioner can raise objections and request that the measure be considered at a College meeting.

A third mode of decision-making is empowerment, whereby the Commission empowers an individual Commissioner to make a decision, while respecting the principle of collective responsibility. There is finally the possibility of delegating decision-making to Directors General and heads of service, who act on behalf of the Commission, which is used for routine business.

(C) COMMISSION BUREAUCRACY

There has been much carping over the years about the size of the Brussels bureaucracy. This is largely based on ignorance of the facts. In 2010 the Commission employed approximately 24,000 full-time officials, with a further 6,000 people on temporary contracts. The permanent officials who work in the Commission, and who form the Brussels bureaucracy, are organized as follows.

Directorates-General (DG) cover the major internal areas over which the Commission has responsibility. There are now DGs for the following areas:[33] Agriculture and Rural Development; Budget; Climate Action; Communication; Communications Networks, Content and Technology; Competition; Economic and Financial Affairs; Education and Culture; Employment, Social Affairs and Inclusion; Energy; Environment; Eurostat; Financial Stability, Financial Services and Capital Markets Union; Health and Food Safety; Humanitarian Aid and Civil Protection; Human Resources and Security; Informatics; Internal Market, Industry, Entrepreneurship, and SMEs; International Cooperation and Development; Interpretation; Joint Research Centre; Justice and

---

[29] Art 247 TFEU.
[30] Art 17(6) TEU.
[31] Art 246 TFEU.
[32] Nugent (n 3) 94.
[33] http://ec.europa.eu/about/ds_en.htm.

Consumers; Maritime Affairs and Fisheries; Migration and Home Affairs; Mobility and Transport; Neighbourhood and Enlargement Negotiations; Regional and Urban Policy; Research and Innovation; Secretariat-General; Service for Foreign Policy Instruments; Taxation and Customs Union; Trade; and Translation. There are also units which provide General Services across the spectrum of Commission activities. These include the European Anti-Fraud Office (OLAF),[34] the Legal Service, and the Internal Audit Service.

There are essentially four layers within the Commission bureaucracy.[35] There is the Commissioner who has the portfolio for that area. There is the Director General who is the head bureaucrat of a particular DG, with responsibility to the Commissioner, and there is commonly a Deputy Director General. There are also Directors. A DG will have a number of Directorates, each of which will normally be headed by a Director who is responsible to the Director General or the Deputy Director General. The final part of the administrative organization is the Head of Division or Unit. These Divisions or Units are parts of Directorates. Each Division or Unit will have a Head, who will be responsible to the relevant Director.

Decisions and draft legislative proposals will normally emanate from a lower part of this hierarchy, upwards towards the College of Commissioners. There will be detailed discussion of the legislative process later.[36] Suffice it to say for the present that a proposal will normally originate within the relevant DG. Outside experts will often be used at this formative stage, and there will be consultation with national civil servants. The draft proposal will then pass up through the DGs to the cabinets of the relevant Commissioners, and on to the weekly meeting held by the *chefs de cabinet*. From there it will proceed to the College of Commissioners, which may accept it, reject it, or suggest amendments. Matters are more complex when a proposed measure affects more than one area, and hence more than one DG may be involved.

It is, moreover, not uncommon for the different DGs involved with a measure to have a 'different angle' on the problem. The term 'multi-organization' has been used to describe the priorities of different parts of the administration.[37] It is for this reason that consultations within the Commission will precede the meeting of the College of Commissioners. Formal meetings will be held by the *chefs de cabinet*, with input from members of the cabinet with specialist knowledge, the object being to reach agreement before the College convenes. There will also be informal exchanges between opposite numbers at all levels of the bureaucracy, including the Commissioners themselves, members of differing cabinets, and officials who work in DGs. The Secretariat-General will also play an important role in coordinating the drafting of legislative initiatives within the Commission as a whole.

The basic principle within the Commission is for positions and promotions to be based upon merit, determined by competitive examination. This meritocratic principle is qualified by the fact that Member States seek to ensure that their own nationals are properly represented, particularly in the senior posts. For this reason it has been traditional for an informal quota regime to operate in the allocation of such jobs,[38] although its legality is doubtful, since the Court has held that job allocation should be decided on merit.[39]

---

[34] This office is still at present part of the Commission, although it has an individual independent status for its investigative functions and is significantly more independent than the anti-fraud unit which it replaced, http://ec.europa.eu/dgs/olaf/index_en.html.

[35] Nugent (n 3) 138–142; A Stevens with H Stevens, *Brussels Bureaucrats? The Administration of the European Union* (Palgrave, 2001) ch 8.

[36] Ch 5.

[37] L Cram, 'The European Commission as a Multi-Organisation: Social Policy and IT Policy in the EU' (1994) 1 JEPP 194.

[38] Nugent (n 3) 174–176.

[39] Case 105/75 *Giuffrida v Council* [1976] ECR 1395.

(D) POWERS OF THE COMMISSION

The powers of the Commission are set out in Article 17 TEU:

> 1. The Commission shall promote the general interest of the Union and take appropriate initiatives to that end. It shall ensure the application of the Treaties, and of measures adopted by the institutions pursuant to them. It shall oversee the application of Union law under the control of the Court of Justice of the European Union. It shall execute the budget and manage programmes. It shall exercise coordinating, executive and management functions, as laid down in the Treaties. With the exception of the common foreign and security policy, and other cases provided for in the Treaties, it shall ensure the Union's external representation. It shall initiate the Union's annual and multiannual programming with a view to achieving interinstitutional agreements.
>
> 2. Union legislative acts may only be adopted on the basis of a Commission proposal, except where the Treaties provide otherwise. Other acts shall be adopted on the basis of a Commission proposal where the Treaties so provide.

The Treaty Articles have never been good at conveying the reality of the Commission's role. A 'bare' reading of Article 211 EC, the predecessor to Article 17 TEU, did little to convey the role played by the Commission. Article 17 TEU fares a little better in this respect, but still does not convey the full extent of the Commission's powers.

(i) *Legislative Power*

The Commission plays a central part in the legislative process, the details of which are discussed below.[40] The Commission is accorded the right of legislative initiative by Article 17(2) TEU, which places it in the forefront of policy development. Most proposals will have to be approved by the Council and the European Parliament, but the Commission's right of initiative has enabled it to act as a 'motor of integration' for the EU. The Council is, however, *de facto* the catalyst for many legislative initiatives.

A second way in which the Commission impacts on the legislative process is that it develops the overall legislative plan for any single year.[41] The agenda-setting aspect of the Commission's work is significant in shaping the EU's priorities for the forthcoming year. This role is both affirmed and qualified by Article 17(1) TEU, which is framed in terms of the Commission initiating the annual and multi-annual programme with a view to achieving inter-institutional agreement.

The Commission also affects EU policy in a third way, by developing general policy strategies. This is exemplified by the Commission's White Paper on the Completion of the Internal Market,[42] which shaped the Single European Act (SEA); Commission initiatives contributed to the development of Economic and Monetary Union; the Commission's Community Charter of the Fundamental Social Rights of Workers[43] (the Social Charter) was important in the debates about Community social policy; the Commission White Paper on European Governance affected debates about institutional reform;[44] and President Juncker's policy strategy document when taking office.[45]

---

[40] Ch 5.

[41] Commission Work Programme 2015, A New Start, COM(2014) 910 final.

[42] COM(85) 310.

[43] Ch 11 below.

[44] European Governance: A White Paper, COM(2001) 428, and Communication from the Commission on the Future of European Union—European Governance: Renewing the Community Method, COM(2001) 727.

[45] A New Start for Europe, My agenda, for Jobs, Growth, Fairness and Democratic Change, 15 July, 2014.

A fourth way in which the Commission exercises legislative power is through its capacity, in certain limited areas, to enact EU norms without the formal involvement of any other EU institution.[46]

Finally, the Commission exercises delegated power.[47] This is expressly contemplated by Article 290 TFEU. The Council and European Parliament delegate power to the Commission to make further regulations within particular areas.[48]

(ii) *Administrative Power*

The Commission has significant administrative responsibilities. This is reflected in Article 17(1) TEU, which states that the Commission shall manage programmes. Policies and legislation, once made, have to be administered. This will commonly be through shared administration, using national agencies.[49] The Commission will maintain a general supervisory overview, to ensure that the rules are properly applied within the Member States. There can be difficulties in executing this role successfully, as will be seen below.[50] It has also become increasingly common for the Commission to exercise direct administrative responsibility for the implementation of certain EU policy.[51]

(iii) *Executive Power*

The Commission possesses responsibilities of an executive nature. Two are of particular importance: those relating to finance and those concerning external relations.

The Commission plays an important role in the EU's budget. It also has significant powers over expenditure, particularly in relation to agricultural support, which takes a substantial share of the Union's annual budget, and structural policy, which is designed to assist poorer regions to convert or adjust declining industries, and combat long-term unemployment.

The Commission also exercises executive powers in the sphere of external relations. Nugent explains.

N Nugent, The Government and Politics of the European Union[52]

First, the Commission is centrally involved in determining and conducting the EU's external trade relations ... [T]he Commission represents and acts on behalf of the EU both in formal negotiations, such as those that are conducted under the auspices of the World Trade Organisation (WTO), and in the more informal and explanatory exchanges that are common between, for example, the EU and the USA over world agricultural trade, and between the EU and Japan over access to each other's markets.

Second, the Commission has important negotiating and managing responsibilities in respect of the various special external agreements that the EU has with many countries and groups of countries. . . .

Third, the Commission represents the EU at, and participates in the work of, a number of important international organizations ...

Fourth, the Commission has responsibilities for acting as a key point of contact between the EU and non-member States. Over 160 countries have diplomatic missions accredited to the EU. . . . The EU, for

---

[46] Ch 5 below.
[47] Ch 4 below.
[48] Chs 4, 5 below.
[49] P Craig, *EU Administrative Law* (Oxford University Press, 2nd edn, 2012) ch 4.
[50] Ch 17 below.
[51] Craig (n 49) ch 2.
[52] (Oxford University Press, 6th edn, 2006) 186–187.

its part, maintains an extensive network of diplomatic missions abroad, numbering over 130 delegations and offices, and these are staffed by Commission employees.

Fifth,...the Commission is entrusted with important responsibilities with regard to applications for EU membership. Upon receipt of an application the Council normally asks the Commission to carry out a detailed investigation of the implications and to submit an opinion. If and when negotiations begin, the Commission, operating within Council-approved guidelines, acts as the EU's main negotiator, except on showpiece ministerial occasions or when particularly sensitive or difficult matters call for an inter-ministerial resolution of differences....

(iv) *Judicial Power*

The Commission possesses two kinds of judicial powers, the foundation being Article 17(1) TEU, which provides that the Commission shall ensure the application of the Treaties and the law made pursuant thereto, and that it shall oversee the application of Union law under the control of the Court of Justice, the CJEU.

The Commission brings actions against Member States when they are in breach of EU law.[53] The action is brought under Article 258 TFEU and assumes the form of *Commission v UK*, etc. Recourse to formal legal action will be a last resort and will be preceded by Commission efforts to resolve the matter through negotiation.

The Commission also acts in certain areas as investigator and initial judge of a Treaty violation, whether by private firms or by Member States. The two most important areas are competition policy and state aids. The Commission's adjudicative powers provide it with a significant tool for development of EU policy, and its decision is reviewable by the General Court.

(E) DOWNFALL OF THE SANTER COMMISSION AND SUBSEQUENT REFORM

There had been concern for some time about fraud and mismanagement, particularly in areas such as the Common Agricultural Policy.[54] This culminated in the setting up of a Committee of Independent Experts, under the auspices of the European Parliament and the Commission. The Committee produced its first report in March 1999,[55] the concluding paragraph of which stated that it was 'becoming difficult to find anyone who has even the slightest sense of responsibility' within the Commission.[56] The Report had an immediate, dramatic effect: the Commission resigned. The principal problem revealed by the Committee's Report was not fraud by the Commission. It was the difficulty of maintaining control over those to whom power had been contracted out,[57] which is an endemic problem for all systems of public administration.[58]

---

[53] Ch 12 below.

[54] D Spence, 'Plus Ça Change, Plus C'est La Même Chose? Attempting to Reform the European Commission' (2000) 7 JEPP 1.

[55] Committee of Independent Experts, First Report on Allegations regarding Fraud, Mismanagement and Nepotism in the European Commission, 15 Mar 1999, [1.4.2].

[56] Ibid [9.4.25].

[57] P Craig, 'The Fall and Renewal of the Commission: Accountability, Contract and Administrative Organization' (2000) 6 ELJ 98.

[58] P Craig, *Administrative Law* (Sweet & Maxwell, 7th edn, 2012) ch 5; M Freedland, 'Government by Contract and Private Law' [1994] PL 86.

Romano Prodi took over as Commission President. He introduced a new Code of Conduct for Commissioners,[59] and set up the Task Force for Administrative Reform (TFRA). The TFRA produced a White Paper,[60] which was heavily influenced by valuable recommendations in the Second Report of the Committee of Independent Experts.[61] The general theme of the White Paper was the need for the Commission to concentrate on its core functions such as policy conception, political initiative, and enforcing EU law. Activities would be delegated to other bodies, so as to enable the Commission to concentrate on its core activities.[62] 'Externalization' was to be used only where it was the most efficient option; it would not be used at the expense of accountability; and there would have to be sufficient internal resources to ensure proper control. There was to be a new type of implementing body, and there were recommendations about financial control. The 2002 Financial Regulation adopted many of these ideas, providing a constitutional framework for much EU administration.[63] The idea that there should be a new breed of agency to oversee work contracted out was accepted,[64] and a number of such agencies were created [65]

(F) ROLE OF THE COMMISSION

The Commission has always been the political force most committed to integration.[66] It must perforce work with the Council and the European Parliament, and the pace of EU development has not always been steady because of this inter-institutional dimension.[67]

There is literature that sees the Commission's influence as in decline, as exemplified by its relatively low impact on the negotiations leading to the Treaty of Nice and the Constitutional Treaty.[68] A more positive picture has, however, been advanced by other writers, who focus on the continuing importance of the Commission bureaucracy.[69] It should moreover be noted that the Commission's power has been increased as a result of the measures enacted to combat the EU financial crisis.[70] The degree of power wielded by the Commission and the best way to explain the extent of Commission influence is therefore debated by political scientists. The following extract presents a spectrum of views.

[59] The Formation of the Commission, 12 July 1999. See also Operation of the Commission, 12 July 1999.

[60] Reforming the Commission, COM(2000) 200.

[61] Committee of Independent Experts, Second Report on Reform of the Commission, Analysis of Current Practice and Proposals for Tackling Mismanagement, Irregularities and Fraud, 10 Sept 1999

[62] Reforming the Commission (n 60) Part I, 6.

[63] Council Regulation (EC, Euratom) No 1605/2002 of 25 June 2002 on the Financial Regulation applicable to the General Budget of the European Communities [2002] OJ L248/1.

[64] Council Regulation (EC) No 58/2003 of 19 December 2002 laying down the Statute for Executive Agencies to be entrusted with certain tasks in the management of Community Programmes [2003] OJ L11/1.

[65] Craig (n 49) ch 2.

[66] See, eg, the Commission's communication prior to the Laeken European Council, The Future of European Union—European Governance: Renewing the Community Method, COM(2001) 727.

[67] See Chs 1, 5.

[68] H Kassim and A Menon, 'EU Member States and the Prodi Commission' in D Dimitrakopoulos (ed), *The Changing European Commission* (Manchester University Press, 2004) ch 5.

[69] See, eg, L Hooghe and H Kassim, 'The Commission's Services' in J Peterson and M Shackleton (eds), *The Institutions of the European Union* (Oxford University Press, 3rd edn, 2012) ch 8; T Christiansen, 'The European Commission: The European Executive between Continuity and Change' in J Richardson (ed), *European Union: Power and Policy-Making* (Routledge, 3rd edn, 2006) ch 5; M Rhinard and B Vaccari, 'The Study of the European Commission' (2005) 12 JEPP 387.

[70] Ch 20 below.

J Peterson, The College of Commissioners[71]

If the Commission really was so weak, intergovernmentalist accounts of EU politics…could be marshalled to explain why. First, it makes little difference who is Commission President. Second, the Commission is only powerful when and where national preferences converge. Third, the Commission is only empowered to the extent that member governments want to ensure the 'credibility of their commitments to each other'…There is little dispute, among scholars as well as practitioners, that the Commission has traditionally had little influence over most 'history-making' decisions about the broad sweep of European integration.

In contrast, institutionalist theory, now firmly established as the 'leading theoretical approach in EU studies'…paints a portrait of the Commission that is often powerful in day-to-day policy debates…According to this view, policy decisions in complex systems such as the EU are difficult to reverse, and policy often becomes locked into existing paths and 'path dependent'…

Some variants of institutionalism combine insights from rational choice and principal–agent theories…They hold that the principal authorities in EU politics—the member governments themselves—make rational choices to delegate tasks to the EU institutions, which then become their agents in specific policy areas. This body of theory sheds light on the tendency for the EU to make policy by means other than the traditional 'Community method' of legislating, according to which only the Commission can propose…

Increased affinity for new policy modes is…reflected in the creation of a variety of new regulatory agencies…EU governments increasingly seem to want new kinds of agents—not just the Commission—to whom they can delegate cooperative policy tasks. Usually, however, the Commission retains the job of identifying and seeking to solve coordination problems within policy networks of… private actors, consumer and environmental groups, and national and European agencies.

Advocates of multi-level governance as an approach to understanding the EU have long contended that the Commission enjoys a privileged place at 'the hub of numerous highly specialized policy networks of technical experts' even retaining 'virtually a free hand in creating new networks'…

3 THE COUNCIL

(A) COMPOSITION

Article 16(2) TEU states that the Council shall consist of a representative of each Member State at ministerial level, who is authorized to commit the government of that state.[72] The members of the Council are, therefore, politicians as opposed to civil servants, but the politician can be a member of a regional government where this is appropriate. The Council meets when convened by the President of the Council, or at the request of a member or the Commission.[73] Council meetings are more transparent than hitherto, as a result of changes introduced in June 2006.[74] The Lisbon Treaty provides that Council meetings are divided into two parts, those dealing with legislative and non-legislative acts respectively. When a Council formation meets in its legislative capacity it must meet in public.[75]

---

[71] Peterson and Shackleton (n 69) 117–118; D Rometsch and W Wessels, 'The Commission and the Council of Ministers' in G Edwards and D Spence (eds), *The European Commission* (Longman, 1994) 203.

[72] M Westlake and D Galloway, *The Council of the European Union* (Harper, 3rd edn, 2004); F Hayes-Renshaw and H Wallace, *The Council of Ministers* (Palgrave, 2nd edn, 2006).

[73] Art 237 TFEU.

[74] Brussels European Council, Presidency Conclusions, 15–16 June 2006, Annex 1.

[75] Art 16(8) TEU.

Council meetings are arranged by subject matter with different ministers attending from the Member States, and are regulated by the Council's Rules of Procedure.[76] There are at present ten such Council configurations, having been reduced from the twenty-two that prevailed in the 1990s. The General Affairs Council (GAC) deals with matters that affect more than one EU policy and also prepares the agenda for the European Council. The Foreign Affairs Council is chaired by the High Representative for Foreign Affairs and Security Policy, and national foreign ministers will normally attend. It deals with external relations and matters relating to the Common, Foreign and Security Policy. The Economic and Financial Affairs Council (Ecofin), by way of contrast, is concerned with matters such as the budget, Economic and Monetary Union, and financial markets, and is attended by national finance ministers. There is a Council dealing with matters concerning Justice and Home Affairs.

The other Council configurations deal with sectoral issues: Transport, Telecommunications and Energy; Employment, Social Policy, Health and Consumer Affairs; Agriculture and Fisheries; Competitiveness; Environment; and Education, Youth, Culture and Sport. The national ministers responsible for these matters attend such meetings, and are supported by national officials with expertise in the relevant area. The Commission attends Council meetings and has a particular role in relation to the GAC.[77]

(B) PRESIDENCY OF THE COUNCIL

There was considerable contestation in the debates that led to the Constitutional Treaty and Lisbon Treaty as to who should hold the Presidency of the Council.[78] The regime in the Lisbon Treaty is that the High Representative of the Union for Foreign Affairs presides over the Foreign Affairs Council (FAC).[79] The European Council decides by qualified majority on the list of other Council formations, and the Presidency of these formations.[80] The Presidency of Council formations other than the FAC must be in accord with the principle of equal rotation.[81]

A Draft Decision was included in the Lisbon Treaty, which embodies a 'team system' for the Presidency of Council formations other than the FAC.[82] The essence of this schema was that the Presidency of the Council, other than the FAC, was held by pre-established groups of three Member States for a period of eighteen months. The groups are made up on a basis of equal rotation among the Member States, taking into account their diversity and geographical balance within the Union. Each member of the group in turn chairs for a six-month period all Council configurations, except the FAC. The other members of the group assist the Chair in its responsibilities on the basis of a common programme. It is open to members of the team to decide on alternative arrangements among themselves.

The President, seven months before taking office, sets the dates for Council meetings in consultation with the Presidencies preceding and following its term of office.[83] Every eighteen months

---

[76] Council Decision 2009/937/EU of 1 December 2009 adopting the Council's Rules of Procedure [2009] OJ L325/35.
[77] Art 16(6) TEU.
[78] P Craig, *The Lisbon Treaty: Law, Politics, and Treaty Reform* (Oxford University Press, 2010) ch 2.
[79] Art 18(3) TEU.
[80] Art 16(6) TEU, Art 236 TFEU.
[81] Art 16(9) TEU.
[82] Lisbon Treaty, Declaration 9; Council 16517/09, Council Decision laying down measures for the implementation of the European Council Decision on the exercise of the Presidency of the Council, and on the chairmanship of preparatory bodies of the Council, Brussels, 30 Nov 2009; Council 16520/09, Decision of the Council (General Affairs) establishing the list of Council configurations in addition to those referred to in the second and third subparagraphs of Article 16(6) of the Treaty on European Union, Brussels, 26 Nov 2009; Council Dec 2009/937 (n 76) Art 1(4).
[83] Council Dec 2009/937 (n 76) Art 1(2).

the three Presidencies due to hold office prepare, in consultation with the Commission, the High Representative, and the President of the European Council, a draft programme of Council activities for that period, which has to be endorsed by the GAC.[84] The incoming Presidency establishes, at least one week before taking office, indicative provisional agendas for Council meetings for the next six-month period, based on the eighteen-month programme and after consulting the Commission.[85] During the actual six-month tenure, the President sets the provisional agenda for each Council meeting, which must be sent to other Council members and the Commission at least fourteen days before the meeting.[86] The agenda is divided into legislative activities and non-legislative activities, and each part is further divided into Part A, covering matters that can be approved without discussion, and Part B, those that require deliberation.[87] The provisional agenda is formally adopted at the Council meeting.[88]

The position of President of the Council has assumed greater importance in recent years,[89] for a number of reasons.[90] Strong central management became more necessary to combat the centrifugal tendencies within the Council. The growing complexity of the EU's decision-making structure necessitated more coordination between the institutions. The scope of EU power increased, demanding greater leadership in the Council. The Council's wish to be more proactive in the development of EU policy required initiatives organized by the President. Westlake and Galloway capture the importance of the position when they state that 'the Presidency is neither an institution nor a body, but a function and an office which has become vital to the good working of the Council'.[91] The President may develop policy initiatives within areas of concern either to the Council, or to the Member State that holds the Presidency.

While the Presidency therefore gives considerable power to the incumbent, the office is not without its stresses.[92] Presidencies must since 1989 draw up their programmes and present them to the Commission and the EP. Six months is a short time in which to get things done. The other Member States will consider the use to which the office has been put. If a country tries to use its Presidency to achieve goals that do not accord with majority sentiment in the Council and which are too narrowly nationalistic, then the criticism is likely to be particularly harsh.[93]

The Presidency of the Council has however altered significantly post the Lisbon Treaty. This is because prior to the Lisbon Treaty the President of the Council also held the Chair of the European Council. This is no longer so. There is a separate President of the European Council, who holds office for two-and-a-half years, renewable once.[94] The policy pursued by the country that holds the Presidency of the Council must therefore cohere with, or take into account, the more general EU strategy of the President of the European Council. The need for synergy in this respect has been recognized by the institutional players.[95]

---

[84] Ibid Art 2(6).
[85] Ibid Art 2(7).
[86] Ibid Art 3(1).
[87] Ibid Art 3(6).
[88] Ibid Art 3(7).
[89] E Kirchner, *Decision-Making in the European Community: The Council Presidency and European Integration* (Manchester University Press, 1992).
[90] Westlake and Galloway (n 72) ch 18.
[91] Ibid 326.
[92] T Christiansen, 'The Council of Ministers, Facilitating Interaction and Developing Actorness in the EU' in Richardson (n 69) 155–159.
[93] Westlake and Galloway (n 72) 334–337.
[94] Art 15(5) TEU.
[95] Council Dec 2009/937 (n 76) Art 2(6).

(c) COMMITTEE OF PERMANENT REPRESENTATIVES

The Lisbon Treaty provides that the work of the Council is to be prepared by the Committee of Permanent Representatives (Coreper), which shall carry out the tasks assigned to it by the Council.[96] Coreper is also empowered to adopt procedural decisions in cases provided for in the Council's rules of procedure. It does not, however, have the power to take formal substantive decisions,[97] but in practice Coreper 'has evolved into a veritable decision-making factory'.[98]

Coreper is staffed by senior national officials and operates at two levels. Coreper II is the more important and consists of permanent representatives who are of ambassadorial rank. It deals with the more contentious matters, such as economic and financial affairs, and external relations. It also performs an important liaison role with the national governments. Coreper I is composed of deputy permanent representatives and is responsible for issues such as the environment, social affairs, the internal market, and transport.

Coreper plays an important part in EU decision-making,[99] because it considers draft legislative proposals that emanate from the Commission, and helps to set the agenda for Council meetings.[100] The agenda is divided into Parts A and B: the former includes those items which Coreper has agreed can be adopted by the Council without discussion; the latter covers topics which do require discussion. It has been estimated that approximately 70–80 per cent of all Council decisions prepared by Coreper and/or working groups are then taken formally through the Council as 'A' points.[101] Decision-making within Coreper tends to be consensual, even where the formal voting rules specify qualified majority,[102] and Lewis notes that 'from a Janus-faced perspective, they act as both, and simultaneously, state agents and supranational entrepreneurs'.[103]

A large number of working groups, approximately 150, feeds into Coreper. They are the lifeblood of the Council, and examine legislative proposals from the Commission. They are composed of national experts from the Member States or from the Permanent Representations. In addition to these working groups the Council receives input from specialist committees established under the Treaty and from committees created by EU legislation.[104] There can be 'turf battles' between Coreper and other preparatory bodies, such as the Political and Security Committee.[105]

(d) COUNCIL SECRETARIAT

In addition to Coreper the Council also has its own General Secretariat, under the responsibility of a Secretary-General, which provides direct administrative support to it.[106] The Secretariat has a staff of about 2,800, and of these roughly 250 are 'A' grade, diplomatic level. It provides administrative service to the Council, Coreper, and the working parties. It prepares documentation, gives legal advice, undertakes translation, processes decisions, and takes part in the preparation of agendas. It will also work closely with the staff of the President of the Council, helping to smooth conflicts.

---

[96] Art 16(7) TEU, Art 240(1)TFEU.

[97] Case C–25/94 *Commission v Council* [1996] ECR I–1469.

[98] J Lewis, 'National Interests: The Committee of Permanent Representatives' in Peterson and Shackleton (n 69) ch 14.

[99] J Lewis, 'The Methods of Community in EU Decision-Making and Administrative Rivalry in the Council's Infrastructure' (2000) 7 JEPP 261; D Bostock, 'Coreper Revisited' (2002) 40 JCMS 215; Lewis (n 98) ch 14.

[100] Council Dec 2009/937 (n 76) Art 19.

[101] Christiansen (n 92) 162.

[102] Lewis (n 98) ch 14.

[103] Ibid 289.

[104] Hayes-Renshaw and Wallace (n 72) ch 3.

[105] Lewis (n 98) 280–281.

[106] Art 240(2) TFEU.

The Secretary-General is an important figure and the Council Secretariat has become more important over the years, especially in relation to EU Foreign and Defence Policy, Treaty negotiation,[107] and legal drafting.[108]

(E) POWERS OF THE COUNCIL

The Lisbon Treaty provides scant guidance as to the powers of the Council. Article 16(1) TEU merely provides that:

> The Council shall, jointly with the European Parliament, exercise legislative and budgetary functions. It shall carry out policy-making and coordinating functions as laid down in the Treaties.

This provision does little to convey the reality of the Council's powers. The Council exercises an important role in the decision-making process in seven ways.

The Council has to vote approval of virtually all Commission legislative initiatives before they become law. The vote will be by unanimity, qualified, or simple majority depending upon the particular Treaty Article, although it is deemed to act by qualified majority unless the Treaty stipulates to the contrary.[109] The draft Commission proposal will be scrutinized by Coreper and the working parties.

The Council has become more proactive in the legislative process through the use of Article 241 TFEU. This states that the Council may by simple majority request the Commission to undertake any studies which the Council considers desirable for the attainment of the common objectives, and to submit to it any appropriate proposals. If the Commission does not do so it must provide reasons. The Council has used this power to frame specific proposals that it wishes the Commission to shape into concrete legislation.[110] The Council has also used opinions and resolutions as a way of pressuring the Commission into generating legislative proposals.[111]

The Council can delegate power to the Commission, enabling the latter to pass further regulations within a particular area.[112] The Treaty rules will be analysed below.[113]

The increasing complexity of the EU's decision-making process has necessitated greater inter-institutional collaboration between the Commission, the Parliament, and the Council. This assumes various guises, from informal discussions concerning the shape of the legislative agenda to the use of Inter-Institutional Agreements.[114]

The Council, together with the EP, plays a major role in relation to the EU's budget, on which many initiatives depend.

The Council concludes agreements on behalf of the EU with third states or international organizations.

It has significant powers in relation to the Common Foreign and Security Policy (CFSP). Thus, it will be the Council which takes the necessary decisions for defining and implementing the CFSP in

---

[107] D Beach, 'The Unseen Hand in Treaty Reform Negotiations: The Role and Impact of the Council Secretariat' (2004) 11 JEPP 408.

[108] Christiansen (n 92) 164–167.

[109] Art 16(3) TEU.

[110] Sir Leon Brittan, 'Institutional Development of the European Community' [1992] PL 567.

[111] Nugent (n 52) 193.

[112] Art 290 TFEU.

[113] Ch 4.

[114] Ch 5.

the light of the guidelines of the European Council.[115] The Council has also played a major role in relation to the Area of Freedom, Security and Justice.

(f) ROLE OF THE COUNCIL

The Council represents national interests and always has. Whether the framers of the Rome Treaty would have been surprised by the interrelation between Commission and Council since the inception of the Community is unclear. They hoped that the EEC would herald an era of greater collaboration in which sectional, national interests would diminish in relation to the collective interests of the Community. The original EEC decision-making structure certainly bore testimony to the central role accorded to the Commission, as is evident from the range of its powers. Clearly, the Council had to approve legislation, but the Commission was in the driving seat. This was because of the Commission's power to set the legislative agenda, because of its institutional resources for the development of Community policy, and because, while Council consent was required for the passage of legislation, unanimity was required for Council amendments to Commission proposals.

It would be wrong to depict the Commission and the Council as perpetually at odds with each other throughout the Community's history.[116] But it would be equally mistaken to view the two institutions as coexisting in perfect harmony. There have been real tensions between the federal pro-integration perspective of the Commission, and the more cautious, intergovernmental perspective of the Council. The Treaty framers might have hoped that these tensions would be short-lived.[117] If this was so it was too optimistic a forecast. There have been institutional changes, often initially outside the letter of the Treaty, whereby the Council strengthened its position in relation to the Commission. This 'temporal' perspective on decision-making will be charted below.[118] It suffices here to note that the development of a veto power in the Council, the importance of Coreper, the creation of committees to oversee power delegated to the Commission, and the evolution of the European Council all played a part in this process.

The balance of power within the EU is however dynamic, not static. The institutions' formal powers and the actual way they interrelate have altered across time. The SEA was the catalyst for a change of attitude by the Member States as represented in the Council. There was a growing recognition that threat of the veto if a measure did not conform to a state's interests was too negative. The SEA also made the European Parliament a more active force in decision-making than hitherto. These developments did not mean that relationships between the Council and the Commission, or for that matter between the Council and the Parliament, were always smooth. It did mean that the inter-institutional relationships changed. Thus, as Christiansen notes, 'the Council may not (yet) be a supranational institution in its own right, but it has certainly moved on from being purely a site of decision-making and the forum for bargaining among representatives of national governments for which it was originally conceived'.[119] The same point is echoed by Hayes-Renshaw, who states that despite the Council being the EU's intergovernmental institution *par excellence*, it is, in reality, 'a unique blend of the intergovernmental and the supranational'.[120] This conclusion is also evident in the following extract.

---

[115] Arts 24–26 TEU.

[116] T Christiansen, 'Intra-Institutional Politics and Inter-Institutional Relations in the EU: Towards Coherent Governance?' (2001) 8 JEPP 747.

[117] Ch 1.

[118] Ch 5.

[119] Christiansen (n 92) 148.

[120] Peterson and Shackleton (n 69) 92.

F Hayes-Renshaw and H Wallace, The Council of Ministers[121]

The Council remains the fulcrum of the decision-making, and legislative process of the EU. This reflects the stubborn determination of member governments in the EU to maximize their involvement in framing the decisions and shaping the legislation that would have a bearing on their polities...Yet, to view the importance of the Council as the victory of intergovernmentalism over supranationalism, or to expect the Council to be able to 'run' the EU, is to misunderstand the institutional constellation of the EU. The Council shares and diffuses power between countries, between different kinds of interests and constituencies, and between national and EU levels of governance. The Council cannot act alone, but is dependent on intricate relationships with other EU institutions. Since the mid-1990s, however these relationships have changed a good deal. The European Parliament (EP) has gained considerable power as co-legislator with the Council, the Commission has lost ground in what used to be the classic 'Council–Commission tandem', and the Council has gained a good deal more direct executive power in newer areas of EU collective policy-making. All these factors have made the Council both more interesting as an object of study and more diverse in its ways of operating.

4 THE EUROPEAN COUNCIL

(A) COMPOSITION

The European Council[122] has evolved over the years. Meetings of heads of government took place during the 1960s, but they were institutionalized in 1974 at the Paris summit. They continued to be held during the 1970s and 1980s, even though there was no formal remit in the Treaty until the SEA. The governing provision is now Article 15 TEU:

1. The European Council shall provide the Union with the necessary impetus for its development and shall define the general political directions and priorities thereof. It shall not exercise legislative functions.

2. The European Council shall consist of the Heads of State or Government of the Member States, together with its President and the President of the Commission. The High Representative of the Union for Foreign Affairs and Security Policy shall take part in its work.

3. The European Council shall meet twice every six months, convened by its President. When the agenda so requires, the members of the European Council may decide each to be assisted by a minister and, in the case of the President of the Commission, by a member of the Commission. When the situation so requires, the President shall convene a special meeting of the European Council.

4. Except where the Treaties provide otherwise, decisions of the European Council shall be taken by consensus.

Meetings of the European Council were in the past held in the country holding the Presidency of the Council, but are now normally held in Brussels. The European Council is mentioned on other

---

121 Hayes-Renshaw and Wallace (n 72) 321.
122 S Bulmer and W Wessels, *The European Council* (Macmillan, 1987); P de Schoutheete and H Wallace, *The European Council* (Notre Europe, 2002); P Ludlow, *The Making of the New Europe: The European Council in Brussels and Copenhagen 2002* (EuroComment, 2004); P de Schoutheete, 'The European Council' in Peterson and Shackleton (n 69) ch 3; J Werts, *The European Council* (Harper, 2008); U Puetter, *The European Council and the Council: New Intergovernmentalism and Institutional Change* (Oxford University Press, 2014).

occasions within the Lisbon Treaty. Thus, for example, it has a prominent role within the CFSP, and in the context of politically sensitive matters, such as coordination of the economic policies of the Member States.

(B) PRESIDENCY OF THE EUROPEAN COUNCIL

Prior to the Lisbon Treaty the Member State that held the Presidency of the Council also chaired the European Council for the same period. The single most divisive issue in the decade of Treaty reform concerned the locus of executive power in the EU and whether the pre-existing regime should be retained.[123] There were two main positions.

The prominent version of the 'single hat' view was that there should be one President for the Union; the office of President should be connected formally and substantively with the locus of executive power within the EU; and the President of the Commission should hold this office. The Presidency of the European Council should continue to rotate on a six-monthly basis. The real 'head' of the Union would be the President of the Commission, whose legitimacy would be increased by election.

The prominent version of the 'separate hats' view was that there should be a President of the Commission and a President of the European Council, and that executive power would be exercised by both. The Presidency of the European Council would be strengthened, and would not rotate between Member States on a six-monthly basis. It was felt that this would not work within an enlarged EU, and that greater continuity of policy would be required. This view was advocated by some larger states, but was opposed by some smaller states, which felt that the Presidency of the European Council would be dominated by the larger Member States.

The 'separate hats' view prevailed. The Lisbon Treaty, following the Constitutional Treaty, provided that the European Council should elect a President, by qualified majority, for two-and-a-half years, renewable once; that the European Council should define the general political directions and priorities of the EU; and gave the President of the European Council increased powers within the Council.[124] The first incumbent of the new position was Herman Van Rompuy, who was previously the Belgian Prime Minister.

(C) RATIONALE

Member States' interests are already represented in the Council, and we must therefore press further to understand the rationale for the European Council. It was in part due to disagreements between the Member States themselves. These would normally be resolved through the Council, but if they were particularly severe on important issues, such as the budget, then resolution might be possible only through the heads of government themselves. The European Council was also due to the need for a focus of authority at the highest political level, in order that general EU strategy could be planned, and that its response to broader world problems could be properly focused.

(D) POWERS

The relative paucity of Treaty references to the European Council should not lead one to doubt its importance. It plays a central role in shaping EU policy, establishing the parameters within which the other institutions operate. As Schoutheete states, 'management of the Union could not be assured

---

[123] Craig (n 78) ch 3.
[124] Art 15(5)–(6) TEU.

without a top-level institution of this type: the European Council has played a fundamental role in European integration and will continue to do so'.[125] The issues commonly considered by the European Council can be grouped into the following categories.

The *European Council is central to the development of the Union*. Major changes in the Treaties will be preceded by an IGC, and the catalyst for its creation will normally be a European Council meeting. The European Council will also affirm the consequential Treaty changes,[126] and it was central to debates about the Constitutional Treaty and the Lisbon Treaty.

The *European Council will normally confirm important changes in the institutional structure of the EU*. The final decision on the enlargement of the Parliament following German unification was taken by a summit of the European Council.

The *European Council can provide the focus for significant constitutional initiatives that affect the EU*. Inter-Institutional Agreements between the three major institutions will often be made or finalized at a summit meeting. The Inter-Institutional Agreement on Subsidiarity and the Declaration on Democracy, Transparency and Subsidiarity were made at European Council meetings.

The *European Council will consider the state of the European economy*,[127] in part because Treaty provisions concerning closer economic union demand growing convergence between national economic policies, and in part because of the centrality of economic issues to the very health of the EU. Thus, the European Council frequently takes initiatives to combat unemployment, promote growth, and increase competitiveness, part of what is known as the Lisbon agenda.[128]

Conflict resolution is another issue addressed by the European Council. This was one of the rationales for its evolution, and continues to be important. For example, budgetary matters, 'who contributes how much, and who gets what financial benefits', continued to cause conflict between the Member States in the early 1980s, and then once again in the later 1980s.

The *European Council plays a role in the initiation/development of policy strategies*. Examples of this include the adoption of the Social Charter in 1989; policies aimed to combat problems concerning drugs and terrorism;[129] and the extension of the 'open method of coordination' to a range of social and economic policies.[130]

The *European Council is central in external relations*. It will, for example, consider important international negotiations, such as those with the World Trade Organization (WTO). It will be the European Council that issues declarations relating to more general international affairs, such as the civil war in what was Yugoslavia, or the conflicts in Lebanon, Iraq, and Syria.

The *European Council will consider new accessions to the EU*. Thus the European Council affirmed that Bulgaria and Romania should be admitted to the EU in January 2007, and debated more generally the EU's approach to membership and enlargement.[131]

(E) ROLE OF THE EUROPEAN COUNCIL

The European Council is a classic example of change in the original institutional structure of the Treaty to accommodate political reality. It evolved from a series of *ad hoc* meetings outside the letter

---

125 Schoutheete (n 122) 57.
126 8 Dec 2000.
127 See, eg, Luxembourg Extraordinary European Council, 20 Nov 1997; Stockholm European Council, 24 Mar 2001.
128 Lisbon European Council, Presidency Conclusions, 23–24 Mar 2000; Nice European Council, Presidency Conclusions, 7–9 Dec 2000; European Council, Presidency Conclusions, 22–23 Mar 2005.
129 Brussels Extraordinary European Council, 21 Sept 2001.
130 (N 128).
131 Brussels European Council, Presidency Conclusions, 15–16 June 2006, [52]–[53].

of the Treaty to a more structured pattern of summits. Treaty-recognition was originally accorded in the SEA and has been modified by later Treaty amendments.

The European Council is central to the EU's decision-making process. The reality is that no important developments internally or externally occur without having been considered by the European Council. The concluding resolutions do not have the force of law. They nonetheless provide the framework in which the other institutions consider specific policy issues. In the words of Westlake and Galloway, 'it is no exaggeration to say that, since 1975, most of the major political decisions of the European Community have been taken in the European Council'.[132]

The relations between the European Council and other EU institutions have evolved. The early European Council summits were viewed with suspicion by the Commission, since they were normally secret and the Commission was usually excluded. Matters are very different today. The European Council has been the institutional mechanism whereby the Commission can secure broad agreement from Member States for major initiatives.[133] The European Council's agenda is prepared by the GAC.[134] The Commission President is a member of the European Council, and many European Council initiatives are the result of Commission suggestions fed into the agenda prepared by the GAC. The President of the European Parliament has, since 1988, addressed a plenary session of the European Council.

The key issue in the post-Lisbon world is the relationship between the President of the European Council, the President of the Commission, and the country that holds the Presidency of the Council for a six-month period. The interplay between them shapes the policies and priorities of the EU. It was argued by opponents of the Lisbon regime that this would lead to confusion and divided responsibility, and that it would increase intergovernmentalism and reduce the supranational dimension of the EU. The elevation of the President of the Commission to be the 'sole' President of the EU would however have generated very real tensions and problems. The reality is that executive authority in the EU has always been divided, and in that respect the Lisbon Treaty represents continuity with, rather than departure from, past practice. There are moreover reasons why the three institutional players should seek consensus, rather than conflict.[135]

5 HIGH REPRESENTATIVE OF THE UNION FOR FOREIGN AFFAIRS AND SECURITY POLICY

(A) POWERS

The High Representative of the Union for Foreign Affairs and Security Policy is not listed in Article 13 TEU and is therefore not an EU institution in the formal sense of the term. It is nonetheless an important position, which must be considered in this chapter.

There were debates in the Convention on the Future of Europe as to the changes that should be made concerning institutional responsibility for external relations.[136] The Constitutional Treaty created the post of EU Minister for Foreign Affairs, who was to 'conduct' the Union's common foreign and security policy.[137] The nomenclature changed in the Lisbon Treaty, because some Member States

---

[132] Westlake and Galloway (n 72) 177.
[133] Ibid 179–180.
[134] Art 16(6) TEU; Council Dec 2009/937 (n 76) Arts 2(3).
[135] Craig (n 78) ch 3.
[136] CONV 459/02, Final Report of Working Group VII on External Action, Brussels, 16 Dec 2002, 19–23.
[137] Art I–28 CT.

were unhappy about the 'statist' connotations of the title 'EU Minister for Foreign Affairs',[138] which was therefore altered in the Lisbon Treaty to be High Representative of the Union for Foreign Affairs and Security Policy.[139]

The substance of the provisions in the Lisbon Treaty is, however, the same as in the Constitutional Treaty. Thus the High Representative is appointed by the European Council by qualified majority, with agreement of the Commission President.[140] The incumbent is one of the Vice-Presidents of the Commission, and is responsible for external relations and for coordinating other aspects of the Union's external action.[141] The High Representative conducts the EU's Common Foreign and Security Policy,[142] takes part in the work of the European Council,[143] chairs the FAC,[144] and is also a Vice-President of the Commission. The High Representative therefore wears 'two hats', or perhaps three if one regards the role of chairing the FAC as distinct from the other functions.

(B) ROLE OF THE HIGH REPRESENTATIVE

The idea that executive power within the Union is shared between the European Council and the Commission is personified in this post. It has been argued that the triple hats worn by the High Representative could lead to institutional schizophrenia, with the incumbent being subject to con-flicting loyalties.[145] There are also legal grounds for concluding that the institutional loyalty owed by the High Representative to the Commission is limited, and constrained by her responsibilities in the FAC and the European Council.[146] We should not, however, too readily assume that the Commission will be weakened by the creation of the new post. The High Representative is Vice-President within the Commission, with responsibility for external relations. The lessons and ideas generated by this 'front-line' work will inevitably impact on the proposals contributed by the High Representative to the more strategic development of common foreign policy, as decided by the European Council and fleshed out by the FAC. This is of course a 'two-way street'. The influence will operate the other way, such that the overall strategic focus of the European Council will impact on the way the High Representative discharges her responsibilities in external relations within the Commission.

6 EUROPEAN PARLIAMENT

The story of the European Parliament is one of gradual transformation from a relatively powerless Assembly under the 1952 ECSC Treaty to the considerably strengthened institution it is today.[147] The history is considered in Chapter 1, and its role in the legislative processes is examined in Chapter 5.

---

138 Brussels European Council, 21–22 June 2007, Annex 1, [3].

139 Art 18 TEU.

140 Art 18(1) TEU.

141 Art 18(4) TEU.

142 Art 18(2) TEU.

143 Art 15(2) TEU.

144 Art 18(3) TEU.

145 Y Devuyst, 'The European Union's Institutional Balance after the Treaty of Lisbon: "Community Method" and "Democratic Deficit" Reassessed' (2008) 39 Georgetown Jnl Int Law 247, 294–295.

146 Art 18(4) TEU; A Dashwood and A Johnston, 'The Institutions of the Enlarged EU Under the Regime of the Constitutional Treaty' (2004) 41 CMLRev 1481, 1504.

147 R Corbett, *The European Parliament's Role in Closer Integration* (Palgrave, 1998); B Rittberger, *Building Europe's Parliament: Democratic Representation Beyond the Nation State* (Oxford University Press, 2005); D Judge and D Earnshaw, *The European Parliament* (Palgrave, 2nd edn, 2008); R Corbett, F Jacobs, and M Shackleton, *The European Parliament* (Harper, 8th edn, 2011).

The Assembly was given few powers under the ECSC Treaty and under the original EEC and Euratom Treaties. It was intended to exercise consultative and supervisory powers, but not to play any substantial legislative role.

However, although the elite 'government of technocrats' established under the ECSC Treaty was not replicated in the EEC Treaty, the institutions set up by the latter were not a model of democratic organization. We saw in Chapter 1 how the influence of the Parliament grew, with the two budgetary treaties of 1970 and 1975, and after the transition to direct elections with the 'cooperation' and 'assent' procedures under the SEA and the 'co-decision' procedure under the Maastricht Treaty 1992,[148] which was strengthened and extended under the Amsterdam Treaty and the Nice Treaty.[149] The European Parliament now exercises substantial powers of a legislative, budgetary, and supervisory nature. While changes in the legislative process have enhanced the power of the only directly elected European institution, the problems of the EU's democratic legitimacy are not thereby resolved.[150] The 'demos' question is a complex one,[151] and the issue of democratic legitimacy will be considered below.[152]

(A) COMPOSITION AND FUNCTIONING

The Parliament sits in Strasbourg, but there is a secretariat based in Luxembourg and certain sessions and committee meetings take place in Brussels to facilitate contact with the Commission and Council.[153] Article 14(2) TEU states that:

> The European Parliament shall be composed of representatives of the Union's citizens. They shall not exceed seven hundred and fifty in number, plus the President. Representation of citizens shall be degressively proportional, with a minimum threshold of six members per Member State. No Member State shall be allocated more than ninety-six seats.
>
> The European Council shall adopt by unanimity, on the initiative of the European Parliament and with its consent, a decision establishing the composition of the European Parliament, respecting the principles referred to in the first subparagraph.

After much wrangling,[154] a Statute regulating important aspects of the rights and duties of Members of the European Parliament (MEPs) was enacted in 2005.[155] The Statute took effect from the parliamentary term beginning in 2009 and deals with important matters of principle: MEPs shall be free and independent and agreements concerning the resignation from office of an MEP before the end

---

[148] P Raworth, 'A Timid Step Forwards: Maastricht and the Democratisation of the European Community' (1994) 19 ELRev 16.

[149] A Dashwood, 'The Constitution of the European Union after Nice: Law-Making Procedures' (2001) 26 ELRev 215.

[150] D Beetham and C Lord, *Legitimacy and the EU* (Longman, 1998); C Lord, *Democracy in the European Union* (Sheffield University Press, 1998).

[151] JHH Weiler, *The Constitution of Europe* (Cambridge University Press, 1999); P Schmitter, *How to Democratize the European Union... And Why Bother?* (Rowman & Littlefield, 2000); E Smith, *National Parliaments as Cornerstones of European Integration* (Kluwer, 1996).

[152] Ch 5 below.

[153] Case C–345/95 *France v Parliament* [1997] ECR I–5215, on the holding of plenary sessions in Strasbourg.

[154] Corbett, Jacobs, and Shackleton (n 147) 59–69.

[155] Decision 2005/684/EC of the European Parliament of 28 September 2005 adopting the Statute for Members of the European Parliament [2005] OJ L262/1; Decision of the Bureau of 19 May and 9 July 2008 concerning implementing measures for the Statute for Members of the European Parliament [2008] OJ C159/1; Decision of the Bureau of the European Parliament of 11 and 23 November 2009, 14 December 2009, 19 April 2010 and 5 July 2010 amending the Implementing Measures for the Statute for Members of the European Parliament [2010] OJ C180/1.

of the parliamentary term are null and void; they shall be entitled to table proposals for EU acts; and can access the EP's files. The Statute also regulates practical matters relating to pay, insurance, and the like. The issue of pay has been of particular significance, since hitherto this was determined by national rates of pay, which differed markedly as between Member States.

The number of seats per country varies, but the 'representativeness' of the European Parliament has nonetheless been criticized because the number of MEPs for each state is not strictly proportionate to population size, and the smaller countries are disproportionately over-represented. A further cause for concern was that, despite holding direct elections since 1979,[156] the uniform electoral procedure originally envisaged was not created.[157] Article 223 TFEU requires the European Parliament to draw up a proposal concerning election of MEPs by direct universal suffrage in accordance with a uniform procedure in all Member States, or in accordance with principles common to all Member States. This has not yet occurred, but there is a Decision specifying that MEPs are to be elected on the basis of proportional representation; that elections shall be by direct universal suffrage; and that they shall be secret and free. Member States may set a threshold for the allocation of seats, provided it does not exceed 5 per cent of votes cast at national level.[158]

The Parliament's term is five years, like that of the Commission.[159] Following the Maastricht Treaty provisions on citizenship, citizens of the EU resident in any Member State gained the right to vote and to stand as candidates in European Parliament elections.[160] The turnout at EP elections has however been low,[161] which is worrying, given that the traditional EU discourse on democracy relies on the democratic legitimacy of the European Parliament. There is moreover significant disparity in voter turnout between different Member States.

MEPs sit according to political grouping, rather than nationality, the largest being, respectively, the centre-right European People's Party (Christian Democrats and European Democrats) with 221 seats after the 2014 elections, and the Group of the Progressive Alliance of Socialists and Democrats in the European Parliament with 191. The other parties are the European Conservatives and Reformists with 70 MEPs; the Alliance of Liberals and Democrats for Europe with 67 MEPs; the European United Left–Nordic Green Left with 52; the Greens–Free Alliance with 50; and the Europe of Freedom and Democracy Group with 48. There were 52 non-attached members.

Article 224 TFEU deals with European political parties. It provides that the European Parliament and Council acting in accordance with the ordinary legislative procedure shall lay down the regulations governing political parties at European level, and in particular the rules regarding their funding.[162] While the absence of properly constituted European-wide political parties has long been regretted by advocates of a genuine European political space, even this small step towards their establishment was not uncontentious.

The Parliament elects its own President, together with fourteen Vice-Presidents, for two-and-a-half-year terms, and collectively they form the Bureau of Parliament.[163] The Bureau is the regulatory

---

[156] Dec 76/787 [1976] OJ L278/1.

[157] Corbett, Jacobs, and Shackleton (n 147) 14–16.

[158] Council Decision 2002/772/EC, Euratom of 25 June 2002 and 23 September 2002 amending the Act concerning the election of representatives of the European Parliament by direct universal suffrage, annexed to Decision 76/787/ ECSC, EEC, Euratom [2002] OJ L283/1.

[159] Art 14(3) TEU.

[160] Art 22(2) TFEU.

[161] M Franklin, 'European Elections and the European Voter' in Richardson (n 69) ch 11.

[162] Regulation (EU, Euratom) No 1141/2014 of the European Parliament and of the Council of 22 October 2014 on the statute and funding of European political parties and European political foundations [2014] OJ L317/1; Regulation (EU, Euratom) No 1142/2014 of the European Parliament and of the Council of 22 October 2014 amending Regulation (EU, Euratom) No 966/2012 as regards the financing of European political parties [2014] OJ L317/28.

[163] Rules of Procedure of the European Parliament, 8th Parliamentary Term, 2015, rule 24.

body responsible for the Parliament's budget and for administrative, organizational, and staff matters.[164] There are also five 'Quaestors', responsible for administrative and financial matters directly concerning members, who assist the Bureau in an advisory capacity.[165] The 'Conference of Presidents' consists of the President together with the leaders of the various political groups.[166] It is the political governing body of the Parliament. It draws up the agenda for plenary sessions, fixes the timetable for the work of parliamentary bodies, establishes the terms of reference and size of parliamentary committees and delegations, and liaises with other EU institutions and with national parliaments.[167]

The Parliament has standing committees on matters including foreign affairs; human rights; security and defence; development; international trade; budgets; budgetary control; economic and monetary affairs; employment and social affairs; environment, public health and food safety; industry, research and energy; internal market and consumer protection; transport and tourism; regional development; agriculture and rural development; fisheries; culture and education; legal affairs; civil liberties, justice and home affairs; constitutional affairs; women's rights and gender equality; and petitions. Sub-committees and temporary committees or committees of inquiry can also be established. The committees are vital to the EP, since they consider legislative proposals from the Commission.[168] They can also produce own-initiative reports.[169]

(B) POWERS

(i) *Legislative Power*

The legislative process will be considered below.[170] It is sufficient for present purposes to say that the EP's role has strengthened over time. Prior to the SEA the general rule was that the EP only had a right to be consulted on legislation, and that was only where the particular Treaty Article so specified. The SEA introduced the cooperation procedure, which brought the EP into the legislative process more fully than hitherto. The co-decision procedure was introduced by the Maastricht Treaty, and in effect made the EP a co-equal partner, or something close thereto,[171] with the Council in the areas where it applied.[172]

It has been renamed the ordinary legislative procedure in the Lisbon Treaty[173] and its remit has been extended to approximately forty further areas. The co-equal status of the EP and Council is affirmed in Article 14(1) TEU, which now states that the EP shall, jointly with the Council, exercise legislative and budgetary functions. There are in addition certain areas where the assent of the EP is required for legislation. The EP now has a veto power over delegated acts,[174] but the reality of this new regime is uncertain, as will be seen below.[175]

---

[164] Ibid rule 25.

[165] Ibid rules 18, 24.

[166] Ibid rule 26.

[167] Ibid rule 27.

[168] Ibid rules 43–48.

[169] C Neuhold, 'The "Legislative Backbone" Keeping the Institution Upright? The Role of the European Parliament Committees in the EU Policy-Making Process', European Integration online Papers, Vol 5 (2001) No 10.

[170] Ch 5.

[171] A Kreppel, 'What Affects the European Parliament's Legislative Influence? An Analysis of the Success of EP Amendments' (1999) 37 JCMS 521.

[172] Art 251 EC.

[173] Art 289 TFEU, Art 294 TFEU.

[174] Art 290 TFEU.

[175] Ch 4.

The changes in the EP's role in the legislative process, most especially through what is now the ordinary legislative procedure, have brought it from the fringes of the EU to become a major player in the shaping of legislation. Its role has been further enhanced through regular meetings held by Council, Commission, and EP in inter-institutional conferences, and through the EP's greater contribution to the framing of the overall legislative agenda.

The EP made frequent use of litigation in order to defend its role in the legislative process,[176] and to contest the choice of legislative procedure used for a particular measure.[177] The ECJ held, after some hesitation,[178] that the EP could be a plaintiff in annulment proceedings, although only where its prerogatives had been infringed.[179] The Court also famously included the Parliament as a respondent in annulment proceedings even though only the Council and the Commission were mentioned under what was Article 173 EEC at that time.[180] The judicial developments were gradually incorporated into the Treaty following successive Treaty amendments. Thus, for example, the EP has full *locus standi* alongside the Commission, the Council, and the Member States to bring annulment proceedings.[181]

The EP's role in relation to the Common Foreign and Security Policy is smaller.[182] It is now the High Representative that is charged with consulting the European Parliament on the main aspects of the CFSP, and must take its views into account. The European Parliament can ask questions of the Council, and make recommendations to the Council and High Representative.

(ii) *Dismissal and Appointment Power*

The Commission's accountability to the Parliament has gradually been strengthened. The EP has always had the power to censure the Commission and require its resignation.[183] The latter power has never formally been used, though various motions of censure have been tabled, including during the period prior to the resignation of the Santer Commission in 1999.

Since the Maastricht Treaty the EP has also had the right to participate in the Commission's appointment. Article 14(1) TEU states that the EP shall elect the President of the Commission, but this must be read with Article 17(7) TEU, which provides for European Council influence over the candidate put before the EP.

The formal regime is thus that the European Council, acting by qualified majority, taking into account the EP elections and after having held appropriate consultations, proposes to the EP a candidate for President of the Commission. The candidate is then elected by the EP by a majority of its component members. If the candidate does not obtain the required majority, the European Council, acting by a qualified majority, shall within one month propose a new candidate, who shall be elected by the European Parliament following the same procedure.

The regime was however modified in substance as a result of the 2014 parliamentary elections, where candidates supported by the leading EP parties canvassed overtly for the position of Commission

---

176 Case 138/79 *Roquette Frères v Council* [1980] ECR 3333; Case 139/79 *Maizena v Council* [1980] ECR 3393.

177 See, eg, Case C–22/96 *European Parliament v Council (Telephonic Networks)* [1998] ECR I–3231; Case C–42/97 *European Parliament v Council (Linguistic Diversity)* [1999] ECR I–869; H Cullen and A Charlesworth, 'Diplomacy by Other Means: The Use of Legal Basis Litigation as a Political Strategy by the European Parliament and Member States' (1999) 36 CMLRev 1243.

178 Case 302/87 *Parliament v Council (Comitology)* [1988] ECR 5616.

179 Case C–70/88 *Parliament v Council (Chernobyl)* [1990] ECR I–2041; Case C–187/93 *Parliament v Council (Transfer of Waste)* [1994] ECR I–2857.

180 Case 294/83 *Parti Ecologiste 'Les Verts' v Parliament* [1986] ECR 1339, [23].

181 Art 263 TFEU.

182 Art 36 TEU.

183 Art 234 TFEU.

President. It was accepted by the European Council, albeit after some discussion, that the results of the election should be honoured and that the candidate of the party that secured most votes should become Commission President. It is very likely that this will continue in future EP elections. The EP committees will in addition question nominated Commissioners about their designated area, and this has led to persons nominated as Commissioners being replaced.[184]

(iii) *Supervisory Power*

The EP monitors the activities of the other institutions, principally the Commission, through the asking of questions and the establishment of committees of inquiry. The long-standing practices permitting the setting-up of committees of inquiry and the right to petition the EP were given Treaty status at Maastricht, and are now provided for under Articles 226 and 227 TFEU.[185]

The Maastricht Treaty also provided for the appointment by the Parliament of an Ombudsman. The Ombudsman is to receive complaints from Union citizens or resident third-country nationals or legal persons, concerning 'instances of maladministration in the activities of Union institutions, bodies, offices or agencies'[186] as well as to 'conduct inquiries for which he finds grounds, either on his own initiative or on the basis of complaints submitted to him direct or through a member of the European Parliament'.[187] The Ombudsman is appointed for the duration of the Parliament, and in the case of serious misconduct or non-fulfilment of the conditions of the office the CJEU may, at the request of the EP, dismiss the office holder.[188]

The EU Courts acting in their judicial role are excluded from the Ombudsman's jurisdiction, and the Ombudsman cannot undertake an own-initiative inquiry in relation to facts that are subject to legal proceedings. However the major limitation on the Ombudsman's jurisdiction is that only EU and not national institutions are subject thereto.

The EU bodies that are subject to the Ombudsman's jurisdiction must supply information requested and give access to files, except where grounds of secrecy are pleaded. The Ombudsman is empowered under Article 228 TFEU to conduct own-initiative inquiries, as exemplified by the 1996 inquiry into public access to documents held by a number of Community institutions.[189] The Ombudsman sends a report to the Parliament and to the institution under investigation, and the complainant is informed of the outcome. The Ombudsman has also adopted a number of special reports following the responses of the institutions to his draft recommendation on a complaint, and has advised that his recommendations be adopted by Parliament as resolutions, or on occasion, such as in relation to the need for a Code of Good Administration, that an administrative regulation should be enacted.

The Ombudsman has been a success and the office is increasingly seen as a source of administrative norms rather than simply a mediation facility for individual complaints.[190] Reference is made to the

---

184 In the case of members of the Court of Auditors, and the President, Vice-President, and Executive Board of the European Central Bank, the Parliament is to be consulted by the Council and the Member States, but its approval is not required, Arts 283, 286 TFEU.

185 E Marias, 'The Right to Petition the European Parliament after Maastricht' (1994) 19 ELRev 169.

186 Art 228(1) TFEU; K Heede, *The European Ombudsman: Redress and Control at Union Level* (Kluwer, 2000); P Bonnor, *The European Ombudsman: A Novel Rule-Source in Community Law* (PhD, Florence EUI, 2001).

187 Art 228(1) TFEU.

188 Art 228(2) TFEU.

189 [1998] OJ C44/1.

190 P Bonnor, 'The European Ombudsman: A Novel Source of Soft Law in the EU' (2000) 25 ELRev 39; I Harden, 'A l'écoute des griefs des citoyens de l'Union européenne: la mission du Médiateur européen' [2001] RTDE 573.

Ombudsman in Article 43 of the EU Charter of Fundamental Rights. The Ombudsman has referred frequently to the fundamental right to good administration contained in Article 41 of the Charter. The annual reports from the Ombudsman contain a wealth of valuable information about the complaints and their resolution.

(iv) *Budgetary Power*

The EP also has important powers in relation to the budget. It used its power over the budget to pressure for more general changes in the inter-institutional allocation of power, and conflicts not infrequently ended up in the Court.[191] The procedure for adoption of the budget is complex and is contained in Article 314 TFEU, which is a variant of the ordinary legislative procedure.

(c) ROLE OF THE EUROPEAN PARLIAMENT

The EP has undoubtedly become of greater importance in EU decision-making since the SEA. Its legislative, supervisory, and budgetary powers have increased, as has its power over the appointment of the Commission. The EP's influence has been most notable over primary legislation, and it has had less impact on either history-making decisions, such as Treaty revision, or policy-implementation, such as the passage of secondary rules made via Comitology. The change in the EP's power is nonetheless marked.

R Corbett, F Jacobs, and M Shackleton, The European Parliament[192]

The European Parliament's role in the Community's legislative procedure has increased from having, initially, no role whatsoever, to having a consultative role, to being a co-legislator with the Council. Parliament has demonstrated its ability to initiate new legislation in areas of concern to the public, to force substantial amendments to major legislative proposals and to oblige the Council to review important elements of several of the common positions it has adopted.

The European Parliament is not a sovereign Parliament in the sense of its word being final. On the other hand, it is not a Parliament whose powers are in practice exercised to legitimize a government's legislative wishes. It is an independent institution whose members are not bound to support a particular governing majority and which does not have a permanent majority coalition...

The European Parliament is now a clearly identifiable part of an institutional triangle. This fact in itself is remarkable in historical terms. The term 'institutional triangle' was virtually unused two decades ago when most commentators referred to a bicephalous Community made up of the Commission and the Council. Now the argument is rather one about preserving and developing the equal status that the Parliament has won with regard to the other two institutions and of making European electorates aware of the contribution that the Parliament is increasingly making to the content of European laws affecting us all.

---

[191] See, eg, Case 34/86 *Council v European Parliament* [1986] ECR 2155; Case 377/87 *European Parliament v Council* [1988] ECR 4017; Case C–284/90 *Council v European Parliament* [1992] ECR I–2277.

[192] Corbett, Jacobs, and Shackleton (n 147) 245.

This leaves open the reason why the EP has been able to increase its power in this manner. Auel and Rittberger[193] argued that the driving force was the need to alleviate the legitimacy deficit. Input legitimacy connotes the idea that political choices are legitimate because they reflect the 'will of the people', which is normally identified through the legislature. Output legitimacy captures the idea that the political choices thus made effectively promote the welfare of that community.[194] Transfers of competence from Member States to the EU thereby created an asymmetry between input and output legitimacy, and hence a legitimacy deficit, since the normal mechanism for input legitimacy, through national parliaments, was reduced as increasing areas were regulated by the EU. One response was to foster closer involvement of national parliaments in EU decision-making.[195] Another response to this legitimacy deficit was to increase the power of the EP.

K Auel and B Rittberger, The European Parliament, National Parliaments and European Integration[196]

[W]e argued that political elites have—since the SEA—gradually empowered the European Parliament's legislative powers and thus its capacity to influence European policy-making. Even though the decisions by member states to increase the legislative powers of the European Parliament were all but uncontroversial, the introduction and transfer of sectoral policy decisions to the European level triggered what we coined a democratic 'legitimacy deficit': European political elites came to perceive that the centralisation of policy-making tasks at the European level undermined the power of domestic parliaments to control and influence their respective governments in European policy-making. The legislative empowerment of the European Parliament was thus considered to serve as a mechanism to 'compensate' for domestic 'de-parliamentarisation'.

7 COURTS

Prior to the Lisbon Treaty the Community Courts comprised the Court of Justice (ECJ), the Court of First Instance (CFI), and judicial panels.[197] The nomenclature has been altered by the Lisbon Treaty. The term 'Court of Justice of the European Union' includes the Court of Justice, the General Court (the successor to the CFI), and specialized courts (the new name for judicial panels). Article 19(1) TEU provides that:

The Court of Justice of the European Union shall include the Court of Justice, the General Court and specialised courts. It shall ensure that in the interpretation and application of the Treaties the law is observed.

---

[193] K Auel and B Rittberger, '*Fluctuant nec Merguntur*. The European Parliament, National Parliaments and European Integration' in Richardson (n 69) 125–129. The argument is developed in more detail in Rittberger (n 147).

[194] F Scharpf, *Governing in Europe: Effective and Democratic?* (Oxford University Press, 1999) 6–7.

[195] Auel and Rittberger (n 193) 129–136.

[196] Ibid 136–137.

[197] R Dehousse, *The European Court of Justice* (Macmillan, 1998); A Arnull, *The European Union and its Court of Justice* (Oxford University Press, 2nd edn, 2006).

(A) COURT OF JUSTICE

Article 19(1) TEU states that there shall be one judge per Member State in the CJEU. They are appointed 'by common accord of the Governments of the Member States',[198] after consultation with a panel that reports on the suitability of the person to perform the function of a CJEU judge.[199] Judges and Advocates General of the Court must be chosen from persons whose independence is beyond doubt, who possess the qualifications required for appointment to the highest judicial offices in their respective countries, or are jurisconsults of recognized competence.[200] The term of office is six years, but the judge can be reappointed. The appointments are staggered, so that there will be a partial replacement of judges every three years.[201] The Court elects its President from amongst its own judges, and a Vice-President,[202] and appoints its Registrar.[203]

The CJEU is assisted by Advocates General.[204] The qualifications for selection, method of appointment, and conditions of office of the Advocate General (AG) are the same as for the CJEU judges. The AG's duty is principally 'to make, in open court, reasoned submissions on cases', Article 252 TFEU. An Opinion of the AG is not required in every case.[205]

Certain Member States have appointed academics as CJEU judges, whereas others, such as the UK and Ireland, have nominated advocates or existing domestic judges. A judge or AG who, in the unanimous opinion of the other judges and AGs, no longer fulfils the conditions and obligations of office may be removed.[206] Judges may not hold any other political or administrative office while members of the Court and, apart from their normal replacement, their period of office may terminate on death, resignation, or on removal from office.[207]

The CJEU may sit as a full Court, a 'Grand Chamber' composed of fifteen judges, or in Chambers, in accordance with rules laid down by the Statute.[208] It sits as a full Court either where the case is regarded as exceptionally important, or where the subject matter so warrants, such as an action for dismissal of the Ombudsman or a Commissioner.[209] The Grand Chamber is used when a Member State or an institution that is party to the proceedings so requests, and in particularly complex or important cases.[210] The great majority of cases are heard in Chambers of three or five judges,[211] which is vital to the Court's functioning, given its increasing case load.

The CJEU's jurisdiction is specified in the Treaties, and many of the heads of jurisdiction will be considered in subsequent chapters. Suffice it to say for the present that the main provisions governing its jurisdiction are Article 19 TEU and Articles 251–281 TFEU. International agreements between Member States may also confer jurisdiction on the CJEU.

---

[198] Art 253 TFEU.

[199] Art 255 TFEU.

[200] Art 19(2) TEU, Art 253 TFEU.

[201] Art 253 TFEU.

[202] Regulation (EU, Euratom) No 741/2012 of the European Parliament and of the Council of 11 August 2012 amending the Protocol of the Statute of the Court of Justice of the European Union and Annex I thereto [2012] OJ L228/1; Decision 2012/671/EU of the Court of Justice of 23 October 2012 concerning the judicial functions of the Vice-President of the Court [2012] OJ L300/47.

[203] Art 253 TFEU.

[204] Art 252 TFEU.

[205] Protocol (No 3) On the Statute of the Court of Justice of the European Union, Consolidated Version, 1 July 2013, Art 20; Art 281 TFEU contains the mechanism for amendment of the Statute.

[206] Ibid Statute Art 6.

[207] Ibid Statute Art 4.

[208] Art 251 TFEU.

[209] Statute (n 205) Art 16.

[210] Ibid.

[211] Ibid.

(B) GENERAL COURT

The CFI[212] was established in 1988 pursuant to the SEA.[213] Initially the CFI had a derivative institutional status, and was described in the EC Treaty as being 'attached to the Court of Justice'. This was altered by the Nice Treaty, and the Lisbon Treaty, as we have seen, now provides that the Court of Justice of the European Union shall include the General Court (GC), the new name for the CFI, and accords it responsibility within the sphere of its jurisdiction for the task of ensuring that the law is observed in the interpretation and application of the Treaty.[214]

The GC comprises 'at least' one judge per Member State, thus distinguishing it from the CJEU.[215] Pressures of workload required an increase in the number of GC judges, although there were protracted debates about the number and method of choice. There are no separate AGs on the GC, although a judge may be called upon to perform the task of an AG.[216] The members of the GC shall be chosen from 'persons whose independence is beyond doubt and who possess the ability required for appointment to high judicial office'.[217] They are appointed by common accord of the Member States for six years renewable,[218] after consultation with the judicial panel that advises on judicial appointments.[219] The GC elects its own President from amongst its judges, and appoints its Registrar.[220] It sits in Chambers of three and five judges, or sometimes as a single judge,[221] and approximately 75 per cent of cases are heard by Chambers of three judges. It may also sit as a Grand Chamber or full Court when the complexity or importance of the case demands it.[222]

There is an appeal to the CJEU within two months from the GC's decision.[223] The appeal is limited to questions of law, and this covers 'lack of competence of the General Court, a breach of procedure before it which adversely affects the interests of the appellant as well as the infringement of Union law by the General Court'.[224]

The rationale for the creation of the Court was to relieve the burden on the CJEU. It was initially given jurisdiction over staff cases, competition cases brought by individuals against the Community institutions, and certain cases under the ECSC Treaty. Gradually the Council transferred to it other categories of case. The GC's jurisdiction is now determined by Article 256 TFEU. This will be examined in detail later. It is sufficient to say here that the GC has jurisdiction over most, although not all, direct actions.[225] Direct enforcement actions against Member States under Articles 258 and 259 TFEU remain, however, under the jurisdiction of the CJEU, although this can be changed through amendment of the Statute. The GC can hear actions against decisions of specialized courts, and the GC's rulings can be reviewed by the CJEU only in exceptional circumstances, 'where there is a serious risk of the unity or consistency of Union law being affected'.[226]

---

[212] Known in French as the *Tribunal de Première Instance*, which explains the T used before the case number when a case is registered with the CFI/General Court.

[213] Council Decision 88/591 [1988] OJ L319/1.

[214] Art 19(1) TEU.

[215] Art 19(2) TEU.

[216] Statute (n 205) Art 49.

[217] Art 254 TFEU.

[218] Art 254 TFEU.

[219] Art 255 TFEU.

[220] Art 254 TFEU.

[221] Council Decision 1999/291 [1999] OJ L114/52; Statute (n 205) Art 50.

[222] Ibid Art 50.

[223] Ibid Art 56.

[224] Ibid Art 58.

[225] The principal categories of direct actions are: annulment actions, Art 263 TFEU; actions for failure to act, Art 265 TFEU; and damages actions, Art 340 TFEU.

[226] Art 256(2) TFEU.

Indirect actions begin in national courts, which seek a preliminary ruling from the CJEU on EU law pursuant to Article 267 TFEU. The national court then decides the case in the light of that ruling. Prior to the Nice Treaty such cases were the preserve of the ECJ. The Nice Treaty changed this and the schema has been carried over to the Lisbon Treaty. Thus the GC can be empowered to decide on preliminary rulings under Article 267 TFEU 'in specific areas laid down by the Statute',[227] subject to controls by the CJEU. The Nice IGC specified in Declarations 12 and 13 that attention should be given as soon as possible to the delineation of such areas, but there has nonetheless been no move to make this a reality by specifying the areas in which the GC would have power over preliminary rulings.[228]

(c) SPECIALIZED COURTS

The establishment of specialized courts, hitherto judicial panels, is governed by Article 257 TFEU. The principal rationale for this development, which dates from the Nice Treaty, was to ease the workload of the CJEU and GC. The proposal to create a system of decentralized or regional EU courts was not taken up,[229] but the creation of a third jurisdictional level below the CJEU and the GC was the most significant structural reform of the EU judicial system since the establishment of the GC. A European Union Civil Service Tribunal has been created to adjudicate on staff cases.[230]

Article 257 TFEU stipulates that the European Parliament and the Council, acting via the ordinary legislative procedure, may establish specialized courts attached to the GC to hear at first instance certain classes of action in specific areas. The European Parliament and the Council act either on a proposal from the Commission after consultation with the Court of Justice, or at the request of the Court of Justice after consultation with the Commission. Decisions given by specialized courts are normally subject to appeal only on law, subject to the caveat that there can be appeal on fact if the regulation establishing a particular specialized court so provides. The members of the specialized courts are chosen from persons whose independence is beyond doubt and who possess the ability required for appointment to judicial office. They are appointed by the Council, acting unanimously.

(d) REFORM OF THE COURT SYSTEM

Reform of the EU Court system was long-awaited and oft-proposed, but reactions to the Nice Treaty amendments to the 'judicial architecture' were rather muted.

JHH Weiler, The Judicial Après-Nice[231]

The actual outcome of the Conference in this area too, as with the political institutions, is an inability to break away from the scheme of the original Treaties. At the core of this architecture, and its most important feature by any perspective one may care to adopt, is the Preliminary Reference and the

---

[227] Art 256(3) TFEU.

[228] Ch 13.

[229] H Rasmussen, 'Remedying the Crumbling EC Judicial System' (2000) 37 CMLRev 1071; JP Jacqué and J Weiler, 'On the Road to European Union: A New Judicial Architecture: An Agenda for the Intergovernmental Conference' (1990) 27 CMLRev 185.

[230] Council Decision 2004/752/EC, Euratom of 2 November 2004, establishing the European Union Civil Service Tribunal [2004] OJ L333/7.

[231] G de Búrca and JHH Weiler (eds), *The European Court of Justice* (Oxford University Press, 2001) 217–218.

Preliminary Ruling. This procedure has remained substantially unchanged for half a century. A Court of First Instance with new-found dignity, Judicial Panels and all the rest notwithstanding, Europe continues to drive in its rusty and trusted 1950 model with the steering wheel firmly in the hands of the Court of Justice.

Put differently, the IGC was not willing to engage in either profound rethinking or profound re-engineering of the judicial function in view of a much changed polity to the one in which the current system was set.... And yet the context in which the judicial system is situated has changed radically in the last fifty years. The increase of size from six Member States to a potential of twenty-six is really only part of the problem, and possibly not even the most important part. Not a limited jurisdiction over some technical areas but a complex polity with jurisdiction ranging from human rights to monetary policy to difficult aspects of immigration and even citizenship.... And then the Court itself: no longer an instance for dispute settlement, but a judicial giant which has successfully positioned itself at the constitutional centre of Europe, a Europe in which national legal orders suddenly feel under threat.

Space precludes detailed elaboration of the changes that might be made to the EU's judicial architecture, although this will be examined in part when discussing preliminary rulings.[232] Suffice it to say for the present that overhaul of the judicial architecture, and the division of jurisdiction between the CJEU and GC for both direct and indirect actions, would be desirable.[233] The Constitutional Treaty and the Lisbon Treaty had less impact on the EU Courts than on the other institutions. The Courts' role within the new constitutional scheme was considered only relatively late in the Convention proceedings, when a Discussion Circle was set up and it worked under severe time constraints. There was little consideration given to the general division of jurisdiction between the ECJ, CFI, and national courts and the Discussion Circle focused on a number of more discrete legal issues. The overall judicial architecture in the Constitutional Treaty and Lisbon Treaty therefore largely replicated the existing Treaties.[234]

(E) ADVOCATE GENERAL

The CJEU's decision-making is assisted by the office of AG. The AG is a full member of the Court and participates at the oral stage of the judicial hearing. The AG's most important task is to produce a written opinion, the 'reasoned submissions' mentioned in Article 252 TFEU, for the Court. This opinion is produced before the Court makes its decision. An AG does not have to be involved in every case and the Statute determines when this is required.[235]

The written opinion sets out the AG's view of the law, and recommends how the case should be decided. This opinion does not bind the Court, but is very influential, and is often followed by the Court. The AG's opinion is intended to constitute impartial and independent advice, and in practice it tends to be a comprehensive, reasoned account of the law governing all aspects of the case. It will often shed light on a CJEU judgment that is difficult to interpret.

---

[232] Ch 13.

[233] P Craig, *EU Administrative Law* (Oxford University Press, 2nd edn, 2012) ch 10.

[234] Craig (n 78) ch 4.

[235] Statute (n 205) Art 20 provides that where the ECJ 'considers that the case raises no new point of law, the Court may decide, after hearing the Advocate-General, that the case shall be determined without a submission from the Advocate-General'.

(F) PROCEDURE BEFORE THE COURT

Procedure before the CJEU and GC is governed by their respective rules of procedure.[236] The procedure before the CJEU takes place in two stages, the written and the oral stages.[237] The written part of the proceedings is normally more important than the oral. At the written stage, all applications, statements of case, defences, and any submissions or relevant documents are communicated to the parties and institutions whose decisions are being contested. The oral stage, by contrast, is limited and short. The *juge-rapporteur*, the judge assigned in a given case, prepares and presents to the Court the 'report for the hearing', which summarizes the facts of the case and the arguments of the parties. The legal representatives may make oral submissions to the Court, which can question them. This has become an important part of the oral proceedings, since it clarifies the issues which the Court considers of significance in the case.

While there is an appeal from judicial panels to the GC and appeals on points of law from the GC to the CJEU, there is no further appeal from the judgments of the CJEU. However, Member States, EU institutions, and parties may under certain conditions contest a judgment delivered without their being heard, where it is prejudicial to their rights.[238] There is also a mechanism whereby any party with an interest in a particular judgment may apply to the Court to construe its meaning where this is in doubt,[239] and revision of a judgment within ten years of its being given can be sought 'only on discovery of a fact which is of such nature as to be a decisive factor' and which was unknown at the time the judgment was given.[240]

The Court, while generally building on its case law, does not consider itself bound by a strict system of precedent.[241] The CJEU may explain the rationale for departure from prior case law, but will not always indicate the cases that have been 'overruled'.[242]

(G) STYLE OF THE COURT'S JUDGMENTS

The style of the CJEU's judgments stands in contrast with the AG's opinions. The CJEU's and GC's judgments are collegiate, representing the single ruling of all judges hearing the case. There are no dissents or separately concurring judgments, and therefore divergent judicial views may be contained within the judgment. This can result in a ruling that is ambiguous on matters of importance. Further difficulties can arise because of the multiplicity of languages used before the Court. Moreover, while the AG's opinion generally considers exhaustively all the legal arguments relevant to the case, the Court may prefer not to commit itself on a specific legal issue until another case arises where it is directly necessary for a decision.

(H) ROLE OF THE COURT

The CJEU has, as noted above, various heads of jurisdiction. Its contribution to EU law has moreover been shaped through use of Article 19(1) TEU, which provides that it 'shall ensure that in the interpretation

---

[236] N Brown and T Kennedy, *The Court of Justice of the European Communities* (Sweet & Maxwell, 5th edn, 2000); K Lenaerts, 'The European Court of First Instance: Ten Years of Interaction with the Court of Justice' in D O'Keeffe and A Bavasso (eds), *Judicial Review in EU Law* (Kluwer, 2000) 97.

[237] Statute (n 205) Art 20.

[238] Ibid Art 42.

[239] Ibid Art 43; Case 69/85 *Re Wünsche* [1986] ECR 947.

[240] Statute (n 205) Art 44.

[241] A Arnull, 'Owning up to Fallibility: Precedent and the Court of Justice' (1993) 30 CMLRev 247.

[242] See, eg, Cases C–267–268/91 *Keck and Mithouard* [1993] ECR I–6097.

and application of the Treaties the law is observed'. This provision now applies to all EU Courts, but it has been the CJEU which made principal use of it. It will be seen in subsequent chapters how the Court utilized this provision to extend review to cover bodies which were not expressly subject to it,[243] and measures which were not listed in the Treaty.[244] In the name of preserving 'the rule of law' the Court has developed principles of a constitutional nature as part of EU law, which bind the EU institutions and Member States when they act within the sphere of EU law.[245] It is the CJEU, as interpreter of the Treaties, which adjudicates on the limits of EU competence as against the Member States.[246]

It has moreover been the Court that fashioned seminal principles of the EU legal order, such as direct effect, supremacy, and state liability in damages. These principles have defined the very nature of the EU, constitutionalizing it and distinguishing it from other international treaties. They were especially significant in the years of so-called institutional malaise or stagnation. The Court rendered the Treaty and EC legislation effective when the provisions had not been implemented as required by the political institutions and the Member States.[247] This was exemplified by the Court's role in the creation of the internal market, requiring removal of national trade barriers, when progress towards completing the single market through legislative harmonization was hindered by institutional inaction.[248]

It is therefore important to view the CJEU's role from a dynamic, rather than static, perspective. It was suggested, after the revival of the political processes of integration leading to the SEA, that the Court should thereafter adopt a 'minimalist' role.[249] The reality is that the Court has not been a consistently 'activist' court at all times, or in all policy spheres. It may, for example, simultaneously create new methods of enforcement,[250] while reducing its intervention in an area where legislative institutions have become more active. The Court is moreover aware of the political environment in which it acts and its judgments are at times influenced by relatively 'non-legal' arguments made by Member States, relating to the financial impact of a ruling, or by critical responses from the public or from national and Union sources.[251]

The Court's jurisprudence cannot be properly understood without an awareness of its approach to interpretation. This is generally described as purposive or teleological.[252] The fact that the documents leading to the making of the original Treaties, known as the *travaux préparatoires*, were not available for thirty years meant these were not used as a source, and this is reflected in the Court's case law.[253] In the case of secondary legislation, declarations and extracts from the minutes have occasionally

---

[243] It subjected the Parliament to judicial review under Art 230 EC in Case 294/83 (n 180) although it was not included in the Treaty as a body subject to review. Conversely, in Case 70/88 (n 179) it allowed Parliament to bring such an action despite not being covered by the Treaty.

[244] Case 22/70 *Commission v Council (ERTA)* [1971] ECR 263.

[245] Chs 11 and 15.

[246] Ch 3.

[247] Ch 7.

[248] Case 8/74 *Procureur du Roi v Dassonville* [1974] ECR 837; Case 120/78 *Rewe-Zentrale AG v Bundesmonopolverwaltung für Branntwein (Cassis de Dijon)* [1979] ECR 649.

[249] T Koopmans, 'The Role of Law in the Next Stage of European Integration' (1986) 35 ICLQ 925.

[250] See, eg, Cases C–6 and 9/90 *Francovich and Bonifaci v Italy* [1991] ECR I–5357; Cases C–46 and 48/93 *Brasserie du Pêcheur SA v Germany* [1996] ECR I–1029.

[251] See, eg, Case C–262/88 *Barber v Guardian Royal Exchange Assurance Group* [1990] ECR I–1889; Case C–450/93 *Kalanke v Freie Hansestadt Bremen* [1995] ECR I–3051; Case C–409/95 *Hellmut Marschall v Land Nordrhein Westfalen* [1997] ECR I–6363.

[252] A Bredimas, *Methods of Interpretation and Community Law* (North Holland, 1978); J Bengoetxea, *The Legal Reasoning of the European Court of Justice* (Oxford University Press, 1993); T Koopmans, 'The Theory of Interpretation and the Court of Justice' in O'Keeffe and Bavasso (n 236) 45; C Kombos, *The ECJ and Judicial Activism: Myth or Reality?* (Sakkoulas, 2010).

[253] See, eg, Case 149/79 *Commission v Belgium* [1980] ECR 3881, 3890; Case 2/74 *Reyners v Belgium* [1974] ECR 631, 666, AG Mayras.

been relied on as aids to interpretation before the Court.[254] However in most cases it has denied the relevance of this material if it does not appear in the text of the legislation.[255]

The Court's teleological or purposive approach is not therefore narrowly historical. The Court rather examines the whole context in which a particular provision is situated, and gives the interpretation most likely to further what the Court considers that provision sought to achieve. This may not be the literal interpretation of the Treaty, or of the legislation, and may not comport with the express language. This aspect of the Court's methodology has attracted criticism, although it has been defended robustly by members of the academic community, by its former personnel, and by some practitioners.

The best known of the Court's early critics was Rasmussen. His thesis was that the Court sought 'inspiration in guidelines which are essentially political of nature and hence, not judicially applicable. This is the root of judicial activism which may be a usurpation of power.'[256] He did not criticize all 'activism', but rather that which he believed to have lost popular legitimacy. There were mixed reactions to Rasmussen's work from an academic community that had largely been supportive of the Court's strategy.[257] Thus Cappelletti argued that Rasmussen's critique lacked an historical dimension, that any constitutional court should have the courage to enforce its 'higher law' against temporary pressures, and that the Court's vision 'far from being arbitrary, is fully legitimate, for it is rooted in the text, most particularly in the Preamble and the first Articles of the EEC Treaty'.[258]

A further attack on the Court came from Sir Patrick Neill, in his 'case study in judicial activism', in which he argued that the Court was a dangerous institution, skewed by its own policy considerations and driven by an elite mission.[259] Advocate General Fennelly however pointed out that the Member States through Treaty revisions have either explicitly or implicitly approved many Court decisions.[260] Advocate General Jacobs, in defence of the Court's 'constitutional' role, argued that it plays an essential role in preserving the balance between the Union and the Member States, and in developing constitutional principles of judicial review.

F Jacobs, Is the Court of Justice of the European Communities a Constitutional Court?[261]

If then, the Court sometimes performs the task of a Constitutional Court, and if it has developed constitutional principles in its case law, we can understand why, in some quarters, the Court's activities have been misunderstood. The Court has sometimes been criticized as a 'political' Court. Such criticisms

---

[254] Case 136/78 *Ministère Public v Auer* [1979] ECR 437, [25]–[26]; Case 131/86 *United Kingdom v Council* [1988] ECR 905, [26]–[27].

[255] See, eg, Case 38/69 *Commission v Italy* [1970] ECR 47, [12]; Case 143/83 *Commission v Denmark* [1985] ECR 427; Case 237/84 *Commission v Belgium* [1986] ECR 1247; Case 306/89 *Commission v Greece* [1991] ECR 5863, [6], [8]; Case C–292/89 *Antonissen* [1991] ECR I–745.

[256] H Rasmussen, *On Law and Policy in the European Court of Justice* (Martinus Nijhoff, 1986) 62.

[257] M Cappelletti (1987) 12 ELRev 3; J Weiler (1987) 24 CMLRev 555; A Toth (1987) 7 YBEL 411.

[258] *The Judicial Process in Comparative Perspective* (Clarendon Press, 1989) 390–391.

[259] *The European Court of Justice: A Case Study in Judicial Activism* (European Policy Forum, 1995). See also T Hartley, 'The European Court, Judicial Objectivity and the Constitution of the European Union' (1996) 112 LQR 95.

[260] N Fennelly, 'Preserving the Legal Coherence within the New Treaty: The ECJ after the Treaty of Amsterdam' (1998) 5 MJ 185, 198.

[261] D Curtin and D O'Keeffe (eds), *Constitutional Adjudication in European Community and National Law* (Butterworths (Ireland), 1992) 25, 32. See also T Tridimas, 'The Court of Justice and Judicial Activism' (1997) 22 ELRev 199; A Arnull, 'The European Court and Judicial Objectivity: A Reply to Professor Hartley' (1996) 112 LQR 95; G Howe, 'Euro-Justice: Yes or No?' (1996) 21 ELRev 187, 191; A Albors-Llorens, 'The European Court of Justice: More than a Teleological Court' (1999) 2 CYELS 373; Kombos (n 252); P Craig, 'The ECJ and *Ultra Vires* Action: A Conceptual Analysis' (2011) 48 CMLRev 395.

are probably based on unfamiliarity with the very notion of constitutional jurisprudence, which, as we have seen, is not familiar in all the Member States, and which requires what may seem novel judicial techniques, different approaches to interpretation, even a different conception of the law. Yet, in the Community system, which is based on the notion of a division of powers, some form of constitutional adjudication is inescapable, if indeed the Community is to be based, as its founders intended, on the rule of law.

It is true that all constitutional courts engage with political issues, but given the unaccountability of courts, the nature and origin of the 'unwritten' values which they promote should be critically scrutinized, as should the extent to which their decisions seem to depart from what their express powers would appear to allow. It is equally important for such judicial decision-making to be fully reasoned.[262]

The Court has overall pursued a policy of legal integration, giving substance to an 'outline' Treaty, thereby enhancing the effectiveness of EU law and promoting its integration into national legal systems. While excessive concentration on the Court should be avoided,[263] its role as an institutional actor in the integration process should be recognized. The nature of this role has been considered by political scientists as well as lawyers.

For liberal intergovernmentalists the central message is that states are the driving forces behind integration, that supranational actors are there largely at their behest, and that such actors have little independent impact on the pace of integration.[264] The supranational institutions are viewed as agents for the Member States, who accord power to such institutions for their own self-interest. Thus the Court's powers are rationalized on the ground that the existence of proper adjudicatory mechanisms at the supranational level can prevent prisoner dilemma and free-rider problems, thereby removing the possibility that the system will be undermined by states seeking to reap the rewards of membership while trying to avoid their obligations.[265]

The idea that the Court can be regarded as an agent of the Member States, with little if any independent impact on integration, will be questioned by lawyers, even if they disagree as to the nature of this impact. It would, to take but one prominent example, be difficult to rationalize the jurisprudence on citizenship in simple principal–agent terms, given that the CJEU's expansive interpretation of the relevant Treaty Articles was often given in the face of fierce opposition from the Member States.[266] It is moreover clear that political scientists who have studied the Court often disagree with liberal intergovernmentalism. Thus Stone Sweet argues against the view that the Court can be regarded as some perfect agent for Member State governments, and contends that Court decisions often produce 'unintended consequences' not readily foreseen by those who designed the EC.[267] In the following extract he adverts to the constitutionalization of the EU, through doctrines developed by the Court, such as direct effect, supremacy, and pre-emption.

[262] U Everling, 'The ECJ as a Decisionmaking Authority' (1994) 82 Mich LR 1294.

[263] T Koopmans, 'The Future of the Court of Justice of the European Communities' (1991) 11 YBEL 15; K Alter and S Meunier-Aitsahalia, 'Judicial Politics in the European Community' (1994) 26 Comparative Political Studies 535, 536.

[264] A Moravcsik, 'Preferences and Power in the European Community: A Liberal Intergovernmentalist Approach' (1993) 31 JCMS 473 and 'Liberal Intergovernmentalism and Integration: A Rejoinder' (1995) 33 JCMS 611, 623–625.

[265] Moravcsik, 'Preferences and Power' (n 264) 512–514. Moravcsik accepts that the ECJ has extended its powers beyond those strictly necessary for the attainment of his theory, but does not regard this as undermining his more general thesis.

[266] Ch 23.

[267] A Stone Sweet, *The Judicial Construction of Europe* (Oxford University Press, 2004) 235.

A Stone Sweet, The Judicial Construction of Europe[268]

There are a number of reasons why the constitutionalization of the Rome Treaty generated an expansive logic of its own, entailing an increasing demand for law, rule clarification, and capacities for monitoring and enforcement. From the beginning the central mission of the EC was to create the conditions for the development of the Common Market. Yet impersonal exchange, across jurisdictional boundaries, is problematic for reasons that social scientists have explored at length…As elsewhere, the success of integration has depended heavily on the extent to which the EC could develop effective organizational capacities: to guarantee property rights, to enforce competition rules, to adjudicate legal claims, to build a European framework for regulating market activities, and so on. At the very least constitutionalization accelerated this process. In my view, one can go further: the ECJ authoritatively reconstituted the Community in ways that linked the demand for and supply of European law and courts to the activities of market actors, and then to all activities governed by EC law. Constitutionalization not only positioned the courts as primary arenas for negative integration; it made them supervisors of positive integration, and creators of a growing corpus of rights which the Court found in the Treaty itself.

…With constitutionalization, the national courts too, developed into privileged sites for deliberation and rulemaking, not least because they are charged with supervising the transposition and implementation of EC law by national authorities…

---

8 THE COURT OF AUDITORS

The Court of Auditors was established by the second Budgetary Treaty of 1975, and came into operation in 1977, replacing the previously existing Auditor of the ECSC and the Audit Board of the Communities. Since the enactment of the Maastricht Treaty, the Court of Auditors has had the status of a Community, now Union, institution. It is governed by Articles 285–287 TFEU.

The Court of Auditors consists of one national from each Member State, appointed by the Council by qualified majority after consulting the Parliament. The term of office is for six years, renewable, and appointments are staggered. The auditors must belong or have belonged in their country to an external audit body, or they must be 'especially qualified for this office',[269] and their independence must be beyond doubt.[270] The conditions of office are strict: members may not engage in any other occupation, paid or unpaid, and even after leaving office they must behave with integrity and discretion as regards the acceptance of certain appointments or benefits.[271] A member of the Court of Auditors can be removed from office only by decision of the CJEU.

The Court of Auditors scrutinizes EU finances and ensures sound financial management. The Court examines the revenue and expenditure of the Union and of EU bodies, offices, and agencies, except where this is precluded by the relevant constituent instrument.[272] The Parliament and the Council are provided by the Court of Auditors with a statement of assurance as to the reliability of the accounts and the legality of transactions and irregularities are to be reported. The annual statement of

---

[268] Ibid 238–239. See also K Alter, *The European Court's Political Power: Selected Essays* (Oxford University Press, 2009).

[269] Art 286(1) TFEU.

[270] Arts 285, 286(1) TFEU.

[271] Art 286(4) TFEU.

[272] Art 287(1) TFEU.

assurance may be supplemented by sectoral assessments on major areas of EU activity.[273] The Court's audit is based on records, but it can also be carried out in the EU institutions, bodies and agencies, and in the Member States, in liaison with the competent national audit body.[274] The Court of Auditors has *locus standi* to bring annulment actions under Article 263 TFEU, similar to that given to the European Central Bank.

The Court of Auditors draws up an annual report, which is adopted by a majority of its members, after the close of each financial year.[275] The report is sent to the other EU institutions and published in the Official Journal together with the replies of the institutions. The Court of Auditors may submit observations on specific questions, or adopt special reports.[276] It can also deliver opinions at the request of another institution, as when it is consulted on legislative proposals.[277]

The Court's reports have often been critical. It has been noted that it is sometimes difficult to show that the Court of Auditors and the Commission are 'on the same side', and that it could easily be accused of being 'anti-Communautaire'.[278] While its relations with the Parliament have been described as 'stable and cooperative',[279] there has been strong criticism of the 'indifference displayed at the Council's highest level to the auditing functions and findings of the European Court of Auditors'.[280] More general assessments of the Court of Auditors vary. Thus, one study suggests that it has an uneasy relationship with the Commission, has come into conflict with the Parliament's budgetary control committee, has been largely ignored by the Council, and remains virtually unknown to most national parliaments, although there have been other more positive appraisals of its evolving institutional role.[281]

9 EU ADVISORY BODIES

The discussion thus far has concerned the bodies listed as EU institutions in Article 13 TEU. There are, however, other institutions that play a role within the EU. Article 300 TFEU specifies two EU advisory bodies, the Economic and Social Committee and the Committee of the Regions.

(A) ECONOMIC AND SOCIAL COMMITTEE

The Economic and Social Committee represents various sectional or functional interests.[282] It consists of 'representatives of organisations of employers, of the employed, and of other parties representative of civil society, notably in socio-economic, civic, professional and cultural

---

[273] Art 287(1)–(2) TFEU.

[274] Art 287(3) TFEU.

[275] Art 287(4) TFEU.

[276] See, eg, Court of Auditors, Special Report 9/2006, concerning translation expenditure incurred by the Commission, the Parliament and the Council [2006] OJ C284/01; Court of Auditors, Special Report 1/2010, Are Simplified Customs Procedures for Imports Effectively Controlled?

[277] Arts 322, 325(4) TFEU.

[278] I Harden, F While, and K Donnelly, 'The Court of Auditors and Financial Control and Accountability in the European Community' (1995) 1 EPL 599.

[279] B Laffan, 'Becoming a "Living Institution": The Evolution of the European Court of Auditors' (1999) 37 JCMS 251, 261.

[280] House of Lords Select Committee on the EU, 'The European Court of Auditors: The Case for Reform' (Report No 12, 2000/2001).

[281] Contrast Harden, While, and Donnelly (n 278) with Laffan (n 279).

[282] S Smismans, *Law, Legitimacy and European Governance: Functional Participation in Social Regulation* (Oxford University Press, 2004).

areas'.[283] The overall number cannot exceed 350 and the Council, acting on a proposal from the Commission, decides on the Committee's composition.[284] The Council, acting by qualified majority, appoints Committee members for five years renewable, on the basis of proposals from Member States.[285] There are three main groups at present representing employers, workers, and other interest groups.

The members of the Economic and Social Committee may not be bound by any mandatory instructions, must be completely independent in the performance of their duties, and must act in the general interest of the EU.[286] The Economic and Social Committee operates via a number of committees. It must be consulted by the Council, Commission, and Parliament where the Treaties so provide, and may also be consulted where the institutions consider it appropriate.[287]

The Economic and Social Committee has not, traditionally, been particularly influential, but its status could be enhanced by the increased institutional attention being paid to the importance of 'civil society' in enhancing EU legitimacy, and by recognition in the Lisbon Treaty of the role of civil society.[288]

(B) COMMITTEE OF THE REGIONS

This Committee was established by the Maastricht Treaty to represent regional and local bodies, in part to counter the idea that the EU was becoming too centralized.[289] The total number of members is 350. The Committee of the Regions consists of representatives of regional and local bodies who either hold a regional or local authority electoral mandate, or are politically accountable to an elected assembly.[290] The Council, acting by qualified majority, appoints the members for a renewable five-year term.[291] They must be independent and act in the Union's general interest.[292] The Parliament, Council, and Commission must consult the Committee of the Regions where the Treaty specifies, and it may be consulted in other instances, in particular where a measure concerns cross-border cooperation.[293] Three main principles lie at the heart of the Committee's work: subsidiarity, proximity, and partnership. These principles inform its contributions to legislative proposals. They also underpin its general studies[294] and those of a more sectoral nature.[295]

[283] Art 300(2) TFEU.
[284] Art 301 TFEU.
[285] Art 302(1) TFEU.
[286] Art 300(4) TFEU.
[287] Art 304 TFEU.
[288] Art 11(2) TEU; 'The ESC: A Bridge between Europe and Civil Society' (Brussels, 2001); 'European Social Dialogue and Civil Dialogue: Differences and Complementarities' (EESC, 2004).
[289] N Roht-Arriaza, 'The Committee of the Regions and the Role of Regional Governments in the European Union' (1997) 20 Hastings I & Comp LJ 413.
[290] Art 300(4) TFEU.
[291] Art 305 TFEU.
[292] Art 300(4) TFEU.
[293] Art 307 TFEU.
[294] See, eg, Committee of the Regions, *The Regional and Local Dimensions in Establishing New Forms of Governance in Europe* (CoR, 2003); Committee of the Regions, *Strengthening Regional and Local Democracy in the European Union* (CoR, 2004); Committee of the Regions, *A New Treaty: A New Role for Regions and Local Authorities* (CoR, 2010).
[295] See, eg, Committee of the Regions, *Services of General Interest in Europe* (CoR, 2005).

10 AGENCIES

Agencies are a prominent feature of modern democratic polities.[296] They facilitate use of experts outside the normal bureaucratic structure; allow the parent department to concentrate on strategic policy; and insulate technical regulatory issues from political change, thereby increasing the credibility of the choices thus made. Agencies have become an important institutional feature of the EU.[297] They deal with areas as diverse as air safety, medicines, border control, food safety, maritime safety, environment, trade marks, and fundamental rights, and are also used in what were the Second and Third Pillars. The Commission's rationale for agency-creation echoes that set out above: agencies 'would make the executive more effective at European level in highly specialized technical areas requiring advanced expertise and continuity, credibility and visibility of public action',[298] thereby enabling the Commission to focus on policy-formation.[299]

The powers accorded to agencies vary.[300] Most have informational and coordinating functions; a few can take individualized decisions; and some have quasi-regulatory powers. None however are true 'regulatory' agencies as that term is normally understood. They do not have powers to make rules and adjudicate in the manner that is common for agencies in the United States, although the EU financial regulatory agencies established post the financial crisis come close in this respect. There are legal and political reasons for the limits on agency powers.

The principal legal constraint is the *Meroni* principle,[301] which stipulated that it was not possible to delegate power involving a wide margin of discretion, since it transferred responsibility by replacing the choices of the delegator for those of the body to whom power was delegated. The Court has however loosened this principle, through its willingness to find that there are sufficient constraints on the exercise of agency power to render it lawful within the Treaty schema.[302]

The Commission provided the political rationale for limiting agency powers. It has been supportive of agencies, but nonetheless wished to adhere to the legal constraints for reasons that transcended the dictates of formal law. This was in order to preserve 'the unity and integrity of the executive function' and to ensure 'that it continues to be vested in the chief of the Commission if the latter is to have the required responsibility *vis-à-vis* Europe's citizens, the Member States and the other

---

[296] M Thatcher and A Stone Sweet, 'Theory and Practice of Delegation to Non-Majoritarian Institutions' (2002) 25 West European Politics 1.

[297] M Everson, 'Independent Agencies: Hierarchy Beaters?' (1995) 1 ELJ 180; A Kreher, 'Agencies in the European Community: A Step Towards Administrative Integration in Europe' (1997) 4 JEPP 225; M Shapiro, 'The Problems of Independent Agencies in the United States and the European Union' (1997) 4 JEPP 276; R Dehousse, 'Regulation by Networks in the European Community: The Role of European Agencies' (1997) 4 JEPP 246; E Vos, 'Reforming the European Commission: What Role to Play for EU Agencies?' (2000) 37 CMLRev 1113; E Chiti, 'The Emergence of a Community Administration: The Case of European Agencies' (2000) 37 CMLRev 309; G Majone, 'Delegation of Regulatory Powers in a Mixed Polity' (2002) 8 ELJ 319; E Chiti, 'Decentralisation and Integration into the Community Administrations: A New Perspective on European Agencies' (2004) 10 ELJ 402; D Geradin and N Petit, 'The Development of Agencies at EU and National Levels: Conceptual Analysis and Proposals for Reform', Jean Monnet Working Paper 01/04, NYU School of Law; P Craig, *EU Administrative Law* (Oxford University Press, 2nd edn, 2012) ch 6; Curtin (n 2) ch 6; M Shapiro, 'Independent Agencies' in Craig and de Búrca (n 2); M Busuioc, *European Agencies: Law and Practices of Accountability* (Oxford University Press, 2013).

[298] The Operating Framework for the European Regulatory Agencies, COM(2002) 718 final, 5.

[299] Ibid 2.

[300] Craig (n 233) ch 6.

[301] Case 9/56 *Meroni & Co, Industrie Metallurgiche SpA v High Authority* [1958] ECR 133, 152.

[302] Case C-270/12 *United Kingdom v Council and Parliament* EU:C:2014:18.

institutions'.[303] The participation of agencies should therefore be 'organised in a way which is consistent and in balance with the unity and integrity of the executive function and the Commission's ensuing responsibilities'.[304]

The Commission has therefore been reluctant to create real regulatory agencies exercising discretionary power through adjudication and rule-making, since if such power could be delegated the Commission's sense of the unity of the executive function vested in it would be undermined. The emphasis placed on the unity and integrity of the executive function located in the President of the Commission was not fortuitous, given that the 2002 Communication was issued during the deliberations of the Convention on the Future of Europe, where the location of executive power was one of the most divisive issues.[305]

The Commission's concern as to the unity of the executive function played out not only in relation to the powers accorded to agencies, but also in relation to agency decision-making structure. The composition of agency boards has been crucial in this respect. The Commission remains concerned about agency decision-making structure, stating that 'the degree of accountability of the Commission cannot exceed the degree of influence of the Commission on the agency's activities'.[306]

In addition to the agencies described above, there are also executive agencies, which are designed to manage some of the non-discretionary functions that fall within the direct administrative responsibility of the Commission, in order to enable the Commission to concentrate on its 'core tasks', while avoiding the problems associated with outsourcing that led to the downfall of the Santer Commission.[307]

11 CONCLUSIONS

i. The EU institutions should not be seen as unitary actors. Each institution has its own distinctive identity and role, but the internal structure and composition of each institution is varied and complex.

ii. The powers of the institutions are formally governed by Treaty provisions, but their actual functioning and interaction are determined by a range of inter-institutional agreements and practices, as well as by significant political developments.

iii. Recent years have witnessed a period of institutional flux, with proposals for reform of the internal working and governance structures of EU administration, following the resignation of the Santer Commission.

iv. The ratification of the Lisbon Treaty resolved in formal legal terms a number of institutional issues that had dominated the debates about Treaty reform for almost a decade. It remains to be seen how these changes affect the individual institutions and the way in which they interact.

---

[303] COM(2002) 718, 1.

[304] Ibid 1, 9.

[305] P Craig, 'European Governance: Executive and Administrative Powers under the New Constitutional Settlement' (2005) 3 I-CON 407.

[306] European Agencies—The Way Forward, COM(2008) 135 final, 8.

[307] Council Regulation (EC) No 58/2003 of 19 December 2002 laying down the statute for executive agencies to be entrusted with certain tasks in the management of community programmes [2003] OJ L11/1; Craig (n 233) ch 2.

v. It will be interesting to see how the division of executive power between the President of the European Commission and the President of the European Council unfolds over time. It should be remembered that both must work with the Council, and that the Member State that holds the Presidency of the Council for six months will also have views as to the priorities that should be accorded to particular policy initiatives.

vi. It will be equally interesting in the post-Lisbon world to see how the further extension of the EP's legislative competence, through the extension of the ordinary legislative procedure to new areas, impacts on the passage of particular legislative initiatives and on the planning of the overall legislative agenda.

12 FURTHER READING

ALTER, K, *The European Court's Political Power: Selected Essays* (Oxford University Press, 2009)

BROWN, N, AND KENNEDY, T, *The Court of Justice of the European Communities* (Sweet & Maxwell, 5th edn, 2000)

BUSUIOC, M, *European Agencies: Law and Practices of Accountability* (Oxford University Press, 2013)

CORBETT, R, *The European Parliament's Role in Closer EU Integration* (Macmillan, 1998)

——, JACOBS, F, AND SHACKLETON, M, *The European Parliament* (Harper, 8th edn, 2011)

CRAIG, P, *The Lisbon Treaty: Law, Politics, and Treaty Reform* (Oxford University Press, 2010)

——*EU Administrative Law* (Oxford University Press, 2nd edn, 2012)

——, AND DE BÚRCA, G (eds), *The Evolution of EU Law* (Oxford University Press, 2nd edn, 2010)

CURTIN, D, *Executive Power in the European Union: Law, Practices, and the Living Constitution* (Oxford University Press, 2009)

DASHWOOD, A, AND JOHNSTON, A, *The Future of the Judicial System of the European Union* (Hart, 2001)

DE BÚRCA, G, AND WEILER, JHH, *The European Court of Justice* (Oxford University Press, 2001)

DEHOUSSE, R, *The European Court of Justice* (Macmillan, 1998)

HAYES-RENSHAW, F, AND WALLACE, H, *The Council of Ministers* (Palgrave, 2nd edn, 2006)

HOOGHE, L, *The European Commission and the Integration of Europe* (Cambridge University Press, 2002)

JUDGE, D, AND EARNSHAW, D, *The European Parliament* (Palgrave, 2nd edn, 2008)

KOMBOS, C, *The ECJ and Judicial Activism: Myth or Reality?* (Sakkoulas, 2010)

NUGENT, N, *The European Commission* (Palgrave, 2001)

PETERSON, J, AND SHACKLETON, M, *The Institutions of the European Union* (Oxford University Press, 3rd edn, 2012)

PIRIS, J-C, *The Lisbon Treaty: A Legal and Political Analysis* (Cambridge University Press, 2010)

POLLACK, M, *The Engines of European Integration: Delegation, Agency, and Agenda Setting in the EU* (Oxford University Press, 2003)

PUETTER, U, *The European Council and the Council: New Intergovernmentalism and Institutional Change* (Oxford University Press, 2014)

RICHARDSON, J (ed), *European Union, Power and Policy-Making* (Routledge, 3rd edn, 2006)

ROSE, R, *Representing Europeans: A Pragmatic Approach* (Oxford University Press, 2013)

SMITH, A (ed), *Politics and the European Commission: Actors, Independence, Legitimacy* (Routledge, 2004)

SPENCE, D (ed), *The European Commission* (Harper, 3rd edn, 2006)

STEVENS, A, WITH STEVENS, H, *Brussels Bureaucrats? The Administration of the European Union* (Palgrave, 2001)

WALLACE, H, POLLACK, M, AND YOUNG, A (eds), *Policy-Making in the European Union* (Oxford University Press, 7th edn, 2014)

WERTS, J, *The European Council* (Harper, 2008)

WESTLAKE, M, AND GALLOWAY, D, *The Council of the European Union* (Harper, 3rd edn, 2004)

3

COMPETENCE

1 CENTRAL ISSUES

i. The general principle has always been that the EU only has the competence conferred by the Treaties. This is what is meant by saying that the EU has attributed competence. Prior to the Lisbon Treaty, it was however difficult to decide on the limits of EU competence. There were no general categories of competence, and thus the limits of competence in a specific area could only be discerned by paying close attention to the detailed Treaty provisions. There could be disagreement as to whether the competence in a particular area was exclusive or shared. These difficulties were compounded by the fact that the real scope of EU competence had to take account of the case law interpreting the relevant Treaty provisions, and legislation made pursuant to those provisions. The difficulties were especially prominent in relation to Treaty Articles that were broadly framed, such as Articles 95 and 308 EC.

ii. The existence and scope of EU competence were therefore key elements in the reforms that culminated in the Lisbon Treaty. There are now categories of competence in the Lisbon Treaty: the EU may have exclusive competence, shared competence, or competence only to take supporting, coordinating, or supplementary action. Legal consequences flow from that categorization. This chapter examines the three principal categories of EU competence, and their implications for the divide between EU and Member State power. There are certain areas of EU competence that do not fall within these categories and they will also be examined within this chapter. The discussion will consider the extent to which the new regime clarifies the scope of EU competence and contains EU power.

iii. The Lisbon Treaty makes provision not only for the existence and scope of EU competence, but also for whether the competence should be exercised. This issue is governed by the principle of subsidiarity, which was initially introduced by the Maastricht Treaty. A revised version of the principle is contained in the Lisbon Treaty and a Protocol attached to the Treaty. The meaning and application of this concept can give rise to problems, as will be seen in the subsequent discussion.

2 IMPETUS FOR REFORM

The EU can only act within the limits of the powers assigned to it. It has in that sense attributed competences. This principle was previously embodied in Articles 5(1) and 7(1) EC and has been reaffirmed by Article 5(2) TEU of the Lisbon Treaty, which states that:

> Under the principle of conferral, the Union shall act only within the limits of the competences conferred upon it by the Member States in the Treaties to attain the objectives set out therein. Competences not conferred upon the Union in the Treaties remain with the Member States.

It was, however, not easy prior to the Lisbon Treaty to specify with exactitude the division of competence between the EU and Member States,[1] and was therefore an issue identified for further inquiry after the Nice Treaty 2000.[2] It was felt that Article 5 EC provided little safeguard against an increasing shift of power from the states to the EU.

We should nonetheless be cautious about the assumption that the 'competence problem' was the result primarily of some unwarranted arrogation of power by the EU to the detriment of states' rights. The reality was that EU competence resulted from the interaction of four variables: Member State choice as to the scope of EU competence, as expressed in Treaty revisions; Council and European Parliament acceptance of legislation that fleshed out the Treaty Articles; the jurisprudence of the EU Courts; and decisions taken by the institutions as to how to interpret and prioritize the power accorded to the EU.[3]

The Laeken Declaration[4] specified in greater detail the inquiry into competence that had been left open after the Nice Treaty 2000. Four principal forces drove the reform process: clarity, conferral, containment, and consideration. The desire for 'clarity' reflected the concern that the Treaty provisions on competences were unclear, jumbled, and unprincipled. The idea of 'conferral' captured not only the idea that the EU should act within the limits of the powers attributed to it, but also carried the more positive connotation that the EU should be accorded the powers necessary to fulfil the tasks assigned to it by the Treaties. The desire for 'containment' reflected the concern that the EU had too much power, and that it should be substantively limited.[5] This argument must be kept in perspective, since a significant factor in the distribution of competence has been the Member States' conscious decision to grant new spheres of competence to the EU. This is where the fourth factor came into play, 'consideration' of whether the EU should continue to have the powers that it had been given in the past. There was however little systematic re-thinking of the areas in which the EU should be able to act, and the emphasis was on clarity, conferral, and containment.

---

[1] A Dashwood, 'The Limits of European Community Powers' (1996) 21 ELRev 113; G de Búrca, 'Setting Limits to EU Competences', Francisco Lucas Pires Working Paper 2001/02; U di Fabio, 'Some Remarks on the Allocation of Competences between the European Union and its Member States' (2002) 39 CMLRev 1289; A von Bogdandy and J Bast, 'The European Union's Vertical Order of Competences: The Current Law and Proposals for its Reform' (2002) 39 CMLRev 227; P Craig, 'Competence: Clarity, Conferral, Containment and Consideration' (2004) 29 ELRev 323; S Weatherill, 'Better Competence Monitoring' (2005) 30 ELRev 23; F Mayer, 'Competences—Reloaded? The Vertical Division of Powers in the EU and the New European Constitution' (2005) 3 I-CON 493; R Schutze, *From Dual to Cooperative Federalism: The Changing Structure of European Law* (Oxford University Press, 2009); L Azoulai (ed), *The Question of Competence in the European Union* (Oxford University Press, 2014).

[2] Treaty of Nice, Declaration 23 [2001] OJ C80/1.

[3] P Craig, 'Competence and Member State Autonomy: Causality, Consequence and Legitimacy' in B de Witte and H Micklitz (eds), *The European Court of Justice and the Autonomy of Member States* (Intersentia, 2011) ch 1.

[4] European Council, 14–15 Dec 2001, [21]–[22].

[5] Mayer (n 1) 504–505.

3 LISBON STRATEGY

(A) CATEGORIES AND CONSEQUENCES

The Lisbon Treaty repeats with minor modifications the provisions in the Constitutional Treaty. The provisions are contained in the TEU and in the TFEU. Thus Article 4 TEU states that competences not conferred on the Union remain with the Member States. Article 5 TEU stipulates that the limits of Union competences are governed by the principle of conferral. It is however the TFEU that contains the main provisions on competence. There are categories of competence that apply to subject matter areas, and legal consequences flow from such categorization. The principal categories are where the EU's competence is exclusive, where it is shared with the Member States, where the EU is limited to supporting/coordinating action, with special categories for EU action in the sphere of economic and employment policy, and Common Foreign and Security Policy (CFSP). Article 2 TFEU provides that:

1. When the Treaties confer on the Union exclusive competence in a specific area, only the Union may legislate and adopt legally binding acts, the Member States being able to do so themselves only if so empowered by the Union or for the implementation of Union acts.

2. When the Treaties confer on the Union a competence shared with the Member States in a specific area, the Union and the Member States may legislate and adopt legally binding acts in that area. The Member States shall exercise their competence to the extent that the Union has not exercised its competence. The Member States shall again exercise their competence to the extent that the Union has decided to cease exercising its competence.

3. The Member States shall coordinate their economic and employment policies within arrangements as determined by this Treaty, which the Union shall have competence to provide.

4. The Union shall have competence, in accordance with the provisions of the Treaty on European Union, to define and implement a common foreign and security policy, including the progressive framing of a common defence policy.

5. In certain areas and under the conditions laid down in the Treaties, the Union shall have competence to carry out actions to support, coordinate or supplement the actions of the Member States, without thereby superseding their competence in these areas.

Legally binding acts of the Union adopted on the basis of the provisions of the Treaties relating to these areas shall not entail harmonisation of Member States' laws or regulations.

6. The scope of and arrangements for exercising the Union's competences shall be determined by the provisions of the Treaties relating to each area.

(B) EXPRESS AND IMPLIED POWER

There are two important points that should be stressed before examining the particular categories of competence, since they apply to the entirety of the subsequent discussion.

First, there can be disagreement as to the ambit of a particular Treaty Article, irrespective of the category of competence that applies to the area, more especially when the Article is cast in broad terms.[6] The ECJ has in general been disinclined to place limits on broadly worded Treaty Articles. It can however do so. In the *Tobacco Advertising* case the ECJ held that a directive relating to tobacco advertising could not be based on Article 95 EC.[7]

---

[6] See, eg, Case C–84/94 *United Kingdom v Council* [1996] ECR I–5755; Case C–233/94 *Germany v European Parliament and Council* [1997] ECR I–2405.

[7] T Hervey, 'Up in Smoke? Community (Anti)-Tobacco Law and Policy' (2001) 26 ELRev 101.

Case C–376/98 **Germany v European Parliament and Council**
[2000] ECR I–8419

[Note Lisbon Treaty renumbering: Arts 57(2), 66, 100a, 164 are now Arts 53(2), 62, 114 TFEU and Art 19 TEU]

Germany sought the annulment of a Directive designed to harmonize the law relating to the advertising and sponsorship of tobacco. The Directive had been based on Articles 57(2), 66, and 100a. Article 100a allows the adoption of harmonization measures for the functioning of the internal market. The ECJ cited Articles 100a, 3(c), and 7a of the EC Treaty. It then continued as follows.

THE ECJ

83. Those provisions, read together, make it clear that the measures referred to in Article 100a(1)…are intended to improve the conditions for the establishment and functioning of the internal market. To construe that article as meaning that it vests in the Community legislature a general power to regulate the internal market would not only be contrary to the express wording of the provisions cited above, but would also be incompatible with the principle embodied in Article 3b…that the powers of the Community are limited to those specifically conferred on it.

84. Moreover, a measure adopted on the basis of Article 100a…must genuinely have as its object the improvement of the conditions for the establishment and functioning of the internal market. If a mere finding of disparities between national rules and of the abstract risk of obstacles to the exercise of fundamental freedoms or of distortions of competition liable to result therefrom were sufficient to justify the choice of Article 100a as a legal base, judicial review of compliance with the proper legal basis might be nugatory. The Court would then be prevented from discharging the function entrusted to it by Article 164…of ensuring that the law is observed in the interpretation and application of the Treaty.

85. So, in considering whether Article 100a was the proper legal basis, the Court must verify whether the measure whose validity is at issue in fact pursues the objectives stated by the Community legislature…

While there are therefore limits to what is now Article 114 TFEU, subsequent case law has shown that the ECJ is willing to accept use of this Article as the legal basis for the enacted measure.[8] This is exemplified by the 2006 *Tobacco Advertising* case,[9] where the ECJ upheld the validity of a revised directive on tobacco advertising, which included, subject to limited exceptions, prohibitions on advertising in the press and radio and constraints on sponsorship by tobacco companies. The Court concluded that this could be adopted under what was Article 95 EC, since there were disparities between national laws on advertising and sponsorship of tobacco products, which could affect competition and inter-state trade.

Secondly, the EU institutions may claim that a particular Treaty Article contains an implied power to make the particular regulation. While the notion of implied power is well known in domestic and international legal systems, its meaning is more contestable. Under the narrower formulation, the existence of a given power implies the existence of any other power that is reasonably necessary for

---

[8] Case C–377/98 *Netherlands v Parliament and Council* [2001] ECR I–7079; Case C–491/01 *The Queen v Secretary of State for Health, ex p British American Tobacco (Investments) Ltd and Imperial Tobacco Ltd* [2002] ECR I–11453; Case C–210/03 *R v Secretary of State for Health, ex p Swedish Match* [2004] ECR I–11893; Case C–270/12 *United Kingdom v European Parliament and Council* EU:C:2014:18.

[9] Case C–380/03 *Germany v European Parliament and Council* [2006] ECR I–11573.

the exercise of the former. Under the wider formulation, the existence of a given objective implies the existence of power reasonably necessary to attain it. The narrow sense of implied power has long been accepted.[10] The ECJ has also embraced the wider formulation. This is exemplified by the following cases.

Cases 281, 283–285 and 287/85 **Germany v Commission**
[1987] ECR 3203

[Note Lisbon Treaty renumbering: Art 118 is now Art 153 TFEU]

The Commission made a decision pursuant to Article 118 by which Member States were to inform the Commission and other Member States of their draft measures concerning entry, residence, equality of treatment, and the integration of workers from non-EC countries into the social and cultural life of their country. There would then be consultation with the Commission and other Member States. This was challenged as being *ultra vires* the Commission. Article 118 concerned collaboration in the social field, and did not expressly give the Commission power to make binding decisions. The ECJ held that migration policy in relation to non-Member States could to some extent fall within Article 118, because of the effects of such migration on the employment situation in the EC.

THE ECJ

27...[I]t must be considered whether the second paragraph of Article 118, which provides that the Commission is to act, *inter alia*, by arranging consultations, gives it the power to adopt a binding decision with a view to the arrangement of such consultations.

28. In that connection it must be emphasised that where an Article of the EEC Treaty...confers a specific task on the Commission it must be accepted, if that provision is not to be rendered wholly ineffective, that it confers on the Commission necessarily and *per se* the powers which are indispensable in order to carry out that task. Accordingly, the second paragraph of Article 118 must be interpreted as conferring on the Commission all the powers which are necessary in order to arrange the consultations. In order to perform that task of arranging consultation the Commission must necessarily be able to require the Member States to notify essential information, in the first place to identify the problems and in the second place in order to pinpoint the possible guidelines for any future joint action on the part of the Member States; likewise it must be able to require them to take part in consultation.

Case 176/03 **Commission v Council**
[2005] ECR I–7879

The Council enacted a Framework Decision under what was the Third Pillar, Title VI TEU, that required Member States to prescribe criminal penalties for certain environmental offences. The Commission argued that the measure should have been enacted under Article 175 EC, since it was concerned with the environment. The ECJ accepted this, and accepted also that, as a general rule, neither criminal law nor criminal procedure fell within Community competence, but then reasoned as follows.

---

[10] Case 8/55 *Fédération Charbonnière de Belgique v High Authority* [1956] ECR 245, 280.

THE ECJ

48. However, [this] does not prevent the Community legislature, when the application of effective, proportionate and dissuasive criminal penalties by the competent national authorities is an essential measure for combating serious environmental offences, from taking measures which relate to the criminal law of the Member States which it considers necessary in order to ensure that the rules which it lays down on environmental protection are fully effective.

The CFI has, however, held that it is only exceptionally that such implicit powers are recognized: they must be necessary to ensure the practical effect of the provisions of the Treaty or the basic regulation at issue.[11]

4 EXCLUSIVE COMPETENCE

(A) BASIC PRINCIPLES

Article 2(1) TFEU establishes the category of exclusive competence, which carries the consequence that only the Union can legislate and adopt legally binding acts. The Member States can only do so if empowered by the Union or for the implementation of Union acts.

The subject matter areas that fall within exclusive competence are set out in Article 3(1) TFEU: customs union; the establishing of the competition rules necessary for the functioning of the internal market; monetary policy for the Member States whose currency is the Euro; the conservation of marine biological resources under the common fisheries policy; and the common commercial policy.

Article 3(2) TFEU states that the Union shall also have exclusive competence for the conclusion of an international agreement when its conclusion is provided for in a legislative act of the Union, or is necessary to enable the Union to exercise its internal competence, or insofar as its conclusion may affect common rules or alter their scope.

(B) AREA EXCLUSIVITY

The areas specified in Article 3(1) that fall within the EU's exclusive competence are limited. We have seen that a pressing concern in the Laeken Declaration and the Convention on the Future of Europe was to contain EU power. The domain of exclusive competence fares well when judged by this criterion, given that only few areas come within this category. This is important because the consequences of inclusion are severe: the Member States have no autonomous legislative competence and they cannot adopt any legally binding act.

The very creation of categories of competence inevitably means that there will be problems of demarcating borderlines between the different categories. Such problems can arise in demarcating between exclusive and shared competence. There are, for example, ambiguities about the relationship between the competition rules, which are a species of exclusive competence, and the internal market, which is shared competence, an issue that arose in connection with the EU unitary patent.[12]

---

[11] Case T–240/04 *French Republic v Commission* [2007] ECR II–4035, [37]; Case T–143/06 *MTZ Polyfilms Ltd v Council* [2009] ECR II–4133, [47].

[12] Cases C–274 and 295/11 *Spain and Italy v Council* EU:C:2013:240, [18]–[24]; P Craig, *The Lisbon Treaty: Law, Politics, and Treaty Reform* (Oxford University Press, 2010) 159–161.

There may also be difficult borderline problems between provisions relating to the customs union and other aspects of the internal market, since the customs union falls within exclusive competence, while the internal market is shared competence. It may be difficult to decide whether a case is concerned with the customs union, tariffs, quotas, and the like, or whether it is really 'about' discriminatory taxation.[13] There can in addition be disputes as to whether an act falls within common commercial policy or the internal market.[14]

(c) CONDITIONAL EXCLUSIVITY

The EU is also accorded exclusive competence to make an international agreement,[15] provided that the conditions in Article 3(2) TFEU are met.

> The Union shall also have exclusive competence for the conclusion of an international agreement when its conclusion is provided for in a legislative act of the Union or is necessary to enable the Union to exercise its internal competence, or insofar as its conclusion may affect common rules or alter their scope.

Article 3(2) TFEU should be read in conjunction with Article 216 TFEU. Article 216 is concerned with whether the EU has competence to conclude an international agreement. Article 3(2) deals with the related, but distinct, issue as to whether that competence is exclusive or not. Article 216 TFEU reads as follows.

> 1. The Union may conclude an agreement with one or more third countries or international organisations where the Treaties so provide or where the conclusion of an agreement is necessary in order to achieve, within the framework of the Union's policies, one of the objectives referred to in the Treaties, or is provided for in a legally binding Union act or is likely to affect common rules or alter their scope.
> 2. Agreements concluded by the Union are binding upon the institutions of the Union and on its Member States.

The catalyst for Article 216 TFEU was the report of the Working Group on External Action. Prior to the Lisbon Treaty the EC Treaty accorded express power to make international agreements in certain limited instances,[16] and this was supplemented by the ECJ's jurisprudence stating when there could be an implied external competence to make an international agreement. The Working Group recommended that there should be a Treaty provision that reflected this case law.[17] This was embodied in the Constitutional Treaty, and taken over into the Lisbon Treaty as Article 216 TFEU. The breadth of Article 216 is readily apparent, and the reality is that it will be rare, if ever, that the EU lacks power to conclude an international agreement. The case law on the scope of the EU's external competence, and the extent to which it is exclusive or parallel with that of the Member States, is complex.[18] Article 3(2)

---

[13] Ch 18.

[14] Case C–137/12 *Commission and European Parliament v Council* EU:C:2013:675.

[15] The EU has legal personality: Art 47 TEU.

[16] Arts 111, 133, 174(4), 181, 310 EC.

[17] CONV 459/02, Final Report of Working Group VII on External Action, Brussels, 16 Dec 2002, [18].

[18] See below, Ch 10; T Tridimas and P Eeckhout, 'The External Competence of the Community and the Case-Law of the Court of Justice: Principle versus Pragmatism' (1994) 14 YBEL 143; A Dashwood and C Hillion (eds), *The General Law of EC External Relations* (Sweet & Maxwell, 2000); P Eeckhout, *External Relations of the European Union: Legal and Constitutional Foundations* (Oxford University Press, 2004); M Cremona, 'The Draft Constitutional Treaty: External Relations and External Action' (2003) 40 CMLRev 1347; P Koutrakos, *EU International Relations Law* (Hart, 2006);

TFEU stipulates three instances in which the EU has exclusive external competence. The interpretation of this provision is by no means easy.[19] The complexity of the case law necessarily means that embodying the principles in a Treaty Article was always going to be difficult. Article 3(2) read together with Article 216 TFEU comes close to eliding the EU's power to act via an international agreement with the exclusivity of that power, an issue which preoccupied much of the case law in this area.

(i) *External Competence and Exclusivity: Pre-Lisbon*

We need therefore to take a brief step back to the pre-Lisbon case law to understand the significance of Article 3(2) TFEU. The ECJ had for some considerable time recognized Community competence to conclude an international agreement where this was necessary to effectuate its internal competence, even where there was no express external competence.[20] The issue of whether this implied external power was exclusive was treated as distinct from the existence of such power. Implied external competence could be exclusive or shared,[21] but the criteria for the divide were not entirely clear.[22] The ECJ's formulations as to when exclusivity could arise were however far-reaching.

Thus in *ERTA* the ECJ held that when the Community acted to implement a common policy pursuant to the Treaty, the Member States no longer had the right to take external action where this would affect the rules thus established or distort their scope.[23] This position was modified in *Kramer*.[24] The ECJ held that the EC could possess implied external powers even though it had not taken internal measures to implement the relevant policy, but that until the EC exercised its internal power the Member States retained competence to act, provided that their action was compatible with Community objectives. The scope of exclusivity was thrown into doubt in the *Inland Waterways* case,[25] where the ECJ held that the EC could have exclusive external competence, even though it had not exercised its internal powers, if Member State action could jeopardize the Community objective sought to be attained.

The ECJ pulled back from the very broad reading of exclusivity in the *Inland Waterways* case in *Opinion 1/94* on the World Trade Organization (WTO) Agreement.[26] It held that exclusive external competence was in general dependent on the actual exercise of internal powers and not their mere existence.[27] The *Inland Waterways* case was distinguished on the ground that the EC's internal objective could not be attained without making an international agreement and internal EC rules could

P Koutrakos, 'Legal Basis and Delimitation of Competence in EU External Relations' in M Cremona and B de Witte (eds), *EU Foreign Relations Law: Constitutional Fundamentals* (Hart, 2008) ch 6; M Cremona, 'Defining Competence in EU External Relations: Lessons from the Treaty Reform Process' in A Dashwood and M Maresceau (eds), *Law and Practice of EU External Relations: Salient Features of a Changing Landscape* (Cambridge University Press, 2008) ch 2; M Cremona, 'External Relations and External Competence of the European Union: The Emergence of an Integrated Policy' in P Craig and G de Búrca (eds), *The Evolution of EU Law* (Oxford University Press, 2nd edn, 2011) ch 9; M Cremona, 'EU External Relations: Unity and Conferral of Powers' in Azoulai (n 1) ch 3.

[19] Cremona, 'Draft Constitutional Treaty' (n 18); Craig (n 1).

[20] (N 18); Case 22/70 *Commission v Council* [1971] ECR 263; Cases 3, 4 and 6/76 *Kramer* [1976] ECR 1279; *Opinion 1/76 On the Draft Agreement Establishing a Laying-up Fund for Inland Waterway Vessels* [1977] ECR 741; *Opinion 2/91 Re the ILO Convention 170 on Chemicals at Work* [1993] ECR I–1061; *Opinion 2/94 Accession of the Community to the European Human Rights Convention* [1996] ECR I–1759.

[21] *Opinion 1/03 Competence of the Community to conclude the new Lugano Convention on jurisdiction and the recognition and enforcement of judgments in civil and commercial matters* [2006] ECR I–1145, [114]–[117].

[22] Cremona, 'External Relations' (n 18); A Dashwood and J Heliskoski, 'The Classic Authorities Revisited' in Dashwood and Hillion (n 18) 3.

[23] Case 22/70 *Commission v Council* (n 20).

[24] Cases 3, 4 and 6/76 *Kramer* (n 20).

[25] *Opinion 1/76 Inland Waterways* (n 20).

[26] *Opinion 1/94 Competence of the Community to Conclude International Agreements Concerning Services and the Protection of Intellectual Property, WTO* [1994] ECR I–5267.

[27] Ibid [77], [88]–[89].

not realistically be made prior to the conclusion of such an agreement.[28] This rationale was held not to apply to the *WTO* case.[29] This reasoning has been followed in later decisions.[30]

Subsequent jurisprudence nonetheless revealed that the ECJ construed broadly the idea of the EC having exercised its powers internally, and that the ECJ was prepared to give a wide interpretation to the circumstances where this gave rise to exclusive external competence for the EC. This was apparent from the 'open skies' litigation, involving Commission actions against several Member States.[31] The Commission alleged that Member States had infringed the Treaty by concluding bilateral 'open skies' agreements with the United States, on the ground that the EC had exclusive external competence in this area. It argued that the EC had exclusive external competence in line with the *ERTA* ruling, because it had exercised its internal competence to some degree within the relevant area. The ECJ accepted this argument. The Council had adopted a package of legislation based on Article 80(2) EC. The ECJ held that the *ERTA* ruling could apply to internal power exercised in this manner, and therefore the EC had an implied external competence. It followed that when the EC made common rules pursuant to this power, the Member States no longer had the right, acting individually or collectively, to undertake obligations towards non-Member States which affected those rules or distorted their scope.

The judgment confirmed the broad reading given to the phrase 'affected those rules or distorted their scope', since it was this that transformed external competence into exclusive external competence. The ECJ, in accord with prior case law, held that this would be so where the international agreement fell within the scope of the common rules, or within an area that was already largely covered by such rules, and this was so in the latter case even if there was no contradiction between the international commitments and the internal rules. EC legislative provisions relating to the treatment of non-Member State nationals, or expressly conferring power to negotiate with non-Member States, gave the EC exclusive external competence.

The same general message emerged from the *Lugano* Opinion:[32] implied external competence could be exclusive or shared, but where the EC had exercised its powers internally, then the ECJ would be inclined to conclude that this gave rise to exclusive external competence, whenever such exclusive competence was needed to 'preserve the effectiveness of Community law and the proper functioning of the systems established by its rules'.[33]

(ii) *External Competence and Exclusivity: Post-Lisbon*

Article 3(2) TFEU specifies three situations in which the EU has exclusive external competence. The first is where conclusion of an international agreement is provided for by a legislative act of the Union. The wording is significant. Article 3(2) TFEU does not state that the Union shall have exclusive external competence where a Union legislative act says that this shall be so. Nor does it state that the EU shall have such exclusive external competence only in the areas in which it has an exclusive internal competence. It states that where the conclusion of an international agreement is provided for in a

---

[28] Ibid [85]–[86].

[29] Ibid [86], [99], [100], [105].

[30] See, eg, *Opinion 2/92 Competence of the Community or one of its Institutions to Participate in the Third Revised Decision of the OECD on National Treatment* [1995] ECR I–521.

[31] Case C–466/98 *Commission v United Kingdom* [2002] ECR I–9427; Case C–467/98 *Commission v Denmark* [2002] ECR I–9519; Case C–468/98 *Commission v Sweden* [2002] ECR I–9575; Case C–469/98 *Commission v Finland* [2002] ECR I–9627; Case C–471/98 *Commission v Belgium* [2002] ECR I–9681; Case C–472/98 *Commission v Luxembourg* [2002] ECR I–9741; Case C–475/98 *Commission v Austria* [2002] ECR I–9797.

[32] *Opinion 1/03 Lugano* (n 21) [114]–[115].

[33] Ibid [131].

legislative act, the Union will have exclusive external competence. Thus express external empowerment to conclude an international agreement is taken to mean exclusive external competence, with the corollary that Member States are pre-empted from concluding any such agreement independently, and from legislating or adopting any legally binding act.

The same elision of external power and exclusive external power is evident in the second situation listed in Article 3(2) TFEU. There is, as we have seen, ECJ jurisprudence that accords the EU competence to conclude an international agreement where this is necessary to effectuate its internal competence, even where there is no express external competence.[34] The effect of Article 3(2) TFEU is nonetheless that the EU has exclusive external competence to conclude an international agreement where it is necessary to enable the Union to exercise its competence internally, irrespective of the type of internal competence possessed by the EU. Taken literally this means that exclusive external competence to conclude an international agreement resides with the Union, where this is necessary for the exercise of internal competence, even where the internal competence is only shared or even where the EU can only take supporting or coordinating action. It might be argued that any EU external competence to make an international agreement must be bounded by the nature of its internal competence in the relevant area. The effect of Article 3(2) TFEU would still be that the EU would have exclusive external competence to conclude an international agreement that was necessary to enable the EU to exercise an internal competence, even where the internal competence only allowed supporting action, provided that the international agreement did not contain provisions that went beyond this type of action.

The third of the situations mentioned in Article 3(2) TFEU is that the EU shall have exclusive competence insofar as the conclusion of an international agreement 'may affect common rules or alter their scope'. This is in accord with the ECJ's case law considered above, such that in many instances where the EU has exercised its power internally it will be held to have an exclusive external competence.[35] A rare exception is the *Pringle* decision,[36] where the CJEU held that the European Stability Mechanism (ESM), an international agreement made by Member States designed to assist states in financial difficulty because of the Euro crisis, did not affect the common rules on economic and monetary union, and therefore did not fall within the EU's exclusive competence pursuant to Article 3(2). It is however clear that the CJEU did not wish to invalidate the ESM as made by the Member States.

Cremona has argued convincingly that Article 3(2) 'conflates the two separate questions of the existence of implied external competence and the exclusivity of that competence',[37] and that the combination of this Article when read with Article 216 TFEU is that implied shared competence could disappear. This does seem to be the outcome of the Treaty provisions, subject to the caveats mentioned above, and it is, as Cremona states, hard to defend in policy terms.[38]

The result is moreover difficult to square with the practical realities in this area. Thus notwithstanding the relatively broad judicial reading given to exclusive external competence, the reality was that prior to the Lisbon Treaty many external powers were shared between the Member States and the EU, through mixed agreements where power to conclude the agreement was shared with the Member States.[39] This might be because the conditions in the case law for the Community's

---

[34] (N 20).

[35] Case C–114/12 *Commission v Council (Convention on the Rights of Broadcasting Organizations)* EU:C:2014:2151; *Opinion 1/13 on the Hague Convention on Child Abduction* EU:C:2014:2292.

[36] Case C–370/12 *Pringle v Government of Ireland, Ireland and the Attorney General* EU:C:2012:756, [100]–[106].

[37] Cremona 'Defining Competence' (n 18) 61.

[38] Ibid 62.

[39] D O'Keeffe and H Schermers (eds), *Mixed Agreements* (Martinus Nijhoff, 1983); M Cremona, 'The Doctrine of Exclusivity and the Position of Mixed Agreements in the External Relations of the European Community' (1982) 2 OJLS 393; M Cremona, 'External Relations of the EU and the Member States: Competence, Mixed Agreements, International Responsibility, and Effects of International Law', EUI Working Paper, Law No 2006/22; Cremona, 'EU External Relations' (n 18).

exclusive external competence were not satisfied, where for example the EC had not adopted sufficient internal measures to accord it exclusive external competence.[40] External competence might also be shared because the EC Treaty did not confer sufficient competence on the EC to ratify the agreement in its entirety, thereby requiring allocation as between the EC and the Member States of the power to conclude the agreement with non-Member States,[41] or where the EC had some competence over the relevant area, but this was limited to laying down minimum requirements, thereby leaving Member States free to apply the rules flowing from the international agreement over and beyond this.[42]

5 SHARED COMPETENCE

(A) BASIC PRINCIPLES

Article 2(2) TFEU defines shared competence. The wording is important and Article 2(2) states that:

> When the Treaties confer on the Union a competence shared with the Member States in a specific area, the Union and the Member States may legislate and adopt legally binding acts in that area. The Member States shall exercise their competence to the extent that the Union has not exercised its competence. The Member States shall again exercise their competence to the extent that the Union has decided to cease exercising its competence.

The areas that fall within shared competence are delineated in Article 4 TFEU. Shared competence is the general residual category, since Article 4(1) provides that the Union shall share competence with the Member States where the Treaties confer on it a competence that does not relate to the categories referred to in Articles 3 and 6 TFEU, which deal respectively with exclusive competence, and that where the Union is restricted to taking action to support, coordinate, or supplement Member State action. This follows also from Article 4(2), which states that shared competence applies in the 'principal areas' listed, implying thereby that the list is not necessarily exhaustive. The idea that shared competence is the default position must nonetheless be read subject to the special category of competence dealing with economic and employment policy, Article 5 TFEU, and that dealing with foreign and security policy, Article 2(4) TFEU, Title V TEU. Article 4 TFEU states that:

> 1. The Union shall share competence with the Member States where the Treaties confer on it a competence which does not relate to the areas referred to in Articles 3 and 6.
> 2. Shared competence between the Union and the Member States applies in the following principal areas:
>   (a) internal market;
>   (b) social policy, for the aspects defined in this Treaty;
>   (c) economic, social and territorial cohesion;
>   (d) agriculture and fisheries, excluding the conservation of marine biological resources;

---

[40] *Opinion 1/94* (n 26) [99]–[105]; *Opinion 2/00 Opinion Pursuant to Article 300(6) EC, Cartegena Protocol* [2001] ECR I–9713, [45]–[46].

[41] *Opinion 2/00* (n 40) [5].

[42] *Opinion 2/91* (n 20) [16]–[21].

(e) environment;

(f) consumer protection;

(g) transport;

(h) trans-European networks;

(i) energy;

(j) area of freedom, security and justice;

(k) common safety concerns in public health matters, for the aspects defined in this Treaty.

3. In the areas of research, technological development and space, the Union shall have competence to carry out activities, in particular to define and implement programmes; however, the exercise of that competence shall not result in Member States being prevented from exercising theirs.

4. In the areas of development cooperation and humanitarian aid, the Union shall have competence to carry out activities and conduct a common policy; however, the exercise of that competence shall not result in Member States being prevented from exercising theirs.

There can be boundary problems between shared competence and the other two principal categories, exclusive competence and the category where the EU is limited to taking supporting, coordinating, or supplementary action. Thus it is, for example, not easy to decide which aspects of social policy come within shared competence. There are also problems in ensuring a fit between Article 4(3) and Article 4(4) TFEU, which assume that the relevant areas fall within shared competence, and the detailed provisions in these areas, many of which are framed in terms of the EU supporting, coordinating, and supplementing Member State action.[43]

(B) PRE-EMPTION

Article 2(2) TFEU stipulates that the Member State can exercise competence only to the extent that the Union has not exercised or has decided to cease to exercise its competence within any such area. Member State action is therefore pre-empted where the Union has exercised its competence, with the consequence that the amount of shared power held by the Member State in these areas may diminish over time. This conclusion must however be qualified in four ways.

First, Member States will lose their competence within the regime of shared power only to the extent that the Union has exercised *its* competence.[44] The scope of the EU's competence can only be determined by considering the detailed provisions that divide power in areas as diverse as social policy, energy, the internal market, and consumer protection. Thus the real limits on Union competence must be found in the detailed provisions which delineate what the EU can do in the diverse areas where power is shared.

Secondly, pre-emption occurs only *to the extent* that the EU has exercised its competence in the relevant area.[45] There are different ways in which the EU can intervene in a particular area.[46] The EU

---

[43] Craig (n 12) 167–171.

[44] Case C–373/11 *Panellinios Syndesmos Viomichanion Metapoiisis Kapnou v Ypourgos Oikonomias kai Oikonomikon* EU:C:2013:567, [26].

[45] Case C–114/12 *Commission v Council* (n 35) [93].

[46] S Weatherill, 'Beyond Preemption? Shared Competence and Constitutional Change in the European Community' in D O'Keefe and P Twomey (eds), *Legal Issues of the Maastricht Treaty* (Chancery Law Publishing, 1994) ch 2; M Dougan, 'Minimum Harmonization and the Internal Market' (2000) 37 CMLRev 853; M Dougan, 'Vive la Différence? Exploring the Legal Framework for Reflexive Harmonisation within the Single Market' (2002) 1 Annual of German and European Law 13.

may choose to make uniform regulations, it may harmonize national laws, it may engage in minimum harmonization, or it may impose requirements of mutual recognition. Thus, for example, where the EU chooses minimum harmonization, Member States will have room for action in that area. The Member States were nonetheless sufficiently concerned about the possible pre-emptive impact of Article 2(2) TFEU to press for the Protocol on Shared Competence,[47] which reinforces the point made above. It provides that where the Union has taken action in an area governed by shared competence, 'the scope of this exercise of competence only covers those elements governed by the Union act in question and therefore does not cover the whole area'. It is nonetheless still possible for Union acts to cover the entire area subject to shared power, provided that the EU could do so under the relevant Treaty provisions.

Thirdly, Article 2(2) TFEU expressly provides for the possibility that the EU will cease to exercise competence in an area subject to shared competence, the consequence being that competence then reverts to the Member States. A Declaration attached to the Treaty[48] specifies different ways in which this might occur.

The final qualification concerns Article 4(3) and Article 4(4) TFEU. They make clear that the Member States can continue to exercise power even if the EU has exercised its competence within these areas. Thus even if the EU has defined and implemented programmes relating to research, technological development, and space, this does not preclude Member States from exercising their competence in such areas. The same reasoning is applied to development cooperation and humanitarian aid.

(c) SCOPE AND VARIATION

Shared competence constitutes the default position in relation to division of competence, but that does not mean that the sharing will be the same in all areas where shared competence applies. The reality is that shared competence is simply an umbrella term, with the consequence that there is significant variation as to the division of competence in different areas of EU law. It follows that the precise configuration of power sharing in areas such as the internal market, consumer protection, energy, social policy, and the environment can only be determined by considering the detailed rules that govern these areas, which are found in the relevant provisions of the TFEU.

The sharing of power in relation to, for example, the four freedoms is very different from the complex world of power sharing that operates within the area of freedom, security, and justice (AFSJ). There are indeed significant variations of power sharing that operate within the overall AFSJ. There is therefore no magic formula that delineates power sharing in any specific area. This is not a criticism, but simply the consequence of the fact that the precise degree of power the EU has been accorded differs between these areas. This is recognized by Article 2(6) TFEU, which states that 'the scope of and arrangements for exercising the Union's competences shall be determined by the provisions of the Treaties relating to each area'.

(d) SHARED COMPETENCE AND RETAINED POWER

It is very important to note that the subject matter that falls within the scope of shared competence, such as the internal market and citizenship, may also have an impact on power retained by Member States.[49] This is because the ECJ interprets the scope of EU power in such areas to mean that even

---

[47] Protocol (No 25).
[48] Declaration 18.
[49] L Boucon, 'EU Law and Retained Powers of Member States' in Azoulai (n 1) ch 8; L Azoulai, 'Introduction: The Question of Competence' in Azoulai (n 1).

though the EU has no competence over matters such as direct taxation, which therefore remain within Member State competence, national rules in these areas must be exercised consistently with the four freedoms that constitute the core of the internal market, or with EU conceptions of citizenship.[50] This interpretation of the EU rules can therefore have a considerable impact on any area that remains within Member State competence.

6 SUPPORTING, COORDINATING, OR SUPPLEMENTARY ACTION

(A) BASIC PRINCIPLES

The third general category of competence in Article 2(5) TFEU allows the EU to take action to support, coordinate, or supplement Member State action, without thereby superseding their competence in these areas, and without entailing harmonization of Member States' laws.[51] While the EU cannot harmonize the law in these areas, it can pass legally binding acts if so empowered by specific Treaty provisions, and the Member States will be constrained to the extent stipulated by such acts. The meaning of supporting, etc action, and hence the precise extent of EU power, varies in the different areas listed, but it is clear that the EU has a significant degree of power in these areas, albeit falling short of harmonization.[52]

The areas that fall within such competence are set out in Article 6 TFEU: protection and improvement of human health; industry; culture; tourism; education, vocational training, youth, and sport; civil protection; and administrative cooperation. Article 6 TFEU gives the impression that the list is finite, but this is belied when reading the TFEU as a whole. It then becomes clear that there are other important areas in which the EU is limited, *prima facie* at least, to supporting, etc action, notably in respect of some aspects of social policy,[53] and certain facets of employment policy.[54]

The creation of categories of competence inevitably means that there will be boundary problems as between them. Thus, for example, regulation of the media might come under the internal market, which is shared competence, or it might be regarded as falling within culture, where only supporting, etc action is allowed. There are moreover difficulties in deciding which aspects of social policy fall within shared competence, and which come within this category.

(B) SCOPE AND VARIATION

It is important to understand the scope of EU power for areas that fall within this category. The meaning of EU action supporting, coordinating, or supplementing action by the Member States varies somewhat in the different areas listed, but the general approach is as follows.

Each substantive area begins with a provision setting out the objectives of Union action. Thus in relation to public health Article 168 TFEU lists, *inter alia*, the improvement of public health, prevention of illness, and the obviation of dangers to health. The EU is to complement national action on

---

[50] See, eg, Case C–246/89 *Commission v United Kingdom* [1991] ECR I–4585, [22]–[24]; Case C–279/93 *Finanzamt Köln-Altstadt v Schumacker* [1995] ECR I–225, [21]; Case C–120/95 *Decker v Caisse de maladie des employés privés* [1997] ECR I–1831, [20]–[23].

[51] R Schutze, 'Co-operative Federalism Constitutionalized: The Emergence of Complementary Competences in the EC Legal Order' (2006) 31 ELRev 167.

[52] See, eg, Art 167 TFEU, culture; Art 168 TFEU, public health; Art 173 TFEU, industry.

[53] Art 153 TFEU.

[54] Art 147 TFEU.

these topics. Member States have an obligation to coordinate their policies on such matters, in liaison with the Commission.[55] The Commission can coordinate action on such matters by exchanges of best practice, periodic monitoring, and evaluation.[56] The EU can also pass laws to establish 'incentive measures' designed to protect human health, and combat cross-border health scourges, subject to the mantra that this shall not entail harmonization.[57] Thus while harmonization is ruled out, the EU still has significant room for intervention through 'persuasive soft law', in the form of guidelines on best practice, monitoring, and the like, and through 'legal incentive measures'.[58] The same combination of soft law and legal incentive measures falling short of harmonization can be found in the other areas within this category.[59]

The scope of EU power within these areas should not however be underestimated. The standard approach under the Lisbon Treaty is for the EU to be empowered to take measures to attain the objectives listed in that area. The language of the empowerment varies. It is sometimes framed in terms of taking 'incentive measures',[60] on other occasions the language is in terms of 'necessary measures',[61] in yet other instances the terminology is 'specific measures'.[62]

The salient point for present purposes is that whatsoever the precise terminology these measures constitute legally binding acts, normally passed in accordance with the ordinary legislative procedure. The boundary of this EU legislative competence is that such legal acts must be designed to achieve the objectives listed for EU involvement in the area. These objectives are however normally set at a relatively high level of generality, with the consequence that the EU is legally empowered to take binding measures provided that they fall within the remit of these broadly defined objectives and do not constitute harmonization of national laws. This is evident in relation to all areas within this category of competence. The scope of EU legislative activity in these areas will be bounded by what is acceptable to the Member States in the Council and the European Parliament, but this does not alter the point being made here.

(c) LEGAL ACTS, HARMONIZATION, AND MEMBER STATE COMPETENCE

Article 2(5) TFEU provides that EU action designed to support, coordinate, or supplement Member State action does not supersede Member State competence. It also states that legally binding acts of the Union adopted on the basis of the provisions specific to these areas cannot entail harmonization of Member States' laws. Thus while the EU cannot harmonize the law in these areas, it can pass legally binding acts on the basis of the provisions specific to these areas. There are three important points that flow from this Treaty provision.

First, where the EU passes such legal acts they will bind the Member States and the competence of the Member States will be constrained to the extent stipulated by the legally binding act. Thus while Member State competence is not *per se* superseded merely because the EU has enacted legally

---

[55] Art 168(2) TFEU.

[56] Art 168(2) TFEU.

[57] Art 168(5) TFEU.

[58] There are also aspects of public health that come within the shared power, where the scope for EU intervention is greater: Art 4(2)(k), Art 168(4) TFEU.

[59] Arts 165(4), 166(4) TFEU, education and vocational training; Art 167 TFEU, culture; Art 173(2)–(3) TFEU, industry; Art 195 TFEU, tourism; Art 196 TFEU civil protection.

[60] Arts 165(4), 166(4) TFEU, education and vocational training; Art 167(5) TFEU, culture; Art 168(5) TFEU, public health.

[61] Art 196(2) TFEU, civil protection.

[62] Art 195(2) TFEU, tourism; Art 173(3) TFEU, industry.

binding acts, it will be constrained to the degree entailed by the EU legal act. It is clear moreover that the EU can pass legislative acts in these areas, where so authorized, provided that they do not entail harmonization.

Secondly, the very meaning of harmonization, which the EU cannot do in relation to this category of competence, is not entirely clear. The proscription of harmonization measures means that a legally binding act made in an area where the EU only has competence to support, coordinate, or supplement Member State action could not be made pursuant to Article 114, since this would be an admission that the objective was to harmonize national law, which is the very thing prohibited by Article 2(5) TFEU. This however takes us only so far. The EU may enact a legally binding act in an area covered by this category of competence, and it may be argued that the enacted measure is tantamount to harmonization of national law, even though it does not bear this imprint on the face of the measure. It would then be for the CJEU to decide whether in substance the contested measure constituted harmonization and was therefore caught by the limit in Article 2(5) TFEU. The line between a legitimate legally binding act that advances the objectives of the areas covered by this category of competence and illegitimate harmonization of national laws may be a fine one in a particular case.

Thirdly, it should not be assumed that the consequences for the Member States of enactment of legally binding acts in these areas will necessarily be less far-reaching than harmonization. The assumption behind Article 2(5) TFEU is that harmonization of national laws is by its very nature more intrusive for Member States than other EU legal norms. This rationale may hold true, but it may not. It depends on the nature of the particular harmonization measure and the non-harmonization legally binding act.

7 ECONOMIC, EMPLOYMENT, AND SOCIAL POLICY

(A) BASIC PRINCIPLES

A division between exclusive, shared, and supporting competence can be understood, notwithstanding the difficulties mentioned above. The creation of a particular head of competence to deal with economic and employment policy however does little to enhance the symmetry of the new scheme. The Lisbon Treaty has a separate category of competence for these matters. Article 2(3) TFEU states that 'the Member States shall coordinate their economic and employment policies within arrangements as determined by this Treaty, which the Union shall have competence to provide'. The detailed rules are then set out in Article 5 TFEU.[63]

> 1. The Member States shall coordinate their economic policies within the Union. To this end, the Council shall adopt measures, in particular broad guidelines for these policies.
> Specific provisions shall apply to those Member States whose currency is the euro.
> 2. The Union shall take measures to ensure coordination of the employment policies of the Member States, in particular by defining guidelines for these policies.
> 3. The Union may take initiatives to ensure coordination of Member States' social policies.

---

[63] The 'fit' between Art 2(3) and Art 5 TFEU is not perfect, insofar as the former refers to economic and employment policy, while the latter also covers social policy. There is moreover a difference in language, in that the EU is enjoined in mandatory language to coordinate economic and employment policy, whereas it is accorded discretion in relation to social policy.

The explanation for this separate category was political. There would have been significant opposition to the inclusion of these areas within shared competence, with the consequence of pre-emption of state action when the EU exercised power within this area. It is equally clear that there were those who felt that the category of supporting, coordinating, and supplementary action was too weak. This was the explanation for the creation of a separate category, and its placement after shared power, but before the category of supporting, coordinating, and supplementary action.

The boundary problems that we have seen in the preceding discussion are evident here too, particularly in relation to social policy. The difficulties in this area are especially marked, since certain aspects of social policy fall within shared competence, although it is not precisely clear which; other aspects appear to fall within the category of supporting, coordinating, and supplementary action, even though they are not within the relevant list; and there is in addition separate provision for social policy in the category being considered here. The reach of Article 5(3) TFEU and its relationship with the more detailed Treaty provisions on social policy are not clear. The most natural 'linkage' would seem to be Article 156 TFEU, which empowers the Commission to encourage cooperation between Member States and facilitate coordination of their action in all fields of social policy, albeit through soft law measures.[64]

(B) CATEGORY AND LEGAL CONSEQUENCE

The Treaty schema for competence in Article 2 TFEU is in general premised on the ascription of legal consequences for EU and Member State power as the result of coming within a particular category. Article 5 TFEU is an exception in this respect, since Article 2(3) TFEU does not spell out the legal consequences of inclusion within this category. It simply provides that the 'Member States shall coordinate their economic and employment policies within the arrangements as determined by this Treaty, which the Union shall have competence to provide'. The legal consequences of inclusion within this category can therefore only be divined by considering the language of Article 5 TFEU, which is couched largely in terms of coordination, and by considering the detailed provisions that apply to these areas. The detailed provisions concerning EU power over, for example, economic policy are considered in a separate chapter.[65]

8 COMMON FOREIGN AND SECURITY POLICY AND DEFENCE

The three-pillar structure that characterized the previous Treaty has not been preserved in the Lisbon Treaty. There are nonetheless distinct rules applicable to foreign and security policy, and this warrants a separate head of competence, which is contained in Article 2(4) TFEU.

> The Union shall have competence, in accordance with the provisions of the Treaty on European Union, to define and implement a common foreign and security policy, including the progressive framing of a common defence policy.

---

[64] The wording of the respective provisions does not however fit perfectly: Art 5(3) is framed in discretionary terms, 'the Union may take initiatives', while Art 156 TFEU is drafted in mandatory language, to the effect that the 'Commission shall' encourage the relevant cooperation and coordination.

[65] Ch 20.

The rules concerning the CFSP are set out in Title V TEU. Decision-making continues to be more intergovernmental and less supranational than in other areas of Union competence.[66] The European Council and the Council dominate decision-making, and the legal instruments applicable to CFSP are distinct from those generally applicable for the attainment of Union objectives.[67]

Article 2(4) does not specify which type of competence applies to the CFSP. In truth none of the categories is a good fit. It is clearly not within exclusive competence, since it is not listed in Article 3 TFEU, and in any event the substance of the CFSP simply does not accord with the idea of exclusive EU competence. Nor is it mentioned in the list of those areas that are subject to supporting, coordinating, or supplementing Member State action in Article 6 TFEU. This would seem to imply that it falls within the default category of shared competence in Article 4 TFEU, even though not mentioned in the non-exhaustive list.

The reality is however that the world of the CFSP does not readily fit within the frame of shared competence, insofar as this connotes pre-emption of Member State action when the EU exercises powers in the area, nor does this idea cohere with Declarations appended to the Lisbon Treaty.[68] If the CFSP is regarded as within shared competence, the point made earlier concerning the need for close examination of the respective powers of the EU and Member States, in order to be clear about the nature of the power sharing, is of especial significance.

9 BROAD TREATY PROVISIONS: THE 'FLEXIBILITY' CLAUSE

The discussion thus far has been concerned with the principal categories of competence established by the Lisbon Treaty. The discussion in this and the following section focuses on two particular Treaty provisions, Articles 352 and 114 TFEU, the successor provisions to Articles 308 and 95 EC.

These provisions are broadly framed, and give the EU wide regulatory competence. Member State concern over the extensive use of these provisions was a principal factor behind Treaty reform in this area, and was reflected in the desire to ensure that EU power was contained. It is therefore important to see how far this has been achieved.

(A) ARTICLE 308 EC

Article 352 TFEU is the successor provision to Article 308 EC. It is important to understand the legal and political background to Article 308 EC in order to understand Article 352 TFEU. Article 308 EC provided that:

> If action by the Community should prove necessary to attain, in the course of the operation of the common market, one of the objectives of the Community and this Treaty has not provided the necessary powers, the Council shall, acting unanimously on a proposal from the Commission and after consulting the European Parliament, take the appropriate measures.

Article 308 was a valuable legislative power, particularly when the Community did not possess specific legislative authority in certain areas. Thus the Article was used to legitimate legislation in areas such as the environment and regional policy, before these matters were dealt with through later

---

[66] Cremona, 'External Relations and External Competence of the European Union' (n 18).
[67] Craig (n 12) ch 10.
[68] Declarations 13 and 14 on the CFSP.

Treaty amendments. Weiler captures the importance of this provision and the manner in which it was interpreted.

J Weiler, The Transformation of Europe[69]

In a variety of fields, including, for example, conclusion of international agreements, the granting of emergency food aid to third countries, and creation of new institutions, the Community made use of Article 235[70] in a manner that was simply not consistent with the narrow interpretation of the Article as a codification of implied powers doctrine in its instrumental sense. Only a truly radical and 'creative' reading of the Article could explain and justify its usage as, for example, the legal basis for granting emergency food aid to non-associated states. But this wide reading, in which all the institutions partook, meant that it would become virtually impossible to find an activity which could not be brought within the objectives of the Treaty.

Article 308 EC required that the power should be used to attain a Community objective. Given, however, the breadth of the Treaty objectives, and given also the ECJ's purposive mode of interpreting Community aims, these 'conditions' did not place a severe constraint on the Council. They were not however entirely devoid of meaning, and the ECJ on occasion held that Article 308 could not be used to legitimate Community action,[71] although in the instant case it should be acknowledged that the ECJ was probably content to reach this conclusion, thereby avoiding subjecting itself to the ultimate authority of the European Court of Human Rights.

The most problematic aspect of Article 308 EC was the condition that the Treaty had not 'provided the necessary powers',[72] and therefore whether another Treaty Article could be used instead of Article 308.[73] This could be of particular significance where a specific Treaty Article provided for more extensive involvement of the European Parliament than did Article 308, which only required consultation with the EP.[74] The other situation in which the choice between Article 308 EC and a more specific Treaty Article could be significant was where there were differences in the voting rules under the respective Articles. Article 308 required unanimity in the Council, whereas many other Treaty provisions demanded only a qualified majority.

(B) ARTICLE 352 TFEU

Article 308 EC was long viewed with suspicion by those calling for a clearer delimitation of Community competences, and in particular by the German *Länder*. The issue was placed on the post-Nice and Laeken agenda for reform of the EU. The Laeken Declaration expressly asked whether Article 308 EC ought to be reviewed, in the light of the twin challenges of preventing the 'creeping expansion of competences' from encroaching on national and regional powers, while allowing

---

[69] (1991) 100 Yale LJ 2403, 2445–2446.

[70] Art 235 EEC was the predecessor provision to Art 308 EC.

[71] *Opinion 2/94 Accession of the Community to the European Human Rights Convention* [1996] ECR I–1759. Cf *Opinion 2/91 ILO Convention 170 on Chemicals at Work* [1993] ECR I–1061.

[72] Case 8/73 *Hauptzollamt Bremerhaven v Massey-Ferguson* [1973] ECR 897.

[73] Case 45/86 *Commission v Council (Tariff Preferences)* [1987] ECR 1493; Case 165/87 *Commission v Council* [1988] ECR 5545; Case C–295/90 *European Parliament v Council* [1992] ECR I–4193; Case C–209/97 *Commission v Council* [1999] ECR I–8067; Case C–377/98 *Netherlands v Parliament and Council* (n 8).

[74] Case 45/86 *Commission v Council* [1987] ECR 1493; Case C–350/92 *Spain v Council* [1995] ECR I–1985; Case C–271/94 *European Parliament v Council (Re the Edicom Decision)* [1996] ECR I–1689.

the EU to 'continue to be able to react to fresh challenges and developments and ... to explore new policy areas'.[75] The Working Group on Complementary Competences recognized the concerns about Article 308. The Group nonetheless recommended the retention of the Article in order that it could provide for flexibility in limited instances.[76] The flexibility clause is now enshrined in Article 352 TFEU:

> 1. If action by the Union should prove necessary, within the framework of the policies defined in the Treaties, to attain one of the objectives set out in the Treaties, and the Treaties have not provided the necessary powers, the Council, acting unanimously on a proposal from the Commission and after obtaining the consent of the European Parliament, shall adopt the appropriate measures. Where the measures in question are adopted by the Council in accordance with a special legislative procedure, it shall also act unanimously on a proposal from the Commission and after obtaining the consent of the European Parliament.
>
> 2. Using the procedure for monitoring the subsidiarity principle referred to in Article 5(3) of the Treaty on European Union, the Commission shall draw national Parliaments' attention to proposals based on this Article.
>
> 3. Measures based on this Article shall not entail harmonisation of Member States' laws or regulations in cases where the Treaties exclude such harmonisation.
>
> 4. This Article cannot serve as a basis for attaining objectives pertaining to the common foreign and security policy and any acts adopted pursuant to this Article shall respect the limits set out in Article 40, second paragraph, of the Treaty on European Union.

Article 352(1) TFEU is framed broadly in terms of the 'policies defined in the Treaties', and attainment of 'one of the objectives set out in the Treaties', with the exception of the CFSP. It can therefore serve as the basis for competence in almost all areas of EU law.[77] The unanimity requirement means however that it will be more difficult to use this power in an enlarged EU, and Article 352 TFEU also requires the consent of the European Parliament, as opposed to mere consultation, as was previously the case under Article 308 EC. It is also important to recognize that the need for recourse to this power will diminish, given that the Lisbon Treaty created a legal basis for action in the areas where Article 308 EC had previously been used.[78] The German Federal Constitutional Court was nonetheless concerned about the scope of Article 352 and stipulated that the exercise of any such competence constitutionally required ratification by the German legislature.[79]

The conditions in Article 352(2)–(4) are novel. The import of Article 352(2) is not entirely clear. Weatherill has argued that uniquely within the Lisbon Treaty it provides national parliaments with the opportunity to contest the existence of competence when legislative action is based on the flexibility clause, as opposed to other contexts where national parliaments can simply challenge on

[75] Laeken Declaration (n 4) 22.

[76] CONV 375/1/02, Final Report of Working Group V on Complementary Competencies, Brussels, 4 Nov 2002, [14]–[18].

[77] See, eg, Case C–270/12 *United Kingdom v European Parliament and Council* EU:C:2013:562, AG Jääskinen; Cases C–103 and 165/12 *European Parliament v Commission and Council* EU:C:2014:334, [110]–[111], AG Sharpston; A Dashwood, 'Article 308 EC as the Outer Limit of Expressly Conferred Community Competence' in C Barnard and O Odudu (eds), *The Outer Limits of European Union Law* (Hart, 2009).

[78] See, eg, Energy, Art 194(2) TFEU; Civil Protection, Art 195(2) TFEU; Economic Aid to Third Countries, Arts 209(1), 212(2) TFEU; Case C–130/10 *European Parliament v Council* EU:C:2012:50, [52].

[79] *Lisbon* case, BVerfG, 2 BvE 2/08, 30 June 2009, [326]–[328], available at www.bverfg.de/entscheidungen/es20090630_2bve000208.html. English translation available at www.bundesverfassungsgericht.de/entscheidungen/es20090630_2bve000208en.html.

grounds of subsidiarity.[80] This may be so. It does not however sit comfortably with the wording of Article 352(2), which is framed in terms of subsidiarity and is not suggestive of national parliamentary power to challenge the existence of competence. The more natural interpretation is that because the flexibility clause entails an exceptional use of EU legislative power, the Commission therefore has an additional obligation, viz to draw this to the attention of national parliaments, in order that they may contest it on the grounds of subsidiarity.

10 BROAD TREATY PROVISIONS: THE HARMONIZATION CLAUSE

The changes made by the Lisbon Treaty to what is now Article 352 TFEU, in particular the fact that express legislative competence is granted in areas where the Article was used hitherto, means that this Article is likely to be less problematic in the future than it was previously.

The Lisbon Treaty has, by way of contrast, done little to alleviate problems of 'competence creep' in the terrain covered by Article 114 TFEU, which has not been changed. It is the main Treaty Article used to enact harmonization measures.

> 1. Save where otherwise provided in the Treaties, the following provisions shall apply for the achievement of the objectives set out in Article 26. The European Parliament and the Council shall, acting in accordance with the ordinary legislative procedure and after consulting the Economic and Social Committee, adopt the measures for the approximation of the provisions laid down by law, regulation or administrative action in Member States which have as their object the establishment and functioning of the internal market.

Concerns about over extensive use of this legislative competence arose because it was felt that the EU was too readily assuming power to harmonize national laws based on mere national divergence, with scant attention being given to the impact, if any, of that divergence on the functioning of the internal market.[81] The ECJ's ruling in the *Tobacco Advertising* case[82] appeared to signal some tightening up in this respect, but subsequent case law[83] revealed that the ECJ is now more willing to find that regulatory competence exists because divergent national laws constitute an impediment to the functioning of the internal market and EU harmonization contributes to the elimination of obstacles to the free movement of goods, or to the freedom to provide services, or to the removal of distortions of competition.[84]

Impact Assessment[85] can, however, be used both politically and legally as a method of checking whether there really is a problem that requires harmonization at EU level.[86] Impact Assessment is a set

---

[80] Weatherill (n 1).

[81] Weatherill (n 1); S Weatherill, 'Competence Creep and Competence Control' (2004) 23 YEL 1.

[82] Case C–376/98 *Germany v European Parliament and Council* [2000] ECR I–8419.

[83] See (nn 8–9); Ch 17 below; D Wyatt, 'Community Competence to Regulate the Internal Market' in M Dougan and S Currie (eds), *50 Years of the European Treaties: Looking Back and Thinking Forward* (Hart, 2009) ch 5; S Weatherill, 'The Limits of Legislative Harmonisation Ten Years after *Tobacco Advertising*: How the Court's Case Law has become a "Drafting Guide"' (2011) 12 German Law Journal 827.

[84] See, for a recent example, Case C–270/12 (n 8).

[85] Impact Assessment, COM(2002) 276 final; Impact Assessment—Next Steps, SEC(2004) 1377; Better Regulation and Enhanced Impact Assessment, SEC(2007) 926; Impact Assessment Guidelines, SEC(2009) 92; http://ec.europa.eu/governance/impact/index_en.htm.

[86] Craig (n 12) 188–192.

of steps to be followed when policy proposals are prepared, alerting political decision-makers to the advantages and disadvantages of policy options by assessing their potential impacts. The results are presented in an Impact Assessment Report.[87] This does not replace political decision-making, which remains the preserve of the College of Commissioners. A typical Impact Assessment will address a range of issues including: the nature and scale of the problem; the views of stakeholders; whether the EU should be involved; the objectives of any such involvement; the main policy options for reaching these objectives, including their relative effectiveness/efficiency; and the likely economic, social, and environmental impacts of those options.

The Impact Assessment is not some panacea that will magically dispel concerns as to 'competence creep' or 'competence anxiety'. It is nonetheless important in addressing these concerns. The Impact Assessment Report considers the very issues that are pertinent to this inquiry. This includes the justification for EU action in terms of, for example, the need for harmonization because of the impact of diverse national laws on the functioning of the internal market. It also includes the subsidiarity calculus, which is a step in the overall Impact Assessment process,[88] with a specific section devoted to verification of the EU's right of action in terms of subsidiarity.[89] The Impact Assessment strategy therefore constitutes a framework within which to address concerns as to competence anxiety. The strategy is not perfect, but it has been improved since its inception, and assessments, both official[90] and academic,[91] have generally been positive, albeit noting room for further improvement.[92] If the data in a particular Impact Assessment Report are felt to be wanting then we should press for further improvement and not be satisfied with exiguous or laconic argument.

The very fact that there is a framework within which these issues are now considered facilitates scrutiny of the justificatory arguments and their adequacy. This should in turn facilitate judicial review.[93] The CJEU should be willing to consider the adequacy of the reasoning for EU legislative action, and to look behind the formal legislative preamble to the arguments derived from the Impact Assessment.[94] The CJEU should be properly mindful of the Commission's expertise as evinced in the Impact Assessment. It should also be cognizant of the precepts in the Treaty, which in the case of Article 114 TFEU condition EU intervention on proof that approximation of laws is necessary for the functioning of the internal market. If the justificatory reasoning in the Impact Assessment is wanting then the CJEU should invalidate the instrument, and thereby signal to the political institutions that the precepts in the Treaty are to be taken seriously.

---

[87] Impact Assessment Guidelines, SEC(2009) 92, 1.1.

[88] Ibid 2.1, 2.3.

[89] Ibid 5.2.

[90] Evaluation of the Commission's Impact Assessment System, Final Report—Executive Summary (Apr 2007, Secretariat-General of the Commission); Impact Assessment Board Report for 2008, SEC(2009) 55; Court of Auditors, Special Report 3/2010, Impact Assessments in the EU Institutions: Do they Support Decision-Making?

[91] European Policy Forum, *Reducing the Regulatory Burden: The Arrival of Meaningful Regulatory Impact Analysis* (City Research Series No 2, 2004); C Radaelli and F de Francesco, *Regulatory Quality in Europe: Concepts, Measures and Policy Processes* (Manchester University Press, 2007); C Cecot, R Hahn, A Renda, and L Schrefler, 'An Evaluation of the Quality of Impact Assessment in the European Union with Lessons for the US and the EU' (2008) 2 Regulation & Governance 405; A Alemanno, 'A Meeting of Minds on Impact Assessment' (2011) 17 EPL 485.

[92] A Meuwese, *Impact Assessment in EU Lawmaking* (Kluwer Law International, 2008).

[93] K Lenaerts, 'The European Court of Justice and Process-Oriented Review' (2013) YEL 3.

[94] The ECJ referred to the impact assessment in Case C–58/08 *The Queen, on the application of Vodafone Ltd v Secretary of State for Business, Enterprise and Regulatory Reform* [2010] ECR I–4999, [45], [55], [58], [65]; Case C–176/09 *Luxembourg v European Parliament and the Council* [2011] ECR I–3727, [65].

11 SUBSIDIARITY

(A) PRE-LISBON

Closely linked to the 'existence' of competence is the principle of subsidiarity, which regulates the 'exercise' of competence. Subsidiarity was introduced in the Maastricht Treaty, and was intended to curb the 'federalist' leanings of the Community. The pre-Lisbon formulation was contained in Article 5 EC:

> The Community shall act within the limits of the powers conferred upon it by this Treaty and of the objectives assigned to it therein.
>
> In areas which do not fall within its exclusive competence, the Community shall take action, in accordance with the principle of subsidiarity, only if and in so far as the objectives of the proposed action cannot be sufficiently achieved by the Member States and can therefore, by reason of the scale or effects of the proposed action, be better achieved by the Community.
>
> Any action by the Community shall not go beyond what is necessary to achieve the objectives of this Treaty.

The requirement in the first paragraph of Article 5 affirmed that the Community only has competence within the areas it has been given power. Article 5 also made it clear that subsidiarity would have to be considered only in relation to areas that did not fall within the Community's exclusive competence, but the problem was that pre-Lisbon there was no simple criterion for determining the scope of the Community's exclusive competence, since the Treaty was not framed in those terms. The Commission took a broad view of exclusive competence,[95] and commentators differed considerably on the issue.[96]

The subsidiarity principle had three components: the Community was to take action only if the objectives of that action could not be sufficiently achieved by the Member States; the Community could better achieve the action, because of its scale or effects; if the Community did take action then this should not go beyond what was necessary to achieve the Treaty objectives. The first two parts of this formulation entailed what the Commission termed a test of comparative efficiency,[97] in the sense of determining whether it was better for action to be taken by the Community or the Member States, while the third part of the formulation brought in a proportionality test.

The 1993 Inter-institutional Agreement on Procedures for Implementing the Principle of Subsidiarity required all three institutions to have regard to the principle when devising Community legislation. This was re-confirmed by the Protocol on the Application of the Principles of Subsidiarity and Proportionality attached to the Amsterdam Treaty,[98] which set out in more detail the subsidiarity calculus.

The idea that matters should be dealt with at the level closest to those affected is fine in principle, but there were many areas in which the comparative efficiency calculus favoured Community action, since realization of the Community objectives often demanded Community action to ensure the

---

[95] Bull EC 10–1992, 116. See 1st Report of Commission on Subsidiarity, COM(94) 533.

[96] AG Toth, 'A Legal Analysis of Subsidiarity' in D O'Keeffe and PM Twomey (eds), *Legal Issues of the Maastricht Treaty* (Chancery, 1994) 39–40; J Steiner, 'Subsidiarity under the Maastricht Treaty' in ibid 57–58; N Emiliou, 'Subsidiarity: Panacea or Fig Leaf?' in ibid ch 5, and 'Subsidiarity: An Effective Barrier Against the "Enterprises of Ambition"?' (1992) 17 ELRev 383.

[97] Commission Communication to the Council and the European Parliament, Bull EC 10–1992, 116.

[98] G de Búrca, 'Reappraising Subsidiarity's Significance after Amsterdam', Jean Monnet Working Paper 7/1999, www.jeanmonnetprogram.org/.

uniformity for attainment of a common market.[99] There were moreover difficulties with the approach in the pre-Lisbon scheme.

A Estella, The EU Principle of Subsidiarity and its Critique[100]

The truth of the matter is that attempting to define *ex ante* criteria of a general and abstract character for the purpose of limiting central intervention stands little hope of success. The reasons for this limitation are functional and can be found in the nature of modern regulatory problems. The functional interconnection between regulatory areas...makes the task of establishing clear dividing lines difficult. Even in those areas in which there seem to be clear reasons in favour of national, or even regional or local, regulation...it will always be possible to argue that due to the close relationship between these areas and the development of the single market, some Community intervention will always be necessary.

Article 5 EC nonetheless had an impact on the existence and form of Community action. The Commission considered whether action really was required at Community level,[101] and if so it would often proceed through directives rather than regulations.

(B) POST-LISBON

(i) *Subsidiarity Principle*

The subsidiarity principle was retained in the Lisbon Treaty, which distinguishes between the existence and the use of competence, the latter being determined by subsidiarity and proportionality.[102] The principles are embodied in Article 5(3)–(4) TEU:[103]

3. Under the principle of subsidiarity, in areas which do not fall within its exclusive competence, the Union shall act only if and insofar as the objectives of the proposed action cannot be sufficiently achieved by the Member States, either at central level or at regional and local level, but can rather, by reason of the scale or effects of the proposed action, be better achieved at Union level.
   The institutions of the Union shall apply the principle of subsidiarity as laid down in the Protocol on the application of the principles of subsidiarity and proportionality. National Parliaments ensure compliance with the principle of subsidiarity in accordance with the procedure set out in that Protocol.
4. Under the principle of proportionality, the content and form of Union action shall not exceed what is necessary to achieve the objectives of the Treaties.
   The institutions of the Union shall apply the principle of proportionality as laid down in the Protocol on the application of the principles of subsidiarity and proportionality.

---

[99] Better Lawmaking 1999, COM(1999) 562 final, 2.
[100] (Oxford University Press, 2002) 113–114.
[101] Better Lawmaking 2000, COM(2000) 772 final, 4–8, 15–21.
[102] Art 5(1) TEU.
[103] J-V Louis, 'National Parliaments and the Principle of Subsidiarity—Legal Options and Practical Limits' in I Pernice and E Tanchev (eds), *Ceci n'est pas une Constitution—Constitutionalization without a Constitution?* (Nomos, 2009) 131–154; G Bermann, 'National Parliaments and Subsidiarity: An Outsider's View' in ibid 155–161; J Peters, 'National Parliaments and Subsidiarity: Think Twice' [2005] European Constitutional L Rev 68; X Grossot and S Bogojevic, 'Subsidiarity as a Procedural Safeguard of Federalism' in Azoulai (n 1) ch 11.

The Lisbon Treaty contains a Protocol on the Application of the Principles of Subsidiarity and Proportionality,[104] which should be read in tandem with the Protocol on the Role of National Parliaments in the EU.[105] The Subsidiarity Protocol applies to only draft legislative acts,[106] and does not cover delegated or implementing acts. It is possible that a detailed delegated act might be felt to infringe subsidiarity, but the Protocol provides no mechanism for checks by national parliaments on such measures.

(ii) *Subsidiarity Calculus*

The Subsidiarity Protocol imposes an obligation on the Commission to consult widely before proposing legislative acts.[107] The Commission must provide a detailed statement concerning proposed legislation so that compliance with subsidiarity and proportionality can be appraised. The statement must contain some assessment of the financial impact of the proposals, and there should be qualitative and, wherever possible, quantitative indicators that the objective can be better attained at Union level.[108] The Commission must submit an annual report on the application of subsidiarity to the European Council, the European Parliament, the Council, and to national parliaments.[109] The CJEU has jurisdiction to consider infringement of subsidiarity under Article 263 TFEU, in actions brought by the Member States, or 'notified by them in accordance with their legal order on behalf of their national Parliament or a chamber of it'.[110]

(iii) *Enhanced Role for National Parliaments*

The most important innovation in the Subsidiarity Protocol is the enhanced role for national parliaments. The Commission must send all legislative proposals to the national parliaments at the same time as to the Union institutions. The national parliaments must also be provided with legislative resolutions of the EP, and positions adopted by the Council.[111] The Protocol provides for varying responses from the EU institutions depending on the number of national parliaments that voice subsidiarity concerns about the proposed legislation.

A national parliament or Chamber thereof may, within eight weeks, send the Presidents of the Commission, European Parliament, and Council a reasoned opinion as to why it considers that the proposal does not comply with subsidiarity.[112] The European Parliament, Council, and Commission must take this opinion into account.[113]

Where non-compliance with subsidiarity is expressed by national parliaments that represent one-third of all the votes allocated to such parliaments, the Commission must review its proposal, the 'yellow card procedure'.[114] The Commission, after such review, may decide to maintain, amend, or withdraw the proposal, giving reasons for the decision.[115]

Where a measure is made in accord with the ordinary legislative procedure, and at least a simple majority of votes given to national parliaments signals non-compliance with subsidiarity, then the

---

[104] Protocol (No 2) On the Application of the Principles of Subsidiarity and Proportionality.
[105] Protocol (No 1) On the Role of National Parliaments in the European Union.
[106] Protocol on Subsidiarity and Proportionality (n 104) Art 3.
[107] Ibid Art 2.
[108] Ibid Art 5.
[109] Ibid Art 9.
[110] Ibid Art 8.
[111] Ibid Art 4.
[112] Ibid Art 6.
[113] Ibid Art 7(1).
[114] Ibid Art 7(2). This threshold is lowered to one-quarter in cases of acts concerning the area of freedom, justice, and security that are based on Art 76 TFEU.
[115] Ibid Art 7(2).

proposal must once again be reviewed, and although the Commission can decide not to amend it, the Commission must provide a reasoned opinion on the matter, and this can, in effect, be overridden by the European Parliament or the Council, the 'orange card procedure'. Thus the EP acting by a majority of votes cast, or 55 per cent of members of the Council, can decide that the legislative proposal is not compatible with subsidiarity and that it should not be given further consideration.

While the Protocol imposes obligations on the Commission to ensure compliance with the principles of subsidiarity and proportionality, national parliaments are afforded a role only in relation to the former and not the latter. The reasoned opinion submitted by the national parliament must relate to subsidiarity. This is regrettable, as Weatherill rightly notes,[116] since it is difficult to disaggregate the two principles, and there is little reason why national parliaments should not be able to proffer a reasoned opinion on proportionality as well as subsidiarity.

(iv) *Political Control: Evaluation*

There are two points to bear in mind when assessing subsidiarity from a political perspective. They are related but distinct.

The first is that there has not surprisingly been discussion as to how far the new controls accorded to national parliaments have really added to their power.[117] The impact of these measures depends in part on the willingness of national parliaments to devote the requisite time and energy to the matter. The national parliament has to submit a reasoned opinion as to why it believes that the measure infringes subsidiarity. It will have to present reasoned argument as to why the Commission's comparative efficiency calculus is defective. This may not be easy. It will be even more difficult for the requisite number of national parliaments to present reasoned opinions in relation to the same Union measure so as to compel the Commission to review the proposal. The Commission is nonetheless likely to take seriously any such reasoned opinion, particularly if it emanates from a larger Member State.[118] The first instance where the requisite number of parliaments was secured to raise a yellow card was in relation to what was known as the 'Monti II' proposal concerning labour law. The Commission withdrew the proposal, albeit without admitting that it violated subsidiarity.[119]

The second point is equally if not more important, albeit much less discussed, which is that subsidiarity can lead to regulatory failure. Subsidiarity can manifest itself in one of three ways: the area may be left to national regulation; part of the area, such as enforcement, may be left to national regulation; the entire area may be subject to EU regulation, but with subsidiarity given voice through discretion left to Member States in relation to various aspects of the policy. The reality is that there will be many areas in which the comparative efficiency calculus in Article 5(3) TFEU favours Union action, more especially in an enlarged EU. While there are surely instances where matters could be better regulated at national level, there are also many instances where giving effect to subsidiarity in one or more of the three ways adumbrated above leads to regulatory failure,[120] as exemplified by the

[116] Weatherill (n 1).

[117] P Kiiver, 'The Early-Warning System for the Principle of Subsidiarity: The National Parliament as a *Conseil d'Etat* for Europe' (2011) 36 ELRev 98; P Kiiver, *The Early Warning System for the Principle of Subsidiarity: Constitutional Theory and Empirical Reality* (Routledge, 2012); A Cygan, 'The Parliamentarisation of EU Decision-Making? The Impact of the Treaty of Lisbon on National Parliaments' (2011) 36 ELRev 48; T van den Brink, 'The Substance of Subsidiarity: The Interpretation and Meaning of the Principle after Lisbon' in M Trybus and L Rubini, *The Treaty of Lisbon and the Future of European Law and Policy* (Edward Elgar, 2012) ch 9.

[118] Annual Report 2010 on Relations Between the Commission and National Parliaments, COM(2011) 345 final.

[119] Annual Report 2012 on Subsidiarity and Proportionality, COM(2013) 566 final, [3]; F Fabbrini and K Granat, 'Yellow Card but no Foul: The Role of the National Parliaments under the Subsidiarity Protocol and the Commission Proposal for an EU Regulation on the Right to Strike' (2013) 50 CMLRev 115.

[120] P Craig, 'Subsidiarity: A Legal and Political Analysis' (2012) 50 JCMS 72; M Emerson, 'Proportionality Needed in the Subsidiarity Debate in the EU—Appraisal of the British and Dutch Initiatives', CEPS No 11, 8 Apr 2014.

sovereign debt and banking crises, a prominent cause being too much regulatory autonomy left to Member States.[121] The reality is also that the business community generally prefers a single regulatory structure rather than a plethora of divergent national regulations, because the latter increase transaction costs and make it more difficult to penetrate other national markets, while consumers are for the most part relatively indifferent as to whether the applicable regulation is national or EU in origin.[122] The continuing tensions in this area are evident from the following extract by the previous Commission President.

JM Barroso, Political Guidelines for the Next Commission[123]

We must kill off the idea that the Member States and the EU level are rivals. Everyone should be working to the same goal—to secure the best results for citizens. Too often, mistrust has been the cause of failings in our system: it contributed to the shortcomings in our system of financial regulation exposed so brutally last year. The question is how best to improve this. That means an effective application of the principle of subsidiarity.

For me, subsidiarity is the translation of a democratic principle, part of a very practical doctrine, aimed at making public policy work to best effect in a Union built on solidarity, and at the most appropriate level. The EU works best when it focuses on its core business. I want to concentrate our limited resources on where we can have most effect, and where we can bring most added value.

At the same time, the continental scale of Europe and the scale of our ambitions points inevitably towards taking the wide view, looking at the bigger picture. This does not mean that the EU always has to make new laws—the Treaties mean we can make laws where this is needed, but they also inspire us to spark debate and spread ideas across the whole vision set out by our founding fathers.

I want to be rigorous about where we need to have common rules and where we need only a common framework. We have not always got the balance right, and we have not always thought through the consequences of diversity in an EU of 27 ...

The Lisbon Treaty puts in place new procedures to allow national parliaments to intervene if they have concerns about subsidiarity. But more importantly, we should develop a much clearer doctrine of how we decide when action needs to be taken at EU level, where the balance should lie between EU-level tools and national level tools, and what expectations should be placed on Member States implementing EU policy in their own countries.

(v) Legal Control: Evaluation

The Protocol provides for recourse to the CJEU for infringement of subsidiarity under Article 263 TFEU, in an action brought by a Member State,[124] and for the action to be notified by the state on behalf of the national parliament. It remains to be seen how the latter works, since there may be

---

[121] P Craig, 'Economic Governance and the Euro Crisis: Constitutional Architecture and Constitutional Implications' in M Adams, F Fabbrini, and P Larouche (eds), *The Constitutionalization of European Budgetary Constraints* (Hart, 2014) ch 2; J de Larosière, The High Level Group on Financial Supervision in the EU (2009, Brussels), paras 102–105.

[122] Business and consumers will have preferences as to the content of the regulatory provisions that are applicable to them, but this is a different issue, and there is no *a priori* reason why they should prefer the content of the national norm merely because it is national.

[123] European Commission, Sept 2009, 40–41, available at http://ec.europa.eu/archives/commission_2010-2014/president/pdf/press_20090903_en.pdf.

[124] The rules on division of competence do not give rise to rights for individuals, Case C–221/10 P *Artegodan GmbH v Commission and Germany* EU:C:2012:216, [75].

instances where the Member State has agreed in the Council to the EU measure, which the national parliament then regards as infringing subsidiarity. It would be odd for the Member State then to contend before the Court that the measure violates subsidiarity. If the legal action is to be a reality the Member State will not simply have to notify the action on behalf of its parliament, but also allow the parliament to argue that the measure does not comply with subsidiarity, even if the Member State does not agree with this.

This still leaves open the central issue, which is the intensity of the judicial review. The ECJ will not lightly overturn EU action for violation of subsidiarity. This is apparent in *procedural* terms from *Germany v European Parliament and Council*.[125] The ECJ held that the duty to give reasons did not require that Community measures contain an express reference to the subsidiarity principle. It was sufficient that the recitals made it clear why the Community institutions believed that the aims of the measure could best be attained by Community action. The difficulty of overturning a measure in *substantive* terms is apparent from the *Working Time Directive* case.[126] The UK argued that the Directive infringed subsidiarity, since it had not been shown that action at Community level would provide clear benefits compared with action at national level. The ECJ disposed of the argument briskly. It held that the Council had responsibility under Article 118a EEC[127] to adopt minimum requirements to contribute to health and safety. The Council had found it necessary to improve the existing level of protection and to harmonize the law in this area, and this necessarily presupposed Community-wide action. A similarly 'light' judicial approach to subsidiarity review is evident in other cases.[128]

There are undoubtedly difficulties with judicial review in this area. If the CJEU continues with very light touch review, it will be open to the criticism that it is effectively denuding the obligation in Article 5(3)–(4) of all content. If, by way of contrast, the CJEU takes a detailed look at the evidence underlying the Commission's claim it will have to adjudicate on what may be a complex socio-economic calculus concerning the most effective level of government for different regulatory tasks.

The difficulty of adjudicating on comparative efficiency would nonetheless be alleviated if the Union courts were to require more from the Commission in procedural terms. The obligation to give reasons could be used to require the Commission to disclose the qualitative and quantitative data that are to inform its reasoning pursuant to the Protocol. This would provide the EU Courts with more to go on, as compared to their present reliance on the exiguous reasoning contained in the Preamble to the contested measure.

The development of Impact Assessment[129] is significant in this context. It includes the subsidiarity calculus,[130] with a specific section devoted to verification of the EU's right of action in terms of subsidiarity.[131] This is a positive step, which facilitates scrutiny as to the justificatory arguments and their adequacy, which should facilitate judicial review. If the justification for EU action contained in the Impact Assessment appears merely formal, scant, or exiguous then the CJEU should not hesitate

---

125 Case C–233/94 *Germany v European Parliament and Council* (n 6) [26]–[28].
126 Case C–84/94 *United Kingdom v Council* (n 6) [46]–[47], [55].
127 Now Art 154 TFEU.
128 Case C–377/98 *Netherlands v Parliament and Council* (n 8); Cases C–154–155/04 *The Queen, on the application of Alliance for Natural Health and Nutri-Link Ltd v Secretary of State for Health* [2005] ECR I–6451, [99]–[108]; Case C–491/01 *British American Tobacco* (n 8) [177]–[185]; Case C–103/01 *Commission v Germany* [2003] ECR I–5369, [46]–[47]; Case T–168/01 *GlaxoSmithKline Services Unlimited v Commission* [2006] ECR II–2969, [201]–[202]; Case T–326/07 *Cheminova A/S v Commission* [2009] ECR II–2685, [250]–[261]; Case C–58/08 *Vodafone* (n 94) [72]–[80]; Case T–526/10 *Inuit Tapiriit Kanatami v Commission* EU:T:2013:215, [85]; Case C–518/07 *Commission v Germany* [2010] ECR I–1885, [52]–[55].
129 (N 85).
130 Impact Assessment Guidelines, SEC(2009) 92, 2.1, 2.3.
131 Ibid 5.2.

so to conclude, thereby indicating that the enhanced role accorded to subsidiarity in the Lisbon Treaty will be taken seriously.

(vi) *Subsidiarity: Evaluation*

Subsidiarity has always been an emotive subject, ever since its introduction in the Maastricht Treaty. This is true just as much for academics as for political players. Thus legal academics have criticized, with justification, the low-intensity judicial review undertaken by EU Courts when dealing with subsidiarity claims. There have been more far-reaching critiques, such as that by Davies,[132] who argued that the subsidiarity inquiry is misplaced, and that the focus should rather be on whether the challenged EU legislation is disproportionate by intruding too far into Member State values in relation to the objective sought to be attained by the EU legislation. Space precludes detailed analysis of these arguments.[133] The following points should nonetheless be borne in mind.

First, there have been few legal challenges based on subsidiarity since its introduction into the Treaty, approximately thirty, which means less than one per year. The real figure is lower than this, since some of the cases duplicate challenges made in other cases;[134] in others the challenge was clearly misplaced, given the nature of the Treaty provisions or EU regulatory scheme;[135] while in yet others the Member State adduced no evidence to substantiate the subsidiarity argument.[136] This leaves approximately twenty cases in over twenty years where there has been a real subsidiarity challenge, and thousands of regulations, directives, and decisions have been enacted during this period. To put this figure in perspective, there will often be more than fifteen challenges in a month on other grounds of judicial review.

Secondly, in a number of the 'real' cases the subsidiarity challenge was opposed by other Member States. Any idea that Member States take a uniform view on subsidiarity in a particular case is untenable. It should also be recognized that some subsidiarity challenges have been brought by private parties and received no support from any Member State. This does not mean that such challenges were therefore misplaced. It does mean that no Member State supported the claim that the relevant EU legislation infringed subsidiarity.

Thirdly, it is by no means clear that the ECJ decisions in the real subsidiarity cases were wrong, or that they would have been different if judicial review had been more intensive. It is too easy to reason from the premise that judicial review *should* be more searching, to the conclusion that the result *would* have been different. The premise is correct, the conclusion is wrong. The result might be different, it might not. Thus even where the reasoning of the Advocate General was considerably more searching than that of the Court, as exemplified by Advocate General Maduro's Opinion in *Vodafone*,[137] the result was the same. The reality is that whether a particular judicial decision was right or wrong can only be determined by looking closely at the contested regulatory scheme and deciding whether it 'passed' the subsidiarity criterion. When judged from this perspective it is not self-evident that any of the challenged regulations should have fallen because of subsidiarity.

Finally, it might be argued in the light of the above that the existing subsidiarity principle is defective, that the focus should be on whether the EU norm violates proportionality by infringing too

---

[132] G Davies, 'Subsidiarity: The Wrong Idea, in the Wrong Place at the Wrong Time' (2006) 43 CMLRev 63.
[133] P Craig, 'Subsidiarity: A Legal and Political Analysis' (2012) 50 JCMS 72.
[134] Case T–326/07 *Cheminova* (n 128).
[135] Case T–65/98 *Van den Bergh Foods Ltd v Commission* [2003] ECR II–4653, [197]–[199]; Case T–420/05 *Vischim Srl v Commission* [2009] ECR II–3841, [221]–[223]; Case C–110/03 *Belgium v Commission* [2005] ECR I–2801, [56]–[58]; Case T–339/04 *France Télécom SA v Commission* [2007] ECR II–521, [77]–[82].
[136] Case C–64/05 P *Sweden v Commission* [2007] ECR I–11389, [74].
[137] Case C–58/08 *Vodafone* (n 94) [27]–[36].

greatly on Member State values, and that if this were so then more cases would be brought by Member States and more might be successful.[138] Space precludes detailed examination of this hypothesis.[139] It is however not clear that any of the existing cases would or should have been decided differently even if this type of analysis had been applied by the EU Courts. There are moreover problems with locating such judicial scrutiny in Article 5(3). If this analysis is to be undertaken it is better done through Article 4(2) TEU, which provides *inter alia* that 'the Union shall respect the equality of Member States before the Treaties as well as their national identities, inherent in their fundamental structures, political and constitutional, inclusive of regional and local self-government'. The scope of application of Article 4(2) will be considered later,[140] but suffice it to say for the present that it could play a role in shaping the subsidiarity inquiry so as not to encroach too greatly on Member State regulatory autonomy.[141]

12 CONCLUSIONS

i.   EU competence is the result of the interaction of four variables: Member State choice as to the scope of EU competence, as expressed in Treaty revisions; Member State and since the SEA European Parliament acceptance of EU legislation; jurisprudence of the EU Courts; and decisions taken by the institutions as to how to interpret and prioritize the power accorded to the EU. We should therefore be cautious about the assumption that the 'competence problem' was the result primarily of some unwarranted arrogation of power by the EU to the detriment of states' rights.

ii. There were two principal objectives driving reform in this area: clarity as to the scope of EU competence and containment of EU power.

iii. The tripartite division in the Lisbon Treaty has gone some way towards greater clarity. The categories of exclusive competence, shared competence, and competence to support, coordinate, or supplement Member State action are helpful in this respect. So too is the fact that the Lisbon Treaty specifies the legal consequences of assignment of a subject matter area to a particular category. There are, however, limits to what can be achieved through categorization. There will necessarily be problems of demarcating the boundaries of each category.

iv. The category of exclusive competence is relatively narrow insofar as it relates to areas that are stipulated as falling within this head of competence, but the scope of exclusive competence in relation to external relations is broader and problematic.

v.   Shared competence is the default position in the Lisbon Treaty. The reality of the divide can, however, only be discerned from the detailed Treaty provisions that govern the particular area, and this may differ significantly as between areas that fall within shared competence. It is also necessary if one wishes to understand what the Member State is allowed to do in any such area

---

[138] Davies (n 132).

[139] Craig (n 133).

[140] L Besselink, 'National and Constitutional Identity Before and After Lisbon' (2010) 6 Utrecht Law Review 36; A von Bogdandy and S Schill, 'Overcoming Absolute Primacy: Respect for National Identity under the Lisbon Treaty' (2011) 48 CMLRev 1417; T Konstadinides, 'Constitutional Identity as a Shield and as a Sword: The European Legal Order within the Framework of National Constitutional Settlement' (2011) 13 CYELS 195; B Guastaferro, 'Beyond the Exceptionalism of Constitutional Conflicts: The Ordinary Functions of the Identity Clause' (2012) 31 YBEL 263; A Arnaiz and C Llivina (eds), *National Constitutional Identity and European Integration* (Intersentia, 2013); E Cloots, *National Identity and the European Court of Justice* (Oxford University Press, 2014).

[141] Guastaferro (n 140) 305–308, 311.

to know whether and how the EU has exercised its power, since the Member States lose their competence to the extent that the EU has exercised its competence.

vi. The recognition in the Lisbon Treaty of the category where the EU supports, coordinates, or supplements Member State action is to be welcomed. There are boundaries on EU competence in these areas, through the proscription on harmonization. The Treaty nonetheless allows persuasive soft law and binding hard law to achieve the objectives for each area. Such measures do not formally supersede Member State competence, but the legal reality is that such legally binding EU acts constrain Member State competence.

vii. The other principal concern driving reform in this area was the desire to contain EU power. This concern was based in large part on the broad use of what are now Articles 114 and 352 TFEU. The Lisbon Treaty renders problems based on Article 352 TFEU less likely in the future: it requires unanimity in the Council; consent from the European Parliament; that national parliaments are specifically alerted to use of this provision; and the EU has been given specific legislative competence in the areas where Article 308 EC was used in the past. The Lisbon Treaty has, by way of contrast, done little to alleviate problems of 'competence creep' in the terrain covered by Article 114 TFEU. Impact Assessment can however be used both politically and legally as a method of checking whether EU harmonization is required.

viii. The strengthening of the role of national parliaments in relation to subsidiarity is to be welcomed. The reality is that the Commission is likely to take seriously subsidiarity concerns voiced by Member States, especially the more powerful, and this is so even if the number of states voicing such concerns does not reach the levels to trigger the response mechanisms in the Protocol on Subsidiarity and Proportionality.

13 FURTHER READING

(a) Books

AZOULAI, L (ed), *The Question of Competence in the European Union* (Oxford University Press, 2014)

CRAIG, P, *The Lisbon Treaty: Law, Politics, and Treaty Reform* (Oxford University Press, 2010) ch 5

DASHWOOD, A, AND HILLION, C (eds), *The General Law of EC External Relations* (Sweet & Maxwell, 2000)

EECKHOUT, P, *External Relations of the European Union: Legal and Constitutional Foundations* (Oxford University Press, 2004)

ESTELLA, A, *The EU Principle of Subsidiarity and its Critique* (Oxford University Press, 2002)

SCHUTZE, R, *From Dual to Cooperative Federalism: The Changing Structure of European Law* (Oxford University Press, 2009)

(b) Articles

BOUCON, L, 'EU Law and Retained Powers of Member States' in L Azoulai (ed), *The Question of Competence in the European Union* (Oxford University Press, 2014)

CRAIG, P, 'Competence: Clarity, Conferral, Containment and Consideration' (2004) 29 ELRev 323

—— 'Competence and Member State Autonomy: Causality, Consequence and Legitimacy' in B DE WITTE and H MICKLITZ (eds), *The European Court of Justice and the Autonomy of Member States* (Intersentia, 2011) ch 1

—— 'Subsidiarity: A Legal and Political Analysis' (2012) 50 JCMS 72

DASHWOOD, A, 'The Limits of European Community Powers' (1996) 21 ELRev 113

DAVIES, G, 'Subsidiarity: The Wrong Idea, in the Wrong Place, at the Wrong Time' (2006) 43 CMLRev 63

DE BÚRCA, G, 'Setting Limits to EU Competences', Francisco Lucas Pires Working Paper 2001/02

—— AND DE WITTE, B, 'The Delimitation of Powers between the EU and the Member States' in A Arnull (ed), *Accountability and Legitimacy in the European Union* (Oxford University Press, 2002)

DI FABIO, U, 'Some Remarks on the Allocation of Competences between the European Union and its Member States' (2002) 39 CMLRev 1289

GROSSOT, X, AND BOGOJEVIC, S, 'Subsidiarity as a Procedural Safeguard of Federalism' in L Azoulai (ed), *The Question of Competence in the European Union* (Oxford University Press, 2014)

MAYER, F, 'Competences–Reloaded? The Vertical Division of Powers in the EU and the New European Constitution' (2005) 3 I-CON 493

SCHUTZE, R, 'Co-operative Federalism Constitutionalized: The Emergence of Complementary Competences in the EC Legal Order' (2006) 31 ELRev 167

VON BOGDANDY, A, AND BAST, J, 'The European Union's Vertical Order of Competences: The Current Law and Proposals for its Reform' (2002) 39 CMLRev 227

WEATHERILL, S, 'Competence Creep and Competence Control' (2004) 23 YEL 1

—— 'Better Competence Monitoring' (2005) 30 ELRev 23

INSTRUMENTS AND
THE HIERARCHY OF NORMS

1 CENTRAL ISSUES

i. This chapter examines two related issues: the EU's legal and non-legal instruments and the hierarchy of norms.

ii. The EU has a number of legal and non-legal instruments that are used to attain Union objectives. The principal legal instruments are regulations, directives, and decisions. These will often be used in conjunction with each other. The foundational provision in an area may be a directive, and regulations and decisions may supplement it. The foundational provision may alternatively take the form of a regulation, which is then supplemented by further regulations, directives, or decisions. The EU also has numerous soft law methods for developing Union policy. Formal and informal law will commonly be used together to attain EU goals.

iii. The Treaties lay down a number of conditions for the legality of such instruments. Thus reasons must be given for all legal acts, and there are requirements concerning publication and signature.

iv. The hierarchy of norms is the second issue addressed in this chapter. This phrase captures the idea that in a legal system there will be a vertical ordering of legal acts, with those lower down the hierarchy being subject to legal acts of a higher status. Prior to the Lisbon Treaty a hierarchy of norms could be discerned. There were, for example, 'primary' regulations, directives, or decisions that laid the legal foundations for policy in a particular area, and these would be supplemented by 'secondary' regulations, directives, or decisions that dealt in greater detail with an issue covered in the primary norm. The secondary norms were clearly subject to the primary norms, and hence lower in the hierarchy.

v. The framers of the Lisbon Treaty felt, however, that it was desirable in terms of simplicity, democratic legitimacy, and separation of powers to have a more definite hierarchy of norms than hitherto. There are now five principal tiers to the hierarchy of norms: the constituent Treaties and Charter of Rights; general principles of law; legislative acts; delegated acts; and implementing acts.

vi. There are however problems with the Lisbon regime, in particular in relation to the distinction between delegated and implementing acts. It is only when these problems have been understood that we can decide whether simplicity, democratic legitimacy, and separation of powers have been attained.

2 INSTRUMENTS

It is important to understand the different types of EU instrument. Article 288 TFEU is the foundational provision:

> To exercise the Union's competences, the institutions shall adopt regulations, directives, decisions, recommendations and opinions.
>
> A regulation shall have general application. It shall be binding in its entirety and directly applicable in all Member States.
>
> A directive shall be binding, as to the result to be achieved, upon each Member State to which it is addressed, but shall leave to the national authorities the choice of form and methods.
>
> A decision shall be binding in its entirety. A decision which specifies those to whom it is addressed shall be binding only on them.
>
> Recommendations and opinions shall have no binding force.

(A) INTRODUCTION

The more particular meaning of these legal acts will be examined below. It is however important to be aware of five points that are relevant to all these instruments.

First, there is no formal hierarchy between these provisions. Regulations are not therefore 'superior' to directives, or vice versa. Regulations, directives, and decisions will often be connected in the development of EU policy in a particular area. There may, for example, be a 'foundational' regulation, and directives or decisions may be made pursuant to this. The 'foundational' provision may equally be a directive or a decision.

Secondly, regulations, directives, and decisions may take the form of legislative, delegated, or implementing acts. The regulations, directives, and decisions do not alter their nature, but their place within the overall hierarchy of norms will depend on whether they are legislative, delegated, or implementing acts.

Thirdly, the Treaties may specify the type of instrument to be used, but will often not do so. Article 296 TFEU states that where the Treaties do not specify the type of act to be adopted, the institutions shall select it on a case-by-case basis, in compliance with the applicable procedures and with the principle of proportionality.

Fourthly, Article 296 TFEU imposes an obligation to give reasons[1] for legal acts, and this includes reference to any proposals, initiatives, recommendations, requests, or opinions required by the Treaties.

Finally, Article 297 TFEU specifies rules for the making of the legal acts in Article 288. Thus where a regulation, directive, or decision takes the form of a legislative act adopted under the ordinary legislative procedure it must be signed by the Presidents of the European Parliament and the Council. Legislative acts adopted under a special legislative procedure are signed by the President of the institution which adopted them. Legislative acts must be published in the Official Journal and enter into force on the date specified therein or, in the absence thereof on the twentieth day following that of their publication.

Where the regulation, directive, or decision is a non-legislative act and does not specify to whom it is addressed, it is signed by the President of the institution which adopted it. Regulations and directives addressed to all Member States, as well as decisions which do not specify to whom they are addressed,

---

[1] Ch 15.

must be published in the Official Journal. They enter into force on the date specified or, in the absence thereof, on the twentieth day following publication. Other directives, and decisions which specify to whom they are addressed, must be notified to the addressee and take effect upon such notification.

(B) REGULATIONS

Regulations are binding in their entirety and directly applicable in all Member States. It is common to think of regulations as akin to legislation made by Member States. There is some force in this analogy, since regulations are measures of general application, applicable to all Member States. The legal reality in the post-Lisbon world is, however, that regulations can be legislative, delegated, or implementing acts.

Regulations are said by Article 288 to be 'directly applicable'. There are two possible interpretations of this term.[2] It might connote the idea that individuals have rights, which they can enforce through national courts. The ECJ has on occasion interpreted directly applicable in this manner.[3] The better view is however that it relates to the way in which international norms enter national legal systems. In Member States with a dualist view of national and international law, this must be done either by the national system transforming the measure into national law, or by a shorter national act adopting the relevant international act. The EU enacts thousands of regulations and if each had to be separately incorporated into each national legal system before it could be legally effective then the EU would grind to a halt. The phrase 'directly applicable' signifies that regulations are part of national legal systems, without the need for transformation or adoption by national legal measures.

Member States may nonetheless need to modify their law in order to comply with a regulation, or they may need to pass consequential legal measures in order to give full effect to what is demanded by the regulation. This does not alter the fact that the regulation itself has legal effect in the Member States independently of any national law, and Member States should not pass measures that conceal the nature of the EU regulation.

Case 34/73 **Variola v Amministrazione delle Finanze**
[1973] ECR 981

The ECJ was asked by a national court whether the provisions of a regulation could be introduced into the legal order of a Member State by internal measures which reproduced the contents of the Community provision 'in such a way that the subject matter is brought under national law'.

THE ECJ

10. The direct application of a Regulation means that its entry into force and its application in favour of those subject to it are independent of any measure of reception into national law.

By virtue of the obligations arising from the Treaty and assumed on ratification, Member States are under a duty not to obstruct the direct applicability inherent in Regulations and other rules of Community law.

---

[2] J Steiner, 'Direct Applicability in EEC Law—A Chameleon Concept' (1982) 98 LQR 229; A Dashwood, 'The Principle of Direct Effect in European Community Law' (1978) 16 JCMS 229.
[3] Ch 7.

> Strict compliance with this obligation is an indispensable condition of simultaneous and uniform application of Community Regulations throughout the Community.
>
> 11. More particularly, Member States are under an obligation not to introduce any measure which might affect the jurisdiction of the Court to pronounce on any question involving the interpretation of Community law or the validity of an act of the institutions of the Community, which means that no procedure is permissible whereby the Community nature of a legal rule is concealed from those subject to it.
>
> Under Article 177 of the Treaty in particular the jurisdiction of the Court is unaffected by any provisions of national legislation which purport to convert a rule of Community law into national law.

An individual may allege that a measure which is called a regulation is really a decision. This arose most commonly when an individual sought to annul a measure because what was Article 230 EC limited the ability of individuals to challenge measures in the form of regulations. The test of whether a measure really is a regulation is one of substance, and not form. The fact that the contested act is called a regulation is not therefore conclusive.[4]

(C) DIRECTIVES

Directives differ from regulations in two important ways. They do not have to be addressed to all Member States, and they are binding as to the end to be achieved while leaving some choice as to form and method to the Member States. The ability to act through directives as well as regulations gives the EU valuable flexibility. The direct applicability of regulations means that they have to be capable of being 'parachuted' into the legal systems of all the Member States just as they are. Normally every 't' must be crossed, and every 'i' must be dotted in regulations, since Member States must not tamper with them. There might however be areas where it was difficult to devise regulations with the requisite specificity, which were suited to immediate impact in the Member States, more especially because the Member States have differing legal systems, and there are variations in the political, administrative, and social arrangements within the Member States.

Directives are particularly useful when the aim is to harmonize the laws within a certain area, or to introduce complex legislative change. This is because discretion is left to Member States as to how the directive is to be implemented. It should not however be thought that directives are vague. They are not. The ends which Member States have to meet will be set out in considerable detail. The force of directives has been increased by ECJ rulings. The Court held that directives have direct effect, enabling individuals to rely on them in actions against the state,[5] and that a Member State can be liable in damages for non-implementation of a directive.[6]

(D) DECISIONS

Article 288 TFEU states that a decision is binding in its entirety, and a decision which specifies those to whom it is addressed is binding only on them. This captures the duality in the use of decisions as legal acts prior to the Lisbon Treaty.

In most instances decisions were used as binding legal acts in relation to specific addressees, as exemplified by the many decisions made in the context of competition and state aids. Some decisions

---

[4] Ch 14.
[5] Ch 7.
[6] Ch 8.

were however of a more generic nature, setting out the legal rules to govern an inter-institutional issue such as Comitology, or providing the legal foundation for Community programmes.[7]

The English version of Article 288 is capable of covering both types of decision. The German and Dutch wording however signifies the generic rather than the individualized version of decision.[8] The individualized sense of decision will however subsist, since it has been an important form of legal act ever since the inception of the EEC.

(E) INTER-INSTITUTIONAL AGREEMENTS

Inter-institutional agreements between the Council, Commission, and the European Parliament have long been an important part of the EU. They are a form of 'constitutional glue' through which the major institutional players can resolve high-level issues, provide guiding principles, or lay the foundations for more concrete legislative action. Such agreements have been made on topics of constitutional significance such as subsidiarity, transparency, the budget, and participation rights.[9]

Article 295 TFEU now provides that the European Parliament, Council, and Commission shall consult each other and by common agreement make arrangements for their cooperation. It also stipulates that they may, in compliance with the Treaties, conclude inter-institutional agreements which may be of a binding nature. There is therefore specific Treaty foundation for rendering inter-institutional agreements binding.

(F) RECOMMENDATIONS, OPINIONS, AND SOFT LAW

Article 288 states that recommendations and opinions have no binding force. While this precludes such measures from having direct effect, it does not immunize them from the judicial process. It is open to a national court to make a reference to the ECJ concerning the interpretation or validity of such a measure.[10]

Recommendations and opinions are, subject to the preceding point, forms of soft law.[11] They are not however the only species of soft law. The Commission has, for example, issued policy guidelines in the area of state aids to indicate how it will exercise its discretion.[12] There are moreover other EU initiatives, such as the open method of coordination, which straddle the divide between soft and hard law.[13]

The admixture of formal and informal law is a common feature of any legal order. This feature has been positively lauded in the EU, rather than seen as a cause for apology or criticism. Thus the Commission in its 2000 Review of the Internal Market Strategy included a neat checklist of the legislative and non-legislative measures it intended to take in order to attain the single market.[14] The same readiness to use the full range of policy instruments was apparent in the Nice European Council.

---

[7] A von Bogdandy, J Bast, and F Arndt, 'Legal Instruments in European Union Law and their Reform: A Systematic Approach on an Empirical Basis' (2004) 23 YBEL 91, 103–106.

[8] B de Witte, 'Legal Instruments and Law-Making in the Lisbon Treaty' in S Griller and J Ziller (eds), *The Lisbon Treaty: EU Constitutionalism without a Constitutional Treaty* (Springer, 2008) 95–96.

[9] Chs 1, 5.

[10] Case C–322/88 *Grimaldi v Fonds des Maladies Professionelles* [1989] ECR 4407.

[11] K Wellens and G Borchardt, 'Soft Law in European Community Law' (1989) 14 ELRev 267; J Klabbers, 'Informal Instruments before the European Court of Justice' (1994) 31 CMLRev 997; L Senden, *Soft Law in European Community Law* (Hart, 2004).

[12] Ch 29.

[13] Ch 6.

[14] COM(2000) 257 final.

In the implementation of the Social Agenda 'all existing Community instruments bar none must be used: the open method of coordination, legislation, the social dialogue, the Structural Funds, the support programmes, the integrated policy approach, analysis and research'.[15] A glance at the Commission's work programme for any year will reveal the interaction between legislative and non-legislative techniques for attaining EU objectives.[16]

The admixture of formal and informal law, while inevitable, can nonetheless give rise to problems. It may be difficult for those affected to understand what the 'law' actually is in a particular area. Recourse to informal law may also prevent the Council and EP from having effective input into the resulting norms.

3 HIERARCHY OF NORMS

(A) RATIONALE

Prior to the Lisbon Treaty the legal acts of the Community were those specified above. Regulations, directives, and decisions could be used either as the 'primary' norm to govern a particular topic, or as a 'secondary' norm made pursuant to the 'primary' norm. The EC Treaty contained however no formal hierarchy of legal acts. This has now changed. The Constitutional Treaty included reform of legal acts and created a hierarchy of norms. The Lisbon Treaty retained a hierarchy of legal acts,[17] although the nomenclature was altered because it was felt by the European Council that the words 'law' and 'lawmaking' in the Constitutional Treaty should be excised on the ground that they carried 'federal' and 'constitutional' resonance.

The provisions in the Constitutional Treaty on the hierarchy of norms followed, with some modifications, the recommendations of Working Group IX on Simplification,[18] but it is instructive to note the cautionary warning of the Group, that 'nothing is more complicated than simplification'.[19] The Working Group sought to attain a number of objectives: simplification, democratic legitimacy, and separation of powers. The hierarchy of norms was said to be 'the consequence of a better separation of powers'.[20] There was to be a clearer delineation between matters that fell to the legislative arm of

---

[15] Nice European Council, 7–9 Dec 2000, Annex 1, [28].

[16] Commission Work Programme 2014, COM(2013) 739 final, Annex.

[17] Von Bogdandy, Bast, and Arndt (n 7); P Craig, 'The Hierarchy of Norms' in T Tridimas and P Nebbia (eds), *European Union Law for the Twenty-First Century: Rethinking the New Legal Order* (Hart, 2004) 75–93; K Lenaerts and M Desomer, 'Towards a Hierarchy of Legal Acts in the European Union? Simplification of Legal Instruments and Procedures' (2005) 11 ELJ 744; J Liisberg, 'The EU Constitutional Treaty and its Distinction between Legislative and Non-Legislative Acts' in B Olsen and K Sorensen (eds), *Regulation in the EU* (Thomson, 2006) 133–168; P Stancanelli, 'Le système décisionnel de l'Union' in G Amato, H Bribosia, and B de Witte (eds), *Genesis and Destiny of the European Constitution* (Bruylant, 2007) 485–543; de Witte (n 8); H Hofmann, 'Legislation, Delegation and Implementation under the Treaty of Lisbon: Typology Meets Reality' (2009) 15 ELJ 482; P Craig, *The Lisbon Treaty: Law, Politics, and Treaty Reform* (Oxford University Press, 2010) ch 7; B Driessen, 'Delegated Legislation after the Treaty of Lisbon: An Analysis of Article 290 TFEU' (2010) 35 ELRev 837; P Craig, 'Delegated Acts, Implementing Acts and the New Comitology Regulation' (2011) 36 ELRev 671; S Peers and M Costa, 'Accountability for Delegated and Implementing Acts after the Treaty of Lisbon' (2012) 18 ELJ 427; J Bast, 'New Categories of Acts after the Lisbon Reform: Dynamics of Parliamentarization in EU Law' (2012) 49 CMLRev 885; J Mendes, 'Delegated and Implementing Rule Making: Proceduralisation and Constitutional Design' (2013) 19 ELJ 22; T Christiansen and M Dobbels, 'Non-Legislative Rule Making after the Lisbon Treaty: Implementing the New System of Comitology and Delegated Acts' (2013) 19 ELJ 42; M Kaeding and A Hardacre, 'The European Parliament and the Future of Comitology after Lisbon' (2013) 19 ELJ 382; P Craig, 'Comitology, Rulemaking and the Lisbon Settlement: Tensions and Strains' in C-F Bergström and D Ritleng (eds), *Rulemaking by the Commission: The New System* (Oxford University Press, 2015).

[18] CONV 424/02, Final Report of Working Group IX on Simplification, Brussels, 29 Nov 2002.

[19] Ibid 1.

[20] Ibid 2.

government and those that were for the executive. We shall consider in due course whether these aims have been realized.

(B) TREATIES AND CHARTER

It is common when discussing the hierarchy of norms to focus on legislative, delegated, and implementing acts, and the hierarchy between them. This is indeed a central part of the subject. It is however incomplete. It is the constituent Treaties, the TEU and TFEU, which sit at the top of the hierarchy of norms in the EU. The Charter of Rights has the same status, since Article 6(1) TEU states that the Charter has the same legal value as the Treaties. The Treaty provisions will themselves be construed in the light of the Charter, in order to give the interpretation that best fits with Charter rights. Any legislative act must, as we have seen in the previous chapter, be made pursuant to some Treaty Article, and the Union Courts will determine the scope and interpretation of such Treaty and Charter provisions.

(C) GENERAL PRINCIPLES

The point made in the preceding section is important and obvious. The subject matter in this section is less obvious for those who are not yet familiar with EU law. The second tier of the hierarchy of norms belongs to what are known as general principles of law.[21] They sit below the constituent Treaties, and may be used when interpreting particular Treaty Articles. They sit above legislative, delegated, and implementing acts: general principles can be used not only to interpret such acts, but also as a ground for invalidation if a particular legislative, delegated, or implementing act contravenes these principles.

The general principles have been largely fashioned by the Union Courts. They have read principles such as proportionality, fundamental rights, legal certainty, legitimate expectations, equality, the precautionary principle, and procedural justice into the Treaty, and used them as the foundation for judicial review under Articles 263 and 267 TFEU. This is examined in more detail below,[22] but the role played by such principles must be understood here.

All developed legal systems embody principles of judicial review, which will normally be part of administrative law, and provide the basis for legal challenges to governmental action. These principles may be developed by the courts. They may be laid down by statute or code. They may be formed from an admixture of the two.

In the EU, the Treaty forms the starting point for elaboration of the grounds of review. Article 263(2) TFEU stipulates that judicial review shall be available for lack of competence, infringement of an essential procedural requirement, infringement of the Treaties or of any rule of law relating to their application, or misuse of powers. The influence of French juristic thought is clearly imprinted on these grounds of review. Article 263 TFEU nonetheless accorded the ECJ, and later the CFI (now the General Court), considerable latitude in fashioning the principles of judicial review.

The ECJ's role was facilitated by the broad wording of Article 263(2), especially the third ground of review, 'infringement of the Treaties or any rule of law relating to their application'. The intent might simply have been to ensure that Commission decision-making complied not only with the primary Treaty Articles, but also regulations, directives, etc, passed pursuant thereto. If this had been the intent it could however have been expressed far more simply. The intent might alternatively have been to capture compliance not only with secondary legislation, but also with other rules of law relating to

---

[21] T Tridimas, *The General Principles of EU Law* (Oxford University Press, 2nd edn, 2006); P Craig, *EU Administrative Law* (Oxford University Press, 2nd edn, 2012).

[22] Ch 15.

the application of the Treaty that might be developed by the Courts. In any event, the very ambiguity in the phrase and the fact that the *travaux préparatoires* for the Rome Treaty were not available for thirty years provided the ECJ with a window through which to justify the imposition of administrative law principles as grounds of review.

Article 19 TEU (ex Article 220 EC) was also important in this respect. It charged the Union Courts with the duty of ensuring that in the interpretation and application of the Treaty the law should be observed. This might have been interpreted in a limited manner to connote the idea that, for example, Commission decisions should be made within the limits of the primary Treaty Articles and secondary legislation. The word 'law' within this Article was however open to a broader interpretation that was used by the ECJ to fashion a system of general principles through which the legality of Union and Member State action could be determined.

The judicial task of elaborating principles of judicial review was further facilitated by more specific Treaty Articles, which made reference to, for example, non-discrimination. It was then open to the ECJ to read these particular Treaty references as indicative of a more general principle of equal treatment and non-discrimination that underpinned the legal order.[23]

In developing these concepts the ECJ and the CFI drew upon Member State administrative law doctrine. They did not systematically trawl through the legal systems of each Member State in order to find common principles. The approach was to consider principles in the major national legal systems, to use those that were best developed, and to fashion them to the EU's own needs.[24] German law was perhaps the most influential. It was German jurisprudence on, for example, proportionality and legitimate expectations that was of principal significance for the development of EU law in these areas.

The general principles afford the EU Courts considerable power over the interpretation of Treaty Articles and the interpretation and validity of other Union acts, as will be apparent from discussion throughout this book. The EU Courts also have considerable power over whether to recognize a new general principle of EU law, as exemplified by the following cases.

Cases T–74, 76, 83–85, 132, 137 and 141/00 **Artegodan GmbH and Others v Commission**
[2002] ECR II–4945

[Note Lisbon Treaty renumbering: Arts 6, 152, 153, 174, 175 EC are now
Arts 11, 168, 169, 191, 192 TFEU]

The case concerned marketing authorizations issued for drugs to control obesity. The Commission withdrew the authorizations pursuant to Directive 65/65 on the basis of scientific advice that the drugs might be harmful to health. The applicants sought annulment of the Commission decisions, and the CFI considered the status of the precautionary principle in EU law.

THE CFI

181. [W]here there is scientific uncertainty, it is for the competent authority to assess the medicinal product in question in accordance with the precautionary principle. It is therefore appropriate to recall the origin and content of that principle before explaining its effect on the rules of evidence in connection with the system of prior authorisation of medicinal products.

---

[23] Cases 117/76 and 16/77 *Ruckdeschel v Hauptzollamt Hambourg-St Annen* [1977] ECR 1753, [7].
[24] Case 14/61 *Hoogovens v High Authority* [1962] ECR 253, 283–284, AG Lagrange.

182. As regards environmental matters, the precautionary principle is expressly enshrined in Article 174(2) EC, which establishes the binding nature of that principle. Furthermore, Article 174(1) includes protecting human health among the objectives of Community policy on the environment.

183. Therefore, although the precautionary principle is mentioned in the Treaty only in connection with environmental policy, it is broader in scope. It is intended to be applied in order to ensure a high level of protection of health, consumer safety and the environment in all the Community's spheres of activity. In particular, Article 3(p) EC includes 'a contribution to the attainment of a high level of health protection' among the policies and activities of the Community. Similarly, Article 153 EC refers to a high level of consumer protection and Article 174(2) EC assigns a high level of protection to Community policy on the environment. Moreover, the requirements relating to that high level of protection of the environment and human health are expressly integrated into the definition and implementation of all Community policies and activities under Article 6 EC and Article 152(1) EC respectively.

184. It follows that the precautionary principle can be defined as a general principle of Community law requiring the competent authorities to take appropriate measures to prevent specific potential risks to public health, safety and the environment, by giving precedence to the requirements related to the protection of those interests over economic interests. Since the Community institutions are responsible, in all their spheres of activity, for the protection of public health, safety and the environment, the precautionary principle can be regarded as an autonomous principle stemming from the abovementioned Treaty provisions.

185. It is settled case-law that, in the field of public health, the precautionary principle implies that where there is uncertainty as to the existence or extent of risks to human health, the institutions may take precautionary measures without having to wait until the reality and seriousness of those risks become fully apparent...Prior to the enshrinement in case-law of the precautionary principle, on the basis of the Treaty provisions, that principle was implicitly applied in the review of proportionality...

The CFI was therefore willing to extrapolate from limited Treaty references to the precautionary principle, and from mention of the principle in some case law, and enshrine it as a general principle of law. It is nonetheless clear that the EU Courts have considerable discretion as to whether to recognize a new general principle of law.[25]

(D) LEGISLATIVE ACTS

Article 289 TFEU is the governing provision that deals with legislative acts. It provides as follows.

1. The ordinary legislative procedure shall consist in the joint adoption by the European Parliament and the Council of a regulation, directive or decision on a proposal from the Commission. This procedure is defined in Article 294.

2. In the specific cases provided for by the Treaties, the adoption of a regulation, directive or decision by the European Parliament with the participation of the Council, or by the latter with the participation of the European Parliament, shall constitute a special legislative procedure.

3. Legal acts adopted by legislative procedure shall constitute legislative acts.

4. In the specific cases provided for by the Treaties, legislative acts may be adopted on the initiative of a group of Member States or of the European Parliament, on a recommendation from the European Central Bank or at the request of the Court of Justice or the European Investment Bank.

---

[25] Compare Case C–101/08 *Audiolux SA ea v Groupe Bruxelles Lambert SA (GBL)* [2009] ECR I–9823.

The basic premise of Article 289 TFEU is that legislative acts are legal acts adopted by a legislative procedure. The legal acts that can be legislative are regulations, directives, or decisions: provided that they are adopted by a legislative procedure they will be legislative acts for the purposes of the Lisbon Treaty. The default position is that this will be the ordinary legislative procedure, which is the successor to co-decision. A special legislative procedure is however mandated in certain instances.[26]

The important point to note is that the definition of a legislative act is purely formal. This follows from the wording of Article 289(3) TFEU: any legal act, whether in the form of a regulation, directive, or decision, which is enacted in accordance with the ordinary or special legislative procedure is a legislative act for the purposes of the Lisbon Treaty. This formalism is symmetrical: any legal act enacted by the ordinary or special legislative procedure is by definition a legislative act; and if a legal act is not enacted in this manner then it does not constitute a legislative act. There are two consequences of this formalism.

The first is that the content of the act is not relevant to its status as a legislative act. If a legislative procedure is prescribed for the enactment of a legal act then it is by definition a legislative act, notwithstanding that the content of the measure might well be regarded as administrative in nature. The converse is equally true. If the Lisbon Treaty does not prescribe a legislative procedure for the passage of a legal act then it is not a legislative act, even if judged by its content it lays down rules of general application that would in substantive terms be regarded as legislative in nature.

The second consequence of the formalistic approach is that the only legal acts that constitute legislative acts for the purposes of the Lisbon Treaty are those made in accordance with the ordinary or special legislative procedure as defined in Article 289(1)–(2) TFEU, including in the case of the latter the requirement that this special procedure is mandated in the specific cases provided for by the Treaties. This gives rise to problems because certain Treaty Articles do not specify the ordinary or special legislative procedure, and hence the acts made thereunder are *prima facie* not legislative acts,[27] even though the measures enacted under the predecessor provisions of the EC Treaty clearly were legislative in nature.

(e) DELEGATED ACTS

Article 290 TFEU defines the new category of delegated act, and sets the conditions and controls over the making of such acts.

> 1. A legislative act may delegate to the Commission the power to adopt non-legislative acts of general application to supplement or amend certain non-essential elements of the legislative act.
>
> The objectives, content, scope and duration of the delegation of power shall be explicitly defined in the legislative acts. The essential elements of an area shall be reserved for the legislative act and accordingly shall not be the subject of a delegation of power.
>
> 2. Legislative acts shall explicitly lay down the conditions to which the delegation is subject; these conditions may be as follows:
>
> (a) the European Parliament or the Council may decide to revoke the delegation;
>
> (b) the delegated act may enter into force only if no objection has been expressed by the European Parliament or the Council within a period set by the legislative act.
>
> For the purposes of (a) and (b), the European Parliament shall act by a majority of its component members, and the Council by a qualified majority.
>
> 3. The adjective 'delegated' shall be inserted in the title of delegated acts.

[26] Ch 5.
[27] See, eg, Arts 103, 109 TFEU; Craig, *The Lisbon Treaty* (n 17) ch 7.

The Lisbon Treaty established two categories of act below that of legislative acts: delegated and implementing acts. The procedure for the making of such acts will be considered in the subsequent chapter. The present discussion is concerned with the nature of delegated and implementing acts and the criteria for the divide between them. The rationale for the divide was to distinguish between secondary measures that were 'legislative' in nature, delegated acts, and those that could be regarded as more 'executive', implementing acts. The difficulties of this divide were however never fully thought through in the deliberations on the Constitutional or Lisbon Treaty, and it is doubtful whether the objective has been realized.

A brief word by way of background to the pre-Lisbon position is necessary to understand the current regime. Prior to the Lisbon Treaty there was no divide between what are now termed delegated and implementing acts. The standard pattern was a 'primary' regulation or directive that governed a policy area, which was complemented by 'secondary' legal measures that 'implemented' the primary rules in accordance with Article 202 EC. This admixture of primary and secondary rules is common in legal systems. The Council recognized from the outset of the EEC that not everything could be done by primary regulation and that it would need to delegate power to the Commission to make secondary norms. The Council was however unwilling to accord the Commission a blank cheque, because it realized that regulatory choices and contentious issues could be resolved through such measures, the devil being in the detail.

This was the rationale for the birth of what became known as Comitology, whereby national technocrats would sit with the Commission when it made these secondary measures, with the possibility of sending them to the Council in accordance with the management and regulatory committee procedures if the national technocrats disagreed with the Commission's proposal. These committee procedures will be analysed below.[28] Suffice it to say for the present that they gave technocrats who were Member State representatives input into the making of the secondary measure. The committees' power flowed from the fact that if they disagreed with the Commission's proposal it could be referred back to the Council, which could then veto the measure.

The European Parliament was not happy with this regime, because although it had some role in the Comitology process, it was very much dominated by Council and Member State interests. The Commission opposed Comitology seeing it as an unwarranted constraint on its executive autonomy. The front line Directorates-General might have been content working with national technocrats, but the higher levels within the Commission were never happy with management and regulatory committees. The strategy was to devise some method whereby it could be freed from these limitations.[29] It advocated a regime of *ex ante* and *ex post* constraints on non-legislative acts of the kind that are now contained in Article 290 TFEU. Comitology in its pre-Lisbon form therefore no longer operates in relation to delegated acts, although some 'advisory' committees composed of national experts continue to exist in relation to delegated acts, and a revised form of Comitology operates in relation to implementing acts. Article 290 now governs delegated acts, which have a number of features.

First, they are described as 'non legislative acts of general application'. They are, however, only non-legislative in the formal sense that they are not legislative acts, because they have not been made by the ordinary or special legislative procedure. Many such delegated acts will nonetheless be legislative in nature. This view is reinforced by the fact that they are said to be of general application, and can supplement or amend certain non-essential elements of legislative acts, and because there is a separate

---

[28] Ch 5.

[29] European Governance, COM(2001) 428 final, [20]–[29]; Institutional Architecture, COM(2002) 728 final, [1.2], [1.3.4]; Proposal for a Council Decision Amending Decision 1999/468/EC Laying Down the Procedures for the Exercise of Implementing Powers Conferred on the Commission, COM(2002) 719 final, 2; Final Report of Working Group IX on Simplification, CONV 424/02, Brussels, 29 Nov 2002, 12.

provision dealing with administrative decisions.[30] The reality is therefore that a delegated act will often be what would be regarded as secondary or delegated legislation. This was recognized by the Working Group, which depicted these acts as a new category of legislation.[31] It was also acknowledged by the European Parliament's Committee on Legal Affairs, whose report was based on the premise that delegation was a 'delicate operation', whereby the Commission was instructed to exercise a power that was 'intrinsic to the legislator's own role'.[32]

Secondly, the legislative act must define the objectives, content, scope, and duration of the delegation of power. This is reinforced by the injunction that the essential objectives of an area must be reserved to the legislative act, and cannot be delegated. These requirements are policed by the Union Courts, although judicial review to determine whether the essential elements of an area were adequately laid down in the primary act has not hitherto been intensive or searching.[33]

Thirdly, the delegated act can 'amend or supplement' non-essential elements of the legislative act. Any general measure that amends or supplements a legislative act must be a delegated act made under Article 290, not Article 291. The meaning of amend and supplement is therefore crucial, because different controls operate under Articles 290 and 291. The two categories should be mutually exclusive, as accepted by the Commission.[34] The term 'amend' denotes a delegated act that formally changes some non-essential element of the legislative act. The word 'supplement' is not subject to such ready definition,[35] but it has in the past been used in a symmetrical manner with 'amend', such that the former connotes the addition of non-essential elements, while the latter captures the deletion thereof.[36] This interpretation was evident in the 2009 Commission Communication.[37] The difficulty of this divide will become apparent below when discussing implementing acts.

The fourth feature of delegated acts is that they are subject to the controls specified in Article 290: the EP or the Council is empowered to revoke the delegation and can veto the particular delegated act. The efficacy of these controls will be analysed below.[38]

(f) IMPLEMENTING ACTS

Article 291 defines the new category of implementing act, which can be made pursuant to a legislative act or a delegated act. This follows from Article 291, which specifies that implementing acts can be made pursuant to any legally binding Union act.

> 1. Member States shall adopt all measures of national law necessary to implement legally binding Union acts.
>
> 2. Where uniform conditions for implementing legally binding Union acts are needed, those acts shall confer implementing powers on the Commission, or, in duly justified specific cases and in the cases provided for in Articles 24 and 26 of the Treaty on European Union, on the Council.

---

[30] Art 288 TFEU.

[31] Final Report of Working Group IX (n 29) 8.

[32] Committee on Legal Affairs, On the Power of Legislative Delegation, A-7 0110/2010, Rapporteur J Sjazer, Preamble C.

[33] Ch 5.

[34] Implementation of Article 290 of the Treaty on the Functioning of the European Union, COM(2009) 673 final, [2.2].

[35] Ibid [2.3].

[36] 2006/512/EC: Council Decision of 17 July 2006 amending Decision 1999/468/EC laying down the procedures for the exercise of implementing powers conferred on the Commission [2006] OJ L200/11.

[37] COM(2009) 673 (n 34) [2.3].

[38] Ch 5.

3. For the purposes of paragraph 2, the European Parliament and the Council, acting by means of regulations in accordance with the ordinary legislative procedure, shall lay down in advance the rules and general principles concerning mechanisms for control by Member States of the Commission's exercise of implementing powers.

4. The word 'implementing' shall be inserted in the title of implementing acts.

It is important once again to take a step back in order to understand the change made by the Lisbon Treaty. We have already seen that pre-Lisbon the making of secondary measures was governed by Article 202 EC, which was framed so as to allow delegation of power to the Commission for the 'implementation' of rules laid down by the Council, subject to the Comitology procedure. There was significant variation as to the secondary measures concluded pursuant to Article 202 EC. In reality there was a spectrum of secondary norms, with 'pure' rule-making at one end, 'pure' implementation at the other, and many measures falling between the two. This did not however matter pre-Lisbon since the same Treaty provision, Article 202 EC, applied to all such measures.[39]

The term 'implementation' as used in Community legislation and official websites thus covered what are now termed delegated acts, as well as the terrain now covered by implementing acts. Thus the standard format in EC legislation was to empower the Commission to make 'implementing provisions', 'implementing rules', or 'determine detailed rules', subject to Comitology, and the paradigm application was through rule-making or decision-making that amended or supplemented the primary legal norm.[40] The same terminology was evident on official websites, where the term 'implementing provisions' carried the broad connotation used in Community legislation.[41]

The post-Lisbon world requires us to distinguish between delegated acts and implementing acts. Delegated acts are of general application and amend or supplement the legislative act. Implementing acts will normally be of general application, since Article 291 specifies their use in circumstances where uniform conditions for implementing legally binding acts are needed. The key distinguishing feature is therefore that implementing acts execute the legislative act without amendment or supplementation. Consider the Commission's approach to this issue.

Implementation of Article 290 of the Treaty on the Functioning of the European Union
COM(2009) 673 final

Firstly, it believes that by using the verb 'amend' the authors of the new Treaty wanted to cover hypothetical cases in which the Commission is empowered formally to amend a basic instrument. Such a formal amendment might relate to the text of one or more articles in the enacting terms or to the text of an annex that legally forms part of the legislative instrument. It makes little difference whether the annex contains purely technical measures; as soon as the Commission is empowered to amend an annex containing measures of general application, the regime of delegated acts must be applied.

Secondly, the Commission wishes to stress the importance that should be attached to the verb 'supplement', the meaning and scope of which are less specific than those of the verb 'amend'.

---

[39] The nature of the secondary measure could after 2006 impact on the precise version of the Comitology procedure.

[40] Craig, *The Lisbon Treaty* (n 17) 271.

[41] See, eg, http://ec.europa.eu/competition/antitrust/legislation/regulations.html; http://ec.europa.eu/information_society/policy/ecomm/implementation_enforcement/index_en.htm; http://ec.europa.eu/internal_market/services/services-dir/implementation_en.htm.

> The Commission believes that in order to determine whether a measure 'supplements' the basic instrument, the legislator should assess whether the future measure specifically adds new non-essential rules which change the framework of the legislative act, leaving a margin of discretion to the Commission. If it does, the measure could be deemed to 'supplement' the basic instrument. Conversely, measures intended only to give effect to the existing rules of the basic instrument should not be deemed to be supplementary measures.

The Commission captures the criterion that must be applied to distinguish delegated and implementing acts. There are, however, three difficulties with this criterion, which call into question the plausibility of the divide between delegated and implementing acts.[42]

First, there is 'the language problem': all secondary measures involve some addition to the primary act. Many thousands of secondary measures have been enacted since the inception of the EEC. In the paradigm case they bring greater exactitude to the meaning of an Article of the primary act. Thus, for example, there might be a complex primary act dealing with agriculture, and a secondary measure specifies in greater detail one part of the primary act relating to, for example, the requirements for the independence of agencies that pay money pursuant to the primary regulation. Such measures clearly 'add something' to the primary act. This will be equally true for any measure classified as an implementing act in the post-Lisbon world, since the very specification of uniform conditions of implementation will be 'adding something' to the enabling provision in the legislative or delegated act. The key issue is therefore whether what is added will be regarded as amending or supplementing the primary act. This demands the following evaluation.

It might be considered that the Article in the legislative act has sufficiently resolved the relevant issues, the conclusion being that the secondary measure, while obviously imbuing the Article of the legislative act with greater detail, does not supplement it by adding any 'new' non-essential element so as to trigger the need for recourse to Article 290, the conclusion being that Article 291 can be used. It might in other instances be concluded that the relevant Article in the legislative act is less definitive, the conclusion being that while it has provided sufficient guide as to essential principles, the secondary measure has nonetheless supplemented it by the addition of 'new' non-essential elements, the conclusion being that Article 290 must be used.

The divide between the terrain of delegated and implementing acts will turn on the preceding determination. It is difficult to regard this as satisfactory. It is bound to generate inter-institutional disputes as to whether recourse should be had to Article 290 or 291 TFEU. It calls into question the normative foundation for the differential controls that operate in relation to delegated and implementing acts. There will inevitably be instances where juxtaposition of acts reveals scant reason as to why the 'supplementation' of the legislative act in the one instance should be regarded as a 'new' non-essential element, such that a delegated act is required, while in other instances this is not so, such that an implementing act can be used.

Secondly, the preceding difficulty is exacerbated by the 'time problem'. It is not possible to decide conclusively whether a secondary measure falls into the category of delegated or implementing acts according to the foregoing criterion until it is made, more especially because any draft measure may be changed prior to final enactment. However the choice between delegated and implementing act has to be made at an early stage, because the procedures for their making are very different.[43]

---

[42] Craig, *The Lisbon Treaty* (n 17); Craig, 'Delegated Acts' (n 17).
[43] Title V TEU.

Delegated acts are subject to the *ex ante* and *ex post* controls described above exercised by the Council or European Parliament; implementing acts are subject to a revised version of the Comitology procedure. The danger is that once the Commission has decided that a measure should be classified as, for example, an implementing act, and the revised Comitology process has been engaged, it will be loathe to admit that any changes made by this process involve 'supplementation' of the legislative act via the introduction of 'new' non-essential elements, since this would mean that the act should be regarded as a delegated act.

Thirdly, it is clear that the ECJ is unwilling to become deeply embroiled in adjudicating on the nature of the divide between delegated and implementing acts as is apparent in the following case.

Case C-427/12 **Commission v European Parliament and Council**
EU:C:2014:170

A legislative act had been enacted concerning biocidal products and empowered the Commission to make implementing regulations pursuant to Article 291. The Commission contended that Article 290 should rather be used, because the regulation supplemented the legislative act and thus should be regarded as a delegated act. It contended that the choice as between a delegated and an implementing act should be based on objective factors that were amenable to judicial review and that the respective scopes of Articles 290 and 291 TFEU were mutually exclusive. The Commission argued that if the purpose was to adopt non-essential rules of general application, which completed the normative framework of the legislative act, then those rules supplemented the legislative act and had to be made via Article 290. If however the purpose was merely to give effect to the rules already laid down in the basic act while ensuring uniform conditions of application within the EU then Article 291 could be used.

THE CJEU

38. When the EU legislature confers, in a legislative act, a delegated power on the Commission pursuant to Article 290(1) TFEU, the Commission is called on to adopt rules which supplement or amend certain non-essential elements of that act. In accordance with the second subparagraph of Article 290(1) TFEU, the objectives, content, scope and duration of the delegation of power must be explicitly defined in the legislative act granting such a delegation. That requirement implies that the purpose of granting a delegated power is to achieve the adoption of rules coming within the regulatory framework as defined by the basic legislative act.

39. By contrast, when the EU legislature confers an implementing power on the Commission on the basis of Article 291(2) TFEU, the Commission is called on to provide further detail in relation to the content of a legislative act, in order to ensure that it is implemented under uniform conditions in all Member States.

40. It must be noted that the EU legislature has discretion when it decides to confer a delegated power on the Commission pursuant to Article 290(1) TFEU or an implementing power pursuant to Article 291(2) TFEU. Consequently, judicial review is limited to manifest errors of assessment as to whether the EU legislature could reasonably have taken the view, first, that, in order to be implemented, the legal framework which it laid down regarding the system of fees referred to in Article 80(1) of Regulation No 528/2012 needs only the addition of further detail, without its non-essential elements having to be amended or supplemented and, secondly, that the provisions of Regulation No 528/2012 relating to that system require uniform conditions for implementation.

The Court concluded in paragraph 40 that it would only review the legislative choice between delegated and implementing acts if there was a manifest error. This approach obviated the need for it to give clear guidance on the division between the two kinds of act. The Court however elides two distinct issues, these being the legislature's power to use both delegated and implementing acts, and whether the conditions for the application of the respective types of act have been met.

It is true that the legislature has 'discretion' as to the former issue, but only in the reductionist sense that the Lisbon Treaty makes provision for both delegated and implementing acts, with the consequence that it is open to the EU legislature in the legislative act to choose whether further rules should be made pursuant to Article 290 or Article 291. This provides however no foundation for the conclusion that the EU legislature has 'discretion' as to the latter issue, which is whether the conditions for the application of Article 290 or Article 291 have been met in any particular instance. Thus the fact that the EU legislature may take the view that, for example, an implementing act will suffice for rules made pursuant to the legislative act because they only add some further detail that does not thereby amend or supplement its non-essential elements does not 'make it so'.

It can be accepted that when reviewing the choice made by the legislature the Court should consider the reasons why it chose to proceed via a delegated act rather than an implementing act, or vice versa. This is however to say no more than that when exercising judicial review a Court should be properly informed as to the reasoning that underpinned the decision of the body being reviewed. It provides no foundation for the conclusion that the body subject to review has 'discretion' as to whether the conditions for the application of delegated or implementing acts are met, with the consequence that the Court uses only light touch review for manifest error.

The real lesson from this case is that the analytical divide between delegated and implementing acts is fragile. The CJEU was faced with a choice. It could choose to give guidance as to the nature of this divide, but this would lead to the analytical criterion set out above, or something analogous as suggested by the Commission in the instant case. This would then invite frequent challenges as to whether an act fell on the right or wrong side of this analytical divide, a scenario that the Court would not welcome. The Court therefore chose the alternative route, which was to avoid close analytical scrutiny of the dichotomy between the two types of act through recourse to the intensity of review, manifest error being said to be warranted because of the 'discretion' possessed by the legislature. This will discourage claimants from challenging the correctness of the use of delegated or implementing acts, because of the difficulty of proving manifest error.

This cannot however conceal the paradox that besets this area. The distinction between delegated and implementing acts was adopted because it was felt to be important constitutionally and pragmatically. The paradox is that it is the very problematic nature of this divide which led the Court to back away from addressing the substantive distinction between the two types of act, and to sidestep the issue by assigning 'discretion' as to its application to the EU legislature, to be policed only through light touch review for manifest error.

(G) INCOMPLETE CATEGORIZATION

The discussion thus far has considered the schema of legal acts in the Lisbon Treaty and the problems presented by this novel regime. There are however two respects in which the Lisbon categorization is incomplete.

First, certain acts do not seem to fit the preceding categories. We have seen that legislative acts, delegated acts, and implementing acts can in principle take the form of regulations, directives, or decisions, subject to the caveats noted above. We have also seen that each type of legal act has its own criteria. Legislative acts are defined formally in accordance with the procedure for their enactment. Delegated acts must be made pursuant to a legislative act, they must be of general application, and amend or supplement non-essential elements of the legislative act. Implementing acts are premised on the need for uniform conditions of implementation.

This leaves an interesting inquiry as to acts that do not fit these categories. Consider, for example, a standard administrative decision addressed to a particular person, which falls within the definition of decision in Article 288 TFEU. It will not be a legislative act if it is not made by a legislative procedure. It will not be a delegated act, since these can only be made pursuant to a legislative act and must be of general application. It will not be an implementing act, since the paradigm administrative decision addressed to a particular person has nothing to do with uniform conditions for implementation as that term is used in Article 291. We might conclude that such decisions cannot legally be made. This would however lead to very considerable practical difficulties and would fly in the face of Article 288, which clearly contemplates a decision addressed to a particular person. The alternative is to accept that such decisions can be legally made, but to acknowledge that they may not fit into the categories of legislative, delegated, or implementing act, the corollary being that the hierarchy of legal acts composed of these categories does not capture the ways in which legal norms are made in the post-Lisbon world.

Secondly, while the Lisbon Treaty dismantled the formal pillar system, there are nonetheless distinct rules concerning the legal acts that can be used for the Common Foreign and Security Policy (CFSP).[44] Article 25 TEU provides that the Union shall conduct the CFSP through a number of measures. General guidelines must be defined, this being a matter for the European Council.[45] Decisions should be adopted defining actions to be undertaken by the Union, positions to be taken by the Union, and arrangements for the implementation of the preceding decisions. These decisions are taken primarily by the Council on the basis of the general guidelines decided by the European Council.[46] It is however unclear whether the term 'decision' used in this context bears the same meaning as in Article 288 TFEU, although this seems doubtful given the specific contexts in which the decision is used in relation to the CFSP. Legislative acts cannot be undertaken in relation to the CFSP.[47]

4 CONCLUSIONS

i. The EU has three principal types of formal legal norms at its disposal, regulations, directives, and decisions. In most instances the EU can choose which type of legal provision to use.

ii. EU policy in any particular area will be made by various formal legal norms. A basic regulation can be made more concrete through further regulations, or through directives or decisions. The foundational provision may alternatively be a directive or even a decision, which can then be complemented by secondary norms cast in terms of regulations, directives, or decisions. These formal legal norms will be supplemented by a variety of soft law devices.

iii. The Lisbon Treaty instituted a more formal hierarchy of legal norms than existed hitherto. There are now five categories within this hierarchy: the constituent Treaties, TEU and TFEU, and the Charter of Rights; general principles of law; legislative acts; delegated acts; and implementing acts. There are four points to note about this hierarchy.

---

[44] Ch 10.
[45] Arts 26(1), 42(2) TEU.
[46] Arts 26(2), 28, 29, 42(4), 43 TEU.
[47] Art 31 TEU.

iv. First, the elaboration of general principles of law lies principally with the Union Courts. This gives them considerable power to decide what constitutes a general principle of EU law, and how it should be applied. This is important because general principles shape the interpretation of Treaty provisions and other Union acts, and because they are also a ground for invalidation of legislative, delegated, and implementing acts.

v. Secondly, certain elements within this hierarchy are defined in purely formal terms. Thus, for example, the definition of legislative acts is formal in the sense that it connotes acts made in accordance with a legislative procedure, irrespective of the nature of the measure enacted. The definition of delegated acts is also formal, insofar as they are said to be non-legislative, since this simply means that these acts have not been made in accordance with the procedure for legislative acts.

vi. Thirdly, the distinction between delegated and implementing acts is problematic. The rationale was to distinguish between secondary measures that were 'legislative' in nature, delegated acts, and those that could be regarded as more purely 'executive', implementing acts. The difficulties of realizing this divide were however never fully thought through. The distinction turns on a criterion that is questionable in terms of principle and very difficult to apply, 'the language problem', and this difficulty is exacerbated by the 'time problem'. The consequence is that different control mechanisms will be applied to secondary measures, where the distinction between the measures is a fine one, judged by the criterion demanded by the Treaty provisions. This is not satisfactory, nor is the CJEU's decision to engage in only minimal review.

vii. Fourthly, the hierarchy of norms is incomplete, in the sense that there are certain legal acts that do not readily fall within any of these categories.

5 FURTHER READING

Bast, J, 'New Categories of Acts after the Lisbon Reform: Dynamics of Parliamentarization in EU Law' (2012) 49 CMLRev 885

Christiansen, T, and Dobbels, M, 'Non-Legislative Rule Making after the Lisbon Treaty: Implementing the New System of Comitology and Delegated Acts' (2013) 19 ELJ 42

Craig, P, *The Lisbon Treaty: Law, Politics, and Treaty Reform* (Oxford University Press, 2010) ch 7

——— 'Delegated Acts, Implementing Acts and the New Comitology Regulation' (2011) 36 ELRev 671

——— 'Comitology, Rulemaking and the Lisbon Settlement: Tensions and Strains' in C-F Bergström and D Ritleng (eds), *Rulemaking by the Commission: The New System* (Oxford University Press, 2015)

De Witte, B, 'Legal Instruments and Law-Making in the Lisbon Treaty' in S Griller and J Ziller (eds), *The Lisbon Treaty: EU Constitutionalism without a Constitutional Treaty* (Springer, 2008) 79

Driessen, B, 'Delegated Legislation after the Treaty of Lisbon: An Analysis of Article 290 TFEU' (2010) 35 ELRev 837

Hofmann, H, 'Legislation, Delegation and Implementation under the Treaty of Lisbon: Typology Meets Reality' (2009) 15 ELJ 482

Lenaerts, K, and Desomer, M, 'Towards a Hierarchy of Legal Acts in the European Union? Simplification of Legal Instruments and Procedures' (2005) 11 ELJ 744

MENDES, J, 'Delegated and Implementing Rule Making: Proceduralisation and Constitutional Design' (2013) 19 ELJ 22

STANCANELLI, P, 'Le système décisionnel de l'Union' in G Amato, H Bribosia, and B de Witte (eds), *Genesis and Destiny of the European Constitution* (Bruylant, 2007) 485

VON BOGDANDY, A, BAST, J, AND ARNDT, F, 'Legal Instruments in European Union Law and their Reform: A Systematic Approach on an Empirical Basis' (2004) 23 YBEL 91

5

LEGISLATION AND DECISION-MAKING

1 CENTRAL ISSUES

i.   The previous chapters focused on the scope of EU competence, and the forms of EU action, including the hierarchy of norms. The present chapter will consider the process by which the EU enacts legislation and makes decisions.

ii. The chapter begins by considering the making of legislative acts. This includes the Treaty rules and practice concerning the initiation of the legislative process, and the way in which the ordinary legislative procedure, in which the Council and EP act as co-legislators, has come to occupy centre stage. The rationale for and use of the special legislative procedure are then explained.

iii. The focus then shifts to the making of delegated acts. There are perennial problems of reconciling the need for the expeditious passage of detailed regulatory norms with some measure of legislative oversight. The Lisbon Treaty made significant changes in this respect, which are explained and evaluated.

iv. The discussion concerning delegated acts is followed by analysis of the way in which implementing acts are made. The problem of maintaining the division between delegated acts and implementing acts is highlighted, and the difficulties with the making of such acts are explicated.

v.   It is equally important to understand the way in which legislation and policy are made in practice. The planning of the overall legislative agenda, and the passage of particular regulations or directives, involves interaction between EU institutions, interest groups, national parliaments, and national bureaucracies.

vi. There is a rich debate about democracy and legitimacy within the EU. An understanding of the issues involved in this discourse is a condition precedent for having something meaningful to say about it.

2 LEGISLATIVE INITIATIVE: PRINCIPLE AND PRACTICE

The basic principle under the Lisbon Treaty is that the Commission has the right of legislative initiative, thereby formalizing the pre-existing legal position. This had hitherto been the case because Treaty Articles generally stipulated that Community legislation could only be made at the initiative of the Commission. The Commission retained its 'gold standard', the right of legislative initiative, which was formalized in the Lisbon Treaty: Union legislative acts may only be adopted on the basis of a Commission proposal, except where the Treaties provide otherwise.[1]

The reality prior to the Lisbon Treaty was nonetheless that many legislative initiatives originated in the Council or the European Council. The legislative process for such measures was formally initiated by the Commission, but the impetus for their introduction often lay with the Council. The Council thus made liberal use of the power to request the Commission to undertake studies the Council considered 'desirable for the attainment of the common objectives, and to submit to it any appropriate proposals'.[2]

The position of the European Parliament in relation to legislative initiation has in formal terms remained the same under the Lisbon Treaty. It can under Article 225 TFEU request the Commission to submit any appropriate proposal on matters on which it considers that a Union act is required for the purpose of implementing the Treaties. If the Commission does not submit a proposal, it must inform the European Parliament of the reasons.[3] The Commission hitherto has not accepted that it must automatically pursue a matter referred to it in this manner, but the Framework Agreement on relations between the Parliament and Commission signed in 2000 included a provision under which the Commission committed itself to undertake 'a prompt and sufficiently detailed response' to such requests.[4]

The EP's Rules of Procedure specify how it uses Article 225. The normal route for a request to the Commission is that there is an own-initiative report of the responsible EP committee,[5] which forms the basis for a resolution of the EP requesting the Commission to submit a proposal. It may indicate a deadline for submission of the proposal. The alternative route is that an individual MEP can be the catalyst for use of Article 225. The proposal is submitted to the EP President, who then refers it to the appropriate EP committee. If the EP committee is supportive, its report then forms the basis for the resolution of the EP requesting that the Commission submit the proposal. The EP's resolution must indicate the appropriate legal basis and be accompanied by detailed recommendations as to the content of the required proposals, which must respect fundamental rights and subsidiarity.

The EP's influence on Commission legislative initiatives may become more significant in the light of the changes discussed in an earlier chapter,[6] whereby candidates for Commission President campaign directly as the chosen candidate for a particular EP party. The candidate for Commission President will therefore have to secure support from the majority within the European Parliament. This may well entail discussion not only of the candidate's overall vision for the EU, but more detailed specification of the legislative programme for the forthcoming years.

An innovation introduced by the Lisbon Treaty was the citizens' initiative. Article 11(4) TEU provides that no fewer than one million citizens who are nationals of a significant number of Member States may take the initiative of inviting the European Commission, within the framework of its powers, to submit any appropriate proposal on matters where citizens consider that a legal act of the Union is required for the purpose of implementing the Treaties. The procedures and conditions required for such a citizens' initiative are to be determined in accordance with Article 24 TFEU.[7]

---

[1] Art 17(2) TEU. There are limited instances where a legislative act can be initiated at the request of a group of Member States, or pursuant to a recommendation from the European Central Bank, or at the request of the CJEU: Art 289(4) TFEU.

[2] Art 241 TFEU.

[3] Art 225 TFEU.

[4] Framework Agreement on relations between the European Parliament and the Commission, C5–349/2000 [2001] OJ C121/122, [4]. The Agreement was revised in 2005 [2006] OJ C117/123.

[5] Rules of Procedure of the European Parliament (8th Parliamentary Term, Jan 2015) Rules 46, 52.

[6] Ch 2.

[7] Regulation (EU) No 211/2011 of the European Parliament and of the Council of 16 February 2011 on the citizens' initiative [2011] OJ L65/1. See Ch 23 for further discussion.

3 LEGISLATIVE ACTS: THE ORDINARY
LEGISLATIVE PROCEDURE

(A) PRE-LISBON

Prior to the Lisbon Treaty there were numerous legislative procedures, the principal difference being the degree of power afforded to the European Parliament. The European Parliament was given the smallest role in the legislative process in the Rome Treaty: subject to limited exceptions, it had only a right to be consulted, and this was so only where a particular Treaty Article so provided.

Subsequent Treaty amendments increased the EP's role in the legislative process. The cooperation procedure introduced by the Single European Act (SEA) 1986 was particularly important.[8] It began the transformation of the legislative process, giving the EP significant input into the legislative process for the first time.[9] The previous reality encapsulated in the maxim that the 'Commission proposes, the Council disposes' changed. There were now three players in the game, which had wide-ranging ramifications. The Commission recognized the need for increased inter-institutional cooperation. It had to draft proposals with an eye to what would 'play' with the EP as well as the Council.[10] Coreper, the gatekeeper for the Council, had to consider the views of the EP, as well as the Council and Commission.[11] The EP's powers in the legislative process were 'transformed from the weak and essentially unconstructive power of delay to a stronger and potentially constructive role in the drafting of legislation'.[12]

The most significant increase in the power of the EP was through the co-decision procedure introduced by the Maastricht Treaty, which prevented a measure being adopted without the approval of the Council and the EP.[13] The subject matter areas to which the co-decision procedure applies were extended by later Treaty reforms.

(B) ORDINARY LEGISLATIVE PROCEDURE

This process was continued in the Lisbon Treaty. The EU was mindful of the complexity of the legislative procedures and the damaging effect on its legitimacy.[14] The Lisbon Treaty simplified matters in this respect. The European Parliament and the Council are said to exercise legislative and budgetary functions jointly.[15] This is embodied in Article 14(1) TEU, which provides that the European Parliament shall, jointly with the Council, exercise legislative and budgetary functions. This provision is replicated in relation to the Council in Article 16(1) TEU.

The cooperation procedure has been repealed. The co-decision procedure is now deemed to be the ordinary legislative procedure,[16] and this procedure consists in the joint adoption by the

---

[8] Art 252 EC.

[9] D Earnshaw and D Judge, 'The European Parliament and the Sweeteners Directive: From Footnote to Inter-Institutional Conflict' (1993) 31 JCMS 1; R Corbett, 'Testing the New Procedures: The European Parliament's First Experience with its New "Single Act" Powers' (1989) 27 JCMS 4.

[10] M Westlake, *The Commission and the Parliament: Partners and Rivals in the European Policy-Making Process* (Butterworths, 1994) 37–39.

[11] J Lewis, 'National Interests, Coreper' in J Peterson and M Shackleton (eds), *The Institutions of the European Union* (Oxford University Press, 2nd edn, 2006) ch 14.

[12] Westlake (n 10) 39.

[13] Art 251 EC; A Dashwood, 'Community Legislative Procedures in the Era of the Treaty on European Union' (1994) 19 ELRev 343.

[14] P Craig, 'Democracy and Rulemaking within the EC: An Empirical and Normative Assessment' (1997) 3 ELJ 105.

[15] Arts 14(1) and 16(1) TEU.

[16] Arts 289 and 294 TFEU.

European Parliament and the Council of a regulation, directive, or decision on a proposal from the Commission.[17] It is always necessary to look at a particular Treaty Article, which will specify the legislative procedure applicable in that area. The reach of the ordinary legislative procedure has been extended to cover more areas than hitherto, including, for example, agriculture,[18] services,[19] asylum and immigration,[20] the structural and cohesion funds,[21] and the creation of specialized courts.[22] The European Parliament and the Council must meet in public when considering and voting on a draft legislative act.[23] The ordinary legislative procedure is set out in Article 294 TFEU and, as the name suggests, it is the normal method for making EU legislation.

1. Where reference is made in the Treaties to the ordinary legislative procedure for the adoption of an act, the following procedure shall apply.

2. The Commission shall submit a proposal to the European Parliament and the Council.

FIRST READING

3. The European Parliament shall adopt its position at first reading and communicate it to the Council.

4. If the Council approves the European Parliament's position, the act concerned shall be adopted in the wording which corresponds to the position of the European Parliament.

5. If the Council does not approve the European Parliament's position, it shall adopt its position at first reading and communicate it to the European Parliament.

6. The Council shall inform the European Parliament fully of the reasons which led it to adopt its position at first reading. The Commission shall inform the European Parliament fully of its position.

SECOND READING

7. If, within three months of such communication, the European Parliament:

    (a) approves the Council's position at first reading or has not taken a decision, the act concerned shall be deemed to have been adopted in the wording which corresponds to the position of the Council;

    (b) rejects, by a majority of its component members, the Council's position at first reading, the proposed act shall be deemed not to have been adopted;

    (c) proposes, by a majority of its component members, amendments to the Council's position at first reading, the text thus amended shall be forwarded to the Council and to the Commission, which shall deliver an opinion on those amendments.

8. If, within three months of receiving the European Parliament's amendments, the Council, acting by a qualified majority:

    (a) approves all those amendments, the act in question shall be deemed to have been adopted;

    (b) does not approve all the amendments, the President of the Council, in agreement with the President of the European Parliament, shall within six weeks convene a meeting of the Conciliation Committee.

[17] Art 289(1) TFEU.
[18] Art 43(2) TFEU.
[19] Art 56 TFEU.
[20] Arts 77–80 TFEU.
[21] Art 177 TFEU.
[22] Art 257 TFEU.
[23] Art 15(2) TFEU.

9. The Council shall act unanimously on the amendments on which the Commission has delivered a negative opinion.

CONCILIATION

10. The Conciliation Committee, which shall be composed of the members of the Council or their representatives and an equal number of members representing the European Parliament, shall have the task of reaching agreement on a joint text, by a qualified majority of the members of the Council or their representatives and by a majority of the members representing the European Parliament within six weeks of its being convened, on the basis of the positions of the European Parliament and the Council at second reading.

11. The Commission shall take part in the Conciliation Committee's proceedings and shall take all necessary initiatives with a view to reconciling the positions of the European Parliament and the Council.

12. If, within six weeks of its being convened, the Conciliation Committee does not approve the joint text, the proposed act shall be deemed not to have been adopted.

THIRD READING

13. If, within that period, the Conciliation Committee approves a joint text, the European Parliament, acting by a majority of the votes cast, and the Council, acting by a qualified majority, shall each have a period of six weeks from that approval in which to adopt the act in question in accordance with the joint text. If they fail to do so, the proposed act shall be deemed not to have been adopted.

14. The periods of three months and six weeks referred to in this Article shall be extended by a maximum of one month and two weeks respectively at the initiative of the European Parliament or the Council.

SPECIAL PROVISIONS

15. Where, in the cases provided for in the Treaties, a legislative act is submitted to the ordinary legislative procedure on the initiative of a group of Member States, on a recommendation by the European Central Bank, or at the request of the Court of Justice, paragraph 2, the second sentence of paragraph 6, and paragraph 9 shall not apply.

In such cases, the European Parliament and the Council shall communicate the proposed act to the Commission with their positions at first and second readings. The European Parliament or the Council may request the opinion of the Commission throughout the procedure, which the Commission may also deliver on its own initiative. It may also, if it deems it necessary, take part in the Conciliation Committee in accordance with paragraph 11.

(c) ORDINARY LEGISLATIVE PROCEDURE: STAGES IN THE PROCESS

(i) *First Reading*

It is important to understand the stages in Article 294 TFEU. It is the Commission that submits its proposal to the EP and the Council.[24] There is no time limit for the first reading, either for the EP or

---

[24] Art 294(2) TFEU. Where, exceptionally, this is not so, the ordinary legislative procedure is modified: Art 294(15) TFEU.

the Council. The references to three-month and six-week time limits in other parts of the process can be extended by one month and two weeks respectively at the initiative of the EP or Council.[25]

The EP has two readings, the first of which occurs when the EP adopts its position and communicates this to the Council.[26] The legislative proposal will initially be considered by the relevant EP committee. Before this committee proceeds to the final vote on a proposal for a legislative act, it asks the Commission to state its position on amendments to the proposal adopted by the committee. It also asks the Council to comment.[27] If the Commission is not in a position to make such a statement, or declares that it is not prepared to accept all the amendments adopted by the committee, then the committee may postpone the final vote.[28] The amendments proposed by the relevant EP committee are then considered and voted on by the EP in plenary session. It is the resolution that results from this vote that constitutes the EP's position that is then sent to the Council.[29] It is possible, although rare, for the EP to reject the Commission proposal at first reading stage.[30] Where the Commission proposal is approved, subject to amendments adopted in the EP plenary session, the vote on the draft legislative resolution is postponed until the Commission has stated its position on each of the EP's amendments.[31] If the Commission states that it does not intend to adopt all the EP's amendments, the EP may decide to postpone the vote and refer the matter back to the relevant committee.[32] Subject to this, the EP's position is then sent to the Council.

If the Council approves the EP's position the legislative act is adopted in the wording that corresponds to the position of the EP.[33] This is subject to the caveat that as long as the Council has not acted, the Commission can alter its proposal at any time prior to the adoption of a Union act.[34] This power is important, since it gives the Commission the legal foundation for continuing involvement in the enactment of legislative acts under the ordinary legislative procedure, even at the first reading stage. The power can be used by the Commission if it does not like alterations to the original proposal made by the EP, more especially if it feels that the Council might agree with such amendments. The EP may however request that the proposal should be referred back to it if the Commission substantially amends its proposal, except where this is done to accommodate the EP's position.[35]

The Council may not agree with the EP's position at first reading. The Council may not approve all the EP's first-reading amendments, or it may have other amendments of its own. If this happens the Council communicates a reasoned explanation of its position to the EP, and the Commission also informs the EP of its position.[36]

(ii) *Second Reading*

The ordinary legislative procedure then moves to the second reading. The Council's position is communicated to the relevant EP committee, which will attempt to broker compromise between the

---

[25] Art 294(14) TFEU.

[26] Art 294(3) TFEU.

[27] Rules of Procedure of the European Parliament (n 5) Rule 58(1). There is provision for a simplified procedure, whereby the Chair of the EP Committee proposes that the legislative act shall be adopted without amendment, or with amendments drafted by the Chair and the rapporteur of the Committee, Rule 50.

[28] Ibid Rule 58(2).

[29] Ibid Rule 59.

[30] Ibid Rule 60.

[31] Ibid Rule 61.

[32] Ibid Rule 61.

[33] Art 294(4) TFEU.

[34] Art 293(2) TFEU.

[35] Rules of Procedure of the European Parliament (n 5) Rule 63.

[36] Art 294(5)–(6) TFEU.

Council, Commission, and EP.[37] The EP has the following options, which can be used within three months. It can approve the position taken by the Council, in which case the act is adopted in the format that corresponds to the wording of the Council's position. This also occurs if the EP takes no action at second reading.[38] The EP may reject the Council's first reading position by a majority of its component members, in which case the act is deemed not to have been adopted.[39] The EP's third option is to propose by a majority of its members second-reading amendments to the Council's position.

The EP has imposed limits on the second-reading amendments that it will propose: they are only admissible if they seek to restore wholly or in part the EP's first-reading position, or to reach a compromise between the EP and Council, or to amend part of the Council's position that was not included in the initial proposal, or to take account of a new fact situation.[40] The amended text is forwarded to the Council and Commission, which deliver an opinion on the amendments.[41]

The ball is then back in the Council's court. It may within three months approve the EP's amendments, in which case the text is adopted in that format.[42] This is subject to the caveat that the Council must act unanimously in relation to amendments on which the Commission has expressed a negative opinion.[43] The Council may, alternatively, not approve all of the EP's second-reading amendments, in which case the Conciliation Committee comes into operation.[44]

(iii) *Conciliation*

The Conciliation Committee is composed of equal numbers from the EP and Council, and the Commission is fully involved. The object is to secure agreement on a joint text, but if this cannot be achieved within six weeks the act is deemed not to have been adopted.[45] If the Conciliation Committee is successful the agreed text must be approved within six weeks by the EP and the Council, failing which the act is deemed not to have been adopted.[46]

(D) ORDINARY LEGISLATIVE PROCEDURE: PRACTICAL OPERATION

The ordinary legislative procedure in Article 294 has been successful in practice, subject to the important caveat made below, in that it has accommodated the differing interests that have a stake in the legislative process, the EP, Council, and Commission.[47] The emphasis throughout the procedure is on compromise and dialogue, so as to facilitate the successful passage of the legislative

---

[37] Rules of Procedure of the European Parliament (n 5) Rule 66.

[38] Art 294(7)(a) TFEU.

[39] Art 294(7)(b) TFEU.

[40] Rules of Procedure of the European Parliament (n 5) Rule 69.

[41] Art 294(7)(c) TFEU.

[42] Art 294(8)(a) TFEU.

[43] Art 294(9) TFEU.

[44] Art 294(8)(b) TFEU.

[45] Art 294(10)–(12) TFEU.

[46] Art 294(13) TFEU.

[47] A Dashwood, 'Community Legislative Procedures in the Era of the TEU' (1994) 19 ELRev 343; D Earnshaw and D Judge, 'From Co-operation to Co-decision: The European Parliament's Path to Legislative Power' in J Richardson (ed), *European Union: Power and Policy-Making* (Routledge, 1996) ch 6; S Boyron, 'The Co-Decision Procedure: Rethinking the Constitutional Fundamentals' in P Craig and C Harlow (eds), *Lawmaking in the European Union* (Kluwer, 1998) ch 7; A Dashwood, 'European Community Legislative Procedures after Amsterdam' (1998) 1 CYELS 25; A Maurer, *Co-Governing after Maastricht: The European Parliament's Institutional Performance 1994–99*, EP Working Paper, POLI 104, 1999; http://ec.europa.eu/codecision/statistics/index_en.htm.

act. This is reflected in the EP's Rules of Procedure, and it is evident in the Joint Declaration[48] and Framework Agreement between the EP and Commission[49] appended to those Rules of Procedure. In the first decade of co-decision, the predecessor to the ordinary legislative procedure, 20 per cent of the Parliament's second-reading amendments to the Council's common position were accepted in their entirety during the conciliation procedure, 70 per cent were the subject of a compromise, and only 12 per cent were rejected.[50]

It is important to understand that not all the stages of Article 294 will be gone through for any particular legislative act. During the parliamentary session 1999–2004, 115 co-decision dossiers, 28 per cent, were concluded at first reading; 200 dossiers, 50 per cent, at second reading; and 84 dossiers, 22 per cent, through conciliation.[51]

It is equally important to understand that the practical operation of Article 294 has been modified in practice through the institutionalization of trilogues, which contain representatives from the Council, EP, and Commission, normally no more than ten from each institution, the aim being to facilitate compromise.[52] They originated as informal meetings that preceded formal meetings of the Conciliation Committee, and have been common since the mid-1990s. Trilogues now feature at all stages of the ordinary legislative procedure,[53] and are increasingly used to broker inter-institutional compromise at first reading and prior to second reading, thereby limiting the potential for meaningful dialogue by a broader range of members of the European Parliament and Council.[54]

The scale of this change is brought home from the Report of the Vice-Presidents responsible for Conciliation. The contrast with the figures from the EP session 1999–2004 is striking. Thus in the period 2004–2009 72 per cent of legislative acts were concluded at first reading, with another 10.8 per cent at early second reading, largely as a result of increased use of such informal negotiations.[55] The trend continued in the seventh parliamentary session 2009–2014, in which 85 per cent of dossiers were agreed at first reading, with another 8 per cent concluded at early second reading. There were 1,500 trilogues that related to approximately 350 ordinary legislative procedure files.[56] This raised concerns that 'deals' were being done in secret, with no readily available documents, and because 'the process removes meaningful debate, disagreements, options, votes from both the Committee meetings and the plenary session'.[57]

These concerns have been recognized and there have been amendments to the EP Rules of Procedure. A formal committee decision is now required before trilogue negotiations are opened,

---

[48] Joint Declaration of the European Parliament, the Council and the Commission of 13 June 2007 on practical arrangements for the co-decision procedure (Article 251 of the EC Treaty) [2007] OJ C145/5. The Joint Declaration can now be found as Rules of Procedure of the European Parliament (n 5) Annex XIX.

[49] Rules of Procedure of the European Parliament (n 5) Annex XIII.

[50] A Dashwood, 'The Constitution of the European Union after Nice: Law-Making Procedures' (2001) 26 ELRev 215, 219.

[51] European Parliament, Conciliations and Co-decision: A Guide to how Parliament Co-legislates, DV/547830EN. doc, 2004, 7.

[52] Code of conduct for negotiating in the context of the ordinary legislative procedure, Rules of Procedure of the European Parliament (n 5) Annex XX; Joint Declaration (n 48) [8], [12]–[15], [23]; M Shackleton and T Raunio, 'Codecision since Amsterdam: A Laboratory for Institutional Innovation and Change' (2003) 10 JEPP 171, 177–179.

[53] Joint Declaration (n 48) [8].

[54] D Curtin, 'The Council of Ministers: The Missing Link?' in L Verhey, P Kiiver, and S Loeffen (eds), *Political Accountability and European Integration* (Europa Law Publishing, 2009) ch 12.

[55] Activity Report 1 May–13 July 2009 of the Delegations to the Conciliation Committee, CM\787539EN.doc; http://ec.europa.eu/codecision/statistics/index_en.htm.

[56] Activity Report on Codecision and Conciliation 14 July 2009–30 June 2014 (7th Parliamentary Term), http://www.europarl.europa.eu/code/information/activity_reports/activity_report_2009_2014_en.pdf.

[57] T Bunyan, 'Abolish 1st and 2nd Reading Secret Deals—Bring Back Democracy "Warts and All"', 6, available at www.statewatch.org/analyses/no-84-ep-first-reading-deals.pdf.

normally pursuant to the report adopted in committee, but exceptionally prior to this.[58] The changes to enhance accountability are as follows: the decision to enter into trilogue negotiations requires an absolute majority of committee members, and must define the mandate and composition of the negotiating team; documentation indicating the respective positions of the institutions involved and possible compromise solutions must be circulated to the negotiating team in advance; the negotiating team must report back to the committee after each trilogue; the committee must be informed of the final compromise; and the agreed text must be formally voted on in committee and, if approved, tabled for consideration in plenary. These changes are to be welcomed, although they do not fully meet the concerns that *de facto* the real legislative decisions/compromises are being made by a relatively small group.

(E) ORDINARY LEGISLATIVE PROCEDURE: POWER DYNAMICS

There has been disagreement about the particular 'power dynamics' that operate within Article 294 and disagreement also about the relative power of the EP under co-decision and other legislative procedures.[59]

It is nonetheless clear that the EP has used its veto power under Article 294 sparingly. This does not mean that such power is ineffective. Decision-making under the shadow of the veto was common within the Council when the Luxembourg Accords imposed a *de facto* unanimity requirement, notwithstanding that actual use of the veto was relatively rare. So too here, the rare use of the veto by the EP does not alter the fact that the EP must accept the measure if it is to become law. The EP's power is further enhanced in relation to the Council because Article 294 read with Article 293(1) TFEU requires unanimity in the Council if it seeks to amend a Commission proposal,[60] while requiring only a qualified majority where the Council accepts amendments from the EP.

It is more difficult to generalize about the nature of the amendments that the EP manages to secure. There is research indicating that the EP amendments modify the Commission proposal, but do not significantly alter it.[61] This is to some extent unsurprising, since most important draft legislative proposals will have been discussed with the EP and Council/Coreper before the formal Article 294 procedure is initiated, thereby accommodating diverse opinion at that early stage. Where this dialogic process still leaves major differences of view, the EP and indeed Council may well propose more far-reaching amendments to the formal legislation, as exemplified by the extensive EP amendments to the Services Directive, forcing the Commission to modify the measure significantly.[62]

It is also important not to overlook the power of the Commission within the Article 294 procedure. It has the power to withdraw a proposed measure before it is adopted and submit a modified version,

---

[58] Rules of Procedure of the European Parliament (n 5) Rules 73–74.

[59] G Tsebelis and G Garrett, 'Legislative Politics and the European Union' (2000) 1 EUP 9; C Crombez, 'Co-decision: Towards a Bicameral European Union' (2000) 1 EUP 363; B Steunenberg, 'Seeing What You Want to See: The Limits of Current Modelling on the European Union' (2000) 1 EUP 368; R Corbett, 'Academic Modelling of the Co-decision Procedure: A Practitioner's Puzzled Reaction' (2000) 1 EUP 373; G Garrett and G Tsebelis, 'Understanding Better the EU Legislative Process' (2001) 2 EUP 353; R Corbett, 'A Response to a Reply to a Reaction (I Hope Someone is Still Interested)' (2001) 2 EUP 361.

[60] Subject to exceptions in Art 294(10), (13) TFEU.

[61] A Kreppel, 'Moving beyond Procedure: An Empirical Analysis of European Parliament Legislative Influence' (2002) 35 Comparative Political Studies 784.

[62] Proposal for a Directive of the European Parliament and of the Council, on services in the internal market, COM(2004) 2 final/3; EP Committee on the Internal Market and Consumer Protection, Report on the Proposal for a Directive of the European Parliament and of the Council, on services in the internal market, A6–0409/2005, Rapporteur Evelyne Gebhardt; Amended Proposal for a Directive of the European Parliament and of the Council, on services in the internal market, COM(2006) 160 final.

or refuse to proceed again if it feels that any such measure will be amended in ways to which it is fundamentally averse. These are admittedly rather blunt tools, but useful nonetheless. In any event the Commission has more 'fine-tuned' modes of influence. Thus it will routinely respond in detail to, for example, proposed EP amendments, indicating which it feels able to accept and which not. This will often form the foundation for dialogue between Commission and EP as to what will be acceptable to both players. The Commission moreover has the 'leverage' that EP second-reading amendments in relation to which the Commission has delivered a negative opinion can be accepted by the Council only if there is unanimity.[63]

(F) ORDINARY LEGISLATIVE PROCEDURE: NORMATIVE FOUNDATIONS

Article 294 has a secure normative foundation. The EP has long pressed for a co-equal role in the legislative process with the Council. The modifications introduced by the Maastricht and Amsterdam Treaties went a considerable way to achieving this through the co-decision procedure. The Lisbon Treaty continued this process. The change in nomenclature from co-decision to the ordinary legislative procedure emphasized that legislative authority was shared between the EP and Council. The extension of the ordinary legislative procedure to new areas was a natural development, building on earlier Treaty reform. It enhanced the legitimacy of EU legislation and its democratic credentials by enabling the EP to have input into the making of legislation in these areas.

4 LEGISLATIVE ACTS: SPECIAL LEGISLATIVE PROCEDURE

Article 289(2) TFEU provides for what is termed a special legislative procedure. This applies in the specific cases provided for by the Treaties. The special legislative procedure takes the form of a regulation, directive, or decision adopted by the EP with the participation of the Council, or by the Council with the participation of the EP. Legal acts adopted by the special legislative procedure constitute legislative acts.[64] It should however be noted that the general 'passerelle' clause of the Lisbon Treaty provides that where the TFEU requires the special legislative procedure, the European Council may adopt a unanimous decision with the consent of the EP allowing for the adoption of such acts in accordance with the ordinary legislative procedure, which takes effect if there is no opposition from a national parliament.[65]

It is only by looking at particular Treaty provisions that one can understand what the special legislative procedure means. In most instances it signifies that the legal act is adopted by the Council unanimously, combined with a requirement of consent of, or more commonly consultation with, the EP.[66] In a few instances, notably those concerned with the organization of the EP, the special legislative procedure signifies that the EP adopts the legal act after approval from the Council.[67]

The pre-Lisbon case law will remain relevant in those areas where the special legislative procedure provides for a legislative act to be adopted by the Council after consultation with the EP, insofar as that jurisprudence specifies what consultation demands. Thus it is clear that the Council must wait

---

[63] Art 294(9) TFEU.
[64] Art 289(3) TFEU.
[65] Art 48(7) TEU.
[66] Art 48 TEU; Arts 19, 21, 22, 23, 25, 64, 77(3), 81(3), 83(2), 86(1), 87(3), 89, 113, 115, 118, 126, 127(6), 153(2), 182(4), 192, 194(3), 203, 218(6), 223(1), 262, 308, 311, 312(2), 314, 333(2), 349, 352 TFEU.
[67] Arts 223(2), 226, 228(4) TFEU.

for the Parliament's opinion. If it does not the measure may be annulled.[68] The EP may have to be re-consulted where there are important changes to the measure, not prompted by the EP itself, after the initial consultation and prior to its adoption by the Council.[69] Nonetheless, a bare requirement to consult the European Parliament is all that is required. The Council is not bound to adopt the Parliament's opinion. Particular Treaty Articles can also stipulate that the Committee of the Regions or the Economic and Social Committee should be consulted.

The special legislative procedure may also stipulate that a measure should be adopted by the Council acting unanimously with the consent of the EP, as opposed to consultation. There are several Treaty Articles framed in this manner, and not surprisingly they deal with sensitive issues over which the EU has competence, such as additions to citizens' rights, establishment of a European Public Prosecutor, creation of a uniform method for electing MEPs, and aspects of the EU's finances.[70] It should also be noted for the sake of clarity that the EP's consent may be required for the adoption of other measures, the distinguishing feature being that such measures are not said to be enacted by a special legislative procedure and do not therefore constitute legislative acts for the purposes of Article 289 TFEU.[71]

The EP's Rules of Procedure indicate the process used in deciding whether to consent to a measure.[72] The EP takes its decision on the basis of a recommendation from the committee responsible for approving or rejecting the measure. The general principle is that the EP's decision is by a single vote, and no amendments are tabled. The majority required for the adoption of the consent is that specified in the relevant Article of the TEU or TFEU. Special rules apply in the case of consent required for international agreements, accession treaties, determination of a serious and persistent breach of common principles by a Member State, and certain other cases.[73]

5 LEGISLATIVE ACTS: COUNCIL VOTING REQUIREMENTS

(A) PRE-LISBON

Prior to the Lisbon Treaty, the EC Treaty provided that the Council should vote by unanimity, simple majority, or qualified majority. The areas to which qualified-majority voting applied were increased over time.

These formal legal powers were for some time overshadowed by the Luxembourg Compromise. This was the result of a political crisis in the Community in the mid-1960s, and coincided with the shift to qualified-majority voting in the Council. In essence the Compromise provided that when majority voting applied to a topic which concerned the important interests of states, they should attempt to

---

[68] Case 138/79 *Roquette Frères v Council* [1980] ECR 3333; Case C–65/93 *European Parliament v Council (Re Generalized Tariff Preferences)* [1995] ECR I–643; Case C–156/93 *European Parliament v Commission (Re Genetically Modified Micro-organisms in Organic Products)* [1995] ECR I–2019; Case C–658/11 *European Parliament v Council* EU:C:2014:2025.

[69] Case C–388/92 *European Parliament v Council* [1994] ECR I–2067; Case C–417/93 *European Parliament v Council (Re Continuation of the TACIS Programme)* [1995] ECR I–1185; Case C–21/94 *European Parliament v Council (Re Road Taxes)* [1995] ECR I–1827. Where the changes are either technical or in accordance with the Parliament's wishes re-consultation may not be necessary: Case 41/69 *ACF Chemiefarma v Commission* [1970] ECR 661; Case 817/79 *Buyl v Commission* [1982] ECR 245; Case C–331/88 *R v Minister of Agriculture, Fisheries and Food and Secretary of State for Health, ex p FEDESA* [1990] ECR I–4023.

[70] See, eg, Arts 19(1), 25(2), 86(1), 223(1), 311, 352 TFEU.

[71] See, eg, Arts 7, 14(2), 48(3), 48(7), 49, 50(2), TEU; Arts 82(2)(d), 83(1) para 3, 86(4), 218(6)(a)(i)–(iv), 312(2), 329(1), 352 TFEU.

[72] Rules of Procedure of the European Parliament (n 5) Rule 99.

[73] Ibid Rules 108, 81, 83.

reach a solution acceptable to all, and France added the rider that discussion should continue until unanimity was attained. The Compromise fostered a climate in which majority voting prejudicial to the interests of a particular state was avoided. The 'threat' that a Member State would exercise a *de facto* veto power did not enhance the speed of Community decision-making.

The Luxembourg Compromise was not formally abolished, because it never formally existed in legal terms. However, the climate in the Community post-1986 rendered it less likely that states would attempt to use such power.[74] Subsequent Treaty amendments generally required greater use of qualified-majority voting, and reflected a shift in Member State perceptions about the nature of the Community, which made it less likely that exclusively national interests would be regarded as a valid rationale for a veto. Moreover, Member States acknowledged that qualified-majority voting had to be extended in an expanded Union. Unanimity would often be synonymous with inaction, since one state out of twenty-eight would often object. The very fact that use of the veto is now less readily accepted than hitherto means that Member States will exert more pressure at other points of the decision-making system, so as to ensure that the measure is acceptable to them. The Council will however search for consensus even where the formal voting rules provide for a qualified majority,[75] and approximately 80 per cent of decisions are taken consensually.

(B) POST-LISBON

The Lisbon Treaty provides for different rules on voting by the Council. The Treaty can prescribe unanimity in the Council, although abstentions do not prevent the adoption of such acts.[76] It may specify that the Council should vote by simple majority, which signifies a majority of its component members.[77] The general rule under the Lisbon Treaty is, however, that Council voting is by qualified majority, unless the Treaty provides otherwise, and approximately 80 per cent of EU legislation is enacted in this way.[78]

The Lisbon Treaty embodies a general 'passerelle' clause enabling modification to the voting rules in the Council. Article 48(7) TEU states that where the TFEU or Title V of the TEU provides for the Council to act by unanimity in a given area or case, the European Council may adopt a decision authorizing the Council to act by a qualified majority in that area or in that case, subject to the caveat that this cannot apply to decisions with military implications or those in the area of defence. The European Council makes such decisions by unanimity after obtaining the consent of the European Parliament, which shall be given by a majority of its component members. Any such initiative taken by the European Council must be notified to the national parliaments. If a national parliament makes known its opposition within six months of the date of such notification, the decision shall not be adopted. In the absence of opposition, the European Council may adopt the decision.

The Lisbon Treaty increased the areas to which qualified-majority voting applies, although unanimity is still required in over seventy areas. There was considerable disagreement about the requirements for a qualified majority in the Council and the shift from unanimity to qualified majority. The requirements for a qualified majority have always been a battleground between small, medium-sized, and large Member States.

---

[74] M Westlake, *The Council of the European Union* (Cartermill, 1995) 91–111.

[75] W Nicoll, 'Representing the States' in A Duff, J Pinder, and R Pryce (eds), *Maastricht and Beyond: Building the European Union* (Routledge, 1994) 193–194.

[76] Art 238(4) TFEU.

[77] Art 238(1) TFEU.

[78] Art 16(3) TEU.

The provisions in the Lisbon Treaty on the definition of a qualified majority are complex. The basic rule that will operate from 1 November 2014 is set out in Article 16(4) TEU. A qualified majority is defined as at least 55 per cent of the members of the Council, comprising at least fifteen of them and representing Member States comprising at least 65 per cent of the population of the Union. A blocking minority must include at least four Council members, failing which the qualified majority shall be deemed attained. There are therefore three criteria to be taken into account for a qualified majority: a certain percentage of Member States in the Council; a certain number of Member States; and a certain percentage of the EU's population.

The default rule defining a qualified majority is, however, subject to exceptions. Thus, where the Council does not act on a proposal from the Commission or the High Representative for Foreign Affairs the qualified majority must be 72 per cent of the members of the Council, comprising 65 per cent of the EU's population.[79] It is therefore more difficult for the Council to adopt a measure in the relatively rare instances where it does not act on a proposal from the Commission or from the High Representative. There are also separate rules specifying the requirements for a qualified majority where not all Member States vote in the Council.[80]

The rules that operate until 31 October 2014, and the transitional rules applicable between 1 November 2014 and 31 March 2017, are set out in a Protocol attached to the Lisbon Treaty.[81] Between 1 November 2014 and 31 March 2017, when an act is to be adopted by qualified majority a member of the Council can request that it be adopted in accordance with the qualified majority as defined under the rules in the Nice Treaty.[82]

It has been estimated that the voting rules in the Lisbon Treaty will increase the probability of securing the passage of legislation through the Council as compared with those under the Nice Treaty.[83] The demographic component of the new rules also increases the relative power of the larger Member States in the Council.[84] The significance of this depends however on voting behaviour post-Lisbon. Thus academic study has shown that voting in the Council has been relatively rare, even in areas where qualified-majority voting operates, and that decision-making by consensus has been the norm. The authors accept that voting rules remain significant, in part because they provide the 'shadow' against which consensus operates in the Council and preliminary bodies such as Coreper. This does not alter the fact that explicit voting has been rare and that when it occurs the dissentient is often a single state.[85]

The shift towards qualified-majority voting in more areas raised, not surprisingly, critiques of loss of sovereignty through surrender of the national veto that accompanies unanimity. The most obvious response is that unanimity renders decision-making excessively difficult in a Union of twenty-eight Member States.

There is in addition a less obvious, but equally important response. The assumption that unanimity is the best protection of national sovereignty is based implicitly on the argument that sovereignty is best safeguarded by maximizing veto points and inaction. This may be true, but it may not. It is

---

[79] Art 238(2) TFEU.

[80] Art 238(3) TFEU.

[81] Protocol (No 36) On Transitional Provisions, Title II. See also Declaration 7, which contains a Draft Council Decision concerning transitional arrangements.

[82] Protocol (No 36), Art 3.

[83] R Baldwin and M Widgrén, 'Council Voting in the Constitutional Treaty. Devil in the Details', CEPS Policy Brief (No 53, July 2004) 6–7.

[84] Ibid; Y Devuyst, 'The European Union's Institutional Balance after the Treaty of Lisbon: "Community Method" and "Democratic Deficit" Reassessed' (2008) 39 Georgetown Jnl Int Law 247, 302–303.

[85] F Hayes-Renshaw, W van Aken, and H Wallace, 'When and Why the EU Council of Ministers Votes Explicitly' (2006) 44 JCMS 161.

axiomatic that if a veto power exists it resides with every Member State. Whether unanimity is the best protector of national sovereignty depends therefore on whether a state believes that maximizing the possibility of inaction through multiple veto points is better for the national interest than a qualified-majority voting rule which increases the possibility of action, with some attendant risk that the particular state will be forced to accept a measure that it dislikes. This in turn depends on whether a state believes that if there is a unanimity rule it is more likely to be 'vetoed against', thereby preventing action which it believes to be desirable, than it is to be an 'exerciser of the veto' itself.

A state may decide on this calculus that the national interest is better protected via qualified majority than unanimity. This was part of the rationale for the UK Conservative Party's acceptance of the important shift from unanimity to qualified majority in the EU's history, through acceptance in the SEA of Article 95 EC, which became the principal vehicle for single market legislation. The unanimity rule in Article 94 impeded market liberalization desired by the Conservative Party, hence the willingness to sacrifice the veto for the enhanced possibility of Community action.

6 DELEGATED ACTS: ENACTMENT AND CONTROL

(A) PRE-LISBON: THE RATIONALE FOR COMITOLOGY

The schema of legal acts in the Lisbon Treaty was considered in the previous chapter.[86] It will be recalled that the Lisbon Treaty distinguishes between legislative acts, delegated acts, and implementing acts. The impact of the Lisbon Treaty on the making of delegated acts can only be appreciated by understanding the previous law.

Delegation of power to make regulations has been present since the inception of the EEC. There are many areas of policy, such as agriculture, which require numerous regulations, often passed quickly to cope with changing market circumstances. If the standard methods of enacting legislation were to be applied the process would grind to a halt, since the relevant acts could not be enacted with sufficient speed. This explains why the Council, through a 'parent regulation', authorized the Commission to enact more specific regulations in a particular area.

The Council was not, however, willing to give the Commission a blank cheque to regulate in this manner. It made the exercise of delegated power subject to institutional constraints, in the form of committees through which Member State interests could be represented. This was so because there might be disagreements between the states as to the content of the detailed regulations that should be made; and because the Council was wary of the federalizing tendencies of the Commission, with the consequence that it was unwilling to delegate power without checks to ensure the representation of Member State interests.

The Council's 'solution' was to condition the exercise of delegated power on the approval of a committee composed of Member State representatives. This system came to be known as Comitology.[87] There was no express warrant for such committees in the original EEC Treaty, and their legality was challenged before the Court. It upheld the validity of the committee system, reasoning that if the Treaty gave power to the Council to delegate to the Commission, then it could do so subject to conditions.[88]

---

[86] Ch 4.

[87] C Joerges and E Vos (eds), *EU Committees: Social Regulation, Law and Politics* (Hart, 1999); M Andenas and A Türk (eds), *Delegated Legislation and the Role of Committees in the EC* (Kluwer, 2000); C-F Bergström, *Comitology: Delegation of Powers in the European Union and the Committee System* (Oxford University Press, 2005); P Craig, *EU Administrative Law* (Oxford University Press, 2nd edn, 2012) ch 5.

[88] Case 25/70 *Koster* [1970] ECR 1161.

The SEA modified Article 202 EC in order to provide a secure foundation for this regime. This was followed shortly thereafter by the Comitology Decision, which rationalized the committee structure.[89] This Decision was revised in 1999, and gave an increased role to the EP in the making of these Comitology regulations, although it did not place the EP on an equal footing with the Council.[90] The 1999 Comitology Decision was itself revised in 2006, with enhanced powers being given to the EP.[91] The Comitology Decision embodied a regime of committee oversight, the nature of which depended on the type of committee procedure that was chosen for a particular area. The committees were composed of Member State representatives and chaired by the Commission.

Under the *management committee procedure*[92] the Commission submitted a proposal, and the committee voted in the same manner as the Council itself, but the Commission had no vote. The Commission adopted measures that applied immediately. However, if the measure *was not in accordance* with the opinion of the committee, the Commission had to communicate this to the Council. The Council could then take a different decision within three months. Thus the committee had to vote against the measure for it to be sent back to the Council.

The *regulatory committee procedure*[93] gave Member State representatives more power, because in effect the measure had to be referred back to the Council unless the committee voted in favour of it. There was also a *regulatory procedure with scrutiny*[94] introduced in 2006. The novelty of this procedure was that it accorded a greater role to the EP in cases where the primary legislation was made under the co-decision procedure and provided for the adoption of measures of general scope designed to amend or supplement non-essential elements of that instrument.

There was also an *advisory committee procedure*,[95] which, as the name would suggest, meant that the national representatives gave advice on the Commission proposal. The Commission was not bound by this opinion, although it took the 'utmost account' of it.

(B) POST-LISBON DELEGATED ACTS: DEMISE OF COMITOLOGY

The Lisbon Treaty made significant changes in the way in which delegated acts are made and overseen. Article 290 TFEU is the relevant Treaty provision.

> 1. A legislative act may delegate to the Commission the power to adopt non-legislative acts of general application to supplement or amend certain non-essential elements of the legislative act.
>
> The objectives, content, scope and duration of the delegation of power shall be explicitly defined in the legislative acts. The essential elements of an area shall be reserved for the legislative act and accordingly shall not be the subject of a delegation of power.
>
> 2. Legislative acts shall explicitly lay down the conditions to which the delegation is subject; these conditions may be as follows:
>
> (a) the European Parliament or the Council may decide to revoke the delegation;

---

[89] Dec 87/373 [1987] OJ L197/33.

[90] Council Decision 99/468 laying down the procedures for the exercise of implementing powers conferred on the Commission [1999] OJ L184/23; K Lenaerts and A Verhoeven, 'Towards a Legal Framework for Executive Rule-Making in the EU? The Contribution of the New Comitology Decision' (2000) 37 CMLRev 645.

[91] Council Decision 2006/512/EC of 17 July 2006 amending Decision 1999/468/EC laying down the procedures for the exercise of implementing powers by the Commission [2006] OJ L200/11.

[92] Council Decision 99/468 (n 90) Art 4.

[93] Ibid Art 5.

[94] Ibid Art 5a.

[95] Ibid Art 3.

(b) the delegated act may enter into force only if no objection has been expressed by the European Parliament or the Council within a period set by the legislative act.

For the purposes of (a) and (b), the European Parliament shall act by a majority of its component members, and the Council by a qualified majority.

3. The adjective 'delegated' shall be inserted in the title of delegated acts.

It is necessary to understand the political background that led to Article 290.[96] The Commission regarded the Comitology regime as an unwarranted constraint on its executive autonomy. It could tolerate purely advisory committees, but it was not happy with management and regulatory committees. Its strategy for over twenty years was to devise some method whereby it could be freed from these limitations.[97] It advocated a regime of constraints on non-legislative acts of the kind that are now contained in Article 290 TFEU, with the hope that this might lead to the demise of management and regulatory committees. The EP was also unhappy with Comitology, since the original Comitology schema concentrated power on Member State representatives and the Council. Subsequent modifications to the regime increased the EP's role within Comitology, notably through the creation of the regulatory procedure with scrutiny, but it did not give the EP institutional parity with the Council.

Article 290 TFEU makes no mention of Comitology, although Article 291 TFEU makes provision for a version of Comitology in relation to implementing acts, as we shall see below. The reality was nonetheless that Comitology was used pre-Lisbon in relation to what are now termed delegated acts, and not just in relation to implementing acts as they are defined in the Lisbon Treaty.[98] It is unlikely that the Member States appreciated the possible demise of Comitology in the terrain where it has been used for nearly fifty years. This may seem surprising, but it is less so when it is recognized that there was scant deliberation about the proposals for legal acts within the plenary sessions of the Convention on the Future of Europe, because of time constraints and because the subject matter was felt to be too technical.

The institutional deliberations concerning Article 290 TFEU have been premised on the assumption that old-style management and regulatory committees do not operate in the post-Lisbon world. Scrutiny of delegated acts may be undertaken through advisory committees of national experts and committees of the European Parliament.[99] The details of the new arrangements were embodied in a Common Understanding between the institutions,[100] but this should not mask the differences between the Commission, Council, and European Parliament as to the role of such committees in enacting delegated acts,[101] which is reflected in the difficulties of securing agreement on a revised version of the Common Understanding.[102]

---

[96] P Craig, *The Lisbon Treaty: Law, Politics, and Treaty Reform* (Oxford University Press, 2010) 48–66, 260–263.

[97] European Governance, COM(2001) 428 final, [20]–[29]; Institutional Architecture, COM(2002) 728 final, [1.2], [1.3.4]; Proposal for a Council Decision Amending Decision 1999/468/EC Laying Down the Procedures for the Exercise of Implementing Powers Conferred on the Commission, COM(2002) 719 final, 2; Final Report of Working Group IX on Simplification, CONV 424/02, Brussels, 29 Nov 2002, 12.

[98] This was implicitly acknowledged by the Committee on Legal Affairs, On the Power of Legislative Delegation, A-7 0110/2010, Rapporteur J Sjazer, 12–13.

[99] Implementation of Article 290 of the Treaty on the Functioning of the European Union, COM(2009) 673 final; Council 17477/09, Implementation of the Treaty of Lisbon, Art 290, Art 291, Brussels, 11 Dec 2009; Committee on Legal Affairs, A-7 0110/2010 (n 98).

[100] Common Understanding on Delegated Acts, Council 8753/1/11, Brussels, 14 Apr 2011.

[101] Craig (n 96) 267–269.

[102] P Craig, 'Comitology, Rulemaking and the Lisbon Settlement: Tensions and Strains' in C-F Bergström and D Ritleng (eds), *Rulemaking by the Commission: The New System* (Oxford University Press, 2015).

It is therefore necessary to understand the two types of control that operate within Article 290. There is an *ex ante* constraint, to the effect that the legislative act must lay down the essential principles on the relevant topic. The *ex post* controls that can be exercised by the Council or the European Parliament are revocation of the delegation or veto of the delegated act.

(c) EVALUATION

(i) *Pre-Lisbon*

The effectiveness of the Lisbon controls on delegated acts will be considered below. It is best seen against the background of the previous debate concerning Comitology.[103]

Rational choice institutionalists regarded it as an exemplification of the principal–agent thesis. Member State principals delegate four functions to supranational agents: monitoring compliance; the resolution of incomplete contracts among principals; the adoption of regulations in areas where the principals would be biased or uninformed; and setting the legislative agenda so as to avoid the 'endless cycling' that would otherwise result if this power were exercised by the principals themselves.[104] The principals try however to ensure that the agents do not stray from the preferences of the principals. Thus on this view Comitology constituted a control mechanism whereby Member State principals exerted control over supranational agents. The Member State principals recognized the need for delegation of power over secondary norms to the supranational agent, the Commission, but did not wish to give it a blank cheque, hence the creation of committees through which Member State preferences could be expressed, with the threat of recourse to the Council if agreement could not be reached with the Commission. It is assumed that the representatives on Comitology reflect their Member States' preferences and bargain within the committees.[105] The variants of committee procedure reflect the Member States' ability to impose the degree of control that best suits their interests.

The Comitology regime was also defended, most prominently by Joerges and Neyer, who saw it in terms of deliberative supranationalism.[106] They contended that the national delegates on the committees often regarded themselves as part of a team dealing with a transnational problem. Comitology was portrayed as a network of European and national actors, with the Commission acting as coordinator. The national participants in the deliberative process were willing to call their own preferences into question in searching for a Community solution. This central core of the deliberative supranationalism thesis had some force.

There were nonetheless problems with this view of Comitology, which related to the constraints placed on consensual deliberation, the role accorded to the EP, and the exclusion from the rule-making process of others who might legitimately wish to have a voice on the resultant rule.[107] Concerns were raised about the exclusion of the EP, the undemocratic nature of the process, the lack of accountability and transparency, and the corporatist nature of the process. Thus Weiler, while acknowledging the importance of Joerges and Neyer's insights concerning the deliberative style of Comitology,[108] was nonetheless troubled by the decisional autonomy of Comitology. Committee members might be

---

[103] See (n 87).

[104] M Pollack, *The Engines of Integration: Delegation, Agency, and Agenda Setting in the EU* (Oxford University Press, 2003) 6.

[105] Ibid ch 2.

[106] C Joerges and J Neyer, 'From Intergovernmental Bargaining to Deliberative Political Processes: The Constitutionalization of Comitology' (1997) 3 ELJ 273.

[107] Craig (n 87).

[108] J Weiler, 'Epilogue: "Comitology" as Revolution—Infranationalism, Constitutionalism and Democracy' in Joerges and Vos (eds) (n 87) 347.

unaware of 'the profound political and moral choices involved in their determinations and of their shared biases',[109] and that the shared understandings that prevail between the committee members might mean that 'moral premises are presumed but not discussed'.[110]

(ii) Post-Lisbon

It might be felt in the light of the above that the demise of Comitology in relation to what are now termed delegated acts is not to be regretted. Any such conclusion is dependent in part on the efficacy of the post-Lisbon controls over delegated acts.[111]

The *ex ante* constraint, to the effect that the legislative act must lay down the essential principles on the relevant topic, was a condition in the CJEU's prior case law, but it was not interpreted rigorously.[112] It is therefore doubtful whether it will furnish much by way of control in this area.

The *ex post* controls that can be exercised by the Council or the European Parliament are revocation of the delegation, or veto of the delegated act. This has increased the European Parliament's power over delegated acts, but not that of the Council, which could under the previous regime veto a secondary norm pursuant to the Comitology procedures. The limits of this aspect of the new regime must moreover be firmly borne in mind.

First, neither the Council nor the European Parliament has any formal right to amend a delegated act, but only the power to veto. While this threat might act as a lever to secure amendment, this does not alter the fact that Article 290 gives no such formal power.

Secondly, exercise of the veto power is dependent on understanding the proposed measure. Member State representatives on the Council have neither the time nor expertise to perform this task unaided. The European Parliament committees might develop such expertise, but they have however hitherto drawn on informational resources from Comitology committees. This explains the emphasis placed by the European Parliament on information flows concerning delegated acts to its own committees in order that they can exercise adequate scrutiny over such acts.[113]

Thirdly, these difficulties are more pronounced, given that the European Parliament and Council have to raise any such objection within a short period specified by the legislative act, which will normally be somewhere between two and three months.

Finally, the very nature of the divide between delegated and implementing acts that lies at the heart of the Lisbon schema is very problematic, and thus it can be fortuitous whether a measure is characterized as delegated and subject to the controls in Article 290, or implementing and subject to the controls in Article 291.

---

[109] Ibid 348.

[110] Ibid 349.

[111] P Craig, 'Delegated Acts, Implementing Acts and the New Comitology Regulation' (2011) 36 ELRev 671; R Schütze, '"Delegated Legislation" in the (New) European Union: A Constitutional Analysis' (2011) 74 MLR 661; S Peers and M Costa, 'Accountability for Delegated and Implementing Acts after the Treaty of Lisbon' (2012) 18 ELJ 427; J Bast, 'New Categories of Acts after the Lisbon Reform: Dynamics of Parliamentarization in EU Law' (2012) 49 CMLRev 885; J Mendes, 'Delegated and Implementing Rule Making: Proceduralisation and Constitutional Design' (2013) 19 ELJ 22; T Christiansen and M Dobbels, 'Non-Legislative Rule Making after the Lisbon Treaty: Implementing the New System of Comitology and Delegated Acts' (2013) 19 ELJ 42; M Kaeding and A Hardacre, 'The European Parliament and the Future of Comitology after Lisbon' (2013) 19 ELJ 382; Craig (n 102).

[112] Case 25/70 *Koster* (n 88); Case 23/75 *Rey Soda v Cassa Conguaglio Zucchero* [1975] ECR 1279, [10], [14]; Case 121/83 *Zuckerfabrik Franken v Hauptzollamt Wurzburg* [1984] ECR 2039; Case 46/86 *Romkes v Officier van Justitie* [1987] ECR 2685, [16]; Cases C–296 and 307/93 *France and Ireland v Commission* [1996] ECR I–795, [17]–[20]; Case C–417/93 *European Parliament v Council* [1995] ECR I–1185, [30]; Case C–156/93 *European Parliament v Commission* [1995] ECR I–2019, [18]–[25]; Case C–303/94 *European Parliament v Council* [1996] ECR I–2943.

[113] Committee on Legal Affairs, A-7 0110/2010 (n 98) 10.

7 IMPLEMENTING ACTS: ENACTMENT AND CONTROL

(A) THE LISBON SCHEMA

Article 291 TFEU is the Treaty provision dealing with implementing acts.

> 1. Member States shall adopt all measures of national law necessary to implement legally binding Union acts.
> 2. Where uniform conditions for implementing legally binding Union acts are needed, those acts shall confer implementing powers on the Commission, or, in duly justified specific cases and in the cases provided for in Articles 24 and 26 of the Treaty on European Union, on the Council.
> 3. For the purposes of paragraph 2, the European Parliament and the Council, acting by means of regulations in accordance with the ordinary legislative procedure, shall lay down in advance the rules and general principles concerning mechanisms for control by Member States of the Commission's exercise of implementing powers.
> 4. The word 'implementing' shall be inserted in the title of implementing acts.

The difficulties of distinguishing delegated and implementing acts were considered above.[114] The present focus is on the controls relating to enactment of such measures. Prior to the Lisbon Treaty there was no formal distinction between delegated and implementing acts. Comitology was created as a method of Member State control over all secondary acts, including what are now delegated acts.[115] A revised version of Comitology however exists in relation to implementing acts, pursuant to Article 291(3) TFEU.

Regulation 182/2011 embodies the new Comitology regime under Article 291.[116] There are two procedures, the advisory procedure and the examination procedure, although the Regulation also makes provision for implementing acts to be immediately applicable on grounds of urgency.[117] The Commission submits a draft of the implementing act to the committee composed of Member State representatives, chaired by the Commission.[118] The Commission can revise the measure in the light of the committee discussion at any time before the committee has delivered its opinion.[119] The committee gives its opinion within a time limit set by the Commission.

The advisory procedure is the default procedure, in the sense that it is to be used except when the examination procedure is mandated.[120] Under the advisory procedure, the Commission decides on the implementing measures 'taking the utmost account of the conclusions'[121] from the committee deliberations.

The examination procedure applies in relation to implementing acts of general scope.[122] It also applies to other acts that relate to:[123] programmes with substantial implications; agriculture and

---

[114] Ch 4.
[115] Craig (n 96) ch 7.
[116] Regulation (EU) No 182/2011 of the European Parliament and of the Council of 16 February 2011 laying down the rules and general principles concerning mechanisms for control by Member States of the Commission's exercise of implementing powers [2011] OJ L55/13; Craig, 'Delegated Acts, Implementing Acts and the New Comitology Regulation' (n 111).
[117] Ibid Art 8.
[118] Ibid Art 3(2)–(3).
[119] Ibid Art 3(4).
[120] Ibid Art 2(3).
[121] Ibid Art 4(2).
[122] Ibid Art 2(2)(a).
[123] Ibid Art 2(2)(b).

fisheries; environment, security and safety or protection of the health or safety of humans, animals, or plants; common commercial policy; and taxation. This is subject to the caveat that the advisory procedure may be used even in these cases where it is considered to be 'duly justified'.[124] The new rules on the examination procedure provide for different outcomes depending on whether the committee votes in favour of the draft measure, against it, or delivers no opinion.

The implementing act will be passed if the committee delivers a *positive opinion*,[125] voting in accordance with the rules for qualified majority laid down in Article 16(4)–(5) TEU.[126] If it gives a *negative opinion* the Commission cannot adopt the acts. It can however submit a revised version to the committee, or submit the original version to the appeal committee.[127] The Commission can also adopt the acts even where there has been a negative opinion if adoption without delay is necessary to avoid creating a significant disruption of the markets in the area of agriculture, or a risk for the financial interests of the Union within the meaning of Article 325 TFEU. The Commission must then immediately submit the adopted acts to the appeal committee, and if it delivers a negative opinion on the adopted acts, the Commission must then repeal them. Where the appeal committee delivers a positive opinion or delivers no opinion, the acts shall remain in force.[128] There is in addition provision enabling the Commission to adopt the draft act in cases of urgency.[129] If the committee that examined the draft act *delivers no opinion*, the default position is that the Commission can adopt the implementing act, save for certain types of case where *prima facie* it cannot do so.[130] However even in these instances it can submit a revised version of the draft measure to the committee, or take the original version to the appeal committee.

The Commission emphasized in its original proposal that control was to be exercised by the Member States, and that neither the Council nor the European Parliament was accorded a direct role on the committees, although they could have access to information about the proceedings.[131] This is reflected in the Regulation.[132] It provides that where the basic act is adopted under the ordinary legislative procedure, the EP or the Council may at any time indicate to the Commission that it considers a draft implementing act to exceed the implementing powers provided for in the basic act. The Commission has a duty to review the draft act, taking account of the views of the EP and Council. It is not however obliged to withdraw the act, but must rather inform the EP and the Council whether it intends to maintain, amend, or withdraw the draft implementing act. There are also provisions concerning information on Comitology committees and documentation to be made available to the EP and Council.[133]

(B) EVALUATION

The Lisbon reforms relating to the hierarchy of norms were designed to simplify the pre-existing regime, but may well have created increased legal and institutional complexity. There are four reasons why this is so.

---

[124] Ibid Art 2(3).
[125] Ibid Art 5(2).
[126] Ibid Art 5(1).
[127] Ibid Art 5(3).
[128] Ibid Art 7.
[129] Ibid Art 8.
[130] Ibid Art 5(4).
[131] COM(2010) 83 final, 3.
[132] Reg 182/2011 (n 116) Art 11.
[133] Ibid Art 10.

First, the divide between delegated and implementing acts is inherently problematic for the reasons considered in the previous chapter. The divide turns on whether the act amends or supplements the legislative act, in which case it must be a delegated act, or whether it does not do so, in which case it is an implementing act. This distinction is fraught with difficulty for the reasons given above.[134]

Secondly, it will not be clear whether a particular act falls into one category or another until it is made. Thus the mere fact that the primary legislative act makes provision for enactment of, for example, implementing acts pursuant to an article of the legislation cannot tell us whether a particular implementing act is lawful or not. This is because it is only by studying the particular 'implementing act' that one can decide whether it in fact supplements or amends the legislative act and therefore should have been made as a delegated act.

Thirdly, the distinction between delegated and implementing acts is nonetheless crucial under the Lisbon Treaty, since very different procedures and controls are prescribed in the two instances. The EP has no formal role in the committees established under Article 291. Nor indeed in formal terms does the Council, although the fact that the committee representatives are from the Member States may lead to some connection with ministerial representatives in the Council.

Finally, the Lisbon regime will lead to greater institutional complexity. There will be Comitology committees established pursuant to Article 291. There will however also be a whole world of advisory committees created by the Council and/or EP pursuant to Article 290, in order to enable these institutions to decide whether they should exercise their veto power, and there is no formal mechanism for such committees to be known or listed.

P Craig, Comitology, Rulemaking and the Lisbon Settlement: Tensions and Strains[135]

The divide between delegated and implementing acts is at the heart of the Lisbon settlement. The analytical and temporal difficulties that beset this distinction however remain. They have not been removed through judicial clarification in the years since the Lisbon Treaty came into effect. It is unclear how far the EU legislature gives systematic considered thought as to whether delegated or implementing acts should be used, and insofar as it does so the choice can be affected as much if not more by political considerations as by the analytical nature of the distinction between the two types of act. The effluxion of time has revealed moreover the constitutional, institutional and conceptual tensions considered above, and the way in which issues of legal form can impact on the normative assumptions underlying the divide between Article 290 and Article 291. It would be tempting but mistaken to identify a clear institutional winner from the new schema. The truth is that all institutional players have lost out in some respects.

For the European Parliament, the hope was parity with the Council in relation to Article 290, and the excision of Comitology committees on which Member State representatives dominated from this terrain. The reality is that it has formal parity with the Council under Article 290, but the Common Understanding has brought advisory expert committees back into this area on which national representatives are still dominant. There is the additional fact that so much rulemaking now occurs via Article 291 and the European Parliament has less input into this new Comitology regime than it did in relation to the old one. For the Commission, the ideal was to remove what it felt were unwarranted

---

[134] Ch 4.
[135] Bergström and Ritleng (n 102).

Comitology constraints from Article 290, thereby reinforcing its executive autonomy over this area, albeit subject to the controls contained therein. The reality is that some Member State input was retained directly through the Common Understanding 2011, a feature that will be further enhanced if the 2014 version takes effect, and indirectly through the provisions for rulemaking in the new agency regulations. There is the additional fact that the new Comitology regime under Article 291 places as many constraints on the Commission as did the old, and that is so notwithstanding that in formal terms the national representatives on the committees are formally separate from those in the Council. From the perspective of the Council, the initial loss was the demise of the Comitology regime from Article 290, although it has since been seeking to recover ground through the Common Understanding and if the revised version does come into effect the committee system under Article 290 will come ever closer to the formalization that existed prior to the Lisbon Treaty and to that which operates under Article 291.

8 ENHANCED COOPERATION: CONDITIONS AND USE

The discussion thus far has been predicated on the assumption that legislation and other Union acts are made with the participation of all twenty-eight Member States. There was provision prior to the Lisbon Treaty whereby certain states could, subject to conditions, adopt acts even though not all Member States took part.[136] The political reality pre-Lisbon was however that while there was some flexibility in the application of Treaty Articles,[137] the provisions on enhanced cooperation did not provide the foundation for such initiatives.

The Lisbon Treaty modified the provisions on enhanced cooperation, so as to render them easier to use in a Union of twenty-eight Member States. Article 20 TEU authorizes enhanced cooperation in accordance with detailed conditions set out in the TFEU. It stipulates that such cooperation shall aim to further the objectives of the EU, protect its interests, and reinforce the integration process. There must be a minimum of nine Member States wishing to participate in order for enhanced cooperation to be used. The pre-Lisbon rules required eight out of fifteen states to participate, so the post-Lisbon number of nine out of twenty-eight is a significant relaxation in this respect. The cooperation must be open at any time to all Member States, in accordance with Article 328 TFEU. It is emphasized in Article 20(2) TEU that enhanced cooperation is a last resort, to be used where the Council has established that the objectives of such cooperation cannot be attained within a reasonable period by the EU as a whole.

All members of the Council can participate in its deliberations, but only those members representing Member States participating in enhanced cooperation take part in the vote, in accordance with the rules in Article 330 TFEU. The acts adopted in the framework of enhanced cooperation bind only participating Member States, and they do not in formal terms constitute part of the *acquis* that has to be accepted by candidate states for accession to the EU. The conditions for such cooperation are contained in Articles 326–327 TFEU, read together with Article 20 TEU.

---

[136] Arts 43–45 EU, Art 11 EC.
[137] F Tuytschaever, *Differentiation in European Union Law* (Hart, 1999); G de Búrca and J Scott (eds), *Constitutional Change in the EU: From Uniformity to Flexibility?* (Hart, 2000).

Article 326

Any enhanced cooperation shall comply with the Treaties and Union law.

Such cooperation shall not undermine the internal market or economic, social and territorial cohesion. It shall not constitute a barrier to or discrimination in trade between Member States, nor shall it distort competition between them.

Article 327

Any enhanced cooperation shall respect the competences, rights and obligations of those Member States which do not participate in it. Those Member States shall not impede its implementation by the participating Member States.

The detailed rules concerning creation of enhanced cooperation are found in Articles 328 and 329 TFEU. The Lisbon provisions on enhanced cooperation also contain two passerelle clauses concerning voting rules and voting procedures respectively.[138] The Lisbon Treaty in addition contains provisions relating to enhanced cooperation in other areas, such as judicial cooperation in criminal matters and police cooperation.[139] The provisions on enhanced cooperation have been used post-Lisbon. They have also given rise to unsuccessful legal challenges.[140]

9 EU DECISION-MAKING: PROCESS AND REALITY

(A) THE TEMPORAL DIMENSION

The discussion thus far has focused on the legislative procedures. To stop there would give only an imperfect grasp of the EU legislative process. We need to press further to understand the way in which EU decision-making works. There are different dimensions to this inquiry, one of which is temporal in nature: the way in which the role of the EU institutions in the decision-making process has developed over time. What follows does not purport to be a thorough historical analysis, but rather a thematic one. A central theme is the development of institutional structures outside the strict letter of the Treaty, as a response to tensions between the Council and Commission, since they embodied different conceptions of the Community.

The Council perceived it principally in intergovernmental terms, and this had both a substantive and a procedural dimension. In substantive terms, the Council was unclear precisely how far it wished to travel down the road of European integration. In procedural terms, intergovernmentalism connoted the idea that Member State interests should not readily be sacrificed to the Community good, and that the Council, as representative of those interests, should retain control over the development of Community policy.

The Commission had a more federalist conception of the Community. In substantive terms, it manifested itself in a commitment to attain Community goals as expeditiously as possible. In procedural

---

[138] Art 333 TFEU.
[139] Art 82 TFEU.
[140] Cases C–274 and 295/11 *Spain and Italy v Council* EU:C:2013:240; Case C–209/13 *UK v Council* EU:C:2014:283.

terms, the Commission's vision naturally inclined to use of majority voting, with the consequence that the interests of a Member State might have to be sacrificed to achieve the greater Community good.

The original Rome Treaty divided power between Council and Commission, but in many respects the Commission was in the driving seat as regards development of Community policy. This is evident from the Commission's right of legislative initiative; from the many other functions it was given; and from the fact that the voting rules, while requiring Council consent to a measure, also required unanimity for Council amendment.[141] The message was that while the Council had to consent to legislation, it was not easy to alter the Commission's draft.

The first twenty years or so of the Community were marked by *de facto* changes in Community decision-making. The unifying theme was the increased dominance of the Council over the Commission, and the limiting of the federalist tendencies within the Commission by the intergovernmental impulses of the Council. Institutional developments outside the strict letter of the Treaty were the vehicle through which this was achieved.

The Luxembourg Accords were one such development. They were the prime example of negative intergovernmentalism: Member States could block measures they disliked which they felt touched their vital interests. Statistics on the usage of this power are only part of the story, since threat of the veto shaped the Commission's policies.[142]

The Council's intergovernmental orientation also had a more positive side to it. The Luxembourg Accords were fine if the ultimate objective was to veto a measure. But the Member States also desired more finely-tuned tools through which to influence legislation they wished to be enacted. The growing influence of Coreper, the establishment of management and regulatory committees, the increased use of Article 208 EC, and the evolution of the European Council were all features of positive intergovernmentalism. They increased Member State influence over Community legislation in complementary ways.

Coreper and the management/regulatory committees enabled the Council to have more formalized input into emergent legislation. Article 208 became a useful vehicle whereby the Council could suggest Community action, while the European Council enabled Member States to discuss general issues of Community concern, outside the framework of the Council. The results were often 'binding', by laying down the parameters of future Community action, whether in relation to the size of the Common Agricultural Policy (CAP) budget, or the timetable for closer economic union.

These developments contributed to the Euro-sclerosis that beset the Community during much of the 1970s, which had implications for the ECJ's role. This story has been told most fully in the important work of Joseph Weiler.[143] He explains how impediments to attainment of Community objectives through the political process led to the growing importance of normative supranationalism. The doctrines of direct effect, the supremacy of Community law, and pre-emption were central in this respect, enabling the Court to develop EC law, notwithstanding the difficulties in securing enactment through the legislative process.[144]

Many of the institutional developments that initially occurred outside the strict letter of the Treaty were accorded legal status through Treaty revisions: the management and regulatory committee structure attained a more secure footing by revision of Article 202 EC; the European Council was recognized by the SEA; and Coreper was accorded a more formal status in Article 207 EC. It should,

---

[141] Art 250(1) EC.

[142] K Neunreither, 'Transformation of a Political Role: Reconsidering the Case of the Commission of the European Communities' (1971–2) 10 JCMS 233.

[143] J Weiler, 'The Community System: The Dual Character of Supranationalism' (1981) 1 YBEL 267, and 'The Transformation of Europe' (1991) 100 Yale LJ 2403, 2412–2431.

[144] P Craig, 'Once Upon a Time in the West: Direct Effect and the Federalization of EEC Law' (1992) 12 OJLS 453.

moreover, be noted that matters have changed since the 1970s and that the divide between institutions that are supranational and those that are intergovernmental is not as sharp as it might once have been.[145]

(B) THE INTER-INSTITUTIONAL DIMENSION

(i) *Planning the Legislative Agenda*

The institutional reforms in the SEA had a mixed impact on Community decision-making. They expedited decision-making by extending qualified-majority voting, but also made the legislative process more complex, since Parliament now had power through the cooperation procedure. It became clear that there would have to be more inter-institutional cooperation in planning the overall legislative programme.[146] The system now operates as follows.[147]

The Commission on entering office publishes a five-year programme, setting out the strategic objectives for that period at a relatively high level of generality.[148] The annual planning cycle begins with the Annual Policy Strategy (APS), which is designed to integrate decisions about priorities and resources more closely together.[149] The APS gives an annual strategic framework at Commission level and defines, early in the previous year, political priorities and initiatives for the following year. It also allocates the financial and human resources to these priority initiatives and establishes the overall resource framework. The President of the Commission presents the annual policy strategy to the Council and the European Parliament, launching a dialogue on the various policy areas with the other institutions. Based on the annual policy strategy and the dialogue with the European Council, Council, and the European Parliament, and taking into account progress in the budgetary process and operational planning, the College determines the Commission's work programme for the following year. The revised APS thus forms the basis for the Commission's more detailed Work Programme for a particular year,[150] which will list the legislative and non-legislative measures to be introduced to attain the objectives agreed in the modified APS. This is presented to the Council and EP, normally in November.

Each Directorate-General (DG) establishes Annual Management Plans (AMPs) on the basis of the preceding framework in order to show how it will contribute towards attainment of the Commission's overall annual work programme.[151] Thus the AMP translates the priority initiatives and the strategic objectives of the Commission into concrete operations and provides an instrument enabling the management to plan and report on all the activities and resources of each DG. Each DG will also present an Annual Activity Report (AAR), which mirrors the AMP in the sense of monitoring how far objectives have been realized.[152]

---

[145] See Ch 1.

[146] M Westlake, *The Commission and the Parliament: Partners and Rivals in the European Policy-Making Process* (Butterworths, 1994) 19–21.

[147] http://ec.europa.eu/atwork/planning-and-preparing/index_en.htm.

[148] Strategic Objectives 2005–2009: Europe 2010, A Partnership for European Renewal, Prosperity, Solidarity, and Security, COM(2005) 12 final; J-C Juncker, A New Start for Europe: My Agenda for Jobs, Growth, Fairness and Democratic Change (Strasbourg, 15 July 2014), http://ec.europa.eu/priorities/docs/pg_en.pdf.

[149] Annual Policy Strategy for 2007, Boosting Trust through Action, COM(2006) 122 final; Annual Policy Strategy for 2009, COM(2008) 72 final; Annual Policy Strategy for 2010, COM(2009) 73 final.

[150] Commission Legislative and Work Programme 2007, COM(2006) 629 final; Commission Legislative and Work Programme 2009, Acting now for a better Europe, COM(2008) 712 final; Commission Work Programme 2015, A New Start, COM(2014) 910 final.

[151] http://ec.europa.eu/atwork/synthesis/amp/index_en.htm.

[152] http://ec.europa.eu/atwork/planning-and-preparing/synthesis-report/index_en.htm.

The cycle ends with Synthesis Reports by the Commission, which assess policy progress, the way in which resources were used, and proposals for remedying deficiencies revealed in the individual reports from the DGs.[153]

Impact assessment is now a prominent feature of the Commission's legislative planning.[154] It is designed to identify and assess the problem and the objectives pursued. It identifies the main options for achieving the objective and analyses their likely impacts in the economic, environmental, and social fields. Impact assessment is regarded as an aid to political decision, not a substitute for it. It informs decision-makers of the impact of proposals, while leaving it to them to take the decisions. Thus, 'impact assessment identifies the likely positive and negative impacts of proposed policy actions, enabling informed political judgments to be made about the proposal and identify trade-offs in achieving competing objectives'.[155] Impact assessment is applied to all major initiatives included in the Commission's Annual Policy Strategy or Work Programme.

(ii) *Inter-Institutional Agreements*

An important vehicle for more formal inter-institutional cooperation is the Inter-Institutional Agreement or Declaration.[156] It functions as 'constitutional glue'[157] for the Community, exemplified by the 1993 Inter-Institutional Agreement on Subsidiarity, and the 1993 Inter-Institutional Declaration on Democracy, Transparency, and Subsidiarity. Such agreements have also been made in relation to, for example, budgetary discipline, codification, implementation of the budget, and Comitology, and they often form the basis for subsequent hard law. Thus the Inter-Institutional Declaration on Democracy, Transparency and Subsidiarity was the catalyst for legislation on transparency in the Commission and Council.[158] Article 295 TFEU now makes express provision for inter-institutional agreements, and provides that they can be binding.

(iii) *The Making of Particular Policies*

We now consider the ways in which the institutions interact in the making of specific legislation. The content of legislative proposals will normally have been flagged in the Commission's legislative agenda. The Commissioner will assume overall responsibility for a proposal within that area, and it will have been fashioned by the relevant DG, including discussion with interest groups, national experts, and senior civil servants. When those directly involved with the proposed measure have given their approval, the draft will be sent to the cabinet of the Commissioner. When the Commissioner is satisfied with the draft it will then be submitted to the College of Commissioners. Legislative proposals, once formulated, require the endorsement of the whole Commission. The College of Commissioners will normally meet weekly.

The role of groups of national experts and civil servants in policy-formation is an interesting one. The framing of the proposal will involve close collaboration with a wide variety of groups. This occurs

---

[153] See, eg, Synthesis of the Commission's Management Achievements in 2009, COM(2010) 281 final; Synthesis of the Commission's Management Achievements in 2013, COM(2013) 342 final.

[154] http://ec.europa.eu/atwork/planning-and-preparing/impact-assessment/index_en.htm.

[155] Impact Assessment, COM(2002) 276 final, 2; Impact Assessment Guidelines, SEC(2009) 92, http://ec.europa.eu/smart-regulation/impact/commission_guidelines/commission_guidelines_en.htm.

[156] J Monar, 'Interinstitutional Agreements: The Phenomenon and its Dynamics after Maastricht' (1994) 31 CMLRev 693.

[157] Westlake (n 146) 101.

[158] Council Dec 93/731 [1993] OJ L340/43; Commission Dec 94/90 [1994] OJ L46/58.

before the proposal begins its formal legislative journey. Bureaucracies at national and Union level may well become more interlocked.

W Wessels, Administrative Interaction[159]

By participating in Community decision-making the national civil servants gain 'access' to and 'influence' on EC decision-making and implementation, thus also increasing their weight inside their respective national systems. The same general cost–benefit calculation applies to Community officials who gain access and influence on 'national' domains by opening their policy cycles to the national colleagues—although traditional federalists and supranationalists would argue that this is an unacceptable loss in autonomy and independence of the EC bureaucracy. This cost–benefit analysis by civil servants (*mutatis mutandis* by heads of State, ministers and interest groups, but not by national parliamentarians) creates a major dynamic for European integration leading not to a transfer of loyalty by national officials to a new centre but to cooperation of officials into a new system of shared government. This stage of State evolution is characterized by an increasing degree of cooperation, in vertical terms between different governmental levels, and in horizontal terms, among several groups of actors. The 'multi-level' interactions of civil servants of several national and international administrations thus reinforce trends towards specific forms of the 'sharing' or 'fusion' of powers between 'bureaucrats and politicians' which non-EC-related studies have identified.

Interest groups also have input into policy-formation. Given that the maxim of lobbyists is to 'shoot where the ducks are' we should therefore expect interest groups to organize themselves at a European level.[160] Successful lobbying is dependent on developing good advance intelligence; watching the national agenda; maintaining good links with national administrations; maintaining close contacts with Commission officials; presenting rational arguments; being cooperative; developing a European perspective; and not ignoring the implementation process.[161] Many Euro-associations have been formed to foster this process, but the Commission's attitude towards them has been ambivalent.[162]

The Commission has developed principles to govern its dealings with interest groups. There is a register for such groups,[163] which must subscribe to a code of conduct.[164] It uses Green Papers and the like as a mechanism for eliciting their views. The Commission also demands certain standards from such groups. Interest-group pressure at the EU level is to be expected. This does not mean we should be complacent. Profit-making groups outnumber non-profit groups by a significant margin, and their resources are much larger. The costs of organizing at the European level may be especially onerous for the voluntary/non-profit sector. Powerful groups are likely to make their voices heard irrespective of whether formal participatory rights exist, but this is not obviously so for those with less financial muscle.

When a Commission proposal has been formulated it will make its way to the Council, and normally to the European Parliament. Coreper is of crucial importance for Council involvement. Before any

---

[159] W Wallace (ed), *The Dynamics of European Integration* (RISIA/Pinter, 1990) 230.

[160] See, eg, S Mazey and J Richardson, *Lobbying in the EC* (Oxford University Press, 1992); RH Pedler and MPCM Van Schendelen (eds), *Lobbying the European Union: Companies, Trade Associations and Issue Groups* (Dartmouth, 1994).

[161] S Mazey and J Richardson, 'Pressure Groups and Lobbying in the EC' in J Lodge (ed), *The European Community and the Challenge of the Future* (Pinter, 2nd edn, 1993) 44.

[162] Ibid 38–39. See also, S Mazey and J Richardson, 'Interest Groups and EU Policy-Making: Organizational Logic and Venue Shopping' in J Richardson (ed), *European Union: Power and Policy-Making* (Routledge, 3rd edn, 2006) ch 12.

[163] http://ec.europa.eu/transparency/regexpert/.

[164] http://ec.europa.eu/transparencyregister/info/about-register/codeOfConduct.do?locale=en.

measure is seen by the Council, it will have been thoroughly examined by working groups that assist Coreper, as well as by Coreper I or II. These working groups are composed of national officials and experts from Member States, plus a member of the Commission. They may be permanent or *ad hoc*. There may be 200–250 such groups at any one time.[165] They examine the Commission proposal and prepare a report. This will indicate the areas on which agreement has been reached ('Roman I points') and all other points ('Roman II points'). The latter will then be discussed within Coreper.

Coreper also helps to set the Council's agenda. Issues on which there is agreement within Coreper are on the 'A list' and adopted without discussion. If agreement within Coreper has not been possible then such issues are placed on the 'B list', indicating that debate and decision by the Council are required. Members of Coreper will attend Council meetings as advisers to their national ministerial representatives. Coreper will also negotiate with the EP should the Conciliations Committee be convened pursuant to the co-decision procedure.

The Council Presidency will coordinate meetings of the different sectoral Councils, and mediate conflicts between the Member States, between the Member States and the Commission, and between the Council and the Parliament.

The EP's role in the passage of legislation is equally important, with the main part of the work being undertaken by standing committees. The appropriate committee will make the initial draft report on legislation submitted to the Parliament pursuant to Article 289 TFEU. The responsibility for drawing up the committee report is given to a *rapporteur*, who will present the draft report to the committee. It will normally have four parts: suggested amendments to the Commission proposal; a Draft Legislative Resolution; an Explanatory Statement; and any relevant annexes. The committee will advise the MEPs how to vote in the plenary session, and the *rapporteur* will usually act as the committee's spokesperson. The preceding discussion revealed the emphasis placed on dialogue and the search for consensus at the various stages of the ordinary legislative procedure.[166]

10 EU DEMOCRACY: ARGUMENT AND EVALUATION

The democratic legitimacy of decision-making within the EU has long been debated.[167] This has been particularly so since the Maastricht Treaty, as reflected in the institutional reports which led to the 1996 IGC[168] and the rich vein of academic literature, much of which is concerned with the EU's 'democratic deficit'.[169] While views differ on this issue, the following account, developed from

---

[165] F Hayes-Renshaw, C Lequesne, and P Mayor Lopez, 'The Permanent Representations of the Member States to the European Communities' (1989) 27 JCMS 119, 132.

[166] Pp 126–133.

[167] The discussion draws in part on P Craig, 'Integration, Democracy and Legitimacy' in P Craig and G de Búrca (eds), *The Evolution of EU Law* (Oxford University Press, 2nd edn, 2011) ch 2.

[168] Craig (n 14); G de Búrca, 'The Quest for Legitimacy in the European Union' (1996) 59 MLR 349.

[169] See, just in terms of books, S Garcia (ed), *European Identity and the Search for Legitimacy* (Pinter, 1993); J Hayward (ed), *The Crisis of Representation in Europe* (Frank Cass, 1995); A Rosas and E Antola (eds), *A Citizens' Europe: In Search of a New Order* (Sage, 1995); R Bellamy, V Bufacchi, and D Castiglione (eds), *Democracy and Constitutional Culture in the Union of Europe* (Lothian Foundation Press, 1995); S Andersen and K Eliassen (eds), *The European Union: How Democratic Is It?* (Sage, 1996); R Bellamy and D Castiglione (eds), *Constitutionalism in Transformation: European and Theoretical Perspectives* (Blackwell, 1996); R Bellamy (ed), *Constitutionalism, Democracy and Sovereignty: American and European Perspectives* (Avebury, 1996); F Snyder (ed), *Constitutional Dimensions of European Economic Integration* (Kluwer, 1996); R Dehousse (ed), *Europe: The Impossible Status Quo* (1997); D Curtin, *Postnational Democracy: The European Union in Search of a Political Philosophy* (Kluwer, 1997); P Craig and C Harlow (eds), *Lawmaking in the European Union* (Kluwer, 1998); J Weiler, *The Constitution of Europe* (Cambridge University Press, 1999); C Hoskyns and M Newman (eds), *Democratizing the European Union* (Manchester University Press, 2000); B Laffan, R O'Donnell, and M Smith, *Europe's Experimental Union: Rethinking Integration* (Routledge, 2000); F Mancini, *Democracy and*

Joseph Weiler's summary of the democratic deficit,[170] is reasonably representative. It is important to understand that the phrase 'democratic deficit' has a number of different features which must be distinguished.

(A) THE NATURE OF THE ARGUMENT

An important critique of EU decision-making is that it is 'unresponsive to democratic pressures'. It is a cardinal feature of democratic regimes that voters can change the government.[171] This is not the case within the EU. Legislative power is divided between the Council, Commission, and Parliament. It is only the Parliament that is directly elected. A change in the Parliament's composition through European elections will not, therefore, necessarily lead to major shifts in EU policy, since it is only one part of the legislature, although the recent changes in EP elections whereby the Commission President is the candidate for a particular party in the EP has alleviated albeit not cured this problem.

A second facet of the democracy deficit argument concerns 'executive dominance'. The transfer of competence to the EU enhances the power of the executive at the expense of national parliaments. This is because of the dominance of the Council and European Council in the EU's decision-making process, and the difficulty experienced by national parliamentary bodies in exercising real control over EU decisions. While the existence of the EP alleviates this problem by providing a directly elected forum at the European level, it does not remove it. This is because of its limited powers, lack of voter interest in EP elections, and the absence of a developed party system within the EU.

A third feature of the democracy deficit argument is the 'by-passing of democracy argument'. This critique was applied most frequently to the complex committee structure, known generally as Comitology. We have seen that many technical, but important, regulations were made by committees established pursuant to delegation of power to the Commission. Technocrats and national interest groups have dominated this decision-making to the exclusion of more regular channels of democratic decision-making, such as the European Parliament and even the Council.

There is, fourthly, what may be termed the 'distance issue'. Many matters have been transferred to Brussels from the nation state, thereby further removing them from the citizen.

A fifth aspect of democracy deficit can be termed the 'transparency and complexity issue'. Traditionally much EU decision-making, particularly in the Council, has taken place behind closed doors. In addition the very complexity of the legislative procedures has meant that it is difficult for anyone, other than an expert, to understand them.

There is, sixthly, the 'substantive imbalance issue'. Writers from the left argue that the democratic deficit should also encompass the imbalance between labour and capital, which they claim has been exacerbated by the freeing up of the European market.

There is, finally, the 'weakening of judicial control issue'. A number of legal systems possess courts with power over the constitutionality of primary legislation. The transfer of competence to the EU means that such powers are thereby reduced in scope.

Constitutionalism in the European Union (Hart, 2000); K Neunreither and A Wiener (eds), *European Integration after Amsterdam: Institutional Dynamics and Prospects for Democracy* (Oxford University Press, 2000); R Prodi, *Europe As I See It* (Polity, 2000); K Nicolaïdis and R Howse (eds), *The Federal Vision: Legitimacy and Levels of Governance in the United States and the European Union* (Oxford University Press, 2001); W Van Gerven, *The European Union: A Polity of States and Peoples* (Hart, 2005).

[170] J Weiler, U Haltern, and F Mayer, 'European Democracy and its Critique' in J Hayward (ed), *The Crisis of Representation in Europe* (Frank Cass, 1995) 32–33; J Weiler, 'European Models: Polity, People and System' in Craig and Harlow (n 47) ch 1.

[171] A Follesdal and S Hix, 'Why there is a Democratic Deficit in the EU: A Response to Majone and Moravcsik' (2006) 44 JCMS 533, 534–537.

(B) EVALUATION: THE EMPIRICAL FRAME OF REFERENCE

We live by and through language. The very language of democratic deficit is powerful in its imagery. It speaks to some base point from which we are deviating, an impression reinforced by the analogy with budget deficit. Democracy cannot however be measured in the same way as a budget. Any assessment of the democratic deficit argument must be partly empirical and partly theoretical. The discussion that follows does not mean that democracy within the EU is incapable of improvement. It does mean that we must be fair when assessing EU democracy in comparison to national regimes, and in comparison to what would be the case if the EU did not exist. The empirical frame of reference is by comparison with the position as it would be if matters were still dealt with at national level. This requires us to assess the reality of decision-making within national polities, and postulate what the locus of decision-making would be if there was no EU.

(i) *Comparison with National Polities*

The first step of the argument takes us into familiar territory. Executives tend to dominate most modern domestic polities. The degree of dominance varies, but the general proposition nonetheless holds true. The idea that national parliaments really control the emergence or content of legislative norms rarely comports with reality. The force of the 'executive dominance' critique of EU decision-making appears weaker when viewed in this light.

It is, moreover, by no means self-evident that the EP has less power over the content of legislation than do national parliaments. Most important EU legislation is now subject to the ordinary legislative procedure. The EP has had a pretty good strike rate at getting its amendments accepted,[172] and trilogues help to ensure that EP concerns are reflected in the final version of the legislative act. It might be argued that the amendments were minor, or ones that the Council was willing to accept. The former can only be tested by a detailed study of the various legislative acts in question. The latter is simply reductionist. The Council must of course accept the amendments since otherwise the legislation will not become law, but this does not prove that the EP exercised no power. The reality is that many national parliaments struggle to impose changes in draft legislation that are not executive-sponsored.

An understanding of the reality of national decision-making is also important when considering the Comitology problem and the 'bypassing of the normal democratic process'. There was a real problem here for the EU. The legitimation of secondary norms is however an endemic problem for all domestic political systems. The UK, for example, has not satisfactorily resolved the need for the expeditious passage of secondary norms and the need to ensure effective legislative oversight. Indeed, many norms of a legislative nature are not seen by the UK legislature at all. The Lisbon Treaty has in any event had a marked impact, as seen above, on the types of act that are subject to such committee procedures.

(ii) *Comparison with International Polities*

The second step of the argument takes us into less familiar terrain. The assumption commonly made is that if the EU did not exist then the matters within its competence would be dealt with at national level. Decisions would be made closer to the people, hence alleviating the 'distance problem', and national parliaments would have greater control, hence mitigating the 'executive dominance' problem.

---

[172] Westlake (n 10) 39; S Boyron, 'The Co-decision Procedure: Rethinking the Constitutional Fundamentals' in Craig and Harlow (n 47) ch 8; Maurer (n 47) 21–29.

The conclusion does not follow from the premise. The pressures for some form of international coordination would still be present, even if the EU never existed. An enduring insight from integration theory is that cross-border flows of goods create international policy externalities, which in turn create incentives for policy coordination.[173] The key issue then becomes not whether states interact, but how. They can do so by *ad hoc* international agreements, involving two or more parties. Some more permanent form of international cooperation will often be preferred, thereby reducing the bargaining and transaction costs of *ad hoc* coordination. This is especially so when the number of parties becomes larger, and the issues on which they seek to coordinate become broader.

The real contrast is, therefore, between how issues such as 'distance', 'executive dominance', 'transparency', and the like play out in these differing forms of international coordination. There is little room for doubt here, since the people fare less well when matters are regulated through a series of *ad hoc* international agreements than they do when they are regulated through the EU. This is so for a number of reasons: international agreements normally include no forum such as the EP; such agreements are made, run, and terminated by the executive; and national parliaments normally exercise minimal control, they may have to give approval to the agreement, but any parliamentary supervision thereafter will usually be relatively marginal.

(c) EVALUATION: THE NORMATIVE FRAME OF REFERENCE

(i) *Four Contrasting Approaches*

We can now consider the theoretical aspect of the democracy deficit argument. What divides commentators is that they accord varying significance to different aspects of democracy when judging the EU. This can be seen by contrasting four approaches in the literature.

Moravcsik's defence of the EU from the allegation that it suffers from a democratic deficit is premised on democracy in terms of *checks and balances*.[174] Viewed from this perspective he maintains that 'constitutional checks and balances, indirect democratic control via national governments, and the increasing powers of the European Parliament are sufficient to ensure that EU policy-making is, in nearly all cases, clear, transparent, effective and politically responsive to the demands of European citizens'.[175] He points to mechanisms for direct and indirect democratic accountability in the EU, via the EP and via the Council and European Council.[176] He rightly notes that insofar as the EU makes decisions in certain areas that are insulated from direct political contestation this bears close analogy to areas in which analogous methods of decision-making are used in nation states.[177] Thus for Moravcsik, the 'classic justification for democracy is to check and channel the arbitrary and potentially corrupt power of the state',[178] and the centrality of this theme to Moravcsik's argument is reflected in the fact that his focus is on the substantive, administrative, and procedural constraints on EU power.

---

[173] A Moravcsik, 'Preferences and Power in the European Community: A Liberal Intergovernmentalist Approach' (1993) 31 JCMS 473, 485; W Wessels, 'The Modern West-European State and the European Union: Democratic Erosion or a New Kind of Polity?' in Andersen and Eliassen (n 169) ch 4; G Majone, 'The European Community Between Social Policy and Social Regulation' (1993) 31 JCMS 153 and 'The Rise of the Regulatory State in Europe' (1994) West European Politics 1; Craig (n 167).

[174] A Moravcsik, 'In Defence of the "Democratic Deficit": Reassessing Legitimacy in the European Union' (2002) 40 JCMS 603.

[175] Ibid 605.

[176] Ibid 609–610.

[177] Ibid 613–614.

[178] Ibid 606.

Moravcsik's thesis has however been challenged by writers such as Weiler,[179] Bellamy,[180] and Follesdal and Hix[181] who are more concerned with *input aspects* of democracy. They contend that the EU suffers from the disjunction between power and electoral accountability, which constitutes an important element of the democratic deficit critique of the EU. Thus, for example, Follesdal and Hix contend that a democratic polity requires contestation for political leadership and over policy, this being an essential element of even the 'thinnest' theories of democracy, and that this has been absent from the EU. They argue that democracy requires procedures that regulate competition for control over political authority, and that the preferences of citizens who participate in elections determine the outcome, such that the government is responsive to the majority or to as many as possible.[182] They contend that these features are lacking in the EU since there is no institutionalized opposition, and scant opportunity to present an alternative set of policy outcomes to those currently espoused by the Commission, Council, and EP. Such electoral contests are moreover integral to the formation of voter preferences on policy issues.[183]

A Follesdal and S Hix, Why there is a Democratic Deficit in the EU: A Response to Majone and Moravcsik

Currently there are several constitution-like and institutional features that insulate the EU from political competition. Most fundamentally, there is no electoral contest for political leadership at the European level or the basic direction of the EU policy agenda. Representatives at the EU level are elected, and so can formally be 'thrown out'. However, the processes of electing national politicians and even the members of the European Parliament are not contests about the content or direction of EU policy. National elections are about domestic political issues, where the policies of different parties on issues on the EU agenda are rarely debated. Similarly, as discussed, European Parliament elections are not in fact about Europe, but are 'second-order national contests'. They are fought by national parties on the performance of national governments, with lower turnout than national elections, and hence won by opposition and protest parties. At no point, then, do voters have the opportunity to choose between rival candidates for executive office at the European level, or to choose between rival policy agendas for EU action, or to throw out elected representatives for their policy positions or actions at the EU level.

While commentators such as Weiler and Follesdal and Hix disagree with certain tenets of Moravcsik's argument, their view has in turn been challenged by Menon and Weatherill.[184] The basis of this disagreement reflects once again differences of view as to the factors that should be prioritized when thinking about democracy in the EU. Menon and Weatherill argue that *output legitimacy* is especially important in this regard. They contend that using state paradigms to measure EU legitimacy is falsely to assume that the EU is seeking to become a state, and that insofar as there may be some virtue in drawing on state practice when thinking about the legitimacy of the EU this must be

---

[179] Weiler (n 170).

[180] R Bellamy, 'Democracy without Democracy? Can the EU's Democratic "Outputs" be Separated from the Democratic "Inputs" provided by Competitive Parties and Majority Rule?' (2010) 17 JEPP 2.

[181] Follesdal and Hix (n 171).

[182] Ibid 547.

[183] Ibid 552.

[184] A Menon and S Weatherill, 'Democratic Politics in a Globalising World: Supranationalism and Legitimacy in the European Union', LSE, Law, Society and Economy Working Papers 13/2007.

done while fully cognizant of the failure of the state to live up to its own ideals.[185] They argue that the effectiveness of the EU is dependent on the Commission and CJEU acting as 'vigorous autonomous institutions'.[186]

Output legitimacy is seen as particularly important.[187] Effectiveness is a 'source of legitimacy',[188] and hence these institutions should not be tied to traditional ways of thinking about democratic accountability within nation states. Menon and Weatherill contend moreover that supranationalism can provide a cure for democratic failings of nation states, through legally enforceable obligations that require the state to respect interests that would normally have little or no voice within national decision-making.[189] They are sceptical about arguments designed to address the EU democracy deficit that focus on input legitimacy, such as election of the Commission President, increase in EP control over the executive, and initiatives designed to enhance the electoral accountability and mandate of the EU institutions in accord with voter preferences.[190]

The fourth of the contrasting approaches to democracy and the EU is different yet again. It comes from the work of Nicolaïdis,[191] who starts from the premise that the EU legitimacy deficit will not be addressed by tinkering with its institutions, and that democracy within Europe should be perceived in terms of democratic interdependence. To this end she articulates a concept of 'demoicracy', which has the following connotation.

K Nicolaïdis, European Demoicracy and Its Crisis[192]

European demoicracy is a Union of peoples, understood both as states and as citizens, who govern together but not as one. It represents a third way against two alternatives which both equate democracy with a single demos, whether national or European. As a demoicracy-in-the-making, the EU is neither a Union of democratic states, as 'sovereignists' or 'intergovernmentalists' would have it, nor a Union-as-a-democratic state to be, as 'federalists' would have it. A Union-as-demoicracy should remain an open-ended process of transformation which seeks to accommodate the tensions inherent in the pursuit of radical mutual opening between separate peoples.

To this end Nicolaïdis articulates ten more specific guiding principles that inform her concept of demoicracy. They are: 'autonomy', capturing the idea that Member States should have the right of entry and exit, and that they should remain masters of the Treaty; 'safeguards' to ensure equality of states within the EU; 'plurality' to counter the drift to majoritarianism inherent in modern democratic logic; 'transnationalism' meaning in this context that a demoicracy should give priority to transnational rights and obligations, but guard against coercive assimilation; 'equivalence' connoting a preference for mutual recognition rather than harmonization; 'mediation' whereby those within the nation state translate and own EU policy; 'empowerment', which addresses the desirability of subsidiarity; 'complementarity' between national and EU forms of accountability; 'co-citizenship', meaning the coexistence of national and EU conceptions of citizenship; and 'diversity' the commitment to

---

185 Ibid 2.
186 Ibid 2.
187 Ibid 6–9.
188 Ibid 3.
189 Ibid 3, 10–15, 18.
190 Ibid 4–5, 20–22, 24.
191 K Nicolaïdis, 'European Democracy and Its Crisis' (2013) 51 JCMS 351.
192 Ibid 353.

which in a demoicracy 'should serve as a mental beacon to resist the pull to oneness—be it one people, one state, one voice on the world stage or one story for the EU'.[193]

(ii) *Evaluation: Input Democracy and the EU*

Space precludes detailed consideration of these contending arguments.[194] The following points can nonetheless be made here. The Lisbon Treaty has alleviated but not cured the concerns about input democracy. Council transparency has been improved. The European Parliament has been empowered through extension of the ordinary legislative procedure to new areas. The EP also has greater control over the appointment of the Commission President than hitherto, more especially in the light of the way in which the 2014 EP elections were conducted, in which the respective candidates for Commission President campaigned as the chosen candidate for a particular party in the EP. Thus, while the European Council retains ultimate power over choice of Commission President, it is unlikely to attempt to force a candidate on the EP other than the person who represents the winning party in EP elections. Insofar as the EU has been depicted as a polity in which policy is divorced from party politics, a formal linkage between the dominant party/coalition in the EP and the appointment of the Commission President serves to strengthen the connection between policy and party politics. This alleviates the disjunction of power and responsibility that has underpinned earlier critiques.

There are nonetheless obstacles that subsist to a closer link between policy and politics in the EU, even after the Lisbon Treaty reforms. The EU policy agenda is not exclusively in the hands of the EP and/or Commission. The Council and the European Council have input both *de jure* and *de facto*. The Commission President is only one member of the Commission team, and the other Commissioners will not necessarily be of the same political persuasion as the President or the dominant party in the EP. The absence of a developed party system at the EU level is also important in this respect. EU elections have hitherto been fought by national political parties in which national political issues often predominate, with the result that there was little by way of a clear political agenda on EU issues that was proffered for the voters to choose from. It remains to be seen how far the way in which the 2014 elections were conducted will affect this. It should moreover be acknowledged that disposition of power in the EU is premised on the twin conceptions of legitimacy now embodied in Article 10 TEU: the people are represented through the European Parliament and the Member States in the Council and the European Council. This very division of power means that it is not possible for the people directly to vote out those in power and substitute a party with different policies, since Member State representatives in the Council and European Council are not chosen in this manner.

It would in theory be possible to have a regime in which the people voted directly for two constituent parts of the legislature, the EP and Council, and for the President of the Commission and the President of the European Council. The political reality is that radical change of this kind was not on the political agenda in the debates on the Constitutional and Lisbon Treaties. However even if such a system were to be introduced it would not ensure that the people could exercise electoral control over the direction of EU policy, since the European Council would still be populated by heads of state, who would continue to have a marked influence over the policy agenda, and in addition members of the Commission, with diverse political views, would still be chosen by their Member States. When considering the democracy problems within the EU we should therefore be mindful of causality.

---

[193] Ibid 365.
[194] See Craig (n 167) for more detailed discussion.

P Craig, The Financial Crisis, the EU Institutional Order and Constitutional Responsibility[195]

It is noteworthy that the discourse concerning democracy deficit is normally presented as a critique of the EU. It is the EU qua real and reified entity that suffers from this infirmity, the corollary being that blame is cast on it. The EU is of course not blameless in this respect, but nor are the Member States, viewed collectively and individually. The present disposition of EU institutional power is the result of successive Treaties in which the principal players have been the Member States. There may well be debate as to the relative degree of power wielded by Member States and the EU institutions in the shaping and application of EU legislation, but there is greater consensus on the fact that Member States tend to dominate at times of Treaty reform. The inter-institutional distribution of power is the result of hard fought battles, the results of which are embodied in Treaty amendment. Thus insofar as the present arrangements divide EU policymaking de facto and de jure between the Commission, Council, European Parliament and European Council, this is reflective of power balances that the Member States shaped and were willing to accept. This is readily apparent when considering the initial Rome Treaty and any of the five major Treaty reforms since then. It is powerfully exemplified by the debates concerning institutional reforms in the Constitutional Treaty, which were then taken over into the Lisbon Treaty.

(iii) *Evaluation: Output Legitimacy and the EU*

There are then obstacles to the full realization of input conceptions of democracy in the EU. It can also be acknowledged that legitimacy judged in terms of output is a significant consideration. We should nonetheless be cautious about Menon and Weatherill's contention that because the EU is not a state input democracy is therefore unnecessary or inappropriate at EU level, and that such matters should be addressed at national level.

The EU may not be a state, but it nonetheless has political authority over a wide range of areas. The days when its sole focus was economic have long gone. It exercises significant power over political, social, and economic issues, ever more so with the increasing EU activity in relation to the Area of Freedom, Security, and Justice, and it is more difficult to judge the efficacy of such initiatives in output terms, by way of comparison with market-making. The legislative and executive initiatives undertaken by the EU in this and other areas have never been apolitical. This is true even in relation to core market-making activities. The very balance between the political and the social within the EU has been contested. A glance at the Commission's detailed legislative agenda for any one year, or the longer term plans, reveals strikingly the political choices and value judgements that are inherent in EU decision-making. So too do the choices made by other institutional players, such as the European Council. It is for this very reason that commentators remain concerned about input democracy and the connection, or absence thereof, between political power and electoral accountability. This concern is warranted, notwithstanding the fact that there may be some activities undertaken by nation states that are not subject to the full rigours of the democratic process.

(iv) *Evaluation: Demoicracy and the EU*

There is much to be said for Nicolaïdis' conception of demoicracy, seeking as it does to steer a course between those who equate democracy with a single national or EU demos. It is moreover difficult to

---

[195] F Fabbrini and E Hirsch Ballin (eds), *What Form of Government for the Eurozone?* (Hart, 2015).

disagree with guiding principles such as autonomy, equivalence and the like, at least when they are set at 'headline level'.

There is however room for considerably more contestation when we give concrete application to such principles, for it is here that the devil is truly in the detail. Thus there will, for example, be diverse views on the implications of 'autonomy' for Member State rights to enter and exit, and as to whether the states should be conceived as masters of the Treaty, including what that should entail in terms of decision-making rules. There will equally be differences of view as to the balance between harmonization and mutual recognition that should flow from attachment to 'equivalence', as to the degree of subsidiarity that can and should flow from 'empowerment', and as to the limits of 'plurality'.

(D) EVALUATION: THE SHADOW OF THE FINANCIAL CRISIS

It is important to consider the implications of the financial crisis for democracy in the EU. The issue has been touched on above, and will be considered again below.[196] Suffice it to say the following in this context.

The financial crisis has increased the EU's powers insofar as it led to measures that strengthened centralized control over national economic policy, in order to prevent a recurrence of the crisis. This has led to: increased EU political and economic intrusion in those Member States that encountered particular financial problems; all Eurozone countries are subject to close scrutiny over their national budgets; and non-Eurozone countries are also subject to many such controls. The bottom line is that many matters of macro-economic policy that were hitherto felt to be within the sphere of national sovereignty are now subject to significantly greater control. The constraints placed on national budgets have in turn placed pressure on social policy at national and EU level.

It is also arguable that the financial crisis increased the power of executive institutions at national and EU level at the expense of parliamentary bodies, at least insofar as the making of measures to combat the crisis is concerned. This was particularly so insofar as some measures to combat the crisis were taken outside the confines of the Lisbon Treaty. By way of contrast it should be noted that some EU provisions have increased national parliamentary power by, for example, obliging Member States to provide budgets that are independently verified, which thereby facilitates greater parliamentary oversight.

It is nonetheless important when reflecting on the impact of the crisis for debates concerning EU democracy to recognize that the problems flowed in significant part because the original Treaty provisions stipulated that the EU would have broad powers over monetary union, but far less over economic union. This schema was flawed from the outset, and the Member States were its principal architects. Thus while the EU institutions were not blameless over their handling of the crisis, nor were the Member States, individually or collectively.

11 CONCLUSIONS

i.   Institutional balance between the Commission, Council, and European Parliament has always characterized decision-making within the EU.[197] That balance is dynamic, not static, and it has changed over time. The increase in the EP's power has been a principal feature in that institutional dynamic.

---

[196] See above, pp 22–23, 737–741.
[197] P Craig, 'Institutions, Power, and Institutional Balance' in P Craig and G de Búrca (eds), *The Evolution of EU Law* (Oxford University Press, 2nd edn, 2011) ch 3.

ii. The legitimacy of EU decision-making is now founded on the Council, as representing state interests, and the EP as representing the interests of the peoples of Europe: Article 10 TEU. The Commission, which is increasingly accountable to the EP, seeks to ensure that the goals laid down in the Treaties are met.

iii. The 'message' that emerged from the Lisbon Treaty concerning democracy within the EU was mixed. Those who hoped that it would signal a significant shift to a more parliamentary regime were disappointed. The EP's power over primary legislation was increased. However state interests in the Council and European Council were also reinforced through creation of the longer term Presidency of the European Council and increase in its power.

iv. The reality was therefore that the Lisbon Treaty embodied a regime in which executive and legislative powers were shared between the European Council, Council, EP, and Commission. The sharing of such power has been a principal theme of the Community, and in this respect the Lisbon Treaty represented continuity with the past, even if the power sharing differed in points of detail.

v. Discussion of EU democracy is important. It is however equally important when doing so to be aware of the empirical and theoretical dimension to such discourse.

vi. The empirical dimension requires us to be objective when comparing democracy within the EU with the reality of its operation at national level. We must be equally realistic as to what would happen if the EU did not exist. Not all powers presently exercised by the EU would return to the nation state. Many such issues would be dealt with through bilateral or multilateral international agreements, which are dominated by national executives and do not fare especially well when judged by precepts of democracy.

vii. It is also important to be aware of the theoretical assumptions that underpin any particular version of the democratic critique. The disagreements within the large literature on this topic are often explicable because commentators regard different aspects of democracy as central when evaluating the EU.

12 FURTHER READING[198]

ANDENAS, M, AND TÜRK, A (eds), *Delegated Legislation and the Role of Committees in the EC* (Kluwer, 2000)

ANDERSON, S, AND ELIASSEN, K (eds), *The European Union: How Democratic Is It?* (Sage, 1996)

BELLAMY, R (ed), *Constitutionalism, Democracy and Sovereignty: American and European Perspectives* (Avebury, 1996)

——— AND CASTIGLIONE, D (eds), *Constitutionalism in Transformation: European and Theoretical Perspectives* (Blackwell, 1996)

———, BUFACCHI, V, AND CASTIGLIONE, D (eds), *Democracy and Constitutional Culture in the Union of Europe* (Lothian Foundation Press, 1995)

CHRISTIANSEN, T, AND KIRCHNER, E, *Committee Governance in the European Union* (Manchester University Press, 2000)

CRAIG, P, *The Lisbon Treaty: Law, Politics, and Treaty Reform* (Oxford University Press, 2010)

---

[198] The volume of material means that only books have been listed here.

——AND HARLOW, C (eds), *Lawmaking in the European Union* (Kluwer, 1998)

CURTIN, D, *Postnational Democracy: The European Union in Search of a Political Philosophy* (Kluwer, 1997)

DEHOUSSE, R (ed), *Europe: The Impossible Status Quo* (Macmillan, 1997)

HAYWARD, J (ed), *The Crisis of Representation in Europe* (Frank Cass, 1995)

HOSKYNS, C, AND NEWMAN, M (eds), *Democratizing the European Union* (Manchester University Press, 2000)

JOERGES, C, AND VOS, E (eds), *EU Committees: Social Regulation, Law and Politics* (Hart, 1999)

MANCINI, F, *Democracy and Constitutionalism in the European Union* (Hart, 2000)

NEUNREITHER, K, AND WIENER, A (eds), *European Integration after Amsterdam: Institutional Dynamics and Prospects for Democracy* (Oxford University Press, 2000)

NICOLAÏDIS, K, AND HOWSE, R (eds), *The Federal Vision: Legitimacy and Levels of Governance in the United States and the European Union* (Oxford University Press, 2001)

PIRIS, J-C, *The Lisbon Treaty: A Legal and Political Analysis* (Cambridge University Press, 2010)

PRODI, R, *Europe As I See It* (Polity, 2000)

RICHARDSON, J (ed), *European Union: Power and Policy-Making* (Routledge, 3rd edn, 2006)

VAN GERVEN, W, *The European Union: A Polity of States and Peoples* (Hart, 2005)

WALLACE, H, POLLACK, M, AND YOUNG, R (eds), *Policy-Making in the European Union* (Oxford University Press, 7th edn, 2014)

WEILER, J, *The Constitution of Europe* (Cambridge University Press, 1999)

WESTLAKE, M, *The Commission and the Parliament: Partners and Rivals in the European Policy-Making Process* (Butterworths, 1994)

DECISION-MAKING AND NEW FORMS OF GOVERNANCE

1 CENTRAL ISSUES

i. The aim of this chapter is to introduce the debate over new forms of governance in the EU, and to provide an account of the apparent shift towards greater use of these over time. The discussion will include the reasons suggested for the spread of new modes of governance, as well as some of the debates to which it has given rise.

ii. The language of 'new' forms of governance in the EU is broadly speaking used to refer to a move away from reliance on hierarchical modes towards more flexible modes as the preferred method of governing. These terms will be explained further in the chapter.

iii. There has been considerable debate over the newness or otherwise of these moves, with a range of other terms such as networked governance, reflexive governance, and experimentalist governance used. While acknowledging the contestation over the novelty or otherwise of 'new modes', the chapter suggests that there have been certain changes in preferred governing modes over the last decade or two in the EU, and it outlines the main contours of those changes.

iv. A number of examples of new governance instruments and methods will be given, in particular the 'new approach to harmonization' and the 'open method of coordination'. A number of other EU governance reform initiatives related to the new governance debate will also be discussed, such as the introduction and elaboration of the subsidiarity and proportionality principles, the 'better regulation' initiative, and the Commission White Paper on Governance and its follow-up.

v. While new forms of governance have been more prominent in certain fields such as environmental policy, employment, and social policy, there is also discussion of these governance trends in other issue areas, such as education, corporate governance, and competition enforcement.[1]

---

[1] See, eg, S Deakin, 'Reflexive Governance and European Company Law' (2009) 15 ELJ 224; P Zumbansen, '"New Governance" in European Corporate Law Regulation as Transnational Legal Pluralism' (2009) 15 ELJ 246; B Lange and N Alexiadou, 'New Forms of European Union Governance in the Education Sector? A Preliminary Analysis of the Open Method of Coordination' (2007) 6 European Educational Research Journal 321; I Maher, 'Regulation and Modes of Governance in EC Competition Law: What's New in Enforcement?' (2008) 31 Fordham Int LJ 1713.

2 HIERARCHY, CLASSIC COMMUNITY METHOD, AND NEW GOVERNANCE

The previous chapters have introduced the main instruments and processes used by the EU for making law and policy. We have seen that there is a wide range of such instruments and processes, binding and non-binding, formal and informal, with a fairly complex categorization and hierarchy of instruments and norms. This extensive array of tools and the multiplicity of processes, both formal and informal, for adopting them raise the question of what is meant by 'new' forms of governance.

There has been a lively debate in the EU and elsewhere in recent decades about new forms and modes of governance. Official EU actors and the Commission have referred expressly to the use of new or 'alternative' regulatory mechanisms and forms of governance.[2] Several key EU actors therefore wished to suggest something distinctive about certain ways of making policy, and a number of extensive research projects on the subject were funded.[3] This discussion on new forms of governance is not however unique to the EU, but is part of a broader debate about a shift from 'government' to 'governance', both within states and internationally.[4] Further, while any assertion of novelty in political systems is often a rhetorical or strategic device, the fact that there is a desire to be seen to do something differently usually means that there has been recognition of the inadequacy of past practice, and even a change in rhetoric can lead to substantive change.

The academic and policy literature on new governance in the EU has grown not only in size but in complexity.[5] There have been intense debates over the difference between 'instruments', 'processes', and 'modes', debates over the meaning of 'hard' and 'soft' law, and debates over the meaning of 'law' itself.[6] There are definitions of new governance by reference to actors, instruments, governance attributes,[7] architecture,[8] overall 'modes',[9] or by reference to various combinations of these.[10] The result is a dizzying and often confusing picture for those seeking to grasp the essentials of the debate and a broad overview of what is at stake.

Partly for that reason, this chapter, while acknowledging the inevitable simplification involved in identifying one primary point of analysis for the debate, will emphasize one core and unifying theme, which is *the shift away from hierarchical governance*. In other words, when it comes to the concrete question of what is distinctive about certain forms of EU governing as compared with others, we

---

[2] See, eg, the Commission's White Paper on European Governance, COM(2001) 428, which generated an extensive debate and a series of governance reform initiatives by the Commission.

[3] See, eg, NEWGOV at www.eu-newgov.org; CONNEX at www.mzes.uni-mannheim.de/projekte/typo3/site/file-admin/docs_pdfs/connex_flyer.pdf; REFGOV at http://refgov.cpdr.ucl.ac.be/ which were funded under the EU's Sixth Framework Programme for research.

[4] For some notable examples from a vast literature see J Jordana and D Levi-Faur (eds), *The Politics of Regulation Institutional and Regulatory Reforms for the Age of Governance* (Edward Elgar, 2004); A Héritier, M Stolleis, and F Scharpf (eds), *European and International Regulation after the Nation State: Different Scopes and Multiple Levels* (Nomos, 2004); R Rhodes, *Understanding Governance* (Open University Press, 1997).

[5] For an excellent discussion of complexity and confusion within the debate see C Kilpatrick and K Armstrong, 'Law, Governance and New Governance: The Changing Open Method of Coordination' (2007) 13 CJEL 649.

[6] See, eg, N Walker and G de Búrca, 'Reconceiving Law and New Governance' (2007) 13 CJEL 519.

[7] J Scott and D Trubek, 'Mind the Gap: Law and New Approaches to Governance in the European Union' (2002) 8 ELJ 1.

[8] C Sabel and J Zeitlin, 'Learning from Difference: The New Architecture of Experimentalist Governance in the European Union' (2008) 14 ELJ 271.

[9] H Wallace, 'An Institutional Anatomy and Five Policy Modes. Policy-Making in the European Union' in H Wallace, W Wallace, and M Pollack (eds), *Policy-Making in the European Union* (Oxford University Press, 5th edn, 2005) 49.

[10] C Knill and A Lenschow, 'Modes of Regulation in the Governance of the European Union: Towards a Comprehensive Evaluation', European Integration Online Paper No 7 (2003); P Dabrowksa, *Hybrid Solutions for Hybrid Products: EU Governance of GMOs* (PhD Thesis, EUI Florence, 2006).

suggest that the core of the debate on new governance concerns a move away from hierarchical forms of governing.[11]

The concept of hierarchical governing used here implies a number of different things. It implies that policies come from 'above' or from the centre, and thus are top-down. It implies that the policies are relatively complete, in the sense that they do not leave much room for discretion on the part of those to whom the policies apply, and thus are prescriptive. It implies moreover that prescriptions are obligatory for those to whom they apply, and thus are binding, generally allowing for compulsory legal enforcement.

Within this broad concept of hierarchical governance, many of the dimensions and features used by other commentators in their analyses of new governance are implicated. The emphasis on central governmental *actors* is clearly one, the degree of detail and prescriptive nature of *instruments* is another, and the use of binding measures with reliance on *legal enforceability* is another. Another common description of certain forms of hierarchical governance which refers to the overall style of the governing mode, rather than to actors, instruments, or processes, is the term *command-and-control-type regulation*.

In an influential article on the rise of new governance and its relationship with law in the EU, the 'Classic Community Method' (CCM) of lawmaking was identified by Scott and Trubek as a benchmark against which new forms of governance can be measured.[12] They explain this benchmark CCM as the exercise of legislative power by the EU following the Commission's exercise of its almost exclusive right of initiative, leading to the adoption of legislation by the Council and Parliament, resulting in a binding uniform rule that is subject to the jurisdiction of the CJEU. We can see in this definition the three elements of hierarchical governance set out above: top-down governing by the central institutional actors leading to binding, uniform rules. Formally speaking, with the disappearance of the European Community after the enactment of the Lisbon Treaty, the CCM no longer exists, even though the ordinary legislative procedure reflects most of the same procedural elements. But the CCM serves as a notional ideal-type of the kind of classic centralized lawmaking with which new governance modes are compared. New governance modes have also been contrasted not just with the CCM, but also with typical intergovernmental modes.[13] While very different from the CCM and the ordinary EU legislative procedure, intergovernmental modes are certainly hierarchical in the top-down sense, albeit privileging state actors more than supranational EU actors. Furthermore, while EU intergovernmental decision-making does not generally lead to detailed prescriptive measures, it often results, as under the CFSP, in the adoption of binding measures that are obligatory for the Member States.

The broad argument of this chapter that there has been some move away from hierarchical governing in the EU does not mean that there is little reliance today on top-down, binding, or detailed legal measures. The ordinary legislative procedure is alive and well, as are many other forms of hierarchical EU governance, intergovernmental and otherwise. A 'move away' implies less reliance, but it does not mean the disappearance of hierarchical modes of governance. Nor does a 'move away' imply that there has in the past been an exclusive reliance on hierarchical governing, but rather that this was officially understood in many instances to be the preferred mode or the more effective mode. There has always been, as indicated above, a multiplicity of different processes of lawmaking and policy-making

---

[11] See, however, B Eberlein and A Newman who argue that hierarchy can also be an important resource for 'new' networked governance arrangements: 'Escaping the International Governance Dilemma? Incorporated Transgovernmental Networks in the European Union' (2008) 21 Governance 25.

[12] Scott and Trubek (n 7).

[13] P Zysk, *New Governance and New Terrorism in the EU: The Beauty and the Beast* (PhD Dissertation, EUI Florence, 2006).

in the EU, not all of which could be described as hierarchical. However, the discussion of new forms of governance implies that *some* shift has occurred, that one mode of governing is no longer assumed to be the preferred or the predominant mode, and that other modes and forms have come to the fore and are increasingly promoted, tested, and used. Finally, it may be the case that new governance forms are more readily used in certain areas of policy than others. While there is some empirical evidence for this, with social and environmental policy being two particularly notable fields in this respect, the argument of this chapter is that the tendency to promote new forms of governance seems to be a more general one in the EU, and that all policy areas are potential candidates.

We suggest that the shift towards new modes of governance is characterized by *a move away from hierarchical governing towards more flexible forms of governance*. A shift away from hierarchical governance does not mean that the main institutional actors are not centrally involved in policy-making, but rather that they share that space with other stakeholders, whether states, regional actors, private actors, non-governmental organizations, or others. Policies adopted in accordance with new governance modes are not generally created and imposed top-down. Rather, those to whom they are to be applied are involved in their shaping and application. The move towards more flexible forms of governance does not necessarily mean that there is no legal commitment to the policies that emerge in this way. Some new forms of governance may be wholly voluntaristic, but many others are not. The difference in emphasis as between traditional hierarchical forms of governance and alternative governance modes, even when the latter result in binding legal acts, is that there is likely to be greater room for input, adaptation, and revision on the part of those administering the policies or those to whom they are applicable. It also implies that policy-making is less likely to be rigidly prescriptive or difficult to revise.

In giving an overview of the emergence of new forms of governance in the EU, there is a multitude of examples which could be cited and developments which could be examined. However, given the constraints of space, this chapter will focus on three issues in particular. The first and most specific is the 'new approach to harmonization' which came to prominence in the 1980s as part of the EU's single market programme, and which exemplifies aspects of the move away from hierarchy and towards greater flexibility.[14] The second is the set of developments that were marked by the EU's adoption of the 'Lisbon Agenda' in 2000.[15] A form of policy coordination that became known as the Open Method of Coordination (OMC) was introduced as part of this strategy, and this gave rise to a vast literature, much of which is concerned with its analysis as a new mode of governance.[16] The third does not analyse a development within particular policy fields, but rather examines the more general official emphasis on the need for change in the character of EU regulation and policy-making over the last decade or so. This emphasis can be discerned in a number of related governance initiatives, including the formal introduction of the principles of subsidiarity and proportionality into policy-making by the Maastricht and Amsterdam Treaties;[17] and the Commission's 'better regulation' initiative, which reveals the influence of related public-management theories that resonate with many aspects of new governance, and also the Commission's 2001 White Paper on Governance.[18]

[14] See also Ch 17 for discussion.

[15] Conclusions of the Lisbon European Council Presidency, Mar 2000; The Community Lisbon Programme, COM(2000) 330.

[16] For an excellent collection and classification of the extensive OMC literature until 2010 see the OMC Forum at the EU Center of the University of Wisconsin, Madison, available at http://eucenter.wisc.edu/OMC/index.htm.

[17] See also Ch 3, Section 11, for discussion.

[18] European Governance: A White Paper, COM(2001) 428. For analysis see the collection of papers published as part of an online symposium, 'Mountain or Molehill: A Critical Analysis of the Commission White Paper on Governance', Jean Monnet Working Paper 6/01.

3 THE NEW APPROACH TO HARMONIZATION

We will see in subsequent chapters that the early approach to common-market harmonization involved the attempt to prescribe the desired result through detailed regulation, and that the shortcomings of this approach were gradually recognized.[19] These included the length of time it took to secure agreement on detail, the cumbersome nature of the legislative process, and the need for ongoing updating of the detail. During the 1980s, the Commission decided, as part of the broader relaunch of the internal market, to adopt a 'new approach' to harmonization and to the use of standards in removing 'technical barriers to trade'.[20] The main elements of the new approach were set out by the Council in an annex to its Resolution adopted in 1985:[21]

> The following are the four fundamental principles on which the new approach is based:
> — legislative harmonization is limited to the adoption, by means of Directives based on Article 100 of the EEC Treaty, of the essential safety requirements (or other requirements in the general interest) with which products put on the market must conform, and which should therefore enjoy free movement throughout the Community,
> — the task of drawing up the technical specifications needed for the production and placing on the market of products conforming to the essential requirements established by the Directives, while taking into account the current stage of technology, is entrusted to organizations competent in the standardization area,
> — these technical specifications are not mandatory and maintain their status of voluntary standards,
> — but at the same time national authorities are obliged to recognize that products manufactured in conformity with harmonized standards (or, provisionally, with national standards) are presumed to conform to the 'essential requirements' established by the Directive. (This signifies that the producer has the choice of not manufacturing in conformity with the standards but that in this event he has an obligation to prove that his products conform to the essential requirements of the Directive.)
> In order that this system may operate it is necessary:
> — on the one hand that the standards offer a guarantee of quality with regard to the 'essential requirements' established by the Directives,
> — on the other hand that the public authorities keep intact their responsibility for the protection of safety (or other requirements envisaged) on their territory.

The new approach to harmonization reveals some shift away from the three dimensions of hierarchical governance set out earlier: the monopoly of central institutional actors, the degree of prescriptive detail, and the formally compulsory nature of the norms. Several elements can be noted in this new approach to harmonization.

The first is that although directives continue to be used to set the basic requirements, they are to be limited to the setting of 'essential requirements' that are necessary to ensure public safety and other general interests, thereby reducing the degree of detail and prescriptiveness in the legislation.

---

[19] See Ch 17 on the single market, Ch 19 on quantitative restrictions on the free movement of goods, and Ch 22 on freedom of establishment and services.

[20] Technical Harmonisation and Standardisation: A New Approach, COM(1985) 19.

[21] [1985] OJ C136/1.

Secondly, the task of setting technical standards for the products that have to meet these essential requirements is to be carried out not by the EU legislative institutions themselves, but by European standardization bodies, which are known as CEN and CENELEC, which act with the agreement of the Commission. Thus we see the devolution of aspects of policy-making to bodies other than the formal EU lawmaking institutions, in this case to private standard-setting organizations composed of representatives of national standard-setting organizations, which are in turn generally financed by industry and by governments.

Thirdly, the standards set by these bodies are not compulsory, but remain voluntary. However, manufacturers are given an incentive to abide by the standards set because if their products are certified as being in conformity with them, they benefit from the presumption that they meet the essential requirements of the directive and are entitled to enjoy freedom of movement across the EU market.

The new approach to harmonization has been subsequently revised.[22] There have been difficulties with the process of standard-setting and the standardization bodies,[23] and with the national bodies carrying out conformity assessments.[24] The Commission nonetheless has retained the new approach, which it regards as efficient and successful,[25] and legislation has been enacted to address problems and improve the schema.[26]

It provides a good example of an early instance of new governance, a form of regulation that moved deliberately away from traditional hierarchical lawmaking to a more experimental and flexible one. The new approach has been regularly updated and modernized, and recently the Commission and the Council have undertaken a review of the processes of standardization underpinning the new approach, both within the EU and in the context of European engagement in global standardization bodies and processes.[27]

4 THE LISBON AGENDA AND THE OPEN METHOD OF COORDINATION

In 2000, the European Council at its Lisbon summit introduced a new ten-year set of policy priorities and goals for the EU which dominated the policy agenda for many years afterwards,[28] and has been followed by the Europe 2020 strategy.[29] The overarching aim of the Lisbon Agenda, the 'new strategic goal', was to improve the EU's competitiveness and economic performance *vis-à-vis* the United States, through a range of ambitious policy goals organized along two axes, economic and social.

---

[22] For discussion of the 2008 legislative package 'modernizing' the new approach see Ch 17.

[23] Efficiency and Accountability in Standardization under the New Approach, COM(1998) 291; Council Conclusions of March 2002 on Standardisation [2002] OJ C66/01.

[24] H Schepel, *The Constitution of Private Governance* (Hart, 2005).

[25] Enhancing the Implementation of the New Approach Directives, COM(2003) 240.

[26] See, eg, Regulation (EU) No 1025/2012 of the European Parliament and of the Council of 25 October 2012 on European standardisation [2012] OJ L316/12.

[27] See, eg, Towards an increased contribution from standardization to innovation in Europe, COM(2008) 133; Modernising ICT Standardisation in the EU: the Way Forward, COM(2009) 324; Report of the Expert Panel on Review of the European Standardisation System, at http://ec.europa.eu/enterprise/policies/european-standards/files/express/exp_384_express_report_final_distrib_en.pdf; The annual Union work programme for European standardization for 2015, COM(2014) 500.

[28] There was a mid-term review and relaunch in 2005 of the 'Lisbon Strategy': Working together for growth and jobs: A new start for the Lisbon Strategy, COM(2005) 24; Presidency Conclusions of the Spring European Council, Brussels, 2005.

[29] See the European Council Conclusions, June 2010, http://ec.europa.eu/europe2020/index_en.htm.

The economic goals included shifting to a 'dynamic, knowledge-based economy' and information society, establishing a European area for research and innovation, developing a business-friendly environment, undertaking further internal-market liberalization reforms, integrating financial markets, and coordinating macro-economic policies. The social goals, under the broad umbrella of 'modernizing the European Social model and building an active welfare state', included training and education for the knowledge society, developing an active employment policy, modernizing social protection, pension reform, and promoting social inclusion through anti-poverty measures.

A new policy instrument was introduced alongside these substantive goals, under the name of the Open Method of Coordination. The reality was that the OMC, which was first named in the Lisbon conclusions, drew on two existing policy-coordination processes introduced into the EC Treaty at Maastricht and Amsterdam, in the fields of economic and employment policy respectively. The European Council Conclusions at Lisbon described the method as follows:[30]

Putting Decisions into Practice: A More Coherent and Systematic Approach

Implementing a new open method of coordination

37. Implementation of the strategic goal will be facilitated by applying a new open method of coordination as the means of spreading best practice and achieving greater convergence towards the main EU goals. This method, which is designed to help Member States to progressively develop their own policies, involves:

— fixing guidelines for the Union combined with specific timetables for achieving the goals which they set in the short, medium and long terms;

— establishing, where appropriate, quantitative and qualitative indicators and benchmarks against the best in the world and tailored to the needs of different Member States and sectors as a means of comparing best practice;

— translating these European guidelines into national and regional policies by setting specific targets and adopting measures, taking into account national and regional differences;

— periodic monitoring, evaluation and peer review organised as mutual learning processes.

38. A fully decentralised approach will be applied in line with the principle of subsidiarity in which the Union, the Member States, the regional and local levels, as well as the social partners and civil society, will be actively involved, using variable forms of partnership. A method of benchmarking best practices on managing change will be devised by the European Commission networking with different providers and users, namely the social partners, companies and NGOs.

The four elements set out above comprise the key features of the OMC, although the exact nature of each element (guidelines, measured against benchmarks and indicators, translated into local policies, accompanied by learning-oriented monitoring and evaluation) has varied depending on the policy area in question, and comprises a range of sub-elements. OMC-type processes have been proposed for a range of reasons: sometimes to overcome a political blockage where agreement on some more conventional measure cannot be found; sometimes where formal, legal competence is lacking; and sometimes because it is considered to be the most suitable instrument for achieving the policy goals in question.

---

[30] Lisbon European Council, Presidency Conclusions, 24 Mar 2000.

The origins and broader significance of this policy instrument are discussed below, in an extract from a paper by the woman who is generally credited with being the architect of the OMC, and who was adviser to the Portuguese Presidency of the EU in the lead-up to the Lisbon Council.

João Rodrigues, The Open Method of Coordination as a New Governance Tool[31]

The political construction of Europe is a unique experience. Its success has been dependent on the ability to combine coherence with respect for diversity and efficiency with democratic legitimacy. This entails using different political methods depending on policies and the various institutional processes. For good reasons, various methods have been worked out which are placed somewhere between pure integration and straightforward co-operation.

...

Policies aimed at building the single market, such as monetary policy or competition policy are, logically, based on a stricter method of coordination in relation to the principles to be observed. However, there are other policies which concentrate more on creating new skills and capacities for responding to structural changes. They involve learning more quickly and discovering appropriate solutions. Such policies have resulted in the formulation of strategic guidelines at European level for coping with structural change and which are more open to national diversity.

As a matter of fact the main source of inspiration of the open method of coordination was that of the Luxembourg process regarding European employment strategy. This method was created to overcome a strong political difficulty identified in the preparation of the special European Council of Luxembourg on employment in 1997, because it was impossible to adopt a common target for unemployment reduction, as a counterpart of the common targets for inflation, deficit and debt reduction. But, under the political pressure of this Summit, it became possible to adopt common qualitative guidelines instead. After that, a process was organized whereby Member States emulate each other in applying them, stimulating the exchange of best practices, and defining specific targets while taking account of national characteristics. The European Commission presents the proposal of European guidelines, organises the follow-up and can make recommendations to Member States. Despite some difficulties, the results obtained have been stimulating and encouraging as it is proved by the current National action plans for employment adopted by all Member States. Three years later, the definition of the open method of coordination was expressly undertaken during the preparation of the Lisbon European Council in order to develop the European dimension in new policy fields, namely information society, research, enterprise policy, education and fighting social exclusion...

A. The purpose of the open method of coordination is not to define a general ranking of Member States in each policy but rather to organise a learning process at European level in order to stimulate exchange and the emulation of best practices, and in order to help Member States improve their own national policies.

B. The open method of coordination uses benchmarking as a technique but it is more than benchmarking. It creates a European dimension by defining European guidelines and it encourages management by objectives by adapting these European guidelines to national diversity.

C. The open method of coordination is a concrete way of developing modern governance using the principle of subsidiarity.

D. The open method of coordination can foster convergence on common interest and on some agreed common priorities while respecting national and regional diversities. It is an inclusive method for deepening European construction.

---

[31] In M Telò (ed), 'L'evoluzione della governance europea', Special Issue of 'Europa/Europe', Rome, No 2–3, 2001, 96.

E. The open method of coordination is to be combined with the other available methods depending on the problem to be addressed. These methods can range from integration and harmonisation, to co-operation. The open method of coordination itself takes an intermediate position in this range of different methods. It is an instrument to be added to a more general set of instruments.

...

The open method of coordination can also become an important tool to improve transparency and democratic participation.

Following the Lisbon summit, the OMC was extended to a broad range of policy areas beyond those initially proposed. The point has been made that there is no one single OMC and that it represents a 'cookbook' of recipes, with variants on a theme, rather than a single recipe.[32] Indeed, since the formal introduction by Lisbon of the OMC, many OMC-like processes, or elements of the OMC process, have been applied to a wide range of EU policies and issue areas. Apart from the two pre-existing areas of economic policy coordination and the European employment strategy, OMCs were introduced also in the fields of social exclusion, pensions, and health care, and similar mechanisms were introduced in the fields of research, education, enterprise, and the information society. Some combination of broad common guidelines with local or national elaboration, reporting obligations, peer review, feedback, and development of best practices can be found in many areas of EU policy. The three elements identified in our introductory discussion of the EU's move away from hierarchical governance towards new forms of governance can be seen in the architecture of the OMC as it was introduced by the Lisbon summit.

The first is the shift away from central, top-down governing. As envisaged at Lisbon, the OMC was supposed to involve a fully decentralized approach in line with the principle of subsidiarity in which the Union, the Member States, the regional and local levels, as well as the social partners and civil society, will be actively involved, using variable forms of partnership. While the extent to which OMC processes have been participatory and decentralized has been seriously questioned, there are clearly areas in which participation has been more extensive than in others.[33]

The second element we can see is the move away from the adoption of complete prescriptive policies. In this sense, the OMC architecture is premised on the setting of general guidelines or goals, which are translated into national plans by state and regional actors. It is readily apparent from a critical perspective that the greater the number, and the more detailed the nature of the objectives, targets, and indicators set, the less flexible and the less of a departure from traditional hierarchical governance the particular OMC instrument will be. However, at least as far as its design is concerned, the OMC is clearly intended to promote flexibility and openness, and to facilitate interaction between levels of governance in framing and developing policies.

The third element is the absence of, or a significantly reduced role for, binding instruments and compulsory legal enforcement. While binding rules and legal enforcement play a role within some of the Treaty-based coordination processes, such as economic policy coordination,[34] nonetheless in most of the OMCs legally enforceable or binding norms are scarcely present, or have a less prominent role.

---

[32] J Zeitlin, 'Introduction: The Open Method of Coordination in Question' in J Zeitlin and P Pochet with L Magnusson (eds), *The Open Method of Coordination in Action: The European Employment and Social Inclusion Strategies* (PIE-Peter Lang, 2005), citing Belgian Minister Frank Vandenbroucke.

[33] For critical discussion of the role of civil society in OMC inclusion processes see K Armstrong, 'Tackling Social Exclusion Through OMC: Reshaping the Boundaries of EU Governance' in T Börzel and R Cichowski (eds), *The State of the European Union: Law, Politics, and Society* (Oxford University Press, 2003) 170; K Armstrong, 'Inclusive Governance? Civil Society and the OMC' in S Smismans (ed), *Civil Society and Legitimate European Governance* (Edward Elgar, 2005); K Armstrong, *Governing Social Inclusion—The Law and Politics of EU Co-ordination* (Oxford University Press, 2010).

[34] W Schelkle, 'Hard Law in the Shadow of Soft Law in EU Economic Governance' (2007) 13 CJEL 705.

Like the new approach to harmonization discussed above, the vast literature generated by the OMC contains much that is critical. Criticism has focused on the empirical question of whether the OMC has 'delivered', and on whether it can be said to have policy-steering effects.[35] Other criticisms have focused on normative questions, such as whether it lives up to its original promise of inclusiveness and participation,[36] whether social priorities are subordinated to economic and competitiveness concerns,[37] whether there has been a turn from politics to managerialism,[38] and whether the OMC has functioned primarily as a bureaucratic means of adjusting to the new reality of EMU.[39] Others have launched a more full-fronted challenge to the method as a whole, questioning its empirical effectiveness and cautioning about its impact on the EU institutional balance, and on democracy, rights, and the rule of law in general.[40]

We shall return to some of these criticisms at the end of the chapter. For now, the significance of the OMC is in the fact that it was a policy instrument specifically designed and introduced as an alternative to hierarchical, prescriptively detailed, and binding lawmaking. It was intended as a more flexible instrument that would simultaneously facilitate a degree of policy coordination and also accommodate diversity between the states. Despite its shortcomings in delivering on the strategic goals of the Lisbon summit, OMC-like processes, or processes with some of the features of the OMC, continue to be adopted in a range of very different policy fields, and not only in the original fields identified for this purpose at Lisbon.

5 GENERAL EU GOVERNANCE REFORM INITIATIVES

The preceding sections have given two specific examples of what are sometimes called new forms of governance in the EU. This section, rather than giving another example of a specific instrument or process, outlines a number of more general EU developments and reform initiatives over the last decade or so, which reflect elements of the shift in the preferred mode of governance from hierarchical to

[35] See, eg, M Citi and M Rhodes, 'New Modes of Governance in the EU: Common Objectives versus National Preferences', European Governance Papers No 07/01 (2007); A Moravcsik, 'In Defence of the Democratic Deficit: Reassessing Legitimacy in the EU' (2002) 40 JCMS 603. For more measured accounts of the likely influence of various OMCs see, M Heidenreich and G Bischoff, 'The Open Method of Co-ordination: A Way to the Europeanization of Social and Employment Policies?' (2008) 46 JCMS 497; P Copeland and B ter Haar, 'The (In)Effectiveness of the European Employment Strategy' (2010) available at http://euce.org/eusa/2011/papers/7b_copeland.pdf.

[36] See, eg, S Smismans, 'New Modes of Governance and the Participatory Myth', European Governance Paper 06/01 (2006); 'Efficient and Democratic Governance in a Multi-Level Europe', Final Report of CONNEX, 2008; C Scott, 'Governing Without Law or Governing Without Government? New-ish Governance and the Legitimacy of the EU' (2009) 15 ELJ 160.

[37] M Dawson, 'The Ambiguity of Social Europe in the Open Method of Coordination' (2009) 34 ELRev 55. For arguments as to how to anchor social-policy objectives more firmly within the OMC see J Zeitlin, 'Towards a Stronger OMC in a More Social Europe 2020: A New Governance Architecture for EU Policy Coordination' in E Marlier and D Natali (eds), *Europe 2020: Towards a More Social EU?* (Peter Lang, 2010); A Renewed Commitment to Social Europe: Reinforcing the Open Method of Coordination for Social Protection and Social Inclusion, COM(2008) 418; Opinion of the European Economic and Social Committee, Effective Governance of the Renewed Lisbon Strategy [2009] OJ C175/03.

[38] M Dawson, 'Transforming into What? New Governance in the EU and the "Managerial Sensibility" in Modern Law' (2010) 2 Wisconsin L Rev 389.

[39] D Chalmers and M Lodge, 'The Open Method of Coordination and the European Welfare State', Discussion Paper 11/2003, CARR, London School of Economics.

[40] V Hatzopoulos, 'Why the Open Method of Coordination is Bad for You: A Letter to the EU' (2007) 13 ELJ 309. For more measured arguments about the impact of the OMC on the rule of law see C Joerges, 'Integration Through De-Legislation?' (2008) 33 ELRev 291.

more flexible modes. The first of these is the development of subsidiarity and proportionality in EU law and policy.

(A) SUBSIDIARITY AND PROPORTIONALITY

We saw in Chapter 3 that the subsidiarity principle was formally introduced by the Maastricht Treaty, and that it was inserted into Article 5 TEU (ex Article 5 EC), together with the principle of conferral and the proportionality principle. This was so for a variety of reasons, including a general concern that the EU should not regulate 'unnecessarily'. The guidelines developed in relation to subsidiarity and proportionality, which were initially contained in the European Council Conclusions at Edinburgh in 1992[41] and which led to the subsequent adoption of an inter-institutional agreement on the application of subsidiarity and proportionality, were eventually codified as primary Treaty law in a Protocol added by the Amsterdam Treaty to the EC Treaty.[42] Like the Edinburgh guidelines on which it was based, the Amsterdam Protocol does not focus on the narrow legal definition of subsidiarity, but offers guidelines as to what kind of action should be taken. Further, although the principles of subsidiarity and proportionality are conceptually distinct, the Edinburgh and Amsterdam Protocol guidelines blur this distinction in a useful way:

> 6. The form of [EU] action shall be as simple as possible, consistent with satisfactory achievement of the objective of the measure and the need for effective enforcement. The [EU] shall legislate only to the extent necessary. Other things being equal, directives should be preferred to regulations and framework directives to detailed measures. Directives as provided for in Article [*288 TFEU*], while binding upon each Member State to which they are addressed as to the result to be achieved, shall leave to the national authorities the choice of form and methods.
>
> 7. Regarding the nature and the extent of [EU] action, [EU] measures should leave as much scope for national decision as possible, consistent with securing the aim of the measure and observing the requirements of the Treaty. While respecting [EU] law, care should be taken to respect well established national arrangements and the organisation and working of Member States' legal systems. Where appropriate and subject to the need for proper enforcement, [EU] measures should provide Member States with alternative ways to achieve the objectives of the measures.
>
> ...
>
> 9. Without prejudice to its right of initiative, the [EU] should:
>
> — except in cases of particular urgency or confidentiality, consult widely before proposing legislation and, wherever appropriate, publish consultation documents;
>
> — justify the relevance of its proposals with regard to the principle of subsidiarity; whenever necessary, the explanatory memorandum accompanying a proposal will give details in this respect. The financing of [EU] action in whole or in part from the [EU] budget shall require an explanation;

Although the Amsterdam Treaty Protocol has now been replaced by a shorter Lisbon Treaty Protocol on subsidiarity and proportionality,[43] which devotes more space to the new political control mechanism and omits the guidelines quoted above,[44] the Commission declared that it will continue

---

[41] Available at www.europarl.europa.eu/summits/edinburgh/a1_en.pdf.

[42] G de Búrca, 'Reappraising Subsidiarity's Significance after Amsterdam', Jean Monnet Working Paper 7/1999, available at www.jeanmonnetprogram.org/.

[43] Protocol (No 2) on the application of the principles of subsidiarity and proportionality [2008] OJ L115/ 206.

[44] Ch 3, Section 11(b)(iii).

to use these guidelines and recommends that other actors do so.[45] Several features of the guidelines are noteworthy for present purposes.

First, the general tenor of all of the provisions suggests a move away from hierarchical governance, as we have defined it earlier in the chapter. The very essence of the subsidiarity and proportionality principles is that of restraint as regards the need for regulation and restraint in both the form and the content of regulation. Paragraphs 6–9 above in particular introduce a range of guidelines as to the form and nature of action. The form of action should be as 'simple' as possible; where legislation is chosen directives are to be preferred to regulations, and framework directives are to be preferred to detailed measures.

Secondly, the degree of prescriptiveness of legislation should be reduced. While directives are binding as to their aim, they leave greater room for discretion in their implementation than other measures such as regulations. This point is emphasized further in the recommendation that directives should ideally be 'framework' in nature rather than being detailed measures. There is also an emphasis on leaving room for 'lower' levels of governing to have as much scope for action as possible, and in the more recent Lisbon Treaty Protocol the regions are for the first time mentioned.[46] These features are broadly consistent with a shift away from hierarchical governance, and away from the dominance of centralized, top-down EU action.

Thirdly, the provision for extensive Commission consultation before proposing legislation demonstrates a concern for the involvement of other actors in lawmaking, even if the formal initiative still rests with the Commission.

Finally, even though the two measures listed, directives and regulations, are legally binding, these are suggested as options only where the EU has decided to 'legislate', and paragraph 7 appears to envisage other possibilities, by referring in general terms to EU 'measures' which leave as much scope for national decision as possible. Further, while the Lisbon Treaty Protocol contemplates judicial enforcement at the initiative of states, parliaments, and to some extent regions, arguably the most important enforcement mechanisms it introduces are political and administrative rather than judicial.[47]

Thus the guidelines and the successive Protocols on subsidiarity and proportionality based on these guidelines reflect the promotion of a move away from hierarchical governance. There is an emphasis away from centrally-dominated, detailed, prescriptive legislation, and reference is made instead to the need for broad consultation, to the desirability of leaving greater space for national action, and to the desirability of facilitating alternative ways of achieving broadly agreed aims.

It is nonetheless difficult to appraise the relative success or failure of the efforts to promote a culture of subsidiarity within EU policy-making.[48] The requirement to justify the relevance of proposals with regard to the principle of subsidiarity has led to the insertion of a formalistic 'subsidiarity recital' in most legislation, and more generally there has been much scepticism about the operation of subsidiarity as a principle.[49] Yet it is undoubtedly true that an increasing number of framework directives, as well as many other less prescriptive forms of EU action, have been adopted in recent years in important policy fields, such as water quality, air quality, waste management, eco-design requirements, discrimination in employment, health and safety of workers, and electronic communications. It may

---

[45] COM(2010) 547.

[46] See Arts 2 and 5 of the Lisbon Treaty Protocol on the application of the principles of subsidiarity and proportionality.

[47] Ch 3, Section 11(b).

[48] For the most recent three annual Commission reports on subsidiarity and proportionality adopted as part of the better lawmaking initiative, see COM(2014) 506, COM(2013) 566, and COM(2012) 373.

[49] G Davies, 'Subsidiarity: The Wrong Idea, in the Wrong Place, at the Wrong Time' (2006) 43 CMLRev 63; A Estella, *The Principle of Subsidiarity and its Critique* (Oxford University Press, 2004). See also the discussion in Ch 3, Section 11.

be that the choice of instrument is increasingly being made in consciousness of, even if not always in deference to, the kind of guidance given in the Edinburgh guidelines and Amsterdam Protocol.

(B) BETTER REGULATION AND THE COMMISSION'S WHITE PAPER ON GOVERNANCE

The EU's 'better regulation' initiative has its origins in the same guidelines on subsidiarity and proportionality adopted at Edinburgh in 1992, but this initiative addresses other and more specific issues such as overall simplification of the legislative environment,[50] conducting regulatory impact assessments in particular on business,[51] and the use of alternatives to regulation. This last aspect is of particular interest in the context of assessing the move to new forms of governance.[52]

According to the Commission, the better regulation initiative has three key objectives: promoting the design and application of better regulation tools at the EU level; working more closely with Member States to ensure better regulation principles are consistently applied throughout the EU; and reinforcing constructive dialogue between stakeholders and all regulators at EU and national levels.

In 2003, the European Parliament, Council, and Commission published an Inter-Institutional Agreement on better lawmaking, in which they focused on a number of different issues, including the need for greater transparency of the formal lawmaking process, as well as the need to respect subsidiarity, proportionality, and democracy. A section of the Agreement focused specifically on 'alternative methods of regulation', and in particular the practices of 'co-regulation' and 'self-regulation':

European Parliament, Council and Commission Interinstitutional Agreement on Better Law-making[53]

Use of alternative methods of regulation

16. The three Institutions recall the Community's obligation to legislate only where it is necessary, in accordance with the Protocol on the application of the principles of subsidiarity and proportionality. They recognise the need to use, in suitable cases or where the Treaty does not specifically require the use of a legal instrument, alternative regulation mechanisms.

17. The Commission will ensure that any use of co-regulation or self-regulation is always consistent with Community law and that it meets the criteria of transparency (in particular the publicising of agreements) and representativeness of the parties involved. It must also represent added value for the general interest. . . .

— Co-regulation

18. Co-regulation means the mechanism whereby a Community legislative act entrusts the attainment of the objectives defined by the legislative authority to parties which are recognised in the field

---

[50] See, eg, Simplifying and Improving the Regulatory Environment, COM(2002) 278; First Progress Report on the Strategy for Simplification of the Regulatory Environment, COM(2006) 689; Strategic Review, COM(2006) 689; Implementing the Community Lisbon programme: A strategy for the simplification of the regulatory environment, COM(2005) 535.

[51] Action Programme for Reducing Administrative Burdens in the EU, COM(2007) 23; Impact Assessment, SEC(2007) 84; Better Regulation and Enhanced Impact Assessment, SEC(2007) 926.

[52] G Van Calster, 'An Overview of Regulatory Innovation in the European Union' (2009) 11 CYELS 289, for a critical overview of many of these initiatives.

[53] [2003] OJ C321/01.

(such as economic operators, the social partners, non-governmental organisations, or associations). This mechanism may be used on the basis of criteria defined in the legislative act so as to enable the legislation to be adapted to the problems and sectors concerned, to reduce the legislative burden by concentrating on essential aspects and to draw on the experience of the parties concerned.

...

20. In the context defined by the basic legislative act, the parties affected by that act may conclude voluntary agreements for the purpose of determining practical arrangements. The draft agreements will be forwarded by the Commission to the legislative authority. In accordance with its responsibilities, the Commission will verify whether or not those draft agreements comply with Community law (and, in particular, with the basic legislative act).

At the request of *inter alia* the European Parliament or of the Council, on a case-by-case basis and depending on the subject, the basic legislative act may include a provision for a two-month period of grace following notification of a draft agreement to the European Parliament and the Council. During that period, each Institution may either suggest amendments, if it is considered that the draft agreement does not meet the objectives laid down by the legislative authority, or object to the entry into force of that agreement and, possibly, ask the Commission to submit a proposal for a legislative act.

21. A legislative act which serves as the basis for a co-regulation mechanism will indicate the possible extent of co-regulation in the area concerned. The competent legislative authority will define in the act the relevant measures to be taken in order to follow up its application, in the event of non-compliance by one or more parties or if the agreement fails. These measures may provide, for example, for the regular supply of information by the Commission to the legislative authority on follow-up to application or for a revision clause under which the Commission will report at the end of a specific period and, where necessary, propose an amendment to the legislative act or any other appropriate legislative measure.

— Self-regulation

22. Self-regulation is defined as the possibility for economic operators, the social partners, non-governmental organisations or associations to adopt amongst themselves and for themselves common guidelines at European level (particularly codes of practice or sectoral agreements). As a general rule, this type of voluntary initiative does not imply that the Institutions have adopted any particular stance, in particular where such initiatives are undertaken in areas which are not covered by the Treaties or in which the Union has not hitherto legislated. As one of its responsibilities, the Commission will scrutinise self-regulation practices in order to verify that they comply with the provisions of the EC Treaty.

23. The Commission will notify the European Parliament and the Council of the self-regulation practices which it regards, on the one hand, as contributing to the attainment of the EC Treaty objectives and as being compatible with its provisions and, on the other, as being satisfactory in terms of the representativeness of the parties concerned, sectoral and geographical cover and the added value of the commitments given. It will, nonetheless, consider the possibility of putting forward a proposal for a legislative act, in particular at the request of the competent legislative authority or in the event of a failure to observe the above practices.

A number of key features are noteworthy for the purposes of this chapter in this description of co-regulation and self-regulation.[54]

---

[54] The Commission maintains a database of EU self-regulation and co-regulation initiatives: see www.eesc.europa.eu/?i=portal.en.self-and-co-regulation. For an analysis of EU self-regulation and co-regulation see www.eu-newgov.org/database/DELIV/D04D69_Limits_of_self-regulation.pdf.

In relation to co-regulation, while a legislative framework is initially adopted by the EU, the 'attainment of the objectives' is entrusted to the relevant stakeholders in the field.[55] Those actors then draw up voluntary agreements which are notified to the Commission. Here we see a departure from the three elements of hierarchical governance identified earlier: lawmaking is not to be a top-down process involving only the central government actors; details are not prescribed in the framework legislative act, but are left to the stakeholders to flesh out; and the agreement adopted by the stakeholders is voluntary. As far as enforcement is concerned, it seems that the framework legislation will make provision for 'follow-up' in the event of non-compliance or failure of the agreement, and that such follow-up can ultimately involve a formal enforcement option if the Commission reports to this effect and proposes an amendment to the legislative act or another legislative measure. Further, the formal legislative process remains a default policy-making option, where this is provided for in the framework legislation and where the voluntary agreement fails to meet its objectives. Thus co-regulation is envisaged as a kind of alternative regulation in the shadow of traditional lawmaking. An example of a kind of co-regulation can be seen in the context of the implementation of the Services Directive 2006/123.[56] Article 37(1) provides for 'the drawing up at Community level, particularly by professional bodies, organisations and associations, of codes of conduct aimed at facilitating the provision of services or the establishment of a provider in another Member State'.[57]

Self-regulation, a more radically decentralized option, is defined as the adoption by the relevant economic or other actors of common guidelines at European level.[58] It clearly involves a move away from centralized top-down regulation and from the adoption of prescriptive, binding norms. It may be asked whether it involves any form of EU governance at all, 'new' or otherwise. The answer to this would seem to be that in areas in which the EU has competence to act, but chooses to promote or permit self-regulation instead, the Commission retains a role in scrutinizing self-regulatory practices to check whether they are compatible with EU law requirements. It will report to the other EU lawmaking institutions on the representativeness of the parties involved, and the 'value' and coverage of the commitments made. Further, as in the case of co-regulation, formal legislation remains a default option in the event of failure to follow the practices agreed.

While extensive use has not been made of co-regulation or self-regulation, the Commission has proposed or facilitated these in a number of areas,[59] such as in the field of internet safety[60] and mobile phone safety[61] in relation to children, and in other audiovisual sectors. A self-regulation agreement was also adopted by the European Advertising Standards Alliance, and approved by the Commission.[62] The main critique in relation to this particular form of EU governance concerns its effectiveness, but there is no evidence that more hierarchical forms of regulation are effective or feasible for the kinds of areas in which co-regulation or self-regulation is being proposed.

The better regulation initiative formed part of the Commission's broader governance reform agenda in the late 1990s. In 2001, following several years of consultation and discussion on the need for reform

---

[55] For criticism of the EU's conception of co-regulation as being excessively narrow and 'top-down' see P Verbruggen, 'Does Co-Regulation Strengthen EU Legitimacy?' (2009) 15 ELJ 425.

[56] Ch 22, Section 7.

[57] See http://ec.europa.eu/internal_market/services/services-dir/conduct_en.htm.

[58] F Cafaggi (ed), *Reframing Self-Regulation in European Private Law* (Kluwer Law International, 2006).

[59] For a list of areas in which they have been used see www.eesc.europa.eu/?i=portal.en.self-and-co-regulation. See also, for the suggestion that the conception of co-regulation should be broadened to include subjects such as the social dialogue, Verbruggen (n 55).

[60] http://ec.europa.eu/digital-agenda/en/self-regulation-and-stakeholders-better-internet-kids.

[61] http://ec.europa.eu/digital-agenda/self-regulation-better-internet-kids.

[62] www.easa-alliance.org/.

of EU governance,[63] the Commission adopted its White Paper on European Governance, which drew on a large array of working papers and background documents. According to the Commission, the Paper was intended to make a set of recommendations on how to enhance democracy in Europe and increase the legitimacy of the institutions. It is in some respects an unfocused document, but many of the issues with which it deals are related to the kind of governance reforms discussed in this chapter.[64]

European Governance: A White Paper[65]

There needs to be a stronger interaction with regional and local governments and civil society. Member States bear the principal responsibility for achieving this. But the Commission for its part will:

— establish a more systematic dialogue with representatives of regional and local governments through national and European associations at an early stage in shaping policy,

— bring greater flexibility into how Community legislation can be implemented in a way which takes account of regional and local conditions.

. . .

The Commission will:

— promote greater use of different policy tools (regulations, 'framework directives', co-regulatory mechanisms),

— simplify further existing EU law and encourage Member States to simplify the national rules which give effect to EU provisions.

. . .

A complementary response at EU level is needed in three areas to build a better partnership across the various levels:

— *involvement in policy shaping.* At EU level, the Commission should ensure that regional and local knowledge and conditions are taken into account when developing policy proposals. For this purpose, it should organise a systematic dialogue with European and national associations of regional and local government, while respecting national constitutional and administrative arrangements. . .

— *greater flexibility.* Local conditions can make it difficult to establish one set of rules that covers the whole of the Union, without tying up the legislation in excessive complexity. There should be more flexibility in the means provided for implementing legislation and programmes with a strong territorial impact, provided the level playing field at the heart of the internal market can be maintained.

The Commission is also in favour of testing whether, while respecting the existing Treaty provisions, the implementation of certain EU policies could be better achieved by target-based, tripartite contracts. Such contracts should be between Member States, regions and localities designated by them for that purpose, and the Commission. . . . The area of environmental policy might be a candidate for this pilot approach. Furthermore, the Commission has already committed itself to a more decentralised approach in future regional policy.

. . .

---

[63] For an earlier stage of the governance reform discussion stimulated by the Commission see N Lebessis and J Paterson, 'Evolution in Governance: What Lessons for the Commission? A First Assessment' (European Commission Forward Studies Unit, 1997).

[64] For a later White Paper on Multilevel Governance adopted by the Committee of the Regions see [2009] OJ C211/01.

[65] COM(2001) 428.

Better policies, regulation and delivery

The European Union's policies and legislation are getting increasingly complex. The reluctance of Council and European Parliament to leave more room for policy execution to the Commission means that legislation often includes an unnecessary level of detail...

The level of detail in EU legislation also means that adapting the rules to technical or market changes can be complex and time-consuming. Overall the result is a lack of flexibility, damaging effectiveness...

...

Achieving improvements depends on seven factors:

— first, proposals must be prepared on the basis of *an effective analysis* of whether it is appropriate to intervene at EU level and whether regulatory intervention is needed...

— second, *legislation is often only part of a broader solution* combining formal rules with other non-binding tools such as recommendations, guidelines, or even self-regulation within a commonly agreed framework. This highlights the need for close coherence between the use of different policy instruments and for more thought to be given to their selection,

— third, the *right type of instrument* must be used whenever legislation is needed to achieve the Union's objectives:

— the *use of regulations* should be considered in cases with a need for uniform application and legal certainty across the Union. This can be particularly important for the completion of the internal market and has the advantage of avoiding the delays associated with transposition of directives into national legislation,

— '*framework directives*' should be used more often. Such texts are less heavy-handed, offer greater flexibility as to their implementation, and tend to be agreed more quickly by Council and the European Parliament. Whichever form of legislative instrument is chosen, *more use should be made of 'primary' legislation* limited to essential elements (basic rights and obligations, conditions to implement them), leaving the executive to fill in the technical detail via implementing 'secondary' rules,

— fourth, under certain conditions, implementing measures may be prepared within the *framework of co-regulation*. Co-regulation combines binding legislative and regulatory action with actions taken by the actors most concerned, drawing on their practical expertise. The result is wider ownership of the policies in question by involving those most affected by implementing rules in their preparation and enforcement. This often achieves better compliance, even where the detailed rules are non-binding.

Many of the Commission's suggestions reflect a move away from hierarchical governance. There is emphasis on the need to involve actors other than the main EU legislative organs, and on reducing the detail and prescriptiveness of legislation. There is mention of the need for a mixture of policy instruments, including a range of non-traditional instruments such as tripartite contracts,[66] and including some of the regulatory methods discussed above, such as co-regulation, the OMC, recommendations, and guidelines.

The White Paper initiative was criticized on the grounds that few concrete proposals for change emerged, and the Commission appeared to be primarily concerned with defending its own role. Nevertheless, the White Paper did advance several of the themes that originated in the subsidiarity

---

[66] A framework for target-based tripartite contracts and agreements between the Community, the states and regional and local authorities, COM(2002) 709.

and proportionality guidelines, and subsequently in the better regulation initiative, and clearly manifested the thinking of the Commission on the issue of governance reform.[67]

More recently in the context of the better regulation initiative the Commission introduced the idea of 'smart regulation', which emphasizes the flexible nature of legislation, and the fact that the way it is interpreted and amended in the light of experience is crucial.[68] This idea of flexibility and reflexivity, the capacity to be interpreted and adapted in the light of experience, is emphasized in the scholarly literature on new governance, especially in the literature on experimentalist and reflexive governance.[69]

6 APPRAISING THE MOVE TOWARDS NEW FORMS OF GOVERNANCE

There are two issues that will be briefly addressed in the ensuing discussion. First, the reasons for the rise of new governance methods in the EU will be considered. Secondly, some of the main appraisals and critiques of new governance will be discussed.

J Scott and D Trubek, Mind the Gap: Law and New Governance in the EU[70]

Why do we see increasing use of New Governance in the EU?

'[N]ew governance' covers a number of very disparate mechanisms each of which has its own particular history. Most, if not all, have emerged as pragmatic forms of accommodation between emerging needs of the Union and available mechanisms for policy making. While detailed histories of all these mechanisms are not available, six factors seem to explain the new governance trend.

a. Increasing complexity and uncertainty of the issues on the agenda

New governance can be seen as a way of coping with complex problems under conditions of uncertainty and thus the trend to new governance may well reflect the increasing salience of such complex problems on the Union's agenda. We can see this within the Union's traditional areas of competence as well as in some of the newer areas it is engaging with. Thus, for example, the unexpected complexities involved in 're-regulation' under the Single Market led to the emergence of the comitology system, and as the Union moves into new areas such as employment and social exclusion it starts to tackle problems that have stymied many Member States for years and for which no easy or uniform solution exists.

b. Irreducible diversity

Not only are many of the problems the Union is now dealing with highly complex; they also may simply not allow for uniform solutions. This is certainly true of many of the issues confronted by the European Employment Strategy (EES) OMC. The underlying systems of industrial relations and social protection

---

[67] For recent developments in the better regulation initiative see Regulatory Fitness and Performance Programme (REFIT): State of Play and Outlook, COM(2014) 368, and http://ec.europa.eu/smart-regulation/index_en.htm.

[68] Smart Regulation in the EU, COM(2010) 543; Strengthening the foundations of Smart Regulation—improving evaluation, COM(2013) 686; http://ec.europa.eu/smart-regulation/index_en.htm.

[69] See, eg, C Sabel and J Zeitlin (eds), *Experimentalist Governance in the European Union—Towards a New Architecture* (Oxford University Press, 2010); O De Schutter and J Lenoble (eds), *Reflexive Governance—Redefining the Public Interest in a Pluralistic World* (Hart, 2010).

[70] (N 7).

of the fifteen Member States vary tremendously, and there is rarely one solution that will work effectively in all these diverse settings...

c. New approaches to public administration and law

The trend to new governance has undoubtedly been influenced by developments in the fields of public administration and law. One can see elements of some of the practices we are calling new governance in domestic administrative law and public administrative practice in Europe and the United States. In these fields, there has been a growing recognition of the limits of traditional top-down regulatory approaches, and repeated calls for things like power sharing, participation, management by objectives, and experimentation.

d. Competence 'creep'

Some of the new approaches may have been adopted to deal with areas where legal authority for EU level action is limited or non-existent. This may well be true of some of the areas to be covered by future OMCs. While the EES has a treaty base, there is no explicit treaty base for such areas as social exclusion and pensions. In such cases, new governance may or may not be the best available approach to policy making, but it may be the only way the Union can play a role in a particular domain.

e. Legitimacy

New Governance often reflects an effort to secure legitimacy for EU policy making. The social dialogue seems to solve some of the democratic deficit problems in the area it covers by essentially delegating law making authority to representatives of the parties to be affected by these laws....

f. Subsidiarity

...While the pressure [*suggested above*] may well have impelled the Union towards new approaches had there been no independent subsidiarity doctrine, the strength of this doctrine and the political forces behind it certainly added impetus to the trend.

A slightly different, although broadly complementary, account of the reasons for the rise, or to use their terms, the 'explosion', of new governance forms in the EU is given by Sabel and Zeitlin. They provide an account of new governance in the EU as a form of experimentalism, and explain it in terms of an architecture with four key features: first, the setting of framework goals by the EU institutions and the states; secondly, freedom on the part of lower-level authorities or units to pursue those goals as they see fit; thirdly, a requirement that these lower-level authorities report regularly on their performance and participate in some form of mutually comparative peer review; and fourthly, periodic review of the framework goals and of the processes by those who established them.

**C Sabel and J Zeitlin, Learning from Difference: The New Architecture
of Experimentalist Governance in the EU**[71]

Given the growing recognition of the need to learn from diversity in order to harmonize, coordinate, and revise regulatory rules without imposing an unworkable uniformity, the new architecture took shape roughly between the mid-1980s and 2000, i.e. between the Single European Act and the

---

[71] (2008) 14 ELJ 271.

Lisbon Summit. For purposes of exposition, and with no pretension to taxonomic comprehensiveness or precision, we can say that the architecture was elaborated more or less independently in three domains: re-regulation of privatized network infrastructure, public health and safety, and social-solidarity [*The authors also refer to Justice and Home Affairs as a fourth domain*]. . . .

From roughly the turn of the millennium onwards, as we will see, the new architecture became available not only as a response to catastrophic breakdowns in regulatory capacity (food safety, maritime safety/pollution) or the threat of these (financial market supervision), but also as a means for unblocking rule-making in domains that had become stalemated by struggles between proponents of (traditional) centralization and (traditional) decentralization (competition policy, state aid). In this most recent period, innovations associated with one of the three originating domains of the new architecture are more and more often proposed for others (such as OMCs in occupational health and safety and fundamental rights or councils of national regulators attached to agencies in drug authorization and maritime safety—to mention only examples that we discuss below). This suggests that the actors perceive commonalities to the problems arising in the three domains, and for that reason are confident that variants of the problem-solving architecture that address these commonalities in one setting can be adapted to address them in others.

Notice that the possibility or scope conditions for experimentalist governance are distinct and much broader than the historical contexts from which the new architecture emerged in particular policy-sectors and in the EU more generally. The possibility conditions for experimentalist governance are arguably quite minimal: strategic uncertainty, meaning that policy makers recognize that they cannot rely on their strategic dispositions (e.g. more market vs. more plan) to guide action in a particular domain (or equivalently that they do not know *how* to achieve their declared goals); and a multi-polar or polyarchic distribution of power, in which no single actor has the capacity to impose her own preferred solution without taking into account the views of the others. . . . Together these conditions open up the possibility for transforming distributive bargaining into deliberative problem-solving through the institutional mechanisms of experimentalist governance.

Thus while Scott and Trubek emphasize the complexity of problems, the need to accommodate diversity, the lack of legal powers, the search for new ways of making policy-making more legitimate, and the political influence of the subsidiarity concept as reasons which explain the increasing adoption of new governance mechanism, Sabel and Zeitlin focus additionally on actual or potential crisis, the breakdown of regulatory authority, as well as the existence of uncertainty as to how to address problems in a situation of mutual interdependence. It is certainly evident from sources such as the Lisbon conclusions that there was a great deal of uncertainty about how to tackle a variety of the EU's social and economic problems, while documents such as the White Paper on Governance clearly reveal the anxiety of the Commission and other EU institutional actors in relation to the EU's perceived legitimacy and in relation to the effectiveness of its regulatory capacity and performance.

The verdict as to whether new governance methods have been successful in addressing complex EU social and economic problems where other methods of regulation have proven inadequate has been mixed. Many critics have focused on the question of effectiveness, since it is difficult to prove particular concrete results for some of the softer policy instruments, including the OMC. Evaluations of the impact, influence, and effectiveness of such instruments differ significantly.[72] Further, others have taken the view that, given the admitted inadequacies of command-and-control-type regulation in so many relevant fields, criticisms of new governance for not demonstrating adequate results are

---

[72] See, eg, Citi and Rhodes (n 35); Moravcsik (n 35). For strong counter-arguments see J Zeitlin, 'The Open Method of Coordination in Action: Theoretical Promise, Empirical Realities, Reform Strategy' in Zeitlin and Pochet with Magnusson (n 32). For some more recent evaluations see M Heidenreich and G Bischoff, 'The Open Method of Co-ordination: A Way to the Europeanization of Social and Employment Policies?' (2008) 46 JCMS 497; Copeland and ter Haar (n 35).

misdirected and premature. A separate argument is that some of the virtues of new governance methods are in the novel processes, and not just in their policy outcomes: the virtues of greater participation, for example, or the virtues of knowledge-creation and experimentation as goods in themselves; or the virtues of reflexivity and revisability in the face of changing circumstances.

Another set of critiques has focused less on the ineffectiveness of new governance mechanisms, and more on the assumption that they have an adverse impact on a range of constitutional values: on the institutional balance in the EU, on the rule of law, on fundamental rights, and on democracy itself.[73] Other analyses have focused on specific aspects of the legitimacy critique,[74] such as the problem of accountability,[75] and the problem of democratic or other forms of participation.[76] One robust response to these critiques is the suggestion that new governance modes may well necessitate some productive re-conceptualization of settled understandings of 'the institutional balance', legal values, and even of democracy, in particular in the non-state context of the EU.[77]

7 CONCLUSIONS

i. The topic of new governance modes in the EU is a lively and contested one. The rise of new regulatory methods is viewed by some with scepticism and distrust.

ii. There has been a concerted emphasis in the EU over the past two decades in particular on the need to reform governance in ways which depart from traditional, hierarchical forms of lawmaking and policy-making. Specific regulatory initiatives such as the New Approach and the OMC, as well as broader governance-reform initiatives such as the better regulation strategy and the operationalization of the principles of subsidiarity and proportionality, attest to this.

iii. The verdict thus far on the significance, impact, and legitimacy of new governance modes is mixed. Nevertheless, the rise of 'new', 'reflexive', or 'experimentalist' governance methods has given rise to a whole range of interesting and complex new research questions, as well as a set of challenges to traditional conceptions of law and legal regulation. Empirically based appraisals of the operation of new governance modes in various fields are beginning to appear, but as yet there is no firm consensus on the question of their influence and effectiveness.

8 FURTHER READING

The literature on new governance is vast, and for that reason the list of further reading includes only a selective range of electronic resources, books, and journal issues, in particular those with some legal focus, and does not list any individual papers or articles.

---

73 Hatzopoulos (n 40).

74 Scott (n 36).

75 Y Papadopoulos, 'Problems of Democratic Accountability in Network and Multilevel Governance' (2007) 13 ELJ 469; A Benz, 'Accountable Multilevel Governance by the Open Method of Coordination?' (2007) 13 ELJ 505; C Harlow and R Rawlings, 'Promoting Accountability in Multilevel Governance: A Network Approach' (2007) 13 ELJ 542; Dawson (n 38).

76 'Efficient and Democratic Governance in a Multi-Level Europe', Final Report of CONNEX, 2008. See also the literature cited at (n 36).

77 C Sabel and W Simon, 'Epilogue' in G de Búrca and J Scott (eds), *Law and New Governance in the EU and the US* (Hart, 2006). See more generally the essays in the special issue of the Columbia J European L (2007) vol 13.

(a) Websites

CONNEX at www.mzes.uni-mannheim.de/projekte/typo3/site/fileadmin/docs_pdfs/connex_flyer.
pdf

NEWGOV at www.eu-newgov.org/

REFGOV at http://refgov.cpdr.ucl.ac.be/

> While the three Commission-funded research projects listed above have officially ended, their results are still available online.

OMC Forum at http://eucenter.wisc.edu/OMC/index.htm (not updated since 2009)

(b) Journal Issues

Special Issue of (2002) 8 ELJ

Special Issue of (2004) 11 JEPP

Special Issue of (2007) 29 J European Integration

Special Issue of (2007) 13 ELJ

Special Issue of (2007) 13 Columbia J European L

Special Issue of (2009) 15 ELJ

Special Issue of (2010) 4 Wisconsin L Rev

(c) Books

ARMSTRONG, KA, *Governing Social Inclusion—The Law and Politics of EU Co-ordination* (Oxford University Press, 2010)

BACHE, I, *Europeanization and Multilevel Governance: Cohesion Policy in the European Union and Britain* (Rowman & Littlefield, 2008)

CAFAGGI, F (ed), *Reframing Self-Regulation in European Private Law*, Private Law in European Context Series (Kluwer Law International, 2006)

DE BÚRCA, G, AND SCOTT, J (eds), *Law and New Governance in the EU and the US* (Hart, 2006)

DE SCHUTTER, O, AND LENOBLE, J (eds), *Reflexive Governance: Redefining the Public Interest in a Pluralistic World* (Hart, 2010)

JORDAN, A, AND SCHOUT, A, *The Coordination of the European Union: Exploring the Capacities of Networked Governance* (Oxford University Press, 2008)

KOHLER-KOCH, B, AND LARAT, F (eds), *European Multi-Level Governance: Contrasting Images in National Research* (Edward Elgar, 2009)

SABEL, CF, AND ZEITLIN, J (eds), *Experimentalist Governance in the European Union—Towards a New Architecture* (Oxford University Press, 2010)

SCOTT, J, *Environmental Protection: European Law and Governance* (Oxford University Press, 2009)

TÖMMEL, I, AND VERDUN, A (eds), *Innovative Governance in the European Union: The Politics of Multilevel Policymaking* (Lynne Rienner, 2009)

ZEITLIN, J, POCHET, P, with MAGNUSSON, L (eds), *The Open Method of Coordination in Action: The European Employment and Social Inclusion Strategies* (PIE-Peter Lang, 2005)

THE NATURE AND EFFECT OF EU LAW: DIRECT EFFECT AND BEYOND

1 CENTRAL ISSUES

i. The doctrine of 'direct effect' applies in principle to all binding EU law including the Treaties, the Charter of Fundamental Rights, general principles, secondary legislation, and international agreements. The most problematic issues for many years concerned directives and international agreements.[1] In recent years the direct effect of general principles of EU law and of the provisions of the Charter of Fundamental Rights has been pleaded before the CJEU. Current uncertainties concern the possible horizontal direct effect of general principles and of Charter provisions.

ii. The meaning of direct effect remains contested. In a broad sense it means that provisions of binding EU law which are sufficiently clear, precise, and unconditional to be considered justiciable *can be invoked and relied on* by individuals before national courts. There is also a 'narrower' or classical concept of direct effect, which is defined in terms of the capacity of a provision of EU law to *confer rights* on individuals.

iii. While directives can be enforced directly by individuals against the state after the time limit for their implementation has expired (vertical direct effect), resulting where necessary in the disapplication of conflicting domestic law, the CJEU has ruled that they cannot of themselves impose obligations on individuals (no horizontal direct effect). The rationale for this limitation on direct effect of directives is however contestable.

iv. This is more especially so given that other legal mechanisms have been developed by the Court to give effect to directives which have not properly been implemented or are not being properly applied. First, the Court has interpreted the concept of the 'state' broadly for the purposes of vertical direct effect. Secondly, there is an obligation on national courts to interpret domestic law, as far as possible, in conformity with directives (indirect effect, or the principle of harmonious interpretation) after the time limit for their implementation has expired. Thirdly, during the period after adoption of a directive but before the time limit for implementation has expired, all organs of the state, including courts, must refrain from adopting any measure or interpretation

---

[1] The legal effect of international agreements is considered in Ch 10, since the distinct issues concerning the direct effect of international agreements can best be understood in the context of the international relations of the EU more generally.

liable seriously to compromise the result prescribed by the directive. Fourthly, a directive can in certain cases be legally invoked in proceedings between private parties (incidental effect) so long as the directive does not in itself impose a legal obligation on one of the parties. Fifthly, a general principle of EU law that covers the same ground as a directive can in certain circumstances bind private parties. Finally, where a regulation refers to a directive and makes compliance with the directive conditional on receipt of benefits under the regulation this can bind private parties.

v. The number of qualifications to the rule that directives do not have horizontal direct effect, and the difficulties of each exception, has made this area of law increasingly complex and difficult to understand.

2. DIRECT EFFECT: A GUIDE

The topic dealt with in this chapter is central to EU law. It has been developed by the ECJ and its jurisprudence has become more complex over the years. The discussion in this section is designed to help the reader navigate some of the difficulties.

(1) The starting point is the distinction between *public and private enforcement*. The Treaty has an express mechanism for *public enforcement* in Article 258 TFEU, allowing the Commission to sue Member States before the Court for breach of EU law. This compulsory jurisdiction was unusual, since most international treaties contain no such mechanism. However, the Commission lacked the capacity to prosecute more than a tiny fraction of possible infringements; the remedy under Article 169 EEC (now Article 258 TFEU), the original version of public enforcement, was weak; and the Article could not be used against private individuals.[2]

(2) The ECJ therefore took the bold step of legitimating *private enforcement* of EU law. It held that Treaty Articles could on certain conditions have direct effect, such that individuals could rely on them before their national courts and challenge national action for violation of EU law. This brought individuals into the EU legal order. The domestic effect of an international treaty had traditionally been determined by the constitutional law of each state party to that treaty. In countries which adopt a dualist approach to international law, international agreements bind only the states at an intergovernmental level and, in the absence of implementation, cannot be directly domestically enforced by citizens.[3] Yet the ECJ ruled that the EEC Treaty was different from other treaties.

(3) From the outset, however, there was *uncertainty about the exact meaning of the term direct effect*.[4] The ECJ's case law supports both a broad or a narrow definition of direct effect.[5] The broader definition, which can arguably be derived from *Van Gend en Loos*, can be expressed as *the capacity of a provision of EU law to be invoked before a national court*.[6] This is sometimes referred to as

---

[2] P Craig, 'Once upon a Time in the West: Direct Effect and the Federalization of EEC Law' (1992) 12 OJLS 453.

[3] D Wyatt, 'New Legal Order or Old' (1982) 7 ELRev 14.

[4] See the earlier discussion of differences in meaning between the terms 'direct applicability' and 'direct effect', which the ECJ used interchangeably: T Winter, 'Direct Applicability and Direct Effects' (1972) 9 CMLRev 425; Case 131/79 *Santillo* [1980] ECR 1585, 1608–1609, AG Warner; Case C–253/00 *Muñoz v Frumar Ltd* [2002] ECR I–7289, AG Geelhoed; P Eleftheriadis, 'The Direct Effect of Community Law: Conceptual Issues' (1996) 16 YBEL 205.

[5] S Prechal, 'Does Direct Effect Still Matter?' (2000) 37 CMLRev 1047 and *Directives in EC Law* (Oxford University Press, 2nd edn, 2005); M Lenz, D Tynes, and L Young, 'Horizontal What? Back to Basics' (2000) 25 ELRev 509; C Hilson and T Downes, 'Making Sense of Rights: Community Rights in EC Law' (1999) 24 ELRev 121.

[6] In Case 26/62 *Van Gend en Loos* [1963] ECR 13 the ECJ ruled that Art 12 should be interpreted 'as producing direct effects and creating individual rights', thus implying that the latter followed from, but was not necessarily a condition for, the former.

'objective' direct effect.[7] The normal consequence of a legal provision being invoked, as in *Van Gend en Loos*, is that it confers a legal right on the individual who invokes it, but this is not, on the broader definition, an essential component of direct effect. The narrower 'classical' definition of direct effect is usually expressed in terms of the *capacity of a provision of EU law to confer rights on individuals which they may enforce before national courts*. This is sometimes referred to as 'subjective' direct effect. The degree of difference between these formulations depends however on the definition of 'right' being used. If what is meant is simply the *right to invoke* EU law in a national court,[8] then there is little difference between the narrow and the broad notions of direct effect.[9] In many other cases, however, the ECJ has gone beyond the simple reference to a right to invoke, and has indicated that an individual litigant can rely before a national court on the substantive right, such as the right to be free from discrimination based on nationality.[10] Moreover if the 'conferral of rights on individuals' involves the entitlement to a particular remedy[11] or the imposition of a corresponding duty or liability on another party,[12] then there may be a relevant difference between the broad and the narrow definitions. In reality, the Court seems to use the language of 'conferral of rights' in the context of direct effect in several different senses. This ambiguity in the meaning of direct effect is not of purely academic interest, but has important practical implications.[13]

(4) In the next stage the ECJ, having established that Treaty Articles could have direct effect, *expanded the concept* in two ways: the conditions for direct effect were subtly loosened, and the refined doctrine was applied to regulations and decisions as well as Treaty Articles.

(5) The *judicial focus then shifted to directives*. Many observers doubted whether directives could have direct effect, since they did not meet the original conditions laid down in *Van Gend*. The ECJ nonetheless held that directives were capable in principle of direct effect. Controversially, however, it ruled that directives were only capable of *vertical direct effect*, meaning that they could only be raised against the state or a state entity. They were not capable of having *horizontal direct effect*, in the sense that they could not impose obligations on a private party.

(6) The *vertical/horizontal distinction applied to directives has generated a complex jurisprudence that is difficult for litigants and national courts*. The ECJ has fashioned numerous ways in which, even though directives do not have horizontal direct effect, they can impact on national law. Thus the Court has adopted a broad definition of the state; it has developed a doctrine of 'indirect effect' or obligation of harmonious interpretation; and it has introduced the concept of 'incidental horizontal effects', whereby a directive can preclude reliance on a provision of national law that is inconsistent with the provisions of the directive even in an action between

---

[7] W Van Gerven, 'Of Rights, Remedies and Procedures' (2000) 37 CMLRev 501; D Edward, 'Direct Effect, the Separation of Powers and the Judicial Enforcement of Obligations' in *Scritti in Onore di Giuseppe Federico Mancini, vol II: Diritto dell' Unione Europea* (Guiffrè, 1998) 423.

[8] Case C–63/99 *Gloszczuk* [2001] ECR I–6369; Case C–257/99 *Barkoci and Malik* [2001] ECR I–6557; Case C–235/99 *Kondova* [2001] ECR I–6427; Case C–268/99 *Jany* [2001] ECR I–8615; Case C–327/02 *Panayotova* [2004] ECR I–11055, [18].

[9] A related question, if the narrower 'subjective' definition is adopted, concerns *who* can invoke the rights conferred by a directly effective provision of law: see Cases C–87–89/90 *Verholen* [1991] ECR I–3757; C–72/95 *Kraaijeveld* [1996] ECR I–5403, [57]–[60]; C–240–244/98 *Océano Grupo Editorial v Rocio Murciano Quintero* [2000] ECR I–4491; C–230/97 *Awoyemi* [1998] ECR I–6781. Also Cases C–83/11 *Muhammad Sazzadur Rahman and Others* EU:C:2012:519, [25]; C–165–167/09 *Stichting Natuur en Milieu and Others* EU:C:2011:348, [99]–[100]; and C–115/09 *Bund für Umwelt und Naturschutz Deutschland, Landesverband Nordrhein-Westfalen eV* EU:C:2011:289.

[10] Case 57/65 *Lütticke v Hauptzollamt Sarrelouis* [1966] ECR (Sp Ed) 205.

[11] Prechal, 'Does Direct Effect Still Matter?' (n 5); M Ruffert, 'Rights and Remedies in European Community Law: A Comparative View' (1997) 34 CMLRev 307; Van Gerven (n 7).

[12] Hilson and Downes (n 5).

[13] Thus, eg, the ECJ has held that even though directives do not give rise to rights between private parties they can nonetheless be invoked in certain ways before national courts.

private parties. This is premised on the primacy of EU law and entails a distinction between a directive 'excluding' inconsistent national law; and a directive having a 'substitution' effect.[14] The tenability of this distinction is questionable, as will be seen below. The ECJ has also held that general principles of law can bind private parties and that the content of the general principle can be drawn from a directive. It has also decided that directives can be enforced horizontally when they are referred to in regulations.

(7) Developments in the case law on direct effect are still ongoing. In particular, the question whether provisions of the Charter of Fundamental Rights may have direct effect between private parties has been raised but not yet answered by the Court.

(8) It is clear that direct effect in the classic 'subjective' sense of the capacity of a provision of EU law to confer rights on individuals that they may enforce before national courts, is increasingly just one way for Union law to impact on national law. The principle of harmonious interpretation, incidental horizontal effect, and the combined effect of different sources and rules of EU law provide different ways in which EU law can impact on national legal systems.[15]

3 DIRECT EFFECT OF PRIMARY LAW: TREATY ARTICLES, GENERAL PRINCIPLES, AND THE CHARTER OF FUNDAMENTAL RIGHTS

(A) THE FOUNDATIONS: DIRECT EFFECT OF TREATY PROVISIONS IN *VAN GEND EN LOOS*

The ECJ first articulated its doctrine of direct effect in 1963 in what remains the most famous of all of its rulings.[16]

Case 26/62 NV Algemene Transporten Expeditie Onderneming van Gend en Loos v Nederlandse Administratie der Belastingen
[1963] ECR 1

[Note Lisbon Treaty renumbering: Art 12 is now Art 30 TFEU, Art 169 is now Art 258 TFEU, Art 170 is now Art 259 TFEU, and Art 177 is now Art 267 TFEU]

Van Gend en Loos imported a quantity of chemicals from Germany into the Netherlands. It was charged with an import duty which had allegedly been increased (by changing the tariff classification from a lower to a higher tariff-heading) since the coming into force of the EEC Treaty, contrary to Article 12. On appeal against payment before the Dutch Tariefcommissie, Article 12 was raised in argument and two questions were referred to the ECJ. The first was 'whether Article 12 of the EEC

---

[14] Case C–244/98 *Océano Grupo* (n 9) [26]–[39], AG Saggio; Case C–287/98 *Luxemburg v Linster* [2000] ECR I–6917, [57]–[90], AG Leger.

[15] K Lenaerts and T Corthaut, 'Of Birds and Hedges: The Role of Primacy in Invoking Norms of EU Law' (2006) 31 ELRev 287; S Robin-Olivier, 'The Evolution of Direct Effect in the EU: Stocktaking, Problems, Projections' (2014) 12 ICON 165

[16] See M Rasmussen, 'Revolutionizing European Law: A History of the *Van Gend en Loos* Judgment' (2014) 12 ICON 136 and JHH Weiler '*Van Gend en Loos*: The Individual as Subject and Object and the Dilemma of European Legitimacy' (2014) 12 ICON 94.

Treaty has direct application within the territory of a Member State; in other words, whether nationals of such a State can, on the basis of the Article in question, lay claim to individual rights which the courts must protect'. Observations were submitted to the Court of Justice by the Belgian, German, and Dutch governments. Belgium argued that the question was whether a national law ratifying an international treaty would prevail over another law, and that this was a question of national constitutional law which lay within the exclusive jurisdiction of the Dutch court. The Dutch government argued that the EEC Treaty was no different from a standard international treaty, and that the concept of direct effect would contradict the intentions of those who had created the treaty.

THE ECJ

To ascertain whether the provisions of an international treaty extend so far in their effects it is necessary to consider the spirit, the general scheme and the wording of those provisions.

The objective of the EEC Treaty, which is to establish a Common Market, the functioning of which is of direct concern to interested parties in the Community, implies that this Treaty is more than an agreement which merely creates mutual obligations between the contracting states. This view is confirmed by the preamble to the Treaty which refers not only to governments but to peoples. It is also confirmed more specifically by the establishment of institutions endowed with sovereign rights, the exercise of which affects Member States and also their citizens. Furthermore, it must be noted that the nationals of the states brought together in the Community are called upon to cooperate in the functioning of this Community through the intermediary of the European Parliament and the Economic and Social Committee.

In addition the task assigned to the Court of Justice under Article 177, the object of which is to secure uniform interpretation of the Treaty by national courts and tribunals, confirms that the states have acknowledged that community law has an authority which can be invoked by their nationals before those courts and tribunals. The conclusion to be drawn from this is that the Community constitutes a new legal order of international law for the benefit of which the states have limited their sovereign rights, albeit within limited fields, and the subjects of which comprise not only Member States but also their nationals. Independently of the legislation of Member States, Community law therefore not only imposes obligations on individuals but is also intended to confer upon them rights which become part of their legal heritage. These rights arise not only where they are expressly granted by the Treaty, but also by reason of obligations which the Treaty imposes in a clearly defined way upon individuals as well as upon the Member States and upon the institutions of the Community....

The wording of Article 12 contains a clear and unconditional prohibition which is not a positive but a negative obligation. This obligation, moreover, is not qualified by any reservation on the part of states which would make its implementation conditional upon a positive legislative measure enacted under national law. The very nature of this prohibition makes it ideally adapted to produce direct effects in the legal relationship between Member States and their subjects.

The implementation of Article 12 does not require any legislative intervention on the part of the states. The fact that under this Article it is the Member States who are made the subject of the negative obligation does not imply that their nationals cannot benefit from this obligation....

It follows from the foregoing considerations that, according to the spirit, the general scheme and the wording of the Treaty, Article 12 must be interpreted as producing direct effects and creating individual rights which national courts must protect.

In addition the argument based on Articles 169 and 170 of the Treaty put forward by the three governments which have submitted observations to the court in their statements of case is misconceived. The fact that these Articles of the Treaty enable the Commission and the Member States to bring before the court a state which has not fulfilled its obligations does not mean that individuals cannot plead these obligations, should the occasion arise, before a national court...

A restriction of the guarantees against an infringement of Article 12 by Member States to the procedures under Article 169 and 170 would remove all direct legal protection of the individual rights of their nationals. There is the risk that recourse to the procedure under these articles would be ineffective if it were to occur after the implementation of a national decision taken contrary to the provisions of the Treaty.

The vigilance of individuals concerned to protect their rights amounts to an effective supervision in addition to the supervision entrusted by Articles 169 and 170 to the diligence of the Commission and of the Member States.

Van Gend en Loos was a ground-breaking judgment. The strong interventions made on behalf of three governments, constituting half of the existing Member States, indicated that the concept of direct effect, understood as the *immediate enforceability by individual applicants of those provisions in national courts*, probably did not accord with the understanding of those states of the obligations they assumed when they created the EEC. The ECJ nonetheless held that Treaty Articles could in principle have direct effect.

It *reasoned partly from the text of the Treaty*. It pointed to the Preamble which makes reference to citizens as well as to states, and argued that the preliminary ruling procedure established in what is now Article 267 TFEU envisaged that parties before national courts could plead and rely on points of Community law.[17] The ECJ pointed also to the fact that citizens were envisaged as having a role to play under the Treaties through the European Parliament. This textual 'evidence' for direct effect is not particularly strong. The ECJ's argument based on Article 267 TFEU is nonetheless interesting. We do not have the *travaux préparatoires* and hence we do not know what the Treaty framers intended with this provision. If however individuals could not invoke EU law in national courts through Article 267 then it could only ever be used if the parties to the case were both public bodies, and there is nothing in the wording of Article 267 to indicate any such limitation. The ECJ replayed this same argument when it justified the direct effect of directives.[18]

The ECJ's *reasoning was also characterized by a vision of the kind of legal community that the Treaties seemed designed to create*. The case provides an early example of the ECJ's teleological methodology, which involves the Court reading the text, and the gaps therein, in such a way as to further what it determines to be the underlying and evolving aims of the Community enterprise as a whole. The ECJ's vision for the EEC was very different from that advanced by the Member States.

It held that the Community was not to be regarded as simply a compact between states, but was also concerned with the peoples of those states. The famous language of a 'new legal order of international law' was designed to introduce the idea that individuals could derive rights from the EEC Treaty, even if that was not normally the case.

The ECJ also rejected the other argument of the Member States. It held that public enforcement of EEC law through the Commission via what is now Article 258 TFEU did not preclude private enforcement via direct effect. Thus the Court developed the concept of direct effect principally in view of the kind of legal system it considered necessary to carry through the ambitious economic and political programme outlined in the Treaties. The ECJ considered that strong enforcement was needed to ensure that Member States complied with the provisions to which they had agreed. Automatic internalization of Treaty rules within national legal systems would strengthen the effectiveness of

---

[17] Note, however, that it is not a corollary of this reasoning that preliminary references can only be made in relation to directly effective provisions of EU law, despite the occasional attempt by governments to argue this: see, eg, C–416/10 *Križan* EU:C:2013:8, [56] and C–370/12 *Pringle* EU:C:2012:756, [89].

[18] See the discussion of Case 41/74 *Van Duyn v Home Office* [1974] ECR 1337 below.

Community norms as well as aiding the Commission in its Article 258 enforcement function by involving individuals and all levels of the national court system directly in their implementation. Consider in this respect the view of Pierre Pescatore, a former judge of the Court.

P Pescatore, The Doctrine of 'Direct Effect': An Infant Disease of Community Law[19]

It appears from these considerations that in the opinion of the Court, the Treaty has created a Community not only of States but also of peoples and persons and that therefore not only Member States but also individuals must be visualised as being subjects of Community law. This is the consequence of a democratic ideal, meaning that in the Community, as well as in a modern constitutional State, Governments may not say any more what they are used to doing in international law: *L'Etat, c'est moi*. Far from it; the Community calls for participation of everybody, with the result that private individuals are not only liable to burdens and obligations, but that they have also prerogatives and rights which must be legally protected. It was thus a highly political idea, drawn from a perception of the constitutional system of the Community, which is at the basis of *Van Gend en Loos* and which continues to inspire the whole doctrine flowing from it.

(B) THE CONDITIONS FOR DIRECT EFFECT: BROADENING THE CONDITIONS

The ECJ in *Van Gend en Loos* established the initial conditions for a Treaty Article to have direct effect. It established the requirement, familiar from international law, that a provision be essentially 'self-executing'. Thus the criteria which were met by Article 12 EEC and which enabled it to have direct effect were that it was: *clear, negative, unconditional, containing no reservation on the part of the Member State, and not dependent on any national implementing measure.* Subsequent case law however broadened and loosened these initial conditions.

The condition that the Treaty Article should be *clear and unconditional, containing no reservation on the part of the Member States*, was soon qualified. In *Salgoil*, the ECJ held that the existence of Member State discretion to limit the free movement of goods on the grounds set out in Article 36 TFEU did not preclude the direct effect of Article 34 TFEU, since the cases coming within Article 36 were exceptional and did not undermine the clear obligation in Article 34.[20] Similarly in *Van Duyn*[21] the ECJ rejected the argument that what is now Article 45(3) TFEU, which allows limitations to the free movement of workers on grounds of public policy, public security, or public health, prevented Article 45 from having direct effect, because 'the applications of these limitations is subject to judicial control'.[22] The idea that direct effect could apply even where Member States possess discretion, because the exercise thereof could be judicially controlled, represented a significant juridical shift in thinking about direct effect.

The *idea that direct effect was precluded where further measures were required at national level* was also modified. Instead, provided the *basic principle* governing the relevant area was sufficiently

---

[19] (1983) 8 ELRev 155, 158.

[20] Case 13/68 *SpA Salgoil v Italian Ministry of Foreign Trade* [1968] ECR 453. See recently, for the direct effect of Art 29 concerning quantitative restrictions on exports, Case C–161/09 *Kakavetsos-Fragkopoulos AE Epexergasias kai Emporias Stafidas* EU:C:2011:110.

[21] Case 41/74 *Van Duyn v Home Office* [1974] ECR 1337.

[22] Ibid [7]; Case C–156/91 *Hansa Fleisch Ernst Mundt GmbH & Co KG v Landrat des Kreises Schleswig-Flensburg* [1992] ECR I–5567, [15].

certain, it could have direct effect, notwithstanding the absence of implementing measures at Community or national level.[23] Thus Article 49 TFEU, for example, provided that restrictions on freedom of establishment of Community nationals in states other than that of their nationality were to be abolished 'within the framework of the provisions set out below'. This framework was to have included a general programme and a set of directives to liberalize the activities of employed and self-employed persons, but few of these had been adopted by the time the *Reyners* case arose in 1973.

Case 2/74 **Reyners v Belgium**
[1974] ECR 631

[Note Lisbon Treaty renumbering: Arts 52, 54, and 57 are now Arts 49, 50, and 53 TFEU]

Reyners was a Dutch national who obtained his legal education in Belgium, but was refused admission to the Belgian Bar (as *avocat*) because he lacked Belgian nationality. He challenged the Belgian legislation before the Conseil d'Etat, which referred several questions to the ECJ, including whether Article 52 was directly effective in the absence of implementing directives under Articles 54 and 57. The Belgian Government argued that Article 52 merely laid down a principle that was to be complemented by secondary legislation, and that it was not for the Court to exercise a discretionary power reserved to the legislative institutions of the Community and the Member States.

THE ECJ

24. The rule on equal treatment with nationals is one of the fundamental legal provisions of the Community.

25. As a reference to a set of legislative provisions effectively applied by the country of establishment to its own nationals, this rule is, by its essence, capable of being directly invoked by nationals of all the other Member States.

26. In laying down that freedom of establishment shall be attained at the end of the transitional period, Article 52 thus imposes an obligation to attain a precise result, the fulfilment of which had to be made easier by, but not made dependent on, the implementation of a programme of progressive measures.

27. The fact that this progression has not been adhered to leaves the obligation itself intact beyond the end of the period provided for its fulfilment....

...

29. It is not possible to invoke against such an effect the fact that the Council has failed to issue the directive provided for by Articles 54 and 57 or the fact that certain of the directives actually issued have not fully attained the objective of non-discrimination required by Article 52.

30. After the expiry of the transitional period the directives provided for by the Chapter on the right of establishment have become superfluous with regard to implementing the rule on nationality, since this is henceforth sanctioned by the Treaty itself with direct effect.

Thus the basic principle of non-discrimination was deemed to be directly effective, even though the conditions for genuine freedom of establishment were far from being achieved. Whereas many cases on direct effect concern the enforcement of obligations against a Member State which has failed

---

[23] Case C–268/06 *Impact v Minister for Agriculture and Food* [2008] ECR I–2483, [66]–[67].

to implement EU requirements properly, the *Reyners* case shows the Court employing direct effect to compensate for insufficient action on the part of the EU legislative institutions.

A similar use of direct effect to 'trigger' proper implementation of a Treaty provision can be seen in the second *Defrenne* judgment,[24] which relaxed further the original *Van Gend en Loos* criteria for direct effect. While in *Reyners* the terms of Article 49 seemed to envisage further implementing measures, Article 141 EC (now Article 157 TFEU) in *Defrenne* appeared to lack sufficient precision to be directly enforced by a national court. Article 141 at that time required states to ensure 'the application of the principle that men and women should receive equal pay for equal work'. Neither the Commission nor the states considered the provision to be directly effective or legally complete, on the basis that the term 'principle' was not very specific and the terms 'pay' and 'work' were not defined.[25] The Court, however, identified the *principle* of Article 141 at the time, that of equal pay for equal work, and held it to have direct effect.

The Court's concern was to ensure that the EU's aims were not ignored either by reluctant Member States or by sluggish EU institutions, during the years of so-called legislative sclerosis which followed the Luxembourg Accords.[26] This story has been told most fully by Weiler, who has explained how impediments to attainment of Community objectives through the political process, decisional supranationalism, led to the growing importance of normative supranationalism.[27] The doctrines of direct effect and the supremacy of Community law were central in this respect, enabling the ECJ to develop EU law, notwithstanding the difficulties in securing enactment through the legislative process. If a national court was unsure of the exact meaning of the relevant provision, the ECJ was more than willing to clarify its scope through the preliminary ruling procedure.

The original conditions for direct effect have therefore been loosened in the years since *Van Gend en Loos*, although there are certainly cases where the ECJ finds that a Treaty Article does not have direct effect.[28] The current position can be summarized as follows: *a Treaty Article will be accorded direct effect provided that it is sufficiently clear, precise, and unconditional to be invoked by individuals.*[29] This criterion clearly leaves the EU Courts with considerable room for manoeuvre. A provision of EU law can be relied on by an individual and applied by a court where it sets out an obligation in unconditional and unequivocal terms.[30]

(C) TREATY ARTICLES: VERTICAL AND HORIZONTAL DIRECT EFFECT

In most instances the claimant will seek to use direct effect vertically, against the state or an emanation of the state. However, the ECJ has also ruled that Treaty Articles can have horizontal direct effect, such as to impose an obligation on a private party.[31]

---

[24] Case 43/75 *Defrenne v Société Anonyme Belge de Navigation Aérienne* [1976] ECR 455.

[25] Ibid 485, AG Trabucchi.

[26] Ch 1.

[27] J Weiler, 'The Community System: The Dual Character of Supranationalism' (1981) 1 YBEL 267, and 'The Transformation of Europe' (1991) 100 Yale LJ 2403, 2412–2431.

[28] Case T–191/99 *Petrie v ALLS I/CDFL* [2001] ECR II–3677, [34]–[35]: Art 255 EC was not unconditional and required further implementation before it could be relied upon for a precise result; Case 126/86 *Zaera v Institutio Nacionale de la Seguridad Social* [1987] ECR 3697, [10]–[11], the promotion of accelerated living standards in Art 2 EC did not confer rights on individuals; Case C–379/09 *Maurits Casteels* EU:C:2011:131, where Art 42 TFEU lacked direct effect.

[29] Pescatore (n 19) 176–177; Lenaerts and Corthaut (n 15) 311.

[30] Cases C–246–249/94 *Cooperativa Agricola Zootecnica S Antonio v Amministrazione delle Finanze dello Stato* [1996] ECR I–4373, [19]; C–317/05 *Pohl-Boskamp GmbH & Co KG v Gemeinsamer Bundesausschuss* [2006] ECR I–10611, [41]; C–194/08 *Gassmayr v Bundesminister für Wissenschaft und Forschung*, EU:C:2010:386, [45].

[31] See also Case 43/75 *Defrenne v SABENA* [1976] ECR 455. For a critique of these developments see H Schepel, 'Constitutionalizing the Market, Marketising the Constitution, and to Tell the Difference: On the Horizontal

Case C–438/05 **International Transport Workers' Federation and Finnish Seamen's Union
v Viking Line ABP and OÜ Viking Line Eesti**
[2007] ECR I–10779
[Note Lisbon Treaty renumbering: Art 43 EC is now Art 49 TFEU]

The dispute arose between trade unions and Viking Line, a shipping company, concerning rates of pay. The unions sought to prevent Viking from shifting its legal base to Estonia, because this would result in lower rates of pay for seamen as compared with what they earned when Viking was legally based in Finland. Viking argued, *inter alia*, that the unions' labour action violated the Treaty provisions on freedom of establishment. The ECJ therefore considered whether these provisions had horizontal direct effect.

THE ECJ

56. By that question, the referring court is asking in essence whether Article 43 EC is such as to confer rights on a private undertaking which may be relied on against a trade union or an association of trade unions.

57. In order to answer that question, the Court would point out that it is clear from its case-law that the abolition, as between Member States, of obstacles to freedom of movement for persons and freedom to provide services would be compromised if the abolition of State barriers could be neutralised by obstacles resulting from the exercise, by associations or organisations not governed by public law, of their legal autonomy (*Walrave and Koch*, paragraph 18; *Bosman*, paragraph 83; *Deliège*, paragraph 47; *Angonese*, paragraph 32; and *Wouters and Others*, paragraph 120).

58. Moreover, the Court has ruled, first, that the fact that certain provisions of the Treaty are formally addressed to the Member States does not prevent rights from being conferred at the same time on any individual who has an interest in compliance with the obligations thus laid down, and, second, that the prohibition on prejudicing a fundamental freedom laid down in a provision of the Treaty that is mandatory in nature, applies in particular to all agreements intended to regulate paid labour collectively (see, to that effect, Case 43/75 *Defrenne* [1976] ECR 455, paragraphs 31 and 39).

59. Such considerations must also apply to Article 43 EC which lays down a fundamental freedom.

. . .

62. This interpretation is also supported by the case-law on the Treaty provisions on the free movement of goods, from which it is apparent that restrictions may be the result of actions by individuals or groups of such individuals rather than caused by the State (see Case C–265/95 *Commission v France* [1997] ECR I–6959, paragraph 30, and *Schmidberger*, paragraphs 57 and 62).

66. In the light of those considerations, the answer to the second question must be that Article 43 EC is capable of conferring rights on a private undertaking which may be relied on against a trade union or an association of trade unions.

(D) GENERAL PRINCIPLES OF EU LAW

Another source of primary EU law is the general principles of EU law. This category of EU law derives from the case law of the ECJ in the 1970s, long before the drafting of the EU Charter of Fundamental

Application of the Free Movement Provisions in EU Law' (2012) 18 ELRev 177. Compare P Caro de Sousa, 'Horizontal Expression of Vertical Desires: Horizontal Effect and the Scope of the EU Fundamental Freedoms' (2013) 2 Cambridge Journal of International and Comparative Law 479.

Rights. Article 6(3) TEU now proclaims that 'fundamental rights, as guaranteed by the ECHR and as they result from the constitutional traditions common to the Member States, shall constitute general principles of the Union's law'. While general principles of law have often been invoked in combination with other sources of EU law in domestic litigation, or as a ground of review under Article 263 TFEU in litigation against the EU, and hence have been implicitly treated as having at least vertical direct effect, the question whether a general principle of law could have horizontal direct effect was not expressly addressed until more recently.

In *Mangold*, however, the ECJ declared that there was a general principle of non-discrimination on grounds of age in EU law and that when hearing a dispute concerning age discrimination which involved the provisions of a directive whose time limit for being brought into force had not yet expired, national courts must set aside national law which conflicts with that principle.

Case C–144/04 **Mangold v Rüdiger Helm**
[2005] ECR I–9981

THE ECJ

74. [D]irective 2000/78 does not itself lay down the principle of equal treatment in the field of employment and occupation. Indeed, in accordance with Article 1 thereof, the sole purpose of the directive is 'to lay down a general framework for combating discrimination on the grounds of religion or belief, disability, age or sexual orientation', the source of the actual principle underlying the prohibition of those forms of discrimination being found, as is clear from the third and fourth recitals in the preamble to the directive, in various international instruments and in the constitutional traditions common to the Member States.

75. The principle of non-discrimination on grounds of age must thus be regarded as a general principle of Community law. Where national rules fall within the scope of Community law, which is the case with Paragraph 14(3) of the TzBfG, as amended by the Law of 2002, as being a measure implementing Directive 1999/70...and reference is made to the Court for a preliminary ruling, the Court must provide all the criteria of interpretation needed by the national court to determine whether those rules are compatible with such a principle (Case C–442/00 *Rodríguez Caballero* [2002] ECR I–11915, paragraphs 30 to 32).

76. Consequently, observance of the general principle of equal treatment, in particular in respect of age, cannot as such be conditional upon the expiry of the period allowed [to] the Member States for the transposition of a directive intended to lay down a general framework for combating discrimination on the grounds of age, in particular so far as the organisation of appropriate legal remedies, the burden of proof, protection against victimisation, social dialogue, affirmative action and other specific measures to implement such a directive are concerned.

77. In those circumstances it is the responsibility of the national court, hearing a dispute involving the principle of non-discrimination in respect of age, to provide, in a case within its jurisdiction, the legal protection which individuals derive from the rules of Community law and to ensure that those rules are fully effective, setting aside any provision of national law which may conflict with that law (see, to that effect, Case 106/77 *Simmenthal* [1978] ECR 629, paragraph 21, and Case C–347/96 *Solred* [1998] ECR I–937, paragraph 30).

The ruling was controversial since it seemed to require national courts to give immediate effect to the terms of a directive and to set aside conflicting national law even before the time limit allowed to Member States under the directive had expired, but the Court achieved this result by focusing on the legal effect of the general principle of EU law rather than on the directive.[32] The implications of the case for the horizontal direct effect of directives is discussed further below.[33]

The Court reaffirmed the core of its *Mangold* ruling about the legal effects of general principles in *Kücükdeveci*.[34] Here the Court specified more precisely that the general principle of non-discrimination will apply and require the setting aside of conflicting national law only when the case 'falls within the scope of EU law'.[35] One of the ways in which it may be brought within the scope of EU law is by the terms of a directive, as in *Kücükdeveci* itself. Yet the Court in *Kücükdeveci* insisted that although the principle of non-discrimination on grounds of age was given specific expression in a directive in that case, it was not the directive but rather the general principle of non-discrimination 'which must be the basis of the examination of whether EU law precludes national legislation such as that at issue in the main proceedings'.[36]

It is not clear which other general principles of law may be found by the Court to be directly effective. In *Römer* the CJEU implied—without actually saying so—that the principle of non-discrimination on grounds of sexual orientation may be a general principle of EU law, but backed away from the most controversial element of *Mangold* by clarifying that the case would not fall within the scope of EU law until the time limit for implementation of the relevant directive in the case had expired.[37] Nevertheless, the central proposition that a general principle of law (and certainly the general principle of non-discrimination) may be invoked by individuals in order to set aside conflicting national laws whenever the case falls within the scope of EU law has by now been firmly asserted in several cases by the Court, including in horizontal cases between private parties.[38]

While some have praised the development and lauded the potential impact of this somewhat qualified doctrine of the direct effect of general principles,[39] others have cautioned about the complexity and uncertainty introduced by the move.[40] One major uncertainty is created by the difficulty of discerning what exactly brings a case within the 'scope of EU law' for the purposes of the direct effect of general principles of law, and whether interaction with the provisions of a directive will be necessary for this to occur. The Court's case law is far from clear on this.[41] It is also unclear which

---

[32] For some of the cases in which the AG questioned the reasoning in *Mangold*, see Case C–321/05 *Kofoed v Skatteministeriet* [2007] ECR I–5795, [67], AG Kokott; Cases C–55–56/07 *Othmar Michaeler v Amt für sozialen Arbeitsschutz and Autonome Provinz Bozen* [2008] ECR I–3135, [14]–[29], AG Ruiz-Jarabo Colomer; Case C–411/05 *Félix Palacios de la Villa v Cortefiel Servicios SA* [2007] ECR I–8531, [79]–[100], AG Mazák.

[33] See below pp 220–221.

[34] Case C–555/07 *Kücükdeveci v Swedex GmbH & Co KG* EU:C:2010:365. See also Cases C–250–268/09 *Georgiev* (n 101). For comment see F Fontanelli, 'General Principles of the EU and a Glimpse of Solidarity in the Aftermath of *Mangold* and *Kücükdeveci*' (2011) 17 EPL 225; P Cabral and R Neves, 'General Principles of EU Law and Horizontal Direct Effect' (2011) 17 EPL 437; M de Mol, 'The Novel Approach of the CJEU on the Horizontal Direct Effect of the Principle of Non-Discrimination' (2011) 18 Maastricht Journal of European and Comparative Law 109; E Muir, 'Of Ages in—and Edges of—EU Law' (2011) 48 CMLRev 39.

[35] Case C–555/07 *Kücükdeveci* EU:C:2010:365, [23]. For a case which was held not to fall within the scope of EU law for the purposes of the application of the principle of non-discrimination on grounds of age, see Case C–427/06 *Bartsch* [2008] ECR I–7245.

[36] Ibid [27].

[37] Case C–147/08 *Römer* EU:C:2011:286, [59]–[63]; Case C–427/06 *Bartsch* (n 35) [18]. For criticism of the CJEU's strategy of avoidance and ambiguity in *Römer*, see L Pech, 'Between Judicial Minimalism and Avoidance: The Court of Justice's Side-Stepping of Fundamental Constitutional Issues in *Römer* and *Dominguez*' (2012) 49 CMLRev 1841.

[38] Apart from Cases C–555/07 *Kücükdeveci* and C–147/08 *Römer*, see also Case C–476/11 *HK Danmark* EU:C:2013: 590 and Cases C–501–506, 540 and 541/12 *Specht* EU:C:2014:2005, [89].

[39] See Cabral and Neves (n 34).

[40] See S Robin-Olivier, 'The Evolution of Direct Effect in the EU: Stocktaking, Problems, Projections' (2014) 12 ICON 165. Also de Mol (n 34).

[41] Compare, eg, Cases C–144/04 *Mangold* [2005] ECR I–9981 and C–427/06 *Bartsch* (n 35).

general principles may be sufficiently precise in their content to be capable of direct effect.[42] A further complexity is created by the impact of this development on the CJEU's continued rejection of the horizontal direct effect of directives. This aspect will be discussed further below. For now, we move on to consider another and related source of primary EU law whose direct effect has also been raised before the CJEU: the Charter of Fundamental Rights.

(E) THE CHARTER OF FUNDAMENTAL RIGHTS

The Charter of Fundamental Rights became formally binding in late 2009, and since then its provisions have been invoked many times before the CJEU. The Charter enjoys the same binding legal status as the EU Treaties, and is part of the primary law of the EU. Article 51 of the Charter provides that its provisions are addressed to the EU institutions, and to the Member States when implementing Union law. Hence it would seem to follow logically that where a provision of the Charter is clear, precise, and unconditional, it would have direct effect just as Treaty provisions do. The vertical effect of the Charter has certainly been evident in a number of cases before the CJEU, in which parties have successfully invoked its provisions to challenge EU law[43] or national law.[44] While the Court has not used the language of direct effect in relation to the Charter, it has allowed provisions of the Charter to be successfully invoked to challenge conflicting EU or domestic law.

It was less clear, however, whether the Court would accept that provisions of the Charter could have horizontal direct effect in cases between private parties. On the one hand, as we have seen above, Treaty provisions have been held to be horizontally directly effective, and the Charter enjoys the same legal status as the Treaties.[45] On the other hand, like many international human rights instruments including the ECHR, the provisions of the Charter seem to be expressed in terms of the obligations and duties of Member States and of EU institutions rather than private parties.[46]

The possible horizontal effect of provisions of the Charter has been raised before the CJEU in a number of cases, and was discussed at length by Advocate General Trstenjak in *Dominguez*, but the Court chose not to address the issue there.[47] In the *AMS* case, the direct effect of Article 27 of the EU Charter, concerning the right of workers to information and consultation, was raised in a case between two private parties.

Case C–176/12 Association de médiation sociale (AMS) v Union locale des syndicats CGT, Laboubi and others
EU:C:2014:2

According to Article L.1111-3 of the French Labour Code, workers employed on certain types of contracts, including those maintained by AMS (a private body), were excluded from the calculation of the number of employees for the purposes of representation. Using this rule, AMS took the view that it did not reach

---

[42] For a case which establishes a different point about the legal effect of general principles of EU law, namely their applicability to the EU institutions and the obligation to interpret EU staff regulations in their light, see Case C–579/12 RX-II *Strack* EU:C:2013:570, concerning the principle of entitlement to paid annual leave.

[43] See, eg, Cases C–293 and 594/12 *Digital Rights Ireland v Minister for Communications et al* EU:C:2014:238.

[44] See, eg, Case C–617/10 *Åklagaren v Hans Åkerberg Fransson* EU:C:2013:105.

[45] (N 31) above.

[46] Note, however, that AG Cruz Villalón in Case C–167/12 *AMS* EU:C:2013:491 compared the Charter to a Constitution, rather than to a human rights instrument, and was prepared to contemplate the horizontal application of the Charter provisions in accordance with the constitutional analogy.

[47] Case C–282/10 *Dominguez* EU:C:2011:559, AG Trstenjak.

the minimum threshold of fifty employees which would make the appointment of a union representative compulsory under the Labour Code. Despite this, a trade union created a work council within the AMS, and appointed an AMS employee, Mr Laboubi, as the representative. In litigation initiated by AMS before the French courts, the compatibility of Article L.111-3 with EU Directive 2002/14 and with Article 27 of the Charter was raised. The Cour de Cassation made a preliminary reference to the CJEU, asking amongst other things whether Article 27 of the Charter could be invoked between the parties. The CJEU began by ruling that despite the discretion left to Member States under the Directive, the obligation contained therein to take account of *all* employees when calculating thresholds was directly effective against the state, and that the relevant provision of the French Labour Code was thus incompatible with the Directive. However, the Directive could not be invoked horizontally against AMS, which is a private body, and national law in this case could not be read *contra legem* under the principle of harmonious interpretation. The Court then turned to the question whether Article 27 of the Charter could be invoked instead against AMS, since the case fell within the scope of EU law for the purposes of the application of the Charter.

THE CJEU

44. It must also be observed that Article 27 of the Charter, entitled 'Workers' right to information and consultation within the undertaking', provides that workers must, at various levels, be guaranteed information and consultation in the cases and under the conditions provided for by European Union law and national laws and practices.

45. It is therefore clear from the wording of Article 27 of the Charter that, for this article to be fully effective, it must be given more specific expression in European Union or national law.

46. It is not possible to infer from the wording of Article 27 of the Charter or from the explanatory notes to that article that Article 3(1) of Directive 2002/14, as a directly applicable rule of law, lays down and addresses to the Member States a prohibition on excluding from the calculation of the staff numbers in an undertaking a specific category of employees initially included in the group of persons to be taken into account in that calculation.

47. In this connection, the facts of the case may be distinguished from those which gave rise to *Kücükdeveci* in so far as the principle of non-discrimination on grounds of age at issue in that case, laid down in Article 21(1) of the Charter, is sufficient in itself to confer on individuals an individual right which they may invoke as such.

48. Accordingly, Article 27 of the Charter cannot, as such, be invoked in a dispute, such as that in the main proceedings, in order to conclude that the national provision which is not in conformity with Directive 2002/14 should not be applied.

49. That finding cannot be called into question by considering Article 27 of the Charter in conjunction with the provisions of Directive 2002/14, given that, since that article by itself does not suffice to confer on individuals a right which they may invoke as such, it could not be otherwise if it is considered in conjunction with that directive.

Unlike the Advocate General, therefore, who addressed the question of horizontal direct effect directly, and who also argued that Article 27 could be invoked together with an EU Directive against a private party,[48] the Court made no definitive pronouncement on the issue, and gave no clear indication whether a provision of the Charter which is more specific and precise than Article 27 might be invoked between private parties.[49] It is interesting also to note that the more precise provisions of

[48] See n 46. Note that the AG considered Art 27 of the Charter to be a 'principle' rather than a 'right', in the terms of Art 52(5) of the Charter, another issue which the Court did not address.

[49] For some of the commentaries on the case, see D Leczykiewicz, 'Horizontal Application of the Charter of Fundamental Rights' (2013) 38 ELRev 479; N Lazzerini, '(Some of) the Fundamental Rights Granted by the Charter May

the Directive could not compensate for the more open-ended provisions of Article 27 of the Charter, given the lack of horizontal direct effect of the Directive. Although it may be tempting to read paragraphs 46–49 as implying that other provisions of the Charter may be invoked between private parties, either by themselves or in conjunction with a Directive (as in *Kücükdeveci*), where they are sufficiently precise, especially since the CJEU has already effectively held this in relation to the general principle of non-discrimination, it may be rash to do so. This is partly because the Court refrains in those paragraphs from referring to the fact that the dispute is between private parties, and addresses itself mainly to the lack of specificity in Article 27 of the Charter. This means that we must wait until a future case is decided in which the Court addresses the issue of horizontal direct effect of the Charter more directly.

4 DIRECT EFFECT OF SECONDARY LAW: REGULATIONS AND DECISIONS

The principal types of EU legal act are set out in Article 288 TFEU, and were analysed in an earlier chapter.[50] All binding forms of EU law are capable of direct effect, and while other types of non-binding law are not said to have direct effect, they are influential in other ways and may have what has become known as indirect effect through the principle of harmonious interpretation.[51]

(A) REGULATIONS

We saw in *Van Gend* that the textual basis for the conclusion that Treaty provisions could have direct effect was not compelling. However, Article 288 TFEU provides that a regulation 'shall be binding in its entirety and directly applicable in all Member States'. Policy considerations aside, this language seems to envisage that regulations will immediately become part of the domestic law of Member States, without needing transposition. If they are immediately part of the domestic law of Member States there is no reason why, so long as their provisions are sufficiently clear, precise, and relevant to the situation of an individual litigant,[52] they should not be capable of being relied upon and enforced by individuals before their national courts.[53] The key issue will be whether the particular article of the regulation on which the individual relies is sufficiently clear, precise, and certain for direct effect.

The direct effect of regulations was affirmed in the *Slaughtered Cow* case, where the ECJ chastised the Italian Government for choosing a method of implementing a regulation which cast doubt on the legal nature and direct applicability of that measure. It held that all methods of implementation were contrary to the Treaty 'which would have the result of creating an obstacle to the direct effect

---

Be a Source of Obligations for Private Parties: *AMS*' (2014) 51 CMLRev 907; E Frantziou, 'Case C–176/12 *Association de Médiation Sociale*: Some Reflections on the Horizontal Effect of the Charter and the Reach of Fundamental Employment Rights in the European Union' (2014) 10 EuConst 332.

[50] Ch 4.

[51] See, eg, Case 322/88 *Salvatore Grimaldi v Fonds des Maladies Professionelles* [1989] ECR 4407.

[52] Case C–403/98 *Azienda Agricola Monte Arcosu v Regione Autonoma della Sardegna* [2001] ECR I–103, in which the provisions of a reg were not sufficiently precise and therefore could not be directly relied upon. Compare Case C–278/02 *Herbert Handlbauer GmbH* [2004] ECR I–6171, [24]–[35].

[53] See AG Geelhoed's discussion of the relationship between the direct applicability of provisions of a reg and their direct effect in terms of the capacity of individuals to invoke and derive rights from those provisions, in Case C–253/00 (n 4).

of Community Regulations and of jeopardizing their simultaneous and uniform application in the whole of the Community'.[54] In *Muñoz*[55] the ECJ stated that 'owing to their very nature and their place in the system of sources of Community law, regulations operate to confer rights on individuals which the national courts have a duty to protect'.[56]

A national measure enacted to give effect to a regulation will not however necessarily be invalid, and in some cases may positively be *required* by the regulation.[57] In *Amsterdam Bulb*, the ECJ ruled that it is only if a national measure alters, obstructs, or obscures the direct effect or nature of the regulation that it will constitute a breach of EU law.[58] Further, any implementing measures must remain within the parameters set by the regulation and by EU law.[59] One concern is that a Member State's implementation of a regulation could, by concealing its EU origins, undermine or ignore the particular qualities of EU law such as its precedence over conflicting national law or the requirement of adequate remedies for breach. It is also possible that the content of a regulation could be adversely affected by national implementing measures. In *Stichting El Asqa* the CJEU found that a national measure freezing the funds of a person who was also subject to a freezing of funds imposed by an EU regulation could 'affect the scope of that regulation', due to possibly divergent definitions under national and EU law of key provisions shared by the two measures.[60]

Finally, it should be noted that the direct effect of regulations obliges not only the courts but also relevant administrative authorities to give immediate effect to EU law in practice.[61] This is sometimes known as 'administrative direct effect' and is discussed below in relation to directives.[62]

(B) DECISIONS

The Treaty wording in relation to decisions has been altered. Article 249 EC previously stated that 'a decision shall be binding in its entirety on those to whom it is addressed'. Article 288 TFEU now states that:

> A decision shall be binding in its entirety. A decision which specifies those to whom it is addressed shall be binding only on them.

---

[54] Case 39/72 *Commission v Italy* [1973] ECR 101, [17]; Case 34/73 *Fratelli Variola SpA* [1973] ECR 981. This was reiterated more recently in Cases C–4 and 27/10 *Bureau national interprofessionnel du Cognac* EU:C:2010:131, [61], concerning the interaction of a Reg on marks of geographical indication with national measures implementing an EU trade mark Dir, where the CJEU ruled that the direct applicability and entry into force of a Reg must be 'independent of any measure of reception into national law, strict compliance with that obligations being an indispensable condition for the simultaneous and uniform application of Regulations throughout the EU'.

[55] Case C–253/00 *Muñoz* (n 4) [27]; Case C–379/04 *Dahms GmbH v Fränkischer Weinbauverband eV* [2005] ECR I–8723, [13].

[56] And in Case C–375/09 *Tele 2 Polska* EU:C:2011:270, the CFEU ruled that since, according to Art 288 TFEU, Art 5 of Competition Regulation 1/2003 is directly applicable in all states, it precludes a rule of national law requiring the national competition authority to terminate an Art 102 TFEU procedure.

[57] Cases C–403/98 *Azienda Agricola Monte Arcosu* (n 52) [26]; C–592/11 *Ketelä* EU:C:2012:673, [35]; and C–24/13 *Dél-Zempléni Nektár Leader Nonprofit kft* EU:C:2014:40, [14].

[58] Case 50/76 *Amsterdam Bulb BV v Produktschap voor Siergewassen* [1977] ECR 137. See also Cases C–113/02 *Commission v Netherlands* [2004] ECR I–9707, [16]; C–316/10 *Danske Svineproducenter* EU:C:2011:863, [40]–[43]; C–24/13 *Dél-Zempléni Nektár Leader Nonprofit kft* EU:C:2014:40, [17], [29]; and C–135/13 *Malom I* EU:C:2014:327, [65]–[66] on the criteria with which national measures implementing a Reg should comply if they are to comply with EU law, including general principles of EU law and the Charter of Rights.

[59] Case C–316/10 *Danske Svineproducenter*, ibid, and Case C–592/11 *Anssi Ketelä* EU:C:2012:673, [36]–[37].

[60] Cases C–539 and 550/10 P *Stichting Al-Aqsa* EU:C:2012:711.

[61] Case C–606/10 *ANAFE* EU:C:2012:348, [75].

[62] (N 103) and text.

The relevance of this change and the different forms of decision were considered in an earlier chapter.[63] The ECJ in *Grad* had little hesitation in holding that decisions could be directly effective, despite the fact that Article 249 EC made no reference to their 'direct applicability'.[64] In an often-repeated phrase, the Court ruled that it did not follow from this 'that other categories of legal measures mentioned in that Article can never produce similar effects', and it relied on the principle of effectiveness to conclude that decisions could in suitable cases be invoked by individuals before national courts.[65]

The ECJ in this judgment discussed direct effect in terms of the right of an individual to 'invoke the obligation' created by a decision before a national court, ie the broad notion of invocability, but also spelt out in some detail the substance of that obligation, the more precise notion of conferral of rights. As with other categories of EU law, however, it is necessary to show that the particular provision of the decision invoked is sufficiently certain, precise, and unconditional for direct effect.[66]

The paradigm case will involve an individual who invokes a decision against a Member State: vertical direct effect. The Court has been reluctant to conclude that a decision addressed to a Member State can produce obligations enforceable against private parties: horizontal direct effect. Thus in *Carp*[67] the Court held that a decision addressed to Member States specifying the conformity procedures applicable to certain building materials did not impose obligations on private parties. This conclusion is reinforced by the wording of Article 288 TFEU, which now states that a decision which specifies those to whom it is addressed is binding only on them. A decision can however be addressed to a private party, in which case it will bind the addressee, and this is reinforced by the wording of Article 288. In such cases the decision may create horizontal direct effect between private parties.[68]

5 DIRECTIVES: DIRECT EFFECT

(A) DIRECT EFFECT OF DIRECTIVES

(i) *Foundations: Van Duyn and Ratti*

The key reason given by the Court for the direct effect of Treaty provisions was that the fundamental aims of the Treaty would be seriously hampered if its provisions could not be domestically enforced by those affected. The explanation for the direct effect of regulations was more straightforwardly textual: Article 288 TFEU specifically provided for their direct applicability, from which the Court deduced that they had the capacity to be invoked by individuals before national courts and to confer rights on them. In the case of decisions, the ECJ took the view that, since they were intended to be binding upon addressees, there was no reason why they should not be directly enforced before a national court where their provisions were sufficiently clear.

The position of directives under the Treaty is different. Under Article 288, a directive 'shall be binding as to the result to be achieved, upon each Member State to which it is addressed, but shall leave to the national authorities the choice of form and methods'. National implementation of directives is specifically envisaged by the Treaty for the following reason. The directive is one of the main EU harmonization instruments used to coordinate Member States' laws. The directive may be a compromise

---

63 Ch 4.

64 Case 9/70 *Franz Grad v Finanzamt Traunstein* [1970] ECR 825.

65 Ibid [5]; Case 249/85 *Albako Margarinefabrik Maria von der Linde GmbH & Co KG v Bundesanstalt für Landwirtschaftliche Marktordnung* [1987] ECR 2345, [17]; Case C–156/91 *Hansa Fleisch* (n 22) [15].

66 See, eg, Case C–18/08 *Foselev Sud-Ouest SARL v Administration des douanes et droits indirects* [2008] ECR I–8745.

67 Case C–80/06 *Carp Snc di L Moleri eV Corsi v Ecorad Srl* [2007] ECR I–4473, [19]–[21].

68 Ibid [58], AG Trstenjak.

between Member States on a complex matter, and may leave discretionary options to states. Eventual implementation need not be uniform in every Member State, although the actual aim of the directive must be properly secured in each.

It follows that some of the criteria for direct effect laid down in the early case law—precision, unconditionality, no need for implementation—are missing. A directive may leave discretion to Member States; it will always require implementing measures; and it might not be sufficiently precise to allow for proper national judicial enforcement.

On the other hand, the aims of legal integration and effectiveness which underpinned the ECJ's original articulation of direct effect of Treaty provisions may be equally applicable to directives. Many important areas of EU policy rely on the proper implementation of EU directives, and Member States frequently fail to implement directives or fail to do so properly. The ECJ therefore held that directives could in principle have direct effect. It gave three reasons for this, two in *Van Duyn*, and the third in *Ratti*.

Case 41/74 **Van Duyn v Home Office**
[1974] ECR 1337

[Note Lisbon Treaty renumbering: Arts 48, 177, and 189 are now Arts 45, 267, and 288 TFEU]

THE ECJ

12. [I]t would be incompatible with the binding effect attributed to a directive by Article 189 to exclude, in principle, the possibility that the obligation which it imposes may be invoked by those concerned. In particular, where the Community authorities have, by directive, imposed on Member States the obligation to pursue a particular course of conduct, the useful effect of such an act would be weakened if individuals were prevented from relying on it before their national courts and if the latter were prevented from taking it into consideration as an element of Community law. Article 177, which empowers national courts to refer to the Court questions concerning the validity and interpretation of all acts of the Community institutions, without distinction, implies furthermore that these acts may be invoked by individuals in the national courts. It is necessary to examine, in every case, whether the nature, general scheme and wording of the provision in question are capable of having direct effects on the relations between Member States and individuals.

The first reason given by the ECJ is functional: directives are binding and will be more effectively enforced if individuals can rely on them. This exemplifies the theme set out above: private enforcement via direct effect complements public enforcement under Article 258, thereby strengthening the overall effectiveness of EU law.

The second reason is textual: Article 177, now Article 267 TFEU, allows national courts to refer questions concerning any EU measure to the ECJ, including directives, and this implies that such acts can be invoked by individuals before national courts. The ECJ had, as we have seen, used this reasoning in *Van Gend* in relation to treaty provisions.

The third rationale, articulated in the *Ratti* case,[69] is the estoppel argument: Member States were precluded by their failure to implement a directive properly from refusing to recognize its binding effect in cases where it was pleaded against them. Thus, the argument is as follows. The Member State should have implemented the directive. If it had done so the individual would have been able

---

[69] Case 148/78 *Pubblico Ministero v Tullio Ratti* [1979] ECR 1629, [23].

to rely on the national implementing law. The Member State had committed a wrong by failing to implement the directive, and could not rely on that wrongdoing so as to deny the binding effect of the directive itself after the date for implementation. Where necessary, a conflicting national law should be disapplied.[70]

(ii) *Subsequent Application: Sufficiently Clear and Precise Provisions of a Directive*

The net effect of these rulings was that directives were capable in principle of having direct effect. The key issue was whether the particular provision of the directive was sufficiently clear, precise, and unconditional to be capable of being applied directly by a national court.[71] The fact that Member States can choose the means of achieving the result required by a directive does not preclude direct effect where the content of the individual's right can be determined with sufficient precision from the directive.[72]

In *Van Duyn*, Directive 64/221 allowed Member States to take measures restricting the movement of non-nationals on grounds such as public policy, without defining the permissible range of public-policy concerns. The ECJ ruled that by providing that measures taken on public-policy grounds had to be based on the personal conduct of the individual, the Directive had limited the discretionary power conferred on states. The obligation imposed was clear, precise, and legally complete.

In most,[73] though not all,[74] later cases the Court has ruled that the existence of discretion would not prevent a directive from being directly relied upon by an individual. Hence the individual can rely on a directive where a Member State has fully exercised its discretion on implementation;[75] where the state has chosen to exercise or not to exercise a particular discretionary option;[76] where a clear and precise obligation can be separated out from other parts of a directive;[77] or where a clear obligation of result can be identified.[78] Further even where the provisions of a directive are insufficiently precise to have direct effect in terms of specifying a particular outcome, they may entitle individuals to

[70] Case C–462/99 *Connect Austria Gesellschaft für Telekommunikation GmbH v Telekom-Control-Kommission and Mobilkom Austria AG* [2003] ECR I–5197, [40]; Case C–591/10 *Littlewoods Retail Ltd and Others* EU:C:2012:478, [33].

[71] (N 30); Cases C–226/07 *Flughafen Köln/Bonn GmbH v Hauptzollamt Köln* [2008] ECR I–5999, [22]–[23]; C–152–154/07 *Arcor AG & Co KG v Bundesrepublik Deutschland* [2008] ECR I–5959, [39]–[44]; C–471–472/07 *AGIM v Belgium* EU:C:2010:9, [25]–[29]. Compare Cases C–165–167/09 *Stichting Natuur en Milieu and Others* EU:C:2011:348, [75] on provisions of an environmental dir held to be too programmatic and flexible to have direct effect.

[72] Case C–138/07 *Belgische Staat v Cobelfret NV* [2009] ECR I–731, [61].

[73] Cases C–72/95 *Kraaijeveld* (n 9) [59]; C–287/98 *Linster* (n 14) [37]–[39]; Case C–363/05 *JP Morgan Fleming Claverhouse Investment Trust plc v The Commissioners of HM Revenue and Customs* [2007] ECR I–5517, [61]–[62]; C–176/12 *Association de médiation sociale* EU:C:2014:2, [33]; C–468 and 469/10 *ASNEF & FECEMD* EU:C:2011:777, [52]–[54]; contrast Case C–365/98 *Brinkmann* [2000] ECR I–4619.

[74] Case C–157/02 *Rieser Internationale Transporte GmbH v Autobahnen- und Schnellstraßen-Finanzierungs- AG (Asfinag)* [2004] ECR I–1477.

[75] Case C–441/99 *Riksskatteverket v Gharehveran* [2001] ECR I–7687.

[76] Cases C–303/98 *SIMAP v Valencia Sindicatode Médicos Asistencia Pública* [2000] ECR I–7963; C–453 and 462/02 *Finanzamt Gladbeck v Linneweber* [2005] ECR I–1131; C–76/97 *Tögel* [1998] ECR I–5357; C–241/97 *Försäkringsaktiebolaget Skandia* [1999] ECR I–1951; C–621/10 and 129/11 *Balkan and Sea Properties ADSITs & Provadinvest OOD* EU:C:2012:248.

[77] Case C–346/97 *Braathens Sverige AB v Riksskatteverket* [1999] ECR I–3419; Case C–292/02 *Meiland Azewijn BV v Hauptzollamt Duisburg* [2004] ECR I–7905; Cases C–465/00 and 138–139/01 *Rechnungshof v Österreichischer Rundfunk* [2003] ECR I–4989; CD Classen, Note (2004) 41 CMLRev 1377.

[78] Case C–476/01 *Criminal proceedings against Felix Kapper* [2004] ECR I–5205, concerning Dir 91/439 on recognition of driving licences, and Case C–595/12 *Napoli* EU:C:2014:128, concerning Arts 14 and 15 of the Equal Treatment Dir 2006/54.

obtain judicial review to determine whether the state has remained within the parameters set by the directive.[79]

More controversially, in *Kortas*, the ECJ ruled that the possibility for a Member State to derogate from a harmonizing directive under Article 95(4) EC did not prevent the directive from having direct effect, nor preclude an individual from relying directly on its provisions, even where a Member State had sought permission for such a derogation and the Commission had unreasonably failed to respond to its request.[80]

(iii) *Direct Effect: Time Limits for Implementation*

The general principle is that the direct effect of a directive operates from the deadline specified for implementation of the directive.[81] The result of *Van Duyn*, *Ratti*, and subsequent case law is that although Article 288 does not declare directives to be directly applicable, so that they do not automatically become part of national law upon adoption, they may produce 'similar effects' to regulations after the time limit for their implementation has expired and the state has not properly implemented them.

The ECJ has moreover made it clear that directives may have an impact even before the implementation period has passed. Thus in *Inter-Environnement Wallonie* it held that although states are not obliged to implement a directive before the period for its transposition has expired, they must, during that period as well as during any transitional period allowed by the directive, *refrain* from adopting any measures liable to compromise seriously the result prescribed by the directive.[82] On the other hand, it is in general for the national court—following guidelines established by the ECJ—to assess whether the national measure in question is liable seriously to compromise the attainment of the result sought by the directive.[83] Further, while directives do not in principle apply retroactively to factual situations occurring before the time limit for the enactment of their provisions has expired,[84] pre-existing national law which is capable of being interpreted in conformity with the directive has been held by the Court to fall within its scope.[85]

The obligation to take steps to avoid compromising the result prescribed by a directive applies to all state entities, including national courts, which must refrain before the implementation period

[79] Cases C–83/11 *Muhammad Sazzadur Rahman and Others* EU:C:2012:519, [25] and C–165–167/09 *Stichting Natuur en Milieu* EU:C:2011:348, [99]–[100].

[80] Case C–319/97 *Kortas* [1999] ECR I–3143. The ECJ held that an action against the Commission for breach of its obligations under Art 265 TFEU was the appropriate remedy. The CJEU in Case C–589/12 *GMAC UK plc* EU:C:2014:2131, [44]–[49] also rejected the Member State's attempt to argue that an individual's reliance on the direct effect of a tax dir was either inappropriately selective, or abusive.

[81] Case 8/81 *Becker v Finanzamt Münster-Innenstadt* [1982] ECR 53; Case C–316/93 *Vaneetveld v Le Foyer SA* [1994] ECR I–763, [18]–[19]; Case C–156/91 *Hansa Fleisch* (n 22) [20]; Case C–141/00 *Ambulanter Pflegedienst Kügler GmbH v Finanzamt für Körperschaften I in Berlin* [2002] ECR I–6833, [52]–[60]; Case C–246/06 *Navarro v Fondo de Garantía Salarial (Fogasa)* [2008] ECR I–105, [25]–[30]; Case C–138/08 *Hochtief AG v Közbeszerzések Tanácsa Közbeszerzési Döntöbizottság* [2009] ECR I–9889, [24]–[30].

[82] Case C–129/96 *Inter-Environnement Wallonie ASBL v Région Wallone* [1997] ECR I–7411; Cases C–378–380/07 *Kiriaki Angelidaki and Others v Organismos Nomarchiakis Autodioikisis Rethymnis* [2009] ECR I–3071, [206]; Cases C–165–167/09 *Stichting Natuur en Milieu* EU:C:2011:348, [78]–[80]. On transitional periods, see Case C–43/10 *Nomarchiaki Aftodioikisi Aitoloakarnanias* EU:C:2012:560, [57]–[59] and Cases C–186 and 209/11 *Stanleybet International* EU:C:2013:33, [38]–[42].

[83] Case C–119/09 *Société fiduciaire nationale d'expertise comptable* EU:C:2011:208, [19]. For a case in which the CJEU itself ruled that the national measure was *not* liable to do so, see Case C–599/12 *Jetair NV* EU:C:2014:144, [36]–[37].

[84] See Case C–477/09 *Defossez* EU:C:2011:134 on a dir concerning protection of employees in the event of insolvency. For a case involving the CJEU's rejection of Germany's attempt to use, to the detriment of an individual, the discretion provided for in a dir after the time limit for implementation of the dir had expired but before the state had actually implemented it, see Case C–297/12 *Criminal proceedings against Filev & Osmani* EU:C:2013:569.

[85] Case C–2/10 *Azienda Agro-Zootecnica Franchini Sarl* EU:C:2011:502, [70].

has passed from interpreting national law so as to prejudice the attainment of the objectives of the directive.[86] The direct effect of directives was also bolstered by *Marks & Spencer*, in which the ECJ declared that even after a Member State implemented a directive correctly into national law, an individual could continue to rely directly on the provisions of the directive against the state so long as it was not being properly *applied* in practice.[87]

(B) THE VERTICAL/HORIZONTAL DISTINCTION

The ECJ had thus far expanded direct effect. In *Marshall* however it held that the direct effect of a directive could be pleaded only against the state, but not against an individual.[88]

Case 152/84 **Marshall v Southampton and South-West Hampshire Area Health Authority (Teaching)**
[1986] ECR 723

[Note Lisbon Treaty renumbering: Arts 189 and 191 are now Arts 288 and 297 TFEU]

Helen Marshall was dismissed after 14 years' employment by the respondent health authority on the ground that she had passed 60, and the Authority's policy required female employees to retire at 60 and male employees at 65. Marshall argued that her dismissal violated the 1976 Equal Treatment Directive, and the national court asked the ECJ whether she could rely on the Directive against the Health Authority. Advocate General Slynn suggested that to give 'horizontal effect' to directives by allowing them to impose obligations directly on an individual would 'totally blur the distinction between directives and regulations' established by the Treaty.[89]

THE ECJ

48. With regard to the argument that a directive may not be relied upon against an individual, it must be emphasized that according to Article 189 of the EEC Treaty, the binding nature of a directive, which constitutes the basis for the possibility of relying on the directive before a national court, exists only in relation to 'each Member State to which it is addressed'. It follows that a directive may not of itself impose obligations on an individual and that a provision of a directive may not be relied upon as such against such a person.

A number of rationales have been suggested as to why directives should only have vertical and not horizontal direct effect.

The reason given by the ECJ in *Marshall* was *textual*, based on the wording of Article 288. This reasoning is unconvincing. The wording of Article 288 merely signifies that a Member State is bound by a directive only if mentioned therein as being bound, by way of contrast to regulations that bind all Member States. It says nothing one way or the other as to whether, if a particular

---

[86] Cases C–261 and 299/07 *VTB-VAB NV v Total Belgium NV* [2009] ECR I–2949, [38]–[39].

[87] Case C–62/00 *Marks & Spencer plc v Commissioners of Customs & Excise* [2002] ECR I–6325, [22]–[28]; noted by M Ruffert (2003) 40 CMLRev 729; S Drake (2003) 28 ELRev 418.

[88] Moreover, a dir, even if pleaded by an individual only against the state, cannot of itself result in the imposition of a civil obligation on another individual: Case C–201/02 *Wells v Secretary of State for Transport, Local Government and the Regions* [2004] ECR I–723, [57]–[58].

[89] [1986] ECR 723, 734.

Member State is bound by a directive, the directive might also impose an obligation on a private individual. Further, the Court's textual fidelity in this context contrasts with its approach to the direct effectiveness of certain Treaty Articles which, like directives, are also explicitly addressed only to the Member State, and yet have been held to be horizontally directly effective. In the first *Defrenne* case, the ECJ dismissed the argument that what is now Article 157 could be relied upon only as against the state, ruling that since 'Article 119 is mandatory in nature, the prohibition on discrimination between men and women applies not only to the action of public authorities, but also extends to all agreements which are intended to regulate paid labour collectively, as well as to contracts between individuals'.[90] The same reasoning has been applied to other Treaty Articles.[91]

A *rule-of-law* argument was initially also used against the horizontal direct effect of directives, since directives were not required, until after the Maastricht Treaty, to be notified or published in the Official Journal.[92] The great majority of directives were however published and the requirement of publication is now contained in Article 297 TFEU. Moreover, all directives contain a time limit for their implementation, thus reducing the rule-of-law concern.

A third argument is that *horizontal direct effect of directives would erode the distinction between regulations and directives*. The argument is however problematic. Insofar as it has force it is equally true of the vertical direct effect of directives. To accord direct effect to directives does not however in reality erode the distinction between regulations and directives. The key distinction between the two instruments is that Member States are intended to have choice as to form and methods of implementation for directives. Giving direct effect to directives, whether vertical or horizontal, is not intended to take away this choice. It is merely expressive of the fundamental proposition that if such implementing measures have not been enacted within the required time then the binding ends stipulated in the directive can still be enforced, provided that they are sufficiently clear and precise.

The final argument adduced against horizontal direct effect is *legal certainty*. This was the rationale given in *Wells*,[93] although it is unconvincing. First, if directives were to be capable of horizontal direct effect this would only apply if the relevant provisions were sufficiently clear, precise, and unconditional. Secondly, the meaning of legal certainty in this context is unclear, since the ECJ has provided no elaboration or plausible explanation for why it prohibits the horizontal direct effect of directives.[94] Thirdly, there are very real problems of legal certainty with the doctrine of indirect effect and incidental effect, which are the major qualifications to the absence of horizontal direct effect of directives.[95]

Yet despite widespread academic criticism and numerous opinions given by Advocates General in favour of horizontal direct effect, the Court has continued to insist that directives should have only vertical direct effect. The ruling in *Marshall* was expressly confirmed ten years later in the *Dori* case.[96]

---

90 Case 43/75 *Defrenne* (n 24).
91 See, eg, Case C–281/93 *Angonese v Cassa di Risparmio di Bologna* [2000] ECR I–4134, [32]–[36]; Case C–438/05 *Viking Line*, Section 3(c) above.
92 See AG Slynn in Case 152/84 [1986] ECR 723; also Case C–192/89 *Sevince v Staatssecretaris van Justitie* [1990] ECR I–3461, [24].
93 Case C–201/02 *Wells* (n 88) [56]. This paragraph of *Wells* is cited also in Cases C–397–403/01 *Pfeiffer* [2004] ECR I–8835, [108] and C–152–154/07 *Arcor AG & Co KG* [2008] ECR I–5959, [35].
94 P Craig, 'The Legal Effect of Directives: Policy, Rules and Exceptions' (2009) 34 ELRev 349, 353–354.
95 Ibid 360–364.
96 Case C–91/92 *Dori v Recreb Srl* [1994] ECR I–3325; Case C–201/02 *Wells* (n 88) [56].

6 DIRECTIVES: ENHANCING THEIR LEGAL EFFECTS

The ECJ has however developed a number of doctrinal devices or strategies that have reduced the impact of the decision to deny horizontal direct effect to directives. These developments have rendered this area of the law increasingly complex. Six such devices or strategies are outlined below. The first is the adoption of a broad definition of the state for the purposes of vertical direct effect, thereby blurring the clarity of the line between horizontal and vertical effect. The second is the principle of harmonious interpretation or indirect effect. The third is the doctrine of 'incidental horizontal effects'. The fourth is the interaction between general principles and directives. The fifth is the interaction between certain regulations and directives, and the sixth is the doctrine of state liability for breach of EU law. These six strategies will be described further below.

(A) A BROAD CONCEPT OF THE STATE

The first way in which the ECJ has lessened the impact of the lack of horizontal direct effect is to adopt a broad understanding of the 'state' for the purposes of vertical direct effect.[97] In *Marshall* the Court concluded that the complainant could rely on the provisions of this Directive as against the Health Authority, since it could be regarded as an organ of the state.[98]

> 49. In that respect it must be pointed out that where a person involved in legal proceedings is able to rely on a directive as against the State he may do so regardless of the capacity in which the latter is acting, whether employer or public authority. In either case it is necessary to prevent the State from taking advantage of its own failure to comply with Community law....
>
> 51. The argument submitted by the United Kingdom that the possibility of relying on provisions of the directive against the respondent *qua* organ of the State would give rise to an arbitrary and unfair distinction between the rights of State employees and those of private employees does not justify any other conclusion. Such a distinction may easily be avoided if the Member State concerned has correctly implemented the directive into national law.[99]

The *Foster* case remains the primary ruling on the concept of the 'state' for the purposes of vertical direct effect.

Case C–188/89 **Foster and Others v British Gas plc**
[1990] ECR I–3313

The plaintiffs were employed by British Gas, whose policy was to require women to retire at 60 and men at 65. British Gas was at the time a nationalized industry with responsibility for and a monopoly of the gas-supply system in Great Britain. The plaintiffs sought to rely on the provisions of the 1976 Equal Treatment Directive and the House of Lords asked the ECJ whether British Gas was a body of the kind against which the provisions of the Directive could be invoked.

---

[97] D Curtin, 'The Province of Government: Delimiting the Direct Effect of Directives in the Common Law Context' (1990) 15 ELRev 195; E Szyszczak, '*Foster v British Gas*' (1990) 27 CMLRev 859.

[98] See also Case C–438/99 *Jiménez Melgar v Ayuntamiento de Los Barrios* [2001] ECR I–6915, [32]–[33]; Case C–147/08 *Römer* EU:C:2011:286, [55].

[99] Case 152/84 *Marshall* (n 92). See also R Mastroianni, 'On the Distinction Between Vertical and Horizontal Direct Effect of Directives: What Role for the Principle of Equality?' (1999) 5 EPL 417.

THE ECJ

18. On the basis of those considerations, the Court has held in a series of cases that unconditional and sufficiently precise provisions of a directive could be relied on against organizations or bodies which were subject to the authority or control of the State or had special powers beyond those which result from the normal rules applicable between individuals.

19. The Court has accordingly held that provisions of a directive could be relied on against tax authorities (the judgments in Case 8/81 *Becker* [1982] ECR 53, Case 221/88 *ECSC* v. *Busseni* [1990] ECR I–495), local or regional authorities (judgment in Case 103/88 *Costanzo* [1989] ECR 1839), constitutionally independent authorities responsible for the maintenance of public order and safety (judgment in Case 222/84 *Johnston* v. *Chief Constable of the RUC* [1986] ECR 1651), and public authorities providing public health services (judgment in Case 152/84 *Marshall* [1986] ECR 723).

20. It follows from the foregoing that a body, whatever its legal form, which has been made responsible, pursuant to a measure adopted by the State, for providing a public service under the control of the State and has for that purpose special powers beyond those which result from the normal rules applicable in relations between individuals, is included in any event among the bodies against which the provisions of a directive capable of having direct effect may be relied upon.

It is evident from paragraph 20 that the Court considered a company in the position of British Gas to be an organ of the state. However, it is not entirely clear what kind of control the state must have over a body for it to be part of the state, and *Foster* does not provide an exhaustive definition. In some cases the ECJ has left it in the hands of national courts to apply the general criteria articulated in *Foster*,[100] while in other cases the ECJ itself has ruled that a particular body clearly satisfied those criteria for the purposes of invoking a directive against it.[101]

A broad range of bodies has been included in the state for these purposes, including local authorities, regions, nationalized industries, privatized undertakings, and universities. The Court has made clear that all such authorities have an obligation within the limits of their power to apply the provisions of the directive, and refrain from applying conflicting provisions of national law,[102] something which has been referred to as 'administrative direct effect'.[103] The broad interpretation of what constitutes an organ of the state seems at odds with the refusal to extend the direct enforceability of directives to relations between non-state entities and individuals, more especially because state organs and domestic administrations that play no part in the formal implementation of EU legislation are bound to apply the provisions of directives in practice.

[100] Cases C–343/98 *Collino & Chiappero v Telecom Italia* [2000] ECR I–6659; C–253–258/96 *Kampelmann v Landschaftsverband Westfalen-Lippe* [1997] ECR I–6907, [47]; T–172 and 175–177/98 *Salamander v Parliament & Council* [2000] ECR II–2487, [60]; C–356/05 *Farrell v Whitty, Minister for the Environment, Ireland* [2007] ECR I–3067, [37]–[44]; C–282/10 *Dominguez* EU:C:2012:33, [38]–[40]; C–425/12 *Portgás* EU:C:2013:829, [28]–[31]; C–614/11 *Kuso* EU:C:2013:544.

[101] Cases C–419/92 *Scholz v Opera Universitaria di Cagliari* [1994] ECR I–505; C–157/02 *Rieser* (n 74) [22]–[29]; C–180/04 *Vassallo v Azienda Ospedaliera Ospedale San Martino di Genova* [2006] ECR I–7251, [26]; C–53/04 *Marrosu and Sardino v Azienda Ospedaliera Ospedale San Martino di Genova* [2006] ECR I–7213; C–6/05 *Medipac-Kazantzidis AE v Venizeleio-Pananeio (PE.S.Y. KRITIS)* [2007] ECR I–4557, [43]; C–250 and 268/09 *Georgiev v Tehnicheski universitet—Sofia, filial Plovdiv* EU:C:2009:549; C–361/12 *Carmela Carratù* EU:C:2013:830. For a General Court ruling, see Case T–370/09 *GDF Suez SA* EU:T:2012:333.

[102] Case 103/88 *Fratelli Costanzo SpA v Comune di Milano* [1989] ECR 1839, [31]; Case C–243/09 *Günter Fuß v Stadt Halle* EU:C:2010:609, [61].

[103] B de Witte, 'Direct Effect, Supremacy and the Nature of the Legal Order' in P Craig and G de Búrca (eds), *The Evolution of EU Law* (Oxford University Press, 2nd edn, 2011) ch 12; Cases C–246–249/94 *Cooperativa Agricola Zootecnica* (n 30). For a case involving such 'administrative direct effect' in the context of an EU Reg, see Case C–606/10 *ANAFE* EU:C:2012:348.

The reality is that the *Foster* test embodies an unusual inverse principle of state or vicarious responsibility, whereby a body that might be regarded in some way as connected with the state is held responsible as an agent for a failing of the state itself, even though it had no control over the relevant event. This is so despite the fact that the degree of special power/state control may vary considerably; the 'agent' for these purposes often has no power over implementation of the directive; and the connection between the existence of the special power/state control and the institution's responsibility under the directive is far from self-evident.

Advocate General Jacobs has noted that the very broad interpretation of the state meant that directives could be enforced even against commercial enterprises where there was some element of state participation or control, 'notwithstanding that they might be in direct competition with private sector undertakings against which the same directives are not enforceable'.[104] The ECJ's thesis is in effect that the 'price' to be paid by, for example, the nationalized industry for whatever powers it has been given by the Member State is that the relevant industry should be subject to whatever duties flow from a directive.[105]

Finally, the ECJ has also made it clear that vertical direct effect is not precluded even if the application of the directive against the Member State will be certain to lead to adverse consequences for the individual, so long as it does not lead to the direct imposition of a legal obligation on the individual.[106] This has been referred to as a 'triangular' situation.[107]

Case C–201/02 The Queen, on the application of Delena Wells v Secretary of State for Transport, Local Government and the Regions
[2004] ECR I–723

The case concerned Directive 85/337. It required assessment of the effects of public and private projects on the environment before planning consent was given. Planning permission was given for mining operations without such an assessment. Wells sought the revocation of the planning consent on the ground that the Directive had not been complied with.

THE ECJ

55. According to the United Kingdom Government, acceptance that an individual is entitled to invoke Article 2(1) of Directive 85/337, read in conjunction with Articles 1(2) and 4(2) thereof, would amount to 'inverse direct effect' directly obliging the Member State concerned, at the request of an individual, such as Mrs Wells, to deprive another individual or individuals, such as the owners of Conygar Quarry, of their rights.

56. As to that submission, the principle of legal certainty prevents directives from creating obligations for individuals. For them, the provisions of a directive can only create rights (see Case 152/84 *Marshall* [1986] ECR 723, paragraph 48). Consequently, an individual may not rely on a directive against a Member State where it is a matter of a State obligation directly linked to the performance of another obligation falling, pursuant to that directive, on a third party (see, to this effect, Case C–221/88 *Busseni*

---

[104] Case C–316/93 *Vaneetveld* (n 81) [31], AG Jacobs.

[105] An interesting twist on the vertical direct effect scenario can be seen in Case C–425/12 *Portgás* EU:C:2013:829, [33]–[38], in which the CJEU ruled that the provisions of a dir could be relied upon by a state enforcement body against a private undertaking which satisfied the *Foster* criteria.

[106] See also Case C–244/12 *Salzburger Flughafen GmbH* EU:C:2013:203, [44]–[47].

[107] See also Case C–152–154/07 *Arcor* (n 71).

[1990] ECR I–495, paragraphs 23 to 26, and Case C–97/96 *Daihatsu Deutschland* [1997] ECR I–6843, paragraphs 24 and 26).

57. On the other hand, mere adverse repercussions on the rights of third parties, even if the repercussions are certain, do not justify preventing an individual from invoking the provisions of a directive against the Member State concerned (see to this effect, in particular, Case 103/88 *Fratelli Costanzo* [1989] ECR 1839, paragraphs 28 to 33, *WWF and Others*, cited above, paragraphs 69 and 71, Case C–194/94 *CIA Security International* [1996] ECR I–2201, paragraphs 40 to 55, Case C–201/94 *Smith & Nephew and Primecrown* [1996] ECR I–5819, paragraphs 33 to 39, and Case C–443/98 *Unilever* [2000] ECR I–7535, paragraphs 45 to 52).

58. In the main proceedings, the obligation on the Member State concerned to ensure that the competent authorities carry out an assessment of the environmental effects of the working of the quarry is not directly linked to the performance of any obligation which would fall, pursuant to Directive 85/337, on the quarry owners. The fact that mining operations must be halted to await the results of the assessment is admittedly the consequence of the belated performance of that State's obligations. Such a consequence cannot, however, as the United Kingdom claims, be described as 'inverse direct effect' of the provisions of that directive in relation to the quarry owners.

(B) 'INDIRECT EFFECT': PRINCIPLE OF HARMONIOUS INTERPRETATION

(i) *Obligation to Interpret National Law in Conformity with Directives*

The second and most important way in which the ECJ has encouraged the effectiveness of directives, despite denying the possibility of direct horizontal enforcement, is by developing a principle of harmonious interpretation which requires national law to be interpreted 'in the light of' directives. *Von Colson* is a leading authority.

Case 14/83 **Von Colson and Kamann v Land Nordrhein-Westfalen**
[1984] ECR 1891

[Note Lisbon Treaty renumbering: Art 189 is now Art 288 TFEU]

The ECJ ruled that the Equal Treatment Directive on which the plaintiffs relied in their claim of unlawful sex discrimination was not sufficiently precise to guarantee them a specific remedy of appointment to a post, but it went on to rule on what effect the Directive's aims might nonetheless have on the interpretation of national law.

THE ECJ

26. However, the Member States' obligation arising from a directive to achieve the result envisaged by the directive and their duty under Article 5 of the Treaty to take all appropriate measures, whether general or particular, to ensure the fulfillment of that obligation, is binding on all the authorities of Member States including, for matters within their jurisdiction, the courts. It follows that, in applying the national law and in particular the provisions of a national law specifically introduced in order to implement Directive No 76/207, national courts are required to interpret their national law in the light of the

wording and the purpose of the Directive in order to achieve the result referred to in the third paragraph of Article 189.

...

28. ...It is for the national court to interpret and apply the legislation adopted for the implementation of the directive in conformity with the requirements of Community law, in so far as it is given discretion to do so under national law.

The Court in *Von Colson* expressly identified the national courts as organs of the state with responsibility for fulfilment of EU obligations, and encouraged the German court to supplement the domestic legislation, which did not on its face seem to provide an adequate remedy, by reading it in conformity with the Directive's requirement to provide a real and effective remedy.[108] The case also makes clear that the doctrine of harmonious interpretation, or 'indirect effect', does not require the provisions of a directive to satisfy the specific justiciability criteria (clarity, precision, unconditionality) for direct effect.[109]

The principle has been strengthened over time, with the Court declaring it to be 'inherent in the system of the Treaty', derived from the obligation in Article 4(3) TFEU, and an aspect of the requirement of full effectiveness of EU law,[110] which applies not only to national courts, but to all competent authorities called upon to interpret national law.[111] Further, the principle of harmonious interpretation is no longer presented as a second best, a strategy to be followed by national courts only when a directive lacks direct effect or is invoked against a private party, but as a first strategy to try to give effect to a directive through the interpretation of national law, even where a directive could be invoked against the state to set aside conflicting national law.[112]

The date at which the interpretive obligation arose was initially unclear, with some Advocates General arguing that it should apply even before the time limit for implementing the directive had expired.[113] The general principle is, as seen above, that vertical direct effect of a directive becomes operative when the time limit for implementation has expired,[114] subject to the duty to refrain in the period prior to expiration of the time limit from taking measures liable seriously to compromise the result prescribed by the directive.[115] In *Adeneler*, the ECJ confirmed a similar rule for the obligation of harmonious interpretation, stating that where a directive 'is transposed belatedly, the general obligation owed by national courts to interpret domestic law in conformity with the directive exists only once the period for its transposition has expired'.[116] The Court went on to rule that the obligation on the state to refrain, even before expiry of the time limit, from measures liable to compromise the result sought by the directive meant that from the date when the directive entered into force, national courts must refrain as far as possible from interpreting domestic law in a manner which might seriously

---

[108] For a similar case involving the principle of harmonious interpretation and the obligation to provide an effective remedy for sexual orientation discrimination, see Case C–81/12 *Asociaţia Accept* EU:C:2013:275.

[109] Cases T–237/08 *Abadía Retuerta, SA v OHIM* EU:T:2010:185, [67]; C–98/09 *Sorge v Poste Italiane SpA* EU:T:2010:185, [49]–[55].

[110] Cases C–160/01 *Mau* [2003] ECR I–4791, [34]; C–397–403/01 *Pfeiffer* (n 93) [114].

[111] Case C–218/01 *Henkel KGaA* [2004] ECR I–1725, [60].

[112] See, eg, Cases C–282/10 *Dominguez* EU:C:2012:33, [23]; C–124/12 *AES-3C Maritza East 1 EOOD* EU:C:2013:488, [52]–[53]; C–142/12 *Hristomir Marinov* EU:C:2013:292, [37]–[39]; C–306/12 *Spedition Welter GmbH* EU:C:2013:650; C–97/11 *Amia SpA* EU:C:2012:306, [30]; C–621/10 and 129/11 *Balkan and Sea Properties ADSITs & Provadinvest OOD* EU:C:2012:248, [62].

[113] See M Klamert, 'Judicial Implementation of Directives and Anticipatory Indirect Effect: Connecting the Dots' (2006) 43 CMLRev 1251.

[114] (N 81).

[115] Case C–129/96 *Inter-Environnement Wallonie* (n 82) [45]; Case C–157/02 *Rieser* (n 74) [66].

[116] Case C–212/04 *Konstantinos Adeneler et al v Ellinikos Organismos Galaktos (ELOG)* [2006] ECR I–6057, [115]; also Cases C–457–460/11 *VG Wort* EU:C:2013:426, [26].

compromise, after the period for transposition had expired, attainment of the objective pursued by that directive.[117]

(ii) Vertical and Horizontal Application of the Obligation

Von Colson concerned a directive which had been inadequately implemented,[118] and the case was brought against a state employer. Later cases however established that the obligation requires a national court to interpret national law in the light of an inadequately implemented or a non-implemented directive even in a case against an individual, thus clearly sidestepping the prohibition on horizontal direct effect.

The *Marleasing* case concerned a 'horizontal' situation involving two private parties before a domestic court, where the interpretation of national law in the light of an unimplemented directive would not impose penal liability, but was likely to affect its legal position in a disadvantageous way.[119] This judgment confirmed that an unimplemented directive could be relied on to influence the interpretation of national law in a case between individuals.

Case C–106/89 **Marleasing SA v La Comercial Internacionale de Alimentacion SA**
[1990] ECR I–4135

[Note Lisbon Treaty renumbering: Arts 5 and 189 EC are now Arts 4(3) TEU and 288 TFEU]

The plaintiff company brought proceedings against La Comercial to have the defendant company's articles of association declared void as the company was created for the sole purpose of defrauding creditors. The provisions of the relevant Council Directive did not include this 'lack of cause' as a ground for the nullity of a company, whereas the Spanish Civil Code provided for the ineffectiveness of contracts for lack of cause. The Spanish court referred the case to the ECJ, asking whether the Council Directive could have direct effect between individuals so as to preclude the declaration of nullity of a company on grounds other than those set out in the Directive.

THE ECJ

7. However, it is apparent from the documents before the Court that the national court seeks in substance to ascertain whether a national court hearing a case which falls within the scope of Directive 68/151 is required to interpret its national law in the light of the wording and the purpose of that directive in order to preclude a declaration of nullity of a public limited company on a ground other than those listed in Article 11 of the directive.

8. In order to reply to that question, it should be observed that, as the Court pointed out in its judgment in Case 14/83 *Von Colson and Kamann* v. *Land Nordrhein-Westfalen* [1984] ECR 1891, paragraph 26, the Member States' obligation arising from a directive to achieve the result envisaged by the directive and their duty under Article 5 of the Treaty to take all appropriate measures, whether general or particular, to ensure the fulfilment of that obligation, is binding on all the authorities of Member States including, for matters

---

[117] Ibid [123].

[118] See also Case C–421/92 *Habermann-Beltermann v Arbeiterwohlfahrt, Bezirksverband* [1994] ECR I–1657. Note that a dir does not need to be transposed into domestic law in precisely the same words as the dir in order to be properly implemented: Case C–337/13 *Almos Agrárkülkereskedelmi Kft* EU:C:2014:328, [21].

[119] G Betlem, 'The Principle of Indirect Effect of Community Law' (1995) 3 ERPL 1; M Amstutz, 'In-Between Worlds: *Marleasing* and the Emergence of Interlegality in Legal Reasoning' (2005) 11 ELJ 766.

within their jurisdiction, the courts. It follows that, in applying national law, whether the provisions in question were adopted before or after the directive, the national court called upon to interpret it is required to do so, as far as possible, in the light of the wording and the purpose of the directive in order to achieve the result pursued by the latter and thereby comply with the third paragraph of Article 189 of the Treaty.

(iii) *The Scope of the Interpretive Obligation*

There are three related points to note about the scope of the interpretive obligation.

First, it is clear from *Marleasing* and subsequent case law that the obligation of harmonious interpretation applies even where the national law *pre-dates* the directive and has no specific connection with it. In *Marleasing* there was no domestic implementing legislation which could be interpreted in the light of the Directive, but only domestic law pre-dating the Directive.

Secondly, it is clear from cases such as *Pfeiffer* that the interpretive obligation applies not only to national law that implements the directive, but to the national legal system as a whole.[120]

Cases C–397–403/01 **Pfeiffer and others v Deutsches Rotes Kreuz, Kreisverband Waldshut eV**
[2004] ECR I–8835

The case concerned the interpretation of directives on health and safety at work and working time. The claimants were workers employed by the defendant, the German Red Cross. They argued that they had been required to work in excess of 48 hours per week, in violation of the Directive. The ECJ reiterated that directives cannot have horizontal direct effect, but held that the interpretive obligation from *Von Colson* was applicable.

THE ECJ

115. Although the principle that national law must be interpreted in conformity with Community law concerns chiefly domestic provisions enacted in order to implement the directive in question, it does not entail an interpretation merely of those provisions but requires the national court to consider national law as a whole in order to assess to what extent it may be applied so as not to produce a result contrary to that sought by the directive (see, to that effect, *Carbonari*, paragraphs 49 and 50).

116. In that context, if the application of interpretative methods recognised by national law enables, in certain circumstances, a provision of domestic law to be construed in such a way as to avoid conflict with another rule of domestic law or the scope of that provision to be restricted to that end by applying it only in so far as it is compatible with the rule concerned, the national court is bound to use those methods in order to achieve the result sought by the directive.

...

118. In this instance, the principle of interpretation in conformity with Community law thus requires the referring court to do whatever lies within its jurisdiction, having regard to the whole body of rules of national law, to ensure that Directive 93/104 is fully effective, in order to prevent the maximum weekly working time laid down in Article 6(2) of the directive from being exceeded (see, to that effect, *Marleasing*, paragraphs 7 and 13).

---

[120] See also Case C–12/08 *Mono Car Styling SA, in liquidation v Dervis Odemis* [2009] ECR I–6653, [64]; Case C–98/09 *Sorge* (n 109) [51]; Case C–239/09 *Seydaland Vereinigte Agrarbetriebe GmbH & Co KG v BVVG Bodenverwertungs- und -verwaltungs GmbH*, EU:C:2010:778, [50].

Thirdly, although the interpretive obligation is a strong one, it does not require an interpretation of national law that it cannot bear, that is *contra legem*, or that violates a fundamental principle of domestic law. There has been an active debate about how strongly national courts are encouraged to interpret otherwise clear provisions of national law so as to comply with the directive.[121] The Treaty obligation on national courts to take all measures possible to comply with EU law clearly constrains the interpretive discretion those courts would otherwise have under national law. The Court has moreover regularly emphasized the strength of the interpretive obligation.[122]

At the same time, however, the Court has generally left it to national courts to decide whether an interpretation in conformity with a directive is possible,[123] or whether it would result in a *contra legem* reading. In *Wagner-Miret*, the Court accepted that the Spanish legislation in question could not be interpreted in such a way as to give effect to the result sought by the applicants,[124] and the Court in various other cases has accepted the limits of interpretation articulated by the national court or apparent in the terms of the legislation.[125]

However, on occasion, as in *Pupino*, even though the ECJ deferred to the ultimate assessment of the national court, the judgment expressly suggested that an interpretation in conformity with the directive or framework decision seemed possible.[126] Similarly in *Lopez Da Silvo Jorge* concerning the EU framework decision on an arrest warrant, the ECJ ruled firmly that the national court must draw on principles and provisions of domestic law such as the principle of non-discrimination so as to interpret domestic law in conformity with the framework decision, pending its proper implementation by the legislature.[127] And in *Deutsche Lufthansa* the CJEU rejected the interpretation of national law offered by the national court on the basis that it was contrary to the purpose of the EU framework agreement, thus implicitly indicating that an interpretation in conformity with EU law would have been possible.[128]

---

[121] Case 262/88 *Barber v Guardian Royal Exchange* [1990] ECR 1889, 1937, AG Van Gerven; Cases C–63–64/91 *Jackson v Chief Adjudication Officer* [1992] ECR I–4737, [29], AG Van Gerven; Case C–271/91 *Marshall (No 2)* [1993] ECR I–4367, [10], AG Van Gerven.

[122] Cases C–397–403/01 *Pfeiffer* (n 93) [118]; C–268/06 *Impact* (n 23) [100]–[101]; C–406/08 *Uniplex (UK) Ltd v NHS Business Services Authority* EU:C:2010:45, [45]–[48]; C–282/10 *Dominguez* EU:C:2012:33, [31]–[32]; and in *Marleasing*, despite declaring that national courts must read national law in conformity with a relevant dir only 'in so far as possible', the ECJ held that the Spanish court was *precluded* from interpreting national law in a way which did not comply with the provisions of the Dir.

[123] In Case C–18/13 *Maks Pen EOOD* EU:C:2014:69, [37]–[39] the CJEU agreed that EU law would not, in principle, require a national court to disregard a principle of national law prohibiting 'reformatio in peius', but did not accept that an interpretation in conformity with EU law would have such an effect in this case. In Case C–177/10 *Rosado Santana* EU:C:2011:557, [60], the CJEU was careful to say that it was not for itself, the CJEU, to rule on the interpretation of provisions of national law. However, where national legislation transposing the dir uses exactly the words contained in the dir, harmonious interpretation is required: Case C–306/12 *Spedition Welter GmbH* EU:C:2013:650, [31]–[32].

[124] Case C–334/92 *Wagner Miret v Fondo de Garantía Salarial* [1993] ECR I–6911, [22].

[125] Cases C–91/92 *Dori* (n 96) [27]; C–192/94 *El Corte Inglés v Cristina Blázques Rivero* [1996] ECR I–1281, [22]; C–111/97 *Evobus Austria v Niederösterreichischer Verkehrsorganisations* [1998] ECR I–5411, [18]–[21]; C–131/97 *Carbonari v Università degli Studi di Bologna* [1999] ECR I–1103, [48]–[50]; C–81/98 *Alcatel Austria v Bundesministerium für Wissenschaft und Verkehr* [1999] ECR I–7671, [49]–[50]; C–282/10 *Dominguez* EU:C:2012:33, [25]; C–351/12 *OSA—Ochranný svaz autorský pro práva k dílům hudebním o.s.* EU:C:2014:110, [43]; C–501–506, 540 and 541/12 *Specht* EU:C:2014:2005, [89]–[91]; and C–176/12 *AMS* EU:C:2014:2, [39]–[40].

[126] Case C–105/03 *Pupino* [2005] ECR I–5285, [47]–[49]. See also Case C–185/97 *Coote v Granada Hospital* [1998] ECR I–5199; Case C–168/00 *Leitner v TUI Deutschland* [2002] ECR I–2631, AG Tizzano; Case C–60/00 *Carpenter v Home Secretary* [2002] ECR I–6279, [41], AG Stix Hackl.

[127] Case C–42/11 *João Pedro Lopes Da Silva Jorge* EU:C:2012:517, [53]–[58].

[128] Case C–109/09 *Deutsche Lufthansa AG* EU:C:2011:129, [51]–[57].

(iv) *The Results of the Interpretive Obligation: Criminal Liability*

While the obligation of harmonious interpretation cannot result in the imposition or aggravation of criminal liability on an individual, it may result in other adverse repercussions for the individual. This flows from the principle of non-retroactivity of penal liability articulated by the ECJ in *Kolpinghuis Nijmegen*.[129] In this case, the Dutch prosecution authorities sought to use the provisions of an unimplemented directive against the defendant. The ECJ in *Kolpinghuis Nijmegen*, after reiterating the principle of interpretation in paragraph 26 of *Von Colson*, declared that:

> [T]he obligation on the national court to refer to the content of the directive when interpreting the relevant rules of its national law is limited by the general principles of law which form part of Community law and in particular the principles of legal certainty and non-retroactivity . . . a directive cannot, of itself and independently of a law adopted for its implementation, have the effect of determining or aggravating the liability in criminal law of persons who act in contravention of the provisions of that directive.[130]

(v) *The Results of the Interpretive Obligation: Non-Criminal Liability*

There has been more debate as to the relationship between the duty of harmonious interpretation and non-criminal liability, in particular the implications for individuals. In *Arcaro* the ECJ ruled:[131]

> However, that obligation of the national court to refer to the content of the directive when interpreting the relevant rules of its own national law reaches a limit where such an interpretation leads to the imposition on an individual of an obligation laid down by a directive which has not been transposed, or, more especially, where it has the effect of determining or aggravating, on the basis of the Directive and in the absence of a law enacted for its implementation, the liability in criminal law of persons who act in contravention of that directive's provisions (see *Kolpinghuis Nijmegen*, cited above).[132]

The case was concerned with criminal liability. The Court seemed however to suggest a narrowing of the principle of interpretation such that where an interpretation of national law in the light of a directive amounted to 'the imposition on an individual of an obligation laid down in the directive',[133] it went too far and was neither permitted nor required by EU law. This was reiterated in *Kofoed*,[134] a case concerned with tax, not criminal law. This suggests that a distinction has to be made between the 'imposition of an obligation' on an individual, which is not permitted, and the creation of other kinds of legal disadvantage or detriment for that party falling short of a legal obligation, which is permitted.[135] In *Hessen v Frank Mücksch*, for example, which concerned the imposition of planning restrictions by a local authority on a commercial entity, the ECJ ruled that the local authority must

---

129 Cases 80/86 *Kolpinghuis Nijmegen* [1987[ECR 3969; C–60/02 *X* [2004] ECR I–651, [54]–[64].

130 Ibid [13]–[14]. See also, Cases C–74 and 129/95 *Criminal Proceedings against X* [1996] ECR I–6609; Case C–384/02 *Knud Grøngaard and Allan Bang* [2005] ECR I–9939, [30].

131 Case C–168/95 *Arcaro* [1996] ECR I–4705.

132 Ibid [42]. See also Case C–105/03 *Pupino* (n 126) [45]–[47].

133 P Craig, 'Directives: Direct Effect, Indirect Effect and the Construction of National Legislation' (1997) 22 ELRev 519.

134 Case C–321/05 *Kofoed v Skatteministeriet* [2007] ECR I–5795, [45].

135 See AG Jacobs in Case C–456/98 *Centrosteel v Adipol* [2000] ECR I–6007, [31]–[35], who suggested that *Arcaro* should be confined to the issue of the imposition of criminal obligations.

follow the principle of harmonious interpretation even when it had no discretion in the exercise of its powers, and that the state was entitled 'to impose on individuals an interpretation in keeping with the Directive'.[136] The interpretation being 'imposed' on an individual in this case was an interpretation of the national planning law in question which would prohibit the siting of Mücksch's garden centre close to a chemical plant, since this siting would contravene an EU directive.

It seems clear that the interpretive obligation may lead to the imposition on an individual of civil liability which would not otherwise have existed.[137] The exact nature of the civil liability or civil obligation will depend upon the case, and the 'correct characterization' will depend on the change to pre-existing national law caused by reading it in the light of the directive.[138] But it is clear that if pre-existing national law is interpreted differently because of the interpretive obligation, the corollary is that the obligations on the private party will alter, and this may well lead to civil liabilities or obligations that would not have existed hitherto, even if they are not 'directly' imposed by the directive.[139]

In *Centrosteel*,[140] for example, an Italian company claimed for payment under a commercial agency contract with the defendant Adipol, an Austrian company. The latter argued that the contract was void because of Centrosteel's failure to comply with the Italian legal requirement of compulsory registration of commercial agents. Centrosteel counter-argued that Directive 86/653 as interpreted by the ECJ[141] only required an agency contract to be written, and precluded a law such as the Italian registration requirement. The ECJ held that the national court must interpret national law in the light of the Directive,[142] with the result that Adipol would be under a legal obligation to pay the amount due under the contract with Centrosteel. If Italian law were not read in the light of the Directive, however, and if the agency contract were rendered void for violation of Italian registration law, Adipol would not be under this obligation. This kind of effect has been referred to as the 'exclusionary effect' of a directive: it prevents conflicting national law from being enforced, but it does not amount to a 'substitution effect' since it is the commercial contract and not the directive itself which imposes obligations on the parties. We shall return to the soundness of this distinction later.

(vi) *Summary*

i. The doctrine of indirect effect is in practical terms the most important qualification to the principle that directives do not have horizontal direct effect. It is however problematic for private defendants in terms of legal certainty, which is paradoxical given that concerns about legal certainty are said to underpin the rule that directives should not have horizontal direct effect.

ii. A company seeking to determine whether it should follow national law or a non-implemented directive has a difficult task. If directives had horizontal direct effect, the company would simply compare relevant national law with the directive, and in the event of inconsistencies it would determine whether the provisions of the directive were sufficiently precise and unconditional.

---

[136] Case C–53/10 *Hessen v Frank Mücksch* EU:C:2011:585, [34].

[137] See AG Kokott in Case C–321/05 *Kofoed* (n 134) fn 45. See, however, the more cautious Opinion of AG Colomer in Cases C–392 and 422/04 *i-21 Germany GmbH and ISIS Multimedia Net GmbH & Co KG v Bundesrepublik Deutschland* [2006] ECR I–8559, [87]–[91].

[138] Craig (n 94) 362–364.

[139] See, eg, Case C–291/13 *Sotiris Papasavvas* EU:C:2014:2209, [54]–[56] concerning civil actions for defamation between private parties in the context of electronic commerce.

[140] Case C–456/98 *Centrosteel* (n 135).

[141] Case C–215/97 *Bellone v Yokohama* [1998] ECR I–2191.

[142] Case C–456/98 *Centrosteel* (n 135) [19]; see also Cases C–240–244/98 *Océano Grupo* (n 9); J Stuyck, Note (2001) 38 CMLRev 719.

Assuming that they were, the company would follow the directive, which under the principle of primacy would take priority over conflicting domestic law.

iii. Given the lack of horizontal direct effect, the company must not only identify any possible inconsistencies between national law and the directive. It must examine all provisions of the directive, even those which are not sufficiently precise or certain for direct effect. It must then make a rough guess as to whether a national court would feel able to read national law to be in conformity with the directive. It would be very difficult to predict the outcome of any litigation, since the duty of harmonious interpretation demands that national courts consider all national law in deciding whether compatibility with the provisions of the directive can be attained. Further, uncertainties remain as to the extent to which the principle of harmonious interpretation can lead to the imposition of legal obligations on a private defendant.

(c) INCIDENTAL HORIZONTAL EFFECTS

(i) *The Doctrine*

The third development which has lessened the impact of the *Marshall/Dori* no-horizontal-direct-effect-of-directives rule is case law which permits the use of unimplemented directives in certain cases between private parties. This development, which is most evident in *CIA Security*[143] and *Unilever Italia*,[144] is complex and confusing. Like the cases concerning indirect effect, it is often difficult to distinguish these cases convincingly from direct horizontal effect.

The following cases suggest that directives can have a limited form of horizontal effect when they do not directly impose legal obligations on individuals. The essence of these cases is that an individual can plead a directive in an action against another individual, and it can affect the outcome of the case even if it does not directly impose obligations on the private defendant. This is the kind of 'exclusionary' effect referred to by Advocate General Saggio in the *Océano* case: the directive is invoked in a case between individuals to preclude the application of a conflicting provision of national law, and the result is that one of the parties to the case is subject to a legal liability or disadvantage to which it would not have been subject had the offending national law been applied.[145]

Case C–194/94 **CIA Security International SA v Signalson SA and Securitel SPRL**
[1996] ECR I–2201

CIA Security brought proceedings against the defendants before the Belgian commercial courts asking for orders requiring them to cease unfair trading practices. CIA argued that the two companies had libelled it by claiming that the alarm system which it marketed had not been approved as required under Belgian legislation. CIA agreed that it had not sought approval but argued that the Belgian legislation was in breach of Article 28 EC and had not been notified to the Commission as required by Directive 83/189 on technical standards and regulations. The national court asked the ECJ whether the Directive was sufficiently clear and precise to be directly effective before the national court, and whether a national court should refuse to apply a national measure which had not been communicated as required by the Directive. The ECJ began by ruling that the national regulation should indeed have been notified under the Directive.

---

[143] Case C–194/94 *CIA Security International SA v Signalson SA and Securitel SPRL* [1996] ECR I–2201.
[144] Case C–443/98 *Unilever Italia SpA v Central Food SpA* [2000] ECR I–7535.
[145] Case C–244/98 (n 9).

THE ECJ

44. [A]rticles 8 and 9 of Directive 83/189 lay down a precise obligation on Member States to notify draft technical regulations to the Commission before they are adopted. Being, accordingly, unconditional and sufficiently precise in their content, those articles may be relied on by individuals before national courts.

45. It remains to examine the legal consequences to be drawn from a breach by Member States of their obligation to notify and, more precisely, whether Directive 83/189 is to be interpreted as meaning that a breach of the obligation to notify, constituting a procedural defect in the adoption of the technical regulations concerned, renders such technical regulations inapplicable so that they may not be enforced against individuals.

The Court ruled that part of the aim of the Directive was to protect the free movement of goods by preventive control,[146] and that it would enhance the effectiveness of that control to provide that a breach of the obligation to notify would render the un-notified domestic rule inapplicable to individuals.[147] The ECJ did not mention *Dori* or *Marshall* and did not advert to the fact that this was a case between private parties. However, although CIA relied on the Directive primarily against the application of the state's technical regulation concerning approval of alarm systems, this changed the legal outcome before the national court: the defendant could now be liable for unfair trading, because its argument that CIA had marketed its alarm system in breach of Belgian law fell away, since the Belgian law was contrary to the Directive. Thus, although the Directive did not itself impose a legal obligation on the defendants, it removed the protection of the national technical regulation and exposed them to potential liability under other provisions of national law.

The issue of indirect horizontal reliance on directives in disputes involving private parties is also apparent in other cases.[148] The crucial factor is that one party suffers a legal detriment and the other party gains a legal advantage from the terms of an unimplemented directive.[149] The common factor, shared also by the *Océano, Centrosteel*, and *Pfeiffer* cases on indirect effect discussed above, seems to be that the directive does not *of itself* impose an obligation on another individual, and that the obligation is imposed by some other provision of national or private law. This incidental effect of directives is apparent in *Unilever*.[150]

---

[146] This factor was used to limit the application of the *CIA Security* ruling in the later case of Case C–226/97 *Lemmens* [2000] ECR I–3711. See also Case C 307/13 *Ivansson* EU:C:2014:258.

[147] Attempts to invoke Dir 83/189 [1983] OJ L109/8 were not however successful in Cases C–425–427/97 *Albers* [1999] ECR I–2947; Case C–37/99 *Donkersteeg* [2000] ECR I–10223; Case C–314/98 *Sneller's Autos v Algemeen Directeur van de Dienst Wegverkeer* [2000] ECR I–8633; Case C–278/99 *Van der Burg* [2001] ECR I–2015. Moreover the obligation imposed on Member States by various dirs to notify the Commission of national rules could not be invoked by individuals to challenge national legislation in Case C–235/95 *AGS Assedic Pas-de-Calais v François Dumon* [1998] ECR I–4531, [32]–[33]; Case 280/87 *Enichem Base v Comune di Cinisello Balsamo* [1989] ECR 2491, [22]–[24].

[148] Case C–441/93 *Panagis Pafitis v Trapeza Kentrikis Ellados AE* [1996] ECR I–1347; Case C–129/94 *Criminal Proceedings Against Rafael Ruiz Bernáldez* [1996] ECR I–1829; Case C–77/97 *Österreichische Unilever GmbH v Smithkline Beecham* [1999] ECR I–431.

[149] For a different view, which sees the cases as being about 'disguised vertical direct effect' in which a private party is precluded from benefiting from the state's substantive breach of an EC dir, see M Dougan, 'The "Disguised" Vertical Direct Effect of Directives' (2000) 59 CLJ 586.

[150] S Weatherill, 'Compulsory Notification of Draft Technical Regulations: The Contribution of Directive 83/189 to the Management of the Internal Market' (1996) 16 YBEL 129; S Weatherill, 'A Case Study in Judicial Activism in the 1990s: The Status before National Courts of Measures Wrongfully Un-notified to the Commission' in D O'Keeffe and A Bavasso (eds), *Judicial Review in EU Law* (Kluwer, 2000) 481.

Case C–443/98 **Unilever Italia SpA v Central Food SpA**
[2000] ECR I–7535

The Directive was invoked to prevent the enforcement of a national regulation which, although properly notified, had been adopted in breach of a standstill clause under Directive 83/189. The contract was for delivery of a quantity of olive oil, and the olive oil delivered by the plaintiff was labelled in a way which complied with EC law, but not with the contested Italian labelling legislation. Thus it was a case where reliance by one party on the terms of the Directive in order to have national law disapplied would result in the imposition of contractual obligations on the defendant, which would not have been imposed had the national law been applied. Advocate General Jacobs evidently had doubts about the *CIA Security* ruling, and argued that the offending national legislation should not be rendered unenforceable in private contractual proceedings of this kind. He contended that such unenforceability would give rise to considerable legal uncertainty, and that it would be unjust since it would penalize individuals for the state's failure.[151] The ECJ however disagreed and did not address the Advocate General's arguments.[152] Having recalled in paragraphs 40–43 its reasoning in *CIA Security* about the aim of Directive 83/189 and why it should render unenforceable any national regulations adopted in breach thereof, the Court continued:

THE ECJ

45. It is therefore necessary to consider, secondly, whether the inapplicability of technical regulations adopted in breach of Article 9 of Directive 83/189 can be invoked in civil proceedings between private individuals concerning contractual rights and obligations.

46. First, in civil proceedings of that nature, application of technical regulations adopted in breach of Article 9 of Directive 83/189 may have the effect of hindering the use or marketing of a product which does not conform to those regulations.

47. That is the case in the main proceedings, since application of the Italian rules is liable to hinder Unilever in marketing the extra virgin olive oil which it offers for sale.

48. Next, it must be borne in mind that, in *CIA Security*, the finding of inapplicability as a legal consequence of breach of the obligation of notification was made in response to a request for a preliminary ruling arising from proceedings between competing undertakings based on national provisions prohibiting unfair trading.

49. Thus, it follows from the case-law of the Court that the inapplicability of a technical regulation which has not been notified in accordance with Article 8 of Directive 83/189 can be invoked in proceedings between individuals for the reasons set out in paragraphs 40 to 43 of this judgment. The same applies to non-compliance with the obligations laid down by Article 9 of the same directive, and there is no reason, in that connection, to treat disputes between individuals relating to unfair competition, as in the *CIA Security* case, differently from disputes between individuals concerning contractual rights and obligations, as in the main proceedings.

50. Whilst it is true, as observed by the Italian and Danish Governments, that a directive cannot of itself impose obligations on an individual and cannot therefore be relied on as such against an individual (see Case C–91/92 *Faccini Dori* [1994] ECR I–3325, paragraph 20), that case-law does not apply where non-compliance with Article 8 or Article 9 of Directive 83/189, which constitutes a substantial procedural defect, renders a technical regulation adopted in breach of either of those articles inapplicable.

---

[151] See his subsequent Opinion in Case C–159/00 *Sapod Audic v Eco Emballages SA* [2002] ECR I–5031, [62].

[152] S Weatherill, 'Breach of Directives and Breach of Contract' (2001) 26 ELRev 177.

51. In such circumstances, and unlike the case of non-transposition of directives with which the case-law cited by those two Governments is concerned, Directive 83/189 does not in any way define the substantive scope of the legal rule on the basis of which the national court must decide the case before it. It creates neither rights nor obligations for individuals.

The ECJ attempted in two ways to distinguish this case from the prohibited 'horizontal direct effect' cases such as *Dori* and *Marshall*. The first was by emphasizing the particular aim of Directive 83/189 and the rationale outlined in *CIA Security* for declaring national rules which breach this Directive to be unenforceable. Its second and more important argument, for general purposes, was that the Directive itself created no individual rights and imposed no obligations on individuals.

This is the now familiar 'exclusionary effect' argument: that the Directive can be invoked in cases between individuals in order to have national law disapplied, so long as the Directive does not create new law, new rights, or new obligations to be applied. Rather it leaves a 'void' which is filled by other provisions of national law, in this case, of national contract law.

(ii) *Summary*

i. The ECJ has consistently refused to depart from the clear *Marshall/Dori* rulings that a directive cannot be invoked by an individual so as to impose a direct obligation on another individual. Yet cases such as *CIA Security* and *Unilever Italia* demonstrate that directives can be enforced horizontally between the parties, provided that this can be rationalized in terms of an exclusionary, rather than substitutionary effect. This distinction has been articulated principally in the Opinions of Advocates General and in the academic literature, but it seems to underlie the Court's jurisprudence on incidental horizontal effect.

ii. The central idea is that directives can, even in actions between private parties, have an 'exclusionary' impact, excluding inconsistent national law. This is said to flow from the primacy of EU law. The result is then said to be justified on the basis of the national law that subsists in the absence of that part of national law that has been excluded by the directive. This is distinguished from a 'substitution' effect, which connotes the idea that the directive will in itself mandate certain novel legal consequences within the national legal order, where it contains no such provisions. This can, so the argument goes, only occur in actions against the state where the conditions for direct effect have been met. This distinction is however problematic for five reasons.

iii. First, the very determination of whether a case is to be regarded as one of 'exclusion' or 'substitution' can be contestable, and depends on the identification of some 'default rule' of the national legal system that will govern the matter, once the provision that is inconsistent with the directive is excluded.[153]

iv. Secondly, the distinction between 'exclusion', combined with the residual application of national law, and 'substitution', entailing the application of 'new' rules derived from the directive, cannot mask the reality that in both instances it is the directive that mandates the outcome and this constitutes a new legal status quo within the national legal system.

v. Thirdly, the very fact that the directive does not impose obligations directly on the individual, but nonetheless has the legal effects on private law relations exemplified by *Unilever*, is more burdensome for the private firm which may have no knowledge of the breach of the obligation by the state.[154]

---

[153] See, eg, Cases C–240–244/98 *Océano Grupo* (n 9) [39], AG Saggio who talks of the exclusion of the incompatible rule being filled by application by 'analogy or recourse to general principles of national law if those national provisions comply with the principles on which the directive is based'.

[154] The consequent injustice was noted by AG Jacobs in Case C–443/98 *Unilever* (n 144) [101].

vi. Fourthly, the argument is premised on the unspoken assumption that to 'exclude' national law that is inconsistent with a directive is somehow less intrusive or less far-reaching in its consequences for the individual than 'substitution' of something new within the national legal order. There is no reason why this has to be so.

vii. Finally, the exclusionary effect of a directive is said to be based on the primacy of EU law. It is however unclear why, if primacy really is the driving imperative, it should not also demand *substitution* even in horizontal cases.

(D) INTERACTION WITH GENERAL PRINCIPLES OF LAW

(i) *Doctrine*

A fourth qualification to the principle that directives do not have horizontal direct effect is to be found in case law concerned with general principles of law, as we have seen above. In *Mangold*, the ECJ ruled, despite the fact that the time limit for implementation of a provision of the Framework Employment Directive 2000/78 had not yet expired and that this was a case between private parties, that the applicant could rely directly on the EU general principle against age discrimination in order to challenge the provisions of a fixed-term contract set by his employer.[155] We also saw that, despite a strong critical reaction against the *Mangold* ruling, the CJEU in later cases such as *Kücükdeveci* and *HK Danmark* affirmed the core assertion that individuals could invoke the general principles of EU law to set aside conflicting provisions of national law even in cases between private parties.[156] The unquestionable effect of these rulings is to render some of the obligations contained in a directive immediately applicable in an action between private parties, albeit via a general principle of EU law.

(ii) *Summary*

i. Two critiques of this case law can be made. If the Treaty framers truly believed that precise and unconditional obligations from a directive should not be imposed on an individual, it is difficult to explain why they would think it acceptable for an individual to be bound by obligations from a general principle of law, where: the existence of the general principle might be uncertain; where the substance of the obligation was found in the directive; where it was questionable whether the provisions of the directive met the conditions for direct effect; where some other provisions from the directive were read into, or applied through, the general principle; and where it was unclear in advance which provisions of the directive would be read into the general principle.

ii. Secondly, there are problems of legal certainty. This critique is not premised on the assumption that general principles should never be applicable as between individuals.[157] The principal arguments denying horizontal direct effect to directives, however, have been the wording of the Treaty and legal certainty. Yet it is not clear why these problems suddenly become less apparent when the obligation on the private party is formally derived from a general principle of law. Indeed, as we have seen above, horizontal effect introduced via general principles may create even greater problems of legal certainty—including the difficulty of determining which general

---

[155] (N 34) and text.

[156] (Nn 34 and 38.) Note, however, that the ECJ backed away from its assertion in the *Mangold* case that an individual could rely directly on the general principle even before the expiry of the time limit for implementing the dir, which brought the issue 'within the scope of EU law': Case C–147/08 *Römer* EU:C:2011:286, [61]–[62].

[157] For discussion of these questions see, eg, Editorial, 'The Scope of Application of General Principles of Union Law: An Ever Expanding Union?' (2010) 47 CMLRev 1589; K Lenaerts and J Gutierrez-Fons, 'The Constitutional Allocation of Powers and General Principles of EU Law' (2010) 47 CMLRev 1629.

principles are likely to have direct effect, and which provisions of directives are to be seen as giving further effect to them.

(E) REGULATIONS CONDITIONAL ON COMPLIANCE WITH DIRECTIVES

(i) *Doctrine*

The qualification to the *Marshall* ruling considered here is considerably less controversial than that which arises from the interaction between general principles and directives, even though it may be of significant practical importance for private defendants. The basic precept is that while directives cannot have horizontal direct effect, they may do so when benefits under a regulation are made conditional on compliance with a directive.

Cases C–37 and 58/06 **Viamex Agrar Handels GmbH and Zuchtvieh-Kontor GmbH (ZVK) v Hauptzollamt Hamburg-Jonas**
[2008] ECR I–69

Payment of export refunds for live animals was dealt with through Regulation 615/98, which however conditioned payment on compliance with Directive 91/628. The Directive laid down rules to protect the welfare of live animals during transit. The German authorities refused to pay the refunds because of non-compliance by the exporter with the 24-hour rest period for animals prescribed by the Directive.

THE ECJ

25. [T]he Finanzgericht Hamburg observes, in essence, that Regulation No 615/98 and Directive 91/628 pursue different objectives and that a regulation cannot thus refer in global terms to a directive which is, moreover, 'regrettably vague'.

26. It must be emphasised in this regard that the simple fact that payment of export refunds for live bovine animals is subject under Regulation No 615/98 to compliance with a number of conditions laid down in legislation pursuing objectives which are specific to that legislation cannot of itself be regarded as a ground of invalidity in relation to that regulation since, as was stated at paragraphs 22 to 24 above, objectives thus pursued are not only perfectly legitimate but also constitute obligations to which, under Community law, all the Member States and institutions are continuously and permanently subject in the formulation and implementation of the common agricultural policy.

27. It is true that, according to settled case-law, a directive cannot of itself impose obligations on an individual (see, inter alia, Case 152/84 *Marshall* [1986] ECR 723, paragraph 48; Joined Cases C–397/01 to C–403/01 *Pfeiffer*...paragraph 108; Joined Cases C–387/02, C–391/02 and C–403/02 *Berlucsoni*...paragraph 73; and Case C–80/06 *Carp*...paragraph 20).

28. However, it cannot be precluded, in principle, that the provisions of a directive may be applicable by means of an express reference in a regulation to its provisions, provided that general principles of law and, in particular, the principle of legal certainty, are observed.

29. Moreover, the purpose of the general reference made by Regulation No 615/98 to Directive 91/628 is to ensure, for the purposes of the implementation of Article 13(9) of Regulation No 805/68, compliance with the relevant provisions of that directive on the welfare of live animals and, in particular, the protection of animals during transport. That reference, which lays down the conditions for the grant of refunds, cannot therefore be interpreted as covering all the provisions in Directive 91/628 and, in particular, those provisions which have no connection with the principle objective pursued by that directive.

(ii) *Summary*

i. There is much to be said for this substantive decision, since few would argue that exporters should not comply with rules on animal welfare. There are nonetheless two difficulties with the reasoning.

ii. First, the textual reconciliation with *Marshall* is not undertaken by the ECJ. It would presumably be that while a directive cannot 'itself' impose obligations on private parties, it can do so when it is referred to in a regulation, since the latter can have horizontal as well as vertical direct effect, and that the Treaty framers would be content with this. This argument is by no means self-evidently true, more especially when combined with the second difficulty.

iii. Secondly, the decision in *Viamex* is questionable in terms of legal certainty. The ECJ used that concept when considering which provisions of the Directive were made applicable through the Regulation, since, as the referring court noted, the Regulation appeared to make payment of the refunds conditional on compliance with the entirety of the Directive. The ECJ's response in paragraph 29 was that notwithstanding the general reference to the Directive, the only provisions made binding were those relating to the purpose of the Regulation, viz, those provisions of the Directive concerning welfare of live animals in transit. This makes sense in substantive terms. It nonetheless generates considerable legal uncertainty for the private party, who, faced by such a regulation making general reference to a directive, would have to divine which provisions of the directive were 'truly' intended to impose obligations on it.[158] There can moreover be considerable difficulties concerning the 'fit' between the regulation and the directive, thereby increasing legal uncertainty for private parties.[159]

(F) STATE LIABILITY IN DAMAGES

A final way for an individual to enforce a directive despite the prohibition on horizontal direct effect is to sue the Member State in damages, pursuant to the *Francovich* ruling, for loss caused by the state's failure to implement a directive.[160] Rather than attempting to enforce the directive against the private party on whom the obligation would be imposed if the directive were properly implemented, the individual can instead bring proceedings for damages against the state. The significance of *Francovich* will be discussed in the next chapter. For now, it is generally mentioned by the Court as a last resort, after the possibilities of direct effect and harmonious interpretation have been deemed unavailable in the case. It should be noted that few successful actions have so far been brought, although perhaps the very existence of the cause of action has provided further incentive for Member States to implement directives properly and on time.[161]

7 CONCLUSIONS

i. Provisions of EU law can be invoked by individuals before national courts provided that they are sufficiently clear, precise, and unconditional. This is known as 'direct effect'. Normally, though not always, this means that they are capable of conferring rights on individuals.

---

[158] The rule binding the defendant in *Viamex* was contained in point 48(5) of Chap VII of the Annex to Dir 91/628.

[159] Case C–207/06 *Schwaninger Martin Viehhandel—Viehexport v Zollamt Salzburg, Erstattungen* [2008] ECR I–5561.

[160] Cases C–6 and 9/90 *Francovich and Bonifaci v Italy* [1991] ECR I–5357.

[161] Note, however, that, a state cannot import *Francovich* criteria (lack of serious fault on its part) into a simple action based on the vertical direct effect of a clear provision of EU law: see Cases C–259 and 260/10 *The Rank Group plc* EU:C:2010:470, [70]. For a recent report on domestic *Francovich* actions, see 'Bottom Up or Rock Bottom Harmonization? Francovich State Liability in National Courts', in B Van Leeuwen and R Condon (eds), EUI Department of Law Research Paper No LAW 2015/3.

ii. The legal effect of directives is complex. They have vertical but not horizontal direct effect. The Court has however crafted a growing number of qualifications to the proposition that directives do not have horizontal direct effect. The result is that directives can still have 'legal effect' on private parties in a wide and sometimes confusing variety of ways.

iii. The resultant body of law is complex and difficult to understand even for the expert, let alone the ordinary private defendant. Complexity in law is sometimes inevitable, but complexity is not warranted in this area of the law, nor has it been justified.

iv. The complex case law is the result of two conflicting impulses. The Court seems, on the one hand, to have locked itself into the proposition that directives cannot have horizontal direct effect, even though the legal rationale for this position is highly contestable. The Court is determined, on the other hand, to promote the effectiveness of directives in a variety of complex legal ways regardless of their proper domestic implementation, even though this makes the prohibition on horizontal direct effect look hollow.

v. The consequence is considerable legal uncertainty for private defendants. This is paradoxical given that one of the reasons advanced for not having horizontal direct effect is that it would be problematic in terms of legal certainty. The reality is that when judged in such terms the private defendant fares worse under the present law than if horizontal direct effect existed.

vi. The only real winners in all this are the lawyers, in the sense that it is virtually impossible for the private defendant to navigate this terrain without legal advice, but what may be good for lawyers does not translate into overall social good.

8 FURTHER READING

(a) Books

PRECHAL, S, *Directives in EC Law* (Oxford University Press, 2nd edn, 2005)

PRINSSEN, J, *Direct Effect: Rethinking a Classic of EC Legal Doctrine* (Europa Law Publishing, Hogendrop Papers, 2002)

(b) Articles

BETLEM, G, 'The Doctrine of Consistent Interpretation: Managing Legal Uncertainty' (2002) 22 OJLS 397

CRAIG, P, 'The Legal Effect of Directives: Policy, Rules and Exceptions' (2009) 34 ELRev 349

CURTIN, D, 'The Province of Government: Delimiting the Direct Effect of Directives in the Common Law Context' (1990) 15 ELRev 195

DASHWOOD, A, 'From *Van Duyn* to *Mangold* via *Marshall*: Reducing Direct Effect to Absurdity?' (2006–7) 9 CYELS 81

DE WITTE, B, 'Direct Effect, Supremacy and the Nature of the Legal Order' in P Craig and G de Búrca (eds), *The Evolution of EU Law* (Oxford University Press, 2nd edn, 2011) ch 12

DOUGAN, M, 'When Worlds Collide! Competing Visions of the Relationship between Direct Effect and Supremacy' (2007) 44 CMLRev 931

LECZYKIEWICZ, D, 'Horizontal Application of the Charter of Fundamental Rights' (2013) 38 ELRev 479

MASTROIANNI, R, 'On the Distinction Between Vertical and Horizontal Direct Effect of Directives: What Role for the Principle of Equality?' (1999) 5 EPL 417

PRECHAL, S, 'Does Direct Effect Still Matter?' (2000) 37 CMLRev 1047

ROBIN-OLIVIER, S, 'The Evolution of Direct Effect in the EU: Stocktaking, Problems, Projections' (2014) 12 I-CON 165

VAN GERVEN, W, 'Of Rights, Remedies and Procedures' (2000) 37 CMLRev 501

WEATHERILL, S, 'Breach of Directives and Breach of Contract' (2001) 26 ELRev 177

8

THE APPLICATION OF EU LAW: REMEDIES IN NATIONAL COURTS

1 CENTRAL ISSUES

i. The CJEU has developed the requirement of effectiveness of EU law, including the principle of effective judicial protection, as a general legal principle. This requirement includes an obligation on national courts to ensure they give adequate effect to EU law in cases arising before them. The Court has increasingly cited the ECHR and the Charter of Fundamental Rights to underscore the principle of effective judicial protection as a fundamental right, and has emphasized the duty of loyal cooperation in Article 4(3) TEU as a basis for the obligations of effective enforcement of EU law.

ii. Article 19 TEU outlines the role of the CJEU, and specifies that 'Member States shall provide remedies sufficient to ensure effective legal protection in the fields covered by Union law'. Article 47 of the Charter of Fundamental Rights, which enjoys the same legal status as the EU Treaties, provides that '[e]veryone whose rights and freedoms guaranteed by the law of the Union are violated has the right to an effective remedy before a tribunal in compliance with the conditions laid down in this Article'.

iii. Beyond these broad provisions, EU law does not lay down any general scheme of substantive or procedural law governing remedies for its enforcement. Sectoral legislation addressing remedial issues in various issue areas of EU law exists,[1] and there have been moves towards more ambitious harmonization and coordination projects in civil law, criminal law, and contract law.[2]

---

[1] Examples can be found in the fields of public procurement, environmental law, intellectual property, consumer protection, and most recently competition law. For the latter, see Dir 2014/104 on certain rules governing actions for damages under national law for infringements of the competition law provisions of the Member States and of the EU [2004] OJ L349/1.

[2] Art 81 TFEU governs the adoption of measures concerning judicial cooperation in civil matters with a view to eliminating obstacles to the cross-border functioning of *civil proceedings*: see E Storskrubb, *Civil Procedure and EU Law* (Oxford University Press, 2008) and Z Vernadacki, 'Civil Procedure Harmonization in the EU: Unravelling the Policy Considerations' (2013) 9 Journal of Contemporary European Research 297. Arts 82–86 TFEU govern the harmonization of *criminal law measures*: see the report and Resolution of 22 May 2012 of the European Parliament, 'Report on an EU Approach to Criminal Law' A7-0144/2012, and the research summarized at: 'Justice and Home Affairs after the Stockholm Program', http://epthinktank.eu/2014/06/25/justice-and-home-affairs-af ter-the-stockholm-programme/. For reviews of the various proposals and attempts to harmonize in the field of European *contract law* see J Devenney and M Kenny, *The Transformation of European Private Law* (Cambridge

iv. Early CJEU case law emphasized a principle of national procedural autonomy, whereby EU law would be enforced according to the procedures and rules established by national law, and there was no requirement to create new remedies. This was subject to two further conditions: (i) rights deriving from EU law must be subject to the same procedures as rights deriving from national law (equivalence) and (ii) national rules and procedures should not render the exercise of EU rights impossible in practice (practical possibility).

v. The Court in later cases also articulated a stronger requirement of adequacy and effectiveness in the domestic enforcement of EU law, going beyond practical possibility, and based on the principle of sincere cooperation in Article 4(3) TEU. In a number of cases the CJEU required national courts to make available a particular type of remedy (eg restitution or interim relief), regardless of whether this would be available under national law.

vi. The most famous judgment in which the CJEU ruled that EU law requires national courts to provide a *specific* form of remedy is *Francovich*, in which the principle of state liability to provide compensation for breaches of EU law was introduced. The scope of this EU 'right to reparation' from the state was subsequently expanded and clarified, and a parallel principle of individual liability for breaches of EU law, at least in the field of competition law, was introduced.

vii. While the idea of national procedural autonomy remains important, the qualifications of equivalence and effectiveness operate as powerful doctrinal tools directing national courts to undertake a case-by-case appraisal of national rules. National courts are expected to engage in a context-specific proportionality analysis of any restrictive provisions of national law and to disapply these whenever necessary to give effect to EU law.

viii. More pronounced intervention by the CJEU into the arena of national procedural and remedial law, sometimes in conjunction with EU legislative intervention, can be seen in particular sectors such as competition law, anti-discrimination and—particularly in the context of mortgage repayment and repossession proceedings during the recent EU economic crisis—consumer protection.

2 THE PRINCIPLES OF NATIONAL PROCEDURAL AUTONOMY, EQUIVALENCE, AND PRACTICAL POSSIBILITY

(A) WHERE NO RELEVANT EU RULES EXIST: NATIONAL LAW DETERMINES THE CONDITIONS FOR ENFORCEMENT OF EU RIGHTS

Early in its case law the CJEU ruled that it was for the national legal system to determine how the interests of a person adversely affected by an infringement of EU law were to be protected.[3]

University Press, 2013) and K Gutman, *The Constitutional Foundations of European Contract Law* (Oxford University Press, 2014). A 'European Law Institute' was founded in 2011 with a view, amongst other things, 'to draft, evaluate or improve principles and rules which are common to the European legal systems' http://www.europeanlawinstitute.eu/.

[3] Case 6/60 *Humblet v Belgium* [1960] ECR 559; Case 13/68 *Salgoil v Italian Ministry for Foreign Trade* [1973] ECR 453.

Case 33/76 **Rewe-Zentralfinanz eG and Rewe-Zentral AG v
Landwirtschaftskammer für das Saarland**
[1976] ECR 1989

[Note Lisbon Treaty renumbering: Art 5 EEC is now Art 4(3) TFEU]

The applicant companies applied for a refund, including interest, of charges they had paid in Germany for import inspection costs, which had been imposed in violation of the Treaty. The national time limit for contesting the validity of national administrative measures had passed, and the case was referred to the CJEU to see whether EU law required that they be granted the remedy sought.

THE ECJ[4]

Applying the principle of cooperation laid down in Article 5 of the Treaty, it is the national courts which are entrusted with ensuring the legal protection which citizens derive from the direct effect of the provisions of Community law.

Accordingly, in the absence of Community rules on this subject, it is for the domestic legal system of each Member State to designate the courts having jurisdiction and to determine the procedural conditions governing actions at law intended to ensure the protection of the rights which citizens have from the direct effect of Community law, it being understood that such conditions cannot be less favourable than those relating to similar actions of a domestic nature...

...In the absence of such measures of harmonisation the right conferred by Community law must be exercised before the national courts in accordance with the conditions laid down by national rules.

The position would be different only if the conditions and time-limits made it impossible in practice to exercise the rights which the national courts are obliged to protect.

This is not the case where reasonable periods of limitation of actions are fixed.

It has been suggested that 'procedural competence'[5] or 'national procedural responsibility' are better terms than 'procedural autonomy' since both the case law and now Article 19(1) TEU clearly emphasize the responsibility of Member States, where there are no relevant EU rules, for determining the procedural conditions under which EU rights are to be protected.[6] Nevertheless, the term 'national procedural autonomy' continues to be widely used, including by the CJEU.

(B) THE PRINCIPLES OF EQUIVALENCE
AND PRACTICAL POSSIBILITY

Two EU requirements were then imposed by the CJEU: first, the principle of *equivalence* or non-discrimination, meaning that the remedies and forms of action available to ensure the observance of national law must be made available in the same way to ensure the observance of EU law;[7] and

---

[4] [1976] ECR 1989, 1997.

[5] This has been suggested by numerous authors including W van Gerven, M Dougan, and C Kakouris. See also J Delicostopoulos, 'Towards European Procedural Primacy in National Legal Systems' (2003) 9 ELJ 599.

[6] Case 45/76 *Comet BV v Produktschap voor Siergewassen* [1976] ECR 2043; Case 179/84 *Bozetti v Invernizzi* [1985] ECR 2301.

[7] For criticism of the conflation of 'procedures' and 'remedies' see C Kilpatrick, 'The Future of Remedies in Europe' in C Kilpatrick, T Novitz, and P Skidmore (eds), *The Future of Remedies in Europe* (Hart, 2000) 1, 4.

secondly, the principle of *practical possibility*, meaning that national rules and procedures should not make the exercise of an EU right impossible in practice.[8]

(c) NO OBLIGATION TO CREATE NEW REMEDIES (UNLESS...)

Subject to these two requirements, the early case law provided that procedures and remedies for breach of EU law were primarily a matter for the Member States. In the absence of EU rules to that effect, the states were not required to provide remedies which would not be available under national law. In *Rewe-Handelsgesellschaft Nord v Hauptzollamt Kiel* (the 'butter-buying cruises' case), the CJEU was asked whether a trader had a right under EU law to require a national court to compel his third party competitor to comply with EU obligations.[9] The Court ruled:

> [I]t must be remarked first of all that, although the Treaty has made it possible in a number of instances for private persons to bring a direct action, where appropriate, before the Court of Justice, it was not intended to create new remedies in the national courts to ensure the observance of Community law other than those already laid down by national law.[10]

However, the 'no new remedies' rule has been qualified by the Court in various ways. Even in some of its early rulings concerning the repayment of charges levied in breach of EU law, the CJEU effectively insisted that a right to repayment must in principle be available under national law, on the basis that this flowed directly from the substantive provisions of EU law in question.[11] In *San Giorgio* the Court ruled:

> 12. In that connection it must be pointed out in the first place that entitlement to the repayment of charges levied by a member state contrary to the rules of Community law is a consequence of, and an adjunct to, the rights conferred on individuals by the Community provisions prohibiting charges having an effect equivalent to customs duties or, as the case may be, the discriminatory application of internal taxes.[12]

This line of case law concerning unlawfully levied charges can be read as imposing a particular remedy,[13] or insisting as a matter of EU law on the availability of a particular remedy within national legal systems.[14] Nonetheless, even in these repayment cases the Court continues to emphasize the

---

[8] In Case 309/85 *Barra v Belgium* [1988] ECR 355 the Court considered that national legislation restricting repayment of a fee which had been charged in breach of EU law would render the exercise of EU rights impossible in practice; see also Case C–62/00 *Marks & Spencer v Commissioners of Customs and Excise* [2002] ECR I–6325.

[9] Case 158/80 *Rewe-Handelsgesellschaft Nord mbH v Hauptzollamt Kiel* [1981] ECR 1805.

[10] Ibid [44].

[11] See, eg, Case 199/82 *Amministrazione delle Finanze dello Stato v San Giorgio* [1983] ECR 3595; Cases C–192–218/95 *Comateb v Directeur Général des Douanes et Droits Indirects* [1997] ECR I–165. There is an extensive case law on the recovery of unlawfully levied charges, and in particular on the compatibility with EU law of different versions of the defence of 'passing on': see (n 243), and also Case C–309/06 *Marks & Spencer plc v Commissioners of Customs & Excise* [2008] ECR I–2283; Case C–524/04 *Test Claimants in the Thin Cap Group Litigation* [2007] ECR I–2107; Case C–446/04 *Test Claimants in the FII Group Litigation* [2006] ECR I–11753; Case C–201/05 *Test Claimants in the CFC and Dividend Group Litigation* [2008] ECR I–02875.

[12] Case 199/82 *San Giorgio* (n 11).

[13] M Dougan, 'Cutting your Losses in the Enforcement Deficit: A Community Right to the Recovery of Unlawfully Levied Charges?' (1998) 1 CYELS 233.

[14] The national legal system nonetheless retains some discretion in deciding on the exact system for repayment of charges: Cases C–10–22/97 *Ministero delle Finanze v IN.CO.GE.'90 Srl* [1998] ECR I–6307, [28], where the CJEU rejected the Commission's argument about the appropriate national remedy.

primary role of the national legal system in laying down the conditions governing the grant of such a remedy, so long as they satisfied the 'twin principles' of equivalence and practical possibility. As Advocate General Warner said in *Ferwerda*:[15]

To that one might object that, if so, there will be a lack of uniformity in the consequences of the application of Community law in the different Member States. The answer to that objection is...that this Court cannot create Community law where none exists: that must be left to the Community's legislative organs.

Further, despite some strikingly interventionist later cases, the CJEU has continued to insist, notably in the important *Unibet* ruling in 2007, that EU law does not, in principle, require the creation of new national remedies.

40. Although the EC Treaty has made it possible in a number of instances for private persons to bring a direct action, where appropriate, before the Community Court, it was not intended to create new remedies in the national courts to ensure the observance of Community law other than those already laid down by national law...
41. It would be otherwise only if it were apparent from the overall scheme of the national legal system in question that no legal remedy existed which made it possible to ensure, even indirectly, respect for an individual's rights under Community law.[16]

The CJEU ruled in *Unibet* that there was no need for Swedish law to provide a self-standing action to challenge the compatibility of a national provision with EU law, since there were other domestic legal remedies available which enabled the compatibility question to be raised indirectly and which complied with the twin principles.

3 EMERGENCE OF REQUIREMENTS OF PROPORTIONALITY, ADEQUACY, AND EFFECTIVE JUDICIAL PROTECTION

In addition to cases concerning *remedies sought by individuals against the state* for violation of EU law, cases have also arisen concerning *state responses to breaches of EU law by individuals* (enforcement of EU law by the state against individuals[17] or enforcement of EU law by individuals against individuals).

In *Sagulo*, the Court ruled that while states were entitled to impose reasonable penalties for infringements of administrative requirements governing EU residence permits by migrant workers, the penalties must not be *disproportionate* to the offence in question and must not constitute an obstacle to the exercise of fundamental EU rights such as freedom of movement.[18] On the other hand, Member

---

[15] Case 265/78 *Ferwerda v Produktschap voor Vee en Vlees* [1980] ECR 617, 640. Here the Court accepted that the systematic application of the principle of legal certainty could make it practically impossible for the authorities to recover money granted in breach of an EC reg.

[16] Case C–432/05 *Unibet Ltd v Justitiekanslern* [2007] ECR I–2271. The qualification to the 'no-new-remedies' principle in [41] is clearly significant, and the Court in *Unibet* indicated that if an individual were forced to be subject to administrative or criminal proceedings with possible penalties as the sole form of legal remedy for challenging the compatibility of national law with EU law, this would not constitute effective judicial protection.

[17] See, eg, in the employment context, Case C–362/13 *Fiamingo and Others* EU:C:2014:2044; Cases C–22/13, C–61–63/13 and C–418/13 *Mascolo* EU:C:2014:2401.

[18] Case 8/77 *Sagulo, Brenca and Bakhouche* [1977] ECR 1495, [12]–[13]; Case 77/81 *Zuckerfabrik Franken* [1982] ECR 681.

States are *required* by EU law—more specifically by Article 4(3) TEU—to take 'all effective measures to sanction conduct which affects the financial interests' of the EU.[19] Moreover the states may impose criminal penalties even where EU legislation provides only for civil sanctions, so long as any penalties imposed satisfy the principle of equivalence and are 'effective, proportionate and dissuasive'.[20]

Other cases concern the adequacy and deterrent effect of national penalties for breaches by private parties of fundamental EU rules.[21] In *Von Colson*, the Court was asked to rule on the compatibility with EU law of national sanctions designed to remedy breaches of rights enjoyed by individuals under the Equal Treatment Directive (at the time Directive 75/207).[22] The plaintiffs had been discriminated against on grounds of sex in applying for posts as prison workers, but they were told that they were entitled, by way of remedy, only to 'reliance loss', such as the costs of travel to the interview, and not compensation or appointment to the post. The Court ruled:

> 23. Although…full implementation of the directive does not require any specific form of sanction for unlawful discrimination, it does entail that that sanction be such as to guarantee real and effective judicial protection.
>
> …
>
> 28. It should, however, be pointed out to the national court that although Directive No 76/207/EEC, for the purpose of imposing a sanction for the breach of the prohibition of discrimination, leaves the Member States free to choose between the different solutions suitable for achieving its objective, it nevertheless requires that if a Member State chooses to penalize breaches of that prohibition by the award of compensation, then in order to ensure that it is effective and that it has a deterrent effect, that compensation must in any event be adequate in relation to the damage sustained and must therefore amount to more than purely nominal compensation such as, for example, the reimbursement only of the expenses incurred in connection with the application.

The Court in *Von Colson* derived from the Equal Treatment Directive the more robust requirement of *adequacy and effectiveness* of national remedies, and added these to the established principles of practical possibility, equivalence and non-discrimination,[23] and proportionality of penalties. In *Kelly* and *Meister*, the CJEU ruled that a refusal of disclosure of relevant information on the part of a defendant in an employment discrimination case might be such as to undermine the effectiveness of the Directive, and could help to establish a presumption of indirect discrimination.[24] Rulings such as *Johnston*,[25] *Heylens*,[26] and *Panayotova*[27] confirmed that the stronger requirement to provide adequate and effective remedies was a general one, extending beyond sex discrimination law. In *Heylens*, a Belgian football trainer's diploma was refused recognition by the French authorities

---

[19] Case C–186/98 *Nunes and de Matos* [1999] ECR I–4883.

[20] Ibid. Where the penalty is imposed by the state under legislation which of itself is in breach of EU law, the penalty is automatically also invalid, and no question of its proportionality arises: Case C–13/01 *Safalero Srl v Prefetto di Genova* [2003] ECR I–8679. On the proportionality of penalties against corporations for breach of disclosure requirements under EU law, see Case C–418/11 *Textdata Software* EU:C:2013:588.

[21] See also Case 68/88 *Commission v Greece* [1989] ECR 2965; Cases C–378–380/07 *Kiriaki Angelidaki and Others* [2009] ECR I–03071, [159]–[176].

[22] Case 14/83 *Von Colson and Kamann v Land Nordrhein-Westfalen* [1984] ECR 1891.

[23] For cases in which national procedural rules on security for costs were found to be indirectly discriminatory, not as compared with equivalent EU law claims, but in relation to traders from other Member States, see Case C–43/95 *Data Delecta* [1996] ECR I–4661, [12]; Case C–323/95 *Hayes v Kronenberger* [1996] ECR I–1711, [13].

[24] Case C–104/10 *Kelly v NUI* EU:C:2011:506 and Case C–415/10 *Meister v Speech Design* EU:C:2012:217.

[25] Case 222/84 *Johnston v Chief Constable of the RUC* [1986] ECR 1651.

[26] Case 222/86 *UNECTEF v Heylens* [1987] ECR 4097.

[27] Case C–327/02 *Panayotova v Minister voor Vreemdelingenzaken en Integratie* [2004] ECR I–11055.

where he worked, and the CJEU, drawing on the right to an effective judicial remedy in Articles 6 and 13 ECHR, ruled:

> [S]ince free access to employment is a fundamental right which the Treaty confers individually on each worker in the Community, the existence of a remedy of a judicial nature against any decision of a national authority refusing the benefit of that right is essential in order to secure for the individual effective protection for his right.[28]

According to the Court, this right to effective judicial review generally requires the giving of reasons for the curtailment of an EU right and the opportunity to defend that right under the best possible conditions.

4 DEVELOPMENT OF THE 'EFFECTIVENESS' REQUIREMENT

(A) A STRONG INITIAL REQUIREMENT

A robust line of cases in the early 1990s highlighted the tension between the emphasis on national procedural autonomy and the requirement that national remedies must secure the effectiveness of EU rights.

In *Dekker*, the applicant sought damages before the Dutch courts against an employer who, in breach of the EU Equal Treatment Directive, refused to employ her on grounds of her pregnancy. Citing *Von Colson* on the Directive's requirement of effective judicial protection, the CJEU ruled that to subject a claim for redress to a requirement of 'fault' on the part of the employer, or to a defence of justification or another ground of exemption, would undermine the Directive.[29] The fact that the Directive itself required access to a judicial remedy may account in part for the strength of the ruling, but the judgment marked a further dilution of the principle of national procedural autonomy, especially since the national rule did not discriminate between situations involving EU law and those involving domestic law, and the requirement of fault might not render the exercise of the EU right 'impossible' in practice.

In *Cotter and McDermott* the Court ruled that to permit reliance by the national authorities on a domestic law principle against unjust enrichment to deny married women payment of social welfare benefits for dependants which had previously been paid to married men but denied to married women in breach of EU sex discrimination law would allow the authorities to use their own unlawful conduct to undermine the Directive.[30] The desire to prevent the state profiting from its own wrong seems to have played as much a part in the Court's reasoning as the desire not to weaken the effectiveness of the Directive.[31]

In *Emmott*, the applicant sought retrospective payment of a disability benefit for the period in which EU Directive 79/7 on sex discrimination in social security had remained unimplemented in Ireland.[32] She had been told by the government department that no decision could be made in her case

---

[28] Case 222/86 *Heylens* (n 26) [14].

[29] Case C–177/88 *Dekker v Stichting voor Jong Volwassenen (VJV) Plus* [1990] ECR I–3941, [26].

[30] Case C–377/89 *Cotter and McDermott v Minister for Social Welfare* [1991] ECR I–1155, [21].

[31] Contrast Case 68/79 *Hans Just I/S v Danish Ministry for Fiscal Affairs* [1980] ECR 501, in which the state was not obliged to repay taxes it had imposed in breach of Community law, if that would unjustly enrich a trader who had passed on the cost of the tax to third parties. See also Cases C–192–218/95 *Comateb* (n 11); Case C–453/99 *Courage Ltd v Crehan* [2001] ECR I–6297, [30]; Cases C–295–298/04 *Manfredi v Lloyd Adriatico Assicurazion SpA et al* [2006] ECR I–6619. The difference in the way the unjust enrichment argument was treated in these cases on the one hand and in *Cotter* on the other is not always easy to understand. For further cases on this subject see (n 243).

[32] Case C–208/90 *Emmott v Minister for Social Welfare* [1991] ECR I–4269.

pending the CJEU's ruling in *Cotter and McDermott*, but when she finally applied for judicial review of the decisions relating to her benefits the department pleaded that her delay in initiating proceedings constituted a bar to the action. Having set out the principle of national procedural autonomy and the conditions of equivalence and practical possibility, the Court ruled that given the 'particular nature of directives', a Member State could not, where an individual sought to rely on the provisions of a directive, invoke against that individual a national time limit for bringing proceedings until the directive was properly implemented.[33]

On the issue of suspension of national time limits pending the proper implementation of a directive, the *Emmott* ruling was subsequently confined largely to the facts of the case, turning on the misleading conduct of the national authorities.[34] However, the CJEU gave robust remedial rulings in a number of other discrimination cases.[35] More generally it seemed after *Factortame I, Cotter*, and *Emmott*, that the requirement that remedies for breach of EU law should be effective had become stronger and had modified considerably the basic notion of national procedural autonomy. The deference implicit in earlier rulings was replaced by an expectation that national courts would be creative in deciding which national rules should be disapplied in order to enforce EU law more effectively.

A consequence of this creativity was a greater degree of uncertainty for both national courts and litigants. In *Marshall II*, the complainant was faced with a domestic statutory ceiling on awards of compensation for discrimination in breach of EU law. The question was whether the national court should ignore or override the statutory limit even though it did not render the exercise of her right 'practically impossible'.

Case C–271/91 Marshall v Southampton and South-West Hampshire Area Health Authority (II)
[1993] ECR I–4367

Following the ECJ's ruling in Case 152/84 *Marshall (No 1)*,[36] the case was remitted to the Industrial Tribunal, which assessed compensation at £18,405 including a sum of £7,710 by way of interest. Under UK legislation, however, the maximum amount of compensation which could be awarded was £6,250, and it was unclear whether the Industrial Tribunal had power to award interest. The House of Lords asked the ECJ whether such an applicant was entitled to full reparation for the loss sustained, and whether Article 6 of Directive 76/207 could be relied on to challenge national legislation limiting the amount of compensation to be awarded.

THE ECJ

23. . . . Article 6 does not prescribe a specific measure to be taken in the event of a breach of the prohibition of discrimination but leaves Member States free to choose between the different solutions suitable for achieving the objective of the Directive, depending on the different situations which may arise.

---

[33] Ibid [21], [23].

[34] Notably, the Commission tried to revive *Emmott* and give it a broader reading in a 2003 Communication: COM(2002) 725, 'Better Monitoring of the Application of Community Law', fn 36.

[35] The CJEU ruled that following the disapplication of an offending national law and pending the adoption of non-discriminatory rules, the appropriate interim remedy would be to level upwards to the existing EU rule: Case 286/85 *McDermott and Cotter* [1987] ECR 1453; Case C–33/89 *Kowalska* [1990] ECR I–2591, [20]; Case C–18/95 *Terhoeve* [1999] ECR I–345, [57].

[36] See Ch 7.

24. However, the objective is to arrive at real equality of opportunity and cannot therefore be attained in the absence of measures appropriate to restore such equality when it has not been observed. As the Court stated in paragraph 23 in *Von Colson*, cited above, those measures must be such as to guarantee real and effective judicial protection and have a real deterrent effect on the employer.

25. Such requirements necessarily entail that the particular circumstances of each breach of the principle of equal treatment should be taken into account. In the event of discriminatory dismissal contrary to Article 5(1) of the Directive, a situation of equality could not be restored without either reinstating the victim of discrimination or, in the alternative, granting financial compensation for the loss and damage sustained.

26. When financial compensation is the measure adopted in order to achieve the objective indicated above, it must be adequate, in that it must enable the loss and damage actually sustained as a result of the discriminatory dismissal to be made good in full in accordance with the applicable national rules.

...

30. It also follows from that interpretation that the fixing of an upper limit of the kind at issue in the main proceedings cannot, by definition, constitute proper implementation of Article 6 of the directive, since it limits the amount of compensation *a priori* to a level which is not necessarily consistent with the requirement of ensuring real equality of opportunity through adequate reparation for the loss and damage sustained as a result of discriminatory dismissal.

31. With regard to the second part of the second question relating to the award of interest, suffice it to say that full compensation for the loss and damage sustained as a result of discriminatory dismissal cannot leave out of account factors, such as the effluxion of time, which may in fact reduce its value. The award of interest, in accordance with the applicable national rules, must therefore be regarded as an essential component of compensation for the purposes of restoring real equality of treatment.

Here, two national rules governing remedies—a substantive rule imposing a ceiling on damages and a jurisdictional rule concerning the power to award interest—had to be disapplied by the national court in order to provide an effective remedy for breach of EU law.

Marshall II contrasts with earlier case law of the Court, in particular the decisions in *Humblet*[37] and *Roquette*.[38] In those cases the CJEU had ruled that it was for the Member States to decide whether or not to award interest on the reimbursement of sums wrongly levied under Community law, whereas in *Marshall II* it was not open to the Member State to refuse to pay interest. While later cases like *Sutton* narrowed the scope of *Marshall II* in some respects, by treating compensation for dismissal as distinct from repayment of social security arrears,[39] other cases like *Evans* have affirmed and extended it by declaring that where compensation or restitution is required by a particular directive, national law must not exclude factors such as the effluxion of time which affect the value of the compensation or restitution.[40]

Another important case which starkly illustrated the tension between the 'no new remedies' rule and the emerging principle of effectiveness was *Factortame I*.[41] The Court, drawing on its earlier *Simmenthal* ruling,[42] insisted on the priority of the requirement of effectiveness over settled principles of UK law to rather dramatic effect, since the national rule in question was a basic principle ('no

---

[37] Case 6/60 (n 3).
[38] Case 26/74 *Société Roquette Frères v Commission* [1976] ECR 677.
[39] Case C–66/95 *R v Secretary of State for Social Security, ex p Eunice Sutton* [1997] ECR I–2163.
[40] Case C–63/01 *Evans* [2003] ECR I–14447, [67]–[71]. On whether costs are recoverable see Case C–472/99 *Clean Car Autoservice GmbH v Stadt Wien* [2001] ECR I–9687, [27]–[31].
[41] Case C–213/89 *R v Secretary of State for Transport, ex p Factortame Ltd* [1990] ECR I–2433.
[42] Case 106/77 *Amministrazione delle Finanze dello Stato v Simmenthal SpA* [1978] ECR 629.

interim relief against the Crown') which, according to the House of Lords, prohibited absolutely the grant of the particular remedy.

Case C–213/89 R v Secretary of State for Transport, ex parte Factortame Ltd and Others
[1990] ECR I–2433

[Note Lisbon Treaty renumbering: Art 5 EEC is now Art 4(3) TEU]

Factortame and other companies, whose directors and shareholders consisted mainly of Spanish nationals, did not satisfy the new registration conditions introduced by the 1988 Merchant Shipping Act. They argued that these conditions, including a 75 per cent nationality requirement for directors and shareholders, breached EU law, and they sought interim relief pending final judgment. When the case reached the House of Lords it was held that interim relief was precluded both by the common law rule prohibiting the grant of an interim injunction against the Crown and by the presumption that an Act of Parliament is in conformity with EU law until a decision on its compatibility has been given. However, the House of Lords referred the case to the ECJ to see whether interim relief was required as a matter of EU law.

THE ECJ

13. The House of Lords…found in the first place that the claims by the appellants in the main proceedings that they would suffer irreparable damage if the interim relief which they sought were not granted and they were successful in the main proceedings were well founded. However, it held that, under national law, the English courts had no power to grant interim relief in a case such as the one before it….

...

17. [T]he preliminary question raised by the House of Lords seeks essentially to ascertain whether a national court which, in a case before it concerning Community law, considers that the sole obstacle which precludes it from granting interim relief is a rule of national law, must disapply that rule.

...

19. In accordance with the case-law of the Court, it is for the national courts, in application of the principle of cooperation laid down in Article 5 of the EEC Treaty, to ensure the legal protection which persons derive from the direct effect of provisions of Community law….

20. The Court has also held that any provision of a national legal system and any legislative, administrative or judicial practice which might impair the effectiveness of Community law by withholding from the national court having jurisdiction to apply such law the power to do everything necessary at the moment of its application to set aside national legislative provisions which might prevent, even temporarily, Community rules from having full force and effect are incompatible with those requirements, which are the very essence of Community law (judgment of 9 March 1978 in Case 106/77 *Simmenthal* [1978] ECR 629).

21. It must be added that the full effectiveness of Community law would be just as much impaired if a rule of national law could prevent a court seised of a dispute governed by Community law from granting interim relief in order to ensure the full effectiveness of the judgment to be given on the existence of the rights claimed under Community law. It follows that a court which in those circumstances would grant interim relief, if it were not for a rule of national law, is obliged to set aside that rule.

The emphasis in *Factortame* was firmly on the requirement of effectiveness of EU law, rather than on the primary role of national procedural law. The CJEU left it to the House of Lords to specify the conditions under which interim relief should be granted,[43] but made clear that a rule which prohibited absolutely the grant of interim relief would be unacceptable.[44]

(B) A MORE CAUTIOUS APPROACH

Immediately after *Marshall II* in 1993, however, the CJEU seemed to withdraw from the boldness of its rulings in *Dekker, Factortame I, Emmott,* and *Marshall II.* The case of *Steenhorst-Neerings* concerned an action for retrospective payment of several years of disability benefit, covering the period when the Directive on sex discrimination in social security had not been properly implemented into Dutch law.[45] Dutch law provided that such benefits should not be payable retroactively for more than one year. The CJEU however distinguished the case from *Emmott,* despite the similarities between the two, ruling that the one-year period for retroactive payment was not a time limit for bringing proceedings, and did not operate (as in *Emmott*) as an absolute bar on bringing an action. Instead, it satisfied the twin conditions of equivalence and practical possibility, and more particularly it served a legitimate purpose including 'preserving financial balance...in a scheme in which claims submitted by insured persons in the course of a year must in principle be covered by the contributions collected during that same year'.[46]

Clearly the circumstances in *Steenhorst-Neerings* were similar to those in *Emmott,* where a plaintiff who had been prevented from claiming a right under EU law, in circumstances of sex discrimination, now confronted a restriction which substantially reduced the effectiveness of the available remedy. The broader principle articulated in *Emmott,* that a Member State cannot rely on domestic rules to limit an applicant's claim to rights under a directive until that directive has been properly implemented, was abandoned. Later case law, including *Texaco A/S,*[47] *Fantask A/S,*[48] *BP Supergas,*[49] and *Spac,*[50] suggests that the fact that the state itself was at fault in *Emmott* and had led the applicant to make the error in question was highly relevant to the ruling in the case.[51]

Confirming the trend of *Steenhorst-Neerings,* the CJEU in *Johnson II* ruled that 'the solution adopted in *Emmott* was justified by the particular circumstances of that case, in which a time-bar had the result of depriving the applicant of any opportunity whatever to rely on her right to equal treatment under the directive'.[52] *Steenhorst-Neerings* had represented a retreat not only from *Emmott,* but

---

[43] The precise conditions under which interim relief against a provision of national law which implemented Community law should be available were later specified by the CJEU in Cases C–143/88 and C–92/89 *Zuckerfabrik Süderdithmarschen* [1991] ECR I–415; Case C–334/95 *Kruger GmbH* [1997] ECR I–4517; Cases C–453/03, 11, 12 and 194/04 *ABNA* [2005] ECR I–10423.

[44] Similarly in *Unibet* (n 16), the CJEU ruled that while interim relief had to be available where the effectiveness of the main judgment on the existence of EU rights depended upon it, the conditions for the grant of interim relief were (at least where the compatibility of national law with EU law is being challenged) for national law to determine, subject to the requirements of equivalence and effectiveness.

[45] Case C–338/91 *Steenhorst-Neerings* [1993] ECR I–5475.

[46] Ibid [23].

[47] Cases C–114–115/95 *Texaco* EU:C:1997:371.

[48] Case C–188/95 *Fantask A/S v Industriministeriet* [1997] ECR I–6783; Case C–88/99 *Roquette Frères v Direction des Services Fiscaux du Pas-de-Calais* [2000] ECR I–10465.

[49] Case C–62/93 *BP Supergas v Greece* [1995] ECR I–1883, [55]–[59], AG Jacobs; Case C–2/94 *Denkavit International BV* [1996] ECR I–2827, [74], AG Jacobs; J Coppel, 'Time up for *Emmott*?' (1996) 25 ILJ 153.

[50] Case C–260/96 *Ministero delle Finanze v Spac* [1998] ECR I–4997, [31].

[51] M Hoskins, 'Tilting the Balance: Remedies and National Procedural Rules' (1996) 21 ELRev 365. See also Cases C–326/96 *Levez v Jennings Ltd* [1998] ECR I–7835, [34]; and C–327/00 *Santex SpA v Unita Socio Sanitaria Locale n. 42 di Pavia* [2003] ECR I–1877.

[52] Case C–410/92 *Johnson v Chief Adjudication Officer* [1994] ECR I–5483, [26]; Case C–114–115/95 *Texaco A/S v Havn* [1997] ECR I–4263, [48]; Case C–90/94 *Haahr Petroleum v Havn* [1997] ECR I–4085, [51]–[52].

also from the principle of adequacy of compensation for sex discrimination established in *Marshall II*. This was reinforced in *Johnson II*, where the Court ruled that, even in the absence of state concerns to ensure administrative convenience and financial balance, a provision restricting to one year the retroactive effect of a claim for a non-contributory incapacity benefit was compatible with EU law.[53] In *Sutton* the Court had to deal directly with the scope of its ruling in *Marshall II*, and confined it further by introducing a distinction between dismissal on grounds of sex and the discriminatory denial of social security benefits.

Case C–66/95 R v Secretary of State for Social Security, ex parte Eunice Sutton
[1997] ECR I–2163

The applicant successfully challenged the refusal to grant her an invalid care allowance under national law, on the basis that this contravened Directive 79/7 on equal treatment in social security. She was awarded arrears of benefit, but was refused interest because national law did not provide for the payment of interest on social security benefits. On a reference to the ECJ, she argued that Article 6 of Directive 79/7 was almost identically worded to Article 6 of Directive 76/207 in *Marshall II*, both being concerned with equal treatment, and that interest should therefore be awarded just as in the earlier case.

THE ECJ

23. That interpretation cannot be adopted. The judgment in *Marshall II* concerns the award of interest on amounts payable by way of reparation for loss and damage sustained as a result of discriminatory dismissal. As the Court observed in paragraph 31 of that judgment, in such a context full compensation for the loss and damage sustained cannot leave out of account factors, such as the effluxion of time, which may in fact reduce its value. The award of interest, in accordance with the applicable national rules, must therefore be regarded as an essential component of compensation for the purposes of restoring real equality of treatment.

24. By contrast, the main proceedings concern the right to receive interest on amounts payable by way of social security benefits. Those benefits are paid to the person concerned by the competent bodies, which must, in particular, examine whether the conditions laid down in the relevant legislation are fulfilled. Consequently, the amounts paid in no way constitute reparation for loss or damage sustained and the reasoning of the Court in its judgment in *Marshall II* cannot be applied to a situation of that kind.

. . .

27. . . . Amounts paid by way of social security benefit are not compensatory in nature, with the result that payment of interest cannot be required on the basis either of Article 6 of Directive 76/207 or of Article 6 of Directive 79/7.

Sutton thus suggests that the requirements imposed by EU law on the availability of national remedies may depend on the nature of the right at stake and on the EU measure which has been breached.[54]

---

[53] Case C–410/92 *Johnson* (n 52); Case C–394/93 *Alonso-Pérez v Bundesanstalt für Arbeit* [1995] ECR I–4101. Contrast Case C–246/96 *Magorrian and Cunningham v Eastern Health and Social Services Board* [1997] ECR I–7153; Case C–78/98 *Preston v Wolverhampton Healthcare NHS Trust* [1999] ECR I–3201.

[54] The cases concerning repayment of sums wrongly paid are instructive, since not all repayment cases are subject to the same analysis. Contrast some of the cases concerning unduly paid agricultural subsidies with those concerning improperly paid state aid: compare, eg, Case C–24/95 *Land Rheinland-Pfalz v Alcan Deutschland* [1997] ECR I–1591 on state aid with Case C–298/96 *Oelmühle Hamburg v Bundesanstalt für Landwirtschaft und Ernährung* [1998] ECR I–4767 and Case C–366/95 *Landbrugsministeriet—EF-Direktoratet v Steff-Houlberg Export* [1998] ECR I–2661 on agricultural subsidies. See also Case C–113/10 *Zuckerfabrik Jülich AG* EU:C:2012:591 on reimbursement of agricultural levies.

Payment of arrears of social security benefits was distinguished from 'compensation for loss or damage', so that there was no requirement of full or adequate compensation for the former under national law.

Finally, even if there is a requirement of adequate compensation for damage caused by a breach of a particular directive, such as the Equal Treatment Directive, a ceiling on damages will not always be impermissible. A maximum upper limit on damages is acceptable in certain cases, such as a case of sex discrimination in access to employment, where the claimant would not have been successful in obtaining the job even in the absence of discrimination, so that the loss sustained is more limited.[55]

(c) WHEN SPECIFIC REMEDIES MUST BE MADE AVAILABLE

Despite drawing back from the full implications of the specific rulings in *Emmott* and *Marshall II* however, the CJEU did not retreat from the robust requirement of adequate and effective national remedies, and has built on the precedent of the repayment cases[56] and the *Factortame I* case[57] to rule that in certain circumstances national law must provide for a particular kind of remedy for violation of EU law.

In *Metallgesellschaft & Hoechst*, in which the plaintiffs challenged the imposition of advance corporation tax (ACT) on subsidiaries whose parent companies were not resident within the Member State, the CJEU ruled that it was for the national court to classify the nature of an action brought, whether as an action for restitution or an action for compensation for damage.[58] The national court argued that it was not clear whether English law even provided for restitution for damage arising from loss of the use of sums of money where no principal sum was due, but the CJEU responded that in an action for restitution, the 'principal sum' due was precisely the amount of interest which would have been generated by the sum, use of which was lost as a result of the premature levy of the tax. In other words, the very substance of the plaintiffs' claim was the interest which would have accrued had they not been subject to discriminatory advance taxation. The CJEU ruled:

> Consequently, Article 52 [*now Art 49 TFEU*] of the Treaty entitles a subsidiary resident in the United Kingdom and/or its parent company having its seat in another Member State to obtain interest accrued on the ACT paid by the subsidiary during the period between the payment of ACT and the date on which MCT became payable, and that sum may be claimed by way of restitution.[59]

While restitution was not a remedy unknown to the English legal system, the CJEU brushed aside the national court's argument that restitution might not be available in these circumstances by characterizing the claim as damage flowing directly from the breach of Article 49 TFEU. On the question whether full compensation equal to the sum claimed by the plaintiffs had to be paid, the CJEU referred to the difference between *Marshall II* (in which interest was held to be an essential component of compensation to restore equality of treatment) and *Sutton* (in which interest was deemed not to be an essential component of the right to obtain arrears of benefits), and deemed *Metallgesellschaft* to be analogous to *Marshall II*, with interest as an essential component of the claim.

---

[55] Case C–180/95 *Draehmpaehl v Urania Immobilienservice* [1997] ECR I–2195. The principle of this judgment was incorporated into Art 18 of the amended Equal Treatment Dir 2006/54 [2006] OJ L204/23, as an exception to the rule that there can be no prior upper limit on damages set by national law.

[56] See (nn 11–12).

[57] See Section 3(b) above.

[58] Case C–410/98 *Metallgesellschaft & Hoechst v Inland Revenue* [2001] ECR I–4727.

[59] Ibid [89].

This robust ruling on the obligation of a national court to provide a specific substantive remedy was echoed in the rulings in *Courage*,[60] *Manfredi*,[61] and *Muñoz*.[62] In *Courage*, the CJEU ruled that an action in damages against another party for breach of Article 81 EC, now Article 101 TFEU, must in principle be available to an individual before national courts.[63] In *Manfredi*, also concerning breach of EU competition law, the Court ruled that injured parties must be able to seek compensation not only for actual loss, but also for loss of profit.[64] In *Muñoz*, the full effectiveness of the EU rules on quality standards was held to require that a civil action based on non-compliance with these rules should be available.[65]

In these cases, the Court focused primarily not on the procedural autonomy of the national legal system, but instead on the nature or importance of the substantive EU right in issue, for example non-discrimination under Article 49 TFEU in *Factortame* and *Metallgesellschaft*, equal treatment in employment in *Marshall II*, competition law rules in *Courage, Manfredi, Donau Chemie*,[66] and *Eco Swiss China Time*,[67] and quality standards and fair trading in *Muñoz*.[68]

The Court's choice to emphasize the substantive EU right at issue, in particular where detailed EU legislation on the substance exists, seems to increase the likelihood that it will indicate a need to override or disapply a restrictive national rule. Conversely, in cases in which the Court begins by emphasizing the presumptive legitimacy of national remedial rules, such as *Steenhorst-Neerings, Sutton*, and *Johnston II*, such an outcome is correspondingly less likely. Another suggestion which has been offered to distinguish the cases in which the Court emphasizes the substance of the EU right as compared with those in which it emphasizes the legitimacy of national rules is that the former cases are those concerned with 'remedial rights' such as damages, injunctions, compensation, and access to court, whereas the latter concern 'ancillary procedural rights' governing the remedial rights such as interest, fair time limits, legal aid, and evidentiary rules.[69]

It is also evident that in certain sectors, particularly cases concerning competition law rights,[70] and also in consumer protection cases (notably in the context of bank and mortgage repayment and

---

[60] Case C–453/99 *Courage* (n 31).

[61] Cases C–295–298/04 *Manfredi* (n 31).

[62] Case C–253/00 *Muñoz y Cia SA and Superior Fruiticola SA* [2002] ECR I–7289. See also Cases C–145–149/08 *Club Hotel Loutraki & Aktor ATE* EU:C:2008:306, [78]–[80], where the CJEU ruled that effective judicial protection of a tenderer whose tender had been blocked by the unlawful decision of an administrative authority which affected the procurement process required that he must be able to bring an action for compensation before the national courts.

[63] Case C–453/99 (n 31) [25]–[28]. For critical analysis, see E Hjelmeng, 'Competition Law Remedies: Striving for Coherence or Finding New Ways?' (2013) 50 CMLRev 1007 and K Havu, 'Horizontal Liability for Damages in EU Law—The Changing Relationship of EU and National Law' (2012) 18 ELJ 407. See also Case C–557/12 *Kone AG v OBB Infrastruktur* EU:C:2014:1317 on national causation rules in an action for compensation for breach of EU competition law provisions.

[64] Cases C–295–298/04 (n 31) [100].

[65] Case C–253/00 (n 62) [30]–[32]. Compare Case C–13/01 *Safalero* (n 20) where the CJEU held there was no obligation on a state to permit an affected third party importer to challenge the confiscation of goods held by another, where that third party had the right to bring proceedings for a declaration of incompatibility of the seizure with EC law. Compare also Case C–216/02 *Österreichischer Zuchtverband für Ponys, Kleinpferde und Spezialrassen v Burgenländische Landesregierung* [2004] ECR I–10683.

[66] Case C–536/11 *Donau Chemie* EU:C:2013:366, concerning national rules on access by third parties to documents in the file as part of competition (leniency) proceedings.

[67] Case C–126/97 *Eco Swiss China Time Ltd v Benetton International NV* [1999] ECR I–3055; Case C–234/04 *Kapferer v Schlank & Schick* [2006] ECR I–2585, on consumer protection in contract law.

[68] For an argument that the uncertainty in the case law on national judicial protection is attributable to 'an uncertainty regarding the exact content of these rights in need of remedial protection' see T Eilmansberger, 'The Relationship between Rights and Remedies in EC Law: In Search of the Missing Link' (2004) 41 CMLRev 1199.

[69] J Engström, *The Europeanization of Remedies and Procedures through Judge-Made Law* (PhD, EUI, 2009).

[70] Apart from *Courage v Crehan* and *Eco Swiss China Time* (nn 60 and 67) respectively, see recently Case C–439/08 *Vebic VZW* EU:C:2010:739; Case C–199/11 *Otis I* EU:C:2012:684; Case C–360/09 *Pfleiderer* EU:C:2011:389; Case C–536/11 *Donau Chemie* EU:C:2013:366; Case C–557/12 *Kone AG v OBB Infrastruktur* EU:C:2014:1317 for robust rulings on national enforcement of EU competition provisions.

repossession proceedings during the EU economic crisis)[71] the Court has insisted on particularly strong procedural protection for EU rights.

5 THE CURRENT APPROACH: BALANCING EFFECTIVE JUDICIAL PROTECTION AND NATIONAL PROCEDURAL AUTONOMY

The position currently reached in the field of national remedies for EU rights can be summarized as follows: it requires national courts to strike an appropriate, proportionality-based, case-by-case balance between the requirement of effective judicial protection for EU law rights and the application of legitimate national procedural and remedial rules. In deciding whether a national rule or principle could undermine the exercise of an EU law right, national courts must weigh the requirements of effectiveness and equivalence in the light of the aim and function of the national rule, bearing in mind also the importance and objective of the EU right in question. This approach was first articulated clearly in the cases of *Peterbroeck*[72] and *Van Schijndel*,[73] concerning the authority of national courts to raise points of EU law of their own motion.

(A) EFFECTIVENESS

In this section some clusters of cases dealing with certain kinds of national procedural rule will be outlined briefly to illustrate what guidance the CJEU has given to national courts on how to undertake this balancing task.

(i) *The Authority of National Courts to Consider EU Law of their own Motion*

Cases C–430–431/93 **Van Schijndel & Van Veen v Stichting Pensioenfonds voor Fysiotherapeuten** [1995] ECR I–4705

The applicants argued that the appeal court whose ruling they sought to challenge ought to have considered, if necessary of its own motion, the compatibility of a compulsory Pension Fund provision with EU competition law. They had not themselves previously raised any point of EU law. Under Dutch law, the national court could not raise such points of law of its own motion. On a reference, the ECJ was asked whether the national court must apply provisions of EU law even where the party to the proceedings had not relied on them. The ECJ referred first to the principle of national procedural autonomy, qualified by the principles of equivalence and practical effectiveness:

---

[71] For recent examples of strong CJEU consumer protecting rulings involving national procedural law, see Case C–169/14 *Sánchez Morcillo and Abril García* EU:C:2014:2099; Case C–415/11 *Aziz v Catalunyacaixa* EU:C:2013:164; Case C–472/11 *Banif plus Bank ZRT* EU:C:2013:88; Case C–618/10 *Banco Español de Crédito SA* EU:C:2012:349; Case C–449/13 *CA Consumer Finance SA v Ingrid Bakkaus* EU:C:2014:2464; V Trstenjak, 'Procedural Aspects of European Consumer Protection Law and the Case Law of the CJEU from the Perspective of Insurance Law' (2013) 21 ERPL 451.

[72] Case C–312/93 *Peterbroeck, Van Campenhout & Cie v Belgian State* [1995] ECR I–4599.

[73] Cases C–430–431/93 *Van Schijndel & Van Veen v Stichting Pensioenfonds voor Fysiotherapeuten* [1995] ECR I–4705.

THE ECJ

19. For the purposes of applying those principles, each case which raises the question whether a national procedural provision renders application of Community law impossible or excessively difficult must be analysed by reference to the role of that provision in the procedure, its progress and its special features, viewed as a whole, before the various national instances. In the light of that analysis the basic principles of the domestic judicial system, such as the protection of the rights of the defence, the principle of legal certainty and the proper conduct of procedure must, where appropriate, be taken into consideration.

20. In the present case, the domestic law principle that in civil proceedings a court must or may raise points of its own motion is limited by its obligation to keep to the subject matter of the dispute and to base its decision on the facts put before it.

21. That limitation is justified by the principle that, in a civil suit, it is for the parties to take the initiative, the court being able to act of its own motion only in exceptional cases where the public interest requires its intervention. That principle reflects conceptions prevailing in most of the Member States as to the relations between the State and the individual; it safeguards the rights of the defence; and it ensures proper conduct of proceedings by, in particular, protecting them from the delays inherent in examination of new pleas.

22. In those circumstances, the answer to the second question must be that Community law does not require national courts to raise of their own motion an issue concerning the breach of provisions of Community law where examination of that issue would oblige them to abandon the passive role assigned to them by going beyond the ambit of the dispute defined by the parties themselves and relying on facts and circumstances other than those on which the party with an interest in application of those provisions bases his claim.

While *Van Schijndel* indicated that the principle of judicial passivity was compatible, on the facts, with the exercise of the EU right, the opposite conclusion was reached soon afterwards in the *Peterbroeck* case.[74] In *Peterbroeck*, where similar aims of legal certainty and the proper conduct of procedure underpinned a procedural provision of the Belgian Tax Code preventing both the parties and the court from raising a point of EU law after sixty days, the application of the rule was held by the CJEU to render the exercise of the EU right excessively difficult.[75] The different outcomes of these rulings indicate clearly that each national provision governing enforcement of an EU right before national courts must be examined and weighed not in the abstract, but in the specific circumstances of each case, to see whether it renders the exercise of that right excessively difficult. The rationale underpinning *Van Schijndel* was later affirmed and reasserted in *van der Weerd*, in which the CJEU ruled that the national court was *not* required to raise the relevant point of EU law of its own motion where the parties had had a genuine opportunity to raise the point themselves before a national court.[76]

In *Kraaijeveld*, the Court indicated that EU law does not confer a *general* power on national courts to consider points of EU law of their own motion but, pursuant to the equivalence principle, if they have a discretion or obligation to raise points of national law of their own motion they must also apply such discretion or obligation to points of EU law.[77] Similarly in *Fazenda Pública*, the Court linked the

---

[74] (N 72).

[75] This was apparently because no court or tribunal in the proceedings had had an opportunity to raise the point of EU law so as to make a reference to the CJEU. See also Case C–327/00 *Santex* (n 51), for a case in which a plea which would otherwise have been inadmissible on grounds of delay may have to have been considered by the national court due to the conduct of the defendant public authority.

[76] Cases C–222–225/05 *van der Weerd and Others* [2007] ECR I–4233.

[77] Case C–72/95 *Aannemersbedrijf PK Kraaijeveld BV v Gedeputeerde Staten van Zuid-Holland* [1996] ECR I–5403.

power, and 'in certain cases' the obligation, of national courts to make a reference to the CJEU with their power or obligation to raise points of EU law of their own motion.[78] In *Eco Swiss China Time* concerning competition law rules the Court also ruled that, since national courts were required to permit an application for annulment of an arbitration award on grounds of failure to observe national public policy rules, they must similarly raise a point based on breach of Article 101 TFEU,[79] giving EU competition law rules the same status as national public policy rules.

The CJEU in *Océano* however went beyond the equivalence requirement by declaring that the aims of the Unfair Contract Terms Directive would not be ensured if the consumer were obliged to raise the unfair nature of such terms, and that the national court *must have the power* to evaluate terms of this kind of its own motion.[80] This formulation, stronger than that of the earlier cases, was linked by the Court to the facts of *Océano* which concerned EU consumer protection law.[81] Similarly in *Banif Plus Bank*, which also concerned EU consumer protection legislation, the CJEU ruled that a national court which has decided of its own motion that a contractual term is unfair must be in a position (subject to the requirements of *audi alteram partem*) to inform the parties of this;[82] and in *Banco Español de Crédito* that a national procedural rule which does not allow a national court to examine, of its own motion, the unfairness of the contractual term unless the consumer has already lodged an objection, is precluded by EU law.[83]

By comparison, in *van der Weerd* the CJEU ruled that there was no breach of either the equivalence or the effectiveness principle.[84] In terms of equivalence, the provisions of the EU Directive on control of foot-and-mouth disease in issue, unlike EU competition rules or rules on consumer protection,[85] did not have the same status as public policy rules, so that national courts were not required to raise the point of their own motion. In terms of effectiveness, the Court in *van der Weerd* found no violation of this principle, and distinguished the situations in *Océano* and *Eco Swiss China Time* where the parties had no real opportunity to raise the point of EU law themselves before the national courts.[86]

(ii) *Legal Certainty and* Res Judicata

In the case of *Kühne and Heitz*, the CJEU ruled that a national administrative body had to re-open a decision that had become final following a national court ruling which was based on a misunderstanding of EU law.[87] This was affirmed in *Kempter*, in which the CJEU ruled that an obligation of review would arise where the contested administrative decision which had become final was based on a misinterpretation of EU law adopted without any preliminary reference being made to the CJEU on the question.[88] The obligation would arise even where the parties themselves had not raised the point

---

[78] Case C–446/98 *Fazenda Pública v Camara Municipal do Porto* [2000] ECR I–11435, [48].

[79] Case C–126/97 *Eco Swiss* (n 67) [36]–[37].

[80] Cases C–240–244/98 *Océano Grupo Editorial v Rocio Murciano Quintero* [2000] ECR I–4491, [26]. See also Case C–397/11 *Jőrős* EU:C:2013:340.

[81] Case C–473/00 *Cofidis* [2002] ECR I–10875; Case C–168/05 *Mostaza Claro* [2006] ECR I–10421; Case C–429/05 *Rampion* [2007] ECR I–8017; Case C–243/08 *Pannon* [2009] ECR I–4713; Case C–40/08 *Asturcom Telecomunicaciones v Cristina Rodríguez Nogueira* [2009] ECR I–9579; Case C–227/08 *Martín Martín v EDP Editores SL* EU:C:2009:792; Case C–215/11 *Szyrocka* EU:C:2012:794; Case C–488/11 *Asbeek Brusse* EU:C:2013:341.

[82] C–472/11 *Banif plus Bank ZRT* EU:C:2013:88.

[83] Case C–618/10 *Banco Español de Crédito SA* EU:C:2012:349; Case C–488/11 *Asbeek Brusse* EU:C:2013:341.

[84] (N 76) [75]–[77].

[85] Case C–40/08 *Asturcom* (n 81) [52].

[86] (N 76) [40].

[87] Case C–453/00 *Kühne and Heitz* [2004] ECR I–837; R Caranta, Note (2005) 42 CMLRev 179. See more recently Case C–249/11 *Byankov* EU:C:2012:608 where an EU citizen challenged an administrative ban on leaving Bulgaria which had become final.

[88] Case C–2/06 *Willy Kempter KG v Hauptzollamt Hamburg-Jonas* [2008] ECR I–411.

of EU law before the national court, at least in circumstances where national courts were permitted to raise rules of national law of their own motion and therefore should equally have been in a position to raise the relevant point of EU law.[89]

The subsequent *Kapferer* ruling seemed to limit the scope of *Kühne and Heitz*, by underscoring the legitimacy of the principle of *res judicata* and the finality of national judicial proceedings,[90] and by distinguishing the situation of a national court in *Kapferer* from that of national administrative bodies in *Kühne and Heitz* and *Kempter*. However, in *Lucchini*, concerning recovery of unlawful state aid, the CJEU went further and ruled that EU law precluded a national rule on *res judicata* from being applied by a court to prevent the recovery of aid which had been found by the Commission to be definitively incompatible with EU law.[91] But the Court in *Lucchini* stressed the distinctiveness of the state aid context, in which the Commission rather than the national courts or authorities has the ultimate authority to rule on the compatibility of state aid, and the Court in the subsequent *Pizzarotti* case emphasized that the *Lucchini* judgment had been given 'in a highly specific situation'.[92] In *Pizzarotti*, the Court ruled that EU law 'does not require a judicial body automatically to go back on a judgment having the authority of *res judicata* in order to take into account the interpretation of a relevant provision of EU law adopted by the Court after delivery of that judgment'.[93] Yet in the *Olimpiclub* judgment the Court ruled that a national court could not rely on the principle of *res judicata* in the context of VAT, since this would excessively undermine the effectiveness of EU VAT rules.[94]

Although the facts of these cases are all slightly different, some relying on the distinction between national courts and national administrative authorities, and others depending on the final authority of the Commission to rule on state aid cases, or on the negative effects for the domestic taxation system of a judicial ruling incompatible with EU law being treated as final, taken together these (undoubtedly confusing) rulings demonstrate that the domestic law principle concerning the finality of judicial proceedings, the principle of *res judicata*, will at times be required to give way to the need to take a binding ruling of EU law into consideration.[95]

(iii) *Limitation Periods*

The general position laid down by the CJEU is that reasonable national limitation periods are, in principle, compatible with EU requirements.[96] However, reasonable limitation periods may be rendered incompatible with EU law where the effective protection of EU rights is negatively affected by other factors,[97] for example: where the date on which the period begins to run is unclear; or commences

---

[89] Ibid [44]–[46].

[90] Case C–234/04 *Kapferer* (n 67); on *res judicata* see also Case C–126/97 *Eco Swiss* (n 67); Case C–118/00 *Larsy* [2001] ECR I–5063; Case C–201/02 *Wells v Secretary of State for Transport* [2004] ECR I–723.

[91] Case C–119/05 *Lucchini* [2007] ECR I–6199; A Biondi, Note (2008) 45 CMLRev 1459.

[92] Case C–213/13 *Pizzarotti* EU:C:2014:335, [61].

[93] Ibid [60].

[94] Case C–2/08 *Amministrazione dell'Economia e delle Finanze v Fallimento Olimpiclub Srl* [2009] ECR I–7501.

[95] For commentary on the confusion generated by the cases, see A Kornezov, 'Res Judicata of National Judgments Incompatible with EU Law: Time for a Major Rethink?' (2014) 51 CMLRev 809.

[96] Case C–542/08 *Friedrich G Barth* EU:C:2010:193, where a three-year limitation on bringing an action to recover length-of-service increments (based on Case C–224/01 *Köbler* [2003] ECR I–10239) was acceptable; Cases C–95 and 96/07 *Ecotrade SpA* [2008] ECR I–3457, where the effectiveness of EU law was not infringed merely because the national tax authority had a longer period in which to recover unpaid VAT than the period granted to taxable persons for the exercise of their right to deduct. See also Cases C–89 and 96/10 *Q-Beef* EU:C:2011:555 in which the setting of different time limits for different types of action was in principle compatible with EU law, and Case C–429/12 *Pohl* EU:C:2014:12 on a thirty-year time period in an employment age-discrimination dispute.

[97] In Case C–69/08 *Raffaello Visciano* [2009] ECR I–6741, the CJEU ruled that Dir 80/987 on the protection of employees in the event of the insolvency of their employer did not preclude a limitation period of one year, but it

before the applicant knew or should have known of the violation;[98] where the limitation period applies retroactively;[99] where the operation of the time limit makes it effectively impossible to obtain a refund due[100] or to deduct VAT;[101] or the national court has too much discretion in determining whether proceedings were brought 'promptly'.[102]

In *Manfredi* the CJEU declared that a national rule under which the limitation period begins to run from the day on which an anti-competitive agreement or concerted practice is adopted could make it practically impossible to exercise the right to seek compensation for the harm caused, particularly if the limitation period is also a short one and not capable of being suspended.[103] In *Marks & Spencer*[104] and *Grundig Italiana*,[105] the Court ruled that although national legislation reducing the period within which repayment of sums collected in breach of Community law may be sought is not in itself incompatible with the effectiveness principle, the new limitation period must remain reasonable and must include adequate transitional arrangements.[106]

The diversity of national time limits across the EU means that the Court generally grants considerable latitude in determining what is reasonable, but it is nonetheless clear that some kind of comparative judgement is being made by the CJEU with reference to the practices of other Member States.[107]

(iv) *Rules of Evidence and Causation*

In *Boiron*, a case concerning state aid, the question was whether national rules placing the burden of proof for demonstrating overpayment of competitors on an economic operator complied with the principle of effectiveness.[108] The CJEU ruled that where the national court found that this

emphasized two factors which were liable to undermine its effectiveness: first, uncertainty as to when the limitation period starts to run; and, secondly, the classification of the benefit by the national court as social security, which would change the applicable time limit. Compare Case C–96/10 *Q-Beef* EU:C:2011:555 on the commencement of the time period. See also Case C–349/07 *Sopropé-Organizações de Calçado Lda* [2008] ECR I–10369, on whether a period of eight to fifteen days allowed for recovery of a customs debt was sufficient.

[98] Case C–246/09 *Susanne Bulicke v Deutsche Büro Service GmbH* EU:C:2010:418, [40]–[41]; Case C–445/06 *Danske Slagterier v Bundesrepublik Deutschland* [2009] ECR I–2119, [49]–[56]. Compare Case C–452/09 *Iaia* EU:C:2010:54 where reliance on the expiry of the time limit was reasonable even though the state had committed a violation of EU law. In the context of public procurement, see Case C–161/13 *Idrodinamica Spurgo Velox* EU:C:2014:307 and Case C–19/13 *Fastweb* EU:C:2014:2194. In the context of a discrimination claim in an employment competition dispute, see Case C–177/10 *Rosado Santana* EU:C:2011:557.

[99] Case C 62/00 (n 8) [39]–[42]; Case C–30/02 *Recheio-Cash & Carry SA v Fazenda Publica/Registo Nacional de Pessoas Colectivas* [2004] ECR I–6051, where a 90-day limitation period was reasonable even though applicable to taxes paid at a time when the EU Dir had not been transposed; Case C–241/06 *Lämmerzahl GmbH v Freie Hansestadt Bremen* [2008] ECR I–8415, where the Public Procurement Remedies Dir precluded a national limitation from being applied in such a way that a tenderer was refused access to a review of the procurement procedure where the specifications had not been clearly stated; in Case C–406/08 *Uniplex* (n 102), the limitation period could start to run only from the date on which the claimants knew, or ought to have known, of the alleged infringement of the provisions they wished to challenge. Also Case C–603/10 *Pelati* EU:C:2012:639.

[100] Case C–427/10 *Banca Antoniana Popolare Veneta* EU:C:2011:844.

[101] Case C–284/11 *EMS-Bulgaria Transport OOD* EU:C:2012:458.

[102] Case C–406/08 *Uniplex (UK) Ltd v NHS Business Services Authority* EU:C:2010:45, [40]–[43].

[103] Cases C–295–298/04 *Manfredi* (n 31).

[104] Case C–62/00 *Marks & Spencer* (n 8).

[105] Case C–255/00 *Grundig Italiana SpA v Ministero delle Finanze* [2002] ECR I–8003.

[106] In *Grundig Italiana* [37]–[42], a 90-day transitional limitation period was unreasonable and insufficient, given that it replaced a previous five-year period for preparing and submitting proceedings. See also Case C–262/09 *Meilicke* EU:C:2011:438.

[107] Case C–30/02 *Recheio-Cash & Carry* (n 99) [22].

[108] Case C–526/04 *Laboratoires Boiron SA v URSSAF de Lyon* [2006] ECR I–7529.

evidentiary requirement rendered it excessively difficult for the operator to produce the necessary proof, that court was required 'to use all procedures available to it under national law, including that of ordering the necessary measures of inquiry, in particular the production by one of the parties or a third party of a particular document' to comply with the EU requirement of effective judicial protection.[109]

Steffenson concerned a directive on control of foodstuffs which required a second opinion on the analysis of a sample of foodstuffs to be obtained in circumstances such as those of the case, where a manufacturer was fined for misleading quality-labelling.[110] A second opinion had not been obtained in the case, and the question was whether the sample could be introduced in evidence despite the violation of the Directive's second-opinion requirement. Under German law, evidence obtained by an irregular administrative procedure could nonetheless be admitted in legal proceedings and evaluated on that basis. The CJEU gave extensive guidance to the national court on how to apply the effectiveness requirement, drawing on ECHR jurisprudence concerning the 'adversarial principle' and the right to a fair hearing.[111] *Steffensen* thus introduced yet another important factor, respect for ECHR (and now EU Charter) rights, into the matrix which national courts must consider when weighing the effectiveness of remedies for EU rights in the context of national procedural rules.[112]

The CJEU in *Unitrading* ruled that in the absence of EU legislation governing the concept of proof in customs proceedings, any type of evidence admissible under the procedural law of the Member States in similar customs proceedings would in principle be admissible, subject always to the requirements of effectiveness and equivalence.[113]

In *Kone*, the CJEU had to consider whether the Austrian legal conception of a 'causal relationship' as a necessary element of a successful claim in compensation by an individual who had suffered economic damage as a result of 'umbrella pricing' by a defendant who was not actually part of a cartel, was compatible with the EU requirement of principles of effectiveness.[114] The defendant, while not contracting with any member of the cartel, operated a pricing policy which was a result of the price-distorting cartel, and the applicant sought damages for loss suffered through the higher prices charged. While the CJEU ultimately left it for the national court to decide whether an adequate causal link had been established on the facts of the case for the purposes of the domestic cause of action, the Court ruled emphatically that:

> The full effectiveness of Article 101 TFEU would be put at risk if the right of any individual to claim compensation for harm suffered were subjected by national law, categorically and regardless of the particular circumstances of the case, to the existence of a direct causal link while excluding that right because the individual concerned had no contractual links with a member of the cartel, but with an undertaking not party thereto, whose pricing policy, however, is a result of the cartel that contributed to the distortion of price formation mechanisms governing competitive.[115]

The ruling has drawn critical attention for its interference into national rules and procedures governing antitrust damages cases.[116]

---

[109] Ibid [57].
[110] Case C–276/01 *Joachim Steffensen* [2003] ECR I–3735.
[111] Case C–276/01 (n 110) [68]–[79].
[112] Ch 11; Case C–344/08 *Rubach* [2009] ECR I–7033.
[113] Case C–437/13 *Unitrading* EU:C:2014:2318.
[114] Case C–557/12 *Kone AG v OBB Infrastruktur* EU:C:2014:1317.
[115] Ibid [33].
[116] See http://howtocrackanut.blogspot.nl/2014/06/when-cjeu-opens-umbrella-lawyers-and.html.

(v) *Access to Court*

We have seen that even in early cases like *Heylens*,[117] and more recently in the *Kadi*[118] and *ZZ*[119] cases even where national security concerns were implicated, the CJEU emphasized the importance of access to judicial control and to a judicial remedy for the vindication of EU law rights,[120] identifying it as a fundamental right guaranteed under the ECHR and the Charter of Fundamental Rights.[121] However, the Court has also accepted the imposition of reasonable national restrictions and preconditions on the fundamental right of access to court.

In *Upjohn* the Court ruled that EU law did not require the availability of a domestic judicial review procedure under which national courts would be competent to substitute their assessment of the facts and the scientific evidence found for that of the national decision-making body, provided that those courts were empowered effectively to apply the principles of EU law when conducting judicial review.[122] In *Evans* a system of national redress which provided for a combination of administrative review, arbitration (including appropriate procedural rights), and appellate judicial review for accident compensation claims was held to satisfy the requirement of effective protection.[123] In *Schneider*, the right was satisfied by the existence of an action for state liability before the civil courts, even if a parallel action before the administrative courts was limited in terms of the factual review which could be carried out.[124] The fact that all claims relating to EU agricultural aid had to be brought before a single court jurisdiction in Bulgaria did not violate the principle of effectiveness,[125] nor did territorial jurisdiction rules in Spain which required actions for an injunction brought by consumer protection associations to be brought before the courts where the defendant is established.[126]

In *Alassini*,[127] the requirement of prior implementation of an out-of-court settlement procedure before having recourse to legal proceedings did not, subject to a range of conditions concerning matters such as costs and delay,[128] infringe the principles of effectiveness or equivalence in the context of the Universal Service Directive. Similar rulings were given in the *Tele2*[129] and *Mono Car Styling*[130] cases, in which the ECHR and the Charter of Rights were again cited as the basis for the principle of effective judicial protection. In *Mono Car Styling*, the Court accepted that national

---

[117] (N 28).

[118] Cases C–402 and 415/05 P *Kadi and Al Barakaat International Foundation v Council and Commission* [2008] ECR I–6351.

[119] Case C–300/11 *ZZ v Secretary of State for the Home Department* EU:C:2013:363.

[120] On the right to judicial review see also Case C–228/98 *Dounias v Ypourgio Oikonomikon* [2000] ECR I–577, [64]–[66]; Case C–424/99 *Commission v Austria* [2001] ECR I–9285; Case C–1/99 *Kofisa Italia* [2001] ECR I–207; Case C–226/99 *Siples* [2001] ECR I–277; Case C–75/08 *R (Mellor) v Secretary of State for Communities and Local Government* [2009] ECR I–3799 on the fact that judicial review presupposes the right to be given reasons.

[121] Case C–185/97 *Coote v Granada Hospitality Ltd* [1998] ECR I–5199; Case C–432/05 *Unibet* (n 16); Case C–23/12 *Zakaria* EU:C:2013:24; Case C–562/12 *Liivimaa Lihaveis MTÜ* EU:C:2014:2229.

[122] Case C–120/97 *Upjohn v The Licensing Authority* [1999] ECR I–223, [33]–[36].

[123] Case C–63/01 *Evans v Secretary of State for the Environment, and the Motor Insurers' Bureau* [2003] ECR I–14447; Case C–506/04 *Wilson* EU:C:2006:587, on the requirements of independence and impartiality of effective judicial protection.

[124] Case C–380/01 *Gustav Schneider v Bundesminister für Justiz* [2004] ECR I–1389.

[125] Case C–93/12 *Agrokonsulting-04* EU:C:2013:432.

[126] Case C–413/12 *Asociación de Consumidores Independientes de Castilla y León* EU:C:2013:800.

[127] Cases C–317–320/08 *Rosalba Alassini and others* EU:C:2008:510.

[128] Ibid [53]–[60].

[129] In Case C–426/05 *Tele2 Telecommunication GmbH v Telekom-Control-Kommission* [2008] ECR I–68, a national provision which, in the context of prior non-adversarial market-analysis proceedings, granted party status only to companies formerly having significant power on the relevant market was ruled not to be contrary to the principle of effective judicial protection underpinning Art 4 of Dir 2002/21 on electronic communications networks.

[130] Case C–12/08 *Mono Car Styling SA, in liquidation v Dervis Odemis* [2009] ECR I–6653.

rules imposing various conditions on the right of action granted to workers affected by collective redundancy did not undermine the fundamental principle of effective judicial protection.[131] In *Commission v Greece*, however, a provision of national law concerning tax exemption could deprive individuals of effective judicial protection under EU law where it induced them, for the purposes of avoiding criminal proceedings, to refrain from seeking the legal remedies provided for as a matter of course by national law.[132] In *Janecek* and *ClientEarth* too, the CJEU gave strong rulings on the requirement of individual access to court to enforce particular obligations on national authorities in the context of an environmental directive.[133] In *DEB*, the CJEU ruled that the principle of effective judicial protection in Article 47 of the Charter required that it should be possible for legal (as opposed to natural) persons to rely on that principle, and required that legal aid granted may cover dispensation from advance payment of the costs of proceedings and the assistance of a lawyer.[134] It was for national courts, ultimately, to determine whether or not the conditions for granting legal aid constituted a disproportionate limitation on the right of access to court.[135] The requirement of access to court did not, however, require in the *Pohotovost* case that a consumer association should be able to intervene in a domestic case in support of a consumer against whom an arbitration award was being enforced.[136]

(B) EQUIVALENCE

We have already seen examples of the requirement of equivalence in the cases on *res judicata* where the CJEU ruled that if a national court may raise certain points of national law of its own motion, it must also have a power to raise similar points of EU law.[137] However, it is often unclear what exactly the requirement of 'equivalence' entails, or when causes of action may be deemed sufficiently similar or comparable to require 'equivalent' treatment.[138] In many cases the Court merely states, after reiterating that national rules must comply with the principle of equivalence, that there is nothing on the file submitted by the national court to suggest any violation of that principle.

---

[131] Ibid [50]–[52]. Compare Case C–268/06 *Impact v Minister for Agriculture and Food and Others* [2008] ECR I–2483, where the CJEU ruled that the principle of effectiveness required that a specialized court which was established by legislation transposing Dir 1999/70 on the framework agreement on fixed-term work to hear claims based on infringement of that legislation must also have jurisdiction to hear an applicant's claims arising directly from the Dir itself between the date of the deadline for transposing the Dir and the date on which the transposing legislation entered into force, where the requirement to bring a separate claim based on the Dir before an ordinary court would involve procedural disadvantages liable to render excessively difficult the exercise of the EU rights; see also Cases C–378–380/07 *Kiriaki Angelidaki* (n 21).

[132] Case C–156/04 *Commission v Greece* [2007] ECR I–4129.

[133] Case C–237/07 *Janecek* [2008] ECR I–6221; Cases C–404–13 *R (ClientEarth) v Secretary of State for Environment* EU:C:2014:2382. See also Case C–416/10 *Križan* EU:C:2013:8 as regards access to information and decision-making in the context of environmental proceedings; J Jans, 'Harmonization of National Procedural Law by the Back Door?' in M Bulterman, L Hancher, A McDonnell, and H Sevenster (eds), *Views of European Law from the Mountain* (2009) 267–275; on national *locus standi* rules see Cases C–87–89/90 *Verholen v Sociale Verzekeringsbank* [1991] ECR I–3757, [24].

[134] Case C–279/09 *DEB v Bundesrepublik Deutschland* EU:C:2010:811.

[135] Ibid [60]–[62].

[136] Case C–470/12 *Pohotovost* EU:C:2014:101.

[137] See in particular Cases C–222–225/05 *van der Weerd* (n 76) [29]–[32]; Case C–488/11 *Asbeek Brusse* EU:C:2013:341, and the cases discussed at (nn 88–92) and text.

[138] See, eg, Case C–93/12 *Agrokonsulting-04* EU:C:2013:432, in which Polish provisions concerning agricultural payments on the one hand, and property rights on the other hand, were not comparable for these purposes, and Case C–361/12 *Carratu* EU:C:2013:830 on the non-comparability of fixed-term and permanent workers for the purposes of rules on compensation for termination.

Edis concerned the repayment of charges which had been paid but were not due under EU law, where national law imposed a time limit of three years for bringing proceedings for repayment for such charges. This was less favourable than the ordinary time limits governing actions between individuals for repayment of sums paid but not due.

Case C-231/96 **Edis v Ministero delle Finanze**
[1998] ECR I-4951

36. Observance of the principle of equivalence implies, for its part, that the procedural rule at issue applies without distinction to actions alleging infringements of Community law and to those alleging infringements of national law, with respect to the same kind of charges or dues (see, to that effect, Joined Cases 66/79, 127/79 and 128/79 *Amministrazione della Finanzo dello Stato* v. *Salumi* [1000] ECR 1237, paragraph 21). That principle cannot, however, be interpreted as obliging a Member State to extend its most favourable rules governing recovery under national law to all actions for repayment of charges or dues levied in breach of Community law.

37. Thus, Community law does not preclude the legislation of a Member State from laying down, alongside a limitation period applicable under the ordinary law to actions between private individuals for the recovery of sums paid but not due, special detailed rules, which are less favourable, governing claims and legal proceedings to challenge the imposition of charges and other levies. The position would be different only if those detailed rules applied solely to actions based on Community law for the repayment of such charges or levies.

Similar rulings were given in the cases of *Spac*,[139] *Aprile*,[140] *Dilexport*,[141] *Roquette*,[142] *Pontin*,[143] and *Bulicke*,[144] affirming the acceptability of national time limits which were not the most favourable within the national remedial system, but which applied equally to actions based on EU law and 'similar' actions based on national law.[145] On the other hand the CJEU has also ruled that national courts cannot rely on the principle of equivalence with national procedures to avoid other EU law requirements such as the freedom to make preliminary references to the Court of Justice,[146] or indeed the provisions of the Customs Code.[147]

While the CJEU has frequently stated that it is for the national court to determine the question of equivalence,[148] it has intervened at times to indicate that the application of a particular national rule does not satisfy that principle, or that the principle of equivalence is not applicable on the facts,[149] or to suggest what other rules of domestic law might provide a comparator for the purposes of considering 'equivalence'.[150] In *Eman and Sevinger*, concerning violation of the right to vote in European

---

[139] Case C-260/96 *Spac* (n 50).

[140] Case C-229/96 *Aprile v Amminstrazione delle Finanze dello Stato* [1998] ECR I-7141.

[141] Case C-343/96 *Dilexport v Amministrazione delle Finanze dello Stato* [1999] ECR I-579.

[142] Case C-88/99 *Roquette Frères* (n 48).

[143] Case C-63/08 *Virginie Pontin v T-Comalux SA* [2009] ECR I-10467; Case C-591/10 *Littlewoods Retail* EU:C:2012:478.

[144] Case C-246/09 *Susanne Bulicke v Deutsche Büro Service GmbH*, 8 July 2010, [27]-[34].

[145] See also Case C-96/10 *Q-Beef* EU:C:2011:555 and Case C-427/10 *Banca Antoniana Popolare Veneta* EU:C:2011:844; Case C-470/12 *Pohotovost* EU:C:2014:101; Cases C-29 and 30/13 *Global Trans Lodzhistik OOD* EU:C:2014:140.

[146] Case C-112/13 *A* EU:C:2014:2195, [45].

[147] Cases C-129 and 130/13 *Kamino International Logistics BV* EU:C:2014:2041, [77].

[148] Case C-261/95 *Palmisani v INPS* [1997] ECR I-4025, [33]; Case C-326/96 *Levez* (n 51) [39]; Case C-177/10 *Rosado Santano* EU:C:2011:557.

[149] Case C-56/13 *Érsekcsanádi Mezőgazdasági Zrt* EU:C:2014:352.

[150] Case C-213/13 *Pizzarotti* EU:C:2014:335, [55]-[57].

Parliament elections, the CJEU proposed that the national court 'may usefully refer to the detailed rules for legal redress laid down in cases of infringement of the national rules in the context of elections to the institutions of the Member State'.[151] In *Weber's Wine World*, the Court gave a clear indication of what would be likely to violate the equivalence requirement,[152] and in *Pontin*, a case concerning the dismissal of a pregnant employee, the CJEU suggested, even while leaving the ultimate decision to the national court, that a fifteen-month time limit for bringing an action for reinstatement as compared with a two-month time limit for bringing an action for damages would not seem to comply with the equivalence principle.[153] In *Club Hotel Loutraki*, the CJEU found that the principle of equivalence was violated due to the differences between domestic actions for compensation in the field of public service contracts governed by EU law and domestic actions for compensation for other unlawful action on the part of state actors.[154] And in *Vale* the principle of equivalence was breached where Member State authorities refused to record and register a company from the Member State of origin as 'predecessor in law' to a company which had engaged in a cross-border conversion, while recording the predecessor in law of a company which had made a domestic conversion.[155]

In *Levez*, an employee sought damages for arrears in payment which had been denied to her in breach of the EU equal pay rules. The CJEU had ruled that the two-year limit on arrears of damages in Industrial Tribunal proceedings could not be applied to her on account of the role played by her employer's deception in the delay.[156] However, the UK argued that the time limit should nonetheless apply to her case, because an alternative full remedy before the county court in an action for deceit against her employer and in an action based on the Equal Pay Act had been open to her, so that the exercise of her right was not rendered ineffective in practice. The CJEU accepted the effectiveness point, but went on to consider the requirement of equivalence and gave firm guidance to the national court on how to apply this.[157]

Case C–326/96 **Levez v Jennings Ltd**
[1998] ECR I–7835

43. In order to determine whether the principle of equivalence has been complied with in the present case, the national court—which alone has direct knowledge of the procedural rules governing actions in the field of employment law—must consider both the purpose and the essential characteristics of allegedly similar domestic actions (see *Palmisani*, paragraphs 34 to 38).

44. Furthermore, whenever it falls to be determined whether a procedural rule of national law is less favourable than those governing similar domestic actions, the national court must take into account the role played by that provision in the procedure as a whole, as well as the operation and any special features of that procedure before the different national courts (see, *mutatis mutandis, Van Schijndel and Van Veen*, paragraph 19).

[*The ECJ rejected the UK's argument that the equivalence requirement was satisfied by the fact that a claim under the Equal Pay Act (which was intended to implement EC law) was comparable to a claim based directly on Article 157 TFEU, and continued as follows.*]

---

[151] Case C–300/04 *Eman and Sevinger v College van burgemeester en wethouders van Den Haag* [2006] ECR I–8055.
[152] Case C–147/01 *Weber's Wine World* [2003] ECR I–11365.
[153] (N 143).
[154] Cases C–145 and 149/08 *Club Hotel Loutraki AE v Ethnico Symvoulio Radiotileorasis*, 6 May 2010, [75]–[77].
[155] Case C–378/10 *VALE Építési* EU:C:2012:440.
[156] Case C–326/96 *Levez* (n 51).
[157] See also Case C–78/98 *Preston* (n 53).

49. Secondly, it is necessary to consider the possibilities contemplated by the order for reference. It is there suggested that claims similar to those based on the Act may include those linked to breach of a contract of employment, to discrimination in terms of pay on grounds of race, to unlawful deductions from wages or to sex discrimination in matters other than pay.

50. If it transpires, on the basis of the principles set out in paragraphs 41 to 44 of this judgment, that a claim under the Act which is brought before the County Court is similar to one or more of the forms of action listed by the national court, it would remain for that court to determine whether the first-mentioned form of action is governed by procedural rules or other requirements which are less favourable.

51. On that point, it is appropriate to consider whether, in order fully to assert rights conferred by [EU] law before the County Court, an employee in circumstances such as those of Mrs Levez will incur additional costs and delay by comparison with a claimant who, because he is relying on what may be regarded as a similar right under domestic law, may bring an action before the Industrial Tribunal, which is simpler and, in principle, less costly.

52. Also of relevance here is the fact mentioned by the national court that the rule at issue applies solely to claims for equal pay without discrimination on grounds of sex, whereas claims based on 'similar' rights under domestic law are not limited by the operation of such a rule, which means that such rights may be adequately protected by actions brought before Industrial Tribunals.

Ultimately, it was for the national court to determine whether the alternative remedy available to her would entail procedural rules or conditions less favourable than those applicable to similar domestic actions. In other words, the CJEU has developed the same context-specific balancing approach for national courts to assess the 'equivalence' of domestic rules as it did for assessing their 'effectiveness' in *Peterbroeck* and *Van Schijndel*.

In *Dounias*, the CJEU declared that it was for the national court to scrutinize domestic procedures not only to determine whether they were comparable, but also to detect whether there was any inherent discrimination in their *application* in favour of domestic claims.[158] In *Manfredi*, the Court ruled that if in similar domestic actions it is possible to award specific damages such as exemplary or punitive damages, it must also be possible to award them in actions based on EU rules.[159]

It has been argued that an excessive emphasis on the need for *effective* rather than *equivalent* protection of EU rights could actually lead to a reverse form of discrimination in favour of EU law.[160] This notion of genuine equality of remedies for EU rights and national law rights is also mirrored by another development in CJEU case law pointing to the need for parity between national-level and EU-level remedies for the enforcement of EU rights. In other words, EU law should not demand better enforcement of EU law from the national legal orders than it is prepared to provide itself at the European level.[161] And in *Bergaderm*, in an action for damages brought against the EU before the CJEU, the Court ruled that the conditions under which Member States may incur liability for damage

---

[158] Case C–228/98 *Dounias* (n 120) 65. In this case the Court seemed to suggest that the equivalence principle should be considered first, and only then the effectiveness principle: [60]. See also Cases C–392 and 422/04 *i-21 Germany GmbH and Arcor AG* [2006] ECR I–8559, [68]–[69], on the need for equivalence in the application of rules to EU and domestic law claims.

[159] Cases C–295–298/04 *Manfredi* (n 31) [99].

[160] See, eg, AG Jacobs in Cases C–430–431/93 *Van Schijndel* (n 73), and AG Léger in Case C–66/95 *Sutton* (n 39).

[161] See, eg, Case C–120/97 *Upjohn* (n 122) [33], where EU law did not require Member States to establish a more extensive review of national decisions revoking marketing authorizations for medicinal products than that carried out by the CJEU in similar cases.

to individuals caused by a breach of EU law could not, in principle, differ from those governing the liability of the EU in similar circumstances.[162]

(C) THE EFFECT OF THE PLAINTIFF'S CONDUCT ON THE RIGHT TO AN EFFECTIVE REMEDY

In *Dionysios Diamantis*, the CJEU ruled that a national court may refuse to permit a plaintiff to rely on EU rights if such reliance constitutes an abuse of those rights.[163] However, the CJEU in *Rechberger* rejected Austria's argument that the misconduct of a relevant third party could constitute a defence to an action for damages brought against the state for breach of EU law.[164] In *Courage* the Court ruled that an individual could not be prohibited from relying on Article 101 TFEU simply because he had been party to an anti-competitive agreement, but that EU law did not prohibit a national rule preventing such a party from relying on his own unlawful actions to obtain damages where he bears significant responsibility for the distortion of competition.[165] And in *Manfredi*, the Court ruled that the requirements of effectiveness and equivalence did not prevent national courts from taking steps to ensure that the protection of EU rights did not entail the unjust enrichment of those claiming them.[166]

The CJEU has also considered the impact of a plaintiff's failure to mitigate losses on the availability and extent of national remedies. In *Metallgesellschaft* the Court dismissed the UK's argument that the plaintiffs should have refused to comply with a national tax rule which infringed their EU rights and should have relied on the direct effect of EU rights, rather than paying the tax and challenging it afterwards.[167] The Court also ruled in *Danske Slagterior* that EU law would not preclude national legislation from refusing to provide reparation for loss to an individual who had wilfully or negligently failed to avail himself of a legal remedy which would have averted such loss, provided that recourse to the legal remedy in question could reasonably be expected.[168] Thus reasonable national rules governing the responsibility of parties to show due diligence in mitigating their losses are compatible with EU law so long as they are applied equally to claims based on EU law.[169]

6 SUMMARY

i.   While early CJEU case law emphasized the autonomy and primary responsibility of the national legal system in the absence of EU harmonization of remedies, this approach yielded over time to a stronger insistence on the effectiveness of EU law, on effective judicial protection as a fundamental right, and on the national courts' duty of loyal cooperation.

---

[162] Case C–352/98 P *Bergaderm v Commission* [2000] ECR I–5291, [41], drawing on Cases C–46 and 48/93 *Brasserie du Pêcheur* [1996] ECR I–1029, [42]; M de Visser, 'The Concept of Concurrent Liability and its Relationship with the Principle of Effectiveness' (2004) 11 MJ 47.

[163] Case C–373/97 *Dionysios Diamantis v Elliniko Dimosio* [1999] ECR I–1705, [42]–[44], in which the CJEU however ruled that some of the impugned conduct would not amount to an abuse of rights under the Second Company Dir.

[164] Case C–140/97 *Rechberger v Austria* [1999] ECR I–3499.

[165] Case C–453/99 *Courage* (n 31) [24], [36].

[166] Cases C–295–298/04 *Manfredi* (n 31) [99]. For further discussion of unjust enrichment see (nn 30–31) and text.

[167] Case C–397/98 *Metallgesellschaft Ltd v Inland Revenue* [2001] ECR I–1727, [99]–[107].

[168] Case C–445/06 *Danske Slagterior v Germany* [2009] ECR I–2119, [63]–[64]. Compare Case C–429/09 *Fuß v Stadt Halle* EU:C:2009:178, [75]–[86].

[169] This is the case for claims against the EU institutions before the CJEU: Case T–178/98 *Fresh Marine Company v Commission* [2000] ECR II–3331, [121].

ii. While certain strands of case law—mainly those in which the CJEU focuses on a particular substantive EU law right, often an EU legislative right—require *specific* national remedies to be made available, and particularly in certain sectors such as competition, consumer, and environmental law, many other cases continue to emphasize the primary responsibility of the national legal system, subject only to the principles of equivalence and effectiveness.

iii. Over time the Court has developed a highly context-specific balancing approach, which requires the importance of the EU right to be weighed against the scope and purpose of the national rule, taking all the circumstances of the case into account. And while the Court sometimes gives firm guidance on the requirements of effectiveness and equivalence, it often leaves it to the national court to assess and apply these to the facts of the case. This results in a substantial continuing flow of litigation.

7 THE PRINCIPLE OF (STATE) LIABILITY FOR BREACH OF EU LAW

(A) ORIGINS OF THE PRINCIPLE

We have seen that despite its early 'no new remedies' rule in *Rewe-Handelsgesellschaft*, the CJEU in cases such as *San Giorgio* on the repayment of charges,[170] *Factortame I* on interim relief,[171] *Heylens* on judicial review,[172] *Muñoz* on civil remedies,[173] and *Courage* on damages,[174] required national courts in certain circumstances to ensure the availability of specific remedies.

However, the most distinctive of the Court's interventionist rulings which required the availability of a particular remedy as a matter of EU law is the *Francovich* judgment. This ruling established the principle of state liability to pay compensation for breach of EU law.

Cases C–6 and 9/90 **Francovich and Bonifaci v Italy**
[1991] ECR I–5357

[Note Lisbon Treaty renumbering: Art 5 EEC is now Art 4(3) TEU]

The applicants brought proceedings against Italy for the government's failure to implement Directive 80/987 on the protection of employees in the event of their employer's insolvency. No steps had been taken pursuant to the Directive to guarantee payment of wages owed by employers, and they argued that the state was liable to pay them the sums owed. The CJEU ruled that although the provisions of the Directive lacked sufficient precision to be directly effective, they nevertheless clearly intended to confer rights of which these individuals had been deprived through the state's failure to implement them.

---

[170] Case 199/82 (n 11).
[171] Case C–213/89 *The Queen v Secretary of State for Transport, ex p Factortame Ltd* [1990] ECR I–2433.
[172] Case 222/86 *Heylens* (n 26).
[173] Case C–253/00 *Muñoz* (n 62).
[174] Case C–453/99 *Courage* (n 31).

THE ECJ

29. The national court thus raises the issue of the existence and scope of a State's liability for harm resulting from the breach of its obligations under Community law....

(a) The existence of State liability as a matter of principle

30. It must be recalled first of all that the EEC Treaty has created its own legal system which is an integral part of the legal systems of the Member States and which their courts are bound to apply; the subjects of that legal system are not only the Member States but also their nationals. Just as it imposes obligations on individuals, Community law is also intended to create rights which become part of their legal patrimony; those rights arise not only where they are expressly granted by the Treaty but also by virtue of obligations which the Treaty imposes in a clearly defined manner both on individuals and on the Member States and the Community institutions: see Case 26/62 *Van Gend en Loos* and Case 6/64 *Costa* v. *ENEL*.

. . .

32. Furthermore, it has been consistently held that the national courts whose task it is to apply the provisions of Community law in cases within their jurisdiction must ensure that those rules have full effect and protect the rights which they confer on individuals: see in particular Case 106/77 *Simmenthal* and Case C–213/89 *Factortame*.

33. It must be held that the full effectiveness of Community rules would be impaired and the protection of the rights which they grant would be weakened if individuals were unable to obtain compensation when their rights are infringed by a breach of Community law for which a Member State can be held responsible.

34. The possibility of compensation by the Member State is particularly indispensable where, as in this case, the full effectiveness of Community rules is subject to prior action on the part of the State and consequently individuals cannot, in the absence of such action, enforce the rights granted to them by Community law before the national courts.

35. It follows that the principle of State liability for harm caused to individuals by breaches of Community law for which the State can be held responsible is inherent in the system of the Treaty.

36. Further foundation for the obligation on the part of Member States to pay compensation for such harm is to be found in Article 5 EEC, under which the Member States are required to take all appropriate measures, whether general or particular, to ensure fulfilment of their obligations under Community law. Among these is the obligation to nullify the unlawful consequences of a breach of Community law....

Contrasting with its early statement that the Treaty did not intend to create new remedies,[175] the CJEU ruled that the principle of state liability is inherent in the Treaty, indicating that an action for compensation against the state for breach of EU law must be available.[176] *Francovich* also required the provision by national courts of a damages remedy for breach of an EU measure which lacked direct effect.[177] This represented an important additional move towards enhancing the effectiveness of unimplemented directives,[178] by presenting an alternative remedy for cases where national law could not otherwise be construed compatibly with an unimplemented directive.[179]

---

[175] Dougan argues that while the Court intended to develop a Community system of liability of public authorities and a right to reparation, it did not necessarily intend to create a specific 'Community remedy in damages': see 'The Francovich Right to Reparation: Reshaping the Contours of Community Remedial Competence' (2000) 6 EPL 103.

[176] M Ross, 'Beyond *Francovich*' (1993) 56 MLR 55; P Craig, '*Francovich*, Remedies and the Scope of Damages Liability' (1993) 109 LQR 595.

[177] D Curtin, 'State Liability under Private Law: A New Remedy for Private Parties' (1992) 21 ILJ 74.

[178] Ch 7.

[179] See, eg, Case C–334/92 *Wagner Miret v Fondo de Garantía Salarial* [1993] ECR I–6911; Case C–54/96 *Dorsch Consult Ingenieurgesellschaft mbH v Bundesbaugesellschaft Berlin mbH* [1997] ECR I–4961; Case C–81/98 *Alcatel Austria v Bundesministerium für Wissenschaft und Verkehr* [1999] ECR I–7671; Case C–111/97 *Evobus Austria*

Despite the importance of the principle established, however, *Francovich* gave only minimal guidance for the future.[180] Three basic conditions were established for breaches involving a state's non-implementation of a *directive*: the conferral upon an individual of specific rights,[181] the content of which must be identifiable under the directive, and a causal link between the state's breach and damage to the individual.[182] For further conditions, the Court fell back on the familiar principle of national procedural autonomy.[183]

(B) CLARIFYING AND EXTENDING THE PRINCIPLE

An opportunity for clarification came in the joined cases of *Brasserie du Pêcheur* and *Factortame III*, in which a series of questions was referred from the German Bundesgerichtshof and the English High Court respectively.[184]

Cases C–46/93 and C–48/93 **Brasserie du Pêcheur SA v Germany, and R v Secretary of State for Transport, ex parte Factortame Ltd and Others**
[1996] ECR I–1029

[Note Lisbon Treaty renumbering: Arts 5 and 164 EC are now Arts 4(3) and 19(1) TEU respectively and Arts 30, 52, 189, and 215 EC are now Arts 34, 49, 288, and 340 TFEU respectively]

The *Factortame* reference arose from the same factual background as *Factortame I* (above) and *II*, in which Spanish fishermen had invoked Article 52 EC to challenge the UK's conditions for registration as a British vessel.[185] They sought damages for losses caused by the UK's breach of the Treaty. Simultaneously, in a case arising from litigation finding Germany's beer purity laws to be in breach of Article 30 EC, a French brewery which suffered losses when it was forced to cease exports to Germany sought compensation from the German state. It was argued before the ECJ that compensation should not be available for breach of directly effective EU law, since national remedies would already be available.

THE ECJ

19. That argument cannot be accepted.
20. The Court has consistently held that the right of individuals to rely on the directly effective provisions of the Treaty before national courts is only a minimum guarantee and is not sufficient in itself to

---

[1998] ECR I–5411; Case C–258/97 *Hospital Ingenieure Krankenhaustechnik Planungs-Gesellschaft mbH (HI) v Landeskrankenanstalten-Betriebsgesellschaft* [1999] ECR I–1405; Case C–131/97 *Carbonari v Università degli Studi di Bologna* [1999] ECR I–1103.

[180] For a fundamental challenge to the very concept of state liability see C Harlow, 'Francovich and the Problem of the Disobedient State' (1996) 2 ELJ 199.

[181] Compare Case C–22/02 *Peter Paul et al v Bundesrepublik Deutschland* [2004] ECR I–9425.

[182] Cases 6 and 9/90 *Francovich* [1991] ECR I–5357, [39]–[40b].

[183] Ibid [42]–[43].

[184] N Emiliou, Note (1996) 21 ELRev 399; Harlow (n 180); J Convery, 'State Liability in the UK after *Brasserie du Pêcheur*' (1997) 34 CMLRev 603; P Craig, 'Once More unto the Breach: The Community, the State and Damages Liability' (1997) 105 LQR 67; P Oliver, Note (1997) 34 CMLRev 635.

[185] Case C–221/89 *R v Secretary of State for Transport, ex p Factortame* [1991] ECR I–3905, known as *Factortame II*.

ensure the full and complete implementation of the Treaty....The purpose of that right is to ensure that provisions of Community law prevail over national provisions. It cannot, in every case, secure for individuals the benefit of rights conferred on them by Community law and, in particular, avoid their sustaining damage as a result of a breach of Community law attributable to a Member State. As appears from paragraph 33 of the judgment in *Francovich*, the full effectiveness of Community law would be impaired if individuals were unable to obtain redress when their rights were infringed by a breach of Community law.

...

22. It is all the more so in the event of an infringement of a right directly conferred by a Community provision upon which individuals are entitled to rely before the national courts. In that event, the right to reparation is the necessary corollary of the direct effect of the Community provision whose breach caused the damage sustained.

[*The CJEU rejected the German Government's argument that a general right to reparation under Community law could be created only by legislation, and defended its own role as interpreter of the Treaty.*]

27. Since the Treaty contains no provisions expressly and specifically governing the consequences of breaches of Community law by Member States, it is for the Court, in pursuance of the task conferred on it by Article 164 of the Treaty of ensuring that in the interpretation and application of the Treaty, the law is observed, to rule on such a question in accordance with generally accepted methods of interpretation, in particular by reference to the fundamental principles of the Community legal system and, where necessary, general principles common to the legal systems of the Member States.

28. Indeed it is to the general principles common to the laws of the Member States that the second paragraph of Article 215 of the Treaty refers as the basis of the non-contractual liability of the Community for damage caused by its institutions or by its servants in the performance of their duties.

29. The principle of non-contractual liability of the Community expressly laid down in Article 215 of the Treaty is simply an expression of the general principle familiar to the legal systems of the member states that an unlawful act or omission gives rise to an obligation to make good the damage caused. That provision also reflects the obligation on public authorities to make good damage caused in the performance of their duties.

Rather than drawing only on the principle of effectiveness and on Article 4(3) TFEU (ex Article 10 EC), as it had done in *Francovich*, the CJEU here situated the principle of state liability in the context of the Treaty provisions on liability of EU institutions under Article 340 TFEU, which in turn are expressly based on the general principles common to the Member States. This reasoning seems intended to legitimate the development of the principle of state liability, deriving it from well-established principles of the national legal orders rather than a creation of the CJEU.

Drawing on international law principles, and on its case law under Article 258 TFEU, the Court ruled that the state is liable whichever of its organs is responsible for the breach and regardless of the internal division of powers between constitutional authorities.[186] In later cases it added that Member States are not required to change the distribution of powers and responsibilities between public bodies, that reparation for damage caused within federal states does not have to be provided by the federal

---

[186] R Davis, 'Liability in Damages for a Breach of Community Law: Some Reflection on the Question of Who to Sue and the Concept of "the State"' (2006) 31 ELRev 69.

state,[187] and that states are permitted though not required to impose liability on individual officials responsible for the breach as well as on the state.[188]

In a notable development, the Court ruled in *Köbler* that the principle of state liability applies even to violations of EU law by national courts of final appeal. The case concerned the failure of the Austrian Verwaltungsgericht (Supreme Administrative Court) to refer to the CJEU the question whether a particular long-service increment for university professors at Austrian universities was contrary to the Treaty provisions on free movement of workers. An earlier ruling of the CJEU on a similar question had seemed to indicate that it would violate Article 45 TFEU, but in *Köbler* the Verwaltungsgericht adopted a factual classification which it had rejected in the earlier case, ie that the increment was a reward for loyalty which could be justified under Article 45.

Case C–224/01 Gerhard Köbler v Republik Österreich
[2003] ECR I–10239

33. In the light of the essential role played by the judiciary in the protection of the rights derived by individuals from Community rules, the full effectiveness of those rules would be called in question and the protection of those rights would be weakened if individuals were precluded from being able, under certain conditions, to obtain reparation when their rights are affected by an infringement of Community law attributable to a decision of a court of a Member State adjudicating at last instance.

34. It must be stressed, in that context, that a court adjudicating at last instance is by definition the last judicial body before which individuals may assert the rights conferred on them by Community law. Since an infringement of those rights by a final decision of such a court cannot thereafter normally be corrected, individuals cannot be deprived of the possibility of rendering the State liable in order in that way to obtain legal protection of their rights.

35. Moreover, it is, in particular, in order to prevent rights conferred on individuals by Community law from being infringed that under the third paragraph of Article 234 EC a court against whose decisions there is no judicial remedy under national law is required to make a reference to the Court of Justice.

36. Consequently, it follows from the requirements inherent in the protection of the rights of individuals relying on Community law that they must have the possibility of obtaining redress in the national courts for the damage caused by the infringement of those rights owing to a decision of a court adjudicating at last instance.

The CJEU dismissed a range of arguments by several intervening governments which objected to the extension of state liability to the conduct of courts of last instance, including arguments based on the principle of legal certainty, *res judicata*, the independence and authority of the judiciary, and more practical problems like the absence of a competent national court to adjudicate on the conduct of a court of last instance.[189] The CJEU drew support for its dismissal of these objections from the fact that under the ECHR system, state reparation can be obtained for infringements of the Convention stemming from a decision of a national court of last instance. The *Köbler* ruling was later reinforced in *Traghetti del Mediterraneo*, and several years later again in *Commission v Italy*, where the CJEU

---

[187] Case C–302/97 *Konle v Austria* [1999] ECR I–3099, [61]–[64]. The Court also ruled in Case C–424/97 *Haim v Kassenzahnärztztliche Vereinigung Nordrhein* [2000] ECR I–5123, [31]–[32] that in states without a federal structure reparation for damage caused to individuals can be made by a public law body legally distinct from the state, or an autonomous territorial body with delegated powers.

[188] Case C–470/03 *AGM-COS.MET Srl v Suomen valtio and Tarmo Lehtinen* [2007] ECR I–2749.

[189] Case C–224/01 [2003] ECR I–10239, [37]–[50]; C Classen, Note (2004) 41 CMLRev 813.

condemned Italian legislation which sought substantially to restrict state liability for damage caused by a last instance court.[190]

Following *Brasserie du Pêcheur*, and particularly the reasoning in paragraph 22 of that judgment, the question arose whether liability to compensate for violation of EU law would be extended also to violations by *private* parties.[191] The issue arose in the *Courage* case, in which the CJEU reiterated its famous 'new legal order' reasoning from *Van Gend en Loos*. The Court went on to emphasize the fundamental nature of the prohibition on anti-competitive agreements in Article 101 TFEU, breach of which would render any such agreement automatically void.

Case C–453/99 **Courage Ltd v Crehan**
[2001] ECR I–6297

[Note Lisbon Treaty renumbering: Arts 85 and 86 EC are now Arts 101 and 102 TFEU]

23. Thirdly, it should be borne in mind that the Court has held that Article 85(1) of the Treaty and Article 86 of the EC Treaty produce direct effects in relations between individuals and create rights for the individuals concerned which the national courts must safeguard . . .

. . .

25. As regards the possibility of seeking compensation for loss caused by a contract or by conduct liable to restrict or distort competition, it should be remembered from the outset that, in accordance with settled case-law, the national courts whose task it is to apply the provisions of Community law in areas within their jurisdiction must ensure that those rules take full effect and must protect the rights which they confer on individuals . . .

26. The full effectiveness of Article 85 of the Treaty and, in particular, the practical effect of the prohibition laid down in Article 85(1) would be put at risk if it were not open to any individual to claim damages for loss caused to him by a contract or by conduct liable to restrict or distort competition.

27. Indeed, the existence of such a right strengthens the working of the Community competition rules and discourages agreements or practices, which are frequently covert, which are liable to restrict or distort competition. From that point of view, actions for damages before the national courts can make a significant contribution to the maintenance of effective competition in the Community.

28. There should not therefore be any absolute bar to such an action being brought by a party to a contract which would be held to violate the competition rules.

The *Courage* case, bolstered by subsequent rulings in *Manfredi*, *Kone*, and *Pfleiderer*,[192] is significant in requiring that national law must provide an action for damages against a private party for breach of the Treaty competition law rules, but the extent of its application to other Treaty provisions such as those on free movement or discrimination remains uncertain.[193] Following years of

---

[190] Case C–173/03 *Traghetti del Mediterraneo SpA v Italy* [2006] ECR I–5177; Case C–379/10 *Commission v. Italy* EU:C:2011:775.

[191] AG Van Gerven in Case C–128/92 *Banks v British Coal* [1994] ECR I–1209, and again extra-judicially in 'Bridging the Unbridgeable: Community and National Tort Laws after *Francovich* and *Brasserie*' (1996) 45 ICLQ 507, 530–532.

[192] Cases C–295–298/04 *Manfredi* (n 31); Case C–557/12 *Kone AG v OBB Infrastruktur* EU:C:2014:1317; Case C–360/09 *Pfleiderer* EU:C:2011:389.

[193] W Van Gerven, '*Crehan* and the Way Ahead' (2006) 17 EBLR 269; S Drake, 'Scope of *Courage* and The Principle of "Individual Liability" for Damages' (2006) 26 ELRev 841; N Reich, 'Horizontal Liability in EC Law: Hybridization of Remedies for Compensation in Case of Breach of EC Rights' (2007) 44 CMLRev 705; F Marcos and A Sánchez Graells, 'Towards a European Tort Law? Damages Actions for Breach of EC Antitrust Rules' (2008) ERPL 469; K Apps, 'Damages claims against Trade Unions after *Viking* and *Laval*' (2009) 34 ELRev 141; R Nazzini, 'Potency and Act of

Commission consultation and proposals, the Council in 2014 adopted a Directive on rules governing actions for damages under national law for breach of competition law.[194] The Commission has also issued a consultation and subsequently a recommendation on common principles for collective redress mechanisms at national level for breach of EU rights, including but not only limited to competition claims, and mentioning specifically consumer protection, environment protection, protection of personal data, financial services legislation, and investor protection as suitable issue areas for collective redress.[195]

(c) THE CONDITIONS FOR STATE LIABILITY

Having affirmed the basic principle of state liability, the CJEU in *Brasserie du Pêcheur* elaborated on the conditions for liability, drawing on Article 340 TFEU governing liability of the EU institutions. In the Court's words, the conditions under which states incur liability for breach of EU law cannot differ from those governing the liability of the EU in similar circumstances.[196]

Cases C–46 and 48/93 **Brasserie du Pêcheur SA v Germany**
[1996] ECR I–1029

[Note Lisbon Treaty renumbering: Arts 189 and 215 EC are now Arts 288 and 340 TFEU]

43. The system of rules which the Court has worked out with regard to Article 215 of the Treaty, particularly in relation to liability for legislative measures, takes into account, inter alia, the complexity of the situations to be regulated, difficulties in the application or interpretation of the texts and, more particularly, the margin of discretion available to the author of the act in question.

44. Thus, in developing its case-law on the non-contractual liability of the Community, in particular as regards legislative measures involving choices of economic policy, the Court has had regard to the wide discretion available to the institutions in implementing Community policies.

45. The strict approach taken towards the liability of the Community in the exercise of its legislative activities is due to two considerations. First, even when the legality of measures is subject to judicial review, exercise of the legislative function must not be hindered by the prospect of actions for damages whenever the general interest of the Community requires legislative measures to be adopted which may adversely affect individual interests. Second, in a legislative context characterized by the exercise of a wide discretion, which is essential for implementing a Community policy, the Community cannot incur liability unless the institution concerned has manifestly and gravely disregarded the limits on the exercise of its powers.

46. That said, the national legislature—like the Community institutions—does not systematically have a wide discretion when it acts in a field governed by Community law. Community law may impose

---

the Principle of Effectiveness: The Development of Competition Law Remedies and Procedures in Community Law' in C Barnard and O Odudu (eds), *Outer Limits of European Union Law* (Hart, 2009); E Hjelmeng, 'Competition Law Remedies: Striving for Coherence or Finding New Ways?' (2013) 50 CMLRev 1007; K Havu, 'Horizontal Liability for Damages in EU Law—The Changing Relationship of EU and National Law' (2012) 18 ELJ 407.

[194] The Commission followed up with a White Paper on Damages for Breach of the EC Antitrust Rules, COM(2008) 165, and a Dir was eventually signed into law in late 2014: see http://ec.europa.eu/competition/antitrust/actionsdamages/damages_directive_final_en.pdf.

[195] Commission Recommendation of 11 June 2013 [2013] OJ L201/60.

[196] The CJEU however indicated that national law could, if so desired, set stricter liability conditions: see [66], and also Case C–524/04 *Thin Cap* (n 11) and Case C–429/09 *Fuß* (n 168).

upon it obligations to achieve a particular result or obligations to act or refrain from acting which reduce its margin of discretion, sometimes to a considerable degree. This is so, for instance, where, as in the circumstances to which the judgment in *Francovich* relates, Article 189 of the Treaty places the Member State under an obligation to take, within a given period, all the measures needed in order to achieve the result required by a directive. In such a case, the fact that it is for the national legislature to take the necessary measures has no bearing on the Member State's liability for failing to transpose the directive.

47. In contrast, where a Member State acts in a field where it has a wide discretion, comparable to that of the Community institutions in implementing Community policies, the conditions under which it may incur liability must, in principle, be the same as those under which the Community institutions incur liability in the comparable situation.

. . .

51. In such circumstances, Community law confers a right to reparation where three conditions are met: the rule of law infringed must be intended to confer rights on individuals; the breach must be sufficiently serious; and there must be a direct causal link between the breach of the obligation resting on the State and the damage sustained by the injured parties.

. . .

53. . . . Those conditions correspond in substance to those defined by the Court in relation to Article 215 in its case-law on liability of the Community for damage caused to individuals by unlawful legislative measures adopted by its institutions.

. . .

55. As to the second condition, as regards both Community liability under Article 215 and Member State liability for breaches of Community law, the decisive test for finding that a breach of Community law is sufficiently serious is whether the Member State or the Community institution concerned manifestly and gravely disregarded the limits on its discretion.

56. The factors which the competent court may take into consideration include the clarity and precision of the rule breached, the measure of discretion left by that rule to the national or Community authorities, whether the infringement and the damage caused was intentional or involuntary, whether any error of law was excusable or inexcusable, the fact that the position taken by a Community institution may have contributed towards the omission, and the adoption or retention of national measures or practices contrary to Community law.

57. On any view, a breach of Community law will clearly be sufficiently serious if it has persisted despite a judgment finding the infringement in question to be established, or a preliminary ruling or settled case law of the Court on the matter from which it is clear that the conduct in question constituted an infringement.

In *Brasserie* the CJEU suggested that the national authorities must have known that the German beer designation rules were in breach of EU law given earlier CJEU rulings to this effect.[197] The Court also indicated that while the existence of a prior CJEU ruling finding an infringement of EU law would suggest that a subsequent similar infringement constitutes a sufficiently serious breach, such a ruling would not be *necessary* to establish a sufficiently serious breach.[198] Similarly, parts of the Merchant Shipping Act's conditions for registration were *prima facie* incompatible with EU law,

---

[197] The referring German court, upon receiving the CJEU ruling in *Brasserie du Pêcheur*, ultimately awarded no damages at all to the plaintiffs even as regards the provisions governing the designation '*bier*', on the basis that there had been no direct causal connection between Germany's sufficiently serious breach and the damage suffered: see [1997] 1 CMLR 971; Oliver (n 184) 657; E Deards, Note (1997) 22 ELRev 620.

[198] Cases 46 and 48/93 *Brasserie du Pêcheur* (n 162) [91]–[95]. Indeed, the *Danske Slagterior* ruling (n 168) indicates that litigants should not wait for an ECJ ruling under Art 258 TFEU before bringing a *Francovich*-type action for damages, and that national law is not required to provide for a suspension of the time limit for an action in damages while the CJEU ruling is awaited.

whereas others might have appeared to be capable of justification.[199] In assessing the question of 'sufficient seriousness' the UK court was encouraged to consider the existing legal disputes over the common fisheries policy, the fact that the Commission had made its attitude known in good time to the UK, and 'the assessments as to the state of certainty of EU law made by the national courts in the interim proceedings brought'.[200] In *Fuß*, the fact that the breach occurred 'in obvious disregard of the Court's case law' made it a sufficiently serious one.[201] However, the fact that the national court in *Ogieriakhi* had not considered it necessary to make a reference to the CJEU did not in itself imply that the breach was not sufficiently serious for the purposes of state liability.[202]

The CJEU indicated that the question of causation of damage was ultimately for the national courts to decide,[203] although in later cases including *Leth* and *Kone*, it gave clear legal guidance as to causation.[204]

On the crucial question of the *standard* of liability, while the CJEU did not respond directly to a question from the German Government on the meaning of 'fault', the Court made clear that the concept of 'sufficiently serious breach', which arguably carries connotations of fault, was all that could be required by domestic law:[205] this position was strongly affirmed by *Köbler*, *Traghetti*, and *Commission v Italy*, concerning state liability arising from the action of national courts. In *Köbler* the CJEU ruled that, regard being had to 'the specific nature of the judicial function' and the legitimate requirements of legal certainty,[206] state liability in cases of judicial breach was governed by the same conditions (conferral of rights on individuals, a sufficiently serious breach, and a causal link between the state's breach and damage to the individual) and by the same standard of liability as any other state violation of EU law. As far as the standard is concerned, liability can be incurred only 'in the exceptional case where the court has manifestly infringed the applicable law'.[207] The CJEU in *Köbler* repeated the content of paragraphs 56 and 57 of *Brasserie du Pêcheur*, but added one further indicator of manifest breach by a national court of last instance: non-compliance by the court in question with its obligation to make a preliminary reference to the CJEU.

In *Traghetti del Mediterraneo*, Italian legislation sought to restrict state liability arising from damage caused by a last instance court by excluding liability where the infringement was the result of an interpretation of law or an assessment of facts or evidence, and by limiting liability solely to cases of intentional fault and serious misconduct by the national court.[208] The CJEU rejected the claim that the impugned legislation struck a fair balance between effective judicial protection and

---

[199] The House of Lords ultimately upheld the finding of the Divisional Court and Court of Appeal that the breach was sufficiently serious to give rise to liability in damages. For the domestic judgments on this issue see [1997] Eu LR 475, [1998] 1 All ER 736, [1999] All ER 640 (CA), [2000] 1 AC 524 (HL), and finally the Div Ct ruling in [2001] 1 WLR 942.

[200] Cases 46 and 48/93 *Brasserie du Pêcheur* (n 162) [63]. Compare Case C–318/13 *X* EU:C:2014:2133, in which the CJEU gave the national court mixed guidance on what factors to take into account, noting both that the CJEU had not yet ruled on the scope of the provision under dispute, nor had infringement proceedings been brought against the Member States, but that similar provisions in a related sex equality directive had been found to violate EU law principles.

[201] Case C–429/09 *Fuß* EU:C:2010:7.

[202] Case C–244/13 *Ogieriakhi* EU:C:2014:2068.

[203] Ibid [65]. See also Case C–140/97 *Rechberger* (n 164) [72]–[73]; Case C–127/95 *Norbrook Laboratories Ltd v Ministry of Agriculture Fisheries and Food* [1998] ECR I–1531.

[204] Case C–319/96 *Brinkmann Tabakfabriken GmbH v Skatteministeriet* [1998] ECR I–5255 [29]; Case C–94/10 *Danfoss* EU:C:2012:591; Case C–420/11 *Leth* EU:C:2013:166; Case C–557/12 *Kone AG v OBB Infrastruktur* EU:C:2014:1317; M Tomulic Vehovec, 'The Cause of Member State Liability' (2012) 20 ERPL 851.

[205] Cases 46 and 48/93 *Brasserie du Pêcheur* (n 162) [76]–[79]; Case C–424/97 *Haim* (n 187); Case C–429/09 *Fuss* (n 168) [65]–[70].

[206] Case C–224/01 *Köbler* (n 96) [53].

[207] Ibid [52]–[53]; B Beutler, 'State Liability for Breaches of Community Law by National Courts: Is the Requirement of a Manifest Infringement of the Applicable Law an Insurmountable Obstacle?' (2009) 46 CMLRev 773.

[208] Case C–173/03 *Traghetti del Mediterraneo* (n 190); Case C–379/10 *Commission v Italy* EU:C:2011:775; G Anagnostaras, 'Erroneous Judgments and the Prospect of Damages' (2006) 31 ELRev 735; M Rodriguez, 'State Liability for Judicial Acts in European Community Law' (2005) 11 CJEL 605.

legal certainty and the independence of the judiciary. On the requirement of showing intentional fault and serious misconduct by the national court, the CJEU ruled:

> [A]lthough it remains possible for national law to define the criteria relating to the nature or degree of the infringement which must be met before State liability can be incurred for an infringement of Community law attributable to a national court adjudicating at last instance, under no circumstances may such criteria impose requirements stricter than that of a manifest infringement of the applicable law, as set out in paragraphs 53 to 56 of the *Köbler* judgment.[209]

Similarly, the exclusion of liability for an interpretation of law or assessment of facts or evidence by the national court of last instance 'would render meaningless' the principle laid down in *Köbler*, since a manifest infringement of EU law could readily arise from either of these two kinds of judicial activity, especially when carried out by a court of last instance.[210]

On the facts of *Köbler*, the CJEU ruled that although it was normally for the national court to apply the law to the facts of the case, it had enough information in this case to give guidance on whether the conditions for state liability were fulfilled.[211] The issue was whether the Austrian Verwaltungsgericht had 'manifestly infringed' EU law by failing to re-refer the question of the compatibility of a long-service increment with Article 45 TFEU to the CJEU. The Verwaltungsgericht had initially referred the question to the Court, but had subsequently withdrawn it on the suggestion of the CJEU registrar, who assumed it had been resolved in Professor Köbler's favour by the earlier *Schöning-Kougebetopoulou*[212] ruling, which had found a similar long-service increment to be incompatible with Article 45 TFEU. However, the Verwaltungsgericht then decided to re-classify the long-service increment as a loyalty bonus under national law, possibly in order to avoid the application of the *Schöning-Kougebetopoulou* ruling. The CJEU nonetheless took a benign view of the action of the Verwaltungsgericht and ruled that in failing to re-refer the question under Article 267 TFEU,[213] its infringement of EU law was not sufficiently manifest to attract state liability.[214]

In *British Telecom*,[215] the CJEU agreed that the UK had mis-implemented a public procurement directive, but concluded that it did not amount to a 'sufficiently serious breach' since the provision was not clear and precise, the UK's interpretation was made in good faith and in keeping with the aims and wording of the directive, and no guidance had been available from past rulings of the CJEU or the Commission. A similar ruling was given in *Denkavit*, in relation to the incorrect transposition by Germany of a company taxation directive, where almost all other Member States had adopted the same interpretation of the directive as Germany and there was no existing case law on the provision concerned.[216] Other rulings have followed suit.[217]

Where EU law leaves considerable discretion to the national authorities, state liability will depend on a finding of manifest and grave disregard for the limits of that discretion.[218] Conversely, in

---

[209] Case C–173/03 [44].

[210] Ibid [34]–[40]. See the follow-up proceedings brought by the Commission against Italy for the same infringement: Case C–379/10 *Commission v Italy* EU:C:2011:775.

[211] Case C–224/01 *Köbler* (n 96) [101].

[212] Case C–15/96 *Kalliope Schöning-Kougebetopoulou v Freie und Hansestadt Hamburg* [1998] ECR I–47.

[213] Interestingly, although the provision of EU law violated by the Austrian court was Art 267 TFEU (ex Art 234 EC), the provision which the CJEU analysed in order to determine whether the first condition of liability (conferral of rights on individuals) was satisfied was Art 45 TFEU (ex Art 39 EC), on the free movement of workers.

[214] Case C–224/01 *Köbler* (n 96) [121]–[124].

[215] Case C–392/93 *R v HM Treasury, ex p British Telecommunications plc* [1996] ECR I–1631.

[216] Cases C–283, 291 and 292/94 *Denkavit International v Bundesamt für Finanzen* [1996] ECR I–5063, [51]–[52].

[217] Case C–319/96 *Brinkmann* (n 204) [30]–[32]; Case C–127/95 *Norbrook* (n 203).

[218] Case C–278/05 *Robins and Others v Secretary of State for Work and Pensions* [2007] ECR I–1053; Cases C–501, 506, 540 and 541/12 *Specht* EU:C:2014:2005.

Dillenkofer,[219] concerning Germany's failure to implement the Package Holidays Directive 90/314, the CJEU ruled that *Francovich* had established that non-transposition of a directive within the prescribed time limit *of itself* amounted to a sufficiently serious breach.[220] Similarly in *Lomas*, the refusal of the UK to grant export licences for live sheep to Spain, on the ground that Spanish slaughterhouses were not complying with the terms of an EU directive, constituted a sufficiently serious breach, given the lack of discretion left to states under the directive, the clarity of the Treaty provision breached, and the absence of a properly verified justification.[221] Similar rulings were given in *AGM-COS.MET*[222] and *Synthon BV*[223] in which there was no room for state discretion.[224]

(D) STATE LIABILITY AND THE NATIONAL REMEDIAL FRAMEWORK

While *Brasserie du Pêcheur/Factortame III* provided guidance on the conditions governing state liability, many issues were left to be governed by national law, subject to the familiar principles of equivalence and effectiveness.[225] In other words, while the core conditions of state liability for breach of EU law are determined by EU law,[226] the action for compensation is provided within the framework of domestic legal systems, with varying procedural and substantive rules on matters such as time limits, causation, mitigation of loss, and assessment of damages.[227]

Concerning the *effectiveness* principle, the CJEU in *Brasserie/Factortame* ruled that German law limiting the liability of the state exercising its legislative function, and English law requirements such as 'abuse of power' or proof of misfeasance in public office, would make it excessively difficult to obtain reparation. Concerning the extent of reparation, the Court ruled that 'reparation for loss or damage caused to individuals as result of breaches of Community law must be commensurate with the loss or damage sustained'.[228] This requirement of commensurability is strong, recalling the ruling in *Marshall II*,[229] and any restrictions imposed on the extent of damages available must be reasonable. Rules on mitigation of loss are acceptable,[230] but the total exclusion of loss of profits or the restriction of damages to certain specific interests such as property,[231] or the imposition of restrictive additional conditions for the recovery of losses other than property,[232] would violate

---

[219] Cases C–178–179 and 188–190/94 *Dillenkofer v Germany* [1996] ECR I–4845, [21]–[23]. For a case involving mis-implementation, rather than non-implementation, of the Package Holiday Dir which also constituted a sufficiently serious breach see Case C–140/97 *Rechberger* (n 164) [51]–[53].

[220] Cases C–178–179 and 188–190/94 *Dillenkofer* (n 219) [21]–[23].

[221] Case C–5/94 *R v Ministry of Agriculture, Fisheries and Food, ex p Hedley Lomas* [1996] ECR I–2553, [28]–[29]; Case C–118/00 *Larsy v INASTI* [2001] ECR I–5063; Case C–150/99 *Stockholm Lindöpark Aktiebolag v Sweden* [2001] ECR I–493.

[222] Case C–470/03 *AGM-COS.MET Srl v Suomen valtio and Tarmo Lehtinen* (n 188).

[223] Case C–452/06 *R, ex p Synthon BV v Licensing Authority of the Department of Health* [2008] ECR I–7681.

[224] Compare Case C–63/01 *Evans* (n 40) [82]–[88].

[225] For discussion of the procedural conditions prevailing in different Member States see C Kremer, 'Liability for Breach of EC Law' (2003) 22 YBEL 203; H Xanathi, 'Effective Judicial Protection at the National Level Against Breaches of EC Law' (2005) 5 EJLR 409.

[226] Case C–300/04 *Eman* (n 151) [70].

[227] In Case C–228/98 *Dounias* (n 120) the exceptional availability of witness evidence in proceedings to establish state liability was deemed compatible with the principles of equivalence and effectiveness. See also Case C–118/00 *Larsy* (n 221).

[228] Cases 46 and 48/93 (n 162) [82]. In C–429/09 *Fuß* (n 168), the CJEU ruled that it was for national law, subject to the requirements of effectiveness and equivalence, to determine whether reparation should consist of time off in lieu rather than financial compensation, and to lay down the method for calculating the reparation.

[229] Case C–271/91 *Marshall v Southampton and South-West Hampshire Area Health Authority II* [1993] ECR I–4367.

[230] Case C–445/06 *Danske Slagterier* (n 168).

[231] Cases 46 and 48/93 *Brasserie du Pêcheur* (n 162) [84]–[88].

[232] Case C–470/03 *AGM* (n 188) [90]–[96] concerning a Finnish rule subjecting the right to compensation for damage other than damage to persons or property to the condition that the damage result either from a criminal offence or from the exercise of public authority, or there are 'especially serious reasons' for awarding compensation.

the effectiveness principle.[233] Although the CJEU rejected the German Government's request for a temporal limit on the effects of the *Brasserie* ruling, the Court indicated that Germany could take account, within the framework of its *national* law on liability, of temporal concerns such as the principle of legal certainty.[234]

Certain other restrictive conditions on the action for damages have been held to be contrary to the principle of effectiveness, such as the provision making a public sector worker's right to reparation for the damage suffered due to the state's infringement of the EU Working Time Directive conditional on a prior application having been made to his employer in order to secure compliance with that provision.[235] In a trilogy of Italian cases concerning claims arising out of the *Francovich* litigation, the CJEU found national provisions limiting the availability of compensation for the state's prior breach of EU law to be excessively restrictive.[236] This breach was the failure to implement Directive 80/987 on the protection of employees following their employer's insolvency, and the CJEU found various provisions of the legislation limiting the period from which wage claims could be made to be excessively restrictive.[237]

Concerning the principle of *equivalence*, the Court in *Palmisani* left it to the national court to decide whether the one-year time limit set by Italian legislation for a claim for compensation for failure to implement Directive 80/987 was in compliance.[238] The general time limit for cases of non-contractual liability brought under the Italian Civil Code was five years, and the CJEU distinguished between claims for wages under the national law implementing the Directive (a social security benefit) and claims for damages for loss caused by the late implementation of the Directive, which were governed by the Italian compensation scheme set up by the later measure (compensation for the state's non-implementation). For this reason, it might be inappropriate to compare the time limit for actions under the compensation scheme with the time limit for social security claims in national law, rather than with the ordinary system of non-contractual liability.[239] It was for the Italian court to determine the issue of 'equivalence', although the CJEU suggested that this principle might have been violated by the legislation at issue.[240] In *Transportes Urbanos*, on the other hand, the requirement of exhaustion of domestic remedies before bringing a claim in damages for breach of EU law was clearly considered by the CJEU to violate the equivalence principle, since it did not apply to claims in damages for breach of the domestic Constitution.[241]

---

[233] On mitigation of loss and economic loss in general see Case C–410/98 *Metallgesellschaft* (n 58) [91]; Cases C–295–298/04 *Manfredi* (n 31). As regards exemplary damages in English law, the CJEU in *Brasserie du Pêcheur* ruled that such an award could not be ruled out in the case of the state's breach of EU law in similar circumstances to those which would give rise to an award in an action founded on domestic law: Cases 46 and 48/93 *Brasserie du Pêcheur* (n 162) [89].

[234] Cases 46 and 48/93 *Brasserie du Pêcheur* (n 162) [98].

[235] Case C–429/09 *Fuß* (n 168). See also Case C–94/10 *Danfoss* EU:C:2012:591 concerning passing-off rules and whether they undermined the effectiveness of the action for compensation.

[236] Cases C–94–95/95 *Bonifaci and Berto v IPNS* [1997] ECR I–3969; Case C–261/95 *Palmisani* (n 148); Case C–373/95 *Maso and Gazzetta v IPNS* [1997] ECR I–4051; Dougan (n 175).

[237] The Court also ruled that while retroactive application of the measures adopted should be sufficient to ensure the adequacy of reparation, this would not necessarily be so if employees could demonstrate otherwise: Cases C–94–95/95 *Bonifaci and Berto* (n 236) [51]–[53].

[238] Case C–261/95 (n 148).

[239] See also Case C–69/08 *Visciano* (n 97) [41]–[42].

[240] Case C–261/95 (n 148) [39]; Cases C–52 and 53/99 *ONP v Camarotto* [2001] ECR I–1395; Case C–470/04 *N v Inspecteur van de Belastingdienst Oost/kantoor Almelo* [2006] ECR I–7409.

[241] Case C–118/08 *Transportes Urbanos y Servicios Generales SAL v Administración del Estado* EU:C:2010:39.

(E) STATE LIABILITY AS A RESIDUAL REMEDY?

What advantages are there for an individual to choose the EU-mandated action for compensation rather than another existing national remedy to enforce EU law?[242]

There was some suggestion in cases like *Société Comateb*[243] and *Sutton*[244] that where a national remedy is unsatisfactory due to the existence of a legitimate national procedural restriction, an action in damages against the state might provide an alternative remedy which is not affected by that particular restrictive national rule. In each case, having conceded that restrictions on the availability of national remedies were potentially legitimate, the CJEU went on to consider the possible liability of the state in damages.[245] One reading of the cases is that they assume that a *Francovich*-style action for compensation may prove to be a more effective remedy than others available under national law. This assumption has, however, been criticized on the basis that an action based on *Francovich* requires the establishment of additional onerous conditions, such as a sufficiently serious breach and causation of loss.[246]

On the other hand the CJEU in *Stockholm Lindöpark* rejected the argument that the availability of a *Francovich*-style action for damages should be precluded by the fact that a separate action under national law could be based on the direct effect of EU law.[247] And in *Wells*, the CJEU left it to the national court to decide which kind of remedy would be available and appropriate for a violation of EU environmental impact assessment law, for example whether revocation or compensation.[248] In *Transportes Urbanos*, the CJEU was asked whether EU law permitted a national rule requiring prior exhaustion of domestic remedies before bringing an action for state liability in damages for breach of EU law.[249] The Court found on the facts of the case that the principle of equivalence was violated, since the exhaustion of remedies rule did not apply to actions for damages for breach of the national constitution, but it left open the question whether such a prior exhaustion rule would violate the effectiveness principle in a case where there was equivalence between the treatment of damages actions based on EU law and national constitutional law.

[242] Oliver (n 184) and Deards (n 197) question whether the action for damages may be made subsidiary to other national remedies; G Anagnostraras, 'State Liability and Alternative Courses of Action: How Independent Can an Autonomous Remedy Be?' (2002) 21 YBEL 355.

[243] Cases C–192–218/95 *Comateb* (n 11) concerning the principle of unjust enrichment as a barrier to the repayment of charges wrongly levied. For further discussion of the case law on repayment of charges and 'passing off', see Dougan (n 13). Compare *Comateb,* where the CJEU accepted the compatibility in principle of such an unjust enrichment rule with the effectiveness principle with Case C–147/01 *Weber's Wine World* (n 152) where the CJEU ruled that a presumption of unjust enrichment, on the sole basis that the charge was passed on to third parties, would make the exercise of EU rights excessively difficult in practice. See also Case C–309/06 *Marks & Spencer* (n 11) on *partial* passing-on, and three groups of Test Claimants cases: Case C–201/05 *CFC* (n 11); Case C–524/04 *Thin Cap* (n 11); Case C–446/04 *FII Group Litigation* (n 11); Case C–94/10 *Danfoss* EU:C:2012:591. For a case on the topic brought by the Commission against a Member State, rather than by an affected individual, see Case C–129/00 *Commission v Italy* [2003] ECR I–14637.

[244] Case C–66/95 *Sutton* (n 39), concerning the non-availability of interest on arrears of social security owed under Dir 79/7. Similarly in Case C–90/96 *Petrie v Università degli Studi di Verona et Camilla Bettoni* [1997] ECR I–6525, the CJEU ruled that although applicants for teaching posts who had been subject to an unlawful discriminatory condition could not insist that they must be eligible for appointment to these posts under national law, that did not mean that they could not seek compensation under the conditions laid down in *Brasserie du Pêcheur.*

[245] Case C–261/95 *Palmisani* (n 148) also lends some support to the hypothesis that, eg, an action for damages against the state for loss caused by the mis-implementation of a dir would also have to include loss caused by the effluxion of time, even where such loss could not be recovered as interest in an action for repayment of arrears under national law.

[246] Dougan (n 175).

[247] Case C–150/99 *Stockholm Lindöpark* (n 221) [35].

[248] Case C–201/02 *Wells* (n 90) [67]–[69].

[249] Case C–118/08 *Transportes Urbanos* (n 241).

According to Prechal (now CJEU judge), state liability for breach of EU law is indeed 'a sort of residual remedy ... a second rank alternative' to the direct or indirect effect of EU rights and their enforcement at national level.[250] She suggests that EU law may even require litigants, as a way of mitigating their loss, to rely first on the direct or indirect effect of an EU right before seeking state compensation. Case law since *Francovich*, in her view, confirms the subsidiary and complementary character of state liability as a kind of 'safety net' where other devices fail. Certainly the question of the national court to the CJEU in one of the *Test Claimants in the FII Group Litigation* cases suggests that litigants may also perceive the action for damages against the state as a second-best to a domestic claim for repayment of taxes.[251] Dougan also argues that the CJEU tends to use state liability as a cure for inadequate domestic remedies.[252] These commentators have questioned whether the Court's tendency to present state liability as a panacea where national remedies are lacking might have the perverse effect of lowering the effectiveness of national protection.

8 CONCLUSIONS

i. Responding to the lack of a harmonized system of EU remedies, the CJEU's intervention to stimulate incremental national procedural alignment has prompted differing reactions. Some applaud the Court for treading a difficult path between the need to respect national legal autonomy, and the competing need to promote effective enforcement of EU law.

ii. Others caution against the effects of such reactive, *ad hoc*, and haphazard judicial lawmaking and argue for a more systematic, politically legitimate, and carefully considered political approach to the effectiveness of EU law and the creation of an EU system of procedures and remedies.[253] Yet, given the difficulty of EU legislative harmonization or even coordination in these fields, other than in very specific sectors, it has been suggested that incremental reform through the Court's case law may in some respects be desirable.[254]

iii. It has also been argued that remedial harmonization may simply be a task for which the CJEU is inherently unsuited.[255] The contribution of the CJEU's case law in most sectors has been described as promoting a form of negative rather than positive harmonization, setting limits and boundaries for national systems rather than prescribing harmonized solutions.[256] Even in more densely integrated sectors such as competition law and state aid, judicially-led harmonization has been described as minimum rather than full harmonization.

iv. The lack of EU legislative activity may reflect a clear political objection on the part of Member States to harmonizing or even coordinating domestic procedures in this respect, or it may simply reflect the difficulty, complexity, and ambition of the task which would be involved.[257]

---

[250] S Prechal, 'Direct Effect and State Liability: What's the Difference After All?' (2006) 17 EBLR 299.

[251] The national court in its third question asked: 'In the circumstances described ..., does the company paying the ACT have a claim for the repayment of the tax unduly levied (*San Giorgio* ...) or only a claim for damages (*Brasserie du Pêcheur and Factortame*)?', Case C–35/11 *Test Claimants in the FII Group Litigation* EU:C:2012:707, [35].

[252] M Dougan, *National Remedies before the Court of Justice* (Hart, 2004) ch 5.

[253] F Snyder, 'The Effectiveness of European Community Law' (1993) 56 MLR 19, 50–53.

[254] C Himsworth, 'Things Fall Apart: The Harmonisation of Community Judicial Protection Revisited' (1997) 22 ELRev 291, 307.

[255] Dougan (n 252).

[256] Ibid chs 6 and 7.

[257] C Harding, 'Member State Enforcement of European Community Measures: The Chimera of "Effective" Enforcement' (1997) 4 MJEL 5.

v. Member States may also be resistant to the prospect of EU interference—whether legislative or judicial—with their systems of private law, which reflect implicit but fundamental social and cultural choices.[258] Nonetheless, the extensive moves to activate the EU's 'area of freedom, security and justice', including coordination of civil procedural law across the Member States, may indicate a shift in this respect.[259] While remedial 'harmonization' in its strong form may be off the agenda, other more gradual forms of mutual alignment—prompted perhaps by measures such as the Commission's recommendation on collective redress—may well emerge.

9 FURTHER READING

(a) Books and Reports

DOUGAN, M, *National Remedies before the Court of Justice* (Hart, 2004)

KILPATRICK, C, NOVITZ, T, AND SKIDMORE, P (eds), *The Future of Remedies in Europe* (Hart, 2000)

VAN LEEUWEN, B, AND CONDON, R, Bottom Up or Rock Bottom Harmonization? Francovich State Liability in National Courts EUI Deparment of Law Research Paper No Law 2015/3

(b) Articles

ANAGNOSTARAS, G, 'Erroneous Judgments and the Prospect of Damages: The Scope of the Principle of Governmental Liability for Judicial Breaches' (2006) 31 ELRev 735

ARNULL, A, 'The Principle of Effective Judicial Protection in EU Law: An Unruly Horse?' (2011) 36 ELRev 51

DOUGAN, M, 'The *Francovich* Right to Reparation: Reshaping the Contours of Community Remedial Competence' (2000) 6 EPL 103

———— M, 'The Vicissitudes of Life at the Coalface: Remedies and Procedures for Enforcing Union Law before the National Courts' in P Craig and G de Búrca (eds), *The Evolution of EU Law* (Oxford University Press, 2nd edn, 2011)

DRAKE, S, 'Scope of Courage and the Principle of "Individual Liability" for Damages' (2006) 6 ELRev 841

HAVU, K, 'Horizontal Liability for Damages in EU Law—The Changing Relationship of EU and National Law' (2012) 18 ELJ 407

PRECHAL, S, 'Member State Liability and Direct Effect: What's the Difference After All?' (2006) 17 EBLR 299

TOMULIC VEHOVEC, M, 'The Cause of Member State Liability' (2012) 20 ERPL 851

TRSTENJAK, V, AND BEYSEN, E, 'European Consumer Protection Law: *Curia semper dabit remedium*?' (2011) 48 CMLRev 95

VAN CLEYNENBREUGEL, P, 'Judge-Made Standards of National Procedure in the Post-Lisbon Constitutional Framework' (2012) 37 ELRev 90

WATTEL, P, 'National Procedural Autonomy and Effectiveness of EC Law' (2008) 35 LIEI 109

---

[258] D Caruso, 'The Missing View of the Cathedral: The Private Law Paradigm of European Legal Integration' (1997) 3 ELJ 3; H Collins, 'European Private Law and the Cultural Identity of States' (1995) 3 ERPL 353.

[259] See the various developments, many spearheaded, promoted, or supported by the EU, in the field of private law, civil law, and criminal law, mentioned at (n 2).

THE RELATIONSHIP BETWEEN EU LAW AND NATIONAL LAW: SUPREMACY

1 CENTRAL ISSUES

i. The doctrine of supremacy of EU law had no formal basis in the Treaty, but was developed by the Court on the basis of its conception of the 'new legal order'. The Court ruled that the aim of creating a uniform common market between different states would be undermined if EU law could be made subordinate to national law.

ii. The validity of EU law can therefore, according to the CJEU, never be assessed by reference to national law. National courts are required to give immediate effect to EU law, of whatever rank, in cases which arise before them, and to ignore or to set aside any national law, of whatever rank, which could impede the application of EU law. Thus, according to the CJEU, any norm of EU law takes precedence over any provision of national law, including the national constitutions.

iii. The requirement to 'set aside' conflicting national law does not entail an obligation to nullify national law, which may continue to apply in any situation which is not covered by a conflicting provision of EU law.

iv. Most national courts do not accept the CJEU's view as regards the supremacy of EU law. While they accept the requirements of supremacy in practice, most regard this as flowing from their national constitutions rather than from the authority of the EU Treaties or the CJEU, and they retain a power of ultimate constitutional review over measures of EU law. There are moreover new challenges flowing from the introduction in the Lisbon Treaty of provisions safeguarding national identity.

2 FIRST DIMENSION: SUPREMACY FROM THE ECJ'S PERSPECTIVE

(A) FOUNDATIONS

The EEC Treaty contained no provision dealing with the supremacy of Community law over national law. A supremacy clause was incorporated in the Constitutional Treaty, and a

Declaration on primacy was included in the Lisbon Treaty, the effect of which will be considered below. Notwithstanding the absence of any explicit provision in the Rome Treaty, the ECJ enunciated its vision of supremacy in the early years of the Community. It touched on the issue in *Van Gend en Loos*[1] when it stated that the Community constituted a new legal order of international law for the benefit of which the states had limited their sovereign rights, but the ECJ's primary focus was on direct effect. The supremacy doctrine was however at the forefront of the decision in *Costa*.

Case 6/64 **Flaminio Costa v ENEL**
[1964] ECR 585, 593

[Note Lisbon Treaty renumbering: Arts 5, 7, 177, and 189 are now
Arts 4(3) TEU, 18, 267, and 288 TFEU]

THE ECJ

By contrast with ordinary international treaties, the EEC Treaty has created its own legal system which, on the entry into force of the Treaty, became an integral part of the legal systems of the Member States and which their courts are bound to apply.

By creating a Community of unlimited duration, having its own institutions, its own personality, its own legal capacity and capacity of representation on the international plane and, more particularly, real powers stemming from a limitation of sovereignty or a transfer of powers from the States to the Community, the Member States have limited their sovereign rights, albeit within limited fields, and have thus created a body of law which binds both their nationals and themselves.

The integration into the laws of each Member State of provisions which derive from the Community, and more generally the terms and the spirit of the Treaty, make it impossible for the states, as a corollary, to accord precedence to a unilateral and subsequent measure over a legal system accepted by them on the basis of reciprocity. Such a measure cannot therefore be inconsistent with that legal system. The executive force of Community law cannot vary from one State to another in deference to subsequent domestic laws, without jeopardizing the attainment of the objectives of the Treaty set out in Article 5(2) and giving rise to the discrimination prohibited by Article 7.

The obligations undertaken under the Treaty establishing the Community would not be unconditional, but merely contingent, if they could be called into question by subsequent legislative acts of the signatories. . . .

The precedence of Community law is confirmed by Article 189, whereby a regulation 'shall be binding' and 'directly applicable in all Member States'. This provision, which is subject to no reservation, would be quite meaningless if a State could unilaterally nullify its effects by means of a legislative measure which could prevail over Community law.

It follows from all these observations that the law stemming from the Treaty, an independent source of law, could not, because of its special and original nature, be overridden by domestic legal provisions, however framed, without being deprived of its character as Community law and without the legal basis of the Community itself being called into question.

---

[1] Case 26/62 *NV Algemene Transport- en Expeditie Onderneming van Gend en Loos v Nederlandse Administratie der Belastingen* [1963] ECR 1.

> The transfer by the states from their domestic legal system to the Community legal system of the rights and obligations arising under the Treaty carries with it a permanent limitation of their sovereign rights, against which a subsequent unilateral act incompatible with the concept of the Community cannot prevail.

What comes across most strongly is the teleological rather than textual approach in the Court's judgment, with emphasis on the aims of the EU and the spirit of the Treaties. The Court deployed a number of arguments to justify its conclusion that EU law should be accorded supremacy over national law.

First, there is what may be termed a contractarian argument. The essence of this argument is that EU law should be accorded primacy because it flowed from the agreement made by the Member States when they joined the EU. We see this argument in the Court's statement that the Treaty created its own legal order, which immediately became 'an integral part' of the legal systems of the Member States. The argument is more explicit in the ECJ's statement that the Member States transferred to the new Union institutions 'real powers stemming from a limitation of sovereignty' and thereby limited their sovereign rights. The Court however made no reference to the constitution of any particular Member State to see whether such a transfer or limitation of sovereignty was contemplated, or was possible in accordance with that constitution.

A second aspect of the judgment is functional, capturing the idea that the very aims of the Treaty could not be achieved unless primacy was accorded to EU law. Thus the Court states that the aims of the Treaty were integration and cooperation, and their achievement would be undermined by one Member State refusing to give effect to a Union law which should uniformly and equally bind all.

A third argument is egalitarian. If Member State law could unilaterally take precedence over EU law then that would lead to discrimination in the application of EU law as between the Member States, and would mean also that a state was taking the benefits of EU law without accepting all the burdens.

A final strand is analytical in nature: the obligations undertaken by the Member States in the Treaty would be 'merely contingent' rather than unconditional if they were to be subject to later legislative acts by the states. Thus the Court adverts to what is now Article 288 TFEU, which provides that regulations are directly applicable, and concludes that this would be meaningless if states could negate the effect of EU law by subsequent inconsistent legislation. This textual argument is, however, of limited efficacy, since Article 288 refers only to the direct applicability of regulations, while the Court sought to establish a general principle of the supremacy of all binding EU law. Moreover, direct applicability refers to the way in which Union law becomes part of the national legal system without the need for implementing measures, but does not resolve the priority between this law and other forms of national law.

(B) AMBIT

While the conceptual basis for the supremacy of EU law was set out in *Costa*, the ambit of the principle became clearer in later decisions.

(i) *Supremacy Principle Applicable Against All National Law*

In the following case, the Court ruled that the legal status of a conflicting national measure was not relevant to the question whether EU law should take precedence.[2] Not even a fundamental rule of

---

[2] See also Case C–473/93 *Commission v Luxembourg* [1996] ECR I–3207, [38].

national constitutional law could be invoked to challenge the supremacy of a directly applicable EU law. This ruling gave rise to a potentially serious conflict in the relationship between the German Federal Constitutional Court and the ECJ. While the latter has sought to avoid a direct constitutional conflict with a national court,[3] it has never retreated from its claims.

Case 11/70 Internationale Handelsgesellschaft mbH v Einfuhr- und Vorratsstelle für Getreide und Futtermittel
[1970] ECR 1125

The applicant argued that a Community regulation under which a deposit would be forfeited if the goods were not exported within the period of time set was contrary to principles of national constitutional law, including freedom of action and of disposition, economic liberty, and proportionality.

THE ECJ

3. Recourse to the legal rules or concepts of national law in order to judge the validity of measures adopted by the institutions of the Community would have an adverse effect on the uniformity and efficacy of Community law. The validity of such measures can only be judged in the light of Community law. In fact, the law stemming from the Treaty, an independent source of law, cannot because of its very nature be overridden by rules of national law, however framed, without being deprived of its character as Community law and without the legal basis of the Community itself being called into question. Therefore the validity of a Community measure or its effect within a Member State cannot be affected by allegations that it runs counter to either fundamental rights as formulated by the constitution of that State or the principles of a national constitutional structure.

The Court faced the opposite kind of argument in *Ciola*, where the Austrian Government argued that the principle of primacy should not automatically apply 'to specific individual administrative acts'.[4] The Court dismissed this argument, reaffirming that any provision of national law which conflicted with directly effective EU law should not be applied. Thus the principle of primacy is required whenever directly effective EU law is concerned, and regardless of whether fundamental national constitutional norms or minor administrative acts are at issue. More recently, the Court qualified its reasoning in *Ciola* by admitting that, under specific circumstances, supremacy needs to be accommodated with domestic limitations of the period of time during which certain administrative acts may be repealed or judicially contested.[5]

(ii) *Supremacy Principle Applicable to National Laws that Pre-Date and Post-Date EU Law*

The ECJ in *Simmenthal* developed further its supremacy doctrine by making clear that it applied irrespective of whether the national law pre-dated or post-dated the EU law. An EU measure rendered inapplicable any conflicting provision of national law and prevented the adoption of new national law that would conflict with Union law.

---

[3] See, eg, Case C–446/98 *Fazenda Pública v Câmara* [2000] ECR I–11435, [36]–[38].
[4] Case C–224/97 *Ciola v Land Vorarlberg* [1999] ECR I–2517, [24].
[5] Case C–453/00 *Kühne & Heitz* [2004] ECR I–837; Case C–2/06 *Willy Kempter AG* [2008] ECR I–411. See Ch 13 for discussion.

Case 106/77 **Amministrazione delle Finanze dello Stato v Simmenthal SpA**
[1978] ECR 629

The respondent company, which had imported beef from France into Italy, brought an action before the Pretore claiming repayment of the fees which had been charged to it for a veterinary inspection at the frontier, on the basis that the charge was incompatible with EC law. The ECJ, on a preliminary reference, ruled that such charges were indeed contrary to the Treaty. When the Pretore therefore ordered repayment of the amounts with interest, the Italian fiscal authorities objected that the national court could not simply refuse to apply a national law which conflicted with Community law, but must first bring the matter before the Italian Constitutional Court to have the Italian law declared unconstitutional. The Pretore therefore referred the case again to the ECJ, asking whether in these circumstances the national law must be disregarded forthwith without waiting until it was set aside by the appropriate constitutional authority.

THE ECJ

17. Furthermore, in accordance with the principle of the precedence of Community law, the relationship between provisions of the Treaty and directly applicable measures of the institutions on the one hand and the national law of the Member States on the other is such that those provisions and measures not only by their entry into force render automatically inapplicable any conflicting provision of current national law but—in so far as they are an integral part of, and take precedence in, the legal order applicable in the territory of each of the Member States—also preclude the valid adoption of new national legislative measures to the extent to which they would be incompatible with Community provisions.

18. Indeed any recognition that national legislative measures which encroach upon the field within which the Community exercises its legislative power or which are otherwise incompatible with the provisions of Community law had any legal effect would amount to a corresponding denial of the effectiveness of obligations undertaken unconditionally and irrevocably by Member States pursuant to the Treaty and would thus imperil the very foundations of the Community.

...

21. It follows from the foregoing that every national court must, in a case within its jurisdiction, apply Community law in its entirety and protect rights which the latter confers on individuals and must accordingly set aside any provision of national law which may conflict with it, whether prior or subsequent to the Community rule.

The reasoning in *Simmenthal* was forcefully reaffirmed in later cases,[6] such as *Winner Wetten*.[7] The ECJ also considered whether provisions of national law held incompatible with EU law could be maintained provisionally in force during the period necessary for the domestic authorities to redress the violation, by analogy with Article 264 TFEU which allows the Court to suspend the annulment of an EU measure pending the adoption of a new measure. The ECJ neither confirmed nor excluded that possibility,[8] but made it clear that if it were to be recognized, a national court could make use of it only 'where overriding considerations of legal certainty involving all the interests [at stake], public as well as private', justified it, and only during the period of time 'necessary in order to allow such illegality to be remedied'.[9] The Court found that these criteria were not met in the case.

---

[6] See, eg, Case C–18/11 *Commissioners for Her Majesty's Revenue and Customs v Phillips Electronics* EU:C:2012:532, [38]; Case C–112/13 *A v B* EU:C:2014:2195, [37].

[7] Case C–409/06 *Winner Wetten v Bürgermeisterin der Stadt Bergheim* [2010] ECR I–8015.

[8] Ibid [67].

[9] Ibid [66]; see also, Cases C–186 and 209/11 *Stanleybet International Ltd* EU:C:2013:33, [38].

(c) THE NATIONAL BODIES THAT MUST APPLY
THE SUPREMACY DOCTRINE

The cases considered thus far laid the foundations for the supremacy doctrine and determined its ambit. They did not however address a separate issue, this being which national courts could apply the supremacy doctrine. This was of special concern in many civil law countries, where it was often only the Constitutional Court which could, according to national law, declare a national law to be unconstitutional. This issue arose in *Simmenthal*, where the Italian tax authorities questioned the Pretore's order awarding the repayment of fees that had been charged under an existing national law before it had been adjudicated upon by the Constitutional Court.

Case 106/77 **Amministrazione delle Finanze dello Stato v Simmenthal SpA**
[1978] ECR 629

THE ECJ

21. It follows from the foregoing that every national court must, in a case within its jurisdiction, apply Community law in its entirety and protect rights which the latter confers on individuals and must accordingly set aside any provision of national law which may conflict with it, whether prior or subsequent to the Community rule.

22. Accordingly any provision of a national legal system and any legislative, administrative or judicial practice which might impair the effectiveness of Community law by withholding from the national court having jurisdiction to apply such law the power to do everything necessary at the moment of its application to set aside national legislative provisions which might prevent Community rules from having full force and effect are incompatible with those requirements which are the very essence of Community law.

23. This would be the case in the event of a conflict between a provision of Community law and a subsequent national law if the solution of the conflict were to be reserved for an authority with a discretion of its own, other than the court called upon to apply Community law, even if such an impediment to the full effectiveness of Community law were only temporary.

24. The first question should therefore be answered to the effect that a national court which is called upon, within the limits of its jurisdiction, to apply provisions of Community law is under a duty to give full effect to those provisions, if necessary refusing of its own motion to apply any conflicting provision of national legislation, even if adopted subsequently, and it is not necessary for the court to request or await the prior setting aside of such provision by legislative or other constitutional means.

The clear message from the ECJ was that, even if the Constitutional Court was the only national court empowered to pronounce on the constitutionality of a national law, where a conflict between national law and EU law arose before another national court, that court must give immediate effect to Union law without awaiting the prior ruling of the Constitutional Court.

The *Simmenthal* principle has been affirmed many times,[10] and was extended in *Factortame*.[11] UK law did not at that time allow interim relief to be claimed against the Crown. The ECJ reiterated the *Simmenthal* ruling on the need for effectiveness and the automatic precedence of directly effective

---

[10] See, eg, Case C–409/06 *Winner Wetten* (n 7); Case C–314/08 *Krzysztof Filipiak v Dyrektor Izby Skarbowej w Poznaniu* [2009] ECR I–11049; Cases C–188–189/10 *Melki and Abdeli* EU:C:2010:363.

[11] Case C–213/89 *R v Secretary of State for Transport, ex p Factortame Ltd and Others* [1990] ECR I–2433.

EU law over national law, and then stated[12] that 'the full effectiveness of Community law would be just as much impaired if a rule of national law could prevent a court seized of a dispute governed by Community law from granting interim relief in order to ensure the full effectiveness of the judgment to be given on the existence of the rights claimed under Community law'. It followed that a court which in those circumstances would grant interim relief if it were not for a rule of national law was obliged to set aside that rule. The *Simmenthal* principle was further extended in *Larsy*, where the ECJ ruled that not only national courts, but also the relevant administrative agencies, in this case a national social insurance institution, should disapply conflicting national laws in order to give effect to the primacy of EU law.[13]

The *Simmenthal* principle was of great significance both practically and conceptually. The supremacy of EU law penetrated throughout the national legal system and was to be applied by all national courts in cases that fell within their jurisdiction. It was not necessary for an individual to fight her way to the national Constitutional Court. The national court seized of the dispute could itself refuse to apply provisions of national law that conflicted with EU law.

The application of this principle was forcefully exemplified in *Elchinov*, where the ECJ held that a national rule that rendered a lower court bound by rulings from higher national courts could not prevent the former from exercising its discretion to seek a ruling under Article 267 where it felt that the higher court's decision was contrary to EU law, and the lower court would then be bound to follow the ECJ's ruling even where it differed from that of the higher national court.[14]

The principle was evident also in *Filipiak*.[15] The ECJ ruled that national courts could not be prevented from respecting the principle of the primacy of Union law and from setting aside provisions of national law that conflicted with Union law because of the judgment of the national Constitutional Court, which had deferred the date on which those provisions, held to be unconstitutional, were to lose their binding force. Similarly in *Melki*[16] the ECJ ruled that EU law precluded Member State legislation which established an interlocutory procedure for the review of the constitutionality of national laws, insofar as the priority nature of that procedure prevented, both before submission of a question on constitutionality to the national Constitutional Court and after its decision, all other national courts from referring to the ECJ under Article 267 TFEU. The ECJ did however set out certain conditions on which such a procedure could be compatible with EU law.[17]

(D) IMPACT ON NATIONAL LAW

We have seen that according to the Court an EU measure renders inapplicable any conflicting provision of national law and prevents the adoption of new national law that would conflict with EU law. Two points should be made by way of further clarification.

---

[12] Ibid [21].

[13] Case C–118/00 *Larsy v INASTI* [2001] ECR I–5063, [52]–[53]; Case C–198/01 *CIF v Autorità Garante della Concorrenza del Mercato* [2003] ECR I–8055; Case C–341/08 *Peterson* [2010] ECR I–47; Case C–606/10 *ANAFE* EU:C:2012:348, [75]; M Bobek, 'Thou Shalt Have Two Masters; The Application of European Law by Administrative Authorities in the New Member States' (2008) 1 Review of European Administrative Law 62.

[14] Case C–173/09 *Elchinov* [2010] ECR I–8889, [25]–[31]; Case C–396/09 *Interedil* [2011] ECR I–9915, [37]–[39]; Case C–416/10 *Križan* EU:C:2013:8, [68].

[15] Case C–314/08 *Krzysztof Filipiak* (n 10) [84]–[85]; Case C–147/08 *Römer v Freie und Hansestadt Hamburg* EU:C:2011:286, [54].

[16] Cases C–188–189/10 *Melki* (n 10); Case C–112/13 *A v B* (n 6) [37]–[38]; Case C–457/09 *Chartry* EU:C:2011:101, [20].

[17] M Bossuyt and W Verrijdt, 'The Full Effect of EU Law and of Constitutional Review in Belgium and France after the *Melki* Judgment' (2011) 7 EuConst 355.

First, the *Simmenthal* principle does not require the national court to invalidate or annul the provision of national law that conflicts with EU law, but rather to refuse to apply it, and considerations of legal certainty may mean that the inapplicability of the national law will not expose those who relied on it to penalties.[18] This distinction between disapplying and nullifying national law was emphasized in the *IN.CO.GE '90* case. The ECJ rejected the Commission's argument that the incompatibility of EU law with a subsequently adopted rule of national law must render the national rule non-existent.[19]

It cannot therefore, contrary to the Commission's contention, be inferred from the judgment in *Simmenthal* that the incompatibility with Community law of a subsequently adopted rule of national law has the effect of rendering that rule of national law non-existent. Faced with such a situation, the national court is, however, obliged to disapply that rule, provided always that this obligation does not restrict the power of the competent national courts to apply, from among the various procedures available under national law, those which are appropriate for protecting the individual rights conferred by Community law.

Secondly, it is clear from *Kapferer*[20] that a national court is not always obliged to review and set aside a final judicial decision which infringes EU law. The ECJ recognized the importance of the principle of *res judicata*, whereby judicial decisions that have become definitive can no longer be called into question. EU law did not therefore require a national court to disapply domestic rules of procedure conferring finality on a decision, even if to do so would enable it to remedy an infringement of EU law by the decision at issue. The relevant national procedural rules must however comply with the principles of equivalence and effectiveness.[21] The ECJ has nevertheless limited the possibility of circumventing supremacy through reliance on the principle of *res judicata*. In *Lucchini*,[22] the Court held that EU law precluded the application of a provision of national law laying down the principle of *res judicata* where this would prevent the recovery of state aid granted in breach of EU law.

Following *Lucchini*, it was uncertain whether *Kapferer* was still good law. In *Fallimento Olimpiclub Srl*, however, the Court distinguished both cases.[23] Recalling the principle in *Kapferer*, the ECJ held that EU law did not require a national court to disapply domestic rules of procedure conferring finality on a decision, even if to do so would make it possible to remedy an infringement of Union law in the contested decision.[24] The Court distinguished *Lucchini*, interpreting it as a 'highly specific' case where the Commission had exclusive competence to assess the compatibility of state aid with the common market.[25] The ECJ nonetheless held that the effectiveness of EU law would be impaired if the principle of *res judicata* deprived national courts not only of the possibility of reopening a final judicial decision made in breach of EU law, but also of rectifying that infringement in subsequent cases presenting the same fundamental issue.[26]

---

[18] Case C–198/01 *CIF* (n 13).

[19] Cases C–10–22/97 *Ministero delle Finanze v IN.CO.GE.'90 Srl* [1998] ECR I–6307, [21]; Case C–314/08 *Krzysztof Filipiak* (n 10) [83].

[20] Case C–234/04 *Kapferer v Schlanck and Schick* [2006] ECR I–2585.

[21] Ch 8.

[22] Case C–119/05 *Ministero dell'Industria, del Commercio e dell'Artigianato v Lucchini SpA* [2007] ECR I–6199.

[23] Case C–2/08 *Amministrazione dell'Economia e delle Finanze and Agenzia delle entrate v Fallimento Olimpiclub Srl* [2009] ECR I–7501. The case concerned an incorrect interpretation of the EU rules in relation to VAT by an Italian judge, and the impact of this judgment on subsequent procedures concerning different tax years.

[24] Ibid [22]–[23].

[25] Ibid [25].

[26] Ibid [29]–[32].

(E) DECLARATION 17 ON PRIMACY

The primacy of EU law over national law has been developed by the EU Courts and has not hitherto been enshrined in the Treaties. The Constitutional Treaty did bite this particular constitutional bullet. Article I–6 CT provided that:

> The Constitution and law adopted by the institutions of the Union in exercising competences conferred on it shall have primacy over the law of the Member States.

This provision was dropped from the Lisbon Treaty at the behest of the European Council in 2007, the rationale being that this would, with other changes, thereby diminish its 'constitutional character'.[27] It was replaced in the Lisbon Treaty by a Declaration concerning primacy.[28]

> The Conference recalls that, in accordance with well settled case law of the Court of Justice of the European Union, the Treaties and the law adopted by the Union on the basis of the Treaties have primacy over the law of Member States, under the conditions laid down by the said case law.
> The Conference has also decided to attach as an Annex to this Final Act the Opinion of the Council Legal Service on the primacy of EC law as set out in 11197/07 (JUR 260).

The opinion of the Council Legal Service appended to the Declaration was brief, reiterating the basic *communautaire* view on the topic.

> It results from the case-law of the Court of Justice that primacy of EC law is a cornerstone principle of Community law. According to the Court, this principle is inherent to the specific nature of the European Community. At the time of the first judgment of this established case law (*Costa/ENEL*, 15 July 1964, Case 6/64) there was no mention of primacy in the treaty. It is still the case today. The fact that the principle of primacy will not be included in the future treaty shall not in any way change the existence of the principle and the existing case-law of the Court of Justice.

It might be argued that dropping the primacy clause from the Lisbon Treaty was unwise, because its removal might cause some national courts to doubt the continuing validity of the supremacy principle. This is unlikely, and any such danger is outweighed by the problems with Article I–6 CT, which was crucially ambiguous.[29] The phrase 'shall have primacy over the law of the Member States' could have been interpreted to mean, following the ECJ's jurisprudence, that supremacy operated over all national law, including provisions in a national constitution. It could alternatively have been read so as to accord primacy to EU law over national law, but not the national constitution. It would have been perfectly possible to have drafted Article I–6 'symmetrically' so as to read that 'the Constitution and law adopted by the institutions of the Union in exercising competences conferred on it shall have primacy over the *constitution* and law of the Member States', thereby removing the ambiguity.

Such a formulation was not chosen in the Convention on the Future of Europe because it would have been very controversial, with the consequence that it would have been more difficult to secure

---

[27] Brussels European Council, 21–22 June 2007, Annex 1, [4].

[28] Declaration 17 Concerning Primacy.

[29] P Craig, 'The Constitutional Treaty and Sovereignty' in C Kaddous and A Auer (eds), *Les Principes Fondamentaux de la Constitution Européene/The Fundamental Principles of the European Constitution* (Dossier de Droit Européen No 15, Helbing & Lictenhahn/Bruylant/LGDJ, 2006) 117–134.

agreement on the Constitutional Treaty in the Convention and the subsequent IGC. It would in addition have created serious problems in some national Constitutional Courts, which might either have decided that according primacy to EU law over the national constitution was not constitutionally possible, or that it would require a constitutional amendment.

It might be argued that primacy of EU law over all national law has been the 'law' as far as the ECJ is concerned ever since the early 1970s. This may well be true, but the legal reality is that it has not been generally accepted by national courts. This 'disjunction' was almost certainly acknowledged by Union and national courts. Neither side was however spoiling for the ultimate fight on the issue, which is why 'constitutional tolerance' prevented constitutional crisis. This was possible in part precisely because there was no hard-edged Treaty provision embodying the ECJ's view. If Article I–6 CT had been brought into the picture this would have changed.

This still leaves open the status of the supremacy principle under the Lisbon Treaty. This will very likely continue much as it had under the EC Treaty. The CJEU continues to espouse its version of primacy, using the Declaration appended to the Lisbon Treaty to reinforce this. The Declaration however suffers from the very same infirmity that pervaded Article I–6 CT. It too is framed in terms of EU law having 'primacy over the law of the Member States', which once again is ambiguous as to whether it covers all national law, including the constitution, or whether the latter is excluded. It could be argued that the broader construction should be given, because the Declaration states that such primacy is to operate 'under the conditions laid down by the said case law'. This refers to the CJEU's jurisprudence, under which all EU law has primacy over all national law, including national constitutions.

It is nonetheless very unlikely that national Constitutional Courts will be persuaded to forget their previous concerns, and accept that EU law prevails over national constitutions, based on a Declaration appended to the Treaties. The 'disjunction' of view between EU and national judiciaries will therefore continue under the new legal order. It is unlikely that either side will be eager to pick a fight, although changes of judicial personnel can lead to altered perspectives in this respect.

There is moreover nothing to suggest that the Lisbon Treaty has 'resolved' the *Kompetenz-Kompetenz* issue, as to who is to decide on the ultimate boundary of Union competences.[30] Nor is there anything in the Lisbon Treaty that strengthens the CJEU's claim to be the ultimate decider in such instances. There is no doubt that the CJEU would have the authority to pronounce on a disputed issue as to whether the EU has competence to act or not, pursuant to its general jurisdiction to interpret EU law in Article 19 TEU. This does not however mean that its judgment would be conclusive in this respect. Moreover the wording of Article 5(2) TEU, which is framed in terms of the Union acting within the limits of the competences conferred on it by the Member States and competences not conferred on the EU remaining with the Member States, does nothing to bolster the claims of the EU to decide on the ultimate boundaries of competence.

---

[30] N MacCormick, *Questioning Sovereignty* (Oxford University Press, 1999); C Schmid, 'From Pont d'Avignon to Ponte Vecchio: The Resolution of Constitutional Conflicts between the EU and the Member States through Principles of Public International Law' (1998) 18 YBEL 415; M Kumm, 'Who is the Final Arbiter of Constitutionality in Europe?: Three Conceptions of the Relationship between the German Federal Constitutional Court and the European Court of Justice' (1999) 36 CMLRev 351; N Walker, 'The Idea of Constitutional Pluralism' (2002) 65 MLR 317; N Walker, 'Late Sovereignty in the European Union' in N Walker (ed), *Sovereignty in Transition* (Hart, 2003) ch 1; M Maduro, 'Contrapunctual Law: Europe's Constitutional Pluralism in Action' in Walker ibid ch 21; A von Bogdandy, 'Pluralism, Direct Effect, and the Ultimate Say: On the Relationship between International and Domestic Constitutional Law' (2008) 6 I-CON 397; K Jaklic, *Constitutional Pluralism in the EU* (Oxford University Press, 2014).

(F) RELATION WITH DIRECT EFFECT

It is important to understand the relationship between supremacy and direct effect. The key issue is whether direct effect is a condition precedent for EU law to have supremacy over national law. Consider in this respect Dougan's insightful analysis.

M Dougan, When Worlds Collide! Competing Visions of the Relationship between Direct Effect and Supremacy[31]

The 'primacy' model treats primacy or supremacy as a 'constitutional fundamental' of the European Union, permeating all relations between national law and Community law...Its basic outlines can be summarized as follows.

Supremacy is capable of producing certain legal effects within the national legal systems, independently of the principle of direct effect, and without reference to the latter's threshold criteria (such as the need for the relevant Community norm to be clear, precise and unconditional). In particular the principle of supremacy is capable, in itself, of producing *exclusionary effects* within the domestic legal order—understood as the setting aside of national rules that are incompatible with a (by definition) hierarchically superior norm of Community law...For these purposes the principle of direct effect is neither necessary nor even relevant: its threshold criteria have no particular function to perform, since the question is not whether the relevant Community norm is clear, precise and unconditional; but merely whether there exists an incompatibility between a rule of Community law and a rule of national law.

However...that is conceptually distinct from the phenomenon of *substitutionary effects*—understood as the direct and immediate application of Community law, so as to create rights or obligations derived from the EC Treaty, which did not already exist in the national legal system. This is the proper domain of direct effect: here the threshold criteria of clarity, precision and unconditionality serve to identify which norms of Community law are apt for direct and immediate application in the national legal system, (although supremacy still has a role to play, of course, should national law prove incompatible with the novel rights or obligations just deduced from the relevant Community measure). Unsurprisingly this 'primacy' model thus aligns supremacy with notions of invocability and judicial review over the validity of national law; whereas direct effect is more closely associated with the creation and enforcement of subjective individual rights.

By contrast, the 'trigger' view sees supremacy, at the outset, as little more than a remedy to be administered by the domestic courts in the resolution of disputes involving Community law...

In particular, the practical remedy afforded by supremacy is available in those individual cases involving a conflict between Community law and national law; but that remedy can only be invoked when Community law has been rendered cognizable before the domestic courts, by satisfying the threshold criteria for enjoying direct effect. Under this model, direct effect encompasses not only the creation and enforcement of subjective individual rights, but any situation in which Community norms produce independent effects within the national legal systems...

The important point, for present purposes, is that direct effect enjoys a monopoly over rendering Community norms justiciable before the national courts; its threshold criteria act as a trigger, and thus a necessary precondition, for the principle of supremacy. The 'primacy' model, by postulating the freestanding potency of the supremacy principle in situations demanding no more than the exclusionary effect of Treaty norms, seems to short-circuit this entire theoretical framework.

[31] (2007) 44 CMLRev 931, 932–935. Italics in the original.

Four points can be made about the relationship between supremacy and direct effect in the light of this analysis.

First, in terms of positive law, it is clear that the primacy model best explains the case law on incidental horizontal effect considered above.[32] Supremacy has been used to exclude national law that is inconsistent with EU law, even though the EU provision does not have horizontal direct effect as between the parties to the case. The very distinction between exclusion and substitution effect is however problematic.[33]

Secondly, in terms of positive law, the distinction between the two models was important more generally pre-Lisbon because direct effect did not exist in relation to what were the Second and Third Pillars. This prompted inquiry as to whether supremacy could operate in these areas in the absence of direct effect. The ECJ applied the principle of indirect effect to the Third Pillar in *Pupino*,[34] but never conclusively answered the supremacy issue. Arguments were made premised on the primacy model to suggest that supremacy could operate in the Second and Third Pillars, even in the absence of direct effect.[35] The issue is no longer a live one insofar as the Third Pillar has been folded into the main fabric of the Treaties, and hence the normal principles of direct effect can apply in this area. While the Second Pillar dealing with Common Foreign and Security Policy no longer formally exists, the rules that apply to the CFSP are distinct. The relationship between direct effect and supremacy in this area is therefore still a live one.[36]

Thirdly, in conceptual terms, it should be recognized that whether a provision is intended to accord rights to individuals in the strict sense of being sufficiently clear, precise, and unconditional is conceptually distinct from the issue of supremacy. There is nothing odd in principle with an EU norm being regarded as supreme, with the correlative obligation on national authorities to disapply conflicting national law, even if the norm does not fulfil the conditions for direct effect *stricto sensu*.

Fourthly, in normative terms, the primacy model places supremacy in the driving seat, with direct effect being relevant only in relation to substitution effects, while the trigger model places direct effect in the driving seat, with supremacy being the remedial manifestation of using directly effective EU rights in national courts. This is a real difference. It can nonetheless be overstated. The more cases are characterized as being about substitution effects, the more the primacy model demands direct effect *stricto sensu* as a trigger for supremacy. The more the trigger model broadens direct effect by embracing not only subjective rights produced by clear, precise, unconditional EU law, but also 'any situation in which Community norms produce independent effects within the national legal systems',[37] the less stringent does the trigger become, and the greater the prominence accorded to supremacy.

(G) CONCLUSION

The supremacy of EU law and the requirement that national courts must ensure its practical effectiveness are established in a consistent line of CJEU case law.[38] There are certain Treaty provisions which some may view as a partial dilution of the supremacy principle, such as Article 351 TFEU, which relieves Member States of the obligation to ensure the primacy of EU law in certain circumstances,[39]

---

[32] Pp 216–220.

[33] Pp 218–220.

[34] Case C–105/03 *Criminal Proceedings against Maria Pupino* [2005] ECR I–5283.

[35] K Lenaerts and T Corthaut, 'Of Birds and Hedges: The Role of Primacy in Invoking Norms of EU Law' (2006) 31 ELRev 287, 289–291.

[36] P Craig, *The Lisbon Treaty: Law, Politics, and Treaty Reform* (Oxford University Press, 2010) ch 10.

[37] Dougan (n 31) 934.

[38] See also Cases C–7 and 9/10 *Kahveci and Inan* EU:C:2012:180, [37].

[39] Art 351 TFEU provides a limited exception to the obligation of Member States to ensure the supremacy of EU law, where conflicting state obligations arise from agreements concluded with non-Member States before the entry

or Article 347 TFEU, which appears to carve out an area within which the Member States retain a degree of sovereignty.[40] Nonetheless, these provisions are of limited scope, and the basic principle of supremacy articulated by the CJEU is a broad and general one. Nevertheless, this constitutes only one part of the supremacy story. Ultimately, the acceptance and application of the primacy of EU law are dependent on the Member States.

J Weiler, The Community System: The Dual Character of Supranationalism[41]

As in the case of 'direct effect' the derivation of supremacy from the Treaty depended on a 'constitutional' rather than international law interpretation. The Court's reasoning that supremacy was enshrined in the Treaty was contested by the governments of Member States in this case and others. Acceptance of this view amounts in effect to a quiet revolution in the legal orders of the Member States....

It follows that the evolutionary nature of the doctrine of supremacy is necessarily bi-dimensional. One dimension is the elaboration of the parameters of the doctrine by the European Court. But its full reception, the second dimension, depends on its incorporation into the constitutional orders of the Member States and its affirmation by their supreme courts. It is relatively easy to trace the evolution of the Community dimension of the doctrine....

As regards the second dimension, the evolutionary character of the process is more complicated. It should be remembered that in respect of the original Member States there was no specific constitutional preparation for this European Court-inspired development.

3 SECOND DIMENSION: SUPREMACY FROM THE PERSPECTIVE OF THE PRE-2004 MEMBER STATES

The evolutionary nature of acceptance of supremacy noted by Weiler is still evident today. There is a continuing tension between national accounts of EU law and the CJEU's account. Constitutional conflicts continue to arise in specific cases, and it remains for national courts to resolve cases arising before them involving a conflict between EU and national law.[42] For reasons of space, only four pre-2004 Member States are discussed.[43] The discussion begins with Germany, which has the most extensive case law in this area, articulated primarily by the German Federal Constitutional Court. This is followed by Italy, where it has once again been the Constitutional Court that has been at the forefront in articulating acceptance of EU supremacy and the limits of this. The discussion then turns to France, where for many years it was the leading private and public law courts that responded albeit differently to EU claims concerning supremacy. The discussion within this section concludes with the UK, a common law system without a written constitution, but with a strong tradition of parliamentary

---

into force of the Treaty: Case C–158/91 *Ministère Public and Direction du Travail et de l'Emploi v Levy* [1993] ECR I–4287; Case C–13/93 *Office Nationale de l'Emploi v Minne* [1994] ECR I–371; Case C–124/95 *R, ex p Centro-Com Srl v HM Treasury and Bank of England* [1997] ECR I–81; Case C–55/00 *Gottardo v INPS* [2002] ECR I–413; J Klabbers, 'Moribund on the Fourth of July? The Court of Justice on the Prior Agreements of the Member States' (2001) 26 ELRev 187 and C Hillion, Note (2001) 38 CMLRev 1269.

40 P Koutrakos, 'Is Article 297 EC a "Reserve of Sovereignty"' (2000) 37 CMLRev 1339.

41 (1981) 1 YBEL 267, 275–276.

42 M Claes, *The National Courts' Mandate in the European Constitution* (Hart, 2006).

43 A-M Slaughter, A Stone Sweet, and J Weiler (eds), *The ECJ and National Courts: Doctrine and Jurisprudence* (Hart, 1998); K Alter, *Establishing the Supremacy of European Law: The Making of an International Rule of Law in Europe* (Oxford University Press, 2001); Walker, *Sovereignty in Transition* (n 30).

sovereignty, where the ordinary courts established the UK's response to EU supremacy. It is helpful to frame the subsequent discussion by distinguishing four particular issues that can arise in any Member State concerning supremacy.

i. The first is whether the Member State accepts the supremacy of EU law, assuming that the EU acts within its proper sphere of competence. The general answer to this question is affirmative, subject to the qualifications flowing from the following three issues.

ii. Assuming an affirmative answer to the first question, the second issue is the conceptual basis on which the Member State accords supremacy to EU law. It may choose to do so because it accepts the Court's *communautaire* reasoning in *Costa*, or because of a provision within its own national legal order. For most Member States it is the latter rather than the former that provides the conceptual foundation for acceptance of supremacy.

iii. The third important issue is whether the national legal order places limits on its acceptance of EU law supremacy derived from its own national constitution and/or national fundamental rights. The CJEU regards the supremacy of EU law as operating against all types of national law, including the national constitution, such that any norm of EU law trumps any norm of national law. This is not generally accepted by Member States.

iv. The final issue is known as *Kompetenz-Kompetenz*, who has ultimate authority to define the allocation of competence as between the EU and the Member States. The CJEU under Article 19 TEU regards this as its task, whereas virtually all national constitutional or supreme courts determine such questions ultimately by reference to their own national constitutional provisions, although they will treat the CJEU's view with respect.

(A) GERMANY

(i) *Acceptance of Supremacy*

There is a rich jurisprudence concerning the relationship between EU law and German law, in which the German courts have articulated different limits to the supremacy of EU law. It is therefore all the more important to be clear that, subject to such limits, the German courts accept the supremacy of EU law. This is evident from the following extract, a decision of the Federal Constitutional Court in the *Honeywell* ruling 2010.[44]

> 53. The law of the European Union can only develop effectively if it supplants contrary Member State law. The primacy of application of Union law does not lead to a situation in which contrary national law is null and void. Member States' law can, rather, continue to apply if and to the degree that it retains an objective area of provision beyond the field of application of pertinent Union law. By contrast, contrary Member States' law is in principle inapplicable in the field of application of Union law. The primacy of application follows from Union law because the Union could not exist as a legal community if the uniform effectiveness of Union law were not safeguarded in the Member States (see fundamentally ECJ Case 6/64 *Costa/ENEL* <judgment of 15 July 1964> [1964] ECR 1251 para. 12). The primacy of application also corresponds to the constitutional empowerment of Article 23.1 of the Basic Law, in accordance with which sovereign powers can be transferred to the European Union (see BVerfGE 31, 145 <174>; 123, 267 <402>). Article 23.1 of the Basic Law permits with the transfer of sovereign powers—if provided for and demanded by treaty—at the same time their direct exercise within the

---

44 BVerfG, 2 BvR 2661/06, 6 July 2010.

Member States' legal systems. It hence contains a promise of effectiveness and implementation corresponding to the primacy of application of Union law.

54. ...Unlike the primacy of application of federal law, as provided for by Article 31 of the Basic Law for the German legal system, the primacy of application of Union law cannot be comprehensive.

(ii) *Conceptual Basis for Acceptance of Supremacy*

The preceding extract provides guidance on the conceptual basis on which the German courts accept the supremacy of EU law over national law. It is evident from the *Honeywell* extract that supremacy is based primarily on what is now Article 23.1 of the German Constitution, which is specifically concerned with the EU and allows for transfer of sovereign powers. Reliance on provisions of the German Constitution has been the dominant rationale for the acceptance of EU supremacy within Germany.[45] The Federal Constitutional Court nonetheless also expressly adverts to the ECJ's functional argument in *Costa*: primacy of application of EU law is demanded because 'the Union could not exist as a legal community if the uniform effectiveness of Union law were not safeguarded in the Member States'.

(iii) *Limits to Acceptance of Supremacy: Fundamental Rights*

The German courts have however laid down limits to the acceptance of EU supremacy. The Federal Constitutional Court noted in paragraph 54 of the *Honeywell* ruling that the primacy of application of EU law could not be comprehensive. It is the nature of those limits that has been subject to most debate, judicial and extra-judicial. Three types of limit are evident in the German courts' case law. They relate to fundamental rights, competence, and constitutional identity. The German courts initially focused on fundamental rights as a limit to acceptance of the supremacy of EU law.

Internationale Handelsgesellschaft mbH v Einfuhr- und Vorratsstelle für Getreide und Futtermittel
[1974] 2 CMLR 540

The facts are those set out in Case 11/70 before the ECJ.[46] On receiving the ECJ's ruling, the German Administrative Court[47] decided, in the face of the ECJ's conflicting judgment, that the Community's deposit system breached basic principles of German constitutional law, and requested a ruling from the Federal Constitutional Court, the Bundesverfassungsgericht (BVerfG). This judgment, known as the '*Solange I*' decision (so long as), was given by the BVerfG in 1974.

THE BUNDESVERFASSUNGSGERICHT (BVERFG)[48]

Article 24 of the Constitution deals with the transfer of sovereign rights to inter-state institutions. This...does not open the way to amending the basic structure of the Constitution, which forms the

---

[45] A Voßkuhle, 'Multilevel Cooperation of the European Constitutional Courts: *Der Europäische Verfassungsgerichtsverbund*' (2010) 6 EuConst 175, 190–191; Arts 24 and 25 of the German Constitution have also been relevant in this respect.

[46] See below p 269.

[47] [1972] CMLR 177, 184.

[48] [1974] 2 CMLR 540, 549–550.

basis of its identity, without a formal amendment to the Constitution, that is, it does not open any such way through the legislation of the inter-state institution. Certainly, the competent Community organs can make law which the competent German constitutional organs could not make under the law of the Constitution and which is none the less valid and is to be applied directly in the Federal Republic of Germany. But Article 24 of the Constitution limits this possibility in that it nullifies any amendment of the Treaty which would destroy the identity of the valid constitutional structure of the Federal Republic of Germany by encroaching on the structures which go to make it up....

The part of the Constitution dealing with fundamental rights is an inalienable essential feature of the valid Constitution of the Federal Republic of Germany and one which forms part of the constitutional structure of the Constitution. Article 24 of the Constitution does not without reservation allow it to be subjected to qualifications. In this, the present state of integration of the Community is of crucial importance. The Community still lacks a democratically legitimated Parliament directly elected by general suffrage which possesses legislative powers and to which the Community organs empowered to legislate are fully responsible on a political level. It still lacks in particular a codified catalogue of fundamental rights, the substance of which is reliably and unambiguously fixed for the future in the same way as the substance of the Constitution....

Provisionally, therefore, in the hypothetical case of a conflict between Community law and...the guarantees of fundamental rights in the Constitution...the guarantee of fundamental rights in the Constitution prevails as long as the competent organs of the Community have not removed the conflict of norms in accordance with the Treaty mechanism.

The highest German court therefore refused to recognize the unconditional supremacy of EU law because of the possible impact of Union law on basic rights enshrined in the German Constitution. It held that what was Article 24 of the Constitution could not cover a transfer of power to amend an 'inalienable essential feature' of the German constitutional structure, such as its protection for fundamental rights. The BVerfG would not abandon its jurisdiction to decide which legislative transfers would alter an unalterable feature of the Constitution, and the protection of fundamental rights in the German Constitution would prevail over EU law in the event of conflict.

In 1986, however, in a case in which an EC import licensing system was challenged despite an ECJ ruling on its validity,[49] the BVerfG delivered its so-called *Solange II* judgment, which qualified the 1974 *Solange I* judgment to a considerable extent. Solange means 'so long as' and it refers to the statement of the BVerfG that so long as the EU had not removed the possible 'conflict of norms' between EU law and national constitutional rights, the German court would ensure that those rights took precedence.

Re Wünsche Handelsgesellschaft
[1987] 3 CMLR 225

Having considered various changes in Community law since the 1974 decision, including the ECJ's development of protection for fundamental rights, the adoption of various declarations on rights and democracy by the Community institutions,[50] and the fact that all EC Member States had acceded to the European Convention on Human Rights, the BVerfG in *Solange II* ruled as follows.[51]

---

[49] Case 345/82 *Wünsche Handelsgesellschaft v Germany* [1984] ECR 1995.
[50] Ch 11.
[51] *Re Wünsche Handelsgesellschaft* [1987] 3 CMLR 225, 265.

THE BUNDESVERFASSUNGSGERICHT (BVERFG)

In view of these developments, it must be held that, *so long as* the European Communities, and in particular the case law of the European Court, generally ensure an effective protection of fundamental rights as against the sovereign powers of the Communities which is to be regarded as substantially similar to the protection of fundamental rights required unconditionally by the Constitution, and in so far as they generally safeguard the essential content of fundamental rights, the Federal Constitutional Court will no longer exercise its jurisdiction to decide on the applicability of secondary Community legislation cited as the legal basis for any acts of German courts or authorities within the sovereign jurisdiction of the Federal Republic of Germany, and it will no longer review such legislation by the standard of the fundamental rights contained in the Constitution.

The *Solange II* decision rendered a clash between EU law and national law over fundamental rights less likely. It should nonetheless be recognized that the court in *Solange II* did not surrender jurisdiction over fundamental rights, but only stated that it would not exercise that jurisdiction as long as the present conditions concerning protection of fundamental rights by the ECJ prevailed.[52] The Federal Constitutional Court preserved its final authority to intervene if real problems concerning the protection of fundamental rights in EU law arose.

It is nonetheless clear that the German courts are reluctant to exercise the jurisdiction which they retain. This is exemplified by the Federal Constitutional Court's ruling concerning a claim that Community regulations concerning bananas interfered with the right to pursue a trade and the right to property as protected by the German Constitution. The BVerfG deemed the reference inadmissible.[53] The Federal Constitutional Court stated that it had already declared itself satisfied, in its *Solange II* and *Maastricht* decisions, with the fact that human rights protection within the EU legal order was generally comparable to the level of human rights protection under the German Basic Law. Consequently, constitutional complaints attacking secondary EU law on the basis of German fundamental rights would be inadmissible *ab initio* if they did not argue that the general level of European human rights protection, including ECJ case law since *Solange II*, fell below the necessary level, as compared to German levels of protection.[54]

(iv) *Limits to Acceptance of Supremacy: Competence and the Ultra Vires Lock*

The BVerfG articulated a competence-based limit to its acceptance of EU supremacy in the so-called '*Maastricht* judgment', when the constitutionality of the state's ratification of the Maastricht Treaty was challenged.

Brunner v The European Union Treaty
[1994] 1 CMLR 57

The BVerfG decided that ratification of the Maastricht Treaty was compatible with the German Constitution, but it ruled not just on Germany's constitutional competence to ratify the TEU, but also on

---

[52] J Frowein, '*Solange II*' (1988) 25 CMLRev 201, 203–204.

[53] Decision of 7 June 2000; A Peters, 'The *Bananas* Decision 2000 of the German Federal Constitutional Court: Towards Reconciliation with the ECJ as regards Fundamental Rights Protection in Europe' (2000) 43 German Yearbook of International Law 276; C Schmid, 'All Bark and No Bite: Notes on the Federal Constitutional Court's "*Banana* Decision"' (2001) 7 ELJ 95; M Aziz, 'Sovereignty Lost, Sovereignty Regained: The European Integration Project and the BVerfG', Robert Schuman Centre Working Paper, EUI 2001/31.

[54] Voßkuhle (n 45) 192–193.

what the future position would be if the Community attempted to exercise powers which were not clearly provided for in the Treaties. The judgment provoked a great deal of comment.[55] Affirming the sovereignty of the German state, the Federal Constitutional Court made clear that it would not relinquish its power to decide on the compatibility of Community law with the fundamentals of the German Constitution and would continue to exercise a power of review over the scope of Community competence.

THE BUNDESVERFASSUNGSGERICHT (BVERFG)

48. There is . . . a breach of Article 38 of the Constitution if an Act that opens up the German legal system to the direct validity and application of the law of the (supranational) European Communities does not establish with sufficient certainty the intended programme of integration. If it is not clear to what extent and degree the German legislature has assented to the transfer of the exercise of sovereign powers, then it will be possible for the European Community to claim functions and powers that were not specified. That would be equivalent to a general enablement and would therefore be a surrender of powers, something against which Article 38 of the Constitution provides protection.

. . .

55. The Federal Republic of Germany, therefore, even after the Union Treaty comes into force, will remain a member of a federation of States, the common authority of which is derived from the Member States and can only have binding effects within the German sovereign sphere by virtue of the German instruction that its law be applied. Germany is one of the 'Masters of the Treaties' which have established their adherence to the Union Treaty concluded 'for an unlimited period' with the intention of long-term membership, but could ultimately revoke that adherence by a contrary act. The validity and application of European law in Germany depends on the application-of-law instruction of the Accession Act. Germany thus preserves the quality of a sovereign state in its own right.

. . .

99. Inasmuch as the Treaties establishing the European Communities, on the one hand, confer sovereign rights applicable to limited factual circumstances and, on the other hand, provide for Treaty amendments . . . this distinction is also important for the future treatment of the individual powers.

Whereas a dynamic extension of the existing Treaties has so far been supported on the basis of an open-handed treatment of Article 235 of the EEC Treaty as a 'competence to round off the Treaty' as a whole, and on the basis of considerations relating to the 'implied powers' of the Communities, and of Treaty interpretation as allowing maximum exploitation of Community powers (*effet utile*), in future it will have to be noted as regards interpretation of enabling provisions by Community institutions and agencies that the Union Treaty as a matter of principle distinguishes between the exercise of a sovereign power conferred for limited purposes and the amending of the Treaty, so that its interpretation may not have effects that are equivalent to an extension of the Treaty. Such an interpretation of enabling rules would not produce any binding effects for Germany.

This was a long and powerful judgment which warned the EU institutions and the ECJ that Germany's acceptance of the supremacy of EU law was conditional. The BVerfG emphasized that the EU should not stray beyond the powers expressly conferred upon it in the Treaties by the Member States. Thus, even if German courts have accepted that, within its proper sphere of application, Union

---

[55] M Herdegen, 'Maastricht and the German Constitutional Court: Constitutional Restraints for an Ever Closer Union' (1994) 31 CMLRev 235; U Everling, 'The *Maastricht* Judgment of the German Federal Constitutional Court and its Significance for the Development of the European Union' (1994) 14 YBEL 1; M Zulegg, 'The European Constitution under Constitutional Constraints: The German Scenario' (1997) 22 ELRev 19; JHH Weiler, 'Does Europe Need a Constitution? Reflections on Demos, Telos and the German *Maastricht* Decision' (1995) 1 ELJ 219; N MacCormick, 'The *Maastricht*-Urteil: Sovereignty Now' (1995) 1 ELJ 259; J Kokott, 'German Constitutional Jurisprudence and European Integration' (1996) 2 EPL 237 and 413.

law should be given precedence over national law, the BVerfG asserted its jurisdiction to review the actions of European 'institutions and agencies', which presumably included the ECJ, to ensure that they remained within the limits of their powers and did not transgress the basic constitutional rights of German inhabitants.

Some of the more contentious aspects of the judgment concerned the BVerfG's comments about the nature of national democracy, and about the need for national democratic legitimation to express the 'spiritual, social and political' homogeneity of a people.[56] However, other sections of the judgment appear more open to the possibility that the EU could develop the conditions of political openness and the 'free interaction of social forces, interests and ideas' necessary for full democratic legitimation,[57] so that, presumably, a wider range of powers and competences could be transferred by Germany to the EU without breaching the basic principle of democracy guaranteed by the Constitution.

After the *Maastricht* decision of the BVerfG there was a more concrete challenge to the supremacy of EU law in a much-litigated dispute concerning the EU's banana import regime.[58] The message from the *Honeywell* ruling was however that the BVerfG would not lightly conclude that the EU had acted beyond its competence and hence *ultra vires*.[59]

---

2 BvR 2661/06, 6 July 2010

THE BUNDESVERFASSUNGSGERICHT (BVERFG)

54. Unlike the primacy of application of federal law, as provided for by Article 31 of the Basic Law for the German legal system, the primacy of application of Union law cannot be comprehensive (see BVerfGE 73, 339 <375>; 123, 267 <398>).

55. As autonomous law, Union law remains dependent on assignment and empowerment in a Treaty. For the expansion of their powers, the Union bodies remain dependent on amendments to the Treaties which are carried out by the Member States in the framework of the respective constitutional provisions which apply to them and for which they take responsibility . . . The applicable principle is that of conferral (Article 5.1 sentence 1 and Article 5.2 sentence 1 TEU). The Federal Constitutional Court is hence empowered and obliged to review acts on the part of the European bodies and institutions with regard to whether they take place on the basis of manifest transgressions of competence or on the basis of the exercise of competence in the area of constitutional identity which is not assignable (Article 79.3 in conjunction with Article 1 and Article 20 of the Basic Law) . . . and where appropriate to declare the inapplicability of acts for the German legal system which exceed competences.

56. The obligation incumbent on the Federal Constitutional Court to pursue substantiated complaints of an *ultra vires* act on the part of the European bodies and institutions is to be coordinated with the task which the Treaties confer on the Court of Justice, namely to interpret and apply the Treaties, and in doing so to safeguard the unity and coherence of Union law (see Article 19.1 (1) sentence 2 TEU and Article 267 TFEU).

---

[56] [44]–[46] of the judgment, and the comments of Weiler about the *völkish* nature of this view of the demos (n 55).

[57] [41]–[42].

[58] Case C–280/93 *Germany v Commission* [1994] ECR I–4873; Case C–466/93 *Atlanta Fruchthandelsgesellschaft v Bundesamt für Ernährung* [1995] ECR I–3799; Order of the Federal Tax Court, 9 Jan 1996, 7 EuZW 126 (1996); U Everling, 'Will Europe Slip on Bananas? The *Bananas* Judgment of the Court of Justice and National Courts' (1996) 33 CMLRev 401; N Reich, 'Judge-Made Europe à la Carte' (1996) 7 EJIL 103.

[59] M Payandeh, 'Constitutional Review of EU Law after *Honeywell*: Contextualizing the Relationship between the German Constitutional Court and the EU Court of Justice' (2011) 48 CMLRev 9.

57. If each Member State claimed to be able to decide through their own courts on the validity of legal acts of the Union, the primacy of application could be circumvented in practice, and the uniform application of Union law would be placed at risk. If, however, on the other hand the Member States were to completely forgo *ultra vires* review, disposal of the treaty basis would be transferred to the Union bodies alone, even if their understanding of the law led in the practical outcome to an amendment of a Treaty or to an expansion of competences. That in the borderline cases of possible transgression of competences on the part of the Union bodies—which are infrequent, as should be expected according to the institutional and procedural precautions of Union law—the constitutional and the Union law perspective do not completely harmonise, is due to the circumstance that the Member States of the European Union also remain the masters of the Treaties subsequent to the entry into force of the Treaty of Lisbon, and that the threshold to the federal state was not crossed (see BVerfGE 123, 267 <370–371>). The tensions, which are basically unavoidable according to this construction, are to be harmonised cooperatively in accordance with the European integration idea and relaxed through mutual consideration.

58. *Ultra vires* review may only be exercised in a manner which is open towards European law...

59. (1) The Union understands itself as a legal community; it is in particular bound by the principle of conferral and by the fundamental rights, and it respects the constitutional identity of the Member States... According to the legal system of the Federal Republic of Germany, the primacy of application of Union law is to be recognised and it is to be guaranteed that the control powers which are constitutionally reserved for the Federal Constitutional Court are only exercised in a manner that is reserved and open towards European law.

60. This means for the *ultra vires* review at hand that the Federal Constitutional Court must comply with the rulings of the Court of Justice in principle as a binding interpretation of Union law. Prior to the acceptance of an *ultra vires* act on the part of the European bodies and institutions, the Court of Justice is therefore to be afforded the opportunity to interpret the Treaties, as well as to rule on the validity and interpretation of the legal acts in question, in the context of preliminary ruling proceedings according to Article 267 TFEU. As long as the Court of Justice did not have an opportunity to rule on the questions of Union law which have arisen, the Federal Constitutional Court may not find any inapplicability of Union law for Germany...

61. *Ultra vires* review by the Federal Constitutional Court can moreover only be considered if it is manifest that acts of the European bodies and institutions have taken place outside the transferred competences... A breach of the principle of conferral is only manifest if the European bodies and institutions have transgressed the boundaries of their competences in a manner specifically violating the principle of conferral (Article 23.1 of the Basic Law), the breach of competences is in other words sufficiently qualified... This means that the act of the authority of the European Union must be manifestly in violation of competences and that the impugned act is highly significant in the structure of competences between the Member States and the Union with regard to the principle of conferral and to the binding nature of the statute under the rule of law...

This ruling renders it far more difficult for a claimant to sustain a challenge to the supremacy of EU law based on the argument that the EU exceeded its competence and hence acted *ultra vires*.[60] The BVerfG makes clear that it will regard any such action as inadmissible unless the ECJ has been given the opportunity to rule on the issue: paragraph 60. The BVerfG also stresses in paragraph 61 that *ultra vires* review requires the claimant to show that any excess of power by the EU was 'manifestly' in violation of its competence and that the impugned act was 'highly significant' in the structure of competence between the Member States and the EU. It is noteworthy that Judge Landau dissented on

---

[60] Voßkuhle (n 45) 194–195.

the grounds that the majority judgment made it excessively difficult to conclude that the EU had acted *ultra vires*, and that the majority had in this respect departed from the *Lisbon* ruling considered below.

Thus, in the same way that the BVerfG softened its fundamental rights qualification to acceptance of EU supremacy, it also qualified the *ultra vires* lock that it initially enunciated in the *Brunner* case. Matters can however change in this area, as exemplified by the BVerfG's first reference to the CJEU, concerning the legality of action by the European Central Bank during the Euro-crisis, where its conception of what constituted *ultra vires* action was a good deal 'tougher' than that evident from the *Honeywell* ruling.[61]

(v) *Limits to Acceptance of Supremacy: The Identity Lock*

A related, but distinct, limit to the acceptance of EU supremacy within the German legal order was fashioned in the BVerfG's ruling on the compatibility of the Lisbon Treaty with the German Constitution. In its *Lisbon* decision, the BVerfG reiterated the existence of the *ultra vires* lock, based on excess of competence, although it should be noted that the *Honeywell* ruling considered above is more recent. The BVerfG in the *Lisbon* ruling however also articulated what has become known as the 'identity lock'. The following extract begins after the BVerfG had reaffirmed its authority to engage in *ultra vires* review.

---

2 BvE 2/08, 30 June 2009

THE BUNDESVERFASSUNGSGERICHT (BVERFG)

240. Furthermore, the Federal Constitutional Court reviews whether the inviolable core content of the constitutional identity of the Basic Law pursuant to Article 23.1 third sentence in conjunction with Article 79.3 of the Basic Law is respected...In this respect, the guarantee of national constitutional identity under constitutional and under Union law goes hand in hand in the European legal area. The identity review makes it possible to examine whether, due to the action of European institutions, the principles under Article 1 and Article 20 of the Basic Law, declared inviolable in Article 79.3 of the Basic Law, have been violated. This ensures that the primacy of application of Union law only applies by virtue and in the context of the constitutional empowerment that continues in effect.

...

249. European unification on the basis of a treaty union of sovereign states may, however, not be achieved in such a way that not sufficient space is left to the Member States for the political formation of the economic, cultural and social living conditions. This applies in particular to areas which shape the citizens' living conditions, in particular the private sphere of their own responsibility and of political and social security, protected by fundamental rights, as well as to political decisions that rely especially on cultural, historical and linguistic perceptions and which develop in public discourse in the party political and parliamentary sphere of public politics. Essential areas of democratic formative action comprise, *inter alia*, citizenship, the civil and the military monopoly on the use of force, revenue and expenditure including external financing and all elements of encroachment that are decisive for the realisation of fundamental rights, above all in major encroachments on fundamental rights such as deprivation of liberty in the administration of criminal law or placement in an institution. These important areas also

---

[61] BVerfG, 2 BvR 2728/13, 14 Jan 2014; J Bast, 'Don't Act Beyond Your Powers: The Perils and Pitfalls of the German Constitutional Court's *Ultra Vires* Review' (2014) 15 German Law Journal 167; M Kumm, 'Rebel Without a Good Cause: Karlsruhe's Misguided Attempt to Draw the CJEU into a Game of "Chicken" and What the CJEU Might Do About It' (2014) 15 German Law Journal 203.

include cultural issues such as the disposition of language, the shaping of circumstances concerning the family and education, the ordering of the freedom of opinion, press and of association and the dealing with the profession of faith or ideology.

...

252. Particularly sensitive for the ability of a constitutional state to democratically shape itself are decisions on substantive and formal criminal law (1), on the disposition of the monopoly on the use of force by the police within the state and by the military towards the exterior (2), fundamental fiscal decisions on public revenue and public expenditure, the latter being particularly motivated, *inter alia*, by social policy considerations (3), decisions on the shaping of living conditions in a social state (4) and decisions of particular cultural importance, for example on family law, the school and education system and on dealing with religious communities (5).

The BVerfG's *Lisbon* judgment is long and contains much else that is relevant to the relationship between the German and EU legal orders. It generated significant academic comment,[62] much of which was critical of the identity lock fashioned in the case.

D Halberstam and C Möllers, The German Constitutional Court says 'Ja zu Deutschland!'[63]

For quite a long time a strange commonplace in German constitutional scholarship has been the lack of any *Staatsaufgabenlehre*, that is, a theory of what necessary tasks the state must fulfill. It was hoped that scholars might define this field in a purely conceptual effort without any reference to the necessarily open democratic process. This dream of a conceptual deduction of the being or essence of the state *Wesen* and its agendas never took concrete form. Instead, it remained a nostalgic sentiment about what might have been a complete theory of the state.

It is no accident that such a theory has never been written. In a different context, the United States Supreme Court has also struggled with, and retreated from, comprehensively defining what constitutes traditional areas of state regulation. An open democratic process makes it difficult to define in any comprehensive way what areas of legislation form the state's 'necessary' tasks. To be sure, any such theory would, indeed, help us draw meta-constitutional lines around the power of the state. Any such doctrine could then protect the state from various forms of disaggregation, privatization, as well as Europeanization and internationalization. Still, in Germany, the dream of a *Staatsaufgabenlehre* project has long been forgotten.

Forgotten? Suddenly and without precedent the Court's *Lisbon Case* develops its own *Staatsaufgabenlehre*. The Court defines five areas in which the state must take a role: Criminal law (substantial and procedural), war and peace, public expenditures and taxation, welfare, and culture and religion. These tasks are, according to the Court, 'especially sensitive for the ability of a constitutional state to democratically shape itself.' But is there any theory or argument behind this list? We find none in the opinion. The Court merely refers to its own imagination of past sovereignty. The opinion asserts that '*seit jeher*,' 'since ever,' the state has fulfilled these tasks as an expression of its sovereignty.

---

[62] F Schorkopf, 'The European Union as an Association of Sovereign States: Karlsruhe's Ruling on the Treaty of Lisbon' (2009) 10 German LJ 1219; D Halberstam and C Möllers, 'The German Constitutional Court says "Ja zu Deutschland!"' (2009) 10 German LJ 1241; D Thym, 'In the Name of Sovereign Statehood: A Critical Introduction to the *Lisbon* Judgment of the German Constitutional Court' (2009) 46 CMLRev 1795; F Mayer, 'Rashomon in Karlsruhe: A Reflection on Democracy and Identity in the European Union' (2011) 9 I-CON 757.

[63] (N 62) 1249–1250.

This is obviously not the case. The welfare function of the European nation state has often been described as the beginning of the end of the idea of sovereignty, as the point of dissolution of the state into society. Religion was a decisive topic of the Westphalian Treaty System that stands at the very beginning of the modern concept of sovereignty in Public International Law, a concept the Court otherwise explicitly endorses. Religion did not belong to state sovereignty at the very moment of its invention. On the other hand, what about the omission of Civil Law in the list? Despite the fact that German BGB, the Civil Code, was the central codification of the newly founded German nation-state, the Court does not even mention this area of law as being special to the German state's identity or sovereignty. And what about the control over currency—a field that often has been mentioned as a classical prerogative of the state? From either a historical or a systematic perspective, the list makes no sense.

Then again, why does the Court classify just the five areas on its list as necessary parts to state sovereignty? The answer is simple. The 'theory' of the Court is a *post hoc* argument in support of a preordained result.

(vi) *Limits to Acceptance of Supremacy: Locks, Limits, and Consequences*

The German jurisprudence has provided much food for thought concerning limits to the acceptance of EU supremacy in one Member State. A few words by way of reflection may be helpful in assessing this case law.

The simplest facts are the easiest to forget. All actions have consequences. This trite proposition applies just as much to legal decisions as to any other. If a legal system decides to apply locks then it must determine their content and how to apply them. This trite proposition leads to a less obvious one. The very language of locks is indicative of asymmetrical power: someone imposes constraints on someone else. The reality is more complex, at least in this context. The reason is not hard to divine. The creator of the lock has to live with the very constraint that it has fashioned. Tough talk, whether by national courts or legislators, leading to 'tight locks', has consequences for the author. The tighter the lock, the more demanding it is for the creator, not just for the person or institution constrained. It is fine if the creator of the lock really does wish to follow through the implications of its constraint. It is problematic if the creator becomes equivocal about the content and application of the lock that it has created. It then has to find ways of 'backing off' or 'softening' the constraint that it has devised, without thereby losing credibility and opening itself to the criticism that its tough talk is not matched by tough action.

The German jurisprudence reveals how the imposition of locks can be controversial or problematic, in terms of content and application. Thus, in terms of content, we have seen that the empirical and conceptual foundation of the identity lock has been questioned by German scholars. The application of any such locks is equally important. The national court should be wary of condemning the CJEU for 'activist' interpretation of the kind that the national court itself regularly engages in at domestic level.[64] The German courts have in any event softened limits to the acceptance of EU supremacy based on fundamental rights and competence/*ultra vires*, rendering it far more difficult for a claimant to succeed on these grounds.

It remains to be seen how the identity lock is applied in subsequent case law. Claimants are likely to challenge EU legislation before the German courts on the ground that it transgresses one of the identity limits listed in the judgment. The *Lisbon* ruling may then prove a dilemma for the German Federal Constitutional Court which created the identity lock. The BVerfG will be faced with a difficult choice. It can take the identity lock seriously, with the consequence that it thereby comes into repeated

---

[64] P Craig, 'The ECJ and *Ultra Vires* Action: A Conceptual Analysis' (2011) 48 CMLRev 395.

conflict with the EU in relation to the five areas listed in the judgment. It can, alternatively, soften the application of the identity lock in ways analogous to the modification of the *ultra vires* lock, with the consequence that it is criticized for not 'taking locks seriously'. It remains therefore to be seen whether its 'bark is worse than its bite'. The following extract, from the President of the Federal Constitutional Court, indicates that the BVerfG may well attempt to soften this lock too, although its future approach can be difficult to predict.[65]

A Voßkuhle, Multilevel Cooperation of the European Constitutional Courts: Der Europäische Verfassungsgerichtsverbund[66]

Just as only the Federal Constitutional Court can exercise the concrete review of statutes according to Article 100 of the Basic Law, which protects the parliamentary legislature, so too is it solely for the Federal Constitutional Court to review whether the inviolable core content of the constitutional identity of the Basic Law pursuant to Article 23(1) third sentence in conjunction with Article 79(3) of the Basic Law is respected. This review power, which is rooted in German constitutional law, is at the same time corroborated by European Union law, as it goes 'hand in hand' with the protection of national constitutional identity and the principle of sincere cooperation in accordance with the European Union Treaty in its Lisbon version. Thus, the 'bridge' between Union law and German national law continues to be secured by the railing of continuing German constitutional empowerment. However, the Federal Constitutional Court, when exercising this review, will continue to observe the principle of the Basic Law's openness towards European integration, thereby continually taking into account the responsibility for integration which is due by the court as it is by all other German constitutional bodies.

(vii) *Summary*

i. The German courts accept the supremacy of EU law, subject to the limits considered above.

ii. The conceptual foundation for acceptance of supremacy is primarily Articles 23.1, 24, and 25 of the German Constitution, but the German Federal Constitutional Court has also adverted to some aspects of the *communautaire* reasoning of the ECJ.

iii. The German courts continue to possess jurisdiction where EU law impinges on fundamental rights protected by the German Constitution, but any claimant will have to show that the protection afforded by EU law is generally deficient before the German courts will exercise their jurisdiction.

iv. The German courts also regard themselves as possessing the ultimate *Kompetenz-Kompetenz* to decide whether EU action is within the scope of EU competence.[67] The case law indicates that this power would only be exercised where the EU institution clearly acted in excess of competence accorded by the Treaties, and then only after the CJEU has been given the opportunity to rule on the contested EU provision. There are however indications of a tougher line in some recent decisions.[68]

---

[65] See, eg, BVerfG, 2 BvR 2728/13, 14 Jan 2014; BVerfG, 2 BvR 1390/12, 18 Mar 2014; E Vranes, 'German Constitutional Foundations of, and Limitations to, EU Integration: A Systematic Analysis' (2013) 14 German Law Journal 75; C Calliess, 'The Future of the Eurozone and the Role of the German Federal Constitutional Court' (2012) 31 YBEL 402; H Detters, 'National Constitutional Jurisprudence in a Post-National Europe: The *ESM* Ruling of the German Federal Constitutional Court and the Disavowal of Conflict' (2014) 20 ELJ 204.

[66] (N 45) 196.

[67] See, eg, BVerfG, 2 BvR 1390/12, 18 Mar 2014, [160].

[68] See, eg, BVerfG, 2 BvR 2728/13, 14 Jan 2014, [17]–[31].

v. The German courts have also fashioned a limit to acceptance of EU law, where this impinges on constitutional identity.

(B) ITALY

(i) *Acceptance of Supremacy*

The Italian courts signalled acceptance of the supremacy of EU law, albeit subject to qualification, at a relatively early stage.

Frontini v Ministero delle Finanze
[1974] 2 CMLR 372

The plaintiff brought proceedings to challenge the applicability of increased agricultural levies, which had been imposed by EC Regulation, on the import of meat into Italy. Frontini argued that the Regulation was inapplicable in Italy, and the case was transmitted to the Italian Constitutional Court to determine the constitutional legitimacy of the Italian EEC Treaty Ratification Act 1957. That Act made Article 249 of the Treaty, providing for the direct applicability of Community regulations, effective in Italy.

THE COURT[69]

The EEC Treaty Ratification Act 1957, whereby the Italian Parliament gave full and complete execution to the Treaty instituting the EEC, has a sure basis of validity in Article 11 of the Constitution whereby Italy 'consents, on condition of reciprocity with other states, to limitations of sovereignty necessary for an arrangement which may ensure peace and justice between the nations' and then 'promotes and favours the international organizations directed to such an aim'....

... It is hardly necessary to add that by Article 11 of the Constitution limitations of sovereignty are allowed solely for the purpose of the ends indicated therein, and it should therefore be excluded that such limitations of sovereignty, concretely laid out in the Rome Treaty, signed by countries whose systems are based on the principle of the rule of law and guarantee the essential liberties of citizens, can nevertheless give the organs of the EEC an unacceptable power to violate the fundamental principles of our constitutional order or the inalienable rights of man. And it is obvious that if ever Article 189 had to be given such an aberrant interpretation, in such a case the guarantee would always be assured that this Court would control the continuing compatibility of the Treaty with the above mentioned fundamental principles.

Frontini was followed in 1984 by *Granital,*[70] in which the Italian Constitutional Court accepted that, in order to give effect to the supremacy of EU law, Italian courts must be prepared where necessary to disregard conflicting national law and to apply EU law directly. The national law would not be abrogated, but rather ignored insofar as the field in which it operated had been pre-empted by EU law. The national provisions would however survive and still govern the relevant subject matter in areas beyond the scope of the EU norm.

A pro-European stance of the Italian courts is also evidenced by the fact that the Corte Costituzionale decided in 2008 that it was a 'court or tribunal of a Member State' for the purposes of making a

---

[69] [1974] 2 CMLR 372, 384.
[70] Dec 170 of 8 June 1984 in *SpA Granital v Amministrazione delle Finanze.* For an unofficial translation see G Gaja (1984) 21 CMLRev 756.

reference to the ECJ under Article 267 TFEU, thereby reversing its position in this regard,[71] and this trend has been continued in subsequent case law.[72]

(ii) *Conceptual Basis for Acceptance of Supremacy*

The conceptual basis for acceptance of the supremacy of EU law is a live issue in all Member States. The Italian courts have grounded such acceptance, as is evident from *Frontini*, on Article 11 of the Italian Constitution, which provides that 'Italy agrees, on conditions of equality with other States, to the limitations of sovereignty that may be necessary to a world order ensuring peace and justice among the Nations'. This formed the basis for the Italian courts' acceptance of the supremacy of EU law, although, as in the case of other Member States, this acceptance has not been unconditional.[73]

(iii) *Limits to Acceptance of Supremacy*

It is clear from *Frontini* that, while accepting the direct effect of EU law and confirming Italy's constitutional competence to ratify the Treaties, the Constitutional Court expressed similar reservations to those of the German BVerfG, and confirmed that it would continue to review the exercise of power by the 'organs of the EEC' to ensure that there was no infringement of fundamental rights or of the basic principles of the Italian constitutional order. Moreover in *Granital* the Italian Constitutional Court was prepared to adjudicate not simply on questions of conflict between specific EU measures and fundamental Italian constitutional rights, but also on the division of competence between national law and EU law.[74] The possibility of conflict was demonstrated in *Fragd*,[75] in which the Italian Constitutional Court considered that an EU measure would not be applied in Italy if it contravened a fundamental principle of the Italian Constitution concerning human rights protection.

G Gaja, New Developments in a Continuing Story: The Relationship between EEC Law and Italian Law[76]

While the *Frontini* decision by the Constitutional Court has often been viewed as a significant example of the willingness on the part of national courts to subject EEC legislation to constitutional rules concerning the protection of fundamental rights, little has happened so far to justify this evaluation....

In *Spa Fragd* v. *Amministrazione delle Finanze*, the Court examined whether a system, such as that applying to preliminary rulings on validity of Community acts, whereby a declaration of invalidity may not produce any effect in the proceedings before the referring court, is consistent with the constitutional principles on judicial protection...The Constitutional Court's main aim was to try and support the view that, as a matter of Community law, rulings should always have some effects in those proceedings. Possibly as a way of persuading the Court of Justice of the need to accept this solution, the

---

[71] Decs 102 and 103/2008.

[72] Order No 207, 2013; O Pollicino, 'From Partial to Full Dialogue with Luxembourg: The Last Cooperative Step of the Italian Constitutional Court' (2014) 10 EuConst 143.

[73] The Corte Costituzionale denied that the revised Art 117(1) of the Italian Constitution replaced Art 11 as the constitutional basis for EU law in Italy: Decs 348 and 349/2007.

[74] R Petriccione, 'Italy: Supremacy of Community Law over National Law' (1986) 11 ELRev 320.

[75] *Spa Fragd v Amministrazione delle Finanze*, Dec 232 of 21 Apr 1989 (1989) 72 RDI.

[76] (1990) 27 CMLRev 83, 93–94.

Constitutional Court also viewed the problem from the perspective of the constitutional protection of fundamental rights. The Court said:

...

In substance, everyone's right to have a court and judicial proceedings for each dispute would be emptied of its essential content if, when a court doubts the validity of a rule which should be applied, the answer came from the court to whom the question has to be referred that the rule is in fact void, but that this should not be relevant for the dispute before the referring court, which should nevertheless apply the rule that is declared to be void.

Contrary to the State Attorney's view, one could not invoke the primary need for the uniform application of Community law and for certainty of law against the possible violation of a fundamental right.

...

Unlike *Frontini*, the *Fragd* decision shows that the Constitutional Court is willing to test the consistency of individual rules of Community law with the fundamental principles for the protection of human rights that are contained in the Italian Constitution. This significantly widens the way for the exercise by the Constitutional Court of a control which has hitherto been only theoretical.

(iv) *Summary*

i. The Italian courts have accepted the supremacy of EU law, subject to the qualifications mentioned below.

ii. The supremacy of EU law is based on Article 11 of the Italian Constitution, and not the *communautaire* reasoning of the ECJ.

iii. The Italian courts do not accept that EU law has primacy over the Italian Constitution, and they retain ultimate authority over the issue of whether EU law infringes fundamental rights.

iv. It seems moreover that the Italian courts regard themselves as possessing the ultimate *Kompetenz-Kompetenz*, being prepared in principle to adjudicate on the division of competence between national law and EU law.[77]

(c) FRANCE

(i) *Acceptance of Supremacy*

We can begin by addressing the first of the issues set out above: whether the national legal system accepts the supremacy of EU law. The French courts now accept the supremacy of EU law, but it took some time before all French courts did so.

The French judicial system is divided between the administrative courts and the ordinary courts. In 1970 the supreme administrative court, the Conseil d'Etat, in effect rejected the supremacy of EU law over national law.[78] In *Semoules*,[79] it ruled that since it had no jurisdiction to review the validity of French legislation, it could not find such legislation to be incompatible with EU law, and could not accord priority to the latter. This was so notwithstanding the fact that the French Constitution

---

[77] P Ruggeri Laderchi, 'Report on Italy' in Slaughter *et al* (n 43) ch 5, points out the procedural problems for Italian courts wishing to exercise a form of *ultra vires* review of EU acts. See also A Adinolfi, 'The Judicial Application of Community Law in Italy (1981–1997)' (1998) 35 CMLRev 1313, 1314–1325.

[78] D Pollard, 'The Conseil d'Etat is European—Official' (1990) 15 ELRev 267, 268–270 and 'European Community Law and the French Conseil d'Etat' (1992–1995) 30 Irish Jurist 79.

[79] Dec of 1 Mar 1968 in *Syndicat Général de Fabricants de Semoules de France* [1970] CMLR 395.

provided for the primacy of certain international treaties over domestic law, since the Conseil d'Etat held that decisions on the constitutionality of legislation were for the Conseil Constitutionnel, the Constitutional Council, to make before the legislation was promulgated.

A doctrinal 'split' occurred when the supremacy of EU law over French law was accepted in 1975 in *Café Jacques Vabres* by the Cour de Cassation,[80] the highest of the ordinary judicial courts, in a case concerning a conflict between Article 90 EC and a later provision of the French Customs Code. Following the suggestion of the Procureur Général, the Cour held that the question was not whether it could review the constitutionality of a French law. Instead, when a conflict existed between an 'internal law' and a properly ratified 'international act' that had entered the internal legal order, the Constitution itself accorded priority to the latter. Respect for the principle of the primacy of international treaties should not be left to the Conseil Constitutionnel, since it was the duty of the ordinary courts before which such problems actually arose to do justice in the case.

It was not until 1989 that the Conseil d'Etat finally abandoned its so-called 'splendid isolation' and decided, in its capacity as an electoral court, to adopt the same position as the Conseil Constitutionnel and the Cour de Cassation.[81]

Raoul Georges Nicolo
[1990] 1 CMLR 173

The applicants were French citizens who brought an action for the annulment of the European Parliament elections in France in 1989, on the ground that the right to vote and to stand had been given to French citizens in the non-European overseas departments and territories of France. It was argued that the French statutory rule under challenge—Act 77–729—was contrary to the EEC Treaty.

COMMISSAIRE FRYDMAN[82]

However, the whole difficulty is then to decide whether, in conformity with your settled case law, you should dismiss this second argument by relying on the 1977 Act alone, without even having to verify whether it is compatible with the Treaty of Rome, or whether you should break fresh ground today by deciding that the Act is applicable only because it is compatible precisely with the Treaty.

In this connection we know that you held, in the famous divisional decision of 1 March 1968, *Syndicat Général des Fabricants de Semoules de France* that an administrative court cannot accord treaties precedence over subsequent legislation which conflicts with them and that this case law applies to Community rules just as much as to ordinary international conventions....

The theoretical foundation of those decisions, which clearly does not take the form of an objection to the principle of the superiority of treaties over statutes, which is expressly stated by Article 55, should rather be sought in your wish to uphold the principle that it is not for the administrative courts to review the validity of legislation....

On the other hand I believe it is possible to take the view that...Article 55 of itself necessarily enables the courts, by implication, to review the compatibility of statutes with treaties. Indeed, we must

---

[80] Dec of 24 May 1975 in *Administration des Douanes v Société 'Cafés Jacques Vabre' et SARL Weigel et Cie* [1975] 2 CMLR 336.

[81] Dec of 20 Oct 1989 in *Nicolo*. It has been suggested that earlier decisions of the Conseil Constitutionnel, which indicated that it was for the other French courts to ensure that international treaties were applied, acted as a spur to the Conseil d'Etat to reverse its original position, P Oliver, 'The French Constitution and the Treaty of Maastricht' (1994) 43 ICLQ 1, 10.

[82] [1990] 1 CMLR 173, 177, 178.

attribute to the authors of the Constitution an intention to provide for actual implementation of the supremacy of treaties which they embodied in that provision....

On this basis, therefore, I propose that you should agree to give treaties precedence over later statutes.

...I am aware that the Court of Justice of the European Communities—which, as we know, gives the Community law absolute supremacy over the rules of national law, even if they are constitutional—has not hesitated for its part to affirm the obligation to refuse to apply in any situation laws which are contrary to Community measures.

I do not think you can follow the European Court in this judge-made law which, in truth, seems to me at least open to objection. Were you to do so, you would tie yourself to a supranational way of thinking which is quite difficult to justify, to which the Treaty of Rome does not subscribe expressly and which would quite certainly render the Treaty unconstitutional, however it may be regarded in the political context....

I therefore suggest that you should base your decision on Article 55 of the Constitution and extend its ambit to all international agreements.

The Conseil d'Etat, although it did not expressly adopt the Commissaire's view, appeared to accept the premise underlying that view. It ruled that the French statutory rules were not invalid on the ground that they were 'not incompatible with the clear stipulations of the abovementioned Article 227(1) of the Treaty of Rome'.[83] By 1989 both the Cour de Cassation and the Conseil d'Etat were therefore willing in principle to accord primacy to EU law over national law.

The Conseil d'Etat has, since *Nicolo*, recognized the primacy of both EU regulations and directives.[84] Its jurisprudence concerning directives was nonetheless complex. This stemmed from its 1978 ruling in *Cohn-Bendit* that directives could not be used to challenge an individual administrative act.[85] The Conseil d'Etat developed an increasing number of qualifications to this basic proposition, which allowed directives to be relied on in a number of situations.[86] It then ruled in 2009 in *Mme Perreux* that a directive can indeed be relied on to challenge an individual administrative act, provided that the time for implementation of the directive had passed and provided also that the provisions of the directive were sufficiently certain and precise.[87]

The Conseil d'Etat's willingness to engage in dialogue with the ECJ is moreover exemplified by its 2007 *Arcelor* ruling.[88] The case concerned a Directive establishing an emission trading scheme under the Kyoto Protocol. The claimants alleged that the rights to property and to trade freely, and the principle of equality, as guaranteed by the French Constitution, were infringed by the decree implementing the Directive into French law. The Conseil d'Etat, instead of ruling on the legality of the decree under French constitutional law, referred the case to the ECJ, after observing that the fundamental rights in question were afforded similar protection under EU law.

---

[83] Pollard, 'The Conseil d'Etat is European' (n 78) 271, 273–274.

[84] *Boisdet* [1991] 1 CMLR 3, on a reg which was adopted after the French law, and *Rothmans and Philip Morris* and *Arizona Tobacco and Philip Morris* [1993] 1 CMLR 253 on a dir adopted before the French law; H Cohen, Note (1991) 16 ELRev 144; P Roseren, 'The Application of Community Law by French Courts From 1982 to 1993' (1994) 31 CMLRev 315, 342.

[85] Dec of 22 Dec 1978 in *Ministre de l'Intérieur v Cohn Bendit*.

[86] C Charpy, 'The Status of (Secondary) Community Law in the French Legal Order: The Recent Case-Law of the *Conseil Constitutionnel* and the *Conseil d'Etat*' (2007) 3 EuConst 436; C Charpy, 'The Conseil d'Etat Abandons its *Cohn Bendit* Case-Law; Conseil d'Etat, 30 October 2009, *Mme Perreux*' (2010) 6 EuConst 123, 125–126; R Mehdi, 'French Supreme Courts and European Union Law: Between Historical Compromise and Accepted Loyalty' (2011) 48 CMLRev 439.

[87] *Mme Perreux*, 30 Oct 2009.

[88] *Société Arcelor Atlantique et Lorraine et autres*, 8 Feb 2007; Case C–127/07 *Société Arcelor Atlantique et Lorraine and Others v Premier ministre, Ministre de l'Écologie et du Développement durable and Ministre de l'Économie, des Finances et de l'Industrie* [2008] ECR I–9895.

(ii) *Conceptual Basis for Acceptance of Supremacy*

In the case of France, the initial conceptual basis for acceptance of supremacy of EU law was Article 55 of the French Constitution and not the ECJ's *communautaire* reasoning in *Costa*. In *Café Jacques Vabres* the Procureur Général tried to persuade the Cour de Cassation to adopt the ECJ's reasoning, and to base the supremacy of Union law on the very nature of the EU legal order. The Cour de Cassation however grounded its decision on Article 55 of the French Constitution. The Conseil d'Etat's ruling in *Nicolo* also rested on Article 55 of the French Constitution, which provided for the superiority of international treaties over national law, and in this case Commissaire Frydman discouraged the Conseil d'Etat from subscribing to the ECJ's 'supranational way of thinking'. The Conseil d'Etat and the Conseil Constitutionnel have also based the duty to implement EU law, and the supremacy of EU law over national law, on Article 88–1 of the French Constitution.[89]

(iii) *Limits to Acceptance of Supremacy*

We have seen that from the ECJ's perspective all EU law is supreme over all national law. This has not been accepted by the French courts. The Conseil d'Etat has not recognized the primacy of EU law over the Constitution itself.[90] EU law ranks above statute, but below the Constitution. This coheres with the views of the Conseil Constitutionnel[91] and the Cour de Cassation.[92] This nonetheless leaves the national courts with considerable interpretive discretion in deciding whether there is indeed a clash between EU law and a provision of the French Constitution.[93]

C Charpy, The Status of (Secondary) Community Law in the French Internal Order[94]

Unquestionably, the reasoning of the *Conseil constitutionnel* and that of the *Conseil d'Etat* emphasizes the principle of the supremacy of the Constitution *vis-à-vis* Community law. They consider that the constituent power has incorporated in Article 88-1 of the Constitution the duty to implement directives and, more generally, the existence of the Community legal order integrated into the internal legal order. Thus, it is the Community legal order which is integrated into the national order, and not the other way around. Community law only can be effective in France by virtue of the constituent power's will. The Constitution remains the norm determining the relationship between the legal systems involved and thus has precedence over all other norms. In other words, because they are inscribed in the Constitution, the duty to implement Community law and the principle of its primacy do not alter the place of the Constitution at the top of the hierarchy of norms.

---

[89] Which provides that France shall participate in the EU 'constituted by States that have freely chosen, by virtue of the Treaties that establish them, to exercise some of their powers in common'.

[90] *Sarran and Levacher*, 30 Oct 1998; *Syndicat National de l'Industrie de Pharmaceutique*, 3 Dec 2001; C Richards, '*Sarran et Levacher*: Ranking Legal Norms in the French Republic' (2000) 25 ELRev 192; V Kronenberger, 'A New Approach to the Interpretation of the French Constitution in Respect of International Conventions' (2000) 47 Netherlands International Law Review 323.

[91] Dec No 2010–605 DC, 12 May 2010; Dec No 2007–560 DC, 20 Dec 2007; C Richards, 'The Supremacy of Community Law before the French Constitutional Court' (2006) 31 ELRev 499; Charpy, 'The Status of (Secondary) Community Law in the French Legal Order' (n 86) 458–462.

[92] *Mlle Fraisse*, 2 July 2000.

[93] See, eg, *Jeremy F*, Dec No 2013–314 QPC of 14 June 2013.

[94] (2007) 3 EuConst 436, 459; F-X Millet, 'How Much Lenience for How Much Cooperation? On the First Preliminary Reference of the French Constitutional Council to the Court of Justice' (2014) 51 CMLRev 195.

(iv) *Summary*

i. The French courts now generally accept, subject to what is said below, the supremacy of EU law over national law.

ii. The supremacy accorded to EU law is however not by virtue of the inherent nature of EU law as the Court of Justice would have it, 'but under the authority of their own national legal order'.[95] Articles 55 and 88–1 of the French Constitution have provided the conceptual foundation for the acceptance of supremacy in France.

iii. The French courts do not accept that EU law takes precedence over the Constitution.

iv. There has not been a clear case in the French courts raising the issue of *Kompetenz-Kompetenz*, but the predominant academic view is that this would be regarded as residing in the French courts.

(D) THE UNITED KINGDOM

(i) *Acceptance of Supremacy*

The central obstacle to acceptance by the UK of the supremacy of EU law is the constitutional principle of parliamentary sovereignty, which in its traditional formulation holds that Parliament has the power to do anything other than to bind itself for the future.[96] This means that if there is a clash between a later and an earlier norm then the latter is taken to be impliedly repealed or disapplied by the former. Moreover, the UK's dualist approach to international law means that international treaties ratified by the UK are not part of the domestic law of the UK, and in order to be enforceable at the domestic level they must be incorporated by an Act of Parliament. In theory, therefore, the sovereignty principle makes it very difficult for the supremacy of EU law over later UK legislation to be guaranteed, since the Act of Parliament which incorporates EU law and makes it domestically binding seems vulnerable to any later Act of Parliament that contravenes or contradicts it, expressly or impliedly.

It was nevertheless decided, after the EC Treaties were ratified by the UK in 1972, to give internal legal effect to Community law by means of an Act of Parliament: the European Communities Act 1972, section 2(1) of which provides:

> All such rights, powers, liabilities, obligations and restrictions from time to time created or arising by or under the Treaties, and all such remedies and procedures from time to time provided for by or under the Treaties, as in accordance with the Treaties are without further enactment to be given legal effect or used in the United Kingdom shall be recognised and available in law, and be enforced, allowed and followed accordingly; and the expression 'enforceable Community right' and similar expressions shall be read as referring to one to which this subsection applies.

Section 2(1) makes the concept of direct effect a part of the UK legal system. It deems law which under the EU Treaties is to be given immediate legal effect to be directly enforceable in the UK. Thus UK courts are directed by section 2(1) to enforce any directly effective EU measures. There is no need

---

[95] B de Witte, 'Community Law and National Constitutional Values' (1991) 2 LIEI 1, 4.

[96] P Craig, 'United Kingdom Sovereignty after *Factortame*' (1991) 11 YBEL 221; P Craig, 'Britain in the European Union' in J Jowell, D Oliver, and C O'Cinneide (eds), *The Changing Constitution* (Oxford University Press, 8th edn, 2015) ch 4.

for a fresh act of incorporation to enable UK courts to enforce each EU Treaty provision, regulation, or directive that has direct effect under EU law.

Section 2(2) provides for the implementation of EU obligations, even when they are intended to replace national legislation and Acts of Parliament, by means of an Order in Council or statutory instrument rather than by primary legislation only. Section 2(4) then provides:

> The provision that may be made under subsection (2) above includes, subject to Schedule 2 to this Act, any such provision (of any such extent) as might be made by Act of Parliament, and any enactment passed or to be passed, other than one contained in this Part of this Act, shall be construed and have effect subject to the foregoing provisions of this section; ...

The Schedule to which the provision refers sets out a number of powers, such as increasing taxation or legislating retroactively, which cannot be exercised by Order in Council or by delegated legislation, even if they are necessary to comply with an EU obligation. For these powers it seems an Act of Parliament will be needed. But the part of section 2(4) which has received most attention is the clause beginning 'any enactment passed or to be passed', which became prominent when the courts sought a way to reconcile new obligations under EU law with the traditional approach to statutory interpretation. Section 3 of the Act makes CJEU decisions on EU law authoritative in UK courts.

> For the purposes of all legal proceedings any question as to the meaning or effect of any of the Treaties, or as to the validity, meaning or effect of any Community instrument, shall be treated as a question of law (and, if not referred to the European Court, be for determination as such in accordance with the principles laid down by and any relevant decision of the European Court or any court attached thereto).

The leading decision on the relationship between EU law and UK law is *Factortame*, which will be considered below. Prior to that decision the judicial approach varied. The predominant approach, despite early judicial comments to the contrary,[97] was to use principles of construction to assume that when Parliament enacted the 1972 European Communities Act it intended any inconsistency with EU law to be resolved by giving primacy to EU law,[98] provided that there was no indication that Parliament expressly intended to depart from a provision of EU law, the assumption being that if the latter were to occur then the courts would follow the will of Parliament.[99] Thus where an apparently conflicting provision of English law was capable of being read in conformity with EU law, this was the proper approach to take.[100] In some cases the courts assumed that this approach would only apply where the provision of EU law was directly effective.[101] However in *Litster*,[102] *Pickstone*,[103] and *Webb*[104] the House of Lords was prepared to construe domestic statutes in conformity with EU law which was not directly effective, even where that construction was not in accordance with the literal or *prima facie* meaning of the statutes. This was so even where

---

[97] *Felixstowe Dock and Railway Company v British Transport and Docks Board* [1976] 2 CMLR 655.
[98] *Shields v E Coomes (Holdings) Ltd* [1979] 1 All ER 456, 461.
[99] *Macarthys v Smith* [1979] 3 All ER 325, 329.
[100] *Garland v British Rail* [1983] 2 AC 751, 771.
[101] *Duke v GEC Reliance Ltd* [1988] AC 618, 638.
[102] *Litster v Forth Dry Dock Co Ltd* [1990] 1 AC 546.
[103] *Pickstone v Freemans* [1989] AC 66.
[104] *Webb v EMO* [1993] 1 WLR 49.

the national statute was introduced to implement a non-directly effective directive. We can now consider *Factortame*.[105]

Factortame Ltd v Secretary of State for Transport (No 2)
[1991] 1 AC 603

The applicants were companies incorporated under UK law, but the majority of the directors and share-holders were Spanish. The companies were in the business of sea fishing and their vessels were registered as British under the Merchant Shipping Act 1894. The statutory regime was altered by the Merchant Shipping Act 1988. Vessels that had been registered under the 1894 Act had to register under the new legislation. Ninety-five vessels failed to meet the new criteria and the applicants argued that the 1988 Act was incompatible with Articles 52, 58, and 221 of the EC Treaty. The first *Factortame* case[106] was concerned with whether interim relief should be available against the Crown, in order to protect the applicants' financial interests if they were prevented from fishing pending the final judgment. The ECJ ruled that the absence of such relief was itself a breach of Community law.[107] This was accepted by the House of Lords in *Factortame (No 2)*, from which the following extract is taken.

LORD BRIDGE[108]

Some public comments on the decision of the Court of Justice, affirming the jurisdiction of the courts of member states to override national legislation if necessary to enable interim relief to be granted in protection of rights under Community law, have suggested that this was a novel and dangerous invasion by a Community institution of the sovereignty of the United Kingdom Parliament. But such comments are based on a misconception. If the supremacy within the European Community of Community law over the national law of member states was not always inherent in the EEC Treaty it was certainly well established in the jurisprudence of the Court of Justice long before the United Kingdom joined the Community. Thus, whatever limitation of its sovereignty Parliament accepted when it enacted the European Communities Act 1972 was entirely voluntary. Under the terms of the 1972 Act it has always been clear that it was the duty of a United Kingdom court, when delivering final judgment, to override any rule of national law found to be in conflict with any directly enforce-able rule of Community law. Similarly, when decisions of the Court of Justice have exposed areas of United Kingdom statute law which failed to implement Council directives, Parliament has always loyally accepted the obligation to make appropriate and prompt amendments. Thus there is nothing in any way novel in according supremacy to rules of Community law in those areas to which they apply and to insist that, in the protection of rights under Community law, national courts must not be inhib-ited by rules of national law from granting interim relief in appropriate cases is no more than a logical recognition of that supremacy.

The acceptance by UK courts of the supremacy of EU law was further evidenced by the *EOC* case where the House of Lords stated that there was no constitutional barrier to an applicant before any UK court, and not just the House of Lords, seeking judicial review of primary legislation which was alleged to be in breach of EU law.

---

[105] Craig (n 96); W Wade, 'Sovereignty—Revolution or Evolution?' (1996) 112 LQR 568; T Allan, 'Parliamentary Sovereignty: Law, Politics and Revolution' (1997) 113 LQR 443; D Nicol, *EC Membership and the Judicialization of British Politics* (Oxford University Press, 2001) ch 7.
[106] *Factortame Ltd v Secretary of State for Transport* [1990] 2 AC 85.
[107] (N 11).
[108] [1991] 1 AC 603, 658.

Equal Opportunities Commission v Secretary of State for Employment
[1994] 1 WLR 409

[Note Lisbon Treaty renumbering: Arts 7, 52, and 177 are now Arts 18, 49, and 267 TFEU]

The Equal Opportunities Commission (EOC) considered that the Employment Protection (Consolidation) Act of 1978 on part-time workers was contrary to Community law. In a letter from the Secretary of State for Employment to the EOC, the Secretary refused to accept that the UK was in breach of EC law. The EOC sought judicial review of the Secretary of State's decision. The Secretary of State argued that the English court had no jurisdiction to declare that the UK or the Secretary of State was in breach of any obligations under Community law.

LORD KEITH[109]

The question is whether judicial review is available for the purpose of securing a declaration that certain United Kingdom primary legislation is incompatible with Community law.... In the *Factortame* series of cases...the applicants for judicial review sought a declaration that the provisions of Part II of the Merchant Shipping Act 1988 should not apply to them on the ground that such application would be contrary to Community law, in particular Articles 7 and 52 of the EEC Treaty.... The Divisional Court, under Article 177 of the Treaty, referred to the Court of Justice of the European Communities a number of questions, including the question whether these restrictive conditions were compatible with Articles 7 and 52 of the Treaty. The European Court...answered that question in the negative, and although the final result is not reported, no doubt the Divisional Court in due course granted a declaration accordingly. The effect was that certain provisions of United Kingdom primary legislation were held to be invalid in their purported application to nationals of Member States of the European Community, but without any prerogative order being available to strike down the legislation in question, which of course remained valid as regards nationals of non-member States. At no stage in the course of the litigation, which included two visits to this House, was it suggested that judicial review of legislation was not available for obtaining an adjudication upon the validity of the legislation in so far as it affected the applicants.

The *Factortame* case is thus a precedent in favour of the EOC's recourse to judicial review for the purpose of challenging as incompatible with Community law the relevant provisions of the 1978 Act.

The following extract summarizes the position in UK law concerning the acceptance of the supremacy of EU law.

P Craig, Britain in the European Union[110]

The substantive impact of *Factortame, EOC, Thoburn* and *HS2* may be described as follows.

First, the relationship between EU law and national law in terms of supremacy is to be decided by the UK courts as a matter of UK constitutional law, taking account of any statutes enacted by Parliament.

Secondly, in doctrinal terms these decisions mean that the concept of *implied repeal*, or *implied disapplication*, under which inconsistencies between later and earlier norms were resolved in favour

---

[109] [1994] 1 WLR 409, 418–419.
[110] Craig, 'Britain in the European Union' (n 96) 119–120.

of the former, will, subject to what is said below, no longer apply to clashes concerning EU and national law...

Thirdly, if Parliament wishes to derogate from its EU obligations then it should do so *expressly and unequivocally*. The reaction of our national courts to such an unlikely eventuality remains to be seen. In principle two options would be open to the national judiciary. Either they could choose to follow the latest will of Parliament, thereby preserving some remnant of traditional orthodoxy on sovereignty. Or they could argue that it is not open to our legislature to pick and choose which obligations to subscribe to while still remaining within the EU....

Fourthly, the supremacy of EU law over national law *operates in areas where EU law is applicable*, as is made clear from the dictum of Lord Bridge set out above... The problem being addressed here is often referred to as *Kompetenz-Kompetenz*: who has the ultimate authority to decide whether a matter is within the competence of the EU? The CJEU may well believe that it is the ultimate decider of this issue. However, national courts may not always be content with this arrogation of authority...

(ii) *Conceptual Basis for Acceptance of Supremacy*

While the UK courts have accepted the supremacy of EU law, it is now clear that the conceptual foundation for this rests on domestic constitutional law. Thus while Lord Bridge in *Factortame (No 2)* adverted to ECJ reasoning to justify according supremacy to EU law, as exemplified by his reference to supremacy being inherent in the nature of the Treaty, he also premised the UK's acceptance of supremacy on the 1972 European Communities Act.

It was the domestic acceptance of supremacy that was emphasized in *Thoburn*.[111] Laws LJ held that the constitutional relationship between the UK and the EU was not to be decided by the ECJ's jurisprudence, which could not itself entrench EU law within national law. The constitutional relationship between the EU and the UK, including the impact of EU membership on sovereignty, was to be decided by the common law in the light of any domestic statutes. The common law had, said Laws LJ, modified the traditional concept of sovereignty, by creating exceptions to the doctrine of implied repeal. Ordinary statutes were subject to the doctrine of implied repeal. What Laws LJ referred to as 'constitutional statutes', which conditioned the legal relationship between citizen and state in some overarching manner, or which dealt with fundamental constitutional rights, were not subject to the doctrine of implied repeal. The repeal of such a statute, or its disapplication in a particular instance, could occur only if there were some 'express words in the later statute, or by words so specific that the inference of an actual determination to effect the result contended for was irresistible'.[112] The European Communities Act 1972 was regarded as just such a constitutional statute.

This approach was affirmed by the Supreme Court in *HS2*, where Lord Reed made clear that application of the supremacy doctrine in UK law 'itself depends upon the 1972 Act', with the consequence that a conflict between national and EU law 'has to be resolved by our courts as an issue arising under the constitutional law of the United Kingdom'.[113] The Supreme Court also endorsed the idea of constitutional statutes.[114]

The following extract considers the ways in which supremacy of EU law has been conceptualized in the UK.

---

[111] *Thoburn v Sunderland City Council* [2003] QB 151.
[112] Ibid [63].
[113] *R (HS2 Action Alliance Ltd) v Secretary of State for Transport* [2014] UKSC 3, [79], [203]–[205]; P Craig, 'Constitutionalizing Constitutional Law: HS2' [2014] PL 373.
[114] Ibid [207].

P Craig, Britain in the European Union[115]

Commentators have been divided as to how best to conceptualize the impact of the courts' jurisprudence.

It is possible to rationalize what the courts have done as a species of *statutory construction*. . . . All would agree that if a statute can be reconciled with an EU norm through construing the statutory words without unduly distorting them then this should be done, more especially when the statute was passed to effectuate a directive. However the species of statutory construction being considered here is more far-reaching. On this view accommodation between national law and EU law is attained through a rule of construction to the effect that inconsistencies *will* be resolved in favour of the latter *unless* Parliament has indicated clearly and unambiguously that it intends to derogate from EU law. The degree of linguistic inconsistency between the statute and the EU norm is not the essential point of the inquiry. Provided that there is no unequivocal derogation from EU law then it will apply, rather than any conflicting domestic statute. . . . The construction view is said to leave the essential core of the traditional view of legal sovereignty intact, in the sense that it is always open to a later Parliament to make it unequivocally clear that it wishes to derogate from EU law. . . . This approach is, however, problematic. . . .

A second way to conceptualize what the courts have done is to regard it as a *technical legal revolution*. This is the preferred explanation of Sir William Wade who sees the courts' decisions as modifying the ultimate legal principle or rule of recognition on which the legal system is based. On this view the 'rule of recognition is itself a political fact which the judges themselves are able to change when they are confronted with a new situation which so demands'. Such choices are made by the judiciary at the point where the law 'stops'.

There is however a third way in which to regard the courts' jurisprudence. This is to regard decisions about supremacy as being based on *normative arguments of legal principle the content of which can and will vary across time*. . . . On this view there is no *a priori* inexorable reason why Parliament, merely because of its very existence, must be regarded as legally omnipotent. The existence of such power, like all power, must be justified by arguments of principle which are normatively convincing. Possible constraints on Parliamentary omnipotence must similarly be reasoned through and defended on normative grounds. This approach fits well with the reasoning of Lord Bridge in the second *Factortame* case.

(iii) *Limits to Acceptance of Supremacy*

The discussion thus far has shown that notwithstanding initial concerns about reconciling EU membership and UK sovereignty, the UK has in reality experienced fewer problems in accepting EU supremacy than many other Member States. There are nonetheless judicial and legislative limits to this acceptance.

In judicial terms, there are statements in *Thoburn* that the European Communities Act 1972 might not give overriding effect to an EU measure that was repugnant to a fundamental or constitutional right guaranteed by UK law.[116] This has been reinforced more recently in the *HS2* case, where the Supreme Court held that it was at the very least arguable that 'there may be fundamental principles, whether contained in other constitutional instruments or recognised at common law, of which Parliament when it enacted the European Communities Act 1972 did not either contemplate or authorise the abrogation'.[117]

---

[115] Craig, 'Britain in the European Union' (n 96) 121–123.
[116] *Thoburn* (n 111).
[117] *HS2* (n 113) [207].

In legislative terms, the European Union Act 2011 introduced a far-reaching regime of statutory and referendum 'locks'. Space precludes detailed examination, which can be found elsewhere.[118] Suffice it to say the following for present purposes. The European Union Act 2011 is not, subject to what will be said below, directly concerned with constraints on the supremacy of EU law. It does however contain far-reaching limits to the acceptance of Treaty change and certain other EU decisions within the UK.

It contains a regime of referendum and statutory locks. Section 2 deals with Treaty amendment pursuant to the ordinary revision procedure in Article 48(2)–(5) TEU, and specifies that there must be an Act of Parliament plus a positive vote in a national referendum, unless the exemption condition applies. Section 3 sets the same conditions for Treaty change undertaken through the Simplified Revision Procedure in Article 48(6) TEU, unless the exemption or significance condition applies. The exemption condition renders a referendum unnecessary if the Treaty change does not fall within section 4 of the Act, but this will rarely occur given the breadth of that section. The significance condition makes a referendum unnecessary if the change made by the Simplified Revision Procedure comes within only section 4(1)(i) or (j),[119] and such change is not significant for the UK.

Section 6 is concerned primarily with changes to Treaty voting rules and procedure for enacting legislation pursuant to passerelle provisions in the TEU and TFEU. In such instances the minister cannot vote in favour of such change unless the EU draft decision is approved by Act of Parliament, plus a positive vote in a national referendum. Section 7 stipulates that a minister may not confirm approval of certain EU decisions unless they are approved by Act of Parliament. Section 8 is concerned with decisions made pursuant to Article 352 TFEU. A minister cannot vote in favour of an Article 352 draft decision unless it is approved by Act of Parliament, or in one of the other ways specified in section 8(4)–(5). Section 9 requires parliamentary approval for certain other decisions made pursuant to the Treaties.

The obligation to hold a referendum is determined by section 4(1), which covers every conceivable case of extension of competence and/or conferral of power, more especially because section 4(2) states that extension of competence includes the removal of a limitation on a competence. The only caveat is section 4(4), which obviates the need to hold a referendum in certain instances, including accession of new Member States. The substantive obligation to hold a referendum is reinforced by the procedural duty in section 5(3), which requires the minister to state whether in his opinion the Treaty amendment or Article 48(6) decision falls within section 4.

There was much debate during the passage of the legislation concerning what was termed the 'sovereignty clause', in section 18. It provides in effect that 'it is only by virtue of an Act of Parliament that directly applicable or directly effective EU law…falls to be recognised and available in law in the United Kingdom'. The legal reality is that section 18 says nothing about the supremacy of EU law over national law in the UK, and is not therefore concerned with 'sovereignty as primacy'. It is concerned with 'sovereignty as dualism'. It reiterates that in a dualist country such as the UK there must be an Act of Parliament which adopts or transforms the EU Treaty into UK law. The European Communities Act 1972, in particular section 2(1), is the gateway for EU law becoming part of UK law. There is moreover no 'legal fight' with the EU *vis-à-vis* this issue, since the application of EU law within a national legal order is predicated on that legal order being part of the EU, as determined by the constitutional requirements of that state.

---

[118] P Craig, 'The European Union Act 2011: Locks, Limits and Legality' (2011) 48 CMLRev 1881.

[119] European Union Act 2011, s 4(1)(i): the conferring on an EU institution or body of power to impose a requirement or obligation on the United Kingdom, or the removal of any limitation on any such power of an EU institution or body; (j) the conferring on an EU institution or body of new or extended power to impose sanctions on the United Kingdom.

(iv) *Limits to Acceptance of Supremacy: Locks, Limits, and Consequences*

There are significant legal problems concerning the interpretation of the European Union Act 2011, and its compatibility with EU law.[120] There are in addition very real political difficulties that flow from the legislation. It is worth recalling what was said when discussing the German jurisprudence: actions have consequences and locks impose demands on their creator. The 'Germanic locks' were fashioned by the Federal Constitutional Court, which has power to soften them through subsequent interpretation if it chooses.

The zeal for a referendum before Treaty change can be accepted in the UK may well come to haunt subsequent UK governments, more especially because the mandatory provisions of the 2011 legislation cannot be softened in the same way. It can, to be sure, be amended, but this does not change the force of the preceding point. It mandates a referendum for pretty much every conceivable Treaty change, large or small. It is doubtful whether our European partners will view with equanimity the prospect of 'sitting on' draft decisions while the UK enacts the relevant statute and organizes the referendum. It is equally doubtful whether they will be content with the delays and possible vetoes on Treaty reform when such amendment is deemed necessary.

This adverse reaction is likely to be heightened if such changes are prevented by a negative vote in a referendum when the voter turn-out is small. It is doubtful whether significant numbers of voters will exercise their franchise in relation to many of the issues on which a referendum is mandated by the Act. The task facing those charged with engaging voters to participate in a referendum on whether, for example, a shift to qualified-majority voting in relation to enhanced cooperation should be approved will be difficult indeed. The political reality is that voter turn-out will often be low, maybe embarrassingly so. If the vote is negative on a 10 per cent total turnout and blocks the desired change our Treaty partners will not be pleased, nor will they think the result has much in the way of legitimacy. The legal reality under what will be the EU Act is nonetheless that a referendum must be held, unless Parliament expressly disapplies it in a particular instance. The UK populace may well feel that the cost of a referendum, which is approximately £30–40 million, would be money better spent on schools, education, or health in a time of financial stringency. The 2011 Act may well prove the truth of the old adage: be careful what you wish for because it may just come true.

(v) *Summary*

i. Notwithstanding early doubts whether UK courts would be able to accommodate the supremacy of EU law, they have done so. A clash between national law and EU law will be resolved in favour of the latter. It is however unclear what the UK courts would do if Parliament sought expressly to derogate from a provision of EU law while still remaining in the EU.

ii. The conceptual foundation for acceptance of the supremacy of EU law is grounded in UK constitutional law and the 1972 European Communities Act, although there has been some recognition of the ECJ's own reasoning.

iii. While the UK does not have a written constitution the courts have indicated limits to acceptance of EU supremacy, and the European Union Act 2011 imposes constraints before proposed Treaty reform and certain other EU decisions can take effect within the UK.

iv. There has been no UK case directly raising the issue of *Kompetenz-Kompetenz*. The decisions according supremacy to EU law are however premised on the assumption that the EU is acting within the scope of its authority. If this were to arise the UK courts would probably regard

---

[120] Craig (n 118).

themselves as possessing the ultimate *Kompetenz-Kompetenz*, while at the same time according respect to the views of the CJEU on the relevant matter.

4 SECOND DIMENSION: SUPREMACY FROM THE PERSPECTIVE OF THE POST-2004 MEMBER STATES

(A) CENTRAL AND EAST EUROPEAN STATES

The judicial approach in the new Member States from Central and Eastern Europe is not uniform, and space precludes examination of all such jurisprudence. The rationale for considering this case law in a separate section from the pre-2004 Member States is that there are some distinct considerations at play. They are brought out by Sadurski, who notes that post-communist countries joined the EU in part to provide a secure foundation for democracy and human rights. He points to the paradox that their constitutional courts have resisted the supremacy of EU law on the ground that it might endanger domestic constitutional protection of such rights.[121] In the following extract he seeks to explain the fact that such courts have engaged in reasoning analogous to that of the German courts in the *Solange* cases.

W Sadurski, 'Solange Chapter 3': Constitutional Courts in Central Europe—Democracy—European Union[122]

The Solange story was well suited to be taken up in Central and Eastern Europe [*CEE*] after accession, for two powerful reasons. First, in nearly all post-communist European States, constitutional courts established themselves as powerful, influential, activist players, dictating the rules of the political game for other political actors...While the powers of the constitutional courts in CEE largely resemble (and often exceed) those of their Western European counterparts, the other branches of CEE States are weaker, more chaotic, disorganized and inefficient compared to those in Western Europe....Accession to the EU provided those courts with yet another opportunity to reinforce their own powers—an opportunity not to be missed: they could easily...assert a right to establish and enforce criteria of democracy, rule of law and human rights protection, which would inform the relationship between the European and national constitutional orders. Such a power would further increase their position vis-à-vis the political branches in their countries, by delineating those aspects of the supremacy of European law which they deemed unacceptable, or by dictating the need to carry out constitutional amendments if certain dimensions of supremacy were to be accepted.

The second reason why the Solange story almost begged for a recurrence in CEE stemmed from the strong sovereignty concerns which were felt and expressed in CEE states prior to accession, and persisted after joining the EU. Elsewhere I have described the situation surrounding this concern as a 'sovereignty conundrum': the often perceived irony that almost immediately after the shaking off of the brutal dominance by the Soviet Union (with its doctrine of 'limited sovereignty' of Warsaw Pact States) and the recovery of their long-missed independence, these countries should accede to a supranational Community in which traditional, strict sovereignty is found to be obsolete and in which

---

121 W Sadurski, '"*Solange* Chapter 3": Constitutional Courts in Central Europe—Democracy—European Union', EUI Working Papers, Law No 2006/40.
122 Ibid 2–4.

they are asked to transfer much of their sovereignty to supranational institutions. . . . The constitutional courts thus found themselves in a situation in which the pull towards rephrasing sovereignty-based objections against the supremacy of EU law, in terms of their role as guardians of constitutional values, was irresistible . . .

(B) POLAND

(i) *Acceptance of Supremacy*

The issues posed by the ECJ's supremacy doctrine are therefore also evident in the jurisprudence of the newer accession countries. Poland can be taken as an example and accepted the supremacy of EU law over national statute.

K 32/09, 24 Nov 2010

The case concerned challenges to the compatibility of various provisions of the Lisbon Treaty with the Polish Constitution.

CONSTITUTIONAL TRIBUNAL

In the statement of reasons for the judgment in the case K 18/04, the Constitutional Tribunal pointed out that, by approving the binding Constitution, the Nation itself decided that it agrees to the possibility of binding the Republic of Poland with the law enacted by an international organisation or international institution, i.e. with the law other than the treaty law. This is carried out within the limits provided for in ratified international agreements. Moreover, the Nation also granted its consent, in the said referendum, to the fact that the said law would be directly binding in the territory of the Republic of Poland, taking precedence over statutes in the event of a clash of laws. The consent to bind the Republic of Poland with the law enacted in accordance with the rules specified in the primary law has been expressed in the Treaty of Accession, accepted by way of a nationwide referendum; and the constitutionality of the Treaty of Accession was the object of assessment carried out by the Constitutional Tribunal in the case K 18/04.

(ii) *Conceptual Basis for Acceptance of Supremacy*

Poland has, like most of the older Member States, grounded the acceptance of supremacy in national constitutional provisions. In the case of Poland this has been primarily based on Article 90(1) of the Constitution, which provides that the 'Republic of Poland may, by virtue of international agreements, delegate to an international organization or international institution the competence of organs of State authority in relation to certain matters'.

(iii) *Limits to Acceptance of Supremacy*

The Polish courts have however articulated firm limits on the acceptance of the supremacy of EU law. Article 8(1) provides that the Constitution shall be the supreme law in Poland, and the Polish courts have made clear that EU law does not take precedence over the Constitution.

Polish Membership of the European Union (Accession Treaty)
K 18/04, 11 May 2005

The Polish Constitutional Tribunal considered the constitutionality of Polish membership of the EU. The Tribunal noted that the Polish Constitution did not have a category of 'supranational organization' and that the Accession Treaty between Poland and the EU should be regarded as a form of international agreement. It then continued as follows.

CONSTITUTIONAL TRIBUNAL

7. Article 90(1) of the Constitution authorizes the delegation of competences of State organs only 'in relation to certain matters'. This implies a prohibition on the delegation of all competences of a State authority organ or competences determining its substantial scope of activity, or competences concerning the entirety of matters within a certain field.

8. Neither Article 90(1) nor Article 91(3) authorize delegation to an international organization of the competence to issue legal acts or take decisions contrary to the Constitution, being the 'supreme law of Poland' (Article 8(1)). Concomitantly, these provisions do not authorize the delegation of competences to such an extent that it would signify the inability of the Republic of Poland to continue functioning as a sovereign and democratic State.

...

11. Given its supreme legal force (Article 8(1)), the Constitution enjoys precedence of binding force and precedence of application within the territory of the Republic of Poland. The precedence over statutes of the application of international agreements which were ratified on the basis of a statutory authorization or consent granted (in accordance with Article 90(3)) via the procedure of a nationwide referendum, as guaranteed by Article 91(2) of the Constitution, in no way signifies an analogous precedence of these agreements over the Constitution.

[*The Court noted the possibility of conflict or collision between Community norms and the Polish Constitution, and continued as follows.*]

13. Such a collision would occur in the event that an irreconcilable inconsistency appeared between a constitutional norm and a Community norm, such as could not be eliminated by means of applying an interpretation which respects the mutual autonomy of European law and national law. Such a collision may in no event be resolved by assuming the supremacy of a Community norm over a constitutional norm. Furthermore, it may not lead to the situation whereby a constitutional norm loses its binding force and is substituted by a Community norm, nor may it lead to an application of the constitutional norm restricted to areas beyond the scope of Community law regulation. In such an event the Nation as the sovereign, or a State authority authorized by the Constitution to represent the Nation, would need to decide on: amending the Constitution; or causing modifications within Community provisions; or, ultimately, on Poland's withdrawal from the European Union.

14. The principle of interpreting domestic law in a manner 'sympathetic to European law'...has its limits. In no event may it lead to results contradicting the explicit wording of constitutional norms or being irreconcilable with the minimum guarantee functions realized by the Constitution. In particular, the norms of the Constitution within the field of individual rights and freedoms indicate a minimum and unsurpassable threshold which may not be lowered or questioned as a result of the introduction of Community provisions.

The approach of the Polish courts is also apparent in the decision of the Constitutional Tribunal concerning the European Arrest Warrant (EAW).[123] The Constitutional Tribunal held that the

---

[123] Polish Constitutional Tribunal, 27 Apr 2005, No P 1/05; noted by D Leczykiewicz, (2006) 43 CMLRev 1181; A Nußberger, 'Poland: The Constitutional Tribunal on the Implementation of the European Arrest Warrant' (2008) 6 I-CON 162.

domestic law giving effect to the EAW was incompatible with Article 55(1) of the Polish Constitution, which prohibited the extradition of a Polish citizen. The Constitutional Tribunal was willing to accept that Article 55(1) should if possible be interpreted to be in conformity with EU law, but nonetheless felt unable to read the legislation giving effect to the EAW as being consistent with Article 55(1). It held that the constitutional prohibition on extradition applied also to the regime of surrender under the EAW. The Constitutional Tribunal acknowledged that the Constitution might have to be amended to ensure compliance with the EU Framework Decision creating the EAW. The time limit for domestic enactment of this Decision had however passed. The Constitutional Tribunal was therefore willing to defer the cancellation of the binding force of the Polish law implementing the EAW for eighteen months, in order to allow the necessary changes to be made to the Constitution.

The Constitutional Tribunal reiterated the supremacy of the Polish Constitution in its *Lisbon* ruling.[124] The judgment is long and complex. Suffice it to say for the present that it contains a delicate blend. There are pro-EU sentiments, and openness to EU norms. There are also statements concerning the limits of conferral of competence on an external institution that could undermine constitutional identity, and affirmation that Article 90 of the Constitution precludes the conferral of competence to an external institution to determine the limits of such competence.

(iv) *Summary*

i. The Polish courts accept the supremacy of EU law over statute, subject to the qualifications below.

ii. The conceptual foundation for this is to be found in provisions of the Polish Constitution, not the *communautaire* reasoning of the CJEU.

iii. The Polish courts do not accept the supremacy of EU law over the Constitution. The ruling on the EAW indicates the priority accorded to the Polish Constitution. The ruling however also indicates the willingness to bring Polish law into line with the demands of EU law, as evidenced by the way in which the Constitutional Tribunal delayed the cancellation of the national law pending possible amendment of the Constitution.

iv. The Polish courts regard themselves as possessing the ultimate *Kompetenz-Kompetenz*.

(c) CZECH REPUBLIC

The Czech Republic can be taken as a second example of the interaction between a post-2004 accession regime and the EU. We shall see that complex forces have shaped the Czech response to the supremacy of EU law.

(i) *Acceptance of Supremacy*

The Czech Constitutional Court has, subject to the qualifications below, accepted the supremacy of EU law. It held that a constitutional principle could be derived from Article 1 paragraph 2 of the Constitution, in conjunction with Article 10 EC, according to which domestic legal enactments, including the Constitution, should be interpreted in conformity with the principles of European integration and the cooperation between Community and Member State organs. If the Constitution, of which the Charter of Fundamental Rights and Basic Freedoms forms a part, could

---

[124] K 32/09, 24 Nov 2010; A Lazowski, 'Half Full and Half Empty Glass: The Application of EU Law in Poland (2004–10)' (2011) 48 CMLRev 503.

be interpreted in several ways, only certain of which led to the attainment of an obligation that the Czech Republic undertook in connection with its membership in the EU, then an interpretation should be selected that supports the carrying out of that obligation, and not an interpretation which precludes it.[125]

(ii) *Conceptual Basis for Acceptance of Supremacy*

The principal conceptual foundation for acceptance of EU law resides in Article 10 of the Czech Constitution. It provides that international agreements that have been duly promulgated and approved by Parliament constitute part of the Czech legal order, and that if the agreement makes provision contrary to a law then it prevails. Article 10a empowers the transfer of certain powers to an international organization.

(iii) *Limits to Acceptance of Supremacy*

The Czech Constitutional Court (CCC) has nonetheless iterated limits on its acceptance of EU supremacy, although it has until recently, not 'activated' those limits.

The CCC has made clear that EU secondary law must be consistent with the Treaties and the Czech constitutional order.[126] Thus EU legal norms had to be consistent with the principles of a democratic-law-based state,[127] since otherwise there would be a conflict with Article 9(2) of the Constitution, which provides that 'the substantive requisites of the democratic, law-abiding State may not be amended', although the CCC accepted that EU fundamental rights' protection sufficed in this respect. The CCC nonetheless emphasized that if EU law could not be interpreted to be in accord with the Constitution then the proper recourse would be for Parliament to amend the Constitution, subject once again to the limits of Article 9(2).[128] The CCC also made clear that it was the final arbiter on issues of Czech constitutionality, and that if EU norms violated the foundations of Czech constitutionality they would not be binding in the Czech Republic.[129]

The CCC exercised this power of *ultra vires* review in the Slovak pensions case,[130] refusing to apply the ECJ's decision in *Landtová*[131] on the ground that its reasoning was predicated on incorrect legal assumptions. The CCC's decision generated, not surprisingly, considerable comment.[132] It is one thing to bark, but quite another to bite. The academic literature however explains the background tensions to the case, which reveal that 'institutional' decisions can be affected by 'personal' factors.

Thus it is clear from the attendant literature that there were in effect three sets of tensions at play. There was long-running discord between the CCC and the Supreme Administrative Court, it being

---

[125] Pl ÚS 66/04.
[126] Pl ÚS 50/04.
[127] Pl ÚS 50/04.
[128] Pl ÚS 66/04.
[129] Pl ÚS 19/08; Pl ÚS 29/09.
[130] Pl ÚS 5/12.
[131] Case C–399/09 EU:C:2011:415.
[132] J Komárek, 'Czech Constitutional Court Playing with Matches: The Czech Constitutional Court Declares a Judgment of the Court of Justice of the EU *Ultra Vires*; Judgment of 31 January 2012, Pl ÚS 5/12, *Slovak Pensions XVII*' (2012) 8 EuConst 323; R Zbíral, 'Czech Constitutional Court, Judgment of 31 January 2012, Pl ÚS 5/12. A Legal Revolution or Negligible Episode? Court of Justice Decision Proclaimed *Ultra Vires*' (2012) 49 CMLRev 1475; M Bobek, '*Landtová, Holubec*, and the Problem of an Uncooperative Court: Implications for the Preliminary Rulings Procedure' (2014) 10 EuConst 54.

the latter that made the reference to the ECJ; there was tension between the CCC and the Czech Government, which argued before the ECJ that a CCC decision was wrong; and there was friction between the CCC and the ECJ, given that the latter snubbed attempts by the former to make its legal views known in the action before the ECJ.

5 CONSTITUTIONAL PLURALISM AND NATIONAL IDENTITY

(A) CONSTITUTIONAL PLURALISM

While the debate over whether there is or can be a final judicial arbiter in Europe remains a live one, different versions of constitutional pluralism are increasingly being proposed as a more attractive alternative to the stalemate of nation-state-centred versus EU-centred monism.[133] The following extracts are from two commentators whose approaches to the constitutional relationship between national law and European law have altered somewhat in recent years. Kirchhof, former judge of the Bundesverfassungsgericht and one of the main architects of the *Maastricht* judgment, expresses a more cooperative and pluralist vision of this relationship than some of his earlier views suggested; while MacCormick's proposed analysis is one of 'legal pluralism under international law', in place of his earlier radically pluralist perspective which saw the answer to fundamental constitutional conflict lying in politics rather than in law.

N MacCormick, Questioning Sovereignty[134]

The doctrine of supremacy of Community law is not to be confused with any kind of all-purpose subordination of Member State law to Community law. Rather, the case is that these are interacting systems, one of which constitutes in its own context and over the relevant range of topics a source of valid law superior to other sources recognized in each of the Member State systems....

On the whole therefore, the most appropriate analysis of the relations of legal systems is pluralistic rather than monistic, and interactive rather than hierarchical. The legal systems of Member States and their common legal system of EC law are distinct but interacting systems of law, and hierarchical relationships of validity within criteria of validity proper to distinct systems do not add up to any sort of all-purpose superiority of one system over another. It follows also that the interpretative power of the highest decision-making authorities of the different systems must be, as to each system, ultimate. It is for the ECJ to interpret in the last resort and in a finally authoritative way the norms of Community law. But equally, it must be for the highest constitutional tribunal of each member State to interpret its constitutional and other norms, and hence to interpret the interaction of the validity of EC law with higher level norms of validity in the given state system....

... The potential conflicts and collisions of systems that can in principle occur as between Community and member States do not occur in a legal vacuum, but in a space to which international law is also relevant. Indeed, it is decisively relevant, given the origin of the Community in Treaties and the continuing normative significance of *pacta sunt servanda*, to say nothing of the fact that in respect of their Community membership and otherwise the states owe each other obligations under international law.... What that signals is that state Courts have no right to assume an absolute superiority of state constitution over international good order, including the European dimension of that good order. This is

---

[133] See (n 30).
[134] (Oxford University Press, 1999) 117–121.

not the same as saying that they must simply defer to whatever the ECJ considers to be mandated by the European constitution.... But in the event of an apparently irresoluble conflict arising between one or more national courts and the ECJ, there would always on this thesis be a possibility of recourse to international arbitration or adjudication to resolve the matter.

P Kirchhof, The Balance of Powers between National and European Institutions[135]

European law would lose its roots and its power to grow by being made autonomous and separate from the Member States, whereas in the close interweaving with Member States' constitutions it gains its identity in a unitary origin and a unitary future...[C]onflicts of norms that may arise are not to be avoided or resolved by a conflict of laws provision whereby one takes primacy over the other and norms are rendered non-legal, but through mutual respect and through 'cooperation'.... The ECJ and the constitutional courts each have adjudicatory responsibility of their own for the success of the European legal community.... Accordingly, it is not just 'open skies' that are above these courts of last instance; a system of balance of powers between the European and Member State courts is developing. Whoever seeks to interpret this system of balance and cooperation as a hierarchy is closing off the way laid down in European integration towards a balance of powers within the judicature.... Adjudicating means establishing the culture of measure, of balance, of co-operation, not dominance, subordination and rejection.

The literature on constitutional pluralism is rich and instructive. The more particular conclusions drawn from such pluralist precepts may nonetheless be contestable. Consider in this respect the following extract from Advocate General Maduro, who relied on such reasoning in defence of the ECJ's *Internationale Handelsgesellschaft* ruling. The case concerned a challenge to an EU directive for conformity with certain provisions in the French Constitution. The Conseil d'Etat sought a preliminary ruling from the ECJ on whether the Directive was compatible with principles of equality.

Case C–127/07 Société Arcelor Atlantique et Lorraine v Premier ministre and others
[2008] ECR I–9895

ADVOCATE GENERAL MADURO

15. It may appear that, in being asked to rule on the conformity of the Directive with the French Constitution, the Conseil d'État was faced with the impossible task of having to reconcile the irreconcilable: how to protect the Constitution within the domestic legal order without breaching the primordial requirement of the primacy of Community law? Those concurrent claims to legal sovereignty are the very manifestation of the legal pluralism that makes the European integration process unique...Far from resulting in a breach of the uniform application of Community law, those claims have prompted the Conseil d'État to seek, through the preliminary ruling procedure, the assistance of the Court of Justice in guaranteeing the observance by Community acts of the values and principles also recognised by its national constitution...In reality, what the Conseil d'État is asking the Court to do is not to verify the conformity of a Community act with certain national constitutional values—which it could

---

[135] (1999) 5 ELJ 225, 227–228, 241. See also Voßkuhle (n 45).

not do anyway—but to review its lawfulness in the light of analogous European constitutional values. It is through this process that what at first sight appeared to be irreconcilable has in fact been reconciled. The European Union and the national legal orders are founded on the same fundamental legal values. While it is the duty of the national courts to guarantee the observance of those values within the scope of their constitutions, it is the responsibility of the Court to do likewise within the Community legal order.

16. Article 6 TEU expresses the respect due to national constitutional values. It also indicates how best to prevent any real conflict with them, in particular by anchoring the constitutional foundations of the European Union in the constitutional principles common to the Member States. Through this provision the Member States are reassured that the law of the European Union will not threaten the fundamental values of their constitutions. At the same time, however, they have transferred to the Court of Justice the task of protecting those values within the scope of Community law. In that connection, the Conseil d'État is correct in assuming that the fundamental values of its constitution and those of the Community legal order are identical. It must be pointed out, however, that that structural congruence can be guaranteed only organically and only at the Community level, through the mechanisms provided for by the Treaty. It is that organic identity which is referred to in Article 6 TEU and which ensures that national constitutions are not undermined, even though they can no longer be used as points of reference for the purpose of reviewing the lawfulness of Community acts. If they could, in so far as the content of the national constitutions and the instruments for protecting them vary considerably, the application of Community acts could be the subject of derogations in one Member State but not in another. Such an outcome would be contrary to the principles set out in Article 6 TEU and, in particular, to the understanding of the Community as a community based on the rule of law. In other words, the effect of being able to rely on national constitutions to require the selective and discriminatory application of Community provisions in the territory of the Union would, paradoxically, be to distort the conformity of the Community legal order with the constitutional traditions common to the Member States. That is why, in *Internationale Handelsgesellschaft*, the Court held that 'the validity of a Community measure or its effect within a Member State cannot be affected by allegations that it runs counter to either fundamental rights as formulated by the constitution of that State or the principles of a national constitutional structure'. The primacy of Community law is therefore indeed a primordial requirement of the legal order of a community based on the rule of law.

17. Article 6 TEU merely makes explicit what was already inherent in that primordial requirement, namely that an examination of the compatibility of Community acts with the constitutional values and principles of the Member States may be carried out only by way of Community law itself and is confined, essentially, to the fundamental values which form part of their common constitutional traditions. Community law having thus incorporated the constitutional values of the Member States, national constitutions must adjust their claims to supremacy in order to comply with the primordial requirement of the primacy of Community law within its field of application. This does not mean that the national courts have no role to play in the interpretation to be given to the general principles and fundamental rights of the Community. On the contrary, it is inherent in the very nature of the constitutional values of the Union as constitutional values common to the Member States that they must be refined and developed by the Court in a process of ongoing dialogue with the national courts, in particular those responsible for determining the authentic interpretation of the national constitutions. The appropriate instrument of that dialogue is the reference for a preliminary ruling and it is in that context that the question raised here must be understood.

It is questionable whether national Constitutional Courts would accept all of this reasoning. The EU has, to be sure, drawn on national constitutional values when framing its own. The CJEU will engage in a dialogue with national courts as to the more particular meaning to be ascribed to such values, although the extent thereof can be questioned.[136] Whether this 'squares the circle' and provides the requisite justification for the 'primordial requirement' of supremacy of EU law over all national law, including the national constitution, is more debatable.

There can be real differences in the interpretation of the general values that are common to the EU and the Member States. It is indeed differences about the particular conception of such values, the way in which rights are balanced, and the weight accorded to them that divides legal systems, and differences of view within those systems. Given that this is so, the 'structural congruence' and 'organic identity' to which Maduro refers may be less readily attainable, or entail greater national constitutional sacrifice, than is evident in the extract. If the national court is content with the CJEU's interpretation of the relevant constitutional values, all well and good. If it is not and the difference of view is serious it may not be willing to sacrifice those values and the interpretation thereof embedded in its national constitution, as attested to by the fact that national constitutional courts continue to conceptualize EU law as lower in the normative hierarchy than the national constitution.

(B) NATIONAL IDENTITY

The Lisbon Treaty recognized national identity as set out in Article 4(2) TEU, which provides that the 'Union shall respect the equality of Member States before the Treaties as well as their national identities, inherent in their fundamental structures, political and constitutional, inclusive of regional and local self-government'. There is a sophisticated academic literature exploring Article 4(2), including its implications for the supremacy of EU law.[137] There is also a linkage, in principle at least, between recognition of national identity and the constitutional pluralism considered above, in that the former has been said to foster the latter.

A von Bogdandy and S Schill, Overcoming Absolute Primacy: Respect for National Identity under the Lisbon Treaty[138]

By focusing national identity on the fundamental political and constitutional structures of Member States, Article 4(2) TEU, we argue, provides a perspective for overcoming the idea of absolute primacy of EU law and the underlying assumption of a hierarchical model for understanding the relationship between EU law and domestic constitutional law, because this provision endorses a pluralistic vision of the relationship between EU law and domestic constitutional law. Article 4(2) TEU should be seen as integrating the thrust of the jurisprudence of numerous domestic constitutional courts on the relationship between EU law and national constitutional law. The revised identity clause in Article 4(2) TEU not only demands the respect for national constitutional identity, but can be understood as permitting domestic constitutional courts to invoke, under certain limited circumstances, constitutional limits to

---

[136] There was, eg, little or no evidence of such dialogue as to the meaning of the particular constitutional value by the ECJ itself in the *Arcelor* case.

[137] L Besselink, 'National and Constitutional Identity Before and After Lisbon' (2010) 6 Utrecht Law Review 36; A von Bogdandy and S Schill, 'Overcoming Absolute Primacy: Respect for National Identity under the Lisbon Treaty' (2011) 48 CMLRev 1417; T Konstadinides, 'Constitutional Identity as a Shield and as a Sword: The European Legal Order within the Framework of National Constitutional Settlement' (2011) 13 CYELS 195; B Guastaferro, 'Beyond the Exceptionalism of Constitutional Conflicts: The Ordinary Functions of the Identity Clause' (2012) 31 YBEL 263; G van der Schyff, 'The Constitutional Relationship between the European Union and its Member States: The Role of National Identity in Article 4(2) TEU' (2012) 37 ELRev 563; A Arnaiz and C Llivina (eds), *National Constitutional Identity and European Integration* (Intersentia, 2013); E Cloots, *National Identity in EU Law* (Oxford University Press, 2015).

[138] (2011) 48 CMLRev 1471, 1419.

the primacy of EU law. At the same time, Article 4(2) TEU, in tandem with the principle of sincere cooperation contained in Article 4(3)TEU, embeds these constitutional limits in an institutional and procedural framework in which domestic constitutional courts and the ECJ interact closely as part of a composite system of constitutional adjudication. This aims at ensuring both respect for EU law and the constitutional identity of the Member States.

It remains to be seen how far this thread is developed or accepted by the CJEU. It took cognizance of Article 4(2) TEU in *Sayn-Wittgenstein*,[139] finding that an Austrian law on the abolition of the nobility was an expression of national identity, which constituted a proportionate restriction on free movement that justified the refusal to recognize all elements of a surname that was lawful in another Member State. In other cases however the CJEU concluded that the restriction based on national identity was disproportionate.[140] The CJEU has moreover rejected arguments based on Article 4(2) TEU, where it concluded that the argument was legally misconceived as a challenge to the EU measure in the instant case.[141]

Von Bogdandy and Schill recognize that national identity does not enjoy absolute protection under EU law, but has to be balanced against the principle of uniform application of EU law, a task to be undertaken by the CJEU and national constitutional courts as parts of a system of composite constitutional adjudication.[142] The result may nonetheless be controversial, as exemplified by *Melloni*.[143] The CJEU denied that Article 53 of the EU Charter authorized a Member State to apply the standard of protection of fundamental rights guaranteed by its constitution when it was higher than that in the Charter. This would, said the CJEU, 'undermine the principle of the primacy of EU law inasmuch as it would allow a Member State to disapply EU legal rules which are fully in compliance with the Charter where they infringe the fundamental rights guaranteed by that State's constitution'.[144] National conceptions of fundamental rights could be applied when a Member State implemented EU law, provided that the level of protection in the Charter, as interpreted by the CJEU, and the primacy, unity, and effectiveness of EU law were not thereby compromised. The CJEU reiterated its settled view that the primacy of EU law applied against all national law, including its constitutional law.[145] Article 4(2) TEU was not raised directly in *Melloni*, but it is difficult to imagine that the result would have been any different if it had been pleaded.

6 CONCLUSIONS

i. The supremacy of EU law still clearly retains its 'bi-dimensional' character, despite the monist view of supremacy asserted by the ECJ in *Simmenthal* and *Internationale Handelsgesellschaft*.

ii. While there are exceptions, most notably in the Netherlands,[146] most Member State courts continue to locate the authority of EU law in the national legal order within the national constitution, and not in the jurisprudence of the Court of Justice or in the sovereignty of the EU.

---

[139] Case C–208/09 *Ilonka Sayn-Wittgenstein v Landeshauptmann von Wien* EU:C:2010:80.

[140] See, eg, Case C–202/11 *Anton Las v PSA Antwerp NV* EU:C:2013:239.

[141] See, eg, Cases C–58–59/13 *Torresi v Consiglio dell'Ordine degli Avvocati di Macerata* EU:C:2014:2088; Case C–151/12 *Commission v Spain* EU:C:2013:690, [37]; Case C–393/10 *O'Brien v Ministry of Justice* EU:C:2012:110, [49].

[142] (2011) 48 CMLRev 1471, 1420.

[143] Case C–399/11 *Stefano Melloni v Ministerio Fiscal* EU:C:2013:107.

[144] Ibid [58].

[145] Ibid [59].

[146] M Claes and B de Witte, 'Report on the Netherlands' in Slaughter *et al* (n 43) ch 6; B de Witte, 'Do Not Mention the Word: Sovereignty in Two Europhile Countries' in Walker (n 30); L Besselink, 'Curing a "Childhood Sickness"? On Direct Effect, Internal Effect, Primacy and Derogation from Civil Rights' (1996) 3 MJ 165.

iii. Further, many higher national courts have asserted the ultimate, albeit residual, role of national courts in ensuring that the proper boundaries of EU competence are respected and in protecting rights which are fundamental within the national legal order.[147]

iv. Thus far, while the residual control of national courts has been firmly asserted as a matter of constitutional theory, it has rarely materialized in practice. Nonetheless, it remains as a clear counterpoint to the CJEU's assertion of the autonomy of EU law, and it may influence the CJEU in showing greater sensitivity to national constitutional concerns.[148] The long-term influence of the identity clause in Article 4(2) TEU remains to be seen.

7 FURTHER READING

(a) Books

ALTER, K, *Establishing the Supremacy of European Law: The Making of an International Rule of Law in Europe* (Oxford University Press, 2001)

CLAES, M, *The National Courts' Mandate in the European Constitution* (Hart, 2006)

CLOOTS, E, *National Identity in EU Law* (Oxford University Press, 2015)

JAKLIC, K, *Constitutional Pluralism in the EU* (Oxford University Press, 2014)

MacCORMICK, N, *Questioning Sovereignty* (Oxford University Press, 1999)

SLAUGHTER, A-M, STONE SWEET, A, AND WEILER, JHH (eds), *The European Court of Justice and National Courts: Doctrine and Jurisprudence* (Hart, 1998)

WALKER, N (ed), *Sovereignty in Transition* (Hart, 2003)

(b) Articles

CHARPY, C, 'The Status of (Secondary) Community Law in the French Legal Order: The Recent Case-Law of the *Conseil Constitutionnel* and the *Conseil d'Etat*' (2007) 3 EuConst 436

CRAIG, P, 'Britain in the European Union' in J Jowell and D Oliver (eds), *The Changing Constitution* (Oxford University Press, 8th edn, 2015) ch 4

——— 'The ECJ and *Ultra Vires* Action: A Conceptual Analysis' (2011) 48 CMLRev 395

DE WITTE, B, 'Direct Effect, Primacy and the Nature of the Legal Order' in P Craig and G de Búrca (eds), *The Evolution of EU Law* (Oxford University Press, 2nd edn, 2011) ch 12

DOUGAN, M, 'When Worlds Collide! Competing Visions of the Relationship between Direct Effect and Supremacy' (2007) 44 CMLRev 931

HALBERSTAM, D, AND MÖLLERS, C, 'The German Constitutional Court says "Ja zu Deutschland!"' (2009) 10 German LJ 1241

LENAERTS, K, AND CORTHAUT, T, 'Of Birds and Hedges: The Role of Primacy in Invoking Norms of EU Law' (2006) 31 ELRev 287

---

[147] See also the decision of the Danish Supreme Court in *Carlsen v Prime Minister*, 6 Apr 1998 [1999] 3 CMLR 854; K Høegh, 'The Danish *Maastricht* Judgment' (1999) 24 ELRev 80, and the decision of the Irish Supreme Court in *Crotty v An Taoiseach* [1987] IR 713.

[148] See, eg, de Witte, 'Community Law and National Constitutional Values' (n 95), and the notion of 'contrapunctual law' in Maduro (n 30).

MADURO, M, 'Contrapunctual Law: Europe's Constitutional Pluralism in Action' in N Walker (ed), *Sovereignty in Transition* (Hart, 2003) ch 21

MEHDI, R, 'French Supreme Courts and European Union Law: Between Historical Compromise and Accepted Loyalty' (2011) 48 CMLRev 439

PAYANDEH, M, 'Constitutional Review of EU Law after *Honeywell*: Contextualizing the Relationship between the German Constitutional Court and the EU Court of Justice' (2011) 48 CMLRev 9

SADURSKI, W, '"Solange Chapter 3": Constitutional Courts in Central Europe—Democracy—European Union', EUI Working Papers, Law No 2006/40

THYM, D, 'In the Name of Sovereign Statehood: A Critical Introduction to the *Lisbon* Judgment of the German Constitutional Court' (2009) 46 CMLRev 1795

VON BOGDANDY, A, 'Pluralism, Direct Effect, and the Ultimate Say: On the Relationship between International and Domestic Constitutional Law' (2008) 6 I-CON 397

—— AND SCHILL, S, 'Overcoming Absolute Primacy: Respect for National Identity under the Lisbon Treaty' (2011) 48 CMLRev 1417

VOßKUHLE, A, 'Multilevel Cooperation of the European Constitutional Courts: *Der Europäische Verfassungsgerichtsverbund*' (2010) 6 EuConst 175

WALKER, N, 'The Idea of Constitutional Pluralism' (2002) 65 MLR 317

WEILER, JHH, 'The Community System: The Dual Character of Supranationalism' (1981) 1 YBEL 267

EU INTERNATIONAL RELATIONS LAW

1 CENTRAL ISSUES

i. A core objective of the EU over the past two decades has been to bring about greater consistency and coherence in its external relations in order to strengthen the EU as a global actor and highlight its international role and identity.

ii. In pursuit of this objective, the Lisbon Treaty introduced several changes into the law on EU external relations. (a) Article 47 TEU formalized the EU's growing practice of entering international agreements by declaring that the EU has legal personality. (b) The three-pillar structure of the EU was formally dissolved, integrating the former Third Pillar (PJCC) into the same framework as all other EU policies, although leaving the Common Foreign and Security Policy (CFSP) separate and distinct, governed by the TEU rather than the TFEU. (c) The office of High Representative of the Union for Foreign Affairs and Security Policy was created. (d) An EU diplomatic corps called the EU External Action Service (EEAS) was created, integrating civil servants and diplomats from the Commission, Council, and Member States. (e) The scope of the EU's exclusive common commercial (external trade) policy (CCP) was widened. (f) EU international action is now based on a common set of values, principles, and objectives. (g) The Treaty codified parts of the CJEU's complex case law on implied external powers.

iii. In the years since the Lisbon Treaty, the effects of several of these changes have begun to appear. The continuation of a distinct institutional and lawmaking regime for the CFSP and the widened scope of the CCP have each given rise to inter-institutional 'legal basis' litigation in this field. Similarly, the provisions of the Treaty codifying the Court's case law on implied exclusive external relations have been tested through litigation. Finally, the EEAS has come into being and its functioning has been subject to appraisal and critique.

iv. The law governing the EU's external competence originated in a complicated body of case law developed over many years by the CJEU. While the express Treaty-based external powers of the former Community were few, the Court early on gave a wide interpretation of the Community's implied powers, sowing the seeds for what became known as the principle of parallelism of internal and external powers.

v. The two important questions dominating this legal doctrine have been: (a) whether a given external power exists and (b) whether it is exclusive to the EU (formerly EC) or shared with the Member States. In the early decades the CJEU consistently answered the first question very broadly, although for some years after *Opinion 1/94* on the World Trade Organization (WTO), the Court interpreted many external EU powers as being shared with the Member States, and gave a less expansive reading to the scope of the EU's CCP. However, more recent rulings suggest the Lisbon Treaty's expansion of the CCP and codification of the Court's earlier case law have emboldened once more the Court to give less cautious readings on the exclusive external powers of the EU, and to affirm its early (*ERTA*) case law.

vi.   The existence of many shared competences has given rise to so-called 'mixed agreements', involving the participation of both the EU and the Member States in the negotiation, conclusion, and implementation of agreements. While this has problematic consequences in terms of efficiency and visibility for international partners, it has been praised as an important source of practical cooperation between the EU and the Member States.

vii.   Unlike the rest of EU law and policy, the CFSP remains governed by a separate set of rules and principles, and is largely excluded from judicial review. However, given the overlap in subject matter between the CFSP and other domains of EU external competence, difficult legal issues have arisen and been litigated before the CJEU. These include the appropriate legal basis for action, the proper delimitation of the scope of each field of action, the involvement of the EP, and the organization of cooperation across fields.

viii. The expansion of the EU's programme of country-based and anti-terrorist sanctions over the years has led to a very significant amount of litigation before the EU General Court and the CJEU challenging the basis for these sanctions, in particular since the seminal *Kadi I* case in 2009.

ix.   The CJEU overall has played an active role in EU international relations law, especially in determining the existence, scope, and nature of EU competences over the years. It has treated international agreements (including mixed agreements) as acts of the EU subject to its jurisdiction. It has ruled that international agreements are a binding and integral part of the EU legal order, and that they may, in principle, have direct effect. However, it has consistently ruled that provisions of the WTO agreements may not be invoked before EU Courts, and it has more recently extended similar reasoning to other categories of international agreement, thereby frequently shielding EU measures from challenges based on international treaties. It has also continued to emphasize the autonomy of the EU legal order when engaging with international institutions, and most recently rejected the proposed accession of the EU to the ECHR for autonomy-related reasons.

2 INTRODUCTION: THE EU AS AN INTERNATIONAL ACTOR AND THE GENERAL PRINCIPLES OF EU EXTERNAL ACTION

(A) THE EU AS AN INTERNATIONAL ACTOR

The European Union has sought, over the last two decades in particular, to shape a role for itself as a significant global actor. While it enjoys substantially more influence in some fields (trade) than others (defence), the EU has developed a substantial network of relations through which it acts to influence international affairs. The EU, despite its recent economic crisis, remains the world's largest trading power and a major donor of development aid and humanitarian assistance. It has been described as many different kinds of power, including a civilian,[1] normative,[2] structural,[3] and market power.[4]

---

[1] F Duchêne, 'Europe's Role in a World Peace' in R Mayne (ed), *Europe Tomorrow: Sixteen Europeans Look Ahead* (Fontana, 1972).

[2] I Manners, 'Normative Power Europe: A Contradiction in Terms?' (2002) 40 JCMS 235.

[3] S Keukeleire and J MacNaughtan, *The Foreign Policy of the European Union* (Palgrave Macmillan, 2008).

[4] C Damro, 'Market Power Europe' (2012) 19 JEPP 682.

These terms reflect the fact that the means the EU deploys are primarily economic, diplomatic, structural, and political rather than strongly coercive in or military in nature. The EU relies primarily on its 'soft power' in the international arena.[5] The Lisbon Treaty did not alter the character of the EU in this respect, although it strengthened the institutional basis for the development of a Common Security and Defence Policy (CSDP).[6]

The EU plays many different roles at the same time. In positive terms it can be described as flexible and multifaceted; in negative terms as somewhat fractured and contradictory. Cremona has identified at least five different roles played by the EU as a global actor: (i) a laboratory and model for other regions; (ii) a market player defending and promoting its own economic interests; (iii) a rule-generator and exporter of norms, operating through a network of agreements with other states and regions; (iv) a force for stabilization, within the EU and beyond; and (v) a magnet and neighbour using the incentive of membership.[7]

(B) THE CONSTITUTIONAL FRAMEWORK AND GENERAL PRINCIPLES OF EU EXTERNAL ACTION

The constitutional structure of EU international relations law prior to the Lisbon Treaty was complex and fragmented, with limited guidance given by EU Treaty provisions. The Lisbon Treaty however introduced a range of provisions designed to define and underscore the role of the EU as a global actor and to strengthen the coherence of its international relations system.[8] Article 3(5) TEU highlights the role of values in EU international relations by declaring that:

> In its relations with the wider world, the Union shall uphold and promote its values and interests and contribute to the protection of its citizens. It shall contribute to peace, security, the sustainable development of the Earth, solidarity and mutual respect among peoples, free and fair trade, eradication of poverty and the protection of human rights, in particular the rights of the child, as well as to the strict observance and the development of international law, including respect for the principles of the United Nations Charter.

Article 205 TFEU, which forms a kind of 'chapeau' to the part of the Treaty (Part V TFEU) dealing with EU external relations other than CFSP, declares that:

> The Union's action on the international scene, pursuant to this Part, shall be guided by the principles, pursue the objectives and be conducted in accordance with the general provisions laid down in Chapter 1 of Title V of the Treaty on European Union.

Chapter 1 of Title V TEU begins with Article 21, which for the first time gathers together, summarizes, and articulates the core objectives of all EU external policies, including the CFSP. As can be seen below, these provisions are intended to contribute to the establishment of an integrated framework and to articulate—alongside the values set out in Article 3(5) TEU—a common, overarching set of principles and objectives for EU international relations:

---

[5] J Nye, *Soft Power: The Means to Success in World Politics* (Public Affairs, 2004).

[6] Art 42 TEU.

[7] M Cremona, 'The Union as a Global Actor: Roles, Models and Identity' (2004) 41 CMLRev 553.

[8] M Cremona, 'Coherence through Law: What Difference Will the Treaty of Lisbon Make?' (2008) 3 Hamburg Review of Social Sciences 11; P Van Elsuwege, 'EU External Action after the Collapse of the Pillar Structure: In Search of a New Balance Between Delimitation and Consistency' (2010) 47 CMLRev 987.

Article 21 TEU

1. The Union's action on the international scene shall be guided by the principles which have inspired its own creation, development and enlargement, and which it seeks to advance in the wider world: democracy, the rule of law, the universality and indivisibility of human rights and fundamental freedoms, respect for human dignity, the principles of equality and solidarity, and respect for the principles of the United Nations Charter and international law.

The Union shall seek to develop relations and build partnerships with third countries, and international, regional or global organisations which share the principles referred to in the first subparagraph. It shall promote multilateral solutions to common problems, in particular in the framework of the United Nations.

2. The Union shall define and pursue common policies and actions, and shall work for a high degree of cooperation in all fields of international relations, in order to:

(a) safeguard its values, fundamental interests, security, independence and integrity;

(b) consolidate and support democracy, the rule of law, human rights and the principles of international law;

(c) preserve peace, prevent conflicts and strengthen international security, in accordance with the purposes and principles of the United Nations Charter, with the principles of the Helsinki Final Act and with the aims of the Charter of Paris, including those relating to external borders;

(d) foster the sustainable economic, social and environmental development of developing countries, with the primary aim of eradicating poverty;

(e) encourage the integration of all countries into the world economy, including through the progressive abolition of restrictions on international trade;

(f) help develop international measures to preserve and improve the quality of the environment and the sustainable management of global natural resources, in order to ensure sustainable development;

(g) assist populations, countries and regions confronting natural or man-made disasters; and

(h) promote an international system based on stronger multilateral cooperation and good global governance.

3. The Union shall respect the principles and pursue the objectives set out in paragraphs 1 and 2 in the development and implementation of the different areas of the Union's external action covered by this Title and by Part Five of the Treaty on the Functioning of the European Union, and of the external aspects of its other policies.

The Union shall ensure consistency between the different areas of its external action and between these and its other policies. The Council and the Commission, assisted by the High Representative of the Union for Foreign Affairs and Security Policy, shall ensure that consistency and shall cooperate to that effect

(c) THE POST-LISBON INSTITUTIONS OF EU INTERNATIONAL ACTION

Following the statement of the principles and goals of EU foreign policy in Article 21 TEU, Article 22 describes the role of some of the key institutional actors of EU external relations, in particular the European Council and the High Representative for Foreign Affairs and Security Policy:

1. On the basis of the principles and objectives set out in Article 21, the European Council shall identify the strategic interests and objectives of the Union.

Decisions of the European Council on the strategic interests and objectives of the Union shall relate to the common foreign and security policy and to other areas of the external action of the Union. Such decisions may concern the relations of the Union with a specific country or region or may be thematic in approach. They shall define their duration, and the means to be made available by the Union and the Member States.

The European Council shall act unanimously on a recommendation from the Council, adopted by the latter under the arrangements laid down for each area. Decisions of the European Council shall be implemented in accordance with the procedures provided for in the Treaties.

2. The High Representative of the Union for Foreign Affairs and Security Policy for the area of common foreign and security policy, and the Commission for other areas of external action, may submit joint proposals to the Council.

The Lisbon Treaty strengthened and highlighted the role of the European Council in international relations, conferring upon it an express mandate to develop the EU's overall foreign policy strategy and the power to adopt binding decisions as well as non-binding frameworks and strategies across the whole field of external relations. The role of the 'semi-permanent' President of the European Council is described in Chapter 2, Section 4(b).

The two important institutional players which were introduced by the Lisbon Treaty in the field of external relations are the High Representative for Foreign Affairs and Security Policy and the EEAS. The office and role of the High Representative are set out and described in Chapter 2, Section 5. As we have seen, the role is complicated by the fact that the holder is simultaneously a member (Vice-President) of the European Commission and Chair of the Foreign Affairs Council, thus serving two rather different masters. The first High Representative, appointed in 2010, was Baroness Catherine Ashton. Reaction to the method of appointment, the role, and the performance of the first High Representative was rather critical, with some of the blame for the EU's perceived underperformance in foreign policy being placed, perhaps somewhat unfairly, on the holder of this new position. The second High Representative, Federica Mogherini, who had brief prior experience as Italian Foreign Minister, was appointed in 2014, and even before she took up the post, the appointment and its process had again attracted criticism. The position itself is undoubtedly a complex and difficult one since, apart from its double or triple-hatted nature, the holder lacks real political power and cannot realistically seek to define or lead the EU's foreign policy. Instead, the High Representative has sought to build consensus amongst states with very different foreign policy positions on many issues, and to manage conflict. Despite its challenges, the institutional potential of the position of High Representative has nonetheless been favourably compared with that of the President of the European Council, given that: (i) the High Representative's position is not limited in time; (ii) the High Representative is given a more independent field of activity in conducting the CFSP and CSDP under Article 18(2) TEU, and explicit powers of initiative such as those in Article 22(2) TEU above; and (iii) the High Representative has the EEAS at her disposal.[9]

The EEAS was formally established in 2010.[10] The description of its function in Article 27(3) TEU is minimal, specifying only that it is to assist the High Representative in fulfilling his or her mandate, and that it shall work 'in cooperation with' the diplomatic services of Member States.[11] The aim, however,

---

[9] C Tomuschat, 'Calling Europe by Phone', Guest Editorial (2010) 47 CMLRev 3.

[10] Council Dec 2010/427/EU of 26 July 2010 [2010] OJ L201/30. For details of the EEAS see http://eeas.europa.eu/background/index_en.htm. See B Van Vooren, 'A Legal-Institutional Perspective on the European External Action Service' (2012) 48 CMLRev 475.

[11] For discussion of the background papers and policy proposals for the establishment and functioning of the EEAS in the years leading up to the Lisbon Treaty see S Vanhoonacker and N Reslow, 'The European External Action Service: Living Forwards by Understanding Backwards' (2010) 15 EFAR 1.

is for the EU diplomatic service to become an important component of EU foreign policy over time, even if its establishment was accompanied by institutional wrangling over its composition, and in particular over the balance between national diplomats (which, it was decided, should number 1/3) and EU civil servants, and by traditional debates over supranational versus intergovernmental influences on the trajectory of the EU. Early appraisals of the first few years of the EEAS—including the report by High Representative Catherine Ashton in 2013[12]—have been modest, suggesting that it remains unclear what exactly the role of the EEAS is, and whether the functioning of 'EU Delegations' around the world is any different from that of the Commission delegations which preceded them. The need for better coordination with the Commission, and the need to develop a common working culture within the EEAS have been identified as areas for improvement.[13] On the positive side, observers have pointed out that it took hundreds of years for national diplomatic services to evolve, and that the EEAS at least creates a structure in which officials from national diplomatic services and from the EU institutions can work together, each learning from and reinforcing the experience and knowledge of the other.

3 EXTERNAL CAPACITY AND EU COMPETENCE

(A) INTERNATIONAL LEGAL PERSONALITY

According to Article 47 TEU, the Union 'shall have legal personality'.[14] We saw in Chapter 9 that the counterpart of this provision in the former EC Treaty (Article 181 EC) was central to the Court of Justice's argument for the autonomy and supremacy of the Community legal system in the 1960s.[15] Article 47 TEU is extremely brief, but Article 335 TFEU elaborates somewhat:

> In each of the Member States, the Union shall enjoy the most extensive legal capacity accorded to legal persons under their laws; it may, in particular, acquire or dispose of movable and immovable property and may be a party to legal proceedings. To this end, the Union shall be represented by the Commission. However, the Union shall be represented by each of the institutions, by virtue of their administrative autonomy, in matters relating to their respective operation.

Notably there is no mention of *international* personality in either of these provisions, unlike the provisions of the former Coal and Steel Treaty and the Euratom Treaty, each of which made express reference to international legal capacity.[16] This makes it all the more striking that the Court in the

---

[12] For the review by the High Representative of the EEAS in 2013, see http://eeas.europa.eu/library/publications/2013/3/2013_eeas_review_en.pdf. For commentary on this review, see 'The 2013 Review of the European External Action Service: A Missed Opportunity? Editorial Comments' (2013) 50 CMLRev 1211, and S Duke, 'Reflections on the EEAS Review' (2014) 19 EFAR 23.

[13] For some external appraisals, see *The New EU Foreign Policy Architecture: Reviewing the First Two Years of the EEAS* (Centre for European Policy Studies, 2013), *The European External Action Service and National Diplomacies* (European Policy Center Issue Paper No 23, 2013), *Review of the European External Action Service: A Commentary on the Report* (Overseas Development Institute, 2013).

[14] This provision ended the decade-long debate over whether the European Union, as opposed to the European Community, enjoyed international legal personality.

[15] Case 6/64 *Costa v ENEL* [1964] ECR 585.

[16] Art 6(2) ECSC Treaty had provided 'In international relations, the Community shall enjoy the legal capacity it requires to perform its functions and attain its objectives'. The Euratom Treaty provides in Art 101(1) that 'The Community may, within the limits of its powers and jurisdiction, enter into obligations by concluding agreements or contracts with a third State, an international organization or a national of a third State'.

early *ERTA* case nonetheless interpreted what was then Article 281 EC as granting the Community international legal personality.[17] The Court in *ERTA* extrapolated from the statement of legal personality to conclude that the then Community's external capacity covers the 'whole extent of the field of the objectives' defined in the first part of the Treaty. However, it distinguished the broad notion of capacity from actual legal authority or competence to enter into an international agreement in a given circumstance. Capacity means that there is the potential for the EU to act, whereas legal authority must be found in the specific conferral of power in another provision of the Treaty.[18]

Under international law, as an organization with international legal personality the EU enjoys the right to be represented and to receive the representatives of third states and organizations, the right to conclude treaties, the right to submit claims or to act before an international court or judge, the right to become party to international conventions, and the right to enjoy immunities. It is also subject to legal obligations and responsibility under international law.

(B) THE NEED FOR A LEGAL BASIS AND THE LIMITS OF EXTERNAL EU COMPETENCE

Being founded on the principle of conferred powers, the EU may act only when there is a legal basis for action provided in the Treaties.[19] The choice of legal basis determines the procedures by which secondary measures are adopted, and the participation of the EU institutions in decision-making.[20] In *Opinion 2/00*, concerning the then Community's signature of the Cartagena Protocol to the Convention on Biological Diversity, the CJEU ruled that the use of an incorrect legal basis was liable to invalidate the EU act concluding the agreement, thereby vitiating the EU's consent to be bound and creating complications both for the EU and at international level.[21] Referring to its case law on the 'objective' choice of legal basis, which specifies that where a measure has more than one purpose and where one purpose is incidental and the other predominant, it should be based on a single legal basis rather than two, the Court added however that where the objectives were inseparably linked, more than one legal basis could be used.[22]

Nevertheless, where an ancillary legal basis has procedural features which are incompatible with the main legal basis, the ancillary basis should be omitted. In the *Conditional Access Services* case, the main legal basis used by the Council to conclude the European Convention on the protection of legal services based on conditional access was Article 207(4) TFEU on the CCP (an exclusive EU competence, involving limited parliamentary involvement), while the ancillary legal basis was Article 114 TFEU on internal market harmonization (which required more extensive parliamentary involvement).[23] The CJEU annulled the decision since Article 207(4) provided a sufficient and appropriate legal basis for the agreement.[24] Similarly the Court dismissed an action by the EP claiming that a decision imposing sanctions on those connected with the Taliban and Al-Qaeda should have been adopted under Article 75 TFEU (which governs economic sanctions

---

[17] Case 22/70 *Commission v Council (AETR/ERTA)* [1971] ECR 263.

[18] The relevance of this distinction can be seen in Declaration 24 which was annexed to the EU Treaties by the Lisbon Treaty and which states that 'the fact that the European Union has a legal personality will not in any way authorise the Union to legislate or to act beyond the competences conferred upon it by the Member States in the Treaties'.

[19] Ch 3.

[20] On external relations and legal basis see P Koutrakos, 'Legal Basis and Delimitation of Competence' in M Cremona and B de Witte (eds), *EU Foreign Relations Law—Constitutional Fundamentals* (Hart, 2008) 171.

[21] *Opinion 2/00 on the Cartegena Protocol* [2001] ECR I–9713.

[22] Ibid [23].

[23] Case C–137/12 *Commission v Council (European Convention on Protection of Legal Services Based on Conditional Access)* EU:C:2013:675.

[24] Ibid.

against non-state entities within the framework of internal market powers), ruling that the procedures under Article 75 were incompatible with those under Article 215 TFEU (which governs sanctions adopted following a decision taken under the CFSP), and that Article 215 was the primary and substantively appropriate legal basis for the measure.[25] And in a number of cases concerning the social security provisions of various EU association agreements, the CJEU ruled that Article 48 TFEU on freedom of movement rather than Article 79 TFEU on immigration policy was the appropriate legal basis. In *United Kingdom v Council (EU–Switzerland Social Security Coordination)* the Court rejected the UK's argument that the Council should have based its decision concerning the replacement of an Annex to the EU–Switzerland Free Movement Agreement on Article 79 TFEU concerning immigration policy (under which the UK can choose to opt out from measures under Protocol 21), rather than on Article 48 TFEU concerning free movement of persons. Part of the reason given by the Court for this ruling was that Switzerland had been effectively equated with a Member State for the purposes of applying EU social security coordination rules.[26]

The ECJ has even declared invalid an EU legislative act which established a position to be taken on an international agreement, on the ground that it did not clearly refer, either explicitly or implicitly, to a specific legal basis for the measure.[27] However, in order to protect third parties and to comply with the Vienna Convention on the Law of Treaties, the Court has ruled that such agreements are nonetheless to be binding on the EU.[28] Assuming that it has competence under another provision of the Treaty to conclude the agreement, the EU is required to act again, this time using the correct legal basis.[29] Further, where the Council has added a number of additional legal bases which are inappropriate and superfluous, the Court will annul the decision *to the extent that* it includes those additional bases, but uphold it insofar as it is founded on an appropriate and sufficient Treaty basis.[30]

The issue of what to do when the EU (or, at the time, the EC) lacks competence altogether arose in the *Passenger Name Records* (PNR) case in which the Parliament challenged the Council's conclusion of an agreement with the United States on the processing and transfer of PNR data, and a Decision of the Commission determining that the US Bureau of Customs and Border Protection provided an adequate level of protection of PNR data under the Data Protection Directive.[31] The PNR Agreement at the time had been concluded on the basis of an internal market provision, Article 95 EC (now Article 114 TFEU), which was also the legal basis for the Data Protection Directive. The Court ruled that although the data would initially be collected by airlines in the course of a normal commercial activity the further use of the data would be for the purpose of safeguarding public security in combating terrorism, and since this use was expressly excluded from the scope of the Directive, the two

---

[25] Case C–130/10 *Parliament v Council (Al-Qaeda Sanctions)* EU:C:2012:472.

[26] Case C–656/11 *UK v Council (EU–Swiss Social Security Coordination)* EU:C:2014:97. A similar ruling was given by the Court on the extension of the rules under the EEA Agreement in Case 431/11 *UK v Council (EEA Agreement)* EU:C:2013:589. Compare the AG's Opinion in Case C–81/13 *UK v Council (EU–Turkey Association Agreement)* EU:C:2014:2114 suggesting that both Art 79 and Art 48 TFEU were inappropriate in this context, but that Art 217 would suffice as legal basis.

[27] Case C–370/07 *Commission v Council (CITES Convention)* [2009] ECR I–8917.

[28] Case C–327/91 *France v Commission (Re EC–US Anti-Trust Agreement)* [1994] ECR I–3641, [25].

[29] Case C–94/03 *Commission v Council (Rotterdam Convention)* [2006] ECR I–1.

[30] See Case C–377/12 *Commission v Council (EU Framework Agreement on Partnership and Cooperation with the Philippines)* EU:C:2014:1903, in which the Court found that Arts 207 and 209 TFEU concerning the CCP and development cooperation policy respectively formed an appropriate legal basis for the adoption of a decision concluding the EU–Philippines Agreement, and annulled the decision to the extent that it added a range of other legal bases including Arts 79(3), 91, 100, and 191(4) TFEU on transport, environment, etc.

[31] Dir 95/46/EC [1995] OJ L281/31.

acts fell outside the scope of European Community competence at the time.[32] As a result, the EU was required to denounce the agreement within a specific period of time, and in accordance with the relevant rules of international law.[33] As we shall see below, the most recent EU–US PNR Agreement, concluded in 2012, is based on Articles 82 and 87 TFEU concerning police and judicial cooperation in criminal matters.

(c) EXPRESS AND IMPLIED COMPETENCE

The two original Treaty provisions which, since 1957, have expressly provided for the conduct of EU international relations are Article 207 TFEU (ex Article 133 EC) on the CCP and Article 217 TFEU (ex Article 310 EC) on the conclusion of agreements 'establishing an association' with the EU. The original Communities were also empowered to maintain relations with other international organizations, in particular the Council of Europe, the OECD, and the organs and specialized agencies of the UN. Further express treaty-making powers were added in 1987 by the SEA in the fields of research, technological development, and the environment, and subsequently by the Maastricht Treaty in 1993 in the fields of development cooperation and economic and monetary policy.

However, from the early 1960s on, the Court apparently took the view that the Community would not be able to develop a sufficiently strong international presence on the basis of its express powers alone. This seems to be the logic underpinning its ruling in *ERTA*, where the Court sought to avoid the prospect of uncoordinated external representation of the Community by its Member States in fields in which they had adopted common internal policies. As we will see below, the Lisbon Treaty seeks to codify the long-standing case law of the CJEU on implied powers. Finally, while the discussion below refers to the competence of the EC, this case law is applicable to the EU now that the EC no longer exists as a separate entity but has been absorbed into the EU.

Case 22/70 Commission v Council (AETR/ERTA)
[1971] ECR 263

[Note Lisbon Treaty renumbering: Art 113 EC is now 207 TFEU, Art 114 EC has been repealed, Art 238 EC is now Art 217 TFEU, and Arts 74 and 75 EC are now Arts 90 and 91 TFEU]

Five out of six Member States of the EEC and a number of other European states which were not EEC members signed a 1962 European Agreement concerning the work of crews of vehicles engaged in international road transport (AETR), but it did not enter into force and negotiations were resumed in 1967. Similar work undertaken at EC level had resulted in the adoption of Council Regulation 543/69 standardizing driving and rest periods of drivers. A year after the adoption of this Regulation, the Member States together concluded the negotiations on a new European Agreement (AETR) with other states. The Commission brought an action for the annulment before the Court of Justice of all legal consequences of the Council proceedings which had led to the Member States adopting the AETR. The Court considered whether the Community had competence to sign the AETR Agreement.

---

[32] The Dir also does not apply to processing operations concerning public security, defence, state security, and the activities of the state in areas of criminal law.

[33] Cases C–317 and 318/04 *European Parliament v Council (PNR)* [2006] ECR I–4721.

THE ECJ

16. Such authority arises not only from an express conferment by the Treaty—as is the case with Articles 113 and 114 for tariff and trade agreements and with Article 238 for association agreements—but may equally flow from other provisions of the Treaty and from measures adopted, within the framework of those provisions, by the Community institutions.

...

23. According to Article 74, the objectives of the Treaty in matters of transport are to be pursued within the framework of a common policy.

24. With this in view, Article 75 (1) directs the Council to lay down common rules and, in addition, 'any other appropriate provisions'.

25. By the terms of subparagraph (a) of the same provision, those common rules are applicable 'to international transport to or from the territory of a Member State or passing across the territory of one or more Member States'.

26. This provision is equally concerned with transport from or to third countries, as regards that part of the journey which takes place on Community territory.

27. It thus assumes that the powers of the Community extend to relationships arising from international law, and hence involve the need in the sphere in question for agreements with the third countries concerned.

28. Although it is true that Articles 74 and 75 do not expressly confer on the Community authority to enter into international agreements, nevertheless the bringing into force, on 25 March 1969, of Regulation No 543/69 of the Council on the harmonization of certain social legislation relating to road transport (OJ L 77, p. 49) necessarily vested in the Community power to enter into any agreements with third countries relating to the subject-matter governed by that regulation...

30. Since the subject-matter of the AETR falls within the scope of Regulation No 543/69, the Community has been empowered to negotiate and conclude the agreement in question since the entry into force of the said regulation.

According to the Court, the fact that by the time the contested decision was taken by the Council on the international road transport agreement, a common policy on social aspects of road transport had already been adopted by the EC, making it possible to imply external powers on the part of the Community. Conversely, the Court ruled that until the internal rules had been adopted those powers remained vested in the Member States.[34]

In the subsequent *Kramer* case concerning fisheries conservation, the Court reiterated this dimension of the *ERTA* judgment. It ruled that external legal authority 'arises not only from an express conferment by the Treaty, but may equally flow *implicitly* from other provisions of the Treaty, from the Act of Accession and from measures adopted, within the framework of those provisions, by the Community institutions'.[35] In the context of *Kramer*, the Court ruled that given the EC's internal power to take any measure for the conservation of the biological resources of the sea, the only way to ensure an effective and equitable conservation was by a system also including non-member countries. Thus, 'it follows from the very duties and powers which Community law has established and assigned to the institutions of the Community on the internal level that the Community has authority to enter into international commitments for the conservation of the resources of the sea'.[36]

---

[34] Case 22/70 *ERTA* [1971] ECR 263, [82].
[35] Cases 3, 4 and 6/76 *Kramer* [1976] ECR 1279, [19]–[20].
[36] Ibid [30].

The subtle difference between the *Kramer* and the *ERTA* rulings is that the *ERTA* principle is based on the actual *adoption* of internal rules. In *Kramer*, however, the Court ruled that the Treaty provisions which explicitly conferred competence on the internal level in this field must, on the grounds of equity and effectiveness, be read as implicitly conferring treaty-making power. This has been described as a 'principle of complementarity' since the external competence of the Community is viewed as necessary to complement its internal competence.[37]

Even after *Kramer*, however, doubts persisted whether international competence existed in the absence of *either* express conferral of external powers *or* the actual adoption of common internal rules. *Opinion 1/76* was the final ambitious step in this expansive articulation of the implied powers doctrine.

Opinion 1/76 (European Laying-up Fund for Inland Waterway Vessels)
[1977] ECR 741

The subject of this Opinion was the legal competence of the EC to sign an international agreement establishing a European laying-up fund for inland waterway vessels. The aim of the proposed scheme was to eliminate disturbances arising from surplus carrying capacity for goods by inland waterway in the Rhine and Moselle basins. This objective could not have been fully achieved by the establishment of common EC transport rules under Article 71 EC, because of the traditional participation of Swiss vessels; therefore Switzerland was brought into the scheme by means of the international agreement. The Court elaborated further on the scope of the implied treaty-making powers of the Community.

THE ECJ

3. [A]uthority to enter into international commitments may not only arise from an express attribution by the Treaty, but equally may flow implicitly from its provisions. The Court has concluded *inter alia* that whenever Community law has created for the institutions of the Community powers within its internal system for the purpose of attaining a specific objective, the Community has authority to enter into the international commitments necessary for the attainment of that objective even in the absence of an express provision in that connection.

4. This is particularly so in all cases in which internal power has already been used in order to adopt measures which come within the attainment of common policies, it is, however, not limited to that eventuality. Although the internal Community measures are only adopted when the international agreement is concluded and made enforceable, as is envisaged in the present case by the proposal for a regulation to be submitted to the Council by the Commission, the power to bind the Community vis-à-vis third countries nevertheless flows by implication from the provisions of the Treaty creating the internal power and in so far as the participation of the Community in the international agreement is, as here, necessary for the attainment of one of the objectives of the Community.

This case has been described as endorsing the principle of parallelism, according to which EU external competence mirrors its internal competence.[38] The upshot is that the EU has competence to enter into an international agreement in a given domain, provided that: (i) the Treaty confers *internal*

---

[37] A Dashwood, 'The Classic Authorities Revisited' in A Dashwood and C Hillion (eds), *The General Law of EC External Relations* (Sweet & Maxwell, 2000).

[38] T Tridimas and P Eeckhout, 'The External Competence of the Community and the Case-Law of the Court of Justice: Principle versus Pragmatism' (1994) 14 YBEL 143.

competence on the EU in that domain for the purpose of attaining a specific objective; and (ii) participation of the EU in the agreement in question is *necessary* for the attainment of that objective. In other words, for the EU to have external competence in a certain field it is not necessary for it to have *exercised* its internal competence in that field. The very existence of such internal competence, together with the necessity to participate in an external agreement in order to achieve the objective for which internal competence was granted, is sufficient.

(D) EXCLUSIVE EU COMPETENCE

Once the existence of EU competence is established, the next important question is whether it is exclusive competence, or whether it is shared with the Member States. Exclusivity means that the competence has been completely transferred by Member States to the EU and that there is no concurrent Member State competence.[39]

The CJEU established the exclusive nature of EU competence as regards the CCP in *Opinion 1/75* as far as the conclusion of international agreements is concerned,[40] and similarly in *Donckerwolcke* as far as the adoption of autonomous or unilateral legislative acts is concerned.[41]

The Court based its assertion of exclusivity on two main factors. The first was the threat which concurrent powers would pose to mutual trust within the EU and thus to the coherence and effectiveness of the defence of EU commercial interests *vis-à-vis* non-member countries. The second was the risk of distortion of competition within a single market brought about by different commercial and trading policies, given the varying degrees of economic strength of the different Member States. Its reasoning here has been described as 'a characteristic mixture of pragmatism and (again) the link between external and internal trade policy'.[42] The same reasoning was echoed in the Court's judgment on the establishment of the common fisheries policy.[43] It follows from these cases that if a particular issue is deemed to fall within the scope of either the CCP or fisheries policy, the EU's competence will be exclusive.

In the early case law the very *existence* of implied powers was closely tied by the Court to their *exclusive* nature. At the same time, the Court developed the doctrine of pre-emption, according to which once the EU had exercised its powers either internally or externally, and the field was thus 'occupied', the Member States were precluded from acting.[44] The rationale was that unilateral action by Member States would be incompatible with the unity of the market and the uniform application of EU law. Although the Court later moved away from the strength of this early position on exclusivity, the Lisbon Treaty subsequently expanded the scope of external exclusive EU competence, even while also adding new non-exclusive and non-pre-emptive external competences.

It is necessary, in order to understand this complicated area of EU law, to trace the journey taken by the Court over time.

---

[39] D O'Keeffe, 'Exclusive, Concurrent and Shared Competence' in Dashwood and Hillion (n 37).

[40] *Opinion 1/75 (Understanding on a Local Cost Standard)* [1975] ECR 1355.

[41] Case 41/76 *Donckerwolcke* [1976] ECR 1921.

[42] M Cremona, 'External Relations and External Competence of the European Union. The Emergence of an Integrated Policy' in P Craig and G de Búrca (eds), *The Evolution of EU Law* (Oxford University Press, 2nd edn, 2011) ch 9.

[43] Case 804/79 *Commission v UK (Sea Fisheries Conservation)* [1981] ECR 1045, [17]–[18]. This case in fact established exclusivity with regard to Art 102 of the Act of Accession.

[44] Cremona (n 42), who argues that this is a stage during which the 'classic' form of pre-emption theory was developed by the Court. External competence was seen as *either* exclusive or concurrent. Concurrent competence at that stage meant 'distinct, discrete compartments for the EC and the Member States' and did not include the concept of complementary action by both in the same field, unless the Member States were acting under a form of authorization from the EU.

Case 22/70 **Commission v Council (AETR/ERTA)**
[1971] ECR 263

[Note Lisbon Treaty renumbering: Art 5 EC is now Art 4(3) TEU]

THE ECJ

17. In particular, each time the Community, with a view to implementing a common policy envisaged by the Treaty, adopts provisions laying down common rules, whatever form these may take, the Member States no longer have the right, acting individually or even collectively, to undertake obligations with third countries which affect those rules.

18. As and when such common rules come into being, the Community alone is in a position to assume and carry out contractual obligations towards third countries affecting the whole sphere of application of the Community legal system.

19. With regard to the implementation of the provisions of the Treaty the system of internal Community measures may not therefore be separated from that of external relations.

20. Under Article 3(e), the adoption of a common policy in the sphere of transport is specially mentioned amongst the objectives of the Community.

21. Under Article 5, the Member States are required on the one hand to take all appropriate measures to ensure fulfilment of the obligations arising out of the Treaty or resulting from action taken by the institutions and, on the other hand, to abstain from any measure which might jeopardize the attainment of the objectives of the Treaty.

22. If these two provisions are read in conjunction, it follows that to the extent to which Community rules are promulgated for the attainment of the objectives of the Treaty, the Member States cannot, outside the framework of the Community institutions, assume obligations which might affect those rules or alter their scope....

...

31. These Community powers exclude the possibility of concurrent powers on the part of Member States, since any steps taken outside the framework of the Community institutions would be incompatible with the unity of the Common Market and the uniform application of Community law.

Following *ERTA*, the ECJ indicated that there were a number of other contexts in which Community competence would be exclusive.

The *first*, which is now a very limited example, is where internal powers could only be effectively exercised *at the same time* as external powers. The Court ruled in *Opinion 1/76* that exclusive external powers could arise at the moment of being exercised, even without there having been any prior exercise of internal powers, so long as internal competence could be effectively exercised only at the same time as external competence,[45] and so long as the conclusion of the international agreement was necessary in order to attain objectives of the Treaty that could not be attained by unilateral rules.[46] This rather convoluted instance has effectively been restricted to the facts of

---

[45] *Opinion 1/76 (European Laying-up Fund for Inland Waterway Vessels)* [1977] ECR 741, [4], [7]; *Opinion 1/94 (WTO Agreement: GATS and TRIPs)* [1994] ECR I–5267, [85].

[46] See, in particular, in the series of 'open skies' cases Case C–467/98 *Commission v Denmark (Open Skies)* [2002] ECR I–9519, [57]; *Opinion 1/94* (n 45) [89].

Opinion 1/76.[47] In later cases, the CJEU has reverted to the stance that the actual adoption of internal legislation is generally a prerequisite for the exclusivity of implied powers.[48]

The *second* context articulated by the Court was where the agreement falls into an area which is already largely covered by EU rules. The Court ruled in its *Opinion 2/91* on the International Labour Organization (ILO) Convention that external EU competence will be exclusive where rules have been adopted in other areas of EU law (apart from common policies such as transport policy in *ERTA*), and particularly in areas where harmonizing legislation has been adopted, even where there is no contradiction between the internal rules and the proposed international rules.[49] The Court relied in making this argument on the principle of loyal cooperation in Article 4(3) TEU which it has used extensively in other fields to promote the effectiveness of EU law.[50] However, the determination of whether a given field has been fully occupied or fully harmonized is far from clear, and requires a definition of the relevant 'field'.

The Court has continued to expand the arena in which Member States are prevented from acting even in the absence of an actual conflict. In the *Greek Maritime Monitoring* case, the Commission brought infringement proceedings against Greece for submitting a proposal on monitoring compliance with the SOLAS Convention to the International Maritime Organization (IMO), within a field of exclusive EU competence.[51] The CJEU ruled that although the proposal submitted by Greece was not itself a binding measure, it could have led to the adoption of new rules by the IMO which in turn could have affected the existing EU regulation implementing the SOLAS Convention. While the Court accepted that the EU's exclusive competence need not preclude Member States from actively participating in the IMO, it ruled that the positions adopted by states within the IMO would first have to be coordinated at EU level, and no state could individually assume obligations likely to affect existing EU rules.[52]

Two other examples of exclusive competence, relating to treatment of non-EU nationals and completely internally harmonized sectors, were referred to in the ECJ's *Opinion 1/94* on the competence of the EU to conclude the General Agreement on Trade in Services (GATS) and the Agreement on Trade-Related Intellectual Property Rights (TRIPs),[53] but these have since been widened further by the Lisbon Treaty. At the time, the Court ruled that competence to conclude the GATS was shared between the EU and the Member States.[54]

Opinion 1/94 represented the first high-profile shift by the Court away from its expansive case law on the exclusive nature of the EU's implied external competence. The line of case law from *ERTA* onwards had consistently widened the sphere of external EU competence and extended its exclusive nature, but *Opinion 1/94*, followed shortly afterwards by *Opinion 2/92*, adopted a more measured tone in relation to exclusivity.

---

[47] The case—on the laying-up fund for inland waterway vessels—allegedly involved a situation in which the achievement of the Treaty objective required the prior conclusion of an international agreement and could not be attained by adopting internal rules: *Opinion 1/94 (WTO)* (n 45) [85]. See also *Opinion 1/03 on the Lugano Convention* [2006] ECR I–1145, [115].

[48] *Opinion 1/94 (WTO)* (n 45) [88]–[89].

[49] *Opinion 2/91 on the ILO Convention* [1993] ECR I–1061, [10]–[11].

[50] *Opinion 2/91* (n 49) [10]; *Opinion 1/03 on the Lugano Convention* (n 47) [119].

[51] Case C–47/07 *Commission v Greece* [2009] ECR I–701.

[52] Ibid [27]–[29].

[53] *Opinion 1/94 on the WTO Agreements (GATS and TRIPs)* [1994] ECR I–5267.

[54] *Opinion 1/94* (n 45) [95]–[96].

Opinion 2/92 (OECD Decision on National Treatment)
[1995] ECR I–521

31. In that regard, the Court has consistently held, most recently in Opinion 1/94..., that the Community's exclusive external competence does not automatically flow from its power to lay down rules at internal level. As the Court pointed out in the AETR judgment..., the Member States whether acting individually or collectively, only lose their right to enter into obligations with non-member countries as and when there are common rules which could be affected by such obligations.

The Court went on to rule that the internal measures adopted by the EU had not covered all the fields of activity to which the OECD decision was related, and that the EU enjoyed exclusive competence only in areas where internal common rules had been adopted.

In *Opinion 1/94* and, more recently in its *Open Skies* rulings,[55] the Court purported to summarize the various situations listed above in which the EU was held to have exclusive external competence. Apart from the lack of clarity in their scope and the debate they have generated, these situations are, according to the Court in *Opinion 1/03* on the Lugano Convention, 'only examples, formulated in the light of the particular contexts with which the Court was concerned'.[56] The CJEU then went on to set out more general guidelines on how to determine whether EU competence in a given instance is exclusive.

Opinion 1/03 (Lugano Convention)
[2006] ECR I–1145

THE ECJ

124. It should be noted in that context that the Community enjoys only conferred powers and that, accordingly, any competence, especially where it is exclusive and not expressly conferred by the Treaty, must have its basis in conclusions drawn from a specific analysis of the relationship between the agreement envisaged and the Community law in force and from which it is clear that the conclusion of such an agreement is capable of affecting the Community rules.

125. In certain cases, analysis and comparison of the areas covered both by the Community rules and by the agreement envisaged suffice to rule out any effect on the former (see Opinion 1/94...; Opinion 2/92..., and Opinion 2/00...).

126. However, it is not necessary for the areas covered by the international agreement and the Community legislation to coincide fully. Where the test of 'an area which is already covered to a large extent by Community rules' (Opinion 2/91...) is to be applied, the assessment must be based not only on the scope of the rules in question but also on their nature and content. It is also necessary to take into account not only the current state of Community law in the area in question but also its future development, insofar as that is foreseeable at the time of that analysis (see, to that effect, Opinion 2/91...).

127. That that assessment must include not only the extent of the area covered but also the nature and content of the Community rules is also clear from the Court's case-law referred to

---

55 Case C–466/98 *Commission v United Kingdom* [2002] ECR I–9427; Case C–467/98 (n 46); Case C–468/98 *Commission v Sweden* [2002] ECR I–9575; Case C–469/98 *Commission v Finland* [2002] ECR I–9627; Case C–471/98 *Commission v Belgium* [2002] ECR I–9681; Case C–472/98 *Commission v Luxembourg* [2002] ECR I–9741; Case C–475/98 *Commission v Austria* [2002] ECR I–9797.

56 *Opinion 1/03* (n 47) [121].

in paragraph 123 of the present opinion, stating that the fact that both the Community rules and the international agreement lay down minimum standards may justify the conclusion that the Community rules are not affected, even if the Community rules and the provisions of the agreement cover the same area.

...

133. It follows from all the foregoing that a comprehensive and detailed analysis must be carried out to determine whether the Community has the competence to conclude an international agreement and whether that competence is exclusive. In doing so, account must be taken not only of the area covered by the Community rules and by the provisions of the agreement envisaged, insofar as the latter are known, but also of the nature and content of those rules and those provisions, to ensure that the agreement is not capable of undermining the uniform and consistent application of the Community rules and the proper functioning of the system which they establish.

Thus the Court here provided a relatively nuanced and context-specific set of guidelines as to the circumstances in which EU competence would be exclusive on the ground that the internal rules adopted by the EU might be adversely affected by an international agreement.

With the apparent intention of codifying the rules on exclusive competences developed in the case law above, the Lisbon Treaty introduced Article 3 TFEU.[57]

1. The Union shall have exclusive competence in the following areas: (a) customs union; (b) the establishing of the competition rules necessary for the functioning of the internal market; (c) monetary policy for the Member States whose currency is the euro; (d) the conservation of marine biological resources under the common fisheries policy; (e) common commercial policy.

2. The Union shall also have exclusive competence for the conclusion of an international agreement when its conclusion is provided for in a legislative act of the Union or is necessary to enable the Union to exercise its internal competence, or in so far as its conclusion may affect common rules or alter their scope.

The Court has so far given a robust reading to the scope of the EU's exclusive competence under Article 3(2) in a number of cases.

In *Commission v Council*, the Commission sought the annulment of a Council decision adopting negotiation directives for a Council of Europe Convention on the Rights of Broadcasting Organizations.[58] The Commission objected to the Council's assumption that the participation of Member States would also be required, and argued that EU competence was exclusive since the international commitments envisaged fell largely within the scope of the common rules already established by the EU. The Court agreed and rejected the argument of the Council and several Member States that the EU's exclusive competence should be more narrowly interpreted since the enactment of the Lisbon Treaty:

---

[57] For criticism of the formulation of this attempt to codify the case law on exclusive external competence, which appeared in the same form in the predecessor Constitutional Treaty, see B de Witte, 'The Constitutional Law of External Relations' in I Pernice and M Poiares Maduro (eds), *A Constitution for the European Union: First Comments on the 2003 Draft of the European Convention* (Nomos, 2004).

[58] Case C–114/12 *Commission v Council (Convention on the Rights of Broadcasting Organizations)* EU:C:2014:2151.

Case C–114/12 Commission v Council (Convention on the Rights of Broadcasting Organizations)
EU:C:2014:2151

64. The first plea is based, in essence, on an infringement of Article 3(2) TFEU.

65. As a preliminary point, it should be noted that, among the various cases of exclusive external competence of the EU envisaged by that provision, only that which is referred to in the last clause of the provision, namely the situation in which the conclusion of an international agreement 'may affect common rules or alter their scope', is relevant in the present case.

66. In that regard, it must be stated that the words used in that last clause correspond to those by which the Court, in paragraph 22 of the judgment in *ERTA* (EU:C:1971:32), defined the nature of the international commitments which Member States cannot enter into outside the framework of the EU institutions, where common EU rules have been promulgated for the attainment of the objectives of the Treaty.

67. Those words must therefore be interpreted in the light of the Court's explanation with regard to them in the judgment in *ERTA* (EU:C:1971:32) and in the case-law developed as from that judgment.

68. According to the Court's case-law, there is a risk that common EU rules might be adversely affected by international commitments, or that the scope of those rules might be altered, which is such as to justify an exclusive external competence of the European Union, where those commitments fall within the scope of those rules (see, to that effect, the judgments in *ERTA*, EU:C:1971:32, paragraph 30; and in *Commission* v *Denmark*, EU:C:2002:625, paragraph 82).

69. A finding that there is such a risk does not presuppose that the areas covered by the international commitments and those covered by the EU rules coincide fully (see, to that effect, Opinion 1/03, EU:C:2006:81, paragraph 126).

70. As the Court has consistently held, the scope of common EU rules may be affected or altered by such commitments also where those commitments fall within an area which is already largely covered by such rules (Opinion 2/91, EU:C:1993:106, paragraph 25; judgment in *Commission* v *Denmark*, EU:C:2002:625, paragraph 82; and Opinion 1/03, EU:C:2006:81, paragraphs 120 and 126).

71. In addition, Member States may not enter into such commitments outside the framework of the EU institutions, even if there is no possible contradiction between those commitments and the common EU rules (see, to that effect, Opinion 2/91, EU:C:1993:106, paragraphs 25 and 26; and the judgment in *Commission* v *Denmark*, EU:C:2002:625, paragraph 82).

72. The above analysis is not affected by the argument of the Council, the Kingdom of the Netherlands and the United Kingdom that, since the entry into force of the Lisbon Treaty, the exclusive external competence of the European Union is viewed in a more restrictive manner.

. . .

74. That said, it is important to note that, since the European Union has only conferred powers, any competence, especially where it is exclusive, must have its basis in conclusions drawn from a specific analysis of the relationship between the envisaged international agreement and the EU law in force, from which it is clear that such an agreement is capable of affecting the common EU rules or of altering their scope (see, to that effect, Opinion 1/03, EU:C:2006:81, paragraph 124).

The Court noted that the Council Decision gave no detail about the content of negotiations for the proposed Convention, and did not identify elements which it considered would fall specifically within either EU or Member State competence. However, having looked at documents of the Council of Europe on the proposed Convention, and at existing EU internal market legislation, the Court concluded that the content of the negotiations fell clearly within an area largely covered by common

EU rules. Hence the Council's Decision was adopted in breach of Article 3(2) TFEU on exclusive external competence.

In its *Opinion 1/13* on the Hague Convention on Child Abduction, the Court continued this robust approach to the EU's exclusive external competence after the Lisbon Treaty. The question for the Court, as in the *Broadcasting Rights Convention* case, was whether there was a risk that a decision to accept the accession of a third state to the Hague Convention would 'affect common [EU] rules or alter their scope' within the meaning of Article 3(2), and hence should fall within exclusive EU and not Member State competence.[59] The Court repeated that it was not necessary, in order for such a risk to exist, that the international agreement should coincide fully with EU common rules, nor that the provisions of the international agreement should conflict with the EU rules. In this case, the fact that an existing EU Regulation (No 2201/2003) largely covered the main Hague Convention procedures, and the fact that the scope and effectiveness of the Regulation could be affected if Member States could individually make separate declarations accepting third-state accessions to the Convention, meant that the EU had exclusive competence.

Another post-Lisbon alteration to the rules on exclusive EU competence was Article 207 TFEU, which broadened the scope of the exclusive competence of the EU in the field of the CCP, expanding it to cover all aspects of trade in services except transport, the commercial aspects of intellectual property, as well as foreign direct investment. In *Daiichi Sanko* the Court was called on to say whether, following the enactment of Article 207 TFEU, Article 27 of the TRIPs Agreement now falls within the competence of the Member States or the EU.[60] Rejecting the more cautious approach of the Advocate General, the Court ruled that Article 27 of TRIPs—and indeed all of the TRIPs Agreement—now falls within the exclusive competence of the EU under the CCP, and noted that the authors of Article 207(1) TFEU 'could not have been unaware that the terms thus used in that provision correspond almost literally to the very title of the TRIPS Agreement'.[61]

(E) SHARED COMPETENCE

Despite the extensive and complex case law on the scope of exclusive competence, and despite the expansion of the scope of the important and extensive CCP by the Lisbon Treaty, a significant part of the EU's external competence remains joint or shared in nature. We saw above that the main fields of EU external and internal competence, apart from CFSP and economic and employment policy coordination, are now categorized and listed in Article 2 TFEU to include: (i) exclusive; (ii) shared; and (iii) supplementary and supporting competences. Article 4 TFEU elaborates on the category of 'shared competence' by indicating that the EU shall share competence with the Member States in fields which are not covered by the exclusive competences mentioned in Article 3, including those in Article 3(2), and it goes on to list a range of fields including the environment, transport, and the area of freedom, security, and justice.

In an analysis fifteen years ago which remains useful post-Lisbon, MacLeod, Hendry, and Hyett identified five situations of joint or shared external competence.[62] The first is where this is expressly determined by the Treaty Article conferring power on the EU. Examples include agreements within the framework of the EMU, development cooperation, and technical cooperation, where Member States have explicitly retained their competence to negotiate in international bodies and to conclude

---

[59] *Opinion 1/13 on the Hague Convention on Child Abduction* EU:C:2014:2292.

[60] Case C–414/11 *Daiichi Sankyo Co Ltd v DEMO Anonimos Viomikhaniki* EU:C:2013:520.

[61] Ibid [55].

[62] I MacLeod, I Hendry, and S Hyett, *The External Relations of the European Communities* (Clarendon Press, 1996) 63–64.

international agreements.[63] The CJEU has ruled that this means that Member States may enter commitments *vis-à-vis* non-Member States either collectively or individually, or jointly with the EU.[64] They may exercise their retained powers either 'collectively in the Council or outside it', and where they act collectively they may adopt acts 'not in their capacity as members of the Council, but as representatives of their governments, and thus collectively exercising the powers of the Member States'.[65]

The second situation is where the EU has a power to adopt common internal rules which has not yet been exercised. An example was the case of the common fisheries policy during the transitional period, or the field of patent law.[66]

The third is where an agreement covers both matters falling within EU competence and matters within Member State competence. The Court ruled to this effect in *Opinion 1/78 (Natural Rubber Agreement)* when it decided that although the field covered by the agreement in question was within the exclusive (CCP) competence of the EU, the financing of this area remained within the competence of the Member States.[67] Since this was a central element of the agreement and the participation of the Member States was required, competence was shared.[68]

The fourth situation is where EU competence derives from the existence of internal 'minimum rules' where Member States are entitled to maintain higher standards which will not 'affect' the scope of the internal EU rules, as we saw in the case of *Opinion 2/91* on ILO Convention No 170.

The fifth situation includes certain fields where EU and Member State competence can coexist without either displacing the other. An example can be found in the field of intellectual property, when the nature of the rights created at the EU level, such as the EU trade mark, is such that they do not necessarily replace national-level intellectual property rights.

Some categories of shared competence can become exclusive through pre-emption by the adoption of EU action, in accordance with the *Lugano* Opinion guidelines and with Article 3(2) TFEU, while other categories of shared competence, such as development cooperation and humanitarian aid, as well as research, technological development, and space, are explicitly deemed by the Treaty to be non-pre-emptive.[69] Similarly, while environmental policy competence is listed as being shared in Article 4(2) TFEU, Article 191(4) indicates that EU external competence in this field is not to be pre-emptive, and shall be 'without prejudice to Member States' competence to negotiate in international bodies and to conclude international agreements'. There are also other areas of EU policy competence, such as culture, education, vocational training, public health, sport, and others, which cannot become exclusive or pre-emptive through exercise in the external domain, because they are expressly categorized as 'supplementary and coordinating competence' in Article 6 TFEU, as well in the specific Treaty provision which outlines the details of the EU's powers in that field.

In other words, the category of shared external competence is a broad and differentiated one, and the exact type of shared competence in any given field may be affected by the case law of the CJEU on the subject, by the Treaty's classification of the competence, and by the terms of the legal basis in the Treaty which outlines the detail of the EU's competence in that field. However, in any case in which competence is shared between the Member States and the EU, each is under a duty to cooperate closely due to the requirement of unity in the international representation of the EU.[70]

---

[63] Arts 219(4), 191(4), and 211 TFEU.

[64] See, eg, Case C–316/91 *European Parliament v Council (EDF)* [1994] ECR I–625, on the Lomé Convention.

[65] Cases C–181 and 248/91 *European Parliament v Council and Commission (Bangladesh)* [1993] ECR I–3685, [12].

[66] Case C–431/05 *Merck Genéricos—Produtos Farmacêuticos Lda v Merck & Co* [2007] ECR I–7001, [39]–[47].

[67] *Opinion 1/78 (International Agreement on Natural Rubber)* [1979] ECR 2871.

[68] See for similar reasoning in relation to the GATS, prior to the adoption of the Lisbon Treaty, *Opinion 1/08 on the Schedules of Specific Commitments annexed to the GATS Agreement* [2009] ECR I–11129.

[69] Art 4(3) and (4), governing humanitarian aid, cooperation, and research and development, provides that 'the exercise of that competence shall not result in Member States being prevented from exercising theirs'.

[70] *Opinion 1/94* (n 45) [108]; *Opinion 1/08* (n 68) [136]; see also the discussion of mixed agreements below.

(F) SUMMARY

i. The constitutional core of EU international relations law, which was shaped over several decades by the CJEU, centres now primarily on the questions of: (a) competence: whether the EU has external competence, either by express grant under the Treaty or as implied from the existence of internal rules or competence; and (b) exclusivity: whether the external competence of the EU in a given field is exclusively held by the EU or is shared with the Member States.

ii. It is a complex and detailed case law which does not enhance the clarity and comprehensibility of the EU's international role. Nonetheless, the basic foundations of the doctrine laid down in *ERTA* in 1971 remain in place, as is evident from *Opinion 1/03* on the Lugano Convention and the post-Lisbon Treaty case law.

iii. The Lisbon Treaty aimed to codify the prior case law by describing the various categories of EU competences—exclusive, shared, supplementary, coordinating, and others—and listing the fields they cover. In post-Lisbon cases thus far, the Court has continued to interpret the scope of the EU's exclusive external competence—including the provision on implied exclusive competence in Article 3(2) TFEU—in a robust and expansive way.

iv. The exact scope and nature of external EU competence cannot be determined from the classification in Articles 3–6 alone, but depends also on the precise terms of Treaty provisions which confer power in a given field, and on the prior legislative activity of the EU in particular fields.

4 FOUR FIELDS OF EU EXTERNAL ACTION

We turn now to a survey of some of the most important external EU policies. Four broad areas of EU external action will briefly be outlined, followed by the special field of the CFSP. The four areas are: (i) the CCP; (ii) association, partnership, cooperation, and neighbourhood policy; (iii) development, technical cooperation, and humanitarian aid; and (iv) the external dimension of other internal policies.

EU international action is now governed by Part V TFEU, entitled 'The Union's External Action'. This Part begins with a 'chapeau clause' in Article 205 TFEU on the principles guiding EU international action,[71] and ends with a solidarity clause in Article 222 governing relations between Member States and the EU in the event of a terrorist attack or natural or man-made disaster. The CFSP is not included within Part V TFEU, but is dealt with separately within the TEU.[72]

The list of fields of action in Part V TFEU does not reflect the full breadth or scope of EU external action. We have seen above how external EU power has been implied, according to a kind of 'parallelism' principle, from internal EU powers and rules. The case law is loosely codified in Article 216(1) TFEU:[73]

The Union may conclude an agreement with one or more third countries or international organisations where the Treaties so provide or where the conclusion of an agreement is necessary in order to achieve, within the framework of the Union's policies, one of the objectives referred to in the Treaties, or is provided for in a legally binding Union act or is likely to affect common rules or alter their scope.

---

[71] See above at Section 2(b).

[72] See Title V, Ch 2, Arts 23–46 TEU.

[73] For criticism of the codification as establishing a potentially wider basis for implied external powers than before see Cremona (n 42).

In other words, every policy of the EU has a potential external dimension, including fields such as social policy, environmental policy, and the area of freedom, security, and justice. Notably, Article 216 TFEU reproduces the textual formula of Article 3(2) TFEU on EU exclusive implied powers, although Article 216 refers only to the existence of external EU competence rather than to its exclusive nature.

(A) THE COMMON COMMERCIAL POLICY (CCP)

The Lisbon Treaty brought significant changes to the CCP. For many years the scope of the CCP was determined primarily by Court rulings, but in recent decades it has been shaped by an interchange between CJEU rulings and Treaty amendments.

The Lisbon Treaty made five important changes. *First*, the distinctions previously drawn between various types of trade in services disappeared, and the CCP now covers trade in services as a whole, meaning a broader scope for the EU's exclusive external competence in this field. *Secondly*, the same is true for the commercial aspects of intellectual property and foreign direct investment.[74] *Thirdly*, transport policy, which is a competence shared between the EU and the Member States under Article 4(2)(g) TFEU, remains outside the scope of the CCP.[75] *Fourthly*, despite the fact that trade in services is now an exclusive EU competence, Article 207(4)(3) TFEU provides exceptionally for unanimity in the field of trade in cultural, audiovisual, social, educational, and health services. *Fifthly*, the EP is finally accorded a full legislative role in the CCP.

Article 206 TFEU sets out the aims of the CCP:

By establishing a customs union . . . the Union shall contribute, in the common interest, to the harmonious development of world trade, the progressive abolition of restrictions on international trade and on foreign direct investment, and the lowering of customs and other barriers.

Article 207(1) TFEU describes the measures to be adopted within the framework of the CCP:

The common commercial policy shall be based on uniform principles, particularly with regard to changes in tariff rates, the conclusion of tariff and trade agreements related to trade in goods and services, and the commercial aspects of intellectual property, foreign direct investment, the achievement of uniformity in measures of liberalisation, export policy and measures to protect trade such as those to be taken in the event of dumping or subsidies.

Article 207(1) TFEU states:

The common commercial policy shall be conducted in the context of the principles and objectives of the Union's external action.

---

[74] The transition from shared to exclusive EU competence in the sphere of foreign direct investment created doubts about the large network of existing bilateral investment treaties (BITs) between Member States and third countries. Case law contributed to the complexity, when the CJEU ruled in Case C–205/06 *Commission v Austria* [2009] ECR I–1301; Case C–249/06 *Commission v Sweden* [2009] I–1335; Case C–118/07 *Commission v Finland* [2009] ECR I–889 that Member States had infringed Art 351 TFEU (ex Art 307 EC) by not taking the necessary steps to ensure the compliance of their BITs with EU law. Following these cases, a Regulation establishing transitional arrangements for bilateral investment agreements between Member States and third countries was adopted to address some of the issues: Regulation (EU) No 1219/2012 [2012] OJ L351/40.

[75] Art 207(5) TFEU.

The institutional framework of the CCP, which was previously quite distinctive, was aligned broadly by the Lisbon Treaty with other EU decision-making processes. The ordinary legislative procedure now applies to the adoption of measures which define the framework for implementing the CCP.[76] The EP eventually became a co-legislator within the CCP, and its consent is now required for the conclusion of an international agreement of the CCP.[77]

The CCP covers both unilateral EU measures, for example anti-dumping instruments, and conventional measures negotiated with third countries and international organizations, such as trade agreements. The Court in 1973 ruled that the proper functioning of the customs union justified a wide interpretation of the powers conferred by the Treaty in this field.[78] The link between the CCP and the original common market project arguably explains many developments in this field, including the Commission's and the Court's determination to establish and expand exclusive EU competence in the early years.[79]

In *Opinion 1/75*, the Court defined the scope of the CCP broadly by reference to the external trade policy of a state,[80] declaring that it was a field which developed progressively, through a combination of internal and external measures, without any priority of one kind over the other.[81] The Court ruled that the defence of the EU's common interest, the need to prevent distortions of competition, and the principle of Member State loyalty to the EU meant that competence must be exclusive.[82] However, while the Court asserted the exclusivity of EU competence in the CCP, it left scope for the gradual implementation of the CCP, during which period Member States were not precluded from acting, provided their activities were regulated by EU law. In *Donckerwolcke* the CJEU ruled that the Member States could deviate from CCP rules, albeit only under 'specific authorization' by the EU.[83]

The Court construed the scope of the CCP dynamically and broadly in the 1970s. In *Opinion 1/78 (Natural Rubber Agreement)*, for example, the CJEU emphasized the complex objectives of commodities agreements, and ruled that the CCP should not be restricted only to the traditional aspects of external trade: 'the Treaty ... does not form a barrier to the possibility of the Community's developing a commercial policy aiming at a regulation of the world market for certain products rather than at a mere liberalization of trade'.[84] The EU was held to have exclusive competence to enter into the agreement, but the role of the Member States in financing the agreement meant that their involvement was also required. This approach towards trade agreements pursuing developmental aims was confirmed in the *General System of Preference (GSP)* judgment.[85]

The international trade policy picture however changed after 1986 with the Uruguay Round of trade negotiations. This brought trade in services, trade-related aspects of intellectual property rights, and trade-related investment measures together with the former General Agreement on Tariffs and Trade (GATT) in the agreements establishing the WTO in 1994. In its *Opinion 1/94* on the WTO Agreement, the CJEU decided that all WTO agreements on trade in goods fell within the EU's CCP.

---

[76] Art 207(2) TFEU.

[77] Art 218(6) TFEU.

[78] Case 8/73 *Hauptzollamt Bremerhaven v Massey-Ferguson GmbH* [1973] ECR 897, [4].

[79] M Cremona, 'EC External Commercial Policy after Amsterdam: Authority and Interpretation within Interconnected Legal Orders' in JHH Weiler (ed), *The EU, the WTO and the NAFTA: Towards a Common Law of International Trade* (Oxford University Press, 2000).

[80] P Koutrakos, *EU International Relations Law* (Hart, 2006) 34, to the effect that this comparison makes the EC's trade policy competence appear potentially unlimited.

[81] *Opinion 1/75 (Understanding on a Local Cost Standard)* [1975] ECR 1355.

[82] For a critique of some of these arguments see P Eeckhout, *External Relations of the European Union. Legal and Constitutional Foundations* (Oxford University Press, 2nd edn, 2011).

[83] Case 41/76 *Donckerwolcke* (n 41) [32].

[84] *Opinion 1/78* [43]–[53].

[85] Case 45/86 *Commission v Council (First GSP Case)* [1987] ECR 1493.

Trade in services were not excluded from the CCP[86] but while some aspects of trade in services fell within the exclusive competence of the EU, others fell within the competence of the states. Transport services fell outside the CCP, as did much of the TRIPs Agreement at the time.[87] The whole WTO Agreement was therefore concluded by the EC as a 'mixed agreement'.

Opinion 1/94 was an important ruling which marked a pause in the expansion of EU competence under the CCP, and in the expansive judicial approach to exclusive EU competence more generally.[88] Subsequent rulings of the Court confirmed this shift and indicated that trade measures would not necessarily always be perceived as trade or commercial policy measures if they pursued other objectives such as environmental policy.[89] Following a number of complex changes made by the Treaties of Amsterdam and Nice to widen further the scope of the CCP,[90] the Lisbon Treaty brought greater clarity and significantly expanded the exclusive external competence of the EU. There is now no distinction between various categories of trade in services: the CCP covers trade in services as a whole as well as the commercial aspects of intellectual property and foreign direct investment. Transport however remains outside the CCP[91] and is a shared competence,[92] which means that trade agreements containing significant provisions on transport will probably continue to be 'mixed' agreements.[93]

Finally, joint involvement of Member States and the EU in the making of agreements is likely to remain in certain sensitive spheres due to the Treaty provisions governing trade in cultural and audiovisual services, and in social, education, and health services which, by way of derogation from the majority voting applicable under the ordinary legislative procedure, preserve Council unanimity where the agreements being negotiated risk 'prejudicing the Union's cultural and linguistic diversity' or 'disturbing the national organization' of social, educational, and health services or prejudicing the responsibility of Member States to deliver them.[94]

Importantly, the EP finally acquired legislative power alongside the Council in the field of the CCP. It is up to the Parliament and the Council, adopting regulations in accordance with the ordinary legislative procedure, to define the framework for implementing the CCP.[95] Further, EP consent is required for the conclusion of international trade agreements.[96]

The European Parliament, as a more frequent champion of transparency, human rights, and other values in EU external trade policy, had long argued for a greater role, while the Council was wary of such an extension. [97] And Parliament has certainly been active in using its new powers under

---

[86] *Opinion 1/94 (WTO Agreement: GATS and TRIPs)* [1994] ECR I–5267, [36]–[41].

[87] These powers could become exclusive under the conditions set in Case 22/70 *ERTA* (n 17).

[88] See also *Opinion 2/92 (Third Revised Decision of the OECD on National Treatment)* [1995] ECR I–521 in which the ECJ confirmed its reasoning in *Opinion 1/94* above.

[89] *Opinion 2/00* (n 21).

[90] For an analysis of this stage of development of the CCP see M Cremona, 'A Policy of Bits and Pieces? The Common Commercial Policy After Nice' (2002) 4 CYELS 61. For litigation to clarify some of the complexities of the new changes, see *Opinion 1/08* on the division of competence between EU and Member States in the conclusion of 'horizontal' transport agreements (n 68), and Case C–13/07 *Commission v Council (Accession of Vietnam to the WTO)* EU:C:2010:327.

[91] Art 207(5) TFEU.

[92] Art 4(2)(g) TFEU.

[93] See *Opinion 1/08* (n 68) [152]–[173], distinguishing the EU's exclusive commercial policy competence from its shared transport policy competence; S Adam and N Lavranos, Note (2010) 47 CMLRev 1523, 1536–1538.

[94] Art 207(4), cl 3, (a)–(b).

[95] Art 207(2) TFEU.

[96] Art 218(6)(b) TFEU.

[97] The Council published an adverse opinion by its legal service on the revised Framework Agreement on relations between the European Parliament and the Commission for the legislative period 2009–2014 [2010] OJ L304/47, citing the provisions on international agreements as being of particular concern, http://register.consilium.europa.eu/pdf/en/10/st15/st15018.en10.pdf.

the CCP.[98] In 2012 Parliament refused its consent to the controversial Anti-Counterfeiting Trade Agreement (ACTA) due to concerns about its impact on civil liberties as well as developing country access to generic medicines, and has been active in the negotiation of several other trade agreements, including the equally controversial proposed Transatlantic Trade and Investment Partnership between the EU and the US (TTIP).

The Court was also called on to rule on the expanded scope of the CCP post-Lisbon. In *Daiichi Sanko*, the CJEU declared that intellectual property rules adopted by the EU would fall within the CCP only if they had a specific link to international trade, but ruled that the provisions of the TRIPs Agreement fall into that category.[99] Importantly, therefore, the entire TRIPs Agreement now falls within the exclusive competence of the EU as part of the CCP. The Court also reaffirmed its holding in earlier cases that an act will fall within the CCP if it 'is essentially intended to promote, facilitate or govern trade and has direct and immediate effects on trade'.[100]

In the *Conditional Access Services* case, the Commission challenged the Council's use of Article 114 TFEU (on internal market harmonization) instead of Article 207(4) TFEU (on the CCP) as the legal basis for its decision concluding a Convention on the legal protection of conditional access services.[101] The Court ruled in favour of the Commission, stating that since the aim of the Convention was to promote trade with non-Member States even if by the means of internal market harmonization, it primarily pursued an objective with a specific connection to the CCP and thus should have been based on Article 207(4).[102] These cases suggest that the Court has taken its cue from the Lisbon Treaty extension of the CCP and is returning to the expansive approach adopted in its pre-*Opinion 1/94* case law to the scope of this policy.

Together with the expansion of the CCP to include intellectual property and investment issues, the widening scope of EU trade policy and the nature of the issues now dealt with within EU trade agreements makes it likely that further litigation will soon come before the CJEU on these matters.[103]

(B) ASSOCIATION, PARTNERSHIP, COOPERATION, AND NEIGHBOURHOOD RELATIONS

Article 217 TFEU provides:

> The Union may conclude with one or more States or international organisations agreements establishing an association involving reciprocal rights and obligations, common action and special procedure.

---

[98] See the Parliament's own appraisal after four years: 'The role of the EP in shaping the EU's trade policy after the entry into force of the Treaty of Lisbon', European Parliament DG for External Policies, (2014) DG EXPO/B/PolDep/Note/2014_54.

[99] Case C–414/11 *Daiichi Sankyo Co Ltd v DEMO Anonimos Viomikhaniki* EU:C:2013:520.

[100] Ibid [41].

[101] Case C–137/12 *Commission v Council* EU:C:2013:675. For a comment on both cases, see L Ankersmit, 'The Scope of the Common Commercial Policy after Lisbon: The Daiichi Sankyo and Conditional Access Services Grand Chamber Judgments' (2014) 41 LIEI 193.

[102] Ibid [66]–[69].

[103] One example is the Commission's decision to seek an opinion from the CJEU on the compatibility of the proposed EU–Singapore Free Trade Agreement: http://europa.eu/rapid/press-release_IP-14-1235_en.htm. The controversy over the inclusion of investment arbitration provisions in the proposed TTIP is another. More generally, on the 'new' era of EU trade agreements, see the special journal issue on European Free Trade Agreements and Fundamental Rights (2014) 20 ELJ 713–869, and the collection edited by M Cremona and T Takács, *Trade Liberalization and Standardization: New Directions in the 'Low Politics' of EU Foreign Policy*, CLEER Working Paper 2013/6.

The power to conclude association agreements was, apart from the CCP, the only express external relations power of the EU until the SEA in 1987. The first association agreements were concluded with Greece and Turkey, and with the African, Caribbean, and Pacific (ACP) countries under the Yaoundé Convention, a few years after the entry into force of the EEC Treaty.[104] Many others have followed since. The association agreements concluded with the states of Central and Eastern Europe were known as 'Europe Agreements', and took account of the fact that these states were likely soon to become EU members. These agreements were extensively invoked before the Court, which ruled consistently that, like other international agreements, they form an integral part of the EU legal order and that the CJEU enjoys broad jurisdiction over their provisions.[105]

The Treaty itself provides no indication of what an association should involve apart from the skeletal provisions of Article 217 TFEU. The initial association agreements indeed included measures covering the entire subject matter of the Treaty.[106] Amongst the most important of the association agreements currently in force are the agreements with the ACP countries, most recently the Cotonou Agreement. Others include the European Economic Area (EEA) Agreement, the Stabilization and Association Agreements with some of the Western Balkans, and the Euro-Mediterranean Agreements. A politically high-profile agreement signed and ratified by the EU was the association agreement with the Ukraine in 2014, the negotiation of which in 2013 gave rise to serious conflict between the Ukraine and Russia and the eventual annexation of Crimea by Russia.

The EU also concludes agreements similar to association agreements but which provide for less intensive forms of integration or a narrower range of fields. Examples are the cooperation and partnership agreements concluded with the countries of the ex-Soviet Union, now members of the Commonwealth of Independent States (CIS), and interregional cooperation agreements with the countries of the Latin American, South-East Asian, and Arab states.

The Lisbon Treaty introduced a new legal basis for the EU to conclude specific agreements with neighbouring countries, establishing a 'special relationship' with the latter and 'aiming to establish an area of prosperity and good neighbourliness, founded on the values of the Union and characterized by close and peaceful relations based on cooperation'.[107] Article 8(1) TEU thus gave Treaty recognition to the policy introduced by the EU in 2004 and known as the European Neighbourhood Policy (ENP).[108] Neighbourhood agreements may contain 'reciprocal rights and obligations' as well as the possibility of undertaking activities jointly.[109] Considering the position of this legal basis in the Treaties, outside the title of the TFEU devoted to EU external action, neighbourhood agreements do not seem to be linked with any particular one of the categories of agreements described above.[110] Although this may

---

[104] [1963] OJ L26/296; [1964] OJ L27/3685; [1964] OJ L93/1430.

[105] Case C–63/99 *Głoszczuk* [2001] ECR I–6369; Case C–235/99 *Kondova* [2001] ECR I–6427; Case C–257/99 *Barkoci and Malik* [2001] ECR I–6557; Case C–268/99 *Jany* [2001] ECR I–8615; Case C–162/00 *Land Nordrhein-Westfalen v Pokrzeptowicz-Meyer* [2002] ECR I–1049.

[106] See for more detailed analysis S Peers, 'EC Frameworks of International Relations: Co-operation, Partnership and Association' in Dashwood and Hillion (n 37); K Lenaerts and E De Smijter, 'The European Community's Treaty Making Competence' (1996) 16 YBEL 1.

[107] Art 8(1) TEU.

[108] The ENP has been described as 'a particularly developed expression of a policy designed to meet the challenge of ensuring coherence between the three EU pillars': M Cremona and C Hillion, 'L'Union fait la force? Potential and Limitations of the European Neighbourhood Policy as an Integrated EU Foreign and Security Policy', EUI Working Paper 2006/39. See also B Van Vooren, *EU External Relations Law and the European Neighbourhood Policy: A Paradigm for Coherence* (Routledge, 2012).

[109] Art 8(2) TEU.

[110] For criticism of the non-use of Art 8(2) TEU in newer Neighbourhood agreements, see M. Comelli, 'Article 8 TEU and the Revision of the European Neighbourhood Policy' in L Serena Rossi and F Casolari (eds), *The EU After Lisbon: Amending or Coping with the Existing Treaties?* (Springer, 2014).

indicate that the EU considers neighbourhood policy as a framework for cooperation with neighbouring countries which are unlikely to become EU members,[111] the ENP to date has been sharply criticized for failing to stabilize the EU's neighbours or to bring them closer to the EU. The revisions of the ENP which the EU has already undertaken have been criticized as insufficient, and arguments for fundamentally resetting the policy have been made.

(c) DEVELOPMENT POLICY, TECHNICAL COOPERATION, AND HUMANITARIAN AID

Prior to the adoption of the Maastricht Treaty in 1993, there was no explicit EU Treaty basis for these three fields. Instead, they had been developed on the basis of other external policies including commercial policy and association, as well by using the residual powers provision in Article 352 TFEU.

We saw in *Opinion 1/78* that the Court accepted the use of trade instruments with a development dimension, although it ruled that the provision of financing by Member States would result in an agreement of the kind at issue being 'mixed'.[112] Following that case, the association and trade legal bases of the Treaty were used for many agreements concluded with developing countries. The Court in the *Bangladesh* case ruled that the EU lacked exclusive competence in the field of humanitarian aid, and that Member States were not precluded from exercising their competence collectively within the Council or outside it.[113] The *Parliament v Council (Lomé IV)* ruling established that EU competence in the field of development was not exclusive, that Member States were entitled to enter into commitments themselves, and that competence to implement the EU's financial assistance was shared between the EU and its Member States.[114]

The Maastricht Treaty subsequently inserted an independent Treaty basis for development policy, now Article 208 TFEU, and the Nice Treaty provided a legal basis for 'economic, financial and technical cooperation' with third states, now Article 212 TFEU. In both of these areas, EU policy is expressly required to contribute to the general objective of developing and consolidating democracy and the rule of law, and to that of respecting human rights and fundamental freedoms.

In *Parliament v Council (European Investment Bank Guarantee)*, the CJEU clarified the relationship between these fields.[115] The Court ruled that it cannot be inferred from the reference to 'third countries' in Article 212 TFEU that all economic, financial, and technical cooperation with developing states may be undertaken on the sole basis of this provision. Otherwise, there would be a risk of this provision being used to circumvent the specific objectives of development cooperation set out in Article 208 TFEU (ex Article 177 EC). Insofar as a measure pursues specific *development* objectives, it must therefore be based on Article 208 TFEU.

In the *EU Philippines Partnership and Cooperation Agreement* case, the Commission challenged the Council's decision to base the conclusion of the partnership and cooperation agreement on a range of Treaty provisions including those concerning transport, the environment, and readmission of third-country nationals, in addition to the main legal bases of Articles 207 and 209 TFEU, covering trade policy and development policy respectively.[116] The Court ruled that the additional legal bases— some of which entailed conflicting procedural provisions—were indeed excessive and superfluous,

[111] See D Cadier, 'Is the European Neighbourhood Policy a Substitute for Enlargement?', LSE Special Report 18 on the Crisis of Enlargement, 2014: www.lse.ac.uk/IDEAS/publications/reports/pdf/SR018/Cadier_D.pdf.

[112] *Opinion 1/78* (n 67).

[113] Cases C–181 and 248/91 (n 65) [14]–[16].

[114] Case C–316/91 *European Parliament v Council* (n 64).

[115] Case C–155/07 *European Parliament v Council* [2008] ECR I–8193.

[116] C–377/12 *Commission v Council (EU–Philippines Partnership and Cooperation Agreement)* EU:C:2014:1903.

since the provisions of the agreement concerning environment, transport, and illegal migration did not constitute objectives distinct from those of development cooperation but were integrated into it.[117]

Following the Lisbon Treaty, the joint legislative powers of the European Parliament were extended beyond the field of development cooperation to include also the field of economic, financial, and technical cooperation.

(D) EXTERNAL DIMENSIONS OF OTHER INTERNAL POLICIES

While the external dimension of many internal policies was initially developed on the basis of the implied powers doctrine and the residual power clause of Article 352, later Treaty amendments provided a range of express external powers.

One of the most important such fields of external EU action is environmental policy. This is a good example of a field in which internal and external activities are often so closely linked that EU internal competence would be limited in effect without its external counterpart.[118] As soon as an explicit environmental policy title was inserted into the EEC Treaty by the SEA, provision was also made for external competence in Article 191(4) TFEU (ex Article 174(4) EC). The Lisbon Treaty added a power for the EU to combat climate change in Article 191(1). External competence in the environmental field is shared with the Member States.[119]

Other areas of EU external policy include education,[120] vocational training,[121] culture,[122] and public health,[123] in which the EU is explicitly required to foster cooperation with third countries and international organizations. These areas are categorized by Article 6 TFEU on competences as supporting, supplementary, or coordinating competences. Other areas providing for cooperation with third countries are trans-European networks under Article 171(3) TFEU and research, technological development, and space under Article 186 TFEU.

In the area of social policy, Article 153 TFEU has been held to confer competence to conclude international agreements, even though the EU's internal legislative competence in the field is defined in rather subsidiary terms. Such external competence, as elaborated in *Opinion 2/91*[124] and now in Article 3(2) TFEU, becomes exclusive where there is EU legislation which could be affected by the provisions of the international agreement.

The operation of the single currency and of monetary union also requires international cooperation. Article 219 TFEU provides for the conclusion of international agreements on an exchange-rate system for the Euro in relation to non-EU currencies.[125]

The field of energy policy was given an express legal basis in Article 194 TFEU by the Lisbon Treaty, and although external competence is not explicitly mentioned, the EU has exercised implied external

---

[117] Ibid [59]–[60].

[118] D Thieme, 'European Community External Relations in the Field of the Environment' (2001) 10 EELR 252.

[119] Art 4(2)(e) TFEU. Art 191(4) TFEU also provides: 'within their respective spheres of competence, the Union and the Member States shall cooperate with third countries and with the competent international organisations. The arrangements for Union cooperation may be the subject of agreements between the Union and the third parties concerned.'

[120] Art 165(3) TFEU.

[121] Art 166(3) TFEU.

[122] Art 167(3) TFEU.

[123] Art 168(3) TFEU.

[124] *Opinion 2/91* (n 49).

[125] For controversy over whether the EU or the ECB (with its own separate legal personality) has external competence in this field see C Zilioli and M Selmayr, 'The External Relations of the Euro Area: Legal Aspects' (1999) 36 CMLRev 273; C Herrmann, 'Monetary Sovereignty over the Euro and External Relations of the Euro Area: Competences, Procedures and Practice' (2002) 7 EFAR 1, 23.

competence, shared between the EU and the Member States, for some time.[126] The issue of EU energy security and energy independence has been particularly salient in recent years.

With regard to policies concerning 'Border checks, asylum and immigration', which are part of Title V of Part III TFEU (the Area of Freedom, Security, and Justice (AFSJ)), there is clearly competence, on the basis of *ERTA* reasoning and Article 3(2) TFEU, to conclude agreements over the whole area.[127] While the EU had already concluded such agreements, an express external competence for the EU to conclude readmission agreements with third countries in relation to third-country nationals who do not fulfil the conditions required by one of the Member States was added by the Lisbon Treaty.[128] More generally, migration issues have been integrated into the EU's overall relations with third countries. Finally, *Opinion 1/03* established that the EU had exclusive competence to conclude the Lugano Convention on jurisdiction and the recognition and enforcement of judgments in civil and commercial matters, a subject covered by Title V of Part III of the TFEU.[129]

The former Third Pillar of the EU governing Police and Judicial Cooperation in Criminal Matters (PJCC) has been integrated into Title V of Part 3 of the TFEU on the AFSJ. [130] Even though the AFSJ legal regime maintains certain specificities in comparison with other fields of EU competence,[131] it is subject to the general rules and principles governing EU international action.[132] The objectives of this policy field include international cooperation in criminal matters, facilitating mutual recognition of judgments, police and judicial cooperation in criminal matters having a cross-border dimension, and perhaps the conclusion of international agreements in fields where common EU rules are established concerning the definition of serious cross-border criminal offences and sanctions.[133]

Even before the Lisbon Treaty, the Union had negotiated and concluded international agreements with third countries or international organizations in the field of PJCC.[134] Since Lisbon, the EU has concluded an agreement with the United States on the processing and transfer of Financial Messaging Data for the purposes of the Terrorist Finance Tracking Programme (the so-called SWIFT Agreement) using Articles 87 and 88 TFEU on police cooperation as a legal basis.[135] The European Parliament unsuccessfully called for the suspension of this agreement following revelations of unlawful surveillance by the US National Security Agency (NSA) in 2013. The EU has also been negotiating a Data Protection 'Umbrella Agreement' with the United States since 2011, and in 2012 concluded a new PNR Agreement with the United States to replace those which had been adopted in 2007 and previously 2004.[136] In 2014 the European Parliament voted to refer the proposed PNR Agreement with Canada to the Court of Justice, with a view to challenging the compatibility of its provisions with the EU Treaties.

---

[126] Art 4(2)(i) TFEU.

[127] M Cremona, J Monar, and S Poli (eds), *External Dimensions of the Area of Freedom, Security and Justice* (Peter Lang-PIE, 2011); M Cremona, 'EU External Action in the JHA Domain: A Legal Perspective', EUI Working Papers, Law 24/2008.

[128] Art 79(3) TFEU.

[129] *Opinion 1/03* (n 47).

[130] See Lisbon Treaty Protocol No 36, Arts 9 and 10 on the transitional phase.

[131] Ch 25.

[132] For a recent overview, see Jorg Monar, 'The EU's Growing External Role in the AFSJ Domain: Factors, Framework and Forms of Action' (2014) 27 Cambridge Review of International Affairs 147.

[133] Arts 82 and 83 TFEU.

[134] The EU began to exercise its contractual powers in this field in 2003 by concluding three agreements: two with the United States on extradition and mutual legal assistance respectively, and one with Iceland and Norway on the application of certain provisions of the EU Convention on Mutual Assistance in Criminal Matters of 2000.

[135] [2010] OJ L195/5.

[136] Agreement between the United States and the EU on the use and transfer of passenger name records to the US Department of Homeland Security [2012] OJ L215/5.

Finally, some of the important agencies in the field of AFSJ such as Europol and Eurojust have been vested with their own powers to conclude agreements with third countries and international organizations,[137] and the borders agency Frontex has a mandate to conclude bilateral cooperation agreements with third countries.[138]

5 THE COMMON FOREIGN AND SECURITY POLICY

The emergence of the EU's CFSP, formerly the Second Pillar, has been examined briefly in Chapter 1. Following the Lisbon Treaty, the CFSP remains separate from the other fields of EU action and is governed by a different set of institutional and procedural rules.

The key differences, reflected in the terms of Article 24(1) paragraph 2 TEU, are that: (i) the institutions which have the primary role in shaping the CFSP are the European Council and the Council; (ii) the Commission's role is secondary and the Parliament is restricted to a mainly consultative role; (iii) no 'legislative acts' can be adopted, but only the range of special CFSP instruments described below; (iv) the CFSP is to be implemented and carried out by the High Representative and by the Member States; and (v) the CJEU lacks jurisdiction over the provisions of the CFSP, except for procedural questions, the boundary-policing provision of Article 40 TEU, and in relation to challenges against individual sanctions in accordance with Article 275 TFEU.

(A) THE SCOPE OF THE CFSP

The Treaty refers to the scope of the CFSP in very wide terms, as covering 'all areas of foreign policy and all questions relating to the Union's security'.[139] Article 23 TEU articulates the requirement of consistency between CFSP action and the principles and objectives governing EU external action more broadly:

> The Union's action on the international scene [in the field of CFSP] shall be guided by the principles, shall pursue the objectives of, and be conducted in accordance with the general provisions [governing EU external action as a whole].

As we saw, the objectives listed in Article 21 TEU governing EU external action include support for democracy, the rule of law, human rights and international law, preservation of peace and security in accordance with the UN Charter, the aims of the Helsinki Final Act, and the Paris Charter. Other Treaty provisions also demonstrate the importance of the CFSP as part of the overall aims of the EU and other external policies. Article 22(1) paragraph 2 TEU declares that:

> Decisions of the European Council on the strategic interests and objectives of the Union shall relate to the common foreign and security policy and to other areas of the external action of the Union.

---

[137] Europol has concluded a wide range of bilateral operational or strategic agreements with other states and international organizations: Council Decision 2009/371/JHA of 6 April 2009 establishing the European Police Office [2009] OJ L121/37, Art 23.

[138] Frontex also concludes 'bilateral working arrangements' with a variety of states: http://frontex.europa.eu/partners/third-countries. For criticism of the ambiguity and impact of these agreements, see M Fink, 'Frontex Working Arrangements: Legitimacy and Human Rights Concerns Regarding "Technical Relationships"' (2012) 28 Merkourios 20.

[139] Art 24 TEU.

However, the distinctiveness of the CFSP is reinforced by Article 40, which governs the relationship between the CFSP and other parts of EU policy. Before the Lisbon Treaty, priority was given to what was then the Community Pillar over the CFSP,[140] but Article 40 TEU now sets the CFSP on an equal footing with all other EU policies and specifies that neither shall affect the other:

Article 40 TEU:

> The implementation of the common foreign and security policy shall not affect the application of the procedures and the extent of the powers of the institutions laid down by the Treaties for the exercise of the Union competences referred to in Articles 3 to 6 of the Treaty on the Functioning of the European Union.
> Similarly, the implementation of the policies listed in those Articles shall not affect the application of the procedures and the extent of the powers of the institutions laid down by the Treaties for the exercise of the Union competences under this Chapter.

Article 24 TEU provides that the CFSP is to include all questions relating to the security of the Union, including the progressive framing of a common defence policy, which may lead to a common defence.

The scope of the CFSP is thus potentially extremely broad,[141] and is described both in terms of its objectives and of the instruments supplied to achieve those objectives. These instruments include *general guidelines* adopted by the European Council, *decisions* adopted by the Council defining specific operational *action* by the Union where it is deemed to be required, *positions* adopted by the Council, which define the approach of the Union to a particular matter of a geographical or thematic nature, and *arrangements* for the implementation of the two latter categories of decisions.[142] Amongst the other instruments mentioned which contribute to building the CFSP are *information and consultation* on any matter of foreign and security policy of general interest and *international agreements*.

There is evidently an overlap of competence between the CFSP and other external policies of the EU, and economic matters may clearly be implicated. Yet since the differences between the procedures, the powers of the institutions, and the guarantees for individuals such as judicial oversight are so important, the borderline between the CFSP and other areas of EU powers is crucial. This was highlighted in two post-Lisbon cases concerning the EU–Mauritius Agreement on the one hand,[143] and the Al Qaeda/Taliban sanctions on the other.[144]

In the *Al-Qaeda Sanctions* case, Parliament challenged the Council's use of a CFSP Common Position under Title V TEU, in conjunction with Article 215(2) TFEU, to enact economic sanctions. Parliament argued that the measure should have been adopted instead under Article 75 TFEU, which is a legal basis devoted to economic sanctions, and located within the internal TFEU provisions concerning the AFSJ.[145] The Court rejected the argument that the imposition of the sanctions was not a

---

[140] The former Art 47 TEU had provided that 'nothing in this Treaty [the TEU] shall affect the Treaties establishing the European Communities or the subsequent Treaties and Acts modifying or supplementing them'. The Court had reinforced this priority in its case law: Case C–91/05 *Commission v Council (ECOWAS)* [2008] ECR I–3651.

[141] For an overview of activities see R Dover, 'The EU's Foreign, Security, and Defence Policies' in M Cini (ed), *European Union Politics* (Oxford University Press, 2007).

[142] Art 25 TEU.

[143] Case C–658/11 *Parliament v Council (EU–Mauritius Agreement)* EU:C:2014:2025.

[144] Case C–130/10 *Parliament v Council (Al-Qaeda Sanctions)* EU:C:2012:472.

[145] Related issues of legal basis and overlapping competences were raised in the famous *Kadi* case concerning the legality of EU anti-terrorist sanctions on individuals, but much of this has been rendered redundant by the insertion of Art 75 TFEU by the Lisbon Treaty. See Cases C–402 and 415/05 P *Kadi & Al Barakaat International Foundation v Council and Commission* [2008] ECR I–6351.

CFSP measure and ruled that 'Article 215(2) TFEU constitutes the appropriate legal basis for measures, such as those at issue in the present case, directed to addressees implicated in acts of terrorism
who, having regard to their activities globally and to the international dimension of the threat they
pose, affect fundamentally the Union's external activity'.[146] And in the *EU–Mauritius Agreement* case,
even though the agreement was broad and covered both CFSP and police and judicial cooperation
issues, the CJEU found the legal basis of Article 37 TEU (on concluding international agreements)
within the CFSP Title to be appropriate.[147]

Quite apart from the different procedures which follow from enacting CFSP measures as compared with other EU measures and policies, there is also a question of how to coordinate the dif-
ferent goals, aims, and other rules which may apply to those policies with those which apply to the
CFSP. In *Centro-Com*, a case pre-dating the creation of the CFSP, concerning action by the Member
States pursuant to a UN Sanctions Regulation against Serbia and Montenegro, the Court ruled that
Member State powers 'must be exercised in a manner consistent with Community law', which in this
case meant that they must respect the provisions of the CCP.[148] That approach was confirmed by the
Court in the *ECOWAS* judgment, in which the Council adopted a joint action (CFSP) on combating
the spread of small arms and light weapons, which also contemplated the provision of assistance to
third countries.[149] The Court ruled that the choice by the Council of the CFSP pillar as the legal basis
for a subsequent implementing decision impinged upon development cooperation competences and
infringed former Article 47 EU.[150] It declared that a measure having legal effects adopted under the
CFSP 'affected' the provisions of the rest of the Treaties for the purposes of Article 47 EU 'whenever it
could have been adopted on the basis of the EC Treaty'.[151]

Article 47 TEU, however, has now been replaced by Article 40 TEU, the so-called 'non-contamination clause',[152] which no longer subordinates the CFSP to other EU policies but rather stipulates that
neither field shall affect the application of the procedures or the extent of exercise of the powers of the
other. Unlike the approach previously adopted by the CJEU in *Centro-Com* and *ECOWAS*, each field
now stands on an equal footing, which, as we have seen from the *EU–Mauritius* and the *Al-Qaeda
Sanctions* cases, creates complexity when a legal measure touching on both CFSP and other EU policy
fields is to be adopted.[153] As was predicted of the new 'non-contamination' clause, the CJEU has to
date interpreted this so as to protect the CFSP and its distinctive autonomous decision-making procedures from encroachment by other policies and procedures of the EU.

(B) THE CONSTITUTIONAL NATURE OF THE CFSP

The TEU establishes binding legal obligations for the Member States to support the Union's
external and security policy actively and unreservedly, in a spirit of loyalty and mutual solidarity. Article 24(3) requires them to work together to enhance and develop their mutual political

---

[146] Case C–130/10 [78].

[147] Case C–658/11 *Parliament v Council (EU–Mauritius Agreement)* EU:C:2014:2025, [44]–[45].

[148] Case C–124/95 *R v HM Treasury and Bank of England, ex p Centro-Com* [1997] ECR I–81, [25].

[149] Case C–91/05 (n 140).

[150] For the text of former Art 47 TEU see (n 140).

[151] Case C–91/05 (n 140) [96].

[152] See S Blockmans and M Spernbauer, 'Legal Obstacles to Comprehensive EU External Security Action' (2013) 18
EFAR 7.

[153] For academic proposals as to how to approach this dilemma see P Van Elsuwege, 'EU External Action after the
Collapse of the Pillar Structure: In Search of a New Balance between Delimitation and Consistency' (2010) 47 CMLRev
987; and 'The Adoption of "Targeted Sanctions" and the Potential for Interinstitutional Litigation after Lisbon' (2011) 7
Journal of Contemporary European Research 488.

solidarity and to refrain from any action contrary to the interests of the Union or likely to impair its effectiveness as a cohesive force in international relations. Further, the principle of sincere cooperation enshrined in Article 4(3) TEU applies also to the Member States when they act within the scope of the CFSP.

While the CFSP system has a mixed record, even since the Lisbon Treaty innovations,[154] it has enabled a reasonable amount of progress to be made towards the coordination of national foreign policies on a range of issues despite the absence of any formal mechanism of supranational enforcement of the various obligations of solidarity and loyalty.

From a constitutional point of view, the legal nature of CFSP instruments is different from that of other EU legislative instruments. Article 25 TEU stipulates that the EU shall conduct the CFSP by defining general guidelines, adopting decisions which define actions and positions to be undertaken by the EU, or adopting decisions defining arrangements for the implementation of such decisions.[155] It has been argued that CFSP instruments are best understood as 'international law decisions' which bear a close affinity to EU law in that they are binding upon both Member States and the EU institutions, and are adopted by the Council as the primary decision-making body.[156] Finally, although this characterization may be contested, it has been suggested that the core features of supranational EU law—primacy, direct effect, and the *ERTA* principles—are not entirely absent from the law of the CFSP.[157]

(c) THE CFSP AND ECONOMIC SANCTIONS

We have seen already that foreign policies based on the CFSP and on other EU policies necessarily overlap, but that difficulties of promoting coordination and consistency between different EU policy fields arise from the different substantive and procedural requirements which apply under different parts of the Treaties.

One example is the treatment of dual-use goods. These are products which can be used for both civil and military purposes, and they are regulated by two different sets of rules: the general EU rules apply in relation to their civil use, and Member States' rules apply with regard to questions of national security.[158] They fall within the scope of the 'public security' exception in Article 36 TFEU which, according to the CJEU in *Aimé Richardt*, covers both a Member State's internal and external security.[159] In *Werner* and *Leifer*, the CJEU ruled that measures which restricted the export of products could not be treated as falling outside the scope of the CCP (a field of exclusive EU competence) on the ground that they had foreign policy and security objectives.[160] Following these rulings, dual-use goods are governed by an EU regulation, with national measures regarding export controls being required to operate within the limits set by this regulation.[161]

[154] N Klein and W Wessels, 'CFSP Progress or Decline after Lisbon?' (2013) 18 EFAR 449.

[155] Art 25 TEU.

[156] R Gosalbo Bono, 'Some Reflections on the CFSP Legal Order' (2006) 43 CMLRev 337, 378.

[157] Ibid.

[158] Art 346(1)(b) TFEU provides that: 'any Member State may take such measures as it considers necessary for the protection of the essential interests of its security which are connected with the production of or trade in arms, munitions and war material; such measures shall not adversely affect the conditions of competition in the internal market regarding products which are not intended for specifically military purposes'.

[159] Case C–367/89 *Criminal Proceedings against Aimé Richardt and Les Accessoires Scientifiques SNC* [1991] ECR I–4621.

[160] Case C–70/94 *Fritz Werner Industrie-Ausrustungen GmbH v Federal Republic of Germany* [1995] ECR I–3189.

[161] Reg 428/2009 [2009] OJ L134/1.

The EU's policy on sanctions (or 'restrictive measures' as they are called in the Treaty), and particularly EU imposition of economic sanctions, is differently organized. An inter-pillar mechanism had existed under the Maastricht Treaty, until the Lisbon Treaty adapted this system in the light of the new institutional structure of the EU.

Article 215 TFEU provides:

> 1. Where a decision, adopted in accordance with Chapter 2 of Title V of the Treaty on European Union, provides for the interruption or reduction, in part or completely, of economic and financial relations with one or more third countries, the Council, acting by a qualified majority on a joint proposal from the High Representative of the Union for Foreign Affairs and Security Policy and the Commission, shall adopt the necessary measures. It shall inform the European Parliament thereof.
>
> 2. Where a decision adopted in accordance with Chapter 2 of Title V of the Treaty on European Union so provides, the Council may adopt restrictive measures under the procedure referred to in paragraph 1 against natural or legal persons and groups or non-State entities.
>
> 3. The acts referred to in this Article shall include necessary provisions on legal safeguards.

In other words, a decision adopted in accordance with the CFSP decision-making process under the TEU is a necessary first step, which is then implemented according to the TFEU procedure outlined above. Notably, Article 215 provides both for 'country sanctions' as well as sanctions imposed on individuals. Articles 75 and 76 however provide for a different procedure involving joint legislative power with the European Parliament when the EU adopts sanctions in the area of freedom, security, and justice, to combat terrorist activities.

The CJEU was confronted with this clash of procedures between Article 215 and Article 75 TFEU in the *Al-Qaeda Sanctions* case, mentioned above, in which the Parliament argued that EU legislation amending earlier anti-terrorist sanctions should have been based on Article 75 with its stronger procedural involvement of the Parliament, rather than on Article 215(1) with very limited parliamentary involvement.[162] The Court rejected this and ruled that the legislation was a CFSP measure and hence was properly based on Article 215. Neither Parliament's attempt to distinguish 'internal' from 'external' terrorism nor its argument that more intensive parliamentary involvement was required where the fundamental rights of individuals were affected, swayed the Court from its conclusion.[163] The case suggests that the scope of application of Article 75 to EU anti-terrorist sanctions with an external dimension is likely to be extremely limited.[164]

Chapter 11 of this book describes some of the legal challenges—which have increased greatly in number in recent years—to the compatibility of EU sanctions, and particularly economic and financial sanctions, with the EU's fundamental rights provisions. Following the early *Bosphorus* case, in which the Court upheld the compatibility of a sanction (seizure of an aircraft) imposed by an EU regulation implementing a UN Security Council resolution with the right to property and the freedom to pursue a commercial activity,[165] a series of cases concerning financial sanctions directed against particular persons and organizations came before the General Court and the CJEU. Beginning with the famous *Kadi I* and *II* cases, the CJEU ruled that the fact that these sanctions were mandated by

---

[162] (N 144).

[163] Ibid [72]–[76] and [83]–[84].

[164] See C Hillion, 'Fighting Terrorism through the EU CFSP' in I Govaere and S Poli (eds), *Management of Global Emergencies, Threats and Crises by the EU* (Brill, 2014).

[165] Case C–84/95 *Bosphorus Hava Yollari Turizm ve Ticaret AS v Minister for Transport, Energy and Communications* [1996] ECR I–3953. This approach was subsequently upheld by the European Court of Human Rights in App No 45036/98 *Bosphorus v Ireland*, judgment of the ECtHR of 30 June 2005. See Ch 11.

the Security Council did not prevent the CJEU from reviewing their compatibility with fundamental rights.[166] Since then, the EU's use of sanctions has continued to expand and diversify, and the Court has also annulled many such measures—both anti-terrorist sanctions as well as political, or country, sanctions—for violation of basic rights such as the right to a fair hearing or access to a judicial remedy.[167]

Apart from economic sanctions, the EU also imposes other kinds of sanctions such as arms embargoes and travel bans, which fall entirely or predominantly under the CFSP, and hence do not raise the same cross-policy consistency and coordination problems.[168]

6 THE CONCLUSION OF INTERNATIONAL AGREEMENTS BY THE EU AND OTHER FORMS OF EU INTERNATIONAL PRACTICE

International agreements are probably the most important form of external lawmaking by the EU, but the international practice of the EU also includes participation in international organizations. Both forms of international activity have important ramifications internally, as well as internationally through the creation of obligations which may entail international responsibility.

(A) EU PROCEDURES FOR CONCLUDING INTERNATIONAL AGREEMENTS

Article 218 TFEU establishes a general procedure for the exercise of treaty-making powers. This provision stipulates the division of tasks between the institutions and the various voting procedures. While the procedure is largely uniform for all international agreements, there are important exceptions for agreements touching on the CFSP. Article 218(2)–(4) provides:

> 2. The Council shall authorise the opening of negotiations, adopt negotiating directives, authorise the signing of agreements and conclude them.
> 3. The Commission, or the High Representative of the Union for Foreign Affairs and Security Policy where the agreement envisaged relates exclusively or principally to the common foreign and security policy, shall submit recommendations to the Council, which shall adopt a decision authorising the opening of negotiations and, depending on the subject of the agreement envisaged, nominating the Union negotiator or the head of the Union's negotiating team.
> 4. The Council may address directives to the negotiator and designate a special committee in consultation with which the negotiations must be conducted.

The first step of the procedure is thus the *negotiation* of an agreement, which is, in principle, the task of the Commission. The Commission generally initiates the whole process, albeit

---

[166] Cases C–402/05 and 415/05 P *Kadi I* (n 145) and Cases C–584/10 P, C–593/10 P and C–595/10 P *Kadi II* EU:C:2013:518.

[167] For a fuller discussion of the expansion of EU sanctions policy and the development of the CJEU's sanctions case law, see C Eckes, 'EU Restrictive Measures Against Natural and Legal Persons: From Counterterrorist to Third Country Sanctions' (2014) 51 CMLRev 869.

[168] For further reading see http://eeas.europa.eu/cfsp/sanctions/index_en.htm. Also I Cameron (ed), *EU Sanctions: Law and Policy Concerning Restrictive Measures* (Intersentia, 2013) and F Giumelli, 'How EU Sanctions Work: A New Narrative', EU Institute for Security Studies Chaillot Paper, 2013.

under the political leadership of the European Council. The directives which form the basis for the Commission's actions are informally known as 'negotiating mandates'. These tend to be general in nature, although the Council sometimes specifies the result which is sought and the margins of the concessions which the Commission is permitted to make. Following the Lisbon Treaty, however, in the case of an agreement which relates exclusively or principally to the CFSP, it is the High Representative who has exclusive power to recommend the opening of negotiations. The Treaty gives little guidance to the Council in designating the negotiator, indicating only that it 'depends on the subject' of the agreement envisaged. While negotiations are normally conducted by the Commission,[169] the Presidency or even the High Representative can be designated as negotiator or head of the negotiating team where an agreement touches on the CFSP.

The second stage of the procedure is the signature and the conclusion of the agreement. In accordance with the terms of Article 218 TFEU the Council exercises this power in conjunction, in most cases, with the European Parliament,[170] as will be outlined further below.[171] Qualified majority in the Council is required for the signing and conclusion of an agreement, just as it is for the opening of the negotiations.[172] However, for both stages there are four exceptional cases in which unanimity is required. The first is when the agreement covers a field for which unanimity is required for the adoption of internal rules. The second is when it concerns an association agreement referred to in Article 217. The third case is where a cooperation agreement is concluded with a country which is officially a candidate for the accession. The fourth is in the case of the agreement on accession of the EU to the ECHR, which would enter into force only after approval by the Member States in accordance with their respective constitutional requirements.[173]

In the case of an agreement which is part of the CCP, the procedure is further modified by Article 207(3) TFEU and involves a specialized Council-appointed committee to assist the Commission in conducting negotiations. Similar committees may be appointed to assist the Commission in the negotiation of other types of agreement.[174] These committees seem intended to ensure control by Member States over the direction of the negotiations.

The institutional procedures may also be varied in the case of agreements concerning monetary or foreign exchange regime matters. According to Article 219(3) TFEU the Council decides, by qualified majority on a recommendation from the Commission and after consulting the ECB, on the arrangements for the negotiation and conclusion of agreements. The Commission is to be 'fully associated with the negotiations'.

Although Article 218 TFEU refers to 'agreements', the CJEU ruled in *Opinion 1/75* that this notion is to be construed broadly as referring to 'any undertaking entered into by entities subject to

---

[169] The most recent Framework Agreement between the European Parliament and the Commission requires the Commission to facilitate a delegation of Members of Parliament as observers within EU delegations, although the Council has challenged this aspect of the Framework Agreement (n 97).

[170] The Council may however decide to delegate the concluding power to the Commission, but only for enacting modifications to an existing agreement and where the latter provides for them to be adopted by a simplified procedure or by a body set up by the agreement. The Council may attach specific conditions to such authorization: Art 218(7).

[171] For discussion of the post-Lisbon arrangements for representation of the EU in the conclusion of international agreements, see M Gatti and P Manzini, 'External Representation of the European Union in the Conclusion of International Agreements' (2012) 49 CMLRev 1703.

[172] All of these acts take the form of decs or sometimes regs.

[173] Art 218(8) TFEU.

[174] These committees, including the Article 207 Committee, are purely advisory and are limited to giving assistance in the negotiation of agreements: Case C–61/94 *Commission v Germany (International Dairy Arrangement)* [1996] ECR I–3989, [14].

international law which has binding force, whatever its formal designation'.[175] The intention of the parties to give the document binding force will be decisive. In *France v Commission*, concerning the EU–US antitrust agreement on the application of competition laws, the Court made clear that the Commission could not adopt a binding document of this kind together with another international actor, outside the procedure provided for in Article 218 TFEU.[176] However, in the *US Regulatory Cooperation* case, the CJEU ruled that where it is clear throughout negotiations that the intention of the parties is not to enter into legally binding commitments, the adoption by the Commission together with an international partner of 'Guidelines' falls outside the scope of Article 218 TFEU (formerly Article 300 EC) and is not precluded by it.[177]

Article 218(9) TFEU provides that the Council may, on a proposal from the Commission or the High Representative, adopt a decision suspending an international agreement concluded by the EU, or establishing the positions to be adopted on the EU's behalf in a body set up by an agreement, when that body may adopt acts having legal effects.[178] In the *Organization of International Wine and Vine (OIV)* litigation, Germany challenged a decision by the Council which had established the position to be adopted on certain non-binding resolutions to be agreed upon by the OIV, which is an organization of forty-six states to which the EU itself is not a party.[179] Germany, supported by several other Member States, argued that this was a matter for Member States to agree amongst themselves albeit in accordance with the EU requirement of sincere cooperation, and that the Council could not impose a position upon Member States to defend in the OIV negotiations. However the Court, disagreeing with the Advocate General, ruled that Article 218(9), despite its language and the fact that the rest of Article 218 applies to binding agreements, was applicable both to international agreements to which only the Member States and not the EU were party, as well as to the non-binding recommendations to be adopted by the organization. This was because non-binding recommendations were capable of 'decisively influencing' the content of legislation if subsequently incorporated into EU laws.[180] This was a surprising ruling which extends the role of the EU in international relations, restricting further the autonomy of Member States within international organizations, even those to which the EU is not party.[181]

A similar procedure to that on suspension in Article 218(9) also applies in relation to the termination of an international agreement. The provisions governing suspension and termination are invoked only in exceptional circumstances, and they tend to serve as instruments of political pressure on third countries.[182]

---

[175] *Opinion 1/75* (n 81) 1359–1360; Case C–327/91 *France v Commission* (n 28). The Court in Case C–327/91 clearly ruled that the term agreement in Art 218 was intended to indicate 'any undertaking entered into by entities subject to international law which has binding force, whatever its formal designation'.

[176] Case C–327/91 *France v Commission* (n 28); Case C–189/97 *European Parliament v Council (EC–Mauritania Fisheries Agreement)* [1999] ECR I–4741.

[177] Case C–233/02 *France v Commission (Guidelines on Regulatory Cooperation and Transparency Concluded with the USA)* [2004] ECR I–2759.

[178] Art 218(9) TFEU.

[179] Case C–399/12 *Germany v Council (OIV)* EU:C:2014:2258.

[180] Case C–399/12 *Germany v Council (Organization of Wine and Vine)* EU:C:2014:2258, [61]–[63].

[181] For critical commentary see C Tournaye, http://voelkerrechtsblog.com/2014/10/21/international-organizations-soon-blocked-by-eus-external-powers/, and S Peers, http://eulawanalysis.blogspot.com/2014/10/in-vino-veritas-cjeu-again-strengthens.html.

[182] M Maresceau, 'Unilateral Suspension and Termination of Bilateral Agreements Concluded by the EC' in M Bulterman, L Hancher, A McDonnell, and H Sevenster (eds), *Views of European Law from the Mountain. Liber Amicorum Piet-Jan Slot* (Kluwer Law International, 2009) 455–466.

(B) MIXED AGREEMENTS

Mixed agreements are a common EU phenomenon, and will remain an integral part of the legal landscape so long as both the EU and the Member States retain treaty-making capacity.[183] Mixed agreements are agreements to which both the EU and the Member States are contracting parties on the basis that their joint participation is required, because not all matters covered by the agreement fall exclusively within EU competence or exclusively within Member State competence. A mixed agreement will also be used in a case where competence over the subject matter of the agreement is shared between the Member States and the EU. Mixed agreements form an integral part of EU law and are binding on both the EU institutions and the Member States.

Discussions of mixity, as with many aspects of EU external relations, are often intricate and confusing. Rosas proposed a detailed typology of mixed agreements on the basis of the nature of the competence involved, distinguishing between 'parallel' and 'shared' competence, with shared competence in turn being divided into 'co-existent' and 'concurrent' competence.[184] While his analysis is helpful, it is clear that any attempt to classify mixed agreements risks oversimplifying the phenomenon, given the complexity of the practice and the variety of international agreements and EU powers involved.[185]

The CJEU has not generally attempted any detailed delineation of areas of competence in the context of mixed agreements. Once exclusive competence is ruled out, the Court generally turns its attention to how best to organize the joint participation of the EU and the Member States, in part because of the dynamic and evolving nature of EU competence.[186] In its ruling on the compatibility with the Euratom Treaty of Member State participation in the Convention on the Physical Protection of Nuclear Materials, the Court held that the division of competence with regard to implementation of the agreement was to be resolved on the basis of the same principles that govern the division of powers concerning the negotiation and conclusion of agreements.[187] The Court emphasized that the duty of cooperation must be observed in all three stages of external action: in the negotiation, conclusion, and execution of mixed agreements.[188] Responsibility for the performance of mixed agreements also follows the respective competences.[189] According to the CJEU, Member States are subject to special duties of action and abstention as soon as a 'concerted common strategy' exists at the level of the EU.[190] The Court has also ruled that whatever difficulties there may be in managing mixed agreements, these difficulties do not provide a reason for altering the classification of competence, or for arguing that it should be exclusive.[191]

As far as negotiation is concerned, the division of competence under a mixed agreement does not, generally, influence participation in negotiations. While the practice is decided on a case-by-case basis, it is generally accepted that the Commission may act as a sole negotiator for the whole agreement according to the mandate given to it by the Council, as occurred in the case of the WTO Agreement. The 'common statement' is usually agreed by consensus and the Commission presents it

---

[183] The literature on mixed agreements is vast. For a recent collection see P Koutrakos and C Hillion, *Mixed Agreements Revisited: The EU and its Member States in the World* (Hart, 2010).

[184] A Rosas, 'The European Union and Mixed Agreements' in Dashwood and Hillion (n 37).

[185] Eeckhout, *External Relations of the European Union* (n 82).

[186] *Ruling 1/78 Euratom (Nuclear Materials)* [1978] ECR 2151, [35].

[187] Ibid [36].

[188] See also Case C–25/94 *Commission v Council (FAO Agreement)* [1996] ECR I–1469, [48].

[189] See however the suggestion by AG Jacobs that there might be a case for joint liability at the international level in Case C–316/91 *Parliament v Council* (n 64) [69].

[190] Case C–246/07 *Commission v Sweden* EU:C:2010:203. See AD Casteleiro and J Larik, 'The Duty to Remain Silent: Limitless Loyalty in EU External Relations?' (2011) 36 ELRev 524.

[191] *Opinion 1/94* (n 45) [107]; *Opinion 2/00* (n 21) [41]; *Opinion 1/08* (n 68) [127].

when competence is exclusive, whereas the Presidency presents the agreed position for matters falling under shared competence.

The phenomenon of mixity has attracted a range of views, with some regarding it as a necessary evil which is rendered all the more problematic by the enlargement of EU membership, while others have praised it as a 'near-unique contribution to true federalism'.[192]

(c) THE ROLE OF THE EUROPEAN PARLIAMENT

Although the power of the European Parliament has been consistently growing in external relations over the years, the most significant changes in this respect were made by the Lisbon Treaty. The Parliament is called upon to act mainly at the stage of conclusion of agreements, which considerably reduces its opportunity for influencing their content. However, a range of informal mechanisms were created to compensate for this, in order to enable the Parliament to be 'regularly and fully informed', including through the participation of MEPs as observers during negotiations, and so that its views could be taken into account.[193]

The position today is that the Council adopts the decision concluding an international agreement after obtaining the Parliament's consent. Under the terms of Article 218(6) such consent is required in five cases: (i) association agreements referred to in Article 217 TFEU; (ii) agreement on EU accession to the ECHR; (iii) other agreements which establish a specific institutional framework by organizing cooperation procedures; (iv) agreements having important budgetary implications for the Union;[194] and finally (v) agreements covering fields of EU competence to which either the ordinary legislative procedure applies or the special legislative procedure where consent by the European Parliament is required. This last category largely reconciles the roles of the European Parliament in the internal decision-making process and in the field of external relations. The most significant impact of this change introduced by the Lisbon Treaty is that no international agreement in the field of the CCP may be concluded without the Parliament's consent, whereas in the past even simple consultation was not required.[195] Further, the categories of international agreement for which mere consultation of the Parliament applies are now the exception.[196] In order to avoid excessive delay, a time limit within which the Parliament is to deliver its opinion in an urgent situation can be set: this time limit is to be agreed between the Parliament and Council in cases in which parliamentary consent is needed, and it can be set unilaterally by the Council in cases where only consultation is required.

According to Article 218(6) TFEU, there is no requirement to consult the Parliament where an agreement 'relates exclusively' to the CFSP. In the *EU–Mauritius Agreement* case, Parliament argued that this exception should be narrowly construed, and that since the EU–Mauritius Agreement also covered issues such as police and development cooperation to which the ordinary legislative procedure would apply internally, the consent of Parliament should be required under

---

[192] JHH Weiler, 'The External Legal Relations of Non-Unitary Actors: Mixity and the Federal Principle' in JHH Weiler, *The Constitution of Europe: Do the New Clothes Have an Emperor?* (Cambridge University Press, 1999).

[193] This was done previously under the so-called Luns-Westerterp procedure and at present under the 2010 Framework Agreement on relations between the European Parliament and the Commission.

[194] This category of agreements has given rise to problems of interpretation, particularly concerning which budgetary implications can be said to be 'important'. See Case C–189/97 *European Parliament v Council* (n 176).

[195] M Cremona, 'Balancing Union and State Interests. Opinion 1/08, Choice of Legal Base and the Common Commercial Policy under the Treaty of Lisbon' (2010) 35 ELRev 678; A Dimopoulos, 'The Effects of the Lisbon Treaty on the Principles and Objectives of the Common Commercial Policy' (2010) 15 EFAR 153; N Lavranos and S Adam, 'How Exclusive is the Common Commercial Policy of the EU After Lisbon?' (2010) 7–8 ELR 263.

[196] See, eg, Art 64(3) TFEU on the adoption of certain restrictive measures in the field of liberalization of capital movements to or from third countries, where only consultation is required.

Article 218(6)(v).[197] The Court disagreed, arguing that the Parliament's approach would introduce considerable uncertainty, and it ruled instead that the substantive legal basis for an agreement should determine which decision-making procedure applies to its conclusion.[198] In this case, since the Agreement was based on Article 37 TEU, the decision-making process applicable to CFSP agreements should apply, meaning that Parliament did not need to be consulted. However, the Court ruled that the Council had breached another obligation under Article 218(10) to keep the Parliament 'immediately and fully informed at all stages of the procedure'—and indeed had not informed Parliament until after the contested decision had already been published in the Official Journal.[199] Underscoring its own jurisdiction to rule on such procedural aspects of the conclusion of CFSP agreements, despite the limitation on its jurisdiction to rule on substantive CFSP matters under Article 24(1) TEU and Article 275 TFEU, the Court ruled that the obligation to keep Parliament informed was an essential procedural requirement, and that the decision concluding the Agreement should consequently be annulled.[200]

(D) THE MEMBER STATES' DUTY OF SINCERE COOPERATION

Although there is no explicit Treaty provision which specifies that the Member States must not enter into negotiations or conclude international agreements which would deviate from the position taken by the EU, it seems that the primacy of EU law, together with Article 4(3) TEU, effectively requires states to abstain from any such action or from enacting any rules conflicting with EU norms.

We have seen that Article 4(3) TEU requires Member States to facilitate the achievement of the Union's tasks and to abstain from any measure which could jeopardize the attainment of the Treaty objectives. This 'duty of sincere cooperation' applies whether the EU's competence is exclusive or shared. It means that, once the EU institutions envisage taking EU action, and once they adopt a decision authorizing the Commission to negotiate a multilateral agreement, the Member States are under a duty to cooperate closely with them in order to 'facilitate the achievement of the EU's tasks and to ensure the coherence and consistency of the action and its international representation'.[201] If on the other hand they negotiate, conclude, ratify, or implement bilateral or multilateral treaties concerned with the same issues without cooperating or consulting with the Commission they will violate EU law.

In infringement proceedings brought by the Commission, the Court ruled that Greece, by submitting to the IMO a proposal for monitoring the compliance of ships and port facilities with the International Convention for the Safety of Life at Sea, had failed to fulfil its obligations under the duty of sincere cooperation.[202] The mere initiation of a procedure that might have led the IMO to adopt a new rule which could affect EU rules was sufficient for the Court to conclude that Greece's proposal amounted to an impermissible exercise by the Member State of an exclusive EU competence. The duty of sincere cooperation is particularly important where, as here, the EU is not a party to an international agreement and the Member States act jointly in the EU's interests.[203] However, even in a field of shared competences such as the negotiation of a mixed environmental agreement, Member States are

---

[197] Case C–658/11 (n 143).

[198] Ibid [57]–[58].

[199] Ibid [76]–[78].

[200] Ibid [86]–[87]. The CJEU however used Art 264 TFEU to maintain the effects of the annulled decision, in order to avoid undermining operations such as the conduct of piracy trials under the EU–Mauritius Agreement.

[201] Case C–266/03 *Commission v Luxembourg (Inland Waterways Agreement)* [2005] ECR I–4805; Case C–433/03 *Commission v Germany (Inland Waterways Agreement)* [2005] ECR I–6985.

[202] Case C–45/07 *Commission v Greece* [2009] ECR I–701.

[203] See also *Opinion 2/91* (n 49) [119].

under duties of action and abstention once the Commission has submitted proposals to the Council which, although not yet adopted by the Council, represent a point of departure for the EU's 'concerted common strategy'.[204]

(E) COOPERATION WITHIN INTERNATIONAL ORGANIZATIONS

The TFEU expressly provides for the establishment of relations with other international entities. Article 220 TFEU refers to the maintenance of all appropriate relations with the organs of the UN and its specialized agencies,[205] the Council of Europe, the OECD, the Organization for Security and Co-operation in Europe (OSCE), and more generally with 'all international organizations'. The maintenance of such relations is the task of the High Representative for CFSP matters[206] and of the Commission in other cases.

Other Treaty provisions mention relations between the EU and 'competent' international organizations in the context of the EMU, education and sport, culture, public health, the environment, and development cooperation. Article 138 TFEU makes provision for the Council to decide on the position of the Union and its representation, at the international level, in relation to issues concerning economic and monetary union. In the context of the CFSP, Article 34 TEU provides that the 'Member States shall coordinate their action in international organizations and at international conferences'.

In *Opinion 1/76*, the CJEU ruled that the powers of the EU to enter international agreements include a power, within the scope of EU competence, to enter agreements establishing international organizations.[207] This was further implicitly confirmed by the ECJ's *Opinion 1/94* where participation in the agreements establishing the WTO was approved. EU participation can take either the form of full membership, as in the WTO example,[208] or the form of observer status, as in the case of the ILO. In many instances, as in the WTO case, the EU participates in the organization alongside the Member States. If membership of the organization in question is open only to states, then the Member States will adopt a common position on the issue for which the EU is competent, and they must act jointly in the Union's interest in accordance with their general duty of cooperation.[209]

7 THE EU AND INTERNATIONAL LAW

As an entity with international legal personality, the EU is the subject of rights and obligations arising under international agreements and under international law. This applies to all areas in which the EU has competence including the CFSP, despite the restricted jurisdiction of the CJEU over this field.

---

[204] Case C–246/07 *Commission v Sweden* (n 190) [91].

[205] On the complexities of EU representation at the UN see A Degrand Guillaud, 'Actors and Mechanisms of EU Coordination at the UN' (2009) 14 EFAR 405 and 'Characteristics of and Recommendations for EU Coordination at the UN' (2009) 14 EFAR 607. The EU's move to gain speaking rights at the UN General Assembly was initially opposed by other regional groupings but was subsequently approved in 2011.

[206] Art 27(2) TEU.

[207] *Opinion 1/76* (n 45); S Marchisio, 'EU's Membership in International Organisations' in E Cannizzaro, *The European Union as an Actor in International Relations* (Kluwer, 2002); R Frid, *The Relations between the EC and International Organizations—Legal Theory and Practice* (Kluwer, 1995).

[208] Other examples include the Food and Agriculture Organization and the European Bank for Reconstruction and Development. In some cases the EU has joined pre-existing international organizations, whereas in other cases it has participated in the agreement creating a new organization.

[209] *Opinion 2/91* (n 49) [1]–[5]. See however Case C–399/12 *Germany v Council (OIV)* EU:C:2014:2258 upholding the power of the Council to decide on the negotiating position to be adopted by Member States in an organization to which the EU is not party.

(A) INTERNATIONAL AGREEMENTS CONCLUDED BY THE EU ARE BINDING UPON IT AND ARE PART OF EU LAW

Article 216(2) TFEU declares that agreements concluded by the Union are binding on the institutions of the Union and on its Member States. The Court has consistently held since the *Haegeman* ruling that once an agreement enters into force, its provisions form an 'integral part' of Community law, now EU law.[210] The CJEU has also ruled that Member States are in violation of their obligations under EU law where they fail to adopt the measures necessary to implement an international agreement concluded by the EU.[211] In other words, agreements entered into by the EU bind the Member States by virtue of their duties under EU law and not international law.

(B) THE EU LEGAL SYSTEM AS AN AUTONOMOUS LEGAL ORDER

When the EU has become a party to an organization or an agreement setting up bodies whose powers may conflict with those of the EU institutions, the Court has been particularly insistent on defending the autonomy of the EU legal order. In *Opinion 1/76*, the CJEU rejected the possibility of establishing a special tribunal composed of six judges from the CJEU and one judge from Switzerland, on the ground that CJEU judges might face a conflict of jurisdiction or allegiance to two different bodies.[212] In *Opinion 1/91* on the EEA Agreement, the proposed conferral of jurisdiction upon a new EEA Court composed of three judges from the CJEU and three from EFTA states was held to be incompatible with EU law.[213] So was the fact that the agreement would introduce a large body of legal rules which would be juxtaposed to a corpus of identically worded EU rules, with all the problems of interpretation and consistency that would follow. This was said to conflict with what was then Article 220 EC[214] and, more generally, with the very foundations of the EU.[215] In *Opinion 1/09* on the creation of a new European and EU patents court, the CJEU ruled that the envisaged agreement establishing the new international court, which would have given exclusive jurisdiction to hear actions brought by individuals in the field of the EU patent to the new court, would deprive the CJEU of its power to give preliminary rulings to national courts on questions of interpretation arising from such disputes, and consequently was incompatible with the EU Treaties.[216]

Most dramatically, however, in its Opinion on the compatibility with the EU Treaties of the Draft Agreement on Accession of the EU to the European Convention on Human Rights, the CJEU declared the provisions of the Draft Agreement to be incompatible with the EU Treaties, in significant part because of the way in which accession to the ECHR would affect the autonomy of EU law.[217] According to the CJEU, no decision of the European Court of Human Rights should have the effect of 'binding the EU and its institutions... to a particular interpretation of the rules of EU law'.[218] However in the

---

[210] Case 181/73 *Haegeman* [1974] ECR 449, [5]; *Opinion 1/91 (EEA Agreement I)* [1991] ECR 6079, [37].

[211] Eg Case C–239/03 *Commission v France (Étang de Berre)* [2004] ECR I–9325.

[212] *Opinion 1/76* (n 45).

[213] *Opinion 1/91* (n 210).

[214] This Art is replaced, in substance, by Art 19 TEU. Art 19 sets out the basic task and role of the CJEU by providing that it 'shall ensure that in the interpretation and application of the Treaties the law is observed'.

[215] Following renegotiation of the agreement, and the replacement of the earlier proposed EEA Court with an EFTA Court consisting only of judges from the EFTA countries, with more limited jurisdiction, the CJEU upheld the compatibility of the revised agreement with the EC Treaty: *Opinion 1/92 (EEA Agreement II)* [1992] ECR I–2821. See also *Opinion 1/00 on the Establishment of a European Common Aviation Area* [2002] ECR I–3493 where the Court underscored the importance of 'the preservation of the autonomy' of the EU legal order.

[216] *Opinion 1/09* EU:C:2011:123.

[217] *Opinion 2/13* delivered on 18 December 2014, [179]–[200]. For the AG's Opinion see EU:C:2014:2475.

[218] Ibid [184].

CJEU's view, the Draft Agreement crucially lacked any provision which would coordinate Article 53 of the Charter (which the CJEU interprets to mean that Member State standards of protection of fundamental rights must not compromise the level of protection provided for by the Charter or the primacy, unity, and effectiveness of EU law) with Article 53 of the ECHR (which allows Council of Europe Member States to lay down *higher* standards of protection of fundamental rights than those guaranteed by the ECHR).[219] Secondly, the CJEU felt there was nothing in the Draft Agreement to guarantee that the operation of the 'mutual trust' requirement between Member States as far as the presumption of compliance with fundamental rights in certain areas of EU law is concerned would not be undermined.[220] Thirdly, the CJEU feared that the operation of the new Protocol 16 to the ECHR, enabling Member State courts to request an advisory opinion from the ECtHR, might undermine the autonomy of EU law and the requirement for certain national courts to make a prior preliminary reference to the CJEU.[221]

The Court found other provisions of the Draft Agreement on Accession, including aspects of the 'co-respondent mechanism', the procedure for prior involvement of the CJEU in cases pending before the ECtHR, and the likelihood of the ECtHR gaining jurisdiction over CFSP acts which are outside the jurisdiction of the CJEU, to be incompatible with EU law. A final hurdle for the Draft Agreement was Article 344 TFEU, which confirms the exclusive jurisdiction of the CJEU, and in accordance with which the Member States undertake not to submit a dispute concerning the interpretation or application of the Treaties to any method of settlement other than those provided for therein. The CJEU ruled in *Opinion 2/13* that the provision made in Article 5 of the Draft Agreement to recognize its role in any dispute between EU Member States or between those states and the EU was insufficient to preserve the exclusive jurisdiction of the CJEU, and that only a provision which expressly excluded the ECtHR's jurisdiction under Article 33 ECHR over disputes between Member States or between Member States and the EU in relation to the application of the ECHR within the material scope of EU law would be compatible with Article 344 TFEU.[222]

The breach of Article 344 also formed the basis of the *Sellafield/MOX Plant* case brought by the Commission against Ireland, in which Ireland had instituted proceedings against the UK before an international arbitral tribunal established by the UN Convention on the Law of the Sea (UNCLOS) for the UK's failure to protect the marine environment in its operation of the MOX nuclear power station on the Irish sea.[223] The CJEU ruled that the breach concerned an area of shared external competence and that the matters covered by the relevant UNCLOS provisions, to which the EU was party, were already largely regulated by EU measures. Pointing out that Article 282 of the UNCLOS actually made it possible to avoid the breach of the CJEU's exclusive jurisdiction and preserve the autonomy of the EU legal system by according precedence to the system of dispute resolution contained in the EU Treaty, the CJEU ruled that the dispute was indeed one covered by the EU Treaty and that Ireland had violated its obligations under Article 259 and 344 TFEU and risked the autonomy of EU law by submitting the dispute to the UNCLOS tribunal instead.[224]

---

[219] Ibid [187]–[190].
[220] Ibid [191]–[195].
[221] Ibid [196]–[199].
[222] Ibid [201]–[214].
[223] Case C–459/03 *Commission v Ireland* [2006] ECR I–4635.
[224] Ibid [124]–[128].

(c) THE EFFECT OF OTHER RULES OF INTERNATIONAL LAW, AND OF INTERNATIONAL AGREEMENTS TO WHICH THE MEMBER STATES ARE PARTY

Article 216(2) TFEU mentions only agreements which have been concluded by the EU, and makes no reference to other rules of international law. However, the CJEU has acknowledged the binding nature of such other rules. Further, as we have seen above, Article 3(5) TEU declares that the EU shall contribute to 'the strict observance and the development of international law, including respect for the principles of the United Nations Charter'. However, the cases in which the CJEU has invoked or applied rules or principles of international law other than international agreements to which it is party remain few in number.[225]

Two decades ago in *Poulsen* the CJEU ruled that the EU must respect international law in the exercise of its powers,[226] and specifically that it was required to comply with the rules of customary international law when adopting a regulation suspending trade concessions resulting from an agreement concluded with a non-member country. Shortly afterwards in *Racke* the Court declared that the rules of customary international law concerning the termination and suspension of treaty relations by reason of fundamental change of circumstances (*rebus sic stantibus*) are binding on the EU institutions and form part of the EU legal order.[227] In a ruling concerning the International Dairy Agreement, the Court drew on the general rule of international law requiring the parties to any agreement to show good faith in its performance.[228] In *Firma Brita*, in which a customs dispute concealed the complex politics of the Middle East, the CJEU ruled that the EU must respect the general principle of international law, also enshrined in Article 34 of the Vienna Convention on the Law of Treaties, concerning the relative effect of treaties, according to which treaties do not impose any obligations, or confer any rights, on non-party states without their consent.[229] No doubt reflecting the highly contested political dispute over Israeli settlements within the Occupied Territories underlying the facts of the case, the judgment has been criticized by some for its 'ill-founded, incomplete, one-dimensional and selective' use of international law,[230] and for raising as many questions as it answered,[231] while others have praised the contribution of the Court as upholding humanitarian law and the rights of the Palestinian people.[232]

Customary international law has been invoked and used in contested ways before the CJEU in other high-profile rulings. In the *Aviation Emissions* case, in which the extension by the EU of its aviation emissions regime to third country airlines which landed in the EU was challenged *inter alia* for violation of the jurisdictional principle of territoriality under customary international law, the CJEU confirmed that it would entertain a challenge to the validity of an EU regulation for incompatibility with principles of customary international law, although the Court found no incompatibility on the facts of the case.[233]

---

[225] For a survey over ten years of the use of international law by the CJEU, see G de Búrca, 'International Law before the Courts: The EU and the US Compared' (2015) 55 Virginia Journal of International Law, forthcoming.

[226] Case C–286/90 *Anklagemyndigheden v Poulsen and Diva Navigation* [1992] ECR I–6019, [9].

[227] Case C–162/96 *Racke GmbH & Co v Hauptzollamt Mainz* [1998] ECR I–3655, [46].

[228] Case C–61/94 *Commission v Germany* (n 174) [30].

[229] Case C–386/08 *Firma Brita* EU:C:2011:347, [44].

[230] G Harpaz and E Rubinson, 'The Interface between Trade, Law and Politics and the Erosion of Normative Power Europe: Comment on *Brita*' (2010) 35 ELRev 551.

[231] I Kornfeld, 'ECJ Holds that West Bank Products are Outside the Scope of the EU–Israel Association Agreement' (2010) 14 ASIL Insight.

[232] C Perrin, 'Products from the Colonies: Labelling or Prohibition?': http://mondoweiss.net/2013/04/products-labeling-prohibition.

[233] Case C–366/10 *ATAA v Secretary of State for Energy and Climate Change* EU:C:2011:864. For commentaries, see B Mayer (2012) 49 CMLRev 1113; E Denza (2012) 37 ELRev 314; A Gattini (2012) 61 ICLQ 977; and G De Baere and C

In the famous *Kadi* litigation, the CJEU ruled that the EU's obligation to respect international law in the exercise of its powers and the special importance attached to resolutions of the UN Security Council under Chapter VII of the UN Charter would not prevent the Court from annulling EU measures implementing a Security Council resolution where those measures violated fundamental rights protected within EU law.[234] According to the ruling of the Court, 'the obligations imposed by an international agreement', even by the UN Charter, 'cannot have the effect of prejudicing the constitutional principles of the EC Treaty'.[235] The Court further ruled that even if the UN Charter were to have primacy over secondary EU acts, it would not have primacy over the EU Treaties or the general principles of EU law.[236] In a most dramatic ruling on the autonomy of the EU legal system and its separateness from the international legal order, the CJEU declared that 'an international agreement cannot affect the allocation of powers fixed by the Treaties or, consequently, the autonomy of the Community legal system'.[237] The *Kadi* case is discussed further in Chapter 11.

As regards international agreements to which the EU is not a party, but which are binding on the Member States, Article 351 TFEU specifies that, in the case of agreements concluded *before* 1 January 1958 (or, for acceding states, before the date of their accession) between Member States and third countries, the rights and obligations arising shall not be affected by the provisions of the TEU or the TFEU. In other words, the pre-existing obligations of states under their international agreements are given some protection. The CJEU has clarified further the conditions for the application of Article 351 TFEU (ex Article 307 EC) in various cases, including in the case of *T. Port*:

> Thus, for a Community provision to be deprived of effect as a result of an international agreement, two conditions must be fulfilled: the agreement must have been concluded before the entry into force of the Treaty and the third country concerned must derive from it rights which it can require the Member State concerned to respect.[238]

In the Bilateral Investment Treaties (BITs) cases, the CJEU ruled that the purpose of Article 351 TFEU was to make it clear, in accordance with the principles of international law, that application of the EU Treaties does not affect the duty of the Member State concerned to respect the rights of third countries under a prior agreement and to perform its obligations.[239] The EU itself, however, is not bound by such previous agreements. Article 351 contains only a duty on the part of the EU institutions not to impede the performance of Member States' obligations stemming from such a prior agreement which confers rights on third countries.[240]

Further, to the extent that such agreements are not compatible with the EU Treaties, the Member States concerned are obliged to take all appropriate steps to eliminate the incompatibilities established. The case below illustrates that the fact that a Member State encounters difficulties in bringing its obligations to a third state in line with its obligations under EU law does not release the state from its obligation to adjust and, where necessary, to denounce the conflicting agreement.[241]

Ryngert (2013) 18 EFAR 389. See also Case C–63/09 *Walz v Clickair SA* [2010] ECR I–4239 on the customary international law principle of state responsibility.

[234] Cases C–402 and 415/05 P (n 145).

[235] Ibid [285].

[236] Ibid [306]–[308].

[237] Ibid [282].

[238] Cases C–364–365/95 *T. Port GmbH & Co v Hauptzollamt Hamburg-Jonas* [1998] ECR I–1023, [61].

[239] Case 205/06, [33]; Case C–249/06, [34]; Case C–118/07 (n 74) [34].

[240] Case 812/79 *Attorney General v Juan C Burgoa* [1980] ECR 2787, [9].

[241] See also Case C–170/98 *Commission v Belgium* [1999] ECR I–5493; Case C–62/98 *Commission v Portugal* [2000] ECR I–5171; Case C–84/98 *Commission v Portugal* [2000] ECR I–5215.

Case C–84/98 **Commission v Portugal**
[2000] ECR I–5215

[Note Lisbon Treaty renumbering: Art 234 EEC is now Art 351 TFEU]

Following its accession to the EU in 1986 Portugal was required to adjust its prior agreement with the Federal Republic of Yugoslavia (FRY) so as to respect Regulation 4055/86 on the freedom of maritime transport services between Member States and third countries, but failed to do so. The Commission brought infringement proceedings against Portugal before the ECJ.

THE ECJ

39. In this case, the Portuguese Government has not succeeded in adjusting the contested agreement by recourse to diplomatic means within the time-limit laid down by Regulation No 4055/86.

40. It must be borne in mind that the Court has already held that, in such circumstances, in so far as denunciation of such an agreement is possible under international law, it is incumbent on the Member State concerned to denounce it (see, to that effect ... *Commission* v *Belgium* [1999] ...).

41. However, the Portuguese Government denies any failure to fulfil its obligations ...

[*The ECJ then ruled that it was not impossible, in the case at hand, for Portugal to respect the rights of the FRY since the agreement itself allowed the parties to denounce it.*]

58. Furthermore, although, in the context of Article 234 of the Treaty, the Member States have a choice as to the appropriate steps to be taken, they are nevertheless under an obligation to eliminate any incompatibilities existing between a pre-Community convention and the EC Treaty. If a Member State encounters difficulties which make adjustment of an agreement impossible, an obligation to denounce that agreement cannot therefore be excluded.

59. As regards the argument that such denunciation would involve a disproportionate disregard of foreign-policy interests of the Portuguese Republic as compared with the Community interest, it must be pointed out that the balance between the foreign-policy interests of a Member State and the Community interest is already incorporated in Article 234 of the Treaty, in that it allows a Member State not to apply a Community provision in order to respect the rights of third countries deriving from a prior agreement and to perform its obligations thereunder. That article also allows them to choose the appropriate means of rendering the agreement concerned compatible with Community law.

...

61. In those circumstances, it must be held that, by failing either to denounce or adjust the contested agreement so as to provide for fair, free and non-discriminatory access by all Community nationals to the cargo-shares due to the Portuguese Republic, as provided for in Council Regulation (EEC) No 4055/86, the Portuguese Republic has failed to fulfil its obligations under Articles 3 and 4(1) of that regulation.

In the BITs cases,[242] the CJEU defined the obligations of Member States under Article 351 TFEU very broadly. The agreements, which had been concluded by Austria, Sweden, and Finland with several third countries, contained provisions guaranteeing the free transfer, without undue delay and in freely convertible currency, of payments connected with an investment. Article 63 TFEU prohibits all restrictions on the movement of capital and on payments between the Member States, and between Member States and third countries, but Articles 64(2), 66, and 75 TFEU empower the EU to adopt measures to restrict such movements which involve direct investment. The BITs in question in these

---

242 (N 74).

cases did not contain any provision allowing for the unilateral suspension of their implementation in the event of the EU exercising that competence. The Court rejected the argument of the states that they could, in the event that the Council decided to exercise its restrictive power under the EU Treaty, negotiate with their third-country partners with a view to suspending, on a temporary basis, the implementation of their bilateral agreements. The CJEU ruled that the time required for such international negotiations would be inherently incompatible with the practical effectiveness of the measures, and that the possibility of relying on international law mechanisms, such as suspension or denunciation of the agreements, would be too uncertain to guarantee that the Council's measures could be effectively applied. The mere risk of difficulties in the implementation of potential future Council measures was sufficient for it to find an infringement by the three Member States concerned.

In the case of the GATT 1947, the ECJ ruled in *International Fruit Company* that the European Community was bound by its provisions, notwithstanding the fact that it was not a party. The Court declared that the Community had assumed the functions inherent in the tariff and trade policy in their entirety on the expiry of the transitional period, and since this is an area governed by the GATT, the provisions of that agreement bound the Community.[243] The CJEU has not however applied this doctrine of so-called 'functional succession' in several subsequent cases involving other international agreements, and has ruled that the EU is not bound by an international agreement where either not all the states were party,[244] or where not all powers in the field covered by the agreement had been transferred by states to the EU.[245]

8 THE LEGAL EFFECT OF INTERNATIONAL AGREEMENTS IN THE EU LEGAL ORDER

One of the major legal topics within EU external relations has been the question of what effect international agreements have within the EU legal order.[246] As we saw, international agreements entered into by the EU have been deemed by the Court to be an integral part of the EU legal order[247] and they are binding upon the EU in accordance with Article 216(2) TFEU. We have also seen in Chapter 7 that most forms of binding EU law have been held by the Court to be in principle capable of having direct effect.

Arguments may be made both for and against the direct legal enforceability of international agreements by private parties before domestic courts. On the one hand, as treaties concluded with other states or international organizations, they can be viewed as traditional international agreements binding only the states or organizations which signed them, having no automatic 'self-executing' quality and conferring neither rights nor obligations on individuals. On the other hand, as agreements entered into by the EU, they can be viewed as sharing some of the key characteristics of EU law, and in particular could be capable of direct effect, of being invoked and enforced by individuals

---

[243] Cases 21–24/72 *International Fruit Company NV v Produktschap voor Groenten en Fruit* [1972] ECR 1219, [14]–[18].

[244] Case C–188/07 *Commune de Mesquer* [2008] ECR I–4501, [85], concerning two international conventions on oil pollution damage.

[245] Case C–366/10 *ATAA v Secretary of State for Energy and Climate Change* EU:C:2011:864, [70]–[71] concerning the International Convention on Civil Aviation since the states had not transferred to the EU all of the powers falling within the scope of the Convention. See also Cases C–402/05 and 415/05 *Kadi* (n 145), where the CJEU did not accept the General Court's view that the EU had effectively succeeded to the obligations of the Member States under the UN Charter in the area of sanctions.

[246] See M Mendez, *The Legal Effect of EU Agreements* (Oxford University Press, 2013).

[247] See (n 210).

whenever sufficiently precise and unconditional. Opting broadly for the approach which would integrate agreements made by the EU into the law of the Member States, the Court held that international agreements can, *under certain circumstances*, be directly effective.

However, we see that in the field of international agreements, a particular set of political and strategic considerations comes into play, and the question whether or not the provisions of a particular agreement can be judicially enforced at the suit of individual litigants is not determined only by reference to the legal criteria first developed in *Van Gend en Loos*.

The issue which dominated this area of law for many years and generated a vast academic literature, namely whether the provisions of the GATT 1947 and the successor WTO agreements could have direct effect, was first raised several decades ago.

Cases 21–24/72 **International Fruit Company v Produktschap voor Groenten en Fruit** [1972] ECR 1219

A Dutch court made a preliminary reference to the ECJ, asking whether it had jurisdiction to rule on the validity of Community regulations in relation to a provision of international law and if so whether the regulations in question were contrary to the GATT.

THE ECJ

7. Before the incompatibility of a Community measure with a provision of international law can affect the validity of that measure, the Community must first of all be bound by that provision.

8. Before invalidity can be relied upon before a national court, that provision of international law must also be capable of conferring rights on citizens of the Community which they can invoke before the courts....

18. It therefore appears that, in so far as under the EEC Treaty the Community has assumed the powers previously exercised by Member States in the area governed by the General Agreement, the provisions of that agreement have the effect of binding the Community.

19. It is also necessary to examine whether the provisions of the General Agreement confer rights on citizens of the Community on which they can rely before the courts in contesting the validity of a Community measure.

20. For this purpose, the spirit, the general scheme and the terms of the General Agreement must be considered.

The Court concluded from various aspects of the GATT, including the 'great flexibility of its provisions', the possibilities of derogation, and the power of unilateral withdrawal from its obligations, that it was 'not capable of conferring on citizens of the Community rights which they can invoke before the courts'. In other words, in terms of the criteria for direct effect laid down in earlier cases, the provisions of GATT were insufficiently precise and unconditional in that the obligations contained therein could be modified, and too great a degree of flexibility was possible. The Court was unwilling to accord direct effect to such international obligations, no doubt in large part because they were being invoked to challenge the legality of EU legislation before a domestic court.[248]

In *Polydor* the Court ruled that a provision of an EU–Portugal trade agreement concerning the free movement of goods, although it was worded identically to a provision of the then EEC Treaty (now

---

[248] This was confirmed in various cases after *Kupferberg* including Case 9/73 *Schlüter v Hauptzollamt Lörrach* [1973] ECR 1135; Case C–469/93 *Amministrazione delle Finanze dello Stato Chiquita Italia* [1995] ECR I–4533.

Article 34 TFEU), was not to be interpreted in the same way and should not be given direct effect, since the agreement with Portugal (at the time a non-Member State) did not have the same aim or purpose as the EEC Treaty of establishing a single market.[249]

In *Kupferberg*,[250] however, a different provision of the same free trade agreement was held to have direct effect, since the provision was unconditional, sufficiently precise, and its direct application was within the *purpose* of the agreement. Notably, unlike in the GATT cases, the effect of declaring the trade agreement in *Kupferberg* to be directly enforceable was to extend the scope of EU rules rather than to challenge or invalidate them. Similarly, the Court has held that provisions of the earlier Lomé Convention governing relations between the EU and the ACP states were directly effective where it was national rather than EU legislation which was being challenged for compatibility with the Convention.[251]

In paragraph 8 of the *International Fruit* judgment, the CJEU seemed to equate direct effect with the possibility of review of legality, and to rule out the latter in the absence of direct effect. However, in the *Nakajima* case, the Court distinguished between the 'direct effect' of the provisions of an international trade agreement in conferring individual rights on the one hand, and the possibility of those provisions being invoked before the CJEU to challenge the compatibility of EU law.[252] Subsequently in *Germany v Commission*, the CJEU made clear that a GATT provision could be invoked for the purposes of alleging the incompatibility of an EU measure in two circumstances only: (i) where the EU *intended* to implement that particular obligation; or (ii) where the EU measure being challenged expressly referred to the particular GATT provision.[253]

In *Ikea Wholesale*, however, the Court appeared to narrow the *Nakajima* and *Germany v Commission* line of reasoning.[254] In earlier case law the CJEU had accepted that the EU intended, in adopting EU anti-dumping legislation, to satisfy the obligations arising from the GATT and the international Anti-Dumping Agreement. Applying the *Nakajima* principle, the validity of the Council regulation imposing definitive anti-dumping duties in the case should be assessed not only in the light of the general EU anti-dumping legislation, but also of the Anti-Dumping Agreement. In *Ikea Wholesale*, however, the Court treated the EU's initial intent to legislate in compliance with the Anti-Dumping Agreement as having been superseded by a later regulation which excluded repayment of duties, in spite of a subsequent report by the dispute settlement body (DSB) of the WTO finding that the EU regulation in question violated the Anti-Dumping Agreement.[255] This means that the political room for manoeuvre left to the EU institutions in implementing the WTO agreements has been expanded further, by enabling them to refuse to follow a DSB ruling on the compatibility of an EU measure with the Anti-Dumping Agreement, even where the EU had previously legislated with the intention of implementing that Agreement. In *Van Parys*, too, the Court refused to apply the *Nakajima* principle

[249] Case 270/80 *Polydor Ltd and RSO Records Inc v Harlequin Record Shops Ltd and Simons Records Ltd* [1982] ECR 329.

[250] Case 104/81 *Hauptzollamt Mainz v CA Kupferberg & Cie KG* [1982] ECR 3641; G Bebr, 'Agreements Concluded by the Community and their Possible Direct Effect: From International Fruit Company to Kupferberg' (1983) 20 CMLRev 35.

[251] Case C–469/93 (n 248).

[252] Case C–69/89 *Nakajima v Council* [1991] ECR 2069, [28]–[29]. For this purpose, according to the Court, the provisions need only be binding on the Community. However, in the case in question the CJEU ruled that the Community anti-dumping rules in issue did not conflict with the Anti-Dumping Code adopted under the GATT. See also Case 70/87 *Fediol v Commission* [1989] ECR 1781, and compare Case C–76/00 P *Petrotub SA and Republica SA v Council* [2003] ECR I–79.

[253] Case C–280/93 *Germany v Commission* [1994] ECR I–4873, and see Case C–76/00 P *Petrotub*, ibid, in which a Council reg was annulled for incompatibility with the GATT/WTO Anti-Dumping Code.

[254] Case C–351/04 *Ikea Wholesale* [2007] ECR I–7723; C Herrmann, Note (2008) 45 CMLRev 1507.

[255] Ibid [35].

to the situation of an EU regulation intended to implement a WTO DSB ruling, and would not assess the validity of the regulation in the light of the WTO rules in question, declaring that the EU had not in this situation intended to implement a 'particular obligation' in the context of the WTO.[256]

Despite this narrowing of the applicability of the *Nakajima* principle, the Court has applied the obligation of harmonious interpretation—ie the principle that EU law should be interpreted in the light of international law and of binding international agreements[257]—to provisions of the GATT and other WTO agreements such as that on Trade-Related Intellectual Property Rights (TRIPs).[258] This has the consequence of enhancing their effectiveness in certain circumstances, although not normally when they are being invoked to challenge EU measures.

It was argued, following the establishment of the WTO and the adoption of GATT 1994, that in view of the more effective means of dispute settlement and enforcement under the new system, the assumptions on which the GATT 1947 had been held to lack direct effect no longer applied.[259] The CJEU confronted this question directly in the *Portugal* case.

Case C–149/96 **Portugal v Council**
[1999] ECR I–8395

Portugal brought an action for annulment of a 1996 Council Decision, arguing *inter alia* that the Decision was in breach of the WTO rules, including provisions of GATT 1994. The Court began by indicating that it was only where an international agreement did not itself settle the question of the effects which its provisions would have within the legal orders of the contracting parties that it would fall to be decided by the courts.

THE ECJ

36. While it is true that the WTO agreements, as the Portuguese Government observes, differ significantly from the provisions of GATT 1947, in particular by reason of the strengthening of the system of safeguards and the mechanism for resolving disputes, the system resulting from those agreements nevertheless accords considerable importance to negotiation between the parties.

[*The CJEU examined the dispute-settlement rules of the WTO, and noted that although they provided for withdrawal of any measures found to be incompatible with WTO rules, they also allowed for compensation to be paid instead as a temporary measure where withdrawal would be impracticable. And if a member of the WTO failed to comply with a recommendation made by the dispute resolution body, that member would be requested to enter negotiations with the other party to the dispute 'with a view to finding mutually acceptable compensation'. The Court continued:*]

40. Consequently, to require the judicial organs to refrain from applying the rules of domestic law which are inconsistent with the WTO agreements would have the consequence of depriving the

---

[256] Case C–377/02 *Van Parys v BIRB* [2005] ECR I–1465, [40]–[41]. This was confirmed by the CJEU in Cases C–120 and 121/06 *FIAMM and Fedon v Council and Commission* [2008] ECR I–6513, [115].

[257] Case C–61/94 *Commission v Germany* (n 174) [52]; Case C–341/95 *Safety Hi-Tech v S & T srl* [1998] ECR I–4355, [20]; Case C–286/90 *Poulsen* (n 226) [9]; Case C–263/08 *Djurgården-Lilla Värtans Miljöskyddsförening* [2009] ECR I–9967, [51].

[258] Case C–53/96 *Hermès International v FHT Marketing Choice* [1998] ECR I–3603; Cases C–300 and 392/98 *Dior v Tuk Consultancy* [2000] ECR I–11307; Case C–245/02 *Anheuser-Busch Inc v Budějovický Budvar, národní podnik* [2003] ECR I–10989, [54]–[57].

[259] See, eg, Case T–228/95 R *S Lehrfreund Ltd v Council and Commission* [1996] ECR II–111, [28], and many cases which followed. There is also a vast and specialized academic literature on this subject.

legislative or executive organs of the contracting parties of the possibility afforded by Article 22 of that memorandum of entering into negotiated arrangements even on a temporary basis.

41. It follows that the WTO agreements, interpreted in the light of their subject-matter and purpose, do not determine the appropriate legal means of ensuring that they are applied in good faith in the legal order of the contracting parties.

42. As regards, more particularly, the application of the WTO agreements in the Community legal order, it must be noted that, according to its preamble, the agreement establishing the WTO, including the annexes, is still founded, like GATT 1947, on the principle of negotiations with a view to 'entering into reciprocal and mutually advantageous arrangements and is thus distinguished, from the viewpoint of the Community, from the agreements concluded between the Community and non-member countries which introduce a certain asymmetry of obligations, or create special relations of integration with the Community, such as the agreement which the Court was required to interpret in *Kupferberg*.

43. It is common ground, moreover, that some of the contracting parties, which are among the most important commercial partners of the Community, have concluded from the subject-matter and purpose of the WTO agreements that they are not among the rules applicable by their judicial organs when reviewing the legality of their rules of domestic law.

44. Admittedly, the fact that the courts of one of the parties consider that some of the provisions of the agreement concluded by the Community are of direct application whereas the courts of the other party do not recognise such direct application is not in itself such as to constitute a lack of reciprocity in the implementation of the agreement (*Kupferberg*, paragraph 18).

45. However, the lack of reciprocity in that regard on the part of the Community's trading partners, in relation to the WTO agreements which are based on 'reciprocal and mutually advantageous arrangements and which must *ipso facto* be distinguished from agreements concluded by the Community, referred to in paragraph 42 of the present judgment, may lead to disuniform application of the WTO rules.

46. To accept that the role of ensuring that those rules comply with Community law devolves directly on the Community judicature would deprive the legislative or executive organs of the Community of the scope for manoeuvre enjoyed by their counterparts in the Community's trading partners.

47. It follows from all those considerations that, having regard to their nature and structure, the WTO agreements are not in principle among the rules in the light of which the Court is to review the legality of measures adopted by the Community institutions.

The Court went on to rule that neither of the two conditions established in the *Nakajima* and *Germany* cases[260] was fulfilled, and so it could not review the legality of the Council decision in the light of the WTO rules.

A number of factors were thus cited by the CJEU as arguments against the direct judicial enforceability of the WTO agreements: first, the agreements themselves do not specify precisely what their own methods of enforcement are to be, given that compensation is permitted in certain circumstances as an alternative to direct enforcement, and that there is scope for negotiation over the recommendations of the WTO dispute-settlement bodies. Secondly, the WTO is still founded on the principle of mutually advantageous negotiations, rather than on clearly and precisely binding legal commitments of the kind to be found in other international agreements entered into by the EU. Such other agreements apparently include those involving an 'asymmetry of obligations', where a guarantee of clear legal enforcement by the EU is given regardless of the lack of direct reciprocity in the relationship with the other party, for example the previous Lomé agreements with the ACP states, as well as those involving special relationships of integration with the EU such as the Portugal free trade agreement

---

[260] See (nn 252–253).

in *Kupferberg*, or the Europe Association Agreements.[261] In other words, lack of reciprocity in obligations and commitments under an international agreement does not itself provide sufficient reason for the CJEU to deny the direct applicability of such an agreement. However, the Court was unwilling to accord such legal effect within the EU legal order to the WTO agreements, given the particular lack of reciprocity in *enforcement* which this would involve—ie the EU Courts giving effect to the obligations contained in these broad-ranging multilateral trade agreements while the other trading partners could enjoy the full 'scope for manoeuvre' expressly permitted under them. The CJEU also commented that the lack of reciprocity in terms of willingness to recognize the direct applicability of the WTO agreements could lead to 'dis-uniform application of WTO rules'.

The *Portugal* judgment generated another avalanche of academic commentary, much of which conceded that while the legal reasoning was less than convincing, the political motivation for the ruling is relatively obvious.[262] For some, this motivation was regrettable;[263] for others it was entirely pragmatic and even laudable, given criticisms of the WTO system for privileging trade liberalization over other social and environmental values.[264]

Since the *Portugal* ruling, the CJEU and the General Court have repeatedly resisted attempts to narrow the scope of the judgment. The CJEU ruled out any remaining uncertainty over the direct effect of provisions of the GATT,[265] and confirmed that the same reasoning applies to other WTO agreements such as TRIPs,[266] and on Technical Barriers to Trade (TBT).[267] The General Court rejected a series of creative legal arguments including attempts to rely on Article 351 TFEU (ex Article 307 EC)[268] or on the principle of *pacta sunt servanda*,[269] or to invoke provisions of the WTO agreements in the context of actions for damages.[270] A number of unsuccessful attempts were also made to invoke the *Nakajima* and *Germany* doctrine,[271] in order to rely on the effects of the ruling of a dispute-settlement panel within the WTO system,[272] specifically by arguing that the EU intended to implement or execute a particular WTO obligation following a dispute-settlement process.[273] Despite rejecting

---

[261] (N 105).

[262] For one example see S Peers, 'Fundamental Right or Political Whim? WTO Law and the ECJ' in G de Búrca and J Scott (eds), *The EU and the WTO: Legal and Constitutional Issues* (Hart, 2001) 111, 120–122.

[263] See, eg, G Zonnekeyn, 'The Status of WTO Law in the Community Legal Order: Some Comments in the Light of the Portuguese Textiles Case' (2000) 25 ELRev 293; S Griller, 'Judicial Enforceability of WTO Law in the EU' (2000) 3 JIEL 441. A long-standing advocate of the justiciability and direct effect of the GATT/WTO Agreements has been E-U Petersmann, 'The Dispute Settlement System of the World Trade Organization and the Evolution of the GATT Dispute Settlement System since 1948' (1994) 31 CMLRev 1157.

[264] A Rosas, '*Portugal v Council*' (2000) 37 CMLRev 797.

[265] Case C–307/99 *OGT v Hauptzollamt Hamburg-St Annen* [2001] ECR I–3159.

[266] Cases C–300 and 392/98 *Dior v Tuk Consultancy* [2000] ECR I–11307; Case C–89/99 *Schieving-Nijstad v Groeneveld* [2001] ECR I–5851, [51]–[55]; Case C–245/02 *Anheuser-Busch* (n 258) [54]–[57]; Case T–279/03 *Galileo International Technology LLC v Commission* [2006] ECR II–1291.

[267] Cases C–27 and 122/00 *The Queen v Secretary of State for the Environment, Transport and the Regions, ex p Omega Air Ltd and others* [2002] ECR I–2569.

[268] Case T–2/99 *T. Port GmbH v Council* [2001] ECR II–2093; Case T–3/99 *Bananatrading GmbH v Council* [2001] ECR II–2093. For pre-*Portugal v Council* cases attempting to use Art 351 TFEU (ex Art 307 EC) in the context of the GATT see Cases C–364 and 365/95 *T. Port* (n 238).

[269] Case T–383/00 *Beamglow Ltd v Parliament, Council and Commission* [2005] ECR II–5459.

[270] Case T–18/99 *Cordis Obst und Gemüse Großhandel v Commission* [2001] ECR II–913; Case T–30/99 *Bocchi Food Trade International v Commission* [2001] ECR II–943; Case T–52/99 *T. Port v Commission* [2001] ECR II–981.

[271] See (nn 252–253). The Commission argued that the *Nakajima* exception should be abolished, or treated as an aspect of the obligation of harmonious interpretation with international law, but the AG rejected the argument and the Court did not address it: Case C–313/04 *Franz Egenberger GmbH Mölkerei und Trockenwerk v Bundesamt für Landwirtschaft und Ernährung* [2006] ECR I–6331.

[272] Previously see Cases T–18/99 *Cordis*, T–30/99 *Bocchi*, and T–52/99 *T. Port* (n 270).

[273] Case T–19/01 *Chiquita Brands International, Inc v Commission of the European Communities* [2005] ECR II–315, [83]–[171].

further attempts of this kind in *IKEA*, and *Biret*, the CJEU in *Biret* seemed to leave open the possibility that a provision of the WTO agreements, including as in this case the Agreement on Sanitary and Phytosanitary Standards (SPS), might be capable of being invoked to challenge the legality of an EU measure in the context of an action for damages, following the expiry of the reasonable period for compliance with its ruling set by a WTO DSB.[274] However the Court in *FIAMM* firmly closed the door on attempts to claim damages based on WTO violations, even those following a DSB ruling, and rejected the argument that a decision of the WTO DSB, as compared with a provision of one of the WTO agreements, could be given 'direct effect'.[275]

In contrast to its reluctance to permit the judicial enforceability of the WTO agreements, the CJEU seemed initially to be more willing to recognize the enforceability of a number of other international agreements, even multilateral agreements, which did not involve special relations of integration with the EU. In the *Biotechnology* case, the CJEU declined to rule on whether the Convention on Biological Diversity (CBD) had created directly effective individual rights in the narrow sense, but confirmed its broader invocability by declaring that, unlike the WTO agreements, the CBD was 'not strictly based on reciprocal and mutually advantageous arrangements' and that courts could therefore review the Community's compliance with the obligations contained therein.[276] Moreover in the case of a regional environmental agreement, the CJEU ruled that the Protocol for the protection of the Mediterranean Sea against pollution from land-based sources, and a later amended Protocol which had been signed by the EU and approximately twenty-one other states in the region was directly effective.[277]

The CJEU in *Racke* ruled that provisions of the EEC–Yugoslavia cooperation agreement of 1980 were directly effective, and could be invoked along with provisions of customary international law to challenge the legality of an EU regulation.[278] Similarly, in a series of cases involving various Europe Association Agreements, the CJEU declared their provisions on freedom of establishment and the free movement of workers to be directly effective.[279] These judgments follow the pattern of similar rulings in which the Court has recognized the direct effect of provisions of EU association or cooperation agreements with third countries,[280] as well as the provisions of secondary decisions adopted by association councils or bodies set up under those agreements.[281] Agreements of this sort fall within the category of those setting up 'special relations of integration' with the EU referred to by the CJEU in paragraph 42 of its ruling in *Portugal v Council*.

---

[274] Case C–94/02 P *Établissements Biret et Cie SA v Council* [2003] ECR I–10565, [54]–[68]; M Mendez, 'The Impact of WTO Rulings in the Community Legal Order' (2004) 29 ELRev 517; A Thies, Note (2004) 41 CMLRev 1661.

[275] Cases C–120 and 121/06 *FIAMM* (n 256) [109]–[133]. The ECJ here also rejected the possibility of liability on the part of the Council or Commission in the absence of unlawful conduct when exercising its legislative powers. For a discussion of the direct effect of WTO provisions more generally, see H Ruiz Fabri, 'Is There a Case—Legally and Politically—For the Direct Effect of WTO Obligations?' (2014) 25 EJIL 151.

[276] Case C–377/98 *Netherlands v Council* [2001] ECR I–7079.

[277] Case C–213/03 *Syndicat professionnel coordination des pêcheurs de l'étang de Berre et de la region v EDF* [2004] ECR I–7357, [31]–[47].

[278] Case C–162/96 (n 227).

[279] (N 105).

[280] For a small sample see Cases C–18/90 *Onem v Kziber* [1991] ECR I–199; C–179/98 *Belgium v Mesbah* [1999] ECR I–7955 on the EEC–Morocco Cooperation Agreement; C–103/94 *Krid v WAVTS* [1995] ECR I–719; C–113/97 *Babahenini v Belgium* [1998] ECR I–813 on the EEC–Algeria Cooperation Agreement; C–37/98 *Savas* [2000] ECR I–2927 on the EU–Turkey Association Agreement—though compare C–221/11 *Demirkan* EU:C:2013:583 and C–91/13 *Essent Energie* EU:C:2014:2206. For discussion see N Tezcan-Idrid and P Van Slot, 'Free Movement of Persons between Turkey and the EU', CLEER Working Paper 2010/2.

[281] There are dozens of cases on these issues. For a small selection see Cases 12/86 *Demirel v Stadt Schwäbisch Gmünd* [1987] ECR 3719; C–192/89 *Sevince* [1990] ECR I–3461; C–237/91 *Kus* [1992] ECR I–6781; C–317 and 369/01 *Abatay* [2003] ECR I–12301, [58]–[59]; C–373/02 *Öztürk* [2004] ECR I–3605, [37]–[68]; C–136/03 *Dörr* [2005] ECR I–4759, [58]–[69]; C–230/03 *Sedef* [2006] ECR I–157, [33]; C–337/07 *Altun* [2008] ECR I–10323, [20]; C–451/11 *Dülger* EU:C:2012:504.

It therefore seemed for many decades that the CJEU, with the exception of the WTO agreements, treated international agreements as capable of having direct effect within the EU legal order. However, in 2008 the Court in *Intertanko* for the first time applied its restrictive reasoning from the GATT/WTO agreements case law to another kind of international agreement.[282] More specifically, the CJEU refused to assess the validity of EU legislation in the light of UNCLOS or the related MARPOL (marine pollution) Convention. The applicant in *Intertanko* had challenged the validity of EU legislation on ship-source pollution, alleging that it violated the provisions of UNCLOS. Returning to its ruling in *International Fruit Company*, the Court declared that UNCLOS does not grant independent rights and freedoms to individuals, and that the nature and broad logic of UNCLOS prevented the Court from assessing the validity of an EU measure in its light.[283]

Notably the Court relied on the argument that UNCLOS does not grant rights to individuals, rather than on the political flexibility maintained by the Convention, in order to conclude that it could not review the legality of EU legislation in the light of UNCLOS. A further notable feature of *Intertanko* is that the Court ignored the distinction which it had drawn earlier in *Nakajima* between the issue of 'conferral of individual rights' and the question whether provisions of an international agreement can be invoked to challenge the validity of EU law.[284]

More generally, the case raised the question whether the CJEU had begun to narrow its previously open approach to the invocability of international agreements. Instead of the GATT/WTO case law standing out as the exception to a general rule of invocability of international agreements binding on the EU, the *Intertanko* ruling may have signalled a shift to the opposite presumption that international agreements cannot normally be invoked to challenge EU acts unless they can satisfy a more demanding criterion of direct effect premised on the conferral of individual rights.

The *Aviation Emissions* and *Z* cases provide further support for the proposition that the Court has narrowed its approach to the invocability of international agreements to challenge EU action. In the *Aviation Emissions* case, the CJEU rejected the invocability of Article 2(2) of the Kyoto Protocol to the United Nations Framework Convention on Climate Change to challenge EU action, since it was not 'unconditional and sufficiently precise so as to confer on individuals the right to rely on it in legal proceedings'.[285] And perhaps most surprisingly of all, given that the Court was dealing with an international human rights treaty designed to empower and confer an array of rights upon persons with disabilities, the Court gave a sweeping ruling in the case of *Z* to the effect that *none* of the provisions of the UN Convention on the Rights of Persons with Disabilities (CRPD) could be considered to be 'unconditional and sufficiently precise... they therefore do not have direct effect in European Union law'.[286] This meant that no provision of the CRPD may be invoked to question the validity of EU law. The Court reached this surprising conclusion by focusing on the fact that Article 4 of the CRPD imposes a wide range of positive obligations on signatory states in their implementation of the Convention, which led the Advocate General to describe the entire agreement as 'programmatic' in nature. Yet the wording of Article 4(1) of the Convention is similar to many provisions of EU directives which have been treated by the CJEU as having direct effect. The peculiar reasoning and conclusion of the Court

---

[282] Case C–308/06 *Intertanko and others* [2008] ECR I–4057.

[283] Ibid [59]–[65]. For discussion, see F Martines, 'Direct Effect of International Agreements of the European Union' (2014) 25 EJIL 129.

[284] See (n 252) and text. The case also left open the question whether Member States, rather than individuals, may challenge the validity of Union legislation in the light of UNCLOS. For comments on *Intertanko* see P Eeckhout, Note (2009) 46 CMLRev 2041; E Denza, Note (2008) 33 ELRev 870; S Adam, P Devisscher, and P Van Elsuwege, Note, CDDE 2009/3–4, 537.

[285] Case C–366/10 *ATAA v Secretary of State for Energy and Climate Change* EU:C:2011:864 (n 233) [77].

[286] Case C–363/12 *Z v A Government Department* EU:C:2014:159.

in the Z case reinforces the impression that the Court has moved to limit the direct invocation of international agreements to challenge EU laws, and seems to be doing so in a range of different and doctrinally inconsistent ways.[287]

The CJEU has, on the other hand, continued to apply the principle of 'indirect effect', or harmonious interpretation, to the provisions of certain international agreements. In addition to the TRIPs and other WTO agreements cited above,[288] the CJEU has also applied the principle of harmonious interpretation to non-trade agreements such as the Aarhus Convention[289] and the Geneva Convention on Refugees.[290] However, it has done this mostly when EU law already made reference to or was intended to implement the international agreement, or when national laws were being interpreted in the light of the international agreement, rather than when the international agreement was being relied upon to challenge EU law.[291]

9 THE ROLE OF THE CJEU
IN EU INTERNATIONAL RELATIONS

It is clear from the above discussion of the CJEU's approach to the effect of international agreements in the EU legal order, as well as its approach to the nature and breadth of EU competence and the scope of the CCP, that the Court has played an active and at times activist role in EU external relations. Below, an overview of the Court's role in the expansive field of international relations will be provided.

(A) PRE-EMPTIVE JURISDICTION: THE ADVISORY OPINION PROCEDURE OF ARTICLE 218(11)

The most distinctive source of CJEU jurisdiction in the field of international relations is the advisory opinion procedure provided for in Article 218(11) TFEU.[292] Article 218(11) stipulates:

> A Member State, the European Parliament, the Council or the Commission may obtain the opinion of the Court of Justice as to whether an agreement envisaged is compatible with the Treaties. Where the opinion of the Court is adverse, the agreement envisaged may not enter into force unless it is amended or the Treaties are revised.

The fact that either a Treaty amendment or a modification of the proposed agreement is required in the case of a negative opinion indicates that the Court's opinions are binding on the institutions. In

---

[287] For a discussion of the differences in the CJEU's treatment of international agreements which are invoked to challenge Member States laws, as compared with international agreements which are invoked to challenge EU law, see M Mendez, *The Legal Effect of EU Agreements* (Oxford University Press, 2013).

[288] (Nn 257–258).

[289] Case C–240/09 *Lesoochranárske zoskupenie (Brown Bears)* [2011] ECR I–1255, concerning the interpretation of national law in the light of Art 9(3) of the Aarhus Convention on access to judicial or administrative procedures. See also Case C–403/12 P *Vereniging Milieudefensie*, pending.

[290] Case C–411/10 *NS v Home Secretary* [2011] ECR I–13905, [75]–[80].

[291] See G de Búrca, 'International Law before the Courts' (n 225).

[292] And Arts 103–105 of the Euratom Treaty. In the past no formal Opinion by an AG was published in Article proceedings, although the Advocates General would be heard together by the Court in closed session. The practice has since changed, and the AG does now give an Opinion. See, eg, the Opinion of AG Jääskinen in *Opinion 1/13 on the Hague Convention on International Child Abduction* EU:C:2014:2292.

its first Opinion, the CJEU outlined the rationale for this advisory procedure, and indicated that the scope of the questions which can form the subject of the request includes questions concerning the competence of the EU (then the EC) to enter the agreement:

Opinion 1/75 (Understanding on a Local Cost Standard)
[1975] ECR 1355

[Note Lisbon Treaty renumbering: Art 228 EC is now Art 218 TFEU]

THE ECJ

The compatibility of an agreement with the provisions of the Treaty must be assessed in the light of all the rules of the Treaty, that is to say, both those rules which determine the extent of the powers of the institutions of the Community and the substantive rules.

It is the purpose of the second subparagraph of Article 228 (1) to forestall complications which would result from legal disputes concerning the compatibility with the Treaty of international agreements binding upon the Community. In fact, a possible decision of the Court to the effect that such an agreement is, either by reason of its content or of the procedure adopted for its conclusion, incompatible with the provisions of the Treaty could not fail to provoke, not only in a Community context, but also in that of international relations, serious difficulties and might give rise to adverse consequences for all interested parties, including third countries.

For the purpose of avoiding such complications the Treaty had recourse to the exceptional procedure of a prior reference to the Court of Justice for the purpose of elucidating, before the conclusion of the agreement, whether the latter is compatible with the Treaty. This procedure must therefore be open for all questions capable of submission for judicial consideration, either by the Court of Justice or possibly by national courts, in so far as such questions give rise to doubt either as to the substantive or formal validity of the agreement with regard to the Treaty.

There is no time limit for the submission of a request under Article 218(11). Moreover, as we have seen above, the term 'agreement' has been interpreted broadly so as to include 'any undertaking entered into by entities subject to international law which has binding force, whatever its legal designation'.[293] On the other hand, the CJEU indicated in its *Opinion 2/94* on accession to the ECHR (a precursor almost twenty years earlier to *Opinion 2/13* on accession to the ECHR) that at least the purpose of the agreement envisaged must be known before the Court is in a position to give an opinion.[294] It was not necessary that the Council should already have adopted a decision to open negotiations, but the Court would need sufficient information concerning the specific arrangements envisaged, such as the proposed mechanism for judicial control under the ECHR. Since no such information was provided for the purpose of *Opinion 2/94*, the Court ruled that it could not give its opinion on that particular point.[295]

Once the EU has expressed its intention to be bound by an agreement, namely once it has concluded the agreement, the CJEU is precluded from continuing with an Article 218(11) procedure. Following its conclusion (even if this takes place after the request for an opinion has been filed) it is no longer an 'envisaged agreement' within the meaning of Article 218(11), the preventive function of the procedure

---

[293] *Opinion 1/75* (n 81).
[294] *Opinion 2/94* [1996] ECR I–1759
[295] Compare the ruling of the CJEU in *Opinion 2/13*, (n 217) and text above.

cannot be achieved, and the ECJ's advisory jurisdiction is excluded.[296] This is clear from *Opinion 1/04* in which the Court refused to provide an opinion on the compatibility with the Treaty of the agreement envisaged with the United States on the exchange of PNR data.[297] The Council had rapidly concluded the agreement only a few weeks after Parliament's request was filed, thereby circumventing the possibility for an advisory opinion, and requiring Parliament to bring a subsequent action for annulment instead.[298] The Parliament has, however, voted to refer the EU–Canada PNR Agreement, whose conclusion now requires the consent of the Parliament, to the CJEU for an opinion on its compatibility with the Treaties.[299]

Once the legal basis on which the EU may act in concluding an agreement has been established, the Court treats it as beyond its jurisdiction to engage in a more precise delineation of competence, particularly since the Article 218(11) procedure is not intended to resolve the difficulties associated with the implementation of an envisaged agreement entailing shared competence.[300]

Although the question is contested, the general exclusion of CJEU jurisdiction over the CFSP would seem to exclude the possibility of the Court providing an opinion on the compatibility of an envisaged agreement which relates exclusively or principally to this field.[301] However, following the logic of its reasoning in the *EU–Mauritius* case in which the Court ruled on the appropriate procedure under Article 318 to be followed when concluding a CFSP agreement, the Court's jurisdiction under Article 40 TEU to ensure that the implementation neither of the CFSP nor of the rest of the EU's policies adversely affects the powers and procedures of the other is likely to provide a basis for an advisory opinion which focuses on questions of procedure and competence.[302]

(B) JURISDICTION OF THE CJEU OVER INTERNATIONAL AGREEMENTS UNDER OTHER EU TREATY PROCEDURES

International agreements entered into by the EU may form the subject matter of a reference for a preliminary ruling on a point of interpretation or validity under Article 267 TFEU. In the first example of such a reference, the CJEU ruled in *Haegeman* that the EU's association agreement with Greece was an act of the institutions within the meaning of Article 267 TFEU.[303] Therefore, the provisions of the Agreement formed an integral part of EU law and the Court had jurisdiction to give preliminary rulings on their interpretation. The Court has also asserted its jurisdiction to interpret acts such as decisions of bodies (like the Turkey–EU Association Council) set up under an agreement[304] as well as non-binding recommendations made under an international agreement.[305]

The CJEU may hear infringement proceedings brought against Member States under Article 258 for violation of their obligations under an international agreement which is binding on the EU.[306]

---

[296] *Opinion 3/94 (Banana Framework Agreement)* [1995] ECR I–4577.

[297] *Opinion 1/04* [2004] OJ C118/1.

[298] Case C–317/03 *Parliament v Council (PNR Agreement)* [2006] ECR I–4721

[299] Vote of the European Parliament of 25 November 2014: www.europarl.europa.eu/news/en/news-room/content/20141121IPR79818/.

[300] *Opinion 2/00* (n 21) [17]–[18].

[301] M Cremona, 'The Union as a Global Actor: Roles, Models and Identity' (2004) 41 CMLRev 571, 572; T Corthaut, 'An Effective Remedy for All? Paradoxes and Controversies in Respect of Judicial Protection in the Field of the CFSP under the European Constitution' [2005] Tilburg Foreign Law Review 124.

[302] Case C–658/11 *Parliament v Council (EU–Mauritius Agreement)* EU:C:2014:2025. For discussion, see above (nn 147 and 198) and text.

[303] Case 181/73 *Haegeman* (n 210) [4]–[6].

[304] Case C–192/89 *Sevince* (n 281).

[305] Case C–188/91 *Deutsche Shell* [1993] ECR I–363.

[306] This is true also even with regard to agreements whose provisions cannot be invoked to challenge the legality of EU acts: Case C–268/94 *Portugal v Council* [1996] ECR I–6177 on the WTO agreements.

International agreements and other provisions of international law are, at least in theory, amongst the rules of law to be taken into account in assessing the validity of EU measures. This was made clear in the *International Fruit Company* case, which has been discussed above in relation to the direct effect of international agreements.[307] By treating international agreements like internal EU acts for these purposes, the Court broadened its jurisdiction to hear actions for annulment and actions for damages brought on the basis of international agreements. However, we have seen above, both from the case law on the GATT/WTO agreements and more recent cases such as *Intertanko* on UNCLOS, *ATAA* on the Kyoto Protocol, and *Z* on the UN Disability Convention, that the Court has begun to narrow the range of international agreements whose provisions may be invoked to assess the validity of EU legislation.[308]

In addition to entertaining actions for the annulment of EU acts alleged to violate international agreements, the Court also hears actions for annulment of an EU decision to conclude an international agreement. The grounds for annulment of a decision concluding an international agreement alleged to violate the Treaty are the same as for internal acts under Article 263(2) TFEU: lack of competence, infringement of an essential procedural requirement, infringement of the Treaties or of any rule of law relating to their application, or misuse of powers. Thus the alleged infringement may arise from the procedure followed for the conclusion of an international agreement,[309] or the substantive provisions of the agreement,[310] or the agreement may be *ultra vires* in the sense that the EU lacked competence to conclude it.[311] The obligation to state reasons means that a specific reference to the legal basis upon which the agreement is concluded is required.[312]

Since international agreements concluded by the EU are binding upon it, violation of their provisions may, at least in theory, form the basis for an action in damages under Article 340 TFEU. Thus far, however, no such action has been successful.

(c) THE CJEU AND MIXED AGREEMENTS

Although the Court's first ruling on the interpretation of an international agreement in the *Haegeman* case concerned a mixed agreement, that fact seemed to play no part in the Court's assessment of its jurisdiction in that case.[313] The mixed nature of the agreement was invoked for the first time in *Demirel*, concerning the EC–Turkey Association Agreement:

> Since the agreement in question is an association agreement creating special, privileged links with a non-member country which must, at least to a certain extent, take part in the Community system, Article 238 must necessarily empower the Community to guarantee commitments towards non-member countries in all the fields covered by the Treaty. Since freedom of movement for workers is, by virtue of Article 48 et seq of the EEC Treaty, one of the fields covered by that Treaty, it follows that commitments regarding freedom of movement fall within the powers conferred on the Community by

---

[307] (N 243).

[308] See (nn 282–286) and text, and also (nn 262–275).

[309] See, eg, Case C–327/91 *France v Commission* (n 28) and Case C–377/12 *Commission v Council (EU–Philippines Partnership and Cooperation Agreement)* EU:C:2014:1903.

[310] Case C–122/95 *Germany v Council* [1989] ECR I–973.

[311] Cases C–317 and 318/04 *European Parliament v Council (PNR)* (n 33).

[312] Case C–370/07 *Commission v Council (CITES Convention)* [2009] ECR I–8917, discussed at (n 27) [37]–[55]. This case concerned a decision establishing the position to be adopted by the EU within an organ created by an international agreement.

[313] P Koutrakos, 'The Interpretation of Mixed Agreements under the Preliminary Reference Procedure' (2002) 7 EFAR 25.

> Article 238. Thus the question whether the Court has jurisdiction to rule on the interpretation of a provision in a mixed agreement containing a commitment which only the Member States could enter into in the sphere of their own powers does not arise.[314]

While this passage seems to suggest that the Court's jurisdiction over mixed agreements covers all issues, with the exception of matters falling within the exclusive competence of the Member States, the question of the Court's jurisdiction in cases where the relevant provisions of the international agreement at issue were concluded on the basis of the Member States' shared powers was not directly addressed in the case.[315]

The point arose in *Hermès*, in which a preliminary reference was made to the CJEU on a question concerning the interpretation of Article 50 of the TRIPs Agreement, concerning the power of judicial authorities to order provisional measures to prevent certain infringements of intellectual property rights.[316] One of the objections raised was that the dispute concerned the application of national trade mark law. The Court replied that it did indeed have jurisdiction, since the provision in question applied also to Community trade marks:

> [W]here a provision can apply both to situations falling within the scope of national law and to situations falling within the scope of Community law, it is clearly in the Community interest that, in order to forestall future differences of interpretation, that provision should be interpreted uniformly, whatever the circumstances in which it is to apply...

Subsequently in *Parfums Christian Dior*, the CJEU extended further the scope of its jurisdiction to rule on the same provision of TRIPs, ruling that since that provision is a procedural one which should be applied in the same way to situations covered by national law as well as situations covered by EU law, only the CJEU is in a position to provide the requisite uniform interpretation.[317] Nevertheless, the Court also indicated that it would not interfere with the jurisdiction of Member State courts to appraise the direct effect of provisions which fall neither within exclusive EU competence nor within exclusive Member State competence, and in respect of which the EU has not yet legislated.[318]

The broad jurisdiction of the Court to rule on the interpretation of mixed agreements was confirmed in two subsequent sets of infringement proceedings brought by the Commission against Member States, involving the Berne Convention for the Protection of Literary and Artistic Works[319] and the Convention for the Protection of the Mediterranean Sea respectively.[320] The Court ruled that mixed agreements had the same status within the EU legal order as purely EU (at the time, Community) agreements 'insofar as the provisions fall within the scope of Community competence', and it repeated that when they ensure compliance with commitments arising from an agreement entered by the EU, Member States are fulfilling an obligation in relation to the EU which has assumed responsibility for its performance.[321] In both cases, the subject matter of the agreements was held to

---

[314] Case 12/86 *Demirel* (n 281).

[315] A Dashwood, 'Preliminary Rulings on the Interpretation of Mixed Agreements' in D O'Keeffe and A Bavaso (eds), *Judicial Review in European Union Law* (Kluwer, 2001) 171.

[316] Case C–53/96 *Hermès International* (n 258).

[317] Cases C–300 and 392/98 *Parfums Christian Dior* [2000] ECR I–11307, [37]–[38].

[318] Ibid [27]–[28].

[319] Case C–13/00 *Commission v Ireland (Berne Convention)* [2002] ECR I–2943.

[320] Case C–239/03 *Commission v France (Etang de Berre)* (n 211). See also Case C–240/09 *Lesoochranárske zoskupenie* EU:C:2011:125, [31]–[35] on Art 9(3) of the Aarhus Convention.

[321] Ibid [25]–[26].

be largely governed by EU law, and the Court ruled that there was a clear EU interest in compliance by the Member States and the EU with the commitments entered.

To sum up, the CJEU has construed its jurisdiction over mixed agreements very broadly, and it seems that only where a particular area falls clearly within the exclusive competence of the Member States under a mixed agreement will the Court actually decline to interpret or enforce it. However, the Court decided in *Merck Genéricos* that in a field in which there is only limited EU legislation, such as patent law, the Member States would remain competent to choose whether or not to give certain direct effect to the provisions of a mixed agreement in that field.[322]

The conclusions of the *Hermès/Dior/Merck* line of case law have been overtaken by the case of *Daiichi Sankyo* insofar as the nature of the TRIPs Agreement is concerned, since the CJEU ruled that the TRIPs Agreement now falls, following the Lisbon Treaty, within the exclusive competence of the EU.[323] Nonetheless, the more general aspects of those previous rulings which concern the jurisdiction of the CJEU over the provisions of mixed agreements remain relevant for other mixed agreements.

(D) THE CJEU AND THE CFSP

The jurisdiction of the Court is expressly excluded from the field of the CFSP.[324] However, Article 275 TFEU contains two major exceptions to the exclusion of CJEU jurisdiction. The first relates to the boundaries between the CFSP and the rest of EU law, which are now governed by Article 40 TEU.[325] The CFSP was created to include all areas of foreign and security policy within its scope, and the possibility of conflict with other parts of EU external competence was therefore quite clear. The terms of Article 40 TEU, which, as indicated above, protect the CFSP and the other parts of EU law against undue encroachment by the other, mean that the CJEU may exercise judicial control over the choice of legal basis and consequently may check that the EU was competent to act as it did, and that the procedural requirements provided in the appropriate Treaty basis have been satisfied. This was confirmed in the *Al-Qaeda Sanctions* and the *EU–Mauritius Agreement* cases, in which the CJEU confirmed and exercised its jurisdiction to rule on procedural as well as legal basis dimensions of the conclusion of CFSP agreements.[326] Indeed, in *EU–Mauritius* the Court declared that the Treaty provisions limiting its jurisdiction with regard to the CFSP should be narrowly construed, given the fundamental task conferred on the Court of ensuring the law is applied:[327]

> 69. As regards, first of all, the question of the Court's jurisdiction to rule on the second plea, it must be noted, as the Council submits, that it is apparent from the final sentence of the second subparagraph of Article 24(1) TEU and the first paragraph of Article 275 TFEU that the Court does not, in principle, have jurisdiction with respect to the provisions relating to the CFSP or with respect to acts adopted on the basis of those provisions.

[322] Case C–431/05 *Merck Genéricos Produtos Farmacêuticos* [2007] ECR I–7001, [46]–[47].
[323] Case C–414/11 *Daiichi Sankyo Co Ltd v DEMO Anonimos Viomikhaniki* EU:C:2013:520. See A Dimopoulos and P Vantsiouri, 'Of TRIPS and Traps: The Interpretative Jurisdiction of the CJEU over Patent Law' (2014) 39 ELRev 210.
[324] Art 24(1) TEU; Art 275 TFEU.
[325] See (n 140) and following text. The CJEU had recognized such a role for itself under the predecessor to Art 40 TEU, which was Art 47 EU: see Case C–170/96 *Commission v Council (Airport Transit Visas)* [1998] ECR I–2763, [16]–[17] and Case C–176/03 *Commission v Council (Environmental Crimes)* [2005] ECR I–7879.
[326] See (nn 145–153) and text; also (nn 200 and 301–302) and text.
[327] Case C–658/11 *Parliament v Council (EU–Mauritius Agreement)* EU:C:2014:2025.

> 70. Nevertheless, the final sentence of the second subparagraph of Article 24(1) TEU and the first paragraph of Article 275 TFEU introduce a derogation from the rule of the general jurisdiction which Article 19 TEU confers on the Court to ensure that in the interpretation and application of the Treaties the law is observed, and they must, therefore, be interpreted narrowly.

The second exception empowers the Court to hear actions brought by natural or legal persons to review the legality of decisions which effectively provide for the imposition of sanctions or 'restrictive measures' against them.[328] This amendment, introduced by the Lisbon Treaty, follows the approach adopted by the CJEU to its own jurisdiction in the earlier *Kadi* case.[329]

There had indeed already been sustained criticism of the lack of adequate judicial control over the law adopted within the CFSP, particularly on account of the consequences for affected individuals.[330] An increasing number of CFSP measures have a quasi-legislative character, in particular with the rapid growth and expansion of EU sanctions law and policy, and the limits of judicial review over the CFSP led to its description as 'patently insufficient from the perspective of the rule of law'.[331]

10 COHERENCE, CONSISTENCY, AND COOPERATION IN THE GOVERNANCE OF EU INTERNATIONAL RELATIONS

One of the key aims of EU foreign policy is said to be the coordination of the variety of different external activities. Consistency is a significant goal in the external relations of an entity like the EU, which still lacks a coherent and recognizable international identity, and it is the task of the Foreign Affairs Council and the High Representative to ensure consistency in the Union's external action.[332] Given the position of the High Representative as Vice-President of the Commission and President of the Foreign Affairs Council, she is assumed to be in a unique position to coordinate the various aspects of EU external action.

The EU seeks to ensure coordination on a number of different levels: first, in the international representation of the EU, secondly, across the different activities of the EU, and, thirdly, between the Member States and the EU.

(A) INTERNATIONAL REPRESENTATION AND THE EU

In order to perform its tasks under the Treaties, the EU has developed extensive diplomatic relations with other subjects of international law. Almost all states have established diplomatic missions to the EU, which are called Representative Missions to the EU, and the EU maintains relations through EU delegations in more than 150 states and international organizations.[333] They are placed under the authority of the High Representative and enjoy customary privileges and immunities under international law. Their task is to communicate the views and to represent the interests of the Union as a

---

[328] Art 274 para 2 provides: 'The Court shall have jurisdiction...to rule on proceedings, brought in accordance with the conditions laid down in the fourth paragraph of Article 263 of this Treaty, reviewing the legality of decisions providing for restrictive measures against natural or legal persons adopted by the Council on the basis of Chapter 2 of Title V of the Treaty on European Union'.

[329] Cases C–402 and 415/05 P (n 145).

[330] P Eeckhout, 'Does Europe's Constitution Stop at the Water's Edge? Law and Policy in the EU's External Relations', 2005 Walter van Gerven Lectures, Leuven.

[331] Ibid.

[332] Arts 16(6) and 18(4) TEU.

[333] Art 221 TFEU. Commission delegations were replaced by Union delegations, following the Lisbon Treaty.

whole. As far as international organizations are concerned, Article 220 TFEU provides that it shall be for the Commission to ensure the maintenance of all appropriate relations with the organs of the UN and its specialized agencies, the Council of Europe, the OECD, the OSCE, and with 'all international organisations'.[334]

Several provisions of the TEU aim at organizing the representation of the interests of the Union internationally. Article 27(2) TEU provides that in matters which come within the scope of the CFSP the Union is represented by the High Representative, who shall express the position of the Union in international organizations and in international conferences. The High Representative and the Member States are responsible for the implementation of CFSP decisions.[335] The High Representative is assisted by the EEAS,[336] which works in cooperation with the diplomatic services of the Member States.[337] Further, the Council may, on a proposal of the High Representative, appoint a special representative with a mandate in relation to particular policy issues.[338]

Article 34 TEU requires Member States to coordinate their action in international organizations and at international conferences as well as to uphold EU common positions in such fora, but, given the institutional complexity of the EU and the elaborate sharing of powers between the EU and the Member States in the field of external relations, this is not a straightforward task.[339] It is for the High Representative to organize this cooperation. In international organizations and at international conferences where not all the Member States participate, those which do take part have particular duties: they must uphold EU common positions and keep the others, as well as the High Representative, informed of any matter of common interest. The Member States which are also members of the UN Security Council are required to 'concert' their practice and to keep the other Member States and the High Representative fully informed. Those Member States which are permanent members of the Security Council must, in the execution of their functions, ensure the defence of the positions and the interests of the Union, even though this is without prejudice to their responsibilities under the provisions of the UN Charter.

Article 35 TEU provides for the cooperation of the diplomatic and consular missions of the Member States and the EU delegations in third countries and international conferences, and their representations to international organizations, in ensuring that the common positions and joint actions adopted by the Council are complied with and implemented.

(B) THE REQUIREMENT OF COHERENCE ACROSS POLICIES

The traditional division in foreign policy between 'high politics' (eg matters of war and peace) and 'low politics' (eg economic and other more 'technical' matters), is arguably legally reflected in the separate legal regimes of the CFSP and the other competences of the EU.[340] The reality of political and economic interaction in a highly globalized world, however, prevails over this kind of formal juridical

---

[334] On the varied nature of EU participation in different international organizations and some of the reasons for that, see T Gehring, 'European Union Actorness in International Insitutions: Why the EU is Recognized as an Actor in Some International Institutions, But Not in Others' (2013) 51 JCMS 849.

[335] Art 24(1) TEU.

[336] See (nn 10–11) above and text.

[337] Art 27(3) TEU.

[338] D Tolksdorf, 'EU Special Representatives: An Intergovernmental Tool in the Post-Lisbon Foreign Policy System?' (2013) 18 EFAR 471.

[339] On the uneven character of EU representation in international organizations see S Gstöhl, '"Patchwork Power" Europe: The EU's Representation in International Institutions' (2009) 14 EFAR 385 and T Gehring (n 334).

[340] On coherence between the CFSP and other EU policies see H Merket, 'The EU and the Security-Development Nexus: Bridging the Legal Divide' (2013) 18 EFAR 83 and M Smith, 'Institutionalizing the Comprehensive Approach to EU Security' (2013) 18 EFAR 25.

delineation.[341] Perhaps it is this mismatch between the constitutional framework and the practical reality of EU international relations that has kept the theme of 'coherence' at the centre of EU attention, such that it has been described as 'the true recurrent theme of European foreign policy'.[342]

Until the entry into force of the Lisbon Treaty, the legal attempt to ensure greater coherence was said to have, at best, mixed results.[343] Article 21(3) TEU now requires the EU to ensure consistency 'between the different areas of its external action and between these and its other policies'.[344] The 'single institutional framework' referred to in the TEU's Preamble is intended to ensure the desired consistency and coherence, and the High Representative has particular responsibility in this regard.

(c) COORDINATION BETWEEN THE MEMBER STATES AND THE EU: COOPERATION AND COMPLIANCE

The effectiveness of EU external activities depends also on ensuring the cooperation, and where necessary the compliance, of Member States. The duty of loyal or sincere cooperation is now to be found in Article 4(3) TEU. The broader application of this obligation is reinforced by Article 24(3) of the TEU, according to which the Member States are under a duty to support the EU's external and security policy 'actively and unreservedly in a spirit of loyalty and mutual solidarity'. Member States are further required to work together to enhance and develop their mutual political solidarity. The TEU stipulates that they shall refrain from any action which is contrary to the interests of the Union or likely to impair its effectiveness as a cohesive force in international relations, and the Council is required to ensure compliance with these principles.

The CJEU has regularly invoked the obligation contained in Article 4(3) TEU together with other provisions to put pressure on the EU institutions and the Member States to act in defence of the EU's common interests.[345] The Court ruled that Member States are required to facilitate the achievement of the EU's tasks and to abstain from any measure which could jeopardize the attainment of the objectives of the Treaty.[346] The Court emphasized that this 'duty of genuine cooperation is of general application and does not depend either on whether the Community [now EU] competence is exclusive, or on any right of the Member State to enter into obligations towards non-member countries'.[347]

The Article 4(3) TEU obligation to comply with EU law imposes legal constraints on the Member States in their external action in a number of ways. It has been held to require Member States to facilitate the application of EU law, and thus not to give effect to a bilateral agreement falling outside the field of application of the Treaties, where giving effect to it would impede the application of a right conferred by EU law and the supremacy of EU law.[348] The *Open Skies* rulings indicate that even where

---

[341] For the waning of the distinction in the context of the EU see J-V Louis, 'The European Union: From External Relations to Foreign Policy?', College of Europe, EU Diplomacy Papers 2/2007.

[342] P Gauttier, 'Horizontal Coherence and the External Competences of the European Union' (2004) 10 ELJ 23, 25. See also M Cremona, 'Coherence Through Law: What Difference will the Treaty of Lisbon Make' (2008) 3 Hamburg Review of Social Sciences 1 and L den Hertog and S Stroß, 'Coherence in EU External Relations: Concepts and Legal Rooting of an Ambiguous Term' (2013) 18 EFAR 373.

[343] Gauttier, ibid 35.

[344] See on this principle I Bosse-Platière, *L'article 3 du Traité UE: Recherche sur une exigence de cohérence de l'action extérieure de l'Union européenne* (Bruylant, 2009).

[345] See, eg, Case 22/70 *ERTA* (n 17); Cases 3, 4 and 6/76 *Kramer* (n 35); *Opinion 2/91* (n 49); *Opinion 1/94* (n 45).

[346] See on the duty of sincere cooperation in the field of external relations, above Section 6(d).

[347] Case C–433/03 *Commission v Germany* (n 201) [64]; Case C–266/03 *Commission v Luxembourg* (n 201) [58].

[348] Case 235/87 *Matteucci v Communauté française de Belgique et al* [1988] ECR 5589, 5611–5612. See also the BITs cases (n 74). While the ECJ used Art 351 TFEU (ex Art 307 EC) to resolve these cases, this Art is a mere expression of the broader principle of sincere cooperation (see on this link the conclusions of AG Poiares Maduro in Case C–205/06 *Commission v Austria* [2009] ECR I–1301, [33]–[43]).

the agreements concluded by the Member States fell largely outside exclusive EU competence, the Member States' treaty-making powers in the field were constrained by the need to comply with the Treaty rules on the right of establishment.[349] We have seen above that not only are the Member States precluded from individual action when an EU agreement exists, but they are also subject to special duties of action and abstention, in particular where the Commission has submitted proposals to the Council which represent the point of departure for concerted EU action.[350]

The international representation of the EU became a particularly salient issue at the time of the Uruguay Round negotiations which led to the establishment of the WTO. In *Opinion 1/94*, the Commission claimed to be the sole spokesperson for the Community and the Member States, on the basis that this was necessary to secure the effective implementation of the WTO agreements. The CJEU ruled that these concerns could not influence the allocation of competence between the EU and Member States, but it also ruled that where the subject matter of an agreement fell within shared EU–Member State competence, close cooperation between them in the process of negotiation, conclusion, and fulfilment of commitments entered into was essential.[351] The obligation to cooperate flowed from the requirement for unity in the international representation of the EU.[352]

In terms of dispute resolution too, Member States are bound by the duty of sincere cooperation: the ECJ ruled in *MOX Plant* that Ireland violated the duty of cooperation by instituting dispute-settlement proceedings against the UK under UNCLOS in relation to matters which fall within EU competence without consulting the Commission.[353]

Finally, it has been argued that the unity of the international presence of the EU and its Member States which is achieved through this kind of cooperation may be greater than the unity resulting from the exclusive competence of the EU, since it operates also when the Member States are exercising their own competences.[354]

11 CONCLUSIONS

i.   The area of external relations has become increasingly important as the EU strives to assert its presence more effectively on the world stage, on issues such as trade, climate change, development, human rights, migration, security, and international terrorism.

ii. One of the crucial issues for the conduct of EU international relations is effective coordination. This includes coordination across policy fields, coordination between the EU and the Member States, and coordination at the level of international representation. Consistency across and between policies has become a constitutional requirement of EU external relations.

iii. In an EU of twenty-eight with several applications for membership pending, the problems of effective coordination and effective international lawmaking are extremely challenging. The EU's

---

[349] Case C–487/98 *Commission v Denmark* [2002] ECR I–9519, [122]–[139]; M Cremona, 'External Relations of the EU and the Member States: Competence, Mixed Agreements, International Responsibility and the Effects of International Law', FIDE Report, 2006.

[350] Case C–266/03 (n 201) [60]; Case C–433/03 (n 201) [66]; Case C–246/07 *Commission v Sweden* (n 190). For critical comment see AD Casteleiro and J Larik, 'The Duty to Remain Silent: Limitless Loyalty in EU External Relations?' (2011) 36 ELRev 524.

[351] *Opinion 1/94* (n 45) [107].

[352] Ibid [108]. The ECJ also referred to *Opinion 1/78* (n 67) [34]–[36] and *Opinion 2/91* (n 49).

[353] Case C–459/03 *Commission v Ireland (MOX Plant)* [2006] ECR I–4635; see also the Opinion of AG Poiares Maduro.

[354] M Cremona, 'Defending the Community Interest: The Duties of Cooperation and Compliance' in Cremona and de Witte (n 20).

ambition of being an influential global player which presents a single face and speaks with a single voice to the outside world is difficult to attain.

iv. The importance of EU external action is reflected in the range of institutional and substantive provisions introduced by the Lisbon Treaty to enhance and streamline the EU's global profile and role.

12 FURTHER READING

CARDWELL, P, *EU External Relations Law and Policy in the Post-Lisbon Era* (TMC Asser Press, 2012)

CREMONA, M, *Developments in EU External Relations Law* (Oxford University Press, 2008)

—— AND DE WITTE, B (eds), *EU Foreign Relations Law: Constitutional Fundamentals* (Hart, 2008)

—— AND MARESCEAU, M (eds), *Law and Practice of EU External Relations* (Cambridge University Press, 2008)

DE BAERE, G, *Constitutional Principles of EU External Relations* (Oxford University Press, 2008)

—— *The EU Common Security and Defence Policy* (Oxford University Press, 2013)

—— AND HILLION, C, *Mixed Agreements Revisited: The EU and its Member States in the World* (Hart, 2010)

EECKHOUT, P, *EU External Relations Law* (Oxford University Press, 2nd edn, 2011)

KUIJPER, PJ, WOUTERS J, HOFFMEISTER, F, DE BAERE, G, and RAMOPOULOS, T, *The Law of EU External Relations* (Oxford University Press, 2013)

MENDEZ, M, *The Legal Effects of EU Agreements* (Oxford University Press, 2013)

SMITH, K, *European Union Foreign Policy in a Changing World* (Polity Press, 3rd edn, 2014)

VAN VOOREN, B, *EU External Relations Law and the European Neighbourhood Policy* (Routledge, 2012)

—— AND WESSEL, R, *EU External Relations Law* (Cambridge University Press, 2014)

HUMAN RIGHTS IN THE EU

1 CENTRAL ISSUES

i. The status of human rights within the EU legal order has changed dramatically since its foundation in the early 1950s. While the draft European Political Community Treaty in 1953 would
have made the European Convention on Human Rights part of the law of the new Communities,
this Treaty was never adopted due to France's rejection of the closely-linked Defence Community
Treaty in 1954. Consequently, the EEC and Euratom Treaties in 1957 omitted any reference to
human rights. Over sixty years later, however, human rights occupy a central position within the
EU legal order. The EU Charter of Fundamental Rights and the general principles of EU law now
rank alongside Treaty provisions as primary norms of EU law,[1] and there is a growing EU case
law dealing with human rights issues.

ii. Three formal sources for EU human rights law are today listed in Article 6 TEU. The first and
most important is the EU Charter of Fundamental Rights which gained binding legal force in
2009. The second is the ECHR, which for decades was treated by the ECJ as a 'special source of
inspiration' for EU human rights principles. The third is the 'general principles of EU law', a
body of legal principles, including human rights, which were articulated and developed by the
ECJ over the years before the Charter of Rights was drafted. General principles are said by the
ECJ to be derived from national constitutional traditions, from the ECHR, and from other international treaties signed by the Member States. These three sources overlap, creating a certain
amount of legal confusion. Other sources of international human rights law have occasionally
been invoked by the ECJ.

iii. The CJEU has made it clear in recent years that the Charter is now the principal basis on
which the EU Courts will ensure that human rights are observed, and the proportion of cases
in which the CJEU has drawn on the ECHR and on the case law of the Strasbourg Court has
declined since the coming into force of the Charter.

iv. Article 6(2) TEU declares that the EU shall accede to the ECHR. The long-discussed idea of EU
accession to the ECHR was intended to introduce a degree of external accountability by ensuring that EU action could be challenged before a non-EU court for compatibility with ECHR
provisions. However, the CJEU dealt a surprising blow to the prospects for EU accession when
it ruled in 2014 that the long-negotiated draft Agreement on Accession of the EU to the ECHR

---

[1] Art 6(1) and (3) TEU, and Cases C–402 and 415/05 P *Kadi & Al Barakaat International Foundation v Council and
Commission (Kadi I)* [2008] ECR I–6351, [308].

was incompatible with the EU Treaties and with the autonomy of the EU legal order in several fundamental ways.

v.   EU human rights standards, including the provisions of the Charter and general principles of law, are binding on the EU and its institutions and bodies in all of their activities, and on the Member States when they are acting within the scope of application of EU law. A stream of cases has come before the CJEU to try to clarify whether particular national laws and actions fall within the scope of application of EU law for this purpose, but further guidance is clearly needed.

vi.   The EU has gradually integrated (or 'mainstreamed') human rights concerns into many of its policies. The most important internally-oriented policy of this kind is EU anti-discrimination law[2] and a second is the field of data protection and privacy. In EU external relations, human rights have featured prominently, if inconsistently.[3] The EU actively promotes its 'human rights and democratization' policy in many countries around the world, and uses human rights clauses in its international trade and development policies. It has imposed a human rights-based 'political conditionality' on candidate Member States, and claims to integrate human rights concerns throughout its Common Foreign and Security Policy. The EU in 2009 concluded its first major international human rights treaty, the UN Convention on the Rights of Persons with Disabilities, with both internal and external policy implications.

vii. Other significant institutional initiatives in the human rights field include the establishment in 1999 of a sanction mechanism for serious and persistent breaches of human rights in Article 7 TEU, and the creation of an EU Fundamental Rights Agency in 2007. However, despite much debate and critique, most recently in relation to the adoption of repressive and anti-democratic measures by the Hungarian Government in recent years, the Article 7 mechanism has not yet been used.

viii. Notwithstanding these extensive developments in the human rights field, the EU's status as a significant human rights actor or organization has been questioned.[4] Critics have suggested that EU attention to human rights often constitutes little more than rhetoric or self-serving instrumentalism.[5] In the fields of immigration and asylum, the EU has been sharply criticized for neglecting and undermining human rights concerns.[6] With thousands of asylum-seekers and refugees dying at Europe's borders and on the seas, the EU Ombudsman opened an investigation into compliance with human rights standards by the EU's border agency, Frontex.[7] Even within the EU, the austerity measures mandated by the EU in response to the Euro-crisis have been

---

[2] Ch 24.

[3] See http://eeas.europa.eu/human_rights/index_en.htm.

[4] P Alston, J Heenan, and M Bustelo (eds), *The EU and Human Rights* (Oxford University Press, 1999), in particular ch 1; A von Bogdandy, 'The European Union as a Human Rights Organization: Human Rights and the Core of the European Union' (2000) 37 CMLRev 1307; A Rosas, 'Is the EU a Human Rights Organization?', CLEER Working Paper 2011/1.

[5] A Williams, *The Irony of Human Rights in the European Union* (Oxford University Press, 2004). For criticisms of the EU from a human rights perspective see Amnesty International, *The EU and Human Rights: Making the Impact on People Count* (2009) and K Roth, 'Filling the Leadership Void: Where is the European Union?' (Human Rights Watch World Report, 2007).

[6] See, eg, Amnesty International, *The Human Cost of Fortress Europe*, 9 July 2014.

[7] Own Initiative Inquiry concerning the means through which FRONTEX ensures respect for human rights in Joint Return Operations, OI/9/2014/MHZ, opened in October 2014.

reported to have had a sharply negative impact on the economic and social rights of the most vulnerable populations.[8]

2 INTRODUCTION

The constitutional framework of the EU today boasts an impressive array of human rights provisions. The Treaties declare that the EU is founded on respect for human rights, they give binding effect to the Charter of Fundamental Rights and Freedoms, and they mandate EU accession to the ECHR. The Treaties require all candidate Member States to adhere to these values and they include a sanction mechanism for existing Member States which seriously and persistently violate such rights. Article 19 TFEU provides a legal basis for a strong EU anti-discrimination regime. The centrepiece of the EU's human rights framework is Article 6 TEU which provides:

> 1. The Union recognises the rights, freedoms and principles set out in the Charter of Fundamental Rights of the European Union of 7 December 2000, as adapted at Strasbourg, on 12 December 2007, which shall have the same legal value as the Treaties.
>
> The provisions of the Charter shall not extend in any way the competences of the Union as defined in the Treaties.
>
> The rights, freedoms and principles in the Charter shall be interpreted in accordance with the general provisions in Title VII of the Charter governing its interpretation and application and with due regard to the explanations referred to in the Charter, that set out the sources of those provisions.
>
> 2. The Union shall accede to the European Convention for the Protection of Human Rights and Fundamental Freedoms. Such accession shall not affect the Union's competences as defined in the Treaties.
>
> 3. Fundamental rights, as guaranteed by the European Convention for the Protection of Human Rights and Fundamental Freedoms and as they result from the constitutional traditions common to the Member States, shall constitute general principles of the Union's law.

These developments however are relatively recent. For many years the European Economic Community was primarily focused on the creation of a common market, even if efforts to broaden the integration project were never entirely off the agenda.[9] It was not until the 1970s that human rights concerns regained formal institutional recognition by the European Community, including by the ECJ and the Member States. The most significant developments came throughout the 1990s with the adoption of the Maastricht and Amsterdam Treaties and the drafting of the EU Charter of Fundamental Rights, followed by the enactment of the Lisbon Treaty.[10] Yet the legacy of the EEC's roots in the common market project retains its significance since, despite the EU's constantly

---

[8] *The European Crisis and its Human Cost* (Caritas Europa, 2014); C Kilpatrick and B de Witte (eds), 'Social Rights in Times of Crisis in the Eurozone: The Role of Fundamental Rights Challenges', EUI Law Department Working Paper 2014/15.

[9] For discussion of the early years of the Communities with regard to human rights, see M Dauses, 'The Protection of Fundamental Rights in the Community Legal Order' (1985) 10 ELRev 398, 399; P Pescatore, 'The Context and Significance of Fundamental Rights in the Law of the European Communities' (1981) 2 HRLJ 295.

[10] For a post-Lisbon overview, see S Douglas-Scott, 'The European Union and Human Rights after the Treaty of Lisbon' (2011) HRLR 1.

changing nature and the recognition of human rights as part of its law and policy, the EU's dominant focus today remains economic.

3 THE ECJ DISCOVERS THE 'GENERAL PRINCIPLES OF EU LAW'

In a series of cases which came before the CJEU in the 1950s and 1960s, the Court initially resisted attempts by litigants to invoke rights and principles recognized by domestic law (eg legitimate expectations, proportionality, and natural justice), and was unwilling to treat them as part of the EU's legal order, even where they were fundamental principles common to the legal systems of most or all Member States.[11] In 1969, however, in the *Stauder* case, the Court announced a change in attitude.[12]

For some years beforehand, anxious discussions had taken place within the European Commission and Parliament about the implications of the doctrine of supremacy of EU law which the Court had pronounced in *Costa v ENEL*,[13] and specifically about the perceived risk that human rights protected under domestic constitutions might be undermined by this doctrine.[14] The Commission President argued that fundamental human rights were part of the 'general principles' of EU law which, although autonomous in source from national constitutions, nevertheless took into account the common legal conceptions of the Member States.[15] Taking its cue from these discussions, the ECJ in *Stauder* responded positively to an argument based on the fundamental right to human dignity, which the applicant alleged was violated by the domestic implementation of an EU provision concerning a subsidized butter scheme for welfare recipients.[16] Having construed the EU measure in a manner consistent with protection for human dignity, the ECJ declared that it 'contains nothing capable of prejudicing the fundamental human rights enshrined in the general principles of Community law and protected by the Court'.[17] In *Stauder* the ECJ thus for the first time affirmed a category of 'general principles of EU law', which included protection for fundamental human rights. Notably, the impetus for this development was the fear of a threat to the supremacy of EU law—a concern which, as we shall see below, continues to animate the Court's development of EU human rights law.[18]

The famous *Internationale Handelsgesellschaft* case followed shortly afterwards, in which the German Federal Constitutional Court was asked to set aside an EU measure concerning forfeiture of an export-licence deposit which allegedly violated German constitutional rights and principles such as economic liberty and proportionality.

---

[11] Case 1/58 *Stork v High Authority* [1959] ECR 17; Cases 36, 37, 38 and 40/59 *Geitling v High Authority* [1960] ECR 423; Case 40/64 *Sgarlata and others v Commission* [1965] ECR 215.

[12] Case 29/69 *Stauder v City of Ulm* [1969] ECR 419.

[13] Case 6/64 *Costa v ENEL* [1964] ECR 585.

[14] See the report by Fernand Dehousse, a Belgian member of the European Parliament, Report on the Supremacy of EC Law over National Law of the Member States, Eur Parl Doc 43 (1965–66) [1965] JO (2923) 14.

[15] Remarks of Walter Hallstein, Eur Parl Deb (79) 218–222 (French Edition) (17 June 1965), discussing the Dehousse Report.

[16] Case 29/69 *Stauder* (n 12). For a similar case more recently see Cases C–92–93/09 *Volker und Markus Schecke GbR v Land Hessen* [2010] ECR I–11063.

[17] Case 29/69 *Stauder* (n 12) [7].

[18] See (nn 110–113) and (n 232) and text.

Case 11/70 Internationale Handelsgesellschaft v Einfuhr- und Vorratstelle für Getreide und Futtermittel
[1970] ECR 1125

THE ECJ

3. Recourse to the legal rules or concepts of national law in order to judge the validity of measures adopted by the institutions of the Community would have an adverse effect on the uniformity and efficacy of Community law. The validity of such measures can only be judged in the light of Community law. In fact, the law stemming from the Treaty, an independent source of law, cannot because of its very nature be overridden by rules of national law, however framed, without being deprived of its character as Community law and without the legal basis of the Community itself being called into question. Therefore the validity of a Community measure or its effect within a Member State cannot be affected by allegations that it runs counter to either fundamental rights as formulated by the constitution of that State or the principles of a national constitutional structure.

4. However, an examination should be made as to whether or not any analogous guarantee inherent in Community law has been disregarded. In fact, respect for fundamental rights forms an integral part of the general principles of Community law protected by the Court of Justice. The protection of such rights, whilst inspired by the constitutional traditions common to the Member states, must be ensured within the framework of the structure and objectives of the Community. It must therefore be ascertained, in the light of the doubts expressed by the Verwaltungsgericht, whether the system of deposits has infringed rights of a fundamental nature, respect for which must be ensured in the Community legal system.

The ECJ upheld the EU measure, ruling that the restriction on the freedom to trade was not disproportionate to the general interest advanced by the deposit system. When the case returned to the German court, however, the national court concluded that the principle of proportionality in German constitutional law had indeed been violated by the EU deposit system. The effect of this and of subsequent cases on the constitutional relationship between EU law and German law is discussed in Chapter 9, but the case also provides an interesting illustration of the difficulty facing the ECJ in seeking to integrate 'common constitutional principles' from the Member States into the EU legal order.

4 THE ECJ DEVELOPS THE GENERAL PRINCIPLES OF EU LAW

The ECJ henceforth both emphasized the autonomy of EU general principles of law as well as their origin in the legal cultures and traditions of the Member States. In *Nold*, concerning the drastic impact on the applicant's right to a livelihood of the EU's regulation of the market in coal, the Court identified international human rights agreements and common national constitutional traditions as the two primary sources of 'inspiration' for the general principles of EU law.

Case 4/73 **Nold v Commission**
[1974] ECR 491

13. As the Court has already stated, fundamental rights form an integral part of the general principles of law, the observance of which it ensures.

In safeguarding these rights, the Court is bound to draw inspiration from constitutional traditions common to the Member States, and it cannot therefore uphold measures which are incompatible with fundamental rights recognized and protected by the Constitutions of those States.

Similarly, international treaties for the protection of human rights on which the Member States have collaborated or of which they are signatories, can supply guidelines which should be followed within the framework of Community law.

Article 6(3) TEU today, which otherwise codifies the ECJ's case law on the general principles of law, mentions only the ECHR and national constitutional traditions as sources of inspiration, and omits express reference to other international human rights instruments. However, the ECJ has continued from time to time to cite international human rights treaties other than the ECHR,[19] and Article 6(3) can certainly be read as an affirmation of the ECJ's 'general principles' case law.[20]

(A) THE ECHR AS A SOURCE OF SPECIAL SIGNIFICANCE FOR THE GENERAL PRINCIPLES OF EU LAW

Prior to the enactment of the Charter of Fundamental Rights, the main international instrument for the protection of human rights drawn upon by the ECJ as a 'special source of inspiration' was the European Convention on Human Rights. From early on the ECJ declared that EU legislation such as that restricting the powers of Member State authorities to limit free movement and residence,[21] as well as legislation on the right to judicial review, protection against sex discrimination, data protection, and privacy rights, were specific EU law manifestations of general principles enshrined in the ECHR.[22] Although the ECJ notably never ruled that the ECHR was formally binding upon the EU, or that its provisions were formally incorporated into EU law,[23] Article 6 TEU has, since 1992, referred expressly to the ECHR. More practically, the ECJ and the CFI[24] routinely cited the 'special

---

[19] See Case C–540/03 *European Parliament v Council* [2006] ECR I–5769, [57] citing the UN Convention on the Rights of the Child, and Case C–354/13 *FOA v Kommunernes Landsforening (Kaltoft)* EU:C:2014:2463, [53] on the UN Convention on the Rights of Persons with Disabilities.

[20] For discussion of the interplay between general principles and the EU Charter in relation to one particular right, see H Hofmann and C Mihaescu, 'The Relation between the Charter's Fundamental Rights and the Unwritten General Principles of EU Law: Good Administration as the Test Case' (2013) 9 EUConst 73.

[21] Case 36/75 *Rutili v Minister for the Interior* [1975] ECR 1219.

[22] Cases 222/84 *Johnston v Chief Constable of the RUC* [1986] ECR 1651, [18]; C–424/99 *Commission v Austria* [2001] ECR I–9285, [45]–[47] on access to judicial protection; C–13/94 *P v S and Cornwall County Council* [1996] ECR I–2143, [18]; C–185/97 *Coote v Granada Hospitality* [1998] ECR I–5199, [21]–[23] on discrimination; C–465/00, 138 and 139/01 *Rechnungshof v Österreichischer Rundfunk* [2003] ECR I–12489, on privacy and data protection.

[23] The Court on the contrary has drawn attention to the fact that the ECHR is not formally incorporated into EU law: eg Case C–501/11 P *Schindler v Commission* EU:C:2013:522, [32] and Case C–617/10 *Åkerberg Fransson* EU:C:2013:105, [44].

[24] See however Cases T–347/94 *Mayr-Melnhof Kartongesellschaft mbH v Commission* [1998] ECR II–1751, [311]; T–112/98 *Mannesmannröhren-Werke v Commission* [2001] ECR II–729, [59], in which the General Court ruled that it had no jurisdiction to 'apply' the ECHR and that it was not part of EU law.

significance' of the ECHR and the rulings of the Court of Human Rights as a key source of inspiration for the general principles of EU law.[25] This allowed the ECJ to continue to assert the autonomy and supremacy of EU law, which, as we shall see below, remains a key concern of the Court.

Further, by treating the ECHR as a source of inspiration rather than a formally binding or fully incorporated bill of rights, the ECJ retained the freedom for EU law to 'go beyond' or diverge from the Convention in certain ways. Examples may be found in the right to lawyer–client confidentiality in *AM & S*[26] and *AKZO*,[27] refugee rights,[28] and data protection.[29] This idea of the ECHR as a 'floor' rather than a 'ceiling' for EU human rights law was maintained by Article 52(3) of the Charter of Fundamental Rights which specifies that the meaning and scope of those Charter rights which correspond to rights guaranteed by the ECHR is to be the same as those laid down by the ECHR,[30] but that 'this provision shall not prevent Union law providing more extensive protection'.

(B) OTHER INTERNATIONAL HUMAN RIGHTS INSTRUMENTS

Apart from the ECHR, the ECJ has rarely drawn on other regional and international instruments, and this neglect has attracted criticism.[31] In *Defrenne v Sabena III*,[32] the ECJ, deeming the elimination of sex discrimination to be a fundamental EU right, drew on the European Social Charter and one of the International Labour Organization Conventions,[33] and it has cited ILO Conventions in various labour law cases. In a challenge brought to the Family Reunification Directive by the European Parliament, the ECJ, while upholding the Directive, drew on the International Covenant on Civil and Political Rights (ICCPR) and on the International Convention on the Rights of the Child, and referred to three other Council of Europe human rights instruments mentioned in the Directive.[34] The UN Convention on Refugees (the Geneva Convention) has regularly been cited in cases dealing with the EU's Directives on minimum standards and reception conditions for asylum-seekers, since the legislation expressly

---

[25] See, eg, Case C–260/89 *ERT v DEP and Sotirios Kouvelas* [1991] ECR I–2925 [41]; *Opinion 2/94 on Accession by the Community to the ECHR* [1996] ECR I–1759, [33]; Case C–299/95 *Kremzow v Austria* [1997] ECR I–2629, [14].

[26] Case 155/79 *AM & S Europe Ltd v Commission* [1982] ECR 1575. AG Warner in his Opinion noted that the ECHR did not provide equivalent protection at the time; although the ECtHR since then has ruled that the absence of lawyer–client confidentiality contributes to a violation of the right to individual petition under Art 34, the right to privacy under Art 8, and the right to a fair trial under Art 6 ECHR.

[27] Case C–550/07 P *Akzo Nobel Chemicals v Commission* [2010] ECR I–8301.

[28] Case C–465/07 *Elgafaji v Staatssecretaris van Justitie* [2009] ECR I–921. Compare Case C–542/13 *M'Bodj v Belgium* EU:C:2014:2452.

[29] Case C–28/08 *Commission v Bavarian Lager* [2010] ECR I–6055.

[30] While the CJEU has not yet focused squarely on the requirement that rights under the Charter and the ECHR should be the 'same', it has looked to relevant ECtHR case law for guidance on the interpretation of Charter Articles in specific cases, eg Cases C–400/10 PPU *JMcB v LE* [2010] ECR I–8965; C–279/09 *DEB v Bundesrepublik Deutschland* [2010] ECR I–13849, [35]–[52]; C–510/11 P *Kone v Commission* EU:C:2013:696, [20]–[22] on effective judicial protection; C–168/13 PPU *Jeremy F* EU:C:2013:358 [43]–[44] on an effective remedy; C–71 and 99/11 *Bundesrepublik Deutschland v Y and C* EU:C:2013:518 on religious freedom; C–334/12 RX–II *Arango Jaramillo v EIB* EU:C:2012:733, [42]–[43] on the right to a Court; C–562/13 *Abida* EU:C:2014:2453, [47]–[53] on refugee rights; C–291/12 *Schwartz v Stadt Bochum* EU:C:2013:670, [27] on data protection; C–34/13 *Kušionová* EU:C:2014:2189, [64] on the right to a home/accommodation; C–398/12 *M* EU:C:2014:1057, [38]–[40] on *ne bis in idem*.

[31] O de Schutter and I Butler, 'Binding the EU to International Human Rights Law' (2008) 27 YBEL 277. See also T Ahmed and I de Jesús Butler, 'The EU and Human Rights: An International Law Perspective' (2006) 17 EJIL 771.

[32] Case 149/77 *Defrenne v Sabena* [1978] ECR 1365.

[33] [1978] ECR 1365, [26]. See also Case 6/75 *Horst v Bundesknappschaft* [1975] ECR 823, 836, where AG Reischl drew on an 'internationally recognized principle of social security as set out in Art 22(2) of International Labour Convention No. 48 on the Maintenance of Migrants' Pension Rights of 1935'.

[34] Case C–540/03 *European Parliament v Council* [2006] ECR I–5769, [37]–[39], [57], [107]. The three Council of Europe instruments were the European Social Charter 1961, the Revised European Social Charter, and the European Convention on the Legal Status of Migrant Workers 1977.

draws on the Geneva Convention.[35] Both the International Covenant on Economic, Social and Cultural Rights (ICESCR)[36] and the ICCPR[37] have been cited by the ECJ in a handful of cases, although the Court was dismissive of an opinion given by the ICCPR's Human Rights Committee,[38] and rejected reliance on the Oviedo Convention on Human Rights and Biomedicine when interpreting an EU directive on the basis that not all Member States had ratified the Convention.[39]

In the famous *Kadi I* case, in which the ECJ annulled the EU's implementation of UN Security Council anti-terrorist asset-freezing resolutions for violating fundamental rights, the CFI cited customary international law and '*ius cogens* rules of international law', as well as principles referred to in the UN Charter,[40] whereas the ECJ cited none of these sources. While the ECJ repeated its statement from *Nold* to the effect that it would look to 'the guidelines supplied by international instruments for the protection of human rights on which the Member States have collaborated or to which they are signatories',[41] in *Kadi I* and *Kadi II* it cited only the EU Charter and the ECHR as sources for the human rights norms applicable in the case.[42]

Further, while many provisions of the EU Charter are themselves based on international human rights instruments,[43] as the explanatory notes to the Charter indicate,[44] those international instruments and the courts or bodies established to interpret them have not yet—apart from the European Convention and Court of Human Rights—been treated as influential or persuasive authority in the interpretation by the ECJ of Charter provisions.[45]

It has been argued that EU fundamental rights standards should be 'indexed' to international human rights standards, not least so as to avoid requiring Member States to choose between their loyalty to EU law and their other international commitments.[46] More generally, the CJEU's emphasis on the EU's constitutional autonomy and its relative disconnection from the wider international human rights system, including through devices such as disconnection clauses[47] and presumptions of mutual

---

[35] See, eg, Cases C–175–179/08 *Aydin Salahadin Abdulla v Germany* [2010] ECR I–364; C–57 and 101/09 *Bundesrepublik Deutschland v B* [2009] ECR I–285; C–31/09 *Bolbol* EU:C:2010:351; C–364/11 *Abed El Karem El Kott* EU:C:2012:826; C–79/13 *Saciri* EU:C:2014:103.

[36] Case C–73/08 *Bressol v Gouvernement de la Communauté française* [2010] ECR I–181 in the context of access of students to higher education.

[37] For a case in which the ECJ cited both the ICCPR and the Convention on the Rights of the Child see Case C–244/06 *Dynamic Medien Vertriebs GmbH v Avides Media AG* [2008] ECR I–505.

[38] Case C–249/96 *Grant v South West Trains Ltd* [1998] ECR I–621, [44]–[47]. For a case involving criminal penalties where the ICCPR was discussed by the General Court, see Case T–48/96 *Acme Industry v Council* [1999] ECR II–3089; and by the Civil Service Tribunal, Case F–29/06, *Arnaldo Rosauros v Commission* EU:F:2011:150.

[39] Case C–237/09 *Belgium v De Fruytier* [2010] ECR I–316.

[40] Case T–315/01 *Kadi v Council and Commission* [2005] ECR II–3649, [228]–[231].

[41] Cases C–402 and 415/05 P *Kadi I* (n 1) [283].

[42] Ibid [333]–[376]. For the subsequent rulings of the General Court and the CJEU on appeal, following the re-listing of *Kadi* by the Commission, see Cases T–85/09 *Kadi v Commission and Council (Kadi II)* [2010] ECR II–5177 and C–584/10 P *Commission v Kadi (Kadi II)* EU:C:2013:518.

[43] Examples are the ICCPR, the ICESCR, the Council of Europe Convention on Human Rights and Biomedicine, the Rome Statute of the International Criminal Court, the UN Convention on the Rights of the Child, the Geneva Convention on Refugees, and the various Social Charters of the EU and the Council of Europe.

[44] The Explanations to the Charter are given interpretative significance by Art 6(1) TEU and Art 52(7) of the Charter. The text of the explanations is available in the Official Journal at [2007] OJ C303/17.

[45] For reliance by the CJEU on interpretations of the ECHR by the Strasbourg Court in cases invoking the Charter of Rights, see the cases at (n 30) above.

[46] See the Network of Independent Experts' Report of the Situation of Fundamental Rights in the EU and its Member States 2002, http://ec.europa.eu/justice/fundamental-rights/files/cfr_cdf_2002_report_en.pdf, 21–24.

[47] Disconnection clauses are used sometimes by the EU when signing regional or international treaties, including human rights treaties. Such clauses provide that the EU and its Member States, in relations between themselves, will apply the rules of EU law rather than the provisions of the relevant treaty. Critics have cautioned that this could lead to the lowering of standards below the 'floor' set by the international instrument. See, eg, Art 40(3) of the Council of Europe Convention on Action Against Trafficking in Human Persons 2005 (CETS no 197).

trust,[48] has given rise to critical comment. The emphasis by the CJEU on the autonomy of the EU legal order in its recent rejection of the draft Agreement on Accession of the EU to the ECHR is only likely to further sharpen those critiques.[49]

(c) NATIONAL CONSTITUTIONAL TRADITIONS

The judgments of the Court have drawn relatively infrequently on national constitutional provisions, despite the symbolic prominence given both by the Court and the EU Treaties to the 'common constitutional traditions' of the states.[50] While occasionally the Advocate General has conducted a survey of national constitutional provisions, the Court has much more rarely cited any specific constitutional provision.[51]

The reasons are to some extent obvious, in that it is more difficult for the ECJ to assert a 'common' approach where a particular right does not appear in every national constitution, whereas an instrument like the ECHR is intended to reflect the collectively shared commitments of all Member States. Further, the fear of compromising the doctrinal supremacy of EU law by appearing to defer to a particular national constitutional provision has animated the ECJ's case law ever since *Costa v ENEL*.[52] This was evident in the case of *Hauer*, in which the referring German Federal Administrative Court declared that an EU agricultural regulation which was incompatible with German fundamental constitutional rights would not be applied. The ECJ in response grounded its decision both in the 'common constitutional traditions' of the states and in the collective commitments of the ECHR.

Case 44/79 **Hauer v Land Rheinland-Pfalz**
[1979] ECR 3727

THE ECJ

14. As the Court declared in its judgment of 17 December 1970, *Internationale Handelsgesellschaft* [1970] ECR 1125, the question of a possible infringement of fundamental rights by a measure of the Community institutions can only be judged in the light of Community law itself. The introduction of special criteria for assessment stemming from the legislation or constitutional law of a particular Member State would, by damaging the substantive unity and efficacy of Community law, lead inevitably to the destruction of the unity of the Common Market and the jeopardizing of the cohesion of the Community.

15. The Court also emphasized in the judgment cited, and later in the judgment of 14 May 1974, *Nold* [1974] ECR 491, that fundamental rights form an integral part of the general principles of the law, the observance of which it ensures; that in safeguarding those rights, the Court is bound to draw inspiration from constitutional traditions common to the Member States, so that measures which are incompatible with the fundamental rights recognized by the Constitutions of those States are unacceptable in

---

[48] In *Opinion 2/13 on EU Accession to the ECHR* EU:C:2014:2454, [192], the CJEU pointed out that—as in the *Melloni* case (n 110)—EU law may require Member States not just to presume that other Member States are observing human rights, but also to refrain in most cases from checking whether other Member States have done so.

[49] Opinion 2/13, ibid.

[50] For a case in which the General Court agreed that national parliamentary traditions could potentially form a source of inspiration for the general principles of EU law, see Cases T–222, 327 and 329/99 *Martinez, Gaulle, Front national and Bonino v European Parliament* [2001] ECR II–2823, [240].

[51] See, eg, Case 17/74 *Transocean Marine Paint v Commission* [1974] ECR 1063, [17].

[52] Case 6/64 [1964] ECR 585.

the Community, and that, similarly, international treaties for the protection of human rights on which the Member States have collaborated or of which they are signatories, can supply guidelines which should be followed within the framework of Community law. That conception was later recognized by the joint declaration of the European Parliament, the Council and the Commission of 5 April 1977, which, after recalling the case law of the Court, refers on the one hand to the European Convention for the Protection of Human Rights and Fundamental Freedoms of 4 November 1950.

. . .

17. The right to property is guaranteed in the Community legal order in accordance with the ideas common to the Constitutions of the Member States, which are also reflected in the first Protocol to the European Convention for the Protection of Human Rights . . .

20. [I]t is necessary to consider also the indications provided by the constitutional rules and practices of the nine member states. One of the first points to emerge in this regard is that those rules and practices permit the legislature to control the use of private property in accordance with the general interest. Thus some constitutions refer to the obligations arising out of the ownership of property (German Grundgesetz, article 14 (2), first sentence), to its social function (Italian Constitution, article 42 (2)), to the subordination of its use to the requirements of the common good (German Grundgesetz, article 14 (2), second sentence, and the Irish Constitution, article 43.2.2*), or of social justice (Irish Constitution, article 43.2.1*) . . .

A further question arising when the 'common constitutional traditions' are cited as a source for EU human rights is whether the ECJ should recognize only those rights shared by all (or most) states, or whether recognition as a fundamental right by even one Member State should suffice (the so-called 'maximum standard' approach) to be part of the general principles of EU law.[53] In *Mannesmannröhren-Werke*, concerning the right to remain silent in the context of competition proceedings, the General Court was dismissive of the 'maximum standard' approach and rejected the argument that a general principle against self-incrimination could be derived from the legal systems of the Member States, even if there was such a principle in German law.[54]

In the case of *AM & S*, not all Member States were happy with the Court's derivation of a principle of lawyer–client confidentiality from a comparative survey of the laws of the Member States, and the French Government in particular argued that the case represented 'an attempt to foist on the EU what was no more than a domestic rule of English law'.[55] However, the Advocate General took the view that a general principle could be distilled from among the various states even if the 'conceptual origin' of the principle and 'the scope of its application in detail' differed as between Member States.[56] In *AKZO*, however, the ECJ refused to extend the EU's general principle of legal professional privilege beyond the context of independent lawyers, despite the fact that a number of Member States have extended the privilege to in-house lawyers, since the Court took the view that there was no 'developing trend' or 'uniform tendency' in this direction across the Member States such as to justify widening the EU's general principle.[57]

In *Omega Spielhallen*, the ECJ abstracted from the *particular conception* of human dignity within German law to a more *general concept* of human dignity shared by all Member States, in order to

[53] L Besselink, 'Entrapped by the Maximum Standard: On Fundamental Rights, Pluralism and Subsidiarity in the European Union' (1998) 35 CMLRev 629 and J Weiler, 'Fundamental Rights and Fundamental Boundaries' in his *The Constitution of Europe* (Cambridge University Press, 1999) ch 3.

[54] Case T–112/98 *Mannesmannröhren-Werke* (n 24) [84].

[55] See AG Warner in Case 155/79 *AM & S* (n 26) 1575, 1631. Case 17/74 *Transocean Marine Paint* (n 51) provides another example of the recognition by the Court of a general principle of Community law where some but not all of the Member States afford protection to the particular right or principle.

[56] Ibid.

[57] Case C–550/07 P *Akzo Nobel* (n 27) [69]–[76].

permit Germany to derogate from EU free movement rules.[58] Yet, even where there may be general consensus amongst the states that a particular abstract right exists, it seems inevitable that there will be disagreement as to how that right should be interpreted and 'translated' into a general principle of EU law. For example, while all Member States recognize the right to life, a handful of the twenty-eight states including Ireland and Malta continue to maintain extremely restrictive national abortion laws, which in Ireland's case partly reflects the constitutional status of the right to life of the foetus. Another example can be seen in the strong protection given by Germany's Grundgesetz to economic rights and to the freedom to pursue a trade or profession, while the constitutions of other states reflect different social priorities. In *Grant* and *D v Council*, the ECJ relied in part on different national legal conceptions of marriage to deny that there had been any breach of the applicants' rights under the general principles of EU law.[59]

In other words, although the idea of 'common constitutional traditions' as a foundation for the general principles of EU law is attractive in principle, the differences between specific national conceptions of particular human rights are often very significant.

5 INSTITUTIONAL AND POLICY DEVELOPMENTS

(A) THE INCLUSION OF HUMAN RIGHTS IN THE TREATY FRAMEWORK

There was, as we saw, no mention of human rights in the ECSC, Euratom, or EEC Treaty in the 1950s and the Court was initially reluctant to entertain rights-based challenges to EU law. Once the Court changed its stance, however, the move to recognize 'general principles of EU law' rapidly gained political approval. It did so initially through a joint declaration of the Parliament, Council, and Commission in 1977,[60] and later through a series of non-binding declarations, charters, and resolutions. Human rights eventually found their way back into the EU Treaties with the amendments introduced by the Maastricht, Amsterdam, Nice, and Lisbon Treaties.

First, Article 6 TEU, which is set out above, lists the various sources of human rights within EU law: the Charter, which is given the same binding status as the Treaties, the ECHR, and common national constitutional traditions which inspire the general principles of EU law. The provisions of the ECHR are thus relevant to EU law in three ways at present: (i) those provisions of the Charter which are based on provisions of the ECHR are to have the 'same' meaning as the ECHR provisions; (ii) the ECHR is one of the main sources of inspiration for the general principles of EU law; and (iii) the provisions of the ECHR will become formally binding on the EU if the EU eventually accedes to the ECHR. By comparison, the provisions of the Charter of Fundamental Rights and the general principles of EU law are already fully binding provisions of EU law, enjoying the same status as provisions of the EU Treaties.

Secondly, following the Amsterdam Treaty, respect for the values on which the EU is founded was made a condition of application for membership of the EU by Article 49 TEU. After the Lisbon

---

[58] Case C–36/02 *Omega Spielhallen- und Automatenaufstellungs-GmbH v Oberbürgermeisterin der Bundesstadt Bonn* [2004] ECR I–9609, [34]–[38]; also Case C–112/00 *Schmidberger v Austria* [2003] ECR I–5659. *Omega Spielhallen* was an easier case for the ECJ to decide, since it did not concern a domestic challenge to the validity of an EU measure, but a state seeking an individual derogation from free movement rules to comply with its constitutional requirements on human dignity. See also Case C–244/06 *Dynamic Medien Vertriebs* (n 37) [44]–[51].

[59] Case C–249/96 *Grant* (n 38); Cases C–122 and 125/99 P *D v Council* [2001] ECR I–4319. Compare however the Court's changing attitude towards sexual orientation discrimination in the later cases of C–267/06 *Maruko* [2008] ECR I–1757; T–58/08 *Commission v Roodhuijzen* [2009] ECR II–3797; and C–267/12 *Hay* EU:C:2013:823.

[60] [1977] OJ C103/1.

Treaty, Article 2 TEU now expresses and expands on the list of values on which the EU is said to be founded:

> The Union is founded on the values of respect for human dignity, freedom, democracy, equality, the rule of law and respect for human rights, including the rights of persons belonging to minorities. These values are common to the Member States in a society in which pluralism, non-discrimination, tolerance, justice, solidarity and equality between women and men prevail.

Article 3 TEU, in setting out the goals and objectives of the EU, adds further to these by declaring that it 'shall combat social exclusion and discrimination, and shall promote social justice and protection, equality between women and men, solidarity between generations and protection of the rights of the child'. In its external relations Article 3(5) declares that the EU shall, amongst other things, 'contribute to peace, security, the sustainable development of the Earth, solidarity and mutual respect among peoples, free and fair trade, eradication of poverty and the protection of human rights, in particular the rights of the child'.

Thirdly, Article 7 TEU, which was also introduced by the Amsterdam Treaty, empowers the Council to suspend some of the voting and other rights of a Member State which is found by the European Council to be responsible for a serious and persistent breach of the principles in Article 2. Article 7 was amended by the Nice Treaty in 2000 to provide for fair procedures to be followed before a negative determination against a Member State is made, and includes the option for the Council to address recommendations to a state which has been found to be clearly at risk of committing a serious breach.[61] However, despite the symbolism of Article 7 TEU, none of the attempts made within the European Parliament to instigate its application have been successful, and its lack of practical use has drawn criticism.[62] Most recently, the failure to instigate the Article 7 procedure in relation to a series of repressive and anti-democratic measures taken by the Hungarian Government has generated a slew of proposals,[63] as well as a communication from the Commission setting out a kind of early warning system to supplement Article 7.[64]

(B) THE FUNDAMENTAL RIGHTS AGENCY

In 2007 an EU Fundamental Rights Agency (FRA) was established, to subsume and replace the previous EU Monitoring Centre for Racism and Xenophobia.[65] There was a debate preceding the establishment of the Agency over whether its powers should include monitoring Member States for the

---

[61] For an account of the 'Haider controversy' which led to the enactment of the Nice amendments see M Merlingen, C Muddle, and U Sedelmeier, 'The Right and the Righteous?: European Norms, Domestic Politics and the Sanctions against Austria' (2001) 39 JCMS 59.

[62] A Williams, 'The Indifferent Gesture: Article 7 TEU, the Fundamental Rights Agency and the UK's Invasion of Iraq' (2006) 31 ELRev 3. See also W Sadurski, 'Adding a Bite to a Bark: A Story of Article 7, the EU Enlargement and Jörg Haider' (2010) 16 CJEL 385.

[63] For a few prominent examples see K Scheppele, 'What the European Commission do when Member States violate Basic Principles of the European Union', http://ec.europa.eu/justice/events/assises-justice-2013/files/contributions/45.princetonuniversityscheppelesystemicinfringementactionbrusselsversion_en.pdf; JW Müller 'Safeguarding Democracy Inside the EU: Brussels and the Future of Liberal Order', Transatlantic Academic Paper 3/2012–13; the Taveres Report of the European Parliament, 'The situation of fundamental rights: standards and practices in Hungary', A7-0229/2013; A von Bogdandy et al, 'Reverse *Solange*: Protecting the Essence of Fundamental Rights against EU Member States' (2012) 49 CMLRev 489; B Bugarič 'Protecting Democracy and the Rule of Law in the European Union: The Hungarian Challenge', LSE 'Europe in Question' Paper no 79/2014.

[64] A New EU Framework to Strengthen the Rule of Law, COM(2014) 158.

[65] Council Regulation (EC) No 168/2007 of 15 February 2007 establishing a European Union Agency for Fundamental Rights [2007] OJ L53/1.

purposes of Article 7 TEU,[66] but the Member States refused to include this within the mandate of the new FRA. Instead, the FRA's remit mainly covers the collection of information, formulating opinions, highlighting good practices, networking with civil society, and publishing thematic reports. The FRA has been active since its establishment and has published influential reports on issues including racism, access to justice, disability, homophobia, the Roma, security and human rights, poverty, migration, data protection, child rights, and violence against women.[67]

(c) EU HUMAN RIGHTS POWERS AND POLICIES

EU Treaty changes since 1997 significantly strengthened the status and role of human rights within the EU legal order, as the provisions of Articles 2, 3, 6, and 7 TEU indicate. Respect for human rights is a condition for the legality of EU measures, and EU laws must be interpreted and construed with a view to respecting human rights. What is less clear, however, is exactly what kind of legal competence the EU possesses to enact laws in the field of human rights protection.

In its first opinion rejecting the compatibility of EU accession to the ECHR in 1996, the ECJ ruled that no specific Treaty provision 'confers on the Community institutions any general power to enact rules on human rights or to conclude international conventions in this field', and that the residual powers clause in Article 235 (now Article 352 TFEU) was subject to certain constitutional limits.[68] The situation has changed since then, in particular as regards external EU competence and the power to conclude international agreements. One striking example of this is the EU's negotiation and conclusion of the UN Convention on the Rights of Persons with Disabilities, the first major international human rights treaty which the EU has concluded.[69] As far as competence to promote human rights *within* the EU is concerned, however, it is not clear exactly how much the situation has changed. Despite the declaration in Article 2 that the EU is founded, *inter alia*, on the value of respect for human rights, and the stipulation in Article 3 that the EU's aim is to promote its values, the EU still requires specific competence under another provision of the Treaties if it is to take concrete action. The Treaties still do not provide the EU with any 'general power to enact rules on human rights'.

Nevertheless, the EU today possesses a powerful human rights tool in the specific field of non-discrimination, since Article 19 TFEU confers competence on the EU to adopt measures combating discrimination on a range of specified grounds. This important field of EU human rights policy is discussed in more detail in Chapter 24. Another significant rights-based field of EU policy since the enactment of Directive 95/46 is data protection. Further, the 'residual powers' provision of Article 352 TFEU can be used (alone or in conjunction with another Treaty provision) as a legal basis for some human rights-related measures, as it was for the enactment of the regulation establishing the EU's external human rights and democratization programme,[70] and for the establishment of the FRA.[71]

Respect for human rights is also now a value of the EU and even a goal which is 'mainstreamed' throughout the external relations of the EU. Following the Lisbon Treaty, Article 3(5) TEU provides

---

[66] The previous 'network of experts on fundamental rights' had informally begun to monitor the Member States' compliance with the Charter for these purposes, but it was replaced by a differently functioning network, FRALEX, within the context of the FRA, which has not been given this power.

[67] See http://fra.europa.eu/en/publications-and-resources/publications. For an interesting report by the FRA on the use of the EU Charter by national courts, see http://fra.europa.eu/sites/default/files/annual-report-2013-charter_en.pdf.

[68] *Opinion 2/94* [1996] ECR I–1795.

[69] G de Búrca, 'The EU in the Negotiation of the UN Disability Convention' (2010) 35 ELRev 174; L Waddington, 'A New Era in Human Rights Protection in the European Community: The Implications the United Nations' Convention on the Rights of Persons With Disabilities for the European Community', University of Maastricht Faculty of Law Working Paper Series 2007, http://papers.ssrn.com/sol3/papers.cfm?abstract_id=1026581.

[70] Regs 975/1999 and 976/1999 [1999] OJ L120/1 and 8.

[71] Reg 168/2007 [2007] OJ L 53/1.

that the EU shall contribute 'to the protection of human rights' in its relations with the wider world, and Article 21(1) TEU provides that the EU's action on the international scene shall be guided by the principles of 'democracy, the rule of law, the universality and indivisibility of human rights and fundamental freedoms, respect for human dignity, the principles of equality and solidarity' amongst others. This gives a Treaty basis to the EU's policy over the past decade to integrate human rights protection into its external relations. The EU's regular practice since 1995 has been to include human rights clauses in external agreements dealing with trade, development, and association relationships,[72] and it has occasionally imposed sanctions or withdrawn trade concessions for human rights violations, as in the cases of Myanmar and Sri Lanka. It has used human rights-based conditionality in the accession process for new Member States,[73] and runs an extensive international human rights and democratization programme known as the EIDHR.[74] These and other EU activities in the field of human rights are outlined each year in the EU's Annual Report on Human Rights.[75]

There is no express Treaty commitment to the protection and promotion of human rights across the EU's internal policies, as there is for external policy. There are however four 'mainstreaming' clauses in Articles 8, 9, 10, and 11 TFEU, which require all EU policies and activities to take account of gender equality, a range of social policy concerns, other grounds of discrimination, and environmental protection respectively, but no general requirement to mainstream human rights. This difference between the emphasis on human rights in external and internal policies has led to criticisms of a double standard in the EU's approach to human rights,[76] which has been acknowledged by the Council of Ministers.[77] Nevertheless, it continues to be a theme in critiques of the EU's human rights policies.[78] On the other hand, the Commission has sought to develop a Charter 'impact assessment' for EU policies, which should help over time to address the double-standard critique.[79] Further, even if the EU lacks any general law-making powers in the field of human rights, many of its specific pieces of legislation set human rights standards in particular areas, such as criminal law, family reunification, refugee law, and data privacy.[80]

The approach of Member States to developing the EU's legal powers in the field of human rights has been equivocal. Although important EU institutions and norms for the protection of human rights have been adopted in recent decades, such as the Charter of Fundamental Rights, Article 19 TFEU (on combating discrimination), and the FRA, Member State governments have simultaneously sought to restrict these new powers and institutions. Thus Article 51 of the Charter declares that no new task or power has been created by its adoption; there has been heated debate over the scope of the Charter's application to Member States, and the FRA was deliberately not given power to monitor Member States for the purposes of Article 7 TEU. The political opposition to EU intervention even when serious human rights abuses may be taking place within a Member State, for example at the time of France's collective expulsion of Roma people in 2010,[81] or Hungary's restrictions on the media and

---

[72] L Bartels, *Human Rights Conditionality in the EU's International Agreements* (Oxford University Press, 2005); U Khaliq, *Ethical Dimensions of the Foreign Policy of the EU: A Legal Analysis* (Cambridge University Press, 2009).

[73] B de Witte and G Toggenburg, 'Human Rights and Membership of the European Union' in S Peers and A Ward (eds), *The EU Charter of Fundamental Rights* (Hart, 2004) 59–82.

[74] For the European Initiative for Democracy and Human Rights, see http://www.eidhr.eu/.

[75] http://eeas.europa.eu/human_rights/docs/index_en.htm.

[76] P Alston and J Weiler, 'A Human Rights Agenda for the Year 2000' in Alston, Heenan, and Bustelo (n 4); A Williams, *EU Human Rights Policies: A Study in Irony* (Oxford University Press, 2004).

[77] See, eg, the Annual Report on Human Rights for 2006, [4.19] in particular.

[78] For discussion see A Williams (n 5).

[79] See most recently COM(2010) 573; and SEC(2011) 567, Operational Guidance in taking account of Fundamental Rights in Commission Impact Assessment.

[80] For discussion see E Muir, 'The Fundamental Rights Implications of EU Legislation: Some Constitutional Challenges' (2014) 51 CMLRev 219.

[81] K Severance, *France's Expulsion of Roma Migrants: A Test Case for Europe* (Migration Policy Institute, 2010), available at www.migrationinformation.org/.

interference with judicial independence,[82] suggests that there is continued resistance on the part of Member States to the EU's development of such a role.

6 THE EU CHARTER OF FUNDAMENTAL RIGHTS[83]

(A) INTRODUCTION

The Charter of Fundamental Rights was first drawn up in 1999–2000, following an initiative of the European Council to 'showcase' the achievements of the EU in this field. The novel Convention process by which the Charter was adopted, which became a model for the Treaty-revision procedure now contained in Article 48 TEU, produced a draft Charter in less than a year.[84] The Charter was then solemnly proclaimed by the Commission, Parliament, and Council and politically approved by the Member States at a European Council summit in December 2000,[85] but its legal status was deliberately left undetermined at the time, pending the outcome of the series of constitutional processes on which the EU had embarked.[86] The horizontal clauses at the end of the Charter were amended slightly during the constitution-drafting process which took place in 2003–2004, but following the failure of the Constitutional Treaty, the legal status of the Charter was not finally resolved until the adoption of the Lisbon Treaty. Article 6 TEU now unequivocally grants it the same legal status as the Treaties themselves.[87]

At the time of the Lisbon Treaty, however, the UK and Poland (with the Czech Republic later to join[88]) negotiated a Protocol which purports to limit the impact of the Charter in those states.[89] The Protocol contains two Articles which read:

Article 1

1. The Charter does not extend the ability of the Court of Justice of the European Union, or any court or tribunal of Poland or of the United Kingdom, to find that the laws, regulations or administrative provisions, practices or action of Poland or of the United Kingdom are inconsistent with the fundamental rights, freedoms and principles that it reaffirms.

---

[82] See (n 63) on developments in Hungary.

[83] There is a vast literature on the Charter. On its origins, see eg (2001) 8(1) MJ and E Eriksen, J Fossum, and A Menéndez (eds), *The Chartering of Europe* (Arena Report No 8/2001). For commentaries see K Feus (ed), *An EU Charter of Fundamental Rights: Text and Commentaries* (Federal Trust, 2000); EU Network of Independent Experts on Fundamental Rights, *Commentary on the Charter* (June 2006); and more recently S Peers, T Hervey, J Kenner, and A Ward, *The EU Charter of Fundamental Rights: A Commentary* (Hart, 2014). The European Commission also publishes an annual report on the application of the Charter: see most recently COM(2014) 224.

[84] G de Búrca, 'The Drafting of the EU Charter of Fundamental Rights' (2000) 25 ELRev 331; J Schönlau, 'Drafting Europe's Value Foundation: Deliberation and Arm-Twisting in Formulating the Preamble to the EU Charter of Fundamental Rights' in Eriksen, Fossum, and Menéndez (n 83).

[85] [2000] OJ C364/1.

[86] For a commentary at the time see B de Witte, 'The Legal Status of the Charter: Vital Question or Non-Issue?' (2001) 8 MJ 81; L Betten, 'The EU Charter of Fundamental Rights: A Trojan Horse or a Mouse?' [2001] International Journal of Comparative Labour Law and Industrial Relations 151.

[87] For a case which firmly applies the Court's case law on primacy to the provisions of the Charter, see Case C–617/10 *Åkerberg Fransson* EU:C:2013:105, [45]–[48].

[88] The European Council on 29–30 Oct 2009 agreed on the text of a new protocol which would apply the provisions of Protocol 30 of the Lisbon Treaty to the Czech Republic. See the Annex to the Presidency Conclusions. See B Dufkova, 'The Legal Status of the Charter of Fundamental Rights within the Member States: The Short Story of the Czech Objection to the Charter', Charles University in Prague Faculty of Law Research Paper No 2015/I/1.

[89] Protocol No 30 to the Lisbon Treaty. See also Declarations 51, 62, and 63 annexed to the Lisbon Treaty, made by the Czech Republic and Poland respectively.

2. In particular, and for the avoidance of doubt, nothing in Title IV of the Charter creates justiciable rights applicable to Poland or the United Kingdom except in so far as Poland or the United Kingdom has provided for such rights in its national law.

Article 2

To the extent that a provision of the Charter refers to national laws and practices, it shall only apply to Poland or the United Kingdom to the extent that the rights or principles that it contains are recognised in the law or practices of Poland or of the United Kingdom.

Whatever the intention of the three signatory states, there has been a debate as to whether the Protocol has anything more than declaratory effect.[90] Article 1 declares that it 'does not extend' the ability of the CJEU to review national measures for compatibility with fundamental rights, but the CJEU had for decades previously exercised jurisdiction to review acts of the Member States within the scope of EU law for compliance with the general principles of EU law. The Protocol does not overturn this earlier case law of the ECJ, and since the contents of the Charter are largely based on the instruments which the ECJ had cited as the inspiration for EU general principles, Article 1(1) appears primarily declaratory. Article 1(2) is designed to support or supplement Article 52(7) of the Charter by deeming Title IV of the Charter (on solidarity rights) not to have created any new justiciable rights in Poland or the UK, but again it can be argued that since the Charter is largely declaratory of what the ECJ had been doing for years under the language of the 'general principles of law', Title IV simply gave the general principles an explicit legal footing.[91]

While some initially referred to the protocol as an 'opt-out', the CJEU soon confirmed the view of the majority of commentators that this was not so. In *NS and ME*, a case concerning the application of EU asylum law in the UK, the CJEU responded to an argument made before the UK courts by the UK Secretary of State that the Charter did not apply in the UK by ruling that: 'Protocol No 30 does not call into question the applicability of the Charter in the United Kingdom or in Poland, a position which is confirmed by the recitals in the preamble to that protocol ... Article 1(1) of Protocol No 30 explains Article 51 of the Charter with regard to the scope thereof and does not intend to exempt the Republic of Poland or the United Kingdom from the obligation to comply with the provisions of the Charter or to prevent a court of one of those Member States from ensuring compliance with those provisions'.[92] Time will tell how the national courts of the three Member States will treat the Protocol.[93]

---

[90] House of Lords Select Committee on the European Union, 10th Report of 2008, [5.84]–[5.111]. Compare V Belling, 'Supranational Fundamental Rights or Primacy of Sovereignty? Legal Effects of the So-Called Opt-Out from the EU Charter of Fundamental Rights' (2012) 18 ELJ 251, who argues that the Protocol has constitutive effect and will limit the extent to which the CJEU can construe the term 'implementing Union law' for the three signatory states.

[91] I Pernice, 'The Treaty of Lisbon and Fundamental Rights' and C Barnard, 'The "Opt-Out" for the UK and Poland from the Charter of Fundamental Rights: Triumph of Rhetoric over Reality?' in S Griller and J Ziller (eds), *The Lisbon Treaty: EU Constitutionalism without a Constitutional Treaty?* (Springer, 2008). See also S Peers, 'The "Opt-Out" that Fell to Earth: The British and Polish Protocol Concerning the EU Charter of Fundamental Rights' (2012) 12 HRLR 375.

[92] Cases C–411 and 493/10 *NS and ME v Minister for Justice* EU:C:2011:865, [119]–[120]. Compare the subsequent reaction of UK High Court Judge Moyston in *AB v Secretary of State for the Home Department* [2013] EWHC 3453 (Admin), and the analysis by V Miller, 'Effects of the EU Charter of Rights in the UK', UK House of Commons Standard Note SN06765, 17 Mar 2014. See also R Clayton and C Murphy, 'The Emergence of the EU Charter of Fundamental Rights in UK Law' [2014] EHRLR 469.

[93] For some evidence from the UK, see (n 92).

(B) CONTENT

The mandate given by the European Council to the Charter-drafting body was to consolidate and render visible the EU's existing 'obligation to respect fundamental rights' rather than to create anything new.[94] Yet the Charter contains several innovative provisions, such as a prohibition on reproductive human cloning, and there are also notable omissions, such as protection for the rights of minorities. Overall the Charter could perhaps best be described as a creative distillation of the rights contained in the various European and international agreements and national constitutions on which the CJEU had for some years already drawn.[95]

Following its lofty Preamble in the name of the 'peoples of Europe', the Charter is divided into seven chapters. The various rights are grouped into six distinct chapters, and the final chapter contains the 'horizontal clauses' or general provisions. The first six chapters are headed: I Dignity, II Freedoms, III Equality, IV Solidarity, V Citizens' Rights, and VI Justice.

The first chapter contains foundational rights such as the right to life, freedom from torture, slavery, and execution.[96] While these might once have appeared anomalous in a Charter addressed primarily to the institutions of an economic union, the EU's current body of policing, criminal, migration, refugee, and anti-terrorism policies suggests that this is no longer so.

The second chapter on freedoms also concentrates on the basic civil and political liberties to be found in the ECHR, such as liberty, association, expression, property, and private and family life,[97] but contains in addition certain fundamental social rights such as the right to education, the right to engage in work, and the right to asylum, as well as a number of provisions which are prominent in the EU context, such as the right to protection of data and freedom to conduct a business.

Chapter III on equality contains a basic equality-before-the-law guarantee, as well as a provision similar (though not identical) to that in Article 19 TFEU, a reference to positive action provisions in the field of gender equality, protection for children's rights, and some weaker provisions guaranteeing 'respect' for cultural diversity, for the rights of the elderly, and for persons with disabilities.

Chapter IV on solidarity contains certain labour rights and reflects some of the provisions of the European Social Charter which have already been integrated into EU law.[98] This chapter contains a mixture of fundamental provisions such as the prohibition on child labour and the right to fair and just working conditions, as well as others which were criticized as insufficiently fundamental to have a place in this Charter, such as the right to a free placement service. This chapter of the Charter was particularly criticized for the weak formulation of many of the rights (including some, such as environmental and consumer protection, which are not formulated as rights or freedoms at all), and because of the phrase 'in accordance with Community law and national laws and practices' which follows them and which seems to undermine the content of the guarantee.

---

[94] The European Council specified the sources on which the new Charter should draw, namely the ECHR; the common constitutional traditions of the Member States; and provisions of the European Social Charter and the Community Charter of Fundamental Social Rights of Workers, 'which go beyond mere objectives': Conclusions of the Cologne European Council, June 1999.

[95] As to whether the Charter can be interpreted 'autonomously' from these other sources (eg in the field of criminal law), see TP Marguery, 'The Protection of Fundamental Rights in European Criminal Law after Lisbon: What Role for the Charter of Fundamental Rights?' (2012) 37 ELRev 444.

[96] For an example of the EU's legislative pursuit of its opposition to the death penalty (citing Arts 2 and 4 of the Charter), see Council Reg (EC) No 1236/2005 and Commission Reg No 1352/2011 concerning trade in certain goods which could be used for capital punishment, torture or other cruel, inhuman or degrading treatment or punishment.

[97] C McGlynn, 'Families and the EU Charter of Fundamental Rights: Progressive Change or Entrenching the Status Quo?' (2001) 26 ELRev 582.

[98] M Gijzen, 'The Charter: A Milestone for Social Protection in Europe?' (2001) 8 MJ 33.

Chapter V contains 'citizens' rights', many of which, unlike the other provisions of the Charter, are not universal but are guaranteed only to EU citizens. These include the rights of EU citizenship in Articles 20–25 TFEU, while the more broadly applicable rights include the right of access to documents and the right to good administration.

Chapter VI, entitled Justice, includes several of the rights of the defence, such as the right to a fair trial, the presumption of innocence, the principle of legality and proportionality of penalties, and the familiar EU right to an effective remedy.

(c) THE 'HORIZONTAL' CLAUSES

The final Chapter VII contains the general clauses which relate to the scope and applicability of the Charter, its addressees, its relationship to other legal instruments, and the 'standard' of protection.

Article 51(1) indicates that the Charter is addressed to the various institutions and agencies of the EU, but to the Member States only when they are 'implementing' Union law. The exact meaning and scope of this phrase has generated considerable debate and analysis.[99] The principle of subsidiarity is mentioned in Article 51(1), although its import in this context is unclear. Article 51 goes on to specify that the EU and the Member States 'respect the rights, observe the principles and promote the application thereof in accordance with their respective powers' and respecting the limits of the EU's powers under the Treaties. There is a tension between the obligation to 'promote' the rights in the Charter and the repeated emphasis on the limits of the EU's powers, which appears also in Article 51(2). Article 51(2) asserts that the Charter does not create any new power or task for the EU nor modify any existing task.[100] Despite the insistence that the Charter is simply a codified or slightly supplemented form of what existed already under prior ECJ jurisprudence, a set of standards against which EU and Member State action within the scope of existing EU policies and powers is to be judged, and not a source of or basis for positive action, the obligation to 'promote' the rights suggests something more proactive. Certainly the proposition in Article 51 that none of the EU's tasks has been 'modified' by the adoption of the Charter seems almost oxymoronic.

Article 52(1), which draws on the jurisprudence of both the ECHR and the ECJ, contains a general 'derogation' clause, indicating the nature of the restrictions on Charter rights which will be acceptable.[101] Any limitation on the exercise of rights and freedoms contained in the Charter must be 'provided for by law' and must respect the essence of those rights and freedoms. Limitations must meet the requirements of proportionality and must be 'necessary and genuinely meet objectives of general interest recognized by the Union,[102] or the need to protect the rights and freedoms of others'.

Article 52(2) addresses the question of overlap between existing provisions of EU law and the provisions of the Charter, providing that rights recognized by the Charter 'for which provision is made in the Treaties shall be exercised under the conditions and within the limits defined by those Treaties'.

---

[99] For fuller discussion see below, (nn 225–227) and text.

[100] The relevant explanatory note to Art 51 reads '[p]aragraph 2 confirms that the Charter may not have the effect of extending the competences and tasks which the Treaties confer on the Union. Explicit mention is made here of the logical consequences of the principle of subsidiarity and of the fact that the Union only has those powers which have been conferred upon it. The fundamental rights as guaranteed in the Union do not have any effect other than in the context of the powers determined by the Treaties. Consequently, an obligation, pursuant to the second sentence of paragraph 1, for the Union's institutions to promote principles laid down in the Charter may arise only within the limits of these same powers.'

[101] For criticism see D Triantafyllou, 'The European Charter of Fundamental Rights and the "Rule of Law": Restricting Fundamental Rights by Reference' (2002) 39 CMLRev 53.

[102] This formulation has been criticized by some who see it as permitting the economic objectives of the EU to be introduced as grounds for limiting the scope of fundamental rights, something which would not be possible under most provisions of the ECHR.

This seems intended to avoid any potential differences in the interpretation of similarly worded provisions of the Charter and of the EU Treaties, most notably the citizenship provisions.

The tricky relationship between the ECHR, other international human rights instruments, national constitutional provisions, and the Charter is addressed in Articles 52(3) and 53.[103] It seems that during the drafting process a heated debate on the proper relationship of the Charter to the Convention was held, as well as on the question whether a right contained in the Charter should necessarily be interpreted in the same way as a similar or identical right contained in the ECHR, and on the proper relationship between the CJEU and the European Court of Human Rights.[104] Article 52(3) relates specifically to the ECHR and aims to promote harmony between the provisions of the ECHR and those of the Charter, while not preventing the EU from developing more extensive protection than is provided for under the Convention:

> In so far as this Charter contains rights which correspond to rights guaranteed by the Convention for the Protection of Human Rights and Fundamental Freedoms, the meaning and scope of those rights shall be the same as those laid down by the said Convention. This provision shall not prevent Union law providing more extensive protection.

This provision does not address the question of the relationship between the two European Courts, the ECtHR and the CJEU, although it seems to have been intended to promote deference—or at least close attention—on the part of the CJEU to the case law of the ECtHR. As we have seen above, the CJEU has indeed drawn on the case law of the ECHR in a range of cases,[105] although it has not done so in others.[106]

The Lisbon Treaty added four further paragraphs to Article 52 of the Charter. Article 52(4) stipulates that the provisions of the Charter derived from national constitutional traditions should be interpreted in harmony with those traditions. Paragraph (6) complements this by stipulating that 'full account' should be taken of national laws and practices as specified in the Charter. Article 52(7), together with Article 6(1) TEU, gives interpretative weight to the explanatory memorandum to the Charter which was drafted by the secretariat to the Charter-drafting Convention.[107]

The most contentious amendment made by the Lisbon Treaty to the Charter as originally adopted in 2000 is contained in Article 52(5), which seeks to distinguish provisions of the Charter containing 'principles', and stipulates that provisions containing 'principles' will be 'judicially cognisable' only when they have been implemented by legislative or executive acts of the EU or the Member

---

[103] See, from a large literature, G Harpaz, 'The European Court of Justice and its Relationship with the European Court of Human Rights: The Quest for Enhanced Reliance, Coherence and Legitimacy' (2009) 46 CMLRev 105; J Callewaert, 'The European Convention on Human Rights and European Union Law: A Long Way to Harmony' [2009] EHRLR 768; P Lemmens, 'The Relationship between the Charter of Fundamental Rights of the EU and the ECHR: Substantive Aspects' (2001) 8 MJ 49; K Lenaerts and E de Smijter, 'The Charter and the Role of the European Courts' (2001) 8 MJ 49; S Parmar, 'International Human Rights Law and the EU Charter' (2001) 8 MJ 351.

[104] P Goldsmith, 'A Charter of Rights, Freedoms and Principles' (2001) 38 CMLRev 1201.

[105] See (n 30).

[106] G de Búrca, 'After the EU Charter of Rights: The Court of Justice as a Human Rights Adjudicator?' (2013) 20 MJ 168; see also the report of the European Parliament DG for Internal Policies: Citizens Rights and Constitutional Affairs, 'Main Trends in the Recent Case Law of the EU Court of Justice and the European Court of Human Rights in the Fields of Fundamental Rights' (2012), http://www.europarl.europa.eu/RegData/etudes/etudes/join/2012/462446/IPOL-LIBE_ET%282012%29462446_EN.pdf.

[107] Art 52(7) reads: 'The explanations drawn up as a way of providing guidance in the interpretation of the Charter of Fundamental Rights shall be given due regard by the courts of the Union and of the Member States'. For a recent commentary by the most influential member of the Charter secretariat, see JP Jacqué, 'The Charter of Fundamental Rights and the CJEU: A First Assessment of the Interpretation of the Charter's Horizontal Provisions' in LS Rossi and F Casolari (eds), The EU After Lisbon (Springer, 2014).

States, and only in relation to interpretation or rulings on the legality of such acts. This amendment seems to have been intended to introduce into the Charter some version of the traditional (and often-criticized) distinction between negatively-oriented civil and political rights and positively-oriented economic and social rights, with a view to rendering the latter largely non-justiciable. The Court has not yet addressed this provision in any detail, although the Advocate General did so in the *AMS* case.[108]

Article 53 of the Charter contains a kind of non-regression clause similar to that contained in Article 53 of the ECHR, which refers not only to the ECHR but also to national constitutions and international agreements:

> Nothing in this Charter shall be interpreted as restricting or adversely affecting human rights and funda-mental freedoms as recognised, in their respective fields of application, by Union law and international law and by international agreements to which the Union, the Community or all the Member States are party, including the European Convention for the Protection of Human Rights and Fundamental Freedoms, and by the Member States' constitutions.

The presence of this clause and the absence of a 'supremacy' clause in the Charter guaranteeing the primacy of EU law prompted some to ask whether the long-established supremacy doctrine was being called into question.[109] In *Melloni*, the CJEU dismissed such an interpretation of Article 53, and categorically reaffirmed the primacy of EU law.[110] In this case the Spanish Constitutional Court asked the CJEU whether Article 53 of the Charter permits a Member State which surrenders an individual pursuant to the EU Arrest Warrant to subject the surrender of a person convicted *in absentia* to an additional condition, in order to avoid undermining a national constitutional right to a fair trial and rights of the defence. The CJEU ruled:

> 56. The interpretation envisaged by the national court at the outset is that Article 53 of the Charter gives general authorisation to a Member State to apply the standard of protection of fundamental rights guaranteed by its constitution when that standard is higher than that deriving from the Charter and, where necessary, to give it priority over the application of provisions of EU law. Such an interpretation would, in particular, allow a Member State to make the execution of a European arrest warrant issued for the purposes of executing a sentence rendered in absentia subject to conditions intended to avoid an interpretation which restricts or adversely affects fundamental rights recognised by its constitu-tion, even though the application of such conditions is not allowed under Article 4a(1) of Framework Decision 2002/584.
> 57. Such an interpretation of Article 53 of the Charter cannot be accepted.
> 58. That interpretation of Article 53 of the Charter would undermine the principle of the primacy of EU law inasmuch as it would allow a Member State to disapply EU legal rules which are fully in compliance with the Charter where they infringe the fundamental rights guaranteed by that State's constitution.

---

[108] Case C–176/12 *AMS* EU:C:2013:491, [43]–[80].

[109] J Liisberg, 'Does the EU Charter of Fundamental Rights Threaten the Supremacy of Community Law?' (2001) 38 CMLRev 1171.

[110] Case C–399/11 *Melloni v Ministerio Fiscal* EU:C:2013:107. For some of the extensive commentaries on *Melloni*, see N de Boer, 'Addressing Rights Divergences Under the Charter: *Melloni*' (2013) 50 CMLRev 1083; M de Visser, 'Dealing with Divergences in Fundamental Rights Standards' (2013) 12 MJ 576; D Sarmiento, 'Who's Afraid of the Charter? The Court of Justice, National Courts and the New Framework of Fundamental Rights Protection in Europe' (2013) 50 CMLRev 1267; L Besselink, 'The Parameters of Constitutional Conflict after "*Melloni*"' (2014) 39 ELRev 531.

> 59. It is settled case-law that, by virtue of the principle of primacy of EU law, which is an essential feature of the EU legal order (see *Opinion 1/91* [1991] ECR I–6079, paragraph 21, and *Opinion 1/09* [2011] ECR I–1137, paragraph 65), rules of national law, even of a constitutional order, cannot be allowed to undermine the effectiveness of EU law on the territory of that State...

The CJEU concluded that although Article 53 left national courts free to apply national standards of protection for fundamental rights, this was subject to the condition that the primacy, unity, and effectiveness of EU law would not be affected. The Framework Decision establishing the arrest warrant was, in the Court's view, precisely intended to reflect a consensus reached by Member States and a 'harmonization' of the procedural rights of a person who had been tried *in absentia*. Allowing Spain to plead its own specific constitutional version of the rights of the defence in order to impose an additional condition on surrender would 'cast doubt on the uniformity of the standard of protection of fundamental rights defined in that framework decision' as well as undermining the principle of mutual trust and recognition between Member States.[111] This interpretation of Article 53 of the Charter as an unequivocal reassertion of the primacy of EU law over national constitutional rights in the event of conflict, rather than a more pluralist vision of coexisting human rights systems, has drawn critical comment,[112] but the CJEU in *Opinion 2/13 on EU accession to the ECHR* clearly confirmed its *Melloni* ruling in this respect.[113]

Finally, Article 54 contains a clause modelled on Article 17 of the ECHR, which provides that no provision of the Charter shall imply the right to engage in any activity aimed at the destruction or excessive limitation of any of the rights contained therein.

7 HUMAN RIGHTS-BASED JUDICIAL REVIEW OF EU ACTION

Since the coming into force of the Charter, the number of cases in which the CJEU has entertained challenges to EU legislation on grounds of human rights violations has grown substantially.[114] Even before the Charter became legally binding, the Court had begun to take fundamental rights claims seriously and to engage with the case law of the European Court of Human Rights in evaluating the validity of EU laws. While litigants enjoyed some success in challenging individual administrative acts of the Commission and other EU actors for violation of rights, the Court for many years was deferential to the EU legislator and slow to annul EU legislation, even in the face of strong fundamental rights challenges.[115] In recent years, however, this has begun to change, particularly in the field of sanctions,[116] and more generally since the coming into force of the Charter.[117]

---

[111] Case C–399/11, ibid [63].

[112] Besselink (n 110).

[113] *Opinion 2/13 on EU Accession to the ECHR* EU:C:2014:2454, [188]. See also Case C–617/10 *Åkerberg Fransson* EU:C:2013:105, [29].

[114] EU judicial processes have also been challenged for their compatibility with fundamental procedural rights: see, eg, Cases C–17/98 *Emesa Sugar v Aruba* [2000] ECR I–665; C–308/07 P *Gorostiaga Atxalandabaso v Parliament* [2009] ECR I–1059, [39]–[50]; C–89/08 P *Commission v Ireland* [2009] ECR I–11245, [50]–[62]; F–45/07 *Mandt v European Parliament* EU:F:2010:72.

[115] For early commentaries on this see A Clapham, 'A Human Rights Policy for the European Community' (1990) 10 YBEL 309, 331; J Coppel and A O'Neill, 'The European Court of Justice: Taking Rights Seriously?' (1992) 29 CMLRev 669.

[116] C Eckes, *EU Counter-Terrorist Policies and Fundamental Rights: The Case of Individual Sanctions* (Oxford University Press, 2010). Following the two *Kadi* cases, there have been dozens of other CJEU and General Court challenges to sanctions imposed by the EU, both anti-terrorist and country sanctions, many of them successful. See (n 136) below and text.

[117] See, eg, Case C–293/12 *Digital Rights Ireland v Minister for Communications* EU:C:2014:238 in which the Data Retention Dir was annulled for violation of Arts 7 and 8 of the Charter.

(A) CHALLENGES TO EU LEGISLATION

Although the Court in the early case of *Nold* had already declared that 'general principles of law' would take precedence, in the event of conflict, over specific Community measures, the ECJ ruled that the rights to property and to a trade or profession were far from absolute, and that limitations in this case were justified by the EU's overall objectives.[118] This approach has characterized many of the cases since concerning property and economic rights,[119] as well as intellectual property.[120]

Since the drafting of the Charter of Fundamental Rights, many other kinds of human rights challenges have been mounted to EU legislation. Cases have been brought to challenge a wide range of EU legislative measures, including the Biotechnology Directive,[121] the Family Reunification Directive,[122] the Framework Decision on an Arrest Warrant,[123] the Money-Laundering Directive,[124] the Audiovisual Media Services Directive,[125] the Biometric Passports Regulation,[126] the Directive on Driving Licences,[127] the Regulation on compensation of passengers for air travel delays,[128] and the Schengen Implementing Convention.[129] In each of these cases, however, the Court, having considered whether the alleged restriction was disproportionate, upheld the EU legislation.

Nevertheless, there have been some notable recent cases in which the CJEU annulled EU legislation for violation of fundamental rights.[130] In *Digital Rights Ireland*, the Data Retention Directive was annulled on the ground that it disproportionately restricted the privacy and data protection guarantees of the Charter of Fundamental Rights.[131] It is in the field of anti-terrorism in the post-9/11

---

[118] Case 4/73 *Nold v Commission* [1974] ECR 491.

[119] See, eg, Cases C–20 and 64/00 *Booker Aquacultur Ltd and Hydro Seafood GSP v The Scottish Ministers* [2003] ECR I–7411; C–37 and 38/02 *Di Lenardo Adriano Srl v Ministero del Commercio con l'Estero* [2004] ECR I–6911; C–453/03, 11, 12 and 194/04 *The Queen, ex p ABNA Ltd v Secretary of State for Health and Food Standards Agency* [2005] ECR I–10423; C–295/03 P *Alessandrini v Commission* [2005] ECR I–5673; C–347/03 *ERSA v Ministero delle Politiche Agricole e Forestali* [2005] ECR I–3785; C–283/11 *Sky Österreich GmbH v Österreichischer Rundfunk* EU:C:2013:28; C–360/10 *SABAM v Netlog* EU:C:2012:85.

[120] eg Case C–360/10 (n 119). For discussion see J Griffith and L McDonough, 'Fundamental Rights and European IP Law—The Case of Article 17(2) of the EU Charter' in C Geiger (ed), *Constructing European Intellectual Property* (Edward Elgar, 2013).

[121] Case C–377/98 *Netherlands v Council and Parliament* [2001] ECR I–7079, challenging the Biotechnology Dir for violation of human dignity.

[122] Case C–540/03 *European Parliament v Council* (n 19) challenging the Family Reunification Dir for violation of the right to respect for family life.

[123] Case C–399/11 *Melloni v Ministerio Fiscal* EU:C:2013:107 challenging the Framework Decision establishing an Arrest Warrant for violation of the right to an effective judicial remedy and a fair trial; also Case C–303/05 *Advocaten voor de Wereld VZW v Leden van de Ministerraad* [2007] ECR I–3633.

[124] Case C–305/05 *Ordre des barreaux francophones et germanophones et al v Council* [2007] ECR I–5305, challenging the Money Laundering Dir for violation of the right to a fair trial and the professional secrecy of lawyers.

[125] Case C–283/11 *Sky Österreich GmbH v Österreichischer Rundfunk* EU:C:2013:28 challenging the Audiovisual Media Services Dir for violation of the right to intellectual property and freedom to conduct a business.

[126] Case C–291/12 *Michael Schwarz v Stadt Bochum* EU:C:2013:670 challenging the Biometric Passports Reg for violation of the right to private life.

[127] Case C–356/12 *Glatzel* EU:C:2014:350 challenging the Driving Licences Dir for violation of the right to non-discrimination.

[128] Case C–12/11 *McDonough v Ryanair* EU:C:2013:43 challenging the EU Reg on compensation for air passengers in the event of delay and cancellation for violation of the right to conduct a business.

[129] Case C–129/14 PPU *Zoran Spasic* EU:C:2014: challenging the Schengen Implementing Convention for violation of the principle of *ne bis in idem*.

[130] In a less high-profile case, C–92–93/09 *Schecke* (n 16) the CJEU annulled the publication rules contained in an EU agricultural subsidies reg for violation of EU data privacy rights and the right of privacy under the EU Charter and the ECHR.

[131] Case C–293/12 *Digital Rights Ireland* (n 117).

era, however, that the Court's willingness to strike down EU laws for disproportionately violating individual rights has been most vividly evident.[132] In an early judgment in this field, in the *Bosphorus* case, the ECJ ruled that the fundamental interests of the international community could justify restrictions of property and trade rights caused by the impounding of a Yugoslav-owned aircraft leased by the applicant, even where the latter appeared to be entirely uninvolved in any activities of the Yugoslav state.[133] However, in a series of important judgments handed down since 2009, most dramatically in *Kadi I*[134] and *Kadi II*,[135] the CJEU and the General Court have struck down a range of EU laws imposing sanctions, including both 'autonomous' EU measures as well as UN-mandated measures, for violating a range of rights, most notably due process (rights of defence) and the right to property.[136]

The *Kadi* cases raised many interesting questions about the relationship of EU law to the international legal order,[137] and became an inspiration for the European Court of Human Rights in its own subsequent case law involving UN-related economic sanctions.[138] For the purposes of this chapter, however, the most significant parts of the judgment are those which deal with the ECJ's treatment of fundamental rights.

---

[132] In another notable terrorism-related case, the ECJ struck down the acts which concluded the EU's agreement with the United States to allow the transfer of passenger data from European airlines to the US security services; the ECJ did not actually rule on the plea concerning violation of fundamental rights, but rather condemned the acts for lacking the correct legal basis: Cases C–317 and 318/04 *European Parliament v Council (PNR)* [2006] ECR I–4721; V Papakonstantinou and P de Hert, 'The PNR Agreement and Transatlantic Anti-Terrorism Cooperation' (2009) 46 CMLRev 885; H Hijmans and A Scirocco, 'Shortcomings in EU Data Protection in the Third and Second Pillars: Can the Lisbon Treaty be Expected to Help?' (2009) 46 CMLRev 1485.

[133] Case C–84/95 *Bosphorus v Minister for Transport* [1996] ECR I–3953, which involved Ireland's implementation of an EU reg which in turn implemented a UN Security Council resolution. See also Case T–184/95 *Dorsch Consult v Council* [1998] ECR II–667, [87]–[88].

[134] Cases C–402 and 415/05 P *Kadi* (n 1) [308]; D Halberstam and E Stein, 'The United Nations, the European Union, and the King of Sweden' (2009) 46 CMLRev 13; A Gattini, Note (2009) 46 CMLRev 191; C Eckes, 'Judicial Review of European Anti-Terrorism Measures—The *Yusuf* and *Kadi* Judgments of the Court of First Instance' (2008) 14 ELJ 74; J Godhino, 'When Worlds Collide: Enforcing United Nations Security Council Asset Freezes in the EU Legal Order' (2010) 16 ELJ 67; T Isiksel, 'Fundamental Rights in the EU after *Kadi* and *Al Barakaat*' (2010) 16 ELJ 551; S Poli and M Tzanou, 'The *Kadi* Rulings: A Survey of the Literature' (2009) 28 YBEL 533; M Cremona, F Francioni, and S Poli (eds), 'Challenging the EU Counter-Terrorism Measures through the Courts', EUI Working Paper 2009/10; J Kokott and C Sobotta 'The *Kadi* Case: Core Constitutional Values and International Law: Finding the Balance' (2012) 23 EJIL 1015.

[135] Cases T–85/09 *Kadi v Commission and Council (Kadi II)* [2010] ECR II–5177 and C–584/10 P *Commission v Kadi (Kadi II)* EU:C:2013:518. T Tridimas, 'Terrorism and the CJEU: Empowerment and Democracy in the EC Legal Order' (2009) 34 ELRev 103.

[136] Prominent examples are Cases T–228/02 *Organisation des Modjahedines du peuple d'Iran (OMPI) v Council* [2006] ECR II–4665; T–256/07 *People's Mojahedin Organization of Iran v Council (PMOI)* [2008] ECR II–3019; C–27/09 P *France v PMOI* EU:C:2011:853; T–318/01 *Othman v Council and Commission* EU:T:2009:187; T–253/04 *KONGRA-GEL v Council* [2008] ECR II–46; T–348/07 *Al-Aqsa v Council*, [2010] ECR II–4575; C–399 and 403/06 P *Hassan and Ayadi v Council and Commission* [2009] ECR I–11393; C–376/10 *Tay Za v Council* EU:C:2012:138; T–496/10 *Bank Mellat v Council* EU:T:2013:39 (currently on appeal); T–565/12 *National Iranian Tanker Company v Council* EU:T:2014:608; and T–400/10 *Hamas v Council* EU:T:2014:1095. Compare Case C–348/12 P *Council v Kala Naft Co* EU:C:2013:776.

[137] For discussion of the international law aspects see Ch 10.

[138] See App No 10593/08 *Nada v Switzerland*, judgment of 12 Sept 2012 and App 5809/08 *Al-Dulimi v Switzerland*, judgment of 26 Nov 2013 (the case has been referred to the Grand Chamber, which should give judgment in 2015).

Cases C-402 and 415/05 P **Yassin Abdullah Kadi and Al Barakaat International Foundation v Council and Commission**
[2008] ECR I-6351

[Note Lisbon Treaty renumbering: Art 6 EU is Art 6 TEU; Art 220 EC is Art 19 TEU; Art 297 EC is Art 347 TFEU; Art 300(7) EC is Art 216(2) TFEU; Art 307 EC is Art 351 TFEU]

The EU adopted a set of legislative measures including regulations designed to implement a series of UN Security Council Resolutions, beginning with Resolution 1267 (1999). These UN Resolutions were adopted in the wake of the 11 September 2001 attacks on the United States, and required all states to freeze the funds and other financial resources of any persons or entities controlled directly or indirectly by the Taliban, or associated with Osama bin Laden or the Al-Qaeda network, and established a Sanctions Committee to ensure their implementation. In 2001 Kadi, together with Yusuf and the Al Barakaat Foundation, who were named on the UN and the EU lists, brought proceedings before the General Court (then CFI) to challenge the EU implementing measures. They argued that the contested EU regulations disproportionately infringed their fundamental rights, in particular their right to the use of their property and the right to a fair hearing. The General Court ruled that it had no jurisdiction to question Resolutions of the UN Security Council, even indirectly, other than for violation of *jus cogens*; and that in this instance there was no violation of *jus cogens*. On appeal, the ECJ took a different approach.

THE ECJ

281. In this connection it is to be borne in mind that the Community is based on the rule of law, inasmuch as neither its Member States nor its institutions can avoid review of the conformity of their acts with the basic constitutional charter, the EC Treaty, which established a complete system of legal remedies and procedures designed to enable the Court of Justice to review the legality of acts of the institutions (Case 294/83 *Les Verts v Parliament* [1986] ECR 1339, paragraph 23).

282. It is also to be recalled that an international agreement cannot affect the allocation of powers fixed by the Treaties or, consequently, the autonomy of the Community legal system, observance of which is ensured by the Court by virtue of the exclusive jurisdiction conferred on it by Article 220 EC, jurisdiction that the Court has, moreover, already held to form part of the very foundations of the Community.

283. In addition, according to settled case-law, fundamental rights form an integral part of the general principles of law whose observance the Court ensures. For that purpose, the Court draws inspiration from the constitutional traditions common to the Member States and from the guidelines supplied by international instruments for the protection of human rights on which the Member States have collaborated or to which they are signatories. In that regard, the ECHR has special significance.

284. It is also clear from the case-law that respect for human rights is a condition of the lawfulness of Community acts (*Opinion 2/94*, paragraph 34) and that measures incompatible with respect for human rights are not acceptable in the Community (Case C-112/00 *Schmidberger* [2003] ECR I-5659, paragraph 73 and case-law cited).

285. It follows from all those considerations that the obligations imposed by an international agreement cannot have the effect of prejudicing the constitutional principles of the EC Treaty, which include the principle that all Community acts must respect fundamental rights, that respect constituting a condition of their lawfulness which it is for the Court to review in the framework of the complete system of legal remedies established by the Treaty.

286. In this regard it must be emphasised that, in circumstances such as those of these cases, the review of lawfulness thus to be ensured by the Community judicature applies to the Community act intended to give effect to the international agreement at issue, and not to the latter as such.

...

304. Article 307 EC may in no circumstances permit any challenge to the principles that form part of the very foundations of the Community legal order, one of which is the protection of fundamental rights, including the review by the Community judicature of the lawfulness of Community measures as regards their consistency with those fundamental rights.

305. Nor can an immunity from jurisdiction for the contested regulation with regard to the review of its compatibility with fundamental rights, arising from the alleged absolute primacy of the resolutions of the Security Council to which that measure is designed to give effect, find any basis in the place that obligations under the Charter of the United Nations would occupy in the hierarchy of norms within the Community legal order if those obligations were to be classified in that hierarchy.

306. Article 300(7) EC provides that agreements concluded under the conditions set out in that article are to be binding on the institutions of the Community and on Member States.

307. Thus, by virtue of that provision, supposing it to be applicable to the Charter of the United Nations, the latter would have primacy over acts of secondary Community law...

308. That primacy at the level of Community law would not, however, extend to primary law, in particular to the general principles of which fundamental rights form part.

...

[*The ECJ went on to rule that the procedure for re-examining the listing of individuals before the UN Sanctions Committee was essentially diplomatic and intergovernmental, and did not offer guarantees of judicial protection. There was no right of representation, no obligation to give reasons or evidence, and no opportunity for judicial review. To grant immunity from jurisdiction to the listing measures within the EU legal order would constitute 'a significant derogation from the scheme of judicial protection of fundamental rights' laid down by the EU Treaties.*]

326. It follows from the foregoing that the Community judicature must, in accordance with the powers conferred on it by the EC Treaty, ensure the review, in principle the full review, of the lawfulness of all Community acts in the light of the fundamental rights forming an integral part of the general principles of Community law, including review of Community measures which, like the contested regulation, are designed to give effect to the resolutions adopted by the Security Council under Chapter VII of the Charter of the United Nations.

...

334. In this regard, in the light of the actual circumstances surrounding the inclusion of the appellants' names in the list of persons and entities covered by the restrictive measures contained in Annex I to the contested regulation, it must be held that the rights of the defence, in particular the right to be heard, and the right to effective judicial review of those rights, were patently not respected.

335. According to settled case-law, the principle of effective judicial protection is a general principle of Community law stemming from the constitutional traditions common to the Member States, which has been enshrined in Articles 6 and 13 of the ECHR, this principle having furthermore been reaffirmed by Article 47 of the Charter of fundamental rights of the European Union, proclaimed on 7 December 2000 in Nice (OJ 2000 C 364, p. 1)....

352. It must, therefore, be held that the contested regulation, in so far as it concerns the appellants, was adopted without any guarantee being given as to the communication of the inculpatory evidence against them or as to their being heard in that connection, so that it must be found that that regulation was adopted according to a procedure in which the appellants' rights of defence were not observed, which has had the further consequence that the principle of effective judicial protection has been infringed.

353. It follows from all the foregoing considerations that the pleas in law raised by Mr Kadi and Al Barakaat in support of their actions for annulment of the contested regulation and alleging breach of their rights of defence, especially the right to be heard, and of the principle of effective judicial protection, are well founded...

357. Next, it falls to be examined whether the freezing measure provided by the contested regulation amounts to disproportionate and intolerable interference impairing the very substance of the fundamental right to respect for the property of persons who, like Mr Kadi, are mentioned in the list set out in Annex I to that regulation...

369. The contested regulation, in so far as it concerns Mr Kadi, was adopted without furnishing any guarantee enabling him to put his case to the competent authorities, in a situation in which the restriction of his property rights must be regarded as significant, having regard to the general application and actual continuation of the freezing measures affecting him.

370. It must therefore be held that, in the circumstances of the case, the imposition of the restrictive measures laid down by the contested regulation in respect of Mr Kadi, by including him in the list contained in Annex I to that regulation, constitutes an unjustified restriction of his right to property...

372. It follows from all the foregoing that the contested regulation, so far as it concerns the appellants, must be annulled.

The ECJ however maintained the relevant Regulation in effect for three months, to allow the EU institutions time to cure the procedural breach and to re-list the applicants. Following the publication and communication to the applicants of summary reasons provided by the UN Sanctions Committee, the Commission adopted a new regulation maintaining the sanctions against Kadi, who promptly brought a further action for annulment.[139] Both the General Court, and the CJEU on appeal, ruled that the evidence offered to justify the sanctions was inadequate, and annulled the Regulation once again.[140]

The *Kadi* cases and many of those which followed are important and raise complex legal issues for the EU and the Member States, and they have generated international controversy, as well as possibly helping to trigger reform of the UN sanctions system, given the global relevance of many of the sanctions.[141] But what is most striking, for the purposes of the present chapter, is that the CJEU and the General Court were less deferential to the EU institutions, and even to international institutions such as the UN Security Council, when considering challenges based on fundamental rights in several of the sanctions cases. Nevertheless, it has also been pointed out that some of the judicial victories (including that of Kadi, whose eventual removal from the UN sanctions list came about due to the intervention of the UN Ombudsperson rather than the EU Courts) have been pyrrhic.[142] Further, developments arising out of the *Kadi* litigation, such as the proposed introduction of rules permitting secret evidence to be heard by the General Court, are likely to create further problems for fundamental rights.[143]

Nevertheless, the stream of high-profile and politically salient anti-terrorist sanctions cases in recent years has shown both the General Court and the ECJ displaying greater willingness to review and to strike down EU legislation for violation of basic rights, and to assert the priority of

[139] Commission Regulation 1190/2008, amending the earlier Regulation 881/2002 to maintain Kadi's name in the relevant Annex [2008] OJ L322/25.

[140] Cases T–85/09 *Kadi v Commission and Council* and C–584/10 P *Commission v Kadi (Kadi II)* (n 135).

[141] For a recent book dedicated to the aftermath of the judgments, see M Avbelj, F Fontanelli, and G Martinico (eds), *Kadi on Trial* (Routledge, 2014). See also P Margulies, 'Aftermath of an Unwise Decision: The UN Terrorist Sanctions Regime after *Kadi II*' (2014) 6 Amsterdam Law Forum 51.

[142] In Case T–348/07 *Al-Aqsa* (n 136) [128]–[132], although the impugned measure was annulled on procedural grounds, the General Court ruled that the domestic court had established as a matter of substance that the applicants had knowledge that their funds were being used for terrorist purposes.

[143] See the draft Rules of Procedure published in Dec 2014: http://data.consilium.europa.eu/doc/document/ST-16724-2014-INIT/en/pdf. For discussion see http://europeansanctions.com/2015/01/22/eu-to-approve-new-court-rules-to-permit-secret-hearings/.

fundamental rights in EU law over secondary EU legislation, and even over the most important norms of international law.

(B) RIGHTS-BASED CHALLENGES TO EU ADMINISTRATIVE ACTION

Rights-based challenges to EU administrative action have also regularly been made. Two particular contexts in which such claims have often been successfully made are those of staff disputes concerning EU bodies and institutions, and competition law proceedings involving the Commission.

(i) *Staff Cases*

In a range of staff and recruitment cases the EU Courts have entertained arguments based on pleas including the violation of freedom of expression,[144] freedom of religion,[145] private and family life,[146] and non-discrimination,[147] and required the EU institutions to amend several of their practices. Administrative proceedings affecting EU staff are subject to the rights of the defence.[148] The EU Civil Service Tribunal (CST), established in 2005, now hears all staff complaints at first instance prior to any appeal to the General Court or CJEU. The CST has ruled that the EU staff regulations and conditions of employment must be read in the light of the provisions of the Charter of Fundamental Rights.[149]

(ii) *Competition Proceedings*

The area of the Commission's enforcement powers in competition proceedings has been a fertile source of litigation, in which general principles of law and fundamental rights—often the cluster referred to as the rights of the defence,[150] including the right to a fair hearing,[151] effective judicial review,[152] and related principles such as non-retroactivity of penal liability,[153] data protection, and

---

[144] Case 100/88 *Oyowe and Traore v Commission* [1989] ECR 4285. Compare the unsuccessful outcome in the colourful case of Case C–274/99 P *Connolly v Commission* [2001] ECR I–1611.

[145] Case 130/75 *Prais v Council* [1976] ECR 1589.

[146] Case T–58/08 *Commission v Roodhuijzen* [2009] ECR II–3797 on the meaning of the term 'non-marital partnership' in the EU Staff Regs. Compare earlier Cases C–122 and 125/99 P *D v Council* (n 59).

[147] Cases C–404/92 P *X v Commission* [1994] ECR I–4737; C–122 and 125/99 P *D* (n 59); C–191/98 P *Tzoanos v Commission* [1999] ECR I–8223; C–252/97 *N v Commission* [1998] ECR I–4871.

[148] In Case C–344/05 P *Commission v De Bry* [2006] ECR I–10915, however, the ECJ ruled that the rights of the defence did not include any obligation on the Commission to give a prior warning to an employee before a staff appraisal.

[149] Case F–51/07 *Bui Van v Commission* EU:F:2008:112.

[150] For some examples, see the principle of *non bis in idem* in Case C–397/03 P *Archer Daniels Midland v Commission* [2006] ECR I–4429, the right of access to documents (specifically to the file containing objections and evidence against a defendant) in Case T–210/01 *GEC v Commission* [2005] ECR II–5575; Cases C–204–219/00 P *Aalborg Portland A/S et al v Commission* [2004] ECR I–123; and the right to challenge findings of fact in Case C–407/08 P *Knauf Gips KG v European Commission* [2010] ECR I–6375, [90]–[92]; more generally the right to effective judicial protection: Case C–272/09 *KME Germany and others v Commission* EU:C:2011:810.

[151] Case C–185/95 P *Baustahlgewebe v Commission* [1998] ECR I–8417 (on the length of time of proceedings), and compare Cases T–213/95 and 18/96 *SCK & FNK v Commission* [1997] ECR II–1739. Other cases outside the competition field which uphold the right to a fair hearing include Cases C–49/88 *Al-Jubail Fertilizer Company v Council* [1991] ECR I–3187 (on anti-dumping); C–7/98 *Krombach v Bamberski* [2000] ECR II–1935 (in the context of the Brussels Convention); and T–83/96 *van der Wal v Commission* [1998] ECR II–545 (on the right of access to documents used in judicial proceedings).

[152] Case C–386/10 P *Chalkor AE Epexergasias Metallon v Commission* EU:C:2011:815; Case C–389/10 P KME *Germany and others v Commission* EU:C:2011:816.

[153] Cases C–189–213/02 P *Dansk Rørindustri et al v Commission* [2005] ECR I–5425. On the size of the penalty imposed see Case T–69/04 *Schunk v Commission* [2008] ECR II–2567.

privacy,[154] or *nullum crimen, nulla poena sine lege*[155]—have frequently been invoked to challenge EU executive action.

The Commission's powers in competition proceedings are very wide, including the authority to investigate and make searches, as well as to impose severe financial penalties, and affected parties have repeatedly called upon the Court to limit and control their exercise by reference to fundamental legal principles.[156] In the early (pre-Charter) case of *Hoechst*, in which the applicant company challenged various decisions of the Commission ordering an investigation into its suspected anti-competitive practices, the Court ruled that the right to inviolability of the home was amongst the general principles of EU law.[157] However, drawing for support on Article 8 ECHR, the Court ruled that this right did not extend to a company's business premises, although companies as well as individuals were entitled under the general principles of EU law to protection against arbitrary interference by public authorities.[158] The Court found on the facts of the case that there had been no breach by the Commission of any of the principles invoked by the applicants. The judgment was criticized on various grounds, including for having overlooked existing case law of the ECtHR,[159] but the ECJ later accepted that Article 8 ECHR, as clarified in subsequent ECtHR case law,[160] did extend to business premises.[161]

Similarly, in relation to the right to a fair trial in Article 6(1) ECHR, the initial decision of the ECJ in *Orkem*,[162] in which it ruled that Article 6 did not confer the right 'not to give evidence against oneself', was at odds with the subsequent ruling of the ECtHR in *Funke*, in which that court indicated that Article 6 protected the right 'to remain silent and not to contribute to incriminating [oneself]'.[163] However the ECJ in *Hüls* and later case law emphasized the significance of the ECHR and the case law of the ECtHR and ruled that the presumption of innocence applies to competition proceedings which may result in fines.[164] The General Court, too, despite its occasional objection to direct reliance on the provisions of the ECHR and the case law of the ECtHR,[165] has been willing to cite and to follow ECtHR

---

154 Case T–474/04 *Pergan Hilfsstoffe für industrielle Prozesse GmbH v Commission* [2007] ECR II–4225.

155 Case T–99/04 *AC-Treuhand AG v Commission* [2008] ECR II–1501; Case T–446/05 *Amann & Söhne GmbH v Commission* [2010] ECR II–1255.

156 For selected examples from a long list see Cases 17/74 (n 51); Cases 209–215/78 *Van Landewyck v Commission* [1980] ECR 3125; Case 136/79 *National Panasonic v Commission* [1980] ECR 2033; Cases 100–103/80 *Musique Diffusion Française v Commission* [1983] ECR 1825; Case 322/81 *Michelin v Commission* [1983] ECR 3461; Case 5/85 *AKZO Chemie v Commission* [1986] ECR 2585; Case 374/87 *Orkem v Commission* [1989] ECR 3283; Case T–11/89 *Shell v Commission* [1992] ECR II–757; Case T–347/94 *Mayr-Melnhof* (n 24); Case C–185/95 P *Baustahlgewebe* (n 151); Case T–112/98 *Mannesmannröhren-Werke* (n 24); Case T–474/04 *Pergan Hilfsstoffe* (n 154); Case T–99/04 *AC-Treuhand* (n 155); Case T–69/04 *Schunk* (n 153); Case C–328/05 P *SGL Carbon AG v Commission* [2007] ECR I–3921; C–199/11 *Europese Gemeenschap v Otis NV and Others* EU:C:2012:684.

157 Cases 46/87 and 227/88 *Hoechst AG v Commission* [1989] ECR 2859.

158 Ibid [17], [19].

159 See in particular the *Chappell* case, App No 10461/83, judgment of 30 Mar 1989.

160 App No 13710/88 *Niemietz v Germany*, judgment of 16 Dec 1992, [31]; App No 44647/98 *Peck v United Kingdom*, judgment of 28 Jan 2003, [57].

161 Case C–94/00 *Roquettes Frères SA v Commission* [2002] ECR I–9011, [29].

162 Case 374/87 (n 156) [30]. The Court did however rule that the 'rights of the defence' in investigative procedures prevented the Commission from compelling a company to provide it with answers which might involve an admission of a breach which it was incumbent on the Commission to prove. See also Case C–60/92 *Otto v Postbank* [1993] ECR I–5683 and Case T–347/94 *Mayr-Melnhof* (n 24).

163 App No 10828/84 *Funke v France*, judgment of 25 Feb 1993, [44]; W van Overbeek, 'The Right to Remain Silent in Competition Investigations' (1994) 15 ECLR 127.

164 Case C–199/92 P *Hüls v Commission* [1999] ECR I–4287, [149]–[150]. See also Cases C–57/02 P *Acerinox v Commission* [2005] ECR I–6689, [87]–[89] and T–59/02 *Archer Daniels Midland Co v Commission* [2006] ECR II–3627. Compare the company law context in Case T–47/02 *Danzer v Council* [2006] ECR II–1779.

165 Case T–112/98 *Mannesmannröhren-Werke* (n 24) [66]–[77].

jurisprudence on the rights of the defence in competition proceedings,[166] and of course more recently the Charter of Fundamental Rights.[167]

(c) CONSTRUING EU LEGISLATION IN CONFORMITY WITH FUNDAMENTAL RIGHTS

Another way in which the EU judiciary has increasingly taken account of fundamental rights is by interpreting EU measures, even when their annulment is not sought, in conformity with such rights. This technique of requiring EU legislation to be interpreted and implemented in compliance with fundamental human rights has the effect both of insulating EU legislation against challenge and, as we shall see below, of imposing human rights obligations, as a matter of EU law, on national authorities.[168] In the famous case of *Google Spain*, for example, the CJEU interpreted the EU Data Processing Directive in the light of Articles 7 and 8 of the Charter in such a way that a 'right to be forgotten' (ie the right to have data concerning oneself deleted from search engines, in certain circumstances) had to be protected by the operator of a search engine.[169]

(d) SUMMARY

i. From the time of the ECJ's acceptance in the early 1970s that fundamental human rights were part of the general principles of EU law until the Charter of Fundamental Rights acquired binding force in 2009, the two main sources of inspiration for those rights have been the ECHR and national constitutional traditions. Other international human rights instruments have played a marginal role. The Charter now dominates as the most important source of fundamental human rights in EU law.

ii. Despite the clear Treaty basis for the various sources of human rights within EU law in Article 6 TEU, their application by the ECJ to the concrete circumstances of specific cases has been more contested. The Court has adopted neither a 'universal standard' based on the highest level of protection given by any single Member State, nor a 'lowest common denominator' approach which would

---

[166] In Case T–99/04 *AC-Treuhand* (n 155) despite the General Court's statement that 'the Court has no jurisdiction to assess the lawfulness of an investigation under competition law in the light of provisions of the ECHR, inasmuch as those provisions do not as such form part of Community law', the Court nonetheless went on to cite and to follow ECtHR case law in [52], [137]–[150]. For a recent discussion, see M Bronckers and A Vallery, 'No Longer Presumed Guilty: The Impact of Fundamental Rights on Certain Dogmas of EU Competition Law' (2011) 43 World Competition 535.

[167] See, eg, Cases T–458/09 and T–171/10 *Slovak Telekom v Commission* [2012] ECR II–145, [67]–[68]; T–348/08 *Aragonesas Industrias y Energía v Commission* EU:T:2011:621, [94]. For some commentaries on the impact of the Charter on EU competition law, see H Andersson, 'Dawn Raids under Challenge' (2014) 35 ECLR 135; W Wils, 'The Compatibility with Fundamental Rights of the EU Antitrust Enforcement System when the Commission Acts as Both Investigator and as First-Instance Decision Maker' (2014) 37 World Competition 5; E Beumer, 'The Interaction between EU Competition Law Procedures and Fundamental Rights Protection' (2014) 7 Yearbook of Antitrust and Regulatory Studies 9; K Lenaerts, 'Due Process in Competition Cases' (2013) 1 Neue Zeitschrift für Kartellrecht 175.

[168] See Case C–578/08 *Chakroun v Minister van Buitenlandse Zaken* [2010] ECR I–1839, [44], [62]–[63] on the protection of family life; also Cases C–275/06 *Promusicae v Telefónica de España SAU* [2009] ECR I–271, [65]–[69] and C–400/10 PPU *JMcB* (n 30) [60] in which the CJEU ruled that Member States had latitude to interpret an EU dir so as to comply with fundamental rights (rights to property, to privacy, to an effective remedy, and the rights of the child respectively); C–300/11 *ZZ v Secretary of State for the Home Department* EU:C:2013:363, [50]–[52], requiring Dir 2000/48 on free movement of citizens to be interpreted in the light of Art 47 of the Charter; C–396/11 *Radu* EU:C:2013:39 and C–168/13 PPU *Jeremy F* EU:C:2013:358, interpreting the decision establishing a European Arrest Warrant in the light of Arts 47 and 48 of the Charter; C–71 and 99/11 *Bundesrepublik Deutschland v Y and C* EU:C:2012:518 interpreting Dir 2004/83 in the light of Art 10 of the Charter; C–277/10 *Martin Luksan v Petrus van der Let* EU:C:2012:65, interpreting Dir 2001/29 in the light of Art 17(1) of the Charter; C–104/10 *Kelly v NUI* EU:C:2011:506, interpreting Dir 97/80 in the light of Art 8 of the Charter; C–112/13 *A v B* EU:C:2014:2195, interpreting Reg 44/2001 in the light of Art 47 of the Charter.

[169] Case C–131/12 *Google Spain v AEPD* EU:C:2014:317

recognize only the common level of protection accorded by all states, but instead a pragmatic case-by-case approach to identify the scope and content of particular rights which are pleaded.

iii. With the enactment of the Charter of Fundamental Rights, the CJEU has increasingly drawn on this instrument, and less on the ECHR or the common constitutional principles of Member States, as the EU's autonomous source of human rights law. In *Melloni* the Court made clear that Article 53 of the Charter does not change its long-standing ruling that fundamental rights under national constitutions cannot call into question the primacy of EU law, which should prevail in the event of conflict.

iv. Until such time as the EU follows the mandate in Article 6(2) TEU and accedes to the ECHR—a prospect which has been further postponed due to the Court's negative *Opinion 2/13* on the draft Accession Agreement—the Convention is not formally binding on the EU.[170] However, even though the Charter has replaced the ECHR as the favoured source of human rights principles in EU law, the CJEU and the General Court continue to cite provisions of the ECHR and sometimes make reference to the case law of the European Court of Human Rights, particularly in cases governed by Article 52(3) of the Charter.[171]

v. The CJEU was formerly reluctant to engage in robust rights-based review of EU policy and legislation. However, with the enactment of the Charter, and the expansion of EU policy activities into the fields of internal and external security, human rights-based challenges against EU action have more recently met with greater success before the CJEU. This is particularly notable in cases challenging economic and financial sanctions imposed by the EU.

vi. The General Court and the Civil Service Tribunal have also entertained many rights-based challenges to administrative action, particularly in the context of EU competition proceedings and staff disputes.

vii. The EU's policy competence in the field of human rights has gradually broadened since the Court first acknowledged the general principles of law. While the EU's legislative competence to enact internal rules on human rights is largely sector-specific, or requires recourse to the residual treaty basis of Art 352 TFEU, human rights feature prominently in EU external relations. Supporting institutions such as the Fundamental Rights Agency have also been created, and debate continues over how to operationalize the sanction mechanism in Article 7 TEU.

8 HUMAN RIGHTS-BASED CHALLENGES TO MEMBER STATE ACTION

Thus far we have mainly examined the role of human rights as standards for assessing the legality of EU action and as constraints on the acts of the EU institutions. However, the ECJ also ruled some decades ago that fundamental rights were binding not only on the EU institutions but *also on the Member States* when they are acting within the scope of application of EU law. And as we have seen, when the Charter of Fundamental Rights was enacted, its provisions were made binding not just on the EU institutions but also on the Member States when 'implementing Union law'. However, the extension of EU fundamental rights review to Member State action remains contentious, not only because

---

[170] For a contrary argument that the EU is already bound, as a matter of EU law, by the provisions of the ECHR, see B de Witte, 'Human Rights' in P Koutrakos (ed), *Beyond the Established Orders: Policy Interconnections Between the EU and the Rest of the World* (Hart, 2011).

[171] (N 30).

it is not always clear whether states are acting within the scope of application of EU law, but also because some Member States remain resistant to the very idea of the CJEU determining standards of human rights protection to be applied to them.[172] The state of the law as regards the circumstances in which Member State action may be reviewed by the CJEU for compliance with EU fundamental rights review (whether the general principles of EU law or the Charter) is outlined below, followed by the question whether the Charter can be directly applied to the conduct of private actors.

(A) MEMBER STATES AS AGENTS OF THE EU: IMPLEMENTING AND APPLYING EU MEASURES

The ECJ first indicated, in the case of *Rutili* in 1975, that when Member States are applying provisions of EU legislation which are based on protection for human rights, they are bound by the general principles of EU law.[173] *Rutili* concerned the provisions of Directive 64/221, whose limitations on the restrictions Member States could impose on the free movement of workers were treated as specific expressions of the general principles enshrined in the ECHR. Similarly in *Johnston v RUC*, the requirement of judicial control in the 1976 Equal Treatment Directive was described by the Court as reflecting a general principle of EU law which meant it should be interpreted as providing the right to an effective remedy.[174] More current examples can be seen in relation to the EU Data Protection Directive 95/46 and Regulation 45/2001 which have been held to reflect rights of privacy protected under the ECHR and the Charter, and to require interpretation and application by national authorities in that light.[175]

Other recent rulings of this kind have been given in relation to EU Directive 2004/83 on minimum standards for refugees, which is based on the UN Geneva Convention and is said by the CJEU to reflect other provisions of the EU Charter including respect for human dignity and the right to asylum.[176] Similarly, if rather more contestedly, the EU's 'Dublin' Regulations 2003/343 and now 604/2013, concerning the determination of the Member State responsible for asylum applications, have been said to ensure full observance of the right to asylum guaranteed by Article 18 of the Charter, and to prevent violations of the prohibition on degrading treatment under Article 4 of the Charter.[177]

---

[172] For contributions by the EU judiciary to some of the extensive literature discussing Art 51 of the Charter and the scope of application of fundamental rights to Member State action, see K Lenaerts, 'Exploring the Limits of the EU Charter of Fundamental Rights' (2012) 8 EUConst 375; A Rosas, 'When is the EU Charter of Fundamental Rights Applicable at National Level?' (2012) 19 Jurisprudence 1271; and C Vadja, The Application of the EU Charter of Fundamental Rights: Neither Reckless nor Timid?', University of Edinburgh Law School Research Paper Series 2014/47, referring also to the reaction of the German Federal Constitutional Court to the CJEU's rulings on Art 51. For a nice overview of the literature and of recent developments in relation to Art 51, including a survey of some national case law on the question, see F Fontanelli, 'The Implementation of European Union Law by Member States under Article 51 of the Charter of Fundamental Rights' (2014) 20 CJEL 193.

[173] Case 36/75 *Rutili* (n 21). See AG Trabucchi in Case 118/75 *Watson and Belmann* [1976] ECR 1185, 1207–1208, for comment on this aspect of the case.

[174] Case 222/84 *Johnston* (n 22). For similar rulings see Cases 222/86 *UNECTEF v Heylens* [1987] ECR 4097; C–185/97 *Coote* (n 22); C–432/05 *Unibet* [2007] ECR I–2271, [37]. See also on access to court, Cases T–111/96 *ITT Promedia NV v Commission* [1998] ECR II–2937; C–279/09 *DEB v Bundesrepublik Deutschland* [2010] ECR I–13849.

[175] Cases C–465/00, 138 and 139/01 *Österreichischer Rundfunk* (n 22) [70]–[72]; C–131/12 *Google Spain v AEPD* EU:C:2014:317; C–73/07 *Tietosuojavaltuutettu v Satakunnan Markkinapörssi Oy* [2008] ECR I–9831.

[176] Cases C–465/07 *Elgafaji* (n 28); C–148/13 *A, B & C v Staatssecretaris van Veiligheid en Justitie* EU:C:2014:2406, [45]–[46], [53]–[54]; C–101/09 *Bundesrepublik Deutschland v B* EU:C:2009:285; C–71 and 99/11 *Bundesrepublik Deutschland v Y and C* EU:C:2012:518; C–175–179/08 *Salahadin Abdulla and Others* [2010] ECR I–1493, [53]–[54]; C–31/09 *Bolbol* [2010] ECR I–5539, [38].

[177] Cases C–411 and 493/10 *NS and Others* [2011] ECR I–13905, [75]–[86]; C–4/11 *Bundesrepublik Deutschland v Puid* EU:C:2013:740, [30]; C–394/12 *Shamso Abdullahi v Bundesasylamt* EU:C:2013:813; C–19/08 *Migrationsverket v Petrosian* [2009] ECR I–495, [4]. See G Mellon, 'The Charter of Fundamental Rights and the Dublin Convention: An Analysis of *N.S. v. Home Secretary*' (2012) 18 EPL 655.

These Regulations have however been the subject of extensive ECHR case law, in which the operation of the EU asylum system has been challenged—and sometimes condemned—for violation of Article 3 ECHR concerning inhuman and degrading treatment.[178]

The upshot of the CJEU rulings, however, is that when Member States are implementing or applying EU measures which are based on or reflect fundamental rights, their action can be scrutinized by the CJEU to ensure they have done everything necessary to avoid violating rights guaranteed under EU law. Thus, for example, they must not return asylum-seekers to a Member State encountering systemic deficiencies and in which they are likely to face inhuman or degrading treatment,[179] they must not require asylum-seekers to undergo 'tests' to prove their sexual orientation,[180] and in determining who qualifies as a refugee they must ensure protection for family life, freedom of religion, and other rights.[181] Further, when applying EU laws which are based on certain fundamental rights, national authorities must also ensure a fair balance between these and other rights protected as part of EU law.[182]

Long before the Charter was enacted, however, the ECJ had already gone beyond the kinds of cases described above, in which EU measures themselves embody a particular right,[183] and had required Member States to ensure that EU fundamental rights are protected *whenever states are implementing an EU measure*, even one which on its face has little to do with rights.[184] Thus in *Wachauf*, a case concerning the regulation of milk production, the ECJ ruled that Member States are bound, when implementing EU law, by all of the same general principles and fundamental rights which bind the EU in its actions.[185] One way of explaining this broader extension of EU fundamental rights review to Member State action is to view Member States as agents of the EU when they implement or enforce EU measures, with the result that they are bound by the range of rights protected as part of EU law.[186] This is a kind of judicial 'human rights mainstreaming' technique, in accordance with which EU legislation is strengthened by the imposition on Member States of an obligation to protect all of the rights guaranteed by the Charter and the general principles of EU law when implementing such measures.[187]

---

[178] See in particular App No 30696/09 *MSS v Belgium and Greece*, Grand Chamber judgment of 21 Jan 2011 and App No 29217/12 *Tarakhel v Switzerland*, Grand Chamber judgment of 4 Nov 2014. For information on other Strasbourg cases concerning the EU's asylum system, see the ECHR's 'Factsheet on the "Dublin" cases', http://www. echr.coe.int/Documents/FS_Dublin_ENG.pdf (updated Jan 2015).

[179] Cases C–411 and 493/10 *NS and Others* [2011] ECR I–13905, [75]–[86]; C–4/11 *Bundesrepublik Deutschland v Puid* EU:C:2013:740, [30].

[180] Case C–148/13 *A, B & C v Staatssecretaris van Veiligheid en Justitie* EU:C:2014:2406.

[181] Cases C–71 and 99/11 *Bundesrepublik Deutschland v Y and C* EU:C:2012:518.

[182] Cases C–468–469/10 *ASNEF and FECEMD v Administración del Estado* EU:C:2011:777, [43]. Also Cases C–275/06 *Promusicae* (n 168); C–314/12 *UPC Telekabel Wien* EU:C:2014:192; C–360/10 *SABAM v Netlog NV* EU:C:2012:85, [42]–[44]; and C–201/13 *Deckmyn and Vrijhejdsfonds* EU:C:2014:2132, [26], [30] on balancing intellectual property rights with other rights; and C–297 and 298/10 *Henning and Mai* [2011] ECR I–7965, [66] on the relationship between the right to collective bargaining and the principle of non-discrimination.

[183] See, eg, Case C–219/91 *Criminal Proceedings against Ter Voort* [1992] ECR I–5495, [33]–[38], on compliance by a Member State with Art 10 ECHR when giving effect to Dir 65/65/EC on the categorization of medicinal products.

[184] In Case 63/83 *R v Kent Kirk* [1984] ECR 2689, [21]–[23], the domestic effect of applying a retroactive provision of an EU fisheries reg to a UK statutory instrument was held to violate the principle of non-retroactivity of penal liability enshrined in Art 7 ECHR. For much recent such non-retroactivity cases, see Cases C–74 and 129/95 *X* [1996] ECR I–6609; Case C–60/02 *X* [2004] ECR I–651; Case C–387/02 *Berlusconi et al* [2005] ECR I–3565.

[185] Case 5/88 *Wachauf v Germany* [1989] ECR 2609, [17]–[19]; Case C–292/97 *Karlsson* [2000] ECR I–2737.

[186] See, eg, Case 249/86 *Commission v Germany* [1989] ECR 1263 on the right to family life in the implementation of EU free movement rules. Also Case C–578/08 *Chakroun* (n 168).

[187] In the challenge to the EU Family Reunification Dir, Case C–540/03 *European Parliament v Council* (n 19) [15]–[23], the ECJ emphasized that the Dir did not in itself violate fundamental rights by leaving discretionary choices to the Member States, because the Dir could not be read as permitting the Member States to use their discretion in such a way as to infringe fundamental rights. See also Case C–101/01 *Lindqvist* [2003] ECR I–12971, [84]–[90].

Examples which pre-date the binding enactment of the Charter include the cases of *Ordre des barreaux francophones et germanophones* concerning the right to a fair trial in the implementation of the Money Laundering Directive;[188] *Spector Photo Group* concerning the presumption of innocence in the implementation of the EU Insider Dealing Directive 2003/6;[189] *Varec* on the rights of the defence under the review procedures put in place to implement the EU Public Procurement Directives;[190] *Chakroun* on the right to family life in the implementation of the EU Family Reunification Directive 2003/86;[191] *Salahadin Abdulla* on protection for the integrity of the person in determining the risk of persecution when assessing applications for refugee status under the EU Directive;[192] *Kabel Deutschland Vertrieb* concerning protection for freedom of expression and media pluralism in the context of the implementation of the Universal Service Directive;[193] *Damgaard* concerning protection for freedom of expression in the context of the prohibition of advertising of medical products under EU Directive 2001/83;[194] *Promusicae* concerning reconciliation of the rights to property, data protection, and private life in the domestic transposition of EU directives on electronic commerce, intellectual property, and electronic communications;[195] *Tietosuojavaltuutettu* concerning data protection and the reconciliation of freedom of expression and privacy rights in the context of the publication of tax information by a Finnish newspaper;[196] and *Aguirre Zarraga* on the rights of the child in considering a custody dispute under EU Regulation 2201/2003.[197] Further, the cluster of cases which deal with national remedies for breach of EU rights, and which describe the right of access to a remedy as a fundamental right which must be provided by domestic law, also fall into this category.[198]

Since the Charter became binding in 2009, many other such cases have been decided. Examples include the actions of Member State authorities in the implementation of the EU Arrest Warrant,[199] the Data Protection Directive,[200] EU intellectual property law,[201] child custody,[202] the rights of long-term residence third-country nationals,[203] anti-discrimination law,[204] recognition and enforcement of judgments,[205] economic sanctions,[206] and free movement measures.[207]

---

[188] Case C–305/05 *Ordre des barreaux francophones* (n 124); M Luchtmann and R van der Hoeven, Note (2009) 46 CMLRev 301.

[189] Case C–45/08 *Specter Photo Group NV v CBFA* [2009] ECR I–12073. Also on the presumption of innocence see Case C–344/08 *Rubach* [2009] ECR I–7033.

[190] Case C–450/06 *Varec v Belgium* [2008] ECR I–581.

[191] Case 578/08 *Chakroun* (n 168).

[192] Cases C–175–179/08 *Salahadin Abdulla et al v Germany*, 2 Mar 2010. See also, on the Refugee Returns Dir 2008/15, Case C–61/11 PPU *El Dridi*, 28 April 2011, [42]–[43].

[193] Case C–336/07 *Kabel Deutschland Vertrieb v Niedersächsische Landesmedienanstalt für privaten Rundfunk* [2008] ECR I–10889.

[194] Case C–421/07 *Damgaard* [2009] ECR I–2629.

[195] Case C–275/06 *Promusicae v Telefónica de España SAU* [2008] ECR I–271.

[196] Case C–73/07 *Tietosuojavaltuutettu v Satakunnan Markkinapörssi Oy* [2008] ECR I–9831, [52]–[62].

[197] Case C–491/10 PPU *Aguirre Zarraga* [2010] ECR I–14247, [60]–[66]; also Case C–394/07 *Gambazzi v Daimler-Chrysler* [2009] ECR I–2563.

[198] See the cases cited at (n 174).

[199] Cases C–396/11 *Radu* EU:C:2013:39; C–168/13 PPU *Jeremy F* EU:C:2013:358; C–399/11 *Melloni v Ministerio Fiscal* EU:C:2013:107.

[200] Case C–131/12 *Google Spain v AEPD* EU:C:2014:317.

[201] Case C–277/10 *Martin Luksan v Petrus van der Let* EU:C:2012:65.

[202] Case C–400/10 PPU *JMcB* (n 30).

[203] Case C–571/10 *Servet Kamberaj v IPES* EU:C:2012:233, [79]–[80].

[204] Case C–104/10 *Kelly v NUI* EU:C:2011:506.

[205] Case C–112/13 *A v B* EU:C:2014:2195.

[206] Case C–314/13 *Užsienio reikalų ministerija v Pevtiev* EU:C:2014:1645, [24]–[26].

[207] Case C–300/11 *ZZ v Secretary of State for the Home Department* EU:C:2013:363.

(B) MEMBER STATES DEROGATING FROM EU RULES OR RESTRICTING EU RIGHTS

Thus far we have considered a variety of situations in which Member States were *implementing* EU measures. However, Member States are also sometimes permitted by the Treaty or by analogous principles developed by the ECJ to *derogate* from or restrict EU rules on public policy or other grounds.

After initial uncertainty in the case law,[208] the ECJ in *ERT* declared that it had a duty to ensure that Member States adequately respected fundamental rights which were part of EU law when they adopted measures derogating from EU law. The case concerned the compatibility with EU law of exclusive rights granted by Greek legislation to ERT, which had the effect of restricting the free movement of services and establishment. The defendant argued that the effect of the legislation on its freedom of expression should also be taken into account by the Court.

Case C–260/89 **Elliniki Radiophonia Tileorassi AE (ERT) v Dimotiki Etairia Pliroforissis and Sotirios Kouvelas**
[1991] ECR I–2925

[Note Lisbon Treaty renumbering: Arts 56 and 66 EC are now Arts 52 and 62 TFEU respectively]

THE ECJ

42. As the Court has held (see Cases C–60 & 61/84 *Cinéthèque*, paragraph 25 and Case C–12/86 *Demirel v. Stadt Schwäbisch Gmünd*, paragraph 28), it has no power to examine the compatibility with the European Convention on Human Rights of national rules which do not fall within the scope of Community law. On the other hand, where such rules do fall within the scope of Community law, and reference is made to the Court for a preliminary ruling, it must provide all the criteria of interpretation needed by the national court to determine whether those rules are compatible with the fundamental rights the observance of which the Court ensures and which derive in particular from the European Convention on Human Rights.

43. In particular, where a Member State relies on the combined provisions of Articles 56 and 66 in order to justify rules which are likely to obstruct the exercise of the freedom to provide services, such justification, provided for by Community law, must be interpreted in the light of the general principles of law and in particular of fundamental rights. Thus the national rules in question can fall under the exceptions provided for by the combined provisions of Article 56 and 66 only if they are compatible with the fundamental rights, the observance of which is ensured by the Court.

44. It follows that in such a case it is for the national court, and if necessary, the Court of Justice to appraise the application of those provisions having regard to all the rules of Community law, including freedom of expression, as embodied in Article 10 of the European Convention on Human Rights, as a general principle of law the observance of which is ensured by the Court.

45. The reply to the national court must therefore be that the limitations imposed on the power of the Member States to apply the provisions referred to in Articles 66 and 56 of the Treaty on grounds of public policy, public security and public health must be appraised in the light of the general principle of freedom of expression embodied in Article 10 of the European Convention on Human Rights.

This ruling extended further the Court's jurisdiction in this sensitive field, namely to review Member State compliance with EU fundamental rights in situations in which they arguably seek to escape the

---

[208] Cases 60 and 61/84 *Cinéthèque v Fédération Nationale des Cinémas Français* [1985] ECR 2605, [25]–[26] in particular, and Case 12/86 *Demirel v Stadt Schwäbisch Gmünd* [1987] ECR 3719, [28].

remit of EU law.[209] And despite arguments made, even by members of the Court itself, to reduce the scope of these rulings,[210] they have been confirmed many times since.[211]

In the field of immigration, for example, there has been a steady stream of rulings concerning the right to family life or due process where states have relied on the public policy or public interest derogation either to expel a migrant who was covered by EU law or to refuse some other family benefit. In cases such as *Orfanopoulos*,[212] *MRAX*,[213] *Baumbast*,[214] *Carpenter*,[215] *Commission v Germany*,[216] *Tsakouridis*,[217] *Ruiz Zambrano*,[218] *ZZ*,[219] *O and S*,[220] and *Ziebell*,[221] the Court has emphasized the requirement on states to take adequate account of the impact of their proposed actions on the right to family life as well as other Charter rights.

Less controversially in *Schmidberger*, the Court confirmed that the protection of human rights *in itself* constitutes a legitimate interest which will justify a restriction on EU free movement rules.[222] Austria had relied on protection for freedom of expression and assembly as a public policy justification for the closure of roads (and trade routes) between Austria and Italy in order to facilitate environmental protests. According to the ECJ, since both the EU and the Member States are required to respect fundamental rights, 'the protection of those rights is a legitimate interest which, in principle, justifies a restriction of the obligations imposed by [EU] law, even under a fundamental freedom guaranteed by the Treaty such as the free movement of goods.'[223] Similarly in *Omega Spielhallen*, Germany successfully pleaded the protection of human dignity as a ground for restricting the marketing in Germany of laser games which simulated the killing of human beings.[224]

---

[209] See Cases C–250/06 *United Pan-Europe Communications Belgium v Belgium* [2007] ECR I–11135 and C–336/07 *Kabel Deutschland* (n 193). And in Case C–368/95 *Vereinigte Familiapress Zeitungsverlags- und Vertriebs GmbH v Heinrich Bauer Verlag* [1997] ECR I–3689, the ECJ clarified that Member States must comply with fundamental rights even when they are not relying on an express Treaty derogation, but on the broader range of public interest justifications developed by the ECJ for 'indistinctly applicable' national measures.

[210] F Jacobs, 'Human Rights in the European Union: The Role of the Court of Justice' (2001) 26 ELRev 331, 337–339. Compare his expansive earlier argument for human rights review of national measures by the ECJ in his opinion as AG in Case C–168/91 *Konstantinidis v Stadt Altensteig* [1993] ECR I–1191, 1211–1212. Also AG Maduro in Case C–380/05 *Centro-Europa 7 Srl* [2008] ECR I–349, [14]–[20].

[211] eg Cases C–370/05 *Festersen* [2007] ECR I–1129 and C–470/03 *AGM-COS.MET Srl v Suomen valtio and Tarmo Lehtinen* [2007] ECR I–2749, [72]–[73].

[212] Cases C–482 and 493/01 *Orfanopoulos and Oliveri v Land Baden-Württemberg* [2004] ECR I–5257, [97]–[100].

[213] Case C–459/99 *MRAX v Belgium* [2002] ECR I–6591, [53], [61], [62].

[214] Case C–413/99 *Baumbast and R v Home Secretary* [2002] ECR I–7091, [72]–[73].

[215] Case C–60/00 *Carpenter v Home Secretary* [2002] ECR I–6279. In this case the ECJ indeed seemed to stretch to fit the facts of the case within the 'scope of application of EU law' for the purpose of fundamental rights review. For a similar stretching approach, see Case C–71/02 *Karner v Troostwijk* [2004] ECR I–3025.

[216] Case C–441/02 *Commission v Germany* [2006] ECR I–3449, [108]–[113].

[217] Case C–145/09 *Land Baden-Württemberg v Tsakouridis* [2010] ECR I–11979.

[218] Case C–34/09 *Ruiz Zambrano v ONEM*, AG's Opinion [2011] ECR I–1177.

[219] Case C–300/11 *ZZ v Secretary of State for the Home Department* EU:C:2013:363.

[220] Cases C–356 and 357/11 *O and S v Maahanmuuttovirasto* EU:C:2012:776.

[221] Case C–371/08 *Ziebell* [2011] ECR I–12735.

[222] Case C–112/00 *Schmidberger v Austria* [2003] ECR I–5659. Also Case C–208/09 *Sayn-Wittgenstein* [2010] ECR I–13693, [84]–[89] on the principle of equality as a public policy justification for restricting citizenship-related rights.

[223] Case C–112/00 *Schmidberger*, ibid [74].

[224] Case C–36/02 *Omega Spielhallen* (n 58); also Case C–208/09 *Sayn-Wittgenstein* [2010] ECR I–13693, [87] and Case C–244/06 *Dynamic Medien* (n 37). In Cases C–341/05 *Laval un Partneri Svenska Byggnadsarbetareförbundet* [2007] ECR I–11767, [101]–[111]; and C–438/05 *International Transport Workers' Federation v Viking* [2007] ECR I–10779, [74]–[90], the fundamental right to strike was taken into account in determining whether a restriction on the free movement of services/establishment caused by collective industrial action could be justified on the basis of the protection of

(c) OTHER KINDS OF MEMBER STATE ACTION 'WITHIN THE SCOPE OF EU LAW'

Doubts soon arose, following the adoption of the Charter of Fundamental Rights, as to whether the drafters had intended to reverse or confine the *ERT/Familiapress* line of jurisprudence, by using narrower language when describing the scope of application of the Charter to Member States. Article 51 of the Charter declares that:

> The provisions of this Charter are addressed to the institutions, bodies, offices and agencies of the Union... and to the Member States only when they are implementing Union law

Yet whatever the intentions of the drafters,[225] the ECJ expressly chose not to read this provision of the Charter narrowly but instead so as to confirm its prior approach.[226] In *Åkerberg Fransson*, the Court drew for support on the Explanations to the Charter, which were given interpretative effect by Article 6(1) TEU and Article 52(7) of the Charter, and which use the wider term 'binding on the Member States when they act within the scope of EU law'.[227] More interestingly still, the factual circumstances of the Member State action in question in *Fransson* amounted neither to an 'implementation of EU law' nor to a 'derogation' from EU law. Could it therefore be covered by Article 51 of the Charter for the purposes of the CJEU's review for compatibility with fundamental rights?

In *Fransson*, the applicant claimed that his prosecution under Swedish law for a tax offence, having been already subject to tax penalties for the same matter, amounted to a violation of the principle of *ne bis in idem* in breach of EU law.[228] The Swedish Government, together with the Commission and four intervening governments, argued to the Court that the situation fell outside the scope of EU law for the purposes of Article 51 of the Charter, since neither the tax penalty nor the criminal prosecution arose from the implementation of EU law. The CJEU began by indicating that Article 51 confirms its previous case law on the scope of application of fundamental rights review:[229]

---

workers. For more recent cases on the right to collective bargaining see Cases C–271/08 *Commission v Germany* [2010] ECR I–7091 and C–297 and 298/10 *Henning and Mai* [2011] ECR I–7965. On freedom of association see Cases C–415/93 *URBSFA v Bosman* [1995] ECR I–4921 and C–235/92 *Montecatini v Commission* [1999] ECR I–4539.

[225] For a comment on this aspect of the original drafting of the Charter in 1999–2000, see G de Búrca, 'The Drafting of the EU Charter of Fundamental Rights' (2000) 25 ELRev 331. Note however that the Charter was subsequently revised during the 2003–2004 Convention and IGC on the Constitutional Treaty, and that it has been proclaimed and adopted by a range of different actors. Discerning the intention of the multiple drafters would be a difficult task.

[226] Case C–617/10 *Åkerberg Fransson* EU:C:2013:105. See also Case C–390/12 *Pfleger* EU:C:2014:281, [35]–[36] and Case C–145/09 *Tsakouridis* (n 217) [52].

[227] Ibid. The Explanations to Art 51 cite Case C–260/89 *ERT* [1991] ECR I–2925 in support of this wider phrasing: see (n 25).

[228] Case C–617/10 (n 226).

[229] For a case in which the ECJ treated the scope of application of Art 51 of the Charter in exactly the same way as the scope of application of other general principles of EU law—notably proportionality—see Case C–206/13 *Cruciano Siragusa v Regione Sicilia* EU:C:2014:126, [34]–[35]. For discussion of this issue of the parallelism of the scope of application of the Charter and the general principles of law, see Rosas (n 172).

C–617/10 Åklagaren v Åkerberg Fransson
EU:C:2013:105

17. It is to be recalled in respect of those submissions that the Charter's field of application so far as concerns action of the Member States is defined in Article 51(1) thereof, according to which the provisions of the Charter are addressed to the Member States only when they are implementing European Union law.

18. That article of the Charter thus confirms the Court's case-law relating to the extent to which actions of the Member States must comply with the requirements flowing from the fundamental rights guaranteed in the legal order of the European Union.

19. The Court's settled case-law indeed states, in essence, that the fundamental rights guaranteed in the legal order of the European Union are applicable in all situations governed by European Union law, but not outside such situations. In this respect the Court has already observed that it has no power to examine the compatibility with the Charter of national legislation lying outside the scope of European Union law. On the other hand, if such legislation falls within the scope of European Union law, the Court, when requested to give a preliminary ruling, must provide all the guidance as to interpretation needed in order for the national court to determine whether that legislation is compatible with the fundamental rights the observance of which the Court ensures (see inter alia, to this effect, Case C–260/89 *ERT* [1991] I–2925, paragraph 42; . . .).

20. That definition of the field of application of the fundamental rights of the European Union is borne out by the explanations relating to Article 51 of the Charter, which, in accordance with the third subparagraph of Article 6(1) TEU and Article 52(7) of the Charter, have to be taken into consideration for the purpose of interpreting it (see, to this effect, Case C–279/09 *DEB* [2010] ECR I–13849, paragraph 32). According to those explanations, 'the requirement to respect fundamental rights defined in the context of the Union is only binding on the Member States when they act in the scope of Union law'.

21. Since the fundamental rights guaranteed by the Charter must therefore be complied with where national legislation falls within the scope of European Union law, situations cannot exist which are covered in that way by European Union law without those fundamental rights being applicable. The applicability of European Union law entails applicability of the fundamental rights guaranteed by the Charter.

22. Where, on the other hand, a legal situation does not come within the scope of European Union law, the Court does not have jurisdiction to rule on it and any provisions of the Charter relied upon cannot, of themselves, form the basis for such jurisdiction (see, to this effect, the order in Case C–466/11 *Currà and Others* [2012] ECR I–0000, paragraph 26).

23. These considerations correspond to those underlying Article 6(1) TEU, according to which the provisions of the Charter are not to extend in any way the competences of the European Union as defined in the Treaties. Likewise, the Charter, pursuant to Article 51(2) thereof, does not extend the field of application of European Union law beyond the powers of the European Union or establish any new power or task for the European Union, or modify powers and tasks as defined in the Treaties (see *Dereci and Others*, paragraph 71).

The Court notably, if predictably, insists that the Charter does not *extend* the scope of application of EU law, but rather *follows* its scope of application. The key sentence in the judgment, which is unfortunately not a particularly helpful one, is that 'the applicability of European Union law entails applicability of the fundamental rights guaranteed by the Charter'. The Court seems to be saying that if EU law is genuinely applicable to the specific facts of the case in respect of which a rights violation is claimed, then the Charter will also be applicable, and the CJEU will have jurisdiction to review whether there has been compliance with its provisions. But that still leaves many questions about when exactly EU law is genuinely applicable to the facts of the case. In *Fransson* itself, the CJEU declined to follow the Opinion of the Advocate General who had advised that the link between the Swedish penalties and EU tax law was insufficient to bring the case within the terms of Article 51 of the Charter.[230] Instead, the CJEU ruled that even though the national laws on the basis of which the tax penalties and criminal proceedings had been brought had not been adopted specifically to implement an EU tax Directive, they were nonetheless designed in part to penalize infringements of the Directive (as well as of national law) in relation to the EU obligation to declare and collect VAT, and this brought them within the scope of application of EU law for the purposes of the Charter.[231]

In subsequent rulings, the CJEU has given further guidance on the scope of Article 51 of the Charter, but still at a level of considerable generality and abstraction. In the *Cruciano Siragusa* and *Julian Hernández* cases, the Court declared that the reason for requiring fundamental rights review of Member State action falling within the scope of EU law is the same as the original reason for requiring fundamental rights review of *EU action* in the early *Handelsgesellschaft* case: namely to ensure the supremacy of EU law. In the Court's words, the scope of Article 51 is intended 'to avoid a situation in which the level of protection of fundamental rights varies according to the national law involved in such a way as to undermine the unity, primacy and effectiveness of EU law.'[232]

In subsequent rulings as to whether national action constitutes 'implementation' within the meaning of Article 51 of the Charter the Court has stated, still rather vaguely, that relevant factors include 'whether that legislation is intended to implement a provision of EU law; the nature of that legislation and whether it pursues objectives other than those covered by EU law, even if it is capable of indirectly affecting EU law; and also whether there are specific rules of EU law on the matter or capable of affecting it.'[233] Somewhat more sharply, the Court insisted that the concept of implementing EU law in Article 51 'presupposes a degree of connection between the measure of EU law and the national measure at issue which goes beyond the matters covered being closely related or one of those matters having an indirect impact on the other'.[234] The fact that a national measure comes within an area in which the EU has powers is of itself insufficient to bring it within the scope of application of EU law and to render the Charter applicable.[235] Thus the fact that national measures may 'indirectly affect' EU law will not be enough to bring the situation within Article 51, while the fact that EU law imposes an *obligation* on the state with regard to the subject matter of the case probably will suffice to bring the situation within the scope of application of EU law.[236] In *NS and ME*, the Court indicated that the fact that a Member State exercises discretion to determine whether or not to avail of an option under asylum legislation does not mean that the situation falls outside the scope of EU law: in this case the UK's decision to examine a claim for asylum which was not its responsibility under the criteria set out in EU Regulation 343/2003 fell within the scope of Article 51 of the Charter, since that option was an integral part of the EU asylum system.[237]

---

[230] Case C–617/10 *Åklagaren v Åkerberg Fransson* EU:C:2012:340, [63] [64].

[231] Ibid [24]–[28]. The CJEU also ruled that the national court was free to apply domestic standards of fundamental rights, since the national law in question was not entirely determined by EU law, so long as these did not compromise the level of protection under the Charter of the unity and consistency of EU law.

[232] Case C–206/13 *Cruciano Siragusa v Regione Sicilia* EU:C:2014:126, [32]; Case C–198/13 *Julian Hernández* EU:C:2014:2055, [47]. There is a clear resonance between this ruling and that of the CJEU in Case C–399/11 *Melloni* (n 110) as to why, despite the language of Art 53 of the Charter, the EU Arrest Warrant could not be reviewed for compliance with Spanish constitutional rights, but only for compliance with Charter provisions.

[233] Cases C–206/13 *Cruciano Siragusa* (n 229) [25]; also Cases C–40/11 *Iida* EU:C:2012:691, [79]; C–87/12 *Ymeraga* EU:C:2013:291, [41].

[234] Cases C–198/13 *Julian Hernández* (n 232) [34]; C–206/13 *Cruciano Siragusa* (n 232) [24].

[235] See Cases C–198/13 *Julian Hernández*, ibid; C–483/09 and C–1/10 *Gueye and Salmerón Sánchez* EU:C:2011:583, [69]–[70] and C–370/12 *Pringle* EU:C:2012:756, [104]–[105], [180]–[181].

[236] See, eg, Case C–617/10 *Åkerberg Fransson* EU:C:2013:105. Compare Cases C–144/95 *Maurin* [1996] ECR I–2909, [11]–[12]; C–206/13 *Cruciano Siragusa* (n 229) [26]. See also K Lenaerts, 'Exploring the Limits of the Charter of Fundamental Rights' (2012) 8 EUConst 375.

[237] Case C–411/10 *NS v Home Secretary* and Case C–493/10 *ME v Refugee Applications Commissioner and Minister for Justice and Law Reform* EU:2011:865, [65]–[68]. Compare Case C–333/13 *Dano* EU:2014:2358 where a Member

It can only be hoped that further case law will lead to better and sharper criteria to determine the contours of this still elusive category of Member State action falling 'within the scope of application of EU law' which amounts neither to a straightforward implementation of EU law nor to a derogation from it.[238]

(D) SITUATIONS FALLING OUTSIDE THE SCOPE OF EU LAW

As we have seen above, the Court in *Fransson* made clear that its pre-Charter case law on situations falling *outside* the scope of EU law also remains relevant. In other words, it follows from Article 51 that the Court has no jurisdiction to review Member State compliance with the Charter in situations which lie beyond the scope of EU law.[239] Yet cases such as *Carpenter*,[240] *Fransson*, *NS*, and others discussed above demonstrate that it is difficult to predict which situations will be deemed to lie 'outside' and which 'inside' the field of application of EU law for the purposes of human rights review.[241]

There has been a steady stream of case law since the Charter gained binding force on the scope of Article 51, and a great many cases have by now been rejected by the CJEU for falling outside the scope of EU law and hence outside its jurisdiction to review state action for compatibility with the Charter.[242] While some of the cases are clearly outside the scope of EU law, or the national referring courts give no explanation as to why they may be considered within the scope of EU law, and hence they are dispensed with promptly by order of the CJEU or left for the national court to decide,[243] others are more complex and borderline cases which require fuller reasoning on the part of the Court. These include situations such as national legislation adopted in the exercise of an exclusive national competence, which grants workers in certain circumstances more extensive protection than that provided under related EU employment law;[244] a Member State's refusal to grant a residence permit to a family member of an EU national who does not satisfy the conditions of residence set by EU legislation;[245] a state's refusal of legal aid to an individual under provisions of national law even where the main proceedings

State's choice as to what constitutes a non-contributory cash benefit for the purposes of EU Reg 883/2004 fell outside the scope of EU law and of Art 51 of the Charter.

[238] For some of the extensive literature, see (n 172).

[239] For one of the earliest pre-Charter cases establishing this point see Case 12/86 *Demirel* (n 208).

[240] Case C–60/00 *Carpenter* (n 215). For some other cases held to fall within the scope of Art 51, despite uncertainty on the part of the referring court or arguments of the parties, see Cases C–156/12 *GREP v Freistaat Bayern* EU:C:2012:342; C–416/10 *Križan and Others* EU:C:2013:8; C–390/12 *Pfleger* EU:C:2014:281; and C–418/11 *Texdata Software* EU:C:2013:588, [71]–[75].

[241] Compare, eg, Cases C–144/95 *Maurin* [1996] ECR I–2909 and C–276/01 *Steffensen* [2003] ECR I–3735, [69]–[78]. For other pre-Charter cases deemed to lie outside the scope of ECJ review for compliance with general principles, see Cases C–299/95 *Kremzow* (n 25); C–291/96 *Grado and Bashir* [1997] ECR I–5531; C–309/96 *Annibaldi v Sindaco del Commune di Guidoma* [1997] ECR I–7493; C–333/09 *Noël v SCP Brouard Daude* [2009] ECR I–205; C–535/08 *Pignataro* [2009] ECR I–50; C–45/03 *Dem'Yanenko* order of 18 Mar 2004. For discussion of the uncertainties in the field of criminal law, see T Marguery, 'EU Fundamental Rights and Member States Action in EU Criminal Law' (2013) 20 MJ 282.

[242] For post-Charter cases see, eg, Cases C–27/11 *Vinkov* EU:C:2012:326, [57]–[59]; C–370/12 *Pringle* EU:C:2012:756, [178]–[180]; C–339/10 *Asparuhov Estov* EU:C:2010:680, [12]–[14]; C–483/09 and C–1/10 *Gueye* EU:C:2011:583, [69]; C–267 and 68/10 *Rossius* EU:C:2011:332, [16]–[20]; C–87/12 *Ymeraga* EU:C:2013:291, [41]–[43]; C–457/09 *Chartry* EU:C:2011:101, [25]; C–314/10 *Pagnoul* EU:C:2011:609, [24]; C–538/10 *Lebrun* EU:C:2011:614, [19]; C–161/11 *Vino* EU:C:2011:420, [22]–[40]; C–5/12 *Betriu Montull v INSS* EU:C:2013:571, [69]–[72]; C–198/13 *Julian Hernández* EU:C:2014:2055, [45]–[48]; C–265/13 *Torralbo Marcos v Korota SA* EU:C:204:187; C–106/13 *Fierro and Marmorale v Ronchi and Scocozza* EU:C:2013:357; C–333/13 *Dano v Leipzig* EU:C:2014:2358, [87]–[91]; C–14/13 *Cholakova* EU:C:2013:374; C–40/11 *Yoshikazu Iida v Stadt Ulm* EU:C:2012:691, [78]–[82]; C–206/13 *Cruciano Siragusa v Regione Sicilia* EU:C:2014:126, [20]–[33].

[243] eg Case C–23/12 *Zakaria* EU:C:2013:24, [39].

[244] Case C–198/13 *Julian Hernández* (n 242) [45].

[245] Case C–40/11 *Yoshikazu Iida v Stadt Ulm* (n 242) [78]–[82].

for which legal aid was sought concerned EU law;[246] and a Member State's definition of what constitutes a 'special non-contributory cash benefit' for the purposes of EU rules on coordination of social security, since the EU rules do not purport to define the national scope of such benefits.[247]

However, it is notable that even where a particular issue has been deemed to lie outside the scope of application of EU law and therefore to be unreviewable by the CJEU for compliance with EU fundamental rights, the CJEU nevertheless often draws the Member State's attention to its 'international' obligations under the ECHR.[248]

(E) HORIZONTAL APPLICATION OF THE CHARTER?

Article 51 of the Charter, as we have seen, declares that the provisions of the Charter are binding on the EU institutions and the Member States, but makes no reference to their effect on individuals. However, since the ECJ had previously declared that Treaty provisions addressed to Member States could also impose obligations on individuals,[249] and had also ruled that general principles of law could in certain circumstances have horizontal direct effect,[250] the question whether the provisions of the Charter might also impose legal obligations on individuals soon arose. The issue came directly before the Court in the *AMS* case.[251] The question was whether Article 27 of the Charter concerning the rights of workers to be consulted could be invoked by an employee against a private employer. While the Court on the facts of the case ruled that Article 27 was insufficiently specific to be able to create an obligation on an employer to include certain categories of worker for the purposes of calculating staff numbers, it left open the larger question of whether a sufficiently precise provision of the Charter could be binding on an individual.[252] This question will certainly return to the Court again before long.

9 THE EU AND THE ECHR

(A) ACCESSION BY THE EU TO THE ECHR

The possible accession of the EU to the ECHR has been a regular part of the EU integration debate at least since the 1970s. The revival of proposals for accession at that time followed from the earlier abandonment of the 1950s federalist blueprint for an EU which was fully integrated with the ECHR system.[253] However, the fact the EU by now has its own Charter of Fundamental Rights which is partly

---

[246] Case C–265–13 *Torralbo Marcos v Korota SA* (n 242).

[247] Case C–333/13 *Dano* (n 242).

[248] See, eg, Cases C–127/08 *Metock* [2008] ECR I–6241, [74]–[79]; C–23/12 *Zakaria* (n 243) [40]; C–87/12 *Ymeraga* EU:C:2013:291 [44].

[249] See, eg, Cases 43/75 *Defrenne v Sabena* [1976] ECR 455; C–281/93 *Angonese v Cassa di Risparmio di Bologna* [2000] ECR I–4134. See more generally, Ch 7.

[250] See Cases C–144/04 *Mangold* [2005] ECR I–9981 and C–555/07 *Kücükdeveci* EU:C:2010:365.

[251] Case C–176/12 *Association de médiation sociale (AMS) v Union locale des syndicats CGT, Laboubi and others* EU:C:2014:2. The facts and an extract from the case are set out in Ch 7, Section 3(e).

[252] Case C–176/12 *AMS* ibid [44]–[49]. See D Leczykiewicz, 'Horizontal Application of the Charter of Fundamental Rights' (2013) 38 ELRev 38 479; N Lazzerini, '(Some of) the Fundamental Rights Granted by the Charter May Be a Source of Obligations for Private Parties: *AMS*' (2014) 51 CMLRev 907; E Frantziou, 'Case C–176/12 *AMS*: Some Reflections on the Horizontal Effect of the Charter and the Reach of Fundamental Employment Rights in the European Union' (2014) 10 EuConst 332; C Murphy, 'Using the EU Charter of Fundamental Rights against Private Parties after *AMS*' [2014] EHRLR 170.

[253] G de Búrca 'The Road Not Taken: The EU as a Global Human Rights Actor' (2011) 105 AJIL 649.

modelled on the ECHR, and a fairly extensive 'domestic' human rights system of its own, raises the question why accession is still considered to be desirable today. There are several possible answers.

First, the EU continues to encounter criticism of its human rights role, and scepticism as to whether its commitment to promoting human rights is genuine. The ECJ has been accused of using human rights discourse in an attempt to extend the influence of EU law over areas which should remain the primary concern of the Member States,[254] and manipulating the rhetorical force of the language of fundamental human rights to promote the integration goals or the internal market goals of the EU.[255] Accession to the ECHR could therefore help to signal the credibility of the EU as far as human rights commitments are concerned.

A related concern for some is that the CJEU should not act as a parallel European Human Rights Court but should leave this task to the ECtHR, a court which was specifically entrusted by the Member States of the Council of Europe with the task of monitoring their compliance with the ECHR.[256] The ECtHR is perceived to have acquired an expertise and a moral stature which the CJEU does not yet share.

A further concern has been that the CJEU's extension of its jurisdiction to review national laws for compliance with fundamental rights raises the possibility of conflict between the pronouncements of the two European Courts on similar issues.[257] While some see any conflict of interpretation between the two Courts as unlikely,[258] others view it as a clear risk.

Finally, the desirability of being able to challenge acts of the EU directly before the ECtHR is perhaps the strongest argument in favour of accession. Accession would mean that the CJEU will no longer be the final official arbiter of the compliance of EU action with human rights. If accession takes place, the EU will have its own judge on the ECtHR, alongside each Council of Europe Member State judge. According to the European Commission, accession will help develop a common culture of fundamental rights in the EU, will reinforce the credibility of the EU's human rights system and external policy, will place the EU's weight behind the Strasbourg system, and will ensure the harmonious development of the case law of the two Courts.[259]

In a first serious political move in this direction, the Court of Justice was asked by the Council in 1994 for its opinion under Article 228(6) EC (now Article 218(11) TFEU) on the compatibility of accession with the EU Treaties. The Court responded that the EU lacked competence under the Treaties, and that an amendment would be necessary.[260] Thirteen years later, Article 6(2) TEU was introduced by the Lisbon Treaty, providing not only competence but a legal obligation ('the EU shall accede') for the EU to accede to the ECHR. Yet while the terms of the Court's *Opinion 2/94* had

---

[254] See, eg, the controversy over the Irish abortion information, Case C–159/90 *SPUC v Grogan* [1991] ECR I–4685, which led to an attempt by the Irish Government to insulate the Irish constitutional prohibition on abortion, and on information and referral services, from the possible impact of EU law: see Protocol No 35 to the TEU and TFEU.

[255] See Coppel and O'Neill (n 115).

[256] See, eg, the argument of the UK Government in Case 118/75 (n 173) 1191. Note that Judge Skouris, President of the CJEU, has been quoted recently in support of this view, declaring that the CJEU is not a 'human rights court': see L Besselink, http://www.verfassungsblog.de/ecj-european-supreme-court-setting-aside-citizens-rights-eu-law-supremacy/#.VOxO-fnF-Yg.

[257] R Lawson, 'Confusion and Conflict? Diverging Interpretations of the ECHR in Strasbourg and Luxembourg' in R Lawson and M de Bloijs (eds), *The Dynamics of the Protection of Human Rights in Europe* (Kluwer, 1994); D Spielman, 'Human Rights Case Law in the Strasbourg and Luxembourg Courts: Inconsistencies and Complementarities' in Alston, Heenan, and Bustelo (n 4).

[258] P van Dijk and G van Hoof, *Theory and Practice of the European Convention on Human Rights* (Kluwer, 3rd edn, 1998) 21; A Rosas, 'The European Court of Justice in Context: Forms and Patterns of Judicial Dialogue' (2007) 1 EJLS 1. See recently K Lenaerts on how the ECtHR had interpreted the principle of *ne bis in idem* in a way which conforms to the CJEU's interpretation: 'Exploring the Limits of the Charter of Fundamental Rights' (2012) 8 EUConst 375, 396.

[259] Commission Press Release IP/10/291 of March 2010.

[260] *Opinion 2/94* [1996] ECR I–1795.

indicated that the Court had concerns about the 'fundamental institutional implications' and 'constitutional significance' of accession, it had not explained the nature of these concerns in any detail.[261] Most observers nonetheless assumed that the Lisbon Treaty's amendment to Article 6(2) TEU had removed any obstacle to accession from the side of the EU.[262] From the side of the Council of Europe, lengthy delays caused by Russia were also finally overcome to allow the enactment of Protocol 14 to the ECHR which amended the statute of the Council of Europe to allow the EU to accede.

It seemed that everything was in place for the EU to succeed, if political negotiations on the text of the accession treaty proceeded smoothly. The Draft Agreement on Accession (DAA) took three years to complete,[263] with hesitations from the UK and France along the way, but by mid-2013 it seemed that most of the sticking points had been overcome.[264] To bring about accession, the DAA would need to be concluded by the Committee of Ministers of the Council of Europe, and unanimously by the Council of Ministers of the EU, as well as gaining the assent of the European Parliament and being ratified by all forty-seven Council of Europe states. Key provisions of the DAA which were drafted to address concerns about the specificity of EU law, which had been voiced by the CJEU during the negotiation process,[265] included: (i) a mechanism for prior involvement of the CJEU to ensure the ECtHR would not rule on the compatibility of an EU act with the Convention until such time as the CJEU had first ruled on the matter; (ii) a co-respondent mechanism to allow the EU to become party to ECHR proceedings against a Member State, where the compatibility of EU law with the ECHR may be at issue; and (iii) a provision to prevent Article 55 ECHR (which prohibits ECHR Member States from bringing disputes arising from the interpretation of the Convention before other dispute-settlement systems) from being interpreted to apply to proceedings before the CJEU, or otherwise lead to a violation of Article 344 TFEU.

These provisions, however, proved insufficient to address the concerns of the CJEU, and in its *Opinion 2/13* on the DAA in December 2014 the Court declared that the DAA was incompatible with Article 6(2) TEU.[266] The Court was not satisfied with the mechanisms provided in the DAA in relation to the three points mentioned above,[267] as well as with a range of other features of the agreement, including the failure to properly clarify the relationship between Article 53 of the Charter and Article 53 of the ECHR;[268] the risk of undermining the principle of mutual trust between Member States within the field of Justice and Home Affairs;[269] the fact that the Strasbourg Court would gain jurisdiction to review EU Common Foreign and Security Policy measures while the CJEU is largely excluded by the TEU from doing so;[270] and the risk that Protocol 16 to the ECHR would enable Member State courts to request interpretative rulings from the ECtHR on matters relating to EU law before the CJEU would have a chance to consider them.[271] The overriding theme of the Court's objections to the

---

[261] Ibid [34]–[35].

[262] For discussion, see JP Jacqué, 'The Accession by the European Union to the European Convention on Human Rights and Fundamental Freedoms' (2011) 48 CMLRev 995.

[263] For a partially successful legal attempt to bring some transparency to the negotiation process, see Case T–331/11 *Besselink v Council* EU:T:2013:91 and EU:T:2013:419.

[264] For the text of the draft agreement and explanatory memorandum, see www.coe.int/t/dghl/standardsetting/hrpolicy/Accession/Meeting_reports/47_1(2013)008rev2_EN.pdf. For discussion of the background: http://www.coe.int/t/dghl/standardsetting/hrpolicy/Accession/default_en.asp.

[265] See, eg, Discussion document of the ECJ on certain aspects of the accession of the EU to the ECHR, Luxembourg, 5 May 2010.

[266] *Opinion 2/13 on EU Accession to the ECHR* EU:C:2014:2454.

[267] On the mechanism for prior involvement of the CJEU see *Opinion 2/13* [236]–[248]; on the co-respondent mechanism, [215]–[235]; on preventing Art 55 ECHR from undermining Art 344 TFEU, [201]–[214].

[268] Ibid [185]–[190].

[269] Ibid [191]–[195].

[270] Ibid [249]–[257].

[271] Ibid [196]–[199].

various 'problematic' provisions of the DAA is the need to preserve the specificity and the autonomy of the EU legal order, as well as the exclusivity of its own jurisdiction.

The Opinion is lengthy and complex, and requires careful reading. Initial reactions have been overwhelmingly critical, with academic commentators describing the Court as 'Humpty Dumpty'[272] and a 'clear and present danger' to the protection of human rights;[273] and the Opinion as 'a bag of coal'[274] and 'a Christmas bombshell'.[275] A leading former European Parliamentarian declared that the EU is 'in deep trouble' with its Court.[276] Thus far at least, defenders of the Opinion have been few.[277] While the Advocate General's Opinion as to the problematic provisions of the DAA was not so different from that of the Court, her advice was ultimately expressed in terms which confirmed the compatibility of the DAA with the Treaties so long as several conditions were ensured as a matter of binding international law. The Court, however, while sharing much of the substance of her Opinion, ruled that the DAA was incompatible with the Treaties, thereby throwing the future of the DAA into doubt, and rendering the future accession of the EU to the ECHR a difficult political task once more. While it seems unlikely—especially in view of the mandatory nature of Article 6(2) TEU—that plans for accession will be shelved, it is difficult to predict at present what the path forward in this respect will be.

(B) INDIRECT REVIEW OF EU ACTS BY THE ECTHR PRIOR TO ACCESSION

In the absence of EU accession to the ECHR, however, while complaints cannot be brought directly against the EU before the Strasbourg Court, the ECtHR has been prepared in a range of circumstances to accept *indirect* complaints against EU acts when they are brought against one or all Member States.[278]

In 1999, the ECtHR ruled in *Matthews v United Kingdom* that, while the Convention did not preclude the transfer by a state of national competences to an international organization such as the EU, the responsibility of states for violations of the ECHR would continue even after such a transfer.[279] Many subsequent cases were brought before the Strasbourg Court involving various forms of EU action, and the ECtHR seemed willing to entertain indirect challenges of this kind including to a Commission decision, a CJEU judgment, and a Common Position of the CFSP, although in most cases

---

[272] AO Neill, http://eutopialaw.com/2014/12/18/opinion-213-on-eu-accession-to-the-echr-the-cjeu-as-humpty-dumpty/.

[273] S Peers, http://eulawanalysis.blogspot.co.uk/2014/12/the-cjeu-and-eus-accession-to-echr.html.

[274] S Johansen, http://blogg.uio.no/jus/smr/multirights/content/opinion-213-a-bag-of-coal-from-the-cjeu.

[275] S Douglas Scott, http://ukconstitutionallaw.org/2014/12/24/sionaidh-douglas-scott-opinion-213-on-eu-accession-to-the-echr-a-christmas-bombshell-from-the-european-court-of-justice/; see also L Besselink, http://www.verfassungsblog.de/en/acceding-echr-notwithstanding-court-justice-opinion-213/#.VOtdOvnF-Yg; and T Lock, http://www.verfassungsblog.de/en/oops-das-gutachten-des-eugh-zum-emrk-beitritt-der-eu/#.VOtgr_nF-Yg.

[276] http://andrewduff.blogactiv.eu/2015/01/07/the-european-union-is-in-deep-trouble-with-its-top-court/.

[277] For a more measured account of the Court's Opinion, see D Halberstam, 'It's the Autonomy, Stupid: A Modest Defence of Opinion 2/13 on EU Accession to the ECHR' available at http://papers.ssrn.com/sol3/papers.cfm?abstract_id=2567591. See also P Gragl, 'The Reasonableness of Jealousy: Opinion 2/13 and EU accession to the ECHR', available at http://papers.ssrn.com/sol3/papers.cfm?abstract_id=2563455.

[278] For decisions of the previously existing Commission on Human Rights on this and on several related questions, see App No 13258/87 *Melcher (M) v Germany*, decision of 9 Feb 1990; App No 21090/92 *Heinz v Contracting States and Parties to the European Patent Convention*, decision of 10 Jan 1994; App No 21072/92 *Gestra v Italy*, decision of 16 Jan 1995; App No 13645/05 *Cooperatieve Producentenorganisatie van de Nederlandse Kokkelvisserij UA v the Netherlands*, decision of 20 Jan 2009.

[279] App No 24833/94 *Matthews v United Kingdom*, judgment of 18 Feb 1999, esp [34]–[35]; R Harmsen, 'National Responsibility for EC Acts under the ECHR: Recasting the Accession Debate' (2001) 7 EPL 625.

it dismissed the challenge for other reasons, such as the lack of a victim or the non-applicability of the substantive right.[280]

The key ruling of the ECtHR concerning its jurisdiction over EU acts, however, is *Bosphorus*.[281] This case was brought by a Turkish company against Ireland for the impounding, without compensation, of an aircraft which the applicant company had leased from the national airline of the former Yugoslavia. The Irish authorities had impounded the aircraft in reliance on an EU regulation, following the interpretation of that regulation by the ECJ on a reference from the Irish Supreme Court,[282] which implemented the UN sanctions regime against the former Yugoslavia during the civil war in the early 1990s. The ECtHR took the view that the alleged violation was committed by Ireland due to the state's compliance with a binding and non-discretionary EU law obligation: in other words, the EU regulation was the real source of the alleged violation. The ECtHR in this case set out the approach which it would adopt when complaints of this kind are brought:

Application No 45036/98 **Bosphorus v Ireland**
Judgment of 30 June 2005

EUROPEAN COURT OF HUMAN RIGHTS

1. The question is therefore whether, and if so to what extent, that important general interest of compliance with EC obligations can justify the impugned interference by the State with the applicant's property rights.

2. The Convention does not, on the one hand, prohibit Contracting Parties from transferring sovereign power to an international (including a supranational) organisation in order to pursue co-operation in certain fields of activity (the *M. & Co.* decision, at p. 144 and *Matthews* at § 32, both cited above). Moreover, even as the holder of such transferred sovereign power, that organisation is not itself held responsible under the Convention for proceedings before, or decisions of, its organs as long as it is not a Contracting Party...

3. On the other hand, it has also been accepted that a Contracting Party is responsible under Article 1 of the Convention for all acts and omissions of its organs regardless of whether the act or omission in question was a consequence of domestic law or of the necessity to comply with international legal obligations...

4. In reconciling both these positions and thereby establishing the extent to which State action can be justified by its compliance with obligations flowing from its membership of an international organisation to which it has transferred part of its sovereignty, the Court has recognised that absolving Contracting States completely from their Convention responsibility in the areas covered by such a transfer would be incompatible with the purpose and object of the Convention: the guarantees of the Convention could be limited or excluded at will thereby depriving it of its peremptory character and undermining the practical and effective nature of its safeguards (*M. & Co.* at p. 145 and *Waite and Kennedy*, at § 67). The State is considered to retain Convention liability in respect of treaty commitments subsequent to the entry into force of the Convention...

---

[280] See, eg, App No 51717/99 *Guérin Automobiles v les 15 Etats de l'UE*, decision of 4 July 2000; App No 56672/00 *DSR-Senator Lines GmbH v the 15 Member States of the EU*, decision of 10 Mar 2004; App Nos 6422/02 and 9916/02 *SEGI v the 15 Member States of the EU*, decision of 23 May 2002; App No 62023/00 *Emesa Sugar v Netherlands*, decision of 13 Jan 2005.

[281] App No 45036/98 *Bosphorus v Ireland*, Grand Chamber judgment of 30 June 2005; S Douglas Scott, Note (2006) 43 CMLRev 243; A Hinarejos Parga, Note (2006) 31 ELRev 251.

[282] Case C–84/95 *Bosphorus v Minister for Transport* [1996] ECR I–3953.

5. In the Court's view, State action taken in compliance with such legal obligations is justified as long as the relevant organisation is considered to protect fundamental rights, as regards both the substantive guarantees offered and the mechanisms controlling their observance, in a manner which can be considered at least equivalent to that for which the Convention provides (see the above-cited *M. & Co.* decision, at p. 145, an approach with which the parties and the European Commission agreed). By 'equivalent' the Court means 'comparable': any requirement that the organisation's protection be 'identical' could run counter to the interest of international co-operation pursued (paragraph 150 above). However, any such finding of equivalence could not be final and would be susceptible to review in the light of any relevant change in fundamental rights' protection.

6. If such equivalent protection is considered to be provided by the organisation, the presumption will be that a State has not departed from the requirements of the Convention when it does no more than implement legal obligations flowing from its membership of the organisation.

However, any such presumption can be rebutted if, in the circumstances of a particular case, it is considered that the protection of Convention rights was manifestly deficient. In such cases, the interest of international co-operation would be outweighed by the Convention's role as a 'constitutional instrument of European public order' in the field of human rights...

7. It remains the case that a State would be fully responsible under the Convention for all acts falling outside its strict international legal obligations. The numerous Convention cases cited by the applicant at paragraph 117 above confirm this. Each case (in particular, the *Cantoni* judgment, at § 26) concerned a review by this Court of the exercise of State discretion for which EC law provided...The *Matthews* case can also be distinguished: the acts for which the United Kingdom was found responsible were 'international instruments which were freely entered into' by it (§ 33 of that judgment)...

8. Since the impugned act constituted solely compliance by Ireland with its legal obligations flowing from membership of the EC (paragraph 148 above), the Court will now examine whether a presumption arises that Ireland complied with its Convention requirements in fulfilling such obligations and whether any such presumption has been rebutted in the circumstances of the present case.

The ECtHR proceeded to survey the EU's system of protection for fundamental rights, and found that the presumption that Ireland complied with its ECHR obligations did indeed arise, on the basis that the EU provided human rights protection 'equivalent' to that of the ECHR system, and there was no dysfunction in the EU's control system such as to rebut that presumption in the case at hand.[283]

Two separate concurring opinions were signed by seven judges in the case, however, expressing certain reservations about the majority approach. They expressed concern about the replacement of a case-by-case review of compliance with a largely abstract review of the organization's general system of 'equivalent protection' for human rights. They also drew attention to the deficiencies in the EU's system of judicial protection due to the limited *locus standi* for private parties before the ECJ, and raised the question whether this amounted to a violation of Article 6(1) ECHR.

Since the *Bosphorus* case, however, the Strasbourg Court has indirectly reviewed EU action for compatibility with the ECHR on numerous occasions, and has shown itself quite willing to conclude that the presumption of equivalence is inapplicable, and to apply its normal standard of review. In cases in which it has condemned the operation of the EU asylum system, the ECtHR held that since the states in question had discretion to decide whether to deal with an asylum application even if it was not their responsibility under the EU regulation, the action was not *strictly* required by EU law

---

[283] See K Kuhnert, '*Bosphorus*—Double Standards in European Human Rights Protection?' (2006) 2 Utrecht Law Review 177 and C Costello, 'The *Bosphorus* Ruling of the ECtHR: Fundamental Rights and Blurred Boundaries in Europe' (2006) 6 HRLR 87.

and hence the presumption of equivalence would not apply.[284] Interestingly, in *Michaud v France*, the ECtHR ruled that since a reference had not yet been made to the CJEU on the compatibility of an EU Money Laundering Directive with Article 8 ECHR, the EU system of human rights had not been given a chance to demonstrate its 'full potential', so that the presumption would not be applied here either.[285] The ECtHR has also been willing to engage with an applicant's argument that the presumption of equivalence had been rebutted by the circumstances of the case.[286] The Court in *Michaud* also elaborated further on the underlying reason for adopting a 'presumption of equivalence' approach in relation to organizations such as the EU, emphasizing that it was 'only where the rights and safeguards it protects are given protection comparable to that afforded by the Court itself' that the Court would reduce the intensity of its supervision of state action taken to comply with the obligations flowing from membership of such organizations.[287]

Where the complaint is brought before the ECtHR in relation to EU action adopted not by an implementing state but by an autonomous EU institution such as the Commission or the Court, it seems that the Strasbourg Court will look to ensure that the act was indeed in some way attributable to the Member State or states against which the action is brought.[288]

There has been speculation as to whether the ECtHR might lessen its degree of deference towards EU action in view of the CJEU's negative ruling in *Opinion 2/13* on EU accession to the ECHR. In this regard, it is interesting to note that the President of the Strasbourg Court, speaking shortly after *Opinion 2/13* had been delivered, expressed disappointment at the Opinion and declared firmly that: 'the important thing is to ensure that there is no legal vacuum in human rights protection on the Convention's territory, whether the violation can be imputed to a State or to a supranational institution.'[289]

(c) MUTUAL INFLUENCE OF THE CJEU AND THE ECTHR PRIOR TO ACCESSION

We have seen above how the CJEU cites and sometimes pays close attention to ECHR rulings, particularly now in cases in which similar rights under the EU Charter are invoked, since Article 52(3) of the Charter stipulates that the meaning and scope of Charter rights which correspond to ECHR rights are to be the same as those laid down by the ECHR.[290] It is certainly evident that the number of cases in which the CJEU hears claims based on fundamental rights, whether the provisions of the Charter or of the ECHR or both, is continually increasing.[291]

---

[284] See, eg, App No 30696/09 *MSS v Belgium and Greece*, Grand Chamber judgment of 21 Jan 2011 and App No 29217/12 *Tarakhel v Switzerland*, Grand Chamber judgment of 4 Nov 2014. For a list of other ECtHR case law on the EU's Dublin asylum system, see www.echr.coe.int/Documents/FS_Dublin_ENG.pdf.

[285] App No 12323/11 *Michaud v France*, judgment of 6 Dec 2012. Compare the case of App 3890/11 *Povse v Austria*, judgment of 18 June 2013, [77]–[83] in which the presumption of equivalence was applied where an Austrian court was enforcing an Italian court order under the terms of the EU Brussels II Reg 2201/2003, and a preliminary reference had already been made to the CJEU.

[286] *Povse v Austria* ibid [84]–[87].

[287] *Michaud v France* (n 285) [104].

[288] See, eg, App 73274/01 *Connolly v 15 Member States*, in which the applicant complained of his dismissal by the EU Commission. The ECtHR mentioned that the *Bosphorus* presumption of equivalence was applicable and had not been rebutted, but also ruled that the act complained of was not attributable to the Member States.

[289] www.echr.coe.int/Documents/Speech_20150130_Solemn_Hearing_2015_ENG.pdf. For a commentary, see T Lock, 'Will the Empire Strike Back? Strasbourg's Reaction to the Accession Opinion', www.verfassungsblog.de/en/will-empire-strike-back-strasbourgs-reaction-cjeus-accession-opinion/.

[290] (N 30).

[291] G de Búrca 'After the EU Charter of Rights: The Court of Justice as a Human Rights Adjudicator?' (2013) 20 MJ 168.

The potential for differences in interpretation between the two Courts on the same issue was evident even from early case law.[292] Compare, for example, the judgment of the ECtHR in *Open Door Counselling*[293] with the Advocate General's opinion in *Grogan*,[294] or the approach of the ECJ in *ERT*[295] with that of the ECtHR in *Lentia v Austria*,[296] or the decision of the ECJ in *Hoechst*[297] with that of the ECtHR in *Niemietz*;[298] or the ECJ in *Orkem*[299] with the ECtHR in *Funke*,[300] and subsequent cases of the ECJ and CFI cases concerning various rights of the defence in EU competition proceedings.[301]

Despite the potential for conflict, however, there has clearly been a desire on the part of both Courts to avoid conflict in their respective case law, and to demonstrate a degree of deference towards one another on similar questions arising before them.[302] This is certainly the approach which Article 52(3) of the Charter encapsulates,[303] and which the Strasbourg Court has also in recent years made many references to,[304] and actively accommodated EU law and the CJEU.[305] The Charter has been cited in many judgments of the ECtHR,[306] which has even followed the lead of the Luxembourg Court in a number of instances.[307] Further, the ECtHR has acted as enforcer of EU law in cases concerning the failure of a national court to make a preliminary reference to the CJEU, finding this under certain circumstances to constitute a violation of Article 6(2) ECHR.[308] The two Courts also hold regular meetings 'to discuss general questions of common interest'.[309]

---

[292] On whether the role of the AG might violate Art 6(2) ECHR on the right to a fair hearing, see Case C–17/98 *Emesa Sugar* (n 114); R Lawson, Note (2000) 37 CMLRev 983; the opinion of the AG in Case C–466/00 *Kaba v Home Secretary* [2003] ECR I–2219; and from the ECHR side, *Vermeulen v Belgium* [1996] I Reports of Judgments and Decisions 224 and App No 39594/98 *Kress v France*, judgment of 11 June 2001 and App no 13645/05 *Cooperatieve Producentenorganisatie van de Nederlandse Kokkelvisserij UA v the Netherlands*, decision of 20 Jan 2009.

[293] App Nos 14234/88 and 14235/88 *Open Door Counselling Ltd and Dublin Well Woman Centre v Ireland*, judgment of 29 Oct 1992.

[294] Case C–159/90 (n 254).

[295] Case C–260/89 *ERT* (n 227).

[296] App Nos 13914/88 etc *Informationsverein Lentia v Austria*, judgment of 24 Nov 1993. See also Case C–23/93 *TV10 SA v Commissariaat voor de Media* [1994] ECR I–4795 and Case C–353/89 *Commission v Netherlands* [1991] ECR I–4069; and the decision of the Commission on Human Rights of 11 Jan 1994 in App No 21472/93 *X v The Netherlands*.

[297] Cases 46/87 and 227/88 *Hoechst AG v Commission* [1989] ECR 2859.

[298] *Niemietz v Germany* (n 160). See however the subsequent decision of the ECJ in Case C–94/00 *Roquette Frères* (n 161) citing the later ECtHR judgment in App No 37971/97 *Colas Est v France*, 16 Apr 2002.

[299] Case 374/87 (n 156).

[300] *Funke v France* (n 163).

[301] See, eg, Cases T–213/95 and 18/96 *SCK* (n 151) [56]–[57]; T–305–335/94 *Limburgse Vinyl Maatschappij NV v Commission* [1999] ECR II–931, [420]; C–185/95 P *Baustahlgewebe* (n 151); Lenaerts and de Smijter (n 103); C–94/00 *Roquettes Frères* (n 161).

[302] ML Pâris-Dobozy. 'Paving the Way: Adjustments of Systems and Mutual Influences between the European Court of Human Rights and European Union Law Before Accession' (2014) 51 Irish Jurist 59.

[303] See (nn 26–29) and text.

[304] For references to EU anti-discrimination law, see App Nos 65731/01 and 65900/01 *Stec v United Kingdom*, judgment of 12 Apr 2006, [58]; App No 57325/00 *DH and Others v Czech Republic*, Grand Chamber judgment of 13 Nov 2007, [85]–[91], [187].

[305] See C Dautricourt, 'A Strasbourg Perspective on the Autonomous Development of Fundamental Rights in EU Law: Trends and Implications', NYU Jean Monnet Working Paper 10/2010.

[306] Prominent examples include App No 28957/95 *Goodwin v United Kingdom*, judgment of 11 July 2002, [100]; App No 34503/97 *Demir and Baykara v Turkey*, judgment of 12 Nov 2008, [47], [150]; App No 10249/03 *Scoppola v Italy*, judgment of 17 Sept 2009; App No 25965/04 *Rantseva v Russia and Cyprus*, judgment of 7 Jan 2010.

[307] Most notably in the anti-terrorism sanctions cases, see App No 10593/08 *Nada v Switzerland*, judgment of 12 Sept 2012 and App 5809/08 *Al-Dulimi v Switzerland*, judgment of 26 Nov 2013 (currently on reference to the Grand Chamber).

[308] See App 17120/09 *Dhabi v Italy*, judgment of 8 July 2014, [31]–[34]. Compare App Nos 3989/07 and 38353/07 *Ullens De Schooten and Rezabek v Belgium*, judgment of 20 Sept 2011 and App No 12323/11 *Michaud v France*, judgment of 6 Dec 2012.

[309] See the reference to a 'regular dialogue' between the two Courts in Declaration No 2 on Art 6(2) TEU; and see the joint communiqué of 24 Jan 2011 issued by the Presidents of the two Courts during the negotiations on EU accession to

Nevertheless, as the European Parliament recently put it in a study of the fundamental rights case law of the two Courts, the CJEU sometimes 'manifestly expressed the preference for the Charter over the Convention, without entering into conflict with the ECHR'.[310] This tendency towards increasing reliance on the Charter as the source of EU human rights law, and towards more autonomous interpretation of the Charter without reference to the ECHR,[311] echoes the wariness of the CJEU in *Opinion 2/13* as regards any arrangement that would tie EU human rights norms too closely, as a matter of law, to the ECHR and particularly to the rulings of the ECtHR.

10 CONCLUSIONS

i.   Human rights occupy an increasingly significant place within EU law and policy today. The Charter of Fundamental Rights has binding legal force. Compliance with human rights standards is a condition for the admission of new Member States, and serious non-compliance forms the basis for the symbolic sanction mechanism in Article 7 TEU. However, there is increasing concern that the Article 7 tool is unusable in practice, and that a more effective mechanism is required.

ii. The case law of the CJEU and the General Court dealing with human rights matters continues to grow exponentially, and covers a wide spectrum of different human rights issues. Since the adoption of the Charter, the CJEU has shown itself willing to strike down EU laws for violation of its provisions.

iii. While national governments remain ambivalent about the EU's role in relation to human rights matters within the EU, the CJEU has taken a broad (if still fuzzy) view of what falls within the scope of EU law for the purposes of Article 51 of the Charter. It has unequivocally asserted the primacy of EU law and of the Charter over national constitutional law in the event of conflict. However, it has not yet clarified whether the Charter can impose obligations on private parties.

iv. While both the Strasbourg and the Luxembourg Courts have sought to avoid conflict between their respective bodies of case law, with Article 52(3) of the Charter promoting deference by the CJEU to the ECtHR, and the ECtHR increasingly accommodating and citing EU law, the CJEU clearly remains very concerned to protect the autonomy of the EU legal order and the exclusivity of its own jurisdiction. This concern demonstrated itself most dramatically in *Opinion 2/13*, in which the CJEU found the draft Agreement on Accession of the EU to the ECHR to be incompatible with the EU Treaties.

11 FURTHER READING

ALSTON, P, HEENAN, J, AND BUSTELO, M (eds), *The EU and Human Rights* (Oxford University Press, 1999)

the ECHR: http://curia.europa.eu/jcms/upload/docs/application/pdf/2011-02/cedh_cjue_english.pdf. For discussion see L Scheeck, 'Competition, Conflict and Cooperation between European Courts and the Diplomacy of Supranational Judicial Networks', Garnet Working Paper 23/07 (2007).

[310] N (106).
[311] De Búrca (n 106).

DZEHTSIAROU, K, KONSTADINIDES, L, LOCK, T, AND O'MEARA, N (eds), *Human Rights Law in Europe: The Influence, Overlaps and Contradictions of the EU and the ECHR* (Routledge, 2014)

FABBRINI, F, *Fundamental Rights in Europe: Challenges and Transformations in Comparative Perspective* (Oxford University Press, 2014)

GRAGL, P, *The Accession of the European Union to the European Convention on Human Rights* (Bloomsbury, 2013)

KOSTA, V, SKOUTARIS, N, AND TZEVELEKOS, V (eds), *The EU Accession to the ECHR* (Hart, 2014)

MORANO-FOADI, S, AND VICKERS, L (eds), *Fundamental Rights in the EU* (Hart, 2015)

PEERS, S, HERVEY, T, KENNER, J, AND WARD, A, *The Charter of Fundamental Rights: A Commentary* (Hart, 2014)

VARJU, M, *European Union Human Rights Law: The Dynamics of Interpretation and Context* (Edward Elgar, 2014)

WILLIAMS, A, *EU Human Rights Policies: A Study in Irony* (Oxford University Press, 2004)

ENFORCEMENT ACTIONS AGAINST MEMBER STATES

1 CENTRAL ISSUES

i.   Article 17(1) TEU entrusts to the Commission the task of ensuring and overseeing the application of EU law 'under the control of the Court of Justice'. One crucial component of the Commission's task is to monitor Member State compliance and to respond to non-compliance.

ii. The TFEU provides for various enforcement mechanisms[1] involving judicial proceedings against the Member States, which are brought either by the Commission or—much less frequently—by a Member State. Article 258 TFEU establishes the general enforcement procedure, giving the Commission broad power to bring infringement proceedings against Member States which it considers to be in breach of their obligations under EU law.[2]

iii. The enforcement procedure performs several functions. It is in part an elite channel for the amicable resolution of disputes involving Member States without recourse to litigation, in part a channel for individuals to complain to the Commission about breaches of EU law, and in part an 'objective' law enforcement tool in the hands of the Commission and Court.[3] It has also been described as a

---

[1] See, eg, Art 108(2) TFEU on state aid, and Art 114(9) TFEU on internal market measures. Under Art 271 the Board of the European Investment Bank and the Council of the European Central Bank have powers similar to those of the Commission under Art 258 TFEU. Art 348 TFEU provides for a different and specialized enforcement procedure where Member States have relied on Art 347 TFEU to derogate from fundamental EU rules: see Case C–120/94 R *Commission v Greece* [1994] ECR I–3037. On the interaction between the derogation in Arts 346 and 347 TFEU (ex Arts 296–298 EC) and the infringement procedure see Cases C–284/05 *Commission v Finland*, C–294/05 *Commission v Sweden*, C–372/05 *Commission v Germany*, C–387/05 *Commission v Italy*, C–461/05 *Commission v Denmark*, all 15 Dec 2009; Case C–38/06 *Commission v Portugal*, 4 Mar 2010; Case C–337/05 *Commission v Italy* [2008] ECR I–2173, and Case C–157/06 *Commission v Italy* [2008] ECR I–7313; M Trybus, Note (2006) 46 CMLRev 973. Another very serious although non-judicial and as yet unused mechanism for monitoring and enforcing EU law is the sanction mechanism under Art 7 TEU, for Member States which seriously and persistently breach the values on which the EU is based. This mechanism is discussed in Ch 11 on human rights in the EU. Finally, Art 126 TFEU provides for a specialized enforcement procedure for the 'excessive deficit procedure' within EU monetary policy, and Art 126(10) explicitly excludes the possibility of recourse to Arts 258–259 TFEU for that purpose.

[2] The original infringement procedure under Art 88 of the Coal and Steel Treaty (which expired at the end of 2002) gave considerably more power to the Commission (then called the High Authority), which was empowered to record the failure of a state to fulfil its obligations, without first bringing the case before the ECJ. However, the state itself could then bring the matter before the Court. A proposal for conferring a similar power on the Commission today was discussed during the negotiations on the Lisbon Treaty and its predecessor Constitutional Treaty, but was dropped. Following the enactment of the Lisbon Treaty, Arts 258–260 TFEU now also govern the Euratom Treaty.

[3] For a discussion of the tensions between all three dimensions see R Rawlings, 'Engaged Elites: Citizen Action and Institutional Attitudes in Commission Enforcement' (2000) 6 ELJ 4.

forum for enhancing the accountability of the different institutional actors involved, in particular the Member States and the Commission,[4] involving also the Parliament and the Ombudsman, if not the Court.

iv. While the Commission has the dominant role in detecting, monitoring, and bringing infringements before the CJEU, it is the Court that has the final say and the ultimate authority on most aspects of the process. This includes whether there has been a violation, what the penalty should be, if any, and whether an infringement has been brought to an end. In recent years, the Court has dismissed complaints brought by the Commission in a sizeable proportion of cases.[5]

v. The general enforcement mechanism came under strain over the decades as the number of infractions and infringement proceedings continued to rise,[6] and various initiatives were introduced to address the resulting problems of overload and delay.[7] Environmental cases account for a high proportion of the overall cases under examination by the Commission as well as of the cases referred to the CJEU,[8] and internal market cases form a significant part of the remainder. The great majority of complaints and investigations are, however, settled without being brought before the Court.

vi. Pursuant to Article 260 TFEU, the Commission may bring proceedings against a state for non-compliance with a previous judgment of the Court finding an infringement against that state under Article 258. Importantly, Article 260 was amended in the 1990s to enable the CJEU to impose a penalty payment on a Member State which has failed to comply with a previous judgment under Article 258. The Commission has however been criticized for under-utilizing this 'more efficient' Article 260 procedure and for resorting excessively instead to Article 258 proceedings.[9] Further, while the potential of Article 260 to enhance the enforcement of EU law is broadly acknowledged, there have been mixed appraisals of its effectiveness in practice as yet.[10]

---

[4] C Harlow and R Rawlings, 'Accountability and Law Enforcement: The Centralized EU Infringement Procedure' (2006) 31 ELRev 447; M Smith, *Centralised Enforcement, Legitimacy and Good Governance in the EU* (Routledge, 2010) 15–18, who identifies five different functions of the general infringement procedure.

[5] Approximately 228 sets of Art 258 infringement proceedings were decided by the Court between 1 Jan 2011 and 31 Dec 2014. Of these, the Commission's action was rejected in its entirety by the Court in thirty-six cases, and was rejected in part (ie some of the allegations against the state dismissed) in a further twenty-nine cases. In other words, the Commission's case was dismissed in whole or in part in 28.5 per cent of the cases that reached the Court. This does not necessarily indicate any frivolity or ill-judgement on the Commission's part, nor any significant tension between Commission and Court, since complaints are dismissed for many reasons, both procedural and substantive, including the difficulty faced by the Commission in obtaining adequate information.

[6] For a useful overview see R Munoz, 'The Monitoring of the Application of Community Law: The Need to Improve the Current Tools and an Obligation to Innovate' (2006) 25 YBEL 395.

[7] For some of these see A Europe of Results: Applying Community Law, COM(2007) 502.

[8] According to the Commission's 31st Annual Monitoring Report, COM(2014) 612 final, one quarter of the cases (334 out of 1,300) under consideration by the Commission in 2013 concerned environmental matters. Further, according to the Commission's Evaluation Reports, COM(2010) 70 and SEC(2011) 1629 on the operation of the first and second years of EU Pilot, a system established by the Commission to coordinate a more efficient response to infringement complaints and queries, over one-third of all complaints and inquiries related to the environment.

[9] P Wennerås, 'Sanctions against Member States under Article 260: Alive but not Kicking?' (2012) 49 CMLRev 145.

[10] P Wennerås, ibid; D Hadroušek, 'Speeding up Infringement Procedures: Recent Developments Designed to Make Infringement Procedures More Effective' (2012) 9 Journal for European Environmental and Planning Law 235; and B Jack, 'Article 260(2) TFEU: An Effective Judicial Procedure for the Enforcement of Judgments?' (2013) 19 ELJ 404.

2 THE FUNCTION AND OPERATION OF THE INFRINGEMENT PROCEDURE

Article 258 TFEU provides:

> If the Commission considers that a Member State has failed to fulfil an obligation under the Treaties, it shall deliver a reasoned opinion on the matter after giving the State concerned the opportunity to submit its observations.
>
> If the State concerned does not comply with the opinion within the period laid down by the Commission, the latter may bring the matter before the Court of Justice of the European Union.

One change introduced by the Lisbon Treaty was to alter the wording of Article 258 so that it refers to the failure to fulfil an obligation under 'the Treaties' rather than solely 'this Treaty', as was the case under the previous EC Treaty.[11] This change reflects the formal abolition of the intergovernmental 'pillars' of the Union by the Lisbon Treaty, and highlights the fact that, with the exception of Chapter 2 of the TEU governing the Common Foreign and Security Policy, the provisions of which are largely excluded from the CJEU's jurisdiction, and Article 126(1) TFEU concerning the excessive deficit procedure,[12] infringement proceedings can now be brought for violation of obligations under both the TEU and the TFEU.

(A) NATURE AND FUNCTION OF THE ARTICLE 258 PROCEDURE

The Commission initiates Article 258 proceedings either in response to a complaint or on its own initiative. Since it has no investigation service, complaints are brought on the basis of information gained from diverse sources, for example through the press, from European Parliament questions or petitions, through direct correspondence from individual or other complainants, or modern technological sources such as databases indicating when Member States have failed to notify implementation of a directive.

The Commission has regularly acknowledged that complaints from citizens constitute a significant source for its detection of infringements, and has suggested that the Article 258 procedure thus contributes to creating a more participatory Community in which citizens can play a role in law enforcement.[13] In 1999 a standard complaint form was designed for individuals' ease of use,[14] and a number of mechanisms have been established by the Commission to enable individuals to

---

[11] Another minor change introduced by the Lisbon Treaty is Art 197 TFEU, which provides that '[e]ffective implementation of Union law by the Member States, which is essential for the proper functioning of the Union, shall be regarded as a matter of common interest', and allows the EU to adopt non-harmonizing legislation to support Member States' administrative capacity.

[12] (N 1) above. Note that there is a debate within German legal scholarship as to whether the Art 7 TEU political mechanism for addressing serious and persistent human rights abuses constitutes *lex specialis* and precludes the Commission from pursuing such infringements under Art 258 TFEU, in part because Art 269 TFEU limits the Court's jurisdiction over Art 7 TEU to procedural questions. Much of the English language literature, by comparison, assumes that infringement proceedings could be brought under Art 258 also for serious and persistent infringements of human rights and other values protected under Art 2 TEU. See Scheppele, Muir, Watson, and Claes (nn 154–155) below. The Commission's recent communication *A new EU Framework to strengthen the Rule of Law*, COM(2014) 158 suggests that the Commission considers Art 258 TFEU to be available as an instrument to pursue such breaches, provided they also constitute breach of a specific EU law provision, and provided the factual circumstances do not fall outside the scope of EU law.

[13] For the Commission's Annual Monitoring Reports see http://ec.europa.eu/atwork/applying-eu-law/infringements-proceedings/annual-reports/index_en.htm.

[14] This is now available online at http://ec.europa.eu/atwork/applying-eu-law/complaint_form_en.htm..

communicate inquiries and complaints, including Europe Direct, Your Europe Advice, Citizen's Signpost, European Citizen Action Service, and European Business Centres.[15]

Nonetheless, the Commission equally asserts that the infringement procedure is not intended primarily to provide individuals with a means of redress, but rather is an 'objective' mechanism for ensuring state compliance with EU law.[16] Cautioning against an over-emphasis on the role of individuals, the Commission has highlighted its discretion in deciding whether to commence infringement proceedings, emphasizing the bilateral rather than trilateral nature of the procedure,[17] and identifying the primary objective as that of bringing offending Member States into line rather than satisfying individual interests.[18]

Given this ambivalent attitude, it is unsurprising to find that the role played by individual complainants varies, although often key in detecting and pursuing infringements.[19] On the one hand, the individual has no say in determining whether or not the Commission actually initiates proceedings against a Member State.[20] On the other hand, since the establishment of the Ombudsman's (albeit currently held by an Ombudswoman!) office, individuals have regularly made complaints about the Commission's procedures, leading to pressure from the Ombudsman on the Commission to make changes and improvements to its practices.[21] After the Ombudsman's own-initiative investigation in 1996,[22] the Commission ceased its previous practice of failing to inform complainants when a case had been terminated, and began to make more frequent use of press releases and to place more information on the internet. In 2002, the Commission issued a communication to the European Parliament on relations with individual complainants, which was updated in 2012, and published a consolidated version of its internal procedural rules governing relations with complainants.[23] These allow the Ombudsman to assess the Commission's performance by reference to its own published commitments, as well as the general principles of transparency and good administration.[24] In 2007, the Commission established an EU Pilot method 'for improved information exchange and problem-solving' putting complainants in direct contact with a Member State's 'central contact point' with a view to resolution of the problem within a fixed deadline, with follow-up by the Commission if no resolution is forthcoming.[25] The EU Pilot scheme is viewed as a significant success by the

---

[15] Some of these are listed at http://ec.europa.eu/atwork/applying-eu-law/complaints_en.htm, and http://europa.eu/youreurope/advice/index_en.htm. Others are described in COM(2007) 502 (n 7). There are also NGOs which help in this respect, including http://www.ecas.org/.

[16] See, eg, 13th Annual Report [1996] OJ C303/8.

[17] COM(2002) 141.

[18] 18th Annual Report, COM(2001) 309.

[19] One example is the role of an Irish NGO, Friends of the Irish Environment, www.friendsoftheirishenvironment.org/ working with a group of crusading pro-bono lawyers including Peter Sweetman and Greg Casey, which has consistently brought information about environmental infringements in Ireland to the attention of the Commission, leading to the initiation of several important infringement proceedings brought against Ireland.

[20] See Cases 247/87 *Star Fruit v Commission* [1989] ECR 291; T–182/97 *Smanor v Commission* [1998] ECR II–271; C–111/11 P *Ruipérez Aguirre and ATC Petition v Commission* EU:C:2011:491.

[21] A search for complaints on the Ombudsman's website relating to the Commission's activities as Guardian of the Treaties under Art 258 TFEU in the period from 1 Jan 2011–31 Dec 2014 yielded 168 results. See www.ombudsman.europa.eu. For a recent Special Report emerging from one of these complaints, see Special Report concerning the inquiry into complaint 2591/2010/GG against the European Commission.

[22] See 303/97/PD, reported in the Ombudsman's Annual Report for 1997; R Mastroianni, 'The Enforcement Procedure under Article 169 of the EC Treaty and the Powers of the European Commission: *Quis Custodiet Custodes*?' (1995) 1 EPL 535; P Kunzlik, 'The Enforcement of EU Environmental Law: Article 169, the Ombudsman and the Parliament' (1997) 6 EELR 46, and Harlow and Rawlings (n 4).

[23] COM(2002) 141, updated in COM(2012) 154.

[24] For a recent complaint which was ultimately referred to the European Parliament, see Case 2591/2010/GG, available at www.ombudsman.europa.eu.

[25] A Europe of Results (n 7) section 2.2.

Commission,[26] although some have questioned whether the Commission is thereby abdicating too much of its function to national authorities.[27]

A major and continuing source of frustration for complainants and other interested parties has been the difficulty in obtaining access to documents relating to the infringement proceedings. The Commission has repeatedly invoked the exception to the EU transparency rules governing 'inspections, investigations and audits',[28] and has generally been supported in this respect by the Ombudsman.[29] In *Petrie*, the General Court underscored the bilateral nature of infringement proceedings in upholding the refusal of access to documents relating to infringement proceedings, pointing out that individuals are not party to such proceedings.[30] A judicial move in the direction of greater transparency came in *Bavarian Lager II*[31] in which the General Court ruled that disclosure of documents relating to infringement proceedings which had been closed six years previously could not jeopardize Commission investigations, and so were not covered by the exception governing inspections.[32] Although the CJEU overturned part of the General Court's judgment on the basis of EU data-protection legislation,[33] its later ruling in *Sweden and API v Commission* affirmed the move towards greater disclosure in the context of infringement proceedings which are closed.[34] In *Sweden/API*, while the CJEU confirmed that there is no third party right of access to pleadings submitted to the Court in judicial proceedings, and that there is a general presumption that disclosure of pleadings lodged by one of the institutions in court proceedings would undermine the protection of those proceedings while they remained pending,[35] this could be overturned by the presentation of evidence that a particular document is not covered by the presumption.[36] Secondly, the CJEU upheld the ruling of the General Court that documents relating to investigations carried out by the Commission in the context of infringement proceedings under Article 258 TFEU would no longer be covered by the exception for the protection of court proceedings in Article 4(2) of Regulation 1049/2001 after the CJEU had delivered its judgment closing those proceedings.[37] Rejecting the Commission's argument that the CFI had misconstrued the relationship between Article 258 and Article 260 (penalty payment) proceedings, the CJEU ruled that these were two distinct procedures and that once the CJEU had found the existence of a breach in the Article 258 procedure, an amicable settlement in the case was no longer possible in the case of that breach. Consequently, it could not be presumed that disclosure of pleadings lodged in a procedure which led to the Article 258

---

[26] For an evaluation of the first and second years of the EU Pilot mechanism see COM(2010) 70 and SEC(2011) 1629, and the Commission also attributes the reduction in the number of infringement proceedings in 2013 to the EU Pilot scheme: see 31st Annual Report on Monitoring the Application of EU Law (2013), COM(2014) 612. See also http://ec.europa.eu/internal_market/scoreboard/performance_by_governance tool/eu pilot/index en.htm.

[27] See Hadroušek (n 10) 251–252, quoting Ludwig Krämer.

[28] Regulation (EC) No 1049/2001 of the European Parliament and of the Council of 30 May 2001 regarding public access to European Parliament, Council and Commission documents [2001] OJ L145/43, Art 4(2).

[29] For the database of complaints made against the Commission in relation to access to documents concerning enforcement of EU law and infringement proceedings and the decisions of the Ombudsman, see www.ombudsman.europa.eu/en/cases/home.faces.

[30] Cases T–191/99 *Petrie v Commission* [2001] ECR II–3677, [70]; T–105/95 *WWF v Commission* [1997] ECR II–313; T–309/97 *Bavarian Lager Company v Commission* [1999] ECR II–3217.

[31] Case T–194/04 *Bavarian Lager v Commission* [2007] ECR II–4523.

[32] Ibid.

[33] Case C–28/08 P *Commission v Bavarian Lager* EU:C:2010:378.

[34] Cases C–514, 528 and 532/07 P *Sweden and API v Commission* EU:C:2009:2, [112]–[127].

[35] Ibid [77]–[102].

[36] Ibid [103]–[104].

[37] Ibid [112]–[123]. However, the general rule that disclosure of documents relating to the pre-litigation procedure could be presumed to undermine those proceedings and therefore is covered by the exception in Art 4(2) of Regulation 1049/2001 was confirmed in Cases C–514 and 605/11 P *LPN and Finland v Commission* EU:C:2013:738.

judgment would undermine investigations which could lead to proceedings being brought under Article 260.[38]

Harlow and Rawlings have suggested that there have been three phases of the infringement procedure over time: a first phase of diplomacy shaped largely by the Commission,[39] a second a more judicialized phase influenced by the jurisprudence of the Court but still dominated by the Commission's negotiation approach, and the third a more clearly legalized phase following the enactment of a provision for pecuniary penalties against states.

C Harlow and R Rawlings, Accountability and Law Enforcement: The Centralized EU Infringement Procedure[40]

Söderman [*the first EU Ombudsman*] portrays the 'citizen who complains' as a 'party in the administrative procedure', who ought to be recognised as such and should enjoy all the procedural safeguards of EC law together with (subject to legal confidentiality) access to the file in accordance with the right to good administration contained in Art.41 of the European Charter of Fundamental Rights. This tripartite analysis, with the Commission presented as arbitrator between two parties, contrasts significantly with the view of Court and Commission of an elite procedure confined to two parties: Commission and Member State....

But just how far can such an approach sensibly go, given the evident need for an efficient procedure and for the Commission to retain effective control of decisions? One need not be an apologist for the Commission to appreciate that complainants are self-selecting and that their concern to vindicate the rule of law is commonly a product of private interest, even if, in some of the cases discussed above, a strong measure of public interest is joined. The dissonance between a Commission policy of stopping at the point of voluntary compliance and a natural concern among complainants with the effects of past infringements is an obvious flashpoint.

(B) OPERATION OF THE PROCEDURE

The infringement procedure can be divided into four distinct stages:

i. The initial *pre-contentious stage* gives the Member State the occasion to explain its position and the opportunity to reach an accommodation with the Commission.

ii. If the matter is not clarified or resolved informally between the two at this stage, the state will be *formally notified* of the specific infringement alleged by means of a letter from the Commission. The state is usually given two months to reply, except in cases of urgency, and the Commission normally decides within a year either to close a case or to proceed.

---

[38] Cases C–514, 528 and 532/07 P *Sweden and API* (n 34) [112]–[123].

[39] For an example of the Court's understanding of this elite negotiation conception of the infringement procedure some decades ago, see its ruling in the case concerning Belgium's interpretation of the 'public service' exception to the Treaty provisions on the free movement of workers in Case 149/79 *Commission v Belgium* [1980] ECR 3881, [23]–[24], in which the Court 'invites the Commission and the Kingdom of Belgium to re-examine the issue between them in the light of the foregoing considerations and to report to the court, either jointly or separately, within a specified period, either any solution to the dispute which they succeed in reaching together or their respective viewpoints, having regard to the matters of law arising from this judgment'.

[40] (2006) 31 ELRev 447.

iii. If, after an exchange with the state, the matter has not been resolved, the Commission may proceed to the stage of issuing a *reasoned opinion*. The reasoned opinion sets out clearly the grounds on which the alleged infringement rests, and marks the beginning of the time period within which the Member State must comply, if it is to avoid the final stage.

iv. The final stage is *referral* of the matter by the Commission *to the Court of Justice*.

The Commission clearly values the 'elite cooperation' dimension of the infringement procedure which enables disputes over enforcement to be resolved at the pre-contentious stage without recourse to the Court. During the mid-1990s, however, following a change of practice by the Commission concerning the issue of letters of formal notice, the number of referrals to the Court rose rapidly.[41] Since then they have stabilized somewhat, and the Commission has suggested that 'in many cases the pre-litigation examination of complaints is enough to prompt the Member States to put the situation right'.[42]

Since 2002, the Commission has drawn attention to a range of 'complementary mechanisms' for resolving non-compliance, such as problem-solving networks like the internal market SOLVIT, national mediation, and national judicial proceedings.[43] Mechanisms of infringement-prevention and management, such as interpretative communications, promotion of peer pressure, notification obligations, transparency campaigns, providing training, exchanges of information and practice, and so-called 'package meetings' with Member States, have also been emphasized.[44]

The EU Pilot scheme for handling complaints and inquiries was introduced to address potential compliance problems at an early stage.[45] The idea was to help Member States with compliance so that the need for recourse to formal infringement proceedings is correspondingly reduced. The Commission also introduced criteria to enable it to prioritize particular kinds of infringement: including those that 'undermine the foundations of the rule of law' or that undermine the 'smooth functioning of the EC legal system', and those involving the incorrect transposal or non-transposal of directives, and these criteria were subsequently refined.[46]

The Commission's conception of the centralized EU enforcement procedure today seems to be of a mechanism to be used in a carefully targeted and strategic manner, ideally as a last-resort mechanism, after other problem-solving efforts and strategies to encourage compliance have failed, and where negotiation and constructive intervention have not succeeded. Apart from the drastically limited time and resources of the Commission in an EU of twenty-eight members, there are pragmatic and political reasons for it to exercise political discretion and not to pursue every known Member State breach to judgment.[47]

Recall too that the enforcement mechanism can be a lengthy and time-consuming process. The Commission stated in 2008 that it took on average fifty months to close a case from the time of a reasoned opinion until its referral to the CJEU,[48] although in its 26th Report in 2009 it declared that

---

[41] See the 13th and 14th Annual Reports for 1995 and 1996 [1996] OJ C303 and [1997] OJ C332 respectively.

[42] See the discussion of statistics in Commission Communication on Better Monitoring of the Application of Community Law, COM(2002) 725.

[43] Ibid.

[44] Ibid. For discussion of the interaction of some of these alternative mechanisms, particularly in the environmental sphere, and Art 258 proceedings, see E Korkea-Aho, 'Watering Down the Court of Justice: The Dynamics between Network Implementation and Article 258 TFEU Litigation' (2014) 20 ELJ 649.

[45] See (nn 25–26) and text. For discussion of some of the critiques of the Pilot scheme, including whether the Commission is abdicating its task of monitoring enforcement of EU law and leaving it to the states, see Hadroušek (n 10) 235.

[46] COM(2007) 502 (n 7). The Commission has emphasized particularly breaches presenting 'the greatest risks, widespread impact for citizens and businesses and the most persistent infringements confirmed by the Court'.

[47] Rawlings (n 3) 26, on selective enforcement.

[48] SEC(2008) 2851, [4.1.1].

the average time taken to process an infringement from opening the file to sending the application to the Court had fallen to twenty-four months. Finally, it is important to remember that enforcement actions successfully brought before the CJEU do not necessarily lead to compliance, even with the additional deterrent of the pecuniary penalty procedure of Article 260 TFEU.

3 RELATIONSHIP BETWEEN 'PUBLIC' AND 'PRIVATE' ENFORCEMENT MECHANISMS

The early rulings of the ECJ which established the principle of direct effect made clear that the public enforcement procedures of Articles 258 and 259 TFEU (then Articles 169 and 170 EEC) provide merely one amongst several legal mechanisms for ensuring the application of Community law. According to the ECJ in *Van Gend en Loos*:[49]

> The vigilance of individuals concerned to protect their rights amounts to an effective supervision in addition to the supervision entrusted by Articles 169 and 170 to the diligence of the Commission and of the Member States.

In *Mölkerei-Zentrale*, however, the ECJ ruled that proceedings brought by an individual were intended to protect individual rights in a specific case, whereas Commission enforcement proceedings were intended to ensure the general and uniform observance of EU law.[50] This meant that the two kinds of proceedings 'have different objects, aims, and effects, and a parallel may not be drawn between them'.[51] Despite the attempts to maintain a clear distinction between the outcome of a preliminary ruling and an enforcement action, however, it is evident that the ECJ by means of preliminary rulings often effectively declares that a Member State is in breach of EU law, leaving little scope for a different conclusion on the part of the referring domestic court.[52] Nevertheless, the two procedures are treated in legal terms as quite distinct.[53]

In particular, the direct effect of an EU provision, and hence the ability of individuals to enforce it before national courts, provides no defence to a Commission action under Article 258 TFEU for failure to implement that provision.[54] Conversely, the ECJ in *Danske Slagterior* rejected attempts to link an individual enforcement action with the public enforcement procedure in a way which would extend the time limit for bringing the individual action.[55]

4 THE COMMISSION'S DISCRETION

There has been much debate over the extent of the Commission's discretion to bring proceedings under Article 258. One risk is that the Commission may use its discretion in a way which is excessively lenient or

---

[49] [1963] ECR 1, 13.

[50] Case 28/67 *Mölkerei-Zentrale Westfalen v Hauptzollamt Paderborn* [1968] ECR 143, 153.

[51] Ibid.

[52] Ch 13.

[53] The ECJ in Case C–508/03 *Commission v UK* [2006] ECR I–3969, [71] rejected the UK's argument that Commission infringement proceedings should be deemed inadmissible on the basis that national judicial proceedings were pending.

[54] Case 29/84 *Commission v Germany* [1985] ECR 1661, [29]; Case 102/79 *Commission v Belgium* [1980] ECR 1473; Case 168/85 *Commission v Italy* [1986] ECR 2945.

[55] Case C–445/06 *Danske Slagterier v Bundesrepublik Deutschland* [2009] ECR I–2119, [27]–[46].

arbitrarily selective with defaulting Member States. Another risk is that enforcement proceedings could be used unfairly or oppressively if there are insufficient procedural constraints on the Commission.

Given the multiple roles of the Commission under the Treaties, there may be political and other reasons leading it to exercise its discretion against bringing infringement proceedings, even where a state is blatantly in violation of EU law.[56] The language of paragraph 2 of Article 258 clearly suggests that, once it has issued a reasoned opinion indicating a breach by a Member State, the Commission has discretion whether or not to bring the matter before the CJEU. And even though paragraph 2 uses mandatory language ('shall') with respect to the decision to issue a reasoned opinion, there is agreement on the fact that the Commission has discretion whether and when to issue a reasoned opinion.[57]

As to the Commission's reasons for bringing proceedings, the Court has repeatedly made clear that proceedings are entirely 'objective', so that it will examine only whether the infringement alleged by the Commission exists, and will not examine the Commission's motives for bringing the action.[58] In the following case, the UK argued that there was a political motive behind the Commission's action:

Case 416/85 **Commission v United Kingdom**
[1988] ECR 3127

9. That argument cannot be upheld. In the context of the balance of powers between the institutions laid down in the Treaty, it is not for the Court to consider what objectives are pursued in an action brought under Article 169 [*now Art 258 TFEU*] of the Treaty. Its role is to decide whether or not the Member State in question has failed to fulfil its obligations as alleged. As the Court held in Case 7/68 *Commission* v. *Italy* [1968] ECR 423, an action against a Member-State for failure to fulfil its obligations, the bringing of which is a matter for the Commission in its entire discretion, is objective in nature.

Conversely, the *absence* of a specific motive or interest on the Commission's part in bringing proceedings against a Member State will not affect the admissibility of the enforcement proceedings either.[59] The Commission acts 'in the general interest', according to the Court, and does not have to have a specific interest, because Article 258 'is not intended to protect that institution's own rights'.[60]

States have enjoyed greater success in arguing that there are *procedural* constraints, such as reasonable time limits, on the Commission's discretion. In an early case, the Court ruled that the Commission's choice of moment to initiate proceedings could not affect their admissibility.[61] However, despite initial reluctance,[62] the ECJ subsequently ruled that there were certain constraints on the Commission's discretion as far as the *length* of time taken by the Commission to bring proceedings in respect of a particular infringement was concerned. In a case in which the Netherlands argued that a period of more than five years for bringing infringement proceedings from the time the first letter was sent to it by the Commission was excessive, the ECJ ruled that although Article 258

---

[56] P Craig, 'Once Upon a Time in the West: Direct Effect and the Federalization of EEC Law' (1992) 12 OJLS 453, 456.
[57] A Evans, 'The Enforcement Procedure of Article 169 EEC: Commission Discretion' (1979) 4 ELRev 442, 445.
[58] See, eg, Case C–200/88 *Commission v Greece* [1990] ECR I–4299, [9]. For another example see the AG's opinion in the *Open Skies* case, dismissing the argument that the Commission's action should be inadmissible on the ground of misuse of procedure, since it had brought this set of infringement proceedings against eight Member States primarily in order to pressurize the Council to open negotiations with the United States: Cases C–466–476/98 *Commission v United Kingdom et al* [2002] ECR I–9855, [29], AG Tizzano.
[59] Case C–431/92 *Commission v Germany* [1995] ECR I–2189, [19]–[22].
[60] Case C–394/02 *Commission v Greece* [2005] ECR I–4713, [15]–[16].
[61] Case 7/68 *Commission v Italy* [1968] ECR 423, 428.
[62] Case 7/71 *Commission v France* [1971] ECR 1003, [5]–[6].

(then Article 169) deliberately laid down no particular time limit for bringing proceedings, excessive delay might nonetheless be prejudicial to the rights of the defence. [63]

In 2006, however, the Court rejected an argument by the UK that, given the length of time which had passed since the particular events which were the subject of the infringement proceedings, the proceedings brought by the Commission would violate the principle of legal certainty and the acquired rights of individuals who had been affected by those earlier events.[64]

Restrictions have also been imposed on the Commission's discretion regarding when to refer a matter to the Court *after* the issuing of a reasoned opinion, rather than on its discretion in commencing the infringement proceedings in the first place, since this could also prejudice a Member State's ability to exercise its rights of defence. In proceedings against Ireland, the ECJ referred to the Commission's 'regrettable behaviour' and reprimanded it for the short length of time it had allowed for compliance with the reasoned opinion. However, the Commission's action was nevertheless admissible since, despite the short time period, the Commission had in fact awaited Ireland's reply before referring the matter to the Court:

> The Court is compelled to state its disapproval of the Commission's behaviour in this regard. It is indeed unreasonable, as Ireland has pointed out, to allow a Member State five days to amend legislation which has been applied for more than 40 years and which, moreover, has not given rise to any action on the part of the Commission over the period which has elapsed since the accession of the Member State in question. Furthermore, it is clear that there was no particular urgency.[65]

The Court ruled that a reasonable period must be allowed, although very short periods could be justified in circumstances of urgency or where the Member State was fully aware of the Commission's views long before the procedure started.[66] A period of four months to respond to a reasoned opinion was adequate where a Member State had three years' prior notice of the Commission's view.[67] A period of seven days for Austria to respond to a formal letter, and fourteen days for responding to a reasoned opinion, were also deemed adequate, since these periods were justified by the urgency of the complaint and the circumstances of the case.[68]

In keeping with its bilateral conception of the infringement procedure, the ECJ has consistently refused to admit actions for 'failure to act' brought by non-privileged parties against the Commission under Article 265 TFEU (formerly Article 232 EC), which seek to require the Commission to initiate infringement proceedings under Article 258. In *Star Fruit* it ruled that:

> It is clear from the scheme of Article 169 of the Treaty [*now Art 258 TFEU*] that the Commission is not bound to commence the proceedings provided for in that provision but in this regard has a discretion which excludes the right for individuals to require that institution to adopt a specific position.[69]

---

[63] Case C–96/89 *Commission v Netherlands* [1991] ECR 2461, [16].

[64] Case C–508/03 (n 53); Case C–475/98 *Commission v Austria* [2002] ECR I–9797.

[65] Case 74/82 *Commission v Ireland* [1984] ECR 317, [12]. See also Case 293/85 *Commission v Belgium* [1988] ECR 305, in which the proceedings were deemed inadmissible due to the shortness of time allowed for responding to the letter of formal notice and reasoned opinion.

[66] Case 74/82, ibid at [14] of the judgment. See also Case C–56/90 *Commission v United Kingdom* [1993] ECR I–4109; Case C–333/99 *Commission v France* [2000] ECR I–1025.

[67] Case C–473/93 *Commission v Luxembourg* [1996] ECR I–3207.

[68] Case C–328/96 *Commission v Austria* [1999] ECR I–7479.

[69] Case 247/87 (n 20) [11]; also Cases C–371/89 *Emrich v Commission* [1990] ECR I–1555 and C–111/11 P *Ruipérez Aguirre and ATC Petition v Commission* EU:C:2011:491. Compare Case C–107/95 P *Bundesverband der Bilanzbuchalter v Commission* [1997] ECR I–947.

Similarly, the Court has dismissed actions for annulment directed by an individual litigant against a 'decision' by the Commission not to commence proceedings against a Member State, again on the basis that this was a matter within the Commission's discretion and that the action sought—the adoption of a reasoned opinion—would not be susceptible to an action for annulment.[70]

Although the lack of a role for individuals in the initiation and conduct of enforcement proceedings has provoked adverse comment, the Commission's discretion in this respect may not be entirely unjustified.[71] As Snyder has argued, the Commission has a long-term view and uses litigation strategically, as just one part of its negotiation process.[72]

The Commission over time has imposed administrative constraints on its own discretion. From 1989 onwards it decided to bring immediate infringement proceedings against a defaulting state as soon as the time limit for implementation of a directive had passed.[73] Since 1990 it has routinely issued letters of formal notice whenever Member States have not notified national measures implementing directives which are due for implementation.[74] As indicated above, the Commission codified its own internal rules governing relations with individual complainants in response to pressure from the Ombudsman.[75] The supervisory role of the European Parliament and the administrative role of the Ombudsman clearly had a positive influence on the Commission's conduct in the infringement procedure, and have strengthened the mechanisms and forms of accountability of the Commission within that process.[76]

5 THE REASONED OPINION

(A) FUNCTION

The reasoned opinion which the Commission is required to issue and to notify to a Member State forms an important part of the pre-judicial procedure under Article 258, and provides the Member State concerned with a measure of protection. Together with the letter of formal notice, the reasoned opinion (sometimes followed by a supplementary reasoned opinion[77]) is the official means by which the Commission communicates to the state the substance of the complaint against it, and specifies a time period within which the violation of EU law must be remedied. It is intended to provide the Member State with a clear statement of the case against it, to 'ensure respect for the principles of natural justice',[78] and to ensure that 'any contentious procedure will have a clearly-defined dispute as its subject matter'.[79]

[70] Case C–87/89 *Sonito v Commission* [1990] ECR I–1981; Case T–201/96 *Smanor v Commission* [1997] ECR II–1081; Case T–182/97 *Smanor* (n 20).

[71] See (n 47); Harlow and Rawlings (n 4); J Weiler, 'The Community System: The Dual Character of Supranationalism' (1981) 1 YBEL 267, 299.

[72] F Snyder, 'The Effectivess of European Community Law' (1993) 56 MLR 19, 30.

[73] 7th Annual Report [1990] OJ C232/6.

[74] 8th Annual Report [1991] 7(e).

[75] COM(2002) 141 and COM(2012) 154 (n 23).

[76] The Commission acknowledges as much in its 2007 Report on Applying Community Law (n 7) when referring to European Parliament reports expressing concern about infringement proceedings.

[77] Cases C–354/99 *Commission v Ireland* [2001] ECR I–7657; C–155/99 *Commission v Italy* [2001] ECR I–4007.

[78] Evans (n 57) 446.

[79] See, eg, Case C–508/10 *Commission v Netherlands* EU:C:2012:243, [34].

(B) FORM AND CONTENT

The obligation to provide reasons is a requirement of general importance in EU law, now enshrined in Article 41(2)(c) of the Charter of Fundamental Rights. Article 296 TFEU requires that legal acts state the reasons on which they are based, and Article 258 contains a specific requirement of reasoning in relation to the opinions issued by the Commission under the infringement procedure. However, although the reasoning requirement is an 'essential procedural requirement' of EU law, breach of which constitutes a ground for annulment of a measure under Article 263 TFEU, the Commission's opinion under Article 258 is not subject to an action for annulment because it lacks binding effect.[80] According to Advocate General Lagrange in an early case:

> No formalism must be demanded of this document, since, as I have said, the reasoned opinion is not an administrative act subject to review by the Court of its legality.[81]

Nonetheless, although a reasoned opinion may not be the subject of an action for annulment, a Member State which is the subject of such an opinion may contest the lack of adequate reasoning in a different way, by raising the matter before the Court if and when the enforcement proceedings reach that stage.[82] In an early case in which Italy challenged the legal form and content of the reasoned opinion, the ECJ ruled that there would be a legally sufficient statement of reasons when the opinion contained a coherent statement of the reasons which led the Commission to believe that the state had failed to fulfil an obligation under the Treaties.[83]

The Commission is not obliged in its reasoned opinion to address or to answer every argument made by the state at the pre-litigation stage, nor to indicate what steps should be taken by the state to remedy the alleged breach.[84] Further, the initial letter of formal notice need not meet particularly strict requirements, since the reasoned opinion is the crucial document which sets out the complaint to which the state must respond. However, the Commission must respond to a state's reply to its letter of formal notice, even if the state is late in replying to the notice.[85] Further, the essence of the complaint must be the same in the formal letter,[86] the reasoned opinion, and in the Commission's application to bring the case before the CJEU.[87] But so long as the Commission sets out clearly and in a coherent way in the reasoned opinion the grounds on which it has relied in concluding that the state has violated Union law, and the particular complaints which will form the subject matter of the proceedings,[88] the reasoning requirement will be satisfied. Notably, the Court has been willing to admit

---

[80] Case 48/65 *First Lütticke Case* (*Alfons Lütticke GmbH v Commission*) [1966] ECR 19.

[81] Case 7/61 *Commission v Italy* [1961] ECR 317, 334, 336.

[82] In Cases C–191/95 *Commission v Germany* [1998] ECR I–5449; C–272/97 *Commission v Germany* [1999] ECR I–2175; and C–198/97 *Commission v Germany* [1999] ECR I–3257, the ECJ dismissed several challenges by Germany to the reasoned opinion on the ground that it had been adopted by the College of Commissioners without having the text of the opinion before them. The Court ruled that it was sufficient for the Commissioners to have available to them, at the time, the information on which the decision to commence proceedings had been based.

[83] Case 7/61 *Commission v Italy* [1961] ECR 317, 327.

[84] Case C–247/89 *Commission v Portugal* [1991] ECR I–3659, [22].

[85] Case C–362/01 *Commission v Ireland* [2002] ECR I–11433, [19].

[86] For a case in which an allegation of breach of the requirement of loyal cooperation in Art 10 EC (now Art 4 TEU) was not admitted by the Court because the formal letter had not referred to it: Case C–371/04 *Commission v Italy* [2006] ECR I–10257. See also Case C–522/09 *Commission v Romania* EU:C:2011:2963.

[87] Cases C–191/95 *Commission v Germany* [1998] ECR I–5449, [54]; C–365/97 *Commission v Italy* [1999] ECR I–7773, [26]; C–480/10 *Commission v Sweden* EU:C:2013:263, [16]–[18].

[88] Case C–328/96 *Commission v Austria* [1999] ECR I–7479, [39]–[41], where part of the Commission's complaint was ruled inadmissible for failure to specify this. Also Case C–252/13 *Commission v Netherlands* EU:C:2014:2312 where the Commission's action was deemed inadmissible for ambiguity and lack of clarity in its claims.

and uphold an allegation by the Commission that the Member State has contravened the 'spirit and scheme' of an EU measure, rather than a specific provision.[89]

Since the reasoned opinion is intended to operate as a procedural protection for the Member State, the Commission is not entitled to amend the substantive content of its submission when the case comes to be heard before the Court, even if both parties wish the Court to consider other aspects of the state's conduct which took place after the date of the reasoned opinion.[90] In such a case, the Commission cannot amend its complaint to include a fresh objection after the reasoned opinion has been issued, but must initiate the entire Article 258 procedure again. This requirement that the content of the reasoned opinion be essentially the same as (although not necessarily identical to[91]) the submissions contained in the Commission's application to the Court has been reiterated many times.[92] However, it will not be sufficient for the Commission when the matter comes before the Court simply to refer in its application to 'all the reasons set out in the letter of formal notice and the reasoned opinion'. Rather the application itself must contain a statement of the grounds on which it is based.[93] A claim by the Commission will not be considered inadmissible merely because the claim in its application to the Court is stated in a more detailed way than it was in the pre-litigation procedure.[94]

On the other hand, where enforcement proceedings brought by the Commission have been found by the CJEU to be inadmissible on the ground that the Commission's application is based on an objection different from that in the reasoned opinion, the Commission is not obliged to recommence the entire pre-litigation procedure but may lodge a fresh application before the Court based on the same objections as the reasoned opinion originally issued.[95] And where EU legislation on which the reasoned opinion was based has been amended prior to the case coming before the CJEU, this does not necessarily mean the Commission has to withdraw the action or issue a new reasoned opinion, so long as the obligations under the amended measure correspond to those arising under the original legislation.[96]

There is one circumstance in which the Court will accept an application made by the Commission which is not the same as it was under the reasoned opinion, and that is where the change *limits* what is contained in the reasoned opinion rather than expanding it in a way which could disadvantage the respondent state.[97] Finally, an extension of the subject matter of the dispute to events which took place *after* the reasoned opinion is acceptable insofar as they are of the same kind and constitute the same conduct as the events to which the opinion referred,[98] or only if the later evidence is not being used to

---

[89] See, eg, Case C–202/99 *Commission v Italy* [2001] ECR I–9319, [23] and Case C–508/10 *Commission v Netherlands* EU:C:2012:243.

[90] Case 7/69 *Commission v Italy* [1970] ECR 111, where Italy had enacted a law, after the date of the reasoned opinion, intended to remedy the alleged violation. Although both Italy and the Commission wished the Member State to take into account the impact of the new law (which the Commission considered to be inadequate to cure the breach), the Court refused to do so.

[91] Case C–433/03 *Commission v Germany* [2005] ECR I–6985, [28]–[29].

[92] Cases 232/78 *Commission v France* [1979] ECR 2729; 124/81; 166/82 *Commission v Italy* [1984] ECR 459; C–350/02 *Commission v Netherlands* [2004] ECR I–6213.

[93] Case C–43/90 *Commission v Germany* [1992] ECR I–1909, [7]–[8]. See also Case C–52/90 *Commission v Denmark* [1992] ECR I–2187.

[94] Case C–281/11 *Commission v Poland* EU:C:2013:855, [57].

[95] Case C–57/94 *Commission v Italy* [1995] ECR I–1249.

[96] Cases C–365/97 (n 87); C–275/04 *Commission v Belgium* [2006] ECR I–9883; C–203/03 *Commission v Austria* [2005] ECR I–935.

[97] Case C–191/95 *Commission v Germany* [1998] ECR I–5449, and for a similar judgment under Art 228 EC see Case C–177/04 *Commission v France* [2006] ECR I–2461.

[98] Cases 42/82 *Commission v France* [1983] ECR 1013, [20]; 113/86 *Commission v Italy* [1988] ECR 607, [11]; C–236/05 *Commission v United Kingdom* [2005] ECR I–10819, [12]–[17].

establish a specific violation, but rather to support the argument that the other violations alleged are part of a general and persistent pattern or practice.[99]

The Commission is not prohibited from responding, during the hearing before the Court, to arguments and defences raised by the respondent Member State, even where it has not made those points in the reasoned opinion itself.[100] Further, the Member State cannot complain of a breach of the right to a fair hearing by the fact that the Commission, in its application to the CJEU, does not take account of facts or defences put forward by the Member State after the expiry of the period set by the reasoned opinion.[101] However, while the Commission is procedurally bound to raise all of the grounds on which it is bringing the case during the pre-litigation procedure, Member States are not similarly bound to raise their defence during the pre-litigation procedure, but may raise new matters as defences before the Court.[102]

(c) CONFIDENTIALITY OF THE REASONED OPINION

In a number of cases, individual complainants who had asked the Commission to bring proceedings against a Member State and who were disappointed by the Commission's failure to do so, subsequently sought disclosure of the reasoned opinion and of other documentation relevant to the investigative proceedings. However, despite a setback for the Commission in the *WWF* case,[103] neither the General Court, the CJEU, nor the Ombudsman[104] has been prepared to require disclosure of a reasoned opinion, a draft reasoned opinion, or any documents relating to the investigative stage of the infringement procedure, before the CJEU has given judgment in Article 258 proceedings. In *WWF*, the General Court ruled, in relation to a Commission investigation into possible breaches of EU law, that:

> [T]he confidentiality which the Member States are entitled to expect of the Commission in such circumstances warrants, under the heading of protection of the public interest, a refusal of access to documents relating to investigations which may lead to an infringement procedure, even where a period of time has elapsed since the closure of the investigation.[105]

And in *Petrie*, which concerned a request for access to a range of documents including letters of formal notice and reasoned opinions, the General Court ruled that:

> This requirement of confidentiality remains even after the matter has been brought before the Court of Justice, on the ground that it cannot be ruled out that the discussions between the Commission and the Member State in question regarding the latter's voluntary compliance with the Treaty requirements may continue during the court proceedings and up to the delivery of the judgment of the Court of Justice. The preservation of that objective, namely an amicable resolution of the dispute between

---

[99] Case C–494/01 *Commission v Ireland* [2005] ECR I–3331, [35]–[37], discussed below at (nn 147–152) and text, and Case C–189/07 *Commission v Spain* [2008] ECR I–195, [29]–[31].

[100] Case 211/81 *Commission v Denmark* [1982] ECR 4547, [16].

[101] Case C–3/96 *Commission v Netherlands* [1998] ECR I–3931.

[102] Case C–414/97 *Commission v Spain* [1999] ECR I–5855. See below (n 166).

[103] See Case T–105/95 (n 30), in which the General Court restricted the Commission's ability to rely on a particular exception to the obligation to provide access to documents as a mandatory general exception rather than an individual discretionary one. For some cases investigated by the Ombudsman into the question of access to documents in such circumstances, see Cases 2219/2008/(JMA)MHZ and 2073/2010/AN.

[104] See (n 29) and text.

[105] (N 103) [62].

the Commission and the Member State concerned before the Court of Justice has delivered judgment, justifies refusal of access to the letters of formal notice and reasoned opinions drawn up in connection with the Article 226 EC [*now Art 258 TFEU*] proceedings.[106]

Access to Commission documents is now governed by Regulation 1049/2001, and Article 4(2) thereof allows the Commission to rely on an exception governing 'protection of the purpose of inspections, investigations and audits' to refuse access to documents relating to infringement proceedings. However, in *Bavarian Lager II*[107] the General Court ruled that disclosure of documents relating to infringement proceedings which had been closed six years previously could not jeopardize Commission investigations, and so were not covered by the exception governing inspections.[108] Further, in *Sweden/API*, the CJEU ruled that documents relating to investigations carried out by the Commission in the context of infringement proceedings under Article 258 would no longer be automatically covered by the exception for the protection of court proceedings in Article 4(2) *after* the CJEU had delivered judgment closing those proceedings, but instead would have to be appraised on a case-by-case basis.[109] The rationale underpinning these rulings would probably apply also to an application for disclosure of the reasoned opinion, once the CJEU had delivered judgment in the Article 258 case in question.

It should be noted that, although it is not required to and cannot be compelled to do so at least until after judgment, the Commission occasionally publishes its reasoned opinions, and more regularly press releases relating to its reasoned opinions,[110] and maintains an electronically accessible list of its decisions on infringement proceedings.[111] However, individuals may have more success in obtaining letters of formal notice or reasoned opinions from national authorities under national freedom-of-information laws, rather than from the Commission.[112]

6 WHY IS AN ENFORCEMENT ACTION ADMISSIBLE AFTER THE BREACH IS REMEDIED?

Once the procedural conditions for bringing Article 258 proceedings have been fulfilled, and the period laid down by the Commission for compliance has expired without an adequate response by the Member State, it is no answer for that state to assert, when the case is heard before the CJEU, that the breach has since been remedied. The CJEU asks only whether the Member State was in breach at the time of the expiry of the period laid down in the reasoned opinion.

The Court's approach here contrasts with its approach to actions brought under Article 265 TFEU against a Union institution for failure to act, where it has held that the procedure is devoid of purpose once the institution has remedied its default.[113] Yet where proceedings have been brought against a

---

[106] Case T–191/99 (n 30) [68]. See also Case T–309/97 *Bavarian Lager v Commission* [1999] ECR II–3217.

[107] Case T–194/04 *Bavarian Lager v Commission* [2007] ECR II–4523.

[108] Ibid. The CJEU overturned part of the General Court's judgment here on the basis of EU data-protection legislation in Case C–28/08 *Commission v Bavarian Lager* EU:C:2010:378.

[109] See (n 34).

[110] For a reference to the Commission's publication of a press release relating to a reasoned opinion see Case C–28/08 (n 33) [20].

[111] http://ec.europa.eu/atwork/applying-eu-law/infringements-proceedings/infringement_decisions/?lang_code=en.

[112] See the Own Initiative Opinion OI/2/2009/MHZ of the Ombudsman on the Commission's role in relation to requests for access to reasoned opinions from national authorities.

[113] Case 377/87 *Council v Parliament* [1988] ECR 4017. The position, however, might be different if it were likely that some party might later wish to seek redress from the institution in question for loss caused by the illegal failure to act.

state under Article 258 TFEU, such actions have been declared admissible by the Court even though the state had remedied its breach by that time. Several reasons have been offered to explain why.

First, the Commission argues that it has a continued interest in bringing the action, not least to prevent states from undermining infringement proceedings by bringing their illegal conduct to an end just before judgment is delivered, and possibly recommencing that same conduct again afterwards.[114] Secondly, it is important for the Court to be able to rule on the legality of breaches of short duration, since these may be no less serious than longer breaches.[115] However, if the effects of a specific infringement have come to an end before the expiry of the period set out in the reasoned opinion,[116] the action before the CJEU will be inadmissible even if the Commission fears that a similar breach is likely to occur again in the future.[117] A third reason for giving judgment even after the breach has been remedied is in order to establish the basis for liability on the part of a defaulting Member State.[118] An individual's action for redress before the national courts—which has been cited by the Commission as 'one of the best ways of combating recidivism'[119]—could derive considerable assistance from a prior finding of the CJEU that the Member State in question had acted in violation of EU law.[120] A prior finding by the CJEU of an infringement is an effective means, even if not a necessary one, of showing the illegality of state action when damages are sought for loss caused by that action.[121]

7 TYPES OF BREACH BY MEMBER STATES OF EU LAW

Article 258 is very general in its description of a Member State violation for the purposes of enforcement proceedings. The Commission must simply consider that a state 'has failed to fulfil an obligation under the Treaties'. This may include actions as well as omissions on the part of states, failure to implement directives, breaches of specific Treaty provisions or of secondary legislation, or of any rule or standard which is an effective part of EU law. Cases involving breaches by Member States in the sphere of the Union's external relations have increasingly come before the Court in recent years.

An interesting example of breach of a Treaty provision by a Member State occurred when Ireland brought dispute-settlement proceedings, involving the interpretation of EU law against the UK in relation to the MOX nuclear recycling plant, to a tribunal under the International Convention on the Law of the Sea, rather than before the ECJ.[122] According to the ECJ, 'a breach of this nature involves a manifest risk that the jurisdictional order laid down in the Treaties and consequently the autonomy of the Community legal system may be adversely affected'.[123]

Certain kinds of breach, for example non-transposition of a directive, are far more often the subject of infringement proceedings than others. The following examples illustrate some of the different sorts of breaches with which the cases are concerned.

---

[114] Case 7/61 *Commission v Italy* [1961] ECR 317, 334, AG Lagrange.

[115] Case 240/86 *Commission v Greece* [1988] ECR 1835, 1844, AG Lenz.

[116] Retroactive legislation to 'cure' an earlier breach will not be accepted by the ECJ: Case C–221/03 *Commission v Belgium* [2005] ECR I–8307.

[117] Cases C–362/90 *Commission v Italy* [1992] ECR I–2353; C–525/03 *Commission v Italy* [2005] ECR I–9405.

[118] Case 240/86 (n 115) [14]; Case C–168/03 *Commission v Spain* [2004] ECR I–8227, [24].

[119] Better Monitoring of the Application of Community Law, COM(2002) 725.

[120] For discussion of the principle of state liability to an individual for breach of EU law, following Cases C–6 and 9/90 *Francovich and Bonifaci v Italy* [1991] ECR I–5357, see Ch 8.

[121] See the attempt in Case T–182/97 *Smanor v Commission* [1998] ECR II–271 to obtain an enforcement ruling from the ECJ for this precise purpose.

[122] Case C–459/03 *Commission v Ireland* [2006] ECR I–4635.

[123] Ibid [154].

(A) BREACH OF THE OBLIGATION OF SINCERE COOPERATION UNDER ARTICLE 4(3) TEU

Case 96/81 **Commission v Netherlands**
[1982] ECR 1791

The Commission brought proceedings against the Netherlands alleging failure to implement certain bathing water Directives and claiming that the Dutch Government had failed to provide information on its compliance with the provisions of one Directive, as required by the terms of the Directive itself. The Commission argued that due to the failure to supply this information, it was entitled to presume that the respondent state had failed to implement the necessary national measures. The breach identified in the application to the Court by the Commission was not however 'failure to comply with the duty to provide information' but rather 'failure to fulfil the obligation to implement the directive'.

THE ECJ

6. It should be emphasized that, in proceedings under Article 169 of the EEC Treaty [*now Art 258 TFEU*] for failure to fulfil an obligation, it is incumbent upon the Commission to prove the allegation that the obligation has not been fulfilled. It is the Commission's responsibility to place before the Court the information needed to enable the Court to establish that the obligation has not been fulfilled, and in doing so the Commission may not rely on any presumption.

However, although the Commission cannot rely on a presumption of breach where a Member State fails to provide information on compliance,[124] the Court has ruled that once the Commission has produced sufficient evidence to show that the Member State appeared to be violating Community law it is incumbent on the state not simply to deny the allegations, but to contest the information produced in a substantive way.[125] Further, even though the burden of proof lies with the Commission to show breach, where the complaint is of inadequate transposition of a directive, it is not necessary for the Commission to demonstrate the harmful effects of the transposing legislation.[126]

In the bathing water case above, the Court went on to say that all Member States had an obligation under Article 10 EC (now Article 4(3) TEU) to facilitate the achievement of the Commission's tasks, including that of monitoring compliance with the Treaty. This particular mode of infringement is frequently invoked by the Commission in enforcement actions where Member State authorities refuse or fail to respond to its requests for information.[127] Clearly, if a Member State is not willing to respond at the pre-litigation stage of an investigation by the Commission for the purposes of infringement proceedings, it will be difficult for the Commission to ascertain whether or not there has been a breach by the state.[128] The Commission's response to this impasse is to initiate separate enforcement proceedings on the basis of a breach of the obligation of cooperation.[129] On the other hand, the CJEU

---

[124] Cases C–217/97 *Commission v Germany* [1999] ECR I–5087; C–221/04 *Commission v Spain* [2006] ECR I–4515.

[125] Cases 272/86 *Commission v Greece* [1988] ECR 4875, [21]; C–508/03 (n 53) [80].

[126] Case C–392/96 *Commission v Ireland* [1999] ECR I–5901.

[127] Case 240/86 (n 115).

[128] For some cases which underscore the importance to the Commission of adequate information, and which highlight the difficulty of bringing Art 258 proceedings without proper sources of information: Cases C–490/09 *Commission v Luxembourg* EU:C:2011:34, [57]–[60]; C–421/12 *Commission v Belgium* EU:C:2014:2064.

[129] For other cases on Art 4(3) TEU (ex Art 10 EC) see, eg, Cases C–35/88 *Commission v Greece* [1990] ECR I–3125; C–48/89 *Commission v Italy* [1990] ECR I–2425; C–374/89 *Commission v Belgium* [1991] ECR I–367; Case 272/86 (n 125).

will not necessarily establish a separate violation of the obligation of sincere cooperation where it has already established a violation of more specific provisions of EU law.[130]

The obligation of sincere cooperation has been held to entail positive obligations on states not just to avoid violating EU law itself, but also to prevent others from frustrating the provisions of the Treaty. In proceedings against France, the ECJ ruled that by failing to take adequate steps to prevent violent and disruptive protests by French farmers which were hindering the free movement of agricultural goods, France had breached its obligations under the Treaty.[131] More generally, the obligation of sincere cooperation will be breached if a Member State fails to penalize those who infringe Union law in the same way as it penalizes those who infringe national law, and in a way which is 'effective, proportionate and dissuasive'.[132] The obligation of sincere cooperation has been prominent in several cases involving EU external relations.[133]

(B) INADEQUATE IMPLEMENTATION OF EU LAW

In many cases, the cause of the Commission's complaint is not the complete failure to transpose or to implement Union legislation, but rather inadequate implementation.[134]

Case 167/73 **Commission v France**
[1974] ECR 359

The French legislature had failed to repeal a provision of the French Code du Travail Maritime under which a certain proportion of the crew of a ship was required to be of French nationality. This nationality requirement was contrary to Community law, but the French Government claimed that directions had been given verbally to the naval authorities to treat Community nationals as French nationals, and that this was sufficient to comply with Community law.

THE ECJ

40. It appears both from the argument before the Court and from the position adopted during the parliamentary proceedings that the present state of affairs is that freedom of movement for workers in the sector in question continues to be considered by the French authorities not as a matter of right but as dependent on their unilateral will.

41. It follows that although the objective legal position is clear, namely, that Article 48 [*then EEC, now Article 45 TFEU*] and Regulation No 1612/68 are directly applicable in the territory of the French Republic, nevertheless the maintenance in these circumstances of the wording of the Code du Travail Maritime gives rise to an ambiguous state of affairs by maintaining, as regards those subject to the law who are concerned, a state of uncertainty as to the possibilities available to them of relying on Community law.

42. This uncertainty can only be reinforced by the internal and verbal character of the purely administrative directions to waive the application of the national law.

---

[130] Case C–334/08 *Commission v Italy* EU:C:2010:414, [75]; Case C–19/05 *Commission v Denmark* [2007] ECR I–8597, [36].

[131] Cases C–265/95 *Commission v France* [1997] ECR I–6959; C–60/01 *Commission v France* [2002] ECR I–5679; Comment, B Kurcz and K Zieleskiewicz (2002) 39 CMLRev 1443.

[132] Case 68/88 *Commission v Greece* [1989] ECR 2979; Case 143/83 *Commission v Denmark* [1985] ECR 427, [8]–[10].

[133] See Section (c) below.

[134] For a discussion of the distinction between failure to transpose and inadequate implementation, see AG Jääskinnen in Case C–525/12 *Commission v Germany* EU:C:2014:449.

In the case of directives, which unlike regulations are not directly applicable, it is always incumbent on the Member States to implement them fully. The fact that directives may have vertical direct effect or be enforced in other ways does not reduce the obligation on states to implement them properly. Article 288 TFEU provides that the manner and form of implementation of directives are a matter for each Member State, but this has not prevented the CJEU from reviewing the *adequacy* of the chosen method of implementation. According to the Court, the state's freedom to decide on the manner of implementation:

> [D]oes not however release it from the obligation to give effect to the provisions of the directive by means of national provisions of a binding nature...Mere administrative practices, which by their nature may be altered at the whim of the administration, may not be considered as constituting the proper fulfilment of the obligation deriving from that directive.[135]

A further objection to state reliance on such 'whimsical' administrative practices is that, quite apart from their uncertainty and alterability, they lack the appropriate publicity to constitute adequate implementation.[136] However, the CJEU has not always condemned Member States which fail to adopt any specific measures to implement a directive, as is evident from the following case concerning freedom of establishment for nurses.

Case 29/84 **Commission v Germany**
[1985] ECR 1661

17. The German Government does not deny that mere administrative practices, which by their nature can be modified as and when the administration pleases and which are not publicized widely enough, cannot be regarded as a proper fulfilment of the obligation imposed on the Member States by Article 189 of the Treaty [*now Art 288 TFEU*], as the Court has consistently held. However, the government claims that that principle cannot be applied in this instance because the administrative practice in question cannot be changed as and when the administration pleases and it has been given sufficient publicity...

[*After summarizing the Commission's counter-argument, the ECJ ruled as follows:*]

22. Faced with those conflicting views, the Court considers it necessary to recall the wording of the third paragraph of Article 189 of the Treaty [*now Art 288 TFEU*], according to which a directive is binding, as to the result to be achieved upon each Member State to which it is addressed, but leaves to the national authorities the choice of form and methods.

23. It follows from that provision that the implementation of a directive does not necessarily require legislative action in each Member State. In particular the existence of general principles of constitutional or administrative law may render implementation by specific legislation superfluous, provided however that those principles guarantee that the national authorities will in fact apply the directive fully and that, where the directive is intended to create rights for individuals, the persons concerned are made fully aware of their rights and, where appropriate, afforded the possibility of relying on them before the national courts.

The ECJ has subsequently ruled that proper transposition is particularly important for individuals to know their rights when those on whom the directive confers rights are nationals of *other* Member States.[137]

---

135 Case 96/81 *Commission v Netherlands* [1982] ECR 1791, [12].

136 Case 160/82 *Commission v Netherlands* [1982] ECR 4637.

137 Cases C–365/93 *Commission v Greece* [1995] ECR I–499, [9]; C–96/95 *Commission v Germany* [1997] ECR I–1653, [34]–[35]; C–162/99 *Commission v Italy* [2001] ECR I–541.

In proceedings brought by the Commission against the UK for improper implementation of the Product Liability Directive 85/374, the ECJ made interesting use of the 'indirect effect' of directives, the obligation on national courts to construe domestic law in accordance with a relevant directive, to dismiss the Commission's application. [138] While the Commission argued that the UK was in breach of the Directive because national courts would be required to interpret national law *contra legem* in order to conform with its requirements, the ECJ simply ruled that there was nothing to suggest that the UK courts would not, if called upon to do so, interpret the relevant national law in the light of the wording and purpose of the Directive so as to give effect to its aim.[139]

Finally, where national legislation has been the subject of different judicial interpretations, some of which are consistent with and others inconsistent with EU law, the ECJ has ruled that such legislation is insufficiently clear to comply with EU law.[140]

(c) BREACHES WHICH INTERFERE WITH EU EXTERNAL RELATIONS

Reflecting the growing activities of the EU in the field of international relations, several infringement proceedings brought by the Commission in recent years concerned conduct by Member States which is alleged to violate an international agreement binding on the EU, or which otherwise violates the obligation of sincere cooperation by jeopardizing EU objectives in the external relations field. In the *Open Skies* cases, the Commission brought proceedings against a number of Member States which had entered bilateral negotiations with the United States on air transport agreements, and the ECJ found that they had infringed the EU's external competence.[141]

In a case concerning the negotiation of issues relating to a mixed environmental agreement, the Court ruled that Sweden had violated the obligation of sincere cooperation and weakened the EU's unity and negotiating stance by its unilateral proposal to list a particular substance before the EU had had time to propose a position on that issue, in an area of shared EU–Member State competence.[142]

In other cases, the Netherlands was condemned for charging excessive and discriminatory fees for residence permits under the EC–Turkey Association Agreement,[143] and Ireland was condemned for failing to adhere to the Berne Convention on copyright.[144] Finally, in an important set of judgments the Court ruled that Sweden and Austria had breached Article 351 TFEU (ex Article 307 EC) by failing to eliminate the incompatibilities between the provisions of the then EC Treaty on the free movement of capital, and the bilateral investment treaties they had concluded with non-Member States prior to their accession to the EU.[145]

---

[138] Case C–300/95 *Commission v United Kingdom* [1997] ECR I–2649.

[139] Contrast Case C–338/91 *Steenhorst-Neerings* [1993] ECR I–5475, in which the ECJ ruled that where a Member State had not implemented a dir properly, the capacity of national courts to read apparently inconsistent national legislation in a way which conformed with the unimplemented dir would not absolve the Member State from the obligation to implement properly.

[140] Case C–129/00 *Commission v Italy* [2003] ECR I–14637, [33].

[141] Cases C–466–476/98 *Commission v United Kingdom et al* [2002] ECR I–9855.

[142] Case C–246/07 *Commission v Sweden* EU:C:2010:203; also Cases C–266/03 *Commission v Luxembourg* [2005] ECR I–4805 and C–433/03 *Commission v Germany* [2005] ECR I–6985, concerning Germany's and Luxembourg's failure to consult the Commission before ratifying a waterways agreement with non-Member States and Case C–45/07 *Commission v Greece* EU:C:2009:81 concerning a monitoring proposal made by Greece to the International Maritime Organization which would have interfered with an EU reg on enhancing ship and port facility security.

[143] Case C–92/07 *Commission v Netherlands* EU:C:2010:228. For a similar case against the Netherlands, but in relation to long-term resident third-country nationals under EU law, see Case C–508/10 *Commission v Netherlands* EU:C:2012:243.

[144] Case C–13/00 *Commission v Ireland* [2002] ECR I–2943.

[145] Cases C–249/06 *Commission v Sweden* [2009] ECR I–1335; C–205/06 *Commission v Austria* [2009] ECR I–1301. Compare Case C–264/09 *Commission v Slovakia* EU:C:2011:580 in which the CJEU ruled that Art 351 TFEU (ex Art 307

(D) SYSTEMIC AND PERSISTENT BREACHES OR GENERAL PRACTICES

The Commission has at times used the infringement procedure to monitor ongoing Member State implementation of a particular set of laws, and in some cases to challenge relatively minor breaches where they are part of a pattern of inadequate implementation and compliance in practice.[146] Even when legislation is properly implemented, a state may be held in breach if an administrative practice infringes EU law, at least in circumstances where the practice is consistent and general.[147] In such cases, according to the Court, the Member State's failure to fulfil obligations can be established only by means of 'sufficiently documented and detailed proof of the alleged practice of the national administration and/or courts', which is different from the kind of evidence usually required when the breach concerns the terms of national legislation.[148]

In a 'pathbreaking'[149] case against Ireland in 2005, the Court ruled that a general administrative practice could be deduced from a selected number of individual infringements, enabling a finding of 'general and persistent breach' to be made against the state.[150] The Commission's proceedings against Ireland cited twelve individual complaints relating to waste disposal which allegedly violated the Waste Directive, and argued that these examples illustrated breaches of a more general nature.[151] The Commission sought judgment not only on the twelve specific complaints but also on the general and persistent nature of Ireland's deficient implementation of the Directive. Ireland counter-argued that the twelve complaints in the reasoned opinion definitively delimited the subject matter of the action against it. The ECJ however supported the Commission's stance and declared, on the basis of an examination of the individual complaints, that Ireland was generally and persistently failing in its obligation to implement the provisions of the Directive correctly.[152] In terms of the burden of proof, the ECJ ruled that once the Commission had adduced sufficient evidence (of individual complaints) to show a persistent and repeated practice of breach, it was up to the state to challenge in detail the evidence provided and the consequences flowing from it. The Commission has since pursued a number of allegations of this kind, not always successfully, but the cases are so far not numerous.[153] It has been suggested that the Commission could make good use of this kind of 'general and persistent' allegation to pursue serious violations by Member States in the field of human rights[154] and anti-discrimination,[155] in part to make up for the difficulties in using the Article 7 TEU procedure, but the Commission has

EC) provided Slovakia with a defence to an action for infringement brought against it, based on its obligations under an investment agreement with Switzerland which pre-dated its EU membership.

[146] Case C–365/97 (n 87); Comment by JC van Haersolte (2002) 39 CMLRev 407. For analysis see Implementing European Community Environmental Law, COM(2008) 773/4, [3.3(b)].

[147] Case C–494/01 (n 99); Case C–441/02 *Commission v Germany* [2006] ECR I–3449

[148] Case C–441/02 (n 147). In this case the ECJ found that the Commission had not proven that the German practice of making expulsion orders against EU citizens was sufficiently consistent and general, rather than being merely a series of isolated cases: [51]–[53].

[149] P Wennerås, 'A New Dawn for Commission Enforcement under Articles 226 and 228 EC' (2006) 43 CMLRev 31.

[150] Case C–494/01 (n 99).

[151] Ibid [20].

[152] Ibid [127], [139], [170], [171], [193].

[153] Case C–135/05 *Commission v Italy* [2007] ECR I–3475, [20]–[22], concerning waste disposal; Case C–88/07 *Commission v Spain* [2009] ECR I–1353 concerning classification of medicinal products; Case C–189/07 *Commission v Spain* [2008] ECR I–195 concerning fisheries inspection; Case C–150/07 *Commission v Portugal* [2009] ECR I–7 concerning payment of own resources to the EU. See Hadroušek (n 10), expressing some scepticism as to whether the potential of this claim of 'general and persistent infringement' can be realized.

[154] K Scheppele, 'What Can the European Commission Do When Member States Violate Basic Principles of the European Union? The Case for Systemic Infringement Actions', http://ec.europa.eu/justice/events/assises-justice-2013/files/contributions/45.princetonuniversityscheppelesystemicinfringementactionbrusselsversion_en.pdf (2013).

[155] M Dawson, E Muir, and M Claes, 'A Toolbox for Legal and Political Mobilization in EU Equality Law' in D Anagnostou, *Rights and Courts in Pursuit of Social Change* (Hart, 2014) 118.

not yet done so.[156] Nevertheless, when the political institutions failed to initiate the Article 7 procedure in response to serious democratic deficiencies and repressive measures introduced by Hungary, the Commission instead brought a number of infringement proceedings against Hungary for specific and distinct violations, including in relation to age discrimination and data processing.[157]

It should be noted that while the Court has made certain allowances for the Commission in adducing proof of general and persistent breaches, it has been fairly stringent in recent years in its requirement that the Commission in other cases should adequately discharge the burden of proof without relying on presumptions.[158]

(E) ACTION BY THE COURTS OF A MEMBER STATE

Failure by a Member State's judiciary to comply with EU law has never formed the basis of an Article 258 judgment against that state, even though the action of national courts is often implicated in a particular breach.[159] Yet the CJEU has regularly ruled that states are responsible even for action and inaction by constitutionally independent organs of the state, and has ruled in *Köbler* that a state may be liable in damages to individuals for breaches of EU law committed by national courts of final appeal.[160] It seems likely that the Commission has deliberately sought to avoid such politically sensitive cases, by bringing infringement proceedings on the basis of the breach of EU law by a national court.[161]

In 2004, however, the Commission took the unprecedented step of issuing a reasoned opinion against Sweden, citing the failure of its supreme court to make references to the ECJ under what is now Article 267 TFEU, and the absence of any law or regulation governing the procedure for making preliminary references.[162] The case did not proceed to judgment since the Swedish Government introduced procedural legislation to resolve the case.

8 STATE DEFENCES IN ENFORCEMENT PROCEEDINGS

Although Member States have not lacked ingenuity or resourcefulness in providing reasons to justify their failure to fulfil Treaty obligations,[163] the Court has rarely been receptive to such attempted

---

[156] See the Commission's own discussion of the possible use of Art 258 TFEU in relation to serious and persistent human rights violations by Member States in its communication COM(2014) 158 (n 12) above.

[157] Case C–288/12 *Commission v Hungary* EU:C:2014:237; Case C–286/12 *Commission v Hungary* EU:2012:687.

[158] Cases C–335/07 *Commission v Finland* [2009] ECR I–9459 concerning treatment of waste water; C–507/03 *Commission v Ireland* [2007] ECR I–9777; C–105/08 *Commission v Portugal* EU:C:2010:345; C–512/08 *Commission v France* EU:C:2010:579 concerning reimbursement of hospital costs from medical treatment abroad; C–110/05 *Commission v Italy* [2009] ECR I–519, [66]; C–525/12 *Commission v Germany* EU:C:2014:2202 on the Water Framework Directive; C–160/08 *Commission v Germany* EU:C:2010:230, [109]–[111] holding that it was sufficient for the Commission to establish the general practice in a particular region of the state.

[159] See, eg, Case C–129/00 (n 140). For discussion see M Taborowski, 'Infringement Proceedings and Non-Compliant National Courts' (2012) 49 CMLRev 1881.

[160] Case C–224/01 *Köbler* [2003] ECR I–10239. See Ch 8 for discussion.

[161] Rawlings (n 3); see however also the warning expressed by the ECJ in Case C–156/04 *Commission v Greece* [2007] ECR I–4129, [52].

[162] Document no C(2004)3899 of 7 Oct 2004, relating to infringement proceedings 2003/2161. The reasoned opinion was made public through the national authorities.

[163] See, eg, Case C–134/10 *Commission v Belgium* EU:C:2011:117, [16], pleading that the national provisions of which the Commission complained were in fact not being effectively applied by Belgium; Case C–165/08 *Commission v Poland* [2009] ECR I–6843, pleading ethical objections to the implementation of EU legislation on genetically modified organisms.

justification.[164] In one case in which an intervening Member State put forward a defence on behalf of the respondent state, the intervention was rejected as inadmissible and the ECJ found a breach of EU law.[165] However, there is nothing to prohibit Member States from introducing defences which they did not raise in the pre-litigation procedure, even though the Commission cannot introduce surprise complaints in the same way.[166] On the other hand, the rules of procedure provide that no new plea in law may be introduced in the course of proceedings unless it is 'based on matters of law or of fact which come to light in the course of the procedure'.[167]

Absence of apparent harm, or the fact that a Member State's infringement has had 'no adverse effects' is not a defence to infringement proceedings.[168] Luxembourg's attempt to plead *res judicata* and *ne bis in idem* on the basis that the Commission had brought a previous case based on the same facts, and its argument that the Commission should have brought Article 260 TFEU penalty proceedings rather than a fresh application under Article 258, was rejected by the ECJ, which ruled that the two sets of complaints were not identical and that the Commission was justified in opening a second procedure.[169] Indeed, the Commission may be *obliged* to bring a second set of infringement proceedings under Article 258 where there is disagreement between the state and the Commission as to whether a prior judgment of the Court has been properly enforced.[170]

One of the few potentially successful defences advanced by a Member State has been a genuine plea of *force majeure*, ie that overwhelming circumstances such as a bomb attack prevented the state from fulfilling its obligations under the Treaties.[171] However, a state cannot argue that the action of one of its independent agencies or institutions constitutes *force majeure*, since the Court has consistently held that a state is responsible for breach, 'whatever the agency of the State whose action or inaction is the cause of the failure to fulfil its obligations, even in the case of a constitutionally independent institution',[172] or in the case of a fraudulent individual.[173] Similarly the Court has consistently ruled that 'a Member State may not plead provisions, practices or circumstances existing in its internal legal system in order to justify a failure to comply with obligations and time limits laid down in Community directives'.[174]

---

[164] Case C–284/05 *Commission v Finland et al* EU:C:2009:778 for an unsuccessful invocation of the 'essential interests of security' under Arts 346–347 TFEU; see (n 1).

[165] Case C–13/00 (n 144), where the UK intervened to argue that the breach alleged constituted a violation of international law obligations and not of EU law. Compare Case C–334/08 *Commission v Italy* EU:C:2010:414, [52]–[55] in which the CJEU allowed Germany's intervention in support of Italy even though the intervention raised a point of defence which had not been raised by Italy.

[166] Case C–414/97 *Commission v Spain* [1999] ECR I–5585

[167] Case C–526/08 *Commission v Luxembourg* EU:C:2010:379, [48]–[50].

[168] Cases C–150/97 *Commission v Portugal* [1999] ECR I–259; C–36/05 *Commission v Spain* [2006] ECR I–10313.

[169] Case C–526/08 *Commission v Luxembourg* EU:C:2010:379, [21]–[35]. See also Case C–529/09 *Commission v Spain* EU:C:2013:31.

[170] Case C–292/11 P *Commission v Portugal* EU:C:2014:3.

[171] Case 33/69 *Commission v Italy* [1970] ECR 93, [16]. However, even in this case the Court was not satisfied that the bomb attack rendered compliance excessively difficult by the time proceedings were brought. See also Cases 70/86 *Commission v Greece* [1987] ECR 3545; C–334/87 *Greece v Commission* [1990] ECR I–2849, [11], for a definition of *force majeure* in other circumstances.

[172] Case 77/69 *Commission v Belgium* [1970] ECR 237, [15].

[173] Case C–334/08 *Commission v Italy* EU:C:2010:414, [46]–[49], where the fraudulent individual was an official within the Italian administration.

[174] Case 280/83 *Commission v Italy* [1984] ECR 2361, [4]; Case 160/82 (n 136); Case 215/83 *Commission v Belgium* [1985] ECR 1039; Case C–298/97 *Commission v Spain* [1998] ECR I–3301; Case C–326/97 *Commission v Belgium* [1998] ECR I–6107. For discussion of the problem of regional non-implementation of EU law within a state, see C Bertolino, 'State Accountability for Violation of EU Law by Regions: Infringement Proceedings and the Right of Recourse' (2013) 5 Perspectives on Federalism 156.

The Court has been similarly dismissive of arguments by Member States that they were not at fault, that the breach was not deliberate,[175] or that it was 'minor'.[176] The Court looks only to see whether or not the infringement has taken place as alleged, and no moral wrongdoing on the part of the state need be shown.[177]

Member States have sometimes argued by way of defence that other Member States are also in breach, as though the obligation to comply with EU law were a reciprocal one which depends on full compliance by other states, but this has been rejected by the ECJ.[178] Since *Van Gend en Loos*[179] the Court has distinguished EU law from other forms and principles of international law,[180] in which the reciprocity principle has a more central role.

Another defence occasionally raised by a Member State is that the EU measure on which the infringement proceedings are based is illegal or invalid. In proceedings against Greece in 1988, however, the Court rejected this argument and ruled that 'a Member State cannot plead the unlawfulness of a decision addressed to it' as a defence in infringement proceedings brought against it for failure to implement that decision.[181] The rationale is that if the Member State wanted to challenge the decision, that state had an opportunity to bring a direct action for annulment under Article 263 TFEU, within two months of the decision being addressed to the state. On the other hand, a plea of illegality might be permitted by way of defence to an action under Article 258 where the EU measure was so gravely flawed as to be legally 'non-existent' and void *ab initio*, or where the earlier measure was not a decision addressed to the Member State in question, but a regulation whose illegality might not have been apparent to the Member State until the Commission brought enforcement proceedings.[182] It is also possible that the Court might also permit the illegality of the decision to be pleaded in Article 258 proceedings in an extreme case where the decision infringes a principle of a constitutional nature.[183]

An interesting situation of this kind arose recently following infringement proceedings brought by the Commission against Sweden and Germany for failure to transpose the data retention Directive 2006/24. This Directive was subsequently declared invalid by the CJEU in preliminary reference proceedings, the *Digital Rights Ireland* case, for violation of the right to respect for private life and protection of personal data in Articles 7 and 8 of the Charter of Fundamental Rights.[184] While the infringement proceedings pending against Germany were promptly withdrawn by the Commission,[185] the case against Sweden had proceeded much further and had already resulted in a lump sum penalty

---

[175] Case 301/81 *Commission v Belgium* [1983] ECR 467, [8]; Case C–385/02 *Commission v Italy* [2004] ECR I–8121, [40].

[176] Case C–43/97 *Commission v Italy* [1997] ECR I–4671.

[177] See however Case C–146/89 *Commission v United Kingdom* [1991] ECR I–3533, in which the Court was sufficiently impressed by the 'exemplary conduct' of the UK in later voluntarily remedying its breach to order each party to bear its own costs.

[178] See, eg, Cases C–146/89 (n 177); C–266/03 *Commission v Luxembourg* [2005] ECR I–4805.

[179] Case 26/62 [1963] ECR 1.

[180] Case 52/75 *Commission v Italy* [1976] ECR 277, [11].

[181] Case 226/87 *Commission v Greece* [1988] ECR 3611, [14] (public sector insurance). For a somewhat similar attempt to plead unlawful conduct on the part of the Commission as a defence to infringement proceedings against the state, see Case C–37/11 *Commission v Czech Republic* EU:C:2012:640, [31]–[36].

[182] See AG Mancini in Case 204/86 *Commission v Greece* [1988] ECR 5323, 5343–5345; Case 226/87 *Commission v Greece* [1988] ECR 3611, 3617. For an unsuccessful attempt to plead the illegality of a dir (rather than a dec) which the state had failed to implement see Case C–74/91 *Commission v Germany* [1992] ECR I–5437.

[183] Cases 6 and 11/69 *Commission v France* [1969] ECR 523; Case 70/72 *Commission v Germany* [1973] ECR 813; Case 156/77 *Commission v Belgium* [1978] ECR 1881.

[184] Case C–293/12 *Digital Rights Ireland v Minister for Communications* and Case C–594/12 *Kärntner Landesregierung* EU:C:2014:238.

[185] The proceedings in Case C–329/12 *Commission v Germany* EU:C:2014:2034 were withdrawn by the Commission after the annulment of the Dir in Case C–293/12 *Digital Rights Ireland* (n 184).

ordered by the CJEU in Article 260 proceedings.[186] It has been suggested that Sweden should be refunded any amount it paid by way of penalty, and that the problem would have been avoided had the state—which had serious reservations about the data retention Directive—been able to plead its invalidity in the course of the infringement proceedings.[187]

9 THE CONSEQUENCES OF AN ARTICLE 258 RULING

A weakness of the Article 258 procedure, at least until the pecuniary penalty provision was intro duced into Article 260 by the Maastricht Treaty, was that the only ruling which the Court could make against a defaulting Member State in Article 258 proceedings was a finding of violation. This indeed remains true even after the introduction of the penalty payment procedure, insofar as the CJEU can-not order the adoption of any specific measures in Article 258 proceedings, nor otherwise dictate the consequences of its judgment in those proceedings.[188] One possibility which has been raised by Member States, however, is that the CJEU might rule that the retroactive effect of its judgment will be limited. In the group of 'own-resources' cases against a number of Member States decided in 2009, the Court refused the requests of the states concerned to limit the retroactive effect of the judgment, but did not rule out the possibility of doing so in a different context.

10 ARTICLE 259

In addition to the Commission's enforcement power under Article 258, Article 259 TFEU provides a means for any Member State to initiate an action against another state which it considers to be in breach of the Treaty. Article 259 provides:

> A Member State which considers that another Member State has failed to fulfil an obligation under the Treaties may bring the matter before the Court of Justice.
>
> Before a Member State brings an action against another Member State for an alleged infringement of an obligation under the Treaties, it shall bring the matter before the Commission.
>
> The Commission shall deliver a reasoned opinion after each of the States concerned has been given the opportunity to submit its own case and its observations on the other party's case both orally and in writing.
>
> If the Commission has not delivered an opinion within three months of the date on which the matter was brought before it, the absence of such opinion shall not prevent the matter from being brought before the Court.

Unlike under Article 258, the Member State bringing the action does not first have to contact the Member State which is the subject of the complaint. Instead the matter must initially be brought by the complainant state before the Commission. The procedure thereafter is similar to that under Article 258, except that in the case of Article 259 both states must be heard and given a chance to make

---

[186] See Case C–185/09 *Commission v Sweden* EU:C:2010:59 for the Art 258 proceedings, followed by Case C–270/11 *Commission v Sweden* EU:C:2013:339 for the Art 260 lump sum penalty Sweden was ordered to pay.

[187] See N Wunderlich and B Hickl, 'Zum Einwand der Grundrechtswidrigkeit von Richtlinien in Vertragsverletzungsverfahren vor dem Europäischen Gerichtshof' (2013) Europarecht 107.

[188] See, eg, Case C–104/02 *Commission v Germany* [2005] ECR I–2689, [48]–[51], concerning whether the Court could order the Member State to pay default interest.

oral and written submissions before the Commission gives its reasoned opinion. The complainant state may bring the case to the CJEU even when the Commission considers that there is no breach.

Article 259 has only rarely been used,[189] no doubt because of the ill-will it could occasion between Member States, and because of their preference for resolving disputes by political means.[190] States also have the option of intervening in a case brought by the Commission to support its allegations, although they more often intervene in support of the Member State. Where political solutions fail, however, and where the Commission chooses not to bring proceedings, states have occasionally had recourse to the Article 259 mechanism.[191] In 2000 Spain brought an action against the UK concerning the way in which the UK extended voting rights in European Parliament elections to residents of Gibraltar.[192] The Commission encouraged the two states to resolve the dispute amicably and declined to issue a reasoned opinion, 'given the sensitivity of the underlying bilateral issue',[193] but the CJEU upheld the conduct of the UK and found against Spain. Similarly, the Court dismissed an action brought by Hungary against Slovakia for refusing to allow the President of Hungary to enter Slovakian territory.[194]

11 ARTICLE 260 TFEU: THE PECUNIARY PENALTY

The provision for a penalty payment to be imposed against a Member State which has failed to comply with a previous enforcement judgment of the Court was first introduced into Article 260 TFEU (then Article 171 EEC) by the Maastricht Treaty. It was intended to give teeth to the infringement procedure, and to provide a sharper incentive for Member States to comply with CJEU rulings against them. Prior to the existence of the penalty payment option, the only way provided under Article 260 to 'enforce' compliance with a judgment against a Member State under Article 258 was by bringing the state before the Court again for a second declaratory ruling. Following its amendment by the Lisbon Treaty in 2009, Article 260 provides:

> 1. If the Court of Justice of the European Union finds that a Member State has failed to fulfil an obligation under the Treaties, the State shall be required to take the necessary measures to comply with the judgment of the Court.
> 2. If the Commission considers that the Member State concerned has not taken the necessary measures to comply with the judgment of the Court, it may bring the case before the Court after giving that State the opportunity to submit its observations. It shall specify the amount of the lump sum or penalty payment to be paid by the Member State concerned which it considers appropriate in the circumstances.

---

[189] Note that Ireland chose to bring proceedings against the UK concerning the MOX nuclear plant before a Tribunal of the International Convention on the Law of the Sea rather than before the ECJ, and was chastised accordingly by the Court in Case C–459/03 *Commission v Ireland* [2006] ECR I–4635 for violating Art 344 TFEU.

[190] In 1984 the procedure was set in motion by the Commission in response to a complaint from France against the Netherlands, which led to a reasoned opinion by the Commission: see Case 169/84 *Cofaz v Commission* [1986] ECR 391, [6].

[191] Case 141/78 *France v United Kingdom* [1979] ECR 2923 (fishing dispute); Cases C–388/95 *Belgium v Spain* [2000] ECR I–3121 (rules of origin for wine); C–364/10 *Hungary v Slovakia* EU:C:2012:630 (freedom of inter-state movement for the Head of State).

[192] Case C–145/04 *Spain v United Kingdom* [2006] ECR I–7917. The UK's action had been a response to the judgment of the European Court of Human Rights in App No 24833/94 *Matthews v United Kingdom*, judgment of 18 Feb 1999.

[193] Case C–145/04 (n 192) [32].

[194] Case C–364/10 *Hungary v Slovakia* (n 191).

> If the Court of Justice finds that the Member State concerned has not complied with its judgment it may impose a lump sum or penalty payment on it.
>
> This procedure shall be without prejudice to Article 259.
>
> 3. When the Commission brings a case before the Court pursuant to Article 258 on the grounds that the Member State concerned has failed to fulfil its obligation to notify measures transposing a directive adopted under a legislative procedure, it may, when it deems appropriate, specify the amount of the lump sum or penalty payment to be paid by the Member State concerned which it considers appropriate in the circumstances.
>
> If the Court finds that there is an infringement it may impose a lump sum or penalty payment on the Member State concerned, not exceeding the amount specified by the Commission. The payment obligation shall take effect on the date set by the Court in its judgment.

Two changes were introduced into Article 260 by the Lisbon Treaty in 2009. The first is that the Commission is no longer obliged, as it previously was under paragraph 2, to issue a reasoned opinion before bringing a Member State before the CJEU for non-compliance with an Article 258 ruling.[195] This amendment is likely to make the penalty procedure somewhat speedier and more efficient. The second change is in the newly-introduced paragraph 3, which provides that the Commission may move directly to seek a pecuniary penalty against a Member State where the state has failed to notify measures transposing an EU directive.[196] In other words, the possibility of imposing a penalty payment on a Member State for breach of EU law is extended beyond the circumstances of non-compliance with an Article 258 ruling of the Court to include another common form of violation. Another notable aspect of the new paragraph 3, which is absent from paragraph 2, is that the Court, in imposing a penalty payment for non-transposition, may not exceed the amount specified by the Commission. It has been noted that the concept of 'failure to notify' is rather a vague one, creating uncertainties as to when Article 258 or Article 260(3) is the correct procedure to use, and widening the scope of the Commission's discretion in a potentially problematic way.[197] At the time of writing, there have been no judgments under Article 260(3) in which a penalty payment was ordered, and although at least fifteen sets of proceedings have been brought under this provision, all were withdrawn by the Commission after implementation of the Directive.[198]

No upper limit to the amount of penalty which can be imposed by the Court in Article 260 proceedings is specified,[199] and the Court is not bound to follow the proposal of the Commission, other than in not exceeding the penalty proposed in cases of non-transposition under paragraph 3. There is no formal mechanism for collection of the payment should a Member State refuse to comply,[200]

---

[195] For discussion of these changes see the Opinion of AG Mázak in Case C–610/10 *Commission v Spain* EU:C:2012:530, an Art 260 case to enforce the judgment in Case C–499/99 *Commission v Spain* [2002] ECR I–6031. Spain argued that the procedure should have been conducted in accordance with the pre-Lisbon Treaty provisions, including a reasoned opinion, but the CJEU disagreed: see EU:C:2012:781.

[196] In 2011 the Commission published a Communication on the implementation of Art 260(3) [2011] OJ C12/1, setting out its policy on the application of the new provision. The Commission stated that it would not be used in the case of non-legislative dirs and—perhaps surprisingly—that it could be used in cases of partial notification and not only total failure to notify.

[197] See S Gáspár-Szilági, 'What Constitutes "Failure to Notify" National Measures?' (2012) 19 EPL 281, and A Sikora, 'Financial Penalties for Non-Execution of the Judgment of the Court of Justice of the EU' in A Lazowski and S Blockmans (eds), *Research Handbook on EU Institutional Law* (Edward Elgar, 2014).

[198] See, eg, Case C–545/12 *Commission v Cyprus* EU:C:2013:329.

[199] Art 261 TFEU, which provides for the imposition of penalties by the Court under regs adopted by the Council and the Parliament, also specifies that the Court's jurisdiction under such legislation may be unlimited.

[200] For a critical analysis see M Theodossiou, 'An Analysis of the Recent Response of the Community to Non-Compliance with Court of Justice Judgments: Art 228' (2003) 27 ELRev 25.

although it is generally assumed that the Commission may withhold payments which may be due to the Member State under other EU law funds. Further, Article 260 provides no possibility for the Commission to seek an injunction from the Court,[201] and the Court may not order a Member State to take specific action in such proceedings.[202] The CJEU has also indicated that it has no jurisdiction under Article 260 to require Member States to comply with its judgment within a specified period of time.[203]

Initially it seemed that, unlike a declaratory judgment under Article 258 which would be given by the CJEU even where the Member State had complied with the Commission's reasoned opinion before judgment, so long as the state had not complied before the expiry of the period laid down in the reasoned opinion, the CJEU would not impose a penalty under Article 260 in circumstances where the Member State had complied before the date of the Article 260 judgment.[204] However, with the introduction of lump sum payments to penalize a state's breach which continues between the date of the initial Article 258 judgment and the date of the Article 260 judgment, the Court made clear that it is entirely appropriate to impose a lump sum payment, although not a periodic penalty, where Member State non-compliance with an earlier judgment has continued after the date set by the Commission in the reasoned opinion, even where it has ceased by the time the Court gives judgment in the Article 260 proceedings.[205] On the other hand, it is clear that the success of Article 260 cases depends largely on the quality of the evidence submitted by the Commission,[206] and there may be invidious effects for individual complainants when the Commission fails to bring sufficient evidence to prove its allegations.[207]

The Commission nowadays makes relatively frequent use of the procedure for proposing pecuniary penalties.[208] In its 2013 annual report, the Commission lamented that no less than 113 judgments (forty of which concerned the environment) given under Article 258 TFEU had still not been fully complied with by the Member States concerned.[209] The number of cases actually referred to the Court

---

[201] Although the Court has a general power to order injunctive measures in interim proceedings under Art 279 TFEU, it does not have these powers under Art 260, when giving judgment in infringement proceedings.

[202] Case C–105/02 *Commission v Germany* [2006] ECR I–9659, [44]–[45].

[203] Case C–473/93 *Commission v Luxembourg* [1996] ECR I–3207, [51]–[52]. However, in Case C–291/93 *Commission v Italy* [1994] ECR I–859, [6], the ECJ ruled that, although Art 260 TFEU (ex Art 228 EC) did not specify the period within which a judgment must be complied with, the interest in the immediate and uniform application of EU law required compliance as soon as possible.

[204] See Case C–119/04 *Commission v Italy* [2006] ECR I–6885, concerning the long-running complaint about nationality discrimination against foreign-language university lecturers, where the Court did not impose the penalty requested by the Commission on the basis that Italy appeared to have substantially complied by the date the Court examined the facts. It has been argued that Italy had not at all complied with the previous judgment, and that the law it had introduced in purported compliance with that earlier judgment had left the affected individuals in a worse position than they were under the original discriminatory employment conditions. See H Rodgers, Parliament Magazine, Feb 2007. Also D Petrie, 'EU's Role in Ghettoisation of Foreign Lecturers in Italy', www.italianinsider.it/?q=node/2168.

[205] See, eg, Case C–304/02 *Commission v France* [2005] ECR I–6263. The Commission had made this suggestion in its memo on the penalty payment: SEC(2005) 1658. See also Cases C–568/07 *Commission v Greece* [2009] ECR I–4504; C–121/07 *Commission v France* [2008] ECR I–9159. Compare Case C–503/04 *Commission v Germany* [2007] ECR I–6153, in which the ECJ imposed neither a lump sum nor a periodic penalty, and Case C–369/07 *Commission v Greece* [2009] ECR I–5703, in which the ECJ imposed both, finding that the breach was continuing at the date of judgment.

[206] See, eg, Case C–457/07 *Commission v Portugal* [2009] ECR I–8091 in which the ECJ dismissed all five complaints brought by the Commission against Portugal for a mixture of procedural and evidentiary reasons.

[207] See above (n 204) on the Italian foreign-language lecturers case. There have been many follow-up questions by MEPs to the Commission in recent years, including E-000936/2013, E-004135/2013, and E-011051/2013 concerning the ongoing discrimination, and a petition has been brought before the petitions committee of the EP.

[208] For earlier criticism of its under-use see European Parliament resolution on the Commission's 21st and 22nd Annual Reports on monitoring the application of Community law (2003 and 2004), P6_TA(2006)0202.

[209] 31st Annual Monitoring Report on 2013, COM(2014) 612 final, p 13.

under Article 260 is significantly lower than the number initiated, and many cases are closed by the Commission when the state complies.[210] It seems that repeated referrals under Article 260 TFEU are sometimes necessary until the Member State eventually complies: this was done in nine out of the 113 Article 260 TFEU cases in 2013, eleven out of 128 in 2012, and eleven out of seventy-seven in 2011.[211] The Commission also now provides a list in its annual reports of all Article 258 judgments with which individual Member States have not yet complied, together with an indication of what action it is taking (under Article 260 or otherwise) against those states.

In 1996, before the development of case law on the calculation of penalties under Article 260, the Commission published guidelines and a memorandum proposing a method for calculation.[212] The Commission argued that the amount should reflect the aim of the sanction, ie to secure effective compliance with EU law as quickly as possible, and that the most appropriate means of achieving this aim would be a periodic penalty running from the date of service of the Court's judgment. The guidelines suggested that penalties should always be deterrent and never purely symbolic. The daily penalty should be calculated on the basis of three criteria: (i) the seriousness of the infringement (including not only failure to comply with a Court judgment, but also the seriousness of the original infringement in terms of both effects and symbolism); (ii) its duration;[213] and (iii) the need to ensure that the penalty itself is a deterrent to further infringements. The method of calculation should involve a uniform flat-rate amount per day of delay to penalize the violation of the principle of legality, multiplied by factors (the coefficient) reflecting the seriousness of the infringement and its duration,[214] and by a factor representing the ability of the Member State to pay and the number of votes it has in the Council.[215] Following several rulings by the Court which built on this non-binding guidance, the Commission amended and supplemented its memorandum in 2005 and 2010, following the ECJ's lead in particular on the issue of lump sum payments, and updated every year in order to reflect annual economic data.[216]

Ever since the Court's first ruling on the pecuniary penalty in 2000,[217] it has repeatedly emphasized that, while agreeing with much of the guidance published by the Commission, the Court is not bound by the Commission's advice.[218] In proceedings against Spain concerning non-compliance with a judgment on the quality of bathing water, the Court rejected the Commission's proposal to impose a daily penalty on Spain, and instead imposed an annual penalty to be assessed on an ongoing basis so as to reflect the progress towards compliance effected by Spain.[219] This was because of the nature of the breach and the difficulty of showing, until a considerable period of time after, that the quality of

---

[210] For cases withdrawn by the Commission once the state had complied, see eg Case C–241/11 *Commission v Czech Republic* EU:C:2013:423; Case C–279/11 *Commission v Ireland* EU:C:2012:834; Case C–407/09 *Commission v Greece* EU:C:2011:196.

[211] See COM(2014) 612 final, COM(2013) 726 final, and COM(2012) 714 final. For a query whether the figures given by the Commission truly reflect the number of cases actually referred to the ECJ see I Kilbey, 'The Interpretation of Article 260 TFEU (ex 228 EC)' (2010) 35 ELRev 370, 383.

[212] See [1996] OJ C242/6 and [1997] OJ C63/2; for discussion see Theodossiou (n 200).

[213] For criticism of the way in which duration is used in the calculation of penalties, see Jack (n 10).

[214] See the Commission's internal decision on the 'duration coefficient' in PV(2001) 1517/2 of 2 Apr 2001.

[215] For criticism of the criteria used to determine ability to pay see I Kilbey (n 211). See also Jack (n 10).

[216] SEC(2005) 1658, SEC(2010) 923. The latter has been revised each year since, with updated macro-economic data: SEC(2011) 1024, C(2012) 6106, C(2013) 8101, and C(2014) 6767. While lump sum payments had not been ruled out in its initial guidelines, the Commission had expressed a strong preference for periodic penalties, and in practice it had never proposed a lump sum penalty to the Court. The case law of the Court prompted the Commission to change its guidelines in this respect.

[217] Case C–387/97 *Commission v Greece* [2000] ECR I–5047.

[218] Ibid [87]–[89]. Although the Court did rule against Greece and imposed a penalty, it reduced the amount of the periodic penalty payment proposed by the Commission.

[219] Case C–278/01 *Commission v Spain* [2003] ECR I–14141; Comment M Ruffert (2004) 41 CMLRev 1387.

bathing water conformed to the limit values set by EU law.[220] In a recent case against Greece involving landfill sites, the Court rejected both the Commission's and the Advocate General's proposal of a daily penalty in favour of a six-monthly penalty in addition to a lump sum, enabling a more proportionate and graduated penalty which would allow account to be taken of Greece's gradual progress towards compliance with the earlier judgment.[221] In proceedings against France involving inadequate implementation of the Products Liability Directive, the Court rejected the Commission's guidelines for calculating the coefficient relating to the duration of the infringement.[222] The Court also raised both the base sum and the coefficient proposed by the Commission in a case against Portugal for non-implementation of a judgment concerning state liability in the field of public contracts.[223] More generally, the CJEU seems to strive to find ways, in the complex process of calculating the pecuniary penalty, to bring a degree of proportionality to bear on the amount imposed, and to take account of progress towards compliance.[224]

The ECJ imposed its first clear stamp on the penalty payment procedure in 2005, by subjecting France to a lump sum penalty payment for a long-standing violation, even though the Commission had not recommended it.[225] The case, in which sixteen other Member States intervened, was brought against France for non-compliance with a judgment dating from 1991 concerning the monitoring and implementation of EU rules on fisheries conservation. Twelve of the intervening states argued that the Treaty text, as well as considerations of policy and principle, militated against the concurrent imposition of a lump sum and a periodic penalty. The Court however dismissed their arguments:

Case C-304/02 **Commission v France**
[2005] ECR I-6263

80. The procedure laid down in Article 228(2) EC [now Art 260(2) TFEU] has the objective of inducing a defaulting Member State to comply with a judgment establishing a breach of obligations and thereby of ensuring that Community law is in fact applied. The measures provided for by that provision, namely a lump sum and a penalty payment, are both intended to achieve this objective.

81. Application of each of those measures depends on their respective ability to meet the objective pursued according to the circumstances of the case. While the imposition of a penalty payment seems particularly suited to inducing a Member State to put an end as soon as possible to a breach of obligations which, in the absence of such a measure, would tend to persist, the imposition of a lump sum is based more on assessment of the effects on public and private interests of the failure of the Member State concerned to comply with its obligations, in particular where the breach has persisted for a long period since the judgment which initially established it.

---

220 The Court did similarly in Case C–304/02 (n 205), varying the periodic penalty proposed by the Commission and imposing it on a half-yearly rather than a daily basis, to allow progress towards compliance to be measured.

221 Case C–378/13 *Commission v Greece* EU:C:2014:2405. See also Case C–196/13 *Commission v Italy* EU:C:2014:2407 and Case C–496/09 *Commission v Italy* EU:C:2011:111483.

222 Case C–177/04 *Commission v France* (n 97).

223 Case C–70/06 *Commission v Portugal* [2008] ECR I–1. The reason given by the ECJ for raising it was that the coefficient proposed by the Commission did not reflect the growth of Portugal's GDP, and hence its ability to pay. Note that Portugal challenged the Commission's enforcement of the penalty which had been imposed by the ECJ in Case 70/06 above. See Case T–33/09 *Portugal v Commission* EU:T:2011:127, which was appealed to the CJEU in Case C–292/11 P *Commission v Portugal* EU:C:2014:3. See (n 234) and text below for discussion.

224 Case C–533/11 *Commission v Belgium* EU:C:2013:659, [70]–[73] on treatment of urban wastewater.

225 Case C–304/02 (n 205). In a subsequent case against France in which the Commission had requested only a periodic penalty and not a lump sum, the ECJ considered whether a lump sum should nonetheless be imposed, but concluded that it should not: Case C–177/04 (n 97).

82. That being so, recourse to both types of penalty provided for in Article 228(2) EC [*now Art 260(2) TFEU*] is not precluded, in particular where the breach of obligations both has continued for a long period and is inclined to persist.

The Court took the view that the absence of any Commission guidelines for the imposition of a lump sum penalty did not lead to any violation of the principle of legal certainty, nor did the fact that the Commission had not proposed the imposition of a lump sum penalty in this particular case present any obstacle to the imposition of such a penalty by the Court. The ECJ declared that the financial penalties should be decided upon 'according to the degree of persuasion needed in order for the Member State in question to alter its conduct'.[226] The rights of defence of the Member State were not affected by its being unable to put forward arguments against a lump sum, in the Court's view, because the Article 228(2) (now Article 260(2) TFEU) procedure was to be viewed as a method of enforcement of the earlier judgment, following a finding, based on *inter partes* proceedings, that a breach of EU law persisted.[227]

The Court's reasoning on the amount of the lump sum penalty was however minimal. In two brief paragraphs the Court simply stated that:

114. In a situation such as that which is the subject of the present judgment, in light of the fact that the breach of obligations has persisted for a long period since the judgment which initially established it and of the public and private interests at issue, it is essential to order payment of a lump sum...

115. The specific circumstances of the case are fairly assessed by setting the amount of the lump sum which the French Republic will have to pay at EUR 20 000 000.

Following the case, the Commission amended its guidelines to refer to the desirability of a lump sum payment where Member States have delayed compliance considerably, and also to the principle of proportionality and equal treatment of the Member States, which had been emphasized by the ECJ in other Article 260 judgments,[228] as well as to the need for sanctions to be foreseeable.[229] The Commission indicated that it would henceforth propose at least a minimum lump sum payment to the Court in every Article 260 case, to reflect 'the principle that any case of persistent non-compliance...in itself represents an attack on the principle of legality'.[230]

The Commission made a range of other recommendations in its 2005 memo, for example proposing that distinct sanctions could be imposed for distinct infringements within the context of a single case, to allow for greater precision and adaptability. It listed certain factors which could aggravate or mitigate the seriousness of a breach for the purposes of calculating the penalty due. Drawing on the Spanish bathing water and French fisheries cases, the Commission proposed to allow for adjustment of sanctions to reflect partial or gradual compliance, and for periods such as six months or a year, rather than only daily penalties. The Court appears to have done so in several cases since.[231]

The Commission in its 2005 memo also proposed a procedure to allow for the suspension of penalties after appropriate verification of compliance with conditions set down by the Court, though such a procedure has not been adopted. Yet the question of how to verify whether a judgment of the Court has been complied with is not an easy one, as recent cases show. On the one

---

[226] Case C–304/02 (n 205) [90]–[91].
[227] Ibid [93].
[228] Case C–378/97 *Commission v Greece* [2000] ECR I–5047; Case C–278/01 (n 219).
[229] SEC(2005) 1658.
[230] Ibid [20].
[231] See n 220 above.

hand, states have unsuccessfully challenged the Commission's decision that they had not complied with a previous judgment[232] while on the other hand the CJEU has dismissed the claim of the Commission in an Article 260 proceedings that a state had failed to comply with a previous judgment.[233] The question whether the Commission has the authority to determine whether a state has complied with an Article 258 judgment, and the question how a dispute between the Commission and the state on that matter should be resolved, were recently addressed in a case brought by Portugal against the Commission to challenge the Commission's decision that it should pay a penalty for non-compliance with a judgment.[234] The General Court annulled the Commission's decision, and the CJEU on appeal ruled that where there was a disagreement between the state and the Commission as to whether the state had fully complied, the Commission must bring the matter back to the CJEU in fresh proceedings under Article 258 and could not take the decision for itself. In reaching this conclusion the CJEU emphasized its own exclusive jurisdiction to determine whether a Member State has complied with EU law:

> The Court of Justice thus enjoys, in this regard, exclusive jurisdiction which is directly and expressly conferred on it by the Treaty and on which the Commission cannot encroach when checking whether there has been compliance with a judgment delivered by the Court of Justice pursuant to Article 260(2) TFEU.[235]

The Court has continued to impose lump sum payments in many of its judgments,[236] and has followed much of the guidance proposed by the Commission as to the calculation of penalties, occasionally imposing both a lump sum and a periodic penalty cumulatively.[237] However, the Court has firmly rejected the Commission's suggestion of the automatic imposition of a lump sum in any case where the Member State has not complied by the date set in the reasoned opinion, and emphasized that the decision whether or not to impose a lump sum (or periodic penalty) lies within the discretion of the Court taking all the relevant circumstances into account.[238] Further, it has been pointed out that the Court has generally imposed lower sums than those proposed both by the Commission and the Advocate General.[239]

The Article 260 mechanism clearly represents the sharp end of the overall enforcement procedure, with a distinctly less diplomatic and more formal legal flavour than the Article 258 stage. This is sharpened further by the Lisbon Treaty's abolition of the requirement of a reasoned opinion by the

---

[232] Shortly after the fisheries judgment, Case C–304/02 *Commission v France* [2005] ECR I–6263, imposing both a lump sum and a six-monthly periodic penalty, France challenged the Commission's claim that France was continuing its failure to comply fully with the original judgment under Art 258 and should pay the periodic penalty, but this challenge was dismissed by the General Court: Case T–139/06 *France v Commission* EU:T:2011:605.

[233] See, eg, Case C–95/12 *Commission v Germany* EU:C:2013:676 in which the CJEU dismissed the Commission's claim that Germany had failed to comply with an earlier judgment of the Court against it. AG Wahl in his opinion cautioned against attempts to ascertain the 'subjective meaning' of a judgment: EU:C:2013:333, [26].

[234] Case T–33/09 *Portugal v Commission* EU:T:2011:127 on appeal to the CJEU in Case C–292/11 P *Commission v Portugal* EU:C:2014:3.

[235] Case C–292/11 P, ibid [50].

[236] Case C–109/08 *Commission v Greece* [2009] ECR I–4657 concerning a prohibition on electronic games outside casinos, in which Greece argued both that the penalty payment was too high and that a lump sum was inappropriate, but the ECJ followed the Commission's proposal and imposed both; Case C–568/07 *Commission v Greece* [2009] ECR I–4505 concerning freedom of establishment for opticians; Case C–121/07 *Commission v France* [2008] ECR I–9159, concerning deliberate release of GMOs.

[237] Case C–369/07 *Commission v Greece* [2009] ECR I–5703, concerning aid to Olympic Airways; Case C–109/08 (n 236); Case C–374/11 *Commission v Ireland* EU:C:2012:827; Case C–610/10, *Commission v Spain* EU:C:2012:781.

[238] See, eg, Case C–121/07 *Commission v France* [2008] ECR I–9159, [61]–[64].

[239] Wennerås (n 9).

Commission, and by the new possibility of seeking a pecuniary penalty for non-transposition of a directive without any prior infringement ruling by the CJEU under Article 258. However, it is also evident that the burden remains on the Commission to marshal the appropriate evidence against the Member State before the CJEU,[240] and that a failure to do so in Article 260 proceedings may even undermine the effect of a previous Article 258 judgment against a state.[241] Further, even though a Member State's GDP and ability to pay is taken into account in calculating the penalty, this issue has been sharpened even more by the effects of the Euro crisis, particularly on the most heavily indebted countries, highlighting the importance of taking into account changes in the situation of those states.[242] Finally, it is clear that many questions remain about the overall coercive or dissuasive impact of pecuniary penalties and their effectiveness in achieving the goals sought, as well as their possible impact on other public and private interests.[243]

12 INTERIM MEASURES

Under Articles 278 and 279 TFEU the CJEU has the power to prescribe interim measures which it considers to be necessary in a case which has been brought before it.[244] Although interim measures may be sought in any case before the CJEU,[245] they may be particularly useful for the Commission to seek at the same time as proceedings under Article 258.[246]

When in Article 258 proceedings a breach is found, the Court simply declares that the Member State has failed to fulfil its obligations, and its ruling does not have any effect on the impugned national rule or provision. Indeed as a general matter, actions before the CJEU do not have suspensory effect.

Article 278 TFEU however provides:

> Actions brought before the Court of Justice of the European Union shall not have suspensory effect. The Court may, however, if it considers that circumstances so require, order that application of the contested act be suspended.

Article 279 then provides:

> The Court of Justice of the European Union may in any cases before it prescribe any necessary interim measures.

---

[240] Case C–457/07 *Commission v Portugal* [2009] ECR I–8091, in which the Commission's Art 260 application was rejected by the Court.

[241] On the long-running saga of foreign-language lecturers in Italy see Case C–212/99 *Commission v Italy* [2001] ECR I–4923; Case C–119/04 *Commission v Italy* (n 204).

[242] Jack (n 10). For a case in which this issue was raised, see Case C–407/09 *Commission v Greece* EU:C:2011:196, [24]–[27].

[243] Jack, ibid.

[244] C Gray, 'Interim Measures of Protection in the European Court' (1979) 4 ELRev 80; G Borchardt, 'The Award of Interim Measures by the ECJ' (1985) 22 CMLRev 203; P Oliver, 'Interim Measures: Some Recent Developments' (1992) 29 CMLRev 7.

[245] See, eg, the Court's dismissal of Greece's objection to an application for interim measures in the context of Art 348 TFEU enforcement proceedings against it: Case C–120/94 R (n 1).

[246] For discussion of the importance of interim measures in environmental cases, see S Grohs, 'Article 258/260 TFEU Infringement Procedures: The Commission Perspective in Environmental Cases' in M Cremona (ed), *Compliance and the Enforcement of EU Law* (Oxford University Press, 2012) 58; Hadroušek (n 10).

The Court's Rules of Procedure specify that such interim measures may not be ordered unless there are circumstances giving rise to urgency, as well as factual and legal grounds which establish a *prima facie* justification for granting the measures sought. The effect of the urgency requirement is that the interim measures requested must be of such a nature as to prevent the injury which is alleged, and that serious and irreparable harm to the applicant's interests must be threatened.[247] Further, the Commission must display diligence in response to a complaint made against a Member State if it is seeking interim measures, given the requirement of urgency, and the CJEU may refuse to order such measures if it has not done so.[248]

13 CONCLUSIONS

i.   Some of the main criticisms of the enforcement procedure over the years, including its lack of bite, the absence of a role for individual complainants, and the elite and unresponsive attitude of the Commission, have gradually been addressed, at least in part. The penalty payment procedure under Article 260 TFEU in particular was introduced to sharpen the coercive effect of the proceedings; and pressure from the Ombudsman and the European Parliament had the effect of encouraging the Commission to follow somewhat more regular and transparent administrative procedures including in its dealings with individual complainants.

ii. The overall enforcement mechanism continues to comprise a mixture of different approaches: parts of it operate in a bilateral and diplomatic dispute-resolution mode, parts of it according to a more formal, judicially-monitored sanction procedure, and parts of it as a quasi-administrative complaints procedure.

iii. The risk of overload led the Commission to propose an array of preventative, alternative, and supplementary mechanisms, including a pilot procedure for dealing with complaints at an early stage. The pilot procedure in particular seems to result in many complaints being addressed at national level without much if any involvement from the Commission.

iv. There has been a gradual growth in recourse to the penalty payment procedure, although its effectiveness in inducing compliance has been questioned, and the provision which was introduced by the Lisbon Treaty to extend the penalty payment procedure for failure to notify the transposition of directives has not yet been tested.

14 FURTHER READING

(a) Books

ANDERSEN, S, *The Enforcement of EU Law: The Role of the European Commission* (Oxford University Press, 2012)

BORZSAK, L, *The Impact of Environmental Concerns on the Public Enforcement Mechanism under EU Law* (Kluwer, 2011)

CREMONA, M (ed), *Compliance and the Enforcement of EU Law* (Oxford University Press, 2012)

---

[247] Case C–76/08 *Commission v Malta* [2009] ECR I–535, concerning the preservation of wild birds from hunting, in which the Court dismissed Malta's argument that the application was inadmissible and ordered interim measures against it. For a case involving several applications for extension of interim measures see Case C–320/03 R *Commission v Austria* [2003] ECR I–7929, [2003] ECR I–11665, and [2004] ECR I–3593.

[248] Case C–87/94 R *Commission v Belgium* [1994] ECR I–1395.

(b) Articles

GÁSPÁR-SZILÁGYI, S, 'What Constitutes "Failure to Notify" National Measures?' (2012) 19 EPL 281

HADROUŠEK, D, 'Speeding Up Infringement Procedures: Recent Developments Designed to Make Infringement Procedures More Effective' (2012) 9 Journal for European Environmental and Planning Law 235

HARLOW, C, and RAWLINGS, R, 'Accountability and Law Enforcement: The Centralized EU Infringement Procedure' (2006) 31 ELRev 447

JACK, B, 'Article 260(2) TFEU: An Effective Judicial Procedure for the Enforcement of Judgments?' (2013) 19 ELJ 404

KILBEY, I, 'The Interpretation of Article 260 TFEU (ex 228 EC)' (2010) 35 ELRev 370

MUNOZ, R, 'The Monitoring of the Application of Community Law: The Need to Improve the Current Tools and an Obligation to Innovate' (2005) 25 YBEL 395

PEERS, S, 'Sanctions for Infringement of EU Law after the Treaty of Lisbon' (2012) 18 EPL 33

RAWLINGS, R, 'Engaged Elites, Citizen Action and Institutional Attitudes in Commission Enforcement' (2000) 6 ELJ 4

TABOROWSKI, M, 'Infringement Proceedings and Non-Compliant National Courts' (2012) 49 CMLRev 1881

WENNERÅS, P, 'Sanctions Against Member States Under Article 260 TFEU: Alive, But Not Kicking?' (2012) 49 CMLRev 145

PRELIMINARY RULINGS

1 CENTRAL ISSUES

i.   Article 267 TFEU is one of the most important Treaty provisions.[1] There would have been few, at the inception of the Treaty, who would have guessed its significance in shaping EU law, and the relationship between the national and EU legal systems. Article 267 TFEU[2] is the 'jewel in the Crown' of the Court's jurisdiction. Prior to the Nice Treaty only the ECJ could give preliminary rulings. This was changed by the Nice Treaty, which has been carried over to the Lisbon Treaty. Article 256(3) TFEU accords the General Court jurisdiction to give such rulings in specific areas laid down by the Statute of the Court of Justice, subject to qualifications considered below. The power to accord the General Court jurisdiction to give preliminary rulings has not, however, been acted on thus far. The CJEU therefore currently hears all Article 267 TFEU cases.

ii. The relationship between national courts and the CJEU is reference-based. It is not an appeal system. No individual has a right of appeal to the CJEU. It is for the national court to make the decision to refer. The CJEU will rule on the issues referred to it, and the case will then be sent back to the national courts, which will apply the Union law to the case at hand.

iii. Article 267 has been of seminal importance for the development of EU law. It is through preliminary rulings that the Court has developed concepts such as direct effect and supremacy.[3] Individuals assert in national courts that the Member State has broken a Union provision, which gives them rights that they can enforce in their national courts. The national court seeks a ruling from the CJEU whether the particular EU provision has direct effect, and the CJEU thereby develops the concept. Article 267 has been the mechanism through which national courts and the CJEU have engaged in discourse on the appropriate reach of EU law when it conflicts with national legal norms.

iv. Article 267 is also an indirect way of testing the validity of EU action for conformity with Union law.[4] An individual can contest the legality of EU law directly before the General Court under

---

[1] Prior to the Lisbon Treaty two variants of the preliminary ruling procedure were applicable to the Area of Freedom, Security, and Justice (AFSJ), which were found in Art 35 EU and Art 68 EC. These variants are no longer applicable, because the AFSJ is now subject to the normal Treaty rules concerning preliminary rulings. There were, however, transitional provisions that limit the legal impact of the Lisbon Treaty on measures concerning Police and Judicial Cooperation in Criminal Matters adopted before its entry into force: Protocol (No 36) On Transitional Provisions, Arts 9–10.

[2] Ex Art 234 EC, Art 177 EEC.

[3] F Mancini and D Keeling, 'From *CILFIT* to *ERT*: The Constitutional Challenge Facing the European Court' (1991) 11 YBEL 1, 2–3.

[4] See pp 533–535.

Article 263 TFEU, but, as will be seen in the next chapter, the rules concerning access to court under Article 263 are restrictive, and therefore raising the validity of EU law before a national court under Article 267 TFEU may be the only way to challenge such a measure.

v.   Article 267 has been the principal vehicle through which the relationship between the national and EU legal systems has been fashioned. The original conception of the relationship was *horizontal* and *bilateral*. It was horizontal in that the ECJ and the national courts were separate but equal. They had differing functions, which each performed within its appointed sphere. It was for the national court to decide whether to refer a matter to the ECJ, which the ECJ would then interpret. It was bilateral in the sense that, in principle, the ECJ's rulings were delivered to the particular national court that made the request. In this sense, there was a series of bilateral relationships between the ECJ and each of the national courts.

vi.   The relationship has become steadily more *vertical* and *multilateral*. It has become more vertical in that developments have emphasized that the ECJ sits in a superior position to that of the national courts. The verticality of the relationship also manifests itself in a less obvious, but equally important, manner. The ECJ has enrolled national courts as enforcers of EU law. They are part of an EU-wide judicial hierarchy,[5] with the Court sitting at its apex. The relationship has become more multilateral, in that judgments given in response to the request for a ruling from one Member State are increasingly held to have either a *de facto* or *de jure* impact on all other national courts.

vii. There has been much discussion about reform of the EU judicial system. This discourse has been driven by the increased workload on the CJEU and General Court, and by the enlargement of the EU.

2 FOUNDATIONS: ARTICLE 267

The Court of Justice of the European Union shall have jurisdiction to give preliminary rulings concerning:

(a) the interpretation of the Treaties;

(b) the validity and interpretation of acts of the institutions, bodies, offices or agencies of the Union;

Where such a question is raised before any court or tribunal of a Member State, that court or tribunal may, if it considers that a decision on the question is necessary to enable it to give judgment, request the Court to give a ruling thereon.

Where any such question is raised in a case pending before a court or tribunal of a Member State against whose decisions there is no judicial remedy under national law, that court or tribunal shall bring the matter before the Court.

If such a question is raised in a case pending before a court or tribunal of a Member State with regard to a person in custody, the Court of Justice of the European Union shall act with the minimum of delay.

---

[5] Report of the Court of Justice on Certain Aspects of the Application of the Treaty on European Union (1995), [11]–[15].

(A) QUESTIONS THAT CAN BE REFERRED

A preliminary reference can be made in two types of case, the first of which concerns *the interpretation of the Treaties*: Article 267(1)(a). It is through Article 267(1)(a) that the Court has given many of its seminal judgments concerning direct effect and supremacy. The CJEU does not, however, pass judgment on the validity of a national law. It interprets the Treaty. The consequence may be that a national law is incompatible with EU law, and the supremacy of EU law will mean that there is an obligation on the national court to redress the situation. The CJEU is nonetheless not directly determining the validity of national law.[6]

Article 267(1)(b) also allows for preliminary references to be made which relate *to the validity and interpretation of acts of the institutions, bodies, offices, or agencies of the EU*. Preliminary references concerning the validity[7] of acts of the institutions, bodies, and the like covers cases such as *ICC*[8] and *Foto-Frost*,[9] where the validity of an EU regulation, directive, or decision is contested before a national court. Preliminary references concerning the interpretation of acts of the institutions cover cases where an individual argues that, for example, an EU regulation gives rise to rights that can be enforced in national courts. References can however be made under Article 267(1)(b) irrespective of whether or not the EU provision is directly effective, in order, for example, to clarify the interpretation of the relevant provision. References may also be made in relation to non-binding acts such as recommendations,[10] and certain agreements with non-Member States.[11] The ECJ has also held that a preliminary reference may be made where a provision of national law is based on or makes some reference to EU law, even if the consequence is that the ambit of EU law is extended by the national provisions.[12]

(B) COURTS OR TRIBUNALS WHICH CAN REFER

Article 267(2) and (3) is framed in terms of courts or tribunals of a Member State, which may or must make a reference. It is for the CJEU to decide whether a body is a court or tribunal for these purposes, and the national categorization is not conclusive.[13] The CJEU will take a number of factors into account: whether the body is established by law, whether it is permanent, whether its jurisdiction is compulsory, whether its procedure is *inter partes*, whether it applies rules of law, and whether it is

---

6 Case C–167/94 R *Grau Gomis* [1995] ECR I–1023; Cases C–37 and 38/96 *Sodiprem SARL v Direction Générale des Douanes* [1998] ECR I–2039; Cases C–10 and 22/97 *Ministero delle Finanze v IN.CO.GE'90 Srl* [1998] ECR I–6307; Recommendations to national courts and tribunals in relation to the initiation of preliminary ruling proceedings [2012] OJ C338/01.

7 This is subject to Art 276 TFEU, which prevents the CJEU from reviewing the validity or proportionality of operations carried out by the police or other law enforcement services of a Member State, or the exercise of the responsibilities incumbent upon Member States with regard to the maintenance of law and order and the safeguarding of internal security.

8 Case 66/80 *International Chemical Corporation v Amministrazione delle Finanze dello Stato* [1981] ECR 1191.

9 Case 314/85 *Firma Foto-Frost v Hauptzollamt Lübeck-Ost* [1987] ECR 4199.

10 Case 322/88 *Salvatore Grimaldi v Fonds des Maladies Professionnelles* [1989] ECR 4407.

11 Case 181/73 *Haegeman v Belgium* [1974] ECR 449; Case C–53/96 *Hermès International v FHT Marketing Choice BV* [1998] ECR I–3603; Cases C–300 and 392/98 *Parfums Christian Dior v Tuk Consultancy BV* [2000] ECR I–11307.

12 Cases C–297/88 and 197/89 *Dzodzi v Belgium* [1990] ECR I–3763; Case C–28/95 *Leur-Bloem v Inspecteur der Belastingdienst/Ondernemingen Amsterdam 2* [1997] ECR I–4161; Case C–217/05 *Confederación Española de Empresarios de Estaciones de Servicio v Compañía Española de Petroleos SA* [2006] ECR I–11987; Case C–139/12 *Caixa d'Estalvis i Pensions de Barcelona v Generalidad de Cataluña* EU:C:2014:174; S Lefevre, 'The Interpretation of Community Law by the Court of Justice in Areas of National Competence' (2004) 29 ELRev 501.

13 Case 43/71 *Politi v Italy* [1971] ECR 1039; Case C–24/92 *Corbiau v Administration des Contributions* [1993] ECR I–1277.

independent.[14] The application of these criteria has not always been straightforward.[15] Thus, for example, it is clear from *Cartesio*[16] that although Article 267 TFEU does not make reference dependent on the proceedings being *inter partes*, such a reference could only be made if there were a case pending before the national court, which led to a decision of a judicial nature. A reference could not, by way of contrast, be made where a national court made what was in essence an administrative decision that did not resolve a legal dispute, since the national court could not be regarded as exercising a judicial function in this instance. The *Broekmeulen* case provides a good example of the Court's general reasoning in this area.

Case 246/80 C Broekmeulen v Huisarts Registratie Commissie
[1981] ECR 2311

[Note Lisbon Treaty renumbering: Art 177 is now Art 267 TFEU]

The case concerned a Dutch body, the Appeals Committee for General Medicine. It heard appeals from another body, which was responsible for registering those who wished to practise medicine in the Netherlands. Both bodies were established under the auspices of the Royal Netherlands Society for the Promotion of Medicine. Although this was a private association, it was indirectly recognized in Dutch law, and it was not possible to practise without registration. The Appeals Committee was not a court or tribunal under Dutch law, but it followed an adversarial procedure and allowed legal representation. Broekmeulen was of Dutch nationality, but had qualified in Belgium. He sought to establish himself as a doctor in the Netherlands, but his application to be registered was refused. The question was whether the Appeals Committee was a court or tribunal for the purposes of Article 177.

THE ECJ

14. A study of the Netherlands legislation and of the statutes and internal rules of the Society shows that a doctor who intends to establish himself in the Netherlands may not in fact practise either as a specialist, or as an expert in social medicine, or as a general practitioner, without being recognised and registered by the organs of the Society...

15. It is thus clear that...the Netherlands system of public health operates on the basis of the status accorded to doctors by the Society and that registration as a general practitioner is essential to every doctor wishing to establish himself in the Netherlands as a general practitioner.

16. Therefore a general practitioner who avails himself of the right of establishment and the freedom to provide services conferred upon him by Community law is faced with the necessity of applying to the Registration Committee established by the Society, and, in the event of his application's being refused, must appeal to the Appeals Committee. The Netherlands Government expressed the opinion that a doctor who is not a member of the Society would have the right to appeal against such a refusal to the ordinary courts, but stated that the point had never been decided by the Netherlands courts.

---

[14] Case C–54/96 *Dorsch Consult Ingenieurgesellschaft mbH v Bundesbaugesellschaft Berlin mbH* [1997] ECR I–4961; Cases C–9 and 118/97 *Proceedings brought by Jokela and Pitkaranta* [1998] ECR I–6267; Case C–407/98 *Abrahamsson and Anderson v Fogelqvist* [2000] ECR I–5539; Case C–195/98 *Österreicher Gewerkschaftsbund, Gewerkschaft Öffentlicher Dienst v Republik Österreich* [2000] ECR I–10497; Case C–178/99 *Salzmann* [2001] ECR I–4421; Case C–53/03 *Syfait v GlaxoSmithKline plc* [2005] ECR I–4609; Case C–506/04 *Wilson v Ordre des avocats du barreau de Luxembourg* [2006] ECR I–8613; Case C–196/09 *Miles v Écoles européennes* EU:C:2011:388; Case C–175/11 *HID and BA v Refugee Applications Commissioner* EU:C:2013:45.

[15] T Tridimas, 'Knocking on Heaven's Door: Fragmentation, Efficiency and Defiance in the Preliminary Ruling Procedure' (2003) 40 CMLRev 9, 27–34.

[16] Case C–210/06 *Cartesio Oktató és Szolgáltató bt* [2008] ECR I–9641, [56]–[57].

Indeed all doctors, whether members of the Society or not, whose application to be registered as a general practitioner is refused, appeal to the Appeals Committee, whose decisions to the knowledge of the Netherlands Government have never been challenged in the ordinary courts.

17. [I]t should be noted that it is incumbent upon Member States to take the necessary steps to ensure that within their own territory the provisions adopted by the Community institutions are implemented in their entirety. If, under the legal system of a Member State, the task of implementing such provisions is assigned to a professional body acting under a degree of governmental supervision, and if that body, in conjunction with the public authorities concerned, creates appeal procedures which may affect the exercise of rights granted by Community law, it is imperative, in order to ensure the proper functioning of Community law, that the Court should have an opportunity of ruling on issues of interpretation and validity arising out of such proceedings.

18. As a result of all the foregoing considerations and in the absence, in practice, of any right of appeal to the ordinary courts, the Appeals Committee, which operates with the consent of the public authorities and with their cooperation, and which, after an adversarial procedure, delivers decisions which are recognised as final, must, in a matter involving the application of Community law, be considered as a court or tribunal of a Member State within the meaning of Article 177 of the Treaty. Therefore, the Court has jurisdiction to reply to the question asked.

It is necessary that the body making the reference be a court or tribunal of a Member State.[17] This can be problematic in, for example, the context of arbitration. Whether an arbitral court or tribunal can be regarded as an emanation of a Member State will depend on the nature of the arbitration. The fact that the arbitral body gives a judgment according to law, and that the award is binding between the parties, will not, however, be sufficient. There must be a closer link between the arbitration procedure and the ordinary court system in order for the former to be considered as a court or tribunal of a Member State.[18]

(c) COURTS OR TRIBUNALS WHICH MUST REFER

Article 267 TFEU draws a distinction between courts or tribunals with a discretion to refer to the CJEU, Article 267(2), and courts or tribunals 'against whose decisions there is no judicial remedy under national law', Article 267(3), which have an obligation to refer, provided that a decision on a question is necessary to enable judgment to be given. The rationale for the duty to refer in Article 267(3) is to prevent a body of national case law that is not in accordance with EU law from being established in any Member State.[19]

There are two views about the type of bodies covered by Article 267(3). According to the abstract theory, it covers only bodies whose decisions are never subject to appeal. According to the concrete theory, the real test is whether the court or tribunal's decision is subject to appeal in the type of case in question.[20]

---

[17] Case C–355/89 *DHSS (Isle of Man) v Barr and Montrose Holdings Ltd* [1991] ECR I–3479; Case C–100/89 *Kaefer and Procacci v France* [1990] ECR I–4647.

[18] Case 102/81 *Nordsee Deutsche Hochseefischerei GmbH v Reederei Mond Hochseefischerei Nordstern AG and Co KG* [1982] ECR 1095; Case C–126/97 *Eco Swiss China Time Ltd v Benetton International NV* [1999] ECR I–3055; Case C–125/04 *Denuit and Cordenier v Transorient-Mosaïque Voyages and Culture SA* [2005] ECR I–923; Case C–377/13 *Ascendi Beiras Litoral e Alta, Auto Estradas das Beiras Litoral e Alta SA v Autoridade Tributária e Aduaneira* EU:C:2014:1754.

[19] Case C–393/98 *Ministerio Publico and Gomes Valente v Fazenda Publica* [2001] ECR I–1327, [17]; Case C–99/00 *Criminal Proceedings against Lyckeskog* [2002] ECR I–4839, [14]–[15]; Case C–458/06 *Skatteverket v Gourmet Classic Ltd* [2008] ECR I–4207, [23].

[20] Difficulties may also arise in circumstances where the judgment in question can be reconsidered in other proceedings: Case 107/76 *Hoffmann-La Roche v Centrafarm* [1977] ECR 957.

Costa[21] suggested that the ECJ favoured the concrete theory. In that case the *giudice conciliatore* (magistrate) made a reference to the ECJ. Although his decisions were capable of being appealed in some instances, there was no right of appeal in the particular case, because the sum involved was relatively small. The ECJ therefore treated the national court as one against whose decision there was no judicial remedy in the actual case at hand.

The concrete theory was affirmed in *Lyckeskog*,[22] although it may still be difficult to decide whether a court's decision is truly final in the particular type of case. The ECJ held that decisions of a national appeal court that could be challenged before a national Supreme Court did not come within Article 267(3), and this was so notwithstanding the fact that the appeal court decision was subject to a prior declaration of admissibility before it could be appealed to the Supreme Court. If a question concerning the interpretation of EU law arose before the Supreme Court it would be under an obligation to refer pursuant to Article 267(3), either when examining admissibility or at a later stage.[23]

This approach was confirmed and applied in *Cartesio*.[24] The ECJ held that a court whose decisions could be appealed on points of law could not be classified as a court or tribunal against whose decisions there was no judicial remedy under national law for the purposes of Article 267(3) TFEU, even though the procedural system under which the dispute was to be decided imposed restrictions with regard to the arguments that could be advanced on appeal. In the instant case the existence of an appeal did not, moreover, suspend the judgment of the court appealed against. This did not, said the ECJ, render the judgment of such a court final for the purposes of Article 267(3), since the lack of suspensory effect did not deprive the parties of the possibility of exercising effectively their right to appeal that decision.

(D) RELATIONSHIP BETWEEN NATIONAL COURTS

The preceding discussion leaves open the relationship between national courts under the preliminary ruling procedure, and more especially the legal tenability of a reference made by a lower national court that is then reversed on appeal by a higher national court. This important issue was considered in *Cartesio*,[25] where the ECJ supported the ability of lower courts to refer to the ECJ, even in the face of a negative decision by a higher national court.[26]

Case C–210/06 **Cartesio Oktató és Szolgáltató bt**
[2008] ECR I–9641

Under Hungarian law it was possible for a lower court decision referring a case to the ECJ to be set aside on appeal, and the lower court could be ordered to resume the domestic law proceedings

THE ECJ

96. In accordance with Article 234 EC, the assessment of the relevance and necessity of the question referred for a preliminary ruling is, in principle, the responsibility of the referring court

---

[21] Case 6/64 [1964] ECR 585, 592.

[22] Case C–99/00 (n 19).

[23] For discussion within the UK see *Chiron Corporation v Murex Diagnostics Ltd* [1995] All ER (EC) 88, 93–94; F Jacobs, 'Which Courts and Tribunals are Bound to Refer to the European Court?' (1977) 2 ELRev 119.

[24] Case C–210/06 *Cartesio* (n 16) [77]–[78].

[25] M Broberg and N Fenger, 'Preliminary References as a Right—But for Whom? The Extent to which Preliminary Reference Decisions can be Subject to Appeal' (2011) 36 ELRev 276.

[26] Case C–416/10 *Križan v Slovenská inšpekcia životného prostredia* EU:C:2013:8, [62]–[73].

alone, subject to the limited verification made by the Court in accordance with the case-law cited in paragraph 67 above. Thus, it is for the referring court to draw the proper inferences from a judgment delivered on an appeal against its decision to refer and, in particular, to come to a conclusion as to whether it is appropriate to maintain the reference for a preliminary ruling, or to amend it or to withdraw it.

97. It follows that, in a situation such as that in the case before the referring court, the Court must—also in the interests of clarity and legal certainty—abide by the decision to make a reference for a preliminary ruling, which must have its full effect so long as it has not been revoked or amended by the referring court, such revocation or amendment being matters on which that court alone is able to take a decision.

98. In the light of the foregoing, the answer to the third question must be that, where rules of national law apply which relate to the right of appeal against a decision making a reference for a preliminary ruling, and under those rules the main proceedings remain pending before the referring court in their entirety, the order for reference alone being the subject of a limited appeal, the second paragraph of Article 234 EC is to be interpreted as meaning that the jurisdiction conferred by that provision of the Treaty on any national court or tribunal to make a reference to the Court for a preliminary ruling cannot be called into question by the application of those rules, where they permit the appellate court to vary the order for reference, to set aside the reference and to order the referring court to resume the domestic law proceedings.

(E) NATIONAL COURT RAISING EU LAW OF ITS OWN VOLITION

The issue of whether national courts can be limited by national procedural rules as to whether they can raise a matter of EU law of their own volition is as follows. In *Peterbroeck* the ECJ held that a national procedural rule which prevented a national court from raising a matter of EU law of its own motion concerning the compatibility of a national law with EU law, even where it had not been raised by the person concerned within the specified time, was contrary to EU law. It was held that the domestic rule could not be justified on the ground of legal certainty or the proper conduct of procedure.[27] This case was distinguished in *Van Schijndel*.[28] The ECJ held that there was no such obligation on national courts if it would oblige the national court to abandon the passive role assigned to it by the domestic procedural rules by going beyond the ambit of the dispute as defined by the parties themselves.

It is nonetheless clear from *Asturcom*[29] that the ECJ may impose a duty to raise a point of EU law, provided that the court has discretion to raise such a point in analogous domestic actions. Thus it held that the Directive on Unfair Contracts should be interpreted to mean that a national court hearing an action for enforcement of an arbitration award that had become final and was made in the absence of the consumer was required to assess of its own motion whether the arbitration clause in a consumer contract was unfair, insofar as under national rules of procedure it could carry out such an assessment in similar actions of a domestic nature.

---

[27] Case C–312/93 *Peterbroeck, Van Campenhout & Cie SCS v Belgium* [1995] ECR I–4599.

[28] Cases C–430–431/93 *Van Schijndel and Van Veen v Stichting Pensioenfonds voor Fysiotherapeuten* [1995] ECR I–4705; Cases C–222–225/05 *van der Weerd v Minister van Landbouw, Natuur en Voedselkwaliteit* [2007] ECR I–4233; Case C–227/08 *Eva Martín Martín v EDP Editores SL* [2009] ECR I–11939, [19]–[20].

[29] Case C–40/08 *Asturcom Telecomunicaciones SL v Cristina Rodríguez Nogueira* [2009] ECR I–9579; Case C–227/08 *Martín* (n 28); Case C–2/06 *Willy Kempter KG v Hauptzollamt Hamburg-Jonas* [2008] ECR I–411, [45]; Case C–488/11 *Brusse v Jahani BV* EU:C:2013:341, [44]–[45].

3 THE EXISTENCE OF A QUESTION: DEVELOPMENT OF PRECEDENT

It is for the national court to decide whether to make a reference. The mere fact that a party before the national court contends that the dispute gives rise to a question concerning the validity of EU law does not mean that the court is compelled to consider that a question has been raised within the meaning of Article 267 TFEU.[30] The national court may conclude that a reference is not required because the EU Courts have already resolved the issue, because there is no doubt as to the validity of the EU measure, or because a decision on the question is not necessary for the case before the national court.

(A) NATIONAL LAW IN BREACH OF EU LAW AND PRIOR CJEU RULINGS

It is clear that Article 267 TFEU is designed to be used only if there is a question to be answered, which falls into one of the categories in Article 267(1). There may be a number of reasons why a 'question' posed by the national court does not necessitate a ruling, the most obvious being that the CJEU has already ruled on the matter.

Cases 28–30/62 **Da Costa en Schaake NV, Jacob Meijer NV and Hoechst-Holland NV v Nederlandse Belastingadministratie**
[1963] ECR 31

[Note Lisbon Treaty renumbering: Arts 12 and 177 are now Arts 30 and 267 TFEU]

The facts in the case were materially identical to those in Case 26/62 *Van Gend en Loos*. The questions asked were also materially identical to those posed in the *Van Gend* case.

THE ECJ

The regularity of the procedure followed by the Tariefcommissie in requesting the Court for a preliminary ruling under Article 177 of the EEC Treaty has not been disputed and there is no ground for the Court to raise the matter of its own motion.

The Commission...urges that the request be dismissed for lack of substance, since the questions on which an interpretation is requested from the Court in the present cases have already been decided...in Case 26/62, which covered identical questions raised in a similar case.

This contention is not justified. A distinction should be made between the obligation imposed by the third paragraph of Article 177 upon national courts or tribunals of last instance and the power granted by the second paragraph of Article 177 to every national court or tribunal to refer to the Court of the Communities a question on the interpretation of the Treaty. Although the third paragraph of Article 177 unreservedly requires courts or tribunals of a Member State against whose decisions there is no judicial remedy under national law—like the Tariefcommissie—to refer to the Court every question of

---

[30] Case C–344/04 *R on the application of IATA and ELFAA v Department of Transport* [2006] ECR I–403, [27]–[28]; Case T–47/02 *Danzer and Danzer v Council* [2006] ECR II–1779, [36]–[37].

interpretation raised before them, the authority of an interpretation under Article 177 already given by the Court may deprive the obligation of its purpose and thus empty it of its substance. Such is the case especially when the question raised is materially identical with a question which has already been the subject of a preliminary ruling in a similar case.

When it gives an interpretation of the Treaty in a specific action pending before a national court, the Court limits itself to deducing the meaning of the Community rules from the wording and spirit of the Treaty, it being left to the national court to apply in the particular case the rules which are thus interpreted. Such an attitude conforms with the function assigned to the Court of ensuring unity of interpretation of Community law within the six Member States....

It is no less true that Article 177 always allows a national court, if it considers it desirable, to refer questions of interpretation to the Court again. This follows from Article 20 of the Statute of the Court of Justice, under which the procedure laid down for the settlement of preliminary questions is automatically set in motion as soon as such a question is referred by a national court.

The Court must, therefore, give a judgment on the present application.

The interpretation of Article 12 of the EEC Treaty, which is here requested, was given in the Court's judgment...in Case 26/62.

[*The Court then repeated the judgment it had given in the case of* Van Gend en Loos. *It continued as follows.*]

The questions of interpretation posed in this case are identical with those settled as above and no new factor has been presented to the Court.

In these circumstances the Tariefcommissie must be referred to the previous judgment.

The ECJ's approach appears clearly in this extract. The national court is still able, in formal terms, to refer a matter to the Court, even where it has ruled on the issue. However, it is clear that such an application must raise some new factor or argument. If it does not do so, then the Court will be strongly inclined to restate the substance of the earlier case. The existence of an earlier ruling can deprive the national court's obligation to refer 'of its purpose and thus empty it of its substance'. The *Da Costa* case, therefore, initiated what is in effect a system of precedent. These seeds have been developed in later cases.[31]

Case 283/81 Srl CILFIT and Lanificio di Gavardo SpA v Ministry of Health
[1982] ECR 3415

[Note Lisbon Treaty renumbering: Art 177 is now Art 267 TFEU]

The plaintiffs alleged that certain duties imposed by Italian law were in breach of Regulation 827/68. The Italian Ministry of Health urged the Italian Court of Cassation, against whose decisions there was no judicial remedy under national law, not to refer the matter to the ECJ, because the answer to the question was so obvious as to remove the need for a reference. The Court of Cassation decided that this contention was itself an issue of Community law. It therefore requested a ruling from the ECJ on whether the obligation to refer imposed in Article 177(3) was unconditional, or whether it was premised

---

31 D Edward, '*CILFIT* and *Foto-Frost* in their Historical and Procedural Context' in M Maduro and L Azoulai (eds), *The Past and Future of EU Law: The Classics of EU Law Revisited on the 50th Anniversary of the Rome Treaty* (Hart, 2010) 173–184; P Craig, 'The Classics of EU Law Revisited: *CILFIT* and *Foto-Frost*' in ibid 185–191; D Sarmiento, '*CILFIT* and *Foto-Frost*: Constructing and Deconstructing Judicial Authority in Europe' in ibid 192–200.

on the existence of reasonable interpretive doubt about the answer which should be given to a question. The ECJ's response to the *acte clair* point will be examined in detail below. The ECJ also gave guidance on the relevance of its prior decisions.

THE ECJ

8. In this connection, it is necessary to define the meaning for the purposes of Community law of the expression 'where any such question is raised' in order to determine the circumstances in which a national court or tribunal against whose decisions there is no judicial remedy under national law is obliged to bring a matter before the Court of Justice.

9. In this regard, it must in the first place be pointed out that Article 177 does not constitute a means of redress available to the parties to a case pending before a national court or tribunal. Therefore the mere fact that a party contends that the dispute gives rise to a question concerning the interpretation of Community law does not mean that the court or tribunal concerned is compelled to consider that a question has been raised within the meaning of Article 177. On the other hand, a national court or tribunal may, in an appropriate case, refer a matter to the Court of Justice of its own motion.

10. Secondly, it follows from the relationship between paragraphs (2) and (3) of Article 177 that the courts or tribunals referred to in paragraph (3) have the same discretion as any other national court or tribunal to ascertain whether a decision on a question of Community law is necessary to enable them to give judgment. Accordingly, those courts or tribunals are not obliged to refer to the Court of Justice a question concerning the interpretation of Community law raised before them if that question is not relevant, that is to say, if the answer to that question, regardless of what it may be, can in no way affect the outcome of the case.

11. If, however, those courts or tribunals consider that recourse to Community law is necessary to decide a case, Article 177 imposes an obligation on them to refer to the Court of Justice any question of interpretation which may arise.

12. The question submitted by the Corte di Cassazione seeks to ascertain whether, in certain circumstances, the obligation laid down by paragraph (3) of Article 177 might none the less be subject to certain restrictions.

13. It must be remembered in this connection that in... *Da Costa* the Court ruled that: 'Although paragraph (3) of Article 177 unreservedly requires courts or tribunals of a Member State against whose decision there is no judicial remedy under national law... to refer to the Court every question of interpretation raised before them, the authority of an interpretation under Article 177 already given by the Court may deprive the obligation of its purpose and thus empty it of its substance. Such is the case especially when the question raised is materially identical with a question which has already been the subject of a preliminary ruling in a similar case.'

14. The same effect, as regards the limits set to the obligation laid down by paragraph (3) of Article 177, may be produced where previous decisions of the Court have already dealt with the point of law in question, irrespective of the nature of the proceedings which led to those decisions, even though the questions at issue are not strictly identical.

15. However, it must not be forgotten that in all such circumstances national courts and tribunals, including those referred to in paragraph (3) of Article 177, remain entirely at liberty to bring a matter before the Court of Justice if they consider it appropriate to do so.

A previous ruling can therefore be relied on even if it did not emerge from the same type of proceedings, and even though the questions at issue were not strictly identical. Provided that the point of law has already been determined by the ECJ, it can be relied on by a national court in a later case, thereby obviating the need for a reference. The national courts were encouraged to rely on these prior rulings where the substance of the legal point had already been adjudicated.[32] Those earlier ECJ rulings became, in that sense, *de facto* precedents for the national courts. This is subject to the qualification in paragraph 15: the national court can still refer if it so wishes, and the application will not be deemed inadmissible, but the Court is likely to give its decision by reasoned order, in which reference is made to its previous judgment or to the relevant case law.[33]

(B) THE VALIDITY OF EU LEGISLATION AND PRIOR CJEU RULINGS

The cases discussed thus far concerned the impact of an earlier ECJ ruling when Member State action has been alleged to violate the Treaty. The ECJ has been even more forceful when the impact of its previous decisions on the validity of EU legislation has been in issue. This is exemplified by the *ICC* case:

Case 66/80 International Chemical Corporation v Amministrazione delle Finanze dello Stato
[1981] ECR 1191

Council Regulation 563/76 was designed to reduce stocks of skimmed-milk powder. It made the grant of Community aid dependent on proof that the recipient had purchased a certain quantity of such skimmed milk held by an intervention agency. Compliance with this obligation was secured by the payment of security that was forfeited if the skimmed milk was not bought. The plaintiff received the Community aid and paid the security, but did not buy the skimmed-milk powder, and hence the national intervention agency did not release the security. In an earlier case the ECJ had found that Regulation 563/76 was invalid, because the price at which the milk powder was to be bought was regarded as disproportionately high.[34] The plaintiff, therefore, took the view that the security could not be forfeited, since it only served to ensure compliance with an obligation (to buy the milk powder), which was invalid. The Italian court requested a ruling on whether the earlier judgment holding the Regulation to be null and void was effective in any subsequent litigation, or whether such a finding was only of relevance in relation to the court which had originally sought the ruling.

THE ECJ

11. The main purpose of the powers accorded to the Court by Article 177 is to ensure that Community law is applied uniformly by national courts. Uniform application of Community law is imperative not only when a national court is faced with a rule of Community law the meaning and scope of which is to be defined; it is just as imperative when the Court is confronted by a dispute as to the validity of an act of the institutions.

12. When the Court is moved under Article 177 to declare an act of one of the institutions to be void there are particularly imperative requirements concerning legal certainty in addition to those concerning the uniform application of Community law. It follows from the very nature of such a declaration that a national court may not apply the act declared to be void without once more creating serious uncertainty as to the Community law applicable.

---

[32] Cases C–428 and 434/06 *Unión General de Trabajadores de La Rioja (UGT-Rioja) v Juntas Generales del Territorio Histórico de Vizcaya* [2008] ECR I–6747, [42]–[43].

[33] Case C–260/07 *Pedro IV Servicios SL v Total España SA* [2009] ECR I–2437, [31].

[34] Case 116/76 *Granaria v Hoofdproduktschap voor Akkerbouwprodukten* [1977] ECR 1247.

13. It follows therefrom that although a judgment of the Court given under Article 177 of the Treaty declaring an act of an institution, in particular a Council or Commission regulation, to be void is directly addressed only to the national court which brought the matter before the Court, it is sufficient reason for any other national court to regard that act as void for the purposes of a judgment which it has to give.

14. That assertion does not however mean that national courts are deprived of the power given to them by Article 177…and it rests with those courts to decide whether there is a need to raise once again a question which has already been settled by the Court where the Court has previously declared an act of a Community institution to be void. There may be such a need in particular if questions arise as to the grounds, the scope and possibly the consequences of the invalidity established earlier.

15. If that is not the case national courts are entirely justified in determining the effect on the cases brought before them of a judgment declaring an act void given by the Court in an action between other parties.

16. It should further be observed, as the Court acknowledged in its judgments…in Joined Cases 117/76 and 16/77, *Ruckdeschel and Diamalt*,[35] and Joined Cases 124/76 and 20/77, *Moulins de Pont-à-Mousson and Providence Agricole*,[36] that as those responsible for drafting regulations declared to be void the Council or the Commission are bound to determine from the Court's judgment the effect of that judgment.

17. In the light of the foregoing considerations and in view of the fact that by its second question the national court has asked, as it was free to do, whether Regulation 563/76 was void, the answer should be that that is in fact the case for the reasons already stated in the judgments of 5 July 1977.

The *ICC* case provides further evidence of the Court's approach to precedent. The national court has discretion to refer a matter to the Court, even if the latter has already given judgment. However, the Court makes it patently clear that, although such a judgment is addressed primarily to the national court which requested the original ruling, it should be relied on by other national courts before which the matter arises. The original ruling will, in this sense, have a multilateral and not merely a bilateral effect. A decision of the ECJ will, therefore, have a precedential impact on all national courts within the EU. The Court has, however, made it clear that national courts cannot themselves find that an EU norm is invalid.

Case 314/85 **Firma Foto-Frost v Hauptzollamt Lübeck-Ost**
[1987] ECR 4199[37]

A national court inquired whether it had the power to declare invalid a Commission decision on the ground that it was in breach of a Community regulation on a certain issue.

THE ECJ

13. In enabling national courts against whose decisions there is a judicial remedy under national law to refer to the Court for a preliminary ruling questions on interpretation or validity, Article 177 did not settle the question whether those courts themselves may declare that acts of Community institutions are invalid.

---

[35] [1977] ECR 1753.

[36] [1977] ECR 1795.

[37] Case C–27/95 *Woodspring DC v Bakers of Nailsea Ltd* [1997] ECR I–1847; Case C–461/03 *Gaston Schul Douane-expediteur BV v Minister van Landbouw, Natuur en Voedselkwalitiet* [2005] ECR I–10513, [15]–[25]; Case C–344/04 *IATA* (n 30) [27]–[32].

14. Those courts may consider the validity of a Community act and, if they consider that the grounds put forward before them by the parties in support of invalidity are unfounded, they may reject them, concluding that the measure is completely valid. By taking that action they are not calling the existence of the Community measure into question.

15. On the other hand, those courts do not have the power to declare acts of the Community institutions invalid. As the Court emphasised in the judgment...(Case 66/80, *International Chemical Corporation...*), the main purpose of the powers accorded to the Court by Article 177 is to ensure that Community law is applied uniformly by national courts. That requirement of uniformity is particularly imperative when the validity of a Community act is in question. Divergences between courts in the Member States as to the validity of Community acts would be liable to place in jeopardy the very unity of the Community legal order and detract from the fundamental requirement of legal certainty.

...

17. Since Article 177 gives the Court exclusive jurisdiction to declare void an act of a Community institution, the coherence of the system requires that where the validity of a Community act is challenged before a national court the power to declare the act invalid must also be reserved to the Court of Justice.

18. It must also be emphasised that the Court of Justice is in the best position to decide on the validity of Community acts. Under Article 20 of the Protocol on the Statute of the Court of Justice of the EEC, Community institutions whose acts are challenged are entitled to participate in the proceedings in order to defend the validity of the acts in question. Furthermore, under the second paragraph of Article 21 of that Protocol the Court may require the Member States and institutions which are not participating in the proceedings to supply all information which it considers necessary for the purpose of the case before it....

19. It should be added that the rule that national courts may not themselves declare Community acts to be invalid may have to be qualified in certain circumstances in the case of proceedings relating to an application for interim measures; however, that case is not referred to in the national court's question.

20. The answer to the first question must therefore be that national courts have no jurisdiction to declare that acts of Community institutions are invalid.

The ECJ, in *Atlanta*,[38] provided guidance on the issue of interim relief raised in paragraph 19. Where a national measure is challenged because of the alleged invalidity of the EU regulation on which it was based, the national court can grant interim relief. Certain conditions must however be met. The national court must have serious doubts about the validity of the EU measure, and must have referred the measure to the Court for a ruling. The interim relief must be necessary to prevent serious and irreparable damage to the applicant. The national court must take due account of the Union interest.[39] It must, moreover, respect any decision of an EU Court already given on the substance of the disputed measure.

(c) CJEU RULINGS AND LEGAL CERTAINTY

The discussion thus far has been concerned with the effect of a prior ruling of the EU Courts for national courts. It is, as we have seen, for the national court to apply that prior ruling. The CJEU

---

[38] Case C–465/93 *Atlanta Fruchthandelsgesellschaft mbH v Bundesamt für Ernährung und Forstwirtschaft* [1995] ECR I–3761; Cases C–143/88 and 92/89 *Zuckerfabrik Süderdithmarschen AG v Hauptzollamt Itzehoe* [1991] ECR I–415; Case C–334/95 *Kruger GmbH & Co KG v Hauptzollamt Hamburg-Jonas* [1997] ECR I–4517.

[39] By considering whether, eg, the EU measure would be deprived of all effectiveness if it were not implemented immediately.

does not, however, delve into the national legal system and determine the validity of national law. It gives an interpretation of the compatibility of national law with EU law, and it is then for the national court to apply that interpretation within its legal system. The general principle is that the CJEU's ruling establishes the law from the time that it entered into force, and should therefore be applied to legal relationships before the ruling was given.[40] This can lead to difficulties concerning legal certainty.[41]

Case C–453/00 **Kühne & Heitz NV v Produktschap voor Pluimvee en Eieren**
[2004] ECR I–837

The applicants were exporters of poultry meat to non-member countries. The product was originally classified under one heading of the common customs tariff, on the basis of which the applicants were paid certain export refunds. The Dutch customs authorities then decided that the product should fall under a different classification and demanded reimbursement of the export refunds. The applicants appealed that decision to a Dutch court, which dismissed the appeal. The applicants did not request a preliminary ruling on the matter. In a subsequent decision involving different parties the ECJ made it clear that reclassification of the product by the Dutch customs authorities was erroneous. The applicants then sought reimbursement of the refunds that they would have received if the Dutch authorities had classified the goods correctly. Under Dutch law administrative bodies could, in principle, re-open a final decision, and could in certain circumstances withdraw the decision. However under Dutch law the finality of an administrative decision would not normally be affected by subsequent judicial decisions, since that could seriously impair legal certainty and give rise to administrative chaos. The ECJ reiterated the general principle that a ruling under Article 267 established the law as it should be understood from the time it entered into force, and that therefore this should be applied by an administrative body to legal relationships before the ruling was given. The issue was whether this should be applied even where the administrative decision had become final.

THE ECJ

24. Legal certainty is one of a number of general principles recognised by Community law. Finality of an administrative decision...contributes to such legal certainty and it follows that Community law does not require that administrative bodies be placed under an obligation, in principle to reopen an administrative decision which has become final in that way.

[*The ECJ then noted that under Dutch law administrative decisions could, subject to certain conditions, be re-opened.*]

28. [T]he circumstances of the main case are the following. First, national law confers on the administrative body competence to reopen the decision...which has become final. Second, that decision became final only as a result of a judgment of a national court against whose decisions there is no judicial remedy. Third, that judgment was based on an interpretation of Community law which, in the light of a subsequent judgment of the Court, was incorrect and which was adopted without a question being referred to the Court for a preliminary ruling in accordance with the conditions provided for in the third paragraph of Article 234 EC. Fourth, the person concerned complained to the administrative body immediately after becoming aware of that judgment of the Court.

---

[40] Case C–455/08 *Commission v Ireland* [2009] ECR I–225, [39].

[41] J Komarek, 'Federal Elements in the Community Judicial System: Building Coherence in the Community Legal System' (2005) 42 CMLRev 9; R Caranta, Note (2005) 42 CMLRev 179.

> 27. In such circumstances, the administrative body concerned is, in accordance with the principle of cooperation arising under Article 10 EC, under an obligation to review that decision in order to take account of the interpretation of the relevant provisions of Community law given in the meantime by the Court. The administrative body will have to determine on the basis of the outcome of that review to what extent it is under an obligation to reopen, without adversely affecting the interests of third parties, the decision in question.

Later cases have fine-tuned the requirements laid down in the preceding case.[42] Thus it is clear from *Kempter*[43] that the third condition in *Kühne & Heitz* does not require the parties to have raised the point of EU law before the national court. It suffices in this respect if either the point of EU law, the interpretation of which proved to be incorrect in the light of a subsequent ECJ judgment, was considered by the national court ruling at final instance or could have been raised by the latter of its own motion.

(D) CONCLUSION

The development of precedent charted above has implications for the relationship between national courts and the CJEU. It modifies the original conception of a horizontal and bilateral relationship. Insofar as CJEU rulings have *de facto* precedential value, they place the Court in a superior position to the national courts. The very existence of a system of precedent is indicative of a shift to a vertical hierarchy between the CJEU and national courts: the CJEU will lay down the legally authoritative interpretation, which will then be adopted by national courts. The creation of precedent serves also to render that relationship less bilateral, and more multilateral, since an earlier CJEU ruling can be relied on by any national court dealing with the point of law that has already been decided by the CJEU.

The importance attached to earlier rulings is both reflected in and reinforced by Article 99 of the Rules of Procedure,[44] which allows the CJEU to give its decision by reasoned order referring to a previous decision or earlier case law where a question referred is identical to one that has already been answered, or where the answer to the question can be clearly deduced from prior case law. Thus if the national court does refer where there is an existing precedent the CJEU may well give judgment by reasoned order that reiterates its previous ruling.

4 THE EXISTENCE OF A QUESTION: THE 'ACTE CLAIR' DOCTRINE

A national court may feel that the answer to the issue is so clear that no reference to the CJEU is required. National courts have, in the past, refused to make a reference for this reason.[45] The conditions in which this is legitimate were considered in *CILFIT*, although the Court is not deprived of

---

[42] Case C–234/04 *Kapferer v Schlanck & Schick GmbH* [2006] ECR I–2585; Cases C–392 and 422/04 *i-21 Germany GmbH and Arcor & Co KG v Germany* [2006] ECR I–8559; Case C–249/11 *Byankov v Glaven sekretar na Ministerstvo na vatreshnite raboti* EU:C:2012:608.

[43] Case C–2/06 *Kempter* (n 29) [44].

[44] Rules of Procedure of the Court of Justice, 25 Sept 2012, http://curia.europa.eu/jcms/upload/docs/application/pdf/2012-10/rp_en.pdf.

[45] See, eg, *Re Société des Pétroles Shell-Berre* [1964] CMLR 462.

jurisdiction to give a ruling, even if the matter does fulfil the following criteria,[46] and a national court can moreover choose to make such a reference even where the criteria are met.[47]

Case 283/81 **Srl CILFIT and Lanificio di Gavardo SpA v Ministry of Health**
[1982] ECR 3415

[Note Lisbon Treaty renumbering: Art 177(3) is now Art 267(3) TFEU]

The facts were set out above. Where a precedent exists, then the relationship between the CJEU and the national court is as set out in the preceding section. The *acte clair* doctrine may however apply where there is no prior EU judicial decision on the point. The extract follows on immediately from that given above.

THE ECJ

16. Finally, the correct application of Community law may be so obvious as to leave no scope for any reasonable doubt as to the manner in which the question raised is to be resolved. Before it comes to the conclusion that such is the case, the national court or tribunal must be convinced that the matter is equally obvious to the courts of the other Member States and to the Court of Justice. Only if those conditions are satisfied may the national court or tribunal refrain from submitting the question to the Court of Justice and take upon itself the responsibility for resolving it.

17. However, the existence of such a possibility must be assessed on the basis of the characteristic feature of Community law and the particular difficulties to which its interpretation gives rise.

18. To begin with, it must be borne in mind that Community legislation is drafted in several languages and that the different language versions are equally authentic. An interpretation of a provision of Community law thus involves a comparison of the different language versions.

19. It must also be borne in mind, even where the different language versions are entirely in accord with one another, that Community law uses terminology which is peculiar to it. Furthermore, it must be emphasised that legal concepts do not necessarily have the same meaning in Community law and in the law of the various Member States.

20. Finally, every provision of Community law must be placed in its context and interpreted in the light of the provisions of Community law as a whole, regard being had to the objectives thereof and to its state of evolution at the date on which the provision in question is to be applied.

21. In the light of all those considerations, the answer to the question submitted...must be that paragraph (3) of Article 177 of the EEC Treaty is to be interpreted as meaning that a court or tribunal against whose decisions there is no judicial remedy under national law is required, where a question of Community law is raised before it, to comply with its obligation to bring the matter before the Court of Justice, unless it has established that the question raised is irrelevant or that the Community provision in question has already been interpreted by the Court or that the correct application of Community law is so obvious as to leave no scope for any reasonable doubt. The existence of such a possibility must be assessed in the light of the specific characteristics of Community law, the particular difficulties to which its interpretation gives rise and the risk of divergences in judicial decisions within the Community.

The implications of *CILFIT* were considered by a number of commentators. References to Article 177 should now be read as to Article 267 TFEU.

---

[46] Cases C–128–131 and 134–135/09 *Boxus and others v Région wallonne* EU:C:2011:667, [32].
[47] Cases C–165–167/09 *Stichting Natuur en Milieu v College van Gedeputeerde Staten van Groningen* [2011] ECR I–4599, [52].

GF Mancini and DT Keeling, From CILFIT to ERT: The Constitutional Challenge Facing the European Court[48]

The correct analysis of *CILFIT* was given by a Danish scholar, Professor Hjalte Rasmussen,[49] who maintains that the judgment was based on an astute strategy of 'give and take'. The Court, recognizing that it could not in any case coerce the national courts into accepting its jurisdiction, concedes something—a great deal in fact, nothing less than the right not to refer if the Community measure is clear—to the professional or national pride of the municipal judge, but then . . . restricts the circumstances in which the clarity of the provision may legitimately be sustained to cases so rare that the nucleus of its own authority is preserved intact (or rather consolidated because it voluntarily divested itself of a part of its exclusive jurisdiction). The objective of the Court is plain: by granting supreme courts the power to do lawfully that which they could in any case do unlawfully, but by subjecting that power to stringent conditions, the Court hoped to induce the supreme courts to use willingly the 'mechanism for judicial cooperation' provided by the Treaty. The result is to eliminate sterile and damaging conflicts and to reduce the risk that Community law might be the subject of divergent interpretations.

Mancini and Keeling therefore saw *CILFIT* as a dialogue between the ECJ and the national courts, with the intent being to rein in the latter. The 'give and take' of *CILFIT* involved the ECJ accepting the *acte clair* doctrine in principle, but placing significant constraints on its exercise in the hope that national courts would play the game and only refuse to refer when matters really were unequivocally clear.

Other writers were, however, more sceptical as to whether the conditions laid down in *CILFIT* really did curb the discretion of national courts. Thus Arnull doubted how far the criteria had practical force and pointed to the fact the ruling could be used 'to justify refusing to make a reference where the national court has formed a view as to how the points of Community law at issue should be resolved'.[50]

Yet others have, however, argued that the conditions in *CILFIT* are too restrictive, and that more discretion should be left to national courts. Thus Advocate General Jacobs argued that national judges should not have to consider all official language versions of EU acts,[51] a view shared by Advocate General Stix-Hackl.[52] This view has been echoed by the Association of the Councils of State and Supreme Administrative Jurisdictions of the EU, which contended that the conditions in *CILFIT* should be relaxed, that they should be applied in a 'commonsense' way, and that comparing all the language versions was no longer realistic or feasible. It argued that *CILFIT* should be applied so that the national court would determine whether the case was worth the burden of a preliminary reference.[53] Rasmussen put an analogous argument, and so more recently have Fenger and Broberg.

---

[48] Mancini and Keeling (n 3) 4.

[49] H Rasmussen, 'The European Court's *Acte Clair* Strategy in *CILFIT*' (1984) 9 ELRev 242.

[50] A Arnull, 'The Use and Abuse of Article 177' (1989) 52 MLR 622, 637. See also A Arnull, 'The Law Lords and the European Union: Swimming with the Incoming Tide' (2010) 35 ELRev 57, 75–79.

[51] Case C–338/95 *Wiener v Hauptzollamt Emmerich* [1997] ECR I–6495.

[52] Case 495/03 *Intermodal Transports BV v Staatssecretaris van Financiën* [2005] ECR I–8151, [98]–[99].

[53] Report of the Association of the Councils of State and Supreme Administrative Jurisdictions of the EU, June 2008, 7; D Sarmiento, 'Amending the Preliminary Reference Procedure for the Administrative Judge' (2009) 2 Review of European Administrative Law 29.

H Rasmussen, Remedying the Crumbling EC Judicial System[54]

The thrust of a *CILFIT II* should be to give the initiative back to the judges of the Member States, trusting them to solve on their own far more questions of interpretation of Community law, including those which are not straightforward. In technical terms, a *CILFIT II* should operate so as to enlarge considerably the scope of the Community acts which are deemed to be *actes clairs*. The job to pin down on paper the demarcation line between those cases which will deserve EC judicial attention...and those classes of cases which the national judges ought to decide on their own responsibility will not be an easy one, but it is as indispensable as difficult.

N Fenger and M Broberg, Finding Light in the Darkness: On the Actual Application of the *Acte Clair* Doctrine[55]

When the Court of Justice laid down the *CILFIT* conditions, the EU differed significantly from the EU of today. This was so not only with regard to the number of Member States and official languages and to the Court's case load and the time that it takes to answer a preliminary question, but also with regard to the EU law system as such. However, today the EU law system has reached a stage where it is considerably less vulnerable than it was a quarter of a century ago. To our mind, there is still a need to limit strictly the possibility for a national court to avoid a preliminary reference in cases concerning general questions of interpretation that go beyond the confines of a single case. Indeed, in such cases there is a genuine need for uniform interpretation that should be established by the Court of Justice. In contrast, taking into consideration both the interests of the parties to the main action and the need to keep the Court's case load at a workable level, it seems less obvious that the same strict conditions should apply in cases where the issue of interpretation is unlikely to arise again, but instead is confined to the particular factual situation before the national court. In this latter situation, we suggest that it should be sufficient for *acte clair* to apply that the national court finds that the result does not give rise to appreciable doubt, but without requiring that the national court is equally convinced that all other courts find the matter to be equally obvious or requiring an examination of all the language versions of the relevant text.

Current indications are however that the Court is content with the formulation in *CILFIT* and shows no inclination to modify the ruling to any significant degree.[56] It is true that in *Intermodal*[57] the ECJ declined to extend the *CILFIT* conditions, holding that a national court was not required to ensure that the matter was equally obvious to bodies of a non-judicial nature, such as administrative authorities. Subject to that caveat, the ECJ reaffirmed the *CILFIT* condition that before declining to refer a national court must be convinced that the matter was so obvious that there was no scope for any reasonable doubt as to the way in which the question should be resolved, and more especially that the matter was equally obvious to other national courts and to the ECJ.[58] The reality in the UK is that the

---

[54] (2000) 37 CMLRev 1071, 1109.

[55] (2011) 30 YBEL 180, 212.

[56] Case C–461/03 *Gaston Schul* (n 37) [16]; Case T–47/02 *Danzer* (n 30) [36]; Cases T–349, 371/06, 14, 15 and 332/07 *Germany v Commission* [2008] ECR II–2181, [67].

[57] Case 495/03 *Intermodal Transports* (n 52) [39].

[58] Ibid [38]–[39].

Supreme Court does not generally consider the *CILFIT* criteria separately, but asks if the answer is 'clear beyond the bounds of reasonable argument'.[59]

(A) SUMMARY

i. The relationship between national courts and the CJEU has been transformed by the development of precedent, *acte clair*, and sectoral delegation of responsibility.

ii. These developments have made national courts EU courts in their own right. They can dispose of cases without the need for a further reference to the CJEU. They can do so where there is an EU decision on the point, where the matter is so clear as to obviate the need for a reference, or where more general responsibility has been delegated to them in a particular area.

iii. The combined effect has been to render the relationship more vertical and multilateral than it was at the inception of the EU.

5 THE DECISION TO REFER: THE NATIONAL COURT'S PERSPECTIVE

The discussion thus far has touched on factors that can influence the national court's decision whether to refer: the existence of a CJEU judgment and the *acte clair* doctrine. We now consider the more general factors that a national court may take into account when making the decision whether to refer. There are two criteria that must be satisfied before a reference may be made.

The first is that the question must be raised before the court or tribunal of the Member State. However, it has been seen that the *CILFIT* case held that a national court may raise a matter of its own motion, even if this has not been done by the parties.[60] The second general criterion is that the national court must consider that a decision on the question is necessary to enable it to give judgment. *CILFIT* makes it clear that even a national court of last resort must believe that this is so before it is obliged to make a reference. It should also be noted that Article 267 does not provide that the reference must be necessary, but that a decision on the question is necessary to enable the national court to give judgment. The danger of confusing these two issues is brought out in the *Bulmer* case, which shows the 'early approach' of the UK courts to the exercise of the discretion accorded to them.

HP Bulmer Ltd v J Bollinger SA
[1974] 2 WLR 202

Bollinger made champagne and claimed that the use of the word champagne by makers of cider, in the form of champagne cider, should be prohibited. Bollinger alleged that the use of the word champagne to describe products other than those which came from the Champagne region in France was contrary to Community law. Bollinger asked that this question of Community law should be referred to the ECJ. The judge at first instance refused to make the reference, and Bollinger appealed to the Court of Appeal. Lord Denning emphasized that the discretion whether to refer was for the national court and

---

[59] *R (Countryside Alliance) v Attorney General* [2007] UKHL 52, [2009] 1 AC 719, [31]; *O'Byrne v Aventis Pasteur* [2008] UKHL 34, [23]–[24].

[60] See also (nn 27, 28).

that it should do so only where the decision on the question was necessary to enable it to give judgment. A reference might not be necessary where there was an existing ECJ judgment on the point or where the matter was *acte clair*.

COURT OF APPEAL: LORD DENNING MR

(2) Guidelines as to the exercise of discretion. Assuming that the condition about 'necessary' is fulfilled, there remains the matter of discretion....

(i) The time to get a ruling. The length of time...before a ruling can be obtained from the European Court. This may take months and months....Meanwhile, the whole action in the English court is stayed until the ruling is obtained. This may be very unfortunate, especially in a case where an injunction is sought or there are other reasons for expedition....

(ii) Do not overload the Court. The importance of not overloading the European Court by references to it. If it were overloaded, it could not get through its work....

(iii) Formulate the question clearly. The need to formulate the question clearly. It must be a question of interpretation only of the Treaty. It must not be mixed up with the facts....

(iv) Difficulty and importance. The difficulty and importance of the point. Unless the point is really difficult and important, it would seem better for the English judge to decide it himself. For in so doing, much delay and expense will be saved....

(v) Expense. The expense of getting a ruling from the European Court....

(vi) Wishes of the parties. The wishes of the parties. If both parties want the point referred...the English court should have regard to their wishes, but it should not give them undue weight. The English court should hesitate before making a reference against the wishes of one of the parties, seeing the expense and delay which it involves.

Lord Denning MR decided on the facts that a reference was not needed for a number of reasons.[61] The judgment was not uncontroversial and the guidelines were criticized. Thus Jacobs argued that there were many situations where time and costs would be saved by an early reference and that cases raising important points of EU law could arise where there was little at stake between the parties.[62] The *Samex* case is more indicative of the 'current approach' of the UK courts, which are more ready to refer.

Customs and Excise Commissioners v ApS Samex
(Hanil Fiber Industrial Co Ltd, third party)
[1983] 1 All ER 1042

An EC Regulation allowed Member States to impose quantitative limits on the import of textiles from certain countries outside the EC. The implementation of the import scheme was left to the Member States, who were to issue import licences up to the quota for each year. The defendant made a contract to buy goods from a non-Member State, which stipulated that the goods had to be shipped by a certain date. The Customs authorities discovered that the goods had been shipped outside the relevant dates, and imposed penalties on the defendant. The latter responded by arguing that the Customs authorities were in breach of the Community Regulation, and sought a reference to the ECJ. Bingham J considered the guidelines set out by Lord Denning MR in *Bulmer*. He then continued as follows.

---

[61] The time and expense involved; the facts had not been fully found; and the point was not a difficult one, [1974] 3 WLR 202, 216–217.

[62] FG Jacobs, 'When to Refer to the European Court' (1974) 90 LQR 486, 492.

> ### HIGH COURT: BINGHAM J
>
> Sitting as a judge in a national court, asked to decide questions of Community law, I am very conscious of the advantages enjoyed by the Court of Justice. It has a panoramic view of the Community and its institutions, a detailed knowledge of the treaties and of much subordinate legislation made under them, and an intimate familiarity with the functioning of the Common Market which no national judge denied the collective experience of the Court of Justice could hope to achieve. Where questions of administrative intention and practice arise the Court of Justice can receive submissions from the Community institutions, as also where relations between the Community and non-Member States are in issue. Where the interests of Member States are affected they can intervene to make their views known....
>
> Where comparison falls to be made between Community texts in different languages, all texts being equally authentic, the multinational Court of Justice is equipped to carry out the task in a way which no national judge, whatever his linguistic skills, could rival. The interpretation of Community instruments involves very often not the process familiar to common lawyers of laboriously extracting the meaning from words used but the more creative process of supplying flesh to a spare and loosely constructed skeleton. The choice between alternative submissions may turn not on purely legal considerations, but on a broader view of what the orderly development of the Community requires. These are matters which the Court of Justice is very much better placed to assess and determine than a national court.

While UK courts sometimes still refer to the guidelines in *Bulmer* they also tend to be more ready to make a reference. Sir Thomas Bingham MR encapsulated the more modern approach.[63]

> [I]f the facts have been found and the Community law issue is critical to the court's final decision, the appropriate course is to refer the issue to the Court of Justice unless the national court can with complete confidence resolve the issue itself. In considering whether it can...the national court must be fully mindful of the differences between national and Community legislation, of the pitfalls which face a national court venturing into what may be an unfamiliar field, of the need for uniform interpretation throughout the Community and of the great advantages enjoyed by the Court of Justice in construing Community instruments. If the national court has any real doubt, it should obviously refer.

6 THE DECISION TO ACCEPT THE REFERENCE: THE CJEU'S PERSPECTIVE

We now turn to consider how the CJEU perceives its role when an issue is referred by a national court. Its approach has altered since the inception of the EEC.

---

[63] *R v International Stock Exchange, ex p Else* [1993] QB 534; *Polydor Ltd v Harlequin Record Shops Ltd* [1980] 2 CMLR 413; *R v Plymouth Justices, ex p Rogers* [1982] 3 WLR 1; *R v Pharmaceutical Society of Great Britain, ex p The Association of Pharmaceutical Importers* [1987] 3 CMLR 951; *R v HM Treasury, ex p Daily Mail and General Trust plc* [1987] 2 CMLR 1; *R v Secretary of State for the National Heritage, ex p Continental Television BV* [1993] 2 CMLR 333; *R v Ministry of Agriculture, Fisheries and Food, ex p Portman Agrochemicals Ltd* [1994] 3 CMLR 18; *Beckmann v Dynamco Whicheloe MacFarlane Ltd* [2000] Pens LR 269; *R (Anderson) v Secretary of State for the Home Department* [2003] 1 AC 837, [91]; *Commissioners of Customs and Excise and Another v Federation of Technological Industries* [2004] EWCA Civ 1020, [88]; *Royal Bank of Scotland Group plc v Commissioners for HM Revenue and Customs* [2007] CSIH 15, [23]–[25]; *The Number (UK) Limited, Conduit Enterprises Limited v Office of Communications, British Telecommunications Plc* [2008] CAT 33, [165]–[171]; *R (Newby Foods Ltd) v Food Standards Agency* [2013] EWHC 1966 (Admin).

(A) THE LIBERAL INITIAL APPROACH

The ECJ's initial approach was very liberal and it would, wherever possible, read the reference so as to preserve its ability to pass judgment on the case. The ECJ was prepared to *correct improperly framed references*. Thus in *Costa* it stated that it had power to extract from a question imperfectly formulated by the national court those questions which really did pertain to the interpretation of the Treaty.[64] This is also exemplified by the *Schwarze* case.

Case 16/65 Firma C Schwarze v Einfuhr- und Vorratsstelle für Getreide und Futtermittel
[1965] ECR 877

[Note Lisbon Treaty renumbering: Arts 173 and 177 are now Arts 263 and 267 TFEU]

Schwarze obtained import licences from the EVSt to import barley. The EVSt fixed the rate of levy which should be paid, pursuant to a Council regulation. The rate of levy was fixed on the basis of a Commission decision. Schwarze argued that the levy rate was too high, and that the Commission decision was illegal. The Finanzgericht therefore submitted a number of detailed questions to the ECJ. France argued that the questions being asked were concerned not with the interpretation of the Treaty, but rather with the validity of Community acts; and that the proper way of challenging such acts was via Article 173, and not via Article 177.

THE ECJ

It appears from the wording of the questions submitted that the Hessisches Finanzgericht is concerned not so much with the interpretation of the Treaty or of an act of a Community institution, as with a preliminary ruling on the validity of such an act under Article 177(1)(b)....

In its comments, the government of the French Republic complains that several of the questions submitted call for more than just an interpretation of the Treaty. The Court of Justice would, in answering these alleged questions of interpretation, actually be ruling on points involving not the interpretation of the Treaty but the validity of acts of the EEC institutions.

The contention of the French Republic that Article 177 cannot be used to obtain from the Court a ruling that such an act is null and void is pertinent. That provision does, however, expressly give the Court power to rule on the validity of such an act. Where it appears that the real object of the questions submitted by a national court is a review of the validity of Community acts rather than an interpretation thereof, the Court of Justice must nevertheless decide the questions immediately, instead of holding the referring court to a strict adherence to form which would only serve to prolong the Article 177 procedure and be incompatible with its true nature. Such a strict adherence to form is conceivable in actions between parties whose respective rights must be determined according to strict rules. It would not, however, be appropriate in the very special area of judicial cooperation provided for in Article 177, where the national court and the Court of Justice—each within its own jurisdiction and with the purpose of ensuring a uniform application of Community law—must together and directly contribute to the legal conclusions. Any other procedure would have the result of letting the national courts rule on the validity of acts of the Community.

---

[64] Case 6/64 *Costa v ENEL* [1964] ECR 585.

The ECJ also *commonly rejected claims that a reference should not be accepted because of the reasons for making it, or the facts on which it was based.* The ECJ emphasized that these matters were for the national court. Thus in *Costa* the ECJ stated that Article 267 'is based on a clear separation of functions between national courts and the Court of Justice'. The ECJ was not empowered to 'investigate the facts of the case or to criticise the grounds and purpose of the request for interpretation'.[65] Similarly in *Pierik*,[66] the ECJ reiterated that Article 267 was based on a clear division of function, which precluded it from judging the relevance of the questions asked, or from determining whether concepts of EU law really were applicable to the case before the national court. The ECJ stressed the point once again in *Simmenthal*,[67] stating that what is now Article 267 was based on a distinct separation of function between national courts and the ECJ, such that the latter did not have jurisdiction to take cognizance of the facts of the case or to criticize the reasons for the reference.

The ECJ's approach during the early years was therefore open and flexible. It clearly did not wish to discourage litigants from having recourse to Community law, more especially because it was through Article 267 TFEU that the ECJ developed doctrines such as direct effect and supremacy. Nor did the ECJ wish to place obstacles in the path of national judiciaries by refusing to answer questions unless they were perfectly framed. This would not have encouraged national judges to make use of novel legal machinery.

(B) THE CJEU ASSERTS AUTHORITY OVER CASES REFERRED

It is clear, notwithstanding the preceding cases, that the CJEU regards itself as having the ultimate authority to decide whether a reference is warranted or not. The seminal case is *Foglia*.

Case 104/79 **Pasquale Foglia v Mariella Novello**
[1980] ECR 745

[Note Lisbon Treaty renumbering: Arts 95 and 177 are now Arts 110 and 267 TFEU]

Foglia made a contract to sell wine to Novello, and the contract stated that Novello would not be liable for any taxes levied by the French or Italian authorities which were contrary to EC law. The goods were carried by Danzas, a general transporter. The contract of carriage also contained a clause stipulating that Foglia would not be liable for charges which were contrary to EC law. Danzas in fact paid a French tax, and this was included in the bill submitted to Foglia, who paid the bill including the amount of the disputed tax, notwithstanding the clause in the contract of carriage which would have entitled him not to do so. Foglia then sought to recover this amount from Novello in an action before an Italian court. The latter refused to pay, relying on the clause in her contract with Foglia which stipulated that she would not be liable for any unlawful charge. Novello argued that the charge was contrary to Article 95. The Italian court sought a preliminary ruling whether the French tax was contrary to Community law. The ECJ noted that the pleadings of Foglia and Novello concerning tax discrimination were essentially identical.

---

[65] Ibid 593.
[66] Case 117/77 *Bestuur van het Algemeen Ziekenfonds, Drenthe-Platteland v G Pierik* [1978] ECR 825.
[67] Case 35/76 *Simmenthal SpA v Ministero delle Finanze* [1976] ECR 1871, [4].

THE ECJ

10. It thus appears that the parties to the main action are concerned to obtain a ruling that the French tax system is invalid for liqueur wines by the expedient of proceedings before an Italian court between two private individuals who are in agreement as to the result to be attained and who have inserted a clause in their contract in order to induce the Italian court to give a ruling on the point. The artificial nature of this expedient is underlined by the fact that Danzas did not exercise its rights under French law to institute proceedings over the consumption tax although it undoubtedly had an interest in doing so in view of the clause in the contract by which it was also bound and moreover of the fact that Foglia paid without protest that undertaking's bill which included a sum paid in respect of that tax.

11. The duty of the Court of Justice under Article 177 of the EEC Treaty is to supply all courts in the Community with the information on the interpretation of Community law which is necessary to enable them to settle genuine disputes which are brought before them. A situation in which the Court was obliged by the expedient of arrangements like those described above to give rulings would jeopardise the whole system of legal remedies available to private individuals to enable them to protect themselves against tax provisions which are contrary to the Treaty.

The ECJ therefore declined to give a ruling, but the Italian judge was undaunted and referred further questions to the ECJ. He asked, in effect, whether the preceding decision was consistent with the principle that it was for the national judge to determine the facts and the need for a reference.

Case 244/80 **Pasquale Foglia v Mariella Novello (No 2)**
[1981] ECR 3045

THE ECJ

12. In his first question the Pretore requested clarification of the limits of the power of appraisal reserved by the Treaty to the national court on the one hand and the Court of Justice on the other with regard to the wording of references for a preliminary ruling and of the appraisal of the circumstances of fact and law in the main action, in particular where the national court is requested to give a declaratory judgment.

...

14. With regard to the first question it should be recalled, as the Court of Justice has had occasion to emphasise in very varied contexts, that Article 177 is based on cooperation which entails a division of duties between the national courts and the Court of Justice in the interest of the proper application and uniform interpretation of Community law throughout all the Member States.

15. With this in view it is for the national court—by reason of the fact that it is seised of the substance of the dispute and that it must bear the responsibility for the decision to be taken—to assess, having regard to the facts of the case, the need to obtain a preliminary ruling to enable it to give judgment.

16. In exercising that power of appraisal the national court, in collaboration with the Court of Justice, fulfils a duty entrusted to them both of ensuring that in the interpretation and application of the Treaty the law is observed. Accordingly the problems which may be entailed in the exercise of its power of appraisal by the national court and the relations which it maintains within the framework of Article 177 with the Court of Justice are governed exclusively by the provisions of Community law.

17. In order that the Court of Justice may perform its task in accordance with the Treaty it is essential for national courts to explain, when the reasons do not emerge beyond any doubt from the file, why they consider that a reply to their question is necessary to enable them to give judgment.

18. It must in fact be emphasised that the duty assigned to the Court by Article 177 is not that of delivering advisory opinions on general or hypothetical questions but of assisting in the administration of justice in the Member States. It accordingly does not have jurisdiction to reply to questions of interpretation which are submitted to it within the framework of procedural devices arranged by the parties in order to induce the Court to give its view on certain problems of Community law which do not correspond to an objective requirement inherent in the resolution of a dispute. A declaration by the Court that it has no jurisdiction in such circumstances does not in any way trespass upon the prerogatives of the national court but makes it possible to prevent the application of the procedure under Article 177 for purposes other than those appropriate for it.

19. Furthermore, it should be pointed out that, whilst the Court of Justice must be able to place as much reliance as possible upon the assessment by the national court of the extent to which the questions submitted to it are essential, it must be in a position to make any assessment inherent in the performance of its own duties in particular in order to check, as all courts must, whether it has jurisdiction. Thus the Court, taking into account the repercussions of its decisions in this matter, must have regard, in exercising the jurisdiction conferred upon it by Article 177, not only to the interests of the parties to the proceedings but also to those of the Community and of the Member States. Accordingly it cannot, without disregarding the duties assigned to it, remain indifferent to the assessments made by the courts of the Member States in the exceptional cases in which such assessments may affect the proper working of the procedure laid down by Article 177.

...

21. The reply to the first question must accordingly be that whilst, according to the intended role of Article 177, an assessment of the need to obtain an answer to the questions of interpretation raised, regard being had to the circumstances of fact and law involved in the main action, is a matter for the national court it is nevertheless for the Court of Justice, in order to confirm its own jurisdiction, to examine, where necessary, the conditions in which the case has been referred to it by the national court.

...

25. The reply to the fourth question must accordingly be that in the case of preliminary questions intended to permit the national court to determine whether provisions laid down by law or regulation in another Member State are in accordance with Community law the degree of legal protection may not differ according to whether such questions are raised in proceedings between individuals or in an action to which the State whose legislation is called in question is a party, but that in the first case the Court of Justice must take special care to ensure that the procedure under Article 177 is not employed for purposes which were not intended by the Treaty.

The important point of principle in *Foglia (No 2)* was that the ECJ would be the ultimate decider of its own jurisdiction. The reasoning is both subtle and dramatic. The judgment began in orthodox fashion in demarcating the role of the national court and the ECJ. A few paragraphs later this was transformed: due regard was to be given to the view of the national court as to whether a response was required to a question, but the ultimate decision rested with the ECJ. If, in order to resolve this issue, further and better particulars were required from the national courts, then these must be forthcoming.

Foglia was therefore not simply about hypothetical cases. It was about the primacy of control over the Article 267 procedure and the nature of the judicial hierarchy, involving EU and national courts, which operates through this Article. The original division of function between national courts and the ECJ may have been separate but equal, as manifested in the idea that the former decide whether to refer, while the latter gives the ruling on the matter placed before it. *Foglia* reshaped that conception. The ECJ was not simply to be a passive receptor, forced to adjudicate on whatever was placed before it.

It would assert some control over the suitability of the reference. The decision in the case, concerning the allegedly hypothetical nature of the proceedings, was simply one manifestation of this assertion of jurisdictional control. The ECJ would, in the future, 'make any assessment inherent in the performance of its own duties in particular in order to check, as all courts must, whether it has jurisdiction' (paragraph 19).

The *Foglia* case generated much comment. Bebr argued against the ruling. References to Article 177 should now be read as to Article 267.

G Bebr, The Existence of a Genuine Dispute: An Indispensable Precondition for the Jurisdiction of the Court under Article 177 EEC Treaty?[68]

In its well-established case law the Court of Justice has always viewed Article 177 as establishing a method of co-operation between the national courts and the Court, based on jurisdictional exclusivity rather than on a hierarchical superiority. Moreover it has systematically refused to review the grounds for questions raised and their relevance to the pending litigation, being obviously anxious to demonstrate that its function is limited to an interpretation of Community rules or to a review of validity of Community acts....

...In this case it took note of several factors from which it inferred that the dispute was fabricated and that, therefore, it lacked jurisdiction...

The fabricated nature of a dispute as a precondition for the admissibility of a referral is a slippery concept, not without dangerous pitfalls. The French government which participated in the preliminary proceedings did not, it may be noted, even contest the jurisdiction of the Court. The Court did so of its own motion. Of course, there may be various shades and degrees to which litigation may appear fabricated. The situation may seldom be clear cut. Litigation in which a private party seeks to obtain a ruling in a test case in which it invokes a directly effective Community rule against a Member State before its own national courts may raise a similar problem; it may also lack the character of a genuine dispute. Who may say with any certainty that the plaintiff entertained the action seriously or whether he merely sought to obtain a decision in a test case which although of negligible interest to him, raised a question of principle?

Not all were however opposed to the decision in *Foglia*. Wyatt argued in favour of the ruling, noting that enforcement actions brought by the Commission under Articles 258 and 259 TFEU are subject to preliminary objections concerning admissibility.

D Wyatt, Foglia (No 2): The Court Denies it has Jurisdiction to Give Advisory Opinions[69]

[A]t bottom the controversy over the Court's decision in *Foglia* v. *Novello*...turns on the simple question whether or not references to the European Court from national courts are subject, before the European Court, to the same preliminary objections as to admissibility as any other claim upon the part of private parties, Member States, or Community institutions, to invoke the Court's jurisdiction. If they are not, then the guardians of the European Court's judicial functions, indeed of its very jurisdiction, within the framework of Article 177 EEC, are national courts, rather than the Court itself. It is not impossible that the draftsmen of the Treaty should have ordained such a thing. Simply improbable, in view of

---

[68] (1980) 17 CMLRev 525, 530–532.
[69] (1982) 7 ELRev 186, 187–188, 190. Italics in the original.

> the departure from principle which it would involve: superior courts are invariably entrusted with the competence to determine their own jurisdiction.
>
> [*Wyatt demonstrated, inter alia, differing ways in which the ECJ determined various jurisdictional issues, such as whether the body making the reference was a court. Later he referred to the reasoning in* Foglia (No 2), *in which the ECJ emphasized that it had no jurisdiction to give advisory opinions.*]
>
> While the Court must be able to place as much reliance as possible upon assessments by national courts of questions referred, it must, it insisted, be in a position to make *itself* any assessment inherent in the performance of its own duties, in particular in order to *check*, as all *courts* must, whether it had jurisdiction. In exercising its *jurisdiction* under Article 177, the Court was bound to consider, not only the interests of the parties to the proceedings, but also the interests of the Community, and of the Member States....
>
> The Court's reasoning is convincing. It affirms its right to determine its own jurisdiction, and contrasts its own essentially judicial functions, with the delivery of advisory opinions. The distinction between a judgment and an advisory opinion is that the former affects the legal position of the parties to a dispute; the latter has no such effect. The capacity to give a *judgment* itself characterises the organ in question as a *court*. The capacity to give legal advice of course has no such corollary...

(c) CASES WHERE THE CJEU HAS DECLINED JURISDICTION

The principle in *Foglia* lay dormant for some time, and attempts to invoke it were unsuccessful.[70] This fuelled the belief that the case was a one-off, and that the principle therein was unlikely to be used. The ECJ however began to use the *Foglia* principle, particularly from the 1990s onwards. The cases fall into a number of categories.

(i) *Hypothetical Cases*

The hypothetical nature of the question provides one example.[71] There are a number of reasons for refusing to give such rulings. They are, in part, practical, since it would be a waste of judicial resources to give a ruling in a hypothetical case, because the problem may never in fact transpire.[72] There are also conceptual problems. If a case really is hypothetical it may be unclear precisely who should be the appropriate parties to the action, and the relevant arguments may not be put. Moreover, if the hypothetical problem becomes 'concrete', it may not do so in exactly the form envisaged by the court's judgment, and hence the precise relevance of that judgment may be unclear.

While there may, therefore, be sound reasons for refusing to give opinions in hypothetical cases, there is also a fine line dividing that type of case from test cases.[73] A function of a legal

---

[70] Case 261/81 *Walter Rau Lebensmittelwerke v De Smedt Pvba* [1982] ECR 3961; Case 46/80 *Vinal SpA v Orbat SpA* [1981] ECR 77; Case C–150/88 *Eau de Cologne and Parfumerie-Fabrik Glockengasse No 4711 KG v Provide Srl* [1989] ECR 3891.

[71] Case C–467/04 *Criminal Proceedings against Gasparini and others* [2006] ECR I–9199.

[72] The wastage of resources argument will also be relevant if the problem has become moot, in the sense that it has been resolved. Whether a problem has become moot can be contentious. Compare Cases C–422–424/93 *Zabala v Instituto Nacional de Empleo* [1995] ECR I–1567, with Case C–194/94 *CIA Security International SA v Signalson SA* [1996] ECR I–2201.

[73] Case C–412/93 *Leclerc-Siplec v TFI Publicité and M6 Publicité* [1995] ECR I–179, AG Jacobs; Case C–200/98 *X AB and Y AB v Riksskatteverket* [1999] ECR I–8261; Case C–458/06 *Skattevet v Gourmet Classic Ltd* [2008] ECR I–4207, [31]–[32].

system is to enable people to plan their lives with knowledge of the legal implications of the choices they make. Test cases enable individuals to gain such knowledge. That the line between advisory opinions/hypothetical judgments and test cases can be a fine one is exemplified by the facts of the *Foglia* case itself.[74] Moreover, it is clear that the mere fact that parties agree on the interpretation they wish to be accorded to EU law does not, in itself, mean that the dispute is not a real one.[75]

(ii) *The Questions Raised Not Relevant to Resolution of the Dispute*

A second reason why the Court may not wish to give a ruling is that the questions raised are not relevant to the resolution of the substantive action in the national court.[76] Thus in *Meilicke*[77] the action was brought by a German lawyer, who challenged a theory of non-cash contributions of capital developed by the German courts on the ground that it was not compatible with the Second Banking Directive. The ECJ cited *Foglia (No 2)*, and declined to give a ruling, because it had not been shown that the issue of non-cash subscriptions was actually at stake in the main action.

In *Corsica Ferries*[78] the ECJ reiterated that it had no jurisdiction to rule on questions that had no relation to the facts or the subject matter of the main action, and decided that only four of the possible eight questions met this criterion. The same concern with relevance was evident in *Monin*,[79] where the ECJ held that it lacked jurisdiction to answer questions that did not involve an interpretation of EU law required for the decision by the national court. It therefore declined to answer questions placed before it by an insolvency judge, given that this judge would not have to deal with these issues in the insolvency itself. The *Dias* case exemplifies the same general point.

---

[74] *Foglia* was not a hypothetical case in the normal sense of that term. It concerned an actual seller of wine whose business was being affected by a current French tax which he believed to be contrary to Community law. The CJEU's argument that the issue should have been resolved by a different route will not withstand examination. Danzas had no incentive to litigate in France, even though it initially paid the tax, since it was a general carrier, and it would make no commercial sense for it to start an expensive action which was of no specific concern to its business. Foglia's decision to pay Danzas, even though it could have resisted payment under the contract, is also readily explicable. If Foglia had resisted payment then either Danzas would have accepted this, swallowed the loss, and still not have pursued the claim in France because it would not have been worthwhile; and/or it would have accepted this, but increased the cost of carriage by the amount of the tax for subsequent journeys and passed it on to Foglia. In either eventuality the legality of the tax under Community law would not have been contested. Even if Danzas had resorted to formal litigation with Foglia, this action would probably have been initiated in Italy, since it would have been an ordinary contract action the governing law of which would probably have been Italian. Compare *Foglia* to Case C–379/98 *PreussenElektra AG v Schhleswag AG* [2001] ECR I–2099, [38]–[46].

[75] Case C–412/93 *Leclerc-Siplec* (n 73); Case C–341/01 *Plato Plastik Robert Frank GmbH v Caropack Handelsgesellschaft mbH* [2004] ECR I–4883; Case C–144/04 *Mangold v Helm* [2005] ECR I–9981.

[76] Case C–134/95 *Unità Socio-Sanitaria Locale No 47 di Biella (USSL) v Istituto Nazionale per l'Assicurazione contro gli Infortuni sul Lavoro (INAIL)* [1997] ECR I–195; Case C–167/01 *Kamer van Koophandel en Fabrieken voor Amsterdam v Inspire Art Ltd* [2003] ECR I–10155; Case C–314/01 *Siemens AG Österreich and another v Hauptverband der österreichischen Socialversicherungstrager* [2004] ECR I–2549; Case C–152/03 *Ritter-Coulais v Finanzamt Gemersheim* [2006] ECR I–1711; Case C–313/07 *Kirtruna SL and Elisa Vigano v Red Elite de Electrodomésticos SA* [2008] ECR I–7907; Case C–180/12 *Stoilov i Ko EOOD v Nachalnik na Mitnitsa Stolichna* EU:C:2013:693, [36]–[38]; Case C–82/13 *Società cooperativa Madonna dei miracoli v Regione Abruzzo* EU:C:2013:655.

[77] Case C–83/91 *Wienand Meilicke v ADV/ORGA F A Meyer AG* [1992] ECR I–4871.

[78] Case C–18/93 *Corsica Ferries Italia Srl v Corpo dei Piloti del Porto di Genova* [1994] ECR I–1783.

[79] Case C–428/93 *Monin Automobiles-Maison du Deux-Roues* [1994] ECR I–1707.

Case C–343/90 **Lourenço Dias v Director da Alfandega do Porto**
[1992] ECR I–4673

[Note Lisbon Treaty renumbering: Art 95 is now Art 110 TFEU]

Dias was a van driver who was prosecuted for modifying his imported vehicle in a manner that altered its categorization for tax purposes without having paid the extra tax. The ECJ was presented with eight detailed questions from the national court concerning the compatibility of the relevant national rules with Article 95. The Portuguese Government argued that the sole basis of the dispute was a narrow question concerning its tax system and that none of the questions actually referred dealt with that issue. The ECJ accepted that national courts were *prima facie* in the best position to decide on the need for a reference, and that therefore, in principle, the ECJ was bound to give a ruling when asked. It then qualified this obligation.

THE ECJ

17. Nevertheless, in Case 244/80 *Foglia (No. 2)*...paragraph 21, the Court considered that, in order to determine whether it has jurisdiction, it is a matter for the Court of Justice to examine the conditions in which the case has been referred to it by the national court. The spirit of cooperation which must prevail in the preliminary ruling procedure requires the national court to have regard to the function entrusted to the Court of Justice, which is to assist in the administration of justice in the Member States and not to deliver advisory opinions on general or hypothetical questions....

18. In view of that task, the Court considers that it cannot give a preliminary ruling...where, *inter alia*, the interpretation requested relates to measures not yet adopted by the Community institutions (see Case 93/78, *Mattheus*...), the procedure before the court making the reference...has already been terminated (see Case 338/85 *Pardini*...) or the interpretation of Community law sought by the national court bears no relation to the actual nature of the case or to the subject-matter of the main action (Case 126/80 *Salonia*...).

19. It should also be borne in mind that...it is appropriate that, before making the reference to the Court, the national court should establish the facts of the case and settle the questions of purely national law....By the same token, it is essential for the national court to explain the reasons why it considers that a reply to its questions is necessary to enable it to give judgment....

20. With this information in its possession, the Court is in a position to ascertain whether the interpretation of Community law which is sought is related to the actual nature and subject-matter of the main proceedings. If it should appear that the question raised is manifestly irrelevant for the purposes of deciding the case, the Court must declare that there is no need to proceed to judgment.

(iii) *Questions Not Articulated Sufficiently Clearly*

A third rationale for refusing to take a case may be that the questions are not articulated clearly enough for the Court to be able to give any meaningful legal response.[80] This should be contrasted with cases where it teases out the real question from a reference that has been imperfectly formulated.[81] The CJEU will not, however, alter the substance of the questions referred to it. Governments and the parties concerned are allowed to submit observations under Article 23 of the Statute of the

---

[80] Case C–318/00 *Bacardi-Martini SAS and Cellier des Dauphins v Newcastle United Football Club* [2003] ECR I–905.
[81] Case C–88/99 *Roquette Frères SA v Direction des Services Fiscaux du Pas-de-Calais* [2000] ECR I–10465.

Court. They are notified of the order of the referring court, and hence it would be wrong for the CJEU to alter the substance of the questions referred.[82]

(iv) *Facts are Insufficiently Clear*

Closely allied to this third rationale is a fourth, where the facts are insufficiently clear for the Court to be able to apply the relevant legal rules. The Court will normally be able to characterize the nature of the legal issue only if the reference has an adequate factual foundation. The ECJ established in *Telemarsicabruzzo* that a national court must provide sufficient factual and legal context in order that the ECJ can respond to the questions referred,[83] and the principle has been applied in subsequent cases.[84]

Case C–567/07 **Minister voor Wonen, Wijken en Integratie v Woningstichting Sint Servatius**
[2009] ECR I–9021

[Note Lisbon Treaty renumbering: Art 87(1) is now Art 107(1) TFEU]

The national court asked whether, when a Member State provides financial resources to undertakings entrusted with the operation of services of general economic interest, the territorial scale of the activities of those undertakings should be limited in order to prevent those resources from constituting unlawful state aid and to prevent the undertakings, when employing those resources in another Member State, from distorting conditions of competition.

THE ECJ

49. [T]he presumption of relevance attaching to questions referred by the national courts for a preliminary ruling can be rebutted only in exceptional cases. Where the questions submitted concern the interpretation of Community law, the Court is in principle bound to give a ruling.

50. It is clear from well-established case-law, however, that the need to provide an interpretation of Community law which will be of use to the national court makes it necessary that the national court define the factual and legislative context of the questions it is asking or, at the very least, explain the factual circumstances on which those questions are based (Joined Cases C–320/90 to C–322/90 *Telemarsicabruzzo...*).

51. It is also important that the national court should set out the precise reasons why it was unsure as to the interpretation of Community law and why it considered it necessary to refer questions to the Court for a preliminary ruling. In that connection, it is essential that the referring court provide at the very least some explanation of the reasons for the choice of the Community provisions which

---

[82] Case C–235/95 *AGS Assedic Pas-de-Calais v Dumon and Froment* [1998] ECR I–4531.

[83] Cases C–320–322/90 *Telemarsicabruzzo SpA v Circostel, Ministero delle Poste e Telecommunicazioni and Ministerio della Difesa* [1993] ECR I–393.

[84] Case C–386/92 *Monin Automobiles v France* [1993] ECR I–2049; Case C–458/93 *Criminal Proceedings against Saddik* [1995] ECR I–511; Case C–316/93 *Vaneetveld v Le Foyer SA* [1994] ECR I–763; Case C–2/96 *Criminal Proceedings against Sunino and Data* [1996] ECR I–1543; Case C–257/95 *Bresle v Préfet de la Région Auvergne and Préfet du Puy-le-Dôme* [1996] ECR I–233; Case C–378/08 *Raffinerie Mediterranee (ERG) SpA v Ministero dello Sviluppo economico* [2010] ECR I–1919; Case C–384/08 *Attanasio Group Srl v Comune di Carbognano* [2010] ECR I–2055; Case C–433/11 *SKP k.s. v Kveta Polhošová* EU:C:2012:702.

it requires to be interpreted and of the link it establishes between those provisions and the national legislation applicable to the dispute in the main proceedings...

52. The information provided in the decision making the reference serves not only to enable the Court to give useful answers, but also to enable the governments of the Member States and other interested parties to submit observations in accordance with Article 23 of the Statute of the Court of Justice...

53. It should also be added that the need for precision, in particular with regard to the factual and legislative context of the main proceedings, applies in particular in the area of competition, which is characterised by complex factual and legal situations...

54. In this instance, the seventh question is based on the premise that...if Servatius used public resources to implement a future project, that would constitute State aid within the meaning of Article 87(1) EC. Neither the decision making the reference nor the observations of the parties to the main proceedings contain any elements which might serve to establish that such an advantage would in fact have been granted in the context of the construction project at issue in the main proceedings—which in any event was not implemented as Servatius did not obtain the necessary prior authorisation.

...

56. Accordingly, the seventh question referred by the national court must be held to be inadmissible.

(D) RECOMMENDATIONS TO NATIONAL COURTS ON PRELIMINARY REFERENCES

The Court has incorporated the results of its case law in Recommendations to National Courts.[85] Paragraph 22 states that the order for reference should contain a statement of reasons which is succinct but sufficiently complete to give the Court a clear understanding of the factual and legal context of the main action. It should include, in particular, a statement setting out the subject matter of the dispute and the essential facts; the relevant national law; identify as accurately as possible the EU provisions relevant to the case; the reasons why the national court referred the matter and the relationship between the provisions of EU law and national provisions applicable to the action; and a summary of the parties' arguments where appropriate.

(E) LIMITS OF THE POWER TO DECLINE A CASE

The CJEU is exerting greater control over the admissibility of references than in the early years of the Community. It has, however, made clear that it will decline to give a ruling only if the issue of EU law on which an interpretation is sought is manifestly inapplicable to the dispute before the national court or bears no relation to the subject matter of that action.[86] The standard formulation now used by the CJEU is that a reference will be deemed inadmissible only where it is quite obvious that the

---

[85] Recommendations to national courts and tribunals in relation to the initiation of preliminary ruling proceedings [2012] OJ C338/01.

[86] Case C–118/94 *Associazione Italiana per il World Wildlife Fund v Regione Veneto* [1996] ECR I–1223; Case C–129/94 *Criminal Proceedings against Bernaldez* [1996] ECR I–1829; Case C–264/96 *ICI Chemical Industries plc (ICI) v Colmer (HM Inspector of Taxes)* [1998] ECR I–4695; Cases C–215 and 216/96 *Bagnasco v BPN and Carige* [1999] ECR I–135; Case C–379/98 *PreussenElektra AG* (n 74) [38]–[39]; Case C–138/05 *Stichting Zuid-Hollandse Milieufederatie v Minister van Landbouw, Natuur en Voedselkwaliktiet* [2006] ECR I–8339; Case C–295/05 *Asemfo v Transformacion Agraria SA* [2007] ECR I–2999.

interpretation of EU law that is sought bears no relation to the actual facts of the main action or its purpose, where the problem is hypothetical, or where the Court does not have before it the factual or legal material necessary to give a useful answer to the questions submitted to it.[87]

Case C–314/08 **Filipiak v Dyrektor Izby Skarbowej w Poznaniu**
[2009] ECR I–11049

The reference concerned the refusal of the Polish tax authorities to grant Filipiak entitlement to tax advantages in respect of the payment of social security and health insurance contributions in the tax year, in the case where the contributions were paid in a Member State other than the state of taxation, even though such tax advantages are granted to taxpayers whose contributions are paid in the Member State of taxation.

THE ECJ

40. According to settled case-law, in proceedings under Article 234 EC, it is solely for the national court before which the dispute has been brought, and which must assume responsibility for the subsequent judicial decision, to determine in the light of the particular circumstances of the case both the need for a preliminary ruling in order to enable it to deliver judgment and the relevance of the questions which it submits to the Court. Consequently, where the questions submitted concern the interpretation of Community law, the Court is in principle bound to give a ruling...

41. Nevertheless, the Court has also held that, in exceptional circumstances, it can examine the conditions in which the case was referred to it by the national court, in order to confirm its own jurisdiction (...Case 244/80 *Foglia*...paragraph 21; *PreussenElektra*, paragraph 39; and *Rüffler*, paragraph 37).

42. The Court may refuse to rule on a question referred for a preliminary ruling by a national court only where it is quite obvious that the interpretation of Community law that is sought bears no relation to the actual facts of the main action or its purpose, where the problem is hypothetical, or where the Court does not have before it the factual or legal material necessary to give a useful answer to the questions submitted to it...

43. In that regard, it is clear from the order for reference that, irrespective of the question of the constitutionality of the provisions at issue in the main proceedings, the dispute in the main proceedings and the first question in the reference relate to the compatibility with Community law of legislation under which the right to a tax reduction on the basis of payment of health insurance contributions and the right to deduct from the basis of assessment social security contributions which have been paid are refused where those contributions have been paid in another Member State.

44. The second question follows on from the first...The national court seeks to ascertain, in essence, whether, in the event that Article 43 EC precludes provisions such as those at issue in the main proceedings, the primacy of Community law obliges the national courts to apply Community law and not to apply the national provisions at issue, and to do so even before the judgment of 7 November 2007 of the Trybunał Konstytucyjny, in which that court held that those provisions were incompatible with certain provisions of the Polish Constitution, comes into effect.

---

[87] Case C–210/06 *Cartesio* (n 16) [67]; Case C–544/07 *Rüffler v Dyrektor Izby Skarbowej we Wrocławiu Ośrodek Zamiejscowy w Wałbrzychu* [2009] ECR I–3389, [38]; Case C–314/08 *Filipiak v Dyrektor Izby Skarbowej w Poznaniu* [2009] ECR I–11049, [42]; Case C–484/08 *Caja de Ahorros y Monte de Piedad de Madrid v Asociación de Usuarios de Servicios Bancarios (Ausbanc)* [2010] ECR I–4785, [19]; Case C–440/08 *Gielen v Staatssecretaris van Financiën* [2010] ECR I–2323, [29]; Case C–470/12 *Pohotovosť sro v Miroslav Vašuta* EU:C:2014:101, [27].

45. In light of the foregoing, it is not manifestly obvious that the interpretation sought bears no relation to the actual facts of the main action or its purpose, that the problem is hypothetical, or that the Court does not have before it the factual or legal material necessary to give a useful answer to the questions submitted to it.

(F) SUMMARY

i. The CJEU will decline to take a case under Article 267 where the question referred is hypothetical, where it is not relevant to the substance of the dispute, where the question is not sufficiently clear for any meaningful legal response, and where the facts are insufficiently clear for the application of the legal rules.

ii. It will, however, decline to give a ruling only if it is quite obvious that the interpretation of EU law that is sought bears no relation to the actual facts of the main action or its purpose, where the problem is hypothetical, or where the Court does not have before it the factual or legal material necessary to give a useful answer to the questions submitted to it.

iii. The rhetoric in Article 267 cases will often be phrased in traditional terms: the judgment will speak of the cooperation between national courts and the CJEU and of the fact that it is for the national court to decide whether to refer or not.[88] This language is still meaningful. The relationship under Article 267 is cooperative.

iv. It is, however, now common for the traditional formula to be supplemented by appropriately drawn caveats which make it clear that the CJEU will not adjudicate if the questions are not relevant, or if they are hypothetical, etc.[89]

v. With changes in the rhetoric have come changes in reality. The cooperation between national courts and the CJEU still exists, but the latter is no longer the passive receptor of anything thrust before it. It has exercised more positive control over its own jurisdiction in the manner redolent of most superior courts.

7 THE DECISION ON THE REFERENCE: INTERPRETATION VERSUS APPLICATION

The preceding discussion has considered whether a reference should be made from the perspective of the national court, and whether the reference should be accepted from the perspective of the CJEU. We now consider the effect of the CJEU's decision when it rules on a reference.

Article 267 gives the CJEU power to interpret the Treaty, but does not empower it to apply the Treaty to the facts of a particular case. The very distinction between interpretation and application is said to characterize the division of authority between the CJEU and national courts: the former interprets the Treaty, the latter apply that interpretation to the facts of a particular case. This distinction is said to differentiate the relationship between national courts and the CJEU from that in a more truly federal, appellate system, where the superior court may well decide the case.

[88] See, eg, Case C–435/97 *World Wildlife Fund (WWF) v Autonome Provinz Bozen* [1999] ECR I–5613.
[89] See, eg, Cases C–332, 333 and 335/92 *Eurico Italia Srl v Ente Nazionale Risi* [1994] ECR I–711.

Theory and reality have not, however, always marched hand in hand. The dividing line between interpretation and application can be perilously thin, more especially because many of the questions submitted to the Court are, by their nature, very detailed, and can only be answered by a specific response. The more detailed is the interpretation provided by the CJEU, the closer it approximates to application. It is moreover common for the CJEU to give 'guidance' to the national court as to how the point of law should be applied in the instant case, and this further diminishes the line between interpretation and application.

Litigants have often argued that the Court should decline to give a ruling because the question posed was not seeking an interpretation, but rather an application, of the Treaty. The Court has not been deterred by such objections. Thus in *Van Gend en Loos*[90] it was argued that the question presented concerning the tariff classification of urea-formaldehyde required, not an interpretation of the Treaty, but rather an application of the relevant Dutch customs legislation. The Court rejected the argument, stating that the question related to interpretation: the meaning to be attributed to the notion of duties existing before the coming into force of the Treaty.

A willingness to respond in detail can be perceived in other cases. *Cristini*[91] was concerned with the meaning of Article 7(2) of Regulation 1612/68, which provides that a Community worker who is working in another Member State should be entitled to the same 'social advantages' as workers of that state. The question put by the French court was whether this meant that a provision which allowed large French families to have reduced rail fares was a social advantage within the ambit of Article 7(2). The ECJ denied that it had power to determine the actual case, but in reality it did just that, and responded to the question by stating that the concept of a social advantage included this fare reduction.

Marleasing[92] provides another example of the detailed nature of the ECJ's rulings. The ECJ produced a detailed response to the question whether Article 11 of Directive 68/151 was exhaustive of the types of case in which the annulment of the registration of a company could be ordered. The judgment furnished the national court with a very specific answer, which simply required the Spanish court to execute the ECJ's ruling.

The Court's willingness to provide very specific answers to questions serves to blur the line between interpretation and application. It also renders the idea of the CJEU and the national courts being separate but equal, each with their own assigned roles, more illusory. The more detailed the CJEU's ruling, the less there is for the national court to do, other than execute the ruling in the instant case.

The CJEU will be particularly motivated to provide 'the answer' where it wishes to maintain maximum control over development of an area of the law, as exemplified by cases concerning damages liability of Member States. Thus it has furnished 'guidance' to the national court on whether there has been a serious breach for the purposes of the test.[93] It has also gone further, and stated that it has sufficient information to dispose of this aspect of the case in its entirety.[94] Tridimas has, in more general terms, discerned three approaches in the CJEU's case law.

---

[90] Case 26/62 [1963] ECR 1.
[91] Case 32/75 *Cristini v SNCF* [1975] ECR 1085, [19].
[92] Case C–106/89 *Marleasing SA v La Comercial Internacional de Alimentacion SA* [1990] ECR I–4135.
[93] Cases C–46 and 48/93 *Brasserie du Pêcheur SA v Germany* [1996] ECR I–1029.
[94] Case C–392/93 *R v HM Treasury, ex p British Telecommunications plc* [1996] ECR I–1631.

T Tridimas, Constitutional Review of Member State Action: The Virtues and Vices of an Incomplete Jurisdiction[95]

One may distinguish three categories of cases depending on the specificity of the ruling. The ECJ may give an answer so specific that it leaves the referring court no margin for manoeuvre and provides it with a ready-made solution to the dispute (*outcome cases*); it may, alternatively, provide the referring court with guidelines as to how to resolve the dispute (*guidance cases*); finally, it may answer the question in such general terms that, in effect, it defers to the national judiciary on the point in issue (*deference cases*).

...

The outcome approach presents some clear advantages. The ECJ ruling concludes the Community law-related aspects of the dispute and avoids further delays and costs...But it is not without disadvantages. Used inappropriately, it may bring the ECJ close to applying the law on the facts thus exceeding its function under the preliminary reference procedure. National courts may resent what they perceive as the usurpation of their own jurisdiction although it appears that, in practice, this is rarely a problem. More importantly, over-zealous specificity may lead the court to be pre-occupied with the facts of the case, encourage over-centralisation, and detract from the Court's fundamental function which is to promote uniform interpretation of the law and oversee the Community's judicial universe. Although it may be favoured by the parties to the dispute, excessive recourse to the outcome approach might in fact reduce rather than help legal certainty. The more specific the ruling, the more difficult it becomes to derive the elements of principle in the judgment and the less the precedential value of its rulings...

The guidance approach, on the other hand, has its own mix of merits and drawbacks. The referring court, and the litigants, may be left with a feeling of incompleteness. The more general and vague the ruling, the higher the risk that national courts will hesitate to make references patriating instead concepts of Community law and thus prejudicing its uniform interpretation. Such drawbacks are extenuated in the case of deference. On the positive side, guidance offers the national courts a stake not only in the application of Community law, which in many cases they will be best equipped to do, but also in the shaping of the Community legal order. In constitutional terms, guidance is a means of inviting the national courts to partake in the construction of the EU edifice and giving them a stake in the articulation of the rule of law. The national judiciaries have the opportunity to mould EU principles to the particularities and sensitivities of their legal system...It should be noted, in this context, that a reference is not a dialogue between the CJEU and the referring court but a conversation with all national polities. A case referred from a court of one Member State may have equally, or even more, profound repercussions in other States. Guidance accommodates experimentation at national level and seems more in keeping with the model of cooperative federalism.

Davies takes however a somewhat different view of the power dynamics under Article 267, seeing the national court as retaining considerably more choice within the reference system.

---

[95] (2011) 9 I-CON 737, 739, 754–755. Italics in the original.

G Davies, Activism Relocated. The Self-Restraint of the European Court of Justice in its National Context[96]

On a reference [the CJEU] can provide an answer which essentially decides on justification and proportionality, and so determines the outcome of the case, but to do this inevitably entails engagement with the specificities of the case, making that answer easier for other judges to distinguish, and less generally applicable. Alternatively, it can answer in abstractions and general principles, providing rules of wide application, but in doing so it must accept that its answers merely guide the national judge, but do not control outcomes. If it tries to finesse this choice, by providing general rules which are also determinative, for example by ruling that broad classes of measures simply cannot be justified, then it risk accusations that it has pre-empted inherently factual and contextual questions, and thereby not just interpreted but applied the law and exceeded its jurisdiction. By allocating judicial functions using the somewhat artificial and unclear distinction between fact and law, interpretation and application, the reference procedure creates a balance of power which it is hard for the Court to escape.

8 DEVELOPMENT OF AN EU JUDICIAL SYSTEM: NATIONAL COURTS AND THE CJEU

The discussion thus far has considered different aspects of the preliminary reference system. It is, however, important to stand back and consider more generally the implications of the development of precedent, the *acte clair* concept, and sectoral delegation of functions to national courts for the EU judicial system.

(A) PRECEDENT

Let us begin by considering precedent. The *Da Costa* decision was a rational step for the ECJ to have taken. Rasmussen correctly pointed out that the authority of the Court's decisions was thereby enhanced, since they became authoritative rulings for national courts.[97] The relationship between national courts and the ECJ was altered. It was no longer bilateral, where rulings were relevant only to the national court that requested them. It became multilateral, in the sense that ECJ rulings had an impact on all national courts. The decision in *CILFIT* to reinforce precedent was similarly significant: the ECJ's rulings were to be authoritative in situations where the point of law was the same, even though the questions posed in earlier cases were different, and even though the types of legal proceeding in which the issue arose differed.

This development of precedent was largely inevitable. The original bilateral conception whereby the Court's rulings were relevant only for the national court that requested them was unrealistic. Taken literally it would have meant that a ruling would have to be given even if the inquiry sought by a national court replicated that in an earlier case already decided by the CJEU. The Court would be 'forced' solemnly to hear the matter, only to reach the same conclusion as it had done previously. A judicial system could not be supposed to exist on such terms. The CJEU would quickly tire of the waste of time and resources. The national courts would not see the sense of a system which placed

---

[96] (2012) 19 JEPP 76, 83.
[97] Rasmussen (n 49).

pressure on them to allow issues to be litigated again where the CJEU had already given a considered judgment.

It is true that the regime of precedent means that a national court might misinterpret past CJEU authority. This does not, however, undermine the rationality of the precedent system, since it leads in aggregate to a more effective regime of EU law. A system of precedent inevitably entails certain 'error costs', the possibility of mistakes by national courts. Precedent also has substantial 'benefits'. Most fundamentally, national courts become enforcers of EU law in their own right. When the Court has decided an issue, national courts apply that ruling without further resort to the CJEU. The national courts are, in this sense, 'enrolled' as part of a network of courts adjudicating on EU law, with the CJEU at the apex of that network. They become 'delegates' in the enforcement of EU law, and part of a broader EU judicial hierarchy. The costs of precedent must, therefore, be weighed against the benefits. These include the increased volume of EU law which can be litigated, mostly correctly, at any one time, and also the important symbolic advantage that flows from the recognition that the national courts are part of an EU judicial hierarchy. It is therefore unsurprising that the Court should have stated in its report for the 1996 IGC that 'national courts are called upon to play a central role as courts with general jurisdiction for Community law'.[98] It should be noted that a study found a high rate of national implementation of CJEU rulings: 96.3 per cent.[99]

(B) *ACTE CLAIR*

Let us now move to *acte clair*. The Court in *CILFIT* had a choice. It could have rejected the *acte clair* doctrine in EU law, the view espoused by Advocate General Capotorti.[100] The Court declined to follow this approach, and instead gave the doctrine limited support. It might be contended, as seen above, that the real objective was to deal it a death-blow, by hedging it around with multiple restrictions or, more moderately, to convince national courts to be responsible when using *acte clair*.

We should, however, distinguish purpose and effect. Thus even if we accept the Mancini/Keeling thesis as to the Court's purpose, the effect is to leave 'clear' cases that fall within these conditions to the national courts. For such cases, the national courts operate once again as the delegates of the CJEU for the application of EU law. The CJEU can then utilize its time to resolve more problematic cases. The conditions in *CILFIT* help to ensure that national courts will not readily regard cases as *acte clair* unless they really are free from interpretive doubt, although it is doubtless true that national courts can interpret these conditions rather differently.[101]

The qualified approval given to the concept can nonetheless be regarded as rational, since the cost/benefit analysis discussed above applies equally here. The fact that a national court might, on occasion, misapply the criteria, intentionally or unintentionally, does not render the exercise a failure. These costs have to be balanced against the benefits: straightforward cases can be disposed of expeditiously by national courts. Moreover, this method of dealing with such cases further emphasizes the role of national courts as but part of a broader judicial hierarchy, with the CJEU at the apex.

There are in addition 'safety' devices built into the system, independently of the conditions in *CILFIT*, so the danger of incorrect interpretation made by national courts becoming embedded should not be overstated. The concern is that a national court may refuse to make a reference, even though the conditions in *CILFIT* are not met. A national court minded to do this intentionally

---

[98] Report of the Court of Justice (n 5) [15].

[99] S Nyikos, 'The Preliminary Reference Process: National Court Implementation, Changing Opportunity Structures and Litigant Desistment' (2003) 4 EUP 397.

[100] [1982] ECR 3415, 3439.

[101] Tridimas (n 15) 41–44; Arnull, 'Law Lords' (n 50) 75–79.

would, however, now be aware of the possibility of damages liability pursuant to *Köbler*.[102] There is the further possibility that the Member State might be subject to an enforcement action under Article 258 TFEU. In any event, the matter might still come before the CJEU via a different court from the same legal system, or from a different legal system. It would also be open to the CJEU to correct aberrant interpretations by national courts, in the context of a case on a related point that has come before it, although the implications of this for prior decisions at national level would be subject to *Kühne*.[103]

(c) SECTORAL DELEGATION

This discussion would be incomplete if it did not take into account what is in effect sectoral delegation of responsibility to national courts: a conscious choice made by the EU to devolve certain enforcement functions to the national courts, as occurred in the context of competition policy.[104]

The rationale for this devolution was instructive. Prior to reforms, the Commission was charged with the initial role in the enforcement of competition policy. It did not, however, possess the resources necessary for this task and therefore called on the national courts. These always played a role in the enforcement of competition law, but this was consciously generalized, so that straightforward competition violations could be dealt with at national level, thereby allowing the Commission and EU Courts to deal with more difficult cases, or those which raised new issues of principle. Such sectoral delegation was facilitated because of the accumulated weight of EU precedent.

9 DEVELOPMENT OF AN EU JUDICIAL SYSTEM: CJEU, GENERAL COURT, AND NATIONAL COURTS

(A) THE CASELOAD PROBLEM

The development of the preliminary ruling system has enrolled national courts as part of the EU judicial system broadly conceived, with both the power and duty to apply EU law in cases that come before them.[105] This has been crucial in making the system 'work'. There are, nonetheless, problems with the current regime which have prompted discussion concerning reform.

The initial catalyst was the Court's increasing workload, which inevitably had implications for the length of time to process a preliminary ruling. The number of preliminary references submitted in 2009 was 302, in 2010 it was 385,[106] and in 2013 it had risen to 450.[107] The CJEU has successfully reduced the time to obtain a reference. At one stage this was taking close to two years, but in 2013 it was 16.3 months, although this was an increase compared to 15.6 months in 2012.

The reduction in the time to secure a preliminary ruling was in part due to changes made to expedite the process. Thus there is now an obligation on the CJEU to decide cases with a minimum of delay

---

[102] Case C–224/01 *Köbler v Austria* [2003] ECR I–10239.

[103] Pp 476–478.

[104] Ch 26.

[105] For analysis of the factors that affect reference rates from different national courts, see M Broberg and N Fenger, 'Variations in Member States' Preliminary References to the Court of Justice—Are Structural Factors (Part of) the Explanation?' (2013) 19 ELJ 488.

[106] Proceedings of the Court of Justice, Annual Report 2010, available at http://curia.europa.eu/jcms/jcms/Jo2_11035/rapports-annuels.

[107] Proceedings of the Court of Justice, Annual Report 2013, available at http://curia.europa.eu/jcms/upload/docs/application/pdf/2014-06/qdag14001enc.pdf.

where a person is in custody.[108] There is provision for expedited hearings in case of urgency.[109] This is however conditional on approval by the President of the Court, and of the fourteen applications made in 2013, none were accepted.[110] Preliminary rulings can be given by reasoned order where the CJEU refers to prior case law in certain types of case: those where the request is identical to a point dealt with by existing case law, or where the answer can clearly be deduced from an existing case, or where the answer admits of no reasonable doubt.[111] The procedure was used thirty-three times in 2013.[112] A case can moreover be decided without an Opinion from the Advocate General,[113] and this power was used in 48 per cent of the judgments delivered in 2013.[114] The reduction in time to secure a preliminary ruling was also in part due to the increase in the number of CJEU judges as a result of enlargement. The net increase of thirteen judges has allowed a greater throughput of cases.

There are, however, reasons to question whether the recent diminution in the time taken for preliminary rulings can be maintained in the coming years. The benefits of extra judges from the newer accession countries may be offset by an increase in the references from those national courts, as lawyers in those countries become more accustomed to using EU law,[115] although practice in this respect is still unfolding.[116] The impact of the Lisbon Treaty is equally important. The fact that the Charter of Rights is now legally binding, and that the Area of Freedom, Security and Justice is now subject to the normal Article 267 procedure, will mean a net increase in preliminary references, more especially because many AFSJ measures are controversial and touch on civil liberties. It has in more general terms been argued that the figures concerning the number of references are in fact surprisingly low, given what might be expected concerning the impact of EU law.[117]

While the primary focus in relation to caseload has been on the CJEU, in recent years the General Court has come under increasing strain. The GC completed 527 cases in 2010, but there were still 1,300 cases pending in December 2010. By 2013 there were 790 new cases, an increase of 30 per cent over the previous year, 702 completed cases, and 1,325 cases pending.

It is therefore important to consider possible reforms to the preliminary ruling system.[118] The range of such reforms was canvassed in two papers prior to the Nice Treaty: one was written by those then in the ECJ and CFI,[119] and will be referred to hereafter as the Courts' paper; the other was produced by a Working Party composed largely of former judges of the ECJ at the behest of the Commission,[120] and

---

[108] Art 267(4) TFEU.

[109] Rules of Procedure of the Court of Justice (n 44) Art 105.

[110] Proceedings of the Court of Justice, Annual Report 2013 (n 107) 10.

[111] Ibid Art 99.

[112] Proceedings of the Court of Justice, Annual Report 2013 (n 107) 10.

[113] Art 252 TFEU; Statute of the Court of Justice of the European Union, Art 20, available at http://curia.europa.eu/jcms/upload/docs/application/pdf/2012-10/staut_cons_en.pdf.

[114] Proceedings of the Court of Justice, Annual Report 2013 (n 107) 10.

[115] M Bobek, 'Learning to Talk: Preliminary Rulings, the Courts of the New Member States and the Court of Justice' (2008) 45 CMLRev 1611.

[116] M Bobek, 'Talking Now? Preliminary Rulings in and from the New Member States' (2014) 21 MJ 781.

[117] M Bobek, 'The Court of Justice, the National Courts and the Spirit of Cooperation: Between Dichtung and Warheit' in A Lazowski and S Blockmans (eds), *Research Handbook on EU Institutional Law* (Edward Elgar, 2014) ch 14.

[118] T Kennedy, 'First Steps Towards a European Certiorari?' (1993) 18 ELRev 121; Rasmussen (n 54); P Craig, 'The Jurisdiction of the Community Courts Reconsidered' in G de Búrca and JHH Weiler (eds), *The European Court of Justice* (Oxford University Press, 2001) ch 6; JHH Weiler, 'Epilogue: The Judicial Après Nice' in ibid 215; C Turner and R Munoz, 'Revising the Judicial Architecture of the European Union' (1999–2000) 19 YBEL 1; A Arnull, 'Judicial Architecture or Judicial Folly? The Challenge Facing the European Union' (1999) 24 ELRev 516; A Dashwood and A Johnston (eds), *The Future of the Judicial System of the European Union* (Hart, 2001); I Pernice, J Kokott, and C Saunders (eds), *The Future of the European Judicial System in Comparative Perspective* (Nomos, 2006).

[119] The Future of the Judicial System of the European Union (Proposals and Reflections) (May 1999), hereafter FJS.

[120] Report by the Working Party on the Future of the European Communities' Court System (Jan 2000), hereafter WP.

it will be referred to as the Due Report after the name of its chairman. The catalyst for the papers was the rise in the number of preliminary references and the strain thereby placed on the ECJ.

(B) LIMITING THE NATIONAL COURTS EMPOWERED TO MAKE A REFERENCE

While there was some 'precedent' for the idea that a preliminary ruling could only be sought by a national court against whose decisions there is no judicial remedy in national law,[121] the Courts' paper and the Due Report came down firmly against any general use of this to limit preliminary rulings.[122] This is unsurprising. The ability of any national court to refer has been central to the development of EU law in practical and conceptual terms.

In practical terms, it has been common for cases raising important points of EU law to come from lower level national courts. To limit the ability to refer would result in cases being fought to the apex of national judicial systems merely to seek a reference to the CJEU. The ability to refer by any national court is also a safeguard against the possibility that the court of final resort may be 'conservative or recalcitrant' and hence reluctant to refer.

In conceptual terms, the ability of any national court to refer has emphasized the penetration of EU law to all points of the national legal system. It is true that even if references were limited to courts of last resort, lower courts could still apply existing EU precedent. The fact that any national court can refer, however, emphasizes that an individual can rely on directly effective EU rights at any point in the national legal system.

(C) A FILTERING MECHANISM BASED ON THE NOVELTY, COMPLEXITY, OR IMPORTANCE OF THE QUESTION

This reform would allow the Court 'to concentrate wholly upon questions which are fundamental from the point of view of the uniformity and development of Community law'.[123] The Due Report advocated some constraints of this kind.[124] It suggested that national courts of final resort should be obliged to refer only questions which are 'sufficiently important for Community law', and where there is still 'reasonable doubt' after examination by lower courts. The idea also received tentative support from the Association of the Councils of State.[125] There are two problems with this suggestion.

First, 'national courts and tribunals might well refrain from referring questions to the Court of Justice, in order to avoid the risk of their references being rejected for lack of interest'.[126] This could jeopardize the machinery for ensuring that EU law is interpreted uniformly in the Member States.

Secondly, those who favour this approach commonly point to the United States where the Supreme Court will decide the cases it is willing to hear. The crucial difference is that the United States is an appellate system, and the EU is a referral system. In the United States, if the Supreme Court declines to hear a case there will be a decision on the point of law from a lower federal court or state court. The situation in the EU is markedly different. The national court has not decided the case. It has referred a question and if the CJEU declines to answer because it is not sufficiently important or novel there is no

---

[121] Art 68 EC.

[122] FJS (n 119) 23–24; WP (n 120) 12–13.

[123] FJS (n 119) 25; Case C–338/95 *Wiener v Hauptzollamt Emmerich* [1997] ECR I–6495, AG Jacobs.

[124] WP (n 120) 14–15.

[125] Association of the Councils of State (n 53) 14. See also T de la Mare and C Donnelly, 'Preliminary Rulings and EU Legal Integration: Evolution and Stasis' in P Craig and G de Búrca (eds), *The Evolution of EU Law* (Oxford University Press, 2nd edn, 2011) ch 13.

[126] FJS (n 119) 25.

decision by a Union Court at all. This places the national court in a difficult position. It could attempt to decide the matter of EU law itself. The national court could alternatively decline to decide the EU point, the effect being that the party who sought to rely on the EU point would be unable to do so, and the case would be decided on the assumption that this point was unproven.

(D) THE NATIONAL COURT PROPOSES AN ANSWER TO THE QUESTION

The national court could include in its reference a proposed reply to the question referred. The advantages were said, in the Courts' paper, to be that it would 'lessen the adverse effect of the filtering mechanism on the co-operation between the national court and the Court of Justice, while the proposed reply could at the same time serve as the basis for deciding which questions need to be answered by the Court of Justice and which can be answered in the terms indicated'.[127] A similar proposal was advanced in the Due Report.[128] This idea has been incorporated in the recommendations to national courts, which states that the referring court may, if it considers itself able, briefly state its view on the answer to be given to the questions referred for a preliminary ruling.[129]

There are, however, limits to how far this proposal can be taken. Most national courts are not specialists in EU law. It is one thing for the national court to identify a question that is necessary for the resolution of the case. It is another thing to be able to answer it. Higher level national courts may be able to furnish some answer to the question posed. This proposal would nonetheless transform the task of such courts. There would have to be detailed argument before the national court of the EU issues in order to provide the judge with the requisite material from which to give an answer to the question posed. Nor is it clear that this proposal would relieve much of the CJEU's workload. Even if national courts are encouraged to provide an answer, the CJEU still has to give the matter detailed consideration, in order to decide whether the question can be answered in the terms indicated by the national court.

(E) TOWARDS AN APPELLATE SYSTEM

A more radical option considered in the Courts' paper would transform the system from one which is reference-based, to one which is more appellate in nature.[130]

> A more radical variant of the system would be to alter the preliminary ruling procedure so that national courts which are not bound to refer questions to the Court of Justice would be required, before making any reference, first to give judgment in cases raising questions concerning the interpretation of Community law. It would then be open to any party to the proceedings to request the national court to forward its judgment to the Court of Justice and to make a reference for a ruling on those points of Community law in respect of which that party contests the validity of the judgment given. This would give the Court of Justice the opportunity of assessing, at the filtering stage, whether it needed to give its own ruling on the interpretation of Community law arrived at in the contested judgment.

The Due Report was however strongly opposed to this change, stating that 'such a proposal would debase the entire system of co-operation established by the Treaties between national courts and the

---

[127] FJS (n 119) 25–26.
[128] WP (n 120) 18.
[129] Recommendations to National Courts (n 85) [24].
[130] FJS (n 119) 26.

Court of Justice'.[131] If this proposal were adopted it would fundamentally alter the current regime from a reference system to an appellate one. This is not an objection in and of itself, but we should nonetheless be aware of the change thereby entailed. The national court would give a decision on the case, and it would then be for the parties to 'require' the national court to make a reference. This was acknowledged in the Courts' paper.[132]

> [S]uch a procedure would involve a fundamental change in the way in which the preliminary ruling system currently operates. Judicial co-operation between the national courts and the Court of Justice would be transformed into a hierarchical system, in which it would be for the parties to an action to decide whether to require the national court to make a reference to the Court of Justice, and in which the national court would be bound, depending on the circumstances, to revise its earlier judgment so as to bring it into line with a ruling by the Court of Justice. From the point of view of national procedural law this aspect of the system would doubtless raise problems which could not easily be resolved.

There are a number of difficulties with this proposal. To require national courts to decide the point of EU law would impose a burden on them that many lower-tier courts would find difficult to discharge. It would be unlikely to relieve the CJEU's caseload, since there would always be an incentive on the losing party to seek a reference to the CJEU.[133] It would seem to involve overruling Foto-Frost,[134] since the national court might well be adjudicating on the validity of an EU law norm. It is, moreover, unclear in the Courts' paper whether the losing party can request or require the national court to refer the matter to the CJEU.[135]

We should also consider the possible advantages of this proposal. An appellate system is more characteristic of a developed federal or confederal legal system, and it could be argued that the EU is ready for such a change. National courts have become more familiar with EU law, and it may be time to move towards an appellate regime where the national court gives judgment on the case, subject to appeal to the CJEU. We should not however go down this road on the assumption that it will thereby radically limit the CJEU's caseload.

(f) CREATION OF DECENTRALIZED JUDICIAL BODIES

The CJEU's burden would be eased if decentralized courts were created. This would also bring legal redress physically closer to citizens, who could obtain a preliminary ruling without travelling to Luxembourg. The Courts' paper and the Due Report were, however, concerned that such decentralized courts would jeopardize the uniformity of EU law,[136] and the Due Report was against this option largely for this reason.[137] The Courts' paper sought to meet this concern by allowing a case to go to the CJEU from a decentralized court.

The creation of regional courts to supplement the EU judicial architecture has been advocated in the past,[138] but has generally been opposed by the GC.[139] The suggestion was not taken up in the

---

[131] WP (n 120) 13.

[132] FJS (n 119) 26.

[133] FJS (n 119) 26.

[134] Case 314/85 Firma Foto-Frost v Hauptzollamt Lübeck-Ost [1987] ECR 4199.

[135] FJS (n 119) 26 is ambiguous in this respect.

[136] FJS (n 119) 28; WP (n 120) 21.

[137] WP (n 120) 21–22.

[138] J-P Jacqué and J Weiler, 'On the Road to European Union—A New Judicial Architecture: An Agenda for the Intergovernmental Conference' (1990) 27 CMLRev 185.

[139] Report of the Court of Justice on Certain Aspects of the Application of the Treaty on European Union—Contribution of the Court of First Instance for the Purposes of the 1996 Intergovernmental Conference, May 1995.

Nice Treaty or the Lisbon Treaty. It may nonetheless be inevitable at some time in the future. If such courts were to be created they should be part of the EU judicial machinery operating at national or regional level.

(G) GENERAL COURT TO HAVE JURISDICTION TO GIVE PRELIMINARY RULINGS

Prior to the Nice Treaty only the ECJ could hear preliminary rulings. The possibility of conferring such jurisdiction on the CFI, now the General Court, was canvassed positively, albeit cautiously, in the Courts' paper.[140] The Due Report was however opposed to this change, except in a limited number of special areas.[141]

The Nice Treaty gave the CFI some power over preliminary rulings and the schema has been taken over in the Lisbon Treaty.[142] There was regrettably no broad-ranging discussion of the EU's judicial architecture. The GC is empowered to hear preliminary rulings in specific areas laid down by the Statute of the Court of Justice. Where the GC believes that the case requires a decision of principle, likely to affect the unity or consistency of EU law, it may refer the case to the CJEU.[143] Preliminary rulings given by the GC can, exceptionally, be subject to review by the CJEU, under the conditions laid down in the Statute, where there is a serious risk of the unity or consistency of EU law being affected.[144]

There is much to be said for the idea that the GC should be able to give preliminary rulings. Some Article 267 TFEU cases involve indirect challenge to the validity of EU norms, where the non-privileged applicants cannot satisfy the standing criteria under Article 263 TFEU. The cases raise issues that would be heard by the GC in a direct action under Article 263. The GC should be able to hear such cases if they emerge indirectly via national courts as requests for preliminary rulings, although it is open to debate whether the current rules concerning onward recourse to the CJEU should be modified.[145] There are, moreover, many Article 267 cases that involve no issue of principle, but are concerned with the detailed interpretation of a particular provision of a regulation or directive. These cases require judicial resolution. They do not require resolution by the CJEU.

There has, however, been no move as yet to activate the power given by Article 256(3) TFEU in order to assign preliminary rulings in certain areas to the General Court.[146] This is in part because it is difficult to decide on the nature of such areas, more especially because there is no necessary correlation between subject matter area and the importance of the point of EU law raised by the case. It might well therefore have been more desirable to give the General Court jurisdiction over all preliminary rulings, subject to the dual mechanisms in Article 256(3) for shifting the case to the CJEU. This would perforce require some increase in the number of judges in the General Court, but this is possible under the Lisbon Treaty.[147] The current reality is however that the caseload pressures on the GC, combined with the difficulties of gaining agreement on the precise terms on which extra judges

---

[140] FJS (n 119) 27.

[141] WP (n 120) 22.

[142] Art 256(3) TFEU.

[143] Art 256(3) TFEU.

[144] Art 256(3) TFEU; Arts 62, 62b of the Statute of the Court of Justice of the European Union.

[145] Compare K Lenaerts, 'The Unity of European Law and the Overload of the CJEU—The System of Preliminary Rulings Revisited' in Pernice, Kokott, and Saunders (n 118) 235 and B Vesterdorf, 'A Constitutional Court for the EU' in Pernice, Kokott, and Saunders (n 118) 87; P Craig, *The Lisbon Treaty: Law, Politics, and Treaty Reform* (Oxford University Press, 2010) ch 4.

[146] Craig (n 145).

[147] Art 19(2) TEU; cf Association of Councils of State (n 53) 15.

would be appointed to the GC,[148] render it unlikely that there will be any move to shift preliminary rulings to the GC.

10 CONCLUSIONS

i. The CJEU is not a fully developed federal Supreme Court, either procedurally or institutionally. In procedural terms, individuals have no right of appeal to the CJEU. The CJEU does not actually decide the case, but rules on the point referred to it. In institutional terms, notwithstanding the creation of the General Court, the EU does not yet have the judicial hierarchy characteristic of federal systems. In countries such as the United States, there is a system of federal courts existing below the Supreme Court, which exercise jurisdiction over a particular area of the country.

ii. The original conception of the relationship between national courts and the CJEU does not however capture reality. It remains cooperative, but many developments have transformed the relationship from *horizontal* and *bilateral*, to *vertical* and *multilateral*. These include: the assertion of EU law supremacy; the development of *de facto* precedent; the *acte clair* doctrine; the sectoral devolution of responsibility to national courts; the CJEU's exercise of control over the cases that it will hear; and the blurring of the line between interpretation and application. These changes evidence the evolution of an EU judicial hierarchy in which the CJEU sits at the apex, as the ultimate Constitutional Court for the EU, assisted by national courts, which apply and interpret EU law.

iii. Reform of the EU's judicial architecture will remain on the agenda, notwithstanding the Lisbon Treaty. There will be continuing efforts to alleviate the workload of both the CJEU and the GC. Whether these can keep pace with the increase of cases remains to be seen.

11 FURTHER READING

(a) Books

Anderson, D, and Demetriou, M, *References to the European Court* (Sweet & Maxwell, 2nd edn, 2002)

Broberg, M, and Fenger, N, *Preliminary References to the European Court of Justice* (Oxford University Press, 2nd edn, 2014)

Craig, P, *The Lisbon Treaty: Law, Politics, and Treaty Reform* (Oxford University Press, 2010) ch 4

——*EU Administrative Law* (Oxford University Press, 2nd edn, 2012) ch 10

Dashwood, A, and Johnston, A (eds), *The Future of the Judicial System of the European Union* (Hart, 2001)

De Búrca, G, and Weiler, JHH (eds), *The European Court of Justice* (Oxford University Press, 2001)

Pernice, I, Kokott, J, and Saunders, C (eds), *The Future of the European Judicial System in Comparative Perspective* (Nomos, 2006)

---

[148] See above, pp 59–61, for discussion of the increase in the number of judges on the GC; P Craig, *UK, EU and Global Administrative Law: Foundations and Challenges* (Cambridge University Press, 2015) ch 3.

(b) Articles

ARNULL, A, 'The Law Lords and the European Union: Swimming with the Incoming Tide' (2010) 35 ELRev 57

BARNARD, C, AND SHARPSTON, E, 'The Changing Face of Article 177 References' (1997) 34 CMLRev 1113

BOBEK, M, 'Learning to Talk: Preliminary Rulings, the Courts of the New Member States and the Court of Justice' (2008) 45 CMLRev 1611

—— 'The Court of Justice, the National Courts and the Spirit of Cooperation: Between Dichtung and Warheit' in A LAZOWSKI and S BLOCKMANS (eds), *Research Handbook on EU Institutional Law* (Edward Elgar, 2014) ch 14

BROBERG, M, AND FENGER, N, 'Variations in Member States' Preliminary References to the Court of Justice—Are Structural Factors (Part of) the Explanation?' (2013) 19 ELJ 488

DAVIES, G, 'Activism Relocated. The Self-Restraint of the European Court of Justice in its National Context' (2012) 19 JEPP 76

DE LA MARE, T, AND DONNELLY, C, 'Preliminary Rulings and EU Legal Integration: Evolution and Stasis' in P Craig and G de Búrca (eds), *The Evolution of EU Law* (Oxford University Press, 2nd edn, 2011) ch 13

DE LA SERRE, E, 'Accelerated and Expedited Procedures before the EC Courts: A Review of the Practice' (2006) 43 CMLRev 783

FENGER, N, AND BROBERG, M, 'Finding Light in the Darkness: On the Actual Application of the *Acte Clair* Doctrine' (2011) 30 YBEL 180

KOMAREK, J, 'Federal Elements in the Community Judicial System: Building Coherence in the Community Legal System' (2005) 42 CMLRev 9

RASMUSSEN, H, 'Remedying the Crumbling EC Judicial System' (2000) 37 CMLRev 1071

SARMIENTO, D, 'Amending the Preliminary Reference Procedure for the Administrative Judge' (2009) 2 Review of European Administrative Law 29

TRIDIMAS, G, AND TRIDIMAS, T, 'National Courts and the European Court of Justice: A Public Choice Analysis of Preliminary Reference Procedure' (2004) 24 International Review of Law and Economics 125

TRIDIMAS, T, 'Knocking on Heaven's Door: Fragmentation, Efficiency and Defiance in the Preliminary Ruling Procedure' (2003) 40 CMLRev 9

—— 'Constitutional Review of Member State Action: The Virtues and Vices of an Incomplete Jurisdiction' (2011) 9 I-CON 737

VESTERDORF, B, 'The Community Court System Ten Years from Now and Beyond: Challenges and Possibilities' (2003) 28 ELRev 303

WEILER, J, 'Epilogue: The Judicial Après Nice' in G de Búrca and JHH Weiler (eds), *The European Court of Justice* (Oxford University Press, 2001) 215

14

REVIEW OF LEGALITY: ACCESS

1 CENTRAL ISSUES

i. The EU develops policy through regulations, directives, and decisions. Any developed legal system must have a mechanism for testing the legality of such measures. This chapter is concerned with access to justice and review of legality by the EU Courts. There are a number of ways in which EU norms can be challenged, but the principal Treaty provision is Article 263 TFEU (ex Article 230 EC).

ii. Five conditions must be satisfied before an act can successfully be challenged. The relevant body must be amenable to judicial review; the act has to be of a kind which is open to challenge; the institution or person making the challenge must have standing to do so; there must be illegality of a type mentioned in Article 263(2); and the challenge must be brought within the time limit indicated in Article 263(6).

iii. The judicial interpretation of Article 230 EC was problematic, and it has in the past been very difficult for individuals to challenge the legality of EU action directly before the EU Courts. Article 263 TFEU was designed to alleviate this difficulty through amendment of Article 230 EC. How far this renders it easier for non-privileged applicants to use Article 263 TFEU will be considered below.

iv. It is also possible for the validity of EU action to be challenged indirectly, via Article 267 TFEU. The interrelationship between direct challenge under Article 263 and indirect challenge is important. The EU Courts defended their narrow interpretation of standing for direct actions by arguing that the Treaty provided a complete system of legal protection through a combination of Articles 263 and 267 TFEU. There are however difficulties with this hypothesis.

2 ARTICLE 263(1): BODIES SUBJECT TO REVIEW

Article 263 TFEU deals with direct challenge to the legality of EU acts. Article 263(1) defines the bodies that are amenable to review.

> The Court of Justice of the European Union shall review the legality of legislative acts, of acts of the Council, of the Commission and of the European Central Bank, other than recommendations and opinions, and of acts of the European Parliament and of the European Council intended to produce legal effects *vis-à-vis* third parties. It shall also review the legality of acts of bodies, offices or agencies of the Union intended to produce legal effects *vis-à-vis* third parties.

It shall for this purpose have jurisdiction in actions brought by a Member State, the European Parliament, the Council or the Commission on grounds of lack of competence, infringement of an essential procedural requirement, infringement of the Treaties or of any rule of law relating to their application, or misuse of powers.

The Court shall have jurisdiction under the same conditions in actions brought by the Court of Auditors, by the European Central Bank and by the Committee of the Regions for the purpose of protecting their prerogatives.

Any natural or legal person may, under the conditions laid down in the first and second paragraphs, institute proceedings against an act addressed to that person or which is of direct and individual concern to them, and against a regulatory act which is of direct concern to them and does not entail implementing measures.

Acts setting up bodies, offices and agencies of the Union may lay down specific conditions and arrangements concerning actions brought by natural or legal persons against acts of these bodies, offices or agencies intended to produce legal effects in relation to them.

The proceedings provided for in this Article shall be instituted within two months of the publication of the measure, or of its notification to the plaintiff, or, in the absence thereof, of the day on which it came to the knowledge of the latter, as the case may be.

Article 263(1) covers acts of the Council and Commission, including legislative acts, and acts of the European Central Bank, other than recommendations and opinions. It also covers acts of the European Parliament, European Council, and EU bodies, offices, or agencies intended to produce legal effects against third parties. The novelty of the Lisbon Treaty is the explicit inclusion of the European Council and EU bodies, offices, or agencies as amenable to judicial review,[1] although prior jurisprudence had already brought agencies within the remit of judicial review.[2]

Article 263(5) stipulates that the acts setting up such EU bodies, offices, and agencies may lay down specific conditions and arrangements concerning actions brought by natural or legal persons against acts of these bodies intended to produce legal effects in relation to them. The nature of such conditions remains to be seen.

3 ARTICLE 263(1): ACTS SUBJECT TO REVIEW

(A) GENERAL PRINCIPLES

Article 263(1) allows the Court to review the legality of acts,[3] other than recommendations and opinions, taken by the institutions listed in Article 263(1).[4] This clearly covers regulations, decisions, and

---

[1] See, eg, Case C–626/11 P *Polyelectrolyte Producers Group GEIE (PPG) and SNF SAS v European Chemicals Agency (ECHA)* EU:C:2013:595.

[2] Case T–411/06 *Sogelma–Societá generale lavori manutenzioni appalti Srl v European Agency for Reconstruction (AER)* [2008] ECR II–2771.

[3] The Court may review acts of the Council which are intended to have legal effects irrespective of whether they have been passed pursuant to Treaty provisions: Case C–316/91 *European Parliament v Council* [1994] ECR I–625. However, decisions adopted by representatives of the Member States acting not as the Council, but as representatives of their governments, and thus collectively exercising the powers of the Member States, are not reviewable under Art 263: Cases C–181 and 248/91 *European Parliament v Council and Commission* [1993] ECR I–3685. It will be for the Court to decide whether a measure really was an act of the institutions or whether it was an act of the Member States acting independently.

[4] The original formulation of Art 173 EEC only formally applied to the Council and the Commission, but the CJEU held that the acts of the European Parliament were also susceptible to review: Case 294/83 *Parti Ecologiste 'Les Verts' v European Parliament* [1986] ECR 1339.

directives, which are listed in Article 288 TFEU. The ECJ has, however, held that this list is not exhaustive, and that other acts which are *sui generis* can also be reviewed, provided that they have binding force or produce legal effects.[5]

Case 22/70 **Commission v Council**
[1971] ECR 263

[Note Lisbon Treaty renumbering: Arts 173 and 228 are now Arts 263 and 218 TFEU]

The Member States acting through the Council adopted a Resolution on 20 March 1970 to coordinate their approach to the negotiations for a European Road Transport Agreement (ERTA/AETR). The Commission disliked the negotiating procedure established in the Resolution, and sought to challenge it before the ECJ under Article 173.

THE ECJ

48. As regards negotiating, the Council decided, in accordance with the course of action decided upon at its previous meetings, that the negotiations should be carried on and concluded by the six Member States, which would become contracting parties to the AETR.

49. Throughout the negotiations and at the conclusion of the agreement, the States would act in common and would constantly coordinate their positions according to the usual procedure in close association with the Community institutions, the delegation of the Member State currently occupying the Presidency of the Council acting as spokesman.

50. It does not appear from the minutes that the Commission raised any objections to the definition by the Council of the objective of the negotiations.

51. On the other hand, it did lodge an express reservation regarding the negotiating procedure, declaring that it considered that the position adopted by the Council was not in accordance with the Treaty, and more particularly with Article 228.

52. It follows from the foregoing that the Council's proceedings dealt with a matter falling within the power of the Community, and that the Member States could not therefore act outside the framework of the common institutions.

53. It thus seems that in so far as they concerned the objective of the negotiations as defined by the Council, the proceedings of 20 March 1970 could not have been simply the expression or the recognition of a voluntary coordination, but were designed to lay down a course of action binding on both the institutions and the Member States, and destined ultimately to be reflected in the tenor of the regulation.

54. In the part of its conclusions relating to the negotiating procedure, the Council adopted provisions which were capable of derogating in certain circumstances from the procedure laid down by the Treaty regarding negotiations with third countries and the conclusion of agreements.

55. Hence, the proceedings of 20 March 1970 had definite legal effects both on relations between the Community and the Member States and on the relationship between institutions.

It is clear from *IBM* that the test as to whether an act is reviewable is one of substance, not form, and that the challenged measure must be final and not preparatory.

---

[5] Case C–57/95 *France v Commission (Re Pension Funds Communication)* [1997] ECR I–1627; Case C–370/07 *Commission v Council (CITES)* [2009] ECR I–8917, [42]. If an EU institution with power to take reviewable decisions delegates that power to another institution, the Court will not be prevented from reviewing the acts of such a delegate.

Case 60/81 International Business Machines Corporation v Commission
[1981] ECR 2639

[Note Lisbon Treaty renumbering: Arts 86 and 173 are now Arts 102 and 263 TFEU]

IBM sought the annulment of a Commission letter notifying it of the fact that the Commission had initiated competition proceedings against it, in order to determine whether it was in breach of Article 86. The letter was accompanied by a statement of objections, with a request that the company reply to it within a specified time. The Commission objected that the impugned letter was not an act challengeable under Article 173.

THE ECJ

9. In order to ascertain whether the measures in question are acts within the meaning of Article 173 it is necessary, therefore, to look to their substance. According to the consistent case-law of the Court any measure the legal effects of which are binding on, and capable of affecting the legal interests of, the applicant by bringing about a distinct change in his legal position is an act or decision which may be the subject of an action under Article 173 for a declaration that it is void. However, the form in which such acts or decisions are cast is, in principle, immaterial as regards the question whether they are open to challenge under that article.

10. In the case of acts or decisions adopted by a procedure involving several stages, in particular where they are the culmination of an internal procedure, it is clear from the case-law that in principle an act is open to review only if it is a measure definitively laying down the position of the Commission or the Council on the conclusion of that procedure, and not a provisional measure intended to pave the way for the final decision.

11. It would be otherwise only if acts or decisions adopted in the course of the preparatory proceedings not only bore all the legal characteristics referred to above but in addition were themselves the culmination of a special procedure distinct from that intended to permit the Commission or the Council to take a decision on the substance of the case.

12. Furthermore, it must be noted that whilst measures of a purely preparatory character may not themselves be the subject of an application for a declaration that they are void, any legal defects therein may be relied upon in an action directed against the definitive act for which they represent a preparatory step.

The applicant failed.[6] The letter was merely the initiation of the competition procedure, a preparatory step leading to the real decision at a later stage. The statement of objections did not, in itself, alter IBM's legal position, although it might indicate, as a matter of fact, that it was in danger of being fined later.[7]

---

[6] See also Cases C–133 and 150/87 *Nashua Corporation v Commission and Council* [1990] ECR I–719; Case C–282/95 P *Guérin Automobiles v Commission* [1997] ECR I–503; Case T–81/97 *Regione Toscana v Commission* [1998] ECR II–2889; Case C–159/96 *Portuguese Republic v Commission* [1998] ECR I–7379; Case C–180/96 *United Kingdom v Commission* [1998] ECR I–2265; Cases T–377, 379, 380/00, 260 and 272/01 *Philip Morris International Inc v Commission* [2003] ECR II–1; Case C–240/92 *Portuguese Republic v Commission* [2004] ECR I–10717; Case C–131/03 P *R J Reynolds Tobacco Holdings Inc v Commission* [2006] ECR I–7795; Case T–195/08 *Antwerpse Bouwwerken NV v European Commission* [2009] ECR II–4439; Cases T–355 and 446/04 *Co-Frutta Soc coop v European Commission* [2010] ECR II–1; Case T–96/10 *Rütgers Germany GmbH v European Chemicals Agency (ECHA)* EU:T:2013:109, [30]; Case C–31/13 P *Hungary v Commission* EU:C:2014:70, [54]–[55].

[7] Compare Case 53/85 *AKZO Chemie BV v Commission* [1986] ECR 1965 and Case C–39/93 P *Syndicat Français de l'Express International (SFEI) v Commission* [1994] ECR I–2681. See also Cases T–10–12 and 15/92 *SA Cimenteries CBR*

(B) NON-EXISTENT ACTS

The general principle is that a reviewable act will have legal effect until it is set aside by the CJEU or the General Court,[8] and the challenge must be brought within the time limit specified in Article 263(6). The exception is where acts are tainted by particularly serious illegality, and are deemed to be 'non-existent', from which three consequences flow: the normal time limits for challenge do not apply, since the act cannot be cloaked with legality by the passage of time; such acts do not have any provisional legal effects; and non-existent acts are not actually susceptible to annulment, because there is no 'act' to annul.

A judicial finding that an act is non-existent will, however, have the same effect in practice as if it had been annulled. Thus in *BASF*[9] the CFI found that a Commission decision in competition proceedings against the PVC cartel was non-existent because: the Commission could not locate an original copy of the decision duly authenticated in the manner required by the Rules of Procedure; it appeared that the Commissioners had not agreed on the precise text of the decision; and it had been altered after it had been formally adopted. The non-existence of a measure should, said the CFI, be raised by the Court of its own motion at any time during the proceedings. The ECJ[10] took a different view on appeal: the defects were not so serious as to make the act non-existent, but the decision was tainted by sufficient irregularity to be annulled.

(C) LIMITATIONS ON REVIEW

(i) *Area of Freedom, Security and Justice*

Prior to the Lisbon Treaty the ECJ had only limited power to review the legality of acts under what was the Third Pillar dealing with Police and Judicial Cooperation in Criminal Matters (PJCC). It was nonetheless creative in the construction of its powers.[11] The Lisbon Treaty has now brought the provisions concerning the Area of Freedom, Security and Justice within the main fabric of the Treaty.[12] The normal principles of judicial review apply to this area, subject to the caveat that the CJEU cannot review the validity or proportionality of operations by the police or law enforcement agencies, or the exercise of responsibilities of Member States with regard to the maintenance of law and order, and the safeguarding of internal security.[13]

(ii) *Common Foreign and Security Policy*

The Lisbon Treaty has 'de-pillarized' the Treaties, but the rules pertaining to the Common Foreign and Security Policy (CFSP) remain distinct. The general principle is that the Union Courts have no jurisdiction over CFSP acts.[14] This is subject to two exceptions.

[1992] ECR II–2667; Case C–25/92 R *Miethke v European Parliament* [1993] ECR I–473; Case C–480/93 *Zunis Holding SA, Finan Srl and Massinvest SA v Commission* [1996] ECR I–1; Case T–120/96 *Lilly Industries Ltd v Commission* [1998] ECR II–2571.

  [8] Case C–137/92 P *Commission v BASF AG* [1994] ECR I–2555.
  [9] Cases T–79, 84–86, 89, 91–92, 94, 96, 98, 102 and 104/89 *BASF AG v Commission* [1992] ECR II–315.
  [10] Case C–137/92 P (n 8).
  [11] Case C–354/04 P *Gestoras Pro Amnistia, Olano and Errasti v Council* [2007] ECR I–1579.
  [12] Arts 67–89 TFEU.
  [13] Art 276 TFEU.
  [14] Art 24 TEU, Art 275 TFEU.

First, the CJEU has jurisdiction to monitor compliance with Article 40 TEU, which provides in essence that exercise of power under the CFSP shall not encroach on competences under the TFEU, and vice versa.

Secondly, the Union Courts can also rule on proceedings, brought in accordance with Article 263(4) TFEU, to review the legality of decisions providing for restrictive measures against natural or legal persons adopted by the Council on the basis of Chapter 2 of Title V of the TEU, which is concerned with the CFSP. It is moreover clear from *Kadi*[15] that review of such measures will not be precluded because they were adopted pursuant to Security Council Resolutions of the United Nations: it was not for the EU Courts to review such Resolutions, but the existence of such Resolutions could not prevent review of Regulations giving effect to them within the EU, since that would offend against the notion that all EU acts were amenable to judicial review.

4 ARTICLE 263(2)–(3): STANDING FOR PRIVILEGED AND QUASI-PRIVILEGED APPLICANTS

Article 263(2) states that the action may be brought by a Member State, the European Parliament, the Council, or the Commission. It appears from this that these applicants are always allowed to bring an action, even where the decision is addressed to some other person or body. EU law does not oblige a Member State to bring an action under Article 263 or 265 TFEU for the benefit of one of its citizens, although EU law does not preclude national law from containing such an obligation.[16]

The status accorded to the European Parliament in review proceedings has altered over time. Prior to the Maastricht Treaty it was not accorded any formal privileged status. In the '*Comitology*' case[17] the ECJ rejected the Parliament's argument that it should have the same unlimited standing as other privileged applicants. The issue was reconsidered in the '*Chernobyl*' case,[18] where the Court took a different view, and held that the EP could have a quasi-privileged status so as to protect its own prerogatives. Article 173(3) EEC was redrafted so as to reflect the legal position in the *Chernobyl* judgment: the Parliament had standing to defend its own prerogatives.[19] The Nice Treaty then added the European Parliament to the list of privileged applicants.

The Court of Auditors, the European Central Bank (ECB), and the Committee of the Regions are covered by Article 263(3) TFEU, so that they have standing only to defend their own prerogatives.

The European Council is included in the bodies amenable to review. It is not, however, listed among either the privileged or quasi-privileged applicants who are entitled to seek judicial review. There is thus an asymmetry built into Article 263 TFEU, which does not apply to the other EU institutions. The European Council is accorded the right to bring an action for failure to act under Article 265 TFEU, which makes the position under Article 263 TFEU look all the more odd. There could be instances in which the European Council might wish to bring an action.[20] The ECJ in the past interpreted the

---

[15] Cases C–402 and 415/05 P *Yassin Abdullah Kadi and Al Barakaat International Foundation v Council and Commission* [2008] ECR I–6351.

[16] Case C–511/03 *Netherlands v Ten Kate Holding Musselkanaal BV* [2005] ECR I–8979.

[17] Case 302/87 *European Parliament v Council* [1988] ECR 5615.

[18] Case C–70/88 *European Parliament v Council* [1990] ECR I–2041. See also Case C–156/93 *European Parliament v Commission* [1995] ECR I–2019; Case C–187/93 *European Parliament v Council* [1994] ECR I–2855; Case C–360/93 *European Parliament v Council* [1996] ECR I–1195.

[19] K Bradley, 'Sense and Sensibility: *Parliament* v *Council* Continued' (1991) 16 ELRev 245; J Weiler, 'Pride and Prejudice—*Parliament* v *Council*' (1989) 14 ELRev 334.

[20] P Craig, *The Lisbon Treaty: Law, Politics, and Treaty Reform* (Oxford University Press, 2010) ch 4.

predecessor to Article 263 TFEU so as to enable the European Parliament to defend its prerogatives, justifying this on the ground that it was necessary to safeguard the institutional balance under the Treaty. It could draw on this precedent and afford the European Council claimant status, at the very least as a quasi-privileged applicant.

Bodies, offices, and agencies of the Union also suffer from the infirmity of being defendants without any separate recognition as applicants. There could be instances in which an EU agency might wish to argue that Union legislation or a delegated act had wrongfully impinged on its terrain, as laid down in its empowering legislation. These bodies, offices, or agencies might seek to bring an action as a non-privileged applicant. Most agencies have legal personality and could therefore count as legal persons for the purposes of Article 263(4) TFEU. They would however then have to satisfy the criteria in Article 263(4), including the test for standing.

5 ARTICLE 263(4): STANDING FOR NON-PRIVILEGED APPLICANTS

Article 263(4) allows a natural or legal person to bring an action in three types of case. The first is straightforward: the addressee of a decision can challenge it before the CJEU or General Court (GC). The second is where the act is of direct and individual concern to the natural or legal person or persons, the assumption being that the person or persons are not the immediate addressees of the act. The third type of case is where there is a regulatory act, which does not entail implementing measures, in which case the claimant must show direct concern, but does not need to prove individual concern.

(A) DIRECT CONCERN

An applicant must show that the act was of direct concern if it is to be accorded standing. The general principle is that a measure will be of direct concern where it directly affects the legal situation of the applicant and leaves no discretion to the addressees of the measure, who are entrusted with its implementation. This implementation must be automatic and result from EU rules without the application of other intermediate rules.[21] It can be difficult to determine whether there is some autonomous exercise of will between the original decision and its implementation.[22]

---

[21] Case C–386/96 *Société Louis Dreyfus & Cie v Commission* [1998] ECR I–2309; Case T–54/96 *Oleifici Italiana SpA and Fratelli Rubino Industrie Olearie SpA v Commission* [1998] ECR II–3377; Case C–486/01 P *National Front v European Parliament* [2004] ECR I–6289, [34]; Case 15/06 P *Regione Siciliana v Commission* [2007] ECR I–2591, [31]; Cases C–445 and 455/07 P *Ente per le Ville Vesuviane v Commission* [2009] ECR I–7993, [45]; Case C–343/07 *Bavaria NV and Bavaria Italia Srl v Bayerischer Brauerbund eV* [2009] ECR I–5491, [43]; Case T–16/04 *Arcelor SA v European Parliament and Council* [2010] ECR II–211, [97]; Case T–95/10 *Cindu Chemicals BV v European Chemicals Agency (ECHA)* EU:T:2013:108, [45]; Cases T–454/10 and 482/11 *Anicav and Agrucon v Commission* EU:T:2013:282, [36].

[22] Case T–12/93 *Comité Central d'Entreprise de la Société Anonyme Vittel v Commission* [1995] ECR II–1247; Case T–96/92 *Comité Central d'Entreprise de la Société Générale des Grands Sources v Commission* [1995] ECR II–1213; Case T–509/93 *Richco Commodities Ltd v Commission* [1996] ECR II–1181; Cases T–172, 175 and 177/98 *Salamander v European Parliament and Council* [2000] ECR II–2487.

Cases 41–44/70 **NV International Fruit Company v Commission**
[1971] ECR 411

[Note Lisbon Treaty renumbering: Art 173 is now Art 263 TFEU]

The Community adopted a Regulation which limited the import of apples from third countries from 1 April 1970 to 30 June 1970. The Regulation provided for a system of import licences, which were granted to the extent to which the Community market allowed. Under this system, a Member State notified the Commission, at the end of each week, of the quantities for which import licences were requested during the preceding week. The Commission then decided on the issue of licences in the light of this information. The challenge was to a Regulation applying this scheme to a particular week. The ECJ found individual concern and then considered whether the applicant was directly concerned.

THE ECJ

23. Moreover, it is clear from the system introduced by Regulation No 459/70, and particularly from Article 2(2) thereof, that the decision on the grant of import licences is a matter for the Commission.

24. According to this provision, the Commission alone is competent to assess the economic situation in the light of which the grant of import licences must be justified.

25. Article 1(2) of Regulation No 459/70, by providing that the 'Member States shall in accordance with the conditions laid down in Article 2, issue the licence to any interested party applying for it', makes it clear that the national authorities do not enjoy any discretion in the matter of the issue of licences and the conditions on which applications by the parties concerned should be granted.

26. The duty of such authorities is merely to collect the data necessary in order that the Commission may take its decision in accordance with Article 2(2) of that regulation, and subsequently adopt the national measures needed to give effect to that decision.

27. In these circumstances as far as the interested parties are concerned, the issue of or refusal to issue the import licences must be bound up with this decision.

28. The measure whereby the Commission decides on the issues of the import licences thus directly affects the legal position of the parties concerned.

29. The applications thus fulfil the requirements of the second paragraph of Article 173 of the Treaty, and are therefore admissible.

The decision in the *International Fruit* case[23] can be compared to the following judgment by the Court.[24]

Case 222/83 **Municipality of Differdange v Commission**
[1984] ECR 2889

The Commission authorized Luxembourg to grant aid to steel firms, on the condition that they undertook reductions in capacity. The applicant municipality argued that it was directly and individually concerned by this Decision, because the reduction in production capacity and closure of factories would lead to a reduction in local taxes.

---

[23] See also Case 207/86 *Apesco v Commission* [1988] ECR 2151, [12]; Cases T–132 and 143/96 *Freistaat Sachsen and others v Commission* [1999] ECR II–3663, [89]–[90]; Cases T–366/03 and 235/04 *Land Oberösterreich and Austria v Commission* [2005] ECR II–4005, [29].

[24] See also, eg, Case 69/69 *Alcan Alumininium Raeren v Commission* [1970] ECR 385; Case 62/70 *Bock v Commission* [1971] ECR 897.

THE ECJ

10. In this case the contested measure, which is addressed to the Grand Duchy of Luxembourg, authorizes it to grant certain aids to the undertakings named therein provided that they reduce their production capacity by a specified amount. However, it neither identifies the establishments in which the production must be reduced or terminated nor the factories which must be closed as a result of the termination of production. In addition, the Decision states that the Commission was to be notified of the closure dates only by 31 January 1984 so that the undertakings affected were free until that date to fix, where necessary with the agreement of the Luxembourg government, the detailed rules for the restructuring necessary to comply with the conditions laid down in the Decision.

11. That conclusion is, moreover, confirmed by Article 2 of the Decision according to which the capacity reductions may also be carried out by other undertakings.

12. It follows that the contested Decision left to the national authorities and undertakings concerned such a margin of discretion with regard to the manner of its implementation and in particular with regard to the choice of factories to be closed, that the Decision cannot be regarded as being of direct and individual concern to the municipalities with which the undertakings affected, by virtue of the location of their factories, are connected.

(B) INDIVIDUAL CONCERN: *PLAUMANN*

Applicants must prove individual concern under Article 263(4) in relation to acts addressed to another person, unless the act is a regulatory act that does not entail implementing measures. The issue can arise either where the legal act takes the form of a decision addressed to another, or where it assumes the form of a regulation or directive. In both instances the applicant must prove that the relevant act was of direct and individual concern and in both types of case *Plaumann* is the legal test for proving individual concern. We must therefore look closely at the test and its application.

(i) *The Test*

Case 25/62 **Plaumann & Co v Commission**
[1963] ECR 95

[Note Lisbon Treaty renumbering: Art 173 is now Art 263 TFEU]

In 1961 the German Government requested the Commission to authorize it to suspend the collection of duties on clementines imported from non-member countries. The Commission refused the request, and addressed its answer to the German Government. The applicant was an importer of clementines, who contested the legality of the Commission's Decision.

THE ECJ

Under the second paragraph of Article 173 of the EEC Treaty 'any natural or legal person may . . . institute proceedings against a decision . . . which, although in the form of . . . a decision addressed to another person, is of direct and individual concern to the former'. The defendant contends that the words 'other person' in this paragraph do not refer to Member States in their capacity as sovereign authorities and that individuals may not therefore bring an action for annulment against the decisions of the Commission or of the Council addressed to Member States.

However the second paragraph of Article 173 does allow an individual to bring an action against decisions addressed to 'another person' which are of direct and individual concern to the former, but this article neither defines nor limits the scope of these words. The words and the natural meaning of this provision justify the broadest interpretation. Moreover provisions of the Treaty regarding the right of interested parties to bring an action must not be interpreted restrictively. Therefore, the treaty being silent on the point, a limitation in this respect may not be presumed.

...

Persons other than those to whom a decision is addressed may only claim to be individually concerned if that decision affects them by reason of certain attributes which are peculiar to them or by reason of circumstances in which they are differentiated from all other persons and by virtue of these factors distinguishes them individually just as in the case of the person addressed. In the present case the applicant is affected by the disputed Decision as an importer of clementines, that is to say, by reason of a commercial activity which may at any time be practised by any person and is not therefore such as to distinguish the applicant in relation to the contested Decision as in the case of the addressee.

For these reasons the present action for annulment must be declared inadmissible.

In *Plaumann* the applicant sought relief against a decision addressed to another. There were also cases where an applicant claimed to be individually concerned by a legal act that took the form of a regulation or a directive. The ECJ made it clear prior to the Lisbon Treaty that a non-privileged applicant could in principle challenge the legality of a directive, even though Article 230(4) EC did not make this explicit. This conclusion has been reinforced by Article 263(4) TFEU, which is framed in terms of challenge to legal acts, and this clearly includes directives. The applicant nonetheless has an uphill struggle to show individual concern.[25] There were initially two tests in the case law: the closed category test[26] and the abstract terminology test. The latter was stricter than the former, and became the general test applied by the Court. It is exemplified by *Calpak*, and many other judgments:[27]

Cases 789 and 790/79 **Calpak SpA and Società Emiliana Lavorazione Frutta SpA v Commission**
[1980] ECR 1949

[Note Lisbon Treaty renumbering: Arts 173 and 189 are now Arts 263 and 288 TFEU]

The applicants were producers of William pears, and they complained that the calculation of production aid granted to them was void. Under the terms of an earlier regulation, production aid was to be calculated on the basis of the average production over the previous three years, in order to avoid the risk of over-production. The applicants alleged that the Commission had abandoned this method of assessing

[25] Case C–298/89 *Gibraltar v Council* [1993] ECR I–3605; Case T–99/94 *Asociación Española de Empresas de la Carne (ASOCARNE) v Council* [1994] ECR II–871, upheld on appeal, Case C–10/95 P [1995] ECR I–4149; Case T–135/96 *UEAPME v Council* [1998] ECR II–2335, [63]; Cases T–172, 175 and 177/98 *Salamander AG v Parliament and Council* [2000] ECR II–2487; Case T–94/04 *EEB v Commission* [2005] ECR II–4919; Case T–16/04 *Arcelor* (n 21) [100]–[123].

[26] Cases 41–44/70 *International Fruit Company BV v Commission* [1971] ECR 411; Case 100/74 *Société CAM SA v Commission* [1975] ECR 1393; Case C–354/87 *Weddel v Commission* [1990] ECR I–3487.

[27] Cases 103–109/78 *Beauport v Council and Commission* [1979] ECR 17; Case 162/78 *Wagner v Commission* [1979] ECR 3467; Case 45/81 *Alexander Moksel Import-Export GmbH & Co Handels KG v Commission* [1982] ECR 1129; Cases 97, 99, 193 and 215/86 *Asteris AE and Greece v Commission* [1988] ECR 2181; Case 160/88 R *Fédération Européenne de la Santé Animale v Council* [1988] ECR 4121; Case C–298/89 *Gibraltar v Council* [1993] ECR I–3605; Case C–309/89 *Codorniu SA v Council* [1994] ECR I–1853.

aid, and had based its aid calculation on one marketing year, in which production was atypically low. The applicants also claimed that they were a closed and definable group, the members of which were known to, or identifiable by, the Commission.

THE ECJ

7. The second paragraph of Article 173 empowers individuals to contest, *inter alia*, any decision which, although in the form of a regulation, is of direct and individual concern to them. The objective of that provision is in particular to prevent the Community institutions from being in a position, merely by choosing the form of a regulation, to exclude an application by an individual against a decision which concerns him directly and individually; it therefore stipulates that the choice of form cannot change the nature of the measure.

8. By virtue of the second paragraph of Article 189 of the Treaty the criterion for distinguishing between a regulation and a decision is whether the measure is of general application or not....

9. A provision which limits the granting of production aid for all producers in respect of a particular product to a uniform percentage of the quantity produced by them during a uniform period is by nature a measure of general application within the meaning of Article 189 of the Treaty. In fact the measure applies to objectively determined situations and produces legal effects with regard to categories of persons described in a generalized and abstract manner. The nature of the measure as a regulation is not called in question by the mere fact that it is possible to determine the number or even identity of the producers to be granted the aid which is limited thereby.

(ii) *The* Plaumann *Test and Decisions: Pragmatic and Conceptual Difficulties*

The *Plaumann* test remains the leading authority after the Lisbon Treaty for those cases where individual concern must be proven. It is therefore important to dwell on the test and its application so as to understand why private applicants have found it so difficult to succeed. The *Plaumann* test effectively prevented virtually all direct actions by private parties to challenge decisions addressed to others,[28] except where the challenged decision had a retrospective impact.[29]

The *test* stipulates that applicants can only be individually concerned by a decision addressed to another if they are in some way differentiated from all other persons, and by reason of these distinguishing features singled out in the same way as the initial addressee. There can however be more than one applicant who is individually concerned. The *application of the test* to the facts is equally important: the applicant failed because it practised a commercial activity that could be carried on by any person at any time. This reasoning can be criticized on both pragmatic and conceptual grounds.

In *pragmatic terms* the application of the test is economically unrealistic. If a limited number of firms is pursuing a trade this is the result of the ordinary principles of supply and demand. If there

---

[28] See, eg, Case 1/64 *Glucoseries Réunies v Commission* [1964] ECR 413; Case 38/64 *Getreide-Import Gesellschaft v Commission* [1965] ECR 203; Case 11/82 *Piraiki-Patraiki* (n 30); Case 97/85 *Union Deutsche Lebensmittelswerke GmbH v Commission* [1987] ECR 2265; Case 34/88 *CEVAP v Council* [1988] ECR 6265; Case 191/88 *Co-Frutta SARL v Commission* [1989] ECR 793; Case 206/87 *Lefebvre Frère et Soeur SA v Commission* [1989] ECR 275; Case T–585/93 *Stichting Greenpeace Council (Greenpeace International) v Commission* [1995] ECR II–2205, upheld on appeal, Case C–321/95 P *Stichting Greenpeace Council (Greenpeace International) v Commission* [1998] ECR I–1651; Case T–117/94 *Associazione Agricoltori della Provincia di Rovigo v Commission* [1995] ECR II–455; Case T–398/94 *Kahn Scheepvaart v Commission* [1996] ECR II–477; Case T–60/96 *Merck & Co Inc v Commission* [1997] ECR II–849; Case T–86/96 *Arbeitsgemeinschaft Deutscher Luftfahrt-Unternehmen and Hapag-Lloyd Fluggesellschaft mbH v Commission* [1999] ECR II–179.

[29] Cases 106 and 107/63 *Alfred Toepfer and Getreide-Import Gesellschaft v Commission* [1965] ECR 405; Case 62/70 *Bock v Commission* [1971] ECR 897; Case 11/82 *Piraiki-Patraiki* (n 30).

were a sudden surge of desire for clementines, the existing firms would normally import more of the produce. The argument that the activity of importing clementines can be undertaken by any person, that the number may alter significantly, and that therefore the applicant is not individually concerned is thus unconvincing. Moreover, even if there were incentives for other traders to enter the relevant industry, this might take time, and might well not occur during the period of application of the contested decision.[30]

The ECJ's reasoning is also open to criticism in *conceptual terms*, since it renders it literally impossible for an applicant to succeed, except in a very limited category of retrospective cases. The *Plaumann* test has to be applied at some point in time. There are only three choices. The relevant question could be asked when the contested determination was made, when the application for review was lodged, or at some future, undefined date. It has been held that the test for standing must be judged when the application for review is lodged.[31] This is sensible. However it is scant comfort to the applicant in a *Plaumann*-type case to be told that standing will be judged at the time the application is lodged, but then to be told the application fails because the activity of clementine-importing could be carried out by anyone at any time. On this reasoning no applicant could ever succeed, subject to the caveat considered below, since it could always be argued that others might engage in the trade at some juncture. This serves, in reality, to shift the focus to choice three: some future, ill-defined date. The possibility of *locus standi* is like a mirage in the desert, ever receding and never capable of being grasped.

The preceding argument might be opposed by contending that the applicant in *Plaumann* was properly rejected, since he was a member of an open rather than closed category of applicants, and hence was not individually concerned. An open category is regarded as one where the membership is not fixed at the time of the decision. A closed category is one in which it is thus fixed.[32] There are however practical and conceptual problems with this reasoning.

In *practical terms*, the language of open categories is used to rule out standing for any applicant, even if there is only a very limited number presently engaged in that trade, on the ground that others might undertake the trade thereafter. If the presence of such notional, future traders renders the category open, this ignores the practical economics that determine those who supply a product.

In *conceptual terms*, to regard any category as open merely because others might notionally undertake the trade leads to bizarre results, since any decision with a future impact would be unchallengeable because the category would be regarded as open. The *Plaumann* test is based on the assumption that some people have attributes that distinguish them from others, and that they possess these attributes when the contested decision is made. The fact that others might acquire these attributes later, by joining that trade, does not mean that they are presently part of that category. The matter can be put quite simply. The fact that I may wish to become striker for England, a great pianist, or a clementine importer does not mean that I currently have the attributes associated with any of these roles in life.

(iii) *The* Plaumann *Test and Regulations/Directives: Pragmatic and Conceptual Difficulties*

The *Plaumann* test led to similar difficulties where the applicant sought to challenge a regulation or a directive. The abstract terminology test placed those who challenged an act in the form of a regulation

---

[30] A point made by the applicants in Case 11/82 *AE Piraiki-Patraiki v Commission* [1985] ECR 207, although ignored by the ECJ.

[31] Case T–16/96 *Cityflyer Express Ltd v Commission* [1998] ECR II–757, [30].

[32] For a recent and rare example of a non-retrospective case where the CJEU was willing to hold that a category was closed, Case C–133/12 P *Stichting Woonlinie v Commission* EU:C:2014:105, where the number of traders was limited by royal decree.

in a difficult position. The purpose of allowing such challenge was to prevent the Community institutions from immunizing matters from attack by the form of their classification. This was the rationale for permitting a challenge when the regulation was in reality a decision, which was of direct and individual concern to the applicant. This required, as acknowledged in *Calpak*, the Court to look behind the *form* of the measure in order to determine whether in *substance* it really was a regulation or not.

The problem with the abstract terminology test was that, rather than looking behind form to substance, it came perilously close to looking behind form to form. A regulation would be accepted as a true regulation if, as stated in *Calpak*, it applied to 'objectively determined situations and produces legal effects with regard to categories of persons described in a generalized and abstract manner'. However, it was always possible to draft norms in this manner, and thus to immunize them from attack, more especially as the Court made clear that knowledge of the number or identity of those affected would not prevent the norm from being regarded as a true regulation.

If a regulation was found to be a 'true regulation' on the basis of the abstract terminology test then traditionally the Court would simply conclude that the applicant was not individually concerned. In *Codorniu* the Union Courts modified this legal stance and accepted that a regulation might be a 'true' regulation as judged by the abstract terminology test, but that nonetheless it might be of individual concern to an applicant.[33] This was a liberalizing move.

However an applicant still had to show individual concern in accordance with the *Plaumann* test. While there were some exceptions,[34] the dominant approach post-*Codorniu* was 'pure *Plaumann*'. Applicants were denied standing because the ECJ and CFI applied the *Plaumann* test in the same manner as in *Plaumann* itself. The fact that the applicant operated a trade which could be engaged in by any other person served to deny individual concern. The possibility of determining the number or identity of the persons to whom a measure applied did not suffice for individual concern.[35] The laudable hope[36] that *Codorniu* might lead to a test for standing based on adverse impact, judged on the facts of the case, was not therefore realized.[37]

(iv) *The* Plaumann *Test: Regulations, Directives, and the Lisbon Treaty*

The Lisbon Treaty changed the wording of what is now Article 263(4). This is relevant for the following reason. Article 230(4) EC was the predecessor to Article 263(4) TFEU, but the wording was subtly different. Article 230(4) stated that a decision addressed to another person might be of individual concern to the applicant, and that an act in the form of a regulation might in reality be a decision that was of direct and individual concern to the applicant. It therefore contained an invitation to look behind the form of the measure to its substance, in the sense that the ECJ or CFI could decide

---

[33] Case C–309/89 *Codorniu SA v Council* [1994] ECR I–1853.

[34] Cases T–480 and 483/93 *Antillean Rice Mills NV v Commission* [1995] ECR II–2305, [70], [76]; Cases T–32 and 41/98 *Government of the Netherlands Antilles v Commission* [2000] ECR II–20; Case T–33/01 *Infront WM AG v Commission* [2005] ECR II–5897.

[35] See, eg, Case T–472/93 *Campo Ebro Industrial SA v Council* [1995] ECR II–421; Case T–489/93 *Unifruit Hellas EPE v Commission* [1994] ECR II–1201; Case T–116/94 *Cassa Nazionale di Previdenza a Favore degli Avvocati e Procuratori v Council* [1995] ECR II–1; Case C–209/94 P *Buralux SA v Council* [1996] ECR I–615; Case T–138/98 *Armement Coopératif Artisanal Vendéen (ACAV) v Council* [2000] ECR II–341; Cases T–38–50/99 *Sociedade Agricola dos Arinhos, Ld v Commission* [2001] ECR II–585; Case T–155/02 *VVG International Handelsgesellschaft mbH v Commission* [2003] ECR II–1949; Case T–139/01 *Comafrica SpA and Dole Fresh Fruit Europe Ltd and Co v Commission* [2005] ECR II–409, [100], [107]–[116]; Case C–362/06 P *Markku Sahlstedt v Commission* [2009] ECR I–2903; Case C–274/12 P *Telefónica SA v Commission* EU:C:2013:852, [47]; Case C–133/12 P *Stichting Woonlinie* (n 32) [45].

[36] A Arnull, 'Private Applicants and the Action for Annulment under Article 173 of the EC Treaty' (1995) 32 CMLRev 7.

[37] A Arnull, 'Private Applicants and the Action for Annulment since *Codorniu*' (2001) 38 CMLRev 7, 51–52.

that a measure in the form of a regulation was in reality a decision that was of direct and individual concern.

Article 263(4) TFEU contains nothing expressly equivalent to this, *and* the structure of the Lisbon Treaty provisions on legal acts renders this more difficult for the following reason. This is in part because the test for a legislative act is formalistic, not substantive, in nature: enactment by a legislative procedure.[38] It is also because there are requirements that must be satisfied for the passage of delegated acts,[39] and thus the consequence of reclassifying a legislative act as a delegated act, or vice versa, would inevitably be to condemn it as invalid, since it would not have been enacted by the proper procedure or subject to the proper conditions. It will therefore be difficult for an individual to contend that the Union Courts should look to the substance of a measure *across* the categories of legal act.

It would still be possible in principle for the Courts to undertake this task *within* a particular category of legal act. Thus an applicant might contend that although a regulation was a legislative act because it was made in accordance with the legislative procedure, it was nonetheless of direct and individual concern. The applicant is however likely to face an uphill task in proving individual concern, given the meaning of this term explained above, and given also the label 'legislative act' attached to such measures. To take another example, an applicant might contend that a delegated act in the form of a regulation was of direct and individual concern to it.

(v) *Individual Concern, Dumping, Competition, and State Aids*

The Court has been more liberal in according standing in certain areas, those concerning anti-dumping, competition, and state aids. The relevant Treaty Articles and regulations had a marked impact on judicial decisions, since the procedure in these areas explicitly or implicitly envisaged a role for the individual complainant, who could alert the Commission to the breach of EU law. The EU interest in these areas was moreover relatively clear, and the Union Courts were therefore receptive to arguments that, for example, a state had infringed EU law by illegal state aid. These areas will be considered in turn.

The EU passes *anti-dumping* regulations to prevent those outside the EU from selling goods within the EU at too low a price, to the detriment of Union traders. Whether a firm is dumping may be controversial. There was the added complication that anti-dumping duties had to be imposed by regulation, as opposed to decision. If, therefore, the Court held that the regulation was not a regulation at all, then the Commission had no power to impose the measure. Three types of applicant might wish to challenge an anti-dumping duty.

The first type is the firm which initiated the complaint about dumping, as exemplified by the *Timex* case[40] where the company that initiated the complaint was unhappy with the resultant regulation because it felt that the anti-dumping duty was too low. The ECJ held that as the principal complainant and a leading watchmaker in the EU it had standing to contest the level of duty imposed.

The second type of applicant is the producer of the product that is subject to the anti-dumping duty. In the *Allied Corporation* case[41] the ECJ confirmed that the producers and exporters who were charged with dumping could also be regarded as individually concerned, at least insofar as they were identified in the measure adopted by the Commission or involved in the preliminary investigation.

---

[38] Art 289 TFEU.

[39] Art 290 TFEU.

[40] Case 264/82 *Timex Corporation v Council and Commission* [1985] ECR 849. Compare Case T–598/97 *British Shoe Corporation Footwear Supplies Ltd v Council* [2002] ECR II–1155.

[41] Cases 239 and 275/82 *Allied Corporation v Commission* [1984] ECR 1005; Case T–155/94 *Climax Paper Converters Ltd v Council* [1996] ECR II–873; Case T–147/97 *Champion Stationery Mfg Co Ltd v Council* [1998] ECR II–4137.

The third category of applicant who might wish to contest the legality of an anti-dumping regulation is the importer of the product against which the anti-dumping duty has been imposed. Some applications were rejected because the importer could challenge the measure indirectly under Article 267 TFEU in an action against the national agency which collected the duty. In *Extramet* the ECJ however held that an importer could have standing because it was the largest importer of the product subject to the anti-dumping measure, the end user of the product, and its business activities were seriously affected by the contested regulation.[42]

A second area in which the ECJ has been more liberal in according standing is *competition policy*, regulated by Articles 101 and 102 TFEU. Under what was Article 3(2) of Regulation 17,[43] a Member State, or any natural or legal person who claimed to have a legitimate interest, could make an application to the Commission, putting forward evidence of a breach of what are now Articles 101 and 102 TFEU.

Case 26/76 **Metro-SB-Großmärkte GmbH & Co KG v Commission**[44]
[1977] ECR 1875

[Note Lisbon Treaty renumbering: Arts 85, 86, and 173 are now Arts 101, 102, and 263 TFEU]

Metro argued that the distribution system operated by SABA was in breach of Article 85 of the Treaty. It initiated a complaint under Article 3(2) of Regulation 17. The Commission decided that certain aspects of the distribution system were not in breach of Article 85, and it was this Decision, addressed to SABA, that Metro sought to annul. The question arose whether Metro could claim to be individually concerned by a Decision addressed to another.

THE ECJ

The contested decision was adopted in particular as the result of a complaint submitted by Metro and it relates to the provisions of SABA's distribution system, on which SABA relied and continues to rely as against Metro in order to justify its refusal to sell to the latter or to appoint it as a wholesaler, and which the applicant had for this reason impugned in its complaint.

It is in the interests of a satisfactory administration of justice and of the proper application of Articles 85 and 86 that natural or legal persons who are entitled, pursuant to Article 3(2)(b) of Regulation No 17, to request the Commission to find an infringement of Articles 85 and 86 should be able, if their request is not complied with wholly or in part, to institute proceedings in order to protect their legitimate interests.

In those circumstances the applicant must be considered to be directly and individually concerned, within the meaning of the second paragraph of Article 173, by the contested decision and the application is accordingly admissible.

---

[42] Case C–358/89 *Extramet Industrie SA v Council* [1991] ECR I–2501; Case T–161/94 *Sinochem Heilongjiang v Commission* [1996] ECR II–695; Case T–2/95 *Industrie des Poudres Sphériques v Council* [1998] ECR II–3939.

[43] The regime for the enforcement of competition policy has now changed: see below, pp 1048–1051.

[44] Case T–37/92 *Bureau Européen des Unions des Consommateurs v Commission* [1994] ECR II–285, although the result was different if the applicant had not taken part in the complaints procedure: Case C–70/97 *Kruidvart BVBA v Commission* [1998] ECR I–7183. See also in relation to mergers Case T–96/92 *Comité Central d'Entreprise de la Société Générale des Grands Sources v Commission* [1995] ECR II–1213; Cases T–528, 542, 543 and 546/93 *Métropole Télévision SA v Commission* [1996] ECR II–649; Case T–158/00 *ARD v Commission* [2003] ECR II–3825.

Similar considerations are apparent in the case law on *state aids*. The provision of such aid is regulated by Articles 107 to 109 TFEU to prevent competition from being distorted by a firm receiving assistance from its government, thereby giving it an unfair advantage against competitors.[45] The Commission decides whether the aid is compatible with the Treaty, and addresses a decision to the state, which can challenge it under Article 263 TFEU. The Treaty was less clear whether complainants could also do so. There was nothing directly comparable in state aids to the complaints procedure that operated in competition law.

Notwithstanding this, the ECJ in *COFAZ*[46] reasoned by analogy from the *Metro* case in competition law and the *Timex* case in anti-dumping. The applicants in *COFAZ* played a comparable role in the procedure under what is now Article 108 TFEU, more especially because Article 108(2) recognized that the undertakings concerned were entitled to submit their comments to the Commission. They were therefore granted standing, subject to the further condition that their position on the market was significantly affected by the aid that was the subject of the contested decision.[47]

(vi) *Individual Concern: Reform and the Courts*

Article 263(4) TFEU amended Article 230(4) EC by providing that individual concern is not required in relation to regulatory acts that do not entail implementing measures. The scope of this exception will be considered below. Before doing so, we should consider attempts at more general reform of the test for individual concern through judicial means.

The very fact that the case law on dumping, competition, and state aids was more liberal cast into sharp relief the restrictive approach that dominated the majority of cases on standing. It is therefore not surprising that the Courts' general jurisprudence on standing for non-privileged applicants was criticized as being too restrictive. The ECJ defended its jurisprudence on the ground that the Treaty provided a comprehensive mechanism for legal protection: applicants who did not have standing for a direct action under Article 263 could test the legality of the measure indirectly through Article 267 TFEU. Advocate General Jacobs questioned this reasoning in the *Extramet* case.[48] In the *UPA* case he subjected the hypothesis to more searching scrutiny, found it to be unconvincing, and suggested that standing should be accorded where the contested measure had a substantial adverse effect on the applicant.

Case C–50/00 **P Unión de Pequeños Agricultores v Council**
[2002] ECR I–6677

[Note Lisbon Treaty renumbering: Arts 230 and 234 are now Arts 263 and 267 TFEU]

An association of farmers, UPA, sought the annulment of Regulation 1638/98, which amended the common organization of the olive oil market. The CFI dismissed the application because the members of the association were not individually concerned by the Regulation under Article 230(4). The UPA

---

[45] Ch 29.

[46] Case 169/84 *Compagnie Française de l'Azote (COFAZ) SA v Commission* [1986] ECR 391; Case T–435/93 *ASPEC v Commission* [1995] ECR II–1281; Case T–380/94 *AIUFFASS v Commission* [1996] ECR II–2169; Case T–88/01 *Sniace, SA v Commission* [2005] ECR II–1165, [56]–[57].

[47] The case law on standing in relation to state aids is complex, see Ch 29 and U Soltesz and H Bielesz, 'Judicial Review of State Aid Decisions—Recent Developments' [2004] ECLR 133.

[48] Case C–358/89 *Extramet* (n 42) [70]–[74], AG Jacobs.

argued that it was denied effective judicial protection because it could not readily attack the measure via Article 234. The following extract contains the Advocate General's summary of his Opinion.

ADVOCATE GENERAL JACOBS

102. ...

(1) The Court's fundamental assumption that the possibility for an individual applicant to trigger a reference for a preliminary ruling provides full and effective judicial protection against general measures is open to serious objections:

— under the preliminary ruling procedure the applicant has no right to decide whether a reference is made, which measures are referred for review or what grounds of invalidity are raised and thus no right of access to the Court of Justice; on the other hand, the national court cannot itself grant the desired remedy to declare the general measure in issue invalid;

— there may be a denial of justice in cases where it is difficult or impossible for an applicant to challenge a general measure indirectly (e.g. where there are no challengeable implementing measures or where the applicant would have to break the law in order to be able to challenge ensuing sanctions);

— legal certainty pleads in favour of allowing a general measure to be reviewed as soon as possible and not only after implementing measures have been adopted;

— indirect challenges to general measures through references on validity under Article 234 present a number of procedural disadvantages in comparison to direct challenges under Article 230 before the Court of First Instance as regards for example the participation of the institution(s) which adopted the measure, the delays and costs involved, the award of interim measures or the possibility of third party intervention.

(2) Those objections cannot be overcome by granting standing by way of exception in those cases where an applicant has under national law no way of triggering a reference for a preliminary ruling on the validity of the contested measure. Such an approach

— has no basis in the wording of the Treaty;

— would inevitably oblige the Community Courts to interpret and apply rules of national law, a task for which they are neither well prepared nor even competent;

— would lead to inequality between operators from different Member States and to a further loss of legal certainty.

(3) Nor can those objections be overcome by postulating an obligation for the legal orders of the Member States to ensure that references on the validity of general Community measures are available in their legal systems. Such an approach would

— leave unresolved most of the problems of the current situation such as the absence of remedy as a matter of right, unnecessary delays and costs for the applicant or the award of interim measures;

— be difficult to monitor and enforce; and

— require far-reaching interference with national procedural autonomy.

(4) The only satisfactory solution is therefore to recognise that an applicant is individually concerned by a Community measure where the measure has, or is liable to have, a substantial adverse effect on his interests. That solution has the following advantages:

— it resolves all the problems set out above: applicants are granted a true right of direct access to a court which can grant a remedy, cases of possible denial of justice are avoided, and judicial protection is improved in various ways;

— it also removes the anomaly under the current case-law that the greater the number of persons affected the less likely it is that effective judicial review is available;

— the increasingly complex and unpredictable rules on standing are replaced by a much simpler test which would shift the emphasis in cases before the Community Courts from purely formal questions of admissibility to questions of substance;

— such a re-interpretation is in line with the general tendency of the case-law to extend the scope of judicial protection in response to the growth of powers of the Community institutions (*ERTA, Les Verts, Chernobyl*);

(5) The objections to enlarging standing are unconvincing. In particular:

— the wording of Article 230 does not preclude it;

— to insulate potentially unlawful measures from judicial scrutiny cannot be justified on grounds of administrative or legislative efficiency: protection of the legislative process must be achieved through appropriate substantive standards of review;

— the fears of over-loading the Court of First Instance seem exaggerated since the time-limit in Article 230(5) and the requirement of direct concern will prevent an insuperable increase of the case-load; there are procedural means to deal with a more limited increase of cases.

(6) The chief objection may be that the case-law has stood for many years. There are however a number of reasons why the time is now ripe for change. In particular:

— the case-law in many borderline cases is not stable, and has been in any event relaxed in recent years, with the result that decisions on admissibility have become increasingly complex and unpredictable;

— the case-law is increasingly out of line with more liberal developments in the laws of the Member States;

— the establishment of the Court of First Instance, and the progressive transfer to that Court of all actions brought by individuals, make it increasingly appropriate to enlarge the standing of individuals to challenge general measures;

— the Court's case-law on the principle of effective judicial protection in the national courts makes it increasingly difficult to justify narrow restrictions on standing before the Community Courts.

The hope that standing rules might be liberalized proved short-lived, since the ECJ declined to follow the lead of Advocate General Jacobs.

Case C–50/00 P Unión de Pequeños Agricultores v Council
[2002] ECR I–6677

The ECJ accepted the principle from *Codorniu* that a true regulation could be challenged, provided the applicant could show individual concern in accordance with the *Plaumann* test. It continued as follows.

THE ECJ

37. If that condition is not fulfilled, a natural or legal person does not, under any circumstances, have standing to bring an action for the annulment of a regulation.

38. The European Community is, however, a Community based on the rule of law in which its institutions are subject to judicial review of the compatibility of their acts with the Treaty and with the general principles of law which include fundamental rights.

39. Individuals are therefore entitled to effective judicial protection of the rights they derive from the Community legal order, and the right to such protection is one of the general principles of law stemming from the constitutional traditions common to the Member States...

40. [T]he Treaty has established a complete system of legal remedies and procedures designed to ensure judicial review of the legality of acts of the institutions...Under that system, where natural or legal persons cannot, by reason of the conditions for admissibility laid down in the fourth paragraph of Article 173 of the Treaty, directly challenge Community measures of general application, they are able, depending on the case, either indirectly to plead the invalidity of such acts before the Community courts under Article 184 of the Treaty or to do so before the national courts and ask them, since they have no jurisdiction themselves to declare those measures invalid..., to make a reference to the Court of Justice for a preliminary ruling on validity.

41. Thus it is for the Member States to establish a system of legal remedies and procedures which ensure respect for the right to effective judicial protection.

42. In that context, in accordance with...Article 5 of the Treaty, the national courts are required, so far as possible, to interpret and apply national procedural rules governing the exercise of rights of action in a way that enables natural and legal persons to challenge before the courts the legality of any decision or other national measure relative to the application to them of a Community act of general application, by pleading the invalidity of such an act.

. . .

44. Finally, it should be added that, according to the system for judicial review of legality established by the Treaty, a natural or legal person can bring an action challenging a regulation only if it is concerned both directly and individually. Although this last condition must be interpreted in the light of the principle of effective judicial protection by taking account of the various circumstances that may distinguish an applicant individually...such an interpretation cannot have the effect of setting aside the condition in question, expressly laid down in the Treaty, without going beyond the jurisdiction conferred by the Treaty on the Community Courts.

45. While it is, admittedly, possible to envisage a system of judicial review of the legality of Community measures different from that established by the founding Treaty and never amended as to its principles, it is for the Member States, if necessary, in accordance with Article 48 EU, to reform the system currently in force.

The ECJ followed this reasoning in subsequent cases.[49] The criteria for standing would not be relaxed even where it was apparent that the national rules did not allow the individual to contest the validity of the measure without having contravened it. The right to effective judicial protection could not, said the ECJ, have the effect of setting aside a condition expressly laid down by the Treaty.

It should be made clear that this traditional interpretation of *Plaumann* continues to apply post the Lisbon Treaty. Thus if an applicant is unable to come within the exception for regulatory acts that do

---

[49] Case C–263/02 P *Commission v Jégo-Quéré & Cie SA* [2004] ECR I–3425, [29]–[39]; Case C–258/02 P *Bactria Industriehygiene-Service Verwaltungs GmbH v Commission* [2003] ECR I–15105; Case T–213/02 *SNF SA v Commission* [2004] ECR II–3047; Case T–231/02 *Gonnelli and AIFO v Commission* [2004] ECR II–1051; Cases T–236 and 241/04 *EEB and Stichting Natuur en Milieu v Commission* [2005] ECR II–4945; Case T–16/04 *Arcelor* (n 21) [100]–[123]; Case T–95/06 *Federación de Cooperativas Agrarias de la Comunidad Valenciana v Community Plant Variety Office (CPVO)* [2008] ECR II–31; Case T–309/02 *Acegas-APS SpA v Commission* [2009] ECR II–1809; Case C–550/09 *Criminal proceedings against E and F* [2010] ECR I–6213, [44]; Case C–583/11 P *Inuit Tapiriit Kanatami v Parliament and Council* EU:C:2013:625, [92]–[96].

not entail implementing measures, either because the act is not a regulatory act *or* because even if it is it does entail implementing measures, then the applicant will still have to prove individual concern in the manner applied in *Plaumann* and subsequent cases. This is exemplified by the *Inuit Tapiriit Kanatami* case considered below,[50] where the CJEU held that the term regulatory act did not cover a legislative act, with the consequence that it was for the applicants to prove that the regulation was of direct and individual concern, as judged by the *Plaumann* test, since 'the prohibition on the placing of seal products on the market laid down in the contested regulation is worded in general terms and applies indiscriminately to any trader falling within its scope'.[51]

(c) INDIVIDUAL CONCERN: LISBON TREATY REFORM

The framers of the Lisbon Treaty amended the rules on standing: individual concern is not required in relation to a regulatory act that is of direct concern and does not entail implementing measures. The significance of this reform depends on the meaning of 'regulatory act' and 'implementing measure'.[52]

(i) *Regulatory Act*

The same term was used in the analogous provision in the Constitutional Treaty.[53] Its meaning was uncertain, but the better view was that it applied only in relation to secondary norms and not to primary legislative acts.[54] There was also uncertainty in relation to the meaning of regulatory act under the Lisbon Treaty. The types of legal act specified by the Lisbon Treaty were considered above.[55] Legislative acts are those enacted by a legislative procedure, and can take the form of a regulation, decision, or directive.[56] A legislative act can delegate power to the Commission to adopt a non-legislative act, which may once again take the form of a regulation, decision, or directive, although it will normally be a regulation.[57] These are termed delegated acts.[58] There is also a separate category of implementing acts.[59]

The term 'regulatory act' did not fit easily with the Lisbon classification of legal acts. It could be construed broadly to cover any legally binding act, whether legislative, delegated, or implementing, provided that it does not entail implementing measures. It could be interpreted more narrowly to cover any legislative, delegated, or implementing act, provided that it takes the form of a regulation or decision that does not entail implementing measures. It could cover only delegated and implementing acts in the form of regulations or decisions, which do not entail implementing measures, or only delegated acts subject to the same condition. The CJEU has held that the term 'regulatory act' does not cover legislative acts.

---

[50] Case C–583/11 P *Inuit Tapiriit Kanatami* (n 49) [71]–[73].

[51] Ibid [73].

[52] S Balthasar, '*Locus Standi* Rules for Challenges to Regulatory Acts by Private Applicants: The New Article 263(4) TFEU' (2010) 35 ELRev 542.

[53] Art III–365(4) CT.

[54] Craig (n 20) ch 4.

[55] Ch 4.

[56] Art 289 TFEU.

[57] Art 290 TFEU.

[58] Art 290(3) TFEU.

[59] Art 291 TFEU.

Case C-583/11 P **Inuit Tapiriit Kanatami v Parliament and Council**
EU:C:2013:625

The claimants challenged a regulation concerning trade in seal products. The General Court rejected the application insofar as it challenged a regulation made as a legislative act pursuant to Article 289 TFEU, concluding that this was not a 'regulatory' act within the scope of Article 263(4) TFEU, and therefore the claimants would have to show individual concern as well as direct concern. The CJEU on appeal upheld the GC's ruling.

THE CJEU

50. [I]t must be observed that, in accordance with the Court's settled case-law, the interpretation of a provision of European Union law requires that account be taken not only of its wording and the objectives it pursues, but also its context and the provisions of European Union law as a whole . . . The origins of a provision of European Union law may also provide information relevant to its interpretation . . .

. . .

53. Next, Article 263 TFEU makes a clear distinction between the right of the European Union institutions and Member States to institute proceedings, on the one hand, and the right of natural and legal persons to do so, on the other . . .

. . .

55. [I]t must be stated that the first two limbs of the fourth paragraph of Article 263 TFEU correspond with those which were laid down, before the entry into force of the Treaty of Lisbon, by the EC Treaty, in the fourth paragraph of Article 230 thereof . . .

. . .

57. [T]he Treaty of Lisbon . . . added to the fourth paragraph of Article 263 TFEU a third limb which relaxed the conditions of admissibility of actions for annulment brought by natural and legal persons. Since the effect of that limb is that the admissibility of actions for annulment brought by natural and legal persons is not subject to the condition of individual concern, it renders possible such legal actions against 'regulatory acts' which do not entail implementing measures and are of direct concern to the applicant.

58. As regards the concept of 'regulatory act', it is apparent from the third limb of the fourth paragraph of Article 263 TFEU that its scope is more restricted than that of the concept of 'acts' used in the first and second limbs of the fourth paragraph of Article 263 TFEU, in respect of the characterisation of the other types of measures which natural and legal persons may seek to have annulled. The former concept cannot, as the General Court held correctly in paragraph 43 of the order under appeal, refer to all acts of general application but relates to a more restricted category of such acts. To adopt an interpretation to the contrary would amount to nullifying the distinction made between the term 'acts' and 'regulatory acts' by the second and third limbs of the fourth paragraph of Article 263 TFEU.

59. Further, it must be observed that the fourth paragraph of Article 263 TFEU reproduced in identical terms the content of Article III-365(4) of the proposed treaty establishing a Constitution for Europe. It is clear from the travaux préparatoires relating to that provision that while the alteration of the fourth paragraph of Article 230 EC was intended to extend the conditions of admissibility of actions for annulment in respect of natural and legal persons, the conditions of admissibility laid down in the fourth paragraph of Article 230 EC relating to legislative acts were not however to be altered . . .

60. In those circumstances, it must be held that the purpose of the alteration to the right of natural and legal persons to institute legal proceedings, laid down in the fourth paragraph of Article 230 EC, was to enable those persons to bring, under less stringent conditions, actions for annulment of acts of general application other than legislative acts.

61. The General Court was therefore correct to conclude that the concept of 'regulatory act' provided for in the fourth paragraph of Article 263 TFEU does not encompass legislative acts.

The consequence of this ruling is that there may be a 'legislative act' that applies to a very narrow group of applicants, which is *de facto* a closed group, where no one could challenge the measure directly because they would not come within the scope of the reformed standing provision. They would hence have to show individual concern and would be unable to do so under existing case law.

The CJEU in *Inuit Tapiriit Kanatami* denied that the preceding analysis was inconsistent with the EU Charter of Fundamental Rights.[60] The claimant argued that the CJEU's interpretation was inconsistent with Article 47 of the Charter, which provides that everyone whose rights and freedoms guaranteed by EU law are violated has the right to an effective remedy before a tribunal in compliance with the conditions laid down in that Article, and with Articles 6 and 13 ECHR. However, the explanatory memorandum stated in relation to Article 47 that there was no intention for this provision to make any change to the rules on standing other than those embodied in what is now Article 263(4) TFEU.[61] The CJEU in *Inuit Tapiriit Kanatami* held that the Treaty provided a complete system of legal protection, based on a combination of Article 263 and Article 267, and that this was consistent with Article 47 of the Charter that was not intended to alter the pre-existing regime of judicial review.[62] This was in line with prior case law,[63] but there is nonetheless something odd about the infringement of an individual right not counting as a matter of individual concern.

(ii) *Implementing Measure*

The novel aspect of Article 263(4) whereby individual concern is not required only applies to a regulatory act that is of direct concern and does not entail implementing measures. It follows that the broader the meaning given to the concept of implementing act, the narrower is the scope of the exception in Article 263(4). Thus even if there is a regulatory act, if there are deemed to be implementing measures then the exception will not apply, and it will be for the claimant to show individual concern in the *Plaumann* sense in order to maintain a direct action. *Telefónica* is the leading case thus far on the meaning of implementing measure, and gives a broad interpretation to that concept.[64]

Case C–274/12 P Telefónica SA v Commission
EU:C:2013:852

The Commission decided that a Spanish financial scheme constituted illegal state aid and issued a Decision to that effect. The Spanish Government was to recover the illegal aid, but this was subject to exceptions for acquisitions made before a certain date. Telefónica SA made two such acquisitions, but also challenged the Commission Decision declaring that the financial scheme was illegal state aid. The Commission argued that Telefónica SA was not individually concerned by the Commission Decision and that the Decision entailed implementing measures and hence the claimant could not benefit from the Lisbon Treaty amendment. Telefónica argued that if any measure that a Member State is required to adopt to give effect to an EU act constitutes an implementing measure then a wide variety of regulatory acts would be automatically excluded from the scope of that provision.

---

[60] [2000] OJ C364/01; [2010] OJ C83/389.

[61] Charte 4473/00, Convent 49, 11 Oct 2000, 41; CONV 828/03, Updated Explanations Relating to the Text of the Charter of Fundamental Rights, 9 July 2003, 41; Explanations Relating to the Charter of Fundamental Rights, 14 Dec 2007 [2007] OJ C303/17.

[62] Case C–583/11 P *Inuit Tapiriit Kanatami* (n 49) [86]–[97].

[63] Case C–258/02 P *Bactria* (n 49) [48]–[51].

[64] See also Case T–601/11 *Dansk Automat Brancheforening v European Commission*, 26 Sept 2014.

THE CJEU

27. As the Advocate General has observed in points 40 and 41 of her Opinion, the concept of a 'regulatory act which…does not entail implementing measures', within the meaning of the final limb of the fourth paragraph of Article 263 TFEU, is to be interpreted in the light of that provision's objective, which, as is clear from its origin, consists in preventing an individual from being obliged to infringe the law in order to have access to a court…

28. It should be explained in this regard, first, that where a regulatory act entails implementing measures, judicial review of compliance with the European Union legal order is ensured irrespective of whether those measures are adopted by the European Union or the Member States. Natural or legal persons who are unable, because of the conditions governing admissibility laid down in the fourth paragraph of Article 263 TFEU, to challenge a regulatory act of the European Union directly before the European Union judicature are protected against the application to them of such an act by the ability to challenge the implementing measures which the act entails.

29. Where responsibility for the implementation of such acts lies with the institutions, bodies, offices or agencies of the European Union, natural or legal persons are entitled to bring a direct action before the European Union judicature against the implementing acts under the conditions stated in the fourth paragraph of Article 263 TFEU, and to plead in support of that action, pursuant to Article 277 TFEU, the illegality of the basic act at issue. Where that implementation is a matter for the Member States, those persons may plead the invalidity of the basic act at issue before the national courts and tribunals and cause the latter to request a preliminary ruling from the Court of Justice, pursuant to Article 267 TFEU…

30. … [A]s the Advocate General has observed in point 48 of her Opinion, the question whether a regulatory act entails implementing measures should be assessed by reference to the position of the person pleading the right to bring proceedings under the final limb of the fourth paragraph of Article 263 TFEU. It is therefore irrelevant whether the act in question entails implementing measures with regard to other persons.

31. … [I]n order to determine whether the measure being challenged entails implementing measures, reference should be made exclusively to the subject-matter of the action and, where an applicant seeks only the partial annulment of an act, it is solely any implementing measures which that part of the act may entail that must, as the case may be, be taken into consideration.

…

33. [T]elefónica's action was concerned solely with challenging the declaration in Article 1(1) of the contested decision that the scheme at issue is partially incompatible with the common market, and did not criticise the recovery of the aid, ordered in Article 4(1) of that decision, or the other directions issued to the Kingdom of Spain in Article 6(2) thereof.

34. [T]he declaration in Article 1(1) of the contested decision that the scheme at issue is partially incompatible with the common market is addressed solely to the Member State to which that decision is addressed, namely the Kingdom of Spain, and therefore the decision is not binding on other persons, in accordance with the fourth paragraph of Article 288 TFEU.

35. [A]rticle 1(1) of the contested decision is concerned exclusively with declaring the scheme at issue incompatible with the common market. It does not define the specific consequences which that declaration has for each taxpayer. Those consequences will be embodied in administrative documents such as a tax notice, which constitutes as such an implementing measure that Article 1(1) of the contested decision 'entails' within the meaning of the final limb of the fourth paragraph of Article 263 TFEU.

The CJEU thus concluded that the Lisbon Treaty exception did not apply irrespective of whether the contested decision was a regulatory act or not. The broad interpretation accorded to the term implementing measure thus narrows the scope of the Lisbon Treaty amendment, and leaves open a series of questions as to what other measures will be regarded as implementing for this purpose.

Regulations are directly applicable: once they are made by the EU they apply within the Member States without the need for transformation or adoption into national law. In that sense regulations should not be regarded as 'entailing' any measure to implement them into the national legal order. The same is true for many decisions, whether they are classic individualized decisions addressed to a particular person, or whether they are decisions of a more generic nature that are concerned with inter-institutional relations. Directives, by way of contrast, specify the ends to be achieved but leave the Member States with the choice of form and methods of implementation. Directives in that sense entail implementing measures.

It might be argued that even regulations or some decisions will lead to the modification of national rules in order that the demands of the regulation/decision are met within the particular Member State, and that where this is so such national measures should be regarded as implementing measures, with the consequence that an applicant could not take advantage of the liberalized standing rules in Article 263(4). The premise is correct, but the conclusion must be wrong.

It is certainly true that even though regulations are directly applicable and hence apply without the need for transformation or adoption, a Member State might still need to modify its prior laws to comply with or fulfil the demands of the regulation. It would nonetheless be regrettable if this were to preclude recourse to the liberalized standing rules under Article 263(4). The possibility of direct challenge of the same regulation would vary from state to state, since whether any particular state needed to modify its national rules, and if so how, would depend on the fit between the demands of the EU regulation and its pre-existing law, which will necessarily differ from state to state.

Such a result would moreover not fit well with the wording of Article 263(4), since it could not be said that the regulatory act 'entailed' implementing measures. The possibility of such national measures would, by way of contrast, be dependent on whether the particular Member State needed to modify its pre-existing rules in order to comply with the demands of the regulation, and that would depend on the national law, not the EU regulatory act itself.

(D) SUMMARY

i.   The premise underlying the CJEU's reasoning as to the balance between direct and indirect modes of challenge will be considered below, after the latter has been explored. The present summary therefore focuses on the current state of the law concerning direct challenge for non-privileged applicants under Article 263 TFEU.

ii.   *Plaumann* remains the test for individual concern. The applicant must show that it has attributes or characteristics which distinguish it from all other persons and mark it out in the same manner as the addressee. The fact that the applicant operates a trade which could be engaged in by any other person will normally serve to deny individual concern, and it is this which makes it almost impossible for most applicants to succeed. The existence of particular factual injury to the applicant will not usually be relevant. Interest groups will not, in general, be in any better position than a private individual.[65]

iii. *Plaumann* can, exceptionally, be interpreted more favourably to the applicant. This may be so where it can be shown that the challenged measure either infringed a right specific to the applicant or was in breach of a duty owed to the applicant. It will be rare for the GC or CJEU to allow a claim merely because of the factual injury suffered by the applicant.

---

[65] See, eg, Case T–601/11 *Dansk Automat Brancheforening* (n 64).

iv. It was clear from *UPA, Jégo-Quéré, Inuit Tapiriit Kanatami* and subsequent cases that the EU Courts were not willing to shift to the more liberal test for standing proposed by Advocate General Jacobs. The rationale for adherence to the status quo was that the Treaty provided a complete system of legal protection for individuals through Articles 263 and 267. There are however, as will be seen below, real difficulties with this view.

v. The Lisbon Treaty reformed the standing rules by providing an exception for cases where individual concern is not required. This is to be welcomed. However an applicant can only make use of this exception if there is a regulatory act that does not entail implementing measures. The CJEU has interpreted regulatory act so that it does not cover legislative acts made pursuant to Article 289 TFEU. It has also interpreted the concept of implementing measures broadly, with the consequence that even if an act is deemed to be regulatory then an individual will not be able to use the Lisbon Treaty amendment because the Court deems that there is an implementing measure, the consequence being that it will be for the claimant to prove individual concern in the manner required by the *Plaumann* test.

6 ARTICLE 267: INDIRECT CHALLENGE TO THE LEGALITY OF EU ACTS

(A) THE RATIONALE FOR USING ARTICLE 267

Article 267 TFEU allows national courts to refer to the CJEU questions concerning the 'validity and interpretation of acts of the institutions, bodies, offices or agencies of the Union'. This provision assumed increased importance for private applicants because of the Court's narrow construction of the standing criteria under what was Article 230 EC.[66] Article 267 is often the only mechanism whereby such parties can contest the legality of Union norms. The limitations and difficulties of indirect challenge will be considered below. The present discussion will focus on the rationale for using Article 267 and the types of Union act that can be challenged.

An individual will often be affected by EU measures through their application at national level.[67] Thus the 'standard' scenario[68] is a Common Agricultural Policy (CAP) regulation which cannot be contested under Article 263, either because the applicant lacks standing or because of the time limit. These regulations will normally be applied by a national intervention agency. The regulation may, for example, require the forfeiture of a deposit given by a trader, who believes that this forfeiture is illegal because it is disproportionate or discriminatory. If the security is forfeited the trader may seek judicial review in the national court, claiming that the regulation is invalid. It will be for the national court to decide whether to refer the matter to the CJEU under Article 267. An alternative scenario is where a regulation demands a levy which the trader believes to be in breach of EU law. The trader's strategy might be to resist payment, be sued by the national agency, and then raise the alleged invalidity of the regulation by way of defence. It is for the national court to decide whether to refer the matter to the CJEU.

---

[66] H Rasmussen, 'Why is Article 173 Interpreted against Private Plaintiffs?' (1980) 5 ELRev 112, 122–127.

[67] C Harding, 'The Impact of Article 177 of the EEC Treaty on the Review of Community Action' (1981) 1 YBEL 93, 96; C Harding, 'Who Goes to Court in Europe? An Analysis of Litigation against the European Community' (1992) 17 ELRev 105.

[68] See, eg, Case 181/84 *R v Intervention Board for Agricultural Produce, ex p ED & F Man (Sugar) Ltd* [1985] ECR 2889; Case C–66/80 *ICC* [1981] ECR 1191.

(B) THE ACTS THAT CAN BE CHALLENGED UNDER ARTICLE 267

Article 267 allows a challenge to the validity of acts of the institutions, bodies, offices, or agencies of the Union. This enables challenge to regulations and directives via the national courts.

The situation with respect to individual decisions is more complex. A person who is not the addressee of an individual decision may contest it through the national courts. Thus, if a decision addressed to a Member State requires certain action to be taken, then an individual affected can contest its validity through the national courts.[69]

This is exemplified by the *Universität Hamburg* case.[70] The Commission issued a decision to all Member States refusing to allow exemption from customs duty in relation to scientific equipment imported from the United States. The German authorities applied this decision, and the applicant contested this before the national court. The ECJ held that the case could be brought via Article 267. It was influenced by the fact that the Commission decision did not have to be published, and that it did not have to be notified to the person applying for the tax exemption, which would have rendered challenge within the time limit under Article 263 virtually impossible. The Court pronounced more generally on the point in *Rau*.[71] It held that the applicants, who were margarine producers, could contest in the national courts the legality of a scheme whereby the Community sold cheap butter on the German market to test consumer reaction. There was no need to ascertain whether or not the applicants had the possibility of challenging the decision directly before the ECJ.

This ruling must, however, be seen in the light of the *TWD* case.[72] The Commission declared aid that Germany had granted to a firm to be incompatible with the common market. The aid had, therefore, to be repaid. The German Government informed the company, and told it also that the Commission's decision could be challenged under Article 263. The company did not do so, but instead sought to raise the legality of the Commission's decision via the German courts. The ECJ held that no indirect challenge was possible, since the company had been informed of its right to challenge under Article 263, and since it would 'without any doubt'[73] have had standing to do so.[74] A challenge under Article 267 will not therefore be possible if the matter could have been raised by a person who had standing under Article 263, and who knew of the matter within the time limits for a direct action. This same principle has been held to preclude reliance by a Member State on Article 267 to challenge a measure addressed to it that it could have challenged under Article 263, but had not done so within the time limits under Article 263(6).[75]

Where it is unclear whether the applicant would have had standing under Article 263 the Court is more willing to admit the indirect action. Thus in *Accrington Beef*[76] it distinguished *TWD*, and

---

[69] Case C–188/92 *TWD Textilwerke Deggendorf GmbH v Germany* [1994] ECR I–833.

[70] Case 216/82 *Universität Hamburg v Hauptzollamt Hamburg-Kehrwieder* [1983] ECR 2771.

[71] Cases 133–136/85 *Walter Rau Lebensmittelwerke v Bundesanstalt für Landwirtschaftliche Marktordnung* [1987] ECR 2289.

[72] Case C–188/92 *TWD* (n 69); Case C–178/95 *Wiljo NV v Belgium* [1997] ECR I–585; Case C–239/99 *Nachi Europe GmbH v Hauptzollamt Krefeld* [2001] ECR I–1197.

[73] Case C–188/92 *TWD*, (n 69) [24].

[74] The Court distinguished *Rau* on the ground that the applicants in that case had in fact brought an annulment action, and that therefore the issue of the time bar under Art 263 and the effect of this on a possible Art 267 action did not arise.

[75] Case C–241/01 *National Farmers' Union v Secretariat Général du Gouvernement* [2002] ECR I–9079, [36].

[76] Case C–241/95 *R v Intervention Board for Agricultural Produce, ex p Accrington Beef Co Ltd* [1996] ECR I–6691. See also Case C–222/04 *Ministero dell'Economia e delle Finanze v Cassa di Risparmio di Firenze SpA* [2006] ECR I–289, [72]–[74]; Cases C–346 and 529/03 *Atzeni v Regione Autonoma della Sardegna* [2006] ECR I–1975, [30]–[34]; Case C–441/05 *Roquette Frères v Ministre de l'Agriculture, de l'Alimentation, de la Pêche et de la Ruralité* [2007] ECR I–1993; Case C–343/09 *Afton Chemical Limited v Secretary of State for Transport* EU:C:2010:419, [19]–[26]; Case C–370/12 *Pringle v Government of Ireland, Ireland and The Attorney General* EU:C:2012:756, [41].

held that the failure to challenge a regulation under Article 263 was no bar to an Article 267 action, since it was not obvious that the Article 263 action would have been admissible. In *Eurotunnel* the Court held that a private party could challenge the validity of provisions of a directive in a national court, since the directive was addressed to Member States and it was not obvious that an action would have been possible under Article 263.[77] The Court is also likely to be more receptive to actions under Article 267 where the applicant would not have known of the relevant measure in time to challenge it under Article 263.[78]

(c) 'A COMPLETE SYSTEM OF LEGAL PROTECTION'

i. The premise underlying the decisions in *UPA* and *Jégo-Quéré* was that the Treaty provided for a complete regime of legal protection in terms of access to court, via Articles 267 and 263 TFEU. The same thesis informed the more recent judgment in *Inuit Tapiriit Kanatami*.[79] There are however real difficulties with this hypothesis.

ii. The Court largely ignored the Advocate General's analysis in *UPA* of the difficulties faced by individuals who seek to use Article 267. They are in part procedural: proceeding via the national court can have implications for participation of the institutions that adopted the contested measure; delays; costs; the award of interim measures; and the possibility of third party intervention. They are in part inherent in the very nature of Article 267: it is a reference system; the applicant must therefore convince the national court that a reference is required; and may have to fight through more than one national court. The difficulties with Article 267 are also substantive: the national court is precluded from invalidating the measure, and hence the applicant has to proceed to the CJEU; and the most the national court can provide pending the CJEU's ruling is interim relief.

iii. The CJEU exhorted national courts, in accordance with what is now Article 4(3) TFEU, to interpret national procedural rules so as to enable applicants to challenge EU norms of general application before the national courts. This strategy is however of limited utility. It cannot resolve the procedural difficulties adverted to above. It cannot overcome, although it may alleviate, the difficulties flowing from the discretionary nature of the Article 267 system.

iv. Indirect challenge via Article 267 also has consequences for the division of competences between the CJEU and the GC. Preliminary rulings are the preserve of the CJEU.[80] Challenges to the validity of EU norms via Article 267 therefore go to the CJEU, while the same issues would be heard by the GC if they were admissible as a direct challenge under Article 263. This increases the CJEU's workload and means that its scarce resources are diverted to answering such preliminary rulings, which will often not involve any point of general importance for EU law.

v. The CJEU's reasoning in *UPA* and *Inuit Tapiriit Kanatami* concerning Article 263 is equally problematic. It held that the boundaries of legitimate Treaty interpretation constrained modification to the traditional case law on direct challenge. The right to effective judicial protection could influence the application of individual concern, but could not, said the CJEU, set aside that condition, which could only be done via a Treaty amendment. This is

---

[77] Case C–408/95 *Eurotunnel SA v Sea France* [1997] ECR I–6315.

[78] See the ground on which the Court distinguished the *Universität Hamburg* case in *TWD* (n 69) [23].

[79] Case C–583/11 P *Inuit Tapiriit Kanatami* (n 49) [92]–[101].

[80] The Nice Treaty qualified this monopoly, but the power to accord the CFI power over preliminary rulings has not been acted on.

with respect unconvincing. The Treaty has always required proof of individual concern. It is the meaning to be given to that phrase that is the question in issue. The crucial issue is not whether the Treaty imposes limits on standing, but whether the interpretation of those limits has been overly restrictive. It is not readily apparent why Advocate General Jacobs' interpretation of individual concern would involve any transgression of the bounds of normal Treaty interpretation, let alone that it would be akin to Treaty amendment through judicial fiat. This is more especially so given that the Court has filled gaps in relation to other parts of Article 263 where this was warranted.[81] The Court gave no explanation as to why it felt that the Advocate General's test would be incompatible with the wording of Article 263. There is in reality no reason why a test framed in terms of substantial adverse impact could not be a legitimate reading of individual concern.

vi. It is true that the general legal status quo concerning the limits of standing was accepted during the discourse that led to the Constitutional Treaty, a point relied on by the CJEU in *Inuit Tapiriit Kanatami*.[82] We should nonetheless treat this with caution. The reality was that discussion about the judicial system during the Constitutional Treaty was very brief, with barely three weeks in which to consider all such matters. There was no time for any broad-ranging consultation or discussion, nor did it take place.

vii. A legal system may have impressive principles of judicial review, but these will be of scant comfort to those who cannot access the system because the standing rules are unduly narrow. It is right in normative terms that those who have suffered some substantial adverse impact should have access to judicial review. This test is no more liberal than that which prevails in most domestic legal orders and is fitting for a legal system based on the rule of law. The idea that the more people are affected by a provision the less chance there is for any challenge is contrary to principle.

viii. The CJEU said nothing about the practical consequences of a more liberal test under Article 263, but one senses concern with possible workload problems. There is however no reason why there should necessarily be any significant net increase in the number of challenges. The very fact that Article 263 has been so restrictive forces applicants to use Article 267. The CJEU has however little control over the range of applicants that can challenge via Article 267 or the type of norm that can be challenged. The consequence of a more liberal interpretation of Article 263 would be to shift some of these cases back to direct challenge, and give the EU Courts scope for control through the determination of whether there was a substantial adverse impact. Moreover, the implicit assumption seems to be that there would be numerous challenges to a regulation by applicants, each of which would claim to have suffered substantial adverse impact. This does not accord with legal or practical reality. Some cases would be joined in a single action. In any event once the CJEU or GC pronounced on the legality of the regulation in relation to one action, that would be the end of the matter. The decision would resolve the issue in relation to any other possible claimant, unless he or she could raise some new legal argument that had not been addressed in the earlier case.

ix. There may well be valid reasons why the EU Courts are wary of intervening too far in the complex discretionary choices made by the EU institutions, and many of the standing cases involve such choices made pursuant to the CAP. The EU Courts can however influence the number of actions that are brought through the standards of review that are applied.[83] This

---

[81] Case C–70/88 *European Parliament v Council* [1990] ECR I–2041; Case 294/83 *Parti Ecologiste 'Les Verts' v European Parliament* [1986] ECR 1339; Case T–411/06 *Sogelma* (n 2).

[82] Case C–583/11 P *Inuit Tapiriit Kanatami* (n 49) [59].

[83] Ch 15.

will impact on the number of actions brought, since applicants will calculate their chances of success before embarking on the expense of litigation. It is of course true that a very strict test for standing may be less demanding on the Court's time. This however comes dangerously close to reductionism, since it says no more than that if a court declines to hear a case it will save more judicial resources than if the case had been heard.

7 ARTICLE 265: FAILURE TO ACT

An action for a wrongful failure to act is provided in Article 265 TFEU:

> Should the European Parliament, the European Council, the Council, the Commission or the European Central Bank, in infringement of the Treaties, fail to act, the Member States and the other institutions of the Union may bring an action before the Court of Justice of the European Union to have the infringement established. This Article shall apply, under the same conditions, to bodies, offices and agencies of the Union which fail to act.
>
> The action shall be admissible only if the institution, body, office or agency concerned has first been called upon to act. If, within two months of being so called upon, the institution, body, office or agency concerned has not defined its position, the action may be brought within a further period of two months.
>
> Any natural or legal person may, under the conditions laid down in the preceding paragraphs, complain to the Court that an institution, body, office or agency of the Union has failed to address to that person any act other than a recommendation or an opinion.

(A) REVIEWABLE OMISSIONS

There is a close relationship between Articles 263 and 265 TFEU. This should be reflected in the omissions that are reviewable under Article 265. It seems, in principle, that the only failures to act which should come within Article 265 are failures to adopt a reviewable act, in the sense of an act which has legal effects. Article 265 refers, however, simply to failure to act. An argument could, therefore, be made that this allows the action to be used in relation to the failure to adopt a non-binding act, such as a recommendation or an opinion. There are, however, conceptual and practical objections to this view, which would create an odd distinction between the action for annulment and that for failure to act.[84] Notwithstanding this the Court stated in *Comitology*[85] that Parliament could bring an Article 265 action for failure to adopt a measure that was not itself a reviewable act. If this is indeed so it will apply only in the context of Article 265(1), since Article 265(3) makes it clear that the action cannot be brought by private individuals with respect to recommendations or opinions.

Article 265 requires the applicant to show that there was an obligation to act. The existence of wide discretionary powers in the Commission will normally preclude such a finding.[86] Article 265 has, moreover, been held to refer to a failure to act in the sense of a failure to take a decision or to define a position. It does not refer to the adoption of a measure different from that desired by the

---

[84] T Hartley, *The Foundations of European Union Law* (Oxford University Press, 7th edn, 2010) 396–398.

[85] Case 302/87 (n 17).

[86] Case 247/87 *Star Fruit Company v Commission* [1989] ECR 291; Case C–301/87 *France v Commission* [1990] ECR I–307; Case T–277/94 *Associazone Italiana Tecnico Economica del Cemento (AITEC) v Commission* [1996] ECR II–351.

applicant.[87] The interrelationship between Articles 263 and 265, and the scope of reviewable omissions, is evident in the *Eridania* case.

Cases 10 and 18/68 Società 'Eridania' Zuccherifici Nazionali v Commission
[1969] ECR 459

[Note Lisbon Treaty renumbering: Arts 173, 175, and 176 are now Arts 263, 265, and 266 TFEU]

The applicants sought the annulment of Commission Decisions granting aid to certain sugar refineries in Italy. They claimed that their competitive position on the sugar market would be deleteriously affected by the grant of such aid. The Court rejected this action because the applicants were not individually concerned by the Decision. The same applicants brought an action under Article 175, arguing that there had been a failure to act, this being the failure to revoke the Decisions in question.

THE ECJ

15. This application concerns the annulment of the implied decision of rejection resulting from the silence maintained by the Commission in respect of the request addressed to it by the applicants seeking the annulment or revocation of the three disputed decisions for illegality or otherwise because they are inappropriate.

16. The action provided for in Article 175 is intended to establish an illegal omission as appears from that Article, which refers to a failure to act 'in infringement of this Treaty' and from Article 176 which refers to a failure to act declared to be 'contrary to this Treaty'.

Without stating under which provision of Community law the Commission was required to annul or revoke the said decisions, the applicants have confined themselves to alleging that those decisions were adopted in infringement of the Treaty and that this fact alone would thus suffice to make the Commission's failure to act subject to the provisions of Article 175.

17. The Treaty provides, however, particularly in Article 173, other methods of recourse by which an allegedly illegal Community measure may be disputed and if necessary annulled on the application of a duly qualified party.

To admit, as the applicants wish to do, that the parties concerned could ask the institution from which the measure came to revoke it and, in the event of the Commission's failing to act, refer such failure to the Court as an illegal omission to deal with the matter would amount to providing them with a method of recourse parallel to that of Article 173, which would not be subject to the conditions laid down by the Treaty.

18. This application does not therefore satisfy the requirements of Article 175 of the Treaty and must thus be held to be inadmissible.

The Court's reference to the use of what is now Article 265 to evade limits placed on Article 263 includes the ability to by-pass the time limits for contesting an action under Article 263.[88]

---

[87] Cases 166 and 220/86 *Irish Cement v Commission* [1988] ECR 6473; Case T–387/94 *Asia Motor France SA v Commission* [1996] ECR II–961; Case T–420/05 *Vischim Srl v Commission* [2009] ECR II–3841, [252]–[255]; Case C–196/12 *Commission and European Parliament v Council* EU:C:2013:753, [22].

[88] See also Cases 21–26/61 *Meroni v High Authority* [1962] ECR 73, 78.

(B) PROCEDURE

Article 265 requires the applicant to call upon the institution to act, since it may not be easy, in the context of an omission, to say when it came into existence and its content. Thus the omission is deemed to have taken place at the end of the first two-month period and its content is defined by the terms of the request. The Treaties do not specify any time limit within which the procedure for failure to act should be initiated. The Court has, however, specified that this procedure must be initiated within a reasonable time.[89] Once the request to act has been made, the institution has a period of two months within which to define its position. If it has not done this, the applicant has a further two months within which to bring the action under Article 265.

(C) STANDING

Article 265, like Article 263, draws a distinction between privileged and non-privileged applicants. The former are identified in Article 265(1), the Member States and other EU institutions. The latter are covered by Article 265(3), which allows a natural or legal person to complain of a failure to address an act, other than a recommendation or an opinion, to that person.[90] Some argued that standing might be accorded for a failure to act only where the act would by its very nature be addressed to the applicant. This view has not prevailed. The ECJ held in *ENU*[91] that standing under Article 148 of the Euratom Treaty, the equivalent of Article 265, would be available to an applicant provided that it was directly and individually concerned: it was not necessary for the applicant to be the actual addressee of the decision.[92] This test, is, however, applied in the same restrictive manner as under Article 263.[93]

8 ARTICLE 277: THE PLEA OF ILLEGALITY

Article 277 TFEU is the relevant Treaty provision.

> Notwithstanding the expiry of the period laid down in Article 263, sixth paragraph, any party may, in proceedings in which an act of general application adopted by an institution, body, office or agency of the Union is at issue, plead the grounds specified in Article 263, second paragraph, in order to invoke before the Court of Justice of the European Union the inapplicability of that act.

(A) THE ACTS THAT CAN BE CHALLENGED

The essence of Article 277 is as follows.[94] An individual may wish, in the course of proceedings initiated for a different reason, to call into question the legality of some other measure. Thus, for example, the applicant may challenge a decision which is of direct and individual concern, in the course of

---

[89] Case 59/70 *Netherlands v Commission* [1971] ECR 639.

[90] AG Toth, 'The Law as it Stands on the Appeal for Failure to Act' (1975) 2 LIEI 65, 85–86.

[91] Case C–107/91 *ENU v Commission* [1993] ECR I–599; Case T–95/96 *Gestevision Telecinco SA v Commission* [1998] ECR II–3407, [58]; Cases T–79/96, 260/97 and 117/98 *Camar Srl and Tico Srl v Commission* [2000] ECR II–2193, [79]; Case T–395/04 *Air One SpA v Commission* [2006] ECR II–1343, [25]. See, however, Case T–277/94 *AITEC* (n 86) [58]; Case T–167/04 *Asklepios Kliniken GmbH v Commission* [2007] ECR II–2379, [45].

[92] Cases T–79/96, 260/97 and 117/98 *Camar* (n 91) [72]–[84].

[93] See, eg, Case T–398/94 *Kahn Scheepvart BV v Commission* [1996] ECR II–477.

[94] M Vogt, 'Indirect Judicial Protection in EC Law: The Case of the Plea of Illegality' (2006) 31 ELRev 364.

which it wishes to raise the legality of a regulation on which the decision is based. Article 277 does not therefore constitute an independent cause of action.[95] Article 277 cannot moreover be used in proceedings before a national court. A declaration of the inapplicability of a regulation pursuant to Article 277 can only be sought in proceedings brought before the Court of Justice under some other provision of the Treaty, and then only incidentally and with limited effect.[96] The most common use of Article 277 is as an additional, incidental challenge in an annulment action brought under Article 263 as exemplified by *Simmenthal*, extracted below.[97]

Moreover the applicant must still meet the time limit for the principal action. Thus while Article 277 allows the applicant incidentally to raise the illegality of a regulation outside the time limits in Article 263, the applicant must still be within those limits in relation to the primary challenge to the decision that is of direct and individual concern.

Article 277 can only be used to challenge acts of general application, such as regulations or directives made pursuant to Article 289 or 290 TFEU, and possibly also generic decisions. There must, moreover, be some real connection between the individual decision which is the subject matter of the action and the general measure the legality of which is being contested.[98] However it is the substance of the measure, and not its form, which is decisive: if the Court decides that the measure is in substance an act of general application Article 277 can be used. This is demonstrated by the *Simmenthal* case:

Case 92/78 Simmenthal SpA v Commission
[1979] ECR 777

[Note Lisbon Treaty renumbering: Arts 173 and 184 are now Arts 263 and 277 TFEU]

The applicant sought to annul a Commission Decision concerning the minimum selling prices for frozen beef. In support of its claim, the applicant wished to use Article 184 to challenge the legality of certain regulations and notices which formed the legal basis of the contested Decision. The Court held that the applicant was directly and individually concerned by the primary Decision, even though it was actually addressed to the Member State. The Court then considered the arguments concerning Article 184.

THE ECJ

34. While the applicant formally challenges Commission Decision No 78/258 it has at the same time criticized, in reliance on Article 184 of the EEC Treaty, certain aspects of the 'linking' system in the form in which it has been implemented pursuant to the new Article 14 of Regulation No 805/68, by Regulation No 2900/77 and No 2901/77 and also by the notices of invitations to tender of 13 January 1978.

. . .

---

[95] Case 33/80 *Albini v Council* [1981] ECR 2141; Case T–154/94 *Comité des Salines de France v Commission* [1996] ECR II–1377; Case C–239/99 *Nachi Europe* (n 72).

[96] Cases 31 and 33/62 *Milchwerke Heinz Wohrmann & Sohn KG and Alfons Lütticke GmbH v Commission* [1962] ECR 501; Cases 87 and 130/77, 22/83, 9 and 10/84 *Salerno and Others v Commission and Council* [1985] ECR 2523, [36]; Case C–239/99 *Nachi Europe* (n 72) [33].

[97] A Barav, 'The Exception of Illegality in Community Law: A Critical Analysis' (1974) 11 CMLRev 366, 375–381; Case T–69/04 *Schunk GmbH and Schunk Kohlenstoff-Technik GmbH v Commission* [2008] ECR II–2567; Case T–15/11 *Sina Bank v Council* EU:T:2012:661, [13].

[98] Cases T–93/00 and 46/01 *Alessandrini Srl v Commission* [2003] ECR II–1635, [76]–[81]; Case C–485/08 P *Claudia Gualtieri v European Commission* [2010] ECR I–3009, [103]–[107]; Case T–58/01 *Solvay v European Commission* [2009] ECR II–4781, [148]; Cases T–394, 408, 453 and 454/08 *Regione autonoma della Sardegna v Commission* [2011] ECR II–6255, [207]; Barav (n 97) 373–374.

36. There is no doubt that this provision (Article 184) enables the applicant to challenge indirectly during the proceedings, with a view to obtaining the annulment of the contested decision, the validity of the measures laid down by Regulation which form the legal basis of the latter.

37. On the other hand there are grounds for questioning whether Article 184 applies to the notices of invitations to tender of 13 January 1978 when according to its wording it only provides for the calling in question of 'regulations'.

38. These notices are general acts which determine in advance and objectively the rights and obligations of the traders who wish to participate in the invitations to tender which these notices make public.

39. As the Court in its judgment…in Case 15/57, *Compagnie des Hauts Fourneaux de Chasse*…, and in its judgment…in Case 9/56, *Meroni*…, has already held in connexion with Article 36 of the ECSC Treaty, Article 184 of the EEC Treaty gives expression to a general principle conferring upon any party to proceedings the right to challenge, for the purpose of obtaining the annulment of a decision of direct and individual concern to that party, the validity of previous acts of the institutions which form the legal basis of the decision which is being attacked, if that party was not entitled under Article 173 of the Treaty to bring a direct action challenging those acts by which it was thus affected without having been in a position to ask that they be declared void.

40. The field of application of the said article must therefore include acts of the institutions which, although they are not in the form of a Regulation, nevertheless produce similar effects and on those grounds may not be challenged under Article 173 by natural or legal persons other than Community institutions and Member States.

41. This wide interpretation of Article 184 derives from the need to provide those persons who are precluded by the second paragraph of Article 173 from instituting proceedings directly in respect of general acts with the benefit of judicial review of them at the time when they are affected by implementing decisions which are of direct and individual concern to them.

42. The notices of invitations to tender of 13 January 1978 in respect of which the applicant was unable to initiate proceedings are a case in point, seeing that only the decision taken in consequence of the tender which it had submitted in answer to a specific invitation to tender could be of direct and individual concern to it.

43. There are therefore good grounds for declaring that the applicant's challenge during the proceedings under Article 184, which relates not only to the above-mentioned regulations but also to the notices of invitations to tender of 13 January 1978, is admissible, although the latter are not in the strict sense measures laid down by Regulation.

(B) THE PARTIES WHO CAN USE ARTICLE 277

Private parties can use Article 277, subject to the qualification that they cannot do so if it is clear that the act could have been challenged via Article 263 as in substance a decision in relation to which the applicant is directly and individually concerned.[99]

Commentators were divided as to whether Article 277 could be used by privileged applicants. Bebr was against privileged applicants using Article 277 because such applicants could challenge any binding act of EU law under Article 263 within the time limit.[100] However, as Barav noted,[101] the

---

[99] Case C–188/92 *TWD* (n 69); Case C–310/97 P *Commission v AssiDomän Kraft Products AB* [1999] ECR I–5363, [60]; Case C–239/99 *Nachi Europe* (n 72) [35]–[37]; Case C–241/01 *National Farmers' Union* (n 75); Case C–441/05 *Roquette Frères* (n 76) [39]–[40]; Case C–343/07 *Bavaria NV* (n 21) [38]–[39].

[100] G Bebr, 'Judicial Remedy of Private Parties against Normative Acts of the European Communities: The Role of the Exception of Illegality' (1966) 4 CMLRev 7.

[101] Barav (n 97) 371.

irregularities in a general act might appear only after the relevant implementation measures had been adopted, and hence the state may not have realized the necessity for challenging the general act until the time limit under Article 263 had passed. The Court has now resolved the matter, concluding that a Member State can invoke Article 277 even if it did not contest the measure within the time limit under Article 263.[102] It reached this conclusion for two reasons.

First, the wording of Article 277 is framed in terms of 'any party' being able to raise the plea of illegality. Secondly, given that Member States are privileged applicants they can always challenge EU acts. If this possibility were to deny Member States recourse to Article 277 then it would never be possible for them to make use of this Article, which would be problematic, since there might be good reasons why the Member State did not seek to challenge the measure within the time limits of Article 263.

9 CONCLUSIONS

i. The rules concerning standing are of considerable importance in any legal system. They constitute the main gateway through which individuals gain access to the principles of judicial review in order to render public decision-making accountable. If therefore the standing rules are drawn too narrowly it will be difficult for individuals to take advantage of these administrative law principles.

ii. The standing rules on direct actions under Article 263 have generated significant case law since the inception of the EEC. In many cases applicants have failed to secure standing, even though they would have done so in many such cases in national legal systems. The primary reason for this 'failure rate' has been the requirement of individual concern as interpreted in the *Plaumann* case, which renders it exceedingly difficult for non-privileged applicants to succeed, even where they have been significantly affected by the contested measure. There are empirical and conceptual problems with this interpretation of individual concern.

iii. The CJEU seeks to justify the status quo by arguing that the Treaty provides a complete system of legal protection, with indirect challenge through Article 267 supplementing direct actions under Article 263. There are, however, difficulties with this hypothesis.

iv. The Lisbon Treaty change to Article 263 whereby individual concern does not have to be shown in relation to regulatory acts that are of direct concern and do not entail implementing measures is welcome. It is however clear from the case law thus far that this new exception to the general rule of needing to prove individual concern will not avail applicants who seek to challenge a legislative act, nor will it avail applicants if there is any form of implementing measure required to give effect to the EU act at national level.

10 FURTHER READING

ALBORS LLORENS, A, 'The Standing of Private Parties to Challenge Community Measures: Has the European Court Missed the Boat?' (2003) 62 CLJ 72

ARNULL, A, 'Private Applicants and the Action for Annulment under Article 173 of the EC Treaty' (1995) 32 CMLRev 7

---

[102] Case C–442/04 *Spain v Council* [2008] ECR I–3517, [22].

———'Private Applicants and the Action for Annulment since *Codorniu*' (2001) 38 CMLRev 7

BALTHASAR, S, '*Locus Standi* Rules for Challenges to Regulatory Acts by Private Applicants: The New Article 263(4) TFEU' (2010) 35 ELRev 542

CRAIG, P, 'Standing, Rights and the Structure of Legal Argument' (2003) 9 EPL 493

———*EU Administrative Law* (Oxford University Press, 2nd edn, 2012) ch 11

ENCHELMAIER, S, 'No-One Slips through the Net? Latest Developments, and Non-Developments, in the European Court of Justice's Jurisprudence on Art 230(4) EC' (2005) 24 YBEL 173

GORMLEY, L, 'Judicial Review: Advice for the Deaf?' (2006) 29 Fordham Int IJ 655

HARLOW, C, 'Towards a Theory of Access for the European Court of Justice' (1992) 12 YBEL 213

TRIDIMAS, T, AND POLI, S, '*Locus Standi* of Individuals under Article 230(4): The Return of Euridice?' in A Arnull, P Eeckhout, and T Tridimas (eds), *Continuity and Change in EU Law: Essays in Honour of Sir Francis Jacobs* (Oxford University Press, 2008) ch 5

VOGT, M, 'Indirect Judicial Protection in EC Law: The Case of the Plea of Illegality' (2006) 31 ELRev 364

WARD, A, *Judicial Review and the Rights of Private Parties in EU Law* (Oxford University Press, 2nd edn, 2007)

WYATT, D, 'The Relationship between Actions for Annulment and References on Validity after *TWD Deggendorf*' in J Lombay and A Biondi (eds), *Remedies for Breach of EC Law* (Wiley, 1996) ch 6

REVIEW OF LEGALITY: GROUNDS OF REVIEW

1 CENTRAL ISSUES

i. The previous chapter considered standing to seek judicial review. If the applicant has standing and is within the time limits for bringing an action it will still have to show why the Union act should be annulled or declared invalid. Four grounds are specified in Article 263 TFEU: lack of competence; infringement of an essential procedural requirement; infringement of the Treaty or any rule of law relating to its application; and misuse of power. The same grounds are relevant for indirect actions under Article 267 TFEU. Judicial review, whether direct through Article 263 or indirect through Article 267, is designed to ensure that decision-making is legally accountable. When reading this chapter the earlier discussion of subsidiarity should not be forgotten.[1] This is in certain respects a general principle of EU law, albeit one which goes principally to the initial legality of Union conduct.

ii. The Union Courts have used the heads of review in Article 263 as the framework through which to develop general principles of law, which function as principles of administrative legality, drawing on concepts found in national legal systems. These include fundamental rights, proportionality, legitimate expectations, non-discrimination, transparency, and more recently the precautionary principle.

iii. The status of general principles of law within the EU's hierarchy of norms was considered within an earlier chapter.[2]

iv. The dividing line between these principles is not absolute: there are certain principles, such as the right to a fair hearing or legal and professional privilege, which some might classify as fundamental rights, while others would regard them as principles of administrative legality.

v. Some principles, such as non-discrimination, have a textual foundation in the Treaty, while others have been developed in Union legislation. However, the ECJ has played a key role in developing all these general principles.

vi. The principles serve a number of functions. They can be used as interpretive guides when construing Treaty provisions and EU legislation. They can also serve as the ground for annulling an

---

[1] Ch 3.
[2] Ch 4.

EU legislative, delegated, or implementing act. They can moreover be the reason why a national rule is found to be in violation of EU law.

2 LACK OF COMPETENCE

The general issue of competence has been considered in detail above, to which reference should be made.[3] The EU institutions must be able to point to a power within the Treaty which authorizes their action. If they cannot do so then the act will be declared void for lack of competence. This ground of review is used relatively rarely. The ECJ has interpreted the EU's powers broadly and purposively, in order to achieve Treaty objectives.

The Lisbon Treaty introduced categories of competence for different subject matter areas. The categories matter, since distinct legal consequences flow from the categorization in terms of the relative power of the Union and Member States. A claimant may therefore argue that the EU lacked competence in the sense that, for example, it acted under the heading of exclusive competence, which would mean that Member States could not take any legally binding act in that area, whereas it should have proceeded via shared competence.

3 INFRINGEMENT OF AN ESSENTIAL PROCEDURAL REQUIREMENT

(A) RIGHT TO BE HEARD

It is for the Union Courts to decide what constitutes an essential procedural requirement. They have read into the Treaty many of the requirements of procedural due process, insofar as this relates to individualized decisions.[4] The right to be heard before an individual measure is taken that would affect a person adversely is included within the Charter of Fundamental Rights.[5]

The Union Courts have imposed a right to be heard as a general rule of EU law, irrespective of whether this was specified in the relevant Treaty Article, regulation, directive, or decision. A hearing is normally required even where no sanction is imposed, provided that there is some adverse impact, or some significant effect, on the applicant's interests.[6] The right to be heard has been held to be part of the fundamental rights jurisprudence.[7] It cannot be excluded or restricted by any legislative

---

[3] See Ch 3.

[4] P Craig, *EU Administrative Law* (Oxford University Press, 2nd edn, 2012) chs 11–12.

[5] Charter of Fundamental Rights of the European Union [2010] OJ C83/2, Art 41(2).

[6] Case 17/74 *Transocean Marine Paint v Commission* [1974] ECR 1063; Case T–450/93 *Lisrestal v Commission* [1994] ECR II–1177; Case C–32/95 P *Commission v Lisrestal* [1996] ECR I–5373; Case T–50/96 *Primex Produkte Import-Export GmbH & Co KG v Commission* [1998] ECR II–3773, [59]; Case C–462/98 P *MedioCurso-Etabelecimento de Ensino Particular Ld v Commission* [2000] ECR I–7183, [36]; Case T–102/00 *Vlaams Fonds voor de Sociale Integratie van Personen met een Handicap v Commission* [2003] ECR II–2433, [59]; Case C–349/07 *Sopropé—Organizações de Calçado Lda v Fazenda Pública* [2008] ECR I–10369, [37].

[7] Case C–49/88 *Al-Jubail Fertilizer v Council* [1991] ECR I–3187, [15]; Cases T–33–34/98 *Petrotub and Republica SA v Council* [1999] ECR II–3837; Case C–458/98 P *Industrie des Poudres Sphériques v Council and Commission* [2000] ECR I–8147, [99]; Case C–141/08 P *Foshan Shunde Yongjian Housewares & Hardware Co Ltd v Council* [2009] ECR I–9147, [83]; Case T–410/06 *Foshan City Nanhai Golden Step Industrial Co, Ltd v Council* [2010] ECR II–879, [109]–[111]; Case T–192/08 *Transnational Company 'Kazchrome' AO v Council* [2011] ECR II–7449, [110].

provision, and the principle must be protected where there is no specific EU legislation and also where legislation exists, but does not take sufficient account of the principle.[8]

The claimant does not have to show that the Commission's decision would have been different, but simply that such a possibility cannot be totally ruled out, since it would have been better able to defend itself had there been no procedural error.[9] Member States must observe these rights when they take decisions within the scope of EU law, even though the EU legislation applicable does not expressly provide for such a procedural requirement.[10]

The Union Courts have also imposed other more particular procedural requirements. They have insisted that notice should be given of the nature of the case and that the individual should have a right to respond.[11] The individual is accorded access to the file in an increasing range of cases,[12] and this is recognized in the Charter of Fundamental Rights.[13] The Union Courts have moreover imposed an obligation to take care when making discretionary determinations in individual cases, which can apply even where the individual is not accorded a hearing.[14]

(B) CONSULTATION AND PARTICIPATION

Where a duty to consult is provided by the Treaty or Union legislation it will be enforced through the courts.[15] The ECJ has, however, consistently resisted claims to procedural rights, such as a right to participate or be consulted, in the making of Union legislation, unless this is expressly provided by a Treaty Article or another EU norm.[16] It has also been generally unwilling to accept that the fact of participation in the making of the legislative measure accords the applicant any enhanced prospects of being given standing to challenge it.[17]

This is regrettable. Participation is one way of imbuing decisions with greater legitimacy. It renders decision-making more accessible to those affected, and enables them to have direct participatory input into the decision reached. The European Council's 1993 Inter-Institutional Declaration on Democracy, Transparency and Subsidiarity proposed the creation of a notification procedure, in which the Commission would publish a brief summary of the draft measure in the Official Journal and there would be a deadline by which interested parties could submit their comments. There is a

---

8 Case T–260/94 *Air Inter SA v Commission* [1997] ECR II–997, [60].

9 Case C–141/08 P *Foshan Shunde Yongjian Housewares* (n 7) [94].

10 Case C–276/12 *Sabou v Finanční ředitelství pro hlavní město Prahu* EU:C:2013:678, [38]; Case C–349/07 *Sopropé* (n 6) [37]; Case C–383/13 PPU *MG and NR v Staatssecretaris van Veiligheid en Justitie* EU:C:2013:533, [35].

11 Cases C–48 and 66/90 *Netherlands and Koninklijke PTT Nederland NV and PTT Post v Commission* [1992] ECR I–565.

12 Case T–7/89 *SA Hercules Chemicals NV v Commission* [1991] ECR II–1711, [53]–[54]; Case T–65/89 *BPB Industries plc and British Gypsum Ltd v Commission* [1993] ECR II–389; Case T–42/96 *Eyckeler & Malt AG v Commission* [1998] ECR II–401; Case T–346/94 *France-Aviation v Commission* [1995] ECR II–2841; Cases C–204, 205, 211, 213, 217 and 219/00 P *Aalborg Portland v Commission* [2004] ECR I–123; Case T–390/08 *Bank Melli Iran v Council* [2009] ECR II–3967, [97]–[104]; Case C–407/08 P *Knauf Gips KG v European Commission* [2010] ECR I–6375, [22]; Case C–139/07 P *European Commission v Technische Glaswerke Ilmenau GmbH* [2010] ECR I–5885, [59].

13 Charter (n 5) Art 41(2)(b).

14 Case C–16/90 *Nolle v Hauptzollamt Bremen-Freihafen* [1991] ECR I–5163; Case C–269/90 *Hauptzollamt München-Mitte v Technische Universität München* [1991] ECR I–5469; Case C–367/95 P *Commission v Sytraval and Brink's France SARL* [1998] ECR I–1719.

15 Case 138/79 *Roquette Frères SA v Council* [1980] ECR 3333.

16 Case C–104/97 P *Atlanta AG v Commission* [1999] ECR I–6983; Case C–258/02 P *Bactria Industriehygiene-Service Verwaltungs GMbH v Commission* [2003] ECR I–15105, [43].

17 Case C–10/95 P *Asociasión Española de Empresas de la Carne (Asocarne) v Council* [1995] ECR I–4149, [39]; Case T–583/93 *Stichting Greenpeace Council (Greenpeace International) v Commission* [1995] ECR II–2205, [56]; Case C–263/02 P *Commission v Jego-Quéré & Cie SA* [2004] ECR I–3425, [47]–[48].

clear analogy between this formulation and the US Administrative Procedure Act 1946, which established a notice and comment procedure for rules made by agencies.

The Commission's response to this idea was, however, limited.[18] It did not bring forward any general measure for the EU akin to the Administrative Procedure Act, and the discussion of participation rights in its report for the 1996 IGC was exiguous to say the least.[19] The Commission has broadened consultation through increasing use of Green and White Papers when important areas of EU policy are being developed.[20]

It has also created Interactive Policy Making (IPM), a principal component of 'Your Voice in Europe',[21] which consists of two internet-based instruments to collect feedback from citizens, consumers, and business, although the number of initiatives subjected to this process is limited. The Commission nonetheless continues to resist the creation of legally enforceable participatory rights as against itself,[22] while at the same time pressing for such rights as against the Member States.[23]

It remains to be seen whether Article 11 TEU introduced by the Lisbon Treaty makes any difference in this respect. It provides that:

1. The institutions shall, by appropriate means, give citizens and representative associations the opportunity to make known and publicly exchange their views in all areas of Union action.

2. The institutions shall maintain an open, transparent and regular dialogue with representative associations and civil society.

3. The European Commission shall carry out broad consultations with parties concerned in order to ensure that the Union's actions are coherent and transparent.

4. Not less than one million citizens who are nationals of a significant number of Member States may take the initiative of inviting the European Commission, within the framework of its powers, to submit any appropriate proposal on matters where citizens consider that a legal act of the Union is required for the purpose of implementing the Treaties.

Article 11 is expressed in mandatory language and legislation has been enacted concerning the citizens' initiative in Article 11(4) TEU.[24] The salient issue is therefore whether this Article will signal any change from the previous position. Article 11 will be relied on by claimants in litigation, and the CJEU will be compelled to face difficult interpretive issues as to the concrete implications drawn from these principles. The CJEU may choose to interpret the Article narrowly, thereby effectively leaving the matter to the political institutions, but this would be problematic. It does not sit well with the wording of Article 11 TEU and would send a very negative message about the nature of participatory democracy in the EU. It would risk turning a provision that was meant to convey a positive feeling

---

[18] Craig (n 4) ch 11; J Mendes, *Participation in EU Rulemaking: A Rights-Based Approach* (Oxford University Press, 2011).

[19] P Craig, 'Democracy and Rule-Making within the EC: An Empirical and Normative Assessment' (1997) 3 ELJ 105.

[20] Towards a Reinforced Culture of Consultation and Dialogue—General Principles and Minimum Standards for Consultation of Interested Parties by the Commission, COM(2002) 704 final; C Quittkat and B Finke, 'The EU Commission Consultation Regime' in B Kohler-Koch, D de Bièvre, and W Moloney, 'Opening EU-Governance to Civil Society—Gains and Challenges', CONNEX Report Series No 5, 2008; B Kohler-Koch, 'Does Participatory Governance Hold its Promises?' in B Kohler-Koch and L Fabrice (eds), 'Efficient and Democratic Governance in the European Union', CONNEX Report Series No 9, 2008.

[21] http://ec.europa.eu/yourvoice/index_en.htm.

[22] COM(2002) 704 (n 20) 10.

[23] See, eg, Council Directive 96/61/EC of 24 September concerning integrated pollution prevention and control [1996] OJ L257/26, Art 4(4).

[24] Regulation (EU) No 211/2011 of the European Parliament and of the Council of 16 February 2011 on the citizens' initiative [2011] OJ L65/1.

about the inclusive nature of the EU and its willingness to engage with its citizenry into one that carried the opposite connotation.

(c) DUTY TO GIVE REASONS

Article 296 TFEU is the successor to Article 253 EC and imposes a duty to provide reasons,[25] breach of which constitutes a violation of an essential procedural requirement for the purposes of review.[26] It imposes a duty to give reasons not only for administrative decisions, but for all legal acts, including legislative, delegated, and implementing acts. This is noteworthy, since many national legal systems do not impose an obligation to furnish reasons for legislative acts, or do so only in limited circumstances.

(i) *Policy Rationale*

There are a number of objectives underlying the duty to give reasons. From the perspective of affected parties, it renders the decision-making process more transparent, so that they can know why a measure has been adopted. From the perspective of the decision-maker, an obligation to give reasons helps to ensure that the rationale for the action has been thought through. From the perspective of the CJEU, the existence of reasons facilitates judicial review by, for example, enabling the Court to determine whether a decision was disproportionate. In the words of the Court:[27]

> In imposing upon the Commission the obligation to state reasons for its decisions, Article 190 is not taking mere formal considerations into account but seeks to give an opportunity to the parties defending their rights, to the court of exercising its supervisory functions and to Member States and to all interested nationals of ascertaining the circumstances in which the Commission has applied the Treaty.

(ii) *Content*

The general principle is that the duty to give reasons must show in a clear and unequivocal manner the reasoning of the author of the act, thereby enabling the persons concerned to ascertain the reasons for it so that they can defend their rights and ascertain whether or not the measure is well founded, and also enable the Court to exercise its power of review.[28] The more particular content of the obligation to give reasons will vary depending on the nature of the measure.[29]

Where it is of a general legislative nature it will be necessary for the EU authority to show the reasoning which led to its adoption, but it will not be necessary for it to go into every point of fact and law.

---

[25] Case 24/62 *Germany v Commission* [1963] ECR 63; Case 5/67 *Beus GmbH & Co v Hauptzollamt München* [1968] ECR 83; Case C–143/95 P *Commission v Sociedade de Curtumes a Sul do Tejo Ld (Socurte)* [1997] ECR I–1; Case T–83/96 *Gerard van der Wal v Commission* [1998] ECR II–545; Case C–370/07 *Commission v Council* [2009] ECR I–8917.

[26] Case C–367/95 P *Commission v Sytraval* (n 14) [67]; Case C–378/00 *Commission v European Parliament and Council* [2003] ECR I–937, [34]; Case C–89/08 P *European Commission v Ireland* [2009] ECR I–11245, [34]–[35]; Case T–177/07 *Mediaset SpA v European Commission* [2010] ECR II–2341, [140].

[27] Case 24/62 (n 25) 69.

[28] Case C–367/95 P *Sytraval* (n 14) [140]; Cases T–228 and 233/99 *Westdeutsche Landesbank Girozentrale and Land Nordrhein-Westfalen v Commission* [2003] ECR II–435, [278]; Case T–177/07 *Mediaset* (n 26) [141]; Case T–319/11 *ABN Amro Group NV v European Commission* EU:T:2014:186, [131].

[29] Case 5/67 *Beus* [1968] ECR 83, 95; Case C–205/94 *Binder GmbH v Hauptzollamt Stuttgart-West* [1996] ECR I–2871; Case C–367/95 P *Sytraval* (n 14); Case T–181/08 *Pye Phyo Tay Za v Council* [2010] ECR II–1965, [93]–[96]; Case T–36/06 *Bundesverband deutscher Banken eV v European Commission* [2010] ECR II–537, [43]–[47]; Case T–637/11 *Euris Consult Ltd v European Parliament* EU:T:2014:237, [31].

Where the essential objective of the measure has been clearly disclosed there is no need for a specific statement of the reasons for each technical choice that has been made.[30]

The Court may demand greater particularity where the measure challenged is of an individual, rather than legislative, nature. Thus in *Germany v Commission*,[31] the Commission made a decision restricting the amount of wine that Germany could import at a lower rate of duty, because there was ample production of wine in the EC and because the grant of the requested quota would lead to serious disturbances on the relevant product market. The ECJ annulled the decision. It held that the Commission's reasoning was insufficiently specific concerning the size of any Community surplus, and that it was unclear from the Commission's decision why there would be serious disturbances in the market.

The content of the duty to provide reasons will also be affected by the extent to which the Court requires the Union institutions to respond to arguments advanced by the parties, what has been termed the dialogue dimension.[32] The ECJ has been cautious in this respect. In the *Sigarettenindustrie* case[33] the Court held that, although Article 253 EC required the Commission to state its reasons, it was not required to discuss all the issues of fact and law raised by every party during the administrative proceedings. It therefore dismissed the claim that the Commission had ignored the applicants' arguments, none of which had featured in the decision. While the Union Courts have affirmed that the Commission is under no obligation to respond to all the parties' arguments, they have also emphasized that the reasons given must suffice to enable it to exercise its judicial review function, and they will annul the decision if it does not withstand examination.[34]

Shapiro explains why the ECJ has been reluctant to move in this direction, and also why, nonetheless, it might be pushed to do so, based on the fostering of participation. The limits to which the EU Courts and political institutions foster dialogue and participation were however noted above.[35] The references to Article 190 should now be read as referring to Article 296 TFEU.

M Shapiro, The Giving Reasons Requirement[36]

The basic reason that the parties push and the ECJ resists dialogue lies in the difference between transparency and participation. Courts are likely to be initially hostile to demands for dialogue. Such requests are the last resort of regulated parties who have no substantive arguments left. Moreover, if dialogue claims are judicially accepted, they lead to a more and more cumbersome administrative process because the regulated parties will be encouraged to raise more and more arguments to which the agency will have to respond. If the only instrumental value for giving reasons is transparency, the courts will resist dialogue demands. One can discover an agency's actions and purposes without the agency rebutting every opposing argument.

. . .

---

[30] Case C–122/94 *Commission v Council* [1996] ECR I–881, [29]; Case C–84/94 *United Kingdom v Council* [1996] ECR I–5755, [74], [79].

[31] Case 24/62 (n 25); Case T–5/93 *Tremblay v Commission* [1995] ECR II–185.

[32] M Shapiro, 'The Giving Reasons Requirement' (1992) U Chic Legal Forum 179, 203–204.

[33] Cases 240–242, 261–262 and 268–269/82 *Stichting Sigarettenindustrie v Commission* [1985] ECR 3831, [88]. See also Case 42/84 *Remia BV and Nutricia BV v Commission* [1985] ECR 2545; Cases T–228 and 233/99 *Westdeutsche Landesbank* (n 28) [280]; Case T–177/07 *Mediaset* (n 26) [142]–[143]; Case T–36/06 *Bundesverband deutscher Banken* (n 29) [44]–[45]; Case C–413/08 P *Lafarge SA v European Commission* [2010] ECR I–5361, [41].

[34] Case T–44/90 *La Cinq SA v Commission* [1992] ECR II–1; Case T–7/92 *Asia Motor France SA v Commission* [1993] ECR II–669.

[35] See above, pp 546–548.

[36] (N 32) 204–205.

If the ECJ sticks closely to transparency as the sole goal of Article 190, the ECJ is unlikely to move towards a dialogue requirement. Yet participation in government by interests affected by government decisions presents an increasingly compelling value in contemporary society, particularly where environmental matters are involved. The ECJ has already, however unintentionally, opened one avenue for linking participation to Article 190 by stating that the Council need not give full reasons to the Member States where they have participated in the decisions. To be sure, these ECJ opinions are transparency-based. They require that those Member States already know what was going on because they were there. Nevertheless they create an opening for counter-arguments from complainants who were not present and claim that, therefore, they need the Commission to be responsive. In short, full transparency can only be achieved through participation or through dialogue as a form of participation.

4 INFRINGEMENT OF THE TREATY OR ANY RULE OF LAW RELATING TO ITS APPLICATION

(A) SCOPE

This ground of review in Article 263 TFEU provided the foundation for the development of the principles of judicial review. Infringement of the Treaty includes all provisions of the constitutive treaties as amended. It is not entirely clear what the phrase 'any rule of law relating to their application' was meant to connote. The intent might have been simply to ensure that decision-making should comply not only with the primary Treaty Articles, but also regulations, directives, and decisions passed pursuant thereto. If this had been the intent it could however have been expressed more simply. The intent might alternatively have been to capture compliance not only with EU legislation, but also with other 'rules of law relating to the application' of the Treaty that might be developed by the Courts. There is some evidence to support this view, but the story is more complex and involves considerable judicial creativity.[37] In any event, the ambiguity in the phrase provided the ECJ with a window through which to justify the imposition of general principles of law, which function as grounds of review.

This strategy was reinforced by what is now Article 19(1) TEU, ex Article 220 EC, which charges the Union Courts with the duty of ensuring that in the interpretation and application of the Treaty the law should be observed. The judicial task of elaborating principles of judicial review was further facilitated by more specific Treaty Articles, which made reference to, for example, non-discrimination. The ECJ read these Articles as indicative of a more general principle of non-discrimination that underpinned the legal order.[38] Moreover Article 2 TEU[39] provides that the Union is founded on the values of respect for human dignity, freedom, democracy, equality, the rule of law, and human rights.

The ECJ developed a rich body of jurisprudence on general principles of law, covering topics such as process rights, fundamental rights, equal treatment and non-discrimination, proportionality, and legal certainty and legitimate expectations.[40] In developing these concepts the ECJ drew on

---

[37] P Craig, *UK, EU and Global Administrative Law: Foundations and Challenges* (Cambridge University Press, 2015) ch 3.

[38] Cases 117/76 and 16/77 *Ruckdeschel v Hauptzollamt Hamburg-St Annen* [1977] ECR 1753, [7].

[39] Ex Art 6 TEU.

[40] K Lenaerts and T Corthaut, 'Judicial Review as a Contribution to the Development of European Constitutionalism' (2002) 22 YBEL 1; K Lenaerts and J Guttierez-Fons, 'The Constitutional Allocation of Powers and General Principles of EU Law' (2010) 47 CMLRev 1629.

national administrative law doctrine. German law was perhaps the most influential in this regard, providing the inspiration for the introduction of proportionality and legitimate expectations into the Community legal order.

The general principles are used in different ways. They function as interpretive guides in relation to primary Treaty Articles and other Union acts. The general principles also operate as grounds of review. The Union Courts cannot invalidate primary Treaty Articles. They can, however, annul other EU acts, and breach of a general principle is ground for annulment. The principles can also be used against national measures that fall within the scope of EU law, although the range of measures caught in this manner is not free from doubt.[41] Breach of a general principle may also form the basis for a damages action. Judicial review for violation of fundamental rights is considered as a separate topic.[42] The discussion in this chapter will consider other important general principles of law.

(B) GENERAL PRINCIPLES OF LAW: PROPORTIONALITY

(i) *Meaning*

The concept of proportionality is most fully developed within German law. It appeared initially in the context of policing, as a ground for challenging measures that were excessive or unnecessary in relation to the objective being pursued.[43] Some notion of proportionality also features within the legal systems of other Member States, although one should be cautious about ascribing the same meaning to the concept whenever the word 'proportionality' is found within different legal systems.[44]

Proportionality is now well established as a general principle of EU law. A version of the principle is enshrined in Article 5(4) TEU, which provides that the content and form of Union action shall not go beyond what is necessary to achieve the objectives of the Treaty, and its requirements are further fleshed out in a Protocol to the Treaty. Proportionality can be used to challenge EU action, and Member State action that falls within the sphere of EU law.

In any proportionality inquiry the relevant interests must be identified, and there will be some ascription of weight or value to those interests, since this is a necessary condition precedent to any balancing operation. There will normally be three stages in a proportionality inquiry: whether the measure was suitable to achieve the desired end; whether it was necessary to achieve the desired end; and whether the measure imposed a burden on the individual that was excessive in relation to the objective sought to be achieved (proportionality *stricto sensu*).

There has been some doubt whether stage three is part of the CJEU's proportionality inquiry.[45] The reality is that the CJEU will consider part three when an applicant addresses an argument concerning this stage of the inquiry. It may not do so where no such specific argument has been raised, more especially where the case can be resolved at one of the earlier stages. Moreover, in some cases the CJEU may distinguish stages two and three of the inquiry, while in others it may in effect 'fold' stage three of the inquiry back into stage one or two. The Court will in addition have to decide how intensively it is going to apply the proportionality test.

---

[41] Ibid; Editorial, 'The Scope of Application of the General Principles of Union Law: An Ever Expanding Union?' (2010) 47 CMLRev 1589.

[42] Ch 11.

[43] J Schwarze, *European Administrative Law* (Sweet & Maxwell, revised 1st edn, 2006) 685–686.

[44] Ibid 680–685.

[45] Craig (n 4) ch 19.

G de Búrca, The Principle of Proportionality and its Application in EC Law[46]

It becomes apparent that in reaching decisions, the Court of Justice is influenced not only by what it considers to be the nature and the importance of the interest or right claimed by the applicant, and the nature and importance of the objective alleged to be served by the measure, but by the relative expertise, position and overall competence of the Court as against the decision-making authority in assessing those factors. It becomes apparent that the way the proportionality principle is applied by the Court of Justice covers a spectrum ranging from a very deferential approach, to quite a rigorous and searching examination of the justification for a measure which has been challenged.

...Courts are generally prepared to adjudicate on issues involving traditionally categorized individual rights, where interference with a discretionary policy decision can be explained not on the ground that it is not the most sensible or effective measure, but on the ground that it unjustifiably restricts an important legally recognized right, the protection of which is entrusted to the court. Courts are accepted as having a legitimate role in deciding on civil liberties and personal rights even in controversial contexts such as euthanasia, abortion and freedom of speech. But in certain specific political contexts, in the case of measures involving, for example, national security, economic policy or national expenditure concerns, courts tend to be considerably more deferential in their review. They are more reluctant to adjudicate if the interest affected is seen as a collective or general public interest rather than an individual right, and if the interest of the State is a mixed and complex one, e.g. in an area involving national economic and social policy choices... The ways in which a court may defer in such circumstances range from deeming the measure to be non-justiciable, to refusing to look closely at the justification for the restrictive effects of the measure, to placing the onus of proof on the challenger who is claiming that the measure is disproportionate. Courts tend to be deferential in their review in cases which highlight the non-representative nature of the judiciary, the limited evidentiary and procedural processes of adjudication, and the difficulty of providing a defined individual remedy in contexts which involve complex political and economic policies.

We can distinguish three broad types of case that may be subject to challenge on grounds of proportionality and the intensity of review may differ in each.[47]

(ii) Challenge to EU Action: Proportionality and Discretionary Policy Choices

The most common type of case is where the individual argues that the policy choice made by the administration is disproportionate. The judiciary is cautious in this type of case: the administrative/political arm of government makes policy choices, and it is recognized that the courts should not overturn these merely because they believe that a different way of doing things would have been better. They should not substitute their judgment for that of the administration. This does not mean that proportionality is ruled out in such instances. It does mean that the courts are likely to apply the concept less intensively than in the other categories, and will overturn the policy choice only if it is clearly or manifestly disproportionate. The guiding principle is, as stated in the *British American Tobacco* case,[48] that this measure of review will be deemed appropriate whenever the EU legislature

[46] (1993) 13 YBEL 105, 111–112.

[47] Craig (n 4) ch 19; T Tridimas, *The General Principles of EU Law* (Oxford University Press, 2nd edn, 2006) ch 3.

[48] Case C–491/01 *R v Secretary of State for Health, ex p British American Tobacco (Investments) Ltd and Imperial Tobacco Ltd* [2002] ECR I–11453, [123]; Case C–210/03 *The Queen, on the application of Swedish Match AB and Swedish Match UK Ltd v Secretary of State for Health* [2004] ECR I–11893, [48]; Case C–344/04 *R (International Air Transport Association and European Low Fares Airline Association) v Department for Transport* [2006] ECR I–403, [80]; Case C–380/03 *Germany v European Parliament and Council* [2006] ECR I–11573, [145]; Case C–266/05 P *Jose Maria Sison v Council* [2007] ECR I–1233, [33]; Case C–558/07 *The Queen, on the application of SPCM SA, and others v Secretary of*

exercises a broad discretion involving political, economic, or social choices requiring it to make complex assessments.

Many of the cases arise from the Common Agricultural Policy (CAP), the objectives of which are set out at a high level of generality in Article 39 TFEU. These objectives can clash, with the result that the Commission and Council will have to make difficult discretionary choices. The Fedesa case provides a good example of such a challenge. The Court frequently emphasized that the EU institutions possessed a wide discretion in the operation of the CAP, and that review would not therefore be intensive.[49] This more deferential approach applies equally to challenges based on proportionality.

Case C–331/88 R v Minister for Agriculture, Fisheries and Food, ex parte Fedesa
[1990] ECR I–4023

Council Directive 81/602 provided that the Council would take a decision as soon as possible on the prohibition of certain hormone substances for administration to animals, but that in the meantime any arrangements made by Member States in relation to such substances would continue to apply. In 1988 Council Directive 88/146 was adopted as an approximating measure, prohibiting the use in livestock farming of certain of these hormonal substances. An earlier identical directive adopted in 1985 had been declared void by the ECJ on grounds of an infringement by the Council of an essential procedural requirement. The applicants were manufacturers and distributors of veterinary medicine who challenged the validity of the national legislative measure implementing the 1988 Directive on the ground that the Directive itself was invalid. They argued that the Directive infringed the principles of legal certainty, proportionality, equality, and non-retrospectivity. The following extract considers proportionality.

THE ECJ

12. It was argued that the Directive infringes the principle of proportionality in three respects. In the first place, the outright prohibition on the administration of the five hormones in question is inappropriate in order to attain the declared objectives, since it is impossible to apply in practice and leads to the creation of a dangerous black market. In the second place, outright prohibition is not necessary because consumer anxieties can be allayed simply by the dissemination of information and advice. Finally, the prohibition in question entails excessive disadvantages, in particular considerable financial losses on the part of the traders concerned, in relation to the alleged benefits accruing to the general interest.

13. The Court has consistently held that the principle of proportionality is one of the general principles of Community law. By virtue of that principle, the lawfulness of the prohibition of an economic activity is subject to the condition that the prohibitory measures are appropriate and necessary in order to achieve the objectives legitimately pursued by the legislation in question; when there is a choice between several appropriate measures recourse must be had to the least onerous, and the disadvantages caused must not be disproportionate to the aims pursued.

14. However, with regard to judicial review of compliance with those conditions it must be stated that in matters concerning the common agricultural policy the Community legislature has a discretionary power which corresponds to the political responsibilities given to it by . . . the Treaty. Consequently,

---

State for the Environment, Food and Rural Affairs [2009] ECR I–5783, [41]–[42]; Case C–58/08 The Queen, on the application of Vodafone Ltd v Secretary of State for Business, Enterprise and Regulatory Reform [2010] ECR I–4999, [51]–[53]; Case T–17/12 Hagenmeyer v European Commission EU:T:2014:234, [104].

[49] See, eg, Case 138/78 Stolting v Hauptzollamt Hamburg-Jonas [1979] ECR 713; Case 265/87 Schräder v Hauptzollamt Gronau [1989] ECR 2237.

the legality of a measure adopted in that sphere can be affected only if the measure is manifestly inappropriate having regard to the objective which the competent institution is seeking to pursue. (See in particular the judgment in Case 265/87, *Schräder* [1989] ECR 2237, paras. 21 and 22).

The applicants had therefore to show that the measure was manifestly inappropriate, and the Court concluded that they had not discharged this burden.[50] The prohibition, even though it caused financial loss to some traders, could not be regarded as manifestly inappropriate.

It would nonetheless be wrong to assume that proportionality when interpreted in this manner has the same meaning as *Wednesbury* irrationality in UK law. The reality is that the former is still generally more exacting than the latter. The CJEU will look closely at the reasoning used when reaching the contested decision and the evidentiary foundation for it, even for cases coming within this category.[51]

(iii) *Challenge to EU Action: Proportionality and Rights*

A second category of case is where an individual argues that her rights have been unduly restricted by Union action. The courts are likely to engage in vigorous scrutiny. Society may well accept that rights cannot be regarded as absolute, but the very denomination of certain interests as Union rights means that any interference should be kept to a minimum. Proportionality is therefore a natural adjunct to the recognition of such rights. Moreover, courts regard it as a proper part of their legitimate function to adjudicate on the boundary lines between state action and individual rights, even though this line may be controversial.

This is exemplified by *Hautala*.[52] The applicant was a Member of the European Parliament (MEP), who sought access to a Council document concerning arms exports. The Council refused to grant access, because this could be harmful to the EU's relations with third countries. It sought to justify this under Article 4(1) of Decision 93/731,[53] governing access to Council documentation. The ECJ held that the right of access to documents was to be broadly construed so as to include access to information contained in the document, not just the document itself. Proportionality required the Council to consider partial access to a document that contained information the disclosure of which could endanger one of the interests protected by Article 4(1). Proportionality also required that derogation from the right of access be limited to what was appropriate and necessary for achieving the aim in view.

Many cases concerning rights and proportionality are however more complex, because the argument arises when challenging an EU discretionary policy choice. The applicant alleges that the discretionary policy infringed property rights, or the right to pursue a profession, trade, or occupation. The EU Courts acknowledge such rights within the Union legal order, but make it clear that they are not absolute and must be viewed in relation to their social function. The CJEU and General Court

---

[50] See also, eg, Case C–8/89 *Zardi v Consorzio Agrario Provinciale di Ferrara* [1990] ECR I–2515; Cases C–133, 300 and 362/93 *Crispoltoni v Fattoria Autonoma Tabacchi* [1994] ECR I–4863; Case C–4/96 *Northern Ireland Fish Producers' Federation and Northern Ireland Fishermen's Federation v Department of Agriculture for Northern Ireland* [1998] ECR I–681; Case C–434/02 *Arnold Andre GmbH & Co KG v Landrat des Kreises Herford* [2004] ECR I–11825, [46]–[56]; Case C–41/03 P *Rica Foods (Free Zone) NV v Commission* [2005] ECR I–6875, [85]–[86]; Case T–158/03 *Industrias Químicas del Vallés, SA v Commission* [2005] ECR II–2425, [136]; Cases C–37 and 58/06 *Viamex Agrar Handels GmbH and Zuchtvieh-Kontor GmbH (ZVK) v Hauptzollamt Hamburg-Jonas* [2008] ECR I–69, [36]; Case T–334/07 *Denka International BV v Commission* [2009] ECR II–4205, [139].

[51] Craig (n 4) ch 19.

[52] Case C–353/99 P *Council v Hautala* [2001] ECR I–9565. See also Case C–353/01 P *Olli Mattila v Council and Commission* [2004] ECR I–1073; Case T–2/03 *Verein für Konsumenteninformation v Commission* [2005] ECR II–1121; Case C–64/05 P *Sweden v Commission* [2007] ECR I–11389, [66].

[53] [1993] OJ L340/43.

will therefore consider whether the restrictions imposed by the measure correspond to objectives of general interest pursued by the Union and whether they constitute a disproportionate and intolerable interference, which impairs the very substance of the rights guaranteed.[54]

Thus in *Hauer*[55] the applicant challenged a Community Regulation limiting the planting of new vines. The Court found that this did not, in itself, constitute an invalid restriction on property rights. It then considered whether the planting restrictions were disproportionate, 'impinging upon the very substance of the right to property'.[56] The Court found that they were not, but in reaching this conclusion it carefully examined the purpose of the general scheme within which the contested Regulation fell. The objects of this scheme were to attain a balanced wine market, with fair prices for consumers and a fair return for producers; the eradication of surpluses; and improvement in the quality of wine. The disputed Regulation, which prohibited new plantings, was part of this overall plan. It was not disproportionate in the light of the legitimate, general Community policy for this area. This policy was designed to deal with an immediate problem of surpluses, while at the same time laying the foundation for more permanent measures to facilitate a balanced wine market.[57]

The preceding decision can be contrasted with *Kadi*,[58] where the applicant sought the annulment of a Regulation freezing the applicant's assets, pursuant to a Security Council resolution to curb Al-Qaeda. The applicant argued that the Regulation constituted a disproportionate infringement of his property rights. The ECJ reiterated its normal approach: property rights were not absolute and hence could be restricted, provided that the restrictions corresponded to objectives of Community public interest and did not constitute a disproportionate and intolerable interference, impairing the very substance of the right so guaranteed.[59] The ECJ concluded that the freezing of funds could not be regarded as *per se* disproportionate, given the importance of the fight against terrorism,[60] but the fact that the Regulation provided no means whereby the applicant could contest his inclusion on the sanctions list meant that it constituted an infringement of his property rights.[61]

(iv) *Challenge to EU Action: Proportionality and Penalties*

A third type of case is where the attack is on the penalty imposed, the claim being that it is excessive. Courts are likely to be reasonably searching in this type of case. This is because penalties can impinge on personal liberties, and because a court can normally strike down a penalty without undermining the relevant administrative policy.

In *Man (Sugar)*[62] the applicant was required to give a security deposit to the Board when seeking a licence to export sugar outside the Community. The applicant was four hours late in completing the relevant paperwork. The Board, acting pursuant to a Community regulation, forfeited the entire

---

[54] Case 265/87 *Schräder HS Kraftfutter GmbH & Co KG v Hauptzollamt Gronau* [1989] ECR 2237, [15]; Case C–280/93 *Germany v Council* [1994] ECR I–4973, [78]; Case C–200/96 *Musik Metronome GmbH v Music Point Hokamp GmbH* [1998] ECR I–1953, [21]; Case C–293/97 *R v Secretary of State for the Environment and Ministry of Agriculture, Fisheries and Food, ex p Standley* [1999] ECR I–2603, [54].

[55] Case 44/79 *Hauer v Land Rheinland-Pfalz* [1979] ECR 3727.

[56] Ibid [23].

[57] See also Case C–491/01 *R v Secretary of State for Health, ex p British American Tobacco (Investments) Ltd and Imperial Tobacco Ltd* [2002] ECR I–11453; Cases C–20 and 64/00 *Booker Aquacultur Ltd and Hydro Seafood GSP Ltd v Scottish Ministers* [2003] ECR I–7411; Cases C–184 and 223/02 *Spain and Finland v European Parliament and Council* [2004] ECR I–7789.

[58] Cases C–402 and 415/05 P *Kadi and Al Barakaat International Foundation* [2008] ECR I–6351.

[59] Ibid [355].

[60] Ibid [363]–[366].

[61] Ibid [368]–[371]. See also Cases C–584, 593 and 595/10 P *Commission v Kadi* EU:C:2013:518.

[62] Case 181/84 *R v Intervention Board, ex p ED & F Man (Sugar) Ltd* [1985] ECR 2889.

deposit of £1,670,370. The Court held that this was too drastic, given the function performed by the system of export licences.[63]

In addition to cases dealing with penalties *stricto sensu* the Court has applied proportionality to scrutinize charges imposed by the EU institutions. Thus in *Bela-Mühle*[64] the Court held that a scheme whereby producers of animal feed were forced to use skimmed milk, rather than soya, in their product in order to reduce a milk surplus was unlawful. Skimmed milk was three times more expensive than soya, and therefore the obligation to purchase the milk imposed a disproportionate burden on the animal feed producers. In *Portugal v Commission*[65] Portugal argued that an export ban on meat products, imposed in response to mad cow disease, was disproportionate. This was because Portugal was not a significant meat exporter, and it was therefore easier to regulate low-volume exports as compared to the large-volume exports from the UK. The ECJ rejected the argument. Beef exports from the UK had not been allowed until the UK had put in place export arrangements of a kind advocated by a health code. This had not been done at the time when the ban was imposed on Portugal.

While the general approach is that set out above there are cases concerned with penalties where the ECJ has applied the manifestly disproportionate test derived from *Fedesa*. This approach seems to be adopted when the penalty is an integral substantive part of a discretionary policy, which is itself subject to the *Fedesa* test.[66]

(v) Challenge to Member State Action: Case Law

There have been many cases dealing with proportionality and Member State action.[67] Proportionality will, for example, often be relevant in equality cases. Thus in *Kreil*[68] it was held that a German rule requiring all armed units in the Bundeswehr to be male contravened the principle of proportionality.

The proportionality principle is also used extensively in cases concerned with free movement. Thus the ECJ insisted that derogation from the principle of free movement of workers can be sanctioned only in cases that pose a genuine and serious threat to public policy, and the measure must be the least restrictive possible in the circumstances.[69] The same principle is evident in cases on freedom to provide services. In *Van Binsbergen*[70] the Court held that residence requirements limiting this freedom might be justified, but only where they were strictly necessary to prevent the evasion by those outside the territory of professional rules applicable to the activity in question. In *Canal*[71] the ECJ considered the legality of national legislation requiring operators of certain television services to register details of their equipment in a national register. It held that such a measure could not satisfy the necessity requirement of the proportionality test if the registration requirement duplicated controls already carried out either in the same state or in another Member State. The same approach is evident in relation to free movement of goods. Thus in the famous *Cassis de Dijon* case[72] the Court decided that a German rule that prescribed the minimum alcohol content for a beverage restricted free movement of

---

[63] Ibid [29]; Case 240/78 *Atalanta Amsterdam BV v Produktschap voor Vee en Vlees* [1979] ECR 2137; Case 122/78 *Buitoni SA v Fonds d'Orientation et de Régularisation des Marchés Agricoles* [1979] ECR 677.

[64] Case 114/76 *Bela-Mühle Josef Bergman KG v Grows-Farm GmbH & Co KG* [1977] ECR 1211.

[65] Case C–365/99 [2001] ECR I–5645.

[66] Case C–94/05 *Emsland-Stärke GmbH v Landwirtschaftskammer Hannover* [2006] ECR I–2619, [53]–[59]; Cases C–37 and 58/06 *Viamex* (n 50) [33]–[36].

[67] Craig (n 4) ch 20; Tridimas (n 47) ch 4.

[68] Case C–285/98 *Kreil v Bundesrepublik Deutschland* [2000] ECR I–69.

[69] Case 36/75 *Rutili v Ministre de l'Intérieur* [1975] ECR 1219; Case 30/77 *R v Bouchereau* [1977] ECR 1999.

[70] Case 33/74 *Van Binsbergen v Bestuur van de Bedrijfsvereniging Metaalnijverheid* [1974] ECR 1299; Case 39/75 *Coenen v Social Economische Raad* [1975] ECR 1547; Case C–140/03 *Commission v Greece* [2005] ECR I–3177.

[71] Case C–390/99 *Canal Satélite Digital SL v Aministación General del Estado and Distribuidora de Televisión Digital SA (DTS)* [2002] ECR I–607; Case C–244/06 *Dynamic Medien Vertriebs GmbH v Avides Media AG* [2008] ECR I–505.

[72] Case 120/78 *Rewe-Zentral AG v Bundesmonopolverwaltung für Branntwein* [1979] ECR 649.

goods. The Court rejected the argument that the rule was necessary to protect consumers from being misled, because the interests of consumers could be safeguarded in less restrictive ways, by displaying the alcohol content on the packaging of the drinks.[73]

The ECJ may pass the application of proportionality back to the national courts, subject to conditions or guidelines as to how the proportionality inquiry should be decided in a particular area. There is justifiable concern about the complexity of some issues that are sent back to national courts to be resolved through a proportionality inquiry.[74]

(vi) *Challenge to Member State Action: Intensity of Review and Balancing of Values*

The case law in this area has been criticized on the ground that the Union Courts have applied proportionality more intensively to Member State action as compared to Union action. There is however a rationale for intensive proportionality review of Member State action. The cases in the preceding section involve situations where there has been a breach of the four freedoms, and the Member State then raises a defence based on the relevant Treaty Article. The four freedoms are central to the very idea of market integration that lies at the economic heart of the EU. They also embody non-economic values. It is therefore unsurprising that the ECJ has closely monitored defences to free movement, including proportionality. Four more particular variables have shaped the Court's review in this type of case.

First, the Court has tended to review more intensively over time. Cases raising similar principles have been subject to more rigorous scrutiny, such that Member State action regarded as lawful in the earlier case has been held unlawful in a later action.[75]

Secondly, the intensity of the Court's review will depend on how seriously it takes the Member State's argument that measures really were necessary to protect, for example, public health. If the ECJ feels that these measures were really a 'front' for a national protective policy, designed to insulate its producers from foreign competition, then the ECJ will subject the Member State's argument to close scrutiny. Thus in *Commission v United Kingdom*[76] the ECJ rejected a claim by the UK Government that a ban on the import of poultry could be justified on grounds of public health, because it felt that the measures were aimed at protecting UK poultry producers from the effects of French imports before Christmas.

Thirdly, the EU Courts have been willing to interpret proportionality in the light of the Member State's values, notwithstanding that those values differ from those of other Member States.[77] This is exemplified by *Omega*.[78] The Bonn police issued an order forbidding the applicant company from

---

[73] See, eg, Case C‑217/99 *Commission v Belgium* [2000] ECR I‑10251; Case C‑473/98 *Kemikalieinspektionen v Toolex Alpha AB* [2000] ECR I‑5681; Case C‑270/02 *Commission v Italy* [2004] ECR I‑1559; Case C‑41/02 *Commission v Netherlands* [2004] ECR I‑11375; Case C‑110/05 *Commission v Italy* [2009] ECR I‑519.

[74] W Van Gerven, 'The Effect of Proportionality on the Actions of Member States of the European Community: National Viewpoints from Continental Europe' in E Ellis (ed), *The Principle of Proportionality in the Laws of Europe* (Hart, 1999) 37–64.

[75] Compare, eg, Case 41/74 *Van Duyn v Home Office* [1974] ECR 1337 with Cases 115 and 116/81 *Adoui and Cornuaille v Belgian State* [1982] ECR 1665. Compare Case 34/79 *R v Henn and Darby* [1979] ECR 3795 with Case 121/85 *Conegate v Customs and Excise Commissioners* [1986] ECR 1007.

[76] Case 40/82 [1982] ECR 2793.

[77] Case C‑384/93 *Alpine Investments BV v Minister van Financiën* [1995] ECR I‑1141, [51]; Case C‑3/95 *Reisebüro Broede v Gerd Sandker* [1996] ECR I‑6511.

[78] Case C‑36/02 *Omega Spielhallen- und Automatenaufstellungs-GmbH v Oberbürgermeisterin der Bundesstadt Bonn* [2004] ECR I‑9609. See also Case C‑124/97 *Läärä, Cotswold Microsystems Ltd and Oy Transatlantic Software Ltd v Finland* [1999] ECR I‑6067; Case C‑67/98 *Questore di Verona v Zenatti* [1999] ECR I‑7289, [33]–[34]; Case C‑277/02 *EU-Wood-Trading GmbH v Sonderabfall-Management-Gesellschaft Rheinland-Pfalz mbH* [2004] ECR I‑11957, [51]; Case C‑244/06 *Dynamic Medien* (n 71) [42]–[52]; Case C‑208/09 *Sayn-Wittgenstein v Landeshauptmann von Wien* [2010] ECR I‑13693, [86]–[91]; Case C‑498/10 *X NV v Staatssecretaris van Financiën* EU:C:2012:635, [37].

allowing laser games that simulated the killing of opponents, because they infringed the right to human dignity in the German Constitution. The ECJ found that the police order limited the freedom to provide services and then considered the public policy justification. It held that the concept of public policy as a derogation from a fundamental freedom must be interpreted strictly. The ECJ accepted, however, that public policy could vary from country to country, and that the national authorities must be accorded a margin of discretion within the limits imposed by the Treaty.

Fourthly, proportionality can require the difficult balancing of social and economic values, as exemplified by *Viking Line*.[79] The case is considered in the discussion of freedom of establishment.[80] Suffice it to say for the present that Viking Line was originally incorporated in Finland. It was obliged under Finnish law and the terms of a collective bargaining agreement to pay its Estonian crew the same wages as those applicable in Finland. Estonian crew wages were lower than those in Finland. Viking Line therefore sought to re-flag one of its ships in Estonia. This was opposed by trade unions, which threatened strike action. Viking Line argued that this was in breach of freedom of establishment. The ECJ accepted that the right to strike was a fundamental right under EU law, but that its exercise had to be reconciled with other Treaty rights and with the principle of proportionality. It was for the national court to decide whether the strike action was proportionate, subject to guidance from the ECJ. While the ECJ acknowledged the social dimension of EU law, it was clear from the ECJ's guidance that strike action could not be objectively justified if it prevented Viking Line from flagging its vessel in a Member State other than that of which the vessel owners were nationals. In this respect the economic value of market integration trumped the social value of worker protection.

(c) GENERAL PRINCIPLES OF LAW: LEGAL CERTAINTY AND LEGITIMATE EXPECTATIONS

The connected concepts of legal certainty and legitimate expectations are found in many legal systems, although their content may vary.[81] These concepts are applied in a number of ways.[82]

(i) *Actual Retroactivity*

The most obvious application of legal certainty is in the context of rules with an actual retroactive effect. Following Schwarze,[83] 'actual retroactivity' covers the situation where a rule is introduced and applied to events which have already been concluded. This can occur either where the date of entry into force precedes the date of publication, or where the regulation applies to circumstances that have been concluded before the entry into force of the measure.

The arguments against allowing such measures to have legal effect are compelling. A basic tenet of the rule of law is that people can plan their lives with knowledge of the legal consequences of their actions. This is violated by measures that were not in force when the events took place. These concerns are particularly marked in the context of criminal penalties, where the effect may be to criminalize activity that was lawful when it was undertaken. The application of retrospective rules may also be

---

[79] Case C–438/05 *International Transport Workers' Federation and Finnish Seamen's Union v Viking Line ABP and OÜ Viking Line Eesti* [2007] ECR I–10779.

[80] Pp 818–819.

[81] S Schonberg, *Legitimate Expectations in Administrative Law* (Oxford University Press, 2000); Craig (n 4) ch 16; Schwarze (n 43) ch 6; Tridimas (n 47) ch 6.

[82] Legal certainty can have implications as to how far an administrative decision that has become final should be re-opened in the light of a subsequent ruling by the Union Courts: pp 476–478.

[83] Schwarze (n 43) 1120.

damaging in commercial circumstances, upsetting the presuppositions on which transactions were based. It is therefore unsurprising that national legal systems take a very dim view of retroactive rules.

The EU is no different in this respect. The basic principle was enunciated in *Racke*.[84] The Commission introduced monetary compensatory amounts for a certain product by a regulation, and then in two further regulations altered the amounts. The later regulations stated that they would apply fourteen days before they were published. The Court held that it was a fundamental principle of the Community legal order that a measure should not be applicable before those concerned could become acquainted with it.[85] The Court then stated that:[86]

> Although in general the principle of legal certainty precludes a Community measure from taking effect from a point in time before its publication, it may exceptionally be otherwise where the purpose to be achieved so demands and where the legitimate expectations of those concerned are duly respected.

The Court has, in accordance with this proviso, upheld the validity of retroactive measures, particularly in the agricultural sphere where they were necessary to ensure market stability, or where the retroactivity placed the individual in a more favourable position.[87] The normal presumption is, however, against the validity of retroactive measures. This manifests itself in both procedural and substantive terms.

In procedural terms, the Court has made it clear that it will interpret norms as having retroactive effect only if this clearly follows from their terms, or from the objectives of the general scheme of which they are a part. The general principle of construction is, therefore, against giving rules any retroactive impact.[88]

In substantive terms, the Court will strike down measures that have a retroactive effect where there is no pressing Union objective that demands this temporal dimension, or where the legitimate expectations of those affected by the measure cannot be duly respected,[89] as the following case shows.

Case 63/83 **Regina v Kent Kirk**
[1984] ECR 2689

> Criminal proceedings were brought in the UK for infringement of fisheries legislation. During the course of these proceedings the question arose whether Council Regulation 170/83 of 25 January 1983, by which, with retroactive effect from 1 January 1983, national measures contravening Community law prohibitions on discrimination were approved by way of transitional arrangements, could also retroactively validate national penal provisions. The ECJ said no, firmly.

---

84 Case 98/78 *Firma A Racke v Hauptzollamt Mainz* [1979] ECR 69. See also Case 99/78 *Weingut Gustav Decker KG v Hauptzollamt Landau* [1979] ECR 101; Case T–115/94 *Opel Austria GmbH v Council* [1997] ECR II–2739; Cases T–225, 255, 257 and 306/06 *Budějovický Budvar, národní podnik v OHIM* [2008] ECR II–3555, [152]; Case T–380/06 *Vischim Srl v Commission* [2009] ECR II–3911, [82]; Case C–146/11 *AS Pimix* EU:C:2012:450, [33]; Cases T–229 and 276/11 *Lord Inglewood v European Parliament* EU:T:2013:127, [32].
85 Case 98/78 *Racke* (n 84) 84.
86 Ibid 86.
87 Case T–7/99 *Medici Grimm KG v Council* [2000] ECR II–2671.
88 Cases 212–217/80 *Salumi* [1981] ECR 2735; Case C–110/03 *Belgium v Commission* [2005] ECR I–2801, [73].
89 Case 224/82 *Meiko-Konservenfabrik v Federal Republic of Germany* [1983] ECR 2539; Case C–459/02 *Willy Gerekens and Association agricole pour la promotion de la commercialisation laitière Procola v État du grand-duc de Luxembourg* [2004] ECR I–7315, [21]–[27]; Cases C–189, 202, 205, 208 and 213/02 P *Dansk Rorindustri A/S v Commission* [2005] ECR I–5425, [202]; Case C–550/09 *Criminal proceedings against E and F* [2010] ECR I–6213, [59].

THE ECJ

20. The Commission...contends that the Member States were empowered to adopt measures such as the Sea Fish Order 1982 by Article 6(1) of Regulation 170/83 of 25 January 1983 which authorises retroactively, as from 1 January 1983, the retention of the derogation regime defined in Article 100 of the 1972 Act of Accession for a further ten years, and which extends the coastal zones from six to twelve nautical miles....

21. Without embarking upon an examination of the general legality of the retroactivity of Article 6(1) of that Regulation, it is sufficient to point out that such retroactivity may not, in any event, have the effect of validating *ex post facto* national measures of a penal nature which impose penalties for an act which, in fact, was not punishable at the time at which it was committed. That would be the case where at the time of the act entailing a criminal penalty, the national measure was invalid because it was incompatible with Community law.

22. The principle that penal provisions may not have retroactive effect is one which is common to all the legal orders of the Member States and is enshrined in Article 7 of the European Convention for the Protection of Human Rights and Fundamental Freedoms as a fundamental right; it takes its place among the general principles of law whose observance is ensured by the Court of Justice.

23. Consequently the retroactivity provided for in Article 6(1) of Regulation 170/83 cannot be regarded as validating *ex post facto* national measures which imposed criminal penalties, at the time of the conduct at issue, if those measures were not valid.

Where there is a pressing Union objective and where the legitimate expectations of those concerned are duly respected, then retroactivity may, exceptionally, be accepted in a non-criminal context. This is exemplified by *Fedesa*.[90] The applicants argued that the Directive was in breach of the principle of non-retroactivity because it was adopted on 7 March 1988 and stipulated that it was to be implemented by 1 January 1988 at the latest. The Court drew a distinction between the retroactive effect of penal provisions and retroactive effect outside the criminal sphere. As to the former, the Court affirmed *Kent Kirk*, but held that the Directive in *Fedesa* did not impose any criminal liability as such. As to the latter, the Court ruled that the Directive did not contravene the principle of non-retroactivity. It had been adopted to replace an earlier Directive that had been annulled. The time frame of the challenged Directive was necessary to avoid a temporary legal vacuum where there would be no Community legislation to back up the Member States' existing implementing provisions. It was for this reason that the Council had maintained the date of the earlier Directive when it passed the later Directive.[91]

(ii) *Legal Certainty, Legitimate Expectations, and Apparent Retroactivity*

Apparent retroactivity covers the situation where legislative acts are applied to events which occurred in the past, but which have not yet been definitively concluded. The moral arguments against allowing laws to have actual retroactive effect are powerful. Cases involving apparent retroactivity are more problematic, because the administration must have the power to alter policy for the future, even though this may have implications for the conduct of private parties, which was planned on the basis

---

[90] Case C–331/88 [1990] ECR I–4023.

[91] The Court held that there was no infringement of the legitimate expectations, because the earlier dir was only annulled because of a procedural defect, and those affected by the national implementing legislation could not expect the Council to change its attitude on the substance of the matter in the dir during the short time between the annulment of the first dir and the notification of the second dir: ibid [47].

of the pre-existing legal regime.[92] The law in this area is complex and only an outline can be provided here. The key elements in the Court's approach are as follows.

First, the protection of legitimate expectations developed initially in relation to the revocation of administrative decisions. The general principle is that favourable decisions bind the administration,[93] although this principle is subject to a number of exceptions.[94]

Secondly, the protection of legitimate expectations also applies to representations.[95] The general principle is that the protection of legitimate expectations extends to any individual who is in a situation from which it is clear that, in giving precise and specific assurances,[96] the Union institutions caused that person to entertain justified hopes.[97] This depends on the nature and wording of the representation.[98] In *CIRFS*[99] the ECJ was willing to accept that the Commission was bound by the terms of its policy framework, and in *IJssel-Vliet*[100] it held that Commission guidelines that had been built into a Dutch aid scheme were binding upon the Dutch Government. Moreover, in *Vlaams Gewest*[101] the CFI held that the guidelines adopted by the Commission had to be applied in accordance with the principle of equal treatment, with the implication that like cases, as defined in the guidelines, had to be treated alike.

Thirdly, the claim will fail where the Court adjudges that the applicant's expectations were not legitimate. This will be so where: the challenged EU activity was designed to close a legal gap to prevent traders from making a speculative profit;[102] the expectations were not reasonable, because the contested measure should have been foreseen;[103] or the applicant had not met the conditions attached to a grant of funding.[104]

Fourthly, the mere fact that a trader is disadvantaged by a change in the law will not give cause for complaint based upon disappointment of legitimate expectations. A trader will not be held to have a legitimate expectation that an existing situation, which is capable of being altered by decisions taken by the institutions within the limits of their discretionary powers, will be maintained.[105] This is particularly so in the context of the CAP, where constant adjustments to meet new market circumstances

---

[92] For a valuable analysis of the justifications for protecting legitimate expectations see Schonberg (n 81) ch 1.

[93] Cases 7/56 and 3–7/57 *Algera v Common Assembly* [1957] ECR 39; Case T–251/00 *Lagardere SCA and Canal+ SA v Commission* [2002] ECR II–4825.

[94] Craig (n 4) ch 18.

[95] Case 54/65 *Chatillon v High Authority* [1966] ECR 185, 196; Case 81/72 *Commission v Council (Staff Salaries)* [1973] ECR 575, 584–585; Case 148/73 *Louwage v Commission* [1974] ECR 81, [12].

[96] Case T–72/99 *Meyer v Commission* [2000] ECR II–2521; Case T–290/97 *Mehibas Dordtselaan BV v Commission* [2000] ECR II–15.

[97] Case T–489/93 *Unifruit Hellas EPE v Commission* [1994] ECR II–1201; Case T–534/93 *Grynberg and Hall v Commission* [1994] ECR II–595; Case T–456/93 *Consorzio Gruppo di Azioni Locale Murgia Messapica v Commission* [1994] ECR II–361; Case T–326/07 *Cheminova A/S v Commission* [2009] ECR II–2685, [81]; Case T–264/07 *CSL Behring GmbH v European Commission and European Medicines Agency (EMA)* [2010] ECR II–4469, [117].

[98] Cases C–189, 202, 205, 208 and 213/02 P *Dansk Rorindustri* (n 89) [209]–[232].

[99] Case C–313/90 *CIRFS v Commission* [1993] ECR I–1125, [34]–[36].

[100] Case C–311/94 *IJssel-Vliet Combinatie BV v Minister van Economische Zaken* [1996] ECR I–5023.

[101] Case T–214/95 *Vlaams Gewest v Commission* [1998] ECR II–717.

[102] Case 2/75 *Einfuhr- und Vorratsstelle für Getreide und Futtermittel v Firma C Mackprang* [1975] ECR 607; Case C–179/00 *Weidacher v Bundesminister für Land- und Forstwirtschaft* [2002] ECR I–501.

[103] Case 265/85 *Van den Bergh en Jurgens and Van Dijk Food Products v Commission* [1987] ECR 1155; Case C–350/88 *Delacre v Commission* [1990] ECR I–395; Case T–489/93 *Unifruit Hellas* (n 97); Cases T–466, 469, 473, 474 and 477/93 *O'Dwyer v Council* [1996] ECR II–2071; Cases T–142 and 283/01 *Organización de Productores de Túnidos Congelados (OPTUC) v Commission* [2004] ECR II–329; Case C–342/03 *Spain v Council* [2005] ECR I–1975, [48]; E Sharpston, 'Legitimate Expectations and Economic Reality' (1990) 15 ELRev 103.

[104] Case T–126/97 *Sonasa—Sociedade Nacional de Segurança Ld v Commission* [1999] ECR II–2793.

[105] Case C–110/97 *Netherlands v Council* [2001] ECR I–8763; Case C–402/98 *ATB v Ministero per le Politiche Agricole* [2000] ECR I–5501; Cases T–64–65/01 *Afrikanische Frucht-Compagnie GmbH v Commission* [2004] ECR II–521, [83]–[84]; Case C–17/03 *Vereniging voor Energie, Milieu en Water v Directeur van de Dienst uitvoering en toezicht energie* [2005] ECR I–4983, [73]–[87].

are required.[106] It may also be so in other areas, such as competition policy, where the CFI emphasized that the Commission has discretion to alter the level of fines.[107]

Fifthly, the individual must be able to point either to a bargain between the individual and the authorities, or to a course of conduct or assurance by the authorities, which can generate the legitimate expectation. The *Mulder* case illustrates the first of these situations.

Case 120/86 Mulder v Minister van Landbouw en Visserij
[1988] ECR 2321

The Community had an excess of milk. In order to reduce this excess it passed Regulation 1078/77, under which producers could cease milk production for a certain period in exchange for a premium for non-marketing of the milk. The applicant made such an arrangement in 1979 for five years. In 1984 he began to plan a resumption of production and applied to the Dutch authorities for a reference quantity of milk, which he would be allowed to produce without incurring the payment of any additional levy. He was refused on the ground that he could not prove milk production during the relevant reference year, which was 1983. This was impossible for Mulder, since he did not produce during that period, because of the bargain struck in 1979. He challenged Regulation 857/84, which was the basis of the Dutch authorities' denial of his quota, arguing that it infringed his legitimate expectations.

THE ECJ

23. It must be conceded...that a producer who has voluntarily ceased production for a certain period cannot legitimately expect to be able to resume production under the same conditions as those which previously applied and not to be subject to any rules of market or structural policy adopted in the meantime.

24. The fact remains that where such a producer, as in the present case, has been encouraged by a Community measure to suspend marketing for a limited period in the general interest and against payment of a premium he may legitimately expect not to be subject, upon the expiry of his undertaking, to restrictions which specifically affect him precisely because he availed himself of the possibilities offered by the Community provisions.

25. However, the regulations on the additional levy on milk give rise to such restrictions for producers who, pursuant to an undertaking entered into under Regulation 1078/77, did not deliver milk during the reference year....Those producers may in fact be denied a reference quantity under the new system precisely because of that undertaking if they do not fulfil the specific conditions laid down in Regulation 857/84 or if the Member States have no reference quantity available.

26. ...There is nothing in the provisions of Regulation 1078/77 or in its Preamble to show that the non-marketing undertaking entered into under that Regulation might, upon its expiry, entail a bar to resumption of the activity in question. Such an effect therefore frustrates those producers' legitimate expectations that the effect of the system to which they had rendered themselves would be limited.

The following cases illustrate the second type of situation, where the legitimacy of the applicant's expectation is based upon some course of conduct by the administration, or an assurance it has given.[108] In *Embassy Limousines*[109] it was held that there was a breach of legitimate expectations where

---

[106] Case C–63/93 *Duff v Minister for Agriculture and Food Ireland and the Attorney General* [1996] ECR I–569; Case C–22/94 *Irish Farmers Association v Minister for Agriculture, Food and Forestry (Ireland) and the Attorney General* [1997] ECR I–1809.

[107] Case T–31/99 *ABB Asea Brown Boveri Ltd v Commission* [2002] ECR II–1881.

[108] Case C–152/88 *Sofrimport Sàrl v Commission* [1990] ECR I–2477.

[109] Case T–203/96 *Embassy Limousines & Services v European Parliament* [1998] ECR II–4239.

a company submitting a tender was encouraged to make irreversible investments in advance of the contract being awarded, and thereby go beyond the risks inherent in making a bid. In *CEMR*[110] it was held that the Commission could not, without infringing the principle of legitimate expectations, reduce the budgetary allocation for a project where the relevant work had been included in the original bid that had been accepted by the Commission. In *CNTA*[111] the applicant made export contracts on the supposition that monetary compensatory amounts, which were payments designed to compensate for fluctuations in exchange rates, would be payable. After the contracts were made, but before they were performed, the Commission passed a regulation abolishing such payments in that sector. The Court held that while these payments could not be said to insulate exporters from all fluctuations in exchange rates, they did shield them from these risks, such that even a prudent exporter might choose not to cover against them:[112]

> In these circumstances, a trader might legitimately expect that for transactions irrevocably undertaken by him because he has obtained, subject to a deposit, export licences fixing the amount of the refund in advance, no unforeseeable alteration will occur which could have the effect of causing him inevitable loss, by re-exposing him to the exchange risk.

Sixthly, even if the applicant is able to prove a *prima facie* legitimate expectation this may be defeated if there is an overriding public interest that trumps the expectation.[113] It is for the defendant to show the overriding public interest. The Union Courts will inquire whether the public interest was overriding.[114] Schonberg has argued that the Union Courts 'will restrict the application of a policy change if there is a *significant imbalance* between the interests of those affected and the policy considerations in favour of the change'.[115] There is force in this view, but the difference between this and a test of proportionality is not clear. Given that proportionality is used to determine whether infringement of a right can be justified, it could also be used to decide whether the trumping of an expectation is warranted.[116]

Finally, the mere fact that an EU decision is unlawful will not necessarily prevent the individual from claiming a legitimate expectation.[117] Unreasonable delay by the administration can operate as a bar to the revocation of an unlawful administrative act.[118] The Union Courts balance the public interest in legality and the private interest in legal certainty. The former does not always trump the latter.[119] The position is however different in relation to unlawful representations, as opposed to unlawful decisions. The former have been held not to generate any legitimate expectations.[120] The Union Courts have provided no explanation for their differential treatment of unlawful decisions and unlawful representations.

---

[110] Cases 46 and 151/98 *Council of European Municipalities and Regions v Commission* [2000] ECR II–167.

[111] Case 74/74 *CNTA SA v Commission* [1975] ECR 533.

[112] Ibid [42].

[113] Craig (n 4) ch 18.

[114] See, eg, Case 74/74 *CNTA* (n 111) [43]; Case C–189/89 *Spagl v Hauptzollamt Rosenheim* [1990] ECR I–4539; Case C–183/95 *Affish BV v Rijksdienst voor de keuring van Vee en Vlees* [1997] ECR I–4315; Case T–155/99 *Dieckmann & Hansen GmbH v Commission* [2001] ECR II–3143.

[115] Schonberg (n 81) 150. Italics in the original.

[116] The UK courts have used proportionality in these circumstances: *Nadarajah v Secretary of State for the Home Department* [2005] EWCA Civ 1363, [68].

[117] Schwarze (n 43) 991–1025; Craig (n 4) ch 18.

[118] Case 15/85 *Consorzio Cooperative d'Abruzzo v Commission* [1987] ECR 1005.

[119] Cases 42 and 49/59 *SNUPAT v High Authority* [1961] ECR 53; Case 14/61 *Hoogovens v High Authority* [1962] ECR 253.

[120] Case 188/82 *Thyssen AG v Commission* [1983] ECR 3721, [11]; Case T–2/93 *Air France v Commission* [1994] ECR II–323, [101]–[102].

(D) GENERAL PRINCIPLES OF LAW: NON-DISCRIMINATION

Equality and non-discrimination are universally recognized principles,[121] but the legal concept of discrimination can be problematic in its application. It is necessary to decide whether people are similarly situated such that a difference in treatment is discriminatory, and whether that apparent difference in treatment can be justified. These difficulties will be explored in later chapters.[122]

(i) *Treaty Foundations*

The principle of non-discrimination, although a general principle and therefore binding on both the EU and the Member States when acting in the scope of application of EU law, is expressly mentioned in a number of Treaty Articles.

i. Equality and non-discrimination are foundational values of the EU: Articles 2 and 3(3) TEU.

ii. There is a general prohibition on non-discrimination on grounds of nationality in Article 18 TFEU, which is reiterated in the free movement context in Articles 45, 49, and 56–57 TFEU.

iii. Equal treatment of men and women is covered in Articles 2 and 3(3) TEU, and in Article 157 TFEU.

iv. Non-discrimination as between producers or consumers in the field of agriculture is dealt with by Article 40(2) TFEU.

v. There are also specific provisions such as Article 110 TFEU, prohibiting discriminatory taxation.

vi. Article 19(1) TFEU,[123] the successor to Article 13 EC, empowers the EU, through a special legislative procedure, to take appropriate action to combat discrimination based on sex, racial or ethnic origin, religion or belief, disability, age, or sexual orientation.[124] Article 19(2) TFEU empowers the EU to adopt non-harmonizing 'incentive measures' by the ordinary legislative procedure. Directives prohibiting discrimination on grounds of race or ethnic origin,[125] and on grounds of religion, belief, disability, age, or sexual orientation in the field of employment,[126] were adopted in 2000. In the same year, an action programme to combat discrimination on all the grounds listed in Article 19 (other than sex) was adopted,[127] and the Commission announced a policy of 'mainstreaming' so as to integrate anti-discrimination considerations such as race and disability in particular into other areas of EU policy formation.[128]

vii. Article 21(1) of the Charter of Fundamental Rights provides that any discrimination based on any ground such as sex, race, colour, ethnic or social origin, genetic features, language,

---

[121] G More, 'The Principle of Equal Treatment: from Market Unifier to Fundamental Right' in P Craig and G de Búrca (eds), *The Evolution of EU Law* (Oxford University Press, 1999) ch 14.

[122] See Chs 21, 22, 24. See, eg, Case C–132/92 *Roberts v Birds Eye Walls Ltd* [1993] ECR I–5579, and on goods see Case C–2/90 *Commission v Belgium (Walloon Waste)* [1992] ECR I–4431, later criticized by AG Jacobs in Case C–379/98 *PreussenElektra AG v Schleswag AG* [2001] ECR I–2099 for the ECJ's reasoning on discrimination.

[123] M Bell, 'The New Article 13 EC Treaty: A Sound Basis for European Anti-Discrimination Law?' (1999) 6 MJ 5; L Waddington, 'Testing the Limits of the EC Treaty Article on Non-Discrimination' (1999) 28 ILJ 133.

[124] M Bell, *Anti-Discrimination Law and the EU* (Oxford University Press, 2002).

[125] Council Directive 2000/43/EC of 29 June 2000 implementing the principle of equal treatment between persons irrespective of racial or ethnic origin [2000] OJ L180/22.

[126] Council Directive 2000/78/EC of 27 November 2000 establishing a general framework for equal treatment in employment and occupation [2000] OJ L303/16.

[127] Council Decision 2000/750/EC of 27 November 2000 establishing a Community action programme to combat discrimination (2001 to 2006) [2000] OJ L303/23.

[128] M Bell, 'Mainstreaming Equality Norms into EU Asylum Law' (2001) 26 ELRev 20.

religion or belief, political or any other opinion, membership of a national minority, property, birth, disability, age, or sexual orientation shall be prohibited. This provision establishes a broad general principle of non-discrimination with an open-ended list of prohibited grounds.

(ii) *Non Discrimination as a 'General' Principle of EU Law*

While the principle of equality and the prohibition of discrimination are therefore found expressly within a number of Treaty Articles,[129] the ECJ held at an early stage that these were merely specific enunciations of the general principle of equality as one of the fundamental principles of EU law,[130] which must be observed by any court.[131] The principle has been applied by the ECJ where there has been arbitrary or unjustifiably unequal treatment of two persons within an area of EU competence,[132] such as in the context of staff policy.[133]

The reach of this general principle can nonetheless be contentious, as exemplified by the case law on discrimination and sexual orientation.[134] The Advocates General in *P v S*[135] and *Grant*[136] argued that, prior to the enactment of what was Article 13 EC, the general principles of Community law imposed a requirement on the EC institutions and the Member States not to discriminate within the areas covered by Community law on arbitrary grounds, such as sexual orientation or gender reassignment. The Court in *P v S* held that Directive 76/207 on equal treatment of men and women in employment was simply the expression, in the relevant field, of the principle of equality, which was a fundamental principle of Community law.

The ECJ was more conservative in *Grant* concerning travel benefits for the same-sex partners of employees. It retreated from this broad principle of equality and decided that discrimination on grounds of sex in EC law did not cover discrimination on grounds of sexual orientation.[137] The Court ruled that ensuring respect for fundamental rights could not extend the scope of the Treaty provisions, which at the time required Member States only to ensure sex equality in employment, beyond the competences of the Community.

The ruling in *D v Council*[138] appeared to reinforce the cautious approach taken in *Grant*. In *D* there was no doubt about competence, since the case concerned the EU's treatment of its own employees. The case concerned the EU's refusal to pay a staff household allowance, which would have been payable to a married employee, to a homosexual employee who was in a stable partnership registered under Swedish law. The Court denied that there had been any discrimination on grounds of sex, and then held, somewhat obscurely, in relation to the claim that there had been discrimination on grounds of sexual orientation, that it was not the sex of the partner that determined whether the household allowance was granted, but the legal nature of the ties between the official and the partner. Thus, while ruling that there had been no unequal treatment on grounds of sexual orientation the Court did not

---

[129] K Lenaerts, 'L'Egalité de Traitement en Droit Communautaire' (1991) 27 CDE 3.

[130] Cases 117/76 and 16/77 *Ruckdeschel v Hauptzollamt Hamburg-St Annen* [1977] ECR 1753, [7].

[131] Case 8/78 *Milac GmbH v Hauptzollamt Freiburg* [1978] ECR 1721, [18]; Case C–442/00 *Caballero v Fondo de Garantía Salarial (Fogasa)* [2002] ECR I–11915, [30]–[32].

[132] Case C–144/04 *Mangold v Helm* [2005] ECR I–9981; Case C–555/07 *Seda Kücükdeveci v Swedex GmbH & Co KG* [2010] ECR I–365.

[133] Cases 75 and 117/82 *Razzouk and Beydoun v Commission* [1984] ECR 1509, [16]–[17]; Case 20/71 *Sabbatini* [1972] ECR 345, [3]; and Case 149/77 *Defrenne v Sabena* [1978] ECR 1365, [26]–[27].

[134] For more detailed treatment in the context of fundamental rights see Ch 11.

[135] Case C–13/94 *P v S and Cornwall County Council* [1996] ECR I–2143, AG Tesauro.

[136] Case C–249/96 *Grant v South-West Trains Ltd* [1998] ECR I–621, AG Elmer.

[137] Ibid [42].

[138] Cases C–122 and 125/99 P *D and Sweden v Council* [2001] ECR I–4319.

actually deny the possible existence of a general principle of EC law prohibiting discrimination on grounds of sexual orientation within its field of application.[139]

(iii) *Justifying Discrimination*

To discriminate means to differentiate or to treat differently. In EU law discrimination on one of the prohibited grounds is impermissible when done without adequate justification, or when there is no relevant difference between two people or situations that would justify a difference in their treatment. These are not easy criteria to apply, since it is not always clear which factors may be taken into account in determining whether two people are 'similarly situated'. Nor is it clear whether, if differences in situation are taken into account to justify discriminatory treatment, this should be seen as a form of justified 'positive discrimination' or should be seen as not discriminatory at all.[140]

A straightforward example of discrimination on grounds of sex would be where a woman was paid a lower wage than a man for doing the same job, and a simple example of nationality discrimination would be where a UK employer refused to hire any employee who was not British. The more difficult situations arise where the discrimination is neither clear nor direct, but is indirect and disguised, or is unintentional but nonetheless discriminatory in its impact. Indirect and disguised discrimination would occur if, for example, a UK employer claimed to hire workers of any nationality so long as they had received their education in the UK, since in practice this requirement would not be fulfilled by most non-UK nationals. Indirect sex discrimination may occur where an employer pays part-time workers less per hour than full-time workers, where the overwhelming majority of part-time workers are women.[141]

In EU law, direct or deliberate disguised discrimination on grounds of sex or nationality is prohibited, subject to fairly limited exceptions, whereas indirect and unintentional discrimination may be justified on a variety of non-exhaustive grounds.[142] Thus in the context of nationality discrimination, a language requirement which is indirectly discriminatory may be justified if it is proportionate and genuinely required for the job.[143] Similarly in the context of sex discrimination, the payment of a higher hourly wage to full-time than to part-time workers may, even where it indirectly discriminates against women, be 'objectively justified' on grounds relating to the needs of the employer.[144] Indirect discrimination was expressly defined for the first time in the context of sex discrimination in the Burden of Proof Directive in 1997,[145] and differently again in the anti-discrimination directives adopted under what was Article 13 EC.[146] In addition to the 'objective justification' requirements, the Directives permitted other specific exceptions to the general non-discrimination principle.

---

[139] See also Case C–423/04 *Richards v Secretary of State for Work and Pensions* [2006] ECR I–3585.

[140] See, eg, Case C–132/92 *Roberts* (n 122); Case C–450/93 *Kalanke v Freie Hansestadt Bremen* [1995] ECR I–3051; Case C–409/95 *Hellmut Marschall v Land Nordrhein-Westfalen* [1997] ECR I–6363.

[141] See Ch 24.

[142] See Chs 21, 22, 23, 24.

[143] Ch 21.

[144] Ch 24.

[145] Council Directive 97/80/EC of 15 December 1997 on the burden of proof in cases of discrimination based on sex [1998] OJ L14/6, Art 2(2).

[146] Council Dir 2000/43/EC (n 125) Art 2(2)(b); Council Dir 2000/78/EC (n 126) Art 2(2)(b).

(E) GENERAL PRINCIPLES OF LAW: TRANSPARENCY

(i) *Development*

Transparency encompasses a number of features, such as the holding of meetings in public, the provision of information, and the right of access to documents.[147] Whether or not transparency can be counted as a general principle of EU law will be considered in due course.

Transparency became of increased importance in EU law after the Maastricht Treaty.[148] The early years of the EEC were weak in terms of democracy, accountability, and accessibility to public scrutiny. There was a greater focus on transparency in the 1990s, not least as a result of the near failure to have the TEU ratified in Denmark and France. This was particularly apparent during the IGC preceding the Amsterdam Treaty.[149] Moreover, a number of Member States, such as the Netherlands, Denmark, and Sweden, increasingly objected to the secrecy surrounding the Council of Ministers, and were dissatisfied with the steps which the Council had taken.[150] The 1993 Inter-Institutional Declaration on Democracy, Transparency and Subsidiarity provided further impetus for reform.[151] The Council and Commission adopted a joint Code of Conduct on access to documents in 1993,[152] which was implemented into their rules of procedure by decision.[153] In 2001 a regulation on access to documents was adopted, which is analysed below.

The European Council agreed an overall policy on transparency in June 2006.[154] All Council deliberations on legislative acts to be adopted by co-decision were, in principle, to be open to the public, as were the votes and explanations of votes by Council members. So too were the initial deliberations on legislative acts other than those adopted by co-decision presented orally by the Commission, with the possibility of subsequent deliberations also being open to the public. The debate on the Commission's annual work programme was also open to the public.

The Commission launched a European Transparency Initiative in 2005.[155] It has brought together a range of issues dealing with transparency including:[156] access to documents; separate registers relating to Comitology, experts, and interest representatives; civil society; and consultation. It includes a transparency register that reveals what interests are being pursued, by whom, and with what budgets. The system is operated jointly by the European Parliament and the European Commission.[157]

---

[147] http://ec.europa.eu/transparency/index_en.htm.

[148] S Peers, 'From Maastricht to Laeken: The Political Agenda of Openness and Transparency in the EU' in V Deckmyn (ed), *Increasing Transparency in the European Union* (EIPA, 2002); A Tomkins, 'Transparency and the Emergence of a European Administrative Law' (1999–2000) 19 YBEL 217.

[149] J Lodge, 'Transparency and Democratic Legitimacy' (1994) 32 JCMS 343; G de Búrca, 'The Quest for Legitimacy in the European Union' (1996) 59 MLR 359.

[150] D Curtin, 'Betwixt and Between: Democracy and Transparency in the Governance of the European Union' in J Winter *et al* (eds), *Reforming the Treaty on European Union: The Legal Debate* (Kluwer, 1996) 95; D Curtin, 'Citizens' Fundamental Right of Access to EU Information: An Evolving Digital Passepartout?' (2000) 37 CMLRev 7.

[151] M Westlake, *The Commission and the Parliament: Partners and Rivals in the European Policy-Making Process* (Butterworths, 1994) 159–161.

[152] Code of Conduct Concerning Access to Council and Commission Documents [1993] OJ L340/41.

[153] Council Decision 93/731/EC of 20 December on public access to Council documents [1993] OJ L340/43; Commission Decision 94/90/ECSC, EC, Euratom of 8 February 1994 on public access to Commission documents [1994] OJ L46/58.

[154] Brussels European Council, 15–16 June 2006, Annex 1.

[155] http://ec.europa.eu/archives/transparency/eti/index_en.htm.

[156] http://ec.europa.eu/transparency/index_en.htm.

[157] http://ec.europa.eu/transparencyregister/public/homePage.do.

(ii) *Lisbon Treaty and EU Legislation*

The Lisbon Treaty makes provision for transparency in a number of ways. The relevant provisions are found in the TEU and the TFEU.

i. Article 1 TEU states that the Lisbon Treaty 'marks a new stage in the process of creating an ever closer union among the peoples of Europe, in which decisions are taken as openly as possible and as closely as possible to the citizen'. This is reiterated in Article 10(3) TEU, which provides that every citizen has the right to participate in the democratic life of the Union, and that decisions shall be taken as openly and as closely as possible to the citizen.

ii. Article 11(2) TEU states that the EU institutions shall maintain an open, transparent, and regular dialogue with representative associations and civil society. This is reinforced by Article 15(1) TFEU, which states that in order to promote good governance and ensure the participation of civil society, the Union's institutions, bodies, offices, and agencies shall conduct their work as openly as possible.

iii. Article 11(3) TEU requires the Commission to carry out broad consultations with the parties concerned in order to ensure that the Union's actions are coherent and transparent.

iv. Article 16(8) TEU imposes an obligation on the Council to meet in public when it deliberates and votes on a draft legislative act. Article 15(2) TFEU renders the EP subject to the same duty.

v. Article 15(3) TFEU[158] deals with access to documents.

> 3. Any citizen of the Union, and any natural or legal person residing or having its registered office in a Member State, shall have a right of access to documents of the Union's institutions, bodies, offices and agencies, whatever their medium, subject to the principles and the conditions to be defined in accordance with this paragraph. General principles and limits on grounds of public or private interest governing this right of access to documents shall be determined by the European Parliament and the Council, by means of regulations, acting in accordance with the ordinary legislative procedure.
>
> Each institution, body, office or agency shall ensure that its proceedings are transparent and shall elaborate in its own Rules of Procedure specific provisions regarding access to its documents, in accordance with the regulations referred to in the second subparagraph.
>
> The Court of Justice of the European Union, the European Central Bank and the European Investment Bank shall be subject to this paragraph only when exercising their administrative tasks.
>
> The European Parliament and the Council shall ensure publication of the documents relating to the legislative procedures under the terms laid down by the regulations referred to in the second subparagraph.

vi. Transparency is also relevant for the Member States. Thus, for example, Treaty Articles on free movement carry an obligation of equal treatment and this has been held to generate an obligation of transparency.[159]

vii. EU legislation frequently imposes an obligation of transparency on EU institutions and/or Member States.

---

[158] Art 255 EC, the predecessor to Art 15(3) TFEU, was held to lack direct effect in Case T–191/99 *Petrie v Commission* [2001] ECR II–3677.

[159] See, eg, Case C–260/04 *Commission v Italy* [2007] ECR I–7083; Case C–203/08 *Sporting Exchange Ltd v Minister van Justitie* [2010] ECR I–4695; Case T–402/06 *Spain v Commission* EU:T:2013:445.

viii. There can be clashes between transparency and Charter rights, such as the protection of personal data.[160]

(iii) *Transparency and Access to Documents*

Access to documents is an important aspect of transparency. The Community enacted a regulation pursuant to Article 255 EC, the predecessor to Article 15(3) TFEU, in 2001,[161] following a number of earlier more specific decisions. Regulation 1049/2001 improved the position on access to documents in several respects, by for example softening the nature of some of the exceptions and requiring a register of documents to be kept.[162] The legislation was implemented by the three EU institutions into their own rules of procedure,[163] and has been applied to EU agencies.[164] The right of access to documents is also enshrined in Article 42 of the Charter of Fundamental Rights.[165]

The European Ombudsman has been central to the development of openness and transparency as broader principles of law.[166] He undertook an own-initiative inquiry into public access to documents addressed to fifteen Community institutions other than the Council and Commission.[167] The Ombudsman concluded that failure to adopt rules governing public access to documents and to make those rules easily available to the public constituted maladministration. The consequence was that most other important EU bodies including the Court of Auditors, the ECB, and agencies adopted rules governing access to documents. The Ombudsman has moreover provided guidance on access to information via the Code of Good Administrative Behaviour.[168]

(iv) *Transparency, Access to Documents, and the Courts*

The ECJ and CFI were generally supportive of transparency even before the Treaty of Amsterdam reforms, but they refrained from far-reaching statements of principle that would enshrine a general right of transparency or access to information. The CFI stressed in *Carvel*[169] that when the Council exercised its discretion whether to release documents it had genuinely to balance the interests of citizens in gaining access to documents with the need to maintain confidentiality of its deliberations. It could not simply adopt a general blanket denial of access to a class of documents.

[160] Cases C–92 and 93/09 *Volker und Markus Schecke GbR and Hartmut Eifert v Land Hessen* [2010] ECR I–11063.

[161] Regulation (EC) 1049/2001 of the European Parliament and of the Council of 30 May 2001 regarding public access to European Parliament, Council and Commission Documents [2001] OJ L145/43.

[162] S Peers, 'The New Regulation on Access to Documents: A Critical Analysis' (2002) 21 YBEL 385; M Broberg, 'Access to Documents: A General Principle of Community Law' (2002) 27 ELRev 194; M de Leeuw, 'The Regulation on Public Access to European Parliament, Council and Commission Documents in the European Union: Are Citizens Better Off?' (2003) 28 ELRev 324.

[163] Council Decision 2002/682/EC, Euratom of 22 July 2002 adopting the Council's Rules of Procedure [2002] OJ L230/7; Commission Decision 2001/937/EC, ECSC, Euratom of 5 December 2001 amending its Rules of Procedure [2001] OJ L345/94.

[164] K Lenaerts, '"In the Union we Trust": Trust Enhancing Principles of Community Law' (2004) 41 CMLRev 317, 321.

[165] [2000] OJ C364/19.

[166] I Harden, 'The European Ombudsman's Efforts to Increase Openness in the Union' in V Deckmyn (ed), *Increasing Transparency in the European Union* (EIPA, 2002) 123.

[167] (616/PUBAC/F/IJH) [1998] OJ C44/9.

[168] European Ombudsman, *European Code of Good Administrative Behaviour*, available at www.ombudsman. europa.eu/en/resources/code.faces.

[169] Case T–194/94 *Carvel and Guardian Newspapers Ltd v Council* [1995] ECR II–2765; Case T–105/95 *WWF UK (World Wide Fund for Nature) v Commission* [1997] ECR II–313.

In *Netherlands v Council*[170] the Dutch Government argued that the principle of openness of the legislative process was an essential requirement of democracy, and that the right of access to information was an internationally recognized fundamental human right. The ECJ confirmed the importance of the right of public access to information and its relationship to the democratic nature of the institutions, but rejected the argument that such a fundamental right should not be dealt with purely as a matter of the Council's internal Rules of Procedure.

In *Hautala*, the ECJ upheld the CFI's decision to annul the Council's refusal to consider granting partial access to politically sensitive documents, but the ECJ declared that it was not necessary for it to pronounce on whether or not EC law recognized a general 'principle of the right to information'.[171]

Nonetheless, despite the failure to articulate a general principle of transparency or a general right of access to information, the Courts played a significant role in elaborating the content of the right of access to information contained in the procedural rules and legislative decisions of the institutions. Thus the CFI and the ECJ annulled a number of decisions of the Council and Commission refusing access to their documents, not on the ground that the institutions had breached a 'general principle of transparency', but on other grounds such as the automatic application of non-mandatory exceptions, the inappropriate use of the authorship rule, the refusal to consider partial access, or the inadequacy of the reasons given for refusal.[172]

(v) *Transparency, Regulation 1049/2001, and the Courts*

The detailed regime for access to documentation is governed by Regulation 1049/2001.[173] It contains provisions defining the institutions covered, the meaning of the term document, the beneficiaries of the scheme, and the exceptions that limit access.

The EU Courts have been willing to protect the reality of access, as exemplified by *Hautala*.[174] This was evident once again in *Verein für Konsumenteninformation*.[175] The applicant sought access to documents held by the Commission concerning a cartel in the banking sector, in order to pursue legal actions in Austria for customers who might have been charged excessive rates of interest. The file was large and the Commission denied the request, stating that partial access was not possible since detailed examination of each document would entail excessive work. The CFI held that the Regulation required the Commission in principle to carry out an individual assessment of the documents requested, except where it was manifestly clear that access should be refused or granted. The refusal to undertake any concrete assessment was therefore manifestly disproportionate.[176]

---

[170] Case C–58/94 *Netherlands v Council* [1996] ECR I–2169, [31]–[36].

[171] Case C–353/99 P *Hautala v Council* [2001] ECR I–9565, [31].

[172] See, eg, Case T–105/95 *WWF* (n 169); Case T–188/97 *Rothmans International v Commission* [1999] ECR II–2463; Case T–174/95 *Svenska Journalistförbundet v Council* [1998] ECR II–2289; Case C–353/99 P *Kuijer v Council* [2000] ECR II–1959; Case T–211/00 *Kuijer v Council* [2002] ECR II–485.

[173] On the Implementation of the Principles in EC Regulation 1049/2001 Regarding Public Access to European Parliament, Council and Commission Documents, COM(2004) 45 final; J Heliskoski and P Leino, 'Darkness at the Break of Noon: The Case Law on Regulation No. 1049/2001 on Access to Documents' (2006) 43 CMLRev 735.

[174] Case C–353/99 P *Hautala* (n 171). See also Case C–41/00 P *Interporc Im- und Export GmbH v Commission* [2003] ECR I–2125, [42]–[44]; Case C–353/01 P *Mattila v Commission* [2004] ECR I–1073, [30]–[32]; Cases T–355 and 446/04 *Co-Frutta Soc coop v European Commission* [2010] ECR II–1, [124]; Case T–300/10 *Internationaler Hilfsfonds eV v European Commission* EU:T:2012:247, [90]–[91]; Case T–380/08 *Netherlands v Commission* EU:T:2013:480, [92]; Case T–301/10 *Sophie in 't Veld v European Commission* EU:T:2013:135, [107], [200]; Case C–127/13 P *Strack v Commission* EU:C:2014:2250, [24]–[31].

[175] Case T–2/03 *Verein für Konsumenteninformation v Commission* [2005] ECR II–1121.

[176] Ibid [100]. The CFI acknowledged that there could be cases where, because of the number of documents requested, the Commission had to retain the right to balance the interest in public access against the burden of work in order to safeguard the interests of good administration. This possibility was however applicable only in exceptional cases.

The CFI acknowledged that the relevant file was large, but nonetheless annulled the Commission's decision.[177]

The effectiveness of any regime for access to information is crucially affected by the exceptions contained in the legislation and their judicial interpretation. The exceptions in Regulation 1049/2001 are listed in Article 4. Most are qualified by provisions allowing access even if the document relates to a protected interest, provided that there is an overriding public interest in disclosure.[178] There are, however, some exceptions that are mandatory: access is prohibited where disclosure would undermine the relevant interest, with no provision allowing access on grounds of public interest.[179]

The Union Courts exercise control in a number of ways. They can determine the legal standard of review; they can decide on the legal meaning of an exception; and they can adjudicate on whether the public interest warranted disclosure. The Union Courts state repeatedly that the exceptions should be interpreted narrowly. There are, however, contestable decisions, where the Union Courts have used the juridical techniques at their disposal sparingly to say the least.

The *Sison* case concerned the standard of judicial review.[180] The ECJ's decision as to the limited scope of review made it difficult for the claimant to succeed.

Case C–266/05 P **Jose Maria Sison v Council**
[2007] ECR I–1233

The applicant's assets were frozen pursuant to a regulation to combat terrorism and he sought access to documentation that had placed him on the relevant list. The Council refused access relying on Article 4(1)(a) of Regulation 1049/2001, on the ground that it would undermine public security and international relations.

THE ECJ

34. Contrary to the appellant's submission, the Court of First Instance, in line with that case-law, correctly held...as regards the scope of the judicial review of the legality of a decision of the Council refusing public access to a document on the basis of one of the exceptions relating to the public interest provided for in Article 4(1)(a) of Regulation No 1049/2001, that the Council must be recognised as enjoying a wide discretion for the purpose of determining whether the disclosure of documents relating to the fields covered by those exceptions could undermine the public interest. The Court of First Instance also correctly held...that the Community Court's review of the legality of such a decision must therefore be limited to verifying whether the procedural rules and the duty to state reasons have been complied with, whether the facts have been accurately stated, and whether there has been a manifest error of assessment or a misuse of powers.

35. In the first place, it must be accepted that the particularly sensitive and essential nature of the interests protected by Article 4(1)(a) of Regulation No 1049/2001, combined with the fact that access must be refused by the institution, under that provision, if disclosure of a document to the public would undermine those interests, confers on the decision which must thus be adopted by the institution a

---

[177] The obligation to assess each document will not however apply where it is clear that access to the file via Reg 1049/2001 conflicts with the policy underlying a different reg: Case C–139/07 P *European Commission v Technische Glaswerke Ilmenau GmbH* [2010] ECR I–5885, [61]–[63].

[178] Reg 1049/2001 (n 161) Art 4(2)–(3).

[179] Ibid Art 4(1).

[180] See also Cases T–391/03 and 70/04 *Franchet and Byk v Commission* [2006] ECR II–2023; Case T–264/04 *WWF European Policy Programme v Council* [2007] ECR II–911; Cases T–355 and 446/04 *Co-Frutta* (n 174).

complex and delicate nature which calls for the exercise of particular care. Such a decision requires, therefore, a margin of appreciation.

36. Secondly, the criteria set out in Article 4(1)(a) of Regulation No 1049/2001 are very general, since access must be refused, as is clear from the wording of that provision, if disclosure of the document concerned would 'undermine' the protection of the 'public interest' as regards, inter alia, 'public security' or 'international relations'.

37. In that regard, it is clear from an examination of the preparatory documents which preceded the adoption of that regulation that various proposals intended to define more precisely the scope of the public-interest exceptions to which Article 4(1)(a) of that regulation refers, which would undoubtedly have enabled the opportunities for judicial review in regard to the institution's assessment to be correspondingly increased, were not accepted.

. . .

46. Moreover, it is clear from the wording of Article 4(1)(a) of Regulation No 1049/2001 that, as regards the exceptions to the right of access provided for by that provision, refusal of access by the institution is mandatory where disclosure of a document to the public would undermine the interests which that provision protects, without the need, in such a case and in contrast to the provisions, in particular, of Article 4(2), to balance the requirements connected to the protection of those interests against those which stem from other interests.

47. It follows from the foregoing that...the particular interest of an applicant in obtaining access to documents cannot be taken into account by the institution called upon to rule on the question whether the disclosure to the public of those documents would undermine the interests protected by Article 4(1)(a) of Regulation No 1049/2001 and to refuse, if that is the case, the access requested.

Sison has however been qualified by subsequent case law, where the CJEU stressed in *Access Info Europe* that it was incumbent on an institution that sought to rely on an exception to explain how disclosure of the document could specifically and actually undermine the interest protected by the exception, and the risk of the interest being undermined had to be reasonably foreseeable and could not be purely hypothetical.[181]

In *Sweden v Commission*[182] it was the legal meaning of an exception to Regulation 1049/2001 that came before the ECJ, and its judgment was more liberal than that of the CFI. The CFI[183] held that Article 4(5) of Regulation 1049/2001, which provides that a Member State may request the Union institution not to disclose a document originating from that Member State without its prior agreement, constituted an instruction from the Member State to the EU institution not to disclose the relevant document. The ECJ on appeal decided that Article 4(5) did not confer on the Member State a general and unconditional right of veto. Article 4(5) must, said the ECJ, be delimited by Article 4(1)–(3), such that the Member State was afforded the opportunity to show why its documents fell within those exceptions. If the Member State felt that this was so there should be a dialogue between it and the EU institutions, in which it was for the Member State to provide reasons to show why the document came within Article 4(1)–(3). It was then for the relevant EU institution to record these reasons, so that an individual seeking access could understand why it had been denied, which would also facilitate any subsequent legal challenge.

---

181 Case C–280/11 P *Council v Access Info Europe* EU:C:2013:671, [31]; Case C–350/12 P *Council v Sophie in 't Veld* EU:C:2014:2039, [52], [64].

182 Case C–64/05 P *Sweden v Commission* [2007] ECR II–11389; Case C–506/08 P *Sweden v MyTravel and Commission* [2011] ECR I–6237, [72]; Case T–545/11 *Stichting Greenpeace Nederland v European Commission* EU:T:2013:523, [27]–[33].

183 Case 168/02 *IFAW Internationaler Tierschutz-Fonds GmbH v Commission* [2004] ECR II–4135.

The *Turco* case concerned the legal meaning of an exception and the judicial approach to the balancing test.[184] The ECJ was again more liberal than the CFI.[185]

Cases C–39 and 52/05 P **Sweden and Turco v Council**
[2008] ECR I–4723

The case concerned the exception for legal advice contained in Regulation 1049/2001,[186] which provides that the institutions shall refuse access to a document where disclosure would undermine the protection of court proceedings and legal advice, unless there is an overriding public interest in disclosure. Turco was refused access to documents from the Council legal service relating to a proposed directive on asylum.

THE ECJ

42. [T]he exception relating to legal advice...must be construed as aiming to protect an institution's interest in seeking legal advice and receiving frank, objective and comprehensive advice.

43. The risk of that interest being undermined must, in order to be capable of being relied on, be reasonably foreseeable and not purely hypothetical.

44. [I]f the Council takes the view that disclosure of a document would undermine the protection of legal advice as defined above, it is incumbent on the Council to ascertain whether there is any overriding public interest justifying disclosure despite the fact that its ability to seek legal advice and receive frank, objective and comprehensive advice would thereby be undermined.

45. In that respect, it is for the Council to balance the particular interest to be protected by non-disclosure of the document concerned against, inter alia, the public interest in the document being made accessible in the light of the advantages stemming...from increased openness, in that this enables citizens to participate more closely in the decision-making process and guarantees that the administration enjoys greater legitimacy and is more effective and more accountable to the citizen in a democratic system.

46. Those considerations are clearly of particular relevance where the Council is acting in its legislative capacity, as is apparent from recital 6 of the preamble to Regulation No 1049/2001, according to which wider access must be granted to documents in precisely such cases. Openness in that respect contributes to strengthening democracy by allowing citizens to scrutinize all the information which has formed the basis of a legislative act. The possibility for citizens to find out the considerations underpinning legislative action is a precondition for the effective exercise of their democratic rights.

...

49. If the Council decides to refuse access to a document which it has been asked to disclose, it must explain, first, how access to that document could specifically and effectively undermine the interest protected by an exception laid down in Article 4...and, secondly, in the situations referred to in Article 4(2) and (3) of that regulation, whether or not there is an overriding public interest that might nevertheless justify disclosure of the document concerned.

---

[184] See also Case T–403/05 *My Travel Group plc v Commission* [2008] ECR II–2027; Cases C–514, 528 and 532/07 *Sweden v API and Commission* [2010] ECR I–8533; Case T–471/08 *Toland v European Parliament* [2011] ECR II–2717; Case C–280/11 P *Access Info Europe* (n 181) [27]–[31]; Cases C–514 and 605/11 *LPN and Finland v European Commission* EU:C:2013:738, [44]–[45]; Case C–365/12 P *European Commission v EnBW Energie Baden-Württemberg AG* EU:C:2014:112, [64]–[65].

[185] Case T–84/03 *Turco v Council* [2004] ECR II–4061.

[186] Reg 1049/2001 (n 161) Art 4(2).

50. It is, in principle, open to the Council to base its decisions in that regard on general presumptions which apply to certain categories of documents, as considerations of a generally similar kind are likely to apply to requests for disclosure relating to documents of the same nature. However, it is incumbent on the Council to establish in each case whether the general considerations normally applicable to a particular type of document are in fact applicable to a specific document which it has been asked to disclose.

...

59. As regards, first, the fear expressed by the Council that disclosure of an opinion of its legal service relating to a legislative proposal could lead to doubts as to the lawfulness of the legislative act concerned, it is precisely openness in this regard that contributes to conferring greater legitimacy on the institutions in the eyes of European citizens and increasing their confidence in them by allowing divergences between various points of view to be openly debated...

...

62. As regards, secondly, the Council's argument that the independence of its legal service would be compromised by possible disclosure of legal opinions issued in the course of legislative procedures, it must be pointed out that that fear lies at the very heart of the interests protected by the exception provided for in the second indent of Article 4(2) of Regulation No 1049/2001. As is apparent from paragraph 42 of this judgment, that exception seeks specifically to protect an institution's interest in seeking legal advice and receiving frank, objective and comprehensive advice.

63. However, in that regard, the Council relied before both the Court of First Instance and the Court on mere assertions, which were in no way substantiated by detailed arguments. In view of the considerations which follow, there would appear to be no real risk that is reasonably foreseeable and not purely hypothetical of that interest being undermined.

64. As regards the possibility of pressure being applied for the purpose of influencing the content of opinions issued by the Council's legal service, it need merely be pointed out that even if the members of that legal service were subjected to improper pressure to that end, it would be that pressure, and not the possibility of the disclosure of legal opinions, which would compromise that institution's interest in receiving frank, objective and comprehensive advice and it would clearly be incumbent on the Council to take the necessary measures to put a stop to it.

The 2001 Regulation was undoubtedly a step forward compared to the pre-existing position, but there was nonetheless concern about its scope and the exceptions. In 2008, the Commission proposed a modified regulation on access to documents,[187] but the European Parliament was not happy with the proposal and suggested numerous amendments.[188] The proposal is currently stalled, and it remains to be seen whether a new regulation emerges and, if so, what form it takes.[189]

(vi) *Conclusion*

Developments such as Treaty Articles on transparency, Regulation 1049/2001, and Article 42 of the Charter of Fundamental Rights led Judge Lenaerts, writing extra-judicially, to conclude that 'it can at present hardly be denied that the principle of transparency has evolved into a general principle of Community law'.[190] This view is reinforced by the ECJ's greater willingness to read EU legislation as subject to transparency, even where there is no explicit mention of this principle in the relevant

[187] Regarding Public Access to European Parliament, Council and Commission documents, COM(2008) 229 final.

[188] On the proposal for a reg of the European Parliament and of the Council regarding public access to European Parliament, Council, and Commission documents, A6–0077/2009, Rapporteur Michael Cashman; T6–0114/2009, PE439/989, 12 May 2010, Rapporteur Michael Cashman.

[189] For detailed analysis see the Statewatch website, www.statewatch.org/foi/observatory–access–reg-2008-2009. htm; European Union Committee, Access to EU Documents, 15th Report 2008–9, HL Paper 108.

[190] Lenaerts (n 164).

articles of the legislation.[191] Even if transparency is regarded as a general principle of EU law, the impact of this on citizens will be crucially dependent on the detailed meaning accorded to the principle. In the post-Lisbon world it remains to be seen how the Treaty provisions dealing with transparency are interpreted both politically and legally.

(F) GENERAL PRINCIPLES OF LAW: PRECAUTIONARY PRINCIPLE

Risk regulation is an important part of the EU's activities, and this often has to be undertaken under conditions of scientific uncertainty. Article 191(2) TFEU mentions the precautionary principle in relation to environmental decision-making, and Article 11 TFEU mandates that environmental protection requirements must be integrated into other EU policies. The EU Courts have however elevated the precautionary principle into a general principle of EU law.

The foundations were laid by the ECJ. In the *BSE* case[192] the UK challenged the legality of a Commission decision banning export of beef from the UK in the wake of mad cow disease. The ECJ stated that when the contested decision was adopted there was great uncertainty as to the risks posed by such produce, and held that 'where there is uncertainty as to the existence or extent of risks to human health, the institutions may take protective measures without having to wait until the reality and seriousness of those risks become apparent'.[193]

It was however the CFI that elevated the precautionary principle to the status of a new general principle of EU law. *Pfizer*[194] and *Artegodan*[195] were the seminal judgments in this respect. The CFI began with the express mention of the precautionary principle in what was Article 174(2) EC concerning environmental policy. It then relied on Article 6 EC,[196] which stipulates that environmental protection must be integrated into the implementation of other Community policies. It followed, said the CFI, that the precautionary principle, being a part of environmental protection, should also be a factor in other Community policies.[197] This conclusion was reinforced through interpretation of other more specific Treaty Articles as requiring a high level of protection for health and consumer protection, with the precautionary principle being the means to ensure this.[198]

The CFI buttressed the argument from the Treaty by drawing on prior case law from the ECJ, such as the *BSE* case, where the existence of the precautionary principle 'has in essence and at the very least implicitly been recognized by the Court of Justice'.[199] The Treaty Articles combined with prior case law provided the foundations for the recognition of a new general principle of EU law.[200]

It follows that the precautionary principle can be defined as a general principle of Community law requiring the competent authorities to take appropriate measures to prevent specific potential risks to public health, safety and the environment, by giving precedence to the requirements related to the

---

[191] Cases C–154 and 155/04 *The Queen, on the application of Alliance for Natural Health and Nutri-Link Ltd v Secretary of State for Health* [2005] ECR I–6451, [81]–[82]; Cases T–246 and 332/08 *Melli Bank plc v Council* [2009] ECR II–2629, [146].

[192] Case C–180/96 *United Kingdom v Commission* [1998] ECR I–2265.

[193] Ibid [99].

[194] Case T–13/99 *Pfizer Animal Health SA v Council* [2002] ECR II–3305.

[195] Cases T–74, 76, 83–85, 132, 137 and 141/00 *Artegodan GmbH v Commission* [2002] ECR II–4945.

[196] Now Art 11 TFEU.

[197] Case T–13/99 *Pfizer* (n 194) [114]; Cases T–74, 76, 83–85, 132, 137 and 141/00 *Artegodan* (n 195) [183].

[198] Ibid.

[199] Case T–13/99 *Pfizer* (n 194) [115].

[200] Cases T–74, 76, 83–85, 132, 137 and 141/00 *Artegodan* (n 195) [184]; Case T–147/00 *Les Laboratoires Servier v Commission* [2003] ECR II–85, [52]; Case T–334/07 *Denka* (n 50) [116]; Case T–326/07 *Cheminova A/S v Commission* [2009] ECR II–2685, [165]–[166].

protection of those interests over economic interests. Since the Community institutions are responsible, in all their spheres of activity, for the protection of public health, safety and the environment, the precautionary principle can be regarded as an autonomous principle stemming from the abovementioned Treaty provisions.

The precautionary principle is used to review the legality of EU action and also that of Member State action when it falls within the sphere of EU law.[201] It should nonetheless be recognized that the meaning and application of the principle are controversial.[202]

5 MISUSE OF POWER

Misuse of power is the final ground of review mentioned in Article 263 TFEU. The concept covers adoption by an EU institution of a measure with the exclusive or main purpose of achieving an end other than that stated, or evading a procedure specifically prescribed by the Treaty for dealing with the circumstances of the case.[203] There is a connection between claims based on misuse of powers and those based on proportionality. The distinguishing feature is that in the former instance the object or purpose sought to be achieved will itself be improper, whereas in the latter instance the objective will be legitimate, and the issue will be whether it was achieved in a disproportionate manner.

The successful use of this head of review is exemplified by *Giuffrida v Council*.[204] The applicant sought the annulment of a decision appointing Martino to a higher grade in the Community service, pursuant to a competition in which he and Martino were the two contestants for the post. He claimed that the competition was in reality an exercise to appoint Martino to the job, the rationale being that Martino had already been performing the duties associated with the higher grade. The Court quashed the appointment, stating that the pursuit of such a specific objective was contrary to the aims of the recruitment procedure and was, therefore, a misuse of power. Internal promotions should be based on selecting the best person for the job, rather than pre-selecting a particular candidate to whom the job would be given.

---

[201] Craig (n 4) ch 21.

[202] See, eg, J Scott and E Vos, 'The Juridification of Uncertainty: Observations on the Ambivalence of the Precautionary Principle within the EU and the WTO' in C Joerges and R Dehousse (eds), *Good Governance in Europe's Integrated Market* (Oxford University Press, 2002) ch 9; E Fisher, 'Precaution, Precaution Everywhere: Developing a "Common Understanding" of the Precautionary Principle in the European Community' (2002) 9 MJ 7; G Majone, 'What Price Safety? The Precautionary Principle and its Policy Implications' (2002) 40 JCMS 89; C Sunstein, 'Beyond the Precautionary Principle' (2003) 151 University of Pennsylvania Law Rev 1003; José Luis da Cruz Vilaça, 'The Precautionary Principle in EC Law' (2004) 10 EPL 369; E Fisher, *Risk Regulation and Administrative Constitutionalism* (Hart, 2007); J Corkin, 'Science, Legitimacy and the Law: Regulating Risk Regulation Judiciously in the European Community' (2008) 33 ELRev 359.

[203] Case C–84/94 *United Kingdom v Council (Re Working Time Directive)* [1996] ECR I–5755; Case T–72/97 *Proderec-Formação e Desinvolvimento de Recursos Humanos, ACE v Commission* [1998] ECR II–2847; Case C–48/96 P *Windpark Groosthusen GmbH & Co Betriebs KG v Commission* [1998] ECR I–2873; Case C–452/00 *Netherlands v Commission* [2005] ECR I–6645, [114]; Cases C–274 and 295/11 *Spain and Italy v Commission* EU:C:2013:240, [33]–[34]; Case T–422/11 *Computer Resources International (Luxembourg) SA v European Commission* EU:T:2014:927, [110].

[204] Case 105/75 [1976] ECR 1395.

6 THE INTENSITY OF REVIEW

The discussion thus far has concentrated on the heads of review, but the intensity of judicial review is equally important. The issue is how far the CJEU will go in reassessing decisions, particularly those involving discretion. The ECSC Treaty contained explicit dictates on the matter.[205] There is no directly analogous provision in the EU Treaty, but the intensity of review has, nonetheless always been an issue.

Judicial review entails challenge to law, fact, and discretion.[206] A paradigm question of law concerns the meaning of a term in a Treaty provision, regulation, directive, or decision. The Union Courts will normally treat the meaning of terms such as state aid, worker, services, goods, capital, agreement, and other such provisions as questions of law. The general approach is to substitute judgment on these issues of law. The EU Courts establish the meaning of the disputed term, and if the challenged interpretation is at variance with this it will be annulled.

The standard of judicial review for fact and discretion is different. The standard formula used by the Courts is that review should be confined to examining whether the exercise of the discretion was vitiated by a manifest error, misuse of power, or clear excess in the bounds of discretion. The intensity with which this standard of review has been deployed has however varied over time and in relation to different subject matter.

The ECJ's early approach was to apply this test with a very light touch, more especially when the provision being reviewed concerned the exercise of discretion in relation to the CAP. The foundational Treaty provisions of the CAP contained various objectives, which necessitated the making of discretionary choices by the Commission and the Council. The ECJ held that the Community institutions had wide discretionary power concerning the definition of the objectives to be pursued and the choice of the appropriate means of action.[207] The ECJ did not wish to second-guess evaluations made by the Community institutions.[208] The choice thus made would be annulled only if the applicant could show manifest error or misuse of power. The ECJ applied this test with a light touch. It would commonly devote only one or two paragraphs to the issue before finding against the applicant.[209]

The Union Courts continue to deploy the same test for the review of fact and discretion in the more modern case law. The applicant must still show manifest error, misuse of power, or clear excess in the bounds of discretion, but in some areas, such as risk regulation competition and fundamental rights,[210] this test is applied with considerably more rigour than hitherto.

Thus in *Pfizer*[211] the applicant challenged a regulation that withdrew authorization for an additive to animal feeding stuffs. The additive was an antibiotic that was added in very small quantities to animal feed to promote growth. The rationale for withdrawal of the authorization was the fear that such additives could reduce the animals' resistance to antibiotics, and that this lessening of resistance could be transmitted to humans. Pfizer argued that it could not be proven in the light of the scientific evidence. The CFI held that judicial review should be confined to examining whether the exercise of the discretion was vitiated by a manifest error, misuse of power, or clear excess in the bounds of

---

[205] Art 33 ECSC.

[206] Craig (n 4) ch 15.

[207] Case 57/72 *Westzucker GmbH v Einfuhr- und Vorratsstelle für Zucker* [1973] ECR 321; Case 78/74 *Deuka, Deutsche Kraftfutter GmbH, BJ Stolp v Einfuhr- und Vorratsstelle für Getreide und Futtermittel* [1975] ECR 421; Case 98/78 *Firma A Racke v Hauptzollamt Mainz* [1979] ECR 69; Case 59/83 *SA Biovilac NV v European Economic Community* [1984] ECR 4057.

[208] Lord Mackenzie Stuart, *The European Communities and the Rule of Law* (Stevens, 1977) 91, 96.

[209] Craig (n 4) ch 15.

[210] Cases C–584, 593 and 595/10 P *Commission v Kadi* EU:C:2013:518, [97]–[141].

[211] Case T–13/99 *Pfizer* (n 194); Case T–70/99 *Alpharma Inc v Council* [2002] ECR II–3495.

discretion,[212] and that where a Community authority was required to make complex assessments, its discretion also applied to some extent to the factual basis of its action.[213] It was not for the CFI to substitute its factual assessment for that of the Community institution, but it should confine its review to manifest error, misuse of power, or clear excess in the bounds of discretion.[214] Notwithstanding this reiteration of orthodoxy, the CFI devoted nearly seventy pages of its judgment to a close assessment of the applicant's arguments concerning fact and discretion in a judgment that spanned nearly 200 pages overall. The CFI ultimately found against the applicants, but it applied the test of manifest error, etc, far more intensively than hitherto. The intensity of review in this area will also be affected by who has the burden of proof under the EU legislation.[215]

This is also evident in judicial review of competition decisions, more especially those concerning mergers. The CFI annulled a number of Commission merger decisions, concluding, after close and exacting scrutiny, that they were tainted by manifest error.[216] The Commission appealed *Tetra Laval* to the ECJ and argued that the CFI had interpreted the test of manifest error in such a way as to be tantamount to substitution of judgment. The ECJ in *Tetra Laval*[217] upheld the CFI's decision.[218]

> Whilst the Court recognises that the Commission has a margin of discretion with regard to economic matters, that does not mean that the Community courts must refrain from reviewing the Commission's interpretation of information of an economic nature. Not only must the Community courts, *inter alia*, establish whether the evidence relied on is factually accurate, reliable and consistent but also whether that evidence contains all the information which must be taken into account in order to assess a complex situation and whether it is capable of substantiating the conclusions drawn from it. Such a review is all the more necessary in the case of a prospective analysis required when examining a planned merger with conglomerate effect.

Space precludes detailed assessment of the broader implications of this judgment. This can be found elsewhere.[219] Suffice it to say for the present that this interpretation of manifest error is a long way from that found in the earlier case law, or from that which continues to be applied in the modern case law concerning common policies, state aids, and the like. There may well be justification for more intensive review in areas such as risk regulation and competition,[220] although this modern jurisprudence still leaves a number of questions unanswered.[221]

The varying intensity of judicial review is also evident in relation to, for example, the application of general principles of law, such as proportionality and non-discrimination. We have already seen that the application of proportionality differs depending upon the type of EU action being reviewed.[222]

---

[212] Ibid [166].

[213] Ibid [168].

[214] Ibid [169].

[215] Case T–334/07 *Denka* (n 50); Case T–326/07 *Cheminova* (n 200).

[216] Case T–342/99 *Airtours plc v Commission* [2002] ECR II–2585; Case T–5/02 *Tetra Laval BV v Commission* [2002] ECR II–4381.

[217] Case C–12/03 P *Commission v Tetra Laval* [2005] ECR I–987.

[218] Ibid [39]. See also Case C–525/04 P *Spain v Commission* [2007] ECR I–9947, [56]–[57]; Case T–201/04 *Microsoft Corp v Commission* [2007] ECR II–3601, [85]–[89]; Case C–413/06 P *Bertelsmann AG and Sony Corporation of America v Independent Music Publishers and Labels Association (Impala)* [2008] ECR I–4951, [145]–[146]; Case T–48/04 *Qualcomm Wireless Business Solutions Europe BV v Commission* [2009] ECR II–2029, [91]–[92]; Case C–290/07 P *European Commission v Scott SA* [2010] ECR I–7763, [65]–[66].

[219] Craig (n 4) ch 15.

[220] Judge B Vesterdorf, 'Certain Reflections on Recent Judgments Reviewing Commission Merger Control Decisions' in M Hoskins and W Robinson (eds), *A True European: Essays for Judge David Edward* (Hart, 2003) ch 10.

[221] Craig (n 4) ch 15.

[222] See above, pp 552–556.

The same holds true for the way in which the EU Courts apply the principle of non-discrimination. This principle is applied more intensively in the context of Article 18 TFEU, especially when used with citizenship in Articles 20–21 TFEU, than it is when the Union Courts review claims for discrimination in the agricultural sphere pursuant to Articles 39–40 TFEU.[223]

7 THE CONSEQUENCES OF ILLEGALITY AND INVALIDITY

It is now necessary to consider the consequences of finding illegality or invalidity. Where the addressee has not challenged[224] a decision within the time limits in Article 263 TFEU, it is definitive as against that person.[225] Article 264 TFEU provides that if the action under Article 263 is well founded, the Court shall declare the act void, although it may find that the illegality affects only part of the measure. The CJEU has power, if it considers it necessary, to state that certain effects of the act declared void shall be considered definitive.[226] Article 266 TFEU complements this by stating that the institution whose act has been declared void or whose failure to act has been declared contrary to the Treaty must take the necessary measures to comply with the judgment. This may involve eradicating the effects of the measure declared void and/or refraining from adopting an identical measure.[227] It does not require the Commission to re-examine identical or similar decisions allegedly affected by the same irregularity, addressed to persons other than the applicant.[228]

The general principle of EU law is that nullity is retroactive: once the act is annulled under Article 263 it is void *ab initio*.[229] Such a ruling has an effect *erga omnes*. In general terms, it is only annulment of lawmaking measures that can produce genuine *erga omnes* effects, affecting the public at large.[230] The meaning of the phrase can be more limited, particularly where decisions are in issue, as is clear from the *Kraft Products* case.[231] The ECJ held that the scope of any annulment could not go further than that sought by the applicants. The *erga omnes* authority of its annulment ruling attached to the operative part and the *ratio decidendi* of its judgment.[232] It did not however entail annulment of an act not challenged before the ECJ, even where it was alleged to be vitiated by the same illegality.

The principle of retroactive nullity can cause hardship, particularly where the measure is a regulation that has been relied on by many, which may be the basis of later measures. This is the rationale

---

[223] Craig (n 4) ch 15.

[224] Normally an act will have to be challenged for its invalidity to be established. There are, however, limited instances in which the act will be treated as absolutely void or non-existent, where the act may be treated as if it were never adopted. In general, however, proceedings will be required to establish the illegality of the act: p 513 above.

[225] Case C–310/97 P *Commission v AssiDomän Kraft Products AB* [1999] ECR I–5363, [57].

[226] The ECJ has power to prescribe interim measures under Art 279 TFEU: Case C–149/95 P(R) *Commission v Atlantic Container Line AB* [1995] ECR I–2165, and it also has power to order the suspension of the contested act: Art 278 TFEU.

[227] Cases 97, 999, 193 and 215/86 *Asteris AE and Hellenic Republic v Commission* [1988] ECR 2181; Cases T–480 and 483/93 *Antillean Rice Mills NV v Commission* [1995] ECR II–2305; Case C–41/00 P *Interporc Im- und Export GmbH v Commission* (n 174) [29]–[30].

[228] Case C–310/97 P (n 225) [56].

[229] Case C–228/92 *Roquette Frères SA v Hauptzollamt Geldern* [1994] ECR I–1445, [17]; Cases T–481 and 484/93 *Vereniging van Exporteurs in Levende Varkens v Commission* [1995] ECR II–2941, [46]; Case T–171/99 *Corus UK Ltd v Commission* [2001] ECR II–2967, [50].

[230] AG Toth, 'The Authority of Judgments of the European Court of Justice: Binding Force and Legal Effects' (1984) 4 YBEL 1, 49.

[231] Case 310/97 P (n 225) [52]–[54].

[232] Case 3/54 *ASSIDER v High Authority* [1955] ECR 63; Case 2/54 *Italy v High Authority* [1954–6] ECR 37, 55.

for Article 264(2), which allows the CJEU to qualify the extent of the nullity.[233] This Article has been used to limit the temporal effect of the Court's ruling. Thus, in *Commission v Council*[234] the Court annulled part of a regulation concerning staff salaries. However, if the regulation had been annulled retroactively then the staff would not have been entitled to any salary increases until a new regulation had been adopted. The Court, therefore, ruled that the regulation should have effect until a new regulation had been promulgated.

A finding of invalidity pursuant to Article 267 TFEU is, in theory, different from a decision made pursuant to Article 263. The former is addressed only to the national court that requested the ruling. However the Court has held that its rulings on Article 267 references concerning validity have an *erga omnes* effect, and provide a sufficient reason for any other national court to regard that act as void.[235] Moreover, the Court has applied the principles of Articles 264 and 266 TFEU, which technically operate only in the context of Articles 263 and 265 TFEU, by analogy to cases arising under Article 267.[236]

Case 112/83 **Société de Produits de Maïs v Administration des Douanes**
[1985] ECR 719

[Note Lisbon Treaty renumbering: Arts 173, 174, 176, and 177 are now
Arts 263, 264, 266, and 267 TFEU]

The case concerned the effects of a ruling by the ECJ on the validity of a regulation, following a reference from the French courts under Article 177.

THE ECJ

16. It should in the first place be recalled that the Court has already held in its judgment...(Case 66/80, *International Chemical Corporation*...) that although a judgment of the Court given under Article 177 of the Treaty declaring an act of an institution, in particular a Council or Commission Regulation, to be void is directly addressed only to the national court which brought the matter before the Court, it is sufficient reason for any other national court to regard that act as void for the purposes of a judgment which it has to give.

17. Secondly, it must be emphasised that the Court's power to impose temporal limits on the effects of a declaration that a legislative act is invalid, in the context of preliminary rulings under indent (b) of the first paragraph of Article 177, is justified by the interpretation of Article 174 of the Treaty having regard to the necessary consistency between the preliminary ruling procedure and the action for annulment provided for in Articles 173, 174 and 176 of the Treaty, which are two mechanisms provided by the Treaty for reviewing the legality of acts of the Community institutions. The possibility of imposing temporal limits on the effects of the invalidity of a Community Regulation, whether under Article 173 or Article 177, is a power conferred on the Court by the Treaty in the interest of the uniform application of Community law throughout the Community....

18. It must be pointed out that where it is justified by overriding considerations the second paragraph of Article 174 gives the Court discretion to decide, in each particular case, which specific

---

[233] The ECJ has extended the principle of Art 264(2) to dirs: Case C–295/90 *European Parliament v Council* [1992] ECR I–4193, and to decs, Case C–22/96 *European Parliament v Council (Telematic Networks)* [1998] ECR I–3231.

[234] Case 81/72 [1973] ECR 575; Case C–41/95 *European Parliament v Council* [1995] ECR I–4411, [43]–[45].

[235] Case 66/80 *International Chemical Corporation v Amministrazione delle Finanze dello Stato* [1981] ECR 1191.

[236] Cases 4, 109 and 145/79 *Société Co-opérative 'Providence Agricole de la Champagne' v ONIC* [1980] ECR 2823; Cases C–38 and 151/90 *R v Lomas* [1992] ECR I–1781.

effects of a Regulation which has been declared void must be maintained. It is therefore for the Court, where it makes use of the possibility of limiting the effect of past events of a declaration in proceedings under Article 177 that a measure is void, to decide whether an exception to that temporal limitation of the effect of its judgment may be made in favour of the party which brought the action before the national court or of any other trader which took similar steps before the declaration of invalidity or whether, conversely, a declaration of invalidity applicable only to the future constitutes an adequate remedy even for traders who took action at the appropriate time with a view to protecting their rights.

The effect of a preliminary ruling which calls into question the compatibility of national law with EU law requires separate consideration. The general principle is that the ruling defines the legal position as it must have been understood from the time when the EU norm came into force.[237] The EU norm must, therefore, be applied by national courts to situations that occurred before the ECJ's ruling was given, provided that an action relating to that rule could have been brought before the courts having jurisdiction. This proposition will be qualified only in exceptional circumstances.[238]

8 CONCLUSIONS

i.   The Union Courts have played the major role in fashioning principles of judicial review to render accountable decision-making by EU institutions and Member States when the latter act in the sphere of EU law. They have to this end developed principles of procedural and substantive judicial review within the framework of the heads of review listed in Article 263 TFEU.

ii. The EU Courts have developed a broad set of general principles of EU law, which continues to develop, as exemplified by the case law on the precautionary principle. The most familiar have been drawn from national constitutional and administrative traditions and have been adapted to the EU context.

iii. A key characteristic of the general principles of EU law is that they function both as aids to interpretation and as grounds for judicial review.

iv. Some principles, such as transparency and the principle of non-discrimination on grounds such as sexual orientation, race, and age, have been implemented and concretized in detailed secondary legislation, and their legal status has been gradually enhanced in this way.

v.   The Charter of Fundamental Rights is now formally binding after the Lisbon Treaty. The fact that it contains rights such as access to documents and freedom from discrimination reinforces the recognition of such principles by the EU Courts and in EU legislation.

vi. The EU Courts have considerable discretion concerning the standard and intensity of review adopted. The case law reveals continuing developments in this regard, as the Union Courts re-evaluate the intensity with which they wish to apply the principles of judicial review which they have created.

---

[237] Cases 66, 127 and 128/79 *Salumi v Amministrazione delle Finanze* [1980] ECR 1237, [9]–[10]; Case C–50/96 *Deutsche Telekom AG v Schröder* [2000] ECR I–743, [43]; Cases C–387, 391 and 403/02 *Criminal proceedings against Silvio Berlusconi* [2005] ECR I–3565, [138], AG Kokott.

[238] Cases C–197 and 252/94 *Société Bautiaa v Directeur des Services Fiscaux des Landes* [1996] ECR I–505; Case 61/79 *Denkavit Italiana* [1980] ECR 1205; Case C–137/94 *R v Secretary of State for Health, ex p Richardson* [1995] ECR I–3407.

9 FURTHER READING

ARNULL, A, *General Principles of EEC Law and the Individual* (Leicester University Press/Pinter, 1990)

BELL, M, *Anti-Discrimination Law and the European Union* (Oxford University Press, 2002)

BERNITZ, U, AND NERGELIUS, J, *General Principles of European Community Law* (Kluwer, 2000)

BUNYAN, T, *Secrecy and Openness in the EU* (Kogan Page, 1999)

CRAIG, P, *EU Administrative Law* (Oxford University Press, 2nd edn, 2012)

DASHWOOD, A, AND O'LEARY, S (eds), *The Principle of Equal Treatment in EC Law* (Sweet & Maxwell, 1997)

DECKMYN, V (ed), *Increasing Transparency in the European Union* (EIPA, 2002)

ELLIS, E (ed), *The Principle of Proportionality in the Laws of Europe* (Hart, 1999)

EMILIOU, N, *The Principle of Proportionality in European Law* (Kluwer, 1996)

GERAPETRITIS, G, *Proportionality in Administrative Law* (Sakkoulas, 1997)

NEHL, N, *Principles of Administrative Procedure in EC Law* (Hart, 1999)

SCHONBERG, S, *Legitimate Expectations in Administrative Law* (Oxford University Press, 2000)

SCHWARZE, J, *European Administrative Law* (Office for Official Publications of the European Communities/Sweet & Maxwell, revised 1st edn, 2006)

TRIDIMAS, T, *The General Principles of EU Law* (Oxford University Press, 2nd edn, 2006)

USHER, J, *General Principles of EC Law* (Longman, 1998)

16

DAMAGES ACTIONS
AND MONEY CLAIMS

1 CENTRAL ISSUES

i.   In any developed legal system there must be a mechanism whereby losses caused by governmental action may be recovered in an action brought by an individual.

ii. Compensation against the EU is governed by Article 340 TFEU[1] (ex Article 288 EC).

iii. The Article leaves the CJEU with considerable room for interpretation,[2] and directs it to consider the general principles common to the laws of the Member States.

iv. The key issue is as to the test for liability where losses are caused by EU acts that are illegal.

v.   It will be seen that the CJEU has fashioned different tests for cases where the challenged act is of a discretionary nature and for those where it is not.

vi. In doing so it has drawn on its jurisprudence on state liability in damages.

2 DISCRETIONARY ACTS

Article 340 TFEU is the Treaty Article that governs damages actions against the EU. This section of the chapter considers the application of Article 340 in relation to discretionary EU acts.

> In the case of non-contractual liability, the Union shall, in accordance with the general principles common to the laws of the Member States, make good any damage caused by its institutions or by its servants in the performance of their duties.

---

[1] The original Treaty Art was numbered Art 215(2) EEC, which was renumbered Art 288(2) EC after the Amsterdam Treaty.

[2] Liability cannot be founded on the primary Treaty Arts, since these do not constitute 'acts of the institutions' but are international agreements: Case T–113/96 *Edouard Dubois et Fils v Council and Commission* [1998] ECR II–125.

(A) THE GENERAL TEST

The cases considered here are those where the decision-maker has a significant element of discretion. The norms challenged will normally be legislative, but an individualized norm, which contains a significant element of discretion, will also be subject to the legal test discussed below.

The norm may not have been annulled because of the restrictive interpretation of *locus standi*. The ECJ's early approach did not augur well for individuals, for it was held in *Plaumann*[3] that annulment of the norm was a necessary condition precedent to using Article 340 TFEU. If this requirement had been retained the Article would have been of little use, given the difficulty for an individual to prove *locus standi* for annulment. The necessity for annulment was, however, generally discarded in later cases, and the action for damages came to be regarded as an independent, autonomous cause of action.[4] This is clear from *Schöppenstedt*.

Case 5/71 **Aktien-Zuckerfabrik Schöppenstedt v Council**
[1971] ECR 975

[Note Lisbon Treaty renumbering: Arts 40 and 215 are now Arts 40 and 340 TFEU]

The applicant claimed that Regulation 769/68, concerning the sugar market, was in breach of Article 40(3) EC because it was discriminatory in the way in which it established the pricing policy for the product.

THE ECJ

11. In the present case the non-contractual liability of the Community presupposes at the very least the unlawful nature of the act alleged to be the cause of the damage. Where legislative action involving measures of economic policy is concerned, the Community does not incur non-contractual liability for damage suffered by individuals as a consequence of that action, by virtue of the provisions contained in Article 215, second paragraph, of the Treaty, unless a sufficiently flagrant violation of a superior rule of law for the protection of the individual has occurred. For that reason the Court, in the present case, must first consider whether such a violation has occurred.

The ECJ decided that no breach of a superior rule of law could be proven on the facts. The test laid down established the general conditions for liability in this area.

---

[3] Case 25/62 *Plaumann v Commission* [1963] ECR 95.

[4] Case 5/71 *Aktien-Zuckerfabrik Schöppenstedt v Council* [1971] ECR 975; Cases 9 and 11/71 *Compagnie d'Approvisionnement de Transport et de Crédit SA et Grands Moulins de Paris SA v Commission* [1972] ECR 391; Case T–178/98 *Fresh Marine Company SA v Commission* [2000] ECR II–3331, [45]–[50]; Cases T–3/00 and 337/04 *Athanasios Pitsiorlas v Council and European Central Bank* [2007] ECR II–4779, [281]–[284]. There may, however, be instances where the failure to proceed with an Art 263 TFEU action will have consequences for an Art 340(2) TFEU action where the individual was directly and individually concerned by the offending norm and could have successfully challenged it under Art 263 TFEU, but either failed to do so entirely or failed to do so within the period for challenge laid down in Art 263: Cases C–199 and 200/94 *Pesqueria Vasco-Montanesa SA (Pevasa) and Compania Internacional de Pesca y Derivados SA (Inpesca) v Commission* [1995] ECR I–3709; Case T–93/95 *Laga v Commission* [1998] ECR II–195; Case C–310/97 P *Commission v AssiDomän Kraft Products AB* [1999] ECR I–5363, [59]; P Mead, 'The Relationship between an Action for Damages and an Action for Annulment: The Return of *Plaumann*' in T Heukels and A McDonnell (eds), *The Action for Damages in Community Law* (Kluwer, 1997) ch 13.

(B) LEGISLATIVE AND NON-LEGISLATIVE DISCRETIONARY ACTS

The ECJ held in *Bergaderm*[5] and *Antillean Rice*[6] that the crucial factor in determining the applicability of the *Schöppenstedt* test was the degree of discretion possessed by the institution in relation to the challenged measure. The general or individual nature of the measure was not a decisive criterion for identifying the limits of its discretion.[7]

This is correct in principle. Many administrative measures involve discretionary choices which are just as difficult as those made in the context of legislative action. The very line between the two can be difficult to draw in substantive terms. This means that the *Schöppenstedt* test can apply to individualized acts that entail a significant element of discretion, and to legislative acts that involve discretionary choice. Many legislative acts will have this feature, but there is no logical reason why all should do so.

It was clear prior to the Lisbon Treaty that whether an act was legislative for the purposes of the *Schöppenstedt* test was dependent on the substance of the measure, and not the legal form in which it was expressed.[8] Thus an applicant in an Article 340(2) action could claim that the measure, although called a regulation, was in reality an administrative decision.[9] The converse was also true: it was possible for a measure to be a decision for some purposes, but a legislative act for the purposes of Article 340(2).[10] Moreover, the mere fact that an applicant had a sufficient interest for a challenge under Article 263 TFEU did not preclude a measure from being legislative for the purposes of the Article 340(2) action.[11]

It is however clear after the Lisbon Treaty that the definition of a legislative act is a matter of form: any act that is passed in accordance with a legislative procedure is a legislative act for the purposes of the Lisbon Treaty, and acts not enacted in accordance with such a procedure do not qualify as legislative acts, irrespective of their substance.[12]

(C) SUPERIOR RULE OF LAW

The case law shows that three differing types of norms can, in principle, qualify as superior rules of law for the protection of the individual.

First, many Treaty provisions fall within this category. A commonly cited ground is the ban on discrimination in Article 40(2) TFEU, in the context of the Common Agricultural Policy (CAP). This is not surprising, given that many damages actions are brought pursuant to CAP regulations.[13]

---

[5] Case C–352/98 P *Laboratoires Pharmaceutiques Bergaderm SA and Goupil v Commission* [2000] ECR I–5291, [46].

[6] Case C–390/95 P *Antillean Rice Mills NV v Commission* [1999] ECR I–769, [56]–[62].

[7] See also Case C–472/00 P *Commission v Fresh Marine A/S* [2003] ECR I–7541, [27]; Case C–312/00 P *Commission v Camar Srl and Tico Srl* [2002] ECR I–11355, [55]; Case C–282/05 P *Holcim (Deutschland) AG v Commission* [2007] ECR I–2941, [47]–[49]; Case C–440/07 P *Commission v Schneider Electric SA* [2009] ECR I–6413, [160]–[161]; Case T–16/04 *Arcelor SA v European Parliament and Council* [2010] ECR–II 211, [141]–[143].

[8] Case C–390/95 P *Antillean Rice Mills* (n 6) [60]; A Arnull, 'Liability for Legislative Acts under Article 215(2) EC' in Heukels and McDonnell (n 4) 131–136.

[9] Case C–119/88 *Aerpo and Others v Commission* [1990] ECR I–2189; Case T–472/93 *Campo Ebro v Commission* [1995] ECR II–421.

[10] Cases T–481/93 and 484/93 *Vereniging van Exporteurs in Levende Varkens v Commission (Live Pigs)* [1995] ECR II–2941; Case C–390/95 P *Antillean Rice* (n 6) [62].

[11] Cases T–480 and 483/93 *Antillean Rice Mills v Commission* [1995] ECR II–2305; Case C–390/95 P *Antillean Rice* (n 6) [62].

[12] Art 289 TFEU. See Ch 4.

[13] See, eg, Case 43/72 *Merkur-Aussenhandels-GmbH v Commission* [1973] ECR 1055; Case 153/73 *Holtz und Willemsen GmbH v Commission* [1974] ECR 675.

A second ground of claim is that a regulation is in breach of a hierarchically superior norm.[14] The regulations made under, for example, the CAP may be made pursuant to a prior network of regulations on the same topic. A third ground is that the Union legislation is held to infringe general principles of law such as proportionality,[15] fundamental rights,[16] legal certainty, or legitimate expectations, although the duty to give reasons does not qualify in this respect.[17]

Superior sometimes seems to be equated with 'important', and sometimes with a more formalistic conception of one rule being higher than another, as in the case of the regulation being in breach of a parent regulation. The rules of the WTO cannot, subject to limited exceptions, be relied on in this context.[18] These various grounds of claim are evident in the *CNTA* case.

Case 74/74 Comptoir National Technique Agricole (CNTA) SA v Commission
[1975] ECR 533

The applicant claimed that it had suffered loss by the withdrawal of monetary compensatory amounts (MCAs) by Regulation 189/72. The system of MCAs was designed to compensate traders for fluctuations in exchange rates. Regulation 189/72, which entered into force on 1 February 1972, abolished these MCAs insofar as they had been applicable to colza and rape seeds, because the Commission decided that the market situation had altered, thereby rendering the MCAs unnecessary. The applicant had, however, entered into contracts before the Regulation was passed, even though these contracts were to be performed after the ending of the scheme. It argued that it had made these contracts on the assumption that the MCAs would still be payable, and that it had set the price on that hypothesis. The sudden termination of the system in this area, without warning, was said by the applicant to have caused it loss. The ECJ began by citing the general principle from the *Schöppenstedt* case.

THE ECJ

17. In this connection the applicant contends in the first place that by abolishing the compensatory amounts by Regulation 189/72 the Commission has infringed basic Regulation 974/71 of the Council.
...
19. It follows from the last sentence of Article 1(2) of Regulation No 974/71 that the option for Member States to apply compensatory amounts may only be exercised where the monetary measures in question would lead to disturbances to trade in agricultural products.

20. As the application of compensatory amounts is a measure of an exceptional nature, this provision must be understood as enunciating a condition not only of the introduction but also of the maintenance of compensatory amounts for a specific product.

21. The Commission has a large measure of discretion for judging whether the monetary measure concerned might lead to disturbances to trade in the product in question.

22. In order to judge the risk of such disturbances, it is permissible for the Commission to take into account market conditions as well as monetary factors.

---

[14] Case 74/74 *Comptoir National Technique Agricole (CNTA) SA v Commission* [1975] ECR 533.

[15] Case T–16/04 *Arcelor* (n 7).

[16] Cases C–120–121/06 P *FIAMM v Council and Commission* [2008] ECR I–6513, [184].

[17] Case 106/81 *Julius Kind KG v EEC* [1982] ECR 2885; Case C–119/88 *Aerpo* (n 9); Cases T–466, 469, 473, 474 and 477/93 *O'Dwyer v Council* [1996] ECR II–207; Cases T–64 and 65/01 *Afrikanische Frucht-Compagnie GmbH v Council and Commission* [2004] ECR II–521, [128].

[18] Case C–149/96 *Portugal v Council* [1999] ECR I–8395; Case T–18/99 *Cordis Obst und Gemüse Grosshandel GmbH v Commission* [2001] ECR II–913; Case T–383/00 *Beamglow Ltd v European Parliament, Council and Commission* [2005] ECR II–5459; Cases C–120–121/06 P *FIAMM* (n 16) [111]–[112].

23. It has not been established that the Commission exceeded the limits of its power thus defined when it considered towards the end of January 1972 that the situation on the market in colza and rape seeds was such that the application of compensatory amounts for those products was no longer necessary.

[*The ECJ then considered whether the withdrawal of the compensatory amounts violated certain general principles of law. It held that Regulation 189/72 was not retroactive, as had been claimed by the applicants. The Court then considered whether this withdrawal had violated the principle of legitimate expectations. It held that the object of the regime for the fixing of refunds in advance on export orders could not be regarded as tantamount to a guarantee for traders against the risk of movements in exchange rates. It continued as follows:*]

41. Nevertheless the application of the compensatory amounts in practice avoids the exchange risk, so that a trader, even a prudent one, might be induced to omit to cover himself against such a risk.

42. In these circumstances, a trader may legitimately expect that for transactions irrevocably undertaken by him because he has obtained, subject to a deposit, export licences fixing the amount of the refund in advance, no unforeseeable alteration will occur which could have the effect of causing him inevitable loss, by re-exposing him to the exchange risk.

43. The Community is therefore liable if, in the absence of an overriding matter of public interest, the Commission abolished with immediate effect and without warning the application of compensatory amounts in a specific sector without adopting transitional measures which would at least permit traders either to avoid the loss which would have been suffered in the performance of export contracts, the existence and irrevocability of which are established by the advance fixing of the refunds, or to be compensated for such loss.

44. In the absence of an overriding matter of public interest, the Commission has violated a superior rule of law, thus rendering the Community liable, by failing to include in Regulation 189/72 transitional measures for the protection of the confidence which a trader might legitimately have had in the Community rules.

The ECJ stated, however, that the Community was not liable to pay the full cost of the MCAs that would have applied to the transactions, but rather that the extent of the applicant's legitimate expectation was merely that of not suffering loss by reason of the withdrawal of the MCAs. In later proceedings it was held that the applicant had not in fact suffered such losses.[19]

(D) FLAGRANT VIOLATION/SERIOUS BREACH

It is evident from *Schöppenstedt* that the individual must prove not only breach of a superior rule of law for the protection of the individual, but also that the breach was flagrant. This term was restrictively construed in the early case law, such that it was difficult for the applicant to succeed, although they did occasionally win.[20] The result of *Bayerische HNL*[21] and *Amylum*[22] was that an applicant had to show that the *effects* of the breach were serious, in terms of the quantum of loss suffered, and also that the *manner* of the breach was arbitrary.

More recent cases have taken a less restrictive interpretation of the term flagrant violation. *Bergaderm* is now the leading modern authority. In *Brasserie du Pêcheur*,[23] the ECJ stated that the

---

[19] Case 74/74 [1976] ECR 797.

[20] Cases 64, 113/76, 167, 239/78, 27, 28 and 45/79 *Dumortier Frères SA v Council* [1979] ECR 3091.

[21] Cases 83, 94/76, 4, 15 and 40/77 *Bayerische HNL Vermehrungsbetriebe GmbH & Co KG v Council and Commission* [1978] ECR 1209.

[22] Cases 116 and 124/77 *Amylum NV and Tunnel Refineries Ltd v Council and Commission* [1979] ECR 3497.

[23] Cases C–46 and 48/93 *Brasserie du Pêcheur SA v Germany; R v Secretary of State for Transport, ex p Factortame Ltd* [1996] ECR I–1029.

test for state liability in damages should not be different from that of the Union under Article 340(2) TFEU.[24] The ECJ's interpretation of the term 'serious breach' in *Brasserie du Pêcheur* therefore shaped the Article 340(2) jurisprudence. This was confirmed by *Bergaderm*, where the ECJ completed the circle by explicitly drawing on the factors mentioned in *Brasserie du Pêcheur* to determine the meaning of flagrant violation for the purposes of Article 340(2).[25]

Case C–352/98 P **Laboratoires Pharmaceutiques Bergaderm SA and Goupil v Commission**
[2000] ECR I–5291

[Note Lisbon Treaty renumbering: Art 215 is now Art 340 TFEU]

This was an appeal from the CFI to the ECJ. The applicant sought damages for losses suffered by the passage of a Directive which prohibited the use of certain substances in cosmetics. It claimed that the Directive should be regarded as an administrative act, since it only concerned the applicant, the consequence being that illegality *per se* would suffice for liability, rather than having to prove a sufficiently serious breach.

THE ECJ

40. The system of rules which the Court has worked out with regard to [Article 215] takes into account, *inter alia*, the complexity of situations to be regulated, difficulties in the application or interpretation of the texts and, more particularly, the margin of discretion available to the author of the act in question (*Brasserie du Pêcheur*, para. 43).

41. The Court has stated that the conditions under which the State may incur liability for damage caused to individuals by a breach of Community law cannot, in the absence of particular justification, differ from those governing the liability of the Community in like circumstances. The protection of the rights which individuals derive from Community law cannot vary depending on whether a national authority or a Community authority is responsible for the damage (*Brasserie du Pêcheur*, para. 42).

42. As regards Member State liability for damage caused to individuals, the Court has held that Community law confers a right to reparation where three conditions are met: the rule of law infringed must be intended to confer rights on individuals; the breach must be sufficiently serious; and there must be a direct causal link between the breach of the obligation resting on the State and the damage sustained by the injured parties (*Brasserie du Pêcheur*, para. 51).

43. As to the second condition, as regards both Community liability under Article 215 . . . and Member State liability for breaches of Community law, the decisive test for finding that a breach of Community law is sufficiently serious is whether the Member State or the Community institution concerned manifestly and gravely disregarded the limits on its discretion (*Brasserie du Pêcheur*, para. 55 . . .).

44. Where the Member State or the institution in question has only considerably reduced, or even no discretion, the mere infringement of Community law may be sufficient to establish the existence of a sufficiently serious breach (*Hedley Lomas*, para. 28).

45. It is therefore necessary to examine whether . . . the Court of First Instance erred in law in its examination of the way in which the Commission exercised its discretion when it adopted the Adaptation Directive.

---

[24] Ch 8.
[25] T Tridimas, 'Liability for Breach of Community Law: Growing Up and Mellowing Down?' (2001) 38 CMLRev 301.

46. In that regard, the Court finds that the general or individual nature of a measure taken by an institution is not a decisive criterion for identifying the limits of the discretion enjoyed by the institution in question.

47. It follows that the first ground of the appeal, which is based exclusively on the categorisation of the Adaptation Directive as an individual measure, has in any event no bearing on the issue and must be rejected.

The change brought about by *Bergaderm* was welcome and has been followed in later cases.[26] The seriousness of the breach will be dependent upon factors such as: the relative clarity of the rule which has been breached; the measure of discretion left to the relevant authorities; whether the error of law was excusable or not; and whether the breach was intentional or voluntary. It is not necessary for a claimant to show arbitrariness.[27] Nor will the possibility of a large number of claimants preclude an Article 340(2) action.[28] The nature of the EU's discretion will inevitably impact on the success of any damages action: the broader and more complex the discretion, the more difficult will it be for the claimant to show the serious breach. This is apparent from recent case law.

Thus in *Arcelor*[29] the claimant sought damages for loss caused by a directive concerned with greenhouse gas emissions. The CFI reiterated the test from *Bergaderm* and held that it was for the claimant to show the serious breach. This required it to show a manifest and serious failure to have regard for the limits of the broad discretion enjoyed by the Union legislature when exercising its environmental powers. The CFI emphasized the breadth of the EC's discretionary power in this area, stating that it required the Union legislature to evaluate 'ecological, scientific, technical and economic changes of a complex and uncertain nature' and to balance 'the various objectives, principles and interests set out in Article 174 EC'.[30]

The same point is evident in *My Travel*,[31] which concerned EU competition law. The CFI held that the concept of a serious breach to establish non-contractual liability did not comprise all errors, even if of some gravity, in the application of competition rules, which were 'complex, delicate and subject to a considerable degree of discretion'.[32] Thus the mere fact that the CFI had annulled a Commission decision holding a concentration incompatible with the common market could not be equated to the finding of a sufficiently serious breach. Mere errors of assessment in the context of an annulment action could not suffice to show a manifest and grave infringement for the purposes of non-contractual liability, since this would inhibit the Commission as a regulator of competition.[33] The CFI emphasized the complex evaluative assessments that had to be made by the Commission in this area, and the discretion it possessed as to how to determine whether a concentration was in breach of the relevant EU legal rules.[34]

---

[26] See cases above (n 7); Case T–341/07 *Sison v Council* [2011] ECR II–7915, [34]–[40]; Case C–221/10 *Artegodan GmbH v Commission and Germany* EU:C:2012:216.

[27] Case C–220/91 P *Stahlwerke Peine-Salzgitter AG v Commission* [1993] ECR I–2393.

[28] Cases C–104/89 and 37/90 *Mulder v Council and Commission* [1992] ECR I–3061.

[29] Case T–16/04 *Arcelor* (n 7).

[30] Ibid [143]; Case T–31/07 *Du Pont de Nemours (France) SAS v Commission*, 12 Apr 2013.

[31] Case T–212/03 *My Travel Group plc v Commission* [2008] ECR II–1967.

[32] Ibid [40].

[33] Ibid [40]–[43].

[34] Ibid [83].

(E) ASSESSMENT

The initial question is whether there are valid reasons for limiting liability under Article 340(2). Views will undoubtedly differ, but we believe that there are good arguments for doing so. Many of the major cases arise out of the CAP, under which the EU has to make difficult discretionary choices, balancing the conflicting variables in Article 39 TFEU. A finding of illegality *per se* should not suffice for a damages action. This would render the decision-makers susceptible to a potentially wide liability, and would run the risk that the Court might 'second-guess' the Council and Commission as to how the variables in Article 39 should be balanced.[35] Analogous considerations have influenced UK courts.[36] It would be feasible to regard illegality *per se* as the appropriate test under Article 340(2) if this were to be taken as proven only where the conduct of the Union institutions was particularly flagrant. This would however incorporate an element of serious breach into the definition of illegality.[37]

If this is accepted, the crucial issue is how to interpret the phrase 'flagrant violation' or 'serious breach'. In the past it was interpreted too restrictively to require something akin to arbitrary action. The approach in *Brasserie du Pêcheur* and *Bergaderm* is more nuanced, and is to be welcomed. It requires attention to the very factors identified in those cases. The mere fact that the general aim being pursued by the EU is legitimate does not shield it from liability, if it can be shown that there was a serious breach in the manner of attaining this end, when judged by the *Brasserie du Pêcheur* criteria.

Where loss has been caused by sufficiently serious illegal action the applicant should not have to prove that the loss was particularly serious. The applicant will have to show that the illegality *caused* the loss, but there should be no requirement over and above this.[38] The ordinary 'economics of litigation' should ensure that claims are, in general, pursued only when it is economically worthwhile to do so.

(F) SUMMARY

i. For an applicant to succeed it is necessary to show that there has been a violation of a superior rule of law for the protection of individuals, that it was manifest and grave, or sufficiently serious, and that it caused the damage.

ii. The key criterion as to whether it is necessary to show that the breach was sufficiently serious is the margin of discretion accorded to the author of the act. Where such discretion exists it will be necessary for the applicant to prove a serious breach. This is so irrespective of whether the measure is general/legislative or individual/administrative in nature.

iii. The factors mentioned in *Brasserie du Pêcheur* and *Bergaderm* which determine whether the breach was sufficiently serious will be determinative in the Article 340(2) case law.

iv. The applicant should not have to show that the loss suffered was serious. It is not part of the *Brasserie du Pêcheur* test, and should not, as a matter of principle, be required.

v. It is no longer fatal to a claim that there are a large number of potential applicants.

---

[35] Cases 83 and 94/76, 4, 15 and 40/77 *Bayersiche HNL* (n 21) 1223–1224, AG Capotorti.
[36] P Craig, 'Once More Unto the Breach: The Community, the State and Damages Liability' (1997) 113 LQR 67.
[37] AG Capotorti (n 35) 1233.
[38] Ibid 1233–1234.

3 NON-DISCRETIONARY ACTS

(A) THE GENERAL PRINCIPLE: ILLEGALITY, CAUSATION, DAMAGE

The discussion thus far has focused on liability in damages for legislative and non legislative acts which involve discretion. The test that applies to liability for non-discretionary acts has been subtly altered.

The traditional approach was that where an act did not entail any meaningful discretionary choice then it would normally suffice to show illegality, causation, and damage.[39] Successful claims were relatively rare. The more recent jurisprudence continues to distinguish between discretionary and non-discretionary acts, but does so within the framework of the sufficiently serious breach test. The modern formulation in *Bergaderm* is that the applicant must prove that the rule of law infringed was intended to confer rights on individuals, there must be a sufficiently serious breach, and a causal link between the breach and the resultant harm. Where however the EU institution has considerably reduced or no discretion, the mere infringement of EU law *may* be sufficient to establish the existence of the sufficiently serious breach.[40]

(B) APPLICATION OF THE GENERAL PRINCIPLE

The Court will inevitably have to decide whether there is discretion such that the applicant must satisfy the sufficiently serious breach test, or whether in the absence of discretion the mere infringement of EU law may suffice for liability.[41]

Case C–390/95 P **Antillean Rice Mills NV v Commission**
[1999] ECR I–769

The applicants challenged aspects of the basic Council Decision which governed the relationship between the overseas countries and territories (OCTs) and the EC. They also challenged a Commission Decision which introduced safeguard measures for rice originating in the Dutch Antilles for breach of the Council Decision. On appeal to the ECJ the applicants argued that the CFI was wrong to have required proof of a sufficiently serious breach, since the contested measures were decisions.

---

[39] Cases 44–51/77 *Union Malt v Commission* [1978] ECR 57; Cases T–481 and 484/93 *Live Pigs* (n 10); Case 26/81 *Oleifici Mediterranei v EEC* [1982] ECR 3057, [16]; Case C–146/91 *KYDEP v Council and Commission* [1994] ECR I–4199; Cases C–258 and 259/90 *Pesquerias de Bermeo SA and Naviera Laida SA v Commission* [1992] ECR I–2901; Case T–175/94 *International Procurement Services v Commission* [1996] ECR II–729, [44]; Case T–178/98 *Fresh Marine* (n 4) [54]; Cases T–79/96, 260/97 and 117/98 *Camar Srl and Tico Srl v Commission* [2000] ECR II–2193, [204]–[205]; Case T–333/03 *Masdar (UK) Ltd v Commission* [2006] ECR II–4377, [59]–[62].

[40] Case C–352/98 P *Bergaderm* (n 5) [42]–[44]; Case C–472/00 P *Fresh Marine* (n 7) [26]–[27]; Case C–312/00 P *Camar* (n 7) [54]–[55]; Cases T–198/95, 171/96, 230/97, 174/98, and 225/98 *Comafrica SpA and Dole Fresh Fruit Europa Ltd & Co v Commission* [2001] ECR II–1975, [134]–[136]; Case T–283/02 *EnBW Kernkraft GmbH v Commission* [2005] ECR II–913, [87]; Case T–139/01 *Comafrica SpA and Dole Fresh Fruit Europe & Co Ltd v Commission* [2005] ECR II–409, [142]; Case T–16/04 *Arcelor* (n 7) [141]; Case C–440/07 P *Schneider* (n 7) [160]; Case T–341/07 *Sison* (n 26) [33]–[40].

[41] Case T–390/94 *Aloys Schröder v Commission* [1997] ECR II–501; Cases T–458 and 523/93 *ENU v Commission* [1995] ECR II–2459; Case T–178/98 *Fresh Marine* (n 4) [57]; Case 79/96 *Camar Srl* (n 39) [206].

THE ECJ

57. It must be noted, first, that it is settled case-law that in a legislative context involving the exercise of a wide discretion, the Community cannot incur liability unless the institution concerned has manifestly and gravely disregarded the limits on the exercise of its powers....

58. Second,...the CFI proceeded on the basis that the Commission enjoyed a wide discretion in the field of economic policy, which means that the stricter criterion of liability must be applied, namely the requirements of a sufficiently serious breach of a superior rule of law for the protection of the individual.

59. It follows that the CFI correctly applied the stricter criterion of liability.

60. The fact that the contested measure is in the form of a decision, and hence in principle capable of being the subject of an action for annulment, is not sufficient to preclude its being legislative in character. In the context of an action for damages, that character depends on the nature of the measure in question, not its form.

...

62. ...[I]t must be stated that the fact they are individually concerned has no effect on the character of the measure in the context of an action for damages, since that action is an independent remedy....

(c) THE MEANING OF ILLEGALITY

It is also important to address the meaning of 'illegality' in this context. In one sense any infringement of law can constitute illegality.[42] It is therefore possible to list types of error which *might* lead to liability, including: failure to gather the facts before reaching a decision, taking a decision based on irrelevant factors, failure to accord appropriate procedural rights, and inadequate supervision of bodies to which power has been delegated. The mere proof of such an error will not, however, always ensure success in a damages action. It is open to a court to construe illegality narrowly, or to define it so as to preclude liability unless there has been some error, or something equivalent thereto. The point is exemplified by the following cases.

Cases 19, 20, 25 and 30/69 **Denise Richez-Parise v Commission**
[1970] ECR 325

The applicants were Community officials who had been given incorrect information concerning their pensions. This information was supplied as a consequence of a request by the Commission to the officials concerned that they should contact the relevant department to obtain information concerning their financial provisions on termination of employment. The information given was based on an interpretation of the relevant regulation which was believed correct at that time. The department which gave the information later had reason to believe that its interpretation of the regulation was incorrect, but no immediate steps were taken to inform the applicants of this. This was done only later, by which time the applicants had already committed themselves as to the way in which they would take their pension entitlements. The applicants sought compensation for their losses.

---

[42] Case T–79/96 *Camar Srl* (n 39) [205].

THE ECJ

36. Apart from the exceptional instance, the adoption of an incorrect interpretation does not constitute in itself a wrongful act.

37. Even the fact that the authorities request those concerned to obtain information from the competent departments does not necessarily involve those authorities in an obligation to guarantee the correctness of the information supplied and does not therefore make them liable for any injury which may be occasioned by incorrect information.

38. However, whilst it may be possible to doubt the existence of a wrongful act concerning the supply of incorrect information, the same cannot be said of the department's delay in rectifying the information.

39. Although such rectification was possible as early as April 1968 it was deferred without any justification until the end of 1968.

...

41. A correction made shortly before or after 16 April, that is to say, before the time when those concerned had to make their decision, would have certainly enabled the defendant to avoid all liability for the consequences of the wrong information. The failure to make such a correction is, on the other hand, a matter of such a nature as to render the Communities liable.

Thus in *Richez-Parise* the ECJ construed illegality for the purposes of damages liability so as to exclude a mere incorrect interpretation of a regulation. Such regulations are often complex, and are open to more than one construction. To render the EU liable in damages whenever such a construction proved to be incorrect would open the EU to strict liability, where the only condition for recovery would be proof that the interpretation was incorrect, even if it was plausible and the decision-maker had taken due care.[43]

The ability to shape illegality for the purposes of damages liability is also apparent in other cases.[44] In *Fresh Marine*[45] the applicant sought damages because the Commission had erroneously decided that the company was in breach of an undertaking it had given in relation to the dumping of salmon. The CFI held that it was not necessary for the applicant to prove a sufficiently serious breach, since the alleged error did not involve complex discretionary choices. A mere infringement of EC law would suffice. However it then defined the relevant error leading to illegality to be the lack of ordinary care and diligence by the Commission, and took account of the applicant's contributory negligence.[46]

(D) SUMMARY

i. The traditional test for liability for non-discretionary acts was proof of illegality, causation, and damage. The more modern case law continues to distinguish between liability for discretionary and non-discretionary acts, but does so from within the framework of the sufficiently serious breach test: where the Union institution has considerably reduced or no discretion, the mere infringement of EU law *may* be sufficient to establish the existence of the sufficiently serious breach.

ii. The General Court and CJEU will decide whether an act, general or individual, falls to be judged by this test, rather than the test discussed in the previous section.

---

[43] See the similar reasoning in relation to state liability in Case C–392/93 *R v HM Treasury, ex p British Telecommunications plc* [1996] ECR I–1631.

[44] Case 145/83 *Stanley George Adams v Commission* [1985] ECR 3539; Case T-341/07 *Sison* (n 26) [33]-[40], [57]-[60].

[45] Case T–178/98 (n 4) [61].

[46] Ibid [57]–[61].

iii. The General Court and CJEU will also have to decide what constitutes illegality for the purposes of liability for non-discretionary acts.

4 OFFICIAL ACTS OF UNION SERVANTS

Article 340 TFEU allows for loss to be claimed where it has been caused either by the EU institutions or by the acts of its servants 'in the performance of their duties'. Not every act performed by a servant will be deemed to be an act in the performance of his or her duties. The matter is rendered more complex by the fact that Article 12 of the Protocol on the Privileges and Immunities of the European Communities stated that 'officials and other servants of the Community shall…be immune from legal proceedings in respect of acts performed by them in their official capacity'.[47]

Case 9/69 **Sayag v Leduc**
[1969] ECR 329

Sayag was an engineer employed by Euratom. He was instructed to take Leduc, a representative of a private firm, on a visit to certain installations. He drove him in his own car, and obtained a travel order which enabled him to claim the expenses for the trip from the Community. An accident occurred and Leduc claimed in the Belgian courts damages against Sayag for the injuries which he had suffered. It was argued that Sayag was driving the car in the performance of his duties, and that therefore the action should have been brought against the Community. Article 188(2) of the Euratom Treaty was equivalent to Article 340(2) TFEU.

THE ECJ

By referring at one and the same time to damage caused by the institutions and to that caused by the servants of the Community, Article 188 indicates that the Community is only liable for those acts of its servants which, by virtue of an internal and direct relationship, are the necessary extension of the tasks entrusted to the institutions.

In the light of the special nature of this legal system, it would not therefore be lawful to extend it to categories of acts other than those referred to above.

A servant's use of his private car for transport during the course of his duties does not satisfy the conditions set out above.

A reference to a servant's private car in a travel order does not bring the driving of such car within the performance of his duties, but is basically intended to enable any necessary reimbursement of the travel expenses involved in this means of transport to be made in accordance with the standards laid down for this purpose.

Only in the rare case of *force majeure*, or in exceptional circumstances of such overriding importance that without the servant's using private means of transport the Community would have been unable to carry out the tasks entrusted to it, could such use be considered to form part of the servant's performance of his duties, within the meaning of the second paragraph of Article 188 of the Treaty.

It follows from the above that the driving of a private car by a servant cannot in principle constitute the performance of his duties within the meaning of the second paragraph of Article 188 of the EAEC Treaty.

---

[47] See now, Protocol (No 7) On the Privileges and Immunities of the European Union, Art 11.

The range of acts done by its servants for which the EU will accept responsibility is therefore narrow,[48] and more limited than that in most Member States. No real justification for the limited nature of this liability is provided by the ECJ. If the EU is not liable then an action can be brought against the servant in a personal capacity, and any such action is brought in national courts and is governed by national law.

However, the Protocol on the Privileges and Immunities of the European Union provides that servants have immunity from suit in national courts in relation to 'acts performed by them in their official capacity'. This language differs from Article 340(2), which speaks in terms of servants acting in 'performance of their duties'. Normally one would expect that where the EU is liable under Article 340(2) because the servant was acting in the performance of his or her duties, then the servant would not be personally liable, since he or she would be acting in an official capacity.

The interrelationship between these two provisions may, nonetheless, be more problematic, and the ECJ has held that the servant's personal immunity and the scope of the EU's liability for the acts of the servant are separate issues.[49] There is however much to be said for the view of Schermers and Swaak that acts of servants in the performance of their duties (leading to EU liability) include, but are not limited to, acts performed by them in their official capacity (leading to the servants' immunity).[50]

It has been assumed thus far that the EU will be liable for the acts of its institutions, and for the acts of its servants, subject to the limitations of the *Sayag* case. Where the EU establishes agencies it is common for the regulation establishing the agency to contain a provision equivalent to Article 340(2).[51] The EU may well be responsible even in the absence of such an express provision where it has delegated functions to an EU body, since the acts of that body, at least those of a governmental nature, will be imputed to the EU.[52]

5 VALID LEGISLATIVE ACTS

(A) THE NATURE OF THE PROBLEM

Individuals may well suffer loss flowing from lawful EU acts, as well as from those tainted with some illegality. This problem can occur in any legal system, but the potential for its occurrence in the EU is particularly marked.

HJ Bronkhorst, The Valid Legislative Act as a Cause of Liability of the Communities[53]

There are many reasons why private individuals may have a particular interest in the existence of a clearly defined principle concerning Community liability for legal acts which result in damage for them . . . Does a fisherman, who, on very short notice, has to make very important changes to his vessel, thus incurring

---

[48] Case T–124/04 *Jamal Ouariachi v Commission* [2005] ECR II–4653.
[49] Case 5/68 *Sayag v Leduc* [1968] ECR 395, 408.
[50] HG Schermers and RA Swaak, 'Official Acts of Community Servants and Article 215(4)' in Heukels and McDonnell (n 4) 177.
[51] P Craig, *EU Administrative Law* (Oxford University Press, 2nd edn, 2012) ch 6.
[52] Case 18/60 *Worms v High Authority* [1962] ECR 195.
[53] Heukels and McDonnell (n 4) 153–154.

substantial financial costs, have an action for compensation even if the Community measures as such cannot be challenged on the ground of illegality?

[P]rivate individuals, operating in the field of the Common Agricultural Policy, may easily suffer financial injury because of the fact that competing producers are favoured by Community measures. Producers of vegetable fats may very well undergo the effects of (uneven) competition if producers of butter or milk powder are able to dispose of large quantities of their products on the European markets with the help of Community subsidies.

The problem of loss being caused by lawful governmental action is not peculiar to the EU. Thus, French law recognizes a principle of *égalité devant les charges publiques*, and German law has the concept of *Sonderöpfer*, whereby loss caused by lawful governmental action can be recovered, albeit in limited circumstances.[54] While there is hardship for individuals in the situations postulated by Bronkhorst, the difficulties of deciding when to grant such compensation should not be underestimated.

PP Craig, Compensation in Public Law[55]

Legislation is constantly being passed which is explicitly or implicitly aimed at benefiting one section of the population at the expense of another. It is a matter of conscious legislative policy. This may be in the form of tax changes or in a decision to grant selective assistance to one particular type of industry rather than another. Any incorporation of state liability arising out of legislation as part of a risk theory would necessitate the drawing of a difficult line. It would be between cases where the deleterious effect on a firm or group was the aim of the legislation or a necessary correlative of it, and where legislation is passed which incidentally affects a particular firm in a serious manner, but where there is no legislative objection to compensating the firm for the loss suffered.

The drawing of such a line in the context of the EU is particularly problematic, given that within, for example, the CAP there will often be 'winners and losers' as the result of attempts to give effect to the conflicting objectives of that policy.

(B) THE CASE LAW

Claims to recover for lawfully caused loss have often been rejected.[56] The leading case is now *Dorsch Consult*.[57]

---

[54] Ibid 155–159.

[55] (1980) 96 LQR 413, 450.

[56] Cases 9 and 11/71 *Compagnie d'Approvisionnement de Transport et de Crédit SA and Grands Moulins de Paris SA v Commission* [1972] ECR 391, [45]; Cases 54–60/76 *Compagnie Industrielle et Agricole du Comté de Loheac v Council and Commission* [1977] ECR 645, [19]; Case 59/83 *SA Biovilac NV v EEC* [1984] ECR 4057, 4080–4081; Case 265/85 *Van den Bergh & Jurgens BV and Van Dijk Food Products (Lopik) BV v EEC* [1987] ECR 1155; Case 81/86 *De Boer Buizen v Council and Commission* [1987] ECR 3677.

[57] Case T–383/00 *Beamglow* (n 18).

Case T–184/95 **Dorsch Consult Ingenieurgesellschaft mbH v Council**
[1998] ECR II–667

The case arose out of the Gulf war. The EC, acting pursuant to a resolution of the United Nations Security Council, passed a regulation banning trade with Iraq. The Iraqi Government retaliated with a law which froze all assets and rights of companies doing business in Iraq, where those companies were based in countries that had imposed the embargo. The applicant was such a company. It argued that it should be compensated by the EC for the loss it had incurred, even if the EC had acted lawfully.

THE CFI

59. At the outset, the Court would point out that if the Community is to incur non-contractual liability as the result of a lawful or unlawful act, it is necessary in any event to prove that the alleged damage is real and the existence of a causal link between that act and the alleged damage. . . .

. . .

80. It is clear from the . . . case law of the Court of Justice that, in the event of the principle of Community liability for a lawful act being recognised in Community law, such liability can be incurred only if the damage alleged, if deemed to constitute a 'still subsisting injury', affects a particular circle of economic operators in a disproportionate manner in comparison with others (unusual damage) and exceeds the economic risks inherent in operating in the sector concerned (special damage), without the legislative measure that gave rise to the alleged damage being justified by a general economic interest (*De Boer Buizen, Compagnie d'Approvisionnement, Biovilac*).

81. As regards the unusual nature of the alleged damage . . . [N]ot only the applicant's claims . . . were affected but also those of all Community undertakings which . . . had not yet been paid. . . .

82. . . . It cannot therefore claim to have suffered special damage or to have made exceptional sacrifice. . . .

83. . . . It is common ground that Iraq . . . was already regarded . . . as a 'high risk country'. In those circumstances, the economic and commercial risks deriving from the possible involvement of Iraq in renewed warfare . . . and the suspension of payment of its debts . . . constituted foreseeable risks inherent in any provision of services in Iraq. . . .

. . .

85. It follows that the risks involved in the applicant's providing services in Iraq formed part of the risks inherent in operating in the sector concerned.

The CFI's judgment in paragraph 80 is framed conditionally: if such liability were to exist then the conditions listed would have to be satisfied. This was stressed on the appeal to the ECJ.[58] It has been emphasized again more recently in *FIAMM*,[59] where the ECJ was even more wary about admitting the existence of any such principle of liability in EU law. It reiterated that no such principle yet existed in EU law and that if it did it would be subject to the stringent conditions set out above. The ECJ noted moreover that there was no consensus in the laws of the Member States as to whether liability for lawful acts of a legislative nature existed.[60]

---

[58] Case C–237/98 P *Dorsch Consult Ingenieurgesellschaft mbH v Council* [2000] ECR I–4549, [19].
[59] Cases C–120–121/06 P *FIAMM* (n 16) [164]–[176].
[60] Ibid [175].

6 CAUSATION AND DAMAGE

(A) CAUSATION

AG Toth, The Concepts of Damage and Causality as Elements of Non-Contractual Liability[61]

[T]he establishment of the necessary causality may give rise to difficult problems in practice. This is particularly so in the field of economic and commercial relations where the cause of an event can usually be traced back to a number of factors, objective as well as subjective, operating simultaneously or successively and producing direct as well as indirect effects. Broadly speaking, it may be said that there is no causality involving liability where the same result would have occurred in the same way even in the absence of the wrongful Community act or omission in question. The converse proposition, i.e., that the requisite causality exists whenever it can be shown that the damage would not have occurred without the Community action, is, however not always correct. Although in theory it is true that any circumstance, near or remote, without which an injury would not have been produced may be considered to be its cause, the fact that a Community act or omission is one only of several such circumstances may not in itself be sufficient to establish a causal connection entailing non-contractual liability. For that purpose, the causality must be 'direct, immediate and exclusive' which it can be only if the damage arises directly from the conduct of the institutions and does not depend on the intervention of other causes, whether positive or negative.

The difficulties of proving that it was the EU's action that caused the loss can be exemplified by *Dumortier*.[62]

Cases 64, 113/76, 167, 239/78, 27, 28 and 45/79 Dumortier Frères SA v Council [1979] ECR 3091

Council regulations provided that production refunds should be payable for maize starch, but that they should be abolished in the case of maize groats and meal (gritz), which were used in the production of beer. This differential treatment had been held to be in breach of what are now Articles 39 and 40 TFEU,[63] and the applicants claimed damages. The subsidies had been restored in the light of the ECJ's decision, but only for the future, and therefore losses had still been suffered in the intervening period. The Court found that there had been a manifest and grave breach by the Community. Some of the applicants claimed that they should be compensated because they were forced to close their factories.

THE ECJ

21. [T]he Council argued that the origin of the difficulties experienced by those undertakings is to be found in the circumstances peculiar to each of them, such as the obsolescence of their plant and

---

61 Heukels and McDonnell (n 4) 192.

62 See also Case T–193/04 *Tillack v Commission* [2006] ECR II–3995; Case T–304/01 *Perez v Council* [2006] ECR II–4857; Case T–42/06 *Bruno Gollnisch v European Parliament* [2010] ECR II–1135, [110]; Case T–88/09 *Idromacchine Srl v Commission* [2011] ECR II–7833.

63 Cases 124/76 and 20/77 *SA Moulins et Huileries de Pont-à-Mousson and Société Coopérative 'Providence Agricole de la Champagne' v Office National Interprofessionnel des Céréales* [1977] ECR 1795.

managerial or financial problems. The data supplied by the parties in the course of the proceedings are not such as to establish the true cause of the further damage alleged. However, it is sufficient to state that even if it were assumed that the abolition of the refunds exacerbated the difficulties encountered by those applicants, those difficulties would not be a sufficiently direct consequence of the unlawful conduct of the Council to render the Community liable to make good the damage.

The applicant must show not only that EU action caused the loss, but also that the chain of causation has not been broken by the Member State or the applicant. The ECJ has held that where the loss arises from an independent/autonomous act by the Member State, the EU is no longer liable.[64] If, however, this conduct has been made possible by an illegal failure of the Commission to exercise its supervisory powers, then this failure will be considered to be the cause of the damage.[65] There may be instances where both the Union and the Member State are responsible. This complex issue will be considered below.

It is not entirely clear what conduct by the individual will break the chain of causation. Negligence, or contributory negligence, will suffice either to defeat the claim or to reduce the award of damages.[66] It has also been held that if the individual ought to have foreseen the possibility of certain events which might cause loss, then the damages claim will be diminished or lost.[67] Moreover, an individual who believes that a wrongful act of the EU caused loss has been encouraged by the Court to challenge the measure through Article 267 TFEU.[68]

(B) DAMAGE

The general objective when awarding compensation for loss in the context of non-contractual liability is to place the victim in the situation that would have pertained if the wrong had not been committed.[69] Although Article 340(2) speaks of the duty of the EU to make good 'any damage', losses will be recoverable only if they are certain and specific, proven and quantifiable.[70]

While the damage claimed must in general be *certain*, the Court held in *Kampffmeyer* that it is possible to maintain an action 'for imminent damage foreseeable with sufficient certainty even if the damage cannot yet be precisely assessed'.[71] The rationale was that it might be necessary to pursue an action immediately in order to prevent even greater damage.

The idea that the damage suffered must be *specific*, in the sense that it affects the applicant's interests in a special and individual way, is to be found in various guises in ECJ decisions. Thus in *Bayerische HNL* the Court emphasized that the effects of the regulation did not exceed the bounds of economic risk inherent in the activity in question.[72] Similar themes concerning the special nature of the burden imposed on a particular trader can be found in the case law concerning possible recovery for lawful

---

[64] Case 132/77 *Société pour l'Exportation des Sucres SA v Commission* [1978] ECR 1061, 1072–1073.

[65] Cases 9 and 12/60 *Vloeberghs v High Authority* [1961] ECR 197, 240; Case 4/69 *Alfons Lütticke GmbH v Commission* [1971] ECR 325, 336–338.

[66] Case 145/83 *Adams* (n 44) 3592; Case T–178/98 *Fresh Marine* (n 4).

[67] Case 59/83 *Biovilac* (n 56); Case T–514/93 *Cobrecaf v Commission* [1995] ECR II–621, 643; Case T–572/93 *Odigitria v Council and Commission* [1995] ECR II–2025, 2051–2052; Case T–184/95 *Dorsch Consult* [1998] ECR II–667.

[68] Cases 116, 124/77 *Amylum* (n 22).

[69] Case C–308/87 *Grifoni v EAEC* [1994] ECR I–341, [40]; Cases C–104/89 and 37/90 *Mulder* (n 28) [51], [63]; Case T–260/97 *Camar Srl v Council* [2005] ECR II–2741, [97].

[70] Toth (n 61) 180–191; Case T–88/09 *Idromacchine Srl* (n 62).

[71] Cases 56–60/74 *Kampffmeyer v Commission and Council* [1976] ECR 711, 741; Case T–79/96 *Camar Srl* (n 39) [207].

[72] Cases 83, 94/76, 4, 15 and 40/77 *Bayerische HNL* (n 21).

governmental action.[73] The question whether an applicant should have to prove abnormal or special damage in a case concerning unlawful Union action has already been discussed.

The injured party will have the onus of *proving* that the damage occurred. In general the individual will have to show that the injury was actually sustained.[74] This may not be easy, and it is not uncommon for cases to fail for this reason.[75]

The damage must also be *quantifiable* if the applicant is to succeed. In order to decide whether the loss is quantifiable, one needs to know what *types* of damage are recoverable. Advocate General Capotorti put the matter as follows:[76]

> It is well known that the legal concept of 'damage' covers both a material loss *stricto sensu*, that is to say, a reduction in a person's assets, and also the loss of an increase in those assets which would have occurred if the harmful act had not taken place (these two alternatives are known respectively as *damnum emergens* and *lucrum cessans*)....The object of compensation is to restore the assets of the victim to the condition in which they would have been apart from the unlawful act, or at least to the condition closest to that which would have been produced if the unlawful nature of the act had not taken place: the hypothetical nature of that restoration often entails a certain degree of approximation....These general remarks are not limited to the field of private law, but apply also to the liability of public authorities, and more especially to the non-contractual liability of the Community.

The ECJ will grant damages for losses actually sustained and will exceptionally award for nonmaterial damage.[77] It is willing in principle to give damages for lost profits, but is reluctant to do so. Thus, in *Kampffmeyer*, while the Court admitted that lost profit was recoverable, it did not grant such damages to traders who had abandoned their intended transactions because of the unlawful act of the Community, even though these transactions would have produced profits.[78] In *CNTA* it was held that lost profits were not recoverable where the claim was based on the concept of legitimate expectations, since that concept only served to ensure that losses were not suffered owing to an unexpected change in the legal position; it did not serve to ensure that profits would be made.[79] However, in *Mulder*,[80] the ECJ was prepared to compensate for lost profit, although it held that any such sum must take into account the income which could have been earned from alternative activities, applying the principle that there is a duty to mitigate loss.

In quantifying the applicant's loss the EU institutions have argued that damages should not be recoverable if the loss has been passed on to the consumers. This was accepted in principle by the ECJ in the *Quellmehl and Gritz* litigation.[81] Toth has justly criticized this reasoning. He points out that whether a firm could pass on a cost increase to consumers would depend upon many variables, which might operate differently for different firms, and which would be difficult to assess. He argues,

---

[73] Case C–237/98 P *Dorsch Consult* (n 58).

[74] Case 26/74 *Roquette Frères v Commission* [1976] ECR 677, 694, AG Trabucchi.

[75] Case 26/68 *Fux v Commission* [1969] ECR 145, 156; Case T–1/99 *T. Port GmbH & Co KG v Commission* [2001] ECR II–465.

[76] Case 238/78 *Ireks-Arkady v Council and Commission* [1979] ECR 2955, 2998–2999.

[77] Case T–84/98 *C v Council* [2000] ECR IA–113, [98]–[103]; Case T–307/01 *Jean-Paul François v Commission* [2004] ECR II–1669, [107]–[111]; Case T–48/01 *François Vainker and Brenda Vainker v European Parliament* [2004] ECR II–197, [180]; Case T–309/03 *Grau v Commission* [2006] ECR II–1173; Case T–88/09 *Idromacchine Srl* (n 62).

[78] Cases 5, 7 and 13–24/66 *Kampffmeyer v Commission* [1967] ECR 245, 266–267; Case T–160/03 *AFCon Management Consultants v Commission* [2005] ECR II–981, [112]–[114].

[79] Case 74/74 (n 14) 550.

[80] Cases C–104/89 and 37/90 [1992] ECR I–3061.

[81] Case 238/78 (n 76) 2974.

moreover, that such an idea is wrong in principle, since it would mean that losses would be borne by consumers, rather than by the institutions which had committed the wrongful act.[82]

7 JOINT LIABILITY OF THE EU AND MEMBER STATES

The joint liability of the Union and the Member States gives rise to complex problems which can be dealt with only in outline.[83] The approach of Oliver, which distinguishes between procedural and substantive issues, will be adopted here.[84]

(A) PROCEDURAL ISSUES

In procedural terms it is not possible for EU non-contractual liability to be decided by national courts. Article 268 TFEU confers this jurisdiction on the ECJ and, while it does not state that this jurisdiction is exclusive, this is implied by Article 274 TFEU.[85] Conversely, it is not possible for an individual to bring a direct action against a Member State before the ECJ, since there is no provision for this in the Treaty.

When an action is brought before the ECJ under Article 340(2), EU law is applied. An action brought against a Member State in the national court will be governed by national law. This will, however, include EU law. The national courts are under an obligation to provide an effective remedy for the enforcement of directly effective EU provisions, and the rights against the state in such actions must be no less favourable than those which exist in domestic matters.[86]

(B) SUBSTANTIVE ISSUES

Joint liability of the EU and the Member States can arise in different situations, two of which will be explored here.

The *first is where the Union has taken inadequate steps to prevent a breach of Union law by national authorities*. This issue arose in *Lütticke* where the Court appeared to accept that, in principle, such an action was possible.[87] However, there are considerable obstacles with any such action. It is doubtful whether the Commission has a duty to bring an action under Article 258 TFEU against a Member State which is in breach of EU law.[88] The position may well be different where the Commission has adopted a more formal measure, which approves of the illegal national action, as in *Kampffmeyer*.

---

[82] Toth (n 61) 189–190.

[83] A Durand, 'Restitution or Damages: National Court or European Court?' (1975–6) 1 ELRev 431; TC Hartley, 'Concurrent Liability in EEC Law: A Critical Review of the Cases' (1977) 2 ELRev 249; W Wils, 'Concurrent Liability of the Community and a Member State' (1992) 17 ELRev 191.

[84] P Oliver, 'Joint Liability of the Community and the Member States' in Heukels and McDonnell (n 4) ch 16.

[85] Art 274 TFEU: 'save where jurisdiction is conferred on the Court of Justice of the European Union by the Treaties, disputes to which the Union is a party shall not on that ground be excluded from the jurisdiction of the courts or tribunals of the Member States': Cases 106–120/87 *Asteris v Greece and EEC* [1988] ECR 5515; Case T–18/99 *Cordis* (n 18) [27].

[86] Oliver (n 84) 289.

[87] Case 4/69 *Alfons Lütticke GmbH v Commission* [1971] ECR 325.

[88] Ch 12.

Cases 5, 7 and 13–24/66 **Kampffmeyer v Commission**
[1967] ECR 245

The case arose from the gradual establishment of a common market in cereals. On 1 October 1963 the German intervention board issued a notice stating that the levy for the import of such products would be zero. On that same day, the applicants applied for import licences for the import of maize from France, with the levy having been set at zero for January 1964. Some of the applicants had actually bought maize from France. The German Government on the same day, 1 October 1963, then suspended the zero-rated import licences for maize. Under Article 22 of Regulation 19 the German Government could refuse such applications only if there was a threat of a serious disturbance to the market in question. Such a decision had to be confirmed by the Commission, and the Commission on 3 October duly authorized this to remain in force until 4 October. This decision was annulled by the ECJ.[89] The applicants then sought compensation from the Commission. Some of them had paid the duties imposed by the German authorities and imported the maize on these terms; others had repudiated their contracts to buy the maize, after the German Government had refused to issue the zero-rated licences. These are the two categories of applicants referred to by the ECJ in the following extract.

THE ECJ

However, with regard to any injury suffered by the applicants belonging to the first and second categories above-mentioned, those applicants have informed the Court that the injury alleged is the subject of two actions for damages, one against the Federal Republic of Germany before a German court and the other against the Community before the Court of Justice. It is necessary to avoid the applicants' being insufficiently or excessively compensated for the same damage by the different assessment of two different courts applying different rules of law. Before determining the damage for which the Community should be held liable, it is necessary for the national court to have the opportunity to give judgment on any liability on the part of the Federal Republic of Germany. This being the case, final judgment cannot be given before the applicants have produced the decision of the national court on this matter, which may be done independently of the evidence asked of the applicants in the first category to the effect that they have exhausted all possible methods of recovery of the amounts improperly paid by way of levy. Furthermore, if it were established that such recovery was possible, this fact might have consequences bearing upon the calculation of the damages concerning the second category. However, the decisive nature of the said evidence required does not prevent the applicants from producing the other evidence previously indicated in the meantime.

It is clear from *Kampffmeyer* that the EU can, therefore, be liable when it has wrongfully authorized a measure taken by a national body. The procedural aspect of the case has, however, been criticized. It has been argued that there was no reason to require the applicants to proceed initially in the German courts, and that the ECJ's rationale for doing so was based implicitly on the assumption that the German authorities were primarily liable, with the Union bearing only a residual liability.[90]

This criticism may be overstated, and it may be necessary to distinguish the claim for the return of the levies paid from the more general tort action. As regards the former, the idea that the primary liability rested with Germany may well have substance, given that it was Germany which imposed the levy and it was Germany to which the funds were paid. As regards the latter, there is no particular reason why the EU's liability should be seen as somehow secondary to that of the Member State.

---

[89] Cases 106 and 107/63 *Toepfer v Commission* [1965] ECR 405.

[90] Oliver (n 84).

The *second situation in which the issue of joint liability may arise is where the Member State applies unlawful Union legislation*. This can arise, for example, in the context of the CAP, where Union regulations will often be applied by national intervention boards. The general rule is that it is the national intervention boards, and not the Commission, which are responsible for the application of the CAP, and that an action must normally be commenced in the national courts.

Case 96/71 **R and V Haegeman Sprl v Commission**
[1972] ECR 1005

[Note Lisbon Treaty renumbering: Art 177 is now Art 267 TFEU]

Haegeman was a Belgian company which imported wine from Greece which was at the time outside the Community. It alleged that it suffered loss because of a countervailing charge imposed on the import of wine from Greece to Belgium. This charge was imposed by a Council regulation and was levied by the Belgian authorities.

THE ECJ

7. Disputes concerning the levying on individuals of the charges and levies referred to by this provision must be resolved, applying Community law, by the national authorities and following the practices laid down by the law of the Member States.

8. Issues, therefore, which are raised during a procedure as to the interpretation and validity of regulations establishing the Communities' own resources must be brought before the national courts which have at their disposal the procedure under Article 177 of the Treaty in order to ensure the uniform application of Community law.

. . .

14. The applicant maintains further that by reason of the defendant's behaviour it has suffered exceptional damage as a result of loss of profit, unforeseen financial outlay and losses on existing contracts.

15. The question of the possible liability of the Community is in the first place linked with that of the legality of the levying of the charge in question.

16. It has just been found that, in the context of the relationship between individuals and the taxation authority which has levied the charge in dispute, the latter question comes under the jurisdiction of the national courts.

17. Accordingly, at the present stage the claim for compensation for possible damage must be dismissed.

The decision in *Haegman* can be criticized since the money levied went into the EU's funds. The sums were imposed by the EU and were collected on its behalf by the Member State. It is nonetheless the case that an action to recover such a charge must be commenced in the national courts, and that this is also so where a trader is seeking payment of a sum to which he believes himself to be entitled under EU law.[91] This principle applies even where the Commission has sent telexes to the national board setting out its interpretation of the relevant regulations.[92] The authorities of a Member State may, however, be able to recover from EU funds where they have paid for losses which are the EU's responsibility.[93]

[91] Case 99/74 *Société des Grands Moulins des Antilles v Commission* [1975] ECR 1531.

[92] Case 133/79 *Sucrimex SA and Westzucker GmbH v Commission* [1980] ECR 1299; Case 217/81 *Compagnie Interagra SA v Commission* [1982] ECR 2233.

[93] Oliver (n 84) 306–308; JA Usher, *Legal Aspects of Agriculture in the European Community* (Oxford University Press, 1988) 104–106, 150–152.

There are, nonetheless, a number of situations in which it is possible to proceed against the EU directly. First, if the Commission sends a telex which is interpreted, in the context of the relevant legislation, as an instruction to the national agency to act in a particular manner, then an action may be brought against the Commission for damages.[94] Secondly, it is possible to proceed against the EU where no action could be brought against any national authority and hence there would be no remedy in the national courts.[95] Thirdly, it is possible to bring an action in the ECJ where the substance of the claim is that the EU has committed a tortious wrong to the applicant. Thus in *Dietz*[96] the essence of the claim was that the EU authorities had introduced a levy without transitional provisions and had thereby caused loss to the applicant in breach of its legitimate expectations. This claim could be pursued in the ECJ since the wrong alleged was entirely directed towards the EU's behaviour, and not that of the Member State.

8 CONTRACT

The discussion thus far has focused on the EU's non-contractual liability under Article 340(2). The Union will obviously also make contracts,[97] and Article 340(1) provides that contractual liability shall be governed by the law applicable to the contract in question.

The meaning of this phrase requires explanation. Contracts are often made between parties in different countries, and therefore it is necessary to determine which law should govern the contract. The body of law dealing with this issue is known as the conflict of laws or private international law. Contracts often have choice-of-law clauses, specifying the law to be applied. The Commission always inserts such a clause in its contracts. It has been held that this clause prevails, and cannot be displaced by arguments that the contract was more closely connected with a different country from that specified in the choice-of-law clause.[98]

It would be possible in principle for a choice-of-law clause to specify EU law as that applicable to the contract. Article 340(1), in contrast to Article 340(2), does not state that the Union is to develop a system of law by drawing on the relevant general principles common to the laws of the Member States, but such a development of contract law may occur in the future.

This can be seen indirectly in staff cases. The Court has characterized contracts of employment of certain Union officials as public law contracts, emphasizing that the work performed was of a governmental nature, with the consequence that the contracts were governed by administrative law. The Court did not state that any system of national administrative law was to be applied.[99]

It can also be seen more directly in initiatives to develop a Common Frame of Reference[100] for contract, which aim to provide the EU with a 'toolbox' of fundamental principles of contract law for the revision of existing and the preparation of new legislation in the area of contract law. To this end, the Commission established an expert group on a Common Frame of Reference, the group's main task

---

[94] Case 175/84 *Krohn & Co Import-Export GmbH & Co KG v Commission* [1986] ECR 753.

[95] Case 281/82 *Unifrex v Commission and Council* [1984] ECR 1969; Case T–167/94 *Nolle v Council and Commission* [1995] ECR II–2589; Case T–18/99 *Cordis* (n 18) [28].

[96] Case 126/76 *Dietz v Commission* [1977] ECR 2431; Case T–18/99 *Cordis* (n 18) [26].

[97] T Heukels, 'The Contractual Liability of the European Community Revisited' in Heukels and McDonnell (n 4) ch 5.

[98] Case 318/81 *Commission v CO.DE.MI. SpA* [1985] ECR 3693.

[99] Case 1/55 *Kergall v Common Assembly* [1955] ECR 151; Cases 43, 45 and 48/59 *Von Lachmüller v Commission* [1960] ECR 463.

[100] http://ec.europa.eu/justice/contract/cesl/background/index_en.htm.

being to deliver a user-friendly and legally certain set of rules, which could serve as a future instrument in European contract law.

If the parties to a contract choose a particular legal system to govern the substance of their contractual obligations, this still leaves open which court will have jurisdiction to determine the dispute. Article 272 TFEU states that the CJEU shall have jurisdiction to give judgment pursuant to any arbitration clause contained in a contract concluded by or on behalf of the Union, whether that contract be governed by public or private law.

9 RESTITUTION

Most legal systems recognize liability in restitution or quasi-contract, in addition to that based on contract or tort. The nature of this liability continues to divide academics, but the better view is that it is distinct from both contract and tort. Restitution is not based upon promise, but rather on unjust enrichment by the defendant, hence its difference from contractual liability. Restitution does not normally require a wrongful act by the defendant, in the sense of fault, and the measure of recovery is normally determined by the extent of the defendant's unjust enrichment rather than the extent of the loss to the plaintiff, hence its difference from most forms of tort liability.

A common restitutionary claim arises from payments made to public bodies when they have no right to the money. This is of considerable importance in the EU.[101] It can arise in two types of situation.

There can, on the one hand, be cases where a Member State has imposed a levy that is illegal under EU law, as exemplified by *Van Gend en Loos*. The matter will be remitted to the national court once the ECJ has found that the levy was in breach of EU law. It will be for the national court to devise a remedy to effectuate the EU right, which will often be return of the sum paid to the national authority.[102]

There may, on the other hand, be instances under, for example, the CAP where money is paid into EU funds where there is no legal obligation to pay the sum. The EU Courts have held that unjust enrichment is a general principle of EU law,[103] and that proof of some independent unlawful act by the defendant is not required.[104] Thus where a fine imposed for breach of the competition rules is annulled there is an obligation to return the money plus interest.[105] The ECJ has also applied restitutionary principles in cases where there has been unjust enrichment by an individual against the EU.[106] It is clearly correct in principle that a remedy should be available in favour of an individual where the EU has been unjustly enriched at his or her expense, as where the EU has imposed an unlawful charge. If a levy imposed by a Member State is recoverable because it is in breach of the Treaty, the same should be true for an illegal charge levied by the EU. The matter is, however, complicated in two different ways.

First, there is the case law discussed above, which has held that, in many such instances, the action should be commenced in the national court against the national collecting agency, even where the funds are treated as EU funds.[107]

---

[101] A Jones, *Restitution and European Community Law* (Mansfield Press, 2000); R Williams, *Unjust Enrichment and Public Law: A Comparative Study of England, France and the EU* (Hart, 2010) chs 6–7.

[102] Ch 8.

[103] Case C–259/87 *Greece v Commission* [1990] ECR I–2845, [26]; Case T–171/99 *Corus UK Ltd v Commission* [2001] ECR II–2967, [55]; Case T–7/99 *Medici Grimm KG v Council* [2000] ECR II–2671, [89]; Case T–28/03 *Holcim (Deutschland) AG v Commission* [2005] ECR II–1357, [127]–[130]; Case C–47/07 P *Masdar (UK) Ltd v Commission* [2008] ECR I–9761, [47]–[50].

[104] Case T–333/03 *Masdar* (n 39) [91]–[93].

[105] Case T–171/99 *Corus* (n 103) [53]–[55].

[106] See, eg, Case 18/63 *Wollast v EEC* [1964] ECR 85; Case 110/63 *Willame v Commission* [1965] ECR 649.

[107] See pp 603–604.

Secondly, there is the difficulty of locating restitutionary claims within the Treaty. The wording of Article 340(2), which requires the EU to 'make good any damage caused' by its institutions, does not fit perfectly with the idea of a restitutionary action. It is, however, framed in terms of 'non-contractual liability', and this is wide enough to cover restitutionary relief. The ECJ affirmed in *Masdar* that it would be contrary to principle if Articles 274 and 340(2) were construed to preclude such recovery.[108]

10 CONCLUSIONS

i. The ECJ's jurisprudence under Article 340 has, in the past, been criticized for being overly restrictive. The case law was, until recently, unclear about the precise criterion for the application of the *Schöppenstedt* test.

ii. It is now clear that the crucial issue is the discretionary or non-discretionary nature of the act. Discretionary acts will be subject to the *Schöppenstedt* test. This requires proof of a breach of a superior rule of law for the protection of the individual; the breach must be sufficiently serious; there must be causation and damage. The factors laid down in the case law on state liability in damages will be directly relevant when deciding whether there has been a sufficiently serious breach under Article 340.

iii. Where the challenged act is not discretionary the traditional test for liability was proof of illegality, causation, and damage. The more modern case law continues to distinguish between liability for discretionary and non-discretionary acts, but does so from within the framework of the sufficiently serious breach test: where the EU institution has considerably reduced or no discretion, the mere infringement of EU law *may* be sufficient to establish the existence of the sufficiently serious breach. It would be regrettable if this shift rendered it more difficult to recover than hitherto.

11 FURTHER READING

(a) Books

HEUKELS, T, AND MCDONNELL, A (eds), *The Action for Damages in Community Law* (Kluwer, 1997)

SCHERMERS, HG, HEUKELS, T, AND MEAD, P (eds), *The Non-Contractual Liability of the European Communities* (Martinus Nijhoff, 1988)

(b) Articles

HARDING, C, 'The Choice of Court Problem in Cases of Non-Contractual Liability under EEC Law' (1979) 16 CMLRev 389

HARTLEY, TC, 'Concurrent Liability in EEC Law: A Critical Review of the Cases' (1977) 2 ELRev 249

HILSON, C, 'The Role of Discretion in EC Law on Non-Contractual Liability' (2005) 42 CMLRev 677

OLIVER, P, 'Enforcing Community Rights in the English Courts' (1987) 50 MLR 881

TRIDIMAS, T, 'Liability for Breach of Community Law: Growing Up and Mellowing Down?' (2001) 38 CMLRev 301

WILS, W, 'Concurrent Liability of the Community and a Member State' (1992) 17 ELRev 191

---

[108] Case C–47/07 P *Masdar* (n 103).

THE SINGLE MARKET

1 CENTRAL ISSUES

i. The single market is central to the EU and is still its principal economic rationale. This chapter considers the forms and techniques of economic integration, the limits of integration prior to 1986, and the subsequent steps taken to complete the single market. There is a substantive and an institutional dimension to this story.

ii. In substantive terms, it is important to understand the economic dimension to the single market. It is equally important to understand that the realization of the single market in economic terms necessarily raises issues about the interrelationship of the economic and social dimensions of EU policy. The single market has been reconceptualized to take account of broader social, consumer, and environmental issues. There are nonetheless continuing tensions between the economic and social dimensions of the single market.

iii. In institutional terms, a subtle mix of legislative, administrative, and judicial initiatives has furthered evolution of the single market. The legislative procedures were changed to facilitate the passage of harmonization legislation. The focus of this legislation altered, through the new approach to harmonization. These developments were facilitated by judicial doctrine, based on mutual recognition, which framed the legislative and administrative initiatives.

2 ECONOMIC INTEGRATION: FORMS AND TECHNIQUES

(A) FORMS OF ECONOMIC INTEGRATION

The discussion in the previous chapters focused on EU institutional law. The remainder of the book is concerned with EU substantive law, although we shall stress the links between the two. It is important to understand the nature of a common market and how it differs from other forms of economic integration.

D Swann, The Economics of the Common Market[1]

Economic integration can take various forms and these can be ranged in a spectrum in which the degree of involvement of participating economies, one with another, becomes greater and greater.

---

[1] (Penguin, 7th edn, 1992), 11–12, italics in the original.

The *free trade area* is the least onerous in terms of involvement. It consists in an arrangement between states in which they agree to remove all customs duties (and quotas) on trade passing between them. Each party is free, however, to determine unilaterally the level of customs duty on imports coming from outside the area. The next stage is the *customs union*. Here tariffs and quotas on trade between members are also removed but members agree to apply a *common* level of tariff on goods entering the union from without. The latter is called the common customs, or common external, tariff. Next comes the *common market* and this technical term implies that to the free movement of *goods* within the customs union is added the free movement of the *factors of production*—labour, capital and enterprise. Finally there is the *economic union*. This is a common market in which there is also a complete unification of monetary and fiscal policy. There would be a common currency which would be controlled by a central authority and in effect the member states would become regions within the union.

Part Three of the TFEU contains many of the fundamental principles for a customs union and common market. It sets out the 'four freedoms': free movement of goods, workers, establishment and the provision of services, and capital. These Articles have social as well as economic objectives. The basic economic aim is the optimal allocation of resources for the EU. This is facilitated by allowing the factors of production to move to the area where they are most valued.

Thus the provisions on the free movement of goods ensure that goods can move freely, with the consequence that those most favoured by consumers will be most successful, irrespective of the country of origin, thereby maximizing wealth-creation in the EU. The same is true for free movement of workers. Labour as a factor of production may be valued more highly in some areas than in others. If there is an excess of supply over demand for labour in southern Italy, and an excess of demand over supply in parts of Germany, labour is worth more in Germany than it is in Italy. The value of labour within the EU is maximized if workers can move to the area where they are most valued. The same idea is applicable to freedom of establishment. If a firm established in the Netherlands believes that it could capture part of the French market, then it should not be prevented by French law that discriminates on grounds of nationality.

(B) TECHNIQUES OF ECONOMIC INTEGRATION

There are two principal techniques that can be used to attain a single market. EU law can prohibit national rules that hinder cross-border trade, because they discriminate against goods or labour, etc, from other Member States, or because they render market access more difficult. This is the classic way in which the four freedoms operate. The approach is essentially negative and deregulatory: EU law prohibits national rules that hinder cross-border trade. This is reinforced through what is known as mutual recognition, which requires a Member State to accept, subject to certain exceptions, goods that have been made in accordance with the regulatory rules of another Member State.

The creation of a single market also requires positive integration. Barriers to integration may flow from diversity in national rules on matters such as health, safety, technical specification, consumer protection, and the like. Many such barriers may only be overcome through harmonization of diverse national laws through an EU directive. This is known as positive integration, which is attained principally through Articles 114 and 115 TFEU, and other more sector-specific Treaty Articles.

3 PRE-1986: LIMITS OF INTEGRATION

Prior to 1986 the process of single market integration had been advanced by legislative and judicial means. The most important *legislative contribution* was harmonization of laws. The existence of divergences in national provisions can create barriers to trade. Article 115 TFEU now provides that:

> Without prejudice to Article 114, the Council shall, acting unanimously in accordance with a special legislative procedure and after consulting the European Parliament and the Economic and Social Committee, issue directives for the approximation of such laws, regulations or administrative provisions of the Member States as directly affect the establishment or functioning of the internal market.

There were, however, difficulties with this legislative mechanism, since it requires unanimity. This difficulty was exacerbated in the 1970s and early 1980s because harmonization directives were drafted in great detail, thereby rendering agreement more problematic. Technical developments meant, moreover, that the Commission was fighting a losing battle: as fast as it enacted a directive to cover one technical problem, so ten more would emerge, resulting from technical innovation and the emergence of new products.

The *judicial contribution* to market integration will be considered in subsequent chapters. Suffice it to say for the present that the ECJ, through Article 258 TFEU and direct effect, interpreted the Treaty so as to promote the single market. Judicial decisions such as *Cassis de Dijon*[2] were of particular importance, by invalidating trade barriers, even if they were not discriminatory, unless they could be justified on certain limited grounds. The decision was of seminal importance, but it was nonetheless essentially negative and deregulatory.

There was therefore still much to be done by the early 1980s. The Community fell behind its agenda in the late 1970s and early 1980s, and single market integration appeared to be no closer. This problem was not lost on the European Council, which, in the early 1980s, considered various techniques for expediting Community initiatives. It was in one such meeting that the seeds of the Single European Act (SEA) were sown. In 1985 the European Council called on the Commission to draw up a detailed programme with a specific timetable for achieving a single market by 1992. The Commission, under the leadership of Jacques Delors, responded.

4 SINGLE EUROPEAN ACT 1986: THE ECONOMICS AND POLITICS OF INTEGRATION

(A) THE ECONOMIC DIMENSION: THE COMMISSION'S WHITE PAPER

The Commission's White Paper addressed the problem in strident tones. It set out to establish the 'essential and logical consequences'[3] of commitment to a single market. The Commission noted that the Community had lost momentum 'partly through recession, partly through a lack of confidence and vision',[4] but it said that the mood had now changed: the 'time for talk has now passed. The time for action has come. That is what this White Paper is about.'[5]

---

[2] Case 120/78 *Rewe-Zentral AG v Bundesmonopolverwaltung für Branntwein* [1979] ECR 649.
[3] COM(85) 310, [3].
[4] Ibid [5].
[5] Ibid [7].

Completing the Internal Market COM(85)310, 14 June 1985[6]

10. For convenience the measures that need to be taken have been classified in this Paper under three headings:
— Part One: the removal of physical barriers
— Part Two: the removal of technical barriers
— Part Three: the removal of fiscal barriers

11. The most obvious example of the first category are customs posts at frontiers... [T]hey continue to exist mainly because of the technical and fiscal divisions between Member States. Once we have removed those barriers, and found alternative ways of dealing with other relevant problems such as public security, immigration and drug controls, the reasons for the existence of the physical barriers will have been eliminated.

...

13. While the elimination of physical barriers provides benefits for traders... it is through the elimination of technical barriers that the Community will give the large market its economic and industrial dimension by enabling industries to make economies of scale and therefore to become more competitive. An example of this second category—technical barriers—are the different standards for individual products adopted in different Member States for health and safety reasons, or for environmental or consumer protection... The general thrust of the Commission's approach in this area will be to move away from the concept of harmonization towards that of mutual recognition and equivalence. But there will be a continuing role for the approximation of Member States' laws and regulations as laid down in Article 100 of the Treaty. Clearly, action under this Article would be quicker and more effective if the Council were to agree not to allow the unanimity requirement to obstruct progress where it could otherwise be made.

[*The Commission explained that the White Paper was not intended to cover every possible issue of relevance to the integration of the Member States' economies. Matters such as the coordination of economic policies and competition policy were relevant in this respect; while other important areas of Community action, such as transport, the environment, and consumer protection, interacted with, and would benefit from, the completion of the internal market. The next extract looks more closely at the Commission's reasoning in relation to the second type of barrier, that arising from differing technical rules.*]

58. [S]ubject to certain important constraints (see paragraph 65), the general principle should be approved that, if a product is lawfully manufactured and marketed in one Member State, there is no reason why it should not be sold freely throughout the Community....

60. Whilst the physical barriers dealt with in Part One impede trade flows and add unacceptable administrative costs (ultimately paid by the consumer), barriers created by different national product regulations and standards have a double-edged effect: they not only add extra costs, but they also distort production patterns; increase unit costs; increase stock holding costs; discourage business cooperation; and fundamentally frustrate the creation of a common market for industrial products....

The Need for a New Strategy

61. The harmonization approach has been the cornerstone of Community action in the first 25 years and has produced unprecedented progress in the creation of common rules on a Community-wide basis. However, over the years, a number of shortcomings have been identified and it is clear that a genuine common market cannot be realised by 1992 if the Community relies exclusively on Article 100

---

[6] References to Arts 30–36 and 100 should now be read as to Arts 34–36 and 115 TFEU.

of the EEC Treaty... Clearly, action under this Article would be quicker and more effective if the Council were to agree not to allow the unanimity requirement to obstruct progress where it could otherwise be made.

63. In principle, ... mutual recognition could be an effective strategy for bringing about a common market in a trading sense. This strategy is supported in particular by Articles 30 to 36 of the EEC Treaty, which prohibit national measures which would have excessively and unjustifiably restrictive effects on free movement.

64. But while a strategy based on mutual recognition would remove barriers to trade and lead to the creation of a genuine common trading market, it might well prove inadequate for the purposes of the building-up of an expanding market based on the competitiveness which a continental-scale uniform market can generate. On the other hand experience has shown that the alternative of relying on a strategy based totally on harmonization would be over-regulatory, would take a long time to implement, would be inflexible and could stifle innovation. What is needed is a strategy that combines the best of both approaches but that, above all, allows for progress to be made more quickly than in the past.

The Chosen Strategy

65. The Commission takes into account the underlying reasons for the existence of barriers to trade, and recognises the essential equivalence of Member States' legislative objectives in the protection of health and safety, and of the environment. Its harmonization approach is based on the following principles:

— a clear distinction needs to be drawn in future internal market initiatives between what it is essential to harmonize, and what may be left to mutual recognition of national regulations and standards; this implies that, on the occasion of each harmonization initiative, the Commission will determine whether national regulations are excessive in relation to the mandatory requirements pursued and, thus, constitute unjustified barriers to trade according to Articles 30 to 36 of the EEC Treaty;

— legislative harmonization (Council Directives based on Article 100) will in future be restricted to laying down essential health and safety requirements which will be obligatory in all Member States. Conformity with this will entitle a product to free movement;

— Harmonization of industrial standards by the elaboration of European standards will be promoted to the maximum extent, but the absence of European standards should not be allowed to be used as a barrier to free movement. During the waiting period while European Standards are being developed, the mutual acceptance of national standards, with agreed procedures, should be the guiding principle.

The Commission's White Paper did not rest content with the enunciation of general strategies. The Annex listed 279 legislative measures, the object being to complete this process by 31 December 1992. The momentum behind the proposals gathered force from economic studies, which estimated that cost savings for the Community of twelve Member States could be somewhere between 70 billion ECU, 2.5 per cent of Gross Domestic Product (GDP) based on a relatively narrow conception of the benefits of removing the remaining internal market barriers, to around 125 to 190 billion ECU, 4.25 to 6.5 per cent of GDP, on the hypothesis of a more competitive, integrated market.[7]

---

[7] M Emerson, M Aujean, M Catinat, P Goybet, and A Jacquemin, *The Economics of 1992: The EC Commission's Assessment of the Economic Effects of Completing the Internal Market* (Oxford University Press, 1988) 1–10; P Cecchini, *The European Challenge 1992: The Benefits of a Single Market* (Gower, 1988).

(B) THE POLITICAL DIMENSION: THE POLITICS OF INTEGRATION

The compelling economic case for reform does not explain why the Commission's initiative suc-ceeded, given that other reforms proposed in the late 1970s and early 1980s failed. There are differing views on who were the key players and why they were willing to accept reform.[8]

Sandholtz and Zysman[9] rejected explanations based on neofunctionalist integration theories and on the domestic politics of the Member States.[10] They argued that the success of the 1992 initiative should instead be viewed in 'terms of elite bargains formulated in response to international structural change and the Commission's policy entrepreneurship'.[11] There were three factors in this regard: the domestic political context, the Commission's initiative, and the role of the business elite.

W Sandholtz and J Zysman, 1992: Recasting the European Bargain[12]

The question is why national government policies and perspectives have altered. Why, in the decade between the mid-1970s and the mid-1980s, did the European governments become open to European-level, market-oriented solutions? The answer has two parts: the failure of national strategies for economic growth and the transformation of the left in European politics. First, the traditional models of growth and economic management broke down. The old political strategies for the economy seemed to have run out. After the growth of the 1960s, the world economy entered a period of stagflation in the 1970s....

...the second aspect of the changed political context was the shift in government coalitions in a number of EC Member States. Certainly the weakening of the left in some countries and a shift from the communist to the market-socialist left in others helped to make possible a debate about market solutions (including unified European markets) to Europe's dilemma....

...

In an era when deregulation—the freeing of the market—became the fad, it made intuitive sense to extend the European market as a response to all ailments....

This was the domestic political soil into which the Commission's initiatives fell. Traditional models of economic growth appeared to have played themselves out, and the left had been transformed in such a way that socialist parties began to seek market-oriented solutions to economic ills. In this setting, the European Community provided more than the mechanisms of intergovernmental negotiation. The Eurocracy was a standing constituency and a permanent advocate of European solutions and greater unity. Proposals from the European Commission transformed this new orientation into policy, and more importantly, into a policy perspective and direction...

...

The third actor in the story, besides the governments and the Commission, is the leadership of the European multinational corporations. The White Paper and the Single European Act gave the appear-ance that changes in the EC market were irreversible and politically unstoppable. Businesses have been acting on that belief. Politically, they have taken up the banner of 1992, collaborating with the Commission and exerting substantial influence on their governments. The significance of the role of business, and of its collaboration with the Commission, must not be underestimated....

---

[8] For an overview of this literature see P Craig, 'Integration, Democracy and Legitimacy' in P Craig and G de Búrca (eds), *The Evolution of EU Law* (Oxford University Press, 2nd edn, 2010) ch 1.

[9] '1992: Recasting the European Bargain' (1989) 42 World Politics 95.

[10] Ibid 97–100.

[11] Ibid 97.

[12] Ibid 108–109, 111–112, 113, 116.

Moravcsik told a different tale. He disagreed with the previous thesis, and argued that the reform was principally due to inter-state bargains between Britain, France, and Germany. This was made possible by the convergence of European economic-policy preferences in the early 1980s, combined with the bargaining leverage which France and Germany used against Britain by threatening a two-track Europe, with Britain in the slow lane. For Moravcsik it was regime theory that best explained the SEA.

A Moravcsik, Negotiating the Single European Act: National Interests and Conventional Statecraft in the European Community[13]

An alternative approach to explaining the success of the 1992 initiative focuses on inter-state bargains between heads of government in the three larger Member States of the EC. This approach, which can be called 'intergovernmental institutionalism', stresses the central importance of power and interests, with the latter not simply dictated by position in the intergovernmental system. . . . Intergovernmental institutionalism is based on three principles: intergovernmentalism, lowest common denominator bargaining, and strict limits on future transfers of sovereignty.

Intergovernmentalism. From its inception, the EC has been based on inter-state bargains between its leading Member States. Heads of government, backed by a small group of ministers and advisers, initiate and negotiate major initiatives in the Council of Ministers or the European Council. Each government views the EC through the lens of its own policy preferences; EC politics is the continuation of domestic politics by other means. . . .

Lowest-common-denominator bargaining. Without a 'European hegemony' capable of providing universal incentives or threats to promote regime formation and without the widespread use of linkages and logrolling, the bargains struck in the EC reflect the relative power positions of the Member States. Small states can be bought off with side-payments, but larger states exercise a de facto veto over fundamental changes in the scope or rules of the core element of the EC, which remains economic liberalization. Thus, bargaining tends to converge toward the lowest common denominator of large state interests. The bargains initially consisted of bilateral agreements between France and Germany; now they consist of trilateral agreements including Britain.

The only tool that can impel a state to accept an outcome on a major issue that it does not prefer to the status quo is the threat of exclusion . . . If two major states can isolate the third and credibly threaten it with exclusion and if such exclusion undermines the substantive interests of the excluded state, the coercive threat may bring about an agreement at a level of integration above the lowest common denominator.

Protection of sovereignty. The decision to join a regime involves some sacrifice of national sovereignty in exchange for certain advantages. Policymakers safeguard their countries against the future erosion of sovereignty by demanding the unanimous consent of regime members to sovereignty-related reforms. They also avoid granting open-ended authority to central institutions that might infringe on their sovereignty, preferring instead to work through intergovernmental institutions such as the Council of Ministers, rather than through supranational bodies such as the Commission and Parliament.

There is no need to decide unequivocally between these two theories. Most would agree that there were two conditions for the success of the new initiatives. There had to be *legislative reform* to facilitate the passage of measures designed to complete the internal market. There had also to be a *new*

---

[13] (1991) 45 International Organization 19, 25–27. Italics in the original.

approach to harmonization, which would expedite the process of breaking down the technical barriers to intra-Community trade. These will be considered in turn.

5 THE INTERNAL MARKET: LEGISLATIVE REFORM AND THE SEA

The European Council endorsed the Commission's White Paper in June 1985. The SEA was signed on 17 February 1986 and entered into force on 1 July 1987. The Act contained new procedures to facilitate legislation to complete the internal market. It should not, however, be thought that the SEA was uncontroversial. The Commission pressed for more far-reaching changes than the Member States were willing to accept. The SEA introduced two major legislative innovations for the single market project. They are now found in Articles 26 and 114 TFEU.

(A) ARTICLE 26: THE OBLIGATION STATED

1. The Union shall adopt measures with the aim of establishing or ensuring the functioning of the internal market, in accordance with the relevant provisions of the Treaties.
2. The internal market shall comprise an area without internal frontiers in which the free movement of goods, persons, services and capital is ensured in accordance with the provisions of the Treaties.
3. The Council, on a proposal from the Commission, shall determine the guidelines and conditions necessary to ensure balanced progress in all the sectors concerned.

We can begin by considering the *content of the obligation* in Article 26(1) TFEU. Article 14 EC, the predecessor to Article 26(1) TFEU, specified that the internal market should be attained by 31 December 1992. This deadline was dropped in Article 26(1), thereby recognizing that establishment of the internal market was an ongoing task, rather than one that could be deemed 'completed' by a particular date.

Article 26(2) *defines the internal market*. It contains a two-part formulation: it was to be an area without internal frontiers, in which there could be free movement of goods, persons, etc. Attainment of an area without internal frontiers can be judged by whether border controls exist on the free movement of goods or persons, etc. It is more difficult to determine how freely goods, persons, and capital can move within the EU, even when border controls have been removed. Attainment of the internal market is not a static objective, since technological developments and economic factors pose new challenges for the internal market ideal.

We must now consider the *legal effect* of Article 26. The Commission, in an early working paper for the Intergovernmental Conference leading to the SEA, intended Article 14 EC to have direct effect and proposed that if national rules on free movement were not removed by the agreed date, then they would automatically be recognized as equivalent. These suggestions 'stunned the participants at the Intergovernmental Conference'.[14] The Commission was forced to modify its suggestions,[15] and the Member States attached a Declaration to Article 14 EC, making clear that the deadline of 31 December 1992 did not create an automatic legal effect. The deadline has been removed from the Lisbon Treaty, and so too has the Declaration.

---

[14] C-D Ehlermann, 'The Internal Market Following the Single European Act' (1987) 24 CMLRev 361, 371.
[15] Ibid 371–372.

It is possible that Article 26 may have *legal effects against the EU itself*,[16] given its mandatory wording. The possibility of using Article 265 TFEU in the event of Commission or Council inaction would depend on whether the criteria for such actions were met.[17] This would not be easy, since it would have to be shown that the measures that it is claimed should have been enacted were defined with sufficient specificity for them to be identified individually, and adopted pursuant to Article 266 TFEU.[18] This will not be so where the relevant institutions possess discretionary power, with consequential policy options, the content of which cannot be identified with precision. A damages claim will be even more difficult to prove.[19]

There is also the possibility that Article 26 may have *legal consequences for the Member States*. This could mean that, even if the relevant EU measures had not been enacted, an individual might argue that Member States' rules which constituted a barrier to the completion of the internal market should not be applied if they were incompatible with Article 26. It would, however, have to be shown that Article 26 fulfilled the conditions for direct effect,[20] the most problematic of which is that there must be no further action required before the norm can have direct effect. The ECJ has been willing to accord direct effect to certain Treaty Articles, notwithstanding the fact that further action is required to flesh out the Article,[21] but it would nonetheless be bold for the Court to hold that Article 26 is directly effective. The Court was reluctant to accord direct effect to Article 14 EC, the predecessor to Article 26 TFEU.[22] The argument for the direct effect of Article 14 was, moreover, premised on the existence of the deadline of 31 December 1992, specified in that Article. The fact that Article 26 TFEU contains no such deadline would make it even more difficult for such an argument to succeed.

(B) ARTICLE 27: THE OBLIGATION QUALIFIED

Article 27 TFEU qualifies Article 26. It requires the Commission, when drawing up proposals pursuant to Article 26, to take into account the extent of the effort that certain economies showing differences in developments will have to sustain during the period of establishment of the internal market, and it may propose appropriate provisions. If the provisions take the form of derogations, they must be temporary and cause the least possible disturbance to the functioning of the common market.[23]

(C) ARTICLE 114(1): FACILITATING THE PASSAGE OF HARMONIZATION MEASURES

A major difficulty in enacting harmonization measures was the unanimity requirement under what is now Article 115 TFEU, which gives a general power to pass directives for the approximation of laws of the Member States that affect the establishment or functioning of the internal market. The SEA

---

[16] Ehlermann (n 14) 372.

[17] Ch 14.

[18] Case 13/83 *European Parliament v Council* [1985] ECR 1513.

[19] Case T–113/96 *Edouard Dubois et Fils SA v Council and Commission* [1998] ECR II–125.

[20] Ch 7.

[21] Ibid.

[22] Case C–378/97 *Criminal Proceedings against Wijsenbeek* [1999] ECR I–6207; Case C–9/99 *Echirolles Distribution SA v Association du Dauphine* [2000] ECR I–8207.

[23] G de Búrca, 'Differentiation within the Core: The Case of the Common Market' in G de Búrca and J Scott (eds), *Constitutional Change in the EU: From Uniformity to Flexibility?* (Hart, 2000) 143–145.

therefore provided in what is now Article 114 TFEU a general legislative power akin to Article 115, without the unanimity requirement. Article 114(1) reads as follows:

> Save where otherwise provided in the Treaties, the following provisions shall apply for the achievement of the objectives set out in Article 26. The European Parliament and the Council shall, acting in accordance with the ordinary legislative procedure and after consulting the Economic and Social Committee, adopt the measures for the approximation of the provisions laid down by law, regulation or administrative action in Member States which have as their object the establishment and functioning of the internal market.

Whereas Article 115 authorizes only the passage of directives, Article 114 empowers enactment of measures, which includes directives but also covers regulations, which are made by the ordinary legislative procedure.[24] Two more general features of Article 114 should be appreciated.

(i) *Article 114: A Residual Provision*

Article 114 is a residual provision. It operates only 'save where otherwise provided in this Treaty'. This means that other, more specific Treaty provisions, such as Articles 43, 50, 53, and 91 TFEU, should be used for measures designed to attain the internal market where they fall within the subject matter areas of those Articles.[25] This can generate boundary-dispute problems about the correct legal basis for EU legislation. Such disputes arose in the past normally because the European Parliament wished to ensure that its legislative rights under Article 114 TFEU were not by-passed by legislation enacted on a different Treaty Article, which gave it less extensive rights in the legislative process.[26]

The general test propounded by the ECJ for the resolution of such boundary disputes was that regard should be had to the nature, aim, and content of the act in question.[27] Where these factors indicated that the measure was concerned with more than one area of the Treaty, then it might be necessary to satisfy the legal requirements of two Treaty Articles.[28] This would not however be insisted upon where the relevant legal bases under the two Articles prescribed procedures that were incompatible,[29] or where one purpose clearly predominated.[30] Boundary disputes are less likely to occur now, since the ordinary legislative procedure, the successor to the co-decision procedure, is applicable to many Treaty Articles.

(ii) *Article 114: The Limits*

Article 114 is broadly framed, but the ECJ confirmed in *Tobacco Advertising* that it has limits.[31] The ECJ struck down a directive[32] designed to harmonize the law relating to the advertising and

---

[24] For an expansive interpretation of 'measures' see Case C–359/92 *Germany v Council* [1994] ECR I–3681.

[25] Case C–388/01 *Commission v Council* [2004] ECR I–4829, [54]–[60]; Case C–533/03 *Commission v Council* [2006] ECR I–1025, [43]–[48].

[26] See, eg, Case 68/86 *United Kingdom v Council* [1988] ECR 855; Case 11/88 *Commission v Council* [1989] ECR 3799; Case C–151/91 *Commission v Council* [1993] ECR I–939; Case C–187/93 *European Parliament v Council* [1994] ECR I–2857.

[27] Case C–300/89 *Commission v Council* [1991] ECR I–2867; Case C–426/93 *Germany v Council* [1995] ECR I–3723; Case C–271/94 *European Parliament v Council* [1996] ECR I–1689.

[28] Case 165/87 *Commission v Council* [1988] ECR 5545.

[29] Case C–388/01 (n 25).

[30] Case C–137/12 *Commission v Council* EU:C:2013:675, [53].

[31] Case C–376/98 *Germany v European Parliament and Council* [2000] ECR I–8419; T Hervey, 'Up in Smoke? Community (Anti)-Tobacco Law and Policy' (2001) 26 ELRev 101.

[32] [1998] OJ L213/9.

sponsorship of tobacco products. It read Article 95 EC in the light of Articles 3(1)(c) and 14 EC and concluded that the measures must be intended to improve the conditions for the establishment and functioning of the internal market.

Article 95 EC did not, as argued by the Commission, Council, and EP,[33] give any general power of market regulation. This would, said the ECJ, be contrary to Articles 3(1)(c) and 14 EC, and be incompatible with the principle in Article 5 EC that the Community's powers were limited to those specifically conferred on it.[34] The ECJ held that a measure enacted pursuant to Article 95 EC must genuinely have as its object the improvement of the conditions for the establishment and functioning of the internal market. If mere disparities between national rules, and the abstract risk of obstacles to the exercise of fundamental freedoms, or distortions of competition, could justify the use of Article 95 EC, then judicial review of compliance with the proper legal basis would be rendered 'nugatory'.[35] Any distortion of competition had to be appreciable, since otherwise 'the powers of the Community legislature would be practically unlimited'.[36] The ECJ had to verify whether a measure enacted under Article 95 EC pursued the objectives stated by the legislature,[37] and whether the distortion of competition which the measure purported to eliminate was appreciable.[38] The ECJ concluded that the Directive had not been validly made under Article 95.

While there are therefore limits to Article 114 TFEU, subsequent case law[39] has shown that the ECJ is willing to accept Article 114 as the legal basis for the enacted measure.[40] This is evident especially in the 2006 *Tobacco Advertising* case,[41] where the ECJ upheld the validity of a revised Directive on tobacco advertising, which included prohibitions on advertising in the press and radio. The Court concluded that this measure could be validly adopted under Article 114, since there were disparities between the relevant national laws on advertising and sponsorship of tobacco products which could affect competition and inter-state trade. The ECJ also stated more generally the circumstances in which Article 114 could be used. The 'criterion' is broad.[42]

It follows ... that when there are obstacles to trade, or it is likely that such obstacles will emerge in the future, because the Member States have taken, or are about to take, divergent measures with respect to a product or a class of products, which bring about different levels of protection and thereby prevent the product or products concerned moving freely within the Community, Article 95 EC authorises the Community legislature to intervene by adopting appropriate measures, in compliance with Article 95(3) EC and with the legal principles mentioned in the EC Treaty or identified in the case law, in particular the principle of proportionality.

---

[33] Case C–376/98 (n 31) [45].

[34] Ibid [83].

[35] Ibid [84].

[36] Ibid [107].

[37] Ibid [85].

[38] Ibid [106].

[39] Case C–377/98 *Netherlands v Parliament and Council* [2001] ECR I–7079; Case C–491/01 *The Queen v Secretary of State for Health, ex p British American Tobacco (Investments) Ltd and Imperial Tobacco Ltd* [2002] ECR I–11453; Case C–210/03 *R v Secretary of State for Health, ex p Swedish Match* [2004] ECR I–11893.

[40] D Wyatt, 'Community Competence to Regulate the Internal Market' in M Dougan and S Currie (eds), *50 Years of the European Treaties: Looking Back and Thinking Forward* (Hart, 2009) ch 5.

[41] Case C–380/03 *Germany v European Parliament and Council* [2006] ECR I–11573.

[42] Ibid [41]. See also Case C–301/06 *Ireland v European Parliament and Council* [2009] ECR I–593, [63]–[64]; Case C–58/08 *R (on the application of Vodafone Ltd) v Secretary of State for Business, Enterprise and Regulatory Reform* [2010] ECR I–4999, [32]–[37]; Case C–518/07 *Commission v Germany* [2010] ECR I–1885.

(D) ARTICLE 114(2)–(10): QUALIFICATIONS TO ARTICLE 114(1)

The remainder of Article 114 qualifies Article 114(1). *Article 114(2)* encapsulates an exception to Article 114(1), by providing that the latter shall not apply to fiscal provisions, to those relating to the free movement of persons, or to those relating to the rights and interests of employed persons. These areas were felt by the Member States to be particularly sensitive, hence their exclusion from Article 114(1). Legislation for these areas will therefore have to be passed under either Article 115, or a more specific Treaty provision.[43]

Article 114(3) instructs the Commission, when proposing measures under Article 114(1) relating to health, safety, environmental protection, and consumer protection, to take as a base a high level of protection, taking into account in particular any new development based on scientific facts. The European Parliament and the Council must also use their respective powers to achieve this objective. Article 114(3) was included to placate countries such as Germany and Denmark, which were concerned that the harmonization measures might not be stringent enough. The wording of Article 114(3) does not, however, compel enactment of a measure in accordance with the standards pertaining in the countries with high levels of protection. It merely requires that a high level of protection should be taken as the base.

Article 114 paragraphs (4)–(9) have received most critical attention. The provisions are complex and therefore should be set out in full:

> 4. If, after the adoption of a harmonisation measure by the European Parliament and the Council, by the Council or by the Commission, a Member State deems it necessary to maintain national provisions on grounds of major needs referred to in Article 36, or relating to the protection of the environment or the working environment, it shall notify the Commission of these provisions as well as the grounds for maintaining them.
>
> 5. Moreover, without prejudice to paragraph 4, if, after the adoption of a harmonisation measure by the European Parliament and the Council, by the Council or by the Commission, a Member State deems it necessary to introduce national provisions based on new scientific evidence relating to the protection of the environment or the working environment on grounds of a problem specific to that Member State arising after the adoption of the harmonisation measure, it shall notify the Commission of the envisaged provisions as well as the grounds for introducing them.
>
> 6. The Commission shall, within six months of the notifications as referred to in paragraphs 4 and 5, approve or reject the national provisions involved after having verified whether or not they are a means of arbitrary discrimination or a disguised restriction on trade between Member States and whether or not they shall constitute an obstacle to the functioning of the internal market.
>
> In the absence of a decision by the Commission within this period the national provisions referred to in paragraphs 4 and 5 shall be deemed to have been approved.
>
> When justified by the complexity of the matter and in the absence of danger for human health, the Commission may notify the Member State concerned that the period referred to in this paragraph may be extended for a further period of up to six months.
>
> 7. When, pursuant to paragraph 6, a Member State is authorised to maintain or introduce national provisions derogating from a harmonisation measure, the Commission shall immediately examine whether to propose an adaptation to that measure.

---

[43] For fiscal provisions Art 113 TFEU requires unanimity in the Council and consultation with the EP; for free movement of persons Art 21(2) TFEU applies the ordinary legislative procedure, except that Art 21(3) applies to provisions relating to social security or social protection, and requires Council unanimity and consultation with the EP; for the rights of employed persons see Arts 46 and 48 TFEU.

8. When a Member State raises a specific problem on public health in a field which has been the subject of prior harmonisation measures, it shall bring it to the attention of the Commission which shall immediately examine whether to propose appropriate measures to the Council.

9. By way of derogation from the procedure laid down in Articles 258 and 259, the Commission and any Member State may bring the matter directly before the Court of Justice of the European Union if it considers that another Member State is making improper use of the powers provided for in this Article.

Article 114(5), (7), and (8) were new provisions introduced by the Treaty of Amsterdam, whereas the other paragraphs modified pre-existing provisions. The inclusion of Article 114(4) gave rise to much critical comment.[44] The genesis of Article 114(4) is evident in the following extract.

C-D Ehlermann, The Internal Market Following the Single European Act[45]

Whereas paragraph 1[46] is the most significant provision of the Single European Act, paragraph 4 is the most problematic. Its purpose is the same as that of the preceding paragraph, namely to protect any Member State in a minority position from being forced to accept the majority line. However, the method devised is completely different. Whereas paragraph 3 is in keeping with the approach followed by the Community in the past, paragraph 4 represents a radical new departure.

It goes back to the fact that the United Kingdom, and later Ireland, wished to safeguard certain special measures connected with their island status against the threat of majority voting. Neither country was satisfied with the safeguard offered by paragraph 3. But they both accepted that retention of the unanimity requirement would have emasculated Article 100a.

The way out of this dilemma was paragraph 4, which was drafted by the European Council itself....

Any assessment of Article 114(4)–(9) must take into account political and legal issues. In *political terms* many of the more dramatic fears about the impact of Article 114(4) have not been borne out. Concerns that Member States would routinely seek to invoke the Article to prevent the application of harmonization measures have proven unfounded.

In *legal terms* the Member State concerns that can trigger Article 114(4) are finite: the matters covered by Article 36 TFEU, plus the environment and working environment. The Treaty of Amsterdam further limited Article 114(4). It had previously been framed in terms of a Member State 'applying' national provisions on one of the specified grounds, but is now framed in terms of 'maintaining' such provisions. A Member State cannot, therefore, invoke the Article to justify *new* national provisions that derogate from the harmonization measure, but only to justify the *retention* of existing provisions.[47] Article 114(5), by way of contrast, deals with the situation where the Member State seeks to *introduce a new national measure* after the adoption of the harmonization directive. The Member State concerns that can trigger Article 114(5) are more limited: there must be new scientific evidence relating to the environment, etc, and there must be a problem specific to that state.[48]

Article 114 paragraphs (4) and (5) are exceptions that derogate from the principles of the Treaty and will therefore be restrictively construed by the Commission and the CJEU. The Member State

---

44 P Pescatore, 'Some Critical Remarks on the "Single European Act"' (1987) 24 CMLRev 9.
45 (N 14) 389.
46 Of Art 100a EEC as it then was, now Art 114 TFEU.
47 Case C–3/00 *Commission v Denmark* [2003] ECR I–2643, [57]–[58].
48 Ibid [57]–[59]; Case T–234/04 *Netherlands v Commission* [2007] ECR II–4589, [58].

has the burden of proving that the conditions for their application exist.[49] The Commission's powers of scrutiny have been reinforced by Article 114(6). Prior to the Treaty of Amsterdam, Article 100a(4) spoke in terms of the Commission 'confirming' the national provisions. Article 114(6) now speaks of the Commission 'approving or rejecting' them. This shift in emphasis has been reinforced by changes to Article 114(4) by the Treaty of Amsterdam, requiring the state to explain the reasons for maintaining the national provisions.[50] The ECJ has, moreover, confirmed that it can judicially review invocation of Article 114(4).[51] The process under Article 114 is not however wholly adversarial. Article 114 paragraphs (7) and (8), introduced by the Treaty of Amsterdam, are designed to facilitate a negotiated solution to the problem.

Article 114(10) is the final qualification to Article 114(1). It provides that harmonization measures may include safeguard clauses authorizing Member States to take, for one of the non-economic reasons in Article 36 TFEU, provisional measures subject to Union control procedures. Recourse to Article 36 is normally precluded when EU harmonization measures have been enacted. The purpose of Article 114(10) is to allow a Member State, subject to the Union control procedure, to adopt temporary measures in the event of a sudden and unforeseen danger to health, life, etc.

6 THE INTERNAL MARKET: THE NEW LEGISLATIVE APPROACH TO MARKETING OF PRODUCTS AND HARMONIZATION

(A) THE RATIONALE FOR THE NEW APPROACH

We noted earlier that the completion of the single market was dependent upon two conditions. There had to be reform of the legislative procedure to facilitate legislation to complete the internal market. There also had to be a new approach to harmonization to make it easier to secure the passage of these measures.

Reforms in the legislative process would not have been sufficient to secure the internal market, even though harmonization measures could now be passed more easily. This was because traditional harmonization techniques had disadvantages.[52] They were slow, and generated excessive uniformity. There was a failure to develop links between harmonization and standardization, thereby leading to inconsistencies and wastage of time. Problems of certification and testing were not sufficiently addressed, and implementation within Member States was imperfect.

The Commission recognized these shortcomings in its White Paper.[53] Thus in its proposals for a New Approach to Technical Harmonization and Standards,[54] the Commission acknowledged that experience had shown the difficulties with the existing approach, which was predicated on attempts to harmonize through detailed technical specification. The Commission admitted that the results of harmonization had been negligible in certain fields, given the multiplicity of national technical regulations and the speed of technological change.

---

[49] Cases C–439 and 454/05 P *Land Oberösterreich and Austria v Commission* [2007] ECR I–7141.

[50] Art 114(5) contains a similar reasoning requirement.

[51] Case C–41/93 *France v Commission* [1994] ECR I–1829; Case C–3/00 (n 47); Case T–234/04 *Netherlands v Commission* (n 48).

[52] J Pelkmans, 'The New Approach to Technical Harmonization and Standardization' (1987) 25 JCMS 249, 252–253; M Egan, *Constructing a European Market* (Oxford University Press, 2001) 78–81.

[53] COM(85) 310, [64].

[54] Bull EC 1–1985.

(B) THE ELEMENTS OF THE NEW APPROACH

The general direction of the new approach to harmonization is apparent in the extract from the Commission's White Paper on Completing the Internal Market. There was to be mutual recognition through the *Cassis de Dijon* principle.[55] National rules that did not come within a mandatory requirement would be invalid; legislative harmonization was to be restricted to laying down health and safety standards; and there would be promotion of European standardization. A number of elements can be identified in the new legislative approach to marketing of products and harmonization.[56]

(i) *Provision of Information: National Rules that might Impede Free Movement*

Member States are obliged to provide information by Directive 83/189,[57] now overtaken by Directive 98/34.[58] This measure, known as the Mutual Information or Transparency Directive, obliges a state to inform the Commission before it adopts any legally binding regulation setting a technical specification, except where it transposes a European or international standard. The Commission then notifies the other states, and adoption of the national measure is delayed for a minimum of three months, in order that possible amendments can be considered. A year's delay can result if the Commission decides to press ahead with a harmonization directive on the issue. The Directive was given added force by the ECJ's decision in the *CIA* case[59] that a national measure which had not been notified in accordance with the Directive could not be relied on.

Pelkmans has shown the importance of this regime for scrutiny of draft national rules that might, if enacted, impede free movement, and the work done by the 98/34 committee in preventing such barriers from becoming a reality.[60] The procedure resolves approximately 95 per cent of cases so as to ensure that the proposed state regulation is consistent with EU law.

(ii) *Provision of Information: Obstacles to Free Movement and Serious Trade Disruption*

A further obligation to furnish information is found in Regulation 2679/98, which requires Member States that have relevant information concerning obstacles to free movement of goods that can lead to serious trade disruption and loss to individuals, and which requires immediate action to prevent any continuation, to notify the Commission.[61] The Member State has an obligation to take all necessary and proportionate action to ensure the free movement of goods and to notify the Commission of the action thus taken.

---

[55] Case 120/78 (n 2).

[56] Enhancing the Implementation of New Approach Directives, COM(2003) 240.

[57] [1983] OJ L109/8; S Weatherill, 'Compulsory Notification of Draft Technical Regulations: The Contribution of Directive 83/189 to the Management of the Internal Market' (1996) 16 YBEL 129.

[58] Directive 98/34/EC of the European Parliament and of the Council laying down a procedure for the provision of information in the field of technical standards and regulations [1998] OJ L204/37; the regime was extended to information services by Dir 98/48/EC [1998] OJ L217/18; The Operation of Directive 98/34 from 2002–2005, COM(2007) 125 final; The Operation of Directive 98/34 in 2009 and 2010, COM(2011) 853 final.

[59] Case C-194/94 *CIA Security International SA v Signalson SA and Securitel SPRL* [1996] ECR I-2201; Case C-443/98 *Unilever v Central Food* [2000] ECR I-7535; Case C-303/04 *Lidl Italia* [2005] ECR I-7865, [23]; Case C-26/11 *Belgische Petroleum Unie VZW v Belgische Staat* EU:C:2013:44, [50].

[60] J Pelkmans, 'Mutual Recognition in Goods. On Promises and Disillusions' (2007) 14 JEPP 699, 705–707.

[61] Council Regulation 2679/98/EC on the functioning of the internal market in relation to the free movement of goods among the Member States [1998] OJ L337/8, but for the weakness of this Reg see Report from the Commission to the Council and European Parliament on the application of Regulation 2679/98, COM(2001) 160 final.

(iii) *Mutual Recognition: Normative Dimension*

Mutual recognition[62] is the core of the CJEU's and Commission's strategy.[63] There are normative and practical dimensions to this strategy, which will be examined in turn. It is generally acknowledged that mutual recognition entails a governance strategy,[64] and embodies a choice as to how to achieve market integration.[65]

Such integration might be furthered by according primacy to host state control, subject to non-discrimination. Thus Member States open their borders to goods from elsewhere, provided that the importers meet the standards of the host country, the only obligation being not to discriminate against such imports. The political sovereignty of the host state remains unchallenged, and it sets the regulatory requirements, but the consequence is that producers based in other countries have to adapt their goods to the requirements of each state into which they wish to sell.

A second strategy for market integration is harmonization at the EU level, thereby overcoming national regulatory diversity. This entails, however, significant negotiation costs and a 'vertical transfer of sovereignty' to the supranational level.[66] Politics remains the mode of setting the regulatory regime, but the politics now take place at the supranational rather than national level.

Mutual recognition constitutes a third mode of market integration. A product lawfully manufactured in a Member State should be capable of being sold in any other Member State. The underlying assumption is that Member States' regulations address 'alternative solutions to the same underlying problems'.[67] Producers no longer have to adapt their goods to each market, and the costs of detailed harmonization are also avoided. It is, however, central to mutual recognition that regulatory control is vested in the home state. This in turn implies a 'horizontal transfer of sovereignty', in the sense that the Member States no longer retain control over the regulatory regime in their own countries. The host state must *prima facie* accept the goods lawfully marketed in accordance with the regulatory requirements of the home state, which requires national governments to trust the regulatory regime of other Member States.[68] This is, however, tempered by the public interest defences that can be made by the host state under Article 36 TFEU, and by the mandatory requirements recognized by the ECJ in its *Cassis* judgment. Harmonization efforts are then concentrated on measures that are still lawful under these.

(iv) *Mutual Recognition: Practical Dimension*

Mutual recognition has been central to EU market integration. The general assumption is that this works just fine. Matters are not so simple. Pelkmans has pointed to the practical difficulties in realizing the ideal.[69] This is largely because the judicial elaboration of mutual recognition in the *Cassis* judgment lacks visibility for many traders, especially small and medium-sized enterprises, with the

---

[62] K Armstrong, 'Mutual Recognition' in C Barnard and J Scott (eds), *The Law of the Single European Market* (Hart, 2002) ch 9; F Kostoris Padoa Schioppa (ed), *The Principle of Mutual Recognition in the European Integration Process* (Palgrave Macmillan, 2005); MP Maduro, 'So Close and Yet So Far: The Paradoxes of Mutual Recognition' (2007) 14 JEPP 814; K Nicolaïdis, 'Trusting the Poles? Constructing Europe through Mutual Recognition' (2007) 14 JEPP 682; Pelkmans (n 60); S Schmidt, 'Mutual Recognition as a New Mode of Governance' (2007) 14 JEPP 667.

[63] http://ec.europa.eu/enterprise/policies/single-market-goods/free-movement-non-harmonised-sectors/mutual-recognition/index_en.htm.

[64] Maduro (n 62); Schmidt (n 62).

[65] Schmidt (n 62).

[66] Ibid 672.

[67] Ibid 672.

[68] Maduro (n 62).

[69] Pelkmans (n 60).

consequence that they adapt their products to the requirements of the host states, even though they are not required to do so under EU law.

This problem was recognized by the Commission,[70] which acknowledged that mutual recognition did not always operate effectively, and made proposals to improve it.[71] There should be increased monitoring of mutual recognition by the Commission, complemented by measures to improve awareness of mutual recognition by producers of goods and services. Member States should deal with requests concerning mutual recognition within a reasonable period of time, and should include mutual recognition clauses in national legislation.

(v) *Mutual Recognition: Control over Member State Derogation*

The Commission has more recently resorted to hard law in order to improve the efficacy of mutual recognition, by imposing tighter controls over Member States' derogations from free movement. The previous approach was based on exchange of information about national measures which derogated from free movement of goods. Decision 3052/95[72] imposed an obligation on a Member State to notify the Commission where it took steps to prevent goods lawfully produced in another Member State from being placed on its market.

This strategy was not, however, successful and it was replaced in 2008[73] by a more strident approach. A Member State that decides to prevent or hinder free movement of goods lawfully marketed in another Member State on grounds listed in Article 36 TFEU, or because of the *Cassis* mandatory requirements, must give written notice to the importer, who has twenty days in which to proffer comments contesting the decision. The Member State then makes a final decision in the light of those comments, and this must be notified to the importer and the Commission. If the Member State abides by its decision to refuse or hinder import it must give reasons. This decision must be open to challenge before national courts. The Member States are, moreover, obliged to establish 'Product Contact Points', which provide information to importers as to the technical rules applicable to particular types of product, and information about the principle of mutual recognition in that Member State.

(vi) *New Approach: Harmonization and Standardization*

The 'New Approach' to legislative harmonization is used for those national rules that survive scrutiny under Article 36 TFEU and/or the *Cassis* mandatory requirements. Where this is so EU harmonization is limited to laying down essential health and safety requirements.[74] Thus far more than thirty such directives have been enacted on the New Approach or principles analogous thereto.[75] Each measure deals with a general product area, such as personal protective equipment, toys, construction products, explosives, medical devices, and the like. A directive can therefore apply to hundreds or

---

[70] Commission Communication to the European Parliament and the Council, Mutual Recognition in the Context of the Follow-up to the Action Plan for the Single Market, 16 June 1999.

[71] Mutual Recognition (n 70) 7–12; Commission interpretative communication on facilitating the access of products to the markets of other Member States: the practical application of mutual recognition [2003] OJ C265/2.

[72] Decision 3052/95/EC of the European Parliament and of the Council establishing a procedure for the exchange of information on national measures derogating from the principle of the free movement of goods within the Community [1995] OJ L321/1.

[73] Regulation (EC) No 764/2008 of the European Parliament and of the Council of 9 July 2008 laying down procedures relating to the application of certain national technical rules to products lawfully marketed in another Member State and repealing Decision No 3052/95/EC [2008] OJ L218/21.

[74] http://europa.eu/legislation_summaries/internal_market/single_market_for_goods/technical_harmonisation/l21001a_en.htm.

[75] www.newapproach.org/.

thousands of products that fall within the relevant generic category. The trading volume of products covered by the major sectors where the new approach has been applied has been estimated to be in excess of €1,500 billion per annum. The essence of this approach is brought out by Pelkmans.

J Pelkmans, The New Approach to Technical Harmonization and Standardization[76]

— harmonization of legislation is limited to the adoption ... of the essential safety requirements ... with which the products brought on the market must comply in order to qualify for free movement in the Community;

— it is the task of the competent (private) standardization organs, given technical progress, to formulate the technical specifications, on the basis of which industry needs to manufacture and market products complying with the fundamental requirements of the directives;

— these technical specifications are not binding and retain their character of voluntary (European) standards;

— but, at the same time, the governments are *obliged to presume* that the products manufactured in accordance with the European standards comply with the 'fundamental requirements' stipulated in the directive. It is this presumption that guarantees business free market access.

When a standard has been approved by the Commission and published in the Official Journal all Member States must accept goods which conform to it. If a Member State disputes whether the standard conforms to the safety objectives set out in the directive, the burden of proof will be on the State to substantiate its contentions. An analogous reversal of the burden of proof operates in the case of producers in the following sense. It is open to producers to manufacture according to specifications other than those laid down. The burden of proof will, however, then be on the producer to show that the goods meet the essential requirements specified in the directive.

European standardization is central to the 'New Approach' to harmonization.[77] It reduces barriers to intra-EU trade and increases the competitiveness of European industry.[78] The principal bodies are the European Committee for Standardization (CEN),[79] the European Committee for Electrotechnical Standardization (CENELEC),[80] and the European Telecommunications Standards Institute (ETSI).[81] These bodies are private organizations, with CEN and CENELEC being non-profit-making technical organizations established under Belgian law in 1961 and 1973 respectively, and ETSI being a non-profit-making organization set up under French law in 1986. They 'ensure that standardization processes take place in parallel with harmonization at Council level and are based on "essential requirements"'.[82] The standardization is very likely to be approved, provided that it complies with the 'essential requirements' laid down in the Directive.

The standard will be drafted by a Technical Committee of the standardization body. Standards may be mandated or unmandated. The former are created when the Commission calls for the standardization bodies to draw up a standard, the latter where the initiative comes from the standardization body itself. Compliance with a mandated standard means that the product is presumed to be safe under the

---

[76] (N 52), italics in the original.

[77] http://ec.europa.eu/enterprise/policies/european-standards/standardisation-policy/index_en.htm.

[78] Pelkmans (n 52) 260; On the Role of European Standardization in the Framework of European Policies and Legislation, COM(2004) 674, [2.2]; Towards an increased contribution from standardisation to innovation in Europe, COM(2008) 133 final.

[79] www.cen.eu/Pages/default.aspx.

[80] www.cenelec.eu/.

[81] www.etsi.org/.

[82] Pelkmans (n 52) 256.

General Product Liability Directive,[83] and that it can, subject to certain qualifications, circulate freely within the EU. The standards are published in the Official Journal.

The Commission published an Action Plan for European Standardisation in 2006, developing ideas canvassed in its 2004 Communication. It has published updated plans in subsequent years. The Action Plans were designed to enhance the use of standardization in different policy areas, and improve its efficiency and coherence, including in this respect strategies to promote the effective participation of interested parties.[84]

It is important to be clear about the relationship between EU harmonization of essential requirements and the standardization process. A directive passed pursuant to the New Approach establishes in general terms the health and safety requirements that the goods must meet. The setting of standards helps manufacturers to prove conformity to these essential requirements, and to allow inspection to test for conformity with them. Promoting EU standards fosters this process by encouraging consensus on the relevant standards in a particular area. Allowing a manufacturer to show that its goods comply with the essential safety requirements, even if they do not comply with the EU standard, provides flexibility.

The New Approach to harmonization has considerable advantages. Directives can be drafted more easily since they are less detailed. The excessive 'Euro-uniformity' of the traditional approach is avoided by combining stipulated safety objectives with flexibility as to the standards through which this compliance can be achieved. The need for unanimity is obviated through Article 114. Harmonization and standardization are related. More EU directives can be made, and hence the gap between EU harmonization and the volume of national technical regulations can be reduced. Incentives for Member States' implementation of directives have been increased through judicial doctrine such as state liability in damages.[85] This is not to say that the New Approach has been problem-free, as will be seen below.[86]

(vii) *New Approach to Harmonization and Standardization: 2008 and 2012 Reforms*

The New Approach was reformed in 2008 to make it more effective. The resulting Decision[87] established certain general principles intended to apply across sectoral legislation in order to foster coherence. It therefore constituted a general horizontal framework for future harmonizing legislation and a reference text for existing legislation, although the specific needs of a particular sectoral area could dictate a different regulatory approach.[88]

The basic principle is that EU harmonization legislation is restricted to setting out the essential requirements determining the level of such protection, subject to the caveat that where recourse to essential requirements is not possible or not appropriate, in view of the objective of ensuring the adequate protection of consumers, public health, and the environment, or other aspects of public

---

[83] Directive 2001/95/EC of the European Parliament and of the Council on general product safety [2002] OJ L11/4, Art 3(2).

[84] On the Role of Standardization (n 78). The Action Plans are available at http://ec.europa.eu/enterprise/policies/european-standards/standardisation-policy/implementation-action-plan/index_en.htm.

[85] Ch 8.

[86] Pp 627–629.

[87] Decision No 768/2008/EC of the European Parliament and of the Council of 9 July 2008 on a common framework for the marketing of products, and repealing Council Decision 93/465/EEC [2008] OJ L218/82. See also Regulation (EC) No 765/2008 of the European Parliament and of the Council of 9 July 2008 setting out the requirements for accreditation and market surveillance relating to the marketing of products and repealing Regulation (EEC) No 339/93 [2008] OJ L218/30.

[88] Dec 768/2008 (n 87) Art 2.

interest protection, detailed specifications may then be set out in the harmonization legislation.[89] Compliance with essential requirements is *prima facie* through compliance with adopted standards, while preserving the possibility of complying by other means.[90] Where harmonization legislation requires conformity assessment in respect of a particular product, the procedures to be used should be chosen from modules specified in Annex II to the Decision.[91]

The Annexes to the Decision set out in detail a 'boilerplate' of provisions that can be used in New Approach directives. These cover: the obligations of the manufacturer, importer, and distributor of goods covered by any such directive; formal objection to harmonized standards; the declaration that the product has been made in conformity with the essential requirements in the directive; affixing of the CE mark; rules relating to conformity assessment bodies; and conformity assessment procedures.

The standardization regime was itself reformed in 2012, through a new Regulation that deals with a range of matters, including provision for transparency, stakeholder participation, planning of the annual EU standardization agenda, and coordination between national, EU, and international standardization initiatives.[92]

(viii) *Harmonization: Minimum and Maximum*

The EU has choices when it enacts harmonization legislation.[93] It may pass legislation that sets minimum standards, which do not preclude Member States from setting more exacting standards. Minimum harmonization enables Member States to maintain more stringent regulatory standards than those prescribed by EU standards, provided that these are compatible with the Treaty. The EU legislation sets a floor and the Treaty a ceiling, with Member States free to pursue their own policies within these boundaries. The EU can alternatively pass maximal legislation that covers the entire area. This entails exhaustive regulation of the given field, with the EU rules setting both the floor and the ceiling of regulatory protection, the corollary being the pre-emption of national action. There is evidence that the Commission now favours maximum harmonization, at least in areas such as consumer policy.[94]

Whether the harmonization measure is intended to preclude any national measures that differ from the EU directive may, however, be a contentious issue. In *Ratti*[95] the ECJ had to decide whether Directive 73/173 on the packaging and labelling of dangerous substances precluded a state from prescribing 'obligations and limitations which are more precise than, or at all events different from, those set out in the directive'. The Italian rules required that more information should be attached to the

---

[89] Ibid Art 3(1).

[90] Ibid Art 3(2).

[91] Ibid Art 4(1).

[92] Regulation (EU) No 1025/2012 of the European Parliament and of the Council of 25 October 2012 on European standardization [2012] OJ L316/12.

[93] A McGee and S Weatherill, 'The Evolution of the Single Market—Harmonisation or Liberalisation' (1990) 53 MLR 578, 582; S Weatherill, 'Beyond Preemption? Shared Competence and Constitutional Change in the European Community' in D O' Keefe and P Twomey (eds), *Legal Issues of the Maastricht Treaty* (Chancery Law Publishing, 1994) ch 2; M Dougan, 'Minimum Harmonization and the Internal Market' (2000) 37 CMLRev 853; S Weatherill, 'Pre-Emption, Harmonization and the Distribution of Competence to Regulate the Internal Market' in C Barnard and J Scott (eds), *The Law of the Single European Market* (Hart, 2002) ch 2; S Weatherill, 'Supply of and Demand for Internal Market Regulation: Strategies, Preferences and Interpretation' in N Nic Shuibhne (ed), *Regulating the Internal Market* (Edward Elgar, 2006) 42–49.

[94] S Weatherill, *EU Consumer Law and Policy* (Edward Elgar, 2nd edn, 2013) ch 1; Proposal for a Directive of the European Parliament and of the Council on Consumer Rights, COM(2008) 614 final; http://ec.europa.eu/consumers/archive/rights/cons_acquis_en.htm.

[95] Case 148/78 *Pubblico Ministero v Ratti* [1979] ECR 1629.

packaging than specified in the Directive. The Court held that the Directive was intended to prevent the state from laying down stricter rules of its own.

It may, by way of contrast, be apparent that the directive only partially regulates the area. In *Grunert*[96] a French producer of food preservative containing lactic and citric acids was prosecuted for selling the preservative for use in the making of certain pork meats. French law prohibited the use of preservatives unless authorized by the national authorities, and the acids used were not on the national list. Directives 64/54 and 70/357 did, however, list the two acids as among those that could be used to protect food against deterioration. This was Grunert's defence. The Directives went on to provide that, subject to certain conditions, they were not to affect provisions of national law specifying the foodstuffs to which the preservatives listed could be added. The ECJ decided therefore that the Member States had discretion as to the foodstuffs to which listed preservatives could be added

7 THE INTERNAL MARKET: TENSIONS AND CONCERNS

The analysis thus far has shown the advantages of the New Approach to harmonization. It would, however, be wrong to imagine that the single market strategy has been problem-free. Commentators have perceived a number of tensions.

(A) CONSUMER INTERESTS AND COMMERCIAL POWER

One concern is whether consumer interests are sufficiently protected in the process of attaining a single market. Many national rules that impede intra-EU trade are designed to protect consumers. This has been recognized in the Treaty, through provisions such as Article 36 TFEU, and in the ECJ's jurisprudence through the *Cassis* mandatory requirements. It has been accepted by the Commission, since harmonization under the New Approach will be necessary where Member States have legitimate health and safety interests. The problem is whether such directives adequately balance consumer and manufacturing interests.

**A McGee and S Weatherill, The Evolution
of the Single Market—Harmonisation or Liberalisation**[97]

It is submitted that there are structural reasons why the New Approach might serve the European consumer ill. The difficulty lies in the privatisation of the standards making process which supports the New Approach. For financial reasons it is likely that business will capture the standardisation process within CEN. Consumer organisations lack resources to participate fully in CEN committee work; in any event, consumer representation is ill-organized and haphazard in several Member States....If standards making becomes the province of business alone, the balance between consumer protection and free trade will be distorted, prejudicing overall public confidence in the Community.

[*The authors return to the theme in their conclusion:*]

---

[96] Case 88/79 *Ministère Public v Grunert* [1980] ECR 1827. See also Case C–11/92 *R v Secretary of State for Health, ex p Gallaher Ltd* [1993] ECR I–3545; Cases C–54 and 74/94 *Cacchiarelli* [1995] ECR I–391; Cases C–320, 328–329 and 337–339/94 *RTI v Ministero delle Poste e Telecomunicazione* [1996] ECR I–6471.

[97] (N 93) 585, 595.

> Not surprisingly, national governments appear to be the most effective at controlling develop-
> ments.... Business and commercial interests have proved less successful in blocking developments,
> but have been highly effective in getting control of the standard-setting process, as in the case of Toy
> Safety, and in ensuring that other provisions take the form which they want. Thus, the EEIG Regulation[98]
> excluded worker participation, the Product Liability Directive allowed for the inclusion of the develop-
> ment risks defence and the Merger Regulation ignores all considerations of social policy. Again, it is
> not surprising to find that the highly motivated, well organised and generously resourced interests at
> work here have proved effective. Far less successful have been the consumer and employee interests,
> whose concerns seem largely to have been overridden. This too need not be a cause for surprise, but
> it is important to ask the fundamental question, what sort of Single Market is being created here? The
> answer seems to be that it is a Market in which business flourishes, relatively free from protective
> regulation, but the legitimate interests of other social groups are at risk of being ignored.

These concerns should be taken seriously.[99] They were addressed in part by the establishment
in 1992 of ANEC, the European Association for the Coordination of Consumer Representation in
Standardization, a body which is independent of the European standards agencies themselves. This
has served to alleviate the concerns expressed above, but not to dispel them. This is especially significant given that the standardization bodies have considerable interpretative latitude in fixing standards that are in accordance with the essential requirements specified in the empowering directive.
The need for transparency and procedural input from affected stakeholders is commensurately all the
more important.

Problems still remain concerning access to the standardization bodies, as recognized by the
Commission,[100] and confirmed by a study undertaken at its behest in 2009.[101] ANEC made a number
of telling observations on the report.[102] It noted in particular that if the European Standardization
System was to respond adequately to real European standards' needs, then the governance bodies and
the technical bodies had to feature representatives of European economic and societal actors with
an equal strength of voice alongside the national delegations; the mere 'observership' of those from
outside national delegations should therefore come to an end in CEN/CENELEC. As Russell, the
Secretary-General of ANEC, astutely observed, 'access may be important. But access without influence is meaningless'.[103] Regulation 1025/2012 has however attempted to address this through new
provisions on stakeholder participation in the standardization process.[104]

---

[98] European Economic Interest Grouping.

[99] Pelkmans (n 52) 263–265; B Farquhar, 'Consumer Representation in Standardisation' (1995) 3 Consumer Law
Journal 56; N Reich, 'Protection of Diffuse Interests in the EEC and the Perspective of Progressively Establishing an
Internal Market' (1988) 11 Jnl Cons Policy 395; K Armstrong and S Bulmer, *The Governance of the Single European
Market* (Manchester University Press, 1998) 157–163; E Vos, *Institutional Frameworks of Community Health and Safety
Regulation: Committees, Agencies and Private Bodies* (Hart, 1999); C Joerges, H Schepel, and E Vos, 'The Law's Problems
with the Involvement of Non-Governmental Actors in Europe's Legislation Processes: The Case of Standardisation',
EUI Working Paper 99/9; European Association for the Coordination of Consumer Representation, ANEC, *Consumer
Participation in Standardisation* (ANEC, 2000); H Schepel, *The Constitution of Private Governance* (Hart, 2005) ch 2.

[100] Commission Green Paper on the Development of Standardization: Action for Faster Technical Integration in
Europe, COM(90) 456 final; The Broader Use of Standardization in Community Policy, COM(95) 412 final; General
Guidelines for the Cooperation between CEN, CENELEC and ETSI and the European Commission and EFTA [2003]
OJ C91/04; COM(2008) 133 (n 78) 8–9.

[101] http://ec.europa.eu/enterprise/policies/european-standards/standardisation-policy/policy-review/access-to-
standardisation/index_en.htm.

[102] Access Study Workshop, ANEC Intervention, 27 Apr 2009, http://ec.europa.eu/enterprise/policies/european-
standards/standardisation-policy/policy-review/access-to-standardisation/index_en.htm.

[103] Ibid 3.

[104] Reg 1025/2012 (n 92) Art 5.

We should moreover recognize that these concerns also exist when regulations about product safety and the like are made at national level. Tensions resulting from the imbalance in power between consumer and commercial interests are not created because harmonization measures are passed at EU rather than national level. They are endemic in most Western-style market economies. Whether consumer interests fare better in the regulatory process at national or EU level will therefore depend on the relative capacities of commercial and consumer interests to influence the legislative process within the EU and the nation state, and the relative costs involved in operating within these differing polities.

(B) THE SINGLE MARKET, MARKET FREEDOM, AND STRUCTURAL BALANCE

A second tension inherent in the single market project is that between an EU free market and its impact on the weaker economies of the Union. The SEA addressed this problem through Article 27 TFEU.[105] Whether this sufficed to meet the difficulty is more contestable.

R Dehousse, Completing the Internal Market: Institutional Constraints and Challenges[106]

At some point…a major challenge will have to be faced, for the objective of market integration itself remains unacceptable, politically speaking, for some Member States if it is not accompanied by specific effort to improve the social and economic cohesion within the Community. It is worth recalling in this respect that economically weaker countries have been reluctant to accept majority voting, precisely because they are those who might suffer most in the short term from the creation of a single market. Of the many problems linked to the completion of the internal market, this one is perhaps the most difficult: unlike the concerns for a high level of health, consumer safety or the environment, this kind of fear cannot be allayed by derogatory measures alone. A parallel in the Community's allocative and redistributive policies has been strongly advocated by recent studies, both from a theoretical and from a practical viewpoint. The Single Act pledges the Community to reinforce its action in favour of backward areas; it even explicitly states that the completion of the internal market should be pursued taking into account the existence of different levels of development within the Community….

However, it fails to give the Community additional means to reach that end. The crucial point is that, at a given stage, progress towards the single European market might be conditioned by the capacity to tackle the problem of structural imbalances: if the Community does not find a way to offer some compensation to those countries which feel they have more to lose, market integration could be severely hampered. More than institutional pragmatism will be needed in order to cut this Gordian knot.

Fulfilment of the single market project can generate macro-economic and social tensions between rich, poor, and middle-class economies within the EU. This should come as no surprise. Reflect on experience within nation states. A market-driven national economic policy will often create regional problems within a particular country, with areas of high unemployment and relative poverty. It is not therefore surprising that a vigorous EU policy of increased competitiveness and breaking down trade

---

[105] See p 615.
[106] R Bieber, R Dehousse, J Pinder, and J Weiler (eds), *1992: One European Market?* (Nomos, 1988) 336.

barriers will produce similar tensions, albeit on a larger scale. Some countries will be concerned about their ability to survive and prosper within this barrier-free, competitive environment. Dehousse is therefore right to point to the connections between the single market project and the need to tackle structural imbalances within the EU. Articles 174–178 TFEU provide the foundation for structural policies to address this problem. The balance between the single market and structural intervention will, however, always be problematic, and that is more especially so after the financial crisis and its implications for several EU Member States.[107]

(c) THE CHALLENGE TO POSITIVE INTEGRATION

The assumption in the earlier part of this chapter was that the single market project required both negative and positive integration, and that insofar as the SEA and subsequent reforms facilitated the latter, by rendering it easier to enact harmonization measures, this was a 'good thing'. Majone has challenged this assumption. He argues that the real costs of such regulations are borne by those who have to comply with them and not by those who make them, and hence that budgetary constraints have limited impact on the regulators, with the consequence that the 'volume, detail and complexity of Community regulations are often out of proportion with the benefits that they may reasonably be expected to produce'.[108] He argues moreover that Member States often enjoy a comparative advantage in devising regulations in areas such as telecommunications, consumer protection, and environmental protection, because they are not tied to the lowest-common-denominator approach that often limits EU regulatory provisions, and because Member States have superior implementation mechanisms to the EU.[109]

Space precludes detailed analysis of this thesis. Suffice it to say for the present that while we should be mindful of the scope and application of EU regulatory competence, Majone's argument in this respect is but part of a broader and controversial thesis concerning the interpretation of EU competence, which is premised on distinctions between positive and negative rights, and between economic and social regulation.[110]

(d) POLITICS, ECONOMICS, AND THE SINGLE MARKET ENTERPRISE

Conceptions of market freedom are not value-free. The meaning of this phrase and the appropriate limits to free markets are contestable. These are key issues that divide political parties. There is sound economic evidence that removing barriers to intra-EU trade will bring economic benefits. There is nonetheless still room for difference of opinion about the desirable scope of protective EU measures, even among those of differing political persuasions who are committed to the European ideal. The politicization which accompanies market integration has been noted by commentators, such as Pelkmans, who states that an internal-market strategy that cuts deeply into the regulatory environment, severely limiting the options available to Member States, cannot pretend to be entirely apolitical.[111] Weiler develops the same theme.

---

[107] See Chs 1, 3 and 20.
[108] G Majone, *Dilemmas of European Integration: The Ambiguities and Pitfalls of Integration by Stealth* (Oxford University Press, 2005) 145.
[109] Ibid 149–150.
[110] Ibid 107–136, 157–158.
[111] J Pelkmans, 'A Grand Design by the Piece? An Appraisal of the Internal Market Strategy' in Bieber, Dehousse, Pinder, and Weiler (n 106) 371.

J Weiler, The Transformation of Europe[112]

It is an article of faith for European integration that the Commission is not meant to be a mere secretariat, but an autonomous force shaping the agenda and brokering the decisionmaking of the Community. And yet at the same time, the Commission, as broker, must be ideologically neutral, not favouring Christian Democrats, Social Democrats or others.

This neutralization of ideology has fostered the belief that an agenda could be set for the Community, and the Community could be led towards an ever closer union among its peoples, without having to face the normal political cleavages present in the Member States. In conclusion, the Community political culture which developed in the 1960s and 1970s led...to an habituation of all political forces to thinking of European integration as ideologically neutral in, or transcendent over, the normal debates on the left–right spectrum. It is easy to understand how this will have served the process of integration, allowing a nonpartisan coalition to emerge around its overall objectives.

1992 changes this in two ways. The first is a direct derivation from the turn to majority voting. Policies can be adopted now within the Council that run counter not simply to the perceived interests of a Member State, but more specifically to the ideology of the government in power. The debates about the European Social Charter and the shrill cries of 'Socialism through the backdoor', as well as the emerging debate about Community adherence to the European Convention on Human Rights and abortion rights are harbingers of things to come....

The second impact of 1992 on ideological neutrality is subtler. The entire program rests on two pivots: the single market plan encapsulated in the White Paper, and its operation through the instrumentalities of the Single European Act....It is not simply a technocratic program to remove the remaining obstacles to the free movement of all factors of production. It is at the same time a highly politicized choice of ethos, ideology and political culture: the culture of 'the market'. It is also a philosophy, at least one version of which—the predominant version—seeks to remove barriers to the free movement of factors of production, and to remove distortion to competition as a means to maximize utility. The above is premised on the assumption of formal equality of individuals. It is an ideology the contours of which have been the subject of intense debate within the Member States in terms of their own political choices....A successful single market requires widespread harmonization of standards and environmental protection, as well as the social package of employees. This need for a successful market not only accentuates the pressure for uniformity, but also manifests a social (and hence ideological) choice which prizes market efficiency and European-wide neutrality of competition above other competing values.

The continuing relevance of this issue was starkly exemplified by the French negative vote in the referendum on the Constitutional Treaty, a result, in part, of the perception that the EU was too dominated by market considerations, thereby endangering traditional French social values. The same theme is apparent in the passage of the Services Directive.[113] It was radically revised because of pressure from the EP, which felt that it jeopardized provision of public services by giving undue weight to market competition. We should nonetheless be mindful of the increased politicization of the Commission as a result of the method for electing the Commission President discussed earlier.[114] The impact that this has on the argument advanced by Joseph Weiler remains to be seen.

[112] (1991) 100 Yale LJ 2403, 2476–2478.
[113] See below, Ch 22.
[114] See above, Chs 2 and 5.

8 THE INTERNAL MARKET: RECONCEPTUALIZATION

The single market project did not magically come to an end in December 1992. There was a continuing flow of internal market legislation post-1992. This was matched by a number of reports that addressed various aspects of the regulatory process.[115]

There were many reports focusing on attainment of the internal market in the economic sense of the term. In 1993 the Commission produced its strategic programme on 'Making the Most of the Internal Market',[116] in which it reviewed issues such as the completion of the legal framework and management of the single market. In 1996 the Commission undertook a wide-ranging study on the 'Impact and Effectiveness of the Single Market'.[117] The study measured the economic gains from the internal market and highlighted areas where further action was required, such as public procurement, tax harmonization, company law, and the transposition of directives. The Commission developed these themes in its 'Single-Market Action Plan',[118] in which it identified four principal goals for the development of the single market: making the rules more effective, dealing with market distortions, removing sectoral obstacles to market integration, and delivering a single market for all citizens. The Amsterdam European Council officially endorsed these goals in 1997. The 1997 Action Plan led to further reports that focused on matters such as making mutual recognition more effective.[119] Single market reform has focused heavily on the services sector, as exemplified by initiatives relating to financial reform,[120] mutual recognition of professional qualifications,[121] and the more general market for services.[122] The financial and banking crisis that began in 2008 led to new initiatives in this area.[123]

A broader conception of the internal market is however also to be found in a number of the papers from the Commission and the European Council. The internal market is conceptualized in more holistic terms, to include not only economic integration, but also consumer safety, social rights, labour policy, and the environment. This material is therefore relevant for the concerns voiced in the previous section. This shift did not occur at any single moment. It developed across time. Certain important steps can nonetheless be identified.

The 1997 Action Plan was significant in this respect. The fourth strategic target was to deliver a single market for the benefit of all citizens. The Commission's introduction to the Action Plan consciously stressed that 'the single market was not simply an economic structure', but included basic standards of health and safety, equal opportunities, and labour law measures.[124] This theme was carried over in the 1997 Action Plan itself. The strategic target of delivering a single market for the benefit of all citizens was particularized through action directed towards protection of social rights, consumer rights, health and the environment, and the right of residence.[125]

---

[115] P Craig, 'The Evolution of the Single Market' in Barnard and Scott (n 62) ch 1.

[116] COM(93) 632 final.

[117] COM(96) 520 final.

[118] Action Plan for the Single Market, SEC(97) 1 final.

[119] Communication from the Commission to the European Parliament and the Council, Mutual Recognition in the Context of the follow-up to the Action Plan for the Single Market, 16 June 1999.

[120] Financial Services—Implementing the Framework for Financial Markets: Action Plan, COM(1999) 232; Financial Services Priorities and Progress, Third Report, COM(2000) 692/2 final; White Paper, Financial Services Policy 2005–2010 (Dec 2005).

[121] Directive 2005/36/EC of the European Parliament and of the Council of 7 September 2005 on the recognition of professional qualifications [2005] OJ L255/22.

[122] An Internal Market Strategy for Services, COM(2000) 888; Directive 2006/123/EC of the European Parliament and of the Council of 12 December 2006 on services in the internal market [2006] OJ L376/36.

[123] Driving European Recovery, COM(2009) 114 final; Regulating Financial Services for Sustainable Growth, COM(2010) 301 final.

[124] Single Market Action Plan sets Agenda, 18 June 1997, 2.

[125] Action Plan (n 118) 9–11.

The Lisbon European Council constituted another important stage in the reconfiguration of the internal-market agenda. The meeting in March 2000 focused on employment, economic reform, and social cohesion. It set a 'new' strategic goal: the Union was to become 'the most competitive and dynamic knowledge-based economy in the world, capable of sustainable economic growth with more and better jobs and greater social cohesion'.[126] Completion of the internal market was one way of achieving this strategy,[127] and modernization of the European social model through an active welfare state was another. This was crucial to ensure that 'the emergence of this new economy does not compound the existing social problems of unemployment, social exclusion, and poverty'.[128] This objective was further particularized in terms of better education, an active employment policy, modernizing social protection, and promoting social inclusion.[129] These commitments were reiterated at the Feira European Council.[130] The same theme permeated the Nice European Council.[131] It considered a 'New Impetus for an Economic and Social Europe'. It approved the European Social Agenda developed by the Commission, which was characterized by the 'indissoluble link between economic performance and social progress'.[132] This link had been forged by the Commission and endorsed by the European Parliament.[133] Economic growth and social cohesion were seen as mutually reinforcing.[134] The Stockholm European Council echoed the same idea. There was 'full agreement that economic reform, employment and social policies were mutually reinforcing';[135] a 'dynamic Union should consist of active welfare states'.[136]

The principal Commission reports concerning the internal market in 2000 developed the ideas of the European Council. Thus the 2000 'Review of the Internal Market Strategy'[137] took the strategic remit of the Lisbon European Council as its starting point. The internal market should be made economically effective, but it should also foster job creation, social cohesion, and safety.[138] The interconnection between the economic and social aspects of the internal market is also apparent in the later report on the 'Functioning of Community Product and Capital Markets'.[139] In economic terms, a properly functioning internal market was the key to prosperity for EU citizens. In social terms, the internal market was seen as the guarantee of rights to safe, high-quality products.[140] The Commission accepted the conclusions of the Internal Market Council of March 2000 that high levels of consumer protection were needed for a well-functioning internal market,[141] and acknowledged that environmental concerns required a 'reinforced, symbiotic integration of environmental policy and economic reforms inside the Internal Market'.[142] The revised Commission Communication on 'Services of General Interest'[143] consciously drew on the conclusions of the Lisbon and Feira European Councils, and stressed the economic and social aspects of such services.

---

[126] Lisbon European Council, 23–24 Mar 2000, [5].
[127] Ibid [5], [16]–[21].
[128] Ibid [24].
[129] Ibid [25]–[34].
[130] Feira European Council, 19–20 June 2000, [19]–[39], [44]–[49].
[131] Nice European Council, 7–9 Dec 2000.
[132] Ibid [15].
[133] Ibid Annex 1, [8]–[9].
[134] Ibid Annex 1, [9], [11].
[135] Stockholm European Council, 23–24 Mar 2001, [2].
[136] Ibid [25].
[137] COM(2000) 257 final.
[138] Ibid 15–17.
[139] Economic Reform: Report on the Functioning of Community Capital and Product Markets, COM(2000) 881 final.
[140] Ibid 3–4.
[141] Ibid 5.
[142] Ibid 5.
[143] Services of General Interest in Europe, COM(2000) 580 final. These are services that public authorities decide should be provided even though ordinary market forces may not do so: [14].

The willingness to consider the internal market in more holistic terms is to be welcomed. The Treaty does not, moreover, preclude taking account of non-market values, such as health and safety, even within internal market legislation, provided that the initial economic hurdle is met.

B de Witte, Non-Market Values in Internal Market Legislation[144]

The conclusion is…that internal market legislation, to be constitutionally valid, *must* satisfy a specific internal market test, in the sense that the authors of the act must make a plausible case that the act either helps to remove disparities between national provisions that hinder the free movement of goods, services or persons, or helps to remove disparities that cause distorted conditions of competition. However these need not be, and cannot logically be, the only purposes of internal market legislation. Such legislation also invariably and legitimately pursues other public policy objectives…Internal market legislation is always *also* about 'something else', and that something else may, in fact, be the main reason why the internal market measure was adopted. The multifaceted nature of internal market legislation is one of the inherent characteristics of that legislation and not a perverse ploy of European actors to extend the range of their competences.

There are, nonetheless, continuing tensions between the economic and social dimensions of the internal market. Thus the priorities in the 'Internal Market Strategy' for 2003–6 were heavily economic in nature.[145] The passage of the Services Directive is a further timely reminder of the tensions that exist between the economic and social dimensions of the internal market. The Commission's proposal[146] was strongly criticized by the EP,[147] on the ground that it was too economic in orientation and jeopardized the provision of public services. The Commission was forced to revise its proposals significantly,[148] as reflected in the final version of the Services Directive.[149] It is also the case that the balance between the economic and social dimensions of the Lisbon Strategy has altered over time. While both remain part of the Strategy,[150] the economic focus has often predominated, although the French rejection of the Constitutional Treaty because it was too economic in its orientation led to some renewed emphasis on the social dimension, albeit still within a 'tight' economic frame.[151] There have been subsequent Commission initiatives designed to facilitate single market integration.[152] In 2009 the President of the Commission asked Mario Monti to report on the single market. The report notes the significant challenges that lie ahead.

---

[144] N Nic Shuibhne (ed), *Regulating the Internal Market* (Edward Elgar, 2006) 75. Italics in the original.

[145] Internal Market Strategy—Priorities 2003–2006, COM(2003) 238; B de Witte, 'Non-Market Values in Internal Market Legislation' in Nic Shuibhne (n 144) 78–79.

[146] Proposal for a Directive of the European Parliament and of the Council, on services in the internal market, COM(2004) 2 final/3.

[147] EP Committee on the Internal Market and Consumer Protection, Report on the Proposal for a Directive of the European Parliament and of the Council, on Services in the Internal Market, A6-0409/2005, Rapporteur Evelyne Gebhardt.

[148] Amended Proposal for a Directive of the European Parliament and of the Council, on services in the internal market, COM(2006) 160 final.

[149] Dir 2006/123/EC (n 122).

[150] Brussels European Council, 8–9 Mar 2007, [1]–[20].

[151] See, eg, J Barroso, 'Alive and Kicking: The Renewed Lisbon Strategy', Brussels, 5 Mar 2007.

[152] A Citizen's Agenda, Delivering Results for Europe, COM(2006) 211 final; A Single Market for Citizens, Interim Report to the 2007 Spring European Council, COM(2007) 60 final; Commission Recommendation of 29 June 2009 on measures to improve the functioning of the single market [2009] OJ L176/17; A Vision of the Internal Market for Industrial Products, COM(2014) 25 final.

Monti Report 2010: A New Strategy for the Single Market, At the Service of Europe's Economy and Society[153]

The report highlights that today the single market is at a critical juncture, as it faces three challenges…The first challenge comes from the erosion of the political and social support for market integration in Europe. The single market is seen by many Europeans—citizens as well as political leaders—with suspicion, fear and sometimes open hostility. Two mutually reinforcing trends are at work: an 'integration fatigue', eroding the appetite for more Europe and for a *single* market; and more recently, a 'market fatigue', with a reduced confidence in the role of the *market*. The single market today is less popular than ever, while Europe needs it more than ever.

The second challenge comes from uneven policy attention given to the development of the various components of an effective and sustainable single market. Some of the difficulties encountered by the single market in recent years can be traced back not only to the incomplete 'welding together' of the national markets into one European market, but also to the unfinished business on two other fronts: the expansion to new sectors to accompany a fast changing economy and the effort to ensure that the single market is a space of freedom and opportunity that works for all, citizens, consumers and SMEs.

A third challenge comes from a sense of complacency that gained strength in the past decade, as if the single market had been really completed and could thus be put to rest as a political priority. The single market was felt to be 'yesterday's business', in need of regular maintenance but not of active promotion. The shift of attention away from the single market was further strengthened by the need to concentrate the EU's political energy on other challenging building blocks of the European construction: monetary union, enlargement and institutional reforms. With the entry into force of the Lisbon Treaty in January 2010, all the three major priorities have been achieved, and there is no reason to deflect attention away from the single market. On the contrary, the correct functioning of the monetary union and of enlargement call the single market back on stage.

The Monti Report is premised on the need for initiatives that will generate a stronger single market, foster consensus about the single market project, and deliver the single market ideal. The Report contains a valuable analysis of the economic challenges facing the single market project, recognizes the tensions between the economic and social dimensions of the single market, and seeks to address them.

The relationship between the economic and the social was however thrown into sharp relief by the financial crisis that was taking hold at the time of the Monti Report. There is little doubt that the social dimension suffered during this period, in part because financial austerity led to cutbacks in social programmes, in part because so much 'political adrenalin' was taken up with enacting the economic measures designed to keep the EU alive during this period. In the words of President Juncker, 'the measures taken during the crisis can be compared to repairing a burning plane whilst flying', with some mistakes made, including 'a lack of social fairness'.[154]

9. CONCLUSIONS

i.   A significant contribution of the SEA and the single market project to the process of European integration was that it jolted the Community out of the Euro-pessimism of the 1970s and early 1980s. If there had been no SEA, the new approach to harmonization might never have taken

---

[153] http://ec.europa.eu/internal_market/strategy/index_en.htm, 6.
[154] J-C Juncker, 'A New Start for Europe: My Agenda for Jobs, Growth, Fairness and Democratic Change', Strasbourg, 15 July 2014, 2.

hold. The SEA laid the foundations for the institutional and substantive changes that occurred later. Causality in international affairs is difficult to determine. But it is doubtful whether the Maastricht Treaty would have been negotiated had the SEA not preceded it.

ii. The focus in the 1980s and early 1990s was, not unnaturally, on the economic dimensions of the single market. Legislative, administrative, and judicial initiatives contributed to the breaking down of the economic barriers to the single market. This is still a central aspect of single market policy.

iii. The focus from the mid-1990s onwards has shifted. The internal market is now felt to embrace broader concerns relating to social, environmental, and consumer policy. This has been a conscious shift by the EU, anxious to avoid the criticism that pursuit of the single market has undercut social, etc, protections within the Member States. There are nonetheless continuing tensions between the economic and social dimensions of the internal market, as revealed by the financial crisis.

10 FURTHER READING

(a) Books

ARMSTRONG, K, *Regulation, Deregulation, Re-Regulation* (Kogan Page, 2000)

——— AND BULMER, S, *The Governance of the Single European Market* (Manchester University Press, 1998)

BARNARD, C, AND SCOTT, J (eds), *The Law of the Single European Market* (Hart, 2002)

BIEBER, R, DEHOUSSE, R, PINDER, J, AND WEILER, J (eds), *1992: One European Market?* (Nomos, 1988)

EGAN, M, *Constructing a European Market* (Oxford University Press, 2001)

JANSSENS, C, *The Principle of Mutual Recognition in EU Law* (Oxford University Press, 2013)

JOERGES, C, AND DEHOUSSE, R (eds), *Good Governance in Europe's Integrated Market* (Oxford University Press, 2002)

MAJONE, G, *Regulating Europe* (Routledge, 1996)

——— *Dilemmas of European Integration: The Ambiguities and Pitfalls of Integration by Stealth* (Oxford University Press, 2005)

NIC SHUIBHNE, N (ed), *Regulating the Internal Market* (Edward Elgar, 2006)

SCHEPEL, H, *The Constitution of Private Governance* (Hart, 2005)

SNYDER, F (ed), *Constitutional Dimensions of European Economic Integration* (Kluwer, 1996)

(b) Articles

ARMSTRONG, K, 'Governance and the Single European Market' in P Craig and G de Búrca (eds), *The Evolution of EU Law* (Oxford University Press, 1999) ch 21

CRAIG, P, 'The Evolution of the Single Market' in C Barnard and J Scott (eds), *The Law of the Single European Market* (Hart, 2002) ch 1

DOUGAN, M, 'Minimum Harmonization and the Internal Market' (2000) 37 CMLRev 853

EHLERMANN, C-D, 'The Internal Market Following the Single European Act' (1987) 24 CMLRev 361

MADURO, MP, 'So Close and Yet So Far: The Paradoxes of Mutual Recognition' (2007) 14 JEPP 814

McGEE, A, AND WEATHERILL, S, 'The Evolution of the Single Market—Harmonisation or Liberalisation' (1990) 53 MLR 578

MORAVCSIK, A, 'Negotiating the Single European Act: National Interests and Conventional Statecraft in the European Community' (1991) 45 International Organization 19

NICOLAÏDIS, K, 'Trusting the Poles? Constructing Europe through Mutual Recognition' (2007) 14 JEPP 602

PELKMANS, J, 'The New Approach to Technical Harmonization and Standardization' (1987) 25 JCMS 249

——— 'Mutual Recognition in Goods. On Promises and Disillusions' (2007) 14 JEPP 699

SANDHOLTZ, W, AND ZYSMAN, J, '1992: Recasting the European Bargain' (1989) 42 World Politics 95

SCHMIDT, S, 'Mutual Recognition as a New Mode of Governance' (2007) 14 JEPP 667

STREIT, M, AND MUSSLER, W, 'The Economic Constitution of the European Community: From "Rome" to "Maastricht"' (1995) 1 ELJ 5

SUN, J-M, AND PELKMANS, J, 'Regulatory Competition and the Single Market' (1995) 33 JCMS 67

WEATHERILL, S, 'New Strategies for Managing the EC's Internal Market' (2000) 53 CLP 595

——— 'Pre-Emption, Harmonization and the Distribution of Competence to Regulate the Internal Market' in C BARNARD and J SCOTT (eds), *The Law of the Single European Market* (Hart, 2002) ch 2

WITTE, B DE, 'Non-Market Values in Internal Market Legislation' in N Nic Shuibhne (ed), *Regulating the Internal Market* (Edward Elgar, 2006) ch 3

18

FREE MOVEMENT OF GOODS: DUTIES, CHARGES, AND TAXES

1 CENTRAL ISSUES

i.   This and the following chapter are concerned with the free movement of goods. This can be impeded in different ways. The most obvious form of protectionism is customs duties, or charges which have an equivalent effect, to make foreign goods more expensive than their domestic counterparts. This is dealt with by Articles 28–30 TFEU. A state may also attempt to benefit domestic goods by taxes that discriminate against imports. This is covered by Articles 110–113 TFEU. These issues will be considered within this chapter.

ii. A state may, however, seek to preserve advantages for its own goods by imposing quotas or measures which have an equivalent effect on imports, thereby reducing imported products. This is dealt with in Articles 34–37 TFEU, analysed in the next chapter.

iii. These two chapters are concerned with Member State action that creates barriers to trade. Such action can also result from aid granted by a Member State to a specific industry, which disadvantages competing products from other Member States. EU law therefore regulates the grant of such aid through Articles 107–109 TFEU.[1] Private parties may also take action that partitions the market along national lines, and hence impedes realization of the single market, such as when firms agree not to compete in each other's markets. EU law addresses both issues in order to prevent private action from recreating barriers to trade analogous in their effect to duties or quotas.[2]

iv. The abolition of customs duties and charges having an equivalent effect is central to the idea of a customs union and a single market. The customs union is a foundation of the EU and essential to the functioning of the single market, with the implication that the 'twenty seven Customs administrations of the EU must act as though they were one'.[3]

v.   The ECJ has therefore interpreted Articles 28–30 strictly in order to ensure that this aim is fulfilled. It looks to the effect of a duty, and not its purpose, and has given a broad reading to 'charges having equivalent effect' to a customs duty. It has allowed only very limited exceptions to these Articles, and any breach will be unlawful *per se*.

---

[1] See Ch 29.
[2] See Chs 26–28.
[3] http://ec.europa.eu/taxation_customs/customs/policy_issues/customs_strategy/index_en.htm.

vi. The prohibition of taxes that discriminate against imports is equally central to the single market ideal. Customs duties apply when goods cross the border, and are caught by Articles 28–30 TFEU. A state may however discriminate against imports through differential taxes when goods are in its country, Articles 110–113 TFEU proscribe such conduct.

vii. The case law concerning Articles 110–113 can be controversial. This is in part because the Treaty language requires the ECJ to make decisions about difficult matters, such as whether goods are similar to each other, or whether a differential tax regime is protective of home state products. It is also in part because tax rules may be used to foster national preferences in relation to matters such as the environment. The ECJ has to adjudicate on whether such rules are compatible with Articles 110–113.

viii. It is essential when reading the materials in this chapter to have some idea of the broader context into which they fit. The discussion of the legal materials will therefore be placed within the context of the more general issues concerning the customs union and taxation respectively.

2 ARTICLES 28–30: DUTIES AND CHARGES

Article 28(1) TFEU[4] is the foundational provision of this part of the Treaty:

> 1. The Union shall comprise a customs union which shall cover all trade in goods and which shall involve the prohibition between Member States[5] of customs duties on imports and exports and of all charges having equivalent effect, and the adoption of a common customs tariff in their relations with third countries.[6]

Article 30 TFEU relates to any customs duties and charges equivalent thereto, whether concerning imports or exports, with no distinction being drawn as to when such duties were imposed:[7]

> Customs duties on imports and exports and charges having equivalent effect shall be prohibited between Member States. This prohibition shall also apply to customs duties of a fiscal nature.

---

[4] Art 28 will almost always be used in conjunction with one of the other Treaty Arts in this area. When it is employed in this manner it will have direct effect: see, eg, Case 18/71 *Eunomia di Porro & Co v Italian Ministry of Education* [1971] ECR 811.

[5] Art 28 prohibits customs duties, etc, even when they are applied within a Member State and are imposed on goods which enter or leave a particular region of that state: Cases C–363, 407, 409 and 411/93 *René Lancry SA v Direction Générale des Douanes* [1994] ECR I–3957; Case C–72/03 *Carbonati Apuani Srl v Commune di Carrara* [2004] ECR I–8027.

[6] The goods which benefit from the provisions on free movement are those which originate in a Member State and those which come from outside the EU but are in free circulation within the Member States: Art 28(2) TFEU. The criteria for goods which come from outside the EU to be in free circulation within the EU are contained in Art 29 TFEU: the goods must have complied with import formalities, and any customs duties and charges must have been paid by the trader and not have been reimbursed.

[7] The old Art 12 EEC prohibited the imposition of *new* customs duties and charges equivalent thereto, while the old Art 13 EEC obliged Member States to abolish *existing* duties within the transitional period, in accordance with Arts 13–15; the old Art 16 EEC concerned the abolition of duties on exports. The passage of time has rendered the distinction between new and existing duties redundant.

(A) DUTIES AND CHARGES: EFFECT NOT PURPOSE

The Court made it clear from the outset that the application of what is now Article 30 TFEU depends upon the effect of the duty or charge, and not on its purpose.

Case 7/68 **Commission v Italy**
[1968] ECR 423

[Note Lisbon Treaty renumbering: Art 169 is now Art 258 TFEU; Art 16 has been repealed, but the substance is now covered by Art 30 TFEU]

Italy imposed a tax on the export of artistic, historical, and archaeological items. The Commission argued that this was in breach of Article 16 EEC, which prohibited duties and charges on exports. Italy argued that the items should not be regarded as goods for the purpose of the customs union and that the purpose of the tax in question was not to raise revenue, but to protect the artistic heritage of the country. The Court rejected these arguments.

THE ECJ

2. The Classification of the Disputed Tax Having Regard to Article 16 of the Treaty

In the opinion of the Commission the tax in dispute constitutes a tax having an effect equivalent to a customs duty on exports and therefore the tax should have been abolished, under Article 16 of the Treaty, no later than the end of the first stage of the common market, that is to say, from 1 January 1962. The defendant argues that the disputed tax does not come within the category, as it has its own particular purpose which is to ensure the protection and safety of the artistic, historic and archaeological heritage which exists in the national territory. Consequently, the tax does not in any respect have a fiscal nature, and its contribution to the budget is insignificant.

Article 16 of the Treaty prohibits the collection in dealings between Member States of any customs duty on exports and of any charge having an equivalent effect, that is to say, any charge which, by altering the price of an article exported, has the same restrictive effect on the free circulation of that article as a customs duty. That provision makes no distinction based on the purpose of the duties and charges the abolition of which it requires.

It is not necessary to analyse the concept of the nature of the fiscal system on which the defendant bases its argument upon this point, for the provisions of the section of the Treaty concerning the elimination of customs duties between the Member States exclude the retention of customs duties and charges having an equivalent effect without distinguishing in that respect between those which are and those which are not of a fiscal nature.

The disputed tax falls within Article 16 by reason of the fact that export trade in the goods in question is hindered by the pecuniary burden which it imposes on the price of the exported articles.

When a tax is caught by Article 30 TFEU as a duty or charge that is of equivalent effect then it is in effect *per se* unlawful. Thus, attempts by Italy to argue that its tax could be defended on the basis of what is now Article 36 TFEU were rejected by the Court, since this can be used as a defence only in relation to quantitative restrictions caught by Article 34 TFEU. It cannot validate fiscal measures prohibited by Article 30 TFEU.

This emphasis on effect as opposed to purpose is clearly justifiable. The peremptory force of Article 30 TFEU would be significantly weakened if a state could argue that a duty or charge should not be prohibited because its purpose was in some sense non-fiscal in nature. Such an argument would, moreover, have required the judiciary to adjudicate on which social policies should be regarded as possessing a legitimate purpose sufficient to take them outside the Treaty.

The ECJ reaffirmed its emphasis on effect rather than purpose in other cases. It also made it clear that the Treaty provisions can be applicable even if the state measure was not designed with protectionism in mind. Thus in *Diamantarbeiders*[8] the Court considered the legality of a Belgian law requiring 0.33 per cent of the value of imported diamonds to be paid into a social fund for workers. The fact that the purpose of the fund was neither to raise money for the exchequer nor to protect domestic industry[9] did not save the charge in question. It was sufficient that the charge was imposed on goods because they had crossed a border.

(B) CHARGES HAVING AN EQUIVALENT EFFECT: GENERAL PRINCIPLES

Article 30 TFEU prohibits not only customs duties, but also charges having an equivalent effect (CEE).[10] The reason is obvious. It is designed to catch protectionist measures that create a similar barrier to trade to customs duties *stricto sensu*. It is therefore unsurprising that the ECJ has interpreted the term expansively.

Case 24/68 **Commission v Italy**
[1969] ECR 193

[Note Lisbon Treaty renumbering: Arts 9 and 12 are now Arts 28 and 30 TFEU;
Arts 13 and 16 have been repealed]

Italy imposed a levy on goods exported to other Member States with the ostensible purpose of collecting statistical material for use in discerning trade patterns. The Court reiterated its holding that customs duties were prohibited irrespective of the purpose for which the duties were imposed, and irrespective of the destination of the revenues which were collected. It then held:

THE ECJ

8. The extension of the prohibition of customs duties to charges having an equivalent effect is intended to supplement the prohibition against obstacles to trade created by such duties by increasing its efficiency.

The use of these two complementary concepts thus tends, in trade between Member States, to avoid the imposition of any pecuniary charge on goods circulating within the Community by virtue of the fact that they cross a national border.

9. Thus, in order to ascribe to a charge an effect equivalent to a customs duty, it is important to consider this effect in the light of the objectives of the Treaty, in the Parts, Titles and Chapters in which Articles 9, 12, 13 and 16 are to be found, particularly in relation to the free movement of goods.

---

[8] Cases 2 and 3/69 *Sociaal Fonds voor de Diamantarbeiders v SA Ch Brachfeld & Sons* [1969] ECR 211. See also Cases 485 and 486/93 *Maria Simitzi v Municipality of Kos* [1995] ECR I–2655; Cases C–441 and 442/98 *Michailidis AE v IKA* [2000] ECR I–7145; Case C–293/02 *Jersey Produce Marketing Association Ltd v States of Jersey and Jersey Potato Marketing Board* [2005] ECR I–9543, [55]–[56]; Case C–72/03 *Carbonati Apuani* (n 5) [30]–[31].

[9] Belgium did not produce diamonds.

[10] R Barents, 'Charges Having an Equivalent Effect to Customs Duties' (1978) 15 CMLRev 415.

> Consequently, any pecuniary charge, however small and whatever its designation and mode of application, which is imposed unilaterally on domestic or foreign goods by reason of the fact that they cross a frontier, and which is not a customs duty in the strict sense, constitutes a charge having equivalent effect within the meaning of Articles 9, 12, 13 and 16 of the Treaty, even if it is not imposed for the benefit of the State, is not discriminatory or protective in effect and if the product on which the charge is imposed is not in competition with any domestic product.
>
> 10. It follows...that the prohibition of new customs duties or charges having equivalent effect, linked to the principle of the free movement of goods, constitutes a fundamental rule which, without prejudice to the other provisions of the Treaty, does not permit of any exceptions.

This test was repeated in *Diamantarbeiders*,[11] making clear that it would bite whether those affected by the charge were all Community citizens, those from the importing state, or only the nationals from the state that was responsible for passing the contested measure. It signalled the Court's intention that the Treaty Articles on customs duties and CEEs were not to be circumvented by the form in which the charge was imposed. They were applicable whether the duty/charge discriminated or not. They had an impact irrespective of whether the product on which the charge was imposed was in competition with domestic goods, and there were no exceptions.[12]

The ECJ's strident approach was unsurprising, given the obstacle presented by customs duties and CEEs to the very notion of a single market. The abolition of such measures goes to the very heart of this ideal. It was a necessary first step in the attainment of market integration. The eradication of customs duties and the like was vital if the broader aims of the common market were to be fulfilled. It is moreover clear that a charge which is imposed not on a product as such, but on a necessary activity in connection with the product, can be caught by Articles 30 and 110 TFEU.[13]

(c) CHARGES HAVING AN EQUIVALENT EFFECT: INSPECTIONS AND THE 'EXCHANGE EXCEPTION'

A common defence is that the charge imposed on imported goods is justified because it is merely payment for a service the state has rendered to the importer, and therefore should not be regarded as a CEE. The Court has been willing to accept this argument in principle. It has, however, been alert to the fact that a state might present a charge in this way when in reality it was seeking to impede imports, or in circumstances where there was no commercial exchange at all. The Court has therefore closely scrutinized such claims from states and has not readily accepted them.

Thus in *Commission v Italy*,[14] considered above, the Italian Government argued that the charge should be seen as the consideration for the statistical information which it collected. The government contended that this information 'affords importers a better competitive position in the Italian market whilst exporters enjoy a similar advantage abroad';[15] and that therefore the charge should be viewed as consideration for a service rendered, and not as a CEE. The Court was unconvinced. It held that the

---

[11] Cases 2 and 3/69 (n 8).

[12] Case 29/72 *Marimex SpA v Italian Finance Administration* [1972] ECR 1309; Case 39/73 *Rewe-Zentralfinanz v Direktor der Landwirtschaftskammer Westfalen-Lippe* [1973] ECR 1039; Case C–130/93 *Lamaire NV v Nationale Dienst voor Afzet van Land- en Tuinbouwprodukten* [1994] ECR I–3215; Case C–16/94 *Dubois et Fils SA v Garonor Exploitation SA* [1995] ECR I–2421; Case C–72/03 *Carbonati Apuani* (n 5) [20]; Case C–234/99 *Niels Nygard v Svineafgiftsfonden* [2002] ECR I–3657, [19].

[13] Case C–206/06 *Essent Netwerk Noord BV v Aluminium Delfzijl BV* [2008] ECR I–5497, [44].

[14] Case 24/68 [1969] ECR 193, [15]–[16].

[15] Ibid [15].

statistical information was beneficial to the whole economy and to the administrative authorities. It then continued in the following vein:[16]

> Even if the competitive position of importers and exporters were to be particularly improved as a result, the statistics still constitute an advantage so general, and so difficult to assess, that the disputed charge cannot be regarded as the consideration for a specific benefit actually conferred.

The same theme is found in other decisions.[17] Even when the charge *is* more directly related to some action taken by the state with respect to specific imported goods, the Court has been reluctant to accept that the charge can be characterized as consideration for a service rendered. This is apparent from the *Bresciani* case.

Case 87/75 **Bresciani v Amministrazione Italiana delle Finanze**
[1976] ECR 129

The Italian authorities imposed a charge for compulsory veterinary and public-health inspections carried out on imported raw cowhides. Was this to be regarded as a CEE or not?

THE ECJ

6. The national court requests that the three following considerations be taken into account:

First, the fact that the charge is proportionate to the quantity of the goods and not to their value distinguishes a duty of the type at issue from charges which fall within the prohibition under Article 13 of the EEC Treaty. Second, a pecuniary charge of the type at issue is no more than the consideration required from individuals who, through their own action in importing products of animal origin, cause a service to be rendered. In the third place, although there may be differences in the method and time of its application, the duty at issue is also levied on similar products of domestic origin.

...

8. The justification for the obligation progressively to abolish customs duties is based on the fact that any pecuniary charge, however small, imposed on goods by reason of the fact that they cross a frontier constitutes an obstacle to the free movement of such goods.

The obligation progressively to abolish customs duties is supplemented by the obligation to abolish charges having equivalent effect in order to prevent the fundamental principle of the free movement of goods within the common market from being circumvented by the imposition of pecuniary charges of various kinds by a Member State.

The use of these two complementary concepts thus tends, in trade between Member States, to avoid the imposition of any pecuniary charge on goods circulating within the Community by virtue of the fact that they cross a national frontier.

9. Consequently, any pecuniary charge, whatever its designation and mode of application, which is unilaterally imposed on goods imported from another Member State by reason of the fact that they cross a frontier, constitutes a charge having an effect equivalent to a customs duty. In appraising a duty of the type at issue it is, consequently, of no importance that it is proportionate to the quantity of the imported goods and not to their value.

---

[16] Ibid [16].
[17] Case 63/74 *W Cadsky SpA v Istituto Nazionale per il Commercio Estero* [1975] ECR 281.

10. Nor, in determining the effects of the duty on the free movement of goods, is it of any importance that a duty of the type at issue is proportionate to the costs of a compulsory public health inspection carried out on entry of the goods. The activity of the administration of the State intended to maintain a public health inspection system imposed in the general interest cannot be regarded as a service rendered to the importer such as to justify the imposition of a pecuniary charge. If, accordingly, public health inspections are still justified at the end of the transitional period, the costs which they occasion must be met by the general public which, as a whole benefits from the free movement of Community goods.

11. The fact that the domestic production is, through other charges, subjected to a similar burden matters little unless those charges and the duty in question are applied according to the same criteria and at the same stage of production, thus making it possible for them to be regarded as falling within a general system of internal taxation applying systematically and in the same way to domestic and imported products.

The ECJ's judgment in *Bresciani* indicates clearly its reluctance to accept arguments that will take pecuniary charges outside the Treaty. In paragraph 9 it rejected the *first* of the Italian arguments: the fact that the charge was proportionate to the quantity of imported goods made no difference, since Article 30 TFEU prohibited *any* charge imposed by reason of the fact that goods crossed a frontier.[18] The rejection of the *second* argument in paragraph 10 was equally significant. The state's argument had some plausibility: if you wish to import a product that requires health inspection, then you, the importer, should bear the cost. The Court's response was, however, unequivocal: the cost of inspections to maintain public health should be borne by the general public. It is doubtful whether this makes sense in micro-economic terms.[19] The ECJ's conclusion was, however, designed to limit exceptions to Articles 28–30 TFEU. This is equally apparent in the Court's response to the state's *third* contention, found in paragraph 11, which required a strict equivalence between the charges levied on domestic and imported goods. Other attempts to employ the exchange argument have not generally proven successful.[20]

(D) CHARGES HAVING AN EQUIVALENT EFFECT: INSPECTIONS AND FULFILMENT OF MANDATORY LEGAL REQUIREMENTS

Where EU legislation *permits* an inspection to be undertaken by a state, the national authorities cannot recover any fees charged from the traders.[21] The Court has, however, accepted that a charge imposed by a state will escape Articles 28–30 TFEU when it is levied to cover the cost of a *mandatory* inspection required by EU law.[22]

---

[18] A charge will be deemed to be a CEE if it is a flat-rate charge which is based on the value of the goods: Case 170/88 *Ford España v Spain* [1989] ECR 2305.

[19] By placing the cost on the general public it means that the importer of the product will not have to bear what is in reality one of the costs of making that product.

[20] See, eg, Case 43/71 *Politi SAS v Italian Ministry of Finance* [1971] ECR 1039; Case 132/82 *Commission v Belgium* [1983] ECR 1649; Case 340/87 *Commission v Italy* [1989] ECR 1483; Case C–209/89 *Commission v Italy* [1991] ECR I–3533; Case C–272/95 *Bundesanstalt für Landwirtschaft und Ernährung v Deutsches Milch-Kontor GmbH* [1997] ECR I–1905.

[21] Case 314/82 *Commission v Belgium* [1984] ECR 1543.

[22] Case 46/76 *Bauhuis v Netherlands* [1977] ECR 5; Case 1/83 *IFG v Freistaat Bayern* [1984] ECR 349; Case C–389/00 *Commission v Germany* [2003] ECR I–2001. The costs of checks carried out pursuant to mandatory obligations imposed by international conventions to which all the Member States are party are treated in the same way: Case 89/76 *Commission v Netherlands* [1977] ECR 1355.

Case 18/87 **Commission v Germany**
[1988] ECR 5427

[Note Lisbon Treaty renumbering: Arts 9–12 and 36 are now Arts 28–30 and 36 TFEU]

German regional authorities charged fees on live animals imported into the country to cover the cost of inspections required by Directive 81/389. The question arose whether they should be regarded as CEEs. The ECJ stated the orthodox proposition that any pecuniary charge imposed as a result of goods crossing a frontier was caught by the Treaty, either as a customs duty or as a CEE. It then recognized an exception to this basic principle.

THE ECJ

6. However, the Court has held that such a charge escapes that classification if it relates to a general system of internal dues applied systematically and in accordance with the same criteria to domestic products and imported products alike (...Case 132/78 *Denkavit* v *France*...), if it constitutes payment for a service in fact rendered to the economic operator of a sum in proportion to the service (...Case 158/82 *Commission* v *Denmark*...), or again, subject to certain conditions, if it attaches to inspections carried out to fulfil obligations imposed by Community law (...Case 46/76 *Bauhuis* v *Netherlands*...).

7. The contested fee, which is payable on importation and transit, cannot be regarded as relating to a general system of internal dues. Nor does it constitute payment for a service rendered to the operator, because this condition is satisfied only if the operator in question obtains a definite specific benefit..., which is not the case if the inspection serves to guarantee, in the public interest, the health and life of animals in international transport....

8. Since the contested fee was charged in connection with inspections carried out pursuant to a Community provision, it should be noted that according to the case law of the Court...such fees may not be classified as charges having an effect equivalent to a customs duty if the following conditions are satisfied:

(a) they do not exceed the actual costs of the inspections in connection with which they are charged;

(b) the inspections in question are obligatory and uniform for all the products concerned in the Community;

(c) they are prescribed by Community law in the general interest of the Community;

(d) they promote the free movement of goods, in particular by neutralizing obstacles which could arise from unilateral measures of inspection adopted in accordance with Article 36 of the Treaty.

9. In this instance these conditions are satisfied by the contested fee. In the first place it has not been contested that it does not exceed the real cost of the inspections in connection with which it is charged.

10. Moreover, all the Member States of transit and destination are required, under, *inter alia*, Article 2(1) of Directive 81/389/EEC...to carry out the veterinary inspections in question when the animals are brought into their territories, and therefore the inspections are obligatory and uniform for all the animals concerned in the Community.

11. Those inspections are prescribed by Directive 81/389/EEC, which establishes the measures necessary...for the protection of live animals during international transport, with a view to the protection of live animals, an objective which is pursued in the general interest of the Community and not a specific interest of individual states.

> 12. Finally, it appears in the preambles to the...directives that they are intended to harmonize the laws of the Member States regarding the protection of animals in international transport in order to eliminate technical barriers resulting from disparities in the national laws....In addition, failing such harmonization, each Member State was entitled to maintain or introduce, under the conditions laid down in Article 36 of the Treaty, measures restricting trade which were justified on grounds of the protection of the health and life of animals. It follows that the standardization of the inspections in question is such as to promote the free movement of goods.

(E) RECOVERY OF UNLAWFUL CHARGES

The general principle[23] is that a Member State must repay charges that have been unlawfully levied.[24] The procedural conditions for such repayment may be less favourable than those applying in actions between private individuals, provided that they apply in the same way to actions based on EU law and national law, and provided also that they do not make recovery impossible or excessively difficult.[25] There is, however, an exception to this general rule for circumstances in which the trader has passed on the loss to customers, since reimbursement could lead to the trader being unjustly enriched.[26] This very exception may itself be qualified where the trader can, nonetheless, show that it has suffered loss.[27] The burden of proving that the duties have not been passed on to others cannot however be placed on the taxpayer.[28]

(F) THE CUSTOMS UNION: THE BROADER PERSPECTIVE

The discussion thus far has focused on the legal issues surrounding Articles 28–30 TFEU, and the limits placed on the capacity of Member States to impose duties or charges when goods cross a frontier. It would, however, be mistaken to believe that this constitutes the entirety of EU law in this area.

The *substantive importance of* customs law is far greater than this.[29] The consequence of the breaking down of customs barriers between Member States is that once goods are in the EU they move freely. The corollary is that 'the ring fence around the single market is only as strong as its weakest link', and that there is no 'second chance' to impose limits on goods coming from a third country.[30] The maintenance of effective customs control for goods coming from outside the EU is important for a number of reasons. Such goods will be subject to a tariff, which is a significant part of the EU's own resources. The EU has, therefore, a strong interest in combating fraud. The fact that there is in effect only ever one customs barrier for goods to enter the EU also has implications for the battle against

---

[23] Ch 8.

[24] Case 199/82 *Amministrazione delle Finanze dello Stato v San Giorgio* [1983] ECR 3595; Case C–310/09 *Ministre du Budget, des Comptes publics et de la Fonction publique v Accor SA* [2011] ECR I–8115; Case C–591/10 *Littlewoods Retail Ltd v Her Majesty's Commissioners of Revenue and Customs* EU:C:2012:478, [24].

[25] Case C–343/96 *Dilexport Srl v Amministrazione delle Finanze dello Stato* [1999] ECR I–579.

[26] K Lasiński-Sulecki, 'Unjust Enrichment in European Union Tax Law: In Search of Balance between the Views of the Court of Justice, the General Principles of EU Law and the Constitutional Principles of EU Member States' (2014) 42 Intertax 2.

[27] Cases C–192–218/95 *Société Comateb v Directeur Général des Douanes et Droits Indirects* [1997] ECR I–165; Case C–309/06 *Marks & Spencer plc v Commissioners of Customs & Excise* [2008] ECR I–283, [41]–[42].

[28] Case C–343/96 *Dilexport* (n 25) [52]; Cases C–441 and 442/98 *Michailidis* (n 8) [38].

[29] Concerning a Strategy for the Customs Union, COM(2001) 51 final; http://ec.europa.eu/taxation_customs/customs/policy_issues/customs_strategy/index_en.htm.

[30] The Changing Role of Customs (EC Commission, 2000), 1.

organized crime, counterfeit goods, and the like. It is clear that customs have a role to play in the fight against terrorism.[31] These objectives are reflected in the 2008 modernized customs code,[32] and in the attendant Commission strategy document.[33]

This led to a number of *organizational initiatives* to meet these new challenges. There is no EU customs service. The EU works through national customs authorities and the object of the 2002 Programme[34] was that these authorities should operate as efficiently and effectively as a single administration,[35] especially in the light of enlargement. Commission initiatives from 2003,[36] endorsed by the Council,[37] were designed to expedite customs checks through increased use of electronic communication.[38] These were combined with initiatives to use customs to combat crime, fraud, and terrorism and the creation of a Customs Security Programme.[39] The 2012 Commission Report identified three challenges in the forthcoming years: completion of the modernization begun in 2003; identifying priorities to be tackled; and reforming the governance and management structures of the customs union.[40] In 2014 the Commission adopted a new risk management plan to protect EU safety and security, while facilitating trade.[41]

3 ARTICLES 110–113: DISCRIMINATORY TAX PROVISIONS

The preceding discussion has focused on Articles 28–30 TFEU. The focus now shifts to discriminatory taxes. Article 110 TFEU is the central provision and has been directly effective since 1 January 1962.[42]

> No Member State shall impose, directly or indirectly, on the products of other Member States any internal taxation of any kind in excess of that imposed directly or indirectly on similar domestic products.
>
> Furthermore, no Member State shall impose on the products of other Member States any internal taxation of such a nature as to afford indirect protection to other products.

[31] http://ec.europa.eu/taxation_customs/customs/policy_issues/customs_strategy/index_en.htm.

[32] Regulation (EC) No 450/2008 of the European Parliament and of the Council of 23 April 2008 laying down the Community Customs Code (Modernised Customs Code) [2008] OJ L145/1.

[33] Strategy for the Evolution of the Customs Union, COM(2008) 169 final; Report on Progress on the Strategy for the Evolution of the Customs Union, COM(2011) 922 final.

[34] Dec 210/97 [1996] OJ L33/24.

[35] Commission Report to the European Parliament and the Council, On the Implementation of the Customs 2000 Programme, Doc XXI/1065/98 EN, [2.1].

[36] A Simple and Paperless Environment for Customs and Trade; On the Role of Customs in the Integrated Management of External Borders, COM(2003) 452 final.

[37] Council Resolution of 5 December 2003, On Creating a Simple and Paperless Environment for Customs and Trade [2003] OJ C305/1.

[38] Decision 70/2008 of the European Parliament and of the Council of 15 January 2008 on a paperless environment for customs and trade [2008] OJ L23/21.

[39] http://ec.europa.eu/taxation_customs/customs/policy_issues/customs_security/index_en.htm; Regulation (EC) No 648/2005 of the European Parliament and of the Council of 13 April 2005, Amending Council Regulation 2913/92 Establishing the Community Customs Code [2005] OJ L117/13.

[40] On the State of the Customs Union, COM(2012) 791 final.

[41] http://europa.eu/rapid/press-release_IP-14-936_en.htm.

[42] Case 57/65 *Alfons Lütticke GmbH v Hauptzollamt Saarlouis* [1966] ECR 205; Case 28/67 *Mölkerei-Zentrale Westfalen/Lippe GmbH v Hauptzollamt Paderborn* [1968] ECR 143; Case 74/76 *Ianelli & Volpi v Meroni* [1977] ECR 557.

(A) THE PURPOSE OF ARTICLE 110

The aim of Article 110 TFEU can be stated quite simply: it is to prevent the objectives of Articles 28–30 from being undermined by discriminatory internal taxation. We have already seen that Articles 28–30 are designed to prevent customs duties, or charges equivalent thereto, from impeding the free flow of goods. The Treaty outlaws such measures when a product crosses a frontier. These provisions would, however, be undermined if a state could prejudice foreign products when they were inside its territory by levying discriminatory taxes, thereby disadvantaging those imported products in competition with domestic goods. Article 110 is designed to prevent this from happening, and this has been recognized by the ECJ, which demands complete neutrality of internal taxation as regards domestic and imported products.[43]

(B) ARTICLE 110(1): DIRECT DISCRIMINATION

Article 110(1) does not stipulate that a Member State must adopt any particular regime of internal taxation. It requires only that whatever system is chosen should be applied without discrimination to similar imported products.

Thus in *Commission v Italy*[44] the Italian Government charged lower taxes on regenerated oil than on ordinary oil. The policy was motivated by ecological considerations, but imported regenerated oil did not benefit from the same advantage. In its defence Italy argued that it was not possible to determine whether imported oil was regenerated or not. This argument was rejected by the ECJ, which held that it was for the importers to show that their oil came within the relevant category, subject to a reasonable standard of proof, and that a certificate from the state of export could be used to identify the nature of the oil. Similarly in *Hansen*[45] the ECJ insisted that a German rule making tax relief available to spirits made from fruit by small businesses and collective farms must be equally applicable to spirits in the same category coming from elsewhere in the EU.[46]

The rules relating to non-discrimination with respect to the payment of taxes will also be broken if the procedure for tax collection treats domestic goods and those which come from another Member State unequally.[47] This is demonstrated by *Commission v Ireland*.[48] In this case, although the tax applied to all goods irrespective of origin, domestic producers were treated more leniently as regards payment, being allowed a number of weeks before payment was actually demanded, whereas importers had to pay the duty directly on importation.

---

[43] Cases 2 and 3/62 *Commission v Belgium and Luxembourg* [1962] ECR 425, 431; Case 252/86 *Gabriel Bergandi v Directeur Général des Impôts* [1988] ECR 1343, 1374; Case C–101/00 *Tulliasiamies and Antti Siilin* [2002] ECR I–7487, [52]; Case C–387/01 *Weigel and Weigel v Finanzlandirektion für Vorarlberg* [2004] ECR I–4981, [66]; Cases C–393/04 and 41/05 *Air Liquide Industries Belgium SA v Ville de Seraing and Province de Liège* [2006] ECR I–5293, [55]–[57]; Case C–313/05 *Maciej Brzeziński v Dyrektor Izby Celnej w Warszawie* [2007] ECR I–513, [27]; Case C–206/06 *Essent Netwerk Noord* (n 13) [40].

[44] Case 21/79 [1980] ECR 1.

[45] Case 148/77 *Hansen v Hauptzollamt Flensburg* [1978] ECR 1787.

[46] See also Case 196/85 *Commission v France* [1987] ECR 1597; Case C–327/90 *Commission v Greece* [1992] ECR I–3033; Case C–375/95 *Commission v Greece* [1997] ECR I–5981.

[47] See, eg, Cases C–290 and 333/05 *Nadasdi v Vam-es Penzugyorseg Eszak-Alfoldi Regionalis Parancnoksaga* [2006] ECR I–10115.

[48] Case 55/79 [1980] ECR 481; Case C–68/96 *Grundig Italiana SpA v Ministero delle Finanze* [1998] ECR I–3775.

(C) ARTICLE 110(1): INDIRECT DISCRIMINATION

Article 110(1) covers indirect as well as direct discrimination. There may well be tax rules that do not explicitly differentiate between the tax liability of goods based on country of origin, but which still place a greater burden on commodities coming from another Member State. The ECJ has emphasized that a tax system will be compatible with Article 110 only if it excludes 'any possibility' of imported products being taxed more heavily than similar domestic goods.[49]

Case 112/84 **Humblot v Directeur des Services Fiscaux**
[1985] ECR 1367

[Note Lisbon Treaty renumbering: Art 95 is now Art 110 TFEU]

French law imposed an annual car tax. The criterion for the amount of tax to be paid was the power rating of the car. Below a 16CV rating the tax increased gradually to a maximum of 1,100 francs. For cars above 16CV in power there was a flat rate of 5,000 francs. There was no French car rated above 16CV, and therefore the higher charge was borne only by those who had imported cars. Humblot was charged the 5,000 francs on a 36CV imported vehicle, and argued that this tax violated Article 95.

THE ECJ

12. It is appropriate in the first place to stress that as Community law stands at present the Member States are at liberty to subject products such as cars to a system of road tax which increases progressively in amount depending on an objective criterion, such as the power rating for tax purposes, which may be determined in various ways.

13. Such a system of domestic taxation is, however, compatible with Article 95 only in so far as it is free from any discriminatory or protective effect.

14. That is not true of a system like the one at issue in the main proceedings. Under that system there are two distinct taxes: a differential tax which increases progressively and is charged on cars not exceeding a given power rating for tax purposes and a fixed tax on cars exceeding that rating which is almost five times as high as the highest rate of the differential tax. Although the system embodies no formal distinction based on the origin of the products it manifestly exhibits discriminatory or protective features contrary to Article 95, since the power rating determining liability to the special tax has been fixed at a level such that only imported cars, in particular from other Member States, are subject to the special tax whereas all cars of domestic manufacture are liable to the distinctly more advantageous differential tax.

15. In the absence of considerations relating to the amount of the special tax, consumers seeking comparable cars as regards such matters as size, comfort, actual power, maintenance costs, durability, fuel consumption and price would naturally choose from among cars above and below the critical power rating laid down by French law. However, liability to the special tax entails a much larger increase in taxation than passing from one category of car to another in a system of progressive taxation embodying balanced differentials like the system on which the differential tax is based. The resultant additional taxation is liable to cancel out the advantages which certain cars imported from other Member States

---

[49] Case C–228/98 *Dounias v Oikonomikon* [2000] ECR I–577, [41]; Case C–265/99 *Commission v French Republic* [2001] ECR I–2305, [40]; Case C–101/00 *Tulliasiamies* (n 43) [52]; Case C–313/05 *Maciej Brzeziński* (n 43) [40]; Case C–402/09 *Ioan Tatu v Statul român prin Ministerul Finanţelor şi Economiei* [2011] ECR I–2711, [35]; Case C–437/12 *X* EU:C:2013:857, [28]–[29].

> might have in consumers' eyes over comparable cars of domestic manufacture, particularly since the special tax continues to be payable for several years. In that respect the special tax reduces the amount of competition to which cars of domestic manufacture are subject and hence is contrary to the principle of neutrality with which domestic taxation must comply.

The *Humblot* case provides a good example of the ECJ's determination to catch indirect as well as direct discrimination. Its reasoning is cogent, demonstrating the way in which such tax provisions can distort the competitive process in the car market. The French authorities duly revised the tax rules in the light of the Court's decision, but the new scheme was challenged and found to be in breach of Community law. Under this new regime the French authorities replaced the 5,000 franc tax for cars above 16CV with nine more specific tax bands, the application of which was dependent on the power of the car. Although this scheme was less obviously discriminatory than that condemned in *Humblot*, the tax rate still increased sharply above 16CV and was therefore condemned in *Feldain*.[50]

(D) ARTICLE 110: NATIONAL AUTONOMY AND FISCAL CHOICES

While the Treaty prohibits indirect as well as direct discrimination the latter cannot be justified, whereas the former may be capable of objective justification, a concept developed in relation to other areas such as free movement of goods, workers, and equal treatment.[51] The Member State can argue that there was some objective policy reason, which is acceptable to the EU, to justify its action, thereby preventing the Treaty provisions from becoming too harsh or draconian in their application. The *Chemial* case exemplifies this judicial approach.

Case 140/79 **Chemial Farmaceutici v DAF SpA**
[1981] ECR 1[52]

Italy taxed synthetic ethyl alcohol more highly than ethyl alcohol obtained from fermentation, even though the products could be used interchangeably. Italy was not a major producer of the synthetic product. The object was to favour the manufacture of ethyl alcohol from agricultural products, and to restrain the processing into alcohol of ethylene, a petroleum derivative, in order to reserve that raw material for more important economic uses. The Court made the following observations on this policy choice.

THE ECJ

13. ...It accordingly constitutes a legitimate choice of economic policy to which effect is given by fiscal means. The implementation of that policy does not lead to any discrimination since although it results in discouraging imports of synthetic alcohol into Italy, it also has the consequence of hampering the development in Italy itself of production of alcohol from ethylene, that production being technically perfectly feasible.

14. As the Court has stated on many occasions...in its present stage of development Community law does not restrict the freedom of each Member State to lay down tax arrangements which differentiate

---

[50] Case 433/85 *Feldain v Directeur des Services Fiscaux* [1987] ECR 3536; Case 76/87 *Seguela v Administration des Impôts* [1988] ECR 2397; Case C–265/99 *Commission v French Republic* (n 49); Case C–402/09 *Ioan Tatu* (n 49).

[51] See Chs 19, 21, 24.

[52] See also Case 46/80 *Vinal SpA v Orbat SpA* [1981] ECR 77.

between certain products on the basis of objective criteria, such as the nature of the raw materials used or the production process employed. Such differentiation is compatible with Community law if it pursues economic policy objectives which are themselves compatible with the requirements of the Treaty and its secondary law and if the detailed rules are such as to avoid any form of discrimination, direct or indirect, in regard to imports from other Member States or any form of protection of competing domestic products.

15. Differential taxation such as that which exists in Italy for denatured synthetic alcohol on the one hand and denatured alcohol obtained by fermentation on the other satisfies these requirements. It appears in fact that that system of taxation pursues an objective of legitimate industrial policy in that it is such as to promote the distillation of agricultural products as against the manufacture of alcohol from petroleum derivatives. That choice does not conflict with the rules of Community law or the requirements of a policy decided within the framework of the Community.

16. The detailed provisions of the legislation at issue before the national court cannot be considered as discriminatory since, on the one hand, it is not disputed that imports from other Member States of alcohol by fermentation qualify for the same tax treatment as Italian alcohol produced by fermentation and, on the other hand, although the rate of tax prescribed for synthetic alcohol results in restraining the importation of synthetic alcohol originating in other Member States, it has an equivalent economic effect in the national territory in that it also hampers the establishment of profitable production of the same product in Italian industry.

The Court predicates its acceptance of the Italian policy on the basis that it does not result in any discrimination, whether direct or indirect. Notwithstanding this, the ECJ's reasoning bears testimony to its willingness to accept objective justifications where the national policy is acceptable from the EU's perspective, even if this benefits domestic traders more than importers. It is clear, as the Court points out, that the Italian policy would hamper an Italian producer that wished to make synthetic ethylene alcohol. However, there was little domestic production of that product, and therefore the Italian tax hit importers harder than firms based in Italy. The same reasoning can be seen in other decisions.

Thus in *Commission v France* the Commission[53] alleged that a French rule which taxed sweet wines produced in a traditional manner at a lower rate than liqueur wines was contrary to what is now Article 110 TFEU. The Court disagreed. It found that there was no direct discrimination on grounds of origin or nationality. Sweet wines made in the natural manner tended to be produced in areas where the growing conditions were less than optimal, since there would often be poor soil and low rainfall. The rationale for the French policy was to provide some fiscal incentives for production in these areas. The Court was willing to accept that this could constitute an objective justification. In *Outokumpu Oy*[54] the ECJ held that it was legitimate for a Member State to tax the same or similar product differentially, provided that this was done on the basis of objective criteria, such as the nature of the raw materials used or the production process employed. Article 110 did not preclude differential tax rates on electricity, where they were based on environmental considerations, provided that there was no discrimination against imports.[55]

It is, moreover, possible for differential tax rates on cars, the *Humblot* case notwithstanding, to escape the prohibition of Article 110. This could be so if the differential rates were to encourage the use of more environmentally friendly models, provided that they did not discriminate against imports. Thus in *Commission v Greece*[56] there was a national fiscal measure that imposed a progressively higher

---

[53] Case 196/85 [1987] ECR 1597.

[54] Case C–213/96 [1998] ECR I–1777.

[55] A Easson, 'Fiscal Discrimination: New Perspectives on Article 95 of the EEC Treaty' (1981) 18 CMLRev 521.

[56] Case C–132/88 [1990] ECR I–1567; Case C–421/97 *Tarantik v Direction des Services Fiscaux de Seine-et-Marne* [1999] ECR I–3633.

tax based on the cylinder capacity of the car. The ECJ held that this would only breach Article 110 if it both discouraged customers from buying highly taxed imported cars and encouraged them to buy domestic cars instead. The mere fact that all cars in the highest tax bracket were imported did not breach Article 110. EU law did not prohibit the use of tax policy to attain social ends, provided that the tax was based on an objective criterion, was not discriminatory, and did not have a protective effect.

(E) THE RELATIONSHIP BETWEEN ARTICLE 110(1) AND (2)

Article 110(1) TFEU prohibits the imposition of internal taxes on products from other Member States in excess of those levied on *similar* domestic products. Thus once the two relevant products are judged similar then Article 110(1) bites, with the consequence that excessive taxes levied on the imported goods are banned. The dividing line between Article 110(1) and (2) may be problematic, since it can be contestable whether goods are deemed to be similar or not.

Article 110(2) is designed to catch national tax provisions that apply unequal tax ratings to goods that may not be strictly similar, but which may nonetheless be in competition with each other. The object is to prevent these differential tax ratings from affording indirect protection to the domestic goods. Thus, wine and beer may not be similar goods, but there may be some competition between them. Economists term this relationship cross-elasticity of demand: as the price of one product rises in relation to another, so consumers switch to the lower-priced product. The extent to which they switch will depend on factors such as the price difference between the products and the degree to which consumers perceive them to be interchangeable. If a state that produces little wine, but much beer, taxes the former considerably more highly than the latter, then wine sellers will be relatively disadvantaged and beer producers afforded indirect protection. The relationship between Article 110(1) and (2) is brought out in the following case.

Case 168/78 **Commission v France**
[1980] ECR 347

[Note Lisbon Treaty renumbering: Arts 9–17 have been replaced by Arts 28–30 TFEU;
Art 95 is now Art 110 TFEU; Art 169 is now Art 258 TFEU]

France had higher tax rates for spirits based on grain, such as whisky, rum, gin, and vodka, than those based on wine or fruit, such as cognac, calvados, and armagnac. France produced very little of the former category of drinks, but was a major producer of fruit-based spirits. The Commission alleged that the French tax regime violated Article 95 EC. The ECJ emphasized the connection between Article 95 EC and Articles 9–17 EC: Article 95 was to supplement the provisions on customs duties and charges by prohibiting internal taxation which discriminated against imported products. It continued as follows.

THE ECJ

5. The first paragraph of Article 95, which is based on a comparison of the tax burdens imposed on domestic products and on imported products which may be classified as 'similar', is the basic rule in this respect. This provision, as the Court has had occasion to emphasize in its judgment...in Case 148/77, *H. Hansen* v. *Haupzollamt Flensburg* [1978] ECR 1787, must be interpreted widely so as to cover all taxation procedures which conflict with the principle of the equality of treatment of domestic products and imported products; it is therefore necessary to interpret the concept of 'similar products'

with sufficient flexibility. The Court specified in the judgment...in the *Rewe* case (Case 45/75 [1976] ECR 181) that it is necessary to consider as similar products those which 'have similar characteristics and meet the same needs from the point of view of consumers'. It is therefore necessary to determine the scope of the first paragraph of Article 95 on the basis not of the criterion of the strictly identical nature of the products but on that of their similar and comparable use.

6. The function of the second paragraph of Article 95 is to cover, in addition, all forms of indirect tax protection in the case of products which, without being similar within the meaning of the first paragraph, are nevertheless in competition, even partial, indirect or potential, with certain products of the importing country. The Court has already emphasized certain aspects of that provision in...Case 27/77, *Firma Fink-Frucht GmbH*...[1978] ECR 223, in which it stated that for the purposes of the application of the first paragraph of Article 95 it is sufficient for the imported product to be in competition with the protected domestic production by reason of one of several economic uses to which it may be put, even though the condition of similarity for the purposes of the first paragraph of Article 95 is not fulfilled.

7. Whilst the criterion indicated in the first paragraph of Article 95 consists in the comparison of tax burdens, whether in terms of the rate, the mode of assessment or other detailed rules for the application thereof, in view of the difficulty of making sufficiently precise comparisons between the products in question, the second paragraph of that Article is based upon a more general criterion, in other words the protective nature of the system of internal taxation.

(F) ARTICLE 110(1) AND (2): THE DETERMINATION OF SIMILARITY

The first step is therefore to determine whether the products are similar. If they are then Article 110(1) applies. If they are not then the tax rules may still be caught by Article 110(2). In an early judgment the ECJ held that products would be regarded as similar if they came within the same tax classification.[57] However, in some cases the ECJ condemned the tax without too detailed an analysis of whether this was because of Article 110(1) or (2). This approach is apparent in the early 'spirits cases', where the Commission alleged that national tax rules on spirits infringed Article 110.[58] The reason the ECJ did not trouble unduly whether the condemnation should be based on Article 110(1) or (2) is apparent in the following extract:

Case 168/78 **Commission v France**
[1980] ECR 347

[Note Lisbon Treaty renumbering: Art 95 is now Art 110 TFEU]

The facts were set out above. The Commission argued that all spirits constituted a single market. France responded by contending that they should be broken down into more specific markets, depending on their composition, physical characteristics, and consumer usages. The ECJ decided that spirits possessed certain generic features, such as high alcohol content; and that they were made from differing materials, and were consumed in different ways.

---

[57] Case 27/67 *Fink-Frucht GmbH v Hauptzollamt München-Landsbergerstrasse* [1968] ECR 327.
[58] Case 169/78 *Commission v Italy* [1980] ECR 385; Case 171/78 *Commission v Denmark* [1980] ECR 447.

THE ECJ

12. Two conclusions follow from this analysis of the market in spirits. First, there is, in the case of spirits considered as a whole, an indeterminate number of beverages which must be classified as 'similar products' within the meaning of the first paragraph of Article 95, although it may be difficult to decide this in specific cases, in view of the nature of the factors implied by distinguishing criteria such as flavour and consumer habits. Secondly, even in cases in which it is impossible to recognize a sufficient degree of similarity between the products concerned, there are nevertheless, in the case of all spirits, common characteristics which are sufficiently pronounced to accept that in all cases there is at least partial or potential competition. It follows that the application of the second paragraph of Article 95 may come into consideration in cases in which the relationship of similarity between the specific varieties of spirits remains doubtful or contested.

13. It appears from the foregoing that Article 95, taken as a whole, may apply without distinction to all the products concerned. It is sufficient therefore to examine whether the application of a given national tax system is discriminatory or, as the case may be, protective, in other words whether there is a difference in the rate or the detailed rules for levying the tax and whether that difference is likely to favour a given national production.

[*The Court then considered various arguments adduced by the French authorities designed to show that the spirits differed in terms of taste, use, and the like.*]

39. After considering all these factors the Court deems it unnecessary for the purposes of solving this dispute to give a ruling on the question whether or not the spirituous beverages concerned are wholly or partially similar products within the meaning of the first paragraph of Article 95 when it is impossible reasonably to contest that without exception they are in at least partial competition with the domestic products to which the application refers and that it is impossible to deny the protective nature of the French tax system within the second paragraph of Article 95.

40. In fact, as indicated above, spirits obtained from cereals have, as products obtained from distillation, sufficient characteristics in common with other spirits to constitute at least in certain circumstances an alternative choice for consumers....

41. As the competitive and substitution relationships between the beverages in question are such, the protective nature of the tax system criticized by the Commission is clear. A characteristic of that system is in fact that an essential part of domestic production, ... spirits obtained from wine and fruit, come within the most favourable tax category whereas at least two types of product, almost all of which are imported from other Member States, are subject to higher taxation under the 'manufacturing tax'.

These early 'spirits' cases demonstrate that the Court was not overly concerned whether a case was characterized as relating to Article 110(1) or (2), if the nature of the products rendered such classification difficult (paragraph 12) and if the Court felt that the tax should be condemned because the goods were in competition and the tax was protective (paragraph 39).

This approach can however be problematic. The consequence of 'globalizing'[59] Article 110(1) and (2) in this manner is that it obscures the appropriate response of the infringing state. A breach of Article 110(1) means that the Member State has to equalize the taxes on domestic and imported goods. Breach of Article 110(2) requires the state to remove the protective effect, but this may not entail equalization of the tax burdens on the respective goods.

Later Courts have been more careful to determine whether the analysis should proceed under Article 110(1) or (2), as exemplified by the *John Walker* case.[60] The issue was whether liqueur fruit wine was similar to whisky for the purposes of Article 110(1). The ECJ analysed the characteristics of the products,

---

[59] Easson (n 55) 521, 535.
[60] Case 243/84 *John Walker v Ministeriet for Skatter og Afgifter* [1986] ECR 875.

their alcohol content and method of manufacture, and consumer perceptions. It decided that the goods were not similar, since they did not possess the same alcohol content, nor was the process of manufacture the same. Further scrutiny of the tax would therefore have to be pursuant to Article 110(2).[61]

The same approach can be perceived in *Commission v Italy*.[62] The Commission brought an action against Italy claiming that its consumption tax on fruit was discriminatory under what is now Article 110. Italy produced large amounts of fruit, such as apples, pears, peaches, plums, and oranges, but almost no bananas, which were imported from France. Italy imposed a consumption tax on bananas that was almost half the import price, and other fruit was not subject to the tax. The Court considered whether bananas and other fruit were similar for the purposes of Article 110(1). It found that they were not, taking account of the objective characteristics of the products, including their organoleptic properties and the extent to which they could satisfy the same consumer need.[63] The Italian tax was therefore examined under Article 110(2).

(G) ARTICLE 110(2): THE DETERMINATION OF PROTECTIVE EFFECT

The Commission brought an enforcement action against the UK for discriminatory taxation of wine with respect to beer. This was more difficult than the other 'spirits' cases, since there is undoubtedly a greater difference between wine and beer than between two spirits. The ECJ therefore initially declined to rule that the UK provisions were in breach of Article 110, and required further information on the nature of the competitive relationship between the two products. Its judgment was finally delivered some years later.

Case 170/78 **Commission v United Kingdom**
[1983] ECR 2265

[Note Lisbon Treaty renumbering: Arts 95 and 169 are now Arts 110 and 258 TFEU]

The UK levied an excise tax on certain wines roughly five times that levied on beer. The tax on wine represented about 38 per cent of the sale price of the product, as compared to the tax on beer which was 25 per cent of the product's price. The UK produces much beer, but very little wine. The Commission claimed that the differential excise tax was in breach of Article 95.

THE ECJ

8. As regards the question of competition between wine and beer, the Court considered that, to a certain extent at least, the two beverages in question were capable of meeting identical needs, so that it had to be acknowledged that there was a degree of substitution for one another. It pointed out that, for the purpose of measuring the possible degree of substitution, attention should not be confined to consumer habits in a Member State or in a given region. Those habits, which were essentially variable in time and space, could not be considered to be immutable; the tax policy of a Member State must not therefore crystallize given consumer habits so as to consolidate an advantage acquired by national industries concerned to respond to them.

---

[61] Cf Case 106/84 *Commission v Denmark* [1986] ECR 833.

[62] Case 184/85 [1987] ECR 2013; Case C–437/12 *X* (n 49) [23].

[63] Bananas do not have the same water content as other fruit, and therefore their thirst-quenching qualities are not the same; and bananas were perceived to have a nutritional value in excess of other fruit: ibid [10].

9. The Court nonetheless recognized that, in view of the substantial differences between wine and beer, it was difficult to compare the manufacturing processes and the natural properties of those beverages, as the Government of the United Kingdom had rightly observed. For that reason, the Court requested the parties to provide additional information with a view to dispelling the doubts which existed concerning the nature of the competitive relationship between the two products.

. . .

11. The Italian Government contended in that connection that it was inappropriate to compare beer with wines of average alcoholic strength or, *a fortiori*, with wines of greater alcoholic strength. In its opinion, it was the lightest wines with an alcoholic strength in the region of 9, that is to say the most popular and cheapest wines, which were genuinely in competition with beer....

12. The Court considers that observation by the Italian Government to be pertinent. In view of the substantial differences in the quality and, therefore, in the price of wines, the decisive competitive relationship between beer, a popular and widely consumed beverage, and wine must be established by reference to those wines which are the most accessible to the public at large, that is to say, generally speaking the lightest and cheapest varieties. Accordingly, that is the appropriate basis for making fiscal comparisons by reference to the alcoholic strength or to the price of the two beverages in question.

[*The Commission, Italy, and the UK differed as regards the criteria which should be used to determine whether the tax on the two products was discriminatory. The Commission argued that assessment of the tax burden should be based on volume plus alcohol content; Italy contended that volume alone should be determinative; while the UK argued that the true basis of comparison was product price net of tax. The ECJ held that none of these tests was sufficient in itself, but that all three could provide 'significant information for the assessment of the contested tax system'.*]

26. After considering the information provided by the parties, the Court has come to the conclusion that, if a comparison is made on the basis of those wines which are cheaper than the types of wine selected by the United Kingdom and of which several varieties are sold in significant quantities on the United Kingdom market, it becomes apparent that precisely those wines which, in view of their price, are most directly in competition with domestic beer production are subject to a considerably higher tax burden.

27. It is clear, therefore,...—whatever criterion for comparison is used, there being no need to express a preference for one or the other—that the United Kingdom's tax system has the effect of subjecting wine imported from other Member States to an additional burden so as to afford protection to domestic beer production...Since such protection is most marked in the case of the most popular wines, the effect of the United Kingdom tax system is to stamp wine with the hallmarks of a luxury product which, in view of the tax burden which it bears, can scarcely constitute in the eyes of the consumer a genuine alternative to the typically produced domestic beverage.

28. It follows...that, by levying excise duty on still light wines made from fresh grapes at a higher rate, in relative terms, than on beer, the United Kingdom has failed to fulfil its obligations under the second paragraph of Article 95 of the EEC Treaty.

This case casts interesting light on the Court's methodology when adjudicating on Article 110(2). Its judgment proceeds in two stages.[64]

At the first stage the ECJ is concerned to establish that there is some competitive relationship between the two products so as to render Article 110(2) applicable at all (paragraphs 8–12). The ECJ rightly accepted that the meaningful comparison was between beer and the cheaper end of the wine market. Product substitutability is central, but consumer preferences are not regarded as immutable, and are affected by the relative tax rates of the two products (paragraph 8). If the varying taxes levied on the commodities serve to place them artificially within separate categories in consumers' eyes, this

---

[64] The same two stages can be perceived in other decisions concerning Art 110(2): Case 184/85 (n 62) [11]–[15].

will reduce the extent to which the public perceives the products to be substitutable. It is this which the Court has in mind when castigating the UK tax policy for stamping wine with the hallmark of being a luxury product which is in a different category from beer (paragraph 27).

At the second stage, the Court then considered whether the tax system was protective of beer. It was willing to apply varying criteria suggested by the parties to decide whether a protective effect had been established or not. It was difficult to contest the conclusion that the UK tax was discriminatory. Where the disparity in tax rates between the two products is less dramatic than that between wine and beer, more finely tuned analysis may be required to determine whether there is any protective effect.[65] Thus it may, for example, be necessary to determine the degree of cross-elasticity between the two products. If this is low, then only a 'large difference in tax burdens will have a protective tendency'.[66] Similarly, if the level of tax is low with respect to the final selling price of the goods, then it will take a very significant tax differential to have any protective impact.

The existence of harmonization will not preclude the application of Article 110 where it is only minimum harmonization. Thus in *Socridis*[67] Community legislation was held to require only that Member States imposed a minimum duty on beer. It did not preclude the application of Article 110 to determine whether a state was being protectionist in its treatment of beer as opposed to wine.

(H) TAXATION: THE BROADER LEGAL PERSPECTIVE

The discussion thus far has been concerned with taxation and Article 110. It is however important to realize that tax issues can be judged for compliance with other Treaty provisions concerning free movement.[68] This is significant because, while the approach under Article 110 is discrimination-based, the case law on free movement has moved beyond this to catch national rules that impede trade even if they are not discriminatory. This has placed the ECJ in something of a dilemma, having to choose whether to preserve coherence in its case law on free movement, even when concerned with fiscal or tax measures, or whether to follow the disparate impact approach in accord with Article 110 when dealing with analogous situations that arise relating to, for example, capital or services.[69] The case law is not entirely clear, but the ECJ has been cautious about applying the full force of its case law on free movement to national fiscal rules, although commentators remain divided as to the 'best' interpretation of this jurisprudence.[70]

---

[65] Case 356/85 *Commission v Belgium* [1987] ECR 3299.

[66] Easson (n 55) 539.

[67] Case C–166/98 *Société Critouridienne de Distribution (Socridis) v Receveur Principal des Douanes* [1999] ECR I–3791.

[68] See, eg, Case C–391/97 *Gschwind* [1999] ECR I–5451 and Case C–527/06 *Renneberg v Staatssecretaris van Financiën* [2008] ECR I–7735, free movement of workers; Case C–376/03 *D v Inspecteur van de Belastingdienst/Particulieren/Ondernerningen/buitenland te Heerlen* [2005] ECR I–5821, free movement of capital; Case C–250/95 *Futura Participations SA v Administration des Contributions* [1997] ECR I–2471 and Case C–284/06 *Finanzamt Hamburg-Am Tierpark v Burda GmbH* [2008] ECR I–4571, freedom of establishment.

[69] See, eg, Case C–134/03 *Viacom Outdoor Srl v Giotto Immobilier SARL* [2005] ECR I–1167; Cases C–544 and 545/03 *Mobistar SA v Commune de Fleron* [2005] ECR I–7723; Case C–76/05 *Herbert Schwarz and Marga Gootjes-Schwarz v Finanzamt Bergisch Gladbach* [2007] ECR I–6849; N Nic Shuibhne (2008) 45 CMLRev 771.

[70] J Snell, 'Non-Discriminatory Tax Obstacles in Community Law' (2007) 56 ICLQ 339; S Kingston, 'The Boundaries of Sovereignty: The ECJ's Controversial Role Applying Internal Market Law to Direct Tax Measures' (2006–7) 9 CYELS 287; S Kingston, 'A Light in the Darkness? Recent Developments in the ECJ's Direct Tax Jurisprudence' (2007) 44 CMLRev 1321; K Banks, 'The Application of the Fundamental Freedoms to Member State Tax Measures: Guarding against Protectionism or Second-Guessing National Policy Choices?' (2008) 33 ELRev 482; A Cordewener, G Kofler, and S van Thiel, 'The Clash between European Freedoms and National Direct Tax Law: Public Interest Defences available to the Member States' (2009) 46 CMLRev 1951; W Haslehner, '"Consistency" and Fundamental Freedoms: The Case of Direct Taxation' (2013) 50 CMLRev 737; S Elwes, 'The Internal Market versus the Right of Member States to Levy Direct Tax—A Clash of Fundamental Principles' (2013) 41 Intertax 15.

(I) TAXATION: THE BROADER POLITICAL PERSPECTIVE

The discussion thus far has concentrated on the legal constraints imposed by the Treaty on the taxation policies of the Member States in order to prevent discrimination against imports. It is important, as in the case of the customs union, to place this material in a broader perspective.[71]

Taxation can be direct or indirect. The paradigm of direct taxation is income tax, while the paradigm of indirect taxation is a tax on sales. The EU does not exercise any general control over direct taxation. This is regarded as central to national sovereignty. EU law will be relevant only to prevent cross-border discrimination, interference with free movement, and the like, although some tax matters have been dealt with through Articles 114 and 115 TFEU, where the conditions therein are satisfied. The sensitivity of tax matters is reflected in the requirement of unanimity, which still prevails after the Lisbon Treaty.[72] EU law has a much greater impact on indirect taxation via Article 113 TFEU. Value Added Tax (VAT) was the first such tax to be harmonized in 1977. This was 'because indirect taxes may create an immediate obstacle to the free movement of goods and the free supply of services within an Internal Market'.[73]

The EU is now striving for a more coherent tax policy.[74] In the context of indirect taxation, this is manifest in proposed improvements to the regimes governing VAT, excise duty, and the like. In the context of indirect and direct taxation, there is the growing realization of the extent to which national tax policy can impact on other EU policies such as employment, the environment, economic and monetary union, health, and consumer protection,[75] and realization of the need to reduce cross-border tax obstacles for EU citizens.[76]

The tension this produces is readily apparent in the Commission's language. It recognized that there is no need for 'across the board harmonization of Member States' tax systems', that Member States are free to choose the 'tax systems they consider most appropriate and according to their preferences'.[77] It cautioned, however, that the level of public expenditure was a matter for national preference, so long as the budget remained in balance. It emphasized that Member States' choices did not take place in isolation and that international aspects should be taken into account. It reaffirmed the need for a high degree of harmonization in relation to indirect taxation. It admitted also that some harmonization of the tax treatment accorded to pay might be necessary,[78] in order to remove obstacles to free movement, as in the case of occupational pensions.

The Commission was candid about the difficulties of securing the passage of EU legislation, given the obstacle of unanimity. It is unsurprising that the Commission has always advocated a shift to qualified-majority voting,[79] all the more so in the light of enlargement. What is particularly interesting is the Commission's willingness to talk openly about other mechanisms for achieving its objectives given the difficulties of securing agreement in the Council.[80] The Commission considered in

---

[71] http://ec.europa.eu/taxation_customs/taxation/gen_info/tax_policy/index_en.htm.

[72] http://ec.europa.eu/taxation_customs/taxation/gen_info/tax_policy/article_6759_en.htm.

[73] Tax Policy in the European Union—Priorities for the Years Ahead, COM(2001) 260 final, [3.1].

[74] Ibid [1].

[75] Tax Policy in the European Union (2000), 8–9; The Key, Taxation and Customs Union, No 15, Mar 2001; Co-ordinating Member States' direct tax systems in the Internal Market, COM(2006) 823.

[76] Removing cross-border tax obstacles for EU citizens, COM(2010) 769.

[77] Tax Policy in the European Union (n 73) [2.4]; http://ec.europa.eu/taxation_customs/taxation/gen_info/tax_policy/index_en.htm.

[78] Ibid [2.4].

[79] http://ec.europa.eu/taxation_customs/taxation/gen_info/tax_policy/index_en.htm.

[80] Tax Policy in the European Union (n 73) [4.1]–[4.4]; http://ec.europa.eu/taxation_customs/taxation/gen_info/tax_policy/index_en.htm.

detail a range of options including greater use of Article 258 TFEU, resort to soft law, and use of the enhanced cooperation procedure.[81]

4 THE BOUNDARY BETWEEN ARTICLES 28–30 AND 110–113

The relationship between Articles 28–30 and Articles 110–113 TFEU has been touched on in the preceding analysis. It is now time to consider this in more detail.

The general principle is that the two sets of Articles are mutually exclusive.[82] They both concern the imposition of fiscal charges by the state. Articles 28–30 bite on those duties or charges levied as a result of goods crossing a border. The duty or charge is exacted at the time of, or on account of, the importation, and is borne specifically by the imported product to the exclusion of similar domestic products.[83] Articles 110–113, by way of contrast, are designed to catch fiscal policy which is internal to the state. They prevent discrimination against goods once they have entered a particular Member State. The Court has construed both sets of provisions so as to ensure that there is no gap between them.

Which set of Treaty Articles is applicable is, however, important, since the result will affect the applicable legal test.[84] If a state fiscal measure is caught by Article 30 TFEU then it will be unlawful, since customs duties or charges are the quintessential barriers to a customs union. If a fiscal measure falls within Article 110 TFEU then the obligation on the state is different. The taxation levels set by the state are not unlawful under the Treaty, and thus the inquiry is whether the tax discriminates against the importer under Article 110(1), or has a protective effect under Article 110(2). In most circumstances there will be little difficulty in determining whether the case should fall under Article 30 or under Article 110. Three situations are however more difficult.

(A) LEVIES IMPOSED ON IMPORTERS

The first problematic type of case is that where a state imposes a levy on an importer. Such a case would normally be decided on the basis of Article 30, and the levy would be deemed to be a CEE. The state would be condemned unless it could show that the levy was consideration for a service given to the importer, or that it was imposed pursuant to mandatory requirements of EU law. Attempts to argue that the levy should instead be considered under Article 110, because domestic producers also had to pay, have not been notably successful, as the *Bresciani* case demonstrates.

In exceptional circumstances the Court may, however, decide that although the charge or levy is taken at the border it is not to be characterized as a CEE within Article 30, but as a tax, the legality of which will be tested under Article 110. In *Denkavit*[85] the applicant was an importer of feedingstuffs from the Netherlands into Denmark. Danish law required that the importer obtain an authorization from the Ministry of Agriculture, *and* charged an annual levy to meet the costs of checking samples of

---

[81] Tackling the corporation tax obstacles of small and medium-sized enterprises in the Internal Market—outline of a possible Home State Taxation Pilot Scheme, COM(2005) 702; Implementing the Community Lisbon Programme: Progress to date and next steps towards a Common Consolidated Corporate Tax Base (CCCTB), COM(2006) 157; Promoting Good Governance in Tax Matters, COM(2009) 201 final.

[82] Case 10/65 *Deutschmann v Federal Republic of Germany* [1965] ECR 469; Case 57/65 *Lütticke* (n 42); Case 105/76 *Interzuccheri SpA v Ditta Rezzano e Cavassa* [1977] ECR 1029.

[83] Case 193/85 *Cooperative Co-Frutta Srl v Amministrazione delle Finanze dello Stato* [1987] ECR 2085, [8]; Cases C–290 and 333/05 *Nadasdi* (n 47) [39]–[42].

[84] Case 105/76 *Interzuccheri* (n 82) [9].

[85] Case 29/87 *Dansk Denkavit ApS v Danish Ministry of Agriculture* [1988] ECR 2965.

the goods. The ECJ held that the requirement of an authorization was caught by what is now Article 34 TFEU,[86] but that it could be justified under Article 36 TFEU. The Court then considered whether the levy was lawful. This levy was imposed on all those engaged in the feedingstuffs trade, whether importers or domestic producers. The ECJ held that it related to a general system of internal dues applied systematically and in accordance with the same criteria to domestic products and imported products alike, and therefore came within Article 110.[87]

The ECJ, however, made it clear in *Michailidis*[88] that a charge levied at the border will be regarded as an internal tax, rather than a CEE, only where the comparable charge levied on national products is applied at the same rate, at the same marketing stage, and on the basis of an identical chargeable event.

(B) IMPORTS TAXED BUT NOT MADE BY THE STATE OF IMPORT

The second type of case in which there can be boundary-line problems between Article 30 and Article 110 is that in which the importing state does not make the imported product, but imposes a tax on it nonetheless. Should this be considered to be a charge within Article 30 or a tax within Article 110? It might be thought that the ECJ would choose the former characterization, since there are no similar domestic goods. This will not always be so, as demonstrated by *Co-Frutta*.

Case 193/85 Cooperative Co-Frutta Srl v Amministrazione delle Finanze dello Stato
[1987] ECR 2085

[Note Lisbon Treaty renumbering: Arts 12, 95, and 177 are now Arts 30, 110, and 267 TFEU]

This was another case which arose from the imposition by Italy of a consumption tax on bananas, even though no such tax was levied on other fruit produced in Italy. This action was brought by a banana importer to test the legality of the tax. The Court considered whether the tax should be viewed as a CEE within Article 12 or as a tax to be assessed under Article 95.

THE ECJ

8. According to established case law of the Court, the prohibition laid down by Articles 9 and 12 of the Treaty in regard to charges having an equivalent effect covers any charge exacted at the time of or on account of importation which, being borne specifically by an imported product to the exclusion of the similar domestic product, has the result of altering the cost price of the imported product, thereby producing the same restrictive effect on the free movement of goods as a customs duty.

9. The essential feature of a charge having an effect equivalent to a customs duty which distinguishes it from an internal tax therefore resides in the fact that the former is borne solely by an imported product as such whilst the latter is borne both by imported and domestic products.

10. The Court has however recognized that even a charge which is borne by a product imported from another Member State, when there is no identical or similar domestic product, does not constitute a charge having equivalent effect but internal taxation within the meaning of Article 95 of the Treaty if it

---

[86] As a measure having equivalent effect to a quantitative restriction, on which see Ch 19.
[87] Case 29/87 *Denkavit* (n 85) [33]. See also Case C–130/93 *Lamaire* (n 12); Case C–90/94 *Haahr Petroleum Ltd v Abenra Havn* [1997] ECR I–4085; Case C–72/03 *Carbonati Apuani* (n 5) [17]–[18]; Case C–387/01 *Weigel* (n 43) [64].
[88] Cases C–441 and 442/98 (n 8) [24].

relates to a general system of internal dues applied systematically to categories of products in accordance with objective criteria irrespective of the origin of the products.

11. Those considerations demonstrate that even if it were necessary in some cases, for the purpose of classifying a charge borne by imported products, to equate extremely low domestic production with its non-existence, that would not mean that the levy in question would necessarily have to be regarded as a charge having an effect equivalent to a customs duty. In particular, that will not be so if the levy is part of a general system of internal dues applying systematically to categories of products according to the criteria indicated above.

12. A tax on consumption of the type at issue in the main proceedings does form part of a general system of internal dues. The 19 taxes on consumption are governed by common tax rules and are charged on categories of products irrespective of their origin in accordance with an objective criterion, namely the fact that the product falls into a specific category of goods. Some of those taxes are charged on products intended for human consumption, including the tax on the consumption of bananas. Whether those goods are produced at home or abroad does not seem to have a bearing on the rate, the basis of assessment or the manner in which the tax is levied. The revenue from those taxes is not earmarked for a specific purpose; it constitutes tax revenue identical to other tax revenue and, like it, helps to finance State expenditure generally in all sectors.

13. Consequently, the tax at issue must be regarded as being an integral part of a general system of internal dues within the meaning of Article 95 of the Treaty and its compatibility with Community law must be assessed on the basis of that Article rather than Articles 9 and 12 of the Treaty.

The ECJ's reasoning makes good sense. If any charge imposed by a state on a product which it did not make at all, or only in negligible quantities, were to be classified as a CEE under Article 30 then the charge would be automatically unlawful,[89] and the importing state could not tax goods which it did not produce itself, since any such tax would be condemned under Article 30. This draconian conclusion would make little social, economic, or political sense, and it is not therefore surprising that the Court avoided this result.[90]

There may be good reasons why a state should choose to tax, for example, a luxury product even if there is no domestic production. The criterion adopted by the ECJ provides a sensible resolution of this problem. If the test propounded by the ECJ is met the charge will not necessarily be regarded as lawful. It will still fall to be assessed under Article 110 TFEU. In the instant case the tax was in fact held to be in breach of what is now Article 110(2), for the same reasons as given in the action brought against Italy by the Commission.[91]

(C) SELECTIVE TAX REFUND

The third type of case arises when a state chooses to make a selective refund of a tax or if it uses the money to benefit a particular group. The position appears to be as follows. If the money from a tax flows into the national exchequer and is then used for the benefit of a particular domestic industry, this could be challenged as a state aid: Articles 107–109 TFEU.[92]

---

[89] Assuming of course that it could not be saved on the ground that it represented consideration for a service, etc.

[90] See also Case 90/79 *Commission v France* [1981] ECR 283; Case C–383/01 *De Danske Bilimportører v Skatteministeriet* [2003] ECR I–6065, [35]–[42].

[91] See p 655 above.

[92] Cases C–78–83/90 *Compagnie Commerciale de l'Ouest v Receveur Principal des Douanes de la Pallice Port* [1992] ECR I–1847.

Classification problems as between Articles 30 and 110 TFEU arise when the money that has been refunded can be linked to what has been levied pursuant to a specific tax. The correct classification will then depend upon whether the refund or other benefit to the national producers wholly or partially offsets the tax. If the former, then the tax will be treated under Article 30, the rationale being that what in effect exists is a charge levied only on the imported or exported product.[93] If, however, the refund or benefit is only partial the matter will fall to be assessed under Article 110, the rationale being that the partial refund in effect means that there could be a discriminatory tax.[94] Barents, summarizing the early case law,[95] identifies three conditions for a charge to be considered under Article 30 rather than Article 110:[96]

> Firstly, the charge must be destined exclusively for financing activities which very largely benefit the taxed domestic product; secondly, there must exist identity between the taxed product and the domestic product benefiting from the charge; and thirdly, the charges imposed on the domestic product must be completely compensated.

This approach is exemplified by *Scharbatke*.[97] There was a challenge to mandatory contributions levied in Germany when slaughtered animals were presented for inspection. The contribution was applied under the same conditions to national and imported products, and the money was assigned to a marketing fund for agricultural, forestry, and food products. The ECJ held that the mandatory contribution constituted a parafiscal charge.[98] Where the resulting revenue benefited solely national products, so that the advantages accruing *wholly* offset the charge imposed on the products, then the charge would be regarded as a CEE within Article 30.[99] If the advantages which accrued only *partially* offset the charges imposed on national products, then the charge might constitute discriminatory internal taxation under Article 110.[100]

5 CONCLUSIONS

i. The Court's decisions on duties and taxation have made a significant contribution to the realization of a single market. The Court's jurisprudence has consistently looked behind the form of a disputed measure to its substance, and the ECJ has interpreted the relevant Articles in the manner best designed to ensure that the Treaty objectives are achieved.

---

[93] Note in this respect that Art 30 expressly includes customs duties of a fiscal nature.

[94] Where the benefits from the activities financed by the charge accrue to both domestic producers and importers, but the former obtain proportionately greater benefits, the charge will fall under Art 30 or Art 110, depending on whether the advantage accruing to domestic producers fully or partially offsets their burdens: Case C–28/96 *Fazenda Publica v Fricarnes SA* [1997] ECR I–4939.

[95] Case 77/76 *Fratelli Cuchi v Avez* [1977] ECR 987; Case 94/74 *Industria Gomma Articoli Vari v Ente Nazionale per la Cellulosa e per la Carta* [1975] ECR 699; Case 105/76 *Interzuccheri* (n 82).

[96] (N 10) 430.

[97] Case C–72/92 *H Scharbatke GmbH v Federal Republic of Germany* [1993] ECR I–5509. See also Cases C–78–83/90 *Compagnie Commerciale* (n 92); Case C–234/99 *Niels Nygard* (n 12) [23]; Case C–517/04 *Visserijbedrijf v Productschap Vis* [2006] ECR I–5015, [18]–[20].

[98] The ECJ held that the charge which was levied might also constitute state aid under Art 107 TFEU.

[99] It is not entirely clear whether *Scharbatke* is intended to modify earlier cases, which had held that in order for the charge to be regarded as a CEE within Art 30 there must, *inter alia*, be a strict coincidence between the product which was being taxed and that which was receiving the benefit: Case 105/76 *Interzuccheri* (n 82).

[100] See also Case 73/79 *Commission v Italy* [1980] ECR 1533; Case C–347/95 *Fazenda Publica v Uniao das Cooperativas Abastecedoras de Leite de Lisboa, URCL (UCAL)* [1997] ECR I–4911.

ii. In relation to the customs union, the main challenges in the years ahead are concerned with the need to forge an efficient and effective customs force from the twenty-eight Member State authorities so as to be able to fight fraud, the import of illegal goods, terrorism, and the like.

iii. In relation to taxation, the issues are more complex. The original Rome Treaty left a considerable degree of autonomy to Member States in the fiscal field, albeit subject to the constraints imposed by Articles 30 and 110. Many of the problems concerning divergences between national taxation systems could only ever be fully resolved if legislative harmonization occurred. Taxation is however regarded as central to national sovereignty, and hence any extension of EU competence over tax is a hotly contested issue.

iv. It should, however, be noted that in this area, as in many others, there is often a link between judicial doctrine and legislative initiatives. The very fact that a challenged national tax policy will, according to the ECJ's decisions in *Chemial*[101] and the *French Sweet Wines* case,[102] be upheld only if the Court deems it to be compatible with the Treaty can lead to paradoxical results. It has been noted[103] that the absence of harmonization has led to the ironic result that the Commission, abetted by the ECJ, has managed to wield perhaps more influence over Member States' tax policies, and thus their economic and social policies, than would be the case if the Council had agreed on a uniform tax regime.

v. The Commission has more recently emphasized the contribution of taxation and customs policy to the implementation of the Lisbon Strategy.[104]

6 FURTHER READING

BANKS, K, 'The Application of the Fundamental Freedoms to Member State Tax Measures: Guarding against Protectionism or Second-Guessing National Policy Choices?' (2008) 33 ELRev 482

BARENTS, R, 'Charges of Equivalent Effect to Customs Duties' (1978) 15 CMLRev 415

——— 'Recent Case Law on the Prohibition of Fiscal Discrimination Under Article 95' (1986) 23 CMLRev 641

CORDEWENER, A, KOFLER G, AND VAN THIEL, S, 'The Clash between European Freedoms and National Direct Tax Law: Public Interest Defences available to the Member States' (2009) 46 CMLRev 1951

DANUSSO, M, AND DENTON, R, 'Does the European Court of Justice Look for a Protectionist Motive Under Article 95?' (1990) 1 LIEI 67

EASSON, A, 'The Spirits, Wine and Beer Judgments: A Legal Mickey Finn?' (1980) 5 ELRev 318

——— 'Fiscal Discrimination: New Perspectives on Article 95 of the EEC Treaty' (1981) 18 CMLRev 521

GRABITZ, E, AND ZACKER, C, 'Scope for Action by the EC Member States for the Improvement of Environmental Protection under EEC Law: The Example of Environmental Taxes and Subsidies' (1989) 26 CMLRev 423

---

[101] Case 140/79 *Chemial Farmaceutici v DAF SpA* [1981] ECR 1.
[102] Case 196/85 [1987] ECR 1597.
[103] J Lonbay, 'A Review of Recent Tax Cases' (1989) 14 ELRev 48, 50.
[104] The Contribution of Taxation and Customs Policies to the Lisbon Strategy, COM(2005) 532 final.

HASLEHNER, W, '"Consistency" and Fundamental Freedoms: The Case of Direct Taxation' (2013) 50 CMLRev 737

KINGSTON, S, 'The Boundaries of Sovereignty: The ECJ's Controversial Role Applying Internal Market Law to Direct Tax Measures' (2006–7) 9 CYELS 287

——— 'A Light in the Darkness? Recent Developments in the ECJ's Direct Tax Jurisprudence' (2007) 44 CMLRev 1321

SNELL, J, 'Non-Discriminatory Tax Obstacles in Community Law' (2007) 56 ICLQ 339

FREE MOVEMENT OF GOODS: QUANTITATIVE RESTRICTIONS

1 CENTRAL ISSUES

i. The discussion in the previous chapter focused on duties and taxes. This is, however, only part of the strategy for a single market. The free movement of goods is dealt with in Articles 34–37 TFEU (ex Articles 28–31 EC). Article 34 is the central provision and states that: 'quantitative restrictions on imports and all measures having equivalent effect shall be prohibited between Member States'. Article 35 contains similar provisions relating to exports, while Article 36 provides an exception for certain cases where a state is allowed to place restrictions on the movement of goods.

ii. It is necessary to understand how Articles 34–37 fit into the general strategy concerning free movement of goods. Articles 28–33 TFEU provide the foundations for a customs union by eliminating customs duties between Member States and by establishing a common customs tariff. It is however also necessary to prevent Member States placing quotas on the amount of goods that could be imported, or restricting their flow by measures that have an equivalent effect to quotas, and that is the object of Articles 34–37.

iii. The ECJ's interpretation of Articles 34–37 has been important in achieving single market integration. It has given a broad interpretation to the phrase 'measures having equivalent effect' to a quantitative restriction (MEQR), and has construed the idea of discrimination to capture both direct and indirect discrimination.

iv. The ECJ also held that Article 34 could apply even where there was no discrimination. The famous *Cassis de Dijon* case[1] decided that Article 34 can bite, subject to certain exceptions, when the same rule applies to domestic goods and imports, where the rule inhibits the flow of goods within the EU. Discrimination is therefore a sufficient, but not necessary, condition for invocation of Article 34. There are, however, six central issues in this area.

v. First, the Court's jurisprudence led to difficult issues about where this branch of EU law 'stops'. Its decision that Article 34 is applicable to trade rules even where they do not discriminate led to difficulties about the outer boundaries of EU law.

vi. Secondly, there is a problem concerning the relationship between negative and positive integration. The Court's approach in *Cassis de Dijon* fostered 'negative integration': indistinctly

---

[1] Case 120/78 *Rewe-Zentral AG v Bundesmonopolverwaltung für Branntwein* [1979] ECR 649.

applicable rules were unenforceable when they hindered cross-border trade unless they came within one of the exceptions. Integration was essentially negative, in the sense that national rules were held not to apply. This can be contrasted with 'positive integration', which resulted from EU legislative measures, stipulating which rules should apply across the Union. There are, as will be seen, important consequences that flow from developing EU policy by these differing strategies.

vii. Thirdly, there is a tension between EU integration and national regulatory autonomy. Article 34 will normally render national regulatory measures inapplicable. It is therefore a tool for policing the borderline between legitimate and illegitimate national regulation, and the nature of this border may well be contestable.[2]

viii. Fourthly, the choice between a 'discrimination approach' and 'a rule of recognition approach' of the kind introduced by *Cassis*' is important for the following reason. The former approach vests control in the host state, normally the country into which the firm is trying to import. Provided that the host state does not discriminate its rules remain lawful. The '*Cassis* approach' reverses the onus: the host state must accept the regulatory provisions of the home state, subject to the exceptions discussed below.

ix. Fifthly, this topic also exemplifies the interconnection between judicial and legislative initiatives for attaining the EU's objectives, a theme stressed throughout this book. It is possible to deal with trade rules that differ between Member States through legislative harmonization, but the process was slow, a difficulty exacerbated by the requirement of unanimity in the Council.[3] The ECJ's jurisprudence constituted an alternative means for ensuring the free flow of goods even in the absence of EU harmonizing legislation. The message was clear: attainment of this central part of EU policy was not to be held up indefinitely by the absence of harmonization legislation. The Court's approach to Article 34 was welcomed by the Commission, which decided that harmonization would be used for those rules that were still lawful under the *Cassis* formula, on the grounds that, for example, they were necessary to protect consumers or safeguard public health. The judicial approach, therefore, caused the Commission to reorient its own legislative programme.

x. Finally, the EU Courts have also maintained tight control over the application of Article 36, which is concerned with defences against a *prima facie* breach of Article 34. The ECJ has interpreted Article 36 strictly to ensure that discriminatory restrictions on the free movement of goods are not easily justified. There are, however, difficulties concerning the relationship between defences to discrimination and defences to indistinctly applicable rules.

2 DIRECTIVE 70/50 AND *DASSONVILLE*

Article 34 will catch quantitative restrictions and all measures that have an equivalent effect, MEQR. It can apply to EU measures,[4] as well as those adopted by Member States. The notion of a quantitative restriction was defined broadly in the *Geddo* case[5] to mean 'measures which amount to a total or partial restraint of, according to the circumstances, imports, exports or goods in transit'. MEQRs are more difficult to define. The Commission and the Court have taken a broad view of such measures.

---

[2] WPJ Wils, 'The Search for the Rule in Article 30 EEC: Much Ado About Nothing?' (1993) 18 ELRev 475, 478; M Maduro, *We the Court, the European Court of Justice and the European Economic Constitution* (Hart, 1998) 54–58.

[3] See Ch 17.

[4] Case C–114/96 *Criminal Proceedings against Kieffer and Thill* [1997] ECR I–3629.

[5] Case 2/73 *Geddo v Ente Nazionale Risi* [1973] ECR 865.

Guidance on the Commission's view can be found in Directive 70/50. This Directive was only applicable during the Community's transitional period, but it continues to furnish guidance on MEQRs. The list of matters which can constitute an MEQR are specified in Article 2 and include:[6] minimum or maximum prices for imported products; less favourable prices for imported products; lowering the value of the imported product by reducing its intrinsic value or increasing its costs; payment conditions for imported products which differ from those for domestic products; conditions in respect of packaging, composition, identification, size, weight, etc, which apply only to imported goods or which are more difficult to satisfy than for domestic goods; the giving of a preference to the purchase of domestic goods as opposed to imports, or otherwise hindering the purchase of imports; limiting publicity in respect of imported goods as compared with domestic products; prescribing stocking requirements which are different from and more difficult to satisfy than those applicable to domestic goods; and making it mandatory for importers of goods to have an agent in the territory of the importing state.

Article 2, therefore, lists a number of ways in which the importing state can discriminate against goods. It should be noted that, even as early as 1970, the Commission was thinking of the potential reach of Article 34 to indistinctly applicable rules, since Article 3 of the Directive, which will be considered below, regulates such rules to some degree. The seminal early judicial decision on the interpretation of MEQRs is *Dassonville*.

Case 8/74 **Procureur du Roi v Dassonville**
[1974] ECR 837

[Note Lisbon Treaty renumbering: Art 36 EEC is now Art 36 TFEU]

Belgian law provided that goods bearing a designation of origin could only be imported if they were accompanied by a certificate from the government of the exporting country certifying their right to such a designation. Dassonville imported Scotch whisky into Belgium from France without being in possession of the certificate from the British authorities. The certificate would have been very difficult to obtain for goods which were already in free circulation in a third country, as in this case. Dassonville was prosecuted in Belgium and argued that the Belgian rule constituted an MEQR.

THE ECJ

5. All trading rules enacted by Member States which are capable of hindering, directly or indirectly, actually or potentially, intra-Community trade are to be considered as measures having an effect equivalent to quantitative restrictions.

6. In the absence of a Community system guaranteeing for consumers the authenticity of a product's designation of origin, if a Member State takes measures to prevent unfair practices in this connection, it is however subject to the condition that these measures should be reasonable and that the means of proof required should not act as a hindrance to trade between Member States and should, in consequence, be accessible to all Community nationals.

7. Even without having to examine whether such measures are covered by Article 36, they must not, in any case, by virtue of the principle expressed in the second sentence of that Article, constitute a means of arbitrary discrimination or a disguised restriction on trade between Member States.

---

[6] Dir 70/50 [1970] OJ L13/29, Art 2(3).

8. That may be the case with formalities, required by a Member State for the purpose of proving the origin of a product, which only direct importers are really in a position to satisfy without facing serious difficulties.

9. Consequently, the requirement by a Member State of a certificate of authenticity which is less easily obtainable by importers of an authentic product which has been put into free circulation in a regular manner in another Member State than by importers of the same product coming directly from the country of origin constitutes a measure equivalent to a quantitative restriction as prohibited by the Treaty.

There are two notable aspects to the ECJ's reasoning. First, it is clear from paragraph 5 that the crucial element in proving an MEQR is its effect, a discriminatory intent is not required. The ECJ takes a broad view of measures that hinder the free flow of goods, and the definition does not require that the rules actually discriminate between domestic and imported goods. *Dassonville* thus sowed the seeds which bore fruit in *Cassis de Dijon*,[7] where the ECJ decided that Article 34 could apply to rules which were not discriminatory. Secondly, the ECJ indicates, in paragraph 6, that reasonable restraints may not be caught by Article 34. This is the origin of what became known as the 'rule of reason', which will be examined below. We now consider the application of Article 34 to cases involving discrimination, both direct and indirect.

3 DISCRIMINATORY BARRIERS TO TRADE

Article 34 can bite if the national rule favours domestic goods over imports, even if the case is confined to products and parties from one Member State.[8] Article 34 can also apply to a national measure preventing import from one to another part of a Member State.[9] There are numerous types of case involving direct or indirect discrimination between domestic and imported goods, and the Treaty prohibition also catches measures that render it more difficult for importers to break into that market.[10]

(A) IMPORT AND EXPORT RESTRICTIONS

The ECJ has always been particularly harsh on discriminatory import or export restrictions. Thus import or export licences are caught by Article 34.[11] So, too, are provisions which subject imported goods to requirements not imposed on domestic products. This is exemplified by *Commission v Italy*,[12] in which the ECJ held that procedures and data requirements for the registration of imported cars, making their registration longer, more complicated, and more costly than for domestic vehicles, were prohibited by Article 34.[13] The same approach is apparent with respect to discriminatory export rules.

---

[7] Case 120/78 *Rewe-Zentral AG* (n 1).

[8] Cases C–321–324/94 *Criminal Proceedings against Pistre* [1997] ECR I–2343; Case C–448/98 *Criminal Proceedings against Guimont* [2000] ECR I–10663.

[9] Case C–67/97 *Criminal Proceedings against Bluhme* [1998] ECR I–8033.

[10] Case 50/85 *Schloh v Auto Contrôle Technique* [1986] ECR 1855.

[11] Cases 51–54/71 *International Fruit Company v Produktschap voor Groenten en Fruit (No 2)* [1971] ECR 1107; Case 68/76 *Commission v French Republic* [1977] ECR 515; Case C–54/05 *Commission v Finland* [2007] ECR I–2473.

[12] Case 154/85 [1987] ECR 2717.

[13] See also Case 4/75 *Rewe-Zentralfinanz v Landwirtschaftskammer* [1975] ECR 843.

Thus in *Bouhelier*[14] a French rule which imposed quality checks on watches for export, but not on those intended for the domestic market, was in breach of Article 35.

(B) PROMOTION OR FAVOURING OF DOMESTIC PRODUCTS

Article 34 prohibits action by a state that promotes or favours domestic products to the detriment of competing imports. This can occur in a number of different ways. The most obvious is where a *state engages in a campaign to promote the purchase of domestic as opposed to imported goods.*

Case 249/81 **Commission v Ireland**
[1982] ECR 4005

[Note Lisbon Treaty renumbering: Arts 30, 92, 93, and 169 are now
Arts 34, 107, 108, and 258 TFEU]

The Irish Government sought to promote sales of Irish goods, the object being to achieve a switch of 3 per cent in consumer spending from imports to domestic products. It adopted a number of measures including: an information service indicating to consumers which products were made in Ireland and where they could be obtained (the Shoplink Service); exhibition facilities for Irish goods; the encouragement of the use of the 'Buy Irish' symbol for Irish goods; and a publicity campaign by the Irish Goods Council to encourage consumers to buy Irish products. The first two of these activities were subsequently abandoned by the Irish Government, but the latter two strategies continued to be used. The Commission alleged that the campaign was an MEQR. Ireland argued that it had never adopted 'measures' for the purpose of Article 30, and that any financial aid given to the Irish Goods Council should be judged in the light of Articles 92 to 93, and not Article 30. The members of the Irish Goods Council were appointed by an Irish Government minister and its activities were funded in proportions of about six to one by the Irish Government and private industry respectively. The ECJ held that the Irish Government was responsible under the Treaty for the activities of the Council even though the campaign was run by a private company, and then continued as follows.

THE ECJ

21. The Irish government maintains that the prohibition against measures having an effect equivalent to quantitative restrictions in Article 30 is concerned only with 'measures', that is to say, binding provisions emanating from a public authority. However, no such provision has been adopted by the Irish government, which has confined itself to giving moral support and financial aid to the activities pursued by the Irish industries.

22. The Irish government goes on to emphasise that the campaign has had no restrictive effect on imports since the proportion of Irish goods to all goods sold on the Irish market fell from 49.2% in 1977 to 43.4% in 1980.

23. The first observation to be made is that the campaign cannot be likened to advertising by private or public undertakings...to encourage people to buy goods produced by those undertakings. Regardless of the means used to implement it, the campaign is a reflection of the Irish government's considered intention to substitute domestic products for imported products on the Irish market and thereby to check the flow of imports from other Member States.

...

---

[14] Case 53/76 *Procureur de la République Besançon v Bouhelier* [1977] ECR 197.

25. Whilst it may be true that the two elements of the programme which have continued in effect, namely the advertising campaign and the use of the 'Guaranteed Irish' symbol, have not had any significant success in winning over the Irish market to domestic products, it is not possible to overlook the fact that, regardless of their efficacy, those two activities form part of a government programme which is designed to achieve the substitution of domestic products for imported products and is liable to affect the volume of trade between Member States.

...

27. In the circumstances the two activities in question amount to the establishment of a national practice, introduced by the Irish government and prosecuted with its assistance, the potential effect of which on imports from other Member States is comparable to that resulting from government measures of a binding nature.

28. Such a practice cannot escape the prohibition laid down by Article 30 of the Treaty solely because it is not based on decisions which are binding upon undertakings. Even measures adopted by the government of a Member State which do not have binding effect may be capable of influencing the conduct of traders and consumers in that State and thus of frustrating the aims of the Community as set out in Article 2 and enlarged upon in Article 3 of the Treaty.

29. That is the case where, as in this instance, such a restrictive practice represents the implementation of a programme defined by the government which affects the national economy as a whole and which is intended to check the flow of trade between Member States by encouraging the purchase of domestic products, by means of an advertising campaign on a national scale and the organization of special procedures applicable solely to domestic products, and where those activities are attributable as a whole to the government and are pursued in an organized fashion throughout the national territory.

The ECJ's reasoning exemplifies its general strategy under Article 34. It looks to substance, not form, rebutting the Irish argument that only formally binding measures are caught by the Article, (paragraphs 21 and 28), and rejecting the argument that, as the campaign appeared to have failed, therefore EU law should be unconcerned with it (paragraph 25).[15]

A second type of case caught by Article 34 is where *a state has rules on the origin-marking of certain goods*.

Case 207/83 **Commission v United Kingdom**
[1985] ECR 1201

[Note Lisbon Treaty renumbering: Arts 30 and 169 are now Arts 34 and 258 TFEU]

The Commission argued that UK legislation which required that certain goods should not be sold in retail markets unless they were marked with their country of origin was in breach of Article 30, as an MEQR. The UK contended that the legislation applied equally to imported and national products, and that this information was important to consumers since they regarded origin as an indication of the quality of the goods. The extract relates to the first of these arguments.

---

[15] The campaign may have had some impact, since the diminution in sales of Irish goods might have been greater had the campaign not existed. Not all measures which promote domestic goods will, however, be caught by the Treaty: Case 222/82 *Apple and Pear Development Council v KJ Lewis Ltd* [1983] ECR 4083. See more recently, J Hojnik, 'Free Movement of Goods in a Labyrinth: Can *Buy Irish* Survive the Crises?' (2012) 49 CMLRev 291.

THE ECJ

17. [I]t has to be recognized that the purpose of indications of origin or origin-marking is to enable consumers to distinguish between domestic and imported products and that this enables them to assert any prejudices which they may have against foreign products. As the Court has had occasion to emphasise in various contexts, the Treaty, by establishing a common market... seeks to unite national markets in a single market having the characteristics of a domestic market. Within such a market, the origin-marking requirement not only makes the marketing in a Member State of goods produced in other Member States in the sectors in question more difficult; it also has the effect of slowing down economic interpenetration in the Community by handicapping the sale of goods produced as the result of a division of labour between Member States.

Member State legislation which contains rules on origin-marking will normally be acceptable only if the origin implies a certain quality in the goods, that they were made from certain materials or by a particular form of manufacturing, or where the origin is indicative of a special place in the folklore or tradition of the region in question.[16]

The Court's clear intent to stamp firmly on national measures that favour domestic over imported products is equally apparent in a third type of case: *public procurement* cannot be structured so as to favour domestic producers.[17]

Case 45/87 **Commission v Ireland**
[1988] ECR 4929

[Note Lisbon Treaty renumbering: Arts 30 and 169 are now Arts 34 and 258 TFEU]

Dundalk Council put out to tender a contract for water supply. One of the contract clauses (4.29) was that tenderers had to submit bids based on the use of certain pipes which complied with a particular Irish standard (IS 188: 1975). One of the bids was based on use of a piping not certified by the Irish authorities, but which complied with international standards. The Council refused to consider it for this reason.

THE ECJ

19. [I]t must first be pointed out that the inclusion of such a clause (as 4.29) in an invitation to tender may cause economic operators who produce or utilize pipes equivalent to pipes certified with Irish standards to refrain from tendering.

20. It further appears... that only one undertaking has been certified by the IIRS[18] to IS 188: 1975 to apply the Irish Standard Mark to pipes of the type required for the purposes of the public works contract at issue. That undertaking is located in Ireland. Consequently, the inclusion of Clause 4.29 had the effect of restricting the supply of the pipes needed for the Dundalk scheme to Irish manufacturers alone.

---

[16] Case 12/74 *Commission v Germany* [1975] ECR 181; Case 113/80 *Commission v Ireland* [1981] ECR 1625.

[17] Case C–21/88 *Du Pont de Nemours Italiana SpA v Unità Sanitaria Locale No 2 Di Carrara* [1990] ECR I–889; Case 72/83 *Campus Oil Ltd v Minister for Industry and Energy* [1984] ECR 2727; Case C–254/05 *Commission v Belgium* [2007] ECR I–4269.

[18] Institute for Industrial Research and Standards.

21. The Irish government maintains that it is necessary to specify the standards to which materials must be manufactured, particularly in a case such as this where the pipes utilized must suit the existing network. Compliance with another standard, even an international standard such as ISO 160: 1980, would not suffice to eliminate technical difficulties.

22. That technical argument cannot be accepted. The Commission's complaint does not relate to compliance with technical requirements but to the refusal of the Irish authorities to verify whether those requirements are satisfied where the manufacturer of the materials has not been certified by the IIRS to IS 188. By incorporating in the notice in question the words 'or equivalent' after the reference to the Irish standard, as provided for by Directive 71/305 where it is applicable, the Irish authorities could have verified compliance with the technical conditions without from the outset restricting the contract to tenderers proposing to utilize Irish materials.

A fourth type of case is where *the discrimination in favour of domestic goods is evident in administrative practice*, as exemplified by *Commission v France*.[19] French law discriminated against imported postal franking machines. The law was changed, but a British company claimed that, notwithstanding this, the French authorities repeatedly refused to approve its machines. The ECJ held that administrative discrimination against imports could be caught by Article 34. It could take the form of delay in replying to applications for approval, or refusing approval on the grounds of various alleged technical faults that were inaccurate.

(c) PRICE FIXING

A state cannot treat imported goods less favourably in law or fact than domestic products through price-fixing regulations.[20]

Case C–531/07 **Fachverband der Buch- und Medienwirtschaft v LIBRO Handelsgesellschaft mbH**
[2009] ECR I–3717

Austrian law provided that an importer of books could not fix a price below the retail price fixed or recommended by the publisher for the state of publication.

THE ECJ

21. In that regard, it should be noted that Paragraph 3(2) of the BPrBG, by prohibiting Austrian importers of German-language books from fixing a retail price below that fixed or recommended by the publisher for the State of publication, less any VAT comprised in it, provides for a less favourable treatment for imported books... since it prevents Austrian importers and foreign publishers from fixing minimum retail prices according to the conditions of the import market, whereas the Austrian publishers are free to fix themselves, for their goods, such minimum retail prices for the national market.

---

[19] Case 21/84 *Commission v France* [1985] ECR 1356.
[20] Case 181/82 *Roussel Laboratoria BV v The State of The Netherlands* [1983] ECR 3849; Case 56/87 *Commission v Italy* [1988] ECR 2919; Case 82/77 *Openbaar Ministerie v Van Tiggele* [1978] ECR 25; Case 65/75 *Riccardo Tasca* [1976] ECR 291.

22. Consequently, such provisions are to be regarded as a measure having equivalent effect to an import restriction contrary to Article 28 EC, in so far as they create, for imported books, a distinct regulation which has the effect of treating products from other Member States less favourably...

23. The German Government contended...that all the considerations concerning the restrictive effects of the Austrian provisions are unfounded because the importation into Austria of books from Germany covers in reality the majority of the Austrian market and that the Austrian market for German-language books cannot be considered independently from the German market. There is, in fact, a single market in which, as the difference in the retail price is minimal, there is no competition between the different editions of the same book sold in those two Member States.

24. These facts, which are, moreover, not contested, cannot be taken into consideration. Even assuming that the publishing houses of German-language books, in particular those established in Germany, are not disadvantaged by the Austrian provisions on the price of imported books, those provisions allow them to exercise control over the prices charged on the Austrian market and also to ensure that those prices are not lower than those charged in the State of publication, such considerations do not allow it to be ruled out that provisions such as those at issue in the main proceedings have the effect of restricting the ability of Austrian importers to compete, as the latter cannot act freely on their market unlike the Austrian publishers who are their direct competitors.

(D) NATIONAL MEASURES VERSUS PRIVATE ACTION

The general principle is that Article 34 applies to state measures,[21] and not those of private parties,[22] and that other Treaty provisions, notably Articles 101 and 102 TFEU, apply to private action that restricts competition.[23] There are three qualifications to this general principle.

First, there may be issues as to what constitutes a state entity. Thus in the '*Buy Irish*'[24] case the ECJ rejected the argument that the Irish Goods Council was a private body and therefore immune from Article 34. The Irish Government's involvement with funding the organization and appointment of its members rendered it public for these purposes, while in the *Apple and Pear Development Council* case[25] the existence of a statutory obligation on fruit growers to pay certain levies to the Council sufficed to render the body public for these purposes. Institutions concerned with trade regulation may come within the definition of the state for these purposes even if they are nominally private, provided that they receive a measure of state support or 'underpinning'.[26]

Secondly, it is clear from the *Fra.bo* case[27] that Article 34 is applicable to standardization and certification activities of a private-law body, where the national legislation considers the products certified by that body to be compliant with national law and that has the effect of restricting the marketing of

---

[21] S Van den Bogaert, 'Horizontality: The Court Attacks?' in C Barnard and J Scott (eds), *The Law of the Single European Market: Unpacking the Premises* (Hart, 2002) ch 5; P Verbruggen, 'The Impact of Primary EU Law on Private Law Relationships: Horizontal Direct Effect under the Free Movement of Goods and Services' (2014) 22 ERPL 201; C Krenn, 'A Missing Piece in the Horizontal Effect "Jigsaw": Horizontal Direct Effect and the Free Movement of Goods' (2012) 49 CMLRev 177.

[22] Case 311/85 *Vereniging van Vlaamse Reisebureaus v Sociale Dienst de Plaatselijke en Gewestelijke Overheidsdiensten* [1987] ECR 3821, [30]; Case C–159/00 *Sapod-Audic v Eco-Emballages SA* [2002] ECR I–5031, [74].

[23] Chs 26–27.

[24] Case 249/81 *Commission v Ireland* [1982] ECR 4005; Case C–325/00 *Commission v Germany* [2002] ECR I–9977.

[25] Case 222/82 (n 15).

[26] Cases 266 and 267/87 *R v The Pharmaceutical Society, ex p API* [1989] ECR 1295.

[27] Case C–171/11 *Fra.bo SpA v Deutsche Vereinigung des Gas- und Wasserfaches eV (DVGW)—Technisch-Wissenschaftlicher Verein* EU:C:2012:453; H van Harten and T Nauta, 'Towards Horizontal Direct Effect for the Free Movement of Goods? Comment on *Fra.bo*' (2013) 38 ELRev 677.

products which are not certified by that body, more especially where the body offers the only possibility for obtaining a compliance certificate for certain products and, by virtue of its authority to certify the products, holds the power to regulate the entry into the market of those products. This is so even though the private body has no government funding, and even though the government has no decisive influence over its activities.

Thirdly, Article 34 can also apply against the state even though private parties have taken the main role in restricting the free movement of goods, as exemplified by *Commission v France*.[28] The Commission brought an action against the French Government for breach of Article 34 TFEU combined with Article 4(3) TEU, because the government had taken insufficient measures to prevent French farmers from disrupting imports of agricultural produce from other Member States. The ECJ held that it was incumbent on a government to take all necessary and appropriate measures to ensure that free movement was respected in its territory, even where the obstacles were created by private parties.[29]

(E) SUMMARY

i.   If a polity decides to embrace a single market, then discriminatory or protectionist measures will be at the top of the list of those to be caught, since they are directly opposed to the single market ideal.

ii. The court entrusted with policing such a regime must be mindful of the many different ways in which a state can seek to discriminate against imported goods.

iii. The ECJ has been aware of this, and has made sure that indirect as well as direct discrimination is caught by Article 34.

4 INDISTINCTLY APPLICABLE RULES: *CASSIS DE DIJON*

(A) FOUNDATIONS: *CASSIS DE DIJON*

The removal of discriminatory trade barriers is a necessary, but not sufficient, condition for single market integration. There are many rules that do not discriminate between goods dependent upon country of origin, but which nevertheless create barriers to trade between Member States.

The Commission appreciated this when framing Directive 70/50.[30] Article 2 was concerned with discriminatory measures. Article 3 provided that the Directive also covered measures governing the marketing of products which deal with shape, size, weight, composition, presentation, and identification, where the measures were equally applicable to domestic and imported products, and where the restrictive effect of such measures on the free movement of goods exceeded the effects intrinsic to such rules.

The possibility that Article 34 could be applied to indistinctly applicable rules was also apparent in *Dassonville*.[31] The definition of an MEQR in paragraph 5 did not require a measure to be discriminatory. The seeds that were sown in Directive 70/50 and *Dassonville* came to fruition in the seminal *Cassis de Dijon* case.

---

[28] Case C–265/95 [1997] ECR I–6959; Case C–112/00 *Schmidberger, Internationale Transporte und Planzuge v Austria* [2003] ECR I–5659, [57]–[59].

[29] See also Regulation 2679/98 of 7 December 1998 on the functioning of the internal market in relation to the free movement of goods among the Member States [1998] OJ L337/8, but for the weakness of this Reg see Report from the Commission to the Council and European Parliament on the application of Regulation 2679/98, COM(2001) 160 final.

[30] Dir 70/50 [1970] OJ L13/29, Art 2(3).

[31] Case 8/74 *Procureur du Roi v Dassonville* [1974] ECR 837.

Case 120/78 **Rewe-Zentral AG v Bundesmonopolverwaltung für Branntwein**
[1979] ECR 649

[Note Lisbon Treaty renumbering: Art 30 is now Art 34 TFEU]

The applicant intended to import the liqueur 'Cassis de Dijon' into Germany from France. The German authorities refused to allow the importation because the French drink was not of sufficient alcoholic strength to be marketed in Germany. Under German law such liqueurs had to have an alcohol content of 25 per cent, whereas the French drink had an alcohol content of between 15 and 20 per cent. The applicant argued that the German rule was an MEQR.

THE ECJ

8. In the absence of common rules relating to the production and marketing of alcohol…it is for the Member States to regulate all matters relating to the production and marketing of alcohol and alcoholic beverages on their own territory.

Obstacles to movement within the Community resulting from disparities between the national laws relating to the marketing of the products in question must be accepted in so far as those provisions may be recognized as being necessary in order to satisfy mandatory requirements relating in particular to the effectiveness of fiscal supervision, the protection of public health, the fairness of commercial transactions and the defence of the consumer.

9. The Government of the Federal Republic of Germany…put forward various arguments which, in its view, justify the application of provisions relating to the minimum alcohol content of alcoholic beverages, adducing considerations relating on the one hand to the protection of public health and on the other to the protection of the consumer against unfair commercial practices.

10. As regards the protection of public health the German Government states that the purpose of the fixing of minimum alcohol contents by national legislation is to avoid the proliferation of alcoholic beverages on the national market, in particular alcoholic beverages with a low alcohol content, since, in its view, such products may more easily induce a tolerance towards alcohol than more highly alcoholic beverages.

11. Such considerations are not decisive since the consumer can obtain on the market an extremely wide range of weakly or moderately alcoholic products and furthermore a large proportion of alcoholic beverages with a high alcohol content freely sold on the German market is generally consumed in a diluted form.

12. The German Government also claims that the fixing of a lower limit for the alcohol content of certain liqueurs is designed to protect the consumer against unfair practices on the part of producers and distributors of alcoholic beverages.

This argument is based on the consideration that the lowering of the alcohol content secures a competitive advantage in relation to beverages with a higher alcohol content, since alcohol constitutes by far the most expensive constituent of beverages by reason of the high rate of tax to which it is subject.

Furthermore, according to the German Government, to allow alcoholic products into free circulation wherever, as regards their alcohol content, they comply with the rules laid down in the country of production would have the effect of imposing as a common standard within the Community the lowest alcohol content permitted in any of the Member States, and even of rendering any requirements in this field inoperative since a lower limit of this nature is foreign to the rules of several Member States.

13. As the Commission rightly observed, the fixing of limits to the alcohol content of beverages may lead to the standardization of products placed on the market and of their designations, in the interests of a greater transparency of commercial transactions and offers for sale to the public.

However, this line of argument cannot be taken so far as to regard the mandatory fixing of minimum alcohol contents as being an essential guarantee of the fairness of commercial transactions, since it is a simple matter to ensure that suitable information is conveyed to the purchaser by requiring the display of an indication of origin and of the alcohol content on the packaging of products.

14. It is clear from the foregoing that the requirements relating to the minimum alcohol content of alcoholic beverages do not serve a purpose which is in the general interest and such as to take precedence over the requirements of the free movement of goods, which constitutes one of the fundamental rules of the Community.

In practice, the principal effect of requirements of this nature is to promote alcoholic beverages having a high alcohol content by excluding from the national market products of other Member States which do not answer that description.

It therefore appears that the unilateral requirement imposed by the rules of a Member State of a minimum alcohol content for the purposes of the sale of alcoholic beverages constitutes an obstacle to trade which is incompatible with the provisions of Article 30 of the Treaty.

There is therefore no valid reason why, provided that they have been lawfully produced and marketed in one of the Member States, alcoholic beverages should not be introduced into any other Member State; the sale of such products may not be subject to a legal prohibition on the marketing of beverages with an alcohol content lower than the limits set by the national rules.

The significance of *Cassis de Dijon* can hardly be overstated, and it is therefore worth dwelling upon the result and the reasoning.

In terms of *result* the Court's ruling affirmed and developed the *Dassonville* judgment. It *affirmed* paragraph 5 of *Dassonville*: what is now Article 34 could apply to national rules that did not discriminate against imported products, but which inhibited trade because they were different from the trade rules applicable in the country of origin. The fundamental assumption was that when goods had been lawfully marketed in one Member State, they should be admitted into any other state without restriction, unless the state of import could successfully invoke one of the mandatory requirements. The *Cassis* judgment encapsulated therefore a principle of *mutual recognition*, paragraph 14(4). The *Cassis* ruling also *built* upon paragraph 6 of *Dassonville*, in which the ECJ introduced the rule of reason: in the absence of harmonization, reasonable measures could be taken by a state to prevent unfair trade practices. Paragraph 8 of *Cassis* developed this idea. Four matters (fiscal supervision, etc) were listed that could prevent a trade rule that inhibited the free movement of goods from being caught by what is now Article 34. This list is not, as will be seen below, exhaustive. The mandatory requirements that constitute the rule of reason are taken into account within the fabric of Article 34, and are separate from what is now Article 36.

The *reasoning* in *Cassis* is as significant as the result. The core is to be found in paragraph 8 of the judgment. The ECJ began by affirming the right of the states to regulate all matters that had not yet been the subject of Community harmonization. Yet within half a dozen lines the whole balance shifted. State regulation of such areas must be accepted, *but* only insofar as these trade rules could be justified by a mandatory requirement listed in paragraph 8. What began by an assertion of states' rights was transformed into a conclusion that required the state to justify the indistinctly applicable rules under the rule of reason.

The ECJ scrutinized closely assertions that the mandatory requirements applied. The German Government's claim in paragraph 10 was weak. The substance of the main claim in paragraph 12 was little better, and was countered in paragraph 13. The point of real substance raised by the German Government was to be found in paragraph 12(3), and it elicited no direct response from the Court. The effect of *Cassis* was deregulatory: it rendered inapplicable trade rules that prevented goods lawfully marketed in one state from being imported into another state. The result might be a common standard based on the country with the least demanding rules, what is often referred to as the 'regulatory race to the bottom'. The implications of this will be considered below.

(B) APPLICATION: THE POST-*CASSIS* JURISPRUDENCE

There were numerous cases applying *Cassis* to various trade rules.[32] In *Déserbais*[33] an importer of Edam cheese from Germany into France was prosecuted for unlawful use of a trade name. In Germany such cheese could be lawfully produced with a fat content of only 34.3 per cent, whereas in France the name Edam was restricted to cheese with a fat content of 40 per cent. The importer relied on Article 34 by way of defence to the criminal prosecution. The ECJ held, in accord with *Cassis*, that the French rule was incompatible with Article 34, and could not be saved by the mandatory requirements.

The same result was reached in *Gilli and Andres*[34] where importers of apple vinegar from Germany into Italy were prosecuted for fraud because they had sold vinegar in Italy that was not made from fermentation of wine. The rule hampered Community trade and did not benefit from the mandatory requirements, since proper labelling could alert consumers to the nature of the product, thereby avoiding consumer confusion.

The same approach was apparent in *Rau*,[35] which was concerned with national rules on packaging rather than content. Belgian law required all margarine to be marketed in cube-shaped packages, irrespective of where it had been made, but it was clearly more difficult for non-Belgian manufacturers to comply without incurring cost increases. The ECJ held that Article 34 was applicable, and that the Belgian rule could not be justified on the basis of consumer protection, since any consumer confusion could be avoided by clear labelling.

(C) INDISTINCTLY APPLICABLE RULES: ARTICLE 35

Article 35 prohibits quantitative restrictions and MEQRs in relation to exports in the same manner as does Article 34 in relation to imports. The ECJ has, however, held that there is a difference between the two provisions. Whereas Article 34 will apply to discriminatory provisions and also to indistinctly applicable measures, Article 35 will, it seems, apply only if there is discrimination.[36] An exporter faced with a national rule on, for example, quality standards for a product to be marketed in that state cannot use Article 35 to argue that such a rule renders it more difficult for that exporter to penetrate other markets. The rationale for making Article 34 applicable to measures which do not discriminate is that they impose a dual burden on the importer, who will have to satisfy the rules in its own state and also the state of import. This will not normally be so in relation to Article 35.[37]

This was established in *Groenveld*.[38] Dutch legislation prohibited all manufacturers of meat products from having in stock or processing horsemeat. The purpose was to safeguard the export of

---

[32] Case 298/87 *Smanor* [1988] ECR 4489; Case 407/85 *Drei Glocken v USL Centro-Sud* [1988] ECR 4233; Case C–362/88 *GB-INNO-BM v Confédération du Commerce Luxembourgeois Asbl* [1990] ECR I–667; Case C–30/99 *Commission v Ireland* [2001] ECR I–4619; Case C–123/00 *Criminal Proceedings against Bellamy and English Shop Wholesale SA* [2001] ECR I–2795; Case C–14/02 *ATRAL SA v Belgium* [2003] ECR I–4431; Case C–170/04 *Klas Rosengren v Riksåklagaren* [2007] ECR I–4071; Case C–265/06 *Commission v Portugal* [2008] ECR I–2245; Case C–443/10 *Philippe Bonnarde v Agence de Services et de Paiement* [2011] ECR I–9327.

[33] Case 286/86 *Ministère Public v Déserbais* [1988] ECR 4907.

[34] Case 788/79 *Italian State v Gilli and Andres* [1980] ECR 2071; Case C–17/93 *Openbaar Ministerie v Van der Veldt* [1994] ECR I–3537.

[35] Case 261/81 *Walter Rau Lebensmittelwerke v de Smedt Pvba* [1982] ECR 3961; Case C–317/92 *Commission v Germany* [1994] ECR I–2039; Case C–369/89 *Groupement des Producteurs, Importeurs et Agents Généraux d'Eaux Minérales Etrangères (Piagème) Asbl v Peeters Pvba* [1991] ECR I–2971.

[36] Case C–12/02 *Criminal Proceedings against Marco Grilli* [2003] ECR I–11585, [41]–[42].

[37] R Barents, 'New Developments in Measures Having Equivalent Effect' (1981) 18 CMLRev 271.

[38] Case 15/79 *PB Groenveld BV v Produktschap voor Vee en Vlees* [1979] ECR 3409; Case 237/82 *Jongeneel Kaas v The State (Netherlands) and Stichting Centraal Organ Zuivelcontrole* [1984] ECR 483; Case 98/86 *Ministère Public v Mathot* [1987] ECR 809; Case C–293/02 *Jersey Produce Marketing Organisation v States of Jersey* [2005] ECR I–9543; Case

meat products to countries that prohibited the marketing of horseflesh. It was impossible to detect the presence of horsemeat within other meat products, and therefore the ban was designed to prevent its use by preventing meat processors from having horsemeat in stock at all. The sale of horsemeat was not actually forbidden in the Netherlands. Nonetheless the Court held that the Dutch rule did not infringe what is now Article 35. The Article was aimed at national measures which had as their specific object or effect the restriction of exports, so as to provide a particular advantage for national production at the expense of the trade of other Member States. This was not the case here, said the Court, since the prohibition applied to the production of goods of a certain kind without drawing a distinction depending on whether such goods were intended for the national market or for export.[39]

It has however been argued that Article 35 should be conceptualized in terms of market access, and that it should be capable of applying to indistinctly applicable rules.[40] It is moreover clear from *Gysbrechts* that the ECJ is willing to find a breach of Article 35 even where the rule applies to all traders if it has a greater effect on exports than on domestic traders.[41] Belgian law prohibited a supplier in a distant selling contract from requiring that the consumer provide his payment card number, even though the supplier undertook not to use it to collect payment before expiry of the period in which the consumer could return the goods. The ECJ cited *Groenveld* for the proposition that Article 35 caught national measures which treated differently the domestic and export trade of a Member State so as to provide an advantage for the domestic market at the expense of trade of other Member States. It noted that the consequences of the prohibition in this case were generally more significant in cross-border sales made directly to consumers, because of the obstacles to bringing legal proceedings in another Member State against consumers who defaulted. The ECJ therefore concluded that even if the prohibition was applicable to all traders active in the national territory, its actual effect was nonetheless greater on goods leaving the market of the exporting Member State than on the marketing of goods in the domestic market of that Member State and was therefore caught by Article 35. It held moreover that although consumer protection could constitute a justification, the challenged rule was disproportionate.

(D) INDISTINCTLY APPLICABLE RULES: THE LIMITS OF ARTICLE 34

Cassis signalled the ECJ's willingness to extend Article 34 to catch indistinctly applicable rules. The difficulty is that all trade rules could be said, directly or indirectly, to affect the free movement of goods in various ways. Thus, as Weatherill and Beaumont note, it could be said that rules requiring the owner of a firearm to have a licence, or spending limits imposed on government departments, reduce the sales opportunities for imported products,[42] even though it would seem absurd to bring such rules within Article 34.

A distinction can however be drawn, as Weatherill and Beaumont note,[43] between what may be termed dual-burden rules and equal-burden rules. *Cassis* is concerned with dual-burden rules. State A imposes rules on the content of goods. These are applied to goods imported from state B, even though such goods have already complied with the trade rules in state B. *Cassis* prevents state

---

C–205/07 *Lodewijk Gysbrechts and Santurel Inter BVBA* [2008] ECR I–9947; Case C–161/09 *Kakavetsos-Fragkopoulos AE Epexergasias kai Emporias Stafidas v Nomarchiaki Aftodioikisi Korinthias* [2011] ECR I–915.

[39] Case 15/79 *Groenveld* (n 38) [7].

[40] Case C–205/07 *Lodewijk Gysbrechts* (n 38) [59]–[61], AG Trstenjak; M Szydło, 'Export Restrictions within the Structure of Free Movement of Goods: Reconsideration of an Old Paradigm' (2010) 47 CMLRev 753.

[41] Case C–205/07 *Lodewijk Gysbrechts* (n 38); W-H Roth, Note (2010) 47 CMLRev 509.

[42] S Weatherill and P Beaumont, *EU Law* (Penguin, 3rd edn, 1999) 608.

[43] Ibid 608–609.

A from imposing its rules in such instances unless they can be saved by the mandatory require-ments. Equal-burden rules are those applying to all goods, irrespective of origin, which regulate trade in some manner. They are not designed to be protectionist. These rules may have an impact on the overall volume of trade, but there will be no greater impact for imports than for domestic products.

A key issue is whether rules of this nature should be held to fall within Article 34, subject to a possible justification, or whether they should be deemed to be outside Article 34 altogether. The result may be the same, in that the rule may be held lawful. The choice is nonetheless important. If these rules are within Article 34 they are *prima facie* unlawful, and the burden is on those seeking to uphold the rule to show objective justification. Both strategies were evident in the ECJ's jurispru-dence prior to *Keck*.[44]

In some cases the ECJ held that rules which did not relate to the *characteristics* of the goods and did not impose a dual burden on the importer, but concerned only the conditions on which all goods were *sold*, were outside Article 34. Thus in *Oebel*[45] the Court held that a rule which prohibited the delivery of bakery products to consumers and retailers, but not wholesalers, at night was not caught, since it applied in the same way to all producers wherever they were established.[46]

In other cases the Court held, however, that Article 34 applied to rules that were not dissimilar to those in the preceding paragraph. Thus in *Cinéthèque*[47] the ECJ held that a French law banning the sale or hire of videos of films during the first year in which the film was released, the objective being to encourage people to go to the cinema and hence protect the profitability of cinematographic produc-tion, was caught by Article 34, even though it did not favour domestic production and did not seek to regulate trade. The ECJ held that the French law could however be justified, since it sought to encour-age the creation of films irrespective of their origin.[48] The same approach to Article 34 is apparent in the *Sunday Trading* cases.

Case 145/88 **Torfaen BC v B & Q plc**
[1989] ECR 3851

B & Q was prosecuted for violation of laws which prohibited retail shops from selling on Sundays, sub-ject to exceptions for certain types of products. B & Q claimed that these laws constituted an MEQR within Article 30. The effect of the laws was to reduce total turnover by about 10 per cent, with a cor-responding diminution of imports from other Member States. But imported goods were in no worse a position than domestic goods, since the reduction in total turnover affected all goods equally.

THE ECJ

11. The first point which must be made is that national rules prohibiting retailers from opening their premises on Sunday apply to imported and domestic products alike. In principle, the marketing of

---

[44] Cases C–267 and 268/91 *Criminal Proceedings against Keck and Mithouard* [1993] ECR I–6097.

[45] Case 155/80 [1981] ECR 1993, [20].

[46] See also Case 148/85 *Direction Générale des Impôts and Procureur de la République v Forest* [1986] ECR 3449, [11]; Case 75/81 *Belgian State v Blesgen* [1982] ECR 1211; Case C–23/89 *Quietlynn Ltd v Southend-on-Sea BC* [1990] ECR I–3059.

[47] Cases 60 and 61/84 *Cinéthèque SA v Fédération Nationale des Cinémas Français* [1985] ECR 2605.

[48] The ECJ's approach can be contrasted with that taken by AG Slynn, who argued that the French law should fall outside Art 34, since it did not impose any additional requirement on importers: ibid 2611.

products imported from other Member States is not therefore made more difficult than the marketing of domestic products.

12. Next, it must be recalled that in its judgment...in Joined Cases 60 and 61/84 (*Cinéthèque*) the Court held, with regard to a prohibition of the hiring of video-cassettes applicable to domestic and imported products alike, that such a prohibition was not compatible with the principle of the free movement of goods provided for in the Treaty unless any obstacle to Community trade thereby created did not exceed what was necessary in order to ensure the attainment of the objective in view and unless that objective was justified with regard to Community law.

13. In those circumstances it is therefore necessary in a case such as this to consider first of all whether rules such as those at issue pursue an aim which is justified with regard to Community law. As far as this question is concerned the Court has already stated in its judgment...in Case 155/80 (*Oebel* [1981] ECR 1993) that national rules governing the hours of work, delivery and sale in the bread and confectionery industry constitute a legitimate part of economic and social policy, consistent with the objectives of public interest pursued by the Treaty.

14. The same consideration must apply as regards national rules governing the opening hours of retail premises. Such rules reflect certain political and economic choices in so far as their purpose is to ensure that working and non-working hours are so arranged as to accord with national or regional socio-cultural characteristics, and that, in the present state of Community law, is a matter for Member States. Furthermore such rules are not designed to govern the patterns of trade between Member States.

15. Secondly, it is necessary to ascertain whether the effects of such national rules exceed what is necessary to achieve the aim in view. As is indicated in Article 3 of Commission Directive 70/50...the prohibition laid down in Article 30 covers national measures governing the marketing of products where the restrictive effect of such measures on the free movement of goods exceeds the effects intrinsic to trade rules.

16. The question whether the effects of specific national rules do in fact remain within that limit is a question to be determined by the national court.

17. The reply to the first question must therefore be that Article 30 of the Treaty must be interpreted as meaning that the prohibition which it lays down does not apply to national rules prohibiting retailers from opening their premises on Sunday where the restrictive effects on Community trade which may result therefrom do not exceed the effects intrinsic to rules of that kind.

The approach in *Torfaen* was identical to that in *Cinéthèque*. The rule was *prima facie* caught by Article 34, but it could escape prohibition if there was some objective justification and the effects of the rule were proportionate, the latter issue to be determined by national courts. Subsequent UK case law revealed the difficulty in applying the test.[49] The ECJ resolved these difficulties by making it clear that Sunday trading rules were proportionate.[50]

The fundamental approach nonetheless remained the same: such rules were *prima facie* within Article 34. The post-*Torfaen* case law simply made things easier for national courts by providing guidance on proportionality. The ECJ's case law provided academics with much material concerning the proper boundaries of Article 34. White distinguished between the characteristics of the goods and selling arrangements, a theme picked up by the ECJ in *Keck*.

49 A Arnull, 'What Shall We Do On Sunday?' (1991) 16 ELRev 112.

50 Case C–312/89 *Union Département des Syndicats CGT de l'Aisne v SIDEF Conforama* [1991] ECR I–997; Case C–332/89 *Ministère Public v Marchandise* [1991] ECR I–1027; Cases C–306/88, 304/90 and 169/91 *Stoke-on-Trent CC v B & Q plc* [1992] ECR I–6457, 6493, 6635; Cases C–418–421, 460–462 and 464/93, 9–11, 14–15, 23–24 and 332/94 *Semeraro Casa Uno Srl v Sindaco del Commune di Erbusco* [1996] ECR I–2975.

E White, In Search of the Limits to Article 30 of the EEC Treaty[51]

[A]s the judgment of the Court in *Cassis de Dijon* clearly shows, Member States are not entitled to require that imported products have the same characteristics as are required of, or are traditional in, domestic products unless this is strictly necessary for the protection of some legitimate interest. There is not, however, the same need to require the rules relating to the circumstances in which certain goods may be sold or used in the importing Member State to be overridden for this purpose as long as imported products enjoy equal access to the market of the importing Member State compared with national goods. In such a case the imported product is not deprived of any advantage it derives from the different legal and economic environment prevailing in the place of production. In fact, any reduction of total sales (and therefore imports) which may result from restrictions on the circumstances in which they may be sold does not arise from disparities between national rules but rather out of the existence of the rules in the importing Member State.

5 INDISTINCTLY AND DISTINCTLY APPLICABLE RULES: *KECK* AND SELLING ARRANGEMENTS

(A) *KECK*: SELLING ARRANGEMENTS

Cases C–267 and 268/91 **Criminal Proceedings against Keck and Mithouard**
[1993] ECR I–6097

[Note Lisbon Treaty renumbering: Arts 30 and 177 are now Arts 34 and 267 TFEU]

Keck and Mithouard (K & M) were prosecuted in France for selling goods at a price which was lower than their actual purchase price (resale at a loss), contrary to French law. The law did not ban sales at a loss by the manufacturer. K & M claimed that the French law was contrary to Community law concerning free movement of goods.

THE ECJ

12. It is not the purpose of national legislation imposing a general prohibition on resale at a loss to regulate trade in goods between Member States.

13. Such legislation may, admittedly, restrict the volume of sales, and hence the volume of sales of products from other Member States, in so far as it deprives traders of a method of sales promotion. But the question remains whether such a possibility is sufficient to characterize the legislation in question as a measure having equivalent effect to a quantitative restriction on imports.

14. In view of the increasing tendency of traders to invoke Article 30 of the Treaty as a means of challenging any rules whose effect is to limit their commercial freedom even where such rules are not aimed at products from other Member States, the Court considers it necessary to re-examine and clarify its case law on this matter.

---

[51] (1989) 26 CMLRev 235, 246–267, italics in the original.

15. In 'Cassis de Dijon' ... it was held that, in the absence of harmonization of legislation, measures of equivalent effect prohibited by Article 30 include obstacles to the free movement of goods where they are the consequence of applying rules that lay down requirements to be met by such goods (such as requirements as to designation, form, size, weight, composition, presentation, labelling, packaging) to goods from other Member States where they are lawfully manufactured and marketed, even if those rules apply without distinction to all products unless their application can be justified by a public-interest objective taking precedence over the free movement of goods.

16. However, contrary to what has previously been decided, the application to products from other Member States of national provisions restricting or prohibiting certain selling arrangements is not such as to hinder directly or indirectly, actually or potentially, trade between Member States within the meaning of the *Dassonville* judgment ... provided that those provisions apply to all affected traders operating within the national territory and provided that they affect in the same manner, in law and fact, the marketing of domestic products and of those from other Member States.

17. Where those conditions are fulfilled, the application of such rules to the sale of products from another Member State is not by nature such as to prevent their access to the market or to impede access any more than it impedes the access of domestic products. Such rules therefore fall outside the scope of Article 30 of the Treaty.

18. Accordingly, the reply to be given to the national court is that Article 30 of the EEC Treaty is to be interpreted as not applying to legislation of a Member State imposing a general prohibition on resale at a loss.

It is clear that the decision was based in part upon the distinction between dual-burden rules and equal-burden rules (paragraphs 15–17).

Cassis-type *rules relating to the goods themselves* were within Article 34 because they would have to be satisfied by the importer *in addition* to any such provisions existing within its own state (paragraph 15). Such rules were by their very nature[52] likely to impede access to the market for imported goods.

Rules concerning selling arrangements, by way of contrast, imposed an equal burden on all those seeking to market goods in a particular territory (paragraph 17). They did not impose extra costs on the importer, their purpose was not to regulate trade (paragraph 12), and they did not prevent access to the market. They were therefore not within Article 34, *provided* that they affected in the same manner in law or fact domestic and imported goods (paragraph 16).

The ECJ's desire to exclude selling arrangements from the ambit of Article 34 is apparent from later case law.[53] In *Tankstation*[54] the Court held that national rules that provided for the compulsory closing of petrol stations were not caught by Article 34. The ECJ concluded that the rules related to selling arrangements that applied equally to all traders. In *Punto Casa*[55] and *Semeraro*[56] the Court reached the same conclusion in relation to Italian legislation on Sunday closing of retail outlets. The same theme is apparent in *Hunermund*,[57] where the ECJ held that a rule prohibiting pharmacists from advertising para-pharmaceutical products they were allowed to sell was not caught by Article 34: the rule was not directed towards intra-Community trade, it did not preclude traders other than

---

[52] Cases C–401 and 402/92 *Criminal Proceedings against Tankstation 't Heustke vof and JBE Boermans* [1994] ECR I–2199, 2220.

[53] In Cases C–401 and 402/92 *Tankstation* (n 52) AG Van Gerven felt that *Cinéthèque* would be decided differently now in the light of *Keck*.

[54] Ibid.

[55] Cases C–69 and 258/93 *Punto Casa SpA v Sindaco del Commune di Capena* [1994] ECR I–2355.

[56] Case C–418/93 *Semeraro* (n 50).

[57] Case C–292/92 *Hunermund v Landesapothekerkammer Baden-Württemberg* [1993] ECR I–6787.

pharmacists from advertising such goods, and it applied evenly as between all traders. The ECJ also held that national provisions restricting the number of outlets for a given product, or imposing a licensing requirement, were outside Article 34. This was either because the rule related to selling arrangements or because the impact was too indirect and uncertain.[58]

(B) *KECK*: STATIC AND DYNAMIC SELLING ARRANGEMENTS

The ECJ's desire to limit Article 34 is readily understandable, but the distinction drawn in *Keck* between rules that go to the nature of the product itself and those which relate to the selling arrangements for that product is problematic. The problem resides in ambiguity about the meaning of the term 'selling arrangements'.

This could connote what may be termed *static selling arrangements*: rules relating to the hours at which shops may be open, the length of time for which people may work, or the type of premises in which certain goods may be sold. *Non-static or dynamic selling arrangements* include the ways in which a manufacturer chooses *to market this specific product*, through a certain form of advertising, free offers, and the like.

The objection to taking the latter out of Article 34 is that they may relate more closely to the definition of the product itself. Legislation that restricted certain forms of advertising or sales promotion might limit intra-EU trade, even if the rules were indistinctly applicable. It might force a producer to adopt sales promotion or advertising schemes that differed as between states, or discontinue an effective scheme.[59] Non-static selling arrangements can therefore form an integral aspect of the goods, in much the same way as do rules relating to composition, labelling, or presentation.

It is, however, clear from *Keck* that the Court regarded some such rules as selling arrangements, and hence as outside Article 34. Thus it admitted that a rule prohibiting sales at a loss deprived traders of a method of sales promotion, and hence reduced the volume of sales, and yet treated this rule as a selling arrangement that was outside Article 34. While in *Hunermund*[60] and *Leclerc-Siplec*[61] a limited ban on advertising was characterized as a method of sales promotion and held to be outside Article 34, and in *Schmidt*[62] a prohibition on doorstep sales of silver jewellery was held *prima facie* to fall outside Article 34.

(c) *KECK* AND SELLING ARRANGEMENTS: TWO QUALIFICATIONS

(i) *Rules Concerning Sales Characterized as Relating to the Product*

It is open to the ECJ to characterize rules which affect selling as part of the product itself,[63] and hence within the ambit of Article 34. This is exemplified by *Familiapress*.[64]

---

[58] Case C–387/93 *Banchero* [1995] ECR I–4663; Case C–379/92 *Peralta* [1994] ECR I–3453; Cases C–140–142/94 *Dip SpA v Commune di Bassano del Grappa* [1995] ECR I–3257.

[59] Case 286/81 *Oosthoek's Uitgeversmaatschappij BV* [1982] ECR 4575. See also Case 382/87 *Buet v Minstère Public* [1989] ECR 1235; Cases C–34–36/95 *Konsumentombudsmannen (KO) v De Agostini (Svenska) Forlag AB and TV-Shop i Sverige AB* [1997] ECR I–3843.

[60] Case C–292/92 (n 57).

[61] Case 412/93 *Société d'Importation Edouard Leclerc-Siplec v TF1 Publicité SA* [1995] ECR I–179.

[62] Case C–441/04 *A-Punkt Schmuckhandels GmbH v Schmidt* [2006] ECR I–2093.

[63] If the national rule requires the alteration of packaging or labelling of the imported products this generally precludes it from being a selling arrangement within *Keck*: Case C–12/00 *Commission v Spain* [2003] ECR I–459, [76]; Case C–416/00 *Morellato v Commune di Padova* [2003] ECR I–9343, [29]–[30]. Compare Case C–159/00 *Sapud Audic* (n 22) [72]–[75].

[64] See also Case C–67/97 *Criminal Proceedings against Bluhme* [1998] ECR I–8033, [21]; Cases C–158 and 159/04 *Alfa Vita Vassilopoulos AE and Carrefour Marinopoulos AE v Elliniko Dimosio and Nomarchiaki Aftodioikisi Ioanninon* [2006] ECR I–8135; Case C–244/06 *Dynamic Medien Vertriebs GmbH v Avides Media AG* [2008] ECR I–505, [24]–[32].

Case C–368/95 **Vereinigte Familiapress Zeitungsverlags-und Vertreibs GmbH v Heinrich Bauer Verlag**
[1997] ECR I–3689

[Note Lisbon Treaty renumbering: Art 30 is now Art 34 TFEU]

Familiapress, an Austrian newspaper publisher, sought to restrain HBV, a German publisher, from publishing in Austria a magazine containing crossword puzzles for which the winning readers would receive prizes. Austrian legislation prohibited publishers from including such prize competitions in their papers. Austria argued that its legislation was not caught by Article 30, since the national law related to a method of sales promotion, and was therefore, according to *Keck*, outside Article 30.

THE ECJ

11. The Court finds that, even though the relevant national legislation is directed against a method of sales promotion, in this case it bears on the actual content of the products, in so far as the competitions in question form an integral part of the magazine in which they appear. As a result, the national legislation in question as applied to the facts of the case is not concerned with a selling arrangement within the meaning of the judgment in *Keck and Mithouard*.

12. Moreover, since it requires traders established in other Member States to alter the contents of the periodical, the prohibition at issue impairs access of the products concerned to the market of the Member State of importation and consequently hinders free movement of goods. It therefore constitutes in principle a measure having equivalent effect within the meaning of Article 30 of the Treaty.

(ii) *Differential Impact in Law or Fact*

The ruling in *Keck* is also subject to a second qualification: even if a national regulation is categorized as being about selling, it will still be caught by Article 34 if it has a differential impact, in law or fact, for domestic traders and importers.[65] This is made clear in paragraph 16 of *Keck* and is exemplified by the following cases.[66]

Cases C–34–36/95 **Konsumentombudsmannen (KO) v De Agostini (Svenska) Forlag AB and TV-Shop i Sverige AB**
[1997] ECR I–3843

[Note Lisbon Treaty renumbering: Arts 30 and 36 are now Arts 34 and 36 TFEU]

The case concerned a Swedish ban on television advertising directed at children under 12 and a ban on commercials for skincare products. It was argued that this was in breach of Article 30, and hence could not be applied in relation to advertising broadcast from another Member State. The ECJ, following

---

[65] The determination of this possible differential impact may be left to the national court: see, eg, Case C–20/03 *Burmanjer* [2005] ECR I–4133; Case C–441/04 *Schmidt* (n 62).

[66] P Koutrakos, 'On Groceries, Alcohol and Olive Oil: More on Free Movement of Goods after *Keck*' (2001) 26 ELRev 391.

Leclerc-Siplec, characterized the Swedish law as one concerning selling arrangements. It then continued as follows.

THE ECJ

40. In…*Keck*…at paragraph 16, the Court held that national measures restricting or prohibiting certain selling arrangements are not covered by Article 30…so long as they apply to all traders operating within the national territory and as long as they affect in the same manner, in law and fact, the marketing of domestic products and of those from other Member States.

41. The first condition is clearly fulfilled in the cases before the national court.

42. As regards the second condition, it cannot be excluded that an outright ban, applying in one Member State, of a type of promotion for a product which is lawfully sold there might have a greater impact on products from other Member States.

43. Although the efficacy of the various types of promotion is a question of fact to be determined in principle by the referring court, it is to be noted that…de Agostini stated that television advertising was the only effective form of promotion enabling it to penetrate the Swedish market since it had no other advertising methods for reaching children and their parents.

44. Consequently, an outright ban on advertising aimed at children less than 12 years of age and of misleading advertising…is not covered by Article 30…, unless it can be shown that the ban does not affect in the same way, in fact and in law, the marketing of national products and of products from other Member States.

45. In the latter case, it is for the national court to determine whether the ban is necessary to satisfy overriding requirements of general public importance or one of the aims listed in Article 36 of the Treaty, if it is proportionate to that purpose and if those aims or requirements could not have been attained or fulfilled by measures less restrictive of intra-Community trade.

Case C–405/98 **Konsumentombudsmannen (KO) v Gourmet International Products AB (GIP)**
[2001] ECR I–1795

[Note Lisbon Treaty renumbering: Art 30 is now Art 34 TFEU]

The Swedish Consumer Ombudsman sought an injunction restraining GIP from placing advertisements for alcohol in magazines. Swedish law prohibited advertising of alcohol on radio and television, and prohibited advertising of spirits, wines, and strong beer in periodicals other than those distributed at the point of sale. The prohibition on advertising did not apply to periodicals aimed at traders such as restaurateurs. GIP published a magazine containing advertisements for alcohol. Ninety per cent of the subscribers were traders, and 10 per cent were private individuals. GIP argued that the advertising ban was contrary to Article 30. It contended that the advertising ban had a greater effect on imported goods than on those produced in Sweden.

THE ECJ

18. It should be pointed out that, according to paragraph 17 of its judgment in *Keck and Mithouard*, if national provisions restricting or prohibiting selling arrangements are to avoid being caught by Article 30 of the Treaty, they must not be of such a kind as to prevent access to the market by products from another state or to impede access any more than they impede the access of domestic products.

19. The Court has also held, in paragraph 42 of...*De Agostini*...that it cannot be excluded that an outright prohibition, applying in one Member State, of a type of product which is lawfully sold there might have a greater impact on products from other Member States.

20. It is apparent that a prohibition on advertising...not only prohibits a form of marketing a product but in reality prohibits producers and importers from directing any advertising messages at consumers, with a few insignificant exceptions.

21. Even without its being necessary to carry out a precise analysis of the facts characteristic of the Swedish situation, which it is for the national court to do, the Court is able to conclude that, in the case of products like alcoholic beverages, the consumption of which is linked to traditional social practices and to local habits and customs, a prohibition of all advertisements in the press, on the radio and on television, the direct mailing of unsolicited material or the placing of posters on the public highway is liable to impede access to the market by products from other Member States more than it impedes access by domestic products, with which consumers are instantly more familiar.

...

25. A prohibition on advertising such as that in issue...must therefore be regarded as affecting the marketing of products from other Member States more heavily than the marketing of domestic products and as therefore constituting an obstacle to trade between Member States caught by Article 30 of the Treaty.

In *de Agostini* and *Gourmet* the advertising ban was total. However the ECJ has also held that limiting market access can fall within Article 34. In *Franzen* Swedish law required a licence for those, including importers, engaged in the making of alcohol, or in wholesaling. This was held to infringe Article 34 since it imposed additional costs on importers and because most licences had been issued to Swedish traders.[67] In *Heimdienst* the ECJ showed that it was willing to consider the proviso to paragraph 16 of *Keck* in relation to a selling arrangement that impeded, rather than prevented, access to the market.[68]

Case C–254/98 **Schutzverband gegen unlauteren Wettbewerb v TK-Heimdienst Sass GmbH**
[2000] ECR I–151

The case concerned an Austrian rule relating to bakers, butchers, and grocers. They could make sales on rounds in a given administrative district only if they traded from a permanent establishment in that district or an adjacent municipality, where they offered for sale the same goods as they did on their rounds. The ECJ classified the rule as one relating to selling arrangements, since it specified the geographical areas in which such operators could sell their goods in this manner. The ECJ found that the legislation had a differential impact on domestic traders and others. Local economic operators would be more likely to have a permanent establishment in the administrative district or an adjacent municipality, whereas others would have to set up such an establishment, thereby incurring additional costs.

---

[67] Case C–189/95 *Criminal Proceedings against Franzen* [1997] ECR I–5909.
[68] See also Case C–322/01 *Deutscher Apothekerverband v 0800 Doc Morris NV and Jacques Waterval* [2003] ECR I–14887, [68]–[75]; Case C–20/03 *Burmanjer* (n 65); Case C–141/07 *Commission v Germany* [2008] ECR I–6935, [37]–[38]; Case C–108/09 *Ker-Optika bt v ÀNTSZ Dél-dunántúli Regionális Intézete* [2010] ECR I–12213.

THE ECJ

29. It follows that the application to all operators trading in the national territory of national legisla-tion such as that in point in the main proceedings in fact impedes access to the market of the Member State of importation for products from other Member States more than it impedes access for domestic products (see to this effect ... *Alpine Investments* ...).

6 INDISTINCTLY AND DISTINCTLY APPLICABLE RULES: PRODUCT USE

The distinction between selling arrangements and product characteristics generated further ques-tions as to how cases concerned with the 'use' of products should be regarded. This issue has arisen in two major cases.

Case C–110/05 **Commission v Italy**
[2009] ECR I–519

Italy prohibited motorcycles, mopeds, etc from towing trailers, even those specifically designed for use with such vehicles. The Commission argued that this was in breach of what is now Article 34 TFEU.

THE ECJ

33. It should be recalled that, according to settled case-law, all trading rules enacted by Member States which are capable of hindering, directly or indirectly, actually or potentially, intra-Community trade are to be considered as measures having an effect equivalent to quantitative restrictions and are, on that basis, prohibited by Article 28 EC (see, in particular, *Dassonville*, paragraph 5).

34. It is also apparent from settled case-law that Article 28 EC reflects the obligation to respect the principles of non-discrimination and of mutual recognition of products lawfully manufactured and marketed in other Member States, as well as the principle of ensuring free access of Community products to national markets (see, to that effect, Case 174/82 *Sandoz* [1983] ECR 2445, paragraph 26; Case 120/78 *Rewe-Zentral* ('*Cassis de Dijon*') [1979] ECR 649, paragraphs 6, 14 and 15; and *Keck and Mithouard*, paragraphs 16 and 17).

35. Hence, in the absence of harmonisation of national legislation, obstacles to the free movement of goods which are the consequence of applying, to goods coming from other Member States where they are lawfully manufactured and marketed, rules that lay down requirements to be met by such goods constitute measures of equivalent effect to quantitative restrictions even if those rules apply to all products alike (see, to that effect, '*Cassis de Dijon*', paragraphs 6, 14 and 15; Case C–368/95 *Familiapress* [1997] ECR I–3689, paragraph 8; and Case C–322/01 *Deutscher Apothekerverband* [2003] ECR I–4887, paragraph 67).

36. By contrast, the application to products from other Member States of national provisions restrict-ing or prohibiting certain selling arrangements is not such as to hinder directly or indirectly, actually or potentially, trade between Member States for the purposes of the case-law flowing from *Dassonville*, on condition that those provisions apply to all relevant traders operating within the national territory and that they affect in the same manner, in law and in fact, the marketing of domestic products and of those from other Member States. Provided that those conditions are fulfilled, the application of such

rules to the sale of products from another Member State meeting the requirements laid down by that State is not by nature such as to prevent their access to the market or to impede access any more than it impedes the access of domestic products (see *Keck and Mithouard*, paragraphs 16 and 17).

37. Consequently, measures adopted by a Member State the object or effect of which is to treat products coming from other Member States less favourably are to be regarded as measures having equivalent effect to quantitative restrictions on imports within the meaning of Article 28 EC, as are the measures referred to in paragraph 35 of the present judgment. Any other measure which hinders access of products originating in other Member States to the market of a Member State is also covered by that concept.

The ECJ held that the Italian rule fell within Article 34, but concluded that it could be justified on grounds of public safety.[69] The Court returned to the issue in the following case.

Case C–142/05 Åklagaren v Percy Mickelsson and Joakim Roos
[2009] ECR I–4273

[Note Lisbon Treaty renumbering: Arts 28 and 30 are now Arts 34 and 36 TFEU]

The ECJ considered whether Article 28 should be interpreted as precluding national regulations which prohibited the use of personal watercraft on waters other than designated waterways.

THE ECJ

24. It must be borne in mind that measures taken by a Member State, the aim or effect of which is to treat goods coming from other Member States less favourably and, in the absence of harmonisation of national legislation, obstacles to the free movement of goods which are the consequence of applying, to goods coming from other Member States where they are lawfully manufactured and marketed, rules that lay down requirements to be met by such goods, even if those rules apply to all products alike, must be regarded as 'measures having equivalent effect to quantitative restrictions on imports' for the purposes of Article 28 EC (see to that effect, Case 120/78 *Rewe-Zentral (Cassis de Dijon)* [1979] ECR 649, . . .). Any other measure which hinders access of products originating in other Member States to the market of a Member State is also covered by that concept (see Case C–110/05 *Commission v Italy* [2009] ECR I–0000, paragraph 37).

25. It is apparent from the file sent to the Court that, at the material time, no waters had been designated as open to navigation by personal watercraft, and thus the use of personal watercraft was permitted on only general navigable waterways. However, the accused in the main proceedings and the Commission of the European Communities maintain that those waterways are intended for heavy traffic of a commercial nature making the use of personal watercraft dangerous and that, in any event, the majority of navigable Swedish waters lie outside those waterways. The actual possibilities for the use of personal watercraft in Sweden are, therefore, merely marginal.

26. Even if the national regulations at issue do not have the aim or effect of treating goods coming from other Member States less favourably, which is for the national court to ascertain, the restriction which they impose on the use of a product in the territory of a Member State may, depending on its scope, have a considerable influence on the behaviour of consumers, which may, in turn, affect the

---

[69] Case C–110/05 [2009] ECR I–519, [69]; see also Case C–433/05 *Criminal proceedings against Lars Sandström* [2010] ECR I–2885.

access of that product to the market of that Member State (see to that effect, *Commission v Italy*, paragraph 56).

27. Consumers, knowing that the use permitted by such regulations is very limited, have only a limited interest in buying that product (see to that effect, *Commission v Italy*, paragraph 57).

28. In that regard, where the national regulations for the designation of navigable waters and waterways have the effect of preventing users of personal watercraft from using them for the specific and inherent purposes for which they were intended or of greatly restricting their use, which is for the national court to ascertain, such regulations have the effect of hindering the access to the domestic market in question for those goods and therefore constitute, save where there is a justification pursuant to Article 30 EC or there are overriding public interest requirements, measures having equivalent effect to quantitative restrictions on imports prohibited by Article 28 EC.

The ECJ accepted, however, that the national rule could be justified for the protection of the environment, provided that certain conditions were met.[70]

7 THE CURRENT LAW: SUMMARY

The academic reaction to the case law on product use has been mixed, with commentators divided as to its impact on the previous law and as to the desirability of the tests used by the ECJ.[71] This area is indeed complex. This section will therefore attempt to summarize the existing law, which will then be assessed in the section that follows.

It is clear from the ECJ's formulation in the two cases on product use that Article 34 covers three types of national rules: those that discriminate, those that impose product requirements, and those that hinder or inhibit market access.[72] National rules concerning sales are not regarded *per se* as inhibiting market access and are only caught insofar as they apply differentially in law or fact to the marketing of domestic products and those from other Member States.[73] It remains to be seen whether selling arrangements disappear as a separate category of case, and are determined simply in terms of market access. Even if this occurs, cases concerned with selling arrangements will remain a prominent type of case in which issues of market access are considered.

The differences of view between commentators as to the current state of the positive law are ultimately explicable according to how one regards the interrelationship between the three types of case covered by Article 34. There are two possible 'readings' of the current law.

---

[70] Case C–142/05 *Åklagaren v Percy Mickelsson and Joakim Roos* [2009] ECR I–4273, [35]–[44].

[71] L Gormley, 'Silver Threads among the Gold…50 Years of the Free Movement of Goods' (2008) 31 Fordham Int LJ 1637; G Davies, '"Process and Production Method"-Based Trade Restrictions in the EU' (2007–8) 10 CYELS; L Prete, 'Of Motorcycle Trailers and Personal Watercrafts: The Battle over *Keck*' (2008) 35 LIEI 133; E Spaventa, 'Leaving *Keck* Behind? The Free Movement of Goods after the Rulings in *Commission v Italy* and *Mickelsson and Roos*' (2009) 34 ELRev 914; P Pecho, 'Good-Bye *Keck*?: A Comment on the Remarkable Judgment in *Commission v Italy*, C–110/05' (2009) 36 LIEI 257; C Barnard, 'Trailing a New Approach to Free Movement of Goods' (2009) 68 CLJ 288; C Barnard, 'Restricting Restrictions: Lessons for the EU from the US?' (2009) 68 CLJ 575; T Horsley, 'Anyone for *Keck*?' (2009) 46 CMLRev 2001; P Wennerås and K Boe Moen, 'Selling Arrangements, Keeping *Keck*' (2010) 35 ELRev 387; M Derlén and J Lindholm, 'Article 28 EC and Rules on Use: A Step Towards a Workable Doctrine on Measures Having Equivalent Effect to Quantitative Restrictions' (2009–10) 16 CJEL 191; J Snell, 'The Notion of Market Access: A Concept or a Slogan?' (2010) 47 CMLRev 437; A Tryfonidou, 'Further Steps on the Road to Convergence among the Market Freedoms' (2010) 35 ELRev 36.

[72] Case C–110/05 *Commission v Italy* (n 69) [34]; Case C–142/05 *Åklagaren* (n 70) [24].

[73] Case C–110/05 *Commission v Italy* (n 69) [36].

The first view regards market access as the overarching principle. On this view discrimination and product requirements are simply the principal examples of national rules that inhibit market access, without thereby precluding the possibility that there may be other cases that can have the same effect. The case law could be read in this manner.[74]

The second view sees market access merely as a residual category. On this view discrimination and product requirements are the primary categories of case that fall within Article 34, with market access simply being used as the criterion to capture other cases that do not fall within the first two. The case law could also be read in this manner.[75]

8 THE CURRENT LAW: ASSESSMENT

The two views as to the reading of the current law are reflected in contrasting normative assessments of what Article 34 ought to cover.

(A) MARKET ACCESS AS OVERARCHING PRINCIPLE

(i) *The Argument*

The view that market access is and should be the overarching principle that determines the reach of Article 34 can be seen in the reaction to the *Keck* decision, which was not generally favourable.[76] It was argued that *Keck* placed too much emphasis on factual and legal equality at the expense of market access. The approach in *Keck* was to deny that rules relating to selling arrangements came within Article 34, provided that such rules did not discriminate in law or fact between traders from different Member States. It was argued that this ignored market access: trading rules could be formally equal, but still inhibit market access, and thus should not be excluded from Article 34.

The concern was voiced judicially by Advocate General Jacobs in *Leclerc-Siplec*.[77] The case concerned a prohibition on television advertising imposed by French law on the distribution sector, in order to protect the regional press by forcing the sector to advertise through that medium. He felt that advertising could be important in breaking down barriers to inter-state trade, and should not always fall outside Article 34.[78]

Advocate General Jacobs' starting point was that all undertakings engaged in legitimate economic activity should have unfettered access to the market. If there was a *substantial* restriction on that access then it should be caught by Article 34. When the measure affected the goods themselves, as in *Cassis*-type cases, then it would be *presumed to have this* substantial impact. If, however, the contested measure affected selling arrangements and was not discriminatory, the substantiality of the impact would depend on: the range of goods affected, the nature of the restriction, whether the impact was direct or indirect, and the extent to which other selling arrangements were available. If

---

[74] Case C–142/05 *Åklagaren* (n 70) [24].

[75] Case C–110/05 *Commission v Italy* (n 69) [34], [37].

[76] N Reich, 'The "November Revolution" of the European Court of Justice: *Keck, Meng* and *Audi* Revisited' (1994) 31 CMLRev 459; D Chalmers, 'Repackaging the Internal Market—The Ramifications of the *Keck* Judgment' (1994) 19 ELRev 385; L Gormley, 'Reasoning Renounced? The Remarkable Judgment in *Keck & Mithouard*' [1994] EBLRev 63; S Weatherill, 'After *Keck*: Some Thoughts on How to Clarify the Clarification' (1996) 33 CMLRev 885; Maduro (n 2) 83–87; C Barnard, 'Fitting the Remaining Pieces into the Goods and Persons Jigsaw?' (2001) 26 ELRev 35.

[77] Case 412/93 (n 61) [38]–[45].

[78] See also AG Jacobs in Case C–384/93 *Alpine Investments* (n 86); AG Lenz in Case C–391/92 *Commission v Greece* [1995] ECR I–1621, 1628–1629.

there was no substantial impact, or the effect on trade was *de minimis*, then such measures would not be within Article 34. The ECJ, however, declined to follow the Advocate General and applied *Keck* to the case.

The approach of Advocate General Jacobs nonetheless influenced the ECJ's later jurisprudence, where it has taken market access more seriously,[79] by considering whether the selling rule could have the same factual impact for the importer. It was not fortuitous that Advocate General Jacobs wrote the Opinions in *de Agostini*[80] and *Gourmet International*,[81] and that the ECJ adopted much of his reasoning. Market access also featured in the product use cases.[82] The approach based on market access has been supported by Advocates General Maduro, Bot, and Trstenjak.[83]

Thus on this view market access is the dominant principle that determines the ambit of Article 34, while recognizing that its application may differ in different types of case. Discriminatory rules are caught not merely because they are protectionist, but because they thereby inhibit access to the relevant market. *Cassis*-type indistinctly applicable product rules are caught because they impose supplementary costs on cross-border activity that impedes market access.[84] Other cases, whether concerned with selling arrangements or product use, are caught insofar as they impede market access.

There was also academic support for the market access approach. Weatherill[85] drew on the reasoning of Advocate General Jacobs, and on jurisprudence concerned with Articles 56 and 45 TFEU.[86] He argued that national measures that applied equally in law and in fact to all goods and services without reference to origin, and which imposed no direct or substantial hindrance to the access of imported goods or services to the market of that Member State should not be caught by Articles 34 and 56 TFEU. The academic argument in favour of market access was reinforced by Barnard.[87]

C Barnard, Fitting the Remaining Pieces into the Goods and Persons Jigsaw?[88]

[A]n approach based on the access to the market provides us with a more sophisticated framework for analysing the goods and persons case law.…[T]his is the approach advocated by Advocate General Jacobs in *Leclerc*. Non-discriminatory measures which directly and substantially impede access to the market (including the extreme case of preventing access to the market altogether) breach the Treaty provision unless they can be justified under one of the public interest grounds or the express derogations and are proportionate (*Schindler*, *Alpine* and *Bosman*). In the case of non-discriminatory measures which do not substantially hinder access to the market the Court will say either that the impediment is too uncertain and remote and so does not breach the Treaty provision at all (*Graf*, *Krantz*), or that the measure has no effect whatsoever on inter-state trade and so is not caught by

---

[79] Cases C–34–36/95 *de Agostini* (n 59); Case C–254/98 *Schutzverband gegen unlauteren Wettbewerb v TK-Heimdienst Sass GmbH* [2000] ECR I–151; Case C–416/00 *Morellato* (n 63) [31]; Case C–98/01 *Commission v United Kingdom and Northern Ireland* [2003] ECR I–4641, [46].

[80] Cases C–34–36/95 *De Agostini* (n 59) [95]–[105].

[81] Case C–405/98 *Konsumentombudsmannen (KO) v Gourmet International Products AB (GIP)* [2001] ECR I–1795.

[82] Case C–110/05 *Commission v Italy* (n 69); Case C–142/05 *Åklagaren* (n 70).

[83] Cases C–158 and 159/04 *Alfa Vita* (n 64) [45] AG Maduro; Case C–110/05 *Commission v Italy* (n 69) [108]–[138] AG Bot; Case C–205/07 *Gysbrechts* (n 38) [59]–[61] AG Trstenjak.

[84] Cases C–158 and 159/04 *Alfa Vita* (n 64) [43]–[45] AG Maduro.

[85] S Weatherill, 'After *Keck*: Some Thoughts on How to Clarify the Clarification' (1996) 33 CMLRev 885.

[86] Case C–384/93 *Alpine Investments BV v Minister van Financiën* [1995] ECR I–1141; Case C–415/93 *Union Royale Belge des Sociétés de Football Association ASBL v Jean-Marc Bosman* [1995] ECR I–4921.

[87] See however Barnard, 'Restricting Restrictions' (n 71) for a more cautious approach.

[88] (2001) 26 ELRev 35, 52.

EC law at all—the outcome is the same. This means that national restrictions on, for example, planning or the green belt, which were introduced for a variety of environmental and social reasons not directly concerned with inter-state trade, can be dealt with adequately. They are not 'certain selling arrangements' in the formal sense, but they are not discriminatory and they do not substantially hinder access to the market. Similarly, national restrictions on the opening hours of shops do not substantially hinder access to the market but merely curtail the exercise of that freedom. However extreme limits on opening hours may well substantially hinder access to the market and so should breach Article 28 and need to be justified.

(ii) *Market Access: Meaning and Application*

Market access may well be the idea underlying free movement, but it is necessary to clarify its meaning. Market access can be viewed from the perspective of both producer and consumer. For the producer, free movement facilitates sales of goods into different national markets, to challenge existing producers in the country of import. Market access is a means to an end, the end being to maximize sales/profits for the individual producer, and to enhance the optimal allocation of resources in the EU. From the perspective of the consumer, free movement increases choice. If Germans are given the option of drinking Dutch beer then some may prefer it to the domestic product.

Given that this is so, it is doubtful whether a rigid distinction can be drawn between dynamic and static selling arrangements so far as market access is concerned. The market-access approach is normally thought to apply to dynamic selling arrangements. There is, however, a reluctance to apply the reasoning to static selling arrangements, in the sense of shop hours, locations, and the like. If, however, 'limitations' on the mode of marketing/advertising are to be regarded as going to market access, then it is difficult to see why this should not also be so in terms of 'limitations' on points of sale. The success of the producer in penetrating new markets may be affected by limitations on where and when goods can be sold as by constraints on marketing.[89] It may be argued that restrictions on where and when goods can be sold would not have a direct and substantial impact on market access. This is, however, contingent on the factual circumstances of the particular case. It cannot be regarded as an *a priori* proposition. It is similarly difficult to maintain a rigid distinction between rules going to access and those that merely affect the volume of sales. A producer perceives rules that limit advertising as detrimental *because* they will lead to a reduction in sales. There is no difference between a rule prohibiting certain forms of marketing or advertising leading to a diminution in sales of 30 per cent and a rule which limits the number or operating hours of shops, leading to the same sales reduction. Both rules can affect the volume of sales and penetration of the new market. Non-discriminatory static selling arrangements may therefore, as Barnard rightly notes, substantially hinder market access.[90]

It is important moreover to be cognizant of the difficulties of applying a test based on market access. Proponents of the test recognize that this can be difficult to estimate.[91] A court may have to take into account the range of goods affected, the existence or not of alternative selling arrangements, and the nature of the restriction itself.[92] This will not be an easy task for the ECJ. It will be

---

[89] This was the argument made, unsuccessfully, in Cases C–418–421, 460–462 and 464/93, 9–11, 14–15, 23–24 and 332/94 *Semeraro* (n 50).

[90] Barnard (n 88) 52.

[91] Weatherill (n 85) 898–901; Barnard (n 88) 55–56; Snell (n 71) 459.

[92] See, for discussion of a *de minimis* test in this context, M Janson and H Kalimo, '*De minimis* Meets "Market Access": Transformations in the Substance—and the Syntax—of EU Free Movement Law?' (2014) 51 CMLRev 523.

even more difficult for national courts,[93] although the ECJ may provide guidance to the national court, as in *Agostini*,[94] or it may go further and state there has been an impediment to market access, as in *Gourmet International*.[95] It is true that the EU and national courts face not dissimilar tasks in competition law, when deciding whether an agreement has an effect on competition. There are, however, real differences between the two areas. In competition law the backdrop to the inquiry is a developed micro-economic theory about cartels that deviate from perfect or imperfect competition. In free movement of goods there is no ready consensus on what comes within the meaning of market access. In competition law private agreements are at stake. In free movement it is national regulations.

(B) MARKET ACCESS AS SLOGAN

(i) *The Argument*

There are, however, other commentators who are sceptical as to whether market access can or should be regarded as the overarching principle for free movement of goods, or more generally for the law of free movement.[96]

Thus Snell argues that if the concern is in reality that imported goods are affected more than domestic products then we should simply speak in terms of factual, legal, or indirect discrimination, or differential impact, the conclusion being that the concept of market access adds little, if anything, to such analysis.[97] He contends that, when pressed, the concept of market access collapses into economic freedom or anti-protectionism. It collapses into economic freedom in the sense that national regulation of economic activity often imposes a burden on cross-border situations, commonly through an impact on profitability. All limits to economic freedom therefore have more or less significant effects on market access, which depend ultimately on their impact on profits, with the consequence that if 'the law were to prohibit each and every hindrance to market access, it would as a matter of logic have to ban all rules limiting the commercial freedom of traders'.[98] Snell maintains that the concept of market access might alternatively collapse into anti-protectionism. Measures that impede new entrants to a market necessarily protect established operators, which usually means domestic actors, the conclusion being that all impediments to market access 'can be portrayed as a weapon in the fight against protectionism'.[99] He concludes in the following vein.

J Snell, The Notion of Market Access: A Concept or a Slogan?[100]

The notion of market access obscures rather than illuminates. The most fundamental question for free movement law remains whether the law is about discrimination and anti-protectionism, in which case a relative or comparative test based on a perceptible disparate impact is appropriate, or whether it is about economic freedom, in which case an absolute test not involving comparisons is necessary. The

---

[93] National courts are intended to apply Art 34 and hence to disapply conflicting national law of their own initiative, subject to the possibility of an Art 267 reference: Case C–358/95 *Tommaso Morellato v Unità Sanitairia Locale (USL) No 11 di Pordenone* [1997] ECR I–1431.

[94] Cases C–34–36/95 (n 59).

[95] Case C–405/98 (n 81).

[96] E Spaventa, *Free Movement of Persons in the European Union* (Kluwer, 2007) 89; Spaventa (n 71) 929.

[97] Snell (n 71) 448–449.

[98] Ibid 468.

[99] Ibid 468.

[100] (2010) 47 CMLRev 437, 470–471.

notion of market access promises that this stark choice does not have to be made. It envisages a third way between anti-protectionism and economic freedom. Yet the more than fifteen years of case law following the ruling in *Keck* has failed to clarify where exactly this middle ground might be between the right not to be discriminated against and the right not to be subjected to unjustified regulation lies. Currently, the Court's analysis in the main seems to focus on the significance of the impact of the measure, with all the uncertainties this approach entails. At the same time, it denies that rules with an insignificant effect fall outside the scope of the Treaty...As a result the precise meaning of market access remains elusive. It may be that the notion of market access simply conceals the need to choose between the competing paradigms of free movement law. If so, the term should be abandoned as an unhelpful slogan.

(ii) *Market Access: Form and Substance*

Snell presents a powerful counter to those who regard market access as the overarching principle. It is nonetheless debatable how far this critique is one of form or substance.

It is common for judges and commentators to seek the background principle that explicates the more detailed rules that apply within a body of law. The background principle embodies the values that the more particular doctrinal rules are designed to effectuate and serves as a reference point when deciding whether there should be incremental extension of those doctrinal rules. The relationship between the background value and the doctrine is symbiotic, in the sense that the former will inform the latter, but doctrinal development may also lead to re-evaluation of the background value or values.

Market access could be said to be the overarching principle in relation to free movement of goods, in the manner articulated in the previous section. Let us imagine that in accord with Snell's argument we drop all mention of the term, and excise it from our jurisprudence. We talk instead, for example, about discrimination, differential impact, or anti-protectionism. It is questionable whether this would be preferable for the following reasons.

First, if discrimination or differential impact were to be regarded as the background value this invites the further inquiry as to why we are concerned about such matters. A response cast in terms of, for example, anti-protectionism likewise prompts the inquiry as to what such protectionism hinders, and such inquiries lead us back in substance to market access, even if we are reluctant to use that precise phrase.

Secondly, it is not self-evident that casting the background value or principle in terms of, for example, anti-protectionism is preferable to market access. The core doctrinal component within free movement of goods is indeed discrimination, direct and indirect. The doctrine was, however, extended in *Cassis* to indistinctly applicable product rules that nonetheless have a differential impact on importers, and it has been applied further in cases on sale and use in the manner considered above. If anti-protectionism were to be regarded as the background value we would then have to acknowledge that its meaning differed in the different parts of doctrine that comprise free movement of goods. Protectionism is a pejorative term, the paradigm being direct discrimination against foreign goods. It is not self-evident that protectionism is an apt background value to capture other doctrinal elements of free movement, or at the very least it would bear a different meaning. Indistinctly applicable rules embody national regulatory choices about particular products, sales, or use, irrespective of who produces them. The existence of such rules can impose extra costs on the importer, hence the decision to bring such rules within the remit of Article 34. It is nonetheless questionable whether such rules should be described as 'protectionist', and if they are so described the term would not bear the same meaning that it has in the paradigm instance of direct discrimination.

Thirdly, there are indubitably problems about the application of the market access test, as we have seen above. The adjudicative difficulties would not be obviated if that concept were to be excised from the law. Insofar as current doctrine requires the analysis of differential impact the difficulties that beset such determinations would remain.

(c) SUMMARY AND CHOICES

i. The case law prior to *Keck* exemplified the difficulties in defining the outer boundaries of Article 34. *Keck* itself was criticized for being overly formalistic, by drawing a distinction between rules relating to the characteristics of the product and those concerning selling arrangements, which is unsatisfactory. This dissatisfaction led to the call to focus on market access. Article 34 now covers three types of national rule: those that discriminate, those that impose product requirements, and those that inhibit market access, although the interrelationship between them is contestable in the manner described above. There are in essence four choices concerning the approach to Article 34.

ii. The first choice is to *use prevention, or direct and substantial hindrance, of access to the market as the background principle for the applicability of Article 34*. This would, subject to the preceding discussion, focus attention on a key background value underlying free movement of goods. The need to consider whether there has been some substantial restriction of market access, however, inevitably entails costs, both for courts applying the test and for private parties who may be uncertain about the legality of their planned conduct.

iii. The second choice is *for a test based on substantial hindrance to market access, subject to presumptions based on the type of case*. This was the approach of Advocate General Jacobs in *Leclerc-Siplec*.[101] When the measure affected the goods themselves, as in *Cassis*-type cases, then it would be presumed to have this substantial impact. If, however, the contested measure affected selling arrangements and was not discriminatory, the substantiality of the impact would depend on a range of factors.

iv. The third choice *would be to persist with the three categories of case currently held to fall within Article 34 and regard market access merely as a residual category and not the overarching principle*.

v. The fourth choice *would be to discard market access and focus instead on discrimination and differential impact as the organizing criteria*. The adjudicative difficulties in deciding on the application of this test would not, however, be less significant than for the other tests.

9 DEFENCES TO DISCRIMINATORY MEASURES: ARTICLE 36

If trade rules are found to be discriminatory[102] they can be saved through Article 36 TFEU:

The provisions of Articles 34 and 35 shall not preclude prohibitions or restrictions on imports, exports or goods in transit justified on grounds of public morality, public policy or public security; the protection of health and life of humans, animals or plants; the protection of national treasures possessing artistic,

---

[101] (N 61).

[102] It may be debatable whether a rule really is discriminatory, and therefore whether it is caught by Art 34 and requires justification under Art 36. See, eg, Case C–2/90 *Commission v Belgium* [1992] ECR I–4431, noted by L Hancher and H Sevenster (1993) 30 CMLRev 351, and D Geradin (1993) 18 ELRev 144.

historic or archaeological value; or the protection of industrial and commercial property. Such prohibitions or restrictions shall not, however, constitute a means of arbitrary discrimination or a disguised
restriction on trade between Member States.

It will come as no surprise to learn that the Court has construed Article 36 strictly. Discriminatory
rules will be closely scrutinized to ensure that the defence is warranted. They must also pass a test of
proportionality: the discriminatory measure must be the least restrictive possible to attain the end in
view. The burden of proof under Article 36 rests with the Member State.[103] Member State application
of the justifications listed in Article 36 is now subject to important new conditions laid down by EU
legislation discussed below.[104]

(A) PUBLIC MORALITY

Two of the main precedents concerned challenges to laws dealing with pornography. In *Henn and
Darby*[105] the ECJ was willing to accept that a UK ban on the import of pornography could be justified
under Article 36, notwithstanding the fact that domestic law did not ban absolutely possession of such
material. The ECJ concluded that the overall purpose of UK law was to restrain pornography, and
that there was no lawful trade in such goods within the UK. However, a different result was reached
in *Conegate*.

Case 121/85 **Conegate Ltd v Commissioners of Customs and Excise**
[1986] ECR 1007

[Note Lisbon Treaty renumbering: Arts 30, 36, and 177 are now Arts 34, 36, and 267 TFEU]

Conegate imported life-size inflatable dolls from Germany into the UK. The invoice for the dolls claimed
that they were for window displays, but the Customs officials were unconvinced, particularly when
they found items described as 'love love dolls'. They seized the goods. Conegate argued that this was
in breach of Article 30. The national court asked whether a prohibition on imports could be justified
even though the state did not ban the manufacture or marketing of the same goods within the national
territory. The ECJ repeated its reasoning from *Henn and Darby* that it was for each Member State to
decide upon the nature of public morality for its own territory. It continued as follows.

THE ECJ

15. However, although Community law leaves the Member States free to make their own assessments of the indecent or obscene character of certain articles, it must be pointed out that the fact that
goods cause offence cannot be regarded as sufficiently serious to justify restrictions on the free movement of goods where the Member State concerned does not adopt, with respect to the same goods
manufactured or marketed within its territory, penal measures or other serious and effective measures
intended to prevent the distribution of such goods in its territory.

---

[103] Case C–17/93 *Openbaar Ministerie v Van der Veldt* [1994] ECR I–3537; Case C–110/05 *Commission v Italy* [2009]
ECR I–519, [62]; Case C–165/08 *Commission v Poland* [2009] ECR I–6843, [53].
[104] Regulation (EC) No 764/2008 of the European Parliament and of the Council of 9 July 2008 laying down procedures relating to the application of certain national technical rules to products lawfully marketed in another Member
State and repealing Decision No 3052/95/EC [2008] OJ L218/21.
[105] Case 34/79 *R v Henn and Darby* [1979] ECR 3795.

16. It follows that a Member State may not rely on grounds of public morality to prohibit the importation of goods from other Member States when its legislation contains no prohibition on the manufacture or marketing of the same goods on its territory.

...

18. In this instance...the High Court took care to define the substance of the national legislation the compatibility of which with Community law is a question which it proposes to determine. Thus it refers to rules in the importing Member State under which the goods in question may be manufactured freely and marketed subject only to certain restrictions...namely an absolute prohibition on the transmission of such goods by post, a restriction on their public display and, in certain areas of the Member States concerned, a system of licensing of premises for the sale of those goods to customers aged 18 years and over. Such restrictions cannot however be regarded as equivalent in substance to a prohibition on manufacture and marketing.

The UK's defence failed. The distinction between *Conegate* and *Henn and Darby* lies in the ECJ's evaluation of whether the banned imported goods were being treated more harshly than similar domestic goods. In *Henn and Darby* the ECJ was willing to find that UK law restrained pornography sufficiently to enable it to conclude that there was no lawful trade in such goods in the UK. In *Conegate*, by way of contrast, the ECJ reached the opposite conclusion. While Member States can determine the public morality applicable within their territory, they cannot place stricter burdens on goods coming from outside than those applied to equivalent domestic goods.

(B) PUBLIC POLICY

Public policy is a ground of justification within Article 36, but the ECJ has resisted attempts to interpret it too broadly. The Court has, for example, rejected arguments that the term 'public policy' can embrace consumer protection. The ECJ has reasoned that since Article 36 derogates from a fundamental rule of the Treaty enshrined in Article 34, it must be interpreted strictly, and cannot be extended to objectives not mentioned therein.[106] A public policy justification cannot therefore be used to advance a separate ground for defence. It is for this reason that relatively few cases contain detailed examination of the public policy argument. The issue was considered in *Centre Leclerc*:

Case 231/83 **Cullet v Centre Leclerc**
[1985] ECR 305

[Note Lisbon Treaty renumbering: Arts 30 and 36 are now Arts 34 and 36 TFEU]

French legislation imposed minimum retail prices for fuel fixed primarily on the basis of French refinery prices and costs. The Court found that this constituted an MEQR within Article 30, since imports could not benefit fully from lower cost prices in the country of origin. The French Government sought to justify its action on the basis of public policy within Article 36. It argued that, in the absence of the pricing rules, there would be civil disturbances, blockades, and violence. Both the Advocate General and the ECJ rejected this argument, but for different reasons.

---

[106] Case 113/80 *Commission v Ireland* [1981] ECR 1625; Case 177/83 *Kohl v Ringelhan* [1984] ECR 3651; Case 229/83 *Leclerc v Au Blé Vert* [1985] ECR 1.

ADVOCATE GENERAL VERLOREN VAN THEMAAT[107]

However, I would add that the acceptance of civil disturbances as justification for encroachments upon the free movement of goods would, as is apparent from experiences of last year (and before, during the Franco–Italian 'wine war') have unacceptably drastic consequences. If roadblocks and other effective weapons of interest groups which feel threatened by the importation and sale at competitive prices of certain cheap products or services, or by immigrant workers or foreign businesses, were accepted as justification, the existence of the four fundamental freedoms of the Treaty could no longer be relied upon. Private interest groups would then, in the place of the Treaty and Community (and, within the limits laid down by the Treaty, national) institutions, determine the scope of those freedoms. In such cases, the concept of public policy requires, rather, effective action on the part of the authorities to deal with such disturbances.

THE ECJ

32. For the purpose of applying Article 36, the French Government has invoked the disturbances to law and order (*ordre public*) and public security caused by violent reactions which should be expected from retailers affected by unrestricted competition.

33. On this point it is sufficient to observe that the French Government has not shown that an amendment of the regulations in question in conformity with the principles set out above would have consequences for law and order (*ordre public*) and public security which the French Government would be unable to meet with the resources available to it.

The Advocate General rejected the French argument on principle, but the ECJ appeared to accept that it could be pleaded under Article 36, while rejecting it on the facts. The ECJ's approach might have been a more diplomatic way of disposing of the point, but the Advocate General is more convincing as a matter of principle. If interest-group pressure leading to potential violence could constitute justification under Article 36 then fundamental EU freedoms would be placed in jeopardy.[108]

(c) PUBLIC SECURITY

Case 72/83 **Campus Oil Ltd v Minister for Industry and Energy**
[1984] ECR 2727

[Note Lisbon Treaty renumbering: Arts 30 and 36 are now Arts 34 and 36 TFEU]

Irish law required importers of petrol into Ireland to buy 35 per cent of their requirements from a state-owned oil refinery at prices fixed by the Irish Government. This rule was held to constitute an MEQR. In defence Ireland relied on public policy and security within Article 36. It argued that it was vital for Ireland to maintain its own oil-refining capacity. The challenged rule was the means of ensuring that its refinery products could be marketed. The ECJ held that recourse to Article 36 would not be possible

---

[107] [1985] 2 CMLR 524, 534.

[108] In Case C–265/95 *Commission v France* [1997] ECR I–6959, the ECJ accepted that serious disruption to public order could justify non-intervention by the police in relation to a specific incident, but that it could not justify any general policy of this nature. See also *R v Chief Constable of Sussex, ex p International Traders' Ferry Ltd* [1997] 2 CMLR 164.

if there were Community rules providing the necessary protection for oil supplies. Certain Community measures existed, but they were not comprehensive. The Court continued as follows.

THE ECJ

31. Consequently, the existing Community rules give a Member State whose supplies of petroleum products depend totally or almost totally on deliveries from other countries certain guarantees that deliveries from other Member States will be maintained in the event of a serious shortfall in proportions which match those of supplies to the market of the supplying State. However, this does not mean that the Member State concerned has an unconditional assurance that supplies will in any event be maintained at least at a level sufficient to meet its minimum needs. In those circumstances, the possibility for a Member State to rely on Article 36 to justify appropriate complementary measures at national level cannot be excluded, even where there exist Community rules on the matter.

[The Court then considered whether the term 'public security' could cover this situation.]

34. It should be stated in this connection that petroleum products, because of their exceptional importance as an energy source in the modern economy, are of fundamental importance for a country's existence since not only its economy but above all its institutions, its essential public services and even the survival of the inhabitants depend upon them. An interruption of supplies of petroleum products, with the resultant dangers for the country's existence, could therefore seriously affect the public security that Article 36 allows States to protect.

35. It is true that, as the Court has held on a number of occasions, most recently in . . . (Case 95/81, Commission v Italy), Article 36 refers to matters of a non-economic nature. A Member State cannot be allowed to avoid the effects of measures provided for in the Treaty by pleading the economic difficulties caused by elimination of barriers to intra-Community trade. However, in the light of the seriousness of the consequences that an interruption in supplies of petroleum products may have for a country's existence, the aim of ensuring a minimum supply of petroleum products at all times is to be regarded as transcending purely economic considerations and thus as capable of constituting an objective covered by the concept of public security.

While the ECJ accepted the public-security argument in *Campus Oil*, the circumstances to which it will be applicable are limited.[109] There is little enthusiasm for extending the reasoning, and in *Centre Leclerc* Advocate General VerLoren van Themaat distinguished *Campus Oil* from the situation in *Centre Leclerc*.[110] Member States can however take certain measures relating to national security pursuant to what are now Articles 346–348 TFEU.

(D) PROTECTION OF HEALTH AND LIFE OF HUMANS, ANIMALS, OR PLANTS

(i) *Health Protection as Real Purpose or Disguised Trade Restriction*

There have been numerous cases in which states have defended measures on this ground. The ECJ closely scrutinizes such claims to determine whether protection of public health is the Member States' real purpose, or whether the measure was designed to protect domestic producers. This is exemplified by *Commission v United Kingdom*.[111] The UK in effect banned poultry meat imports from most other

---

[109] Case C–367/89 *Richardt* [1991] ECR I–4621; Case C–398/98 *Commission v Greece* [2001] ECR I–7915, [29]–[30]; Case C–174/04 *Commission v Italy* [2005] ECR I–4933, [40]–[41].

[110] [1985] 2 CMLR 524, 535–536.

[111] Case 40/82 [1982] ECR 2793; Case 42/82 *Commission v France* [1983] ECR 1013; Case C–434/04 *Criminal proceedings against Jan-Erik Anders Ahokainen and Mati Leppik* [2006] ECR I–9171, [30].

Member States, on the ground that it was necessary to protect public health by preventing the spread of Newcastle disease that affected poultry. The ECJ held that the import ban was motivated more by commercial reasons, to block French poultry, than by public health. The ECJ will also closely examine the arguments concerning public health to determine whether they make sense on the facts.[112]

(ii) *The Determination of Public Health Claims*

The ECJ may have to decide whether a public-health claim is sustainable where there is no perfect consensus on the scientific or medical impact of particular substances. The ECJ's approach is exemplified by the *Sandoz* decision.

Case 174/82 **Officier van Justitie v Sandoz BV**
[1983] ECR 2445

Authorities in the Netherlands refused to allow the sale of muesli bars that contained added vitamins because the vitamins were dangerous to public health. The muesli bars were readily available in Germany and Belgium. It was accepted that vitamins could be beneficial to health, but that excessive consumption could be harmful. Scientific evidence was uncertain as regards the point at which such consumption became excessive, particularly because vitamins consumed in one source of food might be added to those eaten from a different source. There had been some Community legislation which touched on the general issue of food additives.

THE ECJ

15. The above mentioned Community measures clearly show that the Community legislature accepts the principle that it is necessary to restrict the use of food additives to the substances specified, whilst leaving the Member States a certain discretion to adopt stricter rules....

16. As the Court found in its judgment...in Case 272/80 (*Frans-Nederlandse Maatschappij voor Biologische Producten* [1981] ECR 3277), in so far as there are uncertainties at the present state of scientific research it is for the Member States, in the absence of harmonization, to decide what degree of protection of the health and life of humans they intend to assure, having regard however for the requirements of the free movement of goods within the Community.

17. Those principles also apply to substances such as vitamins which are not as a general rule harmful in themselves but may have special harmful effects solely if taken to excess as part of the general nutrition, the composition of which is unforeseeable and cannot be monitored. In view of the uncertainties inherent in the scientific assessment, national rules prohibiting, without prior authorization, the marketing of foodstuffs to which vitamins have been added are justified on principle within the meaning of Article 36 of the Treaty on the grounds of the protection of human health.

18. Nevertheless the principle of proportionality which underlies the last sentence of Article 36 of the Treaty requires that the power of the Member States to prohibit imports of the products in question from other Member States should be restricted to what is necessary to attain the legitimate aim of protecting public health....

19. Such an assessment is, however, difficult to make in relation to additives such as vitamins the above mentioned characteristics of which exclude the possibility of foreseeing or monitoring the quantities consumed as part of the general nutrition and the degree of harmfulness of which cannot be determined with sufficient certainty. Nevertheless, although in view of the present stage of harmonization of

---

[112] Case 124/81 *Commission v United Kingdom* [1983] ECR 203.

national laws at the Community level a wide discretion must be left to the Member States, they must, in order to observe the principle of proportionality, authorize marketing when the addition of vitamins to foodstuffs meets a real need, especially a technical or nutritional one.

20. The first question must therefore be answered to the effect that Community law permits national rules prohibiting without prior authorization the marketing of foodstuffs marketed in another Member State to which vitamins have been added, provided that the marketing is authorized when the addition of the vitamins meets a real need, especially a technical or nutritional one.

The ECJ's approach in *Sandoz* is finely tuned. It will decide whether the public health claim is sustainable in principle. If there is uncertainty about the medical implications of some substance it will,[113] in the absence of harmonization, be for the Member State to decide upon the appropriate degree of protection for its citizens, subject to proportionality.[114] When assessing proportionality the EU Courts will pay special attention to the factual basis of the defence. It is not enough for a Member State simply to assert that a measure is warranted on grounds of public health. The ECJ has demanded evidence or data from Member States to substantiate this claim,[115] even where there may be some scientific uncertainty about the matter.[116] The ECJ will, however, also accept, subject to proportionality, that Member States legitimately differ in the degree of protection that they accord to public health.[117]

(iii) *Health Checks and Double Checks*

A Member State may not ban imports, but it may subject them to checks, even though the goods were checked in the state of origin. This problem of double-checking has arisen frequently, and the ECJ has become stricter over time.

The early approach in *Denkavit*[118] was to urge national authorities to cooperate to avoid dual burdens. National authorities had a duty to ascertain whether the documents from the state of export raised a presumption that the goods complied with the demands of the importing state. The Court admitted, however, that a second set of checks in the state of import might be lawful, provided that the requirements were necessary and proportionate.

The Court's later case law exhibits a healthy scepticism regarding whether a second set of controls is really required. This is evident from *Commission v United Kingdom*[119] concerning UHT milk. The ECJ held that the UK's concerns about the product could be met by less restrictive means than the import ban and marketing system it had instituted. The UK could lay down requirements that imported milk had to meet, and could demand certificates from the authorities of the exporting state.[120] If such certificates were produced then it would be for the authorities within the importing state to ascertain

---

[113] See, however, Case 178/84 *Commission v Germany* [1987] ECR 1227.

[114] See also Case 53/80 *Officier van Justitie v Koniklijke Kaasfabriek Eyssen BV* [1981] ECR 409; Case 94/83 *Albert Heijin BV* [1984] ECR 3263; Case 304/84 *Ministère Public v Muller* [1986] ECR 1511; Case C–62/90 *Commission v Germany* [1992] ECR I–2575; Case C–192/01 *Commission v Denmark* [2003] ECR I–9693, [42]; Case C–24/00 *Commission v France* [2004] ECR I–1277, [49]; Case C–95/01 *Criminal Proceedings against John Greenham and Leonard Abel* [2004] ECR I–1333; Case C–366/04 *Schwarz v Bürgemeister der Landeshauptstadt Salzburg* [2005] ECR I–10139, [30]–[38]; Case C–170/04 *Klas Rosengren* (n 32) [37]–[58].

[115] Case C–270/02 *Commission v Italy* [2004] ECR I–1559.

[116] Case C–41/02 *Commission v Netherlands* [2004] ECR I–11375; Case C–192/01 *Commission v Denmark* (n 114); Case C–24/00 *Commission v France* (n 114); Case C–333/08 *Commission v France* [2010] ECR I–757, [83]–[110].

[117] Case C–141/07 *Commission v Germany* (n 68) [51]; Case C–434/04 *Ahokainen and Mati Leppik* (n 111) [32]–[33].

[118] Case 251/78 *Denkavit Futtermittel v Minister für Ernährung, Landwirtschaft und Forsten des Landes* [1979] ECR 3369.

[119] Case 124/81 *Commission v United Kingdom* [1983] ECR 203.

[120] Ibid [27]–[28].

whether these certificates raised a presumption that the imported goods complied with the demands of domestic legislation. The ECJ concluded that the conditions for such a presumption existed in this case.[121] A similar unwillingness to subject goods to a second set of checks can be seen in the *Biologische Producten* case.[122] Dual checks would not be lawful where they unnecessarily imposed technical tests that had already been done in the state of origin, nor where the practical effect of the tests in the exporting state met the demands of the importing state.[123]

(E) OTHER GROUNDS FOR VALIDATING DISCRIMINATORY MEASURES

The defences for discriminatory rules caught by Article 34 are contained in Article 36. The ECJ has extended Article 34 to indistinctly applicable rules, and created defences that overlap with, but are not identical to, those found in Article 36.[124] The salient issue is therefore whether justification for discriminatory rules is limited to the specific matters listed in Article 36, or whether a rule that is discriminatory might also be defended on a ground listed in *Cassis*.[125] The traditional view was that a Member State could not justify a discriminatory measure on grounds other than those listed in Article 36, even if the justification was in the list that could be invoked for indistinctly applicable measures.

It was questionable whether *Commission v Belgium*[126] was an exception to this proposition. The Commission challenged a Belgian regional decree which banned importation of waste into that area. The decree could be seen as discriminatory, since it did not cover disposal of locally produced waste. Notwithstanding this, the Court allowed environmental protection to be taken into account when considering the legality of the regional decree. The case could, therefore, be seen as allowing justifications to be pleaded that are not found in Article 36. However, the ECJ in effect held that the decree was not discriminatory, notwithstanding appearances to the contrary in the challenged instrument. This was because of the special nature of the subject matter, waste. There were strong arguments, the Court said, for disposing of such material locally, and each area had the responsibility for disposing of its own waste. Thus, although the decree applied only to imports it was not discriminatory.[127]

The relationship between Article 36 and the exceptions in *Cassis* is complicated by the fact that the dividing line between cases involving indirect discrimination and indistinctly applicable rules can be a fine one. This is exemplified by *Commission v Austria*,[128] which concerned an Austrian rule banning lorries in excess of a certain weight from using certain roads in order to protect the environment and air quality. Advocate General Geelhoed acknowledged that it was debatable whether the rule should be regarded as indirectly discriminatory or indistinctly applicable, and accepted that this could have implications for whether protection of the environment could be pleaded by way

---

[121] Ibid [30].

[122] Case 272/80 *Frans-Nederlandse Maatschappij voor Biologische Producten* [1981] ECR 3277.

[123] Ibid [14]–[15]; Case C–400/96 *Criminal Proceedings against Jean Harpegnies* [1998] ECR I–5121; Case C–432/03 *Commission v Portugal* [2005] ECR I–9665, [46].

[124] P Oliver, 'Some Further Reflections on the Scope of Articles 28–30 (ex 30–36)' (1999) 36 CMLRev 738; J Scott, 'Mandatory or Imperative Requirements in the EU and WTO' in Barnard and Scott (n 21) ch 10; P Oliver and W-H Roth, 'The Internal Market and the Four Freedoms' (2004) 41 CMLRev 407, 434–436.

[125] Case 120/78 (n 1).

[126] Case C–2/90 [1992] ECR I–4431.

[127] For indications that protection of the environment can however be raised in discrimination cases see, eg, Case C–203/96 *Chemische Afvalstoffen Dusseldorp BV v Minister van Volkshuisvesting, Ruimtelijke Ordening en Milieubeheer* [1998] ECR I–4075, [50].

[128] Case C–320/03 [2005] ECR I–9871.

of defence. The ECJ implicitly assumed that the Austrian rule was indistinctly applicable and that therefore protection of the environment could constitute an objective justification.

Advocate General Jacobs in *PreussenElektra*[129] questioned whether the list in Article 36 really is exhaustive. He argued that the approach in the *Walloon Waste* case was flawed, in the sense that whether a measure was discriminatory was logically distinct from whether it could be justified. He suggested moreover that there could be good reasons for allowing environmental protection to be pleaded as a justification, even in cases where there was direct discrimination. He argued more generally for a relaxation in the distinction between the justifications that could be pleaded under Article 36 and the rule of reason exceptions to *Cassis*. The ECJ did not, as Advocate General Jacobs suggested, give general guidance on the relationship between Article 36 and the exceptions to *Cassis*. It did however allow the national measure to be justified on environmental grounds.[130]

The ECJ has, more recently, evinced willingness to allow environmental protection to be pleaded as a defence without too close an inquiry into whether this should be rationalized under Article 36 or as a mandatory requirement for the purpose of the *Cassis* exceptions.[131] Advocate General Trstenjak has echoed the earlier suggestions by Advocate General Jacobs that protection of the environment could be a justification even in cases of discrimination,[132] although the discriminatory nature of the measure would affect proportionality. It will be argued more generally below that the same justifications should be applicable irrespective of whether the measure is discriminatory or not, although the application of the justification could be affected by this factor.[133]

(F) THE RELATIONSHIP BETWEEN HARMONIZATION AND ARTICLE 36

EU harmonization measures may make recourse to Article 36 TFEU inadmissible. This will be so where the EU measure is intended to harmonize the area totally. Member State action is thereby preempted. Thus in *Moormann*[134] the ECJ held that harmonization measures for poultry health inspections meant that a state could no longer use Article 36 to legitimate national rules on the matter. In *Commission v Germany*[135] it was held that directives had harmonized the measures that could be taken 'for the detection of a pronounced sexual odour in uncastrated male pigs', thereby preventing Germany from applying different measures.

Many EU measures are, however, not intended to harmonize an area totally. The objective will be minimum harmonization. It will be for the ECJ to decide whether the harmonization

---

[129] Case C–379/98 *PreussenElektra AG v Schleswag AG* [2001] ECR I–2099, [225]–[238]. See also Case C–320/03 *Commission v Austria* [2005] ECR I–9871, [96]–[108], AG Geelhoed.

[130] See also Case C–389/98 *Aher-Waggon GmbH v Bundesrepublik Deutschland* [1998] ECR I–4473.

[131] Case C–524/07 *Commission v Austria* [2008] ECR I–187, [57]; Case C–142/05 *Åklagaren* (n 70) [31]–[32]; Case C–28/09 *Commission v Austria* EU:C:2010:854.

[132] Case C–28/09 *Commission v Austria* EU:C:2010:770, [84]–[91].

[133] See below, p 705.

[134] Case 190/87 *Oberkreisdirektor v Moormann BV* [1988] ECR 4689. See also Case 5/77 *Tedeschi v Denkavit* [1977] ECR 1555; Cases C–277, 318 and 319/91 *Ligur Carni Srl v Unità Sanitaria Locale No XV di Genova* [1993] ECR I–6621; Case C–5/94 *R v Ministry of Agriculture, Fisheries and Food, ex p Hedley Lomas (Ireland) Ltd* [1996] ECR I–2553; Case C–1/96 *R v Minister of Agriculture, Fisheries, and Food, ex p Commission in World Farming Ltd* [1998] ECR I–1251; Case C–322/01 *Deutscher Apothekerverband* (n 68); Case C–443/02 *Nicolas Schreiber* [2004] ECR I–7275; Case C–309/02 *Radlberger Getränkegesellschaft mbH and Co and Spitz KG v Land Baden-Württemberg* [2004] ECR I–11763; Case C–132/08 *Lidl Magyarország Kereskedelmi bt v Nemzeti Hírközlési Hatóság Tanácsa* [2009] ECR I–3841.

[135] Case C–102/96 [1998] ECR I–6871.

measure covers the whole field, or whether it leaves room for national regulatory initiatives.[136] In the case of minimum harmonization, Member States are permitted to 'maintain and often to introduce more stringent regulatory standards than those prescribed by Community legislation, for the purposes of advancing a particular social or welfare interest, and provided that such additional requirements are compatible with the Treaty'.[137] Thus in *de Agostini* it was held that Community directives on 'Television without Frontiers' only partially harmonized the relevant law. They did not preclude national rules to control television advertising designed to protect consumers.[138] In the case of exhaustive harmonization, any national measure relating thereto must be assessed in the light of the harmonizing measure rather than the Treaty provisions.[139] The ECJ will ensure that such national regulations are proportionate and do not constitute a means of arbitrary discrimination.[140] Difficult issues can arise, even in the context of minimum harmonization, as to whether a Member State can impose more stringent welfare standards on goods entering its territory than those in the directive.[141]

10 DEFENCES TO INDISTINCTLY APPLICABLE RULES: THE MANDATORY REQUIREMENTS

(A) THE RATIONALE FOR THE MANDATORY REQUIREMENTS

It is necessary to consider separately defences to indistinctly applicable rules, although it is questionable whether there should be a separate set of defences for discriminatory and non-discriminatory rules. The rationale for the mandatory requirements is that many rules that regulate trade are also capable of restricting trade, yet some serve objectively justifiable purposes. The 'list' of mandatory requirements in *Cassis* is sometimes referred to as the rule of reason, drawing upon *Dassonville* to the effect that, in the absence of EU measures, reasonable trade rules would be accepted in certain circumstances. A similar approach is evident in other areas of EU law.[142] Thus Advocate General VerLoren van Themaat[143] regarded the rule of reason as a general principle of interpretation to mitigate the effects of strict prohibitions laid down in the Treaty provisions on free movement.[144] The burden of proving justification rests on the state relying on the mandatory requirement.[145] Member States' application of the mandatory requirements is now subject to important new conditions laid down by EU legislation discussed below.[146]

---

[136] See, eg, Case C–1/96 *Compassion in World Farming* (n 134); Case C–443/02 *Nicolas Schreiber* (n 134); Case C–309/02 *Radlberger* (n 134).

[137] M Dougan, 'Minimum Harmonization and the Internal Market' (2000) 37 CMLRev 853, 855.

[138] Cases C–34–36/95 *De Agostini* (n 59) [32]–[35].

[139] Case C–324/99 *DaimlerChrysler AG v Land Baden-Württemberg* [2001] ECR I–9897, [32]; Case C–309/02 *Radlberger* (n 134) [53]; Case C–322/01 *Deutscher Apothekerverband* (n 68) [64]; Case C–205/07 *Gysbrechts* (n 38) [33].

[140] Case 4/75 *Rewe-Zentralfinanz* (n 13); Case C–317/92 *Commission v Germany* [1994] ECR I–2039; Case 17/93 *Van der Veldt* (n 103).

[141] Compare Case C–1/96 *Compassion in World Farming* (n 134) with Case C–389/98 *Aher-Waggon* (n 130); Dougan (n 137) 868–884.

[142] See Chs 21, 22, 24.

[143] Case 286/81 *Oosthoek* (n 59).

[144] See also the discussion of the rule of reason in competition law, Ch 26.

[145] Case C–14/02 *ATRAL* (n 32) [67]–[68].

[146] Reg 764/2008 (n 104).

(B) THE RELATIONSHIP BETWEEN THE MANDATORY REQUIREMENTS AND ARTICLE 36

The traditional view has been that the *Cassis* mandatory requirements are separate from the justifications under Article 36, and could be used only for rules that were not discriminatory.[147] The *Cassis* list of mandatory requirements includes matters, such as the protection of consumers and the fairness of commercial transactions, which are not mentioned within Article 36, but the list is not exhaustive. The ECJ's willingness to create a broader category of justifications for indistinctly applicable rules is explicable because discriminatory rules strike at the heart of the EU, and hence justifications should be narrowly confined. The distinction between Article 36 and the mandatory requirements in *Cassis* has, however, come under increasing strain in recent years.

First, there has, as we have seen, been discussion about whether the list in Article 36 should be regarded as exhaustive.[148] It has been argued that there might be instances where, for example, environmental considerations could be pleaded in cases of discrimination.

Secondly, the distinction has also become less tenable because of the difficulty of distinguishing between cases involving indirect discrimination and indistinctly applicable rules.[149] The ECJ may well characterize a case as within the *Cassis* category because it wishes to allow the state to use a mandatory requirement, even though, as in *Aher-Waggon*,[150] the measure appears to be discriminatory or distinctly applicable.

Thirdly, *Keck* contributed to confusion in this respect. Selling arrangements are outside Article 34 provided that they apply to all traders in the national territory, and affect in the same manner, in law and fact, the marketing of domestic and imported products. Later cases have focused on the possible differential impact of national selling arrangements. If this is proven then Article 34 is applicable, subject to possible justifications. In some instances it will not matter whether the justification is considered within the mandatory requirements, or under Article 36, since it is covered by both, as in the case of public health.[151] In other instances it will be relevant, since the alleged justification falls only within the *Cassis* list. The ECJ has equivocated in some cases. Thus in *de Agostini*[152] the ECJ held that the advertising ban might satisfy a mandatory requirement *or* one of the aims listed in Article 36. Consumer protection and fair trading are in the former list, but not the latter.

There is much to be said for simplification. It would be best for the same justifications to be available in principle, irrespective of whether the measure is discriminatory or indistinctly applicable, although greater justification may be required for discriminatory measures. It might be argued that this is not possible, given the wording of Article 36. There is however no reason why phrases within Article 36, such as protection of the health and life of humans, could not be interpreted to include consumer protection and the environment. The ECJ has construed other Treaty provisions in a far more expansive manner when it wished to do so. Moreover, if it was legitimate in *Cassis* to create an open-ended list of mandatory exceptions, not mentioned in the Treaty, then it is difficult to see why it would not be legitimate for the ECJ to read Article 36 to include matters such as the environment or consumer protection.

---

[147] Case 788/79 *Gilli and Andres* (n 34) [6]; Case 113/80 *Commission v Ireland* [1981] ECR 1625, [5]–[8].

[148] See above, pp 702–703.

[149] See, eg, Case C–110/05 *Commission v Italy* (n 69) [35], [37], [59].

[150] See AG Jacobs in Case C–379/98 *PreussenElektra* (n 129) [227], commenting on Case C–389/98 *Aher-Waggon* (n 130).

[151] See, eg, Case C–189/95 *Franzen* (n 67); Case C–405/98 *Gourmet International* (n 81); Case C–322/01 *Deutscher Apothekerverband* (n 68).

[152] Cases C–34–36/95 *De Agostini* (n 59) [45]–[47].

(C) THE MANDATORY REQUIREMENTS: CONSUMER PROTECTION

Case 178/84 **Commission v Germany**
[1987] ECR 1227

German law prohibited the marketing of beer which was lawfully manufactured in another Member State unless it complied with sections 9 and 10 of the Biersteuergesetz (Beer Duty Act 1952), such that drinks could be only sold as '*Bier*' if they were made from barley, hops, yeast, and water. Germany argued that this was necessary to protect consumers, who associated '*Bier*' with these ingredients. The ECJ cited *Dassonville* and *Cassis*, and found that the German rule constituted an impediment to trade.

THE ECJ

31. The German Government's argument that section 10 of the Biersteuergesetz is essential in order to protect German consumers because, in their minds, the designation 'Bier' is inseparably linked to the beverage manufactured solely from the ingredients laid down in section 9...must be rejected.

32. Firstly, consumers' conceptions which vary from one Member State to the other are also likely to evolve in the course of time within a Member State. The establishment of the Common Market is, it should be added, one of the factors that may play a major contributory role in that development. Whereas rules protecting consumers against misleading practices enable such a development to be taken into account, legislation of the kind contained in section 10...prevents it from taking place. As the Court has already held in another context (Case 170/78, *Commission v United Kingdom*), the legislation of a Member State must not 'crystallize given consumer habits so as to consolidate an advantage acquired by national industries concerned to comply with them'.

33. Secondly, in the other Member States of the Community the designations corresponding to the German designation 'Bier' are generic designations for a fermented beverage manufactured from barley, whether malted barley on its own or with the addition of rice or maize. The same approach is taken in Community law as can be seen from heading 22.03 of the Common Customs Tariff. The German legislature itself utilises the designation 'Bier' in that way in section 9(7) and (8) of the Biersteuergesetz in order to refer to beverages not complying with the manufacturing rules laid down in section 9(1) and (2).

34. The German designation 'Bier' and its equivalents in the languages of the other Member States may therefore not be restricted to beers manufactured in accordance with the rules in force in the Federal Republic of Germany.

35. It is admittedly legitimate to seek to enable consumers who attribute specific qualities to beers manufactured from particular raw materials to make their choice in the light of that consideration. However...that possibility may be ensured by means which do not prevent the importation of products which have been lawfully manufactured and marketed in other Member States and, in particular, 'by the compulsory affixing of suitable labels giving the nature of the product sold'...

The ECJ therefore held German law in breach of Article 34. The argument concerning consumer protection was closely scrutinized to determine whether it really 'worked' on the facts of the case, and the ECJ assessed whether the interests of consumers could be safeguarded by less restrictive means: paragraph 35. The same approach is apparent in other cases.[153]

The ECJ has often rejected justifications based on consumer protection by stating that adequate labelling requirements can achieve the national objective with less impact on intra-EU trade. However, even labelling requirements may not escape Article 34. Thus in *Fietje*[154] the ECJ held that the obligation to use a certain name on a label could make it more difficult to market goods coming from other Member States, and would therefore have to be justified on the ground of consumer protection. Labelling requirements which demanded that the purchaser was provided with sufficient information about the product in order to prevent confusion with similar products could, said the Court, be justified, even if the effect was to make it necessary to alter the labels of some imported goods.[155] However, such protection would not be justifiable if the details given on the original labels of the goods contained the same information as required by the state of import, and that information was just as capable of being understood by consumers. Whether there was such equivalence was for the national court to determine.[156]

(D) THE MANDATORY REQUIREMENTS: FAIRNESS OF COMMERCIAL TRANSACTIONS

There is an overlap between consumer protection and the fairness of commercial transactions. This mandatory requirement has been used to justify national rules that seek to prevent unfair marketing practices, such as the selling of imported goods that are imitations of familiar domestic goods. It seems, however, that in order to be justified on this ground the national rule must not prohibit the marketing of goods which have been made according to fair and traditional practices in state A merely because they are similar to goods which have been made in state B.[157]

(E) THE MANDATORY REQUIREMENTS: PUBLIC HEALTH

The traditional view was that only indistinctly applicable rules could take advantage of the mandatory requirements. However, the ECJ has, on occasion, not been too concerned about whether it treats a justification within Article 36 or within the list of mandatory requirements, provided that the justification comes within both lists, more especially where it is unclear whether the impugned rule is discriminatory or indistinctly applicable. Public health is in the list of *Cassis* mandatory requirements and in Article 36. The following extract from the *German Beer* case provides an apt example of this, and the ECJ concluded that the challenged national rule was disproportionate:[158]

---

[153] See, eg, Case 261/81 *Rau* (n 35); Case 94/82 *De Kikvorsch Groothandel-Import-Export BV* [1983] ECR 947; Case C–293/93 *Ludomira Neeltje v Barbara Houtwipper* [1994] ECR I–429; Case C–470/93 *Verein gegen Unwesen in Handel und Gewerbe Köln eV v Mars GmbH* [1995] ECR I–1923; Case C–315/92 *Verband Sozialer Wettbewerb eV v Clinique Laboratoires SNC* [1994] ECR I–317; Case C–14/00 *Commission v Italy* [2003] ECR I–513.

[154] Case 27/80 *Fietje* [1980] ECR 3839.

[155] Ibid [11].

[156] Ibid [12]. See also Case 76/86 *Commission v Germany* [1989] ECR 1021.

[157] Case 58/80 *Dansk Supermarked v Imerco* [1981] ECR 181; Case 16/83 *Karl Prantl* [1984] ECR 1299.

[158] See also Case 53/80 *Koniklijke Kaasfabriek Eyssen* (n 114); Case 97/83 *Criminal Proceedings against Melkunie BV* [1984] ECR 2367.

Case 178/84 **Commission v Germany**
[1987] ECR 1227

[Note Lisbon Treaty renumbering: Arts 36 and 169 are now Arts 36 and 258 TFEU]

A second rule of German law was challenged in the *German Beer* case. Under the German Foodstuffs Act 1974 there was an absolute ban on the marketing of beer which contained additives. The Act prohibited non-natural additives on public-health grounds.

THE ECJ

41. The Court has consistently held (in particular in Case 174/82, *Criminal Proceedings Against Sandoz BV*) that 'in so far as there are uncertainties at the present state of scientific research it is for the Member States, in the absence of harmonization, to decide what degree of protection of the health and life of humans they intend to assure, having regard to the requirements of the free movement of goods within the Community.'

...

43. However, the application to imported products of prohibitions on marketing products containing additives which are authorised in the Member State of production but prohibited in the Member State of importation is permissible only in so far as it complies with the requirements of Article 36 of the Treaty as it has been interpreted by the Court.

44. It must be borne in mind, in the first place, that in its judgments in *Sandoz, Motte* and *Muller*, the Court inferred from the principle of proportionality underlying the last sentence of Article 36 of the Treaty that prohibitions on the marketing of products containing additives authorised in the Member State of production but prohibited in the Member State of importation must be restricted to what is actually necessary to secure the protection of public health. The Court also concluded that the use of a specific additive which is authorised in another Member State must be authorised in the case of a product imported from that Member State where, in view, on the one hand, of the findings of international scientific research, and in particular the work of the Community's Scientific Committee for Food, the Codex Alimentarius Committee of the Food and Agriculture Organisation of the United Nations (FAO) and the World Health Organisation, and, on the other, of the eating habits prevailing in the importing Member State, the additive in question does not present a risk to public health and meets a real need, especially a technical one.

45. Secondly, it should be remembered that, as the Court held in *Muller*, by virtue of the principle of proportionality, traders must also be able to apply, under a procedure which is easily accessible to them and can be concluded within a reasonable time, for the use of specific additives to be authorised by a measure of general application.

[*The Court pointed out that the German rule prohibited all additives; that there was no procedure whereby traders could obtain authorization for a specific additive; and that additives were permitted by German law in beverages other than beer. The German Government argued that such additives would not be needed in the manufacture of beer if it were made in accordance with section 9 of the Biersteuergesetz. The ECJ responded as follows:*]

51. It must be emphasised that the mere reference to the fact that beer can be manufactured without additives if it is made from only the raw materials prescribed in the Federal Republic of Germany does not suffice to preclude the possibility that some additives may meet a technological need. Such an interpretation of the concept of technological need, which results in favouring national production methods, constitutes a disguised means of restricting trade between Member States.

(f) OTHER MANDATORY REQUIREMENTS

The list of mandatory requirements in *Cassis* is not exhaustive. The ECJ stated that the mandatory requirements included *in particular* those mentioned in the judgment.[159] This has been confirmed by later cases. It can, in the absence of harmonization measures, include the protection of the environment.[160]

Case 302/86 **Commission v Denmark**
[1988] ECR 4607

[Note Lisbon Treaty renumbering: Art 30 is now Art 34 TFEU]

Danish law required that containers for beer and soft drinks should be returnable and that a proportion should be re-usable. A national environmental agency had to approve containers to ensure compliance with these criteria. There was also a deposit-and-return system for empty containers. The Danish Government argued that the rule was justified by a mandatory requirement related to the protection of the environment.

THE ECJ

8. The Court has already held in . . . Case 240/83, *Procureur de la République* v *Association de Défense des Brûleurs d'Huiles Usagées* . . . that the protection of the environment is 'one of the Community's essential objectives', which may as such justify certain limitations of the principle of free movement of goods. That view is moreover confirmed by the Single European Act.

9. In view of the foregoing, it must therefore be stated that the protection of the environment is a mandatory requirement which may limit the application of Article 30 of the Treaty.

[*The Commission argued that the Danish laws were disproportionate.*]

13. First of all, as regards the obligation to establish a deposit-and-return system for empty containers, it must be observed that this requirement is an indispensable element of a system intended to ensure the re-use of containers and therefore appears necessary to achieve the aims pursued by the contested rules. That being so, the restrictions which it imposes on the free movement of goods cannot be regarded as disproportionate.

14. Next it is necessary to consider the requirement that producers and importers must use only containers approved by the National Agency for the Protection of the Environment.

[*The Danish Government argued that the number of approved containers had to be limited because otherwise retailers would not take part in the system. This meant that a foreign producer might have to manufacture a type of container already approved, with consequent increases in costs. To overcome this problem the Danish law was amended to allow a producer to market up to 3,000 hectolitres a year in non-approved containers, provided that a deposit-and-return system was established. The Commission argued that the limit of 3,000 hectolitres was unnecessary to achieve the objectives of the scheme.*]

20. It is undoubtedly true that the existing system for returning approved containers ensures a maximum rate of re-use and therefore a very considerable degree of protection of the environment since empty containers can be returned to any retailer of beverages. Non-approved containers, on the other

---

[159] [1979] ECR 649, [8].
[160] See also Case C–379/98 *PreussenElektra* (n 129); Case C–309/02 *Radlberger* (n 134) [75]; Case C–142/05 *Åklagaren* (n 70) [32]; Case C–28/09 *Commission v Austria* (n 131).

hand, can be returned only to the retailer who sold the beverages, since it is impossible to set up such a comprehensive system for those containers as well.

21. Nevertheless, the system for returning non-approved containers is capable of protecting the environment and, as far as imports are concerned, affects only limited quantities of beverages compared with the quantity of beverages consumed in Denmark owing to the restrictive effect which the requirement that containers should be returnable has on imports. In those circumstances, a restriction of the quantity of products which may be marketed by importers is disproportionate to the objective pursued.

22. It must therefore be held that by restricting…the quantity of beer and soft drinks which may be marketed by a single producer in non-approved containers to 3,000 hectolitres a year, the Kingdom of Denmark has failed, as regards imports of those products from other Member States, to fulfil its obligations under Article 30 of the EEC Treaty.

Environmental protection is not the only new addition to this catalogue. In *Familiapress*[161] the ECJ recognized pluralism of the press as a value that could legitimate a national measure that was in breach of Article 34. The offering of prizes for games in magazines could drive out smaller papers which could not afford to make such offers. In *Cinéthèque*[162] the ECJ was willing to recognize that the fostering of certain forms of art could constitute a justifiable objective in EU law. While in *Torfaen*[163] it accepted that rules governing the opening hours of premises pursued a justifiable aim, since they reflected social choices that might differ between Member States.[164] Road safety can also be a justification.[165] It is clear moreover from *Schmidberger* that the protection of fundamental rights can be relevant as justification of an indistinctly applicable measure.

Case C–112/00 Eugen Schmidberger, Internationale Transporte und Planzuge v Austria
[2003] ECR I–5659

The ECJ held that a decision by Austria not to ban a demonstration by an environmental group that led to closure of the Brenner motorway was caught by what is now Article 34 since it impeded trade for the relevant period. The ECJ then considered whether the restriction was justified, since the Austrian Government in allowing the demonstration was influenced by considerations relating to freedom of expression and assembly as enshrined in the ECHR and the Austrian Constitution. The ECJ accepted that fundamental rights were part of the Community legal order, but that these rights and the principles concerning free movement of goods were not absolute.

THE ECJ

81. In those circumstances, the interests involved must be weighed having regard to all the circumstances of the case in order to determine whether a fair balance was struck between those interests.

---

[161] Case C–368/95 *Vereinigte Familiapress Zeitungsverlags- und vertriebs GmbH v Heinrich Bauer Verlag* [1997] ECR I–368.
[162] Cases 60 and 61/84 [1985] ECR 2605.
[163] Case 145/88 [1989] ECR 3851.
[164] While *Cinéthèque* and *Torfaen* would probably now fall outside Art 34, the recognition of these grounds of objective justification could be of relevance in cases that do fall within Art 34 even after *Keck*.
[165] Case C–110/05 *Commission v Italy* (n 69) [60].

82. The competent authorities enjoy a wide margin of discretion in that regard. Nevertheless, it is necessary to determine whether the restrictions placed upon intra-Community trade are proportionate in the light of the legitimate objectives pursued, namely...the protection of fundamental rights.

[*The ECJ emphasized that the demonstrators had sought permission from the Austrian Government, and that the demonstration was limited in scope and time.*]

86. [I]t is not in dispute that by the demonstration, citizens were exercising their fundamental rights by manifesting in public an opinion which they considered to be of importance in society; it is also not in dispute that the purpose of that public demonstration was not to restrict trade in goods of a particular type or from a particular source...

87. [I]n the present case various administrative and supporting arrangements were taken by the competent authorities in order to limit as far as possible the disruption to road traffic....

88. Moreover, it is not in dispute that the isolated incident in question did not give rise to a general climate of insecurity such as to have a dissuasive effect on intra-Community trade flows as a whole....

89. Finally...the competent national authorities were entitled to consider that an outright ban on the demonstration would have constituted unacceptable interference with the fundamental rights of the demonstrators to gather and express peacefully their opinion in public.

[*The ECJ accepted that alternative solutions would have been liable to lead to more serious disruption of trade, such as unauthorized demonstrations.*]

93. [T]he national authorities were reasonably entitled, having regard to the wide discretion which must be accorded to them in the matter, to consider that the legitimate aim of that demonstration could not be achieved in the present case by measures less restrictive of intra-Community trade.

(G) MANDATORY REQUIREMENTS AND HARMONIZATION

An EU harmonization measure may render it impossible for a state to rely on a mandatory requirement.[166] Whether it has this effect will depend upon whether the measure is directed at total or only a minimum harmonization. The previous discussion of this issue is applicable here.[167]

(H) SUMMARY

i. The Court was creative in *Cassis* when it set out the mandatory requirements, and it has shown similar flexibility since then by adding new defences to the list. It has, not surprisingly, interpreted the requirements strictly, obliging Member States to show that a defence is really warranted in the circumstances. There are however two causes for concern.

ii. First, the dividing line between the mandatory requirements and Article 36 is problematic. It has been argued that the same public interest defences should be available irrespective of whether the measure is discriminatory or not. Whether the measure was discriminatory would simply be relevant to the application of the defences to the facts.

iii. Secondly, the decision on whether the mandatory requirements provide a defence for the Member State can involve difficult balancing exercises for the CJEU, and for the national courts, to which many such issues are delegated by the CJEU. This issue will be examined more fully in the following section.

---

[166] See, eg, Case C–383/97 *Criminal Proceedings against Van der Laan* [1999] ECR I–731.
[167] See above, pp 703–704.

11 FREE MOVEMENT OF GOODS AND *CASSIS*: THE BROADER PERSPECTIVE

(A) THE COMMISSION'S RESPONSE TO *CASSIS*

The judgment in *Cassis* was, in part, a response to the Commission's difficulties in securing Member State acceptance of harmonization measures. The judgment rendered indistinctly applicable rules which impeded trade incompatible with Article 34 unless they could be saved by a mandatory requirement, even in the absence of relevant harmonization provisions. *Cassis* therefore fostered single market integration, and obviated the need for many harmonization provisions.

The ECJ's jurisprudence cannot be viewed in isolation. It had an impact upon how other Community institutions perceived their role. The Commission was not slow to respond to the Court's initiative. It published a Communication setting out its interpretation of the *Cassis* decision, and its legislative role in this area.

Commission Communication 3 October 1980 [1980] OJ C256/2

Any product imported from another Member State must in principle be admitted to the territory of the importing Member State if it has been lawfully produced, that is, conforms to rules and processes of manufacture that are customarily and traditionally accepted in the exporting country, and marketed in the territory of the latter.

. . .

Only under very strict conditions does the Court accept exceptions to this principle; barriers to trade resulting from differences between commercial and technical rules are only admissible:

— if the rules are necessary, that is appropriate and not excessive, in order to satisfy mandatory requirements . . . ;

— if the rules serve a purpose in the general interest which is compelling enough to justify an exception to a fundamental rule of the Treaty such as the free movement of goods;

— if the rules are essential for such a purpose to be attained, ie. are the means which are the most appropriate and at the same time least hinder trade.

[*The Commission then set out a number of guidelines in the light of the Court's judgment.*]

— The principles deduced by the Court imply that a Member State may not in principle prohibit the sale in its territory of a product lawfully produced and marketed in another Member State even if the product is produced according to technical or quality requirements which differ from those imposed on its domestic products. Where a product 'suitably and satisfactorily' fulfils the legitimate objective of a Member State's own rules (public safety, protection of the consumer or the environment, etc.), the importing country cannot justify prohibiting its sale in its territory by claiming that the way it fulfils the objective is different from that imposed on domestic products.

In such a case, an absolute prohibition of sale could not be considered 'necessary' to satisfy a 'mandatory requirement' because it would not be an 'essential guarantee' in the sense defined in the Court's judgment.

The Commission will therefore have to tackle a whole body of commercial rules which lay down that products manufactured and marketed in one Member State must fulfill technical or qualitative conditions in order to be admitted to the market of another and specifically in all cases where the trade barriers occasioned by such rules are inadmissible according to the very strict criteria set out by the Court.

> The Commission is referring in particular to rules covering the composition, designation, presentation and packaging as well as rules requiring compliance with certain technical standards.
>
> — The Commission's work of harmonization will henceforth have to be directed mainly at national laws having an impact on the functioning of the common market where barriers to trade to be removed arise from national provisions which are admissible under the criteria set out by the Court.
>
> The Commission will be concentrating on sectors deserving priority because of their economic relevance to the creation of a single internal market.

There are two important themes in the Commission's Communication. The first is the principle of *mutual recognition*.[168] Goods lawfully marketed in one Member State should, in principle, be admitted to the market of any other state. This leads to competition among rules, or regulatory competition. A producer will normally have to comply with the national rules of only one state for its goods to move freely in the EU. Firms are then able to choose between different national regulations. Consumers can choose between the products that comply with those rules. This creates a 'competitive process among the different national rules: the choice of producers of where to produce and of consumers of what to buy will determine the "best rules"'.[169]

The second theme concerns the Commission's enforcement and legislative strategy for trade rules post-*Cassis*. This was to be double-edged. It would tackle trade rules that were *inadmissible* in the light of *Cassis*, by using its powers under Article 258 TFEU against recalcitrant Member States. The harmonization process would be directed towards those trade rules that were *admissible* under the *Cassis* test. *Cassis* therefore caused the Commission to re-orient its legislative programme, and concentrate on national rules that were still valid under the Court's case law. There is now a package of measures,[170] which constitute the 'New Legislative Framework for Marketing of Products',[171] which is considered in the chapter on the single market.[172]

(B) PROBLEMS WITH REALIZING THE *CASSIS* STRATEGY

Mutual recognition is the core of the ECJ's and Commission's strategy.[173] The general assumption is that this works just fine. Matters are not so simple. The Commission's paper on Mutual Recognition[174] emphasized that it did not always operate effectively, and it made proposals to improve it.[175] There

---

[168] K Armstrong, 'Mutual Recognition' in Barnard and Scott (n 21) ch 9; MP Maduro, 'So Close and Yet So Far: The Paradoxes of Mutual Recognition' (2007) 14 JEPP 014; K Nicolaïdis, 'Trusting the Poles? Constructing Europe through Mutual Recognition' (2007) 14 JEPP 682; J Pelkmans, 'Mutual Recognition in Goods. On Promises and Disillusions' (2007) 14 JEPP 699.

[169] Maduro (n 2) 132.

[170] Decision No 768/2008/EC of the European Parliament and of the Council of 9 July 2008 on a common framework for the marketing of products, and repealing Council Decision 93/465/EEC [2008] OJ L218/82; Regulation (EC) No 765/2008 of the European Parliament and of the Council of 9 July 2008 setting out the requirements for accreditation and market surveillance relating to the marketing of products and repealing Regulation (EEC) No 339/93 [2008] OJ L218/30; Reg 764/2008 (n 104).

[171] http://ec.europa.eu/enterprise/policies/single-market-goods/documents/internal-market-for-products/new-legislative-framework/index_en.htm.

[172] Ch 17.

[173] http://ec.europa.eu/enterprise/policies/single-market-goods/free-movement-non-harmonised-sectors/mutual-recognition/index_en.htm.

[174] Mutual Recognition in the Context of the Follow-up to the Action Plan for the Single Market, COM(1999) 299 final; Reg 764/2008 (n 104) recs 4–6.

[175] Mutual Recognition (n 174) 7–12; Commission interpretative communication on facilitating the access of products to the markets of other Member States: the practical application of mutual recognition [2003] OJ C265/2.

should be increased monitoring of mutual recognition by the Commission, complemented by measures to improve awareness of mutual recognition by producers of goods and services. Member States should deal with requests concerning mutual recognition within a reasonable time, and should include mutual recognition clauses in national legislation.

Legislation has been enacted to enhance free movement and mutual recognition. The initial approach[176] was based on exchange of information about national measures that derogated from the free movement of goods. This strategy was not, however, successful and it was replaced in 2008[177] by a more strident approach. A Member State that decides to prevent or hinder free movement of goods lawfully marketed in another Member State on grounds listed in Article 36 TFEU, or because of one of the *Cassis* mandatory requirements, must give written notice to the importer, who has twenty days in which to give comments contesting the decision. The Member State then makes a final decision in the light of those comments, and this must be notified to the importer and the Commission. If the Member State sticks to its decision to refuse or hinder import it must give reasons. This decision must be open to challenge before national courts. The Member States are, moreover, obliged to establish 'Product Contact Points', which provide information to importers about the technical rules applicable to particular types of product and information about the principle of mutual recognition in that Member State.

This Regulation should be viewed in tandem with Directive 98/34[178] on the provision of information on technical standards and regulations. This measure, known as the Mutual Information or Transparency Directive, imposes an obligation on a state to inform the Commission before it adopts any legally binding regulation setting a technical specification. The Commission notifies the other states, and may require that the adoption of the national measure be delayed by up to six months in order that possible amendments can be considered. A further delay can result if the Commission decides to push ahead with a harmonization directive on the issue.

Legislative intervention to secure free movement and mutual recognition has been complemented by judicial initiatives, more especially the obligation to insert mutual recognition clauses in legislation, which derives from the *Foie Gras* case.[179] The French imposed requirements on the composition of *foie gras*. The Commission argued that the French Decree containing the requirements for *foie gras* must also contain a mutual recognition clause in the legislation itself, permitting preparations for *foie gras* that had been lawfully marketed in another Member State to be marketed in France. The ECJ agreed.[180] Henceforth any state which imposes requirements as to product characteristics and the like must also include a mutual recognition clause in the enabling legal instrument, unless the restriction can be justified under Article 36 TFEU.[181] The Commission acknowledged their importance: 'it is through such clauses that not only individuals, but also the competent national authorities and the heads of inspection and control bodies become aware of how mutual recognition has to be applied in a given area'.[182] Such clauses are especially important,

---

[176] Decision 3052/95/EC of the European Parliament and of the Council of 13 December 1995 establishing a procedure for the exchange of information on national measures derogating from the principle of free movement of goods within the Community [1995] OJ L321/1.

[177] Reg 764/2008 (n 104).

[178] Directive 98/34/EC of the European Parliament and of the Council of 22 June 1998 laying down a procedure for the provision of information in the field of technical standards and regulations [1998] OJ L204/37; Case C–194/94 *CIA Security International SA v Signalson SA and Securitel SPRL* [1996] ECR I–2201; The Operation of Directive 98/34 from 2002–2005, COM(2007) 125 final.

[179] Case C–184/96 *Commission v France* [1998] ECR I–6197.

[180] Ibid [28].

[181] Case C–333/08 *Commission v France* (n 116) [61]–[62], AG Mazak.

[182] Mutual Recognition (n 174) 11. See also Council Resolution of 28 October 1999 on Mutual Recognition [2000] OJ C141/5.

given the difficulties that persist with mutual recognition of complex technical products, food-stuffs, and the like.[183]

(c) PROBLEMS FLOWING FROM THE *CASSIS* STRATEGY

The effect of *Cassis* was that policy would be developed through a mixture of adjudication and rule-making. Adjudication by the ECJ pursuant to *Cassis* resulted in negative integration: trade rules would be incompatible with Article 34 unless they could be saved by a mandatory requirement. Rule-making would be used for national rules that survived because of the mandatory requirements, and therefore still posed a problem for market integration. This resulted in positive integration, in the sense that there would be EU rules which would bind all states. There are, however, four problems with this general strategy.

The *first problem* is that it is dependent on agreement as to the outcome of the adjudicative process. If the challenged rule failed the *Cassis* test then it would have to be removed from national law. This conclusion was fine, provided that one agreed with it. The result was less satisfactory if one felt that the trade rule should have been saved by a mandatory requirement. Thus the ECJ has, for example, generally held that national rules on food standards are not saved by the mandatory requirements, because the policy of the importing state can be met by less restrictive rules on product labelling. Weatherill has argued forcefully that the ECJ often takes a robust view of consumers, and has given relatively little attention to the prospects of consumer confusion.[184] Lasa has also argued that labelling requirements, as opposed to food standards, may not adequately protect the consumer.

H-C von Heydebrand u d Lasa, Free Movement of Foodstuffs, Consumer Protection and Food Standards in the European Community: Has the Court of Justice Got it Wrong?[185]

First of all, the Court might simply not be right that consumers are adequately informed through labels. After all, the majority of the consumers apparently do not pay much attention to the information given on the label....

Secondly, the Court's approach can confer an unfair competitive advantage on the importer... The consumer associates with the name or presentation of the product a familiar domestic product of a certain quality which is not met by the imported product, and will therefore perhaps be misled....

Fourthly, the Court's case law, if implemented strictly in the long run, may well result in a 'labelling jungle' which even judges would find difficult to penetrate...

Fifthly, while administrative resources are saved by foregoing harmonization, authorities of the Member States have to struggle with the food standards of the various Member States, since the imported product must still be 'lawfully produced and marketed' in the Member States of export....

---

[183] Second Biannual Report on the Application of the Principle of Mutual Recognition in the Single Market, COM(2002) 419 final.

[184] S Weatherill, 'Recent Case Law Concerning the Free Movement of Goods: Mapping the Frontiers of Market Deregulation' (1999) 36 CMLRev 51.

[185] (1991) 16 ELRev 391, 409–413. See also O Brouwers, 'Free Movement of Foodstuffs and Quality Requirements: Has the Commission Got it Wrong?' (1988) 25 CMLRev 237; C MacMaoláin, 'Waiter! There's a Beetle in my Soup. Yes Sir, that's E120: Disparities between Actual Individual Behaviour and Regulating Food Labelling for the Average Consumer in EU Law' (2008) 45 CMLRev 1147.

Sixthly, depending on the market of the foodstuff in question, mutual recognition can lead to discrimination against manufacturers situated in the importing Member State, if that Member State does not timely adjust the food standard...

More important...the Member State of export can by way of the economic damage caused by inverse discrimination impose de facto its food standard or standard free food law on the Member State of import. Relocation of production to the exporting Member State in an effort to secure market share at home has already occurred in practice....

Seventhly, the preference of the Court for labelling is not sufficiently responsive to the local needs of the people of the importing Member State to define and classify the food they eat according to their conceptions, expectations and habits...

The *second problem* relates to the balancing exercise performed pursuant to Article 36 and the mandatory requirements. The ECJ has to adjudicate on the balance between market integration and the attainment of other societal goals when deciding on the legitimacy of such defences. This can also be problematic for national courts, as is readily apparent from the *Sunday Trading* cases and more recent jurisprudence. Thus in *de Agostini*[186] the national court had to decide whether the advertising ban affected imported goods differentially from domestic goods, whether the ban might satisfy a mandatory requirement, and whether it was proportionate. In *Familiapress*[187] the ban on import of newspapers offering prizes was held to breach Article 34. It was for the national court to decide whether the ban could be saved because it was a proportionate method of preserving press diversity, and whether that objective could be achieved by less restrictive means. The national court was, moreover, required to decide on the degree of competition between papers offering prizes and those small newspapers that could not afford to do so, and to estimate the extent to which sales of the latter would decline if the former could be offered for sale.

The *third problem* concerns the balance between market integration and the protective function played by national rules. EU legislative initiatives may be required to ensure that the protective function of certain trade rules is not lost sight of in the desire to enhance single market integration.[188] Thus consumer groups were worried that trade liberalization could have negative consequences on consumer safety.[189] It is true that safety can be taken into account under the *Cassis* mandatory requirements. There is, however, as Weatherill and Beaumont note, a risk inherent in the *Cassis* line of authority. The risk is 'that the Court has introduced a legal test that tends to tip the balance away from legitimate social protection towards a deregulated (perhaps unregulated) free market economy in which standards of, *inter alia*, consumer protection will be depressed'.[190] Positive harmonization through EU rules may be required to ensure the appropriate level of protection in the relevant area.

The *final problem* concerns the allocation of regulatory competence between the EU and the Member States. The interpretation of Article 34 serves to define the sphere of regulatory competence left to the Member States, and the extent to which EU harmonization is required. This entails important choices.

---

186 Cases C–34–36/95 (n 59).

187 Case C–368/95 (n 161).

188 See, however, Case C–320/93 *Lucien Ortscheit GmbH v Eurim-Pharm Arzneimittel GmbH* [1994] ECR I–5243 for judicial recognition of this problem.

189 K Alter and S Meunier-Aitsahalia, 'Judicial Politics in the European Community: European Integration and the Pathbreaking *Cassis de Dijon* Decision' (1994) 26 Comparative Political Studies 535, 544.

190 (N 42) 600.

M Maduro, We the Court, the European Court of Justice and the European Economic Constitution[191]
[Art 30 should be read as Art 34 TFEU]

The institutional choices, regarding the allocation of regulatory powers, that can be detected in different interpretations of Article 30 [28] and its co-ordination with Treaty rules on harmonisation may be represented in three ideal constitutional models of the European Economic Constitution: the centralised constitutional model, the competitive constitutional model and the decentralised constitutional model. The centralised model reacts to the erosion of national regulatory powers through Article 30 by favouring a process of market integration by means of the replacement of national laws with Community legislation. The competitive model promotes 'competition among national rules', notably through the principle of mutual recognition of national legislation. In the decentralised model, States will retain regulatory powers, but are, at the same time, prevented from developing protectionist policies. These models are heuristic devices. They are all present—and compete with each other—in the European Union.... These, in turn, can be linked with three different visions of the European Economic Constitution and its legitimation.

The first argues that negative integration, deriving from the application of market integration rules, must be followed by positive integration which is legitimised through the development of traditional democratic mechanisms in the European Union.

The second argues for the constitutionalisation of negative integration. No traditional democratic developments are required for the European Union institutions since powers are left to the market.... This vision protects market freedom and individual rights against public power.

The third vision still sees the highest source of legitimacy in national democratic legitimacy. The legitimacy of the European Economic Constitution derives therefrom and is thus conditioned....

The disputes over Article 30 and European regulation are basically disputes over these different economic constitutional models and the different legitimacy they presuppose.

12 CONCLUSIONS

i. The ECJ had certain fundamental choices when interpreting Article 34. It could have limited its remit to measures that were discriminatory or protectionist. It chose not to do so, and extended Article 34 to cover indistinctly applicable rules. Consequences flow from any choice, and this applies as much to those made by courts as other decision-makers.

ii. The *legislative consequence* of *Cassis* was far-reaching. The decision facilitated the creation of a single market. The Commission re-oriented its legislative strategy to concentrate on trade rules that were still lawful in the light of *Cassis* and could be justified by the mandatory requirements. There would be harmonization pursuant to Article 114.

iii. The *judicial consequence* of *Cassis* was equally significant. Litigants challenged all manner of national trade rules claiming that they constituted an impediment, direct or indirect, actual or potential, to EU trade. This led the ECJ to re-think its jurisprudence in *Keck* in an attempt to stem the tide. The distinction between rules going to the characteristics of the goods and those pertaining to selling arrangements proved fragile. The ECJ increasingly brought selling arrangements within Article 34 either by treating them as going to the character of the goods or because they

---

[191] (Hart, 1998) 108–109.

applied unevenly, in fact or law, to imports. Market access has come closer to centre stage in the ECJ's reasoning, as is evident in the case law on product use.

iv. *Cassis* also had a *second-order judicial consequence*. The ECJ had to decide whether a Member State could legitimately plead a mandatory requirement. It was forced to make difficult decisions between the imperatives of market integration and the pursuit of other social goals. National courts are often faced with complex empirical and normative issues when deciding on the application of mandatory requirements.

v. *Cassis* had significant *regulatory consequences*. Member States lost regulatory competence. They could no longer apply national rules to imported goods. These had to be admitted because of mutual recognition unless they could be saved by a mandatory requirement. The EU acquired regulatory competence, since the existence of a proven mandatory requirement brought Article 114 into play.

13 FURTHER READING

(a) Books

BARNARD, C, *The Substantive Law of the EU: The Four Freedoms* (Oxford University Press, 4th edn, 2014)

——— AND SCOTT, J (eds), *The Law of the Single European Market: Unpacking the Premises* (Hart, 2002)

MADURO, MP, *We the Court, The European Court of Justice and the European Economic Constitution* (Hart, 1998)

NIC SHUIBHNE, N, *Regulating the Internal Market* (Edward Elgar, 2006)

——— *The Coherence of EU Free Movement Law, Constitutional Responsibility and the Court of Justice* (Oxford University Press, 2014)

OLIVER, P, AND ENCHELMAIER, S, *Oliver on Free Movement of Goods in the Union* (Hart, 5th edn, 2010)

WOODS, L, *Free Movement of Goods and Services within the European Community* (Ashgate, 2004)

(b) Articles

ARMSTRONG, K, 'Mutual Recognition' in C Barnard and J Scott (eds), *The Law of the Single European Market: Unpacking the Premises* (Hart, 2002) ch 9

BARNARD, C, 'Fitting the Remaining Pieces into the Goods and Persons Jigsaw' (2001) 26 ELRev 35

——— 'Trailing a New Approach to Free Movement of Goods' (2009) 68 CLJ 288

——— AND DEAKIN, S, 'Market Access and Regulatory Competition' in C Barnard and J Scott (eds), *The Law of the Single European Market: Unpacking the Premises* (Hart, 2002) ch 8

BIONDI, A, 'Free Trade, a Mountain Road and the Right to Protest: European Economic Freedoms and Fundamental Individual Rights' [2004] EHRLRev 51

DE BÚRCA, G, 'Unpacking the Concept of Discrimination in EC and International Trade Law' in C Barnard and J Scott (eds), *The Law of the Single European Market: Unpacking the Premises* (Hart, 2002) ch 7

CHALMERS, D, 'Repackaging the Internal Market—The Ramifications of the *Keck* Judgment' (1994) 19 ELRev 385

CONNOR, T, 'Accentuating the Positive: The "Selling Arrangement", the First Decade and Beyond' (2005) 54 ICLQ 127

DAVIES, G, '"Process and Production Method"-Based Trade Restrictions in the EU' (2007–8) 10 CYELS 69

DERLÉN, M, AND LINDHOLM, J, 'Article 28 EC and Rules on Use: A Step Towards a Workable Doctrine on Measures Having Equivalent Effect to Quantitative Restrictions' (2009–10) 16 CJEL 191

DOUGAN, M, 'Minimum Harmonization and the Internal Market' (2000) 37 CMLRev 853

ENCHELMAIER, S, 'The Awkward Selling of a Good Idea, or a Traditionalist Interpretation of *Keck*' (2003) 22 YBEL 249

GORMLEY, LW, 'Silver Threads among the Gold…50 Years of the Free Movement of Goods' (2008) 31 Fordham Int LJ 1637

HILSON, C, 'Discrimination in Community Free Movement Law' (1999) 24 ELRev 445

HORSLEY, T, 'Unearthing Buried Treasure: Art.34 TFEU and the Exclusionary Rules' (2012) 37 ELRev 734

JANSSON, M, AND KALIMO, H, '*De minimis* Meets "Market Access": Transformations in the Substance–and the Syntax—of EU Free Movement Law?' (2014) 51 CMLRev 523

KOUTRAKOS, P, 'On Groceries, Alcohol and Olive Oil: More on Free Movement of Goods after *Keck*' (2001) 26 ELRev 391

KRENN, C, 'A Missing Piece in the Horizontal Effect "Jigsaw": Horizontal Direct Effect and the Free Movement of Goods' (2012) 49 CMLRev 177

MADURO, MP, 'Reforming the Market or the State? Article 30 and the European Constitution: Economic Freedoms and Political Rights' (1997) 3 ELJ 55

——— 'So Close and Yet So Far: The Paradoxes of Mutual Recognition' (2007) 14 JEPP 814

NICOLAÏDIS, K, 'Trusting the Poles? Constructing Europe through Mutual Recognition' (2007) 14 JEPP 682

OLIVER, P, AND ROTH, W-H, 'The Internal Market and the Four Freedoms' (2004) 41 CMLRev 407

PELKMANS, J, 'Mutual Recognition in Goods. On Promises and Disillusions' (2007) 14 JEPP 699

PRETE, L, 'Of Motorcycle Trailers and Personal Watercrafts: The Battle over *Keck*' (2008) 35 LIEI 133

REICH, N, 'The "November Revolution" of the European Court of Justice: *Keck, Meng* and *Audi* Revisited' (1994) 31 CMLRev 459

SCOTT, J, 'Mandatory or Imperative Requirements in the EU and the WTO' in C Barnard and J Scott (eds), *The Law of the Single European Market: Unpacking the Premises* (Hart, 2002) ch 10

SNELL, J, 'The Notion of Market Access: A Concept or a Slogan?' (2010) 47 CMLRev 437

SPAVENTA, E, 'Leaving *Keck* Behind? The Free Movement of Goods after the Rulings in *Commission v Italy* and *Mickelsson and Roos*' (2009) 34 ELRev 914

SZYDŁO, M, 'Export Restrictions within the Structure of Free Movement of Goods: Reconsideration of an Old Paradigm' (2010) 47 CMLRev 753

TRYFONIDOU, A, 'Further Steps on the Road to Convergence among the Market Freedoms' (2010) 35 ELRev 36

WEATHERILL, S, 'After *Keck*: Some Thoughts on How to Clarify the Clarification' (1996) 33 CMLRev 885

——— 'Pre-Emption, Harmonisation and the Distribution of Competence to Regulate the Internal Market' in C BARNARD and J SCOTT (eds), *The Law of the Single European Market: Unpacking the Premises* (Hart, 2002) ch 2

WEILER, JJ, 'From *Dassonville* to *Keck* and Beyond: An Evolutionary Reflection on the Text and Context of the Free Movement of Goods' in P Craig and G de Búrca (eds), *The Evolution of EU Law* (Oxford University Press, 1999) ch 10

WENNERAS, P, AND BOE MOEN, K, 'Selling Arrangements, Keeping *Keck*' (2010) 35 ELRev 387

WHITE, E, 'In Search of the Limits to Article 30 of the EEC Treaty' (1989) 26 CMLRev 235

WILS, WPJ, 'The Search for the Rule in Article 30 EEC: Much Ado About Nothing?' (1993) 18 ELRev 475

WILSHER, D, 'Does *Keck* Discrimination Make any Sense? An Assessment of the Non-Discrimination Principle within the European Single Market' (2008) 33 ELRev 3

FREE MOVEMENT OF CAPITAL AND ECONOMIC AND MONETARY UNION

1 CENTRAL ISSUES

i. This chapter is concerned with free movement of capital and economic and monetary union (EMU).

ii. The discussion begins with the free movement of capital, one of the four freedoms enshrined in the original Rome Treaty. The Treaty Articles were altered radically by the Maastricht Treaty. There is now a growing body of case law on these provisions, which raises similar issues to those encountered in the context of goods, persons, establishment, and services.

iii. The discussion then moves to EMU. There is analysis of the movement towards EMU and the arguments for and against EMU. The position of the European Central Bank (ECB) is analysed. The discussion concludes with analysis of the strains on EMU in the light of the banking and financial crisis.

iv. The Treaties contain provisions on both monetary and economic union. Monetary union means in essence a single currency overseen by the ECB. The meaning of economic union is more diffuse. The essence of the idea is that the health of individual Member State economies can have implications for the overall health of the EU economy and for the value of the single currency, as exemplified by the way in which the Euro crisis was precipitated by concerns over the Greek economy. The Treaties therefore contain provisions to monitor the health of Member States' economies. The extent of these controls is however a sensitive matter, since they entail EU intrusion into domestic economic policy. The weakness of the pre-existing controls was however problematic, and recent legislation has strengthened this oversight.

2 FREE MOVEMENT OF CAPITAL

(A) THE ORIGINAL TREATY PROVISIONS

Articles 67–73 EEC contained the original provisions on free movement of capital,[1] but they were less peremptory than those applicable to free movement of goods, workers, services, and establishment. Thus while Article 67(1) EEC imposed an obligation to abolish progressively restrictions on

---

[1] J Usher, *The Law of Money and Financial Services in the European Community* (Oxford University Press, 1994) 14–16.

capital movements during the transitional period, this was only to the extent necessary to ensure the proper functioning of the common market. This theme was carried over to Article 71, which required Member States to endeavour to avoid the introduction of new exchange restrictions on capital movements. The wording of these Treaty Articles necessarily impacted on the ECJ's approach to this area.[2] The Council enacted various directives pursuant to these Treaty provisions, the most important being Council Directive 88/361.[3]

(B) THE CURRENT PROVISIONS: THE BASIC PRINCIPLE

The Maastricht Treaty completely revised the provisions on free movement of capital, with effect from 1 January 1994.[4] Article 63 TFEU (ex Article 56 EC) now provides:

> 1. Within the framework of the provisions set out in this Chapter, all restrictions on the movement of capital between Member States and between Member States and third countries shall be prohibited.
> 2. Within the framework of the provisions set out in this Chapter, all restrictions on payments between Member States and between Member States and third countries shall be prohibited.[5]

What is now Article 63 was held to have direct effect in *Sanz de Lera*.[6] The ECJ held that it laid down a clear and unconditional prohibition for which no implementing measure was required. The existence of Member State discretion to take all measures necessary to prevent infringement of national law and regulations contained within what is now Article 65(1)(b) TFEU did not prevent Article 63 from having direct effect, because the exercise of such discretion was subject to judicial review. This ruling concerned an action against the state. Treaty Articles often have vertical and horizontal direct effect, and thus can be used against the state and private individuals, and there is nothing in *Sanz de Lera* to indicate the contrary. It would not be difficult, as Usher states,[7] to envisage a situation in which the unilateral conduct of a financial institution could restrict payments between states. This interpretation is reinforced by the fact that Article 63 does not refer only to the state.[8] The argument to the contrary would be derived by way of analogy with Article 34 on the free movement of goods, which has been largely confined to actions against the state.[9]

---

[2] Case 203/80 *Casati* [1981] ECR 2595.

[3] [1988] OJ L178/5.

[4] S Peers, 'Free Movement of Capital: Learning Lessons or Slipping on Spilt Milk?' in C Barnard and J Scott (eds), *The Law of the Single European Market* (Hart, 2002) ch 13; L Flynn, 'Coming of Age: The Free Movement of Capital Case-Law 1993–2002' (2002) 39 CMLRev 773; J Snell, 'Free Movement of Capital: Evolution as a Non-Linear Process' in P Craig and G de Búrca (eds), *The Evolution of EU Law* (Oxford University Press, 2nd edn, 2011) ch 18.

[5] This does not cover national procedural rules governing actions by a creditor seeking payment from a recalcitrant debtor: Case C–412/97 *ED Srl v Italo Fenocchio* [1999] ECR I–3845.

[6] Cases C–163, 165 and 250/94 *Criminal Proceedings against Lucas Emilio Sanz de Lera* [1995] ECR I–4821, [41]–[47]; Case C–101/05 *Skatteverket v A* [2007] ECR I–11531, [20]–[27]; Case C–201/05 *Test Claimants in the CFC and Dividend Group Litigation v Commissioners of Inland Revenue* [2008] ECR I–2875, [90]–[91].

[7] Usher (n 1) 27.

[8] In Case C–464/98 *Westdeutsche Landesbank Girozentrale v Stefan and Republik Österreich* [2001] ECR I–173 a private defendant relied on Art 63, and in Case C–213/04 *Burtscher v Stauderer* [2005] ECR I–10309, the defendant was a private individual, although the case concerned a state measure.

[9] The rationale for this limitation on Art 34 is, however, based in large part on the overlap which would otherwise occur between Art 34 and Arts 101 and 102.

The Treaty provisions do not define movement of capital, but the ECJ held that reference can be made to the non-exhaustive list in Directive 88/361.[10] It will be for the Court to decide, with the aid of the Directive, whether a measure constitutes a restriction on the movement of capital. Thus a national prohibition on the creation of a mortgage in a foreign currency was prohibited by Article 63.[11] The ECJ has held that restrictions on share dealings and 'golden shares'[12] come within Article 63.[13] So too do restrictions on the acquisition and disposal of property,[14] such as requirements of prior administrative authorization.[15] Measures taken by a Member State that are liable to dissuade its residents from obtaining loans or making investments in other Member States constitute restrictions on the movement of capital.[16]

While direct taxation remains within Member States' competence, they must exercise that competence consistently with EU law and avoid discrimination on the grounds of nationality.[17] It is clear moreover that Article 63 covers not only measures that discriminate on grounds of nationality, but also measures that may impede capital movements, even though they are not discriminatory.[18] The ECJ has, by way of contrast, held that a Member State can apply a tax to income, notwithstanding the fact that it has already been taxed in another Member State,[19] with the consequence that double taxation is not contrary to free movement of capital.[20]

Article 63 gives the impression that capital movements within the EU, and between Member States and non-member countries, are treated the same. This is not so, since other Treaty Articles qualify the application of Article 63 to non-member countries. Article 64(1) in effect allows lawful restrictions on capital movements which existed on 31 December 1993 to remain in being, and Article 64(2) only requires the Council to endeavour to achieve free movement with non-member countries to the greatest extent possible. The Council is also empowered under Article 66 to take safeguard measures in exceptional circumstances where capital movements to or from non-member countries cause, or threaten to cause, serious difficulties for the operation of economic and monetary union. Such measures cannot last longer than six months, and can be taken only where strictly necessary.

[10] Case C–222/97 *Proceedings brought by Trummer and Mayer* [1999] ECR I–1661, [21]; Case C–452/01 *Ospelt v Schlossle Weissenberg Familienstiftung* [2003] ECR I–9743; Case C–446/04 *Test Claimants in the FII Group Litigation v Commissioners of Inland Revenue* [2006] ECR I–11753, [174]–[188].

[11] Case C–464/98 *Westdeutsche Landesbank* (n 8).

[12] Cases C–282–283/04 *Commission v Netherlands* [2006] ECR I–9141; Case C–171/08 *Commission v Portugal* [2010] ECR I–6817; Case C–212/09 *Commission v Portugal* EU: C:2011:717; Cases C–105–107/12 *Netherlands v Essent NV* EU:C:2013:677; Case C–250/08 *Commission v Belgium* EU:C:2011:793.

[13] Case C–446/04 *Test Claimants in the FII Group* (n 10); Case C–182/08 *Glaxo Wellcome GmbH & Co KG v Finanzamt München II* [2009] ECR I–8591.

[14] Case C–376/03 *D v Inspecteur van de Belastingdienst/Particulieren/Onderneringen/ buitenland te Heerlen* [2005] ECR I–5821; Case C–443/06 *Erika Waltraud Ilse Hollmann v Fazenda Pública* [2007] ECR I–8491.

[15] Case C–302/97 *Konle v Austrian Republic* [1999] ECR I–3099; Case C–423/98 *Albore* [2000] ECR I–5965; Cases C–515 and 527–540/99 *Reisch v Bürgermeister der Landeshauptstadt Salzburg* [2002] ECR I–2157; Case C–300/01 *Salzmann* [2003] ECR I–4899; Case C–213/04 *Burtscher* (n 8).

[16] Case C–439/97 *Sandoz GmbH v Finanzlandesdirektion für Wien, Niederösterreich und Burgenland* [1999] ECR I–7041, [19]; Case C–478/98 *Commission v Belgium* [2000] ECR I–7587, [18]; Case C–513/03 *Heirs of van Hiltern-van der Heijden* [2006] ECR I–1957, [44].

[17] Case C–80/94 *Wielockx v Inspecteur der Directe Belastingen* [1995] ECR I–2493, [16]; Case C–251/98 *Baars v Inspecteur der Belastingen Particulieren/Ondernemingen Gorinchem* [2000] ECR I–2787, [17]; Cases C–397 and 410/98 *Metallgesellschaft Ltd, Hoechst AG and Hoechst (UK) Ltd v Commissioners of the Inland Revenue and HM Attorney General* [2001] ECR I–1727, [37]; Case C–242/03 *Ministre des Finances v Weidert and Paulus* [2004] ECR I–7379, [12]; Case C–346/04 *Conjin v Finanzamt Hamburg-Nord* [2006] ECR I–6137, [14]–[15].

[18] Case C–367/98 *Commission v Portugal* [2002] ECR I–4731, [44]–[45]; Case C–174/04 *Commission v Italy* [2005] ECR I–4933, [12]; Case C–375/12 *Bouanich v Directeur des services fiscaux de la Drôme*, 13 Mar 2014.

[19] Case C–513/04 *Kerckhaert and Morres v Belgium* [2006] ECR I–10967; Case C–374/04 *Test Claimants in Class IV of the ACT Group Litigation v Commissioners of Inland Revenue* [2006] ECR I–11673; Case C–128/08 *Jacques Damseaux v Belgium* [2009] ECR I–6923; Case C–487/08 *Commission v Spain* [2010] ECR I–4843, [27].

[20] J Snell, 'Non-Discriminatory Tax Obstacles in Community Law' (2007) 56 ICLQ 339, 358–366.

(c) THE CURRENT PROVISIONS: THE EXCEPTIONS

Article 65(1)(a) concerns taxation and constitutes one of the main exceptions to Article 63. It provides that the provisions of Article 63 shall be without prejudice to the right of Member States:

> to apply the relevant provisions of their tax law which distinguish between taxpayers who are not in the same situation with regard to their place of residence or with regard to the place where their capital is invested.

Article 65(1)(a) is expressly made subject to Article 65(3), which stipulates that the measures taken must not constitute a means of arbitrary discrimination or a disguised restriction on the free movement of capital and payments. The ECJ will decide whether, for example, residents and non-residents are in a comparable position, and whether there has been discrimination.[21] For a difference in treatment not to be regarded as arbitrary for the purposes of Article 65(3) it must be objectively justified.[22] The Member State must show, for example, that the differential treatment was intended to protect the integrity of the tax system and was necessary to achieve this end. The ECJ interprets this requirement strictly. Thus in *Verkooijen*[23] it was held that a national provision making the grant of exemption from income tax on dividends paid to shareholders conditional on the company having its seat in the Netherlands was contrary to EU law. The ECJ rejected the defence that the rule was justified to encourage investment in the Netherlands, since such purely economic objectives could not justify a limit placed on a fundamental freedom. The ECJ also rejected arguments that the contested rule was justified on the ground that it was necessary to preserve the cohesion of the Dutch tax system.[24]

Article 65(1)(b) provides that the provisions of Article 63 shall be without prejudice to the right of Member States:

> to take all requisite measures to prevent infringements of national law and regulations, in particular in the field of taxation and the prudential supervision of financial institutions, or to lay down procedures for the declaration of capital movements for purposes of administrative or statistical information, or to take measures which are justified on grounds of public policy or public security.

Article 65(1)(b) is also subject to Article 65(3): the restrictions cannot constitute a means of arbitrary discrimination, etc. Article 65(1)(b) divides into two parts.

The first part covers the whole of the Article apart from the reference to public policy and public security. It has been convincingly argued[25] that this 'relates to the effective administration and enforcement of the tax system and the effective supervision of, for example, banks and insurance companies, rather than to matters of underlying economic policy', the latter being dealt

---

[21] Case C–279/93 *Schumacker* [1995] ECR I–225; Case C–376/03 *D* (n 14); Case C–374/04 *ACT Group Litigation* (n 19) [46]; Case C–446/04 *Test Claimants in the FII Group Litigation* (n 10); Case 375/12 *Bouanich* (n 18) [45].

[22] Usher (n 1) 34.

[23] Case C–35/98 *Staatssecretaris van Financiën v Verkooijen* [2000] ECR I–4071; Case C–512/03 *Blanckaert* [2005] ECR I–7685, [42].

[24] See also Case C–251/98 *Baars* (n 17); Case C–319/02 *Manninen* [2004] ECR I–7477; Case C–265/04 *Bouanich v Skatteverket* [2006] ECR I–923; Case C–386/04 *Centro di Musicologia v Finanzamt München für Körperschaften* [2006] ECR I–8203; Case C–292/04 *Meilicke, Wiede, Stoffler v Finanzamt Bonn-Innenstedt* [2007] ECR I–1835; Case C–43/07 *Arens-Sikken v Staatssecretaris van Financiën* [2008] ECR I–6887.

[25] Usher (n 1) 36.

with under Articles 143 and 144. The Court will inquire closely before accepting this defence. In *Commission v Belgium*[26] the ECJ held that a national rule forbidding Belgian residents from subscribing to securities of a loan on the Eurobond market was caught by Article 63. The Belgian Government argued that the measure was justified under Article 65(1)(b) because it preserved fiscal coherence. This argument was rejected because there was no direct link between any fiscal advantage and disadvantage which should be preserved in order to ensure such coherence. The Belgian Government argued moreover that the contested measure prevented tax evasion by Belgian residents, and ensured effective fiscal supervision. The ECJ disagreed, and held that the national rule was disproportionate: a general presumption of tax evasion could not justify a measure that compromised a Treaty Article.

The second part of Article 65(1)(b) covers public policy and public security. The Court draws on its jurisprudence from other freedoms when interpreting these terms. This exception is interpreted narrowly and the Member State has the burden of proof. The restriction must be justified in terms of national public interest of a kind referred to in Article 65(1), or by grounds of overriding public interest.[27] The restriction must also be proportionate, and will be struck down if a less restrictive measure could have achieved the desired end. In *Scientology International*[28] the ECJ held that a national law requiring prior authorization for capital investments that threatened public policy or security could, in principle, come within Article 65(1)(b). However, the particular French rule, which did not specify further details about the threat to public security, was regarded as too imprecise, and hence could not come within this Article.[29] However in *Commission v Belgium*[30] a national rule vesting the government with a 'golden share' in gas and electricity companies that had been privatized, enabling it to control certain subsequent dispositions of strategic assets, was held to fall within Article 65(1)(b) because it guaranteed energy supplies in the event of a crisis, and hence fell within public security.[31]

Article 65(2) states that the provisions of this Chapter shall be without prejudice to the applicability of restrictions on the right of establishment which are compatible with the Treaty. This Article is once again made subject to Article 65(3). These restrictions therefore include the exception in the case of official activities contained in Article 51.

Articles 143 and 144 contain a different type of qualification from Article 63. These Articles cease to operate from the third stage of EMU, except for states with a derogation, and deal with balance-of-payments crises. The 'strategy' is to look initially to an EU-sponsored solution via Article 143, and then to authorize unilateral action by the state if this is not forthcoming via Article 144.

---

[26] Case C–478/98 (n 16); Case C–315/02 *Lenz v Finanzlandesdirektion für Tirol* [2004] ECR I–7063, [45]–[49]; Case C–334/02 *Commission v France* [2004] ECR I–2229, [27]–[34]; Case C–451/05 *ELISA v Directeur général des impôts and Ministère public* [2007] ECR I–8251, [91]; Case C–540/07 *Commission v Italy* [2009] ECR I–10983, [58]; Case C–39/11 *VBV—Vorsorgekasse AG v Finanzmarktaufsichtsbehörde (FMA)* EU:C:2012:327, [29]–[38].

[27] Cases C–515 and 527–540/99 *Reisch* (n 15) [33]; Case C–213/04 *Burtscher* (n 8) [44]; Case C–174/04 *Commission v Italy* (n 18) [35]; Case C–326/07 *Commission v Italy* [2009] ECR I–2291, [70]; Case C–567/07 *Minister voor Wonen, Wijken en Integratie v Woningstichting Sint Servatius* [2009] ECR I–9021.

[28] Case C–54/99 *Association Eglise de Scientologie de Paris and Scientology International Reserves Trust v Prime Minister* [2000] ECR I–1355; Case C–20/09 *Commission v Portugal* [2011] ECR I–2637.

[29] Case C–423/98 *Albore* (n 15) [17]–[24].

[30] Case C–503/99 [2002] ECR I–4809.

[31] Compare however the different results in Case C–367/98 *Commission v Portugal* (n 18); Case C–483/99 *Commission v France* [2002] ECR I–4781; Cases C–282–283/04 *Commission v Netherlands* [2006] ECR I–9141.

3 EMU AND THE EUROPEAN MONETARY SYSTEM: EARLY ATTEMPTS

A little history is required to set matters in context. In 1969 the heads of state resolved that a plan should be drawn up in relation to EMU.[32] A committee was established chaired by Werner, the Luxembourg Prime Minister. It concluded[33] that EMU would entail either the total convertibility of the Community currencies, free from fluctuations in exchange rates, or that preferably such currencies would be replaced by a single Community currency. The report led to a Council Resolution on the attainment of EMU by stages.[34] Progress was, however, halted as a result of changed economic circumstances.

The Werner Report was premised on the assumption of fixed exchange rates, and this was undermined in the early 1970s.[35] Largely as a result of problems with the US economy,[36] European currencies began to float and there was an urgent need to prevent them from floating too far apart. This was the catalyst for the 'snake', which established that the difference between the exchange rates of two Member States should not be greater than 2.25 per cent. Economic pressures on particular Member States resulted however in departures from the 'snake', such that by 1977 only half of the ten Member States remained within it.[37]

A more general attempt to engender monetary stability occurred in 1978 through the establishment by Resolution of the European Council[38] of the European Monetary System (EMS).[39] There was growing dissatisfaction with floating exchange rates, which were perceived as detrimental to cross-border investment. Foreign currency movements were, moreover, destabilizing European currencies.[40] The EMS instituted the Exchange Rate Mechanism (ERM) and the European Currency Unit (ECU). The ECU rate was determined against a basket of Member State currencies. The ERM operated by setting for each participating state a currency rate against the ECU. These values were collectively determined. When the value of each currency was specified against the ECU it was then possible to determine the worth of any national currency against all other national currencies. These relative values were known as the bilateral central rates. Any participant country would not allow its exchange rate to fluctuate by more than 2.25 per cent above or below these bilateral central rates, with an exceptional band of 6 per cent. When a currency reached its bilateral limits against another currency, intervention was required by the relevant central banks to redress the matter.

The ERM was however thrown into disarray by the currency crises of 1992–1993. Currency dealers speculated that certain weaker currencies could not be sustained within the relatively narrow bands of the ERM. Central banks sought to preserve the integrity of the ERM, but could not resist market pressures. The lira and the pound were suspended from the ERM. Further market pressures led to the widening of the bilateral bands to 15 per cent, and to the devaluation of certain currencies which stayed within the ERM. These measures preserved the ERM in formal terms, but undermined its primary rationale, since they significantly weakened the search for exchange rate stability.

---

[32] For earlier developments, F Snyder, 'EMU Revisited: Are We Making a Constitution? What Constitution Are We Making' in P Craig and G de Búrca (eds), *The Evolution of EU Law* (Oxford University Press, 1999) 421–424.

[33] Bull EC Supp 11–1970.

[34] [1971] OJ C28/1.

[35] Usher (n 1) 138.

[36] D Swann, *The Economics of Europe, From Common Market to European Union* (Penguin, 9th edn, 2000) 204–205.

[37] Ibid 208.

[38] Bull EC 12–1978. This Resolution was reinforced by an Agreement between the national central banks.

[39] Snyder (n 32) 428–433.

[40] Swann (n 36) 209–210.

4 ECONOMIC AND MONETARY UNION: THE THREE STAGES[41]

(A) STAGE ONE AND THE DELORS REPORT

While the Single European Act (SEA) contained no commitment to EMU, it stated in a preamble that in 1972 the heads of state approved the objective of progressing towards EMU. This was the catalyst for bringing the issue back onto the political agenda at the Hanover summit of 1988. A committee, chaired by Jacques Delors, the President of the Commission, was established to assist the European Council, and reported to the Madrid summit in 1989.[42] It recommended that EMU should be approached in three stages.[43]

Stage One was the completion of the internal market, closer economic convergence, and the membership of all states of the ERM. This did not require new Treaty powers. In Stage Two a European System of Central Banks (ESCB) would be created to coordinate national monetary policies and formulate a common monetary policy for the Community. Stage Three would see the locking of exchange rates and a single currency managed by the ESCB. The Delors Report recognized that there would have to be central control over national fiscal policy, since otherwise the action of a particular state could have deleterious consequences for inflation or interest rates in all states.

(B) STAGE TWO AND THE MAASTRICHT SETTLEMENT

The Maastricht Treaty laid the foundations for EMU, and stipulated that the second stage should begin on 1 January 1994. The 'architecture' of the EMU provisions was predicated on a dichotomy between monetary and economic union, which remained largely unchanged in the Lisbon Treaty.

(i) *Monetary Policy*

Monetary union was all about the single currency and the Treaty Articles were powerfully influenced by German ordo-liberal economic thought, which demanded independence of the ECB, governance by experts and the primacy of price stability. These foundational precepts were embodied in the primary Treaty Articles. The independence of the ECB was enshrined in Article 130 TFEU, which stipulates that the ECB shall not take any instruction from EU institutions, Member States, or any other body, and is further affirmed by Article 282(3) TFEU. Governance by experts was stipulated in relation to the decision-making structure of the ECB. The Executive Board is composed of a President, Vice-President, and four other members, who must be recognized experts in monetary or banking matters.[44] The importance of expertise was further emphasized by the ESCB, which is composed of the ECB and the national central banks, although it is the ECB and the national central banks whose currency is the Euro that conduct the EU's monetary policy.[45] Price stability was accorded pride of place in the objectives of EU monetary policy from the outset, now found in Article 127 TFEU.

It was integral to the Maastricht settlement that monetary policy structured in the preceding manner was Europeanized. This was reinforced by mandatory Treaty provisions precluding instructions or interference from any outside party, whether a Member State or another EU institution. The importance of this principle is reflected in the symmetry of Article 130 TFEU. It imposes an obligation on

---

[41] K Dyson and K Featherstone, *The Road to Maastricht: Negotiating Economic and Monetary Union* (Oxford University Press, 1999).

[42] Report on Economic and Monetary Union in the European Community (EC Commission, 1988).

[43] Snyder (n 32) 432–435.

[44] Art 283(2) TFEU.

[45] Art 282(1) TFEU.

the ECB, national central banks, and those involved with their decision-making not to take or seek instructions from any other institution, including EU institutions, bodies, offices or agencies, any government of a Member State, or any other body. It also imposes a duty on EU institutions and Member State governments to respect this principle and not to seek to influence the members of the decision-making bodies of the ECB or of the national central banks in the performance of their tasks.

The very fact that monetary policy lay truly within the domain of the EU was further reinforced by the Lisbon Treaty provisions on competence. Article 3 TFEU stated clearly that monetary policy for those countries that subscribed to the Euro was within the exclusive competence of the EU, with the consequence that only the EU could legislate and adopt legally binding acts, subject to the caveat that the Member States could do so if empowered by the EU or for the implementation of Union acts.[46]

(ii) *Economic Policy*

The Maastricht settlement in relation to economic policy was markedly different. It was built on two related assumptions, preservation of national authority and preservation of national liability.

The former was reflected in the fact that Member States retained fiscal authority for national budgets, subject to oversight and coordination from the EU designed to persuade Member States, with the ultimate possibility of sanctions, to balance their budgets and not run excessive deficits.

The latter, preservation of national liability, was the consequence of the former. It finds its most powerful expression in the no bail-out provision, Article 125(1) TFEU. This provides in essence that the EU should not be liable for, or assume the commitments of, central governments, regional, local, or other public authorities, or other public bodies, and nor should a Member State be liable for, or assume the commitments of, such bodies within another Member State.[47] The message was that national governments retained authority over national economic policy, subject to the Treaty rules designed to persuade them to balance their budgets, the corollary being that if they did not do so then the liabilities remained their own.

This was the 'deal' struck in Maastricht and the principal features were unaltered in the Lisbon Treaty, although the degree of oversight was actually weakened in the intervening years. The Member States recognized the proximate connection between economic and monetary policy. They understood that the economic health of individual Member State economies could have a marked impact on the valuation of the Euro, hence the need for some oversight and coordination of national economic policy. They were however mindful of the policy decisions made in and through national budgets, including those of a redistributive nature, and were unwilling to accord the EU too much control over such determinations, whether at the individual or aggregative level.

(c) STAGE THREE AND THE LEGAL FRAMEWORK

The third stage of EMU had to start no later than 1 January 1999. The Commission and the European Monetary Institute, the forerunner of the ECB, had to report to the Council on the progress made by the states towards EMU. These reports would examine the extent to which the states had made their central banks independent, and whether the convergence criteria had been met, which was a condition precedent for a state to adopt the single currency.[48] Member States that did not fulfil

---

[46] Art 2(1) TFEU.

[47] This injunction was qualified to a limited extent by Art 122(2) TFEU, which allows the Council, on a proposal from the Commission, to grant financial assistance to a Member State that is in difficulty, or is seriously threatened with severe difficulty, caused by natural disasters or exceptional occurrences beyond its control.

[48] Art 140 TFEU.

the criteria were referred to as 'Member States with a derogation'. On the basis of these reports the Council assessed whether each Member State fulfilled the conditions for adoption of a single currency. The Council, meeting as the heads of state or government, had to decide by qualified majority, not later than 31 December 1996, whether a majority of the Member States fulfilled the conditions for the adoption of a single currency. If the date for the beginning of the third stage had not been set by the end of 1997 then the third stage was deemed to start on 1 January 1999.

The formal decision of the Council, meeting as the heads of state or government, that the applicant states, apart from Greece, had met the convergence criteria was made on 2 May 1998. The third stage of EMU duly began on 1 January 1999. The exchange rates of the participating countries were irrevocably set, and the Euro became a currency in its own right, notwithstanding those who doubted whether some states really would meet the convergence criteria,[49] given the high debt levels in Italy and Belgium. The UK negotiated an opt-out Protocol, the import of which is that it was not bound to move to the third stage of EMU even if it met the convergence criteria. On 1 January 2002 the new banknotes and coins were introduced, and national currencies were withdrawn from circulation towards the end of February 2002. There are currently eighteen Member States that have adopted the Euro: Austria, Belgium, Cyprus, Estonia, Finland, France, Germany, Greece, Ireland, Italy, Latvia, Luxembourg, Malta, Netherlands, Portugal, Slovakia, Slovenia, and Spain.

5 EMU: ECONOMIC FOUNDATIONS

It is important before examining the provisions concerning economic and monetary union to understand in outline at least the economic arguments for and against a single currency.[50]

(A) THE CASE FOR EMU

The case for EMU rested on two connected foundations. It was argued that EMU would foster economic growth and engender greater price stability through low inflation.

The argument that EMU would enhance *economic growth* was based on a number of factors, the most important being the *saving of transaction costs*. A single currency removes the cost of exchange-rate conversions when money moves within the EU. The Commission calculated that the total savings would be approximately €25 billion.[51]

An equally important, albeit contested, factor was the *link between the single market and a single currency*. This was captured most vividly in the Commission's slogan of 'one market, one money'.[52] It is possible to have a single market without a single currency, but it was argued that the single market would work better with a single currency. By having a single currency businesses save on 'menu costs', and do not have to maintain different sets of prices for each market. From the manufacturer's perspective, this facilitates marketing strategies for the EU as a whole. From the consumer's perspective, it enables direct price comparisons to be made of products in different countries.

The existence of a single currency was also said to protect against the *costs associated with large exchange-rate changes and competitive devaluation*, which could 'distort the single market by unpredictable shifts of advantage between countries unrelated to fundamentals'.[53] In this sense 'the single

---

[49] Snyder (n 32) 457–463.
[50] P de Grauwe, *Economics of Monetary Union* (Oxford University Press, 10th edn, 2014).
[51] *One Market, One Money* (European Commission, 1990) ch 3.
[52] Ibid; Commission's Work Programme for 1998 (EC Commission, 1997).
[53] C Johnson, *In with the Euro, Out with the Pound* (Penguin, 1996) 47.

market needs a single currency not just to push it forwards, but to stop it sliding backwards'.[54] Such currency fluctuations could slow economic growth by creating uncertainty for business, which was not conducive to investment.[55] The existence of wide price differentials fuelled by different currencies led moreover to attempts by Member States to prevent parallel imports and impede intra-EU trade.

It was argued that a single currency would in addition foster growth by *lowering interest rates and stimulating investment*. Countries would no longer have to raise their interest rates above German levels in order to stop their currencies from falling in relation to the Deutschmark.[56] Investment projects 'will become economic which were not so when they had to earn higher returns to repay expensive borrowed money, compensate for exchange rate uncertainty, and hand out high dividends to share-holders'.[57]

The case for EMU was also based on the argument that it fostered *stable prices and low inflation*. Savers tend to gain from low inflation, since their money retains its purchasing power for longer. Inflation makes it more difficult to maintain long-term business plans, and redistributes income in an arbitrary manner. Businesses incur 'menu costs' when inflation rates are high or constantly changing. The ERM exerted some discipline over inflation rates by the very fact that countries, in effect, linked their exchange rates to the Deutschmark, and limited their use of devaluation. Some countries however overvalued exchange rates, which was in part the rationale for the currency crises in 1992 and 1993. It was argued that EMU offered a better, cheaper, and more stable way of reducing inflation, particularly when monetary policy was run by an independent central bank, which was not subject to short-term political pressures.

(B) THE CASE AGAINST EMU

There were a number of differing arguments made against EMU. These can for the sake of analysis be divided into 'contingent disapproval' and 'outright rejection'.

The essence of the *contingent disapproval argument* was that the Member States were not ready for EMU, since they could not meet the convergence criteria, except by creative accounting that threw the whole enterprise into disrepute. This was exemplified by the letter signed by 155 German university professors, arguing that the time was not yet ripe for EMU,[58] and it was exemplified more recently by the difficulties created for the Euro by the financial crises in Greece, Ireland, and Spain. It is moreover reasonably clear that EMU may well suit some states more than others.

The *outright rejection argument* was more complex, and was part political, part symbolic, and part economic.

In political terms, some argued that a single currency was a major step towards a European super state.[59] Much economic policy was shifted from the domestic to the EU arena. National governments no longer had the ultimate option of devaluation, and parliamentary debates on inflation, interest rates, and unemployment would be largely otiose, since power over such matters would be taken from national polities and given to the ECB. It was argued that this would exacerbate problems of democratic deficit within the EU, given that the demise of national parliamentary power over such matters would not be offset by any meaningful control through the European Parliament.[60]

---

[54] Ibid.
[55] The Impact of Currency Fluctuations on the Internal Market, COM(95) 503 final.
[56] Johnson (n 53).
[57] Ibid 55.
[58] *Financial Times*, 9 Feb 1998.
[59] J Redwood, *The Single European Currency* (Tecla, 1995) 11–12.
[60] Ibid 19–20.

In symbolic terms, a national currency was felt by some to be part of the very idea of nationhood. This point is captured well by Johnson:[61]

> Advocates of monetary and exchange rate autonomy argue that it may not be perfect, but it is preferable to the alternative. The dishonour of a national currency may seem better than its death. Monetary sovereignty is sometimes felt to be part of a national sovereignty, so that giving it up involves a loss of political independence, and ultimately political union. It is almost a case of 'my country, right or wrong'.

In economic terms, it was argued that a single currency would lead to a variety of undesirable consequences. Prices would increase, since businesses would take advantage of the change from national currencies to the Euro to raise prices before consumers were accustomed to the new money.[62] A single currency could moreover create tensions because economic conditions in Member States followed different cycles, and hence removing the possibility of exchange-rate fluctuation eliminated a significant mechanism for economic adjustment between states.

(c) EMU: ECONOMICS, POLITICS, AND LAW

It is readily apparent that the debates about EMU are only in part economic. The economic dimension shades into the political, and these often manifest themselves in legal form.

F Snyder, EMU Revisited[63]

> The legal aspects of EMU are sometimes extremely controversial, either in public or behind the closed doors of diplomatic and monetary negotiations. Legal and other technical debates often act as a kind of shorthand for political disagreement. Competing economic theories frequently play the same role. This was the case long before EMU was set as a priority European Union objective. This does not mean, of course, that all legal aspects of EMU have been or are politically controversial. But, in the future also, political conflicts about EMU are likely often to appear in legal camouflage. This dialectical relationship between politics and law, political discourse and monetary discourse, and political discourse and legal discourse should not be surprising. The driving force in EMU, including its main legal aspects, has always been politics.

6 EMU: MONETARY UNION AND THE ECB

The provisions concerning monetary and economic union are complex. The former will be addressed in this section, the latter in the section which follows. Article 119 TFEU is the lead provision.

> 1. For the purposes set out in Article 3 of the Treaty on European Union, the activities of the Member States and the Union shall include, as provided in the Treaties, the adoption of an economic policy which is based on the close coordination of Member States' economic policies, on the internal market and on the definition of common objectives, and conducted in accordance with the principle of an open market economy with free competition.

---

[61] Johnson (n 53) 87.
[62] Redwood (n 59) 22.
[63] Snyder (n 32) 468.

2. Concurrently with the foregoing, and as provided in the Treaties and in accordance with the procedures set out therein, these activities shall include a single currency, the euro, and the definition and conduct of a single monetary policy and exchange-rate policy the primary objective of both of which shall be to maintain price stability and, without prejudice to this objective, to support the general economic policies in the Union, in accordance with the principle of an open market economy with free competition.

3. These activities of the Member States and the Union shall entail compliance with the following guiding principles: stable prices, sound public finances and monetary conditions and a sustainable balance of payments.

(A) ECB AND ESCB

The ECB together with the national central banks whose currency is the Euro, have the primary responsibility for monetary policy.[64] The ECB has legal personality.[65] It has an Executive Board and a Governing Council. The Executive Board is composed of a President, Vice-President, and four other members, who must be recognized experts in monetary or banking matters. They serve for eight years and the posts are non-renewable.[66] The Governing Council consists of the Executive Board plus the Governors of the national central banks whose currency is the Euro.[67] The President of the ECB is invited to Council meetings for discussion of matters that impact on the ESCB,[68] and for areas falling within its responsibilities the ECB shall be consulted on all proposed Union acts, and all proposals for regulation at national level, and may give an opinion.[69] The President and other members of the Executive Board can be heard before the European Parliament.[70]

The independence of the ECB is enshrined in Article 130 TFEU, which stipulates that the ECB shall not take any instruction from EU institutions, Member States, or any other body, and this is further affirmed by Article 282(3) TFEU. This independence is reflected in the ECB's decision-making structure: the President of the Council and a member of the Commission may participate in meetings of the ECB's Governing Council, but they do not have the right to vote.[71] The ECB has the power to make regulations, take decisions, make recommendations, and deliver opinions.[72] The ECB is entitled, on certain conditions, to impose fines or periodic penalty payments on undertakings for failure to comply with obligations contained in its regulations and decisions.[73]

The ESCB is composed of the ECB and the national central banks, although it is the ECB and the national central banks whose currency is the Euro which conduct the EU's monetary policy.[74] The ESCB is governed by the decision-making bodies of the ECB.[75] The Statute of the ESCB and ECB is attached to the Treaties as a Protocol.[76]

---

[64] Art 282(1) TFEU.
[65] Art 282(3) TFEU.
[66] Art 283(2) TFEU.
[67] Art 283(1) TFEU.
[68] Art 284(2) TFEU.
[69] Art 282(5) TFEU.
[70] Art 284(3) TFEU.
[71] Art 284(1) TFEU.
[72] Art 132(1) TFEU.
[73] Art 132(3) TFEU.
[74] Art 282(1) TFEU.
[75] Arts 129(1), 282(2) TFEU.
[76] Protocol (No 4) on the Statute of the European System of Central Banks and of the European Central Bank.

The third stage of EMU saw the establishment of the Economic and Financial Committee, composed of no more than two members drawn from the Member States, the Commission, and the ECB. This Committee has a number of tasks, including:[77] delivering opinions to the Council or Commission; keeping under review the economic and financial situation of the Member States and the EU; examining the situation regarding free movement of capital; and contributing to the preparation of Council work.

(B) MONETARY POLICY

The objectives of EU monetary policy are set out in Article 127 TFEU. The primary objective of the ESCB is to maintain price stability. Without prejudice to this objective, the ESCB must support the general economic policies of the EU with a view to attaining the objectives set out in Article 3 TEU. The ESCB is to act in accordance with the principle of an open market economy with free competition, and in compliance with the principles in Article 119 TFEU.

The basic tasks of the ESCB are:[78] to define and implement the EU's monetary policy; to conduct foreign-exchange operations; to hold and manage the official foreign reserves of the Member States; and to promote the smooth operation of the payment system. The ECB must be consulted on any EU act in its fields of competence and, subject to certain conditions, by national authorities regarding any draft legislative provision in its fields of competence.[79] The ECB has the exclusive right to authorize the issue of banknotes within the EU, although the actual issue of the notes may also be undertaken by national central banks.[80]

The ESCB is to 'contribute' to the smooth conduct of policies pursued by other competent authorities relating to the prudential supervision of credit institutions and the stability of the financial system.[81] It is in addition open to the Council, acting unanimously after consulting the European Parliament and the ECB, to confer specific tasks on the ECB concerning policies relating to the prudential supervision of credit institutions and other financial institutions with the exception of insurance undertakings.[82]

(C) POLICY ISSUES: CENTRAL BANK INDEPENDENCE

The Treaty places particular emphasis on the independence of the ECB.[83] The degree of independence possessed by national central banks varies.[84] Gormley and de Haan[85] identified five criteria that shape the division of responsibilities between national governments and their central banks.[86]

---

[77] Art 134(2) TFEU.

[78] Art 127(2) TFEU.

[79] Art 127(4) TFEU.

[80] Art 128(1) TFEU.

[81] Art 127(5) TFEU.

[82] Art 127(6) TFEU.

[83] C Zilioli and M Selmayr, *The Law of the European Central Bank* (Hart, 2001).

[84] F Amtenbrink, *The Democratic Accountability of Central Banks* (Hart, 1999) ch 4.

[85] L Gormley and J de Haan, 'The Democratic Deficit of the European Central Bank' (1996) 21 ELRev 95, 97–99; Amtenbrink (n 84) 17–22.

[86] See also R Lastra, 'European Monetary Union and Central Bank Independence' in M Andenas, L Gormley, C Hadjiemmanuil, and I Harden (eds), *European Economic and Monetary Union: The Institutional Framework* (Kluwer, 1997) ch 15; T Daintith, 'Between Domestic Democracy and an Alien Rule of Law? Some Thoughts on the "Independence" of the Bank of England' in ibid, ch 17; L Smaghi, 'Central Bank Independence in the EU: From Theory to Practice' (2008) 14 ELJ 446; R Smits, 'The European Central Bank's Independence and its Relation with the Economic Policy Makers' (2007–2008) 31 Fordham Int LJ 1614; B Krauskopf and C Steven, 'The Institutional Framework of the European System of Central Banks: Legal Issues in the Practice of the First Ten Years of its Existence' (2009) 46 CMLRev 1143.

The first is the ultimate objective of monetary policy, which in many countries is price stability. The second feature is the specification of inflation targets. In some countries this is agreed by the central bank with the government, in others, such as Germany, there is no obligation as such on the Bundesbank to announce or agree to any such targets. The third criterion is the bank's degree of independence and its juridical basis. There will, for example, often be a statute, which stipulates the extent to which the government can give any instructions to its central bank. The fourth criterion is the extent to which the government can override the central bank's view. The final factor is the appointment of bank officials, and the extent to which the government has any real discretion over this matter.

When judged by these criteria the ECB has a high degree of independence. Its independence is enshrined in Articles 130 and 282(3) TFEU. The Treaty establishes the primary and secondary objectives of the ESCB. There is no formal requirement for the ECB to agree with other Union institutions on the specification of price stability in particular economic circumstances, or on inflation targets. Nor is there any formal provision allowing the other EU institutions to override the choices made by the ECB.[87] It should however be noted by way of contrast to the position prior to the Lisbon Treaty that many of the provisions of the Statute of the ESCB and ECB can now be amended through the ordinary legislative procedure, and do not require Treaty amendment.[88]

The Treaty has nonetheless accorded a constitutional status to the ESCB and ECB. This degree of independence was influenced by German desires to have an ECB which mirrored closely the powers and status of the Bundesbank. This sentiment was further strengthened because the ECB would be considering price stability for the EU as a whole. It was therefore important that the short-term interests of certain Member States, or the EU institutions, could not sway the ECB. While political considerations, therefore, played a role in shaping the ESCB, there are also sound economic arguments for central bank independence.

L Gormley and J de Haan, The Democratic Deficit of the European Central Bank[89]

It is widely believed that the success of monetary policy in achieving a stable and low rate of inflation depends very much on the credibility of the monetary authorities. It makes quite a difference whether economic agents believe policy announcements and behave accordingly, or not. If a central bank with a high level of credibility indicates, for instance, that inflation is too high and that it will strive for a reduction, trade unions will take this announcement seriously in bargaining about wage levels. If the credibility of the central bank is low, trade unions may not believe that inflation will come down and demand higher wages, thereby fuelling the inflationary process.

By delegating monetary policy to an independent Central Bank with a clear mandate for price stability the credibility of the monetary authorities can be enhanced. A Central Bank which is independent will not be exposed to the same incentives to create unexpected inflation. The public can assume that the Central Bank will strive for a low level of inflation. Trade unions will lower their wage demands and investors will ask for lower interest rates as their inflationary expectations are reduced. Due to lower inflationary expectations, actual inflation will also decline.

---

[87] The ECB's independence does not render it immune from anti-fraud investigations via OLAF: Case C–11/00 *Commission v ECB* [2003] ECR I–7147.

[88] Art 129(3) TFEU.

[89] Gormley and de Haan (n 85) 110.

There is not, however, only one way to structure a central bank, even given acceptance of independence as an ideal. Numerous factors influence the degree of independence accorded to it. In economic terms, it has been argued that the relationship between a central bank and government should be conceived in terms of a principal/agent contract, whereby the principal, the government, would establish inflation targets and make the agent, the central bank, responsible for attaining them.[90] In political terms, a fully independent central bank, with little provision for policy override by the government may well attain price stability, but at the expense of democratic control. Monetary policy is, in this sense, taken off the normal political agenda, with a corresponding diminution in democratic control.[91]

L Gormley and J de Haan, The Democratic Deficit of the European Central Bank[92]

By now it is well-known that Central Bank independence may improve upon monetary policy. In that sense, the independence of the ESCB and its mandate to strive for price stability are to be applauded, given the virtues of a low and stable rate of inflation. An important problem is how Central Bank independence is related to democratic accountability. Some authors argue that monetary policy should be treated like other instruments of economic policy, like fiscal policy, and should be fully decided upon by democratically elected representatives. Such an approach implies, however, too much a direct involvement of politicians with monetary policy.... Nevertheless, it is respectfully submitted that monetary policy ultimately must be controlled by democratically elected politicians.... Some way or another, the Central bank has to be accountable, and in relation to the ECB, the European Parliament is undoubtedly the appropriate body. National parliaments are, of course, responsible for Central Bank legislation; so too, logically, should the European Parliament be responsible for the legislative framework of the ECB, at least by way of co-decision. In other words, the 'rules of the game' (i. e. the objective of monetary policy) are decided upon according to normal democratic procedures, but the 'game' (monetary policy) is delegated to the Central Bank.

7 EMU: COORDINATION OF ECONOMIC POLICY

Coordination of economic policy is the other limb of EMU. Such coordination has been especially important in the light of monetary union,[93] since the economic health of individual Member States' economies can have a marked impact on the valuation of the Euro, as exemplified by the EU's economic crisis, which is examined below.[94] This is the broad rationale for coordination, two forms of which are embodied in the Treaty.

---

[90] Ibid 111–112.

[91] W Buiter, 'Alice in Euroland' (1999) 37 JCMS 181; O Issing, 'The Eurosystem Transparent and Accountable or "Willem in Euroland"' (1999) 37 JCMS 503.

[92] Gormley and de Haan (n 85) 112. See Amtenbrink (n 84) ch 5 for suggestions on how democratic accountability could be improved.

[93] D Hodson and I Maher, 'The Open Method as a New Mode of Governance: The Case of Soft Economic Policy Co-ordination' (2001) 39 JCMS 719; F Amtenbrink and J de Haan, 'Economic Governance in the European Union' (2003) 40 CMLRev 1075; D Hodson and I Maher, 'Soft Law and Sanctions: Economic Policy Coordination and Reform of the Stability and Growth Pact' (2004) 11 JEPP 798; J-V Louis, 'The Economic and Monetary Union: Law and Institutions' (2004) 41 CMLRev 575; I Maher, 'Economic Governance: Hybridity, Accountability and Control' (2007) 13 CJEL 679; R Goebel, 'Economic Governance in the European Union: Should Fiscal Stability Outweigh Economic Growth in the Stability and Growth Pact?' (2007–2008) 31 Fordham Int LJ 1266.

[94] Council Regulation (EC) No 1467/97 of 7 July 1997 on speeding up and clarifying the implementation of the excessive deficit procedure [1997] OJ L209/6, rec 8.

(A) MULTILATERAL SURVEILLANCE PROCEDURE

The softer version is the multilateral surveillance procedure. Member States are to regard their economic policies as a matter of common concern, and are to coordinate them in the Council.[95] The Council acting on a recommendation from the Commission, formulates a draft for the broad guidelines[96] of the economic policies of the Member States and the EU, and reports this to the European Council. The guidelines are discussed by the European Council, and its conclusion forms the basis for a Council recommendation setting out the broad guidelines.[97] It is then for the Council, on the basis of reports from the Commission, to monitor economic developments in the Member States.[98]

This constitutes the multilateral surveillance. If it becomes apparent that the economic policies of the Member States are not consistent with the broad economic guidelines, or that they risk jeopardizing the proper functioning of EMU, the Commission may address a warning to the relevant Member States. The Council may make the necessary recommendations to the Member State concerned.[99] The Council acts without taking account of the vote of the Member State concerned.[100]

The Treaty provisions have been complemented by the Stability and Growth Pact (SGP). The Regulation[101] provides rules covering the content, submission, examination, and monitoring of the stability and convergence programmes so as to prevent at an early stage the occurrence of excessive government deficit, and to promote the surveillance and coordination of economic policies. The SGP has recently been reformed as will be seen below.

(B) EXCESSIVE DEFICIT PROCEDURE

The harder version of coordination is embodied in the excessive deficit procedure. Member States are under an obligation to avoid excessive deficits.[102] The Commission monitors the budgetary situation and government debt in the Member States to identify 'gross errors'.[103] The Commission must in particular examine compliance with budget discipline on the basis of two criteria.[104]

The first criterion is whether the ratio of the planned or actual government deficit to gross domestic product exceeds a reference value, this being 3 per cent, unless either the ratio has declined substantially and continuously and reached a level that comes close to the reference value, or, alternatively, the excess over the reference value is only exceptional and temporary and the ratio remains close to the reference value. The second criterion is whether the ratio of government debt to gross domestic product exceeds a reference value, this being 60 per cent, unless the ratio is sufficiently diminishing and approaching the reference value at a satisfactory pace. These reference values are specified in the Protocol on the Excessive Deficit Procedure.[105]

The Commission reports where a Member State does not fulfil these criteria, and may do so if it believes that there is a risk of an excessive deficit in a Member State.[106] The Economic and Financial

---

[95] Art 121(1) TFEU.
[96] Council Recommendation 95/326/EC of 10 July 1995 on the broad guidelines of the economic policies of the Member States and of the Community [1995] OJ L191/24.
[97] Art 121(2) TFEU.
[98] Art 121(3) TFEU.
[99] Art 121(4) TFEU.
[100] Art 121(4) TFEU.
[101] Council Regulation (EC) No 1466/97 of 7 July 1997 on the strengthening of the surveillance of budgetary positions and the surveillance and coordination of economic policies [1997] OJ L209/1.
[102] Art 126(1) TFEU.
[103] Art 126(2) TFEU.
[104] Art 126(2) TFEU.
[105] Protocol (No 12), Art 1.
[106] Art 126(3) TFEU.

Committee gives an opinion on this report.[107] Where the Commission considers that there is an excessive deficit, or that it may occur, the Commission must address an opinion to the Member State concerned and inform the Council.[108] It is then for the Council, acting on a proposal from the Commission and having taken account of any observations from the Member State, to decide whether the excessive deficit exists.[109]

Where the Council decides that an excessive deficit does exist, it shall adopt, without undue delay, on a recommendation from the Commission, recommendations addressed to the Member State concerned with a view to bringing that situation to an end within a given period.[110] The general rule is that these recommendations are not made public, but where the Council establishes that the Member State has taken no effective action within the requisite period then the Council may make the recommendations public.[111]

The Treaty then contains provisions specifying what should happen if the Member State fails to put into practice the recommendations of the Council. If this occurs the Council can decide to give notice to the Member State to take, within a specified time limit, measures for the deficit reduction which is judged necessary by the Council in order to remedy the situation, and to submit reports to the Council so that it can examine the adjustment efforts of that Member State.[112]

If the Member State fails to comply with such a decision, the Council may then decide to apply or intensify one or more of the following measures:[113] it can require the Member State to publish additional information, specified by the Council, before issuing bonds and securities; it can invite the European Investment Bank to reconsider its lending policy towards that Member State; it can require the Member State to make a non-interest-bearing deposit of an appropriate size with the Union until the excessive deficit has, in the Council's view, been corrected; and it can impose fines of an appropriate size. The Council must abrogate the preceding decisions and recommendations to the extent that the excessive deficit in the Member State has, in the Council's view, been corrected.[114]

The Treaty provisions on excessive deficit have, like those on surveillance, been complemented by a regulation concerning excessive deficit,[115] this being the other limb of the SGP.

(c) POLICY ISSUES: ECONOMIC POLICY COORDINATION

The frailty of the surveillance and deficit procedures was revealed in relation to the deficits run by France, Germany, Portugal, and Italy in 2002–2003. They undertook to balance their budgets over the medium term, but departed from their corrective programmes. This led to the Commission taking legal action when Ecofin placed the excessive deficit procedure in abeyance for France and Germany.[116] The flouting of the system by France and Germany led to changes to the Stability and Growth Pact Regulations,[117] the net effect being to soften and render more discretionary the multilateral surveillance and excessive deficit procedures.[118]

---

[107] Art 126(4) TFEU.
[108] Art 126(5) TFEU.
[109] Art 126(6) TFEU.
[110] Art 126(7) TFEU.
[111] Art 126(8) TFEU.
[112] Art 126(9) TFEU.
[113] Art 126(11) TFEU.
[114] Art 126(12) TFEU.
[115] Reg 1467/97 (n 94).
[116] 2546th Meeting of the Council of the European Union (Economic and Financial Affairs), Brussels, 25 Nov 2003.
[117] Council Regulation (EC) No 1055/2005 of 27 June 2005 amending Regulation 1466/97 [2005] OJ L174/1; Council Regulation (EC) No 1056/2005 of 27 June 2005 amending Regulation 1467/97 [2005] OJ L174/5; J-V Louis, 'The Review of the Stability and Growth Pact' (2006) 43 CMLRev 85.
[118] W Schelkle, 'EU Fiscal Governance: Hard Law in the Shadow of Soft Law?' (2007) 13 CJEL 705.

The regime for coordination of economic policy was subject to more general strain as a result of the banking and financial crisis that began in 2008.[119] The essence of the problem began with the fact that Greece's rating to repay its debt was downgraded.[120] This then led to problems for the Euro, and to concerns about the budgetary health of some other countries that used the currency. The net impact of these developments was downward pressure on the Euro, which was only alleviated when Euro countries provided a support package for Greece that satisfied the financial markets. The sovereign debt crisis was overlaid by, and interacted with, the banking crisis that affected some lending institutions that were heavily committed to economic sectors, such as housing, which were hit badly by the downturn in the economic markets. The deeper causality underlying these events is contestable.[121] The crisis generated a range of responses from the EU.[122]

(i) *Assistance*

The EU put in place a range of measures to give assistance to Member States that were in severe economic problems as a result of the Euro crisis. The most important common element is conditionality, connoting the basic precept that funds are given on strict conditions concerning reforms that must be put in place by the recipient state.

The assistance was initially provided through the European Financial Stabilisation Mechanism (EFSM), which was financed from the EU budget and from bonds.[123] It was then provided by the European Financial Stability Facility (EFSF), a company established by the Euro countries on 9 May 2010.[124]

The main vehicle for assistance is now the European Stability Mechanism (ESM)[125] which entered into force on 8 October 2012.[126] Article 136 TFEU was amended by the simplified revision procedure, the result being a new paragraph 3, which stated that 'the Member States whose currency is the euro may establish a stability mechanism to be activated if indispensable to safeguard the stability of the euro-area as a whole'.[127] However this amendment was not in force when the ESM was established and could not therefore form the legal basis for the ESM, which therefore took effect as an intergovernmental organization based on an international treaty between the Euro-area Member States. The ESM has a total subscribed capital of €700 billion, €80 billion of which is in the form of paid-in capital provided by the Euro-area Member States in five instalments of €16 billion.

The legality of the ESM was challenged in *Pringle*,[128] where the claimant argued that it was concerned with monetary policy, which fell within the exclusive competence of the EU, with the consequence

---

[119] http://ec.europa.eu/economy_finance/crisis/2010-04_en.htm; H James, H-W Micklitz, and H Schweitzer, 'The Impact of the Financial Crisis on the European Economic Constitution', EUI Law Working Paper, 2010/05.

[120] A valuable summary can be found in P de Grauwe, 'Crisis in the Eurozone and How to Deal With It' CEPS Policy Brief No 204, Feb 2010.

[121] M Maduro, 'A New Governance for the European Union and the Euro: Democracy and Justice', European Parliament, Directorate-General for Internal Policies, Policy Department C: Citizens' Rights and Constitutional Affairs, PE 462.484, 2012, 9–10.

[122] P Craig, 'Economic Governance and the Euro Crisis: Constitutional Architecture and Constitutional Implications' in M Adams, F Fabbrini, and P Larouche (eds), *The Constitutionalization of European Budgetary Constraints* (Hart, 2014) ch 2.

[123] Council Regulation (EU) No 407/2010 of 11 May 2010 establishing a European financial stabilisation mechanism [2010] OJ L118/1.

[124] http://www.efsf.europa.eu/about/index.htm.

[125] http://www.esm.europa.eu/.

[126] Arts 39–40 ESM.

[127] European Council Decision 2011/199 of 25 March 2011 amending Art 136 TFEU with regard to a stability mechanism for Member States whose currency is the euro [2011] OJ L91/1.

[128] Case C–370/12 *Pringle v Government of Ireland, Ireland and the Attorney General* EU:C:2012:756.

that the Member States had no competence to enact legally binding measures in this area. The other principal contention was that the ESM was legally inconsistent with the no bail-out clause contained in Article 125 TFEU. The ECJ rejected the arguments and upheld the legality of the ESM.[129]

The ECB also provided some assistance through, for example, Outright Monetary Transactions (OMTs) which concern transactions in secondary sovereign bond markets 'that aim at safeguarding an appropriate monetary policy transmission and the singleness of the monetary policy.'[130] The legality of these measures was challenged by the German Federal Constitutional Court, its first ever reference to the CJEU. The CJEU's decision has not, at the time of writing, been given. However in *Gauweiler*[131] Advocate General Cruz Villalón concluded that the OMT programme should be regarded as lawful. He rejected the argument that the OMT scheme was economic policy designed to pool debt of certain Member States and thus outside the power of the ECB. He concluded that it could legitimately be regarded as monetary policy, and that it was a proportionate response to the threat posed to the Euro, provided that the ECB refrained from any direct involvement in the financial assistance programmes to which the OMT programme was linked. The Advocate General also concluded that the OMT programme was not in violation of Article 123 TFEU, which prohibits the ECB from purchasing debt instruments from Member States, provided that, in the event of the programme being implemented, the timing of its implementation was such as to permit the formation of a market price in respect of the government bonds.

(ii) *Oversight*

The grant of assistance to Member States in serious financial difficulty has been complemented by increased supervision over national financial institutions. Thus the regulatory apparatus for banking, securities, insurance, and occupational pensions has been thoroughly overhauled,[132] and new measures have been introduced such as the Single Resolution Mechanism, which has increased EU oversight over national banking facilities.

There have also been major changes designed to increase oversight over national economic policy, because of the proximate connection between economic and monetary union. The primary objective was to tighten EU control over national economic policy in order to prevent a recurrence of the sovereign debt and banking crises that precipitated the crisis with the Euro. The legislative framework for economic union was amended through the 'six-pack' of measures in 2011,[133] which were enacted pursuant to Articles 121, 126, and 136 TFEU.[134] The measures were designed to render economic union

---

[129] P Koutrakos, 'Political Choices and Europe's Judges' (2013) 38 ELRev 291; B de Witte and T Beukers, 'The Court of Justice Approves the Creation of the European Stability Mechanism: *Pringle*' (2013) 50 CMLRev 805; A Hinarejos, 'The Court of Justice of the EU and the Legality of the European Stability Mechanism' (2013) 72 CLJ 237; P Craig, '*Pringle*: Legal Reasoning, Text, Purpose and Teleology' (2013) 20 MJ 1; G Beck, 'The Legal Reasoning of the Court of Justice and the Euro Crisis—The Flexibility of the Cumulative Approach and the *Pringle* Case' (2013) 20 MJ 635; P Craig, '*Pringle* and the Nature of Legal Reasoning' (2014) 21 MJ 205.

[130] http://www.ecb.int/press/pr/date/2012/html/pr120906_1.en.html.

[131] Case C–62/14 *Gauweiler and others v Deutsche Bundestag*, 14 Jan 2015.

[132] Regulation (EU) No 1093/2010 of the European Parliament and of the Council of 24 November 2010 establishing a European Supervisory Authority (European Banking Authority) [2010] OJ L331/12; Regulation (EU) No 1095/2010 of the European Parliament and of the Council of 24 November 2010 establishing a European Supervisory Authority (European Securities and Markets Authority) [2010] OJ L331/84; Regulation (EU) No 1094/2010 of the European Parliament and of the Council of 24 November 2010 establishing a European Supervisory Authority (European Insurance and Occupational Pensions Authority) [2010] OJ L331/4.

[133] http://ec.europa.eu/economy_finance/economic_governance/index_en.htm.

[134] Regulation (EU) No 1175/2011 of the European Parliament and of the Council of 16 November 2011 amending Regulation (EC) No 1466/97 on the strengthening of the surveillance of budgetary positions and the surveillance and coordination of economic policies [2011] OJ L306/12; Council Regulation (EU) No 1177/2011 of 8 November 2011 amending Regulation (EC) No 1467/97 on speeding up and clarifying the implementation of the excessive deficit

more effective by tightening the two parts of the schema, surveillance and excessive deficit, the details of which were contained in the Stability and Growth Pact.[135] Further measures, the two-pack, were enacted on 21 May 2013.[136] Space precludes detailed elaboration of these complex provisions. Suffice it to say for the present that they included changes to enhance budgetary oversight by focusing on its timing, the format of national budgetary determinations, and the need for these to be independently verified. Further changes to the surveillance mechanism are substantive and require Member States to make significant progress towards medium-term budgetary objectives (MTO) for their budgetary balances. The EU also strengthened the excessive deficit procedure, the other limb of economic union.

The rules on oversight over national economic policy analysis have also been affected by the Treaty on Stability, Coordination and Governance,[137] hereafter the TSCG, also known as the Fiscal Compact, which was signed by twenty-five contracting states in March 2012.[138] Article 3(1) TSCG contains the 'balanced budget' rule and is the heart of the new Treaty. The budgets of the contracting parties must be balanced or in surplus. This is deemed to be respected if the annual structural balance of the general government is at its country-specific medium-term objective, as defined in the revised SGP, with a lower limit of a structural deficit of 0.5 per cent of gross domestic product at market prices. The contracting parties must ensure rapid convergence towards their respective medium-term objectives, within a time frame set by the Commission. While the obligation to balance the national budget is the core of the TSCG, it is arguable that almost everything therein might have been done under the Lisbon Treaty provisions.[139] It is also important to recognize that the provisions concerning assistance and those concerning oversight are 'joined at the hip', in the sense that grant of assistance under the ESM is conditional from 1 March 2013 on ratification by the applicant state of the Fiscal Compact.

(iii) *Political, Legal, and Economic Concerns*

The financial crisis has cast a serious shadow over the EU and has led to a plethora of political, legal, and economic concerns, which can only be touched on here.[140]

Thus in political terms, it has rocked the EU's defining credo, which was the promise of peace and prosperity. Politicians and academics might engage in complex argument about the relative degree

---

procedure [2011] OJ L306/33; Regulation (EU) No 1173/2011 of the European Parliament and of the Council of 16 November 2011 on the effective enforcement of budgetary surveillance in the euro area [2011] OJ L306/1; Council Directive 2011/85/EU of 8 November 2011 on requirements for budgetary frameworks of the Member States [2011] OJ L306/41; Regulation (EU) No 1176/2011 of the European Parliament and of the Council of 16 November 2011 on the prevention and correction of macroeconomic imbalances [2011] OJ L306/25; Regulation (EU) No 1174/2011 of the European Parliament and of the Council of 16 November 2011 on enforcement measures to correct macroeconomic imbalances in the euro area [2011] OJ L306/8; Results of in-depth reviews under Regulation (EU) No 1176/2011 on the prevention and correction of macroeconomic imbalances, COM(2013) 199 final.

[135] Reg 1466/97 (n 101); Reg 1467/97 (n 94).

[136] Regulation (EU) No 472/2013 of the European Parliament and of the Council of 21 May 2013 on the strengthening of economic and budgetary surveillance of Member States experiencing or threatened with serious difficulties with respect to their financial stability in the euro area [2013] OJ L140/1; Regulation (EU) No 473/2013 of the European Parliament and of the Council of 21 May 2013 on common provisions for monitoring and assessing draft budgetary plans and ensuring the correction of excessive deficit of the Member States in the euro area [2013] OJ L140/11.

[137] P Craig, 'The Stability, Coordination and Governance Treaty: Principle, Politics and Pragmatism' (2012) 37 ELRev 231; S Peers, 'The Stability Treaty: Permanent Austerity or Gesture Politics?' (2012) 8 EuConst 404.

[138] Treaty on Stability, Coordination and Governance in the Economic and Monetary Union, 1–2 Mar 2012, available at www.european-council.europa.eu/eurozone-governance/treaty-on-stability?lang=en.

[139] Craig (n 137); Peers (n 137).

[140] Adams, Fabbrini and Larouche (n 122); C Joerges, 'Law and Politics in Europe's Crisis: On the History of the Impact of an Unfortunate Configuration', EUI Law Working Papers, 2013/09; I Pernice, M Wendel, L Otto, K Bettge, M Mlynarski, and M Schwarz, *A Democratic Solution to the Crisis: Reform Steps Towards a Democratically Based Economic and Financial Constitution for Europe* (Nomos, 2012).

of responsibility for the current malaise. This, however, matters little if at all from the perspective of ordinary citizens, more especially those living in countries affected most dramatically by the Euro-crisis and consequent economic measures imposed under the name of conditionality. For these people it is the EU and the Euro that has failed, and this is so irrespective of political and academic discourse as to the 'real' causes of the crisis. Another political consequence of the crisis has been an increase in EU supervisory power over national economic policy, in order to prevent recurrence of the crisis, with the consequence that national political choice has been further constrained. There are in addition political and social problems caused by the need for national austerity measures to comply with conditionality requirements from EU assistance, which can have a very marked impact on, for example, the funding of national social welfare programmes.

In legal terms, the range of measures enacted pursuant to the financial crisis has exacerbated problems of transparency and complexity that already beset this area. There were prior to the recent reforms three layers of complex legal rules pertinent to control over national economic policy: provisions of the Lisbon Treaty, EU legislation, and the broad economic policy guidelines. The ESM and TSCG add a fourth layer to the existing schema through Treaties operating outside the Lisbon Treaty. This exacerbates difficulties of complexity and transparency, more especially because there is very significant overlap between obligations incumbent on states through the six-pack and two-pack of EU legislation, and those in the TSCG. There are in addition further legal problems concerning, for example, the application of the Charter of Fundamental Rights in this area,[141] and the ability of EU institutions to participate in treaties outside the framework of EU law, such as the ESM and the Fiscal Compact.[142]

In economic terms, the central issues are funding, who pays for the assistance, and moral hazard, the concern that the recipient state will take excessive risks and free ride on the greater fiscal rectitude practised by others. The numbers involved with financial assistance/bail-outs are significant indeed. They are in the billions. The money has come from other Member States, with Germany bearing the principal burden. This is likely to continue for the foreseeable future, given that financing of the ESM is predicated on state contributions. The economic impact of contributions from smaller countries should nonetheless be kept firmly in mind. The aggregate constraints thereby placed on Member State economic freedom are far-reaching.

8 CONCLUSIONS

i. In terms of free movement of capital, there has been a growing body of case law testing the Treaty provisions. This case law should be viewed alongside that dealing with goods, persons, establishment, and services.

ii. In terms of EMU, the financial crisis revealed that the Maastricht architecture, whereby there was an asymmetry between monetary and economic policy, was unsustainable. The controls over national economic policy were not strong enough, even though it is generally recognized that there is an intimate relationship between monetary policy and economic policy, since if countries run long-term budgetary deficits then this will cause the currency markets to take a poor view of the value of the Euro.

---

[141] C Barnard, 'The Charter, the Court and the Crisis', Cambridge Legal Studies Research Paper, 18/2013.
[142] P Craig, '*Pringle* and Use of EU Institutions Outside the EU Legal Framework: Foundations, Procedure and Substance' (2013) 9 EuConst 263.

iii. It is for this reason that one principal dimension of the EU's response to the financial crisis has been the raft of legislation designed to increase control over banking and national budgets to prevent a recurrence of the banking and sovereign debt crisis, with the other principal dimension being the grant of assistance to those countries in dire economic trouble in order to prevent further 'economic contagion' in the Euro area.

iv. The political, legal, and economic consequences of the crisis have been very significant and are unlikely to be short term.

9 FURTHER READING

(a) Books

ADAMS, M, FABBRINI, F, AND LAROUCHE, P (eds), *The Constitutionalization of European Budgetary Constraints* (Hart, 2014)

AMTENBRINK, F, *The Democratic Accountability of Central Banks* (Hart, 1999)

BEAUMONT, P, AND WALKER, N (eds), *The Legal Framework of the Single European Currency* (Hart, 1999)

DAHLBERG, M, *Direct Taxation in Relation to the Freedom of Establishment and the Free Movement of Capital* (Kluwer Law International, 2005)

DE GRAUWE, P, *Economics of Monetary Union* (Oxford University Press, 10th edn, 2014)

DYSON, K, *Elusive Union: The Process of Economic and Monetary Union in Europe* (Longman, 1994)

——— *The Politics of the Euro-Zone: Stability or Breakdown* (Oxford University Press, 2000)

——— AND FEATHERSTONE, K, *The Road to Maastricht: Negotiating Economic and Monetary Union* (Oxford University Press, 1999)

HINAREJOS, A, *The Euro Area Crisis in Constitutional Perspective* (Oxford University Press, 2015)

HINDELANG, S, *The Free Movement of Capital and Foreign Direct Investment: The Scope of Protection in EU Law* (Oxford University Press, 2009)

MULHEARN, C, AND VANE, H, *The Euro: Its Origins, Development and Prospects* (Edward Elgar, 2009)

SWANN, D, *The Economics of Europe: From Common Market to European Union* (Penguin, 9th edn, 2000)

TUORI, K, AND TUORI, K, *The Eurozone Crisis, A Constitutional Analysis* (Cambridge University Press, 2014)

ZILIOLI, C, AND SELMAYR, M, *The Law of the European Central Bank* (Hart, 2001)

(b) Articles

AMTENBRINK, F, AND DE HAAN, J, 'Economic Governance in the European Union: Fiscal Policy Discipline versus Flexibility' (2003) 40 CMLRev 1075

BARNARD, C, 'The Charter, the Court and the Crisis', Cambridge Legal Studies Research Paper, 18/2013

CRAIG, P, 'The Stability, Coordination and Governance Treaty: Principle, Politics and Pragmatism' (2012) 37 ELRev 231

——— 'Economic Governance and the Euro Crisis: Constitutional Architecture and Constitutional Implications' in M ADAMS, F FABBRINI, and P LAROUCHE (eds), *The Constitutionalization of European Budgetary Constraints* (Hart, 2014) ch 2

DE WITTE, B, AND BEUKERS, T, 'The Court of Justice Approves the Creation of the European Stability Mechanism: *Pringle*' (2013) 50 CMLRev 805

JAMES, H, MICKLITZ, H-W, AND SCHWEITZER, H, 'The Impact of the Financial Crisis on the European Economic Constitution', EUI Law Working Paper, 2010/05

JOERGES, C, 'Law and Politics in Europe's Crisis: On the History of the Impact of an Unfortunate Configuration', EUI Law Working Papers, 2013/09

LOUIS, J-V, 'The Economic and Monetary Union: Law and Institutions' (2004) 41 CMLRev 575

PEERS, S, 'The Stability Treaty: Permanent Austerity or Gesture Politics?' (2012) 8 EuConst 404

SCHELKLE, W, 'EU Fiscal Governance: Hard Law in the Shadow of Soft Law?' (2007) 13 CJEL 705

SNELL, J, 'Free Movement of Capital: Evolution as a Non-Linear Process' in P Craig and G de Búrca (eds), *The Evolution of EU Law* (Oxford University Press, 2nd edn, 2011) ch 18

SNYDER, F, 'EMU Revisited: Are We Making a Constitution? What Constitution Are We Making' in P Craig and G de Búrca (eds), *The Evolution of EU Law* (Oxford University Press, 1999) ch 12

——— 'EMU—Integration and Differentiation: Metaphor for European Union' in P CRAIG and G DE BÚRCA (eds), *The Evolution of EU Law* (Oxford University Press, 2nd edn, 2011) ch 22

ZILIOLI, C, AND SELMAYER, M, 'The Constitutional Status of the European Central Bank' (2007) 44 CMLRev 355

FREE MOVEMENT OF WORKERS

1 CENTRAL ISSUES

i. The free movement of persons is one of the four fundamental freedoms of EU law, along with the free movement of goods, services, and capital. This chapter deals primarily with the free movement of employed persons (workers); the next chapter with the free movement of the self-employed and of companies (establishment and services); and the following chapter with the umbrella category of European citizens. The creation of the status of EU citizenship has influenced the development of the law on free movement of workers in various ways.

ii. EU law governing the free movement of workers centres on a number of key questions. These include the scope of Article 45 TFEU, the meaning accorded to 'worker', the rights of intermediate categories such as 'job-seeker', the kinds of restrictions which states may justifiably impose on workers and their families; and the social and other rights which family members enjoy under EU law.

iii. The basic legislative instrument governing the free movement of workers is Regulation 492/2011, which updates and consolidates the original Regulation 1612/68. This is supplemented by (a) the recently adopted Directive 2014/54, which is an enforcement measure intended to facilitate the exercise of the already-existing rights of workers; (b) Decision 2003/8 on the EURES network of public employment services, with a pending proposal for a more ambitious Regulation to create an improved network of employment services;[1] (c) several laws on the coordination of social security, including Regulations 1408/71 and 883/2004, as well as Directive 2014/50; (d) a growing body of soft law and supplementary guidance produced not just by the Commission itself, but also by the network of experts on the free movement of workers which has been in operation for some decades.[2] (e) Finally, Directive 2004/38 on the rights of movement and residence of EU citizens contains many provisions relevant to the free movement of workers. This Directive includes workers and self-employed persons and their families, as well as students and other kinds of non-economically active EU nationals.

---

[1] See COM(2014) 6. For a separate decision on cooperation between public employment services, see Dec 2014/573 [2014] OJ L159/32. For a failed challenge by the European Parliament to the Commission Dec updating Dec 2003/8 on EURES, see Case C–65/13 *Parliament v Commission* EU:C:2014:2289.

[2] See recently Communication on Free Movement of Citizens and Their Families: Five Actions to Make a Difference, COM(2013) 837; Communication Towards a Job Rich Recovery, COM(2012) 173; and also the annual and thematic reports of the Network of Experts on the Free Movement of Persons (2003–2010) which are published on the website of DG Employment, http://ec.europa.eu/social/main.jsp?catId=475&langId=en; as well as the reports of the new network on free movement of workers and social security coordination: http://ec.europa.eu/social/main.jsp?catId=1097&langId=en.

iv. There are economic and social dimensions to the free movement of workers. In economic terms, the rationale is to ensure what economists term the optimal allocation of resources within the EU.[3] The value of labour within the EU is said to be maximized if workers can move to the area or country where they are most valued, in economic terms. Beyond this rationale, it has also been argued that the promotion of mobility of workers helps foster 'an ever closer Union of the peoples of Europe', and is linked with a broader notion of European solidarity.

v. There may be tensions between the various economic and social dimensions. The notion of EU workers as mobile units of production contributing to the economic prosperity of Europe's single market is sometimes at odds with that of EU workers as human beings, exercising a personal right to live in another state and to enjoy equality of treatment for themselves and their families. There are also tensions between the realization of free movement and a Member State's desire to exercise control over entry into its country, especially in relation to the entry of non-EU citizens, who may be family members of the EU worker.

vi. The years since the onset of the economic crisis in the EU have seen these tensions erupt into new political and social challenges to the policy of free movement of workers.[4] On the one hand, objections have been raised by political leaders and others to the risk that EU free-movement law facilitates or promotes 'benefits tourism'.[5] On the other hand, there has been resistance in some states to the full extension of free movement rights to the citizens of newer Member States.[6] Within the UK, there have been political calls for the basic EU principles of free movement of workers to be renegotiated.[7] The Commission has largely resisted such challenges and robustly defended the benefits of the free movement of workers for all states. While helping Member States to tackle alleged abuses in specific areas such as 'marriages of convenience', the Commission has concentrated in recent years on trying to realize free movement rights in practice and to improve their domestic implementation through awareness-raising, information-provision, and procedural support.[8]

2 ARTICLE 45: DIRECT EFFECT

The basic provision is set out in Article 45 TFEU (ex Article 39 EC), which provides as follows:

> 1. Freedom of movement for workers shall be secured within the Union.
> 2. Such freedom of movement shall entail the abolition of any discrimination based on nationality between workers of the Member States as regards employment, remuneration and other conditions of work and employment.

---

[3] Ch 17.

[4] 'Free Movement of Workers in the EU: Salvaging the Dream While Explaining the Nightmare' (2014) 51 CMLRev 729.

[5] 'Britain and Germany demand EU cracks down on 'benefits tourism', *Daily Telegraph*, 24 April 2013, reporting on a letter signed by the home secretaries/ministers for the interior of Austria, Germany, the Netherlands, and the UK and sent to the Commission and the President of the European Council. For a copy of the letter see http://docs.dpaq. de/3604-130415_letter_to_presidency_final_1_2.pdf.

[6] For discussion see the Annual European Reports of the Network of Experts on the Free Movement of Workers in Europe 2010–2011 (2012) and for 2012–2013 (2014), available at http://ec.europa.eu/social/main.jsp?catId=475&langId=en.

[7] For discussion of and a response to some of these concerns, see A Glennie and J Pennington, 'Europe, Free Movement and the UK: Charting a New Course', Institute for Public Policy Research (London, 2014).

[8] See, eg, Free Movement of EU Citizens and Their Families: Five Actions that Make a Difference, COM(2013) 837 and Dir 2014/54.

> 3. It shall entail the right, subject to limitations justified on grounds of public policy, public security or public health:
>
>> (a) to accept offers of employment actually made;
>>
>> (b) to move freely within the territory of Member States for this purpose;
>>
>> (c) to stay in a Member State for the purpose of employment in accordance with the provisions governing the employment of nationals of that State laid down by law, regulation or administrative action;
>>
>> (d) to remain in the territory of a Member State after having been employed in that State, subject to conditions which shall be embodied in regulations to be drawn up by the Commission.
>
> 4. The provisions of this Article shall not apply to employment in the public service.

The Court has repeatedly emphasized the central importance of the twin principles of freedom of movement and non-discrimination on grounds of nationality. Article 45 is said to represent an application, in the specific context of workers, of the general principle in Article 18 TFEU prohibiting discrimination on grounds of nationality.[9]

The ECJ in *Walrave and Koch*[10] held that Article 45 would apply even where the work was done outside the EU, so long as the legal relationship of employment was entered within the EU. In *Boukhalfa*, Article 45 was held applicable where the employment of an EU national was entered into and primarily performed in a non-member country in which the national resided, at least as regards all aspects of the employment relationship which were governed by the legislation of the employing Member State.[11] And in *Petersen* the Court ruled that EU law would apply to professional activities pursued outside the territory of the EU 'as long as the employment relationship retains a sufficiently close link with the European Union', including 'a sufficiently close link between the employment relationship...and the law of a Member State'.[12]

The Court also ruled in *Walrave and Koch*[13] and in *Bosman*[14] that the provisions of Article 45 are not just of 'vertical' direct effect. The rules challenged in these cases were made by international sporting associations, concerning cycling and football respectively, which were neither public nor state bodies. The Court ruled that Article 45 nevertheless applied:

---

[9] For an argument that the principle of non-discrimination on grounds of nationality needs to be strengthened and made comparable to the principle of non-discrimination contained in Art 19 TEU and the other EU anti-discrimination Dirs discussed in Ch 24 of this book, see the Thematic Report of the EU Network of Experts on the Free Movement of Workers on 'Application of Regulation 1612/68' (2011).

[10] Case 36/74 *Walrave and Koch v Association Union Cycliste Internationale* [1974] ECR 1405.

[11] Case C–214/95 *Boukhalfa v BRD* [1996] ECR I–2253. See also Case C–347/10 *Salemink* EU:C:2012:17 in which EU law was held to apply to a worker (and to the Dutch social security law which governed his situation) employed on a gas rig on the continental shelf adjacent to the Netherlands, even though he had moved his residence to Spain.

[12] Case C–544/11 *Petersen* EU:C:2013:124, [41]. The case concerned a Danish citizen resident in Germany and carrying out aid work in Benin which was paid for by his employer, the Danish International Development Agency. For a case concerning employment of an EU national by the European Patent Office, which is an international organization, see Case C–233/12 *Gardella* EU:C:2013:449.

[13] Case 36/74 (n 10). See also Cases C–379/09 *Maurits Casteels* EU:C:2011:131 and C–325/08 *Olympique Lyonnais* [2010] ECR I–2177.

[14] Case C–415/93 *Union Royale Belge des Sociétés de Football Association and others v Bosman* [1995] ECR I–4921, [82]–[84]; Case C–411/98 *Ferlini v Centre Hospitalier de Luxembourg* [2000] ECR I–8081, [50]; Case C–438/05 *International Transport Workers' Federation and Finnish Seamen's Union v Viking Line ABP and OÜ Viking Line Eesti* [2007] ECR I–10779; Case C–94/07 *Andrea Raccanelli v Max-Planck-Gesellschaft zur Förderung der Wissenschaften eV* [2008] ECR I–5939.

Prohibition of such discrimination does not only apply to the action of public authorities but extends likewise to rules of any other nature aimed at regulating in a collective manner gainful employment and the provision of services....

Since, moreover, working conditions in the various Member States are governed sometimes by means of provisions laid down by law or regulations and sometimes by agreements and other acts concluded or adopted by private persons, to limit the prohibitions in question to acts of a public authority would risk creating inequality in their application.[15]

The *Angonese* case subsequently indicated that Article 45 is also horizontally applicable to the actions of individuals who, unlike the associations in *Walrave, Bosman*, and *Olympique Lyonnais* do not have the power to make rules regulating gainful employment, such as an individual employer who refuses to employ someone on the ground of their nationality.[16]

Case C–281/98 **Angonese v Cassa di Riparmio di Bolzano SpA**
[2000] ECR I–4139

[Note Lisbon Treaty renumbering: Arts 48 and 119 are now Arts 45 and 157 TFEU]

Angonese was an Italian national whose mother tongue was German. He applied to take part in a competition for a post with the Cassa di Riparmio bank in Bolzano, Italy. A condition for entry to the competition imposed by the bank was a certificate of bilingualism (in Italian and German) to be issued by the public authorities in Bolzano after an examination held *only* in that province. The national court found as a fact that Angonese was bilingual, and that non-residents of Bolzano could face difficulties obtaining the certificate in time. Angonese argued that the bank's refusal to admit him to the competition due to non-possession of the certificate was contrary to Article 48.

THE ECJ

30. It should be noted at the outset that the principle of non-discrimination set out in Article 48 is drafted in general terms and is not specifically addressed to the Member States.

31. Thus, the Court has held that the prohibition of discrimination based on nationality applies not only to the actions of public authorities but also to rules of any other nature aimed at regulating in a collective manner gainful employment and the provision of services (see... *Walrave*...).

32. The Court has held that the abolition, as between Member States, of obstacles to freedom of movement would be compromised if the abolition of State barriers could be neutralised by obstacles resulting from the exercise of their legal autonomy by associations or organizations not governed by public law (see *Walrave*, paragraph 18... and... *Bosman*... paragraph 83).

33. Since working conditions in the different Member States are governed sometimes by provisions laid down by law or regulation and sometimes by agreements and other acts concluded or adopted by private persons, limiting application of the prohibition of discrimination based on nationality to acts of a public authority risks creating inequality in its application (see *Walrave*, paragraph 19, and *Bosman*, paragraph 84).

---

[15] Case 36/74 *Walrave* (n 10) [17]–[19].

[16] Reg 1612/68 [1968] English Spec Ed Series I, p 475, Art 7(4) supports this reasoning by stipulating that clauses in individual contracts of employment will be void insofar as they discriminate on grounds of nationality. See also Case C–172/11 *Erny* EU:C:2012:399.

34. The Court has also ruled that the fact that certain provisions of the Treaty are formally addressed to the Member States does not prevent rights from being conferred at the same time on any individual who has an interest in compliance with the obligations thus laid down (see...*Defrenne*...). The Court accordingly held...that the prohibition of discrimination applied equally to all agreements intended to regulate paid labour collectively, as well as to contracts between individuals....

35. Such considerations must, *a fortiori*, be applicable to Article 48..., which lays down a fundamental freedom and which constitutes a specific application of the general prohibition of discrimination contained in Article 6 (now...Article 18 TFEU). In that respect, like Article 119...it is designed to ensure that there is no discrimination on the labour market.

36. Consequently, the prohibition of discrimination on grounds of nationality laid down in Article 48...must be regarded as applying to private persons as well.

In *Erny*, the CJEU ruled that Article 45(2), together with Article 7(4) of Regulation 492/2011,[17] applies to rules on 'top-up benefits' in an individual or collective agreement with a private employer which disadvantages an employee residing in a different Member State.[18]

3 ARTICLE 45: WORKER AND THE SCOPE OF PROTECTION

Article 46 TFEU provides for the Parliament and Council to adopt secondary legislation to bring about the freedoms set out in Article 45. A range of directives and regulations were adopted under this provision, many of which were consolidated by Directive 2004/38 on the free movement and residence of EU citizens and their families.[19] Apart from codifying and consolidating the law, a major innovation of Directive 2004/38 was to introduce the right of permanent residence for EU nationals and their families after five years of continuous legal residence in another Member State.

More recently, Regulation 492/2011 was adopted to codify and replace Regulation 1612/68, which fleshes out the basic equal treatment principle and specifies many of the substantive rights and entitlements of workers and their families.[20] This was supplemented in 2014 by an 'enforcement Directive' 2014/54, whose main aim is to give practical effect to the rights established under Article 45 and Regulation 492/2011.[21]

(A) DEFINITION OF 'WORKER': AN EU CONCEPT

Despite the early array of secondary legislation, many of the basic terms were not defined either in the Treaty or in the legislation, but have been shaped by the ECJ, including the meaning of the core term 'worker'. An early issue which the Treaty left unclear was whether 'workers of the Member States' in Article 45(2) covered only nationals of the Member States, or whether it included

---

[17] In fact the case referred to the predecessor Reg 1612/68, but Art 41 of Reg 492/11 now provides that 'References to the repealed Regulation [1612/68] shall be construed as references to this Regulation.'

[18] Case C–172/11 *Erny* EU:C:2012:399.

[19] Directive 2004/38/EC of the European Parliament and of the Council of 29 April 2004 on the right of citizens of the Union and their family members to move and reside freely within the territory of the Member States [2004] OJ L158/77. This Dir replaced Dirs 64/221 and 68/360 and Reg 1251/70.

[20] Regulation 492/2011 on freedom of movement for workers within the Union (codification) [2011] OJ L41/1.

[21] Directive 2014/54/EU on measures facilitating the exercise of rights conferred on workers in the context of freedom of movement for workers [2014] OJ L128/8. See further below.

non-EU nationals resident and working within the EU. The secondary legislation to implement Article 45, in particular Regulation 1612/68 (now Regulation 492/2011), specifically restricted its application to workers who were nationals of the Member States, and that was the interpretation of the Treaty adopted by the ECJ. The position of third-country nationals resident and working in the EU (who are not family members of EU nationals) is now governed in part by secondary legislation.[22]

The Court insisted from the outset that the definition of a 'worker' was a matter for EU law, not national law, in order to avoid the possibility 'for each Member State to modify the meaning of the concept of migrant worker' at will and to 'frustrate the objectives of the Treaty'.[23]

In requiring the term worker to be a Union concept, the Court claimed ultimate authority to define its meaning and scope and conferred on itself a 'hermeneutic monopoly' to counteract possible unilateral restrictions of the application of the rules on freedom of movement by the different Member States.[24] Thus the Court has held that a spouse can be employed by the other spouse as a worker,[25] and that Article 45 can be relied on by the employer,[26] or by a relevant third party,[27] rather than only by the employee. The term has been construed consistently broadly, and the ECJ has presented this freedom as part of the foundations of the EU.

To summarize: any person who pursues employment activities which are effective and genuine, to the exclusion of activities on such a small scale as to be regarded as 'purely marginal and ancillary', is to be treated as a worker.[28] For an economic activity to qualify as employment under Article 45, rather than self-employment under Article 49 TFEU, there must be a relationship of subordination.[29] However, as we shall see the EU concept of worker varies according to the EU law context in which it arises, and the purpose for which the term is invoked.[30]

(B) DEFINITION OF 'WORKER': MINIMUM-INCOME AND WORKING-TIME REQUIREMENTS

A number of cases have been concerned with the interplay between the economic aspect of free movement, as reflected by the level of remuneration received for work done, and the social aspect underlying free-movement policy in terms of its improvement of the quality of life of the individual concerned. This issue arose in *Levin*, in the context of part-time workers.[31]

---

[22] Dir 2003/109. See D Acosto Arcazaro, *The Long-Term Residence Directive as a Subsidiarity Form of EU Citizenship* (Martinus Nijhoff, 2011).

[23] Case 75/63 *Hoekstra v Bestuur der Bedrijfsvereniging voor Detailhandel en Ambachten* [1964] ECR 177, 184.

[24] G Mancini, 'The Free Movement of Workers in the Case-Law of the European Court of Justice' in D Curtin and D O'Keeffe (eds), *Constitutional Adjudication in European Community and National Law* (Butterworths, 1992) 67.

[25] Case C–337/97 *CPM Meeusen v Hoofddirectie van de Informatie Beheer Groep* [1999] ECR I–3289.

[26] Case C–350/96 *Clean Car Autoservice GmbH v Landeshauptmann von Wien* [1998] ECR I–2521; Case C–379/11 *Caves Krier Frères Sàrl* EU:C:2013:798.

[27] Case C–208/05 *ITC Innovative Technology Center GmbH v Bundesagentur für Arbeit* [2007] ECR I–181.

[28] Case C–337/97 *Meeusen* (n 25).

[29] Cases C–268/99 *Jany v Staatssecretaris van Justitie* [2001] ECR I–8615, [34]; C–151–152/04 *Nadin and Durre* [2005] ECR I–11203.

[30] Cases C–256/01 *Allonby v Accrington and Rossendale College* [2004] ECR I–873, [63]; C–138/02 *Collins v Secretary of State for Work and Pensions* [2004] ECR I–2703.

[31] See also Cases C–22–23/08 *Vatsouras and Koupatantze v Arbeitsgemeinschaft (ARGE) Nürnberg 900* [2009] ECR I–4585, [28]–[29].

Case 53/81 **Levin v Staatssecretaris van Justitie**
[1982] ECR 1035

The appellant was a British citizen married to a non-EU national and living in the Netherlands, but whose application for a residence permit had been refused. She argued that she had sufficient income for her own and her husband's maintenance, and that she had taken up part-time employment as a chamber-maid. The Staatssecretaris van Justitie argued that she was not an EU worker because her employment did not provide sufficient means for her support, not being equal at least to the minimum legal wage prevailing in the Netherlands. When the case was referred, the ECJ alluded to its argument in *Hoekstra* that Member States could not unilaterally restrict the scope and meaning of the term worker.

THE ECJ

12. Such would, in particular, be the case if the enjoyment of the rights conferred by the principle of freedom of movement for workers could be made subject to the criterion of what the legislation of the host State declares to be a minimum wage, so that the field of application *ratione personae* of the Community rules on this subject might vary from one Member State to another. The meaning and the scope of the terms 'worker' and 'activity as an employed person' should thus be clarified in the light of the principles of the legal order of the Community.

13. In this respect it must be stressed that these concepts define the field of application of one of the fundamental freedoms guaranteed by the Treaty and, as such, may not be interpreted restrictively.

14. In conformity with this view the recitals to Regulation No 1612/68 contain a general affirmation of the right of all workers in the Member States to pursue the activity of their choice within the Community, irrespective of whether they are permanent, seasonal or frontier workers or workers who pursue their activities for the purpose of providing services. Furthermore, although Article 4 of Directive 68/360 grants the right of residence to workers upon the mere production of the document on the basis of which they entered the territory and of a confirmation of engagement from the employer or a certificate of employment, it does not subject this right to any condition relating to the kind of employment or to the amount of income derived from it.

15. An interpretation which reflects the full scope of these concepts is also in conformity with the objectives of the Treaty which include, according to Articles 2 and 3 [*now Art 3 TEU, which replaced in substance Arts 2 and 3 TEC*], the abolition, as between Member States, of obstacles to freedom of movement for persons, with the purpose *inter alia* of promoting throughout the Community a harmonious development of economic activities and a raising of the standard of living. Since part-time employment, although it may provide an income lower than what is considered to be the minimum required for subsistence, constitutes for a large number of persons an effective means of improving their living conditions, the effectiveness of Community law would be impaired and the achievement of the objectives of the Treaty would be jeopardized if the enjoyment of rights conferred by the principle of freedom of movement for workers were reserved solely to persons engaged in full-time employment and earning, as a result, a wage at least equivalent to the guaranteed minimum wage in the sector under consideration.

...

17. It should however be stated that whilst part-time employment is not excluded from the field of application of the rules on freedom of movement for workers, those rules cover only the pursuit of effective and genuine activities, to the exclusion of activities on such a small scale as to be regarded as purely marginal and ancillary. It follows both from the statement of the principle of freedom of movement for workers and from the place occupied by the rules relating to that principle in the system of the Treaty as a whole that those rules guarantee only the free movement of persons who pursue or are desirous of pursuing a genuine economic activity.

Thus the freedom to take up employment is important not only as a means towards the creation of a single market for the benefit of Member State economies, but as a right for the worker to raise her or his standard of living, even if the worker does not reach the minimum level of subsistence in a particular state (paragraph 15). Moreover, in response to the suggestion that Levin may only have sought work in order to obtain a residence permit to remain in the country, the Court ruled that the purpose or motive of the worker is immaterial, once he or she is pursuing or wishing to pursue a genuine and effective economic activity (paragraph 17).

The ECJ has consistently adopted this kind of response to allegations of 'abuse of rights' in the area of free movement, even while the Council insisted on the inclusion of a new 'abuse of rights' exception in Article 35 of Directive 2004/38. The requirement articulated in *Levin* that work be undertaken as a genuine economic activity was probably a response to Member States' concerns that their social security schemes would become overburdened as a result of migrants entering from other countries whose social benefits systems are less generous, and who do not really intend to engage in effective work. Advocate General Slynn acknowledged this concern, but noted the increasing dependence on part-time work and emphasized that its exclusion from the protection of Article 45 would exclude not only women, the elderly, and disabled who might wish only to work part time, but also women and men who would prefer to work full time but were obliged to accept part-time work. *Levin* thus clarified that part-time workers were covered by free movement, and that it did not matter if workers chose to supplement their income from private sources.

In *Kempf*,[32] the issue was taken a step further. A German national who was living and working in the Netherlands as a music teacher, giving approximately twelve lessons a week, was refused a residence permit. The Dutch and Danish Governments argued that work providing an income below the minimum means of subsistence in the host state could not be regarded as genuine and effective work if the person doing the work claimed social assistance from *public* funds. The Court disagreed, ruling that when a genuine part-time worker sought to supplement earnings below the subsistence level, it was irrelevant whether those supplementary means were derived from property, from the employment of a family member, or even from financial assistance from public funds provided by the state.[33] The state could address any concerns it had about an excessive burden on its social assistance scheme in the criteria it set for access to certain kinds of social assistance, but it could not exclude the part-time employee from the status of 'worker' under EU law. We shall see below, however, that Member State concern about the impact on their social assistance schemes of EU nationals coming in search of work, and the risk of abuse in the form of so-called 'benefits tourism', has resurfaced again even more urgently in recent years.

Nonetheless, the Court has adopted an inclusive reading of the term worker in many cases where the economic dimension of the activity concerned was in question. Thus the practice of sport falls within EU law insofar as it constitutes an economic activity, although the composition of national teams may be a question of purely sporting and not economic interest.[34] And fishermen who are paid a share of the proceeds of sale of their catches can be considered to be 'workers', despite the irregular nature of their remuneration.[35]

A steady stream of cases concerning the concrete application of criteria such as 'genuine and effective work' has continued to flow. In *Lawrie-Blum*,[36] the Court was asked to rule on the compatibility of German measures restricting access for non-nationals to the preparatory service stage which was necessary for qualification as a secondary school teacher. Addressing the question whether a trainee

---

[32] Case 139/85 *Kempf v Staatsecretaris van Justitie* [1986] ECR 1741.

[33] Ibid [14].

[34] Case 36/74 *Walrave* (n 10); Case C–415/93 *Bosman* (n 14); Case 13/76 *Donà v Mantero* [1976] ECR 1333. Compare *Bosman* [120]–[129] and Case C–438/00 *Deutscher Handballbund eV v Maros Kolpak* [2003] ECR I–4135.

[35] Case 3/87 *R v Ministry of Agriculture, Fisheries and Food, ex p Agegate Ltd* [1989] ECR 4459, [33]–[36].

[36] Case 66/85 *Lawrie-Blum v Land Baden-Württemberg* [1986] ECR 2121.

teacher at this stage would qualify as a 'worker' for the purposes of the relevant Treaty provisions, the Court provided a more elaborate three-part definition of the term:

> That concept must be defined in accordance with objective criteria which distinguish the employment relationship by reference to the rights and duties of the persons concerned. The essential feature of an employment relationship, however, is that *for a certain period of time a person performs services for and under the direction of another person in return for which he receives remuneration.*[37]

The Court ruled that a trainee teacher qualified as a worker since, during the period of preparatory service, these three conditions would be fulfilled: she would perform services of economic value, under the direction of the school in question, and would receive a measure of remuneration in return.[38] The fact that the pay was less than a full teacher's salary was immaterial, for the same reasons given in *Levin* and *Kempf*: what mattered was the genuinely economic nature of the work plus remuneration. In *Steymann*, the ECJ pushed the concept of remuneration, and hence of economic activity, a little further.

Case 196/87 Steymann v Staatsecretaris van Justitie
[1988] ECR 6159

Steymann was a German national living in the Netherlands, where he had worked for a short time as a plumber. He then joined the Bhagwan Community, a religious community which provided for the material needs of its members. He participated in the life of the community by performing plumbing work, general household duties, and other commercial activity on the community's premises. His application for a residence permit to pursue an activity as an employed person was refused and the case was referred to the ECJ.

THE ECJ

9. It must be observed *in limine* that, in view of the objectives of the European Economic Community, participation in a community based on religion or another form of philosophy falls within the field of application of Community law only in so far as it can be regarded as an economic activity within the meaning of Article 2 of the Treaty.

...

11. As regards the activities in question in this case, it appears from the documents before the Court that they consist of work carried out within and on behalf of the Bhagwan Community in connection with the Bhagwan Community's commercial activities. It appears that such work plays a relatively important role in the way of life of the Bhagwan Community and that only in special circumstances can the members of the community avoid taking part therein. In turn, the Bhagwan Community provides for the material needs of its members, including pocket-money, irrespective of the nature and the extent of the work which they do.

12. In a case such as the one before the national court it is impossible to rule out *a priori* the possibility that work carried out by members of the community in question constitutes an economic activity within the meaning of Article 2 of the Treaty [*now Art 3 TEU, which replaced in substance Art 2 TEC*]. In so far as

---

[37] Ibid [17], emphasis added.
[38] See also Cases C–357/89 *Raulin v Minister van Onderwijs en Wetenschappen* [1992] ECR I–1027; C–3/90 *Bernini v Minister van Onderwijs en Wetenschappen* [1992] ECR I–1071; C–10/05 *Mattern and Cikotic* [2006] ECR I–3145; C–109/04 *Kranemann v Land-Rheinland Westfalen* [2005] ECR I–2421; C–228/07 *Jörn Petersen v Landesgeschäftsstelle des Arbeitsmarktservice Niederösterreich* [2008] ECR I–6989, [45]; C–94/07 *Andrea Raccanelli* (n 14); C–232/09 *Dita Danosa v LKB Lizings SIA* [2010] ECR I–11405, [39].

> the work, which aims to ensure a measure of self-sufficiency for the Bhagwan Community, constitutes an essential part of participation in that community, the services which the latter provides to its members may be regarded as being an indirect *quid pro quo* for their work.

The fact that the work might be seen in conventional terms as being unpaid did not necessarily mean that it was not effective economic activity. Steymann provided services of value to the religious community which would otherwise have to be performed by someone else, and in return for which his material needs were satisfied.

(c) DEFINITION OF 'WORKER': PURPOSE OF THE EMPLOYMENT

The general rule is that the motive or purpose for which the employment is undertaken will not be relevant in determining whether a person is a worker. Provided that the employment is genuine and not marginal it will be covered by Article 45. There are, however, cases where account has been taken of the purpose of the employment.

In *Bettray* the ECJ considered whether Article 45 would apply to someone undertaking therapeutic work as part of a drug-rehabilitation programme under Dutch social employment law.[39] The aim of the programme was to reintegrate people who were temporarily incapacitated into the workforce. They would be paid a certain amount, and treated, insofar as possible, in accordance with normal conditions of paid employment. The ECJ began by noting that a job was being carried out under supervision and in return for remuneration, and that the low pay from public funds and the low productivity of the worker would not in themselves prevent the application of Article 45. However, unlike in its judgment in *Levin* where the reason for undertaking work was said not to be relevant to its genuineness, the ECJ examined the purpose of the work performed:

> However, work under the Social Employment Law cannot be regarded as an effective and genuine economic activity if it constitutes merely a means of rehabilitation or reintegration for the persons concerned and the purpose of the paid employment, which is adapted to the physical and mental possibilities of each person, is to enable those persons sooner or later to recover their capacity to take up ordinary employment or to lead as normal as possible a life.
>
> It also appears from the order for reference that persons employed under the Social Employment Law are not selected on the basis of their capacity to perform a certain activity; on the contrary, it is the activities which are chosen in the light of the capabilities of the persons who are going to perform them in order to maintain, re-establish or develop their capacity for work. Finally, the activities involved are pursued in the framework of undertakings or work associations created solely for that purpose by local authorities.[40]

Clearly the purpose for undertaking the work was crucial to the ECJ's decision. The fact that the main or sole purpose of the work was to rehabilitate the person, and to find work suited to their capabilities, rather than to meet a genuine economic need, as was the case in *Steymann*, resulted in a ruling against Bettray. The case is open to criticism, because ensuring the mobility of a well-trained workforce would seem to be an important part of the Treaty's aims, and reintegration of people into the workforce through sheltered employment is a part of this. Further, if the *Bettray* ruling were to be applied to the case of sheltered employment for disabled people, this could exclude many disabled people from being workers under EU law.

---

[39] Case 344/87 *Bettray v Staatssecretaris van Justitie* [1989] ECR 1621.
[40] Ibid [17]–[19].

In *Trojani*, however, where a French national worked in Belgium in a reintegration programme run by the Salvation Army, the ECJ seemed to distinguish *Bettray* on the ground that the applicant in that case had apparently been unable for an indefinite period, on account of his drug addiction, to work under normal conditions.

Case C–456/02 **Trojani v CPAS**
[2004] ECR I–7573

18. In this respect, the Court has held that activities cannot be regarded as a real and genuine economic activity if they constitute merely a means of rehabilitation or reintegration for the persons concerned (*Bettray*, paragraph 17).

19. However, that conclusion can be explained only by the particular characteristics of the case in question, which concerned the situation of a person who, by reason of his addiction to drugs, had been recruited on the basis of a national law intended to provide work for persons who, for an indefinite period, are unable, by reason of circumstances related to their situation, to work under normal conditions (see, to that effect, Case C–1/97 *Birden* [1998] ECR I–7747, paragraphs 30 and 31).

20. In the present case, as is apparent from the decision making the reference, Mr Trojani performs, for the Salvation Army and under its direction, various jobs for approximately 30 hours a week, as part of a personal reintegration programme, in return for which he receives benefits in kind and some pocket money.

21. Under the relevant provisions of the decree of the Commission communautaire française of 27 May 1999 on the grant of authorisation and subsidies to hostels (*Moniteur belge*, 18 June 1999, p. 23101), the Salvation Army has the task of receiving, accommodating and providing psycho-social assistance appropriate to the recipients in order to promote their autonomy, physical well-being and reintegration in society. For that purpose it must agree with each person concerned a personal reintegration programme setting out the objectives to be attained and the means to be employed to attain them.

22. Having established that the benefits in kind and money provided by the Salvation Army to Mr Trojani constitute the consideration for the services performed by him for and under the direction of the hostel, the national court has thereby established the existence of the constituent elements of any paid employment relationship, namely subordination and the payment of remuneration.

23. For the claimant in the main proceedings to have the status of worker, however, the national court, in the assessment of the facts which is within its exclusive jurisdiction, would have to establish that the paid activity in question is real and genuine.

24. The national court must in particular ascertain whether the services actually performed by Mr Trojani are capable of being regarded as forming part of the normal labour market. For that purpose, account may be taken of the status and practices of the hostel, the content of the social reintegration programme, and the nature and details of performance of the services.

Thus although the ECJ left it ultimately to the national court to decide whether his employment was real and genuine, it made clear that the fact that social reintegration was the main purpose of the employment would not itself disqualify the employment from being considered as such. Instead, the crucial factor was whether the services 'are capable of being regarded as forming part of the normal labour market'.

In a somewhat different context in *Brown*, the ECJ took into account the purpose behind the employment.[41] The Court indicated that, although someone who engaged in genuine and effective work before leaving to begin a course of study will be considered to be a 'worker' within Article 45, the fact that the

---

[41] Case 197/86 *Brown v Secretary of State for Scotland* [1988] ECR 3205.

work was undertaken purely in order to prepare for the course of study, rather than to prepare for an occupation or employment, would mean that not all of the advantages provided for workers within EU law may be claimed. Brown was a dual national relying on his French nationality in the UK, who had worked for nine months for a company in Scotland as a form of 'pre-university industrial training', before beginning an electrical engineering degree at Cambridge University. The Court ruled that although he was a 'worker', since he satisfied the three criteria in *Lawrie-Blum*, he was not entitled to all the social advantages, in this case a maintenance grant, which would normally be open to workers. This was because his employment was merely 'ancillary' to his desired course of study. This conclusion can be seen as the ECJ's response to Member States' concerns about 'abuse' of the provisions on free movement of workers by those who wished to avail themselves of the generous educational provision in a particular Member State.

We shall see in the later chapter on EU citizenship that the ECJ in *Bidar* changed its position on the specific question of entitlement of a national who moves to study in another Member State to apply for a maintenance grant,[42] and this was confirmed in the case of *LN*.[43] However, *Brown* remains an authority for the proposition that an EU national who undertakes work for a temporary period purely as a means to qualify for an educational course may not be entitled to all the same social advantages as a fully-fledged 'worker' under EU law.

In *Ninni-Oraschi*, the ECJ again reiterated the importance of 'objective' factors such as hours worked and remuneration over other more subjective factors such as motive and conduct, and dismissed as irrelevant the argument that the applicant had 'abused' EU rights in order to gain the status of worker.[44]

Case C–413/01 **Ninni-Orasche v Bundesminister für Wissenschaft, Verkehr und Kunst**
[2003] ECR I–13187

[Note Lisbon Treaty renumbering: Art 48 is now Art 45 TFEU]

28. It should be stated that, with respect to the assessment whether employment is capable of conferring the status of worker within the meaning of Article 48 of the Treaty, factors relating to the conduct of the person concerned before and after the period of employment are not relevant in establishing the status of worker within the meaning of that article. Such factors are not in any way related to the objective criteria referred to in the case-law cited in paragraphs 23 and 24 of this judgment.

29. In particular, the three factors referred to by the national court, namely the fact that the person concerned took up employment as a waitress only several years after her entry into the host Member State, that, shortly after the end of her short term of employment, she obtained a diploma entitling her to enrol at university in that State and that, after that employment had come to an end, she attempted to find a new job, are not linked either to the possibility that the activity pursued by the appellant in the main proceedings was ancillary or to the nature of that activity or of the employment relationship.

30. For the same reasons, nor can the Court accept the argument put forward by the Danish Government that, in order to assess whether activities pursued as an employed person are effective and genuine, it is necessary to take account of the short term of the employment in relation to the total duration of residence by the person concerned in the host Member State, which, in the main proceedings, was two and a half years.

---

[42] Case C–209/03 *Bidar v London Borough of Ealing* [2005] ECR I–2119; Case C–158/07 *Förster v Hoofddirectie van de Informatie Beheer Groep* [2008] ECR I–8507.

[43] Case C–46/12 *LN v Styrelsen for Videregående Uddannelser og Uddannelsesstøtte* EU:C:2013:97, [48].

[44] Cases C–22–23/08 *Vatsouras* (n 31) [29].

31. Finally, as regards the argument that the national court is under an obligation to examine, on the basis of the circumstances of the case, whether the appellant in the main proceedings has sought abusively to create a situation enabling her to claim the status of a worker within the meaning of Article 48 of the Treaty with the aim of acquiring advantages linked to that status, it is sufficient to state that any abusive use of the rights granted by the Community legal order under the provisions relating to freedom of movement for workers presupposes that the person concerned falls within the scope ratione personae of that Treaty because he satisfies the conditions for classification as a worker within the meaning of that article. It follows that the issue of abuse of rights can have no bearing on the answer to the first question.

While the ECJ agreed, as we shall see below, that the national court was entitled to investigate, for the purposes of deciding whether to grant or refuse educational assistance, whether the applicant had taken up and left employment purely in order to gain access to education in the host Member State, this was not relevant to the question whether or not she was a worker under Article 45 as a consequence of the period of employment. The requirement of genuine and effective employment activity 'does not mean, however, that the enjoyment of [free movement of workers] may be made contingent on which objectives are being pursued by a national of a Member State in applying to enter the territory of a host Member State, provided that he pursues or wishes to pursue effective and genuine employment activities'.[45]

(D) DEFINITION OF 'WORKER': THE JOB-SEEKER

The discussion thus far has been concerned with those who have employment of some kind. An important issue is to what extent those *seeking* work are covered by Article 45. In *Royer*, the ECJ had referred to the right 'to look for or pursue an occupation'.[46] The issue was addressed more directly in *Antonissen*, where the Court held that those who are actively seeking work do not have the full status of a worker, but are nonetheless covered by Article 45.

Case C–292/89 **R v Immigration Appeal Tribunal, ex parte Antonissen**
[1991] ECR I–745

[Note Lisbon Treaty renumbering: Art 48 is now Art 45 TFEU]

Antonissen was a Belgian national who had arrived in the UK in 1984, and had attempted unsuccessfully to find work. Following his imprisonment for a drug-related offence, the Secretary of State decided to deport him. Following his appeal, the case was referred to the ECJ where it was argued that only Community nationals in possession of a confirmation of engagement of employment were entitled to a right of residence in another Member State.

THE ECJ

9. In that connection it has been argued that, according to the strict wording of Article 48 of the Treaty, Community nationals are given the right to move freely within the territory of the Member States for the purpose only of accepting offers of employment actually made (Article 48(3)(a) and (b)) whilst the right to stay in the territory of a Member State is stated to be for the purpose of employment (Article 48(3)(c)).

---

[45] Case C–46/12 *LN* (n 43) EU:C:2013:97, [47].
[46] Case 48/75 *Royer* [1976] ECR 497, [31].

10. Such an interpretation would exclude the right of a national of a Member State to move freely and to stay in the territory of the other Member States in order to seek employment there, and cannot be upheld.

...

12. Moreover, a strict interpretation of Article 48(3) would jeopardize the actual chances that a national of a Member State who is seeking employment will find it in another Member State, and would, as a result, make that provision ineffective.

13. It follows that Article 48(3) must be interpreted as enumerating, in a non-exhaustive way, certain rights benefiting nationals of Member States in the context of the free movement of workers and that that freedom also entails the right for nationals of Member States to move freely within the territory of the other Member States and to stay there for the purposes of seeking employment.

Antonissen provides a clear example of the Court's purposive approach, in suggesting a wider scope for Article 45 than the words of the Article convey. The ECJ ruled that the purpose of Article 45 was to ensure the free movement of workers and that a literal interpretation of its terms would hinder that purpose. If nationals could move to another Member State only when they already held an offer of employment, the number of people who could move would be small, and many workers who could seek and find employment on arrival in a Member State would be prevented from so doing. An interesting feature of *Antonissen* was the ECJ's statement that the rights expressly enumerated in Article 45 are not exhaustive. This approach leaves the Court power to adapt the scope of the Article through interpretation.

Nevertheless, the ECJ was clear that the status of an EU national searching for work was not the same as that of an EU national who was actually employed. Member States retain the power to expel a job-seeker who does not have prospects of finding work after a reasonable period of time, without needing to invoke Article 45(3). Moreover, there may be benefits, such as unemployment insurance, that cannot be accessed by someone who has never participated in the employment market.

This was seen in *Commission v Belgium*,[47] and also in *Lebon*, where the ECJ ruled that the social and tax advantages guaranteed to workers under EU law, in particular by Article 7(2) of Regulation 1612/68 (now Regulation 492/2011), were not available to those moving in search of work.[48] In *Collins*, the ECJ confirmed the distinction between fully-fledged workers who can benefit from all provisions of the Regulation concerning social advantages and equality of treatment with national workers, and job-seekers who, although covered by Article 45, can benefit only from the provisions of the Regulation governing access to employment.[49] But the ECJ also departed from the strict implications of the *Lebon* judgment by ruling that when interpreted in the light of EU citizenship, equal treatment in access to employment under Article 45(2) should include the right to apply for a job-seeker's allowance under the same conditions as nationals of the host state, if they are genuinely linked to the employment market of that state.[50]

The *Collins* ruling was confirmed in *Ioannidis* and *Prete*, in which the ECJ ruled that EU nationals seeking employment in another Member State are entitled in principle to a 'tideover allowance' intended specifically to facilitate the transition from education to the employment market, and that a national eligibility condition requiring applicants to have completed their secondary education, or to have undertaken a lengthy period of studies, in the host Member State was contrary to Article 45.[51]

---

[47] Case C–278/94 *Commission v Belgium* [1996] ECR I–4307.
[48] Case 316/85 *Lebon* [1987] ECR 281. Compare Case C–57/96 *Meints v Minister van Landbouw* [1997] ECR I–6689.
[49] Case C–138/02 *Collins* (n 30) [30]–[33]. See also C–22/08 and C–23/08 *Vatsouras and Koupatantze* [2009] ECR I–4585.
[50] Ibid [54]–[73]. The aspects of the judgment which deal with EU citizenship will be considered in Ch 23.
[51] Cases C–258/04 *Office national de l'emploi v Ioannidis* [2005] ECR I–8275 (on the secondary education requirement) and C–367/11 *Déborah Prete* EU:C:2012:668 (on a requirement of completing six years of studies in the host state).

While it was legitimate for states to seek a real link between the claimant and the host state labour market, this requirement would have to be proportionate and could, for example, be satisfied by several years of residence in the host state combined with a substantial period of time spent seeking work, as well as marriage to a national of the host state.[52]

(E) SCOPE OF PROTECTION: NEW MEMBER STATES

Workers as defined in the previous pages have a right to move in accordance with Article 45. This right was, however, qualified in relation to the 2004 enlargement when ten Central and East European states joined. The EU took the unprecedented step of admitting new Members while denying them the immediate right to benefit from one of the four fundamental freedoms. A (three-phased) transitional regime for the free movement of workers from the new states was introduced, giving existing Member States the option of delaying the full implementation of their rights of free movement for up to seven years.[53] While this arrangement was made in order to allay the fears of existing Member States that their labour markets would be flooded with new migrant workers, the effective creation of a 'second-class' membership, however temporary, gave rise to an understandably critical reaction from the new Member States and from other commentators.[54] This transitional regime for the states involved in the 2004 enlargement ended on 30 April 2011.[55] The transitional regime for Bulgaria and Romania, which joined the EU in 2007 ended on 31 December 2013. For the moment, this transitional regime concerns only workers from Croatia, which joined the EU on 1 July 2013. The transitional regime for Croatia will end on 30 June 2020.

4 ARTICLE 45: DISCRIMINATION, MARKET ACCESS, AND JUSTIFICATION

It is clear that rules which directly discriminate on the grounds of nationality will be caught by Article 45.[56] It is equally clear that indirect discrimination, and even impediments to market access which do not depend on a showing of unequal impact,[57] can also lead to infringement of Article 45.[58] Discrimination, whether direct or indirect, will, however, be found only where two groups which are comparable in relevant ways are treated differently, or where groups which are not comparable are treated in the same way.[59]

(A) DIRECT DISCRIMINATION

In proceedings brought by the Commission against France for failing to repeal provisions of the French Maritime Code, which had required a certain proportion of the crew of a ship to be of French nationality,

---

[52] Case C–367/11 *Prete*, ibid.

[53] http://ec.europa.eu/social/main.jsp?catId=466&langId=en.

[54] V Mitsilegas, 'Free Movement of Workers, Citizenship and Enlargement: The Situation in the UK' [2009] Journal of Immigration, Asylum and Nationality Law 223.

[55] For a case concerning the difference between the treatment of third-country nationals, and that of Bulgarian students under the five-year transitional regime in Austria, see Case C–15/11 *Sommer v Landesgeschäftsstelle des Arbeitsmarktservice Wien* EU:C:2012:371.

[56] See, eg, Case C–55/00 *Gottardo v INPS* [2002] ECR I–413.

[57] Case C–415/93 *Bosman* (n 14).

[58] A Castro Oliveira, 'Workers and Other Persons: Step-by-Step from Movement to Citizenship' (2002) 39 CMLRev 77.

[59] Cases C–391/97 *Gschwind v Finanzamt Aachen-Aussenstadt* [1999] ECR I–5451, [21]; C–356/98 *Kaba v Home Secretary* [2000] ECR I–2623; S Peers, 'Dazed and Confused: Family Members' Residence Rights and the Court of Justice' (2001) 26 ELRev 76.

the Court ruled that Article 45 was 'directly applicable in the legal system of every Member State' and would render inapplicable all contrary national law.[60] Further, a state can be held in breach of Article 45 where the discrimination is practised by any public body, including public universities.[61]

While cases involving direct discrimination on grounds of nationality are much less common, such cases do still arise and they raise a strong burden of justification.[62] In *Schiebel*, Austria sought to plead national security as a justification for subjecting a company's authorization to trade in military weapons and munitions to the condition that the managing partner must hold Austrian nationality.[63] Austria invoked Article 346(1)(b) TFEU, which stipulates that the Treaties do not preclude any Member State from taking such measures as it considers necessary for the protection of essential interests of its security. The Court however rejected the argument on the basis that the government had not shown that a nationality condition was either a necessary or a proportionate means to protect the essential interests of Austrian security.

(B) INDIRECT DISCRIMINATION

Indirect discrimination is also prohibited by Article 45, so that a condition of eligibility for a benefit which is more easily satisfied by national than by non-national workers is likely to fall foul of the Treaty. The ECJ has relaxed the requirements for proof of indirect discrimination, ruling in *O'Flynn* that in order for indirect discrimination to be established, it was not necessary to prove that a national measure in practice affected a higher proportion of foreign workers, but merely that the measure was 'intrinsically liable' to affect migrant workers more than nationals.[64] The Court often leaves it up to the national court to determine whether there is, on the facts of the case, an indirectly discriminatory impact.[65]

A common species of indirect discrimination is where benefits are made conditional, in law or fact, on residence, place-of-origin requirements, or place-of-education requirements that can more easily be satisfied by nationals than non-nationals.[66] In *Ugliola*, an Italian worker in Germany challenged a German law under which a worker's security of employment was protected by having periods of military service taken into account in calculating the length of employment.[67] The law in question applied only to those who had done their military service in the Bundeswehr, although the nationality of the worker was irrelevant. The Court stressed that Article 45 allowed for no restrictions on the principle of equal treatment other than in paragraph 3. Germany in this case had created an unjustifiable restriction by 'indirectly introducing discrimination in favour of their own nationals alone', since the requirement

---

[60] Cases 167/73 *Commission v French Republic* [1974] ECR 359; C–185/96 *Commission v Hellenic Republic* [1998] ECR I–6601; C–94/08 *Commission v Spain* [2008] ECR I–160; C–318/05 *Commission v Germany* [2007] ECR I–6957; C–460/08 *Commission v Greece* [2009] ECR I–216.

[61] See, eg, the infamous treatment of foreign-language lecturers in Italian universities: Cases C–212/99 *Commission v Italy* [2001] ECR I–4923 and C–119/04 *Commission v Italy* [2006] ECR I–6885.

[62] See, eg, Case C–155/09 *Commission v Greece* EU:C:2011:22. On nationality restrictions when fielding players in sport see Cases C–415/93 *Bosman* (n 14); C–438/00 *Kolpak* (n 34); C–265/03 *Simutenkov v Ministerio de Educación y Cultura* [2005] ECR I–2579; 13/76 *Donà* (n 34); C–228/07 *Jörn Petersen* (n 38).

[63] Case C–474/12, *Schiebel Aircraft GmbH* EU:C:2014:2139.

[64] Case C–237/94 *O'Flynn v Adjudication Officer* [1996] ECR I–2617; Case C–278/94 *Commission v Belgium* [1996] ECR I–4307.

[65] Cases C-611 and 612/10 *Hudziński & Wawrzyniak* EU:C:2012:339; C–589/10 *Wencel* EU:C:2011:303. The CJEU also often leaves it to the national court to determine whether the facts of the case constitute a non-discriminatory obstacle which hinders free movement, as discussed below: see eg Case C–233/12 *Gardella* EU:C:2013:449, [46].

[66] Cases C–355/98 *Commission v Belgium* [2000] ECR I–1221; C–350/96 *Clean Car* (n 26); C–276/07 *Delay v Università degli studi di Firenze, IPNS* [2008] ECR I–3635; C–258/04 *Ioannidis* (n 51); C–367/11 *Prete* (n 51). In Case C–461/11 *Radziejewski* EU:C:2013:704, a requirement of residence for eligibility for debt relief was contrary to the Treaty.

[67] Case 15/69 *Württembergische Milchverwertung-Südmilch-AG v Salvatore Ugliola* [1970] ECR 363.

that the service be done in the Bundeswehr would clearly be satisfied by a far greater number of nationals than non-nationals.[68]

In *Sotgiu* the German Post Office increased the separation allowance paid to workers employed away from their place of residence within Germany, but did not pay the increase to workers (whatever their nationality) whose residence at the time of their initial employment was abroad, and this was held by the ECJ to be contrary to the Treaty.[69] In *Commission v Belgium*[70] a system of retirement pension points that could be more easily satisfied by workers possessing the nationality of that Member State than by workers from other Member States was indirectly discriminatory, and hence caught by Article 45. In *Zurstrassen*,[71] national rules under which the joint assessment to tax of spouses was conditional on their both being resident on the national territory were incompatible with Article 45.[72] A range of other tax cases in recent years have confirmed that where differential tax treatment of persons who are resident in another Member State is not based on relevant differences in the situation of those persons or their taxable property, that treatment will be caught by the Treaty rules.[73]

Another form of indirect discrimination frequently encountered in the law on free movement more generally is the imposition of a 'double-burden' regulatory requirement, which does not recognize appropriate qualifications or certifications already received in the home state. Such a regulation was held to be contrary to Article 45 in *Commission v Portugal*.[74]

Finally, the imposition of a language requirement for certain posts also constitutes a form of indirect discrimination, since it is likely that a far higher proportion of non-nationals than nationals will be affected by it.[75] However, since such a requirement may well be legitimate, Article 3(1) of Regulation 492/2011 allows for the imposition of 'conditions relating to linguistic knowledge required by reason of the nature of the post to be filled'. The Court considered the scope of this exception in *Groener*, where a Dutch national working in Ireland as a part-time art teacher was rejected for the full-time art teaching post for which she was otherwise selected, because she did not pass an oral examination in the Irish language.[76] The ECJ ruled that even though the teaching was likely to be exclusively in English, the language requirement could, so long as it was not imposed in a disproportionate way, fall within Article 3(1) on account of the policy of the Irish Government to promote the use of Irish as a means of expressing national identity and culture. In *Las*, however, the CJEU ruled that the requirement that employment contracts concluded in Flanders be written in Dutch constituted an impermissible restriction on the free movement of workers.[77] This was because, despite the legitimacy of the Belgian Government's objectives which included the promotion and encouragement of the use of one of the state's official languages,

---

[68] Case C–419/92 *Scholz v Universitaria di Cagliari* [1994] ECR I–505; Case C–15/96 *Kalliope Schöning-Kougebetopoulou v Freie und Hansestadt Hamburg* [1998] ECR I–47; Case C–187/96 *Commission v Hellenic Republic* [1998] ECR I–1095; Case C–278/03 *Commission v Italy* [2005] ECR I–3747; Case C–369/07 *Commission v Germany* [2009] ECR I–7811.

[69] Case 152/73 *Sotgiu v Deutsche Bundespost* [1974] ECR 153. See also Case C–514/12 *Zentralbetriebsrat der gemeinnützigen Salzburger Landeskliniken Betriebs GmbH* EU:C:2013:799 where the taking into account for the purposes of promotion of all non-interrupted periods of service, but only a portion of interrupted periods, was held to be indirectly discriminatory.

[70] Case 35/97 [1998] ECR I–5325.

[71] Case C–87/99 *Zurstrassen v Administration des Contributions Directes* [2000] ECR I–3337.

[72] See also Case C–169/03 *Wallentin v Riksskatteverket* [2004] ECR I–6443; Case C–400/02 *Merida v Bundesrepublik Deutschland* [2004] ECR I–8471; Case C–152/03 *Ritter-Coulais v Finanzamt Germersheim* [2006] ECR I–1711; Case C–329/05 *Finanzamt Dinslaken v Gerold Meindl* [2007] ECR I–1107; Case C–155/09 *Commission v Greece* [2011] ECR I–65.

[73] See, eg, Case C–240/10 *Schulz-Delzers* EU:C:2011:591. Compare Cases C–269/09 *Commission v Spain* EU:C:2012:439 and C–39/10 *Commission v Estonia* EU:C:2012:282 in which there was discriminatory tax treatment caught by the Treaty.

[74] Case C–171/02 *Commission v Portugal* [2004] ECR I–5645.

[75] Cases C–259 and 331–332/91 *Allué and Coonan* [1993] ECR I–4309; Case C–124/94 *Commission v Greece* [1995] ECR I–1457; Case C–90/96 *Petrie v Università degli studi di Verona and Camilla Bettoni* [1997] ECR I–6527.

[76] Case 379/87 *Groener v Minister for Education* [1989] ECR 3967.

[77] Case C–202/11 *Las v PSA Antwerp* EU:C:2013:239.

and the social protection of employees, the measure created obstacles for non-Dutch-speaking workers and employers and constituted a disproportionate hindrance to the establishment of free and informed consent between contracting parties. In the Court's view, less restrictive but equally effective alternative means of achieving the state's objectives were available.[78] Belgium was also brought before the CJEU for imposing a requirement on candidates for posts in the local services in French-speaking or German-speaking regions, where they had not carried out studies in the language concerned, to pass a specific exam set by a particular federal authority.[79] While the general requirement of linguistic competence was justified, the Court ruled that the requirement that candidates must pass this particular exam exclusively administered by one authority was indirectly discriminatory and disproportionate.

(c) OBSTACLES TO ACCESS TO THE EMPLOYMENT MARKET

It was for some time unclear whether Article 45 applied to national measures which restricted the freedom of movement of EU workers, but which were neither directly nor indirectly discriminatory on grounds of nationality. This central issue has arisen in relation to all the 'freedoms', and in each case the CJEU has ruled that even entirely non-discriminatory restrictions may breach the Treaty if they constitute an excessive obstacle to freedom of movement.

The issue was first directly addressed in the context of free movement of workers in the famous *Bosman* ruling, in which the transfer system developed by national and transnational football associations was found to be in breach of Article 45.[80] The system required a football club, which sought to engage a player whose contract with another club had come to an end, to pay money (often substantial) to the latter club. Bosman, who had been employed by a Belgian football club, was effectively prevented from securing employment with a French club. The fact that the transfer system applied equally to players moving from one club to another within a Member State as to players moving between states, and that a player's nationality was entirely irrelevant, did not prevent the system from breaching Article 45. According to the Court in *Bosman*:

> 103. It is sufficient to note that, although the rules in issue in the main proceedings apply also to transfers between clubs belonging to different national associations within the same Member State and are similar to those governing transfers between clubs belonging to the same national association, they still directly affect players' access to the employment market in other Member States and are thus capable of impeding freedom of movement for workers. They cannot, thus, be deemed comparable to the rules on selling arrangements for goods which in *Keck and Mithouard* were held to fall outside the ambit of Article 30 [*now Art 34*] of the Treaty (see also, with regard to the freedom to provide services, Case C–384/93 *Alpine Investments* v. *Minister van Financiën* [1995] ECR I–1141, paras. 36–38).

In the absence of any sufficiently convincing public-interest justification for the rule, it was found by the ECJ to be contrary to Article 45. The existence of an obstacle to the access of workers from one Member State to employment in another Member State was enough to attract the application of Article 45, even in the absence of any discrimination.[81]

---

[78] See E Cloots, 'Respecting Linguistic Identity Within the EU's Internal Market: *Las*' (2014) 51 CMLRev 623; I Urruti, 'Approach of the European Court of Justice on the Accommodation of the European Language Diversity in the Internal Market: Overcoming Language Barriers or Fostering Linguistic Diversity?' (2011–12) 18 CJEL 243.

[79] Case C–317/14 *Commission v Belgium* EU:C:2015:63. See also Case C–281/98 *Angonese* [2000] ECR I–4139.

[80] Case C–415/93 (n 14) [98]–[103], although see the earlier suggestion in Cases 321/87 *Commission v Belgium* [1989] ECR 997, [15]; C–176/96 *Lehtonen v FRBSB* [2000] ECR I–2681; C–325/08 *Olympique Lyonnais SASP v Olivier Bernard and Newcastle UFC* [2010] ECR I–2177, [27]–[37].

[81] L Daniele, 'Non-Discriminatory Restrictions to the Free Movement of Persons' (1997) 22 ELRev 191.

The principle established in *Bosman* has been repeatedly applied in a steady stream of subsequent cases.[82] In *Terhoeve*, the ECJ ruled that provisions, such as a national law concerning the payment of social contributions, which could preclude or deter a national of a Member State from leaving his country of origin in order to exercise his free-movement rights constituted an obstacle to that freedom even if they applied without regard to the nationality of the workers concerned.[83] In *Commission v Denmark*[84] and *Van Lent*,[85] the Court condemned national rules which prohibited workers domiciled in one particular state from using a vehicle registered in another Member State, on the basis that those rules might preclude workers from exercising their right to free movement or might impede access to employment between states.[86]

The fact that non-discriminatory provisions which impede market access can be caught raises concerns about the outer boundaries of Article 45, just as it does in relation to Article 34 on the free movement of goods. In *Graf*, the applicant argued that rules providing that compensation on termination of employment would not be available when the worker voluntarily ended the employment to take up employment elsewhere violated Article 45.[87] The ECJ reiterated the principle from *Bosman* concerning market access, but ruled on the facts that the impugned legislation did not offend this principle. The entitlement to compensation was not dependent on the worker choosing whether or not to stay with his current employer. It was, rather, dependent on a future and hypothetical event, namely the subsequent termination of the contract without this being at his initiative. This was 'too uncertain and indirect' a possibility for the legislation to be regarded as being in breach of Article 45.[88]

Similarly in *Weigel*, the negative tax consequences for an individual who moved from one Member State to another to work did not breach Article 45, even if it might deter the worker from exercising rights of free movement, as it did not place that individual under any greater disadvantage than those already resident and subject to the same tax.[89] In the absence of discrimination, the potentially deterrent effect was not in itself sufficient to be caught by Article 45. And in *Jeltes*, a difference between the benefits provided by the law of the Member State of previous employment and that by the law of the Member State of residence was held not to constitute a restriction on the free movement of workers but simply a result of the lack of harmonization of EU law on the issue.[90]

(D) INTERNAL SITUATIONS

Article 45 does not apply to a so-called 'wholly internal' situation. This is sometimes referred to as a situation of 'reverse discrimination', since its effect is frequently that national workers

---

[82] Case C–385/00 *De Groot v Staatssecretaris van Financiën* [2002] ECR I–11819; Case C–209/01 *Schilling and Fleck-Schilling v Finanzamt Nürnberg-Süd* [2003] ECR I–13389; Case C–137/04 *Rockler v Försäkringskassan* [2006] ECR I–1441; Case C–345/05 *Commission v Portugal* [2006] ECR I–10633; Case C–40/05 *Lyyski v Umeå Universitet* [2007] ECR I–99; Case C–212/06 *Government of Communauté française and Gouvernement wallon v Gouvernement flamand* [2008] ECR I–1683; Case C–325/08 *Olympique Lyonnais* (n 13); Case C–514/12 *Zentralbetriebsrat der gemeinnützigen Salzburger Landeskliniken Betriebs GmbH* EU:C:2013:799.

[83] Case C–18/95 *FC Terhoeve v Inspecteur van de Belastingdienst Particulieren/Onderneminen Buitenland* [1999] ECR I–345, [39]. See also Case C–544/11 *Petersen* EU:C:2013:124, [36].

[84] Case C–464/02 *Commission v Denmark* [2005] ECR I–7929.

[85] Case C–232/01 *Van Lent* [2003] ECR I–11525; Cases C–151–152/04 *Nadin and Durre* [2005] ECR I–11203.

[86] See also Case C–379/09 *Maurits Casteels* EU:C:2011:131, [22]–[23].

[87] Case C–190/98 *Volker Graf v Filzmoser Mashinenbau GmbH* [2000] ECR I–493. See in particular the opinion of AG Fennelly, [32].

[88] Ibid [24]–[25], CJEU's judgment. See MS Jansson and H Kalimo, '*De Minimis* Meets "Market Access": Transformations in the Substance—and the Syntax—of EU Free Movement Law?' (2014) 51 CMLRev 523.

[89] Case C–387/01 *Weigel v Finanzlandesdirektion für Vorarlberg* [2004] ECR I–4981, [50]–[55].

[90] Case C–443/11 *Jeltes* EU:C:2013:224. See also Case C–233/12 *Gardella* EU:C:2013:449, [33]–[35].

cannot claim rights in their own Member State which workers who are nationals of other Member States may claim there. In *Saunders* the ECJ held that since there was 'no factor connecting' the defendant 'to any of the situations envisaged by Community law', she could not rely on Article 45 to challenge an order which effectively excluded her from part of her own national territory.[91]

There have been attempts to circumvent this 'internal situation' barrier to the application of Article 45, by relying on the right to freedom of movement conferred by Article 21 TFEU on European citizens, as something over and above the rights of movement of EU workers, but these have not so far succeeded before the ECJ.[92] It will be seen below that this 'internal situation' approach by the Court has given rise to some invidious results in the context of the rights of workers and their families.[93]

Nevertheless, cases such as *Terhoeve*[94] and *De Groot*[95] make it clear that a worker can rely on Article 45 against his or her own state where that worker has been employed and resided in another Member State.[96] In this case the situation is no longer 'wholly internal'. Such a worker may then claim that he or she has been discriminated against in relation to, for example, social security contributions or taxation, when returning to work in his or her own Member State.

(E) OBJECTIVE JUSTIFICATION

The possible grounds for justifying indirect discrimination are broad, and not confined to the exceptions set out in the Treaty or in secondary legislation.[97] This is well illustrated in a stream of case law concerning apparently discriminatory tax treatment.[98] In *Schumacker*, the Court ruled that indirect discrimination based on the residence of a worker, whereby an EU national employed but not resident in a particular Member State could not benefit from personal tax allowances, could be justified where there was a relevant difference in the position of workers from other Member States and resident workers.[99] Yet while differential tax rules have certainly been held to be capable of justification on grounds of this kind,[100] in many cases the Court on the facts of the case has rejected arguments based on the

---

[91] Case 175/78 *R v Saunders* [1979] ECR 1129; Case 298/84 *Pavlo Iorio v Azienda Autonomo delle Ferrovie dello Stato* [1986] ECR 247; Cases C–225–227/95 *Kapasakalis, Skiathis and Kougiagkas v Greece* [1998] ECR I–4329; Case C–127/08 *Metock and Others v Minister for Justice, Equality and Law Reform* [2008] ECR I–6241; Case C–212/06 *Government of Communauté française* (n 82).

[92] Cases C–64 and 65/96 *Uecker* and *Jacquet v Land Nordrhein-Westfalen* [1997] ECR I–3171; Case C–299/95 *Kremzow v Austria* [1997] ECR I–2629; Case 180/83 *Moser v Land Baden-Württemberg* [1984] ECR 2539. Compare Case C–148/02 *Garcia Avello* [2003] ECR I–11613, discussed further in Ch 23; Case C–34/09 *Ruiz Zambrano* [2011] ECR I–1177.

[93] See, eg, Cases 35 and 36/82 *Morson and Jhanjan v Netherlands* [1982] ECR 3723.

[94] Case C–18/95 *Terhoeve* (n 83).

[95] Case C–385/00 *De Groot* (n 82).

[96] See also Cases C–197 and 203/11 *Libert and Others & All Projects & Developments NV* EU:C:2013:288 where the CJEU rejected the argument of the Belgian Government that this was a wholly internal situation.

[97] Case 152/73 *Sotgiu* (n 69); Case C–237/94 *O'Flynn* (n 64); Case C–176/96 *Lehtonen* (n 80) [51]–[60]; Case C–222/07 *UTECA* [2009] ECR I–1407.

[98] Many of the cases concern personal taxation. See however also on property taxation which discriminated based on whether the property was located in Hungary or another Member State, Case C–253/09 *Commission v Hungary* EU:C:2011:795.

[99] Case C–279/93 *Finanzamt Köln-Altstadt v Roland Schumacker* [1995] ECR I–225; F Vanistendael, 'The Consequences of *Schumacker* and *Wielockx*: Two Steps Forward in the Tax Procession of *Echternach*' (1996) 33 CMLRev 255; E Ros, 'EU Citizenship and Taxation: "Is the European Court of Justice Moving Towards a Citizen's Europe?"' (2014) 23 EC Tax Review 43.

[100] Cases C–300/90 *Commission v Belgium* [1992] ECR I–305; C–204/90 *Bachmann v Belgium* [1992] ECR I–249.

cohesion of the tax system, or on the need to supervise taxation or prevent tax avoidance, as adequate justification.[101]

The ECJ generally undertakes close scrutiny of claims that restrictions are justified, and increasingly demands evidence to support the claim of justification,[102] and an indication of a real connection between the contested measure and the purported justification.[103] In *Terhoeve*[104] the question was whether heavier social security contributions levied on a worker who transferred his residence from one Member State to another to take up work during the course of a year could be justified, but the Court rejected justifications based on the need to simplify and coordinate the levying of such contributions, or technical difficulties preventing other methods of collection.[105] In *Rockler*, arguments based on the supposed financial burden on the national social security scheme were rejected, on the basis that justifications based on purely economic grounds were unacceptable, and that the justification put forward was in any case not proportionate.[106] Similar rulings have been given by the Court in relation to rules against overlapping of social security benefits, or provisions on pension benefits which, although potentially justifiable, were ultimately deemed to be disproportionate or discriminatory in their impact.[107] Compatibility with EU legislation on social security coordination does not guarantee the justifiability of a domestic measure, since the measure may, even if it is in no way discriminatory, nonetheless be contrary to Article 45 if it is disproportionately restrictive of the free movement of workers.[108]

In the case of *Erny*, where the restriction arose not from Member State action but from the terms of a private employer's collective bargaining agreement, the CJEU accepted the importance of the right to negotiate collective agreements as part of the justification for the restriction in question, but ruled that this right could only be exercised in compliance with the principle of non-discrimination.[109]

The following case extract provides a nice illustration of the Court's rigour in assessing justification:

Case C–325/08 Olympique Lyonnais SASP v Olivier Bernard and Newcastle UFC
[2010] ECR I–2177

The case involved challenge to a rule whereby young footballers who were trained by a particular club would then have to pay damages if they signed a contract with a different club. The ECJ held that the rule was caught by Article 45, and then considered whether it could nonetheless be justified.

---

[101] Case C–385/00 *De Groot* (n 82); Case C–169/03 *Wallentin v Riksskatteverket* [2004] ECR I–6443; Case C–52/03 *Ritter-Coulais* (n 72); Case C–150/04 *Commission v Denmark* [2007] ECR I–1163. See also Case C–544/11 *Petersen* EU:C:2013:124 in which the German Government's attempt to plead development policy objectives to justify a tax rule discriminating on the basis of an employer's residence was rejected as insufficiently related to the measure.

[102] See, eg, Case C–73/08 *Bressol v Gouvernement de la Communauté française* [2010] ECR I–2735. N Nic Shuibhne and M Maci, 'Proving Public Interest: The Growing Impact of Evidence in Free Movement Case Law' (2013) 50 CMLRev 965.

[103] See, eg, Cases C–197 and 203/11 *Libert and Others & All Projects & Developments NV* EU:C:2013:288 on the lack of connection between the purported justification (to guarantee sufficient housing for low-income and disadvantaged sections of the local population) and the residence requirement imposed by the contested measure.

[104] Case C–18/95 *Terhoeve* (n 83) [43]–[47].

[105] See also Case C–544/11 *Petersen* EU:C:2013:124.

[106] Case C–137/04 *Rockler* (n 82). See also Case C–514/12 *Zentralbetriebsrat der gemeinnützigen Salzburger Landeskliniken Betriebs GmbH* EU:C:2013:799, [42]–[43].

[107] Cases C–611 and 612/10 *Hudziński & Wawrzyniak* EU:C:2012:339; Case C–379/09 *Maurits Casteels* EU:C:2011:131. Compare Case C–233/12 *Gardella* EU:C:2013:449.

[108] Case C–589/10 *Wencel* EU:C:2011:303, [64].

[109] Case C–172/11 *Erny* EU:C:2012:399. See also Case C–379/09 *Maurits Casteels* EU:C:2011:131 for an unjustified social-security restriction imposed by a private employer under a collective agreement.

THE ECJ

39. In regard to professional sport, the Court has already had occasion to hold that, in view of the considerable social importance of sporting activities and in particular football in the European Union, the objective of encouraging the recruitment and training of young players must be accepted as legitimate (see *Bosman*, paragraph 106).

...

41. In that regard, it must be accepted that, as the Court has already held, the prospect of receiving training fees is likely to encourage football clubs to seek new talent and train young players (see *Bosman*, paragraph 108).

42. The returns on the investments in training made by the clubs providing it are uncertain by their very nature since the clubs bear the expenditure incurred in respect of all the young players they recruit and train, sometimes over several years, whereas only some of those players undertake a professional career at the end of their training, whether with the club which provided the training or another club (see, to that effect, *Bosman*, paragraph 109).

...

44. Under those circumstances, the clubs which provided the training could be discouraged from investing in the training of young players if they could not obtain reimbursement of the amounts spent for that purpose where, at the end of his training, a player enters into a professional contract with another club...

45. It follows that a scheme providing for the payment of compensation for training where a young player, at the end of his training, signs a professional contract with a club other than the one which trained him can, in principle, be justified by the objective of encouraging the recruitment and training of young players. However, such a scheme must be actually capable of attaining that objective and be proportionate to it, taking due account of the costs borne by the clubs in training both future professional players and those who will never play professionally (see, to that effect, *Bosman*, paragraph 109).

46. It is apparent from paragraphs 4 and 6 of the present judgment that a scheme such as the one at issue in the main proceedings was characterised by the payment to the club which provided the training, not of compensation for training, but of damages, to which the player concerned would be liable for breach of his contractual obligations and the amount of which was unrelated to the real training costs incurred by the club.

47. ...the damages in question were not calculated in relation to the training costs incurred by the club providing that training but in relation to the total loss suffered by the club.

48. Under those circumstances, the possibility of obtaining such damages went beyond what was necessary to encourage recruitment and training of young players and to fund those activities.

...

50. A scheme such as the one at issue in the main proceedings, under which a '*joueur espoir*' who signs a professional contract with a club in another Member State at the end of his training period is liable to pay damages calculated in a way which is unrelated to the actual costs of the training, is not necessary to ensure the attainment of that objective.

5 ARTICLE 45(4): THE PUBLIC-SERVICE EXCEPTION

The ECJ has taken an expansive approach to the definition of worker. Conversely, its approach to the limiting clause in Article 45(4), which provides that Article 45 shall not apply to 'employment in the public service', has been correspondingly restrictive. The ECJ has articulated its intention to ensure that the scope of the exception goes no further than is necessary to fulfil the purpose for which it was included in the Treaty.[110] The battle over the scope of the public-service exception has been hard-fought, a fact which has been attributed by Mancini to 'the widespread view that the functioning of the public service is an exercise of full-State sovereignty'.[111]

(A) THE MEANING DETERMINED BY THE COURT, NOT THE MEMBER STATES

Continuing its 'hermeneutic monopoly' over the relevant Treaty terms in Article 45, the ECJ in *Sotgiu* made clear that the Court and not the Member States would decide what constitutes 'employment in the public service':[112]

> It is necessary to establish further whether the extent of the exception provided for by Article 48(4) [*now Art 45(4)*] can be determined in terms of the designation of the legal relationship between the employee and the employing administration.
>
> In the absence of any distinction in the provision referred to, it is of no interest whether a worker is engaged as a workman (*ouvrier*), a clerk (*employé*), or an official (*fonctionnaire*) or even whether the terms on which he is employed come under public or private law.
>
> These legal designations can be varied at the whim of national legislatures and cannot therefore provide a criterion for interpretation appropriate to the requirements of Community law.

Hence the Member States cannot deem a particular post to be 'in the public service' by the name or designation they give to that post, or by the mere fact that the terms of the post are regulated by public law. Further, it is irrelevant, given the need for the 'unity and efficacy' of EU law, whether the state's rules governing nationality as a necessary condition for entry to any post in the public service have constitutional status.[113]

(B) THE ECJ'S TEST FOR PUBLIC SERVICE

In the case extracted below, the Belgian Government, supported by the UK, German, and French Governments, argued that Article 45(4) differed from Article 51 TFEU. The latter provides a similar derogation in the context of freedom of establishment and freedom to provide services, when an activity involves the 'exercise of official authority'. This difference, according to the Belgian Government, was deliberately reflected in the wording of each. Article 51 specifically mentions the exercise of official authority, which implies a *functional* concept, whereas Article 45(4) refers to 'employment in the public service', which is an *institutional* concept. On the latter definition, what is important is the institution within which the worker is employed, rather than the nature of the work itself. The ECJ rejected this argument.

---

[110] Case C–190/98 *Volker Graf v Filzmoser Mashinenbau GmbH* [2000] ECR I–493. See in particular the opinion of AG Fennelly, [32].

[111] Mancini (n 24) 77.

[112] Case 152/73 *Sotgiu* (n 69) [5].

[113] [1980] ECR 3881, [18]–[19]; Case C–473/93 *Commission v Luxembourg* [1996] ECR I–3207, [38].

Case 149/79 **Commission v Belgium**
[1980] ECR 3881

[Note Lisbon Treaty renumbering: Art 48 is now Art 45 TFEU]

Possession of Belgian nationality was required as a condition of entry for posts with Belgian local authorities and public undertakings, regardless of the nature of the duties to be performed. Examples of such posts were those of unskilled railway workers, hospital nurses, and night-watchmen. The Belgian Government argued that, when the Treaties were drafted, there was no Community concept of the objectives and scope of public authorities and that the Member States' governments had wished the conditions of entry to public office to remain their preserve.

THE ECJ

10. That provision *[Art 48(4)]* removes from the ambit of Article 48(1) to (3) a series of posts which involve direct or indirect participation in the exercise of powers conferred by public law and duties designed to safeguard the general interests of the State or of other public authorities. Such posts in fact presume on the part of those occupying them the existence of a special relationship of allegiance to the State and reciprocity of rights and duties which form the foundation of the bond of nationality.

11. The scope of the derogation made by Article 48(4) to the principles of freedom of movement and equality of treatment laid down in the first three paragraphs of the article should therefore be determined on the basis of the aim pursued by that article. However, determining the sphere of application of Article 48(4) raises special difficulties since in the various Member States authorities acting under powers conferred by public law have assumed responsibilities of an economic and social nature or are involved in activities which are not identifiable with the functions which are typical of the public service yet which by their nature still come under the sphere of application of the Treaty. In these circumstances the effect of extending the exception contained in Article 48(4) to posts which, whilst coming under the States or other organizations governed by public law, still do not involve any association with tasks belonging to the public service properly so called, would be to remove a considerable number of posts from the ambit of the principles set out in the Treaty and to create inequalities between Member States according to the different ways in which the State and certain sectors of economic life are organized.

Thus a state cannot bring certain activities within the Treaty derogation simply by including them in the scope of the public law of the state and taking responsibility for their performance.[114] The ECJ held that the aim of the Treaty provision was to permit Member States to reserve for nationals those posts which would require a *specific bond of allegiance and mutuality of rights and duties between state and employee.*

The Court's description of the posts that could be said to require such allegiance and to depend upon the bond of nationality was twofold: (i) they must involve participation in the exercise of powers conferred by public law, and (ii) they must entail duties designed to safeguard the general interests of the state. The notion of 'powers conferred by public law' is rather vague, given the difficulties inherent in defining the scope of public law, but the idea of 'safeguarding the general interests of the State' is somewhat more concrete. It seems that the two requirements are cumulative rather than alternative: a post will benefit from the derogation in Article 45(4) only if it involves *both* the exercise of power conferred by public law *and* the safeguarding of the general interests of the state.[115]

[114] The converse, however, is also true: the application of the Art 45(4) exception is not excluded simply because the employer in question is a private party rather than a public body: Case C–405/01 *Colegio de Oficiales de la Marina Mercante Española v Administracion del Estado* [2003] ECR I–10391.

[115] Cases 66/85 *Lawrie-Blum* (n 36) [27]; C–473/93 *Commission v Luxembourg* (n 113) [18].

Two imperatives seem to drive the ECJ's insistence on the functional as opposed to the institutional test: first, a fear that the institutional approach could immunize large sectors of the economy from the reach of free movement, more especially in countries that take an expansive view of 'state employment'; and, secondly, a desire to break down stereotypes and to encourage Member States to think that employment of a non-national in many public sector jobs should, if that person were best qualified for the position, not be regarded as odd or unnatural.

(c) APPLICATION OF THE ECJ'S TEST

In the *Belgium* case[116] the ECJ ruled that it did not have enough information to identify which of the specified posts fell outside the Treaty derogation. It invited Belgium and the Commission to re-examine and resolve the issue in the light of its judgment, and to report any solution to the ECJ. When they failed to agree on certain posts, the case was brought back to the ECJ which ruled that, with the exception of a limited number, none of the posts satisfied the criteria for the application of the public-service exception.[117]

A further argument advanced by the four governments represented in the *Belgium* case was that certain posts which may not at the outset involve participation in the powers conferred by public law may change, or the holders of such initial posts may subsequently become eligible for careers at a higher grade with duties involving the exercise of public powers. This, too, was rejected by the Court as a reason for treating the initial post as being within the public-service exception, since that exception 'allows Member States to reserve to their nationals, by appropriate rules, entry to posts involving the exercise of such powers and such responsibilities within the same grade, the same branch, or the same class'.[118]

The point was made again by the ECJ in enforcement proceedings brought by the Commission against Italy, concerning laws protecting the security and tenure of researchers at the National Research Council (CNR), which were not applied to non-nationals.[119] Italy argued, first, that the work undertaken by the CNR involved satisfying the general interests of the state and was financed out of public funds. It argued, secondly, that if researchers became established members of staff, they could be promoted to higher managerial positions, which would entail participation in the exercise of public power. The ECJ ruled that only the duties of management or advising the state on scientific and technical questions could constitute 'employment in the public service' within the meaning of Article 45(4),[120] and summarily rejected the second argument by reference to its ruling in the *Belgium* case.[121]

In a later case concerning posts as master and chief mate of merchant ships flying the Spanish flag, however, the Court emphasized that the Article 45(4) exception could be validly invoked only if the rights under powers conferred by public law, for example the exercise of police powers in the event of danger on board, are *in fact exercised on a regular basis* by those holders and do not represent a very minor part of their activities.[122] Member States have continued their attempts to use the exception in numerous other cases,[123] and the Court in turn has continued its strict approach.[124]

---

[116] Case 149/79 *Commission v Belgium* [1980] ECR 3881.

[117] Case 149/79 *Commission v Belgium II* [1982] ECR 1845.

[118] Ibid [21].

[119] Case 225/85 *Commission v Italy* [1987] ECR 2625.

[120] Ibid [9].

[121] Ibid [10].

[122] Case C–405/01 *Colegio de Oficiales de la Marina Mercante Española* (n 114).

[123] Case 66/85 *Lawrie-Blum* (n 36) [28]; Case 33/88 *Allué and Coonan v Università degli Studi di Venezia* [1989] ECR 1591; Case C–213/90 *ASTI v Chambre des Employés Privés* [1991] ECR I–3507; Case C–4/91 *Bleis v Ministère de l'Education Nationale* [1991] ECR I–5627.

[124] See, eg, Case C–270/13 *Haralambidis* EU:C:2014:2185 where the Court ruled that the president of a port authority did not fall within Art 45(4).

There is no secondary legislation which attempts to clarify the concept. The Commission once proposed draft legislation to clarify the derogation, but its proposal was opposed by those who thought that the Member States might take advantage of detailed legislation to undermine the established case law, and also that such legislation could ossify the process of creating a 'citizens' Europe'.[125] Instead, in 1988, the Commission published a guidance document on the sorts of state functions which it considered would or would not fall within that provision.[126] Those which probably would be covered included the armed forces, police, judiciary, tax authorities, and certain public bodies engaged in preparing or monitoring legal acts; and those which probably would not included nursing, teaching, and non-military research in public establishments.

The issue remains fraught with ideological tensions, the underlying debate being about the relevance of nationality in employment. The efforts of the Member States to define the public-service derogation in institutional terms by reference to the 'public sector' have repeatedly failed.[127] The Court has adhered to a rather more difficult but narrower 'functional' approach, which examines closely the character of posts which might be said to require the reciprocal bond of allegiance which is said to be characteristic of nationality. Advocate General Mancini's trenchant opinion in infringement proceedings involving public nursing posts in France exemplifies well the tensions in this field:[128]

> The decisions to which I have referred gave rise to severe criticisms from academic lawyers and, what is more important, they have not been 'taken in' by numerous governments. Such resistance is not surprising if it is borne in mind how deep-rooted is the conviction that the public service is an area in which the State should exercise full sovereignty and how wide-spread is the tendency, in times of high unemployment, to see the public service as a convenient reservoir of posts. Such resistance is a matter for concern and should be tackled head-on before cases similar to the present one multiply....
>
> ...In short, in order to be made inaccessible to nationals of another State, it is not sufficient for the duties inherent in the post at issue to be directed specifically towards public objectives which influence the conduct and action of private individuals. Those who occupy the post must don full battle dress: in non-metaphorical terms, the duties must involve acts of will which affect private individuals by requiring their obedience or, in the event of disobedience, by compelling them to comply. To make a list...is practically impossible; but certainly the first examples which come to mind are posts relating to policing, defence of the State, the administration of justice and assessments to tax.
>
> ...It is a fact that an extremist disciple of Hegel might truly think that access to posts like the ones at issue here [*nursing*] should be denied to foreigners. But anyone who does not regard the State as 'the march of God in the world' must of necessity take the contrary view.

It was suggested, soon after the Maastricht Treaty was adopted, that the provisions on citizenship introduced by that Treaty might reduce the importance of the public-service exception, given the emphasis of the latter on a traditional notion of loyalty between the state and its own nationals, to the exclusion of foreigners.[129] However, the Commission has continued to bring regular infringement proceedings concerning misuse of the public-service exception, which are often vigorously defended by the Member States.[130]

---

[125] Mancini (n 24).

[126] [1988] OJ C72/2.

[127] Case C–473/93 *Commission v Luxembourg* (n 113); Case C–173/94 *Commission v Belgium* [1996] ECR I–3265; Case C–290/94 *Commission v Greece* [1996] ECR I–3285, where the CJEU was asked once again to depart entirely from its previous case law.

[128] Case 307/84 *Commission v France* [1986] ECR 1725, 1727–1733; D O'Keeffe, 'Judicial Interpretation of the Public Service Exception to the Free Movement of Workers' in Curtin and O'Keeffe (n 24) 101–103.

[129] O'Keeffe, ibid.

[130] See the cases at (n 127).

A valuable report by Ziller on the public-service exception found that most Member States had adapted their national rules to comply with the ECJ's functional approach, although there were problems remaining in some cases, and the report made a number of recommendations for improvement.[131] The Commission has continued to assess national trends in this area including through the annual reports of the network of experts on the free movement of workers, and questionnaires distributed through the technical committee on the free movement of workers.[132]

(D) DISCRIMINATORY CONDITIONS OF EMPLOYMENT WITHIN THE PUBLIC SERVICE ARE PROHIBITED

It is clear from *Sotgiu* that Article 45(4) cannot be used to justify discriminatory conditions for employment *within* the public service, but only to restrict admission to public-service employment in the first place. Germany invoked Article 45(4) in an attempt to justify its provisions on separation allowances for post office workers, which worked to the disadvantage of non-nationals, and the ECJ responded:[133]

> The interests which this derogation [*Art 45(4)*] allows Member States to protect are satisfied by the opportunity of restricting admission of foreign nationals to certain activities in the public service.
>
> On the other hand this provision cannot justify discriminatory measures with regard to remuneration or other conditions of employment against workers once they have been admitted to the public service.
>
> The very fact that they have been admitted shows indeed that those interests which justify the exceptions to the principle of non-discrimination permitted by [*Article 45(4)*] are not at issue.

6 DIRECTIVE 2004/38: RIGHT OF ENTRY AND RESIDENCE OF WORKERS AND THEIR FAMILIES

(A) FORMAL REQUIREMENTS FOR WORKERS

Directive 68/360 was originally adopted to facilitate freedom of movement and the abolition of restrictions on employed persons, in part by clarifying the formal requirements relating to the right of entry and residence of non-nationals. This Directive was repealed and replaced by the relevant provisions of Directive 2004/38[134] on the movement and residence of EU citizens and their families, with 'family members' defined in Articles 2 and 3 thereof.

According to the ECJ, Directive 2004/38 aims to facilitate the exercise of the Treaty-derived individual right to move and reside freely within Member States, and to strengthen that right. The consequence is that EU citizens cannot derive lesser rights from Directive 2004/38 than from the instruments

---

[131] J Ziller, 'Free Movement of European Union Citizens and Employment in the Public Sector', available at http://ec.europa.eu/social/main.jsp?catId=465&langId=en. See also Commission Staff Working Document on Free Movement of Workers in the Public Sector, SEC(2010) 1609.

[132] See (n 2). Also P Minderhoud and B Fridriksdottir, 'Report on Posts in the Public Sector Reserved for Nationals Developments in the 27 Member States in 2009–2012' (2013), available at http://ec.europa.eu/social/BlobServlet?docId=10943&langId=en.

[133] Case 152/73 *Sotgiu* (n 69) [4]; Case C–195/98 *Österreicher Gewerkschaftsbund, Gewerkschaft Öffentlicher Dienst v Republik Österreich* [2000] ECR I–10497, [37].

[134] (N 19).

of secondary legislation which it amended or repealed, and the Directive must not be interpreted restrictively.[135]

Article 6 of Directive 2004/38 gives an initial right of entry and residence for up to three months to all EU citizens and their families without any conditions other than presentation of an ID card or passport. The interim status of job-seeker is also recognized in the Preamble to the Directive, which implicitly confirms the ECJ case law on this subject.[136] For periods of residence longer than three months, Article 8 of the Directive provides that workers and their families may be required to register with the host state authorities, and upon presentation of a valid passport or ID card and confirmation of employment (and, in the case of family members, a document attesting to the existence of the relevant family relationship, dependency, etc), to receive a certification of registration as evidence of their underlying right of residence.[137] However, family members who are not EU nationals are to be issued with a 'residence card' under Articles 9 and 10.

Member States are required by Article 4 to grant citizens and their families the right to leave their territory to go and work in other Member States, simply on producing an identity card or passport of at least five years' validity, which their Member State must provide for them and which will be valid throughout the EU and any necessary transit countries between Member States. No exit visa requirement may be imposed. Article 5 sets out similar conditions for the right to enter another Member State: all that is required is a valid identity card or passport and a visa requirement is impermissible, except for certain third-country nationals. The conditions under which a visa can be imposed for family members who are third-country nationals have been tightened up by Article 5(2); they are to be issued free of charge and as soon as possible, and those holding a valid residence card issued by a Member State under Article 9 are exempt from the requirement.

It is made clear in the Directive, as the ECJ had repeatedly emphasized in its case law, that the rights to reside and to work are not conditional upon initial satisfaction of the formalities for which the Directive provides.[138] Various provisions of Directive 2004/38, including Articles 5(5), 8(2), and 9(3), follow this line of case law by referring to the right of states to impose proportionate and non-discriminatory penalties for non-satisfaction of the formal requirements.[139] It is clear that deportation, refusal of entry, or revocation of the right of residence constitutes a disproportionate penalty for failure to fulfil administrative formalities.[140] Even with respect to the right to enter, Article 5(4) of the Directive, following the ECJ ruling in *MRAX*,[141] provides that where the EU national or family member does not have the requisite documents or visas, the Member State shall give them every reasonable opportunity to obtain the documents or to prove their right to movement and residence by other means.

Some confusion was introduced by the ECJ's ruling in *Akrich* that a non-EU national spouse who was not lawfully resident in a Member State could not avail of rights of movement and residence under EU law.[142] The decision was difficult to reconcile with the judgment in *MRAX*,[143] and the ECJ subsequently departed from *Akrich*.

---

[135] Case C–127/08 *Metock* (n 91) [59], [82], [84]; Case C–162/09 *Secretary of State for Work and Pensions v Lassal* [2010] ECR I–9217 [30]–[31]; Case C–145/09 *Land Baden-Württemberg v Tsakouridis* [2010] ECR I–11979, [23]; Case C–507/12 *Jesse Saint Prix* EU:C:2014:2007, [32]–[33].

[136] Dir 2004/38, recs 9 and 16.

[137] This provision was apparently intended to respond to Case 48/75 *Royer* (n 46), which indicated that the residence permit granted under the prior Dir 68/360 did not itself grant rights, but was merely evidence of a pre-existing right under the Treaty.

[138] Case 48/75 *Royer* (n 46).

[139] Case 321/87 *Commission v Belgium* (n 80); Case C–24/97 *Commission v Germany* [1998] ECR I–2133; Case C–215/03 *Oulane v Minister voor Vreemdelingenzaken en Integratie* [2005] ECR I–1215.

[140] Cases 118/75 *Watson and Belmann* [1976] ECR 1185; C–363/89 *Roux* [1991] ECR I–273; C–459/99 *MRAX v Belgium* [2002] ECR I–6591; C–215/03 *Oulane* (n 139).

[141] Case C–459/99 *MRAX* (n 140); Case C–157/03 *Commission v Spain* [2005] ECR I–2911.

[142] Case C–109/01 *Secretary of State for the Home Department v Akrich* [2003] ECR I–9607, [49]–[53].

[143] Case C–459/99 *MRAX* (n 140). In Case C–1/05 *Jia v Migrationsverket* [2007] ECR I–1 the CJEU confined *Akrich* to its own facts.

Case C–127/08 **Metock and Others v Minister for Justice, Equality and Law Reform**
[2008] ECR I–6241

THE ECJ

48. By its first question the referring court asks whether Directive 2004/38 precludes legislation of a Member State which requires a national of a non-member country who is the spouse of a Union citizen residing in that Member State but not possessing its nationality to have previously been lawfully resident in another Member State before arriving in the host Member State, in order to benefit from the provisions of that directive.

49. In the first place, it must be stated that, as regards family members of a Union citizen, no provision of Directive 2004/38 makes the application of the directive conditional on their having previously resided in a Member State.

50. As Article 3(1) of Directive 2004/38 states, the directive applies to all Union citizens who move to or reside in a Member State other than that of which they are a national, and to their family members as defined in point 2 of Article 2 of the directive who accompany them or join them in that Member State. The definition of family members in point 2 of Article 2 of Directive 2004/38 does not distinguish according to whether or not they have already resided lawfully in another Member State.

51. It must also be pointed out that Articles 5, 6(2) and 7(2) of Directive 2004/38 confer the rights of entry, of residence for up to three months, and of residence for more than three months in the host Member State on nationals of non-member countries who are family members of a Union citizen whom they accompany or join in that Member State, without any reference to the place or conditions of residence they had before arriving in that Member State.

. . .

54. In those circumstances, Directive 2004/38 must be interpreted as applying to all nationals of non-member countries who are family members of a Union citizen within the meaning of point 2 of Article 2 of that directive and accompany or join the Union citizen in a Member State other than that of which he is a national, and as conferring on them rights of entry and residence in that Member State, without distinguishing according to whether or not the national of a non-member country has already resided lawfully in another Member State.

55. That interpretation is supported by the Court's case-law on the instruments of secondary law concerning freedom of movement for persons adopted before Directive 2004/38.

56. Even before the adoption of Directive 2004/38, the Community legislature recognised the importance of ensuring the protection of the family life of nationals of the Member States in order to eliminate obstacles to the exercise of the fundamental freedoms guaranteed by the EC Treaty . . .

. . .

58. It is true that the Court held in paragraphs 50 and 51 of *Akrich* that, in order to benefit from the rights provided for in Article 10 of Regulation No 1612/68, the national of a non-member country who is the spouse of a Union citizen must be lawfully resident in a Member State when he moves to another Member State to which the citizen of the Union is migrating or has migrated. However, that conclusion must be reconsidered. The benefit of such rights cannot depend on the prior lawful residence of such a spouse in another Member State (see, to that effect, *MRAX*, paragraph 59, and Case C–157/03 *Commission v Spain*, paragraph 28).

59. The same interpretation must be adopted a fortiori with respect to Directive 2004/38, which amended Regulation No 1612/68 and repealed the earlier directives on freedom of movement for persons . . .

60. [T]he above interpretation of Directive 2004/38 is consistent with the division of competences between the Member States and the Community.

61. It is common ground that the Community derives from Articles 18(2) EC, 40 EC, 44 EC and 52 EC [*now Arts 21(2) TFEU, 46 TFEU, 50 TFEU and 59 TFEU, respectively*]—on the basis of which Directive 2004/38 inter alia was adopted—competence to enact the necessary measures to bring about freedom of movement for Union citizens.

...

63. Consequently, within the competence conferred on it by those articles of the Treaty, the Community legislature can regulate the conditions of entry and residence of the family members of a Union citizen in the territory of the Member States, where the fact that it is impossible for the Union citizen to be accompanied or joined by his family in the host Member State would be such as to interfere with his freedom of movement by discouraging him from exercising his rights of entry into and residence in that Member State.

...

65. It follows that the Community legislature has competence to regulate, as it did by Directive 2004/38, the entry and residence of nationals of non-member countries who are family members of a Union citizen in the Member State in which that citizen has exercised his right of freedom of movement, including where the family members were not already lawfully resident in another Member State.

66. Consequently, the interpretation put forward by the Minister for Justice...that the Member States retain exclusive competence, subject to Title IV of Part Three of the Treaty, to regulate the first access to Community territory of family members of a Union citizen who are nationals of non-member countries must be rejected.

67. Indeed, to allow the Member States exclusive competence to grant or refuse entry into and residence in their territory to nationals of non-member countries who are family members of Union citizens and have not already resided lawfully in another Member State would have the effect that the freedom of movement of Union citizens in a Member State whose nationality they do not possess would vary from one Member State to another, according to the provisions of national law concerning immigration, with some Member States permitting entry and residence of family members of a Union citizen and other Member States refusing them.

68. That would not be compatible with the objective set out in Article 3(1)(c) EC [*now replaced in substance by Art 3(2) and (3) TEU*] of an internal market characterised by the abolition, as between Member States, of obstacles to the free movement of persons. Establishing an internal market implies that the conditions of entry and residence of a Union citizen in a Member State whose nationality he does not possess are the same in all the Member States. Freedom of movement for Union citizens must therefore be interpreted as the right to leave any Member State, in particular the Member State whose nationality the Union citizen possesses, in order to become established under the same conditions in any Member State other than the Member State whose nationality the Union citizen possesses.

The case reveals the tensions between the imperatives of free movement, the ECJ's 'rights-based vision' on the one hand, and Member States' desire to exercise 'first access control' on the entry into their territory of non-nationals, even where they are family members of an EU national, on the other.[144] This is attested to by the fact that ten Member States submitted observations in the case, the decision prompted debate in the Council,[145] and led to heated criticism in some Member States, such as Denmark.[146] The following extract reveals some of the foundational issues raised by the case.

[144] C Costello, '*Metock*: Free Movement and "Normal Family Life" in the Union' (2009) 46 CMLRev 587.
[145] Ibid 607–608.
[146] S Currie, 'Accelerated Justice or a Step Too Far? Residence Rights for Non-EU Family Members and the Court's Ruling in *Metock*' (2009) 34 ELRev 310, 324–325.

Important for TCN rights

S Currie, Accelerated Justice or a Step too Far? Residence Rights for non-EU Family Members and the Court's Ruling in *Metock*[147]

This case illustrates especially clearly the tensions that can arise as a consequence of the extension of residence entitlement to family members of Union citizens. From a legal perspective, when the judgment is considered in light of the case law pre-dating *Akrich* on TCN family members, and subsequent developments which have placed an increasing emphasis on the protection of family life as a fundamental right, *Metock* is not unreasonable. If anything, *Akrich* can be classified as the erroneous judgment due to its apparent contradiction of the case law before it. *Metock* also represents recognition of the reality of family life in the context of mobility and accepts that family relationships which arise in the aftermath of migration are worthy of some protection. In essence, the ruling enshrines a more equitable approach to TCN family members of Union citizens in circumstances of genuine family union. Reasoning on the individual level, this is surely a fair result.

There is a clear disjuncture, though, between the view of *Metock* as a judgment which can be categorised as legally justified and the political reality (or perceived reality) which informs the application of national immigration law. *Metock* has brought to the fore Member State dissatisfaction with the ECJ's claim of Community competence to regulate the residence entitlement of family members and there are clearly questions about compliance in its aftermath. Given the recent finding by the Commission that implementation of Directive 2004/38 is less than meticulous in a significant number of Member States, *Metock* may prove to be the straw that broke the camel's back.

(B) JOB-SEEKERS AND THE UNEMPLOYED

Article 7(3) of Directive 2004/38 governs the position of former workers who, although they have ceased working, nevertheless retain some of the rights of workers for themselves and their families.

It provides that EU citizens who are no longer workers shall retain the status of worker where they are temporarily unable to work as the result of an illness or accident; or where they are involuntarily unemployed after having been employed for more than one year and having registered with the employment office as job-seekers.[148] Where involuntary unemployment follows employment of less than one year, the Directive provides that the status of worker is to be retained for at least six months, if the person registers as a job-seeker. Article 7 also provides, following ECJ case law,[149] that a worker who embarks on vocational training may retain the status of worker, but that in cases where the worker has voluntarily given up employment retention of this status is conditional upon the training being related to the previous employment.

The Directive does not otherwise deal with voluntary unemployment, and so the assumption could reasonably be made that a person will not retain the status of worker if they become voluntarily unemployed unless they are pursuing related vocational training.[150] However, this assumption does not apply in all cases.

---

[147] Ibid 325–326.

[148] See also Case C–379/11 *Caves Krier Frères Sàrl* EU:C:2012:798 on the position of a frontier worker who, having become involuntarily unemployed in a Member State other than the state of residence, finds new employment in that other Member State.

[149] Cases C–3/90 *Bernini* (n 38); C–357/89 *Raulin* (n 38).

[150] In C–413/01 *Ninni-Orasche v Bundesminister für Wissenschaft, Verkehr und Kunst* [2003] ECR I–13187, the CJEU ruled that a worker would not necessarily be considered to be *voluntarily* unemployed upon expiry of a fixed-term contract, since the employee has little or no control over the duration of the contract he or she is offered.

In the first place, as we have seen from *Antonissen* and *Collins*,[151] a person who is seeking work enjoys certain rights under Article 45. By comparison with the category of persons in Article 7(3) who have become involuntarily unemployed in the host Member State, these job-seekers are not 'workers' in the full sense of the term, but they do enjoy a right of residence during the period they are seeking work, and access to certain benefits which are specifically intended to facilitate access to employment.[152] As far as the length of this period of job-seeking is concerned, the ECJ in *Antonissen* left it somewhat flexible, ruling that while the period of six months allowed by the UK seemed reasonable, the right to remain in search of work must continue even after that period so long as the person concerned 'provides evidence that he is continuing to seek employment and that he has genuine chances of being engaged'.[153] Although this is not explicitly governed by the provisions of the Directive, recital 9 concerning the three-month right of residence for all EU citizens declares that it is without prejudice to the 'more favourable treatment applicable to job-seekers as recognized by the case-law of the Court of Justice'.

In the second place, the ECJ has also indicated that rights linked to the status of worker may be retained for some time even when someone is no longer in an employment relationship, although the relevant links with the status of worker will not continue for an excessively lengthy period of time.[154] In *Collins*, the applicant could not rely on the fact that he had been employed as a worker seventeen years previously to claim current entitlement to rights as a worker. However in *Saint Prix*, where a woman voluntarily gave up her employment due to pregnancy less than three months before the birth of her child and returned to work three months after the birth, she did not cease to be a 'worker' during that time even if she was unavailable for employment in that period, 'provided she returns to work or finds another job within a reasonable period after confinement'.[155] The Court ruled firmly that Article 7(3) of the Directive on involuntary unemployment does not 'list exhaustively the circumstances in which a migrant worker who is no longer in an employment relationship may nevertheless continue to benefit from that status'.[156]

(c) THE RIGHT OF PERMANENT RESIDENCE

An important innovation in Directive 2004/38 was the introduction of the right of permanent residence for EU citizens and their families, including non-nationals, who have resided lawfully for a continuous period of five years in the host state. These provisions replace and build on the previous legislation allowing workers or their families under specific conditions to acquire a right of permanent residence in less than three years in the event of retirement, injury, or death.

Articles 16–18 indicate the conditions under which EU citizens may enjoy this right, which clearly covers EU workers and their families. Article 16(3) makes provision for temporary absences and Article 16(4) provides that the right of permanent residence may be lost only through absences of more than two consecutive years. Article 17 details the shorter qualifying period for workers and their families in the event of retirement, incapacity, or death, and Article 18 concerns the right of permanent residence of EU nationals' family members who are not nationals of a Member State, including workers, who have satisfied the five-year legal residence requirement.[157]

---

[151] Case C–292/89 *R v Immigration Appeal Tribunal, ex p Antonissen* [1991] ECR I–745; Case C–138/02 *Collins* (n 30).
[152] Cases C–138/02 *Collins* (n 30); C–258/04 *Ioannidis* (n 51).
[153] Case C–292/89 (n 151) [21].
[154] Case C–138/02 *Collins* (n 30).
[155] C–507/12 *Jesse Saint Prix* EU:C:2014:2007, [39]–[42].
[156] Ibid [38].
[157] Case C–162/09 *Lassal* [2010] ECR I–9217 indicates that periods of residence completed prior to the date of transposition of Dir 2004/38 will count towards the acquisition of the right of residence under Art 16. See also Cases C–147 and 148/11 *Czop and Punakova* EU:C:2012:538.

The administrative formalities are regulated by Articles 19–21. A document certifying permanent residence is to be issued as soon as possible to EU nationals who have verified their duration of residence. Non-EU national family members of workers who enjoy a derivative right of permanent residence are to be given a 'permanent residence card', which is to be automatically renewed every ten years, and the validity of the card will not be affected by absences of less than two consecutive years. Continuity of residence, for any person with the right of permanent residence, will be broken by an expulsion decision which has been enforced against the person.

In *Dias*, the Court ruled that periods of time spent residing in a Member State when the conditions for lawful residence under the Treaty were not satisfied would not count towards the acquisition of permanent residence, even where the applicant had been in possession of a residence permit under the predecessor Directive 68/360.[158] This was because—as the Court had ruled in *Royer* and previous cases[159]—a residence permit cannot in itself grant rights, but can only provide evidence of the underlying right, which in this case did not exist. However, using purposive reasoning, the Court ruled that provided that the period of time during which the person did not satisfy the conditions for lawful residence was less than two years, it should be treated by analogy with absences from the state of less than two years under Article 16(4) of the Directive, and should not affect the acquisition of the right to permanent residence.[160]

(D) CONDITIONS FOR EXERCISE OF THE RIGHT TO RESIDENCE

Articles 22–26 regulate conditions under which the right of residence, including the right of permanent residence, is to be enjoyed. It is to cover the whole of the territory, and importantly includes the right of equal treatment with nationals of the host state within the scope of the Treaty, subject to such exceptions as are provided for by the Treaty or in secondary law.[161] Article 23 guarantees the right to take up employment for EU and non-EU national family members alike, replacing the previous provisions of Regulation 1612/68, which is discussed below.

7 REGULATION 492/2011: SUBSTANTIVE RIGHTS AND SOCIAL ADVANTAGES

(A) REGULATION 492/2011

The main focus thus far has been on the 'negative' effects of Article 45 and associated legislation: the prohibition of discrimination and of barriers to freedom of movement, and the prohibition of entry visas or similar restrictions. The other side of the coin is that this Treaty Article confers positive, substantive rights of freedom of movement and equality of treatment on EU workers. These rights are, to some extent, fleshed out by the secondary legislation, and in particular by Regulation 492/2011, codifying and repealing the previous Regulation 1612/68.[162]

---

[158] Case C–325/09 *Dias* EU:C:2011:498, [48]–[55]. See also Case C–244/13 *Ogieriakhi* EU:C:2014:2068, [31]; Case C–529/11 *Alarape and Tijani* EU:C:2013:290.

[159] (Nn 138–140).

[160] Case C–325/09 *Dias* (n 158) [61]–[66].

[161] This would include exceptions such as 'employment in the public service', benefits such as rewards for war-time loyalty on which the CJEU has ruled, and the right to vote in national elections, which are discussed below.

[162] [2011] OJ L41/1.

The CJEU's approach to Regulation 492/2011 has been similar to that to other free movement legislation, in ruling that the legislation protects and facilitates the exercise of the primary rights conferred by the Treaty, rather than creating rights in itself. However, although the principle of equal treatment, which is now also expressly contained in Article 24 of Directive 2004/38, forms the backbone of the legislation, its degree of detail and specificity goes beyond what is expressed in the Treaty, and requires the Member States to ensure that Union workers enjoy a wide range of the substantive benefits available to nationals. In particular, the Regulation covers the families of EU workers, which are not mentioned in the Treaty chapter.

There are three titles within *Chapter I* of the Regulation: Section 1 (Articles 1–6) on eligibility for employment, Section 2 (Articles 7–9) on equality of treatment within employment, and Section 3 (Article 10) on workers' families. *Chapter II* of the Regulation contains detailed provisions which require cooperation amongst the relevant employment agencies of the Member States, and between the Member States' agencies, the Commission, and the European Coordination Office, on applications for employment and the clearance of vacancies. Chapter III of the Regulation established an Advisory Committee and a Technical Committee made up of Member States' representatives, to ensure close cooperation on matters concerning free movement of workers and employment. Chapters II and III of the Regulation, which were amended several times over the years, have attracted comparatively little legal attention. Yet they can be very significant for a worker seeking to move to another Member State to find employment. Member States' authorities are required to provide information on vacancies, working conditions, and the national labour market, and to cooperate with the Commission in conducting studies on various matters.[163]

However, it is Chapter I of Regulation 492/2011 which has been the subject of most comment and litigation. Article 1 sets out the right of Member State nationals to take up employment in another Member State under the same conditions as its nationals, and Article 2 prohibits discrimination against such workers or employees in concluding and performing contracts of employment. Articles 3 and 4 prohibit certain directly or indirectly discriminatory administrative practices, such as reserving a quota of posts for national workers, restricting advertising or applications, or setting special recruitment or registration procedures for nationals of other Member States, but with an exception for genuine linguistic requirements. Article 5 guarantees the same assistance from employment offices to non-nationals as well as to nationals, and Article 6 prohibits discriminatory vocational or medical criteria for recruitment and appointment. Article 7 fleshes out Article 45(2) of the Treaty by providing for the same social and tax advantages for nationals and non-nationals, for equal access to vocational training, and declares void any discriminatory provisions of collective or individual employment agreements.[164] Article 8 provides for equality of trade-union rights with nationals,[165] and Article 9 for the same access to all rights and benefits in matters of housing.

Prior to the adoption of Directive 2004/38, Article 10 of the Regulation 1612/68 had listed the family members who had the right to install themselves with a worker who was employed in another Member State: these were the spouse and their descendants, who were either under 21 or dependent,[166] and dependent relatives in the ascending line of the worker and spouse.[167] This group was extended by

---

[163] For some of the reports and studies, see (nn 2, 6, 8, and 131). On recent legislation for a network of employment services to integrate labour markets, and to improve the EURES network, see (n 1).

[164] For discussion of the notion of 'social and tax advantages' in Art 7(2), see the paper commissioned by the EU Commission: A Czekaj-Dancewicz, 'Analytical Note on Social and Tax Advantages and Benefits Under EU Law', European Report (2013), available at http://ec.europa.eu/social/BlobServlet?docId=11714&langId=en.

[165] Case C–213/90 *ASTI* (n 123); Case C–118/92 *Commission v Luxembourg* [1994] ECR I–1891; Case C–465/01 *Commission v Austria* [2004] ECR I–8291.

[166] The notion of dependency in Art 10 includes a member of the family who is in fact supported by the worker, whatever the reason for the support: Case 316/85 *Lebon* (n 48).

[167] Case C–1/05 *Jia* (n 143).

Article 2(2) of Directive 2004/38 to include, along with spouses, a partner with whom an EU citizen has a registered partnership under the national legislation of a Member State, if the host Member State treats registered partnerships as equivalent to marriage. Similarly, the under-21 or dependent children of a registered partner and the dependent direct relatives in the ascending line of the registered partner were also included by Article 2(2).

Article 3 of Directive 2004/38 extended the prior provision in Article 10(2) of Regulation 1612/68 which required Member States to 'facilitate entry and residence' for other family members whatever their nationality, who were, in the state of origin, dependants or members of the household of the EU citizen, in this case the worker. Directive 2004/38 added to this that Member States must also facilitate the admission of (i) any family member where serious health issues strictly require personal care of that family member by the EU citizen, and (ii) the partner with whom the Union citizen has a durable relationship, duly attested. Article 3 provides that the obligation of the host state is to 'undertake an extensive examination of the personal circumstances' and to provide a justification for any denial of entry or residence to such persons. The provisions of Directive 2004/38 governing registered partners, and this second-tier category of partners in a 'durable relationship', represent the cautious outcome of a heated legislative debate concerning the definition of family and the need to move beyond traditional definitions by conferring rights also on same-sex and non-marital partners.

Article 23 of Directive 2004/38 grants the right to take up activity as employed persons in the host Member State to *all* family members covered by the Directive, whatever their nationality.[168] Article 24 introduced a new explicit equal treatment guarantee for all EU nationals and their family members who enjoy the right of residence, which clearly includes workers and their families. Article 10 of Regulation 492/2011 provides for equal access for the children of a resident worker to the state's educational courses.

Regulation 1612/68 provoked significant litigation. Indeed, Article 7 of Regulation 1612/68 and now of its successor 492/2011 has probably been the most fruitful provision for workers and their families. The ECJ's rulings on Article 7 illustrate how the initial conferral of limited rights on economic actors has evolved into something more substantial. This is also now reflected in Article 24 of Directive 2004/38, which extended the general equal treatment principle, subject to exceptions provided for in the Treaty and secondary legislation, to all lawfully resident EU nationals and their families.

(B) ARTICLE 7(2) OF REGULATION 492/2011

Initially in *Michel S*, the Court read Article 7(2) in a limited way, ruling that it concerned only benefits connected with employment.[169] Shortly afterwards, however, the ECJ departed from this restrictive interpretation and ruled that Article 7(2) should be read so as to include *all* social and tax advantages, whether or not attached to the contract of employment,[170] that it applied not just to workers but also to surviving family members of a deceased worker, and that although Article 7 refers only to advantages for workers, it covers any advantage to a family member which provides an indirect advantage to the worker.[171] Thus, for example, in *Reina*, an interest-free 'childbirth loan' granted under German law to German nationals in order to stimulate the birth rate of the population was held to be a social advantage

---

[168] The previous and narrower Art 11 of Reg 1612/68 had been interpreted by the CJEU to mean that the non-EU national spouse of an EU migrant worker in a Member State had the right to work only in the Member State in which the spouse was employed: Case C–10/05 *Mattern* (n 38).

[169] Case 76/72 *Michel S v Fonds National de Reclassement Handicapés* [1973] ECR 457.

[170] Case 32/75 *Cristini v SNCF* [1975] ECR 1085, [13].

[171] Case 63/76 *Inzirillo* [1976] ECR 2057; Case 94/84 *Deak* [1985] ECR 1873; Case 152/82 *Forcheri v Belgium* [1983] ECR 2323. For a fuller analysis see the report at (n 164).

within Article 7(2), and available to an Italian couple living and working in Germany.[172] The Court ruled that the loan was a social advantage since its main aim was to alleviate the financial burden on low-income families, even if it was also a part of national demographic policy.

The possible limits to the rights which may be claimed by a worker under Article 7(2) were addressed in the case of *Even*, concerning preferential retirement-pension treatment given in Belgium to nationals who were in receipt of a Second World War service invalidity pension granted by an Allied nation.

Case 207/78 **Ministère Public v Even and ONPTS**
[1979] ECR 2019

THE ECJ

22. It follows from all its provisions and from the objective pursued that the advantages which this regulation extends to workers who are nationals of other Member States are all those which, whether or not linked to a contract of employment, are generally granted to national workers primarily because of their objective status as workers or by virtue of the mere fact of their residence on the national territory and the extension of which to workers who are nationals of other Member States therefore seems suitable to facilitate their mobility within the Community.

23. ...The main reason for a benefit such as that granted by the Belgian national legislation in question to certain categories of national workers is the services which those in receipt of the benefit have rendered in wartime to their own country and its essential objective is to give those nationals an advantage by reason of the hardships suffered for that country.

24. Such a benefit, which is based on a scheme of national recognition, cannot therefore be considered as an advantage granted to a national worker by reason primarily of his status of worker or resident on the national territory and for that reason does not fulfil the essential characteristics of the 'social advantages' referred to in Article 7(2) of Regulation No 1612/68 [*now Reg 492/2011*].

Similarly in *de Vos* the statutory obligation on an employer to continue paying pension insurance contributions on behalf of workers who were absent on military service was held not to be a 'social advantage' to the worker within Article 7(2), since it was an advantage provided by the state as partial compensation for the obligation to perform military service, rather than an advantage granted to workers by virtue of the fact of their residence in the Member State.[173]

By comparison, in *Ugliola*,[174] which concerned the taking into account of military service in calculating seniority at work, the Court found that there was impermissible discrimination under Article 7(2). The difference between the benefit which the employer was required to provide in *Ugliola* and that in *de Vos* is rather difficult to discern, since each was concerned with ensuring that workers who were away on military service would not be disadvantaged as a result. However, the ECJ seemed to treat the obligation to protect a worker's seniority and security of tenure as a condition of employment imposed by the state on employers in *Ugliola*, whereas the obligation on employers to continue paying pension contributions in *de Vos* was treated as part of the state's mechanism for compensating those undergoing military service rather than as being linked to the employment contract.

---

[172] Cases 65/81 *Reina v Landeskreditbank Baden-Württemberg* [1982] ECR 33; C–111/91 *Commission v Luxembourg* [1993] ECR I–817; C–237/94 *O'Flynn* (n 64); C–212/05 *Hartmann v Freistaat Bayern* [2007] ECR I–6303; C–213/05 *Geven v Land Nordrhein-Westfalen* [2007] ECR I–6347.

[173] Cases C–315/94 *De Vos v Bielefeld* [1996] ECR I–1417, [17]–[22]; C–386/02 *Baldinger v Pensionsversicherungsanstalt der Arbeiter* [2004] ECR I–8411. Contrast Case C–131/96 *Romero v Landesversicherungsanstalt* [1997] ECR I–3659.

[174] Case 15/69 (n 67).

While most of the cases discussed above concerned restrictions based directly on nationality, the CJEU has also recently condemned indirectly discriminatory conditions such as residence requirements for the receipt of various social benefits, including disability benefits,[175] and 'portable' higher educational funding for the children of migrant and frontier workers as a breach of Article 7(2).[176] In *Giersch*, a residence requirement for financial aid for higher education studies was also held to breach Article 7(2).[177] While the CJEU accepted the legitimacy in principle of the aim of providing financial aid only to those who may be considered likely to return to Luxembourg after studying to apply their knowledge for the benefit of the country's economic development, the residence requirement was an unnecessarily restrictive way of pursuing this aim since the children of frontier workers could also be considered to have a sufficient degree of attachment to Luxembourg for these purposes.[178]

(c) ARTICLE 7(3) OF REGULATION 492/2011 AND EDUCATIONAL RIGHTS FOR WORKERS

Article 7(3) provides that EU workers shall 'by virtue of the same right and under the same conditions as national workers, have access to training in vocational schools and retraining centres'. The Article has been held to confer equal rights of access for non-national workers to all the advantages, grants, and facilities available to nationals.

This provision was restrictively interpreted by the ECJ in *Lair*, ruling that universities were not 'vocational schools' since the concept of a vocational school referred 'exclusively to institutions which provide only instruction either alternating with or closely linked to an occupational activity, particularly during apprenticeship'.[179] The Court however went on to hold that workers could also invoke the 'social advantages' provision of Article 7(2) to claim entitlement to any advantage available to improve their professional qualifications and social advancement, such as a maintenance grant in an educational institution not covered by Article 7(3).[180] Nonetheless, the Court imposed other limits on the ability of workers to avail of Article 7(2) by ruling that, although they did not have to be in the employment relationship just before or during the course of study, and although states could not require a fixed minimum period of employment,[181] there must be some continuity or link between the previous work and the studies in question.[182] The one exception permitted was where a worker involuntarily became unemployed and was 'obliged by conditions on the job market to undertake occupational retraining in another field of activity'.[183] This case law is confirmed by Article 7(3)(d) of Directive 2004/38. The ECJ also made clear in *Brown* that the employment must not be 'ancillary' to the main purpose of pursuing a course of study.[184]

---

[175] Case C–206/10 *Commission v Germany* EU:C:2011:283.

[176] Case C–542/09 *Commission v Netherlands* EU:C:2012:346. See A Hoogenboom, 'Export of Study Grants and the Lawfulness of Durational Residency Requirements: Comments on Case C–542/09, *Commission v the Netherlands*' (2012) 14 European Journal of Migration and Law 477.

[177] Case C–20/12 *Giersch* EU:C:2013:411.

[178] For critical comment on the CJEU's reasoning on the legitimacy of the aim, as well as on the apparent distinction introduced between migrant workers and frontier workers, see S O'Leary, 'The Curious Case of Frontier Workers and Study Finance: *Giersch*' (2014) 51 CMLRev 601.

[179] Case 39/86 *Lair* [1988] ECR 3161.

[180] Case 235/87 *Matteucci v Communauté Français de Belgique* [1988] ECR 5589; Case C–337/97 *Meeusen* (n 25).

[181] Case 157/84 *Frascogna v Caisse des Dépôts et Consignations* [1985] ECR 1739; Case C–3/90 *Bernini* (n 38); Case C–357/89 *Raulin* (n 38).

[182] Case 39/86 *Lair* (n 179) [37].

[183] Ibid.

[184] Case 197/86 (n 41).

The likely reason for the limits imposed by the ECJ on Article 7(2) and (3) is that the status of worker carries with it a substantial range of social and other benefits for workers and their families, and Member States wish to restrict those claiming such benefits to 'genuine' workers. Member States may fear the prospect of migrants having access to generous educational and other benefits after a short and purely instrumental period of employment.

In *Ninni-Orasche*, however, the ECJ ruled that the conduct of a person who took up short-term employment as a waitress only several years after entering the host Member State, and who shortly after finishing that employment obtained a diploma entitling her to enrol at university in that state, was irrelevant to her status as worker.[185] Echoing its rulings in *Akrich*[186] and *Chen*[187] in which it dismissed the allegations of abuse of rights, the Court ruled that there was no such thing as 'abusively creating' the situation where she became a worker for the purposes of EU law.[188] However, the Court also ruled that, while the fact that the fixed-term contract she had accepted had come to an end did not necessarily make her 'voluntarily unemployed', factors such as the short-term nature of the job and the fact that she obtained the diploma entitling her to enrol at university immediately afterwards might be relevant to the question whether she took up employment with the sole aim of benefiting from the system of student assistance in the host state.

Finally, Article 35 of Directive 2004/38 introduced an exception permitting Member States to refuse or withdraw rights under the Directive 'in the case of abuse of rights or fraud'. The Court's case law so far has not however confirmed any example of abuse or fraud, other than the case of a sham marriage entered for the purpose of gaining EU rights. The Commission recently declared that it would assist Member States in combating fraud, including 'marriages of convenience', and was asked by the Council to gather data on the incidence of such marriages across the Member States.[189]

(D) ARTICLE 10 OF REGULATION 492/2011: EDUCATIONAL RIGHTS FOR CHILDREN

Article 10 (which replaced Article 12 of the prior Regulation 1612/68) provides that 'the children of a national of a Member State who is or has been employed in the territory of another Member State shall be admitted to that State's general educational, apprenticeship and vocational training courses under the same conditions as the nationals of that State, if such children are residing in its territory'. Member States are to encourage 'all efforts to enable such children to attend these courses under the best conditions'.

While the ECJ in *Michel S*[190] interpreted Article 7(2) on educational benefits for *workers* narrowly, in the same case it interpreted Article 10 concerning the children of workers broadly, so that a benefit for disabled nationals was included in Article 10 on access to education for the children of workers.[191] This expansive reading was continued in *Casagrande*,[192] where Article 10 was applied not just to admission to courses but also to any 'general measures intended to facilitate educational attendance', including an educational grant. Article 10 thus places the children of EU workers residing in a Member State in the same position as the children of nationals of that state so far as education is concerned, which means

---

[185] Case C–413/01 *Ninni-Orasche* (n 150).

[186] Case C–109/01 *Akrich* (n 142).

[187] Case C–200/02 *Zhu and Chen v Secretary of State for the Home Department* [2004] ECR I–9925.

[188] Case C–413/01 *Ninni-Orasche* (n 150).

[189] Commission Communication on Free Movement of EU Citizens and their Families: Five Actions to Make a Difference, COM(2013) 837, fn 43. For further discussion of Article 35 of Dir 2004/38 and ECJ case law on the notion of 'abuse', see Ch 23 on Citizenship, p 859, (nn 46–48).

[190] (N 160).

[191] Case C–7/94 *Landesamt für Ausbildungsförderung Nordrhein-Westfalen v Lubor Gaal* [1996] ECR I–1031.

[192] Case 9/74 *Casagrande v Landeshauptstadt München* [1974] ECR 773.

that they enjoy more generous educational rights than their EU worker-parents. Article 10 has been held to require that, where grants are available to the children of nationals to study abroad, these must also be made available to the children of migrant EU workers, even if the studies abroad are to be in the Member State of the child's nationality.[193]

In *Gaal*, the CJEU ruled that the term 'children' in Article 10 of Regulation 492/2011 conferred educational rights on children who were over 21 and non-dependent, even though these were not covered by Article 2(2) of Directive 2004/38 (formerly Article 10 of Regulation 1612/68).[194] The CJEU held that the principle in Article 10 of Regulation 492/2011 required the children of a migrant worker to be able to continue studies in order to complete their education successfully, so long as the children had lived with a parent in the Member State at a time when that parent resided there as a worker[195] and—presumably, although the CJEU does not actually say this—at a time when the child was either dependent or under 21.

In *Echternach and Moritz*, the ECJ ruled that Article 10 covers the child's right to educational assistance even where the working parents have returned to their state of nationality.[196] While the rationale given in *Echternach* was that the child in question was obliged by reason of the noncompatibility of educational systems to remain and to complete the education in the host state, the ECJ moved beyond this in *Baumbast and R*, ruling that it would offend against both the letter and the spirit of Article 10 to limit the rights of children to remain in the host state to complete their education only to situations where they could not complete it in their Member State of origin.[197] The Court continued its expansive ruling in *Baumbast* by declaring that the fact that the parents of the children concerned had meanwhile divorced, the fact that only one parent was a citizen of the Union and that parent had since ceased to be a migrant worker in the host Member State, and the fact that the children were not themselves citizens of the Union were all irrelevant to the enjoyment of the rights under Article 10.[198] It is moreover clear from *Teixeira*[199] that the right of the primary carer to look after the child is derived directly from Article 10 and is not dependent on satisfying the residence conditions in Directive 2004/38.[200]

This case law is now confirmed by Article 12(3) of Directive 2004/38, which also confirms the right of the children, and the right of residence of the carer-parent, to remain and complete their education after the death of the worker-parent. However, in a situation where the worker has left the host state and returned to the Member State of origin in which her children also live, EU law does not confer any right to have her children's studies financed by the former host state under the same conditions as those applying to nationals.[201]

(E) RIGHTS OF FAMILIES AS PARASITIC ON THE WORKERS' RIGHTS

Although the interpretation of 'social advantages' in Article 7 is broad, it is only workers and the family members covered by Directive 2004/38 who may avail themselves of them. In *Lebon*, the ECJ ruled that

---

[193] Case C–308/89 *Di Leo v Land Berlin* [1990] ECR I–4185.

[194] Case C–7/94 *Gaal* (n 191).

[195] See also Cases C–147 and 148/11 *Czop and Punakova* EU:C:2012:538.

[196] Cases 389 and 390/87 *Echternach and Moritz* [1989] ECR 723.

[197] Case C–413/99 *Baumbast and R v Secretary of State for the Home Department* [2002] ECR I–7091.

[198] Ibid [56]–[63].

[199] Case C–480/08 *Teixeira v London Borough of Lambeth* [2010] ECR I–1107; Case C–310/08 *London Borough of Harrow v Nimco Hassan Ibrahim and Secretary of State for the Home Department* [2010] ECR I–1065; P Starup and M Elsmor, Note (2010) 35 ELRev 571.

[200] See also Case C–529/11 *Alarape* EU:C:2013:290, [30]: the question whether an adult child continues to require the carer-parent to look after him or her is to be determined on the facts of the case.

[201] Case C–33/99 *Fahmi* [2001] ECR I–2415.

once the child of a worker reached 21 and was no longer dependent on the worker,[202] benefits to that child could not be construed as an advantage to the worker under Article 7.[203] We have seen moreover how lawfully resident job-seekers are entitled under EU law only to those advantages which are specifically made available for job-seekers nationally.[204]

The creative interpretation given by the ECJ to Article 7(2) is evident also in *Reed*, where the ECJ ruled that the possibility for a migrant worker to have his unmarried companion reside with him could constitute a social advantage under Article 7(2), where the host Member State treated companions in a stable relationship as akin to spouses.[205] This was so even though Reed's companion would not have been covered by Article 10 of Regulation 1612/68 at the time, since it covered only marital spouses. Since the case was decided, however, Directive 2004/38 has been enacted to include registered partners, in states which recognize the status of registered partnerships, within the protected family, and it also requires Member States to facilitate the admission of companions in a 'durable relationship'.

In *Eind*[206] the ECJ ruled that an EU citizen is less likely to travel if he believes that he will not be able to return later to his home Member State with his family. This is so even if the members of the EU citizen's family included a third-country national who did not have a right to reside in the home Member State when he initially left, and it was not material in this respect that the EU national returning home did not intend to engage in economic activity.

Directive 2004/38 also clarified a question which had arisen in *Diatta*[207] and *Singh*[208] concerning the status of a spouse, including a spouse who lacks EU nationality, under Regulation 1612/68. The ECJ in those cases had indicated that, even where the spouses were separated or where a decree nisi of divorce had been granted, the non-working spouse did not lose the right of residence while the marriage was still formally in existence and had not actually been dissolved. The Court in *Baumbast* also ruled that a non-EU national spouse could, even after divorce, continue residing in the host Member State under EU law where the children, whether or not they had EU nationality, were exercising their educational rights under Article 10 of the Regulation and the divorced spouse was their primary carer.[209] And in *Ogieriakhi* the Court ruled that periods of time spent by the non-EU national living separately from his or her EU spouse and with another partner could still qualify towards acquisition of permanent residence.[210]

Article 13(1) of Directive 2004/38 now provides that even after divorce, annulment of marriage, or termination of a registered partnership, the right of residence of the family members who are EU nationals will not be affected. In the case of non-EU national family members, Article 13(2) provides that the right of residence will not be lost where: (i) the marriage or registered partnership has lasted at least three years including one year in the host Member State; or (ii) where the spouse who is not an EU national retains custody of the EU citizen's children; or (iii) where it is warranted by particularly difficult circumstances such as the applicant having been a victim of domestic violence during the marriage/partnership; or (iv) where the non-EU national spouse or partner has the right of access to

---

[202] Case C–1/05 *Jia* (n 143).

[203] Case 316/85 (n 48); Case C–243/91 *Belgium v Taghavi* [1992] ECR I–4401; Case C–33/99 *Fahmi and Cerdeiro-Pinedo Amado* [2001] ECR I–2415. Compare the educational benefits to the child under Art 10 of Reg 492/11 which, as we have seen, can be enjoyed by children over 21 who are not dependent: (n 194).

[204] Case C–138/02 *Collins* (n 30); Case C–258/04 *Ioannidis* (n 51).

[205] Case 59/85 *Netherlands v Reed* [1986] ECR 1283.

[206] Case C–291/05 *Minister voor Vreemdelingenzaken en Integratie v Eind* [2007] ECR I–10719.

[207] Case 267/83 *Diatta v Land Berlin* [1985] ECR 567.

[208] Case C–370/90 *R v Immigration Appeal Tribunal, ex p Secretary of State for the Home Department* [1992] ECR I–4265.

[209] Case C–413/99 *Baumbast* (n 197).

[210] Case C–244/13 *Ogieriakhi* EU:C:2014:2068.

a minor child and where the court has ruled that such access must be in the host Member State, for as long as required.

Article 13 provides that non-EU national family members will retain the right of residence on an exclusively personal basis, and that if they are to go on to qualify for the right of permanent residence they must show that they are themselves workers or self-employed, or have sufficient resources to avoid becoming a burden on the host state and have comprehensive sickness insurance cover in the host state. Article 35 of Directive 2004/38 makes clear, however, that a spouse will not gain any rights of residence or social advantages if the marriage is merely a marriage of convenience or a 'sham'.[211]

(F) FAMILY MEMBERS IN AN INTERNAL SITUATION

The ECJ's approach to the so-called 'wholly internal situation' has been the subject of considerable academic criticism.[212] In *Saunders*[213] the ECJ ruled that a national could not rely on Article 45 in his or her own Member State to challenge a restriction on freedom of movement, since there was no factor connecting the situation with Union law. The impact was harshly illustrated in *Morson and Jhanjan*, where it was held that two Dutch nationals working in the Netherlands had no right to bring their parents, of Surinamese nationality, into the country to reside with them.[214] Had they been nationals of any other Member State working in the Netherlands, they would have been so entitled under Article 2 of Directive 2004/38 (then Article 10 of Regulation 1612/68). However, because they were nationals working in their own Member State 'who had never exercised the right to freedom of movement within the Community', they had no rights under Community law.[215]

This was confirmed in *Uecker and Jacquet*, despite the referring German court's invitation to the ECJ to depart from its previous position.[216] The case concerned two non-EU nationals who came to Germany to live with their spouses, both of whom were German nationals residing and working in Germany. They invoked Article 7 of Regulation 492/2011 (formerly Regulation 1612/68), to claim equal treatment with German nationals in their employment, but the ECJ reiterated its stance on wholly internal situations, despite the national court's suggestion that the reverse discrimination thereby created was in conflict with 'the fundamental principle of a Community moving towards European Union'.[217]

In *Singh*, an Indian national had married a British national, and had travelled with her to Germany where they had both worked for some years before returning to the UK. Although the UK argued that national law and not EU law governed this situation, the ECJ considered that the period of working activity in another Member State made all the difference, and enabled Singh now to claim rights as the spouse of an EU worker:

---

211 Case C–109/01 *Akrich* (n 142) [57]–[58]. See also COM(2013) 837 (n 189).

212 N Nic Shuibhne, 'Free Movement of Persons and the Wholly Internal Rule: Time to Move On?' (2002) 39 CMLRev 731; C Ritter, 'Purely Internal Situations, Reverse Discrimination, *Guimont, Dzodzi* and Article 234' (2006) 31 ELRev 690; C Dautricourt and S Thomas, 'Reverse Discrimination and Free Movement of Persons under Community Law: All for Ulysses, Nothing for Penelope?' (2009) 34 ELRev 443.

213 Case 175/78 (n 91); Case C–212/06 *Government of Communauté française and Gouvernement wallon* (n 82) [33]; Case C–127/08 *Metock* (n 91) [76]–[78].

214 Cases 35 and 36/82 (n 93).

215 Ibid [17].

216 Cases C–64 and 65/96 *Uecker* and *Jacquet* (n 92).

217 Ibid [22].

Case C–370/90 **R v Immigration Appeal Tribunal and Surinder Singh,**
ex parte Secretary of State for the Home Department
[1992] ECR I–4265

THE ECJ

19. A national of a Member State might be deterred from leaving his country of origin in order to pursue an activity as an employed or self-employed person as envisaged by the Treaty in the territory of another Member State if, on returning to the Member State of which he is a national in order to pursue an activity there as an employed or self-employed person, the conditions of his entry and residence were not at least equivalent to those which he would enjoy under the Treaty or secondary law in the territory of another Member State.

20. He would in particular be deterred from so doing if his spouse and children were not also permitted to enter and reside in the territory of his Member State of origin under conditions at least equivalent to those granted them by Community law in the territory of another Member State.

The Court in a later case rejected the suggestion that there was any 'abuse of rights' involved where a couple moved on a temporary basis to work in another Member State in order to avoid the 'internal situation' problem and to acquire rights for a non-EU national in the spouse's Member State of origin.[218] And in *Metock* the Court ruled that Articles 2 and 3 of Directive 2004/38 applied to a national of a non-member country who was the spouse of a Union citizen residing in a Member State whose nationality he did not possess, and who accompanied or joined that EU citizen, irrespective of when and where their marriage took place or how the non-EU national entered the host Member State.[219]

Finally, in *S & G*, the Court transposed its reasoning in the *Carpenter* case from the context of free movement of services to that of free movement of workers,[220] by ruling that a Member State must grant a right of residence to a third-country-national family member of a worker who is a national of that Member State, where the worker is required to travel regularly to another Member State in the course of his professional activities and the refusal of a right of residence to the family member would have a dissuasive effect on the worker's right of free movement.[221]

(g) DIRECTIVE 2014/54

Following extensive consultation and discussion about how to reduce the gap between the rights of EU workers on paper and the realization of those rights in practice,[222] Directive 2014/54 on 'measures facilitating the exercise of rights conferred on workers in the context of freedom of movement of workers' was adopted.[223] The scope of the Directive is the same as that of Regulation 492/2011, and the explanatory memorandum declares that it does not intend to create new rights for migrant workers but to introduce mechanisms to reduce discrimination and make the existing rights more effective. To that effect,

---

[218] Case C–109/01 *Akrich* (n 142) [55]–[56].

[219] Case C–127/08 *Metock* (n 91) [81]–[89].

[220] Case C–60/00 *Carpenter v Home Secretary* [2002] ECR I–6279.

[221] Case C–457/12 *S & G* EU:C:2014:136.

[222] See Commission report VC/2011/0476, 'Study to analyse and assess the socio-economic and environmental impact of possible EU initiatives in the area of freedom of movement for workers, in particular with regard to the enforcement of current EU provisions' (2011), and Commission Staff Working Document, SWD(2013) 149 final.

[223] [2014] OJ L28/8. Interestingly, the working document preceding the Dir explained that a proposal for the most effective option, namely to impose an obligation directly on companies to actively prevent discrimination had not been pursued due to the risk of 'disproportionate costs on companies', SWD(2013) 149, [7.6].

the Directive focuses on three main strategies to improve enforcement, and in doing so it borrows significantly from existing EU directives in the field of anti-discrimination. First, it requires that migrant workers who have been discriminated against or whose rights have not been respected may enforce their rights by a judicial procedure on the same terms as nationals of that state, with support from the social partners or other relevant bodies.[224] Secondly, it requires Member States to designate one or more bodies (whether new or existing bodies) at national level to provide assistance to EU migrant workers and their families, including by providing legal advice, fulfilling an internal coordination role, and acting as a contact point for liaison and cooperation with similar contact points in other Member States.[225] Thirdly, it requires better provision of information about the rights conferred by Article 45 TFEU and Regulation 492/2011 and how these apply in the domestic context, as well as the promotion of dialogue with social partners and non-governmental organizations.[226] The Directive gives Member States a two-year implementation period, and is to be transposed by May 2016.

8 DIRECTIVE 2004/38: PUBLIC POLICY, SECURITY, AND HEALTH RESTRICTIONS

(A) THREE LEVELS OF PROTECTION

Articles 27–33 of Directive 2004/38 govern the restrictions on the right of entry and residence which Member States may impose on grounds of public policy, security, or health. These provisions repeal and replace the previous Directive 64/221, and incorporate much of the relevant jurisprudence of the Court of Justice.

Directive 2004/38 also introduced three different levels of protection against expulsion on these grounds: (i) a general level of protection for all individuals covered by EU law; (ii) an enhanced level of protection for individuals who have already gained the right of permanent residence on the territory of a Member State; and (iii) a super-enhanced level of protection for minors or for those who have resided for ten years in a host state. The Directive additionally simplified the previous requirements of Directive 64/221 by making access to judicial and administrative redress procedures compulsory, and by eliminating references to comparability with national procedures.

(B) ARTICLE 27: GENERAL PRINCIPLES

Article 27(2) sets out the general principles governing the exercise of the exceptions, specifying that all measures adopted on grounds of public policy or security must comply with the principle of proportionality and be based exclusively on the personal conduct of the individual concerned. The Directive makes clear that the public policy, security, and health exceptions cannot be invoked to serve economic ends, and that past criminal convictions are not in themselves grounds for taking such measures. This provision was earlier interpreted in *Santillo* to mean that such convictions may be relied on as a basis for expulsion only where the past conviction in some way provides evidence of a present threat,[227] and that the threat must be assessed by the Member State at the time of the decision ordering expulsion.[228]

---

[224] Art 3.

[225] Art 4.

[226] Arts 5 and 6.

[227] The CJEU in Case 30/77 *Bouchereau* [1977] ECR 1999 also suggested that past conduct alone, rather than the likelihood of future conduct, might be sufficient to indicate that someone is a *present* threat to public policy.

[228] Cases 131/79 *Santillo* [1980] ECR 1585; C–441/02 *Commission v Germany* [2006] ECR I–3449.

Article 27(2) incorporates the case law of the ECJ in various respects. Following *Bouchereau*,[229] it stipulates that the personal conduct of the individual must represent a 'genuine, present, and sufficiently serious threat affecting one of the fundamental interests of society'. General preventative measures, or justifications isolated from the particular facts of the case, are unacceptable.[230] The *Calfa* ruling in particular stipulated that automatic expulsion for commission of a particular offence, without any consideration of whether any specific threat was posed by the individual in question, is prohibited.[231]

Article 27(3) sets a time limit after entry into the host Member State for the latter to seek, and for the Member State of origin to provide, information on an EU national's police record, and stipulates that such information shall not be sought on a routine basis. Article 27(4) provides that upon expulsion the Member State of origin must re-admit the person in question.

Member States nonetheless retain discretion as regards the public-policy exception (and, though perhaps to a lesser extent, the public-security exception[232]) since 'the particular circumstances justifying recourse to the concept of public policy may vary from one country to another and from one period to another'.[233] No 'uniform code of values' is imposed by EU law.[234]

(c) ARTICLE 28: EXPULSION

There is a significant body of case law derived from the original Directive 64/221 concerning the circumstances in which Member States may expel EU nationals or their family members on public-policy or security grounds.

In *Van Duyn*, the ECJ ruled that a Member State need not criminalize an organization whose activities it considers to be socially harmful, in this case the Church of Scientology, in order to justify taking restrictive action against non-national members of the organization on grounds of public policy and security.[235] The case was controversial because it appeared to enable a state to take repressive measures against an EU migrant for conduct that did not give rise to any restriction against nationals of the host state.

Later cases emphasized the need for some kind of comparability, if not exactly equality, in the treatment of nationals and non-nationals as far as such alleged threats to public policy and security were concerned. In *Adoui and Cornuaille*,[236] the ECJ ruled that a Member State may not expel a national of another Member State from its territory or refuse entry by reason of conduct, in this case suspected prostitution, which, when attributable to its own nationals, did not give rise to measures intended to combat such conduct. Similarly in *Rutili*, partial measures of territorial restriction, short of expulsion, could be imposed on EU nationals for reasons of public policy or security only to the same extent that such measures could be imposed against nationals.[237] The Court in *Olazabal* ruled that it was not necessary for identical measures to be taken against nationals and non-nationals,[238] and that a

---

[229] Case 30/77 *Bouchereau* (n 227).

[230] Cases 67/74 *Bonsignore* [1975] ECR 297; 115 and 116/81 *Adoui and Cornuaille* [1982] ECR 1665; C–340/97 *Nazli v Stadt Nürnberg* [2000] ECR I–957; C–482 and 493/01 *Orfanopoulos and others v Land Baden-Württemberg* [2004] ECR I–5257; C–441/02 *Commission v Germany* (n 228); C–383/03 *Dogan v Sicherheitsdirektion für das Bundesland Vorarlberg* [2005] ECR I–6237; C–503/03 *Commission v Spain* [2006] ECR I–1097.

[231] Case C–348/96 *Calfa* [1999] ECR I–11.

[232] See also Case C–474/12 *Schiebel Aircraft GmbH* EU:C:2014:2139, in which Austria unsuccessfully pleaded national security to justify nationality discrimination, albeit relying not on Dir 2004/38 but on Art 346(1)(b) TFEU.

[233] Case 41/74 *Van Duyn v Home Office* [1974] ECR 1337, [18].

[234] Case C–268/99 *Jany* (n 29).

[235] Case 41/74 *Van Duyn* (n 233).

[236] Cases 115 and 116/81 (n 230); Case C–268/99 *Jany* (n 29).

[237] Case 36/75 *Rutili* [1975] ECR 1219.

[238] Case C–100/01 *Ministre de l'Interieur v Olazabal* [2002] ECR I–10981. Also Cases C–65 and 111/95 *Shingara and Radiom* [1997] ECR I–3341.

territorial restriction could be imposed on an EU migrant worker in circumstances in which it could not be imposed on a national, although this may have been reversed by Directive 2004/38.[239] The Court in *Olazabal* also stipulated, however, that a Member State could not adopt measures against a national of another Member State by reason of conduct which, when engaged in by nationals of the first Member State, did not give rise to punitive measures or other genuine and effective measures to combat that conduct.

Article 28 of Directive 2004/38 sets out the substantive and procedural protections for individuals subject to an expulsion order. Article 28(1) builds on existing case law such as *Orfanopoulos*[240] and on ECtHR case law,[241] to provide that Member States must, before making an expulsion decision on public-policy or security grounds, 'take account of considerations such as how long the individual concerned has resided on its territory, his/her age, state of health, family and economic situation, social and cultural integration into the host Member State and the extent of his/her links with the country of origin'. Article 28(2) sets out the enhanced level of protection for EU citizens and their families, irrespective of nationality, who have gained the right of permanent residence, by providing that they may be expelled only for 'serious grounds' of public policy or security. This requirement of 'serious grounds' is additional to the general requirement for all persons established in Article 27(2) that the personal conduct of an individual subject to expulsion must constitute a 'sufficiently serious threat affecting one of the fundamental interests of society'. Article 28(3) provides for an even more stringent level of protection for a minor[242] or an EU citizen and their family who have resided in the host state for the previous ten years, stipulating that an expulsion decision can be taken only 'on imperative grounds of public security'.

In *Tsakouridis*, the ECJ interpreted Articles 27 and 28 of the Directive, and explained the conditions that must be satisfied for an expulsion to be lawful.

Case C–145/09 **Land Baden-Württemberg v Panagiotis Tsakouridis**
[2010] ECR I–11979

THE ECJ

39. [T]he referring court seeks essentially to know whether and to what extent criminal offences in connection with dealing in narcotics as part of an organised group can be covered by the concept of 'imperative grounds of public security' [in]…Article 28(3) of Directive 2004/38, or the concept of 'serious grounds of public policy or public security' [in]…Article 28(2) of that directive.

40. It follows from the wording and scheme of Article 28 of Directive 2004/38…that by subjecting all expulsion measures in the cases referred to in Article 28(3) of that directive to the existence of 'imperative grounds' of public security, a concept which is considerably stricter than that of 'serious grounds' within the meaning of Article 28(2), the European Union legislature clearly intended to limit measures based on Article 28(3) to 'exceptional circumstances', as set out in recital 24 in the preamble to that directive.

---

[239] Art 22 of Dir 2004/38 states that 'Member States may impose territorial restrictions on the right of residence and the right of permanent residence only where the same restrictions apply to their own nationals'.

[240] Cases C–482 and 493/01 (n 230); Case 36/75 *Rutili* (n 237); Case C–459/99 *MRAX* (n 140); Case C–50/06 *Commission v Netherlands* [2007] ECR I–4383. For discussion of the more recent case law on Articles 27 and 28 of the Dir, see Ch 23 on Citizenship, pp 885-887.

[241] See, eg, App No 54273/00 *Boultif v Switzerland*, 2 Aug 2001, which was cited by the CJEU in Cases C–482 and 493/01 *Orfanopoulos* (n 230); App No 47160/99 *Ezzouhdi v France*, 13 Feb 2001.

[242] Except if the expulsion is necessary for the best interests of the child as provided under the 1989 UN Convention on the Rights of the Child.

41. The concept of 'imperative grounds of public security' presupposes not only the existence of a threat to public security, but also that such a threat is of a particularly high degree of seriousness, as is reflected by the use of the words 'imperative reasons'.

42. It is in this context that the concept of 'public security' in Article 28(3) of Directive 2004/38 should also be interpreted.

43. As regards public security, the Court has held that this covers both a Member State's internal and its external security...

44. The Court has also held that a threat to the functioning of the institutions and essential public services and the survival of the population, as well as the risk of a serious disturbance to foreign relations or to peaceful coexistence of nations, or a risk to military interests, may affect public security...

45. It does not follow that objectives such as the fight against crime in connection with dealing in narcotics as part of an organised group are necessarily excluded from that concept.

46. Dealing in narcotics as part of an organised group is a diffuse form of crime with impressive economic and operational resources and frequently with transnational connections...

47. Since drug addiction represents a serious evil for the individual and is fraught with social and economic danger to mankind...trafficking in narcotics as part of an organised group could reach a level of intensity that might directly threaten the calm and physical security of the population as a whole or a large part of it.

...

49. ...[A]n expulsion measure must be based on an individual examination of the specific case (see, inter alia, Metock and Others, paragraph 74), and can be justified on imperative grounds of public security within the meaning of Article 28(3) of Directive 2004/38 only if, having regard to the exceptional seriousness of the threat, such a measure is necessary for the protection of the interests it aims to secure, provided that that objective cannot be attained by less strict means, having regard to the length of residence of the Union citizen in the host Member State and in particular to the serious negative consequences such a measure may have for Union citizens who have become genuinely integrated into the host Member State.

50. In the application of Directive 2004/38, a balance must be struck more particularly between the exceptional nature of the threat to public security as a result of the personal conduct of the person concerned, assessed if necessary at the time when the expulsion decision is to be made...by reference in particular to the possible penalties and the sentences imposed, the degree of involvement in the criminal activity, and, if appropriate, the risk of reoffending...on the one hand, and, on the other hand, the risk of compromising the social rehabilitation of the Union citizen in the State in which he has become genuinely integrated...

51. The sentence passed must be taken into account as one element in that complex of factors. A sentence of five years' imprisonment cannot lead to an expulsion decision, as provided for in national law, without the factors described in the preceding paragraph being taken into account, which is for the national court to verify.

52. In that assessment, account must be taken of the fundamental rights whose observance the Court ensures...in particular the right to respect for private and family life as set forth in Article 7 of the Charter of Fundamental Rights of the European Union and Article 8 of the European Convention for the Protection of Human Rights and Fundamental Freedoms...

53. To assess whether the interference contemplated is proportionate to the legitimate aim pursued, in this case the protection of public security, account must be taken in particular of the nature and seriousness of the offence committed, the duration of residence of the person concerned in the host Member State, the period which has passed since the offence was committed and the conduct of the person concerned during that period, and the solidity of the social, cultural and family ties with the host Member State. In the case of a Union citizen who has lawfully spent most or even all of his childhood and youth in the host Member State, very good reasons would have to be put forward to justify the expulsion measure...

(D) ARTICLE 29: PUBLIC HEALTH

Article 29(1) governs the public-health requirement, and tightens up the provisions of the earlier Directive 64/221 by specifying that the only diseases justifying measures restricting freedom of movement are diseases with epidemic potential as defined by the relevant instruments of the World Health Organization, and other infectious diseases or contagious parasitic diseases if they are the subject of protection provisions applying to nationals of the host Member State. Article 29(2) sets a three-month period following arrival in the host state, after which diseases occurring cannot constitute grounds for expulsion.

Article 29(3) introduces a new provision, apparently in order to combat the practice in some Member States of carrying out medical examinations on beneficiaries of the right to residence, which stipulates that in cases where there are 'serious indications that it is necessary, Member States may, within 3 months of the date of arrival, require persons entitled to the right of residence to undergo, free of charge, a medical examination to certify that they are not suffering from any of the conditions referred to in paragraph 1'. Article 29(3) further stipulates that such medical examinations may not be required as a matter of routine.

(E) ARTICLE 30: NOTIFICATION OF DECISIONS

Article 30 deals with the notification of decisions to the persons concerned, and Article 30(1) incorporates the ruling in *Adoui and Cornuaille*[243] to provide that they must be notified in such a way that the people addressed can comprehend its content and implications. Building on the ECJ's ruling in *Rutili*,[244] Article 30(2) provides that the persons concerned are entitled to full and precise information about the grounds on which their case is based, unless it is contrary to public security to do so. Article 30(3) requires the notification to provide the person with information on how to appeal, the relevant administrative authority or court to which the appeal should be made, the time limit for appeal, and the time limit allowed for the person to leave the territory of the state. It specifies that, save in cases of urgency, the time allowed is not to be less than one month from the date of notification. This minimum period is intended to allow the person to fulfil the necessary formalities for making an appeal.

(F) ARTICLE 31: PROCEDURAL SAFEGUARDS

Article 31 builds on Article 30 by providing for procedural safeguards, simplifying the prior legislation and the complex case law it generated.[245] Article 31(1) provides for 'access to judicial and, where appropriate, administrative redress procedures in the host Member State to appeal against or seek review' of an adverse decision taken on grounds of public policy, public security, or public health.

Article 31(2) of Directive 2004/38 provides, subject to three specific exceptions, for automatic suspension of enforcement of an adverse measure until such time as a decision is taken on a person's application for an interim order to suspend the measure's enforcement.

Article 31(3) incorporates the ruling in *Adoui and Cornuaille*[246] that the judicial or administrative redress procedures must review not only the legality of the decision, but also the facts on which it is

---

[243] Cases 115 and 116/81 (n 230).

[244] Case 36/75 *Rutili* (n 237). For recent case law interpreting Art 30(2) of the Dir, see Case C-300/11 *ZZ* EU:C:2013:363, discussed in Ch 23 on Citizenship, pp 886-887.

[245] Case 48/75 *Royer* (n 46); Case C–175/94 *Gallagher* [1995] ECR I–4253; Case 131/79 *Santillo* (n 228); Case C–357/98 *Yiadom* [2000] ECR I–9265; Case C–136/03 *Dorr v Sicherheitsdirektion für das Bundesland Kärnten* [2005] ECR I–4759. See also Case C–300/11 *ZZ*, ibid.

[246] Cases 115 and 116/81 (n 230).

based, with a view to ensuring its proportionality in the light of considerations including the human-rights criteria listed in Article 28(1).

Article 31(4) builds on the *Pecastaing* case,[247] providing that Member States may exclude an individual from their territory pending the redress procedure, but that they may not prevent such an individual from submitting his or her defence in person, except where such appearance may cause serious public-policy or security difficulties or where the appeal concerns denial of entry to the territory.

(G) ARTICLES 32–33: DURATION OF EXCLUSION ORDERS AND EXPULSION

Article 32 deals with the duration of exclusion orders and reflects various aspects of the ruling in *Adoui and Cornuaille*,[248] as well as in *Calfa*,[249] providing that where someone has been validly excluded on public-policy or security grounds they may apply to have the exclusion order lifted after a reasonable period, and no later than three years from the enforcement of the final exclusion order, by arguing that there has been a material change in the circumstances justifying their exclusion. States must decide on such applications for re-admission within six months, but the applicants have no right of entry to the territory while the application is being considered.

Article 33(1) introduced a new provision which stipulates that expulsion orders may not be issued by the host state as a penalty, or as a legal consequence of a custodial sentence, other than in circumstances which fulfil the conditions set out in Articles 27–29, viz that the person's conduct constitutes a sufficiently serious threat, etc. Finally, Article 33(2) provides that if an expulsion order is enforced more than two years after it was issued, the state must check that the person concerned is still a genuine threat to public policy or security and must assess whether there has been any material change in circumstances since the original order was issued.

9 CONCLUSIONS

i. The free movement of workers is of central importance to the EU, in both economic and social terms. This is reflected in the legislation which fleshes out the basic rights contained in Article 45 and in the ECJ's consistently purposive interpretation of the Treaty Articles and legislation to achieve the EU's objectives in this area. It is also reflected in the number of initiatives adopted by the Commission and other institutions in recent years to 'close the enforcement gap' and try to implement the free movement of workers more effectively in practice.

ii. Directive 2004/38, which covers all EU citizens and not just workers, consolidated, simplified, and replaced much of the prior legislation on the subject. The Directive incorporated and built on the ECJ's expansionist case law by strengthening the substantive rights and procedural protections for migrant workers, widening the category of protected family members, and tightening up the circumstances in which Member States may derogate from or restrict free movement rights. It has also introduced the right of permanent residence, and a provision allowing Member States to restrict rights in the case of abuse or fraud.

iii. The expansion of free-movement law has inevitably led to tensions with Member States. Control over borders and entry has always been sensitive for Member States, and legal reasoning

---

[247] Case 98/79 *Pecastaing v Belgium* [1980] ECR 691.
[248] Cases 115 and 116/81 (n 230), concerning lifelong exclusion orders.
[249] Case C–348/96 (n 231).

concerning the imperatives of free-movement law does not displace the political discomfort that some of these rulings create for the Member States. The free movement of workers has come under particularly heavy fire in recent years, as the economic downturn in Europe has led to political pressure within certain states, and particularly within the UK, to challenge fundamental aspects of free movement, emphasizing particularly the impact of enlargement as well as the fear of benefits tourism.[250]

iv. The Commission has for the most part responded vigorously to such challenges, denying any link between the generosity of a state's welfare benefits and the number of migrants arriving, defending free movement after enlargement, and emphasizing the economic and other benefits of free movement to all EU states.[251] At the same time, it has acknowledged some of the concerns of states and has pledged to help them with some of the practical problems of free movement such as social security coordination, social inclusion and poverty challenges, and applying free movement rules on the ground. New legislation to bolster existing rights has also been introduced, including Directive 2014/54, as well as legislation to improve the network of employment services tasked with helping workers find employment in other Member States.[252]

10 FURTHER READING

(a) Books

BARNARD, C, *The Substantive Law of the EU: The Four Freedoms* (Oxford University Press, 4th edn, 2013)

CARLIER, J-Y, and GUILD, E (eds), *The Future of Free Movement of Persons in the EU* (Bruylant, 2006)

ROGERS, N, and SCANNELL, R, *Free Movement of Persons in the Enlarged European Union* (Sweet & Maxwell, 2nd edn, 2012)

WEISS, F, AND WOOLDRIDGE, F, *Free Movement of Persons within the European Community* (Kluwer, 2nd edn, 2007)

WHITE, R, *Workers, Establishment and Services in the European Union* (Oxford University Press, 2004)

(b) Articles

CARRERA, S, 'What Does Free Movement Mean in Theory and in Practice in an Enlarged EU?' (2005) 11 ELJ 699

COSTELLO, C, '*Metock*: Free Movement and "Normal Family Life" in the Union' (2009) 46 CMLRev 587

DAUTRICOURT, C, AND THOMAS, S, 'Reverse Discrimination and Free Movement of Persons under Community Law: All for Ulysses, Nothing for Penelope?' (2009) 34 ELRev 433

GIUBBONI, S, 'Free Movement of Persons and European Solidarity' (2007) 13 ELJ 360

JANSSON, MS AND KALIMO, H, '*De Minimis* Meets "Market Access": Transformations in the Substance—and the Syntax—of EU Free Movement Law?' (2014) 51 CMLRev 523

---

[250] A conference was organized by the Latvian Presidency of the EU in January 2015 on 'Basic European Rights to Free Movement Under Threat'. Some of the useful background documents are available at www.eesc.europa.eu/?i=portal. en.events-and-activities-eu-free-movement.

[251] COM(2013) 837, fn 23, citing a range of recent empirical studies to support both of these claims.

[252] (N 1).

Nic Shuibhne, N, and Maci, M, 'Proving Public Interest: The Growing Impact of Evidence in Free Movement Case Law' (2013) 50 CMLRev 965

O'Leary, S, 'The Free Movement of Persons and Services' in P Craig and G de Búrca (eds), *The Evolution of EU Law* (Oxford University Press, 2nd edn, 2011) ch 17

Ros, E, 'EU Citizenship and Taxation: "Is the European Court of Justice Moving Towards a Citizen's Europe?"' (2014) 23 EC Tax Review 43

Tryfonidou, A, 'In Search of the Aim of the EC Free Movement of Persons Provisions: Has the Court of Justice Missed the Point?' (2009) 46 CMLRev 1591

FREEDOM OF ESTABLISHMENT
AND TO PROVIDE SERVICES

1 CENTRAL ISSUES

i.   In addition to the category of workers, and the wider category of citizens, the TFEU has two separate chapters on self-employed persons who move on a permanent or temporary basis between Member States. These are the chapters on freedom of establishment and freedom to provide services.

ii. The central principles governing freedom of establishment and the free movement of services are laid down in the TFEU and have been developed through case law. However, a large number of important developments have also been brought about through secondary legislation in sectors such as insurance, public procurement, broadcasting, financial services, electronic commerce, telecommunications, and other 'services of general economic interest'. The relationship in particular contexts between the detailed secondary legislation and the broad general Treaty-based principles is not always clear, apart from the macro-level rule that the Treaty has primacy in the event of conflict over secondary law.[1] However, with the exception of the two general directives mentioned in (iii), this chapter focuses on the broad constitutional principles applicable to every sector rather than on the particularities of the secondary legislation in specific sectors, important though the latter are.

iii. Two important general pieces of secondary legislation dealing with services and establishment were adopted in 2005 and 2006 respectively. In 2005, a consolidating directive on the recognition of professional qualifications replaced most of the previous general and sectoral legislation on this issue.[2] And in 2006, after a lengthy and politically heated debate, a general directive on services in the internal market was adopted.[3]

iv. Articles 49–54 TFEU (ex Articles 43–48 EC) on *freedom of establishment* require the removal of restrictions on the right of individuals and companies to maintain a permanent or settled place of business in a Member State. Establishment is defined as 'the actual pursuit of an economic activity

---

[1] For discussion of this phenomenon across the single market field, including that of services and establishment, see P Syrpis (ed), *The Judiciary, the Legislature and the EU Internal Market* (Cambridge University Press, 2012); and more generally 'The Relationship Between Primary and Secondary Law in the EU' (2015) 52 CMLRev 461.

[2] Directive 2005/36/EC on the recognition of professional qualifications [2005] OJ L255/22. The 2005 Directive has been updated and supplemented by Directive 2013/55 on administrative cooperation through the internal market information (IMI) system.

[3] Directive 2006/123/EC on services in the internal market [2006] OJ L376/36.

through a fixed establishment in another Member State for an indefinite period'.[4] The past decade and a half has seen a series of important cases on corporate mobility in the EU.[5]

v. Articles 56–62 TFEU (ex Articles 49–55 EC) on the *free movement of services* require the removal of restrictions on the provision of services between Member States, whenever a cross-border element is present. This element can result from the fact that the provider is not established in the state where the services are supplied, or that the recipient has travelled to receive services in a Member State other than that in which he or she is established. A movement of services within the scope of Articles 56–57 TFEU (ex Articles 49–50 EC) may also (increasingly frequently in today's world) occur without the provider or the recipient moving, for example where the provision of the service takes place by telecommunication or electronically.[6]

vi. The Treaty provisions governing the free movement of services are said to be residual,[7] in that they apply only insofar as the provisions concerning capital,[8] persons,[9] or goods[10] do not apply. Nonetheless it is often difficult, in contexts such as broadcasting or telecommunications, to separate the issues concerning goods from those concerning services,[11] and several of the Treaty freedoms are often affected by a single national measure.[12]

vii. Although the principle of non-discrimination in Article 18 TFEU (ex Article 12 EC) is an important aspect of these two Treaty chapters,[13] the ECJ has ruled, just as in the case of the other internal market freedoms, that non-discriminatory obstacles are also *prima facie* within the scope of the relevant Treaty provisions.[14] However, the concept of 'discriminatory measures' is not sharply defined, and the distinction between discriminatory and non-discriminatory measures is often unclear.

viii. In addition to the Treaty-based justifications for limiting freedom of movement on grounds of public policy, security, and health, the ECJ has ruled, just as in the cases of goods, workers, and citizens, that a wide range of other public-interest justifications may be invoked by Member States, if they are pursued in a proportionate manner, to restrict the free movement of services and freedom of establishment.

ix. The Court's case law in particular in the field of services has grown ever more voluminous in recent years, in part as the Commission has increasingly pushed to liberalize the services sector

---

[4] Case C–221/89 *R v Secretary of State for Transport, ex p Factortame* [1991] ECR I–3905, [20].

[5] See below Section 3(c) (ii).

[6] Cases C–384/93 *Alpine Investments BV v Minister van Financiën* [1995] ECR I–1141; C–36/02 *Omega Spielhallen- und Automatenaufstellungs-GmbH v Oberbürgermeisterin der Bundesstadt Bonn* [2004] ECR I–9609.

[7] See for an argument that the CJEU does not in fact treat services as 'residual' to the other freedoms: V Hatzopoulos, 'The Court's Approach to Services (2006–2012): From Case Law to Case Load?' (2013) 50 CMLRev 459.

[8] Case C–423/98 *Albore* [2000] ECR I–5965.

[9] See Case C–544/11 *Petersen* EU:C:2013:124, [31]–[33], in which the CJEU decided the case under Art 45 on workers, rather than Art 56 on services.

[10] See however Case C–403/08 *Football Association Premier League* EU:C:2011:631, [77]–[83] where the CJEU decided the case under Art 56 on services instead of Art 34 on goods, since the goods aspect was secondary to the services aspect.

[11] Cases C–390/99 *Canal Satélite Digital v Administración General del Estado* [2002] ECR I–607, [31]–[33]; and C–403/08 *Football Association Premier League* ibid. See T Dreier, 'Online and Its Effect on the "Goods" versus "Services" Distinction' (2013) 44 Int'l Review of Intellectual Property and Competition Law 137. For a separate but similar treatment of the goods and services dimensions of a restriction on alcohol advertising, see Case C–405/98 *Konsumentombudsmannen v Gourmet International Products* [2001] ECR I–1795. For fishing permits as services rather than goods see Case C–97/98 *Jägerskiöld v Gustafsson* [1999] ECR I–7319. For an early case on the relationship between goods and services see Case 155/73 *Sacchi* [1974] ECR 409.

[12] See, eg, Cases C–150/04 *Commission v Denmark* [2007] ECR I–1163; C–522/04 *Commission v Belgium* [2007] ECR I–5701, including the Opinion of AG Stix-Hackl concerning taxation of pension benefits and insurance.

[13] Case 2/74 *Reyners v Belgium* [1974] ECR 631, [15]–[16].

[14] Case C–55/94 *Gebhard* [1995] ECR I–4165.

and remove obstacles to inter-state trade in services, and this has led to calls for more specialised regulation in particular sectors to ease the burden on the Court.[15]

2 DIFFERENCES AND COMMONALITIES BETWEEN THE FREE MOVEMENT OF PERSONS, SERVICES, AND ESTABLISHMENT

(A) COMPARING THE TREATY CHAPTERS

There are several points of similarity between the various chapters on the free movement of persons and services, including also the Treaty provisions on EU citizenship. Advocate General Mayras in *Van Binsbergen* pointed out that the principle of equal treatment on grounds of nationality underpinned the Treaty provisions on workers, services, and establishment alike.[16] They are comparable in that each requires equal treatment for persons who have *settled* in a Member State after exercising their freedom of movement,[17] the essential difference being whether they are working in an employed or a self-employed capacity.[18]

The overlap between workers (Article 45) and temporary service providers (Article 56) can be seen in a series of cases concerning 'posted workers' in which the Court of Justice distinguished the two by ruling that 'workers employed by a business established in one Member State who are temporarily sent to another Member State to provide services do not, in any way, seek access to the labour market in that second State if they return to their country of origin or residence after completion of their work'.[19]

The similarities between establishment and services are evident when considering at what stage a self-employed person providing regular services into or within a Member State may be considered to be sufficiently connected with that state to be established, rather than merely providing services, there.[20] The factors which go to distinguish the temporary provision of services from the exercise of the right of establishment in a Member State were addressed by the ECJ in *Gebhard*:[21]

> 25. The concept of establishment within the meaning of the Treaty is therefore a very broad one, allowing a Community national to participate, on a stable and continuous basis, in the economic life of a Member State other than his State of origin and to profit therefrom, so contributing to economic and social interpenetration within the Community in the sphere of activities as self-employed persons (see *Reyners* para. 21).
>
> 26. In contrast, where the provider of services moves to another Member State, the provisions of the chapter on services, in particular the third paragraph of Article 60, envisage that he is to pursue his activity there on a temporary basis.

---

[15] V Hatzopoulos, 'The Court's Approach to Services (2006–2012): From Case Law to Case Load?' (2013) 50 CMLRev 459.

[16] Case 33/74 *Van Binsbergen v Bestuur van de Bedrijfsvereniging voor de Metaalnijverheid* [1974] ECR 1299.

[17] See, eg, Cases C–345/05 *Commission v Portugal* [2006] ECR I–10633; C–104/06 *Commission v Sweden* [2007] ECR I–671, dealing simultaneously with Arts 45 and 49 TFEU on workers and establishment, and Art 21 on citizenship.

[18] AG Mayras in Case 2/74 *Reyners* (n 13) and the ECJ in Cases C–107/94 *Asscher v Staatsecretaris van Financiën* [1996] ECR I–3089; and C–268/99 *Jany v Staatssecretaris van Justitie* [2001] ECR I–8615, [68]–[70], in the context of the EU–Poland Association Agreement.

[19] Case C–49/98 *Finalarte Sociedade Construçao Civil v Urlaubs- und Lohnausgleichskasse der Bauwirtschaft* [2001] ECR I–7831, [22]–[23].

[20] Case 205/84 *Commission v Germany* [1986] ECR 3755, [22]; Case 33/74 *Van Binsbergen* (n 16) [13]; Opinion of AG Jacobs in Case C–76/90 *Säger v Dennemeyer & Co Ltd* [1991] ECR I–4221.

[21] Case C–55/94 *Gebhard v Consiglio dell'Ordine degli Avvocati e Procuratori di Milano* [1995] ECR I–4165.

> 27. As the Advocate General has pointed out, the temporary nature of the activities in question has to be determined in the light, not only of the duration of the provision of the service, but also of its regularity, periodicity or continuity. The fact that the provision of services is temporary does not mean that the provider of services within the meaning of the Treaty may not equip himself with some form of infrastructure in the host Member State (including an office, chambers or consulting rooms) in so far as such infrastructure is necessary for the purposes of performing the services in question.

The crucial features of establishment are the 'stable and continuous basis' on which the economic or professional activity is carried on, and the fact that there is an established professional base within the host Member State.[22] For the provision of services, the temporary nature of the activity is to be determined by reference to its 'periodicity, continuity and regularity', and providers of services will not be deemed to be 'established' simply by virtue of the fact that they equip themselves with some form of infrastructure in the host Member State.[23] The Court's graduated distinction between establishment and temporary service provision was adopted by the consolidating directive on the recognition of professional qualifications in 2005.[24]

In the past, it was suggested that Article 56 TFEU was more concerned with liberalizing the mobility of services and setting up a single market,[25] and had more in common with the Treaty provisions on free movement of goods[26] than with the Treaty provisions on workers and establishment, which were based primarily on the principle of non-discrimination. In recent years, however, a robust approach has been adopted to the rights of establishment (and workers) too, placing as much emphasis on liberalization and the removal of obstacles as on equal treatment, thereby bringing the law on the different freedoms closer together.[27] It will be evident from the discussion in this chapter that the gradual extension of EU rules to cover genuinely non-discriminatory restrictions on establishment and services has reached increasingly into sensitive areas of national social and economic policy, often with a deregulatory emphasis, and that many controversies have arisen as a result.

(B) ARE THE FREEDOMS HORIZONTALLY APPLICABLE?

We saw in Chapter 21 how the ECJ ruled that the provisions of Article 45 are binding not only on the state but also on private bodies.[28] In the field of services, the Court ruled early on in *Walrave and Koch* that the Treaty rules applied not only 'to the action of public authorities but extends likewise to rules of any other nature aimed at regulating in a collective manner gainful employment and the provision of services'.[29] It remained unclear however, even after the case of *Angonese* in the field of free movement

---

[22] Where a person or company establishes in a Member State to provide services to recipients there for an indefinite period, this does not fall within the Treaty provisions on freedom to provide services: Case C–70/95 *Sodemare v Regione Lombardia* [1997] ECR I–3395.

[23] Case C–215/01 *Schnitzer* [2003] ECR I–14847. Providers of services cannot be made subject to a particular type of mandatory 'employment' relationship, since that would deprive them of their self-employed status: see Cases C–398/95 *SETTG v Ypourgos Ergasias* [1997] ECR I–3091; C–255/04 *Commission v France* [2006] ECR I–5251.

[24] Art 5(2) of Dir 2005/36 [2005] OJ L255/22. According to Hatzopoulos (n 15), the CJEU's more recent rulings on services bring the notion of 'services' under EU law closer to that under the WTO's General Agreement on Trade in Services.

[25] AG Warner in Case 52/79 *Procureur du Roi v Debauve* [1980] ECR 833, 872.

[26] AG Jacobs in Case C–76/90 *Säger* (n 20) 4234–4235, and AG Gulmann in Case C–275/92 *HM Customs and Excise v Schindler* [1994] ECR I–1039, 1059; J Snell, *Goods and Services in EC Law* (Oxford University Press, 2002).

[27] Cases C–212/97 *Centros Ltd v Erhvervs- og Selskabsstyrelsen* [1999] ECR I–1459; C–55/94 *Gebhard* (n 21); C–400/08 *Commission v Spain* [2011] ECR I–1915.

[28] Case C–415/93 *Bosman* [1995] ECR I–4921, [83]–[84]; Case C–281/98 *Angonese v Cassa di Risparmio di Bolzano SpA* [2000] ECR I–4139 [32]; Case C–172/11 *Erny* EU:C:2012:399, [36].

[29] Case 36/74 *Walrave and Koch* [1974] ECR 1405.

of workers which explicitly deemed Article 45 TFEU to be applicable to private persons, whether the Treaty provisions on establishment and services were equally fully horizontally applicable, in the sense of imposing legal obligations on all individuals and not just on powerful, self-regulating collective actors such as sporting organizations, which possess powers akin to public law.[30] In *Wouters* the ECJ applied the *Walrave* ruling to a regulatory measure adopted by the Netherlands Bar Council concerning partnerships between barristers and accountants, but gave no further guidance on the applicability of the Treaty rules to purely individual private conduct.[31] The ECJ returned to this question in the famous *Laval* and *Viking* judgments,[32] where it ruled that Articles 49 and 56 TFEU were applicable to the organization of collective action by trade unions:

Case C–438/05 International Transport Workers Federation (ITF) and Finnish Seamen's Union (FSU) v Viking Line ABP and OÜ Viking Line Eesti
[2007] ECR I–0779

[Note Lisbon Treaty renumbering: Arts 39, 43, and 49 EC are now Arts 45, 49, and 56 TFEU]

THE ECJ

34. Since working conditions in the different Member States are governed sometimes by provisions laid down by law or regulation and sometimes by collective agreements and other acts concluded or adopted by private persons, limiting application of the prohibitions laid down by these [Treaty] articles to acts of a public authority would risk creating inequality in its application (see, by analogy, *Walrave and Koch*, paragraph 19; *Bosman*, paragraph 84; and *Angonese*, paragraph 33).

. . .

57. [T]he Court would point out that it is clear from its case-law that the abolition, as between Member States, of obstacles to freedom of movement for persons and freedom to provide services would be compromised if the abolition of State barriers could be neutralised by obstacles resulting from the exercise, by associations or organisations not governed by public law, of their legal autonomy.

. . .

60. In the present case, it must be borne in mind that . . . the collective action taken by FSU and ITF is aimed at the conclusion of an agreement which is meant to regulate the work of Viking's employees collectively, and, that those two trade unions are organisations which are not public law entities but exercise the legal autonomy conferred on them, inter alia, by national law.

61. It follows that Article 43 EC must be interpreted as meaning that . . . it may be relied on by a private undertaking against a trade union or an association of trade unions.

62. This interpretation is also supported by the case-law on the Treaty provisions on the free movement of goods, from which it is apparent that restrictions may be the result of actions by individuals or

---

[30] Case C–281/98 (n 28). The employer in *Angonese* was a bank, but it might be argued that the field of free movement of workers differs from the other freedoms in that Art 7(4) of Reg 1612/68 expressly applies the Treaty rules to contracts between individual employers and employees. See however also Case C–172/11 *Erny* EU:C:2012:399, [36] where the Court explicitly ruled on the horizontal applicability of Art 45 to individual contracts before going on to address Art 7(4) of the Reg in para [37].

[31] Case C–309/99 *Wouters et al v Algemene Raad van de Orde van Advocaten* [2002] ECR I–1577, [120]; Case C–411/98 *Ferlini v CHL* [2000] ECR I–8081, [50].

[32] Case C–438/05 *The International Transport Workers' Federation and The Finnish Seamen's Union v Viking Line ABP and OÜ Viking Line Eesti* [2007] ECR I–10779; Case C–341/05 *Laval un Partneri Ltd v Svenska Byggnadsarbetareförbundet and others* [2007] ECR I–11767, [98]–[100].

groups of such individuals rather than caused by the State (see Case C–265/95 *Commission* v *France*, paragraph 30, and *Schmidberger*, paragraphs 57 and 62).

63. The interpretation set out in paragraph 61 of the present judgment is also not called into question by the fact that the restriction at issue in the proceedings before the national court stems from the exercise of a right conferred by Finnish national law, such as, in this case, the right to take collective action, including the right to strike.

64. It must be added that, contrary to the claims, in particular, of ITF, it does not follow from the case-law of the Court... that that interpretation applies only to quasi-public organisations or to associations exercising a regulatory task and having quasi-legislative powers.

65. There is no indication in that case-law that could validly support the view that it applies only to associations or to organisations exercising a regulatory task or having quasi-legislative powers. Furthermore, it must be pointed out that, in exercising their autonomous power, pursuant to their trade union rights, to negotiate with employers or professional organisations the conditions of employment and pay of workers, trade unions participate in the drawing up of agreements seeking to regulate paid work collectively.

The case, together with the *Laval* ruling,[33] indicates that the horizontal applicability of the Treaty provisions on establishment and services is not confined to entities exercising a regulatory task or having quasi-legislative powers. However, it remains unclear from the judgments just how far the horizontal applicability of the Treaty rules to 'private parties' extends, and in particular whether there is some threshold requirement as regards the scope, impact, or collective nature of private power before the Treaty rules apply. On the one hand, the reference in paragraph 62 to 'actions by individuals' in the context of free movement of goods could be taken to suggest that no collective dimension will be required,[34] while on the other hand the emphasis in paragraph 65 on the power of trade unions to participate in the collective regulation of labour could be taken to suggest the contrary. Future rulings may reveal how far the Court is prepared to push the scope of the Treaty provisions on the free movement of services and establishment towards full horizontal applicability, but for now some uncertainty remains.[35]

(C) THE 'OFFICIAL AUTHORITY' EXCEPTION

Article 51 TFEU (ex Article 45 EC), which is extended by Article 62 TFEU to cover the chapter on services, states that the provisions of the chapter on freedom of establishment shall not apply 'so far as any given Member State is concerned, to activities which in that State are connected, even occasionally, with the exercise of official authority'. This provision has a similar role to that of the public-service derogation for workers in Article 45(4) TFEU. Advocate General Mayras in *Reyners* defined official authority as implying 'the power of enjoying the prerogatives outside the general law, privileges of official power, and powers of coercion over citizens'.[36]

The wording of Article 51 refers to those 'activities' which are connected with the use of official power, rather than to professions or vocations within which official authority might, under certain

---

[33] Case C–341/05 (n 32).

[34] However, that paragraph refers to the case law on free movement of goods concerning the obligation of the *state* to counter the actions of individuals which restrict the free movement of goods: see Ch 19, Section 3(d).

[35] For a critical comment on the horizontal applicability of the freedoms, see H Schepel, 'Constitutionalising the Market, Marketising the Constitution, and to Tell the Difference: On the Horizontal Application of the Free Movement Provisions in EU Law' (2012) 18 ELJ 177.

[36] Case 2/74 (n 13) 664.

circumstances, be exercised. In *Reyners*, the Court of Justice was asked whether the whole of the legal profession of *avocat* was exempt from the Treaty rules, on the basis that it was 'connected organically' with the public service of the administration of justice.[37] The Court considered that it was possible to exclude a whole profession on the basis of Article 51 only where the activities in question were so closely linked with the profession that it would oblige states to allow non-nationals to exercise, even if only occasionally, functions pertaining to official authority.[38] If, however, the activities connected with the exercise of official authority are separable from the independent professional activity in question taken as a whole, the exception allowed by Article 51 will not apply. In *Reyners* itself the professional activities of an *avocat*, involving regular and official contact and even compulsory cooperation with the courts, were held not to involve the necessary connection with the exercise of official authority, since the discretion of the judicial authority and the free exercise of judicial power were left intact.

The Court has continued to interpret the official-authority exception narrowly in response to Member States' attempts to invoke it for a wide range of professions.[39] In a series of infringement proceedings brought by the Commission against six Member States, the CJEU considered whether the profession of notary, which had been the subject of considerable debate amongst Member States and by the European Parliament in this regard, could be excluded from the scope of the freedom of establishment rules in Article 49.[40] The states argued that since the core of a notary's activities consist in the power to authenticate, which entails the exercise of official authority, it falls within the scope of Article 51(1) TFEU and thereby permits the exclusion of non-nationals. While Advocate General Cruz Villalón accepted this argument, the Court however disagreed, and in a set of lengthy reasoned judgments[41] ruled that the activities of notaries were not connected with the exercise of official authority within Article 51.[42]

(D) THE PUBLIC POLICY, SECURITY, AND HEALTH JUSTIFICATIONS

Article 52 in the chapter on establishment and Article 62 in the chapter on services provide that the provisions of those chapters 'shall not prejudice the applicability of provisions laid down by law, regulation or administrative action providing for special treatment for foreign nationals on grounds of public policy, public security or public health'. In their application to natural persons these derogations are regulated, together with their application to other categories of EU citizen and their families, by the provisions of Directive 2004/38, as well as the general principles of EU law and the Charter of Fundamental

---

[37] Ibid.

[38] Ibid [46].

[39] Cases C–42/92 *Thijssen v Controledienst voor de Verzekeringen* [1993] ECR I–4047 on the post of commissioner of insurance companies; C–306/89 *Commission v Greece* [1991] ECR I–5863 on traffic accident experts; C–272/91 *Commission v Italy* [1994] ECR I–1409 on operating a computerization system for a national lottery; C–263/99 *Commission v Italy* [2001] ECR I–4195 on transport consultants; C–114/97 *Commission v Spain* [1998] ECR I–6717, C–355/98 *Commission v Belgium* [2000] ECR I–1221, C–283/99 *Commission v Italy* [2001] ECR I–4363 on private security activities; C–160/08 *Commission v Germany* [2010] ECR I–3713 on ambulance service activities; C–438/08 *Commission v Portugal* [2009] ECR I–10219 on vehicle inspection; C–372/09 *Peñarroja Fa* EU:C:2011:156 on court translators.

[40] Cases C–61/08 *Commission v Greece* EU:C:2011:340; C–54/08 *Commission v Germany* EU:C:2011:340; C–53/08 *Commission v Austria* EU:C:2011:338; C–51/08 *Commission v Luxembourg* EU:C:2011:336; C–50/08 *Commission v France* EU:C:2011:335; C–47/08 *Commission v Belgium* EU:C:2011:334.

[41] The one exception was Case C–52/08 *Commission v Portugal* EU:C:2011:337, [49]–[56], where the Commission's application was dismissed because it was based solely on non-implementation of Dir 2005/36, at a time when it had not been sufficiently clear to Member States whether or not Dir 2005/36 was applicable to notaries. The subsequent amending Dir 2013/55 explicitly excluded notaries who have been appointed by official act of government from the scope of Dir 2005/36. See further below Section 5(c).

[42] Ibid [81]–[124].

Rights.[43] In their application to companies the derogations are governed by the Treaty,[44] by the general principles of EU law and the Charter of Fundamental Rights, and by the relevant provisions of the Services Directive.[45] The general principles of EU law and the Charter include the principles of non-discrimination and of proportionality, which also govern the justification of public-interest-based restrictions on freedom of movement which have been judicially developed alongside the Treaty grounds for justification. Further, the Court has ruled that Article 52 does not permit a Member State to exclude an entire economic sector from the application of the principles on freedom of establishment and services.[46]

(E) LEGISLATION GOVERNING ENTRY, RESIDENCE, AND EXPULSION

As we see in Chapters 21 and 23, Directive 2004/38 governs the terms and conditions of entry of all EU citizens and their families into a host Member State, as well as their right to remain there after having pursued an economic activity, and the conditions under which their rights may be restricted or revoked.[47] This includes self-employed persons and service providers, so that the discussion of Directive 2004/38 in Chapters 21 and 23 is equally relevant here.

The provisions of the earlier legislation governing self-employed persons, Directive 73/148, which regulated rights of 'abode' and rights of temporary residence for the duration of the services, have been replaced with the simple right of residence for self-employed persons in Article 7(a) of Directive 2004/38. Further, as Chapter 23 on citizenship outlines, even where a self-employed person is no longer engaged in economic activity, the right of residence as an EU citizen continues unless that person has, through lack of sufficient resources, become an unreasonable burden on the host state.

3 THE RIGHT OF ESTABLISHMENT

Article 49 TFEU

Within the framework of the provisions set out below, restrictions on the freedom of establishment of nationals of a Member State in the territory of another Member State shall be prohibited. Such prohibition shall also apply to restrictions on the setting up of agencies, branches, or subsidiaries by nationals of any Member State established in the territory of any Member State.

Freedom of establishment shall include the right to take up and pursue activities as self-employed persons and to set up and manage undertakings, in particular companies or firms within the meaning of the second paragraph of Article 54, under the conditions laid down for its own nationals by the law of the country where such establishment is effected, subject to the provisions of the chapter relating to capital.

Paragraph one requires the *abolition of restrictions* on freedom of primary and secondary establishment, whereas paragraph two provides for the right to pursue self-employed activities *on an equal footing* with the nationals of the Member State of establishment. The reference to capital acknowledges

[43] Ch 21, Section 8.
[44] For examples of the application of Arts 52 and 62 TFEU to companies see Case 3/88 *Commission v Italy* [1989] ECR 4035; Case 352/85 *Bond van Adverteerders v Netherlands* [1988] ECR 2085; Case C–114/97 *Commission v Spain* [1998] ECR I–6717; Case C–355/98 *Commission v Belgium* [2000] ECR I–1221. For a failed attempt see Case C–171/02 *Commission v Portugal* [2004] ECR I–5645.
[45] For further discussion see Section 6(b) below.
[46] Case C–496/01 *Commission v France* [2004] ECR I–2351.
[47] Dir 2004/38 replaced the previous Dir 73/148 in this respect.

that there is a separate chapter on the free movement of capital, which was subject to a different and more gradual regime of liberalization.[48]

Article 49 on its face appears to give rights only to persons in a Member State other than the Member State of their nationality. Secondly, it appears to prohibit discrimination, and to imply that its requirements are satisfied if the person exercising the right of establishment is treated in the same way as a national. However, we shall see that Article 49 has been given a broader reading on these two points: nationals may in appropriate circumstances rely on Article 49 against their own state; and Article 49 prohibits not merely unequal treatment but any unjustified obstacles to freedom of establishment.

Article 50 TFEU originally required the Council to draw up a General Programme for the abolition of restrictions on establishment (which it did in 1961[49]) and to issue directives to achieve freedom for particular activities. Article 53 now requires the European Parliament and the Council to issue directives, acting in accordance with the ordinary legislative procedure, for the mutual recognition of diplomas and other qualifications, and Article 54 places companies in the same position as natural persons for the purpose of the application of this chapter of the Treaty.

(A) THE EFFECT OF ARTICLE 49

In 1974 in *Reyners*, the ECJ ruled that Article 49 TFEU was directly effective, despite the fact that the conditions for direct effect set out in *Van Gend en Loos* were arguably not met,[50] and despite the Council's failure to adopt the necessary implementing legislation envisaged by the Treaty provisions. Such legislation had not been adopted by the time of *Reyners*, partly on account of the slow progress of legislation in the Council in the aftermath of the Luxembourg Accords, and partly on account of the opposition within Member States to the process of opening the professions, and particularly the legal profession, to non-nationals.[51]

Reyners, a Dutch national who had obtained his legal education in Belgium, was refused admission to the Belgian Bar solely because he lacked Belgian nationality. The ECJ ruled that, despite the Treaty requirement that directives should be adopted, Article 49 laid down a precise result to be achieved by the end of the transitional period, namely the requirement of non-discrimination on grounds of nationality. The fulfilment of this result had to be made easier by, but was not dependent on, the implementation of a programme of progressive measures.[52] Thus he could invoke Article 49 directly. The ECJ acknowledged, however, that the directives were nonetheless relevant in that they aimed to make easier the effective exercise of the right of freedom of establishment.[53]

In *Thieffry*, the Court went one step further and ruled that Article 49 could be relied on by an EU national seeking to practise a profession in another Member State where the restriction he faced was based not on nationality but on the adequacy of his qualifications.[54] The case concerned a Belgian national who obtained a doctorate in law in Belgium and practised as an advocate in Brussels, and who subsequently obtained French university recognition of his qualifications as equivalent to a degree in French law, and a certificate of aptitude for the profession of *avocat*. He was however refused admission to the training stage as an advocate at the Paris Bar on the ground that he lacked a degree in French law. According to the ECJ, since he had already obtained what was recognized in France, for both

---

[48] Ch 20.
[49] OJ Spec Ed, Second Ser, IX.
[50] Case 2/74 (n 13); see Ch 7 on direct effect.
[51] Ibid, AG Mayras, 658.
[52] Ibid [26].
[53] Ibid [31].
[54] Case 71/76 *Thieffry v Conseil de l'Ordre des Avocats à la Cour de Paris* [1977] ECR 765.

professional and academic purposes, to be an equivalent qualification, and had satisfied the necessary practical training requirements, the state authorities were not justified in refusing to admit Thieffry to the Bar solely on the ground that he did not possess a French qualification, despite the absence of any EU directives in the field.[55]

In subsequent cases the Court went further still and ruled that Article 49 precluded the competent national authorities from simply refusing, without further explanation, to allow nationals of another Member State to practise their trade or profession on the ground that their qualification was *not* equivalent to the corresponding national qualification. Instead, the Treaty provisions imposed specific, positive obligations on national authorities and professional bodies to take steps to secure the free movement of workers and freedom of establishment, even in the absence of EU or national legislation providing for equivalence or for the recognition of qualifications. In *Heylens* the Court ruled, in the case of a Belgian football trainer working in France who was refused recognition of the equivalence of his Belgian diploma, that Member States were entitled, in the absence of harmonizing directives, to regulate the knowledge and qualifications necessary to pursue a particular occupation. However:

> [T]he procedure for the recognition of equivalence must enable the national authorities to assure themselves, on an objective basis, that the foreign diploma certifies that its holder has knowledge and qualifications which are, if not identical, at least equivalent to those certified by the national diploma. That assessment of the equivalence of the foreign diploma must be effected exclusively in the light of the level of knowledge and qualifications which its holder can be assumed to possess in the light of that diploma, having regard to the nature and duration of the studies and practical training which the diploma certifies that he has carried out.[56]

Further, where employment was dependent on possession of a diploma, it had to be possible for a national of a Member State to obtain judicial review of a decision of the authorities of another Member State, and to ascertain the reasons for refusing to recognize the equivalence of a diploma.

In *Vlassopoulou*, a Greek national who had obtained a Greek law degree and had practised German law for several years in Germany applied for admission to the Bar there. Her authorization to practise was rejected on the ground that she lacked the necessary qualifications because she had not passed the relevant German examinations. The ECJ began by ruling that even the nondiscriminatory application of national qualification requirements could hinder the exercise of freedom of establishment:

> Consequently, a Member State which receives a request to admit a person to a profession to which access, under national law, depends upon the possession of a diploma or a professional qualification must take into consideration the diplomas, certificates and other evidence of qualifications which the person concerned has acquired in order to exercise the same profession in another Member State by making a comparison between the specialized knowledge and abilities certified by those diplomas and the knowledge and qualifications required by the national rules.[57]

Thus the national authorities must consider any education and training received by the holder of the diploma or certificate, and must compare the knowledge and skills acquired with those required by the domestic qualification.[58] If they are found to be equivalent, the state must recognize the qualification,

---

[55] Ibid [17]; Case 11/77 *Patrick v Ministre des Affairs Culturelles* [1977] ECR 1199.

[56] Case 222/86 *UNECTEF v Heylens* [1987] ECR 4097, [13].

[57] Case 340/89 *Vlassopoulou v Ministerium für Justiz, Bundes und Europaangelegenheiten Baden-Württemberg* [1991] ECR 2357, [16].

[58] Also Case C–104/91 *Borrell* [1992] ECR I–3001.

and if they are not so found, the state must assess whether any knowledge or practical training the person may have acquired in the host Member State is sufficient to make up for what was lacking in the qualification.

Vlassopoulou highlights the extent to which the effectiveness of Article 49 was bolstered by the Court in the years following *Reyners*, where the ECJ held that in the absence of legislation only the core non-discrimination requirement of the Article was directly effective. By the time of *Vlassopoulou* it had been held that, despite the diversity of national educational and training systems and the lack of EU coordinating legislation, Article 49 TFEU imposed a precise obligation on national authorities to examine thoroughly the basis for the qualification held by an EU national, to inform the person concerned of the reasons if the qualification was deemed not to be equivalent, and to respect their rights in the process. The effect was that a Member State could no longer simply refuse someone entry to a profession or to practise a trade solely on the ground that he or she lacked the domestic qualification, even where there was as yet no domestic or EU recognition of the equivalence of the foreign qualification.[59]

The approach adopted by the ECJ in *Vlassopoulou* closely reflected the provisions of Council Directive 89/48 on the mutual recognition of higher education diplomas which was adopted around that time,[60] but was not applicable to the facts of *Vlassopoulou*. Directive 89/48 has since been replaced by consolidating Directive 2005/36, which embodies the same approach and the same principles.[61] Further, as we shall see below, the broad principles articulated in the *Vlassopoulou* and *Heylens* cases continue to apply to situations which are not covered by the secondary legislation.

(B) THE SCOPE OF ARTICLE 49

(i) *Discriminatory and Non-Discriminatory Restrictions*

It was noted above that the wording of Article 49 emphasizes the requirement of equal treatment of nationals and non-nationals.[62] Further, apart from the general non-discrimination clause in Article 18 TFEU and the specific non-discrimination requirement in Article 49, Article 24 of Directive 2004/38 on the rights of movement and residence of EU citizens also contains an umbrella equal treatment clause.

In some of its earlier case law, such as *Commission v Belgium*[63] and *Fearon*,[64] the ECJ appeared to suggest that, in the absence of direct or indirect discrimination, rules which restricted the right of establishment would not violate Article 49. However, in keeping with the pattern of its case law on the free movement of goods, services, and workers, the Court has since moved clearly away from the emphasis on unequal treatment.

In *Klopp*, a German lawyer who was refused admission to the Paris Bar on the sole ground that he already maintained an office as a lawyer in another Member State successfully challenged the rule under Article 49, even though the rule applied equally to nationals and non-nationals.[65] The Court ruled that

---

[59] See also Case C–164/94 *Arantis v Land Berlin* [1996] ECR I–135.

[60] See (n 290) and text below.

[61] (N 2) and (nn 301–302).

[62] For some cases in which the ECJ insisted on equality of treatment for persons exercising the right of establishment, see Case 63/86 *Commission v Italy* [1988] ECR 29; Case C–337/97 *Meeusen v Hofddirectie van de Informatie Beheer Groep* [1999] ECR I–3289; Case 197/84 *Steinhauser v City of Biarritz* [1985] ECR 1819; Case 143/87 *Stanton* (n 68); Case 79/85 *Segers* [1986] ECR 2375; Case C–334/94 *Commission v France* [1996] ECR I–1307, [21]; Case C–151/96 *Commission v Ireland* [1997] ECR I–3327.

[63] Case 221/85 *Commission v Belgium* [1987] ECR 719 on clinical biology services.

[64] Case 182/83 *Fearon v Irish Land Commission* [1984] ECR 3677, on a residence requirement for exemption from compulsory purchase of land. See also Cases 305/87 *Commission v Greece* [1989] ECR 1461; C–302/97 *Konle v Austria* [1999] ECR I–2651; and C–197/11 *Libert* EU:C:2013:288 on land restrictions and freedom of movement.

[65] Case 107/83 *Ordre des Avocats v Klopp* [1984] ECR 2971.

Article 49 specifically guarantees the freedom to set up more than one place of work in the EU and there were less restrictive ways, given modern transport and telecommunications, of ensuring that lawyers maintain sufficient contact with their clients and the judicial authorities, and obey the rules of the profession. *Klopp* was not of itself authority for a general proposition that even non-discriminatory rules may breach Article 49, given that Article 49 expressly guarantees the right to secondary establishment which was being denied in that case,[66] but it demonstrated that freedom of establishment requires more than equal treatment in certain circumstances.

In *Wolf*,[67] *Stanton*,[68] and *Kemmler*,[69] the ECJ however ruled that certain indistinctly applicable national rules on social-security exemptions for the self-employed were impermissible, because they constituted an unjustified impediment to the pursuit of occupational activities in more than one Member State, even though the rules contained no direct or indirect discrimination on grounds of nationality.[70] Similarly in cases concerning non-discriminatory registration requirements, the Court found a violation of Article 49 in the absence of objective justification.[71]

The *Gebhard* ruling gave the clearest indication of the Court's broad interpretation of Article 49 TFEU.[72] Here the Court declared that the same principles underpin all of the Treaty provisions on freedom of movement, and stated that the provisions on goods,[73] services,[74] workers,[75] and establishment should be similarly construed. *Gebhard* concerned a German national against whom disciplinary proceedings were brought by the Milan Bar Council for pursuing a professional activity as a lawyer in Italy on a permanent basis. He had set up his chambers using the title *avvocato*, although he had not been admitted as a member of the Milan Bar and although his training, qualifications, and experience had not formally been recognized in Italy. Having established that in the absence of EU rules, Member States may justifiably subject the pursuit of self-employed activities to *bona fide* rules relating to organization, ethics, qualifications, titles, etc, the Court continued:[76]

> It follows, however, from the Court's case law that national measures liable to hinder or make less attractive the exercise of fundamental freedoms guaranteed by the Treaty must fulfil four conditions: they must be applied in a non-discriminatory manner; they must be justified by imperative requirements in the general interest; they must be suitable for securing the attainment of the objective which they pursue; and they must not go beyond what is necessary in order to attain it.

---

[66] See also Case 96/85 *Commission v France* [1986] ECR 1475; Case C–351/90 *Commission v Luxembourg* [1992] ECR I–3945, condemning other similar single-practice rules for doctors, dentists, and vets; Case C–106/91 *Ramrath v Ministre de la Justice* [1992] ECR I–3351; Case C–162/99 *Commission v Italy* [2001] ECR I–541.

[67] Cases 154–155/87 *RSVZ v Wolf* [1988] ECR 3897.

[68] Case 143/87 *Stanton v INASTI* [1988] ECR 3877.

[69] Cases C–53/95 *INASTI v Kemmler* [1996] ECR I–704; C–68/99 *Commission v Germany* [2001] ECR I–1865, concerning social insurance law affecting artists. Compare Case C–249/04 *Allard v INASTI* [2005] ECR I–4535; Case C–565/08 *Commission v Italy*, 29 Mar 2011, in which maximum tariffs applicable to lawyers' fees were held not to restrict the freedom of establishment or to provide services.

[70] Case 143/87 *Stanton* (n 68) [9].

[71] Case 292/86 *Gullung v Conseil de l'Ordre des Avocats* [1988] ECR 111; Case 271/82 *Auer v Ministère Public* [1983] ECR 2727, [18].

[72] Case C–55/94 *Gebhard* (n 21).

[73] Cases 8/74 *Procureur du Roi v Dassonville* [1974] ECR 837; Case 120/78 *Rewe-Zentral v Bundesmonopolverwaltung für Branntwein (Cassis de Dijon)* [1979] ECR 649; C–267 and 268/91 *Keck and Mithouard* [1993] ECR I–6097; C–34–36/95 *de Agostini* [1997] ECR I–3843; C–254/98 *Schutzverband gegen unlauteren Wettbewerb v TK-Heimdienst Sass GmbH* [2000] ECR I–151. See more generally the discussion in Ch 19.

[74] See, eg, Case C–384/93 *Alpine Investments* (n 6); Cases C–369 and 376/96 *Arblade* [1999] ECR I–8453.

[75] Case C–415/93 *Bosman* (n 28) [82]–[84].

[76] Ibid [37].

There is no mention in this paragraph of any requirement of discrimination, direct or indirect. Instead, any national rule *which is liable to hinder or make less attractive the exercise* of the 'fundamental' freedom of establishment (or any of the other fundamental freedoms) may violate the Treaty unless it is justified by an imperative requirement and applied in a proportionate and non-discriminatory manner.[77] Moreover while rules which create 'equally applicable' obstacles to freedom of establishment often impose a heavier burden in practice on non-nationals than on nationals,[78] and hence could be classified as indirectly discriminatory, this is not true of all such rules and some are genuinely equally applicable in law and in fact. The essence of *Gebhard*, adopting an obstacle approach rather than a discrimination approach, has been affirmed by the Court on many occasions since.[79]

A clear example is in the case of *Commission v Spain* concerning a Catalonian retail law involving stringent regulation of larger retail establishments (*hipermercados*), in which the ECJ ruled that:[80]

> the concept of 'restriction' for the purposes of Article 43 EC [*now Art 49 TFEU*] covers measures taken by a Member State which, although applicable without distinction, affect access to the market for undertakings from other Member States and thereby hinder intra-Community trade.

The Court ruled that the Commission had not demonstrated that the legislation had an indirectly discriminatory effect, but that since Article 49 TFEU prohibits even non-discriminatory measures that hinder the exercise of the freedom of establishment, for example by affecting access to the market, the legislation still had to satisfy the requirements of proportionality, which it failed to do in several respects.[81] The strict scrutiny applied by the ECJ to what was agreed to be non-discriminatory Spanish legislation here clearly illustrates the powerfully liberalizing approach adopted by the Court to the economic freedoms of the Treaty.[82]

It should be noted, however, that the discriminatory nature of a restriction is not irrelevant, for several reasons. First, if a restriction on freedom of establishment discriminates directly on grounds of nationality, it will, without further question, fall within the scope of the Treaty prohibition. By comparison, not every non-discriminatory restriction will constitute a sufficient hindrance, by analogy with the case law on goods[83] and on workers, as in *Graf*.[84] An example can recently be seen in the requirement for postal service providers outside the universal service scope to have a mandatory complaints

---

[77] See also Case C–108/96 *MacQuen* [2001] ECR I–837, [26]–[27]. Note that the opposite is also true: even a rule that discriminates on the basis of residence (in this case, corporate residence) will not contravene Art 49 if it is not liable to hinder or make less attractive the exercise of freedom of establishment: Case C–186/12 *Impacto Azul* EU:C:2013:412, [36].

[78] G Marenco, 'The Notion of a Restriction on the Freedom of Establishment and the Provisions of Services in the Case Law of the ECJ' (1991) 11 YBEL 111.

[79] See, eg, Cases C–108/96 *MacQuen* (n 77); C–212/97 *Centros* (n 27) [34]; C–289/02 *AMOK Verlags GmbH v A & R Gastronomie GmbH* [2003] ECR I–15059, [36]; C–8/02 *Leichtle v Bundesanstalt für Arbeit* [2004] ECR I–2641, [32]; C–346/04 *Conijn v Finanzamt Hamburg-Nord* [2006] ECR I–6137; C–433/04 *Commission v Belgium* [2006] ECR I–10653; C–19/92 *Kraus v Land Baden-Württemberg* [1993] ECR I–1663; C–384/08 *Attanasio Group* EU:C:2010:133, [43].

[80] Case C–400/08 *Commission v Spain* (n 27) [64].

[81] The Court of Justice has increasingly made use of the phrase 'access to the market', which is to be found in the *Alpine Investments* case regarding services at (n 6). See, eg, Cases C–518/06 *Commission v Italy* [2009] ECR I–3491; C–89/09 *Commission v France* [2010] ECR I–12941; C–169/07 *Hartlauer Handelsgesellschaft mbH v Wiener Landesregierung and Oberösterreichische Landesregierung* [2009] ECR I–1721. For a book discussing 'market access' approaches to market liberalization in the EU as well as the WTO, see M Klamert, *Services Liberalization in the EU and the WTO: Concepts, Standards and Regulatory Approaches* (Cambridge University Press, 2014).

[82] Compare however Case C–577/11 *DKV Belgium* EU:C:2013:146 in which, although non-discriminatory legislation imposing a system of premium-rate increases on insurance companies was held to constitute a restriction on freedom of establishment, it was justified on the basis of protecting consumers from unexpected sharp increases.

[83] Cases 267 and 268/91 *Keck* (n 73) and the discussion in Ch 19.

[84] Case C–190/98 *Graf v Filzmoser Maschinenbau* [2000] ECR I–493.

procedure.[85] Secondly, at least in certain contexts, if a restriction is directly or deliberately discriminatory, the Member State may rely for justification only on the express justifications on grounds of public policy, security, and health in Article 52 TFEU.[86] By comparison, when the obstacle stems from an equally applicable rule which does not constitute deliberate discrimination, a wider and open-ended range of public-interest grounds, which are referred to *inter alia* as mandatory requirements, imperative requirements, and objective justifications, may be relied upon by the state or the private actor to justify the restrictive measure. It should be noted, however, that the internal-market case law on what constitutes discrimination, whether direct or indirect, and on what kinds of justification are available is very confused.[87] This problem has been discussed in more detail in Chapter 19 in the context of the free movement of goods.[88]

(ii) *Reverse Discrimination and Wholly Internal Situations: When Can Nationals Rely on Article 49 in Their Own Member State?*

It was noted above that the first sentence of Article 49 refers to the situation of nationals of a Member State wishing to establish themselves 'in the territory of another Member State'. A first reading of this sentence suggests that nationals setting up in a self-employed capacity in their own Member State cannot complain under Article 49 about the domestic regulation of those activities. The situation is somewhat more complex, however.

In the first place, a Member State is clearly obliged under both Article 49 and Directive 2004/38 not to restrict its own nationals who wish to *leave* the territory in order to set up an establishment in another Member State.

Secondly, it is obvious that nationals who wish to establish themselves within their own Member State may be disadvantaged if the qualifications they have obtained in another Member State are not recognized by their own state. In *Knoors*, where a Dutch national sought to practise as a plumber in the Netherlands, having obtained training and experience in Belgium, the Dutch Government argued that a national could not rely in his own Member State on Article 49 to gain recognition for qualifications obtained, since he might be seeking to evade the application of legitimate national provisions. The ECJ firmly rejected this argument:[89]

> 24. Although it is true that the provisions of the Treaty relating to establishment and the provision of services cannot be applied to situations which are purely internal to a Member State, the position nevertheless remains that the reference in Article 52 [*now Art 49 TFEU*] to 'nationals of a Member State' who wish to establish themselves 'in the territory of another Member State' cannot be interpreted in such a way as to exclude from the benefit of Community law a given Member State's own nationals when

---

[85] Case C–148/10 *DHL International* EU:C:2011:654, [61]–[63].

[86] Cases 352/85 *Bond van Adverteerders v Netherlands* [1988] ECR 2085, [32]–[33]; C–17/92 *Federación de Distribuidores Cinematográficos v Estado Español et Unión de Productores de Cine y Televisión* [1993] ECR I–2239, [16]; C–484/93 *Svensson and Gustavsson v Ministre du Logement et de l'Urbanisme* [1995] ECR I–3955, [15]; C–341/05 *Laval* (n 32) [116]–[119].

[87] Case C–204/90 *Bachmann v Belgium* [1992] ECR I–249 on the free movement of workers, where the ECJ seemed to say that restrictions which appeared to be discriminatory could be justified without recourse to the specific Treaty exceptions. See also the range of justifications considered by the ECJ for the (arguably directly discriminatory) nationality restrictions in Case C–415/93 *Bosman* (n 28). For a more general discussion of this confusion see J Scott, 'Mandatory Requirements' in C Barnard and J Scott (eds), *Law of the Single European Market* (Hart, 2002) ch 10; and in the context of services, S Enchelmaier, 'Always at Your Service (Within Limits): The ECJ's Case Law on Article 56 TFEU 2006–11' (2011) 36 ELRev 615.

[88] Ch 19.

[89] Case 115/78 *Knoors v Secretary of State for Economic Affairs* [1979] ECR 399; Case 246/80 *Broekmeulen v Huisarts Registratie Commissie* [1981] ECR 2311. Compare however the restrictive approach of the ECJ in the first *Auer* case, Case 136/78 *Ministère Public v Auer* [1979] ECR 437, [20]–[21], and see the later Case 271/82 *Auer* (n 71).

> the latter, owing to the fact that they have lawfully resided on the territory of another Member State and have there acquired a trade qualification which is recognized by the provisions of Community law, are, with regard to their State of origin, in a situation which may be assimilated to that of any other persons enjoying the rights and liberties guaranteed by the Treaty.

We have seen above how in *Heylens* and *Vlassopoulou*, despite the absence of EU legislation, Member States were obliged to consider the equivalence of qualifications obtained in other Member States.[90] Where, however, unlike in *Heylens* and *Vlassopoulou*, the applicant is a national of the host Member State, concerns such as those expressed by the government in *Knoors* about a possible evasion or abuse have occasionally been raised.[91]

Now, however, a national who has obtained a qualification in another Member State and has returned to practise in his or her Member State of origin will probably be covered by the terms of Directive 2005/36 on the recognition of professional qualifications. Further, even where Directive 2005/36 does not cover the facts of the situation, the principles in *Heylens* and *Vlassopoulou* will be applied even when the applicant is a national of the host state.[92] Whenever a national of a Member State has obtained a qualification in another Member State and has returned to practise in the home state, it is no longer deemed a 'wholly internal situation' and the right of establishment in Article 49 applies.[93]

This was clear in *Koller*, in which an Austrian national, after obtaining a law degree in Austria, went to Spain and, after taking additional courses and examinations, had his degree declared equivalent to the Spanish 'Licenciado en Derecho' authorizing him to use the title '*abogado*'.[94] When he later applied for admission to the aptitude test for the profession of lawyer in Austria, his request was refused on the ground that in Spain, unlike in Austria, practical experience was not required in order to pursue the profession of a lawyer. The Austrian Admissions Board concluded that his application was designed to circumvent the requirement for five years' practical experience required by the Austrian rules. The ECJ however held that Koller fell within the scope of Directive 89/48 (the predecessor to Directive 2005/36) and that he could not be refused the option of taking an aptitude test solely on the ground that he had not completed the period of practical experience required by the 'host' state. On the contrary, the ECJ took the view that the very purpose of the aptitude test was 'to ensure that the applicant is capable of exercising the regulated profession in that Member State'.[95] Thus, so long as some 'EU element' is present and the situation is not wholly internal, individuals can rely on Article 49 in their own state.[96]

Conversely, persons who have never exercised the freedom to move within the EU, and where there is no other relevant inter-state element, will have no EU law claim against their state.[97] This

---

[90] See also Case C–108/96 *MacQuen* (n 77).

[91] See, eg, Cases C–61/89 *Bouchoucha* [1990] ECR I–3551; C–330–331/90 *Ministero Fiscal v Lopez Brea* [1992] ECR I–323.

[92] Case C–19/92 *Kraus* (n 79); Case C–234/97 *Fernández de Bobadilla v Museo Nacional del Prado* [1999] ECR I–4773.

[93] Case C–234/97 *De Bobadilla* (n 92) [30]–[34].

[94] Case C–118/09 *Koller* [2010] ECR I–13627.

[95] Ibid. See also Cases C–58 and 59/13 *Torresi* EU:C:2014:2088 for a similar ruling in relation to Dir 98/5 on lawyers' establishment, indicating clearly that this course of action would not amount to fraud or evasion, but simply reliance on the possibility provided by the Dir.

[96] For cases involving a wholly internal situation see Cases 54 and 91/88 and 14/89 *Niño and others* [1990] ECR 3537; 204/87 *Bekaert* [1988] ECR 2029; C–152/94 *Openbaar Ministerie v Geert van Buydner* [1995] ECR I–3981; C–134/94 *Esso Española SA v Comunidad Autónoma de Canarias* [1995] ECR I–4223; C–17/94 *Gervais* [1995] ECR I–4353; C–134/95 *Unità Socio-Sanitaria Locale no 47 de Biella v INAIL* [1997] ECR I–195; C–225–227/95 *Kapasakalis v Greece* [1998] ECR I–4329; E Cannizzaro, 'Producing "Reverse Discrimination" through the Exercise of Competences' (1997) 17 YBEL 29; C Ritter, 'Purely Internal Situations, Reverse Discrimination, *Guimont, Dzodzi* and Article 234' (2006) 31 ELRev 690.

[97] Some establishment cases held to involve wholly internal situations include Case C–139/12 *Caixa d'Estalvis i Pensions de Barcelona* EU:C:2014:174; C–162/12 *Airport Shuttle Express* EU:C:2014:74; C–419/12 *Crono Service* EU:C:2014:81. The CJEU however established a so-called *Guimont* exception, indicating that it may nonetheless provide a ruling for a national

gives rise to the curious phenomenon of 'reverse discrimination' whereby nationals of a Member State find themselves disadvantaged by comparison with other EU nationals within the same Member State. In the *Belgian Social Security* case, the Flemish Government, a federated entity of the Belgian state, had enacted a scheme of care insurance that was available only to those working and residing in either the Dutch-speaking region or the bilingual region of Brussels-Capital.[98] The ECJ ruled that this constituted a restriction under Articles 45 and 59 TFEU, since 'migrant workers, pursuing or contemplating the pursuit of employment or self-employment in one of those two regions, might be dissuaded from making use of their freedom of movement and from leaving their Member State of origin to stay in Belgium, by reason of the fact that moving to certain parts of Belgium would cause them to lose the opportunity of eligibility for the benefits which they might otherwise have claimed'.[99] The ECJ insisted that any EU national working in either of these two regions must be eligible for the scheme, regardless of where in Belgium they resided, with the exception of Belgian nationals living in the French- or German-speaking region who had never exercised their freedom to move. The Court ruled that EU law 'clearly cannot be applied to such purely internal situations'.[100] The consequence is that a Spanish national establishing herself in the French-speaking region and working in the Dutch-speaking region will be able to join the insurance scheme, while her Belgian colleague and neighbour, who has worked and lived all his life in Belgium, will not.

In *Werner*, the ECJ indicated that even if a national was resident in a Member State other than that of his nationality, so long as he maintained his place of establishment and professional practice in his own Member State, he could not rely on Article 49 to challenge tax provisions of his own state which favoured residents over non-residents.[101] By way of contrast, in *Asscher*, a Dutch national residing in Belgium who was a director of companies *both* in Belgium and in the Netherlands, and who, on account of his non-resident status and the level of his earnings outside the Netherlands, was subject within the Netherlands to a considerably higher rate of tax than residents of that state, was entitled to invoke Article 49 against his own Member State.[102] The ECJ ruled this was not an 'internal' situation because his exercise of his Treaty rights of establishment and his dual economic activities in Belgium and the Netherlands had resulted in this unfavourable tax situation, and there was no justification in this case for the differential treatment.[103] Cases such as *Kraus* and *Asscher* indicate clearly that EU law on freedom of establishment is not only about the elimination of unequal treatment of non-nationals or the elimination of protectionism, but also entails a robust attempt to liberalize the 'single market' such that, whatever their nationality, self-employed individuals and companies can set up business in various locations within that market without encountering unnecessary obstacles.

---

court where, eg, national law was being extended to provide the same benefit to nationals as non-national EU persons would enjoy under EU law: see Cases C–448/98 *Guimont* [2000] ECR I–10663; C–393/08 *Sbarigia* [2010] ECR I–6337, [23]; C–84/11 *Susisalo* EU:C:2012:374, [20].

[98] Case C–212/06 *Government of the French Community and Walloon Government v Flemish Government* [2008] ECR I–1683.

[99] Ibid [48].

[100] Ibid [37]–[38].

[101] Case C–112/91 *Werner v Finanzamt Aachen-Innenstadt* [1993] ECR I–429.

[102] Case C–107/94 *Asscher* (n 18).

[103] See also Cases C–80/94 *Wielockx* [1995] ECR I–2493; C–279/93 *Finanzamt Köln-Altstadt v Schumacker* [1995] ECR I–225; C–324/00 *Lankhorst-Hohorst GmbH v Finanzamt Steinfurt* [2002] ECR I–11779; C–383/05 *Talotta v Belgium* [2007] ECR I–2555; C–470/04 *N v Inspecteur van de Belastingdienst Oost/kantoor Almelo* [2006] ECR I–7409. In the context of services see Cases C–484/93 *Svensson and Gustavsson* (n 86); C–294/97 *Eurowings Luftverkehrs AG v Finanzamt Dortmund-Unna* [1999] ECR I–7447, and see the series of cases on corporate taxation at (nn 135–139).

(c) ESTABLISHMENT OF COMPANIES

Article 54 TFEU provides:

> Companies or firms formed in accordance with the law of a Member State and having their registered office, central administration or principal place of business within the Union shall, for the purposes of this Chapter, be treated in the same way as natural persons who are nationals of Member States.
>
> 'Companies or firms' means companies or firms constituted under civil or commercial law, including cooperative societies, and other legal persons governed by public or private law, save for those which are non-profit making.

Although this Article requires companies to be treated in the same way as nationals for the purposes of the Treaty provisions on freedom of establishment, this is not strictly possible, given the differences between natural and legal persons. Further, despite the many company law directives which have been adopted, considerable differences in the way the various Member States regulate companies and their activities remain.

The definition of a company in Article 54 is wide, referring to 'legal persons governed by private or public law'. However, it excludes non-profit-making companies even though non-profit-making economic activities may be covered by Article 49.[104] The exclusion of non-profit-making companies can be compared with the exclusion from the scope of the Treaty of workers who are not remunerated and services which are not provided for remuneration, although it has been subject to criticism.[105]

(i) *When is a Company 'Established' in a Member State?*

It is clear that, so long as a company is formed in accordance with the law of a Member State and has its registered office there and its principal place of business *somewhere* in the EU, it will be established in the first Member State within the meaning of the Treaty. The ECJ made it clear in *Segers* that this would hold true even if the company conducted no business of any kind in that Member State, but instead conducted its business through one of the various forms of secondary establishment, such as a subsidiary, branch, or agency, in another Member State.[106]

This was affirmed in *Centros*, where the ECJ ruled that a company was lawfully established in the UK even though it had never traded there.[107] Further, in the *Insurance Services* case, the Court held that even an office managed for a company by an independent person on a permanent basis would amount to establishment in that Member State.[108] This form of establishment would amount to a secondary establishment, since the registered office or seat of the company and its principal place of business would presumably be elsewhere in the EU. A company has a right of secondary establishment only if it already has its principal place of business or central or registered office within the EU.[109]

---

[104] Case C–70/95 *Sodemare* (n 22). However, the fact that a company is non-profit-making does not mean that it is not engaged in economic activity: see Case C–382/92 *Commission v UK* [1994] ECR I–2435, [45], and see below the cases on cross-border access to health care in the context of services (nn 179–189).

[105] For criticism of the exclusion of non-profit entities, see S Lombardo, 'Some Reflections on Freedom of Establishment of Non-Profit Entities in the European Union' (2013) 14 European Business Organization Law Review 225.

[106] Case 79/85 *Segers* (n 62) [16].

[107] Case C–212/97 *Centros* (n 27).

[108] Case 205/84 (n 20) [21]. Compare Case C–386/04 *Centro di Musicologia Walter Stauffer v Finanzamt München für Körperschaften* [2006] ECR I–8203, [18]–[20].

[109] For interesting cases involving elements of establishment in third countries, but which nonetheless fell within the scope of EU law on freedom of establishment, see Case C–48/11 *A* EU:C:2012:485 and C–80/12 *Felixstowe Dock and Railway Company* EU:C:2014:200, [37]–[41].

(ii) *Court-Led Liberalization in the Absence of EU Harmonization*

While companies are not covered by Directive 2004/38 on citizens (nor by its predecessor Directive 73/148), governing the right of natural persons to leave their Member State, the ECJ ruled in the *Daily Mail* case that companies enjoy similar rights under the Treaty.[110] However, the *Daily Mail* judgment also declared that the Treaty provisions on freedom of establishment did not give companies an unfettered right to move their registered offices or their central management and control to another Member State, whilst retaining an establishment in the first Member State. On the contrary, the Court ruled that the Member State from which the company wishes to move its registered office or central place of administration is entitled to subject the company to certain conditions. In this particular case, the UK could legitimately require a company which wished to transfer its central management and control to the Netherlands to first settle its taxes and even to wind up the company in the UK. The reason given by the Court for this was that the laws of the Member States on what constitutes the place of incorporation or the 'real seat' of the company are not harmonized, and that different Member States may legitimately have different views and different ways of regulating how a transfer of head office may be effected.[111]

The general question underlying *Daily Mail*, ie to what extent a company can rely on Article 49 TFEU when it seeks to set up various forms of establishment in more than one Member State which have different systems of corporate regulation, given the continued absence of EU harmonization, was revisited just over ten years later in *Centros*. This time the restriction was imposed not by the state in which the company had its primary establishment (which was again the UK), but by the state in which the company sought to conduct business through a secondary establishment, which in this case was Denmark.

Case C–212/97 **Centros Ltd v Erhvervs- og Selskabsstyrelsen**
[1999] ECR I–1459

[Note Lisbon Treaty renumbering: Arts 52, 54, and 58 EEC are now Arts 49, 50, and 54 TFEU]

The facts concerned a company which was registered (and therefore had its primary establishment) in the UK, but which had never traded there. It had chosen the UK in which to register because UK law imposed no requirements on limited liability companies as to the provision for, or the paying-up of, a minimum share capital. The main purpose of establishing in the UK was to conduct business in Denmark, the minimum capital requirement laws of which were considerably stricter, through a branch. The Danish Board of Trade and Companies refused to register the branch on the ground that Centros was not in fact seeking to establish a branch in Denmark, but rather a principal establishment, while circumventing legitimate national rules including those on the paying-up of minimum capital. The Danish Government argued that Centros was seeking to abuse EU rights of establishment; and that following the reasoning in *Daily Mail*, the absence of harmonization of national corporate laws would prevent Centros from relying on Article 49 TFEU.

---

[110] Case 81/87 *R v HM Treasury and Commissioners of Inland Revenue, ex p Daily Mail and General Trust PLC* [1988] ECR 5483.

[111] Art 293 EC (ex Art 220 EEC) had originally recognized the need for the adoption of agreements for the mutual recognition of companies and the retention of legal personality in the event of transfer of their seat from one country to another, but the Convention on the Mutual Recognition of Companies, which was adopted pursuant to this Art in 1968, did not come into force: J Wouters, 'European Company Law: *Quo Vadis?*' (2000) 37 CMLRev 257.

THE ECJ

21. Where it is the practice of a Member State, in certain circumstances, to refuse to register a branch of a company having its registered office in another Member State, the result is that companies formed in accordance with the law of that other Member State are prevented from exercising the freedom of establishment conferred on them by Articles 52 and 58 of the [EEC] Treaty.

22. Consequently, that practice constitutes an obstacle to the exercise of the freedoms guaranteed by those provisions.

. . .

24. It is true that according to the case-law of the Court a Member State is entitled to take measures designed to prevent certain of its nationals from attempting, under cover of the rights created by the Treaty, improperly to circumvent their national legislation or to prevent individuals from improperly or fraudulently taking advantage of provisions of Community law....

26. In the present case, the provisions of national law, application of which the parties concerned have sought to avoid, are rules governing the formation of companies and not rules concerning the carrying on of certain trades, professions or businesses. The provisions of the Treaty on freedom of establishment are intended specifically to enable companies formed in accordance with the law of a Member State and having their registered office, central administration or principal place of business within the Community to pursue activities in other Member States through an agency, branch or subsidiary.

27. That being so, the fact that a national of a Member State who wishes to set up a company chooses to form it in the Member State whose rules of company law seem to him the least restrictive and to set up branches in other Member States cannot, in itself, constitute an abuse of the right of establishment. The right to form a company in accordance with the law of a Member State and to set up branches in other Member States is inherent in the exercise, in a single market, of the freedom of establishment guaranteed by the Treaty.

28. In this connection, the fact that company law is not completely harmonised in the Community is of little consequence. Moreover, it is always open to the Council, on the basis of the powers conferred upon it by Article 54(3)(g) of the EC Treaty, to achieve complete harmonisation.

29. In addition, it is clear from paragraph 16 of *Segers* that the fact that a company does not conduct any business in the Member State in which it has its registered office and pursues its activities only in the Member State where its branch is established is not sufficient to prove the existence of abuse or fraudulent conduct which would entitle the latter Member State to deny that company the benefit of the provisions of Community law relating to the right of establishment.

While the principles of law expressed in *Centros* were familiar principles long articulated by the ECJ in the context of freedom of establishment, their application to this factual situation and with this outcome caused considerable surprise, in particular amongst company lawyers, and generated extensive commentary. The fact that the particular manoeuvre engaged in by the company to choose its preferred regulatory environment within the EU internal market (the UK), while conducting all of its business in a different geographic part of the market (Denmark), was not caught by the 'avoidance' or 'abuse' exception was unexpected.[112]

The ECJ ruled that, far from constituting an *abuse* of Article 49, the deliberate choice of a Member State with lenient legislative requirements concerning incorporation in order to enjoy the right of secondary establishment more freely in a Member State with stricter incorporation requirements was

---

[112] For discussion of some of the subsequent, though piecemeal, legislative responses of the EU to the fears of the Member States of abuse of 'letterbox' or brass plate companies, see K E Sørensen 'The Fight Against Letterbox Companies in the Internal Market' (2015) 52 CMLRev 85.

simply an exercise of the rights inherent in the notion of freedom of establishment.[113] Further, the absence of legislative harmonization, which the ECJ in *Daily Mail* had given as a reason for the inapplicability of Article 49 to the case, was deemed irrelevant in *Centros*, and even gave the Court occasion to point out the availability to Member States of the option of adopting EU harmonizing legislation in this area of company law.[114] The Court took the view that there were other options, including under existing EU corporate account and disclosure legislation, available to Member States seeking to protect creditors, to counter fraud, or to prevent unjustified corporate evasion of *legitimate* regulatory requirements, which would be less restrictive than imposing the full range of its company law requirements on a branch the primary establishment of which was lawfully in another Member State.

The case has been described as 'opening the door to competition among national rules as an alternative approach to ensure the completion of the internal market',[115] while others noted that it left the ruling in *Daily Mail* for the moment untouched.[116]

Centros was followed by the *Überseering*[117] and *Inspire Art*[118] rulings which confirmed and extended the *Centros* approach. Überseering was a company incorporated in the Netherlands under Dutch law, where it had its registered office. It then sought to transfer its centre of administration to Germany, and its entire share capital was bought by German shareholders. Unlike the position of the UK in the *Daily Mail* case, the Netherlands did not seek to prevent the company from transferring its administration, or to deny the validity of its continued incorporation under Dutch law. German law, however, would not recognize the legal capacity of a company incorporated in the Netherlands, thus prohibiting it from appearing before the German courts. German law followed the 'company seat principle' rather than the 'incorporation principle' as the relevant factor of connection for a company, and since Überseering had moved its real seat from the Netherlands to Germany, German law would not recognize the company's legal capacity unless it re-incorporated again under German law.

Although the ECJ distinguished *Daily Mail* (where the restriction was imposed by the Member State of incorporation, the UK) on its facts, the reasoning in *Überseering* clearly moves away from the underlying broad rationale in *Daily Mail*. *Überseering* established that, despite the lack of harmonization of the laws governing the connecting factor for incorporation, a company which is legitimately incorporated in one Member State and which moves its centre of administration to another state cannot in those circumstances be denied recognition of its legal personality by the latter. Although objectives such as enhancing legal certainty, protecting creditors and minority investors, and legitimate fiscal requirements could in principle justify rules restricting the freedom of establishment, the German rule in *Überseering* amounted to an outright denial of freedom of establishment and was disproportionate.

The case of *Inspire Art* addressed the question whether a restriction on a company's secondary establishment which is less drastic than an outright denial of the right of establishment might be compatible with Article 49.[119] Dutch legislation sought to impose regulatory requirements concerning minimum

---

[113] For discussion of the ECJ's similar approach to allegations of abuse in the context of the rights of citizenship, and the rights of free movement of workers, see Ch 21 and Ch 23.

[114] For a similar dismissal of the relevance, for the freedom of establishment of companies, of the fact that EU law in the field of cross-border mergers had not been harmonized see Case C–411/03 *Sevic Systems* [2005] ECR I–10805, [26]; P Behrens, Note (2006) 43 CMLRev 1669.

[115] P Cabral and P Cunha, '"Presumed Innocent": Companies and the Exercise of the Right of Establishment under Community Law' (2000) 25 ELRev 157; W-H Roth, Note (2000) 37 CMLRev 147; S Deakin, 'Two Types of Regulatory Competition: Competitive Federalism versus Reflexive Harmonisation. A Law and Economics Perspective on *Centros*' (1999) 2 CYELS 231; A Johnston, 'EC Freedom of Establishment, Employee Participation in Corporate Governance and the Limits of Regulatory Competition' (2006) 6 Journal of Corporate Law Studies 71.

[116] Roth (n 115) 153–155.

[117] Case C–208/00 *Überseering v NCC* [2002] ECR I–9919.

[118] Case C–167/01 *Kamer van Koophandel en Fabrieken voor Amsterdam v Inspire Art Ltd* [2003] ECR I–10155.

[119] Ibid.

share capital and directors' liability on a company which was incorporated in the UK. Once again, while the ECJ accepted that restrictive regulations could in principle be justified in the interests of protecting creditors and investors, or ensuring an effective tax inspection system, the rules at issue were found disproportionate and unnecessary.

While these rulings did not explicitly overturn *Daily Mail*, they seemed to limit its impact and scope significantly.[120] Consequently, the 2008 ruling in *Cartesio* came as something of a surprise.[121] Cartesio, a company formed under Hungarian law, wished to transfer its seat to Italy. However, Hungarian law did not allow a company incorporated in Hungary to transfer its seat abroad while continuing to be subject to Hungarian law. The national court considered that while *Daily Mail* seemed to indicate that Articles 49 and 54 TFEU do not include the right for a company to transfer its central administration to another Member State while retaining its legal personality and nationality of origin, later case law rendered the situation unclear. Contrary to the argument of Advocate General Maduro who saw the Hungarian legislation as an unjustified negation of the freedom of establishment, the ECJ ruled that companies were creatures of national law which existed only by virtue of the national legislation which determined their incorporation and functioning:

Case C–210/06 **Cartesio Oktató és Szolgáltató bt**
[2008] ECR I–9641

[Note Lisbon Treaty renumbering: Arts 43 and 48 EC are now Arts 49 and 54 TFEU]

109. Consequently, in accordance with Article 48 EC, in the absence of a uniform Community law definition of the companies which may enjoy the right of establishment on the basis of a single connecting factor determining the national law applicable to a company, the question whether Article 43 EC applies to a company which seeks to rely on the fundamental freedom enshrined in that article—like the question whether a natural person is a national of a Member State, hence entitled to enjoy that freedom—is a preliminary matter which, as Community law now stands, can only be resolved by the applicable national law. In consequence, the question whether the company is faced with a restriction on the freedom of establishment, within the meaning of Article 43 EC, can arise only if it has been established, in the light of the conditions laid down in Article 48 EC, that the company actually has a right to that freedom.

110. Thus a Member State has the power to define both the connecting factor required of a company if it is to be regarded as incorporated under the law of that Member State and, as such, capable of enjoying the right of establishment, and that is required if the company is to be able subsequently to maintain that status. That power includes the possibility for that Member State not to permit a company governed by its law to retain that status if the company intends to reorganise itself in another Member State by moving its seat to the territory of the latter, thereby breaking the connecting factor required under the national law of the Member State of incorporation.

Cartesio's confirmation of the premise of the *Daily Mail* ruling was unexpected after the series of robust rulings, from *Centros* to *Inspire Art*, which had introduced a mutual recognition principle into

---

[120] M Gelter, '*Centros*, the Freedom of Establishment for Companies, and the Court's Accidental Vision for Corporate Law', Fordham University European Corporate Governance Institute Law Working Paper No 287/2015.

[121] Case C–210/06 *Cartesio Oktató és Szolgáltató bt* [2008] ECR I–9641; M Szydło, Note (2009) 46 CMLRev 703; O Valk, Note (2010) 6 Utrecht LRev 151; G Vossestein, 'Cross-Border Transfer of Seat and Conversion of Companies under the EC Treaty Provisions on Freedom of Establishment' (2009) 6 European Company Law 115; L Burian, 'Personal Law of Companies and Freedom of Establishment' (2008) 61 RHDI 71.

the law on freedom of establishment. While those cases insist that a Member State must recognize the legitimacy of a company's incorporation (and primary establishment) under the law of another Member State and should not impose unnecessary restrictions on the right of secondary establishment, *Cartesio* on the other hand affirmed that the basic rules on what is necessary for incorporation in the first place remain, in the absence of EU harmonization, for the Member State of incorporation to decide.[122]

It seems that these cases do not, however, signal a major retreat by the Court from its insistence on the gradual liberalization of corporate mobility in the absence of EU harmonization. The cases of *Vale* and *National Grid Indus*, following shortly after *Cartesio*, have been less deferential to the Member States, despite using the same language of national regulatory competence in matters of corporate law.

National Grid Indus concerned the compatibility of a Dutch exit tax on the transfer of the seat of a company from the Netherlands to the UK.[123] The company was not prevented from retaining its status as a Dutch company even while transferring its seat, but was subjected to an immediate unrealized capital gains exit tax by the Netherlands. The CJEU ruled that the company could rely on its freedom of establishment in challenging the tax, and that while the tax could in principle be justified by the objective of ensuring the balanced allocation of powers of taxation between the Member States, its imposition was not justified here because of the requirement that it be collected at the very time of the transfer.

The second case was *Vale*, in which a company established under Italian law sought to transfer its registered office to Hungary, so that it would cease to be incorporated under Italian law and become incorporated under Hungarian law.[124] Italy did not seek to prevent the cross-border conversion (ie conversion from the Italian predecessor company to a newly registered Hungarian company), but Hungary refused to register the company or permit the conversion, even though a Hungarian company would have been permitted to do so. The CJEU ruled that while the host state was fully entitled to determine and apply its own law on the incorporation and conversion of companies, Articles 49 and 54 TFEU required it treat domestic conversions and cross-border conversions in an equivalent way, and to take due account of the relevant documents from the Member State of origin.

In all, however, despite the apparently dramatic departure from deference to Member States in the field of corporate establishment (as reflected in the earlier *Daily Mail* ruling) which was signalled by the ECJ in the *Centros* case, it has been suggested that 'the impact of *Centros* has been relatively small' and that 'full-scale regulatory competition has not arrived in Europe'.[125] Instead, it seems that the CJEU's rulings, lacking any deep understanding of business law policies, have brought about other corporate law changes in Europe that were neither intended by the Court nor by policy-makers, as states moved to eliminate the kinds of minimum capital and other requirements which drove their companies to establish in other states.

It remains to be seen whether the establishment (after many decades of efforts) of a European corporate form, the *Societas Europaea* or statute for a European company,[126] will become a more

---

[122] For discussion as to whether companies post-*Cartesio* enjoy the right of establishment by means of an isolated cross-border conversion without moving the real seat of the company, see O Mörsdorf, 'The Legal Mobility of Companies Within the European Union Through Cross-Border Conversion' (2012) 49 CMLRev 629.

[123] Case C–371/10 *National Grid Indus* EU:C:2011:785. For commentaries, see T Biermeyer, F Elsener, and F Timba, 'The Compatibility of Corporate Exit Taxation with European Law' (2012) 9 ECFR 101; K Pantazatou, *National Grid Indus*: the First Case on Companies' Exit Taxation' (2012) 23 EBLR 945; S Peeters, 'Exit Taxation on Capital Gains in the European Union: A Necessary Consequence of Corporate Relocations?' (2013) 10 ECFR 507.

[124] Case C–378/10 *VALE Építési* EU:C:2012:440. For some commentaries, see T Biermeyer, 'Shaping the Space of Cross-Border Conversions in the EU. Between Right and Autonomy' (2013) 50 CMLRev 571; M Krarup, '*Vale*: Determining the Need for Amended Regulation Regarding Free Movement of Companies within the EU' (2013) 24 EBLR 691; J L Hansen 'The *Vale* Decision and the Court's Case Law on the Nationality of Companies' (2013) 10 ECFR 1.

[125] M Gelter, '*Centros*, the Freedom of Establishment for Companies, and the Court's Accidental Vision for Corporate Law', Fordham University European Corporate Governance Institute, Law Working Paper 287/2015.

[126] See Reg 2157/2001 and Dir 2001/86 on the Statute for a European Company. On the background, see V Edwards, 'The European Company—Essential Tool or Eviscerated Dream?' (2003) 40 CMLRev 443. Also more recently the Commission's

popular alternative to facilitate European corporate mobility given the ongoing difficulty of harmonizing national corporate laws.

(iii) *Restrictions on the Freedom of Establishment of Companies: Direct Taxation Rules*

Many of the cases before the ECJ have concerned restrictions or disadvantages imposed by Member States on companies, or on the employees of companies,[127] the registered offices of which were in another Member State. Other cases however have involved restrictions, particularly tax restrictions, imposed by states on companies the registered offices of which are within that state, but which have subsidiaries or branches in other Member States. The compatibility with EU law of tax rules which distinguish between resident and non-resident companies and subsidiaries has generated a vast and complex case law.[128]

In *Commission v France*, the Court drew an analogy between the location of the registered office of a company and the place of residence of a natural person.[129] According to the Court 'it is their corporate seat…that serves as the connecting factor with the legal system of a Member State, like nationality in the case of natural persons'.[130] It ruled that discrimination in tax laws against branches or agencies in a Member State by taxing them on the same basis as companies the registered offices of which are in that state yet not giving them the same tax advantages as such companies was an infringement of Article 49. Neither the lack of harmonization of the tax laws of the different Member States nor the risk of tax avoidance by companies could justify the restriction.[131]

Nevertheless, the ECJ has accepted that a distinction based on the location of the registered office of a company or the place of residence of a natural person may, under certain conditions, be justified in an area such as tax law.[132] In *Futura*, a Member State could impose conditions as regards the keeping of accounts and the location where losses were incurred on a non-resident company, which had a branch but not a main establishment in the state, for the purposes of assessing liability to tax and allowable losses.[133] However, the restrictions imposed by Luxembourg in *Futura* were closely scrutinized for

---

Proposal for a Directive on single-member private limited liability companies (*Societas Unius Personae*), COM(2014) 212, to facilitate cross-border establishment. I Wuisman, 'The *Societas Unius Personae*' (2015) 12 European Company Law 34; H Koster, 'EU Legal Entities: New Options?' (2015) 12 European Company Law 5.

[127] Case 79/85 *Segers* (n 62).

[128] For some overviews, see W Haslehner, '"Consistency" and Fundamental Freedoms: The Case of Direct Taxation' (2013) 50 CMLRev 737; L Cerioni, 'The "Place of Effective Management" as a Connecting Factor For Companies' Tax Residence Within the EU vs. the Freedom of Establishment: The Need for a Rethinking?' (2012) 13 German LJ 1095; K Pantazatou, 'Economic and Political Considerations of the Court's Case Law Post Crisis: An Example from Tax Law and the Internal Market' (2013) 9 Croatian Yearbook of European Law and Policy 77.

[129] Case 270/83 *Commission v France* [1986] ECR 273, [18].

[130] Case C–330/91 *Commerzbank* [1993] ECR I–4017, [18]; Case C–264/96 *ICI v Colmer* [1998] ECR I–4695, [20]; Case C–307/97 *Compagnie de Saint-Gobain v Finanzamt Aachen-Innenstadt* [1999] ECR I–6161, [35]; Cases C–397 and 410/98 *Metallgesellschaft Ltd v Internal Revenue* [2001] ECR I–4727, [42].

[131] Case C–330/91 *R v Inland Revenue Commissioners, ex p Commerzbank AG* [1993] ECR I–4017; Case C–1/93 *Halliburton Services BV v Staatssecretaris van Financiën* [1994] ECR I–1137; Case C–253/03 *CLT-UFA SA v Finanzamt Köln-West* [2006] ECR I–1831; Case C–380/11 *DI. VI. Finanziaria di Diego della Valle & C* EU:C:2012:552.

[132] Case 270/83 *Commission v France* (n 129) [19]; Case C–279/93 *Schumacker* (n 103); Case C–80/94 *Wielockx* (n 103); Case C–107/94 *Asscher* (n 18); Case C–311/97 *Royal Bank of Scotland v Greece* [1999] ECR I–2651. Compare Case C–264/96 *ICI* (n 130); Case C–200/98 *X and Y v Riksskatteverket* [1999] ECR I–8261; Case C–9/02 *de Lasteyrie du Saillant* [2004] ECR I–2409.

[133] Case C–250/95 *Futura Participations SA Singer v Administration des Contributions* [1997] ECR I–2471. For indirect tax discrimination against companies having their principal place of business in other Member States see, eg, Case C–254/97 *Société Baxter v Premier Ministre* [1999] ECR I–4809; Case C–436/00 *X, Y v Riksskatteverket* [2002] ECR I–10829; Case C–334/02 *Commission v France* [2004] ECR I–2229.

proportionality, and the accounting requirement, even in the absence of harmonized EU rules in this area, was excessively restrictive. In *X Holding BV* the Court accepted that legislation preventing a parent company from forming a single tax entity with its subsidiaries in other Member States, while it could do so with resident subsidiaries, was justified by the need to safeguard the allocation of power to impose taxes between Member States.[134]

In recent years there has been a significant stream of important litigation, including the high-profile *Marks & Spencer*[135] and *Cadbury Schweppes*[136] cases and a series of other test cases,[137] to clarify the scope and applicability of Article 49 to a range of corporate taxation laws directed at cross-border situations—governing matters such as tax credits, deductibility of losses (group relief),[138] and taxation of dividends[139]—as applied to companies which are established in more than one Member State. The Court has ruled that while states may in appropriate circumstances treat resident companies differently from non-resident companies, and resident companies with non-resident subsidiaries differently from resident companies with resident subsidiaries, and foreign-sourced dividends differently from domestic-sourced dividends, as far as direct taxation rules are concerned, this is always subject to the requirement of demonstrating reasonable and proportionate justification.[140] Further, if a state treats companies established in another Member State in the same way as companies established in its own jurisdiction for the purposes of taxation of profits, it cannot treat them differently as far as deductibility of losses is concerned.[141] And while goals such as preventing tax avoidance, combating artificial arrangements or tax havens, or preventing companies from benefiting twice from rules governing tax relief are treated as legitimate objectives, the CJEU has continued to apply strict scrutiny to the national laws which claim to be necessitated by such objectives.[142]

(iv) *Restrictions on the Freedom of Establishment of Companies: Vessel Registration Requirements*

A second issue area which has generated a substantial body of case law on freedom of establishment is that dealing with vessel registration.[143] In *Commission v Ireland*, it was held contrary to Article 49 to

---

[134] Case C–337/08 *X Holding BV v Staatssecretaris van Financiën* [2010] ECR I–1215; Also Case C–231/05 *Oy AA* [2007] ECR I–6373.

[135] Case C–446/03 *Marks & Spencer v Halsey* [2005] ECR I–10837.

[136] Case C–196/04 *Cadbury Schweppes plc v Inland Revenue* [2006] ECR I–7995. For a critique of the 'wholly artificial arrangement' criterion introduced by the Court in *Cadbury Schwepppes* see P Tran, '*Cadbury Schweppes plc v Commissioners of Inland Revenue*: Eliminating Harmful Tax Practice or Encouraging Multinational to Shop Around the Bloc?' (2008) 30 Loyola LA Int'l & Comp L Rev 77; and for a critique of the UK legal response to the ruling see A Lyden-Horn, '*Cadbury Schweppes*: A Critical Look at the Future and Futility of UK Controlled Foreign Company Legislation' (2008) 11 Temple Int'l & Comp LJ 191

[137] Cases C–253/03 *CLT-UFA* (n 131); C–347/04 *Rewe-Zentralfinanz v Finanzamt Köln-Mitte* [2007] ECR I–2647; C–374/04 *Test Claimants in Class IV of the ACT Group Litigation v Inland Revenue* [2006] ECR I–11673; C–446/04 *Test Claimants in the FII Group Litigation* [2006] ECR I–11753; C–524/04 *Test Claimants in the Thin Cap Group Litigation v Inland Revenue* [2007] ECR I–2107; C–201/05 *The Test Claimants in the CFC and Dividend Group Litigation v Commissioners of Inland Revenue* [2008] ECR I–2875; C–362/12 *Test Claimants in the Franked Investment Income Group Litigation* EU:C:2013:834.

[138] Case C–18/11 *Philips Electronics UK* EU:C:2012:532.

[139] Cases C–310/09 *Accor* EU:C:2011:581; C–35/11 *Test Claimants in the FII Group Litigation* EU:C:2012:707.

[140] See, eg, Case C–123/11 *A* EU:C:2013:84 on the importance of the principle of equal treatment, as far as possible, of parent companies with resident subsidiaries and those with non-resident subsidiaries.

[141] Case C–48/13 *Nordea Bank Danmark* EU:C:2014:2087.

[142] For recent examples see Cases C–39, 40 and 41/13 *SCA Group Holding et al* EU:C:2014:1758; C–80/12 *Felixstowe Dock and Railway Company* EU:C:2014:200; C–350/11 *Argenta Spaarbank* EU:C:2013:447; C–678/11 *Commission v Spain* EU:C:2014:2434.

[143] Case C–246/89 *Commission v UK* [1991] ECR I–4585; Case C–334/94 *Commission v France* (n 62); Case C–151/96 *Commission v Ireland* (n 62); Case C–299/02 *Commission v Netherlands* [2004] ECR I–9761.

require nationals of other Member States who owned a vessel registered in Ireland to establish a company in Ireland.[144] In *Factortame*, the Court condemned several residency and nationality requirements for the registration of fishing vessels, but permitted a Member State to stipulate as a requirement for registration that a vessel must be managed and its operations directed and controlled from within that Member State.[145]

The most important and controversial ruling to date on this issue however is the *Viking* case, which was discussed above in the context of the 'horizontal' applicability of Article 49 to trade unions.[146]

Case C–438/05 International Transport Workers Federation and Finnish Seamen's Union v Viking Line ABP and OÜ Viking Line Eesti
[2007] ECR I–10779

[Note Lisbon Treaty renumbering: Arts 43 and 137 EC are now Arts 49 and 153 TFEU]

Viking was a company incorporated under Finnish law, which operated the *Rosella* vessel on the route between Tallinn (Estonia) and Helsinki (Finland). The *Rosella* was running at a loss due to competition from Estonian vessels operating on the same route with lower wage costs. Under the Finnish flag, Viking was obliged—under Finnish law and the terms of a collective bargaining agreement—to pay the crew wages at the same level as those applicable in Finland. Consequently, Viking planned to reflag the *Rosella* by registering it in Estonia. FSU, the Finnish union of seamen, together with the international federation of transport workers' unions (ITF), decided to take collective action against the adoption of such a 'flag of convenience' and requested affiliated unions to refrain from entering into negotiations with Viking. Viking argued that the action by FSU and ITF was contrary to its freedom of establishment. FSU and ITF, supported by the Danish and Swedish Governments, argued that the situation did not fall within the scope of the Treaty rules.

THE ECJ

36. [C]ollective action such as that at issue in the main proceedings, which may be the trade unions' last resort to ensure the success of their claim to regulate the work of Viking's employees collectively, must be considered to be inextricably linked to the collective agreement the conclusion of which FSU is seeking.

37. It follows that collective action... falls, in principle, within the scope of Article 43 EC.

. . .

40. In that respect it is sufficient to point out that, even if, in the areas which fall outside the scope of the Community's competence, the Member States are still free, in principle, to lay down the conditions governing the existence and exercise of the rights in question, the fact remains that, when exercising that competence, the Member States must nevertheless comply with Community law...

41. Consequently, the fact that Article 137 EC does not apply to the right to strike or to the right to impose lock-outs is not such as to exclude collective action such as that at issue in the main proceedings from the application of Article 43 EC.

. . .

---

[144] Case 93/89 *Commission v Ireland* [1991] ECR I–4569.
[145] Case C–221/89 *Factortame* (n 4).
[146] Case C–438/05 *Viking Line* (n 32); P Chaumette, 'Reflagging a Vessel in the European Market and Dealing with Transnational Collective Disputes: *ITF & Finnish Seamen's Union v Viking Line*' (2010) 15 Ocean & Coastal LJ 1.

44. Although the right to take collective action, including the right to strike, must therefore be recognised as a fundamental right which forms an integral part of the general principles of Community law the observance of which the Court ensures, the exercise of that right may none the less be subject to certain restrictions. As is reaffirmed by Article 28 of the Charter of Fundamental Rights of the European Union, those rights are to be protected in accordance with Community law and national law and practices. In addition, as is apparent from paragraph 5 of this judgment, under Finnish law the right to strike may not be relied on, in particular, where the strike is *contra bonos mores* or is prohibited under national law or Community law.

45. In that regard, the Court has already held that the protection of fundamental rights is a legitimate interest which, in principle, justifies a restriction of the obligations imposed by Community law, even under a fundamental freedom guaranteed by the Treaty, such as the free movement of goods (see Case C–112/00 *Schmidberger* [2003] ECR I–5659, paragraph 74) or freedom to provide services (see Case C–36/02 *Omega* [2004] ECR I–9609, paragraph 35).

46. However, in *Schmidberger* and *Omega*, the Court held that the exercise of the fundamental rights at issue, that is, freedom of expression and freedom of assembly and respect for human dignity, respectively, does not fall outside the scope of the provisions of the Treaty and considered that such exercise must be reconciled with the requirements relating to rights protected under the Treaty and in accordance with the principle of proportionality (see, to that effect, *Schmidberger*, paragraph 77, and *Omega*, paragraph 36).

47. It follows from the foregoing that the fundamental nature of the right to take collective action is not such as to render Article 43 EC inapplicable to the collective action at issue in the main proceedings.

The ECJ ruled ultimately that the collective action constituted a restriction on Viking's exercise of its right to freedom of establishment in Estonia by making it less attractive or pointless to re-flag there, and that it was for the national court to determine whether the collective action might be justified as a proportionate and necessary means of protecting the rights of workers. The case has been subject to extensive critical analysis.[147]

(D) SUMMARY

i. Article 49 may be invoked by a national in his or her Member State of establishment so long as there is an EU element present. This element often consists of the fact that the individual has obtained a qualification or professional training in another Member State, so long as the situation involves no attempted 'abuse' of EU rights. However, the notion of abuse or evasion of legitimate control, following cases such as *Koller* concerning individuals, and *Centros* and *Cadbury Schweppes* concerning companies, remains underspecified.

ii. The case of *Viking* (and *Laval* for services) controversially extended the horizontal application of the Treaty provisions on establishment to the activities of trade unions, even though they are not public regulatory actors and do not possess quasi-legislative powers, and even where they are acting pursuant to their fundamental right to strike, to impose lock-outs, or other forms of collective action.

---

[147] The EU's EUR-Lex website shows that 92 case notes or commentaries have been published at the time of writing. For more recent overviews and analyses, see C Barnard, 'Free Movement and Labour Rights: Squaring the Circle?', University of Cambridge Legal Studies Research Paper No 23/2013; D Ashiagbor, 'Unravelling the Embedded Liberal Bargain: Labour and Social Welfare Law in the Context of EU Market Integration' (2013) 19 ELJ 303.

iii. Despite the importance of non-discrimination in the field of establishment, the CJEU adopts broadly the same approach to freedom of establishment as it does in other areas of free movement. In other words, any hindrance or measure which renders less attractive the right of establishment in a Member State and any restriction on 'access to the market' for persons seeking to establish themselves, whether or not it has a differential impact on nationals and non-nationals, is caught by the prohibition in Article 49 unless it can be justified.

iv. The law governing establishment of companies is more complex than that governing natural persons, mainly due to the differences between national company laws. Rather than await legislative harmonization at EU level, the CJEU has required host states to permit companies validly incorporated in another state, even under a very different corporate law regime, to exercise rights of secondary establishment in a host state without imposing undue regulatory restrictions. While the cases of *Daily Mail* and *Cartesio* concerning corporate exit from a state indicate that the Member State of incorporation of a company (home state) retains the right to set the basic conditions for acquisition and maintenance of the status as an incorporated entity, a series of other cases including most recently *Vale* and *National Grid Indus* indicate that the Court will carefully scrutinize the justification for a range of other restrictions imposed by states on the cross-border freedom of establishment of companies.

v. Tax restrictions on companies established in more than one Member State, which seek to combine the advantages and minimize the disadvantages of different tax regimes within the different states in which they are established, have been regularly and successfully challenged in recent years.

4 FREE MOVEMENT OF SERVICES

We have seen that the right of establishment entails the pursuit of an economic activity from a fixed base in a Member State for an indefinite period. Freedom to provide services under Article 56 TFEU, on the other hand, entails the carrying out of an economic activity for a temporary period in a Member State in which either the provider or the recipient of the service is not established.

According to the *Insurance Services* case, if a person or an undertaking maintains a *permanent* economic base in a Member State, even if only through an office, it cannot avail itself of the right to provide services in that state but will be governed by the law on freedom of establishment.[148] In *Gebhard*, however, we saw that the ECJ acknowledged that the provision of services did not necessarily cease to be *temporary* simply because the provider might need to equip herself with the necessary infrastructure, for example an office or chambers, to perform those services.[149] The relevant criterion is not the mere existence of an office in a Member State, but rather the temporary vs permanent nature of the economic activities carried on there.

This may prove difficult to establish, especially when certain services, such as the construction of large buildings, take a long time. The Court has held that the fact that services are provided over an extended period, even over several years, does not mean that Article 56 is inapplicable.[150] In *Commission v Portugal* the Court held that the imposition of authorization rules concerning construction activity in Portugal were incompatible with Article 56, since those rules imposed the same requirements on

---

[148] Case 205/84 (n 20) [21]. The earlier decision in Case 39/75 *Coenen v Sociaal-Economische Raad* [1975] ECR 1547 was somewhat contradictory on this point.

[149] Case C–55/94 *Gebhard* (n 21) [27].

[150] Case C–215/01 *Schnitzer* (n 23) [30]. For discussion, see Hatzopoulos (n 7).

the provision of temporary services as were imposed on the establishment of providers of building services.[151] According to the Court, the fact that the provision of construction services generally takes some time and that it may prove difficult to distinguish from the situation in which the provider is actually established in the host Member State does not have the effect of precluding those services from the scope of Article 56 TFEU.

The Court has also ruled that people who direct most or all of their services at the territory of a particular Member State, but maintain their place of establishment outside that state in order to evade its professional rules (the abuse/evasion theory), may in certain circumstances be treated as being established within the Member State, and thus covered not by Article 56 on services but by Article 49 on establishment instead.[152] In such a case the professional rules which were being evaded by the maintenance of an establishment in a different Member State could be applied as though the person were established in the regulating state. Cases in which such an evasion or abuse has been found seem relatively rare, and the onus is firmly on the state to show that a person was seeking to evade legitimate requirements rather than simply exercising their Treaty freedoms.[153]

Article 56 TFEU

Within the framework of the provisions set out below, restrictions on freedom to provide services within the Union shall be prohibited in respect of nationals of Member States who are established in a Member State other than that of the person for whom the services are intended.

The European Parliament and the Council, acting in accordance with the ordinary legislative procedure, may extend the provisions of the Chapter to nationals of a third country who provide services and who are established within the Union.

Article 56 indicates that in order to benefit from the right to provide services, the person in question, natural or legal, must already have a place of establishment within the EU and, if a natural person, must possess the nationality of a Member State.[154] The General Programme on freedom to provide services specified in more detail that the right to provide services was available only to nationals established in the EU, or to companies formed under the laws of a Member State and having their seat, centre of administration, or main establishment within the EU.[155] If only the seat of a company is situated within the EU, then its activity must have a 'real and continuous link' with the economy of a Member State, other than a link of nationality.

Without that economic foothold within the EU, there is no right under EU law for a company or an EU national established *outside* the EU to provide temporary services *within* the EU.[156] A permanent economic base must first be established within a Member State, and from that base the person may provide temporary services in other Member States.

---

[151] Case C–458/08 *Commission v Portugal* [2010] ECR I–11599.

[152] Case 33/74 *Van Binsbergen* (n 16) [13]; Case 205/84 *Commission v Germany* (n 20) [22]. For an example of a justified state restriction to prevent an evasion of domestic rules where a provider of broadcasting services was established outside the Netherlands yet was directing its services at the Netherlands, see Case C–148/91 *Vereniging Veronica Omroep Organisatie v Commissariaat voor de Media* [1993] ECR I–487 and Case C–23/93 *TV10 SA v Commissariaat voor de Media* [1994] ECR I–4795. Contrast Cases C–369 and 376/96 *Arblade* (n 74) [32].

[153] Case C–212/97 *Centros* (n 27) [29]; AG's Opinion in Case C–55/94 *Gebhard* (n 21) [84].

[154] Case C–290/04 *FKP Scorpio Konzertproduktionen GmbH v Finanzamt Hamburg-Eimsbüttel* [2006] ECR I–9461.

[155] The 1961 General Programme (n 49).

[156] Case C–452/04 *Fidium Finanz v Bundesanstalt für Finanzdienstleistungsaufsicht* [2006] ECR I–9521.

Article 57 TFEU

Services shall be considered to be 'services' within the meaning of the Treaties where they are normally provided for remuneration, in so far as they are not governed by the provisions relating to freedom of movement for goods, capital and persons.[157]

'Services' shall in particular include

(a) activities of an industrial character;

(b) activities of a commercial character;

(c) activities of craftsmen;

(d) activities of the professions.

Without prejudice to the provisions of the Chapter relating to the right of establishment, the person providing a service may, in order to do so, temporarily pursue his activity in the Member State where the service is provided, under the same conditions as are imposed by that State on its own nationals.

Article 58 excludes transport services from the chapter on services since transport is dealt with elsewhere in the Treaty,[158] and provides that banking and insurance services connected with capital movements are to be dealt with in line with the Treaty provisions on movement of capital.[159]

As in the chapter on establishment, Article 59 provided for a General Programme to be drawn up, and for directives to be issued by the Council so as to liberalize specific services. The General Programme which was drawn up was similar in many respects to that adopted on establishment, with an emphasis on the abolition of discrimination.

(A) THE EFFECT OF ARTICLE 56 TFEU

The chapter on the free movement of services is very similar to that on establishment, except that the activity in question is pursued on a temporary rather than a permanent basis in a Member State. Shortly after the *Reyners* ruling first established that Article 49 was directly effective, the *Van Binsbergen* case on the direct effect of Article 56 came before the Court.[160] The UK and Irish Governments intervened to argue that, despite the European Court's ruling in *Reyners*, the area of provision of services was subject to even greater problems of control and discipline than that of establishment, that Articles 56 and 57 should not be found to have direct effect, and that the only satisfactory solution was the adoption of directives as provided for by the Treaty.

Case 33/74 **Van Binsbergen v Bestuur van de Bedrijfsvereniging voor de Metaalnijverheid**
[1974] ECR 1299

[Note Lisbon Treaty renumbering: Arts 59, 60, 63, and 66 EC are now Arts 56, 57, 59, and 62 TFEU]

A Dutch national acting as legal adviser to Van Binsbergen in respect of proceedings before a Dutch social security court transferred his place of residence from the Netherlands to Belgium during the course of the proceedings. He was told that he could no longer represent his client since, under Dutch law, only

---

[157] See (nn 7–11) for discussion.
[158] Arts 90–100 TFEU.
[159] Ch 20.
[160] Case 33/74 (n 16).

those established in the Netherlands could act as legal advisers. A reference was made to the ECJ to determine whether Article 56 TFEU (ex Article 59 EC) had direct effect, and whether the Dutch rule was compatible with it.

THE ECJ

20. With a view to the progressive abolition during the transitional period of the restrictions referred to in Article 59, Article 63 has provided for the drawing up of a 'general programme'—laid down by Council Decision of 18 December 1961—to be implemented by a series of directives.

21. Within the scheme of the chapter relating to the provision of services, these directives are intended to accomplish different functions, the first being to abolish, during the transitional period, restrictions on freedom to provide services, the second being to introduce into the law of Member States a set of provisions intended to facilitate the effective exercise of this freedom, in particular by the mutual recognition of qualifications and the coordination of laws with regard to the pursuit of activities as self-employed persons.

22. These directives also have the task of resolving the specific problems resulting from the fact that where the person providing the service is not established, on a habitual basis, in the State where the service is performed he may not be fully subject to the professional rules of conduct in force in that State.

...

24. The provisions of Article 59, the application of which was to be prepared by directives issued during the transitional period, therefore became unconditional on the expiry of that period.

25. The provisions of that article abolish all discrimination against the person providing the service by reason of his nationality or the fact that he is established in a Member State other than that in which the service is to be provided.

26. Therefore, at least as regards the specific requirement of nationality or of residence, Articles 59 and 60 impose a well-defined obligation, the fulfilment of which by the Member States cannot be delayed or jeopardized by the absence of provisions which were to be adopted in pursuance of powers conferred under Articles 63 and 66.

The Court here identified two reasons for the Treaty provisions on the adoption of directives: first, to abolish restrictions and, secondly, to facilitate the freedom to provide services. With regard to the first, where the restriction was a straightforward restriction on the ground of nationality or place of establishment, the Court considered that no directive was necessary and the provisions of Article 56 could be relied on directly. A residence requirement was a particularly straightforward infringement, given that the aim of Article 56 was to abolish state restrictions on the freedom to provide services which were imposed on non-resident providers. More generally, restrictions imposed on the basis of residence are seen as being liable to operate mainly to the detriment of nationals of other Member States, since non-residents are in the majority of cases foreigners.[161]

Notably, the lawyer in *Van Binsbergen* was a national relying on Article 56 in his own Member State. This did not pose any problem because the relevant factor for the application of Article 56 is simply that the provider must be established in a Member State other than that of the person for whom the service is to be provided. The provider may rely on Article 56 as against the state in which he or she is established, so long as the services are provided for persons established in another Member State.[162]

---

[161] Cases C–350/96 *Clean Car Autoservice v Landeshauptmann von Wien* [1998] ECR I–2521; C–224/97 *Ciola v Land Vorarlberg* [1999] ECR I–2517; C–509/12 *Instituto Portuário e dos Transportes Marítimos* EU:C:2012:54.

[162] Cases C–18/93 *Corsica Ferries* [1994] ECR I–1783, [30]; C–379/92 *Peralta* [1994] ECR I–3453, [40]. For a 'purely internal situation' in the services context see Case C–108/98 *RI.SAN v Comune di Ischia* [1999] ECR I–5219.

(B) THE SCOPE OF ARTICLE 56

(i) *The Need for an Inter-State Element*

As with the other freedoms, the Treaty chapter on services does not apply to 'wholly internal situations' where the relevant elements of an activity are confined within a single Member State.[163]

In *Koestler*, which concerned a bank in France carrying out certain stock-exchange orders and account transactions for a customer established in France, the European Court ruled that although both the provider and the recipient of services were established in the same Member State, there was a provision of services within the meaning of Article 57 because the customer moved, before the contractual relationship with the bank was terminated, to establish himself in Germany.[164] Similarly in *Deliège*, in which a Belgian sportswoman had challenged the selection rules of the Belgian Judo Federation, the Court rejected the argument that this was a wholly internal situation, relying on the fact that 'a degree of extraneity may derive in particular from the fact that an athlete participates in a competition in a Member State other than that in which he is established'.[165] Further, in certain sectors such as public procurement, where harmonizing legislation has been adopted, the legislation is made applicable even to wholly internal situations.[166] Finally, the Court's focus has been as much (if not more, in recent times) on the mobility of the service as that of the persons involved.[167]

(ii) *The Freedom to Receive Services*

Article 56 expressly refers to the freedom to *provide* services, and Article 57 to the rights of the *provider* of services, and does not mention the recipient of services. In *Luisi and Carbone*, however, the Court of Justice confirmed that the Treaty covers the situation of recipients as well as providers of services, and that the freedom for the recipient to move was the necessary corollary of the freedom for the provider:

> It follows that the freedom to provide services includes the freedom, for the recipients of services, to go to another Member State in order to receive a service there, without being obstructed by restrictions, even in relation to payments, and that tourists, persons receiving medical treatment and persons travelling for the purposes of education or business are to be regarded as recipients of services.[168]

This was confirmed in subsequent judgments,[169] notably in *Cowan*, in which the Court found that the refusal, under a French criminal compensation scheme, to compensate a British tourist who had been attacked while in Paris constituted a restriction within the meaning of Article 56, without specifying exactly what service he had received.[170]

---

[163] See Case 52/79 *Debauve* (n 25) on broadcasting services. Compare Case 62/79 *Coditel v SA Ciné Vog Films* [1980] ECR 881, [10], [15] and Case 352/85 *Bond van Adverteerders* (n 86) [14]–[15], where there was an inter-state element, in that the substance of the services, the cable television broadcasts, originated in a different Member State.

[164] Case 15/78 *Société Générale Alsacienne de Banque SA v Koestler* [1978] ECR 1971.

[165] Cases C–51/96 and 191/97 *Deliège v Ligue Francophone de Judi et Disciplines Associées ASBL* [2000] ECR I–2549, [59]; S van den Bogaert, Note (2000) 25 ELRev 554.

[166] V Hatzopoulos and T Do, 'The Case Law of the ECJ Concerning the Free Provision of Services: 2000–2005' (2006) 43 CMLRev 923.

[167] See the discussion on the cases concerning cross-border access to health care, below. For more general discussion see V Hatzopoulos, 'Recent Developments of the Case Law of the ECJ in the Field of Services' (2000) 37 CMLRev 43, and Snell (n 26).

[168] Cases 286/82 and 26/83 *Luisi and Carbone v Ministero del Tesoro* [1984] ECR 377, [16].

[169] Cases C–17/00 *De Coster v Collège des Bourgmestre et échevins de Watermael-Boitsford* [2001] ECR I–9445; C–294/97 *Eurowings Luftverkehrs* (n 103); C–158/96 *Kohll v Union des Caisses de Maladie* [1998] ECR I–1931.

[170] Case 186/87 *Cowan v Le Trésor Public* [1989] ECR 195.

(iii) *The Commercial Nature of the Services*

Whether a provision of services falls within Articles 56 to 57 depends not just on the inter-state element, but also on the services being commercial in nature, in that they must be provided *for remuneration*. The European Court has ruled that remunerated services do not lose their economic nature either because the provider is a non-profit making enterprise,[171] or because of an 'element of chance' inherent in the return, or because of the recreational or sporting nature of the services.[172]

The Court ruled further in *Deliège* that 'the mere fact that a sports association or federation unilaterally classifies its members as amateur athletes does not in itself mean that those members do not engage in economic activities'[173] and in *Bond van Adverteerders* that the remuneration does not have to come from the recipient of the services, so long as there is remuneration from some party.[174] In *Deliège* the Court drew on its case law on the free movement of workers concerning economic activity which was not 'marginal or ancillary' and ruled:

> 56. In that connection, it must be stated that sporting activities and, in particular, a high-ranking athlete's participation in an international competition are capable of involving the provision of a number of separate, but closely related, services which may fall within the scope of Article 59 [*now Art 56 TFEU*] of the Treaty even if some of those services are not paid for by those for whom they are performed...
>
> 57. For example, an organiser of such a competition may offer athletes an opportunity of engaging in their sporting activity in competition with others and, at the same time, the athletes, by participating in the competition, enable the organiser to put on a sports event which the public may attend, which television broadcasters may retransmit and which may be of interest to advertisers and sponsors. Moreover, the athletes provide their sponsors with publicity the basis for which is the sporting activity itself.[175]

What is the legal position where the remuneration for the service is provided publicly, by the state? This issue came to prominence in a series of cases concerning cross-border access to medical and healthcare services, which threatened to disrupt the operation of national welfare systems.[176] The question had arisen previously in the context of a course taught under the national educational system in *Humbel*, where the Court of Justice ruled that it did not fall within the scope of the Treaty rules on services:

Case 263/86 Belgium v Humbel
[1988] ECR 5365

> 17. The essential characteristic of remuneration thus lies in the fact that it constitutes consideration for the service in question, and is normally agreed upon between the provider and the recipient of the service.

---

[171] Case C–70/95 *Sodemare* (n 22).

[172] Case C–275/92 *Schindler* (n 26) [33]–[34]. For similar rulings on the concept of an economic activity under Art 45 TFEU see Case 36/74 *Walrave* (n 29); Case C–415/93 *Bosman* (n 28); Cases C–51/96 and 191/97 *Deliège* (n 165); Case C–176/96 *Lehtonen v FRBSB* [2000] ECR I–2681.

[173] Cases C–51/96 and 191/97 (n 165).

[174] Case 352/85 (n 86); Case C–159/90 *SPUC v Grogan* [1991] ECR I–4685 where student distributors of information in Ireland about abortion services in the UK received no remuneration from the providers of the actual service in the second Member State. In the absence of such an economic link between the information ban and the freedom to provide the service, the connection between them was deemed 'too tenuous' to attract the application of Art 56 TFEU.

[175] (N 165).

[176] Cases C–120/95 *Decker* [1998] ECR I–1831 (concerning goods rather than services); C–158/96 *Kohll* (n 169); C–368/98 *Vanbraekel v ANMC* [2001] ECR I–5363; C–157/99 *Geraets-Smits and Peerbooms* [2001] ECR I–5473; C–385/99 *Müller-Fauré* [2003] ECR I–4509; C–372/04 *Watts v Bedford Primary Care Trust* [2006] ECR I–4325; C–444/05 *Stamatelaki v OAEE* [2007] ECR I–3185.

18. That characteristic is, however, absent in the case of courses provided under the national education system. First of all, the State, in establishing and maintaining such a system, is not seeking to engage in gainful activity but is fulfilling its duties towards its own population in the social, cultural and educational fields. Secondly, the system in question is, as a general rule, funded from the public purse and not by pupils or their parents.

19. The nature of the activity is not affected by the fact that pupils or their parents must sometimes pay teaching or enrolment fees in order to make a certain contribution to the operating expenses of the system.

Conversely, the Court in *Wirth* declared that, although most institutions of higher education were financed from public funds, those which sought to make a profit and were financed mainly from private funds, for example by students or their parents, could constitute providers of services within Articles 56 and 57.[177] This was confirmed in *Schwarz*, where the German Government's refusal to grant tax relief to the parents of school-going children on the ground that the private school they attended was established in another Member State amounted to a restriction under Article 56 TFEU.[178]

The distinction between publicly and privately remunerated services on which these cases are based is a difficult one, and the applicability of the reasoning in *Humbel* has been narrowed, as the cases concerning access to cross-border health care demonstrate. In *Kohll*, the Court ruled that treatment provided by an orthodontist established in a different Member State from the applicant amounted to a service provided for remuneration, and that the requirement of prior authorization from the home state's social security institution before the cost would be reimbursed constituted an unjustified restriction on the freedom to receive cross-border services.[179] Together with the subsequent cases of *Geraets-Smits/Peerbooms*,[180] *Inizan*,[181] and *Vanbraekel*,[182] this ruling demonstrates vividly the potentially disruptive effects on national welfare systems of the decision to bring essential and publicly organized services within the scope of the Treaty's free movement provisions.[183]

In *Geraets-Smits/Peerbooms*, the two applicants were insured for their medical costs under a Dutch social insurance scheme for people whose income is below a certain level. Some of the funding in the scheme was derived from individual premiums, some from the state, and some from subsidization by other private insurance funds. Both applicants received medical treatment abroad without prior authorization from the fund, apparently because of the restrictive conditions for authorization which entailed that (i) the treatment must be regarded as 'normal in the professional circles concerned' and (ii) the treatment must be 'necessary', in the sense that adequate care could not be provided without undue delay by a care provider in the home state.

---

[177] Case C–109/92 *Wirth v Landeshauptstadt Hannover* [1993] ECR I–6447; Case C–159/90 *Grogan* (n 174); S O'Leary, Note (1992) 17 ELRev 138; Case C–70/95 *Sodemare* (n 22), in which the ECJ considered the applicability of Art 56 to Italian conditions on the involvement of economic operators in the provision of the state's social welfare services, such as the running of old people's homes.

[178] Case C–76/05 *Schwarz and Gootjes-Schwarz v Finanzamt Bergisch Gladbach* [2007] ECR I–6849; See also Cases C–318/05 *Commission v Germany* [2007] ECR I–6957; C–281/06 *Hans-Dieter and Hedwig Jundt v Finanzamt Offenburg* [2007] ECR I–12231.

[179] Case C–158/96 *Kohll* (n 169). This was decided on the same day as the parallel Case C–120/95 *Decker* (n 176) which concerned a prior authorization requirement from the competent social security institution before reimbursement of spectacles purchased in another Member State could be made. For comment see P Cabral, Note (1999) 24 ELRev 387. For a case concerning non-discriminatory access to medical care under what is now Art 18 TFEU see Case C–411/98 *Ferlini* (n 31).

[180] (N 151); E Steyger, Note (2002) 29 LIEI 97; G Davies, Note (2002) 29 LIEI 27.

[181] Case C–56/01 *Inizan v Caisse primaire d'assurance maladie des Hauts-de-Seine* [2003] ECR I–12403.

[182] Case C–368/98 *Vanbraekel* (n 176).

[183] E Brooks, 'Crossing Borders: A Critical Review of the Role of the European Court of Justice in EU Health Policy' (2012) 105 Health Policy 33.

In addressing whether this kind of prior authorization requirement was prohibited by Articles 56 and 57, the European Court began by reaffirming that Member States retain the power to organize their social security systems, subject to compliance with the rules of EU law.[184] The Court went on to consider the argument made by several governments, citing *Humbel*, that hospital services did not constitute an economic activity when provided free of charge under a sickness insurance scheme.

Case C–157/99 **Geraets-Smits v Stichting Ziekenfonds, Peerbooms v Stichting CZ Groep Zorgverzekeringen**
[2001] ECR I–5473

[Note Lisbon Treaty renumbering: Art 60 EC is now Art 57 TFEU]

55. With regard more particularly to the argument that hospital services provided in the context of a sickness insurance scheme providing benefits in kind, such as that governed by the ZFW, should not be classified as services within the meaning of Article 60 of the Treaty, it should be noted that, far from falling under such a scheme, the medical treatment at issue in the main proceedings, which was provided in Member States other than those in which the persons concerned were insured, did lead to the establishments providing the treatment being paid directly by the patients. It must be accepted that a medical service provided in one Member State and paid for by the patient should not cease to fall within the scope of the freedom to provide services guaranteed by the Treaty merely because reimbursement of the costs of the treatment involved is applied for under another Member State's sickness insurance legislation which is essentially of the type which provides for benefits in kind.

The fact that the hospital treatment was financed directly by the sickness insurance funds on the basis of agreements and pre-set fee scales did not remove such treatment from the ambit of Article 57. The ECJ reiterated that Article 57 did not require the service to be paid for by those for whom it was performed and declared that the payments made by the sickness insurance funds under the contractual arrangements constituted consideration for the hospital services, and represented remuneration for the hospital which was engaged in an activity of an economic character.

Geraets-Smits was followed by the cases of *Müller Fauré*[185] and *Watts*,[186] which confirmed and extended its reasoning. Both cases dealt with a national requirement for prior authorization before travelling to receive medical care in another state. *Watts*, however, concerned the UK's tax-funded National Health Service (NHS) and not the kind of insurance-based health-care systems at issue in the previous cases. The referring court asked the European Court whether Article 56 was applicable to the situation in which the applicant had travelled to another state for medical care and was now seeking reimbursement, despite the fact that the NHS had no fund out of which to pay for health care received in another state, and despite the fact that it had no obligation to pay for private health care obtained *within* the UK.

The Court of Justice's answer was that Article 56 applied where a patient received medical services in a hospital environment for consideration in a Member State other than the state of residence 'regardless of the way in which the national system with which that person is registered and from which reimbursement of the cost of those services is subsequently sought operates'. However, the Court refused

---

[184] Several of the health-care cases involve an interpretation of Reg 1408/71, now Reg 883/2004, on the cross-border coordination of social security, and particularly of Art 22 thereof, but for the purposes of this chapter the focus will be only on the Court's conclusions about the applicability of Art 56 TFEU on the free movement of services.

[185] Case C–385/99 (n 176).

[186] Case C–372/04 (n 176).

to be drawn on the question whether the provision of health-care services by the NHS within the UK amounted to the provision of a commercial service, and stated that there was 'no need in the present case to determine whether the provision of hospital treatment in the context of a national health service such as the NHS is in itself a service within the meaning of those provisions'.

While the outcomes on the facts of these cases may not in themselves be alarming, since the Court in each case acknowledged the importance of the stable financing of national social insurance systems and the justifiability of measures which seek to maintain a balanced and manageable national health-care system, they have undoubtedly opened up to the rigours of the Treaty rules and to cross-border economic activity, some of the core aspects of national welfare systems.[187]

The Court delivered a somewhat more cautious ruling recently in *Commission v Spain*, which did not concern people who travel abroad in order to receive medical treatment, but rather those who travel for other reasons such as travel or education, and the need for medical care arises unexpectedly during their stay.[188] The Court held that the Spanish legislation limiting the level of cover, in such circumstances, to that applicable in the state where the treatment was administered did not amount to a restriction of the freedom to provide services. Distinguishing the case from *Vanbraekel*, where it had ruled that a similar limit on the level of cover would constitute a restriction on the free movement of services where a person had gone abroad specifically to receive scheduled medical treatment, the ECJ ruled that the potential interference with free movement in a case involving unscheduled medical care was too 'uncertain and indirect' to constitute a restriction on the Treaty freedom.[189]

Despite this more careful ruling on the issue of unscheduled medical treatment abroad, the upshot of the Court's rulings remains that Articles 56–57 TFEU apply to any service, however important a public service it may be, which is 'provided for remuneration'.[190] The line between publicly and privately remunerated services remains uncertain. Health-care services, however funded, fall within the scope of the Treaty where a patient who has travelled to another state and paid for health care there seeks reimbursement from their national system. There is no exception from the Treaty rules for state-provided welfare services. One of the consequences of these rulings has been a move by the EU legislature—after three years of contestation and debate—to adopt a directive codifying and clarifying the law on cross-border access to health care.[191]

(iv) *The Scope of the Principle of Equal Treatment for Service Providers and Recipients*

Article 18 TFEU contains a principle of non-discrimination on grounds of nationality within the scope of application of the Treaty, and Article 24 of Directive 2004/38 also contains a general rule of equal treatment for EU citizens who are resident in a host Member State. What does this principle of equal treatment mean in practice for a service provider or recipient in the territory of another Member State? Does it include all social benefits to which a national resident is entitled, as in the case of workers? There is no equivalent, in the field of establishment or services, of Article 7 of Regulation 492/2011

---

[187] See, eg, in Case C–372/04 *Watts* (n 176), how the Court engaged in a detailed review of the way in which the NHS treated waiting lists for the purposes of managing health-care provision.

[188] Case C–211/08 *Commission v Spain* [2010] ECR I–5267.

[189] Ibid [61]–[62]. For critique of this use of the notion that some restrictions are 'too uncertain and indirect' to fall within the scope of the Treaty provision, see S Enchelmaier, 'Always at Your Service (Within Limits): The ECJ's Case Law on Article 56 TFEU 2006–11' (2011) 36 ELRev 615.

[190] G Davies, 'Welfare as a Service' (2002) 29 LIEI 27.

[191] Dir 2011/24 [2011] OJ L88/45. See S De La Rosa, 'The Directive on Cross-Border Healthcare or the Art of Codifying Complex Case Law' (2012) 49 CMLRev 15; M Peeters, 'Free Movement of Patients: Directive 2011/24 on the Application of Patients' Rights in Cross-Border Healthcare' (2012) 19 European Journal of Health Law 29.

(formerly 1612/68) conferring an entitlement to equal treatment in social and tax advantages to workers and their families.

In the *Italian Housing* case, the Court of Justice ruled that the imposition of a nationality requirement for access to reduced-rate mortgage loans and social housing was contrary to Article 49 TFEU on freedom of establishment, but the Italian Government argued that access to publicly built housing could not possibly be relevant to the exercise of the right to provide services, which was precisely the right to provide services without having to have a place of residence in that state. The Court rejected this argument, at least in its absolute form:

Case 63/86 **Commission v Italy**
[1988] ECR 29

18. It is true, as the Italian Government has contended, that in practice not all instances of establishment give rise to the same need to find permanent housing and that as a rule that need is not felt in the case of the provision of services. It is also true that in most cases the provider of services will not satisfy the conditions, of a non-discriminatory nature, bound up with the objectives of the legislation on social housing.

19. However, it cannot be held to be *a priori* out of the question that a person, whilst retaining his principal place of establishment in one Member State, may be led to pursue his occupational activities in another Member State for such an extended period that he needs to have permanent housing there and that he may satisfy the conditions of a non-discriminatory nature for access to social housing. It follows that no distinction can be drawn between different forms of establishment and that providers of services cannot be excluded from the benefit of the fundamental principle of national treatment.

In other words, it may be the case, in certain circumstances, that a host state's denial of access to social housing to a service provider would violate the Treaty.

As far as recipients of services who travel to other states are concerned, we saw above that in *Cowan*, a British tourist in France was refused state compensation for victims of violent crime which was available to nationals and to residents.[192] The Court of Justice cited the general prohibition on discrimination 'within the scope of application of this Treaty' in Article 18 TFEU,[193] and referred to its ruling in *Luisi and Carbone* to the effect that tourists were covered by Article 56 as recipients of services:

When Community law guarantees a natural person the freedom to go to another Member State, the protection of that person from harm in the Member State in question, on the same basis as that of nationals and persons residing there, is a corollary of that freedom of movement. It follows that the prohibition of discrimination is applicable to recipients of services within the meaning of the Treaty as regards protection against the risk of assault and the right to obtain financial compensation provided for by national law when that risk materialises. The fact that the compensation at issue is financed by the Public Treasury cannot alter the rules regarding the protection of the rights guaranteed by the Treaty.[194]

---

[192] Case 186/87 *Cowan* (n 170). See also Case C–164/07 *Wood* [2008] ECR I–4143, which however concerned a resident and not a temporary service-recipient or provider.

[193] For cases in which the Court ruled that Art 18 TFEU could be the basis for a claim of discrimination in treatment, without being linked to another specific Treaty provision, see Cases C–92 and 326/92 *Phil Collins v Imtrat Handelsgesellschaft* [1993] ECR I–5145; C–274/96 *Bickel and Franz* [1998] ECR I–7637; C–411/98 *Ferlini* (n 31); C–628/11 *International Jet Management GmbH* EU:C:2014:171.

[194] [1989] ECR 195, [17]; Case C–45/93 *Commission v Spain* [1994] ECR I–911, concerning free admission to national museums.

Thus, although the state compensation is publicly funded, the provision of compensation is not (following *Humbel*[195]) the commercial service being provided. Instead the relevant services in these cases, although not specifically identified by the ECJ, are presumably services such as hotels and restaurants for which the recipients, as tourists, provide remuneration. If, whilst in the course of a temporary stay in a Member State in order to avail themselves of remunerated services of this nature, such tourists are denied equal treatment in matters such as compensation for assault, and entry fees to museums, they may be able to invoke Article 56.[196]

To conclude, it seems that while there is no express guarantee of equal access to social benefits in the context of the free movement of services, nonetheless the guarantee of equal treatment in Article 18 TFEU and Article 24 of Directive 2004/38 is likely to mean that a person who is temporarily resident in order to provide or receive services is entitled to have equal access to social and other benefits of the host state where there is a sufficient connection between the nature and purpose of the temporary residence and the nature of the social benefit sought.

(v) *Illegal and 'Immoral' Services under Articles 56–57*

Several cases, including a recent stream of rulings on the subject of lotteries and gambling, have raised the question of illegal or 'immoral' services in relation to activities which are lawful in certain states but not in others. Clearly if a person established in a Member State in which a particular activity is lawful wishes to provide services in another Member State in which it is not lawful, the second state may have good reasons for restricting the provision of that service. An initial question is whether such activities, on whose legality the Member States do not agree, can constitute 'services' at all within EU law.

In *Koestler*, the ECJ ruled that Germany's refusal to allow a French bank which had provided services for a German national, including a stock-exchange transaction which was treated as an illegal wagering contract in Germany but not in France, to recover from that client was not contrary to Article 56 if the same refusal would apply to banks established in Germany.[197] Despite the fact that the services were considered illegal in Germany, the Court ruled that the conclusion of the wagering contract could constitute a service, although Germany was justified in restricting that service by refusing to allow the bank to sue for recovery.

In *Grogan*, the Court considered whether the provision of abortion was a service within the meaning of the Treaty, in order to determine whether the restriction in one Member State on information about the provision of abortion in another state was contrary to Article 56.[198] In response to the argument that abortion could not be categorized as a service for the purposes of EU law on the ground that it was immoral, the ECJ ruled that it was not for the Court 'to substitute its assessment for that of the legislature in those Member States where the activities are practised legally'.[199] As *Koestler* indicates however, the fact that abortion constitutes a service within Article 56 does not mean that a Member State in which abortion services are illegal may not prohibit or restrict their provision in its territory by healthcare providers who are established in another Member State. Less clear, even after *Grogan*, is whether

---

[195] Case 263/86 *Belgium v Humbel* [1988] ECR 5365.

[196] For other cases on the provision or receipt of inter-state services see Case C–43/95 *Data Delecta and Forsberg v MSL Dynamics* [1996] ECR I–4661; Case C–323/95 *Hayes v Kronenberger* [1997] ECR I–1171; Case C–122/96 *Saldanha and MTS Securities Corporation v Hiross Holdings* [1997] ECR I–5325 on national procedures requiring non-residents to provide security for costs in litigation, which were held to be capable of having an indirect effect on trade in goods and services between Member States. Compare Case C–177/94 *Perfili* [1996] ECR I–161.

[197] Case 15/78 (n 164).

[198] Case C–159/90 (n 174).

[199] Ibid [20].

a Member State can restrict the access of its citizens to services in another Member State, where those services are prohibited or restricted within the regulating state.[200]

In *Schindler*, the defendants were acting as agents on behalf of a German public lottery, seeking to promote that lottery within the UK, and they were charged with an offence under the UK lotteries legislation. When the case was referred to the European Court, several Member States argued that lotteries were not an 'economic activity' within the meaning of the Treaty, since they were traditionally prohibited or operated by public authorities in the public interest. The Court rejected the argument, ruling that lotteries were services provided for remuneration (the price of the lottery ticket) and that, although they were closely regulated in some Member States, they were not totally prohibited in any.[201] Although the morality of lotteries was 'questionable', they could not be regarded as 'activities whose harmful nature causes them to be prohibited in all the Member States and whose position under Community law may be likened to that of activities involving illegal products'.[202]

Similarly, in a series of cases concerning gambling, despite the fact that these constituted services within the meaning of the Treaty, the Court ruled that 'the morally and financially harmful consequences for the individual and for society associated with betting and gaming, may serve to justify a margin of discretion for the national authorities'.[203] As with all instances of 'objective justification' of Treaty freedoms, the regulation of such services must be carried out in a genuine, non-discriminatory,[204] proportionate, and consistent manner.[205] These cases have given rise to lively national debates on the consistency and coherence of the domestic regulation of gambling, particularly in Sweden, Italy, and Germany, and new cases continue to arise before the Court.[206] The CJEU showed more lenience towards Germany in a case concerning variation in federal regulation across *Länder* within Germany in the regulation of internet gambling, referring in its reasoning to Article 4(2) TEU on the protection of national identity inherent in regional and local structures.[207]

In *Jany*, the Court ruled that the relevant provisions of the EU's Association Agreement with Poland on freedom of establishment and services were to have the same meaning and scope as those under the EU Treaties so that 'the activity of prostitution pursued in a self-employed capacity can be regarded as a service provided for remuneration'.[208] In response to arguments based on the immoral nature of the

---

[200] The AG in *Grogan* (n 174) took the view that the restriction on information in the case in question was proportionate. For an indirect restriction by the UK on access to artificial insemination services in another Member State which was not referred to the ECJ see *R v Human Fertilisation and Embryology Authority, ex p Diane Blood* [1997] 2 CMLR 591.

[201] Case C–275/92 *Schindler* (n 26).

[202] Ibid [32].

[203] Cases C–67/98 *Zenatti* [1999] ECR I–7289; C–42/02 *Lindman* [2003] ECR I–13519; C–6/01 *Anomar* [2003] ECR I–8621; C–243/01 *Gambelli* [2003] ECR I 13031; C 338, 359 and 360/04 *Placanica, Palazzese and Sorricchio* [2007] ECR I–1891; C–447–448/08 *Sjöberg and Gerdin* [2010] ECR I–6921; C–46/08 *Carmen Media Group v Land Schleswig-Holstein* [2010] ECR I–8149; C–64/08 *Ernst Engelmann* [2010] ECR I–8219.

[204] For an example of a non-discriminatory restriction which was compatible with the Treaty provisions, see Case C–176/11 *HIT and HIT LARIX* EU:C:2012:454.

[205] An example of the wide margin of appreciation allowed by the Court is evident in Cases C–316, 358–360 and 409–410/07 *Stoß* [2010] ECR I–8069 which establishes that Member States may impose an authorization requirement for the provision of games of chance, even though the operator, established in another Member State, holds an authorization from its own Member State. See M Schmidl, 'The ECJ and the National Monopoly in the Field of Gambling—Next Round' (2010) European Law Reporter 310; J Mulder, 'A New Chapter in the European Court of Justice Gambling Saga: A Stacked Debt' (2011) 38 LIEI 243.

[206] See Cases C–186 and 209/11 *Stanleybet International v Ypourgos Oikonomias kai Oikonomikon* EU:C:2013:33 on the Greek state monopoly on gambling; Case C–344/13 *Blanco* EU:C:2014:2311 on an Italian income tax on the winnings of gambling obtained in other Member States; Case C–390/12 *Pfleger* EU:C:2014:281 on Austrian criminal penalties for unauthorized gambling machines.

[207] Case C–156/13 *Digibet and Albers* EU:C:2014:1756.

[208] Case C–268/99 *Jany* (n 18).

services, the Court cited its rulings in *Grogan* and *Schindler*, and declared that, 'far from being prohibited in all Member States, prostitution is tolerated, even regulated, by most of those States'.[209]

Somewhat surprisingly in view of the consistent previous case law, the Court in *Josemans* came to a different conclusion as regards the provision of services relating to the marketing of cannabis by so-called marijuana cafés in the Netherlands.[210] The marketing of cannabis in the Netherlands was prohibited but tolerated by law, yet the Court ruled that Article 56 TFEU could not be relied on to challenge municipal legislation which limited access to such cafés to residents only. With regard to the provision of catering services for food and drink in such coffee shops, the Court ruled that although the legislation restricted the free movement of services, this was justified by the need to combat drug tourism. To distinguish the circumstances in *Josemans* (despite the official tolerance of marijuana cafés) from those of previous judgments, the Court emphasized that there was a prohibition in *all* Member States, under both international law and EU law, on the marketing of narcotic drugs, which differentiated it even from the case of prostitution.[211]

The result of these rulings appears to be that provided it is lawful in some Member States, and perhaps even in just one state, a remunerated activity constitutes a service within the meaning of Articles 56–57 TFEU. Nevertheless, Member States remain free to regulate and restrict such services,[212] so long as they do so proportionately and without arbitrary discrimination on grounds of nationality or place of establishment.[213]

(C) JUSTIFYING RESTRICTIONS ON THE FREE MOVEMENT OF SERVICES

(i) *General Requirements*

Alongside the express grounds of justification for measures adopted on the basis of public policy, security, and health considerations contained in Article 52 TFEU, which are made applicable to the field of services by Article 62,[214] the ECJ has developed a justificatory test for workers, services, and establishment alike which is similar to the *Cassis de Dijon* 'rule of reason' in the free movement of goods context.[215] Although in the area of goods these open-ended justifications have generally been referred to as 'mandatory requirements', the term 'imperative requirements' or the generic term 'objective justification' is more often used in the field of services.

The origins of this approach in the services context can be found in the case of *Van Binsbergen*.[216] We saw in that case how various Member States argued that there were greater dangers in the area of services than in the area of establishment, since evasion of national regulation and control would be easier where service providers were not—or were only temporarily—resident in the state where the service was provided.[217] The Court of Justice addressed the issue by indicating that, although the

---

[209] Ibid [57].

[210] Case C–137/09 *Josemans v Burgemeester van Maastricht* [2010] ECR I–13019.

[211] Ibid [76]–[77].

[212] See, eg, Case C–36/02 *Omega* (n 6).

[213] Note that the Court of Justice's initial conclusion in *Schindler* that the UK legislation was justified on public-policy grounds was criticized for ignoring the discrimination practised in favour of national small-scale lotteries, and for applying the proportionality test too loosely: G Straetmans, Note (2000) 37 CMLRev 991 on the subsequent gaming cases, Case C–124/97 *Läärä* [1999] ECR I–6067; Case C–67/98 *Zenatti* (n 203).

[214] See Section 2(d) above.

[215] Ch 19.

[216] Case 33/74 *Van Binsbergen* (n 16); Cases 110–111/78 *Ministère Public v Van Wesemael* [1979] ECR 5; Case 279/80 *Webb* [1981] ECR 3305.

[217] AG Mayras in *Van Binsbergen* (n 16) 1317. These concerns about temporary service provision are to some extent reflected in the distinction between establishment and services in the 2005 Dir on recognition of professional qualifications: Dir 2005/36, Arts 7–9 in particular, and rec 6.

imposition of a residence requirement would probably be excessive in that particular case as a way of ensuring 'observance of professional rules of conduct connected with the administration of justice and with respect for professional ethics', it might not always be so.[218] The test for justification laid down in *Van Binsbergen* contains several conditions which must be satisfied if a restriction on the freedom to provide services is to be compatible with Article 56. These same four conditions indeed apply to justifications for restrictions on the freedom of establishment, just as they do in the field of goods and workers.

First, the restriction must be adopted in pursuit of a legitimate public interest compatible with EU aims. In keeping with the permissible scope of the justifications for limiting other Treaty freedoms, the Court has ruled that an economic aim is not legitimate. Thus the aim of protecting a particular economic sector within a Member State is not legitimate,[219] whereas the maintenance of the financial balance of the social security system with a view to protecting public health is legitimate.[220] In *Finalarte* the Court ruled that the aim of a measure is something to be determined 'objectively' by the national court,[221] although the Court of Justice retains the ultimate role of pronouncing on the legitimacy of the aim. Legitimate aims which have been successfully pleaded as grounds of justification in recent cases include the protection of intellectual property,[222] and protection of the quality of postgraduate education.[223]

Secondly, the restriction must be equally applicable to persons established within the state, and must be applied without discrimination.[224] For example, in a series of cases concerning broadcasting restrictions, the Court held that, although the promotion of cultural policy[225] through ensuring a balance of programmes and restricting the content and frequency of advertisements was a legitimate aim, it must not be pursued in a discriminatory or protectionist manner.[226]

---

[218] Case 33/74 *Van Binsbergen* (n 16) [12]–[14]; Case 39/75 *Coenen* (n 148) [9]; Case C–131/01 *Commission v Italy* [2003] ECR I–1659. For a case in which the protection of creditors and the 'sound administration of justice' was found to be an important objective justifying the imposition of restrictions on the practice of debt collection see Case C–3/95 *Reisebüro Broede v Sandker* [1996] ECR I–6511. On restrictions preventing legal advocates from practising in partnership with accountants see Case C–309/99 *Wouters* (n 31) [97]–[99].

[219] Cases C–398/95 *SETTG v Ypourgos Ergasias* [1997] ECR I–3091, [22]–[23]; C–49/98 *Finalarte* (n 19) [39]; C–221/12 *Belgacom* EU:C:2013:736; C–338/09 *Yellow Cab Verkehrsbetriebs GmbH v Landeshauptmann von Wien* [2010] ECR I–13927 in which the objective of ensuring the profitability of a bus service, as a purely economic objective, could not constitute an overriding reason in the public interest.

[220] See the health-care cases at (n 176) in which the states could not rely on aims of a purely economic nature, and in order to plead the 'risk to the financial balance of the social security system' as a justification, they had to frame the argument as a risk to public health rather than to the economic interests of the state.

[221] Case C–49/98 (n 19) [40]–[41].

[222] Case C–403/08 *Football Association Premier League and Others* EU:C:2011:631; Case C 351/12 *OSA* EU:C:2014:110.

[223] Case C–523/12 *Dirextra Alta Formazione* EU:C:2013:831, concerning a requirement of ten years' experience for a higher education establishment at which students applying for a European Social Fund-financed study grant plan to enrol.

[224] For an example of a discriminatory and inappropriate way of protecting the confidentiality of data by imposing a requirement of state ownership of shares see Cases 3/88 *Commission v Italy* [1989] ECR 4035; C–272/91 *Commission v Italy* (n 39); C–101/94 *Commission v Italy* [1996] ECR I–2691. For other state ownership cases, and prior restrictions on acquisition of share capital, see Case C–244/11 *Commission v Greece* EU:C:2012:694.

[225] For a case in which a cultural policy concerning the deductibility of costs for the repair of listed historic buildings was held to be a legitimate aim, and one which had been proportionately pursued in the case, see Case C–87/13 *X* EU:C:2014:2459.

[226] Case 352/85 (n 86); Case C–288/89 *Gouda v Commissariaat voor de Media* [1991] ECR I–4007; Case C–353/89 *Commission v Netherlands* [1991] ECR I–4069. The subsequent adoption of the Broadcasting Dir 89/552 [1989] OJ L298/23 generated a further spate of litigation: Cases C–222/94 *Commission v United Kingdom* [1996] ECR I–4025; C–11/95 *Commission v Belgium* [1996] ECR I–4115; C–14/96 *Denuit* [1997] ECR I–2785; C–125/06 *Commission v Infront WM AG* [2008] ECR I–1451; C–250/06 *United Pan-Europe Communications Belgium SA and Others v Belgian State* [2007] ECR I–11135; C–195/06 *KommAustria v ORF* [2007] ECR I–8817. In a high-profile series of cases concerning the broadcasting of international football matches, the General Court upheld the decisions of the Commission authorizing the exemption

Thirdly, the restriction imposed on the provider of services must be *proportionate* to the need to observe the legitimate rules in question.[227] The proportionality test entails examining whether the rule is 'suitable' or 'appropriate' in achieving its aim and, although the Court of Justice does not consistently apply this third part of the proportionality test in all cases, whether that aim could be satisfied by other, less restrictive means.[228] In *Van Binsbergen* itself, the Court ruled that the public interest in the proper administration of justice could be ensured by requiring an address for service to be maintained within the state, rather than a residence there. A crucial factor in appraising the proportionality and necessity of any restriction is whether the provider is subject to similar regulation in the Member State in which that person is established.[229] If the requirement duplicates a condition already satisfied, it imposes a 'dual burden' and cannot be justified.[230] Although the proportionality test in principle is for the national court to apply, the Court frequently indicates which requirements or restrictions may be disproportionate in the context of the preliminary reference procedure,[231] or more directly in the context of infringement proceedings under Article 258 TFEU (ex Article 226 EC),[232] such as the series of insurance services cases.[233]

A recent and illustrative example of the Court's approach to the proportionality of particular measures is in a series of cases concerning the regulation of pharmacies and pharmacists, which entailed various restrictive effects on the free movement of services and establishment but were allegedly adopted to protect public health. Citing the importance of public health protection as a value expressed in the EU Charter of Fundamental Rights, the Court gave a series of nuanced rulings, holding that a system of preferential licensing for specific university pharmacies with an educational mandate,[234] prior authorisation requirements, spatial requirements as to distance from existing pharmacies, and population-density requirements for opening a pharmacy were justified if proportionately and transparently implemented.[235]

A *fourth* condition of the test for justification, which was not mentioned in *Van Binsbergen* and has less frequently been highlighted by the ECJ, but which was clearly stated in the *Carpenter* case,[236] is the requirement that the restrictive measure should also respect fundamental rights.[237] In some cases, the

---

of exclusive broadcasting of all World Cup and EURO matches, thus reserving these matches for free-for-air television. The restrictions on the freedom of establishment and to provide services were justified by the protection of the right to information and to ensure wide public access to television broadcasts of events of major importance for society: Cases T–68/08 *FIFA v Commission* [2011] ECR II–349, T–55/08 *UEFA v Commission* [2011] ECR II–271; and T–385/07 *FIFA v Commission* [2011] ECR II–205.

[227] See, eg, the tourist guide cases: Case C–180/89 *Commission v Italy* [1991] ECR I–709; Case C–154/89 *Commission v France* [1991] ECR I–659; Case C–198/89 *Commission v Greece* [1991] ECR I–727; Case C–375/92 *Commission v Spain* [1994] ECR I–923.

[228] For an interesting case concerning alcohol advertising in France, in which the ECJ did not apply a strict proportionality test, see Case C–262/02 *Commission v France* [2004] ECR I–6569.

[229] Case C–272/95 *Guiot and Climatec* [1996] ECR I–1905; Cases C–369 and 376/96 *Arblade* (n 74).

[230] Ch 19, in relation to the free movement of goods.

[231] Case 16/78 *Choquet* [1978] ECR 2293; Case C–193/94 *Skanavi and Chyssanthakopoulos* [1996] ECR I–929 on driving licence requirements. In Case C–49/98 *Finalarte* (n 19) [49]–[52], the Court gave a very directional set of guidelines on how the national court should assess whether the rules are a proportionate restriction. See also Case C–390/99 *Canal Satélite* (n 11) [34]–[42]; Case C–400/08 *Commission v Spain* (n 27).

[232] See, eg, the *Lawyers' Services* case, Case 427/85 *Commission v Germany* [1988] ECR 1123, [26].

[233] Case 205/84 *Commission v Germany* (n 20); Case 206/84 *Commission v Ireland* [1986] ECR 3817; Case 220/83 *Commission v France* [1986] ECR 3663; Case 252/83 *Commission v Denmark* [1986] ECR 3713.

[234] Case C–84/11 *Susisalo and Others* EU:C:2012:374. For a case concerning the justification of restrictions on para-pharmacists from selling prescription-only medicines see Case C–159/12 *Venturini* EU:C:2013:791.

[235] Cases C–570 and 571/07 *Blanco Perez* [2010] ECR I–4629; C–539/11 *Ottica New Line di Accardi Vincenzo* EU:C:2013:591. See R Zahn, 'The Regulation of Healthcare in the European Union: Member States' Discretion or a Widening of EU Law? *Femarbel* and *Ottica New Line*' (2014) 51 CMLRev 1521.

[236] Case C–60/00 *Carpenter v Home Secretary* [2002] ECR I–6279.

[237] Case C–260/89 *ERT v DEP* [1991] ECR I–2925, [42] on freedom of establishment; Case C–370/05 *Festersen* [2007] ECR I–1129 on the free movement of capital.

restrictive measure itself is allegedly adopted in pursuit of the protection of a fundamental right,[238] but in all cases it seems that whatever the aim of the restrictive measure, it must take care not to impinge excessively on other rights protected under the Charter of Fundamental Rights and the general principles of EU law.[239]

The question whether specific restrictions on free movement can be justified is one of the most regularly litigated before the Court. Three lines of case law will be discussed below to exemplify the way in which the Court has dealt with claims that a restriction on the free movement of services was justified. These groups of cases concern the subject of (ii) posted workers, (iii) cross-border access to health care, and (iv) direct taxation rules.

(ii) *Posted Workers*

An important series of European Court rulings on the subject of 'posted workers' concerns the provision of manpower on a temporary basis by a service provider from another Member State. This is a topic which has been governed in part by the Posted Workers Directive.[240] Much of the litigation concerned matters which were not covered by the Directive, so that the Treaty provisions on services were directly applied instead. The case law establishes that preserving the interests of the workforce, ensuring good relations on the labour market, as well as the need to ensure the collection of taxes,[241] and to prevent disturbances on the labour market,[242] are legitimate aims for host Member States to pursue. A host Member State can, in principle, apply its own labour legislation to employees, including non-EU national employees, of a company providing temporary services. The principle of proportionality applies however, so that the imposition of conditions such as a licence requirement is acceptable only if they do not duplicate requirements imposed by the state of establishment (home state), and take account of the relevant evidence and guarantees furnished by the service provider in the home state.[243] In all cases, a claim by the host state that legislative restrictions are intended for the protection of the posted workers must be carefully scrutinized.[244] As has been noted, Directive 96/71 (and indeed the Treaty provisions on services and establishment) is clearly aimed at protecting services rather than protecting workers.[245]

---

[238] The best-known case from the area of free movement of goods is Case C–112/00 *Schmidberger* [2003] ECR I–5659, but in the field of services and establishment some recent cases include Cases C–367/12 *Sokoll-Seebacher* EU:C:2014:68 citing the fundamental freedom to conduct a business under Art 16 of the Charter, and C–570 and 571/07 *Blanco Perez* [2010] ECR I–4629 on the protection of health in Art 35 of the Charter.

[239] For criticism of the lack of clarity in the Court's reasoning on this issue in different cases, see V Hatzopoulos, 'The Court's Approach to Services (2006–2012): From Case Law to Case Load?' (2013) 50 CMLRev 459, 485.

[240] See Dir 96/71 [1997] OJ L18/1. The Commission in 2006 issued a communication with a view to providing guidance on the consequences of the ECJ's case law: COM(2006) 159. A new Dir 2014/67 was adopted in 2014 following the controversial cases discussed below, to supplement the enforcement of Dir 96/71 [2014] OJ L159/11.

[241] Case C–498/10 *X* EU:C:2012:635.

[242] See Case C–307/09 *Vicoplus* EU:C:2011:64 on the transitional period prior to the accession of several of the Central and East European states.

[243] Case 279/80 *Webb* (n 216).

[244] Cases C–113/89 *Rush Portuguesa v Office National d'Immigration* [1990] ECR I–1417; C–43/93 *Vander Elst v Office des Migrations Internationales* [1994] ECR I–3803; C–369 and 376/96 *Arblade* (n 74); C–493/99 *Commission v Germany* [2001] ECR I–8163; C–165/98 *Mazzoleni, Guillame and others* [2001] ECR I–2189; C–164/99 *Portugaia Construções* [2002] ECR I–787; C–445/03 *Commission v Luxembourg* [2004] ECR I–10191; C–244/04 *Commission v Germany* [2006] ECR I–885; C–168/04 *Commission v Austria* [2006] ECR I–9041; C–490/04 *Commission v Germany* [2007] ECR I–6095; C–346/06 *Rüffert v Land Niedersachsen* [2008] ECR I–1989; C–219/08 *Commission v Belgium* [2009] ECR I–9213; C–515/08 *Vítor Manuel dos Santos Palhota* [2010] ECR I–9133; C–498/10 *X* EU:C:2012:635; and C–315/13 *De Clercq* EU:C:2014:2408.

[245] As noted by the EFTA Court decision in Case E–3/12 *Norway v Jonsson* [2013] OJ 277/9, [58], available at www.eftacourt.int/uploads/tx_nvcases/3_12_Judgment_EN.pdf.

The most famous and contested ruling on posted workers to date is that in *Laval*, which came shortly after the *Viking* ruling discussed above.[246] The Court of Justice in *Laval* ruled that industrial action in the form of a blockade by Swedish labour unions against a Latvian company which, due to its considerably lower labour costs, won a construction contract to carry out temporary work in Sweden, where the industrial action was aimed at forcing the company to sign a collective agreement in Sweden containing wage conditions and other terms of employment, was unjustified under Article 56 TFEU.[247] The European Court based its ruling also on the Posted Workers Directive, under which Sweden could have chosen to impose a legislative minimum wage requirement on the Latvian company, or to declare relevant collective agreements to be universally applicable. However, Sweden's labour relations system was designed to be decentralized, entrusting management and labour with the task of setting wage rates through collective negotiations. Further, in the construction sector it required negotiation to take place on a case-by-case basis at the place of work, taking account of the specific qualifications and tasks of the employees concerned.

Case C–341/05 **Laval un Partneri Ltd v Svenska Byggnadsarbetareförbundet ea**
[2007] ECR I–11767

[Note Lisbon Treaty renumbering: Arts 2 and 136 EC are now Arts 3 and 151 TFEU; Art 3 EC has been repealed and replaced by Arts 7 TFEU and 13(1) and 21(3) TEU]

102. The Swedish Government and the defendant trade unions in the main proceedings submit that the restrictions in question are justified, since they are necessary to ensure the protection of a fundamental right recognised by Community law and have as their objective the protection of workers, which constitutes an overriding reason of public interest.

103. In that regard, it must be pointed out that the right to take collective action for the protection of the workers of the host State against possible social dumping may constitute an overriding reason of public interest within the meaning of the case-law of the Court which, in principle, justifies a restriction of one of the fundamental freedoms guaranteed by the Treaty...

104. It should be added that, according to Article 3(1)(c) and (j) EC, the activities of the Community are to include not only an 'internal market characterised by the abolition, as between Member States, of obstacles to the free movement of goods, persons, services and capital', but also 'a policy in the social sphere'. Article 2 EC states that the Community is to have as its task, inter alia, the promotion of 'a harmonious, balanced and sustainable development of economic activities' and 'a high level of employment and of social protection'.

105. Since the Community has thus not only an economic but also a social purpose, the rights under the provisions of the EC Treaty on the free movement of goods, persons, services and capital must be balanced against the objectives pursued by social policy, which include, as is clear from the first paragraph of Article 136 EC, inter alia, improved living and working conditions, so as to make possible their harmonisation while improvement is being maintained, proper social protection and dialogue between management and labour.

...

107. In that regard, it must be observed that, in principle, blockading action by a trade union of the host Member State which is aimed at ensuring that workers posted in the framework of a transnational provision of services have their terms and conditions of employment fixed at a certain level, falls within the objective of protecting workers.

---

[246] (Nn 32–35) above, and text.
[247] Case C–341/05 *Laval un Partneri Ltd v Svenska Byggnadsarbetareförbundet ea* (n 32).

108. However, as regards the specific obligations, linked to signature of the collective agreement for the building sector, which the trade unions seek to impose on undertakings established in other Member States by way of collective action such as that at issue in the case in the main proceedings, the obstacle which that collective action forms cannot be justified with regard to such an objective.

In addition to [*the possibility under the Posted Workers Directive for Sweden to impose, in relation to posted workers, certain specified minimum protections and conditions of employment on a non-discriminatory basis*], their employer is required, as a result of the coordination achieved by Directive 96/71, to observe a nucleus of mandatory rules for minimum protection in the host Member State.

109. Finally, as regards the negotiations on pay which the trade unions seek to impose, by way of collective action such as that at issue in the main proceedings, on undertakings, established in another Member State which post workers temporarily to their territory, it must be emphasised that Community law certainly does not prohibit Member States from requiring such undertakings to comply with their rules on minimum pay by appropriate means (see *Seco and Desquenne & Giral*, paragraph 14; *Rush Portuguesa*, paragraph 18, and *Arblade and Others*, paragraph 41).

110. However, collective action such as that at issue in the main proceedings cannot be justified in the light of the public interest objective referred to in paragraph 102 of the present judgment, where the negotiations on pay, which that action seeks to require an undertaking established in another Member State to enter into, form part of a national context characterised by a lack of provisions, of any kind, which are sufficiently precise and accessible that they do not render it impossible or excessively difficult in practice for such an undertaking to determine the obligations with which it is required to comply as regards minimum pay (see, to that effect, *Arblade and Others*, paragraph 43).

The case generated enormous controversy in Sweden and across Europe. Not only did it involve the disruption of the much-admired Swedish social model, pitting this against the economic freedoms of the Treaty, but it did so in the context of the 'new socio-economic diversity in the Union subsequent to its Eastern Enlargement', bringing to prominence the significant economic disparities between different parts of the European Union.[248] While the judgment has been much criticized, mostly for prioritizing economic free movement over collective labour rights and for the lack of judicial deference in a sensitive domestic field of social and labour policy,[249] it has also divided critics on questions such as whether it can be viewed as enhancing the rights of Latvian workers rather than undermining the rights of Swedish workers. Unlike its 'sister ruling' in *Viking*, above,[250] which was equally criticized for framing collective action as a restriction on freedom of establishment, the Court in *Laval* did not leave it to the national court to apply the proportionality test, but ruled the collective action to be unjustified.

Despite the heated political and public debate which followed the *Viking* and *Laval* cases, the Directive which was eventually adopted in partial response to the controversy, Directive 2014/67, was a fairly weak compromise measure which establishes the possibility for states to adopt measures to 'prevent abuse and circumvention' of the terms of the earlier Posted Workers Directive, and to improve cooperation between national authorities and to strengthen enforcement.[251]

---

[248] C Joerges, 'A New Alliance of De-Legalisation and Legal Formalism? Reflections on Responses to the Social Deficit of the European Integration Project' (2008) 19 Law and Critique 246; N Lindstrom, 'Service Liberalization in the Enlarged EU: A Race to the Bottom or the Emergence of Transnational Political Conflict' (2010) 48 JCMS 1307; U Belavusau, 'The Case of *Laval* in the Context of the Post-Enlargement EC Law Development' (2008) 9 German LJ 2279. For a critical overview, see D Kukovec, *Hierarchies as Law* (Harvard SJD Thesis, 2015).

[249] N Reich, 'Free Movement v. Social Rights in an Enlarged Union—The *Laval* and *Viking* Cases before the ECJ' (2008) 9 German LJ 159; C Kilpatrick, '*Laval*'s Regulatory Conundrum: Collective Standard-Setting and the Court's New Approach to Posted Workers' (2009) 34 ELRev 844. See the collection of essays by M Freedland and J Prassl, *Viking, Laval and Beyond* (Hart, 2015).

[250] (N 32).

[251] [2014] OJ L159/11.

(iii) Cross-Border Health Care

A further example of the Court's treatment of attempts to justify restrictions on the free movement of services is in the line of cases governing access to cross-border health care, discussed above.[252] In *Decker* and *Kohll*, the Court rejected the argument that the financial balance of the social security scheme would be upset, given that the expenses incurred were to be reimbursed at exactly the same rate as that applicable in the home state.[253] In *Leichtle*, the conditions imposed for reimbursement of accommodation and other expenses associated with obtaining a spa health cure in another Member State were deemed to be excessive and thus unjustified.[254]

In *Geraets-Smits*,[255] the Court concluded that the requirement of prior authorization, subject to the conditions of the necessity and 'normality' of the treatment obtained, might be justified in the interests of maintaining a balanced medical and hospital service open to all, or of preventing the risk of the social security system's financial balance being seriously undermined, or for essential public health reasons under Article 52 TFEU.[256] However, the two conditions had to be applied fairly in a non-discriminatory manner, so that the condition that the treatment sought should be 'normal' must, for example, take into account the findings of international medical science, and the condition concerning the 'necessity' meant that authorization should be given unless the same or equally effective treatment can be obtained without undue delay from an establishment with which the insured person's sickness insurance fund has contractual arrangements.[257] A similar ruling was given in *Müller-Fauré*, where the ECJ distinguished between hospital and non-hospital services, holding that the restrictive measures were more readily justified in the case of the former than the latter.[258] In *Watts*, the aim of 'ensuring sufficient and permanent access to a balanced range of high-quality hospital treatment in the State' was a legitimate aim, if applied in a proportionate way.[259] However, the Commission's infringement proceedings against Germany for imposing a range of restrictive durational and reimbursement measures on the receipt of care services in another state were dismissed by the CJEU on the ground that the Commission had failed to prove its case and had merely relied on the previous case law of the Court rather than seeking to prove the specific allegations in this case.[260]

(iv) National Taxation Rules

Just as in the context of freedom of establishment, there has been an increase in recent years in challenges to national taxation rules on the ground that they constitute unjustifiable restrictions on the freedom to provide

---

[252] (N 176); J van de Gronden, 'Cross-Border Health Care in the EU and the Organisation of the National Health Care Systems of the Member States: The Dynamics Resulting from the European Court of Justice's Decisions on Free Movement and Competition Law' (2008–2009) 26 Wis Int'l LJ 705; L Hancher and W Sauter, 'One Step Beyond? From *Sodemare* to *Docmorris*: The EU's Freedom of Establishment Case Law Concerning Healthcare' (2010) 47 CMLRev 117.

[253] Case C–120/95 *Decker* (n 176); Case C–158/96 *Kohll* (n 169).

[254] Case C–8/02 *Leichtle* [2004] ECR I–2641.

[255] Case C–157/99 *Geraets-Smits* (n 176).

[256] See also Case C–368/98 *Vanbraekel* (n 176), where a refusal to make an equivalent payment for hospital treatment received in another Member State with prior authorization was held to be unjustified under the Treaty and under Reg 1408/71.

[257] See also Case C–173/09 *Elchinov v Natsionalna zdravnoosiguritelna kasa* [2010] ECR I–8889.

[258] Case C–385/99 *Müller-Fauré* (n 176); Case C–512/08 *Commission v France* [2010] ECR I–8833 indicating that authorization requirements can also be allowed when applied to extra-mural medical services that imply the use of major medical equipment (such as PET scanners).

[259] Case C–372/04 *Watts* (n 176).

[260] Case C–562/10 *Commission v Germany* EU:C:2012:442, [24], [43], [50], [52].

services. In cases such as *Danner*,[261] *Gerritse*,[262] *FKP*,[263] *Centro Equestre da Lezíria*,[264]and *Commission v Belgium*,[265] the Court of Justice ruled that restrictive tax rules may be justified on grounds such as prevention of fraud or tax avoidance, effective fiscal supervision, and the effective collection of taxes, or on social grounds, but it has regularly rejected the argument on the facts of the case.[266] Further, the Court has indicated clearly that objectives such as the prevention of the erosion of the tax revenue base, or compensation for the low level of tax paid in the company's state of establishment do not constitute legitimate aims.[267]

The Court has also rejected attempts to justify national restrictions where the goals allegedly pursued by such measures were already satisfied by the existence of EU legislation.[268] Conversely, the Court has also indicated that in the absence of coordination of Member States' regulations on a given issue, a national rule will not be deemed to be disproportionate simply because it is stricter than rules applicable in other Member States.[269] Further, EU secondary legislation which implements the provisions on free movement of services in particular sectors or for particular activities must also be interpreted in the light of the fundamental principles laid down in the Treaty and in the case law, including the principles relating to the scope of permissible exceptions and imperative requirements.[270] Finally, the likely interaction of the derogation provisions contained in Article 16(1)(b) and (3) of the Services Directive, discussed below,[271] with the more general public interest justifications developed by the Court raises interesting questions.[272]

(D) NON-DISCRIMINATORY RESTRICTIONS UNDER ARTICLE 56

It has been made increasingly clear in recent years that, in the field of free movement of services, even genuinely non-discriminatory obstacles, as opposed to indirectly discriminatory restrictions, are likely to fall within the scope of Article 56 and to be subjected to the 'objective justification' test. While many of the early cases appeared to involve measures which imposed a heavier burden or a dual burden and thus could have been described as indirectly discriminatory,[273] there were also cases involving rules which did not burden established providers of services any less than non-established providers, and yet which were found to be incompatible with Article 56. In recent years, the Court has explicitly declared that it is not necessary for any kind of discrimination to be established, but simply an impediment to free movement or a restriction on access to the market of another Member State. At the same time, the Court has emphasized the commonality of the principles underpinning all of the internal market freedoms in this respect.[274]

---

[261] Case C–136/00 *Danner* [2002] ECR I–8147.

[262] Case C–234/01 *Gerritse* [2003] ECR I–5933

[263] Case C–290/04 *FKP Scorpio* (n 154).

[264] Case C–345/04 *Centro Equestre da Lezíria Grande Lda v Bundesamt für Finanzen* [2007] ECR I–1425.

[265] Case C–433/04 *Commission v Belgium* (n 79).

[266] Case C–53/13 *Strojírny Prostějov* EU:C:2014:2011.

[267] See, eg, Case C–294/97 *Eurowings Luftverkehrs* (n 103); Case C–422/01 *Försäkringsaktiebolaget Skandia v Riksskatteverket* [2003] ECR I–6817.

[268] See, eg, Case C–158/96 *Kohll* (n 169) [45]–[49].

[269] Case C–108/96 *MacQuen* (n 77); Case C–67/98 *Zenatti* (n 203).

[270] See, eg, Cases C–205/99 *Analir v Administración General de l'Estado* [2001] ECR I–1271; C–470/13 *Generali-Providencia Biztosító* EU:C:2014:2469; C–358/12 *Consorzio Stabile Libor Lavori Pubblici* EU:C:2014:2063.

[271] De Witte (n 315).

[272] In Case C–458/08 *Commission v Portugal* [2010] ECR I–11599, [88] the Court ruled that the obligation on Member States in Art 16(1) of the Services Dir to ensure access to a service activity within its territory by subjecting it only to non-discriminatory and objectively justified requirements 'stems directly from Article 49 EC' (now Art 56 TFEU).

[273] Marenco (n 78); Case C–379/92 *Peralta* (n 162) [51], where, in the absence of any direct or indirect discrimination or any advantage for domestic interests, Art 56 TFEU was held not to apply to a prohibition on discharging harmful chemicals at sea.

[274] Case C–55/94 *Gebhard* (n 21) [37]; Case C–390/99 *Canal Satélite* (n 11) in which the case law on goods and services was treated as being the same. On the convergence of the freedoms see C Barnard, 'Fitting the Remaining Pieces into

The judgment in *Säger* was the first to address the issue of non-discrimination directly.[275] The case concerned German legislation which reserved activities relating to the maintenance of industrial property rights to patent agents.[276] The UK government, citing earlier case law,[277] argued that in the absence of any discrimination, a restriction on the provision of services would not breach Article 56. Advocate General Jacobs responded:

> It does not seem unreasonable that a person establishing himself in a Member State should as a general rule be required to comply with the law of that State in all respects. In contrast, it is less easy to see why a person who is established in one Member State and who provides services in other Member States should be required to comply with all the detailed regulations in force in each of those States. To accept such a proposition would be to render the notion of a single market unattainable in the field of services.
>
> For this reason, it may be thought that services should rather be treated by analogy with goods, and that non-discriminatory restrictions on the free movement of services should be approached in the same way as non-discriminatory restrictions on the free movement of goods under the '*Cassis de Dijon*' line of case-law. That analogy seems particularly appropriate where, as in the present case, the nature of the service is such as not to involve the provider of the service in moving physically between Member States but where instead it is transmitted by post or telecommunications....
>
> [I] do not think that it can be right to state as a general rule that a measure lies wholly outside the scope of [*Article 56 TFEU*] simply because it does not in any way discriminate between domestic undertakings and those established in other Member States. Nor is such a view supported by the terms of [*Article 56 TFEU*]: its expressed scope is much broader. If such a view were accepted, it would mean that restrictions on the freedom to provide services would have to be tolerated, even if they lacked any objective justification, on condition that they did not lead to discrimination against foreign undertakings. There might be a variety of restrictions in different Member States, none of them intrinsically justified, which collectively might wholly frustrate the aims of [*Article 56 TFEU*] and render impossible the attainment of a single market in services. The principle should, I think, be that if an undertaking complies with the legislation of the Member State in which it is established it may provide services in another Member State, even though the provision of such services would not normally be lawful under the laws of the second Member State. Restrictions imposed by those laws can only be applied against the foreign undertaking if they are justified by some requirement that is compatible with the aims of the Community.[278]

The Advocate General's approach was a strongly liberalizing one, since almost any national law which regulates the domestic market even in pursuance of important national policies is potentially subject to rigorous scrutiny by the European Court for justification. Yet this approach has been confirmed by the Court in several judgments, beginning with *Alpine Investments*.[279] The case concerned a Dutch prohibition on cold-calling, ie on the making of unsolicited telephone calls without the prior written consent of the individuals concerned in order to offer financial services, and the prohibition applied both to calls made within the Netherlands and to calls made to other Member States. According to the Court

---

the Goods and Persons Jigsaw' (2001) 26 ELRev 35; T Connor, 'Goods, Persons, Services and Capital in the European Union: Jurisprudential Routes to Free Movement' (2010) 11 German LJ 159.

[275] The first signs were already visible in the *Lawyers' Services* case, concerning the implementation by Germany of Dir 77/249 on the exercise by lawyers of freedom to provide services. See Case 427/85 *Commission v Germany* [1988] ECR 1123; Case 292/86 *Gullung* (n 71); Case C–294/89 *Commission v France* [1991] ECR I–3591; Case C–289/02 *AMOK* (n 79).

[276] Case C–76/90 (n 20).

[277] Case 15/78 *Koestler* (n 164); AG Gulman in Case C–275/92 *Schindler* (n 26).

[278] Case C–76/90 *Säger* (n 20) 4234–4235.

[279] Case C–384/93 *Alpine Investments* (n 6). For criticism see L Daniele, 'Non-Discriminatory Restrictions on the Free Movement of Persons' (1997) 22 ELRev 191; C Hilson, 'Discrimination in Community Free Movement Law' (1999) 24 ELRev 445.

the prohibition deprived the operators of a rapid and direct technique for marketing and for contacting potential clients in other Member States, thus restricting the free movement of services:

> 35. Although a prohibition such as the one at issue in the main proceedings is general and non-discriminatory and neither its object nor its effect is to put the national market at an advantage over providers of services from other Member States, it can, none the less, as has been held (paragraph 28) constitute a restriction on the freedom to provide services.
>
> 36. Such a prohibition is not analogous to the legislation concerning selling arrangements held in *Keck and Mithouard* to fall outside the scope of Article 30 of the Treaty.
>
> 37. According to that judgment, the application to products from other Member States of national provisions restricting or prohibiting, within the Member State of importation, certain selling arrangements is not such as to hinder trade between Member States so long as, first, those provisions apply to all relevant traders operating within the national territory and, secondly, they affect in the same manner, in law and in fact, the marketing of domestic products and of those from other Member States. The reason is that the application of such provisions is not such as to prevent access by the latter to the market of the Member State of importation or to impede such access more than it impedes access by domestic products.
>
> 38. A prohibition such as that at issue is imposed by the Member State in which the provider of services is established and affects not only offers made by him to addressees who are established in that State or move there in order to receive services but also offers made to potential recipients in another Member State. It therefore directly affects access to the market in services in the other Member States and is thus capable of hindering intra-Community trade in services.

Although the reasoning is not altogether clear, the effect of paragraphs 37 and 38 is that a restrictive regulation will not fall outside the scope of Article 56 or 34 TFEU simply because it is non-discriminatory in law and in fact, unless it is *also* a restriction which does not in any way affect the access of the person in question to the market in goods or services of another Member State. If an effect on an individual's access to the market of another Member State can be shown, then, regardless of the equally restrictive effect on situations wholly internal to a Member State, the measure in question will fall within the scope of EU law and require objective justification.[280]

Further, the ruling in *Gebhard* on freedom of establishment, which suggested that the same rules were applicable to all four freedoms and that discrimination is not necessary for a restrictive measure to constitute an impediment to freedom of movement under the Treaty, has since been repeated in several cases concerning services. In a paragraph in *Arblade*, which has been repeated in a number of other rulings,[281] the ECJ declared:

> It is settled case law that Article 59 [now Art 56 TFEU] of the Treaty requires not only the elimination of all discrimination on grounds of nationality against providers of services who are established in another Member State but also the abolition of any restriction, even if it applies without distinction to national providers of services and to those of other Member States, which is liable to prohibit, impede or render less advantageous the activities of a provider of services established in another Member State where he lawfully provides similar services.[282]

---

[280] Not every restrictive measure has been held by the Court to fall within the scope of Art 56. Just as in the case of goods, workers, and establishment, some restrictions are said to be insufficiently direct or significant to be considered liable to have an effect on access to the market: see, eg, Cases C–51/96 and 191/97 *Deliège* (n 165), in which the Judo Federation selection rules for competitions were held not to determine access to the labour market; Case C–190/98 *Graf* (n 84). For criticism of the Court's inconsistency in this area, see S Enchelmaier (n 189).

[281] Case C–165/98 *Mazzoleni and ISA* [2001] ECR I–2189, [22]; Case C–49/98 *Finalarte* (n 19) [28].

[282] Cases C–369 and 376/96 *Arblade* (n 74) [33].

Thus the rules relating to freedom of movement and the internal market have moved away from the earlier emphasis on discrimination and protectionism and focus more on the creation of a single EU market. In that sense any national rules, whether discriminatory or not, which may impede inter-state trade and mobility by affecting the access of goods, persons, or services from one national market to another is in principle caught by EU law and must be justified by the regulating state.

5 GENERAL LEGISLATION TO FACILITATE ESTABLISHMENT AND SERVICES: RECOGNITION OF PROFESSIONAL QUALIFICATIONS

The recognition of qualifications is an important matter for the free movement of services, workers, and establishment alike, and there has been a great deal of litigation before the Court of Justice on this issue. However, in tandem with the developing case law of the Court, there has also been an active legislative programme on recognition of qualifications for many years. The EU moved over time towards a comprehensive mutual-recognition approach, culminating in the adoption of an umbrella Directive 2005/36 consolidating the prior legislation on the recognition of professional qualifications.[283]

(A) THE INITIAL SECTORAL HARMONIZATION/ COORDINATION APPROACH

Initially, the EU legislature pursued a harmonization or coordination approach, which focused on specific sectors of economic or professional life, with a view to reaching agreement between all Member States on the minimum standard[284] of training and education needed for a qualification in that field.[285] These directives mainly covered activities in the medical and health-related sphere—general practitioners, nurses, pharmacists, veterinary surgeons—and also architects, and there were some transitional and other directives on industries such as small craft, food and beverage, wholesale, intermediary, retail, and the coal trade.[286] A directive on lawyers' services was also adopted in 1977,[287] and a directive on the right of establishment for lawyers in 1998.[288]

---

[283] Directive 2005/36 on the Recognition of Professional Qualifications [2005] OJ L255/22. See also Dir 2013/55 [2013] OJ L354/132.

[284] For a case in which Austria was found to violate the sectoral Dirs on dentists' qualifications by recognizing persons as qualified to practise who had not met the minimum training criteria laid down see Case C–437/03 *Commission v Austria* [2005] ECR I–9373.

[285] This has been referred to as 'passive' recognition, since the active recognition work is done by the sectoral legislation and Member States need only passively recognize qualifications which comply with the standards set in that legislation: K Armstrong, 'Mutual Recognition' in C Barnard and J Scott (eds), *The Legal Foundations of the Single Market: Unpacking the Premises* (Hart, 2002) ch 9.

[286] For a case concerning one of the transitional dirs see Case C–58/98 *Corsten* [2000] ECR I–7919; and on pharmacists, Case C–221/05 *McCauley v Pharmaceutical Society of Ireland* [2006] ECR I–6869.

[287] Dir 77/249 [1977] OJ L78/17; Case C–289/02 *AMOK* (n 79). The Commission has initiated a review of the two Lawyers' Dirs: see Final Report: Evaluation of the Legal Framework for the Free Movement of Workers, http://ec.europa.eu/internal_market/qualifications/docs/studies/2013-lawyers/report_en.pdf.

[288] For a challenge to the lawyers' establishment Dir see Case C–168/98 *Luxembourg v Parliament and Council* [2000] ECR I–9131; P Cabral, Note (2002) 39 CMLRev 129; Cases C–351/01 *Commission v France* [2002] ECR I–8101; C–506/04 *Wilson v Ordre des avocats du barreau de Luxembourg* [2006] ECR I–8613; C–193/05 *Commission v Luxembourg* [2006] ECR I–8673.

(B) INTRODUCTION OF THE MUTUAL RECOGNITION APPROACH

It was not easy, however, to gain agreement on the content of such 'harmonizing' sectoral directives, and to get them adopted through the cumbersome EU legislative process. In 1974, the Council expressed the wish that future work on mutual recognition be based on 'flexible and qualitative criteria', and that directives 'should resort as little as possible to the prescription of detailed training requirements'.[289]

The 1984 summit of the European Council at Fontainebleau marked the beginning of a new approach, and the first mutual recognition Directive 89/48 was adopted five years later, providing for 'a general system for the recognition of higher-education diplomas awarded on completion of professional education and training of at least three years' duration'.[290] The Directive differed from previous sectoral directives in several ways.[291]

First, it was intended to apply to all regulated professions for which university-level training of at least three years was required and which was not covered by a specific directive. Secondly, recognition was to be based on the principle of mutual trust, without prior coordination of the preparatory educational and training courses for the various professions in question. The basic principle was that a host Member State may not refuse entry to a regulated profession to a national of a Member State who holds the qualifications necessary for exercise of that profession in another Member State.[292] Thirdly, recognition was granted to the 'end product', ie to fully qualified professionals, including any professional training required in addition to their university diplomas. Fourthly, where there were major differences in education and training, or in the structure of a profession, in different states, the Directive provided for compensation mechanisms in the form either of an adaptation period or an aptitude test.

While the mutual recognition approach has advantages over the time-consuming sectoral harmonization approach, there are also some obvious disadvantages. It does not provide an automatic guarantee to people holding specified qualifications that they will be accepted to practise in any Member State, but merely provides them with a starting point. States remain free, where either the content of the education or training received is inadequate or the structure of the profession it represents is different, to impose the additional requirement of an aptitude test or an adaptation period.[293] By allowing Member States to control and to supervise the process of recognition at each step, this approach is heavily reliant on mutual trust and on the adoption of a non-protectionist attitude by national competent authorities.[294] Nevertheless, it has become the dominant approach, and even the sectors in which harmonization-type directives were adopted have been affected by this approach, most recently under the terms of Directive 2005/36.

The basic thrust of Directive 89/48 was that if an EU national wished to pursue a regulated profession in any Member State, the competent authorities in the Member State could not refuse permission on the ground of inadequate qualifications if the person satisfied certain conditions. The conditions were that the person had pursued the equivalent of a three-year higher education course in the EU and had

---

[289] [1974] OJ C98/1.

[290] [1989] OJ L19/16. For cases involving non-implementation by Member States of Dir 89/48 see Cases C–216/94 *Commission v Belgium* [1995] ECR I–2155; C–365/93 *Commission v Greece* [1995] ECR I–499; C–285/00 *Commission v France* [2001] ECR I–3801; C–145/99 *Commission v Italy* [2002] ECR I–2235.

[291] For a summary see Bull EC 6–1988, 11.

[292] Case C–285/01 *Burbaud v Ministère de l'Emploi et de la Solidarité* [2003] ECR I–8219. For similar cases involving a selection examination imposed in relation to Dir 93/16 on doctors' qualifications see Cases C–232/99 *Commission v Spain* [2002] ECR I–4235; C–10–11/02 *Fascicolo et al* [2004] ECR I–11107.

[293] For a dispute concerning the scope of the professional qualifications of an Italian national seeking recognition as a hydraulic engineer in Spain under the provisions of Dir 89/48 see Case C–330/03 *Colegio de Ingenieros de Caminos, Canales y Puertos v Administración del Estado* [2005] ECR I–801.

[294] J Pertek, 'Free Movement of Professionals and Recognition of Higher Education Diplomas' (1992) 12 YBEL 320. See more generally I Lianos and D Gerard, 'Shifting narratives in European economic integration: trade in services, pluralism and trust', Centre for Law and Governance in Europe Working Paper Series 11/2011.

completed the necessary professional training in order to be qualified to take up the 'regulated profession' in question.[295]

Satisfaction of these conditions did not mean that the person had to be given permission to pursue that profession, but it meant that the competent national authorities could not refuse permission solely on the ground of inadequate qualifications. If the qualifications were considered adequate, then permission to practise should be given. If the duration of the person's training and education was however at least one year less than that required in the host state, the Directive permitted Member States to require certain evidence of professional experience. If, on the other hand, the matters covered by the person's education and training differed substantially from those covered by the host-state qualification, or if the host-state profession comprised specific regulated activities which were not within the profession regulated in the Member State where the qualification was obtained, the Member State was permitted to require the completion of an adaptation period or that an aptitude test be taken.[296]

Directive 89/48 was followed by Directive 92/51, which supplemented and adopted the same approach.[297] The 1992 Directive covered education and training other than the three-year higher-education requirement of Directive 89/48, such as one-year post-secondary courses, qualifying the holder to take up a regulated profession. The third general directive was Directive 99/42, which replaced the series of earlier transitional and other sectoral directives using a mutual recognition approach based on periods of consecutive experience and possession of skills, rather than the possession of formal qualifications or diplomas.[298]

Directives 89/48 and 92/51 were amended in 2001 along with most of the sectoral directives by a general (so-called SLIM) Directive 2001/19/EC.[299] The SLIM Directive simplified the coordination procedure under the general directives and introduced a range of other changes, including extension to the general system of the concept of 'regulated education and training', requiring host states to examine professional experience gained, incorporating some of the ECJ's case law on third-country diplomas, and specifying procedural rights.

(c) DIRECTIVE 2005/36 ON THE RECOGNITION OF PROFESSIONAL QUALIFICATIONS

In 2005, virtually all of the previous legislation, most importantly the three mutual recognition Directives of 1989, 1992, and 1999 and twelve of the sectoral directives (not including the two Lawyers' Directives[300]), was consolidated and replaced by a single Directive 2005/36 on the recognition of professional qualifications. The new Directive maintains the same approach and principles as the earlier mutual recognition legislation.[301]

---

[295] For an 'unregulated' profession see Case C–164/94 *Arantis* (n 59) on geologists, and on a profession which is unregulated in the state in which the qualification was obtained see Case C–149/05 *Price v Conseil des ventes volontaires de meubles aux enchères publiques* [2006] ECR I–7691. For the definition of a 'regulated profession' in Dir 89/48 [1989] OJ L19/16 and Dir 92/51 [1992] OJ L208/25, which includes being governed by the terms of a collective agreement, see Case C–234/97 *De Bobadilla* (n 92) [14]–[21]; Case C–586/08 *Rubino v Ministero dell'Università e della Ricerca* [2009] ECR I–12013; C–372/09 *Peñarroja Fa* EU:C:2011:156 on an 'unregulated' profession under Dir 2005/36.

[296] On the circumstances in which a Member State must permit the partial taking-up of a profession see Case C–330/03 *Colegio de Ingenieros de Caminos* (n 293); Case C–575/11 *Nasiopoulos* EU:C:2013:430.

[297] For a case involving recognition of a teacher's qualifications under both Dir 89/48 and Dir 92/51 see Case C–102/02 *Beuttenbuller v Land Baden-Wurttemberg* [2004] ECR I–5405.

[298] [1999] OJ L201/77.

[299] [2001] OJ L206/1.

[300] These two Lawyers' Dirs govern the recognition of the authorization of lawyers to practise, rather than recognition of their qualifications. Dir 2005/36 thus applies to the recognition of lawyers' qualifications. Dir 2005/35 however leaves unaffected other 'specific legal provisions regarding the recognition of professional qualifications, such as those existing in the field of transport, insurance intermediaries and statutory auditors'. For review of the two lawyers' Directives, see (n 287).

[301] Dir 2005/36 (n 2). For a case prohibiting a state from imposing any additional traineeship requirements on the holder of a professional architectural qualification from another state, see Case C–365/13 *Ordre des architectes* EU:C:2014:280.

Apart from consolidation, the aim of the 2005 Directive was to maintain the guarantees afforded by each of the prior recognition systems, and at the same time 'to create a single, consistent legal framework based on further liberalization of the provision of services, more automatic recognition of qualifications, and greater flexibility in the procedures for updating the Directive'. As with the Services Directive, which is discussed below, the original proposal for the Directive on Recognition of Professional Qualifications was amended and diluted in various ways in response to the concerns of Member States, in particular in relation to controls over the temporary provision of services.

The Directive contained some significant innovations. Three in particular should be mentioned. First, Title II established a more liberalized regime containing detailed procedures and stricter deadlines for decision-making, for the temporary provision of services under the provider's original professional title. Secondly, the part of Title III on establishment dealing with the former general mutual recognition regime introduced the notion of 'common platforms', defined in Article 15 as a set of criteria which make it possible to compensate for the widest range of substantial differences which have been identified between the training requirements in at least two-thirds of the Member States including all the Member States which regulate that profession. Thirdly, Title V provided for close collaboration between the competent administrative authorities of home and host states, involving confidential exchanges of information including in relation to disciplinary action taken or criminal sanctions imposed.[302]

Two other relevant developments in the field of recognition of qualifications were Decision 2241/2004, which introduced a set of European instruments to be used by individuals to describe their qualifications and competences,[303] and the European Qualifications Framework (EQF), intended to act as 'a translation device and neutral reference point for comparing qualifications across different education and training systems and to strengthen co-operation and mutual trust between the relevant stakeholder'.[304]

Directive 2005/36 was updated in 2013 with the adoption of Directive 2013/55, which introduced the 'European Professional Card' to facilitate automatic recognition at the level of the individual professional, and 'Common Training Frameworks' (in line with the existing EQF), as well as seeking to enhance cooperation between national authorities through the use of the Internal Market Information (IMI) System.[305]

(D) SITUATIONS NOT COVERED BY THE LEGISLATION

Despite the comprehensive scope of Directive 2005/36 and the other remaining legislation dealing with mutual recognition of qualifications, there will still be cases and circumstances in which the legislation does not provide a decisive answer. Examples may include the situation of a person seeking to pursue a profession which is unregulated in the host state[306] and other cases which are not covered by the secondary legislation.[307] In such situations, the basic principles outlined by the Court of Justice

---

On the legitimacy under the Dir of the imposition of training requirements in the field of medicine or dentistry, see Case C–492/12 *Conseil national de l'ordre des médecins* EU:C:2013:576.

302 The Court in Case C–475/11 *Konstantinides* EU:C:2013:542 held that rules regulating doctors' fees and prohibiting unprofessional advertising were not covered by Dir 2005/36.

303 Decision 2241/2004 of the European Parliament and Council on a single Community framework for the transparency of qualifications and competences (Europass) [2004] OJ L390/6.

304 COM(2006) 479 and the Recommendation of the European Parliament and Council [2008] OJ C111/01.

305 On the IMI system, see M Lottini, 'An Instrument of Intensified Informal Mutual Assistance: The Internal Market Information System (IMI) and the Protection of Personal Data' (2014) 20 EPL 107.

306 Cases C–164/94 *Arantis* (n 59); C–234/97 *De Bobadilla* (n 92); C–372/09 *Peñarroja Fa* EU:C:2011:156.

307 Cases C–31/00 *Conseil National de l'Ordre des Architectes v Dreessen* [2002] ECR I–663; C–313/01 *Morgenbesser v Consiglio dell'Ordine degli avvocati di Genova* [2003] ECR I–13467.

in *Vlassopoulou*[308] and *Heylens*[309] apply: Article 49 TFEU imposes a requirement on Member State authorities to examine the knowledge and qualifications already recognized or acquired by the person concerned in another Member State, and to give adequate reasons for the non-recognition of any qualification held, as well as access to a judicial remedy.[310] Qualifications obtained by EU nationals outside the EU are covered by Directive 2005/36 to the extent that the holder has at least three years' certified professional experience in the territory of a Member State which has chosen to give due recognition to the third-country qualification.[311] However, apart from EEA nationals, nationals of non-member countries who are established in the EU have no general rights of mutual recognition or permission to practise in a self-employed capacity under EU law, even when they have undergone precisely the same education and training as EU nationals within a Member State. Thus non-EU nationals are protected neither by the Treaty nor by the legislation. In a weak gesture towards recognizing this gap, recital 10 of Directive 2005/36 states that it does not impose any 'obstacle' to the right of Member States to recognize professional qualifications acquired outside the territory of the EU by third-country nationals, but stipulates that all recognition should respect the minimum training conditions for certain professions.

It should also be noted that 'wholly internal situations' are not covered by the Directive, in the sense that the applicant must be seeking to practise in a host state other than the state in which that person's qualification was obtained.[312]

In infringement proceedings brought by the Commission against Greece (and several other Member States) for imposing restrictions on access to the profession of notary, Greece argued to the Court that Directive 2005/36 did not cover notaries.[313] The CJEU however rejected this argument, ruling that the EU legislature when adopting the Directive did not adopt a position of the applicability of Directive 2005/36 to the activities of notaries. Directive 2013/55 however amended Directive 2005/36 to provide that it does not apply to notaries appointed by an official act of government.

6 GENERAL LEGISLATION TO FACILITATE ESTABLISHMENT AND SERVICES: THE SERVICES DIRECTIVE

Late in 2006, following a long and heated political process, Directive 2006/123 on services in the internal market was adopted.[314] Although called the 'Services Directive', in fact the legislation, just like Directive 2005/36 on recognition of qualifications, covers both temporary service provision as well as freedom of establishment. Initially known as the Bolkenstein Directive after the Commissioner who first introduced the proposal, this has been a controversial legislative initiative which was seen by some of its opponents, who dubbed it the Frankenstein Directive, as a threat to the social systems and

---

308 Case 340/89 *Vlassopoulou* (n 57).

309 Cases 222/86 *Heylens* (n 56); C–372/09 *Peñarroja Fa* EU:C:2011:156.

310 Cases C–586/08 *Rubino* (n 295); C–372/09 *Peñarroja Fa* ibid.

311 Art 3(3) of Dir 2006/35. This reflects the general approach which had been taken by the ECJ in relation to earlier dirs in Case C–238/98 *Hocsman v Ministre de l'Emploi* [2000] ECR I–6623; Case C–110/01 *Tennah-Durez v Conseil national de l'ordre des médecins* [2003] ECR I–6239 to the effect that national competent authorities must consider all diplomas or evidence of formal qualifications, and all relevant training and experience, of an EU national seeking to exercise the right of establishment, whether or not they were obtained within the EU. See also the earlier case of Case C–319/92 *Haim v Kassenzahnärztliche Vereinigung Nordrhein* [1994] ECR I–425 on recognition of periods of professional experience in other Member States.

312 Art 2(1) of Dir 2005/36; see Cases C–225–227/95 *Kapasakalis v Greece* [1998] ECR I–4329 for a 'purely internal situation' under Dir 89/48.

313 Case C–61/08 *Commission v Greece* (n 40). Also Case C–52/08 *Commission v Portugal* EU:C:2011:337.

314 Dir 2006/123/EC (n 3).

public-service ethic of many Member States. Some believe that opposition to the Directive played a part in the debate in France which led to a negative outcome in the referendum on the Constitutional Treaty in 2005.

Three particular questions concerning the Directive will be addressed here. In the first place, why was a *general* directive on the liberalization of service-provision in the EU considered to be necessary, so long after the General Programme of the 1960s and more than a decade after the Single Market programme of the 1990s? Secondly, why was the 'country-of-origin' principle which was central to the original proposal for the Directive so controversial? And, thirdly, what are the main significant features of the Services Directive? These questions are addressed in the extract below.

B de Witte, Setting the Scene—How did Services get to Bolkestein and Why?[315]

There was...in the early 1990s, a clear double-track approach to the establishment and functioning of the internal market for services: on the one hand, the most 'obstructed' and economically important sectors had been the subject of sector-specific internal market legislation as part of the 1992 programme, and on the other hand, the European Court of Justice had put in place a 'catch-all' legal regime, which allowed the Commission (in its other capacity of guardian of the Treaty) and interested firms or individuals to tackle national impediments to the services market that had been left in place by the EC legislative programme.

In addition, both elements of this legal strategy were elastic and therefore able to cope, in principle, with future challenges. The *judicial* approach was inherently open-ended, and therefore fit to identify new forms of trade in services as well as newly emerging impediments to such trade; it also covered gaps left even where internal market legislation had been adopted. The *legislative* approach was not exhausted by the deadline set for the 1992 programme, but could be used also later to deal with newly emerging problem sectors...

...

Why and when did the Commission start considering that this double-track approach was not sufficient for the establishment of a 'true' single market of services? One explanation could be the inherent weakness of the judicial limb of the double-track approach. There was a strong suspicion that the European Court of Justice, in its case-law, only dealt with the proverbial tip of the iceberg and that most impediments to trade in services remained hidden under the surface because the Commission failed to identify them in its infringement investigations, because the individual persons or firms suffering from those restrictions failed to take legal action, and because national courts, when confronted with such cases, failed to enforce the Treaty and/or to refer preliminary questions to the European Court of Justice. This suspicion—that many humanly and economically obnoxious impediments to the cross-border provision of services continue to exist in the post-1992 European Community—would seem to be confirmed by the marked increase of services cases before the ECJ in recent years....Whatever the reasons, the growing amount of ECJ cases—assuming that they still only constitute the tip of the iceberg, though perhaps a slightly bigger tip than before—seems to indicate that there are serious problems with the effective application of the internal market rules on services.

[*The author goes on to discuss the most controversial parts of the legislation as it was initially proposed, ie the parts dealing with temporary service-provision and specifically with the country-of-origin principle, rather than the more acceptable part on freedom of establishment which deals mainly with administrative simplification.*]

---

[315] B de Witte, 'Setting the Scene: How did Services get to Bolkestein and Why?', EUI Working Papers 20/2007; C Barnard, 'Unravelling the Services Directive' (2008) 45 CMLRev 323.

As far as provision of services without establishment was concerned, the main emphasis was not on getting rid of administrative formalities but on the much more radical idea that these service providers should in principle be *regulated by the state of origin* and not by the host state…

This element was less obviously necessary, its implications were less clearly spelled out, and it created the virulent opposition which led to a painful retreat in the revised version of 2006.

This 'regulatory competition' part of the Bolkestein draft was more problematic because, unlike the administrative simplification part, it represented a substantive shift compared to the ECJ's case law, and compared to the Commission's own approach in drafting internal market legislation. The case law of the European Court of Justice does not challenge, as a matter of principle, the application of the host country's laws and regulations. The principle of mutual recognition, as adopted by the Court, simply meant that the host state must take into account the laws and regulations to which the service provider is subject in its home state, so as not to create unjustified double burdens. This is not the same thing as imposing, as a matter of principle, the application of the laws of the country of origin.

[*De Witte further points out that the previous, carefully-targeted sector-specific approach of the Commission to the liberalization of services contrasts sharply with the general approach of the Services Directive, and was part of the reason for diluting the original draft. He argues that the final version of the Services Directive adopts instead the 'targeted cross-sector harmonization' approach seen above in the 2005 Directive on recognition of professional qualifications.*]

This time, with the Bolkestein draft, the Commission proposed a regulatory programme applying to the whole range of services (rather than a single one), without an attempt at listing those services…Moreover, the regulatory balance was decidedly tilted away towards deregulation with only a little amount of re-regulation. The basic principle was that the laws of the host country would not apply to the service provision, but instead the laws of the home country in which the service provider was established.

…

The idea of adopting the country of origin approach to regulation without identifying the sectors to which it would apply was the core innovation of the Bolkestein draft, compared to the Commission's earlier internal market policy, but it was also the cause of its troubles. This idea was abandoned in the final version of the Directive. The main innovative content left after the revision of the draft is its programme for 'smooth administration' (chapters II and III of the Directive), which fits better in the tradition of targeted cross-sector harmonisation that had been initiated by the diploma and public procurement directives.

…

As far as the regulation of services is concerned, the country-of-origin clause has been removed, but the price for the removal was the enactment of a highly complex and very confusing Article 16, which, taken as a whole, is reminiscent of the existing case-law of the ECJ on restrictions of services, but with some major differences which are not well explained in the rambling preamble of the Directive. Although the second sentence of Article 16(1) states that the 'Member State in which the service is provided shall ensure free access to and free exercise of a service activity within its territory', this promise of sweeping liberalisation is immediately tempered by the next sentence which makes clear that the host states may continue to apply their laws and regulations, as long as these are non-discriminatory, necessary and proportional—as the Court of Justice has consistently held in its case law on services. So far, Article 16 is only a restatement of existing court-made law. Paragraph 2 of Article 16 adds a number of prohibited requirements which, again, probably correspond to the Court's views of what is permissible, but the specification adds to legal clarity.

However, paragraph 3 of Article 16 attempts (whether deliberately or not) to modify existing services law by specifying which are the acceptable justifications for host country requirements, namely: reasons of public policy, public security, public health, the protection of the environment, and rules on employment conditions. This list is much shorter than the list of mandatory requirements that the Court of

Justice has come to recognize in the course of the years. Neither the text of the Directive nor its preamble explain why the Directive attempts to modify the Court's case law on this point…

So, although the 'revolution' proposed in the Bolkestein draft was turned back by the Council and Parliament, the laborious compromise reached during the codecision procedure seems nevertheless to have produced (whether intentionally or not) a deregulatory shift compared to existing EC services law. This is only one of the many uncertainties raised by the text of the Directive.

In its final form, therefore, the Services Directive accomplished a certain amount of useful administrative simplification and cooperation with a view to reducing obstacles to the free movement of services and establishment. In this sense, it follows the pattern set by Directive 2005/36, which dealt with one particular obstacle, viz the non-recognition of qualifications, and is in the tradition of previous sectoral legislation.

Articles 5–8 of the Services Directive deal with procedural simplification, the setting-up of 'points of single contact', the right to information, and electronic procedures. Articles 9–15 deal with freedom of establishment, covering authorization procedures, and indicating which requirements are prohibited and which are subject to evaluation. Many of these are based directly on ECJ case law, in some cases with more specific detail.

When it comes to temporary service provision, however, we have seen that the retreat from the country-of-origin principle in the Services Directive resulted in a complicated but weakly deregulatory set of provisions in Articles 16–18. One question which was posed in relation to Article 16 was whether the Court would continue to permit Member States to invoke a longer list of grounds for objective justification than the five specific grounds set out in Article 16(3) of the Directive, in keeping with its long-standing interpretation of the Treaty provisions on the free movement of services in this respect.[316] In *OSA*, the Court was asked whether Article 16 precluded a state from adopting a law reserving the collective management of copyright in the territory to a single monopoly collecting society, preventing recipients from using their choice of collecting society from other states.[317] However, the CJEU did not need to consider whether Article 16 might not provide grounds to justify such a restriction, because it ruled instead that Article 16 did not apply to copyright due to the terms of Article 17 of the Directive.

Articles 19–21 of the Directive govern the rights of recipients of services. And finally, Articles 22–27 cover a range of detailed provisions on the 'quality of services' (covering issues such as availability of information, commercial communications, liability insurance, and dispute-settlement).[318]

Articles 28–36 deal with administrative cooperation (covering issues such as supervision, safety alerts, reputational information, and mutual assistance), and Articles 37–43 contain a range of provisions (including a code of conduct, mutual evaluation and review mechanisms, and a Comitology procedure) intended to further the aims of the Directive.

Finally, while the Directive is a general one applicable in principle to all kinds of services, its scope is not comprehensive. Rather it is negatively defined by a series of exclusions of particular kinds of services from its coverage, many of which were again a consequence of parliamentary amendments to

---

[316] One of several arguments in favour of adherence by the Court to its wider, non-exhaustive list of potential justifications is that otherwise the field of services will differ in an apparently arbitrary way from those of goods and workers, where restrictions on free movement can, so long as they are proportionate, be justified on open-ended public interest grounds. Rec 40 to the Dir arguably also supports the broader reading. In Case C–458/08 *Commission v Portugal* (n 151) the Court held that the obligation in Art 16(1) of Dir 2006/123 stems directly from Art 56 TFEU.

[317] Case C–351/12 *OSA* EU:C:2014:110.

[318] In Case C–111/09 *Société fiduciaire nationale d'expertise comptable v Ministre du Budget* [2011] ECR I–2551, the CJEU ruled that Art 24(1) of the Services Dir precludes national legislation which totally prohibits the members of a regulated profession, such as that of qualified accountant, from canvassing.

the initial draft legislation.[319] Apart from the exclusion of sectors already covered by legislation such as financial services, e-communication, and transport, Articles 1–3 contain a range of exclusions: for example, non-economic services of general interest, social services, health care,[320] private security services; explanations of the areas which the Directive 'does not affect' or 'does not concern'; and indications of how it should interact with overlapping legislation such as that on mutual recognition of qualifications. These are in addition to the series of derogations provided for in Articles 17–18. Many of these provisions, which were politically crucial to the adoption process and which were often animated by concerns about the impact of the Directive on the different social-protection systems of Member States,[321] are rather convoluted and unpredictable in their legal effect. To give one example, the declaration in Article 1 that the Directive 'does not affect labour law…which Member States apply in accordance with national law which respects Community law' is circular and confusing.

In all, even if not exactly Frankenstein's monster, the Directive is at best a patchy, complicated, and legally rather unsatisfactory outcome to a fraught and lengthy legislative process.

7 CONCLUSIONS

i. The Court of Justice has increasingly adopted a similar approach to the various Treaty freedoms, including the free movement of services and establishment, such that any national rule which constitutes an inter-state impediment to market access falls in principle within the scope of the free movement rules and requires justification.

ii. Relevant differences remain between temporary service provision, on the one hand, and establishment, on the other. These differences are reflected partly in the more extensive case law on objective justification in the field of services, and partly in the distinction drawn between services and establishment in the two recent directives on recognition of professional qualifications and services in the internal market, with an emphasis on greater liberalization in the case of temporary service provision.

iii. It remains unclear even after the controversial *Laval* and *Viking* cases, which applied the Treaty provisions on establishment and services to collective action by trade unions, whether those provisions will be deemed fully horizontally applicable to all private action.

iv. After years of pursuing a slow sectoral strategy of legislative harmonization of professional qualifications, there was a change of approach in the late 1980s to one of general mutual recognition. In 2005, a single consolidating directive on the recognition of professional qualifications was adopted. This directive, and a supplementary directive adopted in 2013, retained the main elements of previous legislation, but sought to simplify and liberalize further the recognition of entitlement to practise in the case of temporary service providers, and to strengthen the system of recognition for those exercising rights of establishment.

v. Together with Directive 2004/38 on the free movement and residence of EU citizens discussed in Chapters 21 and 23, these directives signify a general move towards legislative consolidation in the field of free movement.

---

[319] See, eg, Case C–197/11 *Libert* EU:C:2013:288, concerning the exclusion from the Dir of rules concerning the development or use of land, town and country planning, building standards.

[320] See Case C–57/12 *Femarbel* EU:C:2013:517 on whether the exclusion of health care and social services from the Dir under Art 2(2)(f) and (j) would cover activities related to the care of elderly persons, and day-care centres.

[321] For similar concerns arising in litigation before the Court see Cases C–341/05 *Laval* and C–438/05 *Viking* (n 32).

vi. Although EU law on establishment and services applies only to economic activity, the case law—in particular on cross-border access to health care—indicates that important or 'special' public services such as health, welfare, and education will not escape the Treaty rules if they are organized and provided through a system which lends itself to market behaviour, and where some kind of remuneration is provided.

8 FURTHER READING

Books

BARNARD, C, *The Substantive Law of the EU: The Four Freedoms* (Oxford University Press, 4th edn, 2013)

CREMONA, M (ed), *Market Integration and Public Services in the European Union* (Oxford University Press, 2011)

HATZOPOULOS, V, *Regulating Services in the European Union* (Oxford University Press, 2012)

HEREMANS, T, *Professional Services in the EU Internal Market: Quality Regulation and Self-Regulation* (Hart, 2012)

KLAMERT, M, *Services Liberalization in the EU and the WTO: Concepts, Standards and Regulatory Approaches* (Cambridge University Press, 2014)

PASCHALIDIS, P, *Freedom of Establishment and Private International Law for Corporations* (Oxford University Press, 2012)

SNELL, J, *Goods and Services in EC Law* (Oxford University Press, 2002)

WEISS, F, AND KAUPA, C, *European Union Internal Market Law* (Cambridge University Press, 2014)

WHITE, R, *Workers, Establishment, and Services in the European Union* (Oxford University Press, 2004)

WIBERG, M, *The EU Services Directive: Law or Simply Policy?* (Asser Press, 2014)

WOODS, L, *Free Movement of Goods and Services within the European Community* (Ashgate, 2004)

CITIZENSHIP OF THE EUROPEAN UNION

1 CENTRAL ISSUES

i.   The Maastricht Treaty first introduced the legal concept of EU citizenship as part of the attempt to move from a mainly economic community to a political union. In addition to providing a stronger Treaty basis for the rights of movement, residence, and equal treatment of EU nationals, and gathering existing entitlements together under the umbrella of citizenship, Articles 20–25 TFEU created a number of novel political and electoral rights.

ii.   The Lisbon Treaty subsequently linked EU citizenship more closely to the prohibition on discrimination on grounds of nationality, and situated EU citizenship in the context of an emphasis on representative and participatory democracy. The Commission has attempted to build on these provisions in recent years, not by introducing new laws but attempting to improve and promote active enjoyment of existing citizenship rights.[1] The Lisbon Treaty introduced an 'agenda-setting' citizens' initiative, which was the subject of implementing legislation in 2011.[2] This popular initiative has attracted significant interest and suggestions for reform[3] as well as critique from civil society.[4]

iii. Directive 2004/38 consolidated and replaced most of the legislation governing the rights of movement and residence of all previous categories of people enjoying such rights under EU law, including workers, the self-employed, job-seekers, students, families, etc, under the title of 'citizens'. However, the ECJ has emphasized that Directive 2004/38 does not eliminate the different EU law categories

---

[1] See, eg, Decision 1093/2012 on the European Year of Citizens (2013) [2012] OJ L325/1; Commission Recommendation 2013/142 on enhancing the democratic and efficient conduct of the elections to the European Parliament and Commission Communication, COM(2013) 126 and the follow-up report, COM(2014) 196; Commission Report under Article 25 TFEU, 'On progress towards effective EU Citizenship 2011–2013', COM(2013) 270; EU Citizenship Report 2013, 'EU citizens: your rights, your future', COM(2013) 269 final; Commission Communication on the consequences of disenfranchisement of Union citizens exercising their right to free movement, COM(2014) 33 final; Commission Communication on 'Citizens' Dialogues as a Contribution to Developing a European Public Space', COM(2014) 173; Commission DG Justice, 'Final Report on the Evaluation of the impact of the free movement of EU citizens at the local level' (Jan 2014).

[2] Regulation (EU) No 211/2011 of the European Parliament and of the Council of 16 February 2011 on the citizens' initiative [2011] OJ L65/1, together with Commission Delegated Reg 887/2013 and Commission Implementing Reg 1179/2011. For the Commission's report on the application of Reg 211/2011 for the first three years, see COM(2015) 145; also http://ec.europa.eu/citizens-initiative/public/initiatives/ongoing for past and present petitions introduced under the initiative.

[3] See the European Parliament report on the first three years of implementation of the citizens' initiative: www.europarl.europa.eu/EPRS/EPRS_IDAN_536343_Implementation_of_the_European_Citizens_Initiative.pdf; also the European Parliament hearing in Feb 2015 on how to reform of the citizen's initiative: www.citizens-initiative.eu/ep-public-hearing/.

[4] See https://euobserver.com/political/127808.

of persons and rights, and that the distinction between economically active and non-economically active EU nationals remains important.

iv. The ECJ's rulings on EU citizenship have been important in several ways. First, the Court established that the Treaty provisions on citizenship create certain autonomous rights, independent of other Treaty provisions governing movement and residence. Secondly, the ECJ linked the provisions on citizenship with the prohibition on discrimination on grounds of nationality in a way which has strengthened the rights and entitlement of EU nationals and their families—both in host Member States and in their own—on matters such as social benefits, taxation, criminal procedures, and dual-nationality situations. However, the Court has at the same time been responsive to Member State concerns in its rulings on access to education for EU citizens in other Member States, and more recently on so-called 'benefits tourism' involving claims made by non-economically active EU citizens to access social welfare benefits in other Member States.

2 INTRODUCTION

The Treaty on European Union first introduced the legal concept of citizenship into EU law,[5] although the idea of European citizenship and the rhetoric of a 'People's Europe' had been in circulation for a long time.[6] The introduction of EU citizenship was greeted at the time with some academic scepticism.[7] Critics focused on the absence of reciprocal duties (other than as a consequence of the ECJ's rulings on horizontal direct effect of certain Treaty provisions[8]), which might give rise to a more active citizenship,[9] ongoing discrimination against resident third-country nationals,[10] and the subjection of citizens' rights of residence to the limiting conditions laid down in earlier directives.

The ECJ has continued to repeat the delphic phrase, first uttered in the *Grzelczyk* case, that: 'Union citizenship is destined to be the fundamental status of nationals of the Member States'.[11] Yet the normative basis for and the exact content of EU citizenship remains ambiguous.[12] Further, the question arises whether EU citizenship has become the primary legal status under EU law for Member States' nationals,

---

[5] C Closa, 'The Concept of Citizenship in the Treaty on European Union' (1992) 29 CMLRev 1137.

[6] See, eg, 'Towards a Citizens' Europe', Bull EC Supp 7–1975, 11, and the report on 'A People's Europe' following the Fontainebleau summit of the European Council, COM(84) 446 final.

[7] See, eg, on the narrow and exclusionary nature of EU citizenship M Everson, 'The Legacy of the Market Citizen' in J Shaw and G More (eds), *New Legal Dynamics of European Union* (Oxford University Press, 1995) 73; C Lyons, 'Citizenship in the Constitution of the European Union: Rhetoric or Reality?' in R Bellamy (ed), *Constitutionalism, Democracy, and Sovereignty: American and European Perspectives* (Avebury, 1996) 96; H D'Oliveira, 'European Citizenship: Its Meaning, Its Potential' in R Dehousse (ed), *Europe after Maastricht* (Law Books in Europe, 1994). For a more recent critique, see A Menendez, 'Which Citizenship? Whose Europe? The Many Paradoxes of European Citizenship' (2014) 15 German LJ 907.

[8] E.g. Cases 43/75 *Defrenne v SABENA* [1976] ECR 455; C–281/98 *Angonese v Cassa di Riparmio di Bolzano SpA* [2000] ECR I–4139; C–341/05 *Laval* [2007] ECR I–11767. Compare D Kochenov, 'EU Citizenship without Duties' (2014) 20 ELJ 482.

[9] J Weiler, 'Citizenship and Human Rights' in J Winter *et al* (eds), *Reforming the TEU: The Legal Debate* (Kluwer, 1996).

[10] Directive 2003/109/EC of 25 November 2003 concerning the status of third-country nationals who are long-term residents [2004] OJ L16/44, Council Decision 2007/435/EC establishing the European Fund for integrating third country nationals; and the Commission Report on the application of Dir 2003/109, COM(2011) 585. See also D Acosta Arcazaro, *The Long Term Residence Directive as a Subsidiary Form of EU Citizenship* (Martinus Nijhoff, 2011) and A Schrauwen, 'Granting the Right to Vote for the European Parliament to Third-Country Nationals' (2013) 19 ELJ 201.

[11] Case C–184/99 *Grzelczyk v Centre public d'aide sociale d'Ottignies-Louvain-la-Neuve* [2001] ECR I–6193, [31].

[12] For a sample from a vast literature, see P Eleftheriadis, 'The Content of European Citizenship' (2014) 15 German LJ 777; W Maas, 'The Origins, Evolution, and Political Objectives of EU Citizenship' (2014) 15 German LJ 797; C O'Brien, 'I Trade, Therefore I Am: Legal Personhood in the European Union' (2013) 50 CMLRev 1643; F Strumia, 'Looking for Substance at the Boundaries: European Citizenship and Mutual Recognition of Belonging' (2013) 32 YBEL 432.

subsuming and rendering residual the other legal categories into which EU law traditionally divided the nationals of EU Member States (worker, student, privileged family member, etc), or whether the practical legal impact of EU citizenship remains supplemental and residual to those other categories. The answer probably lies somewhere in between, as we shall see from the discussion throughout this chapter.

Article 20 TFEU summarizes the main elements of EU citizenship as follows:

1. Citizenship of the Union is hereby established. Every person holding the nationality of a Member State shall be a citizen of the Union. Citizenship of the Union shall be additional to and not replace national citizenship.

2. Citizens of the Union shall enjoy the rights and be subject to the duties provided for in the Treaties. They shall have, inter alia:

(a) the right to move and reside freely within the territory of the Member States;

(b) the right to vote and to stand as candidates in elections to the European Parliament and in municipal elections in their Member State of residence, under the same conditions as nationals of that State

(c) the right to enjoy, in the territory of a third country in which the Member State of which they are nationals is not represented, the protection of the diplomatic and consular authorities of any Member State on the same conditions as the nationals of that State;

(d) the right to petition the European Parliament, to apply to the European Ombudsman, and to address the institutions and advisory bodies of the Union in any of the Treaty languages and to obtain a reply in the same language.

These rights shall be exercised in accordance with the conditions and limits defined by the Treaties and by the measures adopted thereunder.

A number of preliminary points may briefly be noted. First, EU citizenship is expressly made 'additional to' to national citizenship.[13] Indeed, while the notion of EU citizenship poses a challenge to certain dimensions of nationality law, including aspects of dual nationality,[14] and restrictions on the use of surnames,[15] it does not yet displace the centrality of national citizenship in Europe.[16] EU citizenship is contingent upon possession of the nationality of a Member State. EU law does not directly regulate the conditions under which Member States confer nationality,[17] but it indirectly regulates aspects of this process by requiring them to recognize and not to impede enjoyment of the nationality duly granted

---

[13] The original Maastricht Treaty did not contain this provision. The Amsterdam Treaty added a phrase to state that EU citizenship was 'complementary to' national citizenship, and the Lisbon Treaty changed the term 'complementary' to 'additional', at the insistence of Member States: see J Shaw, 'The Treaty of Lisbon and Citizenship', available at http://.fedtrust.co.uk/admin/uploads/PolicyBrief_Citizenship.pdf.

[14] See D Kochenov, 'Double Nationality in the EU: An Argument for Tolerance' (2011) 17 ELJ 323.

[15] Cases C–148/02 *Garcia Avello v Belgium* [2003] ECR I–11613; C–353/06 *Grunkin and Paul v Standesamt Stadt Niebüll* [2008] ECR I–7639; C–208/09 *Sayn-Wittgenstein v Landeshauptmann von Wien* [2010] ECR I–13693; C–391/09, *Runevič-Vardyn* EU:C:2011:291.

[16] See, however, D Kochenov, 'Rounding up the Circle: The mutation of Member States nationalities under pressure from EU citizenship', EUI RSCAS Working Paper 2010/23; G Davies, 'Any Place I Hang My Hat? or: Residence is the New Nationality' (2005) 11 ELJ 43; R Bauböck, 'The Three Levels of Citizenship within the European Union' (2014) 15 German LJ 751.

[17] Declaration No 2 on Nationality of a Member State appended to the Maastricht Treaty confirms that the question whether an individual possesses the nationality of a Member State is determined by reference to the national law of the Member State concerned. This includes the conditions for naturalization. For a survey of naturalization procedures in the EU, see http://eudo-citizenship.eu/docs/policy-brief-naturalisation_revised.pdf.

by another Member State.[18] The *Rottmann* case addressed the question whether the loss or revocation of Member State nationality acquired by deception falls within the scope of EU law, or remains purely a matter of national law.

Case C–135/08 **Rottmann v Freistadt Bayern**
[2010] ECR I–1449

[Note Lisbon Treaty renumbering: Art 17 EC is now Art 20 TFEU]

Rottmann was an Austrian national by birth, who gained German citizenship by naturalization. The naturalization process had the result, under Austrian law, of the loss of his Austrian nationality. When the German authorities discovered he had concealed the fact that serious criminal proceedings were pending against him in Austria, they moved to revoke his newly acquired German nationality. Since revocation would also mean the loss of his EU citizenship and would leave him stateless, Rottmann challenged the decision revoking German nationality and the case was referred to the ECJ.

THE ECJ

42. It is clear that the situation of a citizen of the Union who, like the applicant in the main proceedings, is faced with a decision withdrawing his naturalisation, adopted by the authorities of one Member State, and placing him, after he has lost the nationality of another Member State that he originally possessed, in a position capable of causing him to lose the status conferred by Article 17 EC and the rights attaching thereto falls, by reason of its nature and its consequences, within the ambit of European Union law . . .

45. Thus, the Member States must, when exercising their powers in the sphere of nationality, have due regard to European Union law . . .

48. The proviso that due regard must be had to European Union law does not compromise the principle of international law previously recognised by the Court, and mentioned in paragraph 39 above, that the Member States have the power to lay down the conditions for the acquisition and loss of nationality, but rather enshrines the principle that, in respect of citizens of the Union, the exercise of that power, in so far as it affects the rights conferred and protected by the legal order of the Union, as is in particular the case of a decision withdrawing naturalisation such as that at issue in the main proceedings, is amenable to judicial review carried out in the light of European Union law.

However, the Court went on to rule that the decision to withdraw nationality on the ground of deception might nonetheless be compatible with EU law, if it was a proportionate response to the legitimate interest of a state in protecting the special relationship of solidarity and good faith between it and its nationals, and the reciprocity of rights and duties which form the bond of nationality. The question of proportionality was left to the national court to decide. The *Rottmann* case has generated an avalanche of academic commentary,[19] with some criticizing the ruling for apparently retreating from earlier

---

[18] Cases C–369/90 *Micheletti v Delegación del Gobierno en Cantabria* [1992] ECR I–4239; C–192/99 *R v Secretary of State for the Home Department, ex p Kaur* [2001] ECR I–1237; C–200/02 *Chen v Home Secretary* [2004] ECR I–9925; S Hall, 'Determining the Scope *Ratione Personae* of European Citizenship: Customary International Law Prevails for Now' (2001) 28 LIEI 355; G-R de Groot and N Chun Luk, 'Twenty Years of CJEU Jurisprudence on Citizenship' (2014) 15 German LJ 821.

[19] The EUR-Lex website lists thirty-four case notes and commentaries on *Rottman*: http://eur-lex.europa.eu/legal-content/EN/ALL/?uri=CELEX:62008CJ0135&qid=1428067178987. See also http://eudo-citizenship.eu/citizenship-forum/254-has-the-european-court-of-justice-challenged-member-state-sovereignty-in-nationality-law?start=3.

rulings on the relationship between Member State nationality and EU citizenship such as *Micheletti*,[20] while others hailed it as a seminal case and a far-reaching judgment.[21]

In 2013, a fresh controversy arose over the offer 'for sale' of Maltese citizenship—and hence also the EU citizenship that would flow therefrom—for €650,000.[22] However, despite extensive criticism and arguments that the EU could and should intervene,[23] the Maltese Government eventually amended its 'investor citizenship' scheme under pressure from the Commission.[24]

3 THE RIGHTS OF FREE MOVEMENT AND RESIDENCE OF EU CITIZENS

The provisions of Articles 21–25 TFEU elaborate on the rights summarized in Article 20(2)(a)–(d), beginning with the core rights of free movement and residence.

Article 21

1. Every citizen of the Union shall have the right to move and reside freely within the territory of the Member States, subject to the limitations and conditions laid down in the Treaties and by the measures adopted to give them effect.

2. If action by the Union should prove necessary to attain this objective and the Treaties have not provided the necessary powers, the European Parliament and the Council, acting in accordance with the ordinary legislative procedure, may adopt provisions with a view to facilitating the exercise of the rights referred to in paragraph 1.

3. For the same purposes as those referred to in paragraph 1 and if the Treaties have not provided the necessary powers, the Council, acting in accordance with a special legislative procedure, may adopt measures concerning social security or social protection. The Council shall act unanimously after consulting the European Parliament.[25]

The introduction of these provisions into the EU Treaties has had an impact in a range of ways on the existing body of EU law, which will be described in Section 4 of the chapter below. First, the relevant

---

[20] Case C–369/90 (n 18).

[21] Since the case and the Commission's report on citizenship of the EU, COM(2010) 602, the Commission launched a call for proposals on transnational projects, JUST/2013/FRC/AG, including to 'Facilitate sharing of knowledge and exchange of best practices on acquisition and loss of Union citizenship (BPoC)'.

[22] For a series of commentaries on the Maltese controversy, see http://eudo-citizenship.eu/commentaries/citizenship-forum/990-should-citizenship-be-for-sale.

[23] For European Parliament intervention see www.europarl.europa.eu/news/en/news-room/content/20140110IPR32392/html/EU-citizenship-should-not-be-for-sale-at-any-price-says-European-Parliament. In defence of Malta's action, see D Kochenov, 'EU Citizenship for Real: Its Hypocrisy, its Randomness, its Price' available at http://papers.ssrn.com/sol3/papers.cfm?abstract_id=2385340.

[24] For a joint statement issued by the Commission and the Maltese authorities in Jan 2014, see http://europa.eu/rapid/press-release_MEMO-14-70_en.htm. Also S Carrera, 'How Much Does EU Citizenship Cost?', CEPS Policy Paper in Liberty and Security, 64/2014.

[25] The Lisbon Treaty amended this provision slightly with the effect that provisions concerning passports, identity cards, and residence permits, which were previously excluded from the scope of EU legislative competence under Art 18 EC due to the Treaty provisions in the Area of Freedom, Security and Justice, can be adopted by ordinary legislative procedure rather than requiring the special legislative procedure. Measures on social security or social protection can also now be adopted under this Art, albeit using the special legislative procedure.

parts of Directive 2004/38 which implement various aspects of the Treaty provisions on citizenship will briefly be outlined.

(A) DIRECTIVE 2004/38 ON THE RIGHTS OF FREE MOVEMENT AND RESIDENCE FOR EU CITIZENS AND THEIR FAMILIES

We saw in Chapter 21 that Directive 2004/38[26] consolidated virtually all of the existing legislation on the free movement of persons into a single instrument, repealing and replacing most of the pre-existing laws including the three Residence Directives. It created, according to the Commission, 'a single legal regime for free movement and residence within the context of citizenship of the Union while maintaining the acquired rights of workers'.[27] While in substance Directive 2004/38 did not significantly change the conditions and terms which had been laid down in the three earlier Residence Directives,[28] the Directive implemented a fundamental Treaty-based right of residence for citizens, rather than merely a legislative right.

A full discussion of the main provisions of Directive 2004/38 is contained in Chapter 21. All the main provisions discussed in that context—the initial three-month period of residence, the general right of residence and the right of permanent residence, the reduction in formalities required for entry and residence, the category of family members included, the enhanced procedural and substantive protections in the event of restrictive measures being taken, a general right to equal treatment—apply to all EU citizens and not just to those who are employed or self-employed. The main provisions of the Directive which are specific to EU citizens who are not economically active, or who are students, are set out and briefly discussed below.

The CJEU ruled in *McCarthy*[29] and subsequent case law[30] that Directive 2004/38 provides for the right of residence of an EU citizen and a derived right of residence for his or her privileged family members only where that citizen has *exercised the right of freedom of movement by becoming established* in a Member State other than the Member State of nationality. Articles 20 and 21 TFEU may however in certain circumstances protect the right of residence of a citizen in his or her own state, together with the derived right of her family members.[31]

Article 7(1)(b) and (c) establish the conditions for the right of residence of EU citizens who are neither workers nor self-employed persons. Article 7(1)(b) essentially incorporates the main conditions from the previous Residence Directives, namely that citizens must have sufficient resources for themselves and their family members not to become a burden on the social assistance system of the host Member State during their period of residence, and must have comprehensive sickness insurance cover in the host state. The ECJ has given a number of rulings on the notion of 'dependence' for the purposes

---

[26] Directive 2004/38/EC of the European Parliament and of the Council of 29 April 2004 on the right of citizens of the Union and their family members to move and reside freely within the territory of the Member States [2004] OJ L158/77.

[27] For a report on the impact and effect of Dir 2004/38, see Commission DG Justice, 'Evaluation of the impact of the free movement of EU citizens at the local level' (2014).

[28] Dir 90/366 (replaced later by Dir 93/96) [1993] OJ L317/59; Dir 90/365 [1990] OJ L180/28 and Dir 90/364 [1990] OJ L180/26 covered students who are enrolled in a course of study or vocational training, persons who had previously worked or are retired, and a catch-all category for non-economically active persons who did not previously enjoy rights of movement under EU law respectively.

[29] Case C–434/09 *McCarthy* [2011] ECR I–3375.

[30] Case C–456/12 *O & B* EU:C:2014:135.

[31] See Case C–34/09 *Zambrano v ONEM* [2011] ECR I–1177 and the case law following it discussed in Section 4(b).

of identifying which family members have a derived right of residence,[32] and in relation to the broader category of family members whose admission Member States should 'facilitate'.[33]

Article 7(1)(c) governs students and provides that EU citizens shall enjoy a right of residence where they are enrolled at a recognized educational establishment for the purposes of study, have comprehensive sickness insurance, and can provide an assurance (whether by declaration or otherwise)[34] that they have sufficient resources to avoid becoming a burden on the social assistance scheme.[35] We shall see in Section 4(c) below that the ECJ has required these conditions to be interpreted and applied in a proportionate manner, recognizing that a degree of solidarity between citizens of different Member States had been created by the status of EU citizenship.

Article 8(4) of the Directive elaborates further on the requirement of sufficient resources, providing that no fixed amount may be laid down by Member States, that in any case the amount must not be higher than the eligibility threshold for social assistance or the minimum state social security pension, and that the personal situation of the person concerned must be taken into account.[36]

Article 12 concerns acquisition of the right of permanent residence by the family members of an EU citizen who is deceased or departs from the Member State. The period of time required for acquiring the right of permanent residence has been the subject of interpretation by the ECJ, discussed in Section 4(c)(iv) below. Article 12(2) provides that before acquiring the right of permanent residence, the persons in question (if they are not workers or self-employed) remain subject to the requirements of sufficient resources and adequate sickness insurance. The right of residence of such family members is said to be retained 'exclusively on a personal basis'. Article 13 similarly governs the right of family members to remain, and to gain permanent residence, in the event of divorce, annulment, or termination of a registered partnership, and it contains similar conditions to those in Article 12.[37] Article 14 governs the general initial three-month right of residence for all EU citizens,[38] and subjects it to one condition only: ie that they do not become an unreasonable burden on the social assistance scheme of the host state.[39]

---

[32] On the purely factual requirement of a situation of genuine 'dependence', which must exist at the time the family member seeks to join the EU citizen, see Case C–423/12 *Flora May Reyes* EU:C:2014:16, establishing that a direct descendant who is over 21 does not need to have sought employment in the state of origin in order to demonstrate factual dependence.

[33] On the discretion which Member States enjoy and the steps they may be required to take in relation to those 'dependants' or household members from their state of origin who do not enjoy a derived right of residence under Arts 3(1) and 2(2) but whose entry the state must 'facilitate' under Art 3(2) of the Dir, see Case C–83/11 *Rahman* EU:C:2012:519.

[34] Art 8(3) of the Dir specifies that the Member States cannot require the declaration of sufficient resources to refer to any specific amount.

[35] Art 7(4) limits slightly the category of protected family members of a *student* who can enjoy rights of residence: only the spouse, registered partner, and dependent children of a student are covered, and dependent direct relatives in the ascending line are not included. Instead, Member States are merely required to facilitate the admission of such other relatives under Art 3(2) of Dir 2004/38.

[36] See Case C–408/03 *Commission v Belgium* [2006] ECR I–2647 concerning Belgium's excessively restrictive definition of the sufficient resources condition of the 1990 Residence Dir, which did not take into account the resources of a partner in particular circumstances. The Commission in its Communication on the application of Dir 2004/38, COM(2008) 841, noted that twelve Member States had not correctly implemented the 'sufficient resources' requirement. See more recently Case C–140/12 *Brey* EU:C:2013:565, discussed below.

[37] Arts 13(2) and 14 of the Dir do not cover a third-country national who is not and has not been the spouse or registered partner of an EU citizen, even where she was previously in a relationship with and had a child with an EU citizen: Case C–45/12 *Ahmed* EU:C:2013:390.

[38] Art 39 of the Dir provides that in its report on the application of the legislation after four years, the Commission may submit a proposal on the possibility for extending this initial period of (almost) unconditional residence for all EU citizens, but this seems unlikely to happen in view of Member State fears.

[39] Rec 16 to the Dir sets out three criteria for determining an unreasonable burden: duration, personal situation, and amount, and the Commission's 2009 Communication provides further guidance.

Article 14(3) codifies the case law in *Grzelczyk*[40] and *Trojani*[41] to the effect that expulsion cannot be an automatic consequence of a person's recourse to the social assistance scheme of the host state.[42]

The important provision in Article 24 of the Directive governs the right to equal treatment of all EU citizens in a host Member State. Having set out the right to equal treatment in paragraph 1, paragraph 2 provides by way of derogation that host states are not obliged to confer entitlement to social assistance during the first three months of residence, nor (in the case of job-seekers) during the longer period to which a job-seeker is entitled to reside in search of work.[43] We shall see below in the cases of *Vatsouras* and *Bidar* how the Court has sidestepped this derogation by providing that job-seekers and students may rely instead on Articles 18 and 45 TFEU to gain access to job-seekers' allowances and maintenance grants on the same terms as nationals.[44]

Article 35 of the Directive provides that states may, subject to the procedural safeguards set out in Articles 30 and 31, adopt measures to refuse, terminate, or withdraw any right conferred by the Directive 'in the case of abuse of rights of fraud, such as marriages of convenience'.[45] In *McCarthy* the CJEU ruled that measures adopted under Article 35 must be based on an individual examination of each case.[46] Hence the UK could not invoke Article 35 to justify a measure with a general preventative objective—namely to protect against an alleged risk of systemic abuse or fraud post-*Metock*[47]— which required family members of an EU citizen holding a valid residence card under Article 10 of the Directive to obtain an additional entry permit under national law. Proof of abuse requires, according to the Court, a combination of objective and subjective elements: the objective element is the fact that the purpose of the rules which have been formally followed by the individual has not been achieved, and the subjective element is the intention to obtain an advantage from the EU rule by artificially creating the conditions laid down for obtaining it.[48]

The transposition of Directive 2004/38 was far from straightforward, and the Commission brought dozens of sets of infringement proceedings against various Member States in relation to problems with transposition and implementation after the deadline had expired. Particular controversy was caused by the ECJ ruling in *Metock*, which required several Member States to change their laws which had made the right of residence of third-country family members conditional on prior lawful residence in a Member State.[49] In 2009 the Commission adopted a Communication to provide guidance for its better transposition and application,[50] and established a group of Member States' experts to assist in identifying problems with the Directive, clarifying questions of interpretation, gathering data, and disseminating best practices.

---

[40] (N 11).

[41] (N 95).

[42] See however Case C–333/13 *Dano v Jobseeker Leipzig* EU:C:2014:2358, discussed in Section 4(c) below to the effect that the requirement of adequate resources for the right of residence is a necessary precondition for entitlement to equal access to social benefits, even if its absence does not automatically result in expulsion.

[43] See Case C–333/13 *Dano* ibid and pending Case C–67/14 *Jobcenter Berlin Neuköln v Alimanovic*.

[44] Cases C–22–23/08 *Vatsouras and Koupatantze* [2009] ECR I–4585; Case C–209/03 *Bidar* (n 123).

[45] For Commission action to help implement the provision on sham marriages, see Helping national authorities fight abuses of the right to free movement: Handbook on addressing the issue of alleged marriages of convenience between EU citizens and non-EU nationals in the context of EU law on free movement of EU citizens, COM(2014) 604.

[46] Case C–202/13 *McCarthy* EU:C:2014:2450.

[47] See (n 49).

[48] Case C–456/12 *O & B* EU:C:2014:135, [58]; Case C–364/10 *Hungary v Slovak Republic* EU:C:2012:630, [58].

[49] Case C–127/08 *Metock* [2008] ECR I–6241; see Ch 21 for discussion.

[50] COM(2009) 313.

4 THE IMPACT OF EU CITIZENSHIP LAW

Some of the main effects which the introduction of EU citizenship has had on EU law and policy, and which are explained further in the chapter below, are:

i. The Treaty provisions on citizenship have been held to create an autonomous and directly effective right to move and reside in a Member State, regardless of whether the person concerned falls within any previously existing EU law status category.

ii. Articles 20 and 21 TFEU have had an impact on the prior law concerning 'wholly internal situations', by increasing the extent to which and the circumstances in which individuals can challenge restrictions on the rights they enjoy *within* their own Member State where they have not otherwise exercised EU rights of free movement.

Wholly internal

iii. EU citizens who are neither economically active nor economically self-sufficient, ie who are not covered by any previously recognized EU status category, have invoked Articles 18, 20, and 21 TFEU, to claim entitlement to substantive equality of treatment as compared with nationals of a host Member State in access to social and material benefits. While the ECJ initially recognized this right to equal treatment in certain circumstances, it has more recently declared that EU citizens must first satisfy the conditions of possessing sufficient resources not to constitute an unreasonable burden on the state system, or other conditions for lawful residence under Directive 2004/38, before they can claim equality of treatment in access to social assistance.

iv. Articles 20 and 21 TFEU have however strengthened in various other ways the rights of EU nationals to challenge national restrictions on their movement, residence, entry, exit, and enjoyment of other benefits within the EU.

These four areas of impact of EU citizenship on EU law and policy will be discussed below.

(A) ARTICLE 20 TFEU CREATED AN AUTONOMOUS AND DIRECTLY EFFECTIVE RIGHT OF MOVEMENT AND RESIDENCE

To understand how Article 20 TFEU changed the previous legal situation, it is necessary to understand the prior status-categories for persons moving and residing under EU law. Chapter 21 discussed the categories of worker, former worker, job-seeker, and protected family member, and Chapter 22 discussed the categories of self-employed person and service-recipient. Three other relevant categories are those persons who were formerly covered by the 1990 Residence Directives, as we saw above, namely students, persons who had previously worked or had retired, and a catch-all category of non-economically active citizens.[51] The 1990 Directives had required Member States to grant rights of residence to those three categories of persons and certain of their family members, subject to the important proviso that they had adequate resources not to become a burden on the social assistance schemes of the Member States and were covered by sickness insurance.

The Treaty rights of movement and residence of EU citizens set out in Article 21 TFEU were made *subject to the limitations and conditions laid down in the Treaties and by the measures adopted to give them effect*. Two of the sets of conditions to which this clause refers include: (i) those listed in the Treaty enabling Member States to adopt restrictive measures on grounds of public policy, security, and health; and (ii) the financial and health insurance conditions previously imposed by the Residence Directives, and now by Article 7(1)(b)–(d) of Directive 2004/38, on students and other non-economically active

---

[51] (N 28).

persons, following an initial three-month period of unconditional residence provided by Article 6 of the same Directive.[52]

Article 21 TFEU therefore gave a Treaty basis to the existing rights and limits of EU citizenship. The question whether it went further than this and conferred rights on EU citizens in new situations which would not be covered by the previous provisions of secondary EU legislation arose in the *Baumbast* case.

Case C–413/99 **Baumbast and R v Secretary of State for the Home Department**
[2002] ECR I–7091

[Note Lisbon Treaty renumbering: Arts 17, 18, 48, 52, and 59 EC are now
Arts 20, 21, 45, 49, and 56 TFEU]

Baumbast was a German national married to a Colombian national with two children. He worked and lived in the UK with his family over a three-year period before leaving to work in Asia and Africa. Although he no longer lived with them, he continued to provide for his family, who remained living in the UK and enjoyed health insurance in Germany to which they travelled for health care. The UK refused to renew his and his family's residence permits, and a reference was made to the ECJ to see whether he enjoyed an independent right of residence as an EU citizen under Article 21 TFEU, since he had been found by the relevant national tribunal to be neither a worker nor a person covered by one of the Residence Directives.

THE ECJ

81. Although, before the Treaty on European Union entered into force, the Court had held that that right of residence, conferred directly by the EC Treaty, was subject to the condition that the person concerned was carrying on an economic activity within the meaning of Articles 48, 52 or 59 of the EC Treaty...it is none the less the case that, since then, Union citizenship has been introduced into the EC Treaty and Article 18(1) EC has conferred a right, for every citizen, to move and reside freely within the territory of the Member States.

82. Under Article 17(1) EC every person holding the nationality of a Member State is to be a citizen of the Union. Union citizenship is destined to be the fundamental status of nationals of the Member States...

83. Moreover, the Treaty on European Union does not require that citizens of the Union pursue a professional or trade activity, whether as an employed or self-employed person, in order to enjoy the rights provided...on citizenship of the Union. Furthermore, there is nothing in the text of that Treaty to permit the conclusion that citizens of the Union who have established themselves in another Member State in order to carry on an activity as an employed person there are deprived, where that activity comes to an end, of the rights which are conferred on them by the...Treaty by virtue of that citizenship.

84. As regards, in particular, the right to reside within the territory of the Member States under Article 18(1) EC, that right is conferred directly on every citizen of the Union by a clear and precise provision of the EC Treaty. Purely as a national of a Member State, and consequently a citizen of the Union, Mr Baumbast therefore has the right to rely on Article 18(1) EC.

---

[52] Art 6 of Dir 2004/38 provides for an unconditional three-month period of residence for EU citizens in another Member State, during which the host state cannot impose a requirement of adequate resources or any other requirement save for possession of a valid ID card or passport, but also during which the host state under Art 24(2) of the Dir is entitled to refuse social assistance. See further below.

85. Admittedly, that right for citizens of the Union to reside within the territory of another Member State is conferred subject to the limitations and conditions laid down by the EC Treaty and by the measures adopted to give it effect.

86. However, the application of the limitations and conditions acknowledged in Article 18(1) EC in respect of the exercise of that right of residence is subject to judicial review. Consequently, any limitations and conditions imposed on that right do not prevent the provisions of Article 18(1) EC from conferring on individuals rights which are enforceable by them and which the national courts must protect...

87. As regards the limitations and conditions resulting from the provisions of secondary legislation, Article 1(1) of Directive 90/364 provides that Member States can require of the nationals of a Member State who wish to enjoy the right to reside within their territory that they themselves and the members of their families be covered by sickness insurance in respect of all risks in the host Member State and have sufficient resources to avoid becoming a burden on the social assistance system of the host Member State during their period of residence.

[*The ECJ then found that while Mr Baumbast satisfied the condition requiring adequate resources in the Directive, the adjudicator in the UK had taken the view that he did not satisfy the requirement of having fully adequate sickness insurance.*]

90. In any event, the limitations and conditions which are referred to in Article 18 EC and laid down by Directive 90/364 are based on the idea that the exercise of the right of residence of citizens of the Union can be subordinated to the legitimate interests of the Member States. In that regard, according to the fourth recital in the preamble to Directive 90/364 beneficiaries of the right of residence must not become an unreasonable burden on the public finances of the host Member State.

91. However, those limitations and conditions must be applied in compliance with the limits imposed by Community law and in accordance with the general principles of that law, in particular the principle of proportionality. That means that national measures adopted on that subject must be necessary and appropriate to attain the objective...

...

94. The answer to the first part of the third question must therefore be that a citizen of the European Union who no longer enjoys a right of residence as a migrant worker in the host Member State can, as a citizen of the Union, enjoy there a right of residence by direct application of Article 18(1) EC. The exercise of that right is subject to the limitations and conditions referred to in that provision, but the competent authorities and, where necessary, the national courts must ensure that those limitations and conditions are applied in compliance with the general principles of Community law and, in particular, the principle of proportionality.

On the facts of the case, the ECJ ruled that Mr Baumbast and his family had not become a burden on the host state's public finances, and that given his residence and employment for some years in the EU and the sufficiency of his resources, it would be disproportionate to refuse to recognize his Treaty-based right of residence simply on the ground that his sickness insurance did not cover emergency treatment in the host Member State.

Baumbast thus established that Article 20(1) TFEU confers a directly effective right on EU citizens to reside in a host Member State, regardless of whether they are employed or self-employed. And while the main overall impact of Article 20(1) was to move the rights of residence of such citizens from a legislative footing to a Treaty footing, this move evidently had some significant legal consequences, since the ECJ ruled that the 'limitations and conditions' accepted by the Treaty on the rights of movement and residence must be interpreted and applied in a proportionate way. On the facts of the case, this meant that to read the requirement of 'sickness insurance' in the Directive restrictively would undermine the right of residence conferred directly by the Treaty. More generally, any legislative or other conditions or limitations on the rights of residence and movement of EU citizens must henceforth be interpreted so as to avoid disproportionate interference with the rights.[53]

In *Chen*, the ECJ confirmed that Article 20(1) TFEU confers a directly effective right of residence on EU citizens who do not fall within any other existing EU status category, since the citizen in question in this case was a newborn baby. The key questions raised by the case were: (i) whether the child enjoyed a directly effective right to movement and residence based solely on EU citizenship derived from her Irish nationality; (ii) whether the circumstances amounted to an abuse of rights; and (iii) whether the resources of the mother could be taken into account in determining whether the child had sufficient resources not to become a burden on the social assistance scheme of the state.[54]

Case C–200/02 **Zhu and Chen v Secretary of State for the Home Department**
[2004] ECR I–9925

Mrs Chen was a Chinese national who came to the UK and moved temporarily to Northern Ireland in order to give birth to her child, Catherine, there, with a view to the child obtaining Irish birthright citizenship. Catherine lived with her mother in Wales, UK. The Home Secretary rejected their applications for long-term residence permits on the basis that Catherine was not exercising any EU law rights, and her mother was not covered by EU law. The ECJ began by ruling that this was not a wholly internal situation since, although the child had been born in the UK and had never left the territory, she held the nationality of another state (Ireland). The Court also rejected the argument that a very young child cannot take advantage of the rights of movement and residence. It then moved on to consider whether she enjoyed rights under Article 20(1) TFEU.

THE ECJ

26. As regards the right to reside in the territory of the Member States provided for in Article 18(1) EC [*Art 20(1) TFEU*], it must be observed that that right is granted directly to every citizen of the Union by a clear and precise provision of the Treaty. Purely as a national of a Member State, and therefore as a citizen of the Union, Catherine is entitled to rely on Article 18(1) EC. That right of citizens of the Union to reside in another Member State is recognised subject to the limitations and conditions imposed by the Treaty and by the measures adopted to give it effect . . .

28. It is clear from the order for reference that Catherine has both sickness insurance and sufficient resources, provided by her mother, for her not to become a burden on the social assistance system of the host Member State.

29. The objection raised by the Irish and United Kingdom Governments that the condition concerning the availability of sufficient resources means that the person concerned must, in contrast to Catherine's case, possess those resources personally and may not use for that purpose those of an accompanying family member, such as Mrs Chen, is unfounded.

30. According to the very terms of Article 1(1) of Directive 90/364 it is sufficient for the nationals of Member States to 'have' the necessary resources, and that provision lays down no requirement whatsoever as to their origin . . .

[*The ECJ reiterated paragraphs 91–92 of its ruling in* Baumbast *to the effect that limitations on the exercise of the Treaty rights must be compatible with the principle of proportionality.*]

---

[53] For a different example, see Cases C–396–450/05 *Habelt v Deutsche Rentenversicherung Bund* [2007] ECR I–11895, [78], where a residence requirement imposed on the exportability of benefits accrued during wartime years for the purposes of Reg 1408/71 constituted a restriction on the rights of EU citizens under Art 21 TFEU and not just of EU workers.

[54] For a definition by the CJEU of 'social assistance' for the purposes of determining whether someone may become a burden for the purposes of the Dir, see Case C–140/12 *Brey* EU:C:2013:565, [60]–[61].

33. An interpretation of the condition concerning the sufficiency of resources within the meaning of Directive 90/364, in the terms suggested by the Irish and United Kingdom Governments would add to that condition, as formulated in that directive, a requirement as to the origin of the resources which, not being necessary for the attainment of the objective pursued, namely the protection of the public finances of the Member States, would constitute a disproportionate interference with the exercise of the fundamental right of freedom of movement and of residence upheld by Article 18 EC.

...

[*The ECJ then addressed the argument that Mrs Chen could not rely on EU law because she had abused EU rights by moving to Northern Ireland with the aim of having her child acquire the nationality of another Member State.*]

35. That argument must also be rejected.

36. It is true that Mrs Chen admits that the purpose of her stay in the United Kingdom was to create a situation in which the child she was expecting would be able to acquire the nationality of another Member State in order thereafter to secure for her child and for herself a long-term right to reside in the United Kingdom.

37. Nevertheless, under international law, it is for each Member State, having due regard to Community law, to lay down the conditions for the acquisition and loss of nationality.

38. None of the parties that submitted observations to the Court has questioned either the legality, or the fact, of Catherine's acquisition of Irish nationality.

39. Moreover, it is not permissible for a Member State to restrict the effects of the grant of the nationality of another Member State by imposing an additional condition for recognition of that nationality with a view to the exercise of the fundamental freedoms provided for in the Treaty.

40. However, that would be precisely what would happen if the United Kingdom were entitled to refuse nationals of other Member States, such as Catherine, the benefit of a fundamental freedom upheld by Community law merely because their nationality of a Member State was in fact acquired solely in order to secure a right of residence under Community law for a national of a non-member country.

Finally, the ECJ ruled that Catherine's mother could not be considered a 'dependent relative'[55] for the purposes of deriving a right of residence through her child's EU citizenship, since the reality was that the child was dependent on the mother rather than vice versa. However, the Court ruled that a refusal to grant a right of residence to the parent, whether an EU national or not, who is the carer of a child possessing EU citizenship, and enjoying sufficient resources and health insurance, 'would deprive the child's right of residence of any useful effect'.[56]

Chen thus confirms the *Baumbast* ruling in two ways. First, the rights of movement and residence deriving from EU citizenship under Article 20(1) are directly effective, autonomous, and do not depend on possession of any previously existing EU status category. Secondly, the conditions and limitations which a state may impose on these rights must be interpreted and applied in a proportionate manner which does not unduly restrict their exercise.

Not all of the limits which may be placed on the Treaty rights of EU citizens are to be found in EU law, however. In the unusual case of *Hungary v Slovakia*, one of the rare inter-state infringement proceedings brought under Article 259 TFEU, the CJEU ruled that Slovakia had not infringed Article 21 TFEU in

---

[55] This was regulated by Dir 90/364 at the time, and now by Arts 2(2)(d) and 7(2) of Dir 2004/38. For other cases ruling on the purely factual concept of dependency for the purposes of Dir 2004/38, see Case C–423/12 *Flora May Reyes* EU:C:2014:16; Case C–86/12 *Alokpa* EU:C:2013:645; and Case C–83/11 *Rahman* EU:C:2012:519.

[56] Case C–200/02, [45]. See also Case C–86/12 *Alokpa* EU:C:2013:645; Case C–40/11 *Iida* EU:C:2012:261; and Ch 21 for a similar ruling in Case C–413/99 *Baumbast* [2002] ECR I–7091 concerning the carer-parent of children enjoying educational rights in a Member State after the worker-parent has left the state or has divorced the other. Compare Case C–45/12 *Ahmed* EU:C:2013:390 where the non-EU carer-parent sought access to family benefits.

preventing access by the President of Hungary into its territory.[57] The Court ruled that the fact that an EU citizen was at the time performing the duties of a head of state was sufficient to justify a limitation, based not on EU law but on international law, on the exercise of the right of free movement. Both the *Chen* and *Hungary v Slovakia* rulings also confirm the robust approach adopted by the CJEU in a range of other cases discussed below to allegations that EU rights have been 'abusively' acquired or used.[58]

Thus we see that Article 21 TFEU created a new and directly effective right, and while the most obviously novel element was the conferral of Treaty status on the right of non-economically active persons to move and reside, this was not a purely symbolic change. The limits which states may legitimately impose on the rights of movement and residence of non-economically active persons must be interpreted in the light of their status as citizens, and those limits must be proportionate to the legitimate aim pursued. Further, the fact that EU citizenship rights are also contained in Title V of the Charter of Fundamental Rights provides further reason for treating limits on those rights carefully and reading them restrictively.

(B) DEVELOPMENTS IN THE LAW ON 'WHOLLY INTERNAL SITUATIONS' UNDER THE IMPACT OF ARTICLES 20 AND 21 TFEU

We saw in Chapter 21 that the ECJ has repeatedly held that EU law rights of movement and residence cannot be invoked in a 'wholly internal situation'. The issue arose in the past when workers with Member State nationality sought unsuccessfully to challenge an internal restriction on their freedom of movement within that state, as in *Saunders*,[59] or where a worker who had not previously exercised rights of movement outside their state of nationality sought unsuccessfully to rely on EU law to bring a non-EU national family member to reside with them, as in *Morson and Jhanjan*.[60]

After the Maastricht Treaty introduced the provisions on EU citizenship, attempts were made to challenge the 'wholly internal situation' approach in reliance on the new EU Treaty rights of residence and movement, but the ECJ ruled in *Kremzow*[61] and *Uecker*,[62] the factual contexts of which were broadly similar to those in the cases of *Saunders* and *Morson* respectively, that the provisions on citizenship did not extend the scope of the Treaty to cover these internal situations 'which otherwise had no link' with EU law.

Nevertheless, the ECJ faced continued pressure from scholars, practitioners, and from its own Advocates General in various cases to rethink the judicial stance on 'purely internal situations' in the light of EU citizenship.[63]

Two important categories of case in which the ECJ has increasingly been willing to find that the situation is not wholly internal, where claims are being made by EU nationals against their own Member State are (i) cases involving dual nationality or dual ethnicity and (ii) cases involving family reunification claims on behalf of non-EU national family members.

---

[57] Case C–364/10 *Hungary v Slovak Republic* EU:C:2012:360. See LS Rossi, 'EU Citizenship and the Free Movement of Heads of State: *Hungary v Slovak Republic*' (2013) 50 CMLRev 1451.

[58] See, eg, Cases C–109/01 *Secretary of State for the Home Department v Akrich* [2003] ECR I–9607, [55]–[56]; C–212/97 *Centros Ltd v Erhvervs- og Selskabsstyrelsen* [1999] ECR I–1459; C–196/04 *Cadbury Schweppes* [2006] ECR I–7995; C–413/01 *Ninni-Orasche v Bundesminister für Wissenschaft, Verkehr und Kunst* [2003] ECR I–13187; C–147/03 *Commission v Austria* [2005] ECR I–5969; Case C–364/10 ibid, [56]–[61].

[59] Case 175/78 *R v Saunders* [1979] ECR 1129.

[60] Cases 35 and 36/82 *Morson and Jhanjan v Netherlands* [1982] ECR 3723.

[61] Case C–299/95 *Kremzow v Austria* [1997] ECR I–2629.

[62] Cases C–64 and 65/96 *Uecker and Jacquet v Land Nordrhein-Westfalen* [1997] ECR I–3171.

[63] For discussion, see P Van Elsuwege, 'Shifting the Boundaries? European Union Citizenship and the Scope of Application of EU Law' (2011) 38 LIEI 263; A Lansbergen and N Miller, 'European Citizenship Rights in Internal Situations: An Ambiguous Revolution?' (2011) 7 EuConst 287; A Wiesbrock, 'Union Citizenship and the Redefinition of the "Internal Situations" Rule: The Implications of *Zambrano*' (2011) 12 German LJ 2077.

(i) *Dual Nationality*

In *Garcia Avello*[64] and *Chen*,[65] the ECJ found a cross-border element to which the EU provisions on citizenship would apply even when the applicants had never left the territory of the Member State in which they were born, and were not presently intending to move. In these cases, the person claiming rights as an EU citizen also possessed the nationality of a Member State other than that of the host state. Chen was an Irish national resident in the UK and Garcia Avello was a dual Belgian–Spanish national resident in Belgium.

Garcia Avello concerned a challenge to a Belgian rule prohibiting any change in a registered surname, where Belgian law required the father's surname to be registered but the children wished, given their Spanish nationality, to add the surname of their mother.[66] The children relied on Article 18 TFEU, together with Article 20 TFEU, to claim that they were being discriminated against by comparison with other Belgian nationals. The ECJ ruled that this was not a wholly internal situation, despite the fact that the children were Belgian nationals making a claim against the Belgian state:

> 27. …[A] link with Community law does, however, exist in regard to persons in a situation such as that of the children of Mr Garcia Avello, who are nationals of one Member State lawfully resident in the territory of another Member State.
>
> 28. That conclusion cannot be invalidated by the fact that the children involved in the main proceedings also have the nationality of the Member State in which they have been resident since their birth and which, according to the authorities of that State, is by virtue of that fact the only nationality recognised by the latter. It is not permissible for a Member State to restrict the effects of the grant of the nationality of another Member State by imposing an additional condition for recognition of that nationality with a view to the exercise of the fundamental freedoms provided for in the Treaty (see in particular, to that effect, Case C–369/90 *Micheletti and Others* [1992] ECR I–4239, paragraph 10)…
>
> …

There was discrimination on grounds of their dual Belgian–Spanish nationality against the children, since they were refused the right to bear the surname as it would be determined by Spanish law. The Advocate General and the Court both emphasized the serious professional and personal inconvenience that could result from the discrepancy in surnames given the likely divergences in official documentation as between different Member States. Consequently, Belgium's refusal to allow a change in surname was in violation of both Articles 18 and 20 TFEU.

In the case of *Runevič-Vardyn*, the applicant, who had Lithuanian nationality but belonged to the Polish ethnic minority within Lithuania, together with her Polish husband, was prevented by Lithuanian law from entering their name and surname in official documents other than in roman characters of the Lithuanian language.[67] They had moved to Belgium and sought to have the applicant's birth certificate and their marriage certificate changed to reflect the form of spelling specified by Polish law. Lithuania argued that this should be considered an internal situation, since the rules governing how a person's name should be entered on domestic certificates of civil status fell within the competence of Member States, but the CJEU ruled that this competence had to be exercised in compliance with the Treaty provisions on free movement. Despite the fact that the element of inter-state movement took the

---

[64] Case C–148/02 *Garcia Avello* (n 15).

[65] Case C–200/02 (n 18) [19].

[66] For two other cases concerning restrictions on the use of surnames, but where there was no question of a 'wholly internal situation', see Case C–353/06 *Grunkin and Paul v Standesamt Stadt Niebüll* [2008] ECR I–7639; Case C–208/09 *Sayn-Wittgenstein v Landeshauptmann von Wien* [2010] ECR I–13693.

[67] Case C–391/09, *Runevič-Vardyn* EU:C:2011:291.

case outside the 'wholly internal situation' category, the conclusion of the CJEU as to whether the EU citizenship rights of the applicant had been restricted was rather nuanced:

Case C–391/09 Runevič-Vardyn
EU:C:2011:291

69.... [It] must be held that, when a citizen of the Union moves to another Member State and subsequently marries a national of that other State, the fact that the surname which that citizen had prior to marriage, and her forename, cannot be changed and entered in documents relating to civil status issued by her Member State of origin except using the characters of the language of that latter Member State cannot constitute treatment that is less favourable than that which she enjoyed before she availed herself of the opportunities offered by the Treaty in relation to free movement of persons.

70. Hence, the absence of such a right is not liable to deter a citizen of the Union from exercising the rights of movement recognised in Article 21 TFEU and, to that extent, does not constitute a restriction....

The Court took the same view with regard to the refusal to allow the use of diacritical marks on the marriage certificate, ruling that this was unlikely to give rise to any doubts about identity or authenticity. However, with regard to the applicants' request to add the husband's surname to his wife's name on the marriage certificate, the Court ruled that differences in the spelling of the wife's name on the Lithuanian and Polish documents might possibly give rise to inconvenience in the future, given that a couple moving within the EU may well be required under EU legislation to prove the relationship between them. While an inconvenience of this kind could constitute a restriction under Article 21 TFEU if it were serious, as held in *Garcia Avello* and *Sayn-Wittgenstein*,[68] this had to be weighed against the justification pleaded by Lithuania for refusing to allow the alteration of official documents, namely 'to ensure that the official national language is protected in order to safeguard national unity and preserve social cohesion'. Given the protection in the Charter of Fundamental Rights for cultural and linguistic diversity, and in Article 4(2) TEU for national constitutional identity on the one hand, and the protection under Article 7 of the Charter and Article 8 of the ECHR for personal identity and private life on the other hand, it was for the national court to weigh these different interests and to determine whether the refusal to allow the amendment of the marriage certificate was a disproportionate restriction on their rights under Article 21 TFEU.

An interesting dual-identity, although not dual-nationality, case arose in *Walloon Government*, in which the ECJ ruled that where one of the autonomous communities within Belgium (the Flemish community) excluded Belgian nationals who did not reside either within the jurisdiction of the Flemish community or within another bilingual part of the state from the scope of eligibility for a care insurance scheme, this would remain a 'purely internal situation' unless the Belgian nationals who were excluded had previously *exercised* their rights of movement under EU law to another Member State.[69]

(ii) *Family Reunification Claims*

The most important case in this line of jurisprudence is *Ruiz Zambrano*, which involved the non-EU parents of two EU-citizen children born and resident in Belgium, who had never left that Member

---

[68] Case C–208/09 (n 15).
[69] Case C–212/06 *Government of the French Community and Walloon Government* [2008] ECR I–1683, [37]–[39].

State.[70] Eight Member States intervened to argue that the situation in question should be characterized as 'wholly internal', such that EU law on citizenship was not applicable, but Advocate General Sharpston and the ECJ disagreed. While the Advocate General argued at length that EU citizenship is not wholly bound up with movement between Member States, and that the right of residence and the right to move are *independent* rather than combined rights, the ECJ gave a remarkably brief and minimally reasoned ruling. The essence of the judgment, which focuses on the refusal of residence and a work permit to the parent as an obstacle to the enjoyment of an EU citizen's rights, is contained in the following four paragraphs:

Case C–34/09 **Ruiz Zambrano v ONEM**
[2011] ECR I–1177

THE ECJ

42. In those circumstances, Article 20 TFEU precludes national measures which have the effect of depriving citizens of the Union of the genuine enjoyment of the substance of the rights conferred by virtue of their status as citizens of the Union (see, to that effect, *Rottmann*, paragraph 42).

43. A refusal to grant a right of residence to a third country national with dependent minor children in the Member State where those children are nationals and reside, and also a refusal to grant such a person a work permit, has such an effect.

44. It must be assumed that such a refusal would lead to a situation where those children, citizens of the Union, would have to leave the territory of the Union in order to accompany their parents. Similarly, if a work permit were not granted to such a person, he would risk not having sufficient resources to provide for himself and his family, which would also result in the children, citizens of the Union, having to leave the territory of the Union. In those circumstances, those citizens of the Union would, as a result, be unable to exercise the substance of the rights conferred on them by virtue of their status as citizens of the Union.

45. Accordingly, the answer to the questions referred is that Article 20 TFEU is to be interpreted as meaning that it precludes a Member State from refusing a third country national upon whom his minor children, who are European Union citizens, are dependent, a right of residence in the Member State of residence and nationality of those children, and from refusing to grant a work permit to that third country national, in so far as such decisions deprive those children of the genuine enjoyment of the substance of the rights attaching to the status of European Union citizen.

The case was controversial, in the vein of *Chen* and *Metock*, since it challenged core aspects of Member States' migration policies,[71] and the CJEU drew back significantly from the wider implications of the ruling in the subsequent cases of *McCarthy*[72] and *Dereci*.[73]

In *McCarthy* an EU citizen, who possessed both Irish and British nationality but had only ever lived in the UK, claimed a right of residence deriving from EU law. She sought the EU right of residence in order that her husband, who was a Jamaican national, would enjoy derived residence rights, but the

---

[70] Case C–34/09 *Ruiz Zambrano* (n 31). A vast number of commentaries on the *Zambrano* case have been published. For a sample, see K Hailbronner and D Thym (2011) 48 CMLRev 1253; JT Nowak (2010–11) 17 CJEL 673; U Šadl (2013) 9 EuConst 205; A Wiesbrock (2011) 12 German LJ 2077.

[71] See, eg, the statement issued by the Irish Minister for Justice, Equality and Defence on the implications for Ireland of the ruling of the CJEU in *Zambrano*: www.justice.ie/en/JELR/Pages/PR11000019; and the government's publication of answers to Frequently Asked Questions on *Zambrano*: http://www.inis.gov.ie/en/INIS/Pages/WP11000038.

[72] Case C–434/09 *McCarthy* [2011] ECR I–3375.

[73] Case C–256/11 *Dereci* [2011] ECR I–11315.

CJEU rejected her claim both under Directive 2004/38 and under Article 21 TFEU. The Court—in a holding which has been reiterated in many subsequent cases—ruled that the personal scope of Directive 2004/38 did not cover an EU citizen who has never exercised her right to freedom of movement and has always resided in a Member State of which she was a national, even where she holds the nationality of another Member State. However, the fact that McCarthy had never exercised her right to freedom of movement did not necessarily mean she was in a wholly internal situation as far as Article 21 TFEU was concerned, since *Zambrano* had established that Article 20 TFEU precludes national measures 'which have the effect of depriving Union citizens of the genuine enjoyment of the substance of the rights conferred by virtue of that status' even where they are nationals of the Member State in question and have never exercised rights of free movement.[74] However, the CJEU distinguished *McCarthy* from both *Ruiz Zambrano* and *Garcia Avello*, concluding that UK law in McCarthy's case did not (by comparison with *Zambrano*) have the effect of obliging her to leave the territory of the EU, nor (by comparison with *Garcia Avello*) did it give rise to serious professional inconvenience creating likely obstacles to her exercise of freedom of movement in the future. Thus *McCarthy* established that Article 21 TFEU does not apply to an EU citizen who has never exercised her right to freedom of movement, who has always resided in a Member State of which she is a national, and who is also a national of another Member State, provided that she is not deprived of the genuine enjoyment of the substance of the rights of EU citizenship, and her right of free movement and residence within the territory of the Member States is not impeded.[75]

The crucial factor determining whether the circumstances in *McCarthy* and those in *Ruiz Zambrano* were to be characterized as a wholly internal situation hinged on a relatively slight factual distinction: namely the perceived difference in the degree of dependence and vulnerability of the EU-citizen family member. The fact that the family member for whom the EU citizen was seeking a derivative residence permit in that case was an adult spouse, as compared with the parent of dependent minor children in *Ruiz Zambrano*, may have influenced the Court in reaching a different conclusion in the two cases, even though the right to family life of the EU citizen would be significantly affected by the deportation in both cases. In *Dereci*, the CJEU continued its retreat from the wider implications of *Zambrano*.[76] While repeating the substance of the *Zambrano* ruling to the effect that citizens may rely on Article 20 against their own Member State even where they have not exercised rights of free movement if national measures have the effect of depriving them of the substance of their citizenship rights, the Court implied that this might not be the case for the applicants in *Dereci*, who were the (non-EU national) adult children or spouses of EU citizens in Austria. First, the Court ruled that the 'denial of the substance' of their citizenship rights would occur only where the EU citizen had to leave not just the territory of the Member State of his or her nationality, but also the territory of the EU as a whole.[77] Further, the fact that the EU citizen considered it desirable for economic or family reasons that his or her non-EU national family members should reside with them within the EU did not mean that the EU citizen was being 'forced' to leave EU territory if such a right was not granted,[78] and it seemed here that none of the applicants was dependent for subsistence rights on their EU citizen family member. However, the CJEU left the factual determinations in the case for the national court to make, and added that its ruling was without prejudice to the separate question of whether, if the national court

---

[74] Case C–434/09 *McCarthy* (n 72) [47].

[75] For some of the commentaries on the case, see P Van Elsewuge (2011) 7 EuConst 308; C McCauliff (2013) 36 Fordham Int LJ 1372; N Nic Shuibhne (2012) 49 CMLRev 349; C Taroni (2012) 8 Journal of Contemporary European Research 145.

[76] Case C–256/11 *Dereci* [2011] ECR I–11315. In addition to the commentaries at (nn 70 and 75), see D Kochenov, 'The Right to Have What Rights?' (2013) 19 ELJ 502; A Tryfonidou, 'Redefining the Outer Boundaries of EU Law: The *Zambrano, McCarthy* and *Dereci* Trilogy' (2012) 18 EPL 493.

[77] Case C–256/11 *Dereci* ibid, [66].

[78] Ibid [68].

adjudged that the cases fell within the scope of application of EU law, a right of residence should be granted on the basis of the right to family life in Article 7 of the Charter. Further, even if it fell outside the scope of EU law, the national court 'must' (albeit under ECHR obligations rather than any EU obligation on which the CJEU has jurisdiction to rule) decide the case on the basis of the right to family life under Article 8 ECHR.[79]

Similarly in *Ymeraga*, the CJEU applied its stricter rulings in *McCarthy* and *Dereci* to hold that an EU national who had never exercised his freedom of movement as an EU citizen would not be deprived of the substance of his EU citizenship rights by virtue of the Member State's refusal to grant his third-country national parents a right of residence with a view to bringing about their family reunification in Luxembourg, although as in *Dereci* it was for the national court to take account of the right to family life under the ECHR.[80]

A cluster of other 'family reunification' cases have since followed, testing the boundaries of the internal situation rule. The complex circumstances of *O, S and L* illustrate that the factual question of whether EU citizens (in this case, EU-citizen children with one third-country national parent on whom they are apparently not dependent) would be deprived of the substance of their EU citizenship rights by virtue of the refusal of a residence permit to a third-country national parent, is often difficult to answer, and is ultimately for the national court to determine.[81] And although the CJEU in *O, S and L* declared that the strict test of deprivation of the substance of rights laid down in *Zambrano* would only 'exceptionally' be met, the Court at the same time ruled that it was not necessary for the non-EU national seeking a residence permit to be related by blood to the EU citizen in question. On the other hand, the degree of legal, financial, or emotional dependency of the EU citizen on the third-country national was very important.[82]

The four subsequent family reunification cases of *S & G, Alopka, Iida*, and *O & B* were found not to involve wholly internal situations, although each concerned a claim by EU citizens against their own Member State to acquire derivative residence rights for a third-country national family member. In *S & G*, while the circumstances involved EU nationals claiming a right of residence for a third-country national family member in their own Member State and Directive 2004/38 was not applicable for the same reason as that given in *McCarthy*, the EU citizens had nonetheless engaged their Treaty rights of free movement by regularly travelling to provide services to persons established in other Member States.[83] A refusal to allow the non-EU national family member to live with them would violate their Treaty rights, according to the CJEU, where the grant of residence to that family member was necessary to guarantee the effective exercise of fundamental Treaty freedoms. In *Alopka*, the situation of a non-EU national mother with sole custody and responsibility for her French-EU citizen children, who sought a residence permit to remain with them in Luxembourg where they had lived since their birth, was not a wholly internal situation, since the children were resident in a Member State other than that of their nationality. However, they could only rely on their citizenship rights under the EU Treaty in order to derive a right of residence for their third-country national mother if the criteria established in *Zambrano* were satisfied: namely that the children might otherwise be denied the substance of their citizenship rights. The CJEU doubted that this criterion was satisfied on the facts of the case since they could probably move to live with her in France.[84]

---

[79] Ibid [72]–[73].

[80] Case C–87/12 *Ymeraga* v EU:C:2013:291. See S Iglesias Sanchez, 'Fundamental Rights and Citizenship of the Union at a Crossroads' (2014) 20 ELJ 464.

[81] Cases C–356 and 357/11 *O, S & L* EU:C:2012:776.

[82] Ibid [56].

[83] Case C–457/12 *S & G* EU:C:2014:136.

[84] Ibid [33]–[35].

In *Iida*, where Directive 2004/38 was not applicable because the non-EU national parent seeking a right of residence was not dependent on the EU national child, the situation was not a purely internal one since the child had moved from Germany, her state of nationality, to live in Austria.[85] Nevertheless, and even though Iida could have claimed independent rights as a long-term resident third country national under Directive 2003/109, the CJEU rather surprisingly ruled that the situation fell outside the scope of EU citizenship law since the *Zambrano* test could not be satisfied: there was no risk that a refusal of Iida's right of residence would deprive his daughter of the substance of her EU citizenship rights, since he sought an EU right of residence in Germany rather than in Austria where she was resident.[86] The *Iida* ruling compares interestingly to that in *Schempp*, in which the circumstances of a Member State national who had not exercised the right to freedom of movement was found by the CJEU not to be a wholly internal situation because his former spouse, to whom he continued to pay maintenance, had exercised her right as an EU citizen to move to another Member State, and this affected his tax position within Germany.[87] The recognition by the Court of this continuing cross-border economic element of (former) family life as bringing the case within the scope of EU law, but not the circumstances of ongoing cross-border family life involving one non-EU national in *Iida*, is notable.

Finally, in *O & B*, the situation was not a wholly internal one since although an EU citizen was claiming a right of residence for a non-EU family spouse in his own Member State, he had previously exercised his right of freedom of movement to live in another Member State.[88] Following the cases of *Eind* and *Singh* on the free movement of workers,[89] the CJEU ruled that the refusal to confer a derived right of residence on the family member of an EU citizen who returns to his or her Member State after residing in another Member State with that family member pursuant to and in conformity with EU law, could create an obstacle to the Treaty rights of freedom of movement under Article 21 TFEU.[90] It would constitute such an obstacle, however, only where the period of residence of the EU citizen in the host Member State was 'sufficiently genuine as to enable that citizen to create or strengthen family life in that host state', and a stay of less than three months in the host state without any intention to settle there would not satisfy that criterion.[91]

It is thus evident from the case law discussed above that the introduction of EU citizenship and the rights of movement and residence in Articles 20 and 21 TFEU have placed continued pressure on the notion of a purely internal situation, and have contributed to widening the circumstances in which EU nationals can make citizenship-based claims against their own Member States. Certain factual situations such as those involving dual nationality or—despite the restrictive application of the *Zambrano* test in subsequent cases—family reunification claims, which might otherwise have been considered as purely internal situations, may have a sufficient connection with EU law due to the impact on specific rights enjoyed by virtue of the status of EU citizenship.

---

[85] Case C–40/11 *Iida* EU:C:2012:261.

[86] Strangely, despite the clear cross-border dimension of the EU family life in this case, and applicability of the law on long-term resident third-country nationals, the CJEU held that the situation fell entirely outside the scope of EU law, even for the purposes of the application of Art 51 of the Charter, and no mention was made in this case of the ECHR either. For comment see A Tryfonidou, '(Further) Signs of a Turn of the Tide in the CJEU's Citizenship Jurisprudence, Case C–40/11, *Iida*' (2013) 20 MJ 302.

[87] Case C–403/03 *Schempp v Finanzamt München* [2005] ECR I–6421, [22]–[25].

[88] Case C–456/12 *O & B* EU:C:2014:135.

[89] Case C–291/05 *Eind* [2007] ECR I–10719; Case C–370/90 *R v Immigration Appeal Tribunal and Singh* [1992] ECR I–4265, discussed in Ch 21.

[90] Case C–456/12 (n 88) [46]–[49].

[91] Ibid [51]–[54].

(c) THE IMPACT OF ARTICLES 20 AND 21 ON THE RIGHTS OF EU NATIONALS WHO ARE NEITHER ECONOMICALLY ACTIVE NOR ECONOMICALLY SELF-SUFFICIENT

We have seen that the rights of movement and residence of EU citizens arising from Articles 20 and 21 are subject to the limits and conditions laid down in the Treaties and in secondary legislation. We also saw that Directive 2004/38 imposed two conditions on the freedom of movement and residence of EU nationals who are neither workers nor self-employed, following an initial three-month period during which they enjoy an unconditional right to residence:[92] first, that such persons have sufficient resources to avoid becoming a burden on the social assistance scheme of the state, and, secondly, that they have comprehensive sickness insurance.

Below we examine four (potentially overlapping) groups of cases: (i) the first concerning access to social assistance for *non-economically active persons*; (ii) the second concerning access to social or educational assistance for *students*; and (iii) the third concerning access to various kinds of job-seekers' allowance for *persons seeking work*. In all three, the provisions on citizenship have been invoked to expand the circumstances in which an EU national may be entitled to specific social benefits in a host Member State. However, following an initially more liberal line of case law, there has been less success for the first group of non-economically active citizens, than for the second and third groups of students and job-seekers. The fourth group of cases concerns (iv) EU nationals who have acquired a right of *permanent residence* in an EU Member State other than that of their nationality. This is an enhanced status introduced by Directive 2004/38 which may be enjoyed by all EU citizens who have satisfied certain conditions, and which continues to be enjoyed regardless of whether the person requires social and economic support from the state or not.

(i) *Non-Economically Active Persons*

The early case of *Martínez Sala*, decided before the adoption of Directive 2004/38, concerned a Spanish national who was resident in Germany and had not been working for some time, who was in receipt of social assistance.[93] The case concerned her eligibility for a child-raising allowance under national law, and the CJEU ruled that so long as an EU citizen is lawfully resident within another Member State, he or she is entitled, on a combined reading of Articles 18 and 20(2) TFEU, to equal treatment with Member State nationals in relation to benefits within the scope of the Treaty. The ECJ thus applied the general principle of non-discrimination on grounds of nationality to her purely on the basis of her EU citizenship and her lawful residence in Germany.[94] It was not necessary for there to be involvement in any economic activity as a worker or service provider, nor was it necessary to show preparation for a future economic activity as a student, etc. However, the fact that the ECJ did not base her right to residence on Articles 20–21 TFEU, because it had found that Germany had authorized her residence under the terms of a Council of Europe Convention on social and medical assistance, meant that the Court did not have to confront the limiting conditions referred to in Articles 20–21 TFEU, and especially the requirement under secondary legislation that she should have sufficient resources to avoid becoming a burden on the social assistance scheme of the state.

---

[92] See (n 52) above. This unconditional three-month right of residence is however without entitlement under EU law to social benefits pursuant to Art 24(2) of the Dir.

[93] Case C–85/96 *Maria Martínez Sala v Freistaat Bayern* [1998] ECR I–2691.

[94] *Martínez Sala* thus strengthens the basis for earlier rulings such as Case C–411/98 *Ferlini v Centre hospitalier de Luxembourg* [2000] ECR I–8081, which did not involve EU citizenship, but applied Art 18 TFEU and the principle of non-discrimination on grounds of nationality to a lawfully resident EU national.

In *Trojani*,[95] however, the ECJ directly confronted these limiting conditions since the national court raised the question whether he was entitled to a right of residence under the EU Treaty.[96] Trojani was a French national taking part in a reintegration programme with the Salvation Army in Belgium,[97] who applied for social assistance in the form of a minimum subsistence allowance ('minimex') there. In the first part of the judgment, the ECJ ruled that an EU citizen in Trojani's situation does not derive from Article 20 TFEU (then Article 18 EC) the right to reside in the territory of a Member State of which he is not a national, given his lack of sufficient resources within the meaning of the secondary legislation (which at the time was Directive 90/364).[98] In other words, it was open to Belgium under EU law to deny him a right of residence on the ground that he lacked sufficient resources to avoid becoming a burden on the state. However, the ECJ ruled that since he had apparently already satisfied the conditions for lawful residence according to Belgian law, he could rely on the EU requirement of non-discrimination on grounds of nationality in Article 18 TFEU (ex Article 12 EC) to claim entitlement to a social assistance benefit which was available under national law to national residents.[99] In other words, although he could not derive a right of residence from Article 21 if he lacked sufficient resources within the meaning of the Directive, he was nonetheless entitled, so long as he was lawfully resident on some other basis within the state, to have access to social assistance on the same conditions as nationals under Articles 18 and 21 TFEU.[100] It seemed that if Belgium wanted to deny him access to social benefits, they would have to revoke his residence permit on the ground of lack of sufficient resources, but the ECJ also ruled that recourse to the social assistance system cannot *automatically* lead to revocation of residence permission or deportation. In other words, Member States are not entitled to equate 'recourse to social assistance' with 'lack of sufficient resources'. They must, as recital 16 to Directive 2004/38 suggests, apply the limiting condition in a proportionate manner, and make a proper inquiry into the sufficiency of an EU citizen's resources before moving to revoke his or her residence.

Building on *Trojani*, but drawing directly this time on Directive 2004/38, the CJEU in *Brey* ruled that although Member States are entitled to condition a migrant's entitlement to social benefits on his or her fulfilment of the *domestic* requirements for lawful residence, those requirements must themselves comply with EU law.[101] In this case the requirement imposed by the state for lawful residence was that the migrant must, as soon as the initial unconditional three-month period of residence provided for all EU citizens under Article 6 of Directive 2004/38 has expired, have sufficient resources so as not to apply for a specific social benefit. The CJEU ruled that while eligibility for a particular social assistance benefit could provide an indication that an individual may lack sufficient resources to avoid becoming an unreasonable burden on the host state, the mere fact that a national receives that social benefit is insufficient in itself to prove that he constitutes such a burden. The automaticity of the Austrian legislation in this case, under which the mere fact that Brey had applied for the benefit in question was sufficient to preclude him from receiving it, prevented the national authorities from carrying out an overall assessment of his income and his personal circumstances so as to determine in

---

[95] Case C–456/02 *Trojani v CPAS* [2004] ECR I–7573.

[96] See also Cases C–310/08 *Ibrahim* [2010] ECR I–1065 and C–480/08 *Teixeira* [2010] ECR I–1107 which raised the question whether the non-working parents of EU-citizen children who were pursuing primary education in a host Member State, where the family lacked adequate means of support or health insurance, might enjoy residence rights under EU law. The CJEU however decided the cases on the basis of Art 12 of Reg 1612/68 (now Art 10 of Reg 492/2011) rather than on the basis of EU citizenship rights.

[97] A discussion of his possible status as a worker is contained in Ch 21.

[98] Ibid [32]–[36].

[99] Ibid [41]–[44].

[100] This ruling does not extend to the situation of a third-country national with a residence permit who is not otherwise a protected family member under Dir 2004/38: Case C–45/12 *Ahmed* EU:C:2013:390.

[101] Case C–140/12 *Brey* EU:C:2013:565, [44]–[45]. H Verschueren, 'Free Movement or Benefit Tourism: The Unreasonable Burden of *Brey*' (2014) 16 EJML 147.

a proportionate manner whether and if so how much of a burden he might impose on the state,[102] and hence was contrary to EU law.

The *Sala, Trojani,* and *Brey* cases represented a liberal line of case law which emphasized the obligation on Member States, so long as an EU national was lawfully resident under domestic law, to ensure equal treatment for its own nationals and other EU citizens even with regard to access to social benefits. And while they were fully entitled to condition lawful domestic residence for EU citizens on fulfilment of the criteria set out in Directive 2004/38, namely that they should not become an unreasonable burden on the social assistance system of the host state once the initial three-month period of unconditional right of residence had passed, these criteria had to be carefully and proportionately evaluated, taking account of the fundamental rights of EU citizens. Mere eligibility for a social assistance benefit, or the mere making of an application for a social assistance benefit, would not in themselves be sufficient to prove that the person had or would become an unreasonable burden.

Following the heated transnational political debate over 'benefits tourism' in the EU,[103] however, the CJEU in *Dano* changed direction somewhat, and adopted a more restrictive approach towards the entitlements of non-economically active EU citizens.[104] The tone of the judgment was significantly more cautious and more conciliatory towards Member State concerns than the earlier cases, in particular as seen in the language of paragraphs 76–78. The *Dano* ruling focuses on the entitlement of states to limit the rights of those who have moved in order to take advantage of their welfare systems, rather than on the rights of EU citizens.[105] The progression of the case law from *Sala* to *Brey* had left some room for uncertainty as to the exact circumstances in which a non-economically active EU citizen who was lawfully resident under national law could invoke the principle of non-discrimination on grounds of nationality under EU law, including under Article 24 of Directive 2004/38, to claim equal access to social benefits alongside nationals. This ambiguity was addressed in *Dano*, which involved a non-economically active Romanian woman who had moved with her son to live in Germany for a number of years, had been granted a residence certificate of unlimited duration, and was in receipt of certain basic social benefits. She sought to challenge the rejection of her application for a 'special non-contributory cash benefit' by relying on the prohibition of discrimination on grounds of nationality in Article 18 TFEU and Article 24 of Directive 2004/38.

Case C–333/13 **Dano v Jobseeker Leipzig**
EU:C:2014:2358

THE CJEU

68. Article 24(1) of Directive 2004/38 provides that all Union citizens residing on the basis of the directive in the territory of the host Member State are to enjoy equal treatment with the nationals of that Member State within the scope of the Treaty.

69. It follows that, so far as concerns access to social benefits, such as those at issue in the main proceedings, a Union citizen can claim equal treatment with nationals of the host Member State only if his residence in the territory of the host Member State complies with the conditions of Directive 2004/38.

. . .

---

[102] Ibid [76]–[78].

[103] See Ch 21 (n 5) and text.

[104] Case C–333/13 *Dano v Jobseeker Leipzig* EU:C:2014:2358.

[105] This focus on the motive of the citizen for exercising rights of movement is something which the CJEU has been reluctant in other cases to do. See however Ch 21 (n 41) and text.

71. … . [F]or periods of residence longer than three months, the right of residence is subject to the conditions set out in Article 7(1) of Directive 2004/38 and, under Article 14(2), that right is retained only if the Union citizen and his family members satisfy those conditions. It is apparent from recital 10 in the preamble to the directive in particular that those conditions are intended, inter alia, to prevent such persons from becoming an unreasonable burden on the social assistance system of the host Member State…

…

73. In order to determine whether economically inactive Union citizens, in the situation of the applicants in the main proceedings, whose period of residence in the host Member State has been longer than three months but shorter than five years, can claim equal treatment with nationals of that Member State so far as concerns entitlement to social benefits, it must therefore be examined whether the residence of those citizens complies with the conditions in Article 7(1)(b) of Directive 2004/38. Those conditions include the requirement that the economically inactive Union citizen must have sufficient resources for himself and his family members.

74. To accept that persons who do not have a right of residence under Directive 2004/38 may claim entitlement to social benefits under the same conditions as those applicable to nationals of the host Member State would run counter to an objective of the directive, set out in recital 10 in its preamble, namely preventing Union citizens who are nationals of other Member States from becoming an unreasonable burden on the social assistance system of the host Member State.

75. It should be added that, as regards the condition requiring possession of sufficient resources, Directive 2004/38 distinguishes between (i) persons who are working and (ii) those who are not. Under Article 7(1)(a) of Directive 2004/38, the first group of Union citizens in the host Member State have the right of residence without having to fulfil any other condition. On the other hand, persons who are economically inactive are required by Article 7(1)(b) of the directive to meet the condition that they have sufficient resources of their own.

76. Therefore, Article 7(1)(b) of Directive 2004/38 seeks to prevent economically inactive Union citizens from using the host Member State's welfare system to fund their means of subsistence.

77. As the Advocate General has observed in points 93 and 96 of his Opinion, any unequal treatment between Union citizens who have made use of their freedom of movement and residence and nationals of the host Member State with regard to the grant of social benefits is an inevitable consequence of Directive 2004/38. Such potential unequal treatment is founded on the link established by the Union legislature in Article 7 of the directive between the requirement to have sufficient resources as a condition for residence and the concern not to create a burden on the social assistance systems of the Member States.

78. A Member State must therefore have the possibility, pursuant to Article 7 of Directive 2004/38, of refusing to grant social benefits to economically inactive Union citizens who exercise their right to freedom of movement solely in order to obtain another Member State's social assistance although they do not have sufficient resources to claim a right of residence.

79. To deny the Member State concerned that possibility would, as the Advocate General has stated in point 106 of his Opinion, thus have the consequence that persons who, upon arriving in the territory of another Member State, do not have sufficient resources to provide for themselves would have them automatically, through the grant of a special non-contributory cash benefit which is intended to cover the beneficiary's subsistence costs.

80. Therefore, the financial situation of each person concerned should be examined specifically, without taking account of the social benefits claimed, in order to determine whether he meets the condition of having sufficient resources to qualify for a right of residence under Article 7(1)(b) of Directive 2004/38.

81. In the main proceedings, according to the findings of the referring court the applicants do not have sufficient resources and thus cannot claim a right of residence in the host Member State under Directive 2004/38. Therefore, as has been stated in paragraph 69 of the present judgment, they cannot invoke the principle of non-discrimination in Article 24(1) of the directive.

In *Sala, Trojani,* and *Brey,* the Court had held that so long as EU citizens were lawfully resident within a host Member State according to national law, they could invoke the EU principle of non-discrimination on grounds of nationality to claim equal access to those social benefits which were available to nationals purely on the basis of their nationality or residence. In *Dano,* however, the Court retreated from this position and relied on a stricter reading of Article 24 of the Directive: in order to claim entitlement to social assistance benefits on an equal footing with nationals under Article 18 TFEU and Article 24 of the Directive, the EU citizen must be lawfully resident in compliance with the terms of the Directive and not just under the terms of national law. Hence the possession of lawful national residence, as seemed to be the case in *Sala* and *Trojani,* and to some extent in *Brey,* no longer suffices to ground a claim of equal treatment alongside national residents: it is also necessary for the citizen to satisfy the criteria for lawful residence under Directive 2004/38. These criteria, as we have seen, include, once the three-month initial period of unconditional residence has passed, possession of sufficient resources not to become an unreasonable burden on the host state. Further, while the Court in *Trojani* seemed to imply that the applicant's right of residence would have to be revoked before the host state could deny him equal treatment in access to social benefits, the CJEU in *Dano* indicates that Member States may refuse an EU citizen access to social assistance where she does not meet the criteria established by the Directive, and even where she has already been granted an indefinite residence permit under national law.

Nevertheless, despite this retreat, and even though the terms of the ruling in *Dano* are almost entirely focused on the entitlement of Member States to impose restrictions and limits on the rights of residence and access to benefits of non-economically active EU citizens, key elements of the rulings in *Trojani* and *Brey,* echoed also in *Baumbast*[106] above and *Grzelczyk* below,[107] which emphasized the need for proportionality and respect for fundamental rights on the part of Member States in applying those restrictions and limits, still remain valid.[108]

This means that an important impact of the Treaty provisions on citizenship, and of the Directive adopted to implement them,[109] on the rights of non-economically active EU citizens has been to require Member States, before reaching the conclusion that an EU citizen lacks sufficient resources to avoid becoming an unreasonable burden on the state, to undertake a careful and proportionate overall assessment of the individual circumstances and income of the person in question.[110] Once they have reached this conclusion, however, Member States are entitled to deny that citizen access to social assistance benefits which are available to nationals.

(ii) *Students*

The introduction of EU citizenship has also in certain ways strengthened the rights of students under EU law, by extending the circumstances under which EU nationals pursuing educational courses in states other than that of their nationality are entitled to claim certain social advantages, including

---

[106] Case C–413/99, excerpted at Section 4(a) above.

[107] (Nn 118–122) and text.

[108] See Case C–333/13 *Dano,* [80] on the requirement to carry out a specific examination of the financial circumstances of each individual, and the more detailed description of this requirement in Case C–140/12 *Brey,* [67]–[72].

[109] Note that while *Brey* and *Dano* were decided on the basis of Dir 2004/38 rather than Arts 20–21 TFEU, the CJEU emphasized that the Dir was intended to implement those primary Treaty rights: Case C–140/12 *Brey,* [53]; Case C–333/13 *Dano,* [59]–[61].

[110] In Case C–140/12 *Brey,* [64], [69] the Court seemed to indicate that in calculating the resources available to the applicant and the degree of burden he might cause to the state, the social assistance he was receiving or would receive should be taken into account, while in Case C–333/13 *Dano,* [80] the CJEU ruled that the applicant's financial position was to be assessed without taking account of the benefit claimed.

educational advantages, from either the host state or their home state. This requires a brief discussion of the law relating to students prior to the introduction of EU citizenship.

In *Gravier*, a French national who was studying for a course in strip-cartoon art in Belgium had challenged the requirement of an enrolment fee for non-Belgians.[111] The ECJ ruled that, since the Treaty at the time specified that the EU should lay down principles for developing a common vocational training policy, Belgium was prohibited from discriminating against her under Article 12 EC (now Article 18 TFEU) on grounds of her nationality in access to vocational training. The Court held that, since access to vocational training was likely to promote the free movement of persons, the 'conditions of access to vocational training' fell within the scope of the Treaty, and the enrolment fee for non-nationals was contrary to the requirement of non-discrimination on grounds of nationality.[112]

Given the financial consequences for Member States if they were required to treat all students of EU nationality on an equal footing with national students in conditions of access to vocational training, the *Gravier* ruling clearly had far-reaching potential. However, the ECJ interpreted 'vocational training' expansively in this context,[113] ruling that any form of education, including university education,[114] which prepared for a profession, trade, or employment was included, even if it included 'an element of general education'.[115] The Court decided to limit the financial consequences of *Gravier* for Member States in a different way, by instead restricting the interpretation of what non-discrimination in the 'conditions of access' to vocational training meant. In *Lair* and *Brown* the Court ruled that only grants intended to cover charges relating specifically to *access* to vocational training, such as registration and tuition fees, were covered by the prohibition on discrimination, whereas a maintenance and training grant provided by the state to pursue university study would not be covered.[116]

Subsequently the 1990 Students' Residence Directive provided that while students enjoying the EU right of access to vocational education in a host Member State must also enjoy a right of residence for the duration of their studies, states could subject this to the requirement that they possess sufficient resources to avoid becoming a burden on the state social assistance scheme and that they possess comprehensive sickness insurance.[117]

Against this background, the argument of *Grzelczyk*, who was a French national studying in Belgium, that he was entitled under the Treaty's prohibition of discrimination on grounds of nationality to apply for state social assistance (the non-contributory minimex) seemed unlikely to succeed.[118] However, the influence of EU citizenship on the outcome of the case was once again crucial. The Court ruled that the situation had changed since its ruling in *Brown*, with the introduction of EU citizenship, a new chapter on education and vocational training in the EU Treaty, and the enactment of the Residence Directives since the time of that earlier judgment. As an EU citizen pursuing vocational studies in another Member State, Grzelczyk was entitled to rely on the prohibition on discrimination on grounds of nationality; and the fact that the Students' Residence Directive at the time precluded him from receiving a maintenance

---

[111] Case 293/83 *Gravier v City of Liège* [1985] ECR 593.

[112] For subsequent litigation over discrimination in the Belgian higher education system see Case 42/87 *Commission v Belgium* [1988] ECR 5445; Case C–47/93 *Commission v Belgium* [1994] ECR I–1593.

[113] In particular, the interpretation was much broader than the Court's interpretation of the term 'vocational schools' for workers in Art 7(3) of Reg 1612/68 (now Art 7(3) of Reg 492/2011): Case 39/86 *Lair* [1988] ECR 3161.

[114] Case 24/86 *Blaizot v University of Liège* [1988] ECR 379, [20]. The CJEU drew for support on Art 10 of the Council of Europe's European Social Charter, which treats university education as a form of vocational training. However, the CJEU limited the retroactivity of its ruling in *Blaizot*, because of Belgium's fear that it would throw the financing of university education into chaos.

[115] Case 293/83 *Gravier* (n 111) [30]; Case 263/86 *Belgium v Humbel* [1988] ECR 5365; Case 242/87 *Commission v Council* [1989] ECR 1425.

[116] Case 39/86 *Lair* (n 113) [15]; Case 197/86 *Brown* [1988] ECR 3205.

[117] See also Case C–357/89 *Raulin v Minister van Onderwijs en Wetenschappen* [1992] ECR I–1027.

[118] Case C–184/99 *Grzelczyk v CPAS* [2001] ECR I–6193.

grant, and specified that he should have sickness insurance and sufficient resources not to become a burden on the host state did not necessarily mean that he could not apply for social assistance such as the minimex.[119] The Directive—just as with the successor Directive 2004/38[120] —did not specify any particular amount for 'sufficient resources', but merely required the student to make a declaration of sufficient resources whose truthfulness could only be assessed at that time. Finally, the ECJ ruled, as in *Trojani* and *Brey* above, that while Member States were free to conclude that a student who had recourse to social assistance no longer fulfilled the conditions for a right of residence, and to withdraw the residence permit, this conclusion could not be the automatic consequence of an application for social assistance.[121] Interestingly too, the Court read the Preambles to the various Residence Directives, which provided—as does the Preamble to Directive 2004/38—that the person must not become an unreasonable burden on the public finances of the host state, as an indication that host states could nevertheless be expected to carry a *reasonable* burden. More specifically, the Court ruled that the legislation 'thus accepts a certain degree of financial solidarity between nationals of a host Member State and nationals of other Member States, particularly if the difficulties which a beneficiary of the right of residence encounters are temporary'.[122]

Grzelczyk thus dealt with the issue of access to social security for EU nationals pursuing studies in another Member State, and the Court there drew attention to the fact that the Students' Residence Directive did not establish any right to payment of a maintenance grant. In *Bidar*, however, the Court was confronted with precisely this situation: a student of French nationality applying in the UK for a student maintenance loan or grant to finance the cost of his studies there.[123] The question was whether such maintenance assistance, despite the explicit limiting conditions in the Directive and the earlier case law in *Brown* and *Lair*,[124] fell within the scope of the Treaty for the purposes of discrimination under Article 12 EC (now Article 18 TFEU). The Court followed a similar line of reasoning to that in *Grzelczyk*, and relied on the introduction of EU citizenship and the changes in educational and vocational training competence under the Treaty to depart from its earlier conclusions in *Brown* and *Lair*, and to rule that maintenance grants for students do now fall within the scope of the prohibition of discrimination on grounds of nationality.[125]

The Court in *Bidar* emphasized that its ruling was supported by Directive 2004/38, given the provision in Article 24 of the Directive for equal treatment within the scope of the EU Treaty for all EU citizens residing in the territory of another Member State, and the derogation in Article 24(2) permitting states to restrict eligibility for maintenance grants for students to those who have acquired permanent residence.[126] Hence while students could not rely on the Students' Residence Directive or on Directive 2004/38 to claim a right to a maintenance grant, they could rely on Article 21 TFEU together with Article 18 TFEU for this purpose, on the basis that a maintenance grant could henceforth be considered a benefit falling within the scope of the Treaty.

This was a dramatic ruling, effectively sidelining the restrictive provision which Member States had inserted into Article 24(2) of Directive 2004/38. However, the Court sweetened it somewhat by ruling

---

[119] Ibid [35]–[39].

[120] Art 8(3) of Dir 2004/38 stipulates that Member States may not require this declaration to refer to any specific amount of resources.

[121] (Nn 106–107).

[122] Case C–184/99 *Grzelczyk* (n 118) [46].

[123] Case C–209/03 *Bidar v London Borough of Ealing* [2005] ECR I–2119.

[124] (N 116).

[125] Case C–209/03 *Bidar* (n 123) [31]–[42]. See also Case C–46/12 *LN v Styrelsen for Videregående Uddannelser og Uddannelsesstøtte* EU:C:2013:97, [28]–[29].

[126] See Case C–75/11 *Commission v Austria* EU:C:2012:605 to the effect that the derogation in Art 24(2) of the Dir only covers student grants and student loans, and not other forms of financial assistance to students.

that the host state could decide to limit access to student maintenance grants only to those students who had demonstrated a certain degree of *integration* into the society of that state. A requirement to show a link with the state's employment market would not be acceptable, and the UK requirement that the student must be 'settled' in the UK was also excessively restrictive and disproportionate.[127] Subsequently, however, the ECJ retreated from the boldness of its ruling in *Bidar*. In *Förster*, the Court upheld a (retroactively applicable) condition of five years' prior residence on the right of students to have access to a maintenance grant in the host state, as legitimate and not disproportionate.[128]

In *Morgan and Bucher*, the Court however ruled that Articles 20 and 21 TFEU prohibited German rules limiting the availability of study finance abroad in another Member State to students who had already completed at least one year of the same field of study in Germany.[129] Given their status as EU citizens, the applicants could challenge restrictions imposed by the Member State of their nationality on their freedom to move and study abroad by limiting without adequate justification the availability of study finance to courses which continued studies already begun in Germany. While the Court acknowledged, as in *Bidar* and *Förster*, that it might be legitimate for a Member State to demand a certain degree of integration into its society in order to ensure that the award of financial grants does not become an unreasonable burden, the degree of integration necessary should have been satisfied in the case in question by the fact that the applicants had been raised in Germany and completed their schooling there.[130] Similarly in *Prinz and Seeberger*, a requirement of having obtained permanent residence by having spent three years in the awarding Member State prior to commencing studies was disproportionate, and could not be justified on the ground that it preserved the national educational grant scheme by protecting the state from an unreasonable financial burden.[131] While the aim of preventing such a burden was legitimate, the means of pursuing it was too general and exclusive, to the detriment of other factors which could establish a sufficient degree of integration. In *Elrick* too, the Court rejected as disproportionate a national rule that subjected overseas study finance to the condition that the course in question led to a vocational qualification equivalent to that provided by a vocational school in the state awarding the grant, following a course of at least two years' duration.[132] The state's declared objective of awarding education or training grants for studies pursued abroad only in respect of courses which offered students the highest chance of success in the labour market was legitimate, but the means pursued (the two-year durational requirement) was insufficiently connected to that aim, and was likely to dissuade EU nationals from exercising their rights of free movement and to discourage the Treaty objective of student mobility. Similarly in *Meneses*, a requirement imposed by German legislation of having established a permanent residence on the national territory in order to qualify for study-abroad finance was deemed both over-general, disproportionate, and too exclusive in its specification of the necessary degree of connection between the applicant for a grant and German society.[133] In *Martens*, a rule requiring the applicant for study-abroad finance to have resided for at least three out of the six years preceding his enrolment was deemed both arbitrary and exclusive in its pursuit of the otherwise legitimate aim of ensuring a degree of integration between the granting state and the applicant.[134] In each of

---

[127] Ibid [52]–[63].

[128] Case C–158/07 *Förster v Hoofddirectie van de Informatie Beheer Groep* [2008] ECR I–8507.

[129] Cases C–11 and 12/06 *Morgan and Bucher* [2007] ECR I–9161.

[130] Ibid [43]–[45].

[131] Cases C–523 and 585/11 *Prinz & Seeberger* EU:C:2013:524.

[132] Case C–275/12 *Elrick* EU:C:2013:684. The Opinion of AG Sharpston in *Elrick* EU:C:2013:90 contains a very interesting discussion of the difficulty facing the Court in appraising the legitimacy and proportionality of domestic measures adopted to prevent unreasonable financial burdens on the state, and in disentangling economic objectives from 'reasonable integration' requirements.

[133] Case C–220/12 *Thiele Meneses* EU:C:2013:683.

[134] Case C–359/13 *Martens v Minister van Onderwijs, Cultuur en Wetenschap* EU:C:2015:118.

the cases while the CJEU paid deference to the competence of the Member States in the organization of the financing of higher education and noted that it was open to them not to provide any study-abroad financing at all, it emphasized that once they chose to provide such funding, states must do so in compliance with EU law requirements of non-discrimination and free movement of citizens.[135]

The strongly contested *Commission v Austria* litigation concerned not the availability of study finance or maintenance grants, but rather the imposition by Austria of additional conditions of access to university education on students whose secondary education diplomas were obtained in another Member State.[136] Following earlier cases such as *Commission v Belgium*[137] and *Gravier*,[138] the Court drew on the status of EU citizenship in ruling that this constituted indirect discrimination which could not be justified on any of the various grounds put forward by the Austrian Government. The case caused a political storm within Austria, which as a small country bordering a large neighbour sharing a common language, argued that it was facing an influx of students from Germany, especially in courses like medicine, which threatened to overwhelm the financial and structural equilibrium of its educational system. When Austria did not comply with the judgment but introduced even more restrictive rules, the Commission initiated fresh infringement proceedings against the state, but these were subsequently suspended under an agreement reached between Austria and the Commission due to political pressure over the pending Lisbon Treaty at the time.[139] A parallel legal dispute was brewing with Belgium, but after the Commission also suspended the infringement proceedings it had commenced against Belgium, the issue came before the CJEU via a preliminary reference from a Belgian court in *Bressol*.[140]

In *Bressol* the applicant challenged Belgium's quota system which was designed to restrict the access of non-resident EU citizens into certain medical degree programmes, ostensibly in order to ensure that at least a certain number of Belgian residents would graduate each year with the ultimate objective of protecting public health. The CJEU, mirroring the Commission's retreat from its initial infringement proceedings against Belgium, took a significantly softer stance than it had in the earlier Austrian litigation.[141] The CJEU ruled that although Articles 18 and 21 TFEU *prima facie* prohibit such a quota system for EU citizens based indirectly on nationality, there may be an exception where the national authority can show that it is restricting access of non-resident EU citizens in order to ensure a sufficient supply of national graduates to staff the French Community public health service. Whether there was an actual risk to the health service was to be determined by the national courts, but the CJEU emphasized the need for data and specific evidence to the effect that equal access for non-permanently resident EU nationals is detrimental to the public health service and the quota system would actually ameliorate that problem.[142]

Consequently, while the status of citizenship has been invoked by the CJEU to enhance the rights of access of students in certain circumstances to maintenance grants, social security, travel benefits, and educational courses in host Member States, as well as to study-abroad finance, the Court has at times been responsive to adverse Member State reactions in this field. It has softened some of its strongest

---

[135] See also Case C–75/11 *Commission v Austria* EU:C:2012:605, in which an Austrian scheme for granting reduced fares on public transport only to students whose parents were in receipt of Austrian family allowances was found to violate Arts 18, 20, and 21 TFEU, and Art 24 of Dir 2004/38, since it was a disproportionate way of pursuing the legitimate aim of ensuring a genuine link with the host Member State. See also Case C–20/12 *Giersch* EU:C:2013:411 and Case C–542/09 *Commission v Netherlands* EU:C:2012:346 discussed in Ch 21 in the context of free movement of workers.

[136] Case C–147/03 (n 58).

[137] Case C–65/03 *Commission v Belgium* [2004] ECR I–6427.

[138] Case 293/83 (n 111).

[139] See S Garben, *EU Higher Education Law: The Bologna Process and Harmonization by Stealth* (Kluwer, 2011).

[140] Case C–73/08 *Bressol v Gouvernement de la communauté française* [2010] ECR I–2735.

[141] Case C–147/03 (n 58).

[142] Case C–73/08 *Bressol* (n 140) [64]–[81].

rulings, as the shift in its stance from *Commission v Austria* to *Bressol*, suggests. Nevertheless, despite an apparently similar softening in the Court's shift from *Bidar* to *Förster* as far as its acceptance of certain restrictive conditions on the availability of maintenance grants for students are concerned, the Court has been fairly rigorous in reviewing the proportionality of the various restrictions subsequently imposed by states on the availability of study finance abroad.

(iii) *Job-Seekers*

The cases of *D'Hoop, Collins, Ioannidis*, and *Vatsouras* involved the situation of job-seekers covered by Article 45 TFEU, who wished to apply for job-seekers' allowances.

In *D'Hoop*, the ECJ ruled that a Belgian national who was refused a 'tideover' allowance when seeking her first job on the Belgian job market, purely on the grounds that she had completed her secondary school education in France, had suffered discrimination on the basis of her EU citizenship, and in particular on account of her exercise of the EU right to move and avail herself of educational opportunities in France.[143] The Court ruled that while it might in theory be possible to justify a refusal to grant a tideover allowance to an EU citizen on the basis that there must be a sufficient link between the job-seeker and the host state, the condition which Belgium actually imposed was based on the place where the diploma of completion of secondary education was obtained. This was a disproportionate condition since it did not represent the real and effective degree of connection between the applicant and the Belgian job market. This was taken further still by the Court in *Collins*,[144] in which it relied on the introduction of the provisions of the Treaty on citizenship to depart from its earlier case law in *Lebon*,[145] where it had ruled that job-seekers were entitled to equal treatment only in access to employment and that they were not entitled to the same social and tax advantages enjoyed by workers under Article 45 TFEU or Article 7(2) of Regulation 1612/68 (now 492/2011). The Court in *Collins* ruled that the rights of job-seekers under Article 45 should be interpreted in the light of the more general right to equal treatment of EU citizens. Given this new interpretative framework, the Court ruled, contrary to its prior ruling in *Lebon*, that a job-seeker was henceforth entitled under Article 45 to a 'benefit of a financial nature intended to facilitate access to employment in the labour market of a Member State'. And while it was legitimate for a state to require that a job-seeker has a genuine link with the employment market of the state, a residence condition would have to be applied in a proportionate and non-discriminatory way. *Collins* was then confirmed and applied in subsequent case law.[146]

It remained to be seen, however, whether this case law would survive the introduction of Article 24(2) of Directive 2004/38, which permits Member States, by way of derogation from the equal treatment principle, to limit entitlement to social assistance for migrant EU nationals and their families during the first three months of residence or for the longer period provided for job-seekers in Article 14(4)(b). We have seen how the parallel provision in Article 24(2) permitting Member States to restrict the availability of maintenance grants to students was effectively sidelined by the ECJ in *Bidar*, where it ruled that students could instead rely directly on Articles 18 and 21 TFEU to gain entitlement to a maintenance grant.[147] The ECJ was confronted directly with this question in *Vatsouras*, in which a

---

[143] Case C–224/98 *D'Hoop v Office Nationale de l'Emploi* [2002] ECR I–6191.

[144] Case C–138/02 *Collins v Secretary of State for Work and Pensions* [2004] ECR I–2703.

[145] Case 316/85 *Lebon* [1987] ECR 281.

[146] Case C–258/04 [2005] ECR I–8275, in which it was held that a Greek national seeking his first employment in Belgium could not be refused entitlement to job-seekers' allowance under Belgian law purely on the ground that he completed his secondary education outside Belgium.

[147] Case C–209/03 *Bidar* (n 123). However, the CJEU did subsequently limit the impact of the *Bidar* ruling by allowing Member States instead to impose lengthy integration requirements on students seeking access to maintenance grants under the Treaty: Case C–158/07 *Förster* (n 128).

number of Greek nationals whose economic status was unclear had applied for job-seekers' allowances in Germany. The Court was asked whether the derogation in Article 24(2) of the Directive concerning social assistance for job-seekers was compatible with the commitment to equal treatment for EU citizens under Articles 18 and 21 TFEU.

Cases C–22 and 23/08 **Vatsouras and Koupatantze v Arbeitsgemeinschaft (ARGE) Nürnberg 900**
[2009] ECR I–4585

[Note Lisbon Treaty renumbering: Arts 12 and 39 EC are now Arts 18 and 45 TFEU]

THE ECJ

33. By this question, the referring court asks whether Article 24(2) of Directive 2004/38 is compatible with Article 12 EC, read in conjunction with Article 39 EC.

34. Article 24(2) of Directive 2004/38 establishes a derogation from the principle of equal treatment enjoyed by Union citizens other than workers, self-employed persons, persons who retain such status and members of their families, who reside within the territory of the host Member State.

35. Under that provision, the host Member State is not obliged to confer entitlement to social assistance on, among others, job-seekers for the longer period during which they have the right to reside there.

36. Nationals of a Member State seeking employment in another Member State fall within the scope of Article 39 EC and therefore enjoy the right to equal treatment laid down in paragraph 2 of that provision (Case C–258/04 *Ioannidis* [2005] ECR I–8275, paragraph 21).

37. Furthermore, in view of the establishment of citizenship of the Union and the interpretation of the right to equal treatment enjoyed by citizens of the Union, it is no longer possible to exclude from the scope of Article 39(2) EC a benefit of a financial nature intended to facilitate access to employment in the labour market of a Member State (Case C–138/02 *Collins* [2004] ECR I–2703, paragraph 63, and *Ioannidis*, paragraph 22) . . .

40. It follows that nationals of the Member States seeking employment in another Member State who have established real links with the labour market of that State can rely on Article 39(2) EC in order to receive a benefit of a financial nature intended to facilitate access to the labour market.

41. It is for the competent national authorities and, where appropriate, the national courts not only to establish the existence of a real link with the labour market, but also to assess the constituent elements of that benefit, in particular its purposes and the conditions subject to which it is granted.

42. As the Advocate General has noted in point 57 of his Opinion, the objective of the benefit must be analysed according to its results and not according to its formal structure.

43. A condition such as that in Paragraph 7(1) of the SGB II, under which the person concerned must be capable of earning a living, could constitute an indication that the benefit is intended to facilitate access to employment.

44. In any event, the derogation provided for in Article 24(2) of Directive 2004/38 must be interpreted in accordance with Article 39(2) EC.

45. Benefits of a financial nature which, independently of their status under national law, are intended to facilitate access to the labour market cannot be regarded as constituting 'social assistance' within the meaning of Article 24(2) of Directive 2004/38.

46. In the light of the foregoing, the answer must be that, with respect to the rights of nationals of Member States seeking employment in another Member State, examination of the first question has not disclosed any factor capable of affecting the validity of Article 24(2) of Directive 2004/38.

What the ECJ did in *Vatsouras*, in other words, was to confirm its ruling in *Collins* that the introduction of EU citizenship had the effect of overruling earlier case law such as *Lebon*, by henceforth including within the scope of Article 45(2) TFEU non-discriminatory entitlement to benefits intended to facilitate access to employment. Job-seeker benefits of this kind, according to the ECJ, should not be considered to be 'social assistance' within Article 24(2) of Directive 2004/38. In other words, the impact of EU citizenship in widening the scope of Article 45(2) to include job-seekers' benefits correspondingly limits the scope of Article 24(2) so as to exclude such benefits from the derogation permitted to Member States under the Directive. Yet the *Vatsouras* judgment did not conclude that Article 24(2) was either incompatible with the Treaty or wholly redundant: Member States may arguably continue to rely on Article 24(2) to exclude job-seekers from access to other kinds of 'social assistance', although not from benefits which are objectively construed by the domestic court as 'intended to facilitate access to the labour market' and therefore falling within Article 45 TFEU.[148]

(iv) *EU Citizens who have Acquired a Right of Permanent Residence under Directive 2004/38*

As we saw above, Article 16 of Directive 2004/38 introduced a right of 'permanent residence' in a host EU Member State for EU citizens who have resided legally there for a 'continuous period of five years', and which can only be lost, under Article 16(4), through absence from the host Member State for a period exceeding two consecutive years. This right of permanent residence is not subject to conditions provided earlier in the Directive, including the conditions of possession of adequate resources and sickness insurance in Article 7(1).

In *Lassal*, the CJEU confirmed that the provisions on EU citizenship are applicable as soon as they enter into force and must be applied to the present effects of 'situations arising previously'.[149] The Court ruled that continuous periods of five years' residence completed even *before* the date for transposition of Directive 2004/38 must be taken into account in determining acquisition of the status of permanent residence, although the right itself could not be acquired before the transposition date, and that temporary absences occurring prior to the date of transposition, but after completion of a continuous period of five years, would not affect such acquisition.[150]

The cases of *Ziolkowski and Szeja*[151] and *Dias*[152] established that the period of five years' residence had to be lawful residence under Directive 2004/38, so that only periods of residence completed in compliance with the conditions laid down under Article 7(1) of the Directive (meaning spent as a worker, family member of a worker, as a citizen with sufficient resources, etc) would count towards acquisition of the five years. And in *Onuekwere*, the CJEU ruled that periods of imprisonment in the host Member State could not be taken into consideration in the context of the acquisition of the right of permanent residence by a third-country national family member of an EU citizen who had already acquired that right, and that continuity of residence would be interrupted by such periods of imprisonment in the host Member State, for the purposes of Article 16(2) and (3) of the Directive.[153]

Once they have acquired the right of permanent residence in a Member State, however, EU citizens (and their privileged family members who have resided with them during that period) are entitled to

---

[148] For a pending case on access to social assistance for former workers, see Case C–67/14 *Jobcenter Berlin Neukölln v Alimanovic*.

[149] Case C–162/09 *Secretary of State for Work and Pensions v Lassal* [2010] ECR I–9217, [39].

[150] Ibid.

[151] Cases C–424 and 425/10 *Ziolkowski & Szeja* EU:C:2010:587; for comment see M Jesse (2012) 49 CMLRev 2003.

[152] Case C–325/09 *Dias* [2011] ECR I–6387.

[153] Case C–378/12 *Onuekwere* EU:C:2014:13.

virtually full material equality and equal access to social benefits alongside nationals of the host state, regardless of their lack of resources or health insurance.

(D) ARTICLES 20 AND 21 TFEU HAVE ENHANCED THE RIGHTS OF EU CITIZENS TO CHALLENGE RESTRICTIVE MEMBER STATE MEASURES

The rights of EU Member State nationals and their families have been enhanced in various other ways by the creation of EU citizenship. Apart from: (i) strengthening various other existing rights, and particularly reinforcing the principle of non-discrimination on grounds of nationality and residence; (ii) various protections have been introduced for EU citizens and their families in the event of the adoption by Member States of restrictive measures against them.

(i) *Strengthening Rights of Non-Discrimination*

In *Bickel & Franz*[154] the ECJ emphasized that German and Austrian nationals who were subject to criminal proceedings in Italy and who requested the use of German in the proceedings were exercising their right to free movement as European citizens based on Article 21 TFEU and were entitled not to be discriminated against on grounds of nationality. This was extended in *Rüffer*, where the CJEU ruled that Italian rules which granted the right to use a language (in this case German) other than the official language of that state in civil court proceedings in a specific territorial entity (Bolzano), only to Italian citizens who are domiciled in that entity were in breach of Articles 18 and 21 TFEU.[155]

In cases such as *Turpeinen*,[156] *Pusa*,[157] *N*,[158] *Schwarz and Gootjes-Schwarz*,[159] and *Zanotti*,[160] the Court condemned a number of restrictive or discriminatory measures imposed by Member States as regards access to social or tax benefits as a violation of Article 20 TFEU, regardless of whether the applicants were workers or not.[161] Similarly in *De Cuyper*,[162] *Commission v Sweden*,[163] *Tas-Hagen*,[164] *Nerkowska*,[165] and *Habelt*[166] concerning unemployment, wartime, and other social security benefits, the Court ruled that national residence restrictions were *prima facie* in breach of Article 20 TFEU. In *Gottwald*, however, the imposition of a residence requirement for the issue of an annual toll disc free of charge to disabled persons was held not to constitute an unreasonable or disproportionate restriction on the rights of EU citizens, but was justified by the wish to ensure a connection between the society of the Member State concerned and the recipient of a benefit designed to promote the mobility and integration of disabled persons.[167] In *Stewart*, by comparison, the CJEU ruled that Article 21 precludes

154 Case C–274/96 [1998] ECR I–7637, [15].
155 Case C–322/13 *Rüffer* EU:C:2014:189.
156 Case C–520/04 *Turpeinen* [2006] ECR I–10685.
157 Case C–224/02 *Pusa v Osuuspankkien Keskinäinen Vakuutusyhtiö* [2004] ECR I–5763.
158 Case C–470/04 *N v Inspecteur van de Belastingdienst* [2006] ECR I–7409.
159 Case C–76/05 *Schwarz and Gootjes-Schwarz* [2007] ECR I–6849.
160 Case C–56/09 *Zanotti v Agenzia delle Entrate—Ufficio Roma* [2010] ECR I–4517, [68]–[78].
161 See also Case C–403/03 *Schempp* (n 87), another tax case; Case C–148/02 *Garcia Avello* [2003] ECR I–11613 concerning restrictions on the right to change surnames.
162 Case C–406/04 *De Cuyper v ONEM* [2006] ECR I–6947. Here however the restrictive residence condition was ultimately found to be justifiable on the ground of the need to monitor the circumstances of those in receipt of unemployment benefit.
163 Case C–104/06 *Commission v Sweden* [2007] ECR I–677.
164 Case C–192/05 *Tas-Hagen v Raadskamer WUBO van de Pensioen- en Uitkeringsraad* [2006] ECR I–10451.
165 Case C–499/06 *Nerkowska v Zakład Ubezpieczeń Społecznych Oddział w Koszalinie* [2008] ECR I–3993.
166 Cases C–396–450/05 *Habelt* (n 53) [78].
167 Case C–103/08 *Gottwald v Bezirkshauptmannschaft Bregenz* [2009] ECR I–9117.

a Member State from subjecting the award of youth invalidity benefit to a condition of past presence of the claimant in the state, to the exclusion of any other element which could establish a genuine link between the claimant and the Member State.[168]

(ii) *Enhancing Protection Against Restrictive Measures*

As we have seen in Chapter 21, Article 27 of Directive 2004/38 sets out provisions governing the measures which Member States can take against EU citizens and their families on grounds of public policy, security, and health. This has been the subject of a number of rulings concerning restrictive measures adopted by states to prevent EU or national citizens from leaving their jurisdiction.

In *Gaydarov*,[169] the CJEU ruled that national law restricting an EU citizen who has been convicted of drug trafficking from travelling to another state would not necessarily be contrary to Article 21 TFEU or Article 27 of the Directive provided the other requirements laid down under the Directive and the Court's case law (of sufficient seriousness, proportionality, judicial review, etc) are satisfied.[170] By comparison, in *Byankov*, Article 21 TFEU precluded a provision of national law which restricted the freedom of a national to leave the state on the sole ground that he owed a private debt which exceeded a certain threshold and was unsecured.[171] Article 27(1) could not be invoked to service economic ends; it was not clear whether the state considered that the existence of such a debt could create a threat to public policy, security, or health; and even if the protection of creditors could constitute a sufficiently serious public-policy aim, the absolute nature of the prohibition which made no provision for exception, limitation, or regular review, was disproportionate. The importance of the Treaty provisions on citizenship to the Court's conclusion in the case is clear:

> 81. In view also of the importance which primary law accords to citizenship of the Union (see, inter alia, Case C–135/08 *Rottmann* [2010] ECR I–1449, paragraphs 43 and 56), it must be concluded that ... national legislation such as that described in the order for reference, to the extent that it (i) prevents citizens of the Union from asserting the right conferred on them by Article 21 TFEU to move and reside freely against absolute territorial prohibitions that have been adopted for an unlimited period and (ii) prevents administrative bodies from acting upon a body of case-law whereby the Court has confirmed the illegality, under EU law, of such prohibitions, cannot reasonably be justified by the principle of legal certainty and must therefore be considered, in this respect, to be contrary to the principle of effectiveness and to Article 4(3) TEU.

In *Aladzhov*, however, the CJEU gave a more equivocal ruling on the lawfulness of a Bulgarian prohibition on one of its nationals from leaving Bulgaria's territory because of non-payment of a tax liability of a company of which he was director.[172] While non-payment of tax liability could in certain circumstances, as also recognized by the ECtHR, constitute a public-policy ground of sufficient seriousness to justify a restrictive measure, the prohibition on leaving the territory at issue here would have to satisfy a strict test of necessity and proportionality to be carried out by the national court.

---

[168] Case C–503/09 *Stewart* EU:C:2011:500. See also Case C–522/10 *Reichel-Albert* EU:C:2012:475, where a state which did not permit the taking into account of periods of childraising for the purposes of calculating old-age insurance, purely because the person in question had temporarily established themselves in another Member State, was contrary to Art 21 TFEU.

[169] Case C–430/10 *Gaydarov* [2011] ECR I–11637. These conditions did not however appear from the facts of the case to be met.

[170] See Ch 21, Section 8(b) for a discussion of these requirements.

[171] Case C–249/11 *Byankov* EU:C:2012:608.

[172] Case C–434/10 *Aladzhov* [2011] ECR I–11659.

A case concerning the refusal to permit entry under Article 27, rather than refusal to permit exit, was ZZ.[173] In this case, the serious grounds of public security justifying refusal of entry was the alleged involvement of the applicant in the activities of the Armed Islamic Group some ten years earlier, and while the full reasons were provided to the Special Immigration Appeals Tribunal in the UK, only the more limited publicly available evidence was provided to the applicant. The UK relied on Article 30(2) of Directive 2004/38 which specifies that persons concerned are to be informed, precisely and in full, of the public-policy, security, or health grounds on which the decision in their case is taken, unless that would be contrary to the interests of state security. The CJEU ruled that as a derogation from the procedural rights set out in the Directive, this proviso had to be construed strictly and in the light of the right to an effective remedy in Article 47 of the Charter of Fundamental Rights. Citing Kadi[174] and ECHR case law, the CJEU ruled that Articles 30 and 31 of the Directive require the relevant national court to ensure that any failure by the competent national authority to disclose precisely and fully the grounds on which a decision taken under Article 27 is based and to disclose the related evidence to the applicant is limited to that which is strictly necessary, and that he is in any case informed of the essence of the grounds in a way which takes due account of the necessary confidentiality of the evidence.

The Court has also ruled in a number of cases on the ultra-enhanced protection against expulsion only on 'imperative grounds of public security' which was introduced by Article 28(3)(a) of Directive 2004/38 for EU citizens who had resided in the host Member State for the previous ten years, as well as the enhanced protection against expulsion only on 'serious grounds of public policy or public security' introduced by Article 28(2) for EU citizens who had resided there for the previous five years and acquired permanent residence. In Tsakouridis, the Court was asked whether certain absences from the Member State during the period of ten years would deprive an applicant of ultra-enhanced protection, and whether criminal offences connected with organized drug dealing were sufficient to constitute 'imperative grounds of public security' under Article 28(3), or 'serious grounds of public policy or public security' under Article 28(2).[175] The Court replied that the answers to the question of the length of the period of residence were ultimately for the national courts to determine, taking the reason, nature, and duration of absences into account, and that while offences relating to organized narcotic trafficking could amount to imperative grounds of public security under the Directive, the decision must be proportionate and must respect fundamental rights, and that a balance had to be struck between the exceptional nature of the threat to public security and the risk of compromising the social rehabilitation of the EU citizen in the state in which he had become genuinely integrated. In MG, the Court ruled that the ten-year period of residence referred to in Article 28(3) must, in principle, be continuous and be calculated by counting back from the date of the decision ordering expulsion.[176] Following the principles established in both Tsakouridis and Onuekwere[177] concerning the importance of integration into the host state for the purposes of the enhanced protection conferred by the ten-year period, the Court also ruled that periods of imprisonment could not be taken into account for these purposes and would, in principle, interrupt the continuity of the period of residence required. In PI, the commission of an offence such as the sexual exploitation of children could constitute a particularly serious threat to the fundamental interests of society such as would amount to an 'imperative requirement of public

---

[173] Case C–300/11 ZZ EU:C:2013:363.
[174] Cases C–402 and 415/05 P Kadi & Al Barakaat [2008] ECR I–6351.
[175] Case C–145/09 Land Baden-Württemberg v Tsakouridis [2010] ECR I–11979.
[176] Case C–400/12 MG EU:C:2014:9.
[177] (N 153).

policy' justifying exclusion from a host Member State even after the ten-year period provided for under Article 28(3)(a) had been completed.[178]

Finally, the ECJ in *Commission v Belgium* condemned the disproportionate penalty of automatic deportation imposed by Belgian law for failure to produce the relevant documents needed to obtain a residence permit within the prescribed time limit.[179] And in *Wolzenburg* the Court ruled that when implementing the EU Framework Decision establishing a European Arrest Warrant, Member States were entitled to restrict the ground for optional non-execution of an arrest warrant to their own nationals, and to non-national EU citizens who had demonstrated a sufficient degree of integration by residing continually for five years in the host state and acquiring the right of permanent residence, but they could not impose an additional administrative requirement such as possession of a residence requirement of indefinite duration.[180]

(E) SUMMARY

i. Having discussed the changes brought about by EU citizenship under the four headings above, it seems clear that the introduction of citizenship has bolstered the existing rights of EU nationals and created some new rights both under the Treaty and in secondary legislation. However, it would be an exaggeration to say that citizenship has entirely subsumed the previous legal status categories and become the primary and 'fundamental status' of EU nationals, as the language of the Court at times suggests.

ii. The Court sometimes decides cases on the basis of the claimant's status as an EU citizen or without deciding into which specific status category he or she falls,[181] and often the lens of citizenship is treated by the Court as enhancing the existing legal guarantees of EU law, such as the protections against arbitrary discrimination, criminal prosecution, or expulsion, without addressing the economic or other status of the applicant.[182] In other cases, the Court deals with the issues on the basis of the applicant's economic status as an employed or self-employed person, and expressly sets aside the citizenship-based claim.[183] Importantly, the existence of a recognized economic status under EU law becomes relevant in circumstances in which the individual seeks access to material benefits in a host state, when reliance on the status of citizenship alone renders the rights of the citizen more precarious than if he or she can establish their status as worker or other preferred category.[184]

---

[178] Case C–348/09 *PI* EU:2012:300. For comment see D Kostakopoulou, 'When EU Citizens become Foreigners' (2014) 20 ELJ 447; D Kochenov and B Pirker, 'Deporting the Citizens within the European Union: A Counter-Intuitive Trend in Case C–348/09, *P.I.*' (2012–13) 19 CJEL 369.

[179] Case C–408/03 *Commission v Belgium* [2006] ECR I–2647. See also Case C–50/06 *Commission v Netherlands* [2007] ECR I–4383 in which the Netherlands had violated EU law by applying to EU citizens general legislation relating to foreign nationals which established an automatic connection between a criminal conviction and an expulsion measure.

[180] Case C–123/08 *Dominic Wolzenburg* [2009] ECR I–9621. See L Marin '"A Spectre Is Haunting Europe": European Citizenship in the Area of Freedom, Security and Justice' (2011) 17 EPL 705.

[181] See, eg, Case C–499/06 *Nerkowska* [2008] ECR I–3993 concerning a residence requirement for payment of a benefit for civilian victims of war or repression; Case C–103/08 *Gottwald* (n 167); Cases C–396–450/05 *Habelt* (n 166) [78]; Case C–164/07 *Wood* [2008] ECR I–4143. In *Wood* the CJEU referred to the applicant's status as a worker, but also cited its citizenship-based ruling in *Garcia-Avello* on the prohibition of discrimination on the grounds of nationality. Compare the approaches adopted by the AG and the CJEU in Case C–359/13 *Martens* EU:C:2015:118 and EU:C:2014:2240 concerning study-abroad finance.

[182] See, eg, Case C–145/09 *Tsakouridis* (n 175); Case C–123/08 *Wolzenburg* (n 180).

[183] See, eg, Case C–56/09 *Zanotti* [2010] ECR I–4517, [24]; Case C–287/05 *Hendrix* [2007] ECR I–6909, [62]; Case C–100/01 *Olazabal* [2002] ECR I–10981, [26]; Case C–92/01 *Stylianakis* [2003] ECR I–1291, [18]; Case C–208/05 *ITC* [2007] ECR I–181, [64]–[65].

[184] Cases C–480/08 *Teixeira* and C–310/08 *Ibrahim* (n 96).

iii. The introduction of EU citizenship has changed the law in gradual but significant ways. It has expanded and strengthened existing rights of movement, residence, and non-discrimination including by: (a) introducing an autonomous right to move and reside within the territory of a Member State which does not depend on previously existing free movement rights (*Baumbast, Chen*); (b) shrinking somewhat the scope of the 'purely internal situation' (*Garcia-Avella, Ruiz Zambrano, O, S & L*); (c) granting social rights to non-economically active citizens in certain circumstances where it does not constitute an unreasonable burden for the state (*Gryzlczyk*), although clearly affirming the right of states to limit access to social assistance by EU citizens who do not meet the resource conditions established by secondary legislation (*Dano*); and strengthening the existing social rights of others such as students and job-seekers who are sufficiently 'integrated' in the host state (*Bidar, Förster, Collins, Vatsouras*); (d) introducing the status of permanent residence which entitles the EU citizen to substantial social and material equality alongside nationals (Article 16 of Directive 2004/38) although requiring evidence of social integration in the fulfilment of the five-year period (*Ziolkowski, Onuekwere*); and (e) granting enhanced procedural and other protection (*ZZ*) against repressive (*Tsakouridis*), restrictive (*Byankov, Aladzhov*), or discriminatory (*Zanotti*) state measures, including progressively greater protection against expulsion for permanent residents; and requiring anti-fraud measures to be based on individual rather than general preventative circumstances (*McCarthy*).

5 POLITICAL RIGHTS OF CITIZENSHIP

Thus far we have examined the impact of Articles 20–21 TFEU in some detail. Articles 22–25 also confer a number of rights which, although limited in their range, are of both practical and symbolic importance.

The most important of these are the rights of alien suffrage, and the passive and active electoral rights created for EU citizens in host Member States.[185] Article 22 provides that citizens of the Union[186] shall have the right in a Member State other than that of their nationality to vote and to stand as candidates both in municipal and in European Parliament elections, under the same conditions as nationals.[187] This Article was controversial because of its incompatibility with constitutional provisions in some Member States,[188]

---

[185] For a comprehensive analysis see J Shaw, *The Transformation of Citizenship in the European Union* (Cambridge University Press, 2007).

[186] In Case C–145/04 *Spain v United Kingdom* [2006] ECR I–7917, [78]–[80], the CJEU ruled that the Treaty provisions on citizenship did not prevent Member States from granting rights to vote and stand in European Parliament elections to persons other than EU citizens, in this case residents of Gibraltar. The action by the UK had been necessitated by the judgment of the ECHR in App No 24833/94 *Matthews v UK*, 18 Feb 1999.

[187] Council Directive 93/109/EC of 6 December 1993 laying down detailed arrangements for the exercise of the right to vote and stand as a candidate in elections to the European Parliament for citizens of the Union residing in a Member State of which they are not nationals [1993] OJ L329/34, and more recently Dir 2013/1 [2013] OJ L26/27. On the right to vote and stand in municipal elections see Dir 94/80 [1994] OJ L368, modified by Dir 2006/106. See also Council Decision 2002/772 amending the Act concerning the election of the representatives of the European Parliament by direct universal suffrage [2002] OJ L283/1. For the most recent Commission report on European Parliament elections, including the participation of EU citizens, see COM(2010) 605, and for the most recent report on municipal elections, see COM (2012) 99.

[188] The Fourth Chamber of the Greek Council of State in Feb 2011 (Judgment No 350/2011) ruled that a citizenship law passed in the Greek Parliament on 11 Mar 2010, which allowed foreigners who legally reside in Greece to vote and stand in local elections, was unconstitutional since the constitution in force provided that only Greek citizens were entitled to participate in elections. The Council of State Plenum in 2013 agreed and declared the unconstitutionality of the relevant legislative provisions (Judgment No 460/2013).

and Article 22 allows for the possibility of derogations.[189] In *Eman and Sevinger* the ECJ ruled that although Member States could subject the right to vote and to stand in European Parliament elections to a requirement of residence in the territory in which the elections were held, the principle of equal treatment required that there should not be unjustified differences of treatment of nationals who were in comparable situations.[190] Consequently the provision that a Dutch national resident in a non-Member State had the right to vote and stand in European Parliament elections, but a Dutch national residing in the Netherlands Antilles or Aruba did not, was unjustified under EU law. According to one commentator, it is implicit in this and another ECJ ruling on voting rights in Gibraltar[191] that European citizens have a democratic right to vote for 'their' parliament, and that—even though this is not stated in the Treaty, which provides only for a right of equal treatment for EU citizens in relation to the electoral rights of nationals of a host state—the right to vote in European Parliament elections is in fact a normal incident of EU citizenship.[192]

The take-up and impact of the electoral rights of EU citizens has not been very substantial. In previous reports on the right to vote and stand in municipal elections and European Parliament elections, the Commission noted very low rates of voter registration and low numbers exercising the right to vote in a host state, though with an increase from 2004–2009.[193] The Commission suggested that rates of participation in elections in the Member State of residence may be influenced by the fact that, because double voting is prohibited, EU citizens have to choose whether to vote in their Member State of origin or in the Member State to which they have moved. Significant delays and problems with the transposition of Directive 93/109 on the rights of EU citizens to vote and stand in European Parliament elections in other Member States led to infringement proceedings being brought by the Commission. Eventually, after many years of Commission attempts to introduce changes to Directive 93/109, including a wide-ranging proposal in 2006, the more modest Directive 2013/1 was adopted to make it easier for non-national EU citizens to stand for election in a host state, and shifting the burden of proving their eligibility to stand to the Member States.[194]

In its 2012 report on Directive 94/80 on the right to vote and stand in municipal elections, the Commission noted that the number of EU citizens of voting age residing in a Member State other than their own had increased from 4.7 million (2000) to 8 million (2010), mainly due to enlargement, but that the number of non-national EU citizens actively participating in democratic life at local level by requesting to be registered on the electoral rolls had not grown in proportion as a result.[195] In this and other reports, the Commission has also noted the significance of the EU's problems of political disaffection and the weak quality of democratic participation, and has made various proposals for change and improvement.[196] These include activities carried out during the 2013 European Year of the Citizen,[197] and the launch of a new 'Citizens' Dialogues' instrument.[198]

---

[189] See the Commission's Reports on granting such derogations under the Treaty and Dir 93/109: COM(2003) 31, COM(2005) 382, and COM(2007) 846.

[190] Case C–300/04 *Eman and Sevinger* [2006] ECR I–8055; J Shaw, Comment (2008) 4 EuConst 162.

[191] Case C–145/04 (n 186).

[192] Shaw (n 13).

[193] COM(2010) 605, 5.

[194] Council Dir 2013/1/EU [2013] OJ L26/27.

[195] COM(2012) 99. See also Commission DG Justice, *2011 and 2012 Reports on the Application of the EU Charter of Fundamental Rights* (2012) and (2013).

[196] See, eg, Commission Recommendation 2013/142/EU on enhancing the democratic and efficient conduct of the elections to the European Parliament; Commission Communication addressing the consequences of disenfranchisement of Union citizens exercising their right to free movement, COM(2014) 33; EU Citizenship Report 2013: EU citizens: your rights, your future, COM(2013) 269; Report Under Article 25 TFEU: On progress towards effective EU Citizenship 2011–2013, COM(2013) 270.

[197] Dec 1093/2012 [2012] OJ L325/1. See N Vogiatzis, 'A "European Year of Citizens"? Looking Beyond Decision 1093/2012: Eyeing the European Elections of 2014' (2014) 15 Perspectives on European Politics and Society 571.

[198] Commission Report on Citizens' Dialogues as a Contribution to Developing a European Public Space, COM(2014) 173.

Article 23 TFEU provides that Union citizens have the right, in a third country where their own Member State is not represented, to the protection of the diplomatic authorities of any Member State.[199] The Commission adopted a Green Paper on diplomatic and consular protection of EU citizens in third countries in 2006, and an Action Plan for 2007–2009 to enhance protection in this area.[200] The Lisbon Treaty added a new paragraph to Article 23 providing a legal basis, using a special legislative procedure involving only consultation of the Parliament, for the Council to establish measures necessary to facilitate diplomatic and consular protection.[201] In 2015 Directive 2015/637 was eventually adopted to facilitate protection for unrepresented EU citizens in third countries.[202]

Article 24 TFEU was amended by the Lisbon Treaty to provide for the implementation by the ordinary legislative procedure of the new citizens' initiative which was introduced in Article 11(4) TEU, instituting a process whereby one million Union citizens may invite the Commission to bring forward certain legislative initiatives.[203] A Regulation was adopted in 2011 along with an implementing Regulation, and a delegated Regulation in 2013.[204] There has been praise for the idea of a citizens' initiative but also significant critique of its operation and weakness in practice.[205]

Article 24 TFEU also confirms two previously existing rights under EU law, namely the rights of EU citizens to petition the European Parliament[206] and to apply to the Ombudsman.[207] Article 24 also provides that EU citizens who write to any of the EU institutions in one of the official languages have the right to an answer in that language.

Article 25 requires the Commission to report every three years on the application of these provisions on citizenship.[208] In 2010 the Commission adopted three linked reports on citizenship of the Union, as well as a report on dismantling the obstacles to EU citizens' rights, followed by another Citizenship Report in 2013.[209] Article 25 also allows the Council, with the consent of the Parliament, to 'adopt provisions to strengthen or to add to the rights' of citizenship listed in Article 20(2) TFEU. However, the Council must act unanimously, and Article 25 envisages that such action may require constitutional amendment at the national level.

6 CONCLUSIONS

i. The status of EU citizenship created by EU law has been criticized on various grounds, including the thinness of the rights created and their economic focus, the conditions to which they are subject,

---

[199] Decision 95/553 regarding protection for citizens of the Union by diplomatic and consular representations of the Member States in non-member countries [1995] OJ L314/73, which was repealed and replaced by Dir 2015/637. See (n 202).

[200] COM(2007) 767. See AI Saliceti, 'The Protection of EU Citizens Abroad: Accountability, Rule of Law, Role of Consular and Diplomatic Services' (2011) 17 EPL 91.

[201] Art 35 TEU imposes duties on the diplomatic and consular missions of the EU and the Member States in third countries to provide protection on the basis of EU citizenship, without mentioning Member State nationality.

[202] Council Dir 2015/637 on the coordination and cooperation measures to facilitate consular protection for unrepresented EU citizens in third countries: OJ [2015] L106/1–13.

[203] M Dougan, 'What Are We to Make of the Citizens' Initiative?' (2011) 48 CMLRev 1807; J Pilcher and B Kaufmann (eds), *The European Citizens Initiative: Into New Democratic Territory* (Intersentia, 2010).

[204] Regulation (EU) No 211/2011 of the European Parliament and of the Council of 16 February 2011 on the citizens' initiative [2011] OJ L65/1, together with Commission Delegated Reg 887/2013 and Commission Implementing Reg 1179/2011. The Reg provides that an initiative must include citizens of one-quarter of the EU's Member States, and a method is established for calculating the number of supporters necessary from within each Member State.

[205] See (nn 2–3) on critiques, appraisal of the first three years, and proposals for reform.

[206] See Case C–261/13 P *Schönberger v Parliament* EU:C:2014:2423 on the possibility of judicial review of the Parliament's rejection of a petition.

[207] Non-citizens resident in the EU can also do so: Arts 227 and 228 TFEU.

[208] COM(93) 702, COM(97) 230, COM(2001) 506, COM(2004) 695, COM(2008) 85, and COM(2013)70.

[209] COM(2010) 602, COM(2010) 603, and COM(2010) 605. See also COM(2013) 269 for the 2013 Citizenship Report.

the reinforcement of the distinction between third-country nationals and EU nationals, the limited impact of the new electoral rights, and the reluctant pace of implementation. The legal rights of citizenship have been relatively steadily expanded by the ECJ, often in the face of vocal Member State opposition in cases like *Metock* and *Ruiz Zambrano*, although the Court has responded to Member State anxiety over 'welfare tourism' in cases such as *Dano*.

ii. A broader dimension of the critique of citizenship is that any meaningful idea of European citizenship would require not merely concrete legal and practical measures on the matters examined in this chapter (ie rights of residence, travel, voting), but also deeper political, institutional, and democratic change within the EU.

iii. The non-discrimination clause in Article 18 TFEU clearly strengthens an important dimension of EU citizenship, as do various other aspects of EU law such as the right of access to documents, the right to good administration, and more generally the 'citizens' rights' chapter of the Charter of Fundamental Rights, and the provisions on democratic principles introduced by the Lisbon Treaty into Articles 9–12 TEU.

iv. European citizenship can also be viewed positively in terms of its ongoing potential, even if the political and electoral dimensions of citizenship have been very slow to take hold. A successful future for the EU urgently requires greater political and democratic participation, and the provisions on EU citizenship attempt to lay the groundwork for this.

7 FURTHER READING

(a) Website

European Union Democracy Observatory on Citizenship at http://eudo-citizenship.eu/eu-citizenship

(b) Journal Issues

European Law Journal Volume 13 (2007) Special Issue on EU Citizenship

European Law Journal Volume 20 (2014) Symposium on the Reconceptualization of EU Citizenship

German Law Journal Volume 15 (2014) Special Issue: EU Citizenship 20 Years On

(c) Books

GOUDAPPEL, F, *The Effects of EU Citizenship* (TMC Asser Press, 2010)

GUILD, E, *Legal Elements of European Identity: EU Citizenship and Migration Law* (Kluwer, 2005)

_____ AND PEERS, S, *The EU Citizenship Directive: A Commentary* (Oxford University Press, 2014)

SHAW, J, *The Transformation of Citizenship in the European Union* (Cambridge University Press, 2007)

VAN EIJKEN, H, *EU Citizenship and the Constitutionalization of the European Union* (Europa Law Publishing, 2015)

EQUAL TREATMENT
AND NON-DISCRIMINATION

1 CENTRAL ISSUES

i. EU anti-discrimination law was originally confined to the issue of sex equality in the employment context, but has expanded significantly over the past decade and a half to cover a wide range of grounds and contexts.

ii. There is now an impressive constitutional framework for EU anti-discrimination law. In addition to requiring equal treatment for women and men, the Treaty establishes EU legislative competence to combat discrimination on a range of grounds. The Charter of Fundamental Rights, which enjoys the same status as the EU Treaties, has a chapter devoted to equality. Article 21 of the Charter, which is addressed to the EU institutions and to the Member States within the scope of EU law, prohibits discrimination on *any* ground. Articles 8 and 10 TFEU contain horizontal clauses requiring the EU to promote equality between men and women, and to combat discrimination based on sex, racial or ethnic origin, religion or belief, disability, age, or sexual orientation in all of its policies and activities. Gender mainstreaming is well advanced as an EU policy, and has to some extent spread to other grounds of discrimination. A range of new institutions to promote equality and combat discrimination, including the EU Fundamental Rights Agency, the European Institute for Gender Equality,[1] Equinet,[2] and an array of national equality bodies has been established.

iii. The origins of EU equality law lie in the requirement of equal pay for women and men in Article 157 TFEU, which was first introduced in the EEC Treaty in 1957. Article 157 was later amended to permit the adoption of EU legislation ensuring equal treatment of men and women at work going beyond the field of pay, and to permit forms of 'positive action'. Article 153 TFEU makes equal treatment of men and women in the labour market a sphere of supportive and 'complementary' EU action, allowing for the adoption of 'minimum requirement' directives. There are six major Gender Equality Directives currently in force, and a broad range of other legal and policy measures in this field.

iv. Article 19 TFEU, which was introduced by the Amsterdam Treaty in 1999, provides that the EU may take action to combat discrimination based on sex, racial or ethnic origin, religion or belief, disability, age, or sexual orientation. Two major legislative instruments have been adopted under

---

[1] http://eige.europa.eu/.
[2] http://www.equineteurope.org/. This is the network of national equality bodies and organizations empowered to counteract discrimination in each state across the range of grounds prohibited under EU law.

Article 19: the Race Directive 2000/43 and the Framework Employment Directive 2000/78. In the sphere of criminal law, EU Framework Decision 2008/913/JHA combating racist and xenophobic expression was adopted in 2008. A proposal for a further anti-discrimination directive to extend Directive 2000/78 has been pending since 2008, but has been held up due to political opposition to the measure.

v. There is a significant body of ECJ case law on equality and discrimination. The bulk of this is in the field of sex equality, with a particularly detailed body of jurisprudence on equal pay and social security. However, the expansion of EU anti-discrimination law to cover other grounds since 2000 has mobilized litigation in these other fields, particularly on the issue of age discrimination. There has been some important litigation on disability, and a few cases on sexual orientation and race, but no cases as yet dealing with religious discrimination.

vi. The ECJ has also identified a general principle of equal treatment and non-discrimination. In some cases it has treated EU legislation as an expression of this general principle, and in other cases it has required legislation to be interpreted in the light of the general principle of non-discrimination.

vii. The principle of non-discrimination on grounds of nationality is not covered in this chapter, but is treated in several of the other chapters dealing with EU citizenship, free movement of workers, services, establishment, goods, and capital. The principle of non-discrimination on grounds of nationality is curiously truncated in EU law due to its highly instrumental role in the EU context. It does not, in the absence of specific legislation, extend to discrimination against non-EU nationals, but covers mainly discrimination against EU nationals and certain other privileged categories of family members or long-term residents.

2 EU ANTI-DISCRIMINATION LAW: ORIGINS AND CONTEXT

Originating in the provision on equal pay between men and women in Article 119 of the 1957 EEC Treaty, EU anti-discrimination law for several decades focused almost exclusively on sex equality in the employment context. EU sex discrimination law was divided principally into three parts: equal pay, equal treatment in access to and conditions of employment, and social security. The basic principle of non-discrimination on grounds of sex was common to all three, but they were governed by different bodies of secondary legislation, based on different Treaty Articles. Now, with the exception of state social security and sex equality for self-employed persons, these three are dealt with in one consolidating measure: Directive 2006/54. This consolidating Directive replaces the prior directives on equal pay, equal treatment, occupational social security, and the burden of proof. Apart from the consolidating Directive, there is specific gender equality legislation on state social security (Directive 79/7), on access to and supply of goods and services (Directive 2004/113), on equal treatment as between self-employed men and women (Directive 2010/41), and on pregnancy and parental leave (Directives 92/85 and 2010/18 respectively).

For four decades, EU action in the field of anti-discrimination was largely limited to sex discrimination in the workplace. With the entry into force of the Amsterdam Treaty however, Article 19 TFEU introduced a clear legal basis to take action to combat discrimination on a number of grounds other than sex. Two important pieces of legislation were adopted under Article 19 TFEU: Directive 2000/43, known as the Race Directive, prohibits discrimination on grounds of racial and ethnic origin in a range of contexts.[3] Directive 2000/78, known as the Framework Employment Directive, prohibits

---

[3] Council Dir 2000/43 [2000] OJ L180/22.

discrimination in the field of employment on the grounds of religion, belief, disability, age, and sexual orientation. These cover the remaining grounds listed in Article 19 other than racial or ethnic origin, and sex.

While the list of prohibited grounds of discrimination in Article 21 of the Charter of Fundamental Rights is lengthy and non-exhaustive, the EU has express legislative competence only in relation to the grounds set out in Articles 19 and 157 TFEU. However, in addition to the positive law provisions in the Treaties and in legislation, the ECJ also recognized a general principle of equal treatment in EU law which will be discussed further below.

Over the years, the Treaty framework on equality and the array of legislative measures have been supplemented by a range of softer and supportive policy measures, including the Commission's strategy for equality between men and women (2010–2015),[4] its 'Roadmap' for equality (2006–2010),[5] its action programmes to promote equality in the workplace, and its annual reports on equality between men and women.[6] Within the framework of the 2008 'renewed social agenda',[7] the Commission presented a comprehensive approach to taking action against discrimination and to promote equal opportunities,[8] created an expert group of governmental experts on discrimination,[9] and adopted a number of measures on the integration of the Roma people.[10] A European Disability Strategy 2010–2020 was also adopted.[11]

While gender equality may have been the dominant focus of EU anti-discrimination law for many years, the deeply entrenched economic, social, and political marginalization of the Roma people has in more recent years been recognized as one of the great challenges for EU equality law and policy.[12]

3 EQUAL TREATMENT AND NON-DISCRIMINATION: THE LEGAL FRAMEWORK

The structure of this part of the chapter will be as follows: (1) The Treaty framework for the EU's equal treatment and non-discrimination regime will be briefly outlined. (2) An overview of the original equal pay provision between men and women in Article 157 TFEU and its complex elaboration through case law will be provided. (3) Article 19 TFEU, the two Directives adopted under Article 19, and the proposed new directive to supplement these will be described. (4) Discussion of the six Gender Equality Directives will follow. (5) Finally, an analysis of the general principle of equal treatment elaborated by the ECJ will be provided.

First, the Treaty framework: the principles of equality and non-discrimination are expressed in Articles 2 and 3(3) TEU and Articles 8 and 10 TFEU. Article 2 TEU identifies equality as one of the values on which the EU is founded, and gives specific mention to equality between women and men. Article 3(3) TEU includes the combating of 'social exclusion and discrimination' as well as the promotion of

---

4 COM(2010) 491, http://ec.europa.eu/justice/gender-equality/files/strategy_equality_women_men_en.pdf.

5 See European Network of Equality Bodies (Equinet), *New Directions for Equality between Women and Men*, available at www.equineteurope.org/new-directions-for-equality.

6 http://ec.europa.eu/justice/gender-equality/document/index_en.htm#h2-2.

7 COM(2008) 412 final.

8 COM(2008) 420 final.

9 COM(2008) 3261 final.

10 See http://ec.europa.eu/justice/discrimination/roma/index_en.htm for several of the EU's policy documents concerning the Roma.

11 COM(2010) 636. See also SWD(2014)182 for a report by the Commission on the EU's implementation of the UN Convention on the Rights of Persons with Disabilities.

12 (N 10). See M Dawson and E Muir, 'Individual, Institutional and Collective Vigilance in Protecting Fundamental Rights in the EU: Lessons from the Roma' (2011) 48 CMLRev 751.

'social justice and protection, equality between men and women, solidarity between generations and protection of the rights of the child' amongst the objectives of the Union. Articles 8 and 10 TFEU contain horizontal clauses which effectively require the integration or 'mainstreaming' of gender equality and of non-discrimination on the basis of sex, racial or ethnic origin, religion or belief, disability, age, or sexual orientation within all EU policies.[13]

The Charter of Fundamental Rights, discussed at more length in Chapter 11, contains an entire title on equality, designed to illustrate the status of equal treatment in the EU as a fundamental right. Article 20 declares that everyone is equal before the law. Article 21(1) contains an open-ended prohibition of discrimination:

> 1. Any discrimination based on any ground such as sex, race, colour, ethnic or social origin, genetic features, language, religion or belief, political or any other opinion, membership of a national minority, property, birth, disability, age or sexual orientation shall be prohibited.
> 2. Within the scope of application of the Treaties, and without prejudice to any of their specific provisions, any discrimination on grounds of nationality shall be prohibited.

Despite the breadth and apparently unqualified nature of Article 21(1), its scope must be read together with the horizontal clauses at the end of the Charter. The most important limiting clauses are in Article 51(1) which specifies that the provisions of the Charter apply to the EU but to the Member States 'only when they are implementing Union law', and Article 51(2) which provides that the Charter 'does not extend the field of application of Union law' or 'modify powers and tasks as defined in the Treaties'. It remains to be seen whether the Charter, and Article 21 in particular, impose obligations on private parties not to discriminate as the Court has not yet pronounced on the horizontal effect of the Charter's provisions.[14] However, the general principle of non-discrimination has been held, at least in the context of age and where the relevant implementing directive had not been transposed, to impose obligations directly on private parties.[15]

Equality between men and women is also dealt with in Article 23 of the Charter, which specifies that it must be ensured in all areas, including employment, work, and pay. Finally it should be noted that the Charter, which gained legally binding force with the entry into force of the Lisbon Treaty, is increasingly being cited as a source of rights by the CJEU in non-discrimination cases.

4 THE ORIGINS: ARTICLE 157 TFEU AND THE PRINCIPLE OF EQUAL PAY FOR WOMEN AND MEN

The EEC Treaty from the time of its adoption included the requirement of equal pay for equal work in Article 119 and made it applicable to the Member States. The ECJ soon found this requirement to be directly effective. Later rulings of the ECJ, secondary legislation, and ultimately the Amsterdam Treaty amendments to Article 157 TFEU indicated that not only 'equal work' but also 'work of

---

[13] For the integration of non-discrimination on sexual orientation into EU asylum law, see the interpretation by the CJEU of Dir 2004/83 in Cases C–148–150/13 *A, B, C v Staatssecretaris van Veiligheid en Justitie* EU:C:2014:2406. For the Court's requirement that gender equality be integrated into the context of agricultural support, see Case C– 401/11 *Blanka Soukupová* EU:C:2013:223; and that non-discrimination on grounds of race should be integrated into the context of copyright protection, Case C–201/13 *Deckmyn v Vandersteen and others* EU:C:2014:2132.

[14] Case C–176/12 *AMS* EU:C:2013:491, discussed in Chs 7 and 11.

[15] Case C–144/04 *Mangold* [2005] ECR I–9981 and Case C–555/07 *Kücükdeveci v Swedex GmbH & Co KG* EU:C:2010:365, discussed in Ch 7.

equal value' was covered. The Amsterdam Treaty also added paragraph 3, which provides legislative power for the EU to promote equal treatment for men and women in employment (beyond pay), and paragraph 4 which permits 'positive action' on the part of Member States. Article 157 TFEU now provides:

1. Each Member State shall ensure that the principle of equal pay for male and female workers for equal work or work of equal value is applied.

2. For the purpose of this Article, 'pay' means the ordinary basic or minimum wage or salary and any other consideration, whether in cash or in kind, which the worker receives directly or indirectly, in respect of his employment from his employer.

Equal pay without discrimination based on sex means:

(a) that pay for the same work at piece rates shall be calculated on the basis of the same unit of measurement;

(b) that pay for work at time rates shall be the same for the same job.

3. The European Parliament and the Council, acting in accordance with the ordinary legislative procedure, and after consulting the Economic and Social Committee, shall adopt measures to ensure the application of the principle of equal opportunities and equal treatment of men and women in matters of employment and occupation, including the principle of equal pay for equal work or work of equal value.

4. With a view to ensuring full equality in practice between men and women in working life, the principle of equal treatment shall not prevent any Member State from maintaining or adopting measures providing for specific advantages in order to make it easier for the under-represented sex to pursue a vocational activity or to prevent or compensate for disadvantages in professional careers.

(A) THE SOCIAL AND ECONOMIC UNDERPINNINGS OF ARTICLE 157

The historical explanation for Article 157 TFEU, given the absence of any mention in the Treaty of equal treatment other than in the context of pay, appears to have been France's concern that it would be placed at a competitive disadvantage in observing the principle of equal pay for equal work more than it was observed in other Member States.[16] In other words, concern over unfair treatment of women in the labour market was not the primary motivation for the inclusion of this Article. Nevertheless, Article 157 and the other provisions of EU sex discrimination law are now viewed and interpreted not only as an instrument of economic policy, but also as an important part of EU social policy.[17]

While the equal pay rule was undoubtedly inserted to 'level the playing field' by ensuring that employers in no one Member State would have this competitive advantage over those in another Member State, the ECJ declared in early case law that Article 157 had a social and not just an economic aim. In the first *Defrenne* case, Belgium argued that the aim of this provision was economic only, namely 'to avoid discrepancies in cost prices due to the employment of female labour less well paid for the same work than male labour'.[18] The Court rejected this view in *Defrenne II*.

---

[16] C Barnard, 'The Economic Objectives of Article 119' in D O'Keeffe and T Hervey (eds), *Sex Equality Law in the European Union* (Wiley, 1996).

[17] Case C–50/96 *Deutsche Telekom v Schröder* [2000] ECR I–7.

[18] Case 80/70 *Defrenne v Belgium (Defrenne I)* [1971] ECR 445.

Case 43/75 **Defrenne v Sabena**
[1976] ECR 455

[Note Lisbon Treaty renumbering: Art 119 EEC is now Art 157 TFEU]

THE ECJ

8. Article 119 pursues a double aim.

9. First, in the light of the different stages of the development of social legislation in the various Member States, the aim of Article 119 is to avoid a situation in which undertakings established in States which have actually implemented the principle of equal pay suffer a competitive disadvantage in intra-Community competition as compared with undertakings established in States which have not yet eliminated discrimination against women workers as regards pay.

10. Secondly, this provision forms part of the social objectives of the Community, which is not merely an economic union, but is at the same time intended, by common action, to ensure social progress and seek the constant improvement of the living and working conditions of their peoples, as is emphasized by the Preamble to the Treaty.

...

12. This double aim, which is at once economic and social, shows that the principle of equal pay forms part of the foundations of the Community.

We saw in Chapter 7 that various Member States had avoided the implementation of the equal pay principle for years, eventually arguing unsuccessfully to the ECJ in *Defrenne* that the Treaty provision lacked direct effect. The Court ruled that Article 157 TFEU (ex Article 119 EEC) had been directly effective since the end of the first stage of the transitional period. Nevertheless, the ECJ was swayed by the arguments of the Member States on the serious financial consequences of such a ruling for them, and it declared that in view of the incorrect understanding of the Member States of the effects of this Treaty Article, due in part to the fact that the Commission had not brought earlier infringement proceedings against them, its ruling should have effect only prospectively. Prospective overruling of this kind by the Court has been infrequent, and the cases tend to be those in which there are considerable financial implications for the Member States or their industries.[19]

In *Schröder*, the ECJ was confronted with an apparent conflict between the declared social aim, ensuring fairness to individual women and men, and the economic aim, ensuring equal conditions for competing employers, of Article 157.[20] If the social aim were to take priority, German law could apply the equal pay principle retroactively so as to permit part-time workers access to an occupational pension scheme, whereas if the economic aim were to take priority, Germany, in order to ensure that its firms were not operating under less favourable conditions than those of Member State competitors, should not do so. The ECJ began by repeating the 'double aim' ruling in paragraphs 8–11 of *Defrenne II* (above) and continued:

---

[19] See, eg, Case 262/88 *Barber v Guardian Royal Exchange Assurance Group* [1990] ECR 1889; N Hyland, 'Temporal Limitation of the Effects of the Judgments of the Court of Justice' (1995) 4 IJEL 208. See however Case C–128/93 *Fisscher v Voorhuis Hengelo BV and Stichting Bedrijfspensioenfonds voor de Detailhandel* [1994] ECR I–4583 where the limitation of the effects in time of the *Barber* judgment was held not to apply to the right to join an occupational pension scheme.

[20] Case C–50/96 (n 17); L Besselink, Note (2001) 38 CMLRev 437; E Ellis, Note (2000) 25 ELRev 564.

Case C–50/96 **Deutsche Telekom v Schröder**
[2000] ECR I–743

THE ECJ

56. However, in later decisions the Court has repeatedly held that the right not to be discriminated against on grounds of sex is one of the fundamental human rights whose observance the Court has a duty to ensure (see, to that effect, Case 149/77 *Defrenne III* [1978] ECR 1365, paragraphs 26 and 27, Joined Cases 75/82 and 117/82 *Razzouk and Beydoun* v. *Commission* [1984] ECR 1509, paragraph 16, and Case C–13/94 *P.* v. *S. and Cornwall County Council* [1996] ECR I–2143, paragraph 19).

57. In view of that case-law, it must be concluded that the economic aim pursued by Article 119 of the Treaty, namely the elimination of distortions of competition between undertakings established in different Member States, is secondary to the social aim pursued by the same provision, which constitutes the expression of a fundamental human right.

Thus the social aim of Article 157 TFEU, read in the light of the case law on fundamental human rights, had come to take precedence over its economic rationale.[21] Moreover, while *Schröder* is an equal pay case, the Court's ruling seemed to refer to Article 157 TFEU and the equal treatment principle more generally.

The emphasis on human rights rather than on economic competitiveness as the primary rationale for EU equal treatment law is evident now in the Preambles to recent legislation, including the consolidating Directive 2006/54[22] as well as in the Article 19 anti-discrimination directives.[23]

(B) THE BREADTH OF ARTICLE 157: THE DEFINITION OF PAY

This has proven to be a complex question, despite the guidance given in the Article itself on the meaning of the term 'pay'. The ECJ has given the term a very wide scope, which caused some confusion in relation to the borderline between pay and social security. While some of the Court's rulings appeared to undermine measures adopted by the EU legislative institutions, at other times its rulings appeared responsive to the political context by retreating from earlier expansive positions in the face of obvious dissatisfaction from the Member States or the other institutions.

(i) *Social Security Benefits are Not Pay*

In *Defrenne I*, a case brought against Belgium concerning discrimination in retirement pensions, the ECJ gave an early ruling on the complex relationship between pay and pensions.[24] The ECJ ruled that while 'consideration in the nature of social security benefits' was not in itself excluded from the concept of pay, the employer's contributions to a retirement pension in this case were excluded from the scope of Article 157 for three reasons: first, the pension scheme was directly governed by legislation; secondly, there was no agreement on the scheme within the particular company or occupational branch concerned; and, thirdly, the retirement scheme was *obligatorily* applicable to *general* categories of workers. The determining role of the state and the lack of involvement of the particular employer were crucial: in

---

[21] S Krebber, 'The Social Rights Approach of the European Court of Justice to Enforce European Employment Law' (2006) 27 Comparative Labor Law and Policy Journal 377.

[22] (N 147).

[23] (N 92).

[24] Case 80/70 *Defrenne v Belgium* [1971] ECR 445.

sum, the pension scheme was set up essentially as a matter of social policy and not as a part of the employment relationship in question. The Court's definition of the difference between pay and social security is important, since equal treatment in state social security is not covered by Article 157 TFEU on equal pay but primarily by Directive 79/7, whereas occupational social security is covered in part by Article 157 and in part by Directive 2006/54.

(ii) *Widening the Definition of Pay*

The wide interpretation of pay under Article 157 was already evident in cases such as *Garland*,[25] where the ECJ ruled that the fact that female employees following retirement could no longer enjoy *travel facilities* for their spouses and dependent children, whilst male employees continued to do so, constituted discrimination contrary to the Treaty.[26] Since the travel facilities were benefits conferred in respect of employment, even if after retirement and irrespective of any specific contractual obligation, they were held to constitute pay.[27] In *Kowalska*, a severance grant was covered by Article 157 since it was compensation to which a worker was entitled by reason of her employment, even though it was also paid on termination rather than during the employment relationship.[28] In *Seymour-Smith*, *compensation for unfair dismissal* was held to constitute pay, since it was designed to replace pay to which the employee would have been entitled had she not been unfairly dismissed.[29] And in *Barber* the ECJ ruled that *severance benefits*, including statutory redundancy payments, would constitute pay under Article 157 even though they were required by statute, since the worker was entitled to these benefits upon termination of the employment 'by reason of the existence of the employment relationship'.[30] In *Nimz*, the Court confirmed that the *rules governing the system of salary-classification into grades* were covered by Article 157 on equal pay since they directly governed changes in employees' salaries.[31] The ECJ has also included *statutory sick pay*,[32] *maternity benefit*,[33] and *statutorily required compensation*[34] within the concept of pay. It is generally in the employee's interests that benefits are classified as pay rather than social security, given that Article 157, unlike Directive 79/7, is directly effective both against the state and against private employers.

In contrast, rules governing the calculation of the length of service of public servants for the purposes of determining eligibility for promotion, even while indirectly determining the possibility of access to a higher level of remuneration, were a matter of equal treatment in the conditions of work rather than equal pay.[35] In *Defrenne II* the ECJ had ruled that the fact that the fixing of certain working conditions could have pecuniary consequences was not sufficient to bring such conditions within the scope of the equal pay principles in Article 157, and this point was confirmed again in *JämO*[36] and *Seymour-Smith*,[37]

---

[25] Case 12/81 *Garland v British Rail Engineering Ltd* [1982] ECR 359.

[26] Case C–249/96 *Grant v South-West Trains* [1998] ECR I–621.

[27] On voluntary Christmas bonuses as pay see Case C–333/97 *Lewen v Denda* [1999] ECR I–7243.

[28] Case C–33/89 *Kowalska v Freie und Hansestadt Hamburg* [1990] ECR I–2591, [10].

[29] Case C–167/97 *R v Secretary of State for Employment, ex p Nicole Seymour-Smith* [1999] ECR I–623.

[30] Case 262/88 *Barber* (n 19) [13]–[18].

[31] Case C–184/89 *Nimz v Freie und Hansestadt Hamburg* [1991] ECR I–297.

[32] Case 171/88 *Rinner-Kühn v FWW Spezial-Gebäudereinigung GmbH* [1989] ECR 2743, [7].

[33] Case C–342/93 *Gillespie v Northern Health and Social Services Boards* [1996] ECR I–475; Case C–411/96 *Boyle v EOC* [1998] ECR I–6401; Case C–147/02 *Alabaster v Woolwich plc and Secretary of State for Social Security* [2004] ECR I–3101.

[34] Case C–360/90 *Arbeiterwohlfahrt der Stadt Berlin v Bötel* [1992] ECR I–3589; Case C–457/93 *Kuratorium für Dialyse und Nierentransplantation v Lewark* [1996] ECR I–243; Case C–278/93 *Freers and Speckmann v Deutsche Bundespost* [1996] ECR I–1165.

[35] Case C–1/95 *Gerster v Freistaat Bayern* [1997] ECR I–5253.

[36] Case C–236/98 *Jämställdhetsombudsmannen v Örebro läns landsting* [2000] ECR I–2189, [59]–[60].

[37] Case C–167/97 *Seymour-Smith* (n 29) [36]–[37].

Steinicke,[38] and *Lommers*.[39] Such conditions fell instead to be dealt with under Directive 76/207 (now Directive 2006/54) on equal treatment.

(iii) Bilka *and* Barber: *Occupational Pensions may Constitute Pay*

Some of the most significant developments in relation to the uncertain zone between pay and social security were the rulings on *occupational pensions* in both *Bilka-Kaufhaus* and *Barber*,[40] along with the flood of litigation which followed *Barber*. The ECJ first addressed the issue of occupational pension schemes directly in *Bilka-Kaufhaus*. At the time judgment was given, the Council was considering adopting legislation on occupational social security, which subsequently became Directive 86/378,[41] to supplement Directive 79/7 on statutory social security.

The terms of the 1986 Directive clearly showed that the institutions considered occupational pensions to be a matter of social security rather than pay, so that they were dealt with in a more gradual manner similar to matters of state social security covered by Directive 79/7, rather than under the mandatory strictures of Article 157. However, the ECJ in *Bilka* took a different view, in the context of a supplementary occupational pension scheme *entirely financed by the employer*, and ruled that although the scheme was adopted in accordance with conditions laid down by German law, it was based on an agreement between the employer and the employee staff committee, bringing it within the scope of pay under the Treaty.[42]

By contrast with the statutory pension scheme in *Defrenne I*, the ECJ in this case highlighted three factors: (i) the contractual nature of the pension scheme; (ii) the fact that it was not directly governed by statute but by an agreement between employer and employee; and (iii) it was not financed in part by the public authorities but entirely by the employer. The fact that the employer chose to arrange the scheme in a way which corresponded to the statutory social security scheme was irrelevant, and the benefits paid to employees under the occupational scheme thus constituted 'pay' under Article 157. The fact that employee affiliation to an occupational pension scheme was made compulsory by legislation was also irrelevant.[43] Although the ruling in *Bilka* should have warned the EU institutions that occupational pensions were viewed by the ECJ as pay rather than social security, Directive 86/378 was nonetheless adopted shortly after the case.

The famous *Barber* judgment which followed, however, rendered much of Directive 86/378 redundant, by ruling that even if an occupational pension scheme was 'contracted out', ie where it was set up by an employer in direct substitution for and in fulfilment of the obligations of the statutory scheme, payments of benefits to employees would constitute pay rather than social security.[44] The distinction between social security and pay at issue in the case was particularly important in relation to pensions, because of the exceptions to the equal treatment principle which are allowed under Social Security Directive 79/7 in relation to pensionable age and related benefits.[45] No such exception exists under Article 157 and companies which had operated contracted-out occupational pension schemes had, prior to *Barber*, proceeded on the assumption that they could maintain discriminatory pensionable ages as between men and women.

---

[38] Case C–77/02 *Steinicke v Bundesanstalt für Arbeit* [2003] ECR I–9027.
[39] Case C–476/99 *Lommers v Minister van Landbouw, Natuurbeheer en Visserij* [2002] ECR I–2891.
[40] Case 262/88 *Barber* (n 19); Case 170/84 *Bilka-Kaufhaus GmbH v Karin Weber von Hartz* [1986] ECR 1607.
[41] Council Directive 86/378/EEC of 24 July 1986 on the implementation of the principle of equal treatment for men and women in occupational social security schemes [1986] OJ L225/40.
[42] Case 170/84 *Bilka-Kaufhaus* (n 40) [21]–[22].
[43] Case C–435/93 *Dietz v Stichting Thuiszorg Rotterdam* [1996] ECR I–5223.
[44] Case C–262/88 *Barber* (n 19).
[45] See further below Section 6(b).

The question was whether contracted-out occupational pension schemes were governed by the principle set out in *Defrenne I*,[46] in which case they were social security, or that in *Bilka*,[47] in which case they were pay. Mirroring its reasoning in *Bilka*, the ECJ focused on three features of the contracted-out scheme: first, it was agreed and entirely financed by the employer, not imposed directly by statute;[48] secondly, unlike most social security benefits the scheme was not compulsorily applicable to general categories of employees and, although in conformity with national legislation, was governed by its own rules; and, finally, although it was in substitution for the statutory scheme, its provisions could also go further and provide additional benefits, thereby making it indistinguishable from supplementary schemes such as those in *Bilka*. The fact that the fund was administered by trustees did not prevent the benefits paid from constituting pay, and indeed Article 157 could be relied upon directly as against independent trustees.[49]

Having established that private, contracted-out occupational pension schemes were covered by the equal pay principle, the ECJ in *Barber* ruled that different pension entitlements on redundancy for men and women were in breach of that principle, and that equality had to be ensured with respect to each element of pay.[50] The *Barber* case had serious repercussions throughout the EU, and fundamentally changed the way pension schemes would henceforth have to be organized.[51]

The radical nature of *Barber* met with criticism from employers and the intervening Member States, which had argued strongly against the Court's conclusion in their submissions. They considered that the judgment did not take sufficient account of the social-policy requirements underlying many occupational pension schemes, that it ignored the close link between statutory and occupational pension schemes, and that it involved deliberate judicial by-passing of a legitimate piece of EU legislation: the Occupational Pension Directive of 1986. The ECJ however made one major concession to the concerns of the Member States,[52] and to those of employers who would henceforth have to organize occupational pensions differently, by limiting the retroactivity of its ruling. While the ECJ has regularly insisted that financial consequences alone do not justify limiting the temporal effect of a ruling,[53] it took the view in *Barber* that states and others had reasonably been entitled, in the light of the authorization in the two Social Security Directives to defer implementation of the equal treatment principle in relation to pensionable ages, to consider that Article 157 did not apply to pensions paid under contracted-out schemes.[54] However, the relevant paragraphs of the judgment limiting the retroactive effects of its ruling were somewhat ambiguous, and before the ECJ had the opportunity to clarify its meaning in later case law, the concern aroused by *Barber* had prompted the Member States to annex a Protocol to the then EC Treaty by the Maastricht Treaty, purporting to limit the retroactive effect of the judgment by adopting the more limited of two possible interpretations. The ECJ itself, when later called upon to clarify the

---

[46] Case 80/70 *Defrenne I* (n 18).

[47] Case 170/84 *Bilka-Kaufhaus* (n 40).

[48] The CJEU made it clear subsequently in Case C–200/91 *Coloroll Pension Trustees Ltd v Russell and others* [1994] ECR I–4389, [88], that all benefits payable to an employee under an occupational pension scheme, whether the scheme was contributory or non-contributory, constituted pay within Art 157 TFEU.

[49] Case C–200/91 *Coloroll* ibid [24] and Case C–379/99 *Pensionskasse für die Angestellten der Barmer Ersatzkasse v Menauer* [2001] ECR I–7275.

[50] Case 262/88 *Barber* (n 19) [32]–[34]; Case C–381/99 *Brunnhofer v Bank der österreichischen Postsparkasse AG* [2001] ECR I–4961; Case C–236/98 *JämO* (n 36).

[51] D Curtin, 'Scalping the Community Legislator: Occupational Pensions and *Barber*' (1990) 27 CMLRev 475.

[52] The UK in particular argued that, unless the retroactive effect of the judgment was limited, the increase in costs would run to between £33 and £45 billion, with disastrous effects for the UK economy as a whole.

[53] See, eg, Case C–184/99 *Grzelczyk v CPAS* [2001] ECR I–6193, [50]–[54]; Case C–366/99 *Griesmar v Ministre de l'Economie* [2001] ECR I–9383, [73]–[78].

[54] Case 262/88 *Barber* (n 19) [44]–[45].

meaning of the relevant paragraphs in *Barber*, pragmatically agreed with the version chosen by the states in the Protocol.[55]

(iv) *Post-*Barber *Case Law*

Despite this attempt by Member States to rein in the interpretative autonomy of the ECJ, the Court in subsequent cases reasserted its independence by limiting the potential scope of the Protocol, ruling in *Fisscher* and *Vroege* that it had to be read 'in conjunction with the *Barber* judgment and cannot have a scope wider than the limitation of its effects in time'.[56] This meant that the Protocol related only to *benefits* and not to the *right to join or belong* to an occupational pension scheme. Thus discriminatory conditions governing *membership* of an occupational scheme, such as a full-time requirement or the exclusion of married women, were governed by the ECJ's earlier ruling in *Bilka*,[57] rather than by the Protocol, and the same was later held to be true for other restrictive conditions on participation in occupational pension schemes.[58]

Thus, subject to the application of national time limits for bringing an action,[59] Article 157 could be relied on to challenge a discriminatory exclusion from a pension scheme as from the date of the *Defrenne II* judgment, in which Article 157 was held to be directly effective. However, the right retroactively to join a pension scheme did not mean that workers could avoid paying the value of the past contributions.[60]

The ECJ in *Ten Oever* also ruled that Article 157 covered pension benefits payable not just to an employee, but also to the employee's survivor, in this case a widow's pension, since the crucial factor was that the pension was paid by reason of the employment relationship between the employee and employer.[61] Following from this, the ECJ ruled in *Coloroll*[62] and *Menauer*[63] that Article 157 could be invoked also by the employee's dependants against the employer or the trustees of the pension scheme.[64]

---

[55] Case C–109/91 *Ten Oever v Stichting Bedrijfspensioenfonds voor het Glazenwassers- en Schoonmaakbedrijf* [1993] ECR I–4879, [16]–[19]. See also Case C–166/99 *Defreyn v Sabena* [2000] ECR I–6155 in which the CJEU applied this Protocol.

[56] Cases C–128/93 *Fisscher v Voorhuis Hengelo BV and Stichting Bedrijfspensioenfonds voor de Detailhandel* [1994] ECR I–4583; C–57/93 *Vroege v NCIV Institut voor Volkshuisvesting BV and Stichting Pensioenfonds NCIV* [1994] ECR I–4541; C–7/93 *Bestuur van het Algemeen Burgerlijk Pensioenfonds v Beune* [1994] ECR I–4471.

[57] Case 170/84 *Bilka-Kaufhaus* (n 40).

[58] See also Cases C–435/93 *Dietz v Stichting Thuiszorg Rotterdam* [1996] ECR I–5223, [23]–[25]; C–246/96 *Magorrian and Cunningham v Eastern Health and Social Services Board* [1997] ECR I–7153; C–50/96 *Schröder* (n 17); C–270 and 271/97 *Deutsche Post v Sievers and Schrage* [2000] ECR I–929. Case C–110/91 *Moroni v Collo GmbH* [1993] ECR I–6591 also confirmed that *Barber* applied in the same way to supplementary pension schemes as to contracted-out schemes, thus extending the reasoning in *Bilka* (re the exclusion of part-time workers from a supplementary pension scheme) to the existence of discriminatory pensionable ages *within* such a scheme.

[59] As in the Court's general case law on remedies, the rules relating to national time limits must be no less favourable than for similar actions of a domestic nature and must not render impossible the exercise of the right. See, however, Case C–147/95 *DEI v Efthimios Evrenopoulos* [1997] ECR I–2057.

[60] Case C–128/93 *Fisscher* (n 56) 37. The Court has applied this case law by analogy to membership of a statutory scheme: Cases C–231–233/06 *Jonkman and Others* [2007] ECR I–5149.

[61] See also Case C–147/95 *DEI* (n 59); Case C–50/99 *Podesta v CRICA* [2000] ECR I–4039.

[62] Case C–200/91 *Coloroll* (n 48) [17]–[19].

[63] Case C–379/99 *Menauer* (n 49).

[64] This was sharply criticized by the German Government in the case, which argued that a survivor's pension benefit should be not regarded as pay, since it did not represent consideration for work performed, but reflected social-policy concerns connected to the traditional allocation of men's and women's roles: Case C–109/91 *Ten Oever* (n 55).

(v) Other Kinds of Pension Scheme

In *Beune*,[65] concerning civil service pensions, the ECJ reviewed the criteria it had developed in cases from *Defrenne I* to *Ten Oever* for determining whether a pension scheme constituted pay under Article 157 or social security under Directive 79/7. Ultimately, having considered the criteria of: (i) agreement between employer and employee rather than statutory origin; (ii) the absence of public funding of a scheme; and (iii) the provision of benefits supplementary to state social security benefits, the ECJ concluded that the 'decisive' though not the 'exclusive' criterion was (iv) that set out in Article 157 TFEU itself: that the pension is paid to the worker by reason of the employment relationship between the worker and the former employer.[66] Consequently, even if the civil service pension scheme was affected by 'considerations of social policy, of State organisation, or of ethics or even budgetary preoccupations', factors which would normally point to its classification as a state social security scheme rather than pay, these could not prevail if three other factors were also present: if the pension paid by a public employer: (i) concerned only a particular category of workers rather than general categories; (ii) was directly related to the period of service; and (iii) was calculated, in its amount, by reference to the civil servant's last salary, then it was comparable to a pension paid by a private employer and would constitute pay.[67]

These principles were applied by the ECJ in *Griesmar*[68] and *Mouflin*,[69] where French retirement pensions for civil servants were held to be pay rather than social security, and also to German and Finnish pension schemes in *Schönheit*[70] and *Niemi*[71] respectively. In these cases the ECJ ruled that, whenever the legal criteria of pay and equal work could be identified, an employee could rely directly on Article 157, effectively overriding the relevant provision of the Occupational Pension Directive 86/378 which had purported to allow the postponement until 1993 of the establishment of equal pensionable ages in occupational schemes. However, the limitation on the retroactive effect of *Barber* was held to be applicable to discriminatory age conditions.[72] More recently in *Dittrich*, in relation to sexual orientation rather than gender discrimination, the ECJ ruled that assistance granted to public servants in the event of illness fell within the scope of the Directive as a matter of equal pay, if it was the responsibility of the state, as a public employer (rather than a provider of state social security), to finance it.[73]

(vi) A Limited Retreat from Barber: Employer Contributions to Defined-Benefit Pension Schemes

Among the various other issues raised in post-*Barber* case law was the question whether payments by an employer to a contracted-out occupational pension scheme (rather than payments to an *employee*, as in *Barber*) were covered by Article 157.[74] This question arose because actuarial calculations of the different life expectancies of men and women were used in determining the sums payable by an employer into the scheme.

---

[65] Case C–7/93 *Beune* (n 56); Case C–50/99 *Podesta* (n 61).
[66] Ibid [43]–[44].
[67] Ibid [45].
[68] Case C–366/99 *Griesmar* (n 53). See also Case C–173/13 *Leone v Garde des Sceaux and others* EU:C:2014:2090.
[69] Case C–206/00 *Mouflin v Recteur de l'académie de Reims* [2001] ECR I–10201.
[70] Cases C–4–5/02 *Schönheit and Becker* [2003] ECR I–12575.
[71] Case C–351/00 *Niemi* [2002] ECR I–7007.
[72] Case C–200/91 *Coloroll* (n 48) [71].
[73] Cases C–124, 125 and 143/11 *Dittrich, Klinke and Müller* EU:C:2012:771.
[74] Case C–200/91 *Coloroll* (n 48); Case C–152/91 *Neath v Hugh Steeper Ltd* [1993] ECR I–6935.

Coloroll and *Neath* concerned a 'defined-benefit' pension scheme under which employees would receive a pension for which the criteria were fixed in advance, for example by reference to a fraction of their final year's salary for each year of service.[75] It was held that contributions of *employees* to the scheme must consist of an identical amount for men and women, since, according to the *Worringham* case,[76] employees' contributions were pay within Article 157. However, in such defined-benefit schemes, *employers'* contributions varied over time and were adjusted to take account of the pensions which would have to be paid. As a consequence of using the sex-based actuarial factors in calculating such employers' contributions, the amount which a male employee would receive on redundancy, in the form of a capital sum, transfer benefits, or a deferred pension, would be less than that which a woman would receive. The ECJ ruled that although the pension promised according to fixed criteria constituted pay, neither employer's contributions paid in order to ensure the adequacy of the funds for promised pension, nor the value of those contributions as represented by a lump sum or transfer benefits, would fall within Article 157.[77]

Thus, having gradually broadened the concept of pay, eroding the distinction between pay and occupational social security, but creating a distinction between occupational social security and state social security, the ECJ drew back somewhat in *Neath* and *Coloroll*.[78] The outcome of these and other cases decided after *Barber* was subsequently enacted into legislation, which is now contained in Directive 2006/54.[79] However, the rulings in *Neath* and *Coloroll* on the permissibility of using sex-based actuarial calculations in occupational pensions schemes may have been called into question by the *Test-Achats* ruling prohibiting the use of sex-based actuarial calculations in the field of insurance.[80]

Directive 2006/54 also contains an 'exception' to the scope of the equal treatment principle in occupational pensions which was articulated in the *Coloroll* case, ie that certain pension benefits purchased by *voluntary employees' contributions* to an occupational scheme do not fall within Article 157 and thus do not constitute pay.[81] A range of other specific exceptions are also provided for by the Directive.[82] The legislation additionally incorporates the outcome of the somewhat surprising judgment in *Birds Eye Walls*,[83] which permits Member States to introduce differential treatment between men and women in a bridging pension scheme in order to counterbalance the effects of the state system, which maintains different retirement ages for men and women.[84]

(vii) *Remedying Discrimination in Occupational Pensions*

A major question following *Barber* was how the discrimination identified was to be remedied. In *Coloroll*, the ECJ ruled that, between the date of the *Barber* ruling and the date of entry into force

---

75 Ibid.

76 Case 69/80 *Worringham and Humphreys v Lloyds Bank* [1981] ECR 767.

77 Case C–152/91 *Neath* (n 74) [31]–[32]; Case C–200/91 *Coloroll* (n 48) [80]–[81].

78 Following these cases, Dir 96/97, [1997] OJ L46/20, amended Dir 86/378 largely by enacting the case law of the Court, including *Neath* and *Coloroll*; since *Barber*. Dirs 86/378 and 96/97 have now been replaced by Dir 2006/54 (n 147).

79 Dir 2006/54 (n 147) Art 9 provides that Art 157 TFEU also applies to so-called 'money-purchase' or 'defined-contribution' schemes as opposed to 'defined-benefit' schemes.

80 Case C–236/09 *Association Belge des Consommateurs Test-Achats ASBL v Conseil des Ministres* EU:C:2011:100. See also Case C–476/11 *HK Danmark (Kristensen) v Experian AS* EU:C:2013:590 on the prohibition of age-based discrimination in an employer's contribution to an occupational pension scheme, which was defined by the CJEU as an element of 'pay'.

81 Case C–200/91 *Coloroll* (n 48) [90]–[93]. See Dir 2006/54 (n 147) Art 8(1)(e).

82 Dir 2006/54 (n 147) Art 8(1).

83 Case C–132/92 *Roberts v Birds Eye Walls Ltd* [1993] ECR I–5579.

84 Dir 2006/54 (n 147) Art 8(2).

of measures designed to eliminate discrimination, 'correct implementation of the principle of equal pay requires that the disadvantaged employees should be granted the same advantages as those previous enjoyed by other employees'.[85] In other words, until amending measures were adopted, pension schemes could only 'level up', by giving men the same advantages as women enjoyed. This principle had been first enunciated in *Defrenne II*,[86] in which the ECJ ruled that compliance with the equal pay principle could not be achieved other than by raising the lowest salaries, since Article 157 appeared in the context of the harmonization of working conditions while maintaining an improvement in those conditions.

However, the Court in *Coloroll* took a more limited approach than that in *Defrenne II*, and applied the 'levelling-up' or improvement in conditions of pay only to the transitional stage between the date of the *Barber* ruling and the date on which measures were adopted to comply with it.[87] However, once equalizing measures were adopted, Article 157 'did not then preclude measures to achieve equal treatment by reducing the advantages of the persons previously favoured'.[88] However, EU law had nothing to say about age discrimination between men and women in occupational pension schemes prior to the date of *Barber*, and thus did not provide Member States with a rationale for retroactively reducing the advantages enjoyed by women during that period. The Court also ruled in *Smith* that once an employer took steps for the future to comply with Article 157 TFEU, the achievement of equality could not be made partial or progressive.[89]

Notably, the Court uses the language of 'advantage' in the occupational pensions case law to describe the position of women, since the retirement age for women was generally, being linked to that of state pension schemes, lower than that for men. However, it has been pointed out that the language of 'advantage' or 'favoured group' is hardly appropriate to apply to women in this context, since the less favoured group is 'in reality composed of women, who have worked and contributed to the scheme but receive very low pensions because of the level of pay which they earned during their working life, itself frequently shorter than the men's'.[90]

Finally, it should be said that Directive 2006/54 now incorporates the outcome of the stream of case law from *Barber* onwards, with all of its details and anomalies, virtually without amendment.[91]

5 ARTICLE 19 TFEU AND THE ARTICLE 19 DIRECTIVES[92]

Just over forty years after the EEC Treaty with its equal pay principle entered into force, Article 19 TFEU was introduced by the Amsterdam Treaty. This followed a long campaign by NGOs, European Parliamentarians, and others to empower the EU to address issues of race discrimination and the rise

---

[85] Case C–200/91 *Coloroll* (n 48).

[86] Case 43/75 *Defrenne v Sabena* [1976] ECR 455, [15].

[87] Case C–200/91 *Coloroll* (n 48); Case C–408/92 *Smith v Advel Systems Ltd* [1994] ECR I–4435, [30].

[88] Case C–200/91 *Coloroll* (n 48) [33].

[89] Case C–408/92 *Smith* (n 87) [27]; Case C–28/93 *Van den Akker v Stichting Shell Pensioenfonds* [1994] ECR I–4527, as regards the impermissibility of any advantages for women once a uniform retirement age for men and women is introduced.

[90] D de Vos, 'Pensionable Age and Equal Treatment from Charybdis to Scylla' (1994) 23 ILJ 175, 179.

[91] See N Burrows and M Robison, 'An Assessment of the Recast of Community Equality Laws' (2006) 13 ELJ 186; E Cassell, 'The Revised Directive on Equal Treatment for Men and Women in Occupational Social Security Schemes—The Dog that Didn't Bark' (1997) 26 ILJ 269.

[92] For an appraisal of the impact of the Dirs after ten years, see the Opinion of the Fundamental Rights Agency, *The Situation of Equality in the EU 10 years on from initial implementation of the Equality Directives* at http://fra.europa.eu/en/opinion/2013/fra-opinion-situation-equality-european-union-10-years-initial-implementation-equality.

of xenophobia in Europe.[93] Article 19 does not (unlike Article 21 of the Charter) contain a direct prohibition of discrimination on grounds which it lists, and (unlike the equal pay provision between men and women in Article 157 TFEU) it is not directly effective. Rather it enables the EU to adopt measures to combat discrimination on the grounds listed within the scope of the policies and powers otherwise granted in the Treaties:

> 1. Without prejudice to the other provisions of the Treaties and within the limits of the powers conferred by them upon the Union, the Council, acting unanimously in accordance with a special legislative procedure and after obtaining the consent of the European Parliament, may take appropriate action to combat discrimination based on sex, racial or ethnic origin, religion or belief, disability, age or sexual orientation.

While measures under Article 19(1) require unanimity in the Council, Article 19(2) allows for the adoption by a qualified majority of supportive, non-harmonizing incentive measures to combat discrimination on the grounds set out in paragraph 1.

(A) THE RACE DIRECTIVE 2000/43

Directive 2000/43/EC,[94] which establishes a prohibition of discrimination on grounds of racial or ethnic origin, was the first piece of legislation to be adopted under Article 19. It was adopted in an exceptionally speedy manner in 2000, less than a year after the Treaty of Amsterdam entered into force.[95] There was mounting concern at the time about the resurgence of the far-right in Europe, and the famous 'Haider affair' in Austria arguably played a significant part in explaining the pace and ease with which the legislation was enacted.[96] There was also an intention, reflected in the enactment by the Amsterdam Treaty of the 'sanctions clause' in Article 7 TEU,[97] to send out a signal about the importance of combating racial discrimination to the Central and East European countries which were seeking accession to the EU at the time.[98]

While the jurisdictional limitation in Article 19 TFEU specifies that the EU can act only within the limits of the Union's powers, Article 3 of the Race Directive gives it a wide material scope, including a prohibition on discrimination in relation to social protection, health care, housing, and education. The personal scope of the Directive is also reasonably wide, covering all persons within the EU, including public and private actors alike. The importance of protecting 'all natural persons' against discrimination on grounds of racial or ethnic origin is emphasized in recital 16 of the Preamble. The otherwise broad scope of the Race Directive is, however, limited in respect of third-country nationals, pointing to the troubling issue of the relationship between discrimination, race, and migration in Europe. While non-EU nationals are formally protected from discrimination on grounds of race and ethnic origin whilst

---

[93] For the background to this Treaty provision see M Bell, 'The New Article 13 EC Treaty: A Sound Basis for European Antidiscrimination Law?' (1999) 6 MJ 5; M Bell, *Anti-Discrimination Law and the European Union* (Oxford University Press, 2002).

[94] Council Directive 2000/43/EC of 29 June 2000 implementing the principle of equal treatment between persons irrespective of racial or ethnic origin [2000] OJ L180/22.

[95] On the influence of civil-society grounds and the Starting Line Group NGO in particular on the enactment of the Race Dir see I Chopin, 'The Starting Line: A Harmonised Approach to the Fight against Racism and to Promote Equal Treatment' (1999) 1 EJML 1; J Niessen, 'The Starting Line and the Promotion of EU Anti-Discrimination Legislation: The Role of Policy Oriented Research' (2001) 2 Journal of International Migration and Integration 389.

[96] M Merlingen, C Muddle, and U Sedelmeier, 'The Right and the Righteous?: European Norms, Domestic Politics and the Sanctions against Austria' (2001) 39 JCMS 59.

[97] See Ch 11, Section 7(a).

[98] E Ellis, *EU Anti-Discrimination Law* (Oxford University Press, 2005) 29.

on EU territory, Article 3(2) of the Directive and recital 13 make clear that it does not cover nationality-based discrimination and is 'without prejudice to provisions and conditions relating to the entry into and residence of third-country nationals' and to 'any treatment which arises from the legal status of the third-country national concerned'.

However, the distinction between discrimination based on nationality, discrimination based on religion, and discrimination based on racial or ethnic origin is rather unclear. Further, the Directive itself acknowledges the fact that the very category of 'race' is highly contested and scientifically unfounded, and the legislation avoids attempting to define the notion of discrimination on grounds of racial or ethnic origin.[99] Indeed, the lack of a definition of the prohibited behaviour may add to the familiar difficulties of victims of discrimination in establishing a claim under the Race Directive.[100]

Remarkably few references have so far been made to the ECJ under the Race Directive, and several of the cases which have been referred have been deemed inadmissible by the Court.[101] Further, as though to underscore the difficulty for individuals to bring race discrimination claims before the ECJ, the most important case thus far decided by the Court was brought not by an individual but by a domestic anti-discrimination association.[102] In *Firma Feryn* the Court sidestepped the problem of the Directive's exclusion of nationality discrimination by appearing to treat a public statement by an employer who was seeking to recruit fitters that it 'could not employ immigrants because its customers were reluctant to give them access to their private residences' as equivalent to a statement that it would not employ people of a certain racial or ethnic origin.[103] In *Servet*, however, in which an Albanian national challenged Italy's refusal to grant him a housing benefit on the basis that he was a third-country national, the CJEU ruled firmly that Directive 2000/43 does not cover discrimination based on nationality.[104]

The CJEU eschewed an important opportunity to rule on issues of discrimination against Roma communities when, against the advice of the Advocate General who concluded that the reference was validly made and that a *prima facie* case of indirect discrimination had been established, the Court decided that the body which had made the reference should not be considered as a 'court or tribunal' for the purposes of Article 267 and so refused to give a ruling.[105] And in *Runevič-Vardyn and Wardyn* in which the CJEU was asked whether Lithuanian legislation providing that personal names and surnames in documents indicating the civil status of an individual may be written using only the letters of the national language constituted indirect discrimination on grounds of ethnic origin under Article 2(2)(b) of the Race Directive, the Court ruled that the facts of the case did not fall within the scope of the Directive as laid out by Article 3(1).[106]

Article 2 of the Race Directive identifies four types of prohibited discrimination, namely direct discrimination, indirect discrimination, harassment, and instruction to discriminate. These concepts are

---

[99] Rec 6 of the Dir.

[100] C Brown, 'The Race Directive: Towards Equality for All the Peoples of Europe?' (2002) 22 YBEL 204.

[101] (See n 106). For a case in which the prohibition of discrimination on grounds of race established by the Dir was taken into account in the interpretation of the EU Copyright Dir, see Case C–201/13 *Deckmyn v Vandersteen and others* EU:C:2014:2132, [30].

[102] Case C–54/07 *Firma Feryn* [2008] ECR I–5187.

[103] Case C–54/07 *Firma Feryn* [2008] ECR I–5187, [16], [25], [34]. The CJEU did not directly address the specific question—which was posed to it by the referring Brussels Labour Court in question 4(d) of its reference, at [18] of the judgment—whether a statement of refusal to hire *immigrants*, combined with the failure to hire any employees of a non-indigenous ethnic background, gave rise to a presumption of indirect discrimination on racial or ethnic grounds.

[104] Case C–571/10 *Servet Kamberaj* EU:C:2012:233, [48]–[50].

[105] Case C–394/11 *Belov v CHEZ Elektro Balgaria AD* EU:C:2013:48. For critique, see Mathias Möschel, 'Race Discrimination and Access to the European Court of Justice: *Belov*' (2013) 50 CMLRev 1433.

[106] Case C–391/09 *Runevič-Vardyn and Wardyn* EU:C:2011:291. See also Case C–310/10 *Agafiţei* EU:C:2011:467 which asked whether discrimination in the availability of compensation for prior discrimination against a 'certain socio-professional class' was covered by the Race Dir 2000/43 was deemed inadmissible by the CJEU.

explained further below. Whereas a *prima facie* charge of indirect discrimination can be rebutted by invoking a general 'objective justification' in accordance with Article 2(2)(b), direct discrimination can be justified only on the basis of a limited number of exceptions enumerated in the Directive.[107] These comprise the provision in Article 4 which permits differential treatment based on a 'genuine and determining occupational requirement' which is legitimately and proportionately applied; and the 'positive action' provision in Article 5 which permits the adoption of measures 'to compensate for disadvantages linked to racial or ethnic origin' and in order to ensure 'full equality in practice'.

The Directive also introduces a number of institutional provisions. Article 13 provides for the establishment or designation of a national equality body or agency the tasks of which include the promotion of equal treatment of all persons without discrimination on the grounds of racial or ethnic origin. In addition to their policy work in publishing reports, conducting surveys, and making recommendations, these bodies are to provide independent assistance to victims of discrimination in pursuing their complaints. Article 7 supplements the individual-complaints mechanism by providing that associations and organizations with a legitimate interest, as well as the Article 13 equality bodies, may assist and support victims in any judicial or administrative proceedings to enforce obligations under the Directive. Article 8 introduces a burden-shifting requirement to the effect that once the claimant has introduced facts from which it may be inferred that direct or indirect discrimination has occurred, the burden of proof must shift to the respondent to prove that there has been no breach of the equal treatment rule. In *Meister*, the CJEU rejected the applicant's claim that Article 8 of the Race Directive (or Article 10 of its sister-Directive 2000/78) entitled her, where she was unsuccessful in her application for an advertised job, to be given access to information indicating whether the employer eventually employed another person at the end of the recruitment process.[108] However, the CJEU also ruled that, since the employer had not contested her claim that she was adequately qualified for the job and yet had not been called for an interview, that employer's refusal to grant her access to any information at all was a factor that could be taken into account by the national court in establishing facts from which direct or indirect discrimination might be presumed.[109]

Article 6 indicates that the provisions of the Race Directive are minimum rather than maximum requirements, and introduces a 'non-regression clause' which prevents Member States from relying on the Directive to justify reducing existing protection against discrimination. Finally, effective, proportionate, and dissuasive remedies must be made available to victims of discrimination, and Article 9 requires the establishment of effective measures to prevent retaliation or the victimization of complainants.[110]

(B) THE FRAMEWORK EMPLOYMENT DIRECTIVE 2000/78

The Employment Equality Directive, which followed shortly after the adoption of the Race Directive, is both broader and narrower than the latter. Labelled as a 'Framework' Directive, it is broader in scope in that it covers five grounds of discrimination, but it is narrower in that it is confined, like the earlier Sex

---

[107] See the Opinion of AG Kokott in Case C–394/11 *Belov v CHEZ Elektro Balgaria AD* EU:C:2012:585.

[108] Case C–415/10 *Meister v Speech Design Carrier Systems* EU:C:2012:217.

[109] Ibid [47]. For a similar ruling in the context of the earlier Gender Equality Dirs 76/207 and 202, as well as the Burden of Proof Dir 79/7, see Case C–104/10 *Patrick Kelly v NUI* EU:C:2011:506, [53]–[55] where however the employer had offered some information to the complainant, and the CJEU ruled that the principle of confidentiality must also be taken into account.

[110] The Commission brought infringement proceedings against Poland for inadequate implementation of Art 9 of the Dir, but the case was subsequently withdrawn: Case C–341/10 *Commission v Poland* EU:C:2011:309. In its joint report on the implementation of the two anti-discrimination dirs, the Commission lists a series of infringement proceedings commenced against Member States in respect of these dirs: COM(2014) 2, fns 12–16.

Equality Directives, to labour-market discrimination. Directive 2000/78 prohibits discrimination on the basis of sexual orientation, religious belief, age, and disability in the area of employment.[111]

Article 3(1) defines the scope of the Directive and, like the Race Directive, it applies generally to persons within the EU and to the public and private sectors alike, but with the same limitation as regards nationality-based discrimination.[112] Unlike the Race Directive, the material scope of the legislation is limited to employment-related matters. It covers: (i) conditions for access to employment including selection criteria, recruitment, and promotion; (ii) access to vocational guidance, training, and retraining; (iii) employment and working conditions, including dismissals and pay; and (iv) membership of, and involvement in, workers' or employers' organizations.

There are a number of specific exclusions from the Directive's coverage: Member States may exclude the application of the provisions on age and disability discrimination to employment in the armed forces;[113] and the Directive does not apply to state schemes such as state social security or social protection schemes.[114] Recital 14 of the Preamble also specifies that 'this Directive shall be without prejudice to national provisions laying down retirement ages'. The Court ruled in *Palacios de la Villa* that this recital would not preclude the application of the Directive to national measures affecting the conditions governing termination of employment (in this case a compulsory retirement age), and that it merely confirmed the competence of Member States to establish an applicable retirement age in the first place.[115] Recital 22 also states that 'this Directive shall be without prejudice to national laws on marital status and the benefits dependent thereon'. This provision was discussed in *Maruko*, where the ECJ ruled that once a Member State treated registered life partnerships and marriages as comparable as far as survivors' benefits were concerned, the exclusion of life partners from a scheme of survivor's benefits under an occupational pension scheme amounted to impermissible discrimination on the basis of sexual orientation under the Directive.[116]

As with the Race Directive, Article 2 of the Framework Employment Directive prohibits direct and indirect discrimination, harassment, and instruction to discriminate, and Article 11 requires the introduction of measures to protect against the victimization of complainants. Indirect discrimination, as under the Race Directive, can be 'objectively justified' under Article 2(2)(b). Direct discrimination can be justified only on the basis of one of the exceptions contained in the Directive, but there are a greater number of possible exceptions or justifications for indirect discrimination, some of which vary according to the specific ground of discrimination, in the Framework Employment Directive than in the Race Directive. Article 2(5) provides a generally applicable justification for differential treatment that is necessary for reasons related to public security, public order, prevention of crime, public health, or protection of the rights of others, provided that the measures serve a legitimate objective and are proportionate. Article 4 provides for a 'genuine and determining occupational requirement' exception similar to that contained in the Race Directive. Article 7 contains a positive action provision permitting

---

[111] Council Directive 2000/78/EC of 27 November 2000 establishing a general framework for equal treatment in employment and occupation [2000] OJ L303/16.

[112] Art 3(2) provides that the Dir does not cover differences of treatment based on nationality and is without prejudice to provisions and conditions relating to the entry into and residence of third-country nationals and stateless persons in the territory of Member States, and to any treatment which arises from the legal status of the third-country nationals and stateless persons concerned.

[113] Art 3(4).

[114] Art 3(3). The ECJ in Case C–267/06 *Maruko* [2008] ECR I–1757 ruled that this exclusion does not extend to private occupational pension schemes which, by analogy with the *Barber* case law discussed above (nn 40–42 and text), constitute pay rather than state social security.

[115] Case C–411/05 *Palacios de la Villa* [2007] ECR I–8531, [44]–[45]. For discussion of the many other age discrimination cases focusing on retirement ages, see (nn 297–300) and (nn 346–353) and text.

[116] Case C–267/06 *Maruko* (n 114); also Case C–147/08 *Römer v Freie und Hansestadt Hamburg* EU:C:2011:286; and Cases C–124, 125 and 143/11 *Dittrich, Klinke and Müller* EU:C:2012:771.

the adoption by Member States of preferential measures that 'prevent or compensate for disadvantages' linked to the grounds covered by the Directive, and which seek to ensure full equality in practice. These are discussed further below.

In addition to these general exceptions or justifications, there are a number of more specific exceptions to the prohibition of *direct* discrimination on the grounds of disability, age, and religion. Article 6 permits Member States to adopt differential treatment on the basis of age, where this is objectively and reasonably justified by a legitimate national aim, including legitimate employment-policy, labour-market, and vocational training objectives, and is proportionate. Article 6 sets out some examples of legitimate national measures of this kind. Article 4(2), in the context of the general 'occupational requirement' exception, contains a more specific version of this exception permitting 'churches and other public or private organizations' the ethos of which is based on religion or belief to stipulate (subject to the general principles of EU law and of domestic constitutional law) that a person's religion or belief constitutes an occupational requirement, and to insist that those working for them must act 'with loyalty to the organization's ethos'. There are also specific provisions relating to the remedying of religious discrimination in Northern Ireland. Interestingly, despite the extensive case law of the ECtHR on religious freedom and discrimination, no cases under Directive 2000/78 concerning religious discrimination have yet come before the CJEU.[117]

Article 5 of the Directive contains an important provision on the obligation to provide 'reasonable accommodation' for people with disabilities.[118] The existence of this obligation is recognized also in Article 2(b)(ii), which indicates that measures taken to comply with legislation implementing the obligation of reasonable accommodation will not be considered to be indirectly discriminatory.[119] Article 5 obliges employers to take appropriate measures—which the ECJ has held can include a reduction of working hours[120] —to enable a person with a disability to have access to, participate in, or advance in employment or training, unless such measures would impose a disproportionate burden on the employer.[121] The question whether the burden is disproportionate is to be assessed in the context of the state's disability policy. It has been argued that although the obligation of reasonable accommodation is made explicit only in the context of disability discrimination under the Directive, it is in fact implicit in the test for objective justification of indirect discrimination on all grounds in EU law.[122]

The final procedural and institutional provisions of the Framework Equality Directive are similar to those in the Race Directive. The Directive sets minimum rather than maximum standards, and there is a non-regression clause. There is a burden-shifting provision (which is not to apply in criminal procedures) where the claimant has produced facts from which discrimination may be presumed.[123] Sanctions applicable to infringements must be effective, proportionate, and dissuasive.[124] Member States must promote compliance in other ways too, including through information-dissemination and

---

[117] R Holtmaat, *European Non-Discrimination Law: A Comparison of EU Law and the ECHR in the Field of Non-Discrimination and Freedom of Religion in Public Employment with an Emphasis on the Islamic Headscarf Issue* (Intersentia, 2012).

[118] L Waddington, 'When is it Reasonable for Europeans to be Confused? Understanding when a Disability Accommodation is "Reasonable" from a Comparative Perspective' (2008) 29 Comparative Labor Law and Policy Journal 317.

[119] See Case C–312/11 *Commission v Italy* EU:C:2013:446 in which Italy was found in breach of the obligation to put in place a system requiring employers to provide reasonable accommodation for persons with disabilities.

[120] See Cases C–335 and 337/11 *Ring and Skoube Werge v Dansk almennyttigt Boligselskab* EU:C:2013:222, [57].

[121] In Cases C–335 and 337/11 ibid, [59] the CJEU left it to the national court to assess whether a requirement that an employer should reduce working hours to accommodate an employee with a disability would be an unreasonable burden.

[122] E Howard, 'Reasonable Accommodation of Religion and Other Discrimination grounds in EU Law' (2013) 38 ELRev 360.

[123] See (nn 108–109).

[124] See Case C–81/12 *Asociaţia Accept* EU:C:2013:275.

monitoring, and provision must be made for social dialogue and dialogue with NGOs. States must ensure that associations or organizations with a legitimate interest, including these equality bodies, have the right to engage in judicial or administrative procedures on behalf or in support of the complainant. Notably however, there is no requirement, as there is under the Race Directive, on Member States to establish or designate an equality body or institution charged with promoting equal treatment in these fields.

The ECJ has interpreted the scope of the Framework Employment Directive so as to prohibit discrimination by association, at least in the field of disability. The case of *Coleman* concerned the alleged constructive dismissal of an employee who was not herself disabled, but who had apparently been subjected to adverse treatment by her former employer in connection with the disability of her child.[125] The Court ruled that the prohibition of direct discrimination in Directive 2000/78 is not limited to people who are themselves disabled, but applies also to an employee who is treated less favourably than another employee if the adverse treatment is related to the disability of her child, whose care is provided primarily by that employee. While the case concerned discrimination on grounds of disability, the ruling could equally apply to discrimination by association with the other grounds covered by the Directive:

Case C–303/06 **Coleman v Attridge Law**
[2008] ECR I–5603

51. Where it is established that an employee in a situation such as that in the present case suffers direct discrimination on grounds of disability, an interpretation of Directive 2000/78 limiting its application only to people who are themselves disabled is liable to deprive that directive of an important element of its effectiveness and to reduce the protection which it is intended to guarantee.

More generally, the Framework Employment Directive, unlike the Race Directive, has produced a substantial body of case law, the bulk of it concerning the justifiability of direct age-based discrimination under national law. This case law is discussed below. There have as yet been no cases in relation to religious discrimination, and there is a small but growing number concerning disability discrimination and sexual orientation discrimination.

(i) *Disability Discrimination*[126]

Apart from the *Coleman* case mentioned above concerning discrimination by association, there have been several cases concerning the definition of 'disability' itself, in the absence of a precise definition in the Directive or in the UN Convention on the Rights of Persons with Disabilities, which the EU concluded and ratified.[127] While the ECJ in *Chacón Navas* distinguished illness from disability,[128] it ruled in *Ring and Skouboe Werge* that a disability covered by the Directive could nevertheless *result* from an illness, curable or otherwise, where it 'entails a limitation which results…from physical mental or psychological impairments which in interaction with various barriers may hinder the full and effective

---

[125] Case C–303/06 *Coleman* [2008] ECR I–5603.

[126] For an overview, see C O'Brien, 'Equality's False Summits: New Varieties of Disability Discrimination, "Excessive" Equal Treatment and Economically Constricted Horizons' (2011) 36 ELRev 26.

[127] See SWD(2014)182 for a report by the Commission on the EU's implementation of the UN Convention on the Rights of Persons with Disabilities (CRPD). For discussion of the extent to which the EU and the CJEU are following the CRDP's lead in the development of disability discrimination law in the Framework Directive, see L Waddington, 'Future Prospects for EU Equality Law: Lessons to be Learnt from the Proposed Equal Treatment Directive' (2011) 36 ELRev 163.

[128] Case C–13/05 *Chacón Navas* [2006] ECR I–6467.

participation of the person concerned in professional life on an equal basis with other workers, and the limitation is a long-term one'.[129] Illness which does not result in such a limitation is not covered by the concept of disability in the Directive. In *FOA* the Court ruled that while the Directive does not cover discrimination on grounds of obesity, nevertheless obesity, just like illness, may result in a disability where it entails a limitation of the kind described in *Ring and Skoube Werge*, hindering equal participation in the workplace.[130] In a somewhat harsh ruling in *Z*, the Court rejected the claim that the inability to bear a child due to having being born without a uterus constituted a disability within the meaning of the Directive, since according to the ECJ it did not hinder the woman from participating normally in the workforce.[131] The result was that, even though she was in a disadvantaged position as compared with other women following the birth of a child insofar as she could not take paid maternity or adoptive leave because her child was born by surrogate, the Court decided that this was not discrimination caught by Directive 2000/78.[132]

In *Ring and Skoube Werbe* the CJEU emphasized further that the existence of a disability for the purposes of the Directive does not mean that the person is unable to participate at all in the workforce, but simply that there is a hindrance to participation, and that a finding that there is a disability does not depend on the nature of the accommodation measures which the employer may need to make.[133] Rather the requirement to make reasonable accommodation is, in law, a consequence of and not a condition prior to a finding of disability.

The Court in *Odar* found indirect discrimination on grounds of disability due to the special calculation method used to determine compensation for employees over the age of 54 who were made redundant on operational grounds, which operated to the disadvantage of disabled employees who would be entitled to an early disability pension.[134] And in *Glatzel*, the Court ruled that differential treatment on grounds of disability, in circumstances where the applicant was refused a driving licence on the ground that the visual acuity in one of his eyes did not meet the minimum requirement established by an EU directive (even though his vision was normal when using both eyes together), could be justified as a proportionate pursuit of the legitimate aim of improving road safety.[135]

(ii) *Sexual Orientation*

In *Maruko*, as we have seen, the ECJ indicated that once a Member State treated registered life partnerships and marriages as comparable for the purposes of survivors' benefits, the exclusion of life partners from a scheme of survivor's benefits under an occupational pension scheme constituted discrimination on the basis of sexual orientation.[136] Similar rulings were given in *Römer* as regards a supplementary pension,[137] in *Dittrich* as regards payments for civil servants in the event of illness,[138] and in *Hay* as regards benefits such as special leave and salary bonuses under the terms of a collective agreement.[139]

An important ruling in the field of sexual orientation, which like *Feryn* and *Belov* in the case of race discrimination, illustrates the importance of the role of NGOs and equality bodies in litigating

---

[129] Cases C–335 and 337/11 *Ring and Skouboe Werge v Dansk almennyttigt Boligselskab* EU:C:2013:222.

[130] Case C–354/13 *Fag og Arbejde (FOA)* EU:C:2014:2463.

[131] Case C–363/12 *Z v A Government department* EU:C:2014:159.

[132] The Court also held that there was no discrimination on grounds of sex. Ibid [55]–[57]. See further below.

[133] Cases C–335 and 337/11 *Ring and Skouboe Werge v Dansk almennyttigt Boligselskab* EU:C:2013:222, [44]–[45].

[134] Case C–152/11 *Odar v Baxter Deutschland* EU:C:2012:772.

[135] Case C 356/12 *Glatzel* EU:C:2013:350.

[136] Case C–267/06 *Maruko* (n 114).

[137] Case C–147/08 *Römer v Freie und Hansestadt Hamburg* EU:C:2011:286. See also staff Case F–86/09 *W v Commission* EU:F:2010:125.

[138] Cases C–124/, 125 and 143/11 *Dittrich, Klinke and Müller* EU:C:2012:771.

[139] Case C–267/12 *Hay v Crédit agricole mutuel de Charente-Maritime et des Deux-Sèvres* EU:C:2013:823.

discrimination issues, is *Asociatia Accept*.[140] The case centred on the question whether the homophobic remarks of a leading shareholder of a football club, to the effect that he would never hire a player who was homosexual, could be attributed to the club itself, as well as whether the penalties available were appropriate and sufficient. The CJEU took note of the different and less structured nature of recruitment procedures in the field of football, and ruled that the statements in question were indeed attributable to the club, given the prominent position and leadership role within the club of the shareholder who had made them, and despite the fact that he did not have legal capacity to bind the club. The fact that the club had apparently taken no steps to distance itself from his comments could also contribute to the perception of the public and potential players that the club had a recruitment policy which discriminated on grounds of sexual orientation. On the remedial side the CJEU held that a national rule which made it impossible to impose a fine any later than six months after the discriminatory statements were made was incompatible with the Directive.

(c) THE PROPOSED NEW ARTICLE 19 DIRECTIVE ON EQUAL TREATMENT[141]

We have seen that the two anti-discrimination directives adopted in 2000 differ in their material scope, with Directive 2000/78 covering a wider range of grounds but being confined to the employment context, while the Race Directive prohibits discrimination on grounds of race only, though across a wider range of areas of social and economic life. The alleged 'hierarchy of equality' as between the various EU discrimination directives, and as between the grounds within the Framework Equality Directive, with race and gender equality enjoying (to different degrees) a stronger level of protection than other grounds, has regularly been criticized.[142]

In 2008 the Commission responded to this criticism by proposing legislation under Article 19(1) aiming to 'equalize' standards of protection against discrimination across all of the prohibited grounds in Article 19, namely age, disability, sexual orientation, and religion or belief, though leaving aside race and sex, given the strong existing legislation in these two areas.[143] Given its objective of achieving greater consistency between the different legal instruments, the proposal adopts most of the same terms, definitions, principles, substantive provisions, and exceptions as in the existing Race Directive 2000/78 and the consolidating Gender Equality Directive 2006/54, including positive action, reasonable accommodation, and remedial provisions. The material scope is similar (though not quite identical) to that of the Race Directive, covering social protection, health, education, and access to and supply of goods and services provided in the context of a commercial activity. The proposed directive declares itself to be 'without prejudice' to national laws on marital or family status and reproductive rights, to 'the national content of teaching and the organization of their education system' as well as to the secular nature of the state and its institutions, education, or the status and activities of organizations based on religion or belief.

---

[140] Case C–81/12 *Asociaţia Accept* EU:C:2013:275.

[141] For some analyses of the proposed measure and its context see L Waddington, 'Future Prospects for EU Equality Law: Lessons to be Learnt from the Proposed Equal Treatment Directive' (2011) 36 ELRev 163; E Howard, 'EU Equality Law: Three Recent Developments' (2011) 17 ELJ 785.

[142] L Waddington and M Bell, 'More Equal than Others: Distinguishing European Union Equality Directives?' (2001) 38 CMLRev 587; P Skidmore, 'EC Framework Directive on Equal Treatment in Employment: Towards a Comprehensive Community Anti-Discrimination Policy?' (2001) 30 ILJ 126.

[143] Commission Proposal for a Council Directive implementing the principle of equal treatment between persons irrespective of religion or belief, disability, age or sexual orientation, COM(2008) 426 and the Working Document accompanying the proposal, SEC(2008) 2180.

The Commission based the proposal on Article 19 TFEU, which, as we have seen above, requires the assent of the European Parliament and unanimity in the Council. And although the Commission's draft was approved in 2009 by the Parliament,[144] it has remained stuck in the Council of Ministers due to the unanimity requirement. The German Government in particular has persistently raised objections based on the subsidiarity principle and about the cost to business of the proposed measure, while other governments have opposed the inclusion of 'access to social protection' within its scope, although some states have apparently argued that the provisions on disability in the proposed directive are insufficiently strong. Despite considerable frustration on the part of equality bodies and NGOs with the glacial progress of the legislation,[145] regular discussions of the proposal were continuing in the Council of Ministers at the end of 2014, and a technical working group has apparently made some progress on a number of contested issues.[146]

6 THE GENDER DIRECTIVES

As we have seen EU anti-discrimination law began with a provision on equal pay for men and women for work of equal value, and gender equality policy remains the strongest and best resourced of the EU's anti-discrimination policies. From 1976 on the EU adopted numerous directives tackling specific aspects of gender discrimination. A directive (75/117) on equal pay was adopted in 1975, followed by legislation on equal treatment relating to access to employment, vocational training, promotion, and working conditions (76/207), on equal treatment in state social security (79/7), in occupational security schemes (86/378/EEC), and equal treatment between men and women in a self-employed capacity (86/613). In the decades which followed, further directives were enacted on the protection of pregnancy and maternity (92/85), parental leave (96/34), the burden of proof (97/80), and equality in access to and supply of goods and services (2004/113). Ultimately, not least as a result of ECJ case law, much of this legislation was significantly amended, repealed, and consolidated.

(A) THE 'RECAST' EQUAL TREATMENT DIRECTIVE 2006/54

(i) *General*

As part of the EU's general programme of legislative consolidation, and with a view to 'recasting' the existing legislation on equal pay, equal treatment, occupational social security, and the burden of proof, Directive 2006/54 was adopted.[147] Apart from systematizing the existing legislation and incorporating relevant ECJ rulings, the Directive introduces no major substantive changes. Equal treatment in state social security is still dealt with separately by Directive 79/7, and equal treatment in access to and supply of goods and services by Directive 2004/113. Directive 2006/54 left unamended the Pregnancy Directive 92/85, but the Parental Leave Directive has now been replaced by Directive 2010/18, and Directive 86/613 on equal treatment for self-employed persons has been replaced by Directive 2010/41.

While the relatively unambitious nature of the 2006 consolidation was criticized, it appears that the reason for the selective approach was so that the recast Directive could be adopted on the basis of

---

[144] The Parliament's legislative resolution of 2 Apr 2009, T6–0211/2009, approved the Commission's draft.

[145] See the letter signed by six NGOs in July 2014 on the sixth anniversary of the publication of the initial proposal for the Dir, https://euobserver.com/opinion/124834.

[146] For progress in the legislative procedure, see the European Parliament's legislative observatory: www.europarl.europa.eu/oeil/home/home.do.

[147] Directive 2006/54/EC of the European Parliament and of the Council of 5 July 2006 on the implementation of the principle of equal opportunities and equal treatment of men and women in matters of employment and occupation (recast) [2006] OJ L204/23.

Article 157, without the need to use a more procedurally and substantively onerous legal basis such as Article 153.[148]

Directive 2006/54 now governs equal treatment in access to employment and promotion, vocational training, working conditions including pay, and occupational social security. Title I sets out the purpose and scope of the Directive, defines its key terms, and makes reference to the positive action provision in Article 157(4). Title II contains the main substantive sections. Chapter 1 of Title II deals with pay, Chapter 2 with occupational social security, and Chapter 3 with access to employment and promotion, vocational training, and working conditions. Title III contains the 'horizontal provisions', with a chapter on remedies and enforcement, including adequate compensation, recourse to judicial and conciliation procedures, and the burden of proof; a chapter on the promotion of equal treatment through dialogue, including provision for the establishment of national equality bodies, the promotion of dialogue and adoption of agreements by the social partners, the imposition of positive obligations on the Member States, and dialogue with NGOs; and a final chapter dealing broadly with Member States' compliance, including the requirement of adoption of appropriate penalties, prevention of discrimination, protection against victimization, gender mainstreaming, and dissemination of information. Article 27 of the Directive indicates that it sets minimum conditions only, so that states may adopt more extensive protection, and it contains a qualified non-regression clause.

The core provision of the Directive which applies across the three fields of pay, occupational social security, and employment conditions is the prohibition on direct or indirect discrimination on grounds of sex in the public and private sectors.[149] Discrimination, according to the Directive, includes harassment and sexual harassment,[150] instruction to discriminate, and any less favourable treatment of a woman related to pregnancy or maternity leave. All of the relevant terms, including direct and indirect discrimination and harassment, are defined in Article 2. The reference to discrimination on the basis of 'marital and family status' was omitted from the Directive.[151]

The consolidating Directive tidied up the law of equal treatment by adopting a definition of indirect discrimination which is consistent with other EU equality legislation, and applying the horizontal general provisions on remedies, equality bodies, compliance, information, dialogue, etc to all three fields. EU gender equality legislation was thereby brought into line with the Race Directive and the Framework Employment Equality Directive, discussed above.[152]

(ii) *Equal Pay*

Equal pay was originally governed by Directive 75/117, which was replaced virtually without amendment, other than by being updated in the light of relevant case law, by Directive 2006/54.[153] The basic thrust is to require the elimination of sex discrimination in pay in cases involving the same work or work to which equal value is attributed, and to require job-classification schemes to be free from discrimination.[154] Member States must abolish any such discrimination in legislative or administrative provisions and ensure that any breaches of the equal pay principle in collective agreements or contracts

---

[148] Burrows and Robison (n 91).

[149] Art 14.

[150] These also include 'any less favourable treatment based on a person's rejection of or submission to such conduct'.

[151] See S Koukoulis-Spiliotopoulos, 'The Amended Equal Treatment Directive 2002/73: An Expression of Constitutional Principles/Fundamental Rights' (2005) 12 MJ 327; F Beveridge, 'Gender, the *Acquis* and Beyond' in M Dougan and S Currie (eds), *50 Years of the European Treaties: Looking Back and Thinking Forward* (Hart, 2009) 393.

[152] Dir 2000/78/EC (n 111); Council Dir 2000/43/EC (n 94).

[153] Dir 2006/54 (n 147).

[154] Case 237/85 *Rummler* [1986] ECR 2101 held that the use of criteria such as muscle-demand for the purpose of determining rates of pay was permitted; S Fredman, 'EC Discrimination Law: A Critique' (1992) 21 ILJ 119, 123; Case

are rendered void or amended. There is, as we have seen, a chapter in the consolidating legislation on 'promotion of equal treatment', *inter alia* through dialogue with social partners and NGOs and through the establishment of equality bodies, which replaces the previous and more cursory positive obligation to take appropriate measures to ensure that the equal pay principle is observed.[155] The consolidating Directive also contains more extensive provisions than the earlier Directive on remedies, enforcement, and compliance.[156] These provisions incorporate various aspects of the ECJ's case law, such as the rules that there can be no prior ceiling on damages,[157] that the burden of proof shifts to the defendant where the plaintiff can establish facts which raise a presumption of direct or indirect discrimination,[158] and that penalties must be 'effective, proportionate and dissuasive'.

The ECJ has always ruled that the right to equal pay stems directly from the Treaty, so that the terms of the legislation are to be given the same meaning as those in the Treaty.[159] The Treaty's equal pay provision could also be directly invoked in 'horizontal' cases against an employer, thus avoiding problems concerning the horizontal effect of the Directive. The aim of the Equal Pay Directive was to place the onus on states of putting the principle into practice,[160] something which has been very slow to occur given the significant gender pay gap which persists today.[161]

ECJ jurisprudence indicates that the personal qualities of an employee and the manner in which work was performed could not be conflated and used retrospectively by an employer to argue that the employee was not carrying out work which was similar or equal to that of other employees, for the purposes of explaining a pay differential which existed from the outset.[162] Individual work capacity could however be taken into account in other ways, for example in relation to an employee's career development as compared with that of a more effective colleague, and therefore in *subsequent* postings and pay. The ECJ encountered criticism for stating that professional training could be a valid criterion for ascertaining whether or not employees were engaged in the 'same work', as opposed to treating more extensive qualifications as grounds for justifying a higher level of pay for the same work done.[163]

In 2014, the Commission published a recommendation on strengthening the principle of equal pay through transparency, drawing attention to the fact that after over forty years of EU equal pay legislation women still earn on average 16.2 per cent less than men for each hour worked.[164] The Commission calls on states to ensure that employees can seek and obtain information on pay levels for other employees doing the same work or work of equal value, broken down by gender. States are to report back by the end of 2015, to enable the Commission to decide on the need for further measures.

C–400/93 *Royal Copenhagen, Specialarbejderforbundet i Danmark v Dansk Industri* [1995] ECR I–1275; Case C–236/98 *JämO* (n 36) [48].

[155] See Title III, Ch 2 of Dir 2006/54, and previously see Art 6 of Dir 75/117.

[156] Dir 2006/54 (n 147), Title II, Chs 1 and 3.

[157] Case C–271/91 *Marshall v Southampton and South-West Hampshire Area Health Authority (No 2)* [1993] ECR I–4367; Case C–180/95 *Draehmpaehl v Urania Immobilienservice* [1997] ECR I–2195.

[158] See, eg, Case 109/88 *Handels- og Kontorfunktionærernes Forbund i Danmark v Dansk Arbejdsgiverforening, acting on behalf of Danfoss* [1989] ECR 3199.

[159] Case C–381/99 *Brunnhofer* (n 50) [29]; Case C–309/97 *Angestelltenbetriebsrat der Wiener Gebietskrankenkasse v Wiener Gebietskrankenkasse* [1999] ECR I–2865 on the 'same work'.

[160] See, eg, Case 61/81 *Commission v United Kingdom* [1982] ECR 2601, [9], where the CJEU ruled that in the absence of an adequate job-classification system, a worker had to have a right of access to an appropriate authority to obtain a ruling on whether or not his/her work was of equal value to other work.

[161] See recently Commission Recommendation 2014/124/EU on strengthening the principle of equal pay through transparency.

[162] Case C–381/99 *Brunnhofer* (n 50).

[163] Ibid [78]; Case C–309/97 *Angestelltenbetriebsrat der Wiener* (n 159) [19]. E Ellis, 'The Recent Jurisprudence of the Court of Justice in the Field of Sex Equality' (2000) 37 CMLRev 1403.

[164] 2014/124/EU: Commission Recommendation of 7 March 2014 on strengthening the principle of equal pay between men and women through transparency.

(iii) *Employment Conditions*

Equal treatment between men and women in the field of employment, including access to employment and promotion, vocational training, and working conditions, was originally covered by Directive 76/207,[165] now replaced by the recast Directive 2006/54.[166]

The general rule, as we have seen, is the prohibition of direct and indirect discrimination on grounds of sex. The original Equal Treatment Directive contained three 'exceptions' to this prohibition: an occupational qualification provision, a 'pregnancy and maternity' provision, and a positive action provision. Under the recast Directive, only the occupational qualification provision in Article 14(2) is phrased as an exception, while the other two provisions are affirmatively expressed.

The positive action provision appears in Article 3, covering all matters which fall within the scope of the Directive, and declares that 'Member States may maintain or adopt measures within the meaning of Article 157(4) of the Treaty with a view to ensuring full equality in practice between men and women in working life'. The earlier provision on the protection of women in the event of pregnancy or maternity was replaced by Article 15 of Directive 2006/54, which provides that a woman on maternity leave is to be entitled to return to equivalent employment on no less favourable terms and to benefit from any improvement in working conditions to which she would have been entitled during her absence.[167]

Article 16 provides that the Directive is 'without prejudice to the right of Member States to recognise distinct rights to paternity and/or adoption leave'. The Pregnancy Directive, discussed below, supplies further detail by imposing a requirement to provide a minimum level of employment protection for women who are pregnant, breastfeeding, or who have recently given birth.[168]

In *Hofmann*, it was argued that maternity leave provisions which went beyond what was necessary to protect women before and after childbirth, for example by giving a longer period of leave in order to care for a child, would breach the Directive unless the leave period was made available to men and women alike.[169] However the ECJ rejected this argument, ruling that the provision of a period of extended maternity leave was intended to protect women in connection with the effects of pregnancy and motherhood, and that such leave could legitimately be reserved to the mother 'in view of the fact that it is only the mother who may find herself subject to undesirable pressures to return to work prematurely'.[170] The Court also said that the Equal Treatment Directive was not intended 'to alter the division of responsibility between parents', and that Member States had a measure of discretion as to the social measures they adopt to protect women in the event of pregnancy and maternity. A somewhat similar ruling was given in *Commission v Italy*, concerning national laws giving compulsory maternity leave to the mother of an adopted child under 6 years of age, but not to the father.[171] The ECJ accepted Italy's 'legitimate concern to assimilate as far as possible the conditions of entry of the child into the adoptive family to those of the arrival of a newborn child in the family during the very delicate initial period'.[172]

The dilemma is that these rulings could be said to support the continuation by the Member States of the traditional division of responsibility which entrenches the role of the mother as primary carer,

---

[165] Council Dir 76/207/EEC [1976] OJ L39/40.

[166] (N 147).

[167] See Case C–595/12 *Napoli* EU:C:2014:128 on the exclusion of a woman who was on maternity leave from a vocational training course which was required for promotion.

[168] Dir 92/85 [1992] OJ L348/1.

[169] Case 184/83 *Hofmann v Barmer Ersatzkasse* [1984] ECR 3047.

[170] Ibid [26].

[171] Case 163/82 *Commission v Italy* [1983] ECR 3273.

[172] Ibid [16].

and which, by protecting 'the special relationship between a woman and her child', disincentivizes the father from taking time to develop such a relationship in the period after birth or adoption. On the other hand, had the Court ruled that the Equal Treatment Directive prohibited states from providing special protection for women other than when this was strictly necessary to protect their biological condition during and after pregnancy and childbirth, the states may have chosen to 'equalize down' rather than up by abolishing the more extended maternity leave for women. The Court's case law more recently however has moved in this direction.

In *Roca Álvarez*, the rulings in *Hofmann* and *Italy* appear to be have been read narrowly. The ECJ in this case declared that the Equal Treatment Directive precludes a national measure which provides that female employees are entitled to take leave during the first nine months following the child's birth, while fathers are not entitled to the same leave unless the child's mother is also employed.[173] The Court differentiated *Roca Álvarez* from *Hofmann* by focusing on the purpose of the national legislation in question. Noting that the Spanish law in *Roca Álvarez* had detached the period of leave from the biological fact of breastfeeding, since the leave could be taken by the mother or the father, and was accorded to workers in their capacity as parents rather than to protect the biological condition of women following pregnancy, the ECJ took the view that the imposition of an additional requirement on fathers in order to qualify for the nine-month period of leave would not be permissible under the Directive.

This attempted factual distinction between the earlier cases and *Roca Álvarez* is unconvincing, and there seems instead to have been a certain change in the approach of the Court as regards the role of law in perpetuating traditional gender roles within the family:

Case C–104/09 **Roca Álvarez**
[2010] ECR I–8661

36. However, to hold, as the Spanish Government submits, that only a mother whose status is that of an employed person is the holder of the right to qualify for the leave at issue in the main proceedings, whereas a father with the same status can only enjoy this right but not be the holder of it, is liable to perpetuate a traditional distribution of the roles of men and women by keeping men in a role subsidiary to that of women in relation to the exercise of their parental duties (see, to that effect, *Lommers*, paragraph 41).

While it was clear that the original Equal Treatment Directive permitted Member States to maintain protective provisions favouring women in relation to pregnancy and maternity, it was not clear for some years whether it also *prohibited* measures which discriminated against women on grounds of pregnancy. In a steady line of case law which followed, including *Dekker*[174] and *Hertz*,[175] the ECJ ruled that discrimination on grounds of pregnancy constitutes sex discrimination under the Equal Treatment Directive.

Subsequent cases addressed related questions concerning refusal of employment due to an illness arising from pregnancy, or because of a legislative prohibition on women performing certain work during pregnancy, or because of unavailability for essential work while absent during pregnancy. In *Hertz*,

---

[173] Case C–104/09 *Roca Álvarez* [2010] ECR I–8661, [28]–[31].
[174] Case C–177/88 *Dekker v Stichting Vormingscentrum voor Jong Volwassenen (VJV-Centrum) Plus* [1990] ECR I–3941.
[175] Case C–179/88 *Handels- og Kontorfuntionærernes Forbund i Danmark v Dansk Arbejdsgiverforening* [1990] ECR I–3979.

where a woman was dismissed on account of absence owing to sickness originating in pregnancy, the ECJ rejected the argument that the protection provided by the Directive against dismissal owing to illness caused by pregnancy was unlimited in time.[176] An illness manifesting itself after the maternity leave and not attributable to pregnancy or confinement is covered instead by the general rules applicable in the event of illness.[177]

In *Webb* the ECJ ruled that the dismissal of a woman who discovered, shortly after being employed on a contract of indefinite duration to replace another employee on maternity leave, that she herself was pregnant, would violate the Equal Treatment Directive,[178] and in *Tele Danmark* both the Equal Treatment Directive and the Pregnancy Directive 92/85 were held to prohibit the dismissal of a woman on grounds of pregnancy in the case of a fixed-term contract.[179] In *Busch*, the ECJ ruled that there was no obligation under the Directives on an employee who chose to return to work before the end of her parental leave to inform her employer that she was pregnant again, even though her aim in terminating parental leave and coming back to work was to become eligible for maternity benefit which was at a higher level than the parental leave benefit she received.[180] And in *Paquay* a decision to dismiss on the grounds of pregnancy or the birth of a child was held to violate the Equal Treatment Directive irrespective of the moment when the decision to dismiss was notified.[181]

The Equal Treatment Directive covers some situations that are not covered by the Pregnancy Directive such as that in *Mayr*.[182] Here the ECJ ruled that the dismissal of a female worker on sickness leave who was at an advanced stage of *in vitro* fertilization treatment would violate the Equal Treatment Directive, if the dismissal was essentially based on the fact that the women have undergone such treatment, and even if transfer of the fertilized ova into the women's uterus has not yet taken place, thus precluding application of the Pregnancy Directive. And in *Danosa*,[183] the removal of a member of a company's board of directors on account of pregnancy constituted direct discrimination on grounds of sex, even if the board member was not a 'pregnant worker' within the meaning of Directive 92/85. However, in *Z*, as we saw above,[184] and also in the case of *CD v ST*,[185] the refusal to grant maternity leave to a female worker who as a commissioning mother has had a baby through a surrogate, did not constitute sex discrimination under the Equal Treatment Directive. This was because, in the Court's view, a commissioning father who has a baby through a surrogacy arrangement is treated the same way as a comparable commissioning mother, and is not entitled to paid maternity leave either. Thus the Court has refused to treat having a child through surrogacy as being comparable to giving birth to a child, even if the commissioning mother is breastfeeding.[186] As in the case of adoption, the Court is leaving it to the states to decide what employment and other rights attach to the process of having a baby through surrogacy, subject to the rules on gender equality.

---

[176] Ibid.

[177] For other cases involving pregnancy-related illness or absence see Cases C–400/95 *Larsson v Dansk Handel & Services* [1997] ECR I–2757; C–191/03 *North Western Health Board v McKenna* [2005] ECR I–7631 on equal pay; C–394/96 *Brown v Rentokil Ltd* [1998] ECR I–4185.

[178] Case C–32/93 *Webb v EMO* [1994] ECR I–3567.

[179] Case C–109/00 *Tele Danmark A/S v HK* [2001] ECR I–6993; Case C–438/99 *Jiménez Melgar v Ayuntamiento de Los Barrios* [2001] ECR I–6915.

[180] Case C–320/01 *Busch v Klinikum Neustadt* [2003] ECR I–2041.

[181] Case C–460/06 *Paquay* [2007] ECR I–8511, [42].

[182] Case C–506/06 *Mayr* [2008] ECR I–1017.

[183] Case C–232/09 *Danosa* EU:C:2010:674.

[184] (Nn 131–132).

[185] Case C–363/12 *Z v A Government department* EU:C:2014:159, [52] and Case C–167/12 *CD v ST* EU:C:2014:169, [47]–[50].

[186] Case C–167/12 ibid, [40].

(iv) *Occupational Social Security*

Occupational social security is governed by Title II, Chapter 2, of the recast Equal Treatment Directive 2006/54. Occupational social security schemes are defined broadly as schemes (other than those covered by Directive 79/7), whether membership is optional or compulsory, the purpose of which is to provide workers or self-employed persons in an economic sector or undertaking with benefits intended to supplement or replace those provided by statutory social security schemes. Certain schemes are excluded by Article 8, such as individual contracts for self-employed workers, insurance contracts to which the employer is not a party, and individual options for additional benefits.

Article 6 sets out the personal scope of the Directive, covering the working population (including the self-employed) in terms similar to those of Article 2 of Directive 79/7, except that, in addition to covering those whose work is interrupted by illness, accident, or involuntary unemployment, and to retired and disabled workers or those seeking employment, it also covers interruption by maternity, and those claiming under them. Article 7 sets out the material scope of the Directive, and again the risks covered are almost exactly the same: sickness, invalidity, old age including early retirement, industrial accidents and occupational diseases, and unemployment. Article 7(1)(b) also provides that any other social benefits provided for in an occupational scheme, such as family or survivor's benefits, will fall within the scope of the Directive insofar as they constitute consideration for the worker by reason of the worker's employment. Article 5 sets out the principle of equal treatment in terms virtually identical to those of Article 4 of Directive 79/7, and Article 9 sets out a range of examples of provisions which contravene the principle of equal treatment by discriminating on the basis of sex, or marital or family status.

Article 10 provides for the implementation of the obligations of equal treatment in relation to occupational pension schemes as regards self-employed workers, and the three derogations provided for in Article 11 (concerning pensionable age, survivors' pensions, and actuarial calculations in defined-contribution schemes), which specify matters in relation to which Member States may defer the application of the principle of equal treatment, now apply only in relation to self-employed workers, since as far as employed workers are concerned it is clear since the *Barber* judgment that the equal pay principle applies.

One of the results of repealing the 1986 and 1996 Occupational Social Security Directives and incorporating their provisions into Directive 2006/54 is that this area is now governed by the general ('horizontal') provisions of the Directive, including the positive action provision in Article 3 and the extensive provisions on remedies, promotion of equal treatment, compliance, and dialogue in Title III.

(v) *The Distinction Between Conditions of Work, Pay, and Social Security*

As we have seen, Directive 2006/54[187] seeks to unify the legal principles governing equal pay, occupational social security, and equal treatment in other employment conditions. These three concepts are to be distinguished from state social security, which is governed by Directive 79/7. Social Security Directive 79/7,[188] as we shall see below, allows Member States to maintain certain exceptions to the principle of equal treatment, and permits a more gradual and progressive move towards equality than the legislation on pay and conditions of employment.

The complex relationship between equal treatment in working conditions, pay, and state social security is evident in a series of cases beginning with *Burton*.[189] The ECJ ruled that the maintenance of

---

[187] (N 147).

[188] Council Directive 79/7/EEC of 19 December 1978 on the progressive implementation of the principle of equal treatment for men and women in matters of social security [1979] OJ L6/24.

[189] Case 19/81 *Burton v British Railways Board* [1982] ECR 555.

different age conditions in access to voluntary redundancy was compatible with the Equal Treatment Directive, because the terms of the redundancy scheme had been tied by the employer to the national statutory retirement scheme. The national scheme, which maintained different pensionable ages for men and women, was covered by the exception in Social Security Directive 79/7, and the employer was permitted to arrange a redundancy scheme to correspond with this without breaching the Equal Treatment Directive.

In *Roberts*, however, where the complainant belonged to an occupational pension scheme providing for compulsory retirement with a pension at age 65 for men and 60 for women,[190] the Court decided the case on the basis of the Equal Treatment Directive, thus narrowing the scope of the exception in the Social Security Directive. The imposition of an age limit for compulsory redundancy was not about the terms on which an early pension was *granted* (ie not about social security), but about the terms of *dismissal* (ie about equal treatment). Since the compulsory retirement for reason of redundancy was classified by the ECJ as dismissal, rather than *voluntary* redundancy as in *Burton*, the receipt of a pension was a condition of dismissal within the scope of the Equal Treatment Directive.[191]

The narrowing of the social security exception continued in *Marshall I*.[192] In this case, the Court dealt with a compulsory *retirement* provision which mirrored the different statutory pensionable ages for men and women. The ECJ followed *Roberts* and treated the compulsory retirement as dismissal within the terms of the Equal Treatment Directive, rather than as a consequence of the different statutory pensionable ages falling within the exception in Directive 79/7. In *Hlozek*, the ECJ implicitly overruled *Burton* insofar as it stood as authority for the proposition that benefits paid after termination of the employment relationship, such as voluntary redundancy, do not constitute pay.[193]

The distinction between conditions of work under the Equal Treatment Directive and social security under Directive 79/7 arose also in *Jackson and Cresswell*, where the ECJ held that a scheme of benefits would not be excluded from the scope of the Equal Treatment Directive solely because it was formally part of a national social security system.[194] However, the subject matter of any scheme falling within the Equal Treatment Directive must concern access to employment,[195] access to promotions, vocational training, or conditions of work. An income-support scheme, the purpose of which was to supplement the income of those with inadequate means of subsistence, would not be brought within the scope of the Directive solely by virtue of the fact that the method for calculating eligibility could affect a single mother's ability to take up vocational training or employment.[196]

In *Meyers*, however, family credit, which was an income-related benefit awarded under UK social security legislation, fell within the scope of the Equal Treatment Directive.[197] This was because one of the conditions for its award was that the claimant should be engaged in remunerative work, and because its function was to encourage unemployed workers to accept low-paid work and to keep poorly paid workers in employment, thus concerning access to employment. Since the benefit was 'necessarily linked to a contract of employment' it did not matter that it was not a condition set out in the contract of

---

[190] Case 151/84 *Roberts v Tate & Lyle Industries* [1986] ECR 703; Case 262/84 *Beets-Proper v Van Lanschot Bankiers* [1986] ECR 773.

[191] See also Case C–207/04 *Vergani v Agenzia delle Entrate* [2005] ECR I–7453, concerning tax benefits on the taking of voluntary redundancy, which was held to violate the Equal Treatment Dir and was not saved by Dir 79/7.

[192] Case 152/84 *Marshall v Southampton and South-West Hampshire Area Health Authority (Teaching)* [1986] ECR 723.

[193] Case C–19/02 *Hlozek v Roche Austria Gesellschaft* [2004] ECR I–11491, [36]–[40].

[194] Cases C–63–64/91 *Jackson v Chief Adjudication Officer* [1992] ECR I–4737, [27].

[195] See, eg, Case C–100/95 *Kording v Senator für Finanzen* [1997] ECR I–5289.

[196] Cases C–63–64/91 *Jackson* (n 194) [29]–[30].

[197] Case C–116/94 *Meyers v Adjudication Officer* [1995] ECR I–2131, [19]–[22].

employment, nor that entitlement to the benefit would not be affected by loss of employment or a salary increase for a certain period.[198]

In sum, the disparities between the EU legal regimes governing pay and conditions of work (Directive 2006/54) and social security (Directive 79/7), and the fact that matters of social assistance are left to the Member States, mean that the categorizations within EU sex-discrimination law have regularly given rise to complex litigation.

(B) THE SOCIAL SECURITY DIRECTIVE 79/7

Directive 79/7 was adopted on the basis of the residual powers clause of Article 352 TFEU (ex Article 308 EC) and its purpose was said to be the 'progressive implementation' of the principle of equal treatment for men and women in the field of social security.[199] Unlike with equal pay and equal treatment, Directive 79/7 provided for significant exceptions to the equal treatment principle, and allowed Member States a considerably longer period of time to adapt their laws to its requirements.

Article 2 establishes the personal scope of the Directive, setting out two broad categories of people to which it applies. First, it covers the 'working population', which is subdivided into three categories: (i) those who are employed or self-employed; (ii) those under (i) whose work is interrupted by illness, accident, or involuntary unemployment; and (iii) those who are seeking employment. Secondly, it covers employees and the self-employed who are retired or invalided out. Thus, in keeping with the Equal Pay and Equal Treatment Directives, Directive 79/7 covers only *employment-related* social security.

Directive 79/7 is strictly employment-related, in that it does not cover someone who has never worked. In *Achterberg-te Riele*, the Court also ruled that people who give up work for a reason other than one of the five listed in the Directive, for example to look after children, fall outside its scope. The benefits referred to in Article 3, such as old-age pensions and invalidity allowances, fall within the scope of the Directive only when they are claimed by someone who is within one of the categories of person in Article 2.[200]

These conditions were tightened further in *Johnson I*, where the Court ruled that in order for someone to be covered by the Directive not only must one of the risks listed in the Directive have materialized, but the person in question must have either given up employment or been obliged to give up seeking employment *at the time of materialization of the risk*.[201] This interpretation excludes someone who cannot *seek* employment on account of a disability or illness he or she has suffered.

Once the conditions of the Directive are satisfied by the person seeking a benefit, however, the right to rely on the Directive is not confined to individuals falling within its personal scope, since 'other persons may have a direct interest in ensuring that the principle of non-discrimination is respected as regards persons who are protected'.[202] Thus the claimant's husband who had suffered the effects of discriminatory legislation concerning his spouse could invoke the provisions of the Directive if his spouse came within its personal scope.[203]

Article 3, which sets out the material scope of the Directive, indicates that it does not cover all forms of employment-related social security, but only those statutory schemes which provide protection

---

[198] Ibid [23]. Contrast the opinion of AG Jacobs in Cases C–245 and 312/94 *Hoever and Zachow v Land Nordrhein Westfalen* [1996] ECR I–4895.

[199] Council Directive 79/7/EEC of 19 December 1978 on the progressive implementation of the principle of equal treatment for men and women in matters of social security [1979] OJ L6/24, Art 1.

[200] Cases 48, 106 and 107/88 *Achterberg-te Riele v Sociale Versekeringsbank, Amsterdam* [1989] ECR 1963, [12].

[201] Case C–31/90 *Johnson v Chief Adjudication Officer* [1991] ECR I–3723, [18]–[23].

[202] Cases C–87–89/90 *Verholen v Sociale Versekeringsbank* [1991] ECR I–3757, [22].

[203] See also Case C–200/91 *Coloroll* (n 48) [19], on occupational social security.

against five specified risks, as well as social assistance intended to supplement or replace those statutory schemes. The five categories of risk are sickness, invalidity, old age, accidents at work and occupational diseases, and finally unemployment. Article 3(2) specifies that the Directive will not apply to provisions concerning survivor's benefits or family benefits, except family benefits due in respect of one of the five listed risks. Article 3(3) indicates that occupational social security is not covered.

Although the ECJ initially read Article 3 quite broadly, its scope was later narrowed. In *Drake* the Court found an invalid care allowance to be a benefit falling within the scope of the Directive because it was indirectly of benefit to the disabled person who would receive the care.[204] Later cases however require the link between one of the risks listed and the benefit paid to be strong if the benefit is to fall within the scope of the Directive. In *Smithson* the Court considered that a housing benefit was outside the scope of the Directive even though the criteria for calculating the benefit included two of the listed risks, namely age and invalidity. This was because the link between these criteria and the purpose of the benefit, which was to provide for those whose income was inadequate to cover housing costs, was insufficiently strong to conclude that the housing benefit was intended to protect against the risks of old age or invalidity. The case underlines a distinction between social assistance, including such housing benefit, and social security, and adopts a strict approach to the definition of the latter for the purposes of Directive 79/7.

In *Jackson and Cresswell*, the benefits deriving from a supplementary allowance or income support were not 'directly and effectively' linked to protection against the risk of unemployment.[205] The Court pointed out that the national income-support scheme exempted the applicants from the obligation to be available for work, and the amount of the benefit was set without any consideration of the risks listed in Article 3(1) of the Directive.[206] The Court emphasized the need which the scheme was 'designed' to meet, rather than its 'effect' in meeting one of the risks listed in the Directive. Such an intention-oriented approach, however, risks encouraging Member States to structure their social security and assistance schemes so as to avoid the application of the equal treatment principle to many benefits which provide protection against one or more of the risks set out in the Directive.[207]

In *Hoever and Zachow*, a child-raising allowance intended to secure the maintenance of the family while children were being raised was held to fall outside the material scope of the Directive.[208] Although one effect of the benefit was to help keep people in employment, the ECJ ruled that the intended aim was not to provide direct and effective protection against one of the risks listed in the Directive, and noted that Article 3(2) largely excludes family benefits from its scope. However, although certain benefits, such as survivor's benefits, may be excluded from the Directive's scope, if a benefit such as invalidity benefit which *did* fall within its scope were to be withdrawn on one becoming entitled to a survivor's benefit, this situation would be governed by the Directive.[209]

In *Richardson*, the ECJ ruled that UK national health regulations, which exempted those who qualify for an old-age pension from prescription charges, came within the scope of Directive 79/7, since they were part of a statutory scheme affording direct and effective protection against the risk of sickness, even though they did not strictly form part of national social security rules.[210] Similarly in *Taylor*, a

---

204 Cases 48, 106 and 107/88 *Achterberg-te Riele* (n 200).

205 Cases C–63–64/91 *Jackson* (n 194).

206 Ibid [20]–[21].

207 J Sohrab, 'Women and Social Security Law: The Limits of EEC Equality Law' [1994] JSWFL 5.

208 Cases C–245 and 312/94 *Hoever and Zachow* (n 198). Compare Case C–116/94 *Meyers* (n 197 and text), in which family credit was held to fall within the scope of Dir 76/207 concerning access to employment, since one of its effects was to help keep people in employment. The CJEU did not address Dir 76/207 in its ruling in *Hoever and Zachow*.

209 Case C–338/91 *Steenhorst-Neerings v Bestuur van de Bedrijfsvereniging voor Detailhandel, Ambachten en Huisvrouwen* [1993] ECR I–5475.

210 Case C–137/94 *R v Secretary of State for Health, ex p Richardson* [1995] ECR I–3407.

winter-fuel payment was held to be directly linked to protection against the risk of old age.[211] These cases contrast with *Atkins*, where the ECJ found that a system of concessionary fares on public transport for those who had reached pensionable age fell outside the material scope of the Directive.[212] This was because the purpose or aim of the benefit was to facilitate access to public transport for certain classes of person needing such transport who were less well off financially and, as in *Smithson*, old age and invalidity were merely two of the criteria which could be applied to define the classes of beneficiaries for the concessionary scheme. The ECJ rejected the Commission's argument that Directive 79/7 could extend to measures of 'social protection' of this kind, going beyond the scope of social security proper, so long as they were granted to persons affected by one of the risks listed in the Directive.

The basic principle of equal treatment set out in Article 4(1) provides that there is to be no direct or indirect discrimination on ground of sex, by reference in particular to marital or family status.[213] In *X*, following on from the *Test-Achats* case decided under Directive 2006/54,[214] the Court ruled that Article 4(1) prohibited the use of actuarial evidence based on the different life expectancies of men and women to calculate a social security benefit payable due to an accident at work, which would result in a lower lump-sum payment to similarly situated men than women.[215]

Provisions concerning the protection of women on grounds of maternity are specifically exempted.[216] The Member States are required, as in the other equality directives, to take the necessary measures to ensure that any provisions in breach of the equal treatment principle are abolished, and provide an adequate remedy for those aggrieved.[217]

The permissible exceptions to the scope of the Directive are set out in Article 7(1). Five specific matters are listed which the Member States may choose to exclude from the application of the Directive. The first, which was mentioned above in relation to *Marshall* and *Roberts* on the Equal Treatment Directive, relates to the 'determination of pensionable age for the purposes of granting old-age and retirement pensions and the possible consequences thereof for other benefits'.[218] This has been the subject of much litigation. The second exception concerns advantages in respect of old-age pension schemes for persons who have brought up children and the acquisition of benefit entitlements following periods of interruption of employment due to the bringing up of children. The third concerns the granting of old-age or invalidity benefit entitlements 'by virtue of the derived entitlements of a wife', the fourth the granting of increases in long-term invalidity, old-age, accidents-at-work, and occupational-disease benefits for a dependent wife, and the fifth the consequences of the exercise of a right of option not to acquire rights or incur obligations under a statutory scheme.[219]

However, the justification for maintaining such exceptions must be regularly reviewed. Article 7(2) requires Member States to examine periodically any areas they have excluded, to see whether the justification for exclusion has altered in the light of social developments. Member States must communicate to the Commission the provisions adopted pursuant to Article 7(2) and inform it of their reasons for maintaining existing provisions under Article 7(1), as well as the possibilities for future review of such derogations.

---

[211] Case C–382/98 *R v Secretary of State for Social Security, ex p Taylor* [1999] ECR I–8955.

[212] Case C–228/94 *Atkins v Wrekin District Council and Department of Transport* [1996] ECR I–3633.

[213] For a case on indirect sex discrimination under Dir 79/7 due to the higher contributions required of part-time workers towards a retirement pension, see Case C–385/11 *Elbal Moreno v INSS* EU:C:2012:746. For a different kind of indirect discrimination, see Case C–123/10 *Brachner* [2011] ECR I–10003.

[214] (N 80).

[215] Case C–318/13 *X* EU:C:2014:2133.

[216] Dir 79/7 (n 199) Art 4(2).

[217] Ibid Arts 5 and 6.

[218] Ibid Art 7(1)(a).

[219] Ibid Art 7(1)(b)–(e).

The direct effect of the equal treatment principle in Article 4(1) was confirmed in *FNV*.[220] The prohibition in Article 4(1) was held to be sufficiently precise to be relied upon in a national court, and the exclusion of certain areas in Article 7 did not affect the unconditionality of this prohibition.[221]

(c) THE PREGNANCY DIRECTIVE 92/85

In a move away from the treatment of pregnancy as purely an issue of sex equality, Directive 92/85 was expressly based on Article 138 EC (now Article 153 TFEU) concerning health and safety at work.[222] The Directive was adopted after considerable negotiation and compromise, which included, at the UK's insistence, the setting of the minimum level of pay for workers on maternity leave at the level of sick pay, despite arguments against drawing parallels between sickness and pregnancy.

The Directive introduced a requirement of minimum protection by the Member States for three categories of female workers: pregnant workers, workers who have recently given birth, and workers who are breastfeeding. The Directive is not a 'maximum harmonization' measure, but sets a common floor for Member States, including a non-regression clause which states that the Directive cannot be used to justify any reduction in higher levels of protection already existing.

The Commission is required to draw up guidelines on substances and processes which are considered hazardous or stressful to those three categories of workers. It requires employers to assess the extent to which such women are exposed to specified risks and, under Article 5, to take appropriate action such as adjusting their working hours or conditions, moving them to another job, or granting leave. Article 7 provides that such women cannot be obliged to perform night-work for a period to be set by national law, and the option of day-work or extended maternity leave must be possible. Article 6 provides that pregnant or breastfeeding workers cannot be required to carry out duties involving the risk of exposure to specified substances, and Article 9 stipulates that pregnant workers must be entitled, where necessary, to time off work without loss of pay to attend antenatal examinations.

The core provision on maternity leave is contained in Article 8, which specifies that the three categories of workers shall be given a minimum of fourteen continuous weeks' maternity leave before and/or after confinement,[223] including at least two weeks of compulsory maternity leave.[224] This is bolstered by Article 10, which requires Member States to prohibit the dismissal of such workers during the period of maternity leave, other than in exceptional cases unconnected with pregnancy.[225] The Pregnancy Directive however does not cover the situation of refusal to employ a woman on grounds of pregnancy, and in such a situation the prohibition of discrimination under the Equal Treatment

---

[220] Case 71/85 *Netherlands v FNV* [1986] ECR 3855.

[221] ibid [18]–[21]. The Court has also ruled that Art 4(1) prevents states from extending the discriminatory effects of an old benefit to the criteria for eligibility for a new benefit, under legislation passed after the Dir had been implemented: Cases 384/85 *Borrie Clark v Chief Adjudication Officer* [1987] ECR 2865; 80/87 *Dik v College van Burgemeester en Wethouders* [1988] ECR 1601.

[222] Council Directive 92/85/EEC of 19 October 1992 on the introduction of measures to encourage improvements in the safety and health at work of pregnant workers and workers who have recently given birth or are breastfeeding [1992] OJ L348/1. For a critical analysis of the Dir see V Cromack, 'The EC Pregnancy Directive: Principle or Pragmatism?' [1993] JSWFL 261.

[223] In 2010 the Council rejected a legislative proposal by the Commission to extend the period of paid maternity leave from fourteen to eighteen weeks as being excessively costly and raising subsidiarity concerns: COM(2008) 637. Parliament had proposed an extension to twenty weeks.

[224] In Case C–507/12 *Jesse Saint Prix* EU:C:2014:2007 the CJEU made reference to the duration of the period of maternity leave provided under Art 8 of the Pregnancy Dir in order to determine whether the period of time after birth before which a migrant working woman (who voluntarily gave up her job due to imminent childbirth) returned to the workplace is reasonable, for the purposes of her retaining the status of worker under Art 45.

[225] For an interpretation of the requirement of Member State consent in exceptional cases under Art 10(1) see Case C–438/99 *Melgar* (n 179).

Directive is crucial.[226] In *Boyle*, it was held not to be contrary to Article 8 of the Pregnancy Directive for an employer to specify when the obligatory fourteen-week period of maternity leave should commence, even if the employee was on sick leave at the time of giving birth.[227] In *Z and CD v ST*, the CJEU refused to bring the situation of a commissioning mother having a child through surrogacy within the scope of the Pregnancy Directive, and hence rejected the claim that a commissioning mother would be entitled to paid maternity leave, even if she were breastfeeding, since she had never been pregnant.[228] The Court in these cases asserted that the primary aim of the Directive is to protect the *biological* condition of women during and after pregnancy, and the special relationship between mother and child which follows pregnancy and childbirth. This emphasis on biology over maternity as far as the Pregnancy Directive is concerned was evident also in *Betriu Montull*, in which a father sought to take some of the non-compulsory portion of the period of maternity leave under domestic legislation. The fact that he could not do so under national law did not violate either the Pregnancy Directive or the Equal Treatment Directive.[229]

Article 12 covers the requirement of access to a judicial remedy. Under Article 11, the right to maintenance of payment and other employment rights must be protected in the case of those workers who are on leave in the circumstances specified in Articles 5, 6, and 7. The same is not required in the case of workers who are on maternity leave as provided in Article 8.[230] Instead, Article 11 specifies that they must be entitled to an 'adequate allowance' of not less than the amount of statutory sick pay.[231] It should be noted that the 'special concept of pay' under the Pregnancy Directive is not the same as the concept of pay for the purposes of Article 157 TFEU.[232] The fact that the opportunity was not taken, when the recast Directive 2006/54 was adopted, to align the principles governing pay under Article 157 and under the Pregnancy Directive has been criticized.[233]

Eligibility for the allowance under the Pregnancy Directive can be subjected by national legislation to conditions, other than a condition which requires previous employment of more than twelve months prior to confinement.[234] In *Boyle*, the ECJ ruled that a contractual term under which a higher level of pay than the statutory maternity payment was made conditional on the worker undertaking to

---

[226] For a critique see Cromack (n 222).

[227] Case C–411/96 *Boyle* (n 33). The employer could not, however, make the right to take sick leave during the period of maternity leave conditional on the employee first agreeing to return to work and terminate maternity leave, except in the case where the period of maternity leave in question was an additional period granted by the employer in excess of that required by statute.

[228] Cases C–363/12 *Z v A Government department* EU:C:2014:159 and C–167/12 *CD v ST* EU:C:2014:169.

[229] Case C–5/12 *Betriu Montull v INSS* EU:2013:571, [49]. The national law in question provided that the father of a child could not, even with the consent of the mother, take maternity leave following the compulsory period of maternal leave where the mother was not covered by a national social security scheme, although he could do so where the mother was covered by such a scheme. This did not violate either the Pregnancy or the Equal Treatment Dirs.

[230] In Case C–342/93 *Gillespie* (n 33), on facts which arose before the Dir was applicable, the CJEU ruled that the Treaty did not require a woman on maternity leave to continue to receive full pay, although the amount payable could not be so low as to undermine the purpose of maternity leave in protecting women before and after birth. See also Case C–66/96 *Berit Høj Pedersen v Fællesforeningen for Danmarks Brugsforeninge* [1998] ECR I–7327.

[231] See, however, Case C–194/08 *Gassmayr* [2010] ECR I–6281 in which, even though pregnant workers during maternity leave are entitled to pay which is equivalent to average earnings received during a reference period prior to the beginning of the leave, the employer was not required to include an on-call duty allowance in the calculation of average pay. See also Case C–471/08 *Parviainen* [2010] ECR I–6533 where the CJEU ruled that a pregnant worker who has been temporarily transferred to another job on account of pregnancy is not entitled to a supplementary allowance based on specific functions she no longer performs after the transfer.

[232] In Case C–333/97 *Lewen* (n 27), while a voluntary Christmas bonus given to employees constituted pay within Art 157 TFEU it did not fall within the special concept of pay under Art 11(2)(b) of the Pregnancy Dir in relation to maternity leave.

[233] Burrows and Robison (n 91).

[234] See Case C–65/84 *Roselle v INAMI* EU:C:2014:2473, pending before the CJEU.

return to work after the birth for at least one month was compatible with this provision and also with Article 157 TFEU.[235]

Thus the Pregnancy Directive guarantees only a minimum level of maternity pay, and does not provide a legal guarantee of any higher amount that the employer may choose to pay. Similarly in the case of the period of maternity leave granted: the employer is only required under Article 8 to grant fourteen weeks' leave, and if supplementary leave is also granted, there is nothing in the Pregnancy Directive or the Equal Treatment Directive to prevent the employer from limiting the entitlement to accrual of annual leave to the period of fourteen weeks. However, accrual of annual leave and accrual of occupation pension rights are firmly protected during the fourteen-week period, as basic rights of the employment contract,[236] by Article 11(2)(a).[237]

We shall see below how the 2006 Equal Treatment Directive and other EU equality legislation has been interpreted so as to supplement or complement the Pregnancy Directive in protecting women against suffering adverse consequences as a result of pregnancy and maternity leave. In *Woolwich*, the ECJ referred to its ruling in *Gillespie*[238] that a woman on maternity leave could not usefully rely on Article 157 TFEU to argue for the right to full pay since she was in a different and specially protected legal position, but stated that where a woman is still linked to her employer by a contract of employment or by an employment relationship during maternity leave she is, like any other worker, entitled under Article 157 to benefit from any pay rise awarded between the beginning of the period covered by reference pay and the end of maternity leave.[239] This was in part because, even though maternity pay is not the same as pay for the purposes of Article 157, it is nevertheless equivalent to a weekly payment calculated on the basis of the average pay received by the worker at the time when she was actually working. The thrust of much of this case law is also now reflected in Article 14 of the recast Directive 2006/54, which protects the rights of women returning from maternity leave.

McKenna raised the additional complication of a woman who was absent on pregnancy-related sick leave after the period of her maternity, and who sought to challenge the lower level of sick pay (which was equivalent to that provided for non-pregnancy-related illness) she received during this additional period of sick leave.[240] Here the ECJ ruled that this was not prohibited by Article 157 or the equal pay legislation.

In *Meroni Gómez*, the Court ruled that the Working Time Directive, read together with the Pregnancy Directive and the Equal Treatment Directive, required that a worker be allowed to take her annual leave during a period other than the period of her maternity leave, even if the period of annual leave of the entire workforce happened to coincide with when she was on maternity leave.[241] And in *Sarkatzis Herrero*, the ECJ ruled that, although the case was not covered by the Pregnancy Directive since it did not involve adverse treatment for a woman returning to an existing job from maternity leave, the Equal Treatment Directive was breached where a woman's maternity leave was not taken into account in calculating her seniority, where she had deferred taking up a new post in order to take maternity leave.[242] Finally, in *Mayer* the Occupational Social Security Directives (now replaced by Directive 2006/54)

---

[235] Case C–411/96 *Boyle* (n 33).

[236] Ibid [84]–[87].

[237] See also Case C–333/97 *Lewen* (n 27) [50], on the difference between periods of parenting leave and periods of leave required for the protection of mothers, in relation to the calculation of entitlement to an allowance; Case C–116/06 *Kiiski* [2007] ECR I–7643 on the right to obtain an alteration of the duration of the period of childcare leave at the time of claiming a right to maternity leave.

[238] Case C–342/93 *Gillespie* (n 33).

[239] Case C–147/02 *Woolwich* (n 33).

[240] Case C–191/03 *McKenna* (n 177).

[241] Case C–342/01 *María Paz Merino Gómez v Continental Industrias del Caucho SA* [2004] ECR I–2605.

[242] Case C–294/04 *Sarkatzis Herrero v Imsalud* [2006] ECR I–1513.

prohibited a woman who was on maternity leave from being denied a particular insurance benefit which was part of a supplementary occupational social security scheme, on the ground that she was not in receipt of taxable pay during her maternity leave.[243]

(D) DIRECTIVE 2004/113 ON ACCESS TO AND SUPPLY OF GOODS AND SERVICES

Apart from the broader move towards gender mainstreaming across all areas of EU law and policy, one of the first targeted pieces of 'hard law' on gender equality going beyond the labour market context was Directive 2004/113,[244] which aimed to combat sex discrimination in the access to and supply of goods and services.

The Directive was particularly intended to apply to the field of insurance, and it specifically excludes education and the content of media and advertising from its scope. These exclusions reflect a lively debate which took place when the measure was first proposed, including whether it should apply to ban sex-stereotyping in advertising. The Directive also does not apply to the fields of employment and self-employment.

As in the Article 19 anti-discrimination directives adopted in 2000,[245] the prohibition of discrimination as between women and men in Directive 2004/113 applies to both the public and private sectors. However, unlike the Race Directive in particular, Directive 2004/113 does not have any broader application beyond the fields of access to and supply of goods and services. Contrasting with the Race Directive but in keeping with the provisions of the TFEU on the free movement of services, the term 'services' in Directive 2004/113 refers to commercial services provided for payment. Article 3(1) indicates that the Directive applies to goods and services available to the public, irrespective of the individual situation of the consumer, 'which are offered outside the area of private and family life'. Article 3(2) provides that 'this Directive does not prejudice the individual's freedom to choose a contractual partner as long as an individual's choice of contractual partner is not based on that person's sex'.

The Goods and Services Directive has much in common with the consolidated Equal Treatment Directive 2006/54[246] and with the Article 19 directives adopted in 2000. Thus Article 4 prohibits direct and indirect sex discrimination, including harassment and sexual harassment, as well as adverse treatment on grounds of pregnancy or maternity, and the various directives contain the same definitions of these terms. There is a positive action provision like that contained in the Article 19 directives,[247] and there are also similar provisions on remedies, the burden of proof, compliance, the role of equality bodies, dialogue, non-regression, minimum harmonization, and the dissemination of information.[248] Interestingly, Article 4(5) of the Directive introduces the familiar concept of objective justification, but unlike most of the other legislation with the exception of age discrimination under Directive 2000/78, does not limit it to cases of indirect discrimination. Article 4(5) of Directive 2004/113 provides:

> This Directive shall not preclude differences in treatment, if the provision of the goods and services exclusively or primarily to members of one sex is justified by a legitimate aim and the means of achieving that aim are appropriate and necessary.

---

[243] Case C–356/03 *Mayer v Versorgungsanstalt des Bundes und der Länder* [2005] ECR I–295.
[244] Council Directive 2004/113/EC of 13 December 2004 implementing the principle of equal treatment between men and women in the access to and supply of goods and services [2004] OJ L373/37.
[245] (Nn 94, 111).
[246] (N 147).
[247] Ibid Art 6.
[248] Ibid Arts 8–15.

The examples given in the Preamble to the Directive include single-sex shelters, which can be justified on grounds of protection of victims of violence, and single-sex private clubs, on the grounds of freedom of association.

The Directive was intended in particular to apply to the insurance sector, and Article 5 prohibits the use of sex as a factor in the calculation of premiums and benefits for the purposes of insurance and related financial services in all new contracts concluded after 21 December 2007, insofar as that results in difference in individuals' premiums and benefits. Prior to 21 December 2007, Member States were to be allowed, on the basis of Article 5(2) and subject to review after five years, to permit 'proportionate differences in individual's premiums and benefits where sex is a determining factor in the assessment of the risk, based on relevant and accurate actuarial and statistical data'. The validity of Article 5(2) was successfully challenged in the case of *Test-Achats*[249] on the ground that it conflicted with the sex equality provisions in Articles 21 and 23 of the Charter of Fundamental Rights. The CJEU ruled that, while Member States may use appropriate transitional periods in their application of the principle of equal treatment to the insurance sector, EU law did not allow for the application of unequal treatment without temporal limit.

Case C–236/09 Association belge des Consommateurs Test-Achats v Conseil des ministres
3 March 2011

30. It is not disputed that the purpose of Directive 2004/113 in the insurance services sector is, as is reflected in Article 5(1) of that directive, the application of unisex rules on premiums and benefits. Recital 18 to Directive 2004/113 expressly states that, in order to guarantee equal treatment between men and women, the use of sex as an actuarial factor must not result in differences in premiums and benefits for insured individuals. Recital 19 to that directive describes the option granted to Member States not to apply the rule of unisex premiums and benefits as an option to permit 'exemptions'. Accordingly, Directive 2004/113 is based on the premise that, for the purposes of applying the principle of equal treatment for men and women, enshrined in Articles 21 and 23 of the Charter, the respective situations of men and women with regard to insurance premiums and benefits contracted by them are comparable.

31. Accordingly, there is a risk that EU law may permit the derogation from the equal treatment of men and women, provided for in Article 5(2) of Directive 2004/113, to persist indefinitely.

32. Such a provision, which enables the Member States in question to maintain without temporal limitation an exemption from the rule of unisex premiums and benefits, works against the achievement of the objective of equal treatment between men and women, which is the purpose of Directive 2004/113, and is incompatible with Articles 21 and 23 of the Charter.

33. That provision must therefore be considered to be invalid upon the expiry of an appropriate transitional period.

34. In the light of the above, the answer to the first question is that Article 5(2) of Directive 2004/113 is invalid with effect from 21 December 2012.

Reactions to the judgment have differed as to whether the striking down of Article 5(2) will actually benefit women, or will simply result in the imposition of higher insurance premiums in the name of equality.

---

[249] Case C–236/09 *Test-Achats* (n 80). For a similar question arising in the context of Dir 79/7, see Case C–318/13 *X* EU:C:2014:2133 (n 215).

(E) PARENTAL LEAVE

Following a number of unsuccessful attempts by the Commission to introduce legislation on parental leave, in 1996 a Framework Agreement on parental leave was concluded by the social partners, the main organizations representing confederations of European employers' and employees' representatives, and implemented by Council Directive 96/34.[250] This was replaced in 2009 by a new Framework Agreement which was implemented by Council Directive 2010/18 on parental leave, repealing Directive 96/34.[251]

The 2009 Framework Agreement grants male and female workers a minimum-level individual right to at least four months' parental leave on the grounds of the birth or adoption of a child in order to care for the child, until a given age up to 8 years to be specified by the Member State or the social partners. The right to parental leave is in principle to be granted on a non-transferable basis, but the specific conditions of access and the rules governing the leave are left to the Member States to define by law or by collective agreement.

The Framework Agreement sets out a number of permissible conditions on which Member States may decide, such as whether leave is to be granted on a full-time or part-time basis, whether it is to be subject to a period of work qualification, what notice periods may be required, in what circumstances employers may postpone the grant of leave, and the making of special arrangements for small undertakings.

Workers are to be protected against dismissal on grounds of applying for or taking the permitted parental leave,[252] and they shall have the right to return to the same or an equivalent or similar job at the end of the leave period, without any other of their acquired rights being affected by the leave.[253] Upon return, they shall also have the right to submit a request to change their working hours for a set period of time, which must be considered by the employer, taking into account his own needs and those of the employee. Member States and/or social partners are required to take the necessary measures to protect workers against less favourable treatment or dismissal on the grounds of applying for or taking parental leave. Moreover, the legislation requires the specific needs of parents of adopted children and children with a disability or long-term illness, or, according to the Court in *Chatzi*, the parents of twins,[254] to be taken into account. No provision is made in the Agreement regarding pay or any other allowance, and clause 2(5) specifies that all matters relating to social security are to be determined by the Member States in accordance with national law.[255] The Agreement also provides, in a less detailed clause, that Member States or the social partners shall take 'the necessary measures' to entitle workers to time off work 'on grounds of *force majeure* for urgent family reasons in cases of sickness or accident'.

The Framework Agreement introduces minimum-level rather than maximum-level rights, and contains the usual non-regression clause. The interpretation of provisions of the Agreement is assigned in the first instance to the signatory parties, without prejudice to the role of the Commission, national courts, and the ECJ.

In *Österreichischer Gewerkschaftsbund*, the ECJ ruled that the equal pay provisions of Article 157 TFEU were not violated where Austrian law took account of periods of civilian or military service,

---

[250] Council Directive 96/34/EC of 3 June 1996 on the framework agreement on parental leave concluded by UNICE, CEEP and the ETUC [1996] OJ L145/4, extended to the UK by Dir 97/75 [1998] OJ L10/24.

[251] Council Directive 2010/18/EU implementing the revised Framework Agreement on parental leave concluded by BUSINESSEUROPE, UEAPME, CEEP and ETUC and repealing Directive 96/34/EC [2010] OJ L68/13.

[252] Case C–116/08 *Meerts* [2009] ECR I–10063 on the dismissal of a worker before the end of parental leave without observing the statutory period of notice.

[253] Case C–486/08 *Zentralbetriebsrat der Landeskrankenhäuser Tirols v Land Tirol* [2010] ECR I–3527, [50]–[56] on Dir 96/34.

[254] Case C–149/10 *Chatzi* [2010] ECR I–8489.

[255] See, however, Case C–333/97 *Lewen* (n 27); Case C–537/07 *Gómez-Limón* [2009] ECR I–6525.

which were largely taken by men, but not periods of (nationally-granted) parental leave, which were overwhelmingly taken by women.[256] The Court distinguished maternity leave from parental leave, ruling that the latter was voluntary, and also distinguished it from military and civilian service, ruling that while parental leave served the individual interests of workers and their families, military and civilian service served the national interest.

As we saw above, Article 16 of Directive 2006/54 also now makes reference to the rights of those who have taken paternity (rather than parental) or adoption leave granted by national law to return to jobs and conditions which are equivalent and no less favourable than those they enjoyed before, and to benefit from any improvement in working conditions to which they would have been entitled during their absence. In *Reižneice*, the CJEU ruled that a set of assessment criteria and principles for the abolition of posts due to economic difficulties, which operated to the disadvantage of workers who had taken parental leave, constituted indirect discrimination against women under the Equal Treatment Directive where a much higher number of women than men take parental leave.[257] Conversely in *Leone*, the grant of a pension credit to employees who had taken a period of leave to care for a child, although neutrally phrased to apply to both men and women, constituted indirect sex discrimination against men since the large majority of those who took such leave (including compulsory maternity leave) were women.[258]

(F) DIRECTIVE 2010/41 ON THE SELF-EMPLOYED

The application of the principle of equal treatment between self-employed men and women was originally covered by Directive 86/613/EEC,[259] supplementing the provisions on equal treatment of employed persons in the original Equal Treatment Directive. In 2010 the Council adopted a new directive on self-employed persons, Directive 2010/41/EU, which repealed and replaced Directive 86/613.[260]

Directive 2010/41 was adopted under Article 157(3) TFEU. It supplements the provisions on self-employment activities in a number of existing legal instruments, in particular Directive 79/7 and Directive 2006/54, and does not apply to aspects already covered by those Directives. Article 2 sets out the personal scope of the Directive, providing that it applies to the self-employed as well as their spouses who are not employees or partners, but who participate in the same activities. Life partners recognized by national law who are in the same situation equally fall within the personal scope of the Directive.

Article 3 sets out the principle of equal treatment in a similar way to that in the other Equality and Social Security Directives.[261]

Articles 4–8 set out the 'material scope' of the scheme, which requires Member States to take action to eliminate sex discrimination in a range of matters, such as establishing a business or activity or forming a company.[262] In comparison with Directive 86/613, Directive 2010/41 notably improves the social and maternity protection of female self-employed workers and assisting spouses or life-partners. On the basis of Article 7, Member States must ensure that spouses and life-partners of self-employed

---

[256] Case C–220/02 *Österreichischer Gewerkschaftsbund, Gewerkschaft der Privatangestellten v Wirtschaftskammer Österreich* [2004] ECR I–5907.

[257] Case C–7/12 *Reižneice* EU:C:2013:410. The CJEU also ruled in favour of a female worker who was dismissed after being transferred to another post at the end of her parental leave, where that new post was about to be abolished for economic reasons.

[258] Case C–173/13 *Leone v Garde des Sceaux* EU:C:2014:2090.

[259] Council Dir 86/613/EEC [1986] OJ L359/56.

[260] Council D 2010/41/EU [2010] OJ L180/1.

[261] For a case discussing the concept of indirect discrimination under Dir 86/613 and Dir 76/207 see Case C–226/98 *Jørgensen v Foreningen af Speciallæger* [2000] ECR I–2447.

[262] See Case C–401/11 *Blanka Soukupová* EU:C:2013:658 (AG Jääskinen, fn 18), in which early retirement support for the self-employed was not covered by the scope of the Dir.

workers can benefit from a system of social protection on a mandatory or voluntary basis, provided that a system for social protection for self-employed workers exists under national law. Member States are also required to take the necessary measures to ensure that female self-employed workers and their spouses and life-partners may be granted, on a mandatory or voluntary basis, a 'sufficient' maternity allowance during pregnancy or motherhood for at least fourteen weeks. Article 8(3) stipulates that an allowance is considered to be 'sufficient' for the purpose of the Directive if it guarantees an income at least equivalent to the allowance which the person would receive in the case of illness, the average loss of income or profit in relation to a comparable preceding period, and/or any other family-related allowance established by national law.

7 THE GENERAL PRINCIPLE OF EQUAL TREATMENT AND NON-DISCRIMINATION

Apart from the various sub-regimes of equality law outlined above, the ECJ has increasingly relied on equal treatment as a *general principle* of EU law. As seen above, the principle of equal treatment between men and women is now protected as a fundamental right in Articles 21(1) and 23(1) of the Charter of Fundamental Rights.

Reflecting the origins of EU equality law, the Court first articulated a general principle of equal treatment and non-discrimination between men and women as part of EU law.[263] The Court ruled, originally in *Defrenne III*,[264] and subsequently in *P v S*[265] and *Schröder*,[266] that the elimination of sex discrimination was one of the fundamental personal human rights which had to be protected within EU law. However, at the time of *Defrenne III* in 1978, this principle was held not to be directly applicable against Member States, since the EU had not yet assumed competence in the area of equal treatment at work.[267] Indeed it remains the case, despite the frequent judicial rulings on the fundamental status of the principle of equal treatment on grounds of sex, that the principle may require further legislative implementation to be fully effective in challenging national law or employers' practice.[268]

In *Rinke*, the ECJ ruled that the principle of equal treatment of men and women was a condition for the lawfulness of EU action, so that any EU legislative measure which violated the principle would be illegal.[269] Although they were ultimately held to be justified on objective grounds, the Court found that the terms of two EU directives on the recognition of qualifications for general medical practice did indeed place women at a disadvantage as compared with men.[270] Further, other EU laws and measures must be read in the light of the principle of equal treatment.[271]

---

[263] In Case 20/71 *Sabbatini* [1972] ECR 345; Case 21/74 *Airola* [1972] ECR 221; Cases 75 and 117/82 *Razzouk and Beydoun v Commission* [1984] ECR 1509, the Court held that the EU institutions were bound by the principle of non-discrimination on grounds of sex in the treatment of their staff. See also Case C–37/89 *Weiser* [1990] ECR I–2395, [13]–[14]; Case C–227/04 P *Lindorfer v Council* [2007] ECR I–6767, [51].

[264] Case 149/77 *Defrenne v Sabena* [1978] ECR 1365, [26]–[27].

[265] Case C–13/94 *P v S and Cornwall County Council* [1996] ECR I–2143, [19].

[266] Case C–50/96 *Schröder* (n 17) [56].

[267] Case 149/77 (n 264) [30].

[268] See also on the principle of equal treatment in relation to age Case C–144/04 *Mangold v Rüdiger Helm* [2005] ECR I–9981; Case C–555/07 *Kücükdeveci KG* EU:C:2010:365. On equal treatment in the protection of workers in the event of the insolvency of their employer see Case C–81/05 *Anacleto Cordero Alonso v Fogasa* [2006] ECR I–7569. On equal treatment in relation to unfairly dismissed workers see Case C–246/06 *Josefa Velasco Navarro v Fogasa* [2008] ECR I–105.

[269] Case C–25/02 *Rinke v Ärztekammer Hamburg* [2003] ECR I–8349.

[270] Ibid [32]–[35].

[271] Case C– 401/11 *Blanka Soukupová* EU:C:2013:223.

Following the expansion of EU non-discrimination law beyond gender equality after the Treaty of Amsterdam, the Court began to invoke the general principle of equal treatment outside the area of sex equality. In *P v S* the ECJ declared that the principle underlying Directive 76/207 on sex equality extended to the situation of an employee who was dismissed for undergoing gender reassignment surgery, and later cases reinforced the protection of EU law against transgender discrimination.[272] However, the Court in *Grant* would not extend the principle of equal treatment to the circumstances of sexual orientation discrimination prior to the enactment of Directive 2000/78.[273] More generally, the principle of equal treatment does not extend to situations outside the scope of EU law.[274]

Somewhat controversially, in *Mangold*[275] the ECJ declared and applied a general principle of non-discrimination on grounds of age as a general principle of EU law. Although the period for transposing the Framework Employment Directive into national law had not yet expired in the circumstances of *Mangold*, the ECJ ruled that the general principle of equal treatment in EU law precluded national law from permitting arbitrary discrimination on the basis of age.[276] Effectively, the ECJ invoked and enforced the principle of non-discrimination on the ground of age in a dispute between private parties at a point in time when the implementation period for Directive 2000/78 had not yet expired.

The *Mangold* ruling was controversial and triggered debate over the scope of the general principle of non-discrimination, and the extent to which national legislators are bound by such a principle when drafting employment legislation.[277] As we have seen in Chapter 9, the ruling gave rise to the *Honeywell* case before the German Federal Constitutional Court, questioning whether the ECJ had exceeded EU competence in *Mangold*.[278] The criticism focused on the ECJ's articulation of a general principle of age discrimination in *Mangold*, which seemed to undermine the carefully negotiated provisions of Directive 2000/78/EC,[279] to interfere with the political choices and compromises represented in Member States' social policy,[280] and to create a new EU social right.[281] In *Bartsch* and later cases, however the Court backtracked somewhat on the application of the principle of age discrimination before the expiry of the time limit for implementing the Directive,[282] although it has continued to assert a general principle of non-discrimination on grounds of age.

---

[272] Case C–13/94 *P v S* (n 265); Case C–117/01 *KB v NHS* [2004] ECR I–541, where the CJEU extended protection against discrimination on the basis of transsexuality. Case C–423/04 *Richards v Secretary of State for Work and Pensions* [2006] ECR I–3585.

[273] Case C–249/96 *Grant v South-West Trains* [1998] ECR I–621; Case C–125/99 P *D v Council* [2001] ECR I–4319. Compare later Case F–86/09 *W v Commission* (n 137).

[274] See, eg, Case C–5/12 *Montull v INSS* EU:C:2013:571 in which discrimination between biological and non-biological fathers in relation to the availability of paternity leave was outside the scope of EU law.

[275] Case C–144/04 *Mangold* (n 268) [75]. For a discussion of the approach of the CJEU to the direct effect of this Dir before the time limit had expired, see Ch 8.

[276] The facts and the relevant extract from the *Mangold* judgment are set out in Ch 7, Section 6(c)(i). See D Schiek, 'The CJEU Decision in *Mangold*: A Further Twist on Effects of Directives and Constitutional Relevance of Community Equality Legislation' (2006) 35 ILJ 332.

[277] A Eriksson, 'European Court of Justice: Broadening the Scope of European Non-Discrimination Law' (2009) 7 I-CON 731; M Schmidt, 'The Principle of Non-Discrimination in Respect of Age: Dimensions of the CJEU's *Mangold* Judgment' (2005) 7 German LJ 522.

[278] BVerfG, 2 BvR 2661/06, 6 July 2010.

[279] See, eg, A Masson and C Micheau, 'The *Werner Mangold* Case: An Example of Legal Militancy' (2007) 13 EPL 587; K Riesenhuber, Note (2007) 3 European Review of Contract Law 62.

[280] S Krebber, 'The Social Rights Approach of the European Court of Justice to Enforce European Employment Law' (2006) 27 Comparative Labour Law and Policy Journal 390, 391.

[281] I Eliasoph, 'Switch in Time for the European Community—*Lochner* Discourse and the Recalibration of Economic and Social Rights in Europe' (2007–2008) 14 CJEL 467.

[282] Case C–427/06 *Bartsch* [2008] ECR I–7245; also Case C–147/08 *Römer* EU:C:2011:286.

While later cases sought to rely on this new general principle of non-discrimination on grounds of age, the ECJ focused mainly on the provisions of Directive 2000/78 concerning age discrimination.[283] In *Kücükdeveci*, however, the Court clearly affirmed the core of its ruling in *Mangold* and clarified several aspects of the judgment.[284] *Kücükdeveci* concerned a dispute regarding the appropriate period of notice under German law for the dismissal of an employee who had begun working at a company before the age of 25. Ms Kücükdeveci was employed by Swedex for a period of more than ten years, beginning when she was 18. She was dismissed with one month's notice, instead of the four months that was generally obligatory for the dismissal of employees following ten years of service. According to the relevant German law, periods of employment completed before the age of 25 were not to be taken into account when calculating the notice period in cases of dismissal. While the time limit for implementation of the Directive in this case had, unlike in *Mangold*, expired by the time of her dismissal, this was a dispute between private parties and a non-implemented directive would not normally be given 'horizontal' direct effect under EU law.[285] The ECJ was asked whether the German law was in conformity with EU law and whether the case should be assessed by reference to primary EU law or by reference to Directive 2000/78. Referring to *Mangold* and to the provision on non-discrimination in Article 21(1) of the Charter, the ECJ in *Kücükdeveci* ruled:

> 27. It follows that it is the general principle of European Union law prohibiting all discrimination on grounds of age, as given expression in Directive 2000/78, which must be the basis of the examination of whether European Union law precludes national legislation such as that at issue in the main proceedings.

A national provision such as that concerning the notice period of dismissal was precluded by the principle of non-discrimination on grounds of age, 'as given expression by Directive 2000/78'.

As we saw from Chapter 7, *Mangold* and *Kücükdeveci* effectively confirm the 'direct effect' of the general principle of equal treatment in disputes between private parties, at least in the context of EU legislation giving effect to the principle.[286] The Court in *Römer* further implied, although without saying so expressly, that the principle of non-discrimination on grounds of sexual orientation is a general principle of EU law, even though it retreated from the controversial element of *Mangold* by clarifying that the case would not fall within the scope of EU law until the time limit for implementation of the relevant directive in the case had expired.[287]

The general principle of equal treatment requires that 'comparable situations must not be treated differently and that different situations must not be treated in the same way unless such treatment is objectively justified'.[288] In *Maruko*, followed by similar rulings in *Römer*, *Dittrich*, and *Hay*, it was for the national court to determine whether a surviving spouse and a surviving registered life-partner were in a 'comparable situation' for the purposes of an entitlement to survivor's benefits, supplementary pensions, or other employment benefits under national law or collective agreements.[289] Once the national

---

283 Cases C–227/04 *Lindorfer* [2007] ECR I–6767; C–411/05 *Palacios de la Villa* [2007] ECR I–8531; C–267/06 *Maruko* (n 114); C–427/06 *Bartsch* [2008] ECR I–7245; C–388/07 *Age Concern England* [2009] ECR I–1569; C–88/08 *Hütter* [2009] ECR I–5325; C–499/08 *Andersen* [2010] ECR I–9343; C–45/09 *Rosenbladt* EU:C:2010:601; C–250 and 268/09 *Georgiev* EU:C:2009:549.

284 Case C–555/07 *Kücükdeveci* EU:C:2010:365.

285 Ch 7.

286 See also Case C–476/11 *HK Danmark* EU:C:2013:590 and Cases C–501–506, 540 and 541/12 *Specht* EU:C:2014:2005, [89].

287 Case C–147/08 *Römer* EU:C:2011:286, [59]–[63].

288 Case C–300/04 *Eman and Sevinger* [2006] ECR I–8055, [57]; Case C–227/04 *Lindorfer* (n 263) [63]. For a case alleging discrimination on the basis of marital status see Case C–485/08 P *Gualtieri* [2010] ECR I–3009, [70]–[76].

289 Case C–267/06 *Maruko* (n 114); also Cases F–86/09 *W v Commission* (n 137); C–147/08 *Römer v Freie und Hansestadt Hamburg* EU; C–124, 125 and 143/11 *Dittrich, Klinke and Müller* EU:C:2012:771 and C–267/12 *Hay v Crédit agricole mutuel de Charente-Maritime et des Deux-Sèvres* EU:C:2013:823.

court concluded that they were comparably situated, the exclusion of life-partners from eligibility for the benefits in question was deemed to constitute unlawful discrimination on the basis of sexual orientation under the Framework Employment Directive 2000/78.

The role of the Charter of Fundamental Rights in bolstering the principle of equal treatment in the EU is also evident in recent anti-discrimination cases. We saw in *Test-Achats* that Article 5(2) of Directive 2004/113/EC was ruled invalid on the basis of its conflict with Articles 21 and 23 of the Charter of Fundamental Rights.[290] In *Chatzi*[291] the ECJ ruled that, despite the failure to provide for this in the Parental Leave Directive, the national legislature was required in the light of the principle of equal treatment to establish a parental leave regime which would ensure that the particular needs of parents of twins are duly taken into account.

Case C–149/10 **Chatzi v Ipourgos Ikonomikon**
[2010] ECR I–8489

63. Observance of the principle of equal treatment, which is one of the general principles of European Union law and whose fundamental nature is affirmed in Article 20 of the Charter of Fundamental Rights, is all the more important in implementing the right to parental leave because this social right is itself recognised as fundamental by Article 33(2) of the Charter of Fundamental Rights.

EU equal treatment law has also drawn occasionally on the case law of the ECtHR, although in the field of anti-discrimination law it seems that EU law has influenced the development of ECHR law as much as vice versa. Cases such as *KB v NHS* and *P v S* show the ECJ following the lead of Strasbourg,[292] while cases such as *Stec, Goodwin, DH*, and *Schalk and Kopf* show the ECtHR drawing on EU law and jurisprudence.[293] Nevertheless, despite occasionally looking to one another for inspiration, the two bodies of European anti-discrimination law have developed along quite separate paths and remain different in several important respects.[294]

8 COMMON PROVISIONS AND CONCEPTS OF EU ANTI-DISCRIMINATION LAW

(A) DIRECT AND INDIRECT DISCRIMINATION

(1) *Direct Discrimination*

The recent anti-discrimination directives prohibit four types of discrimination: direct discrimination, indirect discrimination, harassment, and instruction to discriminate. The consolidated Gender Equality Directive 2006/54 also includes any less favourable treatment of a woman related to pregnancy and maternity within the definition of discrimination. The proposed new Equal Treatment Directive

---

[290] Case C–236/09 *Test-Achats* (n 80).

[291] Case C–149/10 *Chatzi* [2010] ECR I–8489; Case C–232/09 *Danosa* EU:C:2010:674, [71].

[292] Case C–117/01 *KB* (n 272) citing App No 28957/95 *Goodwin v United Kingdom*, 11 July 2002 and App No 25680/94 *I v United Kingdom*, 11 July 2002; Case C–13/94 *P v S* (n 265) citing App No 9532/81 *Rees v United Kingdom*, 17 Oct 1986.

[293] App Nos 65731/01 and 65900/01 *Stec v United Kingdom*, 12 Apr 2006; App No 57325/00 *DH and Others v Czech Republic*, 13 Nov 2007; App No 28957/95 *Goodwin* (n 292); App No 30141/04 *Schalk and Kopf v Austria*, 24 June 2006.

[294] See, eg, S Burri, 'Towards More Synergy in the Interpretation of the Prohibition on Sex Discrimination in European Law?' (2013) 9 Utrecht Law Review 80.

if adopted would also, following the provisions of the UN Convention on the Rights of Persons with Disabilities, include denial of reasonable accommodation for persons with disabilities within the definition of discrimination.[295]

Direct discrimination is the most overt form of discrimination and is defined in the same way by the Article 19 directives and by the Recast Gender Equality Directive 2006/54:

> [D]irect discrimination shall be taken to occur where one person is treated less favourably than another is, has been or would be treated in a comparable situation, on any of the [prohibited] grounds.[296]

A finding of direct discrimination is based upon an assessment of the victim's treatment with a (potential) comparator. It is premised on the notion that the complainant was treated in a different way from a similarly situated hypothetical comparator, and that the basis for the differential treatment was the prohibited ground of discrimination.

The ECJ has found direct age discrimination in many cases concerning dismissal or compulsory termination on reaching retirement age such as *Rosenbladt*,[297] *Georgiev*,[298] *Palacios de la Villa*,[299] *Age Concern England*,[300] and *Kleist*,[301] as well as provisions setting a maximum age for recruitment or permission to practise in certain sectors,[302] or introducing age-based criteria for the calculation of pension benefits or job advancement.[303]

With the possible exception of age discrimination, the available grounds of legal justification for direct discrimination are different from and rather narrower than for indirect discrimination.

(ii) *Indirect Discrimination*

Indirect discrimination is a concept which has been discussed in Chapters 19, 21, and 22 in the context of discriminatory restrictions on freedom of movement. Indirect discrimination is a familiar concept in many jurisdictions as a means of confronting and redressing systemic discrimination.

Where a rule or a practice, although apparently neutral, has the effect of disadvantaging a considerably higher percentage of persons sharing the protected characteristics (sex, racial or ethnic origin, sexual orientation, religion, disability, age), that rule or practice is deemed indirectly discriminatory. The concept was initially defined in the early ECJ case law and legislation on the burden of proof,[304] and later in the Article 19 anti-discrimination directives,[305] and the amended Sex Equality Directive in 2002,[306] but these definitions were not uniform. Now, the consolidating Gender Equality Directive 2006/54 has adopted the definition from the anti-discrimination directives and made it generally applicable,

---

[295] (N 143).

[296] Art 2(2)(a) of Dir 2000/78. Art 2 of Dir 2000/43, Dir 2006/54, and the proposed new Equal Treatment Dir contain virtually identical provisions.

[297] Case C–45/09 *Rosenbladt* (n 283).

[298] Cases C–250 and 268/09 *Georgiev* (n 283).

[299] Case C–411/05 *Palacios de la Villa* (n 283).

[300] Case C–388/07 *Age Concern England* (n 283).

[301] Case C–356/09 *Kleist* EU:C:2010:703.

[302] Case C–341/08 *Petersen* [2010] ECR I–47.

[303] Case C–529/13 *Felber v Bundesministerin für Unterricht, Kunst und Kultur* EU:C:2015:20; Case C–530/13 *Schmitzer v Bundesministerin für Inneres* EU:C:2014:2359; Case C–515/13 *Poul Landin v Tekniq* EU:C:2015:115.

[304] Dir 97/80, now repealed.

[305] (Nn 94, 111). See also the proposed Equal Treatment Dir, COM(2008) 426.

[306] Dir 2002/73, now repealed.

abandoning the more complicated definition incorporating reference to statistics which had been used in the Burden of Proof Directive.[307]

The early case law on indirect discrimination concerned the equal pay provision of the Treaty. After a hesitant start when the ECJ seemed to imply that indirect discrimination was not covered by Article 157 TFEU in the absence of further legislation,[308] the Court later ruled clearly that indirect discrimination was covered by the Treaty. In *Jenkins*, although the fact that part-time work was paid at a lower hourly rate than full-time work did not *per se* amount to discrimination, a presumption of discrimination in breach of the Treaty would arise 'if it is established that a considerably smaller percentage of women than of men perform the minimum number of weekly working hours required in order to be able to claim the full-time hourly rate of pay', and no other objective justification existed for the pay differential.[309] The employer's policy of encouraging a greater number of full-time workers was cited as a possible example of legitimate justification.[310] The ECJ ruled that the issue of objective justification was for the national court to weigh, with the onus being on the employer to demonstrate that it was based on something legitimate other than the sex of the worker.

Apart from discrimination against part-time workers, discrimination against those who have taken parental leave, as well as discrimination in favour of those who have taken leave to care for a child, has also been held to constitute indirect discrimination on the basis of sex.[311] On the other hand, discrimination on the basis of the date of recruitment from other employers has been held not to constitute indirect discrimination on the basis of age.[312]

Building on the early case law on equal pay, the two Article 19 directives, the 2006 Gender Equality Directive, and the proposed new Equal Treatment Directive all contain a virtually identical definition of indirect discrimination.

Article 2(1)(b) of Directive 2000/78 provides:

> [I]ndirect discrimination shall be taken to occur where an apparently neutral provision, criterion or practice would put persons having a particular religion or belief, a particular disability, a particular age, or a particular sexual orientation at a particular disadvantage compared with other persons, unless that provision, criterion or practice is objectively justified by a legitimate aim and the means of achieving that aim are appropriate and necessary.

The same definition, although adapted to the specific ground of discrimination covered by the Directives, can be found in Article 2 of both Directive 2000/43 and Directive 2006/54. The remaining Gender Equality Directives also prohibit indirect discrimination, and the ECJ has interpreted them in a similar way.[313]

---

[307] (N 109).

[308] See, eg, Case 149/77 *Defrenne* (n 264) [18]; Case 129/79 *Macarthys Ltd v Smith* [1980] ECR 1275, [14]–[15]; Case C–400/93 *Royal Copenhagen* (n 154) [29]–[38]; Case C–200/91 *Coloroll* (n 48) [103]–[104] on the difficulties of comparisons between employees who are and who are not within the same establishment, for the purposes of showing discrimination; and Case 157/86 *Murphy v Bord Telecom Eireann* [1988] ECR 673 on discrimination where a man was paid the same as a woman for doing work of lower value.

[309] Case 96/80 *Jenkins v Kingsgate (Clothing Productions) Ltd* [1981] ECR 911. AG Warner in the case noted that women constituted 90 per cent of part-time workers in the EU.

[310] Ibid [12].

[311] Case C–7/12 *Reižneice* EU:C:2013:410; Case C–173/13 *Leone v Garde des Sceaux* EU:C:2014:2090.

[312] Case C–132/11 *Tyrolean Airways Tiroler Luftfahrt* EU:C:2012:329.

[313] See, eg, in the context of Art 4(1) of the Social Security Dir 79/7, Case 30/85 *Teuling v Bedrijfsvereniging voor de Chemische Industrie* [1987] ECR 2497. For the interaction of the Framework Agreement on parental leave and the Equal Treatment Dir in prohibiting indirect discrimination against those who have taken parental leave, predominantly women, see Case C–7/12 *Reižneice* EU:C:2013:410.

(iii) *Harassment and Instruction to Discriminate*

Unlike the early equal pay and equal treatment legislation in the field of sex equality, the more recent anti-discrimination directives explicitly prohibit both harassment and any instruction to discriminate.

Harassment is defined in Article 2(3) of Directive 2000/43, Directive 2000/78, and in almost identical terms in Article 2(1)(c) of Directive 2006/54,[314] as:

> Unwanted conduct related to any of the grounds referred to in Article 1 [that] takes place with the purpose or effect of violating the dignity of a person and of creating an intimidating, hostile, degrading, humiliating or offensive environment. In this context, the concept of harassment may be defined in accordance with the national laws and practice of the Member States.

The Court in *Coleman* ruled that the prohibition of harassment is not limited to persons who are themselves disabled, but also covers harassment related to the disability of the child of a person who is not herself disabled.[315]

The prohibition of 'an instruction to discriminate' against any persons on any of the prohibited grounds of discrimination is not further defined in the directives and has not yet been clarified through litigation. All of the directives now also require states to introduce effective measures to prevent retaliation or the victimization of complainants.

(B) EXCEPTIONS AND JUSTIFICATIONS

(i) *Justification for Direct Discrimination: General*

Direct discrimination is more strictly regulated than indirect discrimination, and can be justified only on the basis of one of the limited grounds or exceptions contained in the Treaties or secondary legislation, rather than being capable of a more open-ended 'objective justification'.

One area of exception to this is the field of age discrimination, where Article 6(1) of Directive 2000/78 appears to permit open-ended objective justification for direct age discrimination.[316] The ECJ in *Age Concern England* addressed the question whether there was a difference between the test for objective justification of *indirect discrimination on all grounds* in Article 2(2)(b) and the test for objective justification of *direct age discrimination only* in Article 6(1).[317] Despite the argument of the UK for a single test in the interests of legal certainty, the ECJ, although without giving any detail as to

---

[314] Art 2(1)(d) of Dir 2006/54 also contains a more specific definition of *sexual* harassment as 'any form of unwanted verbal, non-verbal or physical conduct of a sexual nature occurs, with the purpose or effect of violating the dignity of a person, in particular when creating an intimidating, hostile, degrading, humiliating or offensive environment'; K Zippel, 'Gender Equality Politics in the Changing European Union: The European Union Anti-Discrimination Directive and Sexual Harassment', Harvard Center for European Studies Working Paper 134/2006, available at http://aei.pitt.edu/9027/1/Zippel134.pdf.

[315] (N 125).

[316] See also Art 4(5) of Dir 2004/113 on access to and supply of goods and services. Art 6(1) of Dir 2000/78 provides that 'Member States may provide that differences of treatment on grounds of age shall not constitute discrimination, if, within the context of national law, they are objectively and reasonably justified by a legitimate aim, including legitimate employment policy, labour market and vocational training objectives, and if the means of achieving that aim are appropriate and necessary'. Art 6(1)(a) goes on to specify some examples of discriminatory measures which could be justified. In Case C–447/09 *Prigge, Fromm, Lambach v Deutsche Lufthansa AG* EU:C:2011:573, the CJEU ruled that air traffic safety was *not* an objective covered by Art 6(1) of the Dir.

[317] Case C–388/07 *Age Concern England* (n 283).

the differences between them, indicated that the scope and function of Article 2(2)(b) and Article 6(1) are not identical:

Case C–388/07 R (Age Concern England) v Secretary of State for Business, Enterprise and Regulatory Reform
[2009] ECR I–1569

THE ECJ

65. [I]t is important to note that [Article 6] is addressed to the Member States and imposes on them, notwithstanding their broad discretion in matters of social policy, the burden of establishing to a high standard of proof the legitimacy of the aim pursued.

66. Although there is no need in this case to give a ruling on whether that standard of proof is higher than that applicable in the context of Article 2(2)(b) of Directive 2000/78, it must be stated that, if a provision, a criterion or a practice does not constitute discrimination within the meaning of the directive, by reason of an objective justification within the meaning of Article 2(2)(b) thereof, it is as a consequence not necessary to have recourse to Article 6(1) of the directive, which, as is clear from paragraph 62 of this judgment, is intended in particular to permit the justification of certain differences in treatment which, but for that provision, would constitute such discrimination.

The thrust of the ECJ's ruling is that the standard for justifying direct age discrimination under Article 6(1), and consequently the burden of proof, is high, since direct discrimination, unlike indirect discrimination under Article 2(2), is presumptively incompatible with EU law.[318]

Apart from this provision in Article 6 of Directive 2000/78 on age discrimination, the ECJ in some of its early equality case law had also seemed to contemplate the possibility of justifying direct sex discrimination in the field of pay. While the Court never unambiguously declared that *direct* pay discrimination could be 'objectively justified', nonetheless it considered in a number of cases whether men and women who appeared *prima facie* to be paid differently for performing work of equal value might actually have been 'differently situated', such that the unequal pay did not in fact amount to discrimination.

In *Birds Eye Walls*, the payment of different bridging pensions to men and women was held not to constitute discrimination since they were not similarly situated in relevant respects.[319] This was subsequently confirmed in *Hlozek*.[320] In *Abdoulaye*, the ECJ ruled that the situation of a male worker was not comparable to that of a female worker where the advantage granted specifically to the female was designed to offset the occupational disadvantages, inherent in maternity leave, which arise for female workers as a result of being away from work.[321] In *Griesmar*, the ECJ considered the argument that differential service credits for the calculation of retirement pensions for female and not male workers who had children did not constitute discrimination, since the positions of male and female workers were not comparable in this respect.[322] The ECJ however rejected the argument on the basis that their situations

---

[318] See also Case C–477/09 *Prigge* (n 316), for a stricter reading of the legitimate objectives which can be pleaded under Art 6(1).

[319] Case C–132/92 *Birds Eye* (n 83). The case also sat uneasily with the earlier ruling of the CJEU in Case 69/80 *Worringham* (n 76). For criticism see B Fitzpatrick, 'Equality in Occupational Pension Schemes' (1994) 23 ILJ 155.

[320] Case C–19/02 *Hlozek* (n 193).

[321] Case C–218/98 *Abdoulaye v Régie nationale des usines Renault SA* [1999] ECR I–5723, [18]–[20]; C McGlynn, Note (1999) 24 ELRev 202.

[322] Case C–366/99 *Griesmar* (n 53).

could indeed be comparable if the male worker had assumed the task of bringing up his children. *Griesmar* also drew attention to another possible basis for justifying apparently discriminatory pay practices, namely the 'positive action' provision which is discussed in further detail below.

(ii) *Justification for Direct Discrimination: Public Security, Public Order, and Public Health*

In *Johnston* the ECJ rejected the argument that Member States could invoke a general 'public safety' proviso which was applicable across the whole of the Treaty, similar to the specific derogations expressly provided in the context of free movement of persons, services, goods, and in serious military situations.[323]

However, Article 2(5) of the Framework Employment Directive 2000/78 introduced a form of derogation from the prohibition of discrimination for reasons related to the protection of public safety. Notably, however, and reflecting again the uneven nature and scope of EU legal protection against different forms of discrimination, neither the Race Directive 2000/43 nor the consolidated Gender Equality Directive contains any such derogation.

Article 2(5) of Directive 2000/78 provides:

> This Directive shall be without prejudice to measures laid down by national law which, in a democratic society, are necessary for public security, for the maintenance of public order and the prevention of criminal offences, for the protection of health and for the protection of the rights and freedoms of others.

The Court dealt with the derogation on grounds of public health in *Petersen*.[324] A dentist challenged a provision of German law, according to which admission to practise as a panel dentist in the statutory health insurance scheme expired when the dentist reached the age of 68. The dentists concerned were still permitted to practise outside the panel system, although 90 per cent of patients were covered by that scheme. The German Government argued that the difference in treatment was justified on the basis of: (i) the protection of the health of patients covered by the statutory health insurance scheme, given the perceived decline in performance of dentists after a certain age; (ii) the maintenance of the financial balance of the German health-care system; and (iii) the distribution of employment opportunities amongst the generations.

The Court assessed the first two objectives within the context of the public health exception of Article 2(5), and ruled that the measure could be compatible with Article 2(5) if it was intended to prevent a risk of serious harm to the financial balance of the social security system in order to achieve a high level of protection of health. If, on the other hand, the objective was the protection of the health of patients from the point of view of the competence of the dentists, the measure was not justified by this exception, since the means chosen were not necessary to obtain the objective pursued.[325] The Court also underlined the inconsistency of the measure, since the age limit applied only to dentists practising under the panel system, allowing dentists to practise outside that system at any age.

In *Prigge*, while the objective of air traffic safety was undoubtedly linked to public health and safety objectives, the CJEU ruled that a provision of a collective agreement prohibiting pilots from continuing to work as a pilot after the age of 60 was disproportionate to that public health or public safety objective.[326]

---

[323] Case 222/84 *Johnston v Chief Constable of the RUC* [1986] ECR 1651; also Case C–273/97 *Sirdar v Army Board* [1999] ECR I–7403; Case C–285/98 *Kreil v Bundesrepublik Deutschland* [2000] ECR I–69.
[324] Case C–341/08 *Petersen* (n 302).
[325] Ibid [52].
[326] Case C–447/09 *Prigge, Fromm, Lambach v Deutsche Lufthansa AG* EU:C:2011:573.

(iii) *Justification for Direct Discrimination: The Occupational Requirement Exception*

All of the main anti-discrimination directives provide for an occupational requirement exception. Article 4 of Directives 2000/43 and 2000/78 and Article 14(2) of Directive 2006/54 maintain the essence of the occupational qualification exception which was originally contained in the Sex Equality Directive 76/207. Article 4 of Directive 2000/78 provides:

> Member States may provide that a difference of treatment which is based on a characteristic related to any of the grounds [covered] shall not constitute discrimination where, by reason of the nature of the particular occupational activities concerned or of the context in which they are carried out, such a characteristic constitutes a genuine and determining occupational requirement, provided that its objective is legitimate and the requirement is proportionate.

The scope of this occupational requirement provision in the context of gender equality was considered some decades ago in the *Male Midwives* case.[327] The Court found that British legislation which limited access for men to the profession of midwife was in conformity with the occupational requirement exception in Directive 76/207, in view of the fact that 'personal sensitivities' could play an important role in the relationship between midwife and patient (though not, apparently, between gynaecologist and patient). However it seems several decades later that the profession of midwife is open to men across the EU, thus illustrating the evolutionary nature of the occupational qualification exception.[328]

The provision was also considered in *Johnston*, in which the Royal Ulster Constabulary (RUC) sought to justify its decision not to employ women as full-time members of the RUC Reserve.[329] The UK Government argued that if women were permitted to carry and use firearms they would be at greater risk of becoming targets for assassination. The Court accepted the UK's argument without requiring any evidence to support the implication that women could not be trained to use firearms just as safely and effectively as men.[330] Hence the sex of police officers could constitute a 'determining factor' for carrying out certain policing activities.[331] The assessment of the proportionality of the decision was left to the national court.[332]

Similar questions came before the Court in the cases of *Sirdar* and *Kreil*.[333] In *Sirdar*, a woman who was refused employment as a chef with the UK Royal Marines challenged their policy of excluding women from service on the ground that the presence of women was incompatible with the requirement of 'interoperability', ie 'the need for every Marine, irrespective of his specialisation, to be capable of fighting in a commando unit'. The ECJ ruled that this could be justified as an occupational requirement on the basis that the Marine Corps was an exceptional and small force intended to be in the first line of attack.

In *Kreil*, the applicant was challenging a more general prohibition under German law which barred women from military posts involving the use of arms, and allowed them access only to the medical and military-music services. Here the ECJ ruled that, since the occupational requirement derogation in

---

[327] Case 165/82 *Commission v United Kingdom* [1983] ECR 3431.

[328] For discussion see C Barnard, *EU Employment Law* (Oxford University Press, 4th edn, 2012) 365.

[329] Case 222/84 *Johnston* (n 323).

[330] Fredman (n 154) 128; G More, 'Equal Treatment of the Sexes: What does "Equal" Mean?' (1993) 1 Feminist Legal Studies 45, 52–53.

[331] See also Case 318/86 *Commission v France* [1988] ECR 3559, [27].

[332] Case 222/84 *Johnston* (n 323) [39].

[333] Case C–273/97 *Sirdar v Army Board* [1999] ECR I–7403; Case C–285/98 *Kreil v Bundesrepublik Deutschland* [2000] ECR I–69; P Koutrakos, Note (2000) 25 ELRev 433.

Article 2(2) of Directive 76/207 was intended to apply only to specific activities, the scope and breadth of this prohibition exceeded even the discretion given to Member States when adopting measures they consider necessary to guarantee public security.

The *Kreil* judgment was a high-profile one, not least because of the fact that the German Federal Constitution at the time barred women from service involving the use of arms.[334] The relevant constitutional provision was subsequently amended, to provide that women could not be forced to render armed service.

This in turn gave rise to the case of *Dory*, in which a German man challenged the fact that compulsory military service was applicable only to men and not to women. According to Dory, this constituted discrimination as between men and women as regards access to employment, since the need to complete compulsory military service delayed his entry onto the labour market and imposed a disadvantage on him as compared with a similarly situated woman. Rather than treating this case within the context of the occupational requirement exception, however, the ECJ accepted an argument made by the German Government which it had rejected in *Kreil* and earlier cases, namely that the rule in question fell outside the scope of application of EU law.

Case C–186/01 **Dory v Bundesrepublik Deutschland**
[2003] ECR I–2479

39. The decision of the Federal Republic of Germany to ensure its defence in part by compulsory military service is the expression of such a choice of military organisation to which Community law is consequently not applicable.

40. It is true that limitation of compulsory military service to men will generally entail a delay in the progress of the careers of those concerned, even if military service allows some of them to acquire further vocational training or subsequently to take up a military career.

41. Nevertheless, the delay in the careers of persons called up for military service is an inevitable consequence of the choice made by the Member State regarding military organisation and does not mean that that choice comes within the scope of Community law. The existence of adverse consequences for access to employment cannot, without encroaching on the competences of the Member States, have the effect of compelling the Member State in question either to extend the obligation of military service to women, thus imposing on them the same disadvantages with regard to access to employment, or to abolish compulsory military service.

While the reasoning in *Dory* could also have been applied to the 'choice of military organization' adopted by Germany in *Kreil*, the ECJ was presumably motivated in *Dory* by pragmatic concerns. If it had followed the logic of its previous judgments and held that compulsory military service for men only constituted sex discrimination, it would have left Germany with the choice of abolishing compulsory military service altogether, or extending compulsory service also to women. The first would clearly have been seen as a major encroachment by EU law into national military matters, whereas the second would involve taking a controversial option in social terms.[335]

In *Wolf* the ECJ addressed the nature of the occupational requirement provision within the context of the Framework Employment Directive 2000/78.[336] The applicant challenged a German provision setting a maximum age of 30 for the recruitment of officials to intermediate career posts in the professional

---

334 M Trybus, 'Sisters in Arms: EC Law and Sex Equality in the Armed Forces' (2003) 9 ELJ 631.

335 Ibid; M Trybus, Note (2003) 40 CMLRev 1269; G Anagnostaras, Note (2003) 28 ELRev 713.

336 Case C–229/08 *Wolf* [2010] ECR I–1.

fire service. Although the referring court presented the issue as one of the justifiability of direct age discrimination under Article 6(1) of the Directive, the ECJ instead focused on the occupational requirement provision in Article 4(1).[337] The Court emphasized that it is the characteristic related to a ground of discrimination, in this case physical fitness, rather than the ground itself, age, which must constitute a genuine and determining occupational requirement.[338]

The Court held that four familiar conditions must be met for a national measure which restricts or derogates from an EU right or freedom,[339] or which offers objective justification for indirect discrimination,[340] to be justified as an occupational requirement under Article 4(1). First, the objective pursued must be *legitimate*; secondly, the characteristic required must constitute a *genuine and determining* occupational requirement for carrying out the activities in question; thirdly, the characteristic must be *related* to age (or one of the other specified grounds of discrimination); and, fourthly, the national measure must be *necessary and proportionate*.[341] In *Wolf*, the ECJ accepted the statistical data provided by the German Government to show that the physical capacity required to perform fire-fighting activities is related to the age of a person, and it took the view that the four conditions would be satisfied by legislation of this kind.

In *Vital Perez*, by comparison, the Court ruled that while the possession of particular physical capacities could be regarded as a genuine and determining occupational requirement for the purposes of employment as a local police officer, the fixing of an age limit requiring the recruitment only of officers under 30 was disproportionate and therefore was not covered by Article 4(1).[342] Similarly in *Prigge*, while it was in principle a legitimate occupational requirement to require that airline pilots should possess certain physical characteristics (which vary with age), nevertheless in providing that the pilots' employment relationship terminates automatically on reaching age 60, when national and international legislation authorizes the carrying out of piloting activities, under certain conditions, until the age of 65, this provision of a collective agreement was disproportionate and not saved by Article 4(1).[343]

(iv) *Justification for Direct Discrimination: Objective Justification of Direct Age Discrimination*

As we have seen above, Directive 2000/78 contains a specific exception to the prohibition of discrimination on grounds of age in the field of employment. Article 6(1) provides:

> Notwithstanding Article 2(2), Member States may provide that differences of treatment on grounds of age shall not constitute discrimination, if, within the context of national law, they are objectively and reasonably justified by a legitimate aim, including legitimate employment policy, labour market and vocational training objectives, and if the means of achieving that aim are appropriate and necessary.
>
> Such differences of treatment may include, among others:
>
> (a) the setting of special conditions on access to employment and vocational training, employment and occupation, including dismissal and remuneration conditions, for young people, older workers and persons with caring responsibilities in order to promote their vocational integration or ensure their protection;

---

[337] Ibid [32]. On the discretion of the CJEU to reformulate questions referred under the preliminary reference mechanism and to provide a useful answer see Ch 13.

[338] Ibid [35].

[339] See Chs 19, 21, 22, and 23 on justifying restrictions to freedom of movement.

[340] Case C–170/84 *Bilka* (n 40).

[341] Ibid [36].

[342] Case C–416/13 *Mario Vital Pérez v Ayuntamiento de Oviedo* EU:C:2014:2371.

[343] Case C–447/09 *Prigge, Fromm, Lambach v Deutsche Lufthansa AG* EU:C:2011:573.

> (b) the fixing of minimum conditions of age, professional experience or seniority in service for access to employment or to certain advantages linked to employment;
>
> (c) the fixing of a maximum age for recruitment which is based on the training requirements of the post in question or the need for a reasonable period of employment before retirement.

This provision has by now been the subject of extensive litigation. In *Mangold*, the Court considered a provision of German law which authorized the conclusion, without objective reasons, of fixed-term employment contracts with workers aged 52 and above.[344] While the aim of the law, which was to promote the vocational integration of unemployed older workers who might face difficulties in finding work, was held to be a legitimate one within the meaning of Article 6(1), the ECJ ruled that, despite the broad discretion enjoyed by Member States in their choice of social and employment policy measures, the national measure went beyond what was necessary to attain that objective.

Many of the cases arising under Article 6(1) of Directive 2000/78 have concerned the justifiability of compulsory retirement at a certain age on a number of grounds.[345] In *Palacios de la Villa*,[346] an employee challenged the automatic termination of his employment contract upon his reaching the compulsory retirement age as provided for in a collective agreement. Having established that the measure constituted direct discrimination on grounds of age within the scope of Directive 2000/78, the ECJ considered whether it could be justified under Article 6(1), even though the national law in question did not expressly refer to an objective related to a legitimate national-policy, labour-market, or vocational-training objective:

Case C–411/05 Félix Palacios de la Villa v Cortefiel Servicios SA
[2007] ECR I–8531

THE ECJ

56. It cannot be inferred from Article 6(1) of Directive 2000/78 that the lack of precision in the national legislation at issue as regards the aim pursued automatically excludes the possibility that it may be justified under that provision.

...

62. Thus, placed in its context, the single transitional provision was aimed at regulating the national labour market, in particular, for the purposes of checking unemployment.

...

64. The legitimacy of such an aim of public interest cannot reasonably be called into question, since employment policy and labour market trends are among the objectives expressly laid down in the first subparagraph of Article 6(1) of Directive 2000/78 and, in accordance with the first indent of the first paragraph of Article 2 EU and Article 2 EC, the promotion of a high level of employment is one of the ends pursued both by the European Union and the European Community.

65. Furthermore, the Court has already held that encouragement of recruitment undoubtedly constitutes a legitimate aim of social policy (see, in particular, Case C–208/05 [2007] ECR I–181, paragraph

---

344 (N 275).

345 For discussion, see E Dewhurst, 'The Development of EU Case-Law on Age Discrimination in Employment: "Will You Still Need Me? Will You Still Feed Me? When I'm Sixty-Four"' (2013) 19 ELJ 517; D Schiek, 'Age Discrimination Before the CJEU—Conceptual and Theoretical Issues' (2011) 48 CMLRev 777.

346 Case C–411/05 *Palacios de la Villa* (n 283).

39) and that assessment must evidently apply to instruments of national employment policy designed to improve opportunities for entering the labour market for certain categories of workers.

66. Therefore, an objective such as that referred to by the legislation at issue must, in principle, be regarded as 'objectively and reasonably' justifying 'within the context of national law', as provided for by the first subparagraph of Article 6(1) of Directive 2000/78, a difference in treatment on grounds of age laid down by the Member States.

[*The promotion of a high level of employment and the encouragement of recruitment were thus accepted by the Court as legitimate policy objectives. With regard to the proportionality of the measure, the ECJ again emphasized the broad discretion enjoyed by the national authorities in this field and took the view that the measure was probably proportionate.*]

69. As is already clear from the wording, 'specific provisions which may vary in accordance with the situation in Member States', in recital 25 in the preamble to Directive 2000/78, such is the case as regards the choice which the national authorities concerned may be led to make on the basis of political, economic, social, demographic and/or budgetary considerations and having regard to the actual situation in the labour market in a particular Member State, to prolong people's working life or, conversely, to provide for early retirement.

. . .

72. It does not appear unreasonable for the authorities of a Member State to take the view that a measure such as that at issue in the main proceedings may be appropriate and necessary in order to achieve a legitimate aim in the context of national employment policy, consisting in the promotion of full employment by facilitating access to the labour market.

The broad discretion accorded to Member States in *Mangold* and *Palacios de la Villa* was qualified somewhat in *Age Concern England*, in which a British charitable organization challenged a provision of UK law permitting an employer to dismiss workers under the age of 65 when they reached the retirement age fixed by the employer, if such a measure constituted a proportionate means of achieving a legitimate aim.[347] The ECJ clarified that the legitimate policy objectives listed in Article 6(1) were illustrative rather than exhaustive, and ruled that the legitimate aim of a national measure could be inferred from its context if it was not made explicit.[348] However, the ECJ distinguished legitimate employment or social-policy aims of a public nature from 'purely individual reasons particular to the employer's situation such as cost reduction or improving competitiveness', even while acknowledging that there could at times be a close relationship between these.[349] 'Mere generalizations' would risk undermining the effectiveness of the Directive's prohibition against discrimination on grounds of age, and where direct age discrimination was concerned the standard of proof required of the Member States would be high.[350]

In *Petersen*, the German legislation which provided that admission to practise as a panel dentist in the statutory health insurance scheme expired on reaching the age of 68 was a proportionate means of achieving the legitimate aim of improving opportunities for young people entering this particular labour market category.[351] Similarly in *Georgiev*, a law providing for compulsory retirement of university professors who had reached the age of 68 and for fixed-term contracts only beyond the age of 65 was a proportionate means of pursuing the legitimate aim of encouraging recruitment to higher education by offering professorships to younger people.[352] In *Rosenbladt*, a scheme permitting automatic termination of employment contracts on reaching retirement age, which served the legitimate policy aim of

---

347 Case C–388/07 *Age Concern England* (n 283).
348 Ibid [43]–[45].
349 Ibid [46].
350 Ibid [51] and [65]. See also (n 317) and text.
351 Case C–341/08 *Petersen* (n 302).
352 Cases C–250 and 268/09 *Georgiev* (n 283).

promoting a better distribution of work between the generations, was proportionate where the scheme was flexible enough to allow for individual or collective agreements to be made between employers and employees permitting work beyond the retirement age.[353] Similar rulings were given by the Court in *Fuchs and Köhler*[354] and *Hörnfeldt*[355] although in *Dansk Jurist* the denial of availability pay to a civil servant who had been made redundant at 65, when he would have been entitled but not required to retire, was held to be a disproportionate way of pursuing a legitimate state objective.[356]

Perhaps the most famous of the age discrimination cases is that brought by the Commission against Hungary, in which the CJEU found the national scheme requiring the compulsory retirement of judges, prosecutors, and notaries on reaching 62, despite its ostensibly legitimate aim of establishing a more balanced age structure in these professions, to be disproportionate.[357] In fact the firing of judges and prosecutors was widely believed to be part of a political campaign by an authoritarian Hungarian Government to undermine the independence of the judiciary, and the infringement proceedings brought by the Commission was one of the few actions—in the absence of political action by the Council or the invocation of Article 7 TEU sanction mechanisms[358]—taken by the EU to challenge Hungary's increasingly repressive and illiberal policies.[359]

Apart from compulsory retirement, states have sought to justify many other forms of direct age discrimination before the Court and their purported justification appraised. In *Hütter*, the first of a series of such cases,[360] the ECJ held that while the objectives of promoting the integration into the labour market of young people who had pursued vocational education and not treating secondary education less favourably than vocational training were legitimate, national legislation which excluded periods of employment completed before the age of 18 from being taken into account for the purpose of determining the steps at which public servants would be graded was disproportionate to these aims.[361] Similarly in *Kücükdeveci*, discussed above,[362] while the objectives of the national legislation which precluded periods of employment completed before the age of 25 from being taken into account in calculating the notice period for dismissal were legitimate, the means used were neither appropriate nor necessary.[363]

In *Henning and Mai*,[364] and *Specht*,[365] the Court ruled that while the objective of taking into account and rewarding an employee's experience is a legitimate one for the purposes of Article 6(1), a criterion based on length of service would be a more appropriate and proportionate way of achieving this end that a criterion based on age.

The Court has also considered whether national rules which set a specific *minimum* recruitment age or *maximum* age for certain professions can be justified. In *Vital Pérez*, although the CJEU rejected the Spanish Government's claim that the setting of a maximum age for recruitment of local police officers was intended to promote balanced distribution amongst age groups, nevertheless it

---

[353] Case C–45/09 *Rosenbladt* (n 283).

[354] Cases C–159 and 160/10 *Fuchs and Köhler* EU:C:2011:508.

[355] Case C–141/11 *Hörnfeldt* EU:C:2012:421.

[356] Case C–546/11 *Dansk Jurist* EU:C:2013:603.

[357] Case C–286/12 *Commission v Hungary* EU:C:2012:687.

[358] See Ch 11 (nn 82, 63) and text.

[359] For comment see U Belavusau, 'On Age Discrimination and Beating Dead Dogs: *Commission v. Hungary*' (2013) 50 CMLRev 1145.

[360] Eg Case C–530/13 *Schmitzer v Bundesministerin für Inneres* EU:C:2014:2359; Case C–529/13 *Felber v Bundesministerin für Unterricht, Kunst und Kultur* EU:C:2015:20; Case C–515/13 *Poul Landin v Tekniq* EU:C:2015:115.

[361] Case C–88/08 *Hütter* (n 283).

[362] Case C–555/07 *Kücükdeveci* (n 284).

[363] Ibid.

[364] Cases C–297 and 298/10 *Henning and Mai* [2011] ECR I–7965.

[365] Case C–501/12 *Specht and others* EU:C:2014:2005.

ruled that an age requirement could be based on the training requirements of the post and the need for a reasonable period of employment before retirement or transfer.[366] Despite the legitimacy of these aims, however, there was no reasonable connection between the specific age requirement and those aims. Similarly, the imposition by a collective agreement of an age limit of 60 for the employment of pilots in *Prigge*, although adopted in pursuit of a legitimate public safety objective, was disproportionate.[367]

In *HK Danmark*, the Court ruled that the exception in Article 6(2) of the Directive for the setting by the state of an age for *admission* to occupational social security schemes, or for *entitlement to benefits* under such schemes, had to be read strictly, and would not cover age discrimination in the setting of the *amount of contributions* by an employer.[368] The discriminatory setting of the amount of contributions according to age might, however, be justified under Article 6(1), if the national court found it to be a proportionate way of ensuring that a larger proportion of those contributions is set aside to cover the risks of death, incapacity, and serious illness, the occurrence of which is statistically more likely for older workers. Similarly in *Odar*, the age-based criteria used under an occupational pension scheme for calculating compensation for workers who had been made redundant was not justified under Article 2(2), but might be justified under Article 6(1) as a proportionate means of achieving a fair distribution of limited financial resources within a social plan.[369] However, on the facts of the case the scheme in question amounted to unjustified discrimination on grounds of disability.[370]

(v) *Justification for Indirect Discrimination: Objective Justification*

The broadening of the formal criterion of direct discrimination to include less obvious but sometimes more pervasive forms of indirect discrimination was an important development. However, the parallel development of an equally broad concept of objective justification reduced the impact of this expansion. As we have seen above, the definition of indirect discrimination in the Article 19 directives as well as in Directive 2006/54, Article 2(1)(b), now integrates the notion of the absence of 'objective justification' into the definition itself.

Exactly what can constitute objective justification remains unclear. The ECJ often leaves the matter for the national court to decide, raising the likelihood of differences amongst the various Member States' tribunals as to whether an indirectly discriminatory policy is justified. The Court however has given some guidance, by declaring certain grounds of justification to be too general and indicating that others may be sufficient. The bulk of these cases arose in the field of sex equality, beginning with equal pay, but the reasoning is equally applicable now to all of the grounds and forms of discrimination covered by the newer anti-discrimination directives.[371]

In *Bilka*, concerning eligibility of part-time workers for an occupational pension scheme, the ECJ formulated a test for objective justification very similar to the proportionality test developed when it examined state justifications for restrictions on the free movement of goods and services.[372]

---

[366] Case C–416/13 *Mario Vital Pérez v Ayuntamiento de Oviedo* EU:C:2014:2371.

[367] Case C–447/09 (n 343).

[368] Case C–476/11 *HK Danmark (Kristensen) v Experian AS* EU:C:2013:590.

[369] Case C–152/11 *Odar* EU:C:2012:772. For discussion of the 'intersectionality' of different grounds of discrimination with age discrimination see D Schiek, 'Age Discrimination Before the CJEU—Conceptual and Theoretical Issues' (2011) 48 CMLRev 777.

[370] (N 134).

[371] For justification of indirect discrimination on grounds of disability, see Case C–356/12 *Glatzel* EU:C:2013:350.

[372] See in particular Chs 19, 21, and 22.

Case 170/84 **Bilka-Kaufhaus GmbH v Karin Weber von Hartz**
[1986] ECR 1607

[Note Lisbon Treaty renumbering: Art 119 EEC is now Art 157 TFEU]

THE ECJ

33. In its observations Bilka argues that the exclusion of part-time workers from the occupational pension scheme is intended solely to discourage part-time work, since in general part-time workers refuse to work in the late afternoon and on Saturdays. In order to ensure the presence of an adequate workforce during those periods it was therefore necessary to make full-time work more attractive than part-time work, by making the occupational pension scheme open only to full-time workers.

...

36. It is for the national court, which has sole jurisdiction to make findings of fact, to determine whether and to what extent the grounds put forward by an employer to explain the adoption of a pay practice which applies independently of a worker's sex but in fact affects far more women than men may be regarded as objectively justified economic grounds. If the national court finds that the measures chosen by the employer correspond to a real need on the part of the undertaking, are appropriate with a view to achieving the objectives pursued and are necessary to that end, the fact that the measures affect a far greater number of women than men is not sufficient to show that they constitute an infringement of Article 119.

In other words, an indirectly discriminatory measure may be justified if, first, the measure answers a 'real need' of the employer; secondly, the measure is 'appropriate' to achieve the objectives it pursues; and, finally, the measure is 'necessary' to achieve those objectives. In *Bilka*, the ECJ ultimately left the proportionality test for the national court to apply.

In *Rinner-Kühn*, although a legislative exclusion of part-time workers from sick pay provision was *prima facie* contrary to the aim of Article 157 TFEU, such an exclusion could in principle be objectively justified.[373] However, the particular justification offered by the government in this case was inadequate as it was based on generalizations about the relative lack of integration of part-time workers. However, broad characteristics such as length of service or seniority have been accepted by the Court as offering presumptive justification in cases such as *Cadman*.[374]

In *Elsner-Lakeberg* the ECJ accepted that although requiring part-time and full-time workers to exceed their monthly working time by three hours in order to be eligible for excess pay appeared on the surface to constitute equal treatment, it was actually indirectly discriminatory against part-time workers in requiring them to work a higher percentage of their normal monthly hours.[375] It was then for the national court to determine whether this discrimination could be objectively justified.

In *Bötel*,[376] *Lewark*,[377] and *Freers*,[378] the ECJ acknowledged that while the payment of compensation for attending training courses to full-time workers on a more favourable basis than that paid to

---

[373] Case 171/88 *Rinner-Kühn* (n 32). See also Case C–189/91 *Kirsammer-Hack v Nurhan Sidal* [1993] ECR I–6185.

[374] Case C–17/05 *Cadman* (n 381); Case C–486/08 *Zentralbetriebsrat der Landeskrankenhäuser Tirols v Land Tirol* [2010] ECR I–3527, [41]–[46]; Cases C–395 and 396/08 *INPS v Bruno, Pettini, Lotti, Mateucci* [2010] ECR I–5119, [69]–[75], on objective justification under the Framework Agreement on Part-time Work under Dir 97/81.

[375] Case C–285/02 *Elsner-Lakeberg v Land Nordrhein-Westfalen* [2004] ECR I–5861.

[376] Case C–360/90 *Bötel* (n 34).

[377] Case C–457/93 *Lewark* (n 34).

[378] Case C–278/93 *Freers* (n 34).

part-time workers[379] was likely to discriminate indirectly against women, it was nonetheless possible that such discrimination was justified by reference to social-policy aims unrelated to sex.[380] In *Danfoss*, the ECJ considered what kinds of justification for indirect discrimination in the criteria for supplementary pay, criteria such as mobility, training, and length of service, might be acceptable.[381] The ECJ ruled that while the criteria could in principle be neutral, they could also be applied in such a way as to disadvantage women. Further, if mobility meant initiative and enthusiasm, it could in the ECJ's view be a neutral criterion, whereas if it meant adaptability to hours and places of work, it could disadvantage women because of family and household duties for which they so often bear responsibility.

The ECJ in *Kowalska* and *Nimz* ruled that indirect discrimination stemming from a provision in a collective bargaining agreement would breach the Treaty unless objectively justified.[382] The attempt in *Nimz* to offer an *en bloc* justification for rules which discriminate against part-time workers, by asserting that full-time workers were more experienced and acquire abilities and skills more rapidly than part-time workers, was dismissed by the ECJ as reliance on generalizations. It was for the national court in a particular case to assess whether that specific rule was justified or not.[383]

In *Schnorbus*, the ECJ ruled that indirect discrimination against women in access to practical legal training could be objectively justified in order to compensate for the delay occasioned to the careers of men who had undergone compulsory military or civilian service, and the preferential treatment was not disproportionate since it was limited to twelve months maximum.[384] In *JämO*, differences in working hours could constitute objective justification, although the employer would have to demonstrate that this was in fact the case.[385]

In *Hill and Stapleton*, however, discrimination against job-sharers, who were overwhelmingly women, in the method of determining pay progression, could not be justified on a range of unacceptable grounds offered by the Revenue Commissioners, including avoidance of increased costs.[386] The ECJ drew attention in its ruling to the specific type of indirect discrimination involved, discrimination against job-sharers, by noting that job-sharing was overwhelmingly chosen by women seeking to combine work and family responsibilities, and that the protection of women within family life and at work 'in the same way as for men' was a principle recognized by EU law as a 'natural corollary' of the equal treatment principle. The implication seems to be that a stronger onus to justify such indirect discrimination would therefore lie on the defendant whose practices undermined such a principle.

The shortcomings of the indirect discrimination/objective justification tests in the field of sex equality have often been noted,[387] given the male norm on which the concept of discrimination used is generally based, and given the relative ease with which the commercial objectives of the undertaking or employer

---

[379] Whether the basis for payment did in fact give preferential treatment to full-time workers was perhaps open to question: Case C–457/93 *Lewark* (n 34) AG Jacobs; J Shaw, Note (1997) 22 ELRev 256, 259.

[380] Contrast the view of AG Darmon in Case C–278/93 *Freers* (n 34) 1179–1180, who concluded that the national rules were not in the circumstances objectively justifiable.

[381] Case 109/88 *Danfoss* (n 158); Case C–17/05 *Cadman v Health & Safety Executive* [2006] ECR I–9583, [33]–[39].

[382] Case C–33/89 *Kowalska* (n 28); Case C–184/89 *Nimz* (n 31). In Cases C–3/99, 409 and 425/92, 34, 50 and 78/93 *Stadt Lengerich v Helmig* [1994] ECR I–5727, there was no indirect discrimination where collective agreements restricted payment of overtime supplements to cases where the normal working hours fixed for full-time workers were exceeded. Compare Case C–285/02 *Elsner-Lakeberg* (n 375). See also Case C–236/98 *JämO* (n 36) on an 'inconvenient hours' supplement.

[383] Case C–184/89 *Nimz* (n 31) [14].

[384] Case C–79/99 *Schnorbus v Land Hessen* [2000] ECR I–10997.

[385] Case C–236/98 *JämO* (n 36) [61]–[62].

[386] Case C–243/95 *Hill v The Revenue Commissioners and Department of Finance* [1998] ECR I–3739; Case C–77/02 *Steinicke* (n 38); Case C–187/00 *Kutz-Bauer v Freie und Hansestadt Hamburg* [2003] ECR I–2741, although the CJEU decided this case under the Equal Treatment Dir 76/207 rather than as an equal pay case; C McGlynn and C Farrelly, 'Equal Pay and the "Protection of Women within Family Life"' (1999) 24 ELRev 202.

[387] Fredman (n 154) 125.

can defeat a claim of indirect discrimination.[388] On the other hand, rulings such as those in *Hill and Stapleton*, *Seymour-Smith*, and *Kutz-Bauer*[389] show the ECJ adopting a more robust approach to scrutinizing the 'objective justifications' offered by states for indirectly discriminatory legislative measures.

(C) POSITIVE ACTION

Provisions permitting but not mandating 'positive action', sometimes referred to as 'affirmative action', are contained both in the EU Treaties and in secondary legislation. As far as primary law is concerned, Article 157(4) TFEU provides:

> With a view to ensuring full equality in practice between men and women in working life, the principle of equal treatment shall not prevent any Member State from maintaining or adopting measures providing for specific advantages in order to make it easier for the underrepresented sex to pursue a vocational activity or to prevent or compensate for disadvantages in professional careers.

Article 23 of the Charter of Fundamental Rights also allows for the 'maintenance or adoption of measures providing for specific advantages in favour of the under-represented sex'.

The first positive action provision in secondary EU law was to be found in Article 2(4) of the prior Equal Treatment Directive, 76/207. Article 2(4) permitted measures designed to redress inequality between men and women and to 'promote equal opportunity for men and women, in particular by removing existing inequalities which affect women's opportunities'. Article 3 of the recast Gender Equality Directive 2006/54 replaced this provision and aligned it with the terms of Article 157(4) TFEU. Article 3 of Directive 2006/54 now reads:

> Member States may maintain or adopt measures within the meaning of Article 157(4) of the Treaty with a view to ensuring full equality in practice between men and women in working life.

A similar positive action provision is contained in the two Article 19 anti-discrimination directives. Article 5 of Directive 2000/43 and Article 7 of Directive 2000/78 provide:

> With a view to ensuring full equality in practice, the principle of equal treatment shall not prevent any Member State from maintaining or adopting specific measures to prevent or compensate for disadvantages linked to [the protected grounds].

Article 7(2) of Directive 2000/78 contains an additional paragraph in respect of disabled persons, permitting Member States to 'maintain or adopt provisions on the protection of health and safety at work or...measures aimed at creating or maintaining provisions or facilities for safeguarding or promoting their integration into the working environment'.

Article 2(4) was initially read narrowly by the Court, so that a provision of French law which permitted collective agreements to provide special rights for women, including shorter working hours for older women, the obtaining of leave when a child was ill, and the granting of extra days of leave in respect of children, was held to be unjustified.[390] France had not adequately shown that 'the generalized

---

[388] See, eg, Case C–189/91 *Kirsammer-Hack* (n 373); Case C–297/93 *Grau-Hupka v Stadtgemeinde Bremen* [1994] ECR I–5535; T Hervey, 'Small Business Exclusion in German Dismissal Law' (1994) 23 ILJ 267.

[389] Case C–243/95 *Hill* (n 386); Case C–167/97 *Seymour-Smith* (n 29) [71]–[73]; Case C–187/00 *Kutz-Bauer* (n 386) [54]–[60].

[390] Case 312/86 *Commission v France* [1988] ECR 6315.

preservation of special rights for women' would reduce actual instances of inequality in social life.[391] The Commission's argument for condemning the French law acknowledged a danger that EU law might crystallize the existing distribution of domestic labour within the family, since it authorized the maintenance of discriminatory conditions for an indeterminate period and left their removal to the discretion of the two sides of industry.[392]

In *Lommers*, the ECJ upheld the compatibility with Article 2(4) of a scheme set up within a national ministry to tackle the extensive under-representation of women in a situation 'characterised by a proven insufficiency of proper, affordable child-care facilities'.[393] Under the scheme, the ministry made available a limited number of subsidized nursery places to its staff, and reserved those for female staff alone, while permitting male officials access only in individual cases of emergency. The ECJ ruled that this scheme would be acceptable on condition that the emergency exception was construed as allowing any male officials who took care of their children by themselves to have access to the nursery places on the same conditions as female officials. While the situation in *Lommers* was different from that in the *France* case, in that it did not involve the generalized preservation of rights for women, but a specific advantage granted in an attempt to tackle the acknowledged under-representation of women in a particular employment context, the ECJ was nonetheless willing to accept positive action measures even where they were premised on the accurate but role-reinforcing assumption that women would be the primary child-carer in two-parent families.

On the other hand, the ECJ in *Roca Alvarez* ruled that neither Article 157(4) TFEU nor Article 2(4) of the Directive would permit a law which provided that female employees who were mothers could take leave during the first nine months following the child's birth, while male employees who were fathers were not entitled to the same leave unless the child's mother was also an employed person.[394] A measure of this kind was, in the Court's view, liable to perpetuate a traditional distribution of the roles of men and women by keeping men in a role subsidiary to that of women in relation to the exercise of their parental duties.[395]

Some commentators have argued that even if positive action measures of this kind risk perpetuating stereotypes, the law should not ignore an actually existing disadvantage which is broadly shared by members of a group.[396] The differing approaches adopted in *Commission v France, Lommers*, and *Roca Álvarez* suggest that the ECJ continues to grapple with this tension, without taking a consistent stance either for or against positive action measures which could be argued to reinforce traditional roles and responsibilities in particular in relation to childcare. However, when such measures are broad-ranging and general, and when they are legislative rather than specific to one employer, they seem less likely to be saved by the positive action provision.

While the cases discussed above mostly concern schemes providing additional leave or childcare benefits for working women, the most controversial positive action measures have been those which concern access for women to employment or promotion. Positive action schemes of the latter kind were dealt a blow in the mid-1990s by the ECJ ruling in *Kalanke*.[397] In this case the Court ruled that Article 2(4) constituted a derogation from the right to equal treatment which must be strictly interpreted. Consequently, a German regional law which provided, where candidates of different sexes who

[391] Ibid [15].

[392] Ibid [17]. See the similar argument of AG Jacobs at [14] of his Opinion in Case 373/89 *Integrity v Rouvroy* [1990] ECR 4243 concerning 'positive discrimination' in national social security benefits in favour of women, where the Court found a breach of the equal treatment principle in Dir 79/7.

[393] Case C–476/99 *Lommers* (n 39).

[394] Case C–104/09 *Roca Álvarez* [2010] ECR I–8661.

[395] Ibid [36]–[37].

[396] Fredman (n 154) 129.

[397] Case C–450/93 *Kalanke v Freie Hansestadt Bremen* [1995] ECR I–3051.

had been shortlisted for promotion were equally qualified, that priority must to be given to women in sectors where they were under-represented (ie made up less than half of the staff) would breach the Directive. The fact that the Bremen system involved a 'soft' rather than a 'rigid' quota, and was intended to overcome the disadvantages faced by women and the perpetuation of past inequalities, as a result of which few women held senior posts, was insufficient to bring it within Article 2(4):

> 22. National rules which guarantee women absolute and unconditional priority for appointment or promotion go beyond promoting equal opportunities and overstep the limits of the exception in Article 2(4) of the Directive.
>
> 23. Furthermore, in so far as it seeks to achieve equal representation of men and women in all grades and levels within a department, such a system substitutes for equality of opportunity as envisaged in Article 2(4) the result which is only to be arrived at by providing such equality of opportunity.

The *Kalanke* ruling prompted a flood of criticism and comment, not only from women's interest groups and from academic and practising lawyers,[398] but also from the European Commission itself, which issued a communication on the interpretation of the judgment.[399] The Commission took the view that not all quotas would be unlawful, and listed a range of positive action measures which would, in its view, be acceptable despite the ruling. It proposed also an amendment/clarification of the terms of Article 2(4) to provide that a soft quota such as that in issue in *Kalanke* would not be contrary to the Directive, so long as it did not automatically give preference to the under-represented sex, but permitted the assessment of an individual's specific circumstances in a given case.[400]

In the subsequent and similar case of *Marschall*, Advocate General Jacobs suggested that even if individual candidates' circumstances had to be taken into account, a national measure which gave priority to women over men in under-represented sectors where the candidates were equally qualified would still breach the Equal Treatment Directive.[401] He criticized the Commission's proposed clarificatory amendment to Article 2(4) and deemed criticisms of *Kalanke* to be misconceived.[402] However, the ECJ did not follow the Advocate General's Opinion and it narrowed the scope of the *Kalanke* ruling along the lines of the Commission's proposal, by confirming that while a rule guaranteeing 'absolute and unconditional priority' for women was impermissible, a softer quota which allowed for individual consideration of circumstances would fall within the existing terms of Article 2(4).

Marschall concerned a German regional law which provided that where there were fewer women than men in a higher grade post in a career bracket, women were to be given priority for promotion in the event of equal suitability, competence, and professional performance unless reasons specific to an individual male candidate tilted the balance in his favour. In contrast with the *Kalanke* litigation, in which the only intervening Member State was the UK in support of the applicant's challenge against the German law, five governments intervened in *Marschall* to support the compatibility of the positive action legislation with EU law. Only the UK and France opposed it. The ECJ distinguished the rule in *Kalanke* from the *Marschall* rule by reference to its 'saving clause',[403] and adopted a more nuanced view of the 'equal' chances of men and women on the labour market.

---

[398] L Charpentier, Note [1996] RTDE 281; S Dagmar, Note (1996) 25 ILJ 239; S Moore, Note (1996) 21 ELRev 156; A Peters, Note (1996) 2 ELJ 177; S Prechal, Note (1996) 33 CMLRev 45; D Schiek, Note (1996) 25 ILJ 239; L Senden, Note (1996) 3 MJ 146; E Szyszczak, Note (1996) 59 MLR 876; S Fredman, Note (1997) 113 LQR 575.

[399] COM(96) 88.

[400] [1996] OJ C179/8.

[401] Case C–409/95 *Hellmut Marschall v Land Nordrhein Westfalen* [1997] ECR I–6363.

[402] Ibid [47] of his Opinion.

[403] See also the significant role of the 'exceptional clause' in Case C–476/99 *Lommers* (n 39); Case C–380/01 *Schneider v Bundesminister für Justiz* [2004] ECR I–1389, in which the national court had applied the *Kalanke* and *Marschall* rulings to deem an Austrian law which did not contain a savings clause to be incompatible with EU law.

Case C–409/95 **Hellmut Marschall v Land Nordrhein Westfalen**
[1997] ECR I–6363

THE ECJ

29. As the Land and several governments have pointed out, it appears that even where male and female candidates are equally qualified, male candidates tend to be promoted in preference to female candidates particularly because of prejudices and stereotypes concerning the role and capacities of women in working life and the fear, for example, that women will interrupt their careers more frequently, that owing to household and family duties they will be less flexible in their working hours, or that they will be absent from work more frequently because of pregnancy, childbirth and breastfeeding.

30. For these reasons, the mere fact that a male candidate and a female candidate are equally qualified does not mean that they have the same chances.

31. It follows that a national rule in terms of which, subject to the application of the saving clause, female candidates for promotion who are equally as qualified as the male candidates are to be treated preferentially in sectors where they are underrepresented may fall within the scope of Article 2(4) if such a rule may counteract the prejudicial effects on female candidates of the attitudes and behaviour described above and thus reduce actual instances of inequality which may exist in the real world.

32. However, since Article 2(4) constitutes a derogation from an individual right laid down by the Directive, such a national measure specifically favouring female candidates cannot guarantee absolute and unconditional priority for women in the event of a promotion without going beyond the limits of the exception laid down in that provision. (*Kalanke* paras 21 and 22)

33. Unlike the rules at issue in *Kalanke*, a national rule which, as in the case in point in the main proceedings, contains a saving clause does not exceed those limits, if, in each individual case, it provides for male candidates who are equally as qualified as the female candidates a guarantee that the candidatures will be the subject of an objective assessment which will take account of all criteria specific to the individual candidates and will override the priority accorded to female candidates where one or more of those criteria tilts the balance in favour of the male candidate. In this respect, however, it should be remembered that those criteria must not be such as to discriminate against female candidates.

Shortly after *Marschall*, Article 157(4) TFEU was amended to include the provision permitting Member States to adopt positive action 'with a view to ensuring full equality in practice between men and women in working life'. As we have seen above, Article 157(4) refers in formally neutral terms to the permissibility of providing specific advantages for the 'under-represented sex' to pursue vocational training or to compensate for career disadvantages,[404] rather than referring, as previously, to women only.[405] Although the terms of Article 157(4) TFEU, on which the positive action provisions of the more recent anti-discrimination directives are based, are not exactly the same as those of the earlier provision in Article 2(4) of Directive 76/207, the ECJ in both *Abrahamsson*[406] and *Roca Álvarez*[407] reached the same conclusion in the cases under both the Directive and Article 157(4).

---

[404] In Case C–366/99 *Griesmar* (n 53), the CJEU ruled that the predecessor to Art 157(4) (Art 6(3) of the Maastricht Social Policy Agreement) could not be used to justify pay discrimination which consisted of service credits for the calculation of retirement pensions only for female workers who had had children, since this discrimination would not itself offset the disadvantages to which the careers of female civil servants were exposed. See also Case C–173/13 *Leone v Garde des Sceaux and others* EU:C:2014:2090; Case C–46/07 *Commission v Italy* EU:C:2008:618; and Case C–559/07 *Commission v Greece* EU:C:2009:19.

[405] A declaration appended to the Amsterdam Treaty, however, stated that in adopting measures referred to in para 4, the Member States should 'aim at improving the situation of women in working life'.

[406] Case C–407/98 *Abrahamsson v Fogelqvist* [2000] ECR I–5539.

[407] Case C–104/09 *Roca Álvarez* (n 394) and text.

In *Badeck*,[408] the ECJ followed its more permissive post-*Kalanke* approach in finding that a whole series of German public service rules designed to give priority to women in promotion, access to training, and recruitment were compatible with Article 2(4), since they contained sufficient flexibility and non-rigidity to comply with the criteria it had articulated in *Marschall*. Some of the provisions in question in *Badeck* seemed quite strong and even rather strict forms of positive action, for example the quota for training places and the rule on calling women to interview, but the ECJ did not hesitate in exempting them under Article 2(4), finding none to be 'automatic or unconditional' priority rules.

In *Briheche*, however, a French rule which exempted widows who had not remarried and were obliged to work from a rule setting an age limit for entry to competitive civil service examinations was found to constitute discrimination against widowers who had not remarried and were in the same situation.[409] According to the ECJ, such a rule automatically and unconditionally gave priority to women over men, and was not saved by Article 2(4).

In the Swedish case of *Abrahamsson*, the ECJ was asked to consider a practice which, unlike the various German provisions in *Kalanke, Marschall,* and *Badeck*, enabled preference to be given to a candidate of the under-represented sex who, although sufficiently qualified, did not possess qualifications equal to those of other candidates of the opposite sex.[410] The question framed by the ECJ was whether the positive action provision would permit legislation 'under which a candidate for a public post who belongs to the under-represented sex and possesses sufficient qualifications for that post must be chosen in preference to a candidate of the opposite sex who would otherwise have been appointed, where this is necessary to secure the appointment of a candidate of the under-represented sex and the difference between the respective merits of the candidates is not so great as to give rise to a breach of the requirement of objectivity in making appointments'.

Case C–407/98 **Abrahamsson v Fogelqvist**
[2000] ECR I–5539

THE ECJ

46. As a rule, a procedure for the selection of candidates for a post involves assessment of their qualifications by reference to the requirements of the vacant post or of the duties to be performed.

47. In paragraphs 31 and 32 of *Badeck*, cited above, the Court held that it is legitimate for the purposes of that assessment for certain positive and negative criteria to be taken into account which, although formulated in terms which are neutral as regards sex and thus capable of benefiting men too, in general favour women. Thus, it may be decided that seniority, age and the date of last promotion are to be taken into account only in so far as they are of importance for the suitability, qualifications and professional capability of candidates. Similarly, it may be prescribed that the family status or income of the partner is immaterial and that part-time work, leave and delays in completing training as a result of looking after children or dependants in need of care must not have a negative effect.

48. The clear aim of such criteria is to achieve substantive, rather than formal, equality by reducing *de facto* inequalities which may arise in society and, thus, in accordance with Article 141(4) EC, to prevent or compensate for disadvantages in the professional career of persons belonging to the under-represented sex.

---

[408] Case C–158/97 *Badeck v Landesanwalt beim Staatsgerichtshof des Landes Hessen* [1999] ECR I–1875.

[409] Case C–319/03 *Briheche v Ministre de l'Intérieur, Ministre de l'Éducation nationale and Ministre de la Justice* [2004] ECR I–8807.

[410] Case C–407/98 *Abrahamsson v Fogelqvist* (n 406).

49. It is important to emphasise in that connection that the application of criteria such as those mentioned in paragraph 47 above must be transparent and amenable to review in order to obviate any arbitrary assessment of the qualifications of candidates.

50. As regards the selection procedure at issue in the main proceedings, it does not appear from the relevant Swedish legislation that assessment of the qualifications of candidates by reference to the requirements of the vacant post is based on clear and unambiguous criteria such as to prevent or compensate for disadvantages in the professional career of members of the under-represented sex.

51. On the contrary, under that legislation, a candidate for a public post belonging to the under-represented sex and possessing sufficient qualifications for that post must be chosen in preference to a candidate of the opposite sex who would otherwise have been appointed, where that measure is necessary for a candidate belonging to the under-represented sex to be appointed.

52. It follows that the legislation at issue in the main proceedings automatically grants preference to candidates belonging to the under-represented sex, provided that they are sufficiently qualified, subject only to the proviso that the difference between the merits of the candidates of each sex is not so great as to result in a breach of the requirement of objectivity in making appointments.

53. The scope and effect of that condition cannot be precisely determined, with the result that the selection of a candidate from among those who are sufficiently qualified is ultimately based on the mere fact of belonging to the under-represented sex, and that this is so even if the merits of the candidate so selected are inferior to those of a candidate of the opposite sex. Moreover, candidatures are not subjected to an objective assessment taking account of the specific personal situations of all the candidates. It follows that such a method of selection is not such as to be permitted by Article 2(4) of the Directive.

54. In those circumstances, it is necessary to determine whether legislation such as that at issue in the main proceedings is justified by Article 141(4) EC.

55. In that connection, it is enough to point out that, even though Article 141(4) EC allows the Member States to maintain or adopt measures providing for special advantages intended to prevent or compensate for disadvantages in professional careers in order to ensure full equality between men and women in professional life, it cannot be inferred from this that it allows a selection method of the kind at issue in the main proceedings which appears, on any view, to be disproportionate to the aim pursued.

Accordingly, if measures such as job-qualification criteria which indirectly favour the under-represented sex are to be compatible with the positive action provisions of EU law, they must: (i) genuinely be designed to reduce *de facto* inequalities and compensate for career disadvantages; and (ii) be based on transparent and objective criteria which can be reviewed.

There is as yet no case law on the positive action provisions in the three more recent pieces of legislation, the Race Directive, the Framework Employment Directive, and the consolidated Gender Equality Directive, although it seems unlikely that the *Marschall* and *Briheche* cases would be any differently decided under any of the new positive action provisions, and the existence of a savings clause of some kind will probably remain important for the compatibility with EU law of national positive action measures in the field of access to employment or promotion.

(D) REMEDIES

The general subject of remedies has been discussed in Chapter 8, but it is notable how many of the cases on remedies have arisen in the specific context of discrimination.

Like other areas of substantive EU law, the EU equality and anti-discrimination directives do not attempt to harmonize national sanctions and procedures, but they require states to adopt effective remedies and proportionate and dissuasive sanctions for the enforcement of EU anti-discrimination law. In a ruling which could be applied to all of the directives in this field, the CJEU in *Asociata Accept*, in which a football club was claimed to have a homophobic recruitment policy, declared that a purely symbolic sanction would be incompatible with the effective implementation of Directive 2000/78.[411] The Court agreed that, as it had held in *Feryn*,[412] the mere fact that a sanction was not pecuniary need not mean that it was purely symbolic, particularly if it was accompanied by sufficient publicity, but on the facts of *Asociata Accept* it seemed unlikely that the verbal warning issued could be sufficient.

In its 2014 report on the application of the two anti-discrimination directives of 2000, the Commission noted that national courts 'have a tendency to apply the lower scale of sanctions provided for by law in terms of the level and amount of compensation awarded' and indicated that it will closely monitor the standards applied in the use of sanctions and remedies in the Member States.[413]

(i) *Levelling Up or Down*

In *Defrenne II*, the ECJ had appeared to reject the possibility of 'levelling down' salaries in order to comply with the equal pay principle in Article 157 (ex Article 119 EEC):

> In particular, since Article 119 appears in the context of the harmonisation of working conditions while the improvement is being maintained, the objection that the terms of this article may be observed in other ways than by raising the lowest salaries may be set aside.[414]

Subsequently, in the context of social security in *FNV*, the Court, having ruled that Article 4(1) of Directive 79/7 was directly effective from the date on which it should have been implemented, went on to elaborate the proper 'point of reference' pending such proper implementation:

> It follows that until such time as the national government adopts the necessary implementing measures, women are entitled to be treated in the same manner, and to have the same rules applied to them, as men who are in the same situation, since, where the directive has not been implemented, those rules remain the only valid point of reference.[415]

This formula has since been repeated in many other cases concerning transitional measures where there has been previous discrimination, including cases where the discrimination was contained in legislative measures as well as in collective bargaining agreements.[416] However, in *Specht*[417] and *Henning and Mai*[418] the CJEU ruled that the protection of acquired rights provided a justification for the maintenance of certain—though not all[419]—discriminatory elements in the transitional measures which followed the decision to abolish provisions discriminating on grounds of age.

However, once the legislature or the employer responsible for the discrimination takes measures to abolish the discriminatory provisions, there is no 'levelling-up' requirement. While this was not clear

---

[411] Case C–81/12 *Asociaţia Accept* EU:C:2013:275, [64].

[412] Case C–54/07 *Feryn* [2008] ECR I–5187, [39].

[413] COM(2014) 2, 3.5.

[414] Case 43/75 *Defrenne II* (n 86) [15].

[415] Case 71/85 *FNV* (n 220) [22].

[416] See, eg, Case C–377/89 *Cotter and McDermott v Minister for Social Welfare* [1991] ECR I–1155, [18]; Case 102/88 *Ruzius Wilbrink v Bestuur van de Bedrijfsvereniging voor Overheidsdiensten* [1989] ECR 4311, [20]; Case C–184/89 *Nimz* (n 31); Case C–33/89 *Kowalska* (n 28).

[417] Case C–501/12 *Specht and others* EU:C:2014:2005.

[418] Cases C–297 and 298/10 *Henning and Mai* [2011] ECR I–7965.

[419] See in particular Case C–417/13 *ÖBB Personenverkehr AG v Gotthard Starjakob* EU:C:2015:38 and Case C–530/13 *Schmitzer v Bundesministerin für Inneres* EU:C:2014:2359.

from the original *Defrenne II* ruling, the ECJ ruled in *Coloroll* that when action is taken to eliminate sex discrimination, the benefits may be abolished altogether rather than being provided for both sexes.[420]

(ii) *Limitations on Damages*

In *Emmott*,[421] *Cotter*,[422] *Marshall II*,[423] and *Pontin*[424] the ECJ stressed the importance of providing adequate national remedies, and declared that specific national rules—whether procedural or substantive— must be set aside where they have the effect of depriving an aggrieved person of an effective remedy. In *Cotter*, the rule was a principle of unjust enrichment which would have barred the plaintiff's remedy; in *Marshall II* it was a ceiling on damages in a statute and a prohibition on the award of interest by certain tribunals; in *Emmott*, it was a time limit within which proceedings had to be brought; and in *Pontin* it was a fifteen-day time limit for pregnant women dismissed from employment during pregnancy combined with a provision barring pregnant women from obtaining damages that were available to other employees. In *Bulicke*,[425] an age discrimination case decided under Directive 2000/78, the Court held that a period of two months for submitting a claim did not appear liable to render practically impossible or excessively difficult the exercise of rights conferred by EU law, given that the starting point for the time limit was the moment at which the worker has knowledge of the alleged discrimination.[426]

In *Coote*, the ECJ cited Article 6 ECHR in underscoring the fundamental right of access to court, and ruled that the principle of judicial control must extend also to retaliatory measures adopted by an employer in reaction to legal proceedings brought against it for sex discrimination, even after the employment relationship has ended.[427] Further, the requirement to do all that is necessary to give effect to EU equal treatment law applies not just to the national courts, following *Von Colson*,[428] but also to those authorities, such as trustees, who are responsible for the scheme in question.[429]

We have seen in Chapter 8, however, that the principle in *Emmott* was limited by subsequent rulings such as *Johnson II, Texaco A/S*, and *Steenhorst-Neerings*.[430] In these cases the ECJ ruled that national legislation which provided that benefits would not be payable retroactively for more than one year before the date on which they were claimed was compatible with EU law. Subsequently in *Magorrian*, however, the Court ruled that a national measure which provided that the right to be admitted to membership of an occupational pension scheme, from which the applicants had previously been excluded on indirectly discriminatory grounds, should only have effect from a date no earlier than two years before the institution of proceedings was incompatible with EU law, since it would deprive the applicants of an adequate remedy.[431]

---

[420] Case C-200/91 *Coloroll* (n 48) [33]. See also Cases C-137/94 *Richardson* (n 210) [24]; C-280/94 *Posthuma Van Damme* [1996] ECR I-179; C-173/13 *Leone v Garde des Sceaux* EU:C:2014:2090, [77].

[421] Case C-208/90 *Emmott v Minister for Social Welfare* [1991] ECR I-4269.

[422] Case C-377/89 *Cotter* (n 416).

[423] Case C-271/91 *Marshall* (n 157).

[424] Case C-63/08 *Pontin* [2009] ECR I-10467.

[425] Case C-246/09 *Bulicke* EU:C:2010:418, [39]-[41].

[426] For the compatibility with EU law of a thirty-year limitation period for the right to seek a reassessment of the periods of service which must be taken into account in order to fix the reference date for the purposes of advancement, see Case C-429/12 *Pohl v ÖBB-Infrastruktur AG* EU:C:2014:12.

[427] Case C-185/97 *Coote v Granada Hospitality Ltd* [1998] ECR I-5199.

[428] Case 14/83 *Von Colson and Kamann v Land Nordrhein-Westfalen* [1984] ECR 1891.

[429] Case C-200/91 *Coloroll* (n 48) [28].

[430] Case C-338/91 *Steenhorst-Neerings* (n 209); Case C-410/92 *Johnson v Chief Adjudication Officer (No 2)* [1994] ECR I-5483, [26]; Cases C-114-115/95 *Texaco A/S v Havn* [1997] ECR I-4263.

[431] Case C-246/96 *Magorrian* (n 58); Case C-78/98 *Preston v Wolverhampton Healthcare NHS Trust* [2000] ECR I-3201 on the justifiability of a six-month period following the termination of employment within which a claim for membership of an occupational pension scheme must be brought.

The Court distinguished the rules in the various cases on the basis that, whereas those in *Steenhorst-Neerings* and *Johnson II* had merely limited the period in respect of which backdated benefits could be obtained, the rule in *Magorrian* had the effect of preventing the entire record of service of the employees in question from being taken into account for the purpose of calculating the pension benefits which would be payable even after the date of the claim. Moreover in *Levez*, in a kind of compromise between the more generous reasoning in the *Emmott* ruling and the more conservative reasoning underpinning *Steenhorst-Neerings*, the ECJ ruled that a two-year limit on arrears of damages could not be applied to the applicant's case on account of the role played by her employer's deception in the delay occasioned.[432]

The scope of the principle of adequate compensation laid down in *Marshall II* was further circumscribed by the ruling in *Sutton*, where the ECJ distinguished claims for social security arrears, which had been denied on a discriminatory basis, from damages for discriminatory dismissal, and explained why a fixed limitation on the amount recoverable would be compatible with EU law in the former but not the latter situation.[433] On the ECJ's reasoning, an award of damages for discriminatory dismissal was concerned with compensation for harm and the restoration of equal treatment, and thus must be commensurate with the loss suffered, whereas the award of arrears of social security benefits did not constitute reparation or compensation for damage sustained, even where those benefits had been denied in a discriminatory way, so that the sum could more readily be limited or restricted by the state in the interest of matters such as financial balance. In *Draehmpaehl*, however, the Court made clear that the ruling in *Marshall II* did not mean that *any* ceiling on the maximum amount of a compensatory award for discrimination would be in breach of EU law.[434]

(iii) *Broadening the Individual Focus of Remedial Provisions*

Many of these consequences of the ECJ's remedial jurisprudence have been integrated into the anti-discrimination legislation, including in Directive 2006/54 and the Article 19 directives. Indeed, all of the EU anti-discrimination legislation adopted since 2000 exhibits an enhanced emphasis on the active promotion of equal treatment and prevention of discrimination, as well as on questions of compliance, remedies, and enforcement. The traditional, individual-rights-based legal approach to remedies has been broadened to include strategies of equality bodies and other collective actors such as the social partners and NGOs in the endeavour to redress discrimination.[435]

Under the Article 19 directives, judicial or administrative procedures must be made available to all persons who consider themselves to have been discriminated against.[436] Article 7(2) of Directive 2000/43 and Article 9(2) of Directive 2000/78 require Member States to ensure that associations or organizations with a legitimate interest may engage, either on behalf or in support of the complainant, in judicial or administrative procedures. Article 13 of the Race Directive 2000/43 also contains a provision which is not to be found in the Framework Employment Directive 2000/78, which requires Member States to designate or establish bodies for the promotion of equal treatment. The powers of such designated bodies must include the provision of assistance to victims of discrimination in proceedings brought, and they must conduct surveys and publish reports on the situation of racial and

---

[432] Case C–326/96 *Levez v Jennings Ltd* [1998] ECR I–7835; T Connor, Note (1999) 24 ELRev 300.

[433] Case C–66/95 *R v Secretary of State for Social Security, ex p Eunice Sutton* [1997] ECR I–2163.

[434] Case C–180/95 *Draehmpaehl v Urania Immobilienservice* [1997] ECR I–2195. Here a maximum compensatory award of three months' salary could be adequate where the candidate, who had been ruled ineligible for a job on grounds of sex, was less well qualified than the successful candidate and so would not have obtained the job. The ruling is effectively enshrined now in Art 18 of Dir 2006/54.

[435] This has been seen also in the context of the free movement of workers and discrimination on grounds of nationality, with the adoption of Dir 2014/54. See Ch 21 for discussion.

[436] Art 7 of Dir 2000/43 and Art 9 of Dir 2000/78.

ethnic discrimination in their Member State. All of the directives require protection against retaliation or victimization of complainants.

Reflecting the broadening of the anti-discrimination regime to include certain forms of collective as well as individual redress, the ECJ ruled in *Feryn*[437] that the general rule requiring effective, proportionate, and dissuasive sanctions in Article 15 of the Race Directive applies also in cases brought by one of the equality bodies established under Article 13, where there is no identifiable victim. Sanctions in such cases may include a finding of discrimination by the domestic court in conjunction with an adequate level of publicity, a prohibitory injunction, an order to an employer to cease the discriminatory practice, a fine, or an award of damages to the body bringing the proceedings.[438]

(iv) *The Burden of Proof*

One other remedial issue which plays an important role in the anti-discrimination field is the burden of proof. Article 19(1) of Directive 2006/54, which repealed and replaced the prior Burden of Proof Directive, imposes a requirement on Member States to ensure that, where an employee establishes 'facts from which it may be presumed that there has been direct or indirect discrimination', it is for the respondent to prove that there has been no breach of the principle of equal treatment. The Article 19 directives also contain a virtually identical provision. Article 10 of Directive 2000/78[439] provides:

> When persons who consider themselves wronged because the principle of equal treatment has not been applied to them establish, before a court or other competent authority, facts from which it may be presumed that there has been direct or indirect discrimination, it shall be for the respondent to prove that there has been no breach of the principle of equal treatment.

The principle of burden-shifting set out in these legislative provisions was initially laid down by the ECJ in its sex equality case law. In *Danfoss*, discussed above, the employer implemented a system of individual pay supplements in a way that made it impossible for female employees to identify the reasons for a difference between their pay and that of their male colleagues doing the same work.[440] The Court held that where an employer applied a system of pay which was totally lacking in transparency, and where statistical evidence indicated that the average pay for women was less than for men, it was for the employer to provide evidence that the pay difference was not discriminatory.[441] In *Rinner-Kühn*,[442] despite the Advocate General's argument that no presumption of indirect discrimination should arise in the case of national *legislative* provisions, on the ground that they could be presumed to take into account many social, economic, and political circumstances other than the adverse effects on women as compared with agreements made by employers, the ECJ disagreed. While the initial onus was on the employee, save in a case like *Danfoss* where the employer's system was insufficiently transparent, to show that those receiving lower payments were predominantly or disproportionately women, the onus then shifted to the employer to justify such indirect discrimination without the employee having to impute a discriminatory intent or to demonstrate that the pay policy was in some way based on sex.[443]

---

[437] Case C–54/07 *Feryn* [2008] ECR I–5187, [35]–[40].

[438] Ibid [59].

[439] The relevant provision of Dir 2000/43 is Art 8.

[440] Case 109/88 *Danfoss* (n 158).

[441] Ibid [16]. See now Commission Recommendation 2014/124 on strengthening the principle of equal pay through transparency (n 161).

[442] Case 171/88 *Rinner-Kühn v FWW Spezial-Gebäudereinigung GmbH* [1989] ECR 2743.

[443] J Shaw, 'Sick Pay for Cleaners' (1989) 14 ELRev 428, for criticism of the AG's argument and the difficulties it would pose for employees.

It is particularly difficult for complainants to prove discrimination in situations where certain professions are predominantly female while others, who are more highly paid, are predominantly male. The Court dealt with this problem in the *Enderby* case.

Case C–127/92 **Enderby v Frenchay Health Authority and the Secretary of State for Health**
[1993] ECR I–5535

Enderby, who was employed as a speech therapist by the defendant authority, complained of sex discrimination. She argued that members of her profession, which was overwhelmingly a female profession, were paid appreciably less well than members of comparable professions whose jobs were of equal value to hers. She cited the higher pay received by clinical psychologists and pharmacists, since these were professions in which, at an equivalent professional level, there were more men than women. On a preliminary reference, the ECJ, having cited its rulings on the burden of proof in *Bilka* and *Danfoss* (discussed above), continued:

THE ECJ

15. In this case, as both the FHA and the United Kingdom observe, the circumstances are not exactly the same as in the cases just mentioned. First, it is not a question of *de facto* discrimination arising from a particular sort of arrangement such as may apply, for example, in the case of part-time workers. Secondly, there can be no complaint that the employer has applied a system of pay wholly lacking in transparency since the rates of pay of NHS speech therapists and pharmacists are decided by regular collective bargaining processes in which there is no evidence of discrimination as regards either of those two professions.

16. However, if the pay of speech therapists is significantly lower than that of pharmacists and if the former are almost exclusively women while the latter are predominantly men, there is a *prima facie* case of sex discrimination, at least where the two jobs in question are of equal value and the statistics describing that situation are valid.

17. It is for the national court to assess whether it may take into account those statistics, that is to say, whether they cover enough individuals, whether they illustrate purely fortuitous or short-term phenomena, and whether, in general, they appear to be significant.

18. Where there is a *prima facie* case of discrimination, it is for the employer to show that there are objective reasons for the difference in pay. Workers would be unable to enforce the principle of equal pay before national courts if evidence of a *prima facie* case of discrimination did not shift to the employer the onus of showing that the pay differential is not in fact discriminatory.

Although the reference had been made from the national court on the assumption that the two jobs were of equal value, *Enderby* illustrates the problem of establishing indirect discrimination in the sense of showing that work which is performed predominantly by women is undervalued in comparison to work which is performed predominantly by men.[444] In the case of part-time and full-time workers, it is clear that the actual tasks being done are the same, whereas in the case of two distinct types of work and in the absence of a job-classification scheme, it is considerably more difficult to establish this. The same problem is likely to arise in cases of discrimination on the basis of racial or ethnic origin, in situations where there is *de facto* racial segregation rather than sex-segregation in the workforce.

---

444 Case C–236/98 *JämO* (n 36) where a comparison of the pay of midwives and clinical technicians was in issue.

The situation is more complex still in a situation where the average pay of several groups is compared, and where, although the highest paid group consists principally of one category of persons (in this example, women), so also does the lowest paid group. This arose in the *Royal Copenhagen* case, in which it was argued that the system of piecework pay schemes, in which pay depends largely on the individual output of each worker, led to indirect discrimination against women.[445] The ECJ ruled that the mere finding that the average pay, within such a pay scheme, of a group of workers consisting predominantly of women was appreciably lower than the average pay of a group of predominantly male workers carrying out work of equal value would not be sufficient to establish indirect pay discrimination. However, the Court went on to cite its reasoning in *Enderby* and *Danfoss* concerning the situations in which the burden of proof would shift to the employer to establish that there was no discrimination or that it was justified. On the facts of the *Royal Copenhagen* case, the burden of proof might indeed shift if the pay consisted in part of a variable element, depending on each worker's output, and it was not possible to identify the factors determining the unit of measurement used to calculate this variable element.[446]

In the *Meister*[447] and *Kelly*[448] cases concerning Directives 2000/43, 2000/78, and 76/207 respectively, the CJEU ruled that an employer's refusal to grant an unsuccessful job applicant information indicating whether another person had been hired, or possibly other information concerning the recruitment process, might under certain circumstances be a factor to be taken into account by the national court in establishing facts from which direct or indirect discrimination might be presumed.

9 CONCLUSIONS

i. EU anti-discrimination and equality law has undergone significant transformation over the last decade and a half, growing from a narrowly tailored body of law concerned with employment equality between men and women to a broader regime addressing a variety of forms of discrimination on a range of other specified grounds. While the bulk of the legislation, case law, and policy programmes still concern gender equality, the two Article 19 directives are increasingly generating litigation particularly in the field of age discrimination.

ii. The body of EU sex equality law is complex and differentiated, and despite the move towards mainstreaming, remains strongly focused on labour market equality. The core Gender Equality Directive 2006/54 is supplemented by issue-specific legislation on social security, pregnancy, parental leave, part-time work, and access to commercial services. There is a detailed body of case law governing equal pay, which draws subtle and complicated distinctions between pay, social security, and conditions of work, and a large body of case law on many other aspects of gender equality law.

iii. Despite the similarity of many of the provisions and concepts within the Gender Equality Directives and the two Article 19 anti-discrimination directives, the scope and nature of EU equality law are far from uniform. While a general principle of equal treatment has been recognized by the ECJ, and while the Charter of Fundamental Rights contains a broader prohibition of discrimination on any ground, there is specific EU legislative protection only against discrimination on the grounds of sex, race, religious belief, disability, age, and sexual orientation. A kind of hierarchy of protection

---

[445] Case C–400/93 *Royal Copenhagen* (n 154).

[446] Ibid [24]–[27]. The CJEU acknowledged that the employer could deny discrimination by showing that the pay differentials were due, eg, to differences in the worker's choice concerning the rate of work.

[447] Case C–415/10 *Meister v Speech Design Carrier Systems* EU:C:2012:217, [47].

[448] Case C–104/10 *Patrick Kelly v NUI* EU:C:2011:506, [53]–[55].

seems to exist amongst these grounds, with gender and race (in different ways) at the top of the hierarchy, age near the bottom, and sexual orientation, religion/belief, and disability somewhere in between. The Commission's attempt to address the uneven scope of protection by proposing a new Equal Treatment Directive remains stuck in the legislative process. The Council after many years of discussion eventually adopted Framework Decision 2008/913/JHA requiring Member States to criminalize racist and xenophobic speech and expression.

iv. The important common provisions of EU anti-discrimination laws include: (a) the imposition of positive as well as negative obligations on public as well as private actors; (b) a broad prohibition against direct and indirect discrimination, including harassment; (c) permission for 'positive action' measures to be adopted; (d) reversal of the burden of proof on a *prima facie* showing of discrimination; (e) robust remedial requirements, including a more concerted emphasis on dialogue and compliance to supplement other legal remedies, including through the involvement of equality bodies, social partners, and NGOs with an emphasis on collective as well as individual mechanisms. (f) The requirement of reasonable accommodation has so far been introduced only in the field of disability discrimination, though it has been argued that it is implicit in other grounds through the doctrine of objective justification. (g) Most forms of discrimination, even direct discrimination, can be justified on a range of grounds, subject to the requirement of proportionality. The grounds for justifying indirect discrimination, and for justifying all forms of age discrimination, are particularly expansive.

v. The beneficial impact of EU anti-discrimination law is inevitably confined, not only by the limits of the formal concept of equality which has often informed EU lawmaking, and by the emphasis on employment and market-related discrimination, but also by the limits of law's capacity to bring about change in the face of entrenched socio-economic hierarchies, inequalities, prejudices, and exclusion. The continued entrenchment of discrimination against non-EU nationals and the close relationship between race discrimination and migration policy have also drawn criticism.

vi. While some perceive EU law in the anti-discrimination field as being progressive and important in assisting social change, others criticize its ambivalence as regards positive action measures, the unwillingness to extend protection in certain fields and for certain grounds, the market-based focus, and the inconsistent positions taken by the Court on issues relating to the reconciliation of work and family life.

10 FURTHER READING

BELL, M, *Anti-Discrimination Law and the European Union* (Oxford University Press, 2002)

——— *Racism and Equality in the European Union* (Oxford University Press, 2008)

ELLIS, E, and WATSON, P, *EU Anti-Discrimination Law* (Oxford University Press, 2013)

GIVENS, T, AND EVANS CASE, R, *Legislating Equality: The Politics of Antidiscrimination Policy in Europe* (Oxford University Press, 2014)

HOWARD, E, *The EU Race Directive* (Routledge, 2009)

MEENAN, H, *Equality Law in an Enlarged European Union: Understanding the Article 13 Directives* (Cambridge University Press, 2007)

SARGEANT, M, *The Law on Age Discrimination in the EU* (Kluwer, 2008)

SCHIEK, D, AND CHEGE, V, *European Union Non-Discrimination Law: Comparative Perspectives on Multidimensional Equality Law* (Routledge, 2008)

———— AND LAWSON, A, *European Union Non-Discrimination Law and Intersectionality* (Ashgate, 2013)

————, WADDINGTON, L, AND BELL, M, *Cases, Materials and Text on National, Supranational and International Non-discrimination Law* (Hart, 2007)

SOMEK, A, *Engineering Equality: An Essay on European Anti-Discrimination Law* (Oxford University Press, 2011)

TEN BOKUM, N, FLANAGAN, T, AND SANDS, R, *Age Discrimination Law in Europe* (Kluwer, 2009)

WAALDIJK, K, AND BONINI-BARALDI, M, *Sexual Orientation Discrimination in the European Union: National Laws and the Employment Equality Directive* (TMC Asser Press, 2006)

WADDINGTON, L, *From Rome to Nice in a Wheelchair: The Development of a European Disability Policy* (Europa, 2006)

AFSJ: EU CRIMINAL LAW

1 CENTRAL ISSUES

i. The Area of Freedom, Security, and Justice (AFSJ) is now to be found in Title V of Part Three of the TFEU. Prior to the Lisbon Treaty the AFSJ was divided between Title VI EU, which was the Third Pillar, and Title IV EC.[1] The AFSJ was therefore integral to the very idea of the three-pillar structure that characterized the Treaty architecture prior to the Lisbon Treaty.

ii. The subject matter dealt with by these provisions is important and politically sensitive, as it includes police and judicial cooperation in criminal matters, visas, asylum, immigration, and judicial cooperation in civil matters. These are issues of considerable complexity, and it is not therefore possible in this chapter to cover the detailed regulatory regime that pertains in these areas.[2] The approach adopted is therefore as follows.

iii. Section 2 considers the development of the three-pillar structure introduced by the Maastricht Treaty, since it is impossible to understand the current law without an appreciation of the forces that shaped it.

iv. Section 3 deals with the rationale for the subject matter that comprises the AFSJ. The 'official view' is that the policies that make up the AFSJ were 'compensatory measures' made necessary by EU provisions on the free movement of persons, although commentators differ as to how far this provides a full explanation for EU involvement.

v. Section 4 considers the general principles in the Lisbon Treaty that apply to all areas of the AFSJ, including: Treaty objectives, competence, role of the principal EU institutions, judicial role, and an outline of the opt-outs that apply to the UK.

vi. The remainder of the chapter looks in more detail at criminal law and procedure. It would be impossible even within these confines to give detailed treatment to all criminal law measures, since that would require a book in itself. The objective is rather to reveal at a more general level the rationale for the EU's involvement in the criminal sphere, the regulatory techniques used to that end, and the challenges posed by such intervention.

---

[1] In this chapter references to Treaty Arts from the pre-Lisbon TEU will be signified as, eg, Art 35 EU, in order to differentiate them from the TEU provisions of the Lisbon Treaty, which will be represented as, eg, Art 6 TEU.

[2] K Hailbronner, *Immigration and Asylum Law and Policy of the European Union* (Kluwer, 2000); E Guild and C Harlow (eds), *Implementing Amsterdam: Immigration and Asylum Rights in EC Law* (Hart, 2001); E Denza, *The Intergovernmental Pillars of the European Union* (Oxford University Press, 2002); N Walker (ed), *Europe's Area of Freedom, Security, and Justice* (Oxford University Press, 2004); H Toner, E Guild, and A Baldaccini, *EU Immigration and Asylum Law and Policy: Whose Freedom, Security and Justice?* (Hart, 2007); V Mitsilegas, *EU Criminal Law* (Hart, 2009); S Peers, *EU Justice and Home Affairs Law* (Oxford University Press, 3rd edn, 2011).

vii. Thus Section 5 considers the EU's competence over criminal law and procedure prior to the Lisbon Treaty, including the important contributions made by the CJEU. This is followed in Section 6 by a close look at the Lisbon Treaty provisions on criminal law and procedure and on police and judicial cooperation. Section 7 revisits the objectives of the AFSJ in the post-Lisbon world, with specific focus on criminal law and procedure.

viii. Section 8 then considers challenges posed by EU involvement in this area, including those of a political, constitutional, and legal nature. These challenges are exemplified by the European Arrest Warrant, the European Evidence Warrant, the draft European Investigation Order, and the EU rules on organized crime.

2 MAASTRICHT TO LISBON

(A) MAASTRICHT: THREE PILLARS

Intergovernmental cooperation to combat terrorism, cross-border crime, and breach of external frontiers did not begin with the Maastricht Treaty. Thus, for example, the Trevi Group was created in 1975 by the Rome European Council to coordinate the fight against terrorism, and its mandate was extended in 1985 to encompass serious international crimes such as drug trafficking, bank robbery, and arms trafficking. A further prominent example was the Schengen Agreement 1985 to remove border controls among participating states, which was supplemented by the Schengen Implementing Convention 1990.

It was however the Treaty on European Union which formalized the pillar structure. It was signed by the Member States in Maastricht in February 1992 and entered into force in November 1993.[3] The TEU established the 'three-pillar' structure for what was henceforth to be the European Union, with the Communities as the first of these pillars and the EEC Treaty being officially renamed the European Community Treaty.[4] There were originally seven titles in the TEU: Title I included the 'common provisions', which set out the basic objectives of the TEU. Titles II, III, and IV covered the 'First Pillar' amendments to the EEC, ECSC, and Euratom Treaties respectively. Title V created the Second Pillar of the Common Foreign and Security Policy (CFSP), Title VI the Third Pillar of Justice and Home Affairs (JHA), and Title VII contained the final provisions.

The original formulation of the Justice and Home Affairs Pillar under Articles K.1 to K.9 TEU governed policies on matters such as asylum, immigration, and 'third country' nationals, which were later integrated into the EC Treaty by the Treaty of Amsterdam. However, it also included cooperation on a range of international crime issues and various forms of judicial, customs, and police cooperation, including the establishment of a European Police Office (Europol) for exchanging information.[5]

Decision-making under the Third Pillar was more intergovernmental and less supranational. The Council of Ministers was given the role of adopting joint positions and drawing up agreements on the basis of Member State or Commission initiatives, acting unanimously except on matters of procedure or when implementing joint actions or agreed conventions.[6] The Commission was to be 'fully associated' and the Parliament was to be informed, its views to be 'duly taken into consideration', and it could question or recommend matters to the Council.[7] A Coordinating Committee, which became the notorious

---

[3] R Corbett, *The Treaty of Maastricht* (Longman, 1993).
[4] Ch 1.
[5] Art K.1 EU.
[6] Art K.3 EU.
[7] Arts K.4(2) and K.6 EU.

and secretive K-4 Committee, was set up to help the Council, and had a role similar to that of Coreper under the EC Treaty.

(B) AMSTERDAM: THREE PILLARS MODIFIED

A major criticism of the Maastricht Treaty was that unlike foreign and security policy under the Second Pillar, the Third Pillar involved subjects such as immigration, asylum, border controls, and constraints on movement, which touched on fundamental human rights and raised issues similar to those under the free-movement provisions of the EC Treaty.

It was therefore argued that the need for openness and accountability in this policy field was much greater, requiring a full role for the European Parliament and review jurisdiction for the ECJ. Arguments for reform ranged from improving the institutional provisions under the existing JHA to absorbing the Third Pillar entirely into the Community Pillar. What emerged in the Amsterdam Treaty lay between the two, with parts of JHA being incorporated into Title IV EC, and the remaining Third Pillar provisions being subjected to institutional controls closer to those under the Community Pillar.

Thus the major structural substantive change was the incorporation into the Community Pillar of a large part of the former Third Pillar on the free movement of persons, covering visas, asylum, immigration, and judicial cooperation in civil matters, which was shifted to what became Title IV, Articles 61–69 EC. The aim of this title and that of the amended Third Pillar, which covered Police and Judicial Cooperation in Criminal matters (PJCC), were similarly described, both being intended to establish 'an area of freedom, security and justice'. The Area of Freedom, Security, and Justice prior to the Lisbon Treaty was thus comprised of the remodelled Third Pillar and Title IV EC. Further, the *acquis* of the 1985 Schengen Treaty on the gradual abolition of common border checks was integrated by a Protocol to the Amsterdam Treaty into the EU framework.[8]

3 RATIONALE

The three-pillar structure defined the EU's architecture from Maastricht to Lisbon. It is therefore important to reflect on the rationale for its creation.

(A) RATIONALE FOR THE THREE-PILLAR STRUCTURE

Weiler argued that consociationalism was the key to understanding the three-pillar structure.[9] In pluralistic societies functional stability was normally secured by cross-cutting cleavages. This could not, however, explain such stability in societies characterized by cleavages which reinforced each other, leading to divisive conceptions of the public good. Some countries had such reinforcing social cleavage, and yet were stable nonetheless. Consociational theory sought to explain this through the behaviour of a cartel of elites, which rendered the system functional and stable. The 'elites would share a commitment to the maintenance of the system and to the improvement of its cohesion, functionality

---

[8] P Kuijper, 'Some Legal Problems Associated with the Communitarization of Policy on Visas, Asylum and Immigration under the Amsterdam Treaty and Incorporation of the Schengen Acquis' (2000) 37 CMLRev 345; S Peers, 'Caveat Emptor: Integrating the Schengen Acquis into the European Union Legal Order' (1999) 2 CYELS 87.

[9] J Weiler, U Haltern, and F Mayer, 'European Democracy and its Critique' in J Hayward (ed), *The Crisis of Representation in Europe* (Frank Cass, 1995).

and stability'.[10] They would also deliver the agreement or acquiescence of their constituents. Weiler used consociational theory to explain the three-pillar structure.[11] Thus on this view the crucial factor explaining the emergence of the Second and Third Pillars was the sharply segmented nature of the politics in these areas.[12]

There is however an alternative explanation, which was also acknowledged by Weiler. The Member States wished for some degree of international cooperation in these areas, but were not ready for the full supranational machinery of the Community Pillar. Thus the Second and Third Pillars gave the Member States an institutionalized forum in which to discuss these matters, without subjecting themselves to supranational controls. The Member States believed that such cooperation would be beneficial for reasons articulated by international relations theorists.[13] The Member States wished for some established mechanism through which they could cooperate in the areas of Common Foreign and Security Policy and Justice and Home Affairs. Setting up *ad hoc* meetings to discuss such matters is time-consuming and involves heavy 'transaction costs', more especially as the number of players expands. The sensitive nature of the subject matter meant however that Member States preferred the 'default position' of intergovernmentalism, thereby retaining maximum control in their own hands.

(B) RATIONALE FOR SUBJECT MATTER COMPRISING AFSJ

We must also inquire into the rationale for the subject matter included in the AFSJ, and what sense of freedom, security, and justice links this material. We can begin by considering the official rationale, which linked the need for the AFSJ to free movement of persons *and* to the inherently trans-border impact of matters such as immigration and organized crime.

Justice and Home Affairs Council[14]

When the Member States negotiated the Treaty on European Union, they drew up a list of areas of common interest. This ambitious list includes matters relating to asylum, immigration, controls at the Union's external frontiers, drugs, international fraud, civil and criminal justice, customs cooperation and police cooperation, particularly against international crime and terrorism...Why did they decide on such cooperation? What needs did it meet?

The creation of an area of free movement of persons must be accompanied by flanking measures to strengthen external frontiers and asylum and immigration policies...

...

Lifting the frontiers between Member States to permit people to pass freely cannot take place to the detriment of the security of the population, of public order and of civil liberties. To obviate this, flanking compensatory measures were adopted.

---

[10] Ibid 30.

[11] Ibid 29.

[12] Ibid 29.

[13] A Moravcsik, 'Preferences and Power in the European Community: A Liberal Intergovernmentalist Approach' (1993) 31 JCMS 473; A Moravcsik, *National Preference Formation and Interstate Bargaining in the European Community, 1955–86* (Harvard University Press, 1992); M Pollack, *The Engines of European Integration: Delegation, Agency, and Agenda Setting in the EU* (Oxford University Press, 2003); M Pollack, 'International Relations Theory and European Integration', EUI Working Papers, RSC 2000/55.

[14] Available at http://www.consilium.europa.eu.

Strengthening the External Frontiers

By doing away with the frontiers between Member States, the latter were deprived of an important national instrument for controlling and filtering the entry and identity of persons and ensuring internal security within their territory. A person present in one State can cross the frontiers of another state without hindrance . . . To ensure the same level of security without that tool, controls at the external frontiers, ie between a Member State of the Union and a third state, need to be strengthened . . .

. . .

The strengthening of the Union's external frontiers, a measure to compensate for the disappearance of internal frontiers, therefore requires increased cooperation between the interior and justice ministries and, more particularly, the police forces, customs and immigration services.

Immigration and the nationals of third states

Freedom of movement of persons is designed for the citizens of the European Union, ie those holding the nationality of one of the Member States. In an area without frontiers, what happens in the case of nationals of third States legally present in the territory of one of the Member States? . . . These are just some of the new questions to which cooperation in the field of justice and home affairs must provide answers.

Looked at from another angle, the disappearance of internal frontiers also raises the questions of illegal immigration or of illegal residence or employment which the Member States have to resolve together . . .

Asylum

The Member States have to agree on the very concept of political refugee in order to avoid a confusing situation in which one Member State grants asylum where another refuses it. They have to avoid a situation in which applications are made to several States at the same time. They have to cooperate in discussing the minimum guarantees to be granted to asylum applicants in the event of their expulsion and their rights during examination of an asylum application or an appeal . . .

The issues of the strengthening of external frontiers, immigration and asylum, which are all linked to the disappearance of internal frontiers, are very sensitive political questions for each State. They are perceived as directly affecting the sovereignty, security and people of those States. Their political culture, their legal systems and their administrative traditions and practices are often very different. That is why concerted action, comprehension and dialogue in the context of the JHA are proving to be fundamental.

Schengen and the free movement of persons

[T]he Amsterdam Treaty . . . integrates the Schengen acquis into the European Union framework . . .

The Member States of the European Union can no longer tackle certain problems in dispersed order, but must combine their efforts.

Drugs, organised crime, international fraud, trafficking in human beings and the sexual exploitation of children are all problems of great concern to all the Member States of the European Union. These disorders know no frontiers. The aim of the European Union is to become an area of freedom, security and justice, and not an area for all manner of trafficking.

Drugs

[T]he consumption and trafficking of drugs are linked to other problems, such as large-scale crime or money laundering...

Organized crime

Cases of crime, terrorism and fraud can no longer be dealt with solely in a national framework, especially since the creation of a large European market...

The link between the need for the AFSJ, free movement of persons, and the inherently trans-border impact of matters such as immigration, asylum, and organized crime has been echoed by commentators.

S Lavenex and W Wallace, Justice and Home Affairs: Towards a 'European Public Order'?[15]

There were several overlapping rationales for developing common policies within the EU, emerging both from functionalist spill-over from other EU policies, and from new challenges faced by the member states...The requirements of the single market included 'free movement of persons'. Cross-border movements intensified among geographically compact, densely populated countries, as prosperity rose and communication links improved. The success of the 1992 internal market programme in removing controls on goods crossing internal frontiers focused on the remaining controls on people at the EU's internal frontiers. The further surge in border-crossing which the internal market programme encouraged also alerted law enforcement agencies to the need to agree on 'compensatory measures' to maintain public order across the EU for the movement of both the lawful and the unlawful, legal and illegal.

Apart from these functionalist dynamics, new domestic priorities shaped the agenda of evolving cooperation. These included concern about cross-border crime and the international mobility of criminals as well as changing patterns of migration. Tightened controls on immigration from the mid-1970s onwards coincide with increasing flows from outside Europe and a global rise in the number of refugees, leading to a surge of asylum seekers arriving in western Europe...

German concerns and anxieties were a driving force in the development of common policies.

The official explanation for the emergence of the AFSJ has nonetheless been contested. It has been argued that the 'compensatory measures rationale' cannot readily explain the *restrictiveness* of the policies adopted in areas such as migration, asylum, and the like, and that the driving force behind AFSJ has in reality been security.

C Costello, Administrative Governance and the Europeanisation of Asylum and Immigration Policy[16]

[T]he compensatory measures rationale cannot provide an explanation for the restrictiveness of the policies and practices adopted. Bigo...goes so far as to describe '[t]he debate on compensatory measures

---

[15] H Wallace, W Wallace, and M Pollack (eds), *Policy-Making in the European Union* (Oxford University Press, 5th edn, 2005) 460–461.

[16] H Hofmann and A Türk (eds), *EU Administrative Governance* (Edward Elgar, 2006) 289.

and the security deficit created by the opening of the internal borders [as] one of the strongest myths of EU self-presentation'. Any internal market rationale is agnostic as to the restrictiveness or otherwise of external barriers, but simply requires the application of common rules. For example, for internal free trade in goods, there must be a common external tariff and commercial policy, but not of any particular restrictiveness. In contrast in relation to the free movement of persons . . . there are no common immigration rules, but rather a restrictive entry control system. The lie that this system is required by the internal free market movement is revealed in relation to the UK and Ireland's participation in a range of external border control measures without any commitment to the abolition of internal border controls.

It is moreover clear that while the official rationale played a role in the emergence of the AFSJ, this development also provided a 'new' banner through which the legitimacy of the EU could be enhanced. The 1990s was a decade in which the EU's legitimacy came to be increasingly questioned. The Intergovernmental Conference discussions leading to the Amsterdam Treaty were shot through with soul-searching concerning input and output legitimacy. The institutional regime through which the AFSJ was delivered did little to enhance input legitimacy. It nonetheless served as an appropriate vehicle through which it could be argued that the EU fostered output legitimacy. The initial establishment of the EEC had been justified in large part in terms of outcomes, increased peace, and prosperity. It was therefore neither fortuitous, nor surprising, that the AFSJ should be justified in similar terms, more especially because fears relating to crime and the like regularly featured high in Eurobarometer polls for EU citizens. Consider in this respect the following extract from the Tampere European Council in 1999.

Tampere European Council[17]

Towards a Union of Freedom, Security and Justice: The Tampere Milestones

1. From its very beginning European integration has been firmly rooted in a shared commitment to freedom based on human rights, democratic institutions and the rule of law. These common values have proved necessary for securing peace and developing prosperity in the European Union. They will also serve as a cornerstone for the enlarging Union.

2. The European Union has already put in place for its citizens the major ingredients of a shared idea of prosperity and peace: a single market, economic and monetary union, and the capacity to take on global political and economic challenges. The challenge of the Amsterdam Treaty is now to ensure that freedom, which includes the right to move freely throughout the Union, can be enjoyed in conditions of security and justice accessible to all. It is a project which responds to the frequently expressed concerns of citizens and has a direct bearing on their daily lives.

3. This freedom should not, however, be regarded as the exclusive preserve of the Union's own citizens. Its very existence acts as a draw to many others world-wide who cannot enjoy the freedom Union citizens take for granted. It would be in contradiction with Europe's traditions to deny such freedom to those whose circumstances lead them justifiably to seek access to our territory. This in turn requires the Union to develop common policies on asylum and immigration, while taking account the need for a consistent control of external borders to stop illegal immigration and to combat those who organise it and commit related international crimes . . .

4. The aim is an open and secure European Union, fully committed to the obligations of the Geneva Refugee Convention and other relevant human rights instruments . . .

[17] 15–16 Oct 1999, 2–3.

5. The enjoyment of freedom requires a genuine area of justice, where people can approach courts and authorities in any Member State as easily as their own...

6. People have the right to expect the Union to address the threat to their freedom and legal rights posed by serious crime. The joint mobilisation of police and judicial resources is needed to guarantee that there is no hiding place for criminals or the proceeds of crime within the Union.

7. The area of freedom, security and justice should be based on the principles of transparency and democratic control...

8. The European Council considers it essential that in these areas the Union should also develop a capacity to act and be regarded as a significant partner on the international scene...

The discussion thus far has highlighted the rationales for the development of the AFSJ. The extent to which the issues dealt with relating to immigration, border controls, the fight against organized crime, asylum, and the like can be considered to be a *coherent* package has however been contested by Walker.

N Walker, In Search of the Area of Freedom, Security and Justice: A Constitutional Odyssey[18]

To begin with, we might speak of a basic *thematic* coherence in the area of FSJ—a fundamental unity of subject matter. Yet unlike many of the major domains of European law such as the internal market...the subject matter assembled under the AFSJ does not form a 'natural' unity in terms of a clearly defined overall project. Although analogies have often been drawn between the '1992' Single Market project and the AFSJ, the two are not comparable in terms of precision and internal consistency. The '1992' project concerned a well-defined set of objectives directed towards a particular *finalité*...In contrast, the AFSJ, even if part of its initial Maastricht inspiration was the attempt to supply a menu of compensatory measures concerning the control of movements across the EU's external borders and the development of new capacities for the internal monitoring of populations in the light of the supposed 'security deficit' attendant upon the completion of an internal market...has no *finalité* other than continuing adherence to a highly abstract triumvirate of values...

But if there is no clearly defined overall project implicit in the very idea of AFSJ, perhaps there is a kind of *historical* coherence in terms of a tried-and-tested pattern of common treatment...Here, too, only a weak argument can be made. The Treaties tell us that AFSJ is concerned, on the one hand, under Title IV EC, with 'Visas, Asylum, Immigration and Other Policies Relating to Free Movement of Persons',..., and on the other hand under Title VI TEU with 'Provisions on Police and Judicial Cooperation in Criminal Matters'. Yet we need only look at the variety of government departments under which these policies are traditionally organized in various European states to conclude that history lends no obvious coherence to this enterprise...

Another type of coherence, then, might be *institutional* coherence. Is the AFSJ characterized by a distinctive institutional methodology? Evidently, the answer must again be no...Under Amsterdam...there is a clear divide between the communitarized Title IV EC and the more state-centred rump Third Pillar under Title VI EU, even if Title IV EC remains only partly and incrementally communitarized and Title VI EU allows a greater role for EC institutions and instruments than its Maastricht predecessor...

Strikingly, however, institutional diversification has developed hand-in-hand with a new impetus towards *policy* coherence...[T]he post-Amsterdam era is clearly marked by an attempt to *construct* a new kind of policy whole out of diverse parts. To begin with, the very coining of the concept of an Area of Freedom, Security and Justice in the Treaty of Amsterdam is a statement of intent to consider the matters under Title IV EC and Title VI EU as a new policy domain, their new institutional separation

---

18 Walker (n 2) 5–7, italics in the original.

notwithstanding...[T]he special Tampere European Council late in 1999 drew upon the new rhetoric and institutional capability in order to launch an explicit and ambitious programme of action to develop a common policy field within and across four general headings—A Common EU Asylum and Migration Policy; A Genuine European Area of Justice; A Union wide Fight against Crime and Stronger External Action—complete with timetables and milestones.

There is force in this argument. The AFSJ is marked by institutional diversity rather than a distinctive institutional methodology, and the framers of the Amsterdam Treaty did consciously construct a new policy from diverse parts. There is nonetheless also room for disagreement with this thesis, relating to the extent to which the AFSJ is marked by thematic coherence. It is questionable whether the *finalité* of the 1992 internal market project is that much more well-defined than that of the AFSJ. We should remember in this respect that the former is ongoing, notwithstanding the temporal 'end-point' of 1992, and that there is increased contestation as to the balance between the social and the economic in internal market initiatives.[19]

4 LISBON TREATY: GENERAL PRINCIPLES

The Lisbon Treaty has had a marked impact on the Area of Freedom, Security, and Justice. The previous three-pillar system has gone, although distinct rules continue to apply to Foreign and Security Policy.[20] However the provisions concerning the AFSJ have been integrated into the main body of the Treaties. This section examines the general changes made by the Lisbon Treaty.

(A) OBJECTIVES

Article 2 TEU sets out the EU's values, and follows the corresponding provision of the Constitutional Treaty.[21]

The Union is founded on the values of respect for human dignity, freedom, democracy, equality, the rule of law and respect for human rights, including the rights of persons belonging to minorities. These values are common to the Member States in a society in which pluralism, non-discrimination, tolerance, justice, solidarity and equality between women and men prevail.

The EU's objectives are contained in Article 3 TEU, which is close to, although not identical with, the analogous provision of the Constitutional Treaty.[22] The objectives listed in Article 3 TEU bear comparison with those in Article 2 EU of the previous Treaty. There are however differences as to the more precise wording and placing of the objectives. Thus, for example, it is not fortuitous that mention of the area of freedom, security, and justice has 'moved up' the list to become Article 3(2) TEU, thereby signifying its centrality to EU policy. Article 3(2) TEU is framed as follows:

The Union shall offer its citizens an area of freedom, security and justice without internal frontiers, in which the free movement of persons is ensured in conjunction with appropriate measures with respect to external border controls, asylum, immigration and the prevention and combating of crime.

[19] Ch 17.
[20] Ch 10.
[21] Art I-2 CT.
[22] Art I-3 CT.

(B) TREATY ARCHITECTURE

The Lisbon Treaty completed the transition that began with the Amsterdam Treaty. The pillar system introduced by the Maastricht Treaty has been dismantled, although distinct rules still apply to the Common Foreign and Security Policy. The provisions concerning the AFSJ are no longer divided as they were prior to the Lisbon Treaty. They are grouped together in Title V of Part Three of the TFEU, which deals with 'Union Policies and Internal Actions'. Title V is located after those dealing with the internal market, free movement of goods, agriculture and fisheries, and free movement of persons, services, and capital.

The approach to the AFSJ in the Lisbon Treaty follows very closely that in the Constitutional Treaty.[23] Thus it was Working Group X on 'Freedom, Security and Justice'[24] from the Convention on the Future of Europe that strongly advocated de-pillarization, the incorporation of the Third Pillar into the main body of the Treaty, and the abolition of the distinctive categories of legal act that had previously applied to that area.

(C) COMPETENCE

The Lisbon Treaty established categories of competence for different subject matter areas.[25] The AFSJ falls within shared competence.[26] Two points should be noted about this placing, which were elaborated in the earlier discussion.

First, the nature of the power sharing between the EU and the Member States can only be divined by looking at the detailed provisions of the particular area. The divide is not the same in all areas of the AFSJ. It is the particular Treaty provisions and the judicial interpretation thereof that determine the division between Member State and EU competence. This is in reality what we have always had to do to determine the boundaries between state and EU power.

Secondly, Article 2(2) TFEU stipulates that in the context of shared competence the Member State can exercise competence only to the extent that the Union has not exercised, or has decided to cease to exercise, its competence within any such area. This looks like automatic pre-emption of Member State action where the Union has exercised its competence, with the consequence that the amount of shared power held by the Member States will diminish over time. There is truth in this, subject to the following qualifications.

Member States will lose their competence within the regime of shared power only to the extent that the Union has exercised 'its' competence. Precisely what the EU's competence is within these areas can, as noted above, be divined only by considering the detailed provisions in a particular area. The pre-emption of Member State action will moreover occur only 'to the extent' that the EU has exercised its competence in the relevant area. There are different ways in which the EU can intervene in a particular area.[27] The EU may choose to make uniform regulations, it may harmonize national laws, it may engage in minimum harmonization, or it may impose requirements of mutual recognition. The scope for any Member State action will depend on which regulatory technique is used by the EU.[28]

---

[23] Arts III-257–277 CT.

[24] CONV 426/02, Final Report of Working Group X, 'Freedom, Security and Justice', Brussels, 2 Dec 2002.

[25] Ch 3.

[26] Art 4(2)(j) TFEU.

[27] S Weatherill, 'Beyond Preemption? Shared Competence and Constitutional Change in the European Community' in D O'Keefe and P Twomey (eds), *Legal Issues of the Maastricht Treaty* (Chancery Law Publishing, 1994) ch 2; M Dougan, 'Minimum Harmonization and the Internal Market' (2000) 37 CMLRev 853; M Dougan, 'Vive la Différence? Exploring the Legal Framework for Reflexive Harmonisation within the Single Market' (2002) 1 Annual of German and European Law 13; CONV 375/1/02, Final Report of Working Group V on Complementary Competencies, Brussels, 4 Nov 2002, 12–13.

[28] See also Protocol (No 25) On Shared Competence.

(D) ARTICLE 67 TFEU

Article 67 TFEU is the lead provision for this Title of the Lisbon Treaty and it represents both continuity with, and modification of, the previous Treaty Articles.

> 1. The Union shall constitute an area of freedom, security and justice with respect for fundamental rights and the different legal systems and traditions of the Member States.
>
> 2. It shall ensure the absence of internal border controls for persons and shall frame a common policy on asylum, immigration and external border control, based on solidarity between Member States, which is fair towards third-country nationals. For the purpose of this Title, stateless persons shall be treated as third-country nationals.
>
> 3. The Union shall endeavour to ensure a high level of security through measures to prevent and combat crime, racism and xenophobia, and through measures for coordination and cooperation between police and judicial authorities and other competent authorities, as well as through the mutual recognition of judgments in criminal matters and, if necessary, through the approximation of criminal laws.
>
> 4. The Union shall facilitate access to justice, in particular through the principle of mutual recognition of judicial and extrajudicial decisions in civil matters.

Article 67 TFEU is based on Article 29 EU and Article 67 EC. There are however differences, most notably in Article 67(1) TFEU, which now provides that the AFSJ is to be secured with respect for fundamental rights and the different national legal systems and traditions. Article 67(4) is new in terms of its express recognition within the general provision that guides this area.

(E) INSTITUTIONS

The Lisbon Treaty specifies roles for the principal institutional players and for the Member States.

(i) *European Council*

Article 68 TFEU is novel and provides that the European Council shall define the strategic guidelines for legislative and operational planning within the area of freedom, security, and justice. This is however the Treaty catching up with reality, since the European Council had been performing this function for a decade, through the five-year programmes, such as Tampere,[29] Hague,[30] and Stockholm.[31] The Commission and the Justice and Home Affairs Council provide detailed input that fashions the guidelines agreed by the European Council.

(ii) *Council*

The Council is central to all that happens within the AFSJ. It has been the source of many legislative initiatives. It helps to structure the objectives of AFSJ policy, which are then fed into the European Council. Article 74 TFEU empowers the Council to adopt measures to ensure administrative cooperation between the relevant departments of the Member States in the areas covered by this Title, as well as between those departments and the Commission.

---

[29] Tampere European Council, 15–16 Oct 1999.
[30] Brussels European Council, 4–5 Nov 2004.
[31] Council 16484/1/09, Brussels, 25 Nov 2009.

Article 70 TFEU is novel and reflects concern over Member States' implementation of AFSJ policies and the efficacy of mutual recognition. It provides that, without prejudice to the Treaty provisions on enforcement actions,[32] the Council may, on a proposal from the Commission, adopt measures laying down arrangements whereby Member States, in collaboration with the Commission, evaluate the implementation of AFSJ policies, in particular in order to facilitate full application of mutual recognition.

(iii) *Council Committees*

Article 71 TFEU deals with support structures within the Council. The volume and nature of AFSJ initiatives has always necessitated specialist committee support for the Council.[33] There were essentially three layers of such support beneath the Justice and Home Affairs Council. Coreper provided the highest level of support, with the lowest level coming from working groups of specialists,[34] which operated in all major areas of AFSJ policy. There were however also groups that operated between Coreper and the working parties. In relation to the Third Pillar there was the Article 36 Committee, also known as CATS (*Comité de l'Article Trente-Six*). In relation to Title IV EC there was SCIFA, the Strategic Committee on Immigration Frontiers and Asylum, SCIFA + which included national heads of border control, a Committee on Civil Law Matters, and a High Level Working Group on Asylum and Migration.[35]

Article 71 TFEU continues this tradition of committee support. It provides for a standing committee to be set up within the Council in order to ensure that operational cooperation on internal security is promoted and strengthened within the Union. It is, without prejudice to Coreper, to facilitate coordination of the action of Member States' competent authorities. Representatives of the Union bodies, offices, and agencies concerned may be involved in the committee proceedings, and the European Parliament and national parliaments are to be kept informed of the proceedings.

The abbreviation chosen for this new committee is COSI,[36] which prompted comment as to whether the title would match reality. COSI is to facilitate, promote, and strengthen coordination of operational actions between EU Member States in the field of internal security. This coordination role will concern, *inter alia*, police and customs cooperation, external border protection, and judicial cooperation in criminal matters relevant to operational cooperation in the field of internal security. COSI is also to be responsible for evaluating the general direction and efficiency of operational cooperation, so as to identify possible shortcomings and propose recommendations to address them. It can invite representatives from Eurojust, Europol, Frontex, and other relevant bodies to its meetings. COSI is not however to be involved in preparing legislative acts, nor in the conduct of operations. Coreper remains responsible for preparing legislative acts with the help of the different Council working groups.

(iv) *European Parliament*

The ordinary legislative procedure is the norm for areas that fall within the AFSJ. This is to be welcomed, subject to the concerns expressed earlier as to modification of this procedure through use of trilogues.[37] These concerns are especially prevalent in relation to the AFSJ, since the great majority of legislative measures are now subject to these trilogue arrangements, with a consequential loss of transparency and

---

[32] Arts 258, 259, and 260 TFEU.

[33] F Hayes-Renshaw and H Wallace, *The Council of Ministers* (Palgrave, 2nd edn, 2006) 86–87.

[34] H Aden, 'Administrative Governance in the Fields of EU Police and Judicial Co-operation' in Hofmann and Türk (n 16) 351.

[35] Lavenex and Wallace (n 15) 468.

[36] http://ec.europa.eu/dgs/home-affairs/what-we-do/policies/internal-security/cosi/index_en.htm.

[37] Ch 5.

opportunity for democratic input.[38] Article 76 TFEU provides that legal acts passed in relation to crime and police cooperation, and measures enacted pursuant to Article 74 TFEU, can be made on a proposal from the Commission or on the initiative of a quarter of the Member States.

(v) National Parliaments

Article 69 TFEU stipulates that national parliaments ensure that the proposals and legislative initiatives submitted concerning crime and police cooperation comply with the principle of subsidiarity. This provision is new, and reflects the sensitivity of EU involvement in these areas. National parliaments would, however, even in the absence of Article 69, have been able to review such measures for compliance with subsidiarity, pursuant to Article 12 TEU.

(vi) Member States

Articles 72–73 TFEU address the role of the Member States. Article 72 TFEU reiterates the injunction in the previous Treaty that the AFSJ Title shall not affect the exercise of Member State responsibilities with regard to maintenance of law and order and the safeguarding of internal security. This proposition has political resonance and is not without substance, but does not reflect reality. The AFSJ Title is an area of shared competence. This necessarily means that Member State responsibilities for law and order will be circumscribed by EU measures. The nature and degree of this circumscription will perforce depend on the particular measure adopted by the EU. Article 73 TFEU provides that it shall be open to Member States to organize between themselves and under their responsibility such forms of cooperation and coordination as they deem appropriate between the competent departments of their administrations responsible for safeguarding national security.

(F) UNION COURTS

(i) Scope of Jurisdiction

The Lisbon Treaty brought all AFSJ provisions within the normal Treaty structure, with the consequence that the jurisdiction of the Union Courts extends to all EU law unless the Treaties stipulate to the contrary. The injunction that the CJEU shall ensure that in the interpretation and application of the Treaties the law is observed[39] is therefore of general application, save where it is limited by specific Treaty provisions.

The Community Courts' jurisdiction over the Third Pillar had been limited,[40] notwithstanding teleological interpretation which stretched the limits to afford maximum possible judicial oversight. Thus jurisdiction to give preliminary rulings was dependent on a Member State making a declaration accepting such jurisdiction, and it could also specify which national courts should be able to make such a preliminary reference. There were limits on legality review. Enforcement actions by the Commission were not available, and there was no provision for damages. The Community Courts' jurisdiction in relation to the other aspect of the AFSJ, dealing with visas, asylum, immigration, and other policies related to free movement of persons,[41] had also been constrained, since only national courts of last resort could send preliminary rulings to the ECJ.[42]

---

[38] T Bunyan, 'Abolish 1st and 2nd Reading Secret Deals—Bring Back Democracy "Warts and All"', available at www.statewatch.org/analyses/no-84-ep-first-reading-deals.pdf.

[39] Art 19(1) TEU.

[40] Art 35 EU.

[41] Title IV EC.

[42] Art 68(1) EC.

The Lisbon Treaty signalled a major change in this respect. The normal rules on direct and indirect actions are applicable to the AFSJ, subject to transitional provisions considered below. Thus preliminary rulings, legality review, and the other heads of jurisdiction are applicable to the AFSJ in the same manner as to other subject matter that falls within the Treaty.

(ii) *Direct Effect and Supremacy*

The doctrine of direct effect was created and developed by the Court. The Lisbon Treaty does not signal any change in the doctrine, but has implications for its scope of application.

Article 34 EU had provided for a distinct set of legal norms that were used in the context of the Third Pillar, dealing with Police and Judicial Cooperation in Criminal Matters. Framework decisions and decisions were the most important legal norms used in this area, and Article 34(2) EU stated that they did not have direct effect. The Court held that it did not preclude indirect effect.[43]

Article 34 EU has been repealed and the general regime of legal acts specified in the Lisbon Treaty applies to measures in the AFSJ. It will henceforth be possible to argue that a Treaty Article or a legislative, delegated, or implementing act dealing with the AFSJ gives rise to direct effect, provided that it satisfies the criteria for this doctrine to apply.

The supremacy principle was considered in an earlier chapter.[44] There was debate under the preexisting regime as to whether the supremacy of Community law over national law applied in relation to the Third Pillar,[45] although the matter was never ultimately tested in the courts. The de-pillarization resulting from the Lisbon Treaty means that the primacy of EU law will now cover matters that were hitherto part of the Third Pillar and are now shifted to the TFEU. The potential for clashes between Union acts and national constitutional precepts is especially prevalent in this area. This could lead to cases that test the boundaries of the primacy doctrine when the conflict with EU law involves national constitutional provisions.

(iii) *Transitional Provisions*

The Lisbon Treaty contains transitional provisions that are relevant to Union Courts and enforcement.[46] Article 10(1) of the Protocol on Transitional Provisions specified two limits to the powers of the institutions with respect to EU acts in the field of police and judicial cooperation in criminal matters that were adopted before the entry into force of the Lisbon Treaty, but these limits ceased to have effect five years after entry into force of the Lisbon Treaty.[47]

(G) UK AND THE AFSJ

The UK and Ireland negotiated three related opt-outs in the Treaty of Amsterdam that pertained to the AFSJ. These have been preserved and modified in the Lisbon Treaty.[48]

---

[43] Case C–105/03 *Criminal Proceedings against Maria Pupino* [2005] ECR I–5283.

[44] Ch 9.

[45] K Lenaerts and T Corthaut, 'Of Birds and Hedges: The Role of Primacy in Invoking Norms of EU Law' (2006) 31 ELRev 287; A Hinarejos, *Judicial Control in the European Union: Reforming Jurisdiction in the Intergovernmental Pillars* (Oxford University Press, 2009).

[46] Protocol (No 36) On Transitional Provisions, Art 10.

[47] Ibid Art 10(3).

[48] S Peers, 'British and Irish Opt-Outs from EU Justice and Home Affairs (JHA) Law', 3 Nov 2009, available at www.statewatch.org/euconstitution.htm.

(i) Schengen 'Acquis'

The Treaty of Amsterdam brought the Schengen treaties, and implementing measures, the Schengen *acquis*, into the EU legal order, through a Protocol. The Schengen regime abolished internal border controls between the participating states, and established harmonized rules for visas, as well as rules on external border control, illegal migration, and criminal and police cooperation. The UK and Ireland were not bound by the Schengen *acquis*, but the Protocol allowed them to participate in part or all of it, provided that the participating states agreed unanimously that this should be so. Both states have participated in certain aspects of the Schengen regime.

The Lisbon Treaty preserved the Protocol relating to the Schengen regime, together with the option for the UK and Ireland to participate in some or all parts of the regime, subject to unanimous agreement from the participating states.[49] The Protocol has however been amended to give the UK and Ireland a right to opt out of measures building upon parts of the Schengen *acquis*.

(ii) Border Controls

The Treaty of Amsterdam also contained a Protocol that preserved the UK's control over its borders. It was framed in broad terms, in order to preclude Treaty rules or international agreements concluded by the EU from impinging on the UK's control over its borders. This Protocol has been retained in the Lisbon Treaty.[50]

(iii) AFSJ: New and Amended Measures

The Treaty of Amsterdam contained a further Protocol. It provided in essence that the UK and Ireland were not bound by Title IV EC, but that they could choose whether or not to opt in to proposed measures in this area. When a legislative proposal was made, the UK and Ireland had three months to decide whether to opt in to a measure. If they did not do so, they were deemed to have opted out. The UK and Ireland could however opt in to legislation after it was made, subject to permission from the Commission.

The Lisbon Treaty has preserved and extended this Protocol, such that it now applies to the entirety of the AFSJ.[51] The default position is therefore that the UK and Ireland are not bound by measures adopted under the AFSJ Title. This constitutes an extension of the previous Protocol, since the Lisbon Protocol No 21 applies to all AFSJ measures, including those on crime and police cooperation. It is, as before, open to the UK and Ireland to signify that they wish to take part in a proposed measure under this Title, and they can, as previously, choose to opt in after an AFSJ measure has been adopted.

The Lisbon Protocol No 21 extends the UK and Irish opt-out by providing in effect that it applies to amendments to measures in relation to which those states have previously opted in. There are consequential provisions dealing with the situation where the decision to opt out of an amendment to a measure by which they were previously bound would lead to that measure being inoperable as between the other Member States.[52]

---

[49] Protocol (No 19) On the Schengen *Acquis* Integrated into the Framework of the European Union.

[50] Protocol (No 20) On the Application of Certain Aspects of Article 26 of the Treaty on the Functioning of the European Union to the United Kingdom and to Ireland.

[51] Protocol (No 21) On the Position of the United Kingdom and Ireland in respect of the Area of Freedom, Security and Justice, makes special provision for the UK and Ireland.

[52] Protocol (No 21) contains a further extension to the opt-out by providing that the UK and Ireland are not bound by the rules laid down on the basis of Art 16 TFEU, which relate to the processing of personal data by the Member States when carrying out activities which fall within the scope of Ch 4 or Ch 5 of Title V, where the UK and Ireland are not bound by the

(iv) *AFSJ: Opt-Out from Enacted AFSJ Measures*

Further complexity to the special provisions concerning the AFSJ and the UK is to be found in Article 10(4) of Protocol No 36 on Transitional Provisions. It provided in effect that the UK could choose to opt out of Third Pillar acts passed before the Lisbon Treaty, provided that it did so no later than six months before the end of the transitional period after the Lisbon Treaty came into force. This was subject to the caveat that a Third Pillar act amended after the Lisbon Treaty entered into force that was applicable to the UK remained so. Article 10(5) of the Protocol however left the door open to the UK to notify the Council of its wish to participate in acts that ceased to apply to it pursuant to Article 10(4).

The Coalition Government decided to exercise the opt-out, largely as a result of pressure from Tory Eurosceptics, notwithstanding the fact that those affected by the change expressed serious disquiet at the consequences.[53] Space precludes detailed consideration of the complex political manoeuvrings on this issue. Suffice it to say that the government decided to exercise the opt out, but then to opt back into the most important measures, including the European Arrest Warrant.[54]

5 CRIMINAL LAW AND PROCEDURE: PRE-LISBON

The remainder of this chapter will focus on criminal law and procedure as an example of the operation of the AFSJ within a particular substantive area. It is impossible to understand the significance of the Lisbon Treaty on criminal law and procedure without some understanding of the prior legal position.

The EU's express competence over criminal matters was hitherto regulated by the EU Treaty. Article 31(1) EU provided that common action on criminal matters should 'include': facilitating and accelerating cooperation between competent ministries and judicial authorities of the Member States, including, where appropriate, cooperation through Eurojust, in relation to proceedings and the enforcement of decisions; facilitating extradition between Member States; ensuring compatibility in rules applicable in the Member States, as may be necessary to improve such cooperation; preventing conflicts of jurisdiction between Member States; and progressively adopting measures establishing minimum rules relating to the constituent elements of criminal acts and to penalties in the fields of organized crime, terrorism, and illicit drug trafficking. Article 31(2) EU stated that the Council should encourage cooperation through Eurojust in a number of specified ways. Unanimity in the Council was required for decision-making in this area.[55] The Third Pillar thus provided some legislative competence over criminal matters, subject to the unanimity requirement.

It was nonetheless contested whether there was competence to enact measures relating to criminal procedure, since it was not explicitly mentioned in Article 31 EU. The need for such EU initiatives was driven in large part by mutual recognition, which entailed the acceptance by Member States' courts of the judgments by national criminal courts.[56] The creation of the European Arrest Warrant led in turn

---

rules governing the forms of judicial cooperation in criminal matters or police cooperation which require compliance with the provisions laid down on the basis of Art 16.

[53] www.parliament.uk/business/committees/committees-a-z/lords-select/eu-home-affairs-sub-committee-f-/ Publications/; A Hinarejos, JR Spencer, and S Peers, 'Opting Out of EU Criminal Law: What is Actually Involved?', CELS Working Paper, New Series No 1 (2012).

[54] Decision pursuant to Article 10 of Protocol 36 to The Treaty on the Functioning of the European Union, Cm 8671, July 2013; Council 12750/13, UK notification according to Article 10(4) of Protocol No 36 to TEU and TFEU, Brussels, 26 July 2013; Decision pursuant to Article 10(5) of Protocol 36 to the Treaty on the Functioning of the European Union, Cm 8897, July 2014; Council 15398, Notification of the United Kingdom under Article 10(5) of Protocol 36 to the EU Treaties, Brussels, 27 Nov 2014; Council Decision 2014/857/EU [2014] OJ L345/1; Commission Decision 2014/858/EU [2014] OJ L345/6.

[55] Art 34(2) EU.

[56] Mitsilegas (n 2) 101–109.

to calls for procedural protection and defence rights for the person who had been transferred to the Member State issuing the warrant. There were nonetheless serious concerns as to the competence of the EU to enact such measures, and the content thereof.[57]

There was also controversy as to criminal law competence within the Community Pillar, since there was no express Treaty foundation for exercise of such power. A legislative technique used to circumvent this problem was to enact two measures, one adopted under the Community Pillar dealing with the principal regulatory issues, the other made pursuant to the Third Pillar, which contained criminal law measures where these were felt to be necessary to support the regulatory scheme.

This approach was however thrown into question by ECJ decisions, which held that there was some criminal law competence within the Community Pillar.[58] The ECJ had, in its early jurisprudence, placed limits on national criminal law, insofar as it might impede the rules on free movement.[59] It had also positively encouraged the use of national criminal law as a sanction for breach of Community law, where this form of sanction would be used at national level in analogous situations.[60] These decisions were significant, but fell short of ascribing any direct criminal law competence to the EC within the Community Pillar. The Commission nonetheless felt that such competence could be justified in certain circumstances. This was accepted by the ECJ in the *Environmental Crimes* case.[61]

Case C–176/03 **Commission v Council**
[2005] ECR I–7879

The Council enacted a Framework Decision under the Third Pillar, Title VI TEU, that required Member States to prescribe criminal penalties for certain environmental offences. The Commission argued that the measure should have been enacted under Article 175 EC, since it was concerned with the environment. The ECJ found that the principal aim of the Framework Decision was to protect the environment, and that it should have been made under Article 175. It accepted that, as a general rule, neither criminal law, nor criminal procedure fell within Community competence, but then reasoned as follows.

THE ECJ

48. However, [this] does not prevent the Community legislature, when the application of effective, proportionate and dissuasive criminal penalties by the competent national authorities is an essential measure for combating serious environmental offences, from taking measures which relate to the criminal law of the Member States which it considers necessary in order to ensure that the rules which it lays down on environmental protection are fully effective.

The decision was greeted enthusiastically by the Commission, which regarded it as applicable to any sphere of Community action.[62] The Council and Member States were, unsurprisingly, less enamoured by the decision, and were unwilling to accept that it had such a broad reach.[63] The reaction in academic

---

[57] V Mitsilegas, 'The Constitutional Implications of Mutual Recognition in Criminal Matters in the European Union' (2006) 43 CMLRev 1277.
[58] Mitsilegas (n 2) 69–70.
[59] Case 203/80 *Casati* [1980] ECR 2595, [27].
[60] Case 68/88 *Commission v Greece* [1989] ECR 2965.
[61] Case C–176/03 *Commission v Council* [2005] ECR I–7879.
[62] Communication on the implications of the Court's judgment of 13 Sept 2005, COM(2005)583 final/2, [8].
[63] Mitsilegas (n 2) 75–79.

circles was critical, with commentators highlighting the expansion of Community competence on the basis of a generalized notion of effectiveness that was difficult to confine.[64]

The ECJ nonetheless reaffirmed the Community's competence over criminal matters in the *Ship-Source Pollution* case, *Commission v Council*.[65] The Commission argued for a broad reading of the earlier judgment, such that it should be applicable to the sphere of transport, the subject matter in the instant case. The Council, supported by twenty Member States, sought to distinguish and confine the ruling in the *Environmental Crimes* case. The ECJ gave a nuanced judgment.[66] It stated that the contested measure should have been adopted under the Community Pillar, and reiterated the ruling from the earlier decision concerning effectiveness and criminal law. The ECJ nonetheless refrained from holding that this principle was applicable to all spheres of Community policy and also held that the precise sanction should be determined through a Third Pillar measure.

6 CRIMINAL LAW AND PROCEDURE: POST-LISBON

The Lisbon Treaty resolved some issues concerning the scope of EU competence over criminal law, although there are still difficult interpretive problems. The 'thinking' on this issue had however been done in the Convention on the Future of Europe and in Working Group X on 'Freedom, Security and Justice'. The detailed provisions in the Lisbon Treaty merely copied those in the Constitutional Treaty.[67] Article 82 TFEU is now the lead provision in this area.[68]

Article 82(1) provides that judicial cooperation in criminal matters in the Union shall be based on the principle of mutual recognition of judgments and judicial decisions and shall include the approximation of the laws and regulations of the Member States in the areas referred to in Article 82(2) and in Article 83. The European Parliament and the Council, acting by the ordinary legislative procedure, shall adopt measures to: lay down rules and procedures for ensuring recognition throughout the Union of all forms of judgments and judicial decisions; prevent and settle conflicts of jurisdiction between Member States; support the training of the judiciary and judicial staff; and facilitate cooperation between judicial or equivalent authorities of the Member States in relation to proceedings in criminal matters and the enforcement of decisions. The legal acts in this area can be made at the initiative of the Commission or a quarter of the Member States.[69]

(A) CRIMINAL LAW

The EU's competence to enact measures concerning the criminal law is now specified in Article 83 TFEU.

> 1. The European Parliament and the Council may, by means of directives adopted in accordance with the ordinary legislative procedure, establish minimum rules concerning the definition of criminal offences and sanctions in the areas of particularly serious crime with a cross-border dimension resulting from the nature or impact of such offences or from a special need to combat them on a common basis.

---

[64] E Herlin-Karnell, '*Commission v Council*: Some Reflections on Criminal Law in the First Pillar' (2007) 13 EPL 69.

[65] Case C–440/05 *Commission v Council* [2007] ECR I–9097.

[66] S Peers, 'The European Community's Criminal Law Competence: The Plot Thickens' (2008) 33 ELRev 399.

[67] Arts III-270–275 CT.

[68] C Ladenburger, 'Police and Criminal Law in the Treaty of Lisbon. A New Dimension for the Community Model' (2008) 4 EuConst 20.

[69] Art 76 TFEU.

These areas of crime are the following: terrorism, trafficking in human beings and sexual exploitation of women and children, illicit drug trafficking, illicit arms trafficking, money laundering, corruption, counterfeiting of means of payment, computer crime and organised crime.

On the basis of developments in crime, the Council may adopt a decision identifying other areas of crime that meet the criteria specified in this paragraph. It shall act unanimously after obtaining the consent of the European Parliament.

2. If the approximation of criminal laws and regulations of the Member States proves essential to ensure the effective implementation of a Union policy in an area which has been subject to harmonisation measures, directives may establish minimum rules with regard to the definition of criminal offences and sanctions in the area concerned. Such directives shall be adopted by the same ordinary or special legislative procedure as was followed for the adoption of the harmonisation measures in question, without prejudice to Article 76.

Article 83(1) TFEU thus provides that the ordinary legislative procedure should apply to the making of such directives, by way of contrast to unanimity in the Council, which was the decisional rule hitherto. It tightens the pre-existing wording in Article 31 EU, by expressly requiring that EU intervention relates to areas of particularly serious crime that have a cross-border dimension, although this might be regarded as inherent in the earlier formulation. The list of offences in Article 83(1) TFEU has however been broadened by way of comparison to Article 31 EU, and now embraces matters previously listed in Article 29 EU,[70] plus some other matters. Additions to this list can be made only if there is Council unanimity and consent by the European Parliament. The EP issued a cautionary resolution as to the circumstances when Article 83 should be used, stressing the need to show that action really was required at EU level, and that the rights of the accused should be protected in the ensuing legislation.[71]

Article 83(2) TFEU is new and affirms the ECJ's approach in the jurisprudence considered above. The Treaty provision moreover enshrines a broad interpretation of the previous jurisprudence. The EU is empowered to approximate criminal laws and regulations to ensure the effective implementation of a Union policy in an area that has been subject to harmonization measures. This power thus applies to any Union policy that has been harmonized, there being no condition that the relevant Union policy be regarded as referring to 'essential objectives' of the Union. It will be interesting to see the interpretation of the requirement that there has been harmonization of the relevant Union policy. This could well be interpreted liberally, such that relatively minimal substantive harmonization is regarded as sufficient foundation for the approximation of criminal laws and regulations. The Commission makes the initial determination as to whether such approximation is 'essential' to ensure effective implementation of EU policy, subject to acceptance by the Council and European Parliament in the ordinary or special legislative procedure.

Member States' concerns as to possible use of Article 83(1)–(2) furnish the explanation for Article 83(3) TFEU, which enshrines an 'emergency brake'. Thus where a member of the Council considers that a draft directive proposed under Article 83(1)–(2) would affect fundamental aspects of its criminal justice system, it can request that the draft directive should be referred to the European Council. This leads to suspension of the ordinary legislative procedure. If consensus is reached in the European Council within four months, the draft directive is then referred back to the Council, and the ordinary legislative procedure continues. If disagreement persists after four months then the draft directive fails, subject to

---

[70] Art 29 EU did not contain any express power to make minimum rules relating to the constituent elements of offences listed therein, which were not also mentioned in Art 31 EU, although Art 31 did not expressly preclude this.

[71] An EU Approach to Criminal Law, P7_TA(2012)0208 [2013] OJ C264E/2.

the caveat that a minimum of nine Member States can notify the Council, European Parliament, and Commission of their wish to establish enhanced cooperation on the basis of the draft directive. If this occurs, the authorization[72] to proceed with enhanced cooperation is deemed to be granted and the provisions on enhanced cooperation apply.

(B) CRIMINAL PROCEDURE

There were, as seen above, doubts as to EU competence over criminal procedure prior to the Lisbon Treaty. This issue has been addressed through Article 82(2) TFEU.

> To the extent necessary to facilitate mutual recognition of judgments and judicial decisions and police and judicial cooperation in criminal matters having a cross-border dimension, the European Parliament and the Council may, by means of directives adopted in accordance with the ordinary legislative procedure, establish minimum rules. Such rules shall take into account the differences between the legal traditions and systems of the Member States.
>
> They shall concern:
>
> (a) mutual admissibility of evidence between Member States;
>
> (b) the rights of individuals in criminal procedure;
>
> (c) the rights of victims of crime;
>
> (d) any other specific aspects of criminal procedure which the Council has identified in advance by a decision; for the adoption of such a decision, the Council shall act unanimously after obtaining the consent of the European Parliament.
>
> Adoption of the minimum rules referred to in this paragraph shall not prevent Member States from maintaining or introducing a higher level of protection for individuals.

The EU now has explicit competence over criminal procedure, and the Lisbon Treaty has thus settled the controversy that plagued the passage of such measures hitherto. The terms of this competence are nonetheless carefully delineated.

The condition precedent for competence over criminal procedure is that it is necessary to facilitate mutual recognition of judgments and judicial decisions and police and judicial cooperation in criminal matters having a cross-border dimension. The linkage with mutual recognition thereby reaffirms the primary rationale for earlier EU involvement with criminal procedure. The corollary is that 'criminal procedure measures—and the human rights implications which they may have—are thus subordinated to the efficiency logic of mutual recognition'.[73]

There are other limits built into Article 82(2). Thus the EU is only empowered to enact directives which lay down minimum rules, and there is a specific injunction to take account of differences between the legal systems and traditions of the Member States. The addition of any other aspect of criminal procedure requires Council unanimity and the consent of the European Parliament.

Article 82(3) TFEU contains a further limit. The 'emergency brake' mechanism that was considered in relation to criminal law measures is also applicable here. It is therefore open to a Member State to refer a draft directive to the European Council where it believes that it would affect fundamental aspects of its criminal justice system. The procedure thereafter is the same as that described above.

---

[72] Art 20(2) TEU, Art 329(1) TFEU.
[73] Mitsilegas (n 2) 109.

(C) CRIME PREVENTION

The Lisbon Treaty added a new provision that deals directly with crime prevention. Article 84 TFEU provides that the European Parliament and the Council, acting via the ordinary legislative procedure, can establish measures to promote and support the action of Member States in the field of crime prevention, excluding any harmonization of the laws and regulations of the Member States. Article 84 exemplifies the incomplete categorization of competences. It confines the EU to supporting Member State action and excludes harmonization. This would naturally place it within the category of competence dealing with supporting, coordinating, or supplementing Member State action, but it is not included in the relevant list.[74]

(D) CRIMINAL INVESTIGATION AND PROSECUTION

The previous EU Treaty made provision for Eurojust. Article 31(2) EU was framed in terms of the Council 'encouraging cooperation' via Eurojust in a variety of ways, including, for example, the facilitation of coordination between Member States' prosecuting authorities. This sufficed to enable the EU to adopt the Eurojust Decision.[75]

Article 85 TFEU is framed in a similar vein, although there are differences of detail. Thus Article 85(1) states that Eurojust's mission is to support and strengthen coordination and cooperation between national investigating and prosecuting authorities in relation to serious crime affecting two or more Member States, or requiring a prosecution on common bases, on the basis of operations conducted and information supplied by the Member States' authorities and by Europol.

The EU is now empowered to enact regulations via the ordinary legislative procedure to determine Eurojust's 'structure, operation, field of action and tasks', including arrangements for involving the European Parliament and national parliaments in the evaluation of Eurojust's activities.[76] Article 85(1) provides that Eurojust's tasks may include the following.

(a) the initiation of criminal investigations, as well as proposing the initiation of prosecutions conducted by competent national authorities, particularly those relating to offences against the financial interests of the Union;

(b) the coordination of investigations and prosecutions referred to in point (a);

(c) the strengthening of judicial cooperation, including by resolution of conflicts of jurisdiction and by close cooperation with the European Judicial Network.

Eurojust's power can be increased pursuant to Article 85 TFEU. Legislative regulations can be made relating to its tasks, which now include the 'initiation of criminal investigations', which is expressly distinguished from proposing the initiation of prosecutions by national authorities. Eurojust's tasks also cover the resolution of jurisdictional conflicts, as part of the strengthening of judicial cooperation. It remains to be seen whether these provisions serve as the basis for EU regulations that reshape, to some degree, the criminal investigatory process.[77]

---

[74] Art 6 TFEU.

[75] Council Decision 2002/187/JHA of 28 February 2002, setting up Eurojust with a view to reinforcing the fight against serious crime [2002] OJ L63/1.

[76] Art 85(2) TFEU makes clear that formal acts of judicial procedure shall be carried out by the competent national officials in relation to prosecutions, without prejudice to Art 86 TFEU.

[77] Proposal for a Regulation of the European Parliament and of the Council on the European Union Agency for Criminal Justice Cooperation (Eurojust), COM(2013) 535 final; http://ec.europa.eu/justice/criminal/judicial-cooperation/eurojust/index_en.htm.

CRIMINAL LAW AND PROCEDURE: POST-LISBON | 985

(E) CRIMINAL PROSECUTION AND THE EUROPEAN PUBLIC PROSECUTOR

There had, prior to the Lisbon Treaty, been debate and contestation as to whether there should be a European Public Prosecutor, with autonomous power to conduct prosecutions in relation to certain offences that had a marked impact on the EU's financial interests.[78] This provoked considerable opposition from Member States, which regarded the creation of such an office as a further incursion on national sovereignty in a sensitive field. The Lisbon Treaty nonetheless included provision for a European Public Prosecutor in Article 86 TFEU, and the Commission has proposed a regulation to make this a reality.[79]

> 1. In order to combat crimes affecting the financial interests of the Union, the Council, by means of regulations adopted in accordance with a special legislative procedure, may establish a European Public Prosecutor's Office from Eurojust. The Council shall act unanimously after obtaining the consent of the European Parliament.
>
> ...
>
> 2. The European Public Prosecutor's Office shall be responsible for investigating, prosecuting and bringing to judgment, where appropriate in liaison with Europol, the perpetrators of, and accomplices in, offences against the Union's financial interests, as determined by the regulation provided for in paragraph 1. It shall exercise the functions of prosecutor in the competent courts of the Member States in relation to such offences.

Article 86 contains what is in effect an interesting 'emergency accelerator'. It provides that in the absence of Council unanimity, a group of at least nine Member States can request that the draft regulation be referred to the European Council. If this happens, the procedure in the Council is suspended. If consensus is forthcoming in the European Council within four months, the draft regulation is referred back to the Council for adoption. If disagreement persists beyond four months, it is still open to at least nine Member States to notify their wish to the European Parliament, Council, and Commission to establish enhanced cooperation. Authorization to proceed with enhanced cooperation shall be deemed to be granted and the provisions on enhanced cooperation apply.

Article 86(4) TFEU moreover enables the European Council, acting unanimously after obtaining the consent of the European Parliament and consulting the Commission, to adopt a decision amending Article 86(1) in order to extend the powers of the European Public Prosecutor's Office to include serious crime having a cross-border dimension, with relevant amendments to Article 86(2).

(F) CRIME AND POLICE COOPERATION

Article 30 EU dealt with police cooperation, and made provision for cooperation through Europol. The complex rules applicable to Europol and the EU have been expertly examined elsewhere.[80] The Lisbon Treaty builds on and modifies the pre-existing provisions.

Article 87 TFEU embodies the basic principle of police cooperation between Member States' authorities in relation to the prevention, detection, and investigation of crime. Measures can now be enacted pursuant to the ordinary legislative procedure concerning: the collection, storage, processing, analysis,

---

[78] Mitsilegas (n 2) 229–232.

[79] Proposal for a Council Regulation on the establishment of the European Public Prosecutor's Office, COM(2013) 534 final.

[80] Mitsilegas (n 2) 161–187.

and exchange of relevant information; support for staff training; and common investigative techniques in relation to the detection of serious forms of organized crime.[81] It is moreover open to the Council, acting unanimously after consulting the European Parliament, to establish measures concerning operational cooperation between national authorities. This is subject to an 'emergency accelerator' procedure of the kind described above, subject to the caveat that it does not apply to acts that constitute a development of the Schengen *acquis*.

Article 88 TFEU deals with Europol. Its mission is to support and strengthen action by the Member States' police authorities and other law enforcement services and their mutual cooperation in 'preventing and combating serious crime affecting two or more Member States, terrorism and forms of crime which affect a common interest covered by a Union policy'. The reference to forms of crime that affect a common interest covered by a Union policy extends Europol's mandate. Legislative regulations adopted by the ordinary legislative procedure determine Europol's structure, operation, field of action, and tasks, including procedures for scrutiny of Europol's activities by the European Parliament and national parliaments.

Europol's tasks include: collection, storage, processing, analysis, and exchange of information; and coordination, organization, and implementation of investigative and operational action carried out jointly with the Member States' competent authorities or in liaison with Eurojust. This wording lays the foundation for Europol to be granted operational capability, and this is reinforced by the requirement that any such operational action must be carried out in liaison and in agreement with the relevant national authorities, which have exclusive responsibility for application of coercive measures.[82]

7 CRIMINAL LAW AND PROCEDURE: OBJECTIVES

The discussion in the preceding section focused on the Treaty Articles concerning criminal law and procedure. We need however to press further to understand the objectives of EU intervention in this area. The earlier discussion considered in general terms the rationale for the AFSJ. We need now to sharpen the focus to reveal the purpose served by EU intervention in relation to criminal law and procedure. This evolved over time, but now has two discernible strands, as is apparent from Working Group X on 'Freedom, Security and Justice', whose report shaped thinking on the EU's involvement with crime in the Treaty reform process.

The rationale for EU intervention in some instances was the need to combat the cross-border impact of serious crime, which could not be achieved effectively by individual Member States, more especially post-9/11.[83] The need for the approximation of substantive criminal law was pressing because 'certain crimes have a transnational dimension and cannot be addressed effectively by the Member States acting alone'.[84] The cross-border impact of serious crime created therefore externalities in Member States, which demanded collective action. The EU provided an institutional forum for collective action that could be used to fashion appropriate rules, more especially because many such crimes would also have negative effects on the EU economy.

There is also a second rationale for EU intervention in criminal law, which is more closely associated with the efficacy of the internal market and other EU policies. The Working Group touched on this idea when it posited a further reason for EU intervention 'where the crime is directed against a shared

---

[81] The normal rules as to choice of legal base must however be complied with, Case C–43/12 *Commission v European Parliament and Council* EU:C:2014:298.
[82] Art 88(3) TFEU.
[83] Working Group X (n 24) 1, 9.
[84] Ibid 9.

European interest which is already itself the subject of a common policy of the Union...approximation of substantive criminal law should be part of the toolbox of measures for the pursuit of that policy whenever non-criminal rules do not suffice'.[85] The developed version of this idea is now enshrined in Article 83(2) TFEU: approximation of criminal laws is warranted where this is essential to ensure effective implementation of Union policy in an area that has been harmonized.

8 CRIMINAL LAW AND PROCEDURE: CHALLENGES

It is important to appreciate that EU involvement in criminal law has generated significant challenges and tensions.

(A) MEMBER STATE ACCEPTANCE

The first such challenge concerns Member State acceptance of criminal law initiatives. The history of EU intervention in relation to criminal law reveals an interesting duality in the willingness of Member States to realize the Treaty objectives.

The Member States have been at the forefront of the augmentation of EU competence over crime. It was the Member States that agreed to the initial three-pillar structure in the Maastricht Treaty, which gave the EU competence over criminal issues, and to the revisions in the Treaty of Amsterdam. It was the Member States that expressed willingness to bring crime within the main fabric of the Constitutional Treaty and Lisbon Treaty, and to extend the EU's powers in this sphere. It was the Member States once again that fashioned overall policy via the European Council in the Tampere[86] and Hague Programmes.[87]

The Member States' willingness to embrace EU intervention over crime at the 'macro' level must however be balanced by difficulties of realization at the 'micro' level, as attested to by contestation over the content and passage of particular criminal measures. There is no logical inconsistency in this respect. This tension is reflective of the proposition that it is often easier to agree on general principles than on concrete measures to secure their realization. There was thus little difficulty in securing consensus on the desirability of tackling serious cross-border crime, as exemplified by drug trafficking and the like. Decisions as to the particular measures that should be taken to attain this objective were nonetheless often controversial, since they entailed assumptions concerning criminality and incursions into Member State autonomy on which Member States disagreed.

(B) MUTUAL RECOGNITION

The second challenge concerns the regulatory technique used to attain the EU's objectives outlined above. The EU has various regulatory tools at its disposal, but two are of particular significance: approximation of laws and mutual recognition.

Prior to the Lisbon Treaty the formal rules gave prominence to the approximation of laws. Article 34 EU provided that the objectives of the Third Pillar could be attained by framework decisions to approximate Member States' laws and regulations. These measures were analogous to directives, save for the fact that they were said not to have direct effect.

---

[85] Ibid 10.
[86] Tampere European Council, 15–16 Oct 1999.
[87] Brussels European Council, 25–26 Mar 2004.

The late 1990s saw a shift to the principle of mutual recognition. The catalyst was concern about the slow pace of integration post-Maastricht, coupled with Member States' wariness of EU harmonization.[88] This led to suggestions, voiced by the UK Presidency in 1998, that mutual recognition might be the way forward, with analogies drawn to its use to attain the internal market. This suggestion was endorsed by the European Council in the Tampere Programme,[89] and by the Commission.[90]

The centrality of mutual recognition is now firmly embedded in the Lisbon Treaty. Article 82 TFEU, the lead provision in this area, provides that judicial cooperation in criminal matters is to be based on mutual recognition, with approximation of laws denominated for the specific topics delineated in Articles 82(2) and 83 TFEU. This is reinforced by the fact that the new EU competence over criminal procedure in Article 82(2) TFEU is predicated on the need for minimum harmonization in order to facilitate mutual recognition of judgments. The centrality of mutual recognition is apparent in the following extract from the Commission.

Recognition of Decisions between EU Countries[91]

Mutual recognition of judicial decisions is a process by which a decision usually taken by a judicial authority in one EU country is recognised, and where necessary, enforced by other EU countries as if it was a decision taken by the judicial authorities of that latter country.

This is a key concept in the sphere of judicial cooperation, as it helps to overcome the difficulties stemming from the diversity of judicial systems throughout the EU.

Traditional judicial cooperation can be defined as an inter-state relation where one sovereign State makes a request to another sovereign State, which then decides whether or not to comply with it.

Those relations are organised through a variety of legal instruments, agreed either on a bilateral basis or within the framework of international organisations such as the UN or the Council of Europe.

This system is both slow and complex. It no longer corresponds to the reality of today's European area where people circulate easily, with few or no controls.

To a free circulation of people shall correspond a free circulation of judicial decisions. This is where the principle of mutual recognition leads to a real change in the philosophy of judicial cooperation. It means that each national judicial authority should recognise requests made by the judicial authority of another EU country with a minimum of formalities.

Enhanced mutual recognition is to improve the efficiency of cooperation between authorities. It is based on mutual confidence that EU countries have in each others' systems, founded on the common respect of human rights and fundamental freedoms as asserted in the Treaty of the European Union.

The application of mutual recognition to the criminal sphere has not however been unproblematic. Commentators have questioned the analogy with the use of this concept in the internal market. They have rightly pointed to the very real difference between mutual recognition of Member States' regulatory provisions concerning the content of goods for the purpose of enhancing free movement[92] and

---

[88] Mitsilegas (n 2) 116; Mitsilegas (n 57).
[89] Tampere European Council, 15–16 Oct 1999, [33].
[90] Mutual Recognition of Final Decisions in Criminal Matters, COM(2000) 495 final, 2.
[91] http://ec.europa.eu/justice/criminal/recognition-decision/index_en.htm.
[92] Chs 17, 19.

mutual recognition of judicial decisions for the purpose of increasing the applicability of such rulings in other Member States.[93]

C Lavenex, Mutual Recognition and the Monopoly of Force. Limits of the Single Market Analogy[94]

Who benefits from mutual recognition and for what purpose?

...In the single market, mutual recognition facilitates the cross-border flows of economic goods and services. It is an instrument to facilitate economic transactions between societal actors in spite of partly differing state regulations. In the AFSJ, mutual recognition promotes the free movement of judgments and judicial decisions; that is, state acts... In criminal law, the member states accept final judicial decisions, e.g. an arrest warrant or other decisions laying down sanctions issued under the law of that state. Those benefiting from mutual recognition are hence not societal actors but state representatives.

There is thus a fundamental difference in the nature of the flows addressed: in the first case, single market integration, mutual recognition eases the cross-border movement of societal interaction, thus contributing to processes of liberalization and socialization. The private sphere and the rights of individuals engaged in trade and consumption are enhanced while the regulatory scope of the member states is reduced. In the case of judicial co-operation in JHA, in contrast, the introduction of mutual recognition does not expand the rights of individuals vis-à-vis the state. On the contrary, it facilitates the cross-border movement of sovereign acts exercised by states' executives and judicial organs...

What is being mutually recognized?

The second important difference concerns the 'object' that governments agree to mutually recognize and its scope in terms of sovereignty implications for the participating states. In the economic sphere, the object of recognition is another country's rules on products and production methods... In JHA, by contrast, the object of recognition reaches much further as it applies to sovereign acts of the judiciary in their interpretation and application of a whole set of material and procedural laws. By applying mutual recognition, another member state not only recognizes a law as being equivalent but recognizes the judicial act in its interpretation of all relevant provisions in a given case. In other words, mutual recognition not only implies that member states recognize other norms as equivalent to their own but that they accept the need to co-operate in the enforcement of other states' systems of law.

---

[93] S Peers, 'Mutual Recognition and Criminal Law in the European Union: Has the Council Got it Wrong?' (2004) 41 CMLRev 5; Mitsilegas (n 2) ch 3; Mitsilegas (n 57); M Maduro, 'So Close and Yet So Far: The Paradoxes of Mutual Recognition' (2007) 14 JEPP 814.

[94] (2007) 14 JEPP 762, 764–766. See also, S Wolff, 'The Rule of Law in the Area of Freedom, Security and Justice: Monitoring at Home what the European Union Preaches Abroad' (2013) 5 Hague Journal on the Rule of Law 119.

(c) MUTUAL RECOGNITION AND THE EUROPEAN ARREST WARRANT

(i) *Framework Decision and Judicial Interpretation*

The difficulties concerning mutual recognition can be exemplified by experience with the European Arrest Warrant (EAW),[95] which was the first major mutual recognition initiative in this area.[96] The 9/11 terrorist attacks were the immediate catalyst for the EAW, but its reach extends far beyond such offences.

The EAW is a judicial decision issued by a Member State with a view to the arrest and surrender by another Member State of a requested person, for the purposes of conducting a criminal prosecution, or executing a custodial sentence or detention order. Member States are required to execute any EAW on the basis of the principle of mutual recognition.

Article 2(1) provides that an EAW may be issued for acts punishable by the law of the issuing Member State by a custodial sentence or a detention order for a maximum period of at least twelve months or, where a sentence has been passed or a detention order has been made, for sentences of at least four months. The initial EAW regime distinguished between two types of offence. Certain more serious offences listed in Article 2(2) of the Framework Decision that were punishable by at least three years' detention in the issuing state could be the subject of an EAW, irrespective of whether those offences existed in the state that had to execute the warrant. There was no need for verification of double criminality in such instances, meaning that there was no requirement to check that such offences existed in the state that had to execute the warrant. In relation to less serious offences, Article 2(1) and (4) provided that an EAW could be issued, subject to the caveat that it was an offence under the law of the executing state, although this condition could be satisfied whatever the constituent elements of the offence or how it was described. Article 3 listed certain mandatory grounds on which the state required to execute the EAW should not do so; Articles 4 and 4a set out certain optional grounds on which it might refuse to do so; and Article 5 specified guarantees that had to be provided by the state issuing the EAW. The legality of the EAW was challenged in the following case, but the ECJ upheld its legality.[97]

Case C–303/05 **Advocaten voor de Wereld VZW v Leden van de Ministerraad**
[2007] ECR I–3633

The claimant alleged that Article 2(2) of the Framework Decision, by dispensing with the need to verify the double criminality of the offences listed, was contrary, *inter alia*, to the principle of legality in criminal matters. This was because the listed offences were not legally defined, but constituted vague categories

---

[95] Council Framework Decision 2002/584/JHA of 13 June 2002 on the European Arrest Warrant and the surrender procedures between Member States [2002] OJ L190/1; Council Framework Decision 2009/299/JHA of 26 February 2009 amending Framework Decisions 2002/584/JHA, 2005/214/JHA, 2006/783/JHA, 2008/909/JHA and 2008/947/JHA, thereby enhancing the procedural rights of persons and fostering the application of the principle of mutual recognition to decisions rendered in the absence of the person concerned at the trial [2009] OJ L81/24.

[96] S Alegre and M Leaf, 'Mutual Recognition in European Judicial Cooperation: A Step Too Far Too Soon? Case Study—The European Arrest Warrant' (2004) 10 ELJ 200; J Wouters and F Naert, 'Of Arrest Warrants, Terrorist Offences and Extradition Deals: An Appraisal of the EU's Main Criminal Law Measures against Terrorism after "11 September"' (2004) 41 CMLRev 911; J Komárek, 'European Constitutionalism and the European Arrest Warrant: In Search of the Limits of Contrapunctual Principles' (2007) 44 CMLRev 9; A Górski and P Hofmański, *The European Arrest Warrant and its Implementation in the Member States of the European Union* (CH Beck, 2008); D Sarmiento, 'European Union: The European Arrest Warrant and the Quest for Constitutional Coherence' (2008) 6 I-CON 171; V Mitsilegas, 'The Limits of Mutual Trust in Europe's Area of Freedom, Security and Justice: From Automatic Inter-State Cooperation to the Slow Emergence of the Individual' (2012) 31 YBEL 319; E Herlin-Karnell, 'From Mutual Trust to the Full Effectiveness of EU Law: 10 Years of the European Arrest Warrant' (2013) 38 ELRev 79; JR Spencer, 'Extradition, the European Arrest Warrant and Human Rights' (2013) 72 CLJ 250.

[97] D Leczykiewicz, 'Constitutional Conflicts and the Third Pillar' (2008) 33 ELRev 230.

of undesirable conduct. He argued that this violated the requirement that criminal offences should satisfy conditions of precision, clarity, and predictability. The ECJ acknowledged that the principle of the legality of criminal offences was part of EU law and continued as follows.

THE ECJ

50. This principle implies that legislation must define clearly offences and the penalties which they attract. That condition is met in the case where the individual concerned is in a position, on the basis of the wording of the relevant provision and with the help of the interpretative assistance given by the courts, to know which acts or omissions will make him criminally liable…

…

52. [E]ven if the Member States reproduce word-for-word the list of the categories of offences set out in Article 2(2) of the Framework Decision for the purposes of its implementation, the actual definition of those offences and the penalties applicable are those which follow from the law of 'the issuing Member State'. The Framework Decision does not seek to harmonise the criminal offences in question in respect of their constituent elements or of the penalties which they attract.

53. Accordingly, while Article 2(2) of the Framework Decision dispenses with verification of double criminality for the categories of offences mentioned therein, the definition of those offences and of the penalties applicable continue to be matters determined by the law of the issuing Member State, which, as is, moreover, stated in Article 1(3) of the Framework Decision, must respect fundamental rights and fundamental legal principles as enshrined in Article 6 EU, and, consequently, the principle of the legality of criminal offences and penalties.

54. It follows that, in so far as it dispenses with verification of the requirement of double criminality in respect of the offences listed in that provision, Article 2(2) of the Framework Decision is not invalid on the ground that it infringes the principle of the legality of criminal offences and penalties.

The ECJ's reasoning did not fully address the applicant's argument. It is true that the Framework Decision did not seek to harmonize the criminal offences listed in Article 2(2) in respect of their constituent elements, and that the definition of those offences remained a matter for the state issuing the EAW. This did not however meet the substance of the applicant's concern. The Member States have to implement the Framework Decision into their national law. An accused in the executing state will therefore have to determine the constituent elements of the legal definition of the offences listed in Article 2(2) in relation to the state that issues the EAW. This may not be easy to divine, in part because of language issues, and in part because the very definition of those elements may not always be clear.

The ECJ has in its subsequent case law emphasized that Member States are in principle obliged to act on an EAW from the issuing state,[98] an interpretation that is reinforced by the language of Article 1(1), which is framed in terms of 'surrender' of the individual to the issuing state. The Court has ruled that key terms in the Framework Decision will be given an autonomous EU legal meaning.[99] It has signalled that the circumstances in which the executing state can, pursuant to Article 4, legitimately refuse to hand over a person to a state that issued the EAW will be closely controlled by the Union Courts.[100] The fact that the person was not accorded a hearing in the issuing state before the warrant was issued is not

---

[98] Case C–388/08 PPU *Criminal proceedings against Artur Leymann and Aleksei Pustovarov* [2008] ECR I–2993.

[99] Case C–261/09 *Mantello* [2010] ECR I–11477.

[100] Case C–66/08 *Proceedings concerning the execution of a European arrest warrant issued against Szymon Kozłowski* [2008] ECR I–6041.

a ground for refusing to execute the warrant.[101] The Court will however, when interpreting Article 4, give weight to the possibility of increasing the person's chances of reintegrating into society by serving a sentence in the country where he resides.[102]

(ii) Constitutional and Rights-Based Concerns

The implementation and application of the EAW have given rise to constitutional concerns. The new requirement to surrender nationals pursuant to the EAW led to litigation before several constitutional courts and subsequent constitutional amendment, since some Member States' constitutions prohibited *per se* the extradition of nationals. The compatibility of national implementing legislation with the national constitution was challenged in, for example, Germany, Cyprus, Poland, and the Czech Republic.[103]

There have also been related concerns raised as to the EAW regime and human rights. Article 1(3) of the Framework Decision states that it should not have the effect of modifying the obligation to respect human rights contained in Article 6 TEU. The Framework Decision did not, however, make adequate protection of human rights a specific ground *per se* on which a state could refuse to execute a warrant, although recital 12 is more far-reaching in this respect.[104] The inclusion of Article 1(3) did not moreover dispel human rights concerns, as exemplified by the *Advocaten voor de Wereld* case. In addition, even if all EU Member States are bound by the ECHR and the Charter of Fundamental Rights, this does not mean that all twenty-eight legal systems have the same standards of human rights safeguards in the field of criminal law.[105] The problems in this respect became evident in *Melloni*.

Case C–399/11 **Melloni v Ministerio Fiscal**
EU:C:2013:107

The Spanish court asked whether Article 53 of the Charter must be interpreted as allowing the executing Member State of an EAW to make the surrender of a person convicted *in absentia* conditional upon the conviction being open to review in the issuing Member State, in order to avoid an adverse effect on the right to a fair trial and the rights of the defence guaranteed by its constitution. This would, said the CJEU, mean that a Member State could apply the fundamental rights guaranteed by its constitution when that standard was higher than that deriving from the Charter and give it priority over EU law.

THE CJEU

57. Such an interpretation of Article 53 of the Charter cannot be accepted.

58. That interpretation of Article 53 of the Charter would undermine the principle of the primacy of EU law inasmuch as it would allow a Member State to disapply EU legal rules which are fully in compliance with the Charter where they infringe the fundamental rights guaranteed by that State's constitution.

59. It is settled case-law that, by virtue of the principle of primacy of EU law, which is an essential feature of the EU legal order...rules of national law, even of a constitutional order, cannot be allowed

---

[101] Case C–396/11 *Radu* EU:C:2013:39.

[102] Case C–123/08 *Dominic Wolzenburg* [2009] ECR I–9621; Case C–306/09 *IB* [2010] ECR I–10341.

[103] Mitsilegas (n 57) 1294–1299.

[104] Ibid 1291–1292. A number of Member States when implementing the Framework Decision added human rights as grounds for refusal to execute an EAW: ibid 1293. See, eg, Extradition Act 2003, ss 21, 25.

[105] J Vogel and J Spencer, 'Proportionality and the European Arrest Warrant' [2010] Crim LR 474.

to undermine the effectiveness of EU law on the territory of that State (...Case 11/70 *Internationale Handelsgesellschaft* [1970] ECR 1125, paragraph 3,...).

60. It is true that Article 53 of the Charter confirms that, where an EU legal act calls for national implementing measures, national authorities and courts remain free to apply national standards of protection of fundamental rights, provided that the level of protection provided for by the Charter, as interpreted by the Court, and the primacy, unity and effectiveness of EU law are not thereby compromised.

61. However, as is apparent from paragraph 40 of this judgment, Article 4a(1) of Framework Decision 2002/584 does not allow Member States to refuse to execute a European arrest warrant when the person concerned is in one of the situations provided for therein.

62. It should also be borne in mind that the adoption of Framework Decision 2009/299, which inserted that provision into Framework Decision 2002/584, is intended to remedy the difficulties associated with the mutual recognition of decisions rendered in the absence of the person concerned at his trial arising from the differences as among the Member States in the protection of fundamental rights...

63. Consequently, allowing a Member State to avail itself of Article 53 of the Charter to make the surrender of a person convicted *in absentia* conditional upon the conviction being open to review in the issuing Member State, a possibility not provided for under Framework Decision 2009/299, in order to avoid an adverse effect on the right to a fair trial and the rights of the defence guaranteed by the constitution of the executing Member State, by casting doubt on the uniformity of the standard of protection of fundamental rights as defined in that framework decision, would undermine the principles of mutual trust and recognition which that decision purports to uphold and would, therefore, compromise the efficacy of that framework decision.

The following extract reveals some of the broader difficulties concerning constitutional and human rights that relate to the EAW.

V Mitsilegas, The Constitutional Implications of Mutual Recognition in Criminal Matters in the European Union[106]

The application of the mutual recognition principle in criminal matters...has raised a number of constitutional concerns. A major objection has centred on the abolition of the dual criminality requirement, which is seen to constitute breach of the legality principle...As has been noted, constitutionally it is not acceptable to execute an enforcement decision related to an act that is not an offence under the law of the executing state...

A related, but broader concern involves the link between legality and legitimacy of criminal law at the national, and EU, level...Criminal law is fundamental in a society governed by the rule of law, as it contains rules delineating the relationship between the individual and the State...Criminal law and the limits that it sets must be openly negotiated and agreed via a democratic process, and citizens must be aware of exactly what the rules are. However, mutual recognition challenges this framework. Contrary to harmonization, which would involve...a set of concrete EU-wide standards which would be negotiated and agreed by the EU institutions, mutual recognition does not involve a commonly negotiated standard...

...

A related concern...is that the recognition of Warrants with the minimum of formality along with the abolition of the dual criminality requirement will lead to breach of the suspects' rights. Concerns have been focusing in particular on whether the suspect will enjoy ECHR rights in the issuing state, in particular the right to a fair trial and the protection from torture…The mutual recognition measures themselves assume that a high level of confidence between Member States exists, and this has been reiterated by the ECJ. However, debates in national parliaments and the press have shown that this is not necessarily the case.

(iii) *Addressing the Concerns through Harmonization and Proportionality*

Attempts have been made to meet the concerns voiced about the EAW regime through harmonization. This may seem paradoxical, given that mutual recognition was intended to circumvent the difficulties of securing agreement through harmonization. The Commission nonetheless took the view that some criticisms of the EAW regime could be met through harmonized standards that addressed the rights of the defendants when they were sent to the issuing state.[107]

Progress on Commission initiatives launched in 2004[108] was however slow. Member States disagreed about the detailed content of the proposed measures, and there were doubts whether, prior to the Lisbon Treaty, the EU had competence over criminal procedure. In November 2009, the Justice Council however adopted a 'Roadmap' for strengthening the procedural rights of suspected or accused persons in criminal proceedings.[109] It called for the adoption of five measures covering the most basic procedural rights, based on a 'step-by-step' approach. A further impetus came from the Stockholm Programme,[110] which reaffirmed the importance of the rights of the individual in criminal proceedings as a fundamental value of the Union and an essential component of mutual trust between Member States. The Stockholm Programme referred to the 'Roadmap' as an integral part of the multiannual programme and called on the Commission to present the relevant proposals.

Directives dealing with the right to interpretation and translation in criminal proceedings and on the right to information in criminal proceedings have been enacted.[111] The Commission hopes to secure enactment of further measures dealing with: the presumption of innocence and the right to be present at trial;[112] safeguards for children suspected of crime;[113] and on provisional legal aid.[114]

The Commission is moreover mindful of the need for further reforms to the way in which the EAW operates, including a need to ensure that the EAW regime is used proportionately in order that national courts are not beset by calls to execute EAWs for trivial offences.[115] The same idea has been voiced judicially by Advocate General Sharpston,[116] although it was not developed by the CJEU in the instant case.[117]

---

[107] Mitsilegas (n 57) 1304–1307; T Spronken, G Vermeulen, D de Vocht, and L van Puyenbroeck, *EU Procedural Rights in Criminal Proceedings* (Directorate General, Justice and Home Affairs, 2008).

[108] Proposal for a Council Framework Decision on certain procedural rights in criminal proceedings throughout the European Union, COM(2004) 328 final.

[109] [2009] OJ C295/1; http://ec.europa.eu/justice/criminal/criminal-rights/index_en.htm.

[110] [2010] OJ C115/01.

[111] Directive 2010/64/EU of the European Parliament and of the Council of 20 October 2010 on the right to interpretation and translation in criminal proceedings [2010] OJ L280/1; Directive 2012/13/EU of the European Parliament and of the Council of 22 May 2012 on the right to information in criminal proceedings [2012] OJ L142/1; E Smith, 'Running Before We Can Walk? Mutual Recognition at the Expense of Fair Trials in Europe's Area of Freedom, Security and Justice' (2013) 4 New Journal of European Criminal Law 82.

[112] COM(2013) 821 final.

[113] COM(2013) 822 final.

[114] COM(2013) 824 final.

[115] http://ec.europa.eu/justice/criminal/recognition-decision/european-arrest-warrant/index_en.htm.

[116] Case C–396/11 *Radu* EU:C:2012:648.

[117] Case C–396/11 *Radu* (n 101).

(D) MUTUAL RECOGNITION AND THE EUROPEAN EVIDENCE WARRANT

The EAW regime is the best known example of mutual recognition, but is not the only one. Mutual recognition has been used in relation to financial aspects of criminal law enforcement, as exemplified by the measures dealing with execution of orders freezing property and financial penalties.[118]

Mutual recognition has also been used in relation to evidence, leading to a Framework Decision on the European Evidence Warrant (EEW).[119] The initial impetus for the EEW came from the Tampere and Hague Programmes. The measure was seen as an essential component of the EU's criminal law strategy, and one that would complement the EAW and the regimes dealing with execution of orders concerning criminal financial penalties.

The EEW regime has now been replaced by the European Investigation Order (EIO), the rationale being that the existing measures from 2003 and 2008 were too fragmentary in relation to the gathering of evidence.[120] An EIO is a decision issued or validated by a judicial authority of the issuing state to have investigative measures carried out in the executing state to obtain evidence. The evidence may already exist or it may be found pursuant to the investigation. Member States are required to execute the EIO based on mutual recognition. The Directive is said not to modify the obligation to respect the fundamental rights and legal principles as enshrined in Article 6 TEU.[121] An EIO may be sought in relation to a wide range of proceedings, and is not limited to criminal proceedings.[122] The issuing state must indicate the type of investigative measures that it wishes the executing authority to undertake.

There are safeguards built in as to the conditions on which an EIO can be issued. Thus an EIO can only be issued if it is necessary and proportionate for the purposes of the proceedings in relation to which it is sought, and the investigative measures must be capable of being sought in a similar case in the issuing state. If the executing state doubts whether these conditions have been met it can consult the authority in the issuing state, which may withdraw the request.[123] The executing state can refuse to comply with the investigative requests of the issuing authority if they are contrary to the fundamental principles of law of the executing state.[124] It is also open to the executing authority, subject to certain exceptions, to use an investigative procedure other than that specified in the EIO.[125] Article 11 of the Directive specifies the grounds on which the executing state may refuse to recognize an EIO.

> 1. Without prejudice to Article 1(4), recognition or execution of an EIO may be refused in the executing State where:
>
> (a) there is an immunity or a privilege under the law of the executing State which makes it impossible to execute the EIO or there are rules on determination and limitation of criminal liability relating to freedom of the press and freedom of expression in other media, which make it impossible to execute the EIO;

---

[118] Council Framework Decision 2003/577/JHA of 22 July 2003 on the execution in the European Union of orders freezing property or evidence [2003] OJ L196/45; Council Framework Decision 20065/783/JHA of 6 October 2006 on the application of the principle of mutual recognition to confiscation orders [2006] OJ L328/59.

[119] Framework Decision 2008/978/JHA on the European evidence warrant for the purpose of obtaining objects, documents and data for use in proceedings in criminal matters [2008] OJ L350/72.

[120] Directive 2014/41/EU of the European Parliament and of the Council of 3 April 2014 regarding the European Investigation Order in criminal matters [2014] OJ L130/1, rec 6.

[121] Ibid Art 1(4).

[122] Ibid Art 4.

[123] Ibid Art 6.

[124] Ibid Art 9(2).

[125] Ibid Art 10.

(b) in a specific case the execution of the EIO would harm essential national security interests, jeopardise the source of the information or involve the use of classified information relating to specific intelligence activities;

(c) the EIO has been issued in proceedings referred to in Article 4(b) and (c) and the investigative measure would not be authorised under the law of the executing State in a similar domestic case;

(d) the execution of the EIO would be contrary to the principle of *ne bis in idem*;

(e) the EIO relates to a criminal offence which is alleged to have been committed outside the territory of the issuing State and wholly or partially on the territory of the executing State, and the conduct in connection with which the EIO is issued is not an offence in the executing State;

(f) there are substantial grounds to believe that the execution of the investigative measure indicated in the EIO would be incompatible with the executing State's obligations in accordance with Article 6 TEU and the Charter;

(g) the conduct for which the EIO has been issued does not constitute an offence under the law of the executing State, unless it concerns an offence listed within the categories of offences set out in Annex D, as indicated by the issuing authority in the EIO, if it is punishable in the issuing State by a custodial sentence or a detention order for a maximum period of at least three years; or

(h) the use of the investigative measure indicated in the EIO is restricted under the law of the executing State to a list or category of offences or to offences punishable by a certain threshold, which does not include the offence covered by the EIO.

There are provisions for legal remedies to be available in relation to the investigative measures in the EIO, which are equivalent to those in a similar domestic case, but the substantive reasons for issuing the EIO can be challenged only in the issuing state, subject to guarantees of fundamental rights in the executing state.[126] It remains to be seen how the EIO regime works in practice, in particular how far executing states raise objections to an EIO grounded in terms of proportionality or fundamental rights.

(E) SUBSTANTIVE CRIMINAL LAW

(i) *The Broad Reach of EU Criminal Law*

The discussion thus far has focused on EU involvement in criminal law via mutual recognition as it affects aspects of criminal procedure, such as the EAW, the EEW, and the EIO. The analysis has revealed the tensions and concerns resulting from such initiatives.

The EU has, however, also enacted a plethora of detailed measures concerning substantive criminal law.[127] There are now EU measures relating to matters listed in Article 83(1) TFEU: terrorism, trafficking in persons, child pornography and prostitution, drug trafficking, money laundering, corruption, counterfeiting, attacks on information systems, and organized crime. There are also criminal law measures that would now be legitimated under Article 83(2) TFEU or other Treaty provisions, concerning matters such as racism and xenophobia, illegal entry and residence, environmental crime, and the protection of the EU's financial interests.

---

[126] Ibid Art 14.
[127] http://ec.europa.eu/justice/criminal/criminal-law-policy/index_en.htm.

Space precludes examination of all such measures.[128] The concern within this chapter is in any event, as stated at the outset, to reveal at a more general level the rationale for the EU's involvement in the criminal sphere, the regulatory techniques used to that end, and the challenges posed by such intervention. The nature of EU involvement can nonetheless be exemplified by considering its approach to organized crime.

(ii) *EU Criminal Law Initiatives against Organized Crime*

It is readily apparent that cross-border serious crime can create externalities in other Member States, which can be better met by collective action. The EU provides an institutional forum for such collective action to fashion appropriate rules, more especially because many such crimes also have negative effects on the EU economy. This does not mean that development of EU initiatives in this area has been unproblematic.

EU intervention in relation to organized crime with the objective of harmonizing certain aspects of substantive law dates from a Joint Action in 1998, which made it a criminal offence to participate in a criminal organization in the European Union.[129] The Joint Action was broadly framed and was noteworthy for its twin-track approach: it criminalized active participation in such an organization or conspiracy to commit any offence listed in the Joint Action. The use of these divergent approaches to criminalization perforce created a tension, given that the objective was to harmonize the relevant law, but the explanation resides, as Mitsilegas notes,[130] in the need to secure unanimity in the Council in the face of different national legal approaches to organized crime, the conspiracy alternative satisfying the English legal tradition.

The current law dates from a Commission proposal made in 2005.[131] It was designed to take account of developments at the international level, such as the 2000 United Nations Convention on Transnational Organized Crime, the Palermo Convention, and the EU initiatives on terrorism. The Commission proposal concentrated on harmonization of the crime of participation in a criminal organization and removed the alternative conspiracy variant. It also did much to align EU law with the Palermo Convention by, for example, making it criminal to direct a criminal organization and through the definition of an organized crime group. The Commission proposal led to a Third Pillar Framework Decision in 2008 'on the fight against organised crime',[132] which repealed the 1998 Joint Action.

A 'criminal organisation' is defined in Article 1 as a structured association, established over a period of time, of more than two persons acting in concert with a view to committing offences which are punishable by deprivation of liberty or a detention order of a maximum of at least four years or a more serious penalty, to obtain, directly or indirectly, a financial or other material benefit. A 'structured association' is specified as an association that is not randomly formed for the immediate commission of an offence, but it does not require there to be formal roles or tasks for the members thereof. There is inevitably a tension in devising any such definition: if it is drawn too narrowly or formalistically then it is of little use in practical terms, whereas if it is drawn too widely it can lead to problems of legal certainty.[133]

---

[128] Peers (n 2) 780–803; V Mitsilegas, 'The Third Wave of Third Pillar Law: Which Direction for EU Criminal Justice?' (2009) 34 ELRev 523; Towards an EU Criminal Policy: Ensuring the effective implementation of EU policies through criminal law, COM(2011) 573 final; C Harding and J Banach-Gutierrez, 'The Emergent EU Criminal Policy: Identifying the Species' (2012) 37 ELRev 758.

[129] Joint Action 98/733/JHA on making it a criminal offence to participate in a criminal organisation in the Member States of the European Union [1998] OJ L351/1.

[130] Mitsilegas (n 128) 528.

[131] Proposal for a Framework Decision on the fight against organised crime, COM(2005) 6.

[132] Framework Decision 2008/841/JHA on the fight against organised crime [2008] OJ L300/42.

[133] F Calderoni, 'A Definition that Could Not Work: The EU Framework Decision on the Fight against Organised Crime' (2008) 16 European Journal of Crime, Criminal Law and Criminal Justice 265.

The Framework Decision makes provision for penalties for taking part in a criminal organization, specifying a minimum of two years' and a maximum of five years' imprisonment. If a criminal organization commits an offence this is an aggravating circumstance in this regard.

The domain of EU criminal law reveals moreover the enduring truth that the Commission does not always get all that it had hoped for, as determined by its initial proposal. Thus the Framework Decision, by contrast to the Commission's draft, retained the previous duality whereby Member States could choose to criminalize either participation in an organized criminal group or conspiracy. The Framework Decision also refrained from rendering criminal the direction of an organized criminal group, as proposed by the Commission.

It remains to be seen what difference the existence of the 2008 Framework Decision makes in the fight against organized crime. The sceptical view is 'not very much'. The very breadth of the definition of organized crime, combined with the retention of the dual options of participation/conspiracy, may well render the attainment of 'harmonization' more illusory than real. It begs once again in more general terms the rationale for EU involvement in crime, as evidenced by the following extract.

V Mitsilegas, The Third Wave of Third Pillar Law: Which Direction for EU Criminal Justice?[134]

The third wave of EU substantive criminal law demonstrates an effort by the European Union to develop and improve the existing legal framework. The main goal in this context has been to keep abreast of international developments aimed at responding to perceived global security threats such as terrorism and organised crime, while at the same time attempting to send a clear message with regard to European values by taking a strong enforcement stance against racism and xenophobia. In the field of both terrorism and organised crime, the relationship between the Union and international fora is noteworthy: EU legislation largely takes on board and integrates into the Union legal framework internationally agreed standards, which in their turn have been modelled upon or strongly influenced by Union action. This strategy has led, however, to the introduction in the Union legal order of an approach focusing on extensive criminalisation, based on subjective elements, and aiming primarily at prevention. All newly adopted third pillar instruments aiming at harmonisation of substantive criminal law present challenges to the principle of legal certainty.

A persistent feature in attempts to harmonise substantive criminal law at Union . . . level has been the ongoing tension between . . . the quest for meaningful harmonisation, on the one hand, and the respect for state sovereignty and national diversity, on the other . . .

The question which remains, and appears even stronger following recent developments, is *why* European substantive criminal law. Attempts to harmonise seem to aim at a variety of quite disparate objectives . . .

---

9 CONCLUSIONS

i.   The nature of the topics comprised in the AFSJ and the volume of measures enacted bear testimony to its overall importance within the EU polity.

ii. The distinctive nature of the AFSJ stemmed originally from the Member States' unwillingness for the normal EU method to be applied. The Lisbon Treaty has now completed the 'journey' begun in

---

[134] (N 128) 536–537, italics in the original.

the Maastricht Treaty and continued via the Amsterdam Treaty, with the consequence that the AFSJ has been fully integrated into the main body of the Treaty.

iii. It is little surprise, given the nature of the subject matter, that many of the measures enacted have proven controversial. There have been problems concerning effectiveness, complexity, compliance with fundamental rights, and accountability.

iv. The EU bears responsibility in this respect, but so too do the Member States. The measures enacted are dependent in the last resort on what the Member States will accept, and 'all Member States have a contradictory stance regarding closer integration: recognizing the logic that rising cross-border movement and crime require responses that override the boundaries between national jurisdictions, while resisting the adjustments in national practices and the public concessions of sovereignty that this entails'.[135]

10 FURTHER READING

(a) Books

ACOSTA ARCARAZO, D, AND MURPHY, C (eds), *EU Security and Justice Law* (Hart, 2014)

GUILD, E, AND HARLOW, C (eds), *Implementing Amsterdam: Immigration and Asylum Rights in EC Law* (Hart, 2001)

HAILBRONNER, K, *Immigration and Asylum Law and Policy of the European Union* (Kluwer, 2000)

MITSILEGAS, V, *EU Criminal Law* (Hart, 2009)

PEERS, S, *EU Justice and Home Affairs Law* (Oxford University Press, 3rd edn, 2011)

—— AND ROGERS, N, *EU Immigration and Asylum Law* (Martinus Nijhoff, 2006)

TONER, H, GUILD, E, AND BALDACCINI, A (eds), *EU Immigration and Asylum Law and Policy: Whose Freedom, Security and Justice?* (Hart, 2007)

WALKER, N (ed), *Europe's Area of Freedom, Security, and Justice* (Oxford University Press, 2004)

(b) Articles

COSTELLO, C, 'Administrative Governance and the Europeanisation of Asylum and Immigration Policy' in H HOFMANN and A TÜRK (eds), *EU Administrative Governance* (Edward Elgar, 2006) ch 9

FICHERA, M, 'Criminal Law beyond the State: The European Model' (2013) 19 ELRev 174

HERLIN-KARNELL, E, 'From Mutual Trust to the Full Effectiveness of EU Law. 10 Years of the European Arrest Warrant' (2013) 38 ELRev 79

HINAREJOS, A, 'Integration in Criminal Matters and the Role of the Court of Justice' (2011) 36 ELRev 420

LADENBURGER, C, 'Police and Criminal Law in the Treaty of Lisbon. A New Dimension for the Community Model' (2008) 4 EuConst 20

LAVENEX, S, 'Mutual Recognition and the Monopoly of Force: Limits of the Single Market Analogy' (2007) 14 JEPP 762

---

[135] Lavenex and Wallace (n 15) 479.

—— AND WALLACE, W, 'Justice and Home Affairs: Towards a "European Public Order"?' in H Wallace, W Wallace, and M Pollack (eds), *Policy-Making in the European Union* (Oxford University Press, 5th edn, 2005) ch 18

MITSILEGAS, V, 'The Constitutional Implications of Mutual Recognition in Criminal Matters in the European Union' (2006) 43 CMLRev 1277

—— 'The Third Wave of Third Pillar Law: Which Direction for EU Criminal Justice?' (2009) 34 ELRev 523

—— 'The Limits of Mutual Trust in Europe's Area of Freedom, Security and Justice: From Automatic Inter-State Cooperation to the Slow Emergence of the Individual' (2012) 31 YBEL 319

SARMIENTO, D, 'European Union: The European Arrest Warrant and the Quest for Constitutional Coherence' (2008) 6 I-CON 171

SMITH, E, 'Running Before We Can Walk? Mutual Recognition at the Expense of Fair Trials in Europe's Area of Freedom, Security and Justice' (2013) 4 New Journal of European Criminal Law 82

COMPETITION LAW: ARTICLE 101

1 CENTRAL ISSUES

i. Competition law has always been central to the EU. It covers anti-competitive agreements between firms, abuse of a dominant position, and mergers.

ii. Article 101 TFEU is the principal vehicle for control of anti-competitive agreements. Such agreements can be horizontal, made between firms at the same level of the production cycle, such as agreements between cement manufacturers. Vertical agreements are those between firms at different levels of the distribution cycle, such as an agreement between a producer of stereo equipment and a retailer.

iii. The key features of Article 101 are examined in this chapter. These include: the meaning given to the terms agreement and concerted practice; the relationship between Article 101(1) and (3); the extent to which economic analysis does and should take place within Article 101(1); and the interpretation accorded to Article 101(3), including whether non-economic factors can be taken into account.

iv. The discussion then shifts to more detailed examination of vertical agreements. There is controversy about the extent to which these agreements are economically harmful, and about the 'correct' approach for competition policy.

v. The enforcement regime for Articles 101 and 102 has been reformed, and the chapter will conclude with an outline of these reforms.

2 COMPETITION LAW: OBJECTIVES

Competition law has always played an important part in EU law, but its precise role is contestable. A number of differing objectives can be pursued by competition policy.

The primary objective is to *enhance efficiency*, in the sense of maximizing consumer welfare and achieving the optimal allocation of resources. Traditional economic theory indicates that goods and services will be produced most efficiently where there is perfect competition or, more realistically, workable competition.[1] Certain agreements can have a deleterious impact on market efficiency. Thus,

---

[1] F Scherer and D Ross, *Industrial Market Structure and Economic Performance* (Houghton Mifflin, 3rd edn, 1990); S Bishop and M Walker, *The Economics of EC Competition Law: Concepts, Application and Measurement* (Sweet & Maxwell, 3rd edn, 2010); D Gerardin, A Layne-Farr, and N Pettit, *EU Competition Law and Economics* (Oxford University Press, 2012).

for example, a horizontal agreement between cement producers to fix selling prices leads to higher prices for cement, and production of less cement, than would be produced via ordinary competition. There is more disagreement concerning the effects of vertical agreements.

A second objective of competition policy may be *to protect consumers and smaller firms* from large aggregations of economic power, whether in the form of monopolies, or through agreements whereby rival firms coordinate so as to act as one unit.

A third objective is to facilitate the *creation of a single European market*, and to prevent this from being frustrated by private undertakings. EU law prohibits tariffs, quotas, and the like that impede attainment of this goal. The effectiveness of these rules would be undermined if private undertakings could partition the EU market along national lines.

The objectives and priorities of EU competition policy have not remained static across time.[2] Wesseling identifies three phases in the development of EU competition policy.

R Wesseling, The Modernisation of EC Antitrust Law[3]

Initially, the antitrust law provisions were inserted into the Treaty in view of their role in the process of market integration. The antitrust rules were no more than the private counterpart to the rules, enshrined in Articles 28–30 EC....The framers of the Treaty wanted to preclude private undertakings replacing the prohibited public obstacles to inter-state trade. The first period...saw the Commission enforcing the rules with constant reference to ensuring the free flow of goods, thus promoting market integration.

Subsequently, in the second period, antitrust policy was employed to establish a broader Community industrial policy. Exemptions from the antitrust rules were granted to forms of (trans-national) co-operation between undertakings which the Commission considered desirable, to promote either integration (Eurocheque) or broader Community policy aims (for example employment in crisis sectors)....

The momentum created by the Commission's '1992 programme' provided the occasion for expanding the scope of Community antitrust policy even further...the control of corporate mergers and the gradual liberalisation of public economic sectors, both highly political exercises, which commenced by the end of the 1980s, symbolise the altered character of Community antitrust law enforcement.

Although the system was originally devised for promoting market integration, antitrust policy is now also—and mainly—directed at promoting the various other objectives of the Community enshrined in Article 2. Absent a clear hierarchy between those objectives, priorities are selected on a case by case basis....

3 ARTICLE 101: THE TREATY TEXT

Article 101 TFEU (ex Article 81 EC) is the principal weapon to control anti-competitive behaviour by cartels:

1. The following shall be prohibited as incompatible with the internal market: all agreements between undertakings, decisions by associations of undertakings and concerted practices which may

---

[2] I Maher, 'Competition Law and Intellectual Property Rights: Evolving Formalism' in P Craig and G de Búrca (eds), *The Evolution of EU Law* (Oxford University Press, 1999) ch 16; I Maher, 'Competition Law Modernization: An Evolutionary Tale?' in P Craig and G de Búrca (eds), *The Evolution of EU Law* (Oxford University Press, 2nd edn, 2011) ch 23.

[3] (Hart, 2000) 48–49.

affect trade between Member States and which have as their object or effect the prevention, restriction or distortion of competition within the internal market, and in particular those which:

(a) directly or indirectly fix purchase or selling prices or any other trading conditions;

(b) limit or control production, markets, technical development, or investment;

(c) share markets or sources of supply;

(d) apply dissimilar conditions to equivalent transactions with other trading parties, thereby placing them at a competitive disadvantage;

(e) make the conclusion of contracts subject to acceptance by the other parties of supplementary obligations which, by their nature or according to commercial usage, have no connection with the subject of such contracts.

2. Any agreements or decisions prohibited pursuant to this Article shall be automatically void.

3. The provisions of paragraph 1 may, however, be declared inapplicable in the case of:

— any agreement or category of agreements between undertakings,

— any decision or category of decisions by associations of undertakings,

— any concerted practice or category of concerted practices,

which contributes to improving the production or distribution of goods or to promoting technical or economic progress, while allowing consumers a fair share of the resulting benefit, and which does not:

(a) impose on the undertakings concerned restrictions which are not indispensable to the attainment of these objectives;

(b) afford such undertakings the possibility of eliminating competition in respect of a substantial part of the products in question.

4 ARTICLE 101(1): UNDERTAKINGS

Article 101(1) catches agreements and the like made by undertakings, but does not define this term. The EU Courts and competition authorities have taken a broad view. In *Höfner*, the ECJ held that the term undertaking covers any entity engaged in an economic activity regardless of its legal status and the way in which it is financed.[4] This has been held to include: corporations, partnerships, individuals, trade associations, the liberal professions, state-owned corporations, and cooperatives.[5]

It does not, however, cover bodies that pursue an exclusively social objective and do not engage in economic activity, such as bodies entrusted with the management of statutory health insurance and old-age insurance schemes. Whether an undertaking operating in such a field engages in any 'economic' activity so as to fall within Article 101 may require close inquiry into the way in which it operates.[6]

---

[4] Case C–41/90 *Höfner and Elser v Macroton GmbH* [1991] ECR I–1979, [21]; Case C–244/94 *Fédération Française des Sociétés d'Assurance v Ministère de l'Agriculture et de la Pêche* [1995] ECR I–4013; Case T–319/99 *FENIN v Commission* [2003] ECR II–351, [35]–[41], upheld in Case C–205/03 P *FENIN v Commission* [2006] ECR I–6295.

[5] R Whish and D Bailey, *Competition Law* (Oxford University Press, 7th edn, 2012) 83–98.

[6] Cases 159 and 160/91 *Poucet and Pistre v Assurances Générales de France* [1993] ECR I–637; Case C–244/94 *Fédération Française* (n 4); Case C–67/96 *Albany International BV v Stichting Bedrijfspensioenfonds Textielindustrie* [1999] ECR I–5751; Case T–319/99 *FENIN* (n 4); Case C–218/00 *Cisal di Battistello Venanzio & C Sas v INAIL* [2002] ECR I–691; Cases C–264, 306, 354 and 355/01 *AOK Bundesverband and others v Ichthyol-Gesellschaft Cordes, Hermani & Co* [2004] ECR I–2493; Case C–350/07 *Kattner Stahlbau GmbH v Maschinenbau- und Metall- Berufsgenossenschaft* [2009] ECR I–1513; Case C–113/07 P *SELEX Sistemi Integrati SpA v Commission* [2009] ECR I–2207.

State-owned corporations can be undertakings when they operate commercially, but not when they exercise their public law powers.[7] Similarly, a private body vested with public power will only be excluded from Article 101 with respect to its public and not its economic activities.[8] Organizations representing management and labour that conclude a collective agreement are not regarded as undertakings for the purposes of Article 101.[9] This is because the social objectives of such agreements would be undermined if such agreements were subject to Article 101, but collective agreements may still be subject to the rules on freedom of establishment.[10] Employees are, for the duration of their employment relationship, part of the undertakings that employ them, and therefore do not themselves constitute undertakings for the purposes of Article 101.[11]

Firms that are legally distinct may be treated as a single unit because of their close economic link. This may be the case with agreements made between parent and subsidiary, where it is decided that they are, in reality, a single economic unit. The agreement will be regarded as an internal allocation of function within that economic unit.[12] The issue is whether the subsidiary has real autonomy, or whether it merely carries out the instructions of its parent.[13] If Article 101 is inapplicable, it may still be possible to use Article 102.

5 ARTICLE 101(1): AGREEMENTS, DECISIONS, AND CONCERTED PRACTICES

(A) AGREEMENTS

Article 101 requires the existence of an agreement, decision, or concerted practice. If the competition rules operated only when an explicit, formal agreement was made they would be of little practical use, since undertakings would achieve their anti-competitive goals in less formal ways. It is therefore necessary to have provisions to catch less formal species of agreements. The *Quinine Cartel* case provides a good example of this aspect of competition law.

---

[7] Whish and Bailey (n 5) 87-90; Case C–138/11 *Compass-Datenbank GmbH v Republik Österreich* EU:C:2012:449; Case C–327/12 *Ministero dello Sviluppo economico and Autorità per la vigilanza sui contratti pubblici di lavori, servizi e forniture v SOA Nazionale Costruttori—Organismo di Attestazione SpA.* EU:C:2013:827, [27].

[8] Case C–49/07 *Motosykletistiki Omospondia Ellados NPID (MOTOE) v Elliniko Dimosio* [2008] ECR I–4863.

[9] Case C–67/96 *Albany* (n 6); Case C–437/09 *AG2R Prévoyance v Beaudout Père et Fils SARL* [2011] ECR I–973, [29].

[10] Case C–438/05 *International Transport Workers' Federation and Finnish Seamen's Union v Viking Line ABP and OÜ Viking Line Eesti* [2007] ECR I–10779; Case C–271/08 *Commission v Germany* [2010] ECR I–7091.

[11] Case C–22/98 *Criminal Proceedings against Becu* [1999] ECR I–5665.

[12] Case 22/71 *Béguelin Import v GL Import-Export* [1971] ECR 949; Case C–266/93 *Bundeskartellamt v Volkswagen AG and VAG Leasing GmbH* [1995] ECR I–3477, [19]; Case T–145/89 *Baustahlgewebe GmbH v Commission* [1995] ECR II–987.

[13] Case C–73/95 P *Viho Europe BV v Commission* [1996] ECR I–5457, [15]; Case 217/05 *Confederación Española de Empresarios de Estaciones de Servicio v Compañía Española de Petróleos SA* [2006] ECR I–11987; Case C–97/08 P *Akzo Nobel NV v Commission* [2009] ECR I–8237.

Cases 41, 44 and 45/69 **ACF Chemiefarma NV v Commission**
[1970] ECR 661

[Note Lisbon Treaty renumbering: Art 85 is now Art 101 TFEU]

A number of firms agreed to fix prices and divide the market in quinine. They made an agreement to this effect, which affected trade with non-Member States (the export agreement). They also made a gentlemen's agreement, which extended this to sales within the common market.

THE ECJ

110. The gentlemen's agreement, which the applicant admits existed until the end of October 1962, had as its object the restriction of competition within the Common Market.

111. The parties to the export agreement mutually declared themselves willing to abide by the gentlemen's agreement and concede that they did so until the end of October 1962.

112. This document thus amounted to the faithful expression of the joint intention of the parties to the agreement with regard to their conduct in the Common Market.

113. Furthermore it contained a provision to the effect that infringement of the gentlemen's agreement would ipso facto constitute an infringement of the export agreement.

114. In those circumstances account must be taken of this connection in assessing the effects of the gentlemen's agreement with regard to the categories of acts prohibited by Article 85(1).

[*The parties claimed that the gentlemen's agreement ended in October 1962.*]

116. The conduct of the undertakings in the Common Market after 29 October 1962 must...be considered in relation to the following four points: sharing out of domestic markets, fixing of common prices, determination of sales quotas and prohibition against manufacturing synthetic quinidine.

117. The gentlemen's agreement guaranteed protection of each domestic market for the producers in the various Member States.

118. After October 1962 when significant supplies were delivered on one of those markets by producers who were not nationals...there was a substantial alignment of prices conforming to French domestic prices which were higher than the export prices to third countries.

119. It does not appear that there were alterations in the insignificant volume of trade between the other Member States referred to by the clause relating to domestic protection in spite of considerable differences in the prices prevailing in each of those States.

120. The divergences between the domestic legislation of those States cannot by itself explain those differences in price or the substantial absence of trade.

121. Obstacles which might arise in the trade in quinine and quinidine from differences between national legislation governing pharmaceutical products under trade-mark cannot relevantly be invoked to explain those facts.

122. The correspondence exchanged in October and November 1963 between the parties to the export agreement with regard to the protection of domestic markets merely confirmed the intention of those undertakings to allow this state of affairs to remain unchanged.

123. This intention was subsequently confirmed by Nedchem during the meeting of the undertakings concerned in Brussels on 14 March 1964.

124. From those circumstances it is clear that with regard to the restriction on competition arising from the protection of the producers' domestic markets the producers continued after the meeting on 29 October 1962 to abide by the gentlemen's agreement of 1960 and confirmed their common intention to do so.

The *Quinine Cartel* case serves as a good example of the ECJ's approach. Informal agreements can be caught under Article 101 and the mere fact that the parties claim to have terminated them will not be conclusive. The Court examines the facts to determine whether it was economically plausible that the parties' pricing behaviour could have been achieved without collusion.

The Commission and EU Courts therefore take an expansive view of 'agreement'. Thus, in *Polypropylene*,[14] the Commission held that there was a single agreement between firms in the petrochemical industry, which had continued over many years, even though the agreement was oral, even though there were no sanctions for breach, and even though it was not legally binding. An agreement existed if the parties reached a consensus on a plan which limited, or was likely to limit, their commercial freedom by determining the lines of their mutual action or abstention from action in the market. The CFI upheld the Commission in this respect,[15] holding that the firms' pattern of conduct was in pursuit of a single economic aim, the distortion of the market in question. It would therefore be artificial to split this continuous conduct into a number of separate infringements.

The EU Courts have, moreover, held that for there to be an agreement within Article 101 it was sufficient that the undertakings should have expressed their joint intention to conduct themselves on the market in a specific way. Such was the case where there were common intentions between undertakings to achieve price and sales-volume targets.[16] It sufficed for the Commission to show that an undertaking participated in meetings at which an anti-competitive agreement was concluded without opposing it.[17] If an undertaking participated with others in the making of an agreement it could not argue that, because of its limited size, it could not have had a restrictive effect on competition,[18] nor does the undertaking have to be active on the relevant market.[19]

An agreement does, however, require the concurrence of will between at least two parties, as distinct from unilateral measures, although the precise form of this concurrence is not important, provided that it constitutes the faithful expression of the parties' intentions.[20] Unilateral measures do not therefore suffice, but an agreement can be deduced from conduct. However for an agreement to be based on tacit acceptance it is necessary that the manifestation of the wish of one contracting party to achieve an anti-competitive goal constitutes an invitation to the other party, whether

[14] Dec 86/398 [1986] OJ L230/1, [1988] 4 CMLR 347; Dec 89/190, *PVC* [1989] OJ L74/1 [1990] 4 CMLR 345, reversed on other grounds in Case C–137/92 P *Commission v BASF AG* [1994] ECR I–2555; *LdPE* [1989] OJ L74/21, [1990] 4 CMLR 382; *Italian Flat Glass* [1989] OJ L33/44, [1990] 4 CMLR 535.

[15] Case T–7/89 *SA Hercules Chemicals NV v Commission* [1991] ECR II–1711, [262]–[264], upheld on appeal, Case C–51/92 P *Hercules Chemicals NV v Commission* [1999] ECR I–4235; Case T–305/94 *NV Limburgse Vinyl Maatschappij v Commission* [1999] ECR II–93, [773].

[16] Case T–9/89 *Hüls AG v Commission* [1992] ECR II–499; Case T–11/89 *Shell International Chemical Company Ltd v Commission* [1992] ECR II–757; Case T–56/02 *Bayerische Hypo- und Vereinsbank AG v Commission* [2004] ECR II–3495; Case T–18/03 *CD-Contact Data GmbH v Commission* [2009] ECR II–1021, [46]–[48].

[17] Case C–199/92 P *Hüls v Commission* [1999] ECR I–4287, [155]; Cases C–204, 205, 211, 213, 217 and 219/00 P *Aalborg Portland AS v Commission* [2004] ECR I–123, [81]–[86]; Case C–113/04 P *Technische Unie BV v Commission* [2006] ECR I–8831, [114]; Cases C–403 and 405/04 P *Sumitomo Metal Industries Ltd and Nippon Steel Corp v Commission* [2007] ECR I–729, [46]–[48]; Case C–449/11 P *Solvay Solexis SpA v Commission* EU:C:2013:803, [38]; Case T–587/08 *Fresh Del Monte Produce, Inc v European Commission* EU:T:2013:129.

[18] Case T–143/89 *Ferriere Nord SpA v Commission* [1995] ECR II–917; Case T–211/08 *Putters International NV v Commission* [2011] ECR II–3729, [30].

[19] Case T–99/04 *AC-Treuhand AG v Commission* [2008] ECR II–1501, [122].

[20] Case T–41/96 *Bayer AG v Commission* [2000] ECR II–3383; Case C–338/00 P *Volkswagen AG v Commission* [2003] ECR I–9189, [63]–[65]; Cases T–49–51/02 *Brasserie Nationale SA v Commission* [2005] ECR II–3033, [119]; Case C–74/04 P *Commission v Volkswagen AG* [2006] ECR I–6585, [34]–[39]; Case T–99/04 *AC-Treuhand AG* (n 19) [118]; O Black, 'What is an Agreement' [2003] ECLR 504.

express or implied, to fulfil that goal jointly.[21] It has, however, been argued that the concept of agreement should be treated less like the contract law idea of an 'agreement', and more in keeping with the economic objectives of competition policy.[22]

The Commission and Union Courts have also tackled the problems flowing from complex cartels that extend over many years, with multiple participants, by framing the claim in terms of 'agreement and/or concerted practice'. This strategy was upheld in *Limburgse Vinyl*.[23] The CFI stated that where there were complex infringements over many years, involving many parties, the Commission could not be expected to classify the infringement precisely for each undertaking at any given moment. The dual classification designated a complex whole, where some factual elements were relevant to an agreement, others to a concerted practice. This did not mean that the Commission had to prove that there was an agreement and a concerted practice throughout the whole period of the cartel. The ECJ confirmed this approach in *ANIC*,[24] since any other interpretation would have allowed the parties to escape liability through the creation of impossible evidential barriers.[25]

(B) CONCERTED PRACTICE

Firms can be devious. They may well have colluded, but they may have destroyed all paper evidence, or never have committed anything to paper at all. The collusion may be real nonetheless, and the term concerted practice must be able to capture this 'fact' of business life. If, however, the term is interpreted too broadly it may catch parallel pricing that is a rational, natural response of firms in that market. In normal competitive markets, it is unlikely that firms will price at the same level without some collusion, because of differences in cost structures and the like.

This may be different in oligopolistic markets, which have the following characteristics: relatively few sellers, high barriers to entry, little product differentiation, and price transparency, such that price changes are easily detectable by competitors. It has been argued that firms in such markets will naturally price at the same level, not because of any collusion, but because each firm independently recognizes its mutual interdependence. If any firm attempted to increase its market share by cutting prices, this would lead to a similar response from others. There would be a downward spiral of prices, but no increase in market share for any firm. No firm could unilaterally increase price, because its customers would switch trade to a competitor.[26]

If price uniformity really is the result of rational action in an oligopoly, and there is no actual collusion, then it is not sensible to penalize such parties through fines for colluding. The problem is no longer behavioural, since the parties are not engaging in behaviour different from what is normal in that market. The problem is structural, in the sense that this type of market will naturally generate this type of response. This theory has, however, been criticized.

[21] Cases C–2 and 3/01 P *Bundesverband der Arzneimittel-Importeure EV and Commission v Bayer AG* [2004] ECR I–23, [100]–[102].

[22] I Lianos, 'Collusion in Vertical Relations under Article 81 EC' (2008) 45 CMLRev 1027.

[23] Case T–305/94 *NV Limburgse Vinyl* (n 15) [695]–[698].

[24] Case C–49/92 P *Commission v ANIC Partecipazioni SpA* [1999] ECR I–4125; Cases T–202, 204 and 207/98 *Tate & Lyle plc, British Sugar plc and Napier Brown & Co Ltd v Commission* [2001] ECR II–2035; Case T–19/05 *Boliden AB, Outokumpu Copper Fabrication AB and Outokumpu Copper BCZ SA v Commission* [2010] ECR II–1843, [60]–[61]; D Bailey, 'Single Overall Agreement in EU Competition Law' (2010) 47 CMLRev 473.

[25] Cases T–25 etc/95 *Cimenteries CBR SA and others v Commission* [2000] ECR II–491.

[26] G Stigler, 'The Kinked Oligopoly Demand Curve' (1947) 55 J Pol Econ 431.

R Whish and D Bailey, Competition Law[27]

The theory of oligopolistic interdependence has attracted criticism. Four particular problems have been pointed out.

The first is that the theory tends to overstate the interdependence of oligopolists. Even in a symmetrical three-firm oligopoly one firm might be able to steal a march on its rivals by cutting its price if, for example, there would be a delay before the others discovered what it had done: in the meantime the price-cutter may make sufficient profit to offset the cost of any subsequent retaliation....

A second problem is that the theory of oligopoly presents too simplistic a picture of real-life markets. In a symmetrical, stable oligopoly where producers produce identical goods at the same costs interdependence may be strong, but in reality market conditions are usually more complex. The oligopolists themselves will almost inevitably have different cost levels; they may be producing differentiated goods and will usually benefit from at least some consumer loyalty; and their market shares will often not be equal.... Many other factors affect the competitive environment in which oligopolists operate. The concentration of the market on the buying side is also important: the more concentrated it is, the less the oligopolists might compete with one another since it will be relatively easy to detect attempts to attract the custom of particular customers. The transparency of price information is significant: the easier it is to conceal the price of goods from competitors, the less will be the interdependence or mutual awareness of the oligopolists....

A third problem with the theory of interdependence is that it fails to explain why in some oligopolistic markets competition is intense. Firms quite clearly do compete with one another in some oligopolies. Such competition may take various forms. Open price competition may be limited, although price wars do break out periodically in some oligopolistic markets.... Where open price competition is restricted, this does not mean that secret price cutting does not occur. Non-price competition may be particularly strong in oligopolistic markets. This may manifest itself in various ways: offering better quality products and after sales service; striving for a lead in technical innovation and research and development...; and by making large investments in advertising to promote brand image....

A fourth objection to the theory of oligopolistic interdependence is that it does not explain satisfactorily its central proposition, which is that oligopolists can earn supra-competitive profits without explicitly colluding. The interdependence theory says that they cannot increase price unilaterally because they will lose custom to their rivals, and yet to earn supra-competitive profits, prices must have been increased from time to time: how could this have been achieved without explicit collusion? A possible answer to this is that a pattern of price leadership develops whereby one firm raises its price and this acts as a signal for the others to follow suit. Prices therefore remain parallel without conspiracy amongst the oligopolists, although this is not particularly convincing....

Having analysed the economic problems with the term concerted practice we can now consider the leading ECJ decision.

---

27 Whish and Bailey (n 5) 563–565.

Case 48/69 **ICI v Commission**
[1972] ECR 619

[Note Lisbon Treaty renumbering: Art 85 is now Art 101 TFEU]

The Court considered allegations that there had been concerted practices in the dyestuffs industry. The firms argued that any identity of price was the result of the oligopolistic nature of the market. The extract begins with the Court providing a definition of concerted practice.

THE ECJ

64. Article 85 draws a distinction between the concept of 'concerted practices' and that of 'agreements between undertakings' or of 'decisions by associations of undertakings'; the object is to bring within the prohibition of that Article a form of coordination between undertakings which, without having reached the stage where an agreement properly so-called has been concluded, knowingly substitutes practical cooperation between them for the risks of competition.

65. By its very nature, then, a concerted practice does not have all the elements of a contract but may inter alia arise out of coordination which becomes apparent from the behaviour of the participants.

66. Although parallel behaviour may not by itself be identified with a concerted practice, it may however amount to strong evidence of such practice if it leads to conditions of competition which do not correspond to the normal conditions of the market, having regard to the nature of the products, the size and number of the undertakings and the volume of the said market.

67. This is especially the case if the parallel conduct is such as to enable those concerned to attempt to stabilize prices at a level different from that to which competition would have led, and to consolidate established positions to the detriment of effective freedom of movement of the products in the Common Market and of the freedom of consumers to choose their suppliers.

68. Therefore the question whether there was concerted action in this case can only be correctly determined if the evidence upon which the contested decision is based is considered, not in isolation, but as a whole, account being taken of the specific features of the market in the products in question.

[*The Court found that 80 per cent of the dyestuffs market was supplied by ten producers; that these firms possessed differing cost structures; that there were a large number of dyes produced by each firm; that while standard dyes could be replaced by other products relatively easily, this was not the case with specialist dyes; that the market for specialist dyes tended to be oligopolistic; that the Community market in dyestuffs consisted of five separate national markets which had different price levels; and that this division along national lines was in part due to the need to supply local assistance to users of the product, and also to ensure immediate delivery of quantities which were often small. The Court then considered price increases in 1964, 1965, and 1967. It found that in relation to the 1964 and 1965 price increases all the undertakings announced the increases and immediately put them into effect. In 1967 two undertakings announced their intentions of making an increase some time in advance, which allowed the undertakings to observe each other's reactions on the different markets, and to adapt accordingly.*]

101. By means of these advance announcements the various undertakings eliminated all uncertainty between them as to their future conduct and, in doing so, also eliminated a large part of the risk usually inherent in any independent change of conduct on one or several markets.

102. This was all the more the case since these announcements, which led to the fixing of general and equal increases in prices for the markets in dyestuffs, rendered the market transparent as regards the percentage rates of increase.

. . .

104. The fact that this conduct was not spontaneous is corroborated by an examination of other aspects of the market.

105. In fact, from the number of producers concerned it is not possible to say that the European market in dyestuffs is, in the strict sense, an oligopoly in which price competition could no longer play a substantial role.

106. These producers are sufficiently powerful and numerous to create a considerable risk that in times of rising prices some of them might not follow the general movement but might instead try to increase their share of the market by behaving in an individual way.

107. Furthermore, the dividing-up of the Common Market into five national markets with different price levels and structures makes it improbable that a spontaneous and equal price increase would occur on all the national markets.

. . .

109. Therefore, although parallel conduct in respect of prices may well have been an attractive and risk-free objective for the undertakings concerned, it is hardly conceivable that the same action could be taken spontaneously at the same time, on the same national markets and for the same range of products.

. . .

112. In proceeding in this way, the undertakings mutually eliminated in advance any uncertainties concerning their reciprocal behaviour on the different markets and thereby also eliminated a large part of the risk inherent in any independent change of conduct on those markets.

113. The general and uniform increase on those different markets can only be explained by a common intention on the part of those undertakings, first, to adjust the level of prices and the situation resulting from competition in the form of discounts, and secondly, to avoid the risk, which is inherent in any price increase, of changing the conditions of competition.

The ECJ's approach emerges clearly in the above extract.[28] It is apparent from the *Sugar Cartel* case that there can be a concerted practice even though there is no actual 'plan' between the parties. The key idea was that each undertaking should operate independently on the market.[29] Four points should be made about the concept of concerted practice.

First, the burden of proving an infringement of Article 101 rests with the Commission, and the mere existence of parallel conduct will not, in itself, prove a concerted practice. Thus, if the parties can show that, although there is parallel behaviour, there are explanations for what has occurred other than concertation then they may be exonerated.[30] The Court will investigate whether there really is 'room' for the competition rules to operate in a particular context.[31]

Secondly, the Court will not readily accept that uniformity of price is the result of oligopolistic market structure. If the facts do not indicate that the market structure will naturally lead to price uniformity, and if other factors indicate collusion, then the onus may shift to the firms to suggest how the identity of price came about without some concertation.

Thirdly, there can, however, be differences of opinion on which side of the line a case falls. In *Wood Pulp* the Commission concluded that there was a concerted practice by wood pulp producers. It refused to accept that the market was oligopolistic, because of the large number of firms. The fact that they charged similar prices, and altered them uniformly and simultaneously, was itself *prima facie* evidence that they were acting in concert. The ECJ disagreed.[32] It held that

---

[28] See also Case 172/80 *Gerhard Züchner v Bayerische Vereinsbank AG* [1981] ECR 2021.

[29] Cases 40–48, 50, 54–56, 111, 113 and 114/73 *Cooperatiëve Vereniging 'Suiker Unie' UA v Commission* [1975] ECR 1663, 1942; Cases T–202, 204 and 207/98 *Tate & Lyle plc* (n 24); Case T–587/08 *Fresh Del Monte Produce* (n 17).

[30] Cases 29 and 30/83 *Compagnie Royale Asturienne* [1984] ECR 1679.

[31] Cases 40–48 etc/73 *'Suiker Unie'* (n 29) 1916–1924; compare Case C–219/95 P *Ferriere Nord SpA v Commission* [1997] ECR I–4411, and Cases T–202, 204 and 207/98 *Tate & Lyle plc* (n 24).

[32] Cases 89, 104, 114, 116–117 and 125–129/85 *A Ahlström Oy v Commission* [1993] ECR I–1307; Case T–36/91 *Imperial Chemical Industries plc v Commission* [1995] ECR II–1847.

parallel conduct cannot be regarded as proof of concertation unless this constituted the only plausible explanation for the conduct. Article 101 did not deprive firms of the ability to adapt their behaviour intelligently to that of their competitors.[33] It held, moreover, that the parallelism of the prices and the price trends could be explained by the oligopolistic tendencies of the market and the specific circumstances prevailing during the relevant period.[34] The ECJ insisted that rigorous economic analysis is required to determine whether there is another plausible explanation for the parties' conduct. In the absence of overt communication between the parties, the Commission will have to defend its assumptions against experts who can suggest an innocent explanation for the challenged behaviour.[35]

The *Polypropylene* cases provide a good contrast to *Wood Pulp*. In a series of decisions the CFI cited the requirement from the *Sugar Cartel* case that undertakings must behave independently. It held that participation in meetings concerning the fixing of price and sales-volume targets during which information was exchanged between competitors about the prices they intended to charge, their profitability thresholds, the sales volumes they judged to be necessary, or their sales figures constituted a concerted practice. This was because the participant undertakings could not fail to take account of the information thus disclosed in determining their conduct on the market.[36]

Fourthly, there is the issue of whether a concerted practice must have been put into effect. This issue was addressed in *Hüls* and the approach was affirmed in *T-Mobile*.[37]

Case C–199/92 P **Hüls AG v Commission**
[1999] ECR I–4287

[Note Lisbon Treaty renumbering: Art 85 is now Art 101 TFEU]

This was one of the appeals from the CFI to the ECJ resulting from the *Polypropylene* decision of the Commission. The Commission had found that there was a concerted practice of fixing prices on this market. Hüls argued that there was a lack of proof of conduct on the market corresponding to a concerted practice. The ECJ set out the definition of concerted practice, and then continued as follows.

THE ECJ

161. It follows, first, that the concept of a concerted practice...implies, besides undertakings' concerting with each other, subsequent conduct on the market, and a relationship of cause and effect between the two.

162. However, subject to proof to the contrary, which the economic operators concerned must adduce, the presumption must be that the undertakings taking part in the concerted action and

---

33 Ibid [71].

34 Ibid [126]–[127]. The *Juge rapporteur* in *Wood Pulp* was Joliet who had earlier expressed misgivings about the possible impact of the *Dyestuffs* case: R Joliet, 'La Notion de Pratique Concertée et l'Arrêt dans une Perspective Comparative' [1974] CDE 251.

35 G van Gerven and E Varona, 'The *Wood Pulp* Case and the Future of Concerted Practices' (1994) 31 CMLRev 575; F Alese, 'The Economic Theory of Non-Collusive Oligopoly and the Concept of Concerted Practice under Article 81' [1999] ECLR 379.

36 Case T–11/89 *Shell International* (n 16). See also Cases T–202, 204 and 207/98 *Tate & Lyle plc* (n 24); Case T–142/89 *Boël* [1995] ECR II–867; Case T–148/89 *Tréfilunion SA v Commission* [1995] ECR II–1063.

37 Case C–8/08 *T-Mobile Netherlands BV and others v Raad van bestuur van de Nederlandse Mededingingsautoriteit* [2009] ECR I–4529.

remaining active on the market take account of the information exchanged with their competitors for the purposes of determining their conduct on that market. This is all the more true where the undertakings concert together on a regular basis over a long period, as was the case here....

163. Secondly, contrary to Huls's argument, a concerted practice...is caught by Article 81(1) EC, even in the absence of anti-competitive effects on the market.

164. ...it follows from the actual text of that provision that...concerted practices are prohibited regardless of their effect, when they have an anti-competitive object.

165. ...although the very concept of a concerted practice presupposes conduct by the participating undertakings on the market, it does not necessarily mean that that conduct should produce the specific effect of restricting, preventing or distorting competition.

...

166. Consequently, contrary to Huls's argument, the Court of First Instance was not in breach of the rules applying to the burden of proof when it considered that, since the Commission had established to the requisite legal standard that Huls had taken part in polypropylene producers' concerting together for the purpose of restricting competition, it did not have to adduce evidence that their concerting together had manifested itself in conduct on the market or that it had effects restrictive of competition; on the contrary, it was for Huls to prove that that did not have any influence whatsoever on its own conduct on the market.

6 ARTICLE 101(1): OBJECT OR EFFECT OF PREVENTING, RESTRICTING, OR DISTORTING COMPETITION

Article 101(1) requires that the agreement, decision, or concerted practice has the object or effect of preventing, restricting, or distorting competition in the internal market. The interpretation of this phrase has generated a significant body of literature.

(A) NATURE OF THE PROBLEM

Article 101(1) captures all agreements, concerted practices, etc, which have as their object or effect the prevention, restriction, or distortion of competition. However all contracts concerning trade impose some restraints, 'to bind, to restrain is of their very essence',[38] yet it would be absurd if every contract was caught by competition law. Moreover an agreement may have features that both enhance and restrict competition. Imagine that a supplier wishes to break into a new market, and decides to use Brown as its distributor for a particular area. Brown may only be willing to risk marketing the new product if given certain incentives and protection, such that the supplier will not supply other firms in the same area. This is a restriction of competition, but the agreement may enhance competition, since there is a new product on the market. The appropriate response to these issues is contentious. It has been debated whether the EU should follow the approach in the United States, and distinguish between a rule of reason and *per se* rules. A brief glance at US experience is, therefore, necessary in order to understand the diversity of opinion in the EU.

---

[38] *Chicago Board of Trade v US*, 246 US 231 (1918).

(B) EXPERIENCE IN THE UNITED STATES

The preceding dilemma is evident in section 1 of the Sherman Act, which states that every contract, combination, or conspiracy in restraint of trade is illegal. The courts responded by developing the rule of reason. In *Standard Oil v US* White CJ stated that a standard of reason had to be applied to determine whether a restraint was within the Sherman Act, and that only undue or unreasonable restraints should be condemned.[39] The precise meaning of this idea was contested, and still is today.[40] The concept appears to demand a broad inquiry into whether the restrictions increase or decrease competition in the market. The pro- and anti-competitive effects of the agreement are weighed to determine whether it suppresses or promotes competition.[41]

There is, however, continuing disagreement on the effects of particular types of agreement, and therefore whether they should be prohibited. There has also been disagreement on the range of considerations that should be taken into account. For some this should be restricted to economic factors, while others advocate a more wide-ranging inquiry, or are willing to ascribe economic value to social factors.[42]

Per se rules developed from a rule-of-reason analysis. The inquiry demanded by the rule of reason may be time-consuming and costly. With the passage of time the courts came to identify certain types of agreement that were conclusively presumed to be 'without redeeming virtue' and which had a 'pernicious effect on competition'. The courts condemned these without the need for elaborate inquiry into whether they had an impact on the market. The cases within this category were those which were most obviously anti-competitive, such as horizontal price fixing[43] and market division.[44] In these instances proof of the agreement was sufficient to condemn it, obviating the need for more detailed market investigation.[45]

(C) THE ACADEMIC DEBATE IN THE EU

There has been debate about whether we should adopt a rule of reason in EU law. This debate was affected by Article 101(3), whereby agreements that are held to restrict competition can be exempted following an economic analysis. No such provision exists in the United States, thereby rendering the need for some rule-of-reason analysis more necessary. The debate was also affected by the fact that until recently national courts could apply Article 101(1), but not Article 101(3). Korah was an early

---

[39] 221 US 1 (1911).

[40] R Bork, 'The Rule of Reason and the Per Se Concept: Price Fixing and Market Division' (1965) 74 Yale LJ 775 T Piraino, 'Reconciling the Per Se Rule and the Rule of Reason Approaches to Antitrust Analysis' (1991) 45 So Cal L Rev 689 and 'Making Sense of the Rule of Reason: A New Standard for Section 1 of the Sherman Act' (1994) 48 Vand L Rev 1770; O Black, 'Per Se Rules and Rules of Reason: What are They?' [1997] ECLR 145; T Calvani, 'Some Thoughts on the Rule of Reason' [2001] ECLR 201.

[41] *National Society of Professional Engineers v US*, 435 US 679, 691–692 (1978).

[42] Compare R Bork, *The Antitrust Paradox: A Policy at War with Itself* (Basic Books, 1978) with E Fox, 'The Modernization of Antitrust: A New Equilibrium' (1981) 66 Cornell L Rev 1140 and 'The Politics of Law and Economics' (1986) 61 NYULRev 554.

[43] *US v Trenton Potteries Co*, 273 US 392 (1927).

[44] *US v Topco Associates*, 405 US 596 (1972).

[45] Because classification as a price-fixing agreement can have these serious consequences the courts will, on occasion, strive to avoid characterizing a case in this way, if they believe that it has redeeming features, notwithstanding an element of price control: *National Collegiate Athletic Assn v Board of Regents of the University of Oklahoma*, 468 US 85 (1984); *Broadcast Music Inc v Columbia Broadcasting Systems Inc*, 441 US 1 (1979).

advocate of adopting a rule-of-reason analysis in EU law.[46] References to Article 85 EEC should now be read as to Article 101 TFEU.

V Korah, The Rise and Fall of Provisional Validity— The Need for a Rule of Reason in EEC Antitrust[47]

The Community Court and Commission have not developed the same theory of per se offences so brilliantly developed in the early cases under the Sherman Act. Naked restraints on pricing, market sharing, and some kinds of collective boycott...are likely to be condemned with fairly short reasoning if they are found capable of restricting trade between Member States, but more market analysis is required in the case of ancillary restraints. In *Consten & Grundig*, the Court seems to have developed a per se rule against absolute territorial protection conferred by export bans..., and this has been consistently applied by the Commission, despite mounting criticism. For all other restraints, however, the Court seems to be applying a rule of reason, requiring an analysis of the actual or intended effects in the light of market conditions.

The Commission, however, habitually analyzes agreements under Article 85(1) in the formalistic way developed by the German case law...and condemns any restriction on the conduct of the parties, or third parties, provided the restriction has, or may be expected to have, appreciable effects on the market. Only under Article 85(3) does the Commission usually try to balance any pro- and anti-competitive effects.

If national courts adopt the Commission's practice, it is feared that many desirable contracts which restrict only competition that could not take place without such an agreement, or which restrict competition less than they increase it, may not be made. The Commission grants few exemptions.... Important agreements are unlikely to be exempted unless certain clauses are altered. These alterations may help one party more than the other, and the whole contract may have to be renegotiated after the parties have been implementing it, when their relative bargaining power may have been altered as a result of the collaboration. This is a considerable disincentive to notification.

...

There is fear that European firms that may have to compete in world markets may fall behind technologically or have to merge completely, so as to reduce the risk of collaboration. Market analyses are difficult, especially for lawyers and bureaucrats. But if such analyses are not made, agreements that may have overall desirable consequences should not be controlled. This means that national courts will have to be strong in resisting claims that agreements are anti-competitive just because some competitor is harmed.

Whish and Sufrin presented the contrasting view. They argued that the ECJ's case law did not signify acceptance of a rule of reason in EU law, or that differing labels captured what the ECJ was doing better than the adoption of labels from the United States. This will be considered below. They also contended that there were very real differences between the antitrust laws of the United States and the EU, which rendered any transfer of terminology of limited utility.[48]

---

[46] See also R Joliet, *The Rule of Reason in Antitrust Law: American, German and Common Market Laws in Comparative Perspective* (Faculté de Droit, Liège, 1967); M Schecter, 'The Rule of Reason in European Competition Law' [1982] 2 LIEI 1; I Forrester and C Norall, 'The Laicization of Community Law: Self-Help and the Rule of Reason: How Competition Law is and Could be Applied' (1984) 21 CMLRev 11; V Korah, 'EEC Competition Policy—Legal Form or Economic Efficiency' (1986) 39 CLP 85.

[47] (1981) 3 NWJ Int L and Bus 320, 354–355.

[48] (1987) 7 YBEL 12–20.

R Whish and B Sufrin, Article 85 and the Rule of Reason[49]

The call for the adoption of a US-style rule of reason should be resisted and, indeed, there is much to be said for dropping this term (and the terms 'ancillary restraint' and 'per se illegality') from EEC antitrust law altogether, on the basis that they do more to confuse than to clarify. EEC competition law requires its own vocabulary, carefully honed to express its own particular tensions.

One ground for jettisoning the term 'rule of reason' from the vocabulary of EEC competition law is that it is now used in other areas of the law, for example, in the provisions on free movement of goods....

A different reason for abandoning this terminology in EEC competition law is that it invites misleading comparison with antitrust law analysis in the United States. We have suggested above that the context of US antitrust law is so dissimilar from that of the EEC that comparative analysis should be undertaken with great caution.

Quite apart from the issue of terminology, the writers have other doubts about the wisdom of analysing Article 85(1) in a way that relies on an approach similar to that of the Sherman Act. It would not help the cause of certainty.

...

The matter of certainty is, of course, important. It is in no one's interest to retard beneficial collaboration between firms striving to compete in a competitive international market. However, the best answer to this problem is for the Commission to continue to improve its procedures, to publish block exemptions where this is possible, and to develop such notions as objective necessity and potential competition. We also expect its sophistication in dealing with economics to continue to improve, but do not consider that this goes hand in hand with rule-of-reason analysis. This would stifle the proper application of Article 85 which, precisely because of its more ample wording, does not bear the same intellectual burden that the words 'restraint of trade' do in the Sherman Act. We doubt, too, that it would be helpful to draw the national courts further into the application of Article 85 by asking them to undertake extensive economic analysis under Article 85(1). We are happy for them to enforce the competition rules against blatant cartels and abuses of a dominant position. We do not consider them to be appropriate fora for deciding upon complex economic issues.

(D) THE CASE LAW

The academic debate provides a framework within which to evaluate the case law. In reading these materials we should consider whether the Court is balancing the pro- and anti-competitive effects of an agreement to determine whether it is caught within Article 101(1), and how far the terminology of the rule of reason is an apt description of this approach.

Case 56/65 Société La Technique Minière v Maschinenbau Ulm GmbH
[1966] ECR 235

[Note Lisbon Treaty renumbering: Art 85 is now Art 101 TFEU]

The case concerned an exclusive supply contract, whereby STM had the exclusive right to sell in France grading equipment produced by Maschinenbau Ulm (MBU), a German undertaking. The contract did not, however, insulate the French territory: STM could sell the goods outside France, and parallel

[49] Ibid 36–37.

imports could be obtained from other countries. A contract dispute between STM and MBU led the former to argue that this contract was invalid under Article 85.

THE ECJ

Finally, for the agreement at issue to be caught by the prohibition contained in Article 85(1) it must have as its 'object or effect the prevention, restriction or distortion of competition within the Common Market'.

The fact that these are not cumulative but alternative requirements, indicated by the conjunction 'or', leads first to the need to consider the precise purpose of the agreement, in the economic context in which it is to be applied. This interference with competition referred to in Article 85(1) must result from all or some of the clauses of the agreement itself. Where, however, an analysis of the said clauses does not reveal the effect on competition to be sufficiently deleterious, the consequences of the agreement should then be considered and for it to be caught by the prohibition it is then necessary to find that those factors are present which show that competition has in fact been prevented or restricted or distorted to an appreciable extent.

The competition in question must be understood within the actual context in which it would occur in the absence of the agreement in dispute. In particular it may be doubted whether there is an interference with competition if the said agreement seems really necessary for the penetration of a new area by an undertaking. Therefore, in order to decide whether an agreement containing a clause 'granting an exclusive right of sale' is to be considered as prohibited by reason of its object or its effect, it is appropriate to take into account in particular the nature and quantity, limited or otherwise, of the products covered by the agreement, the position and importance of the grantor and the concessionaire on the market for the products concerned, the isolated nature of the disputed agreement or, alternatively, its position in a series of agreements, the severity of the clauses intended to protect the exclusive dealership or, alternatively, the opportunities allowed for other commercial competitors in the same products by way of parallel re-exportation and importation.

Cases 56 and 58/64 **Etablissements Consten SARL and Grundig-Verkaufs-GmbH v Commission**
[1966] ECR 299

[Note Lisbon Treaty renumbering: Art 85 is now Art 101 TFEU]

Grundig granted Consten a sole distributorship for its electronic products in France. Consten had an obligation to take a minimum amount of the product; it had to provide publicity and after-sales service; and undertook not to sell the products of competing manufacturers. Moreover, the French territory was in effect insulated: there was absolute territorial protection. Consten undertook not to sell the goods outside the contract territory. A similar prohibition existed on other Grundig distributors in other countries. Grundig assigned to Consten its trade mark, GINT, which Consten could use against any unauthorized sales in France. In 1961 UNEF bought Grundig goods from sellers in Germany and sold them in France more cheaply than Consten. The latter brought an action for infringement of its trade mark, and UNEF contended that the agreement between Grundig and Consten violated Article 85.

THE ECJ

The applicants and the German Government maintain that since the Commission restricted its examination solely to Grundig products the decision was based upon a false concept of competition...con-
tained in Article 85(1), since this concept applies particularly to competition between similar products
of different makes; the Commission, before declaring Article 85(1) to be applicable, should, by basing
itself upon the 'rule of reason', have considered the economic effects of the disputed contract upon
competition between the different makes. There is a presumption that vertical sole distributorship
agreements are not harmful to competition and in the present case there is nothing to invalidate that
presumption. On the contrary, the contract in question has increased the competition between similar
products of different makes.

The principle of freedom of competition concerns the various stages and manifestations of competition. Although competition between producers is generally more noticeable than that between
distributors of products of the same make, it does not thereby follow that an agreement tending to
restrict the latter kind of competition should escape the prohibition of Article 85(1) merely because it
might increase the former.

Besides, for the purpose of applying Article 85(1), there is no need to take account of the concrete
effects of an agreement once it appears that it has as its object the prevention, restriction or distortion
of competition.

Therefore, the absence in the contested decision of any analysis of the effects of the agreement on
competition between similar products of different makes does not, of itself, constitute a defect in the
decision.

[*The Court considered the system of absolute territorial protection established by the agreement
between Consten and Grundig. It continued as follows:*]

The situation as ascertained above results in the isolation of the French market and makes it possible
to charge for the products in question prices which are sheltered from all effective competition....Since
the agreement thus aims at isolating the French market for Grundig products and maintaining artificially, for products of a very well-known brand, separate national markets within the Community, it is
therefore such as to distort competition in the Common Market.

It was therefore proper for the contested decision to hold that the agreement constitutes an infringement of Article 85(1). No further considerations, whether of economic data...or of the correctness of
the criteria upon which the Commission relied in its comparisons between the situations of the French
and German markets, and no possible favourable effects of the agreement in other respects, can in any
way lead, in the face of the above-mentioned restrictions, to a different solution under Article 85(1).

(i) *Object*

It is clear from the *STM* case that the Court accepted that the words of Article 101 were to be read
disjunctively: if the object of the agreement was anti-competitive then it could be condemned without
pressing further,[50] since 'certain forms of collusion between undertakings can be regarded, by their
very nature, as being injurious to the proper functioning of normal competition'.[51] If one were using
the language of the US courts, such agreements would be *per se* illegal. The anti-competitive nature
of an agreement will be determined by its content, the objectives it seeks to attain, and the economic

---

[50] O Odudu, 'Interpreting Article 81(1): Object as Subjective Intention' (2001) 26 ELRev 60; D Bailey, 'Restrictions of
Competition by Object under Art 101 TFEU' (2012) 49 CMLRev 559.

[51] Case C–209/07 *Competition Authority v Beef Industry Development Society Ltd and Barry Brothers* [2008] ECR
I–8637, [17].

and legal context of which it forms a part.[52] The parties' intention is not a necessary factor, but may be taken into account.[53]

Agreements that are particularly heinous, such as horizontal price fixing, market division, and collective boycotts, are condemned without further analysis of market circumstances.[54] The Union Courts have also regarded agreements that limit parallel trade as having a restrictive object,[55] this being reflective of the Court's concern to prevent partition of markets along national lines.[56] This reading of Article 101 is confirmed by *Ferriere Nord*,[57] and *GlaxoSmithKline*.[58] It is unnecessary to demonstrate any actual effects on the market for such agreements. Proof of the existence of such agreements will suffice.[59] Nor is it necessary to show that consumers are disadvantaged for an agreement to be caught because of its object, since Article 101 has been construed to protect competition as well as the interests of consumers.[60] An agreement may have a restrictive object even if restriction of competition is not its sole aim.[61]

Cases C–501, 513, 515 and 519/06 GlaxoSmithKline Services Unlimited and others v Commission
[2009] ECR I–9291

The case concerned differential pricing whereby GSK made an agreement with Spanish wholesalers which distinguished between prices charged to wholesalers in the case of domestic resale of reimbursable drugs to pharmacies or hospitals and higher prices charged in the case of exports of medicines to any other Member State. The ECJ reaffirmed the approach in the *STM* case that Article 101 embodied a distinction between agreements that had the object of restricting competition and those where it was necessary to consider effect. It continued as follows.

THE ECJ

58. According to settled case-law, in order to assess the anti-competitive nature of an agreement, regard must be had inter alia to the content of its provisions, the objectives it seeks to attain and the economic and legal context of which it forms a part... In addition, although the parties' intention is not a necessary factor in determining whether an agreement is restrictive, there is nothing prohibiting the

---

[52] Ibid [16], [21]; Cases C–501, 513, 515 and 519/06 P *GlaxoSmithKline Services Unlimited v Commission* [2009] ECR I–9291, [58]; Case C–439/09 *Pierre Fabre Dermo-Cosmétique SAS v Président de l'Autorité de la concurrence* [2011] ECR I–9419, [34]; Case C–32/11 *Allianz Hungária Biztosító Zrt v Gazdasági Versenyhivatal* EU:2013:C:160, [33]–[34].

[53] Case C–209/07 *Beef Industry* (n 51) [58].

[54] Case 45/85 *Verband der Sachversicherer eV v Commission* [1987] ECR 405, [39]; Case T–77/92 *Parker Pen Ltd v Commission* [1994] ECR II–549; Case T–66/92 *Herlitz AG v Commission* [1994] ECR II–531; Cases T–374, 375, 384 and 388/94 *European Night Services v Commission* [1998] ECR II–3141, [136]; Case T–213/00 *CMA CGM v Commission* [2003] ECR II–913, [100], [175]–[179], [210]; Cases T–49 and 51/02 *Brasserie Nationale SA v Commission* [2005] ECR II–3033, [85].

[55] Cases C–501/06 P *GlaxoSmithKline* (n 52) [59].

[56] Ibid [61]; Cases C–468–478/06 *Sot Lélos kai Sia EE v GlaxoSmithKline AEVE Farmakeftikon Proïonton* [2008] ECR I–7139, [65].

[57] Case C–219/95 P *Ferriere Nord* (n 31).

[58] Case C–501/06 P *GlaxoSmithKline* (n 52) [55].

[59] Commission Guidelines on the Application of Article 81(3) [2004] OJ C101/97, [21]–[23]; Case C–8/08 *T-Mobile* (n 37) [28]–[29]; Case C–209/07 *Beef Industry* (n 51) [16]–[17]; Cases C–403 and 429/08 *Football Association Premier League Ltd v Media Protection Services Ltd* [2011] ECR I–9083, [135]–[139].

[60] Case C–501/06 P *GlaxoSmithKline* (n 52) [63].

[61] Case C–551/03 *General Motors BV v Commission* [2006] ECR I–3173, [64].

Commission or the Community judicature from taking that aspect into account (see, to that effect, *IAZ International Belgium and Others v Commission*, cited above, paragraphs 23 to 25).

59. With respect to parallel trade, the Court has already held that, in principle, agreements aimed at prohibiting or limiting parallel trade have as their object the prevention of competition . . .

61. The Court has, moreover, held in that regard, in relation to the application of Article 81 EC and in a case involving the pharmaceuticals sector, that an agreement between producer and distributor which might tend to restore the national divisions in trade between Member States might be such as to frustrate the Treaty's objective of achieving the integration of national markets through the establishment of a single market. Thus on a number of occasions the Court has held agreements aimed at partitioning national markets according to national borders or making the interpenetration of national markets more difficult, in particular those aimed at preventing or restricting parallel exports, to be agreements whose object is to restrict competition within the meaning of that article of the Treaty . . .

62. With respect to the Court of First Instance's statement that, while it is accepted that an agreement intended to limit parallel trade must in principle be considered to have as its object the restriction of competition, that applies in so far as it may be presumed to deprive final consumers of the advantages of effective competition in terms of supply or price, the Court notes that neither the wording of Article 81(1) EC nor the case-law lend support to such a position.

63. First of all, there is nothing in that provision to indicate that only those agreements which deprive consumers of certain advantages may have an anti-competitive object. Secondly, it must be borne in mind that the Court has held that, like other competition rules laid down in the Treaty, Article 81 EC aims to protect not only the interests of competitors or of consumers, but also the structure of the market and, in so doing, competition as such. Consequently, for a finding that an agreement has an anti-competitive object, it is not necessary that final consumers be deprived of the advantages of effective competition in terms of supply or price (see, by analogy, *T-Mobile Netherlands and Others*, cited above, paragraphs 38 and 39).

(ii) *Effect*

Where the anti-competitive quality of an agreement is not evident from its object then it is necessary to consider its effects,[62] as emphasized in the *Delimitis* case.[63] The contrast between *STM* and *Consten and Grundig* is instructive. It is clear that the *STM* case countenanced some economic analysis within Article 101(1): the ECJ took into account the fact that the exclusive-supply contract may have been necessary to enable MBU to penetrate the French market, and that this was to be encouraged.

The ECJ's response in *Consten and Grundig* to the argument concerning the rule of reason must be seen in the light of the facts. The parties sought to use that doctrine to legitimate a scheme that gave absolute territorial protection to the French distributor. If one were engaging in a pure economic analysis, which involved trade-offs between the pro- and anti-competitive effects of an agreement, then even absolute territorial protection might be warranted.[64] However, the EU competition rules have

---

[62] Case 23/67 *Brasserie de Haecht SA v Wilkin* [1967] ECR 407; Case 5/69 *Völk v Vervaecke* [1969] ECR 295; Case T-7/93 *Langnese-Iglo GmbH v Commission* [1995] ECR II-1533; O Odudu, 'Interpreting Article 81(1): Demonstrating Restrictive Effect' (2001) 26 ELRev 261.

[63] Case C-234/89 *Delimitis v Henninger Bräu AG* [1991] ECR I-935; Case C-279/06 *CEPSA Estaciones de Servicio SA v LV Tobar e Hijos SL* [2008] ECR I-6681, [43]; Case T-370/09 *GDF Suez v Commission* EU:T:2012:333, [82]-[83].

[64] The protection might be necessary to enable the manufacturer to penetrate a new market, and any reduction in intra-brand competition (competition between distributors of the same product) would be offset by increase in inter-brand competition (competition between those who distribute goods of the same kind, eg different brands of stereo equipment).

been influenced by the desire to create a single market.[65] Agreements that have the effect of partitioning the market along national lines will, therefore, be treated harshly. The *Consten and Grundig* case should not be perceived as rejecting economic analysis within Article 101(1), but rather as indicating that such analysis could not validate absolute territorial protection. Economic analysis is apparent in a number of other decisions.[66]

Case 258/78 LC Nungesser KG and Kurt Eisele v Commission
[1982] ECR 2015

[Note Lisbon Treaty renumbering: Art 85 is now Art 101 TFEU]

The case concerned a contract between INRA, a French research institute specializing in the development of plant seeds, and Eisele, a German supplier of seeds. The contract gave Eisele, and through him Nungesser, absolute territorial protection: INRA would not sell the seed to any other undertaking in Germany, and would prevent third parties from doing so; Eisele could use the plant breeder's rights assigned to him by INRA to prevent third parties selling into Germany. The Commission found that the agreement violated Article 85(1). The applicant argued that the exclusive licence was necessary to enable INRA to enter a new market, and compete with comparable products therein, since no trader would risk launching a new product unless he were given protection from competition from the licensor and from other licensees. The Court distinguished between an open exclusive licence, whereby the owner merely undertook not to compete himself, nor to grant licences to others in the same territory; and an exclusive licence with absolute territorial protection, under which all competition from third parties was eliminated.

THE ECJ

54. That point having been clarified, it is necessary to examine whether, in the present case, the exclusive nature of the licence, in so far as it is an open licence, has the effect of preventing or distorting competition within the meaning of Article 85(1) of the Treaty.

...

56. The exclusive licence which forms the subject-matter of the contested decision concerns the cultivation and marketing of hybrid maize seeds which were developed by INRA after years of research and experimentation and were unknown to German farmers at the time when the cooperation between INRA and the applicants was taking shape. For that reason the concern shown by the interveners as regards the protection of new technology is justified.

57. In fact, in the case of a licence of breeders' rights over hybrid maize seeds newly developed in one Member State, an undertaking in another Member State which was not certain that it would not encounter competition from other licensees for the territory granted to it, or from the owner of the right himself, might be deterred from accepting the risk of cultivating and marketing that product; such a result would be damaging to the dissemination of a new technology and would prejudice competition in the Community between the new product and similar existing products.

58. Having regard to the specific nature of the products in question, the Court concludes that, in a case such as the present, the grant of an open exclusive licence, that is to say a licence which does not

---

[65] Case C–501/06 P *GlaxoSmithKline* (n 52) [63]; G Amato, *Antitrust and the Bounds of Power* (Hart, 1997) 48–49.
[66] Case 262/81 *Coditel SA v Ciné-Vog Films SA* [1982] ECR 3381; Case C–234/89 *Delimitis* (n 63); Cases T–374, 375, 384 and 388/94 *European Night Services* (n 54); Case C–238/05 *Asnef-Equifax v Ausbanc* [2006] ECR I–11125.

affect the position of third parties such as parallel importers and licensees for other territories, is not in itself incompatible with Article 85(1) of the Treaty.

[*In relation to those aspects of the agreement which conferred absolute territorial protection, the Court, however, continued to follow* Consten and Grundig, *and to hold that these were illegal.*]

Closely related to the preceding material is the case law on what are termed ancillary restraints. The jurisprudence indicates that restrictions on the conduct of the parties ancillary, or objectively necessary, to the operation of pro-competitive or non-restrictive agreements cannot be said to restrict competition.[67] Thus, in *Remia*[68] it was held that non-competition clauses included in the sale of an undertaking would not come within Article 101(1), since otherwise the vendor, with his specialist knowledge of the transferred undertaking, could simply win back the custom from the purchaser. Such clauses could, therefore, enhance competition by increasing the number of undertakings on the relevant market. This will, however, exclude only certain clauses from Article 101(1). Thus, in *Remia* the Court held that the non-competition clause must be limited in time and scope.[69] Similar reasoning is evident in *Pronuptia*, although the Court decided that certain of the clauses were not necessary for the integrity of the franchise agreement and hence were caught by Article 101(1).[70]

Case 161/84 **Pronuptia de Paris GmbH v Pronuptia de Paris Irmgard Schillgallis**
[1986] ECR 353

[Note Lisbon Treaty renumbering: Art 85 is now Art 101 TFEU]

The case was concerned with franchising arrangements for wedding apparel. Under the franchise, the franchisor granted the franchisee the exclusive right to use the Pronuptia mark for a certain area; it agreed not to open another shop in that area, or aid any third party to do so; and it assisted the franchisee in setting up the store, providing know-how, etc. In return the franchisee, who remained the owner of the business, agreed to use the Pronuptia name; to pay the franchisor a royalty on turnover; to purchase 80 per cent of its requirements for wedding dresses from the franchisor; to take account of the recommended resale prices proposed by the franchisor; and not to compete with any Pronuptia business. The Court noted the diversity in types of franchise agreement: there were service, production, and distribution franchise agreements. The judgment is directed at distribution franchises.

THE ECJ

15. In a distribution system such as this, an enterprise which has established itself as a distributor in a market and which has thus been able to perfect a range of commercial methods gives independent businessmen the chance, at a price, of establishing themselves in other markets by using its mark

---

[67] A Jones and B Sufrin, *EU Competition Law: Text, Cases, and Materials* (Oxford University Press, 5th edn, 2014) 242–246; Commission Guidelines (n 59) [28]–[31].

[68] Case 42/84 *Remia BV and Verenigde Bedrijven Nutricia NV v Commission* [1985] ECR 2545; Case C–250/92 *Gottrup-Klim Grovvareforeninger v Dansk Landbrugs Grovvareselskab AmbA* [1994] ECR I–5641.

[69] Case 42/84 (n 68).

[70] Case 161/84 [1986] ECR 353, 382–385. This was particularly the case for those clauses which partitioned the market between franchisor and franchisee, or between franchisees themselves. Thus, the obligation on the franchisor not to allow other franchisees to open shops outside their allotted territory was held to fall foul of the *Consten and Grundig* principle. The fact that such a clause might be necessary for any franchisee to make the initial investment was recognized by the Court, but was considered to be of relevance only within Art 101(3).

and the commercial methods which created the franchisor's success....At the same time this system gives businessmen who lack the necessary experience access to methods which they could otherwise only acquire after prolonged effort and research and allows them also to profit from the reputation of the mark....Such a system, which permits the franchisor to take advantage of his success, is not by itself restrictive of competition. For it to function two conditions must be satisfied.

16. First, the franchisor must be able to communicate his know-how to the franchisees and provide them with the necessary assistance in putting his methods into effect, without running the risk that this know-how will aid his competitors, even indirectly. It thus follows that those clauses which are essential to prevent this risk do not constitute restrictions on competition in the sense of Article 85(1). These include the prohibition on the franchisee opening, for the duration of the franchise or for a reasonable period after its termination, a shop with an identical or similar purpose in an area where he could be in competition with one of the members of the network. The same applies to the obligation on the franchisee not to sell his shop without the prior approval of the franchisor: this clause serves to ensure that the benefit of the know-how and assistance provided does not go directly to a competitor.

17. Secondly, the franchisor must be able to take appropriate measures to preserve the identity and reputation of the network which is symbolised by the mark. It thus follows that those clauses which provide a basis for such control as is indispensable for this purpose also do not constitute restrictions on competition in the sense of Article 85(1).

18. This covers then the obligation on the franchisee to apply the commercial methods developed by the franchisor and to utilise the know-how provided.

19. This is also the case with the franchisee's obligation only to sell the merchandise covered by the agreement in premises set up and decorated according to the franchisor's specifications, which have as their purpose to guarantee a uniform image corresponding to specified requirements.

. . .

21. Thanks to the control exercised by the franchisor over the selection of goods offered by the franchisee, the public can find at each franchisee's shop merchandise of the same quality....A clause prescribing that the franchisee can only sell products provided by the franchisor or by suppliers selected by him must, in these circumstances, be considered necessary for the protection of the reputation of the network. It must not, however, operate to prevent the franchisee from obtaining the products from other franchisees.

Notwithstanding the above the CFI in *Métropole Télévision* denied that there is a rule of reason as such within Article 101(1), and it has reiterated this stance in subsequent decisions.[71]

Case T–112/99 **Métropole Télévision (M6), Suez-Lyonnaise des Eaux, France Telecom, and Télévision Française 1 SA (TFI) v Commission**
[2001] ECR II–2459

[Note Lisbon Treaty renumbering: Art 85 is now Art 101 TFEU]

The applicant companies sought to annul a Commission decision relating to the creation of TPS, a company providing digital satellite television for payment. The agreement had an exclusivity clause, whereby the general-interest channels provided by the applicants would be broadcast exclusively by

---

[71] Case T–65/98 *Van den Bergh Foods Ltd v Commission* [2003] ECR II–4653, [107]; Case T–328/03 *O2 (Germany) GmbH & Co OHG v Commission* [2006] ECR II–1231, [65]–[73]; Case T–491/07 *Groupement des cartes bancaires 'CB' v Commission* EU:T:2012:633; Case T–111/08 *MasterCard v Commission* EU:T:2012:260.

TPS. The applicants argued, based on cases such as *Nungesser*, that the Commission should have applied Article 85(1) in the light of the rule of reason to this clause. There were already strong companies on the pay TV market, into which TPS was seeking to gain entry.

THE CFI

72. According to the applicants, as a consequence of the existence of the rule of reason in Community competition law, when Article 85(1)...is applied it is necessary to weigh the pro- and anti-competitive effects of an agreement in order to determine whether it is caught by the prohibition laid down in that article. It should, however, be observed, first of all, that contrary to the applicants' assertions the existence of such a rule has not, as such, been confirmed by the Community courts. Quite the contrary, in various judgments the Court of Justice and Court of First Instance have been at pains to indicate that the existence of a rule of reason in Community law is doubtful (see Case C–235/92, *Montecatini*...[1999] ECR I–4539, paragraph 133...Case T–148/89, *Tréfilunion* [1995] ECR II–1063, paragraph 109).

73. Next, it must be observed that an interpretation of Article 85(1)..., in the form suggested by the applicants, is difficult to reconcile with the rules prescribed by that provision.

74. Article 85...expressly provides, in its third paragraph, for the possibility of exempting agreements that restrict competition where they satisfy a number of conditions....It is only in the precise framework of that provision that the pro- and anti-competitive effects of a restriction may be weighed (see...*Pronuptia* paragraph 24...and *European Night Services* paragraph 136). Article 85(3) would lose much of its effectiveness if such an examination had to be carried out already under Article 85(1)....

75. It is true that in a number of judgments the Court of Justice and the Court of First Instance have favoured a more flexible interpretation of the prohibition laid down in Article 85(1) (see...*STM*...*Nungesser*...*Coditel*...*Pronuptia*...*European Night Services*...).

76. Those judgments cannot, however, be interpreted as establishing the existence of a rule of reason in Community competition law. They are, rather, part of a broader trend in the case law according to which it is not necessary to hold, wholly abstractly and without drawing any distinction, that any agreement restricting the freedom of action of one or more of the parties is necessarily caught by...Article 85(1)....In assessing the applicability of Article 85(1) to an agreement, account should be taken of the actual conditions in which it functions, in particular the economic context in which the undertakings operate, the products or services covered by the agreement and the actual structure of the market concerned....

77....It must, however, be emphasized that such an approach does not mean that it is necessary to weigh the pro- and anti-competitive effects of an agreement when determining whether...Article 85(1)...applies.

[*The CFI then considered whether the exclusivity clause could be considered as a valid ancillary restraint.*]

104. In Community competition law the concept of an ancillary restriction covers any restriction which is directly related and necessary to the implementation of a main operation...

...

106. The condition that a restriction be necessary implies a two-fold examination. It is necessary to establish, first, whether the restriction is objectively necessary for the implementation of the main operation and, second, whether it is proportionate to it...

107. As regards the objective necessity of a restriction, it must be observed that inasmuch as, as has been shown in paragraph 72 et seq above, the existence of a rule of reason in Community competition law cannot be upheld, it would be wrong, when classifying ancillary restrictions, to interpret the requirement for objective necessity as implying a need to weigh the pro- and anti-competitive effects of an agreement. Such an analysis can take place only in the specific framework of Article 81(3) of the Treaty.

...

109. Consequently...examination of the objective necessity of a restriction in relation to the main operation cannot but be relatively abstract. It is not a question of analyzing whether, in the light of the competitive situation on the relevant market, the restriction is indispensable to the commercial success of the main operation, but of determining whether, in the specific context of the main operation, the restriction is necessary to implement that operation. If, without the restriction, the main operation is difficult or even impossible to implement, the restriction may be regarded as objectively necessary for its implementation.

[*The CFI held that the claimants did not satisfy this test.*]

(E) SUMMARY

i. It is clear that the ECJ condemns certain types of agreement because of their object or purpose without any extensive market analysis, and thus effectively proscribes these agreements as *per se* illegal. It is also clear that the Court has engaged in economic analysis within Article 101(1). While it has not employed the language of the rule of reason, there is evidence of a balancing of the pro- and anti-competitive effects of an agreement, subject to the caveats made above.

ii. The Union Courts may choose to undertake this analysis by considering all the clauses of the agreement as a whole, or they might distinguish between the main and ancillary clauses of the agreement. The fact that the Court chooses the latter mode should not disguise the fact that there is some weighing of the pro- and anti-competitive effects of the agreement, as exemplified by *Pronuptia*.

iii. The reasoning in *Métropole* is problematic for two reasons. First, there are problems with the CFI's rationalization of the prior case law. The Union Courts considered the entire economic context since it was only by doing so that it was possible to tell whether, for example, a clause restricting conduct should nonetheless be allowed, because it enabled a party to break into the market, the conclusion being that such restrictions on freedom of action were not restrictive of competition. The Union Courts have, in this sense, balanced the pro- and anti-competitive effects of the agreement.[72] The exclusivity clause in *Métropole* was designed to give subscribers something attractive so as to enable TPS to break into a market where there was strong competition. Secondly, the reasoning assumes that a rule of reason is incompatible with the existence of Article 101(3). It is, however, possible to balance the pro- and anti-competitive effects of an agreement within Article 101(1), and still to preserve a role for Article 101(3).[73]

iv. The Commission has not been enthusiastic about economic analysis in the past, and has been criticized for equating a restriction on conduct with a restriction on competition. This is clearly mistaken, since restriction of competition is an economic concept, which must be assessed in relation to a market. It is unclear how far its approach has changed. In the White Paper on Modernization[74] the Commission stated that it adopted the ECJ's approach in *Nungesser*[75]

---

[72] R Nazzini, 'Article 81 EC between Time Present and Time Past: A Normative Critique of "Restriction of Competition" in EU Law' (2006) 43 CMLRev 487.

[73] R Wesseling, 'The Commission White Paper on Modernisation of EC Antitrust Law: Unspoken Consequences and Incomplete Alternative Options' [1999] ECLR 420.

[74] White Paper on the Modernisation of the Rules Implementing Articles 85 and 86 of the EC Treaty, Comm Programme 99/027, [57]; Commission Guidelines (n 59) [18].

[75] Case 258/78 [1982] ECR 2015.

and *Pronuptia*[76] and balanced the pro- and anti-competitive effects of an agreement within Article 101(1) in relation to some restrictive practices. It however went on to say that any more systematic use of such rule-of-reason analysis under Article 101(1) would mean that Article 101(3) would be 'cast aside'. The Commission said that this would be paradoxical, given that Article 101(3) contains all the elements of a rule of reason.[77] This reasoning, although supported by *Métropole*, has been contested. It has been argued that a more thoroughgoing balancing of pro- and anti-competitive effects within Article 101(1) would be beneficial, and would still leave room for a distinctive role for Article 101(3).[78]

7 ARTICLE 101(1): THE EFFECT ON TRADE BETWEEN MEMBER STATES

In order for Article 101(1) to apply, the agreement, etc, must have an effect on trade between Member States, since otherwise the matter will remain within the jurisdiction of the relevant Member State. The hurdle has not, however, proven difficult for the Court to surmount. It has adopted a broad test. The ECJ held in *STM* that the test was whether it was possible to 'foresee with a sufficient degree of probability on the basis of a set of objective factors of law or of fact that the agreement in question may have an influence, direct or indirect, actual or potential, on the pattern of trade between Member States'.[79]

The focus on potential or indirect effects on trade means that it will be very rare for the EU to lack jurisdiction. Proof that the agreement had an actual impact on trade is not necessary, provided that it was capable of having that effect.[80] The fact that all the parties to the agreement are from one Member State will not preclude application of Article 101(1), since it will increase compartmentalization of the EU along national lines, thereby rendering it more difficult for firms from other states to penetrate that national market.[81] Nor will the Court's jurisdiction be barred merely because the agreement relates to trade outside the EU if it might have an impact on trade within the EU.[82] The Commission has published guidelines indicating when it believes that an agreement is not capable of appreciably affecting trade.[83]

---

[76] Case 161/84 [1986] ECR 353.

[77] White Paper (n 74) [57].

[78] Wesseling (n 73).

[79] Case 56/65 [1966] ECR 235, 249. It is not necessary for each of the restrictions to do so: Case 193/83 *Windsurfing International Inc v Commission* [1986] ECR 611.

[80] Case 19/77 *Miller International Schallplatten GmbH v Commission* [1978] ECR 131; Case C–219/95 P *Ferriere Nord* (n 31). This extends to the situation where the relevant restriction has not been implemented, since the very existence of the restriction can still have a psychological effect which contributes to the partitioning of the market: Case T–77/92 *Parker Pen* (n 54); Case T–66/92 *Herlitz* (n 54).

[81] Case 8/72 *Vereeniging van Cementhandelaren v Commission* [1972] ECR 977; Case 246/86 *Société Coopérative des Asphalteurs Belges (BELASCO) v Commission* [1989] ECR 2117; Case T–66/89 *Publishers Association v Commission (No 2)* [1992] ECR II–1995.

[82] *Franco-Japanese Ballbearings Agreement* [1974] OJ L343/19, [1975] 1 CMLR D8; *French and Taiwanese Mushroom Packers* [1975] OJ L29/26, [1975] 1 CMLR D83.

[83] Commission Guidelines on the effect on trade concept contained in Articles 81 and 82 of the Treaty [2004] OJ C101/81, [44]–[57].

8 ARTICLE 101(1): THE *DE MINIMIS* DOCTRINE

An agreement will not be caught by Article 101(1) if it does not have an appreciable impact on competition or on inter-state trade,[84] but the ECJ also held that an agreement that may affect trade between Member States and that has an anti-competitive object constitutes, by its nature and independently of any concrete effect that it may have, an appreciable restriction on competition.[85] The Commission Notice on this issue does not therefore deal with agreements caught by their object, but gives greater specificity as to when agreements caught by their effect will fall within Article 101 TFEU.[86]

The criterion is that agreements between undertakings do not appreciably restrict competition where the aggregate market share held by the parties to the agreement does not exceed 10 per cent on markets where the parties are actual or potential competitors. The relevant figure is 15 per cent for cases where the parties are not competitors on the relevant markets.[87] In cases where it is difficult to classify the agreement then the 10 per cent threshold applies. Paragraph 10 of the Notice deals with vertical cases, in which competition may be restricted by the cumulative effect of agreements. In such instances, the threshold is reduced to 5 per cent for agreements between both competitors and non-competitors. The Notice further provides that individual suppliers or distributors with a market share not exceeding 5 per cent will, in general, not be considered to contribute significantly to a cumulative foreclosure effect. Moreover, such an effect will be unlikely to exist if parallel networks of agreements having similar effects cover less than 30 per cent of the relevant market. The Notice provides a further buffer, in stipulating that agreements will not be restrictive of competition where the preceding thresholds are not exceeded by more than 2 per cent in two successive years.[88]

However, the benefits of the Notice are excluded if the agreement contains hard-core restrictions listed in paragraph 13, or in any other block exemption, past or future. Thus agreements between competitors cannot contain restrictions as to sale price, limitation of output, or allocation of markets or customers.

9 ARTICLE 101(3): EXEMPTIONS

If an agreement is within Article 101(1) it can gain exemption under Article 101(3), provided that four conditions are satisfied: it must improve the production or distribution of goods or promote technical or economic progress; consumers must receive a fair share of the resulting benefit; it must contain only restrictions which are indispensable to the attainment of the agreement's objectives; and it cannot lead to the elimination of competition in respect of a substantial part of the products in question.

---

[84] Case 5/69 *Völk* (n 62); Case T–77/92 *Parker Pen* (n 54); Case C–180/98 *Pavlov v Stichting Pensioenfonds Medische Specialisten* [2000] ECR I–6451; Case T–199/08 *Ziegler SA v Commission* [2011] ECR II–3507, [44]; Cases T–208–209/08 *Gosselin Group v Commission* [2011] ECR II–3639; Case C–226/11 *Expedia Inc v Autorité de la concurrence* EU:C:2012:795, [16]–[17].

[85] Case C–226/11 *Expedia* (n 84) [37].

[86] Commission Notice on agreements of minor importance which do not appreciably restrict competition under Article 81(1) (de minimis) [2014] OJ C291/01, [13]; Guidance on restrictions of competition 'by object' for the purpose of defining which agreements may benefit from the De Minimis Notice, SWD(2014)198 final.

[87] Ibid [8].

[88] Ibid [11].

The four conditions are cumulative: they must all be fulfilled before an exemption can be granted.[89] There are individual and block exemptions.

(A) INDIVIDUAL EXEMPTION

Prior to 2003 the Commission had the sole power to grant exemptions under Article 101(3), subject to review by the Court. This has now changed with the new scheme for enforcement of competition law, whereby national courts and national competition authorities can apply the entirety of Article 101.[90] The Commission has published guidelines on the application of Article 101(3), which provide a useful frame of reference.[91]

The Commission makes clear that any balancing of the pro- and anti-competitive effect of an agreement should take place within Article 101(3), rather than Article 101(1).[92] All restrictive agreements that are caught by Article 101(1) can in principle be exempted under Article 101(3), but espe cially heinous agreements such as horizontal price fixing are unlikely to satisfy the conditions for exemption.[93]

The *first condition* is that there must be some efficiency gains flowing from the restrictive agreement. The efficiencies may take the form of lower costs, resulting from new production methods, synergies consequent upon integration of existing assets, economies of scale, or cost savings.[94] Efficiency gains may also be qualitative in nature, generating improved products or better research and development.[95] The Commission requires proof of such gains and of the causal link between them and the restrictive agreement.

Commission Guidelines on the application of Article 81(3) of the Treaty[96]

50. The purpose of the first condition of Article 81(3) is to define the types of efficiency gains that can be taken into account...The aim of the analysis is to ascertain what are the objective benefits created by the agreement and what is the economic importance of such efficiencies...

51. All efficiency claims must therefore be substantiated so that the following can be verified:

(a) The nature of the claimed efficiencies;

(b) The link between the agreement and the efficiencies;

(c) The likelihood and magnitude of each claimed efficiency; and

(d) How and when each claimed efficiency would be achieved.

The *second condition* is that consumers receive a fair share of resulting benefits. The Commission's view of this requirement emerges from the following extract.

---

[89] Case T–213/00 *CMA CGM* (n 54) [226].

[90] Council Regulation (EC) No 1/2003 of 16 December 2002 on the implementation of the rules on competition laid down in Articles 81 and 82 of the Treaty [2003] OJ L1/1.

[91] L Kjolbye, 'The New Commission Guidelines on the Application of Article 81(3): An Economic Approach to Article 81' [2004] ECLR 566.

[92] Commission Guidelines (n 59) [11].

[93] Ibid [46].

[94] Ibid [64]–[68].

[95] Ibid [69]–[72].

[96] Ibid [50]–[51].

Commission Guidelines on the application of Article 81(3) of the Treaty[97]

85. The concept of 'fair share' implies that the pass-on of benefits must at least compensate consumers for any actual or likely negative impact caused to them by the restriction of competition found under Article 81(1)...

86. It is not required that consumers receive a share of each and every efficiency gain identified under the first condition. It suffices that sufficient benefits are passed on to compensate for the negative effects of the restrictive agreement...

87. The decisive factor is the overall impact on consumers of the products within the relevant market and not the impact on individual members of this group of consumers. In some cases a period of time may be required before the efficiencies materialize. Until such time the agreement may have only negative effects. The fact that pass-on to the consumer occurs with a certain time lag does not in itself exclude the application of Article 81(3). However the greater the time lag, the greater must be the efficiencies to compensate also for the loss to consumers during the period preceding the pass-on.

The *third condition* concerns the indispensability of the restrictions. This implies a twofold test: the restrictive agreement must be reasonably necessary to achieve the efficiencies; and the individual restrictions of competition that flow from the agreement must also be reasonably necessary for the attainment of those efficiencies.[98] The ECJ will also consider closely whether the restriction is indispensable, as exemplified by *Nungesser*.

Case 258/78 LC Nungesser KG and Kurt Eisele v Commission
[1982] ECR 2015

The facts were set out above. It will be remembered that the Court held that the clauses in the agreement that gave absolute territorial protection were caught by Article 85(1). The Commission had also refused exemption under Article 85(3) for aspects of the agreement because of this territorial protection. The applicants argued that the Court should overturn this part of the Commission's decision.

THE ECJ

76. It must be remembered that under the terms of Article 85(3)...an exemption from the prohibition contained in Article 85(1) may be granted in the case of an agreement between undertakings which contributes to improving the production or distribution of goods or to promoting technical progress, and which does not impose on the undertakings concerned restrictions which are not indispensable to the attainment of those objectives.

77. As it is a question of seeds intended to be used by a large number of farmers for the production of maize, which is an important product for human and animal foodstuffs, absolute territorial protection manifestly goes beyond what is indispensable for the improvement of production or distribution or the promotion of technical progress, as is demonstrated...by the prohibition agreed to by both parties to the agreement, of any parallel imports of INRA maize seeds into Germany even if those seeds were bred by INRA itself and marketed in France.

---

[97] Ibid [85]–[87].
[98] Ibid [73].

> 78. It follows that the absolute territorial protection conferred on the licensee...constituted a sufficient reason for refusing to grant an exemption under Article 85(3)....It is therefore no longer necessary to examine the other grounds set out in the decision for refusing to grant such an exemption.

The *final condition* for exemption is that the agreement should not lead to elimination of competition in respect of a substantial part of the products in question. This reflects the fact that the 'protection of rivalry and the competitive process is given priority over potentially pro-competitive efficiency gains which could result from restrictive agreements'.[99] Whether competition is being eliminated will depend on the degree of competition prior to the agreement and the impact of the restrictive agreement on competition. Thus the 'more competition is already weakened in the market concerned, the slighter the further reduction required for competition to be eliminated within the meaning of Article 81(3)'.[100]

In considering the conditions in the Commission's Notice, one should not lose sight of its overall impact.

P Lugard and L Hancher, Honey I Shrunk the Article! A Critical Assessment of the Commission's Notice on Article 81(3) of the EC Treaty[101]

In clarifying the analytical framework for the application of both Art. 81(1) and (3), the Notice provides useful guidance to national courts, authorities and firms. In addition to several questionable aspects of the analysis...the main concern is that, by significantly raising the threshold in terms of quantification and verification of efficiencies under Art. 81(3), the role of Art. 81(3) in national court proceedings may—paradoxically—be limited. It is not unlikely that national proceedings will in the future increasingly centre around the applicability of Art. 81(1)...Indeed, once the applicability of Art. 81(1) is established, the Notice may not leave much scope to adduce convincingly the extensive evidence required under Art. 81(3). Such an outcome would be at odds with the very purpose underlying the Notice and indeed Regulation 1/2003.

(B) BLOCK EXEMPTION

Article 101(3) allows the Commission to declare the provisions of Article 101(1) inapplicable to a category of agreements. This is the foundation for block exemptions made by the Commission, acting under delegated authority from the Council. The object of such exemptions is to exclude a generic type of agreement from the ambit of Article 101(1), thereby obviating the need for separate and time-consuming individual exemptions. The technique of block exemption is conceptually similar to the evolution of *per se* rules, although the result is to exclude rather than condemn the agreement: experience with individual agreements leads to the conclusion that certain types of agreement, which contain particular terms, warrant exemption. A block exemption encapsulates this conclusion and gives more definite guidance to firms.

---

[99] Ibid [105].
[100] Ibid [107].
[101] [2004] ECLR 410, 420.

Block exemptions have certain common features. They state the reasons for their enactment, set out the substance of the exemption, contain provisions limiting the size of the firms that can take advantage of them, and list the types of clauses that are and are not allowed within the relevant agreement. Such exemptions have been made for a number of areas, including: specialization agreements;[102] research and development;[103] vertical restraints;[104] technology transfer;[105] and franchising.[106] The structure and operation of block exemptions will be examined more closely in the context of vertical restraints.

10 ARTICLE 101: COMPETITION AND NON-COMPETITION CONSIDERATIONS

There has been debate whether the EU Courts should or should not take into account non-competition considerations, in the context of either Article 101(1) and/or Article 101(3).

(A) ARTICLE 101(1)

The general academic consensus is that the EU Courts do and should restrict their analysis within Article 101(1) to considerations that relate to competition. This follows from the preceding analysis of the rule-of-reason debate in the following sense: if there is reluctance to consider the full pro- and anti-competitive effects of an agreement within Article 101(1), then there will be even greater opposition to the inclusion of non-competition considerations in that context.

There is relatively little evidence of such matters being taken into account by the Union Courts, although *Wouters*[107] appears to be an exception in this regard. The Netherlands Bar adopted rules that prevented its members from practising in full partnership with accountants. The ECJ found that this limited production within Article 101(1)(b).[108] It nonetheless concluded that the rules did not violate Article 101(1), because they were to ensure the independence of members of the Bar and hence the sound administration of justice. In that sense the Court appeared to weigh the anti-competitive effect of the rules against the non-economic benefits they were designed to achieve. It has, however, been argued either that the case can be regarded as an instance of 'regulatory ancillarity', in the sense that restraints on competition that are ancillary to a legitimate purpose can be accepted;[109] or that the decision can be seen, by way of analogy with case law on free movement, as one in which the ECJ weighed the impact of non-discriminatory national rules that limited competition against mandatory national public policy.[110]

The ECJ, however, returned to the '*Wouters* theme' in *Meca-Medina*.[111] It held that anti-doping rules adopted by the International Olympic Committee, even if they could be regarded as a decision

---

102 Reg 1218/2010 [2010] OJ L335/43.

103 Reg 1217/2010 [2010] OJ L335/36.

104 Reg 2790/99 [1999] OJ L336/21; Reg 330/2010 [2010] OJ 102/1.

105 Reg 316/2014 [2014] OJ L93/17.

106 Reg 4087/88 [1988] OJ L359/46.

107 Case C–309/99 *Wouters v Algemene Raad van de Nederlandse Orde van Advocaten* [2002] ECR I–1577; A Jones, 'Regulating the Legal Profession: Article 81, the Public Interest and the ECJ's Judgment in *Wouters*' (2008) 19 European Business Law Review 1079.

108 Ibid [90], [94].

109 Whish and Bailey (n 5) 130–131.

110 G Monti, 'Article 81 EC and Public Policy' (2002) 39 CMLRev 1057, 1087–1089.

111 Case C–519/04 P *Meca-Medina and Majcen v Commission* [2006] ECR I–6991, [40]–[56]. Compare Case C–136/12 *Consiglio nazionale dei geologi v Autorità garante della concorrenza e del mercato* EU:C:2013:489.

of an association of undertakings limiting the applicants' freedom of action, did not come within Article 101, since they were justified by a legitimate objective, this being to ensure fair rivalry between athletes in sport, and were proportionate.

(B) ARTICLE 101(3)

Some authors argue that non-competition considerations can be taken into account within Article 101(3).[112] The predominant academic view is, however, that they should not be, more especially so now that national courts apply the entirety of Article 101: if a broad range of non-competition considerations could be taken into account then the criteria that national courts should apply would be uncertain.[113]

R Whish and D Bailey, Competition Law[114]

A narrow view of Article 101(3) is that it permits only agreements that would bring about improvements in economic efficiency: the very wording of Article 101(3), which speaks of improvement to production and distribution and to technical and economic progress, is clearly suggestive of an efficiency standard. Article 101(3), therefore, simply allows a balancing of the restrictive effects of an agreement under Article 101(1) against the enhancement of efficiency under Article 101(3).... The Commission's White Paper on Modernisation...explained Article 101(1) and 101(3) in precisely this way.

...

However, an alternative, and broader view of Article 101(3) is possible: that it allows policies other than economic efficiency to be taken into account when deciding whether to allow agreements that are restrictive of competition. There are many important policies in the Community, for example on industry, the environment, employment, the regions and culture, which go beyond the simple enhancement of efficiency. According to a broad view of Article 101(3), a benefit in terms of any of these policies may be able to 'trump' a restriction of competition under Article 101(1).

[Whish and Bailey review a number of decisions where such factors seem to have had some impact on the Commission's reasoning. They continue as follows:]

It is clear...that a number of factors have been influential in decisions under Article 101(3), not all of which can be considered to be 'narrow' improvements in efficiency. There are significant proponents of the view that Article 101(3) does admit broad, non-competition considerations...

...

This discussion shows that, over a number of years, there has been uncertainty—even confusion—as to the proper application of Article 101(3)...However Regulation 1/2003 makes it necessary to decide on the true content of Article 101(3) because decisions since 1 May 2004 can be made by NCAs[115] and national courts as well as by the Commission itself. These institutions, and the undertakings that enter into agreements that might be challenged under Article 101, need to know the limits of what can be justified under Article 101(3); and the NCAs and national courts, unlike the Commission, are not well-placed to balance a restriction of competition under Article 101(1) against a variety of European Union policies ranging from industrial and environmental policy to social and cultural issues under Article 101(3). It seems reasonable to suppose that NCAs and national courts would have less

---

[112] Monti (n 110); R Wesseling, 'The Draft Regulation Modernising the Competition Rules: The Commission is Married to One Idea' (2001) 26 ELRev 357.

[113] O Odudu, *The Boundaries of EC Competition Law: The Scope of Article 81* (Oxford University Press, 2006) ch 6.

[114] Whish and Bailey (n 5) 157–159.

[115] National Competition Authorities.

difficulty in applying a 'narrow' interpretation of Article 101(3), limited to a consideration of economic efficiencies. These considerations suggest that, in the post-Regulation 1/2003 world, Article 101(3) should be interpreted in a narrow rather than a broad manner, according to standards and by reference to principles that are justiciable in courts of law.

It is absolutely clear from the Commission's *Article 101(3) Guidelines* that it intends Article 101(3) to be applied according to the narrow approach based on economic efficiency...

11 ARTICLE 101: VERTICAL RESTRAINTS

Space precludes detailed analysis of all types of competitive restraint. This section will, therefore, consider one important area of competition policy, that of vertical restraints. Vertical agreements are made between parties at differing levels of the production process, a typical example being a distribution agreement between a manufacturer of a product and a retailer. There is controversy about the extent to which these agreements are economically harmful. There are differing types of vertical restraint. It must be determined whether they are caught by Article 101(1). The criterion used by the ECJ and the Commission has not always been the same, and the Commission has been criticized for taking too formalistic an approach to vertical agreements. In terms of Article 101(3), the EU has primarily used block exemptions to deal with vertical restraints.

(A) THE ECONOMIC DEBATE

There is considerable debate as to whether vertical restraints are economically harmful.[116] Some believe that they are not harmful at all, or only where there is some real market power at the production level. Others believe that vertical restraints may produce a variety of anti-competitive effects, and that therefore they should be scrutinized by competition authorities.

(i) *The First View*

A manufacturer must decide how to market its product. It may decide to establish its own retail outlets; to establish a joint venture with a company that has expertise in the retailing area; to sell its products through any outlet that is willing to stock them; to sell through certain specialized shops, because the product requires sales expertise; or to sell through certain retail outlets, each of which will have exclusive rights for a geographical area, either because retailers demand this, or because it will maximize sales. This list is by no means exhaustive. The argument of those who do not see vertical restraints as harmful has four parts.

First, the manufacturer will choose the most efficient marketing option. It will, for example, give outlets exclusivity only if this leads to greater sales. If the manufacturer is wrong then the market will 'punish' it, through reduced sales. The competition authorities should not try to devise a better marketing strategy for the manufacturer, since this is not their function, and they are less well placed to make this choice.

---

[116] D Neven, P Papandropolous, and P Seabright, *Trawling for Minnows: European Competition Policy and Agreements between Firms* (Centre for Economic Policy Research, 1998); J Lever and S Neubauer, 'Vertical Restraints, Their Motivation and Justification' [2000] ECLR 7.

Secondly, a manufacturer which imposes such restraints will not restrict output to any greater degree than it would otherwise do, and will not take any greater monopoly profit, if such is available, through the presence of a vertical restraint than it would otherwise be able to extract from that market.

Thirdly, any restraints are either outweighed by the pro-competitive effects of the agreement, and/or are necessary to persuade the distributor to market the goods. A producer may wish to enter a new market, but does not have retailing expertise. If the product is to break into the new market it may require advertising, and also a commitment to provide pre- and post-sales service. A retailer may not be willing to undertake this expense unless it is accorded some exclusivity because of the 'free-rider' problem: the retailer will expend money on advertising, pre-sales service, and the like, only to witness the sales being taken by a rival retailer who has not incurred these costs. The grant of exclusivity will restrict intra-brand competition between retailers of the same product, but inter-brand competition will be enhanced by having a new product on the market, and this will control retail prices. A retailer of a brand of car who has exclusivity in a certain area will not be able to raise prices significantly, since there will be competition from other makes of car.

Fourthly, it is argued that vertical restraints should be lawful because they do not produce anti-competitive effects. The nature of these effects will be considered in more detail below. A prominent exponent of the preceding view is Bork.

R Bork, The Antitrust Paradox: A Policy at War with Itself[117]

We have seen that vertical price fixing (resale price maintenance), vertical market division (closed dealer territories), and, indeed, all vertical restraints are beneficial to consumers and should for that reason be completely lawful. Basic economic theory tells us that the manufacturer who imposes such restraints cannot intend to restrict and must (except in the rare case of price discrimination, which the law should regard as neutral) intend to create efficiency. The most common efficiency is the inducement or purchase by the manufacturer of extra reseller sales, service or promotional effort.

The proposal to legalize all truly vertical restraints is so much at variance with conventional thought on the topic that it will doubtless strike many readers as troublesome, if not bizarre. But I have never seen any economic analysis that shows how manufacturer-imposed resale price maintenance, closed dealer territories, customer allocation clauses, or the like can have the net effect of restricting output. We have too quickly assumed something that appears untrue.

Perhaps the ambiguity of the word 'restraint' accounts for some of our confusion on this topic. When the Supreme Court speaks of a restraint it often, or even usually, refers to the manufacturer's control of certain activities of his resellers or to the elimination by the manufacturer of some forms of rivalry among his resellers. There is, of course, nothing sinister or unusual about using 'restraint' in that sense. It is merely a form of vertical integration by contract, a less complete integration than that which would obtain if the manufacturer owned his outlets and directed their activities. It is merely one instance of the coordination of economic activities which is ubiquitous in the economic world and upon which our wealth depends. The important point is that such vertical control never

---

[117] Bork (n 42) 297–298. See also R Bork, 'The Rule of Reason and the *Per Se* Concept in Price Fixing and Market Division II' (1966) 75 Yale LJ 373; JR Gould and BS Yamey, 'Professor Bork on Vertical Price Fixing' (1967) 76 Yale LJ 722; R Bork, 'A Reply to Professors Gould and Yamey' (1967) 76 Yale LJ 731; JR Gould and BS Yamey, 'Professor Bork on Vertical Price Fixing: A Rejoinder' (1968) 77 Yale LJ 936.

creates 'restraint' in that other common meaning, restriction of output. Perhaps, if we are more careful about the ambiguity of the word and make it clear in which sense we use it, our reasoning about antitrust problems, including the problem of vertical restraints, will improve.[118]

(ii) *The Second View*

There are, however, many commentators who perceive possible dangers to the competitive process from such agreements. The principal concerns are as follows.

The first is market foreclosure. If a producer has made exclusive contracts with certain outlets to sell only its product, then it may be difficult for other producers to secure outlets, more especially where the best outlets have been taken, or the number is limited by the nature of the product or by factors such as planning laws.

A second concern is that consumers will be harmed by certain types of vertical restraint, resale-price maintenance being the most commonly cited example, although this has been vigorously contested.[119] Consumer harm is said to be apparent in other ways. Thus, it is argued that systems of selective or exclusive distribution force a 'package' on consumers, which includes the basic price of the product, plus advertising costs, after-sales service, and the like, even though some consumers would prefer to take the product itself and worry about maintenance themselves.

A third disadvantage said to attend vertical agreements is that they can serve as a mask for cartels between producers or distributors. A producer may grant an exclusive distribution right where the distributor has agreed with other distributors of competing products to divide the market horizontally: the consequence will be that inter- as well as intra-brand competition is reduced. It has, however, been questioned whether this actually happens, and whether it is exacerbated by the existence of the vertical agreement. It has also been argued that if this occurred then the horizontal agreement should be the target of the competition authorities.[120]

A final cause for concern with vertical agreements is peculiar to EU competition law, which is not concerned solely with efficiency. The creation of a single European market is also of prime importance. Agreements which divide the market along national or regional lines will, therefore, be treated particularly severely, as exemplified by the Court's continuing opposition to agreements that provide absolute territorial protection.

Comanor expresses the concerns of this second, more cautious, school of thought. He reviews Bork's arguments, but does not believe that vertical agreements should always be regarded as legal.[121]

W Comanor, Vertical Price-Fixing, Vertical Market Restrictions, and the New Antitrust Policy[122]

When vertical restraints are used to promote the provision of distribution services, the critical issue for antitrust purposes remains whether consumers are better served by lower prices and fewer services or by higher prices and more services. In its *Spray-Rite* brief, the Department of Justice suggested that

---

[118] See also F Easterbrook, 'Vertical Arrangements and the Rule of Reason' (1984) 53 Antitrust LJ 135; B Bok, 'An Economist Appraises Vertical Restraints' (1985) 30 Antitrust B 117.

[119] See (n 117).

[120] Bork (n 42) ch 14.

[121] Monti (n 110).

[122] (1985) 98 Harv LRev 983, 1001–1002.

pure vertical restraints always lead to increased consumer welfare. This position is unfounded, and a more hostile treatment of vertical restraints is appropriate.

Because vertical restraints can either enhance or diminish consumer welfare, depending upon the situation, it is tempting to apply the rule of reason on a case-by-case basis.

... Yet it is no easy task to determine whether particular restraints increase or decrease efficiency: the answer depends in each case largely on the relative preferences of different groups of consumers. In the interests of judicial economy, therefore, it may be more expeditious to set general policy standards, even though they will sometimes lead to improper results.

Vertical restraints that concern established products are more likely to reduce consumer welfare. Large numbers of consumers are already familiar with such products and are therefore unlikely to place much value on acquiring further information about them. In this context, stringent antitrust standards should be applied to vertical price and non-price restraints alike. This approach could take the form either of a direct *per se* prohibition, or of a modified rule of reason analysis under which the defendant would be required to demonstrate that the restraints have benefited consumers generally. By contrast, in the case of new products or products of new entrants into the market, vertical restraints are less likely to lessen consumer welfare, because their novelty should create greater demand for information. In these circumstances, the restraints should be permissible, or at the least should be treated more leniently in any modified rule of reason analysis.

(B) THE COMMISSION AND VERTICAL RESTRAINTS

(i) *The Critique of the Commission*

The Commission's approach to vertical restraints has been criticized. References to Article 85 should now be read as to Article 101.

B Hawk, System Failure: Vertical Restraints and EC Competition Law[123]

The most fundamental, and the most trenchant, criticism is that the Commission too broadly applies Article 85(1) to agreements having little or no anticompetitive effects. This criticism rests on three pillars...

Inadequate economic analysis under 85(1)

The majority of Commission decisions fail adequately to consider whether the restraint at issue harms competition in the welfare sense of economics, i.e., effect on price or output. Concomitantly, market power, which should be the threshold issue, frequently is hardly examined (let alone given a central role) or is simply found to exist in a conclusory fashion under the rubric of 'appreciability'.

...

The Commission's rationale under 85(1) is unpersuasive

The...explanation for the inadequate economic analysis under 85(1) lies in the Commission's stubborn (in the face of Court judgments) adherence to the definition of a restriction on competition as

---

[123] (1995) 32 CMLRev 973, 974–975, 977–978, 982; C Bright, 'EU Competition Policy: Rules, Objectives and Deregulation' (1996) 16 OJLS 535.

a restriction on the 'economic freedom' of operators in the marketplace. The principal weaknesses of the Freiburg School notion of restriction on economic freedom are (1) its failure to generate precise operable legal rules, (i.e. its failure to provide an analytical framework); (2) its distance from and tension with (micro) economics which does provide an analytical framework; (3) its tendency to favour traders/competitors over consumers and consumer welfare (efficiency); and (4) its capture under Article 85(1) of totally innocuous contract provisions having no anti-competitive effects in an economic sense.

...

Commission refusal to follow Community Courts

The Court of Justice and the Court of First Instance have taken a more nuanced approach toward vertical arrangements under Article 85(1). The Courts have increasingly required an analysis of economic effects, particularly the possibility of foreclosure. This approach has been largely ignored or distinguished by the Commission, which adheres to its non-economics based application of Article 85(1), i.e. restriction on economic freedom.

(ii) *The Commission's Green Paper*

In part as a result of this criticism, the Commission re-examined its approach in 1996 in a wide-ranging Green Paper on Vertical Restraints.[124] A number of important points emerged from this document.

First, the Commission accepted that the academic consensus on the economic effects of vertical restraints is that market structure is of prime importance. The fiercer the inter-brand competition, the more likely it will be that the pro-competitive and efficiency aspects of the agreement outweigh any anti-competitive effects. This is even more so when market power at the production level is limited and barriers to entry are low.[125]

Secondly, the report made it clear that the desire to create a single market means that vertical restraints that seek to insulate markets through the grant of absolute territorial protection will not be tolerated, under either Article 101(1) or (3).[126]

Thirdly, the Commission accepted[127] that it did not engage in meaningful economic analysis within Article 101(1), but rather reserved such matters for consideration under Article 101(3).

Fourthly, the Commission set out a number of options on which it invited comment. Option 1 was to preserve the then present system, which seemed to mean a broad, formalistic interpretation of Article 101(1), coupled with existing block exemptions.[128] Option 2 was to widen the block exemptions.[129] Option 3 was to develop more focused block exemptions, placing emphasis on market-integration objectives.[130] The final option was to have some economic analysis within Article 101(1), coupled with block exemptions.[131]

---

[124] COM(96) 721 final.
[125] Ibid [82]–[85].
[126] Ibid [276].
[127] Ibid [180], [193], and [216].
[128] Ibid [281].
[129] Ibid [282]–[285].
[130] Ibid [286]–[292].
[131] Ibid [293]–[298].

It is clear that the Commission faced a dilemma. It was aware that many vertical restraints do not have any net anti-competitive impact. It was probably also aware that logically they should not therefore be held to fall within Article 101(1). It was, however, mindful of the costs of extensive economic analysis within Article 101(1).[132]

The Commission presented more concrete proposals in the Follow up to the Green Paper on Vertical Restraints.[133] It concluded that there should be a more economics-based approach to vertical restraints, and that there should be one block exemption for all vertical agreements. The new Regulation was adopted on 22 December 1999, and came fully into force on 1 June 2000.[134] The Regulation expired in May 2010, but the policy has been continued in a new block exemption, which will be analysed below.[135] Before we do so, we should consider the differing kinds of vertical restraint and the extent to which they are caught by Article 101(1).

(c) EXCLUSIVE DISTRIBUTION

In an exclusive distribution agreement (EDA) the producer agrees to supply only to a particular distributor within a particular territory. This may be buttressed by attempts to prevent third parties from selling into the contract territory of the designated distributor, either through contract terms in agreements between the producer and other distributors, and/or by assigning to the designated distributor trade mark rights which will enable the latter to stop such infringements. This type of agreement may be necessary to persuade a distributor to market a new product or to market an existing product in a new area. An EDA may also be beneficial to the producer by facilitating the efficient distribution of its goods, since it will not have to incur transport costs, etc, to multiple sites.

The central issue is whether an EDA will be caught by Article 101(1), and whether it will be exempted under Article 101(3), either individually or pursuant to a block exemption. The applicability of Article 101(1) to an EDA was considered earlier: such an agreement must be considered in its factual, legal, and economic context to determine whether it is caught by Article 101(1).[136] The Commission nonetheless often adopted a more formalistic approach, eschewing the ECJ's contextual approach.

Notwithstanding this divergence between Court and Commission, it is apparent from their combined jurisprudence that certain types of restrictions within an EDA are especially likely to fall within Article 101(1). Thus, export bans which prohibit a distributor from exporting the product outside a designated area will be judged particularly severely, as will any other attempt to establish absolute territorial protection for a distributor.[137] Indirect attempts to attain the same end will also be condemned, as in the case of customer guarantees which are available only if the product is bought from the distributor in that state.[138]

If an EDA is caught by Article 101(1) the parties may seek individual exemption or seek to use the block exemption. The principles that govern individual exemption have been examined above.[139]

---

[132] Ibid [86].

[133] [1998] OJ C365/3, [1999] 4 CMLR 281.

[134] Reg 2790/99 [1999] OJ L336/21.

[135] Reg 330/2010 [2010] OJ L102/1.

[136] Case 56/65 *Société La Technique Minière v Maschinenbau Ulm GmbH* [1966] ECR 235; Case 23/67 *Brasserie de Haecht SA* (n 62); Case T–25/99 *Roberts v Commission* [2001] ECR II–1881; Case T–328/03 *O2 (Germany)* (n 71) [65]–[73].

[137] Cases 56 and 58/64 *Consten and Grundig* [1966] ECR 299; Case 258/78 *Nungesser* (n 75); Case 19/77 *Miller International Schallplatten GmbH v Commission* [1978] ECR 131; Case C–279/87 *Tipp-Ex GmbH & Co KG v Commission* [1990] ECR I–261; Case T–77/92 *Parker Pen* (n 54); Case T–66/92 *Herlitz AG* (n 54).

[138] Case 31/85 *ETA Fabriques d'Ebauches v DK Investments SA* [1985] ECR 3933.

[139] See pp 1027–1029.

There was until recently a separate block exemption for EDAs.[140] This has now been replaced by the general block exemption for vertical restraints, which will be examined below.

(D) SELECTIVE DISTRIBUTION

The approach of the Court and the Commission to selective distribution agreements (SDAs) stands in marked contrast to that adopted towards EDAs. A selective distribution system is one in which the supplier chooses to distribute the goods only through certain outlets, normally those which fulfil certain criteria concerning expertise. There was until recently no block exemption for SDAs as such. They can now come within the new block exemption for vertical restraints, provided that the conditions therein are met. The present discussion will consider whether such agreements fall within Article 101(1).

Case 26/76 Metro-SB-Großmärkte GmbH & Co KG v Commission and SABA
[1977] ECR 1875

[Note Lisbon Treaty renumbering: Art 85 is now Art 101 TFEU]

Metro was a wholesaler of goods in Germany. It operated a system of self-service wholesaling and a cash-and-carry service, which enabled it to undercut the prices charged by other wholesalers. Metro applied to SABA to be allowed to stock the electronic equipment produced by the latter, but SABA refused to supply it, claiming that it did not fulfil the conditions SABA required before supplying its goods. Metro complained to the Commission that SABA's policy was in breach of Article 85(1), but the Commission found in favour of SABA after the latter had amended its terms of trade in certain respects. Metro then sought to have the Commission decision annulled.

THE ECJ

20. ... In the sector covering the production of high quality and technically advanced consumer durables, where a relatively small number of large and medium-scale producers offer a varied range of items which, or so consumers may consider, are readily inter-changeable, the structure of the market does not preclude the existence of a variety of channels of distribution adapted to the peculiar characteristics of the various producers and to the requirements of the various categories of consumers. On this view the Commission was justified in recognising that selective distribution systems constituted, together with others, an aspect of competition which accords with Article 85(1), provided that the resellers are chosen on the basis of objective criteria of a qualitative nature relating to the technical qualifications of the reseller and his staff and the suitability of his trading premises and that such conditions are laid down uniformly for all potential resellers and are not applied in a discriminatory fashion.

21. It is true that in such systems of distribution price competition is not generally emphasised either as an exclusive or indeed as a principal factor.... However, although price competition is so important that it can never be eliminated, it does not constitute the only effective form of competition or that to which absolute priority must in all circumstances be accorded.... For specialist wholesalers

---

140 Reg 1983/83 [1983] OJ L173/1.

and retailers the desire to maintain a certain price level, which corresponds to the desire to preserve, in the interests of consumers, the possibility of the continued existence of this channel of distribution in conjunction with new methods of distribution based on a different type of competition policy, forms one of the objectives which may be pursued without necessarily falling under the prohibition of Article 85(1), and if it does fall thereunder, either wholly or in part, coming within the framework of Article 85(3)....

The significance of *Metro* is that, when the conditions elaborated therein are fulfilled, the SDA is held not to be within Article 101(1).[141] There are, however, limits to the application of this principle.

(i) *First Condition: Nature of the Product*

The product has to be of the kind in relation to which the Court and the Commission believe that it is justifiable to limit price competition and to operate the regime of selective distribution with an element of non-price competition. Such products tend to be those that require specialist sales staff,[142] or goods where brand image is important.[143] Plumbing fittings are, by way of contrast, not deemed to be a technically advanced product which necessitates such a system.[144]

(ii) *Second Condition: Qualitative Criteria*

The *Metro* principle operates to legitimate outlets chosen on qualitative criteria. It can, however, be difficult to determine whether a particular requirement for a distributor to be acceptable to a supplier should be classified as qualitative or not. Subject to this uncertainty, the *Metro* principle does not allow a supplier to impose quantitative limits on those who can distribute the product, or to discriminate as between distributors.[145]

The logic of the distinction drawn between qualitative and quantitative criteria for restrictions on distribution is questionable. Producers will choose the distribution method that they believe best maximizes their sales. Whether they think that this is best achieved by qualitative or quantitative criteria, or a mixture of both, will vary depending upon the nature of the product. The pro- and anti-competitive effects of such distribution strategies will not, however, differ radically depending on which of these criteria is chosen.

[141] Case 210/81 *Demo-Studio Schmidt v Commission* [1983] ECR 3045; Case 107/82 *AEG-Telefunken AG v Commission* [1983] ECR 3151; Case C–376/92 *Metro-SB-Großmärkte GmbH & Co KG v Cartier SA* [1994] ECR I–15; Case T–67/01 *JCB Service v Commission* [2004] ECR II–49, [131]; Case C–439/09 *Pierre Fabre Dermo-Cosmétique SAS v Président de l'Autorité de la concurrence* [2011] ECR I–9419.

[142] Such as electronic equipment: *AEG*; audiovisual equipment: *Demo-Studio Schmidt*; computers: Dec 84/233, *IBM Personal Computers* [1984] OJ L118/24, [1984] 2 CMLR 342. Compare Case C–439/09 *Pierre Fabre Dermo-Cosmétique* (n 141).

[143] Such as ceramic tableware: Dec 85/616, *Villeroy & Boch* [1985] OJ L376/15, [1988] 4 CMLR 461; jewellery: Dec 83/610, *Murat* [1983] OJ L348/20, [1984] 1 CMLR 219; luxury cosmetics: Case T–19/92 *Groupement d'Achat Edouard Leclerc v Commission* [1996] ECR II–1851.

[144] Dec 85/44, *Grohe* [1985] OJ L19/17, [1988] 4 CMLR 612.

[145] Case 107/82 *AEG-Telefunken* (n 141); Cases 25 and 26/84 *Ford v Commission* [1985] ECR 2725; Case T–19/92 *Edouard Leclerc* (n 143); Case C–439/09 *Pierre Fabre Dermo-Cosmétique* (n 141).

JS Chard, The Economics of the Application of Article 85 to Selective Distribution Systems[146]

It should be clear from this discussion of the economic effects of qualitative and quantitative selection criteria that the Commission's attempts to distinguish between the criteria are essentially arbitrary and confusing. To be meaningful, qualitative criteria must have a quantitative effect...while quantitative criteria may have qualitative implications. With regard to the latter aspect for example, in *Omega*, the Commission recognised that the number of concessionaires needed to be limited otherwise no concessionaire could attain a sufficient turnover to be able to undertake service and guarantee commitments. Thus, qualitative and quantitative criteria should be subject to the same analytical procedure.

[*The author suggests that a proper economic analysis along the following lines is required:*]

First, the Commission should examine whether there is direct evidence of collusion between manufacturers and/or distributors of different brands or whether the restriction embraces so large a fraction of the market...as to make cartelisation a plausible motivation for the restriction. If it finds the answer is no...there should be a presumption that the restriction has pro-competitive effects. The parties to the agreements in question can be expected to indicate the alleged pro-competitive effects and the Commission should not query these too closely. It should not be tempted to second-guess business judgments as to what arrangements would or would not provide adequate means for achieving the pro-competitive effects and attach conditions to the granting of negative clearance or exemption under Article 85(3), as its record in this respect does not inspire confidence.

Secondly, if there is some evidence of restrictions in competition between manufacturers and/or distributors, but the evidence is not conclusive,...the Commission should carefully examine whether pro-competitive effects are being achieved,...the burden of justification being shifted firmly onto the defendant....

What evidence there is seems to cast doubt on the likely importance of anti-competitive effects while pro-competitive effects seem likely to be more common...If anti-competitive effects are usually absent, then the greater freedom of manufacturers to choose the distribution arrangements which suit them best will tend to result in the most efficient forms of arrangements being used.

It should, however, be noted that the greater leniency accorded to SDAs as opposed to EDAs may be partially explained by the importance of attaining a single European market. EDAs are more likely to divide the EU along national lines than are SDAs and the ECJ is particularly antagonistic towards such forms of market division.

(iii) *Third Condition: Non-Elimination of Competition through Multiple SDAs*

The compatibility of a particular SDA with Article 101(1) may be affected by the existence of other such SDAs, if the overall impact is to eliminate or unduly restrict competition.

---

[146] (1982) 7 ELRev 83, 97, 100–101. See also C Vajda, 'Selective Distribution in the European Community' (1979) 13 JWTL 409; I Lianos, 'Commercial Agency Agreements, Vertical Restraints, and the Limits of Article 81(1) EC: Between Hierarchies and Networks' (2007) 3 Journal of Competition Law and Economics 625.

Case 75/84 **Metro-SB-Großmärkte GmbH & Co KG v Commission (No 2)**
[1986] ECR 3021

[Note Lisbon Treaty renumbering: Art 85 is now Art 101 TFEU]

The Commission had renewed an exemption for SABA's selective distribution system. Metro, the original objector, contested the renewal of the SDA. In the original decision the Court had intimated that its view (that SDAs were compatible with Article 85(1)), might be different if, in a particular area, the existence of a large number of SDAs similar to that operated by SABA eliminated firms such as Metro from the market. Metro argued that this had occurred, and that therefore the exemption for the SABA SDA should not be renewed.

THE ECJ

40. It must be borne in mind that, although the Court has held in previous decisions that 'simple' selective distribution systems are capable of constituting an aspect of competition compatible with Article 85(1), there may nevertheless be a restriction or elimination of competition where the existence of a certain number of such systems does not leave any room for other forms of distribution based on a different type of competition policy or results in a rigidity in price structure which is not counterbalanced by other aspects of competition between other products of the same brand and by the existence of effective competition between different brands.

41. Consequently, the existence of a large number of selective distribution systems for a particular product does not in itself permit the conclusion that competition is restricted or distorted. Nor is the existence of such systems decisive as regards the granting or refusal of exemption under Article 85(3), since the only factor to be taken into consideration in that regard is the effect which such systems actually have on the competitive situation. Therefore the coverage ratio of selective distribution systems for colour television sets, to which Metro refers, cannot in itself be regarded as a factor preventing an exemption from being granted.

42. It follows that an increase in the number of 'simple' selective distribution systems after an exemption has been granted must be taken into consideration, when application for renewal of that exemption is being considered, only in the special situation in which the relevant market was already so rigid and structured that the element of competition inherent in 'simple' systems is not sufficient to maintain workable competition. Metro has not been able to show that a special situation of that kind exists in the present case.

43. As regards the effect on the market of the existence of selective distribution systems other than 'simple' systems, the Commission in renewing the exemption based itself on the relatively small market share covered by the SABA system and on the fact that that system is distinguished from 'simple' systems only by the existence of obligations pertaining to the promotion of sales. By so doing, it did not misdirect itself in exercising its discretion to assess, within the framework of Article 85(3), the economic context in which the SABA system is situated.

The judgment in *Metro II* builds on the cautionary remarks in the earlier *Metro* case. The situations in which a market analysis is required render it more difficult to predict whether a particular SDA will be caught by Article 101(1). Moreover, it would be unfair if the creation of one further SDA brought it, but not those already existing, within Article 101(1). It would be equally odd if the creation of the most recent SDA had the effect of retrospectively bringing the previous SDAs within the ambit of Article 101(1).

(iv) *Fourth Condition: No Absolute Territorial Protection*

The ECJ will not tolerate an SDA if it operates so as to confer absolute territorial protection. This is apparent from the *BMW* case.[147]

Case C–70/93 **Bayerische Motorenwerke AG v ALD Autoleasing D GmbH**
[1995] ECR I–3439

[Note Lisbon Treaty renumbering: Art 85 is now Art 101 TFEU]

BMW sold its vehicles through a selective distribution system. There was an agreement between BMW and its dealers that the latter were not to deliver vehicles to independent leasing companies that made vehicles available to customers residing or having their seat outside the contract territory of the dealer in question. This was challenged by an independent leasing company, ALD, which had supplied BMW cars in the manner which the agreement was designed to prohibit. Was the agreement caught by Article 85(1)?

THE ECJ

6. BMW claims that the appearance of independent leasing companies...has created an imbalance in its commercial organisation. Those independent companies concentrate on purchasing from certain BMW dealers and lease the vehicles to customers established outside the contract territory of those dealers. Those customers then turn for the customer services and maintenance to the BMW dealer in the contract territory in which they are established. Since those dealers are not involved in the original sales transaction, they do not obtain any profit margin. They therefore complained to BMW about the activities of independent leasing companies which were disturbing the network.

[*As a result of these complaints BMW instituted the agreement which was the subject matter of this action.*]

...

19. As regards the requirement that competition be restricted, it should be noted that, by virtue of the agreement in question BMW dealers are able to supply vehicles of the BMW mark to independent leasing companies only if the vehicles are to be made available to lessees having their seat in the contract territory of the dealer in question. Consequently, only the dealer in whose territory the lessee has its seat is authorised by the manufacturer to supply to ALD vehicles of the BMW mark, to the exclusion of all other BMW dealers. That amounts to absolute territorial protection for the BMW dealer on whose territory the customer of ALD is established. Furthermore, the agreement reduces each dealer's freedom of commercial action in so far as each individual dealer's choice of customer is confined exclusively to those leasing companies which have concluded contracts with lessees established within that dealer's contract territory.

(E) FRANCHISING

A franchise differs from other distribution methods considered thus far. The franchisor allows the franchisee to use intellectual property rights belonging to the former, such as trade names, logos, and the

---

[147] See also Case T–67/01 *JCB* (n 141) [85]; Case T–450/05 *Automobiles Peugeot SA and Peugeot Nederland NV v Commission* [2009] ECR II–2533.

like. The premises on which the goods are sold are owned by the franchisee, who pays a royalty to the franchisor for the use of the trade name, etc. Franchises, therefore, benefit both parties: the franchisor receives a payment for the use of its intellectual property rights; the franchisee can start an independent business with the assurance that the product has been tried and tested elsewhere. It is of the essence of a franchise that the franchisor will require the franchisee to comply with certain standards and methods of sale. Failure to meet such standards by a franchisee can harm both the franchisor and other franchisees by damaging the reputation of the product and trade name. It is also central to the franchising system that the franchisor is able to impose terms to protect the intellectual property rights assigned to the franchisee.

In the seminal *Pronuptia* case the Court held that terms which related to both of the above issues were not caught by Article 101(1). However, other restrictions in the agreement, such as those which divided the market territorially, were examined under Article 101(3).[148] In *Yves Rocher* the Commission held that a franchise agreement under which the franchisor appointed only one franchisee for a particular area, agreed not to compete with the latter in that area, and forbade franchisees from opening more than one shop resulted in a degree of market-sharing which brought the agreement within Article 101(1).[149] The Commission made other decisions that built upon *Pronuptia*.[150] A block exemption, Regulation 4087/88,[151] was passed to cover certain franchise agreements. This was replaced by the general block exemption for vertical restraints.

(f) EXCLUSIVE PURCHASING

Exclusive purchasing agreements (EPAs) are those in which one party agrees to buy all it needs of a product from a particular supplier. Common examples include petrol stations, which stock only one brand of petrol, and tied public houses, which carry only one general brand of beer. Whether EPAs are within the ambit of Article 101(1) requires a market analysis: if the agreement, considered in its legal, factual, and economic context, could have the effect of restricting, preventing, or distorting competition then it will be within Article 101(1).[152]

Case T–7/93 **Langnese-Iglo GmbH v Commission**
[1995] ECR II–1533

[Note Lisbon Treaty renumbering: Art 85 is now Art 101 TFEU]

The CFI considered whether a network of exclusive purchasing agreements was caught by Article 85(1). The Commission had argued that there was no need for any real market analysis to determine whether the agreements restricted competition since the market share covered by the contested agreements

---

[148] Case 161/84 *Pronuptia* (n 70); J Venit, '*Pronuptia*: Ancillary Restraints or Unholy Alliances' (1986) 11 ELRev 213.
[149] Dec 87/14 [1987] OJ L8/49, [1988] 4 CMLR 592, 607.
[150] See, eg, Dec 87/407, *Computerland* [1987] OJ L222/12, [1989] 4 CMLR 259; Dec 88/604, *ServiceMaster Ltd* [1988] OJ L332/38, [1989] 4 CMLR 581.
[151] [1988] OJ L359/46.
[152] Case 23/67 *Brasserie de Haecht* (n 62); Case C–234/89 *Delimitis* (n 63); Case C–393/92 *Municipality of Almelo v NV Energiebedrijf Ijsselmij* [1994] ECR I–1477; Case T–65/98 *Van den Bergh Foods Ltd v Commission* [2003] ECR II–4653, [83]–[84], [91]; Case C–552/03 P *Unilever Bestfoods (Ireland) Ltd v Commission* [2006] ECR I–9091; Case C–279/06 *CEPSA Estaciones de Servicio SA v LV Tobar e Hijos SL* [2008] ECR I–6681. The competition authorities will take account of clauses which, although not constituting an obligation as such on the reseller to purchase all its requirements of a product from a supplier, nonetheless constitute inducements to do so, such as offering discounts to the reseller.

was more than 15 per cent of the relevant market and the turnover of the undertakings concerned was well in excess of the ceilings laid down by the Notice on Agreements of Minor Importance.

THE CFI

98. It must be borne in mind that the Notice is intended only to define those agreements which, in the Commission's view, do not have an appreciable effect on competition or trade between Member States. The Court considers that it cannot however be inferred with certainty that a network of exclusive purchasing agreements is automatically liable to prevent, restrict or distort competition appreciably merely because the ceilings laid down in it are exceeded. Moreover, it is apparent from the actual wording of paragraph 3 of that Notice that it is entirely possible, in the facts of the present case, that agreements . . . which exceed the ceilings indicated affect . . . competition only to an insignificant extent and consequently are not caught by Article 85(1). . . .

99. As to whether the exclusive purchasing agreements fall within . . . Article 85(1) . . . , it is appropriate, according to the case-law, to consider whether, taken together, all the similar agreements entered into in the relevant market and the other features of the economic and legal context of the agreements at issue show that those agreements cumulatively have the effect of denying access to that market for new domestic and foreign competitors. If . . . that is found not to be the case, the individual agreements making up the bundle of agreements as a whole cannot undermine competition within the meaning of Article 85(1). . . . If, on the other hand, such examination reveals that it is difficult to gain access to the market, it is necessary to assess the extent to which the contested agreements contribute to the cumulative effect produced, on the basis that only agreements which make a significant contribution to any partitioning of the market are prohibited (*Delimitis*, paragraphs 23 and 24).

100. It must then be borne in mind, that as the Court of Justice held in . . . *Brasserie de Haecht*, consideration of the effects of an exclusive agreement implied that regard must be had to the economic and legal context of the agreement, in which it might combine with others to have a cumulative effect on competition.

[*The CFI found that the agreements were liable to affect competition appreciably and therefore came within Article 85(1).*]

The parties to an EPA can seek exemption, either on an individual basis or pursuant to the block exemption. There was a specific block exemption, Regulation 1984/83, covering exclusive purchasing.[153] This has now been replaced by the block exemption for vertical restraints.

(G) THE BLOCK EXEMPTION

(i) *The New-Style Block Exemption*

We have already seen the impetus for reform of vertical restraints. Regulation 2790/99[154] was properly regarded as a new-style block exemption.[155] It differed from the previous block exemptions in a number of ways. It was less formalistic than its predecessors, and was more economically oriented. It applied to all species of vertical restraints, with the exception of distribution agreements for motor

---

153 [1983] OJ L173/5.

154 Commission Regulation (EC) No 2790/99 of 22 December 1999 on the application of Article 81(3) of the Treaty to categories of vertical agreements and concerted practices [1999] OJ L336/21.

155 R Whish, 'Regulation 2790/99: The Commission's "New Style" Block Exemption for Vertical Agreements' (2000) 37 CMLRev 887; F Dethmers and P Posthuma de Boer, 'Ten Years On: Vertical Agreements under Article 81' [2009] ECLR 424.

vehicles. It was less prescriptive than the earlier Regulations. These had generally followed a format of having a specific list of white clauses that were allowed and black clauses that were forbidden. The new Regulation did not contain a white list: if conduct was not prohibited it was therefore permitted.

Regulation 2790/99 expired in May 2010 and was replaced by Regulation 330/2010,[156] which must be read in tandem with Commission Guidelines.[157] The recitals to Regulation 330/2010 state that it is possible to define a category of vertical agreements that will normally satisfy the conditions of Article 101(3). These agreements are said to improve economic efficiency by facilitating coordination and reducing distribution costs.[158]

(ii) *Article 1: Definitions*

Article 1 of Regulation 330/2010 provides definitions, the following of which are of particular importance.

> 'vertical agreement' means an agreement or concerted practice entered into between two or more undertakings each of which operates, for the purposes of the agreement or the concerted practice, at a different level of the production or distribution chain, and relating to the conditions under which the parties may purchase, sell or resell certain goods or services.

Article 1(1)(a) is framed in terms of *two or more undertakings*, whereas the old block exemptions applied only to bilateral agreements. It is, however, necessary for *each* of the undertakings to operate, for the purposes of the agreement, at a different level of the production or distribution chain. The fact that Article 1(1)(a) includes the phrase *for the purposes of the agreement* means that it is possible, subject to the limits of Article 2(4), for two firms that are, for example, both cement manufacturers to come within the Regulation. This would be so where one supplies material to the other. Article 1(1)(d) defines non-compete obligation.

> 'non-compete obligation' means any direct or indirect obligation causing the buyer not to manufacture, purchase, sell or resell goods or services which compete with the contract goods or services, or any direct or indirect obligation on the buyer to purchase from the supplier or from another undertaking designated by the supplier more than 80 % of the buyer's total purchases of the contract goods or services and their substitutes on the relevant market, calculated on the basis of the value or, where such is standard industry practice, the volume of its purchases in the preceding calendar year.

(iii) *Article 2: The Core of the Block Exemption*

The core of the block exemption is Article 2. *Article 2(1)* provides that:[159]

> Pursuant to Article 101(3) of the Treaty and subject to the provisions of this Regulation, it is hereby declared that Article 101(1) of the Treaty shall not apply to vertical agreements.
>   This exemption shall apply to the extent that such agreements contain vertical restraints.

---

[156] Commission Regulation (EU) No 330/2010 of 20 April 2010 on the application of Article 101(3) of the Treaty on the Functioning of the European Union to categories of vertical agreements and concerted practices [2010] OJ L102/1.
[157] Guidelines on Vertical Restraints [2010] OJ C130/1.
[158] Reg 330/2010 (n 156) rec 6.
[159] Guidelines (n 157) [5]–[7].

An agreement that does not fall within Article 101(1) will not need to use the block exemption. Subject to this, the exempted agreement can be multilateral.

Article 2(2) applies the block exemption to vertical agreements between an association of undertakings and its members, or its suppliers. All members of the association must however be retailers, and no individual member must have an annual turnover in excess of €50 million.

Article 2(3) makes the block exemption applicable where intellectual property rights are ancillary to the main purpose of the vertical agreement.

Article 2(4) is designed to prevent the block exemption being used by competing undertakings to engage in market division. Competing undertakings are actual or potential suppliers in the same product market.[160] Article 2(4) provides that Article 2(1) shall not apply to vertical agreements between competing undertakings. Article 2(4) then provides that the exemption can apply where such undertakings enter into a non-reciprocal vertical agreement. This can occur where the supplier is a manufacturer and distributor of goods, while the buyer is a distributor not manufacturing goods that compete with the contract goods. It can also occur where the supplier is a provider of services at several levels of trade, while the buyer provides its goods or services at the retail level and is not a competing undertaking at the level of trade where it purchases the contract services.

Article 2(5) states that the block exemption shall not apply to vertical agreements the subject matter of which falls within the scope of any other block exemption.

(iv) *Article 3: The Market Share Cap*

The likelihood of efficiency gains from vertical agreements outweighing anti-competitive effects is said in the recitals to be dependent on the market power of the undertakings concerned, and the Regulation therefore has limits as to the market share of the participating firms.[161] Article 3(1) states that the exemption contained in Article 2 only applies on the condition that the market share held by the supplier does not exceed 30 per cent of the relevant market on which it sells the contract goods or services, and that the market share of the buyer must not exceed 30 per cent of the relevant market on which it purchases the contract goods or services.[162] The method of calculating market share is laid down in Article 7.

(v) *Article 4: The Black List*

The recitals make it clear that certain types of clauses that are regarded as especially anti-competitive will not benefit from the block exemption. These include clauses relating to vertical price fixing and territorial protection.[163] Article 4 excludes the Regulation for vertical agreements which, directly or indirectly, in isolation or combination with other factors under the control of the parties, have as their object any of the following restrictions.

Resale price maintenance is excluded.[164] Maximum selling prices and recommendations as to selling prices are allowed, subject to the caveat that they do not amount to a fixed or minimum sale price, as a result of pressure from, or incentives offered by, any of the parties. It is however open to the parties to seek an individual exemption for such an agreement.[165]

---

[160] Reg 330/2010 (n 156) Art 1(1)(c); Guidelines (n 157) [27].

[161] Reg 330/2010 (n 156) recs 7–8.

[162] Guidelines (n 157) [87]–[92].

[163] Reg 330/2010 (n 156) rec 10.

[164] Ibid Art 4(a); Case C–279/06 *CEPSA* (n 63); Case C–506/07 *Lubricantes y Carburantes Galaicos SL v GALP Energía España SAU* [2009] ECR I–134; Case C–260/07 *Pedro IV Servicios SL v Total España SA* [2009] ECR I–2437.

[165] Guidelines (n 157) [47].

Restrictions on the territory into which, or the customers to whom, the buyer can sell the goods or services are also precluded.[166] This is subject to a number of exceptions.[167] It is permissible to have a restriction on active sales into the exclusive territory or to an exclusive customer group reserved to the supplier, or allocated by the supplier to another buyer, where such a restriction does not limit sales by the customers to the buyer.[168] It is permissible to restrict sales to end users by a buyer operating at the wholesale level of trade, and to restrict sales to unauthorized distributors by the members of a selective distribution system. The final exception is that it is possible to restrict the buyer of components for use from selling them to a customer who would use them to make goods that would compete with those of the supplier.

The restriction of active or passive sales to end users by members of a selective distribution system operating at the retail level is not allowed. This is without prejudice to the possibility of prohibiting a member of the system from operating out of an unauthorized place of establishment.[169] It is important to note that, subject to this condition, selective and exclusive distribution can be combined within one agreement. Such an agreement could still come within the block exemption, provided that it complied with the other conditions laid down therein.[170]

It is not possible to have restrictions of cross-supplies between distributors within a selective distribution system, including between distributors operating at different levels of trade.[171] A selected distributor must therefore be able to buy from any approved distributor.

The final blacklisted provision relates to the supply of components. It is designed to allow end users and independent service providers to obtain spare parts.[172]

(vi) *Article 5: Obligations that Do Not Benefit from the Exemption*

The restrictions in Article 4 prevent the entire vertical agreement from benefiting from the block exemption. Article 5 excludes the benefit of the block exemption from certain terms contained in such an agreement. The agreement may still gain the benefit of the block exemption if the objectionable clause can be severed. There are three types of obligation listed in Article 5.

Non-compete obligations cannot be indefinite or last longer than five years. Obligations not to compete after the term of the agreement are also excluded. This is subject to a qualification allowing such an obligation for one year on sales of competing goods or services from the place of sale that the buyer operated from during the contract, provided that this is necessary to protect the supplier's know-how. The benefit of the block exemption is also excluded from an obligation preventing members of a selective distribution system from selling brands of particular competing suppliers.

(vii) *Article 6: Withdrawing the Benefit of the Regulation*

Article 6 provides limits to the application of the block exemption. It allows the Commission by regulation to declare that, where parallel networks of similar vertical restraints cover more than 50 per cent of a relevant market, this Regulation shall not apply to vertical agreements containing specific restraints relating to that market.[173]

---

[166] Reg 330/2010 (n 156) Art 4(b).
[167] Ibid Art 4(b)(i)–(iv).
[168] Guidelines (n 157) [50].
[169] Reg 330/2010 (n 156) Art 4(c); Guidelines (n 157) [56].
[170] Whish (n 155) 916.
[171] Reg 330/2010 (n 156) Art 4(d).
[172] Ibid Art 4(e).
[173] Reg 330/2010 (n 156) rec 13; Guidelines (n 157) [79]–[82].

The Commission may also[174] withdraw the benefit of Regulation 330/2010 pursuant to Article 29 of Regulation 1/2003.[175] Article 29(1) empowers the Commission to withdraw the benefit of the block exemption where it finds that vertical agreements have effects incompatible with Article 101(3), such as where access to the relevant market is significantly restricted by the cumulative effect of parallel networks of similar vertical restraints.[176] Article 29(2) allows the competition authority of a Member State, where the state has the characteristics of a distinct geographic market, to withdraw the benefit of the block exemption for that state under the same conditions as in Article 29(1).

(H) SUMMARY

i.   There has been fierce debate as to whether vertical agreements are harmful, and if so when.

ii. There has been criticism of the Commission for not talking with the same voice as the ECJ, and for employing a test that equates a restriction of conduct with a restriction of competition.

iii. The degree of difference between the EU Courts and the Commission has diminished more recently. It would, however, be premature to say that the Commission has fully adopted the ECJ's approach to Article 101(1). Moreover, the very approach of the EU Courts has been thrown into some doubt as a result of the CFI's decision in *Métropole*.[177]

iv. The importance of this difference has been lessened by the passage of the general block exemption, which is less formalistic than its predecessors. It should not however be forgotten that the Regulation has a market share cap of 30 per cent. Some commentators feel that this is warranted, since economic theory tells us that it is only when there is some degree of market power that vertical agreements are dangerous.[178] This may well be accepted, but other commentators regard the existing cap as too low, and have characterized the new Regulation as little more than an extended *de minimis* provision.[179]

12 COMPETITION LAW: ENFORCEMENT

(A) THE TRADITIONAL APPROACH AND THE MODERNIZATION WHITE PAPER

The discussion thus far has focused on the central elements of Article 101. The enforcement regime for Articles 101 and 102 was however reformed in 2003. Space precludes detailed treatment of the new regime, but it is nonetheless important to convey the core elements.

The traditional approach to the enforcement of competition law had two foundations. Agreements had, subject to certain exceptions, to be notified to the Commission, and the Commission had a monopoly over the application of Article 101(3). The system was, in this sense, centralized, although

---

[174] These rules were hitherto found in Reg 2790/99 (n 154) Arts 6–7.

[175] Council Regulation (EC) No 1/2003 of 16 December 2002 on the implementation of the rules on competition laid down in Articles 81 and 82 of the Treaty [2003] OJ L1/1.

[176] Guidelines (n 157) [74]–[78].

[177] Case T–112/99 *Métropole Télévision (M6), Suez-Lyonnaise des Eaux, France Télécom, and Télévision Française 1 SA (TFI) v Commission* [2001] ECR II–2459.

[178] Whish (n 155).

[179] M Griffiths, 'A Glorification of De Minimis? The Regulation on Vertical Agreements' [2000] ECLR 241.

there were decentralized aspects. Articles 101 and 102 had direct effect and national courts could therefore apply Article 101(1), but could not grant an individual exemption under Article 101(3).

The traditional approach came under increasing strain. The Commission did not have the resources to deal with all agreements notified to it, nor did it have the resources to adjudicate on anything but a handful of individual exemptions. The Commission therefore encouraged national courts to apply Articles 101 and 102. However, the White Paper on Modernization[180] proposed a thorough overhaul of the enforcement regime, abolishing notification and the Commission's monopoly over Article 101(3). National courts and NCAs would be empowered to apply Article 101 in its entirety and Article 102. The White Paper generated a voluminous literature, which contained all shades of opinion.[181]

(B) THE NEW REGIME

Article 1 of Regulation 1/2003, which implemented the new regime,[182] provides that agreements, etc, caught by Article 101(1) that do not satisfy the conditions of Article 101(3) shall be prohibited, no prior decision to that effect being required. The same principle is applicable to abuse of a dominant position in Article 102. NCAs and national courts can apply the entirety of Articles 101 and 102.[183] The Regulation contains wide-ranging powers of investigation,[184] and far-reaching provisions concerning fines.[185]

There are provisions facilitating cooperation between an NCA and the Commission.[186] NCAs have an obligation to inform the Commission of proceedings begun in the Member States,[187] and the NCAs are also obliged to inform the Commission before they adopt a decision that an infringement of Article 101 or 102 should be brought to an end, and before they accept commitments or withdraw the benefit of a block exemption.[188] The NCAs are 'relieved of their competence' to apply Articles 101 and 102 if the Commission initiates proceedings for adoption of a decision.[189] NCAs cannot make rulings in relation to Articles 101 and 102 that are counter to a decision already reached by the Commission on the same subject matter.[190]

---

[180] White Paper on Modernization of the Rules Implementing Articles 85 and 86 of the EC Treaty, Commission Programme 99/27, 28 Apr 1999.

[181] See, eg, R Wesseling, 'The Commission White Paper on Modernisation of EC Antitrust Law: Unspoken Consequences and Incomplete Treatment of Alternative Options' [1999] ECLR 420; C-D Ehlermann, 'The Modernization of EC Antitrust Policy: A Legal and Cultural Revolution' (2000) 37 CMLRev 537; A Schaub, 'Modernisation of EC Competition Law: Reform of Regulation No. 17' in B Hawk (ed), Fordham Corporate Law Institute (Fordham University, 2000) ch 10; R Whish and B Sufrin, 'Community Competition Law: Notification and Exemption—Goodbye to All That' in D Hayton (ed), *Law's Future(s): British Legal Developments in the 21st Century* (Hart, 2000) ch 8; M Monti, 'European Competition Law for the 21st Century' in B Hawk (ed), Fordham Corporate Law Institute (Fordham University, 2001) ch 15.

[182] Reg 1/2003 (n 175); J Venit, 'Brave New World: The Decentralization and Modernization of Enforcement under Articles 81 and 82 of the EC Treaty' (2003) 40 CMLRev 545; S Kon and A Barcroft, 'Aspects of the Complementary Roles of Public and Private Enforcement of UK and EU Antitrust law: An Enforcement Deficit?' (2008) 1 Global Competition Litigation Review 11.

[183] Reg 1/2003 (n 175) Arts 5 and 6.

[184] Ibid Arts 17–22.

[185] Ibid Arts 23–26; Guidelines on the method of setting fines imposed pursuant to Article 23(2)(a) of Regulation 1/2003 [2006] OJ C210/2.

[186] Reg 1/2003 (n 175) Arts 11–12.

[187] Ibid Art 11(3).

[188] Ibid Art 11(4).

[189] Ibid Art 11(6).

[190] Ibid Art 16(2).

There are also provisions facilitating cooperation between NCAs in different Member States,[191] and a European Competition Network has been established for cooperation between NCAs.[192] Where two or more NCAs have received a complaint, or are acting on their own initiative, against the same agreement, 'the fact that one authority is dealing with the case shall be sufficient grounds for the others to suspend proceedings before them or to reject the complaint'.[193] The Commission may also reject a complaint on the ground that an NCA is dealing with the matter. Where a case has already been dealt with by an NCA, or by the Commission, any other NCA may reject it.[194]

There are separate provisions dealing with cooperation with national courts.[195] National courts may, in proceedings for the application of Articles 101 and 102, ask the Commission for information in its possession, or for its opinion on questions concerning the application of EU competition rules.[196] Member States are obliged to send the Commission copies of judgments applying Article 101 or 102.[197] NCAs may submit written observations to national courts in relation to cases concerning Articles 101 and 102, and may submit oral argument with the permission of the national court. The Commission may do likewise where the coherent application of Articles 101 and 102 so requires.[198] National courts cannot make rulings in relation to Articles 101 and 102 that are counter to a decision already reached by the Commission on the same subject matter, and they must avoid giving decisions that would conflict with a decision contemplated by the Commission in proceedings which it has initiated.[199]

The Commission continues to have enforcement power under the new regime. It can act on a complaint or on its own initiative and find an infringement of Article 101 or Article 102.[200] It can impose behavioural or structural remedies, although the Regulation is framed in favour of the former.[201] The Commission has power, for reasons of the EU public interest, acting on its own initiative, to make a decision either that Article 101(1) is inapplicable to an agreement or that the conditions of Article 101(3) are fulfilled. The Commission has an analogous power in relation to Article 102.[202] The Commission must consult an Advisory Committee on Restrictive Practices and Dominant Positions prior to taking decisions under Article 7, 8, 9, 10, 23, 24(2), or 29(1).[203] The Committee is composed of representatives of the NCAs, and the Commission must take 'utmost account' of its opinion.[204]

The Commission's Reports on the new regime paint a largely positive picture, subject to the caveat that problems flow from divergent national procedures and sanctions.[205] Commentators have

---

[191] Commission Notice on cooperation within the Network of Competition Authorities [2004] OJ C101/43; Joint Statement of the Council and the Commission on the Functioning of the Network of Competition Authorities, available at http://ec.europa.eu/comm/competition/ecn/more_details.html.

[192] http://ec.europa.eu/comm/competition/ecn/more_details.html.

[193] Reg 1/2003 (n 175) Art 13(1).

[194] Ibid Art 13(2).

[195] Commission Notice on the cooperation between the Commission and the courts of the EU Member States in the application of Articles 81 and 82 EC [2004] OJ C101/54.

[196] Reg 1/2003 (n 175) Art 15(1).

[197] Ibid Art 15(2).

[198] Ibid Art 15(3); Case C–429/07 *Inspecteur van de Belastingdienst v X BV* [2009] ECR I–4833.

[199] Ibid Art 16(1).

[200] Ibid Art 7.

[201] Ibid Art 7(1).

[202] Ibid Art 10.

[203] Ibid Art 14(1).

[204] Ibid Art 14(5).

[205] Report on the functioning of Regulation 1/2003, COM(2009) 206 final; Ten Years of Antitrust Enforcement under Regulation 1/2003: Achievements and Future Perspectives, COM(2014) 453.

however expressed continuing concerns about aspects of the current system, including the increased criminalization of competition policy, due process, and compliance with human rights.[206]

(c) JUDICIAL REVIEW

Commission Decisions may be reviewed under Articles 263 and 267 TFEU. The general principles concerning these actions have been considered above.[207] There is appeal from the General Court to the CJEU, but the latter will only review the legal characterization of the facts found by the former and the conclusions drawn from them. The CJEU will not examine the facts or the evidence heard by the General Court in support of the facts.[208]

The applicant will have to show standing under Article 263. This hurdle is less problematic for competition matters than for other issues. The party against whom a competition decision has been made can seek its annulment, and a complainant will normally be accorded standing.[209] There is nonetheless an important issue concerning the range of measures that may be annulled under Article 263. There is little difficulty with formal Commission Decisions, such as findings of infringement. More difficulty has been encountered with less formal measures.[210] The grounds of review are listed in Article 263(2). Thus, for example, failure to authenticate the decision taken by the College of Commissioners in the proper manner constitutes breach of an essential procedural requirement.[211] The General Court has held that review of situations entailing complex economic assessments should be confined to verifying compliance with procedural rules, verifying the material accuracy of facts, and checking to ensure that there has been no manifest error of assessment or misuse of power.[212] Notwithstanding such statements, the intensity of review has increased since the task has been allocated to the General Court.[213]

An action may also be brought against the Commission for failure to act under Article 265 TFEU. However, the Commission is not obliged to proceed with a complaint, and it has discretion whether to use its scarce resources taking account of the Union interest.[214]

The mode of challenging decisions of NCAs or national courts is to seek a preliminary ruling under Article 267 TFEU. Such cases will be heard by the CJEU and the normal rules relating to indirect challenge under Article 267 apply.[215]

---

[206] D Geradin *et al*, 'Towards an Optimal Enforcement of Competition Rules in Europe—Time for a Review of Regulation 1/2003', Global Competition Law Centre, Annual Conference, 11–12 June 2009.

[207] See Chs 14–15.

[208] Case C–8/95 P *New Holland Ford Ltd v Commission* [1998] ECR I–3175.

[209] Case 26/76 *Metro-SB-Großmärkte GmbH & Co KG v Commission* [1977] ECR 1875; Cases 228 and 229/82 *Ford Werke AG v Commission* [1984] ECR 1129; Case T–12/93 *Comité Central d'Entreprise de la Société Anonyme Vittel v Commission* [1995] ECR II–1247.

[210] Case 99/79 *Lancôme v Etos* [1980] ECR 2511; Case 60/81 *IBM v Commission* [1981] ECR 2639; Cases T–125 and 127/97 *The Coca-Cola Company and Coca-Cola Enterprises Inc v Commission* [2000] ECR II–1733; Cases 142 and 156/84 *British American Tobacco Co Ltd and R J Reynolds Inc v Commission* [1987] ECR 4487.

[211] Case C–286/95 P *Commission v Imperial Chemical Industries plc (ICI)* [2000] ECR I–2341, [41]–[43]; Cases C–287–288/95 P *Commission v Solvay SA* [2000] ECR I–2391, [45]–[46].

[212] Case T–44/90 *La Cinq SA v Commission* [1992] ECR II–1; Case T–7/92 *Asia Motor France SA v Commission (No 2)* [1993] ECR II–669; Cases 142 and 156/84 *British American Tobacco* (n 210); Case T–204/03 *Haladjian Frères SA v Commission* [2006] ECR II–3779.

[213] Cases T–79/89 etc *BASF v Commission* [1992] ECR II–315; Cases C–89/85 etc *A Ahlström Oy* (n 32); P Craig, *EU Administrative Law* (Oxford University Press, 2nd edn, 2012) ch 14.

[214] Case T–24/90 *Automec Srl v Commission* [1992] ECR II–2223.

[215] Ch 13.

(D) DAMAGES ACTIONS[216]

The ECJ has confirmed that state liability in damages is in principle available where a state entity is the defendant in an Article 102 action.[217] Damages are also available as a matter of EU law where the defendant is a private party. In *Crehan*[218] the ECJ held that the full effectiveness of Article 101 would be jeopardized if an individual, even a party to the agreement, could not claim damages for loss caused by a contract, or by conduct liable to distort competition. There should not therefore be any absolute bar in national law to such actions, even by parties to the agreement. It was, however, open to national law to prevent a party from being unjustly enriched or profiting from his unlawful conduct. The national court should take into account the respective bargaining strengths of the contracting parties, and the extent to which a contracting party had responsibility for the breach of Article 101.[219]

The Commission has been keen to develop EU rules relating to damages actions as a mechanism for enforcing Articles 101 and 102 in national courts pursuant to Regulation 1/2003. The Commission White Paper[220] laid the foundations[221] for a Directive enacted in 2014.[222] It applies to all damages actions, individual and collective, which are available in the Member States. The Directive renders it easier to access the evidence required for a damages action, establishes a rebuttable presumption that a cartel causes harm, lays down a limitation period of at least five years in which to bring the claim, sets out rules to deal with the problem of passing on, and provides that victims should receive full compensation, including loss of profit and interest.

The issue of how far benefits conferred under a contract which is illegal can be recovered is a complex topic, detailed treatment of which can be found elsewhere.[223] The relevant principles of EU law have been considered above,[224] and the ECJ has confirmed that these principles apply to recovery pursuant to an Article 101 or 102 action, at least where the defendant is a public undertaking.[225]

---

[216] This discussion should be read in conjunction with Ch 8; C Jones, *Private Enforcement of Antitrust Law in the EU, UK and USA* (Oxford University Press, 1999); P Nebbia, 'Damages Actions for the Infringement of EC Competition Law: Compensation or Deterrence?' (2008) 23 ELRev 24; WPJ Wils, 'The Relationship between Public Antitrust Enforcement and Private Actions for Damages' (2009) 32 World Competition 3.

[217] Case C–242/95 *GT-Link A/S v De Danske Statsbaner (DSB)* [1997] ECR I–4449.

[218] Case C–453/99 *Courage Ltd v Crehan* [2001] ECR I–6297, [26]–[36]; Cases C–295–298/04 *Manfredi v Lloyd Adriatico Assicurazione SpA* [2006] ECR I–6619; Case C–557/12 *Kone AG v ÖBB Infrastruktur AG* EU:C:2014:1317.

[219] A Jones and D Beard, 'Co-contractors, Damages and Article 81: The ECJ finally Speaks' [2002] ECLR 246; O Odudu and J Edelman, 'Compensatory Damages for Breach of Article 81' (2002) 27 ELRev 327.

[220] http://ec.europa.eu/competition/antitrust/actionsdamages/index.html; White Paper on damages actions for breach of the EC antitrust rules, COM(2008) 165 final; Green Paper—Damages Actions for Breach of the EC Antitrust Rules, COM(2005) 672 final; J Pheasant, 'Damages Actions for Breach of the EC Antitrust Rules: The European Commission's Green Paper' [2006] ECLR 365; K Bernard, 'Private Antitrust Litigation in the European Union—Why does the EC Want to Embrace what the US FTC is Trying to Avoid?' (2010) 3 Global Competition Law Review 69.

[221] COM(2013) 404 final.

[222] Directive 2014/104/EU of the European Parliament and of the Council of 26 November 2014 on certain rules governing actions for damages under national law for infringements of the competition law provisions of the Member States and of the European Union [2014] OJ L349/1.

[223] A Jones, 'Recovery of Benefits Conferred under Contractual Obligations Prohibited by Article 85 or 86 of the Treaty of Rome' (1996) 112 LQR 606.

[224] See Ch 8.

[225] Case C–242/95 *GT-Link* (n 217).

13 CONCLUSIONS

i. The EU Courts have given a broad reading to Article 101, with the objectives of enhancing effi-ciency and preventing the single market programme from being hindered by private actors. They have therefore read key concepts such as agreement and concerted practice expansively.

ii. The interpretation of Article 101 has also been markedly affected by the extent to which an economic analysis is mandated within Article 101(1). The ECJ has insisted that object and effect should be read disjunctively. Certain agreements will be condemned merely because of proof of their existence. They will be illegal *per se*. Horizontal market division, horizontal price fixing, and boycotts are the classic examples. As far as many other agreements are concerned, a market analysis will be required to determine whether they are within Article 101(1). The General Court and Commission have been more reluctant to embrace a full economic analysis of the pro- and anti-competitive effects of an agreement within Article 101(1).

iii. The jury is still out on whether Article 101(3) should be interpreted according to the narrow or broad view. This issue has been thrown into sharp relief by the devolution of competence over Article 101(3) to national courts and NCAs. It is likely that this will tilt the balance in favour of the narrow view.

iv. The reach of EU competition law has not been the work of the courts alone. The legislature has intervened through measures such as the Merger Regulation. The Commission itself has orchestrated developments in diverse ways, through the passage of block exemptions, the control of mergers, the increased attention paid to competition in the public sector, and the reform of the enforcement mechanisms.

14 FURTHER READING[226]

AMATO, G, *Antitrust and the Bounds of Power* (Hart, 1997)

BELLAMY, C, AND CHILD, G, *European Community Law of Competition* (edited by P Roth and V Rose, Oxford University Press, 7th edn, 2013)

BISHOP, S, AND WALKER, M, *The Economics of EC Competition Law: Concepts, Application and Measurement* (Sweet & Maxwell, 3rd edn, 2010)

BORK, R, *The Antitrust Paradox: A Policy at War with Itself* (Basic Books, 1978)

EZRACHI, A, *EU Competition Law: An Analytical Guide to the Leading Cases* (Hart, 4th edn, 2014)

FAULL, J, AND NIKPAY, A (eds), *The EU Law of Competition* (Oxford University Press, 3rd edn, 2014)

GERBER, D, *Law and Competition in Twentieth Century Europe* (Oxford University Press, 1998)

GOYDER, D, GOYDER, J, AND ALBORS-LLORENS, A, *Goyder's Competition Law* (Oxford University Press, 5th edn, 2009)

HARDING, C, AND JOSHUA, J, *Regulating Cartels in Europe: A Study of Legal Control of Corporate Delinquency* (Oxford University Press, 2003)

JONES, A, AND SUFRIN, B, *EU Competition Law: Text, Cases, and Materials* (Oxford University Press, 5th edn, 2014)

---

[226] There is a voluminous literature on this topic. The references will therefore be confined to books.

KERSE, C, AND KHAN, N, *EU Antitrust Procedure* (Sweet & Maxwell, 6th edn, 2012)

KORAH, V, *An Introductory Guide to EC Competition Law and Practice* (Hart, 9th edn, 2007)

MIDDLETON, K, RODGER, B, AND MACCULLOCH, A, *Cases and Materials on UK and EC Competition Law* (Oxford University Press, 2nd edn, 2009)

MONTI, G, *EC Competition Law* (Cambridge University Press, 2007)

ODUDU, O, *The Boundaries of EC Competition Law: The Scope of Article 81* (Oxford University Press, 2006)

RODGER, B, AND MACCULLOCH, A, *Competition Law and Policy in the EC and UK* (Cavendish, 4th edn, 2009)

WESSELING, R, *The Modernisation of EC Antitrust Law* (Hart, 2000)

WHISH, R, AND BAILEY, D, *Competition Law* (Oxford University Press, 7th edn, 2012)

COMPETITION LAW: ARTICLE 102

1 CENTRAL ISSUES

i.   In the previous chapter we considered the applicability of Article 101. We now focus on the other principal provision concerned with competition policy: Article 102 TFEU (ex Article 82 EC).

ii. The essence of Article 102 is the control of market power, whether by a single firm or, subject to certain conditions, a number of firms. Monopoly power can lead to higher prices and lower output than under more normal competitive conditions, and this is the core rationale for legal regulation.

iii. Article 102 does not, however, prohibit market power *per se*. It proscribes the *abuse* of market power. Firms are encouraged to compete, with the most efficient players being successful. It would therefore be odd if the winner were legally penalized, since it may be more efficient than the competitors.

iv. There are a number of stages in the Article 102 analysis. It is necessary to define the relevant market, since this is a pre-condition for deciding whether a firm is dominant within that market; to determine whether it has abused its dominant position; and whether there are any available defences.

v.   There are difficult issues at each stage of analysis. There can be differences of opinion as to the nature of the product market; what factors other than market share make a firm dominant; whether certain behaviour by a dominant firm should always be regarded as abusive; and the very purpose to be served by Article 102, whether this is primarily to protect competitors or consumers. It is therefore unsurprising that judicial decisions have been criticized on these grounds.

vi. The Commission conducted a review of Article 102. This generated much comment as to the purpose served by this Article, and the extent to which it should be based on legal form or economic effect.

vii. The enforcement of Article 102 is now subject to the reformed regime discussed in the previous chapter, to which reference should be made.[1]

---

[1] See pp 1048–1052.

2 DOMINANT POSITION: DEFINING THE RELEVANT MARKET

Article 102 TFEU provides as follows:

> Any abuse by one or more undertakings of a dominant position within the internal market or in a sub-stantial part of it shall be prohibited as incompatible with the internal market in so far as it may affect trade between Member States.
>
> Such abuse may, in particular, consist in:
>
> (a) directly or indirectly imposing unfair purchase or selling prices or other unfair trading conditions;
>
> (b) limiting production, markets or technical development to the prejudice of consumers;
>
> (c) applying dissimilar conditions to equivalent transactions with other trading parties, thereby placing them at a competitive disadvantage;
>
> (d) making the conclusion of contracts subject to acceptance by the other parties of supplementary obligations which, by their nature or according to commercial usage, have no connection with the subject of such contracts.

Article 102 requires that the undertaking[2] or undertakings be in a dominant position. Dominance must be assessed in relation to three variables: the product market, the geographical market, and the temporal factor.

(A) THE PRODUCT MARKET

A firm will only have market power in the supply of particular goods or services. The narrower the definition of the product market, the easier it is to conclude that an undertaking is dominant under Article 102. Undertakings will therefore often argue that the Commission adopted too narrow a definition of the product.[3] The general approach has been to focus upon *interchangeability*: the extent to which the goods or services are interchangeable with other products.[4] This is addressed by looking at both the demand and supply sides of the market.

From the *demand side* interchangeability requires investigation of cross-elasticities of the product. The basic idea is simple. Cross-elasticity is high where an increase in the price of one product, for example beef, will lead buyers to switch in significant numbers to lamb or pork. The existence of high cross-elasticity indicates that the products are part of the same market. It may, however, be difficult to obtain reliable data on the relative cross-elasticities of different products. In these circumstances the Commission and the Court may well look to related factors to determine whether the products really are interchangeable, including the prices of the respective products and their physical characteristics. For example, wines may vary significantly in price and quality. An increase in the price of a top-quality wine may not lead buyers to switch to low-grade wine, although it may lead them to buy another high-grade wine. The relevance of the physical characteristics of the product is exemplified by *United Brands*, where the Court took into

---

[2] The definition of an undertaking is the same as in the context of Art 101: see pp 1003–1004. It covers any entity engaged in economic activity, regardless of its legal status and the way it is financed: Case T–128/98 *Aéroports de Paris v Commission* [2000] ECR II–3929, [107].

[3] Cases 6 and 7/73 *Istituto Chemioterapico Italiano SpA and Commercial Solvents v Commission* [1974] ECR 223; Case 6/72 *Europemballage Corporation and Continental Can Co Inc v Commission* [1973] ECR 215; Case 85/76 *Hoffmann-La Roche and Co AG v Commission* [1979] ECR 461; Case C–333/94 P *Tetra Pak International SA v Commission* [1996] ECR I–5951.

[4] Case 27/76 *United Brands Company and United Brands Continentaal BV v Commission* [1978] ECR 207.

account the taste, seedlessness, and softness of bananas in order to determine whether they constituted a separate market from other fruits.[5] In *France Télécom*[6] the CFI held that the markets for low- and high-speed internet access were distinct, since there was insufficient substitutability between them.

The degree of product interchangeability may also be affected by factors on the *supply side*. Even if firms are producing differing products it may be relatively simple for a firm to adapt its machinery to make the goods produced by a rival. In these circumstances the two products may be thought to be part of the same market.[7]

The following cases[8] indicate how the Court defines the relevant product market, and the problems that this can entail:

Case 27/76 **United Brands Company and United Brands Continentaal BV v Commission**
[1978] ECR 207

[Note Lisbon Treaty renumbering: Art 86 is now Art 102 TFEU]

United Brands produced bananas, and was accused of a variety of abusive practices, which will be examined below. An initial issue concerned the definition of the relevant product market. UB argued that bananas were part of a larger market in fresh fruit, and produced studies to show that the cross-elasticity between bananas and other fruit was high. The Commission contended that cross-elasticity was low, and bananas were a distinct market because they constituted an important part of the diet for certain consumers, and because they had specific qualities which made other fruits unacceptable as substitutes.

THE ECJ

22. For the banana to be regarded as forming a market which is sufficiently differentiated from other fruits it must be possible for it to be singled out by such special features distinguishing it from other fruits that it is only to a limited extent interchangeable with them and is only exposed to their competition in a way that is hardly perceptible.

23. The ripening of bananas takes place the whole year round without any season having to be taken into account.

. . .

27. Since the banana is a fruit which is always available in sufficient quantities the question whether it can be replaced by other fruits must be determined over the whole of the year for the purpose of ascertaining the degree of competition between it and other fresh fruit.

28. The studies of the banana market on the Court's file show that on the latter market there is no significant long term cross-elasticity any more than . . . there is any seasonal substitutability in general between the banana and all the seasonal fruits, as this only exists between the banana and two fruits (peaches and table grapes) in one of the countries (West Germany) of the relevant geographical market.

29. As far as concerns the two fruits available throughout the year (oranges and apples) the first are not interchangeable and in the case of the second there is only a relative degree of substitutability.

---

[5] Ibid.

[6] Case T–340/03 *France Télécom SA v Commission* [2007] ECR II–107, [78]–[91], upheld on appeal Case C–202/07 P *France Télécom SA v Commission* [2009] ECR I–2369; Case T–427/08 *Confédération européenne des associations d'horlogers-réparateurs (CEAHR) v European Commission* [2010] ECR II–5865.

[7] Case 6/72 *Continental Can* (n 3); Case T–65/96 *Kish Glass & Co Ltd v Commission* [2000] ECR II–1885, [68].

[8] See also Case T–201/04 *Microsoft Corp v Commission* [2007] ECR II–3601, [484]–[485], [531]; Case C–49/07 *Motosykletistiki Omospondia Ellados NPID (MOTOE) v Elliniko Dimosio* [2008] ECR I–4863; Case T–301/04 *Clearstream Banking AG and Clearstream International SA v Commission* [2009] ECR II–3195.

30. This small degree of substitutability is accounted for by the specific features of the banana and all the factors which influence consumer choice.

31. The banana has certain characteristics, appearance, taste, softness, seedlessness, easy handling, a constant level of production which enable it to satisfy the constant needs of an important section of the population consisting of the very young, the old and the sick.

32. As far as prices are concerned two FAO studies show that the banana is only affected by the prices—falling prices—of other fruits (and only of peaches and table grapes) during the summer months and mainly in July and then by an amount not exceeding 20 per cent.

...

34. It follows from all these considerations that a very large number of consumers having a constant need for bananas are not noticeably or even appreciably enticed away from the consumption of this product by the arrival of fresh fruit on the market and that even the seasonal peak periods only affect it for a limited period of time from the point of view of substitutability.

35. Consequently the banana market is a market which is sufficiently distinct from the other fresh fruit market.

Case 322/81 Nederlandsche Banden-Industrie Michelin NV v Commission
[1983] ECR 3461

[Note Lisbon Treaty renumbering: Art 86 is now Art 102 TFEU]

The Commission brought an action against Michelin based on the practice of awarding discounts on tyre sales, which were not related to objective differences in costs, the allegation being that the discounts were granted to tie purchasers to Michelin. Michelin was held to have a dominant position in the market for new replacement tyres for lorries, buses, and similar vehicles. Michelin argued that this definition of the product market was arbitrary and artificial, and that regard should also be had to tyres for cars and vans, and to retreads.

THE ECJ

37. As the Court has repeatedly emphasised... for the purposes of investigating the possibly dominant position of an undertaking on a given market, the possibilities of competition must be judged in the context of the market comprising the totality of the products which, with respect to their characteristics, are particularly suitable for satisfying constant needs and are only to a limited extent interchangeable with other products.

However, it must be noted that the determination of the relevant market is useful in assessing whether the undertaking concerned is in a position to prevent effective competition from being maintained and behave to an appreciable extent independently of its competitors and customers and consumers. For this purpose, therefore, an examination limited to the objective characteristics only of the relevant products cannot be sufficient: the competitive conditions and the structure of supply and demand must also be taken into consideration.

38. Moreover, it was for that reason that the Commission and Michelin NV agreed that new, original-equipment tyres should not be taken into consideration in the assessment of market shares.

Owing to the particular structure of demand for such tyres characterised by direct orders from car manufacturers, competition in this sphere is in fact governed by completely different factors and rules.

39. As far as replacement tyres are concerned, the first point which must be made is that at the user level there is no interchangeability between car and van tyres on the one hand and heavy-vehicle

tyres on the other. Car and van tyres therefore have no influence at all on competition on the market in heavy-vehicle tyres.

40. Furthermore, the structure of demand for each of these groups of products is different. Most buyers of heavy-vehicle tyres are trade users...for whom...the purchase of replacement tyres represents an item of considerable expenditure....On the other hand, for the average buyer of car or van tyres the purchase of tyres is an occasional event....

41. The final point which must be made is that there is no elasticity of supply between tyres for heavy vehicles and car tyres owing to significant differences in production techniques and in the plant and tools needed for their manufacture. The fact that time and considerable investment are required in order to modify production plant for the manufacture of light-vehicle tyres instead of heavy-vehicle tyres or vice versa means that there is no discernible relationship between the two categories of tyre enabling production to be adapted to demand on the market.

...

45. In establishing that Michelin NV has a dominant position the Commission was therefore right to assess its market share with reference to replacement tyres for lorries, buses and similar vehicles and to exclude consideration of car and van tyres.

The nature of the product market may be particularly narrow. Thus in *Hugin*[9] the Commission held Hugin to be in breach of Article 102 by refusing to supply spare parts for its cash registers to Liptons, which competed with Hugin in servicing Hugin's machines. The Commission defined the relevant market as being spare parts for Hugin machines, which were needed by independent repairers. Hugin argued that the proper product market was cash registers in general, which was very competitive. The Court found that users of cash registers would require the services of a specialist to service the machines and upheld the Commission's product definition.[10]

(B) THE GEOGRAPHIC MARKET

The geographic market is defined as the territory in which all traders operate in the same or sufficiently homogenous conditions of competition in relation to the relevant products or services, without it being necessary for those conditions to be perfectly homogenous.[11] In the absence of special factors, the relevant geographic market was held in *Hilti* to be the entire EU.[12] The *United Brands* case provides insights into this aspect of the Court's thinking:

Case 27/76 **United Brands Company and United Brands Continentaal BV v Commission**
[1978] ECR 207

The facts were set out above. UB argued that the Commission misconstrued the geographic market. The Commission had excluded France, Italy, and the UK, because of particular trading conditions which existed there. The applicants accepted this, but contended that trading conditions were also different in each of the other countries that had been treated by the Commission as the relevant geographic market.

---

[9] Case 22/78 *Hugin Kassaregister AB and Hugin Cash Registers Limited v Commission* [1979] ECR 1869; Case 26/75 *General Motors Continental NV v Commission* [1975] ECR 1367.

[10] E Fox, 'Monopolization and Dominance in the US and the EC: Efficiency, Opportunity and Fairness' (1986) 61 Notre Dame LRev 981, 1003–1004.

[11] Case T–83/91 *Tetra Pak v Commission* [1994] ECR II–755, [91], confirmed on appeal in Case C–333/94 P *Tetra Pak* (n 3); Case T–219/99 *British Airways plc v Commission* [2003] ECR II–5917, [108].

[12] Dec 88/138 [1988] OJ L65/19, upheld on appeal, Case C–53/92 P *Hilti AG v Commission* [1994] ECR I–667.

THE ECJ

44. The conditions for the application of Article 86 to an undertaking in a dominant position presuppose the clear delimitation of the substantial part of the Common Market in which it may be able to engage in abuses which hinder effective competition and this is an area where the objective conditions of competition applying to the product in question must be the same for all traders.

45. The Community has not established a common organisation of the agricultural market in bananas.

46. Consequently import arrangements vary considerably from one Member State to another and reflect a specific commercial policy to the States concerned.

[*The Court examined the special arrangements for bananas in France, Italy, and the UK. These arrangements differed in detail, but in general entailed preferential treatment for bananas coming from overseas territories of the three countries, or from the Commonwealth. It continued as follows:*]

51. The effect of the national organisation of these three markets is that the applicant's bananas do not compete on equal terms with the other bananas sold in these States which benefit from a preferential system and the Commission was right to exclude these three national markets from the geographic market under consideration.

52. On the other hand the six other States are markets which are completely free, although the applicable tariff provisions and transport costs are of necessity different but not discriminatory, and in which the conditions of competition are the same for all.

53. From the standpoint of being able to engage in free competition these six States form an area which is sufficiently homogeneous to be considered in its entirety.

In some instances the scope of the geographical market will be relatively straightforward. Thus in *British Telecommunications*,[13] the issue was whether BT had abused its dominant position with regard to message-forwarding agencies in the UK, and hence the geographical market was the UK, within which BT had a monopoly in the provision of telecommunication services. In other instances the scope of the geographical market may be influenced by factors such as transport costs. This was so in *Napier Brown–British Sugar*.[14] The Commission held that in determining whether a UK company had a dominant position in the production and sale of sugar the relevant market was Great Britain, since imports were very limited and acted as a complement to British sugar, rather than an alternative.

(c) THE TEMPORAL FACTOR

Markets have a temporal element. Thus, a firm may possess market power at a particular time of year, during which competition from other products is low because these other products are available only seasonally. Moreover the very definition of the product market will have a temporal dimension, in the sense that technological progress and changes in consumer habits will shift boundaries between markets.[15]

(d) THE COMMISSION NOTICE ON MARKET DEFINITION

The Commission published a Notice on the Definition of the Relevant Market for the Purposes of EU Competition Law.[16] It is important in three related ways.[17]

First, the Commission makes it clear that the definition of the relevant market will be viewed differently depending upon the nature of the competition inquiry: an investigation into a proposed

---

[13] Dec 82/861 [1982] OJ L360/36. On appeal see Case 41/83 *Italy v Commission* [1985] ECR 873.
[14] Dec 88/518 [1988] OJ L284/41.
[15] Dec 92/163, *Elopak Italia Srl v Tetra Pak (No 2)* [1992] OJ L72/1.
[16] [1997] OJ C372/5, available at http://ec.europa.eu/competition/antitrust/legislation/market.html.
[17] W Bishop, 'Editorial: The Modernization of DGIV' [1997] ECLR 481.

concentration is essentially prospective, whereas other types of investigation may be concerned primarily with past behaviour.[18]

Secondly, the Notice signalled a shift in Commission thinking on market definition. The Notice begins in orthodox fashion, by stating that the Commission will inquire into demand substitutability, supply substitutability, and potential competition.[19] The novelty stems from the Commission's detailed indication as to how these principles will be applied. In essence, the Commission adopts what is known as the SSNIP test: 'small but significant and non-transitory increase in prices'. On this test, a relevant market is the narrowest range of products such that a hypothetical monopolist in the relevant product area would find it both possible and worthwhile to institute an SSNIP. If demand substitution would be enough to make the price increase unprofitable because of the resulting loss of sales, then additional product substitutes would be included in the relevant market.[20]

Thirdly, while it is axiomatic that the Commission cannot overrule ECJ decisions, the Commission is nonetheless moving away from some of the benchmarks used by the ECJ. Thus the similarity of product characteristics and intended use, which have featured in case law,[21] are regarded as insufficient to determine whether two products are demand substitutes.[22] The same is true of functional interchangeability,[23] because the responsiveness of customers to price changes may be determined by other considerations.[24] In positive terms, the Commission states that it will consider: evidence of substitution in the recent past or where there have been shocks in the market; the views of customers and competitors; quantitative econometric tests; evidence of consumer preferences where available; barriers and costs entailed in substitution; and whether there are distinct groups of customers for the product.[25]

3 DOMINANT POSITION: MARKET POWER

(A) SINGLE FIRM DOMINANCE

When the Court has defined the relevant market, it then has to decide whether the undertaking is dominant within that sphere. Some measurement of the firm's market power is, therefore, necessary.[26] The legal test was laid down in *United Brands*:[27]

> The dominant position referred to in this Article relates to a position of economic strength enjoyed by an undertaking which enables it to prevent effective competition being maintained on the relevant market by giving it the power to behave to an appreciable extent independently of its competitors, customers and ultimately of its consumers.

---

[18] Commission Notice (n 16) [12].

[19] Commission Notice (n 16) [15]–[24].

[20] Ibid [15]–[18]; see however the reservations expressed about the SSNIP test in the more recent Commission study: DG Competition Discussion Paper on the Application of Article 82 of the Treaty to Exclusionary Abuses (2005), [11]–[17], and Guidance on the Commission's enforcement priorities in applying Article 82 of the EC Treaty to abusive exclusionary conduct by dominant undertakings [2009] OJ C45/7, available at http://ec.europa.eu/competition/antitrust/art82/index.html.

[21] See Case 27/76 *United Brands* (n 4), and Cases 6 and 7/73 *Commercial Solvents* (n 3).

[22] Commission Notice (n 16) [36].

[23] Case 6/72 *Continental Can* (n 3).

[24] Commission Notice (n 16) [36].

[25] Ibid [38]–[43].

[26] D Landes and R Posner, 'Market Power in Antitrust Cases' (1981) 94 Harv LRev 937; R Schmalensee, 'Another Look at Market Power' (1982) 95 Harv LRev 1789.

[27] Case 27/76 [1978] ECR 207, [65]; Case T–128/98 *Aéroports de Paris* (n 2) [147]; Case C–202/07 P *France Télécom* (n 6) [103] ; Case T–336/07 *Telefónica, SA and Telefónica de España, SA v European Commission* EU:T:2012:172, [146]–[150], upheld in Case C–295/12 P, 10 July 2014; Case C–457/10 P *AstraZeneca AB and AstraZeneca plc v European Commission* EU:C:2012:770, [174]–[176].

This test was quoted with approval in *Hoffmann-La Roche*, and the Court then added the following rider:[28]

> Such a position does not preclude some competition, which it does where there is a monopoly or a quasi-monopoly, but enables the undertaking which profits by it, if not to determine, at least to have an appreciable influence on the conditions under which that competition will develop, and in any case to act largely in disregard of it so long as such conduct does not operate to its detriment. A dominant position must also be distinguished from parallel courses of conduct which are peculiar to oligopolies in that in an oligopoly the courses of conduct interact, while in the case of an undertaking occupying the dominant position the conduct of the undertaking which derives profits from that position is to a great extent determined unilaterally. The existence of a dominant position may derive from several factors which, taken separately, are not necessarily determinative but among these factors a highly important one is the existence of very large market shares.

Where there is no statutory monopoly, the Court will consider two types of evidence to determine whether the firm has market power: the market share of the undertaking and whether other factors serve to reinforce its dominance. The test of dominance has been criticized.

J de Azevedo and M Walker, Market Dominance: Measurement Problems and Mistakes[29]

> The legal definition is based on the notion of a firm being able to act to a significant extent independently of its customers, consumers and competitors. Our criticism of the notion of acting independently of customers and consumers is largely conceptual: all firms, whether dominant or not, are constrained by the discipline of the demand curve and so do not act independently of customers or consumers. Our criticism of the notion of acting independently of competitors is largely empirical: it will only rarely be possible to measure this independence, as in general a dominant firm will exercise its market power to the point at which it is constrained from exercising it any further. For instance, a dominant firm may face little pricing constraint at the competitive price level, but for precisely this reason it will raise prices above the competitive price level until prices are high enough that competitors do impose a price constraint.

(i) *Market Share*

An undertaking with a statutory monopoly may be dominant for the purposes of Article 102. The grant of the statutory monopoly confers no immunity from EU competition law, subject to Article 106(2) TFEU.[30] The market share possessed by the undertaking will be central to whether it has market power.[31] Few firms, other than those with a statutory monopoly, will have 100 per cent of the market. Nor is a market share of this size necessary in order for Article 102 to 'bite', but a *de facto* monopoly will lead to a finding of dominance.[32]

---

[28] Case 85/76 *Hoffmann-La Roche* (n 3) [39].
[29] [2003] ECLR 640, 640; F Dethmers and N Dodoo, 'The Abuse of *Hoffmann-La Roche*: The Meaning of Dominance under EC Competition Law' [2006] ECLR 537.
[30] Case 41/83 *Italy v Commission* (n 13).
[31] Commission's enforcement priorities (n 20) [14]–[15]; DG Competition Discussion Paper (n 20) [28]–[32].
[32] Case C–52/07 *Kanal 5 Ltd and TV 4 AB v Föreningen Svenska Tonsättares Internationella Musikbyrå (STIM) upa* [2008] ECR I–9275, [21]–[22].

Thus, in *United Brands* UB's 40–45 per cent of the market was held to be sufficient, although the Court also considered other factors indicative of its dominance.[33] However, in *Hoffmann-La Roche* the Court overturned a Commission finding that the firm was dominant in the market for B3 vitamins, of which it had only 43 per cent. It was not satisfied that there were other factors to sustain its dominance in this market.[34] The Court, however, made it clear that, save in exceptional circumstances, the existence of a very large market share which was held for some time would in itself be indicative of dominance. It would secure for the undertaking the freedom of action that was the hallmark of a dominant position.[35] In the *Akzo* case[36] the ECJ held that a market share of 50 per cent could be said to be very large, and hence indicative of a dominant position, and this finding was repeated in *Irish Sugar*.[37]

It seems moreover that there is a concept of 'super-dominance' emerging, held to be applicable to undertakings with very large market shares. The Commission and Court regard such bodies as having a particular responsibility towards the competitive process.[38]

(ii) *Additional Factors Indicating Dominance: Barriers to Entry*

It can be problematic to determine the other factors that indicate dominance.[39] It is clear that the Court should pay attention to factors other than market share, since even a relatively large market share may be fragile because of the possibility of new market entrants. It must then be considered how far barriers to entry render it difficult for other firms to penetrate this market. There is, however, considerable controversy about the meaning of this concept.

For some, it is a broad idea, embracing almost anything that makes it particularly difficult for a new firm to enter the market. For others, the term has a much narrower construction, since there is concern that matters will be characterized as barriers to entry when they are merely indicative of the superior efficiency of the incumbent firm. The following extract exemplifies this aspect of the argument. There may well be reservations about aspects of Bork's analysis, but similar concerns about the broad meaning accorded to barriers to entry in EU law have been expressed by other writers.[40]

---

[33] Case 27/76 *United Brands* (n 4).

[34] Case 85/76 *Hoffmann-La Roche* (n 3).

[35] Ibid [41], Case T-30/09 *Hilti AG v Commission* [1991] ECR II 1439, [92]; Case T-65/98 *Van den Bergh Foods Ltd v Commission* [2003] ECR II–4653, [154]; Case T–336/07 *Telefónica* (n 27) [149]–[150]; Case C–457/10 P *AstraZeneca* (n 27) [176].

[36] Case C–62/86 *Akzo Chemie BV v Commission* [1991] ECR I–3359, [60].

[37] Case T–228/97 *Irish Sugar plc v Commission* [1999] ECR II–2969, [70], upheld on appeal, Case C–497/99 P *Irish Sugar plc v Commission* [2001] ECR I–5333.

[38] Cases C–395 and 396/96 P *Compagnie Maritime Belge Transports SA v Commission* [2000] ECR I–1365, [137] AG Fennelly; *1998 World Cup* [2000] OJ L5/55, [86]; R Whish and D Bailey, *Competition Law* (Oxford University Press, 7th edn, 2012) 187–189.

[39] Whish and Bailey (n 38) 179–183; A Jones and B Sufrin, *EU Competition Law: Text, Cases, and Materials* (Oxford University Press, 4th edn, 2011).

[40] D Harbord and T Hoehn, 'Barriers to Entry and Exit in European Competition Policy' (1994) 14 International Review of Law and Economics 422; S Turnbull, 'Barriers to Entry, Article 86 and the Abuse of a Dominant Position: An Economic Critique of European Community Competition Law' [1996] ECLR 96; O Arowolo, 'Application of the Concept of Barriers to Entry under Article 82 of the EC Treaty: Is There a Case for Review?' [2005] ECLR 247; J Heit, 'The Justifiability of the ECJ's Wide Approach to the Concept of Barriers to Entry' [2006] ECLR 117.

R Bork, The Antitrust Paradox: A Policy at War with Itself[41]

The concept of barriers to entry is crucial to antitrust debate. Those who advocate extensive and increasing legal intervention in market processes cite the existence of entry barriers as a reason to believe that unassisted market forces very often fail to produce adequate results.... The ubiquity and potency of the concept are undeniable.

Yet it is demonstrable that barriers of the sort these commentators and jurists believe they see do not exist. They are the ghosts that inhabit antitrust theory. Until the concept of barriers to entry is thoroughly revised, it will remain impossible to make antitrust law more rational or, indeed, to restrain the growth of its powerful irrational elements.

We may begin by asking what a 'barrier to entry' is. There appears to be no precise definition, and in current usage a 'barrier' often seems to be anything that makes the entry of new firms into an industry more difficult. It is at once apparent that an ambiguity lurks in the concept, and it is this ambiguity that causes the trouble. When existing firms are efficient and possess valuable plant, equipment, knowledge, skill, and reputation, potential entrants will find it correspondingly more difficult to enter the industry, since they must acquire those things.... But these difficulties are natural; they inhere in the nature of the tasks to be performed. There can be no objection to barriers of this sort. Their existence means only that when market power is achieved by means other than efficiency, entry will not dissipate the objectionable power instantaneously, and law may therefore have a role to play....

The question for antitrust is whether there exist artificial entry barriers. These must be barriers that are not forms of superior efficiency and which yet prevent the forces of the market—entry or the growth of smaller firms already within the industry—from operating to erode market positions not based on efficiency. Care must be taken to distinguish between forms of efficiency and artificial barriers. Otherwise the law will find itself—indeed, it has found itself—attacking efficiency in the name of market freedom. Joe Bain, whose work has done much to popularize the concept, lists among entry barriers such things as economies of scale, capital requirements, and product differentiation.[42] There may be disagreement about two of these barriers, but it is clear that at least one of them, economies of scale, is a form of efficiency. Uncritical adapters of Bain's work have not sufficiently inquired whether the others may not also be efficiencies.

Before examining some claimed entry barriers to determine whether they are efficiencies or artificial clogs upon competition, it should be noted that... an artificial barrier is, of course, an exclusionary practice.... Every barrier will be either a form of efficiency deliberately created or an instance of deliberate predation. There is no 'intermediate case' of non-efficient and unintended exclusion. Failure to bear that in mind leads to serious policy mistakes.

The Court's approach can be exemplified by *Hoffmann-La Roche*.[43] The case was concerned with alleged abusive behaviour in relation to vitamins, and the Court considered whether HLR was dominant. Its market share was taken into account, and the ECJ then evaluated other factors that might indicate market power. The Commission had listed a number of such factors. The ECJ rejected, for example, the fact that HLR had retained its market share, since this might have resulted from effective competitive behaviour.[44] It also rejected the fact that HLR produced a wider range of vitamins than other undertakings, since the Commission itself had found that each group of vitamins constituted a separate market.[45] The following factors were, however, deemed to be of relevance:[46]

[41] (Basic Books, 1978) 310–311.
[42] The reference is to J Bain, *Barriers to New Competition* (Harvard University Press, 1956) ch 1.
[43] Case 85/76 (n 3).
[44] Ibid [44].
[45] Ibid [45]–[46].
[46] Ibid [48]; Case T–219/99 *British Airways* (n 11) [210].

On the other hand the relationship between the market shares of the undertaking concerned and of its competitors, especially those of the next largest, the technological lead of an undertaking over its competitors, the existence of a highly developed sales network and the absence of potential competition are relevant factors, the first because it enables the competitive strength of the undertaking in question to be assessed, the second and third because they represent in themselves technical and commercial advantages and the fourth because it is the consequence of the existence of obstacles preventing new competitors from having access to the market.

The ECJ has persisted in taking a wide view of barriers to entry, as has the Commission.[47] It is questionable whether a number of these factors ought to be regarded as barriers to entry.

Thus, *economies of scale* have been considered to be relevant in assessing the market power of a particular firm,[48] as has the *capital strength* of the undertaking and its access to capital markets.[49] However, as seen above, the former is almost certainly indicative of efficiency. As for the latter, many commentators contend that access to capital is not a barrier to entry, since capital markets accurately reflect the cost of capital to a particular firm, and any inefficiency in this regard is best dealt with through reform of capital markets themselves.

It is equally questionable whether the existence of *vertical integration* should be regarded as a factor indicating dominance.[50] The motivation for a firm to integrate vertically was considered earlier,[51] where it was seen that the rational firm would normally choose to do so only if that was the most efficient method of marketing its product.[52]

It is also doubtful whether *superior technology* should be perceived as a barrier to entry, even though the Court has consistently regarded it in this manner.[53] Any new firm wishing to enter the market should expect to have to expend money on developing technology and know-how. These costs will not necessarily be any greater than for the incumbent firm. *Legal provisions* within Member States which render it more difficult for new firms to break into the market have also been regarded as indicative of dominance.[54]

It is clear that the Court will take into account, in determining dominance, the *conduct of the firm* which is alleged to be the abusive behaviour, notwithstanding the apparent circularity that this entails. Thus, in *Michelin* the Court took account of Michelin's price discrimination as indicative of dominance, even though it noted the circularity thereby involved.[55]

It is difficult to regard the decisions in this area as satisfactory. It may be argued, by way of response, that it is legitimate for the Court to take account of the preceding factors, since it is only seeking to determine whether the firm has some dominance, not whether it has abused that dominance. However, a finding of dominance renders the firm liable to investigation, with attendant costs. Moreover, while the existence of a dominant position is not itself illegal, a firm in such a position is regarded as having a 'special responsibility' not to allow its conduct to impair genuine undistorted competition on the relevant market.

---

[47] DG Competition Discussion Paper (n 20) [38]–[40]; Commission's enforcement priorities (n 20) [17].
[48] Case 27/76 *United Brands* (n 4).
[49] Ibid; Case T–301/04 *Clearstream* (n 8) [146].
[50] Case 27/76 *United Brands* (n 4); Case 85/76 *Hoffmann-La Roche* (n 3).
[51] See pp 1032–1035.
[52] It is, moreover, doubtful whether the existence of vertical integration enables the firm with some dominance to achieve any greater monopoly profit than it would do without the vertical integration.
[53] See, eg, Case 27/76 *United Brands* (n 4); Case 85/76 *Hoffmann-La Roche* (n 3); Case 322/81 *Nederlandsche Banden-Industrie Michelin NV v Commission* [1983] ECR 3461; Case T–301/04 *Clearstream* (n 8) [146].
[54] Case 22/78 *Hugin* (n 9); Case T–30/89 *Hilti* (n 35) [93]; Case C–457/10 P *AstraZeneca* (n 27) [154].
[55] Case 322/81 (n 53).

(B) JOINT DOMINANCE

The discussion thus far proceeded on the assumption that one firm occupies a dominant position. However, Article 102 speaks of an abuse of a dominant position by 'one or more undertakings'. It is clear that this covers the situation, exemplified by *Continental Can* and *Commercial Solvents*, where the dominant position is held by firms that are part of the same corporate group or economic unit.

What has been less clear is whether the phrase also covers oligopolistic markets, in which a number of independent firms operate in a parallel manner. The ECJ appeared to have rejected this in *Hoffmann-La Roche*,[56] when it held that unilateral behaviour by a single firm occupying a dominant position had to be distinguished from interactive behaviour by a number of independent firms, which made up an oligopoly. It however now appears that some species of oligopolistic behaviour can be caught by Article 102.

Cases T–68 and 77–78/89 **Re Italian Flat Glass: Società Italiana Vetro v Commission** [1992] ECR I–1403

[Note Lisbon Treaty renumbering: Arts 85 and 86 are now Arts 101 and 102 TFEU]

A company, Cobelli, a wholesaler of glass, alleged that three producers of flat glass were in breach of the Treaty by maintaining agreed price lists and identical conditions of sale. It also alleged that two of these companies had engaged in practices designed to achieve full control, not only of the production of glass, but also of its distribution, by excluding from the market independent wholesaler-distributors. The Commission found a breach of Article 85 by the producers of the flat glass, and also a breach of Article 86. In relation to the latter, it held that the undertakings had a collective dominant position, that they were able to pursue a commercial policy independent of ordinary market conditions, and that they presented themselves on the market as a single entity, rather than as individual concerns. The CFI partially annulled the findings with respect to Article 85, holding that the Commission had failed to establish the requisite agreement or concerted practice between the three producers. It then considered Article 86.

THE CFI

358. The Court considers that there is no legal or economic reason to suppose that the term 'undertaking' in Article 86 has a different meaning from the one given to it in the context of Article 85. There is nothing, in principle, to prevent two or more independent economic entities from being, on a specific market, united by such economic links that, by virtue of that fact, together they hold a dominant position *vis-à-vis* the other operators on the same market. This could be the case, for example, where two or more undertakings jointly have, through agreements or licences, a technological lead affording them the power to behave to an appreciable extent independently of their competitors, their customers and ultimately of their consumers (*Hoffmann-La Roche*).

...

360. However, it should be pointed out that for the purposes of establishing an infringement of Article 86 EEC, it is not sufficient, as the Commission's agent claimed at the hearing, to 'recycle' the facts constituting an infringement of Article 85, deducing from the finding that the parties to an agreement or to an unlawful practice jointly hold a substantial share of the market, that by virtue of that fact alone they hold a collective dominant position, and that their unlawful behaviour constitutes an abuse of that collective dominant position. Amongst other considerations, a finding of a dominant position,

---

[56] Case 85/76 (n 3) [39].

which is in any case not in itself a matter of reproach, presupposes that the market in question has been defined (Case 6/72, *Continental Can*, Case 322/81, *Michelin*). The Court must therefore examine, first the analysis of the market made in the decision and, secondly, the circumstances relied on in support of the finding of a collective dominant position.

The CFI annulled the Commission's decision on Article 102, since there were errors in its reasoning with respect to market definition and because it had not adduced the necessary proof of a collective dominant position. Notwithstanding this, the CFI's decision was important for its affirmation of the existence of collective dominance.[57] The ECJ endorsed the idea of collective dominance[58] and gave further guidance on its meaning in the following case.[59]

Cases C–395–396/96 P **Compagnie Maritime Belge Transports SA, Compagnie Maritime Belge SA and Dafra Lines A/S v Commission**
[2000] ECR I–1365

[Note Lisbon Treaty renumbering: Art 85 is now Art 101 TFEU]

The members of the liner conference argued that it was wrong of the Commission and the CFI to have concluded that they occupied a collectively dominant position. They contended that the Commission and CFI had, in making this finding, merely 'recycled' facts relating to the existence of a concerted practice.

THE ECJ

41. In order to establish the existence of a collective entity...it is necessary to examine the economic links or factors which give rise to a connection between the undertakings concerned....

42. In particular, it must be ascertained whether economic links exist between the undertakings concerned which enable them to act independently of their competitors, their customers and consumers (see *Michelin*).

43. The mere fact that two or more undertakings are linked by an agreement, a decision...or a concerted practice within the meaning of Article 85(1)...does not, of itself, constitute a sufficient basis for such a finding.

44. On the other hand, an agreement, decision or concerted practice (whether or not covered by an exemption under Article 85(3)...) may undoubtedly, where it is implemented, result in the undertakings

---

[57] M Schodermeier, 'Collective Dominance Revisited: An Analysis of the EC Commission's New Concepts of Oligopoly Control' [1990] ECLR 28; R Whish and B Sufrin, 'Oligopolistic Markets and EC Competition Law' (1992) 12 YBEL 59; D Ridyard, 'Economic Analysis of Single Firm and Oligopolistic Dominance' [1994] ECLR 255; B Rodger, 'Oligopolistic Market Failure: Collective Dominance versus Complex Monopoly' [1995] ECLR 21; C Caffarra and K-U Kuhn, 'Joint Dominance: The CFI Judgment on Gencor/Lonhro' [1999] ECLR 355; R Whish, 'Collective Dominance' in D O'Keefe and A Bavasso (eds), *Judicial Review in European Union Law* (Kluwer, 2000) ch 37; G Monti, 'The Scope of Collective Dominance under Article 82' (2001) 38 CMLRev 131; G Niels, 'Collective Dominance—More Than Just Oligopolistic Independence' [2001] ECLR 168; E Kloosterhuis, 'Joint Dominance and the Interaction between Firms' [2001] ECLR 79; C Withers and M Jephcott, 'Where to Now for EC Oligopoly Control?' [2001] ECLR 295.

[58] Case C–393/92 (n 73); Cases C–140–142/94 *DIP SpA v Commune di Bassano del Grappa* [1995] ECR I–3257, [25]–[26].

[59] Cases T–191 and 212–214/98 *Atlantic Container Line AB v Commission* [2003] ECR II–3275, [594]–[602], [610]; Case C–413/06 P *Bertelsmann AG and Sony Corporation of America v Independent Music Publishers and Labels Association (Impala)* [2008] ECR I–4951, [119].

> concerned being so linked as to their conduct on a particular market that they present themselves as a collective entity vis-à-vis their competitors, their trading partners and consumers.
>
> 45. The existence of a collective dominant position may therefore flow from the nature and terms of an agreement, from the way in which it is implemented and, consequently, from the links or factors which give rise to a connection between undertakings which result from it. Nevertheless, the existence of an agreement or of other links in law is not indispensable to a finding of a collective dominant position; such a finding may be based on other connecting factors and would depend on an economic assessment and, in particular, on an assessment of the structure of the market in question.

The same approach to collective dominance is apparent in the context of mergers. In *Gencor*[60] the CFI held that collective dominance within the Merger Regulation could catch oligopolistic collusion, and that the existence of structural links between the relevant firms was not a necessary condition for collective dominance to apply.

It is still necessary to find that there has been an abuse by the firms that occupy a collective dominant position. The meaning of abuse in this context is difficult.[61] A concerted practice by oligopolists will be caught by Article 101. For Article 102 to be of use collective dominance will have to embrace non-collusive behaviour. However, to condemn parallel pricing behaviour by oligopolists as an abuse under Article 102 would be tantamount to condemning oligopoly *per se*, since this is the rational behaviour of firms in such markets. There is nonetheless still room for the concept of abuse to apply. Thus, if those occupying a collective dominant position seek to drive a competitor from the market, as exemplified by *Compagnie Maritime Belge*, they should properly be caught by Article 102.

4 ABUSE: THREE PROBLEMS OF INTERPRETATION

An undertaking will be condemned only if it has abused its dominant position. The list of abusive practices in Article 102 is not exhaustive. The practices specified are merely examples of abuse.[62] There are three important interpretive issues when considering the meaning of 'abuse'.

(A) WHO IS ARTICLE 102 DESIGNED TO PROTECT?

The first issue is who Article 102 is intended to protect: consumers, competitors, or both?[63] There can be instances where the interests of consumers and competitors clash. Behaviour by a dominant undertaking that injures a competitor will not necessarily injure consumers.[64]

It is common to subdivide the situations to which Article 102 can apply into exploitative and exclusionary abuses.[65] The former signifies behaviour harmful to consumers. The latter, generally, connotes conduct deleterious to competitors, actual or potential. This division should not, however, be treated too rigidly, and in any event the same conduct by the dominant firm may be both exploitative and exclusionary. It is now clear that Article 102 covers both exploitation and anti-competitive behaviour,

---

[60] Case T–102/96 *Gencor Ltd v Commission* [1999] ECR II–753, [276]–[277].

[61] Whish and Bailey (n 38) 579–582.

[62] Case 6/72 *Continental Can* (n 3) [26]; Case C–95/04 P *British Airways plc v Commission* [2007] ECR I–2331, [57].

[63] Whish and Bailey (n 38) 195–197.

[64] Case C–7/97 *Oscar Bronner GmbH & Co KG v Mediaprint Zeitungs- und Zeitschriftenverlag GmbH & Co KG* [1998] ECR I–7791, [58] AG Jacobs.

[65] Whish and Bailey (n 38) 201–210; J Temple Lang, 'Monopolisation and the Definition of Abuse of a Dominant Position under Art. 86 EEC Treaty' (1979) 16 CMLRev 345.

but this was not so apparent at the inception of the Treaty. Some commentators argued strenuously that Article 102 should be restricted to exploitative behaviour harmful to consumers, and that there should be some real link between the harm and the market power of the dominant undertaking.[66] This construction was rendered untenable by *Continental Can*, which will be considered below.

(B) WHAT KINDS OF BEHAVIOUR ARE ABUSIVE?

The second issue relates to the kinds of behaviour held to be abusive. Such behaviour must be distinguished from normal competitive strategy.[67] It would be odd if the ordinary pricing and output decisions of the dominant firm were abusive, since this would mean that we were proscribing dominant market power *per se*. Having said this, it is also clear that Article 102 explicitly prohibits unfair pricing and limits on productive capacity, and that some meaning must, therefore, be ascribed to these terms.

It might be thought that this problem could be overcome if the concept of abuse was confined to practices such as price discrimination, predation, and tying, which look 'bad', even for the firm with dominance. The problem is not so easily resolved since there is considerable disagreement among economists as to whether these activities are always harmful and how this is to be measured. The application of Article 102 can, therefore, be controversial.

The tension in the preceding paragraph is thrown into sharp relief by the Court's jurisprudence, which states that while a finding of dominance does not in itself imply any reproach, the undertaking nonetheless has a 'special responsibility', irrespective of the cause of that position, not to allow its conduct to impair genuine and undistorted competition on the common market.[68] The consequence is that an undertaking in a dominant position may be deprived of the right to adopt a course of conduct which is not itself abusive, and which would be unobjectionable if taken by a non-dominant undertaking.[69] Thus, while it is accepted that a dominant undertaking can take steps to protect its own interests when they are attacked by competitors, it is not allowed to strengthen its dominant position, which will be held to be an abuse.[70] This divide is difficult to apply, more especially given that it has to be judged in the light of the specific circumstances of each case where competition has been weakened.[71]

(C) ABUSE OF WHICH MARKET?

It is clear that abuse of a dominant position in one market may be censured because of the effects that it produces on a different market, even where there is no dominance on the latter market. This is especially so where the dominant undertaking can control access to the other market. This is exemplified by *Aéroports de Paris*.[72] The airport authority controlled access to the supply of catering services and abused its dominant position by discriminatory pricing.

---

[66] R Joliet, *Monopolization and Abuse of a Dominant Position* (Martinus Nijhoff, 1970).

[67] J Temple Lang, 'How can the Problems of Exclusionary Abuses under Article 102 TFEU be Resolved?' (2012) 37 ELRev 136.

[68] Case 322/81 *Michelin* (n 53) [57]; Case T–228/97 *Irish Sugar* (n 37) [112]; Case T–203/01 *Michelin v Commission* [2003] ECR II–4071, [55]; Case T–65/98 *Van den Bergh Foods* (n 35) [157]–[158]; Case C–552/03 P *Unilever Bestfoods (Ireland) v Commission* [2006] ECR I–9091, [136]; Case C–202/07 P *France Télécom* (n 6) [105]; Case C–457/10 P *AstraZeneca* (n 27) [134], [149]; Case C–52/09 *Konkurrensverket v TeliaSonera Sverige AB* [2011] ECR I–527, [23]–[24].

[69] Case 322/81 *Michelin* (n 53) [57]; Case T–51/89 *Tetra Pak v Commission* [1990] ECR II–309, [23]; Case T–111/96 *ITT Promedia NV v Commission* [1998] ECR II–2937, [138]; Case T–301/04 *Clearstream Banking* (n 8) [133].

[70] Case 27/76 *United Brands* (n 4) [189]; Case T–228/97 *Irish Sugar plc* (n 37) [112]; Case T–219/99 *British Airways* (n 11) [241]–[243]; Case T–203/01 *Michelin* (n 68) [54]–[55]; Case T–66/01 *Imperial Chemical Industries Ltd v Commission* [2010] ECR II–2631, [295]; Case T–155/06 *Tomra Systems ASA v Commission* [2010] ECR II–4361, [207].

[71] Case C–333/94 P *Tetra Pak* (n 3) [24]; Cases C–395–396/96 P *Compagnie Maritimes Belge* (n 38) [114].

[72] Case 128/98 (n 2) [164]–[165]; Case T–219/99 *British Airways* (n 11) [127]–[132].

5 ABUSE: PARTICULAR EXAMPLES

(A) ABUSE AND MERGERS

The EU waited a long time for a specific regulation concerning mergers. The ECJ made it clear in the *Continental Can* case that some mergers would, however, be caught by Article 102. The case is also of more general importance for the interpretation of the meaning of abuse.

Case 6/72 **Europemballage Corporation and Continental Can Co Inc v Commission**
[1973] ECR 215

[Note Lisbon Treaty renumbering: Arts 3f, 85, and 86 are now Art 3(3) TEU, Arts 101 and 102 TFEU]

Continental Can (CC) was a US manufacturer of metal packaging which had a presence in Europe through a German firm (SLW), which it acquired in 1969. In 1970 it sought to purchase, through its subsidiary Europemballage, a controlling interest in a Dutch company, TDV. The Commission found that CC had a dominant position in Europe for certain types of packaging through SLW, and that there had been an abuse of that position by the purchase of TDV. CC argued that there had been no abuse.

THE ECJ

20. ...The question is whether the word 'abuse' in Article 86 refers only to practices of undertakings which may directly affect the market and are detrimental to production or sales, to purchasers or consumers, or whether this word refers also to changes in the structure of an undertaking, which lead to competition being seriously disturbed in a substantial part of the Common Market.

21. The distinction between measures which concern the structure of the undertaking and practices which affect the market cannot be decisive, for any structural measure may influence market conditions, if it increases the size and the economic power of the undertaking.

22. In order to answer this question one has to go back to the spirit, general scheme and wording of Article 86, as well as to the system and objectives of the Treaty....

23. Article 86 is part of the chapter devoted to the common rules on the Community's policy in the field of competition. This policy is based on Article 3(f) of the Treaty according to which the Community's activity shall include the institution of a system ensuring that competition in the Common Market is not distorted....

24. But if Article 3(f) provides for the institution of a system ensuring that competition in the Common Market is not distorted, then it requires a fortiori that competition must not be eliminated. This requirement is so essential that without it numerous provisions of the Treaty would be pointless. Moreover, it corresponds to the precept of Article 2 of the Treaty according to which one of the tasks of the Community is 'to promote throughout the Community a harmonious development of economic activities'. Thus the restraints on competition, which the Treaty allows under certain conditions because of the need to harmonise the various objectives of the Treaty, are limited by the requirements of Articles 2 and 3. Going beyond this limit involves the risk that the weakening of competition would conflict with the aims of the Common Market.

25. ...Articles 85 and 86 seek to achieve the same aim on different levels, viz. the maintenance of effective competition within the Common Market. The restraint on competition, which is prohibited if it is the result of behaviour falling under Article 85, cannot become permissible by the fact that such behaviour succeeds under the influence of a dominant undertaking and results in the merger of the

undertakings concerned. In the absence of explicit provisions one cannot assume that the Treaty, which prohibits in Article 85 certain decisions of ordinary associations of undertakings restricting competition without eliminating it, permits in Article 86 that undertakings, after merging into an organic unity, should reach such a dominant position that any serious competition is practically rendered impossible. Such a diverse legal treatment would make a breach in the entire competition law which could jeopardise the proper functioning of the Common Market. If, in order to avoid the prohibitions in Article 85, it sufficed to establish such close connections between the undertakings that they escaped the prohibition of Article 85 without coming within the scope of Article 86, then, in contradiction to the basic principles of the Common Market, the partitioning of a substantial part of the Common Market would be allowed....

26. ...[Article 86] merely gives examples, not an exhaustive enumeration of the sort of abuses of a dominant position prohibited by the Treaty...[T]he provision is not only aimed at practices which may cause damage to the consumer directly, but also at those which are detrimental to them through their impact on an effective competition structure...Abuse may therefore occur if an undertaking in a dominant position strengthens such position in such a way that the degree of dominance reached substantially fetters competition, i. e. that only undertakings remain in the market whose behaviour depends on the dominant one.

27. Such being the meaning and scope of Article 86 of the EEC Treaty, the question of the link of causality raised by the applicants which in their opinion has to exist between the dominant position and its abuse, is of no consequence, for the strengthening of the position of an undertaking may be an abuse and prohibited under Article 86 of the Treaty, regardless of the means and the procedure by which it is achieved, if it has the effects mentioned above.

The decision in *Continental Can* is of seminal importance for Article 102, in terms of both the reasoning and the result. The ECJ's reasoning exemplifies its teleological approach. Reliance is placed on the general principles in the Treaty to guide construction of specific Articles. The competition provisions are read as a whole, and the interpretation of Article 102 is strongly influenced by the desire to avoid any 'gap' in Treaty coverage.

The result of the case signals the ECJ's intent that Article 102 should cover situations where the competitive market structure was placed in jeopardy. The Article included 'behavioural' abuse, which operated directly to the detriment of consumers. It also embraced 'structural' abuse that weakened the competitive market structure. *Continental Can* thus made it apparent that Article 102 would cover exclusionary action where the primary injury was to competitors. This was reinforced by the Court's negation of the need for any real causal link between the dominance and the impugned action: it did not need to be proven that CC's 'economic muscle' had forced the merger on a reluctant undertaking.[73] It sufficed that the merger in fact resulted in damage to the competitive market structure.[74] *Continental Can* received a mixed reception when it first appeared, with certain commentators being critical of the reasoning and result. The Court has, however, persisted in its general approach, as the cases in the following sections will demonstrate.

[73] See also, Case C–393/92 *Municipality of Almelo v NV Energiebedrijf Ijsselmij* [1994] ECR I–1477; Case T–321/05 *AstraZeneca AB and AstraZeneca plc v European Commission* [2010] ECR–II 2805, [267].

[74] P Vogelenzang, 'Abuse of a Dominant Position in Article 86: The Problem of Causality and Some Applications' (1976) 13 CMLRev 61. For a different view about causality see T Eilmansberger, 'How to Distinguish Good from Bad Competition under Article 82: In Search of Clearer and More Coherent Standards for Anti-Competitive Abuses' (2005) 42 CMLRev 49.

(B) ABUSE AND REFUSAL TO SUPPLY

(i) *Refusal to Supply: The Basic Principles*

The obligation on a firm in a dominant position to supply to other firms is exemplified by *Commercial Solvents:*[75]

Cases 6 and 7/73 **Istituto Chemioterapico Italiano SpA
and Commercial Solvents v Commission**
[1974] ECR 223

[Note Lisbon Treaty renumbering: Arts 3f, 85, and 86 are now
Art 3(3) TEU, Arts 101 and 102 TFEU]

Commercial Solvents Corporation (CSC) made raw materials, nitropropane and aminobutanol, which were then used to make ethambutol, a drug for tuberculosis. CSC acquired 51 per cent of an Italian company, Istituto, which bought the raw material from CSC and sold it to another Italian company, Zoja, the latter then using it to manufacture ethambutol-based products. Istituto sought to acquire Zoja, but the negotiations were unsuccessful. Istituto then increased its price to Zoja, and Zoja found an alternative source of supply from other customers of CSC. This alternative source of supply then dried up, principally because CSC instructed those to whom it sold the raw material not to sell it on to firms such as Zoja. CSC then stated that it would no longer sell the raw material, but that it would instead integrate vertically down-market, and use the raw material for its own production of the finished product. When Zoja sought to re-order the raw material from CSC the latter refused to supply.

THE ECJ

25. However, an undertaking being in a dominant position as regards the production of raw material and therefore able to control the supply to manufacturers of derivatives, cannot, just because it decides to start manufacturing these derivatives (in competition with its former customers) act in such a way as to eliminate their competition which, in the case in question, would amount to eliminating one of the principal manufacturers of ethambutol in the Common Market. Since such conduct is contrary to the objectives expressed in Article 3(f) of the Treaty and set out in greater detail in Articles 85 and 86, it follows that an undertaking which has a dominant position in the market in raw materials and which, with the object of reserving such raw material for manufacturing its own derivatives, refuses to supply a customer, which is itself a manufacturer of these derivatives, and therefore risks eliminating all competition on the part of this customer, is abusing its dominant position within the meaning of Article 86. In this context it does not matter that the undertaking ceased to supply in the spring of 1970 because of the cancellation of the purchases by Zoja, because it appears from the applicants' own statement that, when the supplies provided for in the contract had been completed, the sale of aminobutanol would have stopped in any case.

This appears to be a classic case of abusive behaviour: CSC, the dominant firm, teaches Zoja a lesson by making it clear that if the latter seeks an alternative source of supply that later dries up, then Zoja cannot necessarily expect CSC to resume supplies. The case could well have been decided in this way.

---

[75] R Subiotto and R O'Donoghue, 'Defining the Scope of the Duty of Dominant Firms to Deal with Existing Customers under Article 82' [2003] ECLR 683; Commission's enforcement priorities (n 20) [75]–[90]; DG Competition Discussion Paper (n 20) [207]–[224].

However, the Court's reasoning is broader. It specifically addresses the situation where the refusal to supply is based on a desire by the dominant firm to integrate vertically into the finished-product market. This is still deemed an abuse under Article 102.

This is more controversial for the reasons given above.[76] A rational firm will seek to enter the market downstream only if it believes that it can produce the finished product more efficiently than the incumbent firms. If it is correct then the consumer will benefit by the product being cheaper. If it is wrong then it will suffer accordingly. The effect of such vertical integration may be that existing firms making the finished product cannot do so if the dominant firm does not have enough raw materials for its own needs and its rivals.[77] This exemplifies the tension mentioned earlier as to whether Article 102 is intended to protect consumers or competitors/the competitive market structure. There may be situations where actions by a dominant firm may benefit consumers, but harm competitors. *Commercial Solvents* signals that if forced to choose the Court will protect the latter.[78]

Refusal by the dominant firm to supply existing customers will therefore be abusive unless there is some objective justification, as will reduction in supplies to firms in a comparable situation in a way which places them at a comparative disadvantage.[79] Thus in *United Brands* the ECJ held that the dominant firm cannot refuse to meet the orders of a long-standing customer who abides by regular commercial practice.[80] The Union Courts are likely to condemn refusal to supply where, as in *Microsoft*,[81] it precludes competitors of the dominant undertaking from bringing innovative goods or services to market.

It is unclear whether the rules on refusal to supply apply to new customers, as opposed to existing customers. The case law has come close to condemning such refusals, as has the Commission,[82] subject to certain conditions.[83] In *BPB*[84] the CFI held that, in deciding how to allocate supplies in times of shortage, a firm must use an objective criterion, and that favouring loyal customers, even marginally, over others did not meet this test.

A refusal to supply can be justified, but it has not been easy for dominant firms to satisfy the Court that such justification exists.[85]

Cases C–468–478/06 Sot Lélos kai Sia EE and Others v GlaxoSmithKline AEVE Farmakeftikon Proïonton
[2008] ECR I–7139[86]

The action was brought by pharmaceutical wholesalers against GSK for its refusal to supply certain medicinal products. The wholesalers had bought the products for a number of years for resale in Greece and other Member States. The national court asked whether the refusal to supply could be

---

[76] See pp 1032–1035.

[77] The ECJ was not convinced that CSC could not meet its own needs and those of Zoja: [1974] ECR 223, [28].

[78] It may be possible to 'square this circle' by arguing that in the long term the consumer will be better off if there are more competitors at the finished-product-market level; and that if the dominant firm really is more efficient than a firm such as Zoja then the latter will not, in any event, survive.

[79] Case 77/77 *Benzine en Petroleum Handelsmaatschappij BV, British Petroleum Raffinerij Nederland NV and British Petroleum Maatschappij Nederland BV v Commission* [1978] ECR 1513.

[80] Case 27/76 *United Brands* (n 4) [182]–[193].

[81] Case T–201/04 (n 8) [643]–[649], [652]–[656].

[82] Dec 87/500 *Boosey & Hawkes* [1987] OJ L286/36, [1988] 4 CMLR 67.

[83] Commission's enforcement priorities (n 20) [78]–[88]; DG Competition Discussion Paper (n 20) [225]–[236].

[84] Case T–65/89 (n 85), upheld on appeal, Case C–310/93 P *BPB Industries plc and British Gypsum Ltd v Commission* [1995] ECR I–865.

[85] Case T–65/89 *BPB Industries plc and British Gypsum Ltd v Commission* [1993] ECR II–389.

[86] S Kingston, Note (2009) 46 CMLRev 683.

justified because the wholesalers engaged in parallel trade to other Member States. The ECJ repeated orthodoxy that refusal by a dominant undertaking to meet the orders of an existing customer constituted abuse for the purposes of Article 82 EC where, without objective justification, that conduct was liable to eliminate a trading party as a competitor.

THE ECJ

35. With regard to a refusal by an undertaking to deliver its products in one Member State to wholesalers which export those products to other Member States, such an effect on competition may exist not only if the refusal impedes the activities of those wholesalers in that first Member State, but equally if it leads to the elimination of effective competition from them in the distribution of the products on the markets of the other Member States.

36. In this case it is common ground between the parties in the main proceedings that, by refusing to meet the Greek wholesalers' orders, GSK AEVE aims to limit parallel exports by those wholesalers to the markets of other Member States in which the selling prices of the medicinal products in dispute are higher.

37. In respect of sectors other than that of pharmaceutical products, the Court has held that a practice by which an undertaking in a dominant position aims to restrict parallel trade in the products that it puts on the market constitutes abuse of that dominant position, particularly when such a practice has the effect of curbing parallel imports by neutralising the more favourable level of prices which may apply in other sales areas in the Community... or when it aims to create barriers to re-importations which come into competition with the distribution network of that undertaking... Indeed, parallel imports enjoy a certain amount of protection in Community law because they encourage trade and help reinforce competition...

...

[*GSK argued that parallel trade brought only few financial benefits to the consumers.*]

53. In that connection, it should be noted that parallel exports of medicinal products from a Member State where the prices are low to other Member States in which the prices are higher open up in principle an alternative source of supply to buyers of the medicinal products in those latter States, which necessarily brings some benefits to the final consumer of those products.

54. It is true, as GSK AEVE has pointed out, that, for medicines subject to parallel exports, the existence of price differences between the exporting and the importing Member States does not necessarily imply that the final consumer in the importing Member State will benefit from a price corresponding to the one prevailing in the exporting Member State, inasmuch as the wholesalers carrying out the exports will themselves make a profit from that parallel trade.

55. Nevertheless, the attraction of the other source of supply which arises from parallel trade in the importing Member State lies precisely in the fact that that trade is capable of offering the same products on the market of that Member State at lower prices than those applied on the same market by the pharmaceuticals companies.

56. As a result, even in the Member States where the prices of medicines are subject to State regulation, parallel trade is liable to exert pressure on prices and, consequently, to create financial benefits not only for the social health insurance funds, but equally for the patients concerned, for whom the proportion of the price of medicines for which they are responsible will be lower...

(ii) *Refusal to Supply: The Essential Facilities Doctrine*

There has been considerable debate about Article 102 and the essential facilities doctrine. This is the idea that the owner of a facility which is not replicable by the ordinary process of innovation and investment, and without access to which competition on a market is impossible or seriously impeded, has to share it with a rival. There is some indication of this doctrine in the Court's jurisprudence and Commission decisions.

Thus the CFI held that Article 102 applies to a refusal to supply a product which is required by another party to produce a different product, even if the second product is in competition with the first and even if the producer of the first product enjoys an intellectual property right. This was established in *RTE*.[87] RTE was a statutory authority providing broadcasting services, and it reserved the exclusive right to publish a weekly schedule of TV programmes for its channels in Ireland. An Irish company, Magill, sought to publish a weekly guide which would have information on all available channels. RTE claimed that this infringed its copyright in the weekly schedule for its channels. The CFI held that RTE, by reserving the exclusive right to publish its weekly television programme listings, was preventing the emergence of a new product, namely a general television magazine likely to compete with its own magazine, the RTE Guide, and that this constituted a breach of Article 102.

The 'essential facilities doctrine' is also apparent in Commission decisions, as evidenced by the *Sealink* case.[88] Sealink owned the port of Holyhead, and operated a ferry service to Ireland. A rival ferry company claimed that Sealink organized the sailing schedules from Holyhead in the most inconvenient way for the rival company. The Commission held that it was an abuse of Article 102 for the owner of an essential facility to use its power in one market to strengthen its position on another related market. This would occur if it granted its competitors access to the related market on terms which were less favourable than those for its own services without any objective justification.[89] There are, however, dangers in the essential facilities doctrine.

D Ridyard, Essential Facilities and the Obligation to Supply Competitors[90]

It will always be tempting for a liberal-minded competition authority to respond favourably to firms who complain about lack of access to new markets, and there are certain instances where the use of essential facilities can legitimately be used as an aid to market liberalisation. There are many other instances, however, in which an uncritical approach favouring market entry can threaten the incentives to dynamic efficiency that provide the engine for economic and technical progress in workably competitive markets.

... To achieve a better balance, some limiting principles need to be found.... The approach suggested in this article is to recognise that essential facilities, and the obligations on essential facilities owners

---

[87] Cases T–69, 70 and 76/89 *RTE, ITP, BBC v Commission* [1991] ECR II–485, upheld on appeal, Cases C–241 and 242/91 P *Radio Telefis Eireann (RTE) and Independent Television Publications Ltd (ITP) v Commission* [1995] ECR I–743. See also Case T–70/89 *British Broadcasting Corporation and British Broadcasting Corporation Enterprises Ltd v Commission* [1991] ECR II–535; Case 238/87 *Volvo AB v Erik Veng (UK) Ltd* [1988] ECR 6211.

[88] [1992] 5 CMLR 255. See also Dec 88/589, *London European Airways/Sabena* [1988] OJ L317/47; Dec 94/19, Case IV/34.689, *Sea Containers Ltd v Stena Sealink Ports and Stena Sealink Line* [1994] OJ L15/84; Case IV/35.388, *Irish Continental Group v CCI Morlaix* [1995] 5 CMLR 177.

[89] [1992] 5 CMLR 255, [41].

[90] [1996] ECLR 438, 451–452. See also J Temple Lang, 'Defining Legitimate Competition: Companies' Duties to Supply Competitors and Access to Essential Facilities' (1994) 18 Fordham Int LJ 437; P Areeda, 'Essential Facilities: An Epithet in Need of Limiting Principles' (1990) 58 Antitrust LJ 841; M Bergman, 'Editorial: The *Bronner* Case—A Turning Point for Essential Facilities' [2000] ECLR 59; B Doherty, 'Just What Are Essential Facilities?' (2001) 38 CMLRev 397; C Stothers, 'Refusal to Supply as Abuse of a Dominant Position: Essential Facilities in the European Union' [2001] ECLR 256; D Ridyard, 'Compulsory Access under EC Competition Law—A New Doctrine of "Convenient Facilities" and the Case for Price Regulation' [2004] ECLR 669, 673; U Muller and A Rodenhausen, 'The Rise and Fall of the Essential Facility Doctrine' [2008] ECLR 310.

that accompany them, should be identified only in circumstances where competition does not and cannot be expected to operate, and with assets that cannot reasonably be subject to effective competition. The fact that it may be inconvenient or costly for competitors to achieve market access by their own devices is not sufficient. Nor is the fact that the asset owner might be enjoying a high return from its policy of refusing to deal with competitors.

Later decisions have taken a more limited view of the essential facilities doctrine. In *Ladbroke* the CFI made it clear that an action for refusal to supply would be plausible only if the product or service being sought was essential for the exercise of the relevant activity. The supply of TV broadcasts concerning horse racing was not essential for the applicant's business of running betting shops.[91] In *ENS*[92] the CFI held that a product or service could not be considered necessary or essential unless there was no real or potential substitute for it. The same cautionary approach is apparent in *Bronner*.

Case C–7/97 Oscar Bronner GmbH & Co KG v Mediaprint Zeitungs- und Zeitschriftenverlag GmbH & Co KG
[1998] ECR I–7791

Bronner published a newspaper that had 3.6 per cent of the market; Mediaprint published newspapers that had 71 per cent of the market. Bronner claimed that Mediaprint had abused its dominant position by not including Bronner's paper in Mediaprint's home delivery service. Mediaprint argued that the establishment of the service was a considerable financial investment, and that, although it had a dominant position, it was not bound to subsidize competing companies. The ECJ held that the ruling in the *RTE* case turned on the fact that the information on the TV schedules was indispensable for the publication of the TV guide; that RTE's action prevented the appearance of a new product; and that there was no objective justification. The ECJ then held that access to Mediaprint's home delivery service was not indispensable to Bronner's primary business of newspaper production.

THE ECJ

43. In the first place, it is undisputed that other methods of distributing daily newspapers, such as by post and through sale in shops and at kiosks, even though they may be less advantageous for the distribution of certain newspapers, exist and are used by the publishers of those daily newspapers.

44. Moreover, it does not appear that there are technical, legal or even economic obstacles capable of making it impossible, or even unreasonably difficult, for any other publisher of daily newspapers to establish...its own nationwide home-delivery scheme....

45. It should be emphasized in that respect that, in order to demonstrate that the creation of such a system is not a realistic potential alternative and that access to the existing system is therefore indispensable, it is not enough to argue that it is not economically viable by reason of the small circulation of the daily newspaper....

46. For such access to be capable of being regarded as indispensable, it would be necessary at the very least to establish, as the Advocate General has pointed out..., that it is not economically viable to create a second home delivery scheme for the distribution of daily newspapers with a circulation comparable to that of the daily newspapers distributed by the existing scheme.

---

91 Case T–504/93 *Tiercé Ladbroke SA v Commission* [1997] ECR II–923.
92 Cases T–374, 375, 384 and 388/94 *European Night Services Ltd (ENS) v Commission* [1998] ECR II–3141, [208]–[209].

A similarly cautionary approach is apparent in the *IMS* case.[93] The ECJ held that there were three conditions to be met before a dominant undertaking could be required to grant a compulsory licence of data protected by an intellectual property right: the undertaking that requested the licence must intend to offer new services for which there was consumer demand that were not offered by the dominant firm; there must be no objective justification for the refusal to grant the licence; and the result of the refusal to supply the licence is to eliminate all competition on the relevant market. The CFI's reasoning in *Microsoft* was to similar effect.[94] It held that refusal by a dominant undertaking to license a third party to use a product covered by an intellectual property right did not in itself constitute an abuse for the purpose of Article 102. It would be abusive, subject to objective justification, only if the refusal related to a product or service indispensable to the exercise of an activity on a neighbouring market; the refusal excluded any effective competition on that neighbouring market; and it prevented the appearance of a new product for which there was potential consumer demand. The application of these criteria can however be contestable, as evidenced by the *Microsoft* case.

(c) ABUSE AND PRICE DISCRIMINATION

(i) *Price Discrimination: Economic Foundations*

Article 102(c) explicitly prohibits the application of dissimilar trading conditions to equivalent transactions. There is price discrimination where goods are sold or purchased at prices which are not related to differences in costs. Thus, price discrimination can cover the situation in which the same product is sold at different, non-cost-related prices. It can also cover the situation where the goods are sold at the same price, even though there are cost differences.

Discrimination can occur in a variety of ways. It may be *geographical*, whereby the undertaking prices at different levels for different local markets, and then seeks to insulate one from the other in order to prevent arbitrage (reselling) between them. It may assume the form of *discounts* or *rebates* that are not related to cost differences, with the objective of tying customers closer to that producer, thereby rendering it more difficult for competitors. It may also appear as *predatory pricing*: the dominant firm seeks to protect its dominance by dropping its prices to deter a would-be entrant to the market, then raising prices again to reap monopoly profits when it has 'seen the other firm off'.

It is common also to distinguish price discrimination according to the nature of the injured party. *Primary-line injury* refers to harm suffered by a competitor at the same level of the market as the dominant firm, as exemplified by loyalty rebates that make it more difficult for a competitor to break into the market. *Secondary-line injury* is concerned with harm to the purchaser of the product. This is exemplified by uniform delivered pricing, whereby goods are sold at the same price irrespective of the fact that one customer is closer to the factory than the other, and therefore transport costs are different in the two instances.

The term 'price discrimination' suggests that differences in the price at which goods are sold are 'bad'. This is not self-evident in economic terms, or the cure may be worse than the disease. There are three reasons why this is so.

The first concerns *measurement* or *assessment*. Price discrimination is dependent on assessment of production costs, which may be difficult to determine. This is particularly problematic in relation to predatory pricing. If a new firm enters the market then the existing dominant firm will respond in some manner, since this is the essence of competition. It is difficult to decide when this response crosses the line between a 'proper' competitive strategy and 'improper' predation. This is because

---

[93] Case C–418/01 *IMS Health GmbH & Co v NDC Health GmbH & Co KG* [2004] ECR I–5039.
[94] Case T–201/04 *Microsoft* (n 8) [331]–[333].

commentators disagree on the test for predation,[95] its application, and upon the empirical likelihood that it will occur.[96] This has led some to argue that legal intervention can be ineffective or worse than the disease.[97] The court may select the wrong criterion. It may choose the 'correct' criterion, but misapply it to the facts. The very existence of the legal rule may, moreover, have a dampening effect on competition.

The second reason price discrimination is not self-evidently bad relates to *allocative efficiency*. In economic theory monopoly is bad because the monopolist restricts output to a greater extent than under normal competitive conditions, with a consequential misallocation of resources within society. The key issue is whether this misallocation will be greater under a regime requiring the charging of a single price to all customers, or under one which permits price discrimination. This depends upon whether the price discrimination would have the effect of further restricting output, or whether it might actually lead to an increase in output.

W Bishop, Price Discrimination under Article 86:
Political Economy in the European Court[98]

If a monopolist were able to charge each customer exactly that customer's maximum price, then the monopolist would realise very large profits, but output would be identical to that under perfect competition with not a single sale being sacrificed because of higher price. This is called perfectly discriminating monopoly and is very rare, perhaps non-existent.

Much more important is imperfect price discrimination—different prices in a number of different markets or for different classes of customers. British Rail for example discriminates by offering special discounts to students for no reason other than that most of them would not travel by train otherwise, and a little more revenue is better than none at all when it costs virtually nothing to carry an extra passenger outside peak hours.

In *United Brands* the court condemned imperfect price discrimination when practised on a regional basis so as to divide the common market into a number of sub-markets with different, discriminatory prices. However it is not at all clear that imperfect price discrimination generally reduces output below the level that would prevail under simple monopoly. Whether output under imperfectly discriminating monopoly is nearer the perfectly competitive or further from it will depend upon the facts of each case. Unfortunately in any real case the facts are extremely difficult to ferret out—in practice usually impossible to ascertain at all.

Moreover, as several economists have demonstrated, it is conceivable that price discrimination in practice may reduce economic efficiency, i.e. increase the misallocation of money and resources, even if it increases output as compared with output in the absence of discrimination. Probably the best we can do is to adopt one general rule on price discrimination. Many economists guess that price discrimination is probably on balance efficient, assuming that there will be monopoly anyway. Certainly there is no reason to believe that a rule prohibiting it will promote more efficient allocation of resources. Furthermore it is clear that enforcing the prohibition will lead both enforcers and defendants to incur costs that consume real social resources.

---

[95] (N 110).
[96] Bork (n 41) 144–159.
[97] Ibid.
[98] (1981) 44 MLR 282, 287–288. See also Bork (n 41) 394–398; P Muysert, 'Price Discrimination—An Unreliable Indicator of Market Power' [2004] ECLR 353; M Lorenz, M Lubbig, and A Russell, 'Price Discrimination: A Tender Story' [2005] ECLR 355.

The third reason to be cautious about rules against price discrimination relates to *fairness*. This may seem intuitively odd, for many regard price discrimination as unfair. This is less self-evident than is normally thought. Bishop provides a succinct formulation of the counter-argument.

W Bishop, Price Discrimination under Article 86: Political Economy in the European Court[99]

The rule in *United Brands* requires any monopolist who hitherto has discriminated in price between national submarkets to discontinue this practice. Henceforth such a monopolist must charge the same price (with due allowance for cost differences). Generally speaking discriminating monopolists will find it profitable to charge higher prices in higher income countries...than in lower income countries....Suppose these firms are now required to charge only one price. Almost certainly the profit maximising price will lie somewhere between the highest and lowest discriminatory prices that such a firm could charge...consider the effect on income distribution as between high and low income countries. German consumers of (say) bananas get them at a lower price than before. Also some German consumers who did not buy bananas before do buy them now. All these German consumers are better off. Some British consumers who bought before now drop out of the market because the price is too high. Remaining British consumers pay more. All these British consumers are worse off. So, though efficiency effects in this example are ambiguous, distributional effects are quite clear: income is redistributed away from Britain and toward Germany. The general effect of *United Brands* is clear—*it redistributes income away from consumers in the poorer regions of Europe and toward consumers in the richer regions.*

It may be argued that this ignores the importance of the creation of a *single market*, hence the Court's opposition to divisions along national lines. This is not a self-evident justification for all the ECJ's jurisprudence. We can lose sight of substance by concentrating upon form. The rationale for a single market in economic terms was to create greater efficiency:[100]

To that end striking down arrangements in which arbitrary national barriers are preserved is a goal of the Community institutions. But that is very different from charging different prices in geographically separated markets, simply because the markets happen to be different countries. It is also very different when the effect of prohibiting the practice is possibly to induce greater misallocation of resources and certainly to redistribute wealth from the poor to the rich. The common European market was set up *as a means to the opposite ends*, so a general appeal to those means cannot justify the decision.

(ii) *Price Discrimination: The Case Law*

Case 27/76 **United Brands Company and United Brands Continentaal BV v Commission** [1978] ECR 207

The facts were set out above. UB was accused of price discrimination. It shipped bananas from Central America to Europe. Some of these bore the brand name 'Chiquita', and these tended to fetch a higher price. UB sold the goods to ripeners, who sold them to wholesalers, who in turn sold to retailers.

---

[99] Bishop (n 98) 288–289, italics in the original.
[100] Ibid 288–289, italics in the original.

The bananas were landed at two ports, but there were no real differences in unloading costs. The Commission alleged that UB sold the bananas at different prices in different Member States, and that it did so without objective justification. The essence of UB's response was to contend that the price differentials reflected market forces, viz the average anticipated market price in each state; that the Community had not established a single banana market; and that, therefore, it was not possible to avoid differences in the individual supply/demand situations in different countries.

THE ECJ

227. Although the responsibility for establishing the single banana market does not lie with the applicant, it can only endeavour to take 'what the market can bear' provided that it complies with the rules for the regulation and coordination of the market laid down by the Treaty.

228. Once it can be grasped that differences in transport costs, taxation, customs duties, the wages of the labour force, the conditions of marketing, the differences in the parity of the currencies, the density of competition may eventually culminate in different retail selling price levels according to the Member States, then it follows that those differences are factors which UBC only has to take into account to a limited extent since it sells a product which is always the same and at the same place to ripener/distributors who—alone—bear the risks of the consumers' market.

229. The interplay of supply and demand should, owing to its nature, only be applied to each stage where it is really manifest.

230. The mechanisms of the market are adversely affected if the price is calculated by leaving out one stage of the market and taking into account the law of supply and demand as between the vendor and the ultimate consumer and not as between the vendor (UBC) and the purchaser (the ripener/distributor).

231. Thus, by reason of its dominant position UBC...was in fact able to impose its selling price on the intermediate purchaser....

232. These discriminatory prices, which varied according to the circumstances of the Member States, were just so many obstacles to the free movement of goods and were intensified by the clause forbidding the resale of bananas while still green and by reducing the deliveries of the quantities ordered.

233. A rigid partitioning of national markets was thus created at price levels which were artificially different, placing certain distributor/ripeners at a competitive disadvantage, since compared with what it should have been competition had thereby been distorted.

There is much confusion in this extract. The judgment omits any consideration of the general issue whether price discrimination can be beneficial, and the reasoning is punctuated by the mistaken use of concepts. It is, for example, central to the judgment that UB would have to take account of the many factors that differentiated the various retail markets only to a limited extent, and that the risks would instead be borne by the distributors/ripeners: paragraph 228. This is highly questionable. A manufacturer may well bear the risk of differing demand conditions at the retail level. UB almost certainly did bear these risks. If it tried to shift these risks to the distributors, then it would have to give financial inducements to the latter.[101] The Court's references to the markets in which supply and demand is really manifest are equally problematic.[102]

---

[101] Bishop (n 98) 285–286.
[102] Ibid 284–285.

Case 85/76 **Hoffmann-La Roche & Co AG v Commission**
[1979] ECR 461

The case turned on abusive practices by HLR in the vitamins markets, one aspect of this being HLR's practice of giving rebates.

THE ECJ

89. An undertaking which is in a dominant position on a market and ties purchasers—even if it does so at their request—by an obligation or promise on their part to obtain all or most of their requirements exclusively from the said undertaking abuses its dominant position within the meaning of Article 86 of the Treaty, whether the obligation in question is stipulated without further qualification or whether it is undertaken in consideration of the grant of the rebate. The same applies if the said undertaking, without tying the purchasers by a formal obligation, applies, either under the terms of agreements concluded with these purchasers or unilaterally, a system of fidelity rebates, that is to say discounts conditional on the customer's obtaining all or most of its requirements—whether the quantity of its purchases be large or small—from the undertaking in the dominant position.

90. Obligations of this kind...are incompatible with the objective of undistorted competition within the Common Market, because...they are not based on an economic transaction which justifies this burden or benefit but are designed to deprive the purchaser of or restrict his possible choices of sources of supply and to deny other producers access to the market. The fidelity rebate, unlike quantity rebates exclusively linked with the volume of purchases from the producer concerned, is designed through the grant of a financial advantage to prevent customers from obtaining their supplies from competing producers. Furthermore, the effect of fidelity rebates is to apply dissimilar conditions to equivalent transactions with other trading parties in that two purchasers pay a different price for the same quantity of the same product depending on whether they obtain their supplies exclusively from the undertaking in a dominant position or have several sources of supply....

91. For the purpose of rejecting the finding that there has been an abuse of a dominant position the interpretation suggested by the applicant that an abuse implies that the use of the economic power bestowed by the dominant position is the means whereby the abuse has been brought about cannot be accepted. The concept of abuse is an objective concept relating to the behaviour of an undertaking in a dominant position which is such as to influence the structure of the market where, as a result of the very presence of the undertaking in question, the degree of competition is weakened and which, through recourse to methods different from those which condition normal competition in products or services on the basis of the transactions of commercial operators, has the effect of hindering the maintenance of the degree of competition still existing in the market or the growth of that competition.

The ECJ thus reiterated the point made in *Continental Can*: there was no need to prove that the abuse had been brought about by the firm's market power. The concept of abuse was 'objective', and could apply to any behaviour which influenced the 'structure' of the market and weakened competition. The ECJ's antipathy to price discrimination in the form of loyalty rebates emerges clearly in the above extract.[103] This reasoning has been followed in later cases,[104] and it has been held that even

---

[103] D Ridyard, 'Exclusionary Pricing and Price Discrimination Abuses under Article 82—An Economic Analysis' [2002] ECLR 286.

[104] Case 322/81 *Michelin* (n 53); Case T–228/97 *Irish Sugar* (n 37) [111]–[114]; Case T–301/04 *Clearstream* (n 8); Case C–52/07 *Kanal 5* (n 32) [42]–[48]; Case T–155/06 *Tomra Systems ASA v European Commission* [2010] ECR II–4361, [207]–[209]; Case T–286/09 *Intel Corp v European Commission* EU:T:2014:547, [72]–[78].

a quantity rebate system may be contrary to Article 102 if it is not based on economically justified considerations, more especially if it tends, like fidelity rebates, to prevent a customer obtaining supplies from elsewhere.[105] Particular decisions have however been heavily criticized,[106] and there has been a more general call for a principled, economic approach to be applied to the pricing policies of dominant firms.[107] However more recently the ECJ held in the *Post Danmark* case[108] that the fact that a dominant firm charges different prices to those in the same situation did not in itself constitute an exclusionary abuse.

(D) ABUSE AND PREDATORY PRICING

Predatory pricing has already been touched on above. It is now time to focus specifically on this abusive behaviour. *Akzo* is the leading case.

Case C–62/86 Akzo Chemie BV v Commission
[1991] ECR I–3359

[Note Lisbon Treaty renumbering: Art 86 is now Art 102 TFEU]

Akzo, based in the Netherlands, and ECS, a smaller UK firm, both made organic peroxides. Benzoyl peroxide could be used in the flour and the plastics markets. ECS was initially engaged in the flour market, but then moved into the plastics market in 1979 and solicited some of Akzo's customers. Akzo had a meeting with ECS at which it threatened that it would take aggressive action on the flour market unless ECS withdrew from the plastics market. ECS ignored the threats, which Akzo then put into operation. Akzo targeted certain of ECS's customers in the flour market, and offered them prices which were below previous rates and below average total cost. Akzo subsidized these low prices by money drawn from the plastics sector. ECS's business fell significantly as a result. The Court quoted the test of abuse from *Hoffmann-La Roche* set out above,[109] and then reasoned as follows.

THE ECJ

70. It follows that Article 86 prohibits a dominant undertaking from eliminating a competitor and thereby strengthening its position by using methods other than those which come within the scope of competition on the basis of quality. From that point of view, however, not all competition by means of price can be regarded as legitimate.

71. Prices below average variable costs (that is to say, those which vary depending on the quantities produced) by means of which a dominant undertaking seeks to eliminate a competitor must be regarded as abusive. A dominant undertaking has no interest in applying such prices except that of eliminating competitors so as to enable it subsequently to raise its prices by taking advantage of its monopolistic position, since each sale generates a loss, namely the total amount of the fixed costs (that

---

[105] Case C–163/99 *Portugal v Commission* [2001] ECR I–2613; Case T–219/99 *British Airways* (n 11), upheld in Case C–95/04 P *British Airways* (n 62); Case T–203/01 *Michelin* (n 53) [58]–[62], [95].

[106] B Sher, 'Price Discounts and *Michelin II*: What Goes Around Comes Around' [2002] ECLR 482.

[107] J Temple Lang and R O'Donoghue, 'Defining Legitimate Competition: How to Clarify Pricing Abuses under Article 82 EC' (2002) 26 Fordham Int LJ 83.

[108] Case C–209/10 *Post Danmark A/S v Konkurrencerådet* EU:C:2012:172, [30].

[109] See pp 1061–1062.

is to say, those which remain constant regardless of the quantities produced) and, at least, part of the variable costs relating to the unit produced.

72. Moreover, prices below average total costs, that is to say, fixed costs plus variable costs, but above average variable costs, must be regarded as abusive if they are determined as part of a plan for eliminating a competitor. Such prices can drive from the market undertakings which are perhaps as efficient as the dominant undertaking but which, because of their smaller financial resources, are incapable of withstanding the competition waged against them.

The ECJ found Akzo to have violated these principles. It had offered prices to ECS's customers that were lower than Akzo's average total or variable costs, and had done so to remove ECS from the plastics market. Its behaviour was blatant. This should not lead us to underestimate the difficulties predatory pricing presents for competition policy.

First, there is continuing disagreement about the proper definition of predation in economic terms.[110] This ground of challenge may do more harm than good, since the line between vigorous price competition and illegal predation may be a fine one.[111] A dominant firm may feel that it should not pursue price competition too vigorously, lest this should leave it open to allegations of predatory abuse, given that on the *Akzo* test intention is of crucial importance where prices are below average total costs, but above average variable costs.

Secondly, there are those who doubt whether a rational firm would engage in predation. The potential gains from successful predation appear straightforward: the dominant firm lowers its prices, takes a loss in the short term, drives out the smaller firm, and then reaps high monopoly profits. The economic reality is much less certain. For predation to be a rational strategy the future flow of profits has to exceed the present losses incurred as a result of the drop in price. This is more difficult to achieve than might be thought. Predation is, in this sense, a war of attrition, with the outcome to be determined by the combatants' relative losses and reserves: the 'war will be a *Blitzkrieg* only if the predator has greatly disproportionate reserves or is able to inflict very disproportionate losses'.[112]

Thirdly, there are real obstacles to a successful campaign. The losses during the battle will be higher for the predator than the victim. The predator will have to gauge the likelihood of another competitor entering the market, should it seek to reap excessive monopoly profits having disposed of the original combatant.[113] The threat of further predation may constitute a barrier to entry for prospective competitors, but the fact remains that the greater the monopoly profits now reaped by the predator, the greater the incentive for new entrants.

Whether Akzo was behaving rationally depends on whether its present losses were outweighed by future gains.[114] The answer is unclear. The losses to the predator from the campaign will however be lower if it can price discriminate, by charging higher prices to its traditional customers while

---

[110] P Areeda and D Turner, 'Predatory Pricing and Related Practices under Section 2 of the Sherman Act: A Comment' (1975) 88 Harv LRev 697; FM Scherer, 'Predatory Pricing and the Sherman Act: A Comment' (1976) 89 Harv LRev 869; O Williamson, 'Predatory Pricing: A Strategic and Welfare Analysis' (1977) 87 Yale LJ 284; J Brodley and G Hay, 'Predatory Pricing: Competing Economic Theories and the Evolution of Legal Standards' (1981) 66 Cornell L Rev 738; E Mastromanolis, 'Predatory Pricing Strategies in the European Union: A Case for Legal Reform' [1998] ECLR 211.

[111] As recognized by the Commission, DG Competition Discussion Paper (n 20) [94]–[97]; M Gravengaard, 'The Meeting Competition Defence Principle—A Defence for Price Discrimination and Predatory Pricing' [2006] ECLR 658.

[112] Bork (n 41) 147; J Glockner and L Bruttel, 'Predatory Pricing and Recoupment under EC Competition Law—Per se Rules, Underlying Assumptions and the Reality: Results of an Experimental Study' [2010] ECLR 423.

[113] Bork (n 41) 149–155.

[114] R Rapp, 'Predatory Pricing and Entry Deterring Strategies: The Economics of *AKZO*' [1986] ECLR 233.

poaching ECS's customers with lower prices. It appears that Akzo did this, though how long this strategy could have been maintained is more debatable.

The ECJ has continued with its strategy. Thus in *Tetra Pak*[115] it held that Tetra Pak, a world leader in the manufacture of aseptic cartons for liquid and semi-liquid food, had abused its dominant position by its pricing policy on non-aseptic cartons. The company had a dominant position on the market for aseptic cartons, and it had used profits from this market to subsidize sales on the market for non-aseptic cartons, selling the latter at a loss below average variable cost in seven Member States. The ECJ reiterated the holding in paragraphs 72 and 73 of *Akzo*. It was argued that the Commission and CFI should have taken into account whether Tetra Pak had any realistic chance of recouping its losses. This argument was rejected by the ECJ, which held that it must be possible to penalize predation whenever there was a risk that competitors would be eliminated, and that this objective ruled out waiting until such a strategy resulted in the actual elimination of competitors.[116]

This holding was reiterated in *France Télécom*,[117] where the ECJ held that proof of recoupment of loss was not required to find predation under Article 102, although the possibility of such recoupment could be relevant in deciding whether the behaviour was abusive.[118] Moreover in *Deutsche Telekom*[119] the ECJ held that a dominant undertaking could not drive from the market undertakings that were as efficient as the dominant undertaking but which, because of their smaller financial resources, were incapable of withstanding the competition waged against them.

However the approach in *Post Danmark* was more nuanced,[120] the ECJ concluding that low prices would not be considered to be an exclusionary abuse merely because the price was lower than the average total costs attributed to the activity concerned, but higher than the average incremental costs pertaining to that activity. It was necessary to consider whether that pricing policy, without objective justification, produced an actual or likely exclusionary effect, to the detriment of competition and, thereby, of consumers' interests.

(E) ABUSE AND SELECTIVE PRICING

It is clear from cases such as *Irish Sugar*[121] that when judging the legality of a selective pricing policy the General Court and ECJ will take account of the fact that the practice was aimed at eliminating a competitor from the market. This was reaffirmed in the following case.

Cases C–395–396/96 P **Compagnie Maritime Belge Transports SA, Compagnie Maritime Belge SA and Dafra Lines A/S v Commission**
[2000] ECR I–1365

The applicants were members of a liner conference that had a dominant position on certain shipping routes in Africa. They were charged with the lowering of their freight rates in order to drive the only competitor from the market.

---

[115] Case C–333/94 P (n 3).
[116] Ibid [44].
[117] Case C–202/07 P (n 6) [109]–[113].
[118] See also, Case C–52/09 *TeliaSonera Sverige* (n 68) [40]–[45].
[119] Case C–280/08 P *Deutsche Telekom AG v European Commission* [2010] ECR I–9555.
[120] Case C–209/10 *Post Danmark* (n 108) [44].
[121] Case T–228/97 (n 37) [114]; Case T–271/03 *Deutsche Telekom AG v Commission* [2008] ECR II–477.

THE ECJ

117. ...where a liner conference in a dominant position selectively cuts its prices in order deliberately to match those of a competitor, it derives a dual benefit. First, it eliminates the principal, and possibly the only, means of competition open to the competing undertaking. Second, it can continue to require its users to pay higher prices for the services which are not threatened by that competition.

118. It is not necessary, in the present case, to rule generally on the circumstances in which a liner conference may legitimately...adopt lower prices than those of its advertised tariff in order to compete with a competitor who quotes lower prices....

119. It is sufficient to recall that the conduct at issue here is that of a conference having a share of over 90% of the market in question and only one competitor. The appellants have, moreover, never seriously disputed, and indeed admitted at the hearing, that the purpose of the conduct complained of was to eliminate G & C from the market.

6 DEFENCES: OBJECTIVE JUSTIFICATION, PROPORTIONALITY, AND EFFICIENCY

Article 102 has no equivalent to Article 101(3). The Court and Commission[122] have however applied the concepts of objective justification and proportionality to provide some flexibility in what would otherwise be too draconian an application of Article 102.[123] Thus if there is an objective justification for the dominant firm's conduct, and it is proportionate, then it will escape condemnation.[124] While objective justification and proportionality imbue Article 102 with added flexibility, their application is not self-executing. The decision, for example, whether a refusal to supply is objectively justified and proportionate will often reflect certain assumptions concerning the relative importance of protecting competitors and consumers, or the relative significance of single market integration and consumer welfare. The Commission has more recently indicated that an efficiency defence should be available under Article 102, provided that the efficiencies outweigh the negative effects of the relevant conduct.[125]

7 ARTICLE 102: REFORM

In 2005 the Commission undertook a review of Article 102.[126] This was felt to be timely, given the reviews of Article 101 and merger policy, and the disquiet about some decisions under Article 102.

---

[122] DG Competition Discussion Paper (n 20) [77], [84]; Commission's enforcement priorities (n 20) [28]–[31].

[123] A Albors-Llorens, 'The Role of Objective Justification and Efficiencies in the Application of Article 82 EC' (2007) 44 CMLRev 1727.

[124] See, eg, Case 27/76 *United Brands* (n 4); Case T–65/89 *BPB* (n 85); Case T–30/89 *Hilti* (n 35); Case 311/84 *Centre Belge d'Etudes du Marché-Télémarketing (CBEM) v CLT SA* [1985] ECR 3261; Case C–209/10 *Post Danmark* (n 108) [41]–[42].

[125] Commission's enforcement priorities (n 20) [28]–[31]; DG Competition Discussion Paper (n 20); Commissioner Kroes, 'Preliminary Thoughts on Policy Review of Article 82' Speech at the Fordham Corporate Law Institute (Sept 2005) 5, available at http://ec.europa.eu/comm/competition/antitrust/art82/index.html.

[126] DG Competition Discussion Paper (n 20); Dethmers and Dodoo (n 29); B Sher, 'The Last of the Steam-Powered Trains: Modernising Article 82' [2004] ECLR 243; G Niels and H Jenkins, 'Reform of Article 82: Where the Link between Dominance and Effects Breaks Down' [2005] ECLR 605; A Majumdar, 'Whither Dominance' [2006] ECLR 161.

The Discussion Paper led to the Commission issuing Guidance on the Commission's enforcement priorities under Article 102 in December 2008.[127] The Commission's philosophy is to protect consumers, rather than particular competitors, but this requires the safeguarding of the competitive process from foreclosure.[128] The Guidance focused on exclusionary conduct leading to anti-competitive foreclosure, defined as 'a situation where effective access of actual or potential competitors to supplies or markets is hampered or eliminated as a result of the conduct of the dominant undertaking whereby the dominant undertaking is likely to be in a position to profitably increase prices to the detriment of consumers'.[129]

The Commission's Guidance analyses conduct by a dominant undertaking that might lead to such anti-competitive foreclosure, although it is willing to consider arguments that efficiency gains outweigh anti-competitive effects in each type of case.[130] Exclusive dealing, in particular exclusive purchasing obligations, can lead to such foreclosure where it prevents entry or expansion of rival firms,[131] and conditional rebates can have the same impact.[132] Competitive foreclosure can also occur through tying and bundling, whereby customers that buy one product from the dominant undertaking are also required to purchase another product. The Commission signalled its intent to intervene where the tying and tied products are distinct and where the tying practice leads to anti-competitive foreclosure.[133] Predation is a further species of anti-competitive foreclosure that features in the Commission Guidance.[134] So too is refusal to supply, including new customers, where the refusal relates to a product that is objectively necessary to enable competition on a downstream market, the refusal is likely to eliminate competition on the downstream market and consumers will be harmed.[135]

The review also raised broader issues concerning Article 102,[136] the extent to which it should be based on legal form or economic effects, and how far institutional realities limited what the Commission could do.[137] The Discussion Paper stated that 'in applying Article 82, the Commission will adopt an approach which is based on the likely effects on the market',[138] and this is exemplified to some degree by its treatment of particular exclusionary abuses in the later Guidance.[139] Whether this goes far enough for those who advocate an economic-effects approach to Article 102 is less certain. Thus the Economic Advisory Group on Competition Policy (EAGCP) argued for an economics-based approach, whereby assessment would not be undertaken on the form of the particular business practice, tying, exclusive dealing, etc, but on the anti-competitive effects that it generated, and the extent to which they were outweighed by efficiency gains.[140] Similar concerns were voiced by Vickers.

---

[127] Commission's enforcement priorities (n 20); A Ezrachi, 'The European Commission Guidance on Article 82 EC—The Way in which Institutional Realities Limit the Potential for Reform', Oxford Legal Research Paper Series, Paper No 27/2009; L Lovdahl Gormsen, 'Why the European Commission's Enforcement Priorities on Article 82 EC should be Withdrawn' [2010] ECLR 45; M Kellerbauer, 'The Commission's New Enforcement Priorities in Applying Article 82 EC to Dominant Companies' Exclusionary Conduct: A Shift towards a More Economic Approach?' [2010] ECLR 175.

[128] Commission's enforcement priorities (n 20) [6]; DG Competition Discussion Paper (n 20) [1], [4], [55]–[56]; Commissioner Kroes (n 125) 3.

[129] Commission's enforcement priorities (n 20) [19].

[130] Ibid [28]–[31].

[131] Ibid [34]–[36].

[132] Ibid [37]–[45].

[133] Ibid [47]–[62]; Case T–201/04 *Microsoft* (n 8) [842], [859]–[862], [867]–[869].

[134] Ibid [63]–[73].

[135] Ibid [81].

[136] P Akman, 'Searching for the Long-Lost Soul of Article 82 EC' (2009) 29 OJLS 267.

[137] Ezrachi (n 127).

[138] DG Competition Discussion Paper (n 20) [4].

[139] Commission's enforcement priorities (n 20).

[140] Report by EAGCP, 'An Economic Approach to Article 82' (2005), available at http://ec.europa.eu/comm/competition/antitrust/art82/index.html.

J Vickers, Abuse of Market Power[141]

The law on abuse of market power is far from settled. The law in Europe could now develop in either of two broad directions, with emphasis either on form or on economic effect. Form-based evolution of the law would further develop descriptions of conduct for dominant firms to avoid. Economics-based evolution would clarify underlying principles in terms of actual and potential economic effects, develop practically administrable rules and methods explicitly on the basis of those principles, and apply them to cases.

In the competition between economics- and form-based approaches the former has strong advantages. It can align the law with its economic purpose and in an internally consistent manner. It can prevent form from triumphing over substance at the cost of both allowing detrimental conduct and blocking benign conduct. And it can provide clarity at fundamental, rather than superficial level. These advantages will be realized if European competition law on abuse of dominance becomes more firmly anchored to economic principles, and where those principles are practically applicable by competition lawyers and the courts.

To say that the law on abuse of dominance should develop a stronger economic foundation is not to say that rules of law should be replaced by discretionary decision making based on whatever is thought to be desirable in economic terms case by case. There must be rules of law in this area of competition policy, not least for reasons of predictability and accountability. So the issue is not rules versus discretion, but how well the rules are grounded in economics. To that end there is great scope for economic analysis and research to contribute to the development of the law on abuse of dominance. To be effective, however, economics must contribute in a way that competition agencies, and ultimately the courts, find practicable in deciding the cases.

8 CONCLUSIONS

i. It is now generally accepted that Article 102 is to protect consumers rather than particular competitors, and that this requires protection of the competitive process from foreclosure.

ii. Adjudication under Article 102 nonetheless involves difficult problems relating to market definition, the determination of dominance, and the meaning of abuse.

iii. The boundaries of the special responsibility incumbent on dominant firms are not clear from the case law, thereby making it difficult for the dominant firm to know what it is allowed to do.

iv. There is continuing debate as to the detailed ramifications of a shift from legal form to economic effect under Article 102.

v. The enforcement of Article 102 is now subject to the reformed regime discussed in a previous chapter, to which reference should be made.[142]

9 FURTHER READING

(a) Books

BELLAMY, C, AND CHILD, G, *European Union Law of Competition* (edited by P Roth and V Rose, Oxford University Press, 7th edn, 2013)

---

[141] (2005) 115 Economic Journal 244, 259.
[142] See pp 1048–1052.

BISHOP, S, AND WALKER, M, *The Economics of EC Competition Law: Concepts, Application and Measurement* (Sweet & Maxwell, 3rd edn, 2010)

EZRACHI, A (ed), *Article 82: Reflections on its Recent Evolution* (Hart, 2009)

FAULL, J, AND NIKPAY, A (eds), *The EU Law of Competition* (Oxford University Press, 3rd edn, 2014)

GOYDER, D, GOYDER, J, AND ALBORS-LLORENS, A, *Goyder's Competition Law* (Oxford University Press, 5th edn, 2009)

JONES, A, AND SUFRIN, B, *EU Competition Law: Text, Cases, and Materials* (Oxford University Press, 5th edn, 2014)

KORAH, V, *An Introductory Guide to EC Competition Law and Practice* (Hart, 9th edn, 2007)

MIDDLETON, K, RODGER, B, AND MacCULLOCH, A, *Cases and Materials on UK and EC Competition Law* (Oxford University Press, 2nd edn, 2009)

WHISH, R, AND BAILEY, D, *Competition Law* (Oxford University Press, 7th edn, 2012)

(b) Articles

AKMAN, P, 'Searching for the Long-Lost Soul of Article 82 EC' (2009) 29 OJLS 267

—— 'The Role of Intent in the EU Case Law on Abuse of Dominance' (2014) 39 ELRev 316

ALBORS-LLORENS, A, 'The Role of Objective Justification and Efficiencies in the Application of Article 82 EC' (2007) 44 CMLRev 1727

DOHERTY, B, 'Just What Are Essential Facilities?' (2001) 38 CMLRev 397

EILMANSBERGER, T, 'How to Distinguish Good from Bad Competition under Article 82: In Search of Clearer and More Coherent Standards for Anti-Competitive Abuses' (2005) 42 CMLRev 49

EZRACHI, A, 'The European Commission Guidance on Article 82 EC—The Way in which Institutional Realities Limit the Potential for Reform', Oxford Legal Research Paper Series, Paper No 27/2009

GLOCKNER, J, AND BRUTTEL, L, 'Predatory Pricing and Recoupment under EC Competition Law—Per se Rules, Underlying Assumptions and the Reality: Results of an Experimental Study' [2010] ECLR 423

GRAVENGAARD, M, 'The Meeting Competition Defence—A Defence for Price Discrimination and Predatory Pricing' [2006] ECLR 658

HEIT, J, 'The Justifiability of the ECJ's Wide Approach to the Concept of Barriers to Entry' [2006] ECLR 117

HOWARTH, D, AND McMAHON, K, '"Windows Has Performed an Illegal Operation": The Court of First Instance's Judgment in *Microsoft v Commission*' [2008] ECLR 117

KALLAUGHER, J, AND SHER, B, 'Rebates Revisited: Anti-Competitive Effects and Exclusionary Abuse under Article 82' [2004] ECLR 263

KELLERBAUER, M, 'The Commission's New Enforcement Priorities in Applying Article 82 EC to Dominant Companies' Exclusionary Conduct: A Shift towards a More Economic Approach?' [2010] ECLR 175

LORENZ, M, LUBBIG, M, AND RUSSELL, A, 'Price Discrimination: A Tender Story' [2005] ECLR 355

MONTI, G, 'The Scope of Collective Dominance under Article 82' (2001) 38 CMLRev 131

MULLER, U, AND RODENHAUSEN, A, 'The Rise and Fall of the Essential Facility Doctrine' [2008] ECLR 310

RIDYARD, D, 'Essential Facilities and the Obligation to Supply Competitors under UK and EC Competition Law' [1996] ECLR 438

—— 'Exclusionary Pricing and Price Discrimination Abuses under Article 82—An Economic Analysis' [2002] ECLR 286

ROUSSEVA, E, and MARQUIS, M, 'Hell Freezes Over: A Climate Change for Assessing Exclusionary Conduct under Article 102 TFEU' (2013) 4 Journal of European Competition Law and Practice 32

SUBIOTTO, R, AND O'DONOGHUE, R, 'Defining the Scope of the Duty of Dominant Firms to Deal with Existing Customers under Article 82' [2003] ECLR 683

TEMPLE LANG, J, 'How Can the Problems of Exclusionary Abuses under Article 102 TFEU be Resolved?' (2012) 37 ELRev 136

—— AND O'DONOGHUE, R, 'Defining Legitimate Competition: How to Clarify Pricing Abuses under Article 82 EC' (2002) 26 Fordham Int LJ 83

TURNBULL, S, 'Barriers to Entry, Article 86 EC and the Abuse of a Dominant Position: An Economic Critique of European Community Competition Law' [1996] ECLR 96

VICKERS, J, 'Abuse of Market Power' (2005) 115 Economic Journal 244

WHISH, R, 'Collective Dominance' in D O'Keefe and A Bavasso (eds), *Judicial Review in European Union Law* (Kluwer, 2000) ch 37

—— AND SUFRIN, B, 'Oligopolistic Markets and EC Competition Law' (1992) 12 YBEL 59

28

COMPETITION LAW: MERGERS

1 CENTRAL ISSUES

i.   Legal control of mergers is an important component of competition policy. EU regulation of mergers was however a long time coming.[1] Articles 85 and 86 EEC (now Articles 101 and 102 TFEU) made no specific mention of mergers. The Commission attempted to fill this gap as early as 1973.[2] While the Member States recognized that merger control was necessary, they disagreed on the boundary between EU and national merger control, and on the precise form of EU control.

ii. The ECJ partially filled the gap resulting from legislative inaction. Article 102 was invoked in *Continental Can*[3] to catch mergers by a firm in a dominant position. The Court took longer to apply Article 101 to mergers. The traditional orthodoxy was that it did not apply to agreements to acquire ownership. This orthodoxy was shaken in the *BAT* case, where the ECJ indicated its willingness to consider the application of Article 101 to some instances of share acquisition.[4]

iii. Regulation 4064/89 was finally adopted in December 1989.[5] There have been subsequent amendments and the current regime is to be found in Regulation 139/2004 and accompanying provisions.[6] Most concentrations will now be dealt with under this Regulation, but it may still be possible to use Articles 101 and 102 in certain cases.

iv. It is important to understand the policy reasons underlying merger control, which are examined at the outset of this chapter. There are jurisdictional, procedural, and substantive aspects to EU merger policy.

v.   Jurisdictional issues cover the types of concentration that are subject to the Merger Regulation and the interrelationship between merger control at EU and national levels.

---

[1] A Jones and B Sufrin, *EU Competition Law: Text, Cases, and Materials* (Oxford University Press, 5th edn, 2014) 1134–1137.

[2] Commission Proposal for a Regulation of the Council of Ministers on the Control of Concentrations between Undertakings [1973] OJ C92/1.

[3] Case 6/72 [1973] ECR 215.

[4] Cases 142 and 156/84 *British American Tobacco Co Ltd and RJ Reynolds Industries Inc v Commission* [1987] ECR 4487.

[5] [1989] OJ L395/1.

[6] Council Regulation (EC) No 139/2004 of 20 January 2004 on the control of concentrations between undertakings (the EC Merger Regulation) [2004] OJ L24/1.

vi. Procedural issues cover matters such as the way in which notice of a proposed merger must be given and the investigative powers of the Commission.

vii. Substantive issues of merger policy include matters such as the test for determining whether a merger or concentration should be allowed and the extent to which efficiencies produced by the concentration should be taken into account.

2 MERGER CONTROL: THE POLICY RATIONALE

Mergers can be of three kinds. Horizontal mergers are those between companies that make the same products and operate at the same level of the market. Vertical mergers are those between companies that operate at different distributive levels of the same product market. Conglomerate mergers are those between firms which have no connection in any product market. Horizontal mergers are potentially the most damaging to the competitive process.

(A) ARGUMENTS AGAINST MERGERS

A merger can have a *marked impact on competition*. A horizontal merger may enable the new entity to set price and output as a single-firm monopolist. In some countries indices are used to measure the reduction of competition brought about by the merger.[7] The impact of vertical mergers on competition is more controversial.[8] A vertical merger is one form of vertical integration: a company may relate to those down-market in different ways ranging from ordinary contract, through exclusive-distribution arrangements, to vertical merger. Such vertical relationships can be potentially anti-competitive through, for example, foreclosing of outlets to other manufacturers,[9] but commentators also dispute how far these vertical relationships harm competition.[10] This disagreement carries over into vertical merger, since it may, for example, improve distribution of a branded product and hence promote inter-brand competition. There is also disagreement on the impact of conglomerate mergers on competition. Thus, while some see them as dangerous, allowing a wealthy firm to cross-subsidize between products to defeat new entrants, others are sceptical whether such mergers involve any detriment to competition.[11]

S Bishop, A Lofaro, and F Rosati, Turning the Tables: Why Vertical and Conglomerate Mergers are Different[12]

[T]here should be an economic presumption that non-horizontal mergers are pro-competitive. This conclusion derives from a fundamental difference between horizontal and non-horizontal mergers. Whereas horizontal mergers remove a direct competitive constraint and raise the possibility that post-merger prices will increase to the detriment of consumers, non-horizontal mergers do not. Moreover,

---

[7] The best known of these is the Herfindahl–Hirschman Index which is used in the United States.

[8] J Church, 'The Impact of Vertical and Conglomerate Mergers on Competition' (2004), available at http://ec.europa.eu/competition/mergers/studies_reports/studies_reports.html.

[9] G Abbamonte and V Rabassa, 'Foreclosure and Vertical Mergers' [2001] ECLR 214.

[10] See pp 1032–1035.

[11] R Bork, *The Antitrust Paradox* (Basic Books, 1978) ch 12.

[12] [2006] ECLR 403, 406.

> the general impact of a non-horizontal merger is to reduce prices as a result of eliminating externalities and other inefficiencies that might have existed pre-merger. While this is not to say that non-horizontal mergers are always pro-competitive, it does indicate an economic presumption (albeit rebuttable) that such mergers are competitively benign.

Another reason for merger regulation is that mergers have been used to strip the *assets of the acquired firm*, and although this may be in the short-term interests of some shareholders, it may not be in the longer-term public interest. Such concerns have been fuelled by empirical research, which indicates that mergers often do not produce the gains expected of them.[13]

Regional policy constitutes a third rationale for merger control. A merger may lead to the rationalization of existing plants, with consequential effects on unemployment and regional vitality. A government may use merger policy to maintain a balanced distribution of wealth and job opportunities around the country.[14]

(B) ARGUMENTS IN FAVOUR OF MERGERS

Mergers can however enhance economic efficiency in a number of different ways.[15] They can render it easier to reap *economies of scale*. Firms will produce most efficiently when they maximize economies of scale. These are economies that can be reaped by the firm which is at the optimum size for that industry. A certain product may be made most efficiently with a particular piece of machinery, but this machinery may require a specific turnover before it is economically viable. Mergers are one way in which scale economies can be reaped.

Mergers may also enhance *distributional efficiency*. It may, for example, be more efficient for a manufacturing firm which is seeking to extend its operations down-market to merge with an existing distributor, rather than learn the skills of this new area from scratch.

There is also a considerable literature on the relationship between mergers and *managerial efficiency*.[16] The argument is that the threat of a takeover is a spur for management to perform efficiently. The 'market for corporate control' helps to promote economic efficiency: where the shareholders are satisfied with management performance they will not wish to sell to another company.

The Merger Regulation recognizes the inevitability and desirability of mergers within the EU. Thus the third recital to the Regulation acknowledges that the dismantling of internal frontiers will result in major corporate reorganization; while the fourth recital states that this is to be welcomed as one means of increasing the competitiveness of EU industry on world markets.

---

[13] G Newbould, *Management and Merger Activity* (Cruthstead, 1970); G Meeks, *Disappointing Marriage: A Study of the Gains from Mergers* (Cambridge University Press, 1977); A Hughes, 'Mergers and Economic Performance in the UK: A Survey of the Empirical Evidence 1950–1990' in M Bishop and J Kay (eds), *European Mergers and Merger Policy* (Oxford University Press, 1993) ch 1.

[14] There may be a conflict between regional policy and competition policy, particularly where the latter focuses exclusively on the impact of mergers on competition without taking into account other factors.

[15] S Bishop, A Lofaro, F Rosati, and J Young, 'The Efficiency-Enhancing Effects of Non-Horizontal Mergers' (Office for Official Publications of the European Communities, 2005).

[16] F Easterbrook and D Fischel, 'The Proper Role of a Target's Management in Responding to a Tender Offer' (1991) 94 Harv LRev 1161.

3 REGULATION 139/2004: JURISDICTIONAL ISSUES

(A) CONCENTRATION: GENERAL

Regulation 139/2004 is applicable only if there is a concentration. This issue is dealt with in Article 3(1):[17]

> A concentration shall be deemed to arise where a change of control on a lasting basis results from:
>
> (a) the merger of two or more previously independent undertakings or parts of undertakings, or
>
> (b) the acquisition, by one or more persons already controlling at least one undertaking, or by one or more undertakings, whether by purchase of securities or assets, by contract or by any other means, of direct or indirect control of the whole or parts of one or more undertakings.

Article 3(1) must be read in conjunction with Article 3(2):

> Control shall be constituted by rights, contracts or any other means which, either separately or in combination and having regard to the considerations of fact or law involved, confer the possibility of exercising decisive influence on an undertaking, in particular by:
>
> (a) ownership or the right to use all or part of the assets of an undertaking;
>
> (b) rights or contracts which confer decisive influence on the composition, voting or decisions of the organs of an undertaking.

Article 3 paragraphs (1) and (2) bring different situations within the Regulation, and catch concentrations with an EU dimension irrespective of whether the firms are based in the EU.[18] The Commission has made it clear that the determination of whether or not a concentration exists will be based on qualitative rather than quantitative criteria, focusing on the notion of control. It will take account of issues of law and fact in making this determination.[19]

Article 3(1)(a) covers the case of a *complete merger*. Although the Regulation does not define the term merger, it implies the formation of one enterprise from undertakings that were previously distinct. The Commission has made it clear that Article 3(1)(a) can bite in some circumstances where the undertakings retain their separate legal personalities, but create nonetheless a single economic unit.[20]

Article 3(1)(b) captures cases of *change of control*. This is a complex topic, detailed treatment of which can be found elsewhere.[21] The essence of this Article is as follows. A change of control can result in the acquisition of *sole control* by a person or an undertaking. This is exemplified by *Arjomari-Prioux/*

---

[17] M Broberg, 'Improving the EU Merger Regulation's Delimitation of Jurisdiction: Re-Defining the Notion of Union Dimension' (2014) 5 Journal of European Competition Law & Practice 261.

[18] Case T–102/96 *Gencor Ltd v Commission* [1999] ECR II–753.

[19] Commission Consolidated Jurisdictional Notice under Council Regulation (EC) No 139/2004 on the control of concentrations between undertakings [2008] OJ C95/1, [7], hereafter referred to as CJN.

[20] Ibid [10].

[21] Ibid [11]–[90]; M Broberg, 'The Concept of Control in the Merger Control Regulation' [2004] ECLR 741.

Wiggins Teape,[22] where the Commission held that the acquisition of a 39 per cent shareholding in a company was sufficient to give a buyer control, given that the remaining shares were widely dispersed. The CFI emphasized in *Cementbouw Handel*[23] the need to prove that the control gave decisive influence to the acquirer, and this was reiterated in *Aer Lingus*, where the CFI held that acquisition of shares must give the acquirer decisive influence in order for Article 3 to be applicable.[24] The requisite control can, however, be obtained in a series of interdependent stages, even though they are legally distinct.[25] It is also possible for two or more undertakings to acquire *joint control* over another. Thus in *Northern Telecom/Matra Telecommunications*[26] both companies were held to have acquired joint control over Matra SA, because the consent of both parents was necessary for all important business decisions and financial plans. Cases concerning joint control raise difficult questions of how far the Regulation captures joint ventures.

(B) CONCENTRATION: JOINT VENTURES

Joint venture is not a term of art and covers a wide range of business arrangements, from the establishment of a new corporate entity by two competitors to a joint-purchasing scheme or joint research and development. This breadth of coverage causes problems for competition systems. There has been debate about whether joint ventures should be treated by analogy with cartels, and be regarded as essentially a 'behavioural' problem to be dealt with under Article 101, or as a 'structural' problem, to be dealt with under the Merger Regulation.

The approach in the 1989 Regulation was that the structural/concentrative aspects of joint ventures were dealt with under the Merger Regulation, while behavioural/cooperative aspects concerned with the impact on competition of coordination between independent undertakings were considered under Article 101. This caused real difficulties.[27]

The approach has now been modified so that the concentrative and competitive aspects of joint ventures can be considered within the Merger Regulation: the former is dealt with through Article 3(4), the latter through Article 2(4)–(5) of the 2004 Regulation. Hence, the Commission's powers of decision contained in Article 8, and the time limits specified in Article 10, apply to determinations made under Article 2(4). Article 3(4) of Regulation 139/2004 provides that:

> The creation of a joint venture performing on a lasting basis all the functions of an autonomous economic entity shall constitute a concentration within the meaning of paragraph (1)(b).

Article 2(4) of the Regulation states that:

> To the extent that the creation of a joint venture constituting a concentration pursuant to Article 3 has as its object or effect the coordination of the competitive behaviour of undertakings that remain independent, such coordination shall be appraised in accordance with the criteria of Article 81(1) and (3) of the Treaty, with a view to establishing whether or not the operation is compatible with the Common Market.

---

[22] Case IV/M25 [1991] 4 CMLR 854.
[23] Case T–282/02 *Cementbouw Handel & Industrie BV v Commission* [2006] ECR II–319.
[24] Case T–411/07 *Aer Lingus Group plc v European Commission* [2010] ECR II–3691, [63]–[65].
[25] Case T–282/02 *Cementbouw Handel* (n 23).
[26] Case IV/M249.
[27] B Hawk, 'Joint Ventures under EEC Law', Fordham Corporate Law Institute (Fordham University, 1991) 575–576.

Article 2(5) further provides that:

> In making this appraisal, the Commission shall take into account in particular:
> — whether two or more parent companies retain, to a significant extent, activities in the same market as the joint venture or in a market which is upstream or downstream from that of the joint venture or in a neighbouring market closely related to this market,
> — whether the co-ordination which is the direct consequence of the creation of the joint venture affords the undertakings concerned the possibility of eliminating competition in respect of a substantial part of the products or services in question.

The fact remains that a joint venture will be caught by the Merger Regulation only if it results in the creation of an autonomous economic entity which performs functions on a lasting basis. Concentrative joint ventures will lead to the creation of the requisite autonomous economic entity. These joint ventures must operate on a market in the same general way as other undertakings on that market. This means that they must have sufficient financial and other resources to function as a business on a lasting basis.[28] Such joint ventures are known as 'full-function' joint ventures. These conditions will not be met where the joint venture only takes over a specific function of the parents' business activities without access to the market, as in the case of joint ventures relating to research and development.[29] The impact of the parent companies' support on the operational autonomy of the joint venture must be determined in the context of the relevant market. It must be decided whether the joint venture carries out functions normally performed by other undertakings on that market.[30]

A full-function joint venture may also have cooperative features, in the sense that the object or effect of the joint venture is the coordination of the competitive behaviour of independent undertakings. Cooperative features that threaten to restrict competition will be evaluated under Article 2(4). This will not be so if the parent companies transfer their entire business activities to the joint venture. In the converse situation where the parent companies retain their activities in the relevant product and geographic market there is a high probability of such coordination.[31] Various intermediate positions are also possible, such as where the parent companies operate in a market upstream or downstream from that of the joint venture. It can therefore be difficult to distinguish those joint ventures which will be treated as concentrations for the purposes of Article 3(4).[32]

(c) CONCENTRATIONS WITH AN EU DIMENSION

In order for a concentration to be caught by the Merger Regulation it must have an EU dimension. This is defined by Article 1(2) of Regulation 139/2004:

> A concentration has a Community dimension where:
> (a) the combined aggregate world-wide turnover of all the undertakings concerned is more than EUR 5000 million, and

---

[28] CJN (n 19) [92]–[94], [103]–[105].
[29] Ibid [95].
[30] Case T–87/96 *Assicurazioni Generali SpA and Unicredito SpA v Commission* [1999] ECR II–203, [73].
[31] Case IV/M.088 *Elf Enterprise* [1991] OJ C203/14.
[32] Case IV/M72 *Re the Concentration between Sanofi and Sterling Drug Inc* [1992] 5 CMLR M1.

> (b) the aggregate Community-wide turnover of each of at least two of the undertakings concerned is more than EUR 250 million,
>
> unless each of the undertakings concerned achieves more than two-thirds of its aggregate Community-wide turnover within one and the same Member State.

The reach of EU merger control is extended by Article 1(3). It was felt that concentrations which fell below the thresholds in Article 1(2) could nonetheless be examined under the merger laws of Member States, and that this could be costly and lead to conflicting assessments in the different legal systems.[33] By extending the reach of EU merger control to catch such concentrations which could have a significant impact in several Member States, it was hoped that the competitive impact of such concentrations could be considered for the EU as a whole. Article 1(3) provides:

> A concentration that does not meet the thresholds laid down in paragraph 2 has a Community dimension where:
> (a) the combined aggregate world-wide turnover of all the undertakings is more than EUR 2500 million;
> (b) in each of at least three Member States, the combined aggregate turnover of all the undertakings concerned is more than EUR 100 million;
> (c) in each of at least three Member States included for the purposes of point (b), the aggregate turnover of each of at least two of the undertakings concerned is more than EUR 25 million; and
> (d) the aggregate Community-wide turnover of each of at least two of the undertakings concerned is more than EUR 100 million;
>
> unless each of the undertakings concerned achieves more than two-thirds of its aggregate Community-wide turnover within one and the same Member State.

The figures in Article 1(2) and (3) can be revised.[34] Turnover is calculated in accordance with Article 5.[35] The test in Article 1(2) and (3) is purely quantitative: it does not in itself indicate that a merger will be regarded as contrary to the Regulation. The substantive criterion is contained within Article 2, considered below. These definitions can bring many non-EU undertakings within the ambit of the Regulation.[36]

(D) THE RELATION BETWEEN EU AND NATIONAL MERGER CONTROL

(i) *The General Principle: 'One-Stop Shop'*

It is undesirable for the same merger to be subject to investigation under differing regimes at EU and national level. It is therefore central to the Merger Regulation that mergers with an EU dimension should, in general, be investigated only by the Commission. Thus Article 21(1) provides that Regulation 139/2004 alone shall apply to concentrations as defined in Article 3;[37] Article 21(2)

---

[33] CJN (n 19) [126]–[127].

[34] Reg 139/2004 (n 6) Art 1(5).

[35] CJN (n 19) [157]–[205].

[36] See, eg, Case IV/M24 *Mitsubishi Corporation/Union Carbide Corporation* [1992] 4 CMLR M50; Case IV/M69 *Kyowa Bank Limited/Saitama Bank Limited* [1992] 4 CMLR M105.

[37] Subject to exceptions for joint ventures which do not have an EU dimension and which have as their object or effect the coordination of competitive behaviour of undertakings that remain independent.

stipulates that the Commission has sole jurisdiction to take decisions provided for in this Regulation, subject to review by the Union Courts; and Article 21(3) states that, subject to exceptions considered below, no Member State may apply its national legislation to a merger that has an EU dimension. There are, however, exceptions to this general principle.[38] The Commission published a Notice in 2005 articulating the considerations that should be taken into account when deciding on the application of these exceptions to the one-stop shop principle.[39]

(ii) *Protection of National 'Legitimate' Interests: Article 21(4)*

Article 21(4) allows a Member State to take appropriate measures to protect legitimate interests other than those taken into consideration by the Regulation, provided that they are compatible with EU law. Public security, plurality of the media, and prudential rules are listed as legitimate interests for these purposes. Any other public interest must be notified to the Commission, which must inform the Member State of its decision within twenty-five working days.

(iii) *Referral to the Competent Authorities of the Member States by the Commission: Article 4(4)*

Article 4(4) of Regulation 139/2004 provides that undertakings may, prior to notification of a concentration, inform the Commission by reasoned submission that the concentration may significantly affect competition in a market within a Member State that has all the characteristics of a distinct market and should therefore be examined in whole or in part by that Member State.

The Commission transmits this submission to all the Member States. The Member State referred to in the submission can then agree or disagree. Unless the Member State disagrees, the Commission can refer the case to that state for the application of its national competition law, where the Commission considers that such a distinct market exists and that competition in that market may be significantly affected by the concentration.

(iv) *Referral to the Competent Authorities of the Member States by the Commission: Article 9*

When the Regulation was being drafted there was concern that a merger might not be regarded as harmful from the EU perspective, but could still be detrimental at national level. Article 9(1) provides that the Commission can refer a notified concentration to the competent authorities of the Member States. Article 9(2) sets out the conditions.

> Within 15 working days of the date of receipt of the copy of the notification, a Member State, on its own initiative or upon the invitation of the Commission, may inform the Commission, which shall inform the undertakings concerned, that:
>
> (a) a concentration threatens to affect significantly competition in a market within that Member State, which presents all the characteristics of a distinct market, or
>
> (b) a concentration affects competition in a market within that Member State, which presents all the characteristics of a distinct market and which does not constitute a substantial part of the common market.

---

[38] T Soames and S Maudhuit, 'Changes in EU Merger Control: Part I' [2005] ECLR 57.

[39] Commission Notice on Case-Referral in Respect of Concentrations [2005] OJ C56/2.

Article 9(3) states that it is for the Commission to decide whether such a distinct market exists, and also whether there is the relevant threat to competition. The Commission can then either deal with the case itself, or refer the whole or part of the case to the relevant national authorities.[40] The Commission rejected a number of such applications from Member States,[41] but accepted a request from the UK,[42] and greater use has been made of Article 9 since 1996.[43]

(v) *Referral to Commission at Request of Undertakings: Article 4(5)*

Article 4(5) of the Regulation provides a mechanism for undertakings to suggest that a concentration should be considered by the Commission. It is open to such undertakings to suggest that the Commission should consider a concentration as defined in Article 3, which does not have an EU dimension as defined by Article 1, where the concentration is capable of being reviewed under the national competition laws of at least three Member States. This suggestion can be made by the undertakings before any notification to the competent national authorities. If one Member State disagrees within fifteen working days then the case shall not be referred to the Commission. If no such disagreement is forthcoming, then the concentration is deemed to have an EU dimension and is examined by the Commission. In such instances no Member State applies its national law to the concentration.

(vi) *Referral to Commission at Request of Member States: Article 22*

Article 22 provides that one or more Member States may request the Commission to investigate a concentration as defined in Article 3 that does not have an EU dimension within the meaning of Article 1, where it affects trade between Member States and threatens significantly to affect competition within the territory of the Member State or States making the request. The request may come from the competition authority of the Member State.[44] The Commission can then decide to take action where it considers that these criteria are met.[45]

The object of this provision was to provide a mechanism for merger control where none existed at national level. It will be rarely used, given that most states now have their own systems of merger control. The Member State that makes a request cannot control, or define the scope of, the Commission's investigation,[46] and once such a request has been made the Member State can no longer apply its national legislation to the concentration.

(E) RESIDUAL ROLE FOR ARTICLES 101 AND 102 TFEU

We have seen how the ECJ used Articles 101 and 102 to control mergers prior to the Merger Regulation. It is necessary to consider the possible scope of application of these Articles now.[47]

---

[40] This is subject to the proviso that the Commission shall so refer the case where the concentration affects competition in a distinct market in a Member State that does not form a substantial part of the common market, if the Commission considers that such a distinct market is affected.

[41] See, eg, Case IV/M41 *Varta/Bosch* [1991] OJ L320/26; Case IV/M222 *Mannesman/Hoesch* [1993] OJ L114/34.

[42] Case IV/M180 *Streetley plc/Tarmac* [1992] 4 CMLR 343. For examples where the Commission has referred concentrations under Art 9 see, eg, *Rheinmetall/British Aerospace/STN Atlas* [1997] 4 CMLR 987; *REW/Thyssengas/ Bayernwerk/Isarwerke* [1997] 4 CMLR 23.

[43] Jones and Sufrin (n 1) 1159–1163.

[44] Case T–22/97 *Kesko Oy v Commission* [1999] ECR II–3775.

[45] Art 22(3).

[46] Case T–221/95 *Endemol Entertainment Holding BV v Commission* [1999] ECR II–1299.

[47] Jones and Sufrin (n 1) 1171–1172.

As regards the Commission, Article 21(1) of Regulation 139/2004 provides that it alone shall apply to concentrations as defined by Article 3,[48] and that the main implementing regulations concerning Article 101 shall not be applicable. The Regulation cannot however disapply Articles 101 and 102, since these are Treaty provisions, and it may be that the Commission would have power to use these provisions via Articles 104 and 105 TFEU.[49]

As regards national courts, Articles 101 and 102 have direct effect. It might therefore be possible, for example, for an undertaking opposed to a hostile takeover to seek a preliminary reference under Article 267 TFEU, claiming that it was in breach of Article 101 or 102, even if the takeover would not come within the Merger Regulation.[50]

4 REGULATION 139/2004: PROCEDURAL ISSUES

(A) PRIOR NOTIFICATION

In order for merger control to be effective it is necessary for the Commission to be informed about any such acquisition. This is covered by Article 4(1), which deals with pre-notification. It provides that concentrations with an EU dimension must be notified prior to their implementation, and following the conclusion of the agreement, the announcement of the public bid, or the acquisition of the controlling interest. Article 4(3) imposes an obligation on the Commission to publish those notifications that it considers to fall within the ambit of the Regulation. Failure to comply with the duty to pre-notify can lead to fines under Article 14(2)(a). There is a standard form, known as Form CO, which is used for the notification. This form requires the parties to submit certain information to the Commission, including copies of the documentation bringing about the concentration, copies of the accounts of the parties involved, and copies of any reports which have been prepared for the purposes of the concentration.[51]

(B) SUSPENSION PENDING INVESTIGATION

The effectiveness of merger control also demands that a proposed concentration should not be completed pending investigation by the Commission. Article 7(1) provides for the suspension of a concentration before notification, or until it has been declared to be compatible with the common market pursuant to Article 6(1)(b) or Article 8(2), or on the basis of the presumption in Article 10(6). Article 14(2) allows the Commission to impose heavy fines for breach of this obligation. The suspensive effect of notification is, however, qualified by Article 7(3), which allows the Commission to derogate from Article 7(1). The derogation may be made subject to conditions.[52]

(C) INVESTIGATION

There are two stages to the Commission's investigation of notified concentrations.[53] First, there is a preliminary investigation pursuant to Article 6(1), and the Commission can decide that: the

---

[48] Subject to the qualification in (n 37).

[49] Jones and Sufrin (n 1) 1171–1172.

[50] Ibid 1171.

[51] Commission Regulation (EC) No 802/2004 of 7 April 2004 implementing Council Regulation 139/2004 on the control of concentrations between undertakings [2004] OJ L133/1, Arts 2–6, and Annex I.

[52] See, eg, Case IV/M42 *Kelt/American Express* [1991] 4 CMLR 740.

[53] S Maudhuit and T Soames, 'Changes in EU Merger Control: Part 3' [2005] ECLR 144.

concentration is outside the Regulation; that it is within the scope of the Regulation, but is not incompatible with the common market; or that it is within the scope of the Regulation, that there are serious doubts about its compatibility with the common market, and that therefore proceedings must be initiated.[54] These decisions must normally be made within twenty-five working days of the notification, Article 10(1). There is also provision for a simplified procedure in certain types of case.[55]

Secondly, the Commission investigates those concentrations where there are serious doubts about their compatibility with the common market. The Commission has a number of options, listed in Article 8. It can decide that the concentration or concentrative joint venture is not in breach of the relevant substantive criteria, subject to possible modifications,[56] and the Commission has the burden of proof in such instances.[57] If this finding by the Commission is dependent on commitments made by the undertakings, such commitments must eliminate the significant lessening of competition entirely.[58] The Commission may determine that the concentration is incompatible with the common market, because it significantly impedes effective competition, in particular by creating or strengthening a dominant position or because a concentrative joint venture would not benefit from Article 101(3) TFEU.[59] It may demand the reversal of a concentration in certain circumstances,[60] and has power to take interim measures to restore or maintain effective competition in certain instances.[61] The general time limit for such decisions is ninety working days from the initiation of the proceedings,[62] and if this is not complied with then the merger will be deemed to be compatible with the common market.[63] There are rights to be heard before decisions are made,[64] and the list of parties who can be involved in the proceedings is quite broad.[65] The Commission must consult the Advisory Committee on Concentrations, which consists of one or two representatives from Member States, before any decision is made under Articles 8(1)–(6), 14, and 15.[66]

(D) INVESTIGATION AND ENFORCEMENT

The Commission is given broad powers of investigation and enforcement.[67] It can request information: Article 11; conduct on-site investigations: Article 13; and impose considerable fines: Article 14.

---

[54] Reg 139/2004 (n 6) Art 6(2) enables the Commission to decide that a proposed concentration that has been modified no longer raises serious doubts about its compatibility with the common market, and that it therefore can be declared to be compatible with the common market. Conditions can be attached and the decision can be revoked if the conditions are not complied with.

[55] Commission Notice on Simplified Procedure for Treatment of Certain Concentrations under Council Regulation 139/2004 [2005] OJ C56/32.

[56] Reg 139/2004 (n 6) Art 8(1)–(2); Case IV/M190 *Re the Concentration between Nestlé SA and Source Perrier SA* [1993] 4 CMLR M17; a decision finding that the concentration is compatible with the common market may also cover restrictions which are directly related and necessary to the implementation of the concentration: Art 8(1).

[57] Case T–102/96 *Gencor v Commission* [1999] ECR II–753, [318]; Case T–48/04 *Qualcomm Wireless Business Solutions Europe BV v Commission* [2009] ECR II–2029, [89]–[90].

[58] Case T–282/02 *Cementbouw Handel* (n 23).

[59] Reg 139/2004 (n 6) Art 8(3).

[60] Ibid Art 8(4).

[61] Ibid Art 8(5); Case T–411/07 R *Aer Lingus Group plc v Commission* [2008] ECR II–411.

[62] Reg 139/2004 (n 6) Art 10(3). There are a number of exceptions to this basic rule.

[63] Ibid Art 10(6), subject to Art 9.

[64] Ibid Art 18.

[65] Reg 802/2004 (n 51) Art 11; Case T–290/94 *Kayserberg SA v Commission* [1997] ECR II–2137.

[66] Reg 139/2004 (n 6) Art 19(3)–(4).

[67] See, eg, Case C–477/10 P *Commission v Agrofert Holdings* EU:C:2012:394.

A fine of up to 10 per cent of the aggregate turnover of the undertakings concerned may, for example, be imposed where the parties have proceeded with a concentration declared to be incompatible with the common market pursuant to a decision made under Article 8(3).[68]

5 REGULATION 139/2004: THE SUBSTANTIVE CRITERIA

(A) MARKET DEFINITION

Many of the issues encountered in the discussion of Article 102 TFEU are relevant under the Merger Regulation. Thus, it will be necessary to define the relevant market in geographical and product terms, and also in many instances to determine whether there is a dominant position, which has been created or strengthened by the concentration.[69] The Commission makes reference to decisions under Article 102 when adjudicating on the Merger Regulation, and the Commission Notice on the definition of the relevant market for the purposes of EU competition law, considered earlier,[70] applies to the Merger Regulation. There must be a causal link between the creation and strengthening of a dominant position and the impact on competition.[71]

(B) THE TEST

The test for determining whether a concentration is compatible with the common market is in Article 2(1)–(3) of Regulation 139/2004, which should be read in conjunction with Article 2(4) set out earlier:

1. Concentrations within the scope of this Regulation shall be appraised in accordance with the objectives of this Regulation and the following provisions with a view to establishing whether or not they are compatible with the common market.

In making this appraisal, the Commission shall take into account:

(a) the need to maintain and develop effective competition within the common market in view of, among other things, the structure of all the markets concerned and the actual or potential competition from undertakings located either within or outwith the Community;

(b) the market position of the undertakings concerned and their economic and financial power, the alternatives available to suppliers and users, their access to suppliers or markets, any legal or other barriers to entry, supply and demand trends for the relevant goods and services, the interests of the intermediate and ultimate consumers, and the development of technical and economic progress provided that it is to consumers' advantage and does not form an obstacle to competition.

2. A concentration which would not significantly impede effective competition in the common market or in a substantial part of it, in particular as a result of the creation or strengthening of a dominant position, shall be declared compatible with the Common Market.

3. A concentration which would significantly impede effective competition, in the common market or in a substantial part of it, in particular as the result of the creation or strengthening of a dominant position, shall be declared to be incompatible with the common market.

---

[68] Art 14(2)(c).
[69] I Kokkoris, 'The Concept of Market Definition and the SSNIP Test in the Merger Appraisal' [2005] ECLR 209.
[70] See pp 1060–1061.
[71] Cases C–68/94 and 30/95 *France v Commission* [1998] ECR I–1375, [110].

The current formulation in Article 2(2)–(3) differs from that in the earlier Merger Regulation. The original formulation was couched in terms of dominance. Article 2(3) of the 1989 Regulation provided that 'a concentration which creates or strengthens a dominant position as a result of which effective competition would be significantly impeded in the common market or in a substantial part of it shall be declared to be incompatible with the common market'.[72]

Prior to the adoption of the 2004 Regulation there was significant debate as to whether the dominance test contained in the 1989 Regulation should be replaced by a 'substantial lessening of competition' (SLC) test, which has been adopted in some other jurisdictions.[73] The Commission argued that there was little real difference between a dominance test and the SLC test,[74] and some academics questioned the desirability of the change.[75] A number of academics however advocated the SLC test,[76] as did some Member States,[77] one rationale being that concentrations in oligopolistic markets could harm competition, even where there was no dominance and no tacit coordination between the parties.

J Vickers, Merger Policy in Europe: Retrospect and Prospect[78]

[M]ergers in oligopoly settings can reduce competition through non-co-ordinated effects as well as by co-ordinated effects...If erstwhile competitors A and B merge, the market has lost the competition between A and B. If there was a shortage of surrounding competition, this effect could lessen competition substantially in the market as a whole. For example, with A and B no longer competing, C and D might slacken their competitive efforts in the marketplace.

Thus we had what came to be known as the problem of the gap—i.e. the gap between the policy aim of catching all anti-competitive mergers and the ability to catch them by the concept of dominance even as extended to embrace tacit co-ordination between two or more firms. There were three approaches to the problem of the gap:

- denial at least of its practical importance.
- verbal elasticity—give 'dominance' a sufficiently broad meaning in the context of mergers to cover non-coordinated effects as well as coordinated effects and single firm dominance, and
- change the test from dominance to a direct effect on competition formulation.

The outcome of the reform exercise was the change now embodied in Article 2 of Regulation 139/2004. It is broader than the previous formulation, since a concentration can be prohibited if it significantly impedes effective competition, even if it does not create or strengthen a dominant position. This can catch concentrations that will result in non-coordinated effects on oligopolistic markets, even where the firms are not collectively dominant.[79] However Article 2 also states that the significant impediment to competition can arise in particular by the creation or strengthening of a dominant position,

---

[72] Reg 4064/89 (n 5).

[73] I Kokkoris, 'The Reform of the European Merger Control Regulation in the Aftermath of the *Airtours* Case—The Eagerly Expected Debate: SLC v Dominance Test' [2005] ECLR 37.

[74] Green Paper on the Review of Council Regulation 4064/89, COM(2001) 745/6 final, [160]–[167].

[75] S Voigt and A Schmidt, 'Switching to Substantial Impediments to Competition can have Substantial Costs' [2004] ECLR 584.

[76] J Vickers, 'Competition, Economics and Policy' [2003] ECLR 95; Z Biro and M Parker, 'A New EC Merger Test? Dominance v Substantial Lessening of Competition' [2002] Competition Law Journal 157.

[77] K Fountoukakos and S Ryan, 'A New Substantive Test for EU Merger Control' [2005] ECLR 277.

[78] [2004] ECLR 455, 459.

[79] Reg 139/2004 (n 6) rec 25.

thereby preserving the relevance of the prior case law.[80] The reality is, however, that only twenty-four mergers have been prohibited since 1990 and only six since 2004, which is less than 1 per cent of the approximately 5,000 mergers notified.[81]

(c) HORIZONTAL MERGERS: NON-COORDINATED EFFECTS

The Commission's guidelines are binding on it, provided that they are consistent with the Treaty and the Merger Regulation.[82] The guidelines distinguish between non-coordinated and coordinated effects when applying the test in Regulation 139/2004.

Guidelines on the Assessment of Horizontal Mergers[83]

22. There are two main ways in which horizontal mergers may significantly impede effective competition, in particular by creating or strengthening a dominant position:

    (a) by eliminating important competitive constraints on one or more firms, which consequently would have increased market power, without resorting to coordinated behaviour (non-coordinated effects);

    (b) by changing the nature of competition in such a way that firms that previously were not coordinating their behaviour, are now significantly more likely to coordinate and raise prices or otherwise harm effective competition. A merger may also make coordination easier, more stable or more effective for firms which were coordinating prior to the merger (coordinated effects).

    ...

Guidelines on the Assessment of Horizontal Mergers[84]

Non-coordinated effects

24. A merger may significantly impede effective competition in a market by removing important competitive constraints on one or more sellers, who consequently have increased market power. The most direct effect of the merger will be the loss of competition between the merging firms...

25. Generally, a merger giving rise to such non-coordinated effects would significantly impede effective competition by creating or strengthening the dominant position of a single firm, one which, typically, would have an appreciably larger market share than the next competitor post-merger. Furthermore, mergers in oligopolistic markets involving the elimination of important competitive constraints that the merging parties previously exerted upon each other together with a reduction of competitive pressure on the remaining competitors may, even where there is little likelihood of coordination

---

[80] Ibid rec 26; Guidelines on the Assessment of Horizontal Mergers under the Council Regulation on the Control of Undertakings [2004] OJ C31/5, [4].

[81] Towards more Effective Merger Control, COM(2014) 449 final, [6].

[82] Case T–282/06 *Sun Chemical Group BV, Siegwerk Druckfarben AG and Flint Group Germany GmbH v Commission* [2007] ECR II–2149.

[83] (N 80) [22].

[84] Ibid [24], [25], [39].

between the members of the oligopoly, also result in a significant impediment to competition. The Merger Regulation clarifies that all mergers giving rise to such non-coordinated effects shall also be declared incompatible with the common market.

The Commission then listed the relevant factors in deciding whether significant non-coordinated effects would result from a merger: the size of the market share held by the merging firms; whether they were close competitors; the ease with which customers could switch to other suppliers; the ability of the merged entity to hinder expansion by competitors; and whether the merger eliminated an important competitive force. The Commission then considered coordinated effects.[85]

The Commission's approach can be conveyed by reviewing two of its decisions. These remain relevant even though made under the previous Merger Regulation, since dominance is still important under the current Merger Regulation. We can begin by considering an instance in which it cleared the merger.

Case IV/M57 **Re the Concentration between Digital Equipment International and Mannesman Kienzle GmbH**
[1992] 4 CMLR M99

Digital Equipment International (DEIL), a wholly-owned subsidiary of Digital Equipment Corporation (DEC), made an agreement with Mannesman Kienzle (MK) to establish a limited partnership under German law, Digital/Kienzle, which was to be owned as to 65 per cent by DEIL and 35 per cent by MK. The new company was to acquire the computer business of MK, which was then to withdraw from the computer industry (except for printers). MK also agreed not to compete with Digital/Kienzle. DEC had less than 10 per cent of the market for personal computers, and this market was, as a whole, relatively fragmented, with few firms possessing more than 10 per cent. The proposed concentration did not therefore raise serious doubts about its compatibility with the common market in this sphere. DEC was one of the world's largest suppliers of networked computer systems, but MK was very much smaller. The extract which follows concerns the market for workstations. The merger was cleared under Article 6(1)(b) of Regulation 4064/89.

THE COMMISSION

19. The workstation market is the smallest among the four markets mainly affected, but shows the highest annual growth rate (more than 30 per cent). It is also the most concentrated market with DEC, Hewlett Packard and Sun Microsystems holding an aggregate market share of about 80 per cent. DEC's market share has been in the last three years on average 22 per cent.

20. It is unlikely that the concentration will create or strengthen a dominant position because conditions of competition will not significantly change. The workstation market is a fairly new market which developed out of the PC and small computer market during the last 10 years. High market shares on a new developing market are not extraordinary, and they do not necessarily indicate market power. In fact the development of the market shares of the three leading companies over a period of time shows the dynamic nature of this market. There has been constant change including a change of market leadership.

21. DEC acquires with MK only a relatively small vendor and one which is rather insignificant for the maintenance of competition on this market.... Finally, barriers to entry are relatively low for other

---

[85] Ibid [27]–[38].

computer systems manufacturers, especially for those who sell PCs and small multi-user computers. Market entry seems to be feasible even for companies on adjacent markets....

22. Thus, also with regard to the workstation market the concentration does not raise serious doubts as to its compatibility with the Common Market.

At the opposite end of the spectrum we can consider a concentration found to infringe Article 2(3) of the 1989 Merger Regulation.

Case IV/M53 Re the Concentration between Aérospatiale SNI and Alenia-Aeritalia e Selenia SpA and de Havilland
[1992] 4 CMLR M2

Aérospatiale and Alenia controlled the world's largest producer of turbo-prop regional aircraft, ATR, and sought to take over de Havilland, which was the world number two in this market. The Commission found that the product market was regional turbo-prop aeroplanes with between twenty and seventy seats, with sub-markets for aircraft with twenty to thirty-nine seats, forty to fifty-nine seats, and sixty seats and over. The geographical market was the world, excluding China and Eastern Europe.

THE COMMISSION

A. Effect on ATR's Position

27. The proposed concentration would significantly strengthen ATR's position on the commuter markets, for the following reasons in particular:

— high combined market share on the 40 to 59-seat market, and of the overall commuter market
— elimination of de Havilland as a competitor
— coverage of the whole range of commuter aircraft
— considerable extension of customer base.

(a) Increase in Market Shares

...

29. ATR would increase its share of the overall worldwide commuter market of 20 to 70 seats from around 30 per cent to around 50 per cent. The nearest competitor (Saab) would only have around 19 per cent. On the basis of this the new entity would have half the overall world market and more than two and half times the share of its nearest competitor.

30. The combined market share may further increase after the concentration...

Following a concentration between ATR and de Havilland, the competitors would be faced with the combined strength of two large companies. This would mean that where an airline was considering placing a new order, the competitors would be in competition with the combined product range of ATR and de Havilland....

(b) Elimination of de Havilland as a Competitor

31. In terms of aircraft sold, de Havilland is the most successful competitor of ATR....

The parties argue that if the proposed concentration does not proceed, although de Havilland would not be immediately liquidated, its production might be phased out by Boeing so that de Havilland might in any case be eliminated as a competitor in the medium to long term. Without prejudice as to whether such a consideration is relevant pursuant to Article 2 of the Merger Regulation, the Commission considers that such elimination is not probable....

...

(c) Coverage of the Whole Range of Commuter Aircraft

32. The new entity ATR/de Havilland would be the only commuter manufacturer present in all the various commuter markets as defined above.

...

(d) Broadening of Customer Base

33. ATR would significantly broaden its customer base after the concentration. On the basis of deliveries to date, the parties state that ATR has currently delivered commuters to 44 customers worldwide and de Havilland has delivered commuters to 36 other customers, giving a combination of 80 customers in all....

The customer base is an important element of market power for aircraft manufacturers since there is at least to some extent a lock-in effect for customers once their initial choice of aircraft is made.

...

B. Assessment of the Strength of the Remaining Competition

34. In order to be able to assess whether the new combined entity would be able to act independently of its competitors, in view of its strengthened position, it is necessary to assess the current and expected future strength of the remaining competitors.

[*The Commission evaluated the strength of the other competitors and decided that it was questionable whether they could provide effective competition in the medium to long term.*]

...

D. Summary of Effect of the Proposed Concentration on the Commuter Markets

51. The combined entity ATR/de Havilland will obtain a very strong position in the world and Community commuter markets of 40 seats and over, and in the overall world and Community market, as a result of the proposed concentration. The competitors in these markets are relatively weak. The bargaining ability of the customers is limited. The combination of these factors leads to the conclusion that the new entity could act to a significant extent independently of its competitors and customers, and would thus have a dominant position on the commuter markets as defined.

...

E. Potential Entry into the Market

53. In general terms, a concentration which leads to the creation of a dominant position may however be compatible with the Common Market within the meaning of Article 2(2) of the Merger Regulation if there exists strong evidence that this position is only temporary and would be quickly eroded because of high probability of strong market entry.

[*The Commission concluded that there was no realistic potential competition in the commuter markets in the foreseeable future.*]

The Commission's decision to block this merger was not accepted unreservedly. The majority of the Advisory Committee on Concentrations agreed with the Commission. The minority disagreed, stating that the Commission 'is not so much protecting competition but rather the competitors to this proposed concentration',[86] and the decision was also criticized academically by Fox.[87] The Commission later approved a joint venture between Aérospatiale, Alenia, and British Aerospace.[88]

(D) HORIZONTAL MERGERS: COORDINATED EFFECTS AND COLLECTIVE DOMINANCE

The Commission also considers application of the Merger Regulation where there are coordinated effects of the concentration.

Guidelines on the Assessment of Horizontal Mergers[89]

Coordinated effects

39. In some markets the structure may be such that firms would consider it possible, economically rational, and hence preferable, to adopt on a sustainable basis a course of action on the market aimed at selling at increased prices. A merger in a concentrated market may significantly impede effective competition, through the creation or the strengthening of a collective dominant position, because it increases the likelihood that firms are able to coordinate their behaviour in this way and raise prices, even without entering into an agreement or resorting to a concerted practice within the meaning of Article 81 of the Treaty...

40. Coordination may take various forms. In some markets, the most likely coordination may involve keeping prices above the competitive level. In other markets, coordination may aim at limiting production or the amount of new capacity brought to the market. Firms may also coordinate by dividing the market, for instance by geographic area or other customer characteristics, or by allocating contracts in bidding markets.

The idea of coordinated effects, as exemplified by collective dominance, must be seen against the prior case law. The Commission took the view that the 1989 Merger Regulation covered collective dominance where the concentration created or strengthened a dominant position between the parties to the concentration and another party on that market.[90] This was confirmed by the ECJ and CFI.[91]

---

[86] [1992] 4 CMLR M2, 35.

[87] E Fox, 'Merger Control in the EEC—Towards a European Merger Jurisprudence' in B Hawk (ed), Fordham Corporate Law Institute (Fordham University, 1991) ch 28.

[88] [1995] 4 CMLR 377.

[89] (N 80) [39].

[90] Case IV/M190 *Nestlé SA/ Source Perrier SA* [1993] 4 CMLR M17, [112]–[115].

[91] R Whish and B Sufrin, 'Oligopolistic Markets and EC Competition Law' (1992) 12 YBEL 59; A Winckler and M Hansen, 'Collective Dominance under the EC Merger Control Regulation' (1993) 30 CMLRev 787; D Ridyard, 'Economic Analysis of Single Firm and Oligopolistic Dominance' [1994] ECLR 255; C Caffarra and K-U Kuhn, 'Joint Dominance: The CFI Judgment on Gencor/Lonhro' [1999] ECLR 355; R Whish, 'Collective Dominance' in D O'Keefe and A Bavasso (eds), *Judicial Review in European Union Law* (Kluwer, 2000) ch 37.

Cases C–68/94 and 30/95 **France v Commission**
[1998] ECR I–1375

K + S and MdK were proposing to enter into a concentration. Both firms operated in the potash and rock salt markets. The Commission was concerned that as a result of this concentration two entities would enjoy a dominant position: K + S/MdK and another firm, SCPA. The applicants argued that the Merger Regulation did not cover collective dominance. They claimed that the wording of the Merger Regulation did not, in contrast to Article 82, speak in terms of 'one or more undertakings', and that the legislative history of the 1989 Merger Regulation showed that it was not meant to cover such cases.

THE ECJ

166. [I]t cannot be deduced from the wording of Article 2 of the Regulation that only concentrations which create or strengthen an individual dominant position, that is a dominant position held by the parties to the concentration, come within the scope of the Regulation. Article 2 . . . does not in itself exclude the possibility of applying the Regulation to cases where the concentrations lead to the creation or strengthening of a collective dominant position, that is a dominant position held by the parties to the concentration together with an entity not a party thereto.

[*The ECJ found that the legislative history was not conclusive, and therefore that Article 2 should be considered by reference to its purpose and general structure. It considered the recitals to the Regulation and concluded that all concentrations with a Community dimension that could affect the structure of competition within the EC should be within the ambit of the 1989 Regulation.*]

171. A concentration which creates or strengthens a dominant position on the part of the parties concerned with an entity not involved in the concentration is liable to prove incompatible with the system of undistorted competition which the Treaty seeks to secure. Consequently, if it were accepted that only concentrations creating or strengthening a dominant position on the part of the parties to the concentration were covered by the Regulation, its purpose . . . would be partially frustrated . . .

Case T–102/96 **Gencor Ltd v Commission**
[1999] ECR II–753

There was a proposed concentration between two firms in the platinum market. The Commission was concerned that this would lead to a collective dominant position as between them and another firm, the latter being the leading worldwide supplier of platinum and the principal competitor of the two firms that were proposing to concentrate. The CFI followed the ECJ's decision, set out above, and then gave guidance on the relevant factors in judging whether collective dominance existed.

THE CFI

163. In assessing whether there is a collective dominant position, the Commission is therefore obliged to establish, using a prospective analysis of the relevant market, whether the concentration in question would lead to a situation in which effective competition in the relevant market would be significantly impeded by the undertakings involved in the concentration and one or more undertakings which together, in particular because of factors giving rise to a connection between them, are able to adopt a common policy on the market and act to a considerable extent independently of their competitors, their customers and, ultimately, of consumers.

[*The CFI held that the existence of a very large market share could, save for exceptional circumstances, be indicative of dominance: paragraph 205.*]

206. It is true that, in the context of an oligopoly, the fact that the parties hold large market shares does not necessarily have the same significance.... Nevertheless, particularly in the case of a duopoly, a large market share is, in the absence of evidence to the contrary, likewise a strong indication of the existence of a dominant position.

[*The applicants argued that the Commission had ignored the CFI's decision in* Italian Flat Glass.[92] *They claimed that in that case the CFI had required some structural links, through agreements, licences, and the like, as a pre-condition for a finding of collective dominance. The CFI in* Gencor *rejected this argument: paragraphs 273–275. It held that in* Italian Flat Glass *the structural links were regarded as but one way in which collective dominance could be shown.*]

276. Furthermore, there is no reason whatsoever in legal or economic terms to exclude from the notion of economic links the relationship of interdependence existing between the parties to a tight oligopoly within which, in a market with the appropriate characteristics, in particular in terms of market concentration, transparency, and product homogeneity, those parties are in a position to anticipate one another's behaviour and are therefore strongly encouraged to align their conduct in the market, in particular in such a way as to maximise their joint profits by restricting production with a view to increasing prices. In such a context, each trader is aware that highly competitive action on its part designed to increase its market share (for example a price cut) would provoke identical action by the others, so that it would derive no benefit from its initiative....

277. That conclusion is all the more pertinent with regard to the control of concentrations, whose objective is to prevent anti-competitive market structures from arising or being strengthened. Those structures may result from the existence of economic links in the strict sense argued by the applicant or from market structures of an oligopolistic kind where each undertaking may become aware of common interests and, in particular, cause prices to increase without having to enter into an agreement or resort to a concerted practice.

It is clear from *Gencor* that collective dominance can catch oligopolistic collusion, and that the existence of structural links between the relevant firms is not a necessary condition for the concept to apply. In *Airtours*[93] the CFI held that three conditions were necessary for a finding of collective dominance: there must be sufficient market transparency such that the members of the dominant oligopoly can monitor the behaviour of the other members; the tacit coordination must be sustainable over time, with sufficient incentive to comply with the common policy;[94] and the common policy must not be at risk from the foreseeable reaction of competitors and consumers.[95]

In the *Impala* case, the CFI stated that, while the three conditions from *Airtours* must be satisfied, they could be 'established indirectly on the basis of what may be a very mixed series of indicia and items of evidence relating to the signs, manifestations and phenomena inherent in the presence of a collective dominant position'.[96] The case was appealed to the ECJ, which held that it was open to the CFI to regard the evidence in this manner, but that it must sustain its analysis with care and should adopt an approach based on the analysis of such plausible coordination strategies as may exist in the circumstances.[97] The ECJ also provided more general guidance on the conditions in *Airtours*.

[92] See pp 1066–1067.

[93] Case T–342/99 *Airtours plc v Commission* [2002] ECR II–2585, [62].

[94] Caffarra and Kuhn (n 91) 356–357.

[95] The conditions from the *Airtours* case feature in the Horizontal Merger Guidelines (n 80) [41], [49]–[57].

[96] Case T–464/04 *Impala v Commission* [2006] ECR II–2289, [251].

[97] Case C–413/06 P *Bertelsmann AG and Sony Corporation of America v Independent Music Publishers and Labels Association (Impala)* [2008] ECR I–4951, [127]–[129]; J Golding, 'The *Impala* Case: A Quiet Conclusion but a Lasting Legacy' [2010] ECLR 261.

Case C–413/06 P Bertelsmann AG and Sony Corporation of America v Independent Music Publishers and Labels Association (Impala)
[2008] ECR I–4951

Bertelsmann and Sony (B and S) proposed to merge their record businesses. This was opposed by Impala, which argued that it would create a collective dominant position. The Commission found the concentration compatible with the common market, but this decision was annulled by the CFI. B and S appealed to the ECJ, which reaffirmed the decisions in *France v Commission* and *Gencor*.

THE ECJ

122. A collective dominant position significantly impeding effective competition in the common market or a substantial part of it may thus arise as the result of a concentration where, in view of the actual characteristics of the relevant market and of the alteration to those characteristics that the concentration would entail, the latter would make each member of the oligopoly in question, as it becomes aware of common interests, consider it possible, economically rational, and hence preferable, to adopt on a lasting basis a common policy on the market with the aim of selling at above competitive prices, without having to enter into an agreement or resort to a concerted practice within the meaning of Article 81 EC and without any actual or potential competitors, let alone customers or consumers, being able to react effectively.

123. Such tacit coordination is more likely to emerge if competitors can easily arrive at a common perception as to how the coordination should work, and, in particular, of the parameters that lend themselves to being a focal point of the proposed coordination. Unless they can form a shared tacit understanding of the terms of the coordination, competitors might resort to practices that are prohibited by Article 81 EC in order to be able to adopt a common policy on the market. Moreover, having regard to the temptation which may exist for each participant in a tacit coordination to depart from it in order to increase its short-term profit, it is necessary to determine whether such coordination is sustainable. In that regard, the coordinating undertakings must be able to monitor to a sufficient degree whether the terms of the coordination are being adhered to. There must therefore be sufficient market transparency for each undertaking concerned to be aware, sufficiently precisely and quickly, of the way in which the market conduct of each of the other participants in the coordination is evolving. Furthermore, discipline requires that there be some form of credible deterrent mechanism that can come into play if deviation is detected. In addition, the reactions of outsiders, such as current or future competitors, and also the reactions of customers, should not be such as to jeopardise the results expected from the coordination.

[*The ECJ held that these criteria were compatible with those laid down in* Airtours, *which should not be applied mechanistically.*]

...

126. In that regard, the assessment of, for example, the transparency of a particular market should not be undertaken in an isolated and abstract manner, but should be carried out using the mechanism of a hypothetical tacit coordination as a basis. It is only if such a hypothesis is taken into account that it is possible to ascertain whether any elements of transparency that may exist on a market are, in fact, capable of facilitating the reaching of a common understanding on the terms of coordination and/or of allowing the competitors concerned to monitor sufficiently whether the terms of such a common policy are being adhered to...

It should in any event be noted that Regulation 139/2004 reduces the need to prove collective dominance.[98] It encapsulates, as we have seen, both non-coordinated and coordinated effects. The

---

[98] Reg 139/2004 (n 6) Art 2(3).

former can cover oligopolistic behaviour even where there is no coordination or dominance,[99] and thus the fact that it may be more difficult to prove collective dominance will be less important.[100]

(E) VERTICAL AND CONGLOMERATE MERGERS: COORDINATED AND NON-COORDINATED EFFECTS

The Commission also produced guidelines on vertical and conglomerate mergers. Space precludes detailed treatment, but the essence of the approach is as follows.

Guidelines on the Assessment of Non-horizontal Mergers[101]

12. First, unlike horizontal mergers, vertical or conglomerate mergers do not entail the loss of direct competition between the merging firms in the same relevant market...

13. Second, vertical and conglomerate mergers provide substantial scope for efficiencies. A characteristic of vertical mergers and certain conglomerate mergers is that the activities and/ or the products of the companies involved are complementary to each other. The integration of complementary activities or products within a single firm may produce significant efficiencies and be pro-competitive...Vertical integration may...provide an increased incentive to seek to decrease prices and increase output because the integrated firm can capture a larger fraction of the benefits...

14. Integration may also decrease transaction costs and allow for a better co-ordination in terms of product design, the organisation of the production process, and the way in which the products are sold...

...

17. There are two main ways in which non-horizontal mergers may significantly impede effective competition: non-coordinated effects and coordinated effects.

18. Non-coordinated effects may principally arise when non-horizontal mergers give rise to *foreclosure*. In this document, the term 'foreclosure' will be used to describe any instance where actual or potential rivals' access to supplies or markets is hampered or eliminated as a result of the merger, thereby reducing these companies' ability and/or incentive to compete. As a result of such foreclosure, the merging companies...may be able to profitably increase the price charged to consumers. These instances give rise to a significant impediment to effective competition and are therefore referred to hereafter as 'anticompetitive foreclosure'.

19. Coordinated effects arise where the merger changes the nature of competition in such a way that firms that previously were not coordinating their behaviour, are now significantly more likely to coordinate to raise prices or otherwise harm effective competition. A merger may also make coordination easier, more stable or more effective for firms which were coordinating prior to the merger.

---

[99] Horizontal Merger Guidelines (n 80) [25].

[100] S Baxter and F Dethmers, 'Collective Dominance under EC Merger Control—After Airtours and the Introduction of Unilateral Effects is there still a Future for Collective Dominance?' [2006] ECLR 148.

[101] Guidelines on the assessment of non-horizontal mergers under the Council Regulation on the control of concentrations between undertakings [2008] OJ C265/7.

(F) CONCENTRATION AND EFFICIENCIES

Prior to Regulation 139/2004 it was unclear whether efficiencies flowing from a concentration could be taken into account.[102] The argument for considering efficiency gains is that relatively modest cost savings can outweigh the impact of price increases when considering allocative efficiency.[103] The issue has now been clarified. Recital 29 of Regulation 139/2004 states:

> In order to determine the impact of a concentration on competition in the common market, it is appropriate to take account of any substantiated and likely efficiencies put forward by the undertakings concerned. It is possible that the efficiencies brought about by the concentration counteract the effects on competition, and in particular the potential harm to consumers, that it might otherwise have and that, as a consequence, the concentration would not significantly impede effective competition, in the common market or in a substantial part of it, in particular as a result of the creation or strengthening of a dominant position. The Commission should publish guidance on the conditions under which it may take efficiencies into account in the assessment of a concentration.

The Commission published this guidance in the Horizontal Merger Guidelines.[104] Three conditions must be satisfied. First, the efficiencies must benefit consumers in a substantial and timely manner, and must be passed on to the consumer; the greater the potential anti-competitive effect of the concentration, the greater and more likely must be the efficiency savings. The second condition is merger specificity, which connotes the idea that the efficiencies could not be achieved by less anti-competitive alternatives. The third condition is verifiability: the Commission must be satisfied that the efficiencies are likely to materialize and that they should be sufficiently substantial to outweigh the concentration's potential harm to consumers. The fact that efficiencies can be considered is to be welcomed. It should nonetheless be recognized that the hurdles to be surmounted to 'save' a notified concentration on efficiency grounds are significant,[105] although some concentrations have done so.[106]

(G) CONCENTRATIONS AND FAILING FIRMS

The ECJ[107] and Commission[108] have acknowledged that an otherwise problematic merger may be compatible with the common market if one of the merging parties is a failing firm.[109] The central condition is that the deterioration of the competitive structure that follows the merger cannot be said to be caused by the merger, as will be the case where the competitive structure would deteriorate to at least the same extent in the absence of the merger.

---

[102] F Jenny, 'EEC Merger Control: Economies as an Antitrust Defense or an Antitrust Attack?' in B Hawk (ed), Fordham Corporate Law Institute (Fordham University, 1992) 603.

[103] O Williamson, 'Economics as an Antitrust Defense: The Welfare Tradeoffs' (1968) 58 Am Econ Rev 18.

[104] Horizontal Merger Guidelines (n 80) [76]–[88].

[105] L Colley, 'From "Defence" to "Attack"? Quantifying Efficiency Arguments in Mergers' [2004] ECLR 342; M Kocmut, 'Efficiency Considerations and Merger Control—Quo Vadis, Commission' [2006] ECLR 19; H Iversen, 'The Efficiency Defence in EC Merger Control' [2010] ECLR 370.

[106] COMP/M.6570 – *UPS/TNT Express*, 30 Jan 2013; COMP/M.6360 – *Nynas/Harburg*, 2 Sept 2013.

[107] Cases C–68/94 and 30/95 *France v Commission* [1998] ECR I–1375.

[108] Case IV/M.2314 *BASF/Pantochim/Eurodiol* IP/01/984; Case IV/M.2876 *Newscorp/Telepiu* IP/03/478.

[109] I Kokkoris, 'Failing Firm Defence in the European Union: A Panacea for Mergers' [2006] ECLR 494.

Guidelines on the Assessment of Horizontal Mergers[110]

90. The Commission considers the following three criteria to be especially relevant for the application of the 'failing firm defence'. First, the allegedly failing firm would in the near future be forced out of the market because of financial difficulties if not taken over by another undertaking. Second, there is no less anti-competitive alternative than the notified merger. Third, in the absence of a merger, the assets of the failing firm would inevitably exit the market.

(H) THE RELEVANCE OF NON-COMPETITION CONSIDERATIONS

Regulation 139/2004, recital 23, instructs the Commission to place its appraisal within the general framework of the Treaty objectives set out in Article 3 TEU. This would arguably allow the Commission to take broader social considerations into account. The Commission has, nonetheless, taken the view that competition is to be the prime objective of the Regulation.[111] Insofar as such issues are taken into account this may occur in the College of Commissioners.[112]

(I) REMEDIES

Structural and behavioural remedies are available for breach of the Merger Regulation.[113] The principles that govern the Commission's choice of remedies are set out in a Commission Notice.[114] It is also open to the parties to modify a concentration that infringes the Merger Regulation and to offer commitments to the Commission, but to be acceptable such commitments must eliminate the anti-competitive impact of the merger.[115]

6 JUDICIAL REVIEW

Commission decisions under the Merger Regulation are reviewable by the Union Courts, subject to the normal conditions, under Article 263 TFEU.[116] The EU Courts have increased the intensity of judicial review in this area and have imbued review for manifest error with more vigour than hitherto.[117]

---

[110] Horizontal Merger Guidelines (n 80) [90].

[111] Jones and Sufrin (n 1) 1239–1241.

[112] Ibid 1240–1241.

[113] D Went, 'The Acceptability of Remedies under the EC Merger Regulation: Structural versus Behavioural' [2006] ECLR 455; W Wang and M Rudanko, 'EU Merger Remedies and Competition Concerns: An Empirical Assessment' (2012) 18 ELJ 555.

[114] Commission Notice on Remedies Acceptable under Council Regulation (EC) No 139/2004 and under Commission Regulation (EC) No 802/2004 [2008] OJ C267/1.

[115] Case T–282/02 *Cementbouw Handel* (n 23).

[116] Chs 14–15; Case T–177/04 *Easy Jet Co Ltd v Commission* [2006] ECR II–1931; Case T–224/10 *Association belge des consommateurs test-achats ASBL v European Commission* EU:T:2011:588.

[117] Judge B Vesterdorf, 'Certain Reflections on Recent Judgments Reviewing Commission Merger Control Decisions' in M Hoskins and W Robinson (eds), *A True European: Essays for Judge David Edward* (Hart, 2003) ch 10.

This is apparent from decisions such as *Airtours*,[118] *Tetra Laval*,[119] and other cases.[120] Thus in *Tetra Laval* the ECJ stated that:[121]

> Whilst the Court recognises that the Commission has a margin of discretion with regard to economic matters, that does not mean that the Community courts must refrain from reviewing the Commission's interpretation of information of an economic nature. Not only must the Community courts, *inter alia*, establish whether the evidence relied on is factually accurate, reliable and consistent but also whether that evidence contains all the information which must be taken into account in order to assess a complex situation and whether it is capable of substantiating the conclusions drawn from it. Such a review is all the more necessary in the case of a prospective analysis required when examining a planned merger with conglomerate effect.

Space precludes detailed consideration of this topic, which can be found elsewhere.[122] Suffice it to say for the present that the General Court now engages in detailed review of Commission decision-making, and that while this is formally undertaken as review for manifest error, it is clear that the meaning of this head of review has been transformed from that in prior case law. The EU Courts none-theless remain reluctant to find that an error by the Commission in assessing the economic evidence under the Merger Regulation suffices for the purpose of non-contractual liability.[123]

7 CONCLUSIONS

i. Merger policy necessarily entails choices. These choices relate to all the important aspects of merger control.

ii. In *jurisdictional terms*, Regulation 139/2004 contains more sophisticated provisions designed to ensure that a concentration is investigated by the most appropriate authority at EU or national level.

iii. In *procedural terms*, it reflects the need for prompt notification, coupled with adequate inves-tigative powers, in order that the Union controls can be effective. This is balanced against the need for promptness in the application of the EU's powers, since important business deci-sions hang in the balance. The specific time limits under the Merger Regulation serve this imperative.

iv. In *substantive terms*, Regulation 139/2004 encapsulates important economic, social, and political choices, exemplified by the modified test for the application of the Regulation, by the explicit inclusion of an efficiency defence, and by the predominance accorded to competition considerations, to the exclusion, in general, of other social considerations.

---

[118] Case T–342/99 *Airtours plc v Commission* [2002] ECR II–2585.

[119] Case C–12/03 P *Commission v Tetra Laval* [2005] ECR I–987.

[120] Case T–464/04 *Impala* (n 96); Case T–210/01 *General Electric Company v Commission* [2005] ECR II–5575; Case T–282/06 *Sun Chemical* (n 82) [60]; Case T–48/04 *Qualcomm Wireless* (n 57); Case T–145/06 *Omya AG v Commission* [2009] ECR II–145; Case C–413/06 P *Bertelsmann* (n 97) [144]–[145].

[121] Case C–12/03 *Tetra Laval* (n 119) [39].

[122] P Craig, *EU Administrative Law* (Oxford University Press, 2nd edn, 2012) ch 14; S Volcker and C O'Daly, 'The Court of First Instance's *Impala* Judgment: A Judicial Counter-Reformation in EU Merger Control' [2006] ECLR 589; J Killick, 'The *GE/Honeywell* Judgment—In Reality Another Merger Defeat for the Commission' [2007] ECLR 52.

[123] Case T–212/03 *My Travel Group plc v Commission* [2008] ECR II–1967.

v. The EU Courts continue to play an important role in this area, in part through their teleological interpretation of the Merger Regulation, and in part through the increased intensity of judicial review under Article 263 TFEU.

vi. The Commission published a White Paper in 2014 reviewing merger policy. Its principal proposals were for competence to deal with anti-competitive acquisitions of minority shareholdings using a targeted transparency system, and making the case-referral system more efficient by streamlining the Article 4(5) procedure and amending Article 22 so that it enhances adherence to the one-stop shop principle.[124]

8 FURTHER READING

(a) Books

Broberg, M, *The European Commission's Jurisdiction to Scrutinise Mergers* (Kluwer, 3rd edn, 2006)

Cook, J, and Kerse, C, *EC Merger Control* (Sweet & Maxwell, 5th edn, 2009)

Jones, A, and Sufrin, B, *EU Competition Law: Text, Cases, and Materials* (Oxford University Press, 5th edn, 2014)

Whish, R, and Bailey, D, *Competition Law* (Oxford University Press, 7th edn, 2012)

(b) Articles

Bailey, D, 'Standard of Proof in EC Merger Proceedings: A Common Law Perspective' (2003) 40 CMLRev 845

Bishop, S, Lofaro, A, and Rosati, F, 'Turning the Tables: Why Vertical and Conglomerate Mergers are Different' [2006] ECLR 403

Broberg, M, 'Improving the EU Merger Regulation's Delimitation of Jurisdiction: Re-Defining the Notion of Union Dimension' (2014) 5 Journal of European Competition Law & Practice 261

Colley, L, 'From "Defence" to "Attack"? Quantifying Efficiency Arguments in Mergers' [2004] ECLR 342

Golding, J, 'The *Impala* Case: A Quiet Conclusion but a Lasting Legacy' [2010] ECLR 261

Iversen, H, 'The Efficiency Defence in EC Merger Control' [2010] ECLR 370

Killick, J, 'The *GE/Honeywell* Judgment—In Reality Another Merger Defeat for the Commission' [2007] ECLR 52

Kocmut, M, 'Efficiency Considerations and Merger Control—Quo Vadis, Commission' [2006] ECLR 19

Kokkoris, I, 'The Reform of the European Merger Control Regulation in the Aftermath of the *Airtours* Case—The Eagerly Expected Debate: SLC v Dominance Test' [2005] ECLR 37

Vesterdorf, Judge B, 'Certain Reflections on Recent Judgments Reviewing Commission Merger Control Decisions' in M Hoskins and W Robinson (eds), *A True European: Essays for Judge David Edward* (Hart, 2003) ch 10

---

[124] Towards more Effective Merger Control (n 81).

Vickers, J, 'Competition, Economics and Policy' [2003] ECLR 95

——— 'Merger Policy in Europe: Retrospect and Prospect' [2004] ECLR 455

Wang, W, and Rudanko, M, 'EU Merger Remedies and Competition Concerns: An Empirical Assessment' (2012) 18 ELJ 555

Whish, R, 'Collective Dominance' in D O'Keefe and A Bavasso (eds), *Judicial Review in European Union Law* (Kluwer, 2000) ch 37

THE STATE AND
THE COMMON MARKET

1 CENTRAL ISSUES

i.   This chapter is concerned with the way in which the actions of the state can infringe the Treaty. The Treaty contains a number of relevant provisions, including Article 4(3) TEU, and Articles 14, 34, 101, 102, 106, and 107–109 TFEU.

ii. There are valid reasons for controlling state action. Thus, for example, Article 106 is designed to prevent a state from enacting or maintaining in force measures relating to public undertakings, which derogate from other obligations under the Treaty. This provision is required to prevent a state from evading Treaty provisions insofar as these relate to such undertakings. It is equally apparent that the EU must have rules concerning state aids, since if a state were able to give preferential treatment to its own firms then the very idea of a level playing field would be undermined.[1]

iii. While there are valid reasons for EU controls, the topics discussed within this chapter raise important issues concerning the very nature of the EU. Thus the jurisprudence under Article 106 has prompted questions about how far it is possible for a state to entrust certain activities to a public monopoly, or to a private firm which has exclusive rights.

iv. The case law concerning state aids, Articles 107–109, raises broader issues concerning the way in which Union policy is developed in a particular area, and the appropriate balance between market integration and the attainment of other goals, such as regional policy and Union cohesion.

2 THE STATE AND THE MARKET: GENERAL PRINCIPLES

(A) THE GENERAL PRINCIPLE: THE COMPETITION ETHOS

In mixed economic systems it is common for the state to play some role in the marketplace. The rationale for this intervention and its legal form may well vary. It has, for example, been common in the past for utilities either to be nationalized, or to have some privileged monopoly or quasi-monopoly status. Recent thinking has tended to favour a more confined role for the state, as manifested in the privatization of nationalized industries and in the deregulation of sectors of the economy. Notwithstanding

---

[1] C-D Ehlermann, 'The Contribution of EC Competition Policy to the Single Market' (1992) 29 CMLRev 257, 259.

these changes, there continue to be undertakings that remain within public ownership or possess a privileged status in the marketplace.

The basic starting position is Article 345 TFEU, which states that the Treaty shall in no way prejudice the rules in Member States governing the system of property ownership. The mere fact that certain activities are undertaken in the public or the private sphere is not, therefore, contrary to the Treaty. Article 345 has, however, been narrowly interpreted so as, for example, not to prevent limitations on intellectual property rights under EU law.[2] Moreover, Article 173 TFEU provides that the EU and the Member States shall ensure that the conditions necessary for the competitiveness of EU industry exist. The Article is framed in terms of open and competitive markets. Action to attain this end includes encouragement of initiative and development of undertakings throughout the EU, particularly small and medium-sized undertakings.

Thus, while Article 345 supports EU agnosticism as to the regime of ownership within any particular state, the thrust of much else in the Treaty is against the type of dominance that can accompany public ownership. It is also against the grant of any special, beneficial position to firms which may distort competition within the internal market.

(B) THE QUALIFICATION: SERVICES OF GENERAL (ECONOMIC) INTEREST

While the general Treaty ethos is the free interplay of market forces, this is qualified in certain respects by Article 14 TFEU.[3]

> Without prejudice to Article 4 of the Treaty on European Union or to Articles 93, 106 and 107 of this Treaty, and given the place occupied by services of general economic interest in the shared values of the Union as well as their role in promoting social and territorial cohesion, the Union and the Member States, each within their respective powers and within the scope of application of the Treaties, shall take care that such services operate on the basis of principles and conditions, particularly economic and financial conditions, which enable them to fulfil their missions. The European Parliament and the Council, acting by means of regulations in accordance with the ordinary legislative procedure, shall establish these principles and set these conditions without prejudice to the competence of Member States, in compliance with the Treaties, to provide, to commission and to fund such services.

This Article should be read with Protocol No 26 on Services of General Interest, which makes clear that the principles need to be adapted to the different services at stake, and confirms that the Treaty does not affect Member State competence to provide non-economic services of general interest. Moreover, Article 36 of the Charter of Fundamental Rights[4] provides that the Union recognizes and respects access to services of general economic interest as provided for in national laws and practices, in accordance with the Treaties, in order to promote social and territorial cohesion of the EU.

The Commission addressed the concept of services of general interest on a number of occasions,[5] including its White Paper on services of general interest.[6] This concept was, said the Commission,

---

[2] Case 16/74 *Centrafarm BV v Winthrop BV* [1974] ECR 1183.

[3] M Ross, 'Article 16 EC and Services of General Interest: From Derogation to Obligation?' (2000) 25 ELRev 22.

[4] [2007] OJ C303/1.

[5] Services of General Interest in Europe, COM(2000) 580 final; Report to the Laeken European Council, Services of General Interest, COM(2001) 598 final; Green Paper on Services of General Interest, COM(2003) 270; A Quality Framework for Services of General Interest in Europe, COM(2011) 900 final.

[6] White Paper on Services of General Interest, COM(2004) 374 final.

broader than services of general economic interest and covered 'both market and non-market services which the public authorities class as being of general interest and subject to specific public service obligations'.[7] Such services were regarded as 'one of the pillars of the European model of society',[8] reflecting EU values and goals based on 'a common set of elements, including: universal service, continuity, quality of service, affordability, as well as user and consumer protection'[9] Access to such services was perceived as 'an essential component of European citizenship and necessary in order to allow them to fully enjoy their fundamental rights'.[10]

The normal market principles are modified in relation to services of general interest: obligations relating to universal service, continuity, and the like are imposed on those providing the service. This has affected EU legislation and the interpretation of Treaty Articles.

In relation to EU legislation, the directives designed to liberalize markets in energy, telecommunications, and the like are not only concerned with the introduction of competition. They also enable or require Member States to impose public service obligations relating to security, regularity, quality, and price of supply on suppliers.[11]

In relation to the interpretation accorded to Treaty Articles, we shall see that the undertakings most likely to gain exemption under Article 106(2) are those with public service obligations,[12] and that aid granted to offset the cost of public service obligations on an undertaking will, subject to certain conditions, prevent it from being characterized as state aid under Article 107.[13]

Views on the overall impact of the preceding developments differ. Baquero Cruz argues that some of the legislation on utilities still evinces the relative priority given to competition over services of general interest,[14] and Fiedziuk notes the tension between provision of such services and more general EU desires to put matters out to tender.[15] Prosser strikes a more positive note when reflecting on developments relating to such services.

T Prosser, The Limits of Competition Law, Markets and Public Services[16]

Initially they were seen as something of an irritant, limiting the creation of a full internal market. Now a much more positive view is taken, despite only cautious substantive proposals in the 2004 White Paper. Such services are confirmed an essential element of European citizenship and, rather than the main question being that of how their operation can be restricted and remodelled to become compatible with the single market, it is of how their operation can be improved and made both more efficient and more responsive to social values such as those underlying public service.

---

[7] Ibid Annex 1. See also Protocol No 26 on Services of General Interest.

[8] White Paper (n 6) [2.1].

[9] Ibid [2.1].

[10] Ibid [2.1].

[11] See, eg, Directive 2002/22 of the European Parliament and the Council of 7 March 2002 on universal service and users' right relating to electronic communications networks and services (Universal Service Directive) [2002] OJ L108/51; A Quality Framework for Services of General Interest in Europe (n 5).

[12] See p 1127.

[13] See pp 1136–1137; Communication from the Commission on the application of the European Union State aid rules to compensation granted for the provision of services of general economic interest [2012] OJ C8/4.

[14] J Baquero Cruz, 'Beyond Competition: Services of General Interest and European Community Law' in G de Búrca (ed), *EU Law and the Welfare State: In Search of Solidarity* (Oxford University Press, 2005) 207.

[15] N Fiedziuk, 'Putting Services of General Economic Interest up for Tender: Reflections on Applicable EU Rules' (2013) 50 CMLRev 87.

[16] (Oxford University Press, 2005) 172.

3 PUBLIC UNDERTAKINGS AND ARTICLE 106

The interplay between competition and the needs of undertakings that operate services of general economic interest is apparent from Article 106 (ex Article 86 EC), which provides as follows:

1. In the case of public undertakings and undertakings to which Member States grant special or exclusive rights, Member States shall neither enact nor maintain in force any measure contrary to the rules contained in the Treaties, in particular to those rules provided for in Article 18 and Articles 101 to 109.

2. Undertakings entrusted with the operation of services of general economic interest or having the character of a revenue-producing monopoly shall be subject to the rules contained in the Treaties, in particular to the rules on competition, in so far as the application of such rules does not obstruct the performance, in law or in fact, of the particular tasks assigned to them. The development of trade must not be affected to such an extent as would be contrary to the interests of the Union.

3. The Commission shall ensure the application of the provisions of this Article and shall, where necessary, address appropriate directives or decisions to Member States.

(A) ARTICLE 106(1)

(i) *Public Undertaking and Undertakings accorded Special or Exclusive Rights*

Article 106(1) covers two types of undertaking: public undertakings and those to which Member States have granted special or exclusive rights. These will be examined in turn. The scope of the term public undertaking was addressed in the *Transparency Directive* case.

Cases 188–190/80 **France, Italy and the United Kingdom v Commission**
[1982] ECR 2545

[Note Lisbon Treaty renumbering: Art 90 is now Art 106 TFEU]

The Commission, acting pursuant to Article 90(3), enacted Directive 80/723 on the transparency of financial relations between Member States and public undertakings. The object was to make available information on public funds given to public undertakings, and the use to which it had been put. This was necessary to ensure the proper operation of the rules on state aid. Three Member States sought to have the Directive annulled. The ECJ considered the definition of public undertaking contained in the Directive. It acknowledged that the Commission did not set out in the Directive to define 'public undertakings' for the purpose of Article 90, but it nonetheless approved of the definition.

THE ECJ

25. According to Article 2 of the Directive, the expression 'public undertakings' means any undertaking over which the public authorities may exercise directly or indirectly a dominant influence. According to the second paragraph, such influence is to be presumed when the public authorities directly or indirectly hold the major part of the undertaking's subscribed capital, control the majority of the votes, or can appoint more than half of the members of its administrative, managerial or supervisory body.

> 26. As the Court has already stated, the reason for the inclusion in the Treaty of the provisions of Article 90 is precisely the influence which the public authorities are able to exert over the commercial decisions of public undertakings. That influence may be exerted on the basis of financial participation or of rules governing the management of the undertaking. By choosing the same criteria to determine the financial relations on which it must be able to obtain information in order to perform its duty of surveillance under Article 90(3), the Commission has remained within the limits of the discretion conferred upon it by that provision.

The definition of the term public undertaking in the Transparency Directive is not conclusive, but it was approved by the ECJ. The existence of state influence in one of the above ways will therefore be a sufficient reason for an undertaking to be characterized as public. Thus in *Sacchi*[17] the Italian Broadcasting Authority (RAI) was under the control of a state holding company (IRI), the state was represented in its organs and could intervene in its operations.

An undertaking, such as a nationalized industry that has been privatized, but which continues to have a protected position in the relevant area, will also fall within Article 106(1) if a Member State has granted it special or exclusive rights. The rationale is that where the state has relieved an undertaking wholly or partially from the discipline of competition, it must bear responsibility for the consequences.

It is possible for undertakings to be caught by both limbs of Article 106(1). Thus, in *Sacchi* the RAI, as well as being controlled by the state, also possessed a statutory monopoly in relation to broadcasting. In *Muller*[18] the state had power to nominate half the members of the management and supervisory board of a company that controlled port facilities in Luxembourg. The company itself had certain privileges, including that of being consulted before the development of any other port facilities within a particular area was undertaken.

(ii) *The Obligation Flowing from Article 106(1)*

Article 106(1) requires that a Member State shall neither enact nor maintain in force any measure that is contrary to the Treaty. A breach of Article 106(1) presupposes that some other Treaty Article has been broken, as exemplified by the specific reference to Articles 18 and 101–109 TFEU. It is however possible for a Member State to maintain in force a measure that violated another Treaty Article, such as Article 34 TFEU. The way in which Article 106(1) operates can be seen from *Bodson*.

Case 30/87 **Bodson v Pompes Funèbres des Régions Libérées SA**
[1988] ECR 2479

[Note Lisbon Treaty renumbering: Arts 86 and 90 are now Arts 102 and 106 TFEU]

French legislation entrusted the provision of external services for funerals (the carriage of the body after it has been placed in the coffin, the provision of hearses, etc) to local communes. The communes then granted concessions to private undertakings and Pompes Funèbres (PF) held many such concessions. Bodson offered external funeral services at a price significantly lower than that set by PF. PF sought an injunction in the French courts, claiming that Bodson was acting in breach of its exclusive rights resulting from the concession. Bodson argued that PF had abused its dominant position in breach

---

[17] Case 155/73 [1974] ECR 409.
[18] Case 10/71 *Ministère Public of Luxembourg v Muller* [1971] ECR 723.

of Article 86 by charging excessive prices. An issue before the Court concerned the responsibility of the commune under Article 90.

THE ECJ

33. In so far as the communes imposed a given level of prices on the concession holders, in the sense that they refrained from granting concessions for the 'external services' to undertakings if the latter did not agree to charge particularly high prices, the communes are covered by the situation referred to in Article 90(1) of the Treaty. That provision governs the obligations of the Member States—which includes, in this context, the public authorities at the regional, provincial or communal level—towards undertakings 'to which [they] grant special or exclusive rights'. That situation covers precisely the grant of an exclusive concession for the 'external services' for funerals.

34. It follows from that finding that public authorities may not, in circumstances such as those in this case, either enact or maintain in force any 'measure' contrary to the rules of the Treaty. . . . They may not therefore assist undertakings holding concessions to charge unfair prices by imposing such prices as a condition for concluding a contract for a concession.

(iii) *The Court's Expansive Case Law*

We noted above that the Treaty is agnostic in formal terms as to whether economic activity is undertaken by the state or those to whom it has granted special or exclusive rights, as opposed to allowing the free interplay of market forces. Provided that the state itself does not infringe Article 106, and provided that the undertaking does not exercise its exclusive rights so as to constitute an abuse of a dominant position under Article 102, then all will be well. The exclusivity will not infringe Article 102. On this view Article 106 simply preserves parity by ensuring that public undertakings or those to whom exclusive rights are granted do not thereby infringe any Treaty provision.

We have, however, also seen that the thrust of the Treaty more generally favours the application of normal competitive principles. The result of this competitive contest may lead to a firm that is dominant because of its economic prowess. This is one of the reasons that the Treaty does not proscribe monopoly *per se*. The Treaty is, nonetheless, against artificial barriers to competition. This can produce tensions in relation to public undertakings, or those to whom the state has granted special or exclusive rights, because their privileged position is the result not of economic prowess, but of state grant.

The formal way in which the ECJ resolves these tensions is to recognize that the grant of exclusive rights will not *per se* infringe, for example, Article 102, but that the exercise of such rights may do so if it can be said to be abusive. This is fine in principle, but much depends on the more precise meaning given to the idea of abuse. We have already seen the elasticity of this concept in the discussion of Article 102.[19] The point can be put quite simply: the closer the Court comes to regarding the grant of exclusive rights as abusive in and of itself, the more difficult it becomes for a state to organize its economic activities in this manner.

Thus in *Höfner*[20] the ECJ considered the legality of German rules that required certain categories of job-seekers to be placed in contact with potential employers through a state-licensed agency, and the agency was given exclusive powers in the relevant area. The effect of this monopoly was to suppress the activities of independent employment consultants, and contracts they made would be void.

---

[19] Ch 27.
[20] Case C–41/90 *Höfner and Elser v Macrotron GmbH* [1991] ECR I–1979.

The ECJ decided that any state rule that compelled an undertaking to breach Article 102 would be illegal under Article 106(1). It held that the grant of exclusive rights was not *per se* incompatible with Article 106,[21] but that a state violated Article 106(1) if it placed an undertaking in such a dominant position that the very exercise of these exclusive rights could not avoid being abusive. The ECJ concluded that the Member State had created such a situation, because the state-licensed agency was not in a position to satisfy market demand, and the exclusivity could affect nationals of other Member States.[22] The ECJ's willingness to characterize a grant of exclusive rights as abusive within Article 106 is also apparent in the following case.

Case C–179/90 **Merci Convenzionali Porto di Genova SpA v Siderurgica Gabrielli SpA**
[1991] ECR I–5889

[Note Lisbon Treaty renumbering: Arts 30, 85, 86, and 90 are now
Arts 34, 101, 102, and 106 TFEU]

Merci enjoyed the exclusive right to organize dock work in Genoa. It would call upon a dock-work company to unload ships. Siderurgica (S) applied to Merci to have a consignment of steel unloaded, even though the ship's own crew could have performed the task. Merci called upon the relevant Genoa dock-work company to do the job. Delays arose as a result of strikes. S therefore demanded reimbursement from Merci, claiming that the charges were unfair for the services performed. The ECJ reaffirmed that an undertaking having a statutory monopoly over a substantial part of the common market would be regarded as having a dominant position for the purposes of Article 86. It then continued as follows.

THE ECJ

16. It should next be stated that the simple fact of creating a dominant position by granting exclusive rights within the meaning of Article 90(1) EEC is not as such incompatible with Article 86.

17. However, the Court has had occasion to state, in this respect, that a Member State is in breach of the prohibition contained in these two provisions if the undertaking in question, merely by exercising the exclusive rights granted to it, cannot avoid abusing its dominant position (see Case C–41/90, *Höfner*...) or when such rights are liable to create a situation in which that undertaking is induced to commit such abuses (see Case C–260/89, *ERT*...).

18. According to Article 86(2)(a), (b) and (c) EEC, such abuse may in particular consist in imposing on the persons requiring the services in question unfair purchase prices or other unfair trading conditions, in limiting technical development, to the prejudice of consumers, or in the application of dissimilar conditions to equivalent transactions with other trading parties.

19. In that respect it appears from the circumstances described by the national court... that the undertakings enjoying exclusive rights in accordance with the procedures laid down by the national rules in question are, as a result, induced either to demand payment for services which have not been requested, to charge disproportionate prices, to refuse to have recourse to modern technology, which involves an increase in the cost of the operations and a prolongation of the time required for their performance, or to grant price reductions to certain consumers and at the same time to offset such reductions by an increase in the charges to other consumers.

---

[21] Ibid [29].

[22] Ibid [34]; Case C–55/96 *Job Centre coop arl* [1997] ECR I–7119; Case C–258/98 *Criminal Proceedings against Carra* [2000] ECR I–4217; Case C–260/89 *Elliniki Radiophonia Tileorassi AE (ERT) v Dimotiki Etairia Pliroforissis (DEP) and Sotirios Kouvelas* [1991] ECR I–2925.

20. In these circumstances it must be held that a Member State creates a situation contrary to Article 86 EEC where it adopts rules of such a kind as those at issue before the national court, which are capable of affecting trade between Member States as in the case of the main proceedings, regard being had... to the importance of traffic in the Port of Genoa.

21. As regards the interpretation of Article 30 requested by the national court, it is sufficient to recall that a national measure which has the effect of facilitating the abuse of a dominant position capable of affecting trade between Member States will generally be incompatible with that Article, which prohibits quantitative restrictions on imports and all measures having equivalent effect (see Case 13/77, *GB-INNO-BM v ATAB*) in so far as such a measure has the effect of making more difficult and hence of impeding imports of goods from other Member States.

22. In the main proceedings it may be seen from the national court's findings that the unloading of the goods could have been effected at a lesser cost by the ship's crew, so that compulsory recourse to the services of the two undertakings enjoying exclusive rights involved extra expense and was therefore capable, by reason of its effect on the prices of the goods, of affecting imports.

The ECJ's reasoning is instructive.[23] In paragraph 16 the Court reiterated the proposition that the creation of exclusive rights was not itself abusive within Article 106. This was then qualified in paragraph 17. Exclusivity could entail a breach of Articles 106 and 102 either when the exercise of the exclusive rights could not avoid being abusive, or where such rights were liable to create a situation in which the undertaking was induced to commit an abuse. It then applied the latter formulation to the instant case, paragraph 19.

This comes perilously close to regarding the grant of exclusivity as abusive *per se*, because of the ways identified in paragraph 19 in which an undertaking could be induced to commit an abuse. An undertaking can be in breach of Article 102 through charging excessive prices, discriminatory prices, and the like. Any firm with a dominant position has the potential to do this. Whether it actually chooses to behave in this manner is another matter. The message from the Court is, however, that the very grant of the exclusive rights can create a situation in which the undertaking is induced to commit such abuses.

The meaning of the word 'induce' is, however, crucial. The ECJ's reasoning comes close to stating that, because the holder of the exclusive right possessed market power which enabled it to price in an abusive manner, therefore it was induced to do so. On this hypothesis it could always be said that the grantee of exclusivity would be induced to price abusively, with the consequence that exclusive rights would, in effect, be rendered illegal *per se*. It might be argued that this ignores the fact that the holder of the exclusive right had in fact priced in an abusive manner: paragraph 19. If this was indeed so then Merci should have been condemned on this basis alone, since nothing was gained by the language of inducement.

The fact that the Court used the language of inducement was not, however, fortuitous. It wished to make a point about the consequence of forms of economic organization adopted by the state. What is distinctive about the grant of a statutory monopoly is that the grantee obtains a protected sphere of activity, which is immune from the normal rigours of competition. This is by way of contrast to other

---

[23] See also Case C–320/91 P *Procureur du Roi v Paul Corbeau* [1993] ECR I–2533; Case C–18/93 *Corsica Ferries Italia SRL v Corpo dei Piloti di Genova* [1994] ECR I–1783; Case C–323/93 *Société Civile Agricole du Centre d'Insémination de la Crespelle v Coopérative d'Elevage et d'Insémination Artificielle du Départment de la Mayenne* [1994] ECR I–5077; Case C–242/95 *GT-Link A/S v De Danske Statsbaner (DSB)* [1997] ECR I–4449; Case C–451/03 *Servizi Ausiliari Dottori Commercialisti Srl v Calafiori* [2006] ECR I–2941, [23]; Case C–49/07 *Motosykletistiki Omospondia Ellados NPID (MOTOE) v Elliniko Dimosio* [2008] ECR I–4863, [49]–[50]; Case C–553/12 *European Commission v DEI*, 17 July 2014, [39]–[45].

firms with a dominant position. They must always be looking over their shoulder lest new entrants erode their market power. This is a reason why such a firm might decide not to price too highly, since it will act as an incentive for others to enter the market.

The holder of the statutory exclusive right does not have the same rationale for self-restraint, or at least not to the same extent. It is for this reason that such firms might well be induced to charge disproportionate prices, secure in the knowledge that this cannot operate as a carrot to bring others into the market. It is for this reason that the ECJ was particularly concerned about monopoly power in this form. This is readily understandable when looked at from the EU's perspective, but does not alter the fact that the Court's reasoning comes close to regarding the grant of exclusive statutory rights as abusive *per se*.

(iv) *The Court's Current Approach*

The general thrust of the Court's current approach builds on the preceding jurisprudence: the grant of exclusive rights will normally be held *prima facie* to infringe Article 106(1), but the ECJ will then consider whether there is some objective justification for the exclusivity.[24]

In *Traco*[25] it was held that the grant to Poste Italiana of exclusive rights to carry the post violated Article 106(1). Poste Italiana charged any other postal operator charges equivalent to those paid by customers of Poste Italiana, even though it did not carry the mail. It could not therefore avoid abusing its dominant position, was caught by Article 106(1), and had to seek justification under Article 106(2). In *Ambulanz Glockner*[26] a public body refused to renew the applicant's authorization to provide non-emergency transport services for patients. Two other companies had exclusive rights to provide emergency services for patients. The ECJ assumed that the grant of these exclusive rights could violate Article 102(b), limiting markets, in the sense that only these two companies were allowed to provide non-emergency, as well as emergency, transport services. There was therefore *prima facie* a breach of Article 106(1), and the ECJ then considered justification under Article 106(2).[27]

It is thus more difficult than hitherto for a state to organize its economic activities by giving special or exclusive rights to particular firms. Agnosticism as to forms of economic organization has been replaced by a more strident belief in the operation of free markets, unless the state can provide special justification for the privileges accorded.

(B) ARTICLE 106(2)

Article 106(2) has three parts. It begins by emphasizing that undertakings entrusted with the operation of services of a general economic interest, or which have the character of a revenue-producing monopoly, are subject to the Treaty. It then excludes the application of these Treaty rules where the performance of the tasks assigned to such undertakings is liable to be obstructed. This exception is

---

[24] L Hancher, Note (1994) 31 CMLRev 105; L Hancher, 'Community, State and Market' in P Craig and G de Búrca (eds), *The Evolution of EU Law* (Oxford University Press, 1999) ch 20; D Edward and M Hoskins, 'Article 90: Deregulation and EC Law, Reflections Arising from the XVI FIDE Conference' (1995) 32 CMLRev 157; Ehlermann (n 1) 273; L Hancher and P Larouche, 'The Coming of Age of EU Regulation of Network Industries and Services of General Economic Interest' in P Craig and G de Búrca (eds), *The Evolution of EU Law* (Oxford University Press, 2nd edn, 2011) ch 24; G Davies, 'Article 86 EC, the EC's Economic Approach to Competition Law, and the General Interest' (2009) 5 European Competition Journal 549.

[25] Case C–340/99 *TNT Traco SpA v Poste Italiane SpA* [2001] ECR I–4109.

[26] Case C–475/99 *Ambulanz Glockner v Landkreis Südwestpfalz* [2001] ECR I–8089.

[27] See also Case C–67/96 *Albany International BV v Stichting Bedrijfspensioenfonds Textielindustrie* [1999] ECR I–5751; Cases 147–148/97 *Deutsche Post AG v Gesellschaft für Zahlungssyteme mbH and Citicorp Kartenservice GmbH* [2000] ECR I–825; Case C–351/12 *OSA* EU:C:2014:110.

then subject to a proviso that the development of trade must not be affected to such an extent as would be contrary to the interests of the EU.

(i) *The First Step*

The first step is therefore to determine whether an undertaking is of the kind mentioned. The ECJ has stressed that the category of entrusted undertakings should be strictly defined, since Article 106(2) derogates from the Treaty rules.[28] It is irrelevant whether the undertaking is public or private, but the service must have been assigned to it by a public authority.[29]

The *BUPA* case[30] provides guidance on the meaning of services of a general economic interest (SGEI). The GC held that Member States have broad discretion as to what they regard as SGEIs, but that this discretion could not be used arbitrarily so as to remove a particular sector from the ordinary competition rules. It was for the Member State to show that the mission had been granted by an act of a public authority and to provide reasons why it regarded that mission as a SGEI. The provision of a SGEI presumed some general or public interest. It did not mean that the undertaking would have to be accorded exclusive or special rights to carry it out. A SGEI did not have to constitute a universal service in the strict sense of that term, nor did a SGEI have to be offered free of charge or without consideration for profitability. The compulsory nature of the service was however a condition for a SGEI in EU law, in the sense that the undertaking entrusted with the SGEI was required to offer the service to any person requesting it.

(ii) *The Second Step*

The second step in the application of Article 106(2) is to determine whether the exception applies. The ECJ previously held that the exception would apply only if the relevant Treaty prohibitions were incompatible with the performance of the undertaking's assigned tasks.[31]

This is no longer the approach. In *Commission v Netherlands*,[32] the ECJ held that for Article 106(2) to apply it was sufficient if the application of the Treaty rules obstructed the performance, in law or in fact, of the undertaking's special obligations. It was not necessary for the survival of the undertaking to be under threat. It sufficed to show that the exclusive rights were necessary to enable the holder to perform the tasks of general economic interest assigned to it under economically acceptable conditions. The Member State did not have to prove that no other conceivable measure could enable the tasks to be performed under the same conditions.[33]

The ECJ will nonetheless look closely at claims that the exception applies.[34] Thus in *Merci*[35] the ECJ decided that even if dock work were to be regarded as of general economic interest, there was no

---

[28] Case 127/73 *BRT v SABAM* [1974] ECR 313; Case C–242/95 *GT-Link* (n 23); Case C–179/90 *Merci Convenzionali Porto di Genova SpA v Siderurgica Gabrielli SpA* [1991] ECR I–5889, [27].

[29] (N 28); Case 7/82 *GVL v Commission* [1983] ECR 483; Case C–49/07 *MOTOE* (n 23) [45]–[47].

[30] Case T–289/03 *British United Provident Association Ltd (BUPA), BUPA Insurance Ltd and BUPA Ireland Ltd v Commission* [2008] ECR II–81; Cases T–309, 317, 329 and 336/04 *TV 2/Danmark A/S and Others v Commission* [2008] ECR II–2935; Case T–137/10 *CBI v European Commission* EU:T:2012:584; M Ross, 'A Healthy Approach to Services of General Economic Interest? The *BUPA* Judgment of the Court of First Instance' (2009) 34 ELRev 127; W Sauter, Note (2009) 46 CMLRev 269.

[31] Case 155/73 *Sacchi* [1974] ECR 409; Case 311/84 *Centre Belge d'Etudes du Marché-Télémarketing SA v Compagnie Luxembourgeoise de Télédiffusion SA and Information Publicité Benelux SA* [1985] ECR 3261.

[32] Case C–157/94 [1997] ECR I–5699; Case C–438/02 *Criminal Proceedings against Hanner* [2005] ECR I–4551, [47].

[33] Case C–340/99 *TNT Traco* (n 25) [54]; Case C–67/96 *Albany* (n 27) [107].

[34] Case 66/86 *Ahmed Saeed Flugreisen and Silver Line Reisebüro GmbH v Zentrale zur Bekämpfung Unlauteren Wettbewerbs eV* [1989] ECR 803, [56].

[35] Case C–179/90 (n 28) [27].

evidence that this demanded modification of the Treaty rules so as to prevent obstruction in the performance of this task. Similarly in *British Telecom*[36] the Commission decided that practices relating to the transmission of messages breached Article 102. The ECJ rejected the argument that the measures adopted by BT should be exempted from the competition rules because of Article 106(2), since BT failed to establish that the application of these rules would prejudice the accomplishment of its tasks.[37]

The ECJ has been more receptive to use of the exception where the undertaking granted exclusivity has universal service obligations requiring it to perform tasks that are not profitable. The only way that it can do this is to have exclusive rights over the profitable parts of the service, since if it does not other undertakings will 'cream off' those parts.

Thus, in *Corbeau*[38] the ECJ accepted that the Belgian postal service was an entrusted undertaking, and that some restriction on competition might be necessary to enable it to fulfil the duties it was required to perform. If this were not so then other firms could simply 'cream off' the profitable business, since they would have no obligation to perform loss-making activities. This did not, however, serve to exclude all competition. There could, said the Court, be services that could be dissociated from the general public service, which could be offered by other undertakings without threatening the economic stability needed by the holder of the exclusive right. It was for the national court to determine whether the services came within that category.

In *Albany*[39] a company argued that a Dutch law making affiliation to a supplementary pension scheme compulsory was contrary to Article 106. The ECJ held that the exclusivity was justified under Article 106(2). The compulsory pension scheme was obliged to accept all workers without a prior medical examination, and contributions did not reflect risk. If the exclusive right of the fund to manage the supplementary pension scheme were removed, then undertakings with young employees in good health engaged in non-dangerous activities would seek more advantageous terms from private insurers. The departure of these 'good risks' would leave the pension fund with an increased share of 'bad risks'. This would lead to an increase in premiums for these workers, since the fund would not be able to offer pensions at the previous cost.[40]

(iii) *The Third Step*

Even if the exception applies, the third step in Article 106(2) requires that the development of trade must not be affected to such an extent as would be contrary to the interests of the EU. This proviso subjugates Member State interests to those of the Union in the relevant area.

(c) ARTICLE 106(3)

Article 106(3) gives the Commission power to ensure the application of Article 106 through directives or decisions addressed to Member States. It is one of the rare Treaty provisions that confer direct

---

[36] Case 41/83 *Re British Telecommunications: Italy v Commission* [1985] ECR 873, [33].

[37] See also Case C–203/96 *Chemsiche Afvalstoffen Dusseldorp BV v Minister van Volkshuisvesting, Ruimtelijke Ordening en Milieubeheer* [1998] ECR I–4075.

[38] Case C–320/91 P (n 23); Case C–162/06 *International Mail Spain SL v Administración del Estado and Correos* [2007] ECR I–9911; compare Case T–260/94 *Air Inter SA v Commission* [1997] ECR II–997.

[39] Case C–67/96 *Albany* (n 27) [107]–[111].

[40] See also Cases C–115–117/97 *Brentjens' Handelsonderneming BV v Stichting Bedrijfspensioenfonds voor de Handel in Bouwmaterialen* [1999] ECR I–6025, [107]–[111]; Case C–340/99 *Traco* (n 25) [54]–[63]; Case C–475/99 *Ambulanz Glockner* (n 26) [57]–[66]; Cases 147–148/97 *Deutsche Post* (n 27) [50]–[62]; Case C–209/98 *Entreprenørforeningens Affalds/Miljøsektion (FFAD) v Københavns Kommune* [2000] ECR I–3473, [77]–[83]; Case T–289/03 *BUPA* (n 30); Case C–242/10 *Enel Produzione SpA v Autorità per l'energia elettrica e il gas* EU:C:2011:861.

legislative competence on the Commission.[41] The Commission has used this power relatively rarely. The Member States have nonetheless challenged the Commission's competence to proceed in this manner, but the ECJ has commonly rejected such challenges.

Thus in the *Transparency Directive* case,[42] the facts of which were set out above, the Member States argued that the Directive could not be enacted under Article 106(3), which, they said, was limited to dealing with a specific situation in one or more Member States. It did not give any more general legislative power to the Commission. The Court rejected this argument. The term 'directive' in Article 106(3) had the same meaning as in Article 288.[43] The parties also contended that the Directive should have been adopted by the Council pursuant to Article 109. The ECJ disagreed. The specific power to issue directives contained in Article 106(3) was in furtherance of the Commission's duty of surveillance provided for in Article 106.[44]

(D) ARTICLE 106 AND NATIONAL COURTS

We must now consider how far the provisions of Article 106 are directly effective. A distinction must be drawn between Article 106(1) and (2).

Article 106(1) is dependent upon a breach of some other Treaty Article. The ability of an individual to invoke Article 106(1) will therefore depend on whether the other Treaty Article allegedly broken is directly effective. This is exemplified by the *Merci* case.[45] The ECJ held that Articles 34, 45, and 102 have direct effect when they fall to be considered within the framework of Article 106.

Article 106(2) has, as seen above, three parts: the determination of whether a body is an entrusted undertaking, the application of the exception, and the proviso to the exception. The ECJ has long recognized the competence of national courts to answer the first of these questions. In *SABAM*[46] the ECJ affirmed that a national court has the duty of investigating whether an undertaking which invokes Article 106(2) has in fact been entrusted by the Member State with the operation of a service of general economic interest.

There has been more uncertainty about whether a national court can apply the exception. The ECJ's initial response was that Article 106(2) could not be invoked by individuals before national courts, since it did not create rights for individuals,[47] but subsequent case law cast doubt on this proposition. The situation has now been clarified by the *ERT* case.[48] The ECJ held that Article 106(2) renders an undertaking subject to the Treaty rules unless their application is incompatible with the performance of its tasks. It was therefore open to a national court to determine whether the practices of such an undertaking were compatible with, for example, Article 102. The national court could also decide whether those practices, if they were contrary to such a provision, could be justified by the needs of the particular task given to the undertaking.[49] The difficulties that this presents for national courts should not, however, be underestimated.[50]

---

[41] Art 106 can also be enforced through Art 258, and the interpretation of Art 106 can be clarified through Art 267 references.

[42] Cases 188–190/80 *France, Italy and United Kingdom v Commission* [1982] ECR 2545, [4]–[15]. See also Case C–202/88 *France v Commission* [1991] ECR I–1223; Cases C–48 and 66/90 *Netherlands, Koninklijke PTT Nederland NV and PTT Post BV v Commission* [1992] ECR I–565; Case C–107/95 P *Bundesverband der Bilanzbuchhalter eV v Commission* [1997] ECR I–947; Case C–163/99 *Portuguese Republic v Commission* [2001] ECR I–2613.

[43] Cases 188–190/80 (n 42) [7].

[44] Ibid [14].

[45] Case C–179/90 (n 28) [23]; Case C–242/95 *GT-Link* (n 23) [57]; Case C–258/98 *Carra* (n 22) 11.

[46] Case 127/73 (n 28); Case C–218/00 *Cisal di Battistello Venanzio & C Sas v INAIL* [2002] ECR I–691, [19].

[47] Case 10/71 *Muller* (n 18).

[48] Case C–260/89 (n 22) [33]–[34].

[49] The ECJ adopted the same approach to the tasks of the national courts in the cases mentioned in (nn 27 and 40).

[50] See, eg, the task presented to the national courts in Case C–320/91 P *Corbeau* (n 23), discussed by Hancher (1994) 31 CMLRev 105, 119–120.

Should an applicant succeed in bringing a case within the exception, the question remains whether a national court is competent to apply the proviso in Article 106(2). It would be difficult for a national court to perform this task, since it may not have the information on which to make the assessment. On this view it would require a Commission decision made under Article 106(3) to decide the issue.

(E) SUMMARY

i. Article 106 seeks to reconcile a Member State's interest in using certain undertakings as an instrument of social and/or economic policy with the EU's interest in ensuring compliance with the rules on competition and the internal market.

ii. The mere grant of a monopoly, or exclusive rights, will not infringe Article 106(1). It will do so only when the exercise of the exclusive rights could not avoid being abusive, or where such rights were liable to create a situation in which the undertaking was induced to commit an abuse.

iii. It is equally clear that the ECJ has been ready to find that either condition applies, and that therefore Article 106(1) is applicable.

iv. It is then for the state to provide a justification under Article 106(2). It must be shown that the Treaty rules should be excluded because they would obstruct the performance of the tasks assigned to the undertaking. The ECJ will subject such claims to close scrutiny. However, the Court has held the exception applicable to bodies with universal service obligations or the equivalent thereto. Exclusivity in such instances has been held warranted in order that the profitable parts of an activity are not 'creamed off' by the private sector, with the consequence that the body granted exclusive rights is unable to fulfil its remit.

4 THE STATE, ARTICLES 4(3) TEU, 101, 102, AND 34 TFEU

The discussion thus far has focused on Article 106. This is not, however, the only Treaty provision relevant to state action and the EU. The Court has also made important decisions on the basis of Articles 4(3) TEU, 101, 102, and 34 TFEU.[51] The basic principle is that a state may not adopt or maintain in force any measure which would deprive, for example, Article 101 of its effectiveness or prejudice its full and uniform application. A state can be in breach of this obligation when it requires or encourages undertakings to conclude cartels in violation of Article 101, or when it divests its national provisions of their public nature by, in effect, delegating to the firms the responsibility for taking decisions about the boundaries of competition. This jurisprudence is the means by which the ECJ has extended the type of obligation imposed on a state by Article 106 to situations where the undertakings are neither public nor enjoy any specially privileged position. The following cases illustrate the Court's jurisprudence.

In *Vereniging van Vlaamse Reisbureaus*[52] a travel agent was prosecuted for violating a professional code of practice incorporated into Belgian law. The code involved horizontal price fixing, a blatant breach of Article 101. The Court also found that the Belgian state was in breach of Article 4(3) TEU, read together with Article 101, by supporting the cartel through its own legal regime.

---

[51] PJ Slot, 'The Application of Articles 3(f), 5 and 85 to 94 EEC' (1987) 12 ELRev 179; L Gyselen, 'State Action and the Effectiveness of the Treaty's Competition Provisions' (1989) 26 CMLRev 33.

[52] Case 311/85 *Vereniging van Vlaamse Reisbureaus v Sociale Dienst van de Plaatselijke en Gewestelijke Overheidsdiensten* [1987] ECR 3801.

In *Van Eycke*[53] holders of certain Belgian savings accounts had a tax exemption, provided that the bank offered interest rates below that set by the minister in a Royal Decree. Those who held accounts at banks that gave higher interest rates than that in the Royal Decree lost the tax exemption, so it was unattractive for the banks to offer such rates. The effect was to limit price competition between banks. The ECJ held that, although the duty in Articles 101 and 102 is directed towards undertakings, the state itself has an obligation, derived from Article 4(3) TEU, not to introduce measures which render the competition Articles ineffective. This would be the case where national legislation reinforced the effects of agreements that were in breach of Article 101, or where the state deprived its own legislation of its official character by delegating to private traders responsibility for taking decisions affecting the economic sphere.[54] Later attempts to invoke this principle have, however, not been notably successful.[55]

Where the state intervenes not to support an existing agreement which is itself illegal under Article 101, but through an independent measure which undertakings must follow, Article 34 TFEU is the most appropriate provision in relation to goods, and Article 56 TFEU in the case of services.[56]

5 STATE AIDS: POLICY DEVELOPMENT AND REFORM

(A) POLICY DEVELOPMENT

Certain general points should be clarified before discussing the detailed rules on state aids. First, the Commission, as the initial decision-maker, develops the general policy in this area.[57] Its decisions are subject to judicial review, but the EU Courts are mindful of the complex evaluations of social and economic data involved, and they will not, therefore, substitute their view for that of the Commission in relation to determinations made under Article 107(2)–(3). Judicial review is limited to verifying whether the Commission complied with procedural rules, including the provision of reasons; whether the facts on which the decision was based were accurately stated; and whether there was a manifest error of assessment or misuse of power.[58]

Secondly, the Commission has discretion as to the approach to state aids. Thus it has, for example, applied a principle of compensatory justification. Before it will approve aid there must be some contribution by the beneficiary of the aid, over and above the normal play of market forces, to the attainment of Union objectives set out in the derogations from Article 107(3). In general terms, aid

---

[53] Case 267/86 *Van Eycke v NV ASPA* [1988] ECR 4769.

[54] See also Case 229/83 *Leclerc v Au Blé Vert* [1985] ECR 1; Cases 209–213/84 *Ministère Public v Asjes* [1986] ECR 1425; Case C–198/01 *CIF v Autorità Garante della Concorrenza del Mercato* [2003] ECR I–8055.

[55] Case C–2/91 *Wolf Meng* [1993] ECR I–5751; Case C–245/91 *Ohra Schadeverzekeringen NV* [1993] ECR I–5851; Case C–153/93 *Germany v Delta Schiffahrts- und Speditionsgesellschaft mbH* [1994] ECR I–2517; Case C–185/91 *Bundesanstalt für den Güterfernverkehr v Gebrüder Reiff GmbH & Co KG* [1993] ECR I–5801; Cases C–140–142/94 *DIP SpA v Commune di Bassano del Grappa* [1995] ECR I–3257; Case C–70/95 *Sodemare SA, Anni Azzuri Holding SpA and Anni Azzuri Rezzato Srl v Regione Lombardia* [1997] ECR I–3395; Case C–35/99 *Criminal Proceedings against Arduino* [2002] ECR I–1529; Case C–250/03 *Mauri v Ministero della Giustizia* [2005] ECR I–1267; Cases C–94 and 202/04 *Cipolla v Fazari* [2006] ECR I–11421; Case C–393/08 *Emanuela Sbarigia v Azienda USL RM/A* [2010] ECR I–6337.

[56] Case 229/83 *Leclerc* (n 54).

[57] http://ec.europa.eu/competition/state_aid/overview/index_en.html; L Hancher, T Ottervanger, and PJ Slot, *EU State Aids* (Sweet & Maxwell, 4th edn, 2012); A Evans, *EC Law of State Aid* (Oxford University Press, 1997).

[58] Case T–171/02 *Regione Autonoma della Sardegna v Commission* [2005] ECR II–2123, [97]; Cases T–228 and 233/99 *Westdeutsche Landesbank Girozentrale v Commission* [2003] ECR II–435, [282]; Case T–198/01 *Technische Glaswerke Ilmenau GmbH v Commission* [2004] ECR II–2717, [97]; Case T–189/03 *ASM Brescia SpA v Commission* [2009] ECR II–1831, [115]; P Craig, *EU Administrative Law* (Oxford University Press, 2nd edn, 2012) ch 15.

can be designed to restructure an undertaking, to rescue an undertaking, or to help it with operating costs. The Commission has provided guidelines on these.[59] The guidelines for restructuring aid stipulate that viability is restored, that aid is in proportion to the restructuring costs and benefits, that undue distortions of competition are avoided, and that the restructuring plan is fully implemented. Operating aid relieves an undertaking of expenses that it would normally bear in its day-to-day operations, with no technical or structural alteration in the character of the recipient. It is generally regarded as objectionable by the Commission and the Court,[60] and is normally authorized only to cope with specific regional or sectoral problems. The Commission's discretion as to the approach to state aids has been evident more recently in modification of state aid rules in response to the banking and financial crisis.[61]

Thirdly, the Commission can also choose how to develop its substantive policy, whether through formal legislation or through informal rule-making. The Commission has made formal legislation in certain areas. The Council has, pursuant to Article 109 TFEU, delegated power to the Commission to make regulations exempting types of aid from the requirement of notification, and stipulating that it shall be regarded as compatible with the internal market.[62] The Commission has used this power to make formal regulations concerning small and medium-sized enterprises, *de minimis* aid, training aid, and aid for employment.[63] Formal legislation has also been made on procedural matters.[64]

Fourthly, the Commission can choose to develop policy, not only through formal legislation, but also through individual decisions or informal rule-making. Rules and policy frameworks have been made for particular industrial sectors, and in relation to matters such as regional aid, environmental aid, deprived areas, and aid to promote investment of risk capital in small and medium-sized enterprises.[65] It is lawful for the Commission to structure its discretion through guidelines, provided that they do not depart from the Treaty rules.[66] In *CIRFS*[67] the ECJ accepted that the Commission was bound by the terms of its policy framework, and in *Ijssel-Vliet*[68] it held that

[59] Community guidelines on rescuing and restructuring firms in difficulty [2004] OJ C244/2; Guidelines on state aid for rescuing and restructuring non-financial undertakings in difficulty [2014] OJ C249/1; Guidelines on risk finance aid for 2014–2020 [2014] OJ C19/4.

[60] Case T–459/93 *Siemens SA v Commission* [1995] ECR II–1675, upheld on appeal in Case C–278/95 P *Siemens SA v Commission* [1997] ECR I–2507; Case T–214/95 *Vlaams Gewest v Commission* [1998] ECR II–717; Case T–190/00 *Regione Siciliana v Commission* [2003] ECR II–5015, [130].

[61] Communication from the Commission on the application, from 1 January 2012, of State aid rules to support measures in favour of banks in the context of the financial crisis [2011] OJ C356/7; http://ec.europa.eu/competition/state_aid/legislation/temporary.html.

[62] Council Regulation (EC) No 994/98 of 7 May 1998 on the application of Articles 92 and 93 of the Treaty to certain categories of horizontal State aid [1998] OJ L142/1.

[63] Commission Regulation (EU) No 651/2014 of 17 June 2014 declaring certain categories of aid compatible with the internal market in application of Articles 107 and 108 of the Treaty [2014] OJ L187/1, http://ec.europa.eu/competition/state_aid/legislation/block.html.

[64] Council Regulation (EC) No 659/99 of 22 March 1999 laying down detailed rules on the application of Article 93 of the EC Treaty [1999] OJ L83/1.

[65] http://ec.europa.eu/competition/state_aid/legislation/horizontal.html.

[66] Case C–313/90 *CIRFS v Commission* [1993] ECR I–1125, [34]–[36]; Case T–214/95 *Vlaams Gewest* (n 60) [89]; Case T–149/95 *Ducros v Commission* [1997] ECR II–2031, [61]; Case C–288/96 *Germany v Commission* [2000] ECR I–8237, [62]; Case T–171/02 *Regione Autonoma della Sardegna* (n 58) [95]; Case T–17/03 *Schmitz-Gotha Fahrzeugwerke GmbH v Commission* [2006] ECR II–1139, [42]; Cases T–254, 270 and 277/00 *Hotel Cipriani SpA v Commission* [2008] ECR II–3269, [292]–[293]; Cases C–75 and 80/05 P *Germany, Glunz AG and OSB Deutschland GmbH v Kronofrance SA* [2008] ECR I–6619, [59]–[62]; Case C–439/11 P *Ziegler v Commission* EU:C:2013:513, [59]–[60].

[67] Case C–313/90 *CIRFS* (n 66).

[68] Case C–311/94 *Ijssel-Vliet Combinatie BV v Minister van Economische Zaken* [1996] ECR I–5023.

Commission guidelines built into a Dutch aid scheme were binding on the Dutch Government. Moreover, in *Vlaams Gewest*[69] the GC held that the guidelines adopted by the Commission had to be applied in accordance with the principle of equal treatment, with the implication that like cases, as defined in the guidelines, had to be treated alike. Such guidelines are however not formally binding on the EU Courts.[70]

Finally, the variety of instruments used by the Commission can be confusing for users of the system.[71] The reasons for employing such policy documents are part practical, part conceptual, and part political. In practical terms such guidelines help an overburdened administration to cope with increased workload.[72] In conceptual terms they have the advantages associated with rule-making.[73] They 'reduce Member States' room for manoeuvre in giving aid and the controller's margin of discretion, choice and possible arbitrariness';[74] and they facilitate 'the transparency, legal security and credibility which result from strict and consistent enforcement, to the benefit of governments and industry'.[75] In political terms, rule-making by the Commission obviates the need for consent in the Council, which is necessary under Article 109 when formal legislation is enacted. Thus Rawlinson, a principal administrator within the state aids directorate, argued that recourse to Article 109 would make policy-making more protracted.[76] However della Cananea has pointed to the lack of clarity of certain guidelines, and to the fact that the rights of individuals have not always been properly safeguarded.

(B) REFORM

The Commission instituted a consultation exercise in 2005 designed to reform the state aid regime.[77] It reiterated the imperative behind this area of the law: the maintenance of a level playing field between undertakings. The Commission acknowledged that state aid could be legitimate in circumstances of market failure. The more specific reform proposals resonated round that theme. Thus state aid for matters such as innovation, research and development, and risk capital was seen as potentially legitimate where the market failed to provide the requisite incentives to engage in these activities.[78] This led to a new block exemption.[79] The Action Plan also led to improvements related to procedure, and to monitoring and enforcement, which will be considered in the course of the ensuing discussion. Reform of state aid is still ongoing, with further initiatives being planned.[80]

---

[69] Case T–214/95 (n 60) [89].

[70] Case C–310/99 *Italy v Commission* [2002] ECR I–2289, [52].

[71] F Rawlinson, 'The Role of Policy Frameworks, Codes and Guidelines in the Control of State Aid' in I Harden (ed), *State Aid: Community Law and Policy* (Bundesanzeiger, 1993) 59; G della Cananea, 'Administration by Guidelines: The Policy Guidelines of the Commission in the Field of State Aids' in ibid 68–69.

[72] Rawlinson (n 71) 56; Evans (n 57) 408–427.

[73] P Craig, *Administrative Law* (Sweet & Maxwell, 7th edn, 2012) ch 15.

[74] Rawlinson (n 71) 55.

[75] Ibid 57.

[76] Ibid 60; Evans (n 57) 405–408.

[77] State Aid Action Plan, Less and Better Targeted State Aid: A Roadmap for State Aid Reform 2005–2009, COM(2005) 107 final.

[78] Ibid [25], [27], [30].

[79] Comm Reg 651/2014 (n 63).

[80] EU State Aid Modernization, COM(2012) 209 final; http://ec.europa.eu/competition/state_aid/modernisation/index_en.html.

6 STATE AIDS: THE SUBSTANTIVE RULES AND ARTICLE 107

(A) DEFINITION OF STATE AID

Article 107 lays down the test for state aids.[81] It covers aid given to public undertakings within Article 106, subject to Article 106(2), as well as aid given to private firms.[82] Article 107 has three parts. Paragraph (1) establishes the general principle that state aids are incompatible with the internal market. Paragraph (2) provides certain exceptions for situations where the aid will be deemed to be compatible with the internal market. Paragraph (3) lists types of case where the aid may be deemed to be compatible with the internal market. Article 107(1) provides that:

> Save as otherwise provided in the Treaties, any aid granted by a Member State or through State resources in any form whatsoever which distorts or threatens to distort competition by favouring certain undertakings or the production of certain goods shall, in so far as it affects trade between Member States, be incompatible with the internal market.

There are four conditions before something is classified as aid under Article 107. These are cumulative: all must be fulfilled before the Member State measure is caught by Article 107.

(i) *The Definition of State Aid: An Advantage Conferred on the Recipient*

Article 107(1) does not define state aid. The ECJ and Commission have, as might be expected, taken a broad view. The rationale for the aid is not relevant at this stage,[83] and substance, not form, is the criterion when defining aid. The guiding principle is that the measure must confer an advantage to the recipient in order to constitute aid.

The Commission has provided a list of types of aid. These include direct subsidies, tax exemptions,[84] exemptions from parafiscal charges, preferential interest rates, favourable loan guarantees, the provision of land or buildings on special terms, indemnities against losses, preferential terms for public ordering, the deferment of the collection of fiscal or social contributions, and dividend guarantees. This list is illustrative rather than exhaustive.

The ECJ has made it clear that the concept of aid covers not only positive benefits, such as subsidies, but also measures that mitigate the charges an undertaking would normally bear,[85] such as the

---

[81] J-D Braun and J Kühling, 'Article 87 EC and the Community Courts: From Revolution to Evolution' (2008) 45 CMLRev 465; J Luís da Cruz Vilaça, 'Material and Geographic Selectivity in State Aid—Recent Developments' [2009] EStAL 443; L Rubini, 'The "Elusive Frontier": Regulation under EC State Aid Law' [2009] EStAL 277; A Biondi, 'State Aid is Falling Down, Falling Down: An Analysis of the Case Law on the Notion of Aid' (2013) 50 CMLRev 1719.

[82] Case C–387/92 *Banco de Crédito Industrial SA (Banco Exterior de España SA) v Ayuntamiento de Valencia* [1994] ECR I–877; Case T–106/95 *Fédération Française des Sociétés d'Assurances (FFSA) v Commission* [1997] ECR II–229.

[83] Case 173/73 *Italy v Commission* [1974] ECR 709; Case C–241/94 *France v Commission* [1996] ECR I–4187; Case C–251/97 *France v Commission* [1999] ECR I–6639.

[84] Case C–387/92 *Banco de Crédito* (n 82); Cases C–182 and 217/03 *Belgium and Forum 187 ASBL v Commission* [2006] ECR I–5479.

[85] Case C–237/04 *Enirisorse SpA v Sotacarbo SpA* [2006] ECR I–2843, [42]; Case C–222/04 *Ministero dell'Economia e delle Finanze v Cassa di Risparmio di Firenze SpA* [2006] ECR I–289, [131]; Cases C–393/04 and 41/05 *Air Liquide SA v Province de Liège* [2006] ECR I–5293.

supply of goods or services at a preferential rate,[86] a reduction in social security contributions,[87] or tax exemptions.[88]

General measures of economic policy, such as an interest-rate reduction, while benefiting industrial sales, will not in themselves be classified as aid.[89] Thus a non-sectoral measure of general taxation policy remains within the area of state fiscal sovereignty.[90] A measure will, nonetheless, be classified as aid even if it benefits a whole range of undertakings, as in the case of a general export aid,[91] though by way of contrast aid for general infrastructure will not normally constitute aid within Article 107.[92] The dividing line between general measures of economic policy and state aids may however be a fine one.[93]

Particular difficulties have arisen where the state takes a shareholding in a private company. In *Intermills*[94] the ECJ made it clear that no distinction could be drawn between aid granted in the form of loans and aid granted in the form of a holding acquired in the capital of an undertaking. Both could be caught by Article 107(1).[95]

Case C–142/87 **Re Tubemeuse: Belgium v Commission**
[1990] ECR I–959

[Note Lisbon Treaty renumbering: Arts 92 and 93 are now Arts 107 and 108 TFEU]

In 1979 the Belgian Government acquired 72 per cent of the capital holding of Tubemeuse (T), which was in severe financial difficulty following the withdrawal of private shareholders. In 1982 the Commission approved a series of aid measures, but these were not successful and the state then acquired the remaining shares in the firm. Between 1984 and 1986 Belgium initiated a series of measures designed to increase the capital of T. These measures were notified to the Commission, but the Government did not wait for the Commission's approval as required by Article 93(2). The Commission then made a decision that these measures constituted unlawful aid and instructed Belgium to recover the sums. The Belgian Government argued that the measures in 1984–1986 did not constitute state aid, but were rather the normal reaction of any investor whose initial investment (made in 1979 and then in 1982) was at risk. The ECJ reiterated its holding in *Intermills* and then continued as follows.

---

[86] Case C–241/94 *France* (n 83); Case C–387/92 *Banco de Crédito* (n 82); Case C–39/94 *Syndicat Français de l'Express International (SFEI) v La Poste* [1996] ECR I–3547; Case C–143/99 *Adria-Wien Pipeline GmbH and Wietersdörfer & Peggauer Zementwerke GmbH v Finanzlandesdirektion für Kärnten* [2001] ECR I–8365; Case T–301/02 *AEM SpA v Commission* [2009] ECR II–1757.

[87] Case C–75/97 *Belgium v Commission* [1999] ECR I–3671.

[88] Case C–6/97 *Italy v Commission* [1999] ECR I–2981.

[89] Case C–143/99 *Adria-Wien* (n 86) [35].

[90] Case C–308/01 *GIL Insurance Ltd v Commissioners of Customs and Excise* [2004] ECR I–4777, [78]. See however Case C–88/03 *Portugal v Commission* [2006] ECR I–7115.

[91] Case C–75/97 *Belgium v Commission* (n 87).

[92] Case C–225/91 *Matra v Commission* [1993] ECR I–3203.

[93] Case C–6/12 *P Oy* EU:C:2013:525; Case C–452/10 P *BNP Paribas v European Commission* EU:C:2012:366; C Quigley, 'The Notion of a State Aid in the EEC' (1988) 13 ELRev 242, 252–253; M Prek and S Lefevre, 'The Requirement of Selectivity in the Recent Case-Law of the Court of Justice' [2012] EStAL 335.

[94] Case 323/82 *Intermills SA v Commission* [1984] ECR 3809.

[95] See also Cases 296 and 318/82 *The Netherlands and Leeuwarder Papierwarenfabriek BV v Commission* [1985] ECR 809; Case 40/85 *Re Boch: Belgium v Commission* [1986] ECR 2321; Case T–16/96 *Cityflyer Express Ltd v Commission* [1998] ECR II–757; Case T–198/01 *Technische Glaswerke* (n 58) [98]–[99].

THE ECJ

26. In order to determine whether such measures are in the nature of State aid, the relevant criterion is that indicated in the Commission's decision, and not contested by the Belgian government, namely whether the undertaking could have obtained the amounts in question on the capital market.

27. In the event, it can be seen from the contested measure taken together with the other documents before the Court that, in addition to the technical difficulties of its plant, which made necessary the extensive modernisation programme in 1982 carried out with the help of the public authorities and authorised by the Commission, the company has, since 1979, had to face structural financial difficulties. Excessively high production costs, continual operating losses, poor liquidity and heavy indebtedness led to the withdrawal of almost all the private shareholders from the undertaking.

28. Moreover, it is not contested that the seamless steel tubes sector whose production was intended principally for use in oil exploration, was in a state of crisis, marked by considerable surplus capacity in the producing countries and new production capacity in the developing and State trading countries. Furthermore, the restrictions which the United States imposed on the importation of steel tubes into their territory and the fall in world oil prices, which contributed to a reduction in drilling, led to a fall in demand for the tubes in question and therefore to a substantial reduction in their price and in world production. That is the reason why other Member States sought to reduce their production capacity in that sector.

29. Under those circumstances, there is nothing which suggests any error in the Commission's assessment that Tubemeuse's prospects of profitability were not such as to induce private investors operating under normal market economy conditions to enter into the financial transactions in question, that it was unlikely that Tubemeuse could have obtained the amounts essential for its survival on the capital markets and that, for that reason, the Belgian government's support for Tubemeuse constituted State aid.

The ECJ has continued to apply the same test. When capital is invested by a public investor there must be some interest in profitability in the long term, otherwise the investment will be aid for the purposes of Article 107(1).[96] It is important to determine whether the private investor would have entered into the transaction on the same terms as the public investor, and if not on what terms it might have done so.[97] The privatization of an undertaking may also give rise to questions concerning state aid, depending upon the terms of the privatization. The Commission has provided guidelines on this issue.

It is central to the idea of state aid that the recipient gains a financial advantage, directly or indirectly, over its competitors. This will not be so where the assistance is granted to offset public service obligations incumbent on the beneficiary of the aid, provided that the conditions in the *Altmark* case are satisfied.

---

[96] Case C–303/88 *Italy v Commission* [1991] ECR I–1433; Case C–305/89 *Italy v Commission* [1991] ECR I–1635; Case C–42/93 *Spain v Commission* [1994] ECR I–4175; Case T–20/03 *Kahla/Thüringen Porzellan GmbH v Commission* [2008] ECR II–2305; Cases C–533 and 536/12 P *SNCM v Corsica Ferries France*, 4 Sept 2014.

[97] Cases T–228 and 233/99 *Westdeutsche Landesbank* (n 58) [244]–[246]; Case C–73/11 P *Frucona Košice as v European Commission* EU:C:2013:32.

Case C–280/00 **Altmark Trans GmbH and Regierungspräsidium Magdeburg v Nahverkehrsgesellschaft Altmark GmbH**
[2003] ECR I–7747

[Note Lisbon Treaty renumbering: Art 87 is now Art 107 TFEU]

The ECJ considered the compatibility with Article 87 of state measures that accorded assistance to local transport undertakings.

THE ECJ

87. [W]here a State measure must be regarded as compensation for the services provided by the recipient undertakings in order to discharge public service obligations, so that those undertakings do not enjoy a real financial advantage and the measure thus does not have the effect of putting them in a more favourable competitive position than the undertakings competing with them, such a measure is not caught by Article 92(1) of the Treaty.

88. However, for such compensation to escape classification as State aid in a particular case, a number of conditions must be satisfied.

89. First, the recipient undertaking must actually have public service obligations to discharge, and the obligations must be clearly defined...

90. Second, the parameters on the basis of which the compensation is calculated must be established in advance in an objective and transparent manner, to avoid conferring an economic advantage which may favour the recipient undertaking over competing undertakings.

...

92. Third, the compensation cannot exceed what is necessary to cover all or part of the costs incurred in the discharge of the public service obligations, taking into account the relevant receipts and a reasonable profit for discharging those obligations...

93. Fourth, where the undertaking which is to discharge the public service obligations, in a specific case, is not chosen pursuant to public procurement procedure which would allow for the selection of the tenderer capable of providing those services at least cost to the community, the level of compensation needed must be determined on the basis of an analysis of the costs which a typical undertaking, well run and adequately provided with means of transport so as to be able to meet the necessary public service requirements, would have incurred in discharging those obligations, taking into account the relevant receipts and a reasonable profit for discharging the obligations.

The *Altmark* ruling specified that public service compensation would not constitute state aid, and hence would not need to be notified if the conditions laid down were met.[98] This has enabled the Commission to make a Decision[99] and issue a Framework[100] specifying in greater detail the

---

[98] See also Cases C–34 and 38/01 *Enirisorse SpA v Ministero delle Finanze* [2003] ECR I–14243; Case C–451/03 *Serrvizi Ausiliari Dottori Commercialisti Srl v Calafiori* [2006] ECR I–2941; Case C–526/04 *Laboratoires Boiron SA v Urssaf* [2006] ECR I–7529; Cases T–309, 317, 329 and 336/04 *TV 2/Danmark* (n 30); Case T–354/05 *Télévision française 1 SA (TF1) v Commission* [2009] ECR II–471; Case T–189/03 *ASM Brescia SpA v Commission* [2009] ECR II–1831; Case C–140/09 *Fallimento Traghetti del Mediterraneo SpA v Presidenza del Consiglio dei Ministri* EU:C:2010:335; Cases C–197 and 203/11 *Libert v Gouvernement flamand* EU:C:2013:288.

[99] Commission Decision of 20 December 2011 on the application of Article 106(2) of the Treaty on the Functioning of the European Union to State aid in the form of public service compensation granted to certain undertakings entrusted with the operation of services of general economic interest [2012] OJ L7/3.

[100] Communication from the Commission—European Union framework for State aid in the form of public service compensation [2012] OJ C8/15.

requirements to be met if the conditions are to be fulfilled. The Commission wishes to ensure that the ECJ's conditions are strictly adhered to, so that the ruling is not used by Member States to circumvent the application of the state aid rules.

(ii) *Definition of State Aid: 'Member State or through State Resources'*

A second condition for the application of Article 107(1) is that the aid should be granted by a 'Member State or through State resources'.[101] This can include regional as well as central government.[102] It will not suffice that the measure constituting aid was taken by a public undertaking. It has to be shown that the state actually exercised control over the undertaking and was involved in the adoption of the measure.[103] Subject to this, Article 107 can capture advantages granted by a public or private body designated or established by the state.[104]

Cases 67, 68 and 70/85 **Kwekerij Gebroeders Van der Kooy BV v Commission**
[1988] ECR 219

The Commission made a decision that the tariffs charged by Gasunie for gas to certain firms in the horticultural industry were preferential and constituted aid. Gasunie was a company incorporated under private law, but 50 per cent of its shares were held by the Dutch Government, and the tariffs charged by Gasunie were subject to approval by a government minister. It was argued that the fixing of the tariff did not constitute action by the Dutch state.

THE ECJ

32. In the first place, the applicants maintain that…the contested tariff was not imposed by the Dutch State and cannot be regarded as 'aid granted by a Member State or through State resources'.

33. They argue that Gasunie is a company incorporated under private law in which the Dutch State holds only 50% of the share capital and that the tariff is the outcome of an agreement concluded under private law between Gasunie, Vegin and the Landbouwchap, to which the Dutch State is not a party.

34. Turning to the point noted by the Commission that the Minister for Economic Affairs has a right of approval over the tariffs charged by Gasunie, the Dutch Government claims that that is no more than a retrospective supervisory power which is solely concerned with whether the tariffs accord with the aims of Dutch energy policy.

---

[101] Cases C-52–54/97 *Viscido, Scandella and Terragnolo v Ente Poste Italiane* [1998] ECR I-2629; Case C-345/02 *Pearle BV v Hoofdbedrijfschap Ambachten* [2004] ECR I-7139; Cases T-309, 317, 329 and 336/04 *TV 2/Danmark* (n 30); Case C-677/11 *Doux Élevage SNC* EU:C:2013:348; Cases C-399 and 401/10 P *Bouygues SA v European Commission* EU:C:2013:175; Case C-262/12 *Association Vent De Colère* EU:C:2013:851.

[102] Case 323/82 *Intermills* (n 94); Cases T-227, 229, 265, 266 and 270/01 *Territorio Histórico de Álava v Commission* [2009] ECR II-3029.

[103] Case C-482/99 *France v Commission* [2002] ECR I-4397; Case T-442/03 *SIC—Sociedade Independente de Comunicação, SA v Commission* [2008] ECR II-1161.

[104] Case 78/76 *Firma Steinike und Weinlig v Bundesamt für Ernährung und Forstwirtschaft* [1977] ECR 595; Case 290/83 *Re Grants to Poor Farmers: Commission v France* [1985] ECR 439; Case 57/86 *Commission v Greece* [1988] ECR 2855; Case T-358/94 *Compagnie Nationale Air France v Commission* [1996] ECR II-2109. There can be difficulties as to what constitutes a resource granted from the state: Cases C-72–73/91 *Sloman Neptun Schiffahrts AG v Seebetriebsrat Bodo Ziesmer der Sloman Neptun Schiffahrts* [1993] ECR I-887; Cases C-328 and 399/00 *Italy and SIM 2 Multimedia SpA v Commission* [2003] ECR I-4035.

35. As the Court has held..., there is no necessity to draw any distinction between cases where aid is granted directly by the State and where it is granted by public and/or private bodies established or appointed by the State to administer the aid. In this instance, the documents before the Court provide considerable evidence to show that the fixing of the disputed tariff was the result of action by the Dutch State.

36. First of all, the shares in Gasunie are so distributed that the Dutch State directly or indirectly holds 50% of the shares and appoints half of the members of the supervisory board—a body whose powers include that of determining the tariffs to be applied. Secondly, the Minister for Economic Affairs is empowered to approve the tariffs applied by Gasunie, with the result that, regardless of how that power may be exercised, the Dutch Government can block any tariff which does not suit it. Lastly, Gasunie and the Landbouwschap have on two occasions given effect to the Commission's representations to the Dutch Government seeking an amendment of the horticultural tariff....

37. Considered as a whole, these factors demonstrate that Gasunie in no way enjoys full autonomy in the fixing of gas tariffs but acts under the control and on the instructions of the public authorities. It is thus clear that Gasunie could not fix the tariff without taking account of the requirements of the public authorities.

38. It may therefore be concluded that the fixing of the contested tariff is the result of action by the Dutch State and thus falls within the meaning of the phrase 'aid granted by a Member State'....

(iii) *Definition of State Aid: 'Distorts or Threatens to Distort Competition'*

A third condition for the application of Article 107(1) is that the aid distorts or threatens to distort competition by favouring certain undertakings or the production of certain goods. In many cases this will be unproblematic. The grant of, for example, a subsidy will indubitably place the recipient in a more advantageous position. The Court will consider the position of the relevant company prior to the receipt of the aid, and if this has been improved then Article 107 will have been met.[105] It is no 'defence' for the state to argue that the aid is justified because its effect is to lower the costs of an industrial sector which has, in relative terms, higher costs than other such sectors.[106] Nor is it possible for a state to contend that its aid should be excused on the ground that other states made similar payments to firms within those countries.[107]

(iv) *Definition of State Aid: Effect on Inter-State Trade*

The final element in Article 107(1) is that there should be an effect on inter-state trade. If aid strengthens the financial position of an undertaking as compared to others within the EU then inter-Union trade will be affected.[108] The relatively small amount of the aid, or the relatively small size of the recipient undertaking, does not exclude the possibility that EU trade might be affected.[109] The fact that the aid is given to an undertaking that only provides local transport services does not preclude an effect on inter-state trade, since the aid may render it more difficult for transport undertakings from other Member States to penetrate that market.[110] It is not necessary

---

[105] Case 173/73 *Italy v Commission* (n 83).

[106] Ibid.

[107] Case 78/76 *Steinike* (n 104).

[108] Case 730/79 *Philip Morris Holland BV v Commission* [1980] ECR 2671; Cases T–81, 82 and 83/07 *Maas v Commission* [2009] ECR II–2411; Case T–369/06 *Holland Malt BV v Commission* [2009] ECR II–3313.

[109] Case C–142/87 *Re Tubemeuse: Belgium v Commission* [1990] ECR I–959, [43].

[110] Case C–280/00 *Altmark Trans GmbH and Regierungspräsidium Magdeburg v Nahverkehrsgesellschaft Altmark GmbH* [2003] ECR I–7747, [77]–[82].

for the Commission to prove that trade will be affected. It is sufficient to show that trade might be affected.[111]

(B) ARTICLE 107(2)

Article 107(2) lists three types of aid that are deemed compatible with the internal market. Article 107(2)(a) states that 'aid having a social character, granted to individual consumers, provided that such aid is granted without discrimination related to the origin of the products concerned' will be compatible with the internal market. This Article legitimates aid only if there is no discrimination as to the goods' origin. This limits the use of this provision, since most state aid is directed exclusively to a particular firm within the Member State providing the aid.

Article 107(2)(b) legitimates 'aid to make good damage caused by natural disasters or exceptional occurrences'. The rationale for this exception is self-evident, but its limits are somewhat unclear. While the notion of a natural disaster is reasonably apparent, the meaning of exceptional occurrence is considerably vaguer. The Article is construed strictly and will only be held applicable where the economic disadvantage to the state flows directly from the natural disaster of exceptional occurrence.[112]

Article 107(2)(c) makes provision for the special position of Germany, resulting from the division of the country, in order to compensate for the economic disadvantage caused by that division. It does not however allow full compensation for the new *Länder*.[113]

(C) ARTICLE 107(3)

The exceptions in Article 107(3) are discretionary: aid which comes within these categories *may* be deemed compatible with the internal market.

(i) *Article 107(3)(a)*

Article 107(3)(a) states that 'aid to promote the economic development of areas where the standard of living is abnormally low or where there is serious under-employment, and of the regions referred to in Article 349, in view of their structural, economic and social situation' may be considered to be compatible with the internal market.

There is a connection between this provision and Article 107(3)(c), in that both relate to regional development. Article 107(3)(a) can, however, only be used where the problem in an area is especially serious. The seriousness of the regional problem must be judged in an EU and not a national context.[114] To this end the Commission published criteria for deciding on the relative development of different regions as compared to the EU average.[115] The Commission can consider the impact of the aid on the relevant EU markets,[116] and it must be shown that without the planned aid the investment intended to support development of the region would not occur.[117]

---

[111] Cases T–298, 312, 313, 315, 600–607/97, 1, 3–6 and 23/98 *Alzetta Mauro v Commission* [2000] ECR II–2319, [76]–[90]; Case C–310/99 *Italy v Commission* (n 70) [84]–[86]; Case T–211/05 *Italy v Commission* [2009] ECR II–2777, [151]–[155].

[112] Case C–278/00 *Greece v Commission* [2004] ECR I–3997, [81]–[82]; Case T–268/06 *Olympiaki Aeroporia Ypiresies AE v Commission* [2008] ECR II–1091.

[113] Cases C–57 and 61/00 P *Freistaat Sachsen v Commission* [2003] ECR I–9975; Case C–277/00 *Germany v Commission* [2004] ECR I–3925.

[114] Case 248/84 *Germany v Commission* [1987] ECR 4013, [1].

[115] Guidelines on regional State aid 2014–2020 [2013] OJ C209/01.

[116] Case C–114/00 *Spain v Commission* [2002] ECR I–7657, [81].

[117] Cases C–630–633/11 *HGA v Commission* EU:C:2013:387.

Case 730/79 **Philip Morris Holland BV v Commission**
[1980] ECR 2671

[Note Lisbon Treaty renumbering: Art 92(3) is now Art 107(3) TFEU]

The Dutch Government gave aid to a tobacco manufacturer. The Commission found that the aid did not come within Article 92(3)(a), (b), or (c). What follows is an extract from the ECJ's reasoning concerning the general approach to Article 92(3), and its findings on Article 92(3)(a).

THE ECJ

16. According to the applicant it is wrong for the Commission to lay down as a general principle that aid granted by a Member State to undertakings only falls within the derogating provisions of Article 92(3) if the Commission can establish that the aid will contribute to the attainment of one of the objectives specified in the derogations, which under normal market conditions the recipient firms would not attain by their own actions. Aid is only permissible under Article 92(3) of the Treaty if the investment plan under consideration is in conformity with the objectives mentioned in subparagraphs (a), (b) and (c).

17. This argument cannot be upheld. On the one hand it disregards the fact that Article 92(3), unlike Article 92(2), gives the Commission a discretion by providing that the aid which it specifies 'may' be considered to be compatible with the Common Market. On the other hand it would result in Member States being permitted to make payments which would improve the financial situation of the recipient undertaking although they were not necessary for the attainment of the objectives specified in Article 92(3).

18. It should be noted in this connection that the disputed decision explicitly states that the Dutch Government has not been able to give nor has the Commission found any grounds establishing that the proposed aid meets the conditions laid down to enforce derogations pursuant to Article 92(3) of the EEC Treaty.

19. The applicant maintains that the Commission was wrong to hold that the standard of living in the Bergen-op-Zoom area is not 'abnormally low' and that this area does not suffer serious 'under employment' within the meaning of Article 92(3)(a). In fact in the Bergen-op-Zoom region the under-employment rate is higher and the per capita rate lower than the national average in the Netherlands.

...

24. These arguments put forward by the applicant cannot be upheld. It should be borne in mind that the Commission has a discretion the exercise of which involves economic and social assessments which must be made in a Community context.

25. That is the context in which the Commission has with good reason assessed the standard of living and serious under-employment in the Bergen-op-Zoom area, not with reference to the national average in the Netherlands but in relation to the Community level.

(ii) *Article 107(3)(b)*

Article 107(3)(b) states that 'aid to promote the execution of an important project of common European interest or to remedy a serious disturbance in the economy of a Member State' may be considered to be compatible with the internal market.

The first limb has been used for the development of, for example, a common standard for high-definition television and environmental protection, but the ECJ takes the wording of Article 107(3)(b) seriously, as is evident from *Glaverbel*.

Cases 62 and 72/87 **Executif Régional Wallon and Glaverbel SA v Commission**
[1988] ECR 1573

The Belgian Government gave aid to certain glass producers. The applicants argued that the aid could come within Article 92(3)(b), since the new technology made possible by the investment aid would reduce European dependence on US and Japanese producers in the relevant markets.

THE ECJ

21. It should be observed that the categories of aid set out in Article 92(3)... 'may' be considered by the Commission to be compatible with the Common Market. It follows that the Commission enjoys a discretion in the matter.

23. ... The Commission has based its policy with regard to aid on the view that a project may not be described as being of common European interest for the purposes of Article 92(3)(b) unless it forms part of a transnational European programme supported jointly by a number of governments of the Member States, or arises from concerted action by a number of Member States to combat a common threat such as environmental pollution.

In adopting that policy and in taking the view that the investments envisaged in this case did not fulfil the requisite conditions, the Commission did not commit a manifest error of judgment.

24. The two applicants further complain that the Commission failed to give any reasons in the contested decision for its negative assessment....

25. The Court considers that a statement of reasons which is based on a supposedly 'clear' fact must generally be regarded as insufficient. In this case, however, the applicants' arguments cannot be accepted. None of the documents laid before the Court lends any support whatever to the conclusion that the aid at issue might contribute to the implementation of an 'important' project of 'common' European interest. The mere fact that the investments enabled new technology to be used does not make the project one of common European interest; that certainly cannot be the case when, as in this instance, the products have to be sold on a saturated market.

The second limb of this Article concerning serious disturbance to the economy of a Member State will rarely be used, since the economic problem must afflict the whole of the national economy.[118] More specific problems are dealt with under Article 107(3)(a) or (c). The Commission has, however, signalled willingness to use Article 107(3)(b) for problems caused by the financial crisis.[119]

(iii) *Article 107(3)(c)*

Article 107(3)(c) is the most significant of the discretionary exceptions. It provides that 'aid to facilitate the development of certain economic activities or of certain economic areas, where such aid does not adversely affect trading conditions to an extent contrary to the common interest' may be compatible with the internal market.

It allows aid to be legitimated by reference to the needs of an industrial sector, and by reference to economic areas, which can have a national, and not just an EU, dimension.[120] Thus Article 107(3)(c) is the provision through which a state can seek to justify aid to a particular depressed region as judged

---

[118] Cases C–57 and 61/00 P *Freistaat Sachsen* (n 113).

[119] http://ec.europa.eu/competition/state_aid/legislation/temporary.html; Case T–319/11 *ABN Amro Group NV v European Commission* EU:T:2014:186.

[120] Guidelines (n 115).

by national criteria.[121] It is still necessary to consider the impact of the aid on EU trade, and its sectoral repercussions at EU level.[122]

The regional aid must form part of a well-defined regional policy of the state and conform to the principle of geographical concentration. Moreover, given that such aid will benefit regions that are less disadvantaged than those to which Article 107(3)(a) relates, the Commission interprets the geographic scope of the exception and the intensity of the aid strictly. There are two categories of areas that can come within Article 107(3)(c). There are areas that fulfil certain pre-established conditions and that a Member State may therefore designate as 'c' areas without any further justification, known as 'predefined "c" areas'; and areas that a Member State may, at its own discretion, designate as 'c' areas, provided that it demonstrates that such areas fulfil certain socio-economic criteria, known as 'non-predefined "c" areas'.[123]

The EU Courts and Commission have, moreover, made it clear that aid will not normally qualify under this Article unless it is linked to initial investment, to job creation, and/or to restructuring of the activities of the undertaking concerned.[124] The purpose of the aid must be to develop a particular sector or region and not merely a specific undertaking therein.[125]

Case T–20/03 **Kahla/Thüringen Porzellan GmbH v Commission**
[2008] ECR II–2305

The claimants argued that aid given to them should fall within Article 87(3)(c).

THE CFI

267. Essentially, the applicant takes issue with the Commission's finding that the measures from which the applicant benefited between 1994 and the end of 1996 are not compatible with the common market in the light of the 1994 Guidelines on aid for rescuing and restructuring firms in difficulty.

268. First, it must be recalled that, in accordance with settled case-law, Article 87(3) EC confers on the Commission a wide discretion to allow aid by way of derogation from the general prohibition laid down in Article 87(1) EC, since the determination in such a case of the question whether State aid is or is not compatible with the common market raises problems which presuppose the examination and appraisal of complex economic facts and conditions (Case C–39/94 *SFEI and Others* [1996] ECR I–3547, paragraph 36). Since it is not for the Community judicature to substitute its own assessment of the facts, particularly the economic circumstances, for that of the author of the decision, the Court must, in such a context, confine its review to determining whether the Commission complied with the rules governing procedure and the provision of the statement of reasons, whether the facts are accurately stated and whether there has been any manifest error of assessment or misuse of powers...

. . .

270. [T]he Commission may adopt a policy as to how it will exercise its discretion in the form of measures such as the guidelines in question... Therefore, it is in the light of those rules that the contested decision must be examined.

---

[121] Case 248/84 *Germany v Commission* (n 114) [19].

[122] Cases T–126–127/96 *BFM and EFIM v Commission* [1998] ECR II–3437; Cases T–132 and 143/96 *Freistaat Sachsen v Commission* [1999] ECR II–3663.

[123] Guidelines (n 115) [155].

[124] Cases C–278–280/92 *Spain v Commission* [1994] ECR I–4103; Cases T–126–127/96 *BFM* (n 122); Case C–42/93 *Spain v Commission* (n 96); Guidelines (n 115) [6], [31]–[39].

[125] The Commission's general approach was approved in Case 248/84 *Germany v Commission* (n 114).

271. In the present case, the Commission examined the aid granted to the applicant in the light of the 1994 Guidelines on aid for rescuing and restructuring firms in difficulty, which define the criteria to be used in the evaluation of the compatibility of aid for restructuring firms in difficulty.

272. The guidelines stipulate that restructuring aid must be granted under a plan, which is approved only if three substantive conditions are satisfied: the plan must restore the firm's viability, avoid undue distortions of competition and ensure that the aid is in proportion to the restructuring costs and benefits. Therefore, such aid must be linked to a genuine restructuring plan and can only be granted if it can be shown that keeping an undertaking going and returning it to profitability are in the Community's best interest.

273. It is for the Court of First Instance to check whether, in the present case, those requirements were met.

274. It is apparent from the contested decision that, in finding that the conditions laid down in the guidelines on aid for rescuing and restructuring firms in difficulty had not been fulfilled, the Commission relied, first, on the fact that there was no restructuring plan.

275. It must be noted, in this respect, that a restructuring plan must contain precise and reliable information as well as all the explanation for assessing whether it fulfils the substantive conditions laid down in the guidelines on aid for rescuing and restructuring firms in difficulty.

. . .

280. . . . Moreover, aid granted to a firm in difficulty cannot be declared compatible with the common market on the sole ground that restructuring was envisaged, even if the restructuring ends up being successful, as in the present case. It must be stated, in this respect, that in order for the Commission to be in a position to assess whether the aid at issue can encourage the beneficiary undertakings to act in a way that contributes to achieving the aim set out in Article 87(3)(c) EC, it must first check whether the restructuring plan fulfils all the substantive conditions laid down in the guidelines on aid for rescuing and restructuring firms in difficulty.

The Court will, nonetheless, take seriously allegations that the Commission's decision was insufficiently justified.[126]

Case 323/82 Intermills SA v Commission
[1984] ECR 3809

The Commission held that aid granted by the Belgian Government in the form of shareholdings did not qualify for exemption, because it was not directly linked to the restructuring of the undertaking, but was rescue aid, intended to allow the undertaking to meet its financial commitments. Such aid could, said the Commission, do serious damage to competition in the Community. The applicants argued that the aid in the form of shareholdings was not rescue aid, and that it was used to finance the closure of unprofitable factories, combined with the conversion of others to products with a better prospect of profitability.

THE ECJ

33. [T]he criticism raised by the applicants appears to be well founded, inasmuch as the contested decision does indeed contain contradictions and does not make clear the grounds for the Commission's

---

[126] See also Case 248/84 *Germany v Commission* (n 114); Cases 296 and 318/82 *Leeuwarder Papierwarenfabriek* (n 95).

action on certain vital points. Such doubts and contradictions relate both to the economic justification for the aid and the question whether the aid was likely to distort competition within the Common Market.

34. First, as regards the economic justification for the aid, the Commission concedes in the statement of reasons on which its decision is based that the restructuring aimed at by the applicants corresponds, as such, to the Commission's own objectives for the European paper industry. That factor seems to be the chief ground on which the Commission recognised the compatibility with the Treaty of the aid granted in the form of low interest loans and advances.

35. On the other hand, the Commission gave no verifiable reasons to justify its finding that the holding acquired by the public authorities in the capital of the recipient undertaking was not compatible with the Treaty. It merely stated that that holding was 'not directly linked to the restructuring operation' and in view of the losses suffered by the undertaking over several financial years, constituted purely financial 'rescue aid';... In making those assessments...the Commission did not properly explain why its assessment of the restructuring operation in question...called for such a clear-cut distinction between the effect of the aid granted in the form of subsidised loans and the effect of the aid granted in the form of capital holdings.

...

37. In relation to its claim that the contested aid damages competition in the Common Market, the Commission referred to the provisions of Article 92(1) and to the requirement in Article 92(3), according to which aid may be exempted only if it does not adversely affect trading conditions to an extent contrary to the common interest.

38. As regards the first part of that requirement, the relevant paragraphs of the preamble to the decision merely note the objections raised by the Governments of three Member States, two trade associations and an undertaking in the paper industry. Apart from that reference, the decision gives no concrete indication of the way in which the aid in question damages competition.

39. As regards the second part of the requirement, the Commission, having stated that the aid granted in the form of a capital holding is not directly linked to the restructuring of the undertaking but constitutes 'rescue aid', asserts that such aid 'threatens to do serious damage to the conditions of competition, as the free interplay of market forces would normally call for the closure of the undertaking, allowing more competitive firms to develop'. On that point it must be stated that the settlement of an undertaking's debts in order to ensure its survival does not necessarily adversely affect trading conditions to an extent contrary to the common interest, as provided in Article 92(3), where such an operation is, for example, accompanied by a restructuring plan. In this case, the Commission has not shown why the applicant's activities on the market, following the conversion of its production with the assistance of the aid granted, were likely to have such an adverse effect on trading conditions that the undertaking's disappearance would have been preferable to its rescue.

40. On those grounds, the contested decision must be declared void.

(iv) *Article 107(3)(d) and (e)*

Article 107(3)(d) was added by the Maastricht Treaty. It provides that aid to promote culture and heritage conservation may be compatible with the internal market, where such aid does not affect trading conditions and competition in the EU to an extent that is contrary to the common interest.

Article 107(3)(e) constitutes a safety net by providing that such other categories of aid as may be specified by decision of the Council on a proposal from the Commission may be deemed to be compatible with the internal market. A number of directives on aid to shipbuilding have been adopted pursuant to this Article.

(D) THE BLOCK EXEMPTION

The discussion thus far has focused on the individual exemptions under Article 107(2)–(3). A block exemption, part of the state aid reform package, was introduced in 2008, which declares certain categories of aid compatible with the internal market.[127] It was revised in 2014.[128] The principal categories covered by the 2014 block exemption are: regional aid; aid to small and medium-sized enterprises; aid for research, development, and innovation; environmental aid; training aid; aid for local infrastructures; aid for broadband; and aid for disadvantaged and disabled workers. The 2008 Regulation covered approximately 60 per cent of all aid measures, and about 32 per cent of the aid amounts granted each year in the EU. It is estimated that the 2014 Regulation will cover approximately 75 per cent of state aid measures and 66 per cent of the aid amount. The 2014 Regulation encourages aid to stimulate economic growth, job creation, and the like. The exemption thresholds for many measures covered by the 2008 Regulation have been raised, thereby allowing Member States to grant higher aid amounts without prior notification. There have also been efforts to clarify and simplify application of the exemption scheme.

7 STATE AIDS: THE PROCEDURAL RULES AND ARTICLES 108 AND 109

The procedural rules that apply in this area are derived from the relevant Treaty Articles, the case law of the ECJ and GC, and from Regulation 659/99.[129]

(A) REVIEW OF EXISTING STATE AIDS

The EU has an interest in keeping under review aid granted by Member States, even if the Commission has given the green light under Article 107. Article 108(1) provides that:

> The Commission shall, in cooperation with Member States, keep under constant review all systems of aid existing in those States. It shall propose to the latter any appropriate measures required by the progressive development or by the functioning of the internal market.

There are a number of categories of existing aid, derived from ECJ case law[130] and Regulation 659/99.[131]

(1) Aid which existed before the entry into force of the Treaty.

---

[127] Commission Regulation (EC) No 800/2008 of 6 August 2008 declaring certain categories of aid compatible with the common market in application of Articles 87 and 88 of the Treaty (General Block Exemption Regulation) [2008] OJ L214/3.

[128] Commission Regulation (EU) No 651/2014 of 17 June 2014 declaring certain categories of aid compatible with the internal market in application of Articles 107 and 108 of the Treaty [2014] OJ L187/1.

[129] Council Regulation 659/1999 of 22 March 1999 laying down detailed rules for the application of Article 93 of the Treaty [1999] OJ L83/1; Commission Regulation (EC) No 794/2004 of 21 April 2004 implementing Council Regulation (EC) No 659/1999 laying down detailed rules for the application of Article 93 of the EC Treaty [2004] OJ L140/1.

[130] Case C–44/93 *Namur—Les Assurances du Crédit SA v Office National du Ducroire and Belgian State* [1994] ECR I–3829; Cases T–195 and 207/01 *Gibraltar v Commission* [2002] ECR II–2309; Cases T–227, 229, 265, 266 and 270/01 *Territorio Histórico de Álava* (n 102) [228]–[233]; Case T–222/04 *Italy v Commission* [2009] ECR II–1877.

[131] Art 1.

(2) Aid which has been given the green light under Article 107(3).[132] Individual disbursement of aid pursuant to a general aid scheme that has been approved by the Commission counts as existing aid, provided that it comes properly within the general scheme.[133]

(3) Aid which has been notified to the Commission pursuant to Article 108(3), where the Commission has taken no action within the requisite time.

(4) Aid that is not recoverable because the limitation period has expired.

(5) Aid deemed to be existing aid because it did not initially constitute aid, and only became so due to the evolution of the internal market.[134] Where certain measures become aid following the liberalization of an activity by EU law, such measures are considered existing aid after the date fixed for the liberalization.

(B) THE PROCEDURE FOR NEW STATE AIDS: NOTIFICATION AND PRELIMINARY REVIEW

In order for monitoring of state aids to be effective, it is essential for the Commission to be notified of any aid proposal. Article 108 establishes a two-stage procedure.[135] Stage one concerns prior notification of any plan to grant aid and preliminary investigation by the Commission. This is provided for in Article 108(3):

> The Commission shall be informed, in sufficient time to enable it to submit its comments, of any plans to grant or alter aid. If it considers that any such plan is not compatible with the internal market having regard to Article 107, it shall without delay initiate the procedure provided for in paragraph 2. The Member State concerned shall not put its proposed measures into effect until this procedure has resulted in a final decision.

Member States are therefore under a duty to notify the Commission of any aid prior to granting it.[136] This is, however, qualified by the *de minimis* Regulation.[137] Small subsidies do not have to be notified under Article 108(3). Thus aid up to €200,000, granted over any three-year period will not be considered state aid, and loan guarantees are also covered to the extent that the guaranteed part of the loan does not exceed €1.5 million. Subject to this caveat, Member States cannot implement the grant of aid during the period in which the Commission undertakes its initial review of the proposed aid.[138] The Commission must come to some preliminary view within two months. If it does not do so the state is entitled to carry through its aid proposal, after having notified the Commission.[139] The Commission can request further information if it believes that the information supplied is incomplete.[140]

---

[132] The Commission can review an existing aid scheme and decide that it is no longer compatible with the internal market: Reg 659/99 (n 129) Arts 17–18.

[133] Case C–47/91 *Italy v Commission* [1994] ECR I–4635.

[134] Case T–298/97 *Alzetta Mauro v Commission* [2000] ECR II–2319, [143].

[135] Code of Best Practice for the conduct of State aid control procedures [2009] OJ C136/13.

[136] Reg 659/99 (n 129) Art 2.

[137] Commission Regulation (EC) No 1407/2013 of 18 December 2013 on the application of Articles 107 and 108 of the Treaty on the Functioning of the European Union to *de minimis* aid [2013] OJ L352/1.

[138] Case 120/73 *Gebrüder Lorenz GmbH v Germany* [1973] ECR 1471; Case 84/82 *Germany v Commission* [1984] ECR 1451; Cases C–630–633/11 *HGA* (n 117); Reg 659/99 (n 129) Art 3. The Commission must also be notified of any amendment to the aid proposal: Cases 91 and 127/83 *Heineken Brouwerijen BV v Inspecteur der Vennootschapsbelasting* [1984] ECR 3435.

[139] Case 84/82 *Germany v Commission* [1984] ECR 1451; Reg 659/99 (n 129) Art 4(5).

[140] Reg 659/99 (n 129) Art 5.

The Commission at this early stage engages in a preliminary review of the aid proposal.[141] It may decide to approve the aid, in which case it notifies the Member State and the latter implements the aid proposal. The ECJ has emphasized that the preliminary review procedure is 'meant to be just that'.[142] It is to take no more than two months, and if there are difficulties in reaching a decision within this time then the Commission should proceed to the more complete review in Article 108(2). This is important since other parties are entitled to be consulted under Article 108(2), but have no such rights under Article 108(3).[143]

Moreover, the Commission can resolve a case under Article 108(3) only where it is clear that the aid is compatible with the internal market. Where there are serious difficulties in deciding whether aid is compatible with the internal market, the fuller investigation under Article 108(2) should be used.[144]

(c) THE PROCEDURE FOR STATE AIDS: DETAILED INVESTIGATION AND ENFORCEMENT

Stage two is based on the assumption that the Commission has not been able to give the green light to the state aid proposal under Article 108(3). In these circumstances Article 108(2) applies:

> If, after giving notice to the parties concerned to submit their comments, the Commission finds that aid granted by a State or through State resources is not compatible with the internal market having regard to Article 107, or that such aid is being misused, it shall decide that the State concerned shall abolish or alter such aid within a period of time to be determined by the Commission.
>
> If the State concerned does not comply with this decision within the prescribed time, the Commission or any other interested State may, in derogation from the provisions of Articles 258 and 259, refer the matter to the Court of Justice of the European Union direct.

Article 108(2) applies to existing aids in relation to which questions have been raised pursuant to Article 108(1), and to new aids that have not been given the green light pursuant to the preliminary investigation under Article 108(3). If an existing aid is found to be incompatible with the internal market as the result of a review under Article 108(1) then it will be unlawful from the date set for compliance with that decision. In the case of a new aid, the effect of the decision made under Article 108(2) will be to render permanent the temporary prohibition which flows from Article 108(3), unless the Member State can at some future date show that the circumstances have changed. In either eventuality the procedure described in Article 108(2) comes into operation.

A notice is placed in the Official Journal inviting parties concerned to submit their comments. The Commission summarizes the relevant issues of fact and law, setting out its doubts about the compatibility of the aid with the internal market.[145] The phrase 'parties concerned' covers the undertakings receiving aid, and others whose interests may be affected by the grant of the aid, in particular

---

[141] Ibid Art 4.

[142] Case 120/73 *Gebrüder Lorenz* (n 138); Case 84/82 *Germany v Commission* (n 139); Case T–171/02 *Regione Autonoma della Sardegna* (n 58) [31]–[32]; Case T–301/01 *Alitalia—Linee aeree italiane SpA v Commission* [2008] ECR II–1753, [157].

[143] Case C–198/91 *William Cook plc v Commission* [1993] ECR I–2486; Cases T–195 and 207/01 *Gibraltar v Commission* (n 130); Cases C–75 and 80/05 P *Kronofrance* (n 66) [37].

[144] Case C–367/95 P *Commission v Sytraval and Brink's France SARL* [1998] ECR I–1719, [39]; Case C–204/97 *Portugal v Commission* [2001] ECR I–3175, [33]; Case T–158/99 *Thermenhotel Stoiser Franz Gesellschaft mbh & Co KG v Commission* [2004] ECR I–1, [59]–[61]; Case C–431/07 P *Bouygues SA and Bouygues Télécom SA v Commission* [2009] ECR I–2665.

[145] Reg 659/99 (n 129) Art 6.

competitors and trade associations.[146] The participation rights of such parties are, however, limited. They cannot engage in adversarial debate with the Commission in the manner open to the party against which the formal investigation has been initiated.[147] The period for comment will, normally, not exceed one month.[148] Commission findings pursuant to formal investigations are made by decisions. The Commission may decide that the aid is compatible or incompatible with the internal market. It may attach conditions to a positive decision.[149] The Commission can revoke its decision where it was based on incorrect information that was a determining factor in the decision.[150]

The rationale for the more expedited enforcement process contained in the second paragraph of Article 108(2) is that the Commission has already had the opportunity to make its views known, and because the parties themselves have already been heard. While Article 108(2) provides a speedier method of enforcement against a recalcitrant state, the Court has set itself against any further modification of the enforcement process.[151]

(D) EXCEPTIONAL CIRCUMSTANCES: ARTICLE 108(2), PARAGRAPHS 3 AND 4

The third and fourth paragraphs of Article 108(2) make provision for aid to be granted in certain exceptional circumstances in derogation from the provisions of Article 107. The ECJ has construed this provision narrowly.[152]

> On application by a Member State, the Council may, acting unanimously, decide that aid which that State is granting or intends to grant shall be considered to be compatible with the internal market, in derogation from the provisions of Article 107 or from the regulations provided for in Article 109, if such a decision is justified by exceptional circumstances. If, as regards the aid in question, the Commission has already initiated the procedure provided for in the first subparagraph of this paragraph, the fact that the State concerned has made its application to the Council shall have the effect of suspending that procedure until the Council has made its attitude known.
>
> If, however, the Council has not made its attitude known within three months of the said application being made, the Commission shall give its decision on the case.

(E) ARTICLE 109: IMPLEMENTING REGULATIONS

Article 109 empowers the Council on a proposal from the Commission, and after consulting the Parliament, to make any appropriate regulations for the application of Articles 107 and 108, and in

---

[146] Case 323/82 *Intermills* (n 94) [16]; Case C–198/91 *William Cook* (n 143) [24]; Case C–78/03 P *Commission v Aktionsgemeinschaft Recht und Eigentum eV* [2005] ECR I–10737, [31]–[37]; Case T–395/04 *Air One SpA v Commission* [2006] ECR II–1343, [24]–[41]; Case T–167/04 *Asklepios Kliniken GmbH v Commission* [2007] ECR II–2379, [49]; Reg 659/99 (n 129) Art 20(1).

[147] Case C–367/95 P *Sytraval* (n 144) [59]; Cases 74 and 75/00 P *Falck SpA v Commission* [2002] ECR I–7689, [82]; Case T–109/01 *Fleuren Compost BV v Commission* [2004] ECR II–127, [40]–[44]; Cases T–228 and 233/99 *Westdeutsche Landesbank* (n 58) [123]–[125]; Cases T–227, 229, 265, 266 and 270/01 *Territorio Histórico de Álava* (n 102) [269]; Case T–62/08 *ThyssenKrupp Acciai Speciali Terni SpA v European Commission* [2010] ECR II–3229, [162]–[163].

[148] Reg 659/99 (n 129) Art 6(1).

[149] Ibid Art 7.

[150] Ibid Art 9.

[151] Case C–292/90 *British Aerospace plc and Rover Group Holdings plc v Commission* [1992] ECR I–493.

[152] Case C–110/02 *Commission v Council* [2004] ECR I–6333; Case C–121/10 *European Commission v Council* EU:C:2013:784.

particular to determine the conditions under which Article 108(3) shall apply and the categories of aid exempted from this procedure. Article 109 has been used relatively rarely, and the Commission has sought to rely on soft law and adjudication to develop policy in this area.[153] Article 109 was, however, the basis for the Council regulation empowering the Commission to make regulations about certain categories of aid.[154]

(F) CHALLENGE TO COMMISSION DECISIONS

Challenges to Commission decisions will normally be brought under Article 263 TFEU,[155] although they can take the form of actions for failure to act pursuant to Article 265 TFEU.[156] Applicants may be the state that granted the aid, the intended beneficiaries, and competitors. Applicants have to satisfy the requirements of Article 263[157] and show that the action complained of produces legal effects.[158] The time limit of two months will, in general, run from the date when the decision was published in the Official Journal.[159]

The state will have standing, as will a regional body.[160] The intended recipient of the aid has been readily admitted to plead the case,[161] and the Court has afforded standing to interveners who have submitted comments to the Commission and who would be likely to suffer harm if the aid were given.[162] Economic operators that played a significant role in the Article 108(2) procedure have been held to be individually concerned when they have been affected in their capacity as negotiators.[163] The fact that a party has taken part in the Article 108(2) procedure will not, however, suffice for it to be accorded standing under Article 263.[164] Moreover, where an undertaking has not exercised its right to submit comments under Article 108(2), it must prove that it is individually concerned within Article 263(4). The mere fact that the undertaking is in a competitive relationship with the beneficiary of the aid does not necessarily suffice.[165]

An important point concerning the availability of review was affirmed in *William Cook*.[166] We have already seen that interested parties do not have consultation rights under Article 108(3) during the preliminary examination phase, but do have such rights under Article 108(2). This may be problematic if the Commission finds that an aid is compatible with the internal market under Article 108(3), but an interested party believes that the detailed investigation under Article 108(2) should have been

---

[153] Evans (n 57) 405–427.

[154] Council Reg 994/98 [1998] OJ L142/1.

[155] U Soltesz, and H Bielesz, 'Judicial Review of State Aid Decisions—Recent Developments' [2004] ECLR 133. Actions for failure to act under Art 265 will be difficult to sustain, since the applicant must show an obligation to act by the Commission: Case T–277/94 *Associazione Italiana Tecnico Economica del Cemento (AITEC) v Commission* [1996] ECR II–351. The Commission must, however, consider diligently whether it should act on a complaint: Case T–95/96 *Gestevision Telecinco SA v Commission* [1998] ECR II–3407. For the use of Art 277 see Case T–82/96 *Associacão dos Refinadores de Acucar Portugueses (ARAP) v Commission* [1999] ECR II–1889.

[156] Case C–615/11 P *European Commission v Ryanair Ltd* EU:C:2013:310.

[157] Case C–47/90 *Italy v Commission* [1992] ECR I–4145: the Commission's decision to open the Art 108(2) procedure was a reviewable act which could be challenged before the Court.

[158] Case C–400/99 *Italy v Commission* [2001] ECR I–7303, [62]; Case C–521/06 P *Athinaïki Techniki AE v Commission* [2008] ECR I–5829.

[159] Case T–11/95 *BP Chemicals Ltd v Commission* [1998] ECR II–3235.

[160] Case T–288/97 *Regione Autonoma Friuli-Venezia Giulia v Commission* [1999] ECR II–1871.

[161] Case 730/79 *Philip Morris* (n 108); Case 323/82 (n 94).

[162] Case 169/84 *COFAZ v Commission* [1986] ECR 391; Case C–198/91 *William Cook* (n 143); Case T–380/94 *AIUFFASS v Commission* [1996] ECR II–2169.

[163] Case C–313/90 *CIRFS* (n 66).

[164] Case C–106/98 *SNRT-CGT, SURT-CFDT and SNEA-CFE-CGC v Commission* [2000] ECR I–3659.

[165] Case T–11/95 *BP* (n 159).

[166] Case C–198/91 *William Cook* (n 143).

initiated. In *William Cook* the Court held that the *procedural guarantees* in Article 108(2) could be properly safeguarded in such a case only if the parties were able to challenge the Commission decision before the Court.[167] However, if the applicant seeks to contest the *merits* of the decision appraising the aid, the mere fact that it is a party concerned within Article 108(2) will not suffice to render the action admissible. The applicant must still show individual concern within the *Plaumann* test.[168]

The substantive grounds for challenge are set out in Article 263. The legality of a measure is decided on the basis of the facts and law existing when the measure was adopted.[169] It is common for applicants to argue that the Commission's decision is in breach of a general principle of EU law, that the reasoning is defective, or that the Commission has misinterpreted a Treaty Article. However the Court possesses considerable discretion as to the intensity of review under Article 263. The ECJ will often make reference to the Commission's considerable discretion concerning state aids, and will normally overturn such a decision only if the applicant can show a procedural defect, deficiency of reasoning, factual inaccuracy, a manifest error in assessing the facts, or some misuse of power.

(G) AID THAT HAS NOT BEEN NOTIFIED

The consequences of a failure by a Member State to notify in accordance with Article 108(3) must be separately evaluated in relation to the Commission and the national courts.

(i) *Non-Notification and the Commission*

The ECJ held that failure to notify does not in itself render implementation of the aid unlawful.[170] The Commission has the power, after giving the Member State the opportunity for comment, to issue an interim decision requiring the state to suspend immediately the payment of the aid, pending the outcome of the Commission's determination of whether the aid was compatible with the internal market.[171] If in the light of this request for information the state still refused to supply the requisite material, the Commission could then make an assessment of the compatibility of the aid on the basis of the information available to it,[172] although that must be sufficient to conclude that an undertaking benefited from aid.[173] This decision could demand the recovery of aid that had been paid. It was also suggested that the Commission should be able to require immediate repayment of the aid.[174]

These principles have been enshrined in Regulation 659/99. Where the Commission has information from any source regarding alleged unlawful aid, it must examine it without delay.[175] It can request

---

[167] Case C–225/91 *Matra* (n 92); Case C–367/95 P *Sytraval* (n 144) [40]–[41]; Case T–158/99 *Thermenhotel* (n 144) [73]; Case C–78/03 P *Aktionsgemeinschaft Recht und Eigentum* (n 146) [35]; Case T–289/03 *BUPA* (n 30) [73]; Cases C–75 and 80/05 P *Kronofrance* (n 66) [37]–[38]; Case T–375/04 *Scheucher-Fleisch GmbH v Commission* [2009] ECR II–4155, [40]–[43].

[168] Case C–78/03 P *Aktionsgemeinschaft Recht und Eigentum* (n 146) [37]; Case T–395/04 *Air One* (n 146) [32]; Cases C–75 and 80/05 P *Kronofrance* (n 66) [40]; Case C–487/06 P *British Aggregates Association v Commission* [2008] ECR I–10505, [30]; Case T–289/03 *BUPA* (n 30) [74]; K Jürimäe, 'Standing in State Aid Cases: What's the State of Play?' [2010] EStAL 303; H Peytz and T Mygind, 'Direct Action in State Aid Cases—Tightropes and Legal Protection?' [2010] EStAL 331.

[169] Case T–110/97 *Kneissl Dachstein Sportartikel AG v Commission* [1999] ECR II–2881.

[170] Case C–301/87 *France v Commission* [1990] ECR I–307.

[171] Case C–75/97 *Belgium v Commission* (n 87).

[172] Case T–366/00 *Scott SA v Commission* [2007] ECR II–797, [144]; Case T–266/02 *Deutsche Post AG v Commission* [2008] ECR II–1233, [75].

[173] Case C–520/07 P *Commission v MTU Friedrichshafen GmbH* [2009] ECR I–8555, [55]–[57].

[174] Case C–42/93 *Spain v Commission* (n 96), AG Jacobs.

[175] Reg 659/99 (n 129) Art 10(1). The Commission may also re-open a case where aid has been misused: Art 16.

information from the relevant state. The Commission may, after allowing the state to comment, make a decision requiring the state to suspend the aid until the Commission has taken a decision on its compatibility with the internal market. This is termed a 'suspension injunction'.[176] The Commission may, after allowing the state to comment, make a decision requiring the state to recover the aid, pending a decision by the Commission on its compatibility with the internal market. This is known as a 'recovery injunction'.[177]

These injunctions may be ordered only where it is clear that there is aid, it is a matter of urgency, and there is a serious risk of substantial and irreparable damage to a competitor. Non-compliance with either type of injunction can lead to an action before the ECJ.[178] The Commission can make its substantive decisions on such aid by way of preliminary review, or by means of the formal procedure. In either eventuality, the normal time limits do not apply.[179] If the Commission decides that the aid is not compatible with the internal market, it can issue a 'recovery decision'. This obliges the Member State to take all necessary measures to recover the aid from the beneficiary.[180] This shall not be required if it would be contrary to a general principle of EU law.[181]

(ii) *Non-Notification and National Courts*

The duty not to implement aid before notification to the Commission, and before the Commission has undertaken its preliminary investigation under Article 108(3), is directly effective,[182] and there is provision for exchange of information between the Commission and national courts.[183] The national court cannot rule on the compatibility of the aid with the internal market, this being for the Commission, but the national court should, nonetheless, rule aid to be illegal when it has not been notified as required by Article 108(3).[184] The direct effect of Article 108(3) demanded that the rights of the individual should be protected in this manner. A later Commission decision which found that the aid was compatible with Article 107 would not be retrospective in effect.[185] However a national court is not bound to order the recovery of aid implemented contrary to Article 107(3) where the Commission adopted a final decision declaring that aid compatible with the internal market, but the national court must order the aid recipient to pay interest in respect of the period of unlawfulness.[186] The Commission adopted a Notice, which builds on the ECJ's jurisprudence.[187]

---

[176] Ibid Art 11(1).

[177] Ibid Art 11(2).

[178] Ibid Art 12.

[179] Ibid Art 13.

[180] Towards an effective implementation of Commission decisions ordering Member States to recover unlawful and incompatible State aid [2007] OJ C272/05.

[181] Reg 659/99 (n 129) Art 14.

[182] Case 120/73 *Lorenz* (n 138); Cases 91 and 127/83 *Heineken* (n 138); Case C–143/99 *Adria-Wien* (n 86) [26]–[27]; Case C–295/97 *Industrie Aeronautiche e Meccaniche Rinaldo Piaggio SpA v International Factors SpA* [1999] ECR I–3735; Case C–345/02 *Pearle* (n 101) [30]–[32].

[183] Reg 659/99 (n 129) Art 23a.

[184] Case C–354/90 *Fédération Nationale du Commerce Exterieur des Produits Alimentaires v France* [1991] ECR I–5505; Cases C–34 and 38/01 *Enirisorse* (n 98) [42]; Case C–119/05 *Ministero dell'Industria, del Commercio e dell'Artigianato v Lucchini SpA* [2007] ECR I–6199, [48]–[58]; Case T–152/06 *NDSHT Nya Destination Stockholm Hotell & Teaterpaket AB v Commission* [2009] ECR II–1517, [71]–[72].

[185] Case C–368/04 *Transalpine Ölleitung in Österreich GmbH v Finanzlandesdirektion für Tirol* [2006] ECR I–9957.

[186] Case C–199/06 *Centre d'exportation du livre français (CELF) and Ministre de la Culture et de la Communication v Société internationale de diffusion et d'édition (SIDE)* [2008] ECR I–469.

[187] Commission notice on the enforcement of State aid law by national courts [2009] OJ C85/1.

(H) RECOVERY OF UNLAWFUL AID

The Court has, not surprisingly, held that, as a matter of principle, illegal state aids should be repaid, this being the logical consequence of a finding that the aid was unlawful.[188] The peremptory force of this obligation will not easily be deflected by claims that repayment of the aid entails difficulties for the recipient.

Case 52/84 **Commission v Belgium**
[1986] ECR 89

[Note Lisbon Treaty renumbering: Arts 5 and 173 are now Arts 4(3) TEU and 263 TFEU]

The Commission found that the acquisition by a public regional holding company of shares in a firm manufacturing ceramic ware constituted state aid, and ordered that it should be withdrawn since it was incompatible with the common market. The Belgian Government did not contest this decision, but it stressed the serious social consequences of closing down the undertaking, and stated that Belgian law did not allow share capital to be refunded except by way of withdrawal of company profits, and no such profits were available. The Government also requested clarification from the Commission of what it meant by 'withdrawal of aid'. The ECJ held that the Belgian Government was outside the time limit for challenging the decision under Article 173. It then proceeded as follows.

THE ECJ

14. In those circumstances the only defence left to the Belgian Government in opposing the Commission's application for a declaration that it failed to fulfil its Treaty obligations would be to plead that it was absolutely impossible for it to implement the decision properly. In this connection it should be noted that the decision demands the withdrawal from the undertaking of a capital holding of 475 million Bfr . . . ; that demand is sufficiently precise to be complied with. The fact that, on account of the undertaking's financial position, the Belgian authorities could not recover the sum paid does not constitute proof that implementation was impossible, because the Commission's objective was to abolish the aid and, as the Belgian Government itself admits, that objective could be attained by proceedings for winding up the company, which the Belgian authorities could institute in their capacity as shareholder or creditor.

. . .

16. It should be added that the fact that the only defence which a Member State to which a decision has been addressed can raise in legal proceedings such as these is that implementation of the decision is absolutely impossible does not prevent that State—if, in giving effect to the decision, it encounters unforeseen or unforeseeable difficulties or perceives consequences overlooked by the Commission—from submitting those problems for consideration by the Commission, together with proposals for suitable amendments. In such a case the Commission and the Member State concerned must respect the principle underlying Article 5 of the Treaty, which imposes a duty of genuine cooperation on the Member States and Community institutions; accordingly, they must work together in good faith with a view to overcoming difficulties whilst fully observing the Treaty provisions, and in particular the provisions on aid. However, in the present instance none of the difficulties referred to by the Belgian Government is of that nature, and that Government made no proposals whatever to the Commission for the adoption of other suitable measures.

---

[188] Case 310/85 *Deufil GmbH & Co KG v Commission* [1987] ECR 901; Case C–277/00 *Germany v Commission* (n 113) [74]–[76].

The message from the Court was clear. The only exception to the primary obligation to obtain repayment of the illegal aid was where recovery was absolutely impossible,[189] and this was narrowly defined. If the recipient company had to be wound up, so be it. Even where the exception to the primary obligation comes into play, the state is not let off the hook entirely. There is a secondary obligation derived from Article 4(3) TEU, requiring the state to enter into a serious dialogue with the Commission to resolve the problem.

The same uncompromising approach is apparent in other cases,[190] and the national court must cooperate with the Commission in relation to recovery of unlawful aid.[191] The mere fact that the undertaking is bankrupt does not remove the obligation to repay illegal aid.[192] Nor can the recipient of aid plead legitimate expectations. In *Commission v Germany*[193] the ECJ held that a recipient of aid could not have a legitimate expectation that the aid was lawful, unless granted in accordance with Article 108. A diligent businessman should normally be able to determine whether that procedure had been followed. National concepts of legitimate expectations could not be relied upon if the effect was to make it impossible to recover the aid, as where the national doctrine set time limits for the revocation of administrative acts. Similarly in *Lucchini* the ECJ held that EU law precluded reliance on the national concept of *res judicata* if its application prevented recovery of aid in breach of EU law.[194] The ECJ has nonetheless recognized that there may be exceptional circumstances where recovery of aid should not be ordered.[195]

8 STATE AIDS, MARKET INTEGRATION, AND REGIONAL POLICY

(A) POLICY FOUNDATIONS

There have been concerns voiced as to the reasoning and criteria used by the Commission when making its initial determinations concerning state aid, as the following extract reveals.

J Temple Lang, EU State Aid Rules—The Need for Substantive Reform[196]

It is not based on sufficient intellectual rigour or on any clear economic principles, either stating what State aid should be designed and allowed to do, or stating economic tests that aid should always meet if it is to be approved, or even stating for what objectives a rational State aid may legitimately

---

[189] Case C–214/07 *Commission v France* [2008] ECR I–8357.

[190] Case C–142/87 [1990] ECR I–959; Case C–378/98 *Commission v Belgium* [2001] ECR I–5107; Case C–261/99 *Commission v France* [2001] ECR I–2537; Case C–527/12 *European Commission v Germany*, 11 Sept 2014.

[191] Case C–284/12 *Deutsche Lufthansa AG v Flughafen Frankfurt-Hahn GmbH* EU:C:2013:755; Case C–69/13 *Mediaset SpA v Ministero dello Sviluppo economico* EU:C:2014:71.

[192] Cases T–81, 82 and 83/07 *Maas* (n 108) [192]–[193].

[193] Case C–5/89 *Commission v Germany* [1990] ECR I–3437; Case C–24/95 *Land Rheinland-Pfalz v Alcan Deutschland GmbH* [1997] ECR I–1591; Case T–171/02 *Regione Autonoma della Sardegna* (n 58) [64]; Cases T–116 and 118/01 *P & O Ferries (Vizcaya) SA v Commission* [2003] ECR II–2957, [201]–[205], upheld in Cases C–442 and 471/03 [2006] ECR I–4845; Cases T–227, 229, 265, 266 and 270/01 *Territorio Histórico de Álava* (n 102) [310]; Case T–62/08 *ThyssenKrupp* (n 147) [269].

[194] Case C–119/05 *Lucchini* (n 184) [59]–[63].

[195] Case C–354/90 *Fédération Nationale* (n 184); Case C–39/94 *SFEI* (n 86).

[196] [2014] EStAL 440, 449.

be given. The 2012 Modernisation plan envisaged more effective control of 'subsidies leading to inefficient use of resources'. The phrase is ambiguous. It might mean expenditure of taxpayers' money on keeping a company in existence even when it is not likely ever to return to profit. Or it might mean keeping a currently inefficient company in existence even though the effect is to cause its competitors to operate at a lower level of capacity utilization, without any increase in general welfare in the EU as a whole. It is not clear whether the Commission considers that competition is always distorted if an aid causes competitors of the beneficiary to operate at a lower level of capacity utilisation, as would be likely if trade between Member States is affected. The Commission's present efforts to clarify the legal concept of State aid, and therefore the scope of its powers to act in State aid cases, do nothing to clarify the economic principles that the Commission should apply to measures that come within the concept. Those principles are imprecise and confused, even in connection with the key concept of distortion of competition. Also, the Commission does not in practice consistently apply the principles that it claims to follow.

(B) STATE AID AND FREE MOVEMENT

The provisions concerning state aids do not exist in a legal or political vacuum. The ECJ has considered the relationship between them and other Treaty provisions,[197] and this has broader implications for the balance between market integration and regional policy in the EU. The most interesting point of interconnection is the relationship between Articles 107–109 and Article 34.

The Court is willing to apply Article 34 without too delicate an inquiry into whether the measure caught by this Article was an integral part of the aid scheme. In *Commission v France*[198] the Court examined the legality of a measure that gave newspaper publishers tax exemptions on the condition that the papers were printed in France. The Commission argued that this constituted a breach of Article 34. The French Government argued that the measures should be considered under Article 107, since the tax provisions could not be separated from the general aid scheme for the newspaper industry. The ECJ was unconvinced and noted that France had not notified its scheme in accordance with Article 108(3). It then proffered the following strong statement of principle:[199]

[I]t should be pointed out that Articles 92 and 94 cannot, as is clear from a long line of cases decided by the Court, be used to frustrate the rules of the Treaty on the free movement of goods or the rules on the repeal of discriminatory tax provisions. According to those cases, the provisions relating to the free movement of goods, the repeal of discriminatory tax provisions and aid have a common objective, namely to ensure the free movement of goods between Member States under normal conditions of competition. . . . The mere fact that a national measure may possibly be defined as aid within the meaning of Article 92 is therefore not an adequate reason for exempting it from the prohibition contained in Article 30. The argument relating to the Community rules on aid, which the French Republic in any case raised only by way of hypothesis in reply to the observations of the Commission, therefore cannot be accepted.

The Court persisted with this approach.[200] The Court's reasoning has force, but is not unproblematic. It is true that Articles 34 and 107 have in general terms the same objective. Yet the structure

---

197 Cases C–149 and 150/91 *Sanders Adour et Guyomarc'h Nutrition Animale* [1992] ECR I–3899.

198 Case 18/84 [1985] ECR 1339; Case 249/81 *Commission v Ireland* [1982] ECR 4005.

199 Ibid [13]. References to Arts 30 and 92–94 should now be read as to Arts 34 and 107–109.

200 Case C–21/88 *Du Pont de Nemours Italiana SpA v Unità Sanitaria Locale No 2 di Carrara* [1990] ECR I–889; Case C–351/88 *Laboratori Bruneau Srl v Unità Sanitaria Locale RM/24 de Monterotondo* [1991] ECR I–3641; Case C–156/98 *Germany v Commission* [2000] ECR I–6857, [78]; Case C–114/00 *Spain v Commission* [2002] ECR I–7657, [104].

of Articles 107–109 attests to the different way in which this is realized in the context of state aids. These Articles are characterized by Commission discretion, enabling it to weigh certain social and economic variables in deciding whether aid is compatible with the internal market. If Article 34 predominates in the event of overlap with Article 107 then it will rule out the social balancing that occurs in the context of Article 107(3). Concerns of this nature are apparent in the following extract. The case to which the authors refer is the *Du Pont* decision[201] set out above.

JFM Martin and O Stehmann, Product Market Integration versus Regional Cohesion in the Community[202]

First of all, one of the grounds on which the Court of Justice justifies its position is that both sets of rules have a common objective, that is to ensure the free movement of goods under normal conditions of competition. Although this is true, it is only partially so. One should not ignore that there is a second objective underlying Articles 92(3) and 93, namely to grant the Commission the possibility to declare compatible with the EEC Treaty those aids which are intended to close the economic, social and regional gaps existing inside the Community. Therefore, the fact that some competition distorting State aids may be permitted to operate proves that certain exceptions to the free movement of goods and to free competition principles are to be admitted....

Secondly, the relation of both sets of rules... may have certain undesirable consequences. Whereas this position might be justifiable... in those cases in which no prior notification has taken place, applying Article 30 as interpreted in *Dassonville* without engaging in a deeper economic (or other) analysis risks obliterating Articles 92 and 93. After the *Dassonville* definition, almost anything would come under the 'imperium' of Article 30. State aids, by their nature, always have a negative effect on inter-state trade when they strengthen national industry or regions... If one follows strictly the Court's reasoning of giving priority to the application of Article 30... Articles 92 and 93 would lose much of their sense.

...

From an economic point of view the Court's position leads to favouring rapid market integration—represented by the free movement of goods provisions—to the detriment of regional cohesion—represented by the State aids provisions...

(C) NATIONAL AND EU REGIONAL POLICY

While there may be concerns at the too-ready application of Article 34, one must be cautious about the general relationship between national and EU regional aid policy. We must be careful not to condemn the EU for paying insufficient attention to regional problems. Regional[203] and environmental[204] concerns are taken into account within Article 107, and there are EU schemes for regional assistance. The proper limit of national regional assistance is a contestable issue, since such aid can inhibit market integration. Articles 174 and 175 TFEU prioritize greater cohesion within the EU. Attainment of this goal necessitates limits on aid by the richer Member States to regions that may be poor relative to those states, but not in relation to the EU as a whole. Only in this way will cohesion be possible.

---

[201] Case C–21/88 *Du Pont de Nemours* (n 200).

[202] (1991) 16 ELRev 216, 228–230. References to Arts 30, 92, and 93 should be read as to Arts 34, 107, and 108.

[203] F Wishlade, 'Competition Policy or Cohesion Policy by the Back Door? The Commission Guidelines on National Regional Aid' [1998] ECLR 343.

[204] H Vedder, 'The New Community Guidelines on State Aid for Environmental Protection—Integrating Environment and Competition?' [2001] ECLR 365.

It is the larger Member States that spend most on aid to their own industries and regions, and these sums exceed the EU's budget for regional policy. The consequence is that 'strict control of State aid in the central, more prosperous, regions is necessary in the interests of cohesion as well as of competition policy'.[205] In a similar vein the Commission has noted the importance of state aid policy for cohesion, 'by preventing a damaging subsidy race between regions, and by creating the right incentives for growth and jobs, in the least developed regions and elsewhere'.[206] However, persuading the richer Member States to increase their contributions to EU spending in the weaker regions is one thing; getting them to refrain in the name of cohesion from spending so much of their own taxpayers' money locally is quite another.

9 CONCLUSIONS

i. The Treaty undoubtedly places constraints on state behaviour. Some of this is relatively uncontroversial, such as the control of state aids, and is justified by the need to ensure a level playing field between undertakings. In other areas the EU Courts have had to strike a difficult balance between a state's freedom to organize its economic activities and the impact that this might have on the market, as exemplified by the jurisprudence under Article 106. The EU Courts have had to face equally problematic issues concerning the relationship between state aids and free movement of goods.

ii. The ECJ and GC have given a broad reading to the relevant Treaty Articles, enhanced the competitive process, and demanded a justification from the state for the grant of monopoly or privileged status under Article 106.

iii. However, they have also been more willing to recognize the importance of public service obligations, within the context of Article 106(2). This is reflected in EU legislation on liberalization, which has allowed states to impose such obligations on those providing energy, telecommunications, and the like.

10 FURTHER READING

(a) Books

BIONDI, A, EECKHOUT, P, AND FLYNN, J (eds), *The Law of State Aid in the European Union* (Oxford University Press, 2004)

BUENDIA SIERRA, J, *Exclusive Rights and State Monopolies under EC Law* (Oxford University Press, 1999)

EVANS, A, *EC Law of State Aid* (Oxford University Press, 1997)

HANCHER, L, OTTERVANGER, T, AND SLOT, PJ, *EU State Aids* (Sweet & Maxwell, 4th edn, 2012)

HARDEN, I (ed), *State Aid: Community Law and Policy* (Bundesanzeiger, 1993)

PROSSER, T, *The Limits of Competition Law: Markets and Public Services* (Oxford University Press, 2005)

---

[205] A Petersen, 'State Aid and the European Union: State Aid in the Light of Trade, Competition, Industrial and Cohesion Policies' in Harden (n 71) 25.

[206] State Aid Action Plan, COM(2005) 107 final, [40].

Quigley, C, *European State Aid Law and Policy* (Hart, 2nd edn, 2009)

Sauter, W, *Competition Law and Industrial Policy in the EU* (Clarendon Press, 1997)

(b) Articles

Biondi, A, 'State Aid is Falling Down, Falling Down: An Analysis of the Case Law on the Notion of Aid' (2013) 50 CMLRev 1719

Braun, J-D, and Kühling, J, 'Article 87 EC and the Community Courts: From Revolution to Evolution' (2008) 45 CMLRev 465

da Cruz Vilaça, J Luís, 'Material and Geographic Selectivity in State Aid   Recent Developments' [2009] EStAL 443

Davies, G, 'Article 86 EC, the EC's Economic Approach to Competition Law, and the General Interest' (2009) 5 European Competition Journal 549

Fiedziuk, N, 'Putting Services of General Economic Interest up for Tender: Reflections on Applicable EU Rules' (2013) 50 CMLRev 87

Filpo, F, 'The Commission's 2009 Procedural Reform from a Private Party Perspective: Two Steps Forward, One Step Back?' [2010] EStAL 323

Hancher, L, 'Community, State and Market' in P Craig and G de Búrca (eds), *The Evolution of EU Law* (Oxford University Press, 1999) ch 20

——and Larouche, P, 'The Coming of Age of EU Regulation of Network Industries and Services of General Economic Interest' in P Craig and G de Búrca (eds), *The Evolution of EU Law* (Oxford University Press, 2nd edn, 2011) ch 24

Jürimäe, K, 'Standing in State Aid Cases: What's the State of Play?' [2010] EStAL 303

Laprévote, F, 'A Missed Opportunity? State aid Modernization and Effective Third Parties Rights in State aid Proceedings' [2014] EStAL 426

Müller, T, 'Efficiency Control in State aid and the Power of Member States to Define SGEIs' [2009] EStAL 39

Peytz, H, and Mygind, T, 'Direct Action in State Aid Cases—Tightropes and Legal Protection?' [2010] EStAL 331

Ross, M, 'A Healthy Approach to Services of General Economic Interest? The *BUPA* Judgment of the Court of First Instance' (2009) 34 ELRev 127

Rubini, L, 'The "Elusive Frontier": Regulation under EC State Aid Law' [2009] EStAL 277

Temple Lang, J, 'EU State Aid Rules—The Need for Substantive Reform' [2014] EStAL 440

INDEX

Introductory Note

References such as '178–9' indicate (not necessarily continuous) discussion of a topic across a range of pages. Wherever possible in the case of topics with many references, these have either been divided into sub-topics or only the most significant discussions of the topic are listed. Because the entire work is about 'EU law', the use of this term (and certain others which occur constantly throughout the book) as an entry point has been minimized. Information will be found under the corresponding detailed topics.